THIRTY-EIGHTH EDITION

KOVELS'
ANTIQUES
& COLLECTIBLES
PRICE LIST

FOR THE 2006 MARKET
ILLUSTRATED

RANDOM HOUSE REFERENCE
NEW YORK TORONTO LONDON SYDNEY AUCKLAND

Please address inquiries about electronic licensing of any products for use on a network,
in software or on CD-ROM to the Subsidiary Rights Department,
Random House Information Group, fax 212-572-6003.

This book is available for special discounts for bulk purchases for sales promotions or
premiums. Special editions, including personalized covers, excerpts of existing books,
and corporate imprints, can be created in large quantities for special needs. For more
information, write to Random House, Inc., Special Markets/Premium Sales,
1745 Broadway, MD 6-2, New York, NY or email *specialmarkets@randomhouse.com*.

Visit the Random House Reference Web site: *www.randomworks.com*

Library of Congress Catalog Card Number: 83-643618

Printed in the United States of America

ISBN 0-375-72099-5

10 9 8 7 6 5 4 3 2 1

THIRTY-EIGHTH EDITION

BOOKS BY RALPH AND TERRY KOVEL

American Country Furniture, 1780–1875

A Directory of American Silver, Pewter, and Silver Plate

Kovels' Advertising Collectibles Price List

Kovels' American Antiques, 1750–1900

Kovels' American Art Pottery

Kovels' American Silver Marks, 1650 to the Present

Kovels' Antiques & Collectibles Fix-It Source Book

Kovels' Antiques & Collectibles Price List

Kovels' Bid, Buy, and Sell Online

Kovels' Book of Antique Labels

Kovels' Bottles Price List

Kovels' Collector's Guide to American Art Pottery

Kovels' Collectors' Source Book

Kovels' Depression Glass & Dinnerware Price List

Kovels' Dictionary of Marks—Pottery & Porcelain

Kovels' Guide to Selling, Buying, and Fixing
Your Antiques and Collectibles

Kovels' Illustrated Price Guide to Royal Doulton

Kovels' Know Your Antiques

Kovels' Know Your Collectibles

Kovels' New Dictionary of Marks—Pottery & Porcelain

Kovels' Price Guide for Collector Plates, Figurines,
Paperweights, and Other Limited Editions

Kovels' Quick Tips—799 Helpful Hints
on How to Care for Your Collectibles

Kovels' Yellow Pages: A Resource Guide for Collectors

The Label Made Me Buy It: From Aunt Jemima to Zonkers—
The Best-Dressed Boxes, Bottles, and Cans from the Past

INTRODUCTION

This is the thirty-eighth year *Kovels' Antiques & Collectibles Price List* has been published. The book is written by its original authors, Ralph and Terry Kovel. This edition has hundreds of color photographs, product logos, about 45,000 prices, and tips about care. There is a color insert, "A Record-Setting Year," picturing some of the year's highest-priced antiques and collectibles—from a $67,100 Hires Root Beer syrup dispenser to an $8.4-million eighteenth-century Chippendale tea table attributed to John Goddard of Newport, Rhode Island.

READ THIS FIRST

This is a book for the collector. We check prices, visit shops, shows, and flea markets, read hundreds of publications and catalogs, check online services and the Internet, and decide which antiques and collectibles are of most interest to collectors. We concentrate on average pieces in any category. Some high-priced items are included so you will realize that some rarities are very valuable.

Examples of furniture, silver, Tiffany, or art pottery may sell for more than $40,000; we list a few. The highest price in this book is $97,750 for a Tiffany lamp with a turtleback tile shade. Lowest price is 75 cents for a Vernor's Ginger Ale bottle cap. Most pieces listed cost less than $10,000. We also include the weird and the wonderful. This year you can find a handmade wooden artificial leg from Civil War days with a brass fitted bottom and leather laces listed for $1,650. A 1930s one-man band consisting of a washboard, whistle, bells, and noisemakers cost only $875. We have seen only a few vampire-killing kits, and this year one dating from about 1900 sold for $26,400. It is a walnut box holding a stake, crucifix, and pistol. The smallest item is a triangular rhinestone button. Measuring only ½ inch, it sold for $30. The biggest item is a nineteenth-century Aubusson rug 18½ by 16¼ feet that sold for nearly $6,300.

Prices are up in some categories. Pressed glass continues to increase in value. Rare toys set more than thirty-five records this year. More record-setting prices are illustrated in the center of the book. Collectors of modern art have become interested in the newer decorative arts. Furniture from the fifties by "name" designers is up in price again, and furniture from the past ten years by modernist designers like Ron Arad are selling for amazingly high prices, often tens of thousands of dollars. Arts and Crafts and art pottery continue to rise in price. Pottery by Rookwood, Grueby, Ohr, and other well-known potteries continues to be expensive. Works by less-famous makers like Marblehead, Owens, Clewell, and the University of North Dakota are growing in value. Soapstone carvings are up. There is continued interest in garden antiques, from old flowerpots to large fountains. Czechoslovakian pottery and glass sells quickly at middle-range prices. Flower patterns by Hull Pottery are increasing in price. Textiles from the fifties and sixties like Marghab linens or Marimekko prints sell quickly. Less-than-perfect collectibles are selling at about 80 percent of the price of a perfect piece—if they are rare. Arts and Crafts furniture, especially pieces by Gustav Stickley, must have the original finish to sell at a high price. Collectors and dealers were afraid the copies of fifties and sixties furniture for sale at furniture stores would depress prices, but serious collectors still want original examples. Coin-operated machines are up in price. They are often bought to be used, not just admired.

Prices at well-advertised auctions look high when compared to presale estimates, but take a closer look. You'll find estimates in general are lower than they have been in the past. On eBay, estimates are often low because the seller pays a fee to eBay based on the estimated price. In general, Internet-only auction prices are still dropping, but many auction houses are selling on land and online at the same time, giving them an international customer base.

The dealers we have interviewed are concerned that shows appear to have old, not young, customers. Too few new collectors are going to shows and shops. Yet there are crowds at the Modernism shows, toy auctions, and advertising sales. Those under fifty years old are buying what they remember from their childhoods. In the past, buyers wanted items that could have belonged to their grandparents. Hummel figurine prices are very low this year. Fiesta dishes are down in price, too. Royal Doulton figurines and character jugs have dropped slightly.

This book has gotten younger over the past thirty-eight years. Most items in our first book were made before 1860. Today we have pieces made in the 1990s, and there is great interest in furniture, glass, and ceramics made since 1950.

The book is kept at about 825 pages so you can carry it to sales. We have a balanced format—not too many glass, pottery, or collectible items, furniture from the eighteenth through the twentieth centuries, and a few items that sell for over $5,000. Prices are from the American market for the American market. Few European sales are reported. We take the editorial privilege of not including prices we think result from "auction fever." There is a computer-generated index. It includes categories and more. For example, there is a category for Celluloid. Most celluloid is there, but a toy made of celluloid will be listed under Toy and also indexed under Celluloid. There are cross-references in the listings and in the paragraphs. But some searching must be done. For example, Barbie dolls are in the Doll category; there is no Barbie category. When you look at "doll, Barbie" you see Barbie is under "doll, Mattel, Barbie" because most dolls are listed by maker. Where possible, we list the maker at the beginning of an entry, size and age at the end.

All photographs and prices are new, except pattern examples in Depression Glass and Pressed Glass. Antiques pictured are items that were offered for sale. Whenever computer-generated spaces appear, we fill them with new tips about care of collections, security, and other information. Don't discard this book. Old Kovels' price books should be saved for future reference and for tax and appraisal information.

Prices in this book are reports of the general antiques market. Every price is new. We do not estimate or "update" prices. Prices are asking prices; a buyer may have negotiated to a lower selling price. We do not pay dealers and writers to estimate prices. Experience has shown that estimated prices are usually high or low, but rarely accurate. If a price range is given, two identical items were offered for sale at different prices. Price ranges are found only in categories like Pressed Glass, where identical items were made. If the price is from an auction, it includes the buyer's premium, but like all prices, it does not include sales tax. Prices in *Kovels' Antiques & Collectibles Price List* may seem high or low because of regional variations. But each price is one you could have paid for the object somewhere in the United States. Some Internet prices are included, but we find prices there can be misleading. Many non-collectors sell online and know little about the objects they are describing.

If selling your collection, do not expect to get retail value unless you are a dealer. Wholesale prices for antiques are usually 50 percent of retail prices. The antiques dealer must make a profit or go out of business. Internet auction prices are less predictable. Because of the international audience and "auction fever," prices can be higher or lower than retail.

A NOTE TO COLLECTORS

You already know this is a great overall price guide for antiques and collectibles. Each entry is current, every picture is new, all prices are accurate.

But prices change quickly. Important sales produce new record prices. Fakes appear. Rarities are discovered. To keep up, read *Kovels on Antiques and Collectibles*, our monthly newsletter with up-to-date information on collecting. It is filled with color photographs, about forty per issue. The newsletter reports prices, trends, auction results, Internet sales, and other news *as it happens*. For a free sample of *Kovels on Antiques and Collectibles*, fill out and mail the postage-paid postcard at the back of this book. Visit our website, www.kovels.com, for FREE pricing information, lists of publications, sources, and news.

HOW TO USE THIS BOOK

There are rules for using this book. Each listing is arranged in the following manner: CATEGORY (such as Pressed Glass), OBJECT (such as vase), DESCRIPTION (information about size, age, color, and pattern). Some types of glass, pottery, and silver are exceptions to this rule. These are listed CATEGORY, PATTERN, OBJECT, DESCRIPTION. All items are presumed to be in good condition and undamaged, unless otherwise noted. If a maker's name is easily recognized, like Gustav Stickley, we include it near the beginning of the entry. If the maker is obscure, the name may be at the end.

Many general glass entries are in special categories: Glass-Art, Glass-Blown, Glass-Bohemian, Glass-Contemporary, Glass-Midcentury, and Glass-Venetian. Major glass factories are listed under factory names. Well-known types of glass, cut, pressed, Depression, carnival, etc., are in their own categories. You will find silver flatware in either Silver Flatware Plated or Silver Flatware Sterling. There is a section for Silver Plate, which includes coffeepots, trays, and other plated pieces. Solid or sterling silver is listed by country, so look for Silver-American, Silver-Danish, Silver-English, etc. Silver jewelry is listed under jewelry. Most pottery and porcelain is listed by factory name, such as Weller; or by item, such as Calendar Plate; or in sections like Dinnerware or Kitchen; or in a special section, Pottery-Art, Pottery-Contemporary, Pottery-Midcentury, etc.

We make arbitrary decisions. Fishing has its own category, but hunting is part of the category called Sports. We have omitted all guns except toys. It is not legal to sell weapons without a special license, so guns are not part of the general antiques market. Airguns, BB guns, rocket guns, and others are listed in the Toy section. Everything is listed according to the computer alphabetizing system. This means words such as "Mt." are alphabetized as "M-T," not as "M-O-U-N-T." All numerals are before all letters; thus "2" comes before "A."

A butter dish is a "butter." A salt dish is called a "salt" to differentiate it from a saltshaker. It is always "sugar and creamer," never "creamer and sugar." Political collectors often refer to "pinbacks," the round celluloid or tin pins decorated with candidates' names and faces. We use the word "button" instead of "pinback." The word "button" is also used when referring to fasteners on clothing. Where one dimension is given, it is the height; or if the object is round, the dimension is the diameter. The height of a picture is listed before width. Glass is clear unless a color is indicated.

Every entry is listed alphabetically, but idiosyncrasies of language remain. Antiques terms, such as "Sheffield" or "Pratt," have two meanings. Read the paragraph headings to know the meaning used. All category headings are based on the language of the average person, and we use terms like "mud figures" even if not technically correct.

This book does *not* include price listings for fine art paintings, antiquities, stamps, coins, or most types of books. *Big Little Books* and similar children's books *are* included. Comic books are listed only in special categories like Superman, but original comic art and cels *are* listed in their own categories.

Prices for items pictured can be found in the appropriate category. Look for the matching entry with the abbreviation "Illus."

The last computer entries are added in June. Human help finds prices and checks accuracy. We edit more than 55,000 entries down to the approximately 45,000 entries found here. We correct spelling, remove incorrect data, write category paragraphs, and decide on new categories. We proofread copy and prices at least six times, but there will always be some misspelled words and other errors. Information in the paragraphs is updated each year and this year more than thirty updates and additions were made.

Prices are reported from the United States, Canada, and Europe, converted to U.S. dollars. The average rate of exchange between June 2004 and June 2005 was about $0.79 U.S. to $1 Canadian and $1.27 U.S. to ¤1 (one euro). Prices are from auctions, shops, Internet sales, and shows. Every price is checked for accuracy, but we are not responsible for errors.

We cannot answer your letters asking for information. But write if you have requests for categories to be included in future editions or corrections to the paragraphs.

When you see us at shows and flea markets, stop and say hello. Don't be surprised if we ask for your suggestions. You can write to us at P.O. Box 22200-K, Beachwood, Ohio 44122, or visit us at our website, www.kovels.com.

RALPH & TERRY KOVEL
October 2005

ACKNOWLEDGMENTS

We thank those at Random House Reference for working through the unique way we write a price book. Our editor, Mark LaFlaur, guided the book and made sure it was better than ever and on time. He had a challenge this year as we changed to an all-color book. David Naggar, president of the Random House Information Group; Sheryl Stebbins, vice president and publisher of Random House Reference; Beth Levy, associate managing editor; Lisa Montebello, production manager; Fabrizio LaRocca, creative director; Moon Sun Kim, designer; and Oriana Leckert all worked together to create the final book. We are also grateful to former editor Dorothy Harris for her guidance and encouragements. Merri Ann Morrell at Precision Graphics once again solved the problems of forcing data to create printed pages and clear photographs.

The hard work of recording prices, assembling photographs and information, checking and rechecking entries for accuracy, and all other details is done by our staff first. We thank Carmie Amata, Linda Coulter, Grace DeFrancisco, Doris Gerbitz, Marcia Goldberg, Evelyn Hayes, Katie Karrick, Kim Kovel, Liz Lillis, Heidi Makela, Tina McBean, Nancy Saada, Julie Seaman, June Smith, and Cherrie Smrekar. Benjamin Margalit took some of the photographs and managed to show the details and styles that interest collectors. Other pictures came from auctions and dealers. Karen Kneisley has conquered the problems of getting and reproducing pictures using all forms of digital technology. But Gay Hunter keeps us on schedule, reads the copy, keeps up-to-date information for paragraphs, solves hundreds of unexpected problems, and works around the computer glitches. She has survived a year of quick turnarounds, and problems created by the all-color format. This is her twenty-fifth book and her knowledge is encyclopedic. We thank all of them because we know even though our names are on the book, we couldn't do it without their expertise.

THIRTY-EIGHTH EDITION

KOVELS'
ANTIQUES
& COLLECTIBLES

PRICE LIST

FOR THE 2006 MARKET
ILLUSTRATED

A. WALTER made pate-de-verre glass under contract at the Daum glassworks from 1908 to 1914. He started his own firm in Nancy, France, in 1919. Pieces made before 1914 are signed *Daum, Nancy* with a cross. After 1919 the signature is *A. Walter Nancy*.

Bowl, Hermit Crab, Seaweed, Organic Form, Signed, 3 3/4 x 9 In.	4200.00
Box, Cover, Blue, Mottled Ground, Berries, Flowers, Yellow, Green, Red, 5 3/4 x 3 1/2 In.	6000.00
Box, Cover, Blue, Pinecone, Circular, Signed, 2 1/2 x 2 3/4 In.	2880.00
Change Receiver, Lizard, Henri Bere, c.1920, 4 x 8 In.	5975.00
Dish, Blue Fish Swimming, Green, Yellow Swirls, Signed, 7 1/2 x 5 In.	3450.00
Inkwell, Cover, Lizard Stalking Bee, Bunch Of Grapes, Signed, 3 3/4 In.	8337.00
Inkwell, Double, Beetle, Henri Berge, c.1920, 2 1/4 x 6 1/2 In.	3824.00
Jar, Cover, Amber Shaded To Orange, Cat Finial, Round, Straight Sides, 4 In.	1093.00
Paperweight, Butterfly, Multicolored, Spread Wings, Base, Signed, Nancy, 1 1/2 x 4 In.	3000.00
Pen Tray, Brown Beetle, Pinchers, 2 Parts, 9 1/2 In.	2300.00
Tray, Lizard Resting On Blossom, Butterscotch Ground, Signed, 8 3/4 In.	5400.00
Tray, Moth, Blue, Yellow, Green, Brown, c.1910, 5 In.	1150.00
Vase, Green Leaves, Brown Vines, Green Berries, Handles, Signed, 4 1/2 x 7 In.	3600.00

ABC plates, or children's alphabet plates, were most popular from 1780 to 1860, but are still being made. The letters on the plate were meant as teaching aids for children learning to read. The plates were made of pottery, porcelain, metal, or glass. Mugs and other items were also made with alphabet decorations.

Bowl, Tiny Todkins, Playing Baseball, Decal, Gold Rim, D.E. McNicol, W. Va., 8 1/2 In.	32.00
Plate, American Sports, Baseball Running To First Base, 1860, 6 In.	660.00
Plate, Boys On Stilts, Black Transfer, Hand Colored, Embossed Rim, J & G Meakin, 6 In.	50.00
Plate, Boys Playing Marbles, Black Transfer, Hand Colored, Embossed Rim, 5 1/2 In.	115.00
Plate, Dog Wearing Glasses, Framed By Japanese Fan, Green Transfer, Adams, 8 1/4 In.	35.00
Plate, Girls, Umbrella, Brown Transfer, Hand Colored, Embossed Rim, Malkin, 7 In.	65.00
Plate, Horse's Head, Japanese Fan, Mulberry Transfer, Adams & Sons, 6 7/8 In.	65.00
Plate, Hunters, Dogs, Brown Transfer, Ironstone, 6 3/4 In.	175.00
Plate, Man, Automaton, Children, Black Transfer, Embossed Rim, Staffordshire, 5 In.	140.00
Plate, Man, Felled Tree, Little Strokes Fell Great Oaks, Hand Colored, Embossed Rim, 6 In.	45.00
Plate, Mary Had A Little Lamb, Embossed Scene & Rim, Tin, 1870s, 8 In.	40.00
Plate, Mother & Daughter, Brown Transfer, Hand Colored, Embossed Rim, 5 1/2 In.	65.00
Plate, Two Men, One In Cap & Gown, Riddle, Black Transfer, 7 In.	150.00

ABINGDON POTTERY was established in 1908 by Raymond E. Bidwell as the Abingdon Sanitary Manufacturing Company. The company started making art pottery in 1934. The factory ceased production of art pottery in 1950.

Ashtray, Advertising, Embossed Words, Brown Glaze, 5 1/2 In.	30.00
Bookends, Russian Dancers, White Glaze, Paper Label, Early 1930s, 8 1/2 In.	285.00
Bust, Indian Maiden, White Glaze, 5 In.	100.00
Cigarette Box, White Streamlined Base, Black Elephant Cover, 6 x 6 In.	165.00
Cookie Jar, Humpty Dumpty	120.00
Cookie Jar, Humpty Dumpty, Marked, 11 In.	260.00
Cookie Jar, Painted Flowers, No. 697, 7 1/2 In.	75.00
Pitcher, Fern Leaf, Green Matte Glaze, No. 430, 8 In.	100.00
Trinket Dish, Blue Leaf Shape Base, White Flower Cover, 3 x 9 1/2 In.	180.00
Vase, Grecian Urn Shape, Embossed Border, Gray Glaze, 15 1/2 In.	80.00
Vase, Morning Glory, White Glaze, No. 390, 10 In.	80.00
Vase, Red Glaze, Bulbous Base, Tapered Neck, Buttressed Leaf Handles, 1940, 5 In.	240.00
Wall Pocket, Double Morning Glory, Blue Glaze, No. 375, 7 1/2 x 8 1/2 In.	30.00
Wall Pocket, Double Morning Glory, Fawn Glaze, No. 375, 7 1/2 x 8 1/2 In.	35.00

ADAMS china was made by William Adams and Sons of Staffordshire, England. The firm was founded in 1769 and became part of the Wedgwood Group in 1966. The name "Adams" appeared on various items through 1998. All types of tablewares and useful wares were made. Other pieces of Adams may be found listed under Flow Blue and Tea Leaf Ironstone.

Cup & Saucer, Handleless, Adams' Rose, Leaves, 2-Tone, Blue, Spatter	115.00

Mug, Adams' Rose, Straight-Sided, Handle, Child's, 2 1/4 In. 798.00
Pitcher, Adams' Rose, Blue, Red, Paneled, Molded Handle, Spatter, 8 In. 460.00
Plate, Adams' Rose, Rainbow, Blue, Purple Border, Spatterware, 9 5/8 In. 430.00
Platter, Adams' Rose, Blue Spatter, Octagonal, c.1830, 13 1/2 x 8 1/4 In. 1175.00
Soup, Dish, Philadelphia In The Regent Park, 8 7/8 In. 165.00
Waste Bowl, Adams' Rose, Scalloped Edge, 2 3/4 x 5 1/2 In. 1100.00

ADVERTISING containers and products sold in the old country store
are now all collectibles. These stores, with the crackers in a barrel and
a potbellied stove, are a symbol of an earlier, less hectic time. Listed
here are many of the advertising items. Other similar pieces may be
found under the product name, such as Planters Peanuts. We have tried
to list items in the logical places, so large store fixtures will be found
under the Architectural category, enameled tin dishes under Graniteware, paper items in the Paper category, etc. Store fixtures, cases,
signs, and other items that have no advertising as part of the decoration
are listed in the Store category. For information, see *Kovels' Advertising Collectibles Price List.*

Ad, Magazine, Cream Of Wheat, 2 Boys Eating, Edward Brewer, 1923, 10 x 13 In. 22.00
Ashtray, Adolph Coors Co., Golden, Colorado 10.00
Ashtray, Aristocrat Brewery, Tin Lithograph, Round, 4 1/2 In. 33.00
Ashtray, Black & White Scotch Whisky, 2 Dogs, Square, 5 In. 55.00
Ashtray, Budweiser, Bucket, Clip, Metal, Cheinco, 4 1/4 In. 18.00
Ashtray, Coors, A. Coors Co., Golden, Colorado, Embossed, Pottery, 5 3/4 In. 22.00
Ashtray, Corning Glass Works, Smoky Glass, 1960-70, 6 3/4 x 4 3/4 In. 22.00
Ashtray, Dinah's Shack, Palo Alto, California, Black, Gold Accents, Japan, 5 1/4 In. 89.00
Ashtray, Gallagher & Burton Whiskey, Tin Lithograph, Round, 4 1/2 In. 33.00
Ashtray, General Electric, GE Logo, Metal, 1950s, 4 In. Diam. 18.00
Ashtray, Greenfield Recorder, Glass, August 1, 1968, 8 3/4 x 6 3/4 In. 12.00
Ashtray, Harold's Club Casino, Play Longer, Win More, Black Amethyst Glass, 4 In. 12.00
Ashtray, Holiday Inn, World's Innkeeper, Glass, Octagonal, 4 3/4 In. 10.00
Ashtray, Howard Johnson, Orange Roof, Glass, Applied Label, 4 1/2 In. Diam. 14.00
Ashtray, Johnnie Walker, Born 1820, Still Going Strong, Square, 4 In. 41.00
Ashtray, Key City Diner, Phillipsburg, New Jersey, 4 1/4 In. 29.00
Ashtray, Kodak Park Athletic Assoc., Smoky Glass, 1910-60, 5 3/4 x 3 3/4 In. 16.00
Ashtray, Pollits Motel, Air Cooled, Steam Heat, Glass, Oval, Palmyra, Mo., 4 x 3 In. 16.00
Ashtray, S&H Green Stamps, Glass, 6 x 4 x 1 1/2 In. 15.00
Ashtray, Sanka Coffee, 3-Sided, Black Glass, 4 1/2 In. 18.00
Ashtray, Slim Jims, 10 Cents, Make Your Next Drink Taste Better, Phila., Pa. 12.00
Ashtray, Smokey The Bear, Aluminum, Embossed, 4 Different Colors, 4 In., 4 Piece 20.00
Ashtray, Watertown Cream Ale, Watertown Brewery, 3 3/4 x 2 In. 55.00
Ashtray, Woman, Spreads Dress, Art Nouveau, Kenton Hardware, Iron Toys, 6 x 7 In. 138.00
Bag, Leroy Shot & Lead Works, Wind Tower Shot, Eagle, 25 Lb. 72.00
Bag Holder, Red Rock Cola, Enjoy, Red, White, 23 x 19 x 5 In. 330.00
Ball, Borden, Elsie's West Texas State Buffaloes, Plastic, 4 In. 29.00
Banner, Argo Starch, For Best Results, Girl Holding Doll, 18 x 35 In. 220.00
Banner, Blue Lick, Queen Of Health Waters, Cloth, 12 x 48 In. 55.00
Banner, Marble's Specialties For Sportsmen, Felt, Blue, Triangular, 32 x 9 1/2 In. 975.00
Banner, Mayo's Plug, Light & Dark, Rooster, On Crates, Canvas, 32 x 20 In. 275.00
Banner, Schenley, Whiskey, Cesar Romero, Cloth, Wood Dowel, 1950s, 38 x 30 In. 87.00
Banner, Union Leader, Uncle Sam, Best Tobacco Value, Cloth, 35 x 90 In. 220.00
Banner, Victrola, Victor Records, Fabric, Lithograph, 35 In. 825.00
Barrel, Richardson Root Beer, Rich In Flavor, Tap, 26 x 14 In. 165.00
Barrel, Schreiber Brewing, Oak, Red Paint, No Lid, Buffalo, N.Y., 25 1/2 x 18 In. 230.00
Beer Tap, Coors Extra Gold, Acrylic, Gold Tone, Metal Tap Screw, 1980s 18.00
Bench, Star Brand Shoes Are Better, Pierced Back, Painted, Early 1900s 646.00
Bin, Beacon Java Coffee, Boyd, Leeds & Co., Tin, 20 x 13 In. 490.00
Bin, Dwinwll-Wright Co., Boston Coffees, Wood, Paper Labels, 20 x 19 In. 177.00
Bin, King Bee Coffee, Canby, Slanted Lift Top, Stenciled, Painted, Late 1800s, 26 1/4 In. . 440.00
Bin, Mocha Coffee, Tin, Late 1800s, 17 In. 275.00
Bin, Parke's Dry Roast, Tin, Late 1800s, 21 In. 990.00
Bin, Walter McEwan Co., Japanned & Stenciled, 16 x 16 x 16 In. 220.00
Bin, Woods Boston Coffees, Tin, 21 x 20 x 12 In. 220.00

Bin, Woolson's Spice Co., Old Dominion Roast, Orange, Stenciled, Tin, 28 x 19 In. 440.00
Blotter, Chase & Sanborn, Seal Brand Coffee & Tea 7.00
Blotter, Lawson-Cavette Sporting Goods Co., It Pays To Play, May, 1951 .... 9.00
Blotter, Morton Salt, Costs A Family About 2 Cents A Week, Blue Paper 7.00
Blotter, Morton Salt, When It Rains-It Pours, Vegetables Sliding Down Salt Mound 9.00
Blotter, Nestle's, Cherub & Stork, Celluloid, 1910 .... 75.00
Blotter, Shredded Wheat Biscuit, For Your Health & Strength, Easy To Digest 9.00
Blotter, Sneath Glass Co., Teddy Roosevelt, Girl, Hartford City, c.1900, 4 x 9 In. 58.00
Books may be included in the Paper category.
Book Cover, Fresh Up With 7Up, Compliments Of 7Up Bottling Co., 1939 .... 15.00
Booklet, Hires Root Beer, Owl, Parrot, Malvern, Pa., c.1900, 2 1/2 x 5 1/2 In., 8 Pages ... 35.00
Booklet, Kellogg's, Funny Jungleland, Moving Pictures, Premium, 1932, 3 Pages 38.00
Booklet, Kellogg's, Nursery Rhymes, 1931, 8 1/4 x 3 3/4 In., 16 Pages 20.00
Booklet, Red Rose & Blue Ribbon Tea, Space Age, Brooke Bond Album, 1969 .... 12.00
Boot Jack, Musselmans Bootjack Tobacco, Embossed, Cast Iron 230.00
Bottles are listed in their own category.
Bottle Openers are listed in their own category.
Box, see also Box category.
Box, Adams Sweet Fern Chewing Gum, Girl, Flowers In Hair, Cardboard, 9 x 5 In. 95.00
Box, Around The World Candy, Ship, Globe, Cardboard, 1936, 2 3/4 x 2 1/2 In. 34.00
Box, Bixby Best Blacking, Wood, 11 x 11 x 4 In. 55.00
Box, Bromo-Seltzer, Dovetailed, $1.75, 15 1/2 x 12 x 8 1/2 In. 265.00
Box, Cereal, Kellogg's Cocoa Krispies, Snagglepuss, Doll Offer, c.1963, 12 x 17 In. 270.00
Box, Cereal, Kellogg's Raisin Bran, Sonic Wave Gun, Flat, Unused, c.1960, 11 x 16 In. ... 100.00
Box, Cereal, Kellogg's Rice Krispies, H.R. Pufnstuf, Woody Woodpecker, 1970, 8 x 12 In. 175.00
Box, Cereal, Kellogg's Stars, Hillbilly Goat, Flat, c.1963, 11 x 17 In. 235.00
Box, Cereal, Post Honey Comb, Rescue Kit, 1967, 13 x 20 1/2 In. 100.00
Box, Cereal, Post Oat Flakes, Gomer Pyle, 10 Oz., 11 x 16 1/2 In. 175.00
Box, Cereal, Post Sugar Crisp, Sugar Bear, Fun 'n Games, c.1967, 13 x 20 In. 100.00
Box, Cereal, Washington Crisps Corn Flakes, Oversized, Washington, 1900 .... 1870.00
Box, Cigar, King Polly Cigars, Lewistown, Pa., 1910 .... 106.00
Box, Colgan's, Taffee Tolu Gum, Wood, Handle, 17 x 9 x 8 In. 550.00
Box, Colgate, Florient Face Powder, Flowers, Contents, c.1920, 1 1/2 x 3 x 3 In. 49.00
Box, Cool Candy Cigarettes, World Candies Inc., Brooklyn, N.Y., 1960s, 2 3/4 x 1 In. 9.00
Box, Dana's Sarsaparilla, Kind That Cures, Wood, Belfast, Maine, 11 x 9 x 10 In. 99.00
Box, Display, Adams Tutti Frutti Gum, Glass, Card Game, 4 1/2 x 1 1/4 x 10 In. 90.00
Box, Display, Esterbrook Pens, Celebrated Steel Pens, Gold Letters, Wood, 15 x 14 In. 77.00
Box, Display, Fairbank's Fairy Soap, Christmas Box, Lithograph Label, 16 x 16 In. 250.00
Box, Display, Hornady Bullets, 176 Bullets, Molded, 22 1/2 x 17 In. 145.00
Box, Display, Rush Park Seed, Unrivaled Garden Seeds, Dovetailed, 6 x 31 In. 290.00
Box, Dr. Fosters Uterine Applicator, Ladies Friend, Bloomville, Oh., 3 x 6 1/4 In. 470.00
Box, Dr. Hubbards Kidney & Bladder Capsules, They Never Fail, 2 1/2 x 2 1/8 In. 60.00
Box, Dr. McLane's Liver Pills, Fleming Bros. Proprietors, Red, Black, White, 5 x 3 In. 70.00
Box, Dr. Pierce's Favorite Prescription, Wood, Dovetailed, 10 1/2 x 9 In. 265.00
Box, Dr. Starkey & Palen Compound Oxygen, Wood, Brass Clasp, 4 x 6 1/2 In. 145.00
Box, Elysian Complexion Powder, Woman, 3 x 3 In. 90.00
Box, Excelsior Brand Bird Gravel, Color Graphics, Songbirds, Children, 5 x 3 In. 187.00
Box, F.C. Sturtevant Co., Columbia Powdered Tobacco, Poultry, 7 x 4 5/8 In. 99.00
Box, Ford Charcoal Briquets, Cardboard, Family Picnic, Contents, 3 x 7 3/4 In. ..... *Illus* 45.00
Box, Home Brand Oats, Cylindrical, 3 Lb. 7 Oz. 85.00
Box, Ivory Snow, Marilyn Chambers, Early 1970s, 13 Oz., 8 1/2 x 6 In. 80.00
Box, J. Balch & Son, Man With Bellows In Front Of Oven, 2 x 2 5/8 In. 50.00
Box, J.A. Goddard Co., Delicious Brand Oats, Cardboard, Color, 6 1/4 x 4 In., 14 Oz. 55.00
Box, Jergens, Rachel, 3 Women, 1 Oz., 2 1/2 x 2 1/2 x 1 In. 40.00
Box, Kerr Blue Inlay Casting Wax, Contents, 3/4 Oz. 12.00
Box, Lee's Absorbent Gauze, 4 Drawers, Contents, Paper Label, 6 x 9 In. 165.00
Box, Liggets United Chocolate Candy, Little Bits From The East, 3 1/2 x 2 1/2 In. 40.00
Box, Masons Boot Blacking, 8 x 10 1/2 x 2 1/2 In. 45.00
Box, Mrs. Dinsmore's Cough Drops, Woman, 10 Cents, Yellow, 3 3/8 x 2 1/8 In. Diam. ... 100.00
Box, Mrs. Moffat's Shoo Fly Powders, For Drunkenness, 25 Cents, 1 x 2 5/8 In. 290.00
Box, Ney's Hay Rack Clamps, Hinged Lid, Contents, Instructions, Wood, 4 1/2 x 18 In. ... 45.00
Box, No. 2 Formosa Tea, Oval House & River Scene, Wood, 19th Century, 22 In. 3910.00
Box, None Such Mince Meat, Like Mother Used To Make, Wood, 6 x 14 x 6 In. 55.00

Advertising, Box, Ford Charcoal Briquets,
Cardboard, Family Picnic, Contents, 3 x 7 3/4 In.

Advertising, Box, Selected Eggs, One Dozen,
Chicken, Cardboard, 1950s, 2 x 11 x 3 3/4 In.

Box, Popps German Stomach Powder, Chronic Dyspepsia, Chicago, Ill., 2 x 4 In. 255.00
Box, Prof. Branwhites Herbine, Man In Cowboy Hat, McKeesport, 2 7/8 x 1 1/2 In. 20.00
Box, Red Cloud Cigar, Lithograph Labels, Tax Stamp, 1880s 115.00
Box, Selected Eggs, One Dozen, Chicken, Cardboard, 1950s, 2 x 11 x 3 3/4 In. ...... *Illus* 20.00
Box, Stanley No. 7506 Tape Rules, 6 Rules 600.00
Box, Steele, Briggs Famous Seeds, Wood, 3 Hinges, Dovetailed, 11 x 4 1/2 x 22 In. 470.00
Box, Sweet Mist Chewing Tobacco, Cardboard, Tin Lid, Bottom, 10 x 8 x 6 In. 75.00
Box, Turkey Red Cigarette, Woman Wearing Fez, 1910, 3 x 2 x 1/2 In. 535.00
Box, University Oats, Cylindrical, 3 Lb. 7 Oz. 165.00
Box, Whitman, Pleasure Island Chocolates, Cloth Bags, Paper Lithograph, Doily, 1924 ... 145.00
Box, Wood, Mason's Patent No. 30, 1858, Fruit Jars, 13 x 16 1/2 x 8 In. 85.00
Box, Wood, O. & W. Thum Co., Sealed Sticky Fly Paper, 11 1/2 x 17 x 16 In. 59.00
Box, Worlds Par-More Tooth & Gums, Woman, Cardboard, Cylindrical, 3 In. 88.00
Brochure, Zeppelin Airline, Hamburg America Line, Late 1920s, 6 x 9 In., 16 Pages 150.00
Broom Holder, Bond Bread, 2 Porcelain Signs, Wooden, 19 x 14 In. 175.00
Broom Holder, King Oscar, A Good Cigar, Tin, 2-Sided, 30 x 20 In. 300.00
Button, 7Up, Zorro, Celluloid, Pinback, Walt Disney Productions, 1957, 1 1/4 In. 15.00
Button, America's Best Known Baby, Gerber Baby, Black, White, Celluloid, 3 In. 75.00
Button, Bond Bread, First Flight Paris To New York, Celluloid, No. 4 .... 38.00
Button, Borden, Elsie The Cow, Metal, 1 1/2 In. 12.00
Button, Charms Candy, Enamel, 2 1/2 x 3/4 In. 65.00
Button, DuPont, Established 1802, Multicolored, Whitehead & Hoag, Oval, 1 In. 20.00
Button, DuPont, Prosperity Follows Dynamite, Exploding Stump, Brown & Bigelow 68.00
Button, General Electric, GE Logo, Figural Motor, Silver Metal, 2 1/2 x 1 1/2 In. 29.00
Button, George Washington Soda, Red, White, Blue, Celluloid, 7/8 In. 18.00
Button, Golden Guernsey, America's Table Milk, Celluloid, Pinback, Peterboro, N.H. 36.00
Button, High Admiral Cigarettes, Yellow Kid, No. 2, 1894 .... 50.00
Button, High Admiral Tobacco, It's Naughty But It's Nice, Celluloid 35.00
Button, Holsum Bread, I'm Not A Breakfast Battler, Tin, June 56, 2 In. 14.00
Button, Lucas Paint, Best Value Made, Multicolored, Celluloid, 7/8 In. 14.00
Button, Nabisco Golden Anniversary, 1898-1948, Celluloid, Young Boy, 1 1/2 In. 35.00
Button, Pabst, Milwaukee, Red, Black, Gold, White, Celluloid, 7/8 In. 16.00
Button, Pearline Soap, Bell, Hello Give Me Pearline, Celluloid 18.00
Button, Pepsin Gum, Black Boy In Uniform, Walking Stick, Sepia Photo, c.1900, 1 In. ... 25.00
Button, Popeye's Famous Fried Chicken, Black, Yellow, Cream, 1981, 1 1/8 In. 23.00
Button, Quaker Oats, Box, Try Me, 30 Days, Celluloid, 1 1/4 In. 28.00
Button, Simmons Keen Kutter, Ax Head Shape, 10K Gold, Hinged, 1 1/4 In. 340.00
Button, Steiff Toy Animals, Look For Button, Blue, Orange, White, Celluloid, 7/8 In. 140.00
Button, Tokio Cigarettes, Blind-I Can't See You, Blue, White, Premium, 3/4 In. 36.00
Cabinet, American Beauty Iron, Woman Ironing, Oak, Glass, 25 x 12 x 12 In. 950.00
Cabinet, Diamond Dyes, Balloons, Children, Tin Lithograph, 24 1/2 x 15 x 8 In. 1850.00
Cabinet, Diamond Dyes, Court Jester, Women, 27 x 20 x 9 In. 1650.00
Cabinet, Diamond Dyes, Washerwoman, 24 In. 1650.00
Cabinet, Dy-O-La Dyes, For All Goods, Wooden, 16 1/2 x 13 x 8 In. 135.00
Cabinet, Humphrey's Veterinary Remedies, Animals, Tin Lithograph, 28 x 21 x 10 In. 1540.00
Cabinet, Lance, Cracker, Red, 4 Shelves, 18 x 10 x 2 In. 135.00
Cabinet, Mays Seed, Tin, Footed, 29 x 22 x 5 In. 220.00
Cabinet, Putnam Dyes Tints, Colonel Putnam On Horse, Tin, Contents, 14 x 18 In. 220.00
Cabinet, Putnam Dyes Tints, Fadeless, Display, 9 x 15 In. 80.00

Cabinet, Spool, Clark's O.N.T., Oak, Doors, 14 Glass Displays, Turntable, 20 x 23 In. 805.00
Cabinet, Spool, Clark's O.N.T., Walnut, 2 Glass Front Drawers, Brass, 22 x 16 In. 345.00
Cabinet, Spool, Clark's O.N.T., Walnut, 3 Drawers, Porcelain Knobs, 22 x 9 1/2 x 15 In. ... 290.00
Cabinet, Spool, Corticelli, Oak, 2 Drawers, Stenciled Fronts, 14 3/4 x 4 x 9 1/2 In. 86.00
Cabinet, Spool, J. & P. Coats', 2 Glass Sides, Revolving, 23 x 15 In. 2395.00
Cabinet, Spool, J. & P. Coats', Grained Metal, 3 Drawers, Countertop, 19 x 17 x 6 In. 290.00
Cabinet, Spool, J. & P. Coats', Oak, Doors, Glass Displays, Turntable, 20 x 23 In. 865.00
Cabinet, Spool, Merrick's, 6-Cord, Standard Spool Cotton, Wooden 440.00
Cabinet, Spool, Merrick's, Oak, Curved Tambour Door, Glass Panels, 18 x 20 In. 3165.00
Cabinet, Starrett Tools, Oak, Hardware Store, 44 In. 1320.00
Cake Decorating Kit, Swans Down Cake Mix, Football, 1950s 16.00
Calendars are listed in their own category.
Can, American Eagle Co., Old Tar Tobacco, Hinged Lid, 2 1/4 x 3 7/8 In. 99.00
Can, Blue Boar, Rough Cut, 6 In. 110.00
Can, Colgate, Toothpowder, New 15 Cent Size, 1950s 18.00
Can, DeLaval Oil, Centrifugally Clarified & Filtered, Horizontal, 6 x 6 1/2 In. 55.00
Can, Hot Spur Mixture Tobacco, Tin Lithograph, Rooster, 3 3/8 x 4 1/2 x 2 3/8 In. 155.00
Can, Nylotis Baby Powder, Babies, Storks, Tin Lithograph, 4 3/4 x 2 1/4 x 1 1/4 In. 255.00
Can, Old Dutch Cleanser, Girl, Lithograph, Yellow Ground, 6 1/4 In. 55.00
Can, Rawleigh's Talc, Tin Lithograph, Circus Characters, 7 5/8 x 3 x 2 In. 110.00
Can, Two Orphans Cigars, Tin Lithograph, Orphaned Sisters, 50 Count, 5 x 5 In. 255.00
Canisters, see introductory paragraph to Tins in this category.
Cards are listed in the Card category as card, advertising.
Carton, Borden Ice Cream, Elsie The Cow, 1957, Pt. 10.00
Carton, Borden Ice Cream, White House Flavor, 1957, 1/2 Gal. 16.00
Carton, Midwest Ice Cream, Cardboard, Tin Lid, 1950s, 1/2 Gal. 15.00
Case, Display, Boye Needles, Perfect Work Requires A Perfect Needle, 5 Cents, Tin 165.00
Case, Display, Colgan's Gum, Oak, Glass, Countertop, 17 1/2 x 9 1/4 x 8 In. 2090.00
Case, Display, E.C. Simmons, Keen Kutter, Faux Leather, Glass, Hinged, 12 Razors 2285.00
Case, Display, Hibbard Spencer & Bartlett, Metal, Double Top, 6 Knives, 5 3/4 x 4 In. 220.00
Case, Display, J.P. Prowleys California Fruit & Pepsin Chewing Gum, Wood, Glass 495.00
Case, Display, Jones Gum, Curved Glass, Countertop, 9 1/2 x 17 1/2 7 1/2 In. 1045.00
Case, Display, Remington Cutlery, 36 Sections, Wood, c.1922, 11 x 16 x 15 In. 310.00
Case, Display, Tampa Nugget Cigar, 1950s, 22 x 15 x 1 1/4 In. 65.00
Case, Display, Tennyson Cigars, Humidor, Counter, 13 x 9 1/2 In. 220.00
Case, Display, W.R. Case & Sons Cutlery, Etched Glass, Easel Back, 2 x 13 In. 59.00
Case, Ingersoll Watches, Guaranteed, Wooden, 9 1/2 x 12 x 6 3/4 In. 110.00
Catalog, Jim Brown's Farm & Home Supply, Fall & Winter, 1939 .... 55.00
Chair, Salesman's Sample, Harry S. Brown, Furniture Dealer, Pa., Late 1800s, 18 In. 120.00
Change Receiver, see Tip Tray in this category.
Charm, Ideal Dog Food & Good Luck, Verdigris, Metal, 1 In. 85.00
Charm, Roi-Tan Cigars, Car, Shamrock On Door, Gold Tone Metal, 1 1/2 In. 10.00
Cigar Box, Honus Wagner, Supreme Cigar, Hand Made, Long Filler, c.1900 .... 9900.00
Cigar Box, Lid, Star Play, Mahogany, Baseball Game Scene, c.1911 .... 605.00
Cigar Cutter, Artie The Best Cigars, Boy Sitting On Fireplace, Cast Iron, 6 x 7 x 10 In. ... 2640.00
Cigar Cutter, Bauers Kidney Gin, Figural, Pig, Cast Iron, 4 x 7 In. 625.00
Cigar Cutter, Betsy Ross, Cast Iron, Embossed Letters, Patriotic Message, 8 x 6 In. 880.00
Cigar Cutter, Col. J.J. Astor, 5 Cent Cigar, Cast Iron, Clock, Footed Base, 14 x 8 In. 3300.00
Cigar Cutter, Flor Dey Melba, Cast Iron, 6 x 3 1/2 In. 300.00
Cigar Cutter, Las Amantes, Classical Couple, Glass Top, Wood Base, 7 x 8 1/2 x 5 In. 470.00
Cigar Cutter, Red Kamel, Figural, Cast Iron, Embossed Letters, 9 x 8 1/2 In. 600.00
Cigar Cutter, Star Tobacco, Cast Iron, Embossed, 7 x 18 In. 99.00
Cigarette Pack, Players, Magnum Size, Navy Cut, 1940s 30.00
Clicker, Weatherbird, Peters Weatherbird Shoes, Blue Green, Tin 22.00
Clicker, Weatherbird, Rooster, All Leather-For All Weather, Red, Yellow 25.00
Clocks are listed in their own category.
Coaster, Sea View Awnings, Ruffled Edge, 3 In. Diam., 3 Piece 6.00
Coatrack, Whistle, Thirsty, Just Whistle, Wood, 8 x 35 1/2 In. 120.00
Comb, Sunbeam Bread, Reach For Sunbeam, It's Batter Whipped, Blue, Plastic, 5 In. 5.00
Counter Felt, Dead Shot Smokeless, Falling Mallard, 10 1/4 x 11 In. 275.00
Counter Felt, Remington UMC, Arms & Ammunition, 4 Colors, 8 1/2 x 11 1/4 In. 465.00
Counter Felt, Use New DuPont Smokeless, 3-Color Border, 11 1/4 x 13 1/2 In. 245.00
Counter Felt, Winchester Repeating Rifles, 3 Colors, 11 1/2 x 13 1/4 In. 395.00

Coupon Book, Octagon Soap, Premium, 1930 .... 24.00
Crayon Set, Dr Pepper, Pad & Eraser, 1982 .... 12.00
Cuff Links, Mack Trucks, Bulldog, Red, Green, Gold Enamel, Silvertone Metal, 2 Piece ... 29.00
Cup, Cone, Daly's Drive-In Restaurant, Get The Daly Habit, Paper, 6 1/2 In. 7.00
Cup, Dairy Queen Ice Cream, Waxed Paper, 1949, 1 3/4 In. 8.00
Cup, Measuring, Swans Down Cake Flour, Aluminum, Premium, 1 Cup 18.00
Cuspidor, Monogram Cigar, 10 Cents, Porcelain On Tin, 5 x 11 In. 880.00
Decanter, Shot, Barclay 76 Rye, Dry Wheel, Cut Letters, 3 x 2 In. 95.00
Decanter, Shot, Clermont Bourbon, Molded, White Enamel, 3 x 2 In. 165.00
Decanter, Shot, Hearts Of Maryland, Molded, White Enamel, 3 x 2 In. 155.00
Decanter, Shot, Pride Of Ky., Molded, Acid Etched Letters, 3 x 2 In. 98.00
Decanter, Shot, Roosevelt Straight Bourbon, Royal Blue Enamel, Molded, 3 x 2 In. 49.00
Dispenser, Buckeye Root Beer, Ceramic, Original Pump, Cleveland Fruit, 15 In. 2750.00
Dispenser, Buckeye Root Beer, Tree Stump Shape, Pump, 16 x 7 In. 468.00
Dispenser, Douglass Root Beer, Barrel Shape, Ceramic, 15 1/2 In. 415.00
Dispenser, Drink Almond-Smash, Ceramic, Original Pump, 14 In. 11000.00
Dispenser, Drink Birchola, 5 Cents, Ceramic, Original Pump, 14 In. 2750.00
Dispenser, Drink Fowler's Root Beer, 5 Cents, Ceramic, Pump, c.1910, 15 In. 2750.00
Dispenser, Drink Grape-Julep, Ceramic, Original Pump, 14 In. 3575.00
Dispenser, Drink Howel's Cherry-Julep, 5 Cents, Ceramic, Pump, 15 In. 2475.00
Dispenser, Drink Orange-Julep, Ceramic, Original Pump, c.1910, 15 In. 1980.00
Dispenser, Fan-Taz Syrup, Ceramic, Baseball Form, 5 Cents, 16-In. Ball 15400.00
Dispenser, Fowler's Cherry Smash, 5 Cents, Ceramic, Original Pump, c.1900, 16 In. 5500.00
Dispenser, Grapeine Syrup, Brass Base, Top, Engraved, Glass Globe, 39 x 14 1/2 In. 770.00
Dispenser, Green's Muscadine Punch, Barrel Shape, Ceramic, 14 1/2 In. 120.00
Dispenser, Hires Root Beer, 5 Cents, Boy, Mettlach, Villeroy & Boch, 18 1/2 In. 38500.00
Dispenser, Hires Root Beer, Hourglass Form, 1920, 14 3/4 x 8 In. 1185.00
Dispenser, Jersey Creme, Perfect Drink, Original Pump, 12 In. 1870.00
Dispenser, Kirsch's Ice Cream Cone, Clear Glass, Embossed Lid, 8 x 12 In. 440.00
Dispenser, Orange Crush, Ceramic Base, Frosted Glass Globe, 15 1/2 x 8 In. 605.00
Dispenser, Owl's Orange Julep, Figural, Ceramic, Original Pump, 9 x 15 In. 1210.00
Dispenser, Ward's Lemon Crush, Lemon Shape, Ceramic, New Pump, 13 In. 1650.00
Dispenser, Ward's Lime Crush, Lime Shape, Ceramic, New Pump, 13 In. 8800.00
Dispenser, Ward's Orange Crush Syrup, c.1918, 14 3/4 x 8 1/2 In. 1725.00
Dispenser, White King, Embossed, Green Glass, 5 3/4 x 3 In. 65.00
Display, Alka-Seltzer, Tin, 11 In. 105.00
Display, Beech-Nut Chewing Gum, Blue, White, Tin, 11 x 6 In. 165.00
Display, Bicycle & Congress Playing Cards, Die Cut, Cardboard, 11 x 14 In. 1005.00
Display, Bicycle Playing Cards, 12 x 5 x 8 In. 155.00
Display, Bonnie's Hair Net, 15 x 13 x 11 In. 185.00
Display, Bromo-Mint With Caffeine, For Over Indulgence, 10 Cents, 8 3/4 x 8 In. 130.00
Display, Buy Hubley Guns, Metal, 4 Hooks, For Cap Guns, 6 3/4 x 17 x 23 In. 60.00
Display, Clark's Teaberry Gum, Embossed, Clear Glass, Pedestal, 5 x 7 x 4 3/4 In. 99.00
Display, Clark's Teaberry Gum, Embossed, Green Glass, Pedestal, 7 x 3 x 4 In. 210.00
Display, Clark's Teaberry Gum, Vaseline Glass, Pedestal, 7 In. 55.00
Display, Curtiss Baby Ruth, Peppermint Gum, 18 Packages, 6 1/4 x 4 1/2 x 1 In. 660.00
Display, Daisy Air Rifles, Cardboard, Boy With Rifle, 1920s, 49 In. 4400.00
Display, Daisy Air Rifles, Gun Racks, Sliding Doors, Countertop, 36 x 18 1/2 x 15 In. 375.00
Display, DeLaval Separator Oil, Brochure, Tin, 11 x 17 In. 55.00
Display, Dover Electric Iron, Will Not Burn Out, Wooden, 4 Irons 500.00
Display, Hickory Elastic, Wood, Glass, 12 x 8 x 12 In. 82.00
Display, Hubley Mighty Metal Toys, Tin, For Cap Gun & Toys, 6 3/4 x 17 x 23 In. 88.00
Display, Kutie-Vu, 12 Key Chains, On Card, Views Of Naked Women, 1950s 85.00
Display, Leisy's Light Beer, Bottle Shape, Glass, Yellow & Blue Label, 30 In. 110.00
Display, Little Boy Blue, Bluing, 1 Bottle, Self-Serving, Tin, Wall Mount, 19 x 4 In. 100.00
Display, Milk Wagon, Horse, Borden's Farm Products, Milk & Cream, 60 In. 10450.00
Display, P.O.C. Pilsner, Bottle Shape, Glass, Gold, Black & Gold Label, 30 In. 165.00
Display, Pabst Blue Ribbon, Bottle Shape, Glass, White, Blue & Gold, 30 In. 85.00
Display, Remington Boy Scout Knife, 12 Slots, Wood, 1920s, 15 1/2 x 5 In. 925.00
Display, Remington, It's A Beauty, Rifle, Cardboard, Stand-Up, 32 x 13 In. 165.00
Display, Stearn's Electric Paste, 3 Panels, Cardboard, Graphic, 45 x 35 1/2 In. 3450.00
Display, Steinhaus Lager Bottle Shape, Glass, Gold Label, 20 In. 165.00
Display, Union Leader Cut Plug, Cardboard, Uncle Sam, Can Of Tobacco, 12 x 9 In. 880.00

Display, Walnut, Label, Clapp & Baileys Remnants, Box, Counter, 5 x 16 x 16 In. 55.00
Display, Winchester Knives, 12 Sections, Black Box, Counter, 12 1/2 x 4 3/4 In. 1386.00
Display, Winchester Wrenches, W146, Wood, Easel Back, 58 1/4 x 18 In. 2210.00
Display, Yello-Bole, Kay Woodie, 12 Pipes, Wood, 17 x 18 In. 660.00
Display Board, Best Made Cigarette Holders, 12 Holders, 1960s, 6 x 12 In. 23.10
Display Board, Slaymaker Padlox, Cardboard, 12 Locks 65.00
Display Board, Winchester Bullets, Frame, c.1954, 34 1/2 x 50 In. 828.00
Display Board, Yello-Bole, Honey In The Bowl, 16 x 18 In. 110.00
Dolls are listed in their own category.
Door Push, Bireley's Soda, Bottle, Tin Lithograph, Embossed, 12 x 3 In. 190.00
Door Push, Bireley's, Natural Thing To Drink, Bottle, Orange, Tin, 1940, 9 x 4 In. 165.00
Door Push, Braun's Town Talk Bread, Metal, Bronze, 18 1/2 x 3 1/4 In. 90.00
Door Push, Dr Pepper, Red, White, Porcelain, 5 x 13 In. 99.00
Door Push, Duke's Mixture Tobacco, Porcelain, Color Graphics, 8 5/8 x 4 1/4 In. 330.00
Door Push, Fawn Beverage Co., Elmira, N.Y., Tin Lithograph, 9 x 3 3/4 In. 230.00
Door Push, Frings Cigars, 3 Bros., Cuesta Rey, Yellow, Red, Black, Tin, 9 x 3 In. 49.00
Door Push, Henkel's Flour, Please Shut The Door, Cobalt Blue, Porcelain, 8 x 3 In. 90.00
Door Push, Hires, Got A Minute?, Your Invitation To Refresh, Metal, Blue, 32 1/2 In. 100.00
Door Push, Hires, Refreshes Right, Yellow, Red, Black, Porcelain, 33 1/2 In. 20.00
Door Push, Red Rose Coffee & Tea, Red, White, Blue, Tin, 3 x 31 In. 220.00
Door Push, Tip Top Bread, Tin Lithograph, 13 1/2 x 2 1/2 x 1 In. 145.00
Door Push, Tru-Ade, Naturally Delicious, Yellow & Red, Metal, 32 1/2 In. 50.00
Door Push, Ward's Orange Crush, Come In, Bottle, Tin, 1920, 12 x 3 In. 110.00
Envelope, Savage Hammerless Rifles & Ammunition, c.1904 . . . . 1525.00
Fans are listed in their own category.
Fan Pull, Mission Orange Soda, Cardboard, 2-Sided 18.00
Figure, Big Bill Best Bitters, Portly Man, Plaster, c.1900, 15 In. 1675.00
Figure, Big Boy, Bobbin' Head, 1950s, 7 1/2 In. 265.00
Figure, Burger King, Cape, Crown, Hamburger, Ring, Bag, Stand, 1980, 19 1/2 In. 40.00
Figure, Captain Morgan, Rum, Rubberoid, Square Base, 12 1/2 In. 245.00
Figure, Cenol, Insect, Chalkware, Light-Up, Box, 24 In. 815.00
Figure, Christo Cola, Turtle, Celluloid Back, Cast Metal Turtle Base, 1 1/2 In. 155.00
Figure, Corona Coffee, Mule, Composition, 1940s 165.00
Figure, Dr Pepper, Red Devil, Jointed Body, Cardboard, 1900, 27 In. 1035.00
Figure, Kessler Whiskey, Man In Top Hat, Bowling Ball, Chalkware, 14 In. 132.00
Figure, Lowenbrau Beer, Lion, Holding Bottle Of Beer, Gold, Composition, 17 In. 55.00
Figure, Mountain Dew, Willy The Hillbilly, Vinyl, Plush, 1965, 20 In. 165.00
Figure, Mr. Bubble, Rubber, 1970s, 8 x 9 1/2 x 5 In. 25.00
Figure, Mr. Contac, Capsule Form, Face, Legs, Arms, GlaxoSmithKline, 11 3/4 In. 250.00
Figure, Old Smuggler Scotch, Alan Insulated Mfg., 1950s, 10 x 2 x 3 In. 52.00
Figure, Penguin, Dr. Kool, Carrying Doctor's Bag, Chalk, 1940s, 4 1/4 x 2 1/2 In. 138.00
Figure, Penguin, Draught Guinness Sold Here, Rubberoid, 7 In. 162.00
Figure, Pillsbury, Doughboy, Stand, Embossed, Vinyl, Plastic, 1971, 7 1/2 In. 28.00
Figure, Radiotron Man, Wood, Jointed, RCA-Radiotrons, 15 1/2 In. 715.00
Figure, Rainier Brewing, Man, Bobbin' Head, Styrofoam, 1950s, 16 x 5 x 6 1/2 In. 180.00
Figure, Red Goose Shoes, Goose, Chalkware, 11 In. 185.00
Figure, Schmidt's Beer, Waiter, Holding Mugs Of Beer, Cast Spelter, Painted, 13 In. 120.00
Figure, Toucan, My Goodness, My Guinness, Rubberoid, 7 1/4 In. 486.00
Funnel, Lash's Bitters, Copper, Brass Plunger, Metal, 7 x 5 1/2 In. 265.00
Group, Blatz Beer, Catcher, Umpire, Runner, Sliding Home, 16 x 19 x 9 In. 965.00
Hat, Butternut Bread, Peanuts Gang, Paper, 1974 . . . . 15.00
Hat, McDonald's Restaurant, Paper & Mesh, Celluca Mfg., 1950 . . . . 30.00
Hat, Montgomery Hose Co., Fireman's Parade, Blue, Spread Wing Eagle, Banner 9775.00
Hat, Soda Jerk's, Dairylea Ice Cream, Miss Dairylea, Paper, Paperlynen, 1967 . . . . 12.00
Hat, Soda Jerk's, Ted's Root Beer, Laminated Crepe Paper 314.00
Iron, Harvester Foundry First Heat, Feb. 28, 1911, 3 3/4 In. 150.00
Iron, John L. Bobo & Co., Tailors Trimmings, Chicago, Twisted Handle, 2 7/8 In. 825.00
Iron, Jos. M. Hayes, St. Louis Woolen Co., 3 1/2 In. 375.00
Iron, Max & Wertheim Tailors Trimmings, Cleveland, Flat Handle, 3 3/4 In. 375.00
Iron, Safferon Massengill, Bristol Foundry & Machine, 1958 . . . . 10.00
Iron, Stuart, Ferencie HP For Iron Deficiency Anemia, Cylinder Grip, 3 3/4 In. 70.00
Iron, Tailor Sitting On Iron Shaped Base, W.H. Lent Tailor Supplies, New York 1900.00
Jar, Adams Pepsin Tutti-Frutti, Glass, Paper Label, 10 In. 440.00

Jar, Carnation Malted Milk, Tin Lid, Milk Glass, 6 x 6 1/2 In. 165.00
Jar, Faultless Wonder Nipples, Amber Frosted, Baby Bottle Form, 12 1/2 x 5 3/4 In. 3190.00
Jar, Hall Ice Cream Soda, Lime Syrup, Porcelain, 1920s, 10 x 4 In. 85.00
Jar, Lance, Tin Lid, Red, 13 x 9 x 7 In. 93.00
Jar, Lance, Tin Lid, Red, 9 x 8 x 7 In. 110.00
Jar, Lance, Tin Lid, Red, 9 x 9 x 7 In. 104.00
Jar, Lid, Dusseldorfer Style Mustard, Bristol Glaze, Stoneware, c.1900, 4 In. 35.00
Jar, Squirrel Brand Salted Peanuts, Paper Label, Tin Lithograph Lid, 9 x 6 In. 80.00
Jar, Zateks Chocolates, Cover, Footed, 12 x 7 In. 470.00
Jug, Hoffman House, Blended Whiskey, Bristol Glaze, Stencil, Stoneware, c.1906, 2 3/4 In.   99.00
Jug, Microbe Killer, Embossed, Stoneware, 20th May 1890, 12 x 7 In. 330.00
Key Chain, Trojan Powder, Makers Of High Explosives, 2 Chains, 1 1/4 x 3/4 In. 165.00
Kit, TWA Airlines, Welcome Aboard Passenger, 6 1/2 x 9 In. 40.00
Knife, Flamingo Casino & Hotel, Restaurant Ware, Engraved 15.00
Knife Sharpener, Dr. Miles, Anti-Pain Pills, Celluloid, 1 5/8 x 2 3/4 In. 30.00
Label, Cigar, Old King Cole, Embossed, 6 x 10 In. 120.00
Label, Food, Don't Cry Brand Sweet Potatoes, Black Boy, Dice, c.1950, 9 x 9 In. 18.00
Label, Food, Mammy Brand Oranges, Mammy Holding Orange, 1950s, 3 x 8 In. 14.00
Label, Gunpowder, Hazard Powder Co., Shot Shell Box, Red & Black Ink, 2 x 3 5/8 In. . . .   35.00
Label, Gunpowder, Laflin & Rand Powder Co., Orange Extra Sporting, 4 x 1 7/8 In. 17.00
Label, Ola Soda, Family At Seashore, Brooklyn, N.Y., 1935, 3 x 4 In. 12.00
Label, Tobacco, Dick Custer, Hold You Up, Gold Embossed, 6 1/2 x 10 In. 65.00
Label, Tobacco, Elaine, Gold Embossed, 9 1/2 x 9 3/4 In. 60.00
Label, Tobacco, Summer Belle, Embossed, 11 x 10 1/2 In. 60.00
Label, Tobacco, Uncle Sam, La Hilda Cigar Factory, Battleship, Embossed, 4 1/2 In. 30.00
Label, Tobacco, Welcome Nugget, Miner Holding Pick Ax, 10 1/2 x 10 1/2 In. 76.00
Label, Tobacco, Western Bee, Bees Around Hive, Gold Embossed, 6 1/2 x 10 In. 32.00
Lamps are listed in the Lamp category.
Lantern, Sheffield Farms, Milk Wagon, Tin 100.00
Letter Opener, Chicago Sun Times, Silver-Colored Blade, Disc, 1958, 9 In. 10.00
Letter Opener, DuPont Explosives, Giant Powder, Pewter, 9 In. 40.00
Letter Opener, Dutch Boy, Holding Paint Brush, Pure White Lead, Figural, 7 1/4 In. 50.00
Letter Opener, Fuller Brush, Man, Plastic, Pink, 7 1/4 In. 20.00
Letter Opener, Fuller Brush, Man, Red, Plastic 5.00
Letter Opener, Fuller Brush, Man, Woman, Pink, Plastic 8.00
Letter Opener, National Biscuit Special Products, Gold-Colored Metal, 6 3/4 In. 14.00
Letter Opener, Shoot DuPont Standard Loads, Faux Ivory, 1930s, 7 1/2 In. 89.00
Letter Opener, Sioux Valley Grain Co., Embossed & Lithographed Tin, 10 In. 15.00
Letter Opener, Southern Coffin & Casket Co., Casket, Pewter-Colored Metal, 9 In. 30.00
Letter Opener, Tobacco Leaf, Established 1864, Printed Celluloid, Ruler Edge, 6 In. 10.00
Letter Opener, Uneeda Biscuit, Boy In Raincoat, Painted Tin, 8 1/2 In. 12.00
Letter Opener, Wilbert Vault Co., Dagger Shape, Jade Handle, Leather Sheath, 6 In. 25.00
Lunch Box, Dan Patch Tobacco, Handles, 4 1/2 x 7 x 4 1/4 In. 88.00
Lunch Box, Dixie Kid Cut Plug Tobacco, Tin Lithograph, 5 1/4 x 3 3/4 In. 175.00
Lunch Box, Green Turtle Tobacco, 5 1/4 x 7 1/2 x 4 1/4 In. 275.00
Lunch Box, Lorillard's Redicut Tobacco, Break Off A Piece, Tin Lithograph, 7 1/2 x 8 In. .   177.00
Lunch Box, Red Tiger Tobacco, Tin, Handles 55.00
Lunch Box, Union Leader Cut Plug, Tin Lithograph, 5 1/2 x 8 x 4 In. 22.00
Lunch Boxes are also listed in their own category.
Match Striker Card, Wistar's Balsam Of Cherry Night-Time, 4 1/2 x 3 In. 95.00
Matchbook, Bromo-Seltzer, Diamond Match Company, N.Y., 2 x 1 1/2 In. 5.00

Advertising mirrors of all sizes are listed here. Advertising pocket mirrors range in size from 1 1/2 to 5 inches in diameter. Most of these mirrors were given away as advertising promotions and include the name
of the company in the design.

Mirror, Aetna Life Insurance Co., J.C. Barrows, Train, Oval, Pocket 130.00
Mirror, Bromo-Seltzer, Cures All Headaches, Bottle, Minks Badge & Novelty, 2 In. 440.00
Mirror, Bromo-Seltzer, Woman, Cures All Headaches, Celluloid, Oval, 2 3/4 In. 330.00
Mirror, Budweiser, Clydesdale Team & Wagon, Frame, 33 x 57 In.   140.00
Mirror, Burrowes Home Billiard & Pool Table, Celluloid Front, Oval, 2 3/4 In. 818.00
Mirror, Butler's Stylish Clothes, Patriotic, Binghamton, N.Y., Round, 2 1/16 In. 21.00
Mirror, Coon Brand, Collars & Cuffs, Cat In Tree, Bronzed Metal, c.1900, 16 In. 489.00

Mirror, Dr. H.L. Irwin, Dentist, New Concord, Ohio, Jewels, Celluloid, Oval, 2 3/4 In. 130.00
Mirror, Dueber Watch Case, Hampden Watch, Round, 2 In. 40.00
Mirror, Emerson & Fisher Carriage Builders, For The Trade, Cincinnati, Ohio, Pocket 75.00
Mirror, General Accident Of Philadelphia, Pigs, Round, c.1902, 2 1/4 In. 86.00
Mirror, General Offices Knights Of Maccabees Of World, Detroit, Oval, 2 3/4 In. 50.00
Mirror, Gillette Safety Razor, Baby Shaving, Calendar, Round, 1909, 2 1/4 In. 58.00
Mirror, Hardy's Salve, The Kind Your Father Used, Cornish Flat, N.Y., 2 In. 240.00
Mirror, Hobo Kidney & Bladder Remedy, Clears Up The Complexion, Oval, 2 3/4 In. 240.00
Mirror, Hudson Bay Fur Co., Exclusive Furriers, Celluloid, Pocket, Oval, 2 3/4 In. 400.00
Mirror, J.C. Cruttwell, Worrell Mfg Co., St. Louis, Round, 3 In. 628.00
Mirror, L. Stroup Lumber & Roofing, Adjustable Handle, Black, Tin, 7 3/4 In. 65.00
Mirror, Louis Bergdoll Brewing Co., Celluloid, Oval, Pre-Prohibition, 2 3/4 In. 250.00
Mirror, Maxwell House Coffee, Good To Last Drop, Cup, Aluminum, 1 1/2 In. 26.00
Mirror, Minard's Liniment, A Good Thing, Rub It In, Red, Blue, Yellow, 2 In. 240.00
Mirror, Parry Manufacturing Co., Factory, Bastian Bros., Oval, 2 3/4 In. 58.00
Mirror, Pianos & Inner Player Pianos, Tabor Music Co., Wisc., 2 1/8 In. 26.00
Mirror, R.G. Sullivan's, 10 Cent Cigar, Woman, Long Hair, 2 3/4 In. 382.00
Mirror, Rees' Pure High Protein Hog Tankage, Fattens Your Hogs, 1930s, 2 1/4 In. 55.00
Mirror, Runkel's Cocoa, Highest Grade, Woman, Holding Tin, Oval, 2 3/4 In. 259.00
Mirror, Ryan's Pure Beers, Indian, Headdress, Pre-Prohibition, Round 259.00
Mirror, Universal Theaters Concession Co., Handle, 3 1/4 In. 55.00
Mirror, White Fox, No. 2, For Skin & Colds, Celluloid, 1 3/4 In. 240.00
Mirror, White House Shoes, Brown Shoe Co., 1700's Dance Scene, Round, 2 1/4 In. 106.00
Mirror, Wolverine Brass Works, Grand Rapids, Mich., Celluloid, Oval, 2 3/4 In. 20.00
Mirror, Yellow Taxi Co., Celluloid, 3333 Cadillac, Yellow Ground, Detroit, 3 In. 1265.00
Mirror, You Would Look Much Better At The End Of A New No. 5 Cigar, 20 x 20 In. 115.00
Mug, Hires Root Beer, Drink Hires Root Beer, Pointing Boy, Bib, 4 1/4 x 4 1/2 In. . .120.00 to 155.00
Mug, Hires Root Beer, Join Health & Cheer, Pointing Boy, Bowtie, Rose, 5 x 4 In. . .176.00 to 248.00
Pail, Armour Veribest, Peanut Butter, Mother Goose Characters, 12 & 16 Oz. 290.00
Pail, Blue Flame Coffee, 3 Lb. 55.00
Pail, Buckey Pretzels, Cover, Handle, Red, Yellow, Black, 14 1/2 x 12 In. 28.00
Pail, Central Union Cut Plug 45.00
Pail, Chisca Peanut Butter, Indian, Tin Lithograph, Maury-Cole Co., 3 3/8 x 3 3/4 In. 99.00
Pail, Council Cup Coffee, A.W. Fey, Lithograph, 4 Lb., 8 1/2 x 7 1/2 In. 55.00
Pail, Dixie Peanut Butter, Bail Handle, Lid, Kelly Peanut Co., 28 Lb., 12 x 11 In. 77.00
Pail, Dutch Boy, Strictly Pure, Soft Paste White Lead, Bail Handle, 6 1/4 x 7 1/2 In. 28.00
Pail, Gold Flake Peanut Butter, Red, White, 5 Lb., 6 In. 25.00
Pail, Hoody's Peanut Butter, Kid On Seesaw 550.00
Pail, La Turka, Plug Cut, Spaulding & Merrick, Liggett & Myers, 6 x 5 1/2 In. 22.00
Pail, Penns Tobacco, Smoke & Chew, Always The Best, 1 Lb., 6 x 5 1/2 In. 28.00
Pail, Peter Rabbit Peanut Butter, 1 Lb., 4 x 3 3/4 In. 660.00
Pail, Shedd's Peanut Butter, Elf, Red, Yellow, Shedd-Bartush Foods, 5 Lb., 6 1/4 In. 45.00
Pail, Watkins Stock Tonic, Bail Handle, 13 x 12 In. 250.00
Pen, Old Hill Lines, Bullet, Portales, N.M., 3 5/8 In. 22.00
Pennant, Western Flyer, America's Favorite, Boy, Girl, Cardboard, 22 x 13 1/2 In. 55.00
Pin, Heinz, Pickle, Ketchup Bottle, Plastic, Pair 16.00
Pitcher, Bardwell's Root Beer, Pewter Lid, Northface Spout, Stoneware, White's, 14 In. . .   1100.00
Pitcher, Tang, Crisscross Pattern, Lid, 1960s-70s 11.00
Plate, B.H. Douglass' Perfected Capsicum Cough Drops, 6 1/4 In. 80.00
Plate, Fern Brand Chocolates, Amethyst, Carnival Glass, Double Handgrip . . . . . . .600.00 to 775.00
Plate, Woman, Urn, Thomas Porzellan, E.B. Lattorff, Hamburg, 5 3/4 In. . . . . *Illus*   85.00
Platter, Greyhound Bus Lines, Logo, Flowers, Shenango China, 1930-48, 11 3/4 x 8 In. . .   155.00
Platter, Sparks Kidney & Liver, Mrs. Grover Cleveland, Porcelain, 16 1/2 x 11 In. 90.00
Poster, Cycles Rochet, Man On Bike, Car, Plane, Chevalier, France, c.1930, 60 x 42 In. . . .   825.00
Poster, Home Run Cigarettes, Batter & Catcher, Framed, c.1910, 12 x 18 In. 3740.00
Pot Scraper, C.D. Kenny Co. Coffees, Teas, Sugars, Cast Iron, 4 In. 310.00
Pot Scraper, Junket, Makes Milk Into Delicious Dessert, Metal, 2-Sided, 3 x 3 In. 255.00
Pot Scraper, Penn Stoves, Clover, Tin Lithograph, 3 x 3 1/4 In. 154.00
Pot Scraper, Tin, Perfect Scraper, Pat'd. May 21, 89 . . . .   225.00
Pouch, R.J. Reynolds, Stud Tobacco, Cloth, String Tie Tag, 1910, 3 x 2 x 3/4 In. 70.00
Punch Bowl, Bardwell's Root Beer, Stoneware, 19 In. 3575.00
Rack, Brighton Garter, 25 Cents, Wood, 19 In. 1980.00
Rack, Gulf Batteries, Tin, 32 x 24 1/2 In. 66.00

Advertising, Plate, Woman, Urn, Thomas
Porzellan, E.B. Lattorff, Hamburg, 5 3/4 In.

Advertising, Sifter, Steinman & Wellman, Logan,
Ohio, We Can Save You Money, 3 In.

Rack, Ivory Garters, Wood, 4 Product Boxes, 15 x 18 In. 110.00
Rack, Kotex, Nurse, Tin, 13 x 8 In. 165.00
Rack, Life Savers, Tin, 1930s, 18 In. 220.00
Rack, Remington Knives, Wood, Mahogany Finish, 11 Slots, 10 x 33 In. 335.00
Rack, Winchester, 12 Flashlights, 3 Batteries, Wire, 24 3/4 x 14 In. 1880.00
Ring, American Airlines, Junior Pilots 42.00
Sack, Flour, Big Jo Flour, Elephant Holding Sack, Cloth, Frame, 23 1/2 x 19 1/2 In. 176.00
Sack, Flour, Duluth Flour, Black Chef, Paper, Frame, 16 x 12 In. 60.00
Sack, Flour, Red Wing 40.00
Salesman's Sample, Peters Ammunition, Sample Shells, Cardboard, Cloth Cover 239.00
Salt & Pepper Shakers are listed in their own category.
Scales are listed in their own category.
Shaker, Hires, Mechanical, Porcelain, Hand Crank, Metal Cup, Lid, Early 1900s 3300.00
Shaker, Spiller Flour, Flour Fred, England, 9 In. 38.00
Shoehorn, Fuller Brush, Red, Plastic, 4 1/2 In. 6.00
Shot Glass, Commercial Club Rye, 2 1/8 In. 55.00
Shot Glass, Drink Berry's Diamond Wedding Whiskey, Boston, 2 1/8 In. 55.00
Shot Glass, Hayners Lock Box 290, 2 1/8 In. 15.00
Shot Glass, J.F. Cutter Whiskey, S.F., 2 1/8 In. 39.00
Shot Glass, Jesse Moore, 2 1/8 In. 25.00
Shot Glass, O.K. Capitol Whiskey, 2 1/8 In. 44.00
Shot Glass, Old Government, 2 1/8 In. 59.00
Shot Glass, Old I.W. Harper, 2 1/8 In. 39.00
Shot Glass, Old Kirk, S.F., 2 1/8 In. 40.00
Shot Glass, Old Scenter Rye, 2 1/8 In. 45.00
Shot Glass, Sunny Brook Pure Food Whiskey, 2 1/8 In. 39.00
Shot Glass, Zane Club Whiskey, Zanesville, Ohio, 2 1/8 In. 40.00
Sifter, Steinman & Wellman, Logan, Ohio, We Can Save You Money, 3 In. .... *Illus* 30.00
Sign, 7-20-4 Cigar, Porcelain, 12 x 30 In. 440.00
Sign, 7Up, 6-Pack, All Family Drink, Tin, 60 x 35 In. 1540.00
Sign, 7Up, Fresh Up, Light-Up, Revolving, 12 x 14 x 4 In. 770.00
Sign, 7Up, The Uncola, Bottle, Green, White, Red, Yellow, Die Cut, Tin, 70 x 29 In. 300.00
Sign, 7Up, Tin Lithograph, Embossed, Self-Framed, 19 x 13 In. 210.00
Sign, Abadie Cigarette Papers, Ethnic Caricatures, Germany, 1904, 37 x 52 In. 5425.00
Sign, Ace Brand Clover Seed, For Sale Here, Tin, Embossed, 14 x 9 In. 230.00
Sign, Admiration, Cigar That Wins, Woman, Mirror, Tin, Easel Back, 7 1/2 x 5 1/2 In. 275.00
Sign, Akro Agate, Cardboard, Image Of Boy Pointing At Marble Display, 14 In. 4125.00
Sign, Akron Brewing Co, Plywood, Pictures Working Plant, 1905, 36 x 24 In. 460.00
Sign, Anheuser-Busch, Budweiser Girl, Tin, Self-Framed, 37 1/2 x 25 1/2 In. 3300.00
Sign, Armots Rose Cream, Purity, Tin On Cardboard, c.1906, 19 x 13 In. 275.00
Sign, Armour & Co., Hams, Bacon, Woman, Butcher Shop, Tin, Embossed, 30 x 24 In. ... 3850.00
Sign, Art Studio, Hand Crafted, Mixed Materials, 1920s, 35 x 35 In. 220.00
Sign, Arthur's Elixir Of Sulphur, Woman, Dog, Lake, Boat, Paper, 11 5/8 x 8 5/8 In. 94.00
Sign, Ayer's Cherry Pectoral, Santa, Gift To A Friend, Die Cut, Cardboard, 13 x 7 In. 415.00
Sign, Ayer's Sarsaparilla, Old Folks Home, Cardboard, Die Cut, 11 x 8 In. 155.00

Sign, Be Sure With Pure, Blue, White, Porcelain, Bracket, 42 In. Diam. 495.00
Sign, Bears' Honeydew Cigarettes, Porcelain, England, 17 1/2 x 12 1/2 In. 85.00
Sign, Bed & Breakfast, Reverse Etched, Gilt, 14 1/2 x 20 1/2 In. 90.00
Sign, Beech-Nut Chewing Tobacco, Red, White, Blue, Porcelain, 11 x 22 In. 125.00
Sign, Beech-Nut Gum, Ease Tension, Stan Musial, Cardboard, 1950s, 18 x 20 In. 975.00
Sign, Beeman's Pepsin Gum, Satin, Yellow Ground, Red Letters, Gum, 3 x 17 In. 385.00
Sign, Bernard & Co, Distillers Of Old Tom, Multicolored, Frame, 20 1/2 x 26 In. 205.00
Sign, Berry Brothers Varnishes, Wooden, Wagon, Original Box, 19 x 27 In. 300.00
Sign, Bickmore Gall Salve, Cardboard, Easel, 22 x 35 In. 105.00
Sign, Big Chief Soda Water, Indian Chief, Tin, Embossed, 19 1/2 x 27 1/2 In. 440.00
Sign, Big Giant Cola, For A Real Lift, More For Your Money, Tin, 16 Oz., 22 x 11 In. 220.00
Sign, Black-Draught, A Good Laxative, Tin, 2-Sided, Flange, 6 1/2 x 12 In. 130.00
Sign, Blackstone Cigar, Waitt & Bond, Porcelain, 12 x 36 In. 99.00
Sign, Bomba, A Papaya Beverage, 5 Cents, Tin, Embossed, 16 x 24 In. 145.00
Sign, Booster Cigars, Black Man, Woman, Stockings, Paperboard, c.1910, 24 x 16 In. 605.00
Sign, Borden, Flower Basket, 3-Dimensional, Die Cut, Cardboard, 19 x 13 In. 45.00
Sign, Borden, Welcome Home Elsie, Paper, 1980s, 11 x 18 In. 30.00
Sign, Braems Bitters, Bottle, Aluminum, Over Cardboard, Rope Edge, 13 x 7 In. 120.00
Sign, Breinig's Paint, Celluloid, Tin, Color Panels, 1920s, 30 x 36 In. 440.00
Sign, Brookfield Rye, Girl, Diaphanous Gown, Holding Bottle, Tin, 23 x 33 In. 3850.00
Sign, Brown's Vermifuge Comfits Or Worm Lozenges, Frame, c.1890, 13 x 17 In. 330.00
Sign, Budweiser, King Of Bottled Beer, Eagle, Red, Black, White, Tin, 1930s, 20 x 72 In. . . 1100.00
Sign, Bull Durham Smoking Tobacco, Tin Lithograph, Die Cut, 28 1/2 In. . . . . *Illus* 16500.00
Sign, Burma Shave, His Line Was Smooth, Wood, 2-Sided, 12 x 40 In. 55.00
Sign, Butcher, Figural, Steer's Head, Molded Tin, Natural Patina, 20 In. 575.00
Sign, California Insurance Co., San Francisco Fire, Bear, Paper, Oak Frame, 19 x 28 In. . . . 1200.00
Sign, Camel Cigarettes, Camels Never Get On My Nerves, Gloria Wheden, 11 x 22 In. 55.00
Sign, Camel Cigarettes, No Premiums Or Coupons, Porcelain, 12 x 36 In. 205.00
Sign, Camel Cigarettes, Woman, Red Dress, Die Cut, Cardboard, Stand-Up, 30 x 18 In. . . . 35.00
Sign, Campfire Marshmallows, Boy, Sailor Suit, Stone Lithograph, 21 x 14 In. 330.00
Sign, Canoe Club Beverage, Once You Try It, Cardboard, Tin Frame, 14 x 30 In. 300.00
Sign, Carmania, Cunard Steamers, Tin, 27 x 36 In. 990.00
Sign, Carnation Milk, Fresh, Bottle, Red, White, Die Cut, Porcelain, 22 x 23 In. 1160.00
Sign, Carter's Ink, Man, Book, Ink Bottle, Tin, Self-Framed, c.1900, 25 x 19 In. 1320.00
Sign, Castle Hall, 5 Cent Cigar, Best Of All, That's All, 3-Sided Base, 24 In. 440.00
Sign, Catawissa Sparkling Beverages, Dial 2252, Red, White, Tin, 18 x 20 In. 95.00
Sign, Cedarsburg Mutual Insurance, No Smoking, Tin, Embossed, 5 x 23 In. 90.00
Sign, Cello Cola, Tin, Embossed, Reed & Co., Louisville, Wooden Frame, 28 x 27 In. 175.00
Sign, Centilvre Brewing Co., Factory, Paper Lithograph, Mat, Frame, 29 x 40 In. 468.00
Sign, Centlivre Beer, Black Porter, Couple On Train, Nickel Plate, Frame, 24 x 20 In. 605.00
Sign, Centlivre Tonic, Red Cross Nurse, Preparing Extract, 22 x 12 In. 69.00
Sign, Certain-Teed Roofs, Can Take It, They're Millerized, Tin, 13 1/2 x 19 1/2 In. 66.00
Sign, Chancellor Cigar, Cigar Of Quality, Victorian Lady, Cardboard, Frame, 42 x 24 In. . . 5390.00
Sign, Charles E. Poor Painter, Pine, Rectangular, 1800s, 18 3/4 x 77 1/2 In. 1175.00
Sign, Chattanooga Plows, C.F. Morrison, Yellow, Black, Tin, 13 x 19 In. 330.00
Sign, Cherry Smash, Woman, Holds Glass, Die Cut, 2 Piece, 15 x 12 1/2 In. 220.00
Sign, Chiropody, Manicuring Etc., Wood, Oblong, 1800s, 13 x 24 1/2 In. 235.00
Sign, Chum's Confections, Prize In Every Package, Cardboard, 1905, 11 x 14 In. 2475.00
Sign, Clark's O.N.T., Pup On Spool, Die Cut, Cardboard, 9 x 7 1/2 In. 39.00
Sign, Claussens Bread, Slow School Zone, Girl, Wood, Die Cut, 58 x 18 In. 250.00
Sign, Climax Plug Tobacco, Grand Old Chew, Porcelain, Square, 15 x 15 In. 145.00
Sign, Coffee In Every Room, Individually Yours, Green, 2-Sided, 24 x 18 In. 275.00
Sign, Coll's Prescription Delivery Service, White, Green, Wooden, 2-Sided, 45 x 33 In. . . . 55.00
Sign, Colt, Jaguar, Woman, W.F. Powers Co., Spanish, Paper, Store, 1921, 26 x 21 In. 18815.00
Sign, Columbia Grafonolas & Records, Tin, 14 x 21 In. 275.00
Sign, Concord, 5 Cent Cigars, Grapes, Linen, Early 1900s, 55 x 40 In. 880.00
Sign, Consolidated Tours, Member, Porcelain, 2-Sided, 23 x 19 In. 880.00
Sign, Continental Cigar, Washington, Horse, Cardboard, Mat, Frame, 1906, 35 x 28 In. . . . 4950.00
Sign, Coors Extra Gold, Light-Up, Pull Chain, 17 x 12 x 4 In. 70.00
Sign, Copenhagen, Best Chew Ever, Red Ground, White Letters, Porcelain, 22 In. 605.00
Sign, Country Club Ginger Ale, Woman, Snow Outfit, Cardboard, Stand-Up, 18 x 13 In. . . 33.00
Sign, D.M. Ferry & Co. Seeds, Paper On Cardboard, c.1890, 33 x 23 In. 330.00
Sign, Dad's, Ask For, Old Fashioned Root Beer, Metal, 9 x 18 In. 110.00

Sign, Dandro Solvent, Tin Over Cardboard, Self-Framed, 9 1/2 x 13 In. 88.00
Sign, Days Work Chewing Tobacco, A Grand Chew, Paper, 1949, 13 3/4 x 19 In. 65.00
Sign, DeLaval Cream Separators, Red, Tin Lithograph, Gessoed Frame, 40 In. . . . . . . *Illus*   4675.00
Sign, DeLaval Cream Separators, Woman, Kitchen, Child, Tin, Round, c.1907, 26 In. 4400.00
Sign, DeLaval, Separator, Yellow, Porcelain, 26 1/2 x 18 In. 1210.00
Sign, DeLaval, We Use The Cream Separator, Porcelain, 12 x 16 In. 99.00
Sign, DeLaval, We Use The DeLaval Milker, Red & Black On Gray, 15 x 15 In. 138.00
Sign, DeLaval, Woman, Child In Cow Pasture, Tin, Self-Framed, 1905, 26 In. Diam. 2200.00
Sign, Delker Bros., High Grade Buggies, S.H. Findley, Paper, Frame, 8 1/2 x 19 1/2 In. . . .   145.00
Sign, Delphis Cafe, Tile, Medallion, Decorated Border, Poole, 39 x 55 In. 2840.00
Sign, Dennis's Lincolnshire Pig Powders, Tin, Embossed, 10 x 13 1/2 In. 605.00
Sign, Dental Snuff, American Leaders, Eagle, Cardboard, Frame, 16 1/2 x 22 1/2 In. 90.00
Sign, Devilish Good Cigars, Embossed, Tin Lithograph, Hanger, 10 x 14 In. . . . . *Illus*   660.00
Sign, Diehl's Bread, It's Thoroughly Baked, Porcelain, 12 x 24 In. 132.00
Sign, Dingman's Soap, Girl Holding Package, Mat, Frame, 18 x 12 1/2 In. 330.00
Sign, Dobson, Mover, Bay City, Tin Lithograph, Black, Yellow, 24 x 30 In. 248.00
Sign, Dr Pepper, Bottle, 10-2-4, Tin, Embossed, White, Red, Black, 48 x 14 In. 770.00
Sign, Dr Pepper, Certainly, Lady Reaching For Bottle, Cardboard, 30 x 48 In. 40.00
Sign, Dr Pepper, Drink Dr Pepper, Good For Life, 5 Cents, Tin, 12 x 23 In. 247.00
Sign, Dr Pepper, Drink Dr Pepper, Good For Life, Porcelain, 10 1/2 x 26 1/2 In. 120.00
Sign, Dr Pepper, Good For Life, Red, White, Tin, Embossed, 7 x 20 In. 137.00
Sign, Dr Pepper, I Take My Energy Lift Straight, Cowboy, Boy, Cardboard, 16 x 26 In. . . .   550.00
Sign, Dr. A.C. Daniels, Horse, Cat, Dog, Medicines, Tin, 17 x 28 In. 165.00
Sign, Dr. LeGear's Screw Worm, Cow, Easel Back, Die Cut, Cardboard, 17 x 12 In. 33.00
Sign, Dr. LeGear, Man, Horse, Tin, 14 x 18 In. 66.00
Sign, Dr. Mahoney, Gold Lettering On Black, 8 x 26 In. 250.00
Sign, Dr. Miles, Dolly Quincy, Die Cut, Easel Back, c.1902, 22 1/2 x 9 In. 176.00
Sign, Dr. Miles, View 3 Different Angles, Tin Lithograph, Raised Panels, 4 x 18 1/2 In. . . .   1870.00
Sign, Dr. Scholl's Foot Comfort Service, Porcelain, 2-Sided, Flange, 12 x 23 In. 220.00
Sign, Drexel's Bell Cologne, Woman, Paper, Frame, Late 1800s, 39 x 32 In. 385.00
Sign, Drink Barqs, It's Good, Bottle, Tin, Flange, 14 x 21 In. 136.00
Sign, Drink Double Cola, Tin, 2-Sided, Flange, 1947, 15 x 18 In. 1155.00
Sign, Drink Grapette, Bottle, Green, Brown, White, Tin, 39 x 13 In. 715.00
Sign, Drink Holiday, Bottle, Tin, 35 x 35 In. 165.00
Sign, Drink Sealtest Milk, Red, White, Tin, 13 x 18 In. 1100.00
Sign, Dry Goods, Store, Wooden, Bevel Edge, Hand Painted, 11 1/2 x 44 1/2 In. 143.00
Sign, DuPont Dogs, 2 Dogs Looking Sideways, Tin, 1903, 28 x 23 In. 4125.00
Sign, Duralite, W.A. Belcher, Lmbr. Co, Man Holding Paint, Tin, Embossed, 43 x 16 In. . .   146.00
Sign, Durham, 5 Cents, Cow Head, Hanger, Cardboard Lithograph, 2-Sided, 13 In. 310.00
Sign, Dutch Boy, White Lead Paint, Passaic Metal Ware, Tin Lithograph, 10 x 27 In. 440.00
Sign, Eagle, Inn, Granville, Ohio, Sheet Iron, Painted, 2 Bullet Holes, 23 1/2 x 19 1/2 In. . .   489.00
Sign, East India Shipping Co., Masted Ships, Wooden, 3 Panels, Folding, 31 x 40 In. 299.00
Sign, Eat Wheatlet, Children, At Table, Paper, Frame, 18 x 22 In. 440.00
Sign, Ebbert Wagons, Tin Lithograph, Self-Framed, 26 x 18 In. . . . . *Illus*   4675.00
Sign, Ed Price Tailors, Die Cut, Cardboard, Embossed, Easel Back, Germany, 9 x 6 In. 50.00
Sign, Edison Mazda Lamps, Cardboard, Shadowbox, Display, 26 1/2 x 16 x 3 In. 1018.00
Sign, Edison Mazda Light Bulbs, Die Cut, Cardboard, Stand-Up, Parrish, 1920s, 14 x 9 In.   990.00

Advertising, Sign, Bull
Durham Smoking
Tobacco, Tin Lithograph,
Die Cut, 28 1/2 In.

Advertising, Sign, DeLaval
Cream Separators, Red,
Tin Lithograph, Gessoed
Frame, 40 In.

Advertising, Sign, Devilish Good Cigars, Embossed, Tin Lithograph, Hanger, 10 x 14 In.   Advertising, Sign, Ebbert Wagons, Tin Lithograph, Self-Framed, 26 x 18 In.

Sign, Edison Mazda Light Bulbs, Stand-Up Display, Easel Back, c.1930, 18 x 9 In. 385.00
Sign, Egg-O-See, We Serve, Tin, Boy, At Table, Dog, Cats, 16 x 10 In. 990.00
Sign, Egyptienne Straights Cigarettes, Woman, Bonnet, Cardboard, Red, 36 x 24 In. 165.00
Sign, Eisemanns Klondike Head Rub, 10 Cents, Bottle, Cardboard, 8 x 11 In. 155.00
Sign, El Gaurdo, 5 Cent Cigar, Reverse Label On Glass, Early 1900s, 7 x 10 In. 880.00
Sign, El Paterno Cigar, 10 Cents, Tin Lithograph, 2-Sided, Flange, 13 1/2 x 18 1/2 In. 825.00
Sign, Emily Hoar, Seamstress, Riding Habits, Late 1800s, 24 1/2 x 36 In. 4406.00
Sign, Enterprise Stoves & Ranges, Yellow, Black, Tin Lithograph, 2-Sided, 14 x 18 In. 110.00
Sign, Excelsior Beer, Bottle, Celluloid Over Cardboard, 13 x 9 1/2 In. 72.00
Sign, Excelsior Ice Cream, Celluloid Over Cardboard, Self-Framed, 6 x 8 3/4 In. 33.00
Sign, Eye-Gene, For Your Eyes, Enamel, White Letters, Blue Ground, England, 5 x 4 In. . . 39.00
Sign, F. Morse Boot Maker, Man & Woman's Boot, 2-Sided, 23 x 17 3/4 In. 3680.00
Sign, F.W. Woolworth Co., Brass, 4 x 23 In. 220.00
Sign, Fairbanks-Morse Home Water Plant, H.J. Lattin, Tin, Embossed, 13 3/4 x 19 In. 165.00
Sign, Falstaff Bottled Beer, Car, Farm Wagon, Spilled Produce, Tin, 22 x 32 In. 1760.00
Sign, Fargo Way Wild West, Train, Enameled, Porcelain, 8 3/4 x 13 In. 25.00
Sign, Farrier's, Horseshoe, Cleats, Mounting Ring, Laminated, 22 x 18 1/4 x 2 1/4 In. 385.00
Sign, Fatima Cigarettes, Turkish Blend, Woman, Veil, Tin, Round, 19 In. 8250.00
Sign, Ferguson System, Tractor, Porcelain, Blue, White, 41 x 60 In. 5170.00
Sign, Fireman's Insurance Co., Tin, Oak Frame, 20 1/2 x 22 1/2 In. 60.00
Sign, Fletcher's Castoria, Bringing Baby Back To Health, Cardboard, c.1880, 11 In. 354.00
Sign, For Sale, Wooden Shoes, That Fit You, Shoe Shape, Penn., 1890 . . . . 1800.00
Sign, Fresh Eggs For Sale, Southern States Cooperative, Feeds, Tin, 14 x 16 In. 247.00
Sign, Fresh Up, Tin, Domed, Oval, 40 x 31 In. 1430.00
Sign, Frings 3 Bros Cigars, Red, Yellow, Black, Tin, Flange, 12 x 18 In. 330.00
Sign, Frostie, Drink Frostie, Dwarf, Yellow, White, Red, Blue, Tin, 10 x 27 1/2 In. 220.00
Sign, G.P. Government Tea, Superb, Rich, Ripe, Red, White, Porcelain, 24 x 48 In. 137.00
Sign, Gadi White Way, White Shoe Polish, Cleans Instantly, Cardboard, 30 x 20 In. 49.00
Sign, Golden Bridge Root Beer, Remember, Bottle, Yellow, Red, Brown, Tin, 12 x 4 In. . . . 165.00
Sign, Golden Wedding Coffee, Father That's Your Third Cup, Cardboard, 29 x 21 In. 275.00
Sign, Golden West Coffee, Closset & Devers, Portland, Ore., c.1927, 39 x 26 In. 3630.00
Sign, Goldwaites Golden Gum, Paper, Art Nouveau-Style Woman, 22 x 20 In. 350.00
Sign, Good Grape Soda, Tin Lithograph, Embossed, 5 1/2 x 19 1/2 In. 110.00
Sign, Good Grape, In Bottles, Tin, Embossed, c.1930, 5 1/2 x 19 1/2 In. 58.00
Sign, Goodyear Batteries, Blue, Yellow, Porcelain, 2-Sided, Bracket, 27 x 48 In. 190.00
Sign, Granger Pipe Tobacco, Town Crier, Hear Ye Hear Ye, Cardboard, 19 x 15 In. 45.00
Sign, Grape Sparkle, Tin, 12 x 35 In. 660.00
Sign, Great American Insurance, Blue, White, Porcelain, New York, 12 x 18 In. 105.00
Sign, Green Cup Coffee, Clover Farm Stores, Tin, Green, White, Black, 12 x 36 In. 605.00
Sign, Grete's Beauty Shoppe, Wood, Painted, Early 1900s, 13 x 19 1/2 In. 295.00
Sign, Greyhound Lines, Ticket Office, Porcelain, 2-Sided, 30 x 25 In. 9900.00
Sign, Guinness, Ideal Summer Resort, Animals Playing, Gilroy, 12 x 8 In. 445.00
Sign, Gulf, Orange, White, Blue, Light-Up, Round, 21 In. 185.00
Sign, Gulf, Porcelain, Orange Ground, Blue & White Letters, Round, 28 In. 275.00
Sign, Hahne's Porter, Ceramic, Horseshoe, DuBois Brewing, 14 x 10 In. 1100.00
Sign, Hamilton Brown Shoe Store, Porcelain, 8 x 39 In. 198.00
Sign, Happy Hit Cigarettes, El Cigarello De Tabaco Fino, Cardboard, 18 x 12 In. 80.00
Sign, Hartford Fire Insurance Co., Porcelain, Enamel, 12 x 17 1/2 In. 90.00

Sign, Haskell Coffin, Girl, Short Hair, Blue Dress, 29 x 14 In. 386.00
Sign, Hathaway's Bread, Brownie, Tin Lithograph, Wood Frame, 11 1/2 x 34 In. 468.00
Sign, Havana Blossom, Plain, A Mild Chew, Tin, 10 1/2 x 22 In. 250.00
Sign, Heinz Pickle Barrel, 10 Cents Dozen, Cardboard, White Ground, 6 x 10 In. 90.00
Sign, Helmar Turkish Cigarettes, Blue, White, Porcelain, 12 x 27 In. 196.00
Sign, Hershey's Ice Cream, Famous For Quality, Red, Black, Yellow, Tin, 22 x 30 In. 247.00
Sign, Hill, Evans & Co. Pure Malt Vinegar, Tin, Embossed, c.1890, 12 x 9 In. 118.00
Sign, Hills Liver Tickler, Look At Your Tongue, Woman, Mirror, Frame, 12 x 11 In. 220.00
Sign, Hinds Honey & Almond Cream, Girl, Fence, Cardboard, Die Cut, Frame, 11 x 8 In. . . 120.00
Sign, Hires Root Beer, Bottle, Tin, Embossed, Presi Co., Self-Framed, 17 1/2 x 55 In. 413.00
Sign, Hires Root Beer, Drink Hires, Bottle, Green, Red, White, Brown, Tin, 11 x 32 In. 137.00
Sign, Hires Root Beer, Drink Hires, It Hits The Spot, Man, Bottle, Tin, 1918, 9 x 18 In. . . . 1100.00
Sign, Hires Root Beer, Enjoy, Delicious, Healthful, Woman, Glass, Cardboard, 13 x 12 In. . . 121.00
Sign, Hires Root Beer, R-J Root Beer, Real Root Juices, Die Cut Metal, 6 1/4 x 7 3/4 In. . . 66.00
Sign, Hires, R-J Root Beer, With Real Root Juices, Tin, Embossed, 13 1/2 x 39 In. 220.00
Sign, Hoffman & Hiemenz, Carting & Moving, Early 1900s, 15 x 25 In. 380.00
Sign, Hoffman House Cigars, Children, Naked Child, Paperboard, c.1900, 15 x 10 In. 440.00
Sign, Hoffman House Cigars, Satyr, Nymphs, Embossed, c.1896, 15 x 11 1/2 In. 210.00
Sign, Hollingsworth's Candies, For Those Who Love Fine Things, Porcelain, 12 x 24 In. . . 440.00
Sign, Holsum Bakes Real Bread, Blue, Red, White, Yellow, Tin, 60 x 16 In. 550.00
Sign, Home Run Cigarettes, Batter, Catcher, Uniform, Paper, 1910, 12 x 18 In. 3740.00
Sign, Honest Scrap Tobacco, Cat, Dog, Paperboard, Frame, 32 x 24 In. 935.00
Sign, Hood's Ice Cream, Cow, Die Cut, Tin, Multicolored, Flange, 19 x 22 In. 1650.00
Sign, Hood's Old-Fashioned Ice Cream, Metal, 2-Sided, Curb, 33 x 21 In. . . . . *Illus* 1121.00
Sign, Hoodsie Dixies, Now Ready, Free Movie Star Portraits, Paper, 1930s, 6 x 20 In. 75.00
Sign, Hoosier Water Pump, Cow Drinking Water, Woman, Paper, 35 x 23 In. 154.00
Sign, Horton Mfg. Co., Bristol, A Tragedy, Oliver Kemp, Paper, 1911, 23 x 15 In. 1128.00
Sign, Humphrey's Homeopathic Remedies, Nude Woman, Cardboard, 14 x 18 In. 330.00
Sign, Imperial Ice Cream, Silent Movie Star, Paper, Frame, 33 x 18 In. 165.00
Sign, Indian Nickel, Porcelain, Tin, 11 1/4 In. Diam. 25.00
Sign, Infallible Shotgun Powder, Hercules, 2 Ducks, Paper, 30 x 20 In. 462.00
Sign, Iron Clad Hosiery, Copper Wells & Co., Metal, Stand-Up, St. Joseph, 3 x 8 In. 50.00
Sign, Ivorene Cleanser, Elephant, People, Paper, Frame, 10 1/2 x 15 1/2 In. 231.00
Sign, IW Harper, Car, Just Married, Canvas, Frame, 1912, 34 x 46 In. 3300.00
Sign, J. Ruppers Brewery, Brass, Images, Eagle, Hops, 10 x 6 In. 230.00
Sign, J.I. Case Threshing Co., Embossed, Tin Lithograph, 14 x 20 In. . . . . *Illus* 6875.00
Sign, Jeep, Red, White, Blue, Light-Up, 20 x 24 In. 990.00
Sign, JFG Special Coffee, Instant, Blue, White, Brown, Fiberboard, 20 x 10 In. 60.00
Sign, John Deere, General Purpose Farm Tractor, Enameled, Porcelain, 10 x 10 In. 25.00
Sign, John Deere, Worth County Tractor, Green, Black, Porcelain, Light-Up, 34 x 76 In. . . . 3960.00
Sign, Keen Kutter Store, Metal, Glass, Wood, Light-Up, 6 x 30 x 5 In. 865.00
Sign, Kellogg's, Corn Flakes, 1910 World's Best Ear, Die Cut, Paperboard, 11 x 5 In. 77.00
Sign, Kemp's Balsam, Coughs, Colds & Sore Throats, 2-Sided, Octagonal, 10 1/2 In. 145.00
Sign, Kickapoo Joy Juice, Punch In Lunch, Die Cut, Embossed, c.1965, 13 x 9 1/2 In. 120.00
Sign, King Aerator, King System Ventilation, Barn, American Art Works, 19 x 13 In. 345.00
Sign, King No-To-Bac, His Work In America, Paper, Mounted On Board, 18 x 11 In. 290.00
Sign, King Oscar, 5 Cent Cigar, Glass, Reverse Painted, Frame, 20 x 32 In. 990.00

Advertising, Sign, Hood's
Old-Fashioned Ice
Cream, Metal, 2-Sided,
Curb, 33 x 21 In.

Advertising, Sign, J.I. Case Threshing Co.,
Embossed, Tin Lithograph, 14 x 20 In.

Sign, Kist Soda, Brown-Bigelow Glamour Pinup Girl, Celluloid, 18 1/2 x 13 In. 230.00
Sign, Klars Phosfo, Brain & Nerve Food, Made From Grain, Tin, 6 x 10 In. 90.00
Sign, Knickerbocker Beer, Brings You Giants, Russ Hodges, Cardboard, 13 x 19 In. 95.00
Sign, Kodak, Cameras, Film, Red, Yellow, Tin, 2-Sided, 18 x 24 In. 55.00
Sign, La Flor De Erb, 10 Cent Cigar, D.S. Erb & Co., Blue, Yellow, White, Tin, 7 x 14 In. . 165.00
Sign, Ladies Rest Room, Green, White, Tin, 10 1/2 x 9 1/2 In. 85.00
Sign, Lady Borden Ice Cream, Neon, Porcelain, 1952, 42 x 60 In. 1210.00
Sign, Lawrence Barrett Cigar, Mild Havana, 10 Cents, Porcelain, 31 1/2 x 21 In. 220.00
Sign, Lee Overalls, Union-Made, Yellow, Black, Red, Tin, Embossed, 12 x 23 In. 136.00
Sign, Levine's Footwear, For The Family, Shoe, 2-Sided, c.1900, 44 1/2 x 50 In. 705.00
Sign, Liqueur Hanappier, Woman, Blue Dress, Tin, France, 18 x 8 In. 110.00
Sign, Lithiated Lemon Soda, Embossed, 11 1/2 x 29 1/2 In. 198.00
Sign, Lloyds Plate Glass Insurance Company, Glass, Frame, 16 x 32 In. 165.00
Sign, London Assurance, Tin, Self-Framed, 22 x 28 In. 132.00
Sign, London Life Cigarettes, Lawn Party, Tin, Frame, 39 x 27 In. 1650.00
Sign, Lorillards Terrapin Plug Tobacco, Turtle, Tin, Embossed, 14 x 10 In. 330.00
Sign, Louisville Slugger, 54 Baseball Players, Cardboard, c.1958, 22 x 16 In. 2536.00
Sign, Lyons Tea, Porcelain, 2-Sided, Flange, 11 x 15 In. 90.00
Sign, Maine Coast Wood Carving, Rockport, Maine, 3-Masted Schooner, 23 x 36 In. 3165.00
Sign, Mandeville & King, Girl, Smiling, Flowers, Paper, Mat, Frame, 25 x 17 In. 1650.00
Sign, Marquette Life Insurance, Springfield, Ill., Frame, 13 1/2 x 17 In. 20.00
Sign, Mason's Root Beer, Refreshing, Foam-Topped, Tin, Embossed, 17 x 54 In. 165.00
Sign, McCormick-Deering Farm Machines, Yellow, Blue, Tin, Embossed, 5 x 23 In. 55.00
Sign, McNess Products Sold Here, Red, White, Tin, Flange, 16 x 13 1/2 In. 165.00
Sign, Mecca Cigarettes, Woman, Hat, Cardboard, Frame, 1912, 11 x 19 In. 660.00
Sign, Mentholatum, For Vacation Needs, Woman, Multicolored, Cardboard, 40 x 25 In. ... 4950.00
Sign, Merchants Grocers, Independent Service Grocer, c.1880, 20 x 97 1/2 In. 1410.00
Sign, Metropolitan Coal Co., Porcelain, 5 Colors, 14 x 19 In. 209.00
Sign, Milwaukee Binders & Mowers, E.P. Armknecht, Cardboard, 7 x 25 1/2 In. 288.00
Sign, Mirro Aluminum, Woman, Admiring Pan, Die Cut, Easel Back, 40 x 19 1/2 In. 138.00
Sign, Moco Feeds For Turkeys, Green, White, Tin, 6 x 24 In. 77.00
Sign, Model Tobacco, Cigar Store Figure Holds Package, Tin, 15 x 5 3/4 In. 120.00
Sign, Monarch Paint, Martin-Senour, Porcelain, 2-Sided, Flange, 14 x 19 In. 358.00
Sign, Morea Liquid Feeds, Red, Yellow, White, Black, Tin, 2-Sided, 20 x 42 In. 27.00
Sign, Morenci Roller Mills, Gold Lace Flour, Paper Lithograph, c.1890, 16 x 12 In. 120.00
Sign, Mountain Dew, Ya-Hooo, It'll Tickle Your Innards, Tin, 17 x 35 In. 825.00
Sign, Mountain Dew, Ya-Hooo, It'll Tickle Your Innards, Tin, 34 x 57 In. 880.00
Sign, Moxie, Girl, Tin Lithograph, Die Cut, 2 x 2 In. 170.00
Sign, Mrs. Winslow's Soothing Syrup For Children Teething, Cardboard, 13 x 11 In. 187.00
Sign, Munsingwear, Mother, Children, Tin Lithograph, 20 1/2 x 19 In. 605.00
Sign, Murad, Turkish Cigarette, Santa Carrying Large Package, 15 x 10 In. 165.00
Sign, N.J. Zinc Co., Danger, Warning, Electric, Porcelain, Embossed, 12 x 6 In. 220.00
Sign, National Airlines, Red, White, Blue, Porcelain, 12 In. Diam. 80.00
Sign, Nehi Root Beer, Pure Natural Flavors, Bottle, Tin, Embossed, 12 x 30 In. 187.00
Sign, Nehi, Drink Nehi Ice Cold, Embossed, Tin, 8 In. Diam. 175.00
Sign, Nehi, Drink Nehi, Ice Cold, Bottle, Tin, Die Cut, Flange, 13 x 18 In. 105.00
Sign, Nesbitt's, California Orange Sold Here, Bottle, Tin, 13 x 18 In. 660.00
Sign, Netherland Ice Cream, Tin, Dutch Boy & Girl Holding Cone, 1930s, 26 In. 660.00
Sign, New Edison Diamond Disc Phonograph, Tin, 11 x 36 In. 385.00
Sign, New Hampshire Tavern, Marlboro Hotel, Eagle, 2-Sided, 31 x 43 In. 13800.00
Sign, New Yorker Ginger Ale, Bottle, Full Quart, 10 Cents, Tin, 42 x 15 In. 440.00
Sign, Nichol Kola, America's Taste Sensation, 5 Cents, Black, Red, Tin, 33 x 58 In. 165.00
Sign, Nichol Kola, America's Taste Sensation, Bottle, 5 Cents, Tin, 35 1/2 x 12 In. 90.00
Sign, No Smoking, Blue, White, Porcelain, 6 x 18 In. 156.00
Sign, No Smoking, White On Blue, Porcelain, New York Subway 250.00
Sign, No Spitting, Metal, Lithograph, 6 7/8 x 10 In. 145.00
Sign, None Such Condensed Mince Meat, Tin Lithograph, 14 x 20 In. .... *Illus* 9350.00
Sign, Norfolk Tavern, Cream, Gray-Blue Letters, Wood, 2-Sided, 24 x 33 In. 940.00
Sign, Norwich Union Insurance Societies, England, 1800s, 32 x 24 In. 295.00
Sign, NuGrape Soda, Bottle Shape, Die Cut, Tin, 17 x 5 In. 99.00
Sign, NuGrape Soda, Cap, More Fun With, Imitation Grape Flavor, Tin, 36 In. 170.00
Sign, NuGrape Soda, Everybody Likes A Change, Lady In Swimsuit, Frame, 13 x 28 In. .. 95.00
Sign, NuGrape Soda, Suncrest, Deliciously Different, Cardboard, 2-Sided, 11 x 9 In. 70.00

Sign, NuGrape, Made With Welch's Grape Juice, Tin, Embossed, Frame, 20 x 29 In. 257.00
Sign, Ohio Farmers Insurance Co., Organized 1848, Porcelain, 13 1/2 x 18 In. 220.00
Sign, Old Dutch Cleanser, Chases Dirt, 10 Cent Can, Porcelain, Curved, 32 x 23 In. 605.00
Sign, Old Dutch Cleanser, Porcelain, 3 1/2 x 26 In. 145.00
Sign, Old Dutch, Healthful Cleanliness, Girl, Chasing Dirt, Tin Lithograph, 9 x 18 In. 358.00
Sign, Old Gold Cigarettes, Cardboard, 3 Panels, Die Cut, 38 x 51 In. 130.00
Sign, Old Honesty Soap, Blue & White, Porcelain, 7 x 18 In. 440.00
Sign, Old Reliable Coffee, Red Jacket, Box, Tin, H.D. Beach Co., Ohio, 9 x 6 1/2 In. 195.00
Sign, Old Virginia Cheroots, Mildest & Best, Red, Yellow, Black, Paper, 26 x 26 In. 55.00
Sign, Orange Crush, Cardboard, Gardener In Straw Hat, Bottle, 1940s, 36 x 24 In. 495.00
Sign, Orange Crush, Drink O-C Beverages, Crushy Product, Tin, Self-Framed, 17 x 32 In. . 250.00
Sign, Orange Crush, Feel Fresh, Drink Orange Crush, Girl, Bottle, Cardboard, 29 x 41 In. . 137.00
Sign, Orient Insurance Company, Glass, Frame, 20 x 30 In. 110.00
Sign, Orphan Boy Smoking Tobacco, Die Cut, St. Louis, Picture Of Donkey, 13 x 19 In. . . 75.00
Sign, OshKosh B'Gosh, Overalls, Red Ground, Porcelain, 10 x 30 In. 130.00
Sign, Pabst Blue Ribbon, Horse-Drawn Wagon, Paper, Frame, 1904, 18 x 35 In. 110.00
Sign, Paragon Tea, Complexion Of Youth, Girl, Cardboard, S.R. Feil & Co., 5 1/2 x 8 In. . . 120.00
Sign, Peaceful Counsel, Round Oak Stoves, Embossed, 18 x 12 In. 175.00
Sign, Peacock Moreen, Celluloid, Cardboard, 17 x 14 In. 130.00
Sign, Pepo Worm Syrup, 25 Cents At All Druggists, Tin, Embossed, 6 1/2 x 9 In. 95.00
Sign, Pet Milk, Tin, Bubble, 1959, 30 x 36 In. 525.00
Sign, Phelans Paints, Man Holding Can, Red, Yellow, Blue, Tin, Embossed, 47 x 71 In. . . . 192.00
Sign, Philip Morris, Call For, Black, White Letters, Cigarettes, Porcelain, 22 In. 605.00
Sign, Philip Morris, Johnny, Call For Philip Morris, Tin, Self-Framed, 14 x 27 In. 165.00
Sign, Philip Morris, Johnny, Die Cut, Cardboard, Easel Back, 15 x 5 1/4 In. 198.00
Sign, Philip Morris, The Best Resolution, Cardboard, 1940, 28 x 22 In. 85.00
Sign, Phillies Cigars, Only 5 Cents, Blue, Yellow, Brown, Wax Board, Frame, 14 x 42 In. . . 110.00
Sign, Piedmont, Virginia Cigarette, Paper Lithograph, 9 1/2 x 19 1/2 In. 55.00
Sign, Pince-Nez Spectacles, Red & Blue Glass Lenses, Cast Iron, 11 x 22 In. 1880.00
Sign, Piso's Cure For Consumption & Remedy For Catarrh, Paper, 19 x 14 In. 3575.00
Sign, Piso's Remedy For Catarrh, Lake, Boats, Paper, Frame, 19 x 14 In. 3580.00
Sign, Poll-Parrot, Enameled, Green, Yellow & Red, Poll-Parrot Shoes, 1950, 24 In. 2875.00
Sign, Pop Kola, That's It, Bottle, Blue, Yellow, Brown, Tin, 29 x 10 In. 80.00
Sign, Post Toasties, Couple On Swing, Die Cut, Cardboard, 29 x 18 1/2 In. 935.00
Sign, Premier, Mill Behind A Good Cup Of Coffee, Grinder, Cup Of Coffee, 18 x 12 In. . . . 65.00
Sign, Prince Albert Tobacco, Chief Joseph, Tin Lithograph, Frame, 28 x 22 In. 1555.00
Sign, Pure Premium, Be Sure With Pure, Blue, White, Red, Porcelain, 12 x 10 In. 110.00
Sign, Purity Ice Cream, Take Some Home, Red, Yellow, Tin, Flange, 18 x 14 In. 165.00
Sign, Quail Cigars, Die Cut, Paper, 8 x 12 In. 155.00
Sign, Quaker Maid, Milk, First In Quality, Woman, Porcelain, Die Cut, 24 x 41 In. 2750.00
Sign, Railway Express Agency, Depot, Porcelain, Black, Yellow, 72 x 11 1/2 In. 115.00
Sign, RCA Radiotron Tubes, Countertop, Die Cut, Cardboard, Easel Back, 15 x 9 In. 1210.00
Sign, RCA Radiotron Tubes, Countertop, Metal, Lithograph, Carton, 1920s, 6 x 9 In. 90.00
Sign, RCA Victor, His Master's Voice, Canvas Lithograph, Frame, 1901, 27 x 34 In. 310.00
Sign, Reading Battery Service, Tin, Embossed, 14 1/2 x 14 In. 525.00
Sign, Rebel Gas, Flag, Porcelain, Red, White, Blue, 2-Sided, 6 In. Diam. 2640.00
Sign, Recommend & Sell Winchester, Brass, Mounted On Stand, 6 7/8 x 3 In. 230.00
Sign, Red Goose Shoes For Girls & Boys, Red, Yellow, Black, Tin, Embossed, 13 x 19 In. . 185.00
Sign, Red Raven Drink, Victorian Lady Hugging Red Raven, Metal, 1900, 24 In. 2750.00
Sign, Redford's Celebrated Tobaccos, Mat, Frame, c.1910, 19 1/2 x 24 1/2 In. 340.00
Sign, Reid's Flower Seeds, Girl, Woman, Gardening, Paper, Mat, Frame, 14 x 20 In. 1870.00
Sign, Remington UMC, Store, Paper, 1920s, 24 3/4 x 17 In. 3520.00
Sign, Reverse Paint On Glass, Black Ground, 34 x 40 In. 330.00
Sign, Rexall, Amos 'n' Andy, Fresh Air Taxi, Tin Lithograph, 2-Sided, 14 3/4 x 34 In. 240.00
Sign, Rhinelander Butter, We Sell A Lot Of, Tin, 9 x 13 In. 80.00
Sign, Rice's Seeds, True Early Winningstadt, Paper, Mat, Frame, c.1879, 28 x 19 In. 1980.00
Sign, Richmond Cigarette, Woman In Victorian Dress, Paper, Frame, 17 x 14 In. 605.00
Sign, Richmond Stove Co., Armor Clad Warriors, Porcelain, Bracket, 14 3/4 x 17 In. 1785.00
Sign, Rolex, Watches, Blue, White, Gold, Porcelain, 18 x 30 In. 770.00
Sign, Rolling Rock, Cap On Cap, Horse, Rider, Light-Up, 18 x 12 In. 110.00
Sign, Rose-O-Cuba, 5cent Cigars, Tin, Self-Framed, 13 x 36 In. 165.00
Sign, Roxbury Rye, Uncle Sam Guarantees, Paper, Frame, 38 x 28 In. 2475.00

Advertising, Sign, None Such
Condensed Mince Meat, Tin
Lithograph, 14 x 20 In.

Advertising, Sign, Tetley's Teas
Please, Tin Lithograph,
Self-Framed, Hanger, 19 x 13 1/2 In.

Advertising, Sign, Weed Chains,
Cutout, Gas Price Dial, Tin
Lithograph, 23 1/2 x 17 In.

Sign, Royal Crown Cola, Best By Taste Test, Red, Yellow, White, Brown, Tin, 18 x 54 In. . . 275.00
Sign, Royal Crown Cola, Bottle Shape, Die Cut, Tin, 58 x 15 1/2 In. 145.00
Sign, Royal Crown Cola, Bottle, Red, Yellow, Tin, Embossed, Frame, 1936, 36 x 11 In. . . . 190.00
Sign, Royal Crown Cola, Ice Cold, Bottle, Tin, Embossed, 1936, 12 x 30 In. 275.00
Sign, Royal Crown Cola, Santa Singing, Merry Christmas, Paper, 1960s, 24 x 13 In. 55.00
Sign, Royal Crown Cola, Tin, Die Cut, 2-Sided, 1941, 16 x 24 In. 770.00
Sign, Royal Crown Cola, Tin, Die Cut, Embossed, 1952, 58 x 15 1/2 In. 275.00
Sign, Royster, Field Tested Fertilizers, Red, White, Blue, Porcelain, 12 x 36 In. 176.00
Sign, Ruchti Bros. Baby Beef, Porcelain, 1951, 26 x 32 In. 550.00
Sign, Rush Bros., Shoes For Young, Millinocket, Wood, c.1900, 37 1/2 x 13 In. 1175.00
Sign, Salada Tea, Yellow, Brown, Porcelain, 8 x 16 In. 120.00
Sign, Santa Fe Trail Bus Depot, Porcelain, 2-Sided, 1920s, 26 x 23 In. 7150.00
Sign, Sapolin No. 66 Black Stove Pipe & Iron Enamel, Tin Lithograph, 9 x 13 In. 3905.00
Sign, Schaefer Beer, Brooklyn Dodgers, Mounted, Frame, 1955, 27 x 19 3/4 In. 1815.00
Sign, Schlitz, Neon, Flashing, 2 Colors, c.1960, 35 In. 210.00
Sign, Scotch Irish Whiskey, Reverse Paint On Glass, 1800s, 72 In. 220.00
Sign, Scourene Soap, Arrest All Dirt & Cleanse, Policeman, Paper, 13 x 10 In. 65.00
Sign, Sherwin-Williams, Paints, Cover The Earth, Red, Yellow, Porcelain, 30 x 48 In. 185.00
Sign, Snow White Cream Soda, Snow-Covered Trees, Tin, Canada Barker, 14 x 29 In. 60.00
Sign, SOC Credit Card, Wooden, Die Cut Boy, 1973, 48 x 26 In. 495.00
Sign, Squeeze, Bottle, Boy, Girl, Arms Around Each Other, Tin, 21 x 29 In. 490.00
Sign, Squirrel Brand Salted Peanuts, Paperboard, 12 x 11 In. 250.00
Sign, Stanley Rule & Level Co., Improved Carpenter's Tool, Frame, c.1886, 14 x 22 In. . . . 715.00
Sign, Star Laundry, Agency, Danville, Va., Blue, White, Porcelain, 18 x 18 In. 220.00
Sign, State Forest Warden, Please Report Forest Fires Here, Tin, Flange, 10 x 19 In. 220.00
Sign, State Quail Management Area, No Hunting Allowed, Metal, Embossed, 11 x 19 In. . . 110.00
Sign, Stetson Hats, Hunting Scene, Embossed, Paperboard, 20 x 11 1/2 In. 660.00
Sign, Stoneware, American Art Works, Tin, Coshocton, Ohio, 19 x 13 In. 2300.00
Sign, Stoneware, Best Food Container, Boy, Dog, In Kitchen, Tin, c.1910, 19 x 13 In. 1760.00
Sign, Stroh's Bohemian Beer, Fishermen, Frame, 1940s, 19 x 14 In. 385.00
Sign, Sun Spot, Bottled Sunshine, Tin, Embossed, 29 x 20 1/2 In. 110.00
Sign, Sunbeam Bread, Girl, Tin, 1972, 48 x 48 In. 385.00
Sign, Sunbeam Bread, Girl, Tin, Embossed, 1967, 12 x 29 1/2 In. 195.00
Sign, Sunbeam Bread, Girl, Tin, Embossed, Self-Framed, 1956, 47 x 47 In. 990.00
Sign, Sunbeam Bread, Girl, Tin, Embossed, Stout, Self-Framed, 1973, 35 x 71 In. 385.00
Sign, Surety Bonds, Casualty Insurance, Glass, 1950s, 28 x 20 In. 110.00
Sign, Sweet Caporal Cigarettes & Smoking Tobacco, Cardboard, 12 x 9 In. 236.00
Sign, Tar, Liquorice & Tolu Wafers, Pine Tree, Color, Cardboard, 6 5/8 x 4 3/4 In. 110.00
Sign, Telegraph Here Western Union, Blue, Yellow, Porcelain, Flange, 17 x 25 In. 330.00
Sign, Tetley's Teas Please, Tin Lithograph, Self-Framed, Hanger, 19 x 13 1/2 In. . . . . . . *Illus* 4400.00
Sign, The Rexall Store, Blue, White, Porcelain, 8 x 39 In. 115.00
Sign, This Farm Uses Ferguson System, Tractor, Blue, White, Tin, 11 x 22 In. 80.00
Sign, Tiger Skin Rubber Co., Silver Bell Condoms, Tin Lithograph, 1 3/4 x 2 In. 415.00

Sign, Town Cab Co., Want A Cab?, Gold Gilt, Reverse Glass, 11 1/2 x 8 1/2 In. 65.00
Sign, Triple 16 Cola, It's Bigger, It's Better, 16 Oz., Red, White, Brown, Tin, 31 x 12 In. . . .   220.00
Sign, True Fruit Soda, Statue, Fruit, Soda, Tin Lithograph, Self-Framed, 24 x 38 In. 300.00
Sign, Tube Rose Scotch Snuff, It's Mild & Suits Your Taste, Tin, 18 x 28 In. 35.00
Sign, Tuxedo Tobacco, Joy, Frame, 15 x 10 1/4 In. 99.00
Sign, Valley Bell, Quality Checked Dairy Products, Red, Yellow, Black, Tin, 16 x 20 In. . . .   155.00
Sign, Valvoline Marine Products, Tin, Bubble, 1960, 20 x 28 In. 635.00
Sign, Van Heusen Shirts, Sheet Iron, Early 1900s, 7 1/2 x 59 In.   155.00
Sign, Van Houten's Cocoa, Cardboard, Frame, c.1900, 33 x 24 In.   550.00
Sign, Veedol Skater, Tin, Die Cut, Frame, 1956, 17 1/2 x 9 In. 525.00
Sign, Velvet Kind Ice Cream, Thru-Out The South, Porcelain, 2-Sided, 33 1/2 x 23 In. 440.00
Sign, Vernor's, Deliciously Different, Tin, 10 x 30 In. 55.00
Sign, Vigorator Hair Tonic, Tin Lithograph, 5 1/4 x 9 In. 99.00
Sign, W.D. Grover, Undertaker, Tin Lithograph, Embossed, 5 x 19 3/4 In. 155.00
Sign, Waiting For A Kelly Axe, Kelly Axe & Tool, Charleston, W.Va., 1881, 17 x 23 In. . . .   330.00
Sign, Walk-Over Shoes, Man, Boot, Factory, W.A. Schock, Paper, 1920s, 41 x 27 In. 86.00
Sign, Walter's Barber Shop, Wood, Painted Red & White Striped, c.1900, 6 x 40 In. 3200.00
Sign, We Supply Oysters, Mace Woodford & Co., Cambridge, Md., Early 1900s 1058.00
Sign, Weatherbird, Boy Holding Sign, Embossed, Cardboard, 1940-50, 9 x 6 In. 29.00
Sign, Webaco, Credit Cards Honored, Tin, 2-Sided, Flange, Ready Made, 14 x 20 In. 55.00
Sign, Webbers Boot Shop, Goodrich Rubber Footwear, Tin, Me., 1920s, 13 x 39 In. 110.00
Sign, Weed Chains, Cutout, Gas Price Dial, Tin Lithograph, 23 1/2 x 17 In. . . . . *Illus*   4675.00
Sign, Wells Fargo & Co., Express, Porcelain, Flattened, Flange, 23 x 21 In. 58.00
Sign, West End Utica Beer, Reverse Glass, Crimped Metal Frame, 18 x 4 1/2 In. 1660.00
Sign, Western Ammunition, Dog, In Chair, Clothes, Ammunition, Frame, 26 x 20 In. 165.00
Sign, Western Ammunition, Elk Fight, 1920, 27 x 18 In. 825.00
Sign, Whale Inn, Tavern, Textured Gesso, Wooden, Late 20th Century, 18 x 13 In. 230.00
Sign, Whistle, Thirsty?, Just Whistle, Bottle Shape, Die Cut, Cardboard, 30 1/4 x 8 In. 99.00
Sign, Whistle, Thirsty?, Just Whistle, Tin Lithograph, Embossed, 14 x 19 1/2 In. 495.00
Sign, White House Tea, Woman Pouring Tea, Paperboard, 2-Sided, 15 x 10 In. 275.00
Sign, White Orchid Cigar, 5 Cents, You'll Enjoy Every Puff, Tin, Embossed, 10 x 21 In. . .   605.00
Sign, Whitlock Waterflex Cordage, Tin, Embossed, Self-Framed, 13 x 9 In. 55.00
Sign, Wiedmann's Beer, Man, Newspaper, Children, Die Cut, Tin, 13 3/4 x 9 3/4 In. 605.00
Sign, Wieland's Pale Lager, Indian, Tin Lithograph, Self-Framed, 1901, 17 In. 4840.00
Sign, Winchester Ammunition, Metal, Round, Rider Logo, 1970s, 20 In. 160.00
Sign, Wonder Bread, Be A Wonder Winner, Mickey Mantle, Stan Musial, 21 x 44 In. 5500.00
Sign, Worcester Buckeye Farm Implements, Mass., Early 1900s, 12 1/2 x 31 In. 470.00
Sign, Wyandote Cleaner & Cleanser, Indian, Arrow, Self-Framed, 30 x 24 In. 495.00
Sign, Yale, Look For Name, Locks & Hardware, Brass, 4 5/8 x 7 In. 205.00
Sign, Yeast Foam, Delicious Buckwheat Cakes, Chromolithograph, Frame, 15 x 10 In. 110.00
Soap Dish, Gold Dust, Black Baby Looking At Mouse, 2 x 4 In. 59.00
Spoon, Borden, Elsie Ice Cream, Wax Wrapper, Ritwrap-O.W.D. Corp., 2 Piece 5.00
Spoon, Toddle House, Restaurant Ware, Engraved, Marked, International S. Co. 154.00
Stickpin, Moxie, Moxie Girl, Die Cut, Lithograph, c.1900, 2 x 2 In. 100.00
Stove, Simmons Wilson 316, Cast Iron, Salesman's Sample, 18 x 7 In. 6600.00
Stringholder, Dutch Boy, Red Seal Paint, Tin Lithograph, 2-Sided, 25 x 14 In. 1320.00
Stringholder, Heinz, Pickle, Die Cut 5225.00
Stringholder, Red Goose Shoes, Red Goose, Tin Lithograph, 2-Sided, 27 1/2 x 17 In. 1760.00
Tablespoon, Walgreen's Restaurant Ware, Engraved Handle 14.00
Tag, American Navy Brand Tobacco, Tin, 1 3/4 x 1 In. 15.00
Tag, Black Mirah Tobacco, Tin, Late 1800s-Early 1900s 7.00
Tag, Double Cola, Good Luck, Horseshoe, Clover, Tin, 1938, 7 x 4 In. 110.00
Tag, Taylor Brothers, Rich & Ripe Tobacco, Late 1800s-Early 1900s 6.00
Tap Knob, Ball, Black River Ale, Syracuse, N.Y., Black Letters, White Ground, 2 1/2 In. . .   132.00
Tap Knob, Ball, Deer Park Beer, Port Jervis, N.Y., Deer Head, Ivory Ground, 2 1/2 In. 200.00
Tap Knob, Ball, Horse Head, Stars, White Ground, Porcelain Front, 2 1/2 In. 120.00
Teapot, McCormick, Black, White Letters, 16 In. 165.00
Thermometers are listed in their own category.
Tie Bar, Evinrude Motors, Children In Boat, Gold Plated, Enamel, 1950s, 3 x 3 In. 58.00
Tie Bar, Packard Bell, 3 x 1/2 In. 85.00
Tie Bar, Singer, Silvertone, Spring Clip, 1 3/4 In. 18.00
Tie Bar, Smith & Wesson, Gun, Figural, Marked 18.00
Tie Tack, Peppy Flame, 10K EMB, Diamond In Hand, 3/4 In. 38.00

Advertising tin cans or canisters were first used commercially in the United States in 1819 and were called *tins*. The English language is sometimes confusing. Today the word *tin* is used by most collectors to describe many types of containers, including food tins, biscuit boxes, roly poly tobacco containers, gunpowder cans, talcum powder sprinkle-top cans, cigarette flat-fifty tins, and more. Beer Cans are listed in their own category. Things made of undecorated tin are listed under Tinware.

Tin, A&P, Bokar Coffee, 3 3/4 x 2 x 1 1/2 In. 10.00
Tin, A&P, Spanish Nuts, Salted, 2 For 39 Cents, Key Wind, 3 x 3 1/2 In. 25.00
Tin, Air Float, Woman, c.1920 .... 45.00
Tin, Albus Dental Plate, A Babbitt Product, Red, White, Blue, 3 1/8 In. 100.00
Tin, Ames, ABC Salve, 3 1/2 In. Diam. 20.00
Tin, Antikamnia & Quinine Tablets, Green, Black, 2 3/8 x 1 1/2 In. 130.00
Tin, Antikamnia Laxative Tablets, Lithograph, Contents, 1 1/2 x 1 1/4 In. 80.00
Tin, Aunt Nellie's Cream Of Tartar, Tin Lithograph, 2 Oz. 110.00
Tin, Avon, 91st Anniversary Perfumed Talc Pastels, California Perfume, 1977, 5 In. 15.00
Tin, Babcocks Corylopsis Talcum Powder 35.00
Tin, Bagleys Old Colony, Girl, Pocket, 4 1/4 In. 80.00
Tin, Bauer & Back First Aid Kit, Compact, 5 1/2 x 3 1/2 x 1/4 In. 12.00
Tin, Beech-Nut Chewing Tobacco, Quality Made It Famous, 10 x 8 1/2 In. 330.00
Tin, Beech-Nut Coffee, 1 Lb. 22.00
Tin, Belgium Ointment, For Man Or Beast, E.H. Hudfield, 50 Cents, 3 3/4 In. Diam. 90.00
Tin, Berkshire Brand Peanut Butter, 1920s, 5 Lb., 6 1/4 x 5 1/2 In. 65.00
Tin, Bickmorine Powder, Horse, 70 Cents, Old Town Maine, 6 In. 95.00
Tin, Big Ben Tobacco, Brown Horse, Red Ground, Hinged Lid, 4 1/4 In. ....28.00 to 45.00
Tin, Black Cat Virginia Cigarette, Paper Seal, 5 3/4 x 4 1/4 In. 20.00
Tin, Black Cough Drops, Red, Yellow, Bone Eagle & Co., 7 3/8 x 5 In. 190.00
Tin, Blankes Good Times Roasted Coffee, Paper Label, 20 In. 220.00
Tin, Blended Coffee, Paper Label, 5 Lb. 35.00
Tin, Blue Flame Coffee, There's A Witchery In The Flavor, Paper Label, Key Wind, 1 Lb. . 90.00
Tin, Blue Plate Coffee, Blue Willow Pattern On Cup & Saucer, Key Wind, 1 Lb. 45.00
Tin, Blue Spot, 5 Cents, Lithograph, Square, 5 1/2 x 5 In. 70.00
Tin, Bon Olive Oil, For Culinary & Medical Purposes, 1950s, 6 x 3 3/4 x 1 1/2 In. 15.00
Tin, Boston Coffee's Golden Rio, Paper Label, c.1880, 13 x 13 In. 275.00
Tin, Bouquet Coffee, 1 Lb. 165.00
Tin, Browns Bronchial Troches, Paper Label, 3 1/4 x 4 1/2 In. 50.00
Tin, Buckingham Bright Cut Plug Smoking Tobacco, Orange & Blue, 2 x 2 In. 130.00
Tin, Bumble Bee Coffee, Bees On Clover, 1 Lb. 130.00
Tin, Bunny Blend Coffee, Paper Label, Rabbits On Sides, Corbin Sons, 6 x 4 1/2 In. 545.00
Tin, Bunte Marshmallows, 2 x 4 1/4 In. 17.00
Tin, Butter-Nut Coffee, 1 Lb., 5 x 3 In. 12.00
Tin, Butter-Nut Coffee, 10 Cent Coupon Inside, Unopened, 6 Cups, 2 1/4 In. 55.00
Tin, Calumet, Breadbox, Home Comet, Tin, Square, 1889, 12 In. 40.00
Tin, Capitol Mills Coffee 120.00
Tin, Capitol Mills, Pure Coffee, Lincoln, Seyms & Co., Lithograph, 5 1/2 x 5 In. 130.00
Tin, Cedar Brand Talcum Powder, Baby, Contents, c.1907 .... 360.00
Tin, Charles Cookies, Musser Potatoe Chip Co., Mountville, Pa. 11.00
Tin, Chase & Sanborn, Tea, c.1930, 1/2 Lb., 5 x 3 3/4 x 3 3/4 In. 125.00
Tin, Chase Family Coffee, Lithograph, 2 Lb., 9 x 5 In. 55.00
Tin, Chesterfield Cigarettes, Flat, Liggett & Meyers Tobacco Co. 25.00
Tin, Chiclets, 5 1/2 x 4 x 1/2 In. 12.00
Tin, Cigar, Cy Young, Mild Havana Blend, Portrait, Cylindrical, c.1905 .... 3410.00
Tin, Clabber Girl, Paper Label, 1931, 4 x 2 3/4 In. 10.00
Tin, Clover Farm, Cloves, Slide Lid, 1 1/2 Oz., 2 1/2 x 2 1/4 In. 38.00
Tin, Clover Farm, Pumpkin Pie Spice, Slide Lid, Tin, Cleveland, Ohio, 1 1/2 Oz. 45.00
Tin, Co-Re-Ga Denture Adhesive, Sample, Cleveland, Ohio 25.00
Tin, Coach & Four, Pocket, 4 1/4 In. 360.00
Tin, Colman's Mustard, Bull's Head, 4 Oz. 25.00
Tin, Counsellor Cigar, Lithograph, Man, White Beard, 5 x 3 1/2 In. 100.00
Tin, Country Club Talcum Powder, Paper On Cardboard, Tin Lid, 5 1/2 In. 50.00
Tin, Cr. Tartar, Bacon, Stickneys & Co., Albany, N.Y., 15 1b., 9 1/2 x 7 1/2 In. 50.00

Tin, Cream Of Tartar, Gilbert Bros. & Co., 9 x 6 In. 120.00
Tin, Culture Smoking Tobacco, Pocket, 4 1/4 In. 95.00
Tin, Cuticura Talcum Powder, Pottier Drug & Chemical Co., 5 In. 35.00
Tin, Cy Young Cigar, Portrait, Front & Back, c.1910 .... 3410.00
Tin, Daniel Boone Axle Grease, Heals Sores On Man Or Beast, 1 Lb., 4 x 3 1/4 In. 105.00
Tin, Denison's Colonial Inn Brand Coffee, Paper Label, 3 Lb., 8 x 5 1/4 In. 100.00
Tin, Dentapearl Tooth Powder, White, Green, Talcum Puff Co., 4 1/8 In. 405.00
Tin, Derby Peter Pan Peanut Butter, Key Wind, Late 1950s, 1 Lb. 12 Oz. 45.00
Tin, Dill's Best, Paper Stamp On Lid, 4 1/2 In. 65.00
Tin, Dove Brand Rubbed Sage, Turkey, Tin Lithograph, 2 Oz. 99.00
Tin, Dr. Daniel's Liniment Powder, Original Equine Bath, 50 Cents, Blue, 3 x 2 1/2 In. ... 95.00
Tin, Dr. E.L. Graves Tooth Powder, No. 468, Cylindrical, 4 1/4 In. 70.00
Tin, Dr. Edwards Compound Dandelion Tablets, Schenck Chemical Co., 2 7/8 x 2 In. 90.00
Tin, Dr. Lyon's Tooth Powder, Woman, Blue, 2 5/8 In. 70.00
Tin, Dr. Whetzel's Asthma Medicine, Contents, 3 3/8 x 3 1/4 x 1 3/8 In. 35.00
Tin, Droste Holland Candy, Haarlem, Mid 20th Century, 4 1/2 x 7 1/4 x 3 In. 70.00
Tin, Droste's Cocoa, Holland, 4 Oz., 4 1/4 x 2 1/4 In. 30.00
Tin, Edgeworth Tobacco, Crosshatch, Tax Exempt Stamp 330.00
Tin, Electric Salve, Quick & Sure Cure For Burns, 50 Cents, Green, Black, 4 In. Diam. ... 70.00
Tin, Elmer's Candy, Creamy Pecan Pralines, Southern Confections 29.00
Tin, Epicure Shredded Plug Tobacco, 4 In. 255.00
Tin, Euthymol Tooth Powder, Gold, Green, Parke, Davis & Co., 4 In. 550.00
Tin, F.B.G. Coffee, Slip Lid, Paper Label, 1 Lb. 65.00
Tin, First Prize Coffee, Key Wind, 1 Lb. 45.00
Tin, Flying Dutchman, Ship, Blue, Black, Theodorus Niemeyer Ltd., 4 1/4 x 1 1/4 In. 15.00
Tin, Foley's Coffee, Wagon Train, Key Wind 230.00
Tin, Folger's, Golden Gate, Ships, Roses, 5 Lb., 8 1/2 x 7 In. 125.00
Tin, Forest & Stream Tobacco, 4 1/8 In. 155.00
Tin, Frank's Dove Spice, Marjoram, Rubbed, Slide Lid, 1 1/4 Oz. 20.00
Tin, Fresh Oysters, T.A. Treakle & Son, Palmer, Va., Pt., 3 3/4 x 3 1/2 In. 32.00
Tin, G. Washington Instant Coffee, Flat, 3 x 2 x 1/2 In. 30.00
Tin, G. Washington Instant Coffee, Twist Lid, 4 Oz., 3 1/2 In. 35.00
Tin, Game Fine Cut Tobacco, Jno. J. Bagley & Co., 7 x 11 1/2 x 7 1/2 In. 220.00
Tin, Garfield Digestive Tablets, President Garfield, Blue, Gold, 2 7/8 x 1 3/4 In. 30.00
Tin, Gold Dust Tobacco, Tin, Miner Panning For Gold, 2 Men Watching, 4 1/2 In. 3575.00
Tin, Gold-Tex Rubber Co., Condoms, Lithograph, 2 x 2 1/8 x 1/4 In. 275.00
Tin, Grand Union Mustard, Tin, Sliding Lid, 2 3/4 Oz. 10.00
Tin, Granger Laxative Medicine, Purely Vegetable, 25 Cents, 1 5/8 x 1 3/8 x 2 5/8 In. 35.00
Tin, Gre-Solvent, Cleans Hands Clean, Utility Co., New York, 3 1/2 x 2 1/4 In. 20.00
Tin, Great Seal Talcum Powder, Contents 70.00
Tin, H. Anton Bock & Co., Box Shape, Lithograph, 2 x 6 1/2 x 5 1/2 In. 20.00
Tin, Half & Half Tobacco, 3 x 3 In. 32.00
Tin, Haller's Tooth Powder, Woman, No Injurious Ingredients, Cylindrical, 4 3/4 In. 990.00
Tin, Hartz Mountain, Canary, Song Food, 35 Cents, 3 1/2 x 2 1/2 In. 30.00
Tin, Hexamine Tablets, Uric Acid Solvent, Syracuse, N.Y., 1 3/8 In. Diam. 30.00
Tin, Hoadley's, Try Moses Brand Cough Drops, Orange, 2 1/2 x 2 7/8 x 1 5/8 In. 110.00
Tin, Hoffman House Cigar, Man In Tuxedo, Embossed, Red Ground, 5 3/4 x 3 1/2 In. 28.00
Tin, Hoffman's Old Time Blended Coffee, 1 Lb., 4 In. 150.00
Tin, Home Brand Coffee, Mansion, Slip Lid, 1 Lb. 55.00
Tin, Honeymoon, Rum Flavored Tobacco, Hinged Lid, Penn Tobacco Co., 4 1/2 x 3 In. ... 100.00
Tin, Hostess Fruit Cake, Woman Holding Cake, 11 1/4 x 3 1/2 x 3 In. 35.00
Tin, Huberd's Shoe Oil, Screw Lid, Cone Top, 4 1/4 In. 35.00
Tin, Huntley & Palmers Biscuits, Roses, Pink, Yellow, Garden, 3 1/2 x 10 In. 36.00
Tin, Huntley & Palmers, Scottish Tartan, John O'Groats Shortbread, 4 1/2 x 5 In. 49.00
Tin, IGA Potato Chips, Big-Big Can, Red, Yellow, White, 20 Oz., 11 1/4 In. 35.00
Tin, In-Be-Tween Cigaritos, 8 1/4 x 4 x 2 1/2 In. 32.00
Tin, Indian Rifle Gunpowder, Hazard Powder Co., Late 1800s, 2 3/4 In. 880.00
Tin, Ivin's Biscuits, Hinged Lid, Wire Bail, Brass Latch, 5 x 5 In. 40.00
Tin, Ivin's Cheese Flakes, Silhouettes, Red Lid, 12 Oz., 5 x 6 In. 45.00
Tin, J.J. Hillis Teas & Coffee, 12 x 7 In. 22.00
Tin, Jack Sprat Peanut Butter, Lime Green, Jack In Green Outfit, 9 x 10 In. 1180.00
Tin, Jergens Miss Dainty Talcum Powder, Girls, Contents 187.00
Tin, Kan-Tartar Compound, For Baking, Blue Green, Gold Letters, 8 x 5 1/2 In. 32.00

Tin, Keen's Mustard, Lithograph, Multiple Scenes, Unusual Shape, 5 1/2 x 7 x 7 In. 99.00
Tin, Kernel-Fresh, Salted Nuts, Key Wind, c.1950, 3 1/2 In. 75.00
Tin, Kickapoo Indian Salve, Buffalo, 1 3/4 In. Diam. 165.00
Tin, Kroger's Grapefruit Juice, Paper Label, Patent Date 1938, 14 Oz. 10.00
Tin, Lady Orchid Hair Straight, Woman's Profile, New York, 3 In. 12.00
Tin, Lan Tox Tooth Powder, 25 Cents, Aqua, Cylindrical, 4 1/4 In. 580.00
Tin, Lander Powder, Flower Bouquets, Man, Woman In Garden, Gold Trim, 4 In. 28.00
Tin, Lauxes Tablets, Sextonique, Factory, Cumberland Chemical, $2, 2 1/2 x 1 1/2 In. 60.00
Tin, Lilac & Roses Talc, Landers Blended Flower, New York, 1 Lb., 7 3/4 x 3 x 2 In. 45.00
Tin, Lily Of The Valley Coffee, Lithograph, 1 Lb., 6 x 4 1/2 In. 99.00
Tin, Little Elf Coffee, Elf Carrying Tray, Bursley & Co., Fort Wayne, 1 Lb. ....635.00 to 670.00
Tin, Lucky Strike, Cut Plug, R.A. Patterson Tobacco Co., Richmond, Va., 4 x 3 In. 25.00
Tin, Lucky Strike, It's Toasted, Green, Flat Fifty, 6 x 4 In. ....25.00 to 35.00
Tin, Luden's Menthol Cough Drops, Give Quick Relief, Box, 3 3/4 x 2 In. 360.00
Tin, Mad-Ox Herb Tablets, Nature's Health Tablets, United Medicine Co., 1 3/4 x 4 In. ... 120.00
Tin, Marble's Gun Oil, Plastic Spout, Cap, Black, Orange, White, Bear, Moose, 3 Oz. 59.00
Tin, Marble's Nitro Solvent Oil, Lead Spout, Cap, Black, Orange, 3 Oz. 215.00
Tin, Maritana Chewing Tobacco, 2 3/4 x 6 1/2 x 3 1/4 In. 32.00
Tin, Marvens Biscuit, Horse Race, 6 In. 110.00
Tin, Mason Perfumed Talcum Powder, Baby, Contents 305.00
Tin, May Queen Tobacco, Pocket, 2 1/2 x 3 3/4 x 3/4 In. 275.00
Tin, Mellomints, Red Ground, White Letter, 1910, 10 In. 115.00
Tin, Mennen Borated Talcum Powder, Gerhard Mennen, Round ....70.00 to 90.00
Tin, Merck Zinc Stearate, Waterproof Toilet Powder, Sheds Water Like A Duck, 5 In. 36.00
Tin, Mineral Compound For Horses, General Treatment, Red, Square, 3 3/4 x 2 In. 200.00
Tin, Model Tobacco, Paper Label, Nov. 1948, 4 1/2 x 5 3/4 In. 35.00
Tin, Monarch Coffee, Lion, Key Wind, 1 Lb. 35.00
Tin, Morrell's Pride Lard, Heart, Gold Ground, 14 1/2 x 13 In. 120.00
Tin, Mother Hubbard Energy, Energy Wheat Cereal, 5 Lb., 10 x 6 1/2 In. 50.00
Tin, Mother Joy Coffee, A Pleasing Cup For All Occasions, Screw Lid, 1 Lb. 30.00
Tin, Mrs. Van Cotts Excelsior Throat Lozenges, Portrait, 10 Cents 2 1/8 x 1 1/8 In. 200.00
Tin, My Baby's Talcum Powder, Sears Roebuck & Co. 175.00
Tin, National Biscuit Company, Famous Chocolate Wafers, Screw Lid, 10 Oz. 15.00
Tin, Nature's Cure, Celebrated Blood Purifier & Liver Regulator, 3 5/8 x 2 3/4 In. 60.00
Tin, Neal's Anti-Gas Tablets, Hot Air Balloon Shape, Blue, White, 3 1/8 x 2 1/8 In. 100.00
Tin, Nu-Tex Co., Radium Brand Condoms, Lithograph, 1 5/8 x 2 1/8 x 1/4 In. 255.00
Tin, Ol' Sarge Gun Oil, Paper Labels, Screw Cap, 2 Oz., 2 1/2 x 2 1/8 In. 12.00
Tin, Old Judge Coffee, Settles The Question, Lithograph, 1 Lb., 6 x 4 1/4 In. 120.00
Tin, Old Manse Syrup, 11 1/4 x 6 x 3 1/2 In. 90.00
Tin, Old Mansion, Paprika, Slide Lid, 1 Oz., 2 In. 20.00
Tin, One-Spot Flea Killer, Dog Silhouette, Use Before December 1942, 2 x 3 1/2 In. 14.00
Tin, Orange Sporting Gun Powder, 6 x 4 x 1 1/4 In. 149.00
Tin, Orange Wafers, Southern Biscuit Co., 4 1/2 In. 35.00
Tin, Orcico Tobacco, 2 For 5 Cents, Indian, 1919, 5 1/2 In. 236.00
Tin, Pal Jones Clean Cut Tobacco, Image Of George Washington, Blue Ground, 5 In. 138.00
Tin, Palmolive Shaving Stick, Lithograph, Man Using Product, 3 1/2 x 1 1/2 In. 230.00
Tin, Pastime Plug Tobacco, Hunter Shooting Ducks, Dog, 4 x 12 1/2 In. 250.00
Tin, Pennsylvania Dutch Candy, Embossed, Mt. Holly Spring, Pa., 5 1/2 x 4 In. 15.00
Tin, Penny Post, Cut Plug, Handle, 7 x 5 x 5 In. 140.00
Tin, Pep Boys, Handy Bulb Kit, Cadet Batteries, Cornell Tires, 4 x 2 3/4 In. 65.00
Tin, Pepsanels, Mclean's Photo, Dr. J.H. Mclean Medicine Co., 2 1/8 x 1 1/4 In. 190.00
Tin, Petry Retainer, Jacob Petry Inventor, 1 3/4 x 1 1/4 In. 145.00
Tin, Philip Morris' Bond Street Brand Tobacco, Tin Lithograph, Trial Size, 2 x 3 x 7/8 In. . 110.00
Tin, Powers & Weightman Quinine Sulphate, Embossed Lid, 1 Oz., 3 x 2 1/2 In. 120.00
Tin, Pride Of Virginia, Sliced Plug, Hinged Lid, Woman, 1/2 x 4 1/2 x 2 5/8 In. 19.00
Tin, Prince Albert, Long Burning Pipe & Cigarette Tobacco, Crimp Cut, 3 x 4 x 1 In. 16.00
Tin, Punch Mop, 3 1/2 x 7 1/2 In. 33.00
Tin, Pure Stock Cigar, Lithograph, 5 1/2 x 5 In. 66.00
Tin, Qboid Granulated Plug, Hinged Lid, Larus Brother & Co., 4 x 2 3/4 In. 45.00
Tin, Quaker Curry Powder, Slide Lid, Woman, Red, White, Blue, 1 1/2 Oz., 2 5/8 x 2 In. .. 30.00
Tin, Quaker Spice, Marjoram, Pry Lid, Woman, Red, White, Blue, 1 Oz., 2 5/8 x 2 In. 28.00
Tin, Quality Oysters, Freshly Shucked, See-Through Lid, 2 3/4 In. 20.00
Tin, Quest, Positive Deodorant Powder, International Cellucotton Products, 1/2 Oz. 70.00

Tin, Rawleigh's Pure Ground Allspice, Slide Lid, Freeport, Ill., 3 Oz., 3 3/4 In. 16.00
Tin, Rays Seafood Fresh Oysters, 2 3/4 In. 20.00
Tin, Real-Lax, Laxative In Tasty Chocolate, Penna Drug Products, Pittsburgh 10.00
Tin, Red Dot Cigar, Truly Different, Federal Cigar Co., 5 x 5 1/2 In. 35.00
Tin, Red Dot Tobacco, 10 For 50 Cents, Barnes-Smith Co., 3 x 4 3/4 In. 65.00
Tin, Red Jacket Smoking Tobacco, 4 1/2 In. 70.00
Tin, Remington Oil, Lead Spout & Cap, Stencil Painted, Yellow, Red, Black, Silver, 3 Oz. . 90.00
Tin, Rexall Drugs Baby Talc, Pink, Blue, 16 Oz., 7 3/4 In. 36.00
Tin, Richelieu Spice, Whole Cinnamon, Slide Lid, 1 1/2 Oz., 3 3/4 In. 20.00
Tin, Rigby's, Rough Havanas, Rose, Paper Label, 5 x 3 1/2 In. 220.00
Tin, Rivera Brand Coffee, Handle, Sears, 5 Lb. 275.00
Tin, Romeos Condoms 72.00
Tin, Rose Of Cuba Cigar, Gleck Cigar Co., Lithograph, 5 1/2 x 5 1/2 In. 99.00
Tin, Rosekist Popcorn, Um-M-M-M Good, Contents, 1950s, 10 Oz., 5 In. 85.00
Tin, Rupaner Laxative Tablets, Smiling Sun, Flyer, Smile Remedy Co., 1 x 1 3/4 In. 33.00
Tin, Sail Pipe Tobacco, Holland, 14 Oz., 5 1/2 x 5 In. 32.00
Tin, Satin Tooth Powder, Pamphlet, Box, 3 3/4 In. 77.00
Tin, Scull's Ginger, Young Girl, Contents, 4 x 2 1/4 x 1 1/2 In. 187.00
Tin, Seal Of Minnesota Coffee, Knob Top, 1 Lb. 143.00
Tin, Select Lilac Talcum Powder, Contents, c.1907 . . . . 176.00
Tin, Sent-A-Nel Laxative Tablets, Purely Vegetable, Soldier, 2 x 1 1/2 In. 30.00
Tin, Sentinel Utility First Aid Kit, Cleveland, Ohio, 6 1/8 x 3 1/4 x 1 In. 15.00
Tin, Sheridan's Cavalry Conditioning Powder, Cure, For Animals, 5 x 4 In. 575.00
Tin, Silver Buckle Spices, Red Pepper, Cayenne, Twist Lid, 1 1/2 Oz., 2 1/2 In. 25.00
Tin, Sir Walter Raleigh Tobacco, Key Wind, 7 Oz., 4 In. 55.00
Tin, Smith Bros. Cough Drops, S.B., Portraits, 10 Cents, 3 5/8 x 2 1/4 In. 580.00
Tin, Sozodont Tooth Powder, Man Brushing, Van Buskirk Fragrant, Hall & Ruckel, 4 In. . . 525.00
Tin, Spartan, Cream Of Tartar, Slide Lid, 1 1/2 Oz. 22.00
Tin, Sportsman Cigarette Tobacco, Screw Lid, Canada, Port 13-D 30.00
Tin, Stag Tobacco, Red Stag, Hinged Lid, 4 1/2 x 3 In. 60.00
Tin, Steero Chicken Bouillon Cubes, American Kitchen Products, 5/8 Oz., 3 x 1 In. 38.00
Tin, Sterling Tobacco, 11 In. 225.00
Tin, Sunset Trail, 5-Cent Cigar, Couple, Horse, Hinged, Oval, 6 In. 575.00
Tin, Sunshine Biscuit, Cherry Blossoms, 11 x 12 1/2 x 2 3/4 In. 29.00
Tin, Superior's Mixed Nuts, Salted, Always Fresh & Crispy, Key Wind, 3 1/2 In. 16.00
Tin, Sweet Burley Tobacco, Dark, Red, Gold, 10 1/2 In. . . . . .140.00 to 225.00
Tin, Sweet Burley Tobacco, Light, 11 1/2 x 8 1/4 In. 187.00
Tin, Sweet Cuba Chewing Tobacco, Countertop, 14 x 8 In. 435.00
Tin, Sweet Cuba, Fine Cut, Woman, Green, Red, 5 Lb. 220.00
Tin, Sweet Tip Top Tobacco, Paper Label 95.00
Tin, Sykes Comfort Powder, Nurse Cameo Bust, Contents 145.00
Tin, Tac Cut Coffee, Boy On Eagle, 3 Lb., c.1916 . . . . 470.00
Tin, Texel Tape, 5 1/8 In. Diam. 45.00
Tin, Three Knights, Condoms, 1/4 Dozen, Contents, Goodwear Rubber Co., 1930s 138.00
Tin, Traveler Tobacco, Pry Lid, 3 1/2 x 4 1/4 In. 15.00
Tin, Trout Line Tobacco, 3 1/2 In. 275.00
Tin, Tuxedo Tobacco, Pipe, Green, Gold Letters, 4 1/4 x 3 x 1 In. 35.00
Tin, Two Orphans Cigars, 5 x 5 In. 300.00
Tin, U.S. Marine Flake Cut, 4 1/2 In. 302.00
Tin, Unico All Purpose Oil, Plastic Spout, Cap, Red, White, Blue Stencil, 4 Oz. 12.00
Tin, Union Leader, Redi Cut Tobacco, Uncle Sam, c.1917, 4 3/8 x 3 In. 85.00
Tin, Union Leader, Smoking Tobacco, Eagle, P. Lorillard, 4 1/2 x 3 In. 14.00
Tin, Vantines Wisteria Talcum Powder, Oriental Woman 110.00
Tin, Veteran Brand Coffee, Brewster, Gordon Co., Lithograph, 5 3/4 x 4 1/4 In. 90.00
Tin, Violet Flesh Talcum Powder 38.00
Tin, Violin King Harmonica, Artists Brand, Hinged Lid, F.A. Bohm, Germany 65.00
Tin, War Eagle Cigars, 10 Cents, Dark Green, 5 1/4 x 5 In. 385.00
Tin, Watkins Tooth Powder, Embossed, 6 In. 190.00
Tin, Wedding Ring Brand Coffee, Humphrey & Co., Lithograph, 1920s, 6 x 4 In. 198.00
Tin, Wells Tablets, National Drug Co., 3 5/8 x 2 3/4 In. 35.00
Tin, Winchester, New Gun Oil, Yellow, White, Black, Red 40.00
Tin, Yellow Cab Cigar, Taxi, 5 1/2 x 2 1/2 In. 550.00

Advertising tip trays are decorated metal trays less than 5 inches in diameter. They were placed on the table or counter to hold either the bill or the coins that were left as a tip. Change receivers could be made of glass, plastic, or metal. They were kept on the counter near the cash register and held the money passed back and forth by the cashier. Related items may be listed in the Advertising category under Change Receiver.

Tip Tray, Admiral Hopkins Cigars, Germany, 4 In. 125.00
Tip Tray, Angeles Brewing & Malting Co., Polar Background, Seattle, 4 1/4 In. 95.00
Tip Tray, Ballantine & Sons, Ales & Beers, Keg Shape, Tin, 6 In. 100.00
Tip Tray, Bartholomay, Rochester, N.Y., Woman On Bird, Clouds, 4 In. 165.00
Tip Tray, Booth Bros., Dutch Woman & Girl Carrying Water, Blue & White, 4 In. 55.00
Tip Tray, Bubier's Laxative Salz, Tin Lithograph, 4 1/4 In. 110.00
Tip Tray, Cardinal Beer, Woman, Flowers In Hair, Tin Lithograph, 4 1/4 In. 385.00
Tip Tray, Charles Denby Cigar, Factory, Tin Lithograph, Oval, 6 x 4 1/2 In. 120.00
Tip Tray, Christian Feigenspan Brewery, Woman, Ribbon In Hair, Newark, N.J., 4 In. 105.00
Tip Tray, Cigar, Warwick, The Wenham Cigar Co., Tobacco Color, 6 In. 250.00
Tip Tray, DeLaval, Cream Separators, World's Standard, Tin Lithograph, 4 In. 99.00
Tip Tray, Doniphan Vineyards, Bottle, 4 1/4 In. Diam. 60.00
Tip Tray, El Roi-Tan Cigar, Man & Woman, Tin Lithograph, Oval, 4 1/4 x 6 In. 330.00
Tip Tray, Evinrude Rowboat & Canoe Motors, Woman In Boat, 4 In. 245.00
Tip Tray, Feigenspan, P.O.N., Fine Brews, Tin Lithograph, 4 1/2 In. 18.00
Tip Tray, Fort Pitt Beer, Tin Lithograph, 4 1/4 In. 39.00
Tip Tray, Frank Jones Homestead Ale, Emblem In Center, Red & Back, 5 In. 110.00
Tip Tray, Gallagher & Burton, Tin Lithograph, 4 1/4 In. 65.00
Tip Tray, Garland Stoves, Bake The Bread, Roast The Meats That Make The Man, 4 In. ... 230.00
Tip Tray, Geo. W. Schott, Bar Scene, Tin Lithograph, 4 1/4 In. 130.00
Tip Tray, Germania Brewing Co., Woman, Bonnet, Rose Bouquet, 4 1/4 In. 110.00
Tip Tray, Globe, Phillip Nagel Furniture & Undertaking, 4 1/2 In. 190.00
Tip Tray, Goebel, Dutch Girl Carrying Water, Blue & White Ground, 1900s, 4 1/4 In. 30.00
Tip Tray, Gold Seal Urbana Wine Co., Bottle, Lake In Background, Brown Edge, 6 In. 55.00
Tip Tray, Gypsy Hosiery, Gypsy, Campfire, 6 In. 200.00
Tip Tray, Hernan Cortez, Famous Explorer, 6 In. 300.00
Tip Tray, Home Sewing Machine, Grandma Sewing Pants, Boy In Them, 4 In. 175.00
Tip Tray, I.P. Thomas & Son, High Grade Fertilizers, Tin Lithograph, 4 In. 358.00
Tip Tray, Indianapolis Brewing Co., Lieben's Gold Medal Beer, Bottle, Red Ground, 5 In. . 140.00
Tip Tray, Iroquois Beer, Indian Head, Buffalo, 4 In. 60.00
Tip Tray, J. Chr. G. Hupfel Brewing, Beer, Ale, Tin Lithograph, 4 1/4 In. 55.00
Tip Tray, Kellmer Piano, Woman, Flowers, Tin Lithograph, 4 1/4 In. 250.00
Tip Tray, King's, Pure Malt Liquor, Tin Lithograph, Oval, 4 1/4 x 6 In. 55.00
Tip Tray, Monticello Whiskey, Horses, Hounds, Tin Lithograph, Oval, 6 x 4 1/2 In. 120.00
Tip Tray, Moxie, I Just Love Moxie, Don't You, Victorian Woman, 1906, 6 In. .....132.00 to 440.00
Tip Tray, Narragansett Brewing Co., Tin Lithograph, 5 1/2 In. 300.00
Tip Tray, National Beer, I Thank You, Baltimore, Md., Rectangular, 4 x 6 1/4 In. 30.00
Tip Tray, National Brewing Co., Best In The West, Cowboy, Horse, Bottle, 4 In. 1210.00
Tip Tray, National Cigar, Classic Woman, Bands Around Rim, 6 In. 195.00
Tip Tray, Neuweiler's Beer, Tin Lithograph, Rectangular, 7 1/4 x 5 1/4 In. 110.00
Tip Tray, Oldburger, Perfect Beer, United Brewing, Tin Lithograph, 4 In. 77.00
Tip Tray, P. Ballantine & Sons, Ales, Beers, Tin Lithograph, 5 1/2 In. 28.00
Tip Tray, Quick Meal Ranges, Chicks, St. Louis, Mo., Oval, 4 1/2 x 3 1/4 In. 85.00
Tip Tray, Red Raven, Red Raven With Bottle, 1900, 4 In. 175.00
Tip Tray, Red Raven, Victorian Lady With Bird, c.1900, 3 1/2 x 2 1/2 In. ....175.00 to 385.00
Tip Tray, Roi-Tan, Perfect Cigar, Man & Woman At Table With Box, 6 In. 20.00
Tip Tray, Schnecksville State Bank, Woman Fishing, Large Hat, Green & Black, 6 In. 165.00
Tip Tray, Seitz Beer, Spread Wing Eagle, Tin Lithograph, 4 1/4 In. 99.00
Tip Tray, Shawmut Furniture, Woman, Rose In Hair, Tin Lithograph, 4 1/4 In. 198.00
Tip Tray, Smith Wallace Shoes, Woman Portrait, 4 1/4 In. 44.00
Tip Tray, Stollwerck, Red, Gold, Tin Lithograph, 5 In. 66.00
Tip Tray, Tom Moore Cigars, Photo In Center, Green & White, 4 1/4 In. 248.00
Tip Tray, Universal Stoves, Woman Portrait, 4 1/4 In. 33.00
Tip Tray, Urbana Wine Co., Tin Lithograph, Rectangular, 4 1/4 x 6 1/4 In. 120.00

Tip Tray, Welsbach Lamps, 4 1/4 In. 70.00
Tip Tray, White Rock, World's Best Table Water, Girl By Brook, Black & Red, 6 In. 138.00
Tip Tray, Yeungling's, Beer, Porter, Ale, Eagle, Tin Lithograph, 4 1/2 In. 385.00
Tobacco Pouch, None Such, Celebrated, Fine Cut Cavendish, Silver Foil, 3 1/2 x 2 In. 30.00
Token, Sambo's Restaurant, Good For 10 Cent Cup Of Coffee, Wood, Salem, Oregon 5.00
Tray, Tip, see Tip Trays in this category.
Tray, American, Baltimore, Modern Beer, Tin Lithograph, Round, 13 In. 22.00
Tray, Anheuser-Busch, Factory Scene, Tin Lithograph, Oval, 18 3/4 x 15 1/2 In. 385.00
Tray, Arctic Ice Cream, Cream Supreme, Polar Bear, Tin, Round, 13 1/2 In. 1650.00
Tray, Banker Tobacco, Chew Banker, Clean Tobacco, Made For Men, Round, 15 In. 140.00
Tray, Budweiser, Pub Scene, Fox Hunters Enjoying Brew, 10 1/2 x 13 1/4 In. 60.00
Tray, Buffalo Brewing, Tin, Woman In Large Hat, 12 In. 45.00
Tray, Cascade Beer, We Never Disagree About The Purity, Pre-Prohibition, 13 In. 696.00
Tray, Cook's Beer, Ale, Tin Lithograph, Self-Framed, Oval, 13 1/2 In. 176.00
Tray, Crutch Rye, Chrysanthemum Girl, c.1910, 13 1/4 x 10 1/2 In. 130.00
Tray, Drink Koch's Beer, Fred Kock Brewery, Tin, Round, 13 In. 154.00
Tray, Frontenac, Canada's Best, Factory, Tin Lithograph, Montreal, Round, 12 In. ...55.00 to 145.00
Tray, Gallikers Quality Ice Cream, 2 Children, Tin, Round, c.1923, 13 In. 660.00
Tray, Gin Seng, 13 1/4 x 10 1/2 In. 80.00
Tray, Hagerstown, Tin Lithograph, Oval, 13 3/4 x 16 3/4 In. 1320.00
Tray, Hires, Parrot, Orange, Blue, c.1950, 9 x 14 1/4 x 1 In. 30.00
Tray, Horlacher's, Girl Smelling Flower, Tin Lithograph, Oval, 13 3/4 x 16 3/4 In. 2750.00
Tray, Isaac Weil & Son, Monk, Keg, Tin Lithograph, Oval, 13 1/2 x 16 1/2 In. 385.00
Tray, Jersey Cream, Woman, Charles W. Schaump Lithograph, Tin, Round, 12 In. 275.00
Tray, Kuebler Beer, Since 1852, Tin Lithograph, Easton, Pa., Round, 12 In. 187.00
Tray, Labatt's, London, Canada, Established 1832, Round, 12 1/2 In. 50.00
Tray, Local 132, Beer Drivers Union, Submarine Scene, Tin Lithograph, Round, 13 In. 415.00
Tray, Lord Baltimore Cigarets, Tin, Round, 16 In. 440.00
Tray, Melrose Distillers, Metal, N.Y.C., 11 3/4 In. 25.00
Tray, Neff's Ice Cream, Tin Lithograph, Round, 13 1/4 In. 99.00
Tray, Nehi Soda, Woman In Wave, Tin Lithograph, Rectangular, 10 1/2 x 15 1/4 In. 220.00
Tray, NuGrape Soda, Bottle, Tin Lithograph, Rectangular, 10 1/2 x 13 In. 110.00
Tray, NuGrape, A Flavor You Can't Forget, Tin Lithograph, 10 1/2 x 13 1/4 In. 250.00
Tray, Old Crutch Rye, Monk Bottling Whisky, Oval, 16 1/2 x 13 1/2 In. 130.00
Tray, Orange Julep, Woman Holding Drink, 13 1/4 x 10 1/2 In. 165.00
Tray, Peter Doelger, Bottled Beer, Eagle, Tin Lithograph, Oval, 16 3/4 x 13 3/4 In. 440.00
Tray, Sanitary Ice Cream, We Serve, Waitress, Tin, Round, American Art Works, 13 In. ... 1320.00
Tray, St. Pauli Brewery, Bremen, St. Pauli Girl, Tin, Round, 12 In. 6.00
Tray, Stegmaier Brewing Co., Woman, Long Hair, Tin, Round, Wilkes-Barre, Pa., 13 In. .. 85.00
Tray, Stegmaier Brewing, Factory Scene, Wilkes-Barre, Pa., Round, 12 In. 300.00
Tray, Stokely's Finest Foods, Black Border, Rectangular, 10 1/2 x 13 1/4 In. 20.00
Tray, Stroh's, Lager Beer, Detroit, Tin Lithograph, Round, 12 In. 2200.00
Tray, Sunrise Beer, Sunrise Brewing Co., Cleveland, Round, Tin, 1930s, 12 In. 225.00
Tray, Tru-Blue Beer & Ale, Tin Lithograph, Round, 13 In. 45.00
Tray, Walter Brewing Co., Brewery, Eau Claire, Wis., 10 x 14 3/4 In. 330.00
Tray, West End Brewery, Utica, New York, Victorian Woman Wrapped In Flag, 12 In. 550.00
Tray, Yeungling's, Fine Beer, Tin Lithograph, Round, 12 1/4 In. 360.00
Whistle, Foremost Dairy, Bugle Boy, Horn Shape, Plastic, Premium, 1950s, 5 In. 30.00
Whistle, Weatherbird, All Leather Best For Boys & Girls, Rooster, 2 In. 28.00
Whistle, Weatherbird, Happy Days & Happy Feet, Barrel Form, Green, Tin 25.00

AGATA glass was made by Joseph Locke of the New England Glass
Company of Cambridge, Massachusetts, after 1885. A metallic stain
was applied to New England Peachblow and the mottled design characteristic of agata appeared.

Bowl, Corseted, Crimped Trefoil Rim, Mineral Stain, 5 1/2 x 3 1/2 In. 865.00
Bowl, Wild Rose, Crimped, 2 1/2 In. 200.00
Bowl, Wild Rose, Crimped, 3 1/2 In. 259.00
Bowl, Wild Rose, Mineral Stain, 3-Sided Rim, 2 x 5 In. 575.00
Bowl, Wild Rose, Mineral Stain, Crimped Rim, 8 1/4 x 3 1/8 In. 2590.00
Bowl, Wild Rose, Mineral Stain, Cupped Rim, 3 3/8 x 7 1/4 In. 3450.00
Bowl, Wild Rose, Pinched Waist, Mineral Staining, 3 1/2 x 5 1/2 In. .... *Illus* 840.00
Celery Vase, Wild Rose, Mineral Stain, Crimped Rim, 6 3/8 In. 1035.00

Agata, Pitcher,
Wild Rose, 8 1/2 In.

Agata, Vase, Lily,
Salmon Pink Shaded
To Cream, Mineral
Stain, 7 1/4 In.

Agata, Bowl, Wild Rose,
Pinched Waist, Mineral Staining,
3 1/2 x 5 1/2 In.

Creamer, Wild Rose, Applied Reeded Handle, Flattened Circular Body, 2 3/4 In.	750.00
Cruet, Half Sphere Shape, Cream Stopper & Handle, 5 3/4 In.	5465.00
Cruet, Wild Rose, Mineral Stain, Round, Squat, Cream Stopper, 6 In.	1955.00
Finger Bowl, Deep Wild Rose, Mineral Stain, 2 x 5 1/4 In.	460.00
Pitcher, Wild Rose, 8 1/2 In. ....*Illus*	5600.00
Pitcher, Wild Rose, Applied Opal Reeded Handle, Cylindrical, 6 3/4 In.	1150.00
Pitcher, Wild Rose, Cylindrical, Straight Sides, Mineral Stain, 8 1/2 In.	5750.00
Plate, Wild Rose, Mineral Stain, Crimped Rim, 6 3/4 In.	290.00
Sugar & Creamer, Wild Rose, Mineral Stain, Square Mouth, 4 In.	4255.00
Tumbler, Lemonade, Wild Rose Stain, Low Cream Loop Handle, 5 In.	1430.00
Tumbler, Lemonade, Wild Rose, Out Scalloped Band, Cornflowers, Butterfly, 5 In.	1495.00
Tumbler, Pink Shaded To Cream, 3 5/8 In.	633.00
Vase, Lily, Salmon Pink Shaded To Cream, Mineral Stain, 7 1/4 In. ....*Illus*	1380.00
Vase, Lily, Salmon Pink Shaded To Cream, Mineral Stain, Disc Foot, 5 3/4 In.	1380.00
Vase, Lily, Wild Rose, Mineral Stain, 7 In. ....575.00 to 805.00	
Vase, Pale Pink Shaded To Cream, Mineral Stain, Pinched Sides, Folded Rim, 6 1/4 In.	9200.00
Vase, Pink Shaded To Cream, Pinched Sides, Crimped Quatrefoil Rim, 6 In.	1898.00
Vase, Wild Rose Neck, Bulbous Base, Mineral Stain, Pinched Sides, 6 1/4 In.	920.00
Vase, Wild Rose, Mineral Stain, Hobbs Griffin Holder, 10 1/4 In.	6045.00

AKRO AGATE glass was made in Clarksburg, West Virginia, from 1932 to 1951. Before that time, the firm made children's glass marbles, which are listed in this book in the Marble category. Most of the glass is marked with a crow flying through the letter *A*.

Ashtray, Blue, Marbleized, Square, 2 7/8 In.	10.00
Cigarette Set, Red, Marbleized, Ashtrays, 2 3/4-In. Jar, 5 Piece	160.00
Creamer, Transparent Topaz, Interior Panel, 1 1/2 In.	40.00
Cup & Saucer, Green, Marbleized, Octagonal	22.00
Cup & Saucer, Transparent Green, Stippled Band, 1 3/8 In.	30.00
Cup & Saucer, Transparent Topaz, Interior Panel, 1 1/2 In.	40.00
Drink Set, Play-Time, Transparent Green, Stacked Disc, Interior Panel, Box, 7 Piece	175.00
Flowerpot, Blue, Marbleized, 5 1/8 x 6 In.	90.00
Jar, Cover, Apothecary, Black, 6 1/2 In.	43.00
Sugar, Transparent Topaz, Interior Panel, 1 1/2 In.	60.00
Tea Set, Green, 2 Cups, 2 Saucers	65.00
Tea Set, Play-Time, Swirl Lemonade & Green, Box, 1930s, Large, 12 Piece	275.00
Tea Set, Stipple Band, Blue, Large, 17 Piece	795.00
Teapot, Cover, Transparent Topaz, Interior Panel, c.1935, 2 5/8 In.	95.00
Teapot, Opaque Green, Concentric Ring	15.00
Teapot, Transparent Topaz, Stippled Band, c.1935, 2 3/8 In.	42.00
Tumbler, Ivory, Octagonal, 2 In.	20.00

ALABASTER is a very soft form of gypsum, a stone that resembles marble. It was often carved into vases or statues in Victorian times. There are alabaster carvings being made even today.

Bust, Girl In Straw Hat, Curly Hair, 19th Century, 24 In.	350.00
Bust, Young Beauty Adorned With Flowers, American School, c.1890, 14 3/4 In.	750.00
Figurine, Child Reading, 13 1/2 In.	359.00

Figurine, Elizabethan Woman, Holding Flowers, 19th Century, 20 3/8 In. 1058.00
Figurine, Girl With Lamb, Gathering Flowers, 19th Century, Italy, 22 1/4 In. 880.00
Figurine, Woman Bather On Rock, Tying Ribbon In Hair, 20th Century, 18 1/2 In. 1293.00
Urn, Carved, Neoclassical Style, 15 1/4 In. 717.00

ALEXANDRITE is a name with many meanings. It is a form of the
mineral chrysoberyl that changes from green to red under artificial
light. A man-made version of this mineral is sold in Mexico today. It
changes from deep purple to aquamarine blue under artificial light.
The Alexandrite listed here is glass made in the late nineteenth and
twentieth centuries. Thomas Webb & Sons sold their transparent glass
shaded from yellow to rose to blue under the name Alexandrite.
Stevens and Williams had a cased Alexandrite of yellow, rose, and blue.
A. Douglas Nash Corporation made an amethyst-colored Alexandrite.
Several American glass companies of the 1920s made a glass that
changed color under electric lights and this was also called Alexandrite.

Cordial, Applied Stem, Foot, Ribbing, 3 In. 635.00
Decanter, Bulbous Base, Tapered Neck, Cut Stars, Stopper, 8 1/4 In. 35.00
Hat, Ground Pontil, 2 3/4 In. 1265.00

ALUMINUM was more expensive than gold or silver until the 1850s.
Chemists learned how to refine bauxite to get aluminum. Jewelry and
other small objects were made of the valuable metal until 1914, when
an inexpensive smelting process was invented. The aluminum collected today dates from the 1930s through the 1950s. Hand-hammered
pieces are the most popular.

Bowl, Asymmetrical Edges, Cast, Michael Lax, 1960s, 15 x 12 In. 50.00
Bowl, Cover, Spun, Wooden Knob, 8 In., Pair 100.00
Cigarette Box, Rose, Hinged Cover, Marked, World Hand Forged, 5 1/4 x 3 3/4 In. 55.00
Coffee Set, Chrysanthemum, Urn, Creamer, Sugar, Tray, Continental Silver Co. 95.00
Coffee Urn, Hammered Body, Twisted Legs, Electrical Warming Base, 1960s 135.00
Dessert Set, Mixed Colors, Ruffled Bases, Glass Inserts, 3 1/2 In., 6 Piece 45.00
Ice Bucket, Chrysanthemum, No. 705, Continental Silver Co., 12 x 8 In. 160.00
Ice Bucket, Chrysanthemum, Rolled Handles, Continental Silver Co., 10 In. 60.00
Model, Jet, Plastic Lights As Nose Cone, Square Stand, 1950, 12 x 12 x 5 In. 878.00
Popcorn Set, Jewel Tones, 1950s, 5 Piece 55.00
Salad Set, Leaves, Wrought, Bowl, Servers, Continental Silver Co. 65.00
Salesman's Sample, Coal Furnace, Case, 20th Century 489.00
Sandwich Server, Conch Shell, Sections, Mariposa Brillante, 16 In. 80.00
Sugar & Creamer, Tray, Chrysanthemum, Continental Silver Co. 85.00
Tray, Condiments, Glass Insert, No. 462, Rodney Kent, 12 x 5 1/2 In. 65.00
Tray, Embossed World Map, Gold Tint, Arthur Armour, 19 3/4 x 12 1/2 In. 120.00
Tray, Grapes, Arthur Court, 19 x 14 In. 65.00
Tray, Horse, Hammered Background, Palmer Smith, 20 x 14 In. 105.00
Tumbler Set, Mixed Colors, Permahues, 5 1/4 In., 7 Piece 70.00
Tumbler Set, Mixed Colors, Plastic Case, Heller, 5 1/4 In., 8 Piece 60.00
Wastebasket, Dogwood, Wendell August Forge, 10 In. 80.00
Wastebasket, Embossed World Map, Gold Tint, Oval, Arthur Armour, 10 In. 150.00
Wastebasket, Pinecone Design, Wendell August Forge, 11 In. 255.00

AMBER, see Jewelry category.

AMBER GLASS is the name of any glassware with the proper yellow-
brown shading. It was a popular color just after the Civil War and
many pressed glass pieces were made of amber glass. Depression glass
of the 1930s–1950s was also made in shades of amber glass. Other
pieces may be found in the Depression Glass, Pressed Glass, and other
glass categories. All types are being reproduced.

Bowl, Moon & Star, L.E. Smith, 10 In. 30.00
Butter, Cover Only, Dome, Holly, 5 1/8 In. 430.00
Dish, Honey, Cover, Beehive Finial, Footed, Indiana Glass Co., 5 1/2 In. 60.00
Fairy Lamp, Owl, Footed Base, Viking Glass Co., 6 1/2 In. 45.00
Figurine, Dog Dachshund, 5 3/8 In. 40.00

Jug, Cream, Free-Blown, Lily Pad Decoration, 5 1/4 In. 11000.00
Salt & Pepper, Moon & Star, L.E. Smith 30.00
Syrup, Rope & Thumbprint, Metal Cover, Central Glass Co., 6 1/2 In. 50.00
Vase, Baluster, Melon Ribbed, Pilgrim Glass Co., 10 In. 25.00
Vase, Gold Flowers, Label, Lotus, 10 In. 46.00

AMBERETTE pieces are listed in the Pressed Glass category under the pattern name Amberette.

AMBERINA is a two-toned glassware made from 1883 to about 1900. It was patented by Joseph Locke of the New England Glass Company, but was also made by other companies. The glass shades from red to amber. Similar pieces of glass may be found in the Baccarat, Libbey, and Plated Amberina categories. Glass shaded from blue to amber is called *Blue Amberina* or *Bluerina.*

Basket, Applied Amber Feet, Handle, Victorian, 11 In. 230.00
Basket, Optic Ribs, Fold Down Rim, Amber Handle, Side Prunts, 6 1/4 In. 2590.00
Berry Set, Daisy & Button, Hobbs, 10-In. Master, 11 Piece 750.00
Bonbon, Blown Optic, Leaf Shape, Reeded Shell Handle, 1 3/4 x 6 1/2 In. 575.00
Bowl, Deep Ruby To Amber, Diamond Quilted, Notched Rim, Footed, 7 1/4 In. 835.00
Bowl, Diamond-Quilted, Applied Amber Overlay, 5 1/8 In. 2415.00
Celery Vase, Diamond-Quilted, Cylindrical, Scalloped Rim, 6 1/2 In. 175.00
Celery Vase, Inverted Thumbprint, Crimped Rim, Cylindrical, 6 1/2 In. 660.00
Cruet, Honeycomb, Faceted Stopper, 6 1/2 In. 230.00
Cruet, Inverted Thumbprint, Rectangular, Faceted Stopper, 6 3/4 In. 115.00
Mug, Diamond-Quilted, Fuchsia Shaded To Amber, Ribbed, Amber Handle, 3 7/8 In. 1035.00
Pitcher, 5-Petaled Daisies & Leafy Stalks, Reeded Handle, Folded & Ruffled Rim, 5 In. .. 230.00
Pitcher, Inverted Thumbprint, Melon Ribbed, Ground Pontil, Victorian, 8 In. 605.00
Pitcher, Inverted Thumbprint, Optic Ribbed, Oval, Square Mouth, 5 1/2 In. 200.00
Pitcher, Inverted Thumbprint, Ruby Shaded To Amber, Straight Sides, 10 1/2 In. 430.00
Pitcher, Water, Inverted Thumbprint, Crimson To Amber, Bulbous, Square Mouth, 3 In. .. 460.00
Pitcher, Water, Optic Ribbed, Applied Reeded Amber Handle, 8 In. 115.00
Punch Cup, Diamond-Quilted, Applied Reeded Amber Handle, 2 1/2 In. 115.00
Saltshaker, Inverted Thumbprint, Enameled Green Leaves & Flowers, 3 1/4 In. 230.00
Spooner, Diamond-Quilted, Crimped Scalloped Rim, 4 3/4 In. 288.00
Sugar, Coin Spot, Ovoid, Square Mouth, Applied Reeded Handles, 4 In. 374.00
Sugar, Inverted Thumbprint, Applied Reeded Handles, Oval, 4 1/4 In. 520.00
Tankard, Ribbed, Deep Red To Amber, Ribbed, Amber Handle, 6 3/4 In. 575.00
Toothpick, Baby Inverted Thumbprint, Red To Amber, Crimped, Bulbous, 2 1/4 In. 640.00
Toothpick, Diamond-Quilted, Rolled Tricornered Rim, 2 In. 230.00
Toothpick, Square Mouth, 2 1/4 In. ....230.00 to 290.00
Tumbler, Diamond-Quilted, Amber Reeded Handle, 2 1/2 In., 4 Piece 260.00
Tumbler, Lemonade, Amber Handle, 5 1/4 In. 3165.00
Tumbler, Whiskey, Diamond-Quilted, 2 1/4 In. 130.00
Vase, Bud, Ribbed, Rigaree At Neck, 3 1/4 In. 690.00
Vase, Diamond-Quilted, Egg Shape, Tricornered Rim, 3 Reeded Amber Feet, 6 In. 403.00
Vase, Fuchsia To Amber, Flattened Oval Neck, Flared Body, Applied Collar, 3 1/4 In. 980.00
Vase, Inverted Thumbprint, 4 Applied Shells, Double Gourd Form, 4 3/4 In. 2415.00
Vase, Lily, Tricornered, 6 3/4 In. 290.00
Vase, Optic Ribbed, Oval, Pinched Sides, Rigaree Collar, Tricornered Rim, 6 In. 115.00
Water Set, Inverted Thumbprint, 7 Piece 320.00
Wine, Optic Ribbed, 4 3/4 In. 345.00

AMERICAN ART CLAY Company of Indianapolis, Indiana, made a variety of art pottery wares, especially vases, from about 1930 to after World War II. The company used the mark AMACO, as well as the company name. Do not confuse this company with an earlier art pottery firm from Edgerton, Wisconsin, called the American Art Clay Works.

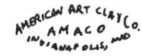

Bust, Girl, Long Hair In Sausage Curls, Tan Glaze, Art Deco 85.00
Vase, Light Green Glaze, Bulbous Base, Pinched Waist, Handles, 5 In. 20.00
Vase, Light Green Glaze, Metallic Streaks, 6 1/2 In. 10.00

AMERICAN DINNERWARE, see Dinnerware.

AMERICAN ENCAUSTIC TILING COMPANY was founded in

Zanesville, Ohio, in 1875. The company planned to make a variety of tiles to compete with the English tiles that were selling in the United States for use in fireplaces and other architectural designs. The first glazed tiles were made in 1880, embossed tiles in 1881, faience tiles in the 1920s. The firm closed in 1935 and reopened in 1937 as the Shawnee Pottery.

Bookends, Cherub, Rabbit, Green Gray, c.1926, 4 1/2 x 5 In. 120.00
Table, Tile Top, 8 4-In. Tiles, Stylized Flowers, 21 x 16 x 8 1/2 In. 441.00
Tile, Classical Woman, Torch, Relief, Yellow, Frame, 18 x 9 In. 1763.00
Tile, Fish, Green, Blue Frothy Matte Ground, Oak Frame, 4 3/4 x 8 1/2 In. 350.00
Tile, Flowers, Turquoise High Glaze, 6 x 6 In., Pair 69.00
Tile, Geometric Design, Tan, Brown, Green, 6 x 6 In. 80.00
Tile, Thistle, Greenish Brown High Glaze, 6 x 6 In. 58.00
Tile, Woman's Profile, c.1892, 4 x 4 In. 130.00
Trivet, 6 3/4 In. 230.00

AMETHYST GLASS is any of the many glasswares made in the dark

purple color of the gemstone called amethyst. Included in this category are many pieces made in the nineteenth and twentieth centuries. Very dark pieces are called *black amethyst* and are listed under that heading.

Console, Controlled Air Bubbles, 1950s, 10 In. 55.00
Decanter, Teardrop Base, Clear Teardrop Stopper, Bischoff, 16 1/2 In. 65.00
Fruit Basket, Openwork, Boston & Sandwich 17600.00
Urn, Square Cut Base, 4 3/4 In. 40.00
Vase, Amethyst Cased In Clear, Twisted Ribs, Chalet Art Glass Co., 8 1/2 In. 135.00
Vase, Hyacinth, Foot, Folded Rim, 8 1/4 In. 575.00
Vase, Stencil Etched Flowers, Baluster Shape, 10 In., Pair 90.00

AMPHORA pieces are listed in the Teplitz category.

ANDIRONS and related fireplace items are included in the Fireplace category.

ANIMAL TROPHIES, such as stuffed animals, rugs made of animal

skins, and other similar collectibles made from animal, fish, or bird parts, are listed in this category. Collectors should be aware of the endangered species laws that make it illegal to buy and sell some of these items. Any eagle feathers, many types of pelts or rugs (such as leopard), ivory, and many forms of tortoiseshell can be confiscated by the government. Related trophies may be found in the Fishing category. Ivory items may be found in the Scrimshaw or Ivory categories.

Bengal Tiger Skin, Black Baise Outline, Anglo-Indian, c.1915, 115 x 77 In. 4370.00
Buffalo, Bison, Full Mounted, Wood Base, c.1950, Life Size, 72 x 108 In. 345.00
Grizzly Bear, 96 In. 2970.00
Horns, Cape Buffalo, Shield Shape Mount, Mahogany, 18 x 39 In. 265.00
Lobster, Mounted, Wood Plaque, Rope Border, New Seashells, 38 x 25 In. 1550.00
Mummy, Cat, Diamond Pattern Wrap, 600 B.C. 13010.00
Mummy, Crocodile, Linen Wrap, Victorian Display Case, c.2000 B.C. 8965.00
Robe, Buffalo, Corduroy Back, Beckman's Furrier, Mt., 1900s-50s, 105 x 80 In. 545.00
Rug, Polar Bear Skin, Pre 1960, 8 Ft. 3 In. 2457.00
Skin, Bear, 20th Century, 62 In. 130.00
Skin, Red Fox, 57 x 19 In. 45.00
Skin, Tiger, 105 x 75 In. 1880.00
Zebra Hide, 10 Ft. 4 In. x 5 Ft. 9 In. 489.00

ANIMATION ART collectibles include cels that are painted drawings

on celluloid needed to make animated cartoons shown in movie theaters or on TV. Hundreds of cels were made, then photographed in sequence to make a cartoon showing moving figures. Early examples made by the Walt Disney Studios are popular with collectors today. Original sketches used by the artists are also listed here. Modern animated cartoons are made using computer-generated pictures. Some of these are being produced as cels to be sold to collectors. Other cartoon art is listed in Comic Art and Disneyana.

Cel, Beauty & The Beast, Dancing In The Ballroom, 1991, 17 x 23 In. 1500.00
Cel, Bugs Bunny & Yosemite Sam, From Hare To Eternity, 20 x 17 In. 710.00
Cel, Flash Gordon & Dale Arden, Running, Frame, 8 1/2 x 9 3/4 In. 345.00
Cel, Lady & The Tramp, Lady & The Tramp Walking, 1955, 10 x 7 In. 1050.00
Cel, Robin Hood, Carrying Toy Dolls, Disney Studios, Frame, 11 x 14 1/2 In. 400.00
Cel, Tom Of Tom & Jerry, MGM Studios, Frame, 7 1/2 x 9 3/4 In. 144.00

ANNA POTTERY was started in Anna, Illinois, in 1859 by Cornwall and Wallace Kirkpatrick. They made many types of utilitarian wares, bricks, drain tiles, and giftware. The most collectible pieces made by the pottery are the pig-shaped bottles and jugs with special inscriptions, applied animals, and figures. The pottery closed in 1894.   *Anna Pottery*

Jug, Shoo Fly, Applied Black Girl At Neck, c.1860, Pt., 6 1/2 In. 7150.00

APPLE PEELERS are listed in the Kitchen category under Peeler, Apple.

ARCHITECTURAL antiques include a variety of collectibles, usually very large, that have been removed from buildings. Hardware, backbars, doors, paneling, and even old bathtubs are now wanted by collectors. Pieces of the Victorian, Art Nouveau, and Art Deco styles are in greatest demand.

Bathtub, Metal, Round, c.1900, 11 x 36 1/2 In. 69.00
Bracket, Mounts, Fleur-De-Lis Terminals, Cast Iron, 24 x 8 In., Pair 805.00
Bracket, Scrolls, 5 Pointed Zinc Stars, Cast Iron, 1800s, 34 1/4 x 65 3/4 In. 470.00
Chimney Cap, Brown Glaze, Square Base, Octagon Body, Scalloped Top, 37 In. 200.00
Chimney Cap, Brown Matte Glaze, Round, Scalloped Top, Octagonal Body, 36 In. 200.00
Chimney Cap, Mottled Brown Glaze, Round, Square Base, Sawtooth Top, 27 In. 405.00
Chimney Cap, Red Brown Matte Glaze, Rectangular Base, Oval Tapered Body, 27 In. 405.00
Chimney Cap, Round Body, Sawtooth Top, Square Base, 30 In. 360.00
Chimney Cap, Stippled Design, Round Top, Scalloped Edge, Square Base, 22 In. 460.00
Column, Burled Veneer, Stepped Bases, Applied Molding, 9 x 9 x 28 In., Pair 230.00
Column, Marble, Rouge, Ivory Veins, Square Top, Fluted, 1900s, 46 x 12 In., Pair 1265.00
Column, Pine, Corinthian Capitals, Fluted Standards, Victorian, 91 x 16 In., Pair 2760.00
Column, Wood, Carved, Black Paint, Raised Moldings, Fluted Post, 41 1/4 In. 144.00
Door, Carved, Mahogany, Paneled, Patriotic, Shield, Eagle, Stars, 74 x 26 In., Pair 3737.00
Door, Cast Iron, Reticulated Inset Panels, France, 97 x 25 1/2 In., Pair 4600.00
Door, Oak Bar Room, Etched Glass, Double Swing Hinges, 47 x 27 1/2 In., Pair 880.00
Door, Oak, Raised Panel, Etched Glass Hunting Scene, 79 x 31 1/2 In. 165.00
Door, Pub, Oak, Etched Window, Wine & Spirit Stores, 83 1/2 x 40 In. 130.00
Door, Wood, Carved, 20 Relief Figures, Dogon, Africa, 25 x 14 In. 264.00
Door Handle, Iron, Heart Shape Ends, Incised Lines, Thumb Latch, 14 x 3 In. 176.00
Door Knob, Backplate, Bronze, Embossed Buds, Guaranty Trust Building, 17 1/2 x 3 In. . . 5580.00
Door Latch, Iron, Incised Lines, Stylized Triangle Decoration, 9 1/2 x 2 In. 165.00
Door Latch, Iron, Scalloped Edges, Slides, 5 3/4 x 2 1/2 In. 50.00
Door Post, Wood, Carved, Woman, Stylized Legs, Holding Breasts, Yoruba, Africa, 52 In. 1060.00
Door Pull, Iron, Tulip Shape Top, Incised Lines, 11 1/2 x 1 3/4 In. 175.00
Doorknob, Backplate, Keyholes, Thumb Latch, Acanthus Leaves, Iron, Pair, 14 x 4 In. . . . 2585.00
Doorknocker, Butterfly, Cast Iron, Waverly Studios, Box, 3 1/2 In. 495.00
Doorknocker, Cast Brass, Spurred, Scrolled, Late 18th Century, 4 1/4 In. 210.00
Doorknocker, Castle, 3 Towers, Cast Iron, No. 680, Hubley, 4 In. 660.00
Doorknocker, Castle, In Woods, No. 630, Hubley, 3 1/2 In. 660.00
Doorknocker, Colonial Lady, Cast Iron, Waverly Studios, Box, 4 1/2 In. 165.00
Doorknocker, Flower Basket, Wicker Basket, Blue Bow, Judd Co., 4 In. 30.00
Doorknocker, Flower Bouquet, Cast Iron, Creations, On Card, 4 In. 55.00
Doorknocker, Gilt Bronze, Imperial Eagle, Square, Germany, c.1900, 4 1/4 In. 750.00
Doorknocker, Girl With Basket, Cast Iron, Hubley, 3 5/8 In. 495.00
Doorknocker, Ivy, Yellow Basket, Cast Iron, No. 123, Hubley, Box, 4 1/2 In. 220.00
Doorknocker, Parrot, In Ring, Leaves, Painted, Iron, 4 In. 39.00
Doorknocker, Pear, Flower Ground, Cast Iron, 3 1/4 In. 195.00
Doorknocker, Rabbit, Eating Cabbage, Cast Iron, Albany, 5 In. 990.00
Doorknocker, Rose, Cast Iron, Hand Painted, 4 5/8 In. 305.00
Doorknocker, Roses & Mixed Flowers, Cast Iron, No. 287, Hubley, Box, 4 In. 220.00
Doorknocker, Ship, Cast Iron, Hubley, 3 1/2 In. 1100.00

Elevator Plate, Louis Sullivan, Stock Exchange Bldg., Chicago, 67 x 18 In. 345.00
Escutcheon Plate, Wrought Iron, Stippled, Openwork, Diamond, Tulips, Pa., 8 1/2 In. 4025.00
Fan Light, Gothic Arched, Green Paint, c.1850, 28 3/4 x 28 In., Pair 1410.00
Fan Light, Radiating Louvers, Wood, Paint, Arched Frame, 1800s, 28 x 78 In. 2233.00
Figure, Head, American Indian, Copper Repousse, Belgium, c.1910, 35 Lbs., 24 x 19 In. . .   2200.00
Finial, Copper, Late 1800s, 43 x 14 In. 1995.00
Finial, Pineapple, Carved, Painted, c.1790, 17 x 13 1/4 In. 9600.00
Finial, Pineapple, Zinc, Hollow, Round Turned Pedestal Base, 30 x 8 In., Pair 1705.00
Finial, Swan, Spread Wings, Giltwood, Neoclassical Style, 14 1/2 In., Pair 2070.00
Fireplace Surround, Louis XVI Style, Carrara Marble, 42 x 53 x 15 In. 2300.00
Fireplace Surround, Oak, Carved, Early 20th Century, 84 x 60 1/2 x 10 3/4 In. 145.00
Fountain, Bronze, Planter-Shape, Ingraham Mfg. Bldg., Conn., 11 x 15 x 11 In. 600.00
Frame, Arched Top, Rosettes, 1/2 Columns, 19th Century, 14 x 12 In. 300.00
Fretwork, Entryway, Oak, Stick & Ball Design, 72 1/4 x 96 1/2 In., 2 Piece 865.00
Fretwork, Entryway, Oak, Stick & Ball Design, Leaf Scrolls, 61 x 104 In. 3910.00
Fretwork, Oak, Stick & Ball Design, Corkscrew Rays, 5 Piece 1035.00
Fretwork, Oak, Stick & Ball Design, Leaf Scrolls, 38 x 20 x 53 In., 3 Piece 865.00
Frontispiece, Deco, Bronze, Brass, Door, Openwork Diamonds, Scrolls, 85 x 90 In. 460.00
Gate, Aesthetic Movement, Iron, Sunflowers, Twisted Stems, c.1885, 83 x 36 In. 750.00
Gate, Entrance, Iron, Arched, Scrolled Flowers, Columns, 99 x 146 In., Pair 3450.00
Gate, Iron, Gilt, Scrolls, Arrows, Crisscross Bars, c.1940, 33 3/4 x 23 In., Pair 3000.00
Gate, Iron, Gilt, Vertical Bars, c.1940, 72 14 x 13 3/4 In., Pair 6600.00
Gate, Iron, Rounded, Tapered Tops, Spear Points, Oval, Scroll, 91 x 37 In., Pair 375.00
Gate, Pine, Gray Paint, Distressed, Hinges, Iron Latch, 35 x 37 1/4 In. 220.00
Hinge, Iron, Fish Shape, Salmon Paint, 18 1/4 In. 330.00
Hinge, Iron, Fishtail Shape, Decorated Beveled Edge, 7 x 5 1/2 In.   39.00
Hinge, Iron, Ram's Horn Shape, Blue Paint, 12 x 5 1/2 In., Pair 415.00
Joint Caps, Georgian, Gilt, Composition, Shell Shape, Acanthus, 10 x 12 In., 4 Piece 880.00
Keystone, Lion, Pendant Ring, Earthenware, c.1900, 17 3/4 x 19 1/2 In. 295.00
Letter Box, Iron, Openwork Sides, Divided Interior, Wood Base, c.1885, 4 x 9 In. 194.00
Mantel, American Federal, Dolphins, Angel Heads, White Paint, c.1810 . . . .   3955.00
Mantel, Blue Paint, New England, c.1800, 48 1/2 x 68 In. 1440.00
Mantel, Cherry, Shell, Fan, Leaf Crest, Beveled Mirror, Shelves, 63 x 12 x 93 In. 2760.00
Mantel, Federal, Green Paint, Faux Grained, Bowed Shelf, Early 1800s, 69 x 85 In. 5750.00
Mantel, Federal, Pine, Dentil Molding, Blue Paint, 58 x 74 In. 1265.00
Mantel, George V, Chinese Lakeside Pavilions, 1700s Style, c.1900, 67 x 40 In. 2185.00
Mantel, Grain Painted, Federal, 19th Century, 55 x 77 x 8 In. 420.00
Mantel, Louis XV Style, Marble, Gray Veined, Carved, c.1900, 43 3/4 x 6 1/2 x 17 In. 6305.00
Mantel, Oak, Mirrored Back, S-Roll Supports, 54 x 11 x 77 1/2 In. 200.00
Mantel, Pine, White Paint, Conn., c.1820, 72 In. 250.00
Mantel, Pine, White Paint, Federal, 55 x 80 x 7 3/4 In. 480.00
Mantel, Poplar, Mortise & Peg, Inset Panels, Hand Painted Doves, Nest, 67 x 59 In. 1955.00
Mantel, Wood, Composition, Ramage & Ferguson, Scotland, c.1790, 58 x 68 In. 25000.00
Niche, Frame, Rounded Arch, Clustered Pillars, Wooden, Gilt, Early 20th Century, 37 In. . .   185.00
Ornament, Cornucopia, Fruit, Cast Iron, 3 Parts, 12 In. 115.00
Ornament, Eagle, Spread Wings, Lead, 1800s, 20 3/4 x 45 1/2 In.   560.00
Overdoor, Carved, Far Eastern Deities, 20th Century, 37 x 83 x 4 In. 750.00
Overmantel Mirror, Aesthetic Revival, Gilt, American, c.1885, 79 1/2 x 60 In., Pair 7765.00
Overmantel Mirror, Carved Giltwood, Divided Panel Mirrors, c.1890, 22 1/2 x 57 In. 546.00
Overmantel Mirror, Empire, Giltwood, Acanthus, Scroll, Crest, 82 x 62 In. 1725.00
Overmantel Mirror, Giltwood, 19th Century, 50 1/2 x 57 1/2 x 5 In. 590.00
Overmantel Mirror, Giltwood, Acorn Drops, Zeus, 3 Parts, 1800s, 84 1/2 x 35 1/2 In. 1880.00
Overmantel Mirror, Giltwood, Carved, Pierced, Leaves, Crest, 45 x 71 In. 230.00
Overmantel Mirror, Giltwood, Carved, Scrolling Frame, Early 1900s, 33 x 37 In. 290.00
Overmantel Mirror, Giltwood, Ebonized, Lancet-Arched Rail, 82 x 49 In. 1840.00
Overmantel Mirror, Giltwood, Gesso, Split Balusters, Rosettes, c.1825, 29 x 70 In. 825.00
Overmantel Mirror, Louis Philippe, Giltwood, Plaster, Flowers, 47 x 40 In. 920.00
Overmantel Mirror, Louis Philippe, Mahogany, 54 1/2 x 42 1/4 In. 865.00
Overmantel Mirror, Louis XVI Style, Beech, Painted, 84 x 54 In., Pair 3220.00
Overmantel Mirror, Louis XVI, Giltwood, Painted, Winged Griffins, 55 x 47 In. 2150.00
Overmantel Mirror, Napoleon III, Cenotaph Shape, Flowers, c.1865, 70 x 47 In. 2300.00
Overmantel Mirror, Napoleon III, Fruitwood, Ebonized, Brass, c.1865, 66 x 52 In. 5060.00

Overmantel Mirror, Napoleon III, Giltwood, 77 x 55 In., Pair 13225.00
Overmantel Mirror, Napoleon III, Giltwood, c.1900, 65 x 50 In. 1840.00
Overmantel Mirror, Napoleon III, Giltwood, Carved, 56 x 38 In. 1725.00
Overmantel Mirror, Napoleon III, Giltwood, Carved, 65 x 43 In. 3450.00
Overmantel Mirror, Napoleon III, Giltwood, Finials, Arched Crest, 71 x 43 In. 2990.00
Overmantel Mirror, Napoleon III, Giltwood, Flowers, c.1865, 71 x 43 In. 3220.00
Overmantel Mirror, Napoleon III, Giltwood, Incised, Carved, 59 x 36 In. 1495.00
Overmantel Mirror, Napoleon III, Giltwood, Mid 19th Century, 50 x 34 In. 1150.00
Overmantel Mirror, Rococo Style, Giltwood, Carved, 3 Parts, c.1890, 39 x 64 In. 470.00
Overmantel Mirror, William IV, Gilt, Black Paint, Rope Carved, c.1835, 32 x 28 In. 920.00
Overmantel Mirror, William IV, Giltwood, Carved, 37 x 48 In. 3220.00
Panel, Acanthus Leaf, Wood, Carved, 1800s, 16 x 35 1/4 In. 1645.00
Panel, Classical, Rosewood, Brass Inlaid, Early 1800s, 13 7/8 x 3 1/4 In., Pair 355.00
Panel, Wood Carving, Bishop Saints, Relief, Germany, 18th Century, 23 x 19 1/2 In., Pair . 865.00
Panel, Wood Carving, Vishnu, Deities, Elephant, Crocodile, India, 39 x 39 In. 1380.00
Pediment, Regency Style, Eagle, Spread Wings, Giltwood, 11 x 25 In. 1725.00
Pediment, Trompe L'Oeil Candelabrum, 5-Light, 1800s, 33 1/2 x 58 In., Pair 3220.00
Post Office Front, Window, Oak Case, M.C. Lane Mfg., 48 x 47 x 11 In. 1210.00
Streetlight, 2 Lamps, Blue, Red, Overhead, 22 x 11 In. 110.00
Tieback, Pansy, Cast Iron, Albany Foundry, 3 In., Pair 110.00
Toilet Tissue Holder, Hickory Bark 250.00
Valance, Louis XVI Style, Giltwood, Carved, Arched Front, 7 1/2 x 70 In. 403.00
Window, Dormer Vent, Tin, Arch & Scroll Design, Early 1900s, 37 x 27 x 56 In. 188.00
Window, Teller, Iron, Flower Rows, Samuel Yellin, 42 x 172 In. 3055.00
Window, Teller, Iron, Flower Rows, Samuel Yellin, 42 x 93 1/2 In. 2468.00
Window, U.S. Post Office, Oak, 43 Boxes, Bars On Windows, 43 x 33 In. 275.00
Window Cornice, Renaissance Revival, Burled Walnut, Giltwood, c.1865, 30 x 63 In. 750.00
Window Screen, Painted, Black & White, Scenic Landscape, 2 x 39 In., Pair 405.00

AREQUIPA POTTERY was produced from 1911 to 1918 by the
patients of the Arequipa Sanatorium in Marin County, north of San
Francisco. The patients were trained by Frederick Hürten Rhead, who
had worked at the Roseville Pottery.

Vase, Baluster, Leaves, Green & Turquoise Glaze, 13 1/2 x 6 1/4 In. 2940.00
Vase, Baluster, Mottled Semimatte Glaze, Purple, Brown, 10 1/2 x 7 1/2 In. 1880.00
Vase, Blue, Cream Glaze, 4 1/2 In. 500.00
Vase, Cabinet, Blue Green & Mauve Matte Glaze, 3 1/2 x 2 1/2 In. 1175.00
Vase, Cabinet, Grape Clusters, Leaves, Squeezebag, Pink Matte Ground, 3 x 2 3/4 In. 3400.00
Vase, Egg Shape, Wreath, Fruit, Caramel Vellum Glaze, 9 1/4 x 5 In. 1528.00
Vase, Flowers, Blue Green Frothy Matte Glaze, 2 1/2 x 4 3/4 In. 2115.00
Vase, Mauve Matte Glaze, Marked, 5 1/2 In. 325.00
Vase, Molded Leaves Form Sides, White Matte, Crackled Glaze, 1912, 11 In. 1200.00
Vase, Mottled Blue Matte, Brown Glaze, Waisted, 4 1/2 In. 590.00
Vase, Mottled Blue, Silver Glaze, Paperweight Form, 3 1/2 In. 529.00
Vase, Squat, Lavender Semimatte Glaze, 7 x 11 In. 940.00
Vase, Squat, Leaves, Chevrons, Blue, Brown Ground, 4 x 4 1/2 In. 1530.00
Vase, Squat, Swirls, Green & Blue Matte Glaze, 4 1/4 x 4 1/4 In. 1765.00
Vase, Stylized Flower, Brown, Green Glaze, 4 1/2 In. 1410.00

ARGY-ROUSSEAU, see G. Argy-Rousseau category.

ARITA is a port in Japan. Porcelain was made there from about 1616.
Many types of decorations were used, including the popular Imari
designs, which are listed under Imari in this book.

Charger, Landscapes, c.1900, 15 1/2 In. 140.00
Dish, 8-Sided, Eggplant, Blue, White, Early 1800s, 4 In., 6 Piece 510.00
Dish, Meandering Flower Border, Flower Vase, Edo Period, 14 1/2 In. 840.00
Dish, Scalloped Rim, Flower Bands, Flower Vase, Edo Period, 14 1/2 In. 654.00
Dish, Scalloped Rim, Peonies, Prunus, Edo Period, 14 In. 610.00
Plate, Leafy Rim, Long Stems, Leaves, 6 Character Mark, c.1885, 8 1/2 In., 9 Piece 1150.00
Plate, Openwork Rim, Dragon, Phoenix, Flowers, Late 1800s, 12 1/2 In. 140.00
Tokuri, Teardrop Shape, Stylized Flowers, Blue, White, 1600s, 8 1/4 In. 1610.00

ART DECO, or Art Moderne, a style started at the Paris Exposition of 1925, is characterized by linear, geometric designs. All types of furniture and decorative arts, jewelry, book bindings, and even games were designed in this style. Additional items may be found in the Furniture category or in various glass and pottery categories, etc.

Ashtray Stand, Cast Iron, Dog Standing Beside Covered Ashtray, 23 1/2 In.	200.00
Bar, Portable, Brown Bakelite, Gold Trimmed Glassware, c.1950, 24 In.	259.00
Bar, Portable, Wood, Metal, Bar Glasses, c.1950, 24 In.	185.00
Cocktail Shaker, Manning Bowman Sportsman	75.00
Gondola, Amusement Park, Metal, Chrome, Vinyl Upholstery, 1930s, 56 x 30 x 40 In.	690.00
Plaque, Lovebirds, Cast Aluminum, Rene P. Chamblen, c.1930, 12 x 9 In.	920.00
Tray, Hammered Brass, Rectangular, 2 Handles, Stamped, 24 In.	127.00
Vase, Blue, Tan Crystalline Glaze, 3 Stepped Handles, Belgium, 8 3/4 In.	69.00
Vase, Orange, White Blown Out Glass, Wrought Iron, Sun Design, 12 In.	1035.00

ART GLASS, see Glass-Art category.

ART NOUVEAU is a style of design that was at its most popular from 1895 to 1905. Famous designers, including Rene Lalique and Emile Galle, produced furniture, glass, silver, metalwork, and buildings in the new style. Ladies with long flowing hair and elongated bodies were among the more easily recognized design elements. Copies of this style are being made today. Many modern pieces of jewelry can be found. Additional Art Nouveau pieces may be found in Furniture or in various glass categories.

Bowl, Cover, Metal Frame, Mistletoe, Peacock Feathers, Lustered Glass, 6 x 8 In.	176.00
Box, Carved Woman, Flowers, Butterflies, France, Square, 7 x 3 In.	825.00
Box, Cover, Wood, Carved Pinecone, Moth, France, 9 In.	1116.00
Jardinere, Pottery, Blue & White, Scroll Decoration, 12 x 18 In.	120.00
Sculpture, Maiden, Flowing Wrap, Raised Arms, Ormolu, 32 In.	2070.00
Vase, Pottery, Female Bust Moldings, Bulbous Leaf Decorated Base, 1900s, 17 x 9 In.	235.00

ARTHUR OSBORNE plaques are found in the Ivorex category.

ARTS & CRAFTS was a design style popular in American decorative arts from 1894 to 1923. In the 1970s collectors began to rediscover Mission furniture, art pottery, metalwork, linens, and light fixtures from this period. The interest has continued. Today everything from this era is collectible, including jewelry, graphics, and silverware. Additional items may be found in the Furniture category, various glass categories, etc.

Bowl, Mottled Green Matte Glaze, Pottery, 9 In.	120.00
Charger, Hammered Metal, Patina, 18 In.	100.00
Vase, Green Matte Glaze, Pottery, 16 x 32 In.	529.00
Vase, Green Matte Glaze, Pottery, Tapered, 9 In.	175.00
Vase, Mottled Green Matte Glaze, Tapering, Bottle Form, Pottery, 10 1/4 In.	200.00
Wastebasket, Cutout Handles, Square, 10 1/2 x 17 In.	500.00

AURENE glass was made by Frederick Carder of New York about 1904. It is an iridescent gold, blue, green, or red glass, usually marked *Aurene* or *Steuben*.

AURENE

Bowl, Blue, 3-Footed, 12 In.	635.00
Bowl, Blue, Ribbed, Signed, 7 x 3 In.	1095.00
Bowl, Blue, Signed, Flared, 8 In.	645.00
Bowl, Centerpiece, Blue, Calcite Pedestal, c.1920, 3 3/4 x 9 3/4 In.	1100.00
Bowl, Centerpiece, Gold, Rolled Rim, Signed, 12 In.	750.00
Bowl, Gold Calcite Interior, 10 In.	520.00
Bowl, Gold, Blown-Out Melon Ribs, Footed, c.1910, 6 1/2 In.	490.00
Bowl, Gold, Red, Signed, 8 In.	1060.00
Bowl, Gold, Ruffled Edge, Signed, 6 In.	230.00
Candlestick, Gold, c.1915, 8 In., Pair	1265.00
Candlestick, Gold, Tulip Shape, Curved Reeded Stem, Petal Base, 12 In.	5175.00
Compote, Gold, Signed, 5 1/4 x 5 1/4 In.	460.00

Compote, Gold, Twist Stem, Applied Cabochons, Signed, 7 In. 1840.00
Cruet, Blue, Applied Gooseneck Spout & Handle, Stopper, Signed, 5 1/4 In. 4025.00
Goblet, Gold, Twist Stem, 6 In. ....290.00 to 500.00
Jar, Cover, Gold, Wide Shoulder, Narrow Rim, Signed, 4 x 2 1/2 In. 900.00
Lamp, Blue, Gold, Baluster Shape, Gilt & Patinated Brass Mounted, 21 In. 2760.00
Nut Dish, Blue, 3 Club Feet, Signed, 1 1/2 x 3 1/2 In. 460.00
Salt, Gold, 1 3/4 In. 430.00
Shade, Gold, Pink Iridescent, Corseted, 4 1/2 x 3 7/8 In. 180.00
Shade, Gold, Ribbed, Bell Form, Signed, 5 In., 4 Piece 750.00
Shade, Gold, Ribbed, Scalloped Rim, Signed, 4 In., 4 Piece 604.00
Shade, Gold, Ribbed, Tulip Form, 5 1/4 In., Pair 201.00
Shade, Green, Gold, Pulled Loops, 5 In. 200.00
Shade, Green, White Zigzag, Applied Border, Lavender Iridescent, 5 1/4 x 4 1/4 In. 4140.00
Sherbet, Underplate, Gold, Signed, 6 In. 290.00
Vase, Blue, Bulbous, Flared, Ruffled Edge, 2 3/4 In. 635.00
Vase, Blue, Raspberry Iridescent, Gold, Green, Signed, 12 In. 660.00
Vase, Blue, Ribbed, Waisted, Ruffled Edge, Ribbed Disc Foot, 5 In. 1495.00
Vase, Blue, Scalloped Rim, 7 In. 1035.00
Vase, Blue, Shouldered, Signed, Steuben, 2 1/2 In. ....646.00 to 750.00
Vase, Blue, Tulip Shape, Footed, 6 1/2 x 8 In. 1495.00
Vase, Bud, Gold, Footed, 6 In. 330.00
Vase, Fan, Blue, Applied White Heart, Vine, Signed, 8 1/4 In. 3600.00
Vase, Gold, 3 Applied Blue Handles, Dimpled Sides, 8 In. 825.00
Vase, Gold, Diamond-Quilted, Signed, 5 1/8 In. 840.00
Vase, Gold, Flared Rim, Footed, Signed, 6 In. 518.00
Vase, Gold, Flower Shape, Flared & Ruffled Edge, Disc Foot, 6 1/4 In. 1150.00
Vase, Gold, Iridescent Green Hooked Feathers, 5 In. 1495.00
Vase, Gold, Pinched Waist, 7 1/4 In. 405.00
Vase, Gold, Raspberry Iridescent Band, Blue Iridescent, 11 3/4 In. 920.00
Vase, Gold, Shouldered, Pink, Blue, 10 1/4 In. 1095.00
Vase, Gold, Urn, 6 1/4 In. 690.00
Vase, Millefiori, Gold, Green, Brown Pulled Leaf, Vine, Signed, 4 In. 3360.00
Vase, Stick, Blue, Circular Foot, Signed, 10 1/4 In. 480.00
Vase, Tree Trunk, 3-Prong, Amber, 6 1/2 In. 294.00
Vase, Tree Trunk, 3-Prong, Blue, 6 1/2 In. 1100.00
Vase, Tree Trunk, 3-Prong, Gold, No. 2749, 6 1/4 In. ....705.00 to 825.00
Vase, Trumpet, Blue, Ribbed, Signed, 6 1/2 In. 1035.00
Vase, Trumpet, Gold, Calcite Interior, Flared, Footed, c.1920, 6 x 7 1/2 In. 230.00
Vase, Trumpet, Gold, Flared Rim, Conical, Circular Foot, 5 7/8 In. 825.00
Vase, Trumpet, Gold, Lily Ruffled Rim, Applied Foot, No. 346, 10 In. 1410.00

AUSTRIA is a collecting term that covers pieces made by a wide variety of factories.
They are listed in this book in categories such as Royal Dux, or Porcelain.

AUTO parts and accessories are collectors' items today. Gas pump globes and license plates are part of this specialty. Prices are determined by age, rarity, and condition. Signs and packaging related to automobiles may also be found in the Advertising category. Lalique hood ornaments will be listed in the Lalique category.

Air Pump, Eco Tireflator, No. 39, Rolling Tire, Pedestal, Pressure Gauge, 52 x 9 x 24 In. ... 1550.00
Ashtray, Winton Auto, Sabina Line, Antique Car, Gold Rim, 1898, 6 In. 8.00
Badge, Gas Station, Texaco, Celluloid Holder For Name, Enameled, Hat 150.00
Badge, Gas Station, White Rose Canadian Refineries, Gold Metal, Enameled, Hat, 3 In. 675.00
Banner, Quaker State Winter Oil, It's A Lucky Day, Horseshoe, Paper, 34 x 57 1/2 In. 880.00
Bottle, Atlantic Motor Oil, Black Top, 15 In. 44.00
Brochure, Oldsmobile, Color Illustrations, 1954, 8 1/2 x 11 In. 65.00
Button, Amoco, Join The American Party, Tin Lithograph, Pinback 15.00
Button, Best Buick Yet, Starry Sky Ground, Round, Late 1930s, 1 1/2 In. 30.00
Button, Browniekar, Omar Motor Co., Newark, N.Y., 1 1/4 In. 380.00
Button, Buick 8 Looks Fine For 39, Buick's The Beauty, 1939, 1 1/4 In. 98.00
Button, Esso For Happy Motoring, Red Ground, Round, 1940, 1 1/4 In. 110.00
Button, Firestone Columbus, Car, Black, White, Celluloid, 1 In. 140.00
Can, Capitan Parlube Motor Oil, 2 Gal., 11 x 9 In. 155.00

Can, Defender Motor Oil, 100% Pure, Paraffin Base, Tin, 2 Gal., 12 x 8 1/2 In. 39.00
Can, Eastlube Motor Oil, 100% Paraffin Base, Tin, 2 Gal., 11 x 8 1/2 In. 28.00
Can, En-Ar-Co Motor Oil, Yellow, Blue, White, Round, 5 Gal. 358.00
Can, Falcon, Motor Oil, Oscar Bryant, Hollis, Oklahoma, Qt., 5 1/2 x 4 In. 17.00
Can, Richmond Motor Oil, Biplane, Horizontal, 6 x 8 In. 55.00
Can, Shamrock Oil, 1960-70, 5 In. 15.00
Can, Sunoco, Motor Oil, Mercury Made, 2 Gal., 12 x 8 1/2 In. 17.00
Card, Esso Gasoline, Scottie In Picnic Basket, Merry Christmas, 1940s, 9 1/2 In. 15.00
Credit Card Holder, Standard Oil, National Credit Card, Red, White, Blue, 10 x 9 In. 22.00
Display, Anco Rain Master Windshield Wipers, For Safer Driving, Tin, 12 x 13 x 8 1/2 In. . 77.00
Display, Schrader Tire Gauge, Red, Black, 15 x 6 In. 165.00
Figure, Fisk Tire, 3-Dimensional, Automation Figure, Moving, Candle, 1920s, 45 In. 4715.00
Figure, Michelin Tires Man, Horsehair & Plaster, 1915, 32 In. 3630.00
Gas Pump, Bowser Cities Service, Globe, Hose, Nozzle, 57 3/4 In. 518.00
Gas Pump, Bowser, Rol-Way, Phillips, Globe, Hose, Nozzle, 58 In. 660.00
Gas Pump, Erie Richfield, Globe, Hose, Nozzle, 58 In. 920.00
Gas Pump, Martin, Schwartz Sinclair, Globe, Hose, Nozzle, 63 In. 900.00
Gas Pump, Sinclair Gasoline, Dino, Globe, 75 x 21 In. 770.00
Gas Pump, Southwest, Gulf, Model No. 30, Globe, Hose, Nozzle, c.1933, 62 In. 865.00
Gas Pump, Texaco, Fire Chief Gasoline, Globe, 75 x 21 In. 800.00
Gas Pump, Tokheim Gulf, Globe, Hose, Nozzle, 58 In. 605.00
Gas Tank, Whiz Emergency Gasoline Tank, Wood, Paper Label, 13 x 9 In. 472.00
Headlight, Twin Service, No. 79124, Extra Reflector, Winchester, Box 139.00
Hood Ornament, Packard, Goddess Of Speed, Marble Base, 8 In. 175.00
License Plate, Arizona, 1938, Yuma County, Black On Yellow 67.00
License Plate, California, 1916, Blue On White, Porcelain, Matching Bear Tag 365.00
License Plate, Massachusetts, 1908, Porcelain 165.00
License Plate, Massachusetts, 1914, Blue On White, Porcelain 60.00
License Plate, New York, 1969, Orange On Blue 70.00
License Plate, Ohio, 1910, White On Maroon 144.00
License Plate, Ohio, 1946, Red On White 40.00
License Plate, Pennsylvania, 1932, Black On Yellow 30.00
License Plate, Wyoming, 1944, Black On Yellow, Bucking Bronco, Soybean Fiberboard .. 310.00
Mug, Lion Gas & Oil, Bill Armstrong Oil Co., Applied Label, 4 In. 25.00
Poster, Mohawk Tire, Mohawks Go Farther, Red, Blue, Cardboard, 1926, 38 x 38 In. 550.00
Pump Plate, Amlico, Regular Gasoline, Porcelain, Round, 10 In. 525.00
Pump Plate, Gloco, Hi'R Octane, Porcelain, 9 x 15 In. 605.00
Pump Plate, Texaco, Porcelain, Black T, Round, 1938, 8 In. 330.00
Rack, Atlantic Lubrication Service, Metal, Wall Mount, Gas Station, 16 x 9 1/2 x 8 1/2 In. . 39.00
Rack, Champion Sprayon, For Beauty & Economy, Yellow, Blue, White, Red, 9 x 17 In. .. 45.00
Rack, STP, Gasoline, Oil Treatment, Quiets Motors, Red, White, Blue, 33 x 16 In. 136.00
Rack, Tiolene Oil, Sealed For Your Protection, Porcelain, 2-Sided, 7 Bottles, 22 x 28 In. ... 2750.00
Rack, Trico Wiper Washer Service, Red, White, Tin, 12 x 14 In. 55.00
Radiator Cap, Pontiac, Indian Head, 3 1/2 In. 176.00
Sign, 400 Pacer, Red, White, Yellow, Ethyl Corporation, 14 x 9 In. 1870.00
Sign, Amalie, Pennsylvania Motor Oil, Red, White, Black, Tin, 12 x 36 In. 165.00
Sign, Authorized Studebaker Service, Porcelain, 2-Sided, Round, 42 In. 2750.00
Sign, B.F. Goodrich, Tin, 1956, 18 x 42 1/2 In. 305.00
Sign, Bear Wheel Alignment Service, Bear, Figural, 2-Sided, Tin, 53 x 36 In. 55.00
Sign, Buick Authorized Service, Porcelain, 2-Sided, Walker Company, Round, 42 In. 4180.00
Sign, Cadillac Service, Porcelain, 2-Sided, Hanging Ring, Round, 60 In. 5500.00
Sign, Champion Spark Plugs, For Better Performance, Blue, Yellow, Porcelain, 60 x 28 In. . 1550.00
Sign, Champion Spark Plugs, Woman On Globe, Tin Lithograph, Oval, 6 1/2 x 4 3/4 In. ... 470.00
Sign, Chevrolet, Super Service, Blue, Yellow, Die Cut, Porcelain, 2-Sided, 42 x 49 In. 2200.00
Sign, Chrysler, Blue, White, Die Cut, Porcelain, 24 x 36 In. 1760.00
Sign, Colonial Gasoline, Minutemen, Red, White, Blue, Porcelain, Oval, 53 x 96 In. 3080.00
Sign, Conoco Bronze Gasoline, Greasing Charts, Tin, 2-Sided, 24 1/2 x 37 1/2 In. 2420.00
Sign, Conoco Travel Bureau, Tin, 2-Sided, 1936, 18 x 24 In. 440.00
Sign, Desoto Plymouth, Approved Service, Red, Blue, Porcelain, 2-Sided, 42 x 45 In. 2650.00
Sign, Edsel Dealership, Green, White, Neon, Porcelain, Columbia, S.C., 52 x 65 x 10 In. ... 12100.00
Sign, Esso Gas, Octagonal, Red, White, Blue, Porcelain, 2-Sided, 30 x 25 1/2 In. 660.00
Sign, Ford Service, Blue, White, Plastic, 10 x 34 In., Pair 220.00
Sign, Ford, Blue, White, Porcelain, Oval, 24 x 48 In. 850.00

Sign, Ford, On Crate, Neon, Blue, White, 36 x 72 In. 3740.00
Sign, Francisco Auto Heater, Family In Car, Self-Framed, Tin, 18 x 40 In. 2200.00
Sign, GMC Trucks, Sales & Service, Porcelain, 2-Sided, Hanging Ring, Round, 42 In. 4675.00
Sign, Goodyear Tires, Porcelain, 94 x 16 In. 715.00
Sign, Goodyear Tires, Porcelain, 96 x 18 In. 220.00
Sign, Harley-Davidson Oil, Porcelain, Yellow Ground, 1930s, 9 x 14 In. 770.00
Sign, Heritage Tires, Eagle, Embossed, Tin, 16 x 48 In. 55.00
Sign, Kendall Motor Oil, Red Ground, Metal, 2-Sided, Round, 24 In. 145.00
Sign, Kendall Motor Oil, Red, White, 2-Sided, Tin, Round, 23 In. 70.00
Sign, Kendall, The 2000 Mile Oil, Refinery Sealed, Black, Red, White, 59 x 34 In. 910.00
Sign, Marvel Engine Protection Service, Black, Red, Yellow, White, Tin, 10 x 16 In. 220.00
Sign, Michelin, Michelin Man In Tire, Black, Yellow, White, Porcelain, 72 x 11 In. 1870.00
Sign, Miller Tires, Geared-To-The-Road, Yellow, Black, 2-Sided, Tin, 26 x 42 In. 660.00
Sign, Mobil, Mobilheat Fuel Oil, With Personal Care, Tin, Wood Frame, 60 x 60 In. 145.00
Sign, Mobil, Pegasus, Die Cut, Porcelain, 36 x 48 In. 5500.00
Sign, Mobilgas, Socony Vacuum, Winged Horse, 2-Sided, Porcelain, 56 x 58 In. 660.00
Sign, Montana Auto Assn., Emergency Service, Porcelain, 2-Sided, Oval, 24 x 36 In. 445.00
Sign, Nash Service Station, Blue, White, Porcelain, 28 x 33 1/2 In. 1650.00
Sign, Oilzum Motor, Tin, Wood Frame, 1975, 36 x 72 In. 495.00
Sign, Packard Approved Service, Neon, Porcelain, Round, 42 In. 4125.00
Sign, Packard, Red, White, Blue, Neon, Porcelain, 36 x 66 In. 4510.00
Sign, Pennzoil Motor Oil, With Z-7, Red, Yellow, Black, Tin, 33 x 48 In. ....295.00 to 495.00
Sign, Pennzoil, Safe Lubrication, Liberty Bell, Tin Lithograph, Self-Framed 300.00
Sign, Pennzoil, Sound Your Z, Tin Lithograph, 2-Sided, Frame, c.1940, 12 x 17 In. 220.00
Sign, Philco Service, Expert, Reliable, Guaranteed, Authorized Member, Tin, 18 x 22 In. ... 55.00
Sign, Phillips 66, Red, Blue, Neon, Die Cut, Porcelain, 42 x 47 In. 3960.00
Sign, Pontiac Service, Authorized, Indian Head, 2-Sided, Porcelain, 42 In. Diam. 1760.00
Sign, Pontiac, Authorized Service, Porcelain, 2-Sided, Walker Company, Round, 48 In. ... 5775.00
Sign, Pure Tiolene Motor Oil, Tin, Die Cut, Flange, 2-Sided, 17 1/2 x 20 In. 660.00
Sign, Pyroil, The Winner, Add To Gas & Oil, Multicolored, Tin Rack, 9 x 18 In. 605.00
Sign, Quaker State Motor Oil, Certified Guaranteed, Green, White, Porcelain, 29 x 27 In. ... 165.00
Sign, Quaker State Motor Oil, Green, White, Die Cut, 2-Sided, Tin, 27 x 29 In. 110.00
Sign, Quaker State, Motor Oil, Green Ground, Bowed Front, Metal, Round, 24 In. 90.00
Sign, Reo Motor Cars, Tin Lithograph, O.F. Seikman, Bartlesville, Okla., 10 x 27 In. 138.00
Sign, Serco Gasoline, White, Red, Tin, Round, 12 In. 50.00
Sign, Shell, Yellow, Red, Porcelain, Die Cut, 48 x 48 In. 2300.00
Sign, Sinclair Gasoline, Porcelain, 14 x 12 In. 110.00
Sign, Sinclair Opaline Motor Oil, Green, White, Tin, 12 x 19 1/2 In. 1360.00
Sign, Sinclair, Dinosaur, Red, White, Green, Porcelain, 43 x 59 In. 220.00
Sign, Studebaker, Authorized Sales & Service, Porcelain, 2-Sided, 48 In. Diam. 1760.00
Sign, Texaco Farm Lubricants, Sold Here, Porcelain, 1956, 30 x 42 In. 2090.00
Sign, Texaco Fire Chief Gasoline, Fireman's Hat, Porcelain, 18 x 12 In. 110.00
Sign, Texaco Service Station, No Smoking, Porcelain, 4 x 23 In. 175.00
Sign, Texaco, Diesel Chief, Tin, Embossed, 10 x 15 In. 415.00
Sign, Texaco, Fire Chief Gasoline, Enameled, Porcelain, 16 x 10 5/8 In. 25.00
Sign, Texaco, Fire Chief Gasoline, Porcelain, Enamel, 18 x 12 In. 80.00
Sign, Texaco, Green T, Red Star, White Ground, Porcelain, Round, 15 In. 495.00
Sign, Texaco, Keyhole, White T, Porcelain, 1954, 18 x 12 In. 385.00
Sign, Texaco, No Smoking, White T, Porcelain, 1941, 4 x 23 In. 250.00
Sign, Texaco, Sky Chief Su-Preme Gasoline, Super-Charged, Petrox, Porcelain, 18 x 12 In. ... 77.00
Sign, Texaco, Star With T, Red, White, Blue, Porcelain, 15 In. Diam. 220.00
Sign, Union 76, Stop Your Motor, No Smoking, Porcelain, 6 x 30 In. 360.00
Sign, Union Minute Man Service, Valvoline, Porcelain, 2-Sided 6820.00
Sign, United Motors Service, Red, Black, White, Porcelain, Oval, 28 x 40 In. 2640.00
Sign, We Install Auto Glass, Curved Parts Service, Green, White, 2-Sided, Tin, 24 x 18 In. . 22.00
Sign, Woco Pep, More Miles, Less Carbon, 2-Sided, Porcelain, 30 x 60 In. 260.00
Sign, Wolf's Head Motor Oil, Curb, Tin, 2-Sided, 1971, 30 x 23 In. 525.00
Sign, Wolf's Head Motor Oil, Finest Of The Fine Since 1879, Tin, Embossed, 80 x 12 In. .. 300.00
Sign, Wolf's Head, 100% Pennsylvania Motor Oil, Red, White, Black, Tin, 1970s, 22 x 17 In. 180.00
Sign, Wolf's Head, Oil & Lubes, 100% Pure, Red, Green, Tin, Flange, 1949, 22 x 17 In. .. 495.00
Song Book, Esso, Allen's Service Center, Salisbury, N.C., Premium, 9 x 6 In., 23 Pages ... 20.00
Thermometer, Gulf, Gulfpride, World's Finest Motor Oil 75.00
Tin, 100% Super Motor Oil, Red, Blue, Major Petroleum Co., 12 In. 45.00

Tin, Mohawk Motor Oil, 2 Gal. 95.00
Tin, Penn-Thrift Oil, 100% Pure Pennsylvania Motor Oil, 2 Gal., 8 x 8 x 7 In. 11.00
Tin, Polarine Transmission Lubricant, Standard Oil, 50 Lb. 330.00
Tin, Standard Oil, Wood Crate, 5 Gal. 38.00
Tin, Sunoco Mercury Oil, 2 Gal. 50.00
Tin, Supreme Auto Oil, Gulf Refining Co., Gal., 6 x 9 x 5 In. 45.00
Tire Cover, Pepsol, Red, White, Round, c.1920, 30 In. 500.00

AUTUMN LEAF pattern china was made for the Jewel Tea Company
beginning in 1933. Hall China Company of East Liverpool, Ohio,
Crooksville China Company of Crooksville, Ohio, Harker Potteries of
Chester, West Virginia, and Paden City Pottery, Paden City, West Virginia, made dishes with this design. Autumn Leaf has remained popular and was made by Hall China Company until 1978. Some other
pieces in the Autumn Leaf pattern are still being made. For more information, see *Kovels' Depression Glass & Dinnerware Price List.*

Baker, 2 3/4 x 7 3/4 In. 19.00
Butter, Cover, 4 x 9 5/8 x 5 1/2 In., 1 Lb. 600.00
Cake Plate, 9 5/8 In. 27.50
Candy Dish, Footed, Metal Base, 4 5/8 x 5 13/16 In. 600.00
Canister, Metal, Plastic Lid 25.00
Casserole, 7 x 3 In. 29.50
Coffeepot, Avocado Handle, Conversation Shape, Taylor, Smith & Taylor, 7 In. 45.00
Coffeepot, Electric, 1950s, 4 Piece 400.00
Coffeepot, Vent Hole In Lid, Gold Bottom Stamp 80.00
Cookie Jar, Tootsie 325.00
Creamer 30.00
Creamer, Ruffled Edge, 1930s, 3 In. 35.00
Drip Bowl, No Lid, 2 3/4 x 5 In. 19.00
Marmalade, Underplate, 1936-76 . . . .   30.00
Mixing Bowl, 5 x 9 In. . . . . .35.00 to 45.00
Mixing Bowl, Mary Danbar, Jewel Homemakers Institute, 4 3/4 x 8 1/2 In. 25.00
Pie Bird, 5 In. 40.00
Plate, Dinner, Mary Dunbar, 9 In. 20.00
Platter, Oval, 14 In. 23.00
Saucer, 6 In. 6.00
Sifter, Metal, Early 1930s 250.00
Soup, Dish, Lug Handles 23.00
Sugar, Cover 24.50
Teapot, Automobile, No. 1543, 1993 . . . .   425.00

AVON bottles are listed in the Bottle category under Avon.

AZALEA dinnerware was made for Larkin Company customers from
1918 to 1941. Larkin, the soap company, was in Buffalo, New York.
The dishes were made by Noritake China Company of Japan. Each
piece of the white china was decorated with pink azaleas.

Bowl, Mayonnaise, Footed, Dish & Scoop, Rising Sun Mark 100.00
Cake Plate, 2 Handles 45.00
Candy Dish, Cover, Hexagonal, 5 1/8 x 3 7/8 In. 850.00
Cup & Saucer, Gold, 1930 . . . .   15.00
Gravy Boat, Underplate 45.00
Plate, Dessert, 7 5/8 In. 10.00
Plate, Salad, 7 1/2 In. 12.00

BACCARAT glass was made in France by La Compagnie des Cristalleries de Baccarat, located 150 miles from Paris. The factory was
started in 1765. The firm went bankrupt and began operating again
about 1822. Cane and millefiori paperweights were made during the
1860 to 1880 period. The firm is still working near Paris making
paperweights and glasswares.

Candlestick, Lime Green Cabochon, Hurricane, Scroll Etched, 27 In. 1725.00
Figurine, Porcupine, Crystal, 3 x 5 In. 155.00

Baccarat, Paperweight, Millefiori, Canes, White Muslin Ground, 2 3/4 In.

Baccarat, Paperweight, Sulphide, George Washington, Cameo, Facets, 1954, 2 5/8 In.

Baccarat, Perfume Bottle, Eduardo, Egyptian Alabastron, Enameled, Clear, c.1927, 4 In.

Liquor Set, Neoclassical, Gilt, Decanter, 10 Cordials, 8 1/2 In., 11 Piece 560.00
Paperweight, Millefiori, Canes, White Muslin Ground, 2 3/4 In. .... *Illus* 1450.00
Paperweight, Millefiori, Red, White, Blue, Green Arrowhead Canes, 2 1/4 In. 520.00
Paperweight, Sulphide, George Washington, Cameo, Facets, 1954, 2 5/8 In. .... *Illus* 275.00
Perfume Bottle, Christian Dior, Diorling, Gilded Bronze, Stopper, Box, c.1963, 7 In. 2585.00
Perfume Bottle, Christian Dior, Miss Dior, Clear, Frosted, Labels, Stand, c.1954, 8 In. ... 646.00
Perfume Bottle, Cologne, Cranberry, Clear Stoppers, 1920s, 4 Piece 750.00
Perfume Bottle, D'Orsay, Le Porte Bonheur, Clear, Frosted, Box, c.1913, 3 1/4 In. 1528.00
Perfume Bottle, Eduardo, Egyptian Alabastron, Enameled, Clear, c.1927, 4 In. ..... *Illus* 16450.00
Perfume Bottle, Elizabeth Arden, It's You, Opaque White, Gilt, Enameled, c.1939, 6 In. ... 4416.00
Perfume Bottle, Myon, Green Cased, Stopper, Enameled Cover, Box, c.1928, 3 1/2 In. 1645.00
Perfume Bottle, Peggy Hoyt, Flowers, Clear, Blue Patina, Engraved Label, c.1920, 4 In. .. 440.00
Perfume Bottle, Ybry, Desir Du Coeur, Pink Cased, Stopper, Enameled, Box, c.1926, 2 In. 1175.00
Perfume Bottle, Ybry, Femme De Paris, Cased, Stopper, Enameled, Box, c.1926, 2 In. ... 1528.00
Perfume Bottle, Ybry, Mon Ame, Purple Cased, Stopper, Enameled, Box, c.1926, 2 In. ... 1645.00
Stemware Set, Cut Glass, 12 Water, 12 Champagne Saucers, 12 Wines, 4 Cordials, Ewer . 1795.00
Tumbler, Multicolored Foil Replica Of Russian Order, Swags, Roundels, c.1885, 4 In. 470.00
Vase, Octagon Shape, Notched Waist, Signed, 9 3/4 In. 300.00

BADGES have been used since before the Civil War. Collectors search for examples of all types, including law enforcement and company identification badges. Well-known prison or law enforcement badges are most desirable. Most are made of nickel or brass. Many recent reproductions have been made.

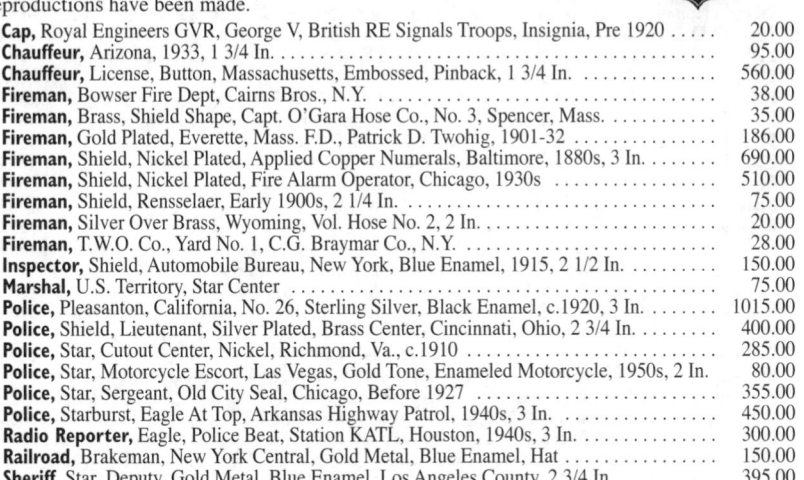

Cap, Royal Engineers GVR, George V, British RE Signals Troops, Insignia, Pre 1920 ..... 20.00
Chauffeur, Arizona, 1933, 1 3/4 In. 95.00
Chauffeur, License, Button, Massachusetts, Embossed, Pinback, 1 3/4 In. 560.00
Fireman, Bowser Fire Dept, Cairns Bros., N.Y. 38.00
Fireman, Brass, Shield Shape, Capt. O'Gara Hose Co., No. 3, Spencer, Mass. 35.00
Fireman, Gold Plated, Everette, Mass. F.D., Patrick D. Twohig, 1901-32 .... 186.00
Fireman, Shield, Nickel Plated, Applied Copper Numerals, Baltimore, 1880s, 3 In. 690.00
Fireman, Shield, Nickel Plated, Fire Alarm Operator, Chicago, 1930s 510.00
Fireman, Shield, Rensselaer, Early 1900s, 2 1/4 In. 75.00
Fireman, Silver Over Brass, Wyoming, Vol. Hose No. 2, 2 In. 20.00
Fireman, T.W.O. Co., Yard No. 1, C.G. Braymar Co., N.Y. 28.00
Inspector, Shield, Automobile Bureau, New York, Blue Enamel, 1915, 2 1/2 In. 150.00
Marshal, U.S. Territory, Star Center 75.00
Police, Pleasanton, California, No. 26, Sterling Silver, Black Enamel, c.1920, 3 In. 1015.00
Police, Shield, Lieutenant, Silver Plated, Brass Center, Cincinnati, Ohio, 2 3/4 In. 400.00
Police, Star, Cutout Center, Nickel, Richmond, Va., c.1910 .... 285.00
Police, Star, Motorcycle Escort, Las Vegas, Gold Tone, Enameled Motorcycle, 1950s, 2 In. 80.00
Police, Star, Sergeant, Old City Seal, Chicago, Before 1927 .... 355.00
Police, Starburst, Eagle At Top, Arkansas Highway Patrol, 1940s, 3 In. 450.00
Radio Reporter, Eagle, Police Beat, Station KATL, Houston, 1940s, 3 In. 300.00
Railroad, Brakeman, New York Central, Gold Metal, Blue Enamel, Hat 150.00
Sheriff, Star, Deputy, Gold Metal, Blue Enamel, Los Angeles County, 2 3/4 In. 395.00

BANKS of metal have been made since 1868. There are still banks, mechanical banks, and registering banks (those that show the total money deposited on the face of the bank). Many old iron or tin banks have been reproduced since the 1950s in iron or plastic. Some old reproductions marked Book of Knowledge or John Wright, or Capron are listed. Pottery, glass, and plastic banks are also listed here. Mickey Mouse and other Disneyana banks are listed in Disneyana. We have added the M-numbers based on *The Penny Bank Book: Collected Still Banks* by Andy and Susan Moore and the R numbers based on *Coin Banks by Banthrico* by James L. Redwine.

3 Little Pigs' House, Tin, Painted Bricks, Red Roof, 3 In.	10.00
3 Stooges, Waiters' Outfits, 3 Top Coin Slots, Ceramic, Japan, 6 3/4 In.	248.00
Alphabet Block, Cast Iron, Gold Color, Multiple Sides, M 1604, 3 7/8 In.	2475.00 to 2750.00
Amish Boy, Black Overalls, Blue Shirt, Black Hat, John Wright, 1970s, M 193, 5 In.	65.00
Apple, Cast Iron, Kyser & Rex, 1880s, M 1621, 3 x 5 1/2 In.	470.00
Armored Truck, Cast Metal, Callen Mfg. Co., 1950s, M 1498, 2 3/4 x 5 1/2 In.	150.00
Auto, Ford Model T, Touring Car, Arcade, c.1923, M 1484, 4 In.	2250.00
Auto, Ford, 1929, 2-Seater, Cast Metal, Tin Coin Trap, Banthrico, 6 In.	75.00
Auto, Ford, 1955, Thunderbird, Cast Metal, Tin Coin Trap, Banthrico, 7 1/8 In.	75.00
Bank Building, Bureaux Caisse, Cast Brass, Slot, Under Eaves, France, M 1136, 8 3/4 In.	330.00
Bank Building, Caisse, Rooster Finial, Brass, France, M 1156, 6 1/4 In.	385.00
Bank Building, Columbia Magic Introduction Co., c.1892, M 1065, 5 In.	165.00
Bank Building, Columbia, Painted White, Cast Iron, Kenton, M 1069, 4 1/2 In.	635.00
Bank Building, Commerce Bank, C Shape, Red, Plastic, New Jersey, 6 x 6 In.	6.00
Bank Building, Crown, Painted, Cast Iron, J. & E. Stevens, M 1226, 3 1/2 In.	165.00
Bank Building, Finial, Cast Iron, Kyser & Rex, M 1158, 5 3/4 x 4 3/8 In.	385.00
Bank Building, General Pershing, Bust, Grey Iron Casting, M 150, c.1918, 7 3/4 In.	165.00
Bank Building, Home Savings, Detroit, Mich., Cast Iron, M 1201, 10 1/2 x 6 1/4 In.	770.00
Bank Building, Home Savings, Dog Finial, J. & E. Stevens, c.1891, M 1126, 5 3/4 x 4 3/8 In.	195.00
Bank Building, Owl On Stump, Cast Iron, M 599, Vindex, 3 5/8 In.	250.00
Bank Building, Presto, Cast Iron, A.C. Williams, M 1168, 3 1/2 In.	28.00
Bank Building, State, Cast Iron, Kenton, M 1080, 4 1/4 In.	358.00
Bank Building, State, Cast Iron, Kenton, M 1080, 5 1/2 In.	275.00
Bank Building, State, Cast Iron, Kenton, M 1080, 5 7/8 In.	305.00
Barney The Dinosaur, Hand Painted, Plastic, Lions Group Co., c.1992	48.00
Barrel, On Hand Cart, Cast Metal, 1930s, M 940, 4 1/4 x 3 In.	125.00
Baseball, National League Bats, Plastic, 1960s, M 1603, 5 3/4 x 4 In.	95.00
Baseball Player, Cast Iron, A.C. Williams, 1910-15, M 18, 5 1/2 In.	495.00
Be Wise & Save Owl, Hand Painted, Plastic, Original Box, 1960s	75.00
Bear, Begging, Standing On Hind Legs, Cast Iron, Gold, A.C. Williams, M 715, 5 3/8 In.	85.00
Bear, In Honey Pot, Painted Silver, Cast Iron, Kyser & Rex, M 696, 2 1/2 x 2 5/8 In.	935.00
Bear, Teddy, Cast Iron, Gold, Arcade, M 694, 2 1/2 x 3 7/8 In.	138.00 to 220.00
Bell, Bailey's Centennial Money Bank, Cast Iron, J.S. Semon, 1876, M 4807, 4 1/2 In.	99.00
Big Boy, Soft Vinyl, Red Checker Overalls, 1973, 9 In.	20.00
Boat, Battleship Maine, Cast Iron, c.1898, M 1440, 5 x 4 1/2 x 2 In.	280.00
Boat, Battleship Maine, Cast Iron, Grey Iron Casting, M 1441, 7 In.	1980.00
Boat, Battleship Maine, J. & E. Stevens, c.1901, M 1439, 6 x 10 1/4 In.	4950.00
Boat, Oregon, Brown, Cast Iron, J. & E. Stevens, M 1452, 6 In.	468.00
Boat, Oregon, Cast Iron, Gray, Red & Gold Trim, J. & E. Stevens, M 1452, 5 1/4 x 6 In.	330.00
Boat, Oregon, Cast Iron, J. & E. Stevens, c.1890s, M 1450, 3 7/8 x 4 7/8 In.	360.00
Boy Bunny, With Pipe, Plastic, Knickerbocker Plastic Co., 11 1/2 In.	95.00
Buddy, Glass Container, Tin Lithograph Figure, Marx, 4 1/4 In.	220.00 to 330.00
Building, Blackpool Tower, Cast Iron, Chamberlain & Hill, 7 3/8 In.	220.00 to 248.00
Building, Columbia, Cast Iron, Kenton, M 1073, 9 In.	1100.00
Building, Cottage, Cast Iron, 5 In. *Illus*	275.00
Building, Cupola, Painted Red, Cast Iron, J. & E. Stevens, M 1145, 5 1/2 In.	143.00
Building, Cupola, Painted, Cast Iron, J. & E. Stevens, M 146, 4 1/8 In.	220.00
Building, Cupola, Red, White, Blue, Cast Iron, J. & E. Stevens, M 1147, 3 1/2 In.	170.00
Building, Independence Hall, Cast Iron, Enterprise Co. *Illus*	660.00
Building, Multiplying, Mirror, J. & E. Stevens, 1880s, M 1184, 6 1/2 In.	1760.00
Building, Palace, Cast Iron, Ives, M 1116, 7 1/2 x 8 x 5 In.	2090.00
Building, Scheut-Missie, Painted Red, Green, Gold, Cast Iron, 4 1/2 In.	143.00
Building, Skyscraper, Cast Iron, Painted Silver & Gold, A.C. Williams, M 1240, 5 1/2 In.	130.00

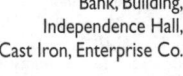

Bank, Building,
Independence Hall,
Cast Iron, Enterprise Co.

Bank, Building, Cottage,
Cast Iron, 5 In.

Building, Statue Of Liberty, Cast Iron, Kenton, M 1165, 6 3/8 In. . . . . .110.00 to 523.00
Building, Tower, Cast Iron, John Harper, M 1208, 9 1/4 In. 578.00
Building, Two Car Garage, Painted Green, White, A.C. Williams, M 1010, 2 1/2 In. 170.00
Building, U.S. Treasury, Painted White, Red, Cast Iron, Grey Iron Casting, M 1053, 3 In. . . 360.00
Building, Victorian House, Silver Finish, J. & E. Stevens, M 1143, 3 1/4 In. 160.00
Cadet Officer, Painted, Cast Iron, Hubley, M 8, 5 3/4 In. 440.00
Camel, Kneeling, Backpack, Cast Iron, Japanned, Kyser & Rex, M 770, 2 1/2 x 4 3/4 In. . . 385.00
Camel, With Saddle, Gold Finish, A.C. Williams, M 767, 7 1/4 In. 330.00
Captain Kidd, Cast Iron, M 38, 6 In. 248.00
Car, Chevy, 1953, Corvette, Cast Metal, Original Box, Banthrico, 7 5/8 In. 75.00
Car, Chrysler New Yorker, 1955 Model, Metal, State Bank, Freeport, Banthrico, 7 3/4 In. . . 248.00
Car, Mercury Monterey, 1954 Model, Metal, Aurora National Bank, Banthrico, 7 5/8 In. . . 248.00
Car, Yellow Cab, Cast Iron, Orange, Black, Arcade, 8 In. 1760.00
Cash Register, Junior, Cast Iron, Nickel Plated, M 930, 4 1/4 In. 176.00
Cash Register, Junior, Cast Iron, Nickel Plated, M 931, 5 1/2 In. 248.00
Cat, Kitty, Seated, Cast Iron, Hubley, 1930s, M 349, 4 3/4 In. 175.00
Cat, Sitting, Soft Hair, Cast Iron, Arcade, M 366, 4 1/4 x 2 7/8 In. 130.00
Charlie The Tuna, Bank On Good Taste, In Star Kist We Trust, Ceramic, Box, 9 x 4 In. 40.00
Chick With Basket, Plastic, Knickerbocker Plastic Co., 9 In. 72.00
Chittenden Bank, Pig, Porcelain, 3 1/2 x 6 1/4 In. 9.00
Chocolate Menier, Tin, L. Revon & Co., France, c.1910 . . . . 248.00
Christmas Stocking, Tree, Snowman, Candy Cane, Train, Ceramic, 6 x 3 In. 30.00
Church, God Loveth A Cheerful Giver, Tin Lithograph, Chein, 1930s, 4 x 3 1/4 x 3 In. 95.00
Cities Service, Koolmotor 5D Oil, Tin, c.1950-60, 2 3/4 x 2 In. 15.00
Citizens Savings & Loan, Umbrella, Plastic, Metal, 1950s, 5 In. 13.00
Clown, Cast Iron, Painted Gold, A.C. Williams, 6 In. 116.00
Cow, Cast Iron, Gold Finish, Cast Iron, A.C. Williams, M 553, 3 3/8 In. 165.00
Curtis Candy, Thrift, Plastic, Metal, Marx Toy Co., 7 3/8 x 3 3/8 x 2 1/8 In. 40.00
Dog, Puppo On Pillow, Cast Iron, Hubley, M 442, 5 5/8 In. 176.00
Dog, Scottie, Standing, Cast Iron, Black, U.S., M 435, 3 1/4 In. 110.00
Dog, Sitting On Treasure Chest, Silvered Metal, Glass Eyes, Denmark, 6 In. 55.00
Dog, Spaniel, Begging, Bristol Glaze, Blue & Green Accents, Early 1900s, 5 1/2 In. 495.00
Dog, Spaniel, Seated, Green Glaze, Early 1900s, 5 In. 358.00
Dog, St. Bernard, Pack, Cast Iron, A.C. Williams, M 437, c.1905, Large, 5 1/2 In. 99.00
Dog, St. Bernard, Pack, Cast Iron, A.C. Williams, M 439, c.1905, Small, 3 3/4 In. 80.00
Dog & Dog House, Tin, 3 x 3 1/4 In. 210.00
Doll's Head, Pot Metal, Mama Sound, Bellows, Semimechanical 275.00
Donkey, Cast Iron, Gold Finish, Red Saddle, A.C. Williams, 7 In. 231.00
Donkey, Cast Iron, Gray, Red Blanket, A.C. Williams, M 500, 6 3/4 x 6 1/4 In. 99.00
Donkey, Cast Iron, With Saddle, Painted Blue, Arcade, M 499, 4 1/2 In. 55.00
Donkey, Cast Iron, With Saddle, Painted Red, Arcade, M 499, 4 1/2 In. 120.00
Drum, Tin, Lithograph, Key Locked Trap, 1940s-50s 45.00
Duck, On Tub, Save For A Rainy Day, Iron, White, Black, Red, Hubley, M 616, 5 3/8 In. . . 165.00
Duck, Silver Plated, Cast Metal, Leonard Silver Plate Co., Blue Eyes, 1960s 50.00
Dutch Girl Holding Flowers, Blue Dress, Cast Iron, Hubley, M 181, 5 1/4 In. 120.00
Dutch Girl Holding Flowers, Green Dress, Cast Iron, Hubley, M 181, 5 1/4 In. 132.00
Eagle, N.R.A., Prudential Insurance, Metal, Painted, Key, M 1410, 5 3/4 x 4 In. 270.00
Elephant, Baby, Cast Iron, Tusks, Tail, Ives, 4 In. 85.00
Elephant, Cast Iron, Blue, Arcade, 4 1/4 In. 275.00
Elephant, Circus, Cast Iron, Hubley, M 462, 3 3/4 In. 390.00

Elephant, On Tub, Cast Iron, Gold Finish, A.C. Williams, M 483, 5 3/8 In. 145.00
Elephant, On Tub, Cast Iron, Silver, Red, Gold, A.C. Williams, M 483, 5 3/8 In. 176.00
Elephant, Raised Coin Slot, Cast Iron, M 475, 4 5/8 In. 475.00
Elephant, Seated, Locket, Porcelain, Germany, c.1930, 3 1/4 In. 55.00
Elephant, Trumpeting, Cast Iron, John Wright, M 482, 7 1/4 x 9 3/4 In. 138.00
Elephant, Trunk Raised, Cast Iron, Painted Red, Art Deco, M 449, 4 3/8 In. . . . . . . .55.00 to 130.00
Elephant, Tucked Trunk, Cast Iron, Painted Blue, Arcade, M 472, 2 3/4 In. 138.00
Elephant, Tucked Trunk, Cast Iron, Painted Green, Arcade, M 472, 2 3/4 In. 138.00
Elephant, With Howdah, Cast Iron, A.C. Williams, 1930s, M 474, 4 7/8 In. 275.00
Elephant, With Howdah, Cast Iron, Painted Green, A.C. Williams, M 359, 3 In. . . . . . .55.00 to 60.00
Elk, Cast Iron, A.C. Williams, c.1900, M 737, 9 x 5 1/2 In. 110.00
English Telephone Booth, Tin Lithograph, Churchill's Candy 50.00
Ertl Truck, Delivery, Cast Metal, 3 11/16 In. 25.00
Ertl Truck, Metal, HP Hood & Sons, Cream, Red Trim, 3 11/16 In. 90.00
Ertl Truck, Metal, Penn State Creamery, Blue, White Stripe, 3 11/16 In. 82.00
Eveready Batteries, Black Cat, Union Carbide, 5 1/2 x 8 1/2 In. 29.00
Eveready Nine Lives Cat, Plastic, 1970s 48.00
Every Copper Helps, Cop, Woman, 2-Sided, Brass, Chamberlain & Hill, c.1910, 4 3/4 In. . 220.00
Farmers Merchant Of New Ulm, House, Plastic, Metal, 3 x 4 In. 60.00
Fido, Cast Iron, Hand Painted, Hubley, 1930s, M 417, 5 In. 250.00
Fisk Tire, Boy, Yawning, Holding Candle, Tire, Time To Retire, Plastic, c.1950, 8 x 3 In. . . 100.00
Fort, Cast Iron, Kenton, M 1172, 4 1/8 In. 440.00
Foxy Grandpa, Cast Iron, John Wright, 1960s 95.00
Franklin Delano Roosevelt, Cast Metal, 1930s 95.00
Gas Pump, Cast Iron, Red, Gold Cast Globe, Arcade, M 1485, 5 3/4 In. 300.00
General Electric, Stack Of U.S. Dollars, Silver, Plastic, 1970, 4 1/2 x 3 In. 18.00
George Washington, Cast Iron, Hand Painted, 1950s-60s, John Wright 150.00
Girl Bunny, Plastic, Red Dress, Knickerbocker Plastic Co., Box, 11 In. 95.00
Graf Zeppelin, Cast Iron, A.C. Williams, M 1428, 6 5/8 In. 165.00
Hole In One, Golfer On Green, Battery Operated, Box, 9 In. 45.00
Hope Chest, Cast Iron, 4 1/2 In. 300.00
Horse, On Tub, Cast Iron, A.C. Williams, c.1920, M 510, 5 1/4 In. . . . . *Illus* 99.00
Horse, Prancing, Cast Iron, Arcade, M 517, 4 1/4 In. 165.00
Horse, Prancing, Oval Base, Cast Iron, A.C. Williams, M 514, 4 3/4 In. 77.00
House, Tin, Key Locked Trap Door, Marklin 2310.00
Howard Johnson, Restaurant, Figural, Orange Roof, Embossed, Plastic, 3 1/2 x 5 In. 29.00
Humpty Dumpty, On Brick Wall, Brass, England, 1920s, 6 In. 110.00
Ice Cream Freezer, Cast Iron, Hand Painted, 1960s 65.00
Ice Cream Freezer, Richmond, Cast Iron, Grey Iron Casting, M 1370, 4 1/4 In. 415.00
Independence Hall Tower, Cannons, Eagle, Cast Iron, Lever Operated Bell, M 1202, 9 In. . . 150.00
Indian Boy, With Rifle, Cast Metal, Anco Toys, 1930s 75.00
Jackie Robinson, Pot Metal, 5 In. 110.00
Leo Chocolate, Tin Lithograph 440.00
Liberty Bell, Carnival Glass, Amber, 1950s 48.00
Liberty Bell, Philadelphia Citizens Committee, Cast Iron, 1941, 3 1/2 In. 80.00
Lion, Tail To The Left, Cast Iron, Hubley, M 763, 3 In. 80.00
Lion, Tail To The Right, Painted Green, Cast Iron, A.C. Williams, M 759, 3 1/2 In. 145.00
Log Cabin, Cast Iron, Japanned, Painted, Kyser & Rex, c.1882, M 1023, 2 1/2 x 3 1/4 In. . . 550.00
Log Cabin, Pottery, Yellow Clay, White, Green Glaze, Houghton Pottery, Dalton, O., 5 In. . . 1725.00
Mailbox, Cast Iron, Green, Hubley, M 841, 5 1/2 In. 140.00
Mailbox, U.S. Mail, Cast Iron, Bronze Finish, Red Letters, M 838, 3 5/8 In. 110.00
Mailbox, U.S. Mail, Cast Iron, Eagle, Silver Finish, Kenton, M 852, 3 5/8 In. 85.00
Mailbox, U.S. Mail, Cast Iron, Silver Color, Red Letters, M 854, 4 1/4 In. 35.00
Mailbox, U.S. Mail, Cast Iron, Trap Door, Bronze Finish, Red Letters, M 835, 4 1/2 In. 95.00
Mailbox, U.S. Mail, Letters, Green, Cast Iron, 4 In. 35.00
Mammy, Hands On Hips, Cast Iron, Painted, Hubley, Box, M 176, 5 1/4 In. 385.00

Mechanical banks were first made about 1870. Any bank with moving
parts is considered mechanical. The metal banks made before World
War I are the most desirable. Copies and new designs of mechanical
banks have been made in metal or plastic since the 1920s. The condition of the paint on the old banks is important. Worn paint can lower a
price by 90%.

Mechanical, Acrobat, Cast Iron, J. & E. Stevens, 1883 Patent . . . . .2475.00 to 5225.00
Mechanical, Artillery, Cast Iron, Gold Finish, 8 x 6 In. 385.00
Mechanical, Artillery, Confederate, Cast Iron, Shepard Hardware . . . . .2100.00 to 2400.00
Mechanical, Artillery, Red Coat, J. & E. Stevens, c.1900 . . . . .1100.00 to 1430.00
Mechanical, Artillery, Union, Cast Iron, Shepard Hardware . . . . .3100.00 to 4400.00
Mechanical, Bad Accident, Cast Iron, J. & E. Stevens, c.1891 . . . . .1320.00 to 2530.00
Mechanical, Bank Building, U.S. Bank, J. & E. Stevens, 1870s 3300.00
Mechanical, Bear, Slot In Chest, Yellow, Cast Iron, Kenton 990.00
Mechanical, Bear, Tree Stump, Cast Iron, H.L. Judd 6 In. 550.00
Mechanical, Bird On Roof, Cast Iron, J. & E. Stevens, 1878 Patent 1980.00
Mechanical, Black Carpet Bagger, Painted, Huge Head, Top Hat, 5 x 4 x 10 In. . .1035.00 to 3165.00
Mechanical, Boy & Bulldog, Brass Casting, H.L. Judd 1100.00
Mechanical, Boy On Trapeze, 1950s 975.00
Mechanical, Boy On Trapeze, Cast Iron, J. Barton Smith, c.1891 . . . . .3300.00 to 9500.00
Mechanical, Boy Robbing Bird's Nest, J. & E. Stevens, 1906 . . . . .4400.00 to 6600.00
Mechanical, Boy Scout Camp, J. & E. Stevens, c.1915 . . . . 4675.00
Mechanical, Boy Stealing Watermelons, Cast Iron, Kyser & Rex 3300.00
Mechanical, Boys Stealing Watermelons, Kyser & Rex, c.1894 . . . . .2750.00 to 3300.00
Mechanical, Bulldog, Brown, Blue Carpet, Cast Iron, J. & E. Stevens, c.1880, 7 In. 660.00 to 2090.00
Mechanical, Bulldog, Brown, Red Carpet, Cast Iron, J. & E. Stevens, 1880 . . . . 715.00
Mechanical, Bulldog, Cast Iron, H.L. Judd, 1870s 770.00
Mechanical, Bulldog, Saving, Man Holds Coin, Ives, Blakeslee, 1878 Patent 5775.00
Mechanical, Butting Buffalo, Cast Iron, Kyser & Rex, c.1888 . . . . 2420.00
Mechanical, Butting Goat, Black, Cast Iron, H.L. Judd 825.00
Mechanical, Cabin, Black Man, Red Shirt, Blue Pants, J. & E. Stevens, 1885 . . . . .468.00 to 1500.00
Mechanical, Cabin, Green, Black Figure, J. & E. Stevens, 1885 Patent 358.00
Mechanical, Calamity, Football, Cast Iron, 1960s 275.00
Mechanical, Calamity, Football, Cast Iron, J. & E. Stevens, c.1906 . . . . 22000.00
Mechanical, Cat & Mouse, Cast Iron, J. & E. Stevens, 1891 Patent . . . . .2750.00 to 3850.00
Mechanical, Chief Big Moon, Cast Iron, J. & E. Stevens, 1899 Patent, 10 In. . . . .1650.00 to 2245.00
Mechanical, Chief Big Moon, Silver Stripe, J. & E. Stevens, c.1899 . . . . 2310.00
Mechanical, Circus, Clown On Dog Drawn Cart, Cast Iron, Shepard, Hardware 6490.00
Mechanical, Clever Dick, Green, Tin, Saalheimer & Strauss, Germany 1045.00
Mechanical, Clown On Globe, Cast Iron, 1960s 275.00
Mechanical, Clown On Globe, Yellow Base, Cast Iron, J. & E. Stevens . . . . *Illus* 3025.00
Mechanical, Clown, J. Chein, c.1939 . . . . 66.00
Mechanical, Coca-Cola Polar Bear, Cast Metal, Ertl Toys 75.00
Mechanical, Coffin, Tin, Windup Key, Yone Toys Of Japan, 1960s 195.00
Mechanical, Columbian Magic Savings Bank, U.S. Safe, Cast Iron, 5 x 5 In. 90.00
Mechanical, Creedmoor, Cast Iron, J. & E. Stevens, 1877 .770.00 to 1210.00
Mechanical, Creedmoor, Cast Iron, Red Pants, J. & E. Stevens, 1877 Patent 330.00
Mechanical, Creedmoor, Cavalier, Cast Iron, J. & E. Stevens, c.1891 . . . . 470.00
Mechanical, Creedmoor, Gray Pants, Cast Iron, J. & E. Stevens, 1877 Patent 825.00

Bank, Horse, On Tub,
Cast Iron, A.C. Williams, c.1920,
M 510, 5 1/4 In.

Bank, Mechanical, Clown On
Globe, Yellow Base, Cast
Iron, J. & E. Stevens

Bank, Mechanical, Elephant
& 3 Clowns, J. & E. Stevens,
1883 Patent

Mechanical, Darktown Battery, Cast Iron, Original Paint, J. & E. Stevens, 10 In. .1840.00 to 5225.00
Mechanical, Dinah, 2150-A, Short Sleeves, John Harper, c.1911 . . . . 935.00
Mechanical, Dinah, Black, Yellow, Cast Iron, John Harper, England, c.1911 . . . . . . .220.00 to 990.00
Mechanical, Dinah, Long Sleeve, Cast Iron, John Harper, c.1911 . . . . 495.00
Mechanical, Dog On Turntable, Building, Cast Iron, H.L. Judd . . . . .575.00 to 2400.00
Mechanical, Eagle & Eaglets, Cast Iron, Painted, J. & E. Stevens, c.1883, 6 In. 450.00
Mechanical, Eagle & Eaglets, Gray, Green, Pat. 1883, J. & E. Stevens, 6 5/8 In. . . . .705.00 to 823.00
Mechanical, Elephant & 3 Clowns, Cast Iron, J. & E. Stevens, 1883 Patent . . . . *Illus* 1650.00
Mechanical, Elephant, Cast Iron, Gold Paint, 10 x 5 In. 80.00
Mechanical, Elephant, Cast Iron, Painted, Capron, 1950s 475.00
Mechanical, Elephant, Howdah Man Pops Out, Cast Iron, 7 x 6 In. . . . . .415.00 to 440.00
Mechanical, Elephant, Howdah, Pull Tail, Trunk Raises, Iron, Hubley, c.1930, 9 In. .195.00 to 220.00
Mechanical, Elephant, Man Pops Out, Cast Iron, Enterprise, Philadelphia, c.1884 . . . . 330.00
Mechanical, Elephant, Moves Trunk, A.C. Williams, c.1905, Small 55.00
Mechanical, Elephant, Pull Tail, Cast Iron, 1960s 65.00
Mechanical, Fisherman, The One That Got Away, 1960s 175.00
Mechanical, Fortune Teller, Tin, Baumgarten 715.00
Mechanical, Frog On Lattice Base, J. & E. Stevens, 1870s . . . . .1800.00 to 2750.00
Mechanical, Frog On Lattice, Green Base, Cast Iron, J. & E. Stevens, 1870s 770.00
Mechanical, Frog On Lattice, Red Base, Cast Iron, J. & E. Stevens, 1870s 1100.00
Mechanical, General Butler, 2571, Cast Iron, J. & E. Stevens, c.1884 . . . . 13750.00
Mechanical, Giant In Tower, Place Coin In Window, Giant Tilts Forward, 1892, 6 In. 4125.00
Mechanical, Girl In Victorian Chair, Cast Iron, W.S. Reed, 1880s 2970.00
Mechanical, Girl Skipping Rope, Cast Iron, J. & E. Stevens, 1890 Patent . . . . .7975.00 to 18700.00
Mechanical, Grenadier, Cast Iron, John Harper, England .495.00 to 770.00
Mechanical, Hall's Liliput, Brown Steps, J. & E. Stevens, 1877 Patent 1100.00
Mechanical, Harlequin, Cast Iron, Second Casting, J. & E. Stevens 16500.00
Mechanical, Harold Lloyd, Tin, 5 1/2 In. 1430.00
Mechanical, Hole In One, Tin, Plastic, Battery Operated, 1950s 175.00
Mechanical, Hoop-La, Cast Iron, John Harper, England . . . . .330.00 to 1430.00
Mechanical, Horse Race, Straight Base, J. & E. Stevens, c.1870 . . . . .2090.00 to 3300.00
Mechanical, Humpty Dumpty, Cast Iron, Shepard Hardware, c.1884 . . . . .1045.00 to 2800.00
Mechanical, I Always Did 'Spise A Mule, Iron, J. & E. Stevens, 1879 . . . . .1100.00 to 4125.00
Mechanical, Independence Hall, Cast Iron, Enterprise 1430.00
Mechanical, Indian & Bear, Cast Iron, J. & E. Stevens 3850.00
Mechanical, Indian & Bear, Cast Iron, Original Paint, Brown Bear, J. & E. Stevens 1380.00
Mechanical, Indian Shooting Bear, J. & E. Stevens, c.1883 . . . . 825.00
Mechanical, Initiating Bank, 1st Degree, Cast Iron, Mechanical Novelty Works, c.1880 . . . 12100.00
Mechanical, Initiating Bank, 2nd Degree, Cast Iron, Mechanical Novelty Works, c.1880 . . . 9625.00
Mechanical, Jolly Nigger, Butterfly Tie, Cast Iron, John Harper . . . . .315.00 to 385.00
Mechanical, Jolly Nigger, Cast Iron, Red Shirt, Shepard Hardware, 6 1/2 In. 345.00
Mechanical, Jolly Nigger, Cast Iron, Shepard Hardware . . . . .358.00 to 440.00
Mechanical, Jolly Nigger, Cast Iron, Sydenham & McOustra, England, 6 In. 385.00
Mechanical, Jolly Nigger, High Hat, Cast Iron, John Harper, c.1882, 8 In. . . . . .690.00 to 950.00
Mechanical, Jolly Nigger, Red Shirt, Aluminum, England 210.00
Mechanical, Jolly Nigger, Red Shirt, J. & E. Stevens 415.00
Mechanical, Jolly Nigger, Rolling Eyes, Holes In Back, Iron, England, 5 1/4 In. . . . .440.00 to 495.00
Mechanical, Jonah & The Whale, Cast Iron, J. & E. Stevens, c.1888 . . . . .1320.00 to 5225.00
Mechanical, Jonah & The Whale, Iron, Shepard Hardware, c.1890, 10 3/8 x 4 In. .1760.00 to 2090.00
Mechanical, Leap Frog, Shepard Hardware, 1890 Patent . . . . .2475.00 to 3850.00
Mechanical, Lion & Monkey, Single Peanut, Kyser & Rex, c.1883, 8 1/2 In. 1320.00
Mechanical, Lion & Two Monkeys, Cast Iron, Kyser & Rex, 1883 Patent . . . . .700.00 to 2860.00
Mechanical, Little Jocko, Steel & White Metal, Ferdinand Strauss, c.1912 . . . . 3850.00
Mechanical, Little Joe, Cast Iron, John Harper, c.1925, 5 x 4 1/2 In. . . . . .330.00 to 525.00
Mechanical, Lucky Wheel, Money Box, Tin, Jacobs & Co. Biscuits, 1920s 495.00
Mechanical, Magic Bank, Building, Man At Door, J. & E. Stevens, c.1876 . . . . . .1150.00 to 1725.00
Mechanical, Magic Bank, Cast Iron, J. & E. Stevens, 1876 Patent 5500.00
Mechanical, Magician, At Table, Cast Iron, J. & E. Stevens . . . . .2640.00 to 5225.00
Mechanical, Mammy & Child, Brown Dress, Cast Iron, Kyser & Rex, 1884 Patent 6050.00
Mechanical, Mason, Brick Layer, Hod Carrier, Iron, Shepard Hardware, 1887 .4125.00 to 15000.00
Mechanical, Merry Go Round, Horse Race, Plastic, Instructions, Crest, 1950s, 5 x 7 In. . . . 265.00
Mechanical, Milking Cow, Cast Iron, J. & E. Stevens, c.1885 . . . . .7700.00 to 19250.00

Mechanical, Minstrel, With Verse, Tin, Saalheimer & Strauss, Germany, c.1928 . . . .330.00 to 415.00
Mechanical, Monkey & Coconut, Iron, J. & E. Stevens, c.1886 . . . . .3080.00 to 4675.00
Mechanical, Monkey & Organ Grinder, 1960s 125.00
Mechanical, Monkey, Organ Grinder, Cast Iron, Hubley, 8 3/4 In. 440.00
Mechanical, Monkey, Tips Hat, Thank You, Tin Lithograph, Chein, 5 1/2 In. . . . . . . .50.00 to 193.00
Mechanical, Monkey, Tray, Uniform, Place Coin Upon My Tail, Tin, Germany, c.1910 . . . . 220.00
Mechanical, Mule Entering Barn, Cast Iron, J. & E. Stevens . . . . .999.00 to 3575.00
Mechanical, New Bank, Painted, Red, Green, Gold, Cast Iron, J. & E. Stevens 1430.00
Mechanical, Novelty Bank, Cast Iron, J. & E. Stevens, c.1873 . . . . .3025.00 to 4125.00
Mechanical, Novelty Bank, Red, Yellow, Blue, Cast Iron, J. & E. Stevens, c.1873 . .770.00 to 891.00
Mechanical, Organ Grinder & Dancing Bear, Kyser & Rex, 1890s . . . . .2588.00 to 6600.00
Mechanical, Organ, Bank, Boy & Girl, Cast Iron, Kyser & Rex, 1882 . . . . .1645.00 to 2090.00
Mechanical, Organ, Bank, Cat & Dog, Kyser & Rex, 1882 . . . . .1100.00 to 1600.00
Mechanical, Organ, Bank, Yellow Jacket, Miniature, Cast Iron, Kyser & Rex, 1881 Patent . 1045.00
Mechanical, Organ, Dancers, Monkey With Cap, Deposits Coin, Kyser & Rex Co., 9 In. . . 1645.00
Mechanical, Owl, Turns Head, Cast Iron, Glass Eyes, J. & E. Stevens, 1880 Patent 1800.00
Mechanical, Owl, Turns Head, Glass Eyes, Cast Iron, Copper, Bronze, Stevens, Pat. 1880 . 7700.00
Mechanical, Paddy & The Pig, Cast Iron, Book Of Knowledge, 1960s 255.00
Mechanical, Paddy & The Pig, Cast Iron, J. & E. Stevens, c.1885 . . . . .1100.00 to 4500.00
Mechanical, Panorama, Painted, Cast Iron, J. & E. Stevens 5225.00
Mechanical, Pelican With Mammy, Cast Iron, J. & E. Stevens 3575.00
Mechanical, Pelican With Rabbit, Cast Iron, Trenton Lock & Hardware, 1878 Patent 6600.00
Mechanical, Pelican, Man Thumbing Nose, Cast Iron, J. & E. Stevens 3300.00
Mechanical, Penny Pineapple, Cast Iron, 1950s 250.00
Mechanical, Pig In Highchair, Iron, Nickel Plated, J. & E. Stevens, c.1897 . . . . . . .495.00 to 770.00
Mechanical, Plantation Darky, Tin, Japanned, Weeden, 1890s . . . . .1430.00 to 2475.00
Mechanical, Presto, Bank Building, Cast Iron, Kyser & Rex, c.1894 . . . . .330.00 to 440.00
Mechanical, Professor Pug Frog's Great Bicycle Feat, Cast Iron, 1960s 275.00
Mechanical, Professor Pug Frog's Great Bicycle, Cast Iron, J. & E. Stevens, c.1886 . . . . . . 5940.00
Mechanical, Punch & Judy, Cast Iron, Shepard Hardware, c.1884 . . . . 3850.00
Mechanical, Punch & Judy, Large Letters, Shepard Hardware, c.1884 . . . . .990.00 to 1650.00
Mechanical, Punch & Judy, Tin Lithograph, Theatre, Die Cut Figures, England, 4 In. 140.00
Mechanical, Rabbit, Cast Iron, Metal Base, 6 In. 550.00
Mechanical, Race Horse, Cast Iron, Hand Painted, 1960s 325.00
Mechanical, Reclining Chinaman, Blue Pants, Cast Iron, J. & E. Stevens, c.1885 6050.00 to 15400.00
Mechanical, Roller Skating, Cast Iron, Kyser & Rex, c.1880 . . . . 12700.00
Mechanical, Rooster, Cast Iron, Kyser & Rex, c.1880 . . . . 275.00
Mechanical, Royal Trick Elephant, Tin, Germany, c.1912 . . . . 1870.00
Mechanical, Santa At Chimney, Cast Iron, Shepard Hardware, 1889 Patent . . . . . .1500.00 to 3520.00
Mechanical, Scotsman, No Verse, Tin, Saalheimer & Strauss 605.00
Mechanical, Sentry, Tin, Lion's Toffee Variant, Germany 1320.00
Mechanical, Sentry, Tin, Saalheimer & Strauss, Germany 660.00
Mechanical, Shoot The Chute, Cast Iron, Second Casting, J. & E. Stevens, Box 3830.00
Mechanical, Smyth X-Ray, Cast Iron, Henry C. Hart, c.1898 . . . . 2750.00
Mechanical, Southern Comfort, Cast Metal, 1950s 215.00
Mechanical, Speaking Dog, Cast Iron, J. & E. Stevens . . . . .770.00 to 1870.00
Mechanical, Speaking Dog, Maroon Base, Cast Iron, Shepard Hardware, c.1885 . .880.00 to 1045.00
Mechanical, Sportsman, Fowler, Man Shooting Bird, Cast Iron, Painted, J. & E. Stevens . . 6600.00
Mechanical, Strike Bowling, Cast Iron, Richards Toys 750.00
Mechanical, Stump Speaker, Black Man, Iron, Shepard Hardware Co., c.1886 . . . .880.00 to 4950.00
Mechanical, Tammany Hall, Cast Iron, 1960s 225.00
Mechanical, Tammany, Brown Pants, Blue Coat, Iron, J. & E. Stevens, 1873 Patent .550.00 to 605.00
Mechanical, Tammany, Cast Iron, J. & E. Stevens, 1873 Patent . . . . .330.00 to 550.00
Mechanical, Tammany, Cast Iron, J. & E. Stevens, Box, 1873 Patent 5225.00
Mechanical, Tammany, Gray Pants, Cast Iron, J. & E. Stevens, 1873 Patent 220.00
Mechanical, Tank & Cannon, Cast Iron, Starkie, Burnley, England 1320.00
Mechanical, Teddy & The Bear, Brown Tree, Cast Iron, J. & E. Stevens, c.1907 . .1210.00 to 3190.00
Mechanical, Teddy & The Bear, Cast Iron, 1960s 275.00
Mechanical, Teddy & The Bear, Gray Tree, Cast Iron, J. & E. Stevens, c.1907 . . . . 1980.00
Mechanical, Tennis Players, Billie Jean King, Bobby Riggs, Battle Of The Sexes, c.1975 . . 1300.00
Mechanical, Toad On Stump, Cast Iron, J. & E. Stevens, 1880s . . . . .750.00 to 1320.00
Mechanical, Trick Dog, Blue, Cast Iron, Solid Base, Hubley, c.1920 . . . . .248.00 to 950.00

Mechanical, Trick Dog, Cast Iron, 6-Part Base, Shepard Hardware ....1045.00 to 7150.00
Mechanical, Trick Dog, Cast Iron, Capron, 1950s 675.00
Mechanical, Trick Pony, Cast Iron, 1970s....................................... 95.00
Mechanical, Trick Pony, Cast Iron, Shepard Hardware, 1885 Patent.............880.00 to 1980.00
Mechanical, Two Frogs, Cast Iron, 1970s 95.00
Mechanical, Two Frogs, Cast Iron, J. & E. Stevens, 1882 Patent ....1058.00 to 5225.00
Mechanical, Uncle Remus, Multicolored, Cast Iron, Kyser & Rex, 1890s ....2310.00 to 6325.00
Mechanical, Uncle Sam, Cast Iron, Mid 20th Century 150.00
Mechanical, Uncle Sam, Cast Iron, Original Paint, Shepard Hardware, c.1886 ....935.00 to 5800.00
Mechanical, William Tell, Aluminum, Sheet Metal, Australia 110.00
Mechanical, William Tell, Cast Iron, J. & E. Stevens, 1896 Patent ....770.00 to 2400.00
Mechanical, World's Fair, Columbus, Cast Iron, J. & E. Stevens, 1893 Patent 6600.00
Mechanical, Zentral Sparkasse, Sheet Metal, Copper, Germany, 1930s ....165.00 to 193.00
Merry-Go-Around, Cast Iron, Grey Iron Casting, M 1614, 4 5/8 In. 660.00
Moody & Sankey, Smith & Egge, M 1228, c.1870 .... 2860.00
Mulligan, Painted, Cast Iron, A.C. Williams, M 177, 5 3/4 In. 248.00
Mutt & Jeff, Cast Iron, Original Paint, A.C. Williams, M 157, 5 1/2 x 2 1/2 In. .....115.00 to 150.00
Organ Grinder, Painted, Cast Iron, Hubley, M 216, 6 3/16 In........................ 145.00
Piano, Upright, Glass, Tin Back, M 838, 3 In...................................... 140.00
Piano Organ, Earthenware, Brown, Austria, c.1900, 4 1/8 In. 140.00
Pig, Cast Iron, Hand Painted, John Wright, 1960s, 10 x 6 In......................... 150.00
Pig, Chalk, Rotund Figure, Fruit Trees, Molded Feet, Late 1800s, 9 In. 3680.00
Pig, Decker's Iowana, Cast Iron, Gold Finish, M 603, 4 3/8 In. 155.00
Pig, Hitler, Save For Victory, Make Him Squeal, Composition, Otis Lawson, M 305, 6 In. . 175.00
Pig, I Made Chicago Famous, Cast Iron, J.M. Harper, M 629, c.1902, 4 In. 210.00
Pig, Wise, Verse, Cast Iron, White, Hubley, M 609, 1930s, 6 5/8 In...............90.00 to 275.00
Pink Pig, Cast Iron, 1960s 65.00
Pirate Chest, On Base, Cast White Metal, M 609, 1950s, 2 5/8 In. 95.00
Pizza Hut, Pizza Pete, Blue Apron, Merit Corp., Wichita, Kan., c.1969, 7 1/2 In.......... 40.00
Policeman, Painted, Cast Iron, Arcade, M 182, 1920s, 5 1/2 In. 470.00
Pool Table, Pool Your Funds, Ceramic, Hand Painted, Glazed, 1950s-60s 75.00
Pram, I'll Have To Ask My Dad, Brass Name Plate, Tin, Brass Wheels, 7 x 7 In. 275.00
Prosperity, Pink, Chein, 1950s 245.00
Rabbit, On Base, Cast Iron, 1884, M 569, 2 1/4 In. 990.00
Rabbit, Seated, Painted, Brown, Cast Iron, Fuzzy White Tail, John Wright, 1960s 65.00
Rabbit, Standing, Cast Iron, Bronze Paint, Lockwood Mfg., c.1900, 6 In. 405.00
Radio, Crosley, Green, Cast Iron, Kenton, M 820, 4 15/16 In. 248.00
Radio, Crosley, Red, Cast Iron, Kenton, 4 15/16 In. 275.00
Radio, Majestic, Cast Iron, Arcade, Box, M 827, 4 1/2 In. 195.00
Red Kettle, Penny Pot, Hand Painted, Ceramic, 1940s-50s 65.00
Refrigerator, Electrolux, Painted, White Metal, M 1335, 1930s 95.00
Refrigerator, Kelvinator, Door Opens, Cast Iron, Arcade, M 1338, 3 7/8 In. 140.00
Register, Beehive, Cast Iron, Nickeled, Register Window, 1890s, M 681, 5 3/8 x 6 1/2 In. . 305.00
Register, Benjamin Franklin Thrift, Tin, Cash Register, 1930s, 2 1/2 In. 175.00
Register, Circus Scenes, Tin Lithograph, Dime, 2 1/2 In............................. 125.00
Register, Elves Rolling Coins To Bank, Tin Lithograph, 1930s, Dime 175.00
Register, Elves Rolling Coins, Tin Lithograph, Dime, 2 1/2 In. 195.00
Register, G.E. Triple Thrift Refrigerators, Tin Lithograph, 1930s, 2 1/2 In., Dime 185.00
Register, Junior, Cast Iron, Nickel Plated, Key, J. & E. Stevens, c.1929, 5 1/4 x 4 5/8 In. ... 165.00
Register, Snow White, Tin, Scene Of Snow White Talking To Dwarfs, 1938, 3 In., Dime .. 110.00
Register, Trunk, Cast Iron, Copper Wash, Pat. 1891, 4 x 5 In., Dime 240.00
Reindeer, Cast Iron, Hand Painted, Turn Pin, Arcade, Early 1900s, M 736, 6 1/4 In. 250.00
Reindeer, Cast Iron, Painted, John Wright, 1970s, M 735, 19 In...................... 150.00
Rooster, Cast Iron, Arcade, M 547, 4 5/8 .... 240.00
Royal Safe Deposit, Cast Iron, Black, Gold Highlights, Kenton, 6 In. 195.00
Rumpelstiltskin, Painted Red Hat, Cast Iron, M 75, 6 In. ....86.00 to 275.00
Safe, 4 Horse Heads, Stenciled, Cast Iron, Lock, Box, 11 In. .... *Illus* 7700.00
Safe, Arabian Safe, Cast Iron, Kyser & Rex, M 882, 4 1/2 In. 140.00
Safe, Army Navy, Cast Iron, 6 In. 660.00
Safe, Bank Of England, Cast Iron, M 870, 4 1/2 In. 990.00
Safe, Bank Of Industry, Cast Iron, Kenton, 5 1/2 In. ....80.00 to 220.00
Safe, Burglar Proof, Cast Iron, Nickel Plated, J. & E. Stevens Co., c.1897, 6 x 5 In. .220.00 to 358.00
Safe, Czar Safe, Cast Iron, Combination Lock, Arcade Toys, 1902 .... 175.00

Look at your home from the viewpoint of a trespasser. Do bushes hide the windows or doors? Are ladders lying around? Can a window be reached by standing on a table or air conditioning compressor? Does your fence hide the burglar from view while he breaks in?

Bank, Safe, 4 Horse Heads, Stenciled, Cast Iron, Lock, Box, 11 In.

Safe, Diamond Safe, 4 Drawers, Key, Cast Iron, Nickel Plated, c.1900, 7 1/2 x 6 1/2 In. 275.00
Safe, Dog, Warriors, Cast Iron, 6 x 4 1/2 In. 440.00
Safe, Egyptian Safe, Cast Iron, 4 1/2 In. 360.00
Safe, Ferris Wheel, State Savings Bank, Cast Iron, Nickel Plated, M 1106, 4 1/2 In. 360.00
Safe, Glass, Cast Iron Top & Bottom, Cylindrical, 3 In. 70.00
Safe, Home Safe, Combination, Cast Iron, 2 1/2 x 3 1/4 In. 80.00
Safe, Home, Painted Silver, Cast Iron, 3 1/4 In. 35.00
Safe, Horse Head, Cast Iron, Nickel Plated, 7 1/2 In. 660.00
Safe, Ideal Security, Cast Iron, 5 1/2 In. . . . . .95.00 to 195.00
Safe, Ideal, Nickeled Cast Iron, Combination Dial, 4 1/8 In. 35.00
Safe, IXL, Cast Iron, Keyser & Rex, M 893, c.1881, 3 1/2 x 2 3/4 In. 55.00
Safe, Keyless Safety Deposit, Cast Iron, 6 In. 220.00
Safe, Pet Safe, Cast Iron, Nickel Plated, 4 1/2 In. . . . . .220.00 to 550.00
Safe, Roller Safe, Cast Iron, Kyser & Rex, M 880, 3 1/2 In. 120.00
Safe, Royal Safe Deposit, Cast Iron, 6 In. . . . . .180.00 to 220.00
Safe, Safe Deposit, Iron, Key Lock Front Door, Shimer Toys, M 888, c.1899, 3 5/8 In. 150.00
Safe, Sport, Cast Iron, Kyser & Rex, M 886, 3 In. 60.00
Safe, Sport, Original Key, Kyser & Rex, Patent Jan. 8, 1882 . . . . 195.00
Safe, Treasure Box, Nickel Plated, Key, 4 x 6 1/2 In. 770.00
Safe, Treasure, Cast Iron, J. & E. Stevens, Pat. 1897, 5 In. 150.00
Safe, Young America, Cast Iron, Kyser & Rex, M 881, 4 1/4 In. 190.00
Santa, Holding Belly, Cast Iron, Hobart, 5 3/4 In. 55.00
Santa, Sleeping In Chair, Black Gloves, Boots, Plaster, Tag, 1950s, M 106, 7 In. . . . . .11.00 to 22.00
Seaman, Sailor Carrying Sack, Earthenware, c.1950, 5 1/2 In. 35.00
Seaman's Bank For Savings, Tin, Cardboard, 1950s 48.00
Seaman's Sailor Savings, Hand Painted, Porcelain, 1940s 65.00
Sharecropper, Black, Cast Iron, A.C. Williams, M 173, 5 1/2 In. 225.00
Shell, 1 1/2 Shell, Nickeled Cast Iron, Ferro Steel Mfg., c.1919, M 1420, 8 In. 33.00
Speedy Alka-Seltzer, Rubber, 1960s, 6 x 2 x 2 1/2 In. 150.00
Stove, Parlor, 1880s Style, Cast Iron, 1950s 175.00
Stove, Parlor, Cast Iron, M 1357, 6 1/4 In. 95.00
Stove, Save Your Money, Buy A Gas Stove, Cast Iron, c.1900, 5 1/2 x 4 x 4 In. 165.00
Sweet Thrift, Tin Lithograph, Glass Panel, Green, Beverly Novelty Co., 6 In. 195.00
Teddy, Theodore Roosevelt, Bust, Painted, Cast Iron, A.C. Williams, M 120, 5 In. 275.00
Telephone, Pressed Steel, Handset, Black, Structo Mfg., 10 1/2 In. 165.00
Transvaal Money Box, Portly Figure, Top Hat, Aluminum, England, M 1647, 6 In. 195.00
Turkey, Cast Iron, A.C. Williams, M 585, Large, 4 1/4 In. 300.00
U.S. Mailbox, Cast Iron, Hand Painted, John Wright, 1960s 95.00
Umbrella, 1/2 Opened, Tin, Save For Rainy Day, M 1279, 6 1/4 x 3 1/4 In. 55.00
Umbrella, Service Savings & Loan Assn., Detroit, Mich., Banthrico, 1970s, Box 27.00
Uncle Sam, Composition, 7 In. 195.00
Uncle Sam's Hat, Tin, Red, White, Blue, Chein, M 1383, 3 1/4 In. 135.00
Wesleyan Chapel, 2 Cherubs, Porcelain, England, 5 7/8 In. 635.00
World War II Doughboy, Cast Iron, Grey Iron Casting, M 48, 7 1/4 In. 220.00
Yellow Kid, Child's Head Shape, Smiling, 1920s, 4 1/2 In. 175.00
Young Negro, Cast Iron, Original Paint, England, M 170, 4 1/2 In. . . . . .220.00 to 345.00
Zeppelin, Graf, Cast Iron, Worn Silver Paint, A.C. Williams, M 1468, 6 3/4 In. 120.00

BANKO is a group of rustic Japanese wares made in the nineteenth and twentieth centuries. Some pieces are made of mosaics of colored clay; some are fanciful teapots. Redware and other materials were also used.

Ginger Jar, Cover, Painted Crane & Flowers, 1930s, 5 In.	300.00
Jar, Potpourri, Pierced Cover, Buddha Finial, Enameled, 3 1/8 In.	200.00
Nodder, Boy With Injured Arm, 1930s, 4 3/8 In.	200.00
Nodder, Man & Wife, 7 3/4 In., Pair	700.00
Teapot, Dog, Figural, Painted, c.1910, 6 In.	350.00
Teapot, Flying Crane, Painted, 1930s, 4 1/4 In.	275.00
Teapot, Quail, Figural, 1920s, 3 1/2 In.	275.00
Wall Pocket, Boy & Girl Climbing, 7 1/2 In.	300.00
Wall Pocket, Origami, Maple Leaf, Ikugawa, Early 1900s, 7 In.	115.00
Wall Pocket, Shield Shape, Woven Sides, Chrysanthemum, 19th Century, 5 1/2 In.	160.00

BARBED WIRE was first patented in 1867. Collectors want eighteen-inch samples.

Havenhill's Long & Narrow Arrow Barbed Wire, Original Card, 1892, 18 In.	14.00
Hodge's Spur Rowel, Rowell Hodge, 1887, 15-Ft. Roll	45.00

BARBER collectibles range from the popular red and white striped pole that used to be found in front of every shop to the small scissors and tools of the trade. Barber chairs are wanted, especially the older models with elaborate iron trim.

Blade Disposal, Figural, Tin & Wood, Red, White, Blue, Key, Bob On Chest, Japan, 9 In.	350.00
Bowl, Brass, Oval, England, 10 In.	115.00
Chair, Horse, Child's, Penn.	14000.00
Chair, Oak, Replaced Leather, Koken, 47 x 29 In.	3300.00
Chair, Pony Head, Child's, 1930s	2100.00
Chair, Salesman's Sample, Koken, 16 x 10 In.	23100.00
Chair, White Porcelain, Hydraulic, Koken, 46 In.	290.00 to 865.00
Display Case, Antiseptic Sterilizer, Wood, Glass Door & Shelves, Etched, 12 x 12 In.	210.00
Pole, Cast Iron, Floor Model, Light-Up, Rotating Insert, 85 In.	1540.00
Pole, Leaded Glass Panels, Red, White, Wall Mount, Koken, c.1910, 33 In.	990.00
Pole, Milk Glass, Red, White, Light-Up, Metal Hanger, Chrome Plates, 1900s, 22 In.	285.00
Pole, Painted, Red, White, Blue Spiral, Gold Turned Ends, 36 In.	990.00
Pole, Pine, Obelisk, Painted, Gilt, Trade Sign, Charles Ehm, Cazenovia, c.1890, 105 In.	45000.00
Pole, Porcelain, Red, White, Blue, Look Better, Feel Better, 48 In.	115.00
Pole, Red & White Stripe Bottom, Red, White, Blue Top, 84 In.	1810.00
Pole, Red, White, Blue Stripes, Half Round, c.1900, 33 In.	1100.00
Pole, Self Standing, Glass Globe Top, Koken Company, St. Louis, 86 In.	2310.00
Pole, Turned, Gilded End Balls, Northeast, c.1875, 29 1/2 x 3 1/4 In.	6600.00
Pole, Turned, Painted, Gilded, Wall Mount, c.1900, 30 1/2 In.	440.00
Pole, Wood, Red, White, Blue, 19th Century, 70 In.	3900.00
Pole, Wood, Turned, Old Paint, Red, Blue, White, Gold Lines, Finials, 35 In.	4310.00
Sign, Assoc. Master Barbers Of America, Pays To Look Well, Celluloid, 6 x 15 In.	120.00
Sign, Barber Shop Union, It Pays To Look Well, Embossed, Tin, Self-Framed, 6 x 15 In.	176.00
Sign, Barber Shop, Ask For Wildroot, Barber Pole, Tin, Embossed, 14 x 40 In.	136.00
Sign, Look Better, Feel Better, Barber Pole, Red, White, Blue, Porcelain, 22 x 9 In.	110.00

BAROMETERS are used to forecast the weather. Antique barometers with elaborate wooden cases and brass trim are the most desirable. Mercury column barometers are also popular with collectors. It is difficult to find someone to repair a broken one, so be sure your barometer is in working condition.

Aneroid, Diamond Shape, Wood Frame, France, 37 x 25 In.	1200.00
Banjo, Clock, Fruitwood, Carved, Leaf Carved Decoration, Late 1800s, 40 x 15 In.	1668.00
Banjo, George III, Mahogany & Ebony, Inlaid, Marked, T. Coibetti, Longon, 42 In.	1150.00
Banjo, Georgian Style, Brass Urn Shape Finial, 20th Century, 37 1/2 x 10 In.	765.00
Banjo, Shoff & Mason, Pediment Top, Acorn Finial, 20th Century, 28 x 7 In.	235.00
Charles X, Carved, Giltwood, Plaster, Eglomise, Lozenge Shape, 25 x 37 In.	1725.00
Desk Top, Louis XVI Style, Bronze, Enamel, Green Onyx, Spread Eagle, 12 1/2 In.	508.00

Louis XVI, Giltwood, Carved, Octagonal, Painted, Gray Blue, White, Gold, 33 x 18 In. 2990.00
Marine, Chelsea, Holosteric, 7 3/4 In. Diam. 1265.00
Marine, JJBM/16 A 22/R.N. Desterro/Lisbon, Brass, Late 1900s, 37 1/2 In. 2300.00
Marine, Welsh Scientific, Chicago, Brass Axis, Copper Glazed Case, 1943, 40 In. 880.00
Paris, Travel, Walnut Case, Sliding Cover, Ebony Stringing, 39 In. 1410.00
Queen Anne Style, Ormolu, Ivory Mount, Walnut, Mahogany Siphon Tube, 41 In. 3220.00
Ship's, Brass, On Gimbals, 38 In. 590.00
Stick, A. Allan, Mahogany, Silver Register Plates, Vernier, Ivory Wheel, 40 In. 5875.00
Stick, Alexander Allan, Edinburgh, Mahogany, Ivory Wheel, 40 In. 5875.00
Stick, English Mahogany, Swan's Neck Pediment, Worthington & Allan, 38 In. 1007.00
Stick, I. Blatt, Mercury, Mahogany Case, Brighton, England, c.1910, 37 In. 560.00
Stick, Mahogany, Arched Face, Thaxter & Bros., Boston, 19th Century, 35 1/2 In. 2940.00
Stick, Maple, Inscribed, C. Wilder, Peterboro, N.H., Pat. June 5, 1860, 39 1/2 In. 2530.00
Stick, Peter Donegan, Mahogany, Broken Arch Pediment, London, c.1820, 38 1/2 In. 1700.00
Stick, Victorian, Rosewood, Ivory, E. & G.W. Blunt, New York, c.1850, 41 In. 2270.00
Thermometer, F. Saltern & Co., Mahogany Veneer Case, London, 38 1/2 In. 546.00
Thermometer, Fox, Bird, Berries, Leaves, Wood, Germany, Post WWI, 28 x 12 1/2 In. . . . 485.00
Thermometer, George III Style, Ebonized Wood Inlay, Mahogany, Stick, 38 In. 1725.00
Thermometer, George III Style, Mahogany, Banjo, Late 19th Century, 38 In. 74800.00
Thermometer, Georgian, Rosewood, Mother-Of-Pearl Inlay, T. Church, c.1820, 41 In. 765.00
Thermometer, Louis XV Style, Ormolu Mounted, Parquetry, Kingwood, 53 In. 5520.00
Wheel, English Rosewood, Cased, Integral Thermometer & Hygrometer, 38 In. 220.00
Wheel, Mahogany Case, Signed, D. Rivolta Edinburgh, England, c.1830, 39 In. 489.00
Wheel, Rosewood, Hygrometer Over Thermometer, Mirror, H. Mayers, c.1875, 38 In. 705.00

BASALT is a special type of ceramic invented by Josiah Wedgwood in
the eighteenth century. It is a fine-grained, unglazed stoneware. The
most common type is black, but many other colors were made.

Bowl, Centerpiece, Gold Rope Border, Interior Floral Band, 15 In. 250.00
Candlestick, Dolphin, Rectangular Base, Shell Border, 8 3/4 In., Pair 635.00
Coffeepot, Pear Shape, Gooseneck Spout, Early1900s, 7 1/2 In. 100.00
Console, Scrolled Base, Fluted, Engine-Turned Border, 10 In., 2 Piece 175.00
Cup, Classical Relief, Man Begging, Woman, Angel, Handleless, 1900s, 2 In. 80.00
Medallion, Bust, Cassandra, Stamped, Late 1700s, 2 x 1 3/4 In. 160.00
Teapot, Hand Painted Flowers, c.1850, 4 x 7 1/4 In. 140.00

BASEBALL collectibles are in the Sports category, except for baseball cards, which
are listed under Baseball in the Card category.

BASKETS of all types are popular with collectors. American Indian,
Japanese, African, Shaker, and many other kinds of baskets can be
found. Of course, baskets are still being made, so the collector must
learn to tell the age and style of the basket to determine the value.

Bread Rising, Rye Straw, Dome Lid, Round, Tapered Sides, Wooden Finial, 8 1/2 x 17 In. . 3410.00
Buttocks, 24 Ribs, Bentwood Handle, Miniature, 2 1/2 In. 290.00
Buttocks, Bentwood Handle, Green Paint, 7 1/4 In. 315.00
Buttocks, Splint, Bentwood Handle, Varnished, 12 1/2 x 6 In. 80.00
Buttocks, Splint, Bentwood Handle, Varnished, 9 x 4 1/2 In. 175.00
Buttocks, Splint, Oak, Bent Wood Handle, 5 3/4 x 7 1/2 In. 45.00
Buttocks, Splint, Oak, Orange Paint, Green Interior, Bentwood Handle, 13 x 16 x 16 In. . . 440.00
Buttocks, Splint, Oak, Reinforced Rim, Bentwood Handle, 6 x 6 In. 745.00
Cheese, Splint, Round Rim, 26 x 7 In. 430.00
Cheese, Splint, Round Rim, Octagonal Base, 1800s, 7 x 22 In. 265.00
Cheese & Fruit, Splint, Oak, Oval, Hexagonal Weave, Waxy Patina, 12 x 20 x 13 3/4 In. . . 489.00
Clam, Iron, Bent Oak, Maine, 19th Century, 14 1/2 x 13 In. 405.00
Clam, Oak, Iron, Square Shape, Jersey Shore, c.1910, 13 1/2 x 15 x 15 1/2 In. 345.00
Coiled, Oak Splint & Straw, Cover, 2 Bentwood Handles, 9 1/2 x 23 x 16 In. 550.00
Egg, Splint, Oak, Patina, 12 x 13 1/2 In. 230.00
Feather, Cover, Side Handles, Oval, Ring Top, Red & Blue Rings, 25 x 16 In. 105.00
Field, Oak Splint & Straw Coil, 2 Willow Bent Handles, Round, 12 x 21 x 24 In. 690.00
Gathering, Splint, Oval Top, Arched Handle, Rectangular Base, Patina, 15 x 10 x 11 In. . . . 115.00
Gathering, Splint, Swing Handle, Green Paint, Round, 16 x 17 1/2 In. 460.00

Hamper, Rye Straw, Fitted Lid, Base, Bulbous, 12 x 16 1/2 In. 1155.00
Hamper, Rye Straw, Lid, Bulbous, 22 x 16 In. 1760.00
Hanging, Splint, 2 Arched Loops, 14 1/2 x 9 1/2 x 10 In. 290.00
Hanging, Splint, Arched Handle, Tapered Sides, 11 x 6 1/2 x 17 In. 430.00
Hanging, Splint, Bentwood Handle, Oak, Red Ocher Paint, 7 1/2 x 7 1/2 In. 275.00
Lacquered, Drop-In Lid, Pegged Handles, Painted, Dragons, Chinese, 14 x 9 x 14 In., Pair 145.00
Laundry, Hawkeye, Burlington Basket, Co., Iowa, 1938, 23 x 18 In. 85.00
Melon, Splint, 34 Ribs, 18 x 16 In. 200.00
Melon, Splint, Pennsylvania, 16 1/2 In. 345.00
Nantucket, Nested, Cherry Handle, Signed, Azuba Scott Howland, c.1970, 12 Piece 4950.00
Nantucket, Purse, Swing Handle, Ebony Plaque, Oval, J.F. Reyes, c.1950, 5 x 7 x 8 In. . . . 3525.00
Nantucket, Splint, Wooden Handle, Ears, 5 x 6 1/4 In. 1150.00
Nantucket, Swing Handle, Lightship, Round, Ash, Wood Base, 5 1/4 x 8 1/2 In. 635.00
Nantucket, Swing Handle, Oval, 5 1/2 In. 1725.00
Nantucket, Swing Handle, Round, Signed, A.E. Cummings, 1889, 4 1/2 x 6 In. 550.00
Nantucket, Wooden Swing Handle, Round, 3 Incised Circles, 3 1/2 x 8 1/2 In. 230.00
Needle, Pine, Coiled Woven, Hard Handle, Out-Turned Rim, 1800s, 10 x 12 In. 230.00
Oriental, Straw, Early 20th Century, 23 x 16 In. 105.00
Pack, Splint, Leather Shoulder Straps, 4 1/4 In. 175.00
Pack, Split Ash, Canvas Straps, 20 1/2 x 15 x 9 In. 136.00
Pack, Split Ash, Canvas Straps, Nickel Plated Hardware, 1/2 Size, 10 x 9 x 6 1/2 In. 69.00
Pie, Lid, Ash Splint, Natural Surface, Late19th Century, 12 x 11 In. 518.00
Potato, Bent Oak Wood Handle, Open Between Splints, Round, 13 1/2 x 15 In. 385.00
Rice, Tight Weave, Chinese, Early 1900s, 28 In. 60.00
Rye Straw, Painted, Lid, Wooden Knob, Salmon Paint, Hanover, Penn., 12 x 18 In. 2970.00
Rye Straw, Round, Tapered Sides, Attached Bentwood Handles, 8 x 14 1/2 In. 1760.00
Rye Straw, Round, Tapered Sides, Openwork Rim, 2 x 6 1/4 In. 550.00
Splint, 2 Rim Handles, Painted, Square Base, 13 x 13 In. 1150.00
Splint, Arched Handle, Blue Paint, Oblong, 16 1/2 x 8 x 14 3/4 In. 400.00
Splint, Arched Handles, Square, Brown Patina, Red & Black Bands, 11 x 12 x 6 In. 115.00
Splint, Ash, Cover, Ring Handles, Goose Down, Mustard Paint, 24 In. 220.00
Splint, Bentwood Handle, Blue Paint, Gray Band, 14 x 10 In. 316.00
Splint, Bentwood Handle, Oak, Reinforced Rim, Round, 3 1/4 x 5 1/2 In. 660.00
Splint, Bentwood Handle, Pink Paint, 9 x 10 x 5 1/4 In. 115.00
Splint, Bentwood Handles, Patina, Round, 13 x 7 3/4 In. 145.00
Splint, Bentwood Swing Handle, Round, 12 x 8 In. 345.00
Splint, Cornucopia Shape, New England, 62 x 24 In. 2300.00
Splint, Cover, Handle, 2 Side Handles, Bulbous Shape, 19 x 10 In. 80.00
Splint, Cover, Handles, Potato Stamp, Alternating Tan, Yellow, 17 x 12 x 9 In. 980.00
Splint, Narrow, Elliptical, Wrapped Handle, Green Paint, c.1850, 16 1/4 In. 1610.00
Splint, Oak Bentwood Handle, Rim, Round, Straight Sides, 13 1/2 x 13 In. 85.00
Splint, Oak, Bent Oak Handle, Tapered Ribs, Red Stained Band, Oval, 6 x 5 1/2 In. 120.00
Splint, Oak, Bentwood Handle, God's Eye, 10 1/2 x 10 x 12 1/2 In. 95.00
Splint, Oak, God's Eye Weave Ends, Bentwood Handle, Round, 10 x 12 In. 95.00
Splint, Oak, Natural Patina, c.1930, 5 1/4 x 6 1/4 In. 175.00
Splint, Oak, Wood Handle, Rim, Varnished, Round, 11 x 11 1/2 In. 440.00
Splint, Pigeon Carrying, Carved M In Handle, Oak, Mountville, Penn., c.1900 . . . . 275.00
Splint, Square, Green Paint, Yellow & Red Geometric Design, 4 x 11 x 11 In. 1210.00
Splint, Upright Handle, Ribbed, Blue Gray Paint, 1800s, 2 3/8 In. 499.00
Splint, Wrapped Handle, Blue & Red Wash In Diagonal Pattern, 11 x 12 In. 750.00
Splint & Coil, 2 Applied Bentwood Handles, Bowl Shape, Tapered, 7 x 16 In. 605.00
Splint & Straw Coil, Split Seam Handles, Round, 14 1/2 x 28 In. 2420.00
Table, Rye Straw, Handle, Green Paint, Oval, 4 5/8 x 7 3/4 x 11 1/2 In. 1320.00

BATCHELDER products are made from California clay. Ernest
Batchelder established a tile studio in Pasadena, California, in 1909 and
expanded until 1916. Then he built a larger factory with a new partner.
The Batchelder-Wilson Company made all types of architectural tiles,
garden pots, and bookends. The plant closed in 1932. In 1936 Batchelder opened Batchelder Ceramics, also in Pasadena, and made bowls,
vases, and earthenware pots. He retired in 1951 and died in 1957.
Pieces are marked *Batchelder Pasadena* or *Batchelder Los Angeles*.

BATCHELDER
LOS ANGELES

Table, Tile Top, 3 Flower & Geometric Tiles, Rectangular Tiles, 19 x 19 x 13 In. 823.00

Tile, Green Matte, 6-Sided, Frame, 6 1/4 x 7 1/4 In. 375.00
Tile, Knight, On Horse, Castle, Blue & Brown Engobe, 7 1/2 In. 940.00
Tile, Knight, On Horse, Tan Gray, Blue Green, Carved, Impressed, Frame, 14 In. 375.00
Tile, Stylized Design, Green High Glaze, 6 In. 530.00
Vase, Mottled Brown Glaze, Shouldered, 8 In. 1530.00

BATMAN and Robin are characters from a comic strip by Bob Kane
that started in 1939. In 1966, the characters became part of a popular
television series. There have been radio and movie serials that featured
the pair. The first full-length movie was made in 1989.

Bank, Ceramic, Hands On Hips, Lego, Japan, Box, 1966, 6 1/2 In. 135.00
Bank, Composition, Hands On Hips, Decals, Lego, Japan, Box, 1966, 6 1/2 In. 90.00
Batcycle, Plastic, On Cardboard, Cellophane Wrap, Irwin Corp., 1966, 8 1/2 x 14 In. 1955.00
Batmobile, Battery Operated, Azrac Hamway, Box, 1972, 4 1/2 x 5 x 13 3/4 In. 925.00
Batmobile, Tin Lithograph, Battery Operated, Alps, Japan, c.1966, 3 x 11 1/2 In. 400.00
Batmobile, Tin Lithograph, Battery Operated, Taiwan, Box, 12 In. 300.00
Batmobile, Tin Lithograph, Friction, Sanka, Japan, 1966, 3 x 9 In. 480.00
Box, Batman Gum Card, 5 Cents, Countertop Display, Topps, c.1966, 3 3/4 x 8 In. 417.00
Box, PEZ Dispenser Display, Cape, 5 1/2 x 7 x 4 1/4 In. 3373.00
Bus, Volkswagen, 1960s, 5 1/2 In. 750.00
Button, Batman, Movie, Summer 89, Yellow Ground, Square, 1989, 2 1/8 In. 12.00
Button, I'm A Batman Crime Fighter, Batman, Robin, Red, Lithograph, 1966, 1 1/2 In. 30.00
Coins, Authentically Engraved, Trade N Play Coins, On Card, 1966 .... 127.00
Game, Batman Electronic Quizz Machine, Lisbeth Whiting Co., Box, c.1966, 9 x 14 In. 155.00
Game, Card, Cardboard, Ideal, Box, 1966, 6 1/2 x 10 1/2 In. 60.00
Goggles, Mask Specs, Bat, Black, Marx, On Card, 1966, 2 3/4 x 6 1/4 In. 165.00
Herald, Batman Movie, Ritz, Woodbury, Tenn., 20th Century Fox, Jan., 1967, 9 x 5 In. ... 115.00
Jeep, Tin, Box, 1960s, 6 In. 990.00
Lamp, Batman, Outside Batcave, Plastic Base, Vinyl Figure, Folding Arm, 14 1/2 x 5 In. .. 50.00
Lobby Card, Tunnel Of Terror, Columbia Pictures, 1949, 11 x 14 In. 236.00
Model Kit, Batplane, Unopened, Aurora, Box, 1966, 5 1/4 x 13 x 1 1/2 In. 175.00
Model Kit, Boat, Imai, Japan, Box, 1960s, 14 x 5-In. Box .... 300.00 to 340.00
PEZ Dispenser, Cape, c.1966, 4 In. 90.00
Photograph, Batmobile, Royal Crest All Star Dairy, ABC Television, 11 x 8 1/2 In. 90.00
Ring, Rubber, Hong Kong, 1960s, 2 1/2 In. 10.00
Robot, Walks, Arms Swing, Tin, Battery Operated, Fairylite, Japan, Box, 1960, 11 1/2 In. . 3490.00
Sign, Slam Bang Vanilla Ice Cream, All Star Ice Cream, Paper, c.1966, 24 x 44 In. 160.00
Soaky, Batman, Robin, Palmolive, 1966, 10 In., Pair 115.00
Toy, Batman Follow The Color Magic Rub-Off, Whitman, Box, c.1966, 8 3/4 x 11 3/4 In. . 40.00

BAUER pottery is a California-made ware. J.A. Bauer bought Paducah Pottery in Paducah, Kentucky, in 1885. He moved the pottery to
Los Angeles, California, in 1909. The company made art pottery after
1912 and dinnerwares marked *Bauer* after 1929. The factory went out
of business in 1962.

Ring, Mixing Bowl, No. 12, Chocolate Brown, Inside Rings 500.00
Vase, Black, Fred Johnson, 5 1/2 In. 295.00
Vase, Fan, Jade, Wavy Line Pattern, Matt Carlton, 6 1/2 In. 450.00

BAVARIA is a region in Europe where many types of porcelain were
made. In the nineteenth century, the mark either included the word
Bavaria. After 1871, the words *Bavaria, Germany,* were used. Listed
here are pieces that include the name *Bavaria* in some form, but major
porcelain makers, such as Rosenthal, are listed in their own categories.

Bowl, Portrait, Hand Painted, Blue Ground, Young Woman, Blue Hat, 8 1/2 In. 95.00
Chocolate Set, Hand Painted Flowers, Pot, Cups, Saucers, 13 Piece 175.00
Pitcher, Hand Painted Grapes, Iridescent Band Around Rim, Gold Handle, 7 1/2 In. 65.00
Pitcher, Tankard, Porcelain, Grape Decoration, Artist Signed, 13 In. 200.00
Plate, 2 Handles, Porcelain, Flowers, 10 In. 10.00
Plate, Hand Painted Red & Pink Roses, Green, Signed, J. Braun, 11 5/8 In. 75.00
Plate, Hand Painted White Roses, Green, Barauther Waldsassen, 10 In. 130.00
Plate, Portrait, Hand Painted, 13 In. 65.00
Sweetmeat Stand, Dresden Style, Schumann, Early 1900s, 6 1/4 In., Pair 145.00

Tea Set, Gold Panels, Colonial Scene, Pot, Cups, Saucer, Sugar, Creamer, 7 Piece 85.00
Teapot, Hand Painted Roses, Butterfly, Melon Shape, Heinrich & Co., 1896, 7 1/2 In. 125.00
Vase, Portrait, Lady With Horse, Gold Frame, Floral Swags, Tirschenreuth, 5 In. 60.00

BEADED BAGS are included in the Purse category.

BEATLES collectors search for any items picturing the four members
of the famous music group or any of their recordings. Because these
items are so new, the condition is very important and top prices are
paid only for items in mint condition. The Beatles first appeared on
American network television in 1964. The group disbanded in 1971.
Ringo Starr and Paul McCartney are still performing. John Lennon
died in 1980. George Harrison died in 2001.

Book, Yellow Submarine, New American Library, 1st Printing, 1968, 128 Pages 90.00
Book Cover, Plastic Display Bag, Glossy Paper, Book Covers Inc., 13 x 10 In., 7 Covers .. 58.00
Button Set, Yellow Submarine, Tin Lithograph, King Features Syndicate, 1968, 4 Piece .. 30.00
Case, Yellow Submarine, Blue Meanie, Metal, Hinged Lid, Enamel, 1968, 3 1/2 x 5 In. ... 275.00
Clock, Alarm, Yellow Submarine, Bells, Windup, Sheffield, 1968 .... 750.00
Clothes Hanger, George, Yellow Submarine, Henderson Haggard, 1968, 18 x 16 1/2 In. 150.00
Clothes Hanger, Paul, Yellow Submarine, Henderson Haggard, 1968, 18 x 16 1/2 In. 175.00
Clothes Hanger, Ringo, Cardboard, Saunders Enterprises, England, 1967, 15 x 16 In. 100.00
Coin Holder, Vinyl, On Display Card, 1964, 12 1/2 x 9 1/2 In., 12 Piece 2300.00
Compass, Beatles Finder, Metal Case, Hinged Lid, NEMS, Seltaeb, Australia, 1964, 3 In. . 150.00
Doll Set, Vinyl, Rooted Hair, Remco Seltaeb, 1964, 4 1/2 In., 4 Piece 350.00
Drum, Lonely Hearts Club Band, Rockola Club, 31 In. Diam. 140.00
Figurine Set, Sgt. Pepper's Costumes, Porcelain, Starshine Inc., 1987, 18 In., 4 Piece 785.00
Game, Flip Your Wig, Milton Bradley, 1964 .... 228.00
Guitar, New Sound, Cut Away, 4 Strings, Selcol, England, 1964, 13 x 8 x 2 1/4 In. 555.00
Hair, Gold Frame, John Lennon, Documents 80.00
Jacket, Beatles Authentic Mod Fashions, Tag, 9th Street East Ltd., NEMS, 1966, 30 In. ... 125.00
Kaboodle Kit, Vinyl, Standard Plastic, NEMS, 1964, 7 x 9 x 4 In. ....500.00 to 675.00
Key Chain Lighter, Plastic, Red, Metal, Permanent Match, Mitsugiri Mfg., c.1966, 1 3/4 In. 29.00
Lunch Box, Metal, Blue, Elmer Lehnhardt, Aladdin, c.1965 .... 1264.00
Lunch Box, Vinyl, Cardboard, Air Flite, NEMS, 1964, 7 x 9 x 4 In. 425.00
Movie Poster, Help!, The Beatles, 1965, 27 x 41 In. 315.00
Nodder Set, Pottery, Coca-Cola Premium, Car Mascot, Japan, 1964, 8 In., Box ....485.00 to 610.00
Note Cards, Yellow Submarine, 5 Designs, Sunshine Card, Box, 1968, 5 x 7 In., 20 Cards . 200.00
Notebook, Yellow Submarine, Vernon Royal, 1968, 7 1/2 x 5 In. 150.00
Ornament Set, Pink & Red Suits, Blown Glass, Western Germany, 7 In., 4 Piece 510.00
Paint Your Own Beatle Kit, Paint By Numbers, Artistic Creations, 1960s 485.00
Pendant, Heart Shape, Photograph, Embossed Roses, Metal Lithograph, NEMS, 2 In. 50.00
Photo Cube, Fan Club, Cardboard, Die Cut, Envelope, Apple Music, 1970, 7 x 12 In. 75.00
Pin, Locket, Yeh, Yeh, Yeh, Die Cut Letter Bar, Celluloid Image, Hinged, 1960s, 1 7/8 In. . 100.00
Pin, Names, Pearl, Drum, Guitar, Gold Luster, Die Cut, NEMS, 1960s, 2 In. 75.00
Poster, Screamer, Caricature, Gordon Currie, Mathews Rotary Press, 22 x 8 In., 4 Piece .. 230.00
Record, All You Need Is Love, Picture Sleeve, No. 5964, Capitol Records, 45 RPM 55.00
Record, I Wanna Hold Your Hand, Picture Sleeve, No. 5112, Capitol Records, 45 RPM ... 65.00
Record, Let It Be, Picture Sleeve, No. 2764, Apple, 45 RPM 65.00
Record Case, Disk Go, Plastic, Round, Blue, Black Pictures, NEMS, Charter Ind., 1966 ... 150.00
Scrapbook, Portraits, Paper, NEMS, Whitman, 13 1/2 x 12 In. 55.00
Sneakers, Low Cut, Lace-Up, Faces, Facsimile Autographs, Wing Dings, c.1964 .... 700.00
Stationery Set, Yellow Submarine, Waves, Unicorn Creations, 1968 .... 145.00
Switch Plate Cover Set, Yellow Submarine, Cardboard, Sealed, DAL Mfg., 1968, 5 Piece . 359.00
Ticket Stub, Civic Center, Baltimore, Md., Sept., 1964, 1 1/2 x 1 3/4 In. 105.00
Tin, With The Beatles Talc, Margo Of Mayfair, Plastic Stopper, 7 In. 200.00
Toy, Arthur A-Go-Go Drummer, Ringo, Vinyl, Plays Drums, Alps, 10 In. 575.00
Tumbler Set, Ringo, George, Paul, John, White, Orange, Yellow, 1964, 5 1/2 In., 4 Piece .. 445.00
Wrapper, Gum Card, Anglo Confectionary, c.1968, 5 1/4 x 6 In. 200.00

BEEHIVE, Austria, or Beehive, Vienna, are terms used in English-
speaking countries to refer to the many types of decorated porcelain
bearing a mark that looks like a beehive. The mark is actually a shield,
viewed upside down. It was first used in 1744 by the Royal Porcelain
Manufactory of Vienna. The firm made porcelains, called *Royal Vienna*

by collectors, until it closed in 1864. Many other German, Austrian, and Japanese factories have reproduced Royal Vienna wares, complete with the original shield or *beehive* mark. This listing includes the expensive, original Royal Vienna porcelains and many other types of beehive porcelain. The Royal Vienna pieces include that name in the description.

Charger, Hand Painted Scene, Cupid & Woman, Royal Vienna, c.1900 .... 920.00
Figurine, Satyr, Drinking From Wineskin, Basket Of Fruit, White Glaze, Vienna, 14 In. ... 345.00
Plaque, Portrait, Man, Woman, Cobalt Blue Border, Gilt Scrolls, Vienna, 21 3/4 In., Pair .. 7360.00
Plate, Marie Antoinette, Portrait, Blue, Gold Decoration, Wagner, Royal Vienna, 9 1/2 In. . 1150.00
Plate, Monk, Edward Grutzner, Royal Vienna Style, Donath, 9 1/2 In. 230.00
Plate, Portrait, Parcel Gilt, Enameled, Claret Ground, Women, Vienna, c.1900, 10 3/4 In... 316.00
Plate, Woman, Long Brown Hair, Gold Gilt Composition Frame, Vienna, 15 x 14 In. 525.00
Plate, Woman, Red Hat, Gold Gilt Composition Frame, Vienna, 16 1/2 x 16 1/2 In. 470.00
Plate Set, Soup, Neoclassical Scenes, Vienna, 9 3/4 In., 9 Piece 7770.00
Platter, Gilt Griffin & Bird Border, Venus, Vulcan's Forge, Oval, Vienna, Early 1800s, 16 In. 4800.00
Tea Caddy, Rinaldo & Almida, Jupiter & Calista, Porcelain, K. Weh, Vienna, c.1900, 6 In. . 240.00
Urn, Cabinet, Bolted, Cupid, Cobalt Blue Ground Gilt Scrolls, Royal Vienna, 1800s, 7 In. . 260.00
Urn, Woman, Gilt Leaves, Burgundy Ground, Square Base, Royal Vienna, c.1900, 35 In. .. 3910.00
Vase, Cover, Bulbous, Geometric Design, Gilt Flower Overlay, Vienna, c.1900, 15 In., Pair 345.00
Vase, Portrait, Picture, Marie Antoinette, Vienna, 7 In............................. 388.00

BEER BOTTLES are listed in the Bottle category under Beer.

BEER CANS are a twentieth-century idea. Beer was sold in kegs or returnable bottles until 1934. The first patent for a can was issued to the American Can Company in September of that year; and Gotfried Kruger Brewing Company, Newark, New Jersey, was the first to use the can. The cone-top can was first made in 1935, the aluminum pop-top in 1962. Collectors should look for cans in good condition, with no dents or rust. Serious collectors prefer cans that have been opened from the bottom.

Anheuser-Busch, Natural Light, Pull Tab, 12 Oz. 10.00
Aristocrat, Red & Black, Gold Chevrons, Flat Top, Steel, 12 Oz. 25.00
Ballantine XXX Ale, Gold, Flat Top, Steel, 12 Oz. 40.00
Berghoff 1887, Walter's Brewing Co., Printed Like Barrel, Pull Tab, Steel, 12 Oz. 15.00
Blue Boar Ale, Blue & White, Flat Top, Steel, 12 Oz. 255.00
Bohio Cerveza Beer, Camden County Beverage Co., Flat Top, Steel, 12 Oz. 760.00
Brown Derby, Flat Top, 12 Oz. 13.00
Brown Derby Lager, Aluminum Pull Tab, Pearl Brewing Company, 12 Oz. 4.99
Brut Super Premium Beer, Lone Star Brewing, Gold, Red, Pull Tab, Steel, 1971, 12 Oz. . 7.50
Budweiser Lager, Anheuser-Busch., Am. Can Co., Flat Top, Steel, Sealed, 12 Oz. 75.00
Burger, Cincinnati, Cone Top, Steel, 12 Oz. 610.00
Burger, Cincinnati, Red & Gold On White, Pull Tab, Steel, 12 Oz. 8.00
Burgermeister King Size, San Francisco, Calif., Gold, Blue, Pull Tab, Steel, 1962, 16 Oz. . 15.00
Carlsberg, Pull Tab, La Brasserie O'Keefe, Montreal, Quebec, 12 Oz. 10.00
Cerveza Tecate, Push Tab, Mexico, 12 Oz. 11.00
Champagne Velvet, Terre Haute Brewing Co., Gold, Cone Top, Crown Cap, Steel, 12 Oz. . 70.00
Colt 45 Power Master, Contents, Heilman Brewery 4.00
Coors, Banquet Waterfall, Push Tab, 12 Oz. 10.00
Coors, Red Stripes, Flat Top, Steel, 1950s, 12 Oz. 20.00
Fort Pitt, Waiter With Mug On Tray, Silver, Flat Top, Steel, 12 Oz. 910.00
Gam, Gambrinus Brewing Co., Cone Top, King, White Background, Steel, 1951, 12 Oz. ... 225.00
Gilley's, Photo Of Gilley, State Of Texas, Pull Tab, Steel, 1970s, 12 Oz. 3.00
Harley-Davidson Heavy Beer, Sturgis, Gold, Pull Tab, Aluminum, 1988, 12 Oz. 5.00
Koehler, Pull Tab, Drained From Bottom, Erie Brewing, Pennsylvania, 12 Oz. 5.00
Labatt Pilsner, Aluminum, Pull Tab, 12 Oz. 9.00
Lifestaff Pale Ale, Rainier Brewing Co., Cone Top, Steel, 1930s, 12 Oz. 325.00
Lucky Lager, Falstaff, Aluminum, Pull Tab, 12 Oz. 5.00
Mark V, Aluminum, Pull Tab, Pittsburgh Brewing Company, 12 Oz. 5.00
Miller High Life, Flat, Rolled, 1940s 30.00
Miss Olde Frothingslosh, Fatima Yechburgh, Pittsburgh Brewing, 1969 ....4.00 to 9.95
Old Export Premium Beer, Cumberland Brewing Co., Pull Tab, Steel, 16 Oz. 20.00
Old German Brand, Queen City Brewing Co., Red, Yellow, Cone Top, Steel, 1934, 12 Oz. 50.00

Olympia, Pull Tab, 12 Oz. 3.00
Pabst Big Cat Malt Liquor, Pull Tab, 12 Oz. 13.00
Pabst Blue Ribbon, Aluminum, Pull Tab, 12 Oz. 3.00
Red Brand Beer, Waldorf, Red On Printed Wood Grain, Flat Top, Steel, 1940s, 12 Oz. 1550.00
Schmidt, Buffalo, Pull Tab, Tin, 12 Oz. 10.00
Shopwell Premium Beer, Colonial Brewing, Red & Gold, Pull Tab, Steel, 1972, 12 Oz. 8.00
White Head Ale, Ebling Brewing Co., Green & Silver, Cone Top, Aluminum, 12 Oz. 315.00
Zobelein's Eastside, Los Angeles Brewing Co., Cone Top, Steel, 12 Oz. 70.00

BELL collectors collect all types of bells. Favorites include glass bells, figural bells, school bells, and cowbells. Bells have been made of porcelain, china, or metal through the centuries.

Brass, Hammered, Dome Shape, Relief Birds & Flowers, Hammer, Oriental, 13 x 10 In. .. 213.00
Brass, Hand, Turned Wood Handle, 11 1/2 In. 105.00
Brass, Hand, Turned Wood Handle, Impressed, No. 6, 8 In. 132.00
Brass, Hand, Turned Wood Handle, Impressed, No. 10, 10 1/4 In. ....94.00 to 145.00
Hand, Brass, Turned Wood Handle, No. 10, 11 In. 145.00
Hotel, Brass, Ivory Tipped Ringer, Early Victorian, 4 1/2 x 3 In. 404.00
Sleigh, Brass, 20 Bells From 3 1/2 To 1 1/2 Inches, Leather Belt, c.1900, 82 In. 145.00
Sleigh, Leather Strap, 19 Graduated Bells, 72 In. 259.00

BELLEEK china was made in Ireland, other European countries, and the United States. The glaze is creamy yellow and appears wet. The first Belleek was made in 1857. All pieces listed here are Irish Belleek. The mark changed through the years. The first mark, black, dates from 1863 to 1890. The second mark, black, dates from 1891 to 1926 and includes the words *Co. Fermanagh, Ireland*. The third mark, black, dates from 1926 to 1946 and has the words *Deanta in Eirinn*. The fourth mark, same as the third mark but green, dates from 1946 to 1955. The fifth mark, green, dates from 1955 to 1965 and has an R in a circle added in the upper right. The sixth mark, green, dates after 1965 and the words *Co. Fermanagh* have been omitted. The seventh mark, gold, was used from 1980 to 1993 and omits the words *Deanta in Eirinn*. The eighth mark, introduced in 1993, is similar to the second mark but is printed in blue. The word *Belleek* is now used only on the pieces made in Ireland even though earlier pieces from other countries were sometimes marked *Belleek*. These early pieces are listed by manufacturer, such as Ceramic Art Co., Haviland, Lenox, Ott & Brewer, and Willets.

Biscuit Jar, Cover, Shamrock Pattern, 6 5/8 In. 390.00
Box, Cover, Acorn, Finial, 3rd Mark, 2 1/2 x 3 1/2 In. 350.00
Figurine, Pig, Green Mark, 3 3/8 In. 225.00
Sugar & Creamer, Cover, Scalloped, Shell Designs, 20th Century, 3 1/2 x 4 1/2 In. 118.00
Tea Set, Neptune Pattern, Teapot, Cups, Saucers, Sugar, Creamer, 7 Piece 1500.00
Tea Set, Shamrock Pattern, Cup, Saucer, Plate, Teapot, 4th Mark, 4 Piece 750.00
Teapot, Limpet Pattern, 2nd Green Mark 295.00
Teapot, Neptune Pattern 850.00
Vase, Figural Owl, Green Mark, 8 1/2 In. 275.00
Vase, Shamrock Pattern, Urn Form, Handles, 1955-65, 8 In. 275.00
Vase, Stump, Bird Nest, 3 Upper & 3 Lower Spouts, Ireland, c.1900, 12 In. 1175.00
Vase, Tapered, Red Poppies, White & Orange Background, Signed, 10 x 4 3/4 In. 180.00
Vase, Trumpet Form, Relief Calla Lily, Black Mark, 10 In. 201.00

BENNINGTON ware was the product of two factories working in Bennington, Vermont. Both the Norton Company and the Lyman Fenton Company were out of business by 1896. The wares include brown and yellow mottled pottery, Parian, scroddled ware, stoneware, graniteware, yellowware, and Staffordshire-type vases. The name is also a generic term for mottled brownware of the type made in Bennington.

Baking Dish, Molded Rim, Rockingham Glaze, Elongated, 1849 Mark, 8 3/4 In. 290.00
Baking Dish, Mottled Green, Flint Enamel, 8-Sided, 1849 Mark, 10 x 12 1/4 In. 750.00
Bottle, Barrel, Coachman, Flint Enamel, Impressed, 10 7/8 In. 345.00
Bottle, Coachman, Holding Mug, Rockingham, Impressed, 10 1/4 In. 345.00
Bottle, Coachman, Wearing Tassels, Holding Flask, Rockingham Glaze, 11 In. 405.00
Bottle, Coachman, Wearing Tassels, Holding Mug, Rockingham Glaze, 9 3/4 In. 175.00

Bottle, Flask, Book, Bennington Battle, Flint Enamel, 4 Qt., 10 3/4 In. 1265.00
Bottle, Flask, Book, Bennington Battle, Flint Enamel, Pt., 5 1/2 In. 805.00
Bottle, Flask, Book, Bennington Companion, Flint Enamel, 10 3/4 In. 1380.00
Bottle, Flask, Book, Departed Spirits, Flint Enamel, Pt., 5 1/2 In. . . . . .460.00 to 520.00
Bottle, Flask, Book, Flint Enamel, Departed Spirits, 2 Qt., 7 3/4 In. 748.00
Bowl, Slope Sides, Rockingham Glaze, 1849 Mark, 11 3/4 In. 230.00
Butter, Dome Cover, Insert, Green & Amber, Bud Finial, Impressed, 7 1/2 In. 1955.00
Candlestick, Flint Enamel, Cylindrical, Molded Rings, 8 1/2 In., Pair 865.00
Candlestick, Flint Enamel, Cylindrical, Molded Rings, 9 1/2 In., Pair 2760.00
Candlestick, Flint Enamel, Olive Green, Brown, Flared, Waisted Stem, 8 1/2 In., Pair 805.00
Chamber Pot, Green & Amber, Scalloped Rib, C-Scroll Handle, Impressed, 9 3/8 In. 575.00
Chamberstick, Ribbed Baluster, Applied Scroll Handle, Flint Enamel, 3 1/4 In. 3105.00
Change Cover, Swiss Lady, Hoop Skirt, Flint Enamel, Mottled Green, 7 In. 8050.00
Churn, Benny Blue, Flower Cornucopia, J. Norton, c.1861, 6 Gal., 19 In. 8250.00
Churn, Spray, Cobalt Blue, E. & L.P. Norton, c.1870, 4 Gal., 17 1/4 In. 805.00
Coffeepot, Helmet Cover, Paneled Baluster, Angular Handle, Flint Enamel, 12 In. 520.00
Coffeepot, Paneled, Angular Handle, Helmet Cover, Flint Enamel, Impressed, 12 1/2 In. . . 920.00
Creamer, Cover, Cow, Rockingham Glaze, 5 1/2 x 7 In. 520.00
Crock, Bird On Twig, Stoneware, Egg Shape, J. Norton & Co., c.1861, 2 Gal., 11 In. 360.00
Crock, Blue Bird On Plume, Stoneware, E. & L.P. Norton, c.1880, 3 Gal., 10 1/2 In. 635.00
Crock, Blue Stylized Leaf, Egg Shape, J. & E. Norton, c.1855, 1 1/2 Gal., 9 1/2 In. 360.00
Crock, Cake, Dotted Reclining Deer, Stoneware, c.1855, 2 Gal., 12 In. . . . . *Illus* 18700.00
Crock, Cobalt Blue Bird, Salt Glaze, E. & L.P. Norton, c.1861, 4 Gal., 13 In. 765.00
Crock, Dotted & Stylized Leaf, E. & L.P. Norton, c.1880, 7 1/2 In. 495.00
Crock, Triple Flower, Blue, Oval, Stoneware, Norton & Fenton, c.1840, 3 Gal., 12 In. 165.00
Figurine, Lion, Standing, Facing Left, Green, Brown, Paw On Ball, Flint Enamel, 11 In. . . 5750.00
Figurine, Lion, Standing, Facing Left, Paw On Ball, Flint Enamel, 7 1/4 x 10 1/2 In. 1610.00
Figurine, Poodle, Flint Enamel, Basket Of Fruit, Coleslaw Lion Clip, 8 1/4 In., Pair 4600.00
Frame, Oval, Rockingham Glaze, 8 3/4 x 9 3/4 In. 489.00
Jar, Canning, Deer, Lying Down, J. & E. Norton, c.1855, 4 Gal. 9350.00
Jar, Canning, Stylized Flower, J. Norton & Co., c.1861, 1 1/2 Gal., 11 In. 2420.00
Jug, Bird, On Plume, Blue, Stoneware, E. & L. P. Norton, c.1880, 1 1/2 Gal., 12 In. 360.00
Jug, Blue Slip, Ball Shape, Stoneware, Oval, L. Norton & Son, c.1835, 2 Gal., 13 1/2 In. . . 360.00
Jug, Blue Thistle Flower, J. & E. Norton, c.1855, 3 Gal., 15 1/2 In. 470.00
Jug, Cobalt Blue Bird, Salt Glaze, J. & E. Norton, 3 Gal., 14 3/4 In. 690.00
Jug, Flower, Blue, Applied Handle, Stoneware, E. & L.P. Norton, Vt., 2 Gal., 13 x 8 In. . . . 385.00
Jug, Flower, Blue, J. & E. Norton, Stoneware, 14 In. 1200.00
Jug, Flowers, Cobalt Blue, Stoneware, J. & E. Norton, Vt., 13 In. 750.00
Jug, Gray, Stoneware, Marked, Norton & Fenton, 1844-47, 11 In. 230.00
Jug, Incised Dove, Flowers, Julius Norton, c.1848, 11 1/2 In. 12650.00
Jug, Peacock, J. & E. Norton, c.1855, 2 Gal., 4 In. 4950.00
Jug, Stoneware, Cobalt Blue Leaves, Strap Handle, 4 x 17 3/4 In. 290.00
Mixing Bowl, Flared Rim, Rockingham Glaze, 1849 Mark, 13 3/4 In. 750.00
Paperweight, Figural, Reclining Spaniel, Graniteware, White Ground, 4 In. 175.00
Pitcher, Alternate Rib, Waisted, Flint Enamel, 1849 Mark, 9 3/4 In. 980.00
Pitcher, Cream, Paneled Baluster, Band, Applied Handle, 1849 Mark A, 5 3/4 In. 145.00
Pitcher, Flint Enamel, 8 Ribs, 8-Sided Base, 1849-58, 5 1/2 In. 295.00
Pitcher, Flint Enamel, Tulip & Heart, Applied Handle, 1849 Mark A, 7 3/4 In. 1840.00
Pitcher, Swirled, Alternate Rib, Waisted, Flint Enamel, 1849 Mark, 9 3/4 In. 1035.00
Pitcher, Tulip & Heart, Paneled Baluster, Curved Handle, Flint Enamel, 10 In. 635.00
Snuff Jar, Cover, Toby, Flint Enamel, Impressed 1849 Mark A, 4 1/4 In. 1095.00
Sugar, Cover, Alternate Rib, Waisted, Branch Loop Handles, Flint Enamel, 6 1/2 In. 460.00
Teapot, Flint Enamel, Alternate Rib, Waisted, Leaf Tip Molded Spout, 5 1/2 In. 290.00

Bennington, Crock,
Cake, Dotted
Reclining Deer,
Stoneware, c.1855,
2 Gal., 12 In.

**Valuable glass should not be
washed in a dishwasher.**

Tobacco Jar, Cover, Alternate Rib, Flint Enamel, 1849 Mark, 7 3/4 In. 430.00
Toby Jug, Benjamin Franklin, Sitting, Boot Handle, Green, 5 3/4 In. 920.00
Washboard, Rockingham, Brown & Yellow, c.1853, 21 3/4 In. 460.00
Water Cooler, Flower Band, Barrel Shape, J. & E. Norton, c.1855, 6 Gal., 15 1/2 In. 1760.00

BERLIN, a German porcelain factory, was started in 1751 by Wilhelm
Kaspar Wegely. In 1763, the factory was taken over by Frederick the
Great and became the Royal Berlin Porcelain Manufactory. It is still in
operation today. Pieces have been marked in a variety of ways.

Charger, Shallow Bowl, Outswept Rim, Painted, Flowers, Mark, 19th Century, 2 x 15 In. ... 345.00
Plaque, A Secret, 2 Peasant Children, Giltwood Frame, Late 1800s, 13 x 8 In. 9600.00
Plaque, Jupiter & Io, Giltwood Frame, Late 1800s, 13 1/8 x 8 In. 12000.00
Plaque, Madonna, Frame, Twist Support, Frame, 20th Century, 16 x 11 1/2 In. 470.00
Plaque, Rape Of Daughters Of Leucippus, Giltwood Frame, Late 1800s, 9 1/4 x 6 3/8 In. . 7800.00
Plaque, St. Rodriguez, Wreath, Cherub, Giltwood Frame, Late 1800s, 18 1/2 x 11 1/4 In. .. 10200.00
Plaque, Stand, Zeppelin, Village, c.1915, 20 1/2 In. 5400.00
Plaque, Woman, Wavy Hair, Oval, Wagner, Giltwood Frame, Late 1800s, 9 x 6 5/8 In. 6000.00
Vase, Wilhelm I, Grisaille, Egg Shape, Octagonal Base, 2 Handles, c.1880, 20 3/4 In. 3600.00

BETTY BOOP, the cartoon figure, first appeared on the screen in
1931. Her face was modeled after the famous singer Helen Kane and
her body after Mae West. In 1935, a comic strip was started. Her dog
was named Bimbo. Although the Betty Boop cartoons ended by 1938,
there was a revival of interest in the Betty Boop image in the 1980s and
new pieces are being made.

Bookends, Betty Boop, Bimbo, Jukebox Center, Pottery, Vendor, 1981 .... 70.00
Cookie Jar, Betty Boop As Carmen Miranda, King Features Syndicate, 1985, 12 In. 300.00
Doll, Wood Body & Arms, Composition Head, Legs, Tag, Cameo Doll Co., 11 1/2 In. 1162.00
Doorstop, Painted, Wooden, 1930s, 13 1/2 x 9 x 3 3/4 In. 187.00
Figurine, Bimbo, Bisque, Painted, Japan, 1930s 2 3/4 In. 30.00
Hosiery, Original 2-Sided Label, Angora Fleece, c.1931, 11 x 4 In. 345.00
Necklace, Balloons, Czechoslovakia, 1930s, 1 x 2 x 7 1/2 In. 1985.00
Necklace, Golf Theme, Czechoslovakia, 1930s, 1 x 1 1/2 x 7 1/2 In. 2645.00
Nodder, Betty Boop As Hula Girl, Pottery, Raffia Skirt, 7 In. 55.00
Nodder, Celluloid, Betty Nods, Heart Shaped Label, Battery Operated, Fleisher Studios ... 1400.00
Puzzle, Betty Boop & Bimbo, Paramount Stars, Fleisher Studios, 1932, 8 1/2 In. 175.00
Soap, Toilet, 3 Bars, Box, Pictorial Products Inc., 1931, 2 3/4 x 5 3/4 x 3/4 In. 150.00
Stringholder, Plaster, Painted, 6 x 7 x 2 1/2 In. 625.00
Toothbrush Holder, Betty Boop On Piano, Pottery, 7 x 4 In. 60.00
Toy, Big Dress-Up Set, Colorforms, Box 40.00
Toy, Jointed, Wood, 1930s, 4 1/4 In. 165.00

BICYCLES were invented in 1839. The first manufactured bicycle
was made in 1861. Special ladies' bicycles were made after 1874. The
modern safety bicycle was not produced until 1885. Collectors search
for all types of bicycles and tricycles. Bicycle-related items are also
listed here.

Advertisement, Columbia, Boycycles & Girlcycles, Foldover, 1930s, 10 1/4 x 20 In. 60.00
Boneshaker, Wooden, Wooden Pedals, Spokes, c.1860, 35-In. Rear, 39-In. Front Wheel ... 3415.00
Brochure, Remington Bicycles, Foldout, 5 Panels, 1901 .... 55.00
Button, 2 Racers, Color, c.1898, 1 1/4 In. 125.00
Button, Hunter Bicycles, Hunter Arms, Dog, Bird In Mouth, Whitehead & Hoag, 7/8 In. .. 265.00
Button, I'm In Plee-Zing Bicycle Contest, Oval, 1930s, 1 1/2 In. 30.00
Button, Major Taylor, Iver Johnson Cycles, Celluloid, 1 1/4 In. 180.00
Button, Orient Cycles, Green Wreath, Linton, Bicycle, c.1899, 1 1/4 In. 40.00
Button, Ride A Fairy Bike, Colson, Child On Tricycle, Red, Green, Black, Celluloid, 1 In. . 65.00
Button, Thomas Cooper, Cyclist, c.1897, 7/8 In. 25.00
CCM, Tandem, Yellow, Black 430.00
Columbia, 5 Star Superb, Girl's, Balloon Tires, Airwheel Whitewalls, 1950 .... 305.00
Columbia, Air Rider, Boy's, Red & Cream, Bookrack, Kickstand, 1940 .... 980.00
Columbia, Expert Model, Radial Wheel, Open Head Badge, Patent 12 1881, 52 In. 4125.00
Columbia, Model 40, Man's, Pneumatic Tire, Hammock Seat, Grip Tires, 1890s 715.00
Columbia, Model 200, Man's, Chainless, Tripe Leaf Spring, Solar Lamp 715.00
Columbia, Superb, Boy's, Maroon & White, Fender Light, 1941 .... 578.00

Elliot Hickory, Model C, c.1892 .... 6270.00
Gedron, Model No. 7, Man's, Split Fame, The Iron Wheel Co., Toledo, Ohio, 1892 ...... 2750.00
Higgins, Girl's, Spring Fork, Balloon Tire, Green & Cream, 1950s 165.00
High Wheel, Child's, Cast Iron, H On Handlebars, 41 In. 3520.00
Indian, Girl's, Pneumatic Tires, Blue & Red, Wooden Rims, Indian Logo, c.1920s 715.00
March-Davis Cycle, The March, Man's, Pneumatic Tires, Downswept Handlebars, Green .. 965.00
Monarch, Silver King, Model M1, Boy's, Silver Finish, 1938 .... 687.00
Norwood, Model 6, Pneumatic Tires, White, Manufactured By Schueter Cycle, 1890s 690.00
Pierce, Lady's, Pneumatic Tires, 1920 .... 220.00
Ribbon, League Of American Wheelmen, N.Y. State Race, 1892, 6 3/4 x 2 In. 35.00
Roadmaster, Supreme, Cleveland Welding Co., Horn, Yellow, Maroon, 1937 .... 8800.00
Schwinn, Aero-Cycle, Red Aluminum, Headlamp, Delta Gangway Horn, 1934 .... 4070.00
Schwinn, Apple Krate, Red, Banana Seat, 1960s 845.00
Schwinn, Challenger, Boy's, Key Locking, Horn Tank, Long Wing Chair Guard, 1940 .... 525.00
Schwinn, Mark IV Jaguar, Boy's, Blue & Chrome, Headlight, West Wind Tires, 1960s 415.00
Shelby Flyer, Hiawatha Arrow, Boy's, Red & Black, Fender Badge, 1939 .... 2850.00
Sherrell Classic, Type 1, Serial 41, Red Paint, 1987 .... 715.00
Standard, Lady's, Maroon, Gold Pinstripes, National Sewing Machine Co., 1895 .... 745.00
Tricycle, Boneshaker, Iron Frame, Wooden Wheels, c.1860, 36-In. Front Wheel 3740.00
Tricycle, Garton, Telephone Repairman, Pressed Steel, Wood Tool Box, Bell, 32 In. 121.00
Tricycle, Junior Tow-Trike, Pressed Steel, Spoke Wheels, AMF, 28 In. 800.00
Tricycle, Mattel, V-Rroom, Pressed Steel, Plastic Engine, Steel Spoke Wheels, 28 In. 66.00
Tricycle, Mattel, V-Rroom, Pressed Steel, Plastic Engine, Steel Spoke Wheels, 35 In. 28.00
Victor Ordinary, Downswept Handlebars, Pear Grips, Black Frame, 54-In. Front Wheel .. 4675.00
Ward's Hawthorn, Boy's, Balloon Tire, Red & White, Rear Carrier, Running Lights, 1940 .. 305.00
Winchester, Boy's, Red, White, 1-Speed, Leatherette Saddle, 23-In. Rims 1035.00
Winchester, No. 25EH, Girl's, 28-In. Tires 660.00

BING & GRONDAHL is a famous Danish factory making fine porcelains from 1853 to the present. Underglaze blue decoration was started in 1886. The annual Christmas plate series was introduced in 1895. Dinnerwares, stoneware, and figurines are still being made today. The firm has used the initials B & G and a stylized castle as part of the mark since 1898.

Figurine, 2 Friends, 4 3/4 In. 150.00
Figurine, Asiatic Pheasants, Standing On Millet, 17 In., Pair 865.00
Figurine, Boy, Walking On Beach, Crab At Feet, Early 20th Century, 7 3/4 In. 128.00
Figurine, Children, Kneeling, Holding Seaweed & Starfish, White, 4 1/2 In., Pair .... *Illus* 130.00
Figurine, Dog, Large, White, 15 1/2 In. 1700.00
Figurine, Headache, 4 1/2 In. 50.00
Figurine, Mother & Child, Seated In Wicker Child, 10 3/4 In. 359.00
Figurine, Ruth, 4 1/4 In. 150.00
Figurine, Tiger, 15 1/2 In. 520.00
Figurine, Titmouse, Optimist, 5 1/8 In. 80.00
Ornament, 1985, Drop, Christmas Eve At Farmhouse 20.00
Ornament, 1986, Drop, Silent Night, Holy Night 30.00
Plate, Christmas, 1895, Behind The Frozen Window, 7 In. ....4000.00 to 6000.00
Plate, Christmas, 1896, New Moon Over Snow-Covered Trees, 7 In. 2500.00
Plate, Christmas, 1897, Christmas Meal Of The Sparrows, 7 In. 1300.00
Plate, Christmas, 1898, Christmas Roses & Christmas Star, 7 In. 850.00
Plate, Christmas, 1899, Crows Enjoying Christmas, 7 In. 1250.00
Plate, Christmas, 1900, Church Bells Chiming, 7 In. 1100.00
Plate, Christmas, 1901, 3 Wise Men From The East, 7 In. 450.00
Plate, Christmas, 1902, Interior Of Gothic Church Jensen, 7 In. 300.00
Plate, Christmas, 1903, Happy Expectation Of The Children, 7 In. 300.00
Plate, Christmas, 1904, View Of Copenhagen From Frederiksberg Hill, 7 In. 125.00
Plate, Christmas, 1906, Sleighing To Church On Christmas Eve, 7 In. 70.00
Plate, Christmas, 1907, Little Match Girl, 7 In. 115.00
Plate, Christmas, 1908, St. Petri Church Of Copenhagen, 7 In. 70.00
Plate, Christmas, 1908, St. Petri Church Of Copenhagen, 12 In. 500.00
Plate, Christmas, 1909, Happiness Over The Yule Tree, 7 In. 70.00
Plate, Christmas, 1909, Happiness Over The Yule Tree, 12 In. 1000.00
Plate, Christmas, 1910, Old Organist, 7 In. 70.00

Do not store opals in a hot, dry place or in water or oil.

Bing & Grondahl, Figurine, Children, Kneeling, Holding Seaweed & Starfish, White, No. 2267, 4 1/2 In., Pair

Plate, Christmas, 1910, Old Organist, 12 In.	2500.00
Plate, Christmas, 1913, Bringing Home The Yule Tree, 7 In.	90.00
Plate, Christmas, 1915, Chained Dog Getting Double Meal, 7 In.	110.00
Plate, Christmas, 1916, Christmas Prayer Of The Sparrows, 7 In.	65.00
Plate, Christmas, 1917, Arrival Of Christmas Boat, 7 In.	70.00
Plate, Christmas, 1920, Hare In Snow, 7 In.	55.00
Plate, Christmas, 1921, Pigeons In Castle Court, 7 In.	55.00
Plate, Christmas, 1925, Child's Christmas, 7 In.	55.00
Plate, Christmas, 1927, Skating Couple, 7 In.	65.00
Plate, Christmas, 1932, Lifeboat At Work, 7 In.	55.00
Plate, Christmas, 1934, Church Bell In Tower, 7 In.	55.00
Plate, Christmas, 1937, Arrival Of Christmas Guests, 7 In.	95.00
Plate, Christmas, 1938, Lighting The Candles, 7 In.	120.00
Plate, Christmas, 1940, Delivering Christmas Letters, 7 In.	220.00
Plate, Christmas, 1942, Danish Farm On Christmas Night, 7 In.	165.00
Plate, Christmas, 1944, Sorgenfri Castle, 7 In.	100.00
Plate, Christmas, 1945, Old Water Mill, 7 In.	130.00
Plate, Christmas, 1946, Commemoration Cross, 7 In.	55.00
Plate, Christmas, 1948, Watchman, Sculpture Of Town Hall, 7 In.	55.00
Plate, Christmas, 1951, Jens Bang, New Passenger Boat, 7 In.	60.00
Plate, Christmas, 1953, Boat Of His Majesty, In Greenland Waters, 7 In.	60.00
Plate, Christmas, 1957, Christmas Candles, 7 In.	95.00
Plate, Christmas, 1958, Santa Claus, 7 In.	65.00
Plate, Christmas, 1959, Christmas Eve, 7 In.	75.00
Plate, Christmas, 1960, Danish Village Church, 7 In.	85.00
Plate, Christmas, 1961, Winter Harmony, 7 In.	70.00
Plate, Christmas, 1964, Fir Tree & Hare, 7 In.	30.00
Plate, Christmas, 1966, Home For Christmas, 7 In.	25.00
Plate, Christmas, 1967, Sharing The Joy Of Christmas, 7 In.	25.00
Plate, Christmas, 1969, Arrival Of Christmas Guests, 7 In.	25.00
Plate, Christmas, 1971, Christmas At Home, 7 In.	17.00
Plate, Christmas, 1974, Christmas In Village, 7 In.	17.00
Plate, Christmas, 1979, White Christmas, 7 In.	25.00
Plate, Christmas, 1982, Christmas Tree, 7 In.	25.00
Plate, Christmas, 1984, Christmas Letter, 7 In.	25.00
Plate, Christmas, 1987, Snowman's Christmas Eve, 7 In.	30.00
Plate, Mother's Day, 1969, Cocker & Pups	250.00
Plate, Mother's Day, 1970, Bird & Chicks	20.00
Plate, Mother's Day, 1973, Duck & Ducklings	15.00
Plate, Mother's Day, 1977, Squirrel & Young	30.00
Plate, Mother's Day, 1983, Raccoon & Young	25.00
Plate, Mother's Day, 1986, Elephant & Calf	30.00
Plate, Mother's Day, 1989, Cow & Calf	45.00
Vase, 7-Sided, Depressed Panels, Green Crystalline Over Moss Green, 3 x 5 In.	545.00
Vase, Boats, Working Harbor, Skyline, Marked, Denmark, Late 1900s, 11 1/2 In.	294.00

BINOCULARS of all types are wanted by collectors. Those made in the eighteenth and nineteenth centuries are favored by serious collectors. The small, attractive binoculars called *opera glasses* are listed in their own category.

Adams, 8 x 40, Brown Leather Neck Strap & Case	26.00
Bausch & Lomb, 7 x 50, Black Pebble Grained Covering, Neck Strap	50.00

Bausch & Lomb, 8 x 56, Leather Case, 1940s 270.00
Le Jockey Club, Paris, Leather Handles, c.1905, 3 x 4 In. 20.00
LeMaire Fabt Paris, Brass & Metal, Marked On Each Eyepiece, 1920s, 2 x 4 In. 50.00
Swift Nighthawk, 7 x 50, Lens Caps, Neck Strap, Hard Leather Case 50.00
Zeiss, 7 x 50, Jena Binoctem 230.00
Zeiss, 7 x 50, U.S. Navy, Black Leather Neck Strap & Case, 1940s 125.00

BIRDCAGES are collected for use as homes for pet birds and as decorative objects of folk art. Elaborate wooden cages of the past centuries can still be found. The brass or wicker cages of the 1930s are popular with bird owners.

Brass, On Stand, 66 In. 259.00
Mahogany, Wire, 2 Brass Drawers, England, 9 x 7 x 6 1/2 In. 195.00
Metal, House Shape, Elk Head Over Door, Painted, Early 1900s, 14 1/2 x 15 x 12 In. 223.00
Parrot, Wood, Multicolored, Turned Columns, Cylindrical, Late 1800s, 34 x 20 In. 353.00
Wire, Glass, Wood, Rotunda, Finial, c.1870, 47 1/2 x 37 x 18 In. 1150.00
Wood, Wire Frame, Painted Turrets, Faux Brick, Victorian, 82 x 69 In. 5750.00
Wood, Wire, Conservatory Shape, Drop Bottom, Continental, c.1900, 17 1/2 In. 50.00

BISQUE is an unglazed baked porcelain. Finished bisque has a slightly sandy texture with a dull finish. Some of it may be decorated with various colors. Bisque gained favor during the late Victorian era when thousands of bisque figurines were made. It is still being made. Additional bisque items may be listed under the factory name.

Candlestick, Boy, Girl, Peach, 12 In., Pair 50.00
Candy Jar, Drum Shape, Bonzo On Lid & Front, Hand Painted, Germany, 6 1/8 In. 193.00
Figurine, 2 Girls, Blue Outfits, One Holds Dove, Other Holds Hand Muff, 10 1/2 In., Pair . 25.00
Figurine, Baby In Bunny Costume, Eggshell, Gebruder Heubach, c.1915, 5 1/2 In. 728.00
Figurine, Baby Riding Bunny, Gebruder Heubach, c.1915, 11 In. 1905.00
Figurine, Baby With Posies, Naked Baby, Standing, Gebruder Heubach, c.1915, 6 1/2 In. .. 530.00
Figurine, Baseball Player, Red & White Striped Shirt, Holding Bat, Germany, 16 In. 2530.00
Figurine, Bathing Beauty & Kitten, Woman Lying On Back, Germany, c.1910, 5 In. 784.00
Figurine, Bonzo, Playing Musical Instruments, G.E. Studdy, Japan, 3 1/8 In., 4 Piece 165.00
Figurine, Boy & Puppy, Side-Glancing Eyes, Germany, c.1920, 3 3/4 In. 112.00
Figurine, Boy On Bunny, Eggshell On Head, Germany, Gebruder Heubach, c.1910, 9 In. ... 1345.00
Figurine, Boy, Girl, Early 20th Century, 10 1/2 In., Pair 259.00
Figurine, Courting Couple, Germany, 17 1/2 In., Pair 105.00
Figurine, Felix The Cat, Seated, Open Mouth, Felix On Chest, 4 In. 165.00
Figurine, Girl Holding Vessel, Boy Holding Ewers, Lavender, Germany, 11 In., Pair 145.00
Figurine, Hand Painted Features, Victorian Style, 18 In., Pair 489.00
Figurine, Power Of Love, Cupid & Lioness, 10 In. 598.00
Figurine, Seated Chubby Baby, Upper-Glancing Eyes, Gebruder Heubach, c.1915, 5 In. 560.00
Figurine, Soccer Boy, Blond Hair, Purple Sweater, Side-Glancing Eyes, c.1900, 10 In. 448.00
Figurine, Uncle Willie, Japan, 3 1/2 x 1 1/2 In. 75.00
Figurine, Warbler, Doughty, Hand Painted, Fitted Wooden Base, c.1963, 8 1/8 & 8 3/4 In. .. 316.00
Figurine, Woman, Standing, Renaissance-Style Dress, Holding Flower, c.1875, 20 In. 410.00
Figurine, Woman, With Goat, Hand Painted Features, Victorian, 18 In. 375.00
Figurine, Young Girl, At Fountain, Painted Features, Germany, c.1900, 10 In. 80.00
Garniture, Figures, Polychromed, Dancing Gypsy Girl & Boy, 18 1/2 In., Pair 2070.00
Group, Amazon On Horseback, Continental, Early 20th Century, 15 1/4 x 16 3/4 In. 660.00
Group, Dark Secret, 2 Black Children, Fence, Gebruder Heubach, c.1910, 7 In. 812.00
Group, Man & Woman Dancing, Germany, 17 In. 150.00
Stringholder, Bonzo, Separates At Neck, Mouth Hole, 5 1/4 In. 99.00

BLACK memorabilia has become an important area of collecting since the 1970s. The best material dates from past centuries, but many recent items are also of interest. F & F is the mark used on plastic made by Fiedler & Fiedler Mold & Die Works, Inc. in the 1930s and 1940s. Objects that picture a black person may also be listed in this book under Advertising, Tin; Bank; Bottle Opener; Cookie Jar; Doll; Salt & Pepper; Sheet Music; Toy; etc.

Ashtray, Figural, Amos 'n' Andy, 8 1/2 x 6 In. 45.00
Ashtray, Screaming Man's Head, Exaggerated Features, Red Lips, Bisque, 1920s, 3 1/2 In.   90.00
Ashtray, Stand, Wooden Figure, Butler, Holding Crimped Tin Tray, Black Coat, 27 In. 575.00

Banner, Aunt Jemima Pancakes, Cloth, 1953, 34 x 57 1/2 In. 385.00
Button, Fight Discrimination, Defend The Bill Of Rights, Clasped Hands, 1950s, 1 1/4 In.   35.00
Button, I Believe In Human Dignity, Blue, White, c.1960, 1 In. 120.00
Button, Malcolm X, Our Black Shining Prince, Freedom By Any Means, 1 3/4 In. 25.00
Button, March On Washington D.C., I Have A Dream Speech, 1963, 2 1/4 In. 52.00
Button, Mississippi Freedom Democratic Party, I Support MFDP, 1964, 1 1/2 In. 105.00
Button, NAACP 40th Anniversary, Book Scale, Blue, Gold, 1949, 3/4 In. 25.00
Button, Pat Bonner-Lyons, Vote Nov. 6, Boston C.P., Black, White, Red, 2 1/4 In. 27.00
Button, Stokely Carmichael, Every Negro Is Potential Black Man, Mid 1960s, 3 In. 845.00
Button, United Black Fund-Support, Black, Cream, Red, c.1970, 1 1/2 In. 53.00
Button, Youth March For Integration, Green, Cream, 1959, 1 1/2 In. 670.00
Cigar Holder, Chicken Thief Boy, Barrel Holder, Bisque, Austria, 6 In. 150.00
Clock, Alarm, Little Black Sambo, Umbrella, Poem, 5 1/2 x 5 In. 167.00
Cookie Jars are listed in the Cookie Jar category.
Doll, Alabama Baby, Cloth, Brown Hair & Eyes, Stitch-Jointed, Ella Smith, c.1910, 25 In. .   880.00
Doll, Babyland Rag, Hand Painted Features, Jointed Shoulders, Hips, Knees, Horsman, 14 In.   1210.00
Doll, Bisque Socket Head, Sleep Eyes, Open Mouth, Teeth, Wood, Composition, 12 In. . . .   715.00
Doll, Boy, Bisque Swivel Head, Sculpted Hair, Peg-Jointed, Germany, c.1890, 3 1/2 In. . . .   440.00
Doll, Brown Eyes, Closed Mouth, Working Crier, Frog Legs, Bye-Lo, 15 In. 220.00
Doll, Chicken Snatcher, Cloth, Stitched Features, 9 In. 80.00
Doll, China Shoulder Head, Painted Eyes, Hair, Cloth Body, Bisque Arms, Legs, 9 1/2 In. .   495.00
Doll, Cloth, Applied Facial Features, Button Eyes, Nappy Hair, Cotton Dress, 23 In. 518.00
Doll, Cloth, Mask Face, Shoulder & Hip Joints, Original Clothes, Bruckner, 13 In. 910.00
Doll, Cloth, Needle Sculpted & Embroidered Features, Yarn Hair, 17 In. 220.00
Doll, Cloth, Needle Sculpted Features, Island Folk Art, 14 In. 468.00
Doll, Cloth, Printed Cotton, Plaid Dress, c.1900, 18 In. 325.00
Doll, Cloth, Stiff Mask Face, Mohair Wig, Girl, Bruckner, 13 1/2 In. 250.00
Doll, Golliwog, Original Clothes, Earrings, 21 1/2 x 7 In. 315.00
Doll, Golliwog, Red Striped Pants, 15 1/2 x 6 In. 145.00
Doll, Golliwog, Stuffed, Turquoise Tuxedo, 17 1/2 x 7 In. 115.00
Doll, Mammy Lou, Cloth, Painted Features, Gray Yarn Hair, Baby Scarlett, c.1940, 13 In. .   935.00
Doll, Man, Bisque Socket Head, Inset Eyes, Wooden Body, 5 1/2 In. 1100.00
Doll, Recknagel, Brown Painted Eyes, Composition Body, Island Costume, Toddler, 9 In. .   135.00
Doll, Sasha, Hard Vinyl, Socket Head, Fleece Hair, 5-Piece, Skirt, England, c.1970, 16 In. .   358.00
Doll, Wax Shoulder Head, Cloth Body, Wax Over Composition Hands, Baby, 17 In. 468.00
Doorstop, Bellhop Carrying Suitcases, 1920s, 7 1/2 In. 770.00
Figurine, Aunt Jemima, Spoon, Iron, Blue Dress, Silver Apron, A.C. Williams, 5 7/8 In. . . .   165.00
Figurine, Golliwog, Cast Iron, Red Pants, Blue Jacket, John Harper, England, 6 1/4 In. 275.00
Figurine, Li'l 8 Ball, Don Roberto Studio, c.1940, 4 1/4 x 2 In. 222.00
Figurine, Mammy, Hands On Hips, Cast Iron, Hubley, 5 1/4 In. 88.00
Figurine, Sharecropper, Toes Visible, Gold Shirt, Iron, A.C. Williams, 5 1/2 In. . . . .138.00 to 220.00
Hearth Brush, Golliwog, Sticking Out Tongue, Wooden, Horsehair Bristles, 22 In. 1065.00
Humidor, Smiling Minstrel, Feathered Cap, Bisque, Austria, 6 1/2 In. 645.00
Inkwell, Blackamoor, Holding Pen, Hinged Torso, Bakelite Quill, Austria, 1890s, 4 In. 225.00
Marionette, U.S. Flag Costume, Papier-Mache Head, Glass Case, c.1840, 30 In. 3500.00
Needlework, Down Where The Cotton Blossoms Grow, Hand Stitched, Frame, 20 x 19 In.   139.00
Nodder, Man, Head Nods, Eyes Roll, Cloth Dressed, Clockwork, 24 In. 1610.00
Pie Vent, Chef, Yellow Outfit, Porcelain 159.00
Pie Vent, Mammy, Red, Brown, White, Blue, Occupied Japan, c.1948, 4 1/2 x 2 1/2 In. . . .   149.00
Pipe, Clay, Black Man's Head, Diamond Registry Mark, 7 1/4 In. 20.00
Place Mat, Aunt Jemima, Story Of Aunt Jemima, Scalloped Edge, 1950, 10 x 14 In. 25.00
Poster, Black Panther Repression, Clenched Fist, May 21, 1970, 15 x 22 In. 40.00
Sheet Music, Coon Coon Coon, 3 Black Men, Top Hats, John Philip Sousa, 1901 . . . .   35.00
Sheet Music, I'se Gwine To Weep No More, Black Man Playing Banjo, 10 1/4 x 14 In. . . .   11.00
Sheet Music, I-N-F-L-U-E-N-Z-A Blues, Black Minstrels, Strutting, 1918 . . . .   40.00
Sheet Music, Oh Baby, I'm Happy Now, George E. Lee's Brunswick Recorders, 1931 . . . .   44.00
Sheet Music, Sing A Good Old Ragtime Song, Black Couple, Smiling, 1909 . . . .   39.00
Sheet Music, That Alabama Jazbo Band, Sophie Tucker, 1918 . . . .   33.00
Smoke Set, Boy Holding Melon, Melons Hold Matches, Cigarettes, Austria, 1880s, 7 In. . .   330.00
Smoke Set, Nubian Queen, Woman In Headdress Reclining, Majolica, Austria, 5 3/4 In. . .   290.00
Spoon, Folk Art, Silver, Shaped Handle, Enameled, Woman Eating Watermelon, 4 In. 430.00
Stringholder, Black Man, Long Tail Coat, Top Hat, Cast Iron, 7 In. 3850.00
Tablecloth, Plantation, Mammy & Children, Flowers, Linen, c.1950, 52 x 49 In. 155.00

Tin, Southern Biscuit, Pre-Civil War Plantation Scene, Mother Serving Cookies, 10 In. ... 40.00
Token, Anti-Slavery, Am I Not A Man & A Brother, Oppression, Copper, c.1795 .... 297.00
Towel, Plantation, Mammy Holding Pie, Boy, New Orleans, Linen, 27 x 15 In. 62.00

BLACK AMETHYST glass appears black until it is held to the light, then a dark purple can be seen. It has been made in many factories from 1860 to the present.

Vase, Ruggle, Silver Overlay, 8 In., Pair 69.00

BLENKO GLASS COMPANY is the 1930s successor to several glassworks founded by William John Blenko in Milton, West Virginia. In 1933, his son, William H. Blenko Sr. took charge. The company made a line of reproductions for Colonial Williamsburg. They are still in business and are best known today for their decorative wares and stained glass.

Bookend, Owl, Embossed, Clear, 9 In. 70.00
Bottle, Water, Flattened Body, Circular Indentation, Tangerine 55.00
Bowl, Oval, Cut Ends, Polished Edges, Blue, Wayne Husted, 1959, 3 1/4 x 7 In. 70.00
Decanter, Amethyst, Bulbous Base, Long Pulled Neck, Tall Stopper, 22 In. 380.00
Decanter, Baluster, Cupped Rim, Green, Lady's Leg Stopper, Husted, Etched Mark, 20 In. 285.00
Decanter, Chess Piece, Turquoise, Wayne Husted, 1959, 22 In. 400.00
Decanter, Cone Shape, Blue, Shot Glass Stopper, Paper Label, 35 In. 280.00
Decanter, Cylindrical, Tangerine, Flame Stopper, 41 In. 460.00
Decanter, Genie, Blue, Teardrop Stopper, Wayne Husted, Etched Mark, 17 In. 150.00
Decanter, Spool, Green, Clear Conical Stopper, Wayne Husted, Etched Mark, 24 In. 265.00
Decanter, Squat, 3 Horizontal Bulges, Red, Flame Stopper, Husted, Late 1950s, 14 In. 400.00
Pitcher, Amethyst, Flat-Sided, Winslow Anderson, 10 In. 75.00
Pitcher, Squat, Nub Handle, Tangerine, Wayne Husted, 3 1/2 x 6 In. 85.00
Pitcher, Straight-Sided, Amethyst, Rosette Base, Lever Handle, 1940s, 11 In. 130.00
Pitcher, Teardrop Body, Orange Peel Texture, Deep Amber, Winslow Anderson, 12 3/4 In. 65.00
Tumbler, Patterned Dimples, Green, 6 Oz., 14 In., 6 Piece 90.00
Vase, Bottle Shape, Amberina, 22 1/4 In. 170.00
Vase, Figural Fish, Amber, 1960s, 8 3/4 x 11 In. 75.00
Vase, Pouch, Green, Irregular Rim, Winslow Anderson, 1953, 11 In. 100.00
Vase, Teardrop Base, Long Neck, Amberina, Bubbled, Joel Philip Myers, 1967, 15 In. 120.00

BLOWN GLASS, see Glass-Blown category.

BLUE GLASS, see Cobalt Blue category.

BLUE ONION, see Onion category.

BLUE WILLOW, see Willow category.

BOCH FRERES factory was founded in 1841 in La Louviere in eastern Belgium. The wares resemble the work of Villeroy & Boch. The factory is still in business.

Bowl, Cover, Stylized Leaves, Crackle Ground, Charles Catteau, c.1925, 5 3/4 In. 224.00
Chamber Pot, Flandria Pattern, Blue Transfer, 5 x 8 In. 18.00
Figurine, Les Patineurs, Skaters, Brown, Pale Blue, Charles Catteau, c.1928, 13 In. 475.00
Figurine, Lion & Snake, White Glaze, Charles Catteau, 13 1/4 In. 355.00
Plate, Napoleon, Battle Of Friedland, Black Transfer, Early 20th Century, 8 In. 70.00
Vase, Bouquet, Green, Gold Outline, Blue High Glaze, Signed, B.K.F., 11 1/2 x 6 In. 315.00
Vase, Brown, Flowers, Matte Glaze, Charles Catteau, Keramis, 7 x 8 In. 345.00
Vase, Egg Shape, Enamel Decoration, Asian Style, Peonies, 10 3/4 In. 441.00
Vase, Stalactites, Blue, Green Angular Areas, Charles Catteau, 1927, 12 1/2 In., Pair 1500.00
Vase, Stylized Hanging Gourds, Brown, Green, Ivory Ground, Stoneware, 11 In. 520.00

BOEHM is the collector's name for the porcelains of Edward Marshall Boehm. In 1953 the Osso China Company was reorganized as Edward Marshall Boehm, Inc. The company is still working in England and New Jersey. In the early days of the factory, dishes were made, but the elaborate and lifelike bird figurines are the best-known ware. Edward Marshall Boehm, the founder, died in 1961, but the firm has continued to design and produce porcelain. Today, the firm makes both limited and unlimited editions of figurines and plates.

Figurine, American Redstart, No. 447, 12 1/2 In. 230.00

Boehm, Figurine,
Towhee, On Stump,
Mushrooms, Fungus,
No. 471, 7 1/2 In.

Boehm, Figurine, Black-
Capped Chickadee, Holly
Branch, No. 439P, 8 3/4 In.

Figurine, Bengal Tiger, No. 500-19, 13 1/2 x 19 In. 980.00
Figurine, Black Grouse, No. 1006, 15 In. 489.00
Figurine, Black-Capped Chickadee, Holly Branch, No. 439P, 8 3/4 In. .... *Illus* 260.00
Figurine, Black-Capped Chickadee, No. 438Y, 8 3/4 In. 175.00
Figurine, Black-Throated Blue Warbler, 11 x 5 1/2 In. 290.00
Figurine, Bobcat With Cubs, 9 x 14 In. 865.00
Figurine, Bobolink, No. 475, 14 3/4 In. 405.00
Figurine, California Quail, No. 433, 7 In. 635.00
Figurine, Calliope Hummingbird With Hibiscus, No. 59, 5 1/4 In. 290.00
Figurine, Carolina Wrens With Sugar Maple, Wood Base, Unmarked, 9 1/2 x 13 In. 1840.00
Figurine, Catbird With Hyacinth, No. 483, 14 1/2 In. 750.00
Figurine, Crested Flycatcher, No. 488, 18 x 14 In. 690.00
Figurine, Dove With Cherry Blossoms, 18 1/4 In. 920.00
Figurine, Downy Woodpeckers, No. 427, 13 1/2 x 5 1/2 In. 460.00
Figurine, Duck With Water Lily, 14 In. 575.00
Figurine, Fledgling Canada Warbler, Marked, 8 1/2 In. 375.00
Figurine, Fledgling Canada Warbler, No. 491, 9 x 7 1/2 In. 345.00
Figurine, Fledgling Great Horned Owl, No. 479B, 7 In. 345.00
Figurine, Goldcrest, On Desert Flower, c.1970, 11 In. 58.00
Figurine, Hibiscus & Monarch Butterfly, No. 159, 11 x 10 1/2 In. 1035.00
Figurine, Hummingbird & Morning Glory, 8 In. 865.00
Figurine, Hummingbird With Orchid, No. 400-08, 5 In. 865.00
Figurine, Indigo Bunting, No. 429W, 10 In. 259.00
Figurine, Kingfisher, Fledgling, c.1970, 6 1/4 In. 81.00
Figurine, Mountain Bluebirds, No. 470, 12 x 15 In. 1150.00
Figurine, Northern Water Thrush, Running Past Mushrooms & Ferns, Marked, 10 In. 1725.00
Figurine, Nuthatch, No. 469I, 10 1/2 x 6 In. 145.00
Figurine, Orchid, Pink, Iridescent Leaves, 4 1/2 In. 81.00
Figurine, Osprey, 26 In. 1265.00
Figurine, Pheasant, Ring-Necked, c.1970, 8 1/2 In. 115.00
Figurine, Prothonotary Warbler, No. 445I, 6 x 6 In. 105.00
Figurine, Raccoons, 12 x 12 In. 690.00
Figurine, Racquet-Tailed Hummingbird, No. 317, 13 1/4 x 12 In. 2415.00
Figurine, Red-Winged Blackbirds, No. 426, 15 1/2 In., Pair 2530.00
Figurine, Robin, No. 472, 13 1/2 x 7 1/2 In. 1610.00
Figurine, Towhee, On Stump, Mushrooms, Fungus, No. 471, 7 1/2 In. .... *Illus* 489.00
Figurine, Tree Sparrow, No. 468F, 8 In. 58.00
Figurine, Tufted Titmice, No. 482, 13 1/2 In. 345.00
Figurine, Tumbler Pigeon, No. 416, 8 1/2 In. 115.00
Figurine, Wood Thrush, Baby, c.1970, 4 1/2 In. 115.00
Figurine, Woodcock, On Stand, No. 413, 10 x 10 In. 460.00
Figurine, Yellow Shafted Flicker, No. 400-16, 13 3/4 In. 805.00

BOHEMIAN GLASS, see Glass-Bohemian.

BONE includes those articles made of bone not listed elsewhere in this
book.

Figurine, Oriental Man, Staff, 20th Century, 9 In. 92.00

Scent Bottle, Carved, Mideastern Figures In Romantic Scenes, India, 7 3/8 In. 69.00
Vase, Figural, Robed Woman, Carved, Hollow, Patina, 11 1/2 In. 115.00

BOOKENDS have probably been used since books became inexpensive. Early libraries kept books in cupboards, not on open shelves. By
the 1870s bookends appeared, especially homemade fret-carved
wooden examples. Most bookends listed in this book date from the
twentieth century. Bookends are also listed in other categories by manufacturer or material. All bookends listed here are pairs.

African American Men, Inset Ears, Figural, Carved Facial Caricatures, 8 In. 58.00
Amish Boy, Amish Girl, Field Ground, 5 1/2 In. 66.00
Boat, Flying, Inlaid Prop Plane, Mahogany, Wedge Form, 6 x 4 x 5 In. 98.00
Boy, Girl Playing On Knees, Bronze, Verdigris, E.B. Parsons, Gorham, 1913, 6 1/2 x 6 In. .   1725.00
Carl Aubock, Austria, c.1949, 5 In. 825.00
Copper, Hammered, Applied Eucalyptus Branches, A. Hairenia, 7 x 6 1/2 In. 1175.00
Copper, Hammered, Rectangular, Clipped Corners, G. Stickley, 5 1/2 x 4 1/4 In. 1528.00
Copper, Hammered, Triangular, Albert Berry, 3 3/4 x 5 1/2 In. 265.00
Dog, Scottie, Cast Iron, Hubley, Box, 5 In. 385.00
Dutch Couple, Kissing, Cast Iron, Hubley, 4 3/4 In. 138.00
Eagle, Pine, Carved, Folk Art, c.1870, 12 In. 425.00
Eagle, Standing On Base, Cast Metal, 7 1/2 x 5 1/2 In. 60.00
Elephant Head, Bronze, Lead Filled, B. Johnson, Gorman Foundry, 6 1/4 In. 2235.00
Flowers, Leaves, Hardstone, Carved, Light Gray, Ivory, 6 1/2 x 4 1/2 x 2 In. 105.00
Flowers In Oval Medallion, Cast Iron, 4 1/2 In. 66.00
Football Players, Cast Iron, 1950s, 6 In. 55.00
Gargoyle, Bird, Green Matte, American Terra Cotta, Chicago, 7 1/4 x 4 3/4 In. 1295.00
Landscape, House, Stream, Trees, Etched, Arts & Crafts, 4 3/4 x 5 In. 206.00
Owl, Standing, Book Base, Compartment, Gilt Bronze, Bergman, 12 In. 3220.00
Priscilla & John Alden, Cast Iron, 1950s, 6 1/4 & 7 In. 250.00
Quail, Cast Iron, Hubley, 6 In. 550.00
Raggedy Ann & Andy, Cast Iron, 6 In. 6600.00
Ship, Brass, 5 In. 80.00
Ship, Ivory & Green Glaze, Tile, Brass Brackets, Moravian, 3 3/4 x 3 3/4 In. 176.00
Terriers, Running, Bronze, Verdigris Patina, E.B. Parsons, Gorham, 6 x 7 3/4 In. 1725.00
Triangular, Butterscotch, Bakelite, Martrix Enterprises, Lake Park, Fl., 5 1/2 In. 104.00
Woman, Bust, Bronze, Art Deco, 8 In. 450.00
Women, Seated, Bronze, Patina, Signed, J. Konti, 9 In. 1998.00

BOOKMARKS were originally made of parchment, cloth, or leather.
Soon woven silk ribbon, thin cardboard, celluloid, wood, silver, tortoiseshell, and metals were used. Examples made before 1850 are
scarce, but there are many to be found dating before 1920.

23rd Psalm, Pink, White Flowers, Green Leaves, Die Cut, Early 1900s, 5 In. 20.00
Airship Akron, Goodyear Zeppelin Corporation, Duralumin, 5 In. . . . . .30.00 to 40.00
Almanack, Booklet At Top, Woman In Feathered Hat, 1876, 7 1/4 x 2 1/6 In. 25.00
Bakery Confections Workers Union, Forget-Me-Not, Heart Finial, Celluloid, 2 1/4 In. . . .   15.00
Cross, Punchwork, On Blue Satin Ribbon, 1850s, 8 x 3 In. 8.00
Dingman Soap, Buffalo, N.Y., Rectangular, Paper, 7 In. 6.00
Good Will Farm, Houghton, Mich., Copper, 4 1/2 In. 20.00
Hershey Park, Penn., Ship's Wheel Finial, Town Scene, Copper, 2 3/4 In. 17.00
Hollingsworth's Candy, Grand Prix, Paris, Die Cut, Paper, 1928, 4 1/2 In. 13.00
Hoyt's German Cologne, Rubifoam, Girl With Bottle, Die Cut, 4 5/8 x 2 In. 10.00
Ivory, Openwork Medallion, Woman Reading Book, Carved, Painted, 1920, 2 1/2 In. 27.00
Libby's Canned Meats Are The Best, Red & Green Flowers, 15 Products, Die Cut, 5 In. . .   25.00
Maltine, Figural Owl, Die Cut, Painted, Celluloid, 3 1/2 In. 13.00
Maltine, Owl, Celluloid, 3 1/2 x 1 3/8 In. 85.00
Mark F. Schwinn Books, West Bend, Wisc., Flowers, Die Cut, Paper 8.00
Michigan College Of Mining & Technology, Ship's Wheel Finial, Copper, 2 3/4 In. 18.00
Shaw Piano Co., Erie, Pa., 2 Girls, Forget-Me-Nots, Gold Border, 2 x 6 In. . . . . *Illus*   2.00
SS Norway, Cruise Shop, Silver Embossed, Green Leather, 1980s, 9 In. 14.00
Star Spangled Banner, Silk, Stevengraph Style, Warner, 10 1/2 x 2 1/2 In. 160.00
Sterling Piano, Girls At River Bank, Die Cut, Embossed, Paper, Victorian, 6 In. 17.00
Sterling Silver, Cactus Finial, Monogram, Frank Whiting Co., 2 5/8 In. 40.00

Bookmark, Shaw
Piano Co., Erie, Pa.,
2 Girls, Forget-Me-
Nots, Gold Border,
2 x 6 In.

Bookmark, Sterling
Silver, Magnifying
Glass, Finial,
Crissford & Norris,
c.1905, 4 In.

Vacuum, don't dust, your
books to prevent the spread
of mold spores. Don't keep
shelves of books near hot-air
vents or radiators. Heat is
bad for books.

Sterling Silver, Magnifying Glass Finial, Crissford & Norris, c.1905, 4 In. . . . . *Illus*	235.00
Stollwerk Gold Brand Chocolate & Cocoa, Celluloid, Bastian Bros., 5 5/8 x 1 5/8 In.	65.00
Valentine, Excuse Me If I Speak My Mind, Die Cut, Embossed, Paper, 6 In.	18.00
Youth's Companion, Woman, Copy Of Magazine In Lap, Die Cut, Paper, 1902, 6 In.	13.00

BOSSONS character wall masks, plaques, figurines, and other decorative pieces are made by W.H. Bossons, Limited of Congleton, England. The company was founded in 1946 and closed in 1996. Dates shown are the date the item was introduced.

BOSSONS

Wall Figure, Parson, 1995	80.00
Wall Mask, Afghan Hound, Series 3, 1968-78, 5 3/4 In.	130.00
Wall Mask, Aviator, No. 199, Box, 1990, 6 In. . . . . .130.00 to 140.00
Wall Mask, Beefeater, Yeoman Of The Guard With Gold Medals	165.00
Wall Mask, Catherine Of Aragon, 1986-94, 6 In.	75.00
Wall Mask, Cavalier, 1962-63, 8 In.	90.00
Wall Mask, Doctor Watson, No. 147, 6 1/2 In.	80.00
Wall Mask, Harry Wheatcroft, 1970, 8 1/2 x 5 In.	500.00
Wall Mask, King Henry VIII, 1985, 7 In.	90.00
Wall Mask, Moriarity, Sherlock Holmes' Nemesis, 6 1/4 In.	100.00
Wall Mask, Welsh Lady, 5 1/2 In.	100.00

BOSTON & SANDWICH CO. pieces may be found in the Lutz and Sandwich Glass categories.

BOTTLE collecting has become a major American hobby. There are several general categories of bottles, such as historic flasks, bitters, household, and figural. ABM means the bottle was made by an automatic bottle machine after 1903. Pyro is the shortened form of the word *pyroglaze*, an enameled lettering used on bottles after the mid-1930s. This form of decoration is also called ACL or applied color label. For more bottle prices, see the book *Kovels' Bottles Price List* by Ralph and Terry Kovel.

Auto, Oil, Skelly Supreme, Paper Label, Embossed Master Metal Pour Top, 14 In.	121.00

Avon started in 1886 as the California Perfume Company. It was not until 1929 that the name *Avon* was used. In 1939, it became Avon Products, Inc. Avon has made many figural bottles filled with cosmetic products. Ceramic, plastic, and glass bottles were made in limited editions.

Avon, 1910 Firefighter, 1975, 6 Oz.	10.00
Avon, Alaskan Moose Aftershave, 1974	14.00
Avon, Snail, Contents, 2 1/2 In.	12.00
Avon, Winnebago Motor Home, 1978, 5 Oz.	16.00
Barber, Amethyst, Bell, Ribs, White Enamel, Pontil, Sheared, Tooled Lip, 7 1/2 In.	123.00
Barber, Amethyst, Vertical Ribs, Enameled Dancing Girl, Cylindrical, 8 3/4 In.	392.00
Barber, Black, Tooled Lip, Label, Pour Stopper, 8 1/8 In.	202.00

Barber, Chas. C. Dissel, Tonic, Milk Glass, Enamel, 11 1/4 In. 230.00
Barber, Cobalt Blue, 3-Color Flowers, Enamel, 8 x 3 1/2 In. 148.00
Barber, Cobalt Blue, Ribs, White Enamel, Pontil, Sheared, Tooled Lip, 8 1/2 In. 157.00
Barber, Cobalt Blue, Ribs, White, Yellow, Orange Enamel, Pontil, Rolled Lip, 7 1/2 In. 157.00
Barber, Cobalt Blue, Ribs, Yellow, Gold, Pontil, Rolled Lip, 7 1/2 In. 179.00
Barber, Cobalt Blue, White Enamel, Girl Smelling Flower, 6 x 3 In. 210.00
Barber, Cut Glass, Flashed Ruby Cut To Clear, Geometric Patterns, Stopper, 7 1/2 In. 230.00
Barber, Emerald Green, Ribs, White Enamel, Pontil, Rolled Lip, 7 1/8 In. 168.00
Barber, Green, White Crane, Leaves, Enamel, c.1870, 8 x 3 In. 178.00
Barber, Hobnail, Cranberry Opalescent, Stopper, 8 In. 224.00
Barber, Mauve, Gold Dots, Fluted, Stretch Neck, 9 x 4 1/2 In. 296.00
Barber, Milk Glass, 3 Cherubs, Dog Head, Pontil, Sheared, Tooled Lip, 7 1/2 In. 202.00
Barber, Milk Glass, Multicolored, Flower, Leaf, Flared Mouth, Cone Shape, 8 1/4 In. 392.00
Barber, Parker's Hair Balsam, Amber, 7 1/2 In. 8.00
Barber, Pink Amethyst, Yellow, Gold, Rolled Lip, Art Nouveau, 1885-1925, 7 3/4 In. 123.00
Barber, R.R. Hean, Tonic, Flowers, Milk Glass, Ground Lip, Screw Cap, 8 7/8 In. 360.00
Barber, Topaz, Ribs, Pink, Yellow, White Flowers, Pontil, Sheared, Tooled Lip, 7 1/2 In. .. 101.00
Barber, Witch Hazel, Purple Amethyst, White Enamel House, Pontil, Rolled Lip, 7 7/8 In. . 235.00
Barber, Yellow Green, Ribs, White, Orange Enamel, Pontil, Tooled Lip, 7 3/4 In. 112.00
Barber, Yellow Green, Ribs, Yellow, White, Orange Flowers, Pontil, Rolled Lip, 7 1/2 In. . 90.00

Beam bottles were made to hold Kentucky Straight Bourbon, made by
the James B. Beam Distilling Company. The Beam series of ceramic
bottles began in 1953.

Avon, 1904 Oldsmobile, 75th Anniversary, Regal China 40.00
Avon, 1934 Duesenberg, Model J, Regal China, 5 3/4 x 18 1/4 In. 100.00
Beam, Arizona, Grand Canyon, Regal China, 1968, 12 In. 12.00
Beam, Atlas Elephant Holding The World, Regal China, 11 In. 19.00
Beam, Barney's Casino Slot Machine, Regal China, 1978, 9 x 8 1/2 In. 30.00
Beam, Elephant Clown, Regal China, 12 1/2 In. 19.00
Beam, Elephant In Top Hat, Regal China, 12 1/4 In. 19.00
Beam, Elephant On Football, Regal China, 10 3/4 In. 19.00
Beam, Elks Centennial Commemorative, Regal China, 1968, 11 In. 20.00
Beam, London Bridge, Regal China, 1971 .... 10.00
Beam, Manitowoc Submarine, Regal China, 1970, 12 In. 17.00
Beam, McCoy, Regal China, 1971, 12 1/2 In. 18.00
Beam, Mortimer Snerd, Regal China, 1976, 11 x 5 In. 35.00
Beam, New York World's Fair, Regal China, 1964, 12 x 6 1/4 In. 20.00
Beam, Pineapple, Hawaiian Open, United Airlines, Regal China, 1972, 10 x 6 In. 20.00
Beam, Police Car, Model A, Porcelain, Blue Body, Plastic Canopy, Box, 15 In. 77.00
Beam, Thailand, Regal China, 1969, 12 In. 16.00
Beam, Train, Tank Car, 1983, 11 x 6 1/4 In. 25.00
Beam, Trout, Regal China, 9 1/4 x 11 1/2 In. 26.00
Beam, Yellow Rose, Green, Regal China, 1969, 12 In. 15.00
Beer, H. Sproatt, Cobalt Blue, Fire Polished Pontil, Applied Collar, 1850-60, 10 In. 400.00
Beer, Haley's California, Yellow Amber, Applied Mouth, Closure Wire, 10 3/4 In. 224.00
Beer, M. Richardson, 12-Sided, Applied Collar, 1850-60 .... 3850.00
Beer, Scarborough Brewery Company, Embossed, Emerald Green, Codd, 9 In. 98.00
Beer, Simon Pure, Buffalo, N.Y., Yellow, Amber, Blob 29.00
Beer, Steinle Brewery, Delphos, Ohio, Paper Label, Amber, 9 1/2 In. 44.00
Bininger, Old Kentucky Bourbon, Blown Molded, Raised Rings, Amber, 1848, 8 1/8 In. .. 235.00
Bininger, Yellow Green, Tapered Collar Mouth, 9 3/4 In. 224.00
Bitters, Atwood's Quinine Tonic, Aqua, Rectangular, 8 1/2 In. 85.00
Bitters, Augauer, Medium Grass Green, Tooled Mouth, Labels, Chicago, 8 1/8 In. .... *Illus* 179.00
Bitters, Ayala Mexican, Amber, Tooled Top, Square Shoulder, M. Rothenberg & Co. 400.00
Bitters, Baker's Orange Grove, Medium Amber, Applied Mouth, 9 1/2 In. 625.00
Bitters, Baker's Orange Grove, Medium Amber, Applied Mouth, 9 In. 100.00
Bitters, Big Bill Best, Reddish Amber, Smooth Base, Tooled Mouth, Labels, 12 In. .. *Illus* 476.00
Bitters, Brown's Celebrated Indian Herb, Gold Amber, 12 1/2 In. 950.00
Bitters, Brown's Celebrated Indian Herb, Medium Amber, Inward Rolled Lip, 12 In. 630.00
Bitters, Brown's Celebrated Indian Herb, Patented 1867, Amber, 12 1/8 In. 840.00
Bitters, Brown's Celebrated Indian Herb, Tobacco Amber, Inward Rolled Lip, 12 In. 680.00
Bitters, Brown's Celebrated Indian Herb, Yellow, 1860-80, 12 1/8 In. 1792.00

Bottle, Bitters, Augauer,
Medium Grass Green,
Tooled Mouth, Labels,
Chicago, 8 1/8 In.

Bottle, Bitters, Big
Bill Best, Reddish
Amber, Smooth Base,
Tooled Mouth,
Labels, 12 In.

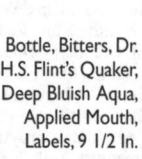

Bottle, Bitters, Dr.
H.S. Flint's Quaker,
Deep Bluish Aqua,
Applied Mouth,
Labels, 9 1/2 In.

Bitters, Caldwell's, Wine & Iron, Medina, N.Y., Medium Amber, Applied Mouth, 10 In. . . . 267.00
Bitters, Cannon's Dyspeptic, Golden Amber, Barrels, Applied Mouth, Square, 9 5/8 In. . . . 5040.00
Bitters, Canteen, Disorders Of Stomach, Blue Green, 1860-70, 9 3/4 In. 3300.00
Bitters, Castilian, Bitters, Cannon, Golden Yellow Amber, Applied Mouth, 10 In. 240.00
Bitters, Clarke's Vegetable, Sherry Wine, Aqua, Tombstone Arch Shoulders, 14 1/4 In. . . . 420.00
Bitters, Congress, William Allens, Purple Amethyst, Semi-Cabin, Pontil, 7 3/4 In. 345.00
Bitters, Constitution, Seward & Bentley, Golden Amber, Red, Sloping Collar, 9 3/8 In. . . . 1600.00
Bitters, Dandelion & Wild Cherry, Aqua, Applied Mouth, 8 7/8 In. 515.00
Bitters, Dingens Napoleon Cocktail, Banjo, Olive, Iron Pontil, 1850-60, 10 In. 7150.00
Bitters, Doctor Fisch's, Lemon Yellow, Applied Mouth, 1870-80, 12 In. 825.00
Bitters, Doyles Hop, Semi-Cabin, Yellow, Green, Tapered Mouth, 10 In. 728.00
Bitters, Dr. A.S. Hopkins, Lady's Leg, Yellow Amber, Applied Mouth, 12 1/4 In. 5500.00
Bitters, Dr. A.S. Hopkins, Union Stomach, Embossed Panel, Applied Top, c.1870, 10 In. . . 880.00
Bitters, Dr. C.D. Warner's, Reading, Mich., Semi-Cabin, Yellow, Amber, 9 7/8 In. 190.00
Bitters, Dr. DeAndries Sarsaparilla, Root Beer, Applied Mouth, Rectangular, 9 3/4 In. . . . 1344.00
Bitters, Dr. H.S. Flint's Quaker, Deep Bluish Aqua, Applied Mouth, Labels, 9 1/2 In. . . *Illus* 952.00
Bitters, Dr. Henley's Wild Grape Root, IXL, Light Green Aqua, Applied Band 2200.00
Bitters, Dr. Henley's Wild Grape Root, IXL, Mossy Emerald, Applied Band 2200.00
Bitters, Dr. J. Hostetter's Stomach, Amber, Square, Applied Top, 8 3/4 In. 32.00
Bitters, Dr. J. Sweets, Strengthening, Aqua, Square, 8 1/2 In. 85.00
Bitters, Dr. Renz's Herb, Light Yellow Green, Square Shoulder, Applied Top, 1868-81 . . . 900.00
Bitters, Dr. Renz's Herb, Olive Green, Applied Top, Square Collar, 1868-81 . . . . 1900.00
Bitters, Dr. Saylor's Rheuma Stomachic, Red Amber, Square, Panels, 8 7/8 In. 1100.00
Bitters, Dr. Stephen Jewett's Celebrated Health, Citron, Pontil, 7 3/8 In. 5500.00
Bitters, Dr. Wilson's Herbine, Aqua, Oval, 6 In. 105.00
Bitters, Drake's Plantation, 4 Log, Green, Applied Tapered Mouth, 10 In. . . . . . .2576.00 to 4200.00
Bitters, Drake's Plantation, 5 Log, Orange Amber, Rolled Lip, 9 1/4 In. 616.00
Bitters, Drake's Plantation, 6 Log, Amber, Applied Tapered Mouth, 10 In. 364.00
Bitters, Drake's Plantation, 6 Log, Applied Sloped Collar, 1860, 9 5/8 In. . . . . *Illus* 1456.00
Bitters, Drake's Plantation, 6 Log, Apricot Puce, Square, Sloping Collar, 10 In. 1344.00
Bitters, Drake's Plantation, 6 Log, Apricot, Strawberry Puce, Collared Mouth, 10 1/8 In. . . 375.00
Bitters, Drake's Plantation, 6 Log, Gasoline Puce, Applied Tapered Mouth, 10 1/4 In. 2576.00
Bitters, Drake's Plantation, 6 Log, Root Beer Amber, Applied Tapered Mouth, 10 1/4 In. . . 112.00
Bitters, Drake's Plantation, 6 Log, Strawberry Puce, Applied Tapered Mouth, 10 In. 392.00
Bitters, Drake's Plantation, 6 Log, Yellow Topaz, Applied Tapered Mouth, 9 7/8 In. 1064.00
Bitters, Fish, W.H. Ware, Patented 1866, Yellow Amber, 11 1/2 In. 530.00
Bitters, Globe, Lighthouse Form, Yellow Amber, Applied Square Mouth, 11 1/8 In. 500.00
Bitters, Granger, Boykin Carmer & Co., Baltimore, Amber, Tooled Lip, 8 3/8 In. 378.00
Bitters, Greeley's Bourbon, Barrel, Amethyst, Applied Mouth, 9 1/2 In. 2688.00
Bitters, Greeley's Bourbon, Barrel, Aqua, Applied Mouth, 9 1/2 In. 4480.00
Bitters, Greeley's Bourbon, Barrel, Chartreuse Green, Applied Mouth, 9 1/4 In. 1904.00
Bitters, Greeley's Bourbon, Barrel, Gray Puce, Applied Square Mouth, 1860-80, 9 In. 532.00
Bitters, Greeley's Bourbon, Barrel, Pink Puce, Square Collared Mouth, 9 1/4 In. 700.00
Bitters, Greeley's Bourbon, Barrel, Smoky Olive Topaz, Applied Mouth, 9 1/8 In. 1070.00
Bitters, Greeley's Bourbon, Barrel, Smoky Topaz, Olive, 9 1/4 In. 308.00
Bitters, Greeley's Bourbon, Barrel, Topaz, Applied Mouth, 9 1/2 In. 5040.00
Bitters, H.P. Herb Wild Cherry, Cabin, Olive Yellow, 10 1/8 In. 6050.00
Bitters, Herkules, Emerald Green, 2 Flat Panels, Tooled Mouth, 7 1/4 In. 1800.00

Bitters, Holtzermann's, Cabin, Golden Amber, Applied Sloping Collar, 9 1/4 In. 2128.00
Bitters, Holtzermann's, Cabin, Yellow Amber, Tooled Mouth, Label, Sample, 4 1/8 In. . . . 378.00
Bitters, John Moffat, Phoenix, Olive Yellow, Pontil, Bubbles, 1840-1860, 5 5/8 In. 880.00
Bitters, Johnson's Indian Dyspeptic, Aqua, Applied Mouth, Open Pontil, 6 1/2 In. 680.00
Bitters, Kimball's Jaundice, Olive Yellow, Applied Sloping Collared Mouth, Pontil, 7 In. . 1100.00
Bitters, McKeever's Army, Drum Base, Cannon Balls, Orange Amber, c.1870, 10 3/8 In. . 3080.00
Bitters, Mishler's Herb, Golden Amber, Applied Top, Square, 8 3/4 In. 85.00
Bitters, National, Ear Of Corn, Yellow Amber, Applied Mouth, c.1870, 12 5/8 In. . .448.00 to 672.00
Bitters, National, Ear Of Corn, Yellow Green, 12 5/8 In. 5500.00
Bitters, Old Homestead, Wild Cherry, Cabin, Amber, Applied Ring, 9 1/2 In. 450.00
Bitters, Old Homestead, Wild Cherry, Cabin, Root Beer Amber, Sloping Mouth, 9 1/2 In. . 420.00
Bitters, Old Sachem & Wigwam Tonic, Apricot Puce, Barrel, Collar Mouth, 9 1/8 In. *Illus* 1456.00
Bitters, Old Sachem & Wigwam Tonic, Yellow Amber, Barrel, Applied Collar, 9 In. 560.00
Bitters, Old Sachem & Wigwam Tonic, Yellow, Apricot, Barrel, 9 3/4 In. 2420.00
Bitters, Reed's, Lady's Leg, Yellow Amber, Double Collar Mouth, 12 3/8 In. 784.00
Black Glass, Green, Mallet, Applied String Lip, Seal, B. Greive, England, 1727, 6 3/8 In. . . 9100.00
Black Glass, Green, Mallet, String Lip, Kick-Up, Seal, E. Herbert, England, 1721, 6 1/2 In 9100.00
Black Glass, Greyhound Under Coronet, Seal, Amber, String Lip, England, c.1700, 7 In. . . 3020.00
Black Glass, Olive Amber, Onion, String Lip, Pontil, Seal, I. Smith, England, 1706, 7 In. . . 9100.00
Black Glass, Olive Green, Mallet, 4-Lobed Pontil, Seal, R. Baker, England, 1729, 7 3/8 In. 3460.00
Black Glass, Olive Green, Onion, Applied Lip, Pontil, Seal, S. Lyne, England, 1728, 5 In. . 3620.00
Black Glass, Yellow Olive, Onion, Sheared Mouth, String Rim, Double Magnum, 12 In. . . 1792.00
Blown, Chestnut, Olive Amber, Bubbles, Pontil, Applied Top, 1820-50, 6 1/2 In. 275.00
Blown, Chestnut, Olive Green, Short Tapered Collar, Open Pontil, New England, 9 In. . . . 420.00
Blown, Chestnut, Olive Yellow, Bubbles, Pontil, Applied Top, 1820-50, 5 3/4 In. 303.00
Blown, Chestnut, Olive Yellow, Rolled Mouth, Pontil, 5 1/2 In. 420.00
Blown, Globular, 24 Ribs, Aqua, Zanesville, 6 3/4 In. 173.00
Blown, Globular, Aqua, Applied Sloping Lip, Kick-Up, Pontil, 8 7/8 In. 55.00
Blown, Globular, Light Green, Applied Rolled Lip, Pontil, 10 In. 242.00
Blown, Globular, Red Amber, Applied Sloping Collar, Solid Handle, Pontil, 6 3/4 In. 66.00
Coca-Cola bottles are listed in the Coca-Cola category.
Cosmetic, Acme Hair Vigor, Label Under Glass, Phil Eismann, Cork, Metal Stopper, 8 In. . 230.00
Cosmetic, Barrow Evans Hair Restorer, Paper Package, 6 1/4 In. 20.00
Cosmetic, Dodge Brothers Melanine Hair Tonic, Amethyst, Double Ring Top, 7 1/2 In. . . . 935.00
Cosmetic, Empire Quinine Hair Tonic, Gal., 12 x 6 1/2 In. 25.00
Cosmetic, Hall's Hair Renewer, Teal Blue, Stopper, Label, 7 3/8 In. 336.00
Cosmetic, Kickapoo Sage Hair Tonic, Cobalt Blue, Tooled Lip, Stopper, 7 3/8 In. 235.00
Cosmetic, T & M Bear Grease Pomade, Blue Green, Inward-Rolled Lip, Pontil, 2 5/8 In. . . 345.00
Cure, Dr. Craig's Original Kidney & Liver Cure For Bright's Disease, Amber, 9 1/2 In. . . . 3850.00
Decanter, Aquamarine, 3-Mold, Bulbous, Applied Collar, Pontil, 1820, 8 1/2 x 5 1/4 In. . . 4200.00
Decanter, Clear, Beehive Shape, 3 Rings, Flared Lip, Pontil, 1820-40, Qt. 29.00
Decanter, Cut Glass, Clear, 2 Rings, Mushroom Stopper, Pt. 69.00
Decanter, Lavender, 15 Ribs, Pontil, Applied Mouth, 1840-60, 6 In. 952.00
Demijohn, Aqua, Basket, Mold Blown, Applied Lip, 13 In. 40.00
Demijohn, Olive Amber, Yellow, Applied Collar Mouth, 1780-1810, 19 1/4 In. 58.00

Bottle, Bitters,
Drake's Plantation,
6 Log, Applied Sloped
Collar, 1860, 9 5/8 In.

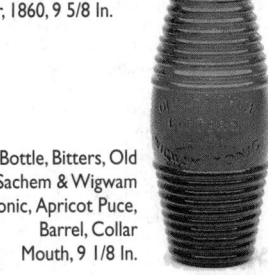

Bottle, Bitters, Old
Sachem & Wigwam
Tonic, Apricot Puce,
Barrel, Collar
Mouth, 9 1/8 In.

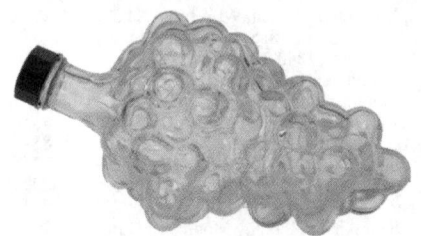

Bottle, Figural,
Coachman,
Bottle, Figural, Bunch Of Grapes,   Bennington, Vermont,
Clear, Black Screw Cap, 6 In.   1840-60, 10 1/2 In.

Demijohn, Olive Green, Applied Aqua Sloped Collar Mouth, Pontil, 1865-75, 3 7/8 In. 131.00
Demijohn, Olive Yellow, Green, Open Pontil, Applied Collar Mouth, c.1800, 19 3/8 In. 246.00
Demijohn, Yellow Amber, Applied Sloped Collar Mouth, Pontil, 1800-20, 12 3/4 In. 158.00
Demijohn, Yellow Green, Rectangular, Applied Sloped Collar Mouth, 8 1/2 x 10 x 6 In. ... 350.00
Demijohn, Yellow Olive Green, Applied Sloped Collar Mouth, Pontil, c.1815, 13 3/4 In. .. 112.00
Figural, 3 Cherubs, Ball Over Heads, Aqua, Pontil, Tooled Lip, France, c.1900, 8 1/2 In. . 138.00
Figural, Artillery Shell, Souviens Toi Siege De Paris, Olive, Paper Label, 1871, 10 In. 285.00
Figural, Baby Face, Feed The Baby, Marble Game, Pontil, Rand Bros., Boston, 4 In. 175.00
Figural, Banjo, Amethyst, 9 1/2 In. 39.00
Figural, Baseball Glove, Ground Lip, Screw Cap, 1885-1910, 5 1/4 In. 240.00
Figural, Baseball, Cobalt Blue, Smooth Base, Ground Lip, 1885-90, 2 3/4 In. 395.00
Figural, Bather, Woman, Clear, Frosted, Pineapple Stopper, Pontil, France, 17 In. 87.00
Figural, Bear, Medallion, Olive Yellow, Sheared Mouth, 10 1/4 In. 308.00
Figural, Bear, Sitting, Olive Green, Applied Face, Tooled Lip, 8 5/8 In. 350.00
Figural, Bear, Sitting, Paw In Air, Teddy's Bear, Blue & White Bisque, c.1910, 7 1/4 In. ... 240.00
Figural, Black Boy, Sitting On Barrel, Embossed, Pontil, Tooled Lip, Germany, 9 In. 680.00
Figural, Black Boy, Sitting On Barrel, Red Amber To Yellow, Tooled Lip, Germany, 9 In. . 540.00
Figural, Bouquet Of Stemmed Roses, Rosebud Stopper, Pontil, Tooled Lip, 12 3/8 In. ... 240.00
Figural, Boy & Girl Climbing Tree, Clear, Frosted, Pontil, Tooled Mouth, France, 12 In. .. 75.00
Figural, Bugle, Ground Lip, Screw Cap, 1885-1910, 8 1/4 In. 220.00
Figural, Bunch Of Grapes, Clear, Black Screw Cap, 6 In. .... *Illus* 10.00
Figural, Car, Mirabel, Aqua, Embossed, Smooth Base, Tooled Lip, 1900-20, 2 7/8 In. 60.00
Figural, Cherub, Clock On Shoulder, Clear, Frosted, Pontil, Glass Stopper, 10 3/4 In. 97.00
Figural, Child, Arms At Sides, Tooled Lip, Britain, 1885-1910, 9 In. 97.00
Figural, Child, Sitting On Barrel, G. & T., Smooth Base, Ground Lip, 1885-1910, 4 7/8 In. 98.00
Figural, Church, Medium Blue Green, Pontil, Applied Mouth, 1885-1915, 6 7/8 In. 900.00
Figural, Coachman, Amber, Van Dunck's Genever, Ware & Schmitz, 8 3/4 In. 112.00
Figural, Coachman, Bennington, Vermont, 1840-60, 10 1/2 In. .... *Illus* 784.00
Figural, Coachman, Medium Amber, J.H. Carter, Applied Mouth, 10 7/8 In. 1820.00
Figural, Coachman, Teal Blue, Ground Lip, 1885-95, 10 1/4 In. 3680.00
Figural, Cockatoo, Black Amethyst, Smooth Base, Ground Lip, c.1885-1910, 13 1/2 In. ... 197.00
Figural, Cottage, Smooth Base, ABM Lip, Screw Cap, c.1920-30, 3 1/4 In. 38.00
Figural, Ear Of Corn, Amber, Gold Paint, Smooth Base, Applied Mouth, c.1875, 9 3/4 In. . 98.00
Figural, Ear Of Corn, Cobalt Blue, Gold & White Paint Traces, Tooled Lip, c.1900, 9 In. .. 499.00
Figural, Ear Of Corn, Turquoise Blue, Sheared, Ground Lip, Footed, c.1895, 8 3/4 In. 252.00
Figural, Ear Of Corn, Yellow Olive, Applied Mouth, 1865-75, 9 7/8 In. 1420.00
Figural, Fish, ABM Lip, Black Paint, Bremer Anker, Cap, 20th Century, 11 1/4 In. 65.00
Figural, Fish, Moravian, Inscribed Scales, Eyes, Fins, Tail, Hole In Side, Pottery, 4 1/2 In. . 4070.00
Figural, Fox, Reading Book, Smooth Base, Ground Lip, Screw Cap, 1885-1910, 4 5/8 In. . 40.00
Figural, Frog, Aqua, Red Paint, Sheared & Polished Lip, 1890-1920, 7 In. 153.00
Figural, Fruit Basket, Multicolored Paint, Tooled Mouth, 1900-25, 7 In. 60.00
Figural, German Helmet, Gesetzlich, Geschutzt, Purple, Pontil Stopper, Ground Lip, 3 In. . 98.00
Figural, Girl, Sitting On Basket, Clear, Frosted, Tooled Lip, Pontil, 8 1/2 In. 87.00
Figural, Grandfather Clock, Merry Christmas, Happy New Year, Label, Houser, 5 5/8 In. ... 197.00
Figural, Grandfather Clock, Original Panel Labels, 1885-1910, 5 1/4 In. 85.00
Figural, Hand Holding Bottle, Cobalt Blue, Frosted Hand, Pontil, Tooled Mouth, 9 5/8 In. . 695.00
Figural, Hand Holding Bottle, Turquoise, Pontil, Tooled Mouth, France, 9 1/2 In. 100.00
Figural, Hand Holding Bottle, Yellow Green, Tooled Mouth, France, c.1900, 9 1/2 In. 175.00

Figural, Hand Holding Mirror, Frosted, Pontil, Tooled Lip, France, 1885-1910, 8 In. 120.00
Figural, Hot Air Balloon, Embossed, Pontil, Tooled Lip, France, 1878, 9 In. 268.00
Figural, House, Medium Amber, Smooth Base, Ground Lip, Screw Cap, 1885-1910, 3 3/8 In. 275.00
Figural, Joan Of Arc, Opening On Base, Tooled Rim, France, 1890-1920, 10 In. 65.00
Figural, Liberty Bell, Amber, Proclaim Liberty, Unto All Inhabitants, c.1900, 5 In. 142.00
Figural, Liberty Bell, Proclaim Liberty, Throughout Land, Sheared, Ground Lip, 3 1/2 In. . 60.00
Figural, Light Bulb, Audubon Utility Mfg. Co., Santa Ana, Calif., Ground Lip, 4 1/2 In. . . . 175.00
Figural, Lighthouse, Frosted, Tooled Mouth, Stopper, France, 1880-1915, 9 1/8 In. 240.00
Figural, Lobster, Holding Fish, Gold Paint, Pontil, Tooled Lip, France, 17 In. 165.00
Figural, Madonna, Holding Child, Pontil, Tooled Lip, 1890-1920 . . . . 76.00
Figural, Man, Leaning On Stick, Beard, Embossed, Ground Lip, Screw Cap, 7 1/2 In. 240.00
Figural, Man, Seated, Mottled 2-Tone Brown, 1875-1900, 9 In. 308.00
Figural, Miss Liberty Coin, United States Of America, Screw Cap, c.1990, 4 1/2 In. 408.00
Figural, Moon Mullins, Brown Glazed Pottery, Stamped, Dickey Clay, 1923-30, 7 In. 317.00
Figural, Oriental Man, Aquamarine, Pontil, Applied Mouth, 1865-75, 10 1/4 In. 1460.00
Figural, Oriental Man, On Barrel, Cobalt Blue, Metal Head, Paint, c.1885, 5 3/4 In. 350.00
Figural, Oriental Man, Sitting, Smooth Base, Ground Lip, 1885-1910, 5 7/8 In. 245.00
Figural, Pierrot, Playing Stringed Instrument, Inside Half-Moon, Star Stopper, 12 In. 275.00
Figural, Pocket Watch, Time To Drink, Smooth Base, Ground Lip, Screw Cap, c.1890, 5 In. 175.00
Figural, Poodle, Sitting, Clear, Frosted, Ground Lip, Removable Head, France, 12 3/4 In. . . 288.00
Figural, Poodle, Sitting, Olive Amber, Tooled, Ground Lip, Removable Head, France, 13 In. 395.00
Figural, Portly Man, Standing, Embossed, Aqua, Tooled Mouth, M. Husted, 11 3/4 In. 1430.00
Figural, Pouch With Drawstring, Yellow Amber, Olive, Sheared Lip, 1885-1915, 2 3/4 In. . 408.00
Figural, Rabbit, Standing, Smooth Base, Ground Lip, 1890-1910, 7 1/2 In. 60.00
Figural, Roasted Turkey, Amber, Smooth Base, Ground Lip, Screw Cap, c.1900, 4 3/4 In. . 72.00
Figural, Senorita, Milk Glass, Paint, M. Quiles-Benetuser, Spain, c.1915, 10 3/4 In. 80.00
Figural, Shoe, N. Antoine & Fils, Sheared & Ground Lip, 1885-1910, 4 In. 242.00
Figural, Shoe, With Protruding Toe, Black, Yellow Toe, Ground Lip, Screw Cap, 5 1/2 In. . 140.00
Figural, Skeleton, White Glaze, Pottery, Removable Head, Cork, c.1885-1915, 10 1/2 In. . . 615.00
Figural, Steamer Trunk, Merry Christmas, Happy New Year, J. Christman, 5 In. 186.00
Figural, Suffragette, Sad Woman, Ground Lip, Screw Cap, England, 1900s-10s, 4 3/4 In. . . 233.00
Figural, Turtle, Horseshoe, Good Luck, Embossed, Ground Lip, Screw Cap, c.1890, 5 In. . 120.00
Figural, Violin, Yellow Amber, Pat Apld. For, Sheared Lip, 1885-1910, 6 1/2 In. 240.00
Figural, Violin, Yellow Amber, Smooth Base, Tooled Lip, 1885-1910, 18 In. 245.00
Figural, Woman, Holding Draped Cloth, Medium Amber, Tooled Lip, 1885-1910, 9 In. . . . 423.00
Flask, 16 Ribs, Swirled To Left, Aqua, Pontil, Sheared & Tooled Lip, Midwestern, 6 In. . . . 300.00
Flask, 20 Diamonds, Amethyst, Flat Cylindrical, Sheared Mouth, Pontil, 5 5/8 x 4 1/4 In. . . 550.00
Flask, 24 Ribs, Golden Amber, Sheared Mouth, Pontil, 5 In. 504.00
Flask, 24 Ribs, Medium Golden Yellow Amber, Sheared Lip, Pontil, Midwestern, 4 In. 400.00
Flask, 24 Ribs, Sapphire Blue, 1820-1840, 6 7/8 In. 1120.00
Flask, 24 Ribs, Swirled To Left, Yellow Amber, Sheared, Midwestern, 4 1/2 In. 518.00
Flask, A. Mayes Wine & Spirit, Hip, Flat, Shouldered, Brown Salt Glaze, 5 1/2 In. 157.00
Flask, Anchor & Resurgam Phoenix, Olive Yellow, Sheared Mouth, Pontil, Pt. 1904.00
Flask, Aqua, Ravenna Glass Co., Pt, 7 In. 230.00
Flask, Boot, Laced Up, Daubed Glaze, Removable Spout, Rockingham, 7 1/4 x 7 In. 405.00
Flask, Boot, White Clay, Blue & Pink Stripes, 3 3/4 In. 316.00
Flask, Byron & Scott, Yellow Amber, Open Pontil, Sheared, Tooled Lip, 1/2 Pt. 308.00
Flask, Cannon, A Little More Grape, Green, Pontil, Sheared, Tooled Lip, 1847-49, Pt. 7280.00
Flask, Cannon, A Little More Grape, Olive Yellow, Pontil, Sheared, Tooled Lip, Pt. 4807.00
Flask, Cannon, A Little More Grape, Pale Aqua Green, Sheared Lip, 7 1/8 In. . . . 154.00
Flask, Chestnut, 10 Diamonds, Blue Aqua, Sheared Mouth, Pontil, Midwestern, 5 1/2 In. . . . 1160.00
Flask, Chestnut, 10 Diamonds, Medium Amber, Sheared & Tooled Lip, Pontil, 4 3/4 In. . . . 1600.00
Flask, Chestnut, 10 Diamonds, Yellow Green, Flared Neck, 5 In. 3575.00
Flask, Chestnut, 18 Broken Ribs, Swirled To Left, Green Aqua, Pontil, Midwestern, 6 In. . . 175.00
Flask, Chestnut, 24 Ribs, Golden Yellow Amber, Pontil, Midwestern, 5 1/4 In. 428.00
Flask, Chestnut, 24 Ribs, Light Emerald Green, Pontil, Sheared Lip, Midwestern, 5 3/4 In. . 290.00
Flask, Chestnut, 24 Ribs, Light Yellow Amber, Tooled Lip, Pontil, Midwestern, 5 In. 495.00
Flask, Chestnut, 24 Ribs, Swirled To Right, Amber, Tooled Lip, Pontil, Midwestern, 5 In. . 515.00
Flask, Chestnut, 24 Ribs, Yellow Amber, Tooled Lip, Pontil, Midwestern, 4 1/2 In. 350.00
Flask, Chestnut, Amber, Applied Tapered Lip, Pontil, 11 In. 358.00
Flask, Chestnut, Elephant, Handle, Golden Amber, 1845-60, Pt. 1792.00
Flask, Chestnut, Olive Green, Applied Mouth, Open Pontil, 1780-1810, 5 3/4 In. 350.00
Flask, Chestnut, Olive Green, Applied Mouth, Open Pontil, 1780-1810, 6 7/8 In. 428.00

Flask, Chestnut, Straw Yellow, Olive, Applied Mouth, Open Pontil, 8 1/8 In. 378.00
Flask, Chestnut, Yellow Olive, Outward Rolled Lip, Open Pontil, 5 5/8 In. 428.00
Flask, Coffin, Opalescent Milk Glass, Tooled Mouth, 1880s-1900s, Pt. 157.00
Flask, Coin, Bryan, Sewall, In Silver We Trust, Tooled Lip, 1896, 5 1/4 In. 1750.00
Flask, Columbia & Eagle, Aqua, Embossed B&W, Pontil, Pt., 6 3/4 In. 413.00
Flask, Columbia & Eagle, Aqua, Pontil, Sheared, Tooled Lip, 1830s-40s, Pt. 1008.00
Flask, Columbia & Eagle, Aquamarine, Inward Rolled Mouth, 1820s-30s, Pt. 1064.00
Flask, Columbia & Eagle, Blue, Aqua, Open Pontil, Sheared, Tooled Lip, 1830s-40s, Pt. .. 448.00
Flask, Corn For The World, Amber Shaded To Brown, Baltimore, Qt., 8 1/2 In. 303.00
Flask, Cornucopia & Urn, Aqua Green, Pt., 7 1/4 In. 230.00
Flask, Cornucopia & Urn, Blue Aqua, Open Pontil, Sheared & Tooled Lip, c.1840, 1/2 Pt. . 316.00
Flask, Cornucopia & Urn, Blue, Green, Open Pontil, Sheared, Tooled Lip, 1835-50, Pt. 1680.00
Flask, Cornucopia & Urn, Dark Olive, Pt. 115.00
Flask, Cornucopia & Urn, Deep Emerald Green, Sheared & Tooled Lip, Pontil, 1/2 Pt. 575.00
Flask, Cornucopia & Urn, Emerald Green, Sheared Mouth, Pontil, Pt. 800.00
Flask, Cornucopia & Urn, Light Green, Iron Pontil, Pt., 6 1/2 In. 413.00
Flask, Cornucopia & Urn, Medium Emerald Green, Sheared & Tooled Lip, Pontil, 1/2 Pt. . 515.00
Flask, Cornucopia & Urn, Olive Green, Applied Collar Mouth, 1/2 Pt. 575.00
Flask, Cornucopia & Urn, Teal Blue, Open Pontil, Applied Ring Mouth, Pt. 870.00
Flask, Cornucopia & Urn, Yellow, Green, Open Pontil, Sheared, Tooled Lip, c.1840, Pt. 2576.00
Flask, Cut Crystal, Engraved, Zipper Cut, Sterling Silver Screw Top, 5 1/2 x 3 x 1 In. 169.00
Flask, Cut Crystal, Round, Sterling Silver Screw Top, 4 1/4 x 3 1/4 In. 169.00
Flask, Double Eagle, Aqua, Plain Lip, Pontil, Qt., 9 1/4 In. 275.00
Flask, Double Eagle, Blue Aqua, Applied Ringed Lip, 1860s-70s, Pt. 258.00
Flask, Double Eagle, Blue Aqua, Open Pontil, Sheared, Tooled Lip, 1835-45, Qt. 308.00
Flask, Double Eagle, Blue Aqua, Pontil, Sheared Mouth, 1840s-60s, 6 3/4 In. 220.00
Flask, Double Eagle, Cobalt Blue, Applied Ringed Mouth, 1855-65, Pt. 3640.00
Flask, Double Eagle, Deep Sapphire Blue, Applied Collar, 1860s-70s, Pt. 4200.00
Flask, Double Eagle, Emerald Green, Pontil, Sheared, Tooled Lip, 1820s-30s, Pt. 5600.00
Flask, Double Eagle, Olive Amber, Applied Ring Mouth, 1865-75, Pt. 476.00
Flask, Double Eagle, Olive Green, Iron Pontil, Applied Mouth, 1855-65, Pt. 840.00
Flask, Duck, Will You Take A Drink, Aqua, Flat Lip With Ring, 1/2 Pt., 6 In. 358.00
Flask, Duck, Will You Take A Drink, Aqua, Flat Lip, Ring Below, Pt., 7 3/4 In. 231.00
Flask, Eagle & Anchor, Apricot Puce, Applied Sloping Collar, Pt. 4000.00
Flask, Eagle & Anchor, Apricot, Applied Double Collared Mouth, 1860-66, Pt. 2016.00
Flask, Eagle & Anchor, Aquamarine, Applied Double Collared Mouth, 1860-66, 1/2 Pt. 672.00
Flask, Eagle & Anchor, Aquamarine, Applied Sloping Collared Mouth, 1860-66, Qt. 1064.00
Flask, Eagle & Anchor, Aquamarine, Double Applied Collar Mouth, Qt. 2000.00
Flask, Eagle & Anchor, Aquamarine, Double Collar Mouth, 1/2 Pt. 400.00
Flask, Eagle & Banner, Aqua, Open Pontil, Qt. 99.00
Flask, Eagle & Banner, Blue Aqua, Open Pontil, Qt. 109.00
Flask, Eagle & Cornucopia, Aqua, Open Pontil, Sheared, Tooled Lip, 1830-40, 1/2 Pt. 392.00
Flask, Eagle & Cornucopia, Blue Aqua, Tooled Lip, Pontil, 1830-40, 1/2 Pt. 360.00
Flask, Eagle & Cornucopia, Deep Olive Green, Pontil, Pt., 6 3/4 In. 132.00
Flask, Eagle & Cornucopia, Golden Amber, Sheared Mouth, Pontil, 1/2 Pt. 1008.00
Flask, Eagle & Cornucopia, Yellow Amber, Pontil Mark, Sheared Mouth, Pt. 201.00
Flask, Eagle & Flag, Aqua, Pontil Mark, Sheared Mouth, Pt. 138.00
Flask, Eagle & Grapes, Golden Amber, Pontil, 1/2 Pt., 5 5/8 In. 231.00
Flask, Eagle & Indian Shooting Bird, Blue, Aqua, Applied Collar Mouth, 1865-75, Qt. 364.00
Flask, Eagle & Indian Shooting Bird, Blue, Aqua, Qt., 9 In. 143.00
Flask, Eagle & Louisville, Blue Aqua, Neck Ring, Pt., 7 3/8 In. 176.00
Flask, Eagle & Lyre, Blue Aqua, Open Pontil, Sheared, Tooled Lip, 1835-45, Pt. 1349.00
Flask, Eagle & Medallion, Yellow Green, Inward Rolled Lip, Pittsburgh, c.1830, Pt. ... *Illus* 31360.00
Flask, Eagle & Willington, Blue, Green, Applied Sloping Collar Mouth, Pt. 2400.00
Flask, Eagle, Olive Yellow, Applied Double Collar, Iron Pontil, Pt. 5600.00
Flask, Eagle, Red Amber, Yellow, Applied Double Collared Mouth, Qt. 2128.00
Flask, Eugene Martin, Opera House Bar, Austin, Tex., Strapped Sides, 1880-1900, Pt. 896.00
Flask, Flora Temple, Blue Green, Applied Mouth, Ring, Pt. 850.00
Flask, Flora Temple, Deep Amber, Applied Lip, Ring Below, 8 1/2 In. 303.00
Flask, Flora Temple, Horse, Harness Trot, Strawberry Puce, Handle, Applied Mouth, Qt. .. 515.00
Flask, Flora Temple, Red Amber, Applied Mouth, Ring, Pt. 325.00
Flask, For Pike's Peak, Prospector & Eagle, Ceredo, Ice Blue, Applied Ring Mouth, Pt. ... 190.00
Flask, For Pike's Peak, Prospector & Eagle, Old Rye, Olive, Collar Mouth, c.1870, Qt. 3600.00

Flask, For Pike's Peak, Prospector & Hunter, Clear, Applied Collar, 1870-75, Pt. 4200.00
Flask, For Pike's Peak, Prospector & Hunter, Olive Yellow, Applied Mouth, Pt. 3920.00
Flask, General Taylor Never Surrenders, Aquamarine, Sheared Mouth, Pontil, Pt. 308.00
Flask, Granite Glass Co., Stoddard, Deep Amber, Double Collar, 1860-80, Pt. 728.00
Flask, Granite Glass Co., Yellow Olive, Sheared Mouth, 1850-60, Pt. 1800.00
Flask, Heart Shape, Stoneware, c.1830, Pt., 7 3/4 In. 145.00
Flask, Horseman & Hound, Citron, 1860-70, Qt. 770.00
Flask, Horseman & Hound, Citron, Applied Double-Collar Mouth, 1860-70, Pt. 616.00
Flask, Horseman & Hound, Puce, Double Ring, 1860-70, Pt. 5500.00
Flask, Horseman & Hound, Teal, Pontil, 1840-60, Qt. 825.00
Flask, Horseman & Hound, Yellow Olive, Applied Ring Mouth, Open Pontil, c.1865, Qt. . . .   910.00
Flask, Horseman & Hound, Yellow, Olive Tint, Applied Double Collar, 8 1/2 In. 880.00
Flask, Hunter & Fisherman, Teal Blue, Calabash, Applied Mouth, c.1850, 9 1/8 In. 489.00
Flask, Jackson & Eagle, Green, Pontil, Sheared, Tooled Lip, 1832-34, Pt. 1568.00
Flask, Jenny Lind & Glassworks, Aqua, Open Pontil, Tapered Mouth, S. Huffsey 1720.00
Flask, Jenny Lind & Glassworks, Olive, Calabash, Pontil, Double Collar, S. Huffsey 2520.00
Flask, Jenny Lind & Lyre, Blue, Aqua, Pontil, Sheared Lip, 1848-53, Qt. 784.00
Flask, Jenny Lind & Lyre, Blue, Aqua, Pontil, Sheared, Tooled Lip, 1848-53, Pt. 1120.00
Flask, Jenny Lind, Calabash, Light Blue, Iron Pontil, Applied Lip, 10 1/4 In. 345.00
Flask, Kossuth & Frigate, Blue Aqua Calabash, Applied Mouth, Iron Pontil, Qt. 345.00
Flask, Kossuth & Tree In Leaf, Yellow, Calabash, Sloping Collar, 1845-60, Qt. 896.00
Flask, Kossuth, Calabash, Yellow, Green, Tree, Leaves, Open Pontil, Qt. 450.00
Flask, Lafayette & Clinton, Medium Yellow Olive, Pontil, Pt., 7 3/8 In. 1155.00
Flask, Lafayette & Clinton, Yellow Olive, Coventry Glassworks, c.1824, Pt. 1904.00
Flask, Lafayette & Clinton, Yellow, Olive, Amber, Pontil, Sheared, Tooled Lip, c.1825, Pt. . .   1456.00
Flask, Lafayette & Eagle, Aqua, Rough Lip, Pt., 6 3/4 In. 330.00
Flask, Lafayette & Liberty, Olive Yellow, Amber, Sheared Mouth, Pontil Scar, 1/2 Pt. 840.00
Flask, Lafayette & Liberty, Olive Yellow, Sheared Mouth, Pontil Scar, Pt. 952.00
Flask, Lafayette & Liberty, Yellow Amber, Sheared Mouth, Pontil, 1/2 Pt. 2688.00
Flask, Lafayette & Masonic, Olive Yellow, Sheared Mouth, Pontil, 1/2 Pt. 4480.00
Flask, Masonic & Eagle, Aquamarine, NEG Co., 1820-40, Pt. 560.00
Flask, Masonic & Eagle, Forest Green, Keene Marlboro, 1820-30, Pt. 1064.00
Flask, Masonic & Eagle, Golden Yellow, Sheared Mouth, Pontil, Pt. 1344.00
Flask, Masonic & Eagle, J. Shepard & Co., Red Amber, 1820-30, Pt. 1344.00
Flask, Masonic & Eagle, Olive Green, Pontil Mark, Sheared Mouth, Pt. 345.00
Flask, Masonic & Eagle, Olive Green, Pontil, Applied Mouth, 1815-30, Pt. 6720.00
Flask, Masonic & Eagle, Olive Yellow, Sheared Mouth, Pontil, Pt., Pair 728.00
Flask, Masonic & Eagle, Purple Amythyst, Sheared, Keene Marlboro, 1815-30, Pt. . . . . *Illus* 47040.00
Flask, Masonic & Eagle, Teal Blue, Pontil, Sheared, Tooled Lip, 1815-30, Pt. 3080.00
Flask, Masonic & Eagle, Yellow Green, Sheared Mouth, Keene Marlboro, c.1825, 1/2 Pt. . . .   1120.00
Flask, Masonic & Eagle, Yellow, Green, Amber Striation, Flared Lip, 1815-25, Pt. 3920.00
Flask, Masonic & Eagle, Yellow, Green, Pontil, Sheared, Tooled Mouth, Pt. 1120.00
Flask, Masonic & Frigate, Franklin, Pale Yellow Green, Pontil, Pt., 6 3/4 In. 440.00

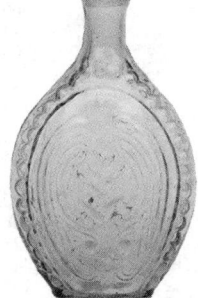
Bottle, Flask, Eagle & Medallion,
Yellow Green, Inward Rolled Lip,
Pittsburgh, c.1830, Pt.

Bottle, Flask, Masonic & Eagle,
Purple Amythyst, Sheared, Keene
Marlboro, 1815-30, Pt.

Bottle, Flask, Scroll, Light
Electric Blue, Double Collar,
Iron Pontil, 1845-60

Flask, Masonic & HS Eagle, Yellow Olive, Keene Marlboro, 1820s-30s, Pt. 5040.00
Flask, Masonic Arch & Eagle, Green Aqua, Sheared & Inward Rolled Lip, Pontil, Pt. 730.00
Flask, Masonic Arch & Eagle, Olive Green, Flared Mouth, Applied Lip, 7 1/2 x 4 x 2 In. ... 468.00
Flask, Masonic Arch & Eagle, Yellow Amber, Sheared & Tooled Lip, Open Pontil, Pt. 317.00
Flask, Masonic Arch & Eagle, Yellow Olive Green, Sheared & Tooled Lip, Pontil, 1/2 Pt. . 400.00
Flask, Monument & Fell's Point, Puce, Striations, Sheared Mouth, Pontil, 1/2 Pt. 1904.00
Flask, Pig, Brown, Stoneware, Bristol Glaze, c.1900, 5 In. 525.00
Flask, Pig, Stoneware, Bristol Glaze, Blue Spots, c.1900, 5 In. 300.00
Flask, Pitkin Type, 18 Broken Ribs, Swirled To Right, Olive, Tooled Mouth, Pontil, 6 In. .. 545.00
Flask, Pitkin Type, 19 Broken Ribs, Swirled To Right, Olive, Tooled Lip, Open Pontil, 6 In. 850.00
Flask, Pitkin Type, 24 Broken Ribs, Swirled To Right, Aqua, Open Pontil, 6 5/8 In. 240.00
Flask, Pitkin Type, 24 Ribs, Swirled To Left, Green, Inward Rolled Mouth, Pontil, 7 In. ... 672.00
Flask, Pitkin Type, 24 Ribs, Swirled To Left, Sheared Mouth, Pontil Scar, 6 5/8 In. 3360.00
Flask, Pitkin Type, 30 Broken Ribs, Swirled To Left, Emerald Green, Pontil, 6 3/8 In. 220.00
Flask, Pitkin Type, 30 Ribs, Swirled To Left, Forest Green, Sheared Mouth, c.1830, 6 In. ... 952.00
Flask, Pitkin Type, 32 Broken Ribs, Swirled To Right, Yellow Green, Pontil, 6 1/4 In. 630.00
Flask, Pitkin Type, 36 Broken Ribs, Swirled To Left, Amber, Open Pontil, 6 In. 680.00
Flask, Pitkin Type, 36 Broken Ribs, Swirled To Right, Olive Amber, 6 3/4 In. 358.00
Flask, Pitkin Type, 36 Broken Ribs, Swirled To Right, Yellow Olive, Open Pontil, 5 In. ... 860.00
Flask, Pitkin Type, 36 Ribs, Swirled To Left, Root Beer Amber, Sheared Mouth, Pontil, 6 In. 1344.00
Flask, Pitkin Type, 36 Ribs, Swirled To Left, Yellow Amber, Sheared, Tooled Lip, 6 In. ... 728.00
Flask, Pitkin Type, 36 Ribs, Swirled To Right, Forest Green, Sheared Mouth, Pontil, 5 In. . 1064.00
Flask, Pitkin Type, 36 Ribs, Swirled To Right, Olive Yellow, Sheared Mouth, Pontil, 6 In. . 1064.00
Flask, Pitkin Type, 36 Ribs, Swirled To Right, Olive Yellow, Sheared, Tooled Lip, 5 In. ... 840.00
Flask, Pumpkinseed, 12 Ribs, Sea Green, Sheared Lip, 1820-40, 1/2 Pt. 79.00
Flask, Pumpkinseed, 20 Ribs, Olive Yellow, Applied Collared Mouth, Pontil, 6 3/4 In. 4760.00
Flask, Pumpkinseed, Deep Amber, Tapered Neck, Sheared Lip, Pontil, 5 In. 165.00
Flask, Sailor & Banjo Player, Olive Yellow, Double-Collar Mouth, 1/2 Pt. 1456.00
Flask, Scroll, Aqua Green, Tooled Lip, Pontil, Qt., 8 7/8 In. 88.00
Flask, Scroll, Aqua, Iron Pontil, Flattened Ring Below Sheared Lip, Qt., 8 1/2 In. 110.00
Flask, Scroll, Corset Waist, Aqua, Pontil, Sheared, Tooled, 1840-50, Pt. 1064.00
Flask, Scroll, Corset Waist, Blue Aqua, Open Pontil, Tooled Lip, J.R. & Son, 7 1/2 In., Pt. . 955.00
Flask, Scroll, Corset Waist, Green Aqua, Open Pontil, Sheared, Tooled Lip, 1840-50, Pt. .. 1120.00
Flask, Scroll, Green, Sheared Mouth, Pontil Scar, 1/2 Pt. 400.00
Flask, Scroll, Light Electric Blue, Double Collar, Iron Pontil, 1845-60 .... *Illus* 3920.00
Flask, Scroll, Medium Amber To Yellow Amber, Sheared Lip, Red Iron Pontil, 1/2 Pt. 1120.00
Flask, Scroll, Medium Blue Green, Pontil, Qt., 8 3/4 In. 176.00
Flask, Scroll, Medium Cobalt Blue, Sheared Lip, Red Iron Pontil, 1845-55, Pt. 3400.00
Flask, Scroll, Moonstone, Lavender Tint, Sheared Mouth, 1845-50, Qt. 2128.00
Flask, Scroll, Moonstone, Pink, Pontil, Sheared, Tooled Lip, 1840-50, Qt. 1904.00
Flask, Scroll, Sapphire Blue, Sheared Mouth, Pontil, 1845-60, Pt. 3920.00
Flask, Scroll, Sapphire Blue, Sheared Mouth, Pontil, 1845-60, Qt. 4807.00
Flask, Scroll, Yellow Olive, Sheared Mouth, 1845-60, Pt. 1568.00
Flask, Scroll, Yellow, Amber, Pontil, Sheared, Tooled Lip, 1840-50, Qt. 1232.00
Flask, Scroll, Yellow, Olive Amber, Pontil, Applied Collar, 1840-50, Qt. 1568.00
Flask, Scroll, Yellow, Olive, Iron Pontil, Sheared Lip, 1840-50, Qt. 3360.00
Flask, Scroll, Yellow, Olive, Pontil, Sheared, Tooled Lip, 1840-50, Pt. 1344.00
Flask, Sheaf Of Rye, Olive Yellow, Sheared Mouth, Pontil Scar, Baltimore, 1/2 Pt. 3000.00
Flask, Sheaf Of Rye, Yellow Orange, Applied Mouth, Baltimore Glass Works, Qt. 1904.00
Flask, Shield & Clasped Hands, Aqua, Applied Double Collar, 9 In. 77.00
Flask, Stiegel Type, Pumpkinseed, Diamond Diaper, Teal Green, Pocket, 5 1/4 In. 440.00
Flask, Stoddard Type, Orange Amber, 1/2 Pt. 19.00
Flask, Success To The Railroad, Aquamarine, Sheared Mouth, Pontil, 1830-1850, Pt. 1344.00
Flask, Success To The Railroad, Blue, Aqua, Open Pontil, Sheared, Tooled Lip, c.1840, Pt. 952.00
Flask, Success To The Railroad, Horse & Cart, Olive Green, Pontil, Sheared Lip, 6 7/8 In. . 190.00
Flask, Success To The Railroad, Medium Blue Green, Pontil, Pt., 6 3/4 In. 88.00
Flask, Success To The Railroad, Olive Green, Pontil, Sheared, Tooled Lip, 1825-35, Pt. ... 728.00
Flask, Success To The Railroad, Olive Yellow, Pontil, Sheared, Tooled Lip, Pt. 448.00
Flask, Success To The Railroad, Yellow Amber, Pontil, Pt., 6 7/8 In. 132.00
Flask, Summer & Winter, Aqua Blue, Applied Slanted Lip, Pontil, Pt. 77.00
Flask, Summer & Winter, Yellow Topaz, Double Collar, 1840-60, Qt. 4200.00
Flask, Sunburst, Aqua Blue, Moonstone Tint, Pontil, 1/2 Pt., 6 3/4 In. 165.00
Flask, Sunburst, Blue Aqua, Sheared & Tooled Lip, Pontil, 1820s-30s, 1/2 Pt. 350.00

Flask, Sunburst, Blue Green, Sheared Mouth, Pontil, 1820s-30s, 1/2 Pt. 1500.00
Flask, Sunburst, Clear, Gray, Amethyst Tint, Sheared Mouth, Pontil, Pt. 2352.00
Flask, Sunburst, Clear, Pontil, Sheared, Tooled Lip, 1815-35, 1/2 Pt. 840.00
Flask, Sunburst, Deep Blue Aqua, Sheared & Tooled Lip, Pontil, 1/2 Pt. 315.00
Flask, Sunburst, Deep Blue Green, Tooled Lip, Pontil, 3/4 Pt., 7 In. 220.00
Flask, Sunburst, Emerald Green, Pontil, Sheared, Tooled Lip, 1815-25, 1/2 Pt. 4480.00
Flask, Sunburst, Emerald Green, Pontil, Sheared, Tooled Lip, 1810-25, Pt. 2800.00
Flask, Sunburst, Forest Green, Inward Rolled Mouth, 1813-30, 1/2 Pt. 2016.00
Flask, Sunburst, Medium Green, Sheared Lip, Pontil, Pt., 8 In. 440.00
Flask, Sunburst, Medium Olive Green, Flared Lip, Pt., 7 3/8 In. 770.00
Flask, Sunburst, Medium To Dark Olive Green, Pontil, 1/2 Pt., 5 3/4 In. 715.00
Flask, Sunburst, Medium Yellow Olive, Sheared Lip, Pontil, Pt., 7 1/2 In. 605.00
Flask, Sunburst, Olive Yellow, Sheared Mouth, 1814-30, 1/2 Pt. 728.00
Flask, Sunburst, Olive Yellow, Sheared Mouth, Pontil Scar, 1/2 Pt. 1120.00
Flask, Sunburst, Yellow Amber, Olive Tone, Sheared Mouth, Pontil, Pt. 728.00
Flask, Sunburst, Yellow Amber, Sheared & Tooled Lip, Pontil, P.W. Keen, 1/2 Pt. 1480.00
Flask, Sunburst, Yellow Olive Amber, Flared Sheared Lip, 1/2 Pt., 5 3/4 In. 715.00
Flask, Sunburst, Yellow Olive, Sheared Mouth, Coventry Glass, 1813-30, Pt. 1456.00
Flask, Sunburst, Yellow, Green, Olive Tone, Sheared Mouth, Pontil, 1/2 Pt. 952.00
Flask, Sunburst, Yellow, Green, Pontil, Sheared, Tooled Lip, 1815-25, 1/2 Pt. 3360.00
Flask, Swirled Broken Ribs, Light Green, Half-Post Neck, 6 In. 230.00
Flask, Taylor & Eagle, Blue, Green, Pontil, Sheared, Tooled Lip, 1840-45, Qt. 2464.00
Flask, Taylor & Fells Point, Olive Yellow, Pontil, Sheared, Tooled Lip, 1847-50, Pt. 4480.00
Flask, Traveler's Companion & Railroad Guide, Aqua Blue, Pontil, 1/2 Pt., 5 3/4 In. 330.00
Flask, Traveler's Companion & Star, Deep Amber, Sheared Lip, 1/2 Pt., 5 3/4 In. 176.00
Flask, Traveler's Companion & Star, Red Amber, 1845-60, 1/2 Pt. 784.00
Flask, Traveler's Companion & Star, Yellow Amber, Iron Pontil, Tooled Lip, 1/2 Pt. 1568.00
Flask, Traveler's Companion, Sheaf Of Grain, Star, Amber, Sloping Collar Mouth, Qt. 275.00
Flask, Traveler's Companion, Sheaf Of Grain, Star, Tobacco Amber, Sloping Collar, Qt. ... 240.00
Flask, Union Glass, Aquamarine, Applied Double-Collar Mouth, Pt. 616.00
Flask, Union, Clasped Hands & Cannon, Aqua, Applied Collar, 1860-70, Pt. 157.00
Flask, Union, Clasped Hands & Eagle, Old Rye, Yellow Green, Applied Ring Mouth, Qt. ... 690.00
Flask, Union, Clasped Hands & Eagle, Yellow Amber, Applied Ring Mouth, 1/2 Pt. 425.00
Flask, Union, Clasped Hands & Eagle, Yellow, Amber, 1860-70, 9 In. 990.00
Flask, Union, Clasped Hands & Eagle, Yellow, Amber, Ringed Mouth, 1/2 Pt. 560.00
Flask, Union, Clasped Hands & Eagle, Yellow, Lorenz & Wightman, 1860-70, Pt. 1232.00
Flask, Washington & Eagle, Green Aqua, Sheared Lip, Pontil, 1830-40, Pt. 306.00
Flask, Washington & Eagle, Green, Aquamarine, Sheared Mouth, Pontil, Pt. 1064.00
Flask, Washington & Eagle, Green, Sheared, Tooled Flared Lip, Pontil, 1830-40, Pt. 4200.00
Flask, Washington & Fells Point, Clear, Smoky Aqua, Pontil, Sheared, Tooled, Qt. 448.00
Flask, Washington & Jackson, Olive Amber, Plain Lip, Pontil, Pt., 6 1/2 In. 303.00
Flask, Washington & Jackson, Olive Yellow, Green, Open Pontil, Pt. 500.00
Flask, Washington & Jackson, Yellow Amber, Olive, Pontil, Sheared, Tooled Lip, 1/2 Pt. .. 616.00
Flask, Washington & Lockport, Aqua, Olive Streak, Pontil, Qt., 7 3/4 In. 22.00
Flask, Washington & Lockport, Deep Blue Green, Pontil, Qt., 8 In. 2860.00
Flask, Washington & Lockport, Medium To Deep Yellow Green, 7 3/4 In. 1760.00
Flask, Washington & Taylor, Blue, Dyottville Glass Works, 1840-60, Pt. 7840.00
Flask, Washington & Taylor, Butterscotch, Pontil, Sheared Lip, 1840-60, Pt. 1210.00
Flask, Washington & Taylor, Cobalt Blue, Dyottville Glass Works, 1840-60, Pt. 4480.00
Flask, Washington & Taylor, Cobalt Blue, Pontil, Applied Mouth, 1848-50, Qt. 3640.00
Flask, Washington & Taylor, Cobalt Blue, Pontil, Sheared, Tooled Lip, 1848-50, Qt. 8960.00
Flask, Washington & Taylor, Dense Burgundy, Square Collar, 1860-80, Qt. 2800.00
Flask, Washington & Taylor, Father Of His Country, Blue Green, Pontil, Qt., 8 1/4 In. 413.00
Flask, Washington & Taylor, Father Of His Country, Teal, Applied Lip, Open Pontil, Qt. .. 325.00
Flask, Washington & Taylor, Frigate, Aquamarine, Albany Glass Works, c.1849, Pt. 672.00
Flask, Washington & Taylor, Gray Puce, Sheared Lip, 1860-80, Pt. 4750.00
Flask, Washington & Taylor, Green, Pontil, Double-Ring Top, 1840-50, 8 5/8 In. 990.00
Flask, Washington & Taylor, Light Green, Open Pontil, Pt. 650.00
Flask, Washington & Taylor, Never Surrenders, Aqua, Open Pontil, Qt. 149.00
Flask, Washington & Taylor, Never Surrenders, Pale Aqua, Pt., 6 3/4 In. 77.00
Flask, Washington & Taylor, Never Surrenders, Sapphire Blue, Qt., 8 1/4 In. 3850.00
Flask, Washington & Taylor, Olive Yellow, Pontil, Applied Double Collar, Pt. 3080.00
Flask, Washington & Taylor, Olive, 6 1/2 In. 259.00

Flask, Washington & Taylor, Orange Amber, Sheared Mouth, 1840-60, Pt. 840.00
Flask, Washington & Taylor, Sapphire Blue, Dyottville Glass Works, 1840-60, Qt. 6160.00
Flask, Washington & Taylor, Sapphire Blue, Soda Style Top, Open Pontil, Qt. 2600.00
Flask, Washington & Taylor, Ship, Yellow Amber, Iron Pontil, Albany Glass Works, Pt. . . . 4760.00
Flask, Washington & Taylor, Teal, Applied Top, Open Pontil, Pt. 650.00
Flask, Washington & Taylor, Yellow Green, Pontil, Sheared Top, 1840-60, Qt. 358.00
Flask, Washington & Taylor, Yellow Topaz, Dyottville Glass Works, 1840-60, Pt. 3360.00
Flask, Washington, Adams & Jefferson, Aqua, Pontil, Sheared, Tooled Lip, 1825-27, Pt. . . . 672.00
Flask, Washington, Adams & Jefferson, Green, Aqua, Pontil, Sheared, Tooled Lip, Pt. 840.00
Food, Blueberry Preserves, Green, Applied Mouth, 10 Flutes, Pontil, Cylindrical, 11 In. . . . 3360.00
Food, Roses Lime Juice, Cylindrical, Embossed, Leaves, Fruit, Brown, England, 13 In. . . . 59.00
Fruit Jar, A. & D.H. Chambers Union, Pittsburgh, Pa., Yellow Olive, Wax Sealer, Qt., 8 In. 990.00
Fruit Jar, A. Stone & Co., Wax Sealer, 9 3/4 In. 1320.00
Fruit Jar, Adlam Patent, Boston, Mass., June 24, 84, Teal, Bail Handle, 1/2 Pt., 4 1/2 In. . . 523.00
Fruit Jar, All Right, Patd Jan 26th 1868, Aqua, Ground Lip, Metal Lid, 7 3/4 In. 110.00
Fruit Jar, All Right, Patd Jan 28th 1868, Aqua, Metal Lid, 7 1/4 In. 88.00
Fruit Jar, Almy, Aqua, Patented Dec. 25, 1877, Star, Screw Lid, 7 In. 99.00
Fruit Jar, Banner, Patd Feby 9th 1864, Press-On Glass Lid, 7 1/2 In. 132.00
Fruit Jar, Beaver, Blue, Glass Insert, Screw Band, 5 5/8 In. 385.00
Fruit Jar, Bloeser, Aqua, Glass Lid, Wire & Metal Clamp, Neck Wire, 8 In. 88.00
Fruit Jar, Cohansey Glass Mf'g. Co., Barrel, Aqua, Wax Sealer, 1/2 Gal., 9 1/8 In. 66.00
Fruit Jar, Cunningham & Co., Pittsburgh, Pa., Deep Aqua, 1/2 Gal., 9 3/4 In. 303.00
Fruit Jar, Eagle, Aqua, Iron Yoke Clamp, 1/2 Gal., 9 3/4 In. 110.00
Fruit Jar, Eagle, Aqua, Smooth Lip, Qt., 7 5/8 In. 88.00
Fruit Jar, Empire, Aqua, Glass Lid, Qt., 8 1/2 In. 77.00
Fruit Jar, F. & J. Bodine, Philadelphia, Pa., Aqua, Tin Lid, Wire Clamp, Qt., 7 In. 66.00
Fruit Jar, Fahnestock Albree & Co., Dark Aqua, Willoughby Stopple, Qt., 8 1/2 In. 358.00
Fruit Jar, Friedley & Cornman's, Aquamarine, Ground Mouth, Iron Rim, 1/2 Gal. 1400.00
Fruit Jar, Gem, Aqua, Glass Insert, Zinc Screw Band, Gal., 12 3/8 In. 880.00
Fruit Jar, Gem, Hero Glass Works, Aqua, Glass Insert, Screw Band, 3 Gal., 17 5/8 In. 3575.00
Fruit Jar, Globe, Red Amber, Glass Lid, Iron Clamp, Qt., 8 In. 132.00
Fruit Jar, Griffen's Patent, Oct 7 1862, Aqua, Glass Lid, Cage-Like Clamp, Qt., 7 In. 66.00
Fruit Jar, Hansee's Palace Home, PH Monogram, Clear, Glass Lid, Wire Clamp, Qt., 7 In. . 44.00
Fruit Jar, Hero Ine, Aqua, Ground Lip, Glass Insert, Screw Band, Pt., 6 5/8 In. 121.00
Fruit Jar, Hero, Aqua, Ground Lip, Glass Insert, Qt., 7 In. 22.00
Fruit Jar, Hero, Aqua, Tin Insert, Screw Band, Qt., 7 1/2 In. 22.00
Fruit Jar, Hero, Honey Amber, Ground Lip, Metal Lid, Qt., 7 1/2 In. 6600.00
Fruit Jar, Johnson & Johnson, New York, Cobalt Blue, Glass Lid, Screw Band, Qt., 7 In. . . 358.00
Fruit Jar, King, Pat. Nov 2 1869, Aqua, Glass Lid, Iron Yoke Clamp, Qt. 121.00
Fruit Jar, Lafayette, Aqua, 3-Piece Glass & Metal Stopper, Qt., 8 1/2 In. 110.00
Fruit Jar, Magic, Star, Golden Amber, Ground Mouth, Glass Lid, Wire Clamp, 1/2 Gal. . . . 1100.00
Fruit Jar, Mansfield Knowlton, May '03 Patent, Aqua, Glass Lid, Metal Screw Cap, Qt. . . . 77.00
Fruit Jar, Mason's Improved, CFJCo, Amber, Glass Insert, 1/2 Gal., 9 In. 187.00
Fruit Jar, Mason's Improved, CFJCo, Aqua, Midget Pt., 6 In. 22.00
Fruit Jar, Mason's Patent Improved, CFJCo, Aqua, Metal Lid, Gal., 12 In. 2310.00
Fruit Jar, Mason's Patent Nov 30th 1858, Dark Aqua, Zinc Lid, Gal., 12 In. 1100.00
Fruit Jar, Mason's Patent Nov 30th 1858, Green, Amber, Milk Glass Insert, 1/2 Gal. 358.00
Fruit Jar, Mason's Patent Nov 30th 1858, Tudor Rose, Ball Blue, Qt., 7 1/4 In. 121.00
Fruit Jar, Millville Atmospheric, Aqua, Glass Lid, Iron Yoke Clamp, 56 Oz., 9 In. 55.00
Fruit Jar, Moore's Patent Dec 3d 1861, Aqua, Glass Lid, Iron Yoke Clamp, Qt., 8 In. 55.00
Fruit Jar, Pansy, Amber, 20 Vertical Panels, Glass Insert, Screw Band, Qt. 220.00
Fruit Jar, Patented Oct. 19 1858, Aqua, Ground Lip, Glass Lid, Lugs Hartell's, Qt., 7 In. . . 44.00
Fruit Jar, Pet, Aqua, Glass Lid, Spring Wire Clamp, 1/2 Gal., 9 7/8 In. 198.00
Fruit Jar, Potter & Bodine's, Air-Tight, Aquamarine, Barrel, Wax Seal Groove, Pontil, Qt. . 1456.00
Fruit Jar, Potter & Bodine's, Air-Tight, Philada, Aqua, Wax Sealer, 1/2 Gal., 8 1/4 In. 66.00
Fruit Jar, Safety Valve, Patd May 21 1895, Emerald Green, Wire Clamp, Pt., 5 3/4 In. 209.00
Fruit Jar, Smalley Full Measure, AGS Monogram, Amber, Qt., 7 1/4 In. 88.00
Fruit Jar, Standard, W. Mc C & Co., Cobalt Blue, Groove Ring Wax Sealer, Qt., 7 1/2 In. . 880.00
Fruit Jar, Star Emblem, Circle Of Fruit, Aqua, Ground Lip, Zinc Insert & Screw Band, Qt. 143.00
Fruit Jar, Sun Trademark, Aqua, Glass Lid, Metal Yoke Clamp, Qt., 7 3/4 In. 99.00
Fruit Jar, The Hero, Honey Amber, Qt. 6600.00
Fruit Jar, Valve Jar Co. Philadelphia, Patd Mar 10th 1868, Aqua, Wire Coil Clamp, Qt. . . . 385.00
Fruit Jar, Van Vliet Jar Of 1881, Aqua, Glass Lid, Metal Yoke Clamp, 1/2 Gal., 7 1/2 In. . . 523.00

Fruit Jar, W. Chrysler, Pat Nov 21, 1865, Aqua, Applied Lip, Qt., 7 3/4 In. 1210.00
Gemel, Chestnut, Deep Blue Green, Applied Rolled Collar, 6-Sided, 5 In. 33.00
Gin, Dark Olive Green, Applied Lip, 12 1/2 In. 345.00
Gin, Olive Amber, Applied Sloping Collared Mouth, Pontil Scar, Square, 17 1/2 In. 2300.00
Gin, Olive Yellow, Square, Tapered, Applied Collared Mouth, 14 7/8 In. 1456.00
Gin, Reed's London Cordial, Deep Blue Aqua, Applied Slope Collar, Iron Pontil, 10 In. ... 350.00
Ginger Beer, A.F. Lawson, Larges & Millport, Blue Transfer, 8 In. 166.00
Ginger Beer, A.W. Buchan & Co., Waverley Potteries, Portobello, Scotland, Sample, 7 In. . 2937.00
Ginger Beer, Anson Brand, Beige, Capped, Logo, Capt. A.C. Anson, Chicago, 7 In. 345.00
Ginger Beer, Bath Brewery Limited, Home Brewed, King, 6 3/4 In. 33.00
Ginger Beer, Binnington & Co., Good Old Fashioned, House, 6 3/4 In. 255.00
Ginger Beer, C.C. Dornat & Co., Barnstable, Tree, Price Bristol, 6 3/4 In. 23.00
Ginger Beer, Corcoran & Co., Carlow, Castle Ruins, Ireland, 6 3/4 In. 685.00
Ginger Beer, Dee Mineral Water Co., Crystal Brewed, Portland Works, Price Bristol, 7 In. . 33.00
Ginger Beer, E.L. Newsomes Ltd., Blackpool, 8 In. 49.00
Ginger Beer, Edmondson & Co., Liverpool, Girl On Swing, 8 In. 20.00
Ginger Beer, G&C Moore Limited, Edinburgh, Green Top, Black Transfer, Buchan, 8 In. ... 137.00
Ginger Beer, Goulds Carisbrooke, Brewed, One Penny, 6 3/4 In. 20.00
Ginger Beer, Grantham, Dale, Street Lamp, Pearson Chesterfield, 8 1/2 In. 78.00
Ginger Beer, H. Firth, Manningham, Sailing Ship, 7 1/4 In. 33.00
Ginger Beer, H.C. Baildon & Son, Chemists, Edinburgh, Buchan, 8 1/2 In. 59.00
Ginger Beer, Holliday & Co., Extra Stout, North Shields, Buchan Portobello, 8 In. 88.00
Ginger Beer, Home Brewery, Renton Street, Sheffield, Wheat Sheaf, 7 1/4 In. ....43.00 to 49.00
Ginger Beer, James Bros. Manufacturers, Manly, Olive Green Top, 7 In. 215.00
Ginger Beer, John Thompson, Stout For Invalids, Blyth, 8 In. 29.00
Ginger Beer, Lee & Green, Buffalo, N.Y., Stoneware, 7 In. 66.00
Ginger Beer, Murphy Bros., Syracuse, N.Y., 7 In. 110.00
Ginger Beer, North & Randall, Blue Top, Bourne Denby, 7 1/4 In. 274.00
Ginger Beer, Phillips & Co., Wellington, Goalie, 8 1/4 In. 88.00
Ginger Beer, Pinks None Nicer, Stoneware, Chichester, 6 3/4 In. 35.00
Ginger Beer, South West Min. Water Co., Bournemouth, Castle, Bristol, 6 3/4 In. 20.00
Ginger Beer, T. Cook & Son, Folkestone & Dover, Foaming Glass, 7 3/4 In. 39.00
Ginger Beer, Victoria Wind Company, Queen Victoria Portrait, Established 1865, 6 1/2 In. . 49.00
Ginger Beer, Wm. Jackson & Co., Newcastle, Man Holding Flag, Bourne Denby, 7 1/4 In. . 20.00
Household, 3 In 1 Lubricant, 15 Cents, Cork Stopper, Box, c.1927, 1 Fl. Oz. 30.00
Household, Formaldehyde For Shoes, Loeffler Drug, Dr. Hanna, Stevensville, Mich., 6 In. . 10.00
Household, George Foster's Jim Dandy Oil, 100 Uses For Home, Farm, Factory, 8 1/2 In. . 10.00
Household, Gold Medal Celery Seed, Shaker Cover, 5 In. 7.50
Household, Race & Sheldons Water Proof Boot Polish, 8-Sided, Emerald Green, 5 5/8 In. . 5040.00
Ink, 6-Sided, Cobalt Blue, Flared Lip, Pontil Base, 2 1/2 In. 133.00
Ink, 8-Sided, Blue, Applied Top, Pontil, 1840-60, 4 In. 385.00
Ink, 12-Sided, Amber, Pontil, Outward-Rolled Lip, 1 5/8 In. 935.00
Ink, 12-Sided, Olive Amber, Pontil, Polished Top, 1830-50, 2 In. 715.00
Ink, 12-Sided, Yellow Olive, Applied Collar, 1830-60, 5 3/4 x 2 3/8 In. 5040.00
Ink, Barrel, Horizontal, Aqua, Sheared Lip, England, 2 x 3 1/2 In. ....29.00 to 49.00
Ink, Birdcage, Embossed M, Aqua, England, 3 1/4 In. 39.00
Ink, Carter's, Cathedral, Cobalt Blue, Qt. 109.00
Ink, Cottage, Aqua, Tiled Roof, Windows, Door, Pen Recess, 2 3/4 In. 266.00
Ink, Derby All British, Triangular, Cobalt Blue, Embossed, Sheared Lip, 2 1/4 In. 53.00
Ink, Dome, Blue, Center Neck, Sheared Lip, Pontil, 3 5/8 x 2 3/4 In. 303.00
Ink, E. Waters, Troy, N.Y., Blue Green, Pontil, Applied Mouth, Fluted, c.1850, 5 1/2 In. ... 1210.00
Ink, Farley's, 8-Sided, Olive Yellow, Sheared Mouth, Pontil, 1 7/8 In. 750.00
Ink, Farley's, 8-Sided, Pontil, Flared Lip, Bubbles, 1840-60, 3 3/4 In. 3025.00
Ink, Farley's, 8-Sided, Yellow Amber, Pontil, Tooled Lip, 1840-60, 1 3/4 In. 1430.00
Ink, Globe, Aqua, Embossed World Map, 3 In. 307.00
Ink, Harrison's Columbian, 8-Sided, Aqua, Applied Mouth, Open Pontil, 3 7/8 In. 105.00
Ink, Harrison's Columbian, 12-Sided, Aqua, Applied Mouth, Open Pontil, 5 3/4 In. 186.00
Ink, Harrison's Columbian, 12-Sided, Aqua, Applied Mouth, Pontil, 11 In. 3600.00
Ink, Harrison's Columbian, 12-Sided, Aqua, Applied Mouth, 1840-60, 6 In. 358.00
Ink, Harrison's Columbian, 12-Sided, Blue, Pontil, Applied Top, 1840-60, 7 3/8 In. 880.00
Ink, Harrison's Columbian, Cobalt Blue, Applied Mouth, Open Pontil, 5 5/8 In. 395.00
Ink, Harrison's Columbian, Cobalt Blue, Inward-Rolled Lip, Open Pontil, 2 In. 505.00
Ink, Harrison's Columbian, Cobalt Blue, Pontil, Hammered, 1840-60, 7 1/8 In. 7700.00

Ink, Harrison's Columbian, Green, Applied Mouth, c.1860, 6 In. 3575.00
Ink, Harrison's Columbian, Yellow Green, Bubbles, 1840-60, 1 3/8 In. 1760.00
Ink, Hoover, Cylindrical, Cobalt Blue, Applied Flared Lip, 5 In. 1650.00
Ink, Hoover, Cylindrical, Olive, Pontil, Applied Flared Lip, 1840-60, 4 1/4 In. 605.00
Ink, House, Domed Roof, Aqua, Rounded-Top Windows, Squared Lip, 2 1/2 x 1 3/4 In. . . . 44.00
Ink, House, Violet Cobalt, Tooled Lip, 1870-90, 4 3/4 In. 935.00
Ink, J. & I.E.M., Igloo, Cobalt Blue, Tooled Top, 1875-90 . . . . 2310.00
Ink, J. & I.E.M., Igloo, Sapphire Blue, Ground Top, 1875-90, 1 3/4 In. 1540.00
Ink, Jones' Empire, N.Y., 12-Sided, Olive Green, Pontil, Applied Top, c.1850, 5 3/4 In. . . . 6050.00
Ink, Lion's Head, Gaping Mouth, Brown, Salt Glaze, Quill Holes, 1 1/2 In. 1105.00
Ink, M & P, New York, Umbrella, 8-Sided, Medium Green, Inward-Rolled Mouth, 2 3/4 In. 728.00
Ink, Olive Yellow, 2-Mold, 7 Rings, Pontil, 1800s-30s, 1 3/8 x 2 1/2 In. 4950.00
Ink, Pitkin-Type, Olive Green, Beveled Corners, Pontil, 1790s-1820s, 1 3/4 In. 1760.00
Ink, Pitkin-Type, Olive Yellow, Disk Mouth, 1790s-1820s, 1 5/8 In. 2090.00
Ink, S. Fine, Cylindrical, Tobacco Amber, Pontil, Flared Lip, 3 1/16 In. 1320.00
Ink, S.O. Dunbar, 12-Sided, Blue Green, Pontil, Sheared Lip, 1840-60, 2 1/8 In. 1760.00
Ink, Sandal, Mans, Light Apple Green, Nen, Embossed, Sheared Lip, England, c.1900, 3 In. 515.00
Ink, Shoe, Aqua, England, 1 3/4 x 4 In. 49.00
Ink, Shoe, Mans, Deep Cobalt Blue, Sheared & Ground Lip, England, 1885-1910, 4 In. . . . 1010.00
Ink, Teakettle, 6-Sided, Cobalt Blue, Gold Paint, Tooled Lip, Brass Cap, 3 1/8 In. 615.00
Ink, Teakettle, 7-Sided, Opaque Lavender, Ground Lip, Hinged Cap, 1875-95, 2 3/4 In. . . . 360.00
Ink, Teakettle, 8 Ribs, Amethyst, Concave Panels, Hinged Cap, 2 In. 680.00
Ink, Teakettle, 8 Ribs, Cobalt Blue, 8 Irregular Panels, Gold Design, Hinged Cap, 2 1/8 In. 350.00
Ink, Teakettle, 8 Ribs, Sapphire Blue Glass, Concave Panels, Brass Ring, 2 In. 515.00
Ink, Teakettle, 8 Ribs, Smoky Purple Glass, Concave Panels, Hinged Cap, c.1885, 2 In. . . . 575.00
Ink, Teakettle, 8-Sided, Green, 2 1/8 x 2 3/8 In. 330.00
Ink, Teakettle, 8-Sided, Opalescent Milk Glass, Flowers, Gold Trim, Pinched Waist, 2 In. . 205.00
Ink, Teakettle, 8-Sided, Opalescent Turquoise, Flowers, Pinched Waist, Hinged Cap, 2 In. . 350.00
Ink, Teakettle, 8-Sided, Opaque Lime Green, Ground Lip, Hinged Cap, c.1885, 2 5/8 In. . . 295.00
Ink, Teakettle, 8-Sided, Opaque White, Opalescence At Top, Applied Upper Font, 3 1/4 In. 88.00
Ink, Teakettle, 10-Sided, Cobalt Blue, Raised Flowers, Ground Lip, Brass Ring, 2 1/8 In. . . 420.00
Ink, Teakettle, 10-Sided, Opalescent Milk Glass, Flowers, Multicolored, Hinged Cap, 3 In. 460.00
Ink, Teakettle, 10-Sided, Opaque Milk Glass, Raised Flowers, Brass Ring, 3 1/8 In. 295.00
Ink, Teakettle, Barrel, Amethyst, Brass Ring, Ground Lip, 1875-95, 2 1/4 In. 920.00
Ink, Teakettle, Barrel, Amethyst, Sheared Lip, Brass Top, 1870-80, 2 1/4 In. 440.00
Ink, Teakettle, Barrel, Cobalt Blue, Ground Mouth, 2 1/8 In. 700.00
Ink, Teakettle, Barrel, Cobalt Blue, Sheared Ground Lip, Brass Ring, 1870-80, 2 1/4 In. . . . 330.00
Ink, Teakettle, Barrel, Dome, Cobalt Blue, Sheared Lip, Brass Ring, 1870-80, 2 1/4 In. . . . 253.00
Ink, Teakettle, Barrel, Dome, Green, Sheared Lip, Brass Ring, 1870-80, 2 1/4 In. 495.00
Ink, Teakettle, Barrel, Green, Sheared Lip, Brass Ring, 1870-80, 2 1/4 In. 660.00
Ink, Teakettle, Barrel, Ice Blue, Brass Ring, Cap, 1875-95, 2 1/8 In. 460.00
Ink, Teakettle, Barrel, Puce, Sheared Ground Lip, Wide Mouth, 1870-80 . . . . 1210.00
Ink, Teakettle, Barrel, Teal, Sheared Mouth, Brass Ring, Lid, 1870-80, 2 1/4 In. 1980.00
Ink, Teakettle, Crown, Brass Ring, 1860-80 . . . . 715.00
Ink, Teakettle, Crown, Cobalt Blue, Sheared Ground Lip, 1860-80, 1 1/2 In. 605.00
Ink, Teakettle, Dome, 10-Sided, Fiery Opalescent, Flowers, Ground Lip, Brass Cap, 3 1/8 In. 505.00
Ink, Teakettle, Dome, Cobalt Blue, Sheared Lip, Brass Ring, 1870-80, 2 1/4 In. 253.00
Ink, Teakettle, Octagonal, Aqua, Upturned Spout, 3 1/2 In. 573.00
Ink, Teakettle, Opaque Clambroth, Hinged Cap, 2 3/8 In. 315.00
Ink, Teakettle, Opaque Lime Green, Ground Lip, Hinged Cap, 1875-95, 2 7/8 In. 515.00
Ink, Teakettle, Opaque Milk Glass, Ground Lip, Hinged Cap, 1875-95, 2 3/4 In. 295.00
Ink, Teakettle, Opaque Turquoise Blue, Hinged Cap, Ground Lip, 1875-95, 2 7/8 In. 515.00
Ink, Teakettle, Square, Purple, Upturned Spout, 2 Pen Rests, Silver Plated Lift-Up Cap, 2 In. 655.00
Ink, Teakettle, Stoneware, Brown Glaze, Chandler & Co., England, 2 1/2 In. 137.00
Ink, Teakettle, Stoneware, Tan Glaze, England, 2 1/2 x 3 In. 39.00
Ink, Teakettle, Yellow, Sheared Ground Lip, 1870-80, 2 In. 385.00
Ink, Tipper, Blue Glass, Octagonal, 1 3/4 In. 82.00
Ink, Umbrella, 5-Sided, Olive Green, Irregular Label Panels, Open Pontil, 2 1/4 In. 5375.00
Ink, Umbrella, 5-Sided, Yellow Amber, Irregular Label Panels, Open Pontil, 2 1/4 In. 690.00
Ink, Umbrella, 8-Sided, Amber, Open Pontil, Tooled Lip, 2 5/8 In. 170.00
Ink, Umbrella, 8-Sided, Blue Green, Open Pontil, Rolled Lip, 2 1/2 In. 345.00
Ink, Umbrella, 8-Sided, Cobalt Blue, Inward-Rolled Lip, 1830-60, 3 x 3 1/4 In. 5320.00
Ink, Umbrella, 8-Sided, Cobalt Blue, Inward-Rolled Lip, Pontil Scar, 2 1/2 In x 2 1/2 In. . . 2200.00

Ink, Umbrella, 8-Sided, Cobalt Blue, Inward-Rolled Lip, Pontil, 2 1/4 In.	2998.00
Ink, Umbrella, 8-Sided, Olive Green, Open Pontil, Rolled Lip, 1840-60, 2 3/8 In.	3680.00
Ink, Umbrella, 8-Sided, Olive Yellow, Inward-Rolled Lip, Pontil Scar, 2 3/8 In.	1064.00
Ink, Umbrella, 8-Sided, Puce Amethyst, Rolled Lip, Pontil, 2 5/8 In.	715.00
Ink, Umbrella, 8-Sided, Red Puce, Open Pontil, Tooled Lip, 1840-60, 2 3/8 In.	3950.00
Ink, Umbrella, 8-Sided, Sapphire Blue, Open Pontil, Tooled Lip, 1840-60, 2 1/2 In.	4200.00
Ink, Umbrella, 8-Sided, Sapphire Blue, Tooled Mouth, 1860-80, 2 5/8 In. . . . . *Illus*	532.00
Ink, Umbrella, 8-Sided, Yellow Amber, Inward-Rolled Lip, Open Pontil, 2 1/2 In.	285.00
Ink, Umbrella, 8-Sided, Yellow Amber, Sheared & Tooled Lip, Open Pontil, 2 3/8 In.	285.00
Ink, Umbrella, 8-Sided, Yellow Green, Olive Tone, Inward-Rolled Mouth, Pontil, 2 1/4 In.	672.00
Ink, Umbrella, 8-Sided, Yellow Green, Sheared & Tooled Lip, Open Pontil, 2 3/8 In.	104.00
Ink, Umbrella, 8-Sided, Yellow Olive Green, Open Pontil, Tooled Lip, 2 3/8 In.	1695.00
Ink, Umbrella, Cobalt Blue, Pontil, Rolled Lip, 1840-60, 2 1/2 In.	1870.00
Ink, Umbrella, Emerald Green, Pontil, Rolled Lip, 1840-60, 2 1/2 In.	1540.00
Ink, Umbrella, Pink, Pontil, Rolled Lip, 1840-60, 2 1/2 In.	2090.00
Ink, Umbrella, Violet Cobalt, Rolled Lip, 1860-80, 2 1/2 In.	1100.00
Ink, Umbrella, Yellow Amber, Pontil, Rolled Lip, 1840-60, 2 1/2 In.	2200.00
Ink, Warren's, Congress, 8-Sided, Olive Yellow, Pontil, Rolled Lip, 1840-60, 2 7/8 In.	3850.00
Ink, Warren's, Congress, 8-Sided, Yellow Green, Pontil, Applied Spout, 1845-60, 7 In.	7150.00
Ink, Waterman's, Paper Label, 15 In.	1650.00
Ink, Wood's Black, Cone, Portland, Green Aquamarine, 1840-60, 2 1/2 In.	504.00
Ink, Zieber & Co.'s, Excelsior, 12-Sided, Emerald Green, Pontil, 1845-60, 5 7/8 In.	13200.00
Ink, Zieber & Co.'s, Excelsior, 12-Sided, Green, Pontil, Applied Top, 1845-60, 7 1/2 In. . .	7150.00
Jar, Apothecary Set, Blue & White, Lid, Reverse Painted Labels, 4 1/2 To 10 In., 7 Piece . .	775.00
Jar, Countertop, Ice Cream Cone, Metal Holder & Cover, 14 x 7 In. . . . . *Illus*	605.00
Jar, Cream, Cover, Amber, Lily Pad, Hollow Ball Finial, 5 3/4 In.	825.00
Jar, Red Amber, Squat, Flared Rim, 5 1/4 In.	140.00
Jar, Storage, Hand Blown, 2 Applied Rings, Pontil, 1800s, 10 x 6 1/2 In.	52.00
Jar, Storage, Kick-Up Base, Pontil, Tin Lid, 11 1/2 x 6 1/2 In.	150.00
Jar, Storage, Olive Green, Flared Rim, 11 3/4 In.	80.00
Jar, Storage, Olive Yellow, Outward Rolled Mouth, Pontil Scar, 6 x 3 1/4 In.	650.00
Jar, Storage, Olive Yellow, Rolled Mouth, Pontil, 14 In.	670.00
Jar, Storage, Olive Yellow, Tooled Collared Mouth, Pontil, 3-Mold, 8 1/4 In.	130.00
Jar, Storage, Yellow Amber, Applied Tooled Collar Mouth, 1860-70, 8 1/2 In.	700.00
Jar, Tobacco, S. Kimball & Co., 8-Sided, Yellow Amber, Ground Lip, Screw Cap, 7 In. . . .	70.00
Jar, Water, Pillar Mold, 8 Ribs, Shaped Handle, 8 1/2 In.	470.00
Jug, Bellarmine, Brown Salt Glaze, Bearded Face, Cartouches, Coat Of Arms, 11 1/4 In. . .	245.00
Jug, Hounds & Horseman, Stag, Windmill, Silver Rim, Cherubs, Salt Glaze, c.1775, 6 In. .	695.00
Jug, Lord Nelson Bust, Tan, Salt Glaze, Handle, Eagle's Head, 3 In.	154.00
Medicine, Apothecary, Coptis Trifolia., Applied Label, Tin Lid, 10 x 6 1/2 In.	297.00
Medicine, Apothecary, Crocus Sat., Fluted Shoulder, Base Recessed Lug, 10 1/2 In.	253.00
Medicine, Apothecary, Green Stopper, Metal Stand, 9 x 4 In.	60.00
Medicine, Apothecary, Green Stopper, Stacking, 13 In.	110.00
Medicine, Apothecary, Hancocks Lozenges, Glass Label, Blown Stopper, Pontil, 10 In. . . .	275.00
Medicine, Apothecary, Liq: Morph: Hyd:, Green, Ribs, Recessed Lug, Stopper, 7 In.	165.00
Medicine, Apothecary, P. Ipec. Et OpII, Recessed Lug, Salt Mouth, Stopper, 8 In.	175.00
Medicine, Apothecary, Pot. Bichr., Applied Gold Label, Tin Lid, Pontil, 11 1/2 x 5 1/2 In. .	220.00

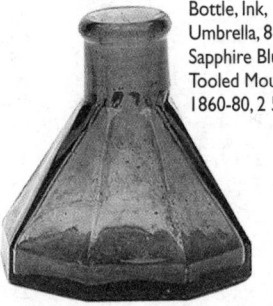

Bottle, Ink,
Umbrella, 8-Sided,
Sapphire Blue,
Tooled Mouth,
1860-80, 2 5/8 In.

Bottle, Jar,
Countertop, Ice
Cream Cone,
Metal Holder &
Cover, 14 x 7 In.

Bottle, Pickle,
Cathedral, 6-Sided,
Apple Green,
Rolled Collar
Mouth, 1860-90,
13 In.

Medicine, Apothecary, Pot. E Sod. Tart, Fluted Shoulder, Base Recessed Lug, 12 1/2 In. . . . 220.00
Medicine, Apothecary, South Carolina, Palm Tree, Amber, Strap Side, c.1895, 1/2 Pt. 955.00
Medicine, Apothecary, South Carolina, Palm Tree, Blue Aqua, Strap Side, Pt. 400.00
Medicine, Apothecary, South Carolina, Palm Tree, C.G. Co., 9 1/4 In. 625.00
Medicine, Apothecary, Syr Limonis, Cobalt Blue, Enamel Shield, Pontil Base, Stopper, 9 In. 210.00
Medicine, Apothecary, Syr: Codeinae, Recessed Lug, Stopper, 9 In. 50.00
Medicine, Apothecary, Tr. Bellad., Amber, Recessed Lug, Veneno, Label, Stopper, 10 In. . . 104.00
Medicine, Apothecary, Tr. Guaiac., Fluted Shoulder, Base Recessed Lug, 8 3/4 In. 198.00
Medicine, Apothecary, Ward & McClelland, Open Pontil, Memphis 425.00
Medicine, Apothecary, Yellow Stopper, 4 Sections, Stacking, Owens-Illinois Mfg., 25 In. . . 330.00
Medicine, Bromo-Kola For Headaches, Clear, Tooled, Ground Lip, Stopper, 7 1/2 In. 134.00
Medicine, Bucklen's Arnica Salve, Clear, Tooled, Ground Lip, Glass Stopper, 10 1/8 In. . . . 280.00
Medicine, Burnett's Cocoaine, Green, c.1860, 7 In. 120.00
Medicine, Carter's Spanish Mixture, Forest Green, Applied Mouth, Ring, Pontil, 8 In. 1456.00
Medicine, Citrate Of Magnesia, Cobalt Blue, Applied Double Collar, 7 1/4 In. 258.00
Medicine, Dent's Desterine, Dog Heads, Contents, Box, Newburgh, N.Y., 4 1/2 In. 232.00
Medicine, Dr. A.C. Daniels Pileozion Wonderworker, 12-Sided, Contents, Box, 5 In. 302.00
Medicine, Dr. Daniels Veterinary Colic Drops, Pamphlet, Box, 3 1/4 In., Pair 55.00
Medicine, Dr. Hobson's Spavin Remedy, Pfeifer Chemical Co., Aqua, Contents, Box, 8 In. 176.00
Medicine, Dr. Kilmer's Female Remedy, Binghamton, N.Y., Aqua, 8 1/2 In. 119.00
Medicine, Dr. King's New Life Pills, Clear, Label Under Glass, Stopper, 13 1/4 In. 448.00
Medicine, Dr. M.M. Fenner's Peoples Remedies, Kidney, Backache Cure, Amber, 10 In. . . 69.00
Medicine, Dr. Swett's Panacea, Olive Amber, Yellow Tone, Sloping Collar, Pontil, 8 In. . . . 13440.00
Medicine, G.W. Merchant Chemist, Lockport, N.Y., Teal Blue, Green, Rectangular 39.00
Medicine, Good Samaritan Ointment Pot, White Glaze, Black Transfer, 1 1/2 In. 777.00
Medicine, Gordon's Hoof Ointment, Hoof Shape, July 20th, 1880, Screw Cap, 5 1/2 In. . . . 650.00
Medicine, H.H. Warner & Co., Tippecanoe, Yellow Amber, Doughnut Mouth, 9 1/8 In. 364.00
Medicine, H.H., The Celebrated Horse Medicine, 1868, Aqua, Paper Label, 7 1/8 In. 580.00
Medicine, Handyside's Consumption Cure, Olive Green, Hexagonal Neck, 11 In. 2251.00
Medicine, Humphrey's Medicine Co., Embossed Horse Head, Square, 4 1/2 x 2 3/4 In. 385.00
Medicine, M.B. Robert's Vegetable, Emerald Green, Open Pontil, Applied Collar, 5 1/2 In. 280.00
Medicine, Mackay's Hoof Ointment, Horse Hoof Shape, Aquamarine, Tooled Lip, 5 In. . . . 800.00
Medicine, Myers Rock Rose, New Haven, Aquamarine, Sloping Collar, 1840-60 . . . . 475.00
Medicine, Poor Man's Friend Ointment Pot, Blue Transfer, White Glaze, 1 1/4 In. 82.00
Medicine, Poor Man's Friend Ointment Pot, Brown Transfer, White Glaze, 1/1/4 In. 225.00
Medicine, Scott & Stewart Syrup, New York, Blue Green, 1845-60, 9 1/2 x 3 1/2 In. 3360.00
Medicine, Sniteman's X-Ray Liniment, Great Horse, Cattle Remedy, Contents, Box, 12 In. 132.00
Medicine, Standard Colic Remedy, Horse Head, Standard Stock Food Co., Omaha, 8 In. . . 252.00
Medicine, Tippers Animal Medicines, Embossed, Brown, Tapered Cylinder, 11 In. 39.00
Medicine, True Daffy's Elixir, Dicey & Co., Aqua, Church Yard, London, 4 3/4 In. 666.00
Medicine, U.S. Army, Medical Department, Caduceus Symbol, Ironstone Plate, 7 1/4 In. . . 17.00
Medicine, Warner's Diabetes Cure, Olive Green, Embossed, 9 1/4 In. 757.00
Medicine, Warner's Safe Cure, Amber, Embossed, London, 9 1/4 In. 23.00
Medicine, Warner's Safe Cure, London, Toronto, Rochester 79.00
Medicine, Warner's Safe Cure, Olive Green, Embossed, London, 9 1/4 In. 92.00
Medicine, Warner's Safe Cure, Red Amber, Embossed, 2 Pt., 11 1/4 In. 1329.00
Medicine, Warner's Safe Cure, Red Amber, Embossed, London, 9 1/2 In. 20.00
Medicine, Warner's Safe Diabetes Cure, Embossed, Olive Green, London, 9 1/4 In. 862.00
Medicine, Warner's Safe Kidney & Liver Cure, Rochester, N.Y., Golden Yellow, Amber . . . 39.00
Medicine, Warner's Safe Nervine, Amber, Embossed, London, 7 1/4 In. 33.00
Medicine, Warner's Safe Nervine, Amber, Embossed, London, 9 1/2 In. 69.00
Medicine, Warner's Safe Nervine, Red Amber, Embossed, London, 7 1/4 In. 59.00
Medicine, Warner's Safe Rheumatic Cure, Amber, Embossed, London, 9 1/2 In. 69.00
Medicine, Watkins Cough Syrup, For Coughs From Colds, 6 1/4 In. 10.00
Milk, Absolutely Pure Milk Protector, Man Milking Cow, c.1885, Pt. 784.00
Milk, Annie Oakley, Gail Harris Rearing On Horse, Pt 22.00
Milk, Augusta Dairies, Staunton, Va., 3 Children Playing In Yard, ACL, Qt. 25.00
Milk, Bartholomay Co. Inc., Rochester, N.Y., Raised Print, Cream Top, 1925, Qt. 55.00
Milk, Blake's Dairy, Heart Trademark, Sacramento, Square, Pt. 10.00
Milk, Borden's, Medium Amber, Ribbed, Embossed, Round, Qt. 2200.00
Milk, Common Sense Milk Jar, Embossed, Round, Thatcher Mfg. Co., Qt. 130.00
Milk, Creamer, Absolutely Pure Milk Protector, Clear, Cylindrical, Lid, Brass Bail 700.00
Milk, Excelsior, Chas. F. Rothenhoefer, Frederick, Md., Embossed, Pt. 25.00

Milk, Freeze & Rissler Dairy, Health & Wealth, Our Milk Is Health, Red Paint, Qt. 18.00
Milk, Gitt's Dairy, Stork Carrying Diapered Baby, Listen Pa!, Paper Cap, 9 1/2 In. 40.00
Milk, Graham Bros. Dairy, Lincoln, Nebr., 1/2 Pt., 6 3/4 In. 14.00
Milk, Lester, Patent Jan. 29, 1878 . . . .   5100.00
Milk, Liberty Dairy, Shillinton, Pa., Raised Letters, Pt., 7 1/2 In. 30.00
Milk, Szeo's Dairy, Bethlehem, Pa., Applied Color Label, Squat, 1/2 Pt. 11.00
Milk, Thatcher's Dairy, Man Milking Cow, Absolutely Pure, Porcelain Top, Embossed, Qt.   25.00
Milk, Uservo Inc., 1/2 Pt., 5 1/2 x 2 1/2 In. 7.00
Milk, Woolman's Buttermilk, Amber, Embossed, Keep Cold In Slug Plate, Qt. 80.00
Mineral Water, A. Hain & Son, Emerald Green, Squat, Iron Pontil, c.1850, 7 In. 935.00
Mineral Water, Buffum & Co., Cobalt Blue, Tenpin Shape, 1860-70, 8 In. 1320.00
Mineral Water, Buffum's, Sarsaparilla & Lemon, Sapphire Blue, 10-Sided, Pontil, 8 In. . . .   935.00
Mineral Water, Caledonia Spring, Wheelock, Vt., Amber, 1860-80, Qt. 694.00
Mineral Water, Chislehurst, Rylands, Barnsley, Aqua, Codd Hamilton Hybrid, 10 In. 69.00
Mineral Water, Clark & White Co., Olive Amber, Pt. 59.00
Mineral Water, Coldbrook Medicinal Spring Water, Yellow Amber, 1860-80, Qt. 560.00
Mineral Water, Congress & Empire Spring Co., Emerald Green, Tapered Shoulder, Qt. . . .   69.00
Mineral Water, Congress & Empire Spring Co., Green, Pt. 48.00
Mineral Water, Congress & Empire Spring Co., Teal Blue, Green, Qt. 79.00
Mineral Water, Congress, Yellow Olive, Sloping Collar, Cylindrical, 1850s-60s, Qt. 448.00
Mineral Water, E. McIntire, Patent, Green, Iron Pontil, Tapered Top, 1840s-50s, 6 7/8 In. .   1430.00
Mineral Water, G.A. Kohl, Blue Green Pony, Pontil, Blob Top, 1850-60, 7 3/8 In. 330.00
Mineral Water, G.A. Kohl, Easton, Pa., Green, Squat, Iron Pontil, Double Taper Top, 7 In.   495.00
Mineral Water, G.H. Goundie, Allentown, Pa., Yellow Green, Squat, Blob Top, 6 3/4 In. . .   165.00
Mineral Water, Geo. W. Felix, Cobalt Blue, Squat, 1850-60, 7 1/4 In. 2200.00
Mineral Water, High Rock Congress Spring, C&W, Teal Blue, Sloping Collar, c.1870, Pt. .   1064.00
Mineral Water, Iodine Spring Water, Olive Golden Amber, Sloping Collar Mouth, Qt. 2100.00
Mineral Water, J. Corwell, Germantown, Yellow Green, Pontil, Double Taper Top, 7 In. . .   825.00
Mineral Water, J. Marbacher, Easton, Pa., Green, Squat, Pontil, 1840-50, 6 3/4 In. 660.00
Mineral Water, J. Marbacher, Easton, Pa., Yellow Green, Squat, 6 1/4 In. 660.00
Mineral Water, J. Steel, Easton, Pa., Green, Squat, Embossed, Pontil, 1840-60, 7 1/4 In. . .   275.00
Mineral Water, J. Steel, Easton, Pa., Yellow Green, Squat, Embossed, Blob Top, 6 7/8 In. .   275.00
Mineral Water, J. Wise, Allentown, Pa., Violet Cobalt, Applied Top, 1870-80, 7 1/4 In. . . .   253.00
Mineral Water, J.& A. Dearborn, New York, Cobalt Blue, 8-Sided, Pontil, Blob Top, 7 In. .   880.00
Mineral Water, John Clarke, Forest Green, Sloping Collar Mouth, 1860-70, Qt. 560.00
Mineral Water, Kissengen, The Spa, Phila., Yellow Olive, 1/2 Pt. 269.00
Mineral Water, Knauss & Lichtenwallner, Sapphire, Blob Top, 1870s-80s, 6 7/8 In. 523.00
Mineral Water, Lynch & Clarke, New York, Yellow Olive, Cylindrical, 1823-33, Qt. 1456.00
Mineral Water, Netherwood & Shaws, Aqua, Embossed, 8 1/2 In.   1443.00
Mineral Water, Poland Spring, Oriental Man, Amber, H. Ricker & Sons, c.1875, 11 In. . . .   2560.00
Mineral Water, Pope, Staplehurst, Crown, Doulton Lambeth, 6 3/4 In. 117.00
Mineral Water, Silver Spring, Barrett & Elers Patent, Codd, Internal Screw, 9 1/4 In. 470.00
Mineral Water, Smith Spencer Limited, Prize Medal, Stratford On Avon, Siphon, 13 In. . . .   53.00
Mineral Water, T.W. Gillett, 8-Sided, Teal, Blob Top, Whittle, 1840-60, 7 1/4 In. 935.00
Mineral Water, W. Heiss Jr., Cobalt Blue, Pontil, Blob Top, 1840-60, 7 1/4 In. 4400.00
Nursing, Baby Feeder, Ceramic, Blue, White Flowers, 7 1/2 In. 573.00
Nursing, Baby Feeder, Ceramic, Blue, White Transfer, Cows, Farmhouse, Trees, 6 1/4 In. .   737.00
Nursing, Baby Feeder, Ceramic, Blue, White, Flowers, Birds, Fruit, 7 1/4 In. 512.00
Nursing, Baby Feeder, Ceramic, White Glaze, Brown Transfer, Oriental Scenes, 6 3/4 In. . .   737.00
Pepper Sauce, Cathedral, 4-Sided, Blue, Aqua, Applied Double Ring, 9 3/4 x 2 3/8 In. . . .   242.00
Pepper Sauce, Tapered Body, Vertical Ribs, Cobalt Blue, England, 7 1/2 In. 255.00
Perfume bottles are listed in their own category.
Pickle, 6-Sided, Green, Outward-Rolled Mouth, Pontil, 1845-60, 13 1/4 In. 532.00
Pickle, Bunker Hill, Lighthouse, Citron, Tooled Mouth, Shilton Foote & Co., 11 In. 3080.00
Pickle, Cathedral, 4-Sided, Blue Green, Rolled Mouth, Iron Pontil, 11 1/2 In. 1008.00
Pickle, Cathedral, 4-Sided, Green, Willington Glass Works, 1860-70, 11 3/4 In. 1232.00
Pickle, Cathedral, 4-Sided, Medium Green, Outward-Rolled Mouth, 1860-80, 11 3/8 In. . .   1120.00
Pickle, Cathedral, 6-Sided, Apple Green, Rolled Collar Mouth, 1860-90, 13 In. . . . . . . *Illus*   616.00
Pickle, Cathedral, 6-Sided, Yarnall Bros., Aquamarine, Applied Collar, c.1870, 13 1/4 In. . .   364.00
Pickle, Cathedral, Blue Aqua, Smooth Base, Rolled Lip, 1860-80, 11 1/2 In. 140.00
Pickle, Cathedral, Green, Applied Lip, 9 1/8 x 2 7/8 In. 523.00
Pickle, Cathedral, Green, Applied Lip, Impressed Character, 1860-80, 11 1/2 In. 413.00
Pickle, Cloverleaf, Olive Amber, Stoddard Glass House, 1860-70, 8 In. 1064.00

Bottle, Poison, Mercury
Oxycyanide, Max
Wocher & Son, Coffin,
Tooled Mouth, 5 In.

Bottle, Sarsaparilla,
Old Dr. J. Townsends,
Light Green, Collar,
Iron Pontil, 9 1/2 In.

Bottle, Sarsaparilla,
Wynkoop's, Sapphire
Blue, Sloped Collar
Mouth, Pontil, 13 In.

Bottle, Scent,
Porcelain, Pineapple Shape,
Gold, Green,
Jacob Petit, 8 In.

Pickle, Cloverleaf, Yellow Amber, Red Tone, Octofoil, Outward-Rolled Mouth, 7 3/4 In. . . 1568.00
Poison, Coffin, Cobalt Blue, Embossed Shield, 1871, 6 1/4 In. 2046.00
Poison, Cyona, Cobalt Blue, Man & Horse, Rectangular, Vertical Ribs, 6 In. 614.00
Poison, Embossed Poisonous, Not To Be Taken, Emerald Green, Raised Dots, 10 1/2 In. . . 532.00
Poison, Fureine Weinflasche, Fureine Literflasche, Olive, Vertical Ribs, Germany, 6 In. . . . 78.00
Poison, Martin, Aqua, Embossed, 7 In. 246.00
Poison, Mercury Oxycyanide, Max Wocher & Son, Coffin, Tooled Mouth, 5 In. . . . . . *Illus* 1120.00
Poison, My-T-Fine, Triangular, Brown, Lucknow Mfg Co., Flemington, 11 1/4 In. 98.00
Poison, Neuraline, Green, Octagonal, Embossed, 1 1/2 In. 450.00
Poison, Property Of Norris Agencies, Brisbane, Brown, Square, Australia, 7 In. 49.00
Poison, Skull, Cobalt Blue, 4 1/4 In. 5225.00
Sarsaparilla, Dr. Guysott's Compound, Aquamarine, Applied Mouth, Pontil, Square, 9 In. . 1232.00
Sarsaparilla, Dr. Guysott's Extract, Blue, Green, Beveled Corners, Square, 8 7/8 In. 2016.00
Sarsaparilla, Dr. Townsend's, Albany, N.Y., Green, Applied Mouth, Pontil, Square, 10 In. . 616.00
Sarsaparilla, Dr. Townsend's, Albany, N.Y., Olive Yellow, Applied Mouth, Pontil, 9 1/4 In. 448.00
Sarsaparilla, Dr. Townsend's, Blue Green, Beveled Corners, Applied Mouth, 9 3/4 In. 616.00
Sarsaparilla, Old Dr. J. Townsend's, Light Green, Collar, Iron Pontil, 9 1/2 In. . . . . . . *Illus* 179.00
Sarsaparilla, Old Dr. Townsend's, New York, Emerald Green, Sloping Top, 9 5/8 In. 1540.00
Sarsaparilla, Wynkoop's, Sapphire Blue, Sloped Collar Mouth, Pontil, 13 In. . . . . *Illus* 43680.00
Scent, 24 Ribs, Teal Blue, Flattened, Tapered, Egg Shape, 2 7/8 In. 176.00
Scent, 26 Ribs, Yellow Amber, Flattened, Tapered, Egg Shape, 3 In. 165.00
Scent, Amethyst, 26 Ribs, Swirled To Right, Egg Shape, Flattened, Tapered, Pontil, 3 In. . . 176.00
Scent, Cameo, Cranberry Cut To Green Flowers, Gilt Metal, Continental, 5 In. 179.00
Scent, Dolphin Shape, Clear, Opaque White Stripes, Cobalt Blue Rigaree, 1 3/4 In. 77.00
Scent, Feathers, Fern, Teal Green, Inward-Rolled Mouth, Pontil, Oval, 2 3/8 In. 2016.00
Scent, Fern, Stopper, Green Ground, Galle, 4 In. 900.00
Scent, Green, Amber, Rose, Lilac, Green Gold, Cobalt Blue Stopper, Signed, Galle, 3 In. . . 5750.00
Scent, Malachite, Molded Rose Garden, Medallions, K. Schlevogt, 6 1/2 In. 316.00
Scent, Opalescent Milk Glass, Screw Cap, 2 1/2 In. 112.00
Scent, Peacock Green, 20 Ribs, Swirled To Right, Egg Shape, Flattened, Pontil, 2 1/4 In. . . 264.00
Scent, Porcelain, Pineapple Shape, Gold, Green, Jacob Petit, 8 In. . . . . *Illus* 1610.00
Scent, Ruby Glass, Silver, Double, Cylindrical, Cover, 4 1/8 In. 176.00
Scent, Sapphire Shaded To Cobalt Blue, Shield Shape, Sunburst, 2 3/4 In. 495.00
Scent, Vertical Optic Rib, Mold Blown, Montgolfier Stopper, Galle, 6 In. 520.00
Seltzer, H. Allison Lincoln, Teal, Dispenser, Embossed, British Syphon Co., 11 In. 94.00
Seltzer, Jacobson Beverages, Lakewood, N.J., 8-Sided, Green 45.00
Seltzer, Johnson & Mason, Plated Metal Tap, Blue, Siphon, Coventry, England, 13 In. 43.00
Seltzer, Soda Latuna 99 Gomez, Balbuena Bonfiglio, Ruby Red 79.00
Seltzer, Soda, Obeal Cuidadela, Pink Amethyst, Argentina 69.00

Snuff, Agate, Cameo, Dragon, Lion, Oval, Floater, Agate Stopper 575.00
Snuff, Agate, Cameo, Rats, Oval, Agate Stopper, 2 1/4 In. 207.00
Snuff, Agate, Carnelian, Beans, Vines, Flowers, Melon Shape, Stopper, 2 3/4 In. 288.00
Snuff, Agate, Chalcedony, Oval, Cream, Tan, Stone Stopper, 2 In. 35.00
Snuff, Agate, Chalcedony, Tan, Coral Stopper, 2 3/4 In. 150.00
Snuff, Agate, Chalcedony, Teardrop, Jade Stopper, 2 1/2 In. 288.00
Snuff, Agate, Chalcedony, White Horse, Gray Body, Oval, Stone Stopper, 2 1/2 In. 748.00
Snuff, Agate, Honey, Chinese Coins, Pilgrim Flask, Jadeite Stopper, 2 In. 230.00
Snuff, Agate, Honey, Flattened Oval, Green Glass Stopper, 2 In. 127.00
Snuff, Agate, Honey, Mask, Mock Ring Handles, Green Glass Stopper, Oval, 3 In. 345.00
Snuff, Agate, Honey, Sage, Deer, Peach Tree, Rectangular, Jadeite Stopper, 2 1/4 In. 259.00
Snuff, Agate, Macaroni, Mask, Ring Handles, Brown, Beige, Tan, Coral Stopper, 2 In. 460.00
Snuff, Agate, Man Watering Tree, Relief, Oval, Coral Stopper, 2 In. 920.00
Snuff, Amber, Mask, Landscape, Mock Ring Handles, Oval, Rose Quartz Stopper, 3 In. ... 374.00
Snuff, Amber, Sage In A Garden, Flask Shape, Green Hardstone Stopper, 2 1/2 In. 176.00
Snuff, Amber, Sages, Figures, Landscape, Mock Ring Handles, Tourmaline Stopper, 2 In. . 1725.00
Snuff, Bamboo, Buddha's Hand Fruit, Leaves, Blossoms, c.1800, 2 1/2 In. 1150.00
Snuff, Chloromelanite, Flowering Tree, Pear Shape, Stone Stopper, 1 1/2 In. 58.00
Snuff, Coconut Shell, Calligraphy, Oval, Coral Stopper, 2 1/2 In. 920.00
Snuff, Coral, Bird, Peony, Relief, Temple Jar, Mother-Of-Pearl Stopper, 2 1/2 In. 920.00
Snuff, Coral, Phoenix, Dragon, Pink, Temple Jar, Stopper, 2 1/2 In. 3450.00
Snuff, Glass, Aventurine, Black Ground, Oval, Coral Stopper, 2 1/2 In. 115.00
Snuff, Glass, Blue, Oval, Lacquered Stopper, 2 3/4 In. 40.00
Snuff, Glass, Forest Green, Sheared Mouth, Pontil Scar, Rectangular, 1800-30, 5 1/8 In. ... 896.00
Snuff, Glass, Olive Yellow, Rectangular, Beveled Corners, 1860-70, 9 1/2 In. 672.00
Snuff, Glass, Olive Yellow, Square, Sheared Flared Mouth, Pontil, Square, 5 x 2 3/8 In. ... 375.00
Snuff, Glass, Overlay, Bat & Shou, Coral Stopper, 2 3/4 In. 115.00
Snuff, Glass, Overlay, Bird, Flowering Tree, Figural Landscape, Glass Stopper, 3 3/4 In. .. 40.00
Snuff, Glass, Overlay, Buddhist Symbols, 7 Colors, Agate Stopper, 2 1/2 In. 1035.00
Snuff, Glass, Overlay, Carp, Lotus, Multicolored, Pear Shape, Coral Stopper, 2 1/2 In. 2185.00
Snuff, Glass, Overlay, Figures, Landscape, Opalescent, Oval, Carnelian Stopper, 2 1/4 In. . 401.00
Snuff, Glass, Overlay, Grasshopper, Snowflake Ground, Green Glass Stopper, 2 1/2 In. ... 575.00
Snuff, Glass, Overlay, Green Frog, Lotus, Opalescent Ground, Green Stopper, 2 3/4 In. ... 1725.00
Snuff, Glass, Overlay, Green, Red Fruit, Peachbloom Ground, Agate Stopper, 2 In. 1495.00
Snuff, Glass, Overlay, Herd Boy, Water Buffalo, Bat Handles, Malachite Stopper, 2 1/4 In. . 316.00
Snuff, Glass, Overlay, Red Carp On Snowflake Ground, Tiger's-Eye Stopper, 2 1/2 In. 1150.00
Snuff, Glass, Overlay, Red Dragon, Opalescent Ground, Rose Quartz Stopper, 3 1/4 In. ... 173.00
Snuff, Glass, Overlay, Red Fish Dragon, Snowflake Ground, Rose Quartz Stopper, 3 In. ... 230.00
Snuff, Glass, Overlay, Stylized Dragon, Blue Ground, Coral Stopper, 2 1/2 In. 288.00
Snuff, Glass, Overlay, Vases, Fruit, Flowers, Fish, Milk White, Jade Stopper, 2 1/2 In. 374.00
Snuff, Glass, Overlay, Zodiac Animals, Snowflake Ground, Green Glass Stopper, 2 1/4 In. . 316.00
Snuff, Glass, Ruby, Faceted, Spade Shape, Jadeite Stopper, 2 In. 3105.00
Snuff, Glass, Rust, Red Ribbons, Clear Body, Flattened Oval, Stained Stopper, 2 1/2 In. ... 316.00
Snuff, Glass, Sapphire Blue, Gourds, Vines, Coral Stopper, 2 1/4 In. 403.00
Snuff, Glass, Splash, Pink, Blue, White, Spade Shape, Stained Red Stopper, 2 1/2 In. 575.00
Snuff, Glass, Square Beveled Corners, Sheared, Flared Mouth, Pontil Scar, 4 3/4 x 3 In. ... 350.00
Snuff, Glass, Tobacco Amber, Tooled Lip, Open Pontil, 1800-30, 4 3/8 In. 72.00
Snuff, Glass, Yellow Green, Tooled Flared-Out Lip, Open Pontil, Square, 1800-30, 4 In. ... 199.00
Snuff, Glass, Yellow, Green, Olive Tone, Flared Mouth, Pontil, 3 3/4 In. 504.00
Snuff, Ivory, Ladybug, 2 Ears Of Corn, Multicolored, Stopper, 2 1/2 In. 1610.00
Snuff, Ivory, Sage, Youth, Crane, Pine Tree, Oval, Stopper, 3 In. 69.00
Snuff, Jade, Brown, Oval, Green Glass Stopper, 2 1/4 In. 207.00
Snuff, Jade, Carved, Chinese Scholars, Prunus Branches, Flying Crane, Ivory Spoon, 3 In. . 956.00
Snuff, Jade, White, Brocade Ribbon, Flattened Oval, Jadeite Stopper, 2 1/2 In. 546.00
Snuff, Jade, White, Carp, Flattened Oval, Glass Stopper, 3 In. 805.00
Snuff, Jade, White, Chih Lung, Dragons, Jadeite Stopper, 2 1/2 In. 2070.00
Snuff, Jade, White, Spade Shape, Rose Quartz Stopper, 2 In. 69.00
Snuff, Jade, Yellow, Medallion, Key Fret Border, Round, Coral Stopper, Stand, 2 1/4 In. ... 9775.00
Snuff, Jadeite, Green, Lavender, Spade Shape, Rose Quartz Stopper, 2 In. 575.00
Snuff, Jadeite, Green, White, Purse Form, Green Glass Stopper, 1 3/4 In. 403.00
Snuff, Jasper, Lion Head Epaulets, Coral Stopper, Flask Shape, 19th Century, 2 1/2 In. 147.00
Snuff, Jasper, Red, Tan, Brown, Oval, Green Jadeite Stopper, 2 1/4 In. 403.00
Snuff, Jasper, Rose Quartz Stopper, 2 In. 115.00

Snuff, Milk Glass, Bat, Cloud, 4 Characters, Red Enamel, Rose Quartz Stopper, 2 3/8 In. ... 374.00
Snuff, Nephrite, Brown Skin, Leaf Carved, Coral Stoppers, Double Gourd, 3 In. 756.00
Snuff, Porcelain, Bird, Flower, 4 Characters, Spade Shape, Glass Stopper, 2 In. 161.00
Snuff, Porcelain, Bird, Prunus, Ring Handles, Oval, Coral Stopper, 2 1/2 In. 115.00
Snuff, Porcelain, Blue, Landscape, Fisherman, Cottage, Mountains, Coral Stopper, 3 In. ... 40.00
Snuff, Porcelain, Chrysanthemum, Teardrop, Ivory Stopper, 2 1/4 In. 81.00
Snuff, Porcelain, Dragons, Phoenix, Exotic Animals, 4 Characters, Jade Stopper, 2 3/4 In. . 575.00
Snuff, Porcelain, Ear Of Corn, Yellow Glaze, Rose Quartz Stopper, 2 3/4 In. 115.00
Snuff, Porcelain, Figural Landscape, Multicolored, Oval, Stone Stopper, 2 1/2 In. 207.00
Snuff, Porcelain, Figural, Blue & White, Green Stone Stopper, 2 1/2 In. 52.00
Snuff, Porcelain, Goddesses Riding Elephant, Foo Dog, Tiger's-Eye Stopper, 2 1/4 In. 29.00
Snuff, Porcelain, Goose, Lotus, Green Glaze, Cylinder, Green Stone Stopper, 3 In. 184.00
Snuff, Porcelain, Grasshopper, Cafe-Au-Lait Ground, Cylindrical, Coral Stopper, 2 3/4 In. . 195.00
Snuff, Porcelain, Horsemen, Cylindrical, Jadeite Stopper, 3 3/4 In. 127.00
Snuff, Porcelain, Mythological Figures, Calligraphy, Double Gourd, Stopper, 2 1/4 In. 1150.00
Snuff, Porcelain, Painted, Boys, Chickens, Flask Shape, Amethyst Stopper, 2 1/2 In. 302.00
Snuff, Porcelain, Passion Flower, 4 Characters, Gold Ground, Double Gourd, 2 3/4 In. 633.00
Snuff, Porcelain, Passion Flower, Aubergine, Green, Yellow, Ceramic Stopper, 2 In. 81.00
Snuff, Porcelain, Roosters, White Ground, Rust, Red, Teardrop, Green Stone Stopper, 3 In. 173.00
Snuff, Porcelain, Tea Dust Glaze, Teardrop, Malachite Stopper, 2 3/4 In. 115.00
Snuff, Puddingstone, Incised Ring, Silver, Teardrop, Coral Stopper, 2 1/4 In. 2415.00
Soda, Brooklyn, Emerald Green, Siphon, Fluted, Waisted, Acid Etched, 12 1/4 In. 51.00
Soda, C. Matchin, Danville, Cobalt Blue, Squat, Pontil, Tapered Top, 1840-60, 6 7/8 In. ... 4950.00
Soda, C.W. Rider, Green Blue, Embossed Tombstone, Hutchinson 6 1/2 In. 3025.00
Soda, Camwal Table Waters, Etched, Pewter Tap, Siphon, England, 26 1/2 In. 1606.00
Soda, D.J. Whelan, Cobalt Blue, Stopper, Hutchinson, 1880, 6 5/8 In. 3850.00
Soda, Devizes, Green, Acid Etched, Siphon, 12 In. 72.00
Soda, Dr Pepper, Commemorative, Texas vs. Oklahoma Football Game, 1973, 16 Oz. 16.00
Soda, Eagle Soda Works, Aqua, 7 In. 22.00
Soda, F. & L. Schaum Baltimore Glassworks, Olive Yellow, Pontil, Taper Top, 7 1/8 In. ... 1430.00
Soda, Frostie Root Beer, Baltimore 28, Md., 12 Oz., 8 In. 9.00
Soda, Ginger Ale, Albert Vonharten, Savannah, Ga., Teal Blue, Blob, 7 1/8 In. 312.00
Soda, Ginger Ale, Edward Moyle, Savannah, Ga., Amber, Applied Mouth, c.1885, 7 In. ... 317.00
Soda, Ginger Ale, Edward Moyle, Savannah, Ga., Deep Amber, Tooled Mouth, 7 3/8 In. .. 212.00
Soda, Ginger Ale, John Ryan, Excelsior, Savannah, Ga., Amber, 1852, 7 3/8 In. 137.00
Soda, Ginger Ale, John Ryan, Excelsior, Savannah, Ga., Lime Green, 1852, 7 3/8 In. 515.00
Soda, Grape Fruit, Sparkling Drink, Shield, Lion, Stoneware, Blue, Inhoud, 3 Liter ...53.00 to 69.00
Soda, Greenock Apothecaries, Pink, Acid Etched, Metal Tap, Siphon, 6 3/4 In. 409.00
Soda, Grimsby, Blue, Fluted, Acid Etched, Siphon, 12 1/2 In. 82.00
Soda, Gruchy & Mayo's Celebrated Soda Water, Hamilton, Olive Green, 8 1/4 In. 69.00
Soda, Haddock & Son, Olive Yellow, Tenpin Form, Applied Mouth, Pontil, 1/2 Pt., 7 In. .. 1792.00
Soda, Hires Root Beer, Syrup, Reverse Glass Label, Metal Cover, 12 In. 220.00
Soda, Hodgson's Soda Water, Bedford Street, Covent Garden, Hamilton, Aqua, 8 1/2 In. .. 20.00
Soda, J.F. Deegan, Yellow Amber, Embossed, Tombstone Shape, Hutchinson, 6 3/8 In. 1045.00
Soda, J.F. Deegan, Yellow Green, Hutchinson, 1880-90, 6 5/8 In. 1650.00
Soda, J.W. Harris, New Haven, Conn., Sapphire Blue, Applied Mouth, Iron Pontil, 1/2 Pt. . 364.00
Soda, Jewsbury & Brown, Pink, Siphon, Pewter Tap, England, 12 In. 215.00
Soda, Job Wragg, Birmingham & Shirley, Etched, Siphon, Green, England, 11 3/4 In. 33.00
Soda, Koca-Nola, Washington Ave., Hutchinson 575.00
Soda, Mason's Root Beer Brown, 10 Oz. 7.50
Soda, Moxie, Ted Williams, Unopened, 7 Oz. 65.00
Soda, Pacific & Puget Sound, Seattle, Wash., Hutchinson 46.00
Soda, Schweppes, Amber, Porcelain Lined, Plated Metal Tap, Siphon, England, 11 3/4 In. . 39.00
Soda, Seltzogene, Ruby Glass, Pewter Tap, Siphon, Double Globe, 17 In. 327.00
Soda, Somarex Casablanca, Green, Embossed, Siphon, Pewter Metal Tap, England, 12 In. . 23.00
Soda, Sparkling Water, Berlin Bottling, M. Singer & Son, N.J., Green, Siphon, 11 In. 19.00
Soda, Standard Bottling Works, Olive Green, Fluted Panels, Hutchinson, 6 5/8 In. 1045.00
Soda, Superior, Charleston Eagle, Yellow Green, Pontil, 1850-60, 7 1/2 In. 1760.00
Soda, T B. Jones & Co., Cobalt Blue, Iron Pontil, Tapered Top, 1840-50, 7 In. 1870.00
Soda, T. Howarth, Pittston, Pa., Olive Amber, Squat, Embossed, 1840-60, 9 In. 3575.00
Soda, Union Glassworks, Teal Blue, Green, Iron Pontil, Squat, Blob 89.00
Target Ball, Amber, 3-Piece Mold, Cork, Feathers, 3 In. 193.00
Target Ball, Amber, 3-Piece Mold, Hand Blown, 2 1/2 In. 83.00

Target Ball, Amber, Diamond, Rough Sheared Mouth, Germany, 2 5/8 In. 415.00
Target Ball, Amethyst, Man Standing With Gun, Crosshatch Ground, Sheared Lip, 3 In. . . 187.00
Target Ball, Black Amethyst, Diamond, Sheared & Ground Lip, Germany, 2 5/8 In. 395.00
Target Ball, Blue, 3-Piece Mold, 3-Dot Pattern Near Lip 116.00
Target Ball, Bogardus, Basket Weave, Yellow, Patd Aprl 10 1877 . . . . .575.00 to 633.00
Target Ball, Bogardus, Hobnail, Medium Amber, Pat'd Apr 10, 1877, 2 3/4 In. 3000.00
Target Ball, Cobalt Blue, 3-Piece Mold, 3 In. 116.00
Target Ball, Cobalt Blue, Squares, Rough Sheared Lip, Australia, 2 5/8 In. 2330.00
Target Ball, Green, Crisscross Embossing, Sheared Lip, 2 3/4 In. 614.00
Target Ball, Green, Square Pattern, Center Band, Sheared Mouth, France, c.1885, 2 5/8 In. 250.00
Target Ball, Ira Paine's Filled Ball, Medium Yellow Amber, Sheared Mouth, 2 5/8 In. 2010.00
Target Ball, N.B. Glassworks, Basket Weave, Light Green, Perth 575.00
Target Ball, N.B. Glassworks, Diamond, Center Band, Sapphire Blue, 2 5/8 In. 136.00
Target Ball, Pink Amethyst, Diamond, Sheared & Ground Lip, Czechoslovakia, 2 1/2 In. . . 452.00
Target Ball, Yellow Amber, 6 Raised Beads On Shoulder, Sheared Lip, c.1885, 2 3/4 In. . . 190.00
Target Ball, Yellow Green, Diamond, Sheared Lip, Czechoslovakia, 2 1/2 In. 128.00
Vinegar, White House, Crackled, Cabbage Rose Pattern, Handles, Cork Stopper, 9 1/2 In. . 30.00
Whiskey, Backbar, Sunny Brook, Pure Food, Gold Medal, Grand Prize, Bulbous 49.00
Whiskey, Backbar, Yellow, 8 Fluted Panels, Laid-On Neck Ring, Pontil, 11 1/2 In. 579.00
Whiskey, Barley Brew, William Gillies, Glasgow, Jug, 3 Men, At Table, Rear Handle, 7 In. 313.00
Whiskey, Bass & Co., Jug, Pub, White, Red, Black Label, 6 3/4 In. 655.00
Whiskey, Beveridge Bros., Jug, Tan, White, Black Transfer, Stag, Thistles, Handle, 8 In. . . 3193.00
Whiskey, Bouquet, Pure Rye, Flowers, Reverse Painted, Late 1800s, 10 In. 1760.00
Whiskey, Bulloch Lade, Jug, Pub, Mottled Blue Glaze, White, Black, Red Print, 5 In. 327.00
Whiskey, Caspers, Made By Honest North Carolina People, Cobalt Blue, 12 1/4 In. 500.00
Whiskey, Claymore Scotch, Jug, Pub, Blue Top, Black Transfer, Crossed Swords, 5 In. 593.00
Whiskey, Daniel Visser & Zonen Schiedam, Cobalt Blue, Applied Seal, Qt., 11 1/4 In. 79.00
Whiskey, E.D. Brown & Co., Orange Amber, Applied Double Tapered Top, 9 3/4 In. 99.00
Whiskey, E.G. Booz's Old Cabin, Philadelphia, Cottage, Amber, Applied Collar, 7 3/4 In. . 800.00
Whiskey, E.O. Middleton & Bros., Pure Rye, Orange, Amber, Squat, Applied Seal, Qt., 9 In. 159.00
Whiskey, E.P. Middleton Wheat Whiskey, Gold Amber, Squat, Applied Seal, Qt., 9 1/2 In. . 149.00
Whiskey, E.P. Middleton Wheat Whiskey, Red, Puce, Squat, Applied Seal, Qt., 9 In. 249.00
Whiskey, Forty Second, Jug, White Glaze, Tan Neck, Black Transfer, 8 In. 1315.00
Whiskey, George's Beers & Wylds Scotch, Jug, Pub, Red, Horse, Black Handle, 4 1/4 In. . . 900.00
Whiskey, Gilmour Thomson's Royal Stag, White, Brown Glaze, Pottery, Scotland, 8 In. . . . 44.00
Whiskey, Glen Garry, Old Highland Whisky, Port Dundas, Jug, Rear Handle, 8 1/4 In. 39.00
Whiskey, Gordon's London Gin, Jug, Pub, Black Transfer, White, 6 3/4 In. 655.00
Whiskey, Gow's Grand Liqueur, Jug, Pub, Blue, Gray Glaze, Black Transfer, 4 1/2 In. 450.00
Whiskey, Greybeard Heather Dew, Mitchell Bros., Port Dundas, Glasgow, Jug, 7 In. 49.00
Whiskey, Haig & Haig, Jug, Pub, Blue Top, Salt Glaze, Lion & Crown, 5 1/2 In. 450.00
Whiskey, J.F.T. & Co., Orange, Amber, Squat, Applied Seal, Qt., 9 1/2 In. 139.00
Whiskey, J.F.T. & Co., Red, Amber, Black, Squat, Applied Seal, Qt., 9 1/2 In. 149.00
Whiskey, J.F.T. & Co., Yellow, Amber, Squat, Applied Seal, Qt., 9 1/2 In. 159.00
Whiskey, J.T. Gayen Altona, Schnapps, Cannon Shape, Sand Amber, Collar, c.1865, 1/2 Pt. . 896.00
Whiskey, Jeroboam Royal Blend, Port Dundas, Glasgow, Jug, Stag, 7 3/4 In. 157.00
Whiskey, Johnnie Walker, Jug, Pub, White, Green Handle, Rim, 6 1/4 In. 1064.00
Whiskey, Keystone Malt Whiskey, Orange, Amber, Oval, Qt., 10 1/2 In. 69.00
Whiskey, M. & J.S. Perrine, Orange Amber, Squat, Applied Seal, Qt. 89.00
Whiskey, Mt. Vernon Rye, Amber, Double Collar, Embossed, Display, 22 3/4 In. 448.00
Whiskey, Neal's Ambrosia, Cobalt Blue, Applied Mouth, Ring, Cylindrical, Seal, 9 1/4 In. . 3080.00
Whiskey, Netter Bros., Clear, Amethyst, Man In Moon, Indian Queen, Qt., 10 In. 49.00
Whiskey, Netter Bros., Golden Amber, Man In Moon, Indian Queen, Qt., 10 In. 79.00
Whiskey, O.B.L. Scotch, Jug, Pub, White, Red, Black Letters, 5 3/4 In. 409.00
Whiskey, Rothschild Bros., Yellow, Amber, Squat, Applied Seal, 1868, Qt., 9 1/2 In. 169.00
Whiskey, S.A. Wertz, Superior Old Rye, Amber, Tapered Shoulder, Squat, Qt., 10 In. 89.00
Whiskey, S.A. Wertz, Superior Old Rye, Red, Amber, Squat, Applied Seal, 9 1/2 In. 139.00
Whiskey, Sanderson's Liqueur Special, Pure Malt, Jug, Side Handle, Portobello, 8 In. 108.00
Whiskey, Selzer & Miller, Orange, Amber, Squat, Applied Seal, 9 1/2 In. 99.00
Whiskey, Sir Edward Lee's, Jug, Pub, Brown, Tan Salt Glaze, Coat Of Arms, Thistles, 6 In. 1023.00
Whiskey, Snow & Co., Jug, Tan Neck, White Glaze, Black Transfer, 7 1/4 In. 737.00
Whiskey, Star, New York, Amber, Applied Lip, Pouring Spout, 8 In. 750.00
Whiskey, Star, W.B. Crowell, 26 Ribs, Amber, Pontil, Applied Mouth, Handle, 8 In. 420.00
Whiskey, Stoneware, Cream, Brown Glaze, Black Transfer, 10 3/4 In. 112.00

Whiskey, Udolpho Wolfe's Aromatic Schnapps, Aqua, Double Taper Top, Pontil, 8 In. 303.00
Whiskey, Watson's Dundee Whisky, Cream, Dark Brown Glaze, Scotland, c.1900, 9 In. ... 120.00
Whiskey, Watson's, Jug, Pub, Blue Luster Glaze, White, Blue Letters, 5 1/4 In. 655.00
Whiskey, Weeks & Gilson, S. Stoddard, N.H., Olive Amber, 1860s-70s, 12 x 3 1/2 In. 1008.00
Wine, Aqua, Flat Bladder, 3 1/2 In. 164.00
Wine, Brown, Graphite, Pontil, Octagonal, Applied Collar, c.1740-60, 10 In. 552.00
Wine, Mallet, Olive Green, Applied String Rim, Pontil, 6 1/4 In. 369.00
Wine, Olive Green, Champagne Shoulder, Applied Collar, String Rim, Seal, 1789, 10 In. ... 1841.00
Wine, Olive Green, Cylindrical, Applied Collar, 3-Piece Mold, 10 1/4 In. 552.00
Wine, Olive Green, Cylindrical, Seal, Applied Collar, 11 1/2 In. 575.00
Wine, Olive Green, Cylindrical, Squat, Seal, 9 3/4 In. 1841.00
Wine, Onion Mallet, Olive Green, Applied String, 5 3/4 In. 1146.00
Wine, Onion, Olive Green, Applied Double Collar, Engraved Crown, Thistle, 10 1/4 In. 552.00
Wine, Onion, Olive Green, Seal, 1720, 7 3/4 In. 2046.00
Wine, Onion, Olive Green, Stipple Engraved, Collar Lip, Pontil, 8 1/4 In. 617.00
Wine, P.C. Brooks, Olive Amber, Cylindrical, Applied Mouth, Ring, Pontil, c.1820, 9 In. ... 1792.00
Wine, T. Reynolds, Black, Olive Amber, Applied String Lip, Seal, 9 3/4 x 4 3/8 In. 2576.00

BOTTLE CAPS for milk bottles are the printed cardboard caps used
since the 1920s. Crown caps, used after 1892 on soda bottles, are also
popular collectibles. Unusual mottoes, graphics, and caps from bottlers
that are out of business bring the highest prices.

Barq's Orange Soda, Black, Orange, Cork Lining, 1940s 5.50
Bell's Orange Drink, Black, Orange, Cork Lining 4.00
Bireley's Chocolate Flavored Beverage, Yellow, Brown, Cork Lining 3.00
Braun's Orange, Black, Orange, Cork Lining 7.00
Coca-Cola, Tour The World, Complete Set, 1962, 100 Piece 60.00
Donald Duck Orange Soda, Red, Silver, Cork Lining 15.00
Howel's Root Beer, White, Brown, Cork Lining, 1940s 1.00
Jamaica Ginger Ale, Black, Green, Cork Lining 6.00
Locust Lane Jersey Farms, Grade A Milk, Howe, Indiana, Aluminum, 1 1/2 In. 5.00
Lyons Cream Soda, Blue, White, Cork Lining 15.00
Pepsi-Cola, Green, Cork Lining, 1920s 40.00
Ritz Root Beer, Top Hat, Cork Lining 45.00
Spiffy Cola, Boy Licking Lips, Yellow, Cork Lining 65.00
Springbrook Dairy, Baby Drinking Milk, Aluminum, Dial 6721, 1 3/4 In. 4.00
Valley View Root Beer, Red, Yellow, Cork Lining 5.50
Vernor's Ginger Ale, Green, Yellow, Cork Lining, Before 1955 .... .75
Welchade, Purple, Yellow, Cork Lining 6.00

BOTTLE OPENERS are needed to open many bottles. As soon as the
commercial bottle was invented, the opener to be used with the new
types of closures became a necessity. Many types of bottle openers can
be found, most dating from the twentieth century. Collectors prize
advertising and comic openers.

Bald Man's Head, 4 Eyes, Mustache, Cast Iron, Wall Mount, 3 3/4 x 3 1/2 In. 88.00
Ballantine Ale & Beer, Metal, Handy Walden, 3 1/2 In. 5.00
Clown Head, Cast Iron, 4 In. 70.00
Codd Bottle, Wood, Cup Type, Smith & Co., Pure Bourne Waters 35.00
Corkscrew, Man, Bottle In Coat, Scarf, Red Nose, Wood, Carved, Hand Painted, 6 In. 20.00
Famous Hot Wiener Lunch, Fish, Pointing Finger, Steel, Spinner, Pa., 3 1/8 In. ......21.00 to 41.00
Fehr's Beer, Bottle Shape, 4 3/8 x 1 In. 10.00
First State Bank, Your Full Service Bank, Plastic, Metal, White, Blue Letters, 12 In. 2.00
Genesee Beer & 12 Horse Ale, Rochester, N.Y., 5 In. 5.00
H.A. Bortner, Bottler, Leg & High Heel Shoe, Phone 623, Hanover, Pa. 38.00
Nehi Quality Drinks, Female Leg, High Heel Shoe, 3 5/8 In. 27.00
Rheingold Beer, Metal, 3 3/4 In. 5.00
Royal Crown Cola, Better Taste Calls For R.C. 5.00
Schmidt Bottling Co., Bottle, Beer Glass, Hanover, Pa., 1912, 3 1/4 In. 20.00
Shottie's Place, Baseball Pitcher, Littlestown, Pa., c.1914, 3 1/4 In. 65.00
Silver Top Bottling, Woman In Swimsuit, Hanover, Pa., 3 In. 29.00
Snyder Auto Garage, Touring Car, Steel, Hanover, Pa., c.1911, 2 7/8 In. 25.00
Sunshine Extra Light, Premium, Wire Type 6.00

BOX 83 **BOX,** Candle

BOXES of all kinds are collected. They were made of thin strips of inlaid wood, metal, tortoiseshell, embroidery, or other material. Additional boxes may be listed in other sections, such as Advertising, Battersea, Ivory, Shaker, Tinware, and various Porcelain categories. Tea Caddies are listed in their own category.

Agate, Figured, Chased Gilt Brass, Carnelian Ball Feet, Russia, Mid 19th Century, 3 x 5 In. ⋯⋯ 575.00
Art Nouveau, Cover, Citrine, Claw Mount, Chased, Gilded, Gilt Interior, c.1912, 4 In. ⋯⋯ 53775.00
Baleen, 3-Finger, Lifting Lid, Copper Tacks, Checked Pincushion, Oval, 4 1/4 x 2 1/2 In. ⋯⋯ 635.00
Ballot, School District No. 16, Letter Slot Top, Pine, Red Graining, 12 x 19 x 11 In. ⋯⋯ 375.00
Ballot, Walnut, 8 Slide Lid Compartments, East Berlin, Penn., 1892, 4 x 8 x 32 In. ⋯⋯ 2200.00
Band, Bentwood Sides, Stenciled & Freehand Gold Decoration, 19 x 14 x 10 In. ⋯⋯ 750.00
Band, Blue Paint, Nailed Construction, Oval, 4 x 5 x 7 In. ⋯⋯ 2530.00
Band, Hat Shape, Wallpaper, Diamond Grid, Flowers, Blue, Yellow, c.1833, 10 In. ⋯⋯ 1380.00
Band, Hat Shape, Wallpaper, Flowers, Yellow Ground, Mr. Hopkin, N.J., 8 3/4 In. ⋯⋯ 3680.00
Band, Joseph Fleeing From Bed, Genesis, Chapter 39, Painted, Oblong, 7 x 12 x 9 In. ⋯⋯ 1150.00
Band, Pine, Bucher Style, Painted, Black Ground, Flowers, Oval, 5 x 6 x 9 In. ⋯⋯ 15950.00
Band, Wallpaper, Block Print, Flowers, Mark Worthley, Boston, 14 x 11 x 11 In. ⋯⋯ 460.00
Band, Wallpaper, Blue, Orange & Black, Newspaper Lined, Oval, 1827, 14 x 15 In. ⋯⋯ 660.00
Band, Wallpaper, Deaf & Dumb Asylum, New York City, Blue, Oblong, 16 In. ⋯⋯ 1610.00
Band, Wallpaper, Figure, Classical Ruins, Oval, c.1835, 12 1/2 x 20 1/2 In. ⋯⋯ 1645.00
Band, Wallpaper, Flower & Medallion Paper, Oval, c.1815, 5 1/2 x 10 1/2 In. ⋯⋯ 1116.00
Band, Wallpaper, Fruit Bowl, Hannah Davis, N.H., Early 1800s, 12 x 16 In. ⋯⋯ 1645.00
Band, Wallpaper, Green, Yellow Block Printed Paper, Courtyard On Lid, Oval, 3 x 1 In. ⋯⋯ 345.00
Band, Wallpaper, House, Man, Waterfall, Blue Ground, Rounded Corners, 11 x 14 x 18 In. 825.00
Band, Wallpaper, Hunting Scene, Cream, Green, Blue, Newspaper Lined, 11 x 14 x 18 In. ⋯ 715.00
Band, Wallpaper, Marble & Moss, Paper Label William Campbell, Worcester, 9 x 6 In. ⋯⋯ 430.00
Band, Wallpaper, Pink Ground, Flowers, German Newsletter Lined, Round, 2 x 3 In. ⋯⋯ 1650.00
Band, Wallpaper, Pink Ground, Flowers, Newspaper Lined, 1 1/2 x 3 x 4 In. ⋯⋯ 715.00
Band, Wallpaper, Poplar, Dome Top, Lancaster County, Penn., 8 x 5 x 5 5/8 In. ⋯⋯ 750.00
Band, Wallpaper, Printed Designs, Tan Ground, Oval, 14 x 11 1/2 x 10 In. ⋯⋯ 230.00
Band, Wallpaper, Salmon, Green, Round, c.1850, 2 1/4 x 1 3/4 In. ⋯⋯ 375.00
Band, Wallpaper, Sewing, Round, 9 Paneled Sides, Marked To Mother Ellin, 5 1/2 x 6 In. ⋯ 1870.00
Band, Wallpaper, Soldier, Historic, France, Deedham, Mass., c.1835, 12 x 7 x 3 In. ⋯⋯ 920.00
Band, Wallpaper, Turks, Flowers, Early 1800s, 11 5/8 x 18 1/4 In. ⋯⋯ 880.00
Band, Wallpaper, Yellow Ground, Pink, Black Flower, Round, 3 1/2 x 4 3/4 In. ⋯⋯ 415.00
Bentwood, 1-Finger, Sponged Paint, Cover, Pencil Label, Lath Ticket Box, Oval, 5 1/2 In. 400.00
Bentwood, Blue Paint, Laced, Seams, Black, Red Leaves, Oval, c.1836, 22 x 13 x 8 In. ⋯ 690.00
Bentwood, Green Paint, Laced Seams, Oval, 17 3/8 x 9 3/4 x 7 3/8 In. ⋯⋯ 145.00
Bentwood, Harvard Type Fingers, Copper Tacks, Oval, 5 3/4 x 2 In. ⋯⋯ 660.00
Bentwood, Laced Seams, Dark Green Paint, Red Interior, Oval, c.1804, 12 x 6 In. ⋯⋯ 290.00
Bentwood, Painted, Black Ground, Pink Flowers, H. Bucher Style, Oval, 3 x 1 1/2 In. ⋯ 660.00
Bentwood, Painted, Decorated, Bird, Flowers, 19th Century, 6 x 16 3/4 In. ⋯⋯ 705.00
Bentwood, Sailing Ship, Lid, Copper Tacks, Label, Brig Hinda, Salem, Round, 6 1/2 In. ⋯ 1035.00
Bentwood, Thick Green & Black Paint, Red Flower, Swags, Oval, 2 1/4 x 1 1/2 In. ⋯⋯ 430.00
Bible, Carved, Flower, Lock Plate, Hinged, Early 18th Century, 8 x 24 x 14 In. ⋯⋯ 600.00
Bible, Chip Carved, Incised Border Panels, Walnut, Wrought Iron Hinges, 17 x 13 x 9 In. ⋯ 115.00
Bible, Old Green Paint, Pine, Applied Molding, Batwing Brass Pulls, 19 x 14 x 7 In. ⋯⋯ 575.00
Birchbark Covered, Tapered Square, Stitched, Lid, Rawhide Strap, 8 1/2 x 14 x 12 In. ⋯⋯ 230.00
Boule, Tortoiseshell Veneer, Brass Leaf Inlay, Brass Lock, 6 1/2 x 3 x 2 1/2 In. ⋯⋯ 690.00
Brassbound, Brass Bail Handles, Mahogany, Pine Bottom, Octagonal, 13 x 15 In. ⋯⋯ 230.00
Bride's, Bentwood, Painted Design, Red Bird, Polka Dots, Leaves, 15 x 9 3/4 x 6 In. ⋯⋯ 1670.00
Bride's, Bentwood, Red Roses, Orange, Blue, Romantic Couple On Lid, 19 x 12 x 7 In. ⋯ 1025.00
Bride's, Brick House, Trees, Finger Lap Construction, Oval, 13 1/2 In. ⋯⋯ 230.00
Bride's, Wood, Multicolored, Lapped Sides, Germany, Oval, Early 1800s, 8 3/8 x 18 In. ⋯ 3173.00
Bronze, Zodiac Design, Patina, Oscar Bach, 7 In. ⋯⋯ 823.00
Candle, Painted, Blue, 3-Finger Pull, Slide Lid, 1820-30, 14 1/2 x 8 1/2 x 3 In. ⋯⋯ 949.00
Candle, Painted, Blue, Carved Initials, H.E.P., New England, 1830 ⋯⋯ 635.00
Candle, Pierced Back, Pine, Dovetailed, Red Paint, Early 1800s, 7 3/4 x 12 x 5 In. ⋯⋯ 1058.00
Candle, Pine, Dovetailed, 2 Walnut Slide Lids, Cutout Handle, New Eng., 12 x 8 x 6 In. ⋯ 460.00
Candle, Pine, Green Paint, 5 x 11 1/2 x 5 In. ⋯⋯ 195.00
Candle, Pine, Painted Flower Designs, Curved Crest, Square Nails, Lift Lid, 12 x 5 x 7 In. ⋯ 5980.00
Candle, Pine, Stenciled Fruit, Ocher Ground, c.1860, 6 x 10 3/4 In. ⋯⋯ 690.00

Candle, Red Paint, Decorated, Incised Hearts, Green Painted Lid, Pine, 13 x 8 x 6 In. 575.00
Candle, Tin, Cylindrical, Hasp, 2 Hanging Tabs, Lift Lid, 12 3/4 In. 230.00
Candle, Tin, Hinged Lid, Early 19th Century, 10 x 5 x 3 In. 460.00
Candle, Wall, Inverted Heart Cutout, Brown Paint, Dovetailed, Ogee Lid, 12 x 6 x 9 In. . . .   1552.00
Candle, Wall, Molded Lid, Walnut, Poplar, 4 Compartments, 11 x 8 x 12 In. 1325.00
Candle, Wall, Pierced Arched Back, Wood, Dovetailed, Early 1800s, 11 x 11 1/2 x 7 In. . . .   1645.00
Candle, Wall, Pine, Poplar, Red Brown Finish, Square Nails, Arched Crest, 10 x 14 In. 259.00
Candle, Wall, Pine, Poplar, Yellow Green Paint, Shallow Tray Top, 11 x 5 x 17 In. 2990.00
Candle, Wall, Poplar, Dovetailed, Tapered Sides, 2 Compartments, 14 1/2 x 9 x 8 In. 315.00
Candle, Wall, Tin, Blue Paint, Shield Shape Back, Hinged Lid, Early 1800s, 7 3/8 x 10 In. .   410.00
Candle, Wall, Walnut, Square Nail Construction, Scalloped Crest, 12 x 5 x 9 In. 750.00
Candle, Walnut, Carved, Dovetailed, Lift Lid, Incised Trees, Star, 13 x 4 1/2 x 4 1/4 In. . . .   690.00
Casket, Napoleon III, Ebony, Bronze Mounted, Cherubs, Maiden, 7 x 12 x 10 In. 1195.00
Chart, Green Paint, Wood, Dovetailed, Hinged Lid, 1800s, 7 x 35 5/8 x 8 In. 410.00
Cigar, Sunset Behind Silhouette Tree, Frame, Mahogany, Black Lacquer, 5 x 5 1/2 In. 220.00
Cigarette, Copper, Silver, Dome Lid, Cedar Lined, Continental, ca.1900, 3 1/4 x 3 x 6 In. . .   2070.00
Cigarette, George V, Nickel, Silver Mount Writing, Tortoiseshell, 2 x 5 x 4 In. 489.00
Collar, Japanese Export, Lacquered, Round, Red Brown, Gold Lacquer Flowers, 8 In. 175.00
Copper, Hammered, Hinged, Fitted Wood Interior, Potter & Mellon, Arts & Crafts 185.00
Cutlery, Mahogany, Slant Lid, Hinged, Velvet Lining, Swing Handles, 11 x 12 x 8 In. 405.00
Cutlery, Stand, Dovetailed, Walnut, 2 Sections, Pierced Handle, 15 5/8 x 10 1/2 x 23 In. . . .   259.00
Decanter, Burl Walnut, Hinged Lid, Sides, Decanters, Cordials, Tray, 10 1/2 x 12 x 9 In. . . .   1610.00
Decanter, Napoleon III, Boulle, Marquetry, Ebonized Wood, Cordials, 10 x 14 x 11 In. . . .   978.00
Desk, Bone Inlay, Ebonized Hardwood, Quill, East India, Early 20th Century, 3 x 9 x 6 In. .   259.00
Desk, Bone, Ebonized Wood, Framed Porcupine Quill, East India, 3 3/4 x 8 3/4 x 7 In. 200.00
Desk, George III, Rosewood, Penwork, Burl, Cartouche, Double Eagle, 6 x 9 x 6 In. 316.00
Desk, Mahogany, Brass Inlay, Slant Front, Hinged Lid, Compartments, 4 x 14 x 10 In. 345.00
Desk, Maple, Arts & Crafts Flower Design, Stained Ground, Slant Lid, 10 x 6 x 6 In. 290.00
Desk, Walnut, Crossbanded, Drop Front, Drawer, Fitted Interior, 18th Century, 17 1/2 In. . .   1095.00
Document, Blue Paint, Flowers, Floral Border, Pine, Dome Top, RM, 11 x 27 x 12 In. 1880.00
Document, Brass Tack, Leather Covered, J. & W. Bailey, Portland, Maine, 9 x 13 x 10 In. .   200.00
Document, Burl Walnut, Parquetry Inlay, Mid 19th Century, 6 x 13 x 8 In. 175.00
Document, Cherry, Dovetailed, Chamfered Lid, Square Cut Nails, Inscription, 12 x 9 In. . .   460.00
Document, Faux Grain, Brass Bail Handle, Painted, Dome Top, New England, 12 In. 2070.00
Document, Geometric Designs, Brass Handle, 1800s, 5 3/4 x 11 1/2 x 6 In. 499.00
Document, George Washington, Horse, Bird's-Eye Maple, Decoupage, 5 x 12 x 6 In. 165.00
Document, Grain Painted, Gilt Stenciled Fruit, Flowers, Pinecone Pendants, 7 x 18 x 8 In. .   2350.00
Document, Leather Cover, Pine, Wire Nails, Brass Bail Handle, Iron Lock, 10 x 7 x 5 In. .   290.00
Document, Putty Painted, Pine, Dome Top, Early 1800s, 5 1/4 x 11 3/8 x 6 1/2 In. 999.00
Document, Red, Green Decoration, Yellow Ground, Dome Top, 19th Century 5175.00
Document, Shield, Stars, Crosses, Stippled Background, Walnut, Pine, Carved, 9 x 6 x 6 In.   175.00
Document, Stencil, Ink, Townscape, Shells, Fruit Baskets, Maple, 5 1/4 x 13 x 8 1/4 In. . . .   1554.00
Document, Tole, Black, Red & Yellow Pinwheels, Dome Top, 7 3/4 x 3 3/8 x 4 5/8 In. 460.00
Document, Tole, Japanned Ground, Painted, Dome Top, Brass Bail Handle, 8 x 4 x 5 In. . .   518.00
Document, Tole, Japanned, Painted Band, Fruit, Leaves, Dome Top, Handle, 8 x 4 x 5 In. .   316.00
Document, Vinegar Painted, Brown Over Pink, Hinged Lid, Latch, Pine, c.1830, 6 x 15 In.   590.00
Document, William & Mary, Oyster Veneer, Cabriole Legs, Walnut, 1600s, 20 x 22 In. . . .   2530.00
Dome Top, Painted, Cats, Vinegar Graining, Wallpaper Lining, Vt., 23 x 13 In. . . . . *Illus* 16675.00
Dresser, Mahogany, Inlaid, Coffin Shape, Top Opening, Early 19th Century, 8 x 12 3/4 In. .   3290.00
Dresser, Mother-Of-Pearl, Silk Lining, Steel Ball Feet, England, 3 1/8 x 7 1/2 x 4 In. 460.00
Dressing Table, Silver Plate Mount, Oblong, Cut Glass, Harvard Pattern, c.1900, 3 x 7 In. .   460.00
Federal, Mahogany, Dome Top, New England, c.1790, 5 1/2 x 12 x 6 In. 3600.00
Federal Period, Mahogany, Satinwood Key Escutcheon, 7 1/2 In. 127.00
Finger Joint Construction, Scrolling Designs, Brown Paint, 1800s, 8 1/2 x 14 3/4 In. 1725.00
Flatware, Cherry, Red Paint, 2 Compartments, 1800s, 11 5/8 x 16 In. 590.00
Formica, Wood, Multicolored, Painted, Applied Metal Hinges, 6 1/2 x 2 1/2 In. 529.00
Gilt Metal, Renaissance Style, Continental, 9 1/4 In. 149.00
Glass, Frosted, Enameled Dutch Scene, Lid, 5 1/2 In. 100.00
Grain Painted, Pine, Dovetailed, 11 3/4 x 8 5/8 x 4 1/4 In. 115.00
Grain Painted, Wavy Decoration, Mustard, Pine, Dovetailed Case, 17 x 12 x 12 In. 230.00
Hepplewhite, Mahogany Veneer, Banded Inlay, Inlay Keyhole, Compartments, 10 x 5 In. .   2415.00
Ivory, Gold Lacquer, Tilting Bevel Mirror, 4 Drawers, 11 x 10 x 13 In. 90.00
Jewelry, Burl Walnut, Brass Inlay, Children's Tales, Art Nouveau, Austria, 6 x 11 1/2 In. . .   3525.00

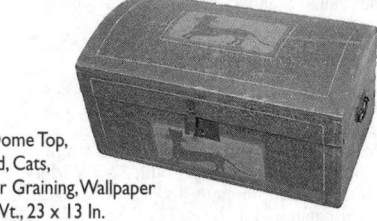

Box, Dome Top,
Painted, Cats,
Vinegar Graining, Wallpaper
Lining, Vt., 23 x 13 In.

Box, Slide Cover, Painted, Tulips, Stars,
Squiggled Centers, Penn., 1792, 11 x 8 In.

Jewelry, Burl, Lift Lid, 2 Handles, Fitted, Art Nouveau, Brass Inlay, 7 1/4 x 13 x 9 1/2 In. .   4995.00
Jewelry, Gilt Bronze, Bas Relief Strapwork, Satin Lining, France, c.1885, 3 x 7 1/4 In. 978.00
Jewelry, Metal, Victorian, 5 1/2 In. 25.00
Jewelry, Metal, Victorian, 10 1/2 In. 125.00
Jewelry, Metal, Victorian, Rectangular, 4 In. 10.00
Jewelry, Napoleon III, Gilt Bronze, Pietra Dura Plaques, Flowers, c.1865, 5 x 7 In. 1495.00
Jewelry, Regency Style, Mahogany, Hinged Lid, Paw Feet, Late 1800s, 7 5/8 x 15 x 8 In. . .   405.00
Jewelry, Restauration Style, Gilt Brass, Cut Glass, France, c.1900, 4 1/2 x 5 1/2 In. 748.00
Jewelry, William IV, Rosewood, Scroll Sawn, Mother-Of-Pearl, c.1835, 5 3/4 x 12 In. 290.00
Jewelry, Wood, Inlaid, Geometric, Lift-Out Tray, England, c.1880, 12 x 8 x 8 In. 1600.00
Jewelry Casket, Russian Style, Silver, Diamond, Enamel, Malachite, 1900s, 2 1/2 x 4 In. . .   550.00
Kindling, Slant Front, Victorian, Brass Clad, Oblong, Tavern Scenes, 15 1/4 x 22 x 15 In. . .   1150.00
Knife, Birch, Canted Sides, Dovetailed, 2 Compartments, Pierced Handle, 14 x 9 In. 375.00
Knife, Black Paint, Serpentine Front, Mahogany Veneer, Molded Trim, 10 x 7 x 15 In. 400.00
Knife, George III, Inlaid Mahogany, Serpentine Front, Brass Handles, Late 1700s, 14 In. . .   2700.00
Knife, George III, Satinwood Inlaid Serpentine, Mahogany, c.1800, 14 3/4 In. 690.00
Knife, Georgian Style, Mahogany, 13 1/2 x 7 1/2 x 8 In. 138.00
Knife, Hepplewhite, Figured Mahogany Veneer, Inlay, Slant Lid, Line Dividers, 15 x 9 In. .   690.00
Knife, Leather, Slant Front, Tooled, Punched Flowers, Paper Lined Slots, 14 x 10 x 7 In. . .   489.00
Knife, Mahogany, Inlaid, Serpentine Lid, England, Late 1800s, 16 x 9 x 12 In. 1840.00
Knife, Mahogany, Serpentine, Hinged Cover, Divided Interior, 14 x 9 x 12 In., Pair 546.00
Knife, Marquetry, Inlaid Satinwood, Serpentine, Hinged Crossbanded Top, 16 In. 546.00
Knife, Pine, Painted, 1800s, 4 x 9 x 13 In. 295.00
Knife, Polychrome Roses, Silver Escutcheon, Satinwood, Serpentine Lid, 14 In., Pair 2300.00
Knife, Relief Carved, Oak, Dovetailed, Scalloped Top, 4 1/2 x 11 x 6 In. 200.00
Knife, Urn Shape, Mahogany, Octagonal, Hinged Lid, Acorn Finial, Pedestal, 24 In., Pair . .   2070.00
Lacquer, Chinese, Red, Curved Top, Tilting Mirror, 8 x 10 x 12 3/8 In. 115.00
Letter, Apple Wood, Hinged Lid, Carved Leather Straps, Buckles, 9 x 5 1/2 x 5 1/2 In. . . .   1500.00
Letter, Edwardian, Satinwood, Painted, Hinged, Slant Top, Divided Interior, 8 x 12 x 5 In.   780.00
Letter, Mahogany, Rosewood, Slant Front, Doors, Drawer, Multiple Slots, 13 x 13 x 10 In.   400.00
Letter, Quillwork, Ivory, Ebony Frame, Hinged Lid, Late 19th Century, 4 x 8 x 6 In. 259.00
Letter, Victorian, Satinwood Veneer, Mahogany, Moldings, Glass Inkwells, 13 x 9 x 11 In.   920.00
Liquor, Pine, Painted, 7 Sections, 19th Century, 8 1/2 x 9 x 13 In.   358.00
Mail, English Style, Cast Iron, 42 x 14 1/2 x 13 1/2 In. 520.00
Middle Eastern Style Star, Banding, Fall Front, 6 Drawers, Lift Lid, 12 x 14 x 10 In. 140.00
Money, Tansu Chest, Elm, Hinged Lid, 3 Drawers, Japan, 1800s, 9 1/2 x 11 3/4 x 8 1/4 In. .   460.00
Moroccan, Openwork, Bail Handle, Quill Banded Top, Quill Base, 5 x 11 x 8 In. 294.00
Painted, Bird, Flowers, Dome Top, Wrought Iron Hasp Lock, Handle, 19 x 13 x 12 In. . . .   460.00
Painted, Flower, Blue Ground, Dome Top, Tin Hinges, N.Y., 1840, 7 3/4 x 4 x 4 3/4 In. . . .   1955.00
Painted, House, Fence, Blue Ground, Hinged Lid, Cutout Hanger, Wall, 1862, 9 x 10 In. . .   1890.00
Painted, Leaves, Swags, Yellow, Red, Dome Top, Wood, Iron Latch, Handles, 8 x 20 In. . .   2235.00
Pantry, Bentwood, Bail Handle, Green Paint, Overlapping Seams, 11 In. 1160.00
Pantry, Bentwood, Blue Paint, Overlapping Seams, Steel Tacks, 11 x 8 1/2 x 5 1/2 In. 520.00
Pantry, Bentwood, Green & Black Paint, 3 Swans, Star, M.J.B., Ink Date, 1880, 6 3/4 In. .   1325.00
Pantry, Bentwood, Lapped, Nailed, Painted, Carved Label Cheese, 9 x 4 In. 290.00
Pantry, Bentwood, Putty Color, Stenciled Cinnamon, Steel Tacks, Wooden Pegs, 10 In. . . .   1035.00
Pantry, Bentwood, Round, Red Ground, Blue, Yellow Tulips, c.1896, 7 3/4 x 3 1/2 In. 2013.00
Pantry, Grain Painted Surface, Harvard Style, Lid, New England, 6 3/4 x 2 3/4 In. 345.00
Pantry, Yellow Paint, Round, Lapped Maple Sides, Pine Top, Base, 1800s, 3 1/2 x 7 5/8 In.   650.00
Pencil, Children Band Scene, Papier-Mache, Divided Interior, France, 2 x 7 3/4 In. 112.00
Pencil, Dixon's Typhonite Eldorado, Master Drawing Pencil, Cardboard, 7 1/4 x 2 In. 10.00

Perfume, Burlwood, Rosewood, Mother-Of-Pearl Panel, Monogram, 4 1/2 x 8 x 5 3/4 In. .   410.00
Photo, Victorian, Gilt Bronze Mounted, Leather, Accordion Style, Handle, 7 x 6 In. 105.00
Pill, Guilloche Amethyst Enamel, Silver, Gilt, London, c.1906, 1 5/8 In. 175.00
Pine, Comb Graining, Dovetailed, Flowers, Slide Lid, c.1815, 11 x 7 x 6 In. 230.00
Pine, Divider, Lift Lid, 24 x 29 1/2 In. 140.00
Pine, Dome Top, Grain Paint, Dovetailed, Hinged Lid, 1800s, 7 x 13 3/4 x 7 1/4 In. 355.00
Pine, Dome Top, Painted Thumbprint Design, John Kelley, 1849, 3 3/4 x 7 x 4 1/4 In. 7800.00
Pine, Dovetailed, Pegged, Compass Point Decorations, Dome Top, Tin Hasp, 4 x 5 x 4 In. .   5225.00
Pine, Grain Painted, Flower, 4 Compartments, Slide Lid, Gouged Finger Pull, 3 x 7 x 4 In.   2200.00
Pine, Grain Painted, Hinged Lid, Turned Feet, Brass Escutcheon, Early 1800s, 7 x 13 x 7 In.   590.00
Pine, Gray & Red Painted, Beveled Lift Lid, New England, 1800s, 72 x 29 x 9 In. . . .   1800.00
Pine, Hinged Lid, Yellow, Blue Wavy Line, Dots, 1800s, 10 5/8 x 24 x 12 In. 940.00
Pine, Lift Lid, Drawer, Faux Grain, Handle, 9 3/4 x 17 x 7 1/2 In. 495.00
Pine, Locking, Painted, Shaped Lift Handle, Green, Initials K.I., 12 x 18 x 14 In. 96.00
Pine, Painted Potted Flowers, Blue, Red, Black, Yellow, Slide Lid, 8 x 16 x 10 In. 415.00
Pine, Painted, Blue Rag Swirls, Red Trim, 2 Compartments, Slide Lid, Knob, 6 x 14 In. . . .   770.00
Pine, Painted, Compass Stars, Rosettes, Incised Checkerboard, 1863, 6 x 13 x 7 In. 5580.00
Pine, Painted, Dovetailed Corners, Slide Lid, Inscription, 1892 In Panel, 16 x 11 x 7 In. . . .   316.00
Pine, Painted, Dovetailed, Wire Hinged Lid, Early 1800s, 5 1/4 x 10 5/8 x 5 3/4 In. 1058.00
Pine, Painted, Green, William Penn & Indian Treaty, Map Of Penn. Inside, 6 x 14 In. 195.00
Pine, Painted, Rectangular, Hinged Lid, Brass Escutcheon, Early 1800s, 8 x 24 x 12 5/8 In. .   529.00
Pine, Red Paint, Scalloped Back, Wall, 11 x 4 x 5 1/2 In. 520.00
Pine, Smoke Decorated, Hinged Lid, Rectangular, 1800s, 4 3/8 x 12 1/8 x 6 In. 765.00
Pine, Sponging, Blue Flower, Dovetailed, Slide Lid, M.H.D. 1866, 19 x 12 In. 690.00
Pine, Staple Hinges, Flowers, Wavy Lines, Dunbury, Penn., c.1863, 10 x 7 In. 230.00
Pipe, Cherry, Tapered, Dovetailed Drawer, 2 Compartments, Connecticut, 6 x 4 x 23 In. . . .   5460.00
Pipe, Pine, Pierced, Shaped Back, Drawer, Red Paint, Early 1800s, 14 1/4 x 5 5/8 In. 2820.00
Pipe, Red Painted, Shaped Backplate, 19th Century, 18 x 4 7/8 In. 1645.00
Pipe, Walnut, Red Paint, Dovetailed, Scalloped Crest, New England, 7 x 5 x 20 In. 8340.00
Poplar, Hinged, Red Ground, White Designs, New England, Early 1800s, 11 x 30 x 13 In. .   1175.00
Poplar, Painted, Landscape, House, Bridges, Dovetailed, Nailed, Brass Lock, 5 x 9 In. 220.00
Poplar, Slide Lid, Black Paint, 4-Section Interior, Square Nails, CM, 9 x 5 1/2 x 2 3/4 In. . .   375.00
Porcelain, Flowers, Basket Ground, Immortals, Chinese, c.1760, 2 3/4 x 2 1/4 x 1 1/2 In. . .   5236.00
Porcelain, Ormolu Mounted, Cobalt Blue, Casket Shape, Grapevines, 15 x 15 x 10 1/2 In. .   865.00
Porcelain, Sevres Style, Hinged, Decorated, Children, Dog, 8 1/2 In. 1016.00
Postage Stamp, Gilt Bronze, Jewels, 3 Chicks, Hinged Lid, Germany, c.1900, 3 1/2 In. . . .   316.00
Powder, Painted Bucolic Scene, Stream, Trees, Silver, Enamel, Edwardian, 2 2/3 x 2 In. . .   1175.00
Quill, Moroccan, Inlaid Porcupine Quills, Ebony Bands, Ivory Circles, 5 x 12 x 8 In. 265.00
Russian Style, Bear, Green, Black, Silver, Cylindrical, 1900s, 2 1/2 x 4 In. 290.00
Salt, Sectioned Drawer, Poplar, Pine, Painted Flowers, Slant Top, 12 x 15 x 10 In. 1210.00
Salt, Wall, Mahogany, Sloping, Hinged Lid, England, c.1800, 12 1/2 x 7 1/2 In. 320.00
Saw, Carpenters, 2 Sections, Handhold, 36 x 12 x 12 In. 115.00
Scriptor, Polychrome, Lift Lid, Slant Front, Transverse Drawer, 10 x 15 x 15 In. 69.00
Seed, Bentwood, Round, Incised Cherry Branch, Scandinavian Verse, Anno 1899, 2 In. . . .   290.00
Slide Cover, Painted, Tulips, Stars, Squiggled Centers, Penn., 1792, 11 x 8 In. . . . . *Illus* 85000.00
Snuff, Benjamin Franklin Bust, Turned Burlwood, Round, c.1800, 2 1/8 In. 410.00
Snuff, First Empire, Carved Horn, Atala Au Tombeau, France, c.1815, 3 x 1 3/4 In. 550.00
Snuff, Gold, Enamel, Women, Children, Rectangular, Cut Corners, Switzerland, c.1820, 4 In.   5400.00
Snuff, Horn, Cork, Silver Overlay Lid, Scotland, 3 3/4 In. 345.00
Snuff, Wood, Shell, Drapery, Grape Leaf, Hunting Horn, Hinged Lid, 1800s, 1 x 3 In. 115.00
Spirits, Mahogany, Dovetailed, Brass Handles, 6 Sections, England, 9 x 11 x 8 In. 115.00
Splint & Taper, Wood, Painted, Lollipop Shape Back, Rectangular, Early 1800s, 13 In. . . .   3525.00
Stationery, Anglo-Indian, Bone Inlaid Hardwood, Cupboard Form, 24 x 15 x 6 In. 635.00
Stationery, Anglo-Indian, Ebony, Porcupine Quill Veneer Panels, Ivory Dot Inlay, 18 In. . .   378.00
Stationery, Rosewood, Brass Inlay, Handles, Scrolls, Leaves, Velvet Lined Interior, 14 In. .   405.00
Storage, Bentwood, Carved & Laced Seams, 21 x 15 x 13 In. 115.00
Storage, Lacquered, Red, Gold, Book Shape, Figures, Chinese, 2 1/2 x 9 x 11 In. 175.00
Storage, Lacquered, Red, Gold, Waved Top, Mirror, Drawers, Chinese, 11 x 10 x 13 In. . . .   200.00
Storage, Painted Red, Hinged Lid, Applied Edge, 3 Interior Dividers, 13 1/2 x 32 x 18 In. .   86.00
Storage, Pine, Sliding Lid, Painted, 7 1/4 x 14 x 9 1/2 In. 220.00
Storage, Scrolling Copperwork, Brass Line Trim, 5 7/8 x 10 x 7 1/2 In. 115.00
Strong, Iron, Rectangular, Hinged Lid, Side Lift Handles, Continental, 26 x 13 In. 1295.00
Strong, Spanish Baroque, Iron, 17th Century, 16 x 25 x 17 In. 3680.00

Sugar, Fruitwood, Drawer, Wrought Iron Cane Cutter, Brass Pull, 14 x 10 x 9 In. 230.00
Tea, 6-Board, Relief Carved Scrolls, Wrought Iron Bail Handles, 18 x 36 In. 690.00
Tibetan, Decorated, Pine, Fruit Compotes, Red, Green Line Borders, 50 x 12 x 10 In. 489.00
Tin, Red & Blue Paint, Wavy Line, Liester, Acorn Knop, c.1840, 4 1/8 x 3 In. 230.00
Tinder, Iron, Brass, Striker, Flint, 1700s 185.00
Tinder, Tin, Round, Finger Loop, Candle Socket, Damper, Flint, Steel, 4 x 4 In. 430.00
Tobacco, Brass, Copper, Rounded, Rectangular, Coat Of Arms, Dutch, 1747, 6 1/4 In. 145.00
Tobacco, Brass, Rounded, Rectangular, Agricultural Scenes, Dutch, 1800, 6 x 3 3/4 In. 150.00
Tobacco, Brass, Rounded, Rectangular, Engraved, 18th Century, 7 In. 195.00
Tobacco, Enameled Flowers, Brass, Gilt Plated, 4 3/4 x 5 1/4 x 5 1/4 In. 259.00
Tobacco, Pewter, Kidney Shape, Hinged Lid, Deer Head, 1799, 3 In. 295.00
Tobacco, White Bone, Black & Charcoal Horn, Tortoiseshell, Dutch, c.1835, 1 x 3 3/4 In. . 230.00
Tortoiseshell, Metal Mounted, Glass Covered, Dome Top, Circle Designs, 1800s, 1 x 3 In. 805.00
Trinket, Norwegian Style, Multicolored, Scrolled Leaf Cameo, c.1850, 9 1/4 In. 430.00
Trinket, Porcelain, Sevres Style, Hinged Lid, Landscape, Blue Ground, 1900s, 6 x 13 x 8 In. 315.00
Trinket, Porcelain, Sevres Style, Hinged Lid, Sarcophagus Shape, 1900s, 6 x 11 x 7 In. ... 315.00
Trinket, Victorian, Mother-Of-Pearl, Inlaid Ebony, c.1880, 4 3/4 x 10 1/2 x 7 1/4 In. 175.00
Tunbridgeware, Walnut, Herringbone Bands, Diamond Shaped Plaque, c.1860, 8 x 5 In. .. 360.00
Valentine, Heart Shape, Walnut, Scalloped, Inlaid Stars, Diamonds, Ink Flowers, 7 x 3 In. . 575.00
Wall, Heart Shaped Crest, Painted Red Rose, Dovetailed, Slant Lid, 10 1/4 x 15 1/2 In. ... 4370.00
Wall, Hinged, Slant Front Lid, Inlaid Mahogany, Oval Patera, 16 x 8 x 6 In. 430.00
Watch Safe, Wood, Carved Man, Woman, Lion On Top, Door On Back, 15 x 10 x 6 In. ... 880.00
Wood, Book, Black, Red & Gilt Arabesque, Geometrics, Drawer, Footed, 1860, 3 x 6 In. .. 235.00
Wood, Burl, Applied Pewter Leaf, Berry, Round, Michael Thoren, 3 3/4 x 2 1/4 In. 175.00
Wood, Carved, Cranes, Cash Coin Ground, Japan, Early 20th Century, 11 In. 380.00
Wood, Carved, Openwork, Arts & Crafts, Rattling Beads, Lift Lid, 5 1/2 x 11 x 6 1/2 In. .. 380.00
Wood, Dovetailed, Inlaid Crossed Flags, Heart Shaped Key Hole, Lift Lid, 5 x 13 x 8 In. .. 440.00
Wood, Edwardian, Carved, Dried Leaf Display Between Glass, c.1900, 4 x 11 x 10 In. 175.00
Wood, Hinged Top, Dovetailed, Locomotive, Strawberries, Peter Ompir, 24 x 7 1/2 In. 1295.00
Wood, Inlaid, 4-Sided, Tapered, 7 1/2 In. 150.00
Wood, Painted, Carved Flowers, Scroll Rim, Blue, Green, Yellow, Red, 4 x 11 x 11 In. 2420.00
Work, Chinese Export, Gilt Black Lacquer, Octagonal, Mid 1800s, 6 x 14 x 11 In. 1955.00
Work, Ebonized Wood, Bone Inlay, Quill, Tray, Anglo-Indian, c.1885, 5 x 11 x 8 In. 345.00
Work, George IV, Brass Mounted, Gilt Japanned, Mandarin's Garden, c.1835, 4 x 9 x 6 In. 1380.00
Writing, George IV, Brass Bound, Compartments, Calamander Wood, c.1845, 15 x 10 In. . 520.00
Writing, George IV, Brass Bound, Rosewood, Tooled Leather, c.1835, 6 1/2 x 17 1/2 In. ... 635.00
Writing, Gilt Tooled, Inlaid Leather, Hinged Lid, Rectangular, England, 5 x 16 x 10 In. ... 230.00
Writing, Regency, Brass Bound, Mahogany, Mid 19th Century, 6 1/2 x 15 3/4 x 9 1/4 In. .. 805.00

BOY SCOUT collectibles include any material related to scouting, including patches, manuals, and uniforms. The Boy Scout movement in the United States started in 1910. The first Jamboree was held in 1937. Girl Scout items are listed under their own heading.

Badge, 5th World Jamboree, Vogelenzang, The Netherlands, Metal, Ribbon, 1937 .... 380.00
Badge, Assistant Scoutmaster, Rectangular, 1915 .... 1200.00
Badge, Merit, Drafting, Square 750.00
Badge, Merit, Tenderfoot Scribe, Combination, Square, 1920s 900.00
Bank, Cast Iron, A.C. Williams, M 45, 5 1/2 In. 130.00
Belt, Woven, Order Of The Arrow Beading, 1913 .... 35.00
Book, Community Boy Leadership, Manual For Scout Leaders, 1921 .... 310.00
Book, Handbook For Boys, 20th Edition, 1919 .... 260.00
Bookends, Be Prepared, Colored Pressed Wood, 5 1/2 In. 45.00
Button, 4th Annual Boy Scout Day, Schuykill County, Celluloid, 1 3/4 In. 174.00
Button, Boy Scouts, White Letters, Green Ground, Celluloid, c.1915, 7/8 In. 40.00
Button, Casper, Wearing Cub Hat, Holding Logo, Lithograph, 1 1/8 In. 12.00
Button, Fund Raiser, I Passed Buck To Boy Scouts, Lithograph, 1957, 1 1/8 In. 20.00
Button, Maverick, Bucking Cow, BSA Brand, Red Ground, 1 1/4 In. 40.00
Button, Parade Of Progress, Boy, I Enrolled One, c.1930, 1 1/4 In. 100.00
Button, Parade Of Progress, I'll Be First Class, c.1932, 1 1/4 In. 80.00
Button, Scout Week, Australia, 1930s, 1 In. 25.00
Button, Scouts, Blue Ground, David Cook, 1930s, 3/4 In. 20.00
Calendar, 1941, A Scout Is Helpful, Norman Rockwell, Full Pad, 8 x 14 In. 65.00
First Aid Kit, Tin, Leather Pouch, c.1928 .... 45.00

Game, Original Box, Playing Board, Milton Bradley No. 4405, 22 x 10 In. 92.00
Hat, Campaign, Felt, Leather Band, Size 7 1/4 . . . .   45.00
Knife, Official, Leather Washer Handle, Aluminum Handle, Sheath, Case, 8 3/8 In. 40.00
Knife, Pocket, Compass In Handle, Can Opener, Spike, Screwdriver 60.00
Knife, Pocket, With Hacket, 5 In. 310.00
Knot Board, 41 Knots, Twisted Hemp Rope, Brass Stud, Plywood Board, 40 x 19 In. 345.00
Marching Group, Cardboard, 42 Figures, McLoughlin Brothers, Box 127.00
Medal, World Jamboree, Contingent, Brass, Red, White, Blue Ribbon, 1920 . . . .   2900.00
Neckerchief, National Conference Delegate, Unami Lodge, 1967 . . . .   200.00
Patch, National Jamboree, Washington, D.C., 1935 . . . .   330.00
Pin, Eagle Scout, Sterling Silver, Red, White & Blue Enameled, 3/4 In. 105.00
Pin, Lapel, Rover Scout, Be Prepared, Sterling Silver, Enameled, 3/4 In. 75.00
Sheet Music, Be Prepared, Song Of The Scouts, 1933 . . . .   55.00
Shoulder Flash, World Jamboree, USA, Red, Navy Felt, 1937 . . . .   2000.00
Uniform, Shirt, Pants, Hat, 1940s, Size 12-14 . . . .   35.00
Watch, Cub Scouts, Leather Band, Plastic Stand, Paperwork, Timex, 1950s 110.00
Watch, Ingersoll, Be Prepared, A Scout Is, 1934, 1 1/4 x 1 1/2 x 8 1/2 In. 275.00
Watch, National Council New York City, Leather Strap, 1935, 1 x 1 1/2 x 8 1/2 In. 200.00

BRADLEY & HUBBARD is a name found on many metal objects.
Walter Hubbard and his brother-in-law, Nathaniel Lyman Bradley,
started making cast iron clocks, tables, frames, lamps, chan-
deliers, sconces, and sewing birds in 1854 in Meriden, Connecticut.
The company became Bradley & Hubbard Manufacturing Company in
1875. Charles Parker Company bought the firm in 1940. Their lamps
are especially prized by collectors.

Ashtray, Rabbit, Cast Iron 385.00
Box, Bronze, Enameled Lid, Fitted Interior, 1 3/8 x 5 x 4 In. 90.00
Chandelier, Gilt Metal, Glass, Late 19th Century, 30 x 14 In. 230.00
Lamp, Double Angle, Clear Globes, Milk Glass Shades, 22 x 35 In. 115.00
Lamp, Electric, 3 Sockets, Embossed Leaves, Ribbed Glass, 25 x 20 In. 2585.00
Lamp, Electric, Slag Glass, 8-Panel Shade, Bronzed Filigree, c.1915, 21 In. 489.00
Lamp, Hanging, Opaque Shade, Blue Bands, Flower Transfers, 14 x 36 In. 115.00
Lamp, Hanging, Opaque Shade, Cottage Transfer, 14 x 46 In. 403.00
Lamp, Hanging, Opaque Shade, Green Blush, Rose Transfer, 14 x 36 In. 230.00
Lamp, Hanging, Opaque Shade, Green Ground, Rosebuds, 13 1/2 x 39 In. 201.00
Lamp, Hanging, Opaque Shade, Landscape Transfer, 14 1/2 x 41 In. 345.00
Lamp, Hanging, Opaque Shade, Pink Blush, Flowers, Brass Font, 14 x 40 In. 259.00
Lamp, Hanging, Opaque Shade, Pink Blush, Roses, 14 x 35 In. 230.00
Lamp, Hanging, Opaque Shade, Red, Yellow Trumpet Flowers, 14 x 40 In. 201.00
Lamp, Hanging, Shaded Blue Opaque Shade, Maroon Mums, 13 x 37 In. 230.00
Lamp, Hemispherical Shade, Landscape, Lake, Chipped Glass, 24 1/2 x 18 In. 2700.00
Lamp, Kerosene, Brass, Grapes, Flowers, Handles, Frosted Shade, 17 In. 173.00
Lamp, Kerosene, Student, Brass Shade, Electrified, 1875-90, 24 In. 1495.00
Lamp, Kitchen, Cast Iron, Opaque Shade, Painted Rose, 13 x 40 In. 230.00
Lamp, Kitchen, Cast Iron, Opaque White Shade, Pink Roses, 13 1/2 x 35 In. 259.00
Lamp, Kitchen, Steel, Opaque White Shade, Satin Font, 11 x 34 In. 201.00
Lamp, Piano, Brass, Telescoping Floor Model, Spiral Shaft, 53 In. 230.00
Lamp, Piano, Kerosene, Wrought & Cast Iron, Tripod Base, 64 In. 259.00
Lamp, Prairie School, Conical Shade, Geometric, 4-Socket Base, 23 x 17 In. 2115.00
Lamp, Ribbed Glass, Flower Border, Bronze Base, 3 Sockets, 22 x 18 In. 1175.00
Lamp, Stained Glass, Slag Glass, Brass, Spider Web On Base, c.1910 . . . .   345.00
Plaque, Wall, Indian, Iron, Full Headdress, Brown Ground, 12 1/2 In. 275.00

BRASS has been used for decorative pieces and useful tablewares
since ancient times. It is an alloy of copper, zinc, and other metals.
Additional brass items may be found under Bell, Candlestick, Tool, or
Trivet.

    Ale Beaker, Hammer Milled Brass, Applied Lip Rim, England, 1700s 250.00
    Altar Candlestand, Stamped, 19th Century, 22 In., Pair 805.00
    Barber's Bowl, England, 18th Century 395.00
    Bed Warmer, Copper, Engraved, Leaves, Flowers, Wood Handle, 1800s, 35 x 12 In. 350.00
    Bed Warmer, Engraved Flower, Turned Wood Handle, 43 In. 196.00

Bed Warmer, Engraved Lid, Central Flower, Scrolls, Wood Handle, 43 3/4 In. 170.00
Bed Warmer, Engraved Lid, Wood Handle, 39 1/2 In. 130.00
Bed Warmer, Pierced, Iron, Turned Wood Handle, England, 17th Century 290.00
Bed Warmer, Pierced, Ring, Sausage Turned Ash Handle, Hearts, Circles, 45 x 14 x 6 In. .. 175.00
Bootjack, Devil 325.00
Bowl, Gondola Shape, Patinated, 1930s, 21 In. 240.00
Candleholder, Processional, Gilt, 14 1/2 In. 140.00
Candleholder, Wrought Iron, Corkscrew Stem, Scroll Feet, Late 19th Century, 8 In., Pair .. 115.00
Candlesnuffer, Stand, George II-III, c.1750, 8 In. 1095.00
Candlesnuffer, Witch's Hat Form, 18th Century 350.00
Candlestand, Tripod Base, Adjustable Holder, Brass Socket, Finial, 22 1/4 x 10 x 10 In. .. 230.00
Cauldron, Low Body, Decorative Band, Loop Handles, 13 x 20 In. 60.00
Chestnut Roaster, England, 19th Century, 23 In. 60.00
Cigar Cutter, Art Deco, Figural Sleeping Nude, Hinted Legs, 2 x 8 1/2 In. 985.00
Cigar Cutter, Figural, Man Sitting On Pot, Cast Iron Base, 1890s, 5 1/4 In. 550.00
Cigar Holder, Hammered, Arts & Crafts, 7 In. 295.00
Cigarette & Match Holder, Automobile Shape, Leather Seats, Germany, c.1910, 4 x 8 In. . 635.00
Clip, Jockey & Horse, Fred Archer & Bendor, England, c.1870, 4 1/4 In. 245.00
Coatrack, Scroll Design, Ball Finial, 79 In. 315.00
Cup, Footed, Lobed Sides, Wiener Werkstatte, c.1920, 2 1/2 In. 2070.00
Dish, Card Players, Clear Head, Quick Eye & Fair Playing, c.1870, 3 1/2 In. 120.00
Dog Collar, Stephen Old's Dog Dash, Padlock, 1700s 650.00
Easel, Table, Rococo Revival Style, c.1900, 10 x 5 x 4 In. 230.00
Figure, Dancer, Egyptian Style, Alabaster Base, Art Deco, 15 1/2 x 4 1/2 In., Pair 325.00
Figure, Dancer, Patinated, Gilt, C. Sullivan, 11 In. 155.00
Frame, Bacchanalian Mask, Scrolling Leaves, Arched Beveled Mirror, 15 x 10 In. 80.00
Gas Fixture, Handing, Swirling Arms, Diamond Shape Lamp, Beveled Panels, 29 x 18 In. . 230.00
Gong, Dragons, Tokugawa Mons, Japan, Early 20th Century, 18 In. 325.00
Humidor, Hammered, Hinged, Trees, Hills, Sponge Holder, Apollo Studios, 4 x 10 3/4 In. . 235.00
Jelly Pot, Hinged Handle, Tapered Body, 19th Century, 9 1/2 x 16 In. 80.00
Kettle Shelf, Wrought Iron, D-Shape, Cast Top, Pierced Scrolling, 13 x 11 x 14 In. 460.00
Kettle Stand, Wrought Iron, Tripod, Column, Painted Black, Pierced, Scalloped, 11 In. 90.00
Ladle, Wrought Iron Handle, Heart Shape Hanger, 20 x 5 3/8 In. 880.00
Mold, Candle, 12-Tube, Pine Rack, Rectangular, Ivory Paint, 10 1/2 x 10 1/2 In. 770.00
Plaque, Gilt Frame, Classical Relief, Huntress With Dog, 19th Century, 22 x 18 In. 190.00
Plate, Alms, Embossed Quatrefoil, Pinecones, Leaves, Germany, 1500s, 13 3/4 In. 1920.00
Reliquary, Gilt, Wood, Dome Lid, Paneled, Jeweled, Saints, Russia, 1977, 12 x 14 x 14 In. 69.00
Salt, Classical Shape, c.1810, 3 In. 155.00
Samovar, Cast Base, Cover, 19 1/2 In. 145.00
Samovar, Imperial Russian, Barrel Shape, 15 In. ....259.00 to 375.00
Samovar, Undertray, Kettle Shape, Handles, 14 1/2 In. 230.00
Sconce, Wall, 2-Arm, 18th Century French Style, Gilt, 9 1/2 In., Pair 355.00
Sconce, Wall, 2-Arm, 18th Century Style, 8 x 11 1/2 In., Pair 378.00
Scribe's Set, Incised, Animal Panels, Calligraphy, 19th Century, 10 In. 160.00
Sculpture, Buddha, Seated In Lotus Position, Elongated Ear Lobes, Tight Curls, 31 1/2 In. 2875.00
Skimmer, Pierced, England, 19th Century, 21 In. 90.00
Skirt Lifter, Man's Hand In Fist Form, Marked, Regd. Nov. 14, 1876, G. MCD, 5 3/4 In. .. 295.00
Station Pointer, Mahogany Case, Oil Bottle, 3 Extensions, Kelvin Hughes, c.1966, 18 In. . 316.00
Tieback, Curtain, Ribbon & Bellflower Design, Flower Medallion, 1880s, 17 In., Pair 510.00
Tieback, Stamped, Sunflower, Acorn Ring, Leaves, c.1835, 4 3/4 x 8 In. 440.00
Tray, Oval, Arts & Crafts, 13 x 9 In. 295.00
Tray, Polychromed, Parcel Giltwood, Butterfly & Flower Center, Gallery, 18 1/4 In. 345.00
Umbrella Stand, 6-Section Compartment, 20th Century, 25 x 12 x 9 In. 190.00
Umbrella Stand, Repousse, Figural Relief, Paw Feet, Liner, Dutch, 19th Century, 29 In. .. 750.00
Vase, Garniture, Neo-Grecque Style, Verdigris Mounted, Black Painted, 21 In., Pair 575.00
Vase, Hammered Leaf, Berry, Arts & Crafts, 12 In. 235.00
Vase, Molded Leaves, 15 x 13 1/2 In. 70.00
Vase, Patinated, WMF, 2 Handles, Embossed Flower Band, c.1910, 19 In. 225.00
Wall Sconce, Arts & Crafts, Aluminum, Spade Motif, 19 x 3 In. 405.00
Wall Sconce, Cast, Bell Flower Drops, Acanthus Leaves, Classical Panels, 17 In., Pair 259.00
Warming Pan, Punch, Chased Decorated, Rooster, Turned Handle, Early 1800s, 43 In. 470.00
Wine Pot, Trumpet Mouth, Animal Spout, Baluster Form, Nepal, 10 1/4 In. 259.00

BRASTOFF, see Sascha Brastoff category.

Bride's Bowl, Cased, Enameled Flowers, Chariot,
Meriden, Frame, 17 1/2 In.

Bride's Bowl,
Jack-In-The-Pulpit,
Meriden, Silver
Plated Frame, 13 In.

BREAD PLATE, see various silver categories, porcelain factories, and pressed glass patterns.

BRIDE'S BASKETS OR BRIDE'S BOWLS were usually one-of-a-kind novelties made in American and European glass factories. They were especially popular about 1880 when the decorated basket was often given as a wedding gift. Cut glass baskets were popular after 1890. All bride's baskets lost favor about 1905. Bride's baskets and bride's bowls may also be found in other glass sections. Check the index at the back of the book.

BRIDE'S BASKET, Lavender, Cased, Decorated, Middletown Plate Co. Frame	350.00
Opalescent, Ruffled Edge, Replated Silver Frame, 1885-95, 11 3/4 In.	350.00
Pink, Cased, Enameled Butterfly, James W. Tufts, Frame	475.00
Pink, Hobnail, Pleated Rim, Applied Clear Handle, 8 x 7 In.	75.00
Shaded Pink, Cased, Thorn Handles, Applied Flowers	215.00
Spanish Lace, Red Trim, Ruffled Edge, Silver Frame, 11 1/4 In.	210.00
Vaseline, Shell & Tassel, Oval, 9 5/8 In.	385.00
White Opal, Cranberry Ruffled Edge, Vaseline Rope Handle, 9 In.	110.00
BRIDE'S BOWL, Cased, Enameled Flowers, Chariot, Meriden, Frame, 17 1/2 In. .... *Illus*	8500.00
Cased, Middletown, Silver Plated Frame, Deer, Acorn Branches, 11 In.	1350.00
Cranberry To Clear, Overshot, Meriden Frame, 1800s, 11 In.	345.00
Jack-In-The-Pulpit, Meriden, Silver Plated Frame, 13 In. .... *Illus*	1050.00
Lavender, Opalescent White, Ruffled, Enameled, Parcel Gilt, Bohemian, 13 x 17 In.	489.00
Pink, Flowers, Leaves, Ruffled Rim, Silver Plated Frame, 9 In.	120.00
Satin, Pink, Silver Plated Frame, Marked USA 1665	300.00

BRISTOL glass was made in Bristol, England, after the 1700s. The Bristol glass most often seen today is a Victorian, lightweight opaque glass that is often blue. Some of the glass was decorated with enamels.

Garniture Set, Candlestick, Vases, White, Enameled Brown Borders, Flowers, 3 Piece	130.00
Goblet, Wine, Enameled Flowers, Leaves, 4 5/8 In.	44.00
Mug, Federal Eagle, Shield, Flowers, Multicolored, Gold Trim, 3 1/2 In.	1190.00
Vase, Classical Portraits, Man, Woman, White, Gold Beading, 12 1/4 In., Pair	100.00
Vase, Dark Green, Gold Iris, Footed, 8 3/4 In.	65.00
Vase, Flowers, Squat Bottom, Flared Neck, White, Gold Trim, 10 In. .... *Illus*	45.00
Vase, Light Blue, Enameled Flowers, Ruffled Rim, 19 1/4 In.	150.00

BRITANNIA, see Pewter category.

BRONZE is an alloy of copper, tin, and other metals. It is used to make figurines, lamps, and other decorative objects. Bronze lamps are listed in the Lamp category. Pieces listed here date from the eighteenth, nineteenth, and twentieth centuries.

Ashtray, Bach, Oscar, Reticulated Base, 10 x 31 In.	176.00
Ashtray, Hurley, E.T., Lobster, Fish, 3 5/8 In.	546.00
Bowl, Fluted, Nude Women, Holding Bowl, Art Deco, 1922, 3 3/4 x 16 In.	5875.00
Bowl, Fountain, Patinated, Round, Chinese, 20th Century, 35 In.	420.00
Bowl, Leaf, Flower, Japan, 9 1/2 In.	127.00
Box, Casket, Gothic Style, Cast, Hinged Lid, Velvet Lined, Footed, 1800s, 7 x 8 x 6 In. ...	980.00

Box, Casket, Repousse Leafy Decoration, Inlaid Copper Lid Rosette, 18th Century, 9 In. . . . 175.00
Box, Grapevine, Fruiting, Cluster Handle, Square, 6 1/4 x 7 1/4 In. 235.00
Box, Hurley, E.T., Seahorse, Seaweed, Cover, 2 3/4 x 4 3/4 In. 1035.00
Box, Hurley, E.T., Seahorses, Round, Cover, 1924, 3 1/8 x 5 3/8 In. 1955.00
Box, Potter Bentley Studios, Applied Art Deco Pewter Handle, 4-Footed, 2 1/2 x 6 x 3 In. . . 175.00
Bust, Aizelin, E., Peasant Woman, F. Barbedienne Foundry, 12 3/4 In. 960.00
Bust, Albert Schweitzer, 20th Century, 14 x 4 1/2 In. 200.00
Bust, Bessin, Paul Lucien, Woman, Daisies In Hair, Stems, Art Nouveau, France, 18 In. . . . 1645.00
Bust, Classical Youth, Verdigris Patina, Beige Marble Base, Late 1800s, 19 In. 3220.00
Bust, Colombo, R., Napoleon, Eagle On Base, Title Plaque, 12 5/8 In. 1060.00
Bust, Escoula, Jean, Girl, Eglantine, Upswept Hair, Apple Blossom Sprig, 17 1/2 In. 500.00
Bust, Napoleon, Resting On Eagle, 22 x 18 x 14 In. 965.00
Bust, Napoleon, Sienna Marble Base, Early 20th Century, 11 In. 1410.00
Bust, Roman Nobleman, Parcel Gilt, Marble Base, Continental, Late 1800s, 32 In. 4600.00
Bust, Salvatore, Victor D., Woman, Face Only, Square Base, Incised Signature, 1922, 4 In. 440.00
Bust, Tereszczuk, P., Madonna, Carved Ivory Face, Incised Signature, 5 5/8 In. 380.00
Bust, Vanderstraeten, Georges, Woman, White Onyx Base, Art Nouveau, Belgium, 7 In. . . 400.00
Bust, Vonnoh, Bessie Potter, Mother & Child, Brown Patina, 6 1/2 In. 5175.00
Bust, Woman With Grape-Leaf Bonnet, Brown Patina, c.1890, 8 In. 375.00
Cachepot, Brandt, Edgar, Eagle, Serpent Handles, c.1925, 5 In. 10755.00
Censer, Church Shape, Chain, Smoke Bell, 13 In. 575.00
Censer, Elephant-Head Feet, Handles, Lotus Pattern Cover, Late 1800s, 8 1/2 In. 235.00
Censer, Goose Shape, Chinese, 1800s, 9 1/4 In. 95.00
Censer, Helmet Shape, Japan, 19th Century, 8 x 7 1/2 x 7 In. 400.00
Censer, Loop Handles, Oval, Squat, Chinese, 3-Footed, 5 3/4 In. 240.00
Censer, Silvered, Repousse, 11 In. 489.00
Cross, Processional, Corpus, Champleve Disc, Angel, Virgin Verso, Spain, 20 In. 430.00
Cross, Processional, Gilt, Silvered, Corpus, Evangelists, Stand, 20th Century, 22 x 16 In. . . 920.00
Cross, Processional, Silvered, Fluted Staff, Germany, 20th Century, 69 In. 460.00
Crucifix, Altar, Silvered, Marble Plinth, Continental, c.1930, 14 In. 750.00
Desk Set, Gilt, Champleve, Double Inkwell, France, c.1900, 7 Piece 1610.00
Dish, Horseshoe Shape, Maiden's Head, Flowing Hair, Art Nouveau, Austria, 7 In. 1910.00
Dish, Maiden Wrapped In Leaf, Gilt, Art Nouveau, 3 x 4 1/4 In. 450.00
Ewer, Napoleon III, Neogrecque Style, Diademed Female Mask, Gilt, c.1865, 10 In., Pair . 230.00
Ewer, Neoclassical, Cavorting Putti, Serpentine Loop Handle, Cherubs, 34 1/2 In., Pair 3525.00
Flag Pole Top, Eagle, Bronze, Brass, Late 1800s, 10 In. 300.00
Humidor, 3 Kneeling American Indians, 3 Bison Heads, Gorham, c.1885, 6 1/2 In. 5175.00
Incense Burner, Campana Shape, Patinated, Everted Rim, Cover, Plinth Base, 6 In. 185.00
Incense Burner, Immortals, Clouds, Elephant Heads, Birds, Lotus, Japan, 1800s, 11 In. . . . 467.00
Incense Burner, Mount Fuji Shape, Dragon Around Base, 19th Century, 7 1/2 x 9 3/4 In. . . 489.00
Incense Burner, Pagoda, Paw Feet, Gilt Openwork, Chinese, 41 x 26 In. 520.00
Jardiniere, Art Deco, Female Nude, Rectangular, Concentric Circles, 4 1/2 x 8 x 6 In. 598.00
Jardiniere, Chinese, Late 19th Century, 15 In. 1076.00
Jardiniere, Geese, Autumn Grasses, Plovers, Silver Wire, Early 1900s, 8 1/2 In. 340.00
Jardiniere, Military Figures, Rectangular, Chinese, 17th Century, 8 1/2 In. 670.00
Mirror, Case, Gold Moon, Black Ground, Kodaiji Lacquer Style, Japan, 1800s, 16 In. 120.00
Note Clip, Owl, Glass Eyes, Gilt, 19th Century, 4 1/2 In. 69.00

Bristol, Vase,
Flowers, Squat
Bottom, Flared
Neck, White,
Gold Trim, 10 In.

Bronze, Sculpture,
Baldwin, Poodle, On
Hind Legs, Wearing
Clown Hat, 8 3/4 In.

Dust your bronze, then try the Chinese method of polishing. Rub the bronze with the palm of your hand. This puts a little oil on the metal.

Pen Wiper, Running Rabbit, Cold Paint, Fur Back, Austria, c.1900, 8 1/2 In. 1295.00
Pipe Holder, Hurley, E.T., Seahorse, 19262 5/8 x 6 3/4 In. 1150.00
Planter, Relief Hawks, Leaves, Cranes, Clouds, Cast, Brown Patina, Oriental, 12 x 13 In. .   430.00
Plaque, Aesthetic Movement, Relief, Flower Maidens, Early 1900s, 12 x 12 In., Pair 705.00
Plaque, Chambellan, Home Front Production, Doehler-Jarvis Corp., Toledo, 33 x 20 In. . . .   345.00
Plaque, Children With Musical Instruments, Golden Brown Patina, Round, 6 In. 90.00
Plaque, Forest Scene, Wild Boar, Incised, Germany, 5 1/2 x 10 1/4 In. 176.00
Plaque, Paolo, C.S., Portrait, John Burroughs, National Art Bronze Works, 5 1/2 x 8 In. . . .   175.00
Plaque, Schmidt, Rudolf, Dancing Couples, Accordion Player, 8 x 11 1/2 In. 1528.00
Plaque, Trade & Industry, Workmen, American Indian, Germany, Frame, 12 x 19 In. 175.00
Reliquary, Cast, Gothic Style, St. Ursula Relic, 7 x 8 x 4 In. 489.00
Reliquary, Gilded, Veil Of The Blessed Virgin Mary Relic, Documentation, 14 3/4 In. 2415.00
Samovar, Extending Spout, Scroll Feet, Electrified, Late 1800s, 36 In. 175.00
Scepter, Faces, Oriental, Paneled Rod, Swirl Designs, Crown Finial, Cast Handle, 20 In. . .   145.00
Sculpture, 2 Arabs In An Interior, Viennese Cold Painted, Early 1900s, 7 3/4 In. 2350.00
Sculpture, 2 Children, Climbing Fence, Brown Patina, Continental, 74 x 84 x 36 In. 2070.00
Sculpture, 2 Giraffes, Art Deco, 9 x 8 In. 380.00
Sculpture, 2 Girls, Playing Leapfrog, 22 1/2 In. 5280.00
Sculpture, 2 Island Natives, Sawing Log, 7 1/2 x 8 1/2 x 6 1/2 In.   90.00
Sculpture, 3 Children, Gilt, Oval Base, Marble Plinth, 15 3/4 In. 1175.00
Sculpture, 3-Headed Deity, Mythical Beast, 6 Arms, Lotus Throne, Tibet, 7 1/8 In. 1120.00
Sculpture, Aizelin, Eugene-Antoine, Nymphe De Diane, Brown Patina, 17 In. 3220.00
Sculpture, American Indian, Headdress, Drum, Marble Plinth, 20th Century, 19 x 8 x 5 In.   470.00
Sculpture, American Indian, On Horseback, Roping, 20th Century, 15 x 24 x 8 In. 265.00
Sculpture, Antelope, Marble Base, Art Deco, 14 In. 880.00
Sculpture, Arab, On Horseback, Marble Base, 11 In. 50.00
Sculpture, Archer, Classical Helmeted Nude, Patinated, Marble Base, 13 x 6 x 3 In. 430.00
Sculpture, Auguste Cesar, Brown Patina, France, 19th Century, 19 In. 2530.00
Sculpture, Bacchante, F. Barbedienne Foundry, 35 3/4 In. 6573.00
Sculpture, Bacque, Daniel-Joseph, Bacchante, Gilt, Ebonized Wood Base, 13 In. 775.00
Sculpture, Baldwin, Poodle, On Hind Legs, Wearing Clown Hat, 8 3/4 In. . . . . *Illus*   595.00
Sculpture, Barye, Antoine-Louis, Lion, Walking, Green Patina, Incised Signature, 15 In. . .   6465.00
Sculpture, Barye, Antoine-Louis, Ostrich, Marble Base, France, 6 x 9 1/2 In. 880.00
Sculpture, Barye, Antoine-Louis, Panther Attacking Antelope, France, 27 1/2 In. 2990.00
Sculpture, Barye, Antoine-Louis, Stag, Walking, Foreleg Raised, Incised, 11 1/4 In. 3290.00
Sculpture, Barye, Antoine-Louis, Wolf, Standing Over Deer, France, 9 x 14 In. 3175.00
Sculpture, Bat Dance, Young Woman, Outstretched Bat Wings, Ivory, Cold Painted, 9 In. .   11950.00
Sculpture, Bazin, Francis Victor, Bird In Flight, Art Deco, 11 In. 1410.00
Sculpture, Bear, Cold Painted, Austria, 4 1/4 In. 420.00
Sculpture, Bearded Dignitary, Gilt, Seated, Chinese, 10 1/2 In. 575.00
Sculpture, Bergman, Golden Pheasant, Cold Painted, 14 1/2 In. 670.00
Sculpture, Bodhisattva Seated Double Lotus, Multicolored, Brocade, Beads, Tibet, 12 In. .   750.00
Sculpture, Bofill, Antoine, Le Travail, Red, Brown Patina, Spain, c.1895, 27 1/2 In. 2760.00
Sculpture, Bologna, Giovanni, Mercury, Putti Frieze, Marble Plinth Base, 29 In. 1495.00
Sculpture, Bonome, Santiago, Femme Elegante, Art Deco Lady, Patinated, 1927, 26 In. . . .   1725.00
Sculpture, Boontard, A., Boy, Swinging, Brown Patina, Continental, 1900s, 99 x 57 x 41 In.   635.00
Sculpture, Bormann, Wilhelm, Child, Cat On Shoulder, Germany, 12 1/2 In. 440.00
Sculpture, Bouret, Eutrope, La Cigale, Veined Green Marble Base, c.1900, 27 In. 1345.00
Sculpture, Bouret, Eutrope, Young Maiden Holding Flowers, 22 1/2 In. 1150.00
Sculpture, Boyer, Emile, Zeus Holding Infant Cupid, 17 1/2 In. 1265.00
Sculpture, Buddha, Amida, Appeasement Mudra, Partial Gilt, Chinese, 18th Century, 6 In.   2820.00
Sculpture, Buddha, Gilt, Thailand, 45 In., Pair 2689.00
Sculpture, Buddha, Gold Lacquer, 19th Century, 8 In. 410.00
Sculpture, Buddha, Holding Beggar's Bowl, 4-Tiered Lotus Base, Gilt, Thailand, 17 In. . . .   400.00
Sculpture, Buddha, Lotus Stand, Southeast Asia, 22 x 16 x 11 In. 9200.00
Sculpture, Buddha, Seated, 2-Tiered Lotus Throne, Tibet, 4 In. 400.00
Sculpture, Buddha, Seated, Brocade Trimmed Robe, Gilt, Chinese, 19th Century, 6 1/4 In.   800.00
Sculpture, Buddha, Seated, Lotus Throne, 3-Character Inscription, Sino-Tibet, 6 3/4 In. . . .   2070.00
Sculpture, Buddha, Seated, Multitiered Throne, Burma, 8 1/2 In. 550.00
Sculpture, Buddha, Seated, Touching Earth, Mirror Inlay, Burma, 1700s, 12 1/4 In. 2185.00
Sculpture, Buddha, Seated, Wearing Crown, Chinese, 17 In. 690.00
Sculpture, Buddha, Standing On 2-Tiered Lotus Throne, Chinese, 20th Century, 18 1/4 In.   575.00
Sculpture, Buddhist Acolyte, Clasped Hands, Lotus Pedestal, Chinese, 19 In. 280.00

Sculpture, Bull, Farmer, Carved Fitted Wood Base, Japan, c.1900, 24 In. 1295.00
Sculpture, Buoy At Sea, Marble Base, 4 x 6 In. 700.00
Sculpture, Cartier, Thomas Francois, Dog & Cat, Marble Base, 1879-1943, 11 1/2 In. 8400.00
Sculpture, Cat, Reclining, Gilt, After Theophile Alexandre Steinlen, 6 In. 1910.00
Sculpture, Charpentier, Black Lacquered Pedestal, France, 1937, 12 x 6 x 5 1/2 In. 1195.00
Sculpture, Charron, Amedee, Winged Fairy With Book, Pedestal, Marble Base, 16 1/2 In. . . 2940.00
Sculpture, Chenrezig, Seated, Lotus Throne, 4 Arms, Double Flame Mandala, Nepal, 6 In. 550.00
Sculpture, Cherub, Playing Lute, Standing On Tiptoes, Stone Pedestal, 9 3/4 In. 1725.00
Sculpture, Cherub, Singing, Playing Tambourine, Green Stone Pedestal, 10 1/4 In. 2070.00
Sculpture, Cherub, With Goose, Dark Brown Patina, 3 x 3 3/4 In. 290.00
Sculpture, Clesinger, Jean Baptiste, Standing Sapho, Red Brown Patina, c.1857, 27 In. . . . 3450.00
Sculpture, Colinet, Claire Jean Roberte, Egyptian Woman, Nude, Seated, Shawl, 11 In. . . . 1880.00
Sculpture, Coloma, Emmanuel De Santa, Soldier On Horseback, Brown Patina, 16 1/2 In. . 1610.00
Sculpture, Cook, R., Dancer Raising Dress, Wood Pedestal, 22 x 12 x 7 In. 910.00
Sculpture, Cook, R., Dancing Girl, Marble Pedestal, 26 x 6 x 8 In. 900.00
Sculpture, Cook, R., Frustration, Wood Pedestal, 22 x 15 x 8 In. 750.00
Sculpture, Cook, R., Man, Walking Sticks, Wood Pedestal, 25 x 9 x 7 1/2 In. 748.00
Sculpture, Couper, William Abram Stevens Hewitt, N.Y.C. Mayor, c.1900, 25 In. 2590.00
Sculpture, Crane, Standing, 19th Century, 93 In. 2300.00
Sculpture, Crane, Variegated Green Patina, 57 In., Pair 1095.00
Sculpture, Crayfish, Articulated, Japan, Early 20th Century, 17 In. 3175.00
Sculpture, Dancer, Holding Snake, Swirling Skirt, Glass Cabochons, Austria, 17 In. 7345.00
Sculpture, Dancer, On Lotus Base, Holding Drum, Gilt Copper, 19th Century, 3 In. 315.00
Sculpture, Dancer, On Marble Column, Outstretched Arms, Dove, Art Deco, 21 x 17 In. . . 2300.00
Sculpture, Dancer, Woman On Foot, Arched Back, Extended Arms, Art Deco, 13 In. 1528.00
Sculpture, Dancing Woman, Faux Ivory Head, Hands, Onyx Base, 1900s, 13 In. 460.00
Sculpture, Deity, In Armor, Seated, Lion Throne, Holding Animal, Chinese, 8 3/4 In. 2875.00
Sculpture, Deity, Seated, Wearing Crown, Wood Throne Stand, Chinese, 15 In. 8050.00
Sculpture, Deity, Standing On Figure, Double Lotus Base, Tibet, 6 3/8 In. 1512.00
Sculpture, Deity, Standing, Holding Scepter, 19th Century, Chinese, 10 1/2 In. 290.00
Sculpture, Delon, F., Bird On Edge Of Bowl, Signed, 7 x 6 In. 1175.00
Sculpture, Devil, Wiener Werkstatte, 3 1/2 In. 235.00
Sculpture, Dignitary, Holding Tablet, Gilt, Multicolored Base, Chinese, 8 1/4 In. 345.00
Sculpture, Dog, Hunting Pose, Cast, Plinth Base, 20th Century, 4 x 8 x 3 1/2 In., Pair 380.00
Sculpture, Dog, Seated, Cast, Marble Plinth, France, 19th Century, 7 In. 316.00
Sculpture, Dog, Seated, Wearing Collar With Pendants, 6 In. 390.00
Sculpture, Dog, Spaniel, Cast, Copper Paint, Stamped, Austria, 11 x 7 In. 520.00
Sculpture, Dogs, Mother, Pup, Japan, 6 1/2 & 8 In., Pair 780.00
Sculpture, Dragon, Holding Crystal Ball, 19th Century, Japan, 12 1/2 In. 1140.00
Sculpture, Dragons, Winged, Writhing, Regency Style, Gilt, Marble Base, 6 x 9 In., Pair . . 1610.00
Sculpture, Duchoiselle, Indian Maiden, Canoe, Marble Base, c.1870, 14 x 18 In. 3450.00
Sculpture, Eagle, Flying, Articulated Wings, Curled, Japan, 1868-1912, 21 1/2 x 15 In. . . . 1610.00
Sculpture, Eagle, Spread Wings, Tree-Stump Base, 44 x 48 In. 2875.00
Sculpture, Eisenberger, Ludwig, Warrior On Horseback, 1895-1920 . . . . 2530.00
Sculpture, Elephant, 2 Tigers Attacking, Ivory Tusks, Signed, Japan, 21 1/2 In. 1208.00
Sculpture, Elephant, Ivory Tusks, Austria, 6 In. 175.00
Sculpture, Engstrom, Torolf, Alskande, Man & Woman Kissing, Sweden, 7 In. 1765.00
Sculpture, Erte, 2 Women, Long Gowns, Multicolored, Marble Base, c.1989, 17 x 19 In. . . 5750.00
Sculpture, Falcon, Removable Wings, Perched On Roost, Japan, c.1890, 19 In. 1090.00
Sculpture, Ferdinand, Pautrot, Bird, Animated Bittern, Eating A Snake, 9 In. 518.00
Sculpture, Figaro, 18th-Century Costume, Cape, Holding Razor, Patinated, 19 In. 2270.00
Sculpture, Fisherman, With Pole, Fish, Signed, Japan, 13 In. 375.00
Sculpture, Foo Dogs, Chinese, 19th Century, 8 1/2 In., Pair 230.00
Sculpture, Foo Dogs, Holding Brocade Ball, Puppy, Gilt, Chinese, 8 In., Pair 290.00
Sculpture, Foo Dogs, Seated, Holding Brocade Ball, Puppy, 19th Century, 15 In., Pair 1095.00
Sculpture, Foo Lions, Foot On Ball, Weathered Green Patina, Glass Eyes, 16 In., Pair 805.00
Sculpture, Gasq, Paul Jean, Baptiste, Winged Goddess, 35 In. 6325.00
Sculpture, Gaudez, A.E., Chevalier On Horse, Serving Girl, France, 32 x 25 In. 6465.00
Sculpture, Gautherin, Jean, Field Worker, Sharpening Scythe, Collins & Co., 13 5/8 In. . . . 705.00
Sculpture, Girl, Bending To Muzzle Of Deer, Art Deco, 23 1/2 x 12 1/2 In. 1175.00
Sculpture, Goddess, Seated, Gilt, Wood Stand, Chinese, 2 3/4 In. 605.00
Sculpture, Gregoire, Jean-Louis, Running Eros, Marble Base, France, c.1885, 22 In. 865.00
Sculpture, Greyhound Dogs, Playing With Ball, 8 x 4 1/2 x 6 1/4 In. 1265.00

Sculpture, Gross, Chaim, Standing Figure, Award Of Learning, Wooden Base, 10 In. 520.00
Sculpture, Guardian Lions, Open Mouths, Detailed Manes, Tails, Chinese, 3 3/4 In., Pair . . 635.00
Sculpture, Hecht, Joseph, Antelope, Incised, c.1937, 17 x 20 x 6 In. 6600.00
Sculpture, Herlinger, Reclining Nude, On Sphinx, Onyx Base, 8 x 10 x 4 1/2 In. 325.00
Sculpture, Hoffman, Malvina, Nude Woman, Green Patina, 9 3/4 In. 3738.00
Sculpture, Horse, Patinated, Oval Base, 15 1/2 x 17 In. 8965.00
Sculpture, Horse, Standing, Detailed Mane, Tail, 7 In. 890.00
Sculpture, Humphreys, Albert, Bear Scratching Back, 1910, 6 1/4 In. 940.00
Sculpture, Humplik, Josef, Atlas, c.1908, 16 1/2 In. 1076.00
Sculpture, Hyatt, Anna V., Ram, Charging, Gorham, 6 3/4 x 8 1/2 x 6 In. 2270.00
Sculpture, Indra, Seated, Coral, Turquoise Inlay, Nepal, 11 In. 570.00
Sculpture, Ironworker, After Gerhard Adolf Janensch, 16 1/2 In. 568.00
Sculpture, Janensch, G.A., Nude, Square Marble Plinth, Brown Patina, Germany, 26 In. . . 1150.00
Sculpture, Joan Of Arc, Kneeling In Prayer, Gilt, 19 1/4 In. 3585.00
Sculpture, Joseph, Explaining Pharaoh's Dream, Brown Patina, Slag Base, 19 In. 1955.00
Sculpture, Jozon, J., Girl's Head, 9 In. 650.00
Sculpture, Kneeling Courtier, Court Robes, Wood Base, Japan, c.1900, 9 1/2 In. 805.00
Sculpture, Konarek, J., Woman, 6 In. 590.00
Sculpture, Kraczkowski, Phil, Sergeant, Northwest Mounted Police, 1885, 21 x 18 In. 1035.00
Sculpture, Lama, Seated, Holding Squirrel, Wearing Gilt Robes, Chinese, 7 In. 259.00
Sculpture, Lambeaux, Jef., Dancing Nude Couple, V. Stevens Foundry, 22 In. 2150.00
Sculpture, Lathrop, G.K., Pekingese Puppy, Marble Base, 3 1/8 x 7 1/4 In. 600.00
Sculpture, Macleod, Woman, Nude, Sitting, Head On Knees, Brown Gold Patina, 6 x 7 In. 863.00
Sculpture, Madrassi, Luca, Woman, With Lute, Brown Patina, France, 27 1/2 In. 2990.00
Sculpture, Malakala, Squatting On Lotus Base, Holding Bell, Vajra, 18th Century, 4 In. . . . 748.00
Sculpture, Marcus Aurelius, Military Uniform, Gilt, Slate Base, Italy, c.1785, 20 In. 1840.00
Sculpture, Marioton, E., Clytie, Classical Draped Woman, Arms Entwined, c.1900, 24 In. . 1765.00
Sculpture, Meijin, With Fan, On Rockery Base, Attendant Rabbit, Chinese, 11 1/2 In. 1610.00
Sculpture, Mene, Pierre Jules, 2 Setters, Leaping, Running, Marble Plinth, 10 In. 1645.00
Sculpture, Mercury, Classical-Style Relief Pedestal, 33 In. 956.00
Sculpture, Merite, E.P., Bird, Marble Base, 5 x 6 In. 380.00
Sculpture, Merman, Swimming, Carrying Shell, France, 19th Century, 7/1 4 x 8 1/2 In. . . . 999.00
Sculpture, Mignon, Leon, Muse Of Music, Patina, 12 In. 430.00
Sculpture, Moigniez, Jules, Setter, Hunting, Crouched In Grass, Incised, 11 1/2 In. 2235.00
Sculpture, Moigniez, Jules, Setter, Pointing, Rounded Rectangular Base, 15 3/4 In. 920.00
Sculpture, Moreau, Auguste, Woman, In Flight, France, 30 1/2 In. 8800.00
Sculpture, Moreau, Classical Woman, Sitting, Green Brown Patina, Late 1800s, 9 1/2 In. . . 630.00
Sculpture, Moreau, Lady Swinging On Branches, 10 1/2 In. 500.00
Sculpture, Mountain Goat, With Chinese Coin, Parcel Gilt Overlay, Chinese, 21 x 16 In. . . 635.00
Sculpture, Mule & Rider, 19th Century, 15 In. 1560.00
Sculpture, Nam, Jacques, Cat, Sitting, Patinated, 15 1/4 x 9 1/2 x 13 1/2 In. 3110.00
Sculpture, Napoleon, Standing, By Column, Square Base, Late 1800s, 14 In. 940.00
Sculpture, Night Watchman, Holding Lantern, Bell, Oblong Base, 23 1/4 In. 1295.00
Sculpture, Nude Male Athlete, Striding, Patinated, 12 x 10 x 5 In. 518.00
Sculpture, Nymph Toasting Satyr, After Claude-Michel Clodion, 16 1/2 In. 1315.00
Sculpture, Osiris, Standing, Holding Flail & Staff, Peaked Cap, 7 1/2 In. 220.00
Sculpture, Pajama Girl, Patinated, Cold Painted, Carved Ivory, Onyx, Marble, 13 1/2 In. . . 3625.00
Sculpture, Pautrot, Ferdinand, Dog, Inscribed Admis Aux Beaux Arts, 12 In. 4315.00
Sculpture, Pheasant, Male Standing Guard Over Female, 3 Chicks, France, 1870 . . . . 4400.00
Sculpture, Picault, E., La Pensee, Winged Female, Standing Over Book, 30 1/2 In. 3680.00
Sculpture, Picault, Emile Louis, Whaler, Brown Patina, Signed, 12 1/4 In. 1840.00
Sculpture, Pina, Alfredo, Banana Seller, Black Patina, 19 3/4 In. 2875.00
Sculpture, Piraino, P., Baby In A Hat, Signed, 9 In. 560.00
Sculpture, Poertzel, Otto, Nude Woman, Standing, Poised, Veined Marble Base, 7 3/4 In. . 380.00
Sculpture, Pradier, Jean Jacques, Sappho, Seated, Brown Patina, 10 In. 1380.00
Sculpture, Pradier, Jean Jacques, Sappho, Silvered, Gilded, c.1848, 17 In. 7360.00
Sculpture, Quan-Ti, Wearing Armor, 4-Footed Platform, Chinese, 10 3/4 In. 748.00
Sculpture, Ring Dancer, Cold Painted, c.1925, 18 1/2 In. 8365.00
Sculpture, Riviere, Theodore, Woman, Cape, 3 In. 590.00
Sculpture, Romantic Couple, Brown Patina, Slate Base, Continental, 15 x 16 x 7 1/2 In. . . 259.00
Sculpture, Saint Christopher, Infant Christ, Wading, Cast, Polychrome, 38 In. 805.00
Sculpture, Sanger, Cat, Stalking, Marble Base, Germany, 13 In. 705.00
Sculpture, Schmidt-Felling, Julius, Dutch Boy & Girl, Mid 1800s, 6 In., Pair 316.00

Sculpture, Schwabauer, Lyle, Break Away, Elk On Rocky Hillside, Cold Painted, 20 In. . . .   630.00
Sculpture, Seagull, Over Waves, Continental, 1900s, 14 x 24 In. 2940.00
Sculpture, Serpent, Art Nouveau, 5 In. 470.00
Sculpture, Shakti, Standing On Lotus Base, Flame Mandala, Tibet, 6 3/4 In. 520.00
Sculpture, Shot Put Thrower, Classical Style, 20th Century, 16 1/2 In. 380.00
Sculpture, Soldier, Riding Horse, Gilt, Black Hardstone, Marble, 16 In. 960.00
Sculpture, Songbird, Seated, Glass Eyes, Oval Base, 1849, 3 5/8 In. 355.00
Sculpture, Spanish Dancer, Gilt, Green Marble Base, 22 In. 765.00
Sculpture, Stag, Leaping, Marble, Black Slate Base, c.1930, 12 x 16 1/2 In. 1380.00
Sculpture, Stupa, Gilt Temple Finial, Semiprecious Gemstones, Tibet, 17th Century, 5 In. .   980.00
Sculpture, Tara, Seated On Lotus Throne, Flowers On Shoulders, 3 1/2 In. 865.00
Sculpture, Tara, Seated On Lotus Throne, Sino-Tibet, 18th Century, 3 In. 690.00
Sculpture, Tara, Seated, In Royal Ease, Double Lotus Throne, Nepal, 19th Century, 6 In. . .   380.00
Sculpture, Tiger, Roaring, Japan, 12 In. 825.00
Sculpture, Tortoise, Inlaid Eyes, Japan, 6 1/4 In. 1495.00
Sculpture, Turtle, Japan, 4 1/2 In. 300.00
Sculpture, Valton, Charles, Hounds, Rounded Rectangular Base, 16 1/2 In., Pair 2070.00
Sculpture, Veeck, Charles, La Fileuse, Silver Patina Trace, 16 In. 115.00
Sculpture, Vela, Vincenzo, Last Days Of Napoleon, Brown Patina, 17 In. 6038.00
Sculpture, Vezin, Charles, Dancer, 1900s, 13 In. 999.00
Sculpture, Villanis, Emmanuel, Elalla-Roukh, Brown Patina, Gilt Highlights, 26 In. 2760.00
Sculpture, Virion, Charles Louis Eugene, Resting Dogs, France, 10 x 17 1/2 In. 1955.00
Sculpture, Waldemann, Oscar, Bear, Marble Base, 4 1/4 In. 550.00
Sculpture, Water Boy, With Water Jugs, Reservoir Base, 19th Century, 22 x 10 x 9 In. 380.00
Sculpture, Water Buffalo, Gilt, Standing, 14 1/4 x 28 In., Pair 259.00
Sculpture, Water Carrier, Female, Nude, Square Marble Base, 8 In.   390.00
Sculpture, Woman Deity, On Lotus Throne, Sino-Tibet, 17th Century, 8 1/4 In. 805.00
Sculpture, Woman Deity, Standing Before Mandala, Calligraphy, Gilt, 9 In. 230.00
Sculpture, Woman, 2 Dogs, Carved Ivory, Painted, Art Deco, France, 25 x 26 In. 26450.00
Sculpture, Woman, Holding Basket Of Grapes, Sampling Fruit, 22 1/4 In. 999.00
Sculpture, Woman, Holding Comedic Mask, Violin, Opera Glasses, Fan, France, 22 In. . . .   2350.00
Sculpture, Woman, In Hoop Skirt, Holding Mirror, Ivory, c.1925, 18 In. 6575.00
Sculpture, Woman, Nude Beside Tree, Holding Seashell Over Head, 20 In. 2300.00
Sculpture, Woman, Victorian, Holding Notebook & Pencil, 19th Century, 9 In. 380.00
Sculpture, Woman, With Lotus Flower, Golden Brown Patina, Green Marble Base, 26 In. . .   1265.00
Sculpture, Woman, With Tambourine, Black Marble Base, 24 In. 489.00
Sculpture, Wyon, Allan G., Egyptian Nude, Kneeling, Arms Outstretched At Sides, 22 In. .   8855.00
Sculpture, Ximenes, Ettore, Archer, Italy, 17 In. 540.00
Sculpture, Young Dionysus, Grand Tour, Patinated, Early 1900s, 14 In. 499.00
Sculpture, Young Girls, Semi-Clad, Carrying Basket, Green Marble Socle, 11 In., Pair 480.00
Sculpture, Zach, Bruno, Seated Nude, Monkey, 17 x 13 x 8 1/2 In.   7640.00
Scuplture, Dallin, Cyrus Edwin, Indian Brave On Horse, Hand At Forehead, 33 x 35 In. . .   4900.00
Sweetmeat Stand, Napoleon III, Louis XVI Style, Gilt, Cut Glass, 2 Tiers, 23 In. 1265.00
Tazza, Art Nouveau, Cast Classical Scenes, Late 1800s, 11 In. 405.00
Tiebacks, Winged Cherubs Riding Cornucopia, Gilt, 19th Century, 13 1/2 In., Pair 630.00
Torchere, Skyscraper, Art Deco, 4 Stepped Feet, 69 In., Pair 2700.00
Tray, Fries, Crane Corners, Whiplash Center, 9 1/4 x 9 1/4 In. 350.00
Tray, Miault, Wheat, France, 11 In. 410.00
Urn, Bulbous, Squat, 2 Angular Handles, 12 x 12 In. 259.00
Urn, Garniture Set, Louis XVI Style, Patina, Parcel Gilt, Flame Shape Cover, 18 In., Pair . .   1380.00
Urn, Phoenix Panels, Waves, Baku-Head Feet, Dome Cover, Japan, Late 1800s, 14 1/4 In. .   700.00
Urn, Regency, Gilt, Ram's-Head Handles, Leaf Carved, 11 1/2 In., Pair 2875.00
Vanetti, Warrior, Chariot, 3 Horses, Rounded Rectangular Base, 13 x 28 In. 3570.00
Vase, Altar, Gilt, 10 To 15 In., 4 Piece 230.00
Vase, Badgers, Inverted Pear Shape, 11 In. 460.00
Vase, Barkley, McClelland, Organic, 8 In. 525.00
Vase, Child, Relief Figure, Marble Base, 12 In. 95.00
Vase, Dragon Heads, Ring Handles, Pear Shape, Footed, Chinese, 1700s, 12 In., Pair 690.00
Vase, Dragons, Fluted, Animal Head Handles, Flared Foot, Chinese, 1800s, 12 In. 210.00
Vase, Dragons, Pearls, 2 Baku-Head Handles, Globular, 3-Footed, Japan, Late 1800s, 9 In.   260.00
Vase, Empire Style, Gilt Mounted, Green Glass, 13 In., Pair 1675.00
Vase, Flowering Lotus, Ribbed Ground, Cast, Calligraphic Inscription, 38 1/2 In. 1725.00
Vase, Garniture Set, Louis Philippe Style, Patinated, Mid 19th Century, 10 1/2 In., Pair . .   2185.00

Vase, Korschann, Charles, Flowers, Gilt, Patinated, Art Nouveau, c.1900, 10 In. 750.00
Vase, Landscape, Peacock, On Branch, Raised Decoration, On Stand, Oriental, 12 x 8 In. .. 510.00
Vase, Mask, Loose Ring Handles, Baluster Form, 18 In. 1200.00
Vase, Moreau, Child, Sitting On Shoulder, Garden Scene, Dragonflies, Bird, 12 In. 2875.00
Vase, Moreau, Elf, Sitting On Broken Branch, Tree Trunk, Flowers, Leaves, 11 3/4 In. 575.00
Vase, Mt. Fuji, Inlaid, Oval, 8 1/2 x 10 In. 575.00
Vase, Napoleon III, Bowl Form, Patinated, Lucite Base, c.1865, 10 In. 865.00
Vase, Potted Deer, Moonlit Landscape, Cylindrical, Sosho, Signed, Japan, 9 1/2 In. 345.00
Vase, Raised Iris & Birds, Cylindrical, Flared Rim, Japan, c.1890, 10 In. 230.00
Vase, Relief Landscape, Cottages, Dragon Handles, Pear Shape, 17 1/2 In. 545.00
Vase, Thistle, Art Nouveau, France, 12 1/2 In. 529.00
Wax Seal, Cherub Drummer, Silvered, Conjoined Initials, After Auguste Moreau, 4 In. 748.00
Wrist Cuff, Flared Ends, Incised Geometric Decoration, Nigerian, Late 1800s, 7 3/8 In. ... 470.00

BROWNIES were first drawn in 1883 by Palmer Cox. They are char-
acterized by large round eyes, downturned mouths, and skinny legs.
Toys, books, dinnerware, and other objects were made with the
Brownies as part of the design.

Book, Brownie Year Book, Palmer Cox, McLoughlin Bros., 1895 .... 500.00
Calendar, Lambertville Rubber Co., Paper, 1903 .... 35.00
Ornament, Christmas Tree, Blown Glass, Annealed Legs, 5 1/2 In. 770.00
Paper Doll, Man Smoking Pipe, V On Chest, Cordova Coffee, 5 In. 45.00
Paper Doll, Man With Horn, Wearing Fez, McLaughlin Coffee, 6 In. 20.00

BRUSH Pottery was started in 1925. George Brush first worked in
1901 in Zanesville, Ohio. He started his own pottery in 1907, but it
burned to the ground soon after. In 1909 he became manager of the
J.W. McCoy Pottery. In 1911, Brush and J.W. McCoy formed the
Brush-McCoy Pottery Co. After a series of name changes, the company became The Brush Pottery in 1925. It closed in 1982. Old Brush
was marked with impressed letters or a palette-shaped mark. Some
new pieces are being marked in raised letters or with a raised mark.
Collectors favor the figural cookie jars made by this company. Because
there was a company named Brush-McCoy, there is great confusion
between Brush and Nelson McCoy pieces. See McCoy category for
more information.

MARK

Cookie Jar, Cow With Cat, Marked, 10 In. 195.00
Cookie Jar, Teddy Bear, Feet Together, 1940s, 11 In. 175.00
Wall Pocket, Branches, Leaves, Brown, 8 1/2 x 3 1/2 In. 118.00

BRUSH MCCOY, see Brush category and related pieces in McCoy categor

BUCK ROGERS was the first American science fiction comic strip. It
started in 1929 and continued until 1967. Buck has also appeared in
comic books, movies, and, in the 1980s, a television series. Any memorabilia connected with the character Buck Rogers is collectible.

Atomic Pistol, Pull Trigger Makes Popping Sound, Gold Metallic, Disney, 1936 .... 875.00
Atomic Pistol U-235, 25th Century, Daisy, Box, 1936, 10 In. 930.00
Book, Big Little Book, Buck Rogers & Super Dwarf, No. 1490, Whitman, Dille, 1943 .... 220.00
Book, Big Little Book, Buck Rogers & The Doom Comet, No. 1178, 1935 .... 190.00
Book, Big Little Book, Buck Rogers 25th Century, No. 742, Whitman, Dille, 1933 .... 165.00
Book, Buck Rogers, War With The Planet Venus, No. 1437, 1938 .... 310.00
Book, Collected Works, Dust Jacket, Chelsea, 1969, 10 3/4 x 14 In., 376 Pages 52.00
Book, Pop-Up, Strange Adventures In The Spider-Ship, 1935 .... 495.00
Book, The Enlarging Ray, 1930s, 4 x 3 In., 8 Pages 65.00
Booklet, Buck Rogers In The 25th Century, Kellogg's, c.1933, 8 x 6 In. 259.00
Folder, Satellite Pioneers, Map Of Solar System, 1958, 8 1/2 x 5 1/2 In., 4 Pages 65.00
Game, Game Of The 25th Century A.D., Board, 1934, 13 1/2 x 9 1/2 In. 920.00
Gun, 25th Century, Handle Cocks, Pressed Steel, Chrome, Daisy, 1930, 9 1/2 In. 190.00
Gun, Sonic Ray, Plastic, Battery Operated, Commonwealth Utilities, Box, 7 1/2 In. 125.00
Gun, Sonic Ray, Plastic, Commonwealth Utilities, Box, 8 In. 275.00
Holster, Leather, Metal Buckle, For Rocket Pistol XZ 35, Daisy, 9 x 30 In. 150.00
Ink Blotter, Newspaper Promo, Chicago Herald-American, c.1946, 8 1/2 x 3 5/8 In. 200.00
Lobby Card, Larry Buster Crabbe, Universal, 1939, 11 x 14 In. 175.00

Lunch Box, Metal, No Thermos 59.00
Map, Solar System, Paper, Linen Mounted, Cocomalt, 1933, 25 1/4 x 18 1/2 In. 1402.00
Movie Serial Herald, Astounding Battles With Amazing Creatures, 1939, 13 x 6 In. 190.00
Pencil Box, Blue Ground, White & Black Graphics, 10 In. 66.00
Pistol, Rocket, XZ-31, Steel, Nickel Plated Pieces, Daisy, 1934, 9 1/2 In. 330.00
Pocket Watch, Buck, Wilma, Chromed Metal Case, Huckleberry Time, 1970s, 2 In. 529.00
Ring, Sylvania TV, Glow, S Logo, Brass Base, Adjustable, c.1953 .... 495.00
Rocket Ship, 25th Century, Sparks, Moves, Tin, Windup, Marx, Box, 12 In. .....2950.00 to 3300.00
Rocket Ship, Tin Lithographed, Buck In Cockpit, Key Wind, 1927, Marx, 12 In. 730.00
Space Ranger Kit, Punch-Out, Makes Hat, Mask, Gun, Figures, Ship, Sylvania, 1952 .... 138.00
Superscope, Plastic, Norton Honer, Box, 9 In. 165.00
Toy, Rocket Police Patrol, Tin Lithograph, Windup, Marx, 12 In. 585.00
Toy, Rocket Police Patrol, Tin Lithograph, Windup, Marx, Box, 12 In. 1540.00
Toy, Space Ship, Tin Lithograph, Windup, Marx, 12 In. ....525.00 to 660.00

BUFFALO POTTERY was made in Buffalo, New York, after 1902.
The company was established by the Larkin Company, famous manufacturers of soap. The wares are marked with a picture of a buffalo and
the date of manufacture. Deldare ware is the most famous pottery
made at the factory. It has either a khaki-colored or green background
with hand-painted transfer designs.

BUFFALO POTTERY, Pitcher, Argyle, Roses, Cobalt Blue, Gold Accent, Mark, 6 1/2 x 8 In. ... 805.00
Pitcher, Chrysanthemum, Embossed Handle, Mark, 7 x 7 1/2 In. 175.00
Pitcher, Cinderella, Coach, Horsemen, Mark, 1908, 5 1/2 x 6 In. 260.00
Pitcher, Dutch, Castle In Landscape, Mother & Daughter Walking, 1907, 6 x 7 In. 230.00
Pitcher, George Washington, Horseback, Battlefield, Cobalt Blue, Mark, 7 1/2 In. 750.00
Pitcher, John Paul Jones, Next To Cannon, On Ship, Cobalt Blue, 1907, 8 1/4 x 7 In. 545.00
Pitcher, Landing Of Roger Williams, 1907, 6 1/2 x 7 In. 920.00
Pitcher, Orchid, Iris, Cobalt Blue, Mark, 6 1/4 x 8 In. 175.00
Pitcher, Pilgrim, Mayflower, Miles Standish, John Alden, Mark, 1908, 9 x 8 In. 690.00
Pitcher, Rip Van Winkle, Dog, Bowling Ball, Pins, 1907, 6 x 6 1/2 In. 260.00
Pitcher, Robin Hood, Sounding Horn, 8 1/4 x 6 In. 345.00
Pitcher, Roosevelt Bears, 4-Sided, Creamware, c.1907, 8 In. 2310.00
Pitcher, The Gunner, Blue Green Glaze, Scroll Handle, 7 In. 230.00
Plate, Dr. Syntax Advertisement For A Wife, Flow Blue, Mark, 1909, 11 x 14 In. 575.00
Plate, Dr. Syntax Disputing His Bill, Flow Blue, Mark, 1909, 9 In. 145.00
Plate, Roosevelt Bears, At Home, School, Circus, Take A Ride, Brown Transfer, 8 x 8 In. .. 3740.00
BUFFALO POTTERY DELDARE, Bowl, Cereal, The Start, E.V.H., Mark, 2 x 6 In. 288.00
Bowl, Fallowfield Hunt The Death, A. Steiner, Mark, 1908, 3 3/4 x 9 In. 375.00
Bowl, Fallowfield Hunt, The Death, 1908, 9 In. 400.00
Calendar Plate, Elves In Seasons, N. Sheehan, 1910, 9 1/4 In. 1380.00
Candlestick, Shieldback, 3 Men Along Boardwalk, Mark, 6 3/4 x 6 In. ....805.00 to 2900.00
Creamer, Breaking Cover, Mark, 1908, 2 3/4 x 4 1/2 In. 260.00
Creamer, Scenes Of Village Life, Sauter, Mark, 1909, 2 3/4 x 4 1/2 In. 260.00
Cup & Saucer, Fallowfield Hunt, EVH, Mark, 1908 .... 290.00
Eggcup, Breaking Cover, Geaton, Signed, 4 x 2 3/4 In. 1150.00
Hair Receiver, Cover, Ye Village Street, L.N., Mark, 3 x 5 In. 200.00
Humidor, Cover, Ye Lion Inn, GHS, Mark, 7 x 6 In. 145.00
Humidor, There Was An Old Sailor, Dowman, Mark, 1909, 7 1/4 x 6 In. 490.00
Jardiniere, Ye Village Street, P. Hall, Mark, 1908, 6 x 8 1/2 In. 920.00
Mug, Breakfast At The 3 Pigeons, Gerhardt, 1909, 4 1/2 x 5 1/4 In. 320.00
Mug, Breaking Cover, Dowlman, Mark, 1909, 3 3/4 x 4 1/2 In. 320.00
Mug, Dr. Syntax Again Filled Up His Glass, Emerald, Mark, 1911, 4 1/2 x 5 1/2 In. 520.00
Mug, Fallowfield Hunt, J.G., Mark, 2 1/2 x 2 3/4 In. 345.00
Pitcher, Fallowfield Hunt, Gerhardt, 1908, 6 x 5 1/2 In. 375.00
Pitcher, Fallowfield Hunt, P. Hall, 1909, 9 x 8 In. 520.00
Pitcher, To Spare An Old Broken Soldier, Signed, AR, 7 3/4 x 7 1/2 In. 460.00
Pitcher, Ye Lion Inn, 8-Sided, Scenic, Signed, A. Roth, 10 In. 400.00
Plaque, An Evening At Ye Lion Inn, W. Foster, 1908, 14 In. 175.00
Plaque, Breakfast At The 3 Pigeons, P. Holland, 1909, 12 1/2 In. 345.00
Plate, Advertising, Hand Painted, Underglaze, 1909, 9 1/4 In. 1265.00
Plate, At Ye Lion Inn, B. Hill, Mark, 1908, 6 1/4 In. 145.00
Plate, Daughter Of The Revolution, Broel, 1909, 9 In. 1495.00

Plate, Dr. Syntax Losing His Way, Emerald, Mark, 1911, 9 In. 635.00
Plate, Dr. Syntax Making A Discovery, Streissel, Emerald, Mark, 1911, 9 3/4 In. 690.00
Plate, Dr. Syntax Presenting A Floral Offering, Emerald, Gerhardt, 1911, 6 1/4 In. 320.00
Plate, Dr. Syntax Soliloquizing, Emerald, H. Robin, 1911, 7 1/4 In. 320.00
Plate, Dr. Syntax, Misfortune At Tulip Hall, Emerald, A. Roth, 1911, 8 1/4 In. 315.00
Plate, Fallowfield Hunt, L. Anna, Mark, 1908, 10 In. 175.00
Plate, Fallowfield Hunt, Steiner, Mark, 1908, 6 1/4 In. 115.00
Plate, Fallowfield Hunt, The Death, E. Dowlman, Mark, 1908, 8 1/2 In. 145.00
Plate, Ye Town Crier, Foster, Mark, 1908, 8 1/2 In. 115.00
Plate, Ye Town Crier, Sned, Mark, 1908, 8 1/2 In. 115.00
Powder Jar, Cover, Ye Village Street, J.G., Mark, 3 x 4 1/2 In. 460.00
Tankard, Dr. Syntax Entertained At College, Emerald, W. Foster, 1911, 10 1/2 x 6 In. 920.00
Tankard, Fallowfield Hunt, A Hunt Supper, Sauter, Mark, 1909, 12 x 7 In. 690.00
Tankard, Great Controversy, Jensen, Mark, 1908, 12 1/2 x 6 In. 750.00
Tile, Traveling In Ye Olden Days, Round, Sheehan, Mark, 6 1/4 In. 175.00
Tray, Calling Card, Ye Lion Inn, Broel, Mark, 1909, 7 3/4 In. 360.00
Tray, Dancing Ye Minuet, L. Anna, Mark, 1909, 12 x 9 1/4 In. 315.00
Tray, Dr. Syntax Mistakes A Gentleman's House For An Inn, Emerald, Mark, 14 x 10 In. . . 1265.00
Tray, Relish, Ye Olden Times, E. Broel, 1909, 12 In. 260.00
Vase, 3 Ladies, L. Streissel, Mark, 1909, 8 x 6 3/4 In. 1265.00
Vase, Ye Village Parson, Ye Village Schoolmaster, L. Winter, 1908, 8 1/2 In. 750.00

BUNNYKINS, see Royal Doulton category.

BURMESE GLASS was developed by Frederick Shirley at the Mt.
Washington Glass Works in New Bedford, Massachusetts, in 1885. It
is a two-toned glass, shading from peach to yellow. Some pieces have
a pattern mold design. A few Burmese pieces were decorated with pictures or applied glass flowers of colored Burmese glass. Other factories made similar glass also called *Burmese*. Related items may be
listed in the Fenton category, the Gunderson category and under Webb
Burmese.

Biscuit Jar, Cover, Pinecone Form, 6 In. 1020.00
Biscuit Jar, Enameled Leaves & Branches, Cherries, Flat Lid, Ivory Finial, 6 In. 750.00
Biscuit Jar, Flowers, 6 In. 800.00
Bowl, 6-Sided, Enameled Flowers, 3 x 4 In. 290.00
Bowl, Jack-In-The-Pulpit, Tight Ruffled Edge, 5 1/2 In. 315.00
Bowl, Optic Ribbed, Tricornered Rim, Crimped & Ruffled Edge, 5 x 9 1/2 In. 400.00
Bowl, Square, Folded Rim, 5 In. 230.00
Candlestick, Applied Berries, Rigaree, 8 1/2 In. 2300.00
Cracker Jar, Oak Leaves, Pastel Flowers, 9 In. 520.00
Creamer, Crimped Top, Gold Enameled Flowers, 5 1/4 In. 1555.00
Creamer, Wishbone Base, Berry Pontil, 4 1/2 In. 920.00
Cruet, Applied Handle, Faceted Stopper, 6 1/2 In. 720.00
Custard Cup, Underplate, 2 1/2 In., 4 Sets 690.00
Hat Form, Ruffled Rim, 2 3/4 In. 345.00
Jar, Cover, Enameled Flowers, Raised Daisies, Oval, 4 In. 400.00
Jar, Cover, Grape, Leaves, Vine Clusters, Oval, 8 1/4 In. 5175.00
Jar, Powder, Enameled, Bulbous, Flared Rim, Yellow Stopper, Glossy, 5 In. 200.00
Lemonade, Optic Pattern, Applied Custard Ring Handle, Mt. Washington, 4 3/4 In. 575.00
Marmalade Jar, Relief Flowers, Gold Trim, Silver Plated Lid & Handle, 3 1/2 In. 635.00
Rose Bowl, Enameled Flowers, 2 1/4 In. 315.00
Rose Bowl, Melon, Ribbed, Leaves, Ivy, 3 1/2 In. 200.00
Salt & Pepper, Pillar Mold, Pastel Flowers, Silver Plated Holder, 6 1/2 In. 575.00
Salt & Pepper, Ribbed, Silver Plated Caps, 4 In. 145.00
Sugar & Creamer, Bulbous, 2 1/2 In. 2990.00
Sugar Shaker, Daisies, Melon Ribbed, 2 1/2 In., Pair 690.00
Sugar Shaker, Queen's Decoration, Flowers, Bulbous, 4 In. 2300.00
Syrup, Asters, Gold Trim, Tapered, Hinged Domed Top, Embossed Flowers, 6 In. 4945.00
Toothpick, Blue & White Flowers, Paneled, 1 1/2 In. 460.00
Toothpick, Diamond-Quilted, 2 1/2 In. 430.00
Toothpick, Diamond-Quilted, Leafy Branches, Raised Red Berries, Trifold Rim, 2 In. 345.00
Toothpick, Diamond-Quilted, Tricornered Rim, Ruffled Edge, 1 3/4 In. 230.00
Toothpick, Hat Shape, Applied Blueberries, Leaves, 2 1/2 In. 805.00

Toothpick, White, Yellow Daisy, Tufts, Gilt Metal Holder, 2 1/2 In. 1150.00
Tumbler, Diamond-Quilted, 3 3/4 In. 230.00
Tumbler, Enameled Roses & Leaves, 3 3/4 In. 1495.00
Tumbler, Juice, Diamond-Quilted, Oak Leaf Branch, Blue Beading, 2 1/2 In. 520.00
Tumbler, Rose Buds, Leafy Stems, 3 3/4 In. 690.00
Vase, Diamond-Quilted, 4-Fold Rim, 4-Footed, Raspberry Prunts, 7 In. 1495.00
Vase, Egyptian Scene, Urn Shape, Squared Handles, 7 In. 775.00
Vase, Enameled Flowers, Petal Rim, Squat, 2 1/2 In. 175.00
Vase, Enameled Rose, Bulbous, Flared & Scalloped Rim, 4 1/4 In. 1440.00
Vase, Jack-In-The-Pulpit, Tightly Ruffled Edge, Footed, 10 In. 520.00
Vase, Lily, Curled & Rolled, 5-Point Star Top, 4 In. 230.00
Vase, Lily, Petal Top, Disc Foot, 8 In. 259.00
Vase, Lily, Ribbed, Trifold Rim, 4 In. 173.00
Vase, Lily, Salmon Petal Rim, Tapered, Footed, 9 In. 290.00
Vase, Lily, Tricornered Rim, 6 3/4 In. 175.00
Vase, Stick, Enameled Hawthorne, Raised Dotted Rim, 8 In. 805.00
Vase, Stick, Pinched Bulbous Base, 6 In. 260.00
Whimsy, Mouse, 4 3/4 x 3 3/4 In. 575.00

BUSTER BROWN, the comic strip, first appeared in color in 1902. Buster and his dog, Tige, remained a popular comic and soon became even more famous as the emblem for a shoe company, a textile firm, and other companies. The strip was discontinued in 1920. Buster Brown sponsored a radio show from 1943 to 1955 and a TV show from 1950 to 1956. The Buster Brown characters are still used by Brown Shoe Company, Buster Brown Apparel, Inc., and Gateway Hosiery.

Bank, Good Luck, Horse, Horseshoe, Buster, Tige, Cast Iron, Arcade, 4 1/8 In. . . . .110.00 to 165.00
Banner, Buster & Tige, For Boys, For Girls, Cloth, Frame, Early 1900s, 9 x 12 In. 165.00
Bowl, Buster & Tige, Running, Porcelain, Elkins, N.Y. 90.00
Button, Buster, Tige, You Can't Buster Brown Hose Supporter, 1920s, 7/8 In. 25.00
Button, Buster, Train Engine, You Can't Buster Brown Hose Supporter, 1920s, 7/8 In. 15.00
Button, Hose Supporter, Buster, Winking, 1900-12, 7/8 In. 40.00
Chewing Gum, Buster Brown Shoes, Buster, Tige, All Have A Chew, 2 7/8 In. 40.00
Clock, Shoes, Lighted, 14 1/2 In. 580.00
Cup, Buster Brown, Tige, Metal, Handle, Homan Mfg. Co., c.1910, 1 7/8 x 3 In. 50.00
Game, Ball Toss, Bliss, 10 x 24 In. 330.00
Iron, Brown Bilt Buster Brown Tread, Electric, Red Handle, Red Cord, 4 5/8 In. 55.00
Keychain Fob, Blue Ribbon Shoes, Silver, Oval 28.00
Pencil Box, 3 Panel Cartoon, Buster Sits On Tack, Germany, Early 1900s, 8 1/2 In. 150.00
Pennant, Buster Brown's Guaranteed Hosiery, Cloth, Frame, 29 In. 220.00
Pin, Hose Supporter, Buster & Tige, Multicolor, Celluloid, 7/8 In. 15.00
Plate, Buster & Tige, Verse, Gold Rim, Baby's, N.C. Co., 6 1/2 In. 125.00
Puzzle, Put Your Feet In Brown Bilt Shoes, Metal Ball, Tin, 2 In. Diam. 55.00
Rug, Buster & Tige, Yellow Ground, Blue Edge, Stars, Mohawk, Round, 47 3/4 In. 170.00
Rug, Buster & Tige, Yellow Ground, Blue Edge, Stars, Mohawk, Round, 53 In. 140.00
Sign, Buster Brown Shoes, Buster, Tige, Plaster Relief, Square, 18 x 17 3/4 In. 175.00
Sign, Buster Brown, Plaster Relief, Winking, Tige, 17 3/4 x 18 In. 175.00
Socks, Buster Brown, Label, Original Box, 1910 . . . . 300.00
Toy, Buster Brown In Cart, Tige Pulling Cart, Cast Iron, 5 x 7 1/2 In. 345.00

BUTTER MOLDS are listed in the Kitchen category under Mold, Butter.

BUTTON collecting has been popular since the nineteenth century. Buttons have been known throughout the centuries, and there are millions of styles. Gold, silver, or precious stones were used for the best buttons, but most were made of natural materials, like bone or shell, or from inexpensive metals. Only a few types are listed for comparison.

Bakelite, Apple With Leaves, Ivory Color, 5/8 In., 4 Piece 30.00
Bakelite, Dog, Scottie, Brown, 1 In. 25.00
Bakelite, Hand, Figural, Tangerine Color, 1940s, 1 1/4 In. 19.00
Brass, Horse's Head, In Horseshoe, Openwork, Brass, 1 In., 6 Piece 120.00
Brass, Little Red Riding Hood, Embossed, Nickel Border, 1 7/16 In. 80.00
Brass, Rebus, Bird With Clock, Time Flies, Cutout, 1 1/4 In. 30.00
Celluloid, Best Atlantic Made, Ship On Ocean, Round, 1 1/2 In. 78.00

Celluloid, Black Scottie Dog, Red, 1930s, 7/8 In. 10.00
Celluloid, Edison Records, Hand Holding Cylinder, Round, 7/8 In. 130.00
Celluloid, Frisco Line, There Is Something To See, Train, 1 3/4 In. 95.00
Celluloid, Steamship, Black Stain, Carved, Cutout, 1/2 In. 20.00
Cinnabar, Floral Carving, 1 5/8 In. 175.00
Enamel, Girl Sewing, Baroque Dress, Cut Steel Border, France, 5/8 In. 80.00
Glass, Acorn, Metal Cap, 19th Century, 1/2 In. 25.00
Glass, Black Satin, Cut Star, Victorian, 1 1/4 In. 10.00
Glass, Hunter & Dog, Reverse Painted, 1/2 In. 8.00
Glass, Lacy Pressed Pattern, Silver Back & Border, 1 1/4 In. 110.00
Ivory, Bust, Cavalier, Glass Eyes, Late 18th Century, 5/8 In. 150.00
Ivory, Classical Nude, Painted, Silver & Marcasite Border, 1790s-1800s, 1 3/8 In. 480.00
Micro Mosaic, Beetle, Brass Back, Round, White Ground, Rose Border, 3/4 In. 518.00
Mother-Of-Pearl, Eiffel Tour, Carved, Gold Details, 1 1/16 In., 7 Piece 870.00
Mother-Of-Pearl, Gold Chanel Logo In Center, 3/4 In., 10 Piece 175.00
Papier-Mache, Painted Flower, Gold Outlining, India, 1950s, 1 1/8 In. 30.00
Pearl, Shirt, Mermaid Pearls, 9 On Card 6.00
Plastic, Shirt, West Germany, 18 On Card 7.00
Porcelain, Hand Painted Roses, Stud Back, 15/16 In. 11.00
Pottery, Jasperware, Blue, Elephant, 1 5/8 In. 20.00
Pottery, Satsuma, Geisha Girls, Boy, Mt. Fuji In Background, Gold Edge, 1 1/8 In. 250.00
Rhinestone, Triangular, Large Center Stone, 1/2 In. 30.00
Sterling Silver, Woman Playing Harp, Embossed, Birmingham, England, 7/8 In. 19.00

BUTTONHOOKS have been a popular collectible in England for
many years but are now gaining the attention of American collectors.
The buttonhooks were made to help fasten the many buttons of the old-
fashioned high-button shoes and other items of apparel.

Bakelite, Tangerine, Flared Handle Ending In Inverted Skyscraper Tip, Art Deco 37.00
Celluloid Handle, Victorian 7.00
Dupont, Ivory Pyralin, 3-In. Handle, 7 1/4 In. 8.00
Ebony Handle, For Gloves, c.1900, 3 1/2 In. 14.00
Steel, Folding, Early 1900s, 2 3/4-In. Long Folded 13.00
Sterling Silver, Amethyst Colored Stone Set In Top, 6 7/8 In. 115.00
Sterling Silver, Scroll Decoration, Foster & Bailey, 5 3/4 In. 38.00

CALENDARS made to hang on the wall or to be displayed on a desk
top have been popular since the last quarter of the nineteenth century.
Many were printed with advertising as part of the artwork and were
given away as premiums. Calendars with guns, gunpowder, or Coca-
Cola advertising are most prized.

1893, Teaberry Elixir, Full Pad, Trade Card 44.00
1894, Prudential Insurance Co., April To June 33.00
1895, Peoples Outfitting, Children, Horse Drawn Carriage, Die Cut, Embossed 99.00
1897, Hood's, Girl, Die Cut, 7 x 4 1/2 In. 132.00
1899, Hood's, American Girl, 9 3/4 x 6 3/4 In. 132.00
1900, Eilers & Bolton, Die Cut, Cardboard, Embossed, 18 x 10 In. 132.00
1901, Coes Fertilizer, Lady By Fence, Frame, 13 x 8 1/4 In. 155.00
1901, Prudential Insurance Co., Woman, Pink Hat, Flowers, Die Cut, 9 x 11 In. 80.00
1901, Union Metallic Cartridge, Boy, Bird, Rifle, Nov. & Dec., Frame, 22 x 35 In. 2677.00
1902, Dr. Miles, Girl Holding Basket Of Flowers, 9 1/2 x 6 1/2 In. 40.00
1904, Singer Sewing Machine, Great West, 17th Century, Discovery, France, 4 Pages 35.00
1905, Dawson Supply Co., Woman At Beach, Frame, 21 1/2 x 18 1/2 In. 45.00
1905, John Mignola & Bro., Die Cut, Cardboard, 10 3/4 x 7 1/4 In. 55.00
1906, Davis Bread, Die Cut, Embossed, Frame, 11 x 7 In. 145.00
1908, Thomas Pinder, Chicago Coffee, Teas & Spices, Boy, Die Cut, 11 1/2 x 8 In. 120.00
1909, DuPont Explosives, Dog With Puppies, Paper, Frame, 29 x 21 In. 275.00
1909, J.D. Newcomer, Child, 2 Dogs, Die Cut, Cardboard, Embossed, 11 x 10 1/2 In. 165.00
1909, Melchior Schmit, Die Cut, Cardboard, Embossed, 12 1/4 x 8 1/4 In. 105.00
1910, McCormick, Girl Kissing Boy, February Through December, 16 x 13 In. 520.00
1911, Boufford & Turcot, Victorian Lady, Die Cut, Cardboard, Embossed, 12 x 8 In. 198.00
1912, Fairest Maidens, Blue Bow, 3 Women, Multicolored, Full Pad, 13 1/4 In. 159.00
1913, Winchester, Hunter, Model 12, Robert B. Robinson, 29 1/2 x 15 1/4 In. 4125.00

1915, Baby Rice Popcorn, Parents Rocking Baby In Cradle, 13 x 7 1/2 In. 35.00
1918, Geo. B. Gehring Grocery Store, Submarine, Frame, 24 1/2 x 21 In. 110.00
1918, Peters Cartridge Co., Hunter, Dog, Puppies, 13 7/8 x 27 In. 840.00
1920, Massachusetts Exterior Scene, Wallace Nutting, Hand Colored, 7 x 12 In. 160.00
1920, Sentinel Fire Insurance, Soldier On Horse, Mountain, 13 x 19 In. 275.00
1921, Hood's, Poppies, 11 x 4 1/2 In. 385.00
1921, Winchester Man, Boy, Dog, Arthur Fuller, October, Frame, 15 x 27 In. 1516.00
1921, Winchester Store, P.L. Cassinelli, Full Pad, 13 1/2 x 8 In. 955.00
1922, Marble's Outing Equipment, Men, Boat, Bear, Frame, Partial Pad, 28 x 33 In. 4850.00
1924, Peter, C. Muss-Arnolt, 15 x 27 1/2 In. 165.00
1924, Winchester, Duck Hunter In Marsh, G. Ryder, 14 x 28 In. . . . . .1469.00 to 2975.00
1927, Hunter, Snowshoes, Full Pad, Frank Stick, Winchester, 10 x 21 In. 1097.00
1927, Nehi Soda, Chero-Cola, 20 x 6 In. 220.00
1928, Western, Lynn Bogue Hunt, 28 1/2 x 15 In. 840.00
1929, Hercules Powder, Dreams, Dogs, Fireplace, LL Edwin Megargee, 29 x 13 In. 1455.00
1929, Mankato Minnesota Shoe Merchant, Indian Maiden, L. Janda, 16 x 10 In. 303.00
1929, Savage Stevens, 2 Men Hunting, Canoe, 36 5/8 x 19 1/8 In.   735.00
1930, Winchester, Full Pad, 26 7/8 x 15 In. 776.00
1933, Peppy Gas, Berry's Atlantic Station, Notebook, Pocket 9.00
1934, Winchester, I Wish I Had Dad's Winchester, Full Pad, Frame, 15 x 27 3/4 In. 4420.00
1936, H.A. Smalley & Co., Fisherman, Full Pad, Frame, 35 x 25 In. 130.00
1937, Brown & Bigelow, Twilight Image, House, Barn, 22 x 16 1/2 In. 160.00
1937, Cheerwine, It's Full Of Good Cheer, Lady, Cardboard, 18 x 11 In. 137.00
1939, Princeton University Store, Tiger, Full Pad, Mat, Frame, 30 x 20 1/2 In. 130.00
1939, Watkins, Girl, Washing, Ironing 140.00
1945, Harrisburg Taxicab & Baggage Co., Paper, June, July, 19 x 14 In. 66.00
1946, Grandma's A Good Skate, Hy Hintermeister, 8 x 10 In. 30.00
1947, Bell Telephone, Illinois, Wallet 5.00
1948, Alberto Varga, Signature, Inscription, 12 Pages, 12 x 8 1/2 In. 690.00
1951, Dr Pepper, A Lift For Life, Lady, Red Hair, 21 x 13 In. 45.00
1954, Betsy Ross Bread, Ty Cobb, Frame, 23 x 11 In. 154.00
1955, Indian Maiden, Hy Hintermeister, 8 x 10 In. 35.00
1955, Marilyn Monroe, Nude, Golden Dreams, Heavy Stock 465.00
1958, Brown & Bigelow, Frankie Frisch, July, 46 x 22 In. 195.00

CAMBRIDGE GLASS Company was founded in 1901 in Cambridge,
Ohio. The company closed in 1954, reopened briefly, and closed again
in 1958. The firm made all types of glass. Their early wares included
heavy pressed glass with the mark *Near Cut.* Later wares included
Crown Tuscan, etched stemware, and clear and colored glass. The firm
used a C in a triangle mark after 1920. Some Cambridge patterns may
be included in the Depression Glass category.

Apple Blossom, Cocktail, Gold Krystol, 3 Oz., 4 Piece 70.00
Apple Blossom, Oil, Gold Krystol, Keyhole Stopper, 2 Oz. 85.00
Apple Blossom, Relish, Gold Krystol, 5 Sections, 12 In. 35.00
Apple Blossom, Relish, Gold Krystol, 5 Sections, Gold Filigree Handle, 12 In. 150.00
Apple Blossom, Vase, Gold Krystol, Ball, Gold Encrusted, 5 In. 190.00
Azurite, Console Set, Gold Trim, 8-In. Candlesticks, 11-In. Bowl 200.00
Bashful Charlotte, Flower Holder, 6 In. 50.00
Blue Swirl, Beverage Set, Pitcher, 9 Tumblers 138.00
Buzz Saw, Basket, Rope Handle, Nearcut 70.00
Buzz Saw, Celery Dish, Nearcut, 11 In. 25.00
Calla Lily, Candlestick, Emerald Green, 6 1/2 In., Pair 180.00
Calla Lily, Candlestick, Mandarin Gold, 6 1/2 In., Pair 85.00
Caprice, Bonbon, Handles, Square, 6 In. 10.00
Caprice, Bowl, 4-Footed, 11 In. 35.00
Caprice, Bowl, Bell, Amethyst, 4-Footed, 12 1/2 In. 300.00
Caprice, Bowl, Cloverleaf, 6 In. 20.00
Caprice, Bowl, Cloverleaf, Moonlight Blue, 6 In. 85.00
Caprice, Bowl, Moonlight Blue, Alpine, Crimped, 3-Footed, 12 1/2 In. 135.00
Caprice, Bowl, Moonlight, Blue, 4-Footed, 13 In. 125.00
Caprice, Bowl, Morning Glory Enamel, 4-Footed, 9 1/2 In. 285.00
Caprice, Candlestick, 3-Light, Moonlight Blue, Alpine, 6 In., Pair 45.00

Caprice, Candlestick, Bobeche Prisms, 7 In., Pair 35.00
Caprice, Candy Box, Cover, Moonlight Blue, 3-Footed, 6 In. 8.00
Caprice, Cheese Stand, 6 In. 210.00
Caprice, Cheese Stand, Moonlight Blue, 6 In. 150.00
Caprice, Cocktail, 3 1/2 Oz. 80.00
Caprice, Compote, Moonlight Blue, 6 In. 115.00
Caprice, Plate, Cabaret, Moonlight Blue, 4-Footed, 11 In. 25.00
Caprice, Relish, Moonlight, Blue, 3 Sections, Handles, 8 In. 25.00
Caprice, Sherbet, 5 Oz. 25.00
Caprice, Tumbler, Blown, La Rosa, 3 7/8 In., 10 Oz. 75.00
Caprice, Vase, Amber, 4 1/4 In. 50.00
Caprice, Vase, Ball, Amber, 8 In. 90.00
Caprice, Vase, Ball, Moonlight Blue, Alpine, Ruffled Edge, 9 In. 525.00
Caprice, Vase, Ball, Ruffled Edge, 9 In. 200.00
Caprice, Vase, Milk Glass, 4 1/2 In. 55.00
Carmen, Cocktail, Martha Washington, 3 1/2 Oz., 4 1/4 In. 75.00
Carmen, Sugar & Creamer, Ball 85.00
Carrara, Doorknob, Nickel Plated, 2 Piece 110.00
Cascade, Candy Box, Cover, Emerald Green, 3-Footed 75.00
Chantilly, Torte Plate, 3-Footed, 13 In. 40.00
Chesterfield, Cordial, Pressed, 1 Oz. 80.00
Cleo, Candlestick, Peach-Blo, 4 In. 35.00
Cleo, Cup & Saucer, Willow Blue 60.00
Cleo, Ice Pail, Light Emerald Green, Tongs, 5 1/2 In. 125.00
Cleo, Plate, Amber, 9 1/2 In. 50.00
Cleo, Platter, Asparagus, Light Emerald Green, 14 1/2 In. 140.00
Cleo, Sandwich Server, Center Handle, Amber, Gold Encrusted, 11 In. 25.00
Cleo, Tray, Willow Blue, 13 In. 140.00
Cleo, Tumbler, Peach-Blo, 10 Oz. 45.00
Corinth, Candlestick, 4 1/2 In., Pair 25.00
Crown Tuscan, Ashtray, Shell, 3-Toed, 4 In. 13.00
Crown Tuscan, Bowl, Oval, 4-Toed, Gold Encrusted Chintz Etch, Signed, 12 In. 40.00
Crown Tuscan, Bowl, Shell, 3-Toed, 10 In. 75.00
Crown Tuscan, Bowl, Shell, 3-Toed, Gold Trim, 10 In. 190.00
Crown Tuscan, Candlestick, Dolphin, Shell, Footed, 4 In., Pair 80.00
Crown Tuscan, Cocktail, Mandarin Gold Stem & Foot, 3 Oz., 4 1/4 In. 155.00
Crown Tuscan, Cocktail, Seafood, Shell, 4 1/2 Oz., 4 Piece 260.00
Crown Tuscan, Compote, Shell, 7 In. 50.00
Crown Tuscan, Plate, Salad, Shell, 7 In. 25.00
Crown Tuscan, Plate, Shell, 14 In. 225.00
Crown Tuscan, Relish, Shell, 3 Sections, 4-Toed, 9 In. 65.00
Crown Tuscan, Sugar, Nautilus, 4 In. 110.00
Crown Tuscan, Urn, Cover, 12 In. 175.00
Crown Tuscan, Vase, Cornucopia, 9 1/2 In. 75.00
Crown Tuscan, Vase, Footed, 10 In. 20.00
Crown Tuscan, Vase, Keyhole Stem, 10 1/2 In. 90.00
Crucifix, Candlestick, 9 In. 300.00
Daisy, Bowl, 4-Footed, Nearcut, 10 In. 25.00
Deauville, Goblet, Gold Krystol, Clear Stem & Foot 55.00
Deauville, Sherbet, Gold Krystol, Clear Stem & Foot 30.00
Decagon, Dish, Mayonnaise, Underplate, Amber 40.00
Decagon, Ice Bucket, Light Emerald Green, Chrome Handle 25.00
Decagon, Sandwich Server, Ebony, Center Handle, 11 In. 20.00
Decagon, Sugar & Creamer, Underplate, Willow Blue 65.00
Diane, Bowl, Flared, 4-Footed, 12 In. 50.00
Draped Lady, Amber, Flower Holder, 8 1/2 In. 150.00
Draped Lady, Console, Flower Frog, Pistachio Green, 10 In. 185.00
Draped Lady, Flower Frog, 8 1/2 In. 45.00
Draped Lady, Flower Frog, Crown Tuscan, 8 1/2 In. 900.00
Draped Lady, Flower Frog, Emerald, 8 1/2 In. 200.00
Ebony, Bowl, Footed, Ram's Head Handles, 8 1/2 In. 85.00
Ebony, Bowl, Gold Band, 9 In. 25.00
Ebony, Candlestick, Doric Column, No. 65, Pair 150.00

Ebony, Vase, Bud, Footed, White Gold, Apple Blossom Encrusted, 10 In. 175.00
Ebony, Vase, Bud, Square, 8 In. 75.00
Elaine, Vase, Bud, Footed, 10 In. 25.00
Emerald Green, Ashtray, Shell, 3-Toed, 4 In. 15.00
Emerald Green, Cheese Stand, Oval, Willow Scene, 5 1/4 In. 105.00
Emerald Green, Compote, 5 1/2 In. 80.00
Emerald Green, Cordial, 1 Oz. 55.00
Everglade, Bowl, Footed, Moonlight Blue, 11 In. 80.00
Everglade, Bowl, Tulip, 14 In. 95.00
Everglade, Candlestick, 2-Light, Moonlight Blue, 4 In. 275.00
Everglade, Candlestick, Willow Blue, 4 In., Pair 70.00
Figurine, Bridge Hound, Amber, Hole For Pencil, 1 3/4 In. 50.00
Georgian, Tumbler, Carmen, 2 1/2 Oz. 25.00
Georgian, Tumbler, Gold Krystol, 9 Oz. 55.00
Gloria, Candy Box, Cover, Gold Krystol, 7 In. 65.00
Gloria, Sandwich Server, Emerald, Center Handle, 11 In. 20.00
Gloria, Tumbler, Iced Tea, Peach-Blo, Footed, 12 Oz., 4 Piece 300.00
Heatherbloom, Jug, Ball, 80 Oz. 140.00
Helio, Bottle, Bitters, Tube Stopper 300.00
Helio, Compote, Footed, 9 1/2 In. 75.00
Helio, Plate, Gold Laurel Wreath, 8 1/2 In. 85.00
Imperial Hunt Scene, Sherbet, Peach-Blo, Emerald Green Foot, 6 Oz. 50.00
Inverted Feather, Banana Stand, Nearcut 175.00
Inverted Feather, Wine, Nearcut, 4 5/8 In., 8 Piece 90.00
Inverted Strawberry, Bowl, Carnival Green, Nearcut, 6 1/2 In. 105.00
Krystolshell, Sugar & Creamer 35.00
Lorna, Tumbler, Royal Blue, 12 Oz. 85.00
Marjorie, Punch Bowl, Nearcut, 13 x 11 In. 85.00
Martha Washington, Bowl, Avocado, Flared, 11 In. 380.00
Martha Washington, Bowl, Experimental, Goldenrod, 9 1/2 In. 525.00
Martha Washington, Cocktail, Willow Blue, 3 1/2 Oz. 70.00
Martha Washington, Cordial, Amber, 1 Oz. 75.00
Martha Washington, Urn, Cover, Forest Green, 9 1/2 In. 40.00
Mt. Vernon, Ice Bucket, Chrome Handle, Tongs 65.00
Mt. Vernon, Lamp, Hurricane, Gold Encrusted, Wildflower, Shade, 18 In. 260.00
Mt. Vernon, Plate, Amber, Tab Handles, 11 1/2 In. 25.00
Mt. Vernon, Relish, 5 Sections, 12 In. 105.00
Nautilus, Decanter, Amber, 40 Oz. 75.00
No. 1125, Bowl, Mystic Blue, 16 In. 150.00
Nude, Brandy, Forest Green, Clear Stem & Foot, 1 Oz., 6 1/2 In. 100.00
Nude, Claret, Carmen, 4 1/2 Oz. 225.00
Nude, Claret, Frosted, Sterling Silver Overlay, 4 1/2 Oz., 6 1/2 In. 2700.00
Nude, Cocktail, Royal Blue, Clear Stem & Foot, 3 Oz., 6 1/2 In. 195.00
Nude, Compote, Amber, Flared, Clear, Stem & Foot, 7 In. 190.00
Nude, Compote, Crown Tuscan, Shell, 5 In. 155.00
Nude, Compote, Crown Tuscan, Shell, 7 In. 200.00
Nude, Compote, Royal Blue, Flared, Clear Stem & Foot, 7 In. 390.00
Nude, Goblet, Carmen, Clear Stem & Foot, 8 Oz., 7 In. 305.00
Pansy, Vase, Emerald Green, 3 In. 35.00
Peach-Blo, Ice Bucket, Chrome Handle, Signed 60.00
Peacock, Tumbler, Nearcut 80.00
Portia, Plate, Luncheon, 8 1/2 In. 20.00
Portia, Plate, Salad, 8 In. 30.00
Portia, Platter, Amber, Handles, 10 3/4 x 12 In. 125.00
Portia, Relish, 8 In. 36.00
Portia, Sherry, 2 Oz. 70.00
Portia, Tumbler, Iced Tea, Footed, 12 Oz., 4 5/8 In. 40.00
Portia, Vase, Crown Tuscan, Gold Encrusted, Footed, 6 In. 80.00
Primrose, Bowl, Black Enamel, Signed, 6 In. 65.00
Primrose, Bowl, Gold Band, Laurel Wreath, 12 In. 45.00
Primrose, Dish, Mayonnaise, Ladle, Footed, 6 1/2 In. 80.00
Primrose, Vase, Bud, Footed, Ruffled Edge, 8 In. 60.00
Pristine, Punch Set, Bowl, Underplate, Cups, Ladle, 16 Piece 190.00

Ribbon, Cracker Jar, Cover, Nearcut 60.00
Rosalie, Tumbler, Mushroom, Peach-Blo, 2 1/2 Oz. 115.00
Rose Chintz, Candlestick, 3-Light, 6 1/2 In. 45.00
Rose Lady, Flower Frog, Peach-Blo, Scalloped Base, 9 1/2 In. 265.00
Rosepoint, Tumbler, Iced Tea, Royal Blue, 12 Oz. 95.00
Rosepoint, Vase, Cornucopia, Crown Tuscan, Gold Encrusted, 9 In. 200.00
Rosepoint, Vase, Crown Tuscan, Gold Encrusted, Footed, 5 In. 130.00
Rosepoint, Vase, Crown Tuscan, Gold Encrusted, Footed, 10 In. . . . . .45.00 to 160.00
Rubina, Bowl, 9 1/2 In., Pair 105.00
Seagull, Flower Frog, 8 1/2 In. 30.00
Shell, Candy Box, Cover, Footed, 6 In. 50.00
Shell, Candy Box, Cover, Milk Glass, Footed, 6 In. 45.00
Shell, Compote, Milk Glass, Enamel Roses, 6 In. 170.00
Shell, Plate, 5 In. 20.00
Stackaway, Ashtray Set, Moonlight Blue, Wooden Base, 5 Piece 35.00
Star, Candleholder, Moonlight Blue, 5 In. 20.00
Swan, Dish, Carmen, 3 In. 75.00
Swan, Dish, Crown Tuscan, 3 In. 30.00
Swan, Dish, Crown Tuscan, 8 1/2 In. 70.00
Swan, Dish, Emerald Green, 6 1/2 In. 90.00
Swan, Dish, Emerald Green, 8 1/2 In. 185.00
Swan, Dish, Gold Krystol, 3 In. 40.00
Tally-Ho, Celery Dish, Gold Encrusted Elaine Etch, 12 In. 45.00
Tally-Ho, Claret, Gold Silk Screen, Carmen, Stem & Foot 100.00
Tally-Ho, Cordial, Carmen, Stem & Foot, 1 Oz. 60.00
Tally-Ho, Punch Mug, 6 Oz. 55.00
Tally-Ho, Relish, 4 Sections, Handles, Gold Encrusted Minerva Etch, 10 In. 50.00
Tally-Ho, Tumbler, Handle, Forest Green, 2 1/2 Oz., 3 Piece 45.00
Wheat Sheaf, Cake Plate, Nearcut, 10 1/2 In. 25.00

CAMBRIDGE POTTERY was made in Cambridge, Ohio, from about
1895 until World War I. The factory made brown glazed decorated artwares with a variety of marks, including an acorn, the name *Cambridge*, the name *Oakwood*, or the name *Terrhea*.

Ewer, Embossed Branches Of Fruit, Brown Glaze, Ruffled Rim, Oakwood, 3 3/4 In. 105.00
Planter, 5 Claw Feet, Oakwood, 7 x 12 In. 295.00

CAMEO GLASS was made in much the same manner as a cameo in
jewelry. Parts of the top layer of glass were cut away to reveal a differ-
ent-colored glass beneath. The most famous cameo glass was made
during the nineteenth century. Signed cameo glass pieces are listed
under the glasswork's name, such as Daum or Galle.

Butter, Cover, Ballerina, Green, 7 1/2 In. 150.00
Flask, Egg Shape, Aubergine, Flowers, Dragonfly, Silver Mounts, c.1890, 6 1/2 In. 6598.00
Scent Bottle, Citrine, Blossoms, Sterling Mounted, England, c.1900, 4 In. 1495.00
Shade, Burgundy, Red Berries, Stylized Leaves, Yellow Ground, Signed, 7 1/4 In. 575.00
Shade, Gold Over Clear, Oak Leaves, Acorns, Satin, 6 1/2 In., Pair 259.00
Tray, Hilly River Bank Scene, Pine Trees, Wood Frame, Handles, Gruber, 10 x 8 In. 1840.00
Vase, Amethyst Flowers, Bands, Frosted & Textured Ground, Gold Trim, Pantin, 9 3/4 In. . . 575.00
Vase, Amethyst To Clear, Elephants, Tropical Trees, Cut Oval Rim, 9 1/2 In. 805.00
Vase, Amethyst, Lilies, Frosted Ground, C. Vessiere, France, 3 In. 290.00
Vase, Baluster Shape, Snapdragons, Pink, Olive, Pink Ground, Arsall, 14 In. 598.00
Vase, Blossoms, Vines, Citrine Overlay, England, c.1900, 8 1/2 In. 2070.00
Vase, Blue Body, White Flowers, Insects, England, c.1900, 8 3/4 In. 2990.00
Vase, Cranberry, White Flowers & Bands, Shouldered, 5 In. 545.00
Vase, Flower Branch, Gold Highlights, Textured, Pinched Sides, S. Denis, 6 In. 230.00
Vase, Flowers, Amber, Art Nouveau, 6 In. 353.00
Vase, Green Over Cranberry, Large Blossoms, Signed, Arsall, 11 In. 863.00
Vase, Hero, Gray, Opaque White, Yellow Overlay, Cut With Flowers, 10 In. 430.00
Vase, Iris, Red, Gold Enameled, Frosted Ground, 9 3/4 In. 780.00
Vase, Long Stem Flowers, Leaves, Amber Satin Ground, France, 12 1/2 In. 230.00
Vase, Magnolia Blossoms, Butterfly, Citrine, England, c.1900, 7 In. 1035.00
Vase, Martele Finish, Overlaid Amber-Stemmed Lilies, Footed, Richardson, 8 In. 460.00

Vase, White Flowers, Blue Ground, England, 7 1/4 In. 805.00
Vase, White Flowers, Dragonfly, Red Ground, England, 4 1/2 In. 1785.00
Vase, White Shaded To Blue, Morning Glories, Cylindrical, Tapered Mouth, 7 1/2 In. 1035.00

CAMPAIGN memorabilia is listed in the Political category.

CAMPBELL KIDS were first used as part of an advertisement for the
Campbell Soup Company in 1906. The kids were created by Grace
Drayton, a popular illustrator of the day. The kids were used in magazine and newspaper ads until about 1951. They were presented again in
1966; and in 1983, they were redesigned with a slimmer, more contemporary appearance.

Dish, Baby On Side, Kids, Alphabet On Rim, Gold Paint, Green Band, 7 1/2 In. 130.00
Doll, Boy & Girl, Soft Vinyl, Accessories, Order Form, Soup Labels, 1972, 10 In., Pr. 150.00
Doll, Campbell Soup Kid, Boy, Composition, Jointed, Unmarked, 12 In. 400.00
Doll, Campbell Soup Kids, Rag Dolls, Original Tags, c.1970, 16 In., Pair 49.00
Doll, Composition, Painted Features, Blue Romper, Chef's Hat, 12 In. 415.00
Doll, Composition, Side-Glancing Eyes, Cotton Romper, Horsman, 12 In. 330.00
Doorstop, Boy & Girl, Dog, Cast Iron, Painted, 10 In. 138.00
Lunch Box, School Scenes, M'm! M'm! Good, 7 3/4 x 6 x 3 In. 13.00
Spoon, Stainless, Campbell Kid Girl Handle, Oneida, Canada 5.00
Spoon Rest, Campbell Kid Chef, White, Red Trim 22.00
Toy, Farm Truck, Pull Toy, Fisher-Price, 9 In. 440.00

CANDELABRUM refers to a candleholder with more than one arm to
hold many candles; a candlestick is designed to hold one candle. The
eccentricity of the English language makes the plural of candelabrum
into candelabra.

2-Light, Brass, Conical Holders, Spiral Branches, Omicron, Jarvie, 10 3/4 x 8 In. 7640.00
2-Light, Brass, Figural, Grecian Shape, Pedestal Base, 19 x 9 In., Pair 765.00
2-Light, Brass, Flattened Urn Finial, Electrified, England, Late 1700s, 16 1/4 In. 410.00
2-Light, Brass, Marble Base, Ship Form, A.M. Greenblatt Studios, Boston, 11 In., Pair 460.00
2-Light, Bronze, Ormolu, Gilt Metal, Putto, Figural, Louis XVI, Marble, 12 In. 1495.00
2-Light, Crystal, Cut Glass Bobeche, 20th Century, 18 1/2 x 13 In., Pair 295.00
2-Light, Gilt Bronze, Bleu Persan Foo Dog Base, France, c.1865, 13 1/2 In., Pair 3220.00
2-Light, Gilt Bronze, Louis XVI Style, Lion Masques, Continental, 12 In., Pair 1150.00
2-Light, Gilt Bronze, Verde Antico Marble, Louis XVI Style, 16 1/2 In. 635.00
2-Light, Gilt, Patinated Bronze, Marble, Louis XVI Style, 9 x 6 x 3 In., Pair 1095.00
2-Light, Iron, Cone Base, Adjustable, Holder, Tabletop, New England, 1800s, 30 x 13 In. . 2990.00
2-Light, Porcelain, Flowers, Branch, Trunk Shape Supports, 8 1/2 In., Pair 200.00
2-Light, Sconce, Eagle, Parcel Gilt, Black Paint, Brass, Neoclassical Style, 44 In., Pair ... 2645.00
2-Light, Sconce, Swan, Giltwood, Neoclassical Style, 21 3/8 In., Pair 1610.00
2-Light, Ship, Antique Brass, Marble Base, A.M. Greenblatt, Boston, Mass., 11 In., Pair .. 460.00
2-Light, Turned Brass, Neoclassical Gilt Brass Applique, Restauration, 17 In. 2185.00
3-Light, Bronze, Oriental Figure, Holding Torchere, Regency Style, 16 In., Pair 2030.00
3-Light, Bronze, Parcel Gilt, Leaf Branches, Putto, Continental, c.1900, 16 In., Pair 2990.00
3-Light, Gilt Bronze, Porcelain, Lily, Putti, Napoleon III Style, France, 20 In., Pair 430.00
3-Light, Gilt Bronze, Putto Supporting Branches, Louis XV Style, 16 In., Pair 2390.00
3-Light, Gilt Bronze, Putto With Roses, Louis XVI Style, Lamp Mount, 15 In., Pair 1315.00
3-Light, Mahogany, Chrome, Ascending Step, France, 15 1/2 In., Pair 800.00
3-Light, Porcelain, Gilt Spelter, Napoleon III Style, Late 19th Century, 12 In. 460.00
3-Light, Sheffield Plate, Leaf Borders, Scroll Branches, c.1825, 20 In., Pair 850.00
3-Light, Sheffield Plate, Vase Shape, Gadroon Base, Shells, c.1815, 20 In., Pair 1560.00
3-Light, Sheffield Plate, Vase Shape, Gadroon Border, Capital Sconce, 22 In., Pair 1200.00
3-Light, Silver Plate, Adam Style, Convertible, England, 18 3/4 In., Pair 489.00
3-Light, Silver Plate, Convertible, Engraved Crests, 17 In., Pair 400.00
3-Light, Silver Plate, Convertible, George II Style, England, Late 1800s, 19 In. 1150.00
3-Light, Silver Plate, Convertible, Lobed Base, Gadroon, Sheffield, 19 In., Pair 570.00
3-Light, Silver Plate, Cotton Reel Sockets, Scrolling Branches, Boulton, 20 In., Pair 1725.00
3-Light, Silver Plate, Gadroon Border, Sheffield, England, 20 1/2 In., Pair 1495.00
3-Light, Silver Plate, Scrolling Branches, Baluster Base, 18 x 17 1/2 In., Pair 200.00
3-Light, Silver Plate, Scrolling Branches, Baluster Shape Stem, 20 In., Pair 1150.00
3-Light, Silver Plate, Scrolling Branches, Baluster Shape Stem, Early 1900s, 14 In., Pair .. 345.00
3-Light, Silver Plate, Shaped Stem, Scrolling Armrests, 14 1/2 x 13 In., Pair 90.00

3-Light, Silver, Ribbed, Ornamented Side Branches, Julius Randahl, 9 1/4 In., Pair 1300.00
3-Light, Silver, Rococo Style, Asymmetrical Tree, Continental, 1900s, 17 In., Pair 9600.00
3-Light, Wood, Iron, Triangle Base, Tabletop, Holder, New England, Early 1800s, 13 In. . . . 1380.00
4-Branch, Nickel Bronze, Deco Style, Marble Base, Austria, 12 1/2 In., Pair 825.00
4-Light, Bisque, 3 Scrolling Branches, Prisms, Man, Woman, 19th Century, 21 In., Pair . . . 315.00
4-Light, Bronze, Gilt Bronze, Victory Figure, Electrified, French Empire, 1800s, 33 In. . . . 980.00
4-Light, Gilt Metal, Porcelain, Continental, 16 In., Pair 570.00
4-Light, Metal Mounted, Porcelain, Bacchanalian Children, 23 1/2 In., Pair . . . . . . .375.00 to 635.00
4-Light, Sheffield Plate, Matthew Boulton, Birmingham, c.1810, 29 In. 1680.00
4-Light, Silver, Paw Feet, Leaves, Shells, Mortimer & Hunt, 1840, 28 3/4 In. 7200.00
5-Light, Barbendienne Incised, Gilt Bronze, Napoleon III, Tripodal, c.1865, 37 In., Pair . . . 3220.00
5-Light, Blackamoor, Wood, Carved, Polychrome, Flower Form, 63 In., Pair 1259.00
5-Light, Brass, Cast Branches, Italy, 20th Century, 20 x 8 In., Pair 80.00
5-Light, Bronze, Glass, Louis XV Style, Electrified, 30 In., Pair 1435.00
5-Light, Bronze, Louis XVI Style, Putto, Holding Flowers, 17 In., Pair 1195.00
5-Light, Bronze, Marble, Louis XVI, Figural, Cherub Supporting Flowers, 29 In. 420.00
5-Light, Bronze, Samurai Warrior, 28 In., Pair 1345.00
5-Light, Gilt Bronze, Marble, 4 Scrolling Branches, Electrified, France, 29 In., Pair 1885.00
5-Light, Gilt Lacquer, Brass Pendant, Electrified, France, c.1865, 20 x 14 In., Pr. 2070.00
5-Light, Gilt Lacquered Brass, Louis Philippe, Column, Bun Feet, 21 x 12 In. 490.00
5-Light, Gilt Metal, Egyptian Revival, Victorian, Urn Shape, 23 In. 450.00
5-Light, Marble, Patinated, Gilt Bronze, Napoleon III Style, c.1900, 26 In., Pair 1610.00
5-Light, Metal, Patinated, Gilt, Marble, Leaf Scroll Branches, Urn, France, 32 In., Pair . . . 1040.00
5-Light, Rococo Revival, Gilt Bronze, 4 Sconces, Acanthus Branches, c.1880, 19 In., Pair . 558.00
5-Light, Silver Plate, Scrolling Branches, Baluster Stem, Late 19th Century, 25 In. 690.00
5-Light, Silver Plate, Scrolling Branches, Convertible Configuration, 24 In. 690.00
5-Light, Silver Plate, Scrolling Branches, Fluted Stem, Boulton, c.1820, 24 In., Pair 1380.00
5-Light, Venetian Glass, Spiraled Ribs, Applied Leaves, Flowers, Gilt, 21 In. 260.00
6-Light, Bronze, 5 Radiating Branches, Fluted Column, 3 Claw Feet, 8 In., Pair 1380.00
6-Light, Gilt Bronze, Louis XV Style, Putto Picking Grapes, 28 In., Pair 1555.00
6-Light, Gilt Bronze, Louis XV Style, Young Boy, Carrying Wheat, 38 In., Pair 2030.00
6-Light, Gilt Bronze, Marble, Napoleon III, 5 Branches, France, 1855-70, 27 In., Pair 1380.00
7-Light, Gilt Bronze, Louis XVI Style, Electrified, 23 In., Pair 2030.00
8-Light, Altar, Gilt Metal, Early 20th Century, 54 In. 58.00
8-Light, Bronze, Hanging, Round Hub, Eight Scrolls, Electrified, 36 x 30 In., Pair 865.00
14-Light, Tinware, Painted, Scrolled Branches, 1900s, 21 1/2 x 40 1/2 In. 470.00
Bronze, Gilt Bronze, Figures Supporting Branches, Early 1800s Style, 35 In., Pair 2686.00
Gilt Metal, Oak Tree, Scrolling Branch Shape, Italy, 22 In., Pair 1495.00
Giltwood, Tripod, Carved, Louis XVI Style, France, c.1900, 60 In. 1265.00
Girandole, 2-Light, Giltwood, Deer, Leaf Scroll, Mirror, c.1815, 37 In. 3525.00
Girandole, 3-Light, Flower Shape Bobeche, Figural Stem, 1800s, 20 In., Pair 201.00
Girandole, 5-Light, Tree Shape, Marble Base, 19th Century, 22 x 17 In., Pair 1265.00
Girandole, 6-Light, Glass, Gilt Bronze, J. & L. Lobmeyr, Vienna, 24 In., Pair 4800.00
Girandole, Brass, Marble, Female-Supported Bobeche, Prisms, Marble, 15 In., Pair 144.00
Girandole, Renaissance Couple, Marble Base, Brass, Prisms, 17 x 14 In., 3 Piece 300.00

CANDLESTICKS were made of brass, pewter, glass, sterling silver, plated silver, and all types of pottery and porcelain. The earliest candlesticks, dating from the sixteenth century, held the candle on a pricket (sharp pointed spike). These lost favor because in times of strife the large church candlesticks with prickets became formidable weapons, so the socket was mandated. Candlesticks changed in style through the centuries, and designs range from classic to rococo to Art Nouveau to Art Deco.

Amber Glass, Scrolling Leafy Molded Design, Early 20th Century, 8 1/2 In., Pair 29.00
Ash Burl, Barrel Shape, Relief Turned Rings, Recessed Socket, 3 x 2 5/8 In. 345.00
Bell Metal, Cylindrical Candle Cup, Vasiform Stem, 18th Century, 4 1/4 In., Pair 410.00
Bell Metal, Waxjack, Urn Finial, 18th Century, 6 In. 440.00
Bilston Enamel, Flower Petal Shape Bobeche, 18th Century, 11 In., Pair 920.00
Birch, Root Base, Scrubbed Top, Red Paint, Maine, c.1850, 26 x 20 x 20 1/2 In. 575.00
Blown Glass, Venetian, Double, Italy, 7 In., Pair 200.00
Brass, Ace Of Diamonds, Push-Up, Victorian, 14 In., Pair 835.00
Brass, Art Nouveau, France, 10 1/2 In. 529.00

Brass, Baluster Form, Octagonal Base, Tall Sockets, Push-Up, England, 12 In., Pair 230.00
Brass, Baluster Stems, Guilloche Bands, France, 10 In., Pair 146.00
Brass, Baluster Stems, Octagonal Base, Scalloped, Step Moldings, 9 In., Pair 690.00
Brass, Baluster Turned Stem, Square Tray Base, Triangular Feet, 5 7/8 In. 259.00
Brass, Banded, Paneled Shaft, 19th Century, 8 1/2 x 3 1/2 In., Pair 50.00
Brass, Beehive, Faceted Columns, Push-Up, 11 In., Pair 305.00
Brass, Brass Collared Plate, Hurricane Shades, Continental, 1900s, 11 In., Pair 316.00
Brass, Capstan, Flared Base, Drip Edge, Tapered Socket, 6 1/4 In. 860.00
Brass, Capstan, Incised Rings, Mid-Drip Pan, 3 1/4 x 3 1/2 In., Pair 1090.00
Brass, Capstan, Urn Shaped Socket, Turned Rings, 4 1/2 x 5 1/4 In. 630.00
Brass, Chamber, Circular Base, Dish Form Base, Push-Up, Georgian, c.1815, 8 In., Pair .. 375.00
Brass, Chamber, Wood Handle, Christopher Dresser, 5 1/2 x 7 1/2 In. 1295.00
Brass, Cotton Reel Sockets, Multi Knopped Stem, Petal Fluted Base, 9 In., Pair 336.00
Brass, Cut Corner, England, c.1735, Pair 695.00
Brass, Dished Base, Cylindrical Standard, Sawtooth Design, Push-Up, England, 7 In. 230.00
Brass, Dished Center, Square Base, England, 8 3/4 In., Pair 230.00
Brass, Empire, Circles & Trelliswork Designs, France, c.1820, 9 In., Pair 645.00
Brass, Flared Rim Bobeches, Tapered, Fluted Column, Paw Foot Base, 12 1/2 x 3 1/2 In. .. 220.00
Brass, Flowers, Germany, 5 1/4 In. 118.00
Brass, Gilt Lacquered, White Marble, Palm Tree Shape, Mid 1800s, 13 In., Pair 290.00
Brass, Gilt, Reticulated, Paw Foot, Louis XVI Style, Lamp Mount, c.1900, 24 In. 1095.00
Brass, Jack-Of-Diamond, Push-Up, 10 3/4 In., Pair 69.00
Brass, Marble, Prisms, Flower Basket Stem Support, c.1870, 15 1/2 In., Pair 259.00
Brass, Mid-Drip, Round, Spun Base, Drip Pan, Baluster Stem, 19th Century, 9 In., Pair ... 230.00
Brass, Open Twist, Lamp Mounting, Pheasant Feather Shade, c.1900, 13 1/2 In., Pair 435.00
Brass, Paneled Stems, Domed Base, Scalloped Edge, Side Push-Up, 7 1/2 In., Pair 1265.00
Brass, Pricket, Drip Pan, Egg Knopped Stem, Continental, c.1800, 17 In., Pair 999.00
Brass, Queen Anne, Removable Bobeche, 18th Century, 10 In., 4 Piece 7050.00
Brass, Queen Anne, Scalloped Edge, Seamed Stem, Socket, 7 In. 315.00
Brass, Queen Anne, Seamed Construction, 7 In. 115.00
Brass, Queen Anne-George I, Ejector, Early 18th Century, 7 In., Pair 865.00
Brass, Reeded Stem, Trefoil Base, Dragons, c.1890, 16 & 9 In., 3 Piece 260.00
Brass, Round Base, Baluster Stem, Hand Threaded Post, 5 x 6 In. 200.00
Brass, Saucer Base, Adjustable Push-Up, 16 3/4 In., Pair 550.00
Brass, Saucer Base, Tooled Column Rings, Push-Up, 4 1/2 In., Pair 175.00
Brass, Scalloped Base, Riveted Stems, 8 In., Pair 550.00
Brass, Scalloped Bobeche, Baluster Stem, Late 1800s, 11 In., Pair 290.00
Brass, Seamed Stem, Socket, Cast Scalloped Edge Base, 6 5/8 In. 259.00
Brass, Square Base, Turned Shaft, Push-Up, 8 3/4 In., Pair 115.00
Brass, Stem Threaded, Saucer Base, 5 1/4 In. 315.00
Brass, Stylized Urn Post, Domed Circular Base, Push-Up, 9 1/4 In., Pair 259.00
Brass, Tapered, Baluster Stem, Threaded Into Petal Bases, 4 1/2 In. 1035.00
Brass, Thin Turnings, Tapered Round Columns, 8 5/8 In., Pair 430.00
Brass, Turned Baluster Stem, Raised Rings Top & Bottom, Square Tray, 6 3/8 In. 345.00
Brass, Turned, Faceted Columns, 12 In., Pair 195.00
Brass, Turned, Faceted Columns, Push-Up, 19th Century, 11 3/4 In., Pair 220.00
Brass, Urn Shape Socket, Tapered Stem, Square Base, England, 10 In., Pair 320.00
Brass, Wide Bobeche, Ringed Cylindrical Candle Cup, 1800s, 9 In., Pair 265.00
Brass, William IV, Weighted, Inverted Lily Shape, Bronze Base, c.1835, 9 1/2 In., Pair 690.00
Bronze, 3 Geese, Art Nouveau, 6 In. 235.00
Bronze, Boy, Holding Knopped Candleholder, Chinese, 1800s, 8 In., Pair 165.00
Bronze, Figural, Don Quixote, Pancho Sanchez, Early 1900s, 10 & 11 In., Pair 295.00
Bronze, Figural, Japanese Cranes, Patinated, Late 19th Century, 21 1/2 In., Pair 520.00
Bronze, Figural, Woman, Standing, Classical Drape, Cornucopia, c.1885, 26 In., Pair 3525.00
Bronze, Flower, Leaf Foot, G. De Feure, c.1900, 14 In. 2390.00
Bronze, Gilt, Louis XIV Style, France, c.1885, 9 1/2 In., Pair 1610.00
Bronze, Iota Model, Bobeche, Jarvie, 14 x 7 In. 4405.00
Bronze, Napoleon III, Neo-Grec Style, Vasiform, Mid 19th Century, 17 In., Pair 750.00
Bronze, Patinated, Gilt, Woman, Classical Robe, Amber Glass, France, 1800s, 11 In., Pair . 1885.00
Bronze, Pricket, Round Drip Pan, Multi Knopped Stems, Bracket Feet, 9 In., Pair 329.00
Bronze, Urn Form, Marble Plinth, Ram's Head, Garlands Swags, 10 x 3 In., Pair 950.00
Bronze, Weighted, Turned Bobeches, 20th Century, 21 1/2 x 5 In., Pair 80.00
Cast Brass, George III, Petal Base, R. Bush, England, c.1765, 7 1/2 In., Pair 4200.00

Rub the base of a candlestick with a little olive oil before lighting a candle. Any wax that drips can easily be peeled off the oiled base.

Candlestick, Chamber, Silver, Snuffer, Ebonized Handle, Christopher Dresser, England, 6 In.

Cast Iron, Curved Finger Hook, Chamber, 2 1/2 x 4 In., Pair 805.00
Chamber, Bronze, Maiden Shape, Art Nouveau, Austria, 7 In. 450.00
Chamber, Silver Plate, Snuffers, Bobeches, England, 7 In., Pair 290.00
Chamber, Silver, Snuffer, Ebonized Handle, Christopher Dresser, England, 6 In. ..... *Illus* 1998.00
Cloisonne, Stork, Oriental, Hold Pricket In Beak, Enameled, Bronze Ground, 33 In., Pair .. 575.00
Copper, Alpha Form, Jarvie, 11 In. 499.00
Copper, Arts & Crafts, Jarvie, 12 In., Pair 825.00
Copper, Delta Form, Jarvie, 14 In. 1000.00
Copper, Hammered, Arts & Crafts, 13 1/2 x 9 In. 635.00
Copper, Hammered, Chamber, Leaf Handle, Square Base, Jauchen's, 5 1/2 x 4 1/2 In. 940.00
Copper, Hammered, Stickley, Applied Bands, 10 1/2 In. 700.00
Copper, Lambda Form, Jarvie, 6 In. 825.00
Copper, Pewter, Dolphin Form, 6 In., Pair 175.00
Engine Turned Brass, Restauration, Early 19th Century, 11 1/2 In., Pair 865.00
Gilt & Patinated Bronze, Louis Philippe, Mounted As Lamp, 11 3/4 In., Pair 635.00
Gilt Brass, Flutes, Leaves, Flower Garlands, France, Late 1800s, 9 1/2 In., Pair 520.00
Gilt Bronze, Marble Coiled, Dragon, Cornucopia Shape, Regency, 1800s, 7 In., Pair 1380.00
Gilt Bronze, Patinated, Restauration Style, Mounted As Lamp, c.1900, 19 In. 1265.00
Gilt Bronze, Polychrome, Anthemion, Palms, Pricket, Continental, 30 In., Pair 920.00
Gilt Bronze, Regency Style, Winged Seated Sphinx, Late 1800s, 8 In., Pair 1150.00
Gilt Bronze, Tripodal, Louis Philippe, Neoclassical Style, 9 1/2 In., Pair 520.00
Gilt Metal, Enameled, Gothic Revival, Hexagonal Sconce, 11 3/4 In., Pair 1000.00
Gilt Wrought Iron, Altar, Baroque, Giltwood, Early 1700s, 49 In. 1095.00
Giltwood, Altar, Neoclassical Style, Columnar, Turned, Paw Footed, Gilt, 25 In., Pair 1095.00
Giltwood, Altar, Neoclassical Style, Vase Shape, Used As Lamp, 1700s, 25 In., Pair 2070.00
Giltwood, Carved, Figural, Angels, Painted Dress, Pricket, 19th Century, 14 In., Pair 3585.00
Giltwood, Pricket, 18th Century Neoclassical Style, c.1900, 19 1/2 In., Pair 1095.00
Giltwood, Renaissance Style, Electrified, Late 1800s, 34 1/2 In., Pair.................. 920.00
Giltwood, Woman, Upright Arm, Scrolled Leaf Branch, Italy, 1800s, 17 In., Pair 3959.00
Glass, Avon 91st Anniversary, Crystal Clear, 6 Coin Shapes, 1977, 4 1/2 In., Pair 30.00
Glass, Caryatid, Canary Yellow, 6-Sided Base, New England Glass Co., 9 3/4 In. 1610.00
Hog Scraper, Brass Ring, Push-Up, Lip Hanger, 4, 6, & 6 In., 3 Piece 520.00
Hog Scraper, Shouldered Brass Band, Push-Up, Lip Hanger, 6 1/2 In. 175.00
Hog Scraper, Soldered Brass Middle Band, Push-Up, Lip Hanger, 12 In. 259.00
Iron, Crimped Tray, C-Form Handle, Chamber, 1800s, 15 1/4 x 10 1/2 In. 2760.00
Ivory, Scrimshaw Decorated, Geisha, Flower, Painted Black Base, 9 3/4 In. 60.00
Metal, Verdigris Patina, Arts & Crafts, 21 1/2 In. 150.00
Milk Glass, Crucifix, 12 In. 25.00
Nickel Silver, Pairpoint, Removable Bobeche, 12 In., Pair 120.00
Parcel Gilt, Black Patinated, Louis Philippe, 10 1/4 x 4 3/4 In., Pair 750.00
Pewter, Baluster Columns, Push-Up, 19th Century, 10 In., Pair 1430.00
Pewter, Turned Shaft, Round Base, Push-Up, 8 1/2 In., Pair 175.00
Pewter, Urn Turned Shafts, Bulbous Base, 18th Century, 5 1/4 In., Pair 705.00
Pine, Altar, Stripped, Carved, Renaissance Style, 36 In., Pair 690.00
Pine, Altar, Tripodal, Carved, Neoclassical Style, Early 19th Century, 27 1/2 In. 805.00
Pine, Gilt, Carved, White Painted, Tripod, Neoclassical, c.1900, Italy, 69 In., Pair 2875.00

Pine, Parcel Silvered, Altar, Acanthine Carved, Italy, c.1815, 29 In., Pair 1610.00
Porcelain, Figural, Twin Light Supports, KPM, 18 x 13 1/2 x 5 1/2 In., Pair 650.00
Porcelain, Gilt Brass Mounted, Rococo Style, Late 19th Century, 9 In., Pair 320.00
Porcelain, Jacob Petit, Paris, Fontainebleau, Rococo Style, Gilt, Applied Bouquets, 10 In. . 1495.00
Rock Crystal, Louis XVI Style, Gilt Bronze, Laurel Leaves, Fluted Cups, 7 1/2 In., Pair ... 980.00
Sheffield Plate, Extinguisher, Circular, Chamber, Creswick, c.1820, 6 1/2 In., Pair 265.00
Silver, Baroque Style, Continental, Late 18th Century, 13 1/2 x 5 In., Pair 1095.00
Silver, Brighton Bun, Traveling, James Garrard, 1897, 3 3/4 In., Pair 3580.00
Silver, Campana Socket, Round Gadroon Base, J. & T. Settle, England, 7 1/2 In., Pair 1150.00
Silver, Chamber, Conical Snuffer, Ebonized Handle, Christopher Dresser, 6 x 7 In. 2000.00
Silver, Corinthian Capital, Fluted Column, W. Cafe, George III, 1765, 12 1/2 In., Pair 4340.00
Silver, Extinguisher, Gadroon Border, Chamber, Bateman, George III, 1807, 3 3/4 In. 615.00
Silver, Flowers, Leaves, Octagonal Socket, 4 Scroll Feet, Dutch, 1851, 13 In., 4 Piece 4150.00
Silver, George I, Taper Stick, Dome Base, Henry Jay, London, 1718, 41 1/4 In., Pair 7800.00
Silver, George II, Taper Stick, Octagonal Baluster, James Gould, London, 4 3/8 In., Pair .. 9600.00
Silver, George II, Taper, Octagonal Baluster, John Cafe, London, c.1744, 4 3/8 In., Pair ... 3600.00
Silver, George III, Adam Style, Sheffield 1804 Mark, Thomas Law, England, 13 In. 2300.00
Silver, George III, Gadroon Border, Scroll Thumbpiece, A. Johnston, 1762, 4 In. 520.00
Silver, George III, Shells, John Roberts & Co., Sheffield, c.1808, 12 5/8 In., 4 Piece 7200.00
Silver, George III, Stepped Octagonal Base, John Perry, England, 1762, 5 1/2 In., Pair 2300.00
Silver, George IV, Square Base, Multi-Knopped Stem, England, c.1829, 11 In., Pair 2435.00
Silver, Inverted Baluster, Engraved Flowers, Birks, Montreal, 10 In., 4 Piece 2760.00
Silver, Leaf Molded Socket, Dolphin Support, H.A. Seethaler, Germany, 10 In., Pair 3020.00
Silver, Multi-Knopped Stem, Square Base, Ebenezer Coker, George III, 1762, 10 In. 1510.00
Silver, Running Animal, Stamped, Hallmark, 12, Austria, 13 1/2 In., Pair 575.00
Silver, Thin Shaft, Tulip Cup, Broad Round Base, Mulholland Bros., 8 1/4 In., Pair 1500.00
Silver Over Bronze, Heintz Silvercrest, 18 1/2 In., Pair 795.00
Silver Plate, Arts & Crafts, WMF, Austria, 10 3/4 In., Pair 499.00
Silver Plate, Columnar, Garland At Base, Sheffield, c.1785, 13 1/4 In., Pair 1035.00
Silver Plate, Flared, Beaded Knop Stem, Acanthus Base, Younge, George IV, 7 In., Pair ... 1035.00
Silver Plate, Gadroon Standard, Tapering, Sheffield, c.1825, 12 1/2 In., Pair 520.00
Silver Plate, Georgian Style, Baluster Stem, Gadrooned Base, Elkington, 10 In., Pair 345.00
Silver Plate, Gilt, Angular, Elsa Tennhardt, 1928, 4 3/4 x 5 x 5 In., Pair 4500.00
Silver Plate, Leaf Capitals, Cluster Columns, J. & W. Deakin, 1897, 5 1/2 In., Pair 470.00
Silver Plate, Oval Base, 6 1/2 In., Pair 127.00
Silver Plate, Reed Cluster, Square Base, Sheffield, c.1820, 12 1/2 In., 4 Piece 1095.00
Silver Plate, Sheffield Plated, Stepped Square Base, England, Late 1700s, 11 In., Pair 270.00
Silver Plate, Sheffield, Copper, Chased Unicorn Design, England, 1800s, 11 In., 4 Piece .. 290.00
Silver Plate, Triangular Stem, Hawksworth, Eyre & Co., Sheffield, c.1870, 12 In., Pair ... 1035.00
Silvered, Altar, Carved, Baroque Style, Paw Feet, Late 18th Century, 75 In. 1095.00
Silvered Wood, Altar, Turned, Leaf Carved, Columnar, Early 19th Century, 30 1/2 In. 635.00
Steel, Brass Band, Hog Scraper, 1800s, 8 In., Pair 1320.00
Sterling Silver, Baluster Shape, Engraved, Initial B, Weighted Base, 12 In., Pair 200.00
Sterling Silver, Square, Art Deco Form, William Nost & Co., 8 1/2 In., Pair 265.00
Sterling Silver, Swirl Base, George III, Removable Bobeche, England, 8 1/2 In., Pair 6000.00
Sterling Silver, Urn Shape Holder, Pedestal Base, Empire 616, 5 In., Pair 115.00
Tin, Conical Base, Black Paint, Mid-Drip Pan, Push-Up, 8 3/4 In. 405.00
Tin, Hollow Notched Column, Crimped Pan, Applied Handle, Push-Up, 8 1/4 In., Pair 145.00
Tin, Oval Saucer Base, Ring Handle, Adjustable Push-Up, 6 1/2 In. 145.00
Tin, Saucer Base, Ring Handle, Adjustable Push-Up, 5 In., Pair 210.00
Tinned Iron, Hog Scraper, Brass Wedding Band, Adjustable, Early 1800s, 12 1/2 In., Pr. .. 3680.00
Tinned Iron, Hog Scraper, Thumb Tab, Circular Base, Early 1800s, 14 1/2 In., Pair 2415.00
Toleware, Chinoiserie, Birds, Shrubs, Ebonized, England, Early 1800s, 7 1/2 In., Pair 285.00
Treenware, Curly Maple, c.1930, 5 x 2 1/4 In., Pair 800.00
White Metal, Bronze, Gilt Finish, Demon Holding Cauldron, Early 1900s, 10 In. 235.00
Wrought Iron, Brass Mounted, Pricket, Baroque Style, Arched Feet, Spain, 59 In., Pair ... 6600.00
Wrought Iron, Circular Beaded Dish Base, Tripod Feet, Samuel Yellin, 10 1/2 In. 3055.00
Wrought Iron, Hog Scraper, Brass Wedding Ring Design, Push-Up, 6 3/4 In. 415.00
Wrought Iron, Hog Scraper, Push-Up, 7 In., Pair 110.00
Wrought Iron, Pagoda Smoke Bell, Adjustable, Holder, Tabletop, 1700s, 38 In. 4830.00
Wrought Iron, Spiral Stick, Turned Base, Push-Up, Lip Hanger, 7 3/4 In. 115.00

CANDLEWICK items may be listed in the Imperial and Pressed Glass categories.

CANDY CONTAINERS have been popular since the late Victorian era. Collectors have long favored the glass containers, but now all types, including tin and papier-mache, are collected. Probably the earliest glass container sold commercially was the Liberty Bell made in 1876 for sale at the Centennial Exposition. Thousands of designs were made until the cost became too high in the 1960s. By the late 1970s, reproductions were being made and sold without the candy. Containers listed here are glass unless otherwise described. A Belsnickle is a nineteenth-century figure of Father Christmas. Some candy containers may be listed in Toy or in other categories.

Amos 'n' Andy, Open Air Taxi, Victory Glass Co., 4 In.	340.00
Asian Woman, Amber Tint, Bisque Shoulder Head, Cone Shape, France, 1890, 9 In.	880.00
Belsnickle, Germany, 5 In.	275.00
Belsnickle, White, Green Chenille Around Hood, 11 In.	1430.00
Box, Paper, Fitted Interior, Gold Leaf Edging, Mirror, 8 Boxes, France, 16 x 10 In.	2260.00
Boy, On Snowball, Googly Eyes, Heubach, Germany, c.1910, 8 In.	605.00
Boy, Seated On Log, Paperweight Eyes, Human Hair, Bisque, France, 12 In.	2310.00
Car, Glass, Rear Trunk & Tire, U.S.A., 5 In.	50.00
Card Box, Appliqued Gilt Border, Drawer, Lined, Hinged Lid, France, c.1860	360.00
Card Box, Rose Paper, Gilt Border, Papier-Mache Claw Feet, Silk Top, c.1860	330.00
Card Box, Rounded Corners, Applique, Gilt Edge, France, c.1860, 10 x 7 In.	550.00
Card Box, Shaped Sides, Gilt Edge, Mirror Top, France, 19th Century, 5 x 3 In.	330.00
Chicken On Oblong Basket, Victory Glass Co., 1930, 3 x 2 3/4 x 1 3/4 In.	60.00 to 65.00
Child On Snowball, Bisque Face, Heubach, Germany, 4 1/2 In.	715.00
Church, Glass Pillars, Japan, 7 In.	45.00
Coach, Cinderella, Wood, Turning Wheels, Velvet Seat, Medallions, Gilt, 1890	2420.00
Cockateel, Stamped Cardboard, Silver Finish, Dresden, 2 In.	1320.00
Dog, Bulldog, Paint, 4 In.	60.00
Dog, Salon, Papier-Mache & White Fur, Amber Eyes, Black Nose, 1890, 9 In.	505.00
Doll, Stork, Bisque Head, Glass Eyes, Mohair, Wooden Torso, 9 1/2 In.	1210.00
Doll's Bed, Mahogany, Inlay, Bronze Mounts, Drawers, Pillows, France, 20 In.	2750.00
Don Quixote, Papier-Mache Head, Painted, Cylindrical, France, c.1890, 10 In.	715.00
Electric Iron, Contents, Cord, Closure, 1940s, 4 In.	90.00
Elf, Seated, Composition, Hand Painted, Germany, 6 In.	385.00
Father Christmas, Composition, Red Coat, Blue Pants, Tree, Germany, 8 In.	1485.00
Father Christmas, Red Coat, Germany, 7 1/4 In.	300.00
Foil, Cone Shape, Flowers, Cutout Semicircles, Purple, Red, 6 In., 5 Piece	30.00
George Washington, Holding Cherry, Ax, Bisque Head, 8 1/2 In.	510.00
Girl On Snowball, Googly Eyes, Heubach, Germany, c.1910, 7 3/4 In.	660.00
Girl With Muff, On Box, Cotton, Bisque Face, Heubach, Germany, 3 1/2 In.	520.00
Greyhound Bus, Glass, 5 In.	110.00
Guitar, Faux Wood, 2 Strings, Papier-Mache, Cardboard, France, c.1890, 6 In.	220.00
Half Doll, China, Painted Features, Molded Hair, Bell Shaped Container, 10 1/2 In.	415.00
Independence Hall, Glass, 5 In.	10.00
Locomotive, Glass, Lithographed Closure, 4 In.	25.00
Lotto Game, Cards, Buttons, Gilt Stencil, Faux Wood, Soldier, France, c.1890, 5 x 4 In.	440.00
Opera Glasses, Glass, 4 In.	50.00
Ornament, Horn Of Plenty, Cardboard, 6 In.	35.00
Owl, Glass, Painted, 5 In.	79.00
Peacock, Papier-Mache Body, Wood Wings & Tail, Continental, 1800s, 6 3/4 In.	590.00
Pere Noel, Composition Face, Cotton Body, 9 In.	165.00
Peter Rabbit, Cloth Clothes, Germany, 1920s	660.00
PEZ, Baseball Glove, Ball & Bat, Made In Austria	150.00
PEZ, Bullwinkle, Yellow Holder & Antlers, Austria, 3 7/8 In.	195.00
PEZ, Donald Duck, Extra Holes In Head, Made In Austria, 1970s	20.00
PEZ, Fred Flinstone, Yellow, With Feet, Marked Made In China, 1992	2.00
PEZ, PEZ Pal Maharahaj, No Feet, Yellow, Green Turban	75.00
PEZ, Santa, No Feet, 4 1/4 In., Marked C 1980 PEZ, Made In Slovenia	5.00
PEZ, Snoopy, With Package Of Candy	6.00
Pig, Papier-Mache, Removable Head, Flocked Finish, Germany, c.1900, 4 1/2 In.	365.00
Rabbit, Basket On Back, Glass Eyes, Flocked, Germany, 1920s, 6 In.	330.00
Rabbit, Brown Flocked, Carrot In Backpack, Glass Eyes, Germany, 1920s	55.00 to 90.00
Rabbit, Eating Carrot, T.H. Strough, 1947, 5 In.	60.00

Candy Container, Santa Claus, Christmas Sprig, 10 In.	Candy Container, Santa Claus, Mica Covered Wood Base, Late 20th Century, 13 In.	Candy Container, Santa Claus, On Reindeer, Glass Eyes, Felt, Papier-Mache, 6 In.

Rabbit, Flocked, Walking, 8 In. 165.00
Rabbit, Glass Eyes, Fur-Like Fabric Covering, Germany, 1920s, 21 In. 3190.00
Rabbit, Mohair, Germany, 1920s, 8 1/2 In. 330.00
Rabbit, Pulling Wagon, Brown Flocked, Germany, c.1920 . . . . 330.00
Rabbit, Sailor Suit, Holding Bowl, Germany, 1920s, 3 1/2 In. 275.00
Rabbit, Seated, Paws Together, Glass, Avor, 6 In. 60.00
Rabbit, Sitting, Brown Flocked, Glass Eyes, Germany, c.1910, 6 1/4 In. 300.00
Rooster, Crowing, Glass, Painted, 6 In. 396.00
Rooster Head, Stamped Cardboard, Dresden, Germany, 3 1/2 In. 3575.00
Santa Claus, Boot, Mesh Bag Container, Composition Face, Japan, 1930s, 6 In. 110.00
Santa Claus, Cardboard House, Bottle Brush Tree, Candy Crafters, Inc., Japan, 1930s 44.00
Santa Claus, Cardboard, Germany, 1930s, 15 In. 110.00
Santa Claus, Christmas Sprig, 10 In. . . . . *Illus* 510.00
Santa Claus, Composition, Fur Beard, Feather Sprig, Basket, Germany, c.1915, 9 In. 660.00
Santa Claus, Composition, Hand Painted, Japan, 4 In. 35.00
Santa Claus, Face, Boat, Celluloid, Foil Covered Cardboard, Japan, 1950s 6.00
Santa Claus, Feather Tree, Fur Beard, Tomato Soup Coat, Germany, c.1920, 12 In. 1650.00
Santa Claus, Glass, Red Robe, Screw Lid, 5 1/8 In. 330.00
Santa Claus, Green Coat, Feather Tree, Papier-Mache, Box, 1930s, 7 In. 135.00
Santa Claus, Holding Basket, Toys, Trees, Wood Base, Germany, Early 1890s, 15 In. 4400.00
Santa Claus, Holding Feather Tree, Rabbit Fur Beard, Germany, 5 1/2 In. 305.00
Santa Claus, Holding Tree, Sack On Back, Japan, c.1930, 9 In. 195.00
Santa Claus, In Boat, Composition, Foil, Pipe Cleaner, Japan, 1930s, 6 1/2 In. 22.00
Santa Claus, In Car, Composition, Celluloid, Cardboard, Chenille, Japan, 1930s 110.00
Santa Claus, In Chimney, Wax, Cardboard, Fanny Farmer Fresh, 6 In. 30.00
Santa Claus, In Mesh Bag, Wicker Basket, Japan, 1930s, 5 In. 55.00
Santa Claus, In Wicker Basket, Celluloid, Composition, Japan, 1930s, 5 In. 35.00
Santa Claus, Mica Covered Wood Base, Late 20th Century, 13 In. . . . . *Illus* 115.00
Santa Claus, Net Bag Body, Chenille Basket, c.1930, 5 x 4 In. 110.00
Santa Claus, Net Bag, Celluloid, Composition, Boots, Japan, 1930s, 7 In. 35.00
Santa Claus, On Chimney, Japan, c.1930, 7 In. 35.00
Santa Claus, On Log, Rabbit Fur Beard, Composition, Germany, 4 In. 140.00
Santa Claus, On Log, Rabbit Fur Beard, Germany, c.1920, 5 In. 165.00
Santa Claus, On Logs, Composition, Hand Painted, Germany, 4 In. 165.00
Santa Claus, On Reindeer, Glass Eyes, Felt, Papier-Mache, 6 In. . . . . *Illus* 1725.00
Santa Claus, On Sled, Celluloid Face, Cardboard Sleigh, Japan, 1930s, 6 In. 195.00
Santa Claus, On Sled, Holly Box, Germany, 6 x 5 In. 140.00
Santa Claus, On Sled, Net Bag, Celluloid, Composition, Japan, 1930s, 6 In. 11.00
Santa Claus, On Sled, Rabbit Fur Beard, Presents, Germany, 6 x 6 In. 275.00
Santa Claus, On Sleigh, Composition, Hand Painted, Germany, 3 3/4 In. 250.00
Santa Claus, On Sleigh, Reindeer, Cotton Batting, Cardboard, Japan, 7 In. 80.00
Santa Claus, On Split Logs, Germany, c.1920 . . . . 195.00
Santa Claus, On Stump, Bisque Face, Crepe Paper, Heubach, Germany, 12 In. 2200.00

Candy Container, Santa Claus, Papier-Mache, Mica Covered Wood Base, Germany, 18 In.

Candy Container, St. Nicholas Pulling Cart, Embossed, Slide Top, 4 In.

Santa Claus, On Wood Pile, Papier-Mache, Felt, Germany, 5 1/2 In. 165.00
Santa Claus, Papier-Mache, Mica Covered Wood Base, Germany, 18 In. . . . . *Illus*   3680.00
Santa Claus, Red Felt Coat, Rabbit Fur Beard, Wood Base, Germany, 1920s, 14 1/2 In. . . .   1650.00
Santa Claus, Tree, Fur Beard, Composition Face, Germany, c.1920, 8 In. 525.00
Santa Claus, Tree, On Box, Papier-Mache, Cardboard, Germany, 1920s, 4 In. 120.00
Santa Claus, Walking, Baby, Basket, Fur Beard, Composition, Germany, 8 In. 1540.00
Santa Claus, White, France, 9 In. 825.00
Ship, Bust Of Admiral Dewey, Milk Glass, 7 In. 15.00
Slipper, Stamped Cardboard, Fabric Bag, Silver Finish, Dresden, 3 1/2 In. 415.00
Snowball, Googly-Eyed Boy & Girl, Heubach, Germany, c.1900, 5 1/2 In. 1100.00
Snowman, Black Hat, Holding Stick, Hard Cotton, Mica, Austria, 6 In. 80.00
Snowman, Black Hat, Venetian Dew Finish, US Zone Germany, 1948-52, 9 In. 220.00
Snowman, Orange Top Hat & Scarf, Holding Stick, Germany, 7 In. 195.00
Snowman, Papier-Mache, Green Hat, Holding Stick, Germany, c.1920, 7 In. 495.00
Snowman & Woman, Umbrella, Composition, 1930s, 4 x 3 1/2 In. 165.00
St. Nicholas Pulling Cart, Embossed, Slide Top, 4 In. . . . . *Illus*   7975.00
Turkey, Japan, 1930s, 8 1/2 In. 138.00
Turkey, Wax, 3 1/2 In. 28.00

CANES and walking sticks were used by every well-dressed man in the nineteenth century, but by World War I the style had changed. Today canes are used by few but the infirm. Collectors prize old canes made with special features, like hidden swords, whiskey flasks, or risqué pictures seen through peepholes. Examples with solid gold heads or made from exotic materials are among the higher-priced canes. See also Scrimshaw.

American Eagle With Shield, Dog, Horse, Snake, Red & Black, Charles Teal, 1817 . . . . . .   640.00
Architect's, Inkwell Top, Rubber Seal, 12-In. Folding Ivory Ruler, 36 In. 750.00
Art Glass, Smoke Color, Twisted Internal Design, 1880, 39 In. 185.00
Art Glass, Smoked, Twisted Internal Design, 19th Century, 39 In.   185.00
Art Glass, Twisted, Amber, Blown, c.1904, 45 1/4 In. 90.00
Bamboo, Silver Band, London Hallmarks, Inscription, Ivory Handle, Gavel, 1919, 36 In. . . .   490.00
Bramble Branch, Carved, Snake On Shaft, Leopard On Handle, 34 1/2 In. 115.00
Diamond Willow, Carved, Beveled Handle, Painted Horse, Leaf Motif, 36 1/2 In. 60.00
Dog Head Handle, Relief Carved Horse, Eagle, Flowers, Fish, Deer, 35 In. 275.00
Engineer's, Silver Top, Malacca Shaft, Cylindrical Calculator Inside, 33 1/2 In. 175.00
Flask, Polychrome Duck Handle, Malacca Shaft, 1900s, 36 In. 460.00
Gun, 32 Caliber, Gutta-Percha, Remington & Sons, J.F. Thomas 1858 Patent, 29 7/8 In. . . .   4025.00
Gun, Dog Head Handle, Gutta-Percha Shaft, 32 Caliber RF, Remington, 27 In. 9200.00
Gun Curio, Antler Handle, Rope Collar, France, 1800s, 36 In. 460.00
Ivory, American Flags, Flowers, Gold Collar, Engraved, Malacca, 1800s, 34 3/4 In. 410.00
Ivory, Boar's Head & Panther, Glass Eyes, Ebony Shaft, 33 In. 940.00
Ivory, Bone, Carved, Dog Handle, Knobbed Top, Glass Eyes, 38 1/2 In. 920.00
Ivory, Carved, Sterling Silver Ferule, 34 3/4 In. 315.00
Ivory, Eagle Head, Exotic Wood Shaft, Gilt Collar, Engraved Dr. E.M. Pierce, 34 In. 705.00
Ivory, Eagle Head, Glass Eyes, Exotic Wood Shaft, Iron Ferrule, 1800s, 36 In. 880.00
Ivory, Fist, Holding Rod, Braided Rope Bracelet, 30 In. 290.00

Ivory, Gold Filled, L-Shape Handle, Embossed, Diamond Band, Early 1900s, 36 In. 175.00
Ivory, Hippopotamus Head, Brass & Bead Eyes, Ivory Top, 36 In. 700.00
Ivory, Rosewood, Hippopotamus, Carved Features, Bead Eyes, Tapered Shaft, 36 In. 690.00
Ivory Handle, Thousand Faces, Bamboo Shaft, Wax & Seal Inside, 36 In. 635.00
Jade, Gemstone, Trumpet Shape Handle, 14K Gold Ferule, Bamboo Shaft, 36 In. 1150.00
Knot Head, Intertwined Knot, Bamboo Style Shaft, 37 In. 115.00
Malacca, Gold Embossed Knob, Top, Leather Wrap, Brass Compartment, 35 In. 115.00
Maple, Carved, Erotic, Woman Standing On Her Head, 19th Century, 37 In. 145.00
Narwhale Tusk, 4 Tusk Sections, Brass Dragon Inset, 38 In. 2300.00
Novelty, Bird Whistle, Ebony Shaft, 1900s, 35 1/2 In. 144.00
Novelty, Boson's Whistle, Silver Plated Brass Top, 36 In. 115.00
Novelty, Brass Balance Gold Scale Inside, Ivory & Silver Handle, 35 1/4 In. 920.00
Novelty, Choir Master's, Silver Top, Malacca Shaft, Pitch Pipe, 1900s, 36 In. 345.00
Novelty, Corkscrew, Engraved Silver Top, Monogram, Continental Touchmarks, 35 In. . . . 800.00
Novelty, Doctor's, Gadget Top, Malacca Shaft, Syringe, Needles, Pills In Cap, 1900s, 36 In. 460.00
Novelty, Doctor's, Silver Top, Partridge Wood Shaft, Syringe, Supplies Inside, 1900s, 36 In. 1495.00
Novelty, Flick Stick, Horn Shaft, 3 1/2-In. Blade, 34 In. 400.00
Novelty, Gambler's, 2-In. Ivory Top, 3 Pairs Of Dice, Wood Shaft, 36 In. 805.00
Novelty, Golf Club Shape, Silver Top, Wood Shaft, Golf Tees Inside, 34 3/4 In. 920.00
Novelty, Hearing Aid, Brass, Partridge Wood Shaft, 35 In. 635.00
Novelty, Ivory, Black Lacquered Shaft, 4 Dice Inside, 2 1/2-In. Top, 36 1/2 In. 375.00
Novelty, Kaleidoscope, Brass, Ebony Shaft, 1900s, 36 In. 259.00
Novelty, Midwife's, Silver Top, Malacca Shaft, Scales To Weigh Baby, 1900s, 36 In. 175.00
Novelty, Round Yardstick Inside, Silver Top, 37 1/8 In. 115.00
Novelty, Scale, Silver Top, Malacca Shaft, Hanging Scales, 1900s, 35 In. 115.00
Novelty, Silver Plated Top, Malacca Shaft, 4 Measuring Rods Inside, 36 1/2 In. 259.00
Novelty, Silver Quail, Partridge Wood Shaft, Pencil Inside, 1800s, 35 1/2 In. 290.00
Novelty, Silver Top, Bamboo Shaft, 4 Ebony Chopsticks, 1900s, 35 In. 115.00
Novelty, Silver Top, Bamboo Shaft, 28 Dominoes Inside, 36 In. 230.00
Novelty, Silver Top, Cigarette Lighter Inside, 34 In. 920.00
Novelty, Silver Top, Mahogany Shaft, Razor & Shaving Brush Inside, c.1890, 35 In. 375.00
Novelty, Silver Top, Malacca Shaft, 5 Dice Inside, Haig Whiskey, 1900s, 34 1/2 In. 345.00
Novelty, Silver Top, Razor, Shaving Brush, c.1900, 36 In. 490.00
Novelty, Silver Whistle, T-Shape Handle, Brass Knob, 33 3/4 In. 225.00
Novelty, Smoker's, Pipe & Stanhope Inside, Wood Shaft, Brass, 35 In. 145.00
Novelty, Tape Measure Top, Brass, Black Wood Shaft, General's Photograph, 35 1/2 In. . . . 520.00
Novelty, Tool Kit, Britton's Patent, Nickel Plated Collar, 8 Tools, c.1894, 35 1/2 In. 1200.00
Novelty, Veterinarian's Thermometer, Silver Top, Brass Tube, England, 35 5/8 In. 800.00
Novelty, Wood, Calculator, Sliding Scales, Otis King's Pocket Calculator, 32 In. . . .290.00 to 460.00
Picnic, Repousse Silver Handle, Oriental Theme, Knife, Chopsticks, Toothpick, 35 1/2 In. . 115.00
Presentation, Ivory Handle, Carved Face, FLT To RL, Ashford Bowdler Ludlow, 38 In. . . 105.00
Scribe's, Collapsible, Pen, Inkwell, Pencil, 3 Sections, Aluminum Ferrules, 33 3/4 In. 180.00
Scribe's, Leather & Brass Knob, Ebony Shaft, Inkwell Top, Pen Inside, 1900s, 36 In. 115.00
Shark Vertebrate, Horn Inserts, 35 In. 145.00
Silver Top, T-Shape Handle, Mask Head, Scrolled Ears, Embossed, 38 In. 230.00
Sword, Alpaca Crook Handle, Wood Shaft, 1900s, 25-In. Blade, 34 In. 405.00
Sword, Diamond Shaped Blade, Silver Colored Top, Burmese Figures, 33 3/4 In. 460.00
Sword, Silver Top, Malacca Shaft, 34 In. 575.00
Walking Stick, Ball, Diamond & Rib Collar, Vine & Berry Shaft, 33 1/2 In. 190.00
Walking Stick, Bird On Dog's Head, Relief Animals On Shaft, Late 1800s, 36 3/4 In. 880.00
Walking Stick, Carved, Serpent, Dog, Fish, Oak Leaves, Acorns, Grapes, 34 In. 115.00
Walking Stick, Cedar, Rabbit, Glass Eyes, Brass Tip, 1920s, 35 In. 280.00
Walking Stick, Fish, Silver, Lignum Vitae, 1800s, 35 1/2 In. 325.00
Walking Stick, Fist, Snake, Cable & Basketweave Shaft, Brass Ferrule, 1800s, 36 In. 1115.00
Walking Stick, Flower Decoration, Gold Cap, Robert Ostland, Continental, 1800s, 34 In. . . 259.00
Walking Stick, Gilt Cap, Engraved Lozenges, Acanthus Scrolls, Steel Tip, 34 In. 145.00
Walking Stick, Hand Grasping Club, Carved, 1931, 34 In. 265.00
Walking Stick, Hand Holding Black Ball, Dotted Shaft, c.1900, 35 In. 440.00
Walking Stick, Ivory, Abraham Lincoln Bust, Lignum Vitae, Silver Collar, 1800s, 39 In. . . 2585.00
Walking Stick, Ivory, Fist, Rope At Wrist, Malacca, Brass Ferrule, c.1800, 31 In. 380.00
Walking Stick, Ivory, Fist, Tapered Shaft, A. Hepburn Inscription, Late 1800s, 31 1/4 In. . . 353.00
Walking Stick, Poacher's Rod, Hollow, Samurai Carving, Fishing Rod Inside, 36 In. 55.00
Walking Stick, Presentation, Gold Head, Louis C. Dilley, Iowa, R.F.S. Co., 1893 . . . . 485.00

Walking Stick, Serpent, Tack Eyes, Carved, Black Paint, Stand, N.Y., 1880-1900, 58 In. ... 1840.00
Walking Stick, Snake Climbing Shaft, Glass Bead Eyes, Black, Yellow Spots, 37 In. 85.00
Walking Stick, Stag Horn, Hoof Detail, Wooden Shaft, 20th Century, 36 In. 35.00
Walking Stick, Walrus Ivory, Sphere, Tapered Malacca Shaft, 1800s, 37 1/2 In. 470.00
Walking Stick, Wood, Corn, Barley, Grape, Eagle, Head Handle, H. Clarke & Sons, 34 In. . 300.00
Walking Stick, Wood, Dog Head Handle, Glass Eyes, Brass Collar, 36 In. 220.00
Walking Stick, Wood, Dog Head, Painted Decoration, Uncarved Shaft, Varnished, 36 In. .. 220.00
Walking Stick, Wood, Lizard & Snake, Stained, Varnished, 33 1/2 In. 660.00
Walking Stick, Wood, Man's Head Handle & Shaft, Bark, Varnished, 34 In. 165.00
Walking Stick, Wood, Snakes, Birds, Animals, Twists, Varnished, Stained, 37 1/2 In. 330.00
Walking Stick, Wood, Snakes, Lizards, Crosshatching, Burnt Decoration, 33 1/2 In. 110.00
Walking Stick, Wood, Vine & Flowers, Initialed S.B.M., Aged Patina, 34 1/2 In. 715.00
Walnut, Tripod Base, Turned, Tapered Legs, Mortised Handle, Virginia, 33 In. 489.00
Whale's Tooth, Set In Silver Cradle, Tapered Malacca Shaft, Marked 1912, 36 In. 460.00
Wood, Black Man's Head, Carved, Painted, Tapering Shaft, Brass Ferrule, 40 In. 2350.00
Wood, Carved Bird Handle, 36 In. 460.00
Wood, Carved Falcon Head Handle, Red Glass Eyes, 34 In. 115.00
Wood, Carved, 2 Snakes, Red, Green, Yellow, Varnished Shaft, Copper Tip, 38 In. 3450.00
Wood, Carved, Adam & Eve, Tree, Civil War Soldier, Made By Luke, c.1816, 40 In. 1495.00
Wood, Carved, Alternating Mexican Hat Type Carving In 15 Sections, 36 In. 390.00
Wood, Carved, American Flag, Spiral Banner, Acorns, Hearts, 34 In. 345.00
Wood, Carved, Bird Handle, Dark Patina, 36 1/2 In. 460.00
Wood, Carved, Boot Handle, Toes Showing, Alligator, Snake, Brass Tip, 36 In. 2875.00
Wood, Carved, Horse Head Handle, Thorns, Snake, Lizard, Tin Tip, Nail Eyes, 33 1/2 In. . 316.00
Wood, Carved, Indian Head Handle, Crowned Coat Of Arms, Names, Initials, 36 In. 315.00
Wood, Carved, L-Shape Handle, Built In Hinged Snuff Box, Oak Leaves, 2 1/4 x 1 In. 345.00
Wood, Carved, Snake, Red Glass Eyes, Burl Knots, Black Paint, 35 In. 170.00
Wood, Carved, Snake, Spiral, Man In Black Waistcoat Handle, 41 In. 1150.00
Wood, Carved, Train, Surveyor's Transit, T.R. Booth, B.B.Ex.A.V.R.R. 1872, 38 In. 805.00
Wood, Fist, Holding Ball, Hand Carved, Coiled Serpent Shaft, Glass Eyes, 35 1/2 In. 750.00
Wood, Knob Shaft, Brass Tip, Standing Lady, Large Hairdo, Hat, Formal Dress, 32 In. 290.00
Wood, Low Relief Eagle & Shield, Fish, Dog, Horse, Charles Teal, N.Y., 35 In. 460.00
Wood, Monkey Head, Carved, 35 1/2 In. 145.00
Wood, Snake, Carved, Painted, 36 In. 635.00

CANTON CHINA is a blue-and-white ware made near the city of
Canton, in China, from about 1785 to 1895. It is hand decorated with
Chinese scenes. Canton is part of the group of porcelains known today
as Chinese Export Porcelain.

Basket, Fruit, Reticulated, Undertray, 2 Piece, Mid 1800s, 8 1/2 In. 795.00
Bowl, Cut Corner, 9 3/4 In. 1265.00
Bowl, Harbor Scenes, Pagodas, Ships, Rain, Cloud Border, 4 3/4 x 9 1/2 In. 750.00
Bowl, Scalloped, Ribbed, 9 3/4 In. 520.00
Bowl, Square Cut Corner, Inside & Outside Decoration, 4 1/2 x 9 In. 1035.00
Bowl, Underplate, Harbor, Ships, Pagodas, 4 x 10 3/4 & 11 1/4 x 4 3/4 In. 690.00
Bowl, Vegetable, 9 1/2 In. 375.00
Cup & Saucer, Landscape, 12 Piece 175.00
Dish, Cover, Pinecone Finial, Rectangular, 1800s, 5 1/8 x 9 3/8 In. 176.00
Dish, Oval, c.1820, 1 1/2 x 7 1/4 x 8 1/2 In. 145.00
Footbath, Hourglass Shape, Landscape Scene Interior, 24 x 15 x 6 In. 345.00
Jug, Slop, Landscape, Handle, Oval, 9 1/2 In. 200.00
Plate, Hot Water, Harbor, Pagodas, Ships, Pouring Spout, 2 1/4 x 10 5/8 In., Pair 545.00
Platter, Cut Corner, 13 1/2 x 10 3/4 In. 200.00
Platter, Cut Corner, 13 x 16 1/4 In. 920.00
Platter, Cut Corner, Rectangular, 17 In. 259.00
Platter, Orange Peel Glaze, 14 3/4 In. 290.00
Platter, Pagodas On Island, Oval, 18 1/4 In. 635.00
Platter, Rectangular, Graduated, Early 20th Century, 15 1/2 In., 2 Piece 120.00
Platter, Water & Landscape, Buildings, Boats, Scalloped Rim, c.1850, Pair 3250.00
Platter, Well & Tree, Cut Corner, 17 x 14 In. 1035.00
Platter, Well & Tree, Octagonal, 17 In. 635.00
Punch Bowl, Orange Butterfly, Iron Red Enamel, Gilding, 1800s, 16 In. 3900.00

Salad Bowl, Cut Corner, 1800s, 4 5/8 x 10 1/2 In. 700.00
Server, Cover, Animal Head Handles, Horn Shape Finial, Pagodas, Ships, 6 10 1/2 In. 635.00
Tea Set, Pear Shape, Teapot, Sugar, Cover, Creamer, 6 In., 3 Piece 230.00
Teapot, Drum Shape, Landscape, 5 1/2 In. 660.00
Teapot, Ferns On Spout, Fruit Finial, 7 1/4 In. 175.00
Teapot, Ferns, Intertwining Handle, Lid, Fruit Finial, 7 1/4 In. 170.00
Tureen, Cover, Oblong, Octagonal, Boar's Head Handles, 1800s, 8 1/2 x 12 3/4 In. 1645.00
Tureen, Cut Corner, Foo Dog Finial Cover, Looped Handles, 9 x 12 x 9 In. 115.00
Vase, Cylindrical, Figures, Birds, Flowers, 1800s, 17 In. 515.00

CAPO-DI-MONTE porcelain was first made in Naples, Italy, from
1743 to 1759. The factory moved near Madrid, Spain, reopened in
1771, and worked to 1834. Since that time, the Doccia factory of Italy
acquired the molds and is using the crown and N mark. Societe
Richard Ceramica is a modern-day firm often referred to as Ginori or
Capo-di-Monte. This company uses the crown and N mark.

Basin, Creamware, Multicolored, Bacchi Decor, c.1915, 2 1/4 x 12 1/2 In. 144.00
Box, Chest Of Drawers Form, Crown Over Shield Mark, 7 3/4 In. 650.00
Box, Oval, Relief Decorated, Aphrodite, Poseidon, Hinged Cover, 4 x 13 x 9 In. 1015.00
Ewer, Classical Relief, Goats Resting, Oval Shape, Gold Ground, Italy, 8 3/4 In. 264.00
Figurine, Young Woman, 13 In. 69.00
Stein, Battle Scene, Inlaid Lid Of Helmet, 1 Liter 755.00
Stein, Festive Scene, Relief, Lion Finial, 1/3 Liter 205.00

CAPTAIN MARVEL was introduced in February 1940 in Whiz comic
books. An orphan named Billy Batson met the wizard, Shazam, and
whenever he said the magic word he was transformed into a superhero.
A movie serial was released in 1940. The comic was discontinued in
1954. A second Captain Marvel appeared in 1966, a third in 1967.
Only the original was transformed by shouting *Shazam.*

Button, Captain Marvel Club, Shazam, Red, White, Blue, Celluloid, 1 In. 49.00
Cap, Military, Silk Screened, Felt, White, 1944, 5 x 10 3/4 In. 550.00
Coloring Book, Fawcett, 1941, 14 3/4 x 10 In., 32 Pages 86.00
Cutout, Flying Captain Marvel, Sensational, Unassembled, Envelope, 7 x 10 In. 35.00
Game, Shazam, Reed & Associates, Box, c.1944, 9 x 12 1/4 In. 160.00
Lobby Card, Scorpion Strikes, Chapter 5, 1941, 11 x 14 In. 135.00
Statuette, Marvel Jr., Plastic, KerKal Plastics, Box, 1946, 6 1/4 In. 865.00
Tie, Hoppy, Marvel Bunny, Synthetic Fabric, 1940s, 11 In. 115.00
Whistle, Magic, Shazam, Cardboard, Die Cut, Fawcett, Penny King, 1940s, 5 x 3 In. 75.00
Wristwatch, Chrome, Red Band, Marvel Importing, Fawcett Pub., 1948 .... 500.00
Wristwatch, Chrome, Red Vinyl Band, Marvel Importing, Box, 1948 .... 565.00
Wristwatch, Green Band, Fawcett Publications, Box, 1948 .... 920.00

CAPTAIN MIDNIGHT began as a radio show in September 1940.
The first comic book appeared in July 1941. Captain Midnight
was really the aviator Captain Albright, who was to defeat the Nazis. A
movie serial was made in 1942 and a comic strip was published for a
short time. The comic book Captain Midnight ended his career in
1948. The radio premiums are the prized collector memorabilia today.

Badge, Decoder, Secret Squadron, Brass, Glossy Photograph, 1942, 2 1/8 In. 76.00
Badge, Decoder, Secret Squadron, Plastic Wheel, 1945, 2 1/2 In. 75.00
Blackout Kit, Lite-Ups, Glows In The Dark, Booklet 180.00
Book, Secret Squadron, Official Manual, Ovaltine Premium, 1967, 4 x 6 In. 35.00
Detect-O-Scope, Cardboard, Metal, Premium, 5 In., 2 Piece 335.00
Folder, Sleeve Insignias Of U.S. Army, Ovaltine Premium, Envelope, 5 1/4 In. 190.00
Handbook, Flight Commander, 1957, 6 x 4 In., 12 Pages 265.00
Keyomatic Decoder With Key, 1949 .... 220.00
Lobby Card, Mistaken Identity, Columbia, 1942, 11 x 14 In. 75.00
Manual, Secret Squadron, Ovaltine Premium, 1949, 6 x 4 1/2 In., 8 Pages 90.00
Manual, Secret Squadron, Ovaltine, Envelope, 1941, 6 x 8 3/4 In., 12 Pages 365.00
Mug, Ovaltine, Heart Of A Hearty Breakfast, Plastic, Red, 1953, 3 1/8 In. ....38.00 to 95.00
Patch, Wings Logo, Insignia Insert, Premium Envelope 140.00

Photograph, Happy Landings, Patsy, Chuck, Skelly Oil, 1939, 6 x 7 3/4 In. 65.00
Poster, Flight Pilot Airlines Map, Skelly Oil, 1940, 11 x 17 In. 225.00
Ring, Ink Stamp, Brass Base, Wing Designs, Ovaltine Premium, 1948 .... 135.00
Ring, Marine Corps Insignia, Eagle, Shield, Brass, Ovaltine, 1942, Adjustable 330.00
Spy Scope, Metal, Plastic, Ovaltine, Mailing Tube, 1947, 3 1/2 In. 525.00
Tumbler, Ovaltine, Plastic, Red, Wander Co., 3 3/4 x 2 3/4 In. 20.00

CARAMEL SLAG, see Imperial Glass category.

CARDS listed here include advertising cards (often called trade cards), greeting cards, baseball cards, playing cards, and others. Color pictures were rare in the nineteenth century, so companies gave away colorful cards with pictures of children, flowers, products, or related scenes that promoted the company name. These were often collected and stored in albums. Baseball cards also date from the nineteenth century when they were used by tobacco companies as giveaways. Gum cards were started in 1933, but it was not until after World War II that the bubble gum cards favored today were produced. Today over 1,000 cards are issued each year by the gum companies. Related items may be found in the Postcard and Movie categories.

Advertising, Anderson's Teas & Coffees, Die Cut Bear, c.1885, 8 In. 28.00
Advertising, Armorside Corsets, 6 Women, Modeling Corsets, 2-Sided 50.00
Advertising, B.T. Babbit's 1776 Brand Soap Powder, Boy, Artist Pallet, c.1885 .... 15.00
Advertising, Babbitt's Soap, A Thing Of Worth Is A Joy Forever, Uncle Sam 10.00
Advertising, Bailie Nicol Jarvie's Hotel, Aberfoyle, Black, White, England, 1860s 33.00
Advertising, Barnett Rowing Machine, Parlor Gymnasium, 2-Sided 88.00
Advertising, Bell's Spiced Seasoning, Praise For All Nations, 3-Panel Folder 44.00
Advertising, Biliousine Patent Medicine, Black Man, Stomach Ache, Watermelon 22.00
Advertising, Brunswick-Balke-Collender Co., Billiard, Pool Tables, c.1910 .... 248.00
Advertising, Buchu-Paiba, Wells' Health Renewer 110.00
Advertising, Burdock Blood Bitters, Invalids, Boy Carrying Books, 4 1/4 x 3 3/8 In. 20.00
Advertising, Capadura Cigars, James Blaine, John Logan Smoking Cigars, 1884, 3 x 5 In. . 75.00
Advertising, Chicago Scale Co., Weighing Cattle 132.00
Advertising, Columbia Bicycles, High Wheeler Bicycle, Tricycle, Red Border, 2-Sided ... 99.00
Advertising, Columbia Yarns, Columbia Guards Sheep, Folder 38.00
Advertising, Daisy Air Rifle, Fletcher Hardware, Latest Parlor Amusement, 5 3/4 x 3 In. .. 405.00
Advertising, Derby & Kilmer Desk Co., Roll & Flat Top Desks, Black & White 33.00
Advertising, Diamond Dyes, Hold-To-Light, Fairy, Sign, Dress Changes Brown To Red ... 22.00
Advertising, Dixon's Stove Polish, Lime Kiln Club, Brother Gardner, Folder 44.00
Advertising, Dr. Miller's Magnetic Balm, Hold-To-Light, Boy, Opens Eyes, Smiles 60.00
Advertising, Dr. Rose's Cough Syrup, Black & White, Woodcut, 1860s 22.00
Advertising, Edwin C. Burt Fine Shoes, Black Children, Shoe, 1880s, 4 3/4 x 2 3/4 In. 25.00
Advertising, Eureka Wringer, Monkeys, Wring Cat's Tail, J.H. Bufford's Sons, c.1850 .... 22.00
Advertising, Fairbank's Twins, History, Chapter 2, Twins, Washtub 44.00
Advertising, Ferris Boots & Shoes, 3-Panel Folder, Orcutt Litho, Chicago 55.00
Advertising, Fleischmann's Yeast, Moonlit Water, Pansies, 1890s, 3 1/2 x 5 1/2 In. 12.00
Advertising, German American Insurance Co, Folder, 1883 .... 44.00
Advertising, Good Morning Coffee Percolator, Manning & Bowman 5.00
Advertising, Grand Union Hotel, N.Y., Black On Gray, Gold Border 39.00
Advertising, Heinz, Pickle Shape, Chef Holding Can Of Soup, Die Cut, London, c.1885 .. 38.00
Advertising, Heinz, Pickle Shape, Girl Holding Can Of Baked Beans, 5 1/4 x 2 In. 55.00
Advertising, Hires, Offer For Ruth & Naomi Lithograph, c.1890s, 5 x 5 7/8 In. 13.00
Advertising, Holmes Brothers Fire Insurance, N.Y., Black & White, 1860s 33.00
Advertising, Hood's, Parthenon, Athens, Greece, Black & White, c.1930, 4 x 6 In. 9.00
Advertising, Humpty Dumpty Bank, Color Lithograph, Just Out, Hit The Season 275.00
Advertising, J.W. Lincoln Wood & Canvas Decoys, Accord, Mass., 5 1/4 x 3 1/4 In. 335.00
Advertising, Jefferson Hotel, Watkins Glen, N.Y., Folder 33.00
Advertising, Lion Coffee, Mocha Java & Rio, 3 Cats On Ball, 5 1/4 x 3 1/2 In. 35.00
Advertising, M.I. Furbish Fly, Fishing Line, Black & White 35.00
Advertising, Magnolia Anti-Friction Metal, Hold-To-Light, Man, Eyes Open, Smiles 72.00
Advertising, Merchant's Gargling Oil, Sepia, Clay & Co., 1878 .... 33.00
Advertising, Mills Restaurant, Box 30.00
Advertising, Milton Bradley Co., Kindergarten Materials, Die Cut 33.00

Although paper is acidic, ink fades, and insects and light cause damage, it is still possible to preserve paper antiques. Keep paper dry, cool, sealed away from oxygen and ultraviolet light. Mylar plastic bags are the best.

Card, Greeting, New Year, Best Wishes, Garden Gate, Moonlight, 3 1/2 In., 20 Piece

Advertising, N.R. Davis & Co. Guns, Green, Black Print, 2-Sided, 5 1/4 x 2 7/8 In. 55.00
Advertising, N.Y. Consolidated Card Co., Men, Cards, Angel Back, Die Cut, Folder 193.00
Advertising, Nat Will Cigars, 2 Dancers Kick Up Legs, Double Kicker, Mechanical 66.00
Advertising, New Departure Coaster Brakes, Calendar, July 1906 .... 33.00
Advertising, New Home Sewing Machine, Children, On High Wheelers, Sepia, Blue 22.00
Advertising, New Household Ranges, Black Man's Face, Winking, 1880s, 5 1/2 x 4 In. ... 35.00
Advertising, Ocean Steamship Company Of Savannah, Ship, City Of Augusta, c.1882 .... 55.00
Advertising, People's Cyclopedia, Salesman, 1885 .... 44.00
Advertising, Pope's Air Pistol, Rifles & Air Pistols Gallery, Capt. Bogardus, c.1875 ...... 83.00
Advertising, Punch & Judy Bank, Color Lithograph 715.00
Advertising, Punch & Judy Toy Savings Bank, Mechanical, Rochester, 3 1/2 x 5 1/2 In. ... 523.00
Advertising, Redwood Portable Range, Black Woman, 1880s, 6 x 4 In. 32.00
Advertising, Rice's Seeds, Log, Multicolored Leaves, 1870s 17.00
Advertising, Rumsey & Co. Pump & Fire Engine Works, Seneca Falls, Flowers, Logo 39.00
Advertising, Schepp's Cocoanut, Monkey, Juggling Coconuts 55.00
Advertising, Speaking Dog Bank, Color Lithograph, Selchow & Righter 550.00
Advertising, T. Jordan, Butcher To Royal Family, Cheltenham, England, Early 1800s 55.00
Advertising, Trick Pony Bank, Color Lithograph 66.00
Advertising, Union Cycle Mfg. Co. Bicycles, Folder 72.00
Advertising, Variety Store, Campaign Badges, Flag, Lanterns, c.1884, 2 3/4 x 4 1/2 In. ... 80.00
Advertising, Villeroy & Boch, Home Furnishings, Worldwide Dealers 77.00
Advertising, Warrior Mower Co., Old & New Ways Of Mowing, Sepia, Gray 39.00
Advertising, Webster Wagon, Hold-To-Light, Wagon In Sky 28.00
Advertising, White Mountain Freezer, Bowl Of Ice Cream, Freezer, Die Cut, Folder 28.00
Advertising, White Swan Soap, Swan Attacking Black Boy 33.00
Advertising, Willard & Lane's Eagle Stove Polish, Black Woman, Children, 5 x 3 In. 25.00
Baseball, Eddie Murray, Rookie, Baltimore Orioles, Topps, 1978 .... 20.00
Baseball, Horace Ford, Big League Chewing Gum, Goudey Gum Co., 1933 .... 25.00
Baseball, Jackie Robinson, Topps, 1952, 3 3/4 x 2 3/4 In. 275.00
Baseball, Roberto Clemente, Pittsburgh Pirates, Topps, 1970 .... 22.00
Baseball, Willie Mays, San Fran. Giants, Topps, 1958 .... 26.00
Baseball, Yogi Berra, New York Yankees, Topps, 1958 .... 22.00
Greeting, New Year, Best Wishes, Garden Gate, Moonlight, 3 1/2 In., 20 Piece ...... *Illus* 20.00
Greeting, Valentine, 6 Hearts, Tulips, Starflower Center, Verses, Pa., c.1820, 10 x 12 In. .. 690.00
Greeting, Valentine, 8 Hearts, Starflower Center, Inscriptions, Pa., 1877, 9 1/4 x 9 In. 1150.00
Greeting, Valentine, Cut, Red, Mustard, Green, 15 3/4 x 15 3/4 In. 920.00
Greeting, Valentine, Cutwork, Our Hearts Are One, Heart Shape, Birds, 1800s, 6 x 7 In. .. 1265.00
Greeting, Valentine, Heart & Hand, Sawtooth Edged Heart, Cut Latticework, 7 3/8 x 4 In. . 1380.00
Greeting, Valentine, Hearts, Lovebirds, Oilcloth, Octagonal, Frame, 1800s, 12 1/2 In. ... 840.00
Greeting, Valentine, Pinprick, Watercolor, Woven, Ribbon Border, Verse, Germany, 2 x 8 In. 460.00
Playing, Anheuser-Busch, Double Deck 36.00
Playing, Edison Mazda Lamps, Contentment, Parrish, c.1928, 3 1/2 x 2 1/2 In. 231.00
Playing, Knuckle Down, 1906, 2 Decks 770.00
Playing, Piedmont Airlines, Hoyle, Unopened 20.00
Playing, Winchester, Sleeve, 1929, 52 Cards 275.00
Trading, Astronauts, Topps, Wax Pack, Unopened, 5 Cents, 3-D Viewer, 1963 .... 725.00

CARDER, see Aurene and Steuben categories.

Carlton Ware,
Pitcher, Poppies,
Yellow Ground,
Gold Trim,
5 1/2 In.

CARLSBAD is a mark found on china made by several factories in
Germany, Austria, and Bavaria. Many pieces were exported to the
United States. Most of the pieces available today were made after
1891.

Plate, Napoleon I & Tsar Alexander At Tilsit, Gilded Border, c.1885, 11 In. 316.00
Plate, Woman By River, Putti In Tree, Scroll & Floral Border, Gold Trim, 11 3/4 In. 150.00
Tray, Woman In Sky, Angels, Cherubs, Swag Border, Gold Trim, Handles, 22 In. 115.00
Vase, Urn Shape, Roses, Pink, Green, Hoofs, Trefoil Base, 3-Footed, 12 1/4 In. 75.00

CARLTON WARE was made at the Carlton Works of Stoke-on-Trent,
England, beginning about 1890. The firm traded as Wiltshaw & Robinson until 1957. It was renamed Carlton Ware Ltd. in 1958. The company went bankrupt in 1995, but the name is still in use.

Ashtray, Flowers, Keg Bitter, Flowers Brewmaster, Shakespeare Bust, 3 1/4 x 9 In. ...41.00 to 51.00
Compote, Stand, Devil's Copse, Stylized Trees, Leaves, Wiltshaw & Robinson, 1930s 604.00
Condiment Set, Floral & Leaf Blade, 4 Eggcups, Salt & Pepper, Toast Rack, Tray 147.00
Lamp, Mandarins Tree, Printed, Painted, Ivory Ground, 1920s, 23 In., Pair 345.00
Pitcher, Poppies, Yellow Ground, Gold Trim, 5 1/2 In. .... *Illus* 65.00
Pub Jug, Dewar's, White Label Whisky, Yellow Ground, 3 1/2 In. 65.00
Pub Jug, Haig, Fine Old Scotch Whisky, Beige Ground, 6 1/4 In. 20.00
Vase, Paradise Bird & Tree, Mottled Red Ground, Wiltshaw & Robinson, 1930s 345.00

CARNIVAL GLASS was an inexpensive, iridescent, pressed glass
made from about 1907 to about 1925. More than 1,000 different patterns are known. Carnival glass is currently being reproduced. Additional pieces may be found in the Northwood category.

Acanthus, Bowl, Aqua 45.00
Acanthus, Chop Plate, Marigold 245.00
Acanthus, Chop Plate, Smoke ....350.00 to 400.00
Acorn, Bowl, Ruffled Edge, Amber, 7 In. ....35.00 to 65.00
Acorn, Bowl, Ruffled Edge, Amberina, 7 In. 225.00
Acorn, Bowl, Ruffled Edge, Amethyst, 7 In. ....50.00 to 75.00
Acorn, Bowl, Ruffled Edge, Aqua, 7 In. ....55.00 to 115.00
Acorn, Bowl, Ruffled Edge, Blue, 7 In. ....60.00 to 70.00
Acorn, Bowl, Ruffled Edge, Ice Blue, 7 In. 135.00
Acorn, Bowl, Ruffled Edge, Lime Green, 7 In. 55.00
Acorn, Bowl, Ruffled Edge, Marigold On Moonstone, 7 In. 350.00
Acorn, Bowl, Ruffled Edge, Marigold, 7 In. ....25.00 to 30.00
Acorn, Bowl, Ruffled Edge, Peach Opalescent, 7 In. 155.00
Acorn, Bowl, Ruffled Edge, Red, 7 In. ....250.00 to 450.00
Acorn Burrs, Berry Bowl, Marigold, 5 In. 15.00
Acorn Burrs, Berry Set, Amethyst, 6 Piece 375.00
Acorn Burrs, Punch Set, Green, 8 Piece 850.00
Acorn Burrs, Spooner, Green 185.00
Acorn Burrs, Tumbler, Amethyst 25.00
Acorn Burrs, Tumbler, Green 60.00
Acorn Burrs, Water Set, Amethyst, 5 Piece 1750.00
Acorn Burrs, Water Set, Marigold, 6 Piece 2000.00

Acorn Burrs & Bark pattern is listed here as Acorn Burrs.
Amaryllis pattern is listed here as Tiger Lily.
American Beauty Roses pattern is listed here as Wreath of Roses.
Apple Blossom Twigs, Plate, Amethyst, 9 In. 175.00
Apple Tree, Pitcher, Water, Marigold 225.00
Apple Tree, Tumbler, Marigold 25.00
April Showers, Vase, Amethyst, 10 In. 35.00
April Showers, Vase, Blue, 9 1/2 In. 20.00
April Showers, Vase, Blue, Squat, 7 In. 60.00
April Showers, Vase, Green, 10 In. 45.00
April Showers, Vase, Lime Green, Marigold Iridescence, 13 In. 95.00
April Showers, Vase, Marigold, 11 In. 25.00
April Showers, Vase, White, 11 1/2 In. 115.00
Argonaut Shell pattern is listed here as Nautilus.
Asters, Cake Plate, Footed, Stem, Marigold, 6 In. 65.00
Australian Emu, Sauce, Ruffled Edge, Marigold . . . . .175.00 to 200.00
Australian Gum Tips, Vase, Amethyst, 8 In. 215.00
Australian Kangaroo, Bowl, Marigold, 9 3/4 In. 200.00
Australian Kangaroo, Bowl, Ruffled Edge, Amethyst, 5 In. .85.00 to 190.00
Australian Kangaroo, Bowl, Ruffled Edge, Marigold, 5 In. .65.00 to 105.00
Australian Kingfisher, Sauce, Ruffled Edge, Marigold 80.00
Australian Kookaburra, Bowl, Marigold, 9 1/2 In. 250.00
Australian Magpie, Bowl, Ruffled Edge, Marigold, 9 In. 175.00
Australian Magpie, Sauce, Ruffled Edge, Marigold, 5 In. 80.00
Australian Plain, Compote, Ruffled Edge, Amethyst 50.00
Australian Shrike, Sauce, Ruffled Edge, Marigold, 5 In. 70.00
Autumn Acorn, Bowl, Marigold, 3-In-1 Edge, 8 1/2 In. 25.00
Autumn Acorn, Plate, Green, 9 In. 700.00
Banded Medallion & Teardrop pattern is listed here as Beaded Bull's-Eye.
Basket, Amethyst 100.00
Basket, Aqua 325.00
Basket, Aqua Opalescent 200.00
Basket, Aqua, Open Edge, 2 Sides Up 45.00
Basket, Blue . . . . .65.00 to 110.00
Basket, Ice Green 75.00
Basket, Ice Green, Open Edge, 2 Sides Up 250.00
Basket, Lime Green, Marigold Overlay, Open Edge, 2 Sides Up 75.00
Basket, Marigold . . . . .45.00 to 95.00
Basket, Open, Ruffled Edge, Red 160.00
Basketweave, Basket, Square, Open Edge, Celestial Blue 185.00
Basketweave, Vase, Marigold, 11 In. 45.00
Basketweave, Vase, White, 11 In. 110.00
Battenburg Lace No. 1 pattern is listed here as Hearts & Flowers.
Battenburg Lace No. 2 pattern is listed here as Captive Rose.
Battenburg Lace No. 3 pattern is listed here as Fanciful.
Beaded Bull's-Eye, Vase, Amber, 11 In. 65.00
Beaded Bull's-Eye, Vase, Amethyst, 8 In. 145.00
Beaded Bull's-Eye, Vase, Amethyst, 10 1/2 In. 185.00
Beaded Bull's-Eye, Vase, Amethyst, Squat, 6 In. 215.00
Beaded Bull's-Eye, Vase, Emerald Green, 10 1/2 In. 2100.00
Beaded Bull's-Eye, Vase, Marigold, 9 In. 45.00
Beaded Bull's-Eye, Vase, Marigold, 11 In. 55.00
Beaded Bull's-Eye, Vase, Marigold, Squat, 7 In. . . . . .70.00 to 115.00
Beaded Cable, Candy Dish, 3-Footed, Light Green, 7 1/2 In. 40.00
Beaded Cable, Rose Bowl, 3-Footed, Aqua Opalescent . . . . .200.00 to 450.00
Beaded Cable, Rose Bowl, 3-Footed, Marigold 20.00
Beaded Cable, Rose Bowl, 3-Footed, Ribbed Interior, Amethyst 60.00
Beaded Medallion & Teardrop pattern is listed here as Beaded Bull's-Eye.
Beaded Shell, Mug, Amethyst . . . . .35.00 to 55.00
Beaded Shell, Mug, Blue 95.00
Beaded Shell, Mug, Marigold 75.00
Beaded Star, Rose Bowl, Marigold 25.00
Beaded Star & Snail pattern is listed here as Constellation.

Birds & Cherries, Bonbon, Marigold 40.00
Birds & Cherries, Compote, Ruffled Edge, Amethyst 85.00
Birds On Bough pattern is listed here as Birds & Cherries.
Birmingham Age Herald, Plate, Amethyst, 9 In. 3300.00
Bishop's Miter, Vase, Blue, 8 In. 450.00
Blackberry, Basket, Ruffled, Open Edge, 2 Sides Up, Amethyst ....30.00 to 40.00
Blackberry, Basket, Ruffled, Open Edge, 2 Sides Up, Aqua 95.00
Blackberry, Basket, Ruffled, Open Edge, 2 Sides Up, Lime Green 85.00
Blackberry, Bowl, Ruffled, Open Edge, Amberina 60.00
Blackberry, Bowl, Ruffled, Open Edge, Red 135.00
Blackberry, Hat, Ruffled, Open Edge, Amethyst ....20.00 to 30.00
Blackberry, Hat, Ruffled, Open Edge, Green 40.00
Blackberry, Hat, Ruffled, Open Edge, Marigold 15.00
Blackberry A pattern is listed here as Blackberry.
Blackberry B pattern is listed here as Blackberry Spray.
Blackberry Spray, Basket, Lime Green, Marigold Iridescence 50.00
Blackberry Spray, Hat, 2 Sides Up, Blue 20.00
Blackberry Spray, Hat, Square, Marigold 12.00
Blackberry Spray, Hat, Square, Red ....105.00 to 245.00
Blackberry Wreath, Bowl, Amethyst, Satin, 8 In. 85.00
Blackberry Wreath, Bowl, Ruffled Edge, Green, 7 In. 60.00
Blossomtime, Compote, Ruffled Edge, Amethyst 175.00
Blossomtime, Compote, Ruffled Edge, Marigold 215.00
Blueberry, Pitcher, Water, Blue 1000.00
Boggy Bayou, Vase, Amethyst, 10 1/2 In. 40.00
Boggy Bayou, Vase, Green, 10 1/2 In. 50.00
Bouquet, Pitcher, Water, Blue 400.00
Broken Arches, Punch Set, Amethyst, 8 Piece 1100.00
Brooklyn Bridge, Bowl, Ruffled Edge, Marigold 200.00
Bull's-Eye & Beads, Vase, Blue, 13 In. 145.00
Bull's-Eye & Beads, Vase, Marigold, 13 In. 25.00
Bull's-Eye & Loop, Vase, Amethyst, 11 In. 275.00
Bulldog, Paperweight, Marigold 325.00
Bushel Basket pattern is listed here as Basket.
Butterflies, Bonbon, Green 75.00
Butterfly, Bonbon, Green 30.00
Butterfly, Bonbon, Green, Threaded Exterior 375.00
Butterfly, Bonbon, Marigold 65.00
Butterfly & Berry, Berry Set, Marigold, 7 Piece 75.00
Butterfly & Berry, Spooner, 3-Footed, Marigold 25.00
Butterfly & Berry, Sugar, Cover, Marigold 45.00
Butterfly & Berry, Tumbler, Vaseline 65.00
Butterfly & Berry, Vase, Blue, 10 In. 30.00
Butterfly & Berry, Vase, Marigold, 10 In. 10.00
Butterfly & Berry, Vase, Red, 8 In. 850.00
Butterfly & Berry, Water Set, Marigold, 5 Piece 105.00
Butterfly & Cable pattern is listed here as Springtime.
Butterfly & Fern, Pitcher, Water, Marigold 205.00
Butterfly & Fern, Water Set, Amethyst, 7 Piece 450.00
Butterfly & Grape pattern is listed here as Butterfly & Berry.
Butterfly & Plume pattern is listed here as Butterfly & Fern.
Butterfly & Stippled Rays pattern is listed here as Butterfly.
Butterfly & Tulip, Bowl, Footed, Square, Amethyst ....1500.00 to 2200.00
Buzz Saw, Cruet, Stopper, Green, 4 In. 250.00
Cactus Leaf Rays pattern is listed here as Leaf Rays.
Captive Rose, Bonbon, Ruffled Edge, Green 160.00
Captive Rose, Bowl, Ruffled Edge, Amethyst 30.00
Captive Rose, Bowl, Ruffled Edge, Blue ....35.00 to 50.00
Captive Rose, Bowl, Ruffled Edge, Green 75.00
Captive Rose, Plate, Amethyst, 9 In. 900.00
Captive Rose, Plate, Blue, 9 In. ....200.00 to 300.00
Captive Rose, Plate, Green, 9 In. 600.00
Captive Rose, Plate, Marigold, 9 In. ....275.00 to 500.00

Carmelia Loop, Vase, Pastel Marigold, 6 In. 115.00
Carolina Dogwood, Bowl, Peach Opalescent . . . . .45.00 to 55.00
Carolina Dogwood, Bowl, Ruffled Edge, Marigold On Milk Glass . . . . .85.00 to 125.00
Cattails & Fish pattern is listed here as Fisherman's Mug.
Cherries & Holly Wreath pattern is listed here as Cherry Circles.
Cherry, Bowl, Amethyst 225.00
Cherry, Plate, Ruffled Edge, Amethyst, 6 1/2 In. 90.00
Cherry, Plate, Ruffled Edge, Peach Opalescent, 6 In. 90.00
Cherry Chain, Chop Plate, Light Marigold 800.00
Cherry Chain, Plate, Marigold, 6 In. . . . . .40.00 to 45.00
Cherry Circles, Bonbon, Marigold 30.00
Christmas, Compote, Amethyst . . . . Illus 3200.00
Christmas, Compote, Marigold 4500.00
Christmas Cactus pattern is listed here as Thistle.
Christmas Plate pattern is listed here as Poinsettia.
Chrysanthemum, Bowl, Footed, Marigold 60.00
Chrysanthemum, Bowl, Ruffled Edge, Footed, Blue . . . . .95.00 to 125.00
Chrysanthemum, Bowl, Ruffled Edge, Red 3400.00
Chrysanthemum, Chop Plate, Amethyst 1650.00
Chrysanthemum, Chop Plate, Smoke 600.00
Chrysanthemum Sprig, Toothpick, 2 3/4 In. 115.00
Chrysanthemum Wreath pattern is listed here as Ten Mums.
Circle Scroll, Vase, Amethyst, 7 In. 215.00
Coin Dot, Bowl, Amethyst . . . . .15.00 to 35.00
Coin Dot, Bowl, Green 10.00
Coin Dot, Bowl, Ruffled Edge, Red 1000.00
Coin Dot, Rose Bowl, Amethyst 35.00
Coin Spot, Compote, Peach Opalescent, 5 In. . . . . .25.00 to 35.00
Coin Spot, Compote, Ruffled Edge, Celeste Blue, 5 In. 500.00
Colonial, Mug, Marigold, Child's 30.00
Colonial, Sugar, Red 85.00
Colonial Lady, Vase, Amethyst, 6 In. 800.00
Columbia, Compote, Ruffled Edge, Amethyst 375.00
Columbia, Compote, Ruffled Edge, Marigold 40.00
Columbia, Plate, Marigold, 8 1/2 In. 145.00
Concave Diamonds, Water Set, Celeste Blue, 7 Piece 250.00
Concord, Bowl, Marigold 105.00
Concord, Bowl, Ruffled Edge, Green 250.00
Concord, Plate, Amethyst, 9 In. . . . . .950.00 to 1700.00
Concord, Plate, Marigold, 9 In. 1000.00
Constellation, Compote, Amethyst 375.00
Constellation, Compote, Marigold 125.00
Constitution pattern is listed here as God & Home.
Corinth, Vase, Aqua, 9 In. . . . . .25.00 to 45.00
Corn, Bottle, Marigold . . . . .275.00 to 475.00
Corn, Bottle, Smoke 475.00
Corn, Vase, Plain Base, Green . . . . Illus 600.00
Corn, Vase, Plain Base, Marigold 400.00

Carnival Glass, Christmas, Compote, Amethyst

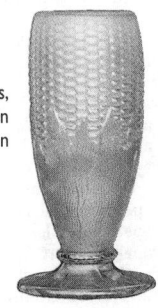

Carnival Glass,
Corn, Vase, Plain
Base, Green

Cosmos & Cane, Compote, Tall Stem, White 1000.00
Cosmos & Cane, Punch Bowl, Ruffled Edge, White 325.00
Cosmos & Cane, Rose Bowl, Honey Amber, Headdress Interior 325.00
Cosmos & Cane, Water Set, Honey Amber, Tankard, 7 Piece 1600.00
Cosmos Variant, Bowl, Ruffled Edge, Blue 40.00
Crab Claw Variant, Water Set, Marigold, 7 Piece 175.00
Curved Star, Vase, Brockwitz, Blue, 7 In. 325.00
Curved Star, Vase, Brockwitz, Marigold, 7 In. 175.00
Dahlia, Pitcher, Water, Marigold 140.00
Daisy & Drape, Vase, Flared, Aqua Opalescent, Butterscotch Iridescence 250.00
Daisy & Drape, Vase, Flared, Blue 850.00
Daisy & Plume, Candy Dish, Blackberry Interior, Footed, Ice Blue 150.00
Daisy & Plume, Rose Bowl, 3-Footed, Marigold 25.00
Daisy Band & Drape pattern is listed here as Daisy & Drape.
Dandelion, Mug, Aqua Opalescent, Butterscotch Iridescence .... .325.00 to 350.00
Dandelion, Tankard, Lavender 500.00
Dandelion, Tumbler, Marigold 35.00
Dandelion, Water Set, Paneled Interior, Amethyst, 5 Piece 275.00
Dandelion, Water Set, Tankard, Amethyst, 5 Piece 1000.00
Dandelion Variant pattern is listed here as Paneled Dandelion.
Diamond & Bows, Vase, Green, Paneled, 7 1/2 In. 95.00
Diamond & Cable pattern is listed here as Fentonia.
Diamond & Column, Amethyst, 10 1/2 In. 20.00
Diamond & Column, Vase, Green, 12 In. 30.00
Diamond & Rib, Vase, Amethyst, 8 In. 10.00
Diamond & Rib, Vase, Green, 11 In. 30.00
Diamond & Sunburst, Wine Set, Amethyst, 7 Piece 500.00
Diamond Band pattern is listed here as Diamonds.
Diamond Lace, Water Set, Amethyst, 7 Piece .... .400.00 to 525.00
Diamond Point, Vase, Amethyst, 9 1/2 In. 80.00
Diamond Point, Vase, Aqua Opalescent, 11 In. 1000.00
Diamond Point, Vase, Marigold, 10 In. 15.00
Diamond Point, Vase, Squat, Amethyst, 5 1/2 In. 30.00
Diamond Point, Vase, Squat, Ice Green, 8 In. 350.00
Diamond Point & Daisy pattern is listed here as Cosmos & Cane.
Diamond Point Columns, Vase, Blue, 15 In. 130.00
Diamonds, Pitcher, Water, Amethyst 110.00
Dogwood & Marsh Lily pattern is listed here as Two Flowers.
Diamonds, Tumbler, Amethyst 170.00
Dogwood Spray, Bowl, Ruffled Edge, Footed, Amethyst 35.00
Dogwood Spray, Bowl, Ruffled Edge, Footed, Marigold 20.00
Dogwood Spray, Bowl, Ruffled Edge, Footed, Peach Opalescent 10.00
Double Dutch, Bowl, Marigold, Footed 20.00
Double Star, Water Set, Green, 7 Piece 265.00
Double Tulip, Vase, Marigold, 10 In. 135.00
Double-Stem Rose, Bowl, Dome Foot, Blue 15.00
Double-Stem Rose, Bowl, Ice Cream, Dome Foot, Peach Opalescent 75.00
Dragon & Lotus, Bowl, Blue, 9 In. .... .50.00 to 75.00
Dragon & Lotus, Bowl, Ice Cream, Amber Opal, 9 In. 800.00
Dragon & Lotus, Bowl, Ice Cream, Amethyst, 9 In. 110.00
Dragon & Lotus, Bowl, Ice Cream, Red, 9 In. .... *Illus* 800.00
Dragon & Lotus, Bowl, Peach Opalescent, 9 In. 200.00
Dragon & Lotus, Bowl, Ruffled Edge, Amber, 9 In. 115.00
Dragon & Lotus, Bowl, Ruffled Edge, Footed, Green 40.00
Dragon & Lotus, Bowl, Ruffled Edge, Footed, Marigold, 9 In. .... .25.00 to 45.00
Dragon & Lotus, Bowl, Ruffled Edge, Vaseline Opalescent, Marigold Iridescence, 9 In. 270.00
Drapery, Candy Dish, White 55.00
Drapery, Rose Bowl, Aqua Opalescent, 5 1/2 In. .... .150.00 to 175.00
Drapery, Vase, Ice Blue, 7 In. 350.00
Drapery, Vase, Ice Green, 8 1/2 In. .... .65.00 to 75.00
Drapery Variant, Vase, Blue, 9 In. 140.00
Egyptian Band pattern is listed here as Round-Up.
Embroidered Mums, Bonbon, Footed, Handle, White 1050.00

Carnival Glass, Dragon & Lotus, Bowl, Ice
Cream, Red, 9 In.

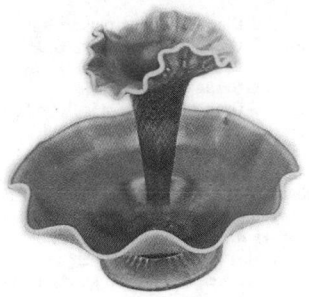

Carnival Glass, Fishnet, Epergne, Peach
Opalescent

Embroidered Mums, Bowl, Cobalt Blue, 8 3/4 In. 475.00
Embroidered Mums, Bowl, Ruffled Edge, Ribbed Back, Aqua Opalescent ..... .2100.00 to 4500.00
Embroidered Mums, Bowl, Ruffled Edge, Ribbed Back, Blue .... .350.00 to 800.00
Embroidered Mums, Bowl, Ruffled Edge, Ribbed Back, Ice Green .... .550.00 to 900.00
Embroidered Mums, Bowl, Ruffled Edge, Ribbed Back, Lavender 1100.00
Embroidered Mums, Bowl, Ruffled Edge, Ribbed Back, Pastel Marigold 575.00
Enameled Lotus, Water Set, Marigold, 6 Piece 175.00
Fan, Gravy Boat, Peach Opalescent 45.00
Fan & Arch pattern is listed here as Persian Garden.
Fanciful, Bowl, Marigold Opalescent, 8 3/4 In. 110.00
Fanciful, Plate, Amethyst, 9 In. .... .750.00 to 850.00
Fanciful, Plate, Blue, 9 In. 275.00
Fantail, Berry Bowl, Footed, Marigold 55.00
Fantail, Bowl, Ruffled Edge, Footed, Blue 175.00
Fantasy pattern is listed here as Question Marks.
Farmyard, Bowl, Ruffled Edge, Square, Amethyst, Silver & Gold Iridescence 600.00
Fashion, Punch Set, Marigold, Ruffled Edge, 10 Piece 145.00
Fashion, Sugar & Creamer, Smoke 85.00
Feather & Heart, Tumbler, Marigold 80.00
Feather & Heart, Water Set, Marigold, 5 Piece 520.00
Feather & Hobstar pattern is listed here as Inverted Feather.
Feathered Scroll pattern is listed here as Feathered Serpent.
Feathered Serpent, Bowl, Ruffled Edge, Blue, 10 In. 145.00
Feathered Serpent, Bowl, Ruffled Edge, Green, 10 In. 95.00
Fenton's Butterfly pattern is listed here as Butterfly.
Fentonia, Spooner, Marigold 75.00
Fentonia, Tumbler, Blue 75.00
Fern Brand Chocolates, Plate, Handgrip, Amethyst 800.00
Field Flower, Tumbler, Marigold 30.00
Field Flower, Water Set, Amethyst, 7 Piece 110.00
File & Fan, Compote, Peach Opalescent 10.00
Fine Cut & Roses, Candy Dish, Green 40.00
Fine Cut & Roses, Candy Dish, Marigold 30.00
Fine Cut & Roses, Rose Bowl, Amethyst 75.00
Fine Cut & Roses, Rose Bowl, Ice Blue 75.00
Fine Rib, Vase, Amberina, 10 In. 225.00
Fine Rib, Vase, Aqua, 10 In. 75.00
Fine Rib, Vase, Marigold, 9 In. 30.00
Fine Rib, Vase, Red, 10 In. .... .275.00 to 325.00
Finecut & Star pattern is listed here as Star & File.
Fish & Flowers pattern is listed here as Trout & Fly.
Fisherman's, Mug, Amethyst .... .35.00 to 65.00
Fishnet, Epergne, Peach Opalescent .... *Illus* 350.00
Fishscales & Beads, Bowl, Crimped Ruffled Edge, Amethyst 135.00
Fishscales & Beads, Plate, Marigold, 7 In. 135.00
Fleur-De-Lis, Bowl, Marigold, Inwald, 8 In. 110.00

Floral & Diamond Point pattern is listed here as Fine Cut & Roses.
Floral & Grape, Pitcher, Water, Blue ....175.00 to 450.00
Floral & Grape, Pitcher, Water, Marigold 85.00
Floral & Grape, Water Set, White, Frosted, 6 Piece 500.00
Floral & Grapevine pattern is listed here as Floral & Grape.
Floral & Optic, Bowl, Footed, Red 105.00
Florentine, Candlestick, Marigold, 8 1/2 In., Pair 35.00
Florentine, Candlestick, Red, 10 In., Pair 600.00
Flower Pot pattern is listed here as Butterfly & Tulip.
Flowering Almonds pattern is listed here as Peacock Tail.
Flowers & Frames, Bowl, Dome Foot, Ruffled Edge, Amethyst 210.00
Fluffy Bird pattern is listed here as Peacock.
Fluffy Peacock, Pitcher, Water, Amethyst 525.00
Fluffy Peacock, Tumbler, Green 10.00
Flute, Sherbet, Amethyst 20.00
Flute, Toothpick, Green 50.00
Flute, Vase, Marigold, 10 In. 20.00
Four Flowers, Bowl, Ice Green 125.00
Four Flowers, Chop Plate, Peach Opalescent 200.00
Four Flowers, Plate, Ice Green, 9 In. 425.00
Four Flowers, Plate, Peach Opalescent, 6 In. ....55.00 to 95.00
Four Pillars, Vase, Aqua Opal, 10 In. 165.00
Four Pillars, Vase, Sapphire, 11 In. 550.00
Four Seventy Four, Goblet, Marigold 25.00
Four Seventy Four, Punch Set, Marigold, 8 Piece 70.00
Four Seventy Four, Vase, Marigold, 10 In. 450.00
Four Seventy Four, Water Set, Marigold, 6 Piece 215.00
Freefold, Vase, Amethyst, 11 In. 70.00
French Knots, Hat, Ruffled Edge, Blue 25.00
Frosted Block, Rose Bowl, Clambroth 50.00
Frosted Block, Rose Bowl, White 10.00
Fruits & Flowers, Bonbon, Footed Handle, Amethyst 75.00
Fruits & Flowers, Bonbon, Footed, Handle, Aqua Opalescent ....250.00 to 500.00
Fruits & Flowers, Bonbon, Footed, Handle, Blue ....130.00 to 165.00
Fruits & Flowers, Bonbon, Footed, Handle, Marigold 65.00
Fruits & Flowers, Plate, Handgrip, Green, 8 In. 125.00
Garland, Rose Bowl, Green 110.00
Garland, Rose Bowl, Marigold 35.00
Gevurtz Brothers, Bowl, Amethyst, Ruffled Edge 850.00
God & Home, Water Set, Blue, 7 Piece 2200.00
Golden Harvest, Wine Set, Amethyst, 5 Piece 185.00
Good Luck, Bowl, Blue, Ruffled Edge, Ribbed 250.00
Good Luck, Bowl, Ribbed Back, Stippled, Green 305.00
Good Luck, Bowl, Ribbed Back, Stippled, Marigold 305.00
Good Luck, Bowl, Ruffled Edge, Basketweave Back, Green 225.00
Good Luck, Bowl, Ruffled Edge, Basketweave Back, Horehound ....500.00 to 550.00
Good Luck, Bowl, Ruffled Edge, Basketweave Back, Marigold ....135.00 to 145.00
Good Luck, Bowl, Ruffled Edge, Ribbed Back, Amethyst ....300.00 to 400.00
Good Luck, Bowl, Ruffled Edge, Ribbed Back, Aqua Opalescent ....650.00 to 1200.00
Good Luck, Bowl, Ruffled Edge, Ribbed Back, Lavender 500.00
Good Luck, Bowl, Ruffled Edge, Ribbed Back, Sapphire 1350.00
Good Luck, Plate, Blue, 9 In. 2200.00
Good Luck, Plate, Ribbed Back, Green, 9 In. 900.00
Gothic Arches, Vase, Marigold, Stretched, 18 In. 130.00
Gothic Arches, Vase, Smoke, 10 In. 650.00
Grape & Cable, Banana Boat, Amethyst 175.00
Grape & Cable, Banana Bowl, Ice Green 500.00
Grape & Cable, Berry Bowl, Green 55.00
Grape & Cable, Bonbon, Amethyst 130.00
Grape & Cable, Bonbon, Stippled, Amethyst 75.00
Grape & Cable, Bonbon, Stippled, Blue 185.00
Grape & Cable, Bonbon, Stippled, Green 100.00
Grape & Cable, Bonbon, Stippled, Marigold 45.00

Grape & Cable, Bowl, Aqua, 7 1/2 In. 30.00
Grape & Cable, Bowl, Centerpiece, 3-Footed, Amethyst, 6 3/4 x 11 In. 550.00
Grape & Cable, Bowl, Footed, Ruffled Edge, Lime Green 80.00
Grape & Cable, Bowl, Fruit, 3-Footed, Marigold, 9 1/2 In. ....100.00 to 125.00
Grape & Cable, Bowl, Fruit, Amethyst 145.00
Grape & Cable, Bowl, Fruit, Ice Green 3100.00
Grape & Cable, Bowl, Green, 8 1/2 In. 30.00
Grape & Cable, Bowl, Pie Crust Edge, Marigold 205.00
Grape & Cable, Bowl, Ruffled Edge, Basketweave Back, Amethyst, 7 In. 185.00
Grape & Cable, Bowl, Ruffled Edge, Red, 7 In. 600.00
Grape & Cable, Bowl, Ruffled Edge, Ribbed, Stippled, Sapphire 1000.00
Grape & Cable, Butter, Cover, Amethyst ....90.00 to 135.00
Grape & Cable, Candlestick, Amethyst, 5 1/2 In., Pair 225.00
Grape & Cable, Cologne, Amethyst, 9 In. 150.00
Grape & Cable, Compote, Cover, Amethyst ....175.00 to 275.00
Grape & Cable, Compote, Cover, Marigold 1050.00
Grape & Cable, Cracker Jar, Amethyst ....250.00 to 295.00
Grape & Cable, Cracker Jar, Marigold ....95.00 to 175.00
Grape & Cable, Decanter Set, Marigold, 5 Piece 475.00
Grape & Cable, Decanter, Amethyst 300.00
Grape & Cable, Dish, Sweetmeat, Amethyst, 8 1/2 In. 175.00
Grape & Cable, Dish, Sweetmeat, Cover, Marigold 3800.00
Grape & Cable, Hatpin Holder, Amethyst ....135.00 to 250.00
Grape & Cable, Hatpin Holder, Marigold ....125.00 to 175.00
Grape & Cable, Hatpin Holder, White 3200.00
Grape & Cable, Humidor, Amethyst 250.00
Grape & Cable, Humidor, Marigold 350.00
Grape & Cable, Perfume Bottle, Amethyst 500.00
Grape & Cable, Pin Dish, Green 85.00
Grape & Cable, Pin Tray, Amethyst 150.00
Grape & Cable, Pitcher, Water, Green 325.00
Grape & Cable, Plate, Amethyst, 9 In. ....80.00 to 100.00
Grape & Cable, Plate, Basketweave Back, Marigold, 9 In. 65.00
Grape & Cable, Plate, Footed, Ice Green, 9 In. 350.00
Grape & Cable, Plate, Marigold, 9 In. ....65.00 to 90.00
Grape & Cable, Plate, Stippled, Emerald Green, 9 In. 2500.00
Grape & Cable, Plate, Stippled, Ribbed Back, Sapphire, 9 In. 1700.00
Grape & Cable, Powder Jar, Ice Green 35.00
Grape & Cable, Punch Set, Amethyst, 14 Piece ....1900.00 to 3000.00
Grape & Cable, Punch Set, Green, 12 Piece 4100.00
Grape & Cable, Punch Set, Marigold, Stippled, 8 Piece 900.00
Grape & Cable, Shot Glass, Amethyst 125.00
Grape & Cable, Tray, Dresser, Amethyst, 11 1/4 In. 350.00
Grape & Cable, Tray, Dresser, Marigold, 11 1/4 In. 100.00
Grape & Cable, Tumbler, Amethyst 50.00
Grape & Cable, Tumbler, Green 10.00
Grape & Cable, Water Set, Amethyst, 7 Piece 300.00
Grape & Cable Variant, Plate, Amethyst, 9 In. 195.00
Grape & Cable Variant, Plate, Marigold, 9 In. 145.00
Grape & Gothic Arches, Table Set, Marigold, 4 Piece 195.00
Grape & Gothic Arches, Water Set, Blue, 5 Piece 350.00
Grape Arbor, Pitcher, Water, Ice Green, Tankard 9500.00
Grape Arbor, Pitcher, Water, Marigold, Tankard ....95.00 to 215.00
Grape Arbor, Pitcher, Water, Tankard, Amethyst 275.00
Grape Arbor, Tumbler, White 70.00
Grape Arbor, Water Set, Ice Blue, Tankard, 7 Piece 1850.00
Grape Arbor, Water Set, Marigold, 5 Piece 225.00
Grape Delight pattern is listed here as Vintage.
Grape Delight, Nut Dish, Gold, 4 1/4 In. 30.00
Grape Delight, Rose Bowl, Amethyst 15.00
Grape Delight, Rose Bowl, Blue 30.00
Grape Leaves, Bowl, Amethyst, 9 In. 40.00
Grape Wreath, Bowl, Ruffled Edge, Green, 7 In. 100.00

Grape Wreath Variant, Sauce, Ruffled Edge, Green 155.00
Grapevine Diamonds pattern is listed here as Grapevine Lattice.
Grapevine Lattice, Bowl, Ruffled Edge, White, 6 In. 55.00
Grapevine Lattice, Pitcher, Water, Marigold 60.00
Grapevine Lattice, Plate, Amethyst, 7 1/2 In. 325.00
Grapevine Lattice, Plate, Marigold, 6 In. 25.00
Grapevine Lattice, Tumbler, Marigold ....10.00 to 15.00
Greek Key, Pitcher, Water, Tankard, Amethyst 2000.00
Greek Key, Plate, Basketweave Back, Amethyst, 9 In. 425.00
Greek Key, Plate, Basketweave Back, Green, 9 In. 750.00
Greek Key, Plate, Ribbed Back, Marigold, 9 In. 750.00
Hanging Cherries, Bowl, Ice Cream, Amethyst, 9 3/4 In. 200.00
Hanging Cherries, Pitcher, Water, Marigold 800.00
Harvest Time pattern is listed here as Golden Harvest.
Hattie, Bowl, Marigold, Round 40.00
Hattie, Chop Plate, Amethyst ....1400.00 to 2100.00
Hattie, Chop Plate, Marigold 2500.00
Heart & Vine, Bowl, 3-In-1 Edge, Amethyst 55.00
Heart & Vine, Bowl, 3-In-1 Edge, Blue 50.00
Heart & Vine, Bowl, 3-In-1 Edge, Green 95.00
Heart & Vine, Bowl, 3-In-1 Edge, Marigold 45.00
Heart & Vine, Plate, Amethyst, 9 In. ....250.00 to 450.00
Heart & Vine, Plate, Blue, 9 In. ....325.00 to 425.00
Hearts & Flowers, Bowl, Ice Blue 70.00
Hearts & Flowers, Bowl, Ruffled Edge, Basketweave Back, Amethyst ....750.00 to 800.00
Hearts & Flowers, Bowl, Ruffled Edge, Ribbed Back, Amethyst 650.00
Hearts & Flowers, Bowl, Ruffled Edge, Ribbed Back, Aqua Opal, Iridescent ....1600.00 to 2000.00
Hearts & Flowers, Bowl, Ruffled Edge, Ribbed Back, Green 950.00
Hearts & Flowers, Bowl, Ruffled Edge, Ribbed Back, Ice Blue 800.00
Hearts & Flowers, Bowl, Ruffled Edge, Ribbed Back, Ice Green 85.00
Hearts & Flowers, Bowl, Ruffled Edge, Ribbed Back, Marigold 500.00
Hearts & Flowers, Bowl, Ruffled Edge, Ribbed Back, White ....175.00 to 200.00
Hearts & Flowers, Compote, Marigold, Ruffled Edge 130.00
Hearts & Flowers, Compote, Ruffled Edge, Amethyst 850.00
Hearts & Flowers, Compote, Ruffled Edge, Aqua Opalescent ....425.00 to 900.00
Hearts & Flowers, Compote, Ruffled Edge, Blue ....450.00 to 650.00
Hearts & Flowers, Compote, Ruffled Edge, Green ....1300.00 to 1400.00
Hearts & Flowers, Compote, Ruffled Edge, Ice Blue 600.00
Hearts & Flowers, Compote, Ruffled Edge, Ice Green 475.00
Hearts & Flowers, Compote, Ruffled Edge, Marigold 225.00
Hearts & Flowers, Compote, Ruffled Edge, Marigold On Custard 4500.00
Hearts & Flowers, Compote, Ruffled Edge, Renninger Blue ....750.00 to 900.00
Hearts & Flowers, Compote, Ruffled Edge, White ....85.00 to 115.00
Hearts & Flowers, Plate, Ribbed Back, Amethyst, 9 In. 2800.00
Hearts & Flowers, Plate, Ribbed Back, Green, 9 In. 1450.00
Hearts & Flowers, Plate, Ribbed Back, Lime Green, 9 In. 1900.00
Hearts & Flowers, Plate, Ribbed Back, Marigold, 9 In. 750.00
Hearts & Flowers, Plate, Ribbed Back, White, 9 In. 1200.00
Heavy Grape, Bowl, Marigold, 7 In. 15.00
Heavy Grape, Bowl, Pastel Marigold, 7 In. 30.00
Heavy Grape, Bowl, Ruffled Edge, Amethyst, 7 In. 20.00
Heavy Grape, Chop Plate, Green 350.00
Heavy Grape, Chop Plate, Marigold ....95.00 to 215.00
Heavy Grape, Plate, Amethyst, 8 In. ....35.00 to 65.00
Heavy Grape, Plate, Green, 8 In. 20.00
Heavy Grape, Plate, Marigold, 8 In. 35.00
Heavy Iris, Water Set, Tankard, Marigold, 6 Piece 1850.00
Heron, Mug, Amethyst 145.00
Heron & Rushes pattern is listed here as Stork & Rushes.
Hobnail, Pitcher, Water, Amethyst 1650.00
Hobnail, Rose Bowl, Amethyst, 4 1/2 In. 200.00
Hobnail Swirl, Vase, Marigold, 10 In. 75.00
Hobstar & Torch pattern is listed here as Double Star.

Hobstar Flower, Compote, Ruffled Edge, Emerald Green 700.00
Hobstar Flower, Compote, Ruffled Edge, Marigold 20.00
Holly, Bowl, Ice Cream, Blue 30.00
Holly, Bowl, Ice Cream, Marigold 25.00
Holly, Bowl, Ice Cream, Vaseline, Marigold Iridescence 135.00
Holly, Bowl, Red, 9 In. 1000.00
Holly, Bowl, Ruffled Edge, Amethyst ....55.00 to 60.00
Holly, Bowl, Ruffled Edge, Black Amethyst 115.00
Holly, Bowl, Ruffled Edge, Blue ....45.00 to 90.00
Holly, Bowl, Ruffled Edge, Green 75.00
Holly, Bowl, Ruffled Edge, Marigold On Moonstone 325.00
Holly, Bowl, Ruffled Edge, Marigold, 8 In. ....25.00 to 40.00
Holly, Bowl, Ruffled Edge, Red, Amberina Base 400.00
Holly, Compote, Blue, Flared 20.00
Holly, Compote, Flared, Lime Green, Marigold Iridescence 60.00
Holly, Compote, Flared, Marigold 10.00
Holly, Compote, Ruffled Edge, Blue 50.00
Holly, Compote, Ruffled Edge, Green 55.00
Holly, Compote, Ruffled Edge, Marigold ....10.00 to 25.00
Holly, Compote, Ruffled Edge, Red 650.00
Holly, Plate, Amethyst, 9 In. ....475.00 to 575.00
Holly, Plate, Black Amethyst, 9 In. 725.00
Holly, Plate, Blue, 9 In. ....200.00 to 275.00
Holly, Plate, Marigold, 9 In. ....30.00 to 65.00
Holly, Plate, White, 9 In. ....125.00 to 250.00
Holly & Berry, Bowl, Ruffled Edge, Amethyst, 7 In. 50.00
Holly Spray pattern is listed here as Holly Sprig.
Holly Sprig, Bonbon, Green, Frosted 85.00
Holly Sprig, Bonbon, Marigold, Frosted 35.00
Holly Sprig, Bowl, Amethyst, 9 1/2 In. 75.00
Holly Whirl, Bowl, Ruffled Edge, Amethyst 75.00
Homestead, Chop Plate, Amethyst ....1100.00 to 2500.00
Homestead, Chop Plate, Smokey Lavender 1300.00
Honeycomb Collar pattern is listed here as Fishscales & Beads.
Horse Medallions pattern is listed here as Horses' Heads.
Horses' Heads, Bowl, Amberina, Ruffled 1100.00
Horses' Heads, Bowl, Footed, Lime Green 225.00
Horses' Heads, Bowl, Footed, Marigold 90.00
Horses' Heads, Bowl, Ruffled Edge, Footed, Green 300.00
Illusion, Bonbon, Marigold ....20.00 to 25.00
Imperial Flute, Tumbler, Marigold 15.00
Imperial Flute, Vase, Amethyst, 11 In. 300.00
Imperial Grape, Berry Set, Green, 7 Piece 50.00
Imperial Grape, Bowl, Marigold, Ruffled Edge, 9 In. 30.00
Imperial Grape, Goblet, Clambroth 10.00
Imperial Grape, Pitcher, Water, Aqua 255.00
Imperial Grape, Plate, Blue, 6 In. ....*Illus* 2100.00

Carnival Glass, Imperial Grape, Plate, Blue, 6 In.

To clean carnival glass, use a soft
brush, room-temperature water, a
sponge, and a gentle detergent.
Window cleaner is also OK.

Imperial Grape, Plate, Green, 9 In. 35.00
Imperial Grape, Punch Set, Marigold, 6 Piece 105.00
Imperial Wide Panel, Vase, Marigold, 10 In. 35.00
Inverted Feather, Cracker Jar, Green 185.00
Inverted Strawberry, Compote, Marigold, Marked, Near Cut 325.00
Inverted Strawberry, Pitcher, Water, Tankard, Amethyst, Marked, Near Cut 1350.00
Inverted Thistle, Water Set, Marigold, 5 Piece 5400.00
Iris, Compote, Ruffled Edge, Amethyst 35.00
Irish Lace pattern is listed here as Louisa.
Isaac Benesch & Sons, Bowl, Ruffled Edge, Amethyst 400.00
Jeweled Heart, Pitcher, Water, Marigold 400.00
Jockey Club, Plate, Handgrip, Amethyst 650.00
Kimberly pattern is listed here as Concave Diamonds.
Kittens, Cup & Saucer, Marigold ....130.00 to 155.00
Kittens, Cup, Blue 300.00
Kittens, Dish, Amethyst, 2 Sides Up 235.00
Kittens, Dish, Blue 65.00
Kittens, Dish, Marigold 70.00
Kittens, Plate, Marigold 105.00
Kittens, Toothpick, Blue 245.00
Kittens, Toothpick, Ruffled Edge, Powder Blue 95.00
Kulor, Vase, Blue, 6 In. 600.00
Kulor, Vase, Marigold, 8 In. 550.00
Labelle Elaine pattern is listed here as Primrose.
Labelle Poppy pattern is listed here as Poppy Show.
Labelle Rose pattern is listed here as Rose Show.
Lattice & Grape, Water Set, Tankard, Marigold, 7 Piece 325.00
Lattice & Grapevine pattern is listed here as Lattice & Grape.
Lattice & Poinsettia, Bowl, Ruffled Edge, Ribbed Back, Footed, Blue 550.00
Lattice & Points, Bowl, Ruffled Edge, White 40.00
Leaf & Beads, Rose Bowl, 3-Footed, Amethyst, Sunflower Interior 115.00
Leaf & Beads, Rose Bowl, 3-Footed, Aqua Opalescent ....145.00 to 200.00
Leaf & Beads, Rose Bowl, 3-Footed, Marigold 50.00
Leaf Chain, Bowl, Ruffled Edge, Red, 7 In. 625.00
Leaf Chain, Bowl, Ruffled Edge, White, 7 In. 45.00
Leaf Chain, Plate, Amethyst, 9 In. 2100.00
Leaf Chain, Plate, Clambroth, 9 In. 50.00
Leaf Chain, Plate, Green, 9 In. 350.00
Leaf Chain, Plate, Marigold, 9 In. 500.00
Leaf Chain, Plate, White, 9 In. 150.00
Leaf Columns, Vase, Amethyst, 10 In. ....85.00 to 145.00
Leaf Columns, Vase, Green, 10 1/2 In. 125.00
Leaf Columns, Vase, Sapphire, 10 In. 300.00
Leaf Columns, Vase, Squat, Amethyst, 6 1/2 In. 95.00
Leaf Columns, Vase, Squat, Green, 6 1/2 In. 145.00
Leaf Medallion pattern is listed here as Leaf Chain.
Leaf Pinwheel & Star Flower pattern is listed here as Whirling Leaves.
Leaf Rays, Nappy, Amethyst 50.00
Lined Lattice, Bowl, Ruffled Edge, White, 6 In. 25.00
Lined Lattice, Vase, Amethyst, 8 In. 195.00
Lined Lattice, Vase, Amethyst, 12 In. 45.00
Lined Lattice, Vase, Footed, Marigold, 12 In. 65.00
Lined Lattice, Vase, White, 10 In. 125.00
Lion, Bowl, Ruffled Edge, Marigold, 6 1/2 In. ....80.00 to 105.00
Little Fishes, Berry Bowl, Footed, Blue 325.00
Little Flowers, Bowl, Amethyst, 8 1/2 In. 30.00
Little Flowers, Bowl, Ice Cream, Marigold, 10 In. 20.00
Little Flowers, Sauce, Ruffled Edge, Blue 45.00
Little Stars, Bowl, Ruffled Edge, Amethyst, Frosted, 7 In. 115.00
Loganberry, Vase, Green 2200.00
Loop & Column pattern is listed here as Pulled Loop.
Looped Petals pattern is listed here as Scales.
Lotus & Daisy, Bowl, 3-Footed, Marigold, 9 1/2 In. 40.00

Lotus & Grape, Bonbon, Aqua 185.00
Lotus & Grape, Bonbon, Lime Green, Marigold Iridescence 75.00
Lotus & Grape, Compote, Red 550.00
Louisa, Bowl, Footed, Ruffled Edge, Amethyst 35.00
Louisa, Rose Bowl, Amethyst 45.00
Luster Flute, Sugar & Creamer, Green 25.00
Luster Rose, Bowl, Centerpiece, Amethyst 375.00
Luster Rose, Fernery, Blue, Footed 75.00
Luster Rose, Pitcher, Water, Helios Green 45.00
Luster Rose, Plate, Footed, Amberina, 9 In. 60.00
Luster Rose, Sugar & Creamer, Marigold 30.00
Luster Rose, Tumbler, Marigold 25.00
Luster Rose, Water Set, Blue, 5 Piece 135.00
Magnolia & Poinsettia pattern is listed here as Water Lily.
Magnolia Drape, Water Pitcher, Enameled, Marigold 35.00
Maine Coast pattern is listed here as Seacoast.
Many Stars, Bowl, Marigold 400.00
Maple Leaf, Table Set, Blue, 4 Piece 200.00
Maple Leaf, Tumbler, Amethyst 10.00
Maple Leaf, Water Set, Marigold, 7 Piece 105.00
Marilyn, Water Set, Amethyst, 7 Piece 1050.00
Maryland pattern is listed here as Rustic.
Melinda pattern is listed here as Wishbone.
Melon & Fan pattern is listed here as Diamond & Rib.
Memphis, Punch Set, Ice Blue, 10 Piece 5700.00
Memphis, Punch Set, Marigold, 7 Piece 450.00
Milady, Pitcher, Water, Tankard, Blue 900.00
Miniature Morning Glory, Vase, Green, 7 In. 65.00
Moonprint, Pitcher, Marigold, Brockwitz 650.00
Morning Glory, Vase, Clambroth, 7 1/2 In. 30.00
Morning Glory, Vase, Funeral, Amethyst, 13 In. ....525.00 to 750.00
Morning Glory, Vase, Funeral, Marigold, 17 In. 250.00
Mums & Greek Key pattern is listed here as Embroidered Mums.
Nautilus, Gravy Boat, Peach Opalescent, 4 x 7 In. 75.00
Nesting Swan, Bowl, Amethyst, 10 In. 200.00
Nesting Swan, Bowl, Green, 10 In. 225.00
Nesting Swan, Bowl, Ruffled Edge, Marigold, 10 In. 125.00
Nine Sixteen, Vase, Blue, 14 In. 50.00
Nine Sixteen, Vase, Marigold, 16 In. 20.00
Nippon, Bowl, Basketweave, Pie Crust Edge, White 250.00
Nippon, Bowl, Ribbed Back, Pie Crust Edge, Amethyst 350.00
Oak Leaf & Acorn pattern is listed here as Acorn.
Octagon, Compote, Amethyst 650.00
Octagon, Cordial, Marigold 75.00
Octagon, Pitcher, Water, Amethyst 500.00
Octagon, Pitcher, Water, Amethyst, Small 1600.00
Octagon, Tumbler, Green 30.00
Octagon, Vase, Marigold, 8 In. 15.00
Octagon, Water Set, Marigold, 7 Piece 170.00
Octagon, Wine Set, Marigold, 6 Piece 85.00
Old Fashion Flag pattern is listed here as Iris.
Open Rose, Bowl, Ruffled Edge, Amethyst, 8 In. 250.00
Open Rose, Bowl, Ruffled Edge, Marigold 35.00
Open Rose, Bowl, Ruffled Edge, Smoke, 5 In. 30.00
Open Rose, Plate, Amber, 9 In. 135.00
Open Rose, Plate, Marigold, 9 In. 85.00
Open Rose, Sauce, Ruffled Edge, Amethyst 60.00
Open Rose, Sauce, Ruffled Edge, Smoke 25.00
Orange Tree, Bowl, Fruit, Footed, Blue 145.00
Orange Tree, Bowl, Fruit, Footed, Marigold 145.00
Orange Tree, Bowl, Ice Cream, Blue 115.00
Orange Tree, Compote, Ruffled Edge, Aqua 185.00
Orange Tree, Hatpin Holder, Blue 175.00

Orange Tree, Hatpin Holder, Marigold 115.00
Orange Tree, Hatpin Holder, White 3100.00
Orange Tree, Loving Cup, Marigold 220.00
Orange Tree, Mug, Blue ....10.00 to 25.00
Orange Tree, Mug, Marigold 10.00
Orange Tree, Mug, Red 150.00
Orange Tree, Plate, Blue, 9 In. 675.00
Orange Tree, Plate, Marigold, 9 In. 135.00
Orange Tree, Plate, White, 9 In. ....120.00 to 170.00
Orange Tree, Punch Set, Marigold, 14 Piece 180.00
Orange Tree, Shaving Mug, Red Slag 300.00
Orange Tree & Scroll, Water Set, Blue, Tankard, 5 Piece 900.00
Oriental Poppy, Pitcher, Tankard, Amethyst 450.00
Oriental Poppy, Pitcher, Tankard, Marigold ....325.00 to 375.00
Oriental Poppy, Tumbler, Marigold 35.00
Oriental Poppy, Water Set, Tankard, Amethyst, 5 Piece 1300.00
Owl, Hatpin Holder, Amethyst 1100.00
Palm Beach, Banana Boat, Amethyst 50.00
Palm Beach, Berry Set, Honey Amber, 6 Piece 275.00
Palm Beach, Butter, Cover, Honey Amber 200.00
Palm Beach, Butter, Cover, White 85.00
Palm Beach, Rose Bowl, White 195.00
Paneled Bachelor Buttons pattern is listed here as Milady.
Paneled Dandelion, Pitcher, Water, Tankard, Amethyst 45.00
Paneled Dandelion, Pitcher, Water, Tankard, Blue 60.00
Paneled Dandelion, Pitcher, Water, Tankard, Green 400.00
Paneled Dandelion, Pitcher, Water, Tankard, Marigold 80.00
Paneled Dandelion, Tumbler, Amethyst 20.00
Paneled Dandelion, Tumbler, Blue ....35.00 to 65.00
Paneled Dandelion, Tumbler, Green ....20.00 to 60.00
Paneled Dandelion, Tumbler, Marigold ....25.00 to 45.00
Pansy, Bowl, Ruffled Edge, Amethyst 65.00
Pansy, Dish, Pickle, Amethyst 75.00
Pansy, Dish, Pickle, Smoke 65.00
Pansy, Nappy, Handle, Amethyst 135.00
Pansy, Nappy, Handle, Marigold 5.00
Pansy, Sugar & Creamer, Honey Amber 30.00
Pansy, Sugar & Creamer, Marigold 10.00
Pansy, Tray, Dresser, Amethyst 575.00
Panther, Bowl, Centerpiece, Ice Cream, Marigold 600.00
Panther, Bowl, Ruffled Edge, Marigold 50.00
Panther, Sauce, Ruffled Edge, Footed, Red 500.00
Panther, Sauce, Ruffled Edge, Marigold 20.00
Parlor Panels, Vase, Clambroth, Squat, 4 In. 375.00
Parlor Panels, Vase, Marigold, 12 In. 95.00
Pastel Swan, Salt, Celeste Blue ....15.00 to 20.00
Pastel Swan, Salt, Peach Opalescent 400.00
Peach, Pitcher, Water, White 500.00
Peach, Tumbler, Electric Blue 70.00
Peach, Tumbler, White, Gold Trim 65.00
Peach, Water Set, Blue, 7 Piece ....1000.00 to 1950.00
Peach, Water Set, White, 5 Piece 850.00
Peacock, Bowl, Ribbed Back, Amethyst 225.00
Peacock, Bowl, Ribbed Back, Lavender 425.00
Peacock, Bowl, Ribbed Back, Marigold 200.00
Peacock, Bowl, Ruffled Edge, Ribbed Back, Green 1000.00
Peacock, Bowl, Ruffled Edge, Ribbed Back, Ice Blue 1300.00
Peacock, Bowl, Ruffled Edge, Ribbed Back, White ....225.00 to 525.00
Peacock & Dahlia, Bowl, Ruffled Edge, Blue, 7 In. 35.00
Peacock & Grape, Bowl, Ruffled Edge, Blue 95.00
Peacock & Grape, Bowl, Ruffled Edge, Marigold ....30.00 to 40.00
Peacock & Grape, Plate, Footed, Green, 9 In. 400.00
Peacock & Grape, Plate, Marigold, 9 In. 250.00

Peacock & Urn, Bowl, Ice Cream, Amethyst 375.00
Peacock & Urn, Bowl, Ice Cream, Ice Green 900.00
Peacock & Urn, Chop Plate, Amethyst 550.00
Peacock & Urn, Compote, Marigold, 5 1/4 In. 25.00
Peacock & Urn, Plate, Blue, 9 In. 1250.00
Peacock & Urn, Plate, Marigold, 9 In. 200.00
Peacock & Urn, Plate, White, 9 In. ....225.00 to 320.00
Peacock & Urn, Sauce, Ice Cream, Aqua Opalescent 1600.00
Peacock & Urn, Sauce, Ice Cream, Blue 85.00
Peacock At The Fountain, Berry Bowl, Ice Green, Master 1150.00
Peacock At The Fountain, Compote, Amethyst 700.00
Peacock At The Fountain, Compote, Ice Blue 600.00
Peacock At The Fountain, Compote, Ruffled Edge, Ice Blue 500.00
Peacock At The Fountain, Compote, White 275.00
Peacock At The Fountain, Creamer, Amethyst 155.00
Peacock At The Fountain, Punch Bowl, Base, Ice Green 6000.00
Peacock At The Fountain, Punch Cup, Ice Blue 60.00
Peacock At The Fountain, Tumbler, Blue 45.00
Peacock At The Fountain, Water Set, Amethyst, 7 Piece 650.00
Peacock Eye & Grape pattern is listed here as Vineyard.
Peacock Garden, Vase, Marigold, 8 In. 400.00
Peacock On Fence pattern is listed here as Peacocks.
Peacock Tail, Bowl, Ruffled Edge, Amethyst, 7 In. 30.00
Peacock Tail, Bowl, Ruffled Edge, Blue, 7 In. 170.00
Peacock Tail, Bowl, Ruffled Edge, Green, 7 In. 35.00
Peacock Tail, Sauce, Ruffled Edge, Green 10.00
Peacocks, Bowl, Pie Crust Edge, Marigold 75.00
Peacocks, Bowl, Pie Crust Edge, Ribbed Back, Blue 600.00
Peacocks, Bowl, Pie Crust Edge, Ribbed Back, Lime Green 1300.00
Peacocks, Bowl, Ribbed Back, Ruffled Edge, Amethyst 450.00
Peacocks, Bowl, Ribbed Back, Ruffled Edge, Aqua 875.00
Peacocks, Bowl, Ruffled Edge, Amethyst 115.00
Peacocks, Plate, Ice Green, 9 In. 225.00
Peacocks, Plate, Ribbed Back, Blue, 9 In. 2000.00
Peacocks, Plate, Ribbed Back, Blue, Electric Highlights, 9 In. 500.00
Peacocks, Plate, Ribbed Back, Horehound, 9 In. 325.00
Peacocks, Plate, Ribbed Back, Ice Blue, 9 In. 950.00
Peacocks, Plate, Ribbed Back, Ice Green, 9 In. 325.00
Peacocks, Plate, Ribbed Back, Lime Green, 9 In. ....400.00 to 500.00
Peacocks, Plate, Ribbed Back, Marigold, 9 In. ....175.00 to 300.00
Peacocks, Plate, Ribbed Back, White, 9 In. 325.00
Peacocks, Plate, Stippled, Electric Blue, 9 In. 2000.00
Peacocks, Sauce, Ruffled Edge, Marigold 65.00
Pebbles, Plate, Marigold On Moonstone, 9 In. 155.00
Persian Garden, Bowl, Ruffled Edge, Peach Opalescent, 11 In. 225.00
Persian Garden, Chop Plate, Amethyst ....*Illus* 1200.00
Persian Garden, Chop Plate, White 3000.00
Persian Garden, Plate, Amethyst, 6 In. 65.00
Persian Garden, Plate, Marigold, 6 In. ....25.00 to 35.00
Persian Medallion, Bonbon, Red ....205.00 to 500.00
Persian Medallion, Bowl, Amethyst, Ruffled Edge, 10 In. ....130.00 to 200.00
Persian Medallion, Bowl, Ice Cream, Blue, 6 In. 45.00
Persian Medallion, Compote, Crimped Ruffled Edge, Blue 125.00
Persian Medallion, Plate, Blue, 6 In. ....40.00 to 65.00
Persian Medallion, Plate, Blue, 9 In. 400.00
Persian Medallion, Plate, Marigold, 6 In. ....60.00 to 75.00
Persian Medallion, Rose Bowl, Square Mouth, Marigold, 4 In. 30.00
Petal & Fan, Bowl, Ruffled Edge, Peach Opalescent 105.00
Petal & Fan, Bowl, Ruffled Edge, White 240.00
Petal & Fan, Plate, Crimped Edge, Amethyst, 6 In. 200.00
Petal & Fan, Sauce, Ruffled Edge, Amethyst 85.00
Peter Rabbit, Bowl, Ice Cream, Blue 1300.00
Peter Rabbit, Plate, Marigold, 9 In. 5750.00

Pine Cone, Plate, Blue, 6 In. 30.00
Pine Cone, Plate, Marigold, 6 In. 175.00
Pine Cone, Sauce, Ruffled Edge, Amethyst 10.00
Pine Cone, Sauce, Ruffled Edge, Blue 15.00
Pine Cone Wreath pattern is listed here as Pine Cone.
Pineapple, Sugar & Creamer, Marigold 35.00
Pineapple Crown, Dish, Oblong, Marigold 15.00
Pinecone, Bowl, Ice Cream, Blue, 7 In. 35.00
Pinecone, Plate, Blue, 6 In. 115.00
Plaid, Bowl, Ruffled Edge, Marigold ....75.00 to 105.00
Plaid, Bowl, Ruffled Edge, Red 1000.00
Plume Panels, Vase, Amethyst, 11 In. ....45.00 to 65.00
Plume Panels, Vase, Blue, 12 In. 105.00
Plume Panels, Vase, Red, 10 In. 800.00
Poinsettia, Pitcher, Milk, Marigold ....30.00 to 80.00
Poinsettia, Pitcher, Milk, Smoke 85.00
Pond Lily, Bonbon, Marigold 35.00
Pony, Bowl, Ruffled Edge, Marigold, 10 In. 35.00
Pony Rosette pattern is listed here as Pony.
Poppy, Compote, Green 1400.00
Poppy, Dish, Pickle, Aqua Opalescent ....1500.00 to 1800.00
Poppy, Dish, Pickle, Blue ....150.00 to 225.00
Poppy Scroll pattern is listed here as Poppy.
Poppy Show, Bowl, Ruffled Edge, Blue 400.00
Poppy Show, Bowl, Ruffled Edge, Ice Blue 1000.00
Poppy Show, Bowl, Ruffled Edge, Ice Green ....900.00 to 1500.00
Poppy Show, Bowl, Ruffled Edge, Marigold 325.00
Poppy Show, Plate, Blue, 9 In. 2400.00
Poppy Show, Plate, Ice Blue, 9 In. ....1050.00 to 1200.00
Poppy Show, Plate, Marigold, 9 In. 850.00
Poppy Show, Vase, Emerald Green 45.00
Poppy Show, Vase, Green, White Cased Interior, Fenton 150.00
Primrose, Bowl, Ruffled Edge, Amethyst 45.00
Primrose, Bowl, Ruffled Edge, Marigold 50.00
Princess Lace pattern is listed here as Octagon.
Pulled Loop, Vase, Amethyst, 10 In. 35.00
Pulled Loop, Vase, Blue, 11 In. 55.00
Pulled Loop, Vase, Squat, White, 5 In. 105.00
Question Marks, Bonbon, Amethyst ....10.00 to 35.00
Question Marks, Bonbon, Marigold 7.50
Question Marks, Candy Dish, Handles, Pedestal Base, Marigold Opalescent, 4 x 7 In. 30.00
Question Marks, Compote, Peach Opalescent, 3 x 6 1/2 In. 60.00
Quill, Pitcher, Water, Marigold 600.00
Raindrops, Bowl, Dome Foot, Peach Opalescent 70.00
Raindrops, Vase, Squat, Amethyst, 6 In. 35.00

Carnival Glass, Persian Garden,
Chop Plate, Amethyst

Carnival Glass, Rose Show, Plate,
Lime Green, 9 In.

Raindrops, Vase, Squat, Blue, 6 In. 40.00
Raspberry, Gravy Boat, Amethyst .... 45.00 to 100.00
Raspberry, Pitcher, Milk, Amethyst .... 165.00 to 195.00
Raspberry, Pitcher, Milk, Green 300.00
Raspberry, Pitcher, Milk, Marigold 150.00
Raspberry, Pitcher, Water, Ice Blue 3000.00
Raspberry, Water Set, Amethyst, 5 Piece 625.00
Rex, Vase, Marigold, 3 In. 315.00
Ribbed Optic, Tumbler, Celeste Blue 40.00
Ribbon Tie, Bowl, 3-In-1 Edge, Blue 75.00
Ribbon Tie, Bowl, Marigold 30.00
Ripple, Vase, Amethyst, 7 3/4 In. 65.00
Ripple, Vase, Amethyst, 11 In. 165.00
Ripple, Vase, Aqua, 11 In. 135.00
Ripple, Vase, Aqua, 14 In. 305.00
Ripple, Vase, Blue, 10 1/2 In. 475.00
Ripple, Vase, Clambroth, 9 In. 20.00
Ripple, Vase, Clambroth, 11 In. 125.00
Ripple, Vase, Green, 8 1/2 In. 125.00
Ripple, Vase, Green, 9 In. 40.00
Ripple, Vase, Green, 11 In. 60.00
Ripple, Vase, Lime Green, 11 1/2 In. 65.00
Ripple, Vase, Lime Green, 15 In. 55.00
Ripple, Vase, Lime Green, Vaseline, Marigold Iridescence, 17 In. 1100.00
Ripple, Vase, Marigold, 4 1/2 In. 135.00
Ripple, Vase, Marigold, 10 In. 25.00
Ripple, Vase, Smoke, 10 In. 80.00
Ripple, Vase, Smoke, 12 In. 155.00
Ripple, Vase, Teal, 10 1/2 In. 145.00
Ripple, Vase, Teal, 11 In. .... 50.00 to 60.00
Rising Sun, Pitcher, Water, Marigold 205.00
Rising Sun, Tumbler, Marigold 40.00
Robin, Water Set, Marigold, 7 Piece 175.00
Robin Red Breast pattern is listed here as Robin.
Rose & Ruffles pattern is listed here as Open Rose.
Rose Garden, Pitcher, Marigold 375.00
Rose Garden, Rose Bowl, Marigold, 6 In. 65.00
Rose Garden, Vase, Fan Shape, Blue, 5 In. 225.00
Rose Garden, Vase, Fan Shape, Blue, 7 1/2 In. 150.00
Rose Garden, Vase, Fan Shape, Blue, 9 In. 250.00
Rose Garden, Vase, Fan Shape, Marigold, 7 1/2 In. 375.00
Rose Show, Bowl, Ruffled Edge, Amethyst 325.00
Rose Show, Bowl, Ruffled Edge, Aqua Opalescent .... 650.00 to 950.00
Rose Show, Bowl, Ruffled Edge, Blue .... 650.00 to 1200.00
Rose Show, Bowl, Ruffled Edge, Electric Blue 1200.00
Rose Show, Bowl, Ruffled Edge, Green .... 1300.00 to 1400.00
Rose Show, Bowl, Ruffled Edge, Ice Blue 850.00
Rose Show, Bowl, Ruffled Edge, Ice Green 1100.00
Rose Show, Bowl, Ruffled Edge, Lime Green 3500.00
Rose Show, Plate, Amethyst, 9 In. 2500.00
Rose Show, Plate, Blue, 9 In. .... 550.00 to 750.00
Rose Show, Plate, Ice Blue, 9 In. 600.00
Rose Show, Plate, Lime Green, 9 In. .... Illus 1900.00
Rose Show, Plate, Marigold, 9 In. 575.00
Rose Show, Plate, White, 9 In. .... 105.00 to 400.00
Roses & Loops pattern is listed here as Double-Stem Rose.
Round-Up, Plate, Blue, 9 In. .... 165.00 to 350.00
Round-Up, Plate, White, 9 In. 150.00
Rustic, Vase, Amethyst, 11 In. 150.00
Rustic, Vase, Cobalt Blue, 21 1/2 In. 1900.00
Rustic, Vase, Marigold, 12 In. 115.00
S-Repeat, Punch Cup, Amethyst 30.00
Sailboat & Windmill pattern is listed here as Sailboats.

Sailboats, Plate, Blue, 6 In. 225.00
Sailboats, Sauce, Green 15.00
Scales, Bowl, Ruffled Edge, Blue Opalescent 90.00
Scales, Plate, Amethyst, 6 In. 35.00
Scroll Embossed, Bowl, Aqua, 9 In. 100.00
Scroll Embossed, Bowl, File Back, Ruffled Edge, Amethyst, 5 In. . . . . .35.00 to 65.00
Scroll Embossed, Bowl, File Back, Ruffled Edge, Marigold, 9 In. 50.00
Scroll Embossed, Compote, Ruffled Edge, Green 30.00
Scroll Embossed, Plate, Amethyst, 9 In. . . . . .300.00 to 825.00
Scroll Embossed, Plate, Marigold, 9 In. 135.00
Sea Lanes pattern is listed here as Little Fishes.
Seacoast, Pin Tray, Green 475.00
Seacoast, Pin Tray, Marigold 400.00
Shell, Plate, Marigold, 9 In. 750.00
Shell, Plate, Smoke, 9 In. 650.00
Shell & Sand, Bowl, Ruffled Edge, Lavender 325.00
Shell & Sand, Bowl, Ruffled Edge, Marigold 45.00
Shell & Sand, Plate, Amethyst, 9 In. . . . . .1400.00 to 1900.00
Shell & Sand, Plate, Green, 9 In. 275.00
Shell & Wild Rose pattern is listed here as Wild Rose.
Singing Birds, Berry Bowl, Amethyst, 5 In. 60.00
Singing Birds, Berry Bowl, Green, 5 In. 25.00
Singing Birds, Berry Set, Green, 5 Piece 400.00
Singing Birds, Mug, Amethyst 60.00
Singing Birds, Mug, Blue 55.00
Singing Birds, Mug, Green . . . . .85.00 to 125.00
Singing Birds, Mug, Ice Blue 475.00
Singing Birds, Mug, Marigold . . . . .25.00 to 40.00
Singing Birds, Pitcher, Water, Amethyst 375.00
Singing Birds, Pitcher, Water, Marigold 400.00
Singing Birds, Tumbler, Amethyst 45.00
Singing Birds, Tumbler, Marigold 45.00
Singing Birds, Water Set, Green, 6 Piece 625.00
Ski Star, Bowl, Ruffled Edge, Amethyst 400.00
Ski Star, Bowl, Ruffled Edge, Peach Opalescent 60.00
Smooth Rays, Bowl, Ruffled Edge, Marigold On Milk Glass 45.00
Soldiers & Sailors, Plate, Illinois, Marigold, 7 In. 2400.00
Spinning Starlet, Vase, Blue 325.00
Spiralex, Vase, Amethyst, 12 In. 25.00
Spring Flowers pattern is listed here as Bouquet.
Springtime, Pitcher, Water, Amethyst 550.00
Springtime, Water Set, Marigold, 6 Piece 900.00
Stag & Holly, Bowl, Ice Cream, Footed, Blue . . . . .150.00 to 230.00
Stag & Holly, Bowl, Ice Cream, Footed, Marigold . . . . .45.00 to 85.00
Stag & Holly, Bowl, Ruffled Edge, Footed, Pink, Marigold Iridescence 105.00
Stag & Holly, Bowl, Ruffled Edge, Footed, Red 900.00
Stag & Holly, Bowl, Ruffled Edge, Marigold 95.00
Stag & Holly, Chop Plate, Marigold, Footed . . . . .500.00 to 750.00
Stag & Holly, Plate, Marigold, Footed, 9 In. 200.00
Star & File, Creamer, Marigold 15.00
Star & File, Spooner, Marigold 50.00
Star Medallion, Pitcher, Milk, Marigold 35.00
Star Of David, Bowl, Amethyst, 9 In. 120.00
Star Of David & Bows, Bowl, Ruffled Edge, Amethyst 75.00
Star Of David Medallion pattern is listed here as Star of David & Bows.
Starburst, Tumbler, Marigold 115.00
Starburst, Vase, Amber, 5 In. 275.00
Starburst, Water Set, Blue, 7 Piece 500.00
Starburst & Diamonds, Vase, Amber, 10 In. 175.00
Starflower, Pitcher, Water, Blue 1800.00
Starflower, Pitcher, Water, Marigold 5500.00
Starlight, Vase, Blue, 6 In. 350.00
Stippled Clematis pattern is listed here as Little Stars.

Stippled Diamond & Flower pattern is listed here as Little Flowers.
Stippled Leaf & Beads pattern is listed here as Leaf & Beads.
Stippled Petals, Bowl, Dome Foot, Ruffled Edge, Peach Opalescent . . . . .25.00 to 40.00
Stippled Posy & Pods pattern is listed here as Four Flowers.
Stippled Rays, Bowl, Crimped Ruffled Edge, Amethyst 35.00
Stippled Rays, Bowl, Marigold, 9 In. 10.00
Stippled Rays, Bowl, Red, 7 In. 175.00
Stippled Rays, Bowl, Ruffled Edge, Red, 7 In. 185.00
Stippled Rays, Creamer, Marigold 5.00
Stippled Rays, Plate, Marigold, 6 In. 25.00
Stippled Rays, Sauce, Marigold 5.00
Stippled Rays, Sauce, Ruffled Edge, Reverse Amberina 95.00
Stippled Strawberry, Bowl, Ruffled Edge, Ribbed Back, Pastel Marigold 175.00
Stork & Rushes, Mug, Blue 400.00
Stork & Rushes, Mug, Marigold 10.00
Stork & Rushes, Pitcher, Water, Amethyst 450.00
Stork & Rushes, Tumbler, Amethyst 50.00
Stork & Rushes, Water Set, Marigold, 7 Piece 350.00
Stork ABC, Dish, Marigold . . . . .25.00 to 40.00
Strawberry, Bonbon, Amber 30.00
Strawberry, Bonbon, Marigold 20.00
Strawberry, Bowl, Amethyst, 8 1/2 In. 70.00
Strawberry, Bowl, Green, 8 1/2 In. . . . . .105.00 to 125.00
Strawberry, Plate, Amethyst, 9 In. . . . . .75.00 to 175.00
Strawberry, Plate, Basketweave Back, Amethyst, 9 In. 175.00
Strawberry, Plate, Basketweave Back, Marigold, 9 In. 155.00
Strawberry, Plate, Marigold, 9 In. 80.00
Strawberry Scroll, Tumbler, Blue 85.00
Stream Of Hearts, Compote, Crimped Ruffled Edge, Marigold 30.00
Sunflower pattern is listed here as Dandelion.
Sunflower & Wheat pattern is listed here as Field Flower.
Sunk Daisy, Bowl, Footed, Marigold, 3 In. 125.00
Sunk Daisy, Bowl, Footed, Marigold, 9 In. 10.00
Target, Vase, Amethyst, 11 In. 25.00
Target, Vase, Blue, 11 In. 30.00
Target, Vase, Marigold On Moonstone, 10 In. 65.00
Target, Vase, Marigold, 10 In. . . . . .5.00 to 10.00
Target, Vase, Marigold, 12 In. 40.00
Target, Vase, Peach Opalescent, 10 In. 50.00
Target, Vase, Peach Opalescent, Squat, 5 In. 60.00
Teardrops pattern is listed here as Raindrops.
Ten Mums, Pitcher, Water, Tankard, Marigold 425.00
Ten Mums, Water Set, Blue, 7 Piece 1300.00
Thin Rib, Vase, Amethyst, 11 In. 45.00
Thin Rib, Vase, Amethyst, 13 In. 165.00
Thin Rib, Vase, Green, 9 In. 30.00
Thistle, Banana Bowl, Amethyst 300.00
Thistle, Banana Bowl, Marigold . . . . .85.00 to 90.00
Thistle, Bowl, 3-In-1 Edge, Green, 8 3/4 In. 60.00
Thistle, Bowl, 3-In-1 Edge, Marigold, 8 3/4 In. 15.00
Thistle, Plate, Green, 9 In. 3700.00
Three Fruits, Bowl, Dome Foot, Ruffled Edge, Green 50.00
Three Fruits, Bowl, Dome Foot, Ruffled Edge, Lime Green 375.00
Three Fruits, Bowl, Pie Crust Edge, Amethyst 80.00
Three Fruits, Bowl, Ruffled Edge, Ribbed Back, Amethyst 75.00
Three Fruits, Plate, Basketweave Back, Amethyst, 9 In. 105.00
Three Fruits, Plate, Basketweave Back, Marigold, 9 In. 65.00
Three Fruits, Plate, Marigold, 9 In. . . . . .75.00 to 95.00
Three Fruits, Plate, Ribbed Back, Stippled, Amethyst, 9 In. 550.00
Three Fruits, Plate, Ribbed Back, Stippled, Aqua Opalescent, 9 In. 2600.00
Three Fruits, Plate, Ribbed Back, Stippled, Marigold, 9 In. 125.00
Tiger Lily, Water Set, Amethyst, 7 Piece 900.00
Tiger Lily, Water Set, Marigold, 7 Piece 165.00

Tree Trunk, Vase, Amethyst, 10 In. ....55.00 to 75.00
Tree Trunk, Vase, Amethyst, 12 In. 305.00
Tree Trunk, Vase, Amethyst, Elephant Foot, 13 In. 1200.00
Tree Trunk, Vase, Aqua Opalescent, 9 1/2 In. 500.00
Tree Trunk, Vase, Aqua Opalescent, Butterscotch Iridescence, 11 In. 850.00
Tree Trunk, Vase, Blue, 10 In. ....75.00 to 180.00
Tree Trunk, Vase, Blue, 12 In. 575.00
Tree Trunk, Vase, Green, 10 In. 150.00
Tree Trunk, Vase, Marigold, 10 In. 40.00
Tree Trunk, Vase, Marigold, 11 In. 375.00
Tree Trunk, Vase, Squat, Amethyst, 6 In. 35.00
Tree Trunk, Vase, Squat, Amethyst, Tricornered, 5 1/2 In. 185.00
Tree Trunk, Vase, Squat, Blue, 8 In. 425.00
Tree Trunk, Vase, Squat, Green, 6 In. ....55.00 to 95.00
Tree Trunk, Vase, Squat, Green, 7 In. ....50.00 to 95.00
Tree Trunk, Vase, Squat, Ice Blue, 6 In. 2400.00
Tree Trunk, Vase, Squat, Marigold, 7 In. 50.00
Tree Trunk, Vase, White, 13 In. 800.00
Trout & Fly, Bowl, Ice Cream, Marigold, Frosted 300.00
Two Flowers, Bowl, Ruffled Edge, Footed, Red 400.00
Vine & Roses, Pitcher, Marigold, 8 1/2 In. 200.00
Vineyard, Pitcher, Water, Marigold 125.00
Vineyard, Tumbler, Marigold 10.00
Vineyard, Water Set, Amethyst, 5 Piece 500.00
Vintage, Bowl, 3-In-1 Edge, Blue, 8 1/2 In. 80.00
Vintage, Bowl, 3-In-1 Edge, Marigold, 8 1/2 In. 20.00
Vintage, Bowl, Amethyst, 7 In. 18.00
Vintage, Bowl, Green, 10 In. 50.00
Vintage, Bowl, Ice Cream, Blue, 10 In. 65.00
Vintage, Bowl, Ruffled Edge, Amethyst ....20.00 to 35.00
Vintage, Bowl, Ruffled Edge, Aqua Opalescent 1600.00
Vintage, Epergne, Blue 145.00
Vintage, Epergne, Green 185.00
Vintage, Fernery, 3-Footed, Blue 40.00
Vintage, Nut Dish, Footed, Amethyst 45.00
Vintage, Plate, Marigold, Pink Iridescence, 9 In. 400.00
Waffle Band pattern is listed here as Luster Flute.
Waffle Block, Basket, Handles, Clambroth 15.00
Waffle Block, Basket, Handles, Marigold 35.00
Water Lily, Berry Bowl, Ruffled Edge, Fluted, Red 700.00
Water Lily, Bowl, 3-Footed, Marigold, 9 3/4 In. 30.00
Water Lily, Sauce, Footed, Ruffled Edge, Marigold 85.00
Water Lily, Sauce, Footed, Ruffled Edge, Powder Blue 85.00
Water Lily, Sauce, Ruffled Edge, Footed, Ice Green 350.00
Water Lily, Sauce, Ruffled Edge, Footed, Lime Green Opalescent 500.00
Water Lily, Sauce, Ruffled Edge, Footed, Red 525.00
Water Lily, Toothpick, Marigold 25.00
Western Thistle, Vase, Marigold, 5 In. 165.00
Whirling Leaves, Bonbon, Handles, Light Marigold 25.00
Wide Panel, Chop Plate, White, 13 In. 30.00
Wide Rib, Vase, Peach Opalescent, 11 In. 45.00
Wild Grapes pattern is listed here as Grape Leaves.
Wild Rose, Bowl, Footed, Marigold 140.00
Wild Rose, Nut Dish, Footed, Green 10.00
Wild Strawberry, Plate, Handgrip, Amethyst, 7 In. 450.00
Wild Strawberry, Plate, Handgrip, Green, 7 In. 155.00
Wild Strawberry, Sauce, Ruffled Edge, Marigold, 6 In. 35.00
Windflower, Bowl, Ruffled Edge, Amethyst 35.00
Windflower, Plate, Marigold, 9 In. 40.00
Windmill, Bowl, Marigold 10.00
Windmill, Dish, Pickle, Marigold 15.00
Windmill, Pitcher, Milk, Marigold ....20.00 to 25.00

Windmill, Pitcher, Water, Marigold, 8 1/4 In. 30.00
Windmill Medallion pattern is listed here as Windmill.
Wishbone, Bowl, Ruffled Edge, Footed, Amethyst, 10 In. 100.00
Wishbone, Bowl, Ruffled Edge, Footed, Ice Blue, 10 In. . . . . .750.00 to 1115.00
Wishbone, Bowl, Ruffled Edge, Footed, Marigold, 10 In. . . . . .105.00 to 120.00
Wishbone, Bowl, Ruffled Edge, Footed, Sapphire, 10 In. 600.00
Wishbone, Bowl, Ruffled Edge, Footed, White, 10 In. .225.00 to 325.00
Wishbone, Bowl, Ruffled Edge, Green, Footed, 10 In. .105.00 to 150.00
Wishbone, Chop Plate, Amethyst 1100.00
Wishbone, Epergne, Marigold 375.00
Wishbone, Plate, Footed, Amethyst, 9 In. 300.00
Wishbone, Plate, Footed, Marigold, 9 In. 1900.00
Wishbone, Tumbler, Amethyst 50.00
Wishbone, Tumbler, Green 45.00
Wishbone, Water Set, Marigold, 7 Piece 950.00
Wishbone & Spades, Bowl, Ruffled Edge, Amethyst, 10 In. 250.00
Wishbone & Spades, Chop Plate, Amethyst 950.00
Wishbone & Spades, Plate, Amethyst, 6 In. 775.00
Wishbone & Spades, Sauce, Amethyst, Ruffled Edge 75.00
Woodpecker, Wall Pocket, Marigold . . . . .55.00 to 105.00
Wreath Of Roses, Compote, Ruffled Edge, Amethyst . . . . .20.00 to 25.00
Wreath Of Roses, Compote, Ruffled Edge, Blue 25.00
Wreath Of Roses, Rose Bowl, Marigold 10.00

CAROUSEL or merry-go-round figures were first carved in the United
States in 1867 by Gustav Dentzel. Collectors discovered the charm of
the hand-carved figures in the 1970s, and they were soon classed as
folk art. Most desirable are the figures other than horses, such as pigs,
camels, lions, or dogs. A jumper is a figure that was made to move up
and down on a pole; a stander was placed in a stationary position.

    Ape, Saddle On Back, Wood, Carved, Painted, 31 x 28 In. 248.00
    Chariot, 2 Benches, Swans, Bird, Snake, Sailor, Parrots, Sunflower, 45 x 72 x 38 In. 1380.00
    Cherub, Wood, Curly Blond Hair, Wings, 45 x 10 In. .2200.00 to 3575.00
    Giraffe, Standing, Wood, Carved, Painted, Platform, 52 x 58 In. 990.00
    Giraffe, Wood, Red Bridle, On Base, 62 x 47 In. 2500.00
    Horse, Front Hooves Up, Carved, Friedrich Heyn, Germany, 55 x 62 In. 1540.00
    Horse, Golden Brown, Black Saddle, Wood, Carved, c.1950, 72 x 72 In. 805.00
    Horse, Gray, Black Mane, Tail, Lower Legs, Leaping, Inside Row, 51 In. 2200.00
    Horse, Jumper, Wood, Painted, Brass Tack Eyes, Horsehair Tail, Stand, c.1900, 56 x 49 In. . 2115.00
    Horse, Rearing, Tan, Blue Harness, Red Saddle, c.1950, 62 x 61 In. 690.00
    Horse, Trotting, Wood, Carved, Painted, Base, 49 x 53 In. 1210.00
    Horse, Wood, White, Roses On Neck, Front Hoof Up, On Base, Outside Row, 57 x 44 In. . . 1430.00
    Mirror, 20-Light, Beveled Glass, Wood, Carved, 23 x 24 In. 880.00
    Plaque, Eagle, Spread Wings, Pine, Silver Paint, Late 1800s, 8 1/4 x 35 In. 560.00
    Plaque, Indian Head, Multicolored Feathers, Cast Iron, 19 1/2 x 11 In. 475.00
    Rounding Board, Dragons, Flowers, Herschell-Spillman, Late 1800s, 22 1/4 x 95 In. 705.00
    Rounding Board, Dragons, Sailboat, Herschell-Spillman, Late 1800s, 22 1/4 x 95 In. 1645.00
    Rounding Board, Tin, Painted, Birds, Flowers, 74 x 18 In. 935.00
    Rounding Board, Tin, Painted, Water, Castle, Flowers, 73 x 18 In. 990.00
    Stag, Leaping, Real Antler Rack, Carved Body, Glass Eyes, Painted, 1900s, 45 x 70 In. . . . 489.00
    Tiger, Wood, Glass Eyes, Gold, Black Stripes, 13 x 55 In. 715.00
    Tiger, Wood, Glass Eyes, Gold, Black Stripes, 15 x 61 In. 715.00
    Tiger, Wood, Glass Eyes, Gold, Black Stripes, 18 x 64 In. 660.00
    Unicorn, Rearing, White, Gray, Blue Harness, Yellow Saddle, c.1950, 54 x 48 In. 635.00

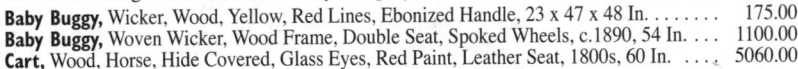

CARRIAGE means several things, so this category lists baby carriages, buggies for adults, horse-drawn sleighs, and even strollers.
Doll-sized carriages are listed in the Toy category.

    Baby Buggy, Wicker, Wood, Yellow, Red Lines, Ebonized Handle, 23 x 47 x 48 In. 175.00
    Baby Buggy, Woven Wicker, Wood Frame, Double Seat, Spoked Wheels, c.1890, 54 In. . . . 1100.00
    Cart, Wood, Horse, Hide Covered, Glass Eyes, Red Paint, Leather Seat, 1800s, 60 In. 5060.00

CASH REGISTERS

CASH REGISTERS were invented in 1884 because an eye on the cash was a necessity in stores of the nineteenth century, too. John and James Ritty invented a large model that resembled a clock and kept a record of the dollars and cents exchanged in the store. John Patterson improved the cash register with a paper roll to record the money. By the early 1900s, elaborate brass registers were made. About World War I, the fancy case was exchanged for the more modern types.

Brandt Automatic Cashier, Polished Cast Aluminum, Griffin, 12 x 11 In.	285.00
National, Brass, Oak Base, 10 1/2 x 16 x 20 1/2 In.	805.00
National, Brass, Oak Base, 25 x 17 x 30 In.	1035.00
National, Model 2, Nickel Plated, 1907, 17 1/2 In.	660.00
National, Model 33, 1895, 17 1/2 In.	440.00
National, No. 542E-4C, Brass, Leafy Casting, Oak Base, 4 Drawers, 28 In.	645.00
National, Serial No. 1527240, Cast Metal Case, Early 20th Century, 17 x 17 x 16 In.	200.00

CASTOR JARS

CASTOR JARS for pickles are glass jars about six inches in height, held in special metal holders. They became a popular dinner table accessory about 1890. Each jar had a top that was usually silver or silver plate. The frame, also of a silver metal, had a handle that arched above the jar and a hook that held a pair of tongs. By 1900, the pickle castor was out of fashion. Many examples found today have reproduced glass jars in old holders. Additional pickle castors may be found in the various Glass categories.

Pickle, Amber Glass, Double, Silver Plated Frame, Tongs, Meriden Quadruple Plate, 9 In.	325.00
Pickle, Amberina, Melon Ribbed, Silver Plated Frame, Wilcox, 12 1/4 In.	2000.00
Pickle, Blue Satin Glass, Enameled, Silver Plate Frame, Acme, 11 1/2 In.	1800.00
Pickle, Cranberry Glass, Enameled Flowers, Silver Plated Frame, Birds Cover, Pelton	895.00
Pickle, Cranberry Opalescent, Swirl, Silver Plate Frame, 12 In.	590.00
Pickle, Daisy & Button, Boat Shape, Amber, Silver Plated Frame, Fork, Wheeled Base	1650.00
Pickle, Daisy & Button, Green, Silver Plated Frame, Bird's Head Tongs, Rogers Smith	975.00
Pickle, Diamond Pattern Insert, Silver Plate Frame, Victorian, 11 3/4 In.	115.00

CASTOR SETS

CASTOR SETS holding just salt and pepper castors were used in the seventeenth century. The sugar castor, mustard pot, spice dredger, bottles for vinegar and oil, and other spice holders became popular by the eighteenth century. These sets were usually made of sterling silver. The American Victorian castor set, the type most collected today, was made of silver plated Britannia metal. Colored glass bottles were introduced after the Civil War. The sets were out of fashion by World War I. Be careful when buying sets with colored bottles; many are reproductions. Other castor sets may be listed in various porcelain and glass categories in this book.

4 Bottles, Clear Ribbed Glass, Georgian Style Silver Plate Frame, Acanthus Feet	425.00
5 Bottles, Clear Glass, Silver Plated Frame, Cherub Handle, Meriden	525.00
5 Bottles, Cranberry Glass, Inverted Thumbprint, Silver Plated Frame	750.00
5 Bottles, Etched Glass, Silver Plated Frame, Covers, Rogers Quadruple Plate	325.00
5 Bottles, New England Pineapple Pattern, Brittania Frame	330.00
6 Bottles, Clear Glass, Silver Plated Frame, Servant's Bell, Wilcox, 9 In.	1295.00

CATALOGS are listed in the Paper category.

CAULDON

CAULDON Limited worked in Staffordshire, Great Britain, and went through many name changes. John Ridgway made porcelain at Cauldon Place, Hanley, until 1855. The firm of John Ridgway, Bates and Co. of Cauldon Place worked from 1856 to 1859. It became Bates, Brown-Westhead, Moore and Co. from 1859 to 1862. Brown-Westhead, Moore and Co. worked from 1862 to 1904. About 1890, this firm started using the words *Cauldon* or *Cauldon ware* as part of the mark. Cauldon Ltd. worked from 1905 to 1920, Cauldon Potteries from 1920 to 1962. Related items may be found in the Indian Tree category.

Bowl, Flow Blue Interior, Flowers, c.1870, 20 1/2 In.	4200.00
Plate, Dessert, Flowers, Tiffany & Co., c.1914, 8 3/4 In., 6 Piece	575.00
Tea Set, Painted Birds, Gold Decoration, 11 Piece	165.00

CELADON is the name of a velvet-textured green-gray glaze used by Chinese, Japanese, Korean, and other factories. The name refers both to the glaze and to pieces covered with the glaze. It is still being made.

Bowl, Footed, 11 1/2 In.	300.00
Box, Brush, Lid, Oriental, Divided Compartment, c.1890, 8 In.	195.00
Brush Washer, Egg Shape, Short Neck, China, Ming Dynasty, 3 1/2-In. Diam.	140.00
Brushpot, Tree Trunk Form, Carved Cranes, Pines, Ju-I Fungus, Red Jade, 5 3/4 In.	1380.00
Figurine, Goat, Resting, Green Jade, 18th Century, 6 3/4 In.	3105.00
Figurine, Immortal Seated On Throne, Mounted As Table Lamp, 9 1/4 In.	1095.00
Plate, Rose Canton Design, Bird, Butterflies, Tree Peony, 10 1/4 In.	210.00
Teabowl, Bell Shape, Chinese, 4 1/4 In.	60.00
Vase, Famille Rose, Flower, Fruit, 14 1/4 In.	405.00
Vase, Incised Landscape, Chinese, c.1900, 18 1/2 In.	

CELLULOID is a trademark for a plastic developed in 1868 by John W. Hyatt. Celluloid Manufacturing Company, the Celluloid Novelty Company, Celluloid Fancy Goods Company, and American Xylonite Company all used Celluloid to make jewelry, games, sewing equipment, false teeth, and piano keys. The name *Celluloid* was often used to identify any similar plastic. Celluloid toys are listed under Toy.

Button, Saturn, Concentric Rings, Yellow, Red Center, 1 7/16 In.	10.00
Dresser Set, Pearlized, Butterscotch & Pale Yellow, Black Rim, 1930s, 10 Piece	310.00
Toilet Set, Amerith Line, Paul T. Frankl, Celluloid Corp., c.1928, 7 1/4-In. Comb, 3 Piece	600.00

CELS are listed in this book in the Animation Art category.

CERAMIC ART COMPANY of Trenton, New Jersey, was established in 1889 by J. Coxon and W. Lenox and was an early producer of American Belleek porcelain. It became Lenox, Inc. in 1906. Do not confuse this ware with the pottery made by the Ceramic Arts Studio of Madison, Wisconsin.

Loving Cup, Song Of Hiawatha, Poem, Gold Highlights, 1897, 6 1/2 In.	300.00
Mug, Pink Luster, Enamel, Drunken Taverners, c.1904, 4 1/2 In.	118.00
Urn, Belleek, Cartouche, Courting Couple, Reticulated Handles & Lid, 12 In.	1150.00
Vase, Belleek, Pink & Yellow Roses, Flared Neck, Pedestal Base, Handles, 12 In.	300.00
Vase, Belleek, Roses, Green Ground, Straight-Sided, 1st CAC Mark, 11 In.	315.00

CERAMIC ARTS STUDIO was founded about 1940 in Madison, Wisconsin, by Lawrence Rabbett and Ruben Sand. Their most popular products were expensive molded figurines. The pottery closed in 1955. Do not confuse these products with those of the Ceramic Art Co. of Trenton, New Jersey.

Bank, Paisley Pig, Yellow, Brown, Green, 1943-53	300.00
Bank, Skunk, Floral Necklace, 4 In.	200.00
Figurine, Balinese Dancer, 9 3/8 In.	85.00
Shelf Sitter, Cowboy, Cowgirl, Bench, 4 1/2 In., 3 Piece	130.00

CHALKWARE is really plaster of Paris decorated with watercolors. One type was molded from Staffordshire and other porcelain models and painted and sold as inexpensive decorations in the nineteenth century. Figures of plaster, made from about 1910 to 1940 for use as prizes at carnivals, are also known as chalkware. Kewpie dolls made of chalkware will be found in their own category.

Bank, Cat, 10 In.	58.00
Bank, Cat, Painted, Late 19th Century, 3 1/2 x 2 1/4 x 5 In., Pair	635.00
Bust, Indian, Red, White, Green, 18 In.	385.00
Compote, Stylized Fruit, Hollow, Yellow, Red, Green, Brown, 13 3/4 x 6 1/2 In.	3630.00
Figurine, Bird, On Pedestal, Painted, Yellow, Brown, Black, Green Base, 6 x 5 In.	990.00
Figurine, Bird, Standing, Hollow, Yellow Bird, Brown, Black, Red, 4 x 2 x 3 In.	1210.00
Figurine, Cat, Reclining, Glass Eyes, Orange Paint, Red Trim, 7 x 14 In.	50.00
Figurine, Cat, Seated, Brown Spots, Red Collar, Painted Face, 5 3/8 In.	2300.00
Figurine, Cat, Seated, Collar, Hollow, Smoke Decorated, Polychrome, 10 x 5 x 5 In.	8800.00
Figurine, Cat, Seated, Painted, Tan, Red, Brown, 3 x 2 In.	1210.00
Figurine, Cat, With Pipe, Red & Black Eyes, Black Dots On Pipe, Yellow Bowtie, 10 In.	230.00

Figurine, Dog, Painted, 1 Seated, 1 Standing, 19th Century, 7 1/2 In., Pair	380.00
Figurine, Dog, Painted, Penn., 5 1/2 x 5 In.	460.00
Figurine, Dog, Poodle, Seated, Painted, Red, Green, Brown, Raised Dot, 6 1/4 x 3 In.	165.00
Figurine, Dog, Poodle, Standing, Polychrome Stylized Design, 7 1/4 x 6 x 3 1/2 In.	275.00
Figurine, Dog, Spaniel, Standing, Brown Ears, Red Collar, Flower Accents, 1800s, 7 x 5 In.	120.00
Figurine, Dove, Incised Wings, Dome Base, Penn., 10 In.	115.00
Figurine, Dove, Painted, Berry Spring, 19th Century, 11 1/2 In., Pair	470.00
Figurine, Dove, Perched, White, Yellow, Green, Brown, Orange, 9 1/2 x 7 1/2 In.	195.00
Figurine, Lady, Standing, White, Brown, Red, Black Polychrome, Hollow, 8 x 3 x 3 In.	825.00
Figurine, Lion, Polychrome Design, 18 3/4 In.	70.00
Figurine, Parrot, On Ball, Hollow, Yellow, Red, Brown Highlights, 8 1/2 x 4 x 3 In.	2310.00
Figurine, Rabbit, Painted, Penn., 5 1/4 x 4 1/4 In.	605.00
Figurine, Rabbit, Seated, Hollow, Yellow, Red, Black Decoration, 5 x 2 1/2 x 4 In.	5500.00
Figurine, Squirrel, Eating Nut, Painted, Red, Brown, Green, 6 x 5 x 2 1/4 In.	275.00
Figurine, Squirrel, Seated, With Nut, Hollow, Smoke Decoration, Painted, 6 1/2 x 3 x 5 In.	1430.00
Figurine, Squirrel, With Nut, Brown Wash Paint, Black Spots, 6 1/4 x 5 1/4 In.	2200.00
Garniture, Compote, Hollow Cast, Fruit, Molded Rosette, 12 In.	259.00
Head, Phrenology, Original Paper Label, Fowler & Wells 129, N.Y., 10 x 5 x 5 In.	1150.00
Plaque, Ram's Head, Painted, Brown, 4 x 3 1/2 x 2 1/2 In.	15.00
Watch Holder, Hollow, Columns, Arch, Applied Angel, Polychrome, 12 x 4 x 8 In.	1100.00

CHARLIE CHAPLIN, the famous comic and actor, lived from 1889 to 1977. He made his first movie in 1913. He did the movie *The Tramp* in 1915. The character of the Tramp has remained famous, and in the 1980s appeared in a series of television commercials for computers. Dolls, candy containers, and all sorts of memorabilia picture Charlie Chaplin. Pieces are being made even today.

Button, Goldwyn Follies Club, Celluloid, Red Rim, 1 1/4 In.	75.00
Button, Portrait, Lithograph, 1920s, 1/2 In.	23.00
Candy Container, Chaplin, Glass Barrel, Metal Slotted Lid, 4 x 3 In.	145.00
Comic Book, Funny Stunts, J. Keeley, 1917, 8 Pages	50.00
Movie Lobby Card, Dog's Life, 1918, 11 x 14 In.	259.00
Movie Lobby Card, Limelight, 1952, 11 x 14 In.	55.00
Photograph, Gold Rush, 1925, 8 x 10 In.	34.00
Pin, Chaplin, Coogan, Enamel & Brass, 1921, 1 In.	5125.00
Toy, Charlie With Cane, Cloth & Tin, Schuco, Box, 7 In.	880.00
Toy, Mechanical, Tin, Flocked Fabric Face, Costume, Cane, Schuco, 1935, 6 In.	395.00
Toy, Twirls Cane While Turning In Circles, Windup, Schuco, Original Box	950.00
Toy, Walking, Mechanical, Wind Up, B&R, Box, 1920s, 8 1/2 In.	1525.00

CHARLIE MCCARTHY was the ventriloquist's dummy used by Edgar Bergen from the 1930s. He was famous for his work in radio, movies, and television. The act was retired in the 1970s.

Bank, Mechanical, Metal, Wooden Jaw, Charlie On Suitcase, 5 1/2 In.	193.00
Button, Edgar Bergen's Charlie McCarthy, Effanbee Play Product, c.1938, 1 In.	75.00
Button, Goldwyn Follies Club, Licensed By Edgar Bergen, 1 1/4 In.	65.00
Doll, Gesso Head, Painted Features, Tuxedo, Metal Steamer Trunk, c.1935, 34 In.	9350.00
Dummy, Composition Shoulder Head, Painted Face, Effanbee, c.1935, 19 In.	1320.00 to 1870.00
Radio, Majestic Charlie McCarthy, Plastic, Small	275.00
Toy, Benzine Buggy, Marx, 1938, 8 In.	468.00 to 660.00
Toy, Benzine Buggy, Windup, Marx, 1930s	475.00
Toy, Mortimer Snerd, Crazy Car, Tin Lithograph, Windup, Marx, 7 1/2 In.	440.00 to 715.00
Toy, Mortimer Snerd, Walker, Tin Lithograph, Windup, Marx, 8 1/2 In.	275.00
Toy, Private Car, Charlie & Mortimer, Tin Lithograph, Windup, Marx, 1939, 16 In.	3300.00
Toy, Walker, Tin Lithograph, Moving Jaw, Marx, Box, 8 1/2 In.	358.00

CHELSEA porcelain was made in the Chelsea area of London from about 1745 to 1784. Some pieces made from 1770 to 1784 may include the letter *D* for *Derby* in the mark. Ceramic designs were borrowed from the Meissen models of the day. Pieces were made of soft paste. The gold anchor was used as the mark but it has been copied by many other factories. Recent copies of Chelsea have been made from the original molds. Do not confuse Chelsea porcelain with Chelsea Grape, a white pottery with luster grape decoration.

Candlestick, Child Holding Basket Of Flowers, Gilt, Anchor Mark, 7 3/8 In., Pair	375.00
Dish, Oval, Fruit, Vines, Flower Bouquet, c.1765, 8 1/2 In.	330.00
Figurine, Youthful Bacchus, Charles Vyse, 1921, 11 In.	2700.00
Pitcher, Applied Apple Blossoms, Blue Green Glaze, 10 x 6 In.	8813.00
Pitcher, Applied Vines, Leaves, Blossoms, Blue Green Glaze, 9 1/2 x 7 1/4 In.	940.00
Plate, Blind Earl Pattern, Rose Branch, Flowers, Scalloped Rim, Gilt, 1765-69, 7 In.	755.00
Vase, Honeycomb, Dark Green Glaze, Blossom Branch, Bottle Shaped, 11 3/4 x 4 1/2 In.	940.00

CHINESE EXPORT porcelain comprises all the many kinds of porcelain made in China for export to America and Europe in the eighteenth, nineteenth, and twentieth centuries. Other pieces may be listed in this book under Canton, Celadon, Nanking, and Rose Medallion.

Basket, Man, Woman, Smelling Rose, Reticulated, Oval, c.1800, 7 1/2 In., Pair	4800.00
Basket, Underplate, Blue, White, Handles, Pierced Border, 1850, 5 x 10 x 9 In.	865.00
Bough Pot, Figures & Birds In Landscape, Square, Flared, Shell Handles, 8 In.	375.00
Bowl, 5-Clawed Dragons, Medallion, Scrolling Lotus, Wooden Stand, 23 1/4 In.	920.00
Bowl, Apple Green Glaze, Crackle Interior, Squat, Oval, 5 1/2 In.	290.00
Bowl, Bird, Flower, Shoe Form, Famille Verte, 5 1/2 In.	635.00
Bowl, Cone Shape, Brown Glaze, Tan Splotches, Henan, 5 In.	300.00
Bowl, Cover, British East India Co., 5 1/4 In.	175.00
Bowl, Figures, Blue Border, c.1780, 6 3/4 In.	690.00
Bowl, Figures, Flower Medallions, Bell Shape, Blue & White, 18th Century, 6 In.	230.00
Bowl, Flowers On Exterior, Single Flower In Center, Lattice Trim, 1 x 4 In.	115.00
Bowl, Flowers, Blue, Gilt, Capt. Nathaniel Howland Sachem Of Boston, 4 In.	2415.00
Bowl, Flowers, Red & Gold Rim, Famille Rose, 11 In.	2300.00
Bowl, Jade, Lobes Radiating From Center Chrysanthemum, 11 3/4 In.	8365.00
Bowl, Lotus Form, Leaves, Stems, Blossoms, White Glaze, 8 In.	220.00
Bowl, Painted, Birds, Butterflies, 4 1/2 x 10 In., Pair	115.00
Bowl, Pine Tree, Peony, Bamboo, Geometric Fretwork, 17 In.	1800.00
Bowl, Polychrome, Enameled, Floral Springs, 19th Century, 9 In.	325.00
Bowl, Sepia Landscape, People Fishing In Pond, 1 3/4 x 8 In.	60.00
Box, Herd Boy, Water Buffalo In Landscape, Blue & White, 3 1/4 In.	185.00
Brushpot, Beehive Shape, Peachbloom, Stylized Dragon, Red, 3 3/4 In.	2629.00
Brushpot, Enameled, Figures Floating On Waves, Blue & White, 6 1/2 In.	120.00
Brushpot, Ivory, Carved, Continuous Dragon Parade, 11 3/4 In.	895.00
Cachepot, Famille Rose, Birds, Flowering Branches, 1800s, 10 1/2 x 11 1/2 In.	230.00
Cachepot, Famille Verte, Flowers, Cylindrical, 1800s, 9 1/2 In.	780.00
Cachepot, Stand, Rose Medallion, Figures In Garden Scene, 22 x 14 In.	200.00
Candlestick, Elephant Shape, 8 1/2 In., Pair	575.00
Charger, Octagonal, Famille Rose, 1740-70	1400.00
Charger, Peonies, Tilework, Tendril Band, Flower & Wave Border, c.1800, 15 In.	610.00
Coffeepot, Famille Rose, Lighthouse Shape Side Handle, c.1795, 9 In.	3450.00
Creamer, Flowers, Helmet Shape, 5 In.	150.00
Creamer, Helmet Shape, Sepia Flowers, Garland Border, 4 1/2 In.	290.00
Creamer, Porcelain, Flowers, Helmet Shape, 5 In.	150.00
Cup & Saucer, Famille Rose, Early 19th Century, 2 1/2 In., 8 Piece	150.00
Cup & Saucer, Figures In Chariot, Grisaille, c.1750	255.00
Cup & Saucer, Grisaille, Biblical Scene, Gilt Trim, Handleless Cup, 4 3/4 In.	240.00
Dish, 6-Character Mark, Club Shape, Sang De Boeuf, 3 3/4 In.	210.00
Dish, Angel & Trumpet, American Eagle, Famille Rose Border, 1800s, 9 1/2 In.	575.00
Dish, Armorial, Famille Verte, Arms Of Friesland, c.1715, 11 3/4 In.	6600.00
Dish, Armorial, Gilt Scrollwork Border, Mid 18th Century, 6 1/4 In.	450.00
Dish, Birds, Chicken, Flowers, Relief Lotus, Leaves, Late 18th Century, 6 In.	345.00
Dish, Blue & White, European Rim, Stylized Floral, Geometric Designs, 8 1/2 In.	575.00
Dish, Boats, Figures, Raised Foot, Multicolored, 10 In.	420.00
Dish, Deer, Pine, Bamboo, Prunus, Multicolored, 4 3/8 In., Pair	230.00
Dish, Entree, Cover, 1000 Butterfly Design, Gilt Pinecone Finial, 10 1/2 x 9 In., Pair	1725.00
Dish, Famille Rose, 1736-95, 8 3/4 In., Pair	805.00
Dish, Famille Verte, Arms Of Amsterdam, c.1715, 9 3/4 In.	7200.00
Dish, Lotus Shape, Raised Leafy Design, 5 1/4 In.	230.00
Dish, Polychrome Bird & Tree, Ribbed Edge, 6 Lobes, Early 18th Century, 6 3/4 In.	140.00
Dish, Vegetable, Cover, Monogram, Pinecone Knop, c.1810, 5 x 8 1/4 x 9 3/8 In.	265.00
Drum Seat, Canton Waterfront, Flowers, Peonies, Butterflies, 1800s, 19 In., Pair	1680.00

Figurine, Dog, Recumbent, Green Glaze, Black Eyes, c.1800, 4 In. 430.00
Figurine, Dog, Seated, Green Glaze, Black Eyes, 4 In. 430.00
Figurine, Foo Dog, Kingfisher Glazed, 9 1/2 In., Pair 748.00
Figurine, Foo Dog, Terra-Cotta, Green Glaze, Facial Features, 12 & 11 In., Pair 275.00
Figurine, Horse, Standing, Head Turned Backwards, Glazed Eyes, 8 & 7 1/2 In. 1610.00
Figurine, Phoenix, Famille Rose Palette, 16 In., Pair 345.00
Figurine, Robed Courtesans Holding Scepters, Plinth, 15 1/2 In., Pair 805.00
Fishbowl, Polychrome, Tripod Carved Stand, Famille Rose, 14 x 16 x 19 In. 520.00
Flask, Moon Shape, Figures, Indigo Scrolling Lotus, Chilong Handles, 18 In., Pair 5975.00
Flask, Moon, Salamander Handles, Flattened Round Body, 19th Century, 8 In. 430.00
Group, 2 Men On Base, Holding Lotus Leaf, Beggar's Bowl, Famille Verte, 7 1/4 In. 431.00
Jar, Blue & White, Figures, Oval, 17th Century, 7 In. 420.00
Jar, Butterfly, Flower, Landscape, Oval, Blue & White, 6 1/2 In. 403.00
Jar, Cover, Blue, White, Foo Dog Finial, Figures, 1800s, 12 3/8 In. 235.00
Jar, Cover, Dome Top, Fruit Finial, Bulbous, Flowers, 7 1/2 In., Pair 259.00
Jar, Cover, Egg Shape, Flowers, Iron Red, Gilt, 1800s, 13 In. 1440.00
Jar, Cover, Peony, Squat, Oval, Blue & White, 18th Century, 3 In. 575.00
Jar, Dome Cover, Blue & White, Prunus Design, Onion Finial, 9 In. 138.00
Jar, Dome Cover, Onion Finial, Flowers, Baluster Form, Multicolored, 12 In., Pair 6000.00
Jar, Elephant Head, Mask Handles, Peony Design, Oval, Blue & White, 7 3/4 In. 575.00
Jar, Foo Dog, Brocade Balls, Elephant Head Handles, Blue & White, 3 In. 345.00
Jar, Foo Dog, Vine, Oval, Blue & White, 5 1/2 In. 316.00
Jar, Fruit & Flower, Oval, Blue & White, 3 In. 58.00
Jar, Wood Cover, Landscape, Blue & White, 9 1/2 In. 575.00
Jar Set, Blue & White, Flowering Branch Decoration, 1900s, 4 x 8 1/2 In. 115.00
Jardiniere, Blue & White, Bell Shape, 19th Century, 16 In. 1554.00
Jug, Cider, Bouquet, Blue & White Borders, Famille Rose, 9 In. 2070.00
Jug, Enameled, Erotic Scene, Courtyard, c.1800, 6 1/4 In. 561.00
Ladle, Blue & White, Flowers, 6-Character Mark, 15 1/2 In. 230.00
Mug, Barrel Shape, Applied Scrolling Handle, Floral Sprays, c.1800, 4 3/4 In. 173.00
Mug, Cylindrical, 2 Vine Handles, 2 Women, At Table, In Courtyard, 1848, 4 In. 187.00
Mug, Figural Reserves, Blue Underglaze, 5 In. 805.00
Mug, Floral Swag, Central Panel, Blue, White, Entwined Handle, 18th Century, 5 In. 1380.00
Mug, Flowers, Bulbous, Cylindrical, Strap Handle, 6 x 4 1/4 In. 345.00
Mug, Flowers, Landscape, Chicken Skin Ground, Entwined Handle, 1700s, 5 1/2 In. 690.00
Mug, Flowers, Polychrome, Barrel Form, 19th Century, 4 1/2 In. 260.00
Mug, Raised Vines, 5 Polychrome Figures, 18th Century, 5 In. 260.00
Necklace, Thousand Sons, Beaded, 14K Gold, Famille Rose, 20th Century, 18 In. 960.00
Pen Box, Ming Style Dragon, Rectangular, Blue & White, 19th Century, 10 In. 546.00
Plaque, Rectangular, Underglaze Blue, Landscape, Figures, c.1800, 14 x 10 In. 980.00
Plate, 3-Masted Ship, American Flag, Green Sea, Gold & Gold Border, 7 1/2 In. 1150.00
Plate, 5-Clawed Dragon, 2 Dragons & Pearls, Blue & White, 10 1/2 In. 1080.00
Plate, Armor, Floral Border, Octagonal, 18th Century 260.00
Plate, Armorial, Cobalt Blue Enameled Band, Flowers, c.1795, 9 3/4 In., Pair 1265.00
Plate, Armorial, Octagonal Rim, Flowers, Chain Band, c.1755, 8 1/2 In. 635.00
Plate, Armorial, Patten, Quartering Hamerton, Gorley, Peake, c.1755, 10 In. 520.00
Plate, Armorial, Reticulated, Flowers, Johnstone, D'Aguilar, c.1810, 8 In., Pair 1495.00
Plate, Blue & White, Flowers, 9 In. 115.00
Plate, Cherry Pickers, Chain Border, c.1750, 9 In. 460.00
Plate, Elias Hasket Derby Service, Hope, Anchor, Spero, 1786, 9 1/4 In. 4200.00
Plate, Famille Rose, Sailing Ships, Sailors, Butterflies, Flowers, 9 1/2 In. 320.00
Plate, Female Nude In Dolphin Chariot, Figures, c.1750, 9 In. 1150.00
Plate, Figures, Landscape, Blue & White, Octagonal, 18th Century, 8 In. 245.00
Plate, Mandarin Center, Kissing Carp Border, Tied Scrolls, 8 1/2 In. 145.00
Plate, Overall Design, Green, Red, Cobalt Blue Flowers, Gilt Accents, 8 1/2 In. 85.00
Plate, Painted, Scenic, Birds, Flowers, Celadon Ground, Early 1800s, 7 In. 115.00
Plate, Peach Medallion, Peonies, Flowering Trees, Famille Rose, 10 1/2 In. 105.00
Plate, Phoenix Medallion, Peonies, Buddhistic Symbols, 18th Century, 13 3/4 In. 430.00
Plate, Polychrome, 3 Figures, Boy Looking At Butterfly, 8 In. 60.00
Plate, Rococo Cartouche, 4 Grisaille Scenes, Inscriptions, c.1770, 11 In., 4 Piece 3600.00
Plate, Seed Form, Apple Green, 9 1/2 In. 169.00
Plate, Ships, Sailors, Butterfly & Flower Border, Famille Rose, 1800s, 9 1/2 In. 316.00
Plate, Soup, Arms Of Dickson, Flower Sprays, Octagonal, 8 1/2 In., Pair 2400.00

Plate, Woman On Rug With Teacup, Being Filled By Man With Teapot, 8 3/4 In. 60.00
Plate Set, Famille Rose, Trees, Flowers, Lotus Petal Border, c.1820, 11 In., 3 Piece 635.00
Platter, Armorial, Arms Of Da Costa, Chain Border, c.1760, 13 In., Pair 9600.00
Platter, Blue & White, Well & Tree, Early 19th Century, 17 In. 359.00
Platter, Cover, Sepia Monogram, Gilt Decorated, Oval, c.1820, 16 In. 805.00
Platter, Dished, Pierced Strainer, Oval, Blue & White, Early 19th Century, 18 In. 420.00
Platter, Famille Rose, Armorial, 1736-95, 11 1/2 In. 865.00
Platter, Famille Rose, Armorial, Chamfered, Rectangular, c.1795, 16 In. 1020.00
Platter, Flower Sprays, Octagonal, Famille Rose, 17 1/2 In. 520.00
Platter, Green Fitzhugh, Chamfered, Rectangular, Floral Sprays, c.1795, 12 In. 450.00
Platter, Green Flower Sprays, 12 1/2 In. 430.00
Platter, Landscape, Buildings, Bridge, Multicolored, Oval, 1700s, 15 1/4 In. 235.00
Platter, Orange Peel Glaze, Painted Rose Designs, Greek Key, 15 x 11 In. 545.00
Platter, Oval, Mandarin Palette, Central Medallion, 14 3/4 In. 2530.00
Platter, Oval, Sprig Border, Crest, 13 1/4 In. 315.00
Platter, Pavilion, River Landscape, Blue & White, c.1800, 12 3/4 In. 290.00
Platter, Roast, Reservoir, Cover, Blue & White, Early 1800s, 15 1/2 In. 1060.00
Platter, Sepia Dragons On Clouds, Green Wave Border, c.1820, 10 1/2 In. 175.00
Pot, Cover, Famille Rose, Handles, 18th Century, 4 1/2 In., Pair 200.00
Punch Bowl, Dragon, Chrysanthemum, Blue & White, c.1900, 15 In. 645.00
Punch Bowl, Famille Rose Exterior, Flower Bouquet Interior, c.1790, 9 In. 2070.00
Punch Bowl, Famille Rose, Figures, Boy, Buffalo, Gilt Ground, c.1785, 15 In. 2280.00
Punch Bowl, Mandarin Pattern, Y-Fret Pattern Ground, Medallion, 11 In. 3220.00
Punch Bowl, Silver, Scalloped Border, Applied Prunus, 1800s, 5 1/2 x 10 In. 1610.00
Punch Bowl, Upswept Rim, Figures, Birds, Flowers, Late 1800s, 5 x 12 In. 635.00
Salt Cellar, Famille Rose, Chamfered, Rectangular, 1 1/2 x 3 1/2 In., Pair 1200.00
Saucer, Flowers, Octagonal, 18th Century, 4 1/4 In. 80.00
Saucer, Mt. Vernon Scene, Hand Painted, Gilt Rim, 1790s, 5 1/2 In. 1580.00
Serving Dish, Cover, Blue & White, Early 19th Century, 16 In. 60.00
Soup, Dish, Peacock, Flower Border, 19th Century, 8 In. 115.00
Spoon Tray, Armorial, Monogram, Diamond Form, c.1800, 7 1/4 In. 240.00
Spoon Tray, Landscape, Blue, White, Gilt Rim, 6-Lobed, 19th Century, 5 In. 230.00
Spoon Tray, Sepia Flowers, 18th Century, 4 3/4 In. 200.00
Tankard, Scenic, Bamboo, Blue Band, Cylindrical, C-Scroll Handle, c.1810, 5 In. 173.00
Tankard, Urn & Flowers, Cylindrical, Strap Handle, c.1780, 5 In.   1150.00
Teapot, Cover, Eagle Decoration, Angular Spout Strap Handle, 10 In. 920.00
Teapot, Cover, Landscape, Drum Form, Blue & White, c.1780, 5 1/2 In. 920.00
Teapot, Dome Cover, Famille Rose, Bulbous Body, Landscape, Figures, 5 1/2 In. 290.00
Teapot, Drum Shape, Flowers, Butterflies, Basketry Carrying Case, 7 In. 160.00
Teapot, Pink, Blue Flowers, Swags, Fruit Finial, 9 1/2 In. 430.00
Tray, Dragons, Peonies, Bamboo Border, Rectangular, Late 1800s, 11 x 14 1/2 In. 690.00
Tureen, Cover, Foo Dog Finial, Flower Branches, 9 1/2 x 12 1/2 x 9 In. 520.00
Tureen, Cover, Oval Platter, Fitzhugh, Blue & White, Early 1800s, 14 In. 180.00
Tureen, Cover, Platter, Blue & White, Rectangular, Early 19th Century, 11 1/2 In. 60.00
Tureen, Cover, Stand, Blue & White, Paneled Oval Shape, 1800s, 17 1/2 In. 2350.00
Tureen, Cover, Tobacco Leaf Pattern, Oval, Scalloped Rim, 1780-90, 11 3/4 In. 4800.00
Tureen, Famille Rose, Pink Roses, Butterflies, Birds, Fruits, Gourds, 15 1/2 x 10 1/2 In. . .   805.00
Tureen, Sauce, Cover, Stand, Oriental Flowers, Rabbits' Heads, c.1775, 7 1/2 In. 3600.00
Tureen, Soup, Cover, 2 Mahouts, Riding Elephants, Flowers, c.1900, 11 In. 1800.00
Tureen, Soup, Cover, Platter, Chinese Hunter, Attendants, 1770-80, 16 3/8 In. 4800.00
Umbrella Stand, Famille Rose, Figures, Flowers, 1900s, 18 In. 259.00
Vase, Bird, Flower, Blue & White, Oval, 18th Century, 3 3/4 In. 140.00
Vase, Cover, Dragons, Flower Form Knop, Loop Handles, Animal Mask, 15 7/8 In. 13800.00
Vase, Cover, Famille Rose, Applied Lion Head Handle, 21 In., Pair 1150.00
Vase, Crackleware, Dragon, Beige Ground, 8 In. 460.00
Vase, Double Gourd, Famille Rose, c.1930, 12 In. 2160.00
Vase, Famille Rose Flask, Animal Figures, Pastel Flowers, c.1870, 10 In. 375.00
Vase, Famille Rose, Birds On Peony Branches, 13 In. 1315.00
Vase, Famille Rose, Bulbous Baluster Shape, Dragons, Foo Dogs, 16 1/2 In., Pair 1150.00
Vase, Famille Rose, Gilt Salamander, Flared Rim, Egg Shape, c.1860, 14 1/2 In. 520.00
Vase, Famille Rose, Peach Tree, Bulbous Body, Elongated Neck, c.1860, 24 In., Pair 1840.00
Vase, Famille Rose, Polychrome, Flowers, 6 1/2 In., 2 Piece 127.00
Vase, Famille Rose, Tapered, Landscape, Oval, 2 Blue Shaped Handles, 13 In. 9560.00

Vase, Famille Verte, Birds, Butterflies, Blossoms, Tapered Square, 20 In. 2629.00
Vase, Famille Verte, Ormolu Mounted, Baluster Shape, 1800s, 10 3/4 In., Pair 2530.00
Vase, Figural Scene, Blue, White, Baluster Shape, 14 1/4 In. 1375.00
Vase, Flowers, Baluster, Scalloped, Flared Rim, 24 3/4 In., Pair 2875.00
Vase, Flowers, Rose Ground, 1800s, 6 In., Pair 115.00
Vase, Flowers, Salmon Red, Gold Ground, Multicolored, Square, 7 1/2 In., Pair 1800.00
Vase, Flying Magpies, Prunus Trees, Black Ground, Famille Verte, 17 1/4 In., Pair 2200.00
Vase, Foo Dog, Butterflies, Bats, Flowers, Blue & White, 11 1/4 In. 2530.00
Vase, Fruit, Flower, Blue & White, 7 1/2 In. 2415.00
Vase, Green Glaze, Scroll, Leaf, Landscapes, 10 In. 570.00
Vase, Landscape, Figures, Blue & White, Transitional, Outswept Rim, c.1660, 10 In. 430.00
Vase, Lotus, Dragon Design, Teardrop, Blue, 11 In. 690.00
Vase, Lotus, Kingfisher, Baluster Form, Red, Blue Underglaze, 19 1/2 In. 3450.00
Vase, Mandarin, Chickenskin, Cover, Foo Dog Finial, Figural Scenes, 14 In. 1380.00
Vase, Molded Flowers, Urn Shape, Late 19th Century, 12 In. 345.00
Vase, Orange Fitzhugh, Compressed Baluster, 1800s, 9 1/8 In. 840.00
Vase, Peach, Bat, Flower & Vine Ground, Flask Form, 10 1/2 In. 660.00
Vase, Persian Flowers, Bulbous Body, Blue & White, Early 1800s, 14 In. 1955.00
Vase, Polychrome Enamel, Flower, Fish, Butterflies, Foo Dog Finial, 20 In., Pair 2990.00
Vegetable, Cover, Orange, Fitzhugh, Gilt Handles & Finial, Oval, Undertray, 8 x 6 1/2 In. . . 920.00
Wine Pot, Lotus, Dragon Handle, Oval, Pink, Green, Lotus Leaf Finial, 5 1/2 In. 259.00

CHINTZ is the name of a group of china patterns featuring an overall
design of flowers and leaves. The design became popular with English
makers about 1928. A few pieces are still being made. The best known
are designs by Royal Winton, James Kent Ltd., Crown Ducal, and
Shelley. Crown Ducal and Shelley are listed in their own sections.

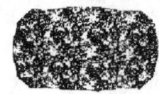

Black Beauty, Teapot, Stacking Sugar, Lord Nelson, 6 In. 490.00
Calico, Pitcher, Royal Crownford, 11 1/2 In. 175.00
Clyde, Teapot, Underplate, Royal Winton, 5 3/4 In. 525.00
DuBarry, Cup & Saucer, James Kent 100.00
Hazel, Tray, Handles, Royal Winton, 11 In. 495.00
Heather, Jam Jar, Cover, Underplate, Lord Nelson, 4 1/2 In. 190.00
Marina, Cup & Saucer, Lord Nelson 130.00
Marina, Vase, Bud, Lord Nelson Pottery 225.00
Marion, Cake Plate, Footed, 8 1/2 In. 375.00
Melody, Plate, Royal Crown, 9 In. 215.00
Old Cottage, Creamer, Royal Winton, 4 In. 215.00
Old Cottage, Trio, Cup, Saucer, Plate, Royal Winton 90.00
Primrose, Cup, Shelley 55.00
Rochelle Ware, Sugar, Cover, James Kent 50.00
Rose, Teapot, Stacking Sugar & Creamer, Lefton 250.00
Rose Time, Cup & Saucer, Lord Nelson 80.00
Rose Time, Salt & Pepper, Tray, Nelsonware 190.00
Royal Brocade, Cup & Saucer, Lord Nelson 58.00
Royal Brocade, Sugar & Creamer, Lord Nelson 175.00
Somerset, Dish, Sweetmeat, Footed, Royal Winton, 3 x 6 In. 160.00
Summertime, Ashtray, Royal Winton 65.00
Summertime, Teapot, Wedgwood 180.00

CHOCOLATE GLASS, sometimes mistakenly called caramel slag,
was made by the Indiana Tumbler and Goblet Company of Greentown,
Indiana, from 1900 to 1903. It was also made at other National Glass
Company factories. Fenton Art Glass Co. also made chocolate glass
from about 1907 to 1915. More recent pieces have been made by
Imperial and others.

Animal Dish, Hen On Nest Cover, Basket Base, Greentown, 5 1/4 In. . . . .*Illus*   415.00
Cactus, Bowl, Scalloped Feet, 8 1/4 In. 50.00
Cactus, Syrup, Dewey Cover, Footed, 6 In. 58.00
Fleur-De-Lis, Celery Vase, 2 Handles, 5 7/8 In. 255.00
Geneva, Bowl, Oval, Footed, 6 x 9 1/4 In. 88.00
Melrose, Compote, 7 In. 145.00
Wild Rose With Bowknot, Saltshaker, 3 1/4 In. 190.00

Chocolate Glass, Animal
Dish, Hen On Nest
Cover, Basket Base,
Greentown, 5 1/4 In.

Christmas, Belsnickle,
Painted, Japan, 3 3/4 In.

CHRISTMAS collectibles include not only Christmas trees and ornaments listed below, but also Santa Claus figures, special dishes, and
even games and wrapping paper. A Belsnickle is a nineteenth-century
figure of Father Christmas. A kugel is an early, heavy ornament made
of thick blown glass, lined with zinc or lead, and often covered with
colored wax. Christmas cards are listed in this section under Greeting
Card. Christmas collectibles may also be listed in the Candy Container
category. Christmas trees are listed in the section that follows.

Angel, Creche, Painted Gesso & Wood, Molded Hair, Wings, 17 In. 2420.00
Baby Jesus, Creche, Painted Gesso & Wood, Glass Eyes, 8 In. 440.00
Bank, Animated Santa Claus, Battery & Coin Operated, Japan, Box, 12 In. 80.00
Bank, Santa Claus, Keystone Nat. Bank, Manheim, Pa., Banthrico, Box, 6 3/4 In. 70.00
Belsnickle, Cardboard, Hand Painted, Stamped, Feather Tree, Germany, 6 In. 220.00
Belsnickle, Cardboard, Hand Painted, Stamped, Red Robe, Feather Sprig, Germany, 7 In. . . 110.00
Belsnickle, Composition, Hand Painted, Gray Robe, Feather Tree, Germany, 7 1/2 In. 415.00
Belsnickle, Composition, Hand Painted, White Robe, Feather Tree, Germany, 9 1/4 In. 770.00
Belsnickle, Composition, Hand Painted, Yellow Robe, Feather Tree, Germany, 4 5/8 In. . . . 415.00
Belsnickle, Composition, Open Coat, Maroon Robe, Germany, 10 In. 3850.00
Belsnickle, Composition, Red, White, Black Paint, Mica Flecks, Feather Tree, 8 3/4 In. . . . 865.00
Belsnickle, Composition, White Mica Base, Feather Tree, Orange, Germany, 10 1/2 In. . . . 2200.00
Belsnickle, Composition, Yellow Robe, Feather Tree Sprig, Germany, 6 In. 220.00
Belsnickle, Green, Hand Painted, Mica Covered, Germany, c.1900, 9 In. 3300.00
Belsnickle, Painted, Japan, 3 3/4 In. . . . . *Illus*   45.00
Belsnickle, Papier-Mache, Blue Robe, Holding Tree, 8 1/2 In. 1045.00
Belsnickle, Papier-Mache, Red Robe, Yellow Highlight, Holding Tree, 9 In. 935.00
Belsnickle, Papier-Mache, White Robe, Holding Tree, 6 In. 745.00
Belsnickle, Papier-Mache, Yellow Robe, Holding Tree, 11 1/8 In. 1020.00
Belsnickle, Red, Cardboard, Mica Covered, 1920s, 9 In. 250.00
Belsnickle, Red, Composition, Germany, c.1900, 6 In. 360.00
Belsnickle, Red, Mica Flecks, Germany, c.1900, 9 In. 275.00
Belsnickle, White, Germany, c.1900, 9 1/2 In. 360.00
Belsnickle, White, Mica Covered, Germany, 9 3/4 In. 605.00
Belsnickle, White, Mica On Coat, Red Chenille Hood Trim, Germany, c.1900, 8 1/2 In. . . . 385.00
Belsnickle, Wood, Hooded Cloak, Penn., 1800s, 26 5/8 x 11 1/2 x 6 In. 1645.00
Belsnickle, Yellow, Gold Flecks, Germany, c.1900, 10 In. 770.00
Book, Night Before Christmas, Moore, McLoughlin, c.1915 . . . . 275.00
Book, Santa Claus & His Works, George Webster, McLoughlin Bros., 1897 . . . . 150.00
Bottle, Figural, Santa Claus, Ground Lip, Aluminum Cap, 1900-25, 3 In. 75.00
Bottle, Figural, Santa Claus, Red Frosted, Ground Lip, Christmas, 1973, 10 3/4 In. 80.00
Bottle, Santa Claus, Original Paint, Smooth Base, Tooled Lip, c.1890-1920, 7 1/2 In. 75.00
Button, Santa Claus, Driving Car, I Am At Bon Marche, Seattle, 1910-12, 1 1/4 In. 100.00
Button, Santa Claus, Flag Cap, Victor & Co., Merry Christmas, 1907-20, 1 1/4 In. 1080.00
Button, Santa Claus, In Chimney, Media Business Men's Association, 1940s, 1 1/4 In. . . . 85.00
Button, Santa Claus, On Roof, Bryant Trott Co., Santa Maria, Calif., c.1930, 1 1/4 In. 75.00
Button & Clicker, Campbell's, Real Christmas Store, 1930s, 1 1/4 & 2 In. 200.00
Candy Containers are listed in the Candy Container category.
Cookie Cutter, Christmas Tree, Aluminum, Loop Handle, 4 x 3 In. 6.00
Cookie Jar, Santa Head, Plastic, Emoire, Tarboro, North Carolina, 1973, 12 In. 100.00

Costume, Santa Claus, Box, 1950s 11.00
Display, Alka-Seltzer, Santa, Tablets In Glass, Cardboard, Stand-Up, Die Cut, 62 x 21 In. .. 55.00
Display, Santa Claus, Airplane, Composition, Wood, Merchants Display & Novelty, 24 In. . 600.00
Display, Santa Claus, Painted Face, Fur Beard, Cloth Suit, Straw Filled, 29 In. 220.00
Doll, Santa Claus, Bisque, Moss Car, Waving American Flag, Germany, c.1900 .... 1650.00
Evergreen Hedge, Feather Tree, Green Wooden Base, Germany, Box, 8 x 8 In. 495.00
Figure, Caroling Gentlemen, Papier-Mache, Marshal Fields Display, 8 In., 45 Piece 220.00
Figure, North Pole Set, Santa's Workshop, Metal, Painted, Germany, 1 To 2 1/2 In. 575.00
Figure, Santa Claus, Clay Face, Cotton Beard, Caribou Fur Trim Suit, Japan, 1930s, 10 In. . 44.00
Figure, Santa Claus, Composition Face, Painted, Felt Clothes, Japan, 14 In. 65.00
Figure, Santa Claus, Composition, Chenille Coat, Cotton Beard, Japan, 1930s, 8 In. 55.00
Figure, Santa Claus, Composition, Painted, Felt Clothes, Basket On Back, Japan, 12 In. ... 100.00
Figure, Santa Claus, Cotton, Papier-Mache Face, Pere Noel Style, 1923, 9 1/2 In. 66.00
Figure, Santa Claus, In Moss Car, Doll, American Flag, Germany, c.1900, 8 x 8 1/2 In. 1650.00
Figure, Santa Claus, In Sleigh, 3 Deer, Candy In Sack, Mica Covered, Japan, 1930s, 12 In. 45.00
Figure, Santa Claus, In Sleigh, Bisque Doll, Tree, Rabbit Fur Beard, 1920s, 9 x 4 3/4 In. .. 66.00
Figure, Santa Claus, In Sleigh, Pipe Cleaners, Japan, 1940 .... 22.00
Figure, Santa Claus, In Sleigh, Reindeer, Celluloid, 4 1/2 In. 11.00
Figure, Santa Claus, In Sleigh, Reindeer, Metal, Painted, 1880s, 1 1/2 x 4 1/2 In. ..... *Illus* 38.00
Figure, Santa Claus, Mask Face, Cloth, Felt Suit, 27 In. 175.00
Figure, Santa Claus, On Skis, Composition, Cardboard, Japan, 1930s, 5 In. 45.00
Figure, Santa Claus, Plastic, Illuminated, Paramount, Box, 1940s, 7 1/4 x 5 x 4 1/2 In. 35.00
Figure, Santa Claus, Store Window Display, Composition, 67 1/2 In. 2090.00
Figure, Santa Claus, Wood, Carved, Natural Finish, 1900s, 26 1/2 In. 290.00
House, Flocked Cardboard, Japan, 13 x 18 In. 175.00
Lamp, Electric, Glass Santa Claus Bulb, 4 1/2 In. 78.00
Lantern, Santa Claus, Milk Glass, Tin Base, Handle, Battery Operated, Japan, 6 1/2 In. ... 55.00
Mold, Chocolate, Father Christmas, Tin, Letang Fils, Paris, Pre World War II, 13 1/2 In. ... 625.00
Mug, Santa Claus, Winking, Porcelain, White, 1950s-60s, 3 In., 4 Piece 30.00
Nativity Scene, Lithograph, 3-D, Die Cut Angels, Germany, c.1900, 16 x 19 x 14 In. 300.00
Nativity Set, Polychrome, Wood Carved, Gilt, Northern Italy, 20th Century, 8 Piece 3680.00
Nodder, Santa Claus, Papier-Mache, Rabbit Fur Trim, Feather Tree, Germany, 1890, 8 In. . 6875.00
Pail, Santa Claus, Sleigh, 6 Pigs, Tin, Gold Color, 1890s, 3 1/4 x 3 1/2 In. 250.00
Pin, Santa Claus, Meet Me At Dunn Tafts, Multicolored, Celluloid, 1 1/4 In. 60.00
Plates that are limited editions are listed in the Collector Plate category or in the correct
factory listing.
Postcard, Happy Christmas Time, Santa Claus, Small Angel, Hold-To-Light, Maileck 230.00
Postcard, Santa Claus, Green Suit, Children, Toy Sack, Mechanical, Head Bobs 430.00
Postcard, Santa Claus, Lighted Tree, Children, Raphael Kirchner 145.00
Puzzle, Santa Claus, On Sleigh, Frame, 1899 .... 300.00
Sign, Santa Claus, Sleigh, Reindeer, Merry Christmas, Cardboard, Germany, 13 x 10 In. ... 80.00
Sign, Santa Claus, Walking, Birds, Merry Christmas, Die Cut, Germany, 14 x 11 In. 70.00
Snow Globe, Glass, Plastic Base, Santa, In Sleigh, Reindeer, 4 Trees, Austria, 7 x 5 In. 30.00
Stocking, Cloth, Art Fabric Mills, Uncut, Frame, 1906, 34 x 22 In. 440.00
Stocking, Net, Unopened, Original Toys, 1950s 55.00
Toothpick Holder, Santa, Red Coat, Yellow Sack, Bisque, 4 In. 35.00
Top, Santa, Dayton Company, Celluloid, 1 1/2 In. 180.00
Toy, Car, Santa Driving, I'm Cookin' With Gas, Plastic, E. Rosen, 5 In. 70.00
Toy, Jolly Santa, Battery Operated, Santa On Skis, Japan, Box, 12 In. 140.00
Toy, Santa Claus, Composition Face, Fur Beard, Fabric Clothes, Squeak, c.1900, 8 In. 358.00
Toy, Santa Claus, Composition, Hand Painted, Red Robe, Roly Poly, Schoenhut, 10 1/2 In. 1980.00
Toy, Santa Claus, Drumming, Eyes Light-Up, Decal, Battery Operated, Alps, 9 1/2 In. 110.00
Toy, Santa Claus, Feather Tree, Rabbit Fur Beard, Basket, Germany, 1920s, 7 In. 330.00
Toy, Santa Claus, Holding Balloons, Bell, Mechanical, Box, Alps, Japan, 1950s 20.00
Toy, Santa Claus, Holding Tree, Molded Sack, Papier-Mache, Japan, 17 In. 275.00
Toy, Santa Claus, Holds Bell, Gifts, Battery Operated, Japan, Box, 8 In. 77.00
Toy, Santa Claus, In Car, Tin Lithograph, Friction, Japan, 5 1/2 In. 80.00
Toy, Santa Claus, On Rotating Globe, Battery Operated, Japan, Box, 15 In. 250.00
Toy, Santa Claus, Sled, Roly Poly Man, Children, Animals, Germany, 1920s, 14 In. 715.00
Toy, Santa Claus, Sleigh & Reindeer, Composition, Painted, Czechoslovakia, 9 In. 220.00
Toy, Santa Claus, Sleigh, Celluloid Reindeer, Cardboard Sleigh, Germany, 1930s, 4 x 8 In. . 140.00
Toy, Santa Claus, Sleigh, Papier-Mache Reindeer, Stamped, Japan, 1930s, 6 In. 45.00
Toy, Santa Claus, Sleigh, Reindeer, Cast Iron, Hubley, 16 In. 2475.00

Christmas, Figure, Santa Claus, In Sleigh,
Reindeer, Metal, Painted, 1880s,
1 1/2 x 4 1/2 In.

Christmas Tree, Light, Church, Pressed
Paper, Cellophane Windows, Open
Back, 3 x 4 1/2 In.

Toy, Santa Claus, Sleigh, Reindeer, Die Cut, Frame, 15 x 20 In. 45.00
Toy, Santa Claus, Sleigh, Reindeer, Wood, Paper Lithograph, R. Bliss, 1890s, 12 In. 1430.00
Toy, Santa Claus, Sleigh, Reindeer, Wood, Paper Lithograph, R. Bliss, c.1890, 17 In. 2750.00
Toy, Santa Claus, Split Log Sled, Toys, 3 Composition Deer, Mica Snow, Germany, 24 In. . .   495.00
Toy, Santa Claus, Velvet Suit, White Belt, Boots, Cotton Beard, Plush, 1950s, 15 In. 20.00
Toy, Santa Claus, Waddler, Tin, Windup, Wells, Box, 5 In. 248.00
Toy, Sparkler, Santa Claus, Tin, 6 In. 165.00
Toy, St. Nicholas, Tin Lithograph, Schuco, Germany, c.1930, 3 3/4 In. 530.00
Trade Stimulator, Rocking Santa's Head, Chimney, Clockwork, 19 1/2 In. 1650.00
Wristwatch, Rudolph Reindeer, Chrome Case, Red Band, Ingersoll, Original Box, 1947 . .   400.00

CHRISTMAS TREES made of feathers and Christmas tree decorations of all types are popular with collectors. The first decorated
Christmas tree in America is claimed by many states, including Pennsylvania (1747), Massachusetts (1832), Illinois (1833), Ohio (1838),
and Iowa (1845). The first glass ornaments were imported from Germany about 1860. Dresden ornaments were made about 100 years ago
of paper and tinsel. Manufacturers in the United States were making
ornaments in the early 1870s. Electric lights were first used on a
Christmas tree in 1882. Character light bulbs became popular in the
1920s, bubble lights in the 1940s, twinkle bulbs in the 1950s, plastic
bulbs by 1955. In this book a Christmas light is a holder for a candle
used on the tree. Other forms of lighting include light bulbs. Other
Christmas memorabilia is listed in the preceding section.

Bells, Of St. Nicholas, Electric, Box, 1957 . . . .   35.00
Bottle Brush, Brown, Green, White, Red Wooden Base, 6 1/2 In. 30.00
Bubble Lights, 9 Lights, Base, 19 In. 80.00
Bubble Lights, Holders, Noma Electric Light Co., 1940s 400.00
Color Wheel, Blue, Green, Red, Yellow, 10 In. 45.00
Feather, Composition Berries, Taped Dowel Rod Trunk, 34 In. 345.00
Feather, Green, Wooden Base, Germany, 38 In. 330.00
Feather, Tree Fence & Stand, Electrical Wiring, 1930s 110.00
Garland, Red & Silver, Aluminum Foil, 108 In. 30.00
Garland, Silver Aluminum Foil, 144 In. 30.00
Glo-Lite, Glass Decorations, Base, 17 In. 22.00
Glo-Lite, Musical Stand, 22 In. 35.00
Holder, Santa, Red Coat, Snow Covered Mountains, Cast Iron, c.1900 . . . .   385.00
Kugel, Cobalt Blue, Germany, 7 In. 120.00
Light, Amber, Diamond, Pain Patent 1882, Anchor, Crown, Sheared, Ground Lip, 3 5/8 In.   95.00
Light, Amber, Harlequin, Sheared & Ground Lip, England, c.1890, 3 3/8 In. 110.00
Light, Amethyst, 12-Diamond, Rolled Lip, Pontil, England, 2 5/8 In. 395.00
Light, Blue Aqua, Pineapple, Sheared Lip, 4 1/8 In. 95.00
Light, Church, Pressed Paper, Cellophane Windows, Open Back, 3 x 4 1/2 In. . . . . *Illus*   15.00
Light, Cobalt Blue, Cluster Of Grapes, Hearn Wright & Co., London, England, 3 7/8 In. . .   130.00
Light, Cranberry Red, 15 Broken Ribs, Outward Rolled Lip, Pontil, 3 1/4 In. 260.00
Light, Diamond, Sheared & Ground Lip, Hanging Wire, Houchin Mfg Co, 3 In. 60.00
Light, Emerald Green, Hobnail, Tooled Lip, England, 1880s-1910s, 3 3/4 In. 170.00

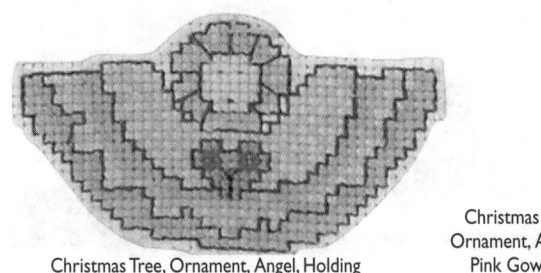

Christmas Tree, Ornament, Angel, Holding
Heart, Cross-Stitch, Velvet, 2 In.

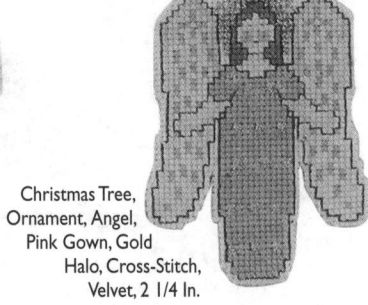

Christmas Tree,
Ornament, Angel,
Pink Gown, Gold
Halo, Cross-Stitch,
Velvet, 2 1/4 In.

Light, Green, 16 Vertical Ribs, Rolled Lip, Pontil, England, 2 1/2 In.	95.00
Light, Light Blue Green, 16 Vertical Ribs, Rolled Lip, Pontil, England, 2 1/2 In.	90.00
Light, Milk Glass, Diamond, Sheared, Ground Lip, Hanging Wire, Houchin Mfg Co, 3 In.	90.00
Light, Pink Amethyst, 15 Ribs, Sheared & Flared Out Lip, Pontil, England, 2 3/4 In.	400.00
Light, Purple Amethyst, Diamond, Rolled Lip, Pontil, England, 2 3/4 In.	252.00
Light, Purple Amethyst, Pointed, Sheared & Ground Lip, England, c.1880, 3 3/8 In.	250.00
Light, Purple, Diamond, Rolled Lip, Pontil, England, 1870-90, 2 7/8 In.	172.00
Light, Ruby Red, Diamond, Ground Lip, 3 5/8 In.	175.00
Light, Sapphire Blue, Diamond, Rolled Lip, Pontil, England, 1870-90, 3 In.	120.00
Light, Sapphire Blue, Diamond, Rolled Lip, Pontil, Hanging Wire, England, 3 In.	95.00
Light, Teal Green, Diamond, Rolled Lip, Pontil, England, 3 1/2 In.	245.00
Light, Yellow Amber, Diamond, Rosette Pattern, Sheared Lip, 4 In.	75.00
Light, Yellow Amber, Harlequin, Sheared & Ground Lip, England, c.1890, 3 3/8 In.	112.00
Light, Yellow Olive, Diamond, Rolled Lip, Pontil, England, 1870-90, 2 5/8 In.	105.00
Light, Yellow Olive, Diamond, Rolled Lip, Pontil, England, 1870-90, 3 1/2 In.	140.00
Light Cover Set, 5 Colors, Plastic, Flowers, 1950-60, 3 In., 16 Piece	50.00
Light Cover Set, Flower Shape, Paper, Silver, Blue, 1940s, 3 In., 3 Piece	30.00
Light Cover Set, Village, Houses, Churches, Plastic, 2 3/4 & 5 1/4 In., 7 Piece	30.00
Light Set, 12 Disney Characters, Mazda, Box, British Thompson Houston Co., 1950s	110.00
Light Set, Bambi & Friends, Mazda, Box, British Thompson Houston Co., 1950s	140.00
Light Set, Flying Saucer Bubble Lites, Noma, Metal Clips, Box, 1940s	66.00
Light Set, Glo-Ray, Noma, Box, 1940s	20.00
Light Set, Mickey Mouse & Friends, Mazda, Box, British Thompson Houston Co., 1950s	175.00
Ornament, Angel, Bell, Playing Accordion, Bisque, Goebel, Germany, 1979	25.00
Ornament, Angel, Bisque, Jointed Body, Yellow Crepe Paper Dress, 6 In.	65.00
Ornament, Angel, Black Face, Germany, Clip-On, 4 In.	99.00
Ornament, Angel, Holding Heart, Cross-Stitch, Velvet, 2 In. *Illus*	2.00
Ornament, Angel, Holds Horn, Composition, Wax, Spun Glass Wings, c.1900, 8 In.	550.00
Ornament, Angel, In Chariot, Dresden Wings, Sebnitz, Germany, 4 3/4 x 4 In.	138.00
Ornament, Angel, On Cloud, Balloon, Wire Wrapped	27.00
Ornament, Angel, On Cloud, Scrap Face, 4 1/2 In.	33.00
Ornament, Angel, On Lyre, Scrap	38.00
Ornament, Angel, Pink Gown, Gold Halo, Cross-Stitch, Velvet, 2 1/4 In. *Illus*	3.00
Ornament, Angel, Scrap, Balloon, Wire Wrapped	35.00
Ornament, Baby's First, Teddy Bear On Rocking Horse, Lenox, Box, 1989	69.00
Ornament, Balloon, Wire Wrapped, Scrap Angel, Stamped, Germany, 6 In.	80.00
Ornament, Bear, Holding Stick, Germany, 4 In.	70.00
Ornament, Belsnickle, Feather Sprig, Gold, Hand Painted, Germany, 1910, 4 In.	176.00
Ornament, Belsnickle, Red Brown, Germany, 1910, 2 In.	220.00
Ornament, Bird, Blown Glass, Pink Beak, Gold Body, Spring Leg Attached To Clip	30.00
Ornament, Blown Glass, Clear Blue Glass, 3 Stripes, 1940s	35.00
Ornament, Boat, Wax Figure, Wire, Cotton Padding, Sebnitz, Germany, 4 x 3 In.	550.00
Ornament, Boy Clown In Moon, Glass, Germany, 3 1/2 In.	120.00
Ornament, Bubble Light Bulbs, Red, Blue, Yellow, 4 1/2 In., 4 Piece	40.00
Ornament, Cat, Sitting, Blown Glass, Pink, 4 1/4 In.	660.00
Ornament, Clown, Blown Glass, Chenille Arms, 5 1/4 In.	415.00
Ornament, Clown, Blown Glass, Hand Painted Face, 4 3/4 In.	32.00

Ornament, Double Balloon, Scrap, Purple Glass, Wire Wrap, 5 In. 120.00
Ornament, Eagle, Flying, Pressed Cardboard, Dresden, 5 3/4-In. Wingspan 358.00
Ornament, Fairy Head, Blown Glass, Flower Petal Hat, 3 3/4 In. 248.00
Ornament, Grape Cluster, Mercury Glass, Green, Germany, 4 3/4 In. 85.00
Ornament, Grape Cluster, Silver Glass, Silver Frost Leaf, East Germany, 3 In. 30.00
Ornament, Green Grape, 4 1/2 In. 335.00
Ornament, Hansom Cab, Pressed Cardboard, Dresden, Germany, 4 1/2 In. 1210.00
Ornament, Heart, Butterfly, Lacquered, Pastel, 1910-19, 3 1/4 x 2 1/2 In. 35.00
Ornament, Horn Of Plenty, Hand Blown Glass, Embossed, 4 1/2 In. 80.00
Ornament, Horse & Rider, Pressed Cardboard, Hand Painted, Dresden, 3 3/4 In. 495.00
Ornament, Hot Air Balloon, Lead Basket, Columbian Air Ship, 1892 Patent, 5 In. 550.00
Ornament, Indian Bust, Germany, 4 In. 300.00
Ornament, Jack-In-The-Box, Tree Trimmer, Yesteryears, Hallmark, 4 1/4 In. 105.00
Ornament, Kitten In Slipper, Blown Glass, White, Red, Gold, 3 3/4 In. 65.00
Ornament, Lantern Shape, Snowmen, Tree, Japan, 5 1/2 In. 22.00
Ornament, Mandolin, Wire Wrapped, Germany, 6 In. 35.00
Ornament, Mary Pickford, Blown Glass, Annealed Legs, Golden Hair, 4 1/4 In. 665.00
Ornament, Owl, Kugel, Heavy Glass, Rose, Silver, Green, 4 1/4 x 3 1/4 In. 275.00
Ornament, Parrot In Ring, Stamped Cardboard, Dresden, 3 5/8 In. 275.00
Ornament, Pea Pod, Hand Stamped Cardboard, Gold Finish, Dresden, 4 1/2 In. 248.00
Ornament, Pig, Stamped Cardboard, Gray, Beige, Dresden, Germany, 3 1/2 In. 775.00
Ornament, Pony, Cotton, Glass Eyes, Wooden Legs, Silver Buckle, Germany, 2 1/2 In. . . . 66.00
Ornament, Poodle, Stamped Cardboard, Germany, 3 3/8 In. 495.00
Ornament, Poulter Pigeon, Stamped Cardboard, Dresden, 3 In. 110.00
Ornament, Red Glass Bead Snake, 11 3/4 In. 295.00
Ornament, Reindeer, Celluloid, Garnet Rhinestone Eyes, Ribbon, 1900-30, 4 1/2 In. 45.00
Ornament, Rifle, Stamped Cardboard, Ribbon Strap, Dresden, 6 1/4 In. 385.00
Ornament, Santa Claus, Composition Head, Cardboard, Wood, Germany, 6 1/2 In. 360.00
Ornament, Santa Claus, In Oak Leaf, Germany, 3 In. 45.00
Ornament, Santa Claus, Pipe Cleaner Body & Hat, Paper Face, Early 1900s, 3 In. 40.00
Ornament, Santa Claus, Pipe Cleaner Legs, Composition Boots, Germany, 5 In. 11.00
Ornament, Santa Claus, Scrap Face, Sprig Tree, Crepe Paper, Cape, Germany, 6 In. 245.00
Ornament, Santa Claus, Tree, Blown Glass, Czechoslovakia, 4 3/4 In. 38.00
Ornament, Santa Claus, Tree, Blown Glass, Poland, 1950s, 3 x 5 In. 25.00
Ornament, Santa Claus, Tree, Mushrooms, Composition, Cardboard, Japan, 3 1/2 In. 65.00
Ornament, Santa Claus, Yellow, Composition, 3 In. 250.00
Ornament, Santa's Fire Engine, Here Comes Santa, No. 7, Hallmark, 1985, 3 In. 95.00
Ornament, Snowman, Cotton, Felt, Paper, Buttons, Scarf, Broom, 2 3/4 In. 30.00
Ornament, Snowman, Papier-Mache, Pipe Cleaner, Painted, Ribbon Scarf, 4 In. 38.00
Ornament, Soldier, Spun Cotton, Composition, Crepe Paper Clothes, Cardboard, 5 In. 20.00
Ornament, Squirrel, Holding Pinecone, Cotton, Germany, 4 In. 415.00
Ornament, Steamship, Cotton, Paper, Wire, Sebnitz, Germany, 5 1/2 In. 770.00
Ornament, Swiss Chalet, Stamped Cardboard, Silver Finish, Dresden, 1 1/2 In. 330.00
Ornament, Tinsel Scrap, Angels, Early 1900s 20.00
Ornament Set, Blue, Silver, Premier Glass Works, New Jersey, Box, 12 Piece 30.00
Ornament Set, Pink, Blue, Green, Black Glitter, Shiny Brite, 9 Piece 45.00
Ornament Set, Shiny Brite, Stained Glass, Space Balls, Box 70.00
Stand, 3-Footed, Albrecht, North Brothers, Early 1900s, 10 In. 65.00
Stand, Cast Iron, 3 Trees On Each Side, 1992, 14 In. 29.00
Stand, Cast Iron, Embossed Scrolls, Buildings, Cherub Turn Screws, Square, 14 In. 95.00
Stand, Cone Shape, Metal, Santa, Chimney, Sleigh, Light-Up, Noma, 1928, 10 x 14 In. . . . 20.00
Stand, Feather Tree, Wood Slat Fence, Square, 13 x 16 In. 110.00
Stand, Santa, Embossed Base, Cast Iron, Germany, 9 1/2 In. 440.00
Stand, Santa, Sleigh, Reindeer, Tin Lithograph, Cast Iron, Noma, 14 In.-Diam. 145.00
Topper, Angel, Bisque Head, Paper Dress, Wings, 9 In. 90.00
Topper, Angel, Spun Glass, Angel Hair, 1950s 90.00
Topper, Santa Claus, Multicolored Globe, Glass Cane, Blown Glass, Box, 4 In. 275.00

CHROME items in the Art Deco style became popular in the 1930s. Collectors are most interested in high-style pieces made by the Connecticut firms of Chase Brass and Copper Company, and Manning Bowman.

Barware, Shaker, 6 Glasses, Bakelite Top, Blue Moon Doric, Chase, 7 Piece 600.00

Barware Set, Server, 14 Piece 69.00
Cocktail Cup Set, 6 Piece 150.00
Cocktail Set, Bowling Pin, Maple, Shaker, 6 Goblets, 15 3/4 In. 1315.00
Cocktail Set, Glass, 9 Piece 95.00
Cocktail Set, Shake A Leg, Frosted, Silvered Glass, Martini Glass, c.1937, 6 Piece 5736.00
Cocktail Shaker, Ruby Glass Leg, Tray & Cups, 1937, 5 Piece 2900.00
Picnic Set, Canister, Trays, Cups, Saucers, Wicker Case, Drew & Sons, London, 13 In. . . . 176.00

CIGAR STORE FIGURES of carved wood or cast iron were used as advertisements in front of the Victorian cigar store. The carved figures are now collected as folk art. They range in size from counter type, about three feet, to over eight feet high.

Highlander, Carved, Painted, Countertop, c.1850, 24 1/2 x 9 1/2 In. 7200.00
Indian, Brown, Black Trim, Wesley's Store, Dover, N.J., c.1925, 50 In. 2995.00
Indian, Carved, Painted, 43 In. 5750.00
Indian, Chief, Buffalo On Chest, Drum Base, Hand Carved, 1900-50, 48 In. 805.00
Indian, Chief, Samuel Robb, New York City, 57 In. 29000.00
Indian, Full Headdress, Holding Cigar & Hatchet, Composition, 73 In. 1320.00
Indian, Headdress, Drum Base, Hand Carved, c.1950, 73 x 14 In. 2070.00
Indian, Maiden, Thomas Brooks, 74 In. 49000.00
Indian, Squaw, Wood, Cross Around Neck, Wood Base, 75 x 20 In. 5500.00
Indian, Standing, Raised Arm, Pine, Old Virginia Cheroots, John Cromwell 23000.00
Indian, Woman, Holding Tobacco Leaves, Metal, Feather Headdress, 28 x 8 In. 4400.00
Indian, Woman, Wood, Multicolored, 1800s, Countertop, 27 1/2 In. . . . . .4994.00 to 6756.00

CINNABAR is a vermilion or red lacquer. Pieces are made with tens to hundreds of thicknesses of the lacquer that is later carved. Most cinnabar was made in the Orient.

Vase, Dragon, 5 Claws, Rectangular, 12 In. 400.00
Vase, Figures, Landscape, Double Gourd, 9 In., Pair 2875.00
Vase, Landscape, Lotus, Hexagonal, Chinese, 1800s, 10 1/4 In. 234.00

CIVIL WAR mementos are important collectors' items. Most of the pieces are military items used from 1861 to 1865. Be sure to avoid any explosive munitions.

Artificial Leg, Wood, Hand Made, Brass Fitted Bottom, Leather Lace 1650.00
Battle Rattle, Oak, 11 x 9 In. 40.00
Bayonet, Scabbard, c.1860, 22 1/2 In. 375.00
Blanket, Saddle, Wool, Leather 1210.00
Bowie Knife, Kenansville, N.C., c.1860, 19 In. 345.00
Broadside, Grand Rally, Columbia City, December 10, 1863, Frame, 11 1/2 x 14 In. 605.00
Candlestick, Tin, Wire, Shield Shaped Support, Painted, Red, White, Blue, c.1863, 9 In. . . 1295.00
Canteen, Model 1859, Flat Sides, Union, Soldier's Name Scratched On, Cover, Sling 405.00
Canteen, Tin, Drum Shape Body, 3 Strap Hoops, c.1860, 9 x 6 In. 635.00
Canteen, Tin, Pattern 1858, Round Body, Spout, 3 Strap Loops, Leather Strap, 9 x 8 In. . . 115.00
Cartridge Box, Leather, Union, Brass Fastener, Crossman Maker, Newark, N.J., c.1863 . . . 75.00
Cartridge Pouch, Leather, Brass Fastener, Copper Rivet Belt Loop, 7 x 4 1/2 x 3 In. 55.00
Cartridge Pouch, Leather, Marked 13, Brass Fastener, 7 x 4 1/2 x 3 In. 46.00
Coat, Officers, Wool, Navy Blue, WHK Initials, Eagle Buttons, Epaulets, Horstmann Co. . 575.00
Comb, Cow Horn, 3 In. 35.00
Crutches, Confederate, c.1863, 51 In., Pair 90.00
Cup, Collapsible, Pewter, Tin Case 50.00
Dice, Bone, Drilled & Blackened Spots 30.00
Drum, Painted, Eagle, Banner, Reg. U.S. Infantry, R. Mein, Drumsticks, 17 In. 7500.00
Drum, Regimental, Wood Frame, Calfskin Head, Photograph, c.1862, 14 5/8 x 18 In. 1530.00

Civil War, Sword, Cavalry Saber, Roby, Wire, Leather, Iron Scabbard, 1860, 35 In.

Civil War, Sword, Staff & Field Officers, Sharkskin Grip, Gilt Twisted Wire, 1862, 32 In.

Drum, Third Maine Reg. Infantry, Eagle, J & G Dennison, Freeport, 15 x 16 In. 3165.00
Holsters, Pommel, For 1851 Navy Size Revolvers, Black Leather, 13 1/2 In. 1440.00
Knife, Side, Confederate, Iron Blade, D-Guard, Curved, Stag Handle, 14-In. Blade 230.00
Microscope, Presentation, Dr. Thomas Carroll, Brass, Mahogany Case, 1863 . . . . 2350.00
Pipe, Handmade, Eagle, 6th Corps Badge, Orrin Dolly, Co., C-121, N.Y.V. 950.00
Pocket Watch, Texas United Confederate Veteran, Inscription, Nickel Case, Elgin 865.00
Pouch, Medics, Leather, Stamped US, Brass Fittings, Belt 120.00
Saber, Confederate, c.1860, 35-In. Blade, 40 1/2 In. 750.00
Saber, Scabbard, Ames, U.S., M.M., 1864 . . . . 825.00
Shield, Wood, Painted, G.W. Morgan, Co. E., 53d. Mass., 1862-65, 13 x 11 In. 4200.00
Sword, Artillery, Etched Oak Leaf & Acorn, Ames, Springfield, 24 In. 935.00
Sword, Cavalry Saber, Roby, Wire, Leather, Iron Scabbard, 1860, 35 In. . . . . *Illus* 2415.00
Sword, Confederate, Brig. Gen. Gracie, Presentation, Scabbard, c.1861, 30 1/4-In. Blade . . 10350.00
Sword, Confederate, Foot Artillery, Hour Glass Blade, Double Edged, 18 5/8-In. Blade . . . 1380.00
Sword, Confederate, Foot Officer's, Snakes, Leather Covered Grip, DeWitt, Ga., 36 In. . . . 4600.00
Sword, Light Cavalry, Model 1860, Brass Guard, Scabbard, Ames, 1864, 34 1/2-In. Blade . 560.00
Sword, Light Cavalry, U.S. Model, Mansfield & Lamb, 1864, 42 1/2 In. 380.00
Sword, Militia, Straight Blade, Etched, Brass Scabbard, 30-In. Blade 2530.00
Sword, Officer's, Presentation, Thos. Hay, Brass Scabbard, France, c.1864 . . . . 2875.00
Sword, Officer's, Scabbard, Hanger, Etched, 36 1/2 In. 605.00
Sword, Presentation, Model 1850, Dennis Flynn, Scabbard, Tiffany, 32-In. Blade 5175.00
Sword, Presentation, Model 1850, Lt. Col. Charles Hammond, Scabbard, 31-In. Blade 4465.00
Sword, Staff & Field Officers, Sharkskin Grip, Gilt Twisted Wire, 1862, 32 In. . . . . . . *Illus* 13800.00

CKAW, see Dedham category.

CLARICE CLIFF was a designer who worked in several English fac-
tories after the 1920s, including A.J. Wilkinson Ltd., Wilkinson's
Royal Staffordshire Pottery, Newport Pottery, and Foley Pottery. She is
best known for her brightly colored Art Deco designs, including the
"Bizarre" line. She died in 1972. Reproductions have been made by
Wedgwood.

Bizarre, Flowerpot, Multicolored Geometric Design, Backstamp, 7 3/4 In. 940.00
Bizarre, Latona, Bowl, Treed Landscape, Backstamp, c.1930, 16 3/8 In. 1645.00
Bizarre, Lotus, Pitcher, 11 1/2 In. 230.00
Bizarre, Nuage, Biscuit Jar, Cover, Square, Multicolored Flowers, c.1930, 5 In. 2115.00
Bizarre, Pitcher, Geometric, 11 3/4 In. 490.00
Bizarre, Vase, Leaves, Multicolored, Backstamp, 20th Century, 7 In. 880.00
Blue Chintz, Bizarre, Jug, Ribbed Body, Multicolored, c.1930, 11 5/8 In. 1880.00
Celtic Harvest, Jug, Newport Pottery, c.1940, 11 In. 140.00
Fantasque, Vase, Flowers, Multicolored, Backstamp, 1900s, 7 3/4 In. 1880.00
Plate, Flower, Brown Stem, Cream Ground, Marked, 8 1/4 x 10 1/4 In. 400.00
Tea Service, Painted, Glazed, Coffeepot, Creamer, Sugar, Cups, Saucer 600.00

CLEWELL ware was made in limited quantities by Charles Walter
Clewell of Canton, Ohio, from 1902 to 1955. Pottery was covered with
a thin coating of bronze, then treated to make the bronze turn different
colors. Pieces covered with copper, brass, or silver were also made.
Mr. Clewell's secret formula for blue patinated bronze was burned
when he died in 1965.

Basket, Copper Clad, Handle, 5 x 5 In. 590.00
Bowl, Copper Clad, Footed, Etched, 2 3/4 x 5 In. 200.00
Vase, Bud, Copper Clad, Flared, Footed, Verdigris Patina, 8 In. 295.00
Vase, Copper Clad, 12 1/2 In. 1645.00
Vase, Copper Clad, Bronze & Verdigris Patina, Spherical, 9 x 7 1/2 In. 2703.00
Vase, Copper Clad, Bulbous, 4 1/2 x 4 1/2 In. 295.00
Vase, Copper Clad, Bulbous, Verdigris Patina, 11 1/4 x 10 1/2 In. 2585.00
Vase, Copper Clad, Original Patina, Bulbous, Marked, 3 1/2 In. 265.00
Vase, Copper Clad, Original Patina, Flared Rim, Marked, 8 1/2 In. 470.00
Vase, Copper Clad, Original Patina, Shouldered, Marked, 4 1/2 In. 380.00
Vase, Copper Clad, Original Patina, Swollen, Footed, Marked, 7 In. 820.00
Vase, Copper Clad, Original Patina, Tapered, 8 1/2 In. 620.00
Vase, Copper Clad, Ruffled Rim, 2 Handles, 5 x 3 1/4 In. 145.00
Vase, Copper Clad, Shouldered, Patina, Marked, 4 In. 520.00

Vase, Copper Clad, Tapered Shape, Incised Mark, 13 In. 3100.00
Vase, Painted Copper Clad, 5 1/2 In. 320.00
Vase, Painted Copper Clad, 6 5/8 In. 920.00
Vase, Painted Copper Clad, Squat Shape, 3 1/2 In. 460.00
Vase, Pottery, Copper Clad, Green & Red Patina, 2 Handles, 6 In. 1175.00
Vase, Pottery, Copper Clad, Green & Red Patina, 9 1/2 In. 1530.00

CLEWS pottery was made by George Clews & Co. of Brownhills Pottery, Tunstall, England, from 1906 to 1961. Additional pieces may be
listed in the Flow Blue category.

Gravy Boat, Repose In The Woods, Don Quixote Series, Blue Transfer, 8 In. 380.00
Plate, Hunting View, Blue Transfer, c.1825, 9 1/4 In. 200.00
Plate, Landing Of General Lafayette, Blue, 9 In. 248.00
Plate, States Border, America & Independence, 11 In. 400.00
Plate, States, Peace & Plenty, Early 1800s, 8 3/4 In. 200.00
Platter, America & Independence, Dock, Building Ships, 18 1/2 In. 2300.00
Platter, Landing Of Lafayette, Blue, Cobridge, England 1400.00
Platter, Landing Of Lafayette, Blue, Early 1900s, 19 In. 1410.00

CLIFTON POTTERY was founded by William Long in Clifton, New
Jersey, in 1905. He worked there until 1909 making lines including
Crystal Patina and *Clifton Indian Ware*. Clifton Pottery made art pot-
tery until 1911 and then concentrated on wall and floor tile. By 1914
the name had been changed to Clifton Porcelain and Tile Company.
Another firm, Chesapeake Pottery, sold majolica marked *Clifton Ware*.

Humidor, Incised, Painted Wave Design, Terra-Cotta Ground, c.1907, 5 1/2 In. 100.00
Vase, Bottle Form, Buff To Celadon Green, Incised Clifton 1905, 10 1/2 In. 850.00
Vase, Bulbous, Crystal Patina, 1906, 6 1/4 In. 325.00
Vase, Crystal Patina, 4 Buttressed Handles, Celadon Matte Crystalline Glaze, 14 x 9 In. . . . 2940.00
Vase, Squat, Green Glaze, Incised Mark, No. 108, 1/2 x 4 In. 440.00
Vase, Squat, Green Matte Glaze, Raised Stylized Design, Marked, 1906, 4 In. 175.00

CLOCKS of all types have always been popular with collectors. The
eighteenth-century tall case, or grandfather's clock, was designed to
house a works with a long pendulum. In 1816, Eli Terry patented a
new, smaller works for a clock, and the case became smaller. The clock
could be kept on a shelf instead of on the floor. By 1840, coiled springs
were used and even smaller clocks were made. Battery-powered electric clocks were made in the 1870s. A garniture set can include a clock
and other objects displayed on a mantel.

Advertising, A&P Coffee, White Metal, Black Numbers, Time To Change To, 1950s 275.00
Advertising, Bell Of Bourbon, Cast Iron, Pot Metal, Bell Shape, 12 x 13 In. 330.00
Advertising, Black Cat Shoe Dressing, Superba Polish, Tin, Nonsuch, Toronto, 23 x 17 In. 7700.00
Advertising, Buffalo, New York, Say It In Neon, Stainless Bezel, c.1940, 33 In. 690.00
Advertising, Buick, Authorized Service, V8, Red, White, Blue, Double Bubble, Round . . . 2800.00
Advertising, Canada Dry, Red, Green, Gold, Double Bubble, Pocket Watch Attachment . . . 1100.00
Advertising, Cities Service, Light-Up, Pam, 14 1/2 In. 330.00
Advertising, Dayton Tires, Horse Head, Light-Up, 15 In. 110.00
Advertising, Dr Pepper, Blue, Red & Pink Numbers, Glass Lens, Square, 15 1/2 In. 80.00
Advertising, Dr Pepper, Distinctively Different, Wood Grain, Square, 15 1/4 In. 100.00
Advertising, Dyola Dyes, Regulator, Oak Case, 34 x 19 In. 495.00
Advertising, Ever-Ready Safety Razor, Wood, Repainted, Bald Man Shaving, 27 In. 904.00
Advertising, Evinrude, Authorized Parts & Service, Red, Yellow, Blue, Double Bubble . . . 2090.00
Advertising, Fairacres Superior Ice Cream, Grand Island, Neb., Late 1940s, 16 In. . . 200.00 to 275.00
Advertising, Firestone, Guaranteed Brake Service, Red, White, Double Bubble, Round . . . 2310.00
Advertising, Ford Parts, Service, Cars, Trucks, Tractors, Double Bubble, Round 3080.00
Advertising, Gem Damaskeene Razor, Man Shaving, Holding Baby, Wood, c.1910, 24 In. . . 1760.00
Advertising, Gem Damaskeene Razor, Wood, New Pendulum, 27 x 22 3/4 In. 2420.00
Advertising, Hastings Piston Rings, Man Holding Ring, Double Bubble, Round 2750.00
Advertising, Hudson Sales & Service, Neon, 20 In. 1980.00
Advertising, Iroquois Beer & Ale, Indian, Metal Case, Square, Electric, 14 1/2 In. 159.00
Advertising, Kist, Drink Kist, Great Taste, Light-Up, Glass, 15 x 15 In. 165.00
Advertising, Lincoln Mercury, Red, White, Black, 15 In. 2100.00

Advertising, Mapl-Flake, Wheat Bran, Tin Lithograph, Battle Creek, 1902, 9 x 6 1/2 In. . . . 2970.00
Advertising, Mohawk Tires, Neon, Octagonal, 18 1/2 In. 990.00
Advertising, Monroe Shock Absorbers, Load Levelers, Bubble, Light-Up, 15 In. 550.00
Advertising, Mopar Parts & Accessories, Yellow, Red, Black, White, 15 In. 1430.00
Advertising, Oldsmobile Service, Blue, Yellow, White, Double Bubble, Round 2750.00
Advertising, Olga Pocahontas Coal, Red, Yellow, Plastic, 15 In. 247.00
Advertising, Orange Crush, Carbonated Beverage, 15 In. 660.00
Advertising, OshKosh B'Gosh, Neon, Octagonal, c.1938, 19 In. 315.00
Advertising, Pearl Beer, Octagon, Neon, 18 1/2 In. . . . . .358.00 to 468.00
Advertising, Phillips 66, First-Class Service, Red, White, Black, Double Bubble, Round . . 2530.00
Advertising, Poll-Parrot Shoes, Parrot On Perch, For Boys, For Girls 2750.00
Advertising, R.C. Royal Crown Cola, Blue Numbers, Glass Lens, Square, 15 1/4 In. 110.00
Advertising, Reading Premium, Friendly Beer For Modern People, Round, 15 In. 155.00
Advertising, Reed's Tonic, Malaria, Indigestion, Gilt Edge, 24 x 10 In. 3025.00
Advertising, Sauers Extract, Regulator, Wood Case, Reverse Painted Glass, 36 In. 1469.00
Advertising, Simmons Liver Regulator, Take In Time, Cast Metal Horseshoe Frame, 7 In. . . 110.00
Advertising, Squirt, Boy, Telechron, 15 In. 1430.00
Advertising, The Times, Twice As Many Pictures, Chicago's Picture Newspaper, 15 In. . . . 88.00
Advertising, Vernors, Deliciously Different, Box, 18 x 18 In. 44.00
Advertising, Whistle Soda, Thirsty?, Just Whistle, Tin, Orange, Blue, Electric, 15 In. 55.00
Alarm, Bugs Bunny On Dial, Metal, Glass, Arm With Carrot Moves, c.1955, 5 x 4 In. 220.00
Alarm, Mattel, Metal, Glass, Black Face On Dial, K.C. Co., Germany, 1925, 4 x 6 In. 1098.00
Anniversary, Mahogany Columns, Red Marble Case, France, c.1890, 17 In. 1790.00
Ansonia, Belgium, Shelf, Iron Case, Winged Griffins, 8-Day, Time & Strike, c.1904, 11 In. 448.00
Ansonia, Carriage, 30-Hour, Time & Strike, Alarm, c.1904, 7 1/2 In. 235.00
Ansonia, Carriage, Petite, Cast Metal, 1-Day, Time Only, c.1904, 4 In. 100.00
Ansonia, Chester, Shelf, 8-Day, Time & Strike, Enameled Iron Case, c.1904, 10 1/2 In. . . . 225.00
Ansonia, Crystal Palace, No. 1 Extra, 8-Day, Time & Strike, Glass Dome, c.1880, 17 In. . . 952.00
Ansonia, Dorval, Regulator, 4-Glass, Beveled, Porcelain Dial, c.1914, 9 In. 950.00
Ansonia, Duke, Regulator, Crystal, Porcelain Dial, 8-Day, Time & Strike, c.1904, 12 In. . . 812.00
Ansonia, Elysian, Regulator, Crystal, Gilded Case, 8-Day, Time & Strike, c.1914, 16 In. . . 728.00
Ansonia, Gallery, 8-Day, Paper Dial, Round, c.1905, 16 1/2 In. 336.00
Ansonia, Gingerbread, Oak Case, Gilt Door Panel, Victorian, 22 In. 185.00
Ansonia, Gloria Swing, Angel With Lyre, Holding Ball Pendulum, c.1890, 28 1/2 In. 4760.00
Ansonia, Huntress, Ball Swing, 8-Day, c.1890, 24 1/2 In. . . . . .3080.00 to 4030.00
Ansonia, Jumper, No. 1, 30-Hour, Bobbing Doll, Teardrop, c.1894, 15 1/2 In. 672.00
Ansonia, La Corsica, Painted, Flowers, Gold Highlights, c.1905, 12 In. 896.00
Ansonia, Marchionesse, Regulator, Crystal, Porcelain Dial, c.1914, 15 3/4 In. 1120.00
Ansonia, Ogee, 2-Weight, Time & Strike, American Eagle, c.1860, 26 In. 106.00
Ansonia, Olympia, 8-Day, Time & Strike, No. 1173, c.1904, 24 In. 420.00
Ansonia, Peconic, Shelf, Porcelain, 8-Day, Time &strike, c.1905, 11 1/2 In. 532.00
Ansonia, Queen Elizabeth, Walnut, c.1880, 37 In. 336.00
Ansonia, Regulator, Crystal, Floral, Gilt Metal, Cast Leaves, Porcelain Dial, c.1914, 16 In. 2800.00
Ansonia, Rosalind, Iron, Enamel, Paper Dial, 8-Day, Time & Strike, c.1890, 12 In. 308.00
Ansonia, Seine, 8-Day, Time & Strike, Enameled Iron Case, c.1894, 18 In. 168.00
Ansonia, Shakespeare, 8-Day, Time & Strike, Spelter Statue, Iron Base, c.1894, 15 In. 448.00
Ansonia, Shelf, Black, Marble, 8-Day, Time & Strike, c.1900, 9 1/2 In. 140.00
Ansonia, Shelf, Cabinet B, Antique Series, c.1894, 18 In. 896.00
Ansonia, Shelf, Mahogany, Pillars, Carved Pediment, 8-Day, Time & Strike, 14 x 11 In. . . . 120.00
Ansonia, Shelf, Spelter Case, Classical Women, 8-Day, Time & Strike, 12 x 12 In. 2390.00
Ansonia, Shelf, Steeple, Mahogany, 8-Day, Time & Strike, Fenn Tablet, c.1865, 20 In. 252.00
Ansonia, Triumph, Walnut, Mirror Side, Cherubs, Faux Burl, 8-Day, c.1890, 24 In. 950.00
Ansonia, Tunis, Shelf, Walnut, 8-Day, Time & Strike, c.1894, 14 In. 140.00
Ansonia, Viscount, Regulator, Crystal, 8-Day, Time & Strike, c.1904, 15 1/4 In. 476.00
Ansonia, Vulcan, Regulator, Crystal, Cast Metal, 8-Day, Time & Strike, c.1914, 12 1/4 In. . 504.00
Art Deco, Porcelain, Woman, Petting Goat, Diamond Shape Face, France, c.1930, 9 In. . . . 200.00
Art Deco, Shelf, Marble, Variegated Brown & Ivory, Bronze Mounts, France, 15 In. 460.00
Arts & Crafts, Copper, Pewter, Embossed, I Mark Time, Dost Thou, c.1900, 15 In. 690.00
Atkins, Shelf, 8-Day Time & Strike, Walnut Veneer, Venetian Style Case, c.1867, 17 In. . . . 168.00
Atkins, Shelf, Centennial, No. 3, Myrtle, Gothic, 30-Hour, Time & Strike, c.1875, 14 In. . . 225.00
Atkins, Shelf, Mahogany, Reverse Painted Eagle, Gilt, 8-Day, Painted Dial, 17 x 12 In. . . . 359.00
Atkins, Shelf, Rosewood, 2 Glass Doors, Eglomise, Wagon Spring Movement, 18 x 13 In. . 3525.00
Atkins, Shelf, Victor, Gothic, 8-Day, Time & Strike, Myrtle, c.1870, 17 1/2 In. 286.00

Atkins & Porter, Shelf, Mahogany, Ogee, Reverse Painted Scene, 26 x 16 In. 375.00
Atkins & Porter, Shelf, Mahogany, Rectangular, Ogee, Tin Dial, Flowers, 26 In. 375.00
Atkins Whiting & Co., Shelf, Rosewood, 30-Day, Lever Spring, c.1852, 19 In. 2910.00
Atmos, Never Wind, Perpetual Running, Swiss, c.1968, 9 In. 420.00
Atmos, Shelf, Perpetual, Swiss, c.1948, 9 In. 450.00
Auguste Bruel, Shelf, 8-Day, Time & Strike, Empire, Columns, Dome, Paris, c.1875, 27 In. 1345.00
Austrian, Porcelain, Cobalt Blue Case, Lever Movement, 8 Scenes, c.1890, 11 1/2 In. 3360.00
Austrian, Portico, 1-Day, Verge Movement, Porcelain Dial, c.1810, 5 1/2 In. 560.00
Balloon, Sheraton Style, Mahogany, Inlay, 2-Train, Half-Strike Chime, 17 1/4 In. 880.00
Banjo, Chelsea, Weight, Pendulum, c.1915, 33 In. 1345.00
Banjo, Eli Terry, Mahogany, Eglomise Scene, Square, Conn., Mid 1800s, 34 3/4 In. 2700.00
Banjo, Federal, Giltwood, Eglomise, Park Scene, Mass., Early 19th Century, 42 1/2 In. . . . 3824.00
Banjo, Federal, Mahogany, Brass Bezel, Eglomise Pendulum Panels, 33 3/4 In. 2115.00
Banjo, Federal, Mahogany, Mahogany Veneer, Flower Eglomise Tablets, Mass., c.1820 . . . 940.00
Banjo, Federal, Mahogany, Roman Numerals, White Sheet-Iron Dial, c.1820, 32 1/2 In. . . . 1495.00
Banjo, Federal, Parcel Gilt, Mahogany, Eglomise Panel, 19th Century, 33 In. 575.00
Banjo, Foster Campos, 8-Day, Moberg Signed Glass, c.1978, 21 In. 925.00
Banjo, Gilbert, Hampshire, 8-Day, Spring Driven, Pendulum, c.1930, 22 In. 110.00
Banjo, Herschede Hall Clock Co., Mahogany, 8-Day, Weight, Mansion, c.1912, 41 1/2 In. . 1290.00
Banjo, Howard, Cherry, Wood Bezel, Battery-Wind Balance Movement, c.1965, 14 In. . . . 260.00
Banjo, Howard, E., U.S. Bicentennial, 13 States In Ribbon, c.1976, 41 1/2 In. 3360.00
Banjo, Killam & Co., Mahogany, Reverse Painted, Brass Eagle Finial, c.1939, 39 x 10 In. . 450.00
Banjo, Mahogany Case, Weight Driven, Boston Area, c.1825, 41 In. 1900.00
Banjo, Mahogany, 8-Day, Time & Strike, Germany, 1935, 33 In. 200.00
Banjo, Mahogany, Acanthus Leaf Scrolls, Carved Finial, Eglomise Panel, 8-Day, 41 In. . . . 5290.00
Banjo, Mahogany, Parcel Gilt, Eglomise Panel, 19th Century, 39 1/2 In. 1175.00
Banjo, Mahogany, Parcel Gilt, Gilded Spread-Wing Phoenix Finial, 34 1/2 In. 705.00
Banjo, Mahogany, Parcel Gilt, Ivory Eglomise Neck Panel, 31 1/2 In. 1528.00
Banjo, Mahogany, Parcel Gilt, Spread-Wing Eagle, Mid 19th Century, 33 1/2 In. 645.00
Banjo, Marble, Ormolu Flower Garland, France, 17 x 7 x 5 1/2 In. 1208.00
Banjo, New Haven, 8-Day, Lever, c.1928, 13 In. 150.00
Banjo, New Haven, Whitney, 8-Day, Time & Strike, Ship, c.1930, 30 1/2 In. 280.00
Banjo, No. 5, Howard, E. & Co., c.1890, 29 In. 4928.00
Banjo, Sessions, Halifax, Mahogany Case, 8-Day, Time & Strike, Sailing Ship, c.1925, 27 In. 85.00
Banjo, Sessions, Model 463-W, Electric, 110v, c.1950, 21 In. 35.00
Banjo, Seth Thomas, Brookfield, Mahogany Case, 8-Day, Time & Strike, c.1958, 29 In. . . . 78.00
Banjo, Waltham, Federal, George Washington, Mt. Vernon, Early 1900s 1645.00
Banjo, Waltham, Hardwood Case, 8-Day, Lever, Independence Hall, Green, c.1932, 8 In. . . 3360.00
Banjo, Waltham, Mahogany Case, No. 1550, 8-Day, Ships & Eagle Tablets, c.1928, 21 In. . 560.00
Banjo, Waltham, Mahogany, 8-Day, Weight, Mount Vernon, G. Washington, c.1930, 42 In. 2070.00
Banjo, Waterbury, Willard, No. 3, Weight Driven, Sailing Ships, Hull, c.1920, 42 1/2 In. . . 2800.00
Banjo, Westminster, 8-Day, Time & Strike, Spring Movement, c.1978, 40 In. 200.00
Banjo, Willard, Simon, Federal, Mahogany, 8-Day, Weight Driven, Boston, c.1805, 30 In. . 9400.00
Barr Mfg. Co., Executive Model, Battery, Weedsport, N.Y., c.1920, 11 In. 280.00
Biedermeier, Shelf, Brass Mounted, Ebonized, Fruit & Lemon Wood, 18 1/2 x 12 In. 1150.00
Bigelow & Kennard, Marble, 8-Day, Time & Strike, French Movement, c.1890, 8 In. 200.00
Bigelow & Kennard, Regulator, Crystal, Brass, Beveled Glass, 12 x 6 x 7 In. 315.00
Birge & Fuller, Steeple On Steeple, Gothic, Wagon Spring Movement, Bristol, 24 x 11 In. . 3290.00
Birge & Ives, Shelf, Mahogany, Parcel Gilt, Gilded Leaf-Carved Crest, 1800s, 36 In. 560.00
Birks, H., Desk, Silver Case, White Enamel Dial, Stylized Leaves, 4 Paw Feet, 1903, 4 In. . 437.00
Black Forest, Cuckoo, 1-Day, 2-Weight, Leaves, Birds, Chicks, Germany, c.1935, 27 In. . . 336.00
Black Forest, Cuckoo, Bavarian Chalet, 30-Hour, Time & Strike, Germany, c.1935, 10 In. . 140.00
Black Forest, Cuckoo, Dancing Figures, Pivoting, Chalet, W. Germany, c.1955, 14 In. 196.00
Black Forest, Cuckoo, Eagle, 30-Hour, Time & Strike, American, c.1900, 20 In. 336.00
Black Forest, Cuckoo, Ebonized Wood, Hare, Pheasant, Stag's Head, Horn, Rifles, 52 In. . 5630.00
Black Forest, Cuckoo, Monk, Monastery, Rustic Case, Burl Wood, c.1860, 24 1/2 In. 1790.00
Black Forest, Cuckoo, Quail, 3-Weight, Quarter Strike, Germany, c.1900, 29 In. 730.00
Black Forest, Cuckoo, Quail, 30-Hour, Quarter Striking, Germany, c.1900, 24 In. 1120.00
Black Forest, Cuckoo, Squirrels, Linden Case, 8-Day, Time & Strike, c.1980, 11 In. 70.00
Boardman, Chauncey, Mahogany, Triple Fusee, 1-Day, Strawberry Tablet, c.1847, 20 In. . . 730.00
Boardman, Chauncey, Shelf, Rosewood, Mahogany, 8-Day, Time & Strike, c.1845, 19 In. . . 1456.00
Boardman & Wells, Ogee, Mahogany, 30-Hour, Time & Strike, Fusee, c.1848, 17 1/2 In. . . 505.00
Boardman & Wells, Shelf, Wood Movement, 30-Hour, Time & Strike, c.1835, 33 In. 310.00

Bonnet & Pottier, Tambour, Marble, Mustard Color, Art Deco, Paris, c.1925, 10 In. 615.00
Boston Clock Co., 8-Day, Lever Movement, Brass, Regulator, Crystal, c.1894, 10 In. 365.00
Boulle, Shelf, Brass Dial, Cherub Finial, Ogee Case, France, Late 1800s, 20 In. 1790.00
Bracket, George III, Mahogany, Dome, Rectangular, Brass Mounts & Handle, 18 In. 4600.00
Bracket, Ivory Inlaid Case, Gilt, Chinese Characters, 2 Bell Chimes, 12 x 10 x 4 In. 1955.00
Bracket, Mahogany Case, Inlaid, Triple Fusee, 2 Chimes, 8-Bell, England, c.1890, 18 In. . . 3470.00
Bracket, Mahogany Case, Inlaid, Triple Fusee, 2 Chimes, 8-Bell, England, c.1890, 24 In. . 5710.00
Bracket, Mahogany, Inlaid, Butterfly, 2 Finials, Rack & Snail Strike, England, 25 x 13 In. . 3100.00
Bracket, Neoclassical, Giltwood, Ribbon Bow, Sphinxes, Sweden, c.1900, 24 x 20 x 5 In. . 1610.00
Bradley & Hubbard, Shelf, Figural, Topsy, Painted, Blinking Eye, c.1880, 17 In. 1880.00
Bradley & Hubbard, Topsy, Blinking Eye, Woman, Dress, c.1860 . . . . 1345.00
Brewster & Ingrahams, Steeple, Mahogany, Time & Strike, c.1845, 20 In. 1456.00
Brewster & Ingrahams, Wall, 8-Day, Cast-Iron Case, c.1847, 16 3/4 In. 1000.00
Bronze, Dome Finial, Scrolling, Lion, Figures, France, Late 1800s, 22 x 13 x 6 In. 430.00
Brown, J.C., Shelf, Gothic, Rosewood, Acorn Side Arms, Reverse Painted, 24 x 15 In. 5580.00
Brown, J.C., Steeple, Triple Fusee, Ripple, Brass Lyre Trim, c.1850, 20 In. 5040.00
Brown, J.E., Shelf, Gothic, Rosewood, Flower Etched Panel, c.1875, 15 In. 5581.00
Bugs Bunny, Stands By Dial, Says Eh, Wake Up, Doc, Plastic, Janex, c.1974, 7 In. 366.00
Carriage, Angle Riche Case, Corinthian Columns, Champleve Enamel, c.1900, 8 In. 3360.00
Carriage, Brass Case, 8-Day, Porcelain Dial, Beveled Glass, H&H, c.1910, 5 3/4 In. 225.00
Carriage, Brass Corniche, Petite Sonnerie, Quarter Repeater, France, c.1900, 7 1/4 In. 1960.00
Carriage, Brass, 8-Day, Time & Strike, 5 Beveled Glass Panes, c.1900, 6 In. 310.00
Carriage, Brass, 8-Day, Time & Strike, Repeater, Square Columns, France, c.1900, 8 In. . . . 1288.00
Carriage, Brass, Figures, Landscape, Pillars, Handle, Barrel Movement, France, 8 In. 5750.00
Carriage, Brass, Scroll Bail Handle, Scalloped Design, 20th Century, 6 x 3 1/2 x 3 In. 153.00
Carriage, Brass, Time & Strike, Repeater, Column Case, Brass Trim, c.1900, 6 In. 560.00
Carriage, Brass, Time & Strike, Repeater, Silvered Lever Platform, c.1900, 5 3/4 In. 517.00
Carriage, Bronze, Enameled Face, Alarm, Repeater, Lifting Handle, France, 7 1/2 In. 1645.00
Carriage, Bronze, Gorge Case, Alarm, Lift Handle, Enameled Dial, c.1900, 4 In. 235.00
Carriage, Bronze, Push Repeater, Enameled Face, Beveled, Handle, France, 6 In. 645.00
Carriage, Bronze, Repeater, Alarm, Beveled Glass, Half-Strike Movement, c.1875, 8 In. . . 1410.00
Carriage, Bronze, Silvered Face, Gorge Case, Alarm, Repeater, Handle, France, 7 In. 705.00
Carriage, Gilt Bronze, Porcelain Chapter Ring, France, c.1890, 5 1/2 In. 489.00
Carriage, Gong, White Enamel Dial, Gilt Brass, Beveled Glass, c.1900, 7 In. 320.00
Carriage, Oval, Bail Handle, Beveled Glass Panels, Roman Numerals, Early 1900s, 4 In. . . 375.00
Cartel, Louis XV Style, Gilt Metal, Round Dial, Cast Leaves, Tied Ribbon, 14 x 7 In. 650.00
Cartel, Louis XVI Style, Vernis Martin Style Case, Ormolu, France, c.1880, 11 In. 1120.00
Cartel, Walnut, Carved, 8-Day, Gong Strike, France, c.1890, 24 In. 500.00
Chandler, A., Gilt Gesso, Wood, Black, Stenciled Flowers, Mirror, 8-Day, 29 x 14 In. 8225.00
Chandler, Abiel, 8-Day, Time & Strike, Mahogany, Rat Trap Movement, c.1832, 33 In. . . . 5640.00
Chelsea, Mahogany Case, Ship's Bell Movement, Dial, c.1908, 21 1/2 In. 1120.00
Chelsea, Shelf, Bicentennial, Brass, Mahogany Base, 8-Day, Time & Strike, c.1976, 9 In. . 390.00
Chelsea, Shelf, Mahogany, Ormolu, Cherubs, 8-Day, Time, House Strike, c.1919, 12 In. . . . 2016.00
Clark, George, Lantern, Georgian Style, Weight-Driven Chime, Pendulum, 4 3/8 x 14 In. . 2235.00
Clarke, Sylvester, Shelf, Classical, Mahogany, Veneer, c.1830, 31 1/2 x 18 1/2 In. 3525.00
Columbia Time, Woody Woodpecker, Alarm, Walter Lantz, Box, 1959, 5 1/2 x 3 x 5 In. . . . 300.00
Columbia Time, Woody Woodpecker, Wall, Riding Horse, No. 535, Box, 9 In. 385.00
Couaillet Freres, Carriage, Brass, Alarm, Leather Travel Case, France, 4 In. 325.00
Cummings, W., Shelf, Mahogany, Stepped Case, Early 19th Century, 34 In. 3819.00
Daniel Pratt & Sons, Shelf, Beehive, 8-Day, Mahogany, Reading, Mass., c.1869, 19 In. . . . 250.00
David Dutton, 30-Hour, Wood Movement, Time & Strike, Alarm, Mirror, c.1835, 32 In. . . 1120.00
Davies, H.J., Mozart As Boy, Iron Case, White Metal Trim, c.1880, 16 In. 250.00
Desk, 2 Coolies Hold Drum, Gilt Metal, 19th Century, 8 In. 230.00
Desk, Art Deco, Semicircular, Brass, Wood Base, Barometer, Thermometer, 5 x 12 x 3 In. . 900.00
Desk, Doxa, Brass, Spherical, Naval Scene, Moving Sailor's Arm, Swiss, c.1940, 2 1/4 In. . 345.00
Desk, Oak Case, Satinwood Inlay, 8-Day, Platform Lever, Swiss, c.1930, 8 1/2 In. 140.00
Desk, Ormolu, Enamel, Silvered Flower Mask, France, c.1890, 9 In. 2800.00
Donne, Charles, Shelf, Lacquer, Balloon Style, Double Fusee, Bell, England, c.1834, 15 In. 1680.00
Dutch Hood, Double, 3 Finials, Female Trumpeters, Atlas, 30-Hour, c.1840, 64 In. 3025.00
Dutton, David, Column, Splat, Mahogany, 30-Hour, Wood Movement, c.1838, 32 In. 218.00
Fair Haven, Regulator, Wall, Oak, Eglomise, Brass, 8-Day, Weight Driven, Vt., Late 1800s 1880.00
Farcot, Conical Pendulum, Alarm, France, c.1890, 7 In. 840.00
Fertbauer, Shelf, Grand Sonnerie, Walnut Veneer, Serpents, Alabaster Urn, c.1810, 12 In. . 1120.00

Figural, Rabbit, Brass, Bearing Clock On Back, 6 5/8 In. 200.00
Figural, Race Car, Clock On Radiator, Die Cast, Tin, White Rubber Tires, Box, 6 1/4 In. .. 1320.00
Figural, Shelf, Resting Warrior, Louis Philippe, Bronze, Gilt, Patinated, 19 x 12 In. 5520.00
Forestville, Column, Cornice, Mahogany, 8-Day, Time & Strike, J.C. Brown, c.1845, 32 In. 1456.00
Forestville, Double Decker, Ogee, Mahogany Veneer, 8-Day, 2-Weight, c.1840, 31 In. 1000.00
Forestville, Ripple Beehive, Rosewood Veneer, c.1845, 20 In. 3360.00
Forestville, Shelf, Empire, Mahogany, Eglomise Door, c.1855, 37 In. 155.00
Forestville, Steeple, Ripple, Mahogany, 8-Day, Time & Strike, J.C. Brown, c.1845 .... 1790.00
French, Empire, Mahogany, 8-Day, Time & Strike, 4 Columns, c.1875, 20 1/2 In. 1680.00
French, Mini Music, Boy, Drum, Trumpet, Bronze, Marble, 8-Day, c.1885, 8 3/4 In. 1120.00
French, Napoleon III, Ormolu, Gilding, Brass, Porcelain Dial, c.1870, 27 1/2 In. 336.00
French, Ormolu, Marble, Running Woman, Torch, Castanets, Jug, Bowl, c.1875, 9 In. 1680.00
French, Shelf, Second Empire, Napoleon III, Bronze, c.1860, 23 x 19 In. 2415.00
Garniture Set, Napoleon III, Onyx, Gilt Bronze, Cloisonne, 15 x 13 1/2 x 9 In., 3 Piece ... 2760.00
Garniture Set, Onyx, Ormolu Mounted, France, c.1880, 18 1/2 x 10 1/4 x 5 In., 3 Piece ... 520.00
Gautier & Albinet, Shelf, Louis XV Style, Gilt Bronze, Paris, c.1880, 25 1/4 In. 6000.00
General Electric, Model No. 7H92, Art Deco, c.1935, 8 In. 127.00
German, Shelf Regulator, Oak Case, 8-Day, Gong Strike, c.1910, 12 In. 112.00
German, Swinger, Berlin Style, Porcelain Dial, 8-Day, Time & Strike, c.1890, 37 In. 280.00
German, Swinging Cat, Monkey, 8-Day, Barrel Top, c.1890, 12 1/2 In. 2520.00
Gibraltar, NRA, We Do Our Part, Electric, 13 x 91/2 x 3 1/2 In. 400.00
Gilbert, Calendar, Steeple, G. B. Owen Patent, c.1866, 17 1/2 In. 785.00
Gilbert, Oak Case, Electric, c.1920, 61 1/2 x 12 1/2 x 6 1/2 In. 90.00
Gilbert, Shelf, Cottage, Mahogany Veneer Case, 30-Hour, Time, Alarm, c.1870, 12 In. 125.00
Gilbert, Wm. L., Regulator, No. 21, Cherry, 8-Day, 1-Weight, Front Pendulum, c.1880 ... 1960.00
Gilbert, Wm. L., Regulator, Wall, Mahogany, 8-Day, Weight Driven, Conn., c.1880 ...... 650.00
Gilbert, Wm. L., Shelf, Joyce, Oak, 8-Day, Time & Strike, Alarm, c.1900, 24 In. 215.00
Gilbert, Wm. L., Shelf, Mahogany, 8-Day, Time & Strike, Arched Top, c.1920, 16 1/4 In. . 336.00
Gilbert, Wm. L., Shelf, No. 413, Porcelain, 8-Day, Time & Strike, c.1898, 10 1/2 In. 616.00
Gilbert, Wm. L., Shelf, Parisian, Walnut, 8-Day, Time & Strike, c.1880, 24 In. 196.00
Gilbert, Wm. L., Shelf, Parlor, Amphion, Walnut Case, Etched, Mirror, c.1885, 25 In. 1900.00
Gilbert, Wm. L., Shelf, Parlor, Walnut, Calliope, Cathedral Gong, c.1885, 25 In. 900.00
Gilbert, Wm. L., Shelf, Tambour, Hardwood Case, 8-Day, Time & Strike, c.1930, 10 In. .. 110.00
Goodwin, E.O., Shelf, Column & Cornice, 8-Day, Time & Strike, Bristol, c.1852, 20 1/2 In. 730.00
Goodwin, E.O., Shelf, Empire, Mahogany, 8-Day, Ft. Stanwix, Congress Hall, c.1852, 21 In. 2016.00
Gubelin, Boudoir, Bronze Argente, Guilloche Enamel, Pedestal, Lucerne, c.1915, 8 1/2 In. . 1380.00
Gustav Becker, Novelty, Old Man, Clock Over Head, Sheet Brass, 30-Hour, c.1870, 8 In. . 476.00
Gustav Becker, Oak Case, Grand Sonnerie, Quarter Strike, 3-Weight, c.1910, 37 In. 890.00
Gustav Becker, Regulator, 2-Weight, Wood Veneer, Rod Strike, c.1890, 32 In. 310.00
Gustav Becker, Vienna Regulator, Walnut, Alt Deutsch Style, 2-Weight, c.1890, 51 In. 645.00
Gustav Becker, Wall, Mahogany, Carved Pillars, 8-Day, Silver & Brass Dial, 32 x 15 In. .. 400.00
Hamburg American, Shelf, Mahogany, Westminster Chime, 8-Day, c.1910, 14 In. 170.00
Hamburg American, Shelf, Oak, Westminster Chime, 8-Day, c.1910, 13 1/2 In. 250.00
Hatch, G.D., Regulator, Figure 8, Wooden Rod, Lift-Off Pendulum, c.1845, 35 In. 3218.00
Hoadley, Silas, Columns, 30-Hour, Wood, Time & Strike, Alarm, c.1835, 39 In. 2240.00
Hopkins & Alfred, Shelf, Half Columns, Eagle Design, Divided Door, Claw Feet, 1820s .. 1455.00
Howard, E. & Co., Arched Top, Half Columns, 8-Day, Hidden Pendulum, 32 x 12 In. 4540.00
Howard, E. & Co., Cherry Case, Reverse Painted Base, Round Face, 8-Day, 36 x 18 In. 2629.00
Howard, E. & Co., Wall, Figure 8, Walnut, Brass Movement, Boston, c.1870, 34 In. 7640.00
Howard, E., Regulator, No. 8, Black Walnut, Figure 8, c.1885, 44 1/2 In. 10080.00
Howard, E., Regulator, No. 10, Walnut, Figure 8, 8-Day, Weight Driven, c.1978, 34 In. ... 2520.00
Howard, E., Regulator, No. 59, Walnut, Vienna Style, 8-Day, Weights, c.1977, 46 In. 1900.00
Howard, Egyptian Pharaoh, Globe, Marble Base, Bell Strike, France, c.1890, 26 In. 670.00
Howard Miller, Asterisk, Enameled Metal, G. Nelson, No. 2213, Marked .... *Illus* 650.00
Howard Miller, Ball, Black Balls, Brass Rods, Center, G. Nelson, 1950s, 14 In. 440.00
Howard Miller, Ball, Brown Balls, G. Nelson, No. 4755, Box, c.1947, 13 In. 1295.00
Howard Miller, Ball, G. Nelson, 1947, Box, 13 In. 1295.00
Howard Miller, Ball, Green Balls, Steel Rods, Center, G. Nelson, 1950s, 14 In. 940.00
Howard Miller, Ball, Multicolored Balls, G. Nelson, No. 4755, c.1947, 13 In. 1528.00
Howard Miller, Ball, Painted Wood, Brass, G. Nelson, No. 4755, Label, 13 1/2 In. 2000.00
Howard Miller, Eye, G. Nelson, c.1954, 29 In. 7050.00
Howard Miller, Kite, Enameled Metal, G. Nelson, No. 2201, Label, 16 1/2 In. .... *Illus* 10620.00
Howard Miller, Kite, G. Nelson, No. 2201, c.1953, 17 x 22 In. 2705.00

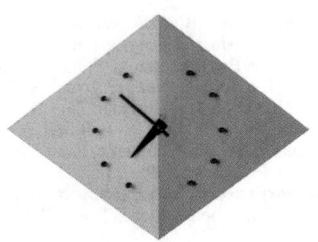

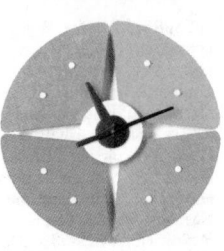

Clock, Howard Miller,
Asterisk, Enameled Metal,
G. Nelson, No. 2213, Marked

Clock, Howard Miller, Kite,
Enameled Metal, G. Nelson,
No. 2201, Label, 16 1/2 In.

Clock, Howard Miller, Paddle,
Wood, Enameled Metal,
G. Nelson, No. 2246, 17 1/2 In.

Howard Miller, Paddle, Wood, Enameled Metal, G. Nelson, No. 2246, 17 1/2 In. . . . . *Illus* 2950.00
Howard Miller, Pretzel, G. Nelson, c.1955, 18 In. 2350.00
Howard Miller, Sunburst, Black, G. Nelson, No. 2202, c.1948, 19 In. 470.00
Howard Miller, Sunburst, G. Nelson, 1948, 19 In. 470.00
Howard Miller, Wall, Nathan George Horwitt, No. 4628, 12 1/2 In. 155.00
Imhoff, Alarm, Gilt Brass Case, 8-Day, Swiss, c.1960, 3 1/2 In. 56.00
Ingersoll, Big Bad Wolf, Alarm, Chrome Bezel, c.1938, 4 1/2 In. 450.00
Ingraham, Admiral Dewey, Shelf, Oak, c.1900, 23 x 14 1/2 In. 345.00
Ingraham, Bristol, Shelf, Alternating Maple & Walnut Veneer, c.1885, 14 1/2 In. 730.00
Ingraham, Gingerbread, Oak Case, Gilt Door Panel, Victorian, 23 In. 160.00
Ingraham, Grecian, Ash Case, 8-Day, Time & Strike, c.1880, 15 In. 420.00
Ingraham, Hartford, School, Pressed Oak, 8-Day, Calendar, c.1911, 32 In. 370.00
Ingraham, Huron, Shelf, Rosewood, 8-Day, Time & Strike, Benj. Boyce, c.1880, 16 In. . . . 840.00
Ingraham, Lilac, Shelf, Walnut, 8-Day, Time & Strike, c.1895, 22 In. 110.00
Ingraham, Oriental, Shelf, Rosewood, 8-Day, Time & Strike, c.1870, 17 1/2 In. 1000.00
Ingraham, Shelf, 30-Hour, Time & Strike, Alarm, Scroll Front, c.1852, 16 1/2 In. . .185.00 to 390.00
Ingraham, Shelf, Wood, Black Paint, Faux Marble, Lion's-Head Handles, 17 x 7 x 13 In. . . 115.00
Ingraham, Tortoiseshell Appearance, 30-Hour, Porcelain Dial, c.1920, 4 1/2 In. 125.00
International Time Recording Co., 2-Jar Pendulum, Endicott, N.Y., c.1920, 66 In. 900.00
Ithaca Calendar Clock Co., Shelf, Library, No. 8, c.1875, 25 In. . . . . .910.00 to 950.00
Ithaca Calendar Clock Co., Wall, Office, No. 4, 30-Day, Rosewood, c.1880, 28 In. 1290.00
Japy Freres, Porcelain, Cobalt Blue, Ormolu Trim, c.1890, 22 In. 950.00
Japy Freres, Shelf, 8-Day, Bell Strike, Silk Suspension, c.1850, 25 In. 785.00
Japy Freres, Shelf, Architectural, Cast Brass, 8-Day, Time & Strike, c.1890, 18 1/2 In. 560.00
Jefferson Electric, Mystery, Desk, Golden Hour, c.1950, 8 In. 110.00
Jerome, Chauncey, Shelf, Ogee, Mahogany Veneer, 30-Hour, Alarm, c.1855, 26 In. 100.00
Jerome & Co., Cottage, Dreadnought, Rosewood, Mahogany, 30-Hour, c.1880, 14 1/4 In. . . 140.00
Jerome & Co., Oscillating, Sphere, Stained Case, Brass Border, c.1883, 10 1/2 In. 825.00
Jerome & Co., Steeple, 8-Day, Alarm, Greenwood Cemetery Tablet, c.1869, 19 In. 500.00
Jeromes Gilbert Grant & Co., Shelf, Mahogany, 30-Hour, Time & Strike, c.1840, 22 In. . . 225.00
John Wanless & Co., Shelf, Balloon, Inlaid Mahogany, Canada, c.1900, 13 1/4 In. 360.00
Johnson, Bracket, Mahogany, Brass Mounted, London, Late 1700s 5840.00
Junghans, Box, Art Nouveau, Birch, Beveled Glass Door, 8-Day, 11 1/2 In. 785.00
Junghans, Cleopatra, Swinging Arm, 8-Day, Germany, c.1910, 15 1/2 In. 1065.00
Junghans, Diana, Swinging Arm, Wood Base, Germany, c.1910, 13 1/2 In. 896.00
Junghans, Figural, Kangaroo, Swinger, Germany, c.1905, 12 1/4 In. 2350.00
Junghans, Mystery, Statue Of Liberty, Bronze Spelter, Germany, c.1905, 18 1/2 In. 3585.00
Junghans, Swinging Arm, Elephant, Wood Base, c.1905, 11 In. 1290.00
Kienzle, 2-Tune, 9-Rod, Chime, Germany, c.1950, 9 x 31 In. 125.00
Kienzle, Tambour, Oak Case, 8-Day, Time & Strike, Gong, Germany, c.1920, 8 In. 60.00
Kroeber, F., Hartford, Shelf, Ebonized, Jacot Pendulum, Cherubs, c.1880, 20 In. 1120.00
Kroeber, F., Parisian, Parlor, Walnut, Jacot Dial, Right Pendulum, 1876, 23 1/2 In. 450.00
Lantern, Brass, Engraved Face, Pierced Hands, Gallery, Bell, R & C, No. 167942, 16 In. . . 350.00
Lantern, Brass, Iron, Wings, Anchor Shaped Bob, 18th Century, Signed, 5 1/2 x 15 In. 4800.00
LeCoultre, Anniversary, Gilt Bronze Case, c.1955, 9 3/4 In. 520.00
LeCoultre, Atmos, Perpetual Wind, Brass Case, c.1955, 9 1/4 In. 390.00
LeCoultre, Atmos, Skeleton Movement, Gilt Brass & Glass Case, Box, 1970s, 9 In. 615.00

LeCoultre, Novelty, Brass Case, Music Box, Bird On Branch, Alarm, 8-Day, c.1960, 5 In. . 170.00
Lenzkirch, Porcelain, Cherubs, Leaves, Musical Themes, Pink, c.1890, 15 1/2 In. 1570.00
LeRoy, A L'Elephant, Louis XVI Style, Bronze, Ormolu, France, c.1860, 22 3/4 In. 8400.00
Liberty & Co., Shelf, Oak, Arched Top, Carved Roses & Branches, Bun Feet, 10 x 15 In. . . . 720.00
Litchfield, Shelf, Papier-Mache, Mother-Of-Pearl, Flower, Time & Strike, c.1850, 19 In. . . . 110.00
Mantel, Bronze, Chelsea, Silvered Dial, Tiffany & Co., Ball Feet, 6 x 8 x 3 In. 645.00
Margaine, Carriage, Brass Corniche Case, Petite Sonnerie, France, c.1900, 6 3/4 In. 785.00
Margaine, Carriage, Time & Strike, Repeater, c.1895, 7 In. 785.00
Margaine, Shelf, Porcelain, Mulberry Ground, Mid 1800s, 15 x 10 In. 1495.00
Marshall Field & Co., Craft Shop, Metal Footed, Etched Roses, Patina, 6 1/2 In. 690.00
McCoy, Heart Beat, 5 x 5 In. 264.00
McKee Glass Co., Tambour, Daisy & Button, Green, 30-Hour, c.1930, 6 1/4 In. 110.00
Meyer, Animated, Double Dog, Woman, Holding 2 Dogs, Austria, c.1870, 10 1/4 In. 3360.00
Meyer, Novelty, Triple Dog, Picnic Basket, Metal Finish, Austria, c.1870, 6 In. 2465.00
Morbier, Crown Wheel, Vertical Rack Strike, 2-Weight, Repeater, 8-Day, c.1850, 59 In. . . . 280.00
Morbier, Hour Repeater, Prayer, Repousse Pendulum, Calendar, France, c.1870, 53 In. 505.00
Morbier, Prayer, Wheat & Harvest Theme, Repeater, Calendar, France, c.1840, 58 In. 670.00
Munger & Benedict, Shelf, 8-Day, Time & Strike, Mirror, Butternut, c.1832, 39 In. 3360.00
Mystery, Bronzed Spelter, Woman, Brise D'Automne, Swinging, France, c.1890, 28 In. . . . 3696.00
Mystery, Harvest, Bronzed Spelter, Swinging, France, c.1890, 29 1/2 In. 3800.00
Mystery, Le Lever Du Jour, Bronzed Spelter, Swinging, France, c.1890, 24 In. 2350.00
Mystery, Swinging Arm, Patinated Spelter, Fleur Du Mai, France, c.1890, 39 In. 5376.00
New Haven, Beehive, 8-Day, Time & Strike & Alarm, c.1860, 19 In. 85.00
New Haven, Cottage, Rosewood, 30-Hour, Time & Strike, c.1870, 13 In. 90.00
New Haven, Genesta, Enameled Iron, Open Escapement, c.1890, 10 In. 125.00
New Haven, Inglewood, Shelf, Mahogany Case, 8-Day, Westminster, c.1930, 12 1/2 In. . . . 196.00
New Haven, Mission Oak, Brass Hands, No. 2849, c.1920, 30 In. 196.00
New Haven, Novelty, Cut Glass, 30-Hour, Buttons, Bows, Flower, c.1915, 5 In. 125.00
New Haven, Occidental, Shelf, Walnut, 8-Day, Time & Strike, c.1911, 24 In. 420.00
New Haven, Regulator, 8-Day, Time & Strike, Scroll Cut Wing, c.1890, 30 In. 515.00
New Haven, Romany, Shelf, 8-Day, Westminster Chime, c.1925, 9 In. 336.00
New Haven, San Pedro, Mission Oak, 8-Day, Gong Strike, c.1913, 19 In. 196.00
New Haven, School, Rosewood, 8-Day, Time & Strike, Calendar, 24 In. 269.00
New Haven, Shelf, Mahogany Case, 11 x 23 In. 80.00
New Haven, Shelf, Mahogany, Chime No. 4, c.1911, 20 In. 390.00
New Haven, Shelf, Marble, Bronze, 8-Day, Time & Strike, Japy Freres, c.1890, 13 1/4 In. . . 225.00
New Haven, Shelf, Ogee, Greenwood Cemetery Entrance, 30-Hour, c.1835, 26 In. 115.00
New Haven, Shelf, Steeple, Walnut Veneer, Greenwood Cemetery, 8-Day, c.1850 . . . . 265.00
New Haven, Tuscan, Shelf, Rosewood, Rose Tablet, 8-Day, Time & Strike, c.1880, 18 In. . . 135.00
North, Norris, Shelf, Mahogany, Pillar & Scroll, Torrington, Conn., c.1820, 30 1/4 In. 8395.00
Novelty, Skull, Rotating Eye, Plastic Base, Germany, c.1920, 4 In. 1345.00
Novelty, Street Light, Drunk Man In Top Hat, Pot Metal, 16 x 7 In. 70.00
Oswald, Dog, Rotating Eye, Wood, Germany, c.1930, 8 In. 615.00
Peck Hayden & Co., Shelf, Column & Cornice, 8-Day, Time & Strike, c.1840, 36 In. 560.00
Pons, Shelf, Empire Style, Carved & Pierced Alabaster, White, France, c.1840, 23 In. 1485.00
Prentiss Improvement Clock Co., Empire, Calendar, Oak Case, 30-Day, c.1895, 37 In. . . . 6160.00
Prihoda, Vienna Regulator, Walnut, 2-Weight, c.1880, 49 In. 1150.00
Raingo Freres, Shelf, Louis XVI Style, Ormolu, France, c.1880, 11 1/2 In. 1000.00
Regulator, Crystal, Brass Case, 8-Day, Time & Strike, Brevete, France, c.1900, 8 1/4 In. . . 250.00
Regulator, Crystal, Onyx, Brass, Bow Front, Corinthian Columns, c.1900, 13 1/2 In. 1510.00
Regulator, Oak Case, Beveled Glass Door, Germany, c.1920, 33 In. 315.00
Regulator, Vienna, 2-Weight, Pendulum, Reeded Ball Pendants, 44 In. 575.00
Regulator, Vienna, Black Walnut, Ebonized Finials, 2-Weight, Germany, c.1885, 44 In. . . . 670.00
Regulator, Vienna, Mahogany, Porcelain Dial, 8-Day, 1-Weight, Germany, 37 x 14 In. 720.00
Regulator, Vienna, Mahogany, Swan's-Neck Top, 1-Weight, 8-Day, Germany, 44 In. 775.00
Regulator, Vienna, Oak, 2-Weight, Gong Strike, Germany, c.1890, 55 In. 2576.00
Regulator, Vienna, Walnut Veneer, Enameled Face, Key Wind, 46 x 17 x 9 1/2 In. 1150.00
Regulator, Vienna, Walnut, 30-Day, 5-Wheel Train, 5-Spoke Pulley, c.1870, 51 In. 3360.00
Regulator, Vienna, Walnut, Carved, Glazed Panel Door, c.1880, 37 x 13 1/4 x 7 In. 230.00
Regulator, Vienna, Walnut, Grande Sonnerie, Fluted Columns, 3-Weight, 8-Day, 54 In. . . . 3585.00
Regulator, Vienna, Walnut, Molded Crown, Applied Carving, c.1890, 31 x 16 x 8 In. 105.00
Regulator, Vienna, Walnut, Turned Decoration, Victorian, 26 In. 315.00
Regulator, Wall, Calendar, Mahogany, Brass Bezel, Wood Pendulum, 32 x 18 x 4 1/2 In. . . 385.00

Regulator, Wall, Spring Driven, 8-Day, Time & Strike, Germany, c.1900, 38 In. 170.00
Riss, E., Regulator, Vienna Oak, Molded Crown, Turned Columns, c.1900, 22 x 12 x 7 In. . 175.00
Saintilan, F., Inlaid Mahogany, Ormolu Trim, Westminster Chime, c.1900, 40 1/2 In. 840.00
Schatz & Sons, Brass Case, Torsion Pendulum, 1000-Day, c.1954, 9 In. 135.00
Serin, Edouard, World Time Globe, Striking, Moon Phases, Porcelain Dial, c.1890, 21 In. . 7000.00
Sessions, Regulator, Oak Case, c.1900, 40 In. 230.00
Sessions, Shelf, Black Wood Case, Faux Marble Pilasters, Leaf Feet, Handles, 18 x 7 In. .. 105.00
Sessions, Star Pointer, Calendar, 8-Day, Octagonal Top, c.1910, 32 1/2 In. 280.00
Sessions, Tambour, Mahogany, 8-Day, Time & Strike, Silvered Dial, c.1927, 10 In. 28.00
Seth Thomas, Black Bakelite Case, 24-Hour Dial, 8-Day, Lever Movement, c.1940, 8 In. . 310.00
Seth Thomas, Brass, Round, Etched, Key Wind, Glass Case, Bell, 10 1/2 x 7 x 3 1/2 In. ... 325.00
Seth Thomas, Calendar, Date, Day, Month, c.1915, 42 In. 978.00
Seth Thomas, Candlestick, 8-Day, Time & Strike, Dome, Porcelain Dial, c.1870, 11 In. ... 1290.00
Seth Thomas, Cherry, Curved Top, Turned Posts, 2 Dials, Calendar, 8-Day, 28 x 16 In. ... 1795.00
Seth Thomas, Dundee, Mahogany, Silvered Dial, c.1917, 10 1/2 In. 135.00
Seth Thomas, Mahogany Case, 8-Bell Sonora, No. 266, c.1905, 18 In. 3640.00
Seth Thomas, Office Calendar, No. 7, Mahogany, 8-Day, Time & Strike, c.1878, 26 In. ... 950.00
Seth Thomas, Parlor Calendar, No. 3, 8-Day, Time & Strike, c.1870, 27 In. 728.00
Seth Thomas, Parlor, Hecla, Walnut, 8-Day, Quarter-Hour Gong, c.1886, 22 1/2 In. 2240.00
Seth Thomas, Parlor, Rosewood, 8-Day, Time & Strike, c.1863, 30 1/2 In. 670.00
Seth Thomas, Regulator, Crystal, 8-Day, Time & Gong, Porcelain Dial, c.1905, 9 1/4 In. .. 420.00
Seth Thomas, Regulator, Crystal, Empire, No. 9, 8-Day, Time & Strike, c.1910, 13 In. 390.00
Seth Thomas, Regulator, Crystal, Empire, No. 23, 8-Day, Time & Strike, c.1909, 11 In. ... 335.00
Seth Thomas, Regulator, Crystal, Empire, No. 63, c.1910, 11 In. 560.00
Seth Thomas, Regulator, Crystal, Orchid, No. 6, 8-Day, Time & Strike, c.1909, 11 In. 450.00
Seth Thomas, Regulator, No. 2, Mahogany, 8-Day, Silk-Screened, 36 x 15 In. ...1195.00 to 1960.00
Seth Thomas, Regulator, No. 2, Rosewood, 1-Weight, c.1865, 34 In. 3810.00
Seth Thomas, Regulator, No. 2, Walnut, c.1888, 34 In. 3360.00
Seth Thomas, Regulator, No. 3, Oak, 72-Beat Movement, c.1890, 44 In. 3920.00
Seth Thomas, Regulator, No. 30, Oak, c.1905, 49 In. 3920.00
Seth Thomas, Regulator, Wall, Walnut, No. 18, Roman Numerals, c.1890, 54 In. 3910.00
Seth Thomas, Rosewood, 30-Hour, Time & Strike, c.1866, 25 In. 420.00
Seth Thomas, School, Mahogany, 8-Day, c.1885, 22 In. 250.00
Seth Thomas, Shelf, Adamantine, Black, 8-Day, Time & Strike, Brass Dial, c.1896, 11 In. . 140.00
Seth Thomas, Shelf, Adamantine, Mottled Tan, 8-Day, Time & Strike, c.1895, 11 In. 225.00
Seth Thomas, Shelf, Classical, Rosewood Veneer, 8-Day, Weight Driven, c.1875 .... 355.00
Seth Thomas, Shelf, Column & Cornice, 8-Day, Shell Columns, c.1870, 32 In. 1090.00
Seth Thomas, Shelf, Column, 8-Day, Spring Driven, Time & Strike, c.1870, 16 In. 170.00
Seth Thomas, Shelf, Column, Shell, 2-Weight, 30-Hour, c.1860, 25 In. 170.00
Seth Thomas, Shelf, Cordova, Oak, 15-Day, Time & Strike, c.1900, 10 3/4 In. 515.00
Seth Thomas, Shelf, Cottage, Rosewood, 8-Day, Time & Strike, c.1884, 14 1/2 In. 310.00
Seth Thomas, Shelf, Federal, Mahogany, Pillar & Scroll, Mt. Vernon, c.1815, 29 In. 765.00
Seth Thomas, Shelf, Gothic, No. 2, Bronze Case, Time & Strike, c.1909, 14 In. 560.00
Seth Thomas, Shelf, Kingsbury, Pillar & Scroll, 8-Day, Time & Strike, c.1928, 17 In. 560.00
Seth Thomas, Shelf, Mahogany, Reeded Sides, 2-Weight, 8-Day, Coiled Gong, 27 x 17 In. 900.00
Seth Thomas, Shelf, Mahogany, Shell & Leaf Crest, Village Green, c.1825, 35 x 17 In. ... 940.00
Seth Thomas, Shelf, No. 66, Mahogany, 4 Bells, Sonora Chime, c.1912, 18 In. 900.00
Seth Thomas, Shelf, Off-Center Pillar & Scroll, 30-Hour, Time & Strike, c.1820, 32 In. ... 3080.00
Seth Thomas, Shelf, Omaha, Walnut, 8-Day, Time & Strike, c.1886, 19 In. 365.00
Seth Thomas, Shelf, Rosewood, Reverse Painted Eagle, 16 x 10 In. 290.00
Seth Thomas, Shelf, Simsbury, Westminster Chime, c.1935, 9 In. 65.00
Seth Thomas, Ship's Bell, Brass, Silvered Dial, Keyholes, Outside Bell, 11 x 6 In. 290.00
Seth Thomas, Ship's Bell, Cast Brass Case, Hinged Bezel, Key Lock, c.1930, 14 In. 3920.00
Seth Thomas, Sonora Chime, No. 57, c.1915, 11 In. 810.00
Seth Thomas, Tory, Shelf, 8-Day, Time & Strike, Porcelain Dial, c.1910, 13 1/2 In. 280.00
Seth Thomas, Wall, Bracket, Oak, Double Dial, Double Spring Movement, c.1922, 30 In. . 670.00
Seth Thomas, Wall, Eclipse, Walnut Case, Alarm, 8-Day, Time & Strike, c.1890, 27 In. ... 505.00
Seth Thomas, Wall, Gallery, Mahogany, 15-Day, c.1909, 25 1/2 In. 2800.00
Seth Thomas, Wall, Lobby, Oak, 15-Day, c.1909, 38 In. 3360.00
Seth Thomas, Wall, Lobby, Oak, 15-Day, Double Spring, c.1890, 30 In. 1850.00
Seth Thomas, Wall, Marcy, Oak, 8-Day, Quarter Strike, 2 Bells, c.1886, 46 In. 3025.00
Seth Thomas, Wall, Queen Anne, Oak, 8-Day, Time Only, c.1900, 36 In. 1176.00
Seth Thomas, Wall, Queen Anne, Walnut, 8-Day, Time & Strike, c.1890, 36 In. 2350.00

Seth Thomas, Wall, Umbria, Oak, 15-Day, c.1909, 40 1/2 In. 1905.00
Shelf, Art Deco, Circassian Walnut, 8-Day, Striking, Germany, c.1950, 9 In. 140.00
Shelf, Art Deco, Marble Side Pieces, Bronze Dog, Square Dial, 8-Day, 11 x 24 In. 96.00
Shelf, Banjo, Walnut, Carved, Mid 19th Century, 29 In. 3408.00
Shelf, Black Marble, 6 Jade Inserts, Vial Mercury Pendulum, c.1890, 19 In. 336.00
Shelf, Black Marble, Porcelain Dial, 8-Day, Time & Strike, France, c.1900, 12 1/2 In. 195.00
Shelf, Brass Dial, Lacquer Case, Chinoiserie, Pagoda, Fluted Canopy, Late 1800s, 13 In. . . 1225.00
Shelf, Brass, Glass, Enamel, Green Onyx, Portrait Pendulum, France, c.1890, 16 In. 2352.00
Shelf, Bronze Dore, Wounded Goddess, Seated, Signed Lepine, c.1830, 21 x 16 x 6 In. . . . 2760.00
Shelf, Bronze Gold Gilt, Cherubs, Swag, Rope Bezel, 8-Day, Time & Strike, c.1880 . . . . . . 2390.00
Shelf, Bronze Mounted, Black Slate, Temple Front, France, c.1885, 11 x 21 x 7 1/2 In. 520.00
Shelf, Bronze Mounted, Rouge Marble, Gothic Arch Shape, White Enameled Dial, 13 In. . . 510.00
Shelf, Bronze, 2-Train Chime Movement, Beveled Glass Sides, c.1920, 9 In. 410.00
Shelf, Chamois, Carved, Rock Formation, Birds, Rabbits, Swiss, c.1890, 33 x 24 In. 5175.00
Shelf, Dirty Time Co., Spiro Agnew, Metal, Box, 3 1/2 x 2 1/2 x 1 1/2 In. 50.00
Shelf, Edwardian Gothic, Mahogany, Arched Case, Inlaid Ribbons, Fans, 12 1/2 In. 115.00
Shelf, Empire, 4 Columns, Brass, Cornice, Gilding, c.1835, 21 In. 1456.00
Shelf, Empire, Mahogany Veneer, Eagle Crest, 17 x 5 x 37 In. 230.00
Shelf, Empire, Mahogany, Ormolu Mounted, Ivory Inlay, 3-Train Movement, 12 In. 750.00
Shelf, Federal, Mahogany, Bird's-Eye Maple, Brass Finials, Eglomise Panel, 32 In. 1035.00
Shelf, Federal, Mahogany, Pillar & Scroll, Brass Movement, Half-Hour Strike, 31 1/4 In. . . 1035.00
Shelf, Federal, Mahogany, White Face, Landscape, Paw Feet, c.1830, 29 x 16 3/4 In. 1380.00
Shelf, Figural, Astronomer, Ormolu, Winged Figure, Telescope, Globe, c.1870, 13 In. 3360.00
Shelf, Figural, Clock Peddler, Polychrome, Man, Hat, Top Coat, Cane, 15 x 8 x 5 In. 290.00
Shelf, Figural, Crusader, Under Glass Dome, Gilt, France, 19th Century, 19 In. 545.00
Shelf, Figural, Lighthouse, Automaton, Thermometers, Barometer, France, c.1885, 16 In. . . 3025.00
Shelf, Figural, Organ Grinder, Monkey, Blinking Eye, Iron, c.1880, 17 1/2 In. 3819.00
Shelf, Figural, Retour Des Champs, Bronzed Figures, Women, Marble Base, c.1900, 25 In. 1035.00
Shelf, Figural, Woman On Crescent Moon, Spelter, Bronze, Onyx, Enamel, 11 x 5 x 24 In. . 315.00
Shelf, Franklin Roosevelt, Man Of Hour, Ship's Wheel, Bronze Luster, Electric, 14 x 9 In. . 104.00
Shelf, French Empire, Panels, Columns, Black Onyx, Ormolu, c.1844, 17 1/2 In. 865.00
Shelf, Gilt Metal, Porcelain, Urn Finial, Classical Shape, c.1890, 17 x 9 x 5 In. 489.00
Shelf, Inlaid Rosewood, Gilt Brass, Enameled Dial, France, 1800s, 18 In. 1700.00
Shelf, Louis XV Style, Gilt, Ebonized Metal, c.1900, 16 1/2 In. 500.00
Shelf, Louis XV Style, Ormolu Putti, Fighting Ducks, Porcelain, 14 1/4 In. 1150.00
Shelf, Louis XV Style, Ormolu, 2-Train Movement, Flower Spray, Stand, 21 1/2 In. 5750.00
Shelf, Louis XVI Style, 2-Train Movement, Woman, Putto, Porcelain, 25 In. 5750.00
Shelf, Louis XVI Style, Bronze, 2-Train Chime, Enameled Dial, Pilasters, c.1880, 16 In. . . 705.00
Shelf, Louis XVI Style, Ormolu, Putti, Striking, Porcelain, 14 x 19 In. 2530.00
Shelf, Mahogany Case, 3-Train, Arched Dial, Westminster, Germany, c.1905, 14 In. 336.00
Shelf, Mahogany, 8-Day, Time & Gong, Germany, c.1910, 11 In. 60.00
Shelf, Mahogany, Quarter Westminster Chime, Germany, c.1905, 12 In. 140.00
Shelf, Maple, Eagle, Spread Wings, Ball Finial, Early 19th Century, 28 1/4 In. 5290.00
Shelf, Marble, Gilt Bronze, Maiden, 2 Cherubs, France, Late 1800s, 13 1/2 In. 1600.00
Shelf, Marble, Ormolu, Brass Works, Single Bell Strike, Flower Swag, France, 18 In. 865.00
Shelf, Moorish Style, Bronze, Continental, 20 In. 720.00
Shelf, Napoleon III, Gilt Metal, Obelisk Shape, Dial Flanked By Wings, 32 x 26 In. 8365.00
Shelf, Napoleon III, Ormolu, Marble, 2-Train Movement, Woman, Putto, 23 In. 1265.00
Shelf, Napoleon III, Ormolu, Onyx, Figural, Woman, Putto, 18 3/4 In. 2530.00
Shelf, Neuchatel Style, Mahogany, 8-Day, Time & Strike, France, c.1910, 16 In. 185.00
Shelf, Onyx, Marble, French Movement, c.1890, 16 1/2 In. 140.00
Shelf, Ormolu Mounted, Marble, Lepine, Paris, c.1850, 27 x 17 x 5 In. 5520.00
Shelf, Ormolu, Onyx, 2-Train Movement, Giltwood Plinth, Medallion, France, 13 1/2 In. . . 460.00
Shelf, Pillar & Scroll, Reverse Painted Glass, American, c.1830, 34 In. 520.00
Shelf, Portico, Classical Style, Satinwood, Rosewood, Gilt Metal, 18 1/2 In. 510.00
Shelf, Portico, Ebony, Molded Crown, Gilt Bronze Swags, 4 Columns, 20 x 11 x 6 In. 800.00
Shelf, Raingo Freres, 4-Glass, Ormolu, Marble, c.1870, 21 In. 4145.00
Shelf, Rococo Revival, Blue & White Faience, 2-Train, Chiming, c.1925, 15 3/4 In. 470.00
Shelf, Rococo Style, Gilt Bronze, Cupid, 8-Day, Time & Strike, France, c.1875, 20 In. 1512.00
Shelf, Steeple, Candle Finials, Wagon Spring, 30-Hour, Time & Strike, c.1848, 22 In. 3190.00
Shelf, Tambour, Oak Case, 8-Day, Gong, Silvered Brass Dial, England, c.1920, 9 In. 60.00
Shelf, Thoroughbred, Bronze, Marble, Silk Thread Movement, France, c.1830, 18 In. 2350.00
Shelf, Victorian, Walnut, Alarm, Silvered Decoration, Cameo Pendulum, 21 In. 175.00

Shelf, Victorian, Walnut, Carved Decoration, Alarm, 22 In. 140.00
Shelf, Victorian, Walnut, Gilt Decorated Door, Alarm Mechanism, 21 In. 130.00
Shelf, Victorian, Walnut, Incised, Carved Decoration, Alarm, 16 In. 90.00
Shelf, Walnut, Cast Metal & Brass Moon Dial, Back Plate, Early 1900s, 18 1/2 x 9 x 5 3/4 In. 175.00
Shelf, Wood, Carved, Lion, Shield, Wheel, Briefcase, Mercury, Caduceus, Pan, 26 x 15 In. 3625.00
Ship's Bell, Chelsea, Brass, Round Case, Silvered Dial, 10 In. 1325.00
Shreve & Co., Carriage, Gilt Bronze, Glazed Panels, Leather Case, France, c.1900, 6 In. ... 460.00
Shreve Crump & Low, Ship's Bell, Chelsea, Brass, Mahogany Stand, Boston, 7 1/4 In. 920.00
Simplex Time Recorder Co., Time Punch, Oak, 8-Day, Model T-10, Mass., c.1935, 31 In. . 950.00
Skeleton, Brighton Pavilion, Passing Strike, England, Mid 20th Century, 14 x 18 In. 670.00
Skeleton, Calendar & Alarm Dials, Dome, Bell In Base, France, c.1880, 7 1/2 In. 2800.00
Skeleton, Single Fusee, Dome, On Base, England, c.1850, 17 In. 1065.00
Skeleton, Single Fusee, Passing Strike, Glass Dome, England, c.1890, 19 1/2 In. 925.00
Skeleton, Striking, Crown Verge Escapement, Mid 19th Century, 26 In. 5040.00
Smith & Goodrich, Beehive, Bristol, 30-Hour Fusee, Time & Strike, c.1847, 20 In. 5150.00
Smith & Goodrich, Shelf, Mahogany, 8-Day, Time Only, c.1845, 12 1/2 In. 785.00
Spencer Wooster & Co., Column, Cornice, Shelf, 8-Day, Time & Strike, c.1840, 34 In. ... 840.00
Sperry & Shaw, Empire, 30-Hour, Time & Strike, 4 Columns, c.1848, 25 3/4 In. 170.00
Steeple, Rosewood, American, Late 19th Century, 20 3/4 x 11 1/2 x 4 1/2 In. 175.00
Swinging Arm, Le Triomphe, Bronzed Spelter, France, c.1890, 26-In. Arm, 34 In. 2575.00
Swinging Doll, Alabaster Case, Porcelain Dial, Dome, c.1890, 15 1/2 In. 785.00
Swinging Doll, Skeleton, 8-Day, Chaff Cutter Escapement, Dome, c.1890, 11 In. 1456.00
Swinging Doll, White Alabaster, Brass Trim, 8-Day, Chaff Cutter, c.1890, 9 1/4 In. 950.00
Tall Case, Caleb Wheaton, Chippendale, Mahogany, Rhode Island, c.1765, 83 In. 18400.00
Tall Case, Carved Leaf Crest, Single Arm Movement, Sweden, c.1800, 79 In. 1725.00
Tall Case, Cherry, Double Scroll Bonnet, Pa., c.1800, 98 1/2 In. 4993.75
Tall Case, Cherry, Double Scroll Pediment, Eagle, Ball Center Finial, c.1800, 90 In. 2350.00
Tall Case, Cherry, Iron Face, Swan's Neck, Brass Rosettes, Spires, 90 1/2 x 20 x 10 1/2 In. 5290.00
Tall Case, Cherry, Mahogany Veneer, Poplar, Early 1800s, 94 1/2 In. .... *Illus* 5940.00
Tall Case, Cherry, Poplar, Mother-Of-Pearl, Heart & Flower Vase Inlay, 94 In. ...... *Illus* 8050.00
Tall Case, Chippendale, Mahogany, Brass Mounted, Moon Phase Lunette, 93 In. 3450.00
Tall Case, Daniel Monroe, Federal, Inlaid Mahogany, c.1810 .... 39100.00
Tall Case, David Smith, Mahogany, Rounded Glass Door, Calendar, Seconds Dials, 82 In. . 598.00
Tall Case, David Williams, Federal, Mahogany, Newport, R.I., c.1810, 92 In. 4780.00
Tall Case, E. Howard, Georgian Style, Mahogany, Electrified, Boston, Early 1900s 2938.00
Tall Case, Elliott, Mahogany, Columns, 9 Tubular Bells, 8-Day, London, c.1890, 95 In. ... 5019.00
Tall Case, Elliott, Mahogany, Glass, Brass Dial, Moon, Chimes, London, c.1900, 89 In. ... 4063.00
Tall Case, Elmer O. Stennes, Pine Case, Westminster Chime, c.1964, 61 In. 1905.00
Tall Case, Father Time, 8-Day, Brass Dial Movement, c.1875, 90 In. 2016.00
Tall Case, Federal, Broken Arch Bonnet, Painted Face, Wag Works, c.1815, 87 In. 3450.00
Tall Case, Federal, Cherry, Arched Top, Glazed Door, Painted Face, Early 1800s, 87 In. ... 2938.00
Tall Case, Federal, Cherry, Broken Pediment, 19th Century, 94 x 18 x 11 In. 1315.00
Tall Case, Federal, Cherry, Rose Basket, Shell Painted Dial, Brass Works, 97 In. 2743.00
Tall Case, Federal, Mahogany, 3 Spire & Ball Finials, Washington Portrait, Flags, 95 In. 9988.00
Tall Case, Federal, Mahogany, Sun & Moon Phase, c.1800, 93 In. 4830.00
Tall Case, Federal, Painted, Decorated Wood Face, Hadley & Plymouth, Mass., 88 x 17 In. 1528.00

Clock, Tall Case,
Cherry, Mahogany
Veneer, Poplar, Early
1800s, 94 1/2 In.

Clock, Tall Case, Cherry,
Poplar, Mother-Of-Pearl,
Heart & Flower Vase
Inlay, 94 In.

Clock, Tall Case,
Parkinson & Frodsham,
Mahogany, Pineapple
Finials, 8 Bells, 88 In.

Tall Case, French Provincial, Fruitwood, Brass Surround, Late 18th Century, 110 In. 2099.00
Tall Case, George II, Walnut, Pewtered Chapter Ring, c.1730, 90 In. 9200.00
Tall Case, George III, Green Japanned, Roman & Arabic Numbers, Dial, c.1780, 88 1/4 In. 8625.00
Tall Case, George III, Inlaid Mahogany, Quarter Strike, Chime, 91 In. 5581.00
Tall Case, George III, Mahogany, 2-Train Movement, Lunar Arch, Date Dial, 88 In. 2350.00
Tall Case, George III, Mahogany, Lord Nelson Scene, Firth, Leeds, c.1785, 95 x 26 In. 8338.00
Tall Case, George III, Mahogany, Satinwood Inlaid, Brass Mount, 20th Century 4140.00
Tall Case, George III, Oak, Broken Arch Pediment, Hand Painted Dial, 93 x 10 x 20 In. ... 1900.00
Tall Case, Hepplewhite, Cherry, Red Wash, Tapered Feet, Raised Panel, 91 In. 2875.00
Tall Case, Herschede, Model 245, Mahogany, 5-Tube, Quarter Chime, c.1951, 86 In. 1790.00
Tall Case, John Stancliffe, Oak, Mahogany Case, Inlaid, Arched Brass Dial, 8-Day, 90 In. . 4370.00
Tall Case, John Walker, Oak, 8-Day, Brass Dial, Rolling Moon, England, c.1850, 86 In. ... 2910.00
Tall Case, M. Thomas, Oak, 8-Day, Arched Brass Dial, Carnarvon, Wales, 86 In. 4140.00
Tall Case, Mahogany Case, England, 19th Century, 62 In. 1610.00
Tall Case, Mahogany Veneer, Fluted Columns, Castle, Ship Arch, England, c.1840, 93 In. . 2910.00
Tall Case, Mahogany, Brass & Silver Dial, Scotland, c.1860, 29 1/2 x 36 x 22 In. 3450.00
Tall Case, Mahogany, Broken Arch Pediment, Paneled Door, c.1840, 90 x 21 x 10 In. 4140.00
Tall Case, Mahogany, Broken Swan's-Neck Pediment, 1800s, 85 x 20 x 10 1/2 In. 2235.00
Tall Case, Mahogany, Quarter Chime, 1800s 3890.00
Tall Case, Major Scholfield, Mahogany, Broken Arch Pediment, 8-Day, Manchester, 91 In. 5290.00
Tall Case, Oak Case, Broken Arch, Rolling Moon, 30-Hour, England, c.1825, 91 In. 1456.00
Tall Case, Oak, Arched Pediment, Brass Face, Chimes, Beveled Glass Panels, 80 In. 1035.00
Tall Case, Organ, Mahogany, Classical Scene, 5-In. Organ Roll, 93 1/2 In. 8800.00
Tall Case, Parkinson & Frodsham, Mahogany, Pineapple Finials, 8 Bells, 88 In. ..... *Illus* 10350.00
Tall Case, Pine, Leavenworth Movement, 30-Hour, Time & Strike, c.1820, 83 In. 336.00
Tall Case, Pine, Wooden Works, Painted Dial, New England, 81 1/2 In. 3840.00
Tall Case, R. Whiting, Hepplewhite, Cherry, Overlapping Door, Winchester, Conn., 90 In. . 1610.00
Tall Case, Riley Whiting, Pine, Flower Dial, 30-Hour, Weight Driven, c.1825, 86 In. 1410.00
Tall Case, Satinwood, Mahogany, Grain Painted Pine, Arched Bonnet Door, 8-Day, 88 In. . 3525.00
Tall Case, Seth Thomas, Federal, Cherry, Mahogany, c.1810, 94 1/2 x 17 3/4 In. 4800.00
Tall Case, Shaker, Pine, 1800s, 77 1/2 x 13 x 7 1/2 In. 10158.00
Tall Case, Silas Hoadley, Cherry, Conn., Early 19th Century, 98 In. 3290.00
Tall Case, Symphonion, Germany, c.1895, 95 In. 9744.00
Tall Case, Walker, Mahogany, Arched Door, Inlaid, 8-Day, Flowers, Bird, c.1805, 86 In. ... 4300.00
Tall Case, Walnut, Double Scrolled Cresting, c.1815, 67 In. 5875.00
Tall Case, Walnut, Inlay, Leaf Cluster, Bracket Feet, 8-Day, New Jersey, c.1810, 90 In. 3930.00
Tall Case, Waterbury, Pillar, Ebony Finish, 8-Day, 2-Weight, Time & Strike, c.1920, 83 In. 336.00
Tall Case, Wignall, Chippendale, Mahogany, Veneer, Ogee Feet, Southport, c.1785, 94 In. . 1035.00
Tall Case, William Bucknell, Mahogany, Inlaid, Arched Dial, 8-Day, Burslem, 91 In. 2185.00
Tall Case, William IV, Satinwood, Ebonized, Bird's-Eye Maple, c.1835, 88 In. 2300.00
Tall Case, Winstanley, Mahogany, 8-Day, Bell, Strike, England, c.1830, 14-In. Dial, 86 In. . 1230.00
Tall Case, Woodley Kington, Chinoiserie, Day, Date, England, c.1815, 89 x 19 1/2 In. 4140.00
Terry, Eli & Samuel, Shelf, Mahogany, Pillar & Scroll, Eglomise Panel, c.1820, 32 In. 3055.00
Terry, Eli, Shelf, Mahogany, Pillar & Scroll, Eglomise Panel, Conn., c.1875, 31 In. 2470.00
Terry & Andrews, Double Steeple, Mahogany, Eglomise Flags, Mid 1800s, 25 1/4 In. 646.00
Terry & Sons, Federal, Mahogany, Pillar & Scroll, Eglomise Panel, 31 x 16 In. 4140.00
Terry & Sons, Shelf, Federal, Mahogany, Pillar & Scroll, c.1820, 31 x 17 1/2 x 4 1/2 In. 5875.00
Terry Clock Co., Iron Case, 30-Hour, Time & Alarm, c.1875, 6 In. 70.00
Terry Clock Co., Iron Case, Black Enamel, 8-Day, c.1875, 9 In. 70.00
Terry Clock Co., Shelf, 30-Hour, Time & Strike, Waterbury, Conn., c.1868, 18 In. 2910.00
Tiffany clocks that are part of desk sets made by Louis Comfort Tiffany are listed in the
Tiffany category. Clocks sold by the store, Tiffany & Co., are listed here.
Tiffany & Co., Shelf, Classical Revival, Parcel-Gilt Bronze, Foo Dog Handles, 19 In. 825.00
Travel, Art Deco, Enamel, Painted, Pink Swags, Blue Ground, Urn Shape, Cover, 7 In. 9560.00
Travel, Hermes, Stainless Steel, Leather, Quartz Movement, Folding Case 235.00
Travel, Movado, Silver Gilt, Enamel, Silvertone Dial, Ball Terminals, Cylindrical Case ... 265.00
United Clock Co., Will Rogers, Cast, Base Metals, 1930s, 14 In. 235.00
Upson Merrimans & Co., 30-Hour, Wood Movement, Time & Strike, c.1832, 27 1/2 In. ... 500.00
Vincenti, Shelf, Marble, 8-Day, Time & Strike, c.1890, 10 3/4 In. 110.00
Vincenti, Shelf, Marble, 8-Day, Time & Strike, c.1910, 9 3/4 In. 140.00
Vincenti, Wall, Cartel, Brass, 8-Day, Bell Strike, c.1890, 25 In. 390.00
Wag-On-Wall, 30-Hour, Time & Strike, Painted Dial, Germany, c.1890, 9 1/2 In. 459.00
Wag-On-Wall, Thomas Dadswell, Engraved, Brass, Weight-Driven, England, Late 1700s .. 650.00

Wall, Bakers, 8-Day, Time & Strike, Ebonized, Reverse Painted, France, c.1890, 24 1/2 In. ... 125.00
Wall, Berlin Style, Walnut, Kienzle Prima Movement, Art Nouveau, c.1910, 31 In. 336.00
Wall, Cartel, Bell Strike, Flowers, Ormolu, Gilt Bronze, France, c.1870, 23 In. 1960.00
Wall, Cherry Veneer, Box, 8-Day, Time & Strike, Beveled Glass, c.1910, 24 3/4 In. 215.00
Wall, Comtoise, 8-Day, Time & Strike, Bakers, Morbier, Spring Driven, c.1890, 25 In. 110.00
Wall, Comtoise, 8-Day, Time & Strike, Morbier, Spring Driven, c.1890, 17 1/2 In. 140.00
Wall, Dovetailed Pine Case, Mirror, Hinge Front, New Hampshire, 38 x 18 In. 1265.00
Wall, Dutch Baroque Style, Walnut, Ebonized Burl Walnut, Ormolu Mount, 30 In. 460.00
Wall, Gothic, Mahogany, Mahogany Veneer, Double Fusee Strike, England, c.1830 ...... 765.00
Wall, Grand Sonnerie, 3-Weight, Quarter Column, North Wind Top, Austria, c.1880, 53 In. 3430.00
Wall, Grand Sonnerie, Walnut, 3-Weight, Austria, c.1875, 49 In. 728.00
Wall, Jockele, Time & Alarm, 2-Weight, 30-Hour, Germany, c.1870, 3 1/2 In. 3136.00
Wall, Mahogany, Fusee Movement, Pendulum, Silk-Screened Dial, c.1880, 16 x 16 In. 179.00
Wall, Porcelain, 8-Day, Brass Pendulum, Pot, Fish, Herbs, Germany, c.1920, 12 1/2 In. ... 280.00
Wall, Regulator, Walnut, Box, Beveled Glass, 2-Weight, Austria, c.1910, 39 In. 420.00
Wall, Regulator, Walnut, Ormolu Mount, Train Movement Strikes Gong, Germany, 39 In. . 1265.00
Waltham, Regulator, No. 16, Oak, 3-Jar Mercury Pendulum, c.1908, 67 1/2 In. 6720.00
Waterbury, Bruno, Black Iron Case, Ormolu Mounts, 19th Century, 13 In. 230.00
Waterbury, Carriage, Conductor, Brass, 30-Hour, Time & Strike, Repeater, c.1893, 5 In. .. 135.00
Waterbury, Cottage, 30-Hour, Pendulum, c.1870, 10 1/2 In. 125.00
Waterbury, Dalton, Shelf, Painted, Black, Faux Marble, 11 1/2 x 14 In. 105.00
Waterbury, Gallery, Oak, Stepped Case, 8-Day, c.1890, 18 In. 1000.00
Waterbury, Regulator, No. 60, Maple, c.1900, 79 1/2 In. 7168.00
Waterbury, Shelf, Mahogany Veneer, Ogee, 8-Day, Alarm, c.1875, 28 In. 310.00
Waterbury, Shelf, Mahogany Veneer, Ogee, Reverse Painted Bird, 8-Day, c.1870 .... 295.00
Waterbury, Valdora, Bronzed Spelter, Enameled Iron Base, c.1905, 13 1/4 In. 280.00
Waterbury, Wall, Cherry, Arched Top, Columns, 8-Day, Time & Strike, 50 x 16 In. 1075.00
Waterbury, Wall, Figure 8, Wood, Batalla Mosaic, 8-Day, Time & Strike, 22 x 13 In. 359.00
Waterbury, Wall, Mahogany, Scalloped Arched Top, 8-Day, Time & Strike, 46 x 16 In. ... 1910.00
Welch, E.N., Briggs Rotary, Bottom Wind, New Dome, c.1870, 7 In. 310.00
Welch, E.N., Briggs Rotary, Brass Movement, c.1878, 7 1/2 In. 476.00
Welch, E.N., Cottage, Rosewood Veneer, 30-Hour, c.1870, 10 In. 60.00
Welch, E.N., Cottage, Rosewood Veneer, Horns Of Plenty, 30-Hour, c.1870, 12 In. 45.00
Welch, E.N., Gallery, Rosewood, 8-Day, Noah Pomeroy Movement, c.1855, 11 In. 900.00
Welch, E.N., Gingerbread, Walnut, Conquistador Glass, Brass Pendulum, c.1885, 23 In. ... 260.00
Welch, E.N., Regulator, Eclipse Calendar, Walnut Case, 8-Day, c.1880, 39 In. 615.00
Welch, E.N., Shelf, Rosewood, 30-Hour, Time & Strike, c.1855, 18 In. 365.00
Welch, E.N., Steeple, Mahogany, 8-Day, Riverboat, Town, c.1857 .... 1512.00
Welch, E.N., Wall, Alexis, Rosewood, 8-Day, c.1885, 22 In. 810.00
Welch, E.N., Wall, Mahogany, Etched Glass Door, 8-Day, c.1890, 40 x 15 In. 600.00
Welch Spring, Gale Drop Calendar, No. 2, Moon Phase Dial, 8-Day, c.1877, 30 In. 8400.00
Welch Spring, Italian, No. 3, Rosewood, Perpetual Calendar, 8-Day, 18 1/4 In. 900.00
Welch Spring, Wall, Mahogany, Days & Months, 8-Day, Time & Strike, 33 x 17 In. 1315.00
Westclox, Mission Novelty, Oak Case, 30-Hour, Time, Alarm, c.1920, 12 In. 70.00
Whiting, Lewis, E., Timby Solar Timepiece, Globe, Mahogany Case, c.1864, 27 In. 4480.00
Winterhalder & Hofmeier, Bracket, Mahogany, 3-Train, Westminster Chime, c.1890, 17 In. 1120.00
Winterhalder & Hofmeier, Shelf, Arts & Crafts, Oak, 8-Day, 2 Gongs, c.1910, 12 In. 340.00
Winterhalder & Hofmeier, Shelf, Oak, 8-Day, Quarter Strike, c.1890, 19 1/2 In. 560.00
Winterhalder & Hofmeier, Walnut, 9 Gongs, Quarter Chime, c.1895, 19 In. 3640.00

CLOISONNE enamel was developed during the tenth century. A
glass enamel was applied between small ribbons of metal on a metal
base. Most cloisonne is Chinese or Japanese. Pieces marked *China* are
twentieth-century examples.

Bowl, Black Ground, Swirls, Flower Roundels, Japan, Late 19th Century, 5 In. 170.00
Box, Cover, Gray, Red Carp, Silver Wire, Japan, 5 1/2 In. 2530.00
Box, Fan Shape, Butterflies, Lavender Foil Ground, 19th Century, 1 3/4 In. 69.00
Box, Flower Shape, Phoenix, Paulownia, Aventurine Ground, 19th Century, 2 1/2 In. 185.00
Box, Lattice Design, On Silver, Cylindrical, Chinese, 1800s, 3 In. 208.00
Box, Opium, Coin, Vase, Blue Ground, Cylindrical, 1800s, 2 1/2 In. 127.00
Box, Opium, Flower Vases, Censer, Cylindrical, Chinese, 1800s, 2 3/4 In. 127.00
Candleholder, Torchere, Patinated Metal, Elephant Shaped Base, Chinese, 75 In. 1315.00
Candlestick, Duck, Cast, Standing On Tortoise Back, Chinese, 14 1/2 In., Pair 2530.00

Censer, Lid, Openwork, Rounded Rectangular, 9 1/4 x 11 x 5 In. 980.00
Charger, Lappet Rim, Cranes, Wisteria, Lotus, Phoenix, Japan, c.1900, 24 1/2 In. 608.00
Charger, Phoenix Medallions, Flower Roundels, Japan, c.1890, 17 1/2 In., Pair 1680.00
Charger, Scalloped Rim, Cartouche Center, Figure, Moorish Arches, Late 1800s, 15 In. ... 175.00
Charger, Scalloped Rim, Cranes, Peonies, Mythical Animals, Lotus, Japan, c.1900 .... 610.00
Cigarette Case, Falconer Amid Trees, Rectangular, Rounded Corners, Russia, 4 1/4 In. ... 1080.00
Figure, Bull, Decorated, Inlaid, Aqua Blue Background, 10 1/2 x 18 x 5 1/2 In. 225.00
Ginger Jar, Egg Shape, Treebark, Sparrow, On Porcelain, Japan, Early 1900s, 8 1/2 In. 1150.00
Incense Burner, 2 Sections, 4 Holes, Ball Finial, 18th Century, 10 x 5 In. 805.00
Incense Burner, 3 Entwined Cranes, God, Shou Lao, Chinese, 28 1/2 In. 1150.00
Jar, Baluster, Dragon, Silver Wires, Royal Blue Ground, Japan, 20th Century, 8 1/2 In. .. 630.00
Jar, Cover, Ball Shape, Flowers, Butterflies, Dragons, Gray Ground, 19th Century, 6 In. ... 430.00
Jar, Cover, Birds, Lotus Blossoms, 7 1/2 In., Pair.................................... 138.00
Jar, Cover, Blossoms, Yellow, Burgundy, Red, Pink, Blue Ground, 15 3/4 In., Pair 460.00
Jar, Cover, Egg Shape, Birds, Flowers, Lotus Finial, Japan, 1880s-1900s, 5 1/2 In. 6170.00
Jar, Cover, Egg Shape, Flowers, Butterflies, Green Ground, 19th Century, 5 In. 230.00
Jar, Cover, Gilt Bronze, Carved Pedestal, 8 1/2 In. 115.00
Jar, Dome Cover, Enamel, Geese, Marsh, Black Ground, Ball Finials, 12 1/2 In., Pair 1150.00
Jar, Egg Shape, Dragon, Scalloped Foot & Mouth Borders, Japan, Early 1900s, 6 In. 375.00
Jardiniere, Bronze Vases, Shou, Blue Ground, c.1800, 2 3/4 In. 120.00
Kovsh, Silver Gilt, Cyrillic Makers Mark, Russia, c.1900, 4 In. 1035.00
Teapot, Egg Shape, Flowers, Black Ground, 19th Century, 3 1/2 In. 69.00
Vase, Baluster Shape, Chrysanthemums, Foo Dogs, Chinese, c.1890, 11 3/4 In., Pair 690.00
Vase, Baluster Shape, Hexagonal, Irises, Japan, c.1915, 18 3/4 In. 935.00
Vase, Bands, Geometric, Flowers, Dragons, Phoenixes, Black Field, Japan, 9 7/8 In., Pair . 259.00
Vase, Birds Amidst Flowering Branches, White Ground, 18 1/2 In. 900.00
Vase, Butterfly, Black Ground, Hexagonal, Japan, 3 1/2 In. 375.00
Vase, Chrysanthemum, 16 Petals, Club Shape, Yellow Ground, 19th Century, 9 3/4 In. ... 460.00
Vase, Chrysanthemum, Lavender Ground, Blue, Red, Japan, 3 1/2 In. 1150.00
Vase, Cloisonne Flowers On Porcelain Treebark, Japan, Early 1900s, 3 1/2 In. 200.00
Vase, Club Shape, Dragon Designs, Black Aventurine Ground, 19th Century, 18 1/2 In. ... 3335.00
Vase, Cranes, Tree, Bulbous, Shouldered, Blue, 5 In. 1175.00
Vase, Dragon, Cobalt Blue Ground, Pink, White, Red, Gold, 9 1/2 In. 25.00
Vase, Dragon, Flowers, Gilt, Black, Amphora Form, Chinese, 18th Century, 12 3/4 In. 2415.00
Vase, Dragon, Green Ground, Japan, 14 1/4 In. 690.00
Vase, Flower Scene, Sky Blue Ground, Early 20th Century, Japan, 8 In. 265.00
Vase, Flowers, Blue Ground, Club, 9 1/2 In. 405.00
Vase, Flowers, Blue Ground, Transparent, Japan, 2 1/2 In. ....105.00 to 115.00
Vase, Flowers, Cylindrical, Musen Shippo, Signed, Japan, 8 1/4 In. 90.00
Vase, Flowers, Cylindrical, Musen Shippo, Signed, Japan, 9 3/4 In. 150.00
Vase, Goldstone Ground, Gray Tree, White, Pink Flowers, Teakwood Stand, 12 1/2 In. 980.00
Vase, Ovoid, Tapered, Scrolling Vines, 4 Buttressed Feet, China, 12 In. 720.00
Vase, Phoenix Amidst Clouds, Japan, 6 In. 130.00
Vase, Pigeon's Blood, Kumeno Teitaru, Japan, 5 In. 85.00
Vase, Porcelain Treebark, Cloisonne Peonies & Birds, Japan, Early 1900s, 7 1/2 In., Pair .. 1380.00
Vase, Purple Poppy, Green Ground, Cylindrical, Japan, c.1980, 13 1/4 In. 1610.00
Vase, Roses, Leaves, Bird, Pink, White, Red Ground, 7 1/4 In. 29.00
Vase, Seed Shape, Butterflies, Black Ground, 19th Century, 4 1/2 In. 400.00
Vase, Stylized Pink & Green Blossoms, Blue Ground, Chinese, c.1900, 22 In. 375.00
Vase, White Crane, Pink Ground, Inverted Pear Shape, Japan, 4 3/4 In. 195.00

CLOTHING of all types is listed in this category. Dresses, hats, shoes,
underwear, and more are found here. Other textiles are to be found in
the Coverlet, Movie, Quilt, Textile, and World War I and II categories.

Beanie, My Favorite Martian, Bell Tipped Antenna, Benay Albee, 1963, 6 1/2 x 7 In. 120.00
Belt, Battlestar Galactica, Leather, 1978, Child's 20.00
Belt, Beaded, Graphic, Relief Faces, Blue Birds, Shells, Cloth Back, Africa, 5 x 40 In. 85.00
Belt, Gold Tone Pyramid Hardware, Hermes, 31 In. 205.00
Bikini, Brown, Pink, Orange, Blue, White, Signature, Emilio Pucci, Size 12 .... 175.00
Bodysuit, Black Lace, Over Red Satin Leotard, Giorgio Sant' Angelo, 1970s, Small 810.00
Bonnet, Calash, Beige Linen, Reed Ribs, Ruffled Brim, Women's, 1790s-1820s 900.00
Boots, Go-Go, White Vinyl, Knee High, Buckles, 2-In. Heels, Italy, Size 10 .... 40.00
Boots, Leather, Stack Heels, Pull Straps, Size 10 .... 40.00

Boots, Saint Nick, Red, Black, Cotton Lining, Unika Rubber Co., Box, Child's, 10 1/2 In. . . 220.00
Cap, Railroad, Blue & White, Cotton, 4 Metal Grommets, Lee Tag, 1940s, 6 7/8 In. 30.00
Cap, Ranger Joe Safety Cap, 4 Stitched Cloth Panels, c.1951, 7 In. 140.00
Cape, Dorothy, Green Wool, Pink Silk Lined Hood, 19th Century, 60 In. 375.00
Chaps, Leather Outers & Belt, Nickel Hardware & Buckle, 1950s, Child's 120.00
Coat, Mink, Full-Length, Reversible, Silk Lining, Belted, Fendi 8225.00
Coat, Mink, Late 20th Century, Women's, Medium . . . . .200.00 to 259.00
Coat, Oriental, Embroidered, Fur Lined, Black Silk, Courtyard Scenes, 1927, 45 In. 230.00
Dress, Cotton, Green, Pink, Blue, Brown, White, Turquoise Belt, Emilio Pucci, Size 10 . . . 120.00
Dress, Paper, Cat, London Poster Dress Company, c.1968 . . . . 499.00
Dress, Silk, Black, Green, Pink, White, Emilio Pucci, Signature, Size 10 . . . . 465.00
Dress, Silk, Brown, Blue, Gray, Ivory, Emilio Pucci, Signature, Size 10 . . . . 275.00
Dress, Silk, Printed, Black, Orange, Pink & White, Labeled Emilio Pucci, Size 10 . . . . 465.00
Dress, Silk, Purple, Green, Blue, Black, Ivory, Signature, Emilio Pucci, Size 10 . . . . 295.00
Dress, Souper, Campbell's Soup, 2 Yellow Bands At Bottom, After Andy Warhol, c.1968 . . 800.00
Girdle, White, Mold 'n Hold Zipper, Blue Metallic Tube, Playtex, Medium, 1950s 55.00
Gloves, Gunsmoke, Black, Red Leather Fringe, Canvas Cuffs, Colt Revolver, Badge 22.00
Gloves, Lace, Fingers Out, Ruffled Wrist, White, 1940s 55.00
Hat, Cowboy, Felt, Inside Band, Labels, Harrelson Costume Company, 1880s 55.00
Hat, Mass. Officer's Militia, Felt, Leather, Eagle, Tassels, Box, c.1815, 9 1/2 x 17 In. 1880.00
Hat, Shako, Felt Body, Leather Binding, Blue & White Pompom, Harding Co., Mass. 115.00
Hat, Western, Red Ryder, Red, Cord Chin Strap, Wood Bolo, C. Stephen, N.Y. 55.00
Jacket, AC Smart Spark Plug, Great Lakes Sportswear, 1970s, Medium 25.00
Jacket, Denim, Indigo, 2 Flapped Pockets, Woven Label, Lee Riders, 1950s, Size 40 . . . . . 380.00
Jacket, Mink, Woman's, Late 20th Century, Medium 345.00
Jacket, Motorcycle, Leather, Tan, Black Sleeves, Bates Of California, 1960s 420.00
Jeans, Denim, Indigo, Zipper Fly, Paper Tags, Tuf-Nut Westerns, 1950s, Size 31 x 30 In. . . 110.00
Riding Attire, Rodeo, Hand Beaded, Wool Challis, Military Style Buttons, 19th Century . . 245.00
Robe, Damask, Blue Field, Dragons, Stylized Ocean, Stripes, Chinese, 1900s, 55 In. 715.00
Robe, Dragon, Chinese, Early 20th Century 355.00
Robe, Silk Needlework, 8 Dragons, 5 Claws, Gold Threadwork, Chinese, Child's 1955.00
Robe, Silk Needlework, Crane Medallions, Red Ground, Chinese, 19th Century 2185.00
Robe, Silk Needlework, Gold, Horse's Hoof Cuffs, Dragon, Bronze Buttons, Chinese 1725.00
Robe, Silk Needlework, Satin Stitch, Flowers, Red, Chinese, 19th Century, Child's 360.00
Robe, Silk, 9 Dragons, 5 Claws, Gold Threads, Blue Ground, Chinese, 19th Century 2070.00
Robe, Silk, Embroidered Flying Crane, Blue Sky, White Clouds, 1900, Medium 625.00
Robe, Silk, Embroidered, Dragon, 5 Claws, Salmon Ground, Chinese, 19th Century 750.00
Robe, Silk, French Knot, Satin Stitch Flowers, Red Brocade Ground 805.00
Robe, Theatrical, Lions, Red Ground, Peonies, Censer, Phoenix, Chinese, 19th Century . . . 2990.00
Scarf, Silk, Histoire Des Cartes Jouer, Face Cards, Ivory, White, Yellow Border, Hermes . . 295.00
Scarf, Silk, Le Carnaval De Venise, City Scenes, Masqueraders, Masks, Ribbons, Hermes . 355.00
Scarf, Yellow Abstract Design, Cream Ground, Emilo Pucci, 1960s, 28 In. 270.00
Shawl, Manilla, Peonies, Buff Ground, Lace Fringe, Chinese, Early 1900s, 46 x 46 In. 140.00
Shoes, High Top High Heels, Lace, Beige, Pointed Toes, c.1910, Size 8AAA 100.00
Shoes, Penny Loafer, Black Leather, G.H. Bass, 1960s, Size 7 . . . . 45.00
Skirt, Quilted, Brown Cotton Twill, Appliqued Velvet Flowers, Embroidered, 34 In. 345.00
Skirt, Silk Embroidered, Flowers, Chinese, 20th Century 45.00
Skirt, Silk Needlework, Blue Peony, Red Ground, Winter, Buddha Symbols, Chinese 290.00
Sleeve Band, Foo Dogs, Phoenix, Dragon, Gold, Blue Ground, 19th Century, Pair 120.00
Slippers, Ball, Satin, Cream, Shaped Covered Medium Heels, New England, 1750 . . . . 2500.00
Suit, Tweed, Checkerboard, Wool, Caped Jacket, Straight Skirt, Jaques Fath, 1950s 2200.00
Sweater, Women's, Navy Blue & Pink, White Flowers, Catalina, 1940s, Medium 55.00
Swimsuit, Right Side Drape, Catalina, 1950s, Large 135.00
Tie, Bret & Bart Maverick, Clip On, Warner Brothers, c.1959, 7 x 4 In. 185.00
Top Hat, Beaver, Leather Box, Lock & Co Hatters, London, 1800s, 15 x 14 x 13 In. 275.00

CLUTHRA glass is a two-layered glass with small air pockets that form white spots. The Steuben Glass Works of Corning, New York, made it in 1920. Kimball Glass Company of Vineland, New Jersey, made Cluthra from about 1925. Victor Durand signed some pieces with his name. Related items are listed in the Steuben category.

Bowl, Shouldered, Pink To Opal, Squat, 5 1/2 In. 690.00
Bowl, White, Pink, 6-Sided, 2 1/4 x 5 In. 230.00

Finger Bowl, Underplate, 6 Sides, 5 In. 1100.00
Lamp, Pink, Reticulated Metal Base, 4-Footed, 25 In. 1035.00
Vase, Amethyst, Art Nouveau, Fleur-De-Lis, Stamped, 4 1/4 x 7 3/4 In. 540.00
Vase, Amethyst, Oval, Optic Ribbed, 4 In. 1840.00
Vase, Green, 8 In. 480.00
Vase, Green, Urn Shape, Signed, Steuben, 8 In. ....520.00 to 1035.00
Vase, White, Rose, 8 1/4 In. 660.00

COALPORT ware has been made by the Coalport Porcelain Works of England from 1795 to the present time. Early pieces were unmarked. About 1810–1825 the pieces were marked with the name *Coalport* in various forms. Later pieces also had the name *John Rose* in the mark. The crown mark has been used with variations since 1881. The date 1750 is printed in some marks, but it is not the date the factory started. Some pieces are listed in Indian Tree.

BONE CHINA
COALPORT
MADE IN ENGLAND
EST. 1750

Cachepot, Stand, Flowers, Yellow Ground, Gilt Trim, Ring Handles, 7 In. 1095.00
Fish Platter, Blue & Gilt Design, White Ground, 19 In., Pair 290.00
Pitcher, Masque Spout, Green, Dragon Head Handle, Early 1800s, 7 In. 230.00
Plate, Fruit & Leaves, On Marble Slap, Gilt Leaf Rims, c.1810, 8 1/2 In., Pair 660.00
Platter, Blue & Gilt Design, White Ground, 18 3/4 In. 200.00

COBALT BLUE glass was made using oxide of cobalt. The characteristic bright dark blue identifies it for the collector. Most cobalt glass found today was made after the Civil War. There was renewed interest in the dark blue glass in the late 1930s and dinnerwares were made.

Bowl Set, Finger, Hand Blown, Bulbous, 3 In. 489.00
Spooner, Bellflower 4500.00
Vase, Paneled, Gilt Trim, 6 Medallions, Hand Painted Flowers, 5 In. 374.00

COCA-COLA was first served in 1886 in Atlanta, Georgia. It was advertised through signs, newspaper ads, coupons, bottles, trays, calendars, and even lamps and clocks. Collectors want anything with the word *Coca-Cola*, including a few rare products, like gum wrappers and cigar bands. The famous trademark was patented in 1893, the *Coke* mark in 1945. Many modern items and reproductions are being made.

Bench, Drink Coca-Cola, Wooden, 29 x 48 In. 550.00
Board, Menu, Die Cut Tin, Be Refreshed, 1957, 16 x 25 In. 130.00
Book Cover, 2 Bottles, Pause-Refreshed, No. 617, 22 x 16 In. 10.00
Bookmark, Heart Shape, Refreshing, Delicious, 5 Cents, 1898 .... 513.00
Bottle, 23rd Olympiad, Los Angeles, 1984, Bird Carrying Torch, 10 x 2 1/4 In. 12.00
Bottle, Jackson, Tenn., Bottling Wks., Amber, Tooled Lip, c.1900, 8 In. 190.00
Bottle Topper, Die Cut, Cardboard Lithograph, US Printing & Litho, 1927, 10 x 7 In. 4345.00
Bowl, Aluminum, 3 Coke Bottles, Attached To Bowl, 1935, 4 x 9 In. 490.00
Box, Pepsin Gum, Wood, Dovetailed, 6 1/2 x 6 x 12 3/4 In. 440.00
Calendar, 1923, Flapper, Girl, Glass Of Coke, Partial Pad, October, 24 1/4 x 12 1/4 In. 315.00
Calendar, 1941, Skating Girl, Thirst Knows No Season, Jan., Feb., 20 1/4 x 14 1/2 In. 195.00
Calendar, 1946, Sprite Boy, 21 x 13 In. 1430.00
Calendar, 1950, Girl Serving Cokes, Hospitality In Your Hands, 22 x 13 In. 55.00
Calendar, 1958, Starts With December 1957, Santa Claus On Cover 195.00
Calendar Holder, Button Top, Tin, 19 1/2 x 8 In. 825.00
Carrier, Wooden, Yellow, Red, 6-Pack 126.00
Clock, Drink Coca-Cola Center, Metal, Round, 18 In. 66.00
Clock, Drink Coca-Cola In Bottles, Oak, Square, Selecto, Chicago, 16 In. 240.00
Clock, Drink Coca-Cola In Bottles, Red, White, Light-Up, 16 In. Diam. 660.00
Clock, Drink Coca-Cola, Please Pay When Served, 9 x 20 In. 660.00
Clock, Drink Coca-Cola, Red, White, Black, Roman Numerals, 15 In. Diam. 1650.00
Clock, Drink Coca-Cola, Serve Yourself, 9 x 19 In. 915.00
Clock, Ideal Brain Tonic, Delicious, Refreshing, Baird, 1893-96, 30 1/2 x 18 1/2 In. 2160.00
Clock, Neon, Neon Clock Company, Tag, 31 x 36 In. 1760.00
Clock, Neon, Round, Spinner Type, Metal, Green Band, Red Numbers, Girl, 1940, 22 In. .. 4400.00
Clock, Please Pay When Served, Light-Up, 9 x 19 1/2 In. 715.00
Clock, Sold Everywhere, 5 Cents, Oak Case, 31-Day, Gilbert, 38 x 16 1/2 In. 375.00

Clock, Sprite, Light-Up, Neon Products, 16 In. 525.00
Clock-Radio, Red, Plastic, Model Of Cooler, Drink Coca-Cola In White Letters, 1950 . . . . 3630.00
Coaster, Sprite Boy, 1950s, 4 Piece 20.00
Coin-Operated Machine, Carton Cooler Co., Cooler, 4 Legs, Bottles, Shelf, 14 x 38 In. . . . 2970.00
Coin-Operated Machine, Drink Coca-Cola In Bottles, Ice Cold, Red, 66 x 25 In. 469.00
Cooler, Sales Sample, Drink Coca-Cola, Ice Cold, Red, Books, 1939, 12 x 8 x 10 In. 3580.00
Crate, 24 Bottles, Drink Coca-Cola, In Spanish, Plastic, Wood, 1950s, 6 x 4 In. 49.00
Crate, Yellow, Red Insignia, Wood, 18 x 12 x 4 In. 65.00
Dispenser, Bottles, Cavalier, Glass Door, c.1960, 57 In. 1610.00
Display, So Easy To Carry Home, Lady, Umbrella, 6-Pack, Cardboard, 1942, 27 x 16 In. . . 2200.00
Door Pull, Refresh Yourself, c.1940, 6 x 3 In. 415.00
Door Push, Have A Coca-Cola, Red Ground, Red & White Letters, Canada 170.00
Festoon, 3 Ladies Lying On The Beach, 1946, 5 Piece 4600.00
Festoon, Howdy Partner, Horns, Rope, Horseshoes, 10 x 106 In. 2310.00
Glass, Wizard Of Oz, 50th Anniversary, Scarecrow, 1989, 6 In. 10.00
Globe, Have A Coke Here, Light-Up, Metal, Plastic, Rotating Base, Neon Products 990.00
Ice Chest, Red, Drink Coca-Cola, Ice Cold, c.1940, 36 In. 750.00
Insert, Return Bottles For Free Lube Job, 1963, 5 3/4 x 4 3/4 In. 5.00
Kickplate, Drink Coca-Cola, Porcelain, Green & Red, 1931, 10 x 30 In. 630.00
Letter Opener, Bellhop, Bottle Cap Hat, Brass, White Metal, Tampico, Mexico, 10 In. . . . 100.00
Lighter, Enjoy Coca-Cola, Bluebird, Music, Plays Dixie, Box, 2 1/4 x 1 1/2 In. 1150.00
Magazine Ad, Lillian Nordica, Coupon, Mat, Frame, 1905, 9 3/4 x 6 1/2 In. 360.00
Menu Board, Fishtail, Robertson Co., 1963, 27 1/2 x 19 1/2 In. 305.00
Menu Board, Good With Food, Fishtail, 1945, 19 x 96 In. 770.00
Mirror, Drink Coca-Cola, Woman, Wide Brimmed Hat, Oval, 1910, 2 7/8 In. 520.00
Pencil, Drink Coca-Cola, Mechanical, Eversharp, U.S.A., 1950s 25.00
Radio-Music Box, Conversion Type, Plastic, Red Figural Cooler, 1950s, 18 In. 1705.00
Sheet Music, Coke Is It, Coke Bottle, 1981 . . . . 32.00
Sign, 2 Bottles, Button, Sprite Boys, Fluted, 2 Panels, c.1950, 16 x 30 1/2 In. 330.00
Sign, 6-Pack, Tin, Die Cut, 1952, 12 x 11 In. 2200.00
Sign, 6-Pack, Tin, Signed Allan Morrison 1948, 16 x 44 In. 880.00
Sign, 6-Pack, Top Button, Tin, 1954, 54 x 16 In. 1430.00
Sign, 12-Pack, Die Cut, 14 x 20 In. 70.00
Sign, Arrow, Self-Framed, Tin Lithograph, c.1950, 18 x 54 In. 385.00
Sign, Barbecue, Here's A Coke For You, Tin, 24 x 77 In. 1045.00
Sign, Betty, Tin Lithograph, Self-Framed, 1914, 41 x 31 In. . . . . .1100.00 to 2860.00
Sign, Blue Bonnet Cafe, Tin, Self-Framed, 1947, 16 x 48 In. 195.00
Sign, Bottle, Cap, Tin, 1948, 54 x 16 In. 715.00
Sign, Bottle, Coca-Cola, Red, Brown, White, Round, 1936, 46 In. 1540.00
Sign, Bottle, White, Brown, Tin, 36 In. 770.00
Sign, Cap With Banner, Tin Lithograph, 36 In. 220.00
Sign, Cap, Bottle, Coca-Cola, Tin, 36 In. Diam. 440.00
Sign, Cap, Bottle, Flange, Tin Lithograph, c.1950, 22 1/2 x 18 1/4 In. 440.00
Sign, Cap, Celluloid Over Cardboard, Easel Stand, c.1950, 9 In. 232.00
Sign, Cap, Coca-Cola, Red, White, Tin, 36 In. Diam. 374.00
Sign, Cap, Drink Coca-Cola, Porcelain, 44 In. 275.00
Sign, Coca-Cola Delicious, Refreshing, Tin, 1963, 24 x 24 In. 193.00
Sign, Coca-Cola In Bottles, Neon, Countertop, c.1939, 12 x 24 In. 6820.00
Sign, Coca-Cola, Girl Holding Out Glass, Tin, Oval, Self-Framed, c.1926, 13 x 19 In. 3520.00
Sign, Counter Dispenser, 2-Sided, Tin Lithograph 935.00
Sign, Counter Dispenser, Porcelain, 2-Sided, c.1941, 25 1/4 x 26 1/4 In. 1100.00
Sign, Curb Service, Sold Here, Ice Cold, Red, Green, Yellow, White, Tin, 28 x 20 In. 330.00
Sign, Delicious & Refreshing, Porcelain, 2-Sided, Metal Frame, Tenn. Enamel, 36 x 60 In. . 3300.00
Sign, Douglas A-20-A Attack Bomber Airplane, Cardboard, World War II, c.1940 . . . . 99.00
Sign, Drink Coca-Cola In Bottles, Button, Arrow, White, Red, Tin, 16 x 24 In. 3190.00
Sign, Drink Coca-Cola In Bottles, Button, Red, White Arrow, Tin, 12 x 20 In. 770.00
Sign, Drink Coca-Cola In Bottles, Light-Up, Metal, Plastic, Round, Neon Products, 16 In. . 880.00
Sign, Drink Coca-Cola While You Wait, Gas Today, Hand On Bottle, Tin, 1926, 15 x 24 In. 10450.00
Sign, Drink Coca-Cola, 2 Glasses Of Coke, Shield Shape, Wood, Metal, 9 x 11 1/2 In. 853.00
Sign, Drink Coca-Cola, 4 Seasons, 4 Ladies, Trolley, Cardboard, 1913, 11 x 21 In. 3960.00
Sign, Drink Coca-Cola, Betty, Woman Holds Bottle, Cardboard, 32 x 56 In. 132.00
Sign, Drink Coca-Cola, Bottle, Tin, Flange, 1946, 21 x 24 In. 275.00
Sign, Drink Coca-Cola, Candy Films, Red, White, Green, Porcelain, 30 x 18 In. 275.00

Sign, Drink Coca-Cola, Coffee, Cup, Spoon, Tin, 16 x 54 In. 990.00
Sign, Drink Coca-Cola, Delicious & Refreshing, Confectionery, Porcelain, 47 x 46 In. 1760.00
Sign, Drink Coca-Cola, Delicious & Refreshing, Fountain Service, Porcelain, 42 x 60 In. ... 715.00
Sign, Drink Coca-Cola, Delicious, Refreshing, Tin, Self-Framed, c.1937, 32 3/4 x 57 In. .. 385.00
Sign, Drink Coca-Cola, Die Cut, Flange, Tin, 2-Sided, 1952, 22 1/2 x 18 In. 935.00
Sign, Drink Coca-Cola, Fountain Service, 2 Spigots, Porcelain, 1941, 14 x 27 In. 1760.00
Sign, Drink Coca-Cola, Fountain Service, Die Cut, Porcelain, 14 x 27 In. 1210.00
Sign, Drink Coca-Cola, Neon Border, Plastic, Button Type, Round, 1960s, 16 In. 550.00
Sign, Drink Coca-Cola, Porcelain, Green Border, Red Ground, 10 x 30 In. 220.00
Sign, Drink Coca-Cola, Red, White, Yellow, Tin, Wood Frame, 1947, 24 x 58 In. 330.00
Sign, Drink Coca-Cola, Script, White Porcelain, 1930s, 18 In. 660.00
Sign, Drink Coca-Cola, White, Red, Silver Base, Light-Up, 21 x 13 x 14 In. 2860.00
Sign, Drink Coca-Cola, Work Refreshed, Tin, 31 x 47 In. 220.00
Sign, Enjoy Frosty Bottles, 3-D, Cardboard, 1937, 26 x 20 In........................ 3850.00
Sign, Enjoy That Refreshing New Feeling, Robertson, 1950, 17 1/2 x 55 1/2 In. 440.00
Sign, Fountain Service, Drink Coca-Cola, Delicious & Refreshing, Porcelain, 1933, 3 x 5 In. 3600.00
Sign, Fountain Service, Porcelain, Die Cut, 1941, 58 x 66 In........................ 11000.00
Sign, Girl, Candle, Hospitality Coca-Cola, Paperboard, Frame, c.1950, 27 x 56 In. 660.00
Sign, Glenn Martin B-26 Fighter Airplane, Cardboard, World War II, c.1940 .... 28.00
Sign, Grumman F4F-3 Fighter Airplane, Cardboard, World War II, c.1940 .... 110.00
Sign, Have A Coke, Neon, Spinner, Countertop, Rounded Octagonal, c.1950, 18 In. 8470.00
Sign, Hot Dogs, Drink Coca-Cola In Bottles, White, Red, Green, Tin, 16 x 54 In. 1100.00
Sign, I'll Bring The Coke, Girl On Phone, Cardboard, Frame, 1946, 20 x 36 In. 1430.00
Sign, Ice Cold, Sign Of Good Taste, Bottle, Fishtail, Tin, 20 x 28 In. 390.00
Sign, Metal Over Cardboard, Bottle, Drink Coca-Cola, Nov. 16, 1915, 6 x 13 In. 590.00
Sign, Metal, Screen Painted Bottle, Logo, Wood Frame, c.1960, 72 x 35 In. 345.00
Sign, New Betty, Drink Coca-Cola, Tin, Self-Framed, 1941, 11 x 35 In. 910.00
Sign, Pause That Refreshes, Woman Holds Bottle, Die Cut, Cardboard, 41 x 32 In. 770.00
Sign, Pick Up 6, For Home Refreshment, 6-Pack, White, Red, Black, Tin, 16 x 50 In. 1980.00
Sign, Policeman Form, School Zone Crossing Guard, Blue Uniform, Red, White, 60 In. 1456.00
Sign, Ponders Ice Cream, Drink Coca-Cola, Silhouette, Porcelain, 1942, 52 x 36 In. 4070.00
Sign, Refreshment Area, White Ground, Gold Border, Tin, Self-Framed, 18 x 24 In. 240.00
Sign, Santa, Helicopter, Train Set, Season's Greetings, Die Cut, Cardboard, 46 x 31 In. 250.00
Sign, Seasons Greetings, Santa Claus, Train, Helicopter, Cardboard, Stand-Up, 48 x 30 In. . 90.00
Sign, Serve Coca-Cola At Home, Girl, Bottle, Houses, 2-Sided, Frame, 20 x 36 In. 715.00
Sign, Serve Yourself A Fresh Drink, Silk Screened Glass, 1930-40, 5 x 15 1/2 In. 990.00
Sign, Sign Of Good Taste, Bottle, Fishtail, Tin, 12 x 32 In. 310.00
Sign, Sign Of Good Taste, Cap On Arrow, Tin, 1960, 12 x 24 In. 1650.00
Sign, Sign Of Good Taste, Fishtail, Bottle, Tin, Robertson, 1950, 31 1/2 x 55 1/2 In. 550.00
Sign, Sign Of Good Taste, Tin, Self-Framed, 1959, 53 x 5 x 17 1/2 In. 415.00
Sign, Slow School Zone, Policeman, Drink Coca-Cola, Cast Iron Base, 1950s 6820.00
Sign, Snowflakes, Fishtail, Cup, Plastic, 10 x 26 In. 250.00
Sign, Take A Case Home Today, Quality Refreshment, Red Carpet, Tin, 28 x 20 In........ 1320.00
Sign, Take Enough Home, Hand Holding Bottle, 3-D, Cardboard, 1952, 14 x 12 In. 440.00
Sign, Take Home A Carton, Tin, Self-Framed, 1937, 18 x 54 In. 1320.00
Sign, Take Home In Carton, Big King Size, 6-Pack, Tin, 28 x 20 In. 1540.00
Sign, Things Go Better With Coke, Ice Cold, Bottle, Tin, 18 x 53 In. 55.00
Sign, Welcome Pause, Girl, Tennis Racket, Cooler, Cardboard, Frame, 1946, 16 x 27 In. ... 1210.00
Sign, Your Choice Of Sizes, Paper, Red, White, Green, 1950s, 27 1/2 x 16 1/2 In. 86.00
Thermometer, 2 Bottles, Die Cut, 16 x 7 In. 70.00
Thermometer, Coke Bottle Shape, Die Cut, Tin, 17 x 5 1/2 In. 88.00
Thermometer, Drink Coca-Cola In Bottles, Round, Red Ground, Tin, 12 In. 88.00
Thermometer, Drink Coca-Cola, Glass, Aluminum, Glass, Round, 1950s, 12 In. 385.00
Thermometer, Drink Coca-Cola, Red, White, 12 In. Diam. 140.00
Thermometer, Enjoy Coca-Cola, Red, White, 18 In. Diam. 990.00
Thermometer, Things Go Better With Coke, White, Red, Green, 18 In. Diam. .....440.00 to 770.00
Tip Tray, 1909, Exhibition Girl, St. Louis World's Fair, Oval, 6 1/4 x 4 1/2 In. .....385.00 to 537.00
Tip Tray, 1910, Coca-Cola Girl, Drink Delicious Coca-Cola, 6 1/4 x 4 1/2 In. ......415.00 to 900.00
Tip Tray, 1913, Hamilton King Girl, Picture Hat, 6 x 4 1/4 In. ....250.00 to 780.00
Tip Tray, 1914, Betty, Bonnet, Pink Ribbon, Oval, 6 x 4 1/4 In. ....175.00 to 248.00
Tip Tray, 1916, Girl With Basket Of Flowers, Oval, 6 x 4 1/4 In. ....138.00 to 200.00
Toy, Car, Ford, 1959 Model, Tin, Friction, Japan, 9 In. 275.00
Toy, Soda Fountain, Plastic, 2 Coca-Cola Glasses, Andy Guard, Box, 1962, 9 In. 94.00

Toy, Truck, Buddy L, 1959 .... 350.00
Toy, Truck, Buddy L, 1961 .... 250.00
Toy, Truck, Cabover, Diecast, Steel Body, Plastic Cases, Smith Miller, 1940s, 13 In. 1430.00
Toy, Truck, Corvair, Pickup, Tin, Friction, KTS, 8 In. 385.00
Toy, Truck, Delivery, Yellow Steel, Rubber Tires, Bottle Rack, Buddy L, 14 In. 176.00
Toy, Truck, GMC, Bottles, Smith Miller, Box 1980.00
Toy, Truck, Japan, Tin, Box, 1956 .... 495.00
Toy, Truck, Marx, 1939, 20 In. 395.00
Toy, Truck, Pressed Steel, 10 Bottles, Metalcraft, 11 In............................ 550.00
Toy, Truck, Pressed Steel, Decals, Metalcraft, 11 In. ....370.00 to 480.00
Toy, Truck, With Cases Of Coke, Plastic, Marx, 10 3/4 In........................... 310.00
Toy, Volkswagon Bus, Tin, Friction, Japan, 8 3/4 In. 149.00
Tray, 1904, Girl, Seated, St. Louis World's Fair, Cascades, Lagoon 537.00
Tray, 1905-07, Topless, Coca-Cola Is Better, Try It, Tin, Round, 12 1/4 In. 7150.00
Tray, 1914, Betty, Passaic Metal Wear Co., Oval, 6 x 4 1/4 In......................... 1868.00
Tray, 1926, Golfing Couple, 13 1/4 x 10 1/2 In. 690.00
Tray, 1928, Bobbed Hair Girl, 13 1/4 x 10 1/2 In. 747.00
Tray, 1930, Bather Girl, 13 1/2 x 10 1/2 In...................................... 199.00
Tray, 1931, Barefoot Boy, Dog, Norman Rockwell Art, 13 1/4 x 10 1/2 In. 1595.00
Tray, 1934, Weismuller & O'Sullivan, 10 1/2 x 13 1/4 In. 850.00
Tray, 1935, Madge Evans, American Art Works, 13 1/4 x 10 In. 165.00
Tray, 1936, Hostess, Evening Gown, American Art Works, 13 1/4 x 10 1/2 In. 465.00
Tray, 1937, Running Girl, On Beach, American Art Works, 13 1/4 x 10 1/2 In. .....369.00 to 890.00
Tray, 1938, Girl At Shade, Yellow Dress, Flaring Hat, 13 1/4 x 10 1/2 In. 220.00
Tray, 1939, Springboard Girl, American Art Works, 13 1/4 x 10 1/2 In................. 360.00
Tray, 1941, Skater Girl, Seated On Log, 13 1/4 x 10 1/2 In. 440.00
Tray, 1942, 2 Girls At Car, 13 1/4 x 10 1/2 In. 150.00
Tray, 1948, Girl With Red Hair, 13 1/2 x 10 1/2 In. 80.00
Tray, 1953, Menu Girl, 13 1/4 x 10 1/2 In. 95.00
Tray, 1972, Betty, Reproduction Of 1914 Tray, 15 x 12 1/4 In. 32.00
Uniform, Coverall Style, Metal Buttons, Patch, 1950s, 6 3/4-In. Hat, Size 40 L 149.00
Vending Machine, Vendo, Model 44, Bottle, Sprite Decal, Restored 3575.00
Vending Machine, Vendo, Model 81, 10 Cents, White Top, Red Bottom, 27 x 59 In. 3905.00
Vending Machine, Vendo, Model No. A23, 10 Cent Deposit, Red Paint, Transfer, 36 In. ... 705.00
Writing Tablet, Flag Of The United Nations, Eisenhower Quote, 1950-60 .... 12.00

COFFEE MILLS

COFFEE MILLS are also called coffee grinders, although there is a
difference in the way each grinds the coffee. Large floor-standing or
counter-model coffee mills were used in the nineteenth-century country store. Small home mills were first made about 1894. They lost
favor by the 1930s. The renewed interest in fresh-ground coffee has
produced many modern electric mills and hand mills and grinders.
Reproductions of the old styles are being made.

Arcade, No. 25, Glass, Wall Canister, Tin Cover, Black Metal Frame, 15 1/2 In. 150.00
Bronson Walton Co., None Such, Steel Body, Wood Base, c.1895, 10 x 5 3/4 In. 110.00
Bronson Walton Co., Old Oak, Japanned Steel Body, Black, 8 x 5 1/4 In. 120.00
Enterprise, Cast Iron, Double Wheel, Pinstripes, Flower Decals, Red Ground, 60 In. 3450.00
Enterprise, No. 00, Wall Mount, Cast Iron, Stenciling, 9 In. 255.00
Enterprise, No. 3, Blue, Black, Flowers, Walnut Drawer, Double Wheel, 15 In. 575.00
Enterprise, No. 7, Wooden Drawer, Eagle Finial, Stenciled, 1899, 25 In. ....748.00 to 805.00
Enterprise, No. 9, Wooden Drawer, Eagle Finial, Stenciled, 17 x 25 x 19 1/2 In. 690.00
Enterprise, No. 12, Decals, Eagle Finial, Reproduction, 25-In. Wheels 1900.00
Enterprise, No. 12 1/2, Tin Drawer, Eagle Finial, Stars, Stripes, 1898, 17 x 37 x 25 In. ... 980.00
Enterprise, No. 100, Wall, Cast Iron, Enamel, Embossed Glass Receiver, c.1917, 14 In. ... 675.00
Enterprise, No. 218, Nickel Plated, Brass Hopper, Eagle Finial, 69 1/2 In. 2245.00
Enterprise, No. 512, Iron Hopper, Orange Paint, Decals, c.1900, 31 In. 770.00
Enterprise, No. 514, Cast Iron, Nickel Plated Hopper, Red Paint, Decals, c.1900, 31 In. ... 1535.00
Enterprise, No. 712, Iron Hopper, Tin Drawer, Eagle Finial, 1901, 36 In. ....865.00 to 1325.00
Golden Rule Coffee, Wall Mount, Cast Iron, Wood, 19 In............................ 530.00
Lane Bros., Swift Mill, No. 15, Iron Hopper, Vermillion, Gold, Black Markings, 30 In. ... 2860.00
Maple, Drawer, Turned Handle, Dovetailed, 10 1/2 x 9 x 7 1/2 In. 220.00
National Specialty, Small, Cast Iron, Wood Base, 10 1/2 In. 195.00
Peugot Freres, No. 0A, Wood Drawer & Handle, 12 x 11 In. 204.00

Peugot Freres, No. 2A, Wood Drawer, Metal Tag, 17 x 16 In. 295.00
Pewter & Iron, Turned Wood Handle, Pine Case, Dovetailed Drawer, 9 1/4 x 7 In. 440.00
Woodruff & Edwards, Elgin, No. 42, Counter, Eagle Finial, Iron Hopper, 28 In. 550.00

COIN-OPERATED MACHINES

of all types are collected. The vending machine is an ancient invention dating back to 200 B.C., when holy water was dispensed in a coin-operated vase. Smokers in seventeenth-century England could buy tobacco from a coin-operated box. It was not until after the Civil War that the technology made modern coin-operated games and vending machines plentiful. Slot machines, arcade games, and dispensers are all collected.

Arcade, A.B.T., Challenger, Shooting, 1 Cent, 1946, 11 x 29 In. 470.00
Arcade, Benedict, House Of Mystery, Penny, On Stand, 64 x 14 In. 3850.00
Arcade, Exhibit Supply, Cupid's Arrow, Penny, c.1929, 16 x 30 In. 770.00
Arcade, Hamilton, E.Z. Aces, Roulette Wheel, 1930s, 30 x 46 x 48 In. 2200.00
Arcade, J.H. Keeney, Baseball, Mickey Mantle, 10 Cent, 17 x 69 In. 1430.00
Arcade, Lila & Edna, Figural, Ball Toss, Floor Model, 43 x 65 In. 525.00
Arcade, Lois, Figural, Ball Toss, Wooden, 22 x 63 In. 415.00
Arcade, Scientific Corp., Batting Practice, 15 Balls, 5 Cent, 77 In. 1100.00
Arcade, United Nations, Graphics On Front Glass, 5 Cent, 24 x 70 In. 275.00
Cigarette, 4 Brands, 15 Cent, 1920s, 32 In. 495.00
Cigarette, Elde Inc., Dial-A-Smoke, 25 Cent, 1940s, 27 x 18 x 6 In. 138.00
Cigarette, Mills, 2 For 1 Cent, Wood, 2 Columns, Oak, Key, 18 x 8 1/2 In. 300.00
Cigarette, Shipman, Makaroff Brand, 1 Cent, Chrome, Metal, 12 1/2 In. 295.00
Gum, Adams, 1 Cent, Yellow Enamel Paint, 22 1/2 x 10 In. 420.00
Gum, Baseball Card, Red Metal, 1 Cent, 1950s, 13 x 13 x 5 1/2 In. 1035.00
Gum, Keller-Coin-Op, 5 Reels, Wooden, 5 Cent, 16 x 12 x 8 In. 3020.00
Gum, Pulver, Cop, 1 Cent, Tasty Chew, Porcelain, Red, 20 In. 770.00
Gum, Pulver, Foxy Grandpa, Kola Pepsin Gum, c.1899, 24 In. 7425.00
Gum, Pulver, Yellow Kid, 1 Cent, Tasty Chew, Porcelain, Red, 20 In. 990.00
Gum, Regal, 5 Cent, Glass Globe, Contents, 1940s, 15 In. 95.00
Gum, Standard, 20 In. 10500.00
Gum, Wrigley's, 1 Cent, Metal, Wall Mount, 4 1/2 x 29 In. 165.00
Gumball, Bingo Ball, 1 Cent, c.1931, 11 x 17 In. 440.00
Gumball, E-Z, Knock A Homerun, 5 Cent, Cast Iron, 16 In. 1650.00
Gumball, Hart, 1 Cent, Glass Ball, Chrome Base, c.1950, 11 In. 190.00
Gumball, Kopper King Selective, Yellow, 1950s, 18 x 8 In. 185.00
Gumball, Masters, 1 Cent, Key, Rectangular 275.00
Gumball, Masters, Chlorophyll Gum, 5 Cent, Thank You, Key 140.00
Gumball, Mills, Wild Deuces, 5 Reel, 4 Cent, 12 x 11 x 8 In. 240.00
Gumball, Victory, 1 Cent, Contents, 1940s 110.00
Horse, Ride Sandy, 10 Cent, Brown & White Paint, Leather Saddle 1790.00
Matches, 1 Cent, Cast Iron, Embossed, 13 1/2 In. 678.00
Matches, Diamond, Beaton & Caldwell, 1 Cent, Drum, Tilted 900.00
Matches, Northwestern, Cigar Cutter, 1 Cent, Cast Iron, 13 In. . . . . .1000.00 to 1870.00
Matches, Smoke Leandro Cigars, 1 Cent, Metal, 13 In. 770.00
Music Box, Polyphon, Double Comb, Walnut Case, 19-In. Disc, 38 In. 3729.00
Music Box, Polyphon, Style 54, Double Comb, Walnut, 20 24 1/2-In. Discs, 85 1/2 In. 22000.00
Music Box, Polyphon, Style 104, Walnut, Upright, 19 19 5/8-In. Discs, 84 In. 17050.00
Music Box, Regina, Double Comb, Oak Case, Discs, 21 x 19 x 13 In. 3190.00
Music Box, Regina, Double Comb, Oak, 30 15 1/2-In. Discs, 96 1/2 In. 18700.00
Music Box, Regina, Orchestral, Style 5, Mahogany, Upright, 18 27-In. Discs, 87 In. 27500.00
Music Box, Symphonion, Eroica, Walnut, 18 3-Disc Sets, 81 In. 38500.00
Pinball, 3 Sporting Designs, Tabletop, Box 110.00
Pinball, Chubbie, Wood Case & Legs, Stoner Corp., Aurora, Ill., 22 x 61 In. 275.00
Pinball, Genco, Subway, 1 Cent, 1934, 34 1/2 x 38 1/2 x 17 1/2 In. 550.00
Pinball, Gottlieb, Universe, Animated Back Screen, c.1955, 66 In. 1840.00
Pinball, Little Monarch, 27 In. 385.00
Pinball, Perky, Williams, Reverse Painted Glass Scoreboard, c.1950 . . . . 220.00
Pinball, Poosh-M-Up Triple Play, Lion, Elephant, Tiger, 22 In. 85.00
Skill, Baker Novelty, Kicker & Catcher, 1 Cent, c.1946 . . . . 550.00
Skill, Daval, Mexican Baseball, 1 Cent, Metal, c.1947, 20 In. 158.00
Skill, J.F. Frantz, Kicker & Catcher, 1 Cent, c.1954 . . . . 440.00

Skill, Marvel, Pop-Up Baseball, 1940s 495.00
Skill, Peo Manufacturing, Bat-A-Ball, 1930s, 16 In. 385.00
Slot, Burham, 3 Reel, Cast Iron, Side Gum Vendor, c.1910, 25 x 18 In. 5225.00
Slot, Caille, Musical, Upright, 5 Cent, Oak Case, c.1900, 64 x 27 x 21 In. 20900.00
Slot, Caille, Silent Sphinx, Aluminum, Oak, 3 Reel, c.1932, 16 x 24 In. 1840.00
Slot, Caille, Superior Jackpot, 25 Cent, c.1930 .... 1900.00
Slot, Jennings, Ciga-Rola, 10 Cent, Cigarettes, c.1945, 60 x 22 In. 1870.00
Slot, Jennings, Club Chief, 5 Cent, c.1945 .... 1210.00
Slot, Jennings, Club Special, 10 Cent, c.1938, 60 x 21 In. 3575.00
Slot, Jennings, Duchess, Double Jack, Aluminum, Oak, 5 Cent, c.1933 .... 1200.00
Slot, Jennings, Dutch Boy, 25 Cent, 3 Reel, c.1929, 25 x 15 x 14 In. 1650.00
Slot, Jennings, Four Star Chief, 5 Cent, 3 Reel, c.1936, 27 x 15 In. 2310.00
Slot, Jennings, Little Duke, 1 Cent, 3 Reel, Art Deco, c.1932, 22 x 13 x 10 In. 2310.00
Slot, Jennings, Standard Chief, 25 Cent, Cast Metal, Oak, c.1946, 26 In. 1245.00
Slot, Jennings, Sun Chief, Console, Dollar, 1947 .... 4400.00
Slot, Jennings, Victoria, 5 Cent, Aluminum, Oak, 24 1/2 x 16 In. 1265.00
Slot, Jennings, Victory Chief, 10 Cent, 3 Reel, Wood Front, c.1942, 28 x 16 In. 1870.00
Slot, Mills, Bursting Cherry, 5 Cent, 3 Reel, c.1937, 26 x 16 In. 1540.00
Slot, Mills, Bursting Cherry, 10 Cent, 3 Reel, c.1937, 26 x 16 In. 1650.00
Slot, Mills, Bursting Cherry, 25 Cent, 3 Reel, c.1937, 26 x 16 In. 1760.00
Slot, Mills, Castle Front, 1 Cent, Oak, Cast Metal, c.1933, 26 x 16 In. 1980.00
Slot, Mills, Castle Front, 5 Cent, c.1933, 26 x 16 x 16 In. 825.00
Slot, Mills, Check Boy, 5 Cent, Oak, Nickel Plated Front, 1907-16, 16 In. ......4510.00 to 6440.00
Slot, Mills, Golden Falls, 25 Cent, 1946 .... 1980.00
Slot, Mills, Golden Nugget, Double, 5 Cent, 1950s 2475.00
Slot, Mills, Horse Head, 5 Cent, 3 Reel, c.1937, 25 x 16 x 15 In. 2420.00
Slot, Mills, Jockey Card, 1 Cent, 5 Reel, Oak, c.1900, 62 x 18 In. 16500.00
Slot, Mills, Liberty Bell, 5 Cent, Cast Iron, 1906-39 .... 7200.00
Slot, Mills, Operator Bell, 3 Reel, Cast Iron, c.1915, 24 x 19 x 15 In. 2640.00
Slot, Mills, Operator Bell, 5 Cent, c.1922 .... 1770.00
Slot, Mills, Poinsettia, 5 Cent, 3 Reel, Gooseneck, c.1928, 25 x 16 In. 1540.00
Slot, Mills, Poinsettia, 25 Cent, 3 Reel, Gooseneck, c.1928, 25 x 16 In. 1870.00
Slot, Mills, Vest Pocket, 5 Cent, 3 Reel, Aluminum, c.1938, 8 x 11 In. ....358.00 to 470.00
Slot, Mills, War Eagle, 5 Cent, 3 Reel, c.1931, 26 x 16 x 15 In. ....1610.00 to 1870.00
Slot, Pace, All Star Comet, 10 Cent, 1936 .... 1210.00
Slot, Pace, Bantam Jak-Pot, Aluminum, Oak, 5 Cent, c.1930 .... 2300.00
Slot, Pace, Bantam Mint, 5 Cent, 3 Reel, Aluminum, c.1933, 20 x 17 In. 2015.00
Slot, Pace, Comet, 5 Cent, 3 Reel, Art Deco, Aluminum, c.1932, 25 x 16 In. 1870.00
Slot, Vendet, Midget, 5 Cent, Aluminum, Glass, c.1932, 9 x 16 x 10 In. 2300.00
Slot, Watling, Brownie Jackpot, 5 Cent, Oak, c.1929, 16 x 27 In. 4125.00
Slot, Watling, Rol-A-Top, Coin Front, 10 Cent, c.1935 .... 3850.00
Slot, Watling, Rol-A-Top, Twin Jackpot, Front Vendor, 25 Cent, c.1939 .... 5310.00
Slot, Watling, Treasury Twin Jackpot, c.1941 .... 5600.00
Slot, Watling, Twin Jack Pot Ball Gum, 1 Cent, 3 Reel, c.1932, 24 x 16 In. 2640.00
Sobriety Test, Booz Barometer, c.1950, 20 x 19 In. 175.00
Sobriety Test, Drinker-Tinker, Tests Your Alcohol Content, 21 x 20 In. 120.00
Stamp, U.S. Postage, 5 & 10 Cent, Uncle Sam, Red, White, Blue, 21 x 8 In. 220.00
Strength Tester, Mercury, 1 Cent, 17 x 52 In. 191.00
Strength Tester, Metal Grip, 1 Cent, Red, Cast Aluminum, 12 In. 145.00
Trade Stimulator, Daval, American Eagle, 1 Cent, 3 Reel, Cast Metal, 8 x 10 In. 275.00
Trade Stimulator, Daval, Free Play, Cigarette Matching, Gumball, 5 Cent, 1946, 12 In. ... 115.00
Trade Stimulator, Daval, Gusher, 5 Cent, c.1946, 9 1/2 x 6 1/2 x 9 In. 255.00
Trade Stimulator, Decatur, Fairest Wheel, Oak, 1895 .... 2300.00
Trade Stimulator, J.F. Frantz, Pot Of Gold, Pinfield, c.1955, 13 x 17 In. 385.00
Trade Stimulator, John M. Wadell, Bicycle, c.1897, 14 In. 1430.00
Trade Stimulator, Kelley, Gum, 1 Cent, Oak, c.1903, 14 x 17 In. 2200.00
Trade Stimulator, Lion Manufacturing, Puritan Baby, 3 Reel, 1928 .... 660.00
Trade Stimulator, Mills, Gumball, Wild Deuces, 5 Cent, 5 Reel, c.1938, 11 In. 240.00
Trade Stimulator, Mills, Tickette, 1940s 220.00
Trade Stimulator, Rock-Ola, Official Sweepstakes, 1 Cent, Oak, 1937, 15 1/2 In. 1760.00 to 2147.00
Trade Stimulator, Stittman & Pitt, Five Card Draw, 1 Cent, Cast Iron, 1894 .... 4100.00
Vending, Buy Blades, 10 Cent, Iron, Table Top, 4 Windows, 18 x 14 In. 140.00
Vending, Condoms, Tease Her, Please Her, 25 Cent, 30 In. 385.00

Vending, Essex, Wood, 36 In. 1210.00
Vending, Lawrence, Candy, Nut Jewel, Double, 5 Cent, 1940s, 14 x 8 In. 58.00
Vending, Mills, Cigar, 1 Cent, 5 Card, 57 x 11 In. 4950.00
Vending, Peanut, 5 Cent, Thank You, Key, 11 In. 140.00
Vending, Price Collar Button, Cast Iron, Stencil, Tag, Key, c.1905, 12 In. 2150.00
Vending, Stollwerck Victoria, Chocolate, Spar Automat, 2 Slots, Penny, c.1920s 770.00
Vending, Ticket, Man In Top Hat, 5 Cent, Zinc, c.1900, 36 x 12 In. 23100.00
Vending, Van Houten, Chocolate Bars, 1 Cent, Wall Mount, 3 1/2 x 26 In. 155.00
Viewing, Caille, Cail-O-Scope, French Doll Baby, 1 Cent, c.1905, 73 x 21 In. 4400.00
Viewing, Exhibit Supply, 5 Cent, Oak Case, 19 x 13 In. 470.00
Viewing, Mills, Mutoscope, Ben Turpin, 1 Cent, Oak, c.1905, 72 x 22 In. 3740.00
Viewing, Mutoscope, Clamshell, Fight Of Century, Iron, c.1900, 65 x 16 In. 5225.00

COLLECTOR PLATES are modern plates produced in limited editions. Some may be found listed under the factory name, such as Bing & Grondahl, Royal Copenhagen, Royal Doulton, and Wedgwood.

Anri, Christmas, 1972, Juan Ferrandiz, Christ In Manger, Box 175.00
Anri, Christmas, 1972, Malfertheiner, Pipers At Alberobello, Frame, Box 65.00
Anri, Christmas, 1974, Malfertheiner, Young Man & Girl, Frame, Box 60.00
Anri, Christmas, 1975, Malfertheiner, Christmas In Ireland, Frame, Box 50.00
Anri, Christmas, 1979, Moss Gatherer, Frame, Box 98.00
Anri, Christmas, 1979, Moss Gatherers Of Villnoess, Wood Frame, 11 1/2 In. 75.00
Anri, Christmas, 1980, Wintry Churchgoing, Frame, 9 In. 90.00
Anri, Father's Day, 1975, Sailing, Wood Frame, 9 In. 45.00
Anri, Mother's Day, 1972, Alpine Mother & Children, Wood Frame, 9 In. 40.00
Anri, Mother's Day, 1972, Juan Ferrandiz, Mother Sewing, 9 In. 85.00
Anri, Mother's Day, 1972, Juan Ferrandiz, Mother Sewing, Box 135.00
Avon, Christmas, Trimming Tree, 6th Edition, Enoch Wedgwood, England, 1978 . . . . 25.00
Avon, Christmas On Farm, 1st Edition, Enoch Wedgwood, 1973, 9 1/4 In. 10.00
Avon, Country Christmas, 8th In Series, Enoch Wedgwood, 1980, 8 1/2 In. 30.00
Bradford Exchange, Gone With The Wind, 1991-93, Complete Set, 12 Piece 150.00
Bradford Exchange, Marilyn Monroe, 1999, Complete Set, 8 Piece 90.00
Degrazia, Flower Boy, Box, 1979, 10 1/2 In. 195.00
Franklin Mint, Easter Parade, Bill Bell 5.00
Franklin Mint, Gunsmoke, Official 40th Anniversary 125.00
Franklin Mint, John Wayne, Tribute Edition, 1993 . . . . 70.00
Gorham, Mother's Day, 1979, Norman Rockwell, Homecoming, Box, 8 1/2 In. 40.00
Kaiser, Little Clowns, L. Trester, Red Mask, 1st Issue, Box, 1981 . . . . 20.00
Kaiser, Yesterday's World, L. Trester, Summer Is Forever, 2nd Issue, Box, 1979 . . . . 45.00
Kaiser, Yesterday's World, L. Trester, Time For Dreaming, 1st Issue, Box, 1978 . . . . 45.00
Knowles, Alice In Wonderland, Complete Set, 4 Piece 50.00
Knowles, Christmas Dream, No. 5, Norman, Rockwell, 1978 . . . . 25.00
Knowles, Classic Fairy Tales, Complete Set, 1991-92, 8 Piece 100.00
Knowles, Eastern Screech Owl, 1990 . . . . 5.00
Knowles, Mother's Day, 1976, Mother's Love, Norman Rockwell, 8 1/2 In. 60.00
Knowles, Mother's Day, 1978, Bedtime, Norman Rockwell 32.00
Knowles, Mother's Day, 1980, Mother's Pride, Norman Rockwell, 8 1/2 In. 22.00
Knowles, Mother's Day, 1982, Cooking Lesson, Norman Rockwell, Box 58.00
Knowles, Mother's Day, 1984, Abby & Lisa, Edna Hibel, Box, 8 1/2 In. 99.00
Knowles, Mother's Day, 1984, Grandma's Courting Dress, Norman Rockwell, Box, 8 1/2 In. 35.00
Knowles, Mother's Day, 1985, Erica & Jamie, Edna Hibel, Box, 8 1/2 In. 300.00
Knowles, Mother's Day, 1985, Mending Time, Norman Rockwell, Box, 8 1/2 In. . . . . .28.00 to 30.00
Knowles, Mother's Day, 1986, Emily & Jennifer, Edna Hibel, Box, 8 1/2 In. 260.00
Knowles, Mother's Day, 1988, Sarah & Tess, Edna Hibel, Box, 8 1/2 In. 250.00
Knowles, Wizard Of Oz, 1977-79, Complete Set, 8 Piece 250.00
Konigszelt, Christmas, 1979, Adoration, Hedi Keller, Box, 9 1/2 In. 36.00
Konigszelt, Christmas, 1980, Flight Into Egypt, Hedi Keller, Box 42.00
Konigszelt, Christmas, 1982, Following The Star, Hedi Keller, Box, 9 1/2 In. 38.00
Konigszelt, Grimm's Fairy Tales, 1981, Rumpelstilzchen, Charles Gehm, Box 20.00
Konigszelt, Grimm's Fairy Tales, 1982, Rapunzel, Charles Gehm, Box, 7 3/4 In. 35.00
Konigszelt, Grimm's Fairy Tales, 1984, Golden Goose, Charles Gehm, Box, 8 In. 28.00
Konigszelt, Sulamith Wulfing, Die Musik, The Music, 1982, 7 3/4 In. . . . . .35.00 to 45.00

If you live near a body of water, be sure to keep silica gel near your stored coins and other metals. The gel absorbs excess moisture. Check once or twice a year to be sure the silica gel does not need to be replaced.

Commemorative, Tin, Queen Elizabeth II,
Duke Of Edinburgh, 4 1/2 x 3 3/4 In.

Porsgrund, Christmas, 1968, Church, 7 In.	150.00
Porsgrund, Christmas, 1970, Flight From Egypt, 7 In.	20.00
Porsgrund, Christmas, 1973, Angels, 7 In.	20.00
Porsgrund, Christmas, 1978, Farm, 7 In.	20.00
Porsgrund, Christmas, 1984, Christmas Sheaf, 7 In.	40.00
Porsgrund, Christmas, 1988, Christmas Snow Is Falling, 7 In.	50.00
Porsgrund, Father's Day, 1971, Fishing With Dad, 5 3/8 In.	8.00
Porsgrund, Father's Day, 1975, Ice Skating With Dad, 5 3/8 In.	20.00
Porsgrund, Mother's Day, 1971, Feeding The Ducks, 5 3/8 In.	8.00
Porsgrund, Mother's Day, 1976, Feeding The Calf, 5 3/8 In.	20.00
Royal Devon, Mother's Day, 1976, Puppy Love, Norman Rockwell, 8 1/2 In.	80.00
Royale Blue Winter China, Christmas Night In A Village, Reco, 1971	42.00
Schmid, Bavarian Christmas, 1971, Christmas In Tyrol, Beerstein, Box, 9 1/2 In.	45.00
Schmid, Christmas, 1972, Christ In Manger, Juan Ferrandiz, 8 In.	175.00
Schmid, Christmas, 1976, Merry Blades, Raggedy Ann, Box, 7 1/2 In.	38.00
Schmid, Christmas, 1977, Christmas Morning, Raggedy Ann, Box, 7 1/2 In.	25.00
Schmid, Mother's Day, 1977, Bouquet Of Love, Raggedy Ann, Box, 7 1/2 In.	30.00
Schmid, My Name Is Star, 1981, Winter, Girl, Bird Feeder, Jessica Zemsky, 8 1/2 In.	25.00

COMIC ART, or cartoon art, is a relatively new field of collecting. Original comic strips, magazine covers, and even printed strips are collected. The first daily comic strip was printed in 1907. The paintings on celluloid used for movie cartoons are listed in this book under Animation Art.

Cartoon, Cannibal Returns Home, Charles Addams, New Yorker, Jan. 31, 1953, 12 x 14 In.	4781.00
Cartoon, Men Find Artifact, With The Antiquarian, Henry Mayer, c.1900, 7 x 7 In.	675.00
Cartoon, People At World's Fair, George Price, New Yorker, 19 1/2 x 16 3/4 In.	1690.00
Drawing, 3 Brownies, Burning Hat, Pen, Ink, Signed Palmer Cox, Mat, Frame, 4 1/2 x 5 In.	650.00
Drawing, Standing Rooster With Large Comb, Arthur B. Frost, 1913, 8 x 6 In.	1690.00
Illustration, Women's Hairdos, John Held, Jr., New York Times, 1920, 4 3/4 x 13 1/4 In.	2700.00
Strip, King Kong, 1933, 11 x 12 In.	115.00
Strip, Krazy & Ignatz, Sunday Page, George Herriman, July 20, 1930, 20 x 18 1/2 In.	6750.00

COMMEMORATIVE items have been made to honor members of royalty and those of great national fame. World's fairs and important historical events are also remembered with commemorative pieces. Related collectibles are listed in the Coronation and World's Fair categories.

Bank, Prince & Princess Of Wales, Zinc Alloy, Robert Brown, 1981, 6 3/4 In.	44.00
Bowl, Barber, Prince William Of Orange, Princess Wilhelmina, Verse, 10 3/4 In.	3910.00
Figure, Prince Of Wales With Dog, Staffordshire, c.1850, 8 In.	315.00
Figure, Queen Victoria, Staffordshire, c.1850, 8 1/4 In.	395.00
Pitcher, Commemorating Early American Naval Heroes, Creamware, 6 1/2 In.	1020.00
Plate, Prince William Of Orange, Princess Wilhelmina, Tree, Creamware, 10 In.	1095.00 to 2185.00
Plate, Prince William V Of Orange, Verse, Black, Red, Creamware, 9 1/2 In., 4 Piece	5060.00

Plate, Queen Victoria Diamond Jubilee, Johnson Bros., England, 1897, 9 3/4 In. 196.00
Tin, Queen Elizabeth II, Duke Of Edinburgh, 4 1/2 x 3 3/4 In. . . . . *Illus*   38.00
Toy, Model, NASA Lunar Module, Marked July 29, 1969, Circular Base, 7 In. 705.00

COMPACTS hold face powder. A woman did not powder her face in
public until after World War I. By 1920, the beauty parlor, permanent
waves, and cosmetics had become acceptable. A few companies sold
cake face powder in a box with a mirror and a pad or puff. Soon the
compact was designed by jewelers and made of gold, silver, and precious materials. Cosmetic companies began to sell powder in attractive
compacts of less valuable metal or plastic. Collectors today search for
Art Deco designs, commemorative compacts from world's fairs or
political events, and unusual examples. Many were made with com-
panion lipsticks and other fittings.

Art Deco, Ring Handle, Powder & Rouge, Silver Metal, 1 3/4 x 2 1/2 In. 75.00
Diamond, Ruby, Enamel, 14K Gold, Russian Style, 1913, 3 x 2 1/2 In. 1265.00
Dorset, Stylized Seashell, Black Enamel, Gold Metal, Round 30.00
Gem Set Flowers, Mirrored Interior, 14K Gold, Shreve, Crump & Low, c.1950 . . . .   646.00
Petit Point, Black With Pink Flowers, West Germany, Square, 3 In. 18.00
Rhinestones, Faux Pearls, Blue Cabochons, Gold Metal, Square, 2 3/4 In. 85.00
Stratton, Flowers, Engraved & Colored, Brushed Silver Metal, Round, 3 1/4 In. 32.00
Tiffany & Co., Scalloped Petals, Engraved Scrolling, 18K Gold 4700.00
Van Cleef & Arpels, Dimpled, Round Compact, Lipstick Cover, Silk Bag, Revlon, 1960s . .   45.00

CONSOLIDATED LAMP AND GLASS COMPANY of Coraopolis,
Pennsylvania, was founded in 1894. The company made lamps, tablewares, and art glass. Collectors are particularly interested in the wares
made after 1925, including black satin glass, Cosmos (listed in its own
category in this book), Martele (which resembled Lalique), Ruba
Rombic (1928–1932 Art Deco line), and colored glasswares. Some
Consolidated pieces are very similar to those made by the Phoenix
Glass Company. The colors are sometimes different. Consolidated
made Martele glass in blue, crystal, green, pink, white, or custard glass
with added fired-on color or a satin finish. The company closed for the
final time in 1967.

Tumbler, Catalonia, Amethyst, 5 1/2 In., 2 Piece 65.00
Vase, Katydid, Amber Wash, 6 3/4 In. 140.00

CONTEMPORARY GLASS, see Glass-Contemporary.

COOKBOOKS are collected for various reasons. Some are wanted for
the recipes, some for investment, and some as examples of advertising.
Cookbooks and recipe pamphlets are included in this category.

Atlanta Cooks For Company, 1971, 303 Pages 15.00
Borden, Eagle Brand Magic Recipes, 1946, 27 Pages . . . . .3.00 to 9.00
Calumet, Recipe Book, 1931, 7 1/2 x 5 In., 31 Pages 5.00

Cookbook, Jell-O, Salad Selector,
3 Recipe Wheels, Plastic Binding,
1980, 9 x 10 1/2 In.

Cookbook, Pillsbury, 3rd Grand
National 100 Prize Winning
Recipes, 1952, 96 Pages

Cookbook, Salad Dressings,
Vegetables On Cover, Paperback,
1925, 27 Pages, 5 3/4 In.

Centenary Favorites, Deliciously Yours, 1986, 344 Pages	10.00
Charleston Receipts, 1958, 330 Pages	10.00
Dr Pepper, Cookin' With Dr Pepper, Recipes, 5 x 8 In.	20.00
Everyday Banana Recipes, Paperback, 1927, 20 Pages	6.00
How To Cook, Granite Iron Ware	30.00
Jell-O, Jack & Mary's Jell-O Recipes, 1937, 23 Pages	35.00
Jell-O, Salad Selector, 3 Recipe Wheels, Plastic Binding, 1980, 9 x 10 1/2 In. .... *Illus*	25.00
Junket, Delicious Quick Desserts, Paperback, 1929, 24 Pages	6.00
Mountain Measures, Hardback, 1983, 336 Pages	10.00
New Cooks, By Illuminating Company, 1953	8.00
Pillsbury, 3rd Grand National 100 Prize Winning Recipes, 1952, 96 Pages .... *Illus*	95.00
Pillsbury Bake-Off, No. 10, 1958, 100 Pages	22.00
Salad Dressings, Vegetables On Cover, Paperback, 1925, 27 Pages, 5 3/4 In. .... *Illus*	10.00
The Compleat Housewife, By E. Smith, London, 1750	595.00

COOKIE JARS with brightly painted designs or amusing figural shapes became popular in the mid-1930s. Many companies made them and collectors search for cookie jars either by design or by maker's name. Listed here are examples by the less common makers. Major factories are listed under their own names in other categories of the book, such as Abingdon, Brush, Hull, McCoy, Red Wing, and Shawnee. See also the Disneyana category.

Bear Policeman, Treasure Craft, 10 In.	100.00
Black, Chef, c.1940, 9 1/2 In.	69.00
Casper The Friendly Ghost, American Bisque, 1961, 13 1/2 In.	575.00
Christmas Tree, California Originals, Marked 873, 12 In.	175.00
Cottage, Wicker Handle, Japan, 6 7/8 x 5 1/4 In.	125.00
Davy Crockett, Regal China, 10 In.	450.00
Elsie The Cow, Head & Shoulders In Barrel, 12 1/4 In.	130.00
Fred & Dino, Flintstones, American Bisque, 14 1/2 In.	550.00
French Chef, Regal China, 1950, 11 In.	275.00
Humpty Dumpty, Abingdon, 11 In.	259.00
Jim Beam Bottle Club, Regal China, 9 1/2 In.	125.00
Lamb, American Bisque	375.00
Lamb, American Bisque, 13 In.	110.00
Lemon Face, Blue Hat, PY, Japan, 6 1/2 In.	115.00
Majorette, Regal China, 11 In.	600.00
Pig, Yellow, Hand Painted, Los Angeles Potteries	95.00
Pig In Baby Diaper, Regal China, 1950s, 11 In.	275.00
Pirate Fox, Twin Winton	230.00
Pot Belly Stove, Twin Winton, 12 1/2 In.	75.00
Quaker Oats, Old Fashioned Quaker Oats, Regal China, 9 1/2 In.	125.00
Raggedy Ann, 11 In.	255.00
Rooster, Twin Winton, 11 1/2 In.	95.00
Saddle, American Bisque, 12 In.	345.00
Sitting Horse, American Bisque, 11 In.	1100.00
Tractor, John Deere Model 750, Enesco	57.00

COORS ware was made by a pottery in Golden, Colorado, a company founded with the help of the Coors Brewing Company. Its founder, John Herold, started the Herold China and Pottery Company in 1910. The company name was changed in 1920, when Herold left. Dishes and decorative wares were produced from the turn of the century until the pottery was destroyed by fire in the 1930s. The name *Coors* is marked on the back. The company is still in business making industrial porcelain. For more information, see *Kovels' Depression Glass & Dinnerware Price List.*

Baker, Rosebud, Rectangular, Blue, 10 7/8 x 7 1/4 In.	135.00
Bowl, Cereal, Rock-Mount, Orange, 6 1/4 In.	25.00
Bowl, Pudding, Coorado, Ivory, 5 3/4 In.	75.00
Cake Plate, Thermo Porcelain, Tulip, 11 In.	85.00
Cake Server, Rosebud, Blue, 10 In.	195.00
Casserole, Cover, Rosebud, Orange, Handles, 8 In.	100.00

Casserole, Cover, Thermo Porcelain, Tulip, Medium 100.00
Crock, Thermo Porcelain, Pure Malted Milk, 7 1/4 In. 90.00
Gravy Bowl, Underplate, Coorado, White 135.00
Mixing Bowl, Coorado, Ivory, Handle, 9 3/4 In. 75.00
Mixing Bowl, Rosebud, Blue, 10 In. 125.00
Mixing Bowl, Rosebud, Orange, Handle, 12 1/4 In. 165.00
Mixing Bowl, Rosebud, Red, 7 In. 85.00
Mortar & Pestle, White, 7-In Mortar, 6 3/4-In. Pestle 95.00
Pie Plate, Coorado, Ivory, 10 3/4 In. 140.00
Pie Plate, Rosebud, Blue, Handles, 10 1/4 In. 90.00
Pitcher, Cover, Rosebud, Green, 5 In. 80.00
Pitcher, Cover, Rosebud, Ivory, 7 1/2 In. 425.00
Pitcher, Tilt Ball, Teal, No. 190, 8 x 7 In. 95.00
Platter, Mello-Tone, Green, Oval, 15 In. 75.00
Platter, Rock-Mount, Green, Oval, 15 In. 75.00
Saucer, Rosebud, Red 12.00
Vase, Beehive, Orange Matte Glaze, White Interior, Art Deco, 1930s, 5 x 4 3/4 In. 85.00
Vase, Berthoud Orange Matte Glaze, White Interior, Handles, Art Deco, 1930s, 8 1/4 In. ... 150.00
Vase, Berthoud, Blue Satin, White Satin Interior, Handles, 8 In. 125.00
Vase, Brighton, White, Green, 8 In. 95.00
Vase, Cripple Creek, Turquoise Matte Glaze, White Interior, Art Deco, 5 3/4 x 4 1/4 In. ... 75.00
Vase, Cripple Creek, Yellow Matte Glaze, White Interior, 5 3/4 x 4 1/4 In. 75.00
Vase, Golden, Yellow Glossy Glaze, White Interior, Handles, 5 1/2 x 6 1/2 In. ...... 85.00 to 145.00
Vase, Minturn, Blue Matte Glaze, White Interior, 8 1/2 In. 115.00
Vase, Orange Matte Glaze, White Interior, Handles, 1930s, 7 1/4 x 8 1/2 In. 175.00
Vase, Vail, Tan Matte Glaze, Turquoise Interior, Bulbous, Ribs, Handles, 1930s, 12 x 5 In. . 525.00
Vase, Vail, White Matte Glaze, Turquoise Interior, Bulbous, Ribs, Handles, 12 x 4 3/4 In. .. 525.00
Water Server, Stopper, Rosebud, 48 Oz., 7 3/8 x 8 1/4 In. 275.00
Water Server, Thermo Porcelain, White, 48 Oz. 100.00

COPELAND pieces listed here are those that have a mark including
the word Copeland used between 1847 and 1976. Marks include
Copeland Spode and Copeland & Garrett. See also Copeland Spode
and Royal Worcester.

Bust, Daphne, Circular Socle Mount, Marked, Parian, c.1865, 14 1/2 In. 705.00
Figurine, Children, Bisque, 2 Resting Girls, Cat, Late 19th Century, 13 x 10 1/2 In. 315.00
Figurine, Comus, Male Leaning On Rock, Goblet, Parian, England, c.1860, 12 1/2 In. 880.00
Figurine, Girl, Reading, Draped Gown, Parian, c.1869, 13 1/4 In. 500.00
Jug, Lotus, Impressed, c.1877, 8 In. 345.00
Pitcher, Blue & White, Rugby Pattern, Jasperware, 7 In. 175.00
Pitcher, Jasperware, Classical Maidens, Marked Copeland England 24, 5 1/2 In. 95.00
Plate Set, Japan Pattern, Octagonal, Wavy Rim, 1851-85, 8 1/4 In., 8 Piece 615.00
Platter, Italian Pattern, Animals & Figural, Architectural Ruins, Blue, c.1835, 18 In. 415.00
Tower, Coffeepot, Spode, Blue Oval Mark, 9 1/2 x 10 In. 58.00

COPELAND SPODE appears on some pieces of nineteenth-century
English porcelain. Josiah Spode established a pottery at Stoke-on-
Trent, England, in 1770. In 1833, the firm was purchased by William
Copeland and Thomas Garrett and the mark was changed. In 1847,
Copeland became the sole owner and the mark changed again. W.T.
Copeland & Sons continued until a 1976 merger when it became Royal
Worcester Spode. Pieces are listed in this book under the name that
appears in the mark. Copeland Spode, Copeland, and Royal Worcester
have separate listings.

COPELAND
SPODE
ENGLAND

Bowl, Reticulated, Scalloped Rim, 4-Footed, 2 Handles, Label, 9 1/2 x 6 1/4 In. 230.00
Dessert Set, Flowers, Garland, Insects, c.1900, 10 9-In. Plates, 12 Piece 660.00
Tea Set, Jasperware, Fox-Hunting Scene, Blue Ground, 5 In., 3 Piece 295.00

COPPER has been used to make utilitarian items, such as teakettles
and cooking pans, since the days of the early American colonists. Copper became a popular metal with the Arts & Crafts makers of the early
1900s, and decorative pieces, like desk sets, were made. Other pieces
of copper may be found in the Arts & Crafts, Bradley & Hubbard,
Kitchen, and Roycroft categories.

Bed Warmer, Brass, Round Bowl, Hinged Cover, Turned Handle, Early 1900s, 42 In. 105.00
Bed Warmer, Hinged Cover, Flowers, Stipple Work, Turned Handle, c.1900, 38 1/2 In. ... 115.00
Boiler, Molded Top, Handle, Oval Body, c.1900, 17 x 25 x 12 In. 200.00
Bowl, Begging Bowl Shape, Red, 6-Character K'ang Hsi Mark, 8 In. 470.00
Bowl, Hammered, Albert Berry Craftshop, 5 1/2 In. 355.00
Bowl, Hammered, Applied Spiral Medallions, Arts & Crafts, 10 In. 460.00
Bowl, Hammered, Arts & Crafts, 5 In. 206.00
Bowl, Hammered, Jarvie, 8 In. 470.00
Box, Stickley Brothers, Footed, Brass, Applied Hinges, Handle, 11 1/2 x 5 In. 1955.00
Box, Tobacco, Engraved Design, Dutch, 1 1/4 x 6 1/4 x 2 In. 126.00
Brandy Warmer, Dovetailed Construction, Wooden Handle, 18th Century 265.00
Cauldron, Candy Maker, 23 1/2 In. 316.00
Chafing Dish, Hammered, Oak, Linear Design, Onondaga Metal Shops, 14 x 14 In. 1175.00
Chamberstick, Enameled Flowers, Arts & Crafts, 8 In. 294.00
Charger, Hammered, Inlaid Flower Design, Silver Rim, Early 1800s, 11 1/2 In., Pair 127.00
Charger, Poppy Pods, Hammered, Arts & Crafts, England, 21 In. 3055.00
Cigar Box, Hammered, Hinged Lid, Cedar Lining, Albert Berry, 4 x 7 x 6 In. 2115.00
Coal Bin, Hammered, G. Stickley, Stylized Spades, Applied Riveted Handles, 13 x 12 In. .. 4115.00
Coal Bin, Hammered, Stylized Spade Design, Riveted Handles, Benedict, 12 x 14 In. 2235.00
Dish, Hammered, Quatrefoil Band, Walter Jennings, 1 1/4 x 7 1/4 In. 2468.00
Figure, Lion, Seated, Molded, Hollow, Erik Kramer, 1900s, 35 1/2 x 22 In. 1410.00
Frame, Hammered, Arts & Crafts, 6 1/2 In. 150.00
Frame, Hammered, Arts & Crafts, Grotesque Bird Design, Inset Stones, 13 In. 980.00
Frame, Hammered, Wheat, Raised, Tooled, Arts & Crafts, 14 In. 999.00
Frame, Raised, Embossed Iris Design, Arts & Crafts, 9 1/2 In. 1095.00
Jardiniere, Hammered, 2 Handles, Embossed Band, Stickley Bros., 6 x 14 1/2 In. 1060.00
Jardiniere, Stickley Bros., No. 418, Hammered, Footed, Geometric Designs, 17 In. 1175.00
Ladle, Hammered, Jarvie, 11 In. 235.00
Lavabo, Brass Hangers, Spout, France, 19th Century, 24 x 13 In., 3 Piece 150.00
Meat Cover, Acanthus Leaf Handle, Domed Body, c.1900, 6 x 10 In & 8 x 14 In., Pair 175.00
Mitten Warmer, Engraved Peacock, Turned Wooden Handle, 9 In. 430.00
Molds are listed in the Kitchen category.
Pan, Oval, Lid, Brass Handles, Tin Lined 13 x 21 1/2 x 5 In. 175.00
Plaque, Egyptian Revival, Silver Inlay, Egyptian Royalty Scenes, Early 1900s, 32 In. 210.00
Plaque, Stickley Brothers, Hammered, 3 Stylized Leaves, 7 1/2 In. 375.00
Teakettle, Dovetailed, Tapered Sides, Gooseneck Spout, Domed Lid, Acorn Finial, 12 In. . 230.00
Teakettle, Gooseneck, Brass Handle, Domed Lid, Partial Stamp, 10 3/4 In. 489.00
Teakettle, Hollow Handle, Brass Urn Finial, Early 1800s, 14 1/2 In. 115.00
Tray, Hammered, Etched Trees, Arts & Crafts, 12 1/2 In. 176.00
Tray, Hammered, Oval, Riveted Handles, G. Stickley, 11 x 23 In. 999.00
Tray, Hammered, Rectangular, Frost, 20 In. 440.00
Tray, Hammered, Riveted Handles, G. Stickley, 17 In. 1116.00
Tray, Hammered, Tooled Designs, Pinched Ends, Old Mission Kopperkdraft, 6 1/2 In. 145.00
Tray, Hand Wrought, Pipes, Tomahawks, Round, Javis, 1906, 7 In. 2100.00
Tray, Handwrought, Stylized Pattern, Pipes, Tomahawks, Round, R. Jarvie, c.1906, 7 In. .. 2100.00
Tray, Incised Tulips, William Arthur Smith Benson, 14 x 23 In. 355.00
Umbrella Stand, Hammered, Flared, Riveted, Handles, Embossed Spades, 25 x 13 In. 1175.00
Vase, Arts & Crafts Hammered, Bulbous Shape, Flared Ruffled Mouth, 8 3/4 In. 12.00
Vase, Bud, Hammered, Embossed TR, Circular, Riveted Base, Jarvie, 11 1/2 x 7 In. 5290.00
Vase, Bulbous, Hammered, Jauchen's Olde Copper Shop, 4 1/4 In. 635.00
Vase, Hammered Flared, Stylized Organic Design, Arts & Crafts, 18 In. 880.00
Vase, Hammered Tooled Designs, Arts & Crafts, 6 In. 295.00
Vase, Hammered, Harry Dixon, 5 1/4 In. 1295.00
Vase, Hammered, Stylized Organic, 8 In. 1116.00
Vase, Japonesque, Cylindrical, Brass & Silver Overlay, Christofle, Early 1900s, 8 In. 6600.00

COPPER LUSTER items are listed in the Luster category.

CORALENE glass was made by firing many small colored beads on
the outside of glassware. It was made in many patterns in the United
States and Europe in the 1880s. Reproductions are made today. Cora-
lene-decorated Japanese pottery is listed in the Japanese Coralene
category.

Vase, 2 Handles, Flowers, Signed, Japan, Feb. 9, 1909, 5 1/2 In. 345.00

Vase, Peacock, Enamel Branches On Reverse, 4 Scrolled Feet, Victorian, c.1900, 8 In. 360.00
Vase, Pink, Allover Gold Branch Design, Bulbous, Crimped & Ruffled Rim, 9 1/2 In....... 288.00

CORKSCREWS have been needed since the first bottle was sealed
with a cork, probably in the seventeenth century. Today collectors
search for the early, unusual patented examples or the figural corkscrews of recent years.

Bone Handle, Serrated Cork Grip Disk, England, 6 In. 69.00
Brass, Carved Bone, Turned Handle, Royal Coat Of Arms, 9 3/4 In. 290.00
Double Lever, Metal, James Heeley & Sons, England, 6 1/2 In. 69.00
Open Frame, Spring Below Wooden Handle, England, 6 In. 59.00
Peg & Worm Type, England, 4 In. 53.00
Rack Type, Side Handles, Wooden Handle, England, 7 1/2 In. 49.00
Rack Type, Wooden Handle, England, 7 1/4 In. 69.00
Scotsman, Painted Body, Head Shape Handle, Bakelite, Leather Pouch, 3 In. 86.00
Sperm Whale's Tooth, Early 19th Century 475.00

CORONATION souvenirs have been made since the 1800s. Pottery,
glass, tin, silver, and paper objects with a picture of the monarchs and
date have been sold at many coronations. The pieces that mention King
Edward VIII, the king who was never crowned, are not rare; collectors
should be sure to check values before buying. Related pieces are found
in the Commemorative category.

Bank, Elizabeth II, Crown Shape, Cast Iron, 1953, 3 1/4 x 3 In. 33.00
Bank, George V, Cast Iron, Sydenham & McOustra, England, 6 5/8 In. ....66.00 to 138.00
Book Match Case, George VI, Queen Elizabeth, Silvered Brass, 1937, 1 3/4 x 2 3/8 In. ... 40.00
Knife, King George VI, Queen Elizabeth, May 12, 1937, 3 In. 45.00
Mug, Queen Mary Commemorative, Moorcroft, Signed, c.1914, 3 3/4 In. 265.00
Tin, Edward VIII, Accession To The Throne, 1936, 2 5/8 x 5 1/4 In. .... *Illus* 80.00
Whiskey Jug, King George V & Queen Mary, Jug, A. Usher, Edinburgh, 1911, 10 In. 120.00

COSMOS is a pressed milk glass pattern with colored flowers made
from 1894 to 1915 by the Consolidated Lamp and Glass Company.
Tablewares and lamps were made in this pattern. A few pieces were
also made of clear glass with painted decorations. Other glass patterns
are listed under Consolidated Lamp and also in various glass categories. In later years, Cosmos was also made by the Westmoreland
Glass Company.

Butter, Cosmos, Cover 155.00
Butter, Cover 330.00
Condiment Set, Salt, Pepper, Mustard, Tray, Metal Center Handle 425.00
Lamp, Kerosene, 9 1/2 In. 475.00
Pitcher, 9 1/8 In. 400.00
Sugar & Creamer 200.00

COVERLETS were made of linen or wool during the nineteenth cen-
tury. Most of the coverlets date from 1800 to the 1880s. There was a
revival of hand weaving in the 1920s and new coverlets, especially
geometric patterns, were made. The earliest coverlets were made on
narrow looms, so two woven strips were joined together and a seam
can be found. The weave structures of coverlets can include summer
and winter, double weave, overshot, and others. Jacquard coverlets
have elaborate pictorial patterns that are made on a special loom or
with the use of a special attachment. Quilts are listed in this book in
their own category.

Double Weave, Blue & White, Leaf & Basket Borders, Medallions, 84 x 79 In. 175.00
Double Weave, Blue & White, Pine Tree Borders, Snowflakes Panels, 88 x 108 In. 310.00
Double Weave, Blue & White, Tulips, Houses, Pears, J. Klein Hamilton, 1856, 75 x 83 In. . 290.00
Double Weave, Blue & White, Tulips, Roses, C. Lochman, Hamburg, Pa., 1842, 98 x 83 In. 2753.00
Double Weave, Blue, Red, Natural, Optical Pattern, 70 x 80 In. 520.00
Double Weave, Blue, Red, White, Flowers, Geometric, York County, Penn., 90 x 84 In. ... 220.00
Double Weave, Blue, Salmon, Natural, Medallions, 1849, 72 x 82 In. 920.00
Double Weave, Blue, White, Red, Flowers, E.E., Aaronsburg Centre, Penn, 1835, 95 x 74 In. 575.00
Double Weave, Brown, Blue, Marked, M. Edith Geesey, York County, 77 x 76 In. 330.00

Coronation, Tin, Edward VIII, Accession To The
Throne, 1936, 2 5/8 x 5 1/4 In.

Coverlet, Jacquard,
Bellflower, Rose,
Catharine Miller,
1841, 88 x 98 In.

Double Weave, Navy Blue On White, Schoolhouse, Flower, 1848, 78 x 110 In.	1035.00
Double Weave, Optical, Navy Blue, Border, 72 x 90 In.	150.00
Jacquard, 5 Colors, Eagle, Liberty Corner Blocks, Medallion, 64 x 80 In.	489.00
Jacquard, 5 Colors, Julia Verdier, Bethel Township, Ohio, c.1840, 72 x 92 In.	1265.00
Jacquard, Agriculture & Manufacturers, Declaration Of Independence, 1827, 73 x 82 In.	1800.00
Jacquard, Bellflower, Rose, Catharine Miller, 1841, 88 x 98 In. . . . . *Illus*	550.00
Jacquard, Birds, Willows, Amanda M. Wiswell, Ohio, 1850, 68 x 76 In.	345.00
Jacquard, Blue & White, Double Rose, Border, c.1840, 91 x 72 In.	540.00
Jacquard, Blue, Green, Red, Bellflower, Stars, Nicklas, Chambersburg, 1853, 93 x 84 In.	330.00
Jacquard, Blue, Green, Red, Tulip Border, T. Weber, N. Emmaus, 1841, 80 x 78 In.	335.00
Jacquard, Blue, Orange, Sunburst, Flowers, Birds, Dan Smith, 1840, 82 x 96 In.	660.00
Jacquard, Blue, Red, Blue Green, Natural, Ohio, 71 x 84 In.	2245.00
Jacquard, Blue, Red, Gold, Natural, Medallions, Ohio, 1853, 76 x 86 In.	1495.00
Jacquard, Blue, Red, Green, Flowers, Geometric, Hausman, Trexlertown, 1857, 94 x 80 In.	440.00
Jacquard, Blue, Red, Green, Natural, 1843, 76 x 84 In.	1210.00
Jacquard, Blue, Red, Green, Natural, Wayne County, Ohio, 72 x 84 In.	545.00
Jacquard, Brick Red, Navy, Blue, Green, Natural, Striped, Tree Borders, 75 x 93 In.	290.00
Jacquard, Flower Filled Urn, Peacocks, Penn., 19th Century, 108 x 84 In.	295.00
Jacquard, Flower Medallion, Penn., Mid 1800s, 76 x 92 In.	646.00
Jacquard, Flowers, Red, Blue, Green, White, John Smith, S. Leman, 1837, 80 x 106 In.	550.00
Jacquard, Flowers, Star, Blue, White, Jacquard, c.1850, 88 x 90 In.	470.00
Jacquard, Green, Red, Natural, No. 23, 1838, Bucks County, Penn., 83 x 94 In.	1120.00
Jacquard, Green, Red, Natural, Stripes, Fringe, 78 x 98 In.	460.00
Jacquard, Green, Salmon, Natural, Ch. S. Meily, Wayne Country, Ohio, 1842, 34 x 34 In.	1840.00
Jacquard, Independence Hall, Eagles, Stars, James Alexander, 1824, 94 x 79 In.	3410.00
Jacquard, Medallions, Hancock County, Ohio, 1864, 70 x 84 In.	545.00
Jacquard, Medallions, Leaves, Flowers, c.1825, 80 x 74 In.	295.00
Jacquard, Memorial Hall Bldg., Red, Eagle, Spread Wing, Flowers, 73 x 82 In.	220.00
Jacquard, Navy & Natural, Floral Medallion, Bird Borders, 1840, 66 x 84 In.	480.00
Jacquard, Potted Tulips, Rose, Lochman, Hamburg, Penn., 1842, 83 x 98 In. . . . . *Illus*	275.00
Jacquard, Red, Green & Navy, Rose & Star Center, Eagle Border, 1848, 73 x 65 In.	635.00
Jacquard, Red, Green, Blue, Bell Flower Rose, Catharine Miller, 1841, 88 x 98 In.	550.00
Jacquard, Red, Green, Blue, Star, Flowers, J. Smith, Millerstown, Pa., 1930, 80 x 104 In.	358.00
Jacquard, Red, Green, Blue, Washington, Horses, Capitol, Schum, Lancaster, Pa., 80 x 82 In.	1870.00

Coverlet, Jacquard,
Potted Tulips, Rose,
Lochman, Hamburg,
Penn., 1842, 83 x 98 In.

Coverlet, Jacquard, Starburst, Tulip, Floral, Charles
Fehr Manufactory, Emmaus, Pa., 84 x 90 In.

Jacquard, Red, Green, Sunburst, Flowers, Fritzinger & Dannerd, Allentown, 92 x 92 In. ...   225.00
Jacquard, Red, Natural, Floral Medallion, Portrait Of George Washington, 1869, 73 x 82 In.   1090.00
Jacquard, Red, Navy Blue, Tan, Floral, Diamond Center, Ohio, 1855, 74 x 82 In. 805.00
Jacquard, Rose, Flowers, Medallion, Penn., 1843, 93 x 76 In. 590.00
Jacquard, Star, Eagles, Trees, Birds, Vines, Blue, White, N.Y. 1841, 86 x 82 In. 500.00
Jacquard, Starburst, Tulip, Floral, Charles Fehr Manufactory, Emmaus, Pa., 84 x 90 In. *Illus*   275.00
Jacquard, Stripes, Blue, Green, Reds, Medallions, 78 x 90 In. 489.00
Jacquard, Sunburst, Red, Natural, Acorn & Oak Leaf Wreath, 76 x 76 In. 230.00
Jacquard, Union, Flowers, Blue, White, Rhoda Hoffman, 1843, 80 x 90 In. 230.00
Overshot, 2 Panel, Geometric, Blue, Red, 1800s, 70 x 90 In. 155.00
Summer & Winter, Blue & White, Signed, S. Balantyne, 1847 ....   770.00

COWAN POTTERY made art pottery and wares for florists. Guy
Cowan made pottery in Rocky River, Ohio, a suburb of Cleveland,
from 1913 to 1931. A stylized mark with the word *Cowan* was used on
most pieces. A commercial, mass-produced line was marked *Lakeware*. Collectors today search for the Art Deco pieces by Guy Cowan,
Viktor Schreckengost, Waylande Gregory, or Thelma Frazier Winter.

Bookends, Elk, Mottled Orange Glaze, Marked, 7 In., Pair 646.00
Bowl, Lavender Wisteria Glaze, Ink Stamp, 4 1/2 x 9 5/8 In. 81.00
Bowl, Octagonal, Stylized Flowers, Oriental Red Glaze, 2 1/2 x 4 1/2 In. 52.00
Candlestick, Figural, Women, Original Ivory, 12 1/2 In., Pair 410.00
Charger, Molded Leaves, Vines, Oriental Red Glaze, 13 In. 259.00
Console, Green Glaze, 3 3/8 x 13 1/4 In. 58.00
Decanter, King, Stopper, Oriental Red Glaze, Waylande Gregory, c.1930, 12 x 4 1/2 In. ...   705.00
Figurine, Bird & Wave, Egyptian Blue, No. 749A, 12 1/4 In. 235.00
Figurine, Dancer, Original Ivory, No. 792, 8 In. 355.00
Figurine, Elephant, Tucked Trunk, Orange Matte, Impressed, Circular Mark, 4 3/4 In. 235.00
Figurine, Horses, Shadow White 290.00
Figurine, Woodland Nymph, Woman Seated On Stump, Ivory Glaze, 1930, 13 7/8 In. 575.00
Humidor, Cover, Oriental Red Glaze, Impressed Mark, 5 3/4 In. 175.00
Lamp, Aztec Style, Black, Tan, Milky Overglaze, 11 3/8 In. 290.00
Lamp, Woman Holding Dove, Egyptian Blue Glaze, 1930, 12 3/4 In. 115.00
Plaque, Polo Player, Horse Under Sun, Russet Brown Glaze, Impressed, 11 1/4 In. 345.00
Trivet, Flowers, Molded, Yellow, Green, Blue Ground, 6-Sided, Mark, 6 In. 175.00
Urn, Lakeware, Peacock Glaze, Impressed Mark 115.00
Vase, Cabinet, Orange Luster Glaze, Stamped, 4 In. 46.00
Vase, Egg Shape, Orange Luster Glaze, 9 In. 80.00
Vase, Fan Shape, Green Glaze, 5 1/8 x 8 In. 240.00
Vase, Fir Green Glaze, 4 5/8 In. 58.00
Vase, Flambe Luster, Gunmetal, Sea Green Glaze, 12 1/2 In. 635.00
Vase, Swan, Impressed, Ivory Glaze, 11 3/4 In. 138.00

CRACKER JACK, the molasses-flavored popcorn mixture, was first
made in 1896 in Chicago, Illinois. A prize was added to each box in
1912. Collectors search for the old boxes, toys, and advertising materials. Many of the toys are unmarked.

Bookmark, Dog, Tin Lithograph, 1930s, 2 3/4 In. 30.00
Box, c.1910, 6 x 3 x 1 3/4 In. 79.00
Fork & Spoon, Prize, Tin, 1930s, 2 In. 10.00
Lunch Box, Metal, No Thermos 49.00
Mug & Bowl, Sailor, Dog, Breakfast Cereal, Plastic, Stamped, Deka, Elizabeth, N.J. 42.00
Puzzle, 2 Birds In Flight, Cardboard, 1 1/4 In. Diam. 10.00
Puzzle, Cowboy, 2 Guns, Cardboard, 1 1/4 In. Diam. 10.00
Puzzle, Daisy, Cardboard, 1 3/4 x 1 1/4 In. 10.00
Puzzle, Donkey, Cardboard, 1 1/2 In. Diam. 10.00
Puzzle, Fish In Bowl, Cardboard, 1 1/2 In. Diam. 10.00
Puzzle, Man Shooting Basketball Hoops, Cardboard, 2 Metal Balls, 1 1/4 In. Diam. 10.00
Puzzle, Mouse & Cheese, Cardboard, 1 3/4 x 1 1/4 In. 10.00
Puzzle, Panda Bear, Cardboard, 1 1/4 In. Diam. 10.00
Puzzle & Mirror, Tin Frame, Cardboard, 6 Balls, Dexterity, Round, c.1910, 1 1/2 In. 45.00
Sign, Cardboard, Color, c.1901, 15 3/4 x 11 3/4 In. 880.00
Toy, Ambulance, Tin, Lithograph, 1930s 75.00

Toy, Fortune Wheel, Sailor Boy Says To Spell Your Name, Tin, Early 1930s, 3/4 In. 65.00
Toy, Horse Drawn Wagon, More You Eat, More You Want, 2 1/4 x 1 In. 125.00
Toy, Train Car, Cast Metal, 1920s, 1 In. 30.00
Whistle, Man, Large Mouth, Gold Colored Tin, 2 1/4 In. 34.00

CRACKLE GLASS was originally made by the Venetians, but most of
the ware found today dates from the 1800s. The glass was heated,
cooled, and refired so that many small lines appeared inside the glass.
It was made in many factories in the United States and Europe.

Cruet, Amber, Bulbous Base, Long Neck, Metal Stopper, Kanawha, 1960s, Pair 45.00
Decanter, Bulbous, Ogee Handle, Tricornered Rim, Ball Stopper, 7 1/2 In. 30.00
Vase, Wall, Pear Shape, Gilt Metal Mount, 19th Century, 6 In. 375.00

CRANBERRY GLASS is an almost transparent yellow-red glass. It
resembles the color of cranberry juice. The glass has been made in
Europe and America since the Civil War. It is still being made, and
reproductions can fool the unwary. Related glass items may be listed in
other categories, such as Northwood, Rubena Verde, etc.

Bottle, Scent, Faceted, Stopper, 7 In. 200.00
Cruet, Clear Applied Handle, Faceted Stopper, 7 In. 250.00
Ewer, Wine, Enameled, Italy, 6 In. 30.00
Lamp, Hobnail, Bulbous Shade, Stem, Gilt Metal, 26 1/2 In., Pair 315.00
Perpetual Fountain, Tufts, 1880s, 20 In. 1320.00
Rose Bowl, Enameled, 3 1/2 In. 65.00
Tumbler, Amber Base, Enameled Gold Women, Urn, Flowers, Victorian, 5 In. 435.00
Vase, Folded Rim, Rigaree, Victorian, 13 In. 160.00

CREAMWARE, or queensware, was developed by Josiah Wedgwood
about 1765. It is a cream-colored earthenware that has been copied by
many factories. Similar wares may be listed under Pearlware and
Wedgwood.

Bowl, Pierced, 2 Handles, 11 1/4 In., Pair 1020.00
Coffeepot, Cover, Lead Glazed, Pear Shape, Brown & Green Glaze, c.1770, 10 3/4 In. 999.00
Jug, Transfer Print, Religion, Faith, Hope & Charity, 10 1/2 In. 600.00
Mug, Success To The Plough, Fleece & Pail, Transfer Print 350.00
Pitcher, Perry, Pike, Canary Ground, 6 1/2 In. 3970.00
Pitcher, Stephen Decatur, Naval Battle, Bombe Shape, Pink Luster Trim, 4 3/4 In. 2645.00
Pitcher, Transfer Print, Admiral Nelson, Battle Of Trafalgar, 9 1/2 In. 500.00
Plate, Basket Weave, Diaper & Lattice Panels, Whieldon Glaze, c.1760, 9 In., Pair 805.00
Plate, Prodigal Son, Harlots, Royal Edge, England, c.1780, 10 In. 1725.00
Teapot, Cover, Aurora, Angels, Twisted Handle, c.1775, 5 In. 2115.00
Teapot, Cover, Lead Glazed, Chintz Decorated, Globular, 5 1/4 In. 1060.00
Tureen, Cover, Stand, Village Scene, Insects, Flowers, Melon Finial, 11 x 15 In. 330.00
Urn, Cover, Stand, Beehive Shape, Basket Weave, c.1800, 12 1/4 In. 1700.00
Vase, Cover, Pierced, Angel Form Handles, Leeds, 10 1/2 In. 540.00
Vase, Relief Decorated, Maidens & Animals At Play, Square, 6 1/2 In., Pair 480.00
Wall Pocket, Cornucopia, Leaf Border, Cupids, Early 1800s, 10 In., Pair 520.00

CREDIT CARDS, credit tokens, metal charge plates, phone cards,
and other similar collectibles that replace money are now part of the
numismatic collecting hobby.

Bank Americard, 1969 .... 10.50
Bloomingdale's, Metal, 1980 .... 15.00
Bullock's, Los Angeles 26 Calif, Before 1963 .... 24.00
Charge Plate, Red Leatherette Case, Cleveland, 1950s 6.00
Esso Gas & Oil, Humble Oil & Refining Co., Plastic, 1962 .... 25.00
Mastercharge, Marine Midland, 1972 .... 20.00

CREIL, France, had a faience factory as early as 1794. The company
merged with a factory in Montereau in 1819. They made stoneware,
mocha ware, and soft paste porcelain. The name *Creil* appears as part
of the mark on many pieces. The Creil factory closed in 1895.

Lavabo, Cover, Neoclassical Design, Blue & White, Faience, Montereau, c.1884 .... 1400.00

Crown Derby, Figurine, Man, Woman, Holding
Baskets, Fruit & Flowers, 7 3/4 In., Pair

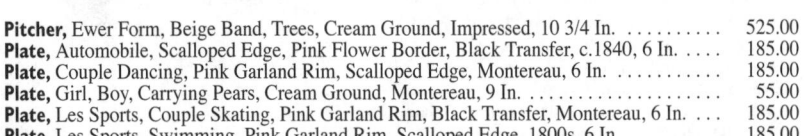

Don't immerse figurines in water.
Many have holes in the bottom
that will let water get inside. It's
difficult to remove the water and it
may drip out and stain a wooden
table or the figurine.

Pitcher, Ewer Form, Beige Band, Trees, Cream Ground, Impressed, 10 3/4 In.	525.00
Plate, Automobile, Scalloped Edge, Pink Flower Border, Black Transfer, c.1840, 6 In.	185.00
Plate, Couple Dancing, Pink Garland Rim, Scalloped Edge, Montereau, 6 In.	185.00
Plate, Girl, Boy, Carrying Pears, Cream Ground, Montereau, 9 In.	55.00
Plate, Les Sports, Couple Skating, Pink Garland Rim, Black Transfer, Montereau, 6 In.	185.00
Plate, Les Sports, Swimming, Pink Garland Rim, Scalloped Edge, 1800s, 6 In.	185.00

CROWN DERBY is the name given to porcelain made in Derby, England, from the 1770s to 1935. Pieces are marked with a crown and the letter *D* or the word *Derby*. The earliest pieces were made by the original Derby factory, while later pieces were made by the King Street Partnerships (1848–1935) or the Derby Crown Porcelain Co. (1876–1890). Derby Crown Porcelain Co. became Royal Crown Derby Co. Ltd. in 1890. It is now part of Royal Doulton Tableware Ltd.

Figurine, Man, Woman, Holding Baskets, Fruit & Flowers, 7 3/4 In., Pair	*Illus*	650.00
Vase, Cover, Pink Ground, Flowers, Leaves, Butterflies, c.1880		1800.00

CROWN DUCAL is the name used on some pieces of porcelain made by A. G. Richardson and Co., Ltd., of Tunstall and Cobridge, England. The name has been used since 1916.

Bowl, Persian Rose, Flowers, Leaves, Charlotte Rhead, 1930s, 10 In.	155.00
Tea Set, Rose Peony, Teapot, Cups, Saucers, Sugar, Creamer, Plate, 8 Piece	575.00
Wall Pocket, Stylized Oak Leaves, 7 In.	35.00

CROWN MILANO glass was made by Frederick Shirley at the Mt. Washington Glass Works about 1890. It had a plain biscuit color with a satin finish. It was decorated with flowers and often had large gold scrolls.

Basket, Enameled, Pansies Interior, Metal Rim & Handle, 5 1/2 x 6 1/2 In.	260.00
Basket, Pansies, Fitted Metal Rim, Signed, 6 x 5 In.	225.00
Biscuit Jar, Cover, Gold Flowers, Vine, Blue Diagonal Stripes, Turtle Finial, 4 x 6 In.	1150.00
Biscuit Jar, Cover, Pink Melon Ribbed, Flowers, Berries, Silver Plated Collar, 9 In.	575.00
Biscuit Jar, Cover, Rust, Cream, Jewels, Starfish, 6 In.	635.00
Biscuit Jar, Embossed Metal Cover, Chrysanthemums, Gold Tracery, Seashell, 10 In.	460.00
Biscuit Jar, Gold Flowers, Applied Jewels, Peach & Cream Stripes, 4 x 5 1/2 In.	805.00
Biscuit Jar, Shaded Butterscotch, Flowers, Gold Scrolled Medallions, 7 In.	315.00
Bowl, Rose, Shaded Blue, Scalloped Rim, Amethyst, Brown Flowers, 4 In.	115.00
Cup & Saucer, Raised Gold Ferns, Shaded Pink	490.00
Dresser Box, Lime, Gold Ginko, Heart Shaped Hinged Cover, 5 1/4 In.	575.00
Ewer, Aquatic Life, Fish, Shells, Coral, Applied Rope Handle, 10 In.	9200.00
Ewer, Shaded Green, Flowers, Twisted, Curled Handle, 10 3/4 In.	2185.00
Hatpin Holder, Mushroom Shape, Pansies, Shaded Blue, 3 1/2 In.	605.00
Jar, Cover, Jeweled Starfish, Gold Encrusted, Hobnail, Squat, 6 In.	1035.00
Jar, Cover, Ribbed, Peach, Sienna, Leaf, Berry, Embossed Crab, 5 1/4 x 6 1/2 In.	1320.00
Jar, Cover, White Flowers, Mottled Apricot & White, Melon Ribbed, 6 x 6 In.	635.00

Marmalade, Pansies, Gold Trim, Hobnail, Round, Squat, Embossed Metal Lid, 6 In. 950.00
Rose Bowl, Shaded Yellow, Chrysanthemums, Scalloped Rim, 6 In. 260.00
Salt, Cockle Shell Form, Ribbed, Enamelrd Flowers, 2 3/4 In. 520.00
Sugar, Cover, Flower Sprays, Gold Scrolls, Squat, 4 In. 635.00
Sugar Shaker, Jonquils, Melon Ribbed, 2 1/2 x 4 In. 230.00
Vase, Bulbous Top, Stick, Salmon, Nine Flying Sea Gulls, 12 In. 3500.00
Vase, Green & Brown Mallard Ducks, Sun, Stars, Bulbous, 11 In. 950.00
Vase, Pink, Yellow, Oval, 9 In. 400.00
Vase, Reverse Trumpet, Shaded Blue, Flower Bouquets, Seaweed, 9 1/2 In. 3740.00
Vase, Stick, Salmon, 9 Flying Sea Gulls, Gold Sunburst & Stars, Bulbous, 12 In. 4025.00

CROWN TUSCAN pattern is included in the Cambridge glass category.

CRUETS of glass or porcelain were made to hold vinegar, oil, and other condiments. They were especially popular during Victorian times and have been made in a variety of styles since the eighteenth century. Additional cruets may be found in the Castor Set category and also in various glass categories.

Cobalt Blue Glass, Derby Shaped Stopper, 6 1/4 In. 220.00
Earthenware, Rooster, Cork, Japan, 1940s 19.00
Faience, Deer, French Faience 135.00
Glass, Clear, c.1900 .... 58.00
Glass, Heisey, Panels & Dots 48.00
Jadite, Strawberries, Hand Painted 25.00
Milk Glass, Westmoreland, Quilt Pattern 30.00
Satin Glass, Yellow, White Bird, Leaves, Camphor Handle, Faceted Stopper, 6 In. 230.00
Set, Porcelain, Duck, Luster, Japan, Pair 35.00

CT GERMANY was first part of a mark used by a company in Altwasser, Germany, in 1845. The initials stand for C. Tielsch, a partner in the firm. The Hutschenreuther firm took over the company in 1918 and continued to use the *CT*.

C.T.

Basket, Hydrangeas, Pink, Lavender, Gold Trim, Scrolled Handle, Oval, Low, 11 3/4 In. .. 50.00
Bowl, Cereal, Flowers, Pink, Blue, Green, White, Yellow, c.1930, 6 1/4 In. 20.00
Bowl, Floral Center, Heavy Gold Border, Embossed Scrolling, Oval, Handles, 13 In. 15.00
Bowl, Floral, Handle, 1920s, 3 1/2 x 11 x 9 In. 55.00
Bowl, Flowers, Blue Border, Scalloped Edge, 1875-1918, 2 x 11 1/4 x 7 1/2 In. 85.00
Compote, Open Lace, Reticulated, Gilded Flowers, Late 1920s 95.00
Cup & Saucer, Demitasse, Pink Irises 5.00
Plate, Bread & Butter, Rose Swags, Gold Trim, Scalloped Rim, 6 1/4 In., 4 Piece 10.00
Plate, Floral, Random, Scalloped Edge, 7 5/8 In. 32.00
Platter, Flowers, 10 In. 20.00

CUP PLATES are small glass or china plates that held the cup while a diner of the mid-nineteenth century drank coffee or tea from the saucer. The most famous cup plates were made of glass at the Boston and Sandwich factory located in Sandwich, Massachusetts. There have been many new glass cup plates made in recent years for sale to gift shops or limited edition collectors. These are similar to the old plates but can be recognized as new.

2 Hunters, Dog, Light Blue, Gun & Bag Border, Staffordshire, 3 7/8 In. 99.00
4-Leaf, Beaded Scrolls, Flower & Scroll Border, 42 Scallops, Opaque Opal, 3 1/2 In. 88.00
4-Leaf, Flowers, Stippled Scroll Border, 63 Scallops Rim, Peacock Blue, 3 9/16 In. 1045.00
4-Plume & C-Scroll, 5-Point Stars, Stippled Star & Leaf Border, Rope Rim, 3 1/2 In. 1870.00
4-Plume Center, Wheat Sheaf & Arch Border, Scalloped Rim, Octagonal, 3 1/2 In. 120.00
4-Scrolled Plume Center, Scrolled Scalloped Rim, Octagonal, 3 1/2 In. 55.00
5-Point Star & Rays, Concentric Rings, 50 Scallops Rim, Amethyst, 3 1/16 In. 220.00
6-Beaded Point Star, 11 Lace Points, 16 Wheat Sheaf Scallops Rim, 3 5/8 In. 45.00
6-Petal Rosette, Trumpet Vine Border, Strawberry-Diamond Rim, 3 7/16 In. 55.00
6-Point Rayed Star, 12-Point Rayed Border, Plain Edge, Blue, 3 1/4 In. 220.00
6-Point Rosette, Leaf & Beaded Diamond Border, 35 Bull's-Eye Rim, 3 1/4 In. 1430.00
7-Petal Rosette, 4 Scrolled Bull's-Eye Border, Stippled, Rope Rim, 3 1/2 In. 3190.00
8-Leaf Rosette, Stippled Border, 17 Wheat Sheaf Scallops Rim, 3 1/4 In. 50.00

8-Leaf Rosette, Stippled Wheat Sheaf Border, 55 Scallops, Peacock Blue, 3 3/8 In. 230.00
8-Petal Rosette, Rings, Stippled Borders, 15 Scallops & Points Rim, Opal, 3 3/4 In. 495.00
8-Triangle Center, Fans, Stippled Border, 10 Scallops Rim, Fiery Opaque Opal, 3 5/8 In. ... 120.00
10-Petal Rosette, 20-Arch Border, Scalloped Rim, Light Green, Octagonal, 3 In. 230.00
12-Point Star, Peacock Feathers, 36 Bull's-Eye & Point Rim, Bright Blue, 3 3/8 In. 3300.00
16-Petal Rosette, Fleur-De-Lis Border, 40 Scallops Rim, Dark Blue, 3 In. 3575.00
16-Petal Rosette, Rope Borders, 24 Scallops & Point Rim, Light Blue Green, 2 7/8 In. ... 80.00
16-Stippled Point Rosette, 10 Scallops Rope Rim, 3 7/16 In. 50.00
18-Rib, Blown, Plain Edge, Amethyst, 3 7/16 In. 198.00
Basket Band, Hanging Leaves, Rosette, Rope Edge & Table Ring, Opal, Fiery Rim, 4 In. . 66.00
Bull's-Eye & Scrolls, Fleur-De-Lis, Trefoils, 66 Scallops Rim, Gray Blue, 3 5/16 In. 100.00
Bull's-Eye Center, 6-Comet Tail Border, 30 Scallops Rim, 3 1/16 In. 190.00
Bunker Hill Monument, Ship's Wheel Border, 53 Scallops, Emerald Green, 3 3/4 In. 1650.00
Eagle, Facing Right, Stippled Porthole Border, 30 Scallops Rim, 3 1/16 In. 242.00
Flower Band, 20 Leaves, Star, Opaque Swirled Blue, Opalescent Outer Rim, 3 5/8 In. 2530.00
Flower Band, 23 Leaves, Star, Opaque Powder Blue, Silvery Sheen, 4 In. 2860.00
Harp, 6 Bull's-Eyes, Stippled Porthole Border, 33 Bull's-Eye Scallops Rim, 3 1/16 In. 4125.00
Heart, Concentric Circles, 14-Heart Border, 73 Scallops Rim, Canary, 3 5/8 In. ....660.00 to 770.00
Hearts, Stippled & Scrolled, Leaves, Rope Edge & Table Ring, Opal, Green Tint, 3 3/4 In. . 275.00
Henry Clay, Fleur-De-Lis Border, 50 Uneven Scallops Rim, 3 7/16 In. 165.00
Irish Harp, 7-Petal Rosette, Stippled Vine, 24 Bull's-Eyes & Points, Blue, 3 7/16 In. 880.00
Lafayette & Washington, Black Transfer, Wood, Staffordshire, 3 3/4 In. 518.00
Lafayette & Washington, Red Transfer, Wood, Staffordshire, 3 3/4 In. 1265.00
Liberty Torch, Stippled Scroll Border, 34 Bull's-Eye Rim, 3 5/16 In. 253.00
Log Cabin, Continuous Floral Vine Border, 55 Uneven Scallops, 3 7/16 In. 935.00
Log Cabin, Forget-Me-Not Border, 66 Scallops Rim, Amber, 3 1/4 In. 358.00
Moses & The Ten Commandments, Red, Shell Border, Staffordshire, 4 In. 176.00
Plow, Acanthus Leaves, 19 Leaf Darts Border, 24 Bull's-Eye & Points Rim, 3 7/16 In. 1320.00
Point & Petal Rosette, 28 Bull's-Eye Stippled Border, 30 Bull's-Eye Scallops, 3 In. 99.00
Point & Petal Rosette, 28 Bull's-Eye Stippled Border, Rope Rim, 3 In. 90.00
Pointed Quatrefoil, Stippled Leaves, Pentagons, 10 Scallops Rope, Green, 3 7/16 In. 1155.00
Prunus Wreath, Medium Dark Blue, Impressed, Rogers, Staffordshire, 4 In. 165.00
Quatrefoil, 12 Stippled Hearts Border, 43 Scallops Rim, Smokey Electric Blue, 3 7/8 In. ... 440.00
Quatrefoil, 12 Stippled Hearts Border, 48 Scallops Rim, Emerald Green, 3 7/8 In. 1595.00
Quatrefoil, 12 Stippled Hearts Border, 63 Scallops Rim, Bright Violet Blue, 3 3/8 In. 358.00
R.H. Miller & Company, Importers Of China, 50 Scallops Rim, 3 7/16 In. 190.00
Rayed Bull's-Eye, 14-Arch Border, 64 Scallops Rim, Deep Cobalt Blue, 3 7/16 In. 132.00
Rayed Star, Graduated Ray Border, 66 Scallops Rim, Honey Amber, 3 1/4 In. 50.00
Rayed Star, Graduated Ray Border, 66 Scallops Rim, Red Amber, 3 1/4 In. 80.00
Roman Rosette, Darts, Diamonds, 9 Serrated Scallops & Points, Blue Green, 3 5/8 In. ... 130.00
Roman Rosette, Rosettes Borders, 8 Serrated Scallops, Light Clambroth, 3 9/16 In. 50.00
Rose & Pansy, Egg & Dart Border, 30 Bull's-Eye Rim, Medium Blue, 3 In. 1760.00
Rosette In Triangle, Scrolled Diamonds, Vine Border, Blue, Opal Edge, 3 7/16 In. 2090.00
Rosette In Triangle, Scrolled Diamonds, Vine Border, Electric Blue, 3 3/8 In. 660.00
Scrolled Star, Stippled Triangles, Rope Edge, Fiery Opalescent, 10 Sides, 3 5/8 In. 1045.00
Sheltered Peasants, Dark Blue, Flower & Fruit Border, Staffordshire, 3 15/16 In. 110.00
Ship, Benjamin Franklin, Anchor & Star Border, 59 Scallops, Amber Stain, 3 7/16 In. 5500.00
Ship, Chancellor Livingston, Stippled Rigging, 63 Scallops, Blue, Opal Edges, 3 7/16 In. .. 5775.00
Ship, Chancellor Livingston, Stippled Rigging, 63 Scallops, Emerald Green, 3 7/16 In. 3850.00
Steamship, Union Glass Works, 41 Eggs & Scallops Rim, 3 1/2 In. 1870.00
Strawberry-Diamond Waffle, 15 Fan Scallops & Flowers Rim, Cobalt Blue, 3 7/16 In. ... 4125.00
Sunburst, Bull's-Eye Center, Plain Border, Scalloped, Lavender, Octagonal, 2 15/16 In. ... 385.00
Target, Concentric Border Rings, Plain Rope Rim On Top, 3 5/16 In. 358.00
Target Center, Narrow Fluted Border, Crossed Flute Rim, Plain Edge, 3 3/4 In. 33.00
Thistle & Leaf, 32 Stippled Oval Border, 24 Bull's-Eye & Point Rim, 3 7/16 In. 66.00
Victoria, Scrolled & Floral Borders, 75 Uneven Scallops Rim, Deep Blue, 3 5/8 In. 523.00

CURRIER & IVES made the famous American lithographs marked
with their name from 1857 to 1907. The mark used on the print
included the street address in New York City, and it is possible to date
the year of the original issue from this information. Earlier prints were
made by N. Currier and use that name from 1835 to 1847. Many
reprints of the Currier or Currier & Ives prints have been made. Some

collectors buy the insurance calendars that were based on the old prints. The words *large*, *small*, or *medium folio* refer to size. The original print sizes were very small (up to about 7 x 9 in.), small (8.8 x 12.8 in.), medium (9 x 14 in. to 14 x 20 in.), large (larger than 14 x 20 in.). Other sizes are probably later copies. Other prints by Currier & Ives may be listed in the Card category under Advertising and in the Sheet Music category. Currier & Ives dinnerware patterns may be found in the Adams or Dinnerware categories.

Abraham Lincoln, Nation's Martyr, Black, White, Mat, Frame, 13 x 10 In.	460.00
American Homestead Autumn, Hand Colored, 7 3/4 x 12 1/2 In.	81.00
Arkansas Traveler, 11 x 14 In.	345.00
Darktown Fire Brigade, A Prize Squirt, Frame, 16 x 20 In.	2450.00
Darktown Fire Brigade, Last Shake, Frame, 15 x 22 In.	300.00
Express Train, Hand Colored, Frame, 1870, 8 x 12 1/2 In.	2400.00
First Ride, Scottish Child, Pony, 13 x 9 1/4 In.	60.00
Futurity Race At Sheepshead Bay, Frame, 1889, 26 x 38 1/2 In.	1530.00
Great Fire At St. John, June 20th 1877, Frame, 11 1/2 x 15 In.	240.00
Harvest, Hand Colored, 8 1/4 x 12 1/2 In.	127.00
Haying Time, First Load, Hand Colored, 1868, 15 3/4 x 24 In.	7800.00
Home In The Wilderness, Frame, 14 x 17 In.	1064.00
Home In The Wilderness, Frame, 17 1/4 x 21 1/2 In.	630.00
Judge Fullerton, Hand Colored, Frame, 1873, 14 x 18 In.	230.00
Lakeside Home, Hand Colored, 9 3/4 x 16 In.	115.00
M'Donough's Victy. On Lake Champlain, Hand Colored, 13 x 18 In.	345.00
Midnight Race On The Mississippi, Frame, 28 x 36 In.	2875.00
Outlet Of Niagara River, Hand Colored, 8 x 12 1/2 In.	105.00
Rising Family, Family Of Snipes, Mat, Frame, 27 x 32 In.	575.00
River Shannon, Hand Colored, 8 1/2 x 12 1/2 In.	138.00
Some Pumpkins, Horse & Locomotive Race, Frame, 11 x 15 In.	170.00
Trotting Mare, American Girl, Frame, 9 1/2 x 13 1/2 In.	139.00
Trotting Mare, Flora Temple, Frame, 10 1/2 x 13 1/4 In.	190.00
Trotting Mare, Lucy, Frame, 1868, 10 1/2 x 15 1/4 In.	139.00
Western Farmer's Home, Hand Coloring, 8 1/4 x 12 1/2 In.	160.00
Winter Morning In The Country, Hand Colored, 1873, 9 x 12 1/4 In.	1200.00

CUSTARD GLASS is a slightly yellow opaque glass. It was first made in England in the 1880s and was first made in the United States in the 1890s. It has been reproduced. Additional pieces may be found in the Cambridge, Fenton, Heisey, and Northwood categories. Custard glass is called Ivorina Verde by Heisey and other companies.

Chrysanthemum Sprig, Berry Set, Blue, Gold Trim, 7 Piece	650.00
Chrysanthemum Sprig, Compote, Blue, Gold Trim	135.00
Chrysanthemum Sprig, Creamer, Blue, Gold Trim	120.00
Chrysanthemum Sprig, Table Set, Blue, Gold Trim, 4 Piece	1125.00
Georgia Gem, Spooner, Enameled Flowers	95.00
Grape & Gothic Arches, Goblet	75.00
Inverted Fan & Feather, Berry Set, Gold & Pink Trim, 7 Piece	950.00
Inverted Fan & Feather, Table Set, Pink & Gold Trim, 4 Piece	575.00
Little Gem, see Georgia Gem pattern in this category.	
Louis XV, Spooner, Gold Trim	110.00
Maize is its own category in this book.	
Ring Band, Tumbler, Souvenir, Ogden, Utah, Gold Trim	80.00

CUT GLASS has been made since ancient times, but the large majority of the pieces now for sale date from the brilliant period of glass design, 1880 to 1905. These pieces have elaborate geometric designs with a deep miter cut. Modern cut glass with a similar appearance is being made in England, Ireland, and the Czech and Slovak republics. Chips and scratches are often difficult to notice but lower the value dramatically. A signature on the glass adds significantly to the value. Other cut glass pieces are listed under factory names.

Berry Bowl, Empire Pattern, Brilliant, 3 1/2 x 8 1/4 In.	805.00
Bottle, Scent, Cane, Star Cut Base, Stopper, 10 In.	230.00

Bowl, Butterfly & Flower, Flared, Reverse Cut Petal Foot, c.1915, 12 x 9 In. 345.00
Bowl, Button, Hobstars, Arches, Brilliant, 9 1/2 In. 150.00
Bowl, Buttons, Arches, Fan, Brilliant, 8 In. 60.00
Bowl, Elmira Pattern, 10 In. 500.00
Bowl, Fruit, Poppies, Shell & Scroll Edge, c.1915, 4 1/2 x 10 In. 865.00
Bowl, Fruit, Russian Pattern, 5 In. 580.00
Bowl, Fruit, Star & Cane, Handles, Hobstar Foot, 6 1/4 x 9 In. 1150.00
Bowl, Fruit, Strawberry-Diamond, Hobstar, Hobstar Base, 10 In. 675.00
Bowl, Hobstar & Arches, Tuthill, c.1910, 8 In. 125.00
Bowl, Hobstar & Diamond, Brilliant, 8 In. 90.00
Bowl, Hobstar & Fan, Oval, Brilliant, 11 3/4 In. 185.00
Bowl, Hobstar, 3 1/2 x 10 1/2 In. 60.00
Bowl, Hobstar, Arches, Allover Hobstar Base, Brilliant, 8 In. 130.00
Bowl, Hobstars, Fan Paneled Rim, Boat Shape, Anglo-Irish, 11 In. 325.00
Bowl, Stand, Strawberry Diamonds, Fluted Borders, Anglo-Irish, Oval, 11 In. 1425.00
Bowl, Strawberry-Diamond, Rolled Rim, Footed, Continental, 1800s, 9 1/2 In. 415.00
Bowl, Thumbprint Rim, Diamond Point Body, England, c.1885, 7 x 8 In. 115.00
Bowl, Underplate, Diamond Panels, Stylized Leaves, 6 x 3 3/4 In. 145.00
Bread Tray, Basket Weave, 12 1/2 In. 500.00
Butter, Cover, Hobstar, Cane, 5 3/4 x 7 3/4 In. 460.00
Candlestick, Hollow Diamond, Dorfinger, 12 In., Pair 1350.00
Candlestick, Russian & Swirl, T.G. Hawkes, 10 In., Pair 2125.00
Candlestick, Silvered Brass Mount, Square Base, Georgian, c.1815, 12 In., Pair 1955.00
Candlestick, Tulip Top, Baluster Stem, 2 Tiers Prisms, Stepped Domed Base, 11 In., Pair . . 1495.00
Celery Vase, Hobstar, Fan, Button Designs, Pitkin & Brooks, Early 20th Century, 12 In. . . 105.00
Celery Vase, Paneled, Baluster Stem, Scalloped Rim, Footed, 9 1/2 In. 265.00
Celery Vase, Strawberry Diamonds & Fans, Rays, Leaf Band, Notched Rim, Footed, 8 In. . 440.00
Cheese Dome, Underplate, Barred Hobstar, Brilliant, Early 20th Century, 5 x 5 In. 290.00
Compote, 6-Hobstar Cover, Teardrop Stem, 10 1/2 In. 850.00
Compote, Cover, Scalloped Rim, Silver Pedestal, Ireland, c.1880, 14 1/2 In., Pair 1380.00
Compote, Diamond & Petal, England, c.1865, 8 3/4 x 9 In. 865.00
Compote, Diamond Cut Sides, Scalloped Edge, Octagonal Stem, 12 x 8 1/4 In. 190.00
Compote, Intaglio Swirls, Brilliant Cutting, Teardrop Stem, Tuthill, 9 In. 750.00
Compote, Strawberry Diamonds & Fans, Medial Knop, Scalloped Rim, Footed, 7 1/2 In. . . 415.00
Creamer, Diamond Point Band, Flutes, Notched Rim & Foot, Ireland, 5 1/4 In. 210.00
Cuspidor, Diamonds, Bands Of Miters, 4 1/2 x 12 In. 410.00
Decanter, Cranberry To Clear, Grapes, Leaves, Stopper, Silver Overlay, 14 In. 2415.00
Decanter, Diamond Point, Honeycomb, Ribs, Star-Cut Stopper, 7 1/2 In. 130.00
Decanter, Grapes, Leaves, Stopper, Silver Overlay, 9 In. 1610.00
Decanter, Green To Clear, Flowers, Star-Cut Base, Stopper, Silver Overlay, 10 In. 3220.00
Decanter, Green, Flowers, Leaves, Vines, Stopper, Silver Overlay, 9 In. 1035.00
Decanter, Green, Pineapples, Leaves, Stopper, Silver Overlay, 11 In. 2300.00
Decanter, Monarch, Ring Handle, 9 In. 1175.00
Decanter, Pinwheels, Zipper Decoration, Bulbous, Ball Stopper, 11 1/2 In. 45.00
Decanter, Star Flake, Bulbous, 7 1/2 x 5 1/4 In., Pair 55.00
Dish, Cranberry To Clear, Hobstar & Fan, 6 In., Pair 720.00
Dish, Sweetmeat, Baluster Shape, Domed Foot, Silver, Russia, c.1846, 11 x 8 3/4 In. 1955.00
Dish, Sweetmeat, Hobnail Border, Oval, Pedestal, Undulating Rim, Anglo-Irish, 6 In., Pair 471.00
Ewer, Hobstar & Sheaf, Gilt Bronze Mount, First Empire Style, c.1900, 17 In., Pair 1610.00
Goblet, Hobstar & Fan, Brilliant, c.1910, 6 In., 12 Piece 750.00
Jar, Dome Cover, Butterfly, Flower, Pear Shape, Flower Finial, 4 1/2 In. 230.00
Jar, Vertical Lines, 10 Panels, Faceted Shoulder Panel, Starburst Design, 6 In., Pair 90.00
Jug, Claret, Bulbous, Duck Bill Spout, Sterling Silver Mount, Continental, 14 x 9 In. 1610.00
Nappy, Pinwheel & Cane, 4 Sections, Applied Handles, 11 In. 70.00
Pitcher, Champagne, Interlaced Hobstar, Brilliant, 19th Century, 11 1/2 In. 400.00
Pitcher, Diamond Point, Fluted Base, Notched Rim & Handle, Ireland, 7 3/4 In. 145.00
Pitcher, Flower Band, Thumbprint, Bulbous, Applied Handle, 7 1/2 In. 60.00
Pitcher, Hobstar, Fern, 11 In. 105.00
Pitcher, Lemonade, Tapering, Hobstar & Bowtie, Brilliant, 8 1/2 In. 315.00
Pitcher, Star & Lozenge, Applied Handle, Bulbous, 8 1/4 In. 200.00
Pitcher, Water, Hobstar & Shaft, Triple Thumbprint Cut Band, Brilliant, 8 In. 230.00
Plate, Engraved Flowers, Leaves, Sterling Silver Edge, 7 In. 85.00

Plate, Flower Blossoms, Leaves, Central Flower, 10 In. 115.00
Plate, Ice Cream, Hobstar & Interlaced Gable, Brilliant, J. Hoare & Co., 8 1/4 In. 635.00
Punch Bowl, Hobstar & Fan, Bell Shape Pedestal, Brilliant, c.1900, 11 x 12 In. 920.00
Punch Bowl, Holland Pattern, Sterling Silver Rim, T.G. Hawkes & Co., 7 x 15 In. 8950.00
Punch Bowl, Mercedes Pattern, Signed, Clark, 14 In. 4950.00
Punch Bowl, Ray & Zipper, Shaped Bowl, 8 x 14 In. 290.00
Punch Bowl & Stand, Hobstar & Feathered Arch, 1900, 14 In. 2070.00
Salt Set, Master, Footed, Navette Shape, Anglo-Irish Style, c.1900, 2 1/2 In., 4 Piece 70.00
Serving Bowl, Interlaced Hobstar, Oval, Brilliant, Late 19th Century, 14 1/4 In. 430.00
Syllabub, Star Whirl, Cover, Brilliant, Silver Ladle 2600.00
Tazza, Flower Engraved, Lattice Work Ground, 7 1/2 In. 225.00
Tazza, Hobstar Base, Brilliant, 7 1/2 In. 350.00
Tray, 13 Hobstars, Handles, 13 1/2 In. 375.00
Tumbler, Hobstar, 4 In. 60.00
Urn, Campana, Strawberry Diamonds, Rolled Rim, Fluted Band, Continental, 9 1/2 In. ... 50.00
Vase, Amethyst To Clear, Gilt Bronze Mounts, Sunflower Base, Russia, 32 x 8 In., Pair ... 2185.00
Vase, Engraved, Ferns, Leaves, Stars, Punties, Flared Rim, 8 1/2 In. 165.00
Vase, Engraved, Flower & Scroll Panels, Star-Cut Foot, Bottle Shape, 7 3/4 In., Pair 275.00
Vase, Flower Center, Meriden, 12 x 8 In. 1875.00
Vase, Fruit & Leaves, Flared, Round Base, 9 1/2 x 9 3/4 In. 115.00
Vase, Greek Key & Punty Bands, Bulbous, Crimped & Curled Handle, 10 In. 360.00
Vase, Hobstar & Cane, 10 In. 545.00
Vase, Hobstar, 32-Point Hobstar Foot, 11 3/4 x 5 In. 1085.00
Vase, Hobstar, Border, 9 1/2 x 5 3/4 In. 645.00
Vase, Hobstar, Serrated Rim, Hobstar Base, 11 In. 460.00
Vase, Orient Pattern, 11 1/2 x 4 1/4 In. 490.00
Vase, Paneled Hobstar, Mid 20th Century, 11 3/4 In. 104.00
Vase, Ruby To Clear, Gold Metal Frame, 4-Footed, Lion's Heads, Leaves, Handles, 25 In. . 900.00
Vase, Trumpet, Amber, Thumbprint, Ellipse, Anglo-Irish Style, c.1900, 12 In. 175.00
Vase, Trumpet, Notched Prism, Silver Plated Mount, Brilliant, 14 1/2 In. 200.00
Water Jug, George III, c.1800, 11 In. 1035.00
Wine, Cranberry Cut To Clear, Strawberry, Diamond Point, 4 3/4 In. 275.00

CUT VELVET is a special type of art glass, made with two layers of
blown glass, which shows a raised pattern. It usually had an acid finish
or a texture like velvet. It was made by many glass factories during the
late Victorian years.

Cracker Jar, Cover, Pink, Silver Plated Collar, Mt. Washington, 11 In. 1020.00
Vase, Cranberry, 4-Fold Ruffled Rim, 7 1/2 In. 300.00

CYBIS porcelain is a twentieth-century product. Boleslaw Cybis came
to the United States from Poland in 1939. He started making porcelains
in Long Island, New York, in 1940. He moved to Trenton, New Jersey,
in 1942 as one of the founders of Cordey China Co. and started his
own Cybis Porcelains about 1950. The firm is still working. See also
Cordey.

Figurine, Madame Butterfly, 20th Century, 13 In. 770.00

CZECHOSLOVAKIA is a popular term with collectors. The name,
first used as a mark after the country was formed in 1918, appears on
glass and porcelain and other decorative items. Although Czechoslovakia split into Slovakia and the Czech Republic on January 1, 1993, the
name continues to be used in some trademarks.

CZECHOSLOVAKIA GLASS, Cocktail Set, Embossed Nudes Base, Alexandrite, Satin, 7 Piece .. 160.00
Cordial, Painted, Hunt Scene, 10 Piece 145.00
Decanter, Liqueur, Ruby Flashed, Etched Pattern, 1920s, 7 Piece 1830.00
Perfume Bottle, Bonzo, Clear Glass, Molded, Silver Finished Rim, 3 1/2 In. 110.00
Perfume Bottle, Ingrid, Malachite Glass, Jeweled Metal Cap, 1920s, 2 1/4 In. ...... *Illus* 95.00
Perfume Bottle, Pink, Satin Clear, Etched Circle Mark, 1920s, 3 3/4 In. .... *Illus* 147.00
Powder Box, Black Cased, Orange Enamel, Cameo, Round, c.1915, 3 x 4 In. 288.00
Vase, Blue In Red & Green Ribbons, Flattened Oval, c.1950, 15 1/2 In. 520.00
Vase, Blue, Spatter, Baluster, Signed, 7 In. 60.00

Czechoslovakia Glass,
Perfume Bottle, Ingrid,
Malachite Glass, Jeweled
Metal Cap, 1920s, 2 1/4 In.

Czechoslovakia Glass, Perfume
Bottle, Pink, Satin Clear, Etched
Circle Mark, 1920s, 3 3/4 In.

Vase, Opalescent Blue, Gold, Purple, Pulled Feathers, Clambroth, 8 3/4 In. 3740.00
Vase, Pink, Internal Rosettes, c.1925, 6 1/2 In. 115.00
Vase, Trumpet, Etched Peacock, Urns, Scrolls, Signed, 7 1/4 In. 100.00
Vase, Woman, Leaves, Flared, Frosted, Cameo, 16 In. 590.00
CZECHOSLOVAKIA POTTERY, Creamer, Bird, Orange, Yellow, Green, Beak Spout, 4 3/4 In. *Illus* 25.00
Dish, Felix The Cat, Baby, Blue Rim, 6 3/4 In. 88.00
Pitcher, Lostro Shape, Art Deco Style ....*Illus* 275.00
Plate, Transfer, Baby's, 5 1/2 In. 69.00

D'ARGENTAL is a mark used in France by the Compagnie des
Cristalleries de St. Louis. The firm made multilayered, acid-cut cameo
glass in the late nineteenth and twentieth centuries. D'Argental is the
French name for the city of Munzthal, home of the glassworks. Later
they made enameled etched glass.

Bowl, Lilies, Citron Yellow, Amber, Frosted, c.1885, 3 1/2 x 3 1/2 In. 575.00
Vase, Brown Berries, Leaves, Shouldered, Mottled, 9 1/2 In. 545.00
Vase, Butterscotch, Burgundy Flowering Branches, Oval, Signed, 8 In. 1100.00
Vase, Cherries On Branches, Citron Ground, Oval, Tapered, Flared Rim, Signed, 8 In. 1035.00
Vase, Citrine, Cherry, Berries, Leaves, c.1900, 5 In. 460.00
Vase, Flowers, Brown, Yellow Ground, Tapered, Signed, 13 In. 120.00
Vase, Flowers, Leaves, Peach Ground, Bottle Shape, Signed, 8 In. 900.00
Vase, Maroon Flowers, Citron Ground, Oval, Tapered, Signed, 5 1/2 In. 575.00
Vase, Red Lilies, Green Ground, 8 In. 1116.00
Vase, Roses, Red, Yellow Ground, Shouldered, 10 In. 940.00
Vase, Sailboat, Water Scene, Blossoms, Leaves, Signed, 13 3/4 In. 1035.00
Vase, Trumpet Vines, Red, Orange, 12 3/4 In. 2115.00

DANIEL BOONE, a pre–Revolutionary War folk hero, was a surveyor, trapper, and frontiersman. A television series, which ran from
1964 to 1970, was based on his life and starred Fess Parker. All types
of Daniel Boone memorabilia are collected.

Action Figure, Accessories, Instructions, Marx, Box, 1965, 12 In. 225.00
Play Set, Fess Parker, Frontier Attack Sticker, No. 5061, Box 660.00

Czechoslovakia Pottery,
Pitcher, Lostro Shape,
Art Deco Style

Czechoslovakia Pottery,
Creamer, Bird, Orange, Yellow,
Green, Beak Spout, 4 3/4 In.

DAUM, a glassworks in Nancy, France, was started by Jean Daum in 1875. The company, now called *Cristalleries de Nancy*, is still working. The *Daum Nancy* mark has been used in many variations. The name of the city and the artist are usually both included.

Bottle, Stopper, Gold Enameled, c.1890, 4 In.	5020.00
Bottle, Swirled Panels, Curly Lines, Gilt Line, Thistle, Stopper, Cameo, 3 In.	980.00
Bowl, Cover, Mottled Orange & Purple, Gold Iridescent Splotches, Signed, 5 1/2 x 9 In.	955.00
Bowl, Figs, Lizard, Purple, Green, Leaf Form, 20th Century, 7 3/4 In.	235.00
Bowl, Leaf, Butterfly, Amethyst, Blue, Brown, Signed, France, 20th Century, 6 7/8 In.	470.00
Bowl, Mountains, Trees, Autumn, Powder Blue, Spangled, Cameo, c.1885, 3 1/2 In.	2185.00
Bowl, Mushrooms, Enameled, Yellow, Brown Ground, Cameo, Signed, 3 3/4 x 2 1/2 In.	2875.00
Bowl, Orange Poppy, Green Leaves, Mottled, Cameo, c.1900, 8 1/2 x 9 In.	6900.00
Bowl, Purple, Leaf Form, Cast Head Pedestal, Signed, France, 20th Century, 8 1/4 x 13 In.	355.00
Bowl, Vines, Blossoms, Multicolored Enameled, Mottled Ground, Cameo, 7 3/4 In.	940.00
Bowl, Winter Landscape, Trees Against An Orange Sky, Signed, 3 3/4 In.	4405.00
Box, Cover, Green, Enameled Flower, Boudoir Scene, Sterling Silver, 4 In.	410.00
Box, Cover, Lake Scene, Trees, Mottled Orange & Yellow, Square, Round Cover, 6 In.	2590.00
Box, Cover, Martele, Enameled Flowers, Gold, Scrolls, c.1895, 5 In.	2760.00
Box, Cover, Purple Violets, Green Leaves, Blue Opal, Cameo, c.1900, 3 1/2 In.	2185.00
Compote, Boat Shape, Blue, Yellow, Red, Amethyst, Fall Scene, Signed, 10 In.	2575.00
Cordial, Swimming Swan, Birch Trees, Blue, Frosted, Signed, 1 3/4 In.	2070.00
Cordial, Winter Scene, Windmills, Church, Trees, Textured Blue Ground, 2 In.	1093.00
Cup & Saucer, Flower, Dragonfly, Gold Enameled, Signed, 2 x 4 1/2 In.	805.00
Decanter, Clear, Gold Enameled, Stopper, Signed, 10 In.	345.00
Figurine, Rearing Horse, Pate-De-Verre, Maurice Legendre, 166/200, 1970s, 14 In.	605.00
Inkwell, Mottled Ground, Carved Cabochons, Insects, Clear Insert, Signed, 3 x 4 1/2 In.	1995.00
Inkwell, Oak Leaves, Frosted Ground, Applied Acorns, Insect, Cameo, Signed, 4 x 4 In.	7500.00
Lamp, Geometric, Mottled Green, Frosted Ground, Bulbous, Pewter, 8 x 11 1/2 In.	1530.00
Lamp, Harbor Scene, Ships, Brown, Black, Mottled Yellow, Enameled, Cameo, 14 In.	12075.00
Lamp, Leaf, Brown, Mottled Orange To Yellow Ground, Cameo, Signed, 22 In.	5465.00
Lamp, Mottled Pink, Yellow, Art Nouveau, Brass Base, 22 In.	980.00
Lamp, Mushrooms, Yellow Mottled Ground, Enameled, Signed, 7 1/2 In.	10065.00
Lamp, Trees, Frosted Ground, Rain Drops, Enameled, Cameo, Signed, 13 In.	35650.00
Lamp, Trees, Lake, Yellow, Amber, Cameo, 14 In.	9990.00
Lamp, Winter Scene, Birch Trees, Mottled Orange To Yellow Ground, Cameo, 28 In.	10350.00
Night-Light, Applied Bugs, Mottled Yellow, Brown, Blue, 3-Footed, 6 1/2 In.	2350.00
Perfume Bottle, Cameo Glass, Clematis, Silver Mounted, Etched, Enameled, c.1890, 6 In.	865.00
Pitcher, Mottle Turquoise, Blue Glass, 2 Applied Red Insects, Handle, 4 1/2 In.	1410.00
Plaque, Woman, Brown Flowing Shawl, Yellow, Oval, Signed, 10 3/4 In.	2070.00
Salt, Cut Panels, Schwarzlot Enameled Scene, Bucket, Case, c.1885, 1 1/2 In., 6 Piece	2990.00
Salt, Flowers, Leaves, Enamel, Green, Red, Yellow, Brown Ground, Cameo, Signed, 2 In.	1020.00
Salt, Winter Scene, Black Birds, Frosted Ground, Signed, 1 x 2 In.	2300.00
Tumbler, Cranberry, Textured, Mistletoe, Gold Trim, Barrel Shape, Signed, 5 In.	430.00
Tumbler, Flowers, Gray, Green Tint, c.1900, 3 3/4 In.	375.00
Tumbler, Gold Enameled, Verse, Intaglio, Fluted, c.1900, 4 1/4 In.	315.00
Tumbler, Winter Scene, Enameled Trees, Black, Brown, White Snow, Cameo, 1 7/8 In.	1035.00
Vase, Amber, Controlled Bubbles, Scroll Handles, c.1930, 4 In.	260.00
Vase, Aqua, Etched, Triangles, Footed, c.1930, 14 1/4 In.	5700.00
Vase, Aqua, Geometric, Etched Lava Finish, 11 1/2 In.	1610.00
Vase, Autumn Scene, Trees, Orange, Yellow Sky, Enameled, Cameo, Signed, 16 In.	5175.00
Vase, Berries & Leaves, Mottled Yellow & Red, Cylindrical, Signed, 5 In.	1320.00
Vase, Berries, Leaves, Green, Amber, Footed, Enameled, Cameo, Signed, 5 In.	940.00
Vase, Blackberries, Green Ground, Enameled, Cameo, 8 1/4 In.	3940.00
Vase, Blue, Applied Black Rim, Foot, Flared, c.1930, 7 1/4 In.	380.00
Vase, Branches, Leaves, Green, Brown, Mottled, Yellow Ground, Flared, Cameo, 6 In.	940.00
Vase, Bud, Blackberries, Yellow, Orange, Green Ground, Square, Cameo, 4 3/4 In.	1315.00
Vase, Bud, Lilies Of The Valley, Cranberry, Frosted, Textured, Cameo, c.1900, 7 1/2 In.	1725.00
Vase, Butterfly, Enameled, Handles, Signed, 4 3/4 In.	2700.00
Vase, Charcoal Flecked, Round, Circles, Etched, c.1930, 9 In.	4500.00
Vase, Circles, Arches, Butterscotch, Etched, c.1930, 12 1/4 In.	6600.00
Vase, Clear, Gold Enalemed Bird Panels, Signed, 8 3/4 In.	1150.00
Vase, Dandelions, Seed Pods, Opal, Enameled, Cameo, c.1900, 3 1/2 In.	2415.00

Vase, Enameled Verse, Amethyst, Parcel Gilt, Handles, c.1915, 4 1/2 In. 690.00
Vase, Flower Garden, Amethyst, Orange, Gold, 2 Handles, Oval, Cameo, 8 x 10 In. 2590.00
Vase, Flowers, Amethyst, Gold Highlights, Opalescent, Signed, 19 In. 4715.00
Vase, Flowers, Brown, Pink, Yellow, Frosted Ground, Flared, Hammered Band, 11 1/2 In. . 1765.00
Vase, Flowers, Burgundy, Blue, Metal Overlay, c.1900, 5 3/4 In. 529.00
Vase, Flowers, Leaves, Turquoise & Purple, Amethyst Ground, Flared, Cameo, 21 In. 3740.00
Vase, Flowers, Leaves, Yellow, Purple Ground, Enameled, Cameo, Signed, 2 In. 920.00
Vase, Flowers, Martele, Cabochon Centers, Opalescent, Amethyst, Oval, 4 x 6 In. 5465.00
Vase, Flowers, Orange, Art Deco, Signed, 9 3/4 In. 1610.00
Vase, Flowers, Stems, Leaves, Blue, Purple, Orange, Cream, Signed, 14 In. 3910.00
Vase, Fruiting Branches, Mountain Ash Tree, Enameled, Cameo, Signed, 2 In. 920.00
Vase, Fuchsia, White To Purple Mottled Ground, Gold Trim, Enameled, Cameo, 6 3/4 In. . . 6900.00
Vase, Geometric, Flower, Enameled, Cameo, Signed, 4 1/4 In. 1000.00
Vase, Girl Holding 4 Geese, Frosted White Ground, Signed, 3 1/4 In. 1610.00
Vase, Gray, Amber, Yellow, Spider Web, Violet Blossoms, Leaves, 1900, 15 In. 2530.00
Vase, Gray, Internally Decorated, Amber, Yellow, Enameled, Cameo, c.1900, 15 In. 2530.00
Vase, Green, Brown, Rose, Sweet Peas, Enameled, Cameo, 19 1/2 In. 6615.00
Vase, Horse Chestnut, Green, Mottled Orange Ground, Cameo, Signed, 7 1/4 In. 1115.00
Vase, Iris, Enameled Verse, Oval, Rose Textured, Cameo, 3 1/4 In. 518.00
Vase, Jade Green, Etched, Shouldered, Flared Rim, c.1930, 11 1/4 In. 5400.00
Vase, Lake Scene, Green, Mottled Red, Orange Ground, Cameo, Signed, 2 1/4 In. 940.00
Vase, Landscape, Brown, Red, Orange, Yellow Ground, Signed, 3 3/4 In. 1295.00
Vase, Landscape, River, Pink, Orange, Brown, 15 In. 4405.00
Vase, Landscape, River, Trees, Blue, Green, Brown, Enameled, Cameo, c.1900, 3 1/2 In. . . . 2070.00
Vase, Landscape, Trees, Lake, Amethyst, Blue, Mottled, 10 3/4 In. 2585.00
Vase, Landscape, Trees, Lake, White Spangled, Frosted, Enameled, Cameo, 10 In. 2530.00
Vase, Landscape, Trees, Purple, Green Lake, Cameo, 12 1/2 x 4 1/4 In. 1645.00
Vase, Landscape, Trees, River, Brown, Yellow, Orange, Oval, Cameo, c.1900, 12 1/4 In. . . . 1265.00
Vase, Landscape, Woods, Lake, Purple, Green, Cameo, 12 1/2 In. 2115.00
Vase, Leaf, Flowers, Mold Blown, Chalice Form, Signed, 10 In. 5175.00
Vase, Leaves, 2 Applied Insects, Flared, Footed, Cameo, 20 In. 3525.00
Vase, Leaves, Berries, Mottled Yellow, Red Ground, Cameo, 3 1/2 In. 646.00
Vase, Lilies Of The Valley, Amethyst, Gray, Cameo, c.1900, 4 1/4 In. 405.00
Vase, Lily, Purple Leaves, Stems, Mottled Lavender To Cream Ground, Cameo, 19 1/2 In. . 6900.00
Vase, Maroon, Light Blue, Trefoils, Vines, Bulbous, White Enameled Flower, 11 3/4 In. . . . 5290.00
Vase, Mottled Blue, Ribbed, Controlled Bubbles, Etched, 7 3/4 In. 825.00
Vase, Mushroom, Orange, Brown, Mottled Ground, Handles, Enameled, Cameo, 6 In. 9775.00
Vase, Ocean Scene, Iridescent, Etched, Seagulls, Tortoises, Gold Enamel, Signed, 7 x 6 In. 8625.00
Vase, Orange Blooms, Leaves, Mottled Ground, Enameled, Cameo, 3 3/4 In. 1554.00
Vase, Orchid, Orange, Burgundy, Frosted Ground, Signed, c.1905, 13 3/4 In. 470.00
Vase, Orchids, Green, Brown, Yellow Mottled Ground, Enameled, Cameo, Signed, 14 In. . 3525.00
Vase, Orchids, Spiked Stems, Leaves, Raspberry, Coral Ground, Cameo, 8 3/8 In. 3565.00
Vase, Oriental Poppy, Flowers, Grasses, Gold, Footed, Enameled, Cameo, Signed, 6 In. . . . 5290.00
Vase, Oriental Scene, Enameled Cranes, Water Lilies, Flowers, Cylindrical, Signed, 8 In. . . 4428.00
Vase, Pinecone, Lake, Square, Cameo, c.1900, 5 1/4 In. 920.00
Vase, Purple Morning Glory, Mottled, Enameled, Cameo, c.1900, 23 In. 9000.00
Vase, Rosehip, Leaves, Baluster, Enameled, Cameo, Signed, 4 In. 900.00
Vase, Seascape, Harbor, Sailboat, Clouds, Signed, 5 3/4 In. 1150.00
Vase, Seascape, Ships, Mottled Green Sea, Crimson, Yellow Sky, Cameo, Signed, 5 3/4 In. 1380.00
Vase, Seascape, Ships, Trees, Mottled Amber, Yellow, Cameo, Signed, c.1910, 6 1/2 In. . . . 1300.00
Vase, Shape, Tree & Lake Scene, Yellow, Red, Brown, Oval, Cameo, 12 In. 1500.00
Vase, Spring Scene, Trees, Leaves, Pink, Elongated, Ear Handles, Enameled, 14 In. 7475.00
Vase, Spring Scene, Trees, Leaves, River, Village, Enameled, Cream Ground, 1 3/4 In. 980.00
Vase, Stick, Leaves, Berries, Enameled, Signed, 2 In. 460.00
Vase, Stick, Martele, Cut Trumpet Flowers, Brown, Yellow, Footed, 13 In. 4315.00
Vase, Stick, Opaque Pink, Green, Brown Mottle, Double Gourd Base, Signed, 16 In. 1440.00
Vase, Stick, Trumpet Flowers, Red, Amber, Mottled, Martele Finish, Cameo, 14 In. 3820.00
Vase, Storm Scene, Cream, Butterscotch, Peach Windblown Trees, Leaves, 16 1/2 In. 4430.00
Vase, Stylized Etched Flowers, Blue Controlled Bubbles, Footed, Cameo, 6 3/4 In. 590.00
Vase, Stylized Flower, Orange, Frosted Pink Ground, Enameled, Cameo, c.1930, 9 In. 705.00
Vase, Summer Scene, Green, Bottle Shape, Engraved, 10 1/2 In. 3050.00
Vase, Thistles, Leaves, Lavender Enameled, Opalescent, Cameo, 19 In. . . . . .6325.00 to 6900.00
Vase, Tobacco Flowers, Leaves, Yellow Ground, Chalice Shape, Cameo, 9 3/4 In. 2530.00

Vase, Trees In Summer, Village, Burnt Orange Sky, Shouldered, Cameo, c.1900, 11 In. ... 8625.00
Vase, Vine, Green, Yellow, Applied Red Cabochon Berries, Enameled, Cameo, 21 1/4 In. ... 9490.00
Vase, Violets, Leaves, Martele, Pink, Frosted, Mottled, Footed, Cameo, 7 3/4 In. 5580.00
Vase, White Flowers, Green Leaves, Orange, Blue Ground, Cameo, 8 In. 8915.00
Vase, Winter Scene, Gray, Amber, Enameled, Cameo, c.1900, 11 3/4 In. 4255.00
Vase, Winter Scene, Pillow, Yellow Ground, Cameo, Signed, 4 3/4 x 5 1/2 In. 2818.00
Vase, Winter Scene, Trees, Church Steeple, Windmill, Pond, Oval, Cameo, 1 3/4 In. 1440.00
Vase, Winter Scene, Trees, Mottled Orange To Yellow, Enameled Snow, Cameo, 20 In. ... 11500.00
Vase, Winter Scene, Village, Windmills, Enameled Figures, Cameo, Signed, 1 5/8 x 2 In. .. 1560.00
Vase, Winter Scene, Windmill, Harbor, Birds, Black Enamel, Asymmetrical, 1 5/8 In. 780.00
Vase, Winter Village Scene, Gray With Blue & Amber, 1910, 8 1/4 In. 6325.00
Vase, Woodland Winter Scene, Double Gourd Form, Enameled, 5 In. 700.00

DAVENPORT pottery and porcelain were made at the Davenport factory in Longport, Staffordshire, England, from 1793 to 1887. Earthenwares, creamwares, porcelains, ironstone, and other ceramics were made. Most of the pieces are marked with a form of the word *Davenport*.

DAVENPORT
LONGPORT
STAFFORDSHIRE

Brush Vase, Saucer, Tea Leaf Ironstone 1250.00
Dessert Service, Countryside Scenes, c.1850, 13 9-In. Plates, 16 Piece 707.00

DAVY CROCKETT, the American frontiersman, was born in 1786 and died in 1836. The historical character gained new fame in 1954 when the Walt Disney television show ran a series of episodes featuring Fess Parker as Davy Crockett. Coonskin caps and buckskins became popular and hundreds of different Davy Crockett items were made.

Award, Shooting, Pinback, Heavy Pot Metal, Early 1940s 28.00
Bank, Pony Express, Golden Star, Wrapper, Lock, Keys, White, Brown 28.00
Belt, Leather, Metal Buckle, Cardboard Package, 6 1/2 x 11 3/4 In. 58.00
Button, Davy Crockett, Frontier Scout, Red Ground, Australia, Mid 1950s, 1 3/4 In. 100.00
Button, Davy, Holding Rifle, Light Green Ground, Lithograph, Round, 3/4 In. 20.00
Button, Davy, Holding Rifle, Trees, Multicolor, Mid 1950s, 1 1/4 In. 40.00
Button, Kiddieland's Davy Crockett Ranger Club, 1 3/8 In. 105.00
Cards, Picture Card Bubble Gum, Wax Pack, Unopened, 5 Cents, Topps, 1956 .... 875.00
Case, Official Dispatch, Imitation Leather 28.00
Clock, Motion Light, Metal, Gold Luster, 1940s, 10 x 6 x 8 In. ....375.00 to 570.00
Clock, Plastic, Davy Riding Bucking Horse, Light-Up, Haddon, 1950s, 11 In. 819.00
Cookie Jar, C. Miller, Regal China, 1955, 10 In. 450.00
Costume, Walt Disney's Official, Box, 1950s 495.00
Figure, Davy Crockett, On Horse, Metal Chain, Breyer Molding Co., c.1950, 9 In. 300.00
Figure, Davy, Horse, Accessories, Ideal, Box, 1950s, 2 1/4 x 4 3/4 x 5 In. ......175.00 to 200.00
Game, Davy Crockett Adventures, Gardner Games, c.1955, 10 1/4 x 13 1/2 In. 120.00
Gun, BB, Powder Horn, Frontier Smoke Rifle, No. 968, Daisy, Box, 32 In. 217.00
Holster, Davy & Rifle, Painted Graphics, 2-Tone Leather, Tan, Brown, Fringe, Single 17.00
Holster Set, Leather, 3 Wood Bullets, Arrow Sales, Box, 12 3/4 In. 100.00
Horseshoe Set, Rubber, 2 Red, 2 Green, No. 703, Box 55.00
Jacket, Iron-On Back Patch, Zipper, Tags, Campus Outer Wear, 1950s 28.00
Knife, Pocket, Fess Parker As Davy Crockett, Plastic, Imperial, c.1955, 2 1/4 In. 120.00
Knife, Pocket, Fess Parker As Davy Crockett, Plastic, Imperial, c.1955, 3 1/4 In. 79.00
Knife, Pocket, Illustrated Grip, Screwdriver, Opener, Blade, Colonial, 3 1/2 In. 176.00
Label, Bread End, Waxed Paper, c.1955, 2 3/4 x 2 3/4 In. 30.00
Lunch Box, Green Border, Hotemp, American Thermos Co., 1955 .... 110.00
Mug, Coffee, D-Handle, Fire King 26.00
Pail, Davy, Horse, Fort, Teepees, Metal Lithograph, Ohio Art, 1955, 7 1/2 x 7 In. 100.00
Pencil Case, Davy Crockett, King Of Frontierland, Ontents, Vinyl, 6 1/2 x 8 1/2 In. 75.00
Ring, Davy Crockett, Rifle On Sides, Aluminum, Adjustable, 1950s 50.00
Scarf, Yellow, Brown & Black Graphics 17.00
Shirt, Tan, Scenes On Lapels & Pocket, Tags, E&W, Size 10 .... 10.00
Shirt, Tan, Tags, However Bros., E&W Sports, Size 10 .... 85.00
Socks, Davy, Rifle, Coonskin Cap, Label, Lambert Hosiery, Child's, 7 1/2 In., Pair 14.00
Sweater, Button Up, Maroon, Puritan Natch 22.00
Toy, Western Set, Rodeo, Plastic, Ajax, 16 In. 110.00
Wrapper, Gum Card, Waxed Paper, 1 Cent, Walt Disney, Topps, 1956, 5 x 6 1/4 In. 195.00
Wristwatch, Green Plastic Case, Decorated Band, U.S. Time, Box, 1957 ....360.00 to 395.00

DE MORGAN art pottery was made in England by William De Morgan from the 1860s to 1907. He is best known for his luster-glazed Moorish-inspired pieces. The pottery used a variety of marks.

Tile, Bird, Facing Right, Leaves, Mahogany Frame, 8 In.	5875.00
Tile, Lion & Snake, Luster, 1900	9780.00

DE VEZ was a signature used on cameo glass after 1910. E. S. Monot founded the glass company near Paris in 1851. The company changed names many times. Mt. Joye, another glass by this factory, is listed in its own category.

Vase, Boats, Mountains, Tall Grasses, Bulbous, Knopped Neck, Cameo, Signed, 7 In.	750.00
Vase, Castle, River, Forest, Mountains, Tapered, Flared Rim, Cameo, Signed, 10 In.	860.00
Vase, Lake, Mountains, Trees, Lobed, Tapered Cylindrical Neck, Signed, 5 1/2 In.	605.00
Vase, Oriental Design, Chrysanthemums, Water, Boat, Knopped Neck, Signed, 7 In.	3250.00
Vase, Pink Shaded To Yellow, Blue Landscape, Sailboats, Mountain, Knopped Neck, 8 In.	805.00
Vase, Red Sailboats, Mountains, Citron Ground, Cylindrical, Pinecone Rim, Signed, 10 In.	690.00
Vase, Sailboats, Snow-Capped Peaks, Citron Ground, Tapered, 10 In.	719.00
Vase, Scenic, Blue, Yellow, Orange, Signed, 6 In.	700.00
Vase, Scenic, Yellow, Pink, Blue, Signed, 10 In.	800.00
Vase, Tall Trees, Blue Lake Scene, Distant Mountains, Forest, Reverse Trumpet, 9 In.	978.00
Vase, Village Below Castle Towers, Tree, Leaves, Mountains, Signed, 7 1/2 In.	920.00
Vase, Village Scene, Lake, Mountains, Boat, Pink, Yellow, Blue, 8 1/2 In.	850.00
Vase, Woodland Scene, Cone Shape, Knopped Neck, 3 1/2 In.	230.00

DECORATED TUMBLERS have been made by Anchor Hocking, Federal, Hazel Atlas, Libbey, and other companies since the 1930s, when the pyroglaze process of printing was introduced. The barware and other glasses feature drinking jokes, characters, or decorative geometric patterns. Swankyswigs are listed in their own category. Decorated tumblers may also be listed in Advertising, Coca-Cola, Pepsi-Cola, and many other categories.

Allen's Red Tame Cherry, Flared, Etched, 5 x 3 In.	50.00
Big Boy, Weighted Bottom, 1936 Logo, 50th Anniversary, 1986, 6 1/2 In.	18.00
Borden, Elsie, Federal Glass, 6 1/8 In., 6 Piece	72.00
Dr Pepper, Good For Life!, 1940s, 3 3/4 x 2 1/4 In.	55.00
Dr Pepper, King Of Beverages, Red Center, White Diamond, 5 5/8 In.	8.00
Klee-Ko Soda, 5 In.	15.00
McDonald's, Big Mac, 2 Sides, Collector Series, 1970s, 5 5/8 In.	5.00
McDonald's, Ronald Jumping Into Fillet O' Fish Lake, 1977, 5 5/8 In.	10.00
Moxie, Embossed, 4 In.	30.00 to 35.00
Sealtest Cottage Cheese, Scarecrow, Corning Glassworks, 1939, 4 3/4 In.	75.00
Welch's, Archie, Jughead Wins Pie-Eating Contest, 1973, 4 1/4 In.	8.00
Welch's, Fred Flintstone Playing Golf, 1962, 5 In.	7.00

DECOYS are carved or turned wooden copies of birds, fish, or animals. The decoy was placed in the water or propped on the shore to lure flying birds to the pond for hunters. Some decoys are handmade; some are commercial products. Today there is a group of artists making modern decoys for display, not for use in a pond.

American Widgeon Drake & Hen, Glass Eyes, Frank Finney, Chincoteague, Va.	750.00
Black Duck, Painted, Tack Eyes, Signed, Impressed DAH D, N.J., 8 x 3 x 2 1/4 In.	230.00
Black Duck, Standard Grade, Glass Eyes, Mason Factory, 1896-1924	178.00
Black-Bellied Plover, Glass Eyes, Carved Bill, Sculpted Body, Herter, 5 x 10 In.	175.00
Black-Bellied Plover, R.J. De La Grange, 9 1/8 In.	230.00
Black-Bellied Plover, Raised Wings, Carved Eye, Oak Bill, On Base, Mark McNair, Va.	725.00
Blue Heron, Glass Eyes, Metal Feet, William Gibian, 33 x 15 x 47 In.	990.00
Bluebill Style, Sink Box, Cast Iron, Upper Bay, c.1900	270.00
Bufflehead, Carved, Applied Glass Eyes, 5 1/2 x 10 1/2 x 5 In.	1150.00
Bufflehead Drake, Carved, Painted, Glass Eyes, 20th Century, 19 1/4 In.	175.00
Bufflehead Drake, Standing, Wood, Glass Eyes, Pine Base, Signed, Lou Reineri, Virginia	165.00
Bufflehead Hen, Glass Eyes, James Lapham, Mass., 1958	1955.00
Canada Goose, Carved Wood, Painted, Eastern North Carolina, Early 1900s, 16 x 21 In.	345.00

Canada Goose, Carved, Painted, c.1900, 13 x 23 3/4 In. 235.00
Canada Goose, Painted, Label, Signed, Josef Wooster, Ashley, Oh., 1982, 6 In. 115.00
Canada Goose, Sheet Iron Body, Wood Head & Breast, Painted, c.1900, 31 x 25 In. 999.00
Canada Goose, Wood Head & Bottom, Cork Body, Lambert Morris, Atlantic, N.C., 1950s . 135.00
Canvasback, Painted Eyes, Carved Bill, Spike Type Steel Weight, Upper Bay, 1920s 145.00
Canvasback Drake, 2-Piece Construction, Glass Eyes, Rasp Carved Head, c.1940 . . . 330.00
Canvasback Drake, Glass Eyes, Mammoth Grade, Pratt Mfg., Joliet, Ill., c.1930, Oversize . 650.00
Canvasback Drake, Painted, Susquehanna River, 17 x 7 In. 495.00
Canvasback Drake & Hen, Glass Eyes, Carved Heads, Simple Paint Pattern 220.00
Canvasback Hen, Carved, Brown, Black, White, Madison Mitchell, Maryland, 15 1/2 In. . . 315.00
Canvasback Hen, Painted Eyes, Carved Bill, Eastern Shore, Maryland, 1950s 150.00
Canvasback Hen, Tie Ye, Original Weight, Will Heverin, Chestertown, Md., 1800s 315.00
Cinnamon Teal, Standing, Glass Eyes, Base, Lou Reineri, Virginia, 10 1/2 x 12 1/2 In. 165.00
Curlew, Carved, Painted, Glass Eyes, 20th Century, 16 In. 235.00
Curlew, Glass Eyes, Driftwood Base, Buzzanco, Mt. Kisco, N.Y., 1977, 15 x 16 In. 150.00
Curlew, Oak Bill, Carved Eyes, Solid Body, Frank Finney, Chincoteague, Va., 18 In. 265.00
Curlew, Wooden, Carved, Gray, White, Tack Eyes, 11 In. 865.00
Dowitcher Shorebird, Glass Eyes, Stand, Steve Morey, New Jersey, 12 1/2 x 12 In. 110.00
Duck, Brown Paint, Blue, White, Black, Relief Carved Wings, Tail Feather Incising, 14 In. 230.00
Duck, Carved Wood, Glass Eyes, Signed, Ken Harris, Woodville, N.Y., 10 1/2 x 3 3/4 In. . . 145.00
Duck, Glass Eyes, Black Paint, Pequaw Honk Club, A.E. Crowell, Mass., 17 1/2 In. 1060.00
Duck, Redhead, Wooden, Painted, Carved, Victor Animal Trap Co., Miss., 8 x 16 In. 145.00
Eider, Carved, Black, White, Green Head Stripe, Yellow Bill, Maine, 17 3/4 In. 230.00
Eider Drake, Mussel, Carved, Painted, 20th Century, 17 1/4 In. 175.00
Eider Drake, Solid, Lead Weight, Stonington, Deer Isle, Maine, c.1900, 19 x 10 In. 275.00
Fish, Catfish, Wood, Carved, Tin Fins, Glass Eyes, White Whiskers, Mottled Brown, 12 In. 290.00
Fish, Crawdad, Tin Pincers, Old Red Paint, Nail Eyes, 7 1/2 In. 115.00
Fish, Frog Shape, Green, White Paint, Tin Appendages, Glass Eyes, 11 In. 200.00
Fish, Orange, Green, Yellow, White, Tin Fins, Glass Eyes, Chub Buchman, 12 In. 345.00
Fish, Snake, Twisted Wire Tongue, Original Paint, Green, Red, Yellow, 12 1/4 . . . . 115.00
Fish, Tin Fins, Brown, White Paint, Original, 10 1/4 In. 200.00
Fish, Tin Fins, Original Paint, Orange, Black, Yellow, 8 In., Pair 230.00
Fish, Turtle, Wooden, Carved, Tin Fins, Glass Eyes, Brown Paint, 9 In. 460.00
Fish, Wood, Tin Fins, Original Paint, Brown Stripes, Tan, White, 7 3/4 In. 200.00
Fish, Wood, Tin Fins, Original Red, Brown, White Paint, 9 1/2 In. 230.00
Fish, Wooden Frog, Tin Front Legs, Tack Eyes, Green & Yellow Paint, 8 1/4 In. 345.00
Flapper, Carved, Yellow, Brown Paint, Cord Moves Hinged Wings, 15 x 6 In. 635.00
Flapper, Yellow Bill, Brown Body, Hinged Wings, Glass Eyes, Bracher, 14 x 9 In. 785.00
Goose, Painted, Carved, Laminated, Lead Weights, 15 x 25 x 8 In. 489.00
Mallard, Carved, Painted, Glass Eyes, Douglas Bane, St. Albans, Maine, 6 1/2 x 16 1/2 In. . 115.00
Mallard Drake, Carved Wood, Painted, Padco Decoy Co., Miss., c.1935, 5 1/2 x 16 In. 105.00
Mallard Drake, Wooden, Painted, Carved, Mason Factory c.1910, 5 1/2 x 15 1/2 In. 175.00
Mallard Drake & Hen, Mounted On Branch, Painted, 2 7/8 In. 575.00
Marbled Godwit, Shorebird, Glass Eyes, Stand, Steve Morey, New Jersey, 16 1/2 x 15 In. . 140.00
Merganser, Carved, Painted, Signed, G.R. Huey, 1910, 6 1/2 x 15 In. 8910.00
Merganser, Green Head, Glass Eyes, Horsehair Comb, Jake Fishmon, Nova Scotia, 16 In. . 290.00
Peep, Carved Eyes, Oak Bill, Raised Carved Wings, Mark McNair, Va., 6 3/4 x 3 In. 365.00
Red-Breasted Merganser Drake, Running, James Lapham, 1957, Miniature 2185.00
Redhead, Carved, Glass Eyes, Branded JCS, 12 3/4 In. 345.00
Ruddy Duck, Glass Eyes, Carved Bill, Dowelled Head, Stevens Factory, c.1890 . . . . 578.00
Scoter, Preening, Raised Wings, Hand Carved, Gus Wilson, Maine, Early 1900s, 16 In. . . . 2070.00
Swan, Canvas, Wire Frame, Carved Bill, Wood Bottom, North Carolina 405.00
Swan, Tack Eyes, Metal Neck Band, Solid Carved, Ken Cargnell, Front Royal, Va., 34 In. . 85.00
Swan, Wood, Carved, Painted, Glass Eyes, c.1900, 22 1/4 x 8 1/2 x 29 In. 355.00
Turtle, Ice Fishing, Minnesota, 1950s 135.00
Widgeon, Standing, Glass Eyes, Open Mouth, Driftwood Base, Frank Finney, Va. 1100.00
Widgeon Drake, Carved Bill, Glass Eyes, Weights, Stippled Paint, Frank Finney, Va. 350.00
Widgeon Drake, Carved, Glass Eyes, Lead Weight, Frank Finney, Chincoteague, Va. 325.00
Widgeon Drake & Hen, Glass Eyes, Carved Bills, Nostrils, A.E. Crowell, Mass. 825.00
Widgeon Drake & Hen, Tie Eyes, Lead Weights, Madison Mitchell, Maryland, 1956 . . . . . 895.00
Widgeon Hen, Glass Eyes, Stippled Paint, Carved Bill, Frank Finney, Chincoteague, Va. . . 490.00
Wood Duck Drake, Wooden, Painted, Signed, Big Sky Carvers, 7 x 13 In. 230.00
Yellowlegs, Glass Eyes, Oak Bill, Frank Finney, Chincoteague, Va. . . . . 165.00 to 240.00

DEDHAM Pottery was started in 1895. Chelsea Keramic Art Works was established in 1872 in Chelsea, Massachusetts, by members of the Robertson family. The factory closed in 1889 and was reorganized as the Chelsea Pottery U.S. in 1891. The firm used the marks *CKAW* and *CPUS*. It became the Dedham Pottery of Dedham, Massachusetts. The factory closed in 1943. It was famous for its crackleware dishes, which picture blue outlines of animals, flowers, and other natural motifs. Chelsea Keramic Art Works and Dedham Pottery pieces are listed here.

Azalea, Plate, Cobalt Blue, 2 Impressed Rabbits, 7 1/2 In.	150.00
Azalea, Plate, Ink Stamp, c.1925, 8 5/8 In.	120.00
Azalea, Plate, Marked, 9 3/4 In.	170.00
Birds In Potted Orange Tree, Plate, Stamp Mark, 10 In.	325.00
Butterfly, Plate, Cobalt Blue, Flowers, Stamp Mark, 8 1/4 In.	350.00
Cat, Dish, Child's, Flared Rim, Stamp Mark, 1 1/8 x 7 3/4 In.	9500.00
Cat, Mug	4730.00
Chick, Bowl, Cobalt Blue, Stamp Mark, 2 x 4 3/4 In.	2400.00
Crab, Plate, Stamp Mark, Impressed Rabbit, 8 1/2 In.	475.00
Dolphin, Plate, Waves, Air Bubbles, Stamp Mark, 8 3/4 In.	1100.00
Duck, Coaster, Duck Swimming In Water, Cobalt Blue, Stamp Mark, 3/4 x 4 In.	500.00
Duck, Plate, Blue Band, Gray, 8 1/2 In.	150.00
Duck, Plate, Blue, Ducks In Pond, Water Lilies, Stamp Mark, Impressed Rabbit, 9 3/4 In.	200.00
Elephant, Bowl, Flared, No. 6, Stamp Mark, 1 3/4 x 4 1/2 In.	550.00
Elephant, Charger, Stamp Mark, 12 In.	2400.00
Elephant, Cup & Saucer, Stamp Mark	600.00
Elephant, Eggcup, Cover, Stamp Mark, 4 1/4 x 5 In.	2600.00
Elephant, Pitcher, No. 2, Stamp Mark, 5 x 6 In.	1300.00
Grape, Bowl, Clusters Of Grapes, No. 1, Stamp Mark, 4 x 9 In.	425.00
Grape, Cup & Saucer, Cobalt Blue, Stamp Mark	175.00
Grape, Plate, Clusters Of Grapes, Cobalt Blue, Stamp Mark, 6 In.	125.00
Grape, Plate, Ink Stamp, c.1925, 8 3/8 In.	176.00
Iris, Plate, Blue Leaves, Impressed Rabbit Mark, 8 1/4 In.	200.00
Iris, Plate, Marked, 10 In.	120.00
Landscape, Plate, Hills, Sailboats, Lake, Sky, Gray Glaze, Stamp Mark, 6 In.	2400.00
Lobster, Plate, Bread & Butter, Blue Ink Stamp, 6 In., Pair	850.00
Lobster, Plate, Impressed Rabbit, 8 1/2 In.	600.00
Log Cabin, Humidor, Cover, Farmhouses, Trees, Incised Mark, No. 13, 6 3/4 x 5 1/2 In.	4000.00
Lotus, Bowl, Embossed Panels Of Lotus Petals, Stamp Mark, 2 x 5 In.	400.00
Magnolia, Plate, 10 In.	120.00
Magnolia, Plate, Cobalt Blue, Crackle Finish, Incised Mark, 7 1/2 In.	200.00
Magnolia, Plate, Cobalt Blue, Maude Davenport, Stamp Mark, Impressed Rabbit, 10 In.	300.00
Magnolia, Plate, Impressed Rabbits, 8 1/2 In.	150.00
Magnolia, Plate, Stamp Mark, Impressed Rabbit, 6 In.	100.00
Moth, Plate, Luna, Broad Wings, Impressed Rabbit, 8 1/2 In.	750.00
Mushroom, Plate, Cobalt Blue, Impressed Rabbit, 8 1/2 In.	100.00
Mushroom, Plate, Cobalt Blue, White Ground, 2 Impressed Rabbits, 10 In.	500.00
Polar Bear, Plate, Cobalt Blue, Bear On Icebergs, Stamp Mark, Impressed Rabbit, 10 In.	650.00
Pond Lily, Plate, Cobalt Blue, Stamp Mark, 2 Impressed Rabbits, 6 In.	175.00
Poppy, Plate, Fringed Petals, Stamp Mark, Impressed Rabbit, 6 In.	650.00
Poppy, Vase, Chartreuse, Red Poppies, Thistles, Flat, Footed, CKAW, 7 1/2 x 6 1/4 In.	425.00
Rabbit, Ashtray, Cobalt Blue, Circular, Stamp Mark, 1 x 3 3/4 In.	125.00
Rabbit, Bowl, Blue Band, Gray Glaze, Marked, 5 1/4 In.	176.00
Rabbit, Bowl, Oval, Stamp Mark, 2 1/2 x 10 1/2 In.	250.00
Rabbit, Candlestick, Flat Rim, Blue Bands, Stamp Mark, 1 3/4 x 3 1/2 In., Pair	250.00
Rabbit, Card Holder, Slot Along Ears, Blue Ink Stamp, 2 1/2 In.	1520.00
Rabbit, Charger, Nature Scene, Etched, Gray Blue Glaze, Hugh Robertson, CKAW, 11 In.	1800.00
Rabbit, Compote, Cobalt Blue, Chalice Form, Handles, Stamp Mark, 3 1/2 x 6 In.	225.00
Rabbit, Creamer, Cylindrical, Cobalt Blue, Stamp Mark, 2 3/4 x 3 In.	275.00
Rabbit, Creamer, Trumpet Neck, Bulbous, White Ground, No. 8, 3 x 3 In.	485.00
Rabbit, Dish, Cover, Blue Band, Gray Glaze, Marked, 9 In.	265.00
Rabbit, Eggcup, Cobalt Blue, Partial Stamp Mark, 2 1/2 x 2 In.	225.00
Rabbit, Mug, Child's, Incised D5, 3 1/2 x 4 1/2 In.	425.00
Rabbit, Nappy, Stamp Mark, 1 3/4 x 6 In.	100.00

Rabbit, Paperweight, Crouching, Oval Base, Stamp Mark, 1 1/2 x 3 1/4 In.	550.00
Rabbit, Pitcher, Bulbous, Stamp Mark, Impressed Rabbit, 8 1/2 x 8 In.	350.00
Rabbit, Pitcher, Stamp Mark, 4 3/4 x 6 In.	375.00
Rabbit, Plate, 1931, 8 1/2 In.	1765.00
Rabbit, Plate, Cobalt Blue, Blue Ink Stamp, 8 1/2 In.	150.00
Rabbit, Salt & Pepper, Bulbous, Cobalt Blue, 2 3/4 x 2 1/2 In.	125.00
Rabbit, Sugar & Creamer, Marked, 4 In.	295.00
Rabbit, Sugar, Cover, No. 2, Stamp Mark, 3 1/8 x 4 1/4 In.	175.00
Rabbit, Tankard, Cobalt Blue, Tapered, Incised Mark, 5 x 6 In.	325.00
Rabbit, Tea Tile, Square, 5 In.	205.00
Snowtree, Plate, Bread & Butter, Deep Blue, Stamp Mark, 6 In.	175.00
Snowtree, Plate, Ink Stamp, c.1925, 8 1/2 In.	120.00
Snowtree, Plate, Stamp Mark, 8 1/2 In.	225.00
Swan, Bowl, Cobalt Blue, No. 2, Stamp Mark, 3 1/2 x 8 In.	500.00
Tapestry Lion, Plate, Stamp Mark, Impressed Rabbit, 8 1/2 In.	1100.00
Turkey, Plate, Cobalt Blue, Stamp Mark, 2 Impressed Rabbits, 6 In.	325.00
Turkey, Plate, Ink Stamp, c.1925, 8 1/2 In.	265.00
Turkey, Tea Tile, Circle Of Turkeys, Cobalt Blue, Stamp Mark, Square, 5 3/4 x 5 3/4 In.	700.00
Turtle, Paperweight, Recessed Panels, 4-Footed, Cobalt Blue, Stamp Mark, 1 1/2 x 3 In.	900.00
Turtle, Plate, Cobalt Blue, Stamp Mark, Impressed Rabbit, 6 In.	1400.00
Vase, Bird, Barbotine, Pillow, Hugh Robertson, Chelsea Keramic Art, 5 1/4 x 4 3/4 In.	880.00
Vase, Black, Charcoal Melt Fissure Flambe, Egg Shape, Chelsea Keramic Art, 5 x 4 In.	880.00
Vase, Lion's Head Ring Handles, Brown, Blue Flambe, Cylindrical, CKAW, 6 3/4 In.	470.00
Vase, Oxblood, Long Tapering Neck, Bulbous Base, Experimental, 7 3/8 In.	2940.00
Vase, Thick, Frothy Glaze, Green, Purple, Experimental, Hugh Robertson, 10 x 5 In.	1410.00
Vase, Volcanic Base, Drip Glaze, Experimental, Hugh Robertson, 6 1/2 x 4 1/2 In.	5290.00

DEGENHART is the name used by collectors for the products of the Crystal Art Glass Company of Cambridge, Ohio. John and Elizabeth Degenhart started the glassworks in 1947. Quality paperweights and other glass objects were made. John died in 1964 and his wife took over management and production ideas. Over 145 colors of glass were made. In 1978, after the death of Mrs. Degenhart, the molds were sold. The D in a heart trademark was removed, so collectors can easily recognize the true Degenhart piece.

Figurine, Owl, Black Amethyst, 3 1/2 In.	5.00
Figurine, Owl, Tomato, 3 1/2 In.	20.00
Figurine, Pooche, Daffodil & Purple Slag, 3 In.	20.00
Figurine, Pooche, Powder Blue Slag, 3 In.	27.00
Figurine, Priscilla, Blue Lady Variant, Semiopaque, 5 1/4 In.	25.00
Figurine, Priscilla, Green Satin, 5 1/4 In.	22.00
Slipper, Daisy & Button, Cat's Head, Light Blue, 5 In.	25.00
Sugar & Creamer, Vaseline, 3 In.	25.00
Toothpick, Colonial Drape, Amber	10.00
Toothpick, Lavender Slag	10.00

DEGUE is a signature acid-etched on pieces of French glass made in the early 1900s. Cameo, mold blown, and smooth glass with contrasting colored rims are the types most often found.

Lampshade, Hanging, Bird, Dahlias, Frosted Ground, Dome Shape, Cameo, 14 In.	1035.00
Vase, Blue & Purple Flowers, Mottled Amethyst, Art Deco, Bulbous, Footed, 20 In.	3450.00
Vase, Cameo Glass, Orange, Red Mottled, Amethyst, Cut With Landscape, Sailboat, 5 In.	319.00
Vase, Green Flowers, Peach Ground, Reverse Trumpet, Tapered, Signed, 4 1/2 In.	489.00

DELATTE glass is a French cameo glass made by Andre Delatte. It was first made in Nancy, France, in 1921. Lighting fixtures and opaque glassware in imitation of Bohemian opaline were made. There were many French cameo glass makers, so be sure to look in other appropriate categories.

Vase, Cameo Glass, Yellow, Mottled, Green, Amethyst, Cut With Flowers, 1920s, 6 In.	1466.00
Vase, Fuchsia Flowers, White, Burgundy Mottling, Egg Shape, Flared Rim, Signed, 11 In.	1150.00
Vase, Purple, Flower, Leaf, Cameo, Signed, 7 1/4 In.	461.00

DELDARE, see Buffalo Pottery Deldare.

DELFT is a tin-glazed pottery that has been made since the seventeenth century. Delft was made in England in the eighteenth century. It is decorated with blue on white or with colored decorations. Most of the pieces sold today were made after 1891, and the name *Holland* usually appears with the Delft factory marks. The word *delft* appears alone on some twentieth century pottery from Asia and Germany.

Bowl, Chinoiserie Figures, Cell Border, 1759, 9 In.	1885.00
Bowl, Openwork Ring Border, Blue Flowers, Scrollwork, Lotus Leaf Panels, 6 5/8 In.	2470.00
Bowl, Painted, Cottages, Green Hills, Willows, White, 10 x 6 In.	575.00
Bowl, Powdered Manganese, Crosshatch Border, Floral Center, Bristol, England, 5 In.	440.00
Bowl, Sloped Sides, Flowers, Leaf Band, Flat Rim, England, 18th Century, 4 5/8 In.	1055.00
Charger, Blue, White, Peacock, Flower Border, 13 1/4 In.	315.00
Charger, Cobalt Blue, Peacock, Butterfly Border, Marked, 12 1/4 In.	800.00
Charger, Dragonfly Medallion, Flowers, Leaves, Bristol, England, 18th Century, 13 In.	1645.00
Charger, Flower Center & Border, Bristol, 18th Century, 13 In.	1060.00
Charger, Flower Garden & Fence Center, Flower Border, Bristol, England, 13 1/4 In.	1060.00
Charger, Hunter & Hounds, Chasing Deer, Hand Painted, 18th Century, 12 In.	1175.00
Charger, Prince William, Center Portrait, Fruit & Flower Border, Holland, 1700s, 13 In.	3055.00
Dish, Scalloped Rim, 1700s, 8 1/2 In.	350.00
Drug Jar, Ex Valer Sylv, Man, Dog, White, Cylindrical, 5 In.	600.00
Figurine, Man, On Horse, Tricornered Hat, Multicolored, Plinth Base, Holland, 8 3/4 In.	2760.00
Figurine, Man, Woman, Seated, Milking Cow, White, 8 1/2 In., Pair	1955.00
Jar, Apothecary, White, Cover, 1700s	295.00
Plaque, 2 Ships Colliding, Harbor, Cobalt Blue, White, Frame, V. Brohn, c.1900, 17 x 11 In.	920.00
Plaque, Cartouche Shape, Enamel, Blue, Windmill Shoreline Scene, Holland, 23 1/2 In.	529.00
Plate, 2 Blue Winged Horses, Crown, Tassels, GPI 1688 In Cartouche, 8 1/2 In.	2700.00
Plate, Multicolored Flower, 9 In.	230.00
Plate, Peony & Rock, Multicolored, c.1770, 8 7/8 In.	380.00
Plate, Prince William V Of Orange, Stylized Oranges, Scrolling Leaves, 8 3/4 In.	805.00
Plate, Prince William V Of Orange, Verse, Oranges, Leaves, Striped Border, 9 In.	690.00
Plate, Prince William V, Fruit & Leaf Border, Holland, Late 1700s, 8 3/4 In.	800.00
Punch Bowl, Chinoiserie Decoration, Figures In Landscape, Blue, White, 12 In.	2300.00
Sauceboat, Handle, Footed, England, 3 1/2 x 6 1/2 In.	660.00
Tankard, Oriental Design, 2 Figures, Landscape, Pewter Foot & Lid, RSF 1696, 8 1/2 In.	1035.00
Tankard, Oriental, Woman, Garden, Pewter Foot & Lid, Engraved CJW 1738, 10 1/2 In.	980.00
Teapot, Globular, Flower & Bird Panels, England, 18th Century, 3 3/4 In.	4400.00
Tile, 2 Spanish Galleons At Sea, Small Ships, Crystalline Glaze, 4 1/8 x 8 3/8 In.	690.00
Tile, Dog, Chasing Deer, Snow, Arts & Crafts Frame, 4 1/4 x 16 1/2 In.	880.00
Tile, Dog, Chasing Deer, Snow, Raised Outline, 4 3/4 x 17 1/4 In.	940.00
Tile, Flamingo, Facing Right, Raised Outline, Frame, 12 x 4 1/2 In.	440.00
Tile, Fleet Of Tall Ships, Raised Outline, 4 x 16 1/2 In.	176.00
Tile, Goose, Flying, White, Green Glass, Blue Water, Marked, Frame, 7 1/2 x 16 In.	475.00
Tile, Peacock, Facing Left, Raised Outline, 4 1/2 x 16 1/2 In.	410.00
Tile, Peacock, Facing Right, Raised Outline, Wood Frame, 4 1/2 x 16 1/2 In.	530.00
Tile, Peacock, Facing Right, White Brick Wall, Raised Outline, 13 x 4 In.	500.00
Tile, Potter At Wheel, Raised Outline, 4 3/4 In.	120.00
Tile, Potters, Working, 50th Anniversary Of Zeelandia, c.1950, 11 1/2 x 8 In.	235.00
Tile, Rooster, White, Blue Ground, Raised Outline, 9 x 4 3/4 In.	355.00
Tile, Swan, Facing Right, Raised Outline, 4 3/4 x 8 3/4 In.	410.00
Tile, Viking Ship, Raised Outline, 4 1/2 x 9 In.	120.00
Tobacco Jar, Scrolled Cartouche, Duinkerke, Flower Basket, Copper Cover, 11 In.	1675.00
Tobacco Jar, Scrolled Cartouche, Rapee, Flower Vase, Baluster, Brass Cover, 9 In.	1315.00
Vase, Blue & White, Garlic Mouth, Tall Neck, Chinese Style, Late 19th Century, 31 In.	430.00
Vase, Blue, White, Baluster Shape, Oriental Landscapes, Borders, c.1882, 13 In., Pair	420.00
Vase, Cherub, Rooster, Applied Fruit Wreath, 2 Centaurs, Urn Shape, Footed, 18 In.	400.00
Vase, Cover, Paneled, Flowers, Leaves, Birds, Red, Blue, Green, Octagonal, 16 3/4 In.	805.00
Vase, Octagonal, Flared Rim, Double Gourd Body, Floral, Early 1800s, 13 In., Pair	2530.00
Wall Pocket, Blue & White, Cornucopia Shape, Raised Peony Border, 18th Century, 8 In.	705.00

DENTAL cabinets, chairs, equipment, and other related items are listed here. Other objects may be found in the Medical category.

Cabinet, Walnut, Pink Marble Shelf, Leaded Glass, 22 x 21 x 74 In.	1035.00

Chair, Folding, Oak, Leather Seat, Southern Novelty Works, c.1890 . . . .   460.00
Forceps, Wrought Iron, 2 Curved Handles, Clenched Fist, Shell, 4 1/2 In. 880.00
Mirror, Standard Dental Laboratories, Laboratory, Chicago, Celluloid, 3 3/8 In. 130.00
Tooth Key, Milliken, Steel Shaft, Removable Claw, Carved Bone Handle, England, 6 In. . .   265.00

DENVER is part of the mark on an American art pottery. William
Long of Steubenville, Ohio, founded the Lonhuda Pottery Company in
1892. In 1900 he moved to Denver, Colorado, and organized the Denver China and Pottery Company. This pottery, which used the mark
Denver, worked until 1905 when Long moved to New Jersey and
founded the Clifton Pottery. Long also worked for Weller Pottery,
Roseville Pottery, and American Encaustic Tiling Company. Do not
confuse this pottery with the Denver White Pottery, which worked
from 1894 to 1955 in Denver.

DENVER
C T &
P Co

Vase, Poppies, Green Matte Vellum Glaze, Squat Top, Denaura, 5 1/2 x 5 In. 3173.00
Vase, Violets, Robin's-Egg Blue Matte Glaze, Squat, Denaura, 2 1/2 x 5 1/4 In. 1410.00

DEPRESSION GLASS was an inexpensive glass manufactured in
large quantities during the 1920s and early 1930s. It was made in many
colors and patterns by dozens of factories in the United States. Most
patterns were also made in clear glass, which the factories called *crystal.* If no color is listed here, it is clear. The name *Depression glass* is a
modern one. For more descriptions, history, pictures, and prices of
Depression glass, see the book *Kovels' Depression Glass & Dinnerware Price List.*

Alice, Cup & Saucer, Jade-Ite 35.00
Anniversary, Berry Bowl, Pink, 4 7/8 In. 15.00
Anniversary, Bowl, Fruit, 9 In. 33.00
Anniversary, Butter, Cover, Pink 95.00
Anniversary, Compote, Pink, 3 Legs, 5 3/4 In. . . . . .17.00 to 23.00
Anniversary, Creamer, Footed, 4 In. 12.00
Anniversary, Plate, Bread & Butter, Pink, 6 1/4 In. 7.00
Anniversary, Plate, Dinner, Gold Trim, 10 In. 6.00
Anniversary, Relish, 4 Sections, Gold Trim, 4 Plastic Spoons, Metal Holder, 11 In. 57.00
Anniversary, Sandwich Server, Iridescent, 12 1/2 In. 16.00
Anniversary, Sherbet, Pink, 3 1/2 In. 22.50
Anniversary, Sugar, Cover 13.00
Anniversary, Vase, Crimped Rim, 6 1/2 In. 14.00
Anniversary, Vase, Pink, 6 1/2 In. 39.00
Anniversary, Wall Vase, 6 1/2 In. 55.00
Anniversary, Wine, Pink, 2 1/2 Oz. . . . . .20.00 to 27.00
Aunt Polly, Butter, Cover, Blue, 4 3/4 x 7 In. 250.00
Aunt Polly, Candy Dish, Blue, Handles, Footed, 5 1/4 In. . . . . .54.00 to 65.00
Aunt Polly, Candy Dish, Green, Handles, Footed, 5 1/4 In. 22.00
Aunt Polly, Candy Dish, Iridescent, Handles, Footed, 5 1/4 In. 30.00
Aunt Polly, Dish, Pickle, Blue, Oval, 7 1/4 In. 42.00
Aunt Polly, Dish, Pickle, Green, Oval, 7 1/4 In. 14.00
Aunt Polly, Plate, Sherbet, Blue, 6 In. . . . . .12.50 to 14.00
Aunt Polly, Sherbet, Blue, 3 1/8 In. . . . . *Illus*   14.00
Aunt Polly, Sherbet, Green, 3 1/8 In. 13.00
Aunt Polly, Sherbet, Iridescent, 3 1/8 In. 10.00
Aunt Polly, Tumbler, 8 Oz., 3 3/4 In. 36.00
Bamboo Optic, Plate, Luncheon, 8 In. 8.00
Basket pattern is listed here as No. 615.
Block pattern is listed here as Block Optic.
Block Optic, Berry Bowl, Green, 4 1/4 In. 16.00
Block Optic, Berry Bowl, Green, 8 1/2 In. 38.00
Block Optic, Bowl, Cereal, Green, 5 1/4 In. 18.00
Block Optic, Bowl, Console, Green, Rolled Edge, 11 3/4 In. 100.00
Block Optic, Bowl, Salad, Green, 7 1/4 In. 130.00
Block Optic, Bowl, Salad, Pink, 7 1/4 In. 155.00
Block Optic, Compote, Mayonnaise, 5 3/8 In. 100.00
Block Optic, Cup & Saucer, Green 20.00

Depression Glass,
Aunt Polly, Sherbet
Blue, 3 1/8 In.

Depression Glass,
Cherry Blossom, Plate,
Dinner, Pink, 9 In.

Depression Glass,
Colonial Fluted, Sherbet
Green

Block Optic, Cup & Saucer, Pink 18.00
Block Optic, Cup, Green, Angled Handle . . . . .8.00 to 9.00
Block Optic, Cup, Green, Beaded Top 12.00
Block Optic, Cup, Green, Plain Handle 7.00
Block Optic, Cup, Pink . . . . .6.00 to 9.00
Block Optic, Goblet, 9 Oz., 5 3/4 In. . . . . .10.00 to 15.00
Block Optic, Goblet, Pink, 9 Oz., 5 3/4 In. 25.00
Block Optic, Ice Tub, Pink, 4 5/8 x 5 3/8 In. 110.00
Block Optic, Pitcher, 80 Oz., 8 In. 80.00
Block Optic, Pitcher, Green, Bulbous, 54 Oz., 7 5/8 In. . . . . .95.00 to 105.00
Block Optic, Plate, Dinner, Green, 9 In. 30.00
Block Optic, Plate, Luncheon, Green, 8 In. 8.00
Block Optic, Plate, Luncheon, Pink, 8 In. 8.00
Block Optic, Plate, Luncheon, Yellow, 8 In. . . . . .9.00 to 10.00
Block Optic, Plate, Sherbet, Green, 6 In. . . . . .3.00 to 7.00
Block Optic, Plate, Sherbet, Luncheon, 8 In. 8.00
Block Optic, Plate, Sherbet, Pink, 6 In. 4.00
Block Optic, Saucer 10.00
Block Optic, Sherbet, 3 1/4 In. 5.00
Block Optic, Sherbet, Green, 5 1/2 Oz., 3 1/4 In. . . . . .6.50 to 10.00
Block Optic, Sherbet, Pink, 5 1/2 Oz., 3 1/4 In. . . . . .7.50 to 10.00
Block Optic, Sherbet, Yellow, 6 Oz., 4 3/4 In. 24.00
Block Optic, Tumbler, Pink, 9 1/2 Oz., 3 3/4 x 2 3/4 In. 15.00
Block Optic, Wine, 4 1/2 In. 20.00
Blue Mosaic, Plate, Dinner, 10 In. 20.00
Bowknot, Berry Bowl, Green, 4 1/2 In. . . . . .30.00 to 33.00
Bowknot, Bowl, Cereal, Green, 5 1/4 In. 38.00
Bowknot, Cup, Green . . . . .12.00 to 15.75
Bowknot, Plate, Salad, Green, 7 In. 18.00
Bowknot, Tumbler, Green, 10 Oz., 5 In. . . . . .17.50 to 25.00
Bowknot, Tumbler, Green, Footed, 10 Oz., 5 In. 35.00
Bubble, Berry Bowl, 8 3/8 In. 8.00
Bubble, Berry Bowl, Forest Green, 3-Footed, 4 1/2 x 8 1/2 In. . . . . .12.00 to 18.00
Bubble, Berry Bowl, Sapphire Blue, 8 3/8 In. 15.00
Bubble, Bowl, Cereal, 5 1/4 In. 8.00
Bubble, Bowl, Forest Green, 3 x 8 1/2 In. 20.00
Bubble, Bowl, Fruit, 4 1/2 In. 4.00
Bubble, Bowl, Fruit, Forest Green, 4 1/2 In. . . . . .6.00 to 8.00
Bubble, Cocktail, Bell Shape, Forest Green, 4 1/2 Oz., 4 1/4 In. 15.00
Bubble, Creamer, Sapphire Blue 35.00
Bubble, Goblet, 14 Oz., 7 In. 10.00
Bubble, Goblet, Forest Green, 9 Oz., 6 In. . . . . .15.00 to 20.00
Bubble, Plate, Dinner, 9 3/8 In. 8.00
Bubble, Platter, Sapphire Blue, 12 In. 14.99
Bubble, Sherbet, Forest Green, White Stem, 6 Oz., 4 In. 10.00
Bubble, Sherbet, Green, 6 Oz., 4 In. 14.00

Bubble, Soup, Dish, 7 3/4 In. 10.00
Bubble, Soup, Dish, Sapphire Blue, 7 3/4 In. 12.00
Bubble, Tumbler, Juice, Footed, Forest Green, 5 1/2 Oz., 4 1/2 In. 14.00
Bubble, Tumbler, Juice, Footed, Forest Green, Bell Shape, 4 Oz., 3 5/8 In. 19.00
Bubble, Tumbler, Juice, Ruby, 5 Oz., 3 3/4 In. 12.00
Bubble, Tumbler, Lemonade, 16 Oz., 5 7/8 In. 18.00
Bullseye pattern is listed here as Bubble.
Cabbage Rose pattern is listed here as Sharon.
Candlewick pattern is listed in the Imperial Glass category.
Caprice pattern is included in the Cambridge Glass category.
Charm, Bowl, Dessert, Jade-Ite, 4 3/4 In. 35.00
Cherry Blossom, Berry Bowl, Pink, 4 3/4 In. 23.00
Cherry Blossom, Bowl, Fruit, 3-Footed, 10 1/2 In. 80.00
Cherry Blossom, Bowl, Fruit, Pink, 3-Footed, 10 1/2 In. 90.00
Cherry Blossom, Bowl, Vegetable, Green, Oval, 9 In. 43.00
Cherry Blossom, Butter, Cover, Pink, 6 In. 75.00
Cherry Blossom, Butter, Pink 12.00
Cherry Blossom, Coaster, 3 1/4 In. 18.00
Cherry Blossom, Creamer, Green, 3 1/2 In. 30.00
Cherry Blossom, Pitcher, Pink, 36 Oz., 6 3/4 In. ....55.00 to 75.00
Cherry Blossom, Plate, Dinner, Green, 9 In. 18.00
Cherry Blossom, Plate, Dinner, Pink, 9 In. ....*Illus* 22.00
Cherry Blossom, Plate, Salad, Pink, 7 In. 35.00
Cherry Blossom, Platter, Green, Oval, 11 In. ....35.00 to 50.00
Cherry Blossom, Relish, 4 Sections, Pink, 13 In. 88.00
Cherry Blossom, Sandwich Server, Pink, Handles, 10 1/2 In. ....40.00 to 70.00
Cherry Blossom, Sherbet, Green 20.00
Cherry Blossom, Sherbet, Pink ....19.00 to 22.50
Cherry Blossom, Soup, Dish, Pink, 7 3/4 In. 113.00
Cherry Blossom, Sugar 33.00
Chinex Classic, Bowl, Cereal, 5 3/4 In. 8.00
Chinex Classic, Bowl, Cereal, Castle, Blue Trim, 5 3/4 In. 15.00
Chinex Classic, Bowl, Vegetable, 7 In. 26.50
Chinex Classic, Bowl, Vegetable, 9 In. 19.00
Chinex Classic, Cake Plate, 11 1/2 In. 7.50
Chinex Classic, Cake Plate, Flowers, 11 1/2 In. 12.00
Chinex Classic, Creamer 10.00
Chinex Classic, Cup & Saucer 8.00
Chinex Classic, Plate, Dinner, 9 3/4 In. ....5.00 to 7.00
Chinex Classic, Plate, Dinner, Castle, Blue Trim, 9 3/4 In. 22.00
Chinex Classic, Plate, Sherbet, 6 1/4 In. 7.00
Chinex Classic, Plate, Sherbet, Castle, Blue Trim, 6 1/4 In. 7.50
Chinex Classic, Saucer, Castle, Blue Trim 6.00
Chinex Classic, Sherbet 18.00
Chinex Classic, Sherbet, Castle, Blue Trim 28.00
Chinex Classic, Soup, Dish, 7 3/4 In. 24.00
Chinex Classic, Soup, Dish, Castle, Blue Trim, 7 3/4 In. ....30.00 to 40.00
Chinex Classic, Sugar 10.00
Christmas Candy, Plate, Luncheon, 8 In. ....13.00 to 14.00
Cloverleaf, Sherbet, Green 9.00
Colonial, Soup, Cream, Green, 4 1/2 In. 100.00
Colonial Block, Powder, Jar, Cover, Frosted 40.00
Colonial Fluted, Creamer, Footed, Green 14.00
Colonial Fluted, Cup, Green 10.00
Colonial Fluted, Grill Plate, Green, 10 3/8 In. 17.00
Colonial Fluted, Sherbet, Green ....*Illus* 17.00
Colonial Fluted, Sugar, Green, Footed 14.00
Crackle, Candleholder, Light Green 33.00
Crackle, Candy Jar, Cover, Medium Green, 4 5/8 In. 31.00
Crackle, Plate, Light Green, 7 In. 12.00
Crackle, Plate, Party, Light Green, Sherbet Well, 8 x 10 In. 16.00
Crackle, Sherbet, Light Green, 3 In. 16.00
Crackle, Sherbet, Pink, 4 1/4 In. 14.00

Crackle, Tumbler, 8 Oz., 4 1/4 In. 12.00
Cube pattern is listed here as Cubist.
Cubist, Bowl, Gold Trim, 4 1/2 In. 6.00
Cubist, Bowl, Green, 7 In. 23.00
Cubist, Butter, Pink 23.00
Cubist, Candy Jar, Cover, Pink 38.00
Cubist, Coaster, Green, 3 1/4 In. 18.00
Cubist, Coaster, Pink, 3 1/4 In. 18.00
Cubist, Creamer, 3 1/2 In. 8.00
Cubist, Creamer, White, 2 5/8 In. 5.00
Cubist, Plate, Sherbet, Pink, 6 In. 9.00
Cubist, Powder Jar, Cover, Pink 39.00
Cubist, Powder Jar, Windsor Cover 30.00
Cubist, Sherbet, Pink 9.00
Cubist, Sugar & Creamer, White, 2 5/8 In. 6.00
Cubist, Sugar, 2 3/8 In. 8.00
Cubist, Sugar, 3 In. 7.00
Cubist, Sugar, Cover, Green, 3 In. 29.00
Cubist, Sugar, Pink, 2 3/8 In. ....7.00 to 8.50
Cubist, Tray, For Sugar & Creamer 8.00
Diamond pattern is listed here as Miss America.
Doric, Berry Bowl, Green, 4 1/2 In. ....8.00 to 14.50
Doric, Berry Bowl, Green, 8 1/4 In. 36.00
Doric, Berry Bowl, Pink, 4 1/2 In. 13.00
Doric, Berry Bowl, Pink, 8 1/4 In. 33.00
Doric, Bowl, Green, Handles, 9 In. 25.00
Doric, Bowl, Vegetable, Pink, Oval, 9 1/2 In. 47.00
Doric, Butter, Green 19.00
Doric, Cake Plate, Pink, 3-Footed, 10 In. 32.00
Doric, Candy Dish, 3 Sections, Delphite, 7 x 6 In. 15.00
Doric, Candy Dish, 3 Sections, Iridescent, 7 x 6 In. ....8.00 to 15.00
Doric, Candy Dish, 3 Sections, Pink, 7 x 6 In. 15.00
Doric, Candy Dish, Teal Green, 3 Sections, Ultramarine, 7 x 6 In. 10.50
Doric, Candy Jar, Cover, Green, 8 In. 60.00
Doric, Candy Jar, Cover, Pink, 8 In. ....48.00 to 75.00
Doric, Creamer, Green 10.00
Doric, Creamer, Pink 18.50
Doric, Cup & Saucer, Green 20.00
Doric, Cup & Saucer, Pink 17.00
Doric, Cup & Saucer, Platinum Trim 33.00
Doric, Grill Plate, Green, 9 In. 18.00
Doric, Grill Plate, Pink, 9 In. ....23.50 to 27.00
Doric, Pitcher, Green, 32 Oz., 5 1/2 In. 60.00
Doric, Plate, Dinner, Green, 9 In. ....18.00 to 25.00
Doric, Plate, Dinner, Pink, 9 In. ....18.00 to 23.00
Doric, Plate, Sherbet, Green, 6 In. 9.00
Doric, Relish, Pink, 4 x 4 In. 25.00
Doric, Salt & Pepper, Pink 50.00
Doric, Saltshaker, Green 22.00
Doric, Saltshaker, Pink 13.00
Doric, Sherbet, Footed, Delphite Blue, 3 5/8 x 3 5/8 In. 8.00
Doric, Sherbet, Green 23.00
Doric, Sherbet, Pink 14.00
Doric, Tray, Handles, Green, 10 In. 53.00
Doric, Tray, Handles, Pink, 10 In. 16.00
Doric, Tumbler, Pink, 9 Oz., 4 1/2 In. 80.00
Doric, Tumbler, Pink, Footed, 10 Oz., 4 In. 45.00
Doric & Pansy, Creamer, Pink, Child's 39.00
Doric & Pansy, Cup 10.00
Doric & Pansy, Cup & Saucer, Ultramarine 35.00
Doric & Pansy, Cup, Ultramarine 17.00
Doric & Pansy, Plate, Salad, Ultramarine, 7 In. 41.00

Doric & Pansy, Plate, Sherbet, Pink, 6 In. 8.00
Doric & Pansy, Plate, Sherbet, Ultramarine, 6 In. 10.00
Doric & Pansy, Saucer, Pink 4.00
Doric & Pansy, Sugar, Pink, Child's 39.00
Double Shield pattern is listed here as Mt. Pleasant.
Early American Prescut, Berry Set, Bowl, Sugar, Creamer, Box, 10 Piece 65.00
Early American Prescut, Bowl, Salad, 10 3/4 In. 12.00
Early American Prescut, Candy Dish, Cover, 5 1/4 In. 12.00
Early American Prescut, Salt & Pepper, Square, 1 3/8 In. 60.00
Early American Prescut, Tray, Rectangular, 6 1/2 x 12 In. 12.00
Fire-King, Bowl, Heat Resistant, 3 x 8 In. 12.00
Fire-King, Casserole, Cornflower, 2 Qt. 12.00
Fire-King, Casserole, Cover, Ivory, Apple, 5 x 9 In. 90.00
Fire-King, Casserole, Wheat, Qt. 12.00
Fire-King, Egg Plate, Milk White, Gold Trim, Scalloped Rim, 10 In. 12.00
Fire-King, Grease Jar, Cover, Ivory, Apples Cherries, 6 In. 80.00
Fire-King, Grease Jar, Cover, Ivory, Stripes, 4 x 5 5/8 In. 78.00
Fire-King, Grease Jar, Cover, Ivory, Tulip, 6 x 5 In. 90.00
Fire-King, Loaf Pan, Cornflower, Qt. 15.00
Fire-King, Measuring Cup, 1 Cup 12.00
Fire-King, Measuring Cup, Red Writing, 2 Cup, 4 1/2 In. 15.00
Fire-King, Mixing Bowl Set, Gay Fad, Peach Blossom, 3 Piece 79.00
Fire-King, Mixing Bowl Set, Jade-Ite, 4 Piece 165.00
Fire-King, Mixing Bowl Set, Jade-Ite, Beaded Edge, 3 Piece 150.00
Fire-King, Mixing Bowl, Apple, Splashproof, 9 1/2 In. 89.00
Fire-King, Mixing Bowl, Ivory, Tulip, Splash Proof, 8 1/2 In. 65.00
Fire-King, Mixing Bowl, Jade-Ite, Beaded Edge, 7 In. 39.00
Fire-King, Mixing Bowl, Jade-Ite, Beaded Edge, 6 In. 65.00
Fire-King, Mixing Bowl, Jade-Ite, Splash Proof, 4 Qt., 6 x 9 1/2 In. 150.00
Fire-King, Mixing Bowl, Jade-Ite, Swedish Modern, 11 In. 175.00
Fire-King, Mixing Bowl, Jade-Ite, Swedish Modern, 2 1/8 x 5 x 6 1/2 In. 80.00
Fire-King, Mixing Bowl, White, Tulip, Splashproof, 7 1/2 In. 65.00
Fire-King, Mixing Bowl, White, Tulip, Splashproof, 9 1/2 In. 65.00
Fire-King, Mug, Stacking, Fired-On Yellow 16.00
Fire-King, Pie Plate, Sapphire Blue, 8 In. 12.00
Fire-King, Platter, Blue Mosaic, Oval, 9 x 12 In. 25.00
Fire-King, Refrigerator Dish, Philbe, Jade-Ite, 3 1/2 x 4 1/2 x 5 In. 65.00
Fire-King, Shaker, Range, Striped, 4 1/2 x 2 1/2 In. 65.00
Fire-King, Sugar, Cover, Wheat, 4 1/4 x 3 1/4 In. 13.00
Fire-King, Vase, Deco, 5 1/4 In. 35.00
Florentine No. 1, Cup 9.00
Florentine No. 1, Plate, Dinner, 10 In. 20.00
Florentine No. 1, Plate, Salad, Gold Trim, 8 1/2 In. 9.00
Florentine No. 1, Salt & Pepper, Green, Footed, 4 In. 38.00
Florentine No. 1, Sherbet, Green 12.00
Florentine No. 2, Creamer, Silver Trim 9.00
Florentine No. 2, Cup, Gold Trim 8.00
Florentine No. 2, Gravy Boat, Yellow, 6 1/4 In. 54.00
Florentine No. 2, Plate, Sherbet, 6 In. 5.00
Florentine No. 2, Sugar, Crystal, Silver Trim 10.00
Florentine No. 2, Tumbler, Yellow, 9 Oz., 4 In. 22.00
Game Birds, Platter, Pheasant, Oval, 9 x 12 In. 65.00
Harp, Cake Stand, Ice Blue, 9 In. 55.00
Hobnail pattern is listed in the Hobnail category.
Homestead, Plate, Pink, 8 In. 12.00
Horizontal Ribbed pattern is listed here as Manhattan.
Horseshoe pattern is listed here as No. 612.
Jane-Ray, Bowl, Desert, Jade-Ite, 4 7/8 In. 14.00
Jane-Ray, Bowl, Vegetable, Jade-Ite, 8 1/4 In. .... 45.00 to 57.00
Jane-Ray, Creamer, Jade-Ite 35.00
Jane-Ray, Cup & Saucer, Jade-Ite 15.00
Jane-Ray, Cup, Jade-Ite 9.00

Jane-Ray, Plate, Dinner, Jade-Ite, 9 1/8 In. . . . . .20.00 to 28.00
Jane-Ray, Plate, Salad, Jade-Ite, 7 3/4 In. 15.00
Jane-Ray, Platter, Jade-Ite, Oval, 12 x 9 In. 28.00
Jane-Ray, Saucer, Jade-Ite . . . . *Illus*   6.00
Jane-Ray, Soup, Dish, 7 5/8 In. 30.00
Jane-Ray, Starter Set, Jade-Ite, Plates, Bowls, Cups, Saucers, 16 Piece 500.00
Jane-Ray, Sugar & Creamer, Jade-Ite, 3 In. 65.00
Jane-Ray, Sugar, Cover, Jade-Ite . . . . .35.00 to 50.00
Knife & Fork pattern is listed here as Colonial.
Leaf & Blossom, Plate, White, Fired-On Yellow, 8 In. 18.00
Line 300 pattern is listed in the Paden City category as Peacock & Wild Rose.
Lorain pattern is listed here as No. 615.
Lorna pattern is included in the Cambridge Glass category.
Madrid, Dinner Set, Amber, 45 Piece 150.00
Manhattan, Candlestick, 2-Light, 4 1/2 In., Pair 40.00
Manhattan, Relish Set, Clear Tray & Center Dish, 5 Royal Ruby Dishes, 7 Piece 95.00
Martha Washington pattern is included in the Cambridge Glass category.
Mayfair Open Rose, Bowl, Green, 11 3/4 In. 110.00
Mayfair Open Rose, Bowl, Pink, 11 3/4 In. 65.00
Mayfair Open Rose, Bowl, Vegetable, Handles, 10 In. 38.00
Mayfair Open Rose, Bowl, Vegetable, Pink, Handles, 10 In. 28.00
Mayfair Open Rose, Bowl, Vegetable, Pink, Handles, 7 In. 65.00
Mayfair Open Rose, Cookie Jar, Cover 57.00
Mayfair Open Rose, Cookie Jar, Cover, Blue 150.00
Mayfair Open Rose, Creamer, Pink 35.00
Mayfair Open Rose, Cup, Blue 45.00
Mayfair Open Rose, Pitcher, Pink, 37 Oz., 6 In. 70.00
Mayfair Open Rose, Plate, Luncheon, 8 1/2 In. 30.00
Mayfair Open Rose, Salt & Pepper, Pink 60.00
Mayfair Open Rose, Sandwich Server, Green, Center Handle, 11 1/2 In. 75.00
Mayfair Open Rose, Sugar, Pink 35.00
Milano, Pitcher, Ball, Aquamarine, 8 1/2 In. 30.00
Milano, Pitcher, Ball, Desert Gold, 8 1/2 In. 18.00
Miss America, Bowl, Cereal, 6 1/4 In. 25.00
Miss America, Bowl, Cereal, Pink, 6 1/4 In. 50.00
Miss America, Bowl, Vegetable, Oval, Pink, 10 In. . . . . .65.00 to 70.00
Miss America, Cake Plate, 12 In. 25.00
Miss America, Candy Jar, No Cover, 7 In. 60.00
Miss America, Celery Dish, Pink, Oval, 10 1/2 In. 45.00
Miss America, Compote, Pink, Footed, 5 In. . . . . .60.00 to 75.00
Miss America, Creamer 25.00
Miss America, Cup & Saucer, Pink . . . . .40.00 to 50.00
Miss America, Grill Plate, Pink, 10 1/4 In. 50.00
Miss America, Plate, Bread & Butter 25.00
Miss America, Plate, Dinner, 10 1/4 In. . . . . .12.50 to 15.00
Miss America, Plate, Salad, 8 1/2 In. 10.00
Miss America, Platter, Oval, 12 1/4 In. 22.50
Miss America, Relish, 4 Sections, Pink, 8 3/4 In. . . . . .25.00 to 80.00
Miss America, Relish, Sections, Round, 11 3/4 In. 26.00
Miss America, Sugar & Creamer 25.00
Miss America, Tumbler, Pink, 10 Oz., 4 1/2 In. 25.00
Moderntone, Ashtray, Pink, 7 3/4 In. 95.00
Moderntone, Berry Bowl, Amethyst, 5 In. 28.00
Moderntone, Berry Bowl, Amethyst, 8 3/4 In. 55.00
Moderntone, Cup & Saucer, Amethyst 20.00
Moderntone, Cup & Saucer, Cobalt Blue . . . . .20.00 to 23.00
Moderntone, Cup & Saucer, Pink 22.00
Moderntone, Custard Cup, Cobalt Blue . . . . .25.00 to 30.00
Moderntone, Plate, Dinner, Cobalt Blue, 8 7/8 In. . . . . .20.00 to 23.00
Moderntone, Soup, Cream, Amethyst, 5 In. 25.00
Moderntone, Sugar & Creamer, Pink 25.00
Moderntone Little Hostess Party, Plate, Pastel Yellow, 5 1/4 In.   10.00
Moderntone Little Hostess Party, Tea Set, 14 Piece 150.00

Moderntone Platonite, Berry Bowl, 8 3/4 In. 35.00
Moderntone Platonite, Cup & Saucer, Burgundy 20.00
Moderntone Platonite, Salt & Pepper 28.00
Moderntone Platonite, Sherbet 4.00
Moderntone Platonite, Sherbet, Fired-On Yellow 9.00
Moderntone Platonite, Sherbet, White 5.00
Moderntone Platonite, Soup, Cream, Burgundy, 5 In. 25.00
Moderntone Platonite, Sugar & Creamer 32.00
Moondrops pattern is listed in the New Martinsville category.
Mt. Pleasant, Bowl, Cobalt Blue, Footed, 4 3/4 In. 30.00
Mt. Pleasant, Candlestick, 2-Light, Cobalt Blue 30.00
Mt. Pleasant, Cup & Saucer, Cobalt Blue 25.00
Mt. Pleasant, Sandwich Server, Black Amethyst, Center Handle, 9 In. 40.00
Mt. Pleasant, Tray, Black Amethyst, Square, Handles, 10 In. 35.00
Mt. Pleasant, Tumbler, Black Amethyst, Footed, 7 Oz., 6 In. 30.00
Mt. Pleasant, Tumbler, Cobalt Blue, Footed, 7 Oz., 6 In. 33.00
Mt. Vernon pattern is included in the Cambridge Glass category.
No. 612, Plate, Salad, Green, 8 3/8 In. 12.00
No. 612, Platter, Green, Oval, 10 3/4 x 8 In. 32.00
No. 612, Relish, 3 Sections, Handles, 3-Footed, Yellow, 7 3/8 x 1 5/8 In. 48.00
No. 612, Sandwich Server, Green, 11 1/2 In. ....20.00 to 25.00
No. 612, Sherbet 13.00
No. 612, Sugar, Green 18.00
No. 612, Sugar, Yellow 20.00
No. 615, Relish, 8 In. 30.00
No. 618, Bowl, Vegetable, Oval, Handles, 10 In. 10.00
No. 618, Plate, Dinner, 9 3/8 In. ....18.00 to 19.50
No. 618, Platter, Closed Handles, 11 1/2 In. 18.00
Old Colony, Bowl, Cereal, 6 3/8 In. 30.00
Old Colony, Cookie Jar, Pink 35.00
Old Colony, Cup & Saucer, Pink 45.00
Old Colony, Relish, 3 Sections, Pink, 10 1/2 In. 30.00
Old Colony, Sugar, Pink 40.00
Old Colony, Tumbler, Pink, 9 Oz., 4 1/2 In. 40.00
Old Florentine pattern is listed here as Florentine No. 1.
Open Rose pattern is listed here as Mayfair Open Rose.
Ovide, Berry Bowl, Platonite, Fired-On Burgundy, 4 3/4 In. 6.00
Ovide, Berry Bowl, Platonite, Fired-On Butterscotch, 4 3/4 In. 6.00
Ovide, Berry Bowl, Platonite, Fired-On Green, 4 In. ....4.00 to 9.00
Ovide, Bowl, Cereal, Fired-On Butterscotch, 5 1/4 In. 5.00
Ovide, Bowl, Cereal, Fired-On Gray, 5 1/4 In. 5.00
Ovide, Bowl, Cereal, Platonite, Fired-On Aqua, 5 1/2 In. 12.00
Ovide, Bowl, Cereal, Platonite, Fired-On Burgundy, 5 1/2 In. 8.00
Ovide, Bowl, Cereal, Platonite, Fired-On Chartreuse, 5 1/2 In. 4.00
Ovide, Bowl, Cereal, Platonite, Fired-On Gray, 5 1/2 In. 12.00
Ovide, Bowl, Cereal, Platonite, Fired-On Green, 5 1/2 In. ....8.00 to 12.00
Ovide, Candy Dish, Cover, Black, 5 3/4 In. 46.00
Ovide, Cocktail, Green 6.00
Ovide, Creamer, Black 10.00
Ovide, Creamer, Green 10.00
Ovide, Creamer, Platonite, Fired-On Chartreuse 6.00
Ovide, Creamer, Platonite, Fired-On Pink 12.00
Ovide, Creamer, Platonite, Fired-On Rust ....6.00 to 11.00
Ovide, Cup & Saucer, Platonite, Black Flower Decal 5.00
Ovide, Cup, Green 5.00
Ovide, Cup, Platonite, Fired-On Burgundy 5.00
Ovide, Cup, Platonite, Fired-On Butterscotch 5.00
Ovide, Plate, Dinner, Platonite, Fired-On Butterscotch, 9 In. ....8.00 to 12.00
Ovide, Plate, Dinner, Platonite, Fired-On Green, 9 In. 4.00
Ovide, Plate, Dinner, Platonite, Fired-On Pink, 9 In. 4.00
Ovide, Plate, Dinner, Platonite, Fired-On Yellow, 9 In. 4.00
Ovide, Plate, Dinner, Platonite, Flying Geese Decal, 9 In. 18.00
Ovide, Plate, Luncheon, Platonite, Fired-On Aqua, 8 In. 10.00

Ovide, Plate, Luncheon, Platonite, Fired-On Burgundy, 8 In. 8.00
Ovide, Plate, Luncheon, Platonite, Fired-On Chartreuse, 8 In. 8.00
Ovide, Plate, Luncheon, Platonite, Fired-On Gray, 8 In. . . . . .3.00 to 8.00
Ovide, Plate, Luncheon, Platonite, Fired-On Green, 8 In. 8.00
Ovide, Platter, Platonite, Fired-On Butterscotch, 9 1/2 x 12 In. 10.00
Ovide, Saucer, Green 3.00
Ovide, Sherbet, Black 11.00
Ovide, Sherbet, Green . . . . .4.00 to 5.00
Ovide, Sherbet, Platonite, Fired-On Green 40.00
Ovide, Sugar & Creamer, Chartreuse 12.00
Ovide, Sugar & Creamer, Platonite 32.00
Ovide, Sugar & Creamer, Platonite, Fired-On Rust 13.00
Ovide, Sugar, Green 10.00
Ovide, Tumbler, Footed, Platonite, Fired-On Rust, 3 5/8 In. 10.00
Parrot pattern is listed here as Sylvan.
Peacock & Wild Rose pattern is listed in the Paden City category.
Petalware, Berry Bowl, Cremax, 9 In. . . . . .25.00 to 35.00
Petalware, Cup & Saucer, Cremax 20.00
Petalware, Cup & Saucer, Cremax, Gold Trim 15.00
Petalware, Cup & Saucer, Monax . . . . 12.00 to 17.50
Petalware, Cup & Saucer, Pink 17.50
Petalware, Cup, Cremax 15.00
Petalware, Mixing Bowl, Pink, Ribbed, Plain Banded Edge, 2 3/4 x 5 1/4 In. 18.00
Petalware, Plate, Dessert, Pink, 6 In., 5 Piece 34.00
Petalware, Plate, Dinner, 9 In. 18.00
Petalware, Plate, Dinner, Cremax, 9 In. . . . . .10.00 to 14.00
Petalware, Plate, Dinner, Florette, 9 In. 24.00
Petalware, Plate, Dinner, Monax, 9 In. 18.00
Petalware, Plate, Dinner, Monax, Regency, 9 In. 13.00
Petalware, Plate, Salad, Monax, 8 In. 13.00
Petalware, Plate, Salad, Monax, Gold Trim, 8 In. 12.00
Petalware, Plate, Salad, Pink, 8 In. 7.00
Petalware, Platter, Oval, 10 x 13 In. 12.00
Petalware, Platter, Pink, Oval, 10 x 13 In. . . . . .25.00 to 33.00
Petalware, Salver, Cremax, 11 In. 22.00
Petalware, Salver, Cremax, Princess Decal, 12 In. 20.00
Petalware, Salver, Cremax, Yellow Rim, 12 In. 26.00
Petalware, Salver, Monax, Gold Trim, 11 In. 18.00
Petalware, Saucer, Cremax, 6 In. . . . . *Illus* 2.00
Petalware, Saucer, Cremax, Floral, Gold Trim 3.50
Petalware, Sherbet, Monax 23.00
Petalware, Soup, Cream, Monax, 4 1/2 In. 13.00
Petalware, Soup, Cream, Monax, Gold Trim, 4 1/2 In. 12.00
Petalware, Sugar & Creamer, Cremax 22.00
Petalware, Sugar, Monax 12.00

Depression Glass,
Jane Ray, Saucer, Jade-ite

Depression Glass,
Petalware, Saucer, Cremax, 6 In.

Depression Glass,
Windsor, Cup, Pink

Pineapple & Floral pattern is listed here as No. 618.
Poppy No. 1 pattern is listed here as Florentine No. 1.
Poppy No. 2 pattern is listed here as Florentine No. 2.
Pretty Polly Party Dishes, see also the related pattern Doric & Pansy.
Primrose, Cake Pan, Round, 8 In. 16.00
Primrose, Creamer 14.00
Primrose, Snack Set, Plates, Cups, Box, 8 Piece 50.00
Prismatic Line pattern is listed here as Queen Mary.
Provincial pattern is listed here as Bubble.
Queen Mary, Plate, Salad, Pink, 8 3/4 In. 65.00
Restaurant Ware, Bowl, Breakfast, Jade-Ite, 16 Oz., 5 In. 170.00
Restaurant Ware, Bowl, Cereal, Jade-Ite, 5 In. 33.00
Restaurant Ware, Bowl, Chili, Jade-Ite, 5 In. 26.00
Restaurant Ware, Platter, Ivory, 9 1/2 In. 35.00
Restaurant Ware, Soup, Dish, Beaded Edge, 7 1/8 In. 38.00
Romanesque, Plate, Green, Octagonal, 8 In. 15.00
Romanesque, Plate, Octagonal, 7 In. 10.00
Romanesque, Sherbet, Amber 12.00
Rope pattern is listed here as Colonial Fluted.
Royal Lace, Berry Bowl, Pink, 10 In. . . . . .33.00 to 45.00
Royal Lace, Bowl, Ruffled Edge, 3-Footed, 10 In. 58.00
Royal Lace, Cookie Jar, No Cover, Green 50.00
Royal Lace, Creamer, Green 15.00
Royal Lace, Creamer, Pink 32.00
Royal Lace, Cup 11.00
Royal Lace, Cup & Saucer 63.00
Royal Lace, Cup & Saucer, Green 45.00
Royal Lace, Cup & Saucer, Pink . . . . .30.00 to 32.00
Royal Lace, Cup, Pink 20.00
Royal Lace, Grill Plate, 10 In. 10.00
Royal Lace, Grill Plate, Green, 10 In. 15.00
Royal Lace, Plate, Dinner, Green, 9 7/8 In. 17.00
Royal Lace, Platter, Oval, Pink, 13 In. 30.00
Royal Lace, Salt & Pepper, Pink 120.00
Royal Lace, Saucer, Green 13.00
Royal Lace, Sugar 12.00
Royal Lace, Sugar & Creamer, Cover, Cobalt Blue 390.00
Royal Lace, Sugar, Pink 15.00
Royal Lace, Tumbler, 5 Oz., 3 1/2 In. 8.00
Royal Ruby, Berry Bowl, 4 1/2 In. 14.00
Royal Ruby, Jam Jar, Notched, Silver Lid, 3 3/4 x 3 1/2 In. 35.00
Sail Boat pattern is listed here as Sportsman Series.
Sandwich, Indiana Sugar & Creamer, Diamond Tray 20.00
Sandwich, Indiana, Snack Set, Cup, Plate 15.00
Sandwich Anchor Hocking, Punch Set, Ivory, 13 Piece 75.00
Sharon, Pitcher, Green, 80 Oz. 500.00
Shell, Bowl, Cereal, Jade-Ite, 6 3/8 In. 35.00
Shell Pink, Dish, Cover, Butterfly, Sections, 6 1/2 In. 138.00
Soreno, Pitcher, Aquamarine, 6 3/4 In. 20.00
Sportsman Series, Cocktail Mixer, Stirrer, Sailboat, Cobalt Blue, 4 1/2 In. . . . . .25.00 to 40.00
Sportsman Series, Cocktail Mixer, Windmill, Cobalt Blue, 4 1/2 In. 40.00
Sportsman Series, Tumbler, Roly Poly, Sailboat, Cobalt Blue, 2 1/2 In. . . . . .10.00 to 12.00
Sportsman Series, Tumbler, Windmill, Hazel Atlas, 4 Oz., 3 1/4 In. 35.00
Swirl Fire-King, Bowl, Vegetable, Golden Anniversary, 7 1/2 In.   20.00
Swirl Fire-King, Bowl, Vegetable, Golden Anniversary, 8 1/8 In.   15.00
Swirl Fire-King, Cup & Saucer, Golden Anniversary, 8 Oz. 14.00
Swirl Fire-King, Cup & Saucer, Pink 35.00
Swirl Fire-King, Plate, Dinner, Jade-Ite, 9 1/8 In. 90.00
Swirl Fire-King, Relish, 3 Sections, White, Golden Anniversary, Round, 9 3/4 In. 14.00
Swirl Jeannette, Bowl, Salad, Pink, Large Rim 38.00
Swirl Jeannette, Candy Dish, Cover, Pink, Footed, 6 1/4 x 6 In. 165.00
Sylvan, Creamer 75.00

Sylvan, Salt & Pepper, Green 400.00
Sylvan, Sugar, Green 375.00
Turquoise Blue, Egg Plate, Gold Trim 35.00
Vertical Ribbed pattern is listed here as Queen Mary.
Wexford, Punch Bowl, 13 3/4 In. 20.00
Wexford, Water Set, 9 Piece 80.00
Whirly Twirly, Tumbler, Juice, Cobalt Blue, 3 In. 25.00
White Ship pattern is listed here as Sportsman Series.
Windmill pattern is listed here as Sportsman Series.
Windsor, Candy Jar, Cover, 7 1/2 In. 6.00
Windsor, Creamer, Pink 14.00
Windsor, Cup, Pink .... *Illus* 5.00
Windsor, Tumbler, Pink, 9 Oz., 4 In. 20.00
Windsor Diamond pattern is listed here as Windsor.

DERBY has been marked on porcelain made in the city of Derby, England, since about 1748. The original Derby factory closed in 1848, but others opened there and continued to produce quality porcelain. The Crown Derby mark began appearing on Derby wares in the 1770s.

Basket, Yellow Mayflowers, Birds, Pierced Trelliswork Sides, Twist Handles, 11 In. 1725.00
Figurine, Child, Holding Basket, Flowered Bocage, Rocaille Base, 5 In., Pair 546.00
Figurine, Young Turk, Scroll Base, Puce, Red, Yellow, Gilt, 1800s, 3 1/2 In. 285.00
Plate, Japan Pattern, Paneled Design, Stylized Flowers, Leaves, 10 In., 14 Piece 2519.00
Vase, Spill, Figures In Rustic Scene, White & Gilt Ground, Flared Rim, 6 1/2 In., Pair 1380.00

DICK TRACY, the comic strip, started in 1931. Tracy was also the hero of movies from 1937 to 1947 and again in 1990, and starred in a radio series in the 1940s and a television series in the 1950s. Memorabilia from all these activities are collected.

Action Figure, The Blank, Playmates, Blister Card, Canada, c.1990, 4 1/2 In. ......140.00 to 185.00
Belt Insert, Tracy Speaking Into Wrist Radio, Plastic, 1970s, 2 In. 15.00
Book, Adventures Of Dick Tracy & Dick Tracy Jr., No. 710, C. Gould, Whitman, 1933 ... 597.00
Book, Caught Racketeers, Hardcover, No. 2, Cupples & Leon, c.1933, 88 Pages 259.00
Book, Coloring, Bonnie Braids, Saalfield, 12 Pages, 10 3/4 In. 9.00
Bracelet, Bangle, 3 Charms, Brass, Link, Quaker Cereal Premium, 1938, 6 3/4 In. 213.00
Button, Dick Tracy, Detective, Read Everyday In Detroit Mirror, c.1932, 1 1/4 In. 155.00
Button, Secret Service Patrol, Blue, Gold, 1 3/8 In. 4.00
Card, Valentine, You Left A Clue, Die Cut, Paper, Unlicensed, 5 3/4 x 4 1/4 In. 35.00
Crimestopper Club Kit, Chicago Tribune, Box, c.1961, 6 x 9 In. 50.00
Game, Chinese Checkers, Envelope, Quaker, 1939, 13 x 13 In. 80.00
Game, Target, Plastic Pistol, Suction Darts, Cardboard Target, Box, Marx 185.00
Gun, Clicker, Black, 1-In. Round Sticker On Left Side, Marx, 1938 .... 90.00
Gun, Clicker, Black, 1-In. Round Sticker On Right Side, Marx, 1938 .... 85.00
Gun, Water, Submachine, Green & Yellow Plastic, Box, Tops, 1951 .... 160.00
Junior Detective Kit, Manual, Decoder, Badge, Card, Ruler, Wall Chart, 1944 .... 190.00
Knife, Pocket, Dick Tracy, Detective, Imperial, 2 1/4-In. Blade, 2 3/4 In. 60.00
Knife, Pocket, Magnifyer, Whistle, Glow-In-The-Dark Handle, Camco, 1956 ....50.00 to 144.00
Lunchbox, Thermos, Aladdin, 1967 .... 50.00
Police Car, Plastic, Siren, Marx, Box, 10 In. 440.00
Poster, Dick Tracy's G-Men, Linen Back, Republic Serial, 1939, 41 x 21 In. 330.00
Ring, Post Raisin Bran, 1948, 2 1/2 In. 30.00
Squad Car, Figures, Dick & Sam Catchum, Siren, Flashing Light, Marx, 1948, 20 In. 745.00
Suspender Set, Handcuff Set, Original Gift Box, 12 x 6 x 1 In. 145.00
Toy, Car, Remote Control, Battery Operated, Linemar, Box, 9 In. 330.00
Toy, Pistol, Siren Police, Marx, Box, c.1934, 8 1/2 In. 600.00
Toy, Squad Car, Police Department, Tin Lithograph, Battery Operated, Green, Marx, 10 In. .. 65.00
Toy, Squad Car, Siren, Flashing Light, Tin, Windup, Marx, Box, 11 In. 495.00
Toy, Squad Car, Tin, Friction, Battery Operated Light, Marx, 20 In. 170.00
Toy, Squad Car, Tin, Friction, Marx, 6 3/4 In. 170.00
Toy, Wrist Radio, 2-Way, Box, c.1967, Pair 90.00
Tumbler, Domino's Pizza, Chester Gould, Glass, 1970s, 6 1/2 In. 100.00

Wristwatch, Chrome Case, Tan Leather Band, New Haven, Chester Gould, 1948 . . . .   200.00
Wristwatch, Chrome, Moving Gun Second Hand, New Haven, Box, 1951 . . . .   735.00
Wristwatch, Chrome, Tan Leather Band, New Haven, Box, Insert, 1948 . . . . .200.00 to 225.00

DICKENS WARE pieces are listed in the Royal Doulton and Weller catego `

DINNERWARE used in the United States from the 1930s through the
1950s is listed here. Most was made in potteries in southern Ohio,
West Virginia, and California. A few patterns were made in Japan,
England, and other countries. Dishes were sold in gift shops and
department stores, or were given away as premiums. Many of these
patterns are listed in this book in their own categories, such as Autumn
Leaf, Azalea, Coors, Fiesta, Franciscan, Hall, Harker, Harlequin, Red
Wing, Riviera, Russel Wright, Vernon Kilns, Watt, and Willow. For more
information, see *Kovels' Depression Glass & Dinnerware Price List.*

Acanthus, Plate, Bread & Butter, Johnson Brothers, 7 1/8 In. 11.00
Accent, Sugar, Cover, Green, E.M. Knowles 15.99
Apple Blossom, Casserole, Cover, Handles, Homer Laughlin 75.00
Arcadia, Cup & Saucer, Johnson Brothers 12.00
Athena, Bowl, Fruit, Johnson Brothers, 5 1/4 In. 11.00
Athena, Gravy Boat, Johnson Brothers 56.00
Athena, Soup, Dish, Johnson Brothers 11.00
Autumn Harvest, Sugar, Taylor Smith & Taylor 15.00
Bali Flower, Platter, Homer Laughlin, 11 1/2 In. 24.00
Ballerina, Cup & Saucer, Burgundy, Universal 7.50
Ballerina, Cup & Saucer, Jade Green, Universal 15.00
Ballerina, Cup & Saucer, Moss Rose, Universal 6.00
Ballerina, Plate, Dinner, Dove Gray, Universal, 10 In. 7.50
Ballerina, Plate, Dinner, Poppies, Universal, 10 In. 6.00
Ballerina, Sugar, Cover, Dove Gray, Universal 15.00
Baltic Ivy, Bowl, Vegetable, Cover, Blue Ridge, 8 In. 40.00
Baroness, Plate, Dinner, Homer Laughlin, 10 In. 24.00
Bells Of Ireland, Cup & Saucer, Harmony House 10.00
Bells Of Ireland, Plate, Dinner, Harmony House, 10 1/2 In. 10.00
Berkshire, Casserole, Cover, Tab Handles, Homer Laughlin 80.00
Betsy Jug, Red Gingham Dress, Hat, Blue Ridge, 8 1/2 In. . . . . .95.00 to 125.00
Big Apple, Bowl, Cereal, Blue Ridge, 6 In. 60.00
Biscayne, Gravy Boat, Salem China 25.00
Bittersweet, Plate, Dinner, Universal, 9 1/4 In. 30.00
Blossom Top, Salt & Pepper, Blue Ridge, 5 1/4 In. 94.00
Blue Belle Bouquet, Platter, Oval, Blue Ridge, 13 x 10 In. 45.00
Blue Ice, Soup, Dish, Johnson Brothers, 7 5/8 In. 12.00
Blue Moon, Plate, Dinner, Blue Ridge, 10 1/2 In. 48.00
Boutonniere, Sugar, No Cover, Taylor Smith & Taylor, 5 1/4 In. 5.00
Briar Rose, Plate, Luncheon, Homer Laughlin, 8 3/4 In. 23.00
Briar Rose, Platter, Oval, Salem China, 11 x 8 1/2 In. . . . . .25.00 to 34.00
Bridal Bouquet, Coffeepot, American Limoges, 8 In. 35.00
Bridal Bouquet, Gravy Boat, Underplate, Tab Handles, American Limoges, 4 3/4 In. 24.00
Brittany, Soup, Dish, Homer Laughlin, 8 1/4 In. 24.00
Brown Tulip, Bowl, Cereal, Skyline Shape, Blue Ridge, 6 In. 8.00
Calico Fruit, Cup & Saucer, Universal 20.00
Calico Fruit, Mixing Bowl, Universal, 6 In. 25.00
Cameo Rose, Bowl, Cereal, Harmony House, 6 1/4 In. 5.00
Cameo Rose, Cup & Saucer, Harmony House 10.00
Cameo Rose, Plate, Dinner, Harmony House, 10 1/4 In. 10.00
Cameo Rose, Plate, Salad, Harmony House, 7 1/2 In. 5.00
Capri, Plate, Dinner, Gray, Harmony House, 10 In. 7.00
Capri, Plate, Dinner, Pink, Harmony House, 10 In. 7.00
Capri, Soup, Dish, Gray, Harmony House, 8 In. 6.00
Capri, Soup, Dish, Pink, Harmony House, 8 In. 7.00
Cattail, Cup & Saucer, Universal 10.50
Cattail, Mixing Bowl, Universal, 8 In. 25.00

Cavalier, Bowl, Homer Laughlin, 11 In. 20.00
Cavalier, Casserole, Cover, Handles, Homer Laughlin, c.1950, 11 In. 20.00
Cavalier, Platter, Gray Border, Gold Trim, Homer Laughlin, 13 In. 25.00
Cavalier, Sauceboat, Homer Laughlin 20.00
Cavalier, Sugar, Cover, Homer Laughlin 20.00
Christmas Tree, Plate, Dinner, Mistletoe, Blue Ridge, 10 1/2 In. 95.00
Cock O' The Walk, Cup & Saucer, Blue Ridge 42.00
Cock O' The Walk, Plate, Bread & Butter, Blue Ridge, 6 1/2 In. 15.00
Colonial White, Platter, Round, Homer Laughlin, 10 In. 20.00
Columbine, Bowl, Vegetable, Square, Homer Laughlin 24.00
Columbine, Cup & Saucer, Homer Laughlin ....15.00 to 16.00
Columbine, Platter, Rectangular, Homer Laughlin, 10 In. 24.00
Crab Apple, Platter, Oval, Blue Ridge, 11 x 15 In. 50.00
Crinoline, Bowl, Cereal, Harmony House, 6 1/2 In. 5.00
Crinoline, Bowl, Fruit, Harmony House, 5 In. 5.00
Crinoline, Creamer, Harmony House 6.00
Crinoline, Cup & Saucer, Harmony House 5.00
Crinoline, Plate, Bread & Butter, Harmony House, 7 In. 5.00
Crinoline, Sugar, Cover, Harmony House 6.00
Currier & Ives, Cake Plate, A Home In The Wilderness, Harker, 12 1/4 In. ....9.00 to 20.00
Currier & Ives, Cake Server, Winter Scene, Man Carrying Firewood, Harker, 9 1/4 In. 20.00
Damask Rose, Bowl, Vegetable, E.M. Knowles, 8 3/4 In. 15.00
Dubarry, Casserole, Cover, Homer Laughlin 75.00
Eggshell Georgian, Cup & Saucer, Countess, Homer Laughlin, 1940s 13.00
Eggshell Georgian, Plate, Dinner, Cashmere, Gold Trim, Homer Laughlin 14.00
Eggshell Georgian, Soup, Dish, Countess, Homer Laughlin, 1950, 8 In. 14.00
Eggshell Nautilus, Casserole, Cover, Aristocrat, Handles, Homer Laughlin 75.00
Eggshell Nautilus, Gravy Boat, Underplate, Aristocrat, Homer Laughlin 75.00
Eggshell Nautilus, Platter, Oval, Lisa, Homer Laughlin, 11 3/4 In. 24.00
Eggshell Nautilus, Teapot, Gold Trim, Homer Laughlin 89.00
English Abbey, Gravy Boat, Taylor, Smith & Taylor 40.00
English Chippendale, Plate, Salad, Pink, Johnson Brothers, 7 In. 25.00
English Village, Cup & Saucer, Salem China, 5 1/2 In. 11.00
English Village, Plate, Dinner, Salem China, 9 3/4 In. 28.00
Evening Song, Creamer, E.M. Knowles 11.00
Fairlane, Gravy Boat, Underplate, Steubenville 12.00
Fairlane, Plate, Dinner, Steubenville, 10 In. 10.00
Ferndale, Cup & Saucer, Harmony House 10.00
Floral Wreath, Platter, Steubenville, 13 In. 35.00
Flower Of The Meadow, Bowl, Vegetable, Oval, Homer Laughlin, 9 In. ....30.00 to 33.00
Flower Of The Meadow, Plate, Dinner, Homer Laughlin, 10 In. 23.00
Flower Of The Meadow, Soup, Dish, Homer Laughlin, 8 In. 23.00
Forsythia, Platter, Gold Trim, E.M. Knowles, 12 1/2 In. 22.00
Fox Grape, Sugar, No Cover, Blue Ridge 80.00
French Peasant, Plate, Man, Blue Ridge, 9 1/4 In. 65.00
Friendly Village, Bowl, Fruit, Johnson Brothers, 5 1/2 In. 12.00
Friendly Village, Chop Plate, Johnson Brothers, 14 In. 150.00
Friendly Village, Mug, Johnson Brothers, 3 1/4 In. 12.00
Friendly Village, Plate, Salad, Square, Johnson Brothers, 8 In. 12.00
Friendly Village, Platter, Oval, Johnson Brothers, 12 In. 45.00
Friendly Village, Tureen, Johnson Brothers, 7 1/2 x 12 3/4 In. 175.00
Fruit Sampler, Sugar & Creamer, Johnson Brothers 15.00
Garland, Platter, Rectangular, Bird, Homer Laughlin, 11 In. 30.00
Georgetown, Plate, Dinner, Salem China, 10 1/4 In. 28.00
Godey Prints, Charger, Green Border, Gold Trim, Salem China, 11 In. 43.00
Golden Wheat, Bowl, Vegetable, Round, Homer Laughlin, 8 1/2 In. 20.00
Golden Wheat, Plate, Dinner, Homer Laughlin, 10 In. 23.00
Golden Wheat, Sauceboat, Homer Laughlin ....20.00 to 29.00
Grapevine, Platter, Oval, E.M. Knowles, 10 x 12 1/2 In. 18.00
Green Eyes, Plate, Bread & Butter, Blue Ridge, 6 In. ....8.00 to 9.00
Hacienda, Bowl, Homer Laughlin, 8 1/4 In. 30.00
Haddon Hall, Soup, Dish, Johnson Brothers, 8 In. 12.00

Harvest, Creamer, Steubenville 15.00
Heirloom, Creamer, Platinum Trim, Harmony House 10.00
Hevella, Plate, Luncheon, Johnson Brothers, 9 In. 12.00
Indian Tree, Creamer, Johnson Brothers 19.99
Indian Tree, Cup & Saucer, Johnson Brothers 12.00
Indian Tree, Soup, Dish, Johnson Brothers, 7 1/2 In. 12.00
Indian Tree, Teapot, Johnson Brothers, 6 x 10 In. 130.00
Jewel, Plate, Salad, Johnson Brothers, 8 In. 12.00
Jubilee, Platter, Misty Gray, Homer Laughlin, 13 In. 32.00
King Charles, Casserole, Cover, Handles, Homer Laughlin, 6 x 7 In. 23.00
Kitchen Kraft, Fork, Green, Homer Laughlin 95.00
Kitchen Kraft, Jar, Cover, Ball Shape, Tulips, Homer Laughlin, 7 x 4 In. 75.00
Kitchen Kraft, Pie Plate, Homer Laughlin, 9 5/8 In. 24.00
Kwaker, Butter, Cover, Homer Laughlin 65.00
Kwaker, Casserole, Cover, Handles, Homer Laughlin, 10 In. 75.00
Kwaker, Dish, Pickle, Homer Laughlin, 5 3/4 x 9 In. 24.00
Kwaker, Sugar, Cover, Homer Laughlin 33.00
Laurella, Platter, Round, Handles, Jade, Universal, 11 3/4 In. 35.00
Leaf Fantasy, Sandwich Set, Gray, Taylor, Smith & Taylor, 2 Piece 14.00
Lexington, Platter, Fairway Shape, Taylor, Smith & Taylor, 11 In.   16.00
Lexington, Sugar, Cover, Fairway Shape, Taylor, Smith & Taylor 14.00
Liberty Blue, Cup, Paul Revere, Enoch Wedgwood 24.00
Liberty Blue, Saucer, Old North Church, Enoch Wedgwood, 5 3/4 In. 24.00
Lu-Ray, Gravy Boat, Windsor Blue, 8 In. 20.00
Lu-Ray, Platter, Sharon Pink, Taylor, Smith & Taylor, 11 1/2 In. 12.00
Lu-Ray, Salt & Pepper, Windsor Blue, Taylor, Smith & Taylor, 3 3/4 In. 20.00
Majestic, Bowl, Vegetable, Brittany Shape, Homer Laughlin, 9 1/2 In. 20.00
Manchester, Bowl, Vegetable, Enoch Wedgwood, 9 1/4 In. 14.95
Manchester, Plate, Bread & Butter, Enoch Wedgwood, 6 In. 4.99
Maple Leaf, Gravy Boat, Salem China, 8 In. 24.00
Marigold, Platter, Oval, Homer Laughlin, 12 In. 16.00
Mary, Bowl, Cereal, Harmony House, 6 In. 6.00
Mary, Cup, Harmony House 8.00
Mary, Gravy Boat, Underplate, Harmony House 65.00
Mary, Plate, Salad, Harmony House, 7 1/2 In. 8.00
Mary, Saucer, Harmony House 8.00
Mexicana, Bowl, Vegetable, Homer Laughlin, 8 1/2 In. 17.00
Mexicana, Jar, Cover, Small, Homer Laughlin 112.00
Mixing Bowl, Homer Laughlin, 6 In. 24.00
Moderne, Plate, Dinner, Harmony House, 10 1/4 In. 9.00
Moderne, Soup, Dish, Harmony House, 7 3/4 In. 6.00
Moderne, Sugar, Harmony House 16.00
Moonglow, Cup & Saucer, Harmony House 6.00
Moonglow, Plate, Dinner, Harmony House, 10 1/4 In. 9.00
Nora, Cup, Harmony House 10.00
Nordic, Plate, Bread & Butter, Johnson Brothers, 6 1/4 In. 11.00
Old Britain Castles, Plate, Dinner, Blue, Johnson Brothers, 10 In. 22.00
Old Britain Castles, Plate, Dinner, Pink, Johnson Brothers, 10 In. 26.00
Old Britain Castles, Soup, Dish, Pink, Johnson Brothers, 8 In. 12.00
Old McDonald's Farm, Canister, Coffee, Horse Cover, Gold Trim, Regal China, 10 In. 235.00
Old McDonald's Farm, Canister, Flour, Grandpa Cover, Gold Trim, Regal China, 10 In. . . .   225.00
Old McDonald's Farm, Creamer, Rooster, Gold Trim, Regal China, 6 In. 135.00
Old McDonald's Farm, Sugar & Creamer, Hen, Rooster, Gold Trim, Regal China 250.00
Old McDonald's Farm, Teapot, Duck Finial, Regal China, 7 1/2 In. 295.00
Olde English Countryside, Mug, Johnson Brothers 12.99
Orient, Soup, Dish, Harmony House, 7 1/2 In. 10.00
Ovenserve, Pie Baker, Homer Laughlin, 10 1/2 In. 30.00
Parsley, Sugar, Cover, Salem China, 3 1/2 In. 35.00
Pastel Rose, Casserole, Cover, Handles, Homer Laughlin 75.00
Periwinkle, Bowl, Vegetable, Steubenville 29.50
Petalware, Bowl, Dessert, W.S. George, 5 1/2 In. 12.00
Petalware, Cup, Pink, W.S. George 12.00

Petalware, Saucer, Blue, W.S. George	12.00
Petalware, Saucer, Green, W.S. George	12.00
Petalware, Soup, Dish, Green, W.S. George, 8 In.	11.50
Petalware, Soup, Dish, Pink, W.S. George, 8 In.	11.50
Petit Point Basket, Casserole, Cover, Salem China, 9 In.	78.00
Petit Point Basket, Coffeepot, Cover, Salem China, 9 1/2 In.	110.00
Petit Point Basket, Trivet, Salem China, 7 1/4 In.	30.00
Piccadilly, Creamer, Homer Laughlin	16.00
Poinsettia, Bowl, Vegetable, Round, Blue Ridge, 9 1/2 In.	35.00
Priscilla, Mixing Bowl, Homer Laughlin, 6 In.	24.00
Provence, Cup & Saucer, Johnson Brothers	14.99
Provence, Soup, Coupe, Johnson Brothers, 7 In.	14.99
Provincial, Salt & Pepper, Flower Center, Blue Border, Johnson Brothers	38.00
Quilted Apple, Cup & Saucer, Skyline Shape, Blue Ridge	56.00
Regency, Cup & Saucer, Johnson Brothers	15.00
Regency, Plate, Luncheon, Johnson Brothers, 9 3/4 In.	13.50
Regency, Sugar, Cover, Johnson Brothers	38.00
Revere, Soup, Dish, Johnson Brothers	12.00
Rhythm, Cup & Saucer, Capri, Homer Laughlin	14.00
Rhythm, Teapot, Magnolia, Homer Laughlin, 4 1/2 x 8 In.	65.00
Rhythm Rose, Bowl, Vegetable, Homer Laughlin, 8 7/8 In.	20.00
Rio Rita, Platter, Taylor, Smith & Taylor, 13 In.	17.50
Riviera, Bowl, Red, Oval, Homer Laughlin, 9 1/8 In.	24.00
Riviera, Bowl, Vegetable, Red, Homer Laughlin, 8 1/4 In.	30.00
Riviera, Butter, Cover Only, Ivory, Homer Laughlin, 1/2 Lb.	70.00
Riviera, Casserole, Cover, Mauve Blue, Homer Laughlin, 10 1/4 In.	85.00
Riviera, Casserole, Cover, Red, Homer Laughlin, 10 1/4 In.	90.00
Riviera, Sugar & Creamer, Cover, Red	22.00
Riviera, Tumbler, Mauve Blue, Homer Laughlin	75.00
Rodeo, Plate, Bread & Butter, Blue, Universal, 6 1/4 In.	8.95
Romance, Bowl, Vegetable, Blue Rim, Platinum Trim, Homer Laughlin, 9 In.	30.00
Rooster, Box, Cover, Blue Ridge, 2 x 4 1/2 In.	75.00
Rosalinda, Soup, Dish, Century Shape, Homer Laughlin, 7 3/4 In.	24.00
Rose, Gravy Boat, Green, E.M. Knowles	15.00
Rose, Pitcher, Milk, Steubenville, 6 1/2 In.	125.00
Rose Chintz, Plate, Bread & Butter, Johnson Brothers, 6 In.	11.00
Rose Marie, Creamer, Blue Ridge	63.00
Rose Point, Platter, Oval, Steubenville, 13 1/4 In.	19.95
Rose Point, Salt & Pepper, Steubenville	25.00
Rose Point, Sugar, Cover, Steubenville	15.95
Rosedawn, Bowl, Fruit, Johnson Brothers, 5 1/2 In.	12.00
Rosedawn, Cup & Saucer, Johnson Brothers	12.00
Rosedawn, Plate, Salad, Square, Johnson Brothers, 8 In.	12.00
Roslyn, Sauceboat, Underplate, Gadroon Edge, E.M. Knowles	25.00
Samantha, Salver, Salem China, 12 In.	25.00
Sculptured Fruit, Jug, Blue Ridge, 32 Oz., 6 3/4 In.	85.00
Sheffield, Bowl, Vegetable, Round, Salem China	25.00
Sheffield, Platter, Oval, Salem China, 11 3/4 x 9 3/8 In.	25.00
Sheffield, Sugar, Cover, Salem China	25.00
Simplicity, Gravy Boat, Salem China	34.00
Skytone, Casserole, Cover, Blue, White Handles, Homer Laughlin	65.00
Skytone, Sugar, Cover, Blue, White Finial, Homer Laughlin	22.00
Summer Chintz, Bowl, Cereal, Johnson Brothers, 6 In.	11.00
Summer Chintz, Soup, Dish, Johnson Brothers	11.00
Symphony, Bowl, Harmony House, 9 1/4 In.	10.00
Symphony, Creamer, Harmony House	8.00
Symphony, Cup & Saucer, Chartreuse, Harmony House	10.00
Symphony, Cup & Saucer, Gray, Harmony House	10.00
Symphony, Cup & Saucer, Pink, Harmony House	10.00
Symphony, Plate, Luncheon, Chartreuse, Harmony House, 9 1/4 In.	17.50
Symphony, Saucer, Gray, Harmony House, 6 1/4 In.	5.00
Symphony, Saucer, Turquoise, Harmony House, 6 1/4 In.	5.00
Symphony, Sugar & Creamer, Salem China	29.00

Symphony, Sugar, Cover, Handles, Harmony House	9.00
Tangerine, Coffeepot, Orange & Green Stripes, Harmony House, 10 In.	35.00
Tangerine, Plate, Bread & Butter, Harmony House, 7 1/2 In.	7.00
Tom & Jerry Set, Homer Laughlin, 7 Piece	65.00
Tom & Jerry Set, Homer Laughlin, 9 1/2-In. Punch Bowl, 7 Piece	60.00
Triumph, Cup & Saucer, Beige, Platinum Trim, Homer Laughlin	22.00
Triumph, Platter, Empire Shape, Platinum Border, Taylor, Smith & Taylor, 11 In.	14.00
Tulip, Salt & Pepper, Blue Ridge, 5 In.	50.00
Tutti Fruit, Cup & Saucer, Blue Ridge	95.00
Virginia Rose, Creamer, Homer Laughlin	25.00
Virginia Rose, Mug, Homer Laughlin	65.00
Virginia Rose, Plate, Dinner, Homer Laughlin, 10 In.	20.00
Virginia Rose, Platter, Homer Laughlin, 15 1/2 In.	32.00
Weathervane, Casserole, Cover, Round, E.M. Knowles, 11 In.	25.00
Wells, Plate, Century, Square, Homer Laughlin, 9 In.	12.99
Wild Strawberry, Bowl, Vegetable, Blue Ridge, 9 1/4 In.	45.00
Wild Strawberry, Platter, Oval, Blue Ridge, 13 In.	75.00
Wild Strawberry, Sugar & Creamer, Cover, Blue Ridge	65.00
Winchester, Plate, Dinner, Johnson Brothers, 10 In.	66.00
Wisteria, Bowl, Fruit, Harmony House	8.00
Woodfield, Cup & Saucer, Chartreuse, Steubenville	7.50
Yellow Jasmine, Plate, Dinner, E.M. Knowles, 10 In.	8.00

DIONNE QUINTUPLETS were born in Canada on May 28, 1934. The publicity about their birth and their special status as wards of the Canadian government made them famous throughout the world. Visitors could watch the girls play; reporters interviewed the girls and the staff. Thousands of special dolls and souvenirs were made picturing the quints at different ages. Emilie died in 1954, Marie in 1970, and Yvonne in 2001. Annette and Cecile still live in Canada.

Calendar, Height & Weight Chart, Envelope, 32 x 9 In.	60.00
Doll, Madame Alexander, Composition Socket Head, Sleep Eyes, c.1935, 6 In.	2860.00
Doll, Madame Alexander, Dr. Dafoe, Composition Socket Head, c.1936, 15 In.	1200.00
Doll, Madame Alexander, Dr. Dafoe, Composition, Painted Features, 1936	1300.00
Handkerchief, Blue Hat, Red Gingham Bows, 9 x 9 In.	25.00
Lamp, Quints In High Chairs, Ceramic, 9 x 4 1/2 In.	254.00
Spoon Set, Silver Plated, Carlton, Box, 5 Piece	80.00
Toy, Shell Water Flower, Box, Japan, 1930s	100.00

DIRK VAN ERP was born in 1860 and died in 1933. He opened his own studio in 1908 in Oakland, California. He moved his studio to San Francisco in 1909 and the studio remained under the direction of his son until 1977. Van Erp made hammered copper accessories, including vases, desk sets, bookends, candlesticks, jardinieres, and trays, but he is best known for his lamps. The hammered copper lamps often had shades with mica panels.

Ashtray Stand, Copper, Hammered, 4 Strands, Hemispherical Base, Top, 30 x 9 In.	1293.00
Bookends, Copper, Hammered, Initials, MES, 6 x 4 1/2 In.	316.00
Bowl, Center, Hammered, Silver Plated, Flower Shape, 1 3/4 x 14 1/2 In.	1175.00
Bowl, Morning Glory Shape, Flared, 3 x 10 1/2 In.	2235.00
Box, Copper, Hammered, Hinged, Riveted Handles, 2 1/2 x 7 x 3 3/4 In.	2705.00
Charger, Hammered, Silver Plated, Flower Shape, 15 1/2 In.	825.00
Lamp, Copper Base, Hammered, Conical Mica & Copper Shade, 21 x 18 In.	12925.00
Lamp, Copper, Hammered, Mica, 4-Paneled Shade, Beanpot Base, 12 x 10 1/2 In.	10575.00
Lamp, Mission Style, Hammered Copper, Mica Shade, Signed, 17 In.	18400.00
Tray, Copper, Hammered, Bronze Patina, 19 In.	590.00
Vase, Copper, Hammered, Bulbous, Rolled Rim, Stamped Windmill, 9 1/2 x 8 In.	5580.00
Vase, Copper, Hammered, Rolled Rim, Dark Patina, 15 3/4 x 9 1/2 In.	12925.00
Vase, Copper, Hammered, Shell Casing Shape, Fluted Rim, 1903, 27 x 7 1/2 In.	8813.00
Vase, Copper, Hammered, Shouldered, 12 1/4 In.	12925.00
Vase, Copper, Hammered, Windmill, 3 1/2 x 4 1/4 In.	1290.00
Vase, Hammered Copper, Patina, 1 3/4 In.	499.00
Vase, Hammered Copper, Patina, 3 1/4 In.	350.00

DISNEYANA is a collector's term. Walt Disney and his company introduced many comic characters to the world. Collectors search for examples of the work of the Disney Studios and the many commercial products modeled after his characters, including Mickey Mouse and Donald Duck, and recent films, like *Beauty and the Beast* and *The Little Mermaid.*

Ashtray, Mickey & Minnie Mouse, Niagara Falls, Canada, Japan, 1930s, 3 1/4 x 4 In.	250.00
Ashtray, Mickey Mouse, Ceramic, Japan, 3 In.	130.00
Ashtray, Mickey Mouse, Germany, 5 In.	415.00
Ashtray, Mickey Mouse, Playing Guitar, Maastricht, Dutch, 1930s, 3 1/2 x 7 1/2 In.	845.00
Badge, Mickey Mouse Club, Metal, Early 1950s, 3 1/2 In.	20.00
Badge, Official Musketeer, Bag, Card, Dan Brechner & Co., 1950s, 3 1/2 In.	35.00
Bank, Mickey Mouse, Aluminum, No. 201, Moore, c.1930s	770.00
Bank, Mickey Mouse, Japan, 1950s, 6 3/4 In.	250.00
Bank, Mickey Mouse, Painted, Cast Iron, No. 196, John Wright, 7 1/2 In.	105.00
Bank, Practical Pig, Saw, Ceramic, Hagen Renaker, 1950s, 6 1/2 x 3 1/2 x 4 In.	580.00
Bank, Snow White, Talking To Dwarfs, Dime Register, Tin, 1938, 3 In.	110.00
Beanie, Mickey Mouse, Theater Club, Yours Truly, Felt, 2-Tone, c.1930, 5 x 8 1/2 In.	350.00
Blotter, Snow White & Seven Dwarfs, RKO's Happy Easter Show, c.1952, 4 x 8 In.	50.00
Book, Donald Duck, Whitman, 1935	800.00
Book, Life Of Donald Duck, Cover, Random House, 1941, 72 Pages	475.00
Book, Mickey Mouse ABC Story, Whitman, 1936	450.00
Book, Mickey Mouse Story Book, McKay, 1931	600.00
Book, Pedro, Grossett & Dunlap, 1943	200.00
Book, Snow White & Seven Dwarfs, Grossett & Dunlap, 1938	275.00
Book, Snow White & Seven Dwarfs, Pop-Up, Prague, c.1960	99.00
Book, Stories From Walt Disney's Fantasia, Random House, 1940	400.00
Book, Walt Disney's Famous Seven Dwarfs, Whitman, 1938	400.00
Box, Mickey & Minnie Mouse, Underwear, Pluto, 8 1/4 x 11 1/4 x 2 In.	325.00
Box, Mickey Mouse Waddler, Cardboard, 8 In.	2750.00
Box, Mickey Mouse, Tin, Lithograph, Mickey, Minnie, Pluto On 5 Sides, 1935	395.00
Box, Pencil, Minnie Mouse, Die Cut, Cardboard, Dixon, 1930s, 8 1/2 In.	250.00
Cake Plate Set, Big Bad Wolf, Cake Plate, 12 Plates, 1930s	385.00
Candy Container, Donald Duck, In Airplane, Composition, 8 x 9 In.	990.00
Candy Container Set, Snow White & Seven Dwarfs, Box	275.00
Card, Dental Appointment, Mickey, Donald, Envelope, Unused, c.1938, 7 x 4 1/4 In.	35.00
Card, Goofy, Christmas, Story Verse, Hallmark, 1946, 6 x 5 In., 8 Pages	45.00
Card, Mickey Mouse, Bubble Gum, Gum Inc., 1935, 20 Cards	4600.00
Card, Mickey Mouse, Chums, Weekly Club, England, 1930s	1725.00
Card, Mickey Mouse, Saturday Matinee Club, Card Stock, c.1935, 4 x 4 1/2 In.	145.00
Cel, see Animation Art category.	
Clock, Alarm, Mickey Mouse, Metal, Square, Electric, Ingersoll, 1933, 4 1/2 In.	480.00
Clock, Alarm, Mickey Mouse, Red Bells, Bayard, France, c.1977, 6 In.	145.00
Clock, Alarm, Pinocchio, Bayard, Box, France, 1964, 4 3/4 x 2 x 3 1/2 In.	150.00
Clock, Pluto, Googly Eyes, Sitting, Red Dial, Plastic Resin, c.1955, 9 x 5 In.	220.00
Comic Book, Snow White & Seven Dwarfs, Dell, 1944	80.00
Creamer, Mickey & Minnie Mouse, China, Faiencerie D'Onnaing, France, 1930s, 3 In. ...	90.00
Cup, Mickey Mouse, Horace Horsecollar, Silver Plate, International Silver, c.1934, 2 In. ..	125.00
Cup & Saucer, Mickey & Minnie Mouse, Crying, Bavarian China, 1930s, 2 1/2 In.	150.00
Cup & Saucer, Mickey Mouse, Walking, Gold Trim, Bavarian China, 1930s, 2 1/2 In.	235.00
Doll, Mickey Mouse, Stuffed, Button Eyes, Toothy Grin, Dean's Rag, England, 6 In.	385.00
Doll, Mickey Mouse, Stuffed, Velvet Outfit, Silk Hands, Charlotte Clark, 12 In.	2750.00
Doll, Mickey Mouse, Stuffed, Velveteen, Dean's Rag, England, 1930s, 8 1/2 In.	250.00
Doll, Mickey Mouse, Velveteen, Charlotte Clark, c.1930, 21 1/2 x 19 x 8 In.	6565.00
Doll, Minnie Mouse, Cowgirl, Stuffed, Knickerbocker, c.1935, 16 1/2 In.	1580.00
Doll, Minnie Mouse, Stuffed, Velveteen, Dean's Rag, England, 1930s, 9 In.	350.00
Doll, Pinocchio, Jointed Wood, Kreuger, Original Tag, c.1939, 16 In.	285.00
Doll, Sleeping Beauty, Blond, Gown, No. 795, Cissette, Alexander, Box, c.1960, 10 In. ...	360.00
Doll, Snow White, Cloth, Mask Face, Original Clothes, Ideal, c.1938, 16 In.	440.00
Drum, Mickey Mouse, Wood, Paper, Noble & Cooley, 1930s, 6 1/2 In.	255.00
Drum, Mickey, Donald, Minnie, Pluto, Ohio Art, 1930s, 6 1/4 x 4 In.	230.00
Egg Holder, Mickey Mouse, Porcelain, 1930s	195.00
Figurine, Donald Duck, Composition, Movable Head, Knickerbocker, c.1935, 5 1/2 In. ...	450.00

Figurine, Donald Duck, Long Bill, Bisque, Hand Painted, Japan, 4 5/8 In. 110.00
Figurine, Dumbo, Hagen Renaker, 1950s, 3 x 4 x 3 1/2 In. 779.00
Figurine, Dumbo, Vernon Kilns, 4 3/4 x 4 3/4 In. 230.00
Figurine, Ferdinand The Bull, Seiberling Rubber Co., 1930s, 6 In. 125.00
Figurine, Jiminy Cricket, China, Beswick, 1950s, 2 x 2 1/2 x 3 3/4 In. 475.00
Figurine, Mademoiselle Upanova, Ceramic, Hagen Renaker, 1985, 4 In. 360.00
Figurine, Mickey & Minnie Mouse Fun-E-Flex, Wood, Borgfeldt, 1930s, 4 1/2 In., Pair . . . 450.00
Figurine, Mickey & Minnie Mouse Fun-E-Flex, Wood, Borgfeldt, 1930s, 7 In., Pair 765.00
Figurine, Mickey Mouse Riding Pluto, Pie-Eyed, Bisque, Japan, 1930s, 2 1/4 x 2 3/4 In. . . 60.00
Figurine, Mickey Mouse, Derby, Striped Pants, Celluloid, 4 In. 325.00
Figurine, Mickey Mouse, Hands On Waist, Cast Iron, France, 1930s, 9 x 6 1/2 In. 2977.00
Figurine, Mickey Mouse, Latex, Black, White Eyes, Red Buttons, Seiberling, 6 In. 35.00
Figurine, Mickey Mouse, Latex, White, Black Eyes, Red Shorts, Seiberling, 1930s, 6 In. . . 305.00
Figurine, Mickey Mouse, Saxophone, Celluloid, 3 In. 125.00
Figurine, Mickey Mouse, Seiberling, 1930s, 3 1/2 In. 95.00
Figurine, Mickey Mouse, Seiberling, 1930s, 6 In. 145.00
Figurine, Mickey Mouse, Sitting On Baby Rattle, Celluloid, 5 In. 325.00
Figurine, Sprite, No. 10, 1940, 4 1/2 In. 275.00
Figurine Set, Lady & Tramp Characters, Plastic, Kellogg's Rice Krispies, 1955, 12 Piece . . 166.00
Figurine Set, Snow White & Seven Dwarfs, Bisque, Borgfeldt, Box, 1930s, 8 Piece 695.00
Figurine Set, Snow White & Seven Dwarfs, Bisque, Japan, c.1938, 6 1/2 In., 8 Piece 950.00
Figurine Set, Snow White & Seven Dwarfs, Celluloid, Foreign, Box, 6 In., 8 Piece 330.00
Figurine Set, Snow White & Seven Dwarfs, Rubber, Sieberling, 1930s, 8 Piece 305.00
Flashlight, Mickey & Minnie Mouse, In Forest, 6 In. 154.00
Game, Mickey & Donald Speedway, Ideal, Box, 1950s, 6 x 19 1/4 x 8 In. 350.00
Game, Mickey Mouse Library Of Games, 6 Games, Russell Mfg., c.1940, 6 x 2 1/2 In. . . . 55.00
Game, Mickey Mouse, Party, Unused, Marks Bros., Box, 1930s, 8 x 10 In. 690.00
Game, Zorro, Parker Brothers, Box, 1966, 9 x 17 x 1 1/2 In. . . . . .45.00 to 115.00
Key Ring Display, Mickey Maus Und Donald Duck, 12 Key Rings, 11 In. 55.00
Lunch Box, Fire Fighters, Dome, Aladdin, c.1969 . . . . .50.00 to 99.00
Lunch Box, Jungle Book, Metal, No Thermos, Aladdin, c.1968 . . . . 59.00
Lunch Box, Magic Kingdom, Metal, No Thermos, Aladdin, c.1980 . . . . .17.00 to 32.00
Lunch Box, Pete's Dragon, Metal, Plastic Thermos, Aladdin, c.1978 . . . . 69.00
Lunch Box, School Bus, Dome, Metal, Aladdin, 1960s, 7 x 9 x 4 1/2 In. . . . . .50.00 to 79.00
Lunch Box, Snow White & Seven Dwarfs, 2 Swing Handles, European 193.00
Lunch Box, Snow White & Seven Dwarfs, Tin, 2 Handles, Belgium, 1930s, 8 In. 500.00
Lunch Box, Snow White, Aladdin, c.1975 . . . . 80.00
Lunch Box, Sport Goofy, Metal, No Thermos, Aladdin, 1983 . . . . 39.00
Lunch Box, Zorro, Metal, Aladdin, c.1960 . . . . 210.00
Movie Poster, Song Of The South, 1946, 1 Sheet, 27 x 41 In. 518.00
Movie Projector, Mickey Mouse, 4 Film Rolls, 11 In. 209.00
Mug, Ludwig Von Drake, RCA Victor Premium, Box, c.1961, 3 1/2 x 7 1/2 In., Pair 50.00
Music Box, Snow White, Heigh Ho, Ceramic, Enesco, 7 1/2 x 5 In. 410.00
Needle Case, Mickey Mouse Playing Saxophone, Voris Original, Germany, 1 5/8 In. 165.00
Night-Light, Donald Duck, Tin, Cardboard, Kiddy Lite, Micro-Lite Co., 1938, 2 1/2 In. . . . 405.00
Night-Light, Mickey Mouse, Tin, Cardboard, Kiddy Lite, Micro-Lite Co., 1938, 2 3/4 In. . . . 305.00
Nodder, Donald Duck, Occupied Japan, 1940s, 4 1/2 x 2 x 3 In. 460.00
Nodder, Pluto, Celluloid, Tag, 8 In. 385.00
Pail, Disney Characters, Tin Lithograph, Ohio Art, 1930s, 5 In. 275.00
Pail, Donald Duck, Angry, Nephews Playing Instruments, Tin Lithograph, 1938, 5 In. 195.00
Pail, Donald Duck, Nephews, Dumbo, Balloons, Japan, 5 1/2 x 5 1/2 In. 45.00
Pail, Donald Duck, Sailing Scene, Mickey, Minnie, Pluto, Ohio Art, 1938, 4 x 4 In. 255.00
Pail, Donald Duck, Tin Lithograph, Ohio Art, 1939, 4 In. 187.00
Pail, Mickey & Minnie Mouse, Pluto, Beach, Tin Lithograph, Ohio Art, 1930s, 4 1/2 In. . . 350.00
Pail, Mickey Mouse, Guitar, Tin Lithograph, Handle, Ohio Art, c.1930, 7 In. 1725.00
Pail, Mickey's Ice Cold Drinks, Pluto, Bail Handle, Ohio Art, 3 In. . . . . *Illus* 250.00
Paint Set, Donald Duck, Paint, 15 Posters, Box, 1937 . . . . 200.00
Pen, Snow White, Ballpoint, Blue Ink, 50th Anniversary, 1980, 6 In. 15.00
Pencil Holder, Mickey Mouse, Movable Arms, Wood, 12 Pencils, Spain, c.1930, 5 1/4 In. . . 300.00
Pencil Holder, Minnie Mouse, Miel Pot, Movable Arms, Wood, Spain, c.1930, 5 3/4 In. . . . 250.00
Pennant, Mickey Mouse, Disneyland, Felt, Red, White, c.1950, 8 3/4 x 4 In. 25.00
Photograph, Walt Disney, Autographed, Inscription, Black & White, 10 x 8 In. 2590.00
Pin, Bambi, Donald Duck's Peanut Butter, Lithograph, 1950s, 3/4 In. 35.00

Disneyana, Pail, Mickey's
Ice Cold Drinks,
Pluto, Bail Handle,
Ohio Art, 3 In.

Disneyana, Toy, Donald Duck,
Xylophone, Pull Toy,
Fisher-Price, 1946-52, 13 In.

Pin, Donald Duck, Donald Duck's Peanut Butter, Lithograph, 1950s, 3/4 In. 56.00
Pin, Mickey Mouse, Follow My Adventures, Buy Buttercup, 12 Cent Loaf, 1 1/4 In. 130.00
Pin, Snow White, Donald Duck's Peanut Butter, Lithograph, 1950s, 3/4 In. 45.00
Pincushion, Mickey Mouse, Holding Red Velvet Cushion, Bisque, Japan, 3 In. 55.00
Placecard Holder, Mickey Mouse, Stringed Instrument, Celluloid, Japan, 1930s, 2 1/4 In. .   175.00
Plate, Mickey Mouse, Enameled, 6 In. 165.00
Plate, Mickey Mouse, Uniform, Holding Gun, Bicentennial, Schmid, 1976, 7 1/2 In. 24.00
Plate, Snow White & Seven Dwarfs, Mother's Day, Schmid, Box, c.1975, 7 1/2 In. 45.00
Playset, Complete Disneyland, No. 4368, Marx, Box 770.00
Playset, Walt Disney's Television Playhouse, No. 3349, Marx, Box 440.00
Poster, Pluto, Sleep Walker, Paper, 31 In. 385.00
Proof Sheet, Donald Duck, Holding Glasses, Juice, 1950s, 14 x 7 1/4 In. 100.00
Puppet, Mickey Mouse, Hand, Cloth, Felt, Steiff, 9 In. 550.00
Puzzle, Snow White, 2 Puzzles, Box, 1938 . . . .   75.00
Radio, Mickey Mouse, Cutout, Wood, Glass Panel, Argentina, 1930s, 8 3/4 x 13 In. 1323.00
Radio, Mickey Mouse, Playing Bass, Wood, Emerson, 1930s, 7 x 5 In. . . . . .1654.00 to 1760.00
Radio, Snow White & Seven Dwarfs, Wood, Lamp, Emerson, c.1935, 7 x 8 In. 3075.00
Ring, Mickey Mouse, Brass, Enamel, 1930s, Child's 40.00
Roller Skates, Mouseketeer, Tin, Ball Bearing, Key, 1950s 70.00
Rug, Donald Duck, Carrying Buckets, Chipmunks, Cotton, Fringed Ends, 21 x 34 In. 66.00
Rug, Goofy, On Go Cart, Rabbit, Fabric, Multicolored, 1950s, 21 x 41 In. 90.00
Rug, Goofy, On Go-Cart Heading Toward A Rabbit, Multicolored Fabric, 1950 . . . .   90.00
Salt & Pepper, Alice In Wonderland, Ceramic, 4 3/4 In. 248.00
Salt & Pepper, Pinocchio, 4 3/4 In. 66.00
Scissors, Mickey Mouse, Tin Lithograph, 2-Sided, WDE, 1937, 3 In. 355.00
Shoehorn, Mickey Mouse, Metal, Spain, 1930s, 4 In. 230.00
Sign, Donald Duck Cola, Paperboard, 26 x 22 In. 650.00
Sign, Mickey Mouse, Saylor's Bread, Cardboard, 1930s, 18 x 12 In. 100.00
Silverware Caddy, Mickey Mouse, Cardboard, Wheels, Rogers & Son, 1930s, 5 x 5 1/2 In.   317.00
Sticker, Mickey Mouse, Kay Kamen Incorporated, On Paper, 2 1/2 In. 75.00
Submarine, Nautilus, 20,000 Leagues Under The Sea, Tin, Box, 10 In. 185.00
Tape Measure, Elmer Elephant, Boxing Gloves, Celluloid, Japan, 1930s, 2 3/8 In. 275.00
Tea Set, Nursery Rhymes, Wade Heath, England, 1930s, 9 Piece 400.00
Teapot, Mary Poppins, Musical, Chim Chim Cheree, Enesco, c.1964, 6 1/2 x 5 1/2 In. 120.00
Tin, Donald Duck, Handles, Australia, 1950s, 5 1/2 x 8 1/2 x 3 1/2 In. 351.00
Tin, Snow White & Seven Dwarfs, Biscuit, Belgium, 1930s, 13 In. 330.00
Tin, Snow White & Seven Dwarfs, Candy, European, 7 In. 80.00
Tin, Snow White & Seven Dwarfs, In Woods, 1939, 12 x 8 x 3 In. 185.00
Toothbrush Holder, 3 Little Pigs, Bisque, Japan, 1930s, 2 x 4 x 3 1/4 In. 150.00
Toothbrush Holder, Donald Duck, Twins, Long Bill, Bisque, Japan, 1930s, 4 x 5 In. 410.00
Toothbrush Holder, Mickey & Minnie Mouse, Bisque, Japan, 1930s, 4 1/2 In. . . . . .170.00 to 275.00
Toothbrush Holder, Mickey Mouse, Wiping Pluto's Nose, Bisque, Japan, 1930s 350.00
Toothbrush Set, Snow White & Seven Dwarfs, S. Maw & Sons, England 1430.00
Toy, 3 Little Pigs & Big Bad Wolf, Metal, Lithograph, Animated, Linemar, 1950, 4 Piece . .   800.00
Toy, 3 Little Pigs Acrobat, Celluloid, Tin, Windup, Japan, Box, 10 In. 1320.00
Toy, 3 Little Pigs, Bisque, Box, 3 1/2-In. Figures, 3 Piece 625.00
Toy, Airplane, Tin, 4 Engines, Linemar, 7 1/2 x 6 In. 275.00

Toy, Car, Parade Roadster, Tin Lithograph, Spring Wind Motor, Marx, Box, 11 In. 825.00
Toy, Car, Television, Tin Lithograph, Friction, Marx, Box, 7 1/2 In. 825.00
Toy, Cinderella, Railcar, Gus & Jaq, Tin, Windup, Wells, Box, 12 x 14 In. 2750.00
Toy, Disneyland, Ferris Wheel, Tin Lithograph, Windup, Chein, 17 In. 250.00
Toy, Disneyland, Ferris Wheel, Tin Lithograph, Windup, Chein, Box, 17 In. ....425.00 to 770.00
Toy, Disneyland, Jeep, Tin Lithograph, Marx, Japan, 1960s, 9 1/2 In. 105.00
Toy, Donald Duck & Goofy, Dancing, On Drums, Tin Lithograph, Marx, 1946, 10 In. 118.00
Toy, Donald Duck & Nephews, Pull Toy, Fisher-Price, 12 In. 275.00
Toy, Donald Duck, Acrobat, Celluloid, Gym-Toys, Windup, Linemar, Box, 12 In. 385.00
Toy, Donald Duck, Animated, Plastic, Windup, Mavco, Box, Postwar, 6 1/2 In. 195.00
Toy, Donald Duck, Car, Flivver, Linemar, 6 In. 250.00
Toy, Donald Duck, Cart, Wings, Pull Toy, Fisher-Price, 1937, 10 In. 990.00
Toy, Donald Duck, Chick Cart, Pull Toy, Fisher-Price, 10 In. 1100.00
Toy, Donald Duck, Choo Choo, Wood, Paper Lithograph, Fisher-Price, 1942, 8 1/2 In. 140.00
Toy, Donald Duck, Doughboy, Pluto, Pull Toy, Fisher-Price, 1942, 13 3/4 In. 990.00
Toy, Donald Duck, Drummer, Plastic, Tin, Windup, Marx, Box, 10 In. 385.00
Toy, Donald Duck, Drummer, Tin, Windup, Linemar, Postwar, 5 1/2 In. 220.00
Toy, Donald Duck, Duet, Goofy, Tin Lithograph, Windup, Marx, 1946, 10 1/2 In. 468.00
Toy, Donald Duck, Duet, Goofy, Tin Lithograph, Windup, Marx, Box, 1946, 10 1/2 In. 685.00
Toy, Donald Duck, Fireman, Climbing, Engine, Linemar, Box, 18 In. 1980.00
Toy, Donald Duck, Fireman, Climbing, Tin Lithograph, Windup, Linemar, 14 In. 240.00
Toy, Donald Duck, Mouth Opens, Metal, Plastic, Windup, Schuco, Box, 1950s 450.00
Toy, Donald Duck, Pulling Minnie Mouse, Celluloid, Tin, Windup, Japan, 6 In. 4675.00
Toy, Donald Duck, Pushing Cart, Pull Toy, 9 x 10 In. 250.00
Toy, Donald Duck, Straight Shooter, Tin, Plastic, Windup, 1950s, 6 In. 275.00
Toy, Donald Duck, Talking, Pull Toy, No. 765, Fisher-Price, Box, c.1955, 8 In. 385.00
Toy, Donald Duck, Tricycle, Celluloid, Japan, Prewar, 4 In. 220.00
Toy, Donald Duck, Tricycle, Celluloid, Paradise Novelty, Japan, Box, Prewar, 6 In. 770.00
Toy, Donald Duck, Umbrella Twirling Overhead, Celluloid, Windup, 1930s, 10 In. 1400.00
Toy, Donald Duck, Whirligig, Celluloid, Red Canopy, Windup, Japan, 10 1/2 In. 3300.00
Toy, Donald Duck, Xylophone, Pull Toy, Fisher-Price, 1946-52, 13 In. .... *Illus* 330.00
Toy, Donald Duck, Xylophone, Pull Toy, Profile, Fisher-Price, 1938-43, 13 In. 550.00
Toy, Dopey & Doc, Hammering Drum, Pull Toy, Fisher-Price, 1938, 12 In. 1540.00
Toy, Dopey, Tin Lithograph, Windup, Marx, Box, 8 In. 550.00
Toy, Goofy, Car, Stock, Tin, Friction, Linemar, 6 In. 220.00
Toy, Goofy, Tricycle, Tin, Lithograph, Windup, Linemar, Box, 4 x 4 In. 680.00
Toy, Goofy, Unicycle, Rubber Ears, Original Paper Label, Linemar, 1950s 685.00
Toy, Goofy, Whirling Tail, Tin, Windup, Linemar, 5 In. 220.00
Toy, Ludwig Von Drake, Go-Cart, Tin, Friction, Vinyl Head, Linemar, 6 In. 220.00
Toy, Mickey & Minnie Mouse, Acrobats, Box, 1930s, 11 x 11 In. 1980.00
Toy, Mickey & Minnie Mouse, Donald Duck, Acrobat, Borgfeldt, Box, Japan, 10 In. 3850.00
Toy, Mickey & Minnie Mouse, Handcar, Composition, Steel, Lionel, 1930s, 9 In. ...495.00 to 700.00
Toy, Mickey & Minnie Mouse, Handcar, Plastic, Windup, Marx, Box 550.00
Toy, Mickey & Minnie Mouse, Handcar, Tin, Windup, Wells, Box, 1930s 1540.00
Toy, Mickey & Minnie Mouse, Piano, Wood, Animated, Marks Bros., 1930s, 10 In. 904.00
Toy, Mickey & Minnie Mouse, Shovel, Tin, Wood Handle, Ohio Art, 1930s, 5 x 15 In. 220.00
Toy, Mickey & Minnie Mouse, Tambourine, Tin, Paper, Noble & Cooley, 1930s, 9 In. 283.00
Toy, Mickey & Minnie Mouse, Trapeze, Celluloid, Windup, G. Borgfeldt 630.00
Toy, Mickey Mouse & Donald Duck, Handcar, Tin, Windup, Wells, Box, 1930s 2750.00
Toy, Mickey Mouse & Pluto, Cyclist, Celluloid, Tin, Windup, Borgfeldt, Box, 8 In. 6325.00
Toy, Mickey Mouse Club, Tambourine, Paper, Tin Lithograph, Red, White, 7 In. 66.00
Toy, Mickey Mouse, Acrobat, Fun-E-Flex, 4 1/2 In. 360.00
Toy, Mickey Mouse, Bubble Bluster, Gun, Kilgore, c.1935, 8 In. 90.00
Toy, Mickey Mouse, Car, Dipsy, Tin Lithograph, Windup, Marx, Box, 6 In. 495.00
Toy, Mickey Mouse, Car, Dipsy, Tin, Windup, Linemar, Box 775.00
Toy, Mickey Mouse, Car, Racing, Metal, Key Wind, c.1930, 4 x 4 In. 585.00
Toy, Mickey Mouse, Choo Choo, No. 485, Fisher-Price, c.1949, 8 1/4 x 7 In. 140.00
Toy, Mickey Mouse, Climbing, Dolly Toy Co., Box, 9 In. 415.00
Toy, Mickey Mouse, Drummer, Paper Lithograph, Fisher-Price, c.1941, 9 In. 248.00
Toy, Mickey Mouse, Drummer, Tin Lithograph, Battery Operated, Linemar, 11 In. 880.00
Toy, Mickey Mouse, Drummer, Tin, Silk Screened, Windup, c.1930, 7 x 3 In. 2930.00
Toy, Mickey Mouse, Drumming, Battery Operated, Remote Control, Linemar, Box, 11 In. . 1695.00
Toy, Mickey Mouse, Fire Department, Rubber, Viceroy Sunruco, Canada, 6 1/2 In. 110.00

Toy, Mickey Mouse, Handcar, Composition, Tin, Windup, Lionel, Box, 1930s, 8 x 6 In. ... 1760.00
Toy, Mickey Mouse, Magician, Battery Operated, Linemar, Box, 10 In. ....1320.00 to 1350.00
Toy, Mickey Mouse, Magician, Battery Operated, Linemar, Japan, 10 In. 660.00
Toy, Mickey Mouse, Melody Railroad, Tin, Plastic, Battery Operated, Box, 7 In. 165.00
Toy, Mickey Mouse, Ride 'Em, Wood, 31 In. 275.00
Toy, Mickey Mouse, Roller Coaster, Fun House, Tin, Windup, Chein, Box, 19 x 8 In. 1045.00
Toy, Mickey Mouse, Roller Skater, Windup, Linemar, Box, 6 1/4 In. ....1850.00 to 3575.00
Toy, Mickey Mouse, Safety Patrol, Paper Lithograph, No. 733, Fisher-Price, Box, 1955 ... 330.00
Toy, Mickey Mouse, Sand Set, Watering Can, Shovel, Sand Pail, Ohio Art, Box 1276.00
Toy, Mickey Mouse, Telephone, Tin Lithograph, Yellow, c.1950, 4 x 8 x 8 In. 220.00
Toy, Mickey Mouse, Top, Tin, Ohio Art, 9 In. 220.00
Toy, Mickey Mouse, Train Set, Circus, Metal, Windup, Lionel, 1930s, 13 Piece 2000.00
Toy, Mickey Mouse, Train, Circus, 3 Cars, Tin, Windup, Wells, Box, 17 x 19 In. 6050.00
Toy, Mickey Mouse, Train, Express, 5 Cars, Tin Lithograph, Windup, Marx, 16 In. ..275.00 to 350.00
Toy, Mickey Mouse, Train, Express, Tin, Windup, Marx, Box 2200.00
Toy, Mickey Mouse, Train, Meteor, 5 Cars, Tin Lithograph, Windup, Marx, 43 In. ..565.00 to 715.00
Toy, Mickey Mouse, Train, Meteor, Engine, 3 Cars, Windup, Marx, 33 In. 775.00
Toy, Mickey Mouse, Trapeze, Celluloid, Metal, Windup, 3-In. Figure 410.00
Toy, Mickey Mouse, Twirling Tail, Plastic, Wire Tail, Windup, Marx, Box, 6 1/2 In. 140.00
Toy, Mickey Mouse, Walker, Celluloid, Windup, 7 1/2 In. 550.00
Toy, Mickey Mouse, Washing Machine, Crank, Agitator, Tin Lithograph, 1930s, 7 1/2 In. ... 978.00
Toy, Mickey Mouse, Xylophone, Tin, Windup, Linemar, 6 In. 440.00
Toy, Mickey The Magician, Raises Hat, Chick Disappears, Tin, Linemar, Box, 10 In. 1350.00
Toy, Minnie Mouse, Holding Nurse Kit, 3 1/4 In. 125.00
Toy, Minnie Mouse, Rocking Chair, Tin, Windup, Box, 6 1/2 In. 660.00
Toy, Minnie Mouse, Rocking Chair, Tin, Windup, Linemar, 1950s, 6 3/4 In. ....375.00 to 495.00
Toy, Oswald The Rabbit, Tin Stroller, 6 In. 250.00
Toy, Pinocchio, Acrobat, Windup, Marx, 1939 .... 450.00
Toy, Pinocchio, Express, Pull Toy, Fisher-Price, c.1940, 10 In. 1210.00
Toy, Pinocchio, Plucky, On Donkey, Wood, Pull Toy, Fisher-Price, 1939, 8 1/2 In. 525.00
Toy, Pinocchio, Waddles Back & Forth While His Eyes Move, Marx, Windup, Box 575.00
Toy, Pinocchio, Walker, Composition, Windup, France, 8 In. 275.00
Toy, Pinocchio, Walker, Moving Eyes, Tin Lithograph, Windup, Marx, 8 1/2 In. 275.00
Toy, Pinocchio, Walker, Moving Eyes, Tin Lithograph, Windup, Marx, Box, 8 1/2 In. 413.00
Toy, Pluto & Goofy, Tin Lithograph, Windup, Mechanical, Linemar, Box, 6 In. 2200.00
Toy, Pluto, Drum Major, Plastic, Windup, Marx, Postwar, 10 1/2 In. 185.00
Toy, Pluto, Fire Truck, Donald Duck, Nephews, Mickey Mouse, Tin, Linemar, 18 In. 990.00
Toy, Pluto, Musical, Animated, Bells, Horn, Metal, Lithograph, Marx, 6 x 3 x 5 In. 365.00
Toy, Pluto, Pull Toy, Wood, Painted, 11 1/2 In. 70.00
Toy, Pluto, Pull Toy, Wood, Paper Lithograph, Chad Valley, England, 11 1/2 In. 510.00
Toy, Pluto, Roll Over, Tin Lithograph, Windup, Marx, Box, 1939, 9 In. 515.00
Toy, Pluto, Roll Over, Tin Lithograph, Windup, Marx, c.1940, 9 In. ....110.00 to 395.00
Toy, Pluto, Roll Over, Tin, Rubber Ears, 1930s 395.00
Toy, Pluto, Standing On Paddle, Moves, Wood, Lacquered, Fisher-Price, c.1950, 5 x 11 In. . 220.00
Toy, Pluto, Tin, Windup, Whirling Tail, New Ears, Linemar, 5 In. 605.00
Toy, Pluto, Unicycle, Tin Lithograph, Windup, Linemar, Box, 5 1/2 In. 1210.00
Toy, Professor Von Drake, Tin, Walker, Windup, Linemar, 6 In. 200.00
Toy, Roller Coaster, Tin Lithograph, Windup, Chein, 19 In. 155.00
Toy, Ship, Plastic, 8 Polyethylene Characters, Ideal, Box, 14 In. 330.00
Toy, Snow White & Seven Dwarfs, Roly Poly, Celluloid, Disney Authorized, Dutch, 2 In. . 575.00
Toy, Television, Plastic, Windup, Automatic Toy Co., Box, 5 In. 45.00
Toy, Truck, Moving, Club Logo, Tin Lithograph, Friction, Linemar, 4 1/4 x 12 1/2 In. 506.00
Toy, Water Pistol, Donald Duck 50.00
Toy, Zorro, Sergeant Garcia, Vinyl, Kestral, c.1958, 35 x 16 In. 140.00
Travel Bag, Zorro, On Tornado, Town, Blue, Vinyl, Zipper, Handles, c.1958, 7 x 12 In. 125.00
Tricycle, Mickey Mouse, Velocipede, Steel, Colson, 1934, 27 x 18 x 34 In. ......1840.00 to 4400.00
Tumbler, Donald Duck, Goofy, Antarctic Trip, 1942, 4 3/8 In. 115.00
Tumbler, Donald Duck, Scoutmaster, Donna Duck, All Star Parade, 1939, 4 3/8 In. 60.00
Tumbler Set, Snow White & Seven Dwarfs, 1938, 4 In., 8 Piece 1200.00
Underwear, Mickey Mouse, Playing Drum, Unopened, 1930s, 5 x 7 3/4 In. 265.00
View-Master Set, Zorro, 3 Reels, Booklet, Envelope, 1958, 4 1/2 In. 45.00
Warming Plate, Donald Duck, 6 In. 70.00
Watch, Pocket, Mickey Mouse, Ingersoll, Insert, Box, c.1940 .... 770.00

Watering Can, Tin Lithograph, Blue Body, Yellow Spout, 3 In. 209.00
Window Display, Dopey, Head Nods, Composition, Papier-Mache, Electric, 24 In. 550.00
Wristwatch, Bambi, Chrome, Animated Ears, Ingersoll, 20th Birthday Box 310.00
Wristwatch, Big Bad Wolf, Pigs, Chrome Case, Pigs Bracelet, Ingersoll, 1934 .... 700.00
Wristwatch, Cinderella, Chrome, Pink Band, U.S. Time, Slipper Box, 1950 .... 400.00
Wristwatch, Cinderella, U.S. Time, Round Box, c.1950 .... 175.00
Wristwatch, Daisy Duck, Chromed Metal, Vinyl Over Leather, U.S. Time, c.1947 .... 320.00
Wristwatch, Donald Duck, Chrome, Blue Vinyl Band, U.S. Time, Box, 1947 .... 820.00
Wristwatch, Goofy, Chrome, 17 Jewel, Runs Backward, Helbros, Box, 1972 .... 765.00
Wristwatch, Mickey Mouse, Black Leather Band, Ingersoll, Box, 1939 .... 914.00
Wristwatch, Mickey Mouse, Gold Plated Case, Leather Band, Ingersoll, Box, 1938 ...... 932.00
Wristwatch, Mickey Mouse, Red Band, Ingersoll, Box, c.1940 .... 80.00
Wristwatch, Pinocchio, Chrome, Luminous Dial, Ingersoll, 20th Birthday Box 509.00
Zorro Set, Black Mask, Ring, Whip & Lariat, 1958 .... 335.00

DOCTOR, see Dental; Medical

DOLL entries are listed by marks printed or incised on the doll, if possible. If there are no marks, the doll is listed by the name of the subject or country or maker. Notice that Barbie is listed under Mattel. G.I. Joe figures are listed in the Toy section. Eskimo dolls are listed in the Eskimo section and Indian dolls are listed in the Indian section. Doll clothes and accessories are listed at the end of this section. The twentieth-century clothes listed here are in mint condition.

A.M., 200, Bisque, Closed Mouth, Googly Eyes, 5-Piece Body, Bunny Suit, 1925, 9 In. ... 950.00
A.M., 248, Bisque Socket Head, Blue Glass Eyes, 5-Piece Composition Body, 11 In. 520.00
A.M., 253, Bisque Socket Head, Googly, 5-Piece Composition Body, c.1925, 6 In. 715.00
A.M., 320, Bisque Socket Head, Googly, 5-Piece Composition Body, c.1925, 10 In. 1155.00
A.M., 323, Bisque Socket Head, Googly Sleep Eyes, 5-Piece Composition Body, 7 In. 385.00
A.M., 323, Googly, Bisque Socket Head, Glass Sleep Eyes, c.1920, 10 In. 1510.00
A.M., 341, Dream Baby, Bisque Flange Head, Blue Sleep Eyes, Cloth Body, 15 In. 95.00
A.M., 341, Dream Baby, Bisque Flange Head, Sleep Eyes, Cloth Body, 16 In. 84.00
A.M., 341, Dream Baby, Bisque Socket Head, Sleep Eyes, Composition Body, 14 In. 358.00
A.M., 341, Dream Baby, Bisque Socket Head, Solid Dome, Composition Body, 18 In. 165.00
A.M., 341, Dream Baby, Bisque Socket Head, Composition Body, 8 In. 84.00
A.M., 345, Bisque Socket Head, Intaglio Eyes, Composition, Wood, c.1910, 10 In. 2200.00
A.M., 351, Black Solid Dome Socket Head, Composition Body, Dressed 303.00
A.M., 353, Bisque Socket Head, Sleep Eyes, Painted, Asian, Composition, Toddler, 10 In. . 358.00
A.M., 370, Bisque Shoulder Head, Blue Sleep Eyes, Riveted Kid Body, Box, 25 In. 275.00
A.M., 370, Bisque Shoulder Head, Blue Sleep Eyes, Kidolene Body, Bisque Hands, 17 In. . 120.00
A.M., 370, Bisque Shoulder Head, Glass Eyes, Open Mouth, Kid Body, 20 In. 176.00
A.M., 370, Bisque Shoulder Head, Sleep Eyes, Open Mouth, Kid Body, 21 In. 154.00
A.M., 372, Kiddiejoy, Bisque Head, Brown Eyes, Kid Body, Bisque Arms, Gussets, 21 In. . 440.00
A.M., 390, Bisque Head, Blue Eyes, Mohair Wig, Composition, Ethnic Clothing, 8 In. 140.00
A.M., 390, Bisque Head, Mohair Wig, Wood, Composition, Jointed, 18 In. 275.00
A.M., 390, Bisque Socket Head, Glass Eyes, Open Mouth, Composition, Flapper, 7 In. 80.00
A.M., 390, Bisque Socket Head, Paperweight Set Eyes, 5-Piece Body, 8 In. 85.00
A.M., 390, Bisque Socket Head, Set Brown Eyes, Wood, Composition, Jointed, 19 In. 330.00
A.M., 390, Bisque Socket Head, Sleep Eyes, 5-Piece Composition Body, 14 In. 85.00
A.M., 390, Bisque Socket Head, Sleep Eyes, Composition, Ball-Jointed, 25 In. 140.00
A.M., 390, Bisque Socket Head, Sleep Eyes, Open Mouth, Composition, Jointed, 21 In. ... 275.00
A.M., 518, Bisque Socket Head, Solid Dome, Sleep Eyes, Composition Body, 12 In. 220.00
A.M., 550, Bisque Socket Head, Blue Glass Sleep Eyes, c.1915, 15 In. 1680.00
A.M., 560, Bisque Head, Sleep Eyes, Open Mouth, Composition Body, Baby, 17 In. 155.00
A.M., 590, Bisque Socket Head, Blue Sleep Eyes, 5-Piece Composition Body, 8 In. 135.00
A.M., 985, Bisque Head, Sleep Eyes, Lashes, Open Mouth, Teeth, Composition, 12 x 18 In. 176.00
A.M., 985, Bisque Socket Head, Sleep Eyes, Composition, Bent Limbs, c.1920, 15 In. 605.00
A.M., 996, Bisque Head, Sleep Eyes, Composition Baby Body, 23 In. 358.00
A.M., 1894, Bisque Head, Glass Paperweight Eyes, Composition Body, Jointed, 15 In. 550.00
A.M., 1894, Bisque Head, Sleep Eyes, Open Mouth, Wig, Composition Body, 18 In. 120.00
A.M., 1894, Bisque Socket Head, Sleep Eyes, Blond Mohair, Composition, Wood, 17 In. .. 120.00
A.M., Baby Gloria, Bisque Solid Dome Head, Sleep Eyes, Cloth Body, Disk Joints, 13 In. . 440.00
A.M., Baby Phyllis, Bisque Flange Head, Blue Sleep Eyes, Cloth Body, 12 In. 336.00
A.M., Baby Phyllis, Bisque Head, Cloth Body, 8 1/2-In. Head 135.00

A.M., Bisque Head, Blue Eyes, Composition Jointed Arms, Legs, 15 In. 70.00
A.M., Bisque Head, Composition Jointed Legs, Arms, 7 In. 59.00
A.M., Bisque Head, Mohair Wig, Jointed Wood, Brown Composition Body, 12 1/2 In. 385.00
A.M., Bisque Head, Movable Eyes, Composition Arms, Legs, 23 In. 88.00
A.M., Bisque Shoulder Head, Sleep Eyes, Open Mouth, Mohair Wig, 20 In. 220.00
A.M., Bisque Socket Head, Blue Sleep Eyes, Button Nose, Mohair, 5-Piece Body, 8 In. 2310.00
A.M., Dream Baby, Bisque Flange Head, Sleep Eyes, Cloth Body, 11 In. 210.00
A.M., Florodora, Bisque Socket Head, Sleep Eyes, 5-Piece Body, Toddler, 13 In. 84.00
A.M., Just Me, Bisque Socket Head, Blue Eyes, Button Nose, Closed Mouth, 10 In. 5150.00
A.M., Just Me, Bisque Socket Head, Glass Sleep Eyes, Mohair Braids, c.1928, 7 In. 1900.00
A.M., Just Me, Bisque Socket Head, Googly Eyes, Composition Body, 7 1/2 In. 330.00
A.M., Just Me, Bisque Socket Head, Mohair Wig, 5-Piece Body, Toddler, c.1925, 10 In. . . .   2420.00
A.M., Lily, Bisque Shoulder Head, Paperweight Eyes, Kidolene Body, 12 In. 22.00
A.M., Lily, Bisque Shoulder Head, Paperweight Eyes, Rivets, Kidolene, 25 In. 100.00
A.M., Queen Louise, Bisque Head, Sleep Eyes, Open Mouth, Composition, 25 In. 130.00
Advertising, Kellogg's, Little Bo Peep, Cloth, Uncut, c.1928, 15 x 13 In. 99.00
Advertising, Nestle, Little Hans, Cloth, Stuffed, 1970, 13 In. 50.00
Advertising, Sweetheart Soap, Composition, Kicks, Waves, Turns Head, 1950s 770.00
Advertising, Tastykake Bakery, Cloth, Shirt, Pants, Apron, Baker's Hat, 1974, 13 In. 14.00
Advertising, Uneeda, Dollikin, Vinyl Socket Head, Curly Hair, Flapper, c.1960, 19 In. 330.00
Advertising, Uneeda, Dollikin, Vinyl Socket Head, Sleep Eyes, Ballerina, c.1960, 19 In. . .   415.00
Advertising, Uneeda, Mommy Dollikin & Baby, Vinyl Socket Head, Box, c.1960, 19 In. . .   415.00
Alexander dolls are listed in this category under Madame Alexander.
Alt Beck & Gottschalck, 698, Bisque Shoulder Head, Sleep Eyes, Mohair, Kid, 16 In. 330.00
Alt Beck & Gottschalck, 890, Bisque Shoulder Head, Sculpted Hair, Muslin, 1885, 21 In. .   990.00
Alt Beck & Gottschalck, 911, Bisque Head, Pierced Ears, Mohair, Composition, 16 In. . . .   825.00
Alt Beck & Gottschalck, 911, Bisque Socket Head, Paperweight Eyes, Cloth Body, 23 In. .   525.00
Alt Beck & Gottschalck, 911, Bisque Socket Head, Paperweight Eyes, Kid, 13 1/2 In. 390.00
Alt Beck & Gottschalck, 990, Bisque Shoulder Head, Muslin Body, c.1885, 16 In. 990.00
Alt Beck & Gottschalck, 1000, China Head, Hair, Cloth Body, 17 1/2 In. 700.00
Alt Beck & Gottschalck, 1034, Bisque Shoulder Head, Sculpted, Kid Body, c.1885, 13 In. .   1430.00
Alt Beck & Gottschalck, 1260, Bisque, Human Hair, Cloth Body, Bisque Limbs, 19 In. . . .   180.00
Alt Beck & Gottschalck, 1352, Bisque Socket Head, Sleep Eyes, Composition, 25 In. 468.00
Alt Beck & Gottschalck, 1361, Bisque Head, Sleep Eyes, Voice Box, Composition, 23 In. .   440.00
Alt Beck & Gottschalck, Bisque Head, Muslin, Scarf, Costume, c.1885, 17 In. . . . . . . *Illus*   1375.00
Amberg, Newborn Babe Twins, Bisque, Blue Sleep Eyes, Cloth Bodies, Squeakers, 1914 . .   500.00
American Character, Annie Oakley, Leather Outfit, Cast Iron Gun, Lasso, c.1950s, 8 In. . .   28.00
American Character, Betsy McCall, Vinyl Socket Head, Sleep Eyes, Gown, c.1958, 24 In.   358.00
American Character, Sweet Sue, Plastic, Sleep Eyes, Vinyl Arms, Box, 18 In. 440.00
American Character, Sweet Sue, Plastic, Sleep Eyes, Walker, Box, c.1955, 18 In. 248.00
American Character, Tressy, Blond, Hair Grows, Booklet, Stand, Box 110.00
American Character, Tressy, Brunette, Hair Grows, Booklet, Stand, Box 130.00
Armand Marseille dolls are listed in this category under A.M.
Arranbee, Cinderella, Plastic Socket Head, Blue Sleep Eyes, Blond, 1952, 20 In. 358.00
Arranbee, Composition, Green Eyes, Human Hair, Gown, Fur Stole, c.1937, 18 In. 470.00
Arranbee, Composition, Sleep Eyes, Human Hair, Dress, Jacket, Hat, c.1940, 17 In. 715.00
Arranbee, Composition, Socket Head, Brown Sleep Eyes, c.1938, 18 In. 560.00
Arranbee, Composition, Socket Head, Human Hair, 5-Piece Body, Child, c.1940, 20 In. . . .   250.00
Arranbee, Debu'teen, Skating, Composition, Blue Sleep Eyes, Human Hair Wig, 18 In. 330.00
Arranbee, Nancy Lee, Plastic, Socket Head, Blue Sleep Eyes, Blond, c.1952, 20 In. 880.00
Arranbee, Nancy Lee, Plastic, Socket Head, Blue Sleep Eyes, Dress, c.1952, 17 In. 578.00
Arranbee, Nancy Lee, Plastic, Socket Head, Blue Sleep Eyes, Fleeced Hair, c.1952, 20 In. .   660.00
Arranbee, Nancy, Composition, Socket Head, Sleep Eyes, Sailor Clothes, c.1940, 19 In. . . .   670.00
Arranbee, Pirate, Composition Socket Head, Sculpted Hair, Closed Mouth, c.1940, 9 In. . .   275.00
Automaton, 2 Musicians, Cello, Bisque, Papier-Mache, Squeeze Box, Hand Crank, 12 In. .   1555.00
Automaton, 5 Musicians, Dancers, Bisque, Wood Base, Musical, Germany, 16 In. 2034.00
Automaton, Artist With Palette, Brush, Turns Head, Paints, Decamps, c.1900, 18 In. 3190.00
Automaton, Baby, Composition, Limbs, Head, Eyes Move, Wood Box, Electric, 20 x 26 In.   480.00
Automaton, Ballerina, Sways, Raises Leg, Turns Head, Twirls, Simon & Halbig, 19 In. . . .   3740.00
Automaton, Bear & Drummer, France, 10 In. 2200.00
Automaton, Bird In Cage, Flutters, Beak Opens, Chirps, Windup, Bontems, c.1880, 20 In.   3520.00
Automaton, Bird Singing, Leather Travel Case, c.1890 . . . .   4025.00
Automaton, Birds In Cage, Head, Feathers Up, Down, Beak Opens, Bontems, 1880, 21 In.   6325.00

Doll, Alt Beck & Gottschalck,
Bisque Head, Muslin, Scarf,
Costume, c.1885, 17 In.

Doll, Automaton, Birds In
Gilded Cage, Chirps, Flowers &
Leaves, 4 Movements, 21 In.

Doll, Automaton, Little Red
Riding Hood, Bisque, 2 Tunes,
Roullet & Decamps, 25 In.

Automaton, Birds In Gilded Cage, Chirps, Flowers & Leaves, 4 Movements, 21 In. . . *Illus*   6325.00
Automaton, Black Man Playing Banjo, Vichy 9075.00
Automaton, Black Smoker, Blows Cigarette Smoke, French Courtier Dress, 17 In. 4800.00
Automaton, Black Smoker, Blows Cigarette Smoke, Turns Head, Bisque, Lambert, 20 In. . . 5750.00
Automaton, Boy, Turns Head To Side, Plays Violin, 2 Tunes, Decamps, c.1900, 18 In. 4400.00
Automaton, Butterfly Catcher, Turns Head, Raises Net, Bisque, 2 Tunes, Lambert, 20 In. . 8625.00
Automaton, Chef, Strikes Copper Saucepan, Turns Head, Bisque Head, Lambert, 16 In. . . 4715.00
Automaton, Child At Piano, Hands Play, Turns Head, Bisque Head, Glass Eyes, 7 1/2 In. . 750.00
Automaton, Chinese Man, Urn, Lid Opens, Raises Arm, Cup To Mouth, 13 In. 6325.00
Automaton, Country Woman, Bird, Basket, Lid Opens, Chick, G. Vichy, 1885, 24 In. 9900.00
Automaton, Dancer On Tightrope, Moves, Balances On Toe, Twirls, c.1910, 18 In. 5060.00
Automaton, Dancing Children, Twirl, Mohair Wigs, Wood, 2 Tunes, c.1880, 16 In. 4950.00
Automaton, Dancing School, Musicians, Dancers, Plays Piano, Violin, c.1880, 25 In. 4400.00
Automaton, Drunkard, Pours Drink, Rolls Eyes, Jaw Opens, Papier-Mache, 26 In. 2415.00
Automaton, Ethiopian Harpist, Black, Head Moves, Strums Harp, Roullet, c.1867, 28 In. . 9900.00
Automaton, Girl, Beats Drum, Clangs Cymbals, Head Turns, Decamps, c.1900, 20 In. 5940.00
Automaton, Girl, Birdcage, Turns Head, Taps, Offers Cherries, Lambert, c.1890, 20 In. . . . 9900.00
Automaton, Girl, Dancer, Twirls, Head, Arms Move, 2 Tunes, Lambert, c.1910, 23 In. 4840.00
Automaton, Girl, Fan, Hankie, Turns, Nods Head, Dabs Face, Lambert, c.1895, 20 In. 5500.00
Automaton, Girl, Feeding Chickens, Raises, Lowers Head, Leans Back, Forth, 18 In. 1200.00
Automaton, Girl, Lifts Mirror, Powders Face, Looks In Mirror, Lambert, c.1900, 20 In. . . . 4840.00
Automaton, Girl, Nods Head, Knits, Bisque Head, Seated, Decamps, c.1895, 17 In. 5500.00
Automaton, Girl, Selling Flowers To Man, Lifts Hand, Head Turns, Bisque Heads, Jumeau   4800.00
Automaton, Girl, With Basket, Bird, Head Side, Up, Down, Lambert, c.1890, 20 In. 5720.00
Automaton, Grandmother, Nods Head, Eyes Open, Close, Knits, Decamps, c.1900, 25 In. . 7150.00
Automaton, Harpist, Plays Strings, Bisque Arms Raise, Lower, Roullet & Decamps 4315.00
Automaton, Hookah Smoker, Musical, Leopold Lambert, France, c.1890, 23 In. 9900.00
Automaton, Little Red Riding Hood, Bisque, 2 Tunes, Roullet & Decamps, 25 In. . . . *Illus* 29700.00
Automaton, Man, Boat, Windmill, Pond, 7 Movements, 2 Tunes, Phalibois, c.1875, 25 In. . 6165.00
Automaton, Man, Turns Head, Nods, Strums Mandolin, J. Roullet, c.1880, 22 In. 9350.00
Automaton, Monkey, Holding Baby, F.A.O. Schwarz, 765 Broadway, 13 x 9 In. 1870.00
Automaton, Monkey, Plays Fiddle, Eyes & Head Move, Birds, Ebonized Base, 14 x 14 In.   1840.00
Automaton, Monkey, Plays Violin, 6 Tunes, Mahogany Base, 16 In. 7700.00
Automaton, Monkey, Smoking Louis Vuitton, France, c.1910 . . . . 3190.00
Automaton, Monkey, Strums Harp, Glass Eyes, Metal Hands, G. Vichy, c.1885, 19 In. . . . 5940.00
Automaton, Mother, Holding Baby, Sways To Music, Nods Head, Bisque, 13 In. 345.00
Automaton, Musketeer, Nods Head, Fires Pistol, Wheel Base, Antoine Vichy, c.1875, 12 In. 3190.00
Automaton, Pastry Chef, Brioche, Lid Opens, Peeks, Hides, Decamps, c.1895, 10 1/2 In. . 5060.00
Automaton, Perfume Sniffer, Turns Head, Lifts Bottle, Douses Hankie, Bisque, 18 In. 3450.00
Automaton, Russian Girl, Serving Tea, Lifts Teapot, Pours, Nods, Lambert, c.1890, 20 In.   6030.00
Automaton, Soldier, Moves Head, Beats Drum, Wooden, c.1850, 32 In. 4620.00
Automaton, Soldier, Turns Head, Lifts Bugle, Bisque Head, Papier-Mache, France, 20 In. . 2875.00
Automaton, Spanish Man, Dances, Shakes Tambourine, Lambert, c.1895, 26 In. 5775.00

Automaton, Waltzing Child, Arms Lift, Falls, Cardboard Container, Steiner, 15 In. 2270.00
Automaton, Waltzing Couple, Twirls, Wax, Papier-Mache, Tunes, Theroude, c.1850, 12 In. 6325.00
Automaton, Waltzing Couple, Twirls, Wax, Papier-Mache, Tunes, Theroude, c.1850, 20 In. 8800.00
Automaton, Waltzing Couple, Woman Swivel Neck, Man Stiff Neck, France, 13 In. 4255.00
Automaton, Woman, Dressing Table, Head Turns, Eyes Flutter, Bisque Head, Hands, 19 In. 3840.00
Automaton, Woman, Plays Mandolin, Nods Head, Eyelids Blink, Decamps, c.1885, 21 In. 5280.00
Automaton, Woman, Plays Mandolin, Turns Head, Glass Eyes, Bisque Hands, 17 In. 1495.00
Automaton, Woman, Plays Piano, Turns Head, Bisque Head, J.B. Scott, c.1880.11 In. 8800.00
Automaton, Woman, Plays Piano, Turns Head, Papier-Mache, Music, Germany, 13 x 10 In. 2703.00
Automaton, Woman, Pours Tea, Head Moves Side To Side, Ethnic Costume, 19 In. 4900.00
Automaton, Woman, Seated, Plays Guitar, Turns, Nods Head, G. Vichy, c.1880, 14 In. . . . 4180.00
Automaton, Woman, Shakes Tambourine, Turns Head, Decamps, c.1900, 18 In. 5280.00
Automaton, Woman, Strums Violin, Glides, Nods, Wheel Base, G. Vichy, c.1875, 22 In. . . 5280.00
Automaton, Woman, Turns Head, Flowers, Bird Chirps, Wheel Base, Vichy, c.1875, 18 In. 5500.00
Automaton, Woman, Turns Head, Nods, Dabs Perfume, Lambert, c.1890, 18 In. 7700.00
Averill, Bonnie Babe, Bisque Flange Head, Dimples, Cloth Body, 20 In. 440.00
Averill, Bonnie Babe, Bisque Flange Head, Sleep Eyes, Cloth Mama Body, 21 In. 1045.00
Averill, Bonnie Babe, Bisque Head, Glass Sleep Eyes, Muslin Body, c.1920, 15 In. 840.00
Averill, Jimmie, Composition, Googly Eyes, Madame Hendren, c.1935, 13 In. 500.00
Averill, Little Cherub, Composition Head, Sleep Eyes, Harriet Flanders, c.1937, 17 In. 330.00
Averill, Lullabye Baby, Composition Flange Head, Cloth Body, Madame Hendren, 12 In. . . 50.00
Averill, Nancy & Sluggo, Cloth, Swivel Head, Stitch-Jointed, 13 In., Pair 945.00
Baby Barry, Mammy Yokum, With Pipe, Al Capp's Dogpatch Family, Vinyl, 1957, 14 In. . 350.00
Bahr & Proschild, 224, Bisque Socket Head, Glass Eyes, Brunette Mohair, c.1885, 14 In. . 2750.00
Bahr & Proschild, 273, Bisque Socket Head, Glass Eyes, Teeth, Composition, Child, 18 In. 250.00
Bahr & Proschild, 300, Bisque Head, Set Eyes, Human Hair, Composition, Wood, 17 In. . . 275.00
Bahr & Proschild, 585, Bisque Head, Sleep Eyes, Open-Close Mouth, Baby, 10 In. 265.00
Bahr & Proschild, 585, Bisque Socket Head, Sleep Eyes, Composition Body, Baby, 13 In. . 385.00
Bahr & Proschild, 585, Bisque Socket Head, Sleep Eyes, Open Mouth, Composition, 19 In. 560.00
Bahr & Proschild, 585, Bisque, Mohair Wig, Composition, Starfish Hands, Toddler, 9 In. . 495.00
Bahr & Proschild, 604, Bisque Head, Sleep Eyes, Composition Body, Baby, 11 1/2 In. . . 275.00
Bahr & Proschild, 604, Bisque Socket Head, Blue Glass Sleep Eyes, c.1915, 28 In. 1230.00
Bahr & Proschild, 604, Bisque Head, Sleep Eyes, Composition Body, Baby, 15 In. . 358.00
Bahr & Proschild, 678, Bisque Socket Head, Glass Sleep Eyes, Composition, Baby, 17 In. 415.00
Barbie dolls are listed in this category under Mattel.
Bartenstein, Wax Over Papier-Mache, 2 Faces, Black & White, Germany, c.1890, 12 In. . . 1210.00
Bawo & Dotter, 213, Bisque Socket Head, Sleep Eyes, Wood, Composition, 16 1/2 In. . . . 5280.00
Belton-Type, 137, Bisque Socket Head, Mohair, Wood, Composition, Jointed, 9 1/2 In. . . . 1320.00
Bergmann dolls are also in this category under S & H and Simon & Halbig.
Bergmann, Bisque Socket Head, Blue Sleep Eyes, Jointed, Wood, Composition, 23 In. . . . 305.00
Bergmann, Bisque Socket Head, Brown Sleep Eyes, Wood, Composition, 1916, 23 In. 305.00
Bild Lilli, Plastic, Blond, Ponytail, Swimsuit, Cylinder, Germany, 7 In. 3190.00
Bisque, Brown Sleep Googly Eyes, Mohair, Jointed Knees, 7 In. 825.00
Bisque, Closed Mouth, Painted Eyes, Edwardian Costume, Belgium, 5 In. 525.00
Bisque, Cobalt Eyes, Pierced Ears, Mohair Wig, Kid Body, Stitched Fingers, 13 In. 1980.00
Bisque, Googly Eyes, Jointed Knees, Elbows, c.1920, 4 1/2 In. 3585.00
Bisque, Socket Head, Brown Complexion, Mohair, Bent Limbs, Baby, 16 In. 1430.00
Bisque, Socket Head, Brown Complexion, Mohair, Jointed, 22 In. 9625.00
Bisque, Socket Head, Brown Complexion, Painted Hair, Sleep Eyes, 8 In. 798.00
Bisque, Swivel Head, Brown Glass Inset Eyes, Blond Mohair Wig, Peg-Jointed, 5 In. 660.00
Bisque Head, Open Mouth, Brown Eyes, 6 1/2 In. 85.00
Bisque Head, Open Mouth, Rolling Eyes, Composition, Jointed Arms, Legs, 25 In. 190.00
Bisque Head, Open Mouth, Teeth, Glass Eyes, Composition, Marked Special, 22 In. 440.00
Bisque Head, Painted Face, Movable Eyes, Composition Jointed Arms, Legs, 20 In. 48.00
Bisque Shoulder Head, Painted Eyes, Blond Hair, Cloth Body, Bisque Limbs, 12 1/2 In. . . 70.00
Bisque Shoulder Head, Painted Eyes, Molded Hair, Cloth Body, 1949, 22 In. 150.00
Black dolls are also included in the Black category.
Borgfeldt, 253, Bisque, Googly Eyes, Smiling, Mohair, 5-Piece Body, Lace Dress, 7 In. . . . 1045.00
Borgfeldt, Bisque Socket Head, Sleep Eyes, Lashes, Open Mouth, Composition, 24 In. 150.00
Borgfeldt, Gladdie, Ceramic Head, Blue Sleep Eyes, Cloth, Helen Jensen, 19 1/2 In. 578.00
Bru Jne, 6, Bisque, Closed Mouth, Pierced Ears, Glass Eyes, Clothing, Bebe, 18 In. 19580.00
Bru Jne, 9, Bisque Head, Mohair Wig, Set Eyes, Composition, Jointed, Walker, 22 In. 3960.00
Bru Jne, 9, Bisque, Closed Mouth, Glass Eyes, Original Label, 24 In. 18700.00

Bru Jne, Bisque Socket Head, Glass Paperweight Eyes, c.1892, Size 13, Bebe, 28 In. 6720.00
Bru Jne, Bisque Swivel Head, Wooden Articulated Body, Inset Eyes, c.1869, 15 In. 7390.00
Bruno Schmidt, Tommy Tucker, Bisque Head, Sleep Eyes, Composition, Jointed, 26 In. . . 1220.00
Buddy Lee, Composition Head, Side-Glancing Eyes, Western Costume, c.1940, 12 In. 580.00
Buddy Lee, Composition, Eyes To Right, Smiling, Jointed, Original Shirt, Pants, 12 In. . . . 578.00
Buddy Lee, Composition, Lee Overalls, Shirt, Cap, 12 In. .250.00 to 403.00
Buddy Lee Set, Lee Jeans, 10 In., 6 Piece 900.00
Butterick, Junior Miss Manikin, Composition, Painted, Pattern, Fabric, Box, 13 In. 220.00
Bye-Lo, Bisque Flange Head, Sleep Eyes, Closed Mouth, Cloth, Celluloid Hands, 13 In. . . . 190.00
Bye-Lo, Bisque Flange Head, Sleep Eyes, Cloth Frog Body, Celluloid Hands, 10 In. 224.00
Bye-Lo, Bisque Flange Head, Sleep Eyes, Cloth Frog Body, Celluloid Hands, 13 In. 250.00
Bye-Lo, Bisque Flange Head, Solid Dome, Celluloid Hands, Frog Legs, 11 In. . . . . .360.00 to 385.00
Bye-Lo, Bisque Flange Head, Solid Dome, Celluloid Hands, Frog Legs, Twins, 9 In. 605.00
Bye-Lo, Bisque Flange Head, Solid Dome, Eyes, Cloth Body, Celluloid Hands, 8 1/2 In. . . . 220.00
Bye-Lo, Bisque Flange Head, Solid Dome, Sleep Eyes, Celluloid Hands, 17 In. 385.00
Bye-Lo, Bisque Head, Cloth Body, Marked, Grace Putnam, Early 20th Century, 12 In. 230.00
Bye-Lo, Bisque Socket Head, Solid Dome Sleep Eyes, Bisque Body, Jointed, 5 In. 440.00
Bye-Lo, Bisque, Blue Painted Eyes, Closed Mouth, Molded Hair, c.1920, 4 1/4 In. 380.00
Bye-Lo, Bisque, Painted Lashes, Closed Mouth, Mohair Wig, Organdy Dress, Slip, 8 In. . . . 385.00
Bye-Lo, Black Wax Flange Head, Muslin Body, Poured Wax Hands, Frog Legs, 15 In. 220.00
Cameo Doll Co., Annie Rooney, Composition, Jointed, c.1925, 17 In. 235.00
Cameo Doll Co., Margie, Composition, Eyes To Left, Wood Arms, Legs, 15 In. 468.00
Chase, Hospital Baby, Stockinette Head, Oil Painted, Weighted Cloth Body, 19 In. 259.00
Chase, Stockinette Head, Oil Painted, Cloth Body, Sateen, Stitched Fingers, 19 In. 415.00
China, Painted, Glazed, Glass Beaded Dress, Boots, 5 In. 248.00
China Shoulder Head, Blue Eyes, Molded Hair, Jointed, Cloth Lower Arms, 1880, 18 In. . 193.00
China Shoulder Head, Flat Top, Cloth Body, Stitch Jointed, Silk Dress, 22 In. 248.00
China Shoulder Head, High Brow, Blue Eyes, Black Hair, Cloth Body, 12 In. 195.00
China Shoulder Head, High Brow, Cloth Body, Sewn-On Clothing.10 In. 305.00
China Shoulder Head, Painted Eyes, Mustache, Cloth Body, Man, Tuxedo, 8 In. 1045.00
China Shoulder Head, Solid Dome, Human Hair, Looped Braids, Bun, Cloth Body, 13 In. . . 330.00
Cloth, Amish, Green Dress, Black Cape, Bonnet, Lancaster County, Pa., 16 In. 690.00
Cloth, Amish, Green Dress, Elizabeth Lapp, Lancaster County, Pa., 1925-30 . . . . 1650.00
Cloth, Amish, Lavender Dress, Apron, Purple Bonnet, Corncob Arms, Legs, Ohio, 15 In. . . 340.00
Cloth, Blue Eyes, Blond Hair, Teeth, Hairbow, 17 In. 95.00
Cloth, Bruckner, Girl, Stiff Mask, Shoulder & Hip Joints, Original Clothes, c.1901, 13 In. . 265.00
Cloth, Bruckner, Sailor Boy, Stiff Mask Face, Jointed Shoulders, Hips, c.1901, 12 1/2 In. . . 300.00
Cloth, Bruckner, Stiff Mask Face, Shoulder & Hip Joints, Baby, c.1901, 11 1/2 In. 220.00
Cloth, Chase, Painted Eyes, Blond Hair, Sateen Body, 16 1/2 In. 295.00
Cloth, Chase, Painted Features, Stitch-Jointed Limbs, c.1900, 20 In. 1430.00
Cloth, Clown, Button Eyes, Pink & White Striped Outfit, 24 In. 55.00
Cloth, Dean's Rag Book Co., Curley Locks, Uncut, 18 x 30 In. 22.00
Cloth, Dean's Rag Book Co., Dolly Varden, Lithograph Face, Excelsior Stuffed 15 In. 470.00
Cloth, Dean's Rag Book Co., Dolly Varden, Printed Oilcloth Face, Jointed, Clothes, 12 In. . 220.00
Cloth, Dean's Rag Book Co., Dolly Varden, Topsyturvy, Masks, White, Black Faces, 9 In. . 800.00
Cloth, Emma Adams, Columbian Exposition, Round Face, Stitch-Jointed, c.1893, 19 In. . . 2200.00
Cloth, Horsman, Babyland Rag, Golfer, Printed Face, Jointed Shoulders, Hips, 14 In. 550.00
Cloth, Horsman, Babyland Rag, Hand Painted Face, Jointed, Dress, Bonnet, 30 In. 990.00
Cloth, Horsman, Babyland Rag, Lithograph Face, Jointed, Original Gingham Dress, 14 In. . 385.00
Cloth, Horsman, Babyland Rag, Red Riding Hood, Stitch-Jointed Shoulder & Hips, 14 In. . 550.00
Cloth, Horsman, Babyland Rag, Topsyturvy, Black, White Child, Muslin, c.1935, 15 In. . . 1430.00
Cloth, Horsman, Babyland Rag, Topsyturvy, Black, White Girl, Original Dress, 12 In. 660.00
Cloth, Horsman, Babyland Rag, Topsyturvy, Happy & Crying Baby, 11 In. . . . . .250.00 to 523.00
Cloth, Kamkins, Auburn Hair, Painted Features, Original Clothes, Girl, 18 In. 1955.00
Cloth, Kamkins, Molded Face, Painted Features, Blond Wig, Snowsuit, Boy, 19 In. 1116.00
Cloth, Kamkins, Molded Face, Painted Features, Blond, Swing Joints, Cloth, Girl, 18 In. . . 999.00
Cloth, Kamkins, Molded Face, Painted Features, Human Hair, Swing Joints, Girl, 19 In. . . 650.00
Cloth, Kamkins, Swivel Head, Painted Eyes, Mohair Wig, Jointed, 19 In. 715.00
Cloth, Oil Painted 3-Piece Head, Eyes, Hair, Stitched Fingers, Separate Thumb, 15 In. 580.00
Cloth, Oil Painted, Felt Body, Swivel Jointed, Stitched Fingers, Original Dress, 14 In. 330.00
Cloth, Photograph Face, Shoulder & Hip Joints, Mitten Hands, Original Clothes, 15 In. . . . 303.00
Cloth, Photograph Face, Shoulder & Hip Joints, Mitten Hands, Original Clothes, 17 In. . . . 330.00
Cloth, Photograph Face, Stitch-Jointed Hips, Mitten Hands, Original Clothes, 12 In. 240.00

Cloth, Red, Black Checkerboard Dress, Black Bonnet, Hand Sewn, Mennonite, 17 1/2 In. .   965.00
Cloth, Woman, Embroidered, Floral Costume, Jamaica, 15 1/2 In. 115.00
Conta & Boehme, China Shoulder Head, Blue Eyes, Black Hair, Cloth Body, 13 In. 495.00
Conta & Boehme, China Shoulder Head, Pierced Ears, Closed Mouth, Wool Dress, 17 In. .   660.00
Cosmopolitan, Little Miss Ginger, Brunette, Clothes, Accessories, Metal Trunk, c.1959 . . .   440.00
Cosmopolitan, Little Miss Ginger, Platinum White Hair, Pajamas, Purse, 1959 . . . .   140.00
Cosmopolitan, Miss Ginger, Brunette, Wedding Gown, c.1959 . . . .   110.00
Cosmopolitan, Miss Ginger, Curly Brunette, 4 Outfits, Gift Box, c.1959 . . . .   415.00
Danel, Bisque Socket Head, Glass Paperweight Eyes, Jointed, Bebe, c.1891, 17 In. 3080.00
Danel, Black Bisque Socket Head, Glass Paperweight Eyes, Paris Bebe, c.1890, 13 In. 4480.00
Deluxe Reading, Sweet Ann, Vinyl Socket Head, Sleep Eyes, Hair, Box, 1950s, 30 In. 110.00
Denamur, Amber Brown Bisque Socket Head, Mohair Wig, France, 20 In. 5225.00
Door Of Hope, Boy, Carved Wood Head, Hands, Hair, Swivel Neck, Cloth Body, 11 In. . . .   560.00
Door Of Hope, Child, Carved Wood Head, Hands, Parted Hair, Cloth Body, 7 In. 705.00
Door Of Hope, Girl, Carved Wood Hands, Silk Costume, Headband, 6 1/2 In. 1610.00
Door Of Hope, Girl, Oriental, Carved, Painted, 7 1/2 In. 1140.00
Door Of Hope, Woman With Bun, Original Clothing, Cloth Mitt Hands, 11 1/2 In. . .460.00 to 575.00
Dressel, Bisque Socket Head, Blue Sleep Eyes, Wood, Composition, 1912, 22 In. 275.00
Dressel, Uncle Sam, Bisque, Pointed Chin & Nose, Wooden Jointed Body, 1900, 13 In. . . .   2300.00
Dressel & Kister, Ballerina, China, Blue Eyes, Gray Hair, Closed Mouth, 7 1/2 In. 440.00
Dressel & Kister, Bisque Head, Sculpted Brown Hair, Muslin, c.1910, 14 In. . . . . *Illus*   1650.00
Dressel & Kister, Glazed Porcelain Shoulder Head, Muslin Body, c.1910, 12 In. 770.00
Eden Bebe, Bisque Socket Head, Paperweight Eyes, Wood, Composition, 20 In. 990.00
Eden Bebe, Papier-Mache Socket Head, Clown, Butterflies On Face, c.1900, 16 In. 825.00
Eegee, Carmen Miranda, Pressed Cloth Face, Painted Features, Gesso Arms, Saltern, 15 In.   495.00
Eegee, Little Debutante, Vinyl, Sleep Eyes, Blond, Dress, Hat, Box, c.1960, 10 In. 330.00
Effanbee, Anne Shirley, Composition Head, Sleep Eyes, Human Hair, c.1937, 14 In. 470.00
Effanbee, Baby Tinyette, Composition Socket Head, Blue Eyes, Painted Hair, c.1937, 6 In. .   440.00
Effanbee, Baby Tinyette, Cowgirl, Composition Socket Head, Painted Hair, c.1935, 8 In. . .   520.00
Effanbee, Baby, Eyes, Composition Flange Head, Sleep Eyes, Molded Hair, Cloth, 22 In. .   185.00
Effanbee, Bubbles, Composition Head, Arms, Legs, Upper Teeth, Cloth Body, c.1924, 18 In.   495.00
Effanbee, Charlie McCarthy, Composition, Monocle, Pull String Mouth, c.1930, 19 In. . . .   150.00
Effanbee, Dy-Dee Baby, Composition Swivel Head, Glassine Sleep Eyes, Box, 15 In. 170.00
Effanbee, Dy-Dee Baby, Rubber, Sleep Eyes, Flannel Diaper, Box, 11 In. 165.00
Effanbee, George & Martha Washington, Composition Head, Jointed, 1940s, 9 In., Pair . . .   710.00
Effanbee, Honey Walker, Hard Plastic, Blue Sleep Eyes, Blond Hair, Box, 19 In. 275.00
Effanbee, Ice Queen, Composition Socket Head, Sleep Eyes, Human Hair, c.1937, 14 In. . .   495.00
Effanbee, Indian Girl, Composition Head, Human Hair, Fringed Skirt, c.1939, 14 In. 630.00
Effanbee, Little Lady, Composition Head, Sleep Eyes, Drum Majorette, c.1937, 17 In. 440.00
Effanbee, Marilee, Composition, Green Sleep Eyes, Open Mouth, 4 Teeth, 1937, 29 In. . . .   955.00
Effanbee, Mary Ann, Composition, Green Sleep Eyes, Blond Human Hair Wig, 19 In. 248.00
Effanbee, Mary Lee, Composition, Sleep Eyes, Human Hair Wig, Gingham Dress, 16 In. . .   250.00
Effanbee, Patricia, Composition Head, Sleep Eyes, Human Hair, Gypsy, c.1937, 14 In. 715.00
Effanbee, Patricia, Composition Socket Head, Coiled Braids, Dancer, c.1933, 14 In. 550.00
Effanbee, Patricia, Composition Socket Head, Human Hair, 5-Piece Body, c.1935, 14 In. . .   420.00
Effanbee, Patsy Ann, Composition Socket Head, Sleep Eyes, Sculpted Hair, c.1935, 19 In. .   935.00
Effanbee, Patsy Ann, Composition, Green Sleep Eyes, Molded Hair, Peach Dress, 19 In. . .   210.00
Effanbee, Patsy Ann, Green Sleep Eyes, Composition Body, 19 In. 660.00
Effanbee, Patsy Baby, Composition Head, Painted Hair, Organdy Gown, c.1937, 10 In. . . .   580.00
Effanbee, Patsy Babyette, Hazel Tin Sleep Eyes, Molded Hair, Box, 9 In. 770.00
Effanbee, Patsy Joan, Brown, Composition, Brown Sleep Eyes, Molded Hair, 17 In. 385.00
Effanbee, Patsy Joan, Composition, Green Sleep Eyes, Molded Hair, 17 In. 220.00
Effanbee, Patsy Joan, Sleep Eyes, Blond Hair Wig, Composition, c.1940, 16 In. . . . .176.00 to 358.00
Effanbee, Patsy Joan, Sleep Eyes, Cloth Body, Composition Arms, Music Box, 17 In. 550.00
Effanbee, Patsy Jr., Composition, Blue Painted Eyes, Molded Hair, Red Coat, 12 In. 130.00
Effanbee, Patsy Jr., Composition, Painted Features, Blue & White Dress, 11 In. 100.00
Effanbee, Patsy Lou, Composition Socket Head, Bobbed Hair, Button Nose, 1935, 21 In. . .   615.00
Effanbee, Patsy Lou, Composition, Green Sleep Eyes, Molded Hair, 22 In. 360.00
Effanbee, Patsy Tinyette, Composition, Brown Painted Eyes, Sailor Outfit, 7 1/2 In. 198.00
Effanbee, Patsy, Blue Painted Eyes, Molded Hair, Vintage Clothing, 14 In. 220.00
Effanbee, Patsy, Composition Socket Head, Googly Eyes, 1935, 13 In. 475.00
Effanbee, Patsy, Composition, Blue Painted Eyes, Cloth Body, 14 1/2 In. 200.00
Effanbee, Patsy, Composition, Brown Sleep Eyes, Brown Wig, Blue Coat, Hat, 14 In. 360.00

Effanbee, Patsy, Composition, Painted Brown Eyes, Molded Hair, Light Blue Dress, 14 In. 155.00
Effanbee, Patsy, Composition, Sleep Eyes, Closed Mouth, Painted Hair, Jointed, 11 In. ... 385.00
Effanbee, Patsy, Composition, Wig, Closed Mouth, Jointed Shoulders, Hips, Baby, 11 In. .. 220.00
Effanbee, Patsy, Quintuplets, Composition Socket Heads, Diapers, Jackets, c.1935, 6 In. .. 1760.00
Effanbee, Patsyette, Black, Brown Painted Eyes, Molded Hair, Hawaiian Costume, 9 In. .. 660.00
Effanbee, Patsyette, Composition, Brown Painted Eyes, 9 1/2 In. 165.00
Effanbee, Patsyette, Composition, Googly Eyes, Blond Mohair, Braids, 1940, 9 1/2 In. 120.00
Effanbee, Patsyette, Composition, Painted Eyes, Mohair, Braids, c.1940, 9 1/2 In. 120.00
Effanbee, Patsyette, Composition, Painted Googly Eyes, Blond Mohair, 1930s, 9 1/2 In. .. 120.00
Effanbee, Patsyette, Composition, Socket Head, Painted Eyes, Box, c.1935, 9 In. 500.00
Effanbee, Rosemary, Composition Shoulder Head, Metal Eyes, Human Hair, Trunk, 21 In. 323.00
Effanbee, Skippy, Composition Socket Head, Blue Eyes, Soldier's Uniform, c.1935, 14 In. 385.00
Effanbee, Skippy, Composition Socket Head, Painted Hair, Cowboy, c.1932, 14 In. 1210.00
Effanbee, Skippy, Composition Socket Head, Red Shirt, Blue Pants, c.1935, 14 In. 469.00
Effanbee, Skippy, Composition, Blue Painted Eyes, Sailor's Uniform, 14 In. 275.00
Effanbee, Suzanne, Bride, Composition, Sleep Eyes, Mohair, Gown, Veil, 14 In. ...120.00 to 147.00
Effanbee, Suzanne, Composition Socket Head, Blue Eyes, Closed Mouth, 1940, 14 In. 725.00
Effanbee, Wee Patsy, Composition Head, Sculpted Hair, Organdy Gown, c.1935, 5 1/2 In. . 521.00
Effanbee, Wee Patsy, Composition, Blue Painted Eyes, Striped Outfit, 5 In. 155.00
Effanbee, Wee Patsy, Composition, Molded & Painted Hair, Jointed, 6 In. 155.00
Fashion, Bisque Head, Paperweight Eyes, Mohair, Kid Body, Gussets, 10 1/2 In. 1210.00
Fashion, Bisque Shoulder Head, Portrait Face, France, c.1867, 18 In. 3300.00
Fashion, Bisque Socket Head, Cork Pate, Kid Over Wood, Nun's Habit, 18 In. 5500.00
Fashion, Bisque Swivel Head, Kid & Wood Body, France, c.1870, 17 In. 4700.00
Fashion, Bisque Swivel Head, Kid, Gusset Joints, Aux Reves De L'Enfance, c.1865, 20 In. 4400.00
Fashion, Bisque, Paperweight Eyes, Pierced Ears, Human Hair, Kid Body, Gussets, 12 In. . 1430.00
Fashion, Wax Shoulder Head, Arms, Painted Features, Velvet, Metallic, Robe, 14 In. 385.00
Fashion, Wax Shoulder Head, Kid Body, Beaded Costume, Hat, Purse, 12 In. 310.00
Franz Schmidt, 1272, Bisque, Solid Dome Socket Head, Sleep Eyes, Composition, 13 In. . 250.00
Franz Schmidt, 1295, Bisque Socket Head, Glass Sleep Eyes, Composition, c.1920, 9 In. . 1155.00
Franz Schmidt, 1295, Bisque Socket Head, Sleep Eyes, Composition Body, Baby, 15 In. .. 300.00
French, Bisque Swivel Head, Blond Mohair Wig, Peg-Jointed, c.1880, 6 In. 2130.00
French, Bisque Swivel Head, Blue Glass Enamel Eyes, Blond Mohair Wig, c.1880, 5 In. .. 3250.00
French, Bisque Swivel Head, Cut Pate, Inset Eyes, Mohair, Kid Body, Jointed, 5 In. 3300.00
French, Bisque Swivel Head, Glass Enamel Inset Eyes, c.1885, 5 1/2 In. 1320.00
French, Bisque Swivel Head, Glass Inset Eyes, Peg Joints, c.1878, 5 In. 4400.00
French, Bisque Swivel Head, Glass Inset Eyes, Peg Joints, c.1882, 5 In. 2090.00
French, Bisque Swivel Head, Glass Inset Eyes, Peg Joints, c.1885, 5 1/2 In. 1540.00
French, Bisque Swivel Head, Glass Inset Eyes, Peg Joints, c.1910, 4 In. 600.00
French, Bisque Swivel Head, Inset Eyes, Accented Nostrils, Kid Body, Jointed, 5 In. 1430.00
French, Bisque Swivel Head, Inset Eyes, Mohair, Kid Body, 5 In. 1980.00
French, Bisque Swivel Head, Shoulder Plate, Blond Mohair, Wood Body, c.1870, 17 In. 3760.00
French, Bisque, Glass Enamel Eyes, Lace Costume, c.1882, 5 1/2 In. 2465.00
French, Black Bisque Socket Head, Wig, Jointed Wood, Composition, Limoges, 13 In. 605.00
French, China Head, Cork Pate, Mohair, Kid Body, Mitten Hands, Stitched Fingers, 11 In. . 1870.00
French, Fortune Teller, Wood, Tuck Comb, Dowel-Jointed, Plaform, c.1850, 11 In. 605.00
French, Governess & Infant, Bisque, Peg-Jointed, c.1882, 5 In. 2576.00
French, Papier-Mache Shoulder Head, Human Hair, Inset Eyes, Kid Body, 14 In. 2310.00
French, Papier-Mache, Glass Eyes, Human Hair, Gusseted Kid Body, 20 In. 1955.00
French, Porcelain Head, Jester Costume, Twirling, Wood Platform, c.1870, 16 In. 1680.00
French, Shepherd Boy, French Bisque Head, Glass Eyes, 5-Piece Body, Sheep, Box, 5 In. . 1210.00
French, Soldier, Bisque Head, Human Hair, Composition, Box, Montreuil, 12 1/2 In. 358.00
Freundlich, W.A.A.C., Composition Head, Sculpted Cap, Military Uniform, c.1940, 15 In. 330.00
Frozen Charlie, China, Painted Blue Eyes, Closed Mouth, Hands In Fists, 15 In. 575.00
Frozen Charlie, China, Painted Blue Eyes, Painted Blond Hair, Arms Held Forward, 14 In. 385.00
Frozen Charlotte, Glazed China, Blond, Antique Fabric Dress, Tatted Collar, c.1870, 5 In. 305.00
G.I. Joe figures are listed in the Toy category.
Gaultier, Bisque Head, Paperweight Eyes, Pierced Ears, Human Hair, Bebe, 23 In. 1540.00
Gaultier, Bisque Head, Paperweight Eyes, Pierced Ears, Mohair, Cork Pate, 12 In. 3575.00
Gaultier, Bisque Shoulder Head, Muslin Over Carton Body, Costume, c.1865, 20 In. 4400.00
Gaultier, Bisque Socket Head, Blue Glass Paperweight Eyes, Bebe, c.1880, 23 In. 4760.00
Gaultier, Bisque Socket Head, Brown Glass Paperweight Eyes, Bebe, c.1880, 27 In. 7390.00
Gaultier, Bisque Socket Head, Glass Enamel Eyes, Ball-Jointed, Bebe, c.1882, 12 In. 3410.00

Gaultier, Bisque Swivel Head, Blue Glass Paperweight Eyes, Kid Body, c.1865, 32 In. ... 5150.00
Gaultier, Fashion, Bisque Swivel Head, Closed Mouth, Paperweight Eyes, 26 In. 1320.00
Gaultier, Fashion, Bisque Swivel Head, Gesland Patent Body, c.1875, 17 In. 5225.00
Gaultier, Fashion, Bisque Swivel Head, Glass Enamel Eyes, Gesland Body, c.1875, 19 In. . 7615.00
Gaultier, Fashion, Bisque Swivel Head, Glass Enamel Eyes, Kid Body, c.1870, 23 In. 3800.00
Gaultier, Fashion, Bisque Swivel Head, Glass Enamel Eyes, Kid Body, c.1875, 15 In. 3410.00
Gaultier, Fashion, Bisque Swivel Head, Wooden Articulated Body, 1870, 17 In. 3960.00
Gaultier, Fashion, Bisque, Gusseted Kid Body, Silk Beaded Outfit, 14 1/2 In. 1495.00
Gebruder Heubach dolls are also in this category under Heubach.
Gebruder Heubach, 6969, Bisque Head, Glass Sleep Eyes, Boy, Pouty, c.1915, 12 In. 1400.00
Gebruder Heubach, 6969, Bisque Head, Glass Sleep Eyes, Girl, Pouty, c.1915, 12 In. 1232.00
Gebruder Heubach, 7407, Bisque, Dimples, Mohair Wig, Wood, Composition, 17 In. 3850.00
Gebruder Heubach, 7602, Bisque Head, Solid Dome, Intaglio Eyes, Composition, 17 In. .. 1100.00
Gebruder Heubach, 7603, Bisque Socket Head, Blue Intaglio Eyes, Closed Mouth, 10 In. . 250.00
Gebruder Heubach, 7604, Bisque Head, Intaglio Eyes, Laughing, Jointed, Toddler, 15 In. . 700.00
Gebruder Heubach, 7663, Bisque Socket Head, Intaglio Eyes, c.1912, 18 In. 1120.00
Gebruder Heubach, 7890, Bisque Socket Head, Glass Inset Eyes, c.1915, 10 In. 1650.00
Gebruder Heubach, 7926, Bisque Head, Arms, Glass Eyes, Mohair, Cloth, Tiara, 21 In. ... 1610.00
Gebruder Heubach, 8192, Bisque Head, Human Hair, Jointed Wood, Composition, 14 In. . 525.00
Gebruder Heubach, 8413, Bisque Socket Head, Blue Glass Sleep Eyes, c.1915, 9 In. 900.00
Gebruder Heubach, 8413, Bisque Socket Head, Blue Glass Sleep Eyes, c.1915, 16 In. 2016.00
Gebruder Heubach, 8636, Bisque Head, Glass Sleep Eyes, Laughing, c.1915, 13 In. 3025.00
Gebruder Heubach, 9832, Bisque Shoulder Head, Black, Intaglio Eyes, Muslin Body, 8 In. 275.00
Gebruder Heubach, Bisque Head, Intaglio Eyes, Composition, Wood, c.1912, 19 In. 1265.00
Gebruder Heubach, Bisque Head, Solid Dome, Intaglio Eyes, Jointed, 12 In. 1650.00
Gebruder Heubach, Bisque, Sculpted Brown Hair, Lace Collar, Dancing, c.1910, 12 In. .. 730.00
Gebruder Heubach, Bisque, Sculpted Hair, Loop-Jointed, c.1916, 9 In. 990.00
Gebruder Heubach, Stuart, Bisque Head, Molded Bonnet, Composition, Toddler, 8 In. ... 495.00
Gebruder Kuhnlenz, 31, Bisque Body, Mohair Wig, Jointed, Taffeta Dress, 5 1/2 In. 300.00
Gebruder Kuhnlenz, 38-27, Bisque Shoulder Head, Gusset-Jointed, Child, c.1885, 17 In. . 770.00
Gebruder Kuhnlenz, 41-29, Bisque Head, Paperweight Eyes, Composition, Child, 20 In. .. 605.00
Gebruder Kuhnlenz, 46-7, Bisque Head, Glass Inset Eyes, Sonnenberg, c.1890, 17 In. 990.00
Gebruder Kuhnlenz, Bisque Head, Glass Eyes, Ethnic, Mohair, Straight Limbs, 5 1/2 In. .. 320.00
Gebruder Kuhnlenz, Bisque Head, Glass Inset Eyes, Composition, Wood, c.1885, 20 In. .. 6875.00
Gebruder Kuhnlenz, Bisque Head, Paperweight Eyes, Wood, Composition, 12 1/2 In. 630.00
Gebruder Kuhnlenz, Black Bisque Socket Head, Brown Glass Sleep Eyes, c.1900, 20 In. . 5264.00
Gebruder Kuhnlenz, Black Bisque Socket Head, Glass Sleep Eyes, Mohair, c.1900, 9 In. .. 952.00
Gebruder Kuhnlenz, Black Bisque Swivel Head, Glass Inset Eyes, c.1900, 5 1/2 In. 560.00
Gebruder Kuhnlenz, Black Bisque Swivel Head, Loop Joints, Germany, c.1890, 3 1/2 In. . 605.00
Gerling, Bisque Head, Pierced Nostrils, Cloth Body, Christening Dress, Baby, 15 In. 550.00
Gerling, Solid Dome Bisque Flange Head, Blue Sleep Eyes, Disk Joints, 18 In. 470.00
German, Bisque Head, Glass Inset Eyes, Sculpted Hair, Muslin Body, c.1870, 21 In. 1760.00
German, Bisque Head, Sculpted Hair, Muslin Body, Leather Arms, c.1870, 25 In. 660.00
German, Bisque Head, Sculpted Hair, Muslin Body, Leather Arms, c.1880, 23 In. 1760.00
German, Bisque Shoulder Head & Hands, Sculpted Hair, Muslin Body, c.1870, 25 In. 935.00
German, Bisque Shoulder Head & Limbs, Sculpted Hair, Muslin Body, c.1875, 17 In. 1540.00
German, Bisque Shoulder Head & Limbs, Sculpted Hair, Muslin Body, c.1880, 18 In. 825.00
German, Bisque Shoulder Head, Blond Hair, Muslin Body, Leather Arms, c.1870, 17 In. .. 1430.00
German, Bisque Shoulder Head, Blond Sculpted Hair, Muslin Body, c.1875, 15 In. 1155.00
German, Bisque Shoulder Head, Blond Sculpted Hair, Muslin Body, c.1875, 16 In. 825.00
German, Bisque Shoulder Head, Brown Glass Inset Eyes, Blond, Muslin, c.1880, 11 In. .. 225.00
German, Bisque Shoulder Head, Glass Eyes, Sculpted Hair, Muslin Body, c.1870, 14 In. .. 605.00
German, Bisque Shoulder Head, Sculpted Eyes & Hair, Muslin Body, c.1880, 20 In. 1320.00
German, Bisque Shoulder Head, Sculpted Hair, c.1870, 16 In. 1045.00
German, Bisque Shoulder Head, Sculpted Hair, Muslin Body, Man, c.1875, 17 In. 605.00
German, Bisque Socket Head, Googly Eyes, Closed Mouth, Mohair, c.1920, 7 3/4 In. 1115.00
German, Bisque Socket Head, Googly Eyes, Closed Mouth, Mohair, Jointed, c.1920, 5 In. . 764.00
German, Bisque Swivel Head, Sculpted Hair, Glass Eyes, Muslin, c.1870, 21 In. .....*Illus* 1760.00
German, Bisque, Blue Glass Inset Eyes, Closed Mouth, Beaded Teeth, c.1915, 7 1/2 In. 448.00
German, Papier-Mache Head, Hands, Muslin Body, Wood Limbs, Tauflinge, c.1865, 24 In. 1430.00
German, Papier-Mache Swivel Head, Neck Socket, Shoulder Plate, Tauflinge, 21 In. 1760.00
German, Papier-Mache, Woman, Black Sculpted Hair, Kid Body, c.1850, 15 In. 1235.00
German, Porcelain Shoulder Head & Limbs, Blond Mohair, Muslin, c.1910, 14 In. 880.00

German, Porcelain Shoulder Head, Sculpted Hair, Muslin, Leather Arms, c.1870, 23 In. . . .	1100.00
German, Porcelain, Oval Face, Black Hair, Muslin Body, Leather Arms, c.1860, 24 In. . . .	2640.00
German, Uncle Sam, Poured Bisque Head, Blue Glass Eyes, Mohair Wig, 12 1/2 In.	1210.00
German, Wax Over Papier-Mache Shoulder Head, Glass Eyes, Muslin, c.1860, 15 In.	330.00
Glad Toy, Dennis The Menace, Vinyl, Cloth Outfit, Box, 15 In.	90.00
Goebel, Bisque Socket Head, Googly Eyes, 5-Piece Composition Body, 7 In.	385.00
Greiner, Composition Head, Cloth Arms & Legs, Printed Dress, Apron, 36 In.	1540.00
Greiner, Papier-Mache Head, Painted Features, Stuffed, Dress, 1858, 31 In.	345.00
Greiner, Papier-Mache Shoulder Head, Blue Eyes, Cloth Body, March '58 Patent, 27 In. . .	635.00
Greiner, Papier-Mache Shoulder Head, Cloth Limbs, Red Plaid Silk Dress, 29 In.	805.00
Grodner Tal, Wood, Egg-Shaped Head, Black Painted Hair, Dowel-Jointed, c.1880, 14 In. .	360.00
Half Dolls are listed in the Pinchushion category.	
Handwerck, 69, Bisque Head, Pierced Ears, Human Hair, Jointed, Composition, 15 In.	495.00
Handwerck, 79, Bisque Head, Pierced Ears, Human Hair, Jointed, Composition, 16 In.	495.00
Handwerck, 79, Bisque Socket Head, Glass Sleep Eyes, Ball-Jointed, c.1900, 36 In.	5390.00
Handwerck, 79, Bisque Socket Head, Sleep Eyes, Composition, Wood, c.1890, 40 In.	4620.00
Handwerck, 99, Bisque Head, Pierced Ears, Human Hair, Wood, Composition, 20 In.	303.00
Handwerck, 99, Bisque Head, Brown Sleep Eyes, Composition, Jointed, 32 In.	880.00
Handwerck, 109, Bisque Head, Human Hair, Jointed Wood, Composition, 16 1/2 In.	495.00
Handwerck, 109, Bisque Head, Mohair Wig, Jointed Wood, Composition, 17 1/2 In.	470.00
Handwerck, 109, Bisque Head, Pierced Ears, Mohair, Curls, Jointed, 23 1/2 In.	440.00
Handwerck, 109, Bisque Socket Head, Sleep Eyes, Human Hair, Wood, Composition, 30 In.	525.00
Handwerck, 119, Bisque Socket Head, Sleep Eyes, Open Mouth, Composition, 26 In.	525.00
Handwerck, Bisque Head, Human Hair, Jointed Wood, Composition, Dress, 21 In.	360.00
Handwerck, Bisque Head, Original Wig, Ball-Jointed, 22 In.	370.00
Handwerck, Bisque Head, Real Lashes, Fur Brows, Earrings, Human Hair, Jointed, 24 In. .	415.00
Handwerck, Bisque Socket Head, Blue Sleep Eyes, Wood, Composition, Jointed, 28 In. . . .	470.00
Handwerck, Bisque Socket Head, Brown Sleep Eyes, Composition, Ball-Jointed, 25 In. . . .	280.00
Handwerck, Bisque, Glass Eyes, Pierced Ears, Human Hair, Composition Body, 29 In.	500.00
Handwerck, Cosmopolite, Bisque Head, Pierced Ears, Mohair Wig, Jointed, Boy, 24 In. . . .	825.00
Hertel Schwab, 148, Bisque Socket Head, Glass Sleep Eyes, Ball-Jointed, c.1912, 16 In. . .	6050.00
Hertel Schwab, 151, Bisque Head, Sleep Eyes, Open Mouth, Composition Body, 17 In. . . .	415.00
Hertel Schwab, 151, Bisque Socket Head, Sleep Eyes, 5-Piece Composition, Baby, 10 In. .	275.00
Hertel Schwab, 152, Bisque Head, Sleep Eyes, Open Mouth, Toddler, Boy, 13 In.	415.00
Hertel Schwab, 152, Bisque Socket Head, Sleep Eyes, Composition Body, Baby, 11 In. . . .	130.00
Hertel Schwab, 152, Bisque Socket Head, Sleep Eyes, Jointed Composition Body, 20 In. . .	468.00
Hertel Schwab, 165, Bisque Socket Head, Googly Eyes, Composition, Toddler, 10 In.	1100.00
Hertel Schwab, 208, Bisque, Mohair Wig, Jointed, Silk Dress, 7 In.	220.00
Hertel Schwab, Bisque Socket Head, Solid Dome, Painted Eyes, Composition, 14 In.	415.00
Heubach dolls are also in this category under Gebruder Heubach.	
Heubach, 250, Bisque Socket Head, Sleep Eyes, Composition, Ball-Jointed, 23 In.	170.00
Heubach, 262, Bisque Head, Solid Dome, Googly, 5-Piece Body, Suit, 7 1/2 In.	798.00
Heubach, 262, Bisque Socket Head, Painted Eyes, Hair, Closed Mouth, c.1915, 9 In.	560.00
Heubach, 320, Bisque Head, Pierced Nostrils, Mohair, Composition, Wood, Boy, 26 In. . . .	578.00

Doll, Dressel & Kister, Bisque Head, Sculpted Brown Hair, Muslin, c.1910, 14 In.

Doll, German, Bisque Swivel Head, Sculpted Hair, Glass Eyes, Muslin, c.1870, 21 In.

Doll, Madame Alexander, Bride, Hard Plastic, Socket Head, Sleep Eyes, c.1950, 18 In.

Heubach, 1900, Bisque Socket Head, Paperweight Set Eyes, Composition Body, 20 In. . . .   85.00
Heubach, 8101, Bisque Socket Head, Painted Intaglio Eyes, Composition, Baby, 7 In. 330.00
Heubach, 8197, Bisque Shoulder Head, Sculpted Hair, Googly Eyes, Muslin, c.1912, 23 In.   6160.00
Heubach, 9573, Bisque Socket Head, Glass Googly Eyes, Papier-Mache, 7 In. . . . . .715.00 to 935.00
Heubach, 9578, Bisque Socket Head, Googly Eyes, Mohair, 5-Piece Body, Toddler, 7 In. . .   1100.00
Heubach, Bisque Head, Real Lashes, Spring Tongue, Mohair, Composition, Baby, 18 In. . .   300.00
Heubach, Bisque Socket Head, Intaglio Eyes, Pouty Mouth, Composition, Girl, 8 1/2 In. . .   200.00
Horsman, Bisque Head, Frowning, Muslin, Composition, Baby, c.1924, 10 In.   1100.00
Horsman, Bisque Socket Head, Set Brown Eyes, Toddler, Fulper, c.1910, 16 In. 140.00
Horsman, Composition Head, Sleep Eyes, Teeth, Mohair Bobbed Wig, Girl, c.1935, 27 In.   495.00
Horsman, Ella Cinders, Composition Head, Painted Features, Muslin Dress, c.1928, 18 In.   1760.00
Horsman, Jackie Coogan, Composition, Painted Eyes, Molded Hair, Cloth, 1920, 14 In. . . .   176.00
Ideal, Bamm Bamm, Vinyl Socket Head, 5-Piece Body, Felt Costume, 12 In. 410.00
Ideal, Betsy McCall, Vinyl Head, Sleep Eyes, Brunette, Taffeta Gown, c.1960, 14 In. 305.00
Ideal, Bonnie Braids, Vinyl & Magic Skin, Toothbrush, Ipana, Wrist Tag, Box, 16 In. 285.00
Ideal, Deanna Durbin, Composition Socket Head, Sleep Eyes, c.1938, 20 In. . . . . . .558.00 to 785.00
Ideal, Jane Withers, Composition, Socket Head, Blue Sleep Eyes, c.1935, 13 In. 645.00
Ideal, Little Miss Revlon, Vinyl Socket Head, Wardrobe, Box, No. 9010, c.1958, 10 In. . . .   1155.00
Ideal, Mary Hartline, Hard Plastic, Blue Sleep Eyes, Closed Mouth, Jointed, 16 In. 185.00
Ideal, Mary Hartline, Plastic, Blue Sleep Eyes, Blond Wig, Shoulder & Hip Joints, 16 In. . .   198.00
Ideal, Mary Hartline, Plastic, Sleep Eyes, Blond Mohair, 5-Piece Body, Box, c.1959, 8 In. .   250.00
Ideal, Miss Revlon, Bride, Vinyl Socket Head, Green Sleep Eyes, 1957, 20 In. 275.00
Ideal, Miss Revlon, Bride, Vinyl Socket Head, Sleep Eyes, No. 0975, Box, c.1957, 20 In. .   470.00
Ideal, Miss Revlon, Vinyl Head, Blue Sleep Eyes, Cherry Jubilee Dress, Box, 17 In. 415.00
Ideal, Miss Revlon, Vinyl Socket Head, Blond, Sleep Eyes, Rosy Cheeks, 1958, 18 In. 1265.00
Ideal, Miss Revlon, Vinyl Socket Head, Blue Sleep Eyes, Flowered Dress, c.1956, 22 In. . .   440.00
Ideal, Miss Revlon, Vinyl Socket Head, Green Sleep Eyes, Pink Nylon Dress, c.1958, 15 In.   495.00
Ideal, Miss Revlon, Vinyl Socket Head, Sleep Eyes, Taffeta Dress, Fur Wrap, 1958, 18 In. .   250.00
Ideal, Miss Revlon, Vinyl, Synthetic Wig, Dress, Fur Stole, Nylon Stockings, 18 In. 330.00
Ideal, Naughty Marietta, Composition Shoulder Head, Cloth Body, 15 In. 100.00
Ideal, Peter Pan, Composition Flange Head, Tin Sleep Eyes, Felt Stuffed Body, 17 In. 305.00
Ideal, Pos'n Misty, Blond, Plastic Telephone Booth Box 100.00
Ideal, Pos'n Tammy, Blond Hair, Bendable Arms & Legs, Curlers, Swing, Box 70.00
Ideal, Samantha, Bewitched, Blond, Red Vinyl Outfit, Shoes 132.00
Ideal, Saucy Walker, Plastic Head, Brunette, Blue Sleep Eyes, Open Mouth, c.1952, 22 In.   495.00
Ideal, Toni, Hard Plastic, Nylon Wig, 15 In. 175.00
Ideal, Toni, Plastic Head, Sleep Eyes, Platinum Hair, Accessories, Box, c.1952, 14 In. 415.00
Ideal, Toni, Plastic Socket Head, Sleep Eyes, 5-Piece Body, Dress, c.1950, 20 In. 880.00
Ideal, Toni, Plastic, Blue Eyes, Brown Wig, c.1948, 14 In. 95.00
Ideal, Toni, Plastic, Blue Sleep Eyes, Accessories, Box, 14 In. 360.00
Imhof, Bisque Head, Set Eyes, Pierced Ears, Tin Body, Walking, Mechanism, 11 In. 330.00
Indian dolls are listed in the Indian category.
Izannah Walker, Cloth, Brown Hair, Muslin Body, Stitch-Jointed, c.1870, 17 In. 5060.00
J.D.K. dolls also may be listed in this category under Kestner.
J.D.K., 154, Bisque Shoulder Head, Sleep Eyes, Kid Body, Gusset Joints, 17 In. 140.00
J.D.K., 154, Bisque Shoulder Head, Sleep Eyes, Kid Body, Gusset Joints, 22 In. 170.00
J.D.K., 164, Bisque Socket Head, Sleep Eyes, Composition Body, Ball-Jointed, 32 In. 730.00
J.D.K., 245, Hilda, Bisque Head, Blue Sleep Eyes, Composition Body, 16 In. 1870.00
J.D.K., 260, Bisque Socket Head, Brown Sleep Eyes, Wood, Composition, Jointed, 27 In. . .   745.00
J.D.K., Bisque Head, Sleep Eyes, Lashes, Open Mouth, Mohair Wig, Composition, 23 In. . .   470.00
Jackie Robinson, Accessories, Allied Grand Doll Mfg., Box, 13 In. 2657.00
Jackie Robinson, Composition, Painted Eyes, Mouth, Dodgers Uniform, c.1950, 13 In. . . .   206.00
Japanese, Ichimatsu, Papier-Mache, Glass Inset Eyes, Late 1800s, 10 In. 660.00
Japanese, Seven Days Babies, Monday Thru Sunday, 1 Piece, Different Poses, 1935, 4 In. .   1230.00
Japanese, Smiling Sam, Tin, Cloth Covered, 9 In. 110.00
Joel Ellis, Wood, Painted Features, Leather & Wood Arms, Jointed, Beaded Boots, 15 In. . .   75.00
Jullien, Bisque Socket Head, Paperweight Eyes, Jointed Body, Bebe, c.1895, 32 In. 2310.00
Jumeau, 3, Bisque, Paperweight Eyes, Mohair Wig, Straight Wrist, 12 In. 3325.00
Jumeau, 13, Triste, Bisque, Paperweight Eyes, Human Hair, Sailor Uniform, 29 In. 6325.00
Jumeau, 1907, Bisque Head, Paperweight Eyes, Composition, Jointed Wood, 20 In. 2090.00
Jumeau, Bisque Head, Paperweight Eyes, Composition Body, Bebe, Size 15, 32 In. 1870.00
Jumeau, Bisque Head, Paperweight Eyes, Swivel Neck, Fringed Mohair, c.1880, 15 In. . . .   2470.00
Jumeau, Bisque Head, Threaded Eyes, Pierced Ears, Composition, Jointed, 19 In. 7425.00

Jumeau, Bisque Socket Head, Blue Glass Enamel Eyes, Mohair Wig, Bebe, c.1878, 15 In. .   5040.00
Jumeau, Bisque Socket Head, Blue Glass Enamel Inset Eyes, Bebe, c.1878, 12 In. 6160.00
Jumeau, Bisque Socket Head, Blue Glass Paperweight Inset Eyes, Bebe, c.1885, 15 In. . . .   6500.00
Jumeau, Bisque Socket Head, Blue Glass Paperweight Inset Eyes, Bebe, c.1888, 18 In. . . .   6945.00
Jumeau, Bisque Socket Head, Brown Glass Enamel Inset Eyes, Bebe, c.1878, 12 In. 8680.00
Jumeau, Bisque Socket Head, Brown Glass Paperweight Eyes, Bebe, c.1882, 18 In. 8400.00
Jumeau, Bisque Socket Head, Closed Mouth, Ball-Jointed, Silk Dress, Portrait, 21 In. . . .   7700.00
Jumeau, Bisque Socket Head, Glass Paperweight Eyes, Bebe, c.1890, Size 1, 9 In. 8960.00
Jumeau, Bisque Socket Head, Paperweight Eyes, Bebe, Box, c.1888, 26 In. 6050.00
Jumeau, Bisque Socket Head, Paperweight Eyes, Composition Body, Bebe, c.1880, 12 In. .   6600.00
Jumeau, Bisque Socket Head, Paperweight Eyes, Composition Body, Bebe, c.1885, 16 In. .   6875.00
Jumeau, Bisque Socket Head, Paperweight Eyes, Composition, Bebe, c.1885, 22 In. 6600.00
Jumeau, Bisque Socket Head, Paperweight Eyes, Composition, Bebe, c.1888, 10 In. 10450.00
Jumeau, Bisque Socket Head, Paperweight Eyes, Cork Pate, Mohair Wig, 1907, 10 In. 2000.00
Jumeau, Bisque Socket Head, Paperweight Eyes, Human Hair Wig, Composition, 22 In. . .   1000.00
Jumeau, Bisque Socket Head, Paperweight Eyes, Pierced Ears, Jointed Body, Tete, 22 In. .   2750.00
Jumeau, Bisque Socket Head, Paperweight Eyes, Wood, Composition, Bebe, 15 1/2 In. . . .   1760.00
Jumeau, Bisque Socket Head, Paperweight Eyes, Wood, Composition, Tete, 20 In. 2860.00
Jumeau, Bisque Socket Head, Paperweight Inset Eyes, Bebe, c.1890, 26 In. 4480.00
Jumeau, Bisque Socket Head, Sleep Eyes, Jointed, Original Costume, Box, c.1900, 16 In. .   1430.00
Jumeau, Bisque Swivel Head, Kid Body, Gusset Jointed, Portrait, c.1875, 30 In. 9900.00
Jumeau, Bisque, Amber Eyes, Composition, Human Hair, Jointed, Bebe, 10 In. 3160.00
Jumeau, Bisque, Long Face, Human Hair, Paperweight Eyes, Ball-Jointed, Bebe, 20 In. . . .   5175.00
Jumeau, Bisque, Paperweight Eyes, Eyelet Dress, Mohair, Leather Shoes, 30 In. 1320.00
Jumeau, Bisque, Paperweight Eyes, Pierced Ears, Jointed, Walking, Kiss Throwing, 23 In.   1210.00
Jumeau, Bisque, Paperweight Eyes, Pierced Ears, Wood, Composition, 23 In. 880.00
Jumeau, Black Bisque Socket Head, Wood, Composition, Jointed, 14 In. 1650.00
Jumeau, Brown Bisque Head, Pierced Ears, Jointed Composition, Mohair Wig, 18 1/2 In. .   1430.00
Jumeau, Fashion, Bisque Head, Paperweight Eyes, Pierced Ears, Human Hair, Kid, 16 In. .   2090.00
Jumeau, Fashion, Bisque Socket Head, Kid Body, Gusset Joints, Poupee Peau, 17 In. 2640.00
Jumeau, Fashion, Bisque Socket Head, Mohair Wig, Kid Body, Gusset Hips, 11 In. 1980.00
Jumeau, Fashion, Bisque Swivel Head, Wood Body, Glass Enamel Eyes, c.1867, 17 In. . . . 14000.00
Jumeau, Fashion, Bisque, Swivel Head, Inset Eyes, Blond Mohair Wig, c.1878, 20 In. 5775.00
Jumeau, Papier-Mache Socket Head, Paperweight Eyes, Jointed, Bebe, 20 In. 935.00
Juno, Metal Shoulder Head, Paperweight Set Eyes, Molded Hair, 21 In. 45.00
K * R, 73, Bisque Socket Head, Sleep Eyes, Composition Body, Ball-Jointed, 29 In. 448.00
K * R, 100, Bisque Head, Painted Features, Hair, Composition, Old Clothes, Baby, 11 In. . .   330.00
K * R, 100, Bisque Socket Head, Painted Eyes, Composition Body, Baby, 10 1/2 In. 330.00
K * R, 100, Bisque Socket Head, Solid Dome, Blue Eyes, Composition Body, Baby, 14 In. .   413.00
K * R, 100, Bisque Socket Head, Solid Dome, Composition Baby Body, 11 In. 165.00
K * R, 101, Bisque Head, Mohair Braids, Jointed Wood, Composition, 11 1/2 In. 1100.00
K * R, 101, Bisque Head, Painted Eyes, Pouty Mouth, Human Hair, Composition, 8 In. . . .   410.00
K * R, 101, Bisque Socket Head, Mohair Wig, Wood, Composition Body, Jointed, 17 In. . .   3300.00
K * R, 112, Bisque Socket Head, Painted Eyes, Wood, Composition Body, c.1912, 13 In. . .   7280.00
K * R, 112, Elise, Bisque Socket Head, Painted Eyes, Ball-Jointed, c.1910, 19 1/2 In. 12320.00
K * R, 114, Bisque Socket Head, Painted Eyes, Wooden Ball-Jointed Body, c.1910, 11 In. .   2970.00
K * R, 114, Gretchen, Bisque, Painted, Chunky Body, Original Clothing, 22 In. 4600.00
K * R, 115A, Bisque, Mohair, Jointed Wood, Composition, Boy, Toddler, 16 In. 3520.00
K * R, 115A, Phillip, Bisque Socket Head, Glass Sleep Eyes, Wood Body, c.1912, 13 In. . .   3300.00
K * R, 116A, Bisque Head, Brown Sleep Eyes, Human Hair, Bent Limbs, Baby, 15 In. 1650.00
K * R, 117N, Bisque, Real Lashes, Human Hair, Jointed Wood, Composition, 21 In. 688.00
K * R, 121, Bisque Head, Sleep Eyes, Mohair Wig, Composition, Wood, 11 In. 743.00
K * R, 121, Bisque Socket Head, Blue Sleep Eyes, Composition Body, Baby, 25 In. 440.00
K * R, 121, Bisque Socket Head, Sleep Eyes, Composition, Ball-Jointed, c.1915, 23 In. . . .   1650.00
K * R, 122, Bisque Head, Cardboard Pate, Sleep Eyes, Mohair, Composition, Baby, 11 In. .   440.00
K * R, 126, Bisque Head, Sleep Eyes, Synthetic Wig, Composition, Baby, 17 In. 235.00
K * R, 126, Black Bisque Socket Head, Sleep Eyes, Composition, Toddler, c.1920, 6 In. . .   935.00
K * R, 127, Bisque Socket Head, Molded Forelock, Bent Limbs, Baby, 12 In. 1430.00
K * R, 127, Bisque Socket Head, Painted Hair, Ball-Jointed, Boy Scout, Toddler, 16 In. . . .   2640.00
K * R, 127, Bisque Socket Head, Sculpted Hair, Composition Body, c.1915, 15 1/2 In. 1210.00
K * R, 131, Bisque Socket Head, Googly Eyes, Blue Glass Sleep, Mohair, 15 In. 6875.00
K * R, 191, Bisque Head, Mohair Wig, Composition Body, Jointed Wood, 18 In. 413.00
K * R, 192, Bisque Socket Head, Glass Eyes, Wood Body, Ball-Jointed, c.1905, 12 In. 880.00

K * R, 192, Bisque Socket Head, Sleep Eyes, 5-Piece Composition Body, 7 1/2 In. 550.00
K * R, 192, Bisque Socket Head, Sleep Eyes, Composition Body, Ball-Jointed, 20 In. 560.00
K * R, 403, Bisque Head, Pierced Ears, Mohair, Composition Body, Jointed Wood, 16 In. . 413.00
K * R, 403, Bisque Head, Sleep Eyes, Open Mouth, Teeth, Mohair, Composition, 20 In. . . . 588.00
K * R, 728, Celluloid Socket Head, Mohair Wig, 5-Piece Body, 22 In. 95.00
K * R, 917, Composition Head, Flirty Eyes, Mohair, Composition, Wood, 13 In. 358.00
K * R, Black Bisque Socket Head, Glass Sleep Eyes, Ball-Jointed, c.1912, 19 In. 1815.00
Karl Hartmann, 29, Bisque Socket Head, Sleep Eyes, Composition, Ball-Jointed, 24 In. . . 140.00
Kathe Kruse, Cloth, Brown Hair, Eyes, Stitch-Jointed Arms, Jointed Legs, c.1915, 17 In. . . 1870.00
Kathe Kruse, Cloth, Hazel Eyes, Round Mouth, Blond, Red Dress, 1950s, 20 In. 1400.00
Kathe Kruse, Cloth, Oil Painted, Bellow-Jointed, 16 In. 855.00
Kathe Kruse, Cloth, Painted Eyes, Blond Mohair, Jointed Neck, Limbs, Girl, c.1930, 14 In. 1998.00
Kathe Kruse, Cloth, Painted Eyes, Hair, Jointed Limbs, 17 In. 2115.00
Kathe Kruse, Cloth, Painted Features & Hair, Brown Eyes, c.1930, 13 In. 3025.00
Kathe Kruse, Cloth, Painted Features & Hair, Green Eyes, Series I, c.1915, 17 In. 3920.00
Kathe Kruse, Cloth, Painted Features, Brown Eyes, Hair, c.1945, 17 In. 1570.00
Kathe Kruse, Plastic Socket Head, Cloth Body, Tab Jointed, Swivel Hips, Girl, 17 In. 425.00
Kathy Kruse, Barbel, Plastic Molded Head, Painted Eyes, Cloth Body, Box, 17 1/2 In. 330.00
Kathy Kruse, Christina, Plastic Molded Head, Painted Eyes, Cloth Body, Box, 18 In. 200.00
Kathy Kruse, Jennifer, Plastic Molded Head, Painted Eyes, Cloth Body, Box, 19 1/2 In. . . . 330.00
Kathy Kruse, Karoline, Plastic Molded Head, Painted Eyes, Cloth Body, Box, 19 In. 300.00
Kathy Kruse, Plastic Molded Head, Painted Eyes, Cloth Body, Box, 18 1/2 In. 385.00
Kathy Kruse, Wilhelm, Plastic Molded Head, Painted Eyes, Brown Wig, Box, 14 In. 155.00
Kaulitz, Composition Socket Head, Wooden Ball-Jointed Body, Girl, c.1910, 13 In. 5060.00
Kestner dolls are also in this category under J.D.K.
Kestner, 133, Bisque Socket Head, Sleep Eyes, Mohair Wig, Composition Body, 6 In. 410.00
Kestner, 143, Bisque Socket Head, Cardboard Pate, Mohair, Composition, Jointed, 13 In. . 660.00
Kestner, 143, Bisque Socket Head, Glass Sleep Eyes, Ball-Jointed, c.1915, 13 In. 715.00
Kestner, 143, Bisque Socket Head, Glass Sleep Eyes, Composition Body, c.1915, 10 In. . . 825.00
Kestner, 143, Bisque Socket Head, Mohair Wig, Jointed Wood, Composition, Dress, 11 In. 660.00
Kestner, 143, Bisque Socket Head, Plaster Pate, Sleep Eyes, Mohair, Composition, 12 In. . 990.00
Kestner, 143, Bisque Socket Head, Sleep Eyes, Blond Mohair, Composition, 9 In. 440.00
Kestner, 143, Bisque Socket Head, Sleep Eyes, Wood, Composition Body, Jointed, 27 In. . 1100.00
Kestner, 146, Bisque Head, Sleep Eyes, Teeth, Mohair, Composition, c.1900, 20 In. 1210.00
Kestner, 150, Bisque, Brown Set Eyes, Human Hair Braids, Jointed, Dressed, 9 In. 400.00
Kestner, 156, Bisque, Sleep Eyes, Open-Close Mouth, Molded Socks, Shoes, 4 1/2 In. . . . 440.00
Kestner, 162, Bisque Head, Sleep Eyes, 4 Teeth, Mohair, Composition, c.1910, 19 In. 1155.00
Kestner, 164, Bisque Head, Mohair Wig, Wood, Composition, Jointed, Dressed, 17 In. . . . 220.00
Kestner, 166, Bisque Shoulder Head, Human Hair Wig, Kid Body, Rivet-Jointed, 20 In. . . . 210.00
Kestner, 167, Bisque Head, Plaster Pate, Mohair, Sleep Eyes, Open Mouth, Teeth, 20 In. . 764.00
Kestner, 168, Bisque Head, Sleep Eyes, Human Hair, Jointed Wood, Composition, 21 In. . 485.00
Kestner, 171, Bisque Head, Sleep Eyes, Composition, Wood, Ball-Jointed, c.1900, 25 In. . 745.00
Kestner, 172, Gibson Girl, Bisque Head, Mohair, Cloth Body, China Feet, 10 1/2 In. 633.00
Kestner, 178, Bisque Socket Head, Painted Brown Eyes, c.1912, 11 In. 4480.00
Kestner, 179, Bisque Head, Brown Sleep Eyes, Open Mouth, Teeth, Acrylic Wig, 23 In. . . 470.00
Kestner, 179, Bisque Socket Head, Blue Upper Glancing Eyes, c.1912, 15 In. 3360.00
Kestner, 180, Bisque Socket Head, Wood, Composition, Painted Blue Eyes, c.1910, 17 In. 3470.00
Kestner, 182, Bisque Socket Head, Closed Mouth, Composition Body, c.1912, 15 In. 4030.00
Kestner, 184, Bisque, Set Eyes, Mohair, Jointed, Silk Dress, Molded Boots, 4 1/2 In. 330.00
Kestner, 196, Bisque Head, Mohair, Fuzzy Brows, Jointed Wood, Composition, 13 1/2 In. . 470.00
Kestner, 211, Bisque Head, Sleep Eyes, 2 Teeth, 5-Piece Composition Body, Baby, 14 In. . 550.00
Kestner, 211, Bisque Socket Head, Blue Glass Sleep Eyes, c.1915, 9 1/2 In. 1300.00
Kestner, 211, Bisque Socket Head, Composition Body, Glass Sleep Eyes, c.1915, 22 In. . . 1175.00
Kestner, 211, Bisque Socket Head, Sleep Eyes, Composition Body, Baby, 24 In. 825.00
Kestner, 221, Bisque Head, Googly Eyes, Mohair, Ball-Jointed, c.1912, 13 In. . . . 5060.00
Kestner, 221, Bisque Socket Head, Googly Brown Sleep Eyes, Mohair, 13 In. 70.00
Kestner, 237, Bisque Socket Head, Mohair, Blue Sleep Eyes, Hip Joints, Toddler, 27 In. . . 5720.00
Kestner, 237, Hilda, Bisque, Glass Eyes, Chunky Body, Straight Wrists, Toddler, 18 In. . . . 2070.00
Kestner, 243, Bisque Socket Head, Mohair, Plaster, Chinese Boy, c.1912, 13 In. 2750.00
Kestner, 243, Bisque Socket Head, Sleep Eyes, Chinese Baby, c.1912, 16 1/2 In. 3695.00
Kestner, 247, Bisque Socket Head, Blue Sleep Eyes, Painted Lashes, Ball-Jointed, 10 In. . . 1980.00
Kestner, 247, Bisque Socket Head, Googly Sleep Eyes, Mohair, Toddler, 18 In. 1540.00
Kestner, 257, Bisque Socket Head, Sleep Eyes, Composition, Bent Limbs, c.1915, 22 In. . . 1020.00

Kestner, 260, Bisque Head, Sleep Eyes, Human Hair, Composition Body, c.1920, 19 In. .. 441.00
Kestner, 262, Catterfelder Puppenfabrik, Bisque Head, Sleep Eyes, Composition, 23 In. ... 450.00
Kestner, 390, Bisque, Blue Eyes, Mohair, Clothing, Accessories, 20th Century, 24 In. 176.00
Kestner, Baby Jean, Bisque Head, Glass Sleep Eyes, Composition, Wood, c.1915, 23 In. ... 3410.00
Kestner, Baby Jean, Bisque Head, Solid Dome, Composition Body, Baby, 17 In. 770.00
Kestner, Bisque Head, Human Hair, Kid Body, Gussets, Child's Dress, 34 In. 1650.00
Kestner, Bisque Head, Overbite, Accented Lips, Human Hair, Cloth, Composition, 20 In. . 385.00
Kestner, Bisque Head, Plaster Pate, Mohair Wig, Composition, Jointed Wood, 12 In. 1210.00
Kestner, Bisque Head, Turned, Kid Body, Bisque Limbs, Gussets, Dressed, 14 In. 330.00
Kestner, Bisque Socket Head, Brown Glass Sleep Eyes, c.1890, 10 1/2 In. 2800.00
Kestner, Bisque Socket Head, Brown Glass Sleep Eyes, Composition Body, c.1890, 9 In. . 3920.00
Kestner, Bisque Socket Head, Glass Inset Eyes, Composition, Wood, c.1885, 27 In. 2970.00
Kestner, Bisque Socket Head, Glass Sleep Eyes, Blond, 6 Ball Joints, c.1890, 15 In. 2200.00
Kestner, Bisque Swivel Head, Mohair Wig, Bisque Body, Jointed, Silk Dress, 4 1/2 In. ... 2530.00
Kestner, Bisque, Painted Features, Closed Mouth, Peg-Jointed Arms, c.1885, 6 In. 715.00
Kestner, Gibson Girl, Bisque Head, Mohair, Kid Body, Jointed, Walking Suit, 20 In. 1650.00
Kestner, Hilda, Bisque Head, Human Hair, Composition, Christening Gown, 20 In. 1100.00
Kestner, Hilda, Bisque Head, Sleep Eyes, Mohair, Composition, Baby, 1914, 16 In. 2200.00
Kestner, Hilda, Bisque Socket Head, Sleep Eyes, Composition Body, Baby, 1914, 20 In. .. 2420.00
Kestner, Hilda, Bisque Socket Head, Solid Dome, Composition Body, Baby, 20 In. 1870.00
Kestner, Hilda, Brown Sleep Eyes, 5-Piece Papier-Mache Body, Baby, c.1912, 22 In. 2640.00
Kestner, Nurse, Bisque, Brown Sleep Eyes, Open Mouth, Jointed, 32 In. 600.00
Kewpie dolls are listed in the Kewpie category.
Kley & Hahn, 72, Bisque Head, Weighted Tongue, Mohair, Composition, Baby, 14 In. 250.00
Kley & Hahn, 158, Bisque Head, Dome, Molded Tongue, Hair, Jointed, 2 Piece Suit, 11 In. 250.00
Kley & Hahn, 250, Bisque Head, Sleep Eyes, Lashes, Blond Mohair, Composition, 22 In. ... 210.00
Kley & Hahn, 282, Bisque Head, Sleep Eyes, Composition Body, Ball-Jointed, 24 In. 200.00
Kley & Hahn, 525, Bisque Socket Head, Dome, Composition Body, Baby, 14 In. 525.00
Kley & Hahn, 680/9, Bisque Head, Hand Painted Face, Open Mouth, Crying, 22 In. 165.00
Kley & Hahn, Walkure, Bisque Socket Head, Blue Sleep Eyes, Wood, Composition, 25 In. . 220.00
Kley & Hahn, Walkure, Bisque Socket Head, Sleep Eyes, Composition, Ball-Jointed, 29 In. 500.00
Kling, 128, Bisque Head, Brown Glass Eyes, Blond Molded Hair, Lady, 19 In. 605.00
Kling, 162, Bisque Shoulder Head, Glass Inset Eyes, Kid Body, Gusset Joints, c.1885, 19 In. 1485.00
Kling, 189, China Shoulder Head, Molded Hair, Cloth Body, Stitch-Jointed, Dress, 22 In. .. 385.00
Kling, 217, Bisque Shoulder Head, Blue Paperweight Eyes, Cloth Body, 15 In. 415.00
Knickerbocker, Baby Dumpling, Composition Socket Head, Large Ears, c.1935, 9 In. 2970.00
Knickerbocker, Dagwood, Composition Head, Large Ears, Black Suit, c.1935, 14 In. 2970.00
Knickerbocker, Little Lulu, Pressed Mask Face, Painted Features, Dress, c.1940, 17 In. ... 580.00
Konig & Wernicke, 1070, Bisque Socket Head, Sleep Eyes, Wood, Composition, 4 In. 385.00
Konig & Wernicke, 4711, Bisque Head, Human Hair, Jointed Wood, Composition, 42 In. .. 1210.00
Konig & Wernicke, Bisque Head, Sleep Eyes, Open Mouth, Composition, Baby, 17 In. ... 353.00
Konig & Wernicke, Bisque Socket Head, Blue Glass Sleep Eyes, Toddler, c.1915, 21 In. .. 1000.00
Krueger, Elves, Pressed Mask Face, Yarn Hair, Oilcloth, Overalls, Hat, c.1938, 6 In., Pair . 408.00
Lenci, 300, Felt Swivel Head, Googly Eyes, Felt Body, Ringlets, c.1930, 17 In. 1568.00
Lenci, American Indian, Felt Swivel Head, Painted Features, Jointed, c.1920, 20 In. 3520.00
Lenci, Boy, Felt, Painted Googly, Mohair Wig, Jointed Neck, Limbs, 1930s, 17 In. ..500.00 to 825.00
Lenci, Boy, Felt, Swivel Head, Checked Pants, Shoulder Yoke, Pails, Dutch, 16 In. 1980.00
Lenci, Equestrienne, Felt Swivel Head, Eyes, Red Jacket, Riding Crop, c.1935, 17 In. 1760.00
Lenci, Girl, Felt Swivel Head, Blue Eyes, Painted Features, Dress, Bonnet, c.1935, 22 In. . 1560.00
Lenci, Girl, Felt Swivel Head, Curly Mohair, Felt Body, Jointed, Stitched Fingers, 16 In. .. 495.00
Lenci, Girl, Felt, Painted Googly Eyes, Curly Inset Mohair Wig, Felt Dress, c.1930, 15 In. . 200.00
Lenci, Mozart, Felt Swivel Head, Blond Mohair Wig, Muslin Body, c.1935, 11 In. 2310.00
Lenci, Mozart, Felt Swivel Head, Ponytail, Felt Costume, 1926, 20 In. 4100.00
Lenci, Piglet, Pink Velvet, 4 Finger White Felt Hand, Overalls, 1940, 10 In. 450.00
Lenci, Puss In Boots, Velvet Head, Green Eyes, Neck Ruffle, Boots, Sword, c.1940, 16 In. . 2090.00
Lenci, Salon Lady, Felt Swivel Head, Painted Face, Braids, Googly Eyes, 1930, 23 In. 670.00
Lenci, Tyrolean, Felt Swivel Head, Googly Eyes, c.1930, 17 In. 3136.00
Lenci, Valtellina, Felt Swivel Head, Painted Eyes, Cloth Body, Felt Arms, 11 In. 360.00
Lenci, Winker, Felt Swivel Head, Cigarette In Mouth, 1921, 12 In. 1065.00
Lenci, Winker, Felt Swivel Head, Painted Eyes, c.1928, 10 1/2 In. ....1000.00 to 1065.00
Lenci, Woman, Felt Swivel Head, Blue Googly Eyes, c.1928, 24 In. 2240.00
Madame Alexander, Alice In Wonderland, Mask Face, Yarn Hair, Muslin, c.1935, 16 In. .. 1045.00
Madame Alexander, American Girl, Plastic, Braids, Dress, Hat, Box, No. 388, 8 In. 220.00

Madame Alexander, Amy, Little Women, Hard Plastic, Tagged Outfit, 15 In. 250.00
Madame Alexander, Amy, Little Women, Mask Face, Mohair, Muslin, c.1935, 16 In. 385.00
Madame Alexander, Amy, Little Women, Plastic Socket Head, No. 1500, c.1952, 15 In. . . .   140.00
Madame Alexander, Amy, Little Women, Plastic, Sleep Eyes, Floss Hair, Box, 14 In. 965.00
Madame Alexander, Annabelle, Maggie Face, Plastic Head, Sleep Eyes, c.1954, 18 In. . . .   990.00
Madame Alexander, Annette Dionne, Composition, Human Hair, 5-Piece, Toddler, 16 In. .   700.00
Madame Alexander, Babs Skater, Plastic Socket Head, Blond, Sleep Eyes, c.1949, 15 In. . . .   1650.00
Madame Alexander, Baby Jane, Composition Head, Mohair, Dress, c.1935, 15 In. 550.00
Madame Alexander, Ballerina, Plastic Socket Head, Tosca Hair, c.1952, 15 In. 385.00
Madame Alexander, Beth, Little Women, Hard Plastic, Tagged Outfit, 15 In. 200.00
Madame Alexander, Billy, Alexander-Kins, Blond, Red & White Outfit, Box, 1959, 8 In. . . .   360.00
Madame Alexander, Binnie Walker, Plastic Socket Head, Sleep Eyes, c.1952, 18 In. 275.00
Madame Alexander, Bride, Alexander-Kins, Blond, No. 483, 1959, 8 In. 385.00
Madame Alexander, Bride, Hard Plastic, Socket Head, Sleep Eyes, c.1950, 18 In. . . . . *Illus*   935.00
Madame Alexander, Bridesmaid, Composition Swivel Head, Sleep Eyes, Mohair, 21 In. . .   85.00
Madame Alexander, Cinderella, Plastic Socket Head, Blue Sleep Eyes, 1950, 15 In. 715.00
Madame Alexander, Cinderella, Plastic Socket Head, Satin Gown, c.1948, 18 In. 633.00
Madame Alexander, Cinderella, Poor, Plastic Socket Head, Sleep Eyes, 1950, 15 In. 690.00
Madame Alexander, Cissette, Blond, Lacy Chemise, No. 700, Box, 1962, 10 In. 770.00
Madame Alexander, Cissette, Blond, Polished Cotton Shirtwaist, No. 810, c.1960, 10 In. . .   1100.00
Madame Alexander, Cissette, Margot, Plastic, Hair Jewel, Clothes, Box, No. 900, 10 In. . .   385.00
Madame Alexander, Cissette, Pink Cotton Sateen Dress, No. 813, Box, 1958, 10 In. 715.00
Madame Alexander, Cissette, Plastic, Blue Sleep Eyes, Box, 9 In. 385.00
Madame Alexander, Cissette, Tosca Hair, Lavender Evening Ensemble, Box, 1957, 10 In. .   660.00
Madame Alexander, Cissy, Blond, Purple Velvet Gown, Ensemble No. 2174, 1956, 20 In. .   2640.00
Madame Alexander, Cissy, Hard Plastic, Vinyl Arms, Jointed Knees, c.1959, 20 In. 525.00
Madame Alexander, Cissy, Plastic Socket Head, Black Velvet Gown, c.1956, 20 In. 2200.00
Madame Alexander, Cissy, Plastic Socket Head, Red Hair, Swimsuit, c.1955, 20 In. 550.00
Madame Alexander, Cissy, Plastic Socket Head, Red Polka Dot Dress, c.1955, 20 In. 2310.00
Madame Alexander, Cissy, Plastic Socket Head, Red Taffeta Ball Gown, c.1956, 20 In. . . .   3190.00
Madame Alexander, Cissy, Plastic Socket Head, Summer Shorts, Halter, c.1955, 20 In. . . .   1595.00
Madame Alexander, Cissy, Queen Elizabeth Coronation, Brunette, 1956, 20 In. 770.00
Madame Alexander, Composition, Straw Hat, Basket, Mid 20th Century, 18 In. 115.00
Madame Alexander, Cynthia, Plastic Socket Head, Black Hair, Sleep Eyes, c.1952, 15 In. .   880.00
Madame Alexander, David Copperfield, Mask Face, Mohair, Muslin, c.1935, 16 In. 385.00 to 770.00
Madame Alexander, Doctor Defoe, Composition Head, Blue Eyes, Gray Hair, 1935, 14 In.   1800.00
Madame Alexander, Dutch Boy, Blond, Bent Leg, Walking Body, No. 777, c.1961, 8 In. . .   195.00
Madame Alexander, Elise, Ballerina, Hard Plastic, Closed Mouth, Jointed, 15 In. 200.00
Madame Alexander, Elise, Bridesmaid, Plastic Head, Tulle Gown, c.1958, 16 1/2 In. 525.00
Madame Alexander, Elise, Plastic Socket Head, Brunette, Dress, c.1960, 16 1/2 In. 440.00
Madame Alexander, Elise, Plastic Socket Head, I. Magnin Costume, c.1958, 16 1/2 In. . . .   635.00
Madame Alexander, First Communion, Alexander-Kins, Brunette, Box, c.1957, 8 In. 580.00
Madame Alexander, Flora McFlimsey, Composition, Freckles, Human Hair, 13 In. 385.00
Madame Alexander, Flora McFlimsey, Composition, Freckles, Human Hair, 15 In. 440.00
Madame Alexander, Flower Girl, Alexander-Kins, Auburn Hair, Box, 8 In. 250.00
Madame Alexander, Groom, Alexander-Kins, Brunette, No. 577, c.1956, 8 In. 990.00
Madame Alexander, Jane Withers, Composition Head, Scottish Outfit, c.1935, 19 In. 4620.00
Madame Alexander, Jane Withers, Composition Socket Head, Mohair, c.1935, 13 In. 2530.00
Madame Alexander, Jane Withers, Composition, Mohair, Tagged Dress, 19 In. 1210.00
Madame Alexander, Jeannie Walker, Composition, Tagged Outfit, 18 In. 470.00
Madame Alexander, Jo, Little Women, Alexander-Kins, Brunette, No. 781, c.1960, 8 In. . .   165.00
Madame Alexander, Jo, Little Women, Brunette Mohair, Muslin Body, c.1935, 16 In. 415.00
Madame Alexander, Jo, Little Women, Hard Plastic, Tagged Outfit, 15 In. 300.00
Madame Alexander, Kelly, Vinyl Head & Body, Blue Sleep Eyes, Box, 1958, 15 In. 330.00
Madame Alexander, Laurie, Little Women, Hard Plastic, Tagged Outfit, 15 In. 220.00
Madame Alexander, Lissy, Bride, Brunette, Wedding Dress, Box, c.1956, 11 1/2 In. 303.00
Madame Alexander, Lissy, Plastic Socket Head, Graduation Costume, c.1955, 12 In. 1980.00
Madame Alexander, Little Genius, Plastic Head, Vinyl, Christening, No. 185, 1960, 7 In. . . .   385.00
Madame Alexander, Little Shaver, Cloth, 11 In. 250.00
Madame Alexander, Little Victoria, Plastic, Tagged Dress, Straw Hat, Shoes, Walker, 8 In.   250.00
Madame Alexander, Little Women Set, Lissy Dolls, Articulated, 1957, 12 In., 5 Piece 908.00
Madame Alexander, Madeline, Vinyl Head, Sleep Eyes, Plastic Body, Taffeta Dress, 17 In.   550.00
Madame Alexander, Maggie Face, Alexander-Kins, Scottish, No. 396, Box, c.1961, 8 In. . .   193.00

Madame Alexander, Maggie Mixup, Carrot-Red Hair, No. 1855, c.1961, 17 In. 600.00
Madame Alexander, Maggie Walker, Plastic Head, Sleep Eyes, Auburn, 1953, 18 In. 880.00
Madame Alexander, Maggie, Plastic Socket Head, Blond, 5-Piece Body, c.1951, 20 In. . . . 495.00
Madame Alexander, Maggie, Plastic Socket Head, Blond, 5-Piece Body, c.1952, 18 In. . . . 965.00
Madame Alexander, Margaret O'Brien, Composition, Mohair, Braids, Jointed, 18 In. 743.00
Madame Alexander, Margaret O'Brien, Plastic Socket Head, 5-Piece Body, c.1946, 14 In. . . 2200.00
Madame Alexander, Margaret O'Brien, Sleep Eyes, Mohair Wig, c.1940, 21 In. 150.00
Madame Alexander, Margaret Rose, Plastic Socket Head, Brunette, Dress, c.1950, 14 In. . . 660.00
Madame Alexander, Margaret Rose, Plastic Socket Head, Brunette, Dress, c.1950, 18 In. . . 880.00
Madame Alexander, Margot, Ballerina, Hard Plastic, Walker, Tagged Outfit, Box, 15 In. . . 500.00
Madame Alexander, Marie, Composition Socket Head, Sculpted Hair, Romper, 1935, 6 In. 440.00
Madame Alexander, Marlo Thomas, That Girl, Vinyl, Brown Eyes, Boots, 1966, 17 In. . . . 200.00
Madame Alexander, Marme, Little Women, Plastic Head, No. 1500, c.1952, 15 In. .110.00 to 200.00
Madame Alexander, McGuffey Ana, Composition Head, Sleep Eyes, Jointed, 20 In. 160.00
Madame Alexander, McGuffey Ana, Composition, Sleep Eyes, Human Hair, 13 In. 550.00
Madame Alexander, McGuffey Ana, Composition, Sleep Eyes, Human Hair, 20 In. 825.00
Madame Alexander, McGuffey Ana, Hard Plastic, Blue Sleep Eyes, Closed Mouth, 14 In. . 465.00
Madame Alexander, McGuffey Ana, Sleep Eyes, Teeth, Human Hair, c.1940, 16 In. 150.00
Madame Alexander, Meg, Little Women, Alexander-Kins, Blond, Box, 1957, 8 In. 275.00
Madame Alexander, Meg, Little Women, Plastic Head, No. 1500, c.1952, 15 In. . . .120.00 to 300.00
Madame Alexander, Nina Ballerina, Strung, Hard Plastic, 17 In. 248.00
Madame Alexander, Nurse, Baby, Plastic, Tagged Clothes, No. 363, 8 In. 415.00
Madame Alexander, Nurse, Composition Head, Sleep Eyes, Mohair Wig, c.1935, 13 In. . . . 1760.00
Madame Alexander, Peggy Bride, Plastic Socket Head, Brunette, c.1950, 20 In. 2310.00
Madame Alexander, Peter Pan, Plastic Socket Head, Green Sleep Eyes, c.1953, 15 In. 440.00
Madame Alexander, Polish Girl, Blond, Walking Style Body, No. 780, c.1961, 8 In. 140.00
Madame Alexander, Prince Charles, Flocked Hair, Bent-Legs, Blue Suit, c.1957, 8 In. 195.00
Madame Alexander, Prince Charming, Plastic Socket Head, Box, c.1950, 15 In. 770.00
Madame Alexander, Prince Philip, Plastic Socket Head, Blue Sleep Eyes, 18 In. 770.00
Madame Alexander, Princess Elizabeth, Composition, Tagged Outfit, 23 In. 140.00
Madame Alexander, Queen Elizabeth, Hard Plastic, Walker, Tagged Outfit, 19 In. 400.00
Madame Alexander, Red Riding Hood, Alexander-Kins, Blond, Box, c.1961, 8 In. 250.00
Madame Alexander, Scarlett O'Hara, Composition, c.1936, 18 In. 520.00
Madame Alexander, Scarlett, Alexander-Kins, Brunette, Green Eyes, c.1973, 8 In. 250.00
Madame Alexander, Shari Lewis, Hard Plastic Head, Vinyl Body, Tagged Outfit, 20 In. . . . 500.00
Madame Alexander, Sleeping Beauty, 1959, 9 In. 95.00
Madame Alexander, Snow White, Composition, Sleep Eyes, Dress, 16 In. 155.00
Madame Alexander, Snow White, Plastic Socket Head, Blue Sleep Eyes, c.1952, 15 In. . . . 580.00
Madame Alexander, Sonja Henie, Composition, Brown Sleep Eyes, Box, 14 In. 600.00
Madame Alexander, Sonja Henie, Composition, Brown Sleep Eyes, Skates, 18 In. 580.00
Madame Alexander, Sonja Henie, Composition, Eyes, Mohair, Skating Costume, 15 In. . . . 1650.00
Madame Alexander, Sonja Henie, Composition, Human Hair, Ski Costume, c.1937, 20 In. . 1320.00
Madame Alexander, Sonja Henie, Composition, Sleep Eyes, Human Hair, Tag, 17 In. 415.00
Madame Alexander, Story Princess, Margaret Face, Plastic Socket Head, 1948, 21 In. 2365.00
Madame Alexander, Susie Q & Bobbie Q, Mask Face, Yarn Hair, Muslin, c.1935, 13 In. . . 1320.00
Madame Alexander, Susie Q, Cloth, Mask Face, Painted Eyes, Yarn Hair, c.1938, 16 In. . . 205.00
Madame Alexander, Susie Q, Cloth, Painted, Yarn Pigtails, Stitch-Jointed, 15 In. 470.00
Madame Alexander, Swedish Girl, Bent Legs, Walking Style Body, No. 492, c.1961, 8 In. . . 55.00
Madame Alexander, Tommy Bangs, Plastic Socket Head, Sleep Eyes, 1952, 15 In. 690.00
Madame Alexander, Wendy Ann, Composition, Socket Head, Glass Eyes, c.1940, 13 In. . . 530.00
Madame Alexander, Wendy Ann, Margaret Face, Plastic Head, Dress, c.1948, 14 In. 1430.00
Madame Alexander, Wendy Ann, Plastic Socket Head, Brunette, c.1952, 15 In. 2310.00
Madame Alexander, Wendy Ann, Plastic Socket Head, Tosca Mohair Wig, c.1950, 15 In. . . 745.00
Madame Alexander, Wendy, Alexander-Kins, Blond, Taffeta Dress, No. 321, 1960, 8 In. . . 935.00
Madame Alexander, Wendy, Alexander-Kins, Hard Plastic, Tagged Outfit, 8 In. 300.00
Madame Alexander, Wendy, Bride, Blond, Pink Wedding Gown, No. 483, 1961, 8 In. 1540.00
Madame Alexander, Winnie Walker, Blue Eyes, Red Dress, Blue Coat, 1953, 8 In. 310.00
Marietta Adams Ruttan, Columbian Exposition, Cloth, Painted Features, c.1893, 28 In. . . 1430.00
Marionette, Cinderella, Pelham Co., England, Box 65.00
Marionette, Gebruder Kuhnlenz, Bisque Head, Mohair, Composition, Wire Limbs, 7 In. . . 385.00
Mary Hoyer, Ballerina, Composition, Red Hair, 5-Piece Body, Pink Outfit, 14 In. 205.00
Mary Hoyer, Composition, 5-Piece Body, Red Hair, Pink Dress, Bonnet, 14 In. 155.00
Mary Hoyer, Plastic, Sleep Eyes, Mohair, Jointed Neck, Limbs, c.1950, 14 In. 295.00

Mattel, Angie 'n Tangie, Dress, Fishnet Stockings, Yellow Yarn Hair, Pretty Pairs 136.00
Mattel, Barbie & Ken, Here Comes The Bride Ensembles, 1964, 11 1/2 & 12 In., Pair 1100.00
Mattel, Barbie, American Girl, Ash Blond Hair, Side Part, 1965, 11 In. 3835.00
Mattel, Barbie, American Girl, Blond, Fab City, c.1960 .... 415.00
Mattel, Barbie, American Girl, Blond, Gold 'n Glamour Ensemble, 1965, 11 1/2 In. 605.00
Mattel, Barbie, American Girl, Blond, Sunday Visit, No. 1675, 1965, 11 1/2 In. 385.00
Mattel, Barbie, American Girl, Blond, Swimsuit, c.1960 .... 358.00
Mattel, Barbie, American Girl, Brunette, Peach Lips, Swimsuit, Turquoise Shoes 310.00
Mattel, Barbie, American Girl, Brunette, Pink Dress, Feather Ruffle, c.1960 .... 495.00
Mattel, Barbie, American Girl, Brunette, Swimsuit, Stand, Tag, Booklet, Box, c.1960 ..... 1210.00
Mattel, Barbie, American Girl, Outdoor Art Show Ensemble, c.1965, 11 1/2 In. 880.00
Mattel, Barbie, American Girl, Platinum Blond, Yellow Lips, Swimsuit, Box 495.00
Mattel, Barbie, Bubble Cut, Auburn, Golden Glory Ensemble, 1961, 11 1/2 In. 195.00
Mattel, Barbie, Bubble Cut, Blond, Black Swimsuit, White Lips, Box, 1962, 11 1/2 In. ... 525.00
Mattel, Barbie, Bubble Cut, Blond, Enchanted Evening Ensemble, 1962, 11 1/2 In. 220.00
Mattel, Barbie, Bubble Cut, Blond, Golden Glory Ensemble, c.1962, 11 1/2 In. 195.00
Mattel, Barbie, Bubble Cut, Blond, Lavender Lips, Red Swimsuit 50.00
Mattel, Barbie, Bubble Cut, Blond, Pink Lips, Wrist Tag, Booklet, Stand, Box 210.00
Mattel, Barbie, Bubble Cut, Blond, Sophisticated Lady Ensemble, 1962, 11 1/2 In. 330.00
Mattel, Barbie, Bubble Cut, Brunette, Career Girl Ensemble, Stand, 1961, 11 1/2 In. 360.00
Mattel, Barbie, Bubble Cut, Brunette, Plantation Belle Ensemble, 1961, 11 1/2 In. 220.00
Mattel, Barbie, Bubble Cut, Strawberry Blond, Red Bathing Suit, 1961-62, 11 1/2 In. 130.00
Mattel, Barbie, Color Magic, Red Hair, Bendable Legs, Accessories, Box, 1966, 11 1/2 In. 1980.00
Mattel, Barbie, Fashion Queen, Japan Costume, c.1963, 11 1/2 In. 220.00
Mattel, Barbie, Funtime, Blond, Cheek Blush, Orange Swimsuit, 1974, Box 170.00
Mattel, Barbie, Hawaiian, Brunette, Hula Skirt, Accessories, No. 7470, Box 60.00
Mattel, Barbie, No. 1, Blond, Ponytail, Striped Swimsuit, Accessories, Booklet, Box 3960.00
Mattel, Barbie, No. 1, Brunette, Ponytail, Swimsuit, 1959, 11 1/2 In. 3960.00
Mattel, Barbie, No. 1, Brunette, Ponytail, Swimsuit, Booklet, Box, 1959, 11 1/2 In. 5720.00
Mattel, Barbie, No. 3, Brunette, Ponytail, Cotton Casual Ensemble, 1960, 11 1/2 In. 360.00
Mattel, Barbie, No. 3, Brunette, Ponytail, Striped Swimsuit, Sunglasses, Shoes, Booklet . 580.00
Mattel, Barbie, No. 3, Brunette, Ponytail, Sweater Girl Costume, Stand, 1960, 11 1/2 In. . 385.00
Mattel, Barbie, No. 4, Blond, Ponytail, Busy Gal Ensemble, Stand, Box, 1960, 11 1/2 In. .. 330.00
Mattel, Barbie, No. 4, Blond, Ponytail, Evening Splendour, Booklet, Box, 11 1/2 In. 2640.00
Mattel, Barbie, No. 4, Brunette, Ponytail, Striped Swimsuit, Red Lips 250.00
Mattel, Barbie, No. 5, Blond, Ponytail, Commuter Set, Hat Box, 1961, 11 1/2 In. 385.00
Mattel, Barbie, No. 6, Blond, Ponytail, Lip Rub, Red-Blue Dress, Stand, Box 210.00
Mattel, Barbie, No. 6, Blond, Ponytail, Red Swimsuit, Stand, Shoes, Box, 1962 .... 165.00
Mattel, Barbie, No. 6, Titian, Ponytail, Stand, Box, 1962 .... 175.00
Mattel, Barbie, Ponytail, Blond, Swirl, Coral Lips, Red Swimsuit, Shoes, Stand, Box 440.00
Mattel, Barbie, Ponytail, Blond, Swirl, Coral Lips, Red Swimsuit, Wrist Tag, Box 680.00
Mattel, Barbie, Ponytail, Blond, Swirl, Pink Lips, White Playsuit, Orange Belt, Shoes 165.00
Mattel, Barbie, Ponytail, Brunette, Black & White Swimsuit, Montgomery Ward 110.00
Mattel, Barbie, Ponytail, Brunette, Black, White Swimsuit, Montgomery Ward, c.1960 ... 190.00
Mattel, Barbie, Ponytail, Swirl, Blond, Modern Art Ensemble, 1964, 11 1/2 In. 300.00
Mattel, Barbie, Ponytail, Swirl, Brunette, Benefit Performance Ensemble, 1964, 11 1/2 In. 495.00
Mattel, Barbie, Talking, Brunette, Bendable Legs, Pink Chiffon Tunic, 1968, 11 1/2 In. ... 220.00
Mattel, Barbie, Talking, Brunette, Swimsuit, Lace Jacket, Real Eyelashes, Box 330.00
Mattel, Barbie, Walk Lively, Blond, Box, c.1971 .... 200.00
Mattel, Beany Boy, Of Beany & Cecil, Propeller On Hat, Says 11 Phrases, 1962, 17 In. ... 325.00
Mattel, Brad, Black Painted Hair, Red Outfit, Box 115.00
Mattel, Brad, Brown Painted Hair, Bendable Legs, Talks, Wrist Tag 60.00
Mattel, Buffy & Mrs. Beasley, Box 140.00
Mattel, Charmin' Chatty, Blond, Get Acquainted Recording, Brochure, Box, 1962, 25 In. . 360.00
Mattel, Charmin' Chatty, Blond, Travels Round World, Accessories, Box, 1962, 25 In. 1045.00
Mattel, Charmin' Chatty, Red Hair, Birthday Party Recording, 1962, 25 In. 165.00
Mattel, Chatty Cathy, Black, Vinyl Head, Sleep Eyes, Rooted Hair, Plastic Body, 20 In. ... 825.00
Mattel, Chatty Cathy, Clothing, Shoehorn, Box, 20 In. 330.00
Mattel, Chatty Cathy, Pigtails, Brown Complexion, Brown Eyes, 1962, 19 In. 990.00
Mattel, Christie, Talking, Oxidized Hair, Coral Lips, Swimsuit, 1968, Box 250.00
Mattel, Donny Osmond, Costume, Microphone, Osbro Productions, Box, 1976, 12 In. 60.00
Mattel, Francie, Twist 'n Turn, Black, Brunette, Pink Lips, Rooted Lashes, Bendable Legs 950.00
Mattel, Francie, Twist 'n Turn, Black, Titian Hair, Pink Lips, Floating-In Outfit 715.00

Mattel, Julia, Twist 'n Turn, Oxidized Red Hair, Dress, Cape, Shoes 95.00
Mattel, Ken, Arabian Nights, Red Velvet Coat, Turban, No. 0774, 1964 .... 310.00
Mattel, Ken, Blond, Flocked, Stand, Box 55.00
Mattel, Ken, Brown Painted Hair, Hawaiian, Surfboard, Accessories, No. 2960, Box 60.00
Mattel, Ken, Brunette, Flocked Hair, Tennis Outfit, Shoes, Tennis Racquet & Balls 155.00
Mattel, Ken, No. 1, Blond, Flocked Hair, Tuxedo, Box, 1961, 12 In. 195.00
Mattel, Ken, No. 2, Blond, Sculpted Hair, Special Date, Box, 1962, 12 In. 140.00
Mattel, Ken, Play Ball, Accessories, 1960s 80.00
Mattel, Ken, Touchdown Football, Accessories, 1960s 75.00
Mattel, Kozmic Kiddles, Purple Gurple 145.00
Mattel, Liddle Biddle Peep, Blond, Dress, Staff, Lamb, Storybook 160.00
Mattel, Liddle Red Riding Hiddle, Blond, Cape, Basket, Wolf, Storybook 150.00
Mattel, Marie Osmond, Costume, Microphone, Osbro Productions, Box, 1976, 12 In. 60.00
Mattel, Midge, Blond Flip Hair, Swimsuit, Box, First Issue, 1963, 11 1/2 In. 360.00
Mattel, Midge, Blond, Peach Lips, Stiff Legs, Suburban Shopper Dress 45.00
Mattel, Midge, Brunette, White Pleated Outfit, Stand, Box 145.00
Mattel, Midge, Red Flip Hair, Ensemble Gift Set, No. 1012, Box, 1963, 11 1/2 In. 3850.00
Mattel, Midge, Red Flip Hair, Mix & Match Set, No. 3807, Sears, Box, 1963, 11 1/2 In. .. 3970.00
Mattel, Midge, Titian Hair, Coral Lips, Orange Blossom Outfit 55.00
Mattel, Midge, Titian, Swimsuit, Stand, Booklet, Box 145.00
Mattel, Pretty Pairs, Lori 'n Rori, Blond, Blue Eyes, Striped Dress, Teddy Bear 77.00
Mattel, Pretty Pairs, Nan 'n Fran, Brown Skin, Hair, Nightgown, Hat, Baby, On Card 90.00
Mattel, Ricky, Red Painted Hair, Striped Jacket, Swim Trunks, Sandals, Box 49.00
Mattel, Skipper, Auburn, Junior Bridesmaid, Nylon Gown, 1965, 9 1/4 In. 140.00
Mattel, Skipper, Blond, Party Pink Costume, Cotton Sundress, 1964, 9 1/4 In. 165.00
Mattel, Skipper, Blond, Quick Curl, Peach Lips, France, No. 4223, 1972, Box 70.00
Mattel, Skipper, Brunette, Silk N' Fancy Outfit, 1964, 9 1/4 In. 140.00
Mattel, Skipper, Growing Up, Houndstooth Skirt, Short Sleeve Shirt, Box 95.00
Mattel, Skipper, New Living, Stand, Box, 1969 .... 99.00
Mattel, Skooter, Blond, Peach Lips, Ship Ahoy Outfit, Boat, Camera 50.00
Mattel, Tutti, Me & My Dog, Brunette, Vinyl Head, Blue Eyes, Box, 1965, 6 1/2 In. 440.00
Mattel, Tutti, Melody In Pink, Blond, Vinyl Head, Posable, Piano, 1965, Box, 6 1/2 In. ... 330.00
Mattel, Tutti, Swing Set, Blond, Vinyl Head, Blue Eyes, Box, 1965, 6 1/2 In. 600.00
Mattel, Twiggy, Blond, Blue Eyes, Bendable Legs, Mod Outfit, 1967, 10 In. 335.00
Mattel, Wayne Gretzky, Great, Le Magnifique, No. 99, Box, 12 In. 60.00
Mego, Cher, Growing Hair, Box 95.00
Mego, Wonder Woman, Lynda Carter, Diana Prince Outfit, Box, 12 In. 330.00
Milliner's, Papier-Mache Head, Molded Hair, Kid Body, Wooden Limbs, 12 1/2 In. 470.00
Milliner's, Wooden, Painted, Jointed Limbs, Blue Checked Dress, 11 1/2 In. 316.00
Milliner's, Wooden, Painted, Jointed Limbs, Striped Dress, White Apron, Bonnet, 16 In. ... 865.00
Minerva, Metal Shoulder Head, Molded Hair, Cloth Body, Germany, 17 In. 112.00
Morimura Bros., Bisque Socket Head, Blue Sleep Eyes, Composition, Wood, 25 In. 248.00
Morimura Bros., Bisque Socket Head, Sleep Eyes, 5-Piece Composition Body, 5 In. 162.00
Muller & Strassburger, Papier-Mache Head, Leipzig, 1850-70 .... 850.00
Nancy Ann Storybook, Plastic, Sleep Eyes, Saran Wig, Walker, 1950, 14 In. 295.00
Norah Wellings, American Indian, Velvet Face, Pigtails, Wooden Ax, c.1935, 12 In. 410.00
Norah Wellings, Baby, Felt Swivel Head, Glass Eyes, Painted Features, c.1935, 23 In. 2530.00
Norah Wellings, Boy, Felt Swivel Head, Mohair, Romper, Coat, c.1935, 32 In. 2970.00
Norah Wellings, Bullfighter, Felt Swivel Head, Painted Features, Mohair, c.1935, 25 In. .. 1980.00
Norah Wellings, Man, Black Velvet Head, Glass Eyes, Sateen Body, c.1935, 16 In. 1100.00
Norah Wellings, Mistress Mary, Felt Swivel Head, Orange Organdy Gown, c.1935, 17 In. . 515.00
Norah Wellings, Royal Guard, Felt Swivel Head, Red & Blue Uniform, c.1935, 34 In. 2530.00
Orsini, Bisque Head & Body, Googly Eyes, Germany, c.1920, 5 In. 2200.00
Paper dolls are listed in their own category.
Papier-Mache, Glass Pupilless Eyes, Cloth Body, Jointed, Stitched Fingers, 19 In. 715.00
Papier-Mache, Japanese Man, Gofum, Enamel Eyes, Straw-Filled, 19th Century, 18 In. ... 519.00
Papier-Mache, Shoulder Head, Painted Eyes, Top Knot, Comb, Kid Body, Wood, 12 In. ... 1210.00
Papier-Mache, Socket Head, Painted Eyes, Cloth Body, Jointed, Composition, 17 In. 200.00
Papier-Mache, Woman, Human Hair, Glass Eyes, Carved Hands, Silk Dress, 14 In. 230.00
Parian, Bride, Bisque Shoulder Head, Painted Eyes, Hair, Cloth Body, Silk Gown, 7 In. ... 440.00
Parian, Bridesmaid, Bisque Head, Painted Hair, Cloth Body, Silk Dress, 7 1/2 In. 660.00
Parian, Man, China Shoulder Head, Painted Eyes, Molded Hair, Tuxedo, 7 3/4 In. 660.00
Phenix, Bisque Head, Paperweight Eyes, Human Hair, Jointed, Bebe, 24 In. 3595.00

Phenix, Bisque Socket Head, Paperweight Eyes, Composition Body, Bebe, c.1890, 14 In. .   4180.00
Philadelphia Baby, Oil Painted Stockinette Head & Body, 21 In. 1100.00
Pincushion dolls are listed in their own category.
Pintel & Godchaux, Bisque Head, Paperweight Eyes, Mohair, Composition, Bebe, 16 In. . .   1650.00
Puppet, Bye-Lo Baby, Bisque, Celluloid, H. Steiner, Grace Putnam, Box, 1923, 10 In. 550.00
Puppet, Gomez, Addams Family, Vinyl Head, Fabric Body, Ideal, 1964, 10 1/2 In. 165.00
Puppet, Hand, Alligator, Steiff, 8 In. 55.00
Puppet, Harold Lloyd, Red Fez, Fabric Body, 1960s, 10 1/2 x 8 1/2 In. 75.00
Puppet, Illya Kuryakin, Rubber, Gilbert, 1960s, 13 In. 95.00
Puppet, Monkey, Mohair, Tin Face, Felt Hands, Schuco, Germany, 7 3/4 In. 55.00
Rabery & Delphieu, Bisque Socket Head, Paperweight Eyes, Bebe, c.1888, 24 In. 4675.00
Raggedy Ann, Shoebutton Eyes, Painted Features, Georgene Novelties, c.1951, 30 In. 880.00
Raggedy Ann, Shoebutton Eyes, Triangle Nose, Yarn Hair, Stitch-Jointed, Volland, 16 In. . .   550.00
Ravca, Peddler Woman, Stockinette, Mohair Wig, Wire-Frame Body, France, 15 In. 660.00
Recknagel, 22-70, Bisque Head, Painted Eyes, Molded Bonnet, Composition, Baby, 9 In. .   330.00
Recknagel, 50, Bisque Socket Head, Googly Intaglio Eyes, 5-Piece Body, 6 1/2 In. 470.00
Recknagel, 57, Bisque Socket Head, Intaglio Eyes, Laughing, Composition Body, 7 In. . . .   470.00
Recknagel, 241, Bisque Flange Head, Sleep Eyes, Cloth Body, 6 1/2 In. 75.00
Rohmer, Bisque, Kid Body, Bisque Arms, Jointed Legs, Gown With Train, 16 In. 3160.00
Roullet & Decamps, Bisque Socket Head, Glass Eyes, Mechanical, Walker, c.1900, 19 In. .   1540.00
Royal Copenhagen, Woman, Porcelain, Muslin, Stitch-Jointed, c.1840, 15 In. 1760.00
Rushton, Mistress Mary, Pressed Mask Face, Mohair, Sateen Body, Taffeta Dress, 14 In. . .   440.00
S & H dolls are also listed here as Bergmann and Simon & Halbig.
S & H, 1023, Bisque Head, Jointed Composition Arms, Legs, Brown Eyes, Dress, 19 In. . .   175.00
S & H, 1468, Flapper Girl, Bisque, Sleep Eyes, Dress, 14 1/2 In. 2470.00
S & H, 9149, Bisque Head, Period Dress, 23 In. 120.00
S.F.B.J., 14, Bisque Socket Head, Paperweight Eyes, Composition Body, Bebe, 31 In. 1008.00
S.F.B.J., 60, Bisque Head, Glass Eyes, Composition, Wood Body, Bleuette, 11 In. 2585.00
S.F.B.J., 60, Bisque Head, Mohair, Composition, Jointed Wood, Satin Outfit, 19 In. 385.00
S.F.B.J., 60, Bisque Head, Pupilless Eyes, Mohair, 5-Piece Body, Alsace Costume, 10 In. . .   385.00
S.F.B.J., 60, Bisque Socket Head, Blue Sleep Eyes, Composition, Wood, Jointed, 22 In. . . .   300.00
S.F.B.J., 230, Bisque Socket Head, Paperweight Eyes, Composition, Wood, Jointed, 23 In. .   740.00
S.F.B.J., 235, Bisque Socket Head, Brown, Glass Inset Eyes, Beaded Teeth, 13 In. 4030.00
S.F.B.J., 236, Bisque Head, Sleep Eyes, Composition, Laughing, Jumeau, Toddler, 15 In. . .   730.00
S.F.B.J., 237, Bisque Head, Sculpted Hair, Composition, Wood, Jointed, c.1912, 16 In. 1210.00
S.F.B.J., 238, Bisque Head, Glass Inset Eyes, Composition, Wood Body, c.1915, 18 In. 2640.00
S.F.B.J., 252, Bisque Head, Glass Sleep Eyes, Jointed Body, Mohair Wig, c.1912, 9 In. 4180.00
S.F.B.J., 252, Bisque Head, Pouty, Composition, Wood, Jointed, Toddler, c.1910, 13 In. 4950.00
S.F.B.J., 301, Bisque Head, Pierced Ears, Human Hair, Composition, Wood, Jointed, 25 In. .   475.00
S.F.B.J., 301, Bisque Socket Head, Composition & Wood Body, Bebe, c.1920, 9 1/2 In. 785.00
S.F.B.J., 301, Bisque Socket Head, Set Blue Eyes, Wood, Composition Body, Jointed, 26 In.   440.00
S.F.B.J., 301, Bisque Socket Head, Sleep Eyes, Composition Body, Bebe, 23 In. 336.00
S.F.B.J., Bisque Head, Pierced Ears, Human Hair, Jointed Wood, Composition, 20 In. 880.00
S.F.B.J., Bisque Head, Pierced Ears, Mohair Wig, Walker, Kissing Mechanism, 19 In. 330.00
S.F.B.J., Bisque Socket Head, Flirty Sleep Eyes, Composition, Walker, Talker, 23 In. 715.00
S.F.B.J., Bisque Socket Head, Glass Flirty Eyes, Walking-Style Body, Bebe, c.1900, 23 In. .   1870.00
S.F.B.J., Bisque Socket Head, Glass Inset Eyes, Bleuette, Model 4, Bebe, c.1922, 11 In. . . .   1680.00
S.F.B.J., Bisque Socket Head, Glass Sleep Eyes, Mariner's Clothes, c.1915, 11 In. 1345.00
S.F.B.J., Peddler, Bisque Head, Glass Eyes, Blond Hair, Antique Clothes, Bebe, 17 In. 635.00
Sayco, Miss America, Vinyl Socket Head, Blond, Sleep Eyes, Fur Wrap, c.1959, 10 In. 110.00
Schilling, Papier-Mache Shoulder Head, Glass Inset Eyes, Kid Body, Box, c.1885, 12 In. . .   1100.00
Schlaggenwald, Morning Glory, China Shoulder Head, Kid Body, 16 3/4 In. 6270.00
Schmitt & Fils, Bisque Socket Head, Glass Enamel Inset Eyes, Bebe, c.1880, 14 In. 10175.00
Schoenau & Hoffmeister, 1906, Bisque Head, Sleep Eyes, Jointed, Composition, 40 In. . . .   1120.00
Schoenau & Hoffmeister, 4900, Bisque Head, Caracul Hair, Uniform, Sword, 9 In. 470.00
Schoenau & Hoffmeister, Hanna, Bisque, Human Hair, Composition, Baby, 16 In. 220.00
Schoenhut, 301, Wood Socket Head, Body, Intaglio Eyes, Mohair, Spring Jointed, 21 In. . .   880.00
Schoenhut, Bisque Head, Wood, Jointed, Original Clothes, Lady Acrobat, 8 1/4 In. 385.00
Schoenhut, Bisque Head, Wood, Jointed, Original Clothes, Lady Rider, 8 3/8 In. 66.00
Schoenhut, Clown, Wood, Hand Painted Face, Diamond Design Clothes, Jointed, 9 In. . . .   195.00
Schoenhut, Jiggs, Wood, Jointed, Painted Features, Original Clothes, Button, 7 1/2 In. . . .   390.00
Schoenhut, Lion Tamer, Wood, Molded Hair, Moustache, Goatee, Jacket, 1909, 8 3/4 In. . .   470.00
Schoenhut, Maggie, Wood, Painted Features, Original Clothes, Jointed, Button, 9 In. 390.00

Schoenhut, Miss Dolly, Wood Socket Head, Decal Eyes, Spring-Jointed, c.1920, 21 In. 825.00
Schoenhut, Miss Dolly, Wood Socket Head, Spring-Jointed, Sailor Outfit, 19 In. 385.00
Schoenhut, Nature Baby, Painted Blue Eyes, Closed Mouth, Wood Body, 16 In. 120.00
Schoenhut, Wood Head, Intaglio Eyes, Human Hair, Jointed, Sailor Suit, Boy, 21 In. 660.00
Schoenhut, Wood Head, Painted Eyes, Carved Hair, Spring-Jointed, Boy, c.1912, 16 In. .. 1455.00
Schoenhut, Wood Head, Painted Eyes, Mohair Wig, Spring-Jointed, Girl, c.1911, 20 In. .. 950.00
Schoenhut, Wood Socket Head, Blue Eyes, Blond Mohair, Spring-Jointed, c.1912, 18 In. . 990.00
Schoenhut, Wood Socket Head, Bobbed Hair, Checkered Dress, 1915, 16 In. 3850.00
Schoenhut, Wood Socket Head, Brunette Mohair, Spring-Jointed, c.1912, 18 In. 1045.00
Schoenhut, Wood Socket Head, Brunette Mohair, Spring-Jointed, c.1913, 12 In. 1430.00
Schoenhut, Wood Socket Head, Brunette Mohair, Spring-Jointed, c.1914, 21 In. 1595.00
Schoenhut, Wood Socket Head, Jointed Shoulders & Hips, Walker, 1913, 14 In. 330.00
Schoenhut, Wood Socket Head, Mohair Wig, Spring-Jointed, c.1912, 21 In. 1870.00
Schoenhut, Wood Socket Head, Sleep Eyes, Jointed Body, Girl, c.1911, 22 In. 440.00
Schoenhut, Wood Socket Head, Spring-Jointed, Girl, 1911, 16 In. 470.00
Schoenhut, Wood, Blue Painted Eyes, Blond Mohair Wig, Jointed Body, Toddler, 14 In. .. 385.00
Schoenhut, Wood, Intaglio Eyes, Carved Hair, Comb Marks, Spring-Jointed, Boy, 16 In. .. 1055.00
Schoenhut, Wood, Jointed, Blue Intaglio Painted Eyes, Blond Wig, Boy, 15 In. 175.00
Schoenhut, Wood, Pouty Painted Eyes, Brown Mohair Wig, Jointed Body, Girl, 14 In. 330.00
Schoenhut, Wood, Pouty, Painted Eyes, Mohair, Toddler, 20th Century, 17 In. 500.00
Shirley Temple dolls are included in the Shirley Temple category.
Simon & Halbig dolls are also listed here under Bergmann and S & H.
Simon & Halbig, 164, Bisque Socket Head, Black Mohair, Asian Woman, 23 In. 4950.00
Simon & Halbig, 550, Bisque Head, Human Hair, Jointed Wood, Composition, 22 In. 288.00
Simon & Halbig, 570, Bisque Socket Head, Blue Sleep Eyes, Wood, Composition, 19 In. .. 360.00
Simon & Halbig, 739, Bisque Head, Inset Eyes, Muslin Body, Stitched, c.1885, 20 In. 1430.00
Simon & Halbig, 739, Bisque Head, Pierced Ears, Caracul, Kid, Cloth Body, 18 In. 880.00
Simon & Halbig, 750, Bisque Shoulder Head, Paperweight Eyes, Kid Body, 17 1/2 In. 635.00
Simon & Halbig, 878, Governess, Child, Bisque Head, Sleep Eyes, Composition, 7 In. 360.00
Simon & Halbig, 881, Bisque Swivel Head, Brown Glass Inset Eyes, c.1885, 7 1/2 In. 3470.00
Simon & Halbig, 886, Bisque, Mohair Wig, Jointed, Original Dress, Bonnet, 9 In. 1650.00
Simon & Halbig, 886, Bisque, Set Eyes, Mohair Wig, Jointed, 7 1/2 In. 1100.00
Simon & Halbig, 890, Bisque Head, Sleep Eyes, Mohair Wig, 5-Piece Body, 6 In. 1100.00
Simon & Halbig, 890, Bisque Swivel Head, Brown Glass Sleep Eyes, c.1895, 6 1/2 In. 1230.00
Simon & Halbig, 908, Bisque Socket Head, Glass Paperweight Eyes, c.1885, 16 In. 1790.00
Simon & Halbig, 929, Bisque Socket Head, Brown Glass Inset Eyes, c.1890, 14 In. 2070.00
Simon & Halbig, 939, Bisque Socket Head, Glass Inset Eyes, 8 Ball Joints, c.1890, 23 In. . 2860.00
Simon & Halbig, 939, Bisque Swivel Head, Glass Eyes, Muslin Body, c.1890, 13 In. 1230.00
Simon & Halbig, 949, Bisque Head, Paperweight Eyes, Pierced Ears, Human Hair, 26 In. .. 2310.00
Simon & Halbig, 949, Bisque Socket Head, Brown Glass Sleep Eyes, c.1890, 10 In. 2530.00
Simon & Halbig, 949, Bisque Socket Head, Glass Inset Eyes, Ball-Jointed, c.1890, 18 In. .. 2860.00
Simon & Halbig, 949, Bisque Socket Head, Glass Inset Eyes, Jointed, c.1890, 9 1/2 In. .. 1815.00
Simon & Halbig, 949, Bisque Swivel Head, Blue Glass Eyes, Muslin Body, c.1890, 12 In. . 1345.00
Simon & Halbig, 949, Bisque Swivel Head, Brown Glass Sleep Eyes, c.1890, 7 In. 1650.00
Simon & Halbig, 969, Bisque Socket Head, Brown Glass Inset Eyes, c.1890, 15 In. 6385.00
Simon & Halbig, 969, Bisque Socket Head, Glass Inset Eyes, Wood Body, c.1890, 16 In. .. 3850.00
Simon & Halbig, 1009, Bisque Head, Jointed Wood, Composition, Dress, 16 1/2 In. 385.00
Simon & Halbig, 1009, Bisque Socket Head, Glass Inset Eyes, Ball-Jointed, c.1885, 19 In. .. 1540.00
Simon & Halbig, 1078, Bisque Head, Mohair Braids, Composition, Ethnic, 8 1/2 In. 275.00
Simon & Halbig, 1078, Bisque Head, Mohair Wig, Composition, 7 1/2 In. 350.00
Simon & Halbig, 1078, Bisque Head, Mohair, Bob Style, Seersucker Dress, 9 In. 470.00
Simon & Halbig, 1079, Bisque Head, Glass Sleep Eyes, Ball-Jointed, c.1900, 18 In. 770.00
Simon & Halbig, 1079, Bisque Head, Glass Sleep Eyes, Ball-Jointed, c.1910, 28 In. 1980.00
Simon & Halbig, 1079, Bisque Head, Human Hair, Jointed Composition, 21 In. 300.00
Simon & Halbig, 1079, Bisque Head, Mohair Curls, Composition, Jointed, 8 In. 385.00
Simon & Halbig, 1079, Bisque Head, Mohair, Composition Body, Jointed Wood, 13 In. ... 440.00
Simon & Halbig, 1079, Bisque Head, Mohair, Composition, Jointed Wood, 18 In. 275.00
Simon & Halbig, 1079, Bisque Head, Sleep Eyes, Composition, Wood, c.1900, 15 In. 825.00
Simon & Halbig, 1079, Bisque Head, Sleep Eyes, Human Hair, Jointed, 21 In. 385.00
Simon & Halbig, 1079, Bisque Head, Sleep Eyes, Jointed Wood, Composition, 17 1/2 In. .. 250.00
Simon & Halbig, 1079, Bisque Head, Sleep Eyes, Pierced Ears, Mohair, Jointed, 30 In. ... 605.00
Simon & Halbig, 1079, Bisque Socket Head, Sleep Eyes, Composition, Wood, 8 In. 413.00
Simon & Halbig, 1079, Bisque, Human Hair, Jointed Wood, Composition, 24 1/2 In. 440.00

Simon & Halbig, 1080, Bisque Shoulder Head, Sleep Eyes, Kid, Composition Body, 19 In.   275.00
Simon & Halbig, 1099, Bisque Socket Head, Amber Tint, Slanted Eyes, Jointed, 15 In. 1870.00
Simon & Halbig, 1129, Bisque Head, Sleep Eyes, Jointed Body, Asian Child, 24 In. 3850.00
Simon & Halbig, 1199, Bisque Head, Mohair, Jointed Wood, Composition, 13 In. 880.00
Simon & Halbig, 1249, Bisque Head, Blue Eyes, Pierced Ears, Mohair, Jointed, 21 1/2 In. .   745.00
Simon & Halbig, 1249, Bisque Head, Pierced Ears, Mohair, Composition, Jointed, 12 In. . .   440.00
Simon & Halbig, 1249, Santa, Bisque Head, Sleep Eyes, Composition, Human Hair, 17 In.   705.00
Simon & Halbig, 1249, Santa, Bisque Head, Sleep Eyes, Open Mouth, Mohair, 22 1/2 In. . .   646.00
Simon & Halbig, 1250, Bisque Head, Synthetic Wig, Kid Body, Rivet Joints, 20 In. 385.00
Simon & Halbig, 1250, Bisque Shoulder Head, Sleep Eyes, Mohair, Kid Body, 23 In. 380.00
Simon & Halbig, 1299, Bisque Head, Pierced Ears, Human Hair, Wood, Composition, 18 In.   720.00
Simon & Halbig, 1299, Bisque Head, Wood, Composition, Child, 32 1/2 In. 2860.00
Simon & Halbig, 1303, Bisque Socket Head, Glass Inset Eyes, Brunette, c.1900, 15 In.   . . .   9350.00
Simon & Halbig, 1329, Bisque Head, Olive Skin, Pierced Ears, Mohair, Asian Child, 15 In.   1540.00
Simon & Halbig, 1329, Bisque Socket Head, Sleep Eyes, Asian Child, c.1900, 11 In. 2016.00
Simon & Halbig, 1329, Bisque, Olive Skin, Pierced Ears, Human Hair, Jointed, 21 In. 2310.00
Simon & Halbig, 1349, Bisque Head, Jointed Wood, Composition Body, Dress, 18 In. 330.00
Simon & Halbig, 1418, Bisque Socket Head, Blue Glass Sleep Eyes, c.1912, 13 In. 12880.00
Simon & Halbig, 1428, Bisque Head, Glass Sleep Eyes, Composition, c.1912, 14 In. 1870.00
Simon & Halbig, 1469, Bisque Socket Head, Blue Glass Sleep Eyes, c.1912, 14 In. 5150.00
Simon & Halbig, 1488, Bisque Head, Chubby Face, Mohair, Ball-Jointed, c.1912, 22 In. . .   5500.00
Simon & Halbig, 1488, Bisque Socket Head, Glass Sleep Eyes, Pouty, c.1912, 11 In. 2465.00
Simon & Halbig, Bisque Head, Glass Eyes, Open Mouth, Teeth, Jointed, 28 In. 385.00
Simon & Halbig, Bisque Head, Inset Eyes, Mohair, Composition, Jointed, c.1880, 12 In. . .   2530.00
Simon & Halbig, Bisque Socket Head, Blue Glass Sleep Eyes, Mohair Wig, c.1910, 19 In. .   1400.00
Simon & Halbig, Bisque Socket Head, Glass Sleep Eyes, Composition, Jointed, 27 In. 825.00
Simon & Halbig, Bisque Socket Head, Revolving, 2 Sculpted Faces, White, Black, 11 In. . . .   3300.00
Simon & Halbig, Bisque Swivel Head, Glass Inset Eyes, Wool Coat, c.1890, 7 In. 2130.00
Simon & Halbig, Bisque Swivel Head, Twill Over Wood Body, c.1885, 10 In. 4070.00
Simon & Halbig, Bisque, Set Eyes, Period Costume, Boy, 6 1/2 In. 920.00
Simon & Halbig, Cook, Printed Cotton Dress, Apron, Mop, Plate & Pie, 6 1/2 In. 1870.00
Sonneberg, 117, Bisque Head, Glass Inset Eyes, Mohair, Composition, Jointed, 16 In. 2420.00
Sonneberg, Bisque Socket Head, Glass Inset Eyes, Composition Body, c.1885, 14 In. 1210.00
Sonneberg, Bisque Socket Head, Wood, Composition, Glass Inset Eyes, c.1885, 22 In. 3250.00
Steiner, Bisque Head, Paperweight Eyes, Synthetic Wig, Composition, Jointed, 14 In. 3080.00
Steiner, Bisque Head, Paperweight Eyes, Teeth, Human Hair, Bebe, 22 In. 2940.00
Steiner, Bisque Head, Turns, Moves Limbs, Key Wind, Gigoteur, Bebe, c.1880, 20 In. 3300.00
Steiner, Bisque Socket Head, Blue Eyes, Ball-Jointed, Wood, Composition Body, 15 In. . .   240.00
Steiner, Bisque Socket Head, Blue Glass Paperweight Eyes, Bebe, c.1888, 18 In. 5710.00
Steiner, Bisque Socket Head, Glass Paperweight Eyes, Bebe, Figure A, c.1888, 14 In. 4950.00
Steiner, Bisque Socket Head, Glass Paperweight Inset Eyes, Figure A, Bebe, c.1890, 8 In. . .   2750.00
Steiner, Bisque Socket Head, Paperweight Eyes, Jointed, Bebe, Figure B, c.1885, 26 In. . .   6325.00
Steiner, Bisque, Paperweight Eyes, Mohair, Walker, Cryer, Gigoteur, 20 In. 2300.00
Superior, Papier-Mache Shoulder Head, Cloth Body, Stitch-Jointed, Fingers, 34 1/2 In. . . .   275.00
Sustrac, Bisque Swivel Head, Glass Eyes, c.1880, 5 1/2 In. 5375.00
Swaine & Co., Lori Baby, Bisque Socket Head, Solid Dome, Composition, 19 In. 715.00
Terri Lee, Hard Plastic, Painted Eyes, Closed Mouth, Mohair, Jointed, c.1950, 16 In. 235.00
Terri Lee, Hard Plastic, Socket Head, Brown Eyes, Closed Mouth, Walker, 1956, 10 In. . . .   210.00
Terri Lee, Mary Jane, Plastic, Socket Head, Sleep Eyes, 1950s, 15 In. 250.00
Terri Lee, Plastic Socket Head, Brown Eyes, Blond Hair, Red Gown, 1950s, 16 In. 590.00
Terri Lee, Plastic Socket Head, Brown Eyes, Cowgirl Outfit, 1950s, 16 In. 1065.00
Terri Lee, Plastic Socket Head, Brown Eyes, Lavender Party Dress, 1950s, 16 In. 310.00
Terri Lee, Plastic Socket Head, Brown Eyes, Yellow Party Dress, 1950s, 16 In. 365.00
Trudy, 3 Faces, Composition Head & Limbs, Cloth Body, Original Clothes, 15 In. 84.00
TynieToy, Father, Mother, Piggity, Wood, Articulated, Original Clothes, 5 1/2 In., Pair 2860.00
Vogue, Brikette, Vinyl, Orange Hair, Green Flirty Sleep Eyes, Sunglasses, 1961, 22 In. 110.00
Vogue, Brikette, Virgin, Carrot-Red Hair, Green Eyes, Italy, 1959, 22 In. 305.00
Vogue, Dora Lee, Composition, Sleep Eyes, Mohair Wig, Jointed, Dress, Box, 11 In. 770.00
Vogue, Ginnette, Nylon Romper, In Shoe-Fly Rocker Baby Chair, c.1960 . . . .   195.00
Vogue, Ginny, Hard Plastic, Blond Braids, Blue Eyes, Checkered Dress, 1950-53, 8 In.   . . .   550.00
Vogue, Ginny, Hard Plastic, Blond Saran Wig, Elastic Strung, c.1952, 7 1/2 In. 150.00
Vogue, Ginny, Hard Plastic, Fleecy Hair, Blue Eyes, Checkered Dress, 1950-53, 8 In. 770.00

Doll, Vogue, Nurse,
Composition,
Mohair Wig,
Original Clothes,
Gold Label, 7 1/2 In.

Doll, Vogue, Robin
Hood, Composition,
Mohair Wig,
Original Clothes,
Box, 7 1/2 In.

Doll, Vogue, Toddles,
Red, Composition,
Molded, Painted
Hair, Original Dress,
Box, 7 1/2 In.

Vogue, Ginny, Hard Plastic, Molded Lashes, Red & White Dress, Walker, 8 In. 120.00
Vogue, Ginny, Hard Plastic, Painted Eyes, Red, White, Green Dress, Red Sweater, 8 In. 200.00
Vogue, Ginny, Hard Plastic, Painted Lashes, Braids, Jointed, Dress, Zipper, Straw Hat, 7 In.   1595.00
Vogue, Ginny, Hard Plastic, Painted Lashes, Dress, Hat, Pin, Center-Snap Shoe, 8 In. 260.00
Vogue, Ginny, Hard Plastic, Painted Lashes, Jointed, Original Dress, 7 1/2 In. 1155.00
Vogue, Ginny, Hard Plastic, Red Hair, Painted Lashes, Elastic Strung, Trunk, 7 In. 150.00
Vogue, Ginny, Ice Skater, Hard Plastic, Painted Lashes, Blond Braids, 8 In. 495.00
Vogue, Ginny, Kindergarten Afternoon Series, Blue Sleep Eyes, 1953, 7 In. 945.00
Vogue, Ginny, Sweetheart, Hard Plastic Head, Sleep Eyes, Taffeta Dress, 1949, 8 In. 740.00
Vogue, Jan, Vinyl Socket Head, Auburn Hair, Sleep Eyes, Swivel Waist, Skirt, 1958, 10 In.   385.00
Vogue, Jan, Vinyl Socket Head, Brunette, Sleep Eyes, Swivel Waist, 1958, 10 1/2 In. 140.00
Vogue, Jeff, Plastic Head, Cabana Suit, No. 6131, 1958, 11 In. 110.00
Vogue, Jeff, Plastic Head, Plaid Shirt, Green Pants & Cap, No. 6463, 1959, 11 In. 85.00
Vogue, Jill, Plastic Head, Auburn Hair, Black Record Hop Skirt, Box, 1957, 10 1/2 In. 385.00
Vogue, Jill, Plastic Head, Blond Angel Coiffure, Flowered Capri Set, 1959, 10 1/2 In. 220.00
Vogue, Jill, Plastic Head, Blond, Sleep Eyes, Sailor Dress, No. 3166, c.1959, 10 In. .138.00 to 165.00
Vogue, Jill, Plastic Head, Brunette, Ponytail, Black Velvet Pants, Box, 1957, 10 1/2 In. 275.00
Vogue, Jill, Plastic Head, Brunette, Sleep Eyes, Riding Outfit, 1958, 10 1/2 In. 195.00
Vogue, Jill, Plastic Head, Reddish Blond, Sleep Eyes, No. 3230, 1959, 10 1/2 In. 360.00
Vogue, Nurse, Composition, Mohair Wig, Original Clothes, Gold Label, 7 1/2 In. . . . . *Illus*   523.00
Vogue, Robin Hood, Composition, Mohair Wig, Original Clothes, Box, 7 1/2 In. . . . . . . *Illus*   468.00
Vogue, Toddles, Blue Painted Eyes To Right, Blond Mohair, 1940s, 7 1/2 In. . . . . . .175.00 to 265.00
Vogue, Toddles, Composition, Painted Eyes To Right, Blond Mohair, 1940s, 7 1/2 In. 265.00
Vogue, Toddles, Hansel & Gretel, Composition, Looking Right, Mohair, Jointed, 7 1/2 In. .   990.00
Vogue, Toddles, Nurse, Composition, Painted Eyes Looking Right, Mohair, 7 1/2 In. 525.00
Vogue, Toddles, Red Riding Hood, Composition, Mohair Wig, Jointed, 7 1/2 In. 305.00
Vogue, Toddles, Red, Composition, Molded, Painted Hair, Original Dress, Box, 7 1/2 In. *Illus*   303.00
Vogue, Toddles, Sailor, Composition, Googly Eyes, Mohair, Jointed Body, Box, 7 1/2 In. . . .   385.00
Vogue, Toddles, Wee Willie Winkie, Composition, Looking To Right, Mohair, 7 1/2 In. . . .   525.00
Wax, Blond Hair, Movable Blue Eyes, 20th Century, 22 In. 235.00
Wax, Blue Glass Enamel Inset Eyes, Muslin, Mohair Inserts, England, c.1880, 18 In. 615.00
Wax, Fashion, Glass Enamel Eyes, Muslin Body, England, c.1875, 14 In. 600.00
Wax, Over Composition, Shoulder Head, Fuzzy Hair, Cloth Body, 24 In. 275.00
Wax, Over Composition, Shoulder Head, Glass Eyes, Mohair Wig, Cloth Body, 27 In. 440.00
Wax, Over Papier-Mache, Blue Glass Sleep Eyes, Muslin Body, Germany, c.1875, 14 In. . .   670.00
Wax, Shoulder Head, Blue Eyes, Muslin Body, Baby, England, c.1880, 18 In. 1456.00
Wax, Shoulder Head, Blue Sleep Eyes, Mohair Wig, Gusseted Kid Body, 16 In. 305.00
Wax, Shoulder Head, Human Hair, Padded Wire Frame Body, Lanvin, Base, 12 In. 250.00
Wax, Shoulder Head, Human Hair, Padded Wire Frame Body, Pheruit, 1904, 12 In. 165.00
Wax, Spanish Lady, Sculpted Hair, Painted Features, Crepe Paper Costume, c.1935, 18 In. .   190.00
Wax Head, Glass Enamel Inset Eyes, Muslin Body, Baby, England, c.1880, 24 In. 1210.00
Wax Head, Glass Enamel Inset Eyes, Muslin Body, England, Child, c.1885, 21 In. 1155.00
Wax Head, Glass Enamel Inset Eyes, Muslin Body, Pine Box, England, c.1854, 20 In. 1540.00
Wax Head, Human Hair, Cloth Body, Man, 19 In. 1210.00
Weiss Kybnert, Composition, Glass Sleep Eyes, Tosca Wig, Jointed, Germany, 21 In. 110.00
Wislizenus, Bisque Socket Head, Googly Eyes, Mohair, 5-Piece Body, Toddler, 5 1/2 In. . .   3960.00

Wooden, Carved Hair, Carved Features, Egg-Shaped Head, Dowel Joints, c.1830, 23 In. .. 2530.00
Wooden, Carved, Georgia, 1920-30 .... 1695.00
Wooden, Nun, Peg, Painted Features, Habit, Leather Box, 3 1/2 In. 200.00
Wooden, Painted, Carved Comb, Pegged Joints, Dress, Silk Panel In Skirt, 8 1/2 In. 1020.00
DOLL CLOTHES, Alexander-Kins, Ballerina Tutu, Pink, Purple, No. 0586, Box, c.1958 ...... 330.00
Barbie, Aboard Ship, Nautical Dress, Vest, Shoes, Camera, No. 1631 .... 60.00
Barbie, All That Jazz, Coat, Dress, Hairpiece, Shoes, No. 1848 .... 90.00
Barbie, American Airlines Stewardess, No. 984, Package, c.1961 .... 305.00
Barbie, American Airlines Stewardess, Uniform, No. 984 .... 50.00
Barbie, Beautiful Bride, Satin Gown, Veil, Shoes, Bouquet, No. 1698 .... 120.00
Barbie, Benefit Performance, Red Tunic, Tulle Skirt, Gloves, Shoes, No. 1667 .... 145.00
Barbie, Black Magic Ensemble, Black Sheath, Cape, Ribbon, Shoes, Gloves, No. 1609 ... 65.00
Barbie, Busy Gal, Jacket, Skirt, Body Shirt, Cap, Belt, Shoes, Glasses, No. 981 .... 65.00
Barbie, Campus Sweetheart, Satin Gown, Tulle Panels, Long Gloves, Pearls, No. 1616 ... 300.00
Barbie, Career Girl, Tweed Jacket, Skirt, Hat, Body Shirt, Long Gloves, Shoes, No. 954 .. 50.00
Barbie, Commuter Set, Navy Jacket, Skirt, Satin Body Shirt, Shoes, Gloves, No. 916 .... 130.00
Barbie, Disco Dater, Satin Dress, Pleated Skirt, Sleeveless Shell, Hanger, No. 1807 ...... 80.00
Barbie, Dressmakers Kit, Zippers, Buttons, No. 1831, Box 25.00
Barbie, Easter Parade, Print Sheath Dress, Black Coat, Short Gloves, Shoes, No. 971 ..... 550.00
Barbie, Fashion Editor, Sheath, Skirt, Print Bodice, Jacket, Cap, Shoes, No. 1635 .... 165.00
Barbie, Fashion Luncheon, Pink Dress, Jacket, Accessories, No. 1656 .... 121.00
Barbie, Formal Occasion, Long White Dress, Fuchsia Gold Lame Cape, Shoes, No. 1697 . 220.00
Barbie, Friday Night Date, Corduroy Jumper, Appliques, Underdress, Shoes, No. 979 .... 45.00
Barbie, Garden Wedding, Pink Strapless Dress, White Lace Gown, Shoes, No. 1658 ...... 80.00
Barbie, Golden Evening, Knit Top, Long Skirt, No. 1610 .... 65.00
Barbie, Golden Glory, Gold Damask Gown, Accessories, No. 1645 .... 105.00
Barbie, In Switzerland, Dress, Bonnet, Shoes, Bouquet, No. 0822 .... 50.00
Barbie, Invitation To Tea, Chiffon Jumpsuit, Vest, Belt, Shoes, Glitter, No. 1632 .... 100.00
Barbie, London Tour, Vinyl Coat, Button, Hat, Handbag, Scarf, Shoes, No. 1661 .... 70.00
Barbie, Lunch On The Terrace, Dress, Hat, Shoes, No. 1649 .... 110.00
Barbie, Mad About Plaid, Coat, Dress, Hat, Belt, Purse, No. 1587 .... 110.00
Barbie, Made For Each Other, Coat, Shirt, Skirt, Boots, Hat, No. 1881 .... 90.00
Barbie, Magnificent Midi, Coat, Dress, Hat Boots, No. 3418 .... 70.00
Barbie, Masquerade, Dress, Hat, Hose, Shoes, Mask, Invitation, No. 944 .... 60.00
Barbie, Maxi 'n Mini, Foil Dress, Shirt, Pants, Belt, Boots, No. 1799 .... 80.00
Barbie, Mood For Music, Sweater, Shirt, Pants, Pearl Necklace, Shoes, No. 940 .... 55.00
Barbie, Music Center Matinee, Shirt, Skirt, Hat, Long White Gloves, No. 1663 .... 175.00
Barbie, Outdoor Life, Checked Coat, Print Pants, Shirt, Hat, Tennis Shoes, No. 1637 ..... 45.00
Barbie, Party Date, Print Dress, Purse, Glitter Shoes, No. 958 .... 45.00
Barbie, Picnic Set, Shirt, Denim Pants, Straw Hat, Bamboo Pole, Basket, Fish, No. 967 ... 95.00
Barbie, Plantation Belle, Dress, Slip, Wide-Brimmed Hat, Purse, Jewelry, No. 966 .... 135.00
Barbie, Print Aplenty, Dress, Earrings, Shoes, No. 1686 .... 75.00
Barbie, Red For Rain, Red Belted Trench Coat, Hat, Boots, No. 3409, Box 55.00
Barbie, Riding In The Park, Jacket, Shirt, Cropped Pants, Boots, Hat, Whip, No. 1688 .... 180.00
Barbie, Solo In The Spotlight, Black Glitter Gown, Gloves, Scarf, Shoes, No. 982 .... 40.00
Barbie, Student Teacher, Dress, Hat, Accessories, No. 1622 .... 135.00
Barbie, Twinkle Togs, Dress, Lame Bodice, Hose, Shoes, No. 1854 .... 90.00
Barbie, Vacation Time, Knit Sweater, Checked Shorts, Flat Shoes, Camera, No. 1623 ..... 65.00
Barbie, White Magic, White Satin Coat, Accessories, No. 1607 .... 75.00
Barbie, Winter Wow, Jacket, Skirt, Fur, Hat, Muff, Belt, Long Gloves, No. 1486 .... 90.00
Barbie, Yellow Mellow, Dress, Hose, Shoes, No. 1484 .... 55.00
Busy Morning, Dress, Hat, Phone, Purse, Shoes, No. 956 .... 115.00
Cissette, Ballerina Tutu, Ivory Satin, Tulle Skirt, Flowers, No. 926, Alexander, c.1960 .... 110.00
Cissette, Cabana Outfit, Blue Cotton, Rosebuds, No. 805, Alexander, Box, c.1957 .... 935.00
Cissette, Dress, Lacy, Taffeta Petticoat, Hat, No 0731, Alexander, Box, c.1957 .... 880.00
Cissette, Gown, Satin, Pink, Tulle Wrap, No. 823, Alexander, Box, 1957 .... 385.00
Cissette, Gown, Velvet Wrap, Petticoat, Stockings, No. 879, Alexander, Box, c.1957 ..... 1100.00
Cissy, Cocktail Ensemble, Tulle, Pale Green, No. 21-54, Alexander, Box, 1957 .... 1650.00
Cissy, Gown, Pink, Taffeta Petticoat, No. 22-61, Alexander, Box, c.1958 .... 935.00
Cissy, Hat, Yellow, Fancy, No. 22-91, Alexander, Box, c.1958 .... 415.00
Cissy, Smoke Blue Coat, Hat, Pink Bows, Flowers, No. 2148, Alexander, Box, c.1957 .... 935.00
Cissy, Suit, Jacket, Skirt, Scarf, Powder Blue, Alexander, Box, c.1958 .... 550.00

Cissy, Summer Ensemble, White Pique, Blouse, Shirt, Shorts, Alexander, Box, 1958 ...... 415.00
Cissy, Sundress, Blue & White Checks, Cotton, Alexander, Box, 1957 .... 688.00
Francie, Check-Mates, Houndstooth Jacket, Skirt, Blouse, Shoes, Purse, No. 1259 .... 77.00
Francie, Combination, Jacket, Shirt, Skirt, Hose, Shoes, Hat, No. 1234 .... 85.00
Francie, Concert In The Park, Dress, Sleeveless Vest, Hat, Purse, Pumps, No. 1256 .... 125.00
Francie, Cool It, Jumper, Gingham Pockets & Hem, Tie Shoes 33.00
Francie, Long On Leather, Coat, Skirt, Shirt, Hose, Boots, Scarf, No. 1769 .... 125.00
Francie, Pazam, Vinyl Raincoat, Culotte Dress, Swimsuit, Hairpiece, Shoes, No. 1213 .... 185.00
Francie, Striped Types, Blue & Red Knit Sweater, Pants, Vest, Shoes, Box, No. 1243 ..... 95.00
Francie, Summer Coolers, Jacket, Shoes, Hairpiece, Hat, Bag, No. 1292 .... 70.00
Francie, Summer Frost, Dress, Shoes, Hat, No. 1276 .... 120.00
Francie, Sweet 'n Swingin', Lace Dress, Coat, Purse, Shoes, No. 1283 .... 130.00
Francie, Tenterrific, Floral Dress, Hat, Hose, Purse, Shoes, No. 1211 .... 110.00
Francie, Victorian Wedding, Satin Lace Gown, Tulle Veil, Bouquet, Shoes, No. 1233 ..... 65.00
Ken, Breakfast At 7, Pajamas, Bathrobe, Slippers, No. 1428 .... 35.00
Ken, Fountain Boy, White Shirt, Hat, Plastic Tray, Napkins, Drinks, No. 1407 .... 105.00
Ken, In Holland, Shirt, Pants, Socks, Shoes, Hat, Scarf, No. 0777, Box 100.00
Ken, Masquerade, Clown Suit, Accessories, No. 794, Box 65.00
Ken, Night Scene, Velour Jacket, Pants, Tie, Cummerbund, Socks, Shoes, No. 1496 ...... 44.00
Ken, Rally Day, Khaki Coat, Red Lining, Map, Car Keys On Chain, No. 788, Box 50.00
Ken, Sea Scene, Jacket, Shirt, Pants, Socks, Shoes, No. 1449 .... 40.00
Skipper, Nifty Knickers, Pants, Vest, Boots, Hanger, Shoes, No. 3291, Box 66.00
Skipper, Sunny Pastels, Striped Dress, Accessories, No. 1910 .... 55.00
Todd, Karo-Mode, Shirt, Pants, Shoes, Hat, No. 9481, Box 33.00
Tutti, Come To My Party, Dress, Shoes, Underwear, Socks, No. 3607, Box 44.00
Tutti, Plantin' Posies, Dress, Underwear, Shoes, Garden Accessories, No. 3609, Box 55.00
Twiggy, Striped Sweater Tank Top, Pants, Belt, Shoes, Hat, Camera 145.00

DONALD DUCK items are included in the Disneyana category.

DOORSTOPS have been made in all types of designs. The vast majority of the doorstops sold today are cast iron and were made from about 1890 to 1930. Most of them are shaped like people, animals, flowers, or ships. Reproductions and newly designed examples are sold in gift shops.

2 Geese, Cast Iron, Hubley, 8 In. 770.00
3 Ducks, Cast Iron, Hubley, 8 1/4 In. 770.00
Anchor, Sailing Ship, Bradley & Hubbard, 11 1/4 In. 220.00
Ann Hathaway's Cottage, Cast Iron, 2-Piece Casting, No. 438, Hubley, 6 x 8 In. 550.00
Ann Hathaway's Cottage, Trees, 6 3/4 x 4 3/4 In. 605.00
Aunt Jemima, Cast Iron, Hubley, 8 1/2 x 5 1/2 In. 975.00
Banjo Player, Blue & Yellow Suit, 6 3/4 In. 1430.00
Basket Of Flowers, Cast Iron, Hubley, 7 In. 99.00
Basket Of Tulips, Mixed Flowers, Cast Iron, 11 In. 1320.00
Bathing Beauties, Art Deco, Hubley, 10 7/8 x 5 1/4 In. 6875.00
Bellhop, Cast Iron, CJO, 8 7/8 x 4 5/8 In. 1210.00
Billy Goat, Black Paint, Full Figure, Cast Iron, 1940s, 5 1/2 x 4 1/2 In. 200.00
Bobby Blake, Teddy Bear, Grace Drayton, Hubley, 9 1/4 In. ....330.00 to 675.00
Caddie, Holding Golf Bag, 8 x 6 In. 3025.00
Cat, Black & White, Seated, Cast Iron, 8 In. 110.00
Cat, Black & White, Seated, Cast Iron, 9 x 6 1/2 In. 275.00
Cat, Black, 4 3/8 x 9 3/4 In. 330.00
Cat, Black, Sitting Front, Glass Eyes, Cast Iron, 12 In. 176.00
Cat, Glass Eyes, Painted, Bronze, 8 x 12 1/2 In. 2500.00
Cat, Gray Tabby, Sitting On Rug, Cast Iron, 9 In. 220.00
Cat, Orange, White Eyes & Whiskers, Cast Iron, Art Deco Style, Hubley, 10 In. 523.00
Cat, Sleeping, Bow, Cast Iron, Copper Electroplate, No. 131, Albany Co., 3 x 10 In. 275.00
Cat, Sleeping, Bronze, National Foundry, 10 In. 460.00
Cat, Sleeping, Bronze, Patina, National Foundry, 9 1/4 In. 460.00
Cat, Sleeping, Gray, Cast Iron, 5 x 12 7/8 In. 1650.00
Cats, Twin White Cat In Dress, Black Cat In Blue Overalls, Hubley, 7 x 5 1/4 In. 550.00
Charleston Dancers, Cast Iron, Hubley, Signed, Fish, 8 7/8 x 5 3/8 In. .... *Illus* 3300.00

Doorstop, Charleston
Dancers, Cast Iron, Hubley,
Signed, Fish, 8 7/8 x 5 3/8 In.

Doorstop, Dog, Boston
Terrier, Cast Iron,
9 5/8 x 11 3/4 In.

Doorstop, Flower Basket,
Cast Iron, Hubley, No. 471,
9 3/4 x 5 1/2 In.

Coach, London Royal Mail, Early 1900s 395.00
Cockatoo, On Stump, Cast Iron, National Foundry, 14 x 4 1/2 In. 440.00
Colonial Woman, Painted, Yellow Dress, Blue Scarf, Painted, Cast Iron, 10 In. 150.00
Colonial Woman, Yellow & Green Dress, 10 1/2 In. 140.00
Cosmos Vase, Cast Iron, No. 455, Hubley, 18 In. . . . . .1870.00 to 2475.00
Cottage, Fence, Flowers, Red Roof, National Foundry, 5 3/4 x 8 In. 99.00
Cottage, Fence, Flowers, White, Green Roof, National Foundry, 7 1/4 In. 138.00
Cottage, In Woods, Flowers, Birdhouse, Wedge Back, 8 1/4 In. 303.00
Cottage, In Woods, Smoking Chimney, Cast Iron, 8 1/4 x 7 1/4 In. 660.00
Cottage, White, Flowers, Hubley, 5 3/4 x 7 1/2 In. 248.00
Daisy Bowl, Black Base, No. 232, Hubley, 7 1/8 x 5 7/8 In. 99.00
Daisy Bowl, No. 452, Hubley, 7 1/2 x 6 In. 303.00
Dapper Dan, Cast Iron, J. Held Jr., c.1920, 7 3/4 In. 165.00
Dog, 2 Scotties, Listen, Cast Iron, Texaco Oil Co., 1930s, 6 x 9 In. 225.00
Dog, Beagle Puppy, Hubley, 8 x 7 1/2 In. 1650.00
Dog, Boston Terrier, Brown & White, Full Figure, 10 x 10 In. 86.00
Dog, Boston Terrier, Cast Iron, 9 5/8 x 11 3/4 In. . . . . *Illus* 330.00
Dog, Boston Terrier, Facing Right, 9 x 9 1/4 In. 138.00
Dog, Boston Terrier, Hubley, 1930s 495.00
Dog, Cocker Spaniel, Cast Iron, No. 487, Hubley, 6 3/4 x 11 In. 440.00
Dog, Cocker Spaniel, Wedge Style, VA Metalcrafters, 7 x 9 In. 303.00
Dog, Dachshund, Cast Iron, No. 8, Taylor Cook, c.1930, 5 1/2 x 7 1/2 In. 880.00
Dog, Dachshund, Hubley, 5 1/2 x 9 1/2 In. 770.00
Dog, Doberman Pinscher, Hubley, 8 x 8 1/2 In. 1320.00
Dog, English Bulldog, Cast Iron, No. 460, Hubley, 4 5/8 x 5 1/2 In. 385.00
Dog, Fox Terrier, Cast Iron, 6 1/2 In. 99.00
Dog, Fox Terrier, Facing Right, Cast Iron, 8 In. 138.00
Dog, French Bulldog, Hubley, 8 In. 193.00
Dog, German Shepherd, Cast Iron, c.1900, 9 1/2 In. 127.00
Dog, German Shepherd, Original Paint, Full Figure, Cast Iron, 9 7/8 In. 230.00
Dog, Greyhound, Bronze Color, 7 In. 303.00
Dog, Laddie Boy, Pres. Harding's Dog, Cast Iron, 6 x 8 In. 495.00
Dog, Pekingese, Cast Iron, Red Brown Paint, 1800s, 9 x 13 3/4 In. 705.00
Dog, Pekingese, Hubley, 9 x 14 1/2 In. 4400.00
Dog, Scottie, Cast Iron, Hubley, 10 In. 220.00
Dog, Sealyham, 9 x 12 In. 1320.00
Dog, Terrier, Between Bushes, 1929, 7 x 8 In. 468.00
Dog, Whimsical, AM Greenblatt Studio, 1927, 9 1/2 In. 523.00
Dogwood, Cast Iron, No. 1260, CJO, 16 1/4 x 7 7/8 In. 385.00
Dolly, Holding Doll, Hand In Pocket, Grace Drayton, Hubley, 9 3/4 In. 4400.00
Duck, White, Blue Sailor Shirt, Cast Iron, 10 In. 110.00
Dutch Boy, Flowers, 1275, Judd Co., 7 1/2 In. 220.00
Dutch Cleanser, Girl Chasing Dirt, Cast Iron, Hubley, 8 3/4 In. 3575.00

Dutch Girl, Carrying Buckets, Cast Iron, Littco Prod. 950.00
Dutch Girl, Cast Iron, Hubley, 9 1/4 In. 193.00
Elephant, Stair Base, 7798, Bradley & Hubbard, 10 1/2 In. 385.00
Elk, Glass Eyes, 15 3/4 x 19 In. 8800.00
English Guard, Cast Iron, Reading Foundry, 13 In. 990.00
Fawn, No. 6, Taylor Cook, 1930, 10 x 6 In. 990.00
Fireplace, Red Bricks, Sword, Cat, Pitcher, Plates 66.00
Fisherman, At Wheel, Yellow Coat, 6 1/4 x 6 In. 468.00
Flapper Girl, Holding Parasol, Cast Iron, Toledo Stove Co., 9 1/2 In. 2475.00
Flower Basket, 475, Hubley, 7 1/4 x 7 In. 138.00
Flower Basket, Cast Iron, 5 1/2 In. 88.00
Flower Basket, Cast Iron, 6 1/2 In. ....66.00 to 165.00
Flower Basket, Cast Iron, Hubley, 9 1/2 In. 358.00
Flower Basket, Cast Iron, Hubley, No. 471, 9 3/4 x 5 1/2 In. .... *Illus* 138.00
Flower Basket, Deco, Cast Iron, Lacs, 12 In. 660.00
Flower Basket, Hubley, 1930s 395.00
Flower Basket, Poppies & Snapdragons, Blue Base, Hubley, 7 1/2 x 7 1/4 In. 110.00
Flower Basket, W.S., 1926 .... 450.00
Flower Vase, Bradley & Hubbard, 11 3/4 In. 660.00
Flower Vase, Cast Iron, Bradley & Hubbard, 9 1/2 In. 470.00
Flower Vase, Cast Iron, Hubley, 10 1/2 In. 413.00
Flower Vase, Marigolds, No. 315, Hubley, 7 1/2 x 8 In. 248.00
Flower Vase, Poppies & Daisies, No. 491, Hubley, 7 1/4 In. 275.00
Flower Vase, Primroses, Hubley, 7 3/8 x 6 1/4 In. 165.00
Flowerpot, Nasturtiums, Black & White Striped Pot, Hubley, 7 1/4 x 6 1/2 In. 99.00
Flowers In Medallion, Oval, No. 859, 10 In. 138.00
Flowers In Urn, Cast Iron, No. 1288, 7 In. 440.00
Football Player, Cast Iron, 11 1/4 x 6 In. .... *Illus* 16500.00
Footmen, Hubley, 9 1/8 In. 1430.00
Footmen, Hubley, 12 1/8 x 8 1/4 In. 5500.00
Frog, Cast Iron, Early 1900s, 7 x 7 In. 75.00
Fruit Basket, Cast Iron, CJO, New England, 10 In. 165.00
Fruit Basket, Cherries, Cast Iron, No. 78, Hubley, 12 x 10 In. 385.00
Fruit Basket, Handle, Albany Foundry, 10 1/8 x 7 1/2 In. 440.00
Giraffe, Hubley, 12 1/2 x 9 In. 10450.00
Girl, Kicking Flowers, 9 3/4 In. 1870.00
Gladiolas, Cast Iron, No. 489, Hubley, 10 x 8 In. 220.00
Gnome, Red Hat, Gray Beard, Green Pants, 11 In. 220.00
Golfer, Club Overhead Swing, 238, Hubley, 7 x 10 In. 1210.00
Golfer, Putting, Plaid Hat, Original Paint, Cast Iron, Flat Back, 8 x 7 In. ....305.00 to 470.00
Griffin, Winged, Shield, Cast Iron, Lusse Bros Inc., c.1920, 7 3/4 x 8 3/4 In. 195.00
Heron, Albany Foundry, 7 1/2 x 5 1/8 In. 825.00
Horse, Dapple Gray, Cast Iron, No. 476, 11 x 7 1/2 In. 275.00
Horse, Percheron, Dapple Gray, Cast Iron, No. 346, Hubley, 7 3/4 x 9 In. 330.00
House, Cape Cod, Cast Iron, Hubley, 5 1/2 x 7 3/4 In. .... *Illus* 303.00
House, Colonial, Brown, Black Roof, Red Chimney, Green Grass, 6 x 9 In. 40.00
House, Nathaniel Green, General, Second Only To Washington, 8 1/4 In. 3025.00

Doorstop, Football
Player, Cast Iron,
11 1/4 x 6 In.

Doorstop, House,
Cape Cod, Cast
Iron, Hubley,
5 1/2 x 7 3/4 In.

House, Sophia Smith, Birthplace, 5 1/4 x 8 1/4 In. 468.00
House, Woman On Steps, Cast Iron, Eastern Specialty Manufacturing, 5 x 8 In. 165.00
Humpty Dumpty, On Brick Wall, Green Bowtie, Red Suit, Cast Iron, 1920s 750.00
Jonquils, Bending In Breeze, Hubley, 7 1/2 x 8 In. 220.00
Kitten, Reclining, Bow, Cast Iron, No. 77, National Foundry, 4 x 8 1/8 In. 990.00
Kittens, In Boot, Hand Painted, Cast Iron 295.00
Koala, No. 5, Taylor Cook, 1930, 7 1/4 x 5 1/2 In. 1650.00
Lady, Hoop Skirt, Cast Iron, National & Albany Foundry, 6 In. 55.00
Lighthouse, Highland, Cape Cod, 7 3/4 x 9 In. 4125.00
Lilies Of The Valley, Cast Iron, No. 189, Hubley, 10 1/2 x 7 1/2 In. 220.00
Little Heiskell Soldier, Cast Iron, 11 In. 110.00
Little Miss Muffet, Cast Iron, No. 121, 7 3/4 x 5 In. 275.00
Little Red Riding Hood, Grace Drayton, Hubley, 9 1/2 x 5 In. 385.00
Little Red Riding Hood, Wolf, Cast Iron, NUYDEA, 7 1/2 x 9 1/2 In. ....1210.00 to 2200.00
Little Red Riding Hood, Wolf, National Foundry, 7 1/4 x 5 3/8 In. 415.00
Lobster, Red, Green Base, 12 1/2 x 6 1/2 In. 1430.00
Mammy, Red Dress, White Apron, Hands On Hips, Hollow, Hubley, 8 1/2 x 4 1/2 In. 385.00
Man, In Chair, With Stein, 9 1/2 x 5 3/4 In. 660.00
Man, In Goat Cart, Porgy, Charleston, S.C., Cast Iron, 6 1/2 x 5 1/4 In. 400.00
Man, With Cane, Bowler Hat, CJO, 7 3/8 In. 1320.00
Man, With Cane, Top Hat, Tuxedo, Hubley, 4 1/2 x 8 In. 1760.00
Man & Girl, Cast Iron, Painted, 14 In. 50.00
Marigolds, Cast Iron, No. 315, Hubley, 7 1/2 x 8 In. 275.00
Mary Quite Contrary, Holding Flowers, Rake, Watering Can, 15 x 8 In. 1760.00
Messenger Boy, Hubley, 10 In. 4950.00
Mexican Guitarist, Cast Iron, No. 951, Littco Production, 12 In. 6600.00
Monkey On Barrel, No. 3, Taylor Cook, 1930, 8 3/8 x 4 7/8 In. 413.00
Mouse, Metal, 3 1/2 x 3 In. 138.00
Nasturtiums, Cast Iron, No. 221, Hubley, 7 1/4 x 6 1/2 In. 220.00
Old Salt, Yellow Rain Gear, Mounted On Wood Base, Cast Iron, 8 In. 28.00
Olive Picker, Hubley, 7 3/4 x 8 3/4 In. 825.00
Owl, On 2 Books, Eastern Specialty, 9 1/2 In. 1210.00
Pansy Bowl, Cast Iron, No. 258, Hubley, 7 x 6 1/2 In. 220.00
Parlor Maid, Serving Cocktails, Hubley, 9 1/2 x 3 1/2 In. 5500.00
Parrot, Cast Iron, 7 3/4 In. 165.00
Parrot, In Ring, Bradley & Hubbard, 13 3/4 x 7 1/4 In. 525.00
Parrot, No. 4, Taylor Cook, 1930, 10 1/2 x 4 7/8 In. 468.00
Parrot, On Stump, Glass Eye, Cast Iron, No. 39, National Foundry, 10 3/8 x 6 3/4 In. 385.00
Peacock, Art Nouveau, Cast Iron, c.1910 .... 165.00
Peacock, Fan Open, Cast Iron, 6 1/4 In. 94.00
Penguin, No. 1, Taylor Cook, 1930, 9 1/2 x 5 3/8 In. 4125.00
Penguin, Top Hat, Hubley, 10 1/2 x 3 3/4 In. 660.00
Petunias & Asters, Cast Iron, No. 470, Hubley, 9 1/2 x 6 1/2 In. 275.00
Pheasant, Cast Iron, Signed, Fred Everett, Hubley, 8 1/2 x 7 1/2 In. ....385.00 to 440.00
Pheasant, Hubley, 8 1/2 x 7 1/2 In. 415.00
Pied Piper, Seated On Mushroom, 7 1/4 x 5 In. 220.00
Pilgrim, 2-Sided Casting, 8 3/4 x 5 3/8 In. 99.00
Pilgrim, Boy, 2-Sided, Full Figure, Cast Iron, CJO, 9 In. 440.00
Poppies, No. 440, Cast Iron, Hubley, 11 In. 220.00
Poppies & Cornflowers, Cast Iron, Hubley, 7 1/4 In. 300.00
Poppies & Daisies, Hubley. 7 1/4 x 6 In. 375.00
Punch, With Dog, Painted, Cast Iron, 12 x 9 In. 296.00
Rabbit, By Fence, Albany Foundry, 7 1/4 In. 715.00
Rabbit, Cast Iron, Bradley & Hubbard, 15 3/8 x 8 3/8 In. 1980.00
Rabbit, Top Hat, Red Coat, Cast Iron, Albany Foundry, 9 7/8 In. 3300.00
Rooster, Crowing, Cast Iron, 12 1/8 In. 360.00
Rooster, Crowing, Cast Iron, W.P. Loth Stove Company, Waynesboro, Pa., 10 In. 275.00
Rose Basket, Cast Iron, No. 737, Lacs, 10 x 11 In. 1870.00
Roses, Cast Iron, No. 445, Hubley, 8 3/4 x 7 7/8 In. 660.00
Sea Nymphs, Cast Iron, No. 151, Albany Foundry, 4 3/8 x 7 5/8 In. 990.00
Soldier, Black, Major Domo, Cast Iron, 8 1/4 x 5 1/4 In. 300.00
Spanish Girl, Shawl, Fan, Hubley, 9 x 5 In. 140.00
Squirrel, On Log, 11 x 9 1/2 In. 300.00

Stagecoach, Wedge Back, 12 3/4 In. 55.00
Steam Engine, Cast Iron, Full Figure, 9 1/2 In. 28.00
Tulip Pot, Cast Iron, National Foundry, 8 1/4 x 7 In. 193.00
Tulip Vase, Cast Iron, No. 443, Hubley, 10 x 8 In. 275.00
Turkey, Cast Iron, 7 In. 495.00
Turkey, Cast Iron, Bradley & Hubbard, 12 In. 4125.00
Turtle, Cast Iron, S In Circle, 2 1/2 x 7 3/4 In. 385.00
Warrior, Beard, Cast Iron, Bradley & Hubbard, 13 1/4 x 7 1/4 In. 660.00
Wolf's Head, Riding Crop, 1880 .... 475.00
Woman, Riding Horse, Side Saddle, Cast Iron, National Foundry, 7 In. 660.00
Woman, Southern Belle, Cast Iron, National Foundry, 11 1/4 x 6 In. 140.00
Woman, Tropical, Carrying Bowl On Head, 12 x 6 1/4 In. 470.00
Zinnias, Cast Iron, Hubley, 9 3/4 x 8 1/2 In. 275.00
Zinnias, Hubley, 7 1/4 x 7 In. 165.00
Zinnias, Wedge Back, LVC Pat. Appl. For, 9 1/4 x 6 In. 468.00

DORCHESTER POTTERY was founded by George Henderson in 1895 in Dorchester, Massachusetts. At first, the firm made utilitarian stoneware, but collectors are most interested in the line of decorated blue and white pottery that Dorchester made from 1940 until it went out of business in 1979.

**DORCHESTER
POTTERY WORKS
BOSTON, MASS.**

Bowl, Grape, Handles, 7 In. 70.00
Casserole, Cover, Blueberry, Handles, 9 In. 180.00
Cookie Jar, Blueberry, 7 3/4 In. 290.00
Dish, Eagle, Star, Striped Blue Border, 1776-1976, CAH/EHH, 8 In. 175.00
Mug, Fruit, 4 3/4 In. 50.00
Pitcher, Daffodils, Deep Blue Ground, CAH & Ricci, 5 x 5 1/2 In. 225.00
Pitcher, Plum, 5 1/2 In. 75.00
Pitcher, Scroll, 7 In. 95.00
Plate, Dinner, Pinecone, 10 1/2 In. 200.00
Plate, Lily Of The Valley, White Blossoms, Blue Ground, CAH & Ricci, 7 1/2 In. 250.00
Sugar & Creamer, Blueberry 50.00

DOULTON pottery and porcelain were made by Doulton and Co. of Burslem, England, after 1882. The name *Royal Doulton* appeared on their wares after 1902. Other pottery by Doulton is listed under Royal Doulton.

Biscuit Jar, Flowers, Embossed Scrolled Mold, Multicolored, c.1890, 6 1/2 In. 200.00
Bowl, Silicon, Applied Geometric Interlacing Frieze, Lambeth, c.1882, 7 1/2 In. 155.00
Crumb Tray, Frog, Turtle, George Tinworth, Elizabeth Atkins, Lambeth, 1880s, 8 1/4 In. ... 3970.00
Cuspidor, Muses En Grisaille, Mustard Ground, Burslem, 12 In. 510.00
Inkwell, Votes For Woman, Virago, Stoneware, Lambeth, c.1913, 3 1/2 In. 3042.00
Jardiniere, Everted Rim, Grazing Cows, Barlow Beere & Adams, Lambeth, c.1887, 7 In. ... 2245.00
Jardiniere, Natural Foliage Ware, 1892-1902, 16 In. .... *Illus* 300.00
Jug, White Flowerhead, Painted Leaves, A. Butler, Lambeth, c.1873, 7 In. 605.00
Loving Cup, Lord Nelson, 2 Handles, Lambeth, c.1905, 6 In. 1000.00
Pitcher, Sterling Silver Mount, Faux Leather Sheath, Stoneware, Lambeth, 1891, 8 In. 575.00
Tankard, Willow, Flow Blue, 15 In. 230.00
Toby Jug, Man, Seated, Holding Jug, Double XX, 2-Tone Brown Glaze, 10 In. 690.00
Vase, Chine, Oval, Flowering Leaves, Spores, Florets, Lambeth, c.1905, 11 3/4 In., Pair ... 475.00

Doulton,
Jardiniere,
Natural
Foliage Ware,
1892-1902, 16 In.

Vase, Embossed Tapestry, Enamel, Slaters Patent, Early 1900s, 11 3/4 In., Pair 345.00
Vase, Flowers, Geometrics, Incised, Brown, Cobalt, Gray Ground, Lambeth, 7 1/2 In. 245.00
Vase, Incised, Painted, Frolicking Horses, Hannah Barlow, Lambeth, c.1872, 7 In. 520.00
Vase, Mums, Enameled, Baluster, Lambeth, 11 x 4 1/2 In., Pair 940.00

DRESDEN china is any china made in the town of Dresden, Germany.
The most famous factory in Dresden is the Meissen factory. Figurines
of eighteenth-century ladies and gentlemen, animal groups, or cherubs
and other mythological subjects were popular. One special type of figurine was made with skirts of porcelain-dipped lace. Do not make the
mistake of thinking that all pieces marked *Dresden* are from the Meissen factory. The Meissen pieces usually have crossed swords marks,
and are listed under Meissen. Some recent porcelain from Ireland,
called *Irish Dresden*, is not included in this book.

Candelabrum, 7-Light, Flower Encrusted, Serpentine, Cupid Form Stem, 26 In. 380.00
Candlestick, Blue, Cherub, Bird, Finger Handle, Shell Shape Base, 6 1/4 In. 85.00
Compote, Flowers, Reticulated Shaped Border, Gold Trim, Footed, 4 1/8 x 8 1/2 In. 70.00
Dish, Sweetmeat, Flowers, Gold Trim, Fluted Edge, 3 Sections, 10 1/4 In. 50.00
Figurine, 2 Couples Playing Billiards, 11 In. 145.00
Figurine, Dancing Lady, 6 x 5 In. 125.00
Figurine, Gentleman Playing Flute, Woman Playing Piano, 10 1/4 In. 200.00
Figurine, Girl, Yellow Bonnet, 4 3/4 x 3 1/2 In. 125.00
Figurine, Lady Playing Mandolin By Table, West Germany, 9 x 7 In. 135.00
Figurine, Monkey, Seated, No Stump, Holding Apple, Carl Thieme, c.1915, 16 1/2 In. 865.00
Figurine, Woman Applying Makeup, 7 In. 175.00
Plate, Courting Scene, Flowers, Yellow & White Panels, Gold Trim, Handles, 11 In., Pair . 85.00
Plate, Woman Seated, Flowers In Hair, Shaped Rim, Flower Sprays, 10 1/4 In. 1150.00
Plate Set, Cobalt Blue Rim, Gilt Enamel, Scrolls, Diapered Cartouches, 9 In., 12 Piece .. 590.00
Punch Bowl, Cover, Boy, Girl, Flower Basket, Ozier Molded Rim, Tavern Scenes, 13 In. ... 1295.00
Teakettle, On Stand, Porcelain, Pastoral Scene, Garland, c.1883, 14 1/4 In. 748.00
Urn, Cover, Toilette Der Venus, Hand Painted, Kaufmann, 5 In. 485.00
Vase, Gourd Form, Courting Scenes, Flowers, Alternating Panels, Gilt, c.1875, 12 In., Pair 520.00
Vase, Ruby, Gold Scrolling, Children Playing, Cylindrical, 4 3/4 In. 920.00

DUNCAN & MILLER is a term used by collectors when referring to
glass made by the George A. Duncan and Sons Company or the Duncan and Miller Glass Company. These companies worked from 1893 to
1955, when the use of the name *Duncan* was discontinued and the firm
became part of the United States Glass Company. Early patterns may
be listed under Pressed Glass.

Canterbury, Bowl, Pink Opalescent, 10 In. 95.00
Canterbury, Candlestick, 2-Light, Chartreuse, Pair 105.00
Canterbury, Candy Dish, Cover 75.00
Canterbury, Celery Dish, 1937-50, 10 1/2 x 6 3/4 In. 33.00
Canterbury, Cornucopia, Chartreuse 85.00
Canterbury, Pitcher, Martini, 32 Oz. 85.00
Canterbury, Relish, 3 Sections & Handles, 8 1/4 In. 26.00
Canterbury, Rose Bowl, Crystal, 3 1/4 x 5 1/4 In. 25.00
Canterbury, Vase, Flared, Blue, Cloverleaf Shape, c.1937, 2 5/8 x 4 1/2 In. 28.00
Canterbury, Wine, 5 In. 10.00
Caribbean, Bowl, Handles, Gold Trim, 6 In. 15.00
Caribbean, Plate, 4-Footed, 12 Oz. 30.00
First Love, Plate, Luncheon, 8 In. 30.00
Hobnail, Ivy Ball, Blue Opalescent, Footed, 7 1/2 In. 95.00
Pall Mall, Swan, Chartreuse, 7 In. 65.00
Pall Mall, Swan, Green Body, Clear Head & Neck, 10 In. 75.00
Sandwich, Basket, 11 1/2 In. 235.00
Sandwich, Bowl, Salad, 12 In. 75.00
Sandwich, Cup 12.00
Sandwich, Plate, Deviled Egg, Pink, 12 In. 85.00
Sandwich, Tumbler, 9 Oz., 4 3/4 In. 20.00
Sandwich, Tumbler, Footed, 10 Oz., 5 1/2 In. 36.00
Spiral Flutes, Bowl, 12 In. 45.00

Spiral Flutes, Cup, After Dinner, Amber 26.00
Spiral Flutes, Cup, Amber 9.00
Spiral Flutes, Plate, Luncheon, Green, 8 3/8 In. 15.00
Spiral Flutes, Vase, Green, 10 3/4 In. 35.00
Sylvan, Candy Dish, Cover, Leaf Form, 8 In. 125.00
Sylvan, Dish, Leaf Form, 7 In. 8.00
Tear Drop, Cocktail, 4 1/2 In. 15.00
Tear Drop, Cordial, 1 Oz. 30.00
Tear Drop, Nut Dish, Sections, Handles, 6 In. 15.00
Tear Drop, Relish, Heart Form, Sections, Handle, 7 1/2 In. 22.00
Tear Drop, Saltshaker, 3 3/4 In. 14.00
Tear Drop, Sugar, 8 Oz. 13.00

DURAND art glass was made from 1924 to 1931. The Vineland Flint
Glass Works was established by Victor Durand and Victor Durand, Jr.,
in 1897. In 1924 Martin Bach, Jr., and other artisans from the Quezal
glassworks joined them at the Vineland, New Jersey, plant to make
Durand art glass.

Bottle, Genie, Silver Blue, Iridescent, Signed, 18 In. 3740.00
Bowl, Centerpiece, Ambergris, Translucent Blue & White Zigzags, Footed, 4 x 10 3/4 In. ... 1150.00
Candlestick, Cranberry, White Pulled Feathers, Ambergris Stem, 5 1/4 x 3 In., Pair 1150.00
Compote, Blue, Amber, Applied Threading, Flared, 5 In. 590.00
Compote, Ruby Bowl, Ruffled Edge, Ribbed Ambergris Stem, Ruby Foot, 6 1/2 In., Pair .. 1380.00
Goblet, Cranberry & White, Pulled Feathers, Ambergris Stem, 6 3/4 In., 5 Piece 230.00
Incense Lamp, Egyptian Revival, Woman, Kneeling, Holding Shade, 12 1/2 x 5 In. 765.00
Lamp, Gold Iridescent, Blue, White Crackle, Embossed Metal Foot, Wired, 10 In. 805.00
Lamp, King Tut, Gold & Orange, 10 In. 890.00
Lamp, King Tut, Orange, Corseted, 4-Footed, Glass Insert, 12 x 29 In. 1725.00
Lamp, King Tut, Platinum, Green Ground, Glass Finial, Linen Shade, 6 1/4 In. 540.00
Lamp, Lady Gay Rose, Pink & White, Round Base, Egg Shape Body, 9 1/2 In. 400.00
Lamp, Threaded, Opal, Gold Iridescent, Blue Pulled Hearts, Bronze Mount, c.1920, 18 In. . 460.00
Lamp, White Iridescent, Variegated Green, Gold Body, Metal Foot, Wired, 10 1/2 In. 2300.00
Torchere, Table, Opal Shade, Pulled Heart & Vine, Gold Threading, Teak Base, 10 In. 575.00
Vase, Blue Iridescent, Allover Gold Threading, Shouldered, Signed, 6 1/2 In. 489.00
Vase, Blue Iridescent, Coils, Flared Rim, Gold Foot, Shape No. 2011, 14 In. 2875.00
Vase, Blue Iridescent, Moorish Crackle Over Ambergris, Shouldered, No. 1712, 10 1/4 In. . 4025.00
Vase, Blue Iridescent, Overall Gold Threading, Shouldered, Signed, 6 1/2 In. 489.00
Vase, Blue Iridescent, Shouldered, 7 In. 750.00
Vase, Blue Iridescent, Shouldered, Pulled Heart & Vine, 6 1/2 In. 1265.00
Vase, Blue Iridescent, Silver Threading, 1924, 8 1/2 In. 530.00
Vase, Blue Iridescent, Threading, Bulbous, No. 1940, 6 3/4 In. 565.00
Vase, Blue Iridescent, White Hearts & Vines, Cylindrical, Shouldered, Flared, 8 1/2 In. ... 920.00
Vase, Blue Iridescent, White Pulled Hearts & Vines, Shouldered, Flared, Signed, 8 1/2 In. . 920.00
Vase, Blue, White Pulled Heart & Vine, Gold, Footed, Signed, 9 In. 1440.00
Vase, Gold Iridescent, Bulbous, Shouldered, Flared Rim, 6 1/4 In. 635.00
Vase, Gold Iridescent, Green Moorish Crackle, 12 In. 5175.00
Vase, Gold Iridescent, Reverse Trumpet, No. 1713, 7 1/4 In. 375.00
Vase, Gold Iridescent, White Cased, Shouldered, 4 1/4 In. 200.00
Vase, King Tut, Blue Iridescent, Waisted Neck, Flared Ruffled Rim, 6 1/2 In. 1610.00
Vase, King Tut, Blue, Orange, Signed, 12 In. 2280.00
Vase, King Tut, Green, Gold Iridescent, Signed, 6 3/4 In. 4315.00
Vase, Lady Gay Rose, Cranberry, White & Pink Pulled Feathers, 1907, 9 3/4 In. 1115.00
Vase, Opal, Blue Iridescent Coils, Cylindrical, Shouldered, Flared Rim, 10 1/2 In. 2070.00
Vase, Opal, Blue Iridescent Coils, Shouldered, Flared Rim, 10 1/2 In. 2070.00
Vase, Orange, Iridescent, Blue Pulled Heart & Vine, Flared Rim, 7 1/4 In. 1150.00
Vase, Peach Iridescent, Pulled Heart & Trailing Vine, Signed, 1924, 8 In. 13450.00
Vase, Pulled Feather, Applied Gold Threading, Shoulder, Flaring Rim, 7 3/4 In. 1175.00
Vase, Silver Blue Iridescent, Bulbous, Cylindrical Neck, c.1920, 4 1/2 In. 290.00
Vase, Stick, Gold Iridescent, Gold Threading, Bulbous Base, 7 In. 400.00
Vase, Trumpet, Blue, Gold, Iridescent, Applied Gold Foot, 14 1/2 In. 1300.00
Vase, Trumpet, Footed, Blue, Gold, 14 1/4 In. 1115.00
Vase, Trumpet, Gold, Iridescent Swirls, Green Ground, Gold Interior, Foot, 10 1/2 In. 2000.00
Wine, Cranberry, Ribbed, Amber Teardrop Stem, Cranberry Disc Foot, 5 1/2 In. 490.00

ELFINWARE is a mark found on Dresden-like porcelain that was sold in dime stores and gift shops. Many pieces were decorated with raised flowers. The mark was registered by Breslauer-Underberg, Inc., of New York City in 1947. Pieces marked *Elfinware Made in Germany* had been sold since 1945 by this importer.

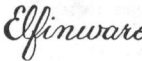

Basket, Rose, Spinach Moss, Forget-Me-Nots, 2 In.	30.00
Figurine, High Heel Shoe, Forget-Me-Nots, 3 In.	110.00
Trinket Box, Forget-Me-Nots, Roses, Bronze Mount, 3 1/2 In.	75.00
Trinket Box, Hen On Nest, 2 1/2 In.	50.00
Trinket Box, Rose On Cover, 5 1/2 In.	35.00

ELVIS PRESLEY, the well-known singer, lived from 1935 to 1977. He became famous by 1956. Elvis appeared on television, starred in twenty-seven movies, and performed in Las Vegas. Memorabilia from any of the Presley shows, his records, and even memorials made after his death are collected.

Belt, Vinyl, Metal Buckle, Song Titles, Elvis Presley Enterprises, 1956, 2 x 31 In.	350.00
Button, Best Wishes Elvis Presley, Elvis In Blue Jacket, 1956, 2 1/2 In.	100.00
Button, Love Me Tender, Gold Record, Silhouette Figure, Playing Guitar, 1956, 7/8 In.	30.00
Card Set, Topps, 1956, 66 Cards	797.00
Collector Plate, Bradford Exchange, 1989, Complete Set, 4 Piece	36.00
Document, Employment Agreement, Truck Driver, Signed, 1952, 9 x 6 1/2 In.	5463.00
Lipstick, Hound Dog, Orange, Goldtone Case, Teen-Ager Lipstick Corp., 1956, 2 1/4 In.	345.00
Lobby Card, Love Me Tender, Yellow Ground, 1956, 11 x 14 In.	160.00
Menu, Las Vegas Hilton, Concerts Sold Out 1970-73, 1974, 8 1/2 x 11 In.	40.00
Movie Poster, Love Me Tender, Introducing Elvis Presley, 1956, 1 Sheet	805.00
Pencil, Cellophane Wrapper, Unopened, 1956, 7 1/2 In., 9 Piece	380.00
Poster, Clambake, United Artists, 1967, 41 x 27 In.	95.00
Poster, Fun In Acapulco, Paramount, 1963, 41 x 27 In.	60.00
Poster, Kissin' Cousins, MGM, 1964, 41 x 27 In.	60.00
Poster, Spinout, MGM, 1966, 41 x 27 In.	100.00
Sheet Music, It's Now Or Never, 1960	56.00
Title Card, Love Me Tender, White Ground, 1956, 11 x 14 In.	250.00

ENAMELS listed here are made of glass particles and other materials heated and fused to metal. In the eighteenth and nineteenth centuries, workmen from Russia, France, England, and other countries made small boxes and table pieces of enamel on metal. One form of English enamel is called *Battersea* and is listed under that name. There was a revival of interest in enameling in the 1930s and a new style evolved. There is now renewed interest in the artistic enameled plaques, vases, ashtrays, and jewelry. Enamels made since the 1930s are usually on copper or steel, although silver was often used for jewelry. Granite-ware is a separate category, and enameled metal kitchen pieces may be included in the Kitchen category.

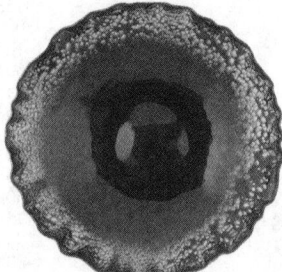

Enamel, Bowl, Green, Speckled White Border, Ruffled Rim, Winter, 6 1/4 In.

Enamel, Vase, Green, Red, Yellow, White, Green Inside, Flared, H. Tishler, 8 x 6 3/4 In.

Erphila, Pitcher, Girl, Holding Flowers, Green Hat, c.1930, 6 In.

Beaker, Nicholas III, Coronation, Tin, Imperial Cipher, Romanov Eagle, 4 x 4 In. 518.00
Bowl, Cover, Red, Green, Abstract, Pink, Doris Hall, 1950 May Show, 4 x 6 In. 150.00
Bowl, Green, Speckled White Border, Ruffled Rim, Winter, 6 1/4 In. .... *Illus* 58.00
Bowl, Leaf Motif, Green, Edward Winter, 5 1/2 In. 58.00
Charger, Woman Gathering Oranges, Thelma Winters, 11 In. 115.00
Cymbals, On Steel, John Puskas, c.1995, 17 x 16 In. 430.00
Desk Set, Guilloche, Silver Gilt, Dove Gray, Faberge, Wood Case, Russia, 3 Piece 2070.00
Desk Set, Lion, Reclining, Flint, Running Blue Glaze, Yellowware, 9 3/4 In. 4255.00
Dish, Hykes, African Woman's Profile, Yellow Ocher Field, Gold Leaf, Copper, 8 In. 69.00
Dish, The Archer, Copper, c.1982, 7 In. 58.00
Inkstand, Champleve, Gilt Bronze Mounted, 2 Handles, France, c.1885, 5 x 7 In. 259.00
Plaque, Nude Female Riding Bull, Aaron Bohrod, Metal, c.1940, 12 1/2 x 12 1/2 In. 1840.00
Tazza, Champleve, Gilt Bronze Mounted, Doves, France, c.1885, 6 1/4 x 6 1/2 In. 405.00
Toilette Set, Gentleman's, Art Deco, Green Guilloche, Copper Gilt Mount, Glass, 3 Piece . 145.00
Tray, Metal, Decorated, Artist Painted Infant Portrait, Continental, 6 1/2 In. 538.00
Vase, Green, Red, Yellow, White, Green Inside, Flared, H. Tishler, 8 x 6 3/4 In. ...... *Illus* 200.00

ERICKSON glass was made in Bremen, Ohio, from 1943 to 1961. Carl and Steven Erickson designed and made free-blown and mold-blown glass. Best known are pieces with heavy ball bases filled with controlled bubbles.

Bookends, Emerald, Pear Shape, Cut & Polished Top, 5 1/2 In. 75.00
Candlestick, Urn Shape, Emerald, Controlled Bubbles, Clear Base, 4 1/2 In., Pair 200.00
Candy Dish, Amber Gold, 4 Pinched-In Sides, Controlled Bubbles, 7 In. 30.00
Decanter, Genie, Aqua, Clear Controlled Bubble Base & Stopper, 13 In. 75.00
Vase, Cone Shape, Clear Controlled Air Bubble Base, 6 1/4 In., Pair 50.00
Vase, Trumpet, Smoke, Clear Controlled Bubble Ball Base, 10 In. 85.00

ERPHILA is a mark found on Czechoslovakian and other pottery and porcelain made after 1920. The mark was used on items imported by Ebeling & Reuss, Philadelphia, a giftware firm that is still operating in Pennsylvania. The mark is a combination of the letters *E* and *R* (Ebel-ing & Reuss) and the first letters of the city, Phila(delphia). Many whimsical figural pitchers and creamers, figurines, platters, and other giftwares carry this mark.

Cigarette Set, Art Deco Woman Figural Jar, Peach Luster, 4 Piece 150.00
Creamer, Yellow, Cat Handle, 5 1/4 In. 70.00
Figurine, Dog, Borzoi, Black & White, 9 In. 175.00
Figurine, Rooster, Green, Gold, Rust, Gold Detail, 7 1/2 In. 15.00
Pitcher, Cat, Stylized, Yellow, Red & Black Details, Tail Handle, 8 1/2 In. 520.00
Pitcher, Girl, Holding Flowers, Green Hat, c.1930, 6 In. .... *Illus* 50.00
Powder Jar, Figural Woman, Green Rococo Ball Gown, 6 In. 60.00
Teapot, Cat, Black & White, Pink Bow, 7 1/2 In. 75.00
Teapot, Chintz, Dorset, Ball Shape, 6 In. 110.00
Teapot, Terrier, Black & White, Pink Ruffled Collar, 7 1/2 In. 225.00
Vase, Classical Nudes, Between Columns, Tan Glaze, 10 In. 75.00

ES GERMANY porcelain was made at the factory of Erdmann Schlegelmilch from 1861 to 1937 in Suhl, Germany. The porcelain, marked *ES Germany* or *ES Suhl*, was sold decorated or undecorated. Other pieces were made at a factory in Saxony, Prussia, and are marked *ES Prussia*. Reinhold Schlegelmilch made the famous wares marked *RS Germany*.

Bowl, Portrait, Mold No. 468, Courting Scene, 10 In. 150.00
Plate, Poppy Decoration, E. Schlegelmilch, Germany, 12 In. 35.00
Plate, Scenic, Allegorical Scene, 3 Women, Cupid, Kauffmann, 9 1/2 In. 81.00

ESKIMO artifacts of all types are collected. Carvings of whale or wal-rus teeth are listed under Scrimshaw. Baskets are in the Basket cate-gory. All other types of Eskimo art are listed here. In Canada and some other areas, the term *Inuit* is used instead of Eskimo.

Basket, Cover, Bird Effigy, Mary T. Coupchiak, 1970s, 3 x 3 1/2 In. 150.00
Basket, Flat Bowl, Radiating Red, Green, Stairstep, 12 1/2 x 2 In. 127.00

Basket, Lid, Hand Woven, Yu'pik, 21 x 17 In. 78.00
Carving, Paddling Kayak, Wood Paddle, Soapstone, Inuit, Mid 1900s, 16 In. 610.00
Cribbage Board, Ivory, Scrimshaw Figures, Marked Cape Prince, 19 1/2 In. 470.00
Figure, Bird, Carved, Long Neck, Stone, Initials, AC E9 1988, 4 3/4 In. 58.00
Figure, Soapstone, Jadite, Anthropomorphic, Raven With Human Face 86.00
Knife, Walrus Bone Handle, Single Edged Steel Blade, Hudson Bay Co., 10 1/2 In. 550.00
Parka, Fur, Badger Skin Collar, Claws, 64 x 42 In. 290.00
Parka, Fur, Sealskin Cutouts, c.1950, 50 x 40 In. 160.00

FABERGE was a firm of jewelers and goldsmiths founded in St. Petersburg, Russia, in 1842, by Gustav Faberge. Peter Carl Faberge, his son, was jeweler to the Russian Imperial Court from about 1870 to 1914. The rare Imperial Easter eggs, jewelry, and decorative items are very expensive today.

Cigarette Case, Silver, Gem, Guilloche Enamel, August Hollming, 1908-17, 3 1/2 In. 7245.00

FAIENCE refers to tin-glazed earthenware, especially the wares made in France, Germany, and Scandinavia. It is also correct to say that faience is the same as majolica or Delft, although usually the term refers only to the tin-glazed pottery of the three regions mentioned.

Bird, Butterfly, Raspberry Bush, Bottle Shape, Pierced Handles, 18 x 8 1/2 In. 1880.00
Dish, Continental, Blue & White, Scalloped Reeded Rim, Architectural Scene, 10 1/2 In. ... 69.00
Jar, Cover, Pottery, 2-Headed Eagle With Shield, c.1920, 10 1/2 In. 193.00
Pitcher, Red Tulips, 6 7/8 In. 290.00
Vase, Apothecary, Blue & White, Marked, Hedera Helix, Cristaux De Lune, 11 In., Pair ... 1265.00
Vase, French Provincial, Green Glaze, Baluster Shape, Southern France, 14 In., Pair 460.00
Water Cooler, 4 Sections, Castle Decoration, Trees, Flowers, 20th Century, 61 1/2 In. 345.00

FAIRINGS are small souvenir china boxes and figurines that were sold at country fairs during the nineteenth century. Most were made in Germany. Reproductions of fairings are being made, especially of the famous *twelve months of marriage* series.

Trinket Box, 3 Girls With Muffs, Conta & Boehme, 1870s, 5 In. 145.00
Trinket Box, Enamel, Busy Harbor, Flowers, White Ground, Hinged Lid, c.1875, 5 1/2 In. . 645.00

FAIRYLAND LUSTER pieces are included in the Wedgwood category.

FAMILLE ROSE, see Chinese Export category.

FANS have been used for cooling since the days of the ancients. By the eighteenth century, the fan was an accessory for the lady of fashion, and very elaborate and expensive fans were made. Sticks were made of ivory or wood, set with jewels or carved. The fans were made of painted silk or paper. Inexpensive paper fans printed with advertising were giveaways in the late nineteenth and early twentieth centuries. Electric fans were introduced in 1882.

Advertising, Air Show, Hotel Sherman, College Inn Chicago, 1910 .... 130.00
Advertising, Burke Drug Co., Come To Us For It, Morganton, N.C., 14 3/4 In. 16.00
Advertising, Excelsior Flour, Indian Chief Black Hawk, Wood Handle, Round, 8 1/2 In. ... 120.00
Advertising, Independent Insurance Co., Addresses, Office Pictures, 1920-75 .... 5.00
Advertising, Moxie, Copyright 1925, 8 x 7 In. 95.00
Advertising, Moxie, Muriel Ostriche, 9 x 8 1/4 In. 54.00
Advertising, Schenck Hardware Store, Winchester, Duck Hunting Scene, 1920s, 9 x 7 In. . 220.00
Advertising, Westinghouse Mazda Lamp, Woman, Dark Hair, Sales Sample, c.1916, 11 In. 145.00
Bone, 15 Carved Spines, Painted Landscape Scene, Chinese, 17 1/2 x 27 x 2 1/2 In. 230.00
Electric, Ceiling, Airplane Shape, Cast Iron, Metal, Wood Propeller, 32 x 34 In. 635.00
Electric, Polar Cub, Desk, Type G, Cat Metal, Tin Blade, 8 In. 100.00
Electric, Winchester, Brass Blades, Felt Bottom, 10 3/4 In. 345.00
Fly, Ray's Country Store, Wood, Paper, 36 In. 396.00
Folding, Watercolor, Gilt, Carved Bone Sticks, Oriental Figures, Birds, Plants, 19 In. 259.00
Ivory, Courting Couples, Flower Urns, Shepherdesses At Well, Continental, 1700s, 21 In. . 435.00
Ivory, Landscapes, Chinese, c.1800, 12 1/2 In. 400.00
Ivory, Painted Figures, Courtyard, Faces, Black Lacquer, Inscribed, 11 In. 1375.00
Ivory, Reserves, Insect End Panel, Chinese, c.1800, 11 1/2 In. 400.00

Mother-Of-Pearl, Paper, Painted, Garden Scene, Shadowbox, Late 1800s, 12 x 22 In. 120.00
Mother-Of-Pearl, Paper, St. George, Dragon, Shadowbox, Velvet Lining, 12 x 22 In. 115.00
Mother-Of-Pearl Inlay, Gilt, Turned Handles, Lacquer, 15 In. 180.00
Needlework, Bird, Flowers, Butterfly, Asian, 1800s, 17 1/2 x 10 1/2 In. 690.00
Painted, Toile, Mother-Of-Pearl, 2 Seated Women, Baskets, Stick, Frame, 18 1/4 In. 175.00
Paper, Ink & Gold Leaf, 2 Manchurian Cranes Flying, Trees, Folding, Noh, Japan, 19 In. .   480.00
Paper, Ink & Gold Leaf, Peony Blossoms, River, Folding, Noh, Frame, 20 In. 480.00
Sandalwood Stays, Painted Figures, Brocade & Ivory Face Collage, Chinese, 1800s 148.00
Silk, Hand Painted, Red Toile, Lace Inserts, Trim, Woman Holding Basket, 25 1/4 In. 115.00

FAST FOOD COLLECTIBLES may be included in several categories, such as Advertising, Coca-Cola, Toy, etc.

FEDERZEICHNUNG, see Loetz category.

FENTON Art Glass Company, founded in Martins Ferry, Ohio, by Frank L. Fenton, is now located in Williamstown, West Virginia. It is noted for early carnival glass produced between 1907 and 1920. Some of these pieces are listed in the Carnival Glass category. Many other types of glass were also made. Spanish Lace in this section refers to the pattern made by Fenton.

Aqua Crest, Vase, Hat, Ruffled Edge, 5 In. 40.00
Bubble Optic, Vase, Pinched, Honey Amber, Ruffled Edge, 8 3/4 In. 62.00
Burmese, Basket, Enameled Landscape, Ruffled Edge, 8 In. 110.00
Burmese, Rose Bowl, Cupped & Crimped Edge, Glossy, 3 1/2 In.   75.00
Burmese, Rose Bowl, Enameled Roses, Satin, 4 In. 90.00
Cactus, Vase, Topaz Opalescent, Pulled Neck, 10 1/2 In. 210.00
Cherry & Blossoms, Beverage Set, Cobalt Blue, Enameled, 7 Piece 207.00
Christmas Plate, Old North Church, Blue Satin, 1976, 8 In. 25.00
Coin Dot, Bride's Basket, Aqua Opalescent, Crimped & Ruffled Edge, 10 In. 85.00
Coin Dot, Tumbler, Cranberry Opalescent, 5 3/8 In. 39.00
Coin Dot, Vase, Hat, Cranberry Opalescent, 3 1/4 x 4 1/2 In. 48.00
Coin Dot, Vase, White, Crimped & Ruffled Edge, 6 In. 75.00
Custard Satin, Candleholder, Water Lily, 5 1/4 In., Pair 42.00
Custard Satin, Candy Dish, Cover, Water Lily, Footed, 7 1/2 In. 35.00
Custard Satin, Compote, Water Lily, Crimped Edge, 5 In. 41.00
Custard Satin, Figurine, Bird Of Happiness, Enameled Roses, 7 In. 32.00
Custard Satin, Vase, Love Birds, 6 5/8 In. 45.00
Custard Satin, Vase, Poppy, Crimped & Ruffled Edge, 6 1/2 In. 41.00
Daisy & Button, Boot, Woman's, Blue, 4 In. 18.00
Daisy & Button, Tray, Dresser, Fan, 10 3/4 In. 25.00
Daisy & Fern, Beverage Set, Topaz Opalescent, 9 1/4-In. Pitcher, 7 Piece 310.00
Dancing Ladies, Vase, Fan, Mandarin Red, 9 1/2 In. 863.00
Diamond Lace, Epergne, 3-Lily, Milk Glass, 9 In. 60.00
Dolphin, Bonbon, Handles, Aqua, 8 3/8 In. 40.00
Dolphin, Candy Dish, Florentine Green, 9 x 5 1/2 In. 200.00
Dolphin, Compote, Handles, Footed, Marigold, 7 In. 80.00

Fenton, Hobnail,
Cruet, Milk Glass,
Fluted Neck, 4 3/4 In.

Custard glass and milk glass can now be repaired by black-light-proof methods. Be very careful when buying antiques.

Hanging Heart, Vase, Red, Cobalt Blue Iridescent Handles, Rolled Rim, 9 1/2 In.	6900.00
Hobnail, Bowl, Footed, Plum Opalescent, Crimped & Ruffled Edge, 8 In.	215.00
Hobnail, Compote, Milk Glass, Scalloped Edge, 5 1/2 In.	18.00
Hobnail, Cookie Jar, Milk Glass, 11 In.	125.00
Hobnail, Cruet, French Opalescent, Clear Stopper	50.00
Hobnail, Cruet, Milk Glass, Fluted Neck, 4 3/4 In. *Illus*	27.50
Hobnail, Dish, Mayonnaise, Underplate, 4 1/2 In.	20.00
Hobnail, Epergne, 3-Lily, Milk Glass, 6 1/2 In.	85.00
Hobnail, Lamp, Gone With The Wind, Cranberry Opalescent, 25 In.	300.00
Hobnail, Plate, Salad, Crescent, French Opalescent, 6 1/2 In.	25.00
Hobnail, Relish, Cloverleaf, 3 Sections, Metal Center Handles, 7 In.	12.00
Hobnail, Salt & Pepper, Milk Glass	18.00
Hobnail, Shoe With Cat, Milk Glass, 6 In.	17.00
Hobnail, Sugar & Creamer, Blue Opalescent	32.00
Hobnail, Vase, Cranberry Opalescent, Bulbous, Crimped & Ruffled Edge, 5 In.	80.00
Hobnail, Vase, Fan, Blue Opalescent, Footed, 8 1/4 In.	45.00
Hobnail, Vase, Green Opalescent, Bulbous, Crimped & Ruffled Edge, 5 In.	115.00
Hobnail, Vase, Topaz Opalescent, Bulbous Base, Ruffled Edge, 5 1/2 In.	110.00
Jade Green, Bowl, Concentric Rings, Cupped Rim, 3-Legged, 6 In.	35.00
Jade Green, Compote, Low Foot, Rolled Edge, 7 3/4 In.	35.00
Jade Green, Console, Rolled & Flared Edge, 9 In.	40.00
Lime Sherbet, Bell, Dinner, Daisy & Button, 6 In.	37.00
Lime Sherbet, Bonbon, Butterfly, Handles, 9 In.	23.00
Lime Sherbet, Compote, Persian Medallion, Crimped & Ruffled Edge, 6 1/2 In.	45.00
Lime Sherbet, Vase, Drape, Bulbous Base, Ruffled Edge, 8 In.	50.00
Lime Sherbet, Vase, Melon Ribbed, Crimped & Ruffled Edge, 5 1/2 In.	25.00
Lime Sherbet, Vase, Peacock, 8 In.	45.00
Mosaic, Vase, Amethyst Iridescent, Red & Yellow Oil Spot, 2 Handles, 11 In.	2645.00
Peach Crest, Vase, Beaded Melon, Ruffled Edge, 6 1/2 In.	45.00
Rose Crest, Vase, Bulbous Base, Pulled Neck, Ruffled Edge, 8 In.	60.00
Silver Crest, Bowl, Crimped & Ruffled Edge, 10 In.	50.00
Silver Crest, Bowl, Tricornered, Ruffled Edge, 7 In.	26.00
Silver Crest, Vase, Beaded Melon, Ruffled Edge, 6 In.	35.00
Silver Crest, Vase, Violets In The Snow, Bulbous, Crimped & Ruffled Edge, 4 1/2 In.	42.00
Thumbprint, Compote, Amber, Ruffled Edge, 5 In.	17.00
Thumbprint, Compote, Colonial Blue, Ruffled Edge, 7 1/2 In.	12.00
Thumbprint, Epergne, 3-Lily, Milk Glass, 9 In.	75.00
Thumbprint, Goblet, Pink, 6 1/2 In.	12.00
Thumbprint, Sugar & Creamer, Pink	35.00
Topaz Opalescent, Plate, Leaf Form, 8 In.	38.00
Vase, Vaseline, Opalescent, 20 In.	160.00
Velva Rose, Dish, Mayonnaise, Footed, 5 3/4 In.	30.00

FIESTA, the colorful dinnerware, was introduced in 1936 by the Homer Laughlin China Co., redesigned in 1969, and withdrawn in 1973. It was reissued again in 1986 in different colors and is still being made. The simple design was characterized by a band of concentric circles, beginning at the rim. Cups had full-circle handles until 1969, when partial-circle handles were made. Harlequin and Riviera were related wares. For more information about Fiesta, its colors and prices, see the book *Kovels' Depression Glass & Dinnerware Price List*.

Chartreuse, Chop Plate, 13 In.	45.00
Chartreuse, Chop Plate, 15 In.	45.00
Chartreuse, Cup & Saucer, After Dinner	364.00
Chartreuse, Eggcup, 3 1/8 In.	160.00
Chartreuse, Mug, 3 1/8 In.	90.00
Chartreuse, Nappy, 8 1/2 In.	28.00
Chartreuse, Plate, 6 In.	6.00
Chartreuse, Plate, 9 In.	14.00
Chartreuse, Plate, Compartment, 10 1/2 In.	34.00
Chartreuse, Soup, Cream	50.00
Cobalt Blue, Ashtray	45.00
Cobalt Blue, Candleholder, Bulb, Pair	50.00

Cobalt Blue, Candleholder, Tripod, Pair 320.00
Cobalt Blue, Carafe 224.00
Cobalt Blue, Casserole, Individual, Kitchen Kraft 90.00
Cobalt Blue, Chop Plate, 15 In. 100.00
Cobalt Blue, Compote, Sweets 120.00
Cobalt Blue, Cup, Tea 35.00
Cobalt Blue, Jar, Cover, Kitchen Kraft, Large 140.00
Cobalt Blue, Marmalade 134.00
Cobalt Blue, Plate, 6 1/4 In. 20.00
Cobalt Blue, Plate, 9 In. 4.25
Cobalt Blue, Plate, Compartment, 12 In. 45.00
Cobalt Blue, Plate, Dinner, 10 In. 33.00
Cobalt Blue, Platter, Oval, 12 In. 90.00
Cobalt Blue, Relish Tray 308.00
Cobalt Blue, Saltshaker, 2 3/4 In. 33.00
Cobalt Blue, Sauceboat 28.00
Cobalt Blue, Teapot, 6 Cup 205.00
Cobalt Blue, Tray, Figure 8 .... 80.00
Cobalt Blue, Vase, Flared, 8 In. 795.00
Forest Green, Ashtray 56.00
Forest Green, Bowl, Fruit, 4 3/4 In. 38.00
Forest Green, Bowl, Fruit, 5 1/2 In. 38.00
Forest Green, Cup, Tea 38.00
Forest Green, Jug, 2 Pt. 78.00
Forest Green, Plate, 9 In. 16.00
Forest Green, Plate, 10 In. 40.00
Forest Green, Platter, 12 In. 39.00
Forest Green, Sauceboat 230.00
Forest Green, Soup, Cream 45.00
Gray, Chop Plate, 15 In. 50.00
Gray, Eggcup 62.00
Gray, Mug ....28.00 to 88.00
Gray, Pitcher, Water, Disk, 2 Qt. 225.00
Gray, Plate, 9 In. 30.00
Gray, Plate, Compartment, 12 In. 45.00
Gray, Soup, Cream 50.00
Green, Saltshaker, Kitchen Kraft 110.00
Ivory, Bowl, Fruit, 4 3/4 In. 35.00
Ivory, Candleholder, Bulb, Pair ....65.00 to 150.00
Ivory, Candleholder, Tripod, Pair ....300.00 to 420.00
Ivory, Coffeepot, Cover 195.00
Ivory, Compote, Sweets 100.00
Ivory, Mixing Bowl, No. 4 .... 125.00
Ivory, Plate, 6 In. ....7.00 to 9.00
Ivory, Plate, 9 In. 18.00
Ivory, Plate, Calendar, 1955, 9 In. 58.00
Ivory, Tumbler, Juice 30.00
Ivory, Vase, Bud 40.00
Light Green, Ashtray 30.00
Light Green, Candleholder, Tripod, Pair ....336.00 to 525.00
Light Green, Coffeepot, Cover 175.00
Light Green, Compote, Sweets ....84.00 to 110.00
Light Green, Creamer, Stick 37.00
Light Green, Cup & Saucer, After Dinner 28.00
Light Green, Eggcup 34.00
Light Green, Jar, Cover, Kitchen Kraft, Medium 160.00
Light Green, Marmalade 179.00
Light Green, Mixing Bowl, Kitchen Kraft, 8 In. 101.00
Light Green, Nappy, 8 1/2 In. 40.00
Light Green, Pitcher, Juice, Disk, 30 Oz. 125.00
Light Green, Plate, Deep, 8 In. 38.00
Light Green, Soup, Onion 448.00
Light Green, Spoon, Kitchen Kraft 62.00

Light Green, Stacking Unit, Kitchen Kraft 50.00
Light Green, Syrup 450.00
Light Green, Tray, Utility 70.00
Medium Green, Ashtray 130.00
Medium Green, Creamer 67.00
Medium Green, Cup & Saucer, Tea 90.00
Medium Green, Mug 105.00
Medium Green, Plate, 6 In. 35.00
Medium Green, Plate, 7 In. 45.00
Medium Green, Plate, 9 In. 80.00
Medium Green, Plate, 10 In. ....67.00 to 120.00
Medium Green, Plate, Deep, 8 In. ....50.00 to 140.00
Medium Green, Platter, Oval, 12 In. ....150.00 to 180.00
Medium Green, Salad, Individual ....67.00 to 112.00
Medium Green, Sugar, Cover 134.00
Red, Bowl, Fruit, 4 3/4 In. ....14.50 to 35.00
Red, Bowl, Fruit, 5 1/2 In. 35.00
Red, Bowl, Fruit, 11 3/4 In. 146.00
Red, Bowl, Salad, Individual, 7 1/2 In. ....56.00 to 67.00
Red, Cake Server, Kitchen Kraft 65.00
Red, Candleholder, Tripod, Pair ....280.00 to 448.00
Red, Carafe ....112.00 to 345.00
Red, Casserole, Cover 205.00
Red, Casserole, Individual, Kitchen Kraft 50.00
Red, Coffeepot, Cover ....146.00 to 240.00
Red, Compote, Sweets 130.00
Red, Cup, Tea 35.00
Red, Fork, Kitchen Kraft 80.00
Red, Jar, Cover, Kitchen Kraft, Large 220.00
Red, Mixing Bowl, Cover Only, No. 1 .... 1100.00
Red, Mustard 280.00
Red, Pitcher, Water, Disk, 2 Qt. 150.00
Red, Salad, Footed 224.00
Red, Sauceboat 85.00
Red, Shaker, Ball, 2 1/2 In. 15.00
Red, Spoon, Kitchen Kraft 50.00
Red, Teapot, 8 Cup 202.00
Red, Tray, Relish 252.00
Red, Tray, Utility 28.00
Red, Tumbler, Water 93.00
Rose, Ashtray 50.00
Rose, Casserole, Cover, 7 3/4 In. ....125.00 to 295.00
Rose, Chop Plate, 15 In. 62.00
Rose, Cup & Saucer, Tea ....30.00 to 37.00
Rose, Jug, 2 Pt. 190.00
Rose, Nappy, 8 1/2 In. 36.00
Rose, Pitcher, Water, Disk 84.00
Rose, Plate, Compartment, 10 1/2 In. 45.00
Rose, Sugar, Cover 85.00
Tray, Relish, Cobalt Blue, Green, Ivory, Red, Turquoise & Yellow 375.00
Turquoise, Ashtray 39.00
Turquoise, Bowl, Dessert, 6 In. 38.00
Turquoise, Candleholder, Bulb, Pair ....100.00 to 250.00
Turquoise, Candleholder, Tripod, Pair 170.00
Turquoise, Carafe 168.00
Turquoise, Casserole, Cover 80.00
Turquoise, Compote, 12 In. 28.00
Turquoise, Cup & Saucer, Tea 22.00
Turquoise, Nappy, 8 1/2 In. 60.00
Turquoise, Pitcher, Water, Disk, 2 Qt. 250.00
Turquoise, Plate, 10 In. 32.00
Turquoise, Plate, Compartment, 10 1/2 In. 30.00
Turquoise, Platter, Oval, 12 In. ....35.00 to 90.00

Turquoise, Syrup 336.00
Turquoise, Tray, Figure 8 .... 90.00
Turquoise, Tray, Utility 22.00
Turquoise, Vase, Bud ....95.00 to 135.00
Yellow, Bowl, Vegetable 25.00
Yellow, Cake Plate, Kitchen Kraft 40.00
Yellow, Candleholder, Tripod, Pair 325.00
Yellow, Carafe ....100.00 to 225.00
Yellow, Compote 78.00
Yellow, Cup & Saucer, After Dinner 85.00
Yellow, Cup & Saucer, Tea 18.00
Yellow, Jug, Cover, Kitchen Kraft, Large 120.00
Yellow, Jug, Cover, Kitchen Kraft, Medium 140.00
Yellow, Mixing Bowl, Cover Over, No. 5 .... 5700.00
Yellow, Mixing Bowl, No. 4 .... 56.00
Yellow, Mug 30.00
Yellow, Mustard 300.00
Yellow, Nappy, 8 1/2 In. 30.00
Yellow, Pitcher, Ice Lip 67.00
Yellow, Plate, 9 In. 9.00
Yellow, Plate, 10 In. 30.00
Yellow, Plate, 12 In. 35.00
Yellow, Plate, Compartment, 10 1/2 In. ....30.00 to 36.00
Yellow, Plate, Deep, 8 1/4 In. 38.00
Yellow, Platter, Oval, 12 In. 30.00
Yellow, Sauceboat ....25.00 to 55.00
Yellow, Stacking Unit, Kitchen Kraft 65.00
Yellow, Teapot, 6 Cup 101.00
Yellow, Tray, Figure 8 .... 100.00
Yellow, Tumbler, Juice 45.00
Yellow, Vase, 8 In. 616.00

FINCH, see Kay Finch category.

FINDLAY ONYX AND FLORADINE are two similar types of glass made by Dalzell, Gilmore and Leighton Co. of Findlay, Ohio, about 1889. Onyx is a patented yellowish white opaque glass with raised silver daisy decorations. A few rare pieces were made of rose, amber, orange, or purple glass. Floradine is made of cranberry-colored glass with an opalescent white raised floral pattern and a satin finish. The same molds were used for both types of glass.

Box, Cover, Round, 4 1/2 x 5 3/4 In. 1093.00
Creamer, Floradine, Bulbous, Applied Camphor Handle, 4 1/2 In. 260.00
Creamer, Silver Flowers, Leaves, Opal Handle, 4 1/2 In. 345.00
Jug, Cased Opal Glass, Silvered Decoration, 4 1/2 In. 374.00
Muffineer, Metal Collar, Screw Lid, 5 1/2 In. 518.00
Pitcher, Platinum Flowers, Opalescent Handle, Bulbous, 7 5/8 In. 288.00
Spooner, Floradine, Light Red, White Flowers, 4 1/4 In. 980.00
Spooner, Floradine, White Flowers, 4 1/4 In. 775.00
Spooner, Platinum Flowers, 4 1/4 In. ....115.00 to 230.00
Sugar, Cover, Ball Finial, Bulbous, 6 In. 431.00
Sugar, Cover, Floradine, Bulbous, 6 In. 345.00
Sugar, Floradine, 4 1/2 In. 1438.00
Sugar Shaker, Floradine, Silver Flowers, Fluted Neck, 5 In. 375.00
Syrup, 6 1/2 In. 546.00
Toothpick, 2 1/8 In. 316.00
Tumbler, Barrel Shape, 3 3/4 In. 201.00

FIREFIGHTING equipment of all types is wanted, from fire marks to uniforms to toy fire trucks. It is said that every little boy wanted to be a fireman or a train engineer 75 years ago and the collectors today reflect this interest.

Alarm, Cast Iron, Maroon Paint, Gamewell Fire Alarm & Telegraph Co., N.Y., 32 In. 880.00

Alarm, Walnut Case, Carved, Gamewell Fire Alarm Telegraph Co., N.Y., 1880s, 37 In. 4140.00
Alarm Box, Cast Iron, Painted, Brass Plaque, For Boston Building, New York, 32 In. 880.00
Alarm Box, Gamewell, Pull Down Lever, Brass Plaque, No. 4 . . . .   95.00
Ax, Parade, Rounded Steel Head, Curved Handle, Stamped Star & C, 36 In. 295.00
Ax, Viking Style, 33 1/2 In. 165.00
Ax, Viking Style, Red Painted Tin, Reservoir Head, C-Handle, 38 1/2 In. 630.00
Ax, Viking Style, Wooden Handle, Painted, 34 1/2 In. 220.00
Banner, Welcome Firemen, Firemen's Scramble, 3 x 5 In. 110.00
Bell, Gong, Center Wind, Turtle, 6 In. 66.00
Bell, Painted, Gray, Hart Hardware Co., Louisville, Kentucky, c.1886, 16 In. 230.00
Belt, Leather, Brass, Black & Red, Brass Buckle, Hydrant, V.F.A. Phil., 38 In. 115.00
Belt, Parade, Leather, Black, Keeper Washington H & L Cogan, Boston 100.00
Belt, Parade, Leather, Black, Randolph, No. 1 . . . .   80.00
Belt, Parade, Leather, White, Black Cutout Letters, Atlas Fire Co., Box 88.00
Bucket, Leather, Blue, Burning Building, 2-Sided, Union Hose Co., No. 2, 9 1/2 In. 23000.00
Bucket, Leather, Painted Black, Gilt Letters, Fountain No. 2, 1801, Handle, 21 1/2 In. 2820.00
Bucket, Leather, Painted Green, Black Letters, L. Tower, Iron Rings, 19 In. 700.00
Bucket, Leather, Painted, Black, Crossed Arrows, Pitch Painted Interior, 12 x 12 In. 110.00
Bucket, Leather, Painted, Black, H.B. Thornton, Saco, Maine, 1817, 13 In. 925.00
Bucket, Leather, Painted, Danvers Fire Society, John Dunn, 1826, 12 1/2 In. 1100.00
Bucket, Leather, Painted, Dark Green, Red Trim, Yellow, c.1831, 9 1/2 In. 1295.00
Bucket, Leather, Painted, Eagle, Spread Wings, Banner, 12 In. 270.00
Bucket, Leather, Painted, J.B. No. 1, Handle, 13 In. 880.00
Bucket, Leather, Painted, L. Tower-3, 14 In. 330.00
Bucket, Leather, Painted, N. Marsten 1815, No. 2, 10 1/2 In. 497.00
Bucket, Leather, Painted, No Handle, 11 1/2 In. 110.00
Bucket, Leather, Painted, Red, D. Wilmarth, No. 56, Handle, 13 1/2 In. 770.00
Bucket, Leather, Painted, Stenciled, E.W. Upham Concord, 12 1/2 In. 330.00
Bucket, Leather, Red Paint, Green Band, New England, 20 In. 345.00
Bucket, Leather, Scrolling Leaf Cartouche, Inscribed, H. Rich, 1827, 11 3/4 In. 1495.00
Bucket, Leather, Tapered Sides, Stitched Joints, Black Letters, John Wood, 13 In. 175.00
Certificate, Fireman Of The City Of New York, W. Mott, 1797, Gilt Frame, 24 x 22 In. . . .   705.00
Cuff, Leather, FD Button, Red, Gold Embroidered Shield, 19th Century, Pair 360.00
Extinguisher, Gorham, Pony 140.00
Extinguisher, Liberty Tin Tube 50.00
Extinguisher, Tin Lithograph, George F. Johnson Co., 22 In. 45.00
Extinguisher, Tin Lithograph, Richmond Chemical Co., 22 In. 35.00
Extinguisher, Universal, Copper, 2 1/2 Gal. 30.00
Fire Mark, Cast Iron, Round, F.I. Co., Mass. 425.00
Fire Mark, Clasped Hands, Date 1776, Gold, Black Paint, Cast Iron, 10 x 10 1/2 In. 835.00
Fire Mark, United Fireman's Insurance, Philadelphia, Iron, c.1870, 9 1/2 x 11 1/4 In. 440.00
Gate, Wrought Iron, Fire Dept, 37 x 38 In. 495.00
Grenade, Cobalt Blue, Horizontal Ribs, c.1880-95, 6 1/4 In. 460.00
Grenade, Harden's Hand, Blue, Segmented, Round, Footed, 1860-1900, 4 3/4 In. 560.00
Grenade, Harden's Hand, Star, Aqua, Sheared & Ground Lip, c.1890, 6 3/4 In. 90.00
Grenade, Harden's Star, Sapphire Blue, Contents, 6 1/2 In. 115.00
Grenade, Hardens Star, Vertical Ribs, Contents, Cobalt Blue, 6 3/4 In. . . . . .88.00 to 92.00
Grenade, Haywards, Hand Fire, Patented Aug. 8, 1871, Cobalt Blue, Ground Lip, 3 In. . . .   340.00
Grenade, Imperial Grenade, Fire Extinguisher, Emerald Green, Foil, England, 6 1/2 In. . . .   520.00
Helmet, Aluminum, Cairns, Yellow, Eye Shields, Matwah F.D. No. 2 . . . .   120.00
Helmet, Black, High Eagle, Globe Fire Co., No. 30 . . . .   660.00
Helmet, Cast Iron, Black, B.F.D. No. 5 On Back Brim, 7 1/2 In. 120.00
Helmet, Leather, Black, Cutout Letters, No. 1, C.W.F., 8 In. 255.00
Helmet, Leather, Black, Shield, Tooled Brim, Community F Co., Cairns & Bros., 14 In. . . .   175.00
Helmet, Leather, Black, White Shield, Paper Label, W.D. Edson, Cairns & Bro. 1880.00
Helmet, Leather, Brass Open Eagle, Engineer, No. 5, W.F.D. 255.00
Helmet, Leather, Cairns, New Yorker, Lynn Front Shield 295.00
Helmet, Leather, Cairns, Short Brim 175.00
Helmet, Leather, Transitional, Open Eagle Finial 190.00
Helmet, Leather, White, High Eagle, Painted, Front V Hose 660.00
Helmet, Leather, White, Red Leather Shield, Eagle, Black Letters, Newburyport, 15 In. . . .   355.00
Helmet, Leather, White, Running Fireman Finial, Cutout Hose, No. 1 . . . . 1100.00
Helmet, Leather, White, South American Style, Friendship 1 Engine & Hose, 6 1/2 In. 715.00

Helmet, Metal, Silver Eagle, Ladder 1 PFD, Cairns & Bros., 14 In. 265.00
Hydrant, Cast Iron, Model 82, Chapman Valve Mfg Co, Boston, c.1890, 33 1/2 In. 150.00
Nozzle, Brass, American La France, Ladder Hook & Shut Off, 18 In. 115.00
Nozzle, Brass, F.D.N.Y., Engine 161 Fireboat, 16 In. 22.00
Nozzle, Brass, Shut Off, C. Callahan, Boston 99.00
Nozzle, Mill, Boston Woven Hose & Rubber Co., 30 In. 55.00
Nozzle, Mill, Henry K. Barnes, Boston, 30 In. 55.00
Nozzle, Mill, Red Wrapping, Boston Woven Hose & Rubber Co., 30 In. 66.00
Nozzle, Straight Steam, Quick Disconnect Cup Link, Rookwood, 33 1/2 In. 66.00
Pick Ax, Painted Red Handle, 35 In. 44.00
Saber, Etched Blades, Original Scabbard, 19th Century, 39 In. 770.00
Shield, Aide To Fire Commissioner, Boston, Leather, Painted, Black, Red, Yellow, 6 In. . . . 380.00
Shield, District Chief 7, Leather, Black, Red On Gray Banner, Crossed Horns, 6 In. 325.00
Trumpet, Brass, Painted Bell, Mouthpiece, 19 In. 330.00
Trumpet, Brass, Workman, 18 In. 290.00
Trumpet, Brass, Workman, Red Tassel, 16 In. 340.00
Trumpet, Brass, Workman, Red Tassel, Painted Mouthpiece, Bell, 14 In. 580.00
Trumpet, Nickel Over Brass, Workmans, Gold Tassel, 19 In. 410.00
Trumpet, Presentation, Neoclassical Relief, Woman, Leaves, Sept. 17, 1870, 23 In. 3408.00
Trumpet, Presentation, Silver Plated, Inscription, Boston Fire, Nov. 9, 1872 . . . . 2115.00
Trumpet, Silver Plated, Engraved, Eagle Helmet, Ladder, Hose, Oct. 15th 1901, 21 In. . . . 120.00
Trumpet, Silver Plated, Etched, Dolphin Tassel Holder, 20 In. 990.00
Trumpet, Silver Plated, Etched, Medallions, Classical Woman, Boston, Sept. 17th 1870 . . . 3400.00

FIREPLACES were used to cook food and to heat the American home
in past centuries. Many types of tools and equipment were used.
Andirons held the logs in place, firebacks reflected the heat into the
room, and tongs were used to move either fuel or food. Many types of
spits and roasting jacks were made and may be listed in the Kitchen
category.

Andirons, Aluminum, Iron, Donald Deskey, c.1935, 17 3/4 x 13 1/2 x 4 3/8 In. 10800.00
Andirons, Bell Metal, Chippendale, Ball & Claw Feet, c.1780, 23 1/2 x 15 3/4 In. 3600.00
Andirons, Bell Metal, Chippendale, Log Stop, Late 18th Century, 23 In. 1795.00
Andirons, Brass Wash, Hammered, Balls, Shafts, Arts & Crafts, 24 1/2 x 13 In. 235.00
Andirons, Brass, Ball Top, Ball Feet, Scalloped Legs, 17 1/4 In. 345.00
Andirons, Brass, Ball Top, Concentric Rings, Shaped Columns, Cabriole Legs, 16 5/8 In. . . . 560.00
Andirons, Brass, Ball Top, Ring Turned Shaft, Square Stepped Base, 15 x 8 In. 440.00
Andirons, Brass, Ball Tops, Swiveling Backs, Bradley & Hubbard, 16 x 8 x 22 1/2 In. 470.00
Andirons, Brass, Baluster Turned Shaft, Ball Feet, Early 19th Century, 16 1/2 In. 235.00
Andirons, Brass, Baroque, Pierced Stylized Finials, 20th Century, 23 x 10 x 23 In. 190.00
Andirons, Brass, Double Acorn Finials, Spur Arches, Iron Rods, 19th Century, 16 In. 375.00
Andirons, Brass, Empire Style, Paw Feet, Scrolled Leaves, Columns, Urn Tops, 28 In. 230.00
Andirons, Brass, Federal Style, Turned, Faceted Tops, 19 1/2 In. 200.00
Andirons, Brass, Federal, Arched Legs, Ball Feet, 18 1/2 In. 520.00
Andirons, Brass, Federal, Baluster Shape, Ball Feet, Early 19th Century, 20 x 19 In. 545.00
Andirons, Brass, Federal, Bright Cut, Wittingham Attribution, c.1810, 22 x 20 In. 7200.00
Andirons, Brass, Federal, Double Lemon Top, Arch Legs, Ball Feet, 17 1/4 In. 690.00
Andirons, Brass, Federal, Double Lemon Top, Arch Spurred Legs, Penny Feet, 18 1/4 In. . . . 805.00
Andirons, Brass, Federal, Iron, Lemon Finial, Urn & Plinth, c.1800, 21 In. 3819.00
Andirons, Brass, Federal, Ringed Stem, Urn Finial, S-Scroll Legs, Ball Feet, 21 1/2 In. . . . 179.00
Andirons, Brass, France, Early 20th Century, 16 In. 175.00
Andirons, Brass, Iron, Acorn Top, Ball Finials, c.1800, 20 x 9 5/8 x 23 1/2 In. 1116.00
Andirons, Brass, Iron, Ball Top, Baluster Shafts, c.1800, 17 x 11 3/4 x 21 1/2 In. 355.00
Andirons, Brass, Iron, Federal, Urn Top, Ball & Claw, Philadelphia, c.1800, 30 x 29 In. . . . 1800.00
Andirons, Brass, Iron, Knife Blade Shaft, c.1785, 22 3/4 x 9 x 16 3/4 In. 999.00
Andirons, Brass, Iron, Lemon Top, Beaded Belts, Cabriole Legs, Ball Feet, 9 x 19 In. 765.00
Andirons, Brass, Iron, Steeple Top, Columnar, Cabriole Legs, J. Davis, Boston, 18 In. 940.00
Andirons, Brass, Iron, Urn Top, Knife Blade Shaft, Arched Legs, Penny Feet, 21 x 9 In. . . . 650.00
Andirons, Brass, Iron, Urn Top, Knife Blade Shaft, c.1785, 19 1/4 x 9 x 16 1/4 In. 500.00
Andirons, Brass, Iron, Urn Top, Slender Column, Cabriole Legs, Late 1700s, 27 In. 2940.00
Andirons, Brass, Queen Anne Style, Acorn Finial, Cabriole Legs, 20 1/2 In. 60.00
Andirons, Brass, Spherical Top, Turned Stem, England, 1800s, 20 In. 259.00
Andirons, Brass, Steeple Top, Ball Feet, Scalloped Legs, 2-Piece Construction, 19 In. 520.00

Andirons, Brass, Steeple Top, Ball Feet, Scalloped Legs, 24 In. 460.00
Andirons, Brass, Steeple Top, Spire & Ball, Hexagon Turned Shaft, Spur Legs, 19 In. 520.00
Andirons, Brass, Turned Finials, Spurred Arching Legs, Ball Feet, 23 In. 400.00
Andirons, Brass, Urn Top, Knife Blade Shaft, c.1885, 18 x 7 3/4 x 12 1/2 In. 645.00
Andirons, Brass, Wrought Iron, Vase Shape, c.1900, 25 x 9 x 17 In. 345.00
Andirons, Bronze, Dolphin Form, Late 19th Century, 13 In. 230.00
Andirons, Bronze, Iron, Neptune & Venus Standing, Baroque Style, c.1865, 27 In. 1150.00
Andirons, Cast Brass, Scrolled Base, Fleur-De-Lis, Ball, Spire Columns, 1900s, 22 1/2 In. . 85.00
Andirons, Cast Iron, Black Paint, Ducks, 4 Seasons Shop, Memphis, Tenn., 14 x 34 1/4 In. 2990.00
Andirons, Cast Iron, Fluted Base, Applied Brass Buttons, Arts & Crafts, 9 x 18 x 27 In. . . . 470.00
Andirons, Cast Iron, George Washington, 14 1/2 x 7 1/2 x 11 1/2 In. 290.00
Andirons, Cast Iron, George Washington, Swagged Plinth, 21 1/2 In. 520.00
Andirons, Cast Iron, Hessian Soldier, Painted, 1800s, 20 x 9 x 20 In. 1195.00
Andirons, Cast Iron, Man, Woman, 10 x 20 x 16 In. 410.00
Andirons, Cast Iron, Scottie Dogs, 11 x 8 x 16 In. 29.00
Andirons, Cast Iron, Squirrel, Seated, Footed Log Base, 16 x 12 x 19 In. 1610.00
Andirons, Cast Iron, Sword Shape, Painted Handles, 8 x 18 x 24 In. 530.00
Andirons, Cast Iron, Woman, Ruffled Skirt, Beaded Necklace, 11 1/2 In. 290.00
Andirons, Fender, Brass, Ball & Turned Support, 20th Century, 17 1/2 & 9 x 43 x 13 In. . . 80.00
Andirons, Fender, Fire Tool Set, Brass, Federal Style, Early 20th Century, 20 x 42 In. 345.00
Andirons, Fender, Scalloped Legs, Ball Feet, Pierced, Early 20th Century; 16 & 27 In. 100.00
Andirons, Gilt Brass, Louis XV, Scrolling Leaves, Early 20th Century, 9 1/2 x 22 In. 115.00
Andirons, Gilt Metal, Neoclassical, Gallery, Pineapple Finial, Leaf Feet, 10 In. 840.00
Andirons, Iron, 9 Diamonds, Removable Log Bars, Arts & Crafts, 17 x 20 1/2 In. 275.00
Andirons, Iron, Brass Blade, Arched Base, Scrolled Feet, Log Stops, 18 3/4 In. 575.00
Andirons, Iron, Brass, Knife Edge, Urn Top, 18th Century, 22 In. 590.00
Andirons, Iron, Female Figures, Painted Black, Mid 19th Century, 11 1/2 x 6 x 6 In. 315.00
Andirons, Iron, Reticulated, Applied Copper Spade Top, 12 x 7 x 9 In. 1760.00
Andirons, Wrought Iron, Arched Base, Penny Feet, Tapered Columns Ball Tops, 19 In. . . . 660.00
Andirons, Wrought Iron, Brass, Knife Blade, Urn Finial, Penny Feet, 23 1/2 In. 489.00
Andirons, Wrought Iron, Copper, Riveted, Pyramid Tops, Arts & Crafts, 24 x 14 x 25 In. . . 2115.00
Andirons, Wrought Iron, G. Stickley, No. 237, Tapering Shafts, c.1905, 24 x 16 x 20 In. . . . 8815.00
Andirons, Wrought Iron, Wallace Nutting, Colonial Curl, c.1920, No. I-400 . . . . 1970.00
Bellows, Painted, Turtleback, Yellow, Green, Orange Flowers, Early 1800s, 18 In. 165.00
Bellows, Shell, Leaves, Red, Green, Gold, On Yellow Ground, Brass Spout, 18 In. 630.00
Bellows, Turtleback, Tulips, Borders, Leather, 18 1/4 In. 200.00
Bellows, Wood, Brass, Leather, Salmon Paint, 19th Century, 15 x 6 1/2 In. 230.00
Bench, Hammered Copper, Leatherette Stools, Arts & Crafts, Early 1900s, 22 x 56 In. 2530.00
Bucket, Fire, Copper Rivets, Wood Bottom, 12 x 10 In. 325.00
Chenet, Andirons, Bronze, Iron, Louis XV Style, Bouhon, c.1900, 16 x 15 x 28 In. 2760.00
Chenet, Andirons, Fender, Bronze, Lion Head Masks, 1800s, 20 x 12 & 36 x 6 In. 520.00
Chenet, Andirons, Gilt Brass, Iron, Napoleon III, Children, c.1865, 9 1/2 x 7 x 14 In. 920.00
Chenet, Andirons, Seated Lion, Gilt Brass Mount, Bronze Patinated, Brass, c.1915, 21 In. . 1610.00
Chenet, Andirons, Wrought Iron, Gilt, Patinated Bronze, Louis XVI Style, c.1900, 19 In. . . . 1265.00
Coal Bin, Aesthetic Revival, Rosewood, Wedgwood, Brass, 1875, 26 x 17 In., Pair 4400.00
Coal Bin, Brass, Urn Shape, Dutch, 23 In. 390.00
Coal Scuttle, Toleware, Painted Flowers, Removable Bucket, 24 x 15 x 10 In. 290.00
Coal Scuttle, Victorian, Brass, Embossed Lid, Brass, Wood Cast Handles, 19 x 13 x 19 In. 200.00
Fender, Arts & Crafts Style, Copper, Hand Hammered, Tulips, 6 1/2 x 50 x 11 In. 60.00
Fender, Brass, Black Wire, Federal, Early 19th Century, 34 In. 720.00
Fender, Brass, Pierced Grapevines, Applied Grape Bunches, Rope Twist, 47 x 13 x 9 In. . . 345.00
Fender, Brass, Pierced, 3 Stepped Feet, 19th Century, 9 x 44 x 8 In. 520.00
Fender, Brass, Wirework, 3 Finials, 12 x 57 x 14 1/2 In. 290.00
Fender, Brass, Wirework, D-Shape, Acorn Finials, 19th Century, 53 3/4 In. 380.00
Fender, Brass, Wirework, Swag, Scroll, Undulating Line, c.1800, 10 x 56 3/4 In. 1880.00
Fender, Louis Philippe, Gilt Bronze Mounted, Steel, Mid 19th Century, 8 1/2 x 52 In. 920.00
Fender, Louis XVI Style, Gilt & Patinated Bronze, Putti, c.1885, 20 x 34 In. 3450.00
Fender, Neoclassical, Bronze, Parcel Gilt, Figures, Medallions, Late 1800s, 9 1/2 x 39 In. . . 1150.00
Fender, Pierced Gallery, Paw Feet, England, c.1900, 5 1/2 x 43 x 9 1/2 In. 260.00
Fender, Serpentine, Vertical Wirework, Brass Rail & Swags, 12 x 51 x 18 In. 5580.00
Fender, Wire, Brass Trimmed, D-Shape, Early 19th Century, 39 x 8 In. 140.00
Fender, Wirework, Brass, Scroll & Scallop Elements, c.1800, 12 1/2 x 49 x 18 In. 1765.00
Fender & Andirons, Brass, Porcelain, 14 x 64 x 12 & 22 x 9 In. 7480.00

Fender & Andirons, Brass, Twist Rods, Fan Drops, Ball Columns, 1900s, 25 x 60 In. 345.00
Kindling Box, Slant Front, Brass Clad, Repousse, Late Victorian, c.1885, 15 1/4 x 22 In. . . 259.00
Log Carrier, Birch Bark, Reindeer, Tree, Owl, Hawk, Rabbits, Penobscot, c.1915, 24 In. . . 1265.00
Log Holder, Copper, Iron, Repousse, Lions, Eagle, Shield, 6 Footed, 14 1/2 x 27 1/8 In. . . . 690.00
Log Holder, Wrought Iron, Copper, Riveted, Arts & Crafts, 15 1/2 x 20 x 20 In. 940.00
Mantel is listed in the Architectural category.
Screen, 4-Panel, Folding, Arched Tops, Mother-Of-Pearl, Black, Red, 36 x 44 x 1 In. 110.00
Screen, Arts & Crafts Style, Painted, Tole, Early 20th Century, 39 1/2 In. 35.00
Screen, Brass, Iron, Wirework, Folding, c.1800, 24 x 76 In. 3175.00
Screen, Brass, Scrolling Leaves, Lions, Mask, Ring Mount, 1600s Style, 56 x 39 In. 1995.00
Screen, Brass, Wire, Scrolled Detail, American, 1800-30, 42 In. 750.00
Screen, Cast Brass, Oval, Scrolled Feet, Wire Mesh Insert, 1900s, 27 x 29 In. 776.00
Screen, Edwardian, Satinwood, Painted, Watercolor On Silk Inset, 42 x 18 x 15 In. 720.00
Screen, French Style, Brass, Wire Mesh Backing, Flower Basket, 1900s, 31 x 27 In. 345.00
Screen, French Style, Walnut, Carved, Scrolled Feet, Fluted Saber Legs, 43 x 22 In. 115.00
Screen, George III Style, Mahogany, Crewelwork, 1900s, 32 x 21 x 14 1/2 In. 175.00
Screen, Les Pins, Wrought Iron, Edgar Brandt, c.1924, 34 x 32 x 14 In. 35850.00
Screen, Mahogany, Needlework, Trestle Base, Stretcher, Late 1800s, 31 x 17 x 11 In. 105.00
Screen, Pole, Chippendale, Brass Mounted, Needlepoint, Tripod, 60 x 21 x 21 In. 375.00
Screen, Pole, Federal Style, Maple, Silk, Embroidered, Urn Finial, 62 x 16 x 15 In. 805.00
Screen, Pole, Papier-Mache Scene, Lacquer, Venice, c.1850, 53 x 14 x 18 In. 400.00
Screen, Pole, Queen Anne, Mahogany, Needlework, England, c.1760, 53 x 16 3/4 In. 1200.00
Screen, Pole, Victorian, Mahogany, Needlepoint, Turned Pedestal, 70 x 19 x 17 In. 490.00
Screen, Pole, Victorian, Mahogany, Needlework Panel, Couple, Landscape, 58 In. 290.00
Screen, Pole, Victorian, Mahogany, Needlework Panel, Hunting Scene, 52 In. 489.00
Screen, Renaissance Revival, Leaded Glass, Tripartite, Early 20th Century, 32 3/4 In. 1058.00
Screen, Renaissance Revival, Walnut, Openwork Cresting, Trestle Base, 44 x 26 1/2 In. . . . 205.00
Screen, Tapestry, Oak Frame, 34 1/2 x 32 In. 185.00
Screen, Victorian, Brass Mounted, Bamboo, Leaf Painted Panel, 40 x 31 In. 150.00
Spit Holder, Wrought Iron, Tripod Base, Diamond Shaped Feet, 35 In. 1380.00
Surround, Carved, Acanthus, Fleur-De-Lis, Continental, 60 x 89 x 14 In. 1265.00
Surround, Cast Iron, Mantel, Molded Cornice, Acanthus Leaf, 55 x 67 x 13 In. 865.00
Surround, Georgian Style, Wood, Carved, Late 1800s, 94 x 61 x 10 In. 690.00
Surround, Heart Pine, Board Shelf, Shaped Brackets, c.1860, 57 x 58 x 8 In. 460.00
Surround, Louis XVI Style, Stepped Cornice, Flowers, Painted, 52 1/2 x 60 In. 475.00
Surround, Salmon, Ivory Marble, Carved Flower Swags, 2 Women, 45 1/2 x 63 x 12 In. . . 1725.00
Tinder Box, Candleholder Top, Flint Striker, Flint, Iron, 1700s 285.00
Tool Set, Brass, Shovel, 2 Pairs Tongs, 33 In. 290.00
Tool Set, Cast Iron, Cast As Medieval Suit Of Armor, 31 In. 300.00
Tool Set, Polished Steel, Whitesmith Made, c.1880, 3 Piece 4500.00
Tool Set, Shovel, Tongs, G. Stickley, 42 In. 825.00
Tool Set, Shovel, Tongs, Iron, Heart Shaped Terminal, 43 In. 405.00
Tool Set, Stand, Wrought Iron, Flower, Scroll Support, 20th Century, 41 1/2 x 19 x 12 In. . 325.00
Tool Set, Wrought Iron, Twisted Stems, Emery Park Inn, 34 1/2 x 12 In., 4 Piece 1645.00

FISCHER porcelain was made in Herend, Hungary, by Moritz Fischer. The factory was founded in 1839 and continued working into the twentieth century. The wares are sometimes referred to as *Herend* porcelain.

MF

Platter, Roasted Meat, Rothschild Birds, Oval, Herend, 1700s Style, 16 In. 200.00
Teapot, Flower Sprays, Turquoise Ground, Gilt Scroll Borders, Herend, Early 1900s, 5 In. . 633.00

FISHING reels of brass or nickel were made in the United States by 1810. Bamboo fly rods were sold by 1860, often marked with the maker's name. Lures made of metal, or metal and wood, were made in the nineteenth century. Plastic lures were made by the 1930s. All fishing material is collected today and even equipment of the past thirty years is of interest if in good condition with original box.

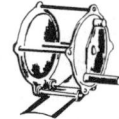

Catalog, Bristol Steel Fishing Rods, 1929, 7 1/4 x 10 In., 40 Pages 100.00
Catalog, Heddon Fishing Tackle, 1955, 5 x 6 3/4 In., 30 Pages 80.00
Catalog, Pflueger Fishing Tackle, No. 151, 1931, 5 1/4 x 8 In., 136 Pages 55.00
Catalog, Pflueger Fishing Tackle, No. 156, Pocket, 1936, 5 1/4 x 8 In., 130 Pages 96.00
Catalog, Pflueger Fishing Tackle, No. 157, 1937, 5 1/4 x 8 In., 130 Pages 58.00
Catalog, Pflueger Fishing Tackle, No. 161, 5 1/4 x 8 In., 118 Pages 50.00

Catalog, Shakespeare Fishing Tackle, No. 31D, 1930-31, 10 1/2 x 7 3/4 In., 82 Pages 60.00
Catalog, South Bend, 1924, 6 1/4 x 5 1/4 In., 68 Pages 185.00
Catalog, South Bend, Boy Holding Big Fish, 1933, 5 1/4 x 6 1/4 In., 100 Pages 175.00
Catalog, South Bend, What Tackle & When, 1931, 5 1/4 x 6 1/4 In., 80 Pages 28.00
Catalog, South Bend, What Tackle & When, 1941, 6 1/4 x 5 1/4 In., 136 Pages 28.00
Catalog, South Bend, What Tackle & When, Full Color, 1950, 6 1/4 x 5 1/4 In. 30.00
Catalog, Weber, Fly Tackle For Fresh Water Fish, Wisconsin, 1938, 6 x 9 In., 96 Pages . . . 29.00
Creel, George Lawrence, Round Woven Wicker, Leather, Strap, 9 1/2 x 14 1/2 x 6 1/2 In. . . 440.00
Creel, George Lawrence, Split Cane, Leather Hinge, Square Hole, 14 1/2 x 6 1/2 x 9 In. . . . 755.00
Creel, George Lawrence, Split Cane, Leather, Brass, 15 x 6 x 10 1/2 In. 460.00
Creel, George Lawrence, Woven Wicker, Leather, Left Hand Hole, 9 x 14 x 6 In. 230.00
Creel, Split Cane, Ash, Wood Top, Oval Hole, Leather Strap, Indian Made, 11 x 7 x 6 In. . . 105.00
Creel, Woven Cane, Leather Trim & Front Pocket, Left Hand Hole, 1950s, 15 x 8 x 7 In. . . 35.00
Display, Line, Mason's Silk Co., Glass Front, Wall Mounting, 22 x 34 x 6 In. 345.00
Display, South Bend, Die Cut, 4 Fold, Multicolor, 30 x 50 In. 2894.00
Display Rack, Winchester Rods, 28 Rod Holes, Oak, Folding, 18 x 48 In. 2059.00
Eel Spear, Stamped, I.T. Frantz, 6 Barbed Tines, Poplar Handle, Wrought Iron, 60 In. 175.00
Envelope, James Heddon's Sons, Fishing Tackle, Postmark, 1937, 3 5/8 x 6 1/2 In. 65.00
Envelope, McLean, Fishing Nets & Tackle, Address, Postmark, 3 1/2 x 6 In. 85.00
Fishing, Rod, Winston, Fly, Bamboo, Cork Hand Hold, Metal Seat, 9 Ft., 2 Piece 316.00
Gaff, Marble's, Automatic, Steel Jaws, Turned Wood Handle, c.1905, 38 1/2 In. 490.00
Knife, Marble's, Safety, 1907-11, 4-In. Blade 285.00
Knife, Marble's, Trout, c.1924, 2-In. Blade, 5 5/8 In. 148.00
License, 1917, Angling, California Citizen, Paper, $1 . . . . 14.00
License, 1927, Minnesota Non-Resident, Button, Celluloid, 1 3/4 In. 86.00
License, 1935, Pennsylvania Resident, Green, Round 13.00
License, 1936, New York Non-Resident, Orange, White, Black, Button, 1936, 1 1/4 In. . . . 55.00
License, 1938, Maryland Resident, Celluloid, Green Ground, Cellomet Products, N.Y. 59.00
License, California, Paper, Expired Dec. 31, 1923, 4 3/8 x 2 3/4 In. 20.00
Lure, Al Foss, Oriental Wiggler, No. 3, Red, White, Glass Eyes, Tin Box 42.00
Lure, Al Sisco, Shurebite, Black, White, Composite Body, Box, 4 In. 20.00
Lure, Charles W. Lane, Wagtail Minnow, Hinged Metal Tail, 3 In. 456.00
Lure, Creek Chub, Dingbat, Glass Eyes, Red Head, White Eyes, 2 In. 46.00
Lure, Creek Chub, Giant Jointed Pikie Minnow, Orange & Red Frog Spot, 6 1/4 In. 28.00
Lure, Creek Chub, Jointed Pike Minnow, Glass Eyes, Pikie Scale, Box, 3 1/2 In. 30.00
Lure, Creek Chub, Jointed Pikie Minnow, 3-Hook Cup Rig, Box, 6 1/4 In. 52.00
Lure, Creek Chub, Jointed Pikie Minnow, Glass Eyes, 4 1/4 In. 25.00
Lure, Creek Chub, Juskie Pikie, No. 2300, Glass Eyes, Box, 6 In. 36.00
Lure, Creek Chub, Plunker, Glass Eyes, Green Scale Finish, 3 In. 14.00
Lure, Creek Chub, Wagtail Glass Eyes, Red Head, White Body, 2-Hook Cup Rig, 2 3/4 In. 11.00
Lure, Creek Chub, Wiggler, 2 Treble Hooks, Hand Painted, Golden Brown, Garret, Ind. . . . 1500.00
Lure, Fred Arbogast, Tin Liz, Gold Scale, Glass Eyes, 2 1/2 In. 29.00
Lure, Heddon, Dowagiac Baby Tadpolly, Green Scale, Glass Eyes, L-Rig, 3 7/8 In. 35.00
Lure, Heddon, Dowagiac Minnow, No. 150, Wood, Glass Eyes, 5 Hooks, Box, 4 In. 87.00
Lure, Heddon, Dowagiac Underwater Minnow, No. 150S, 5 Hooks, Box, 3 5/8 In. 116.00
Lure, Heddon, Game Fisher, 2-Cup Hook Rig, 4 3/4 In. 40.00
Lure, Heddon, Giant Jointed Vamp, Red, White, Box, 7 In. 64.00
Lure, Heddon, Jointed Vamp, No. 7300, Gold Scale, Green Stripes, Painted Eyes, 4 3/4 In. 23.00
Lure, Heddon, Lucky 13, Wood, Glass Eyes, Red Head, 3 Treble Hooks, 1940s, 4 In. 22.00
Lure, Heddon, Surface Minnow, No. 300 Series, c.1925, 3 3/4 x 1 In. 144.00
Lure, Heddon, Wilder-Dilg, Red Body, Painted Eyes, Red Feather Skirt, Box 105.00
Lure, Makinen Tackle Co., Waddle Bug, Frog Spot Paint, Box, 2 3/4 In. 38.00
Lure, Marathon Bait Co., Fish-Hound, Bucktail Skirt, On Card, Box, 4 In. 22.00
Lure, McKenzie, Magic Minnow, Metal, 1930s, 5 In. 28.00
Lure, Mueller-Perry, Crazy Legs, Wood Body, 2 Treble Hooks, Box, 1971, 3 1/2 In. 16.00
Lure, Pachner & Koehler, Bright Eyes, Box, 2 3/4 In. 15.00
Lure, Paw Paw, Baby Jointed Pikie, Tack Eyes, Green Scale Paint, 3 3/4 In. 13.75
Lure, Paw Paw, Chub Minnow, Green Back, Gold Sides, White Belly, 2 5/8 In. 13.75
Lure, Paw Paw, Injured Minnow, 3-Hook Cup Rig, Tack Eyes, Box, 3 1/2 In. 39.00
Lure, Paw Paw, Wotta-Frog, Tack Eyes, Diving Lip, Yellow, Black, Green, 3 1/2 In. 56.00
Lure, Pflueger, Monarch Neverfail Minnow, Glass Eyes, Green Fish Scale Paint, 3 In. 97.00
Lure, Pflueger, Neverfail Minnow, Wire Rig Hardware, Papers, Box, 3 In. 116.00
Lure, South Bend, Bass-Oreno, No. 973, Tack Eyes, 3-Hook Cup Rig, Box, 3 3/4 In. 29.00

Lure, South Bend, Nip-I-Didee, No. 910, 3-Hook Cup Rig, Painted Tack Eyes, Box	58.00
Lure, South Bend, Whirl-Oreno, Black & Yellow Body, Bucktail Shirt, c.1932, 3 In.	78.00
Lure, Winchester, Crusader, No. 29515, Mother-Of-Pearl Spinner, On Card	283.00
Lure, Winchester, Kidney Shape, No. 9633, Nickel Finish, 5 1/2 In.	185.00
Lure, Winchester, Kidney Trolling Bait, No. 9634, Box	460.00
Lure, Winchester, Multi-Wobbler, No. 9201, Glass Eyes, Cup Rig, Box	479.00
Lure, Winchester, Multi-Wobbler, No. 9206, Rainbow Color, Glass Eyes, Box	1404.00
Lure, Winchester, Spinner, No. 9616, Nickel Front, Red Back, 5 1/2 In.	106.00
Lure, Winchester, Tear-Drop Shape, No. 9624, Spinning, 4 1/2 In.	140.00
Minnow Trap, Glass, Hand Blown, Tin Lid, Galvanized Straps, Gal., 10 1/2 x 6 1/2 In.	87.00
Minnow Trap, Orvis, Glass, Wire Frame, Aluminum Cap, 14 x 9 In.	290.00
Net, Ed Cummings, Trout, Laminated Wood, Cotton Net, Early 1950s, 24 x 10 In.	92.00
Net, Winchester, Landing, No. 9433, 2-Piece Bamboo Handle, Collapsible, 48 In.	500.00
Reel, E. Vom Hofe, Trout, Model 360, Perfection, German Silver, Rubber, 2 1/2 x 7/8 In.	7150.00
Reel, E. Vom Hofe, Universal Star, Model 621, Hard Rubber, 1902	530.00
Reel, Fin-Nor, Trout, No. 1, Case, 3 x 7/8 In.	220.00
Reel, Hardy, Trout, St. George Junior, Nickel Silver Line Guide, Bag, Box, 2 1/2 x 5/8 In.	605.00
Reel, Horton, Bluegrass Simplex, No. 33, Nickel, Brass, Single Handle, Bakelite Knob	165.00
Reel, Leonard, Trout, Patent 191813, Bronze, Silver, Raised Pillar, Engraved, 2 x 1 In.	2860.00
Reel, Meek & Sons, Bluegrass, No. 3, Satin Stainless Steel	310.00
Reel, Meek, Casting, Bluegrass, No. 33, Nickel Plated, c.1905, 1 7/8 x 1 5/8 In.	185.00
Reel, Meisselbach, Tripart, No. 580, Nickel, Brass	42.00
Reel, Otto Zwarg, Salmon, German Silver, Rubber, Leather Case, 3 3/8 x 1 3/8 In.	1925.00
Reel, Pezon Et Michel, Trout, Super Parabolic, No. 76, Pouch, Box, 3 x 11/16 In.	410.00
Reel, Shakespeare, Tournament, 1740 HE, Nickel, Silver Plated, Bakelite Knobs	72.00
Reel, Ted Godfrey, Trout, S Handle, Multiplying, Adjustable Drag, 3 1/4 x 7/8 In.	385.00
Reel, Vom Hofe, Trout, Raised Pillar, 1889 Patent, Size No. 3, 2 1/8 In.	1430.00
Reel, Von Lengerke & Antoine, Casting, Club Special, Bakelite Knob, Case, 2 x 2 In.	139.00
Reel, William Mills & Son, Trout, Fairy, Later Model, Nickel Silver, 2 1/16 x 3/4 In.	2090.00
Reel, Winchester, No. 2142	127.00
Reel, Winchester, No. 2830	400.00
Reel, Winchester, No. 4231, Wood Handle, Nickel	200.00
Reel, Winchester, No. 4331, Single Action, Ivory & Bone Knob	167.00
Rod, Bob Summers, Trout, Model 82, 2 Tips, Bag, Tube, 8 Ft. 2 In., 2 Piece	1430.00
Rod, Dickerson, Trout, Model 7012-E, 2 Tips, Bag, Tube, 7 Ft., 2 Piece	3300.00
Rod, Gillum, Trout, 2 Tips, Bag, Tube, 7 Ft., 2 Piece	5775.00
Rod, H.L. Leonard, Trout, Model 38H, 2 Tips, Bag, Tube, 7 Ft., 2 Piece	2200.00
Rod, Heddon, Bass, Expert Model 125, 2 Tips, Bag, Tube, 8 Ft. 6 In., 3 Piece	495.00
Rod, Orvis, Fly, Battenkill, Split Bamboo, Aluminum Tube, 7 1/2 Ft.	600.00
Rod, Orvis, Fly, Madison, Bamboo, Cork, Aluminum Reel Seat, 7 Ft.	275.00
Rod, Orvis, Fly, Ultralight, Tip, Staggered Ferrule, Bag, Tube, 5 Ft. 9 In., 2 Piece	440.00
Rod, Orvis, Salmon, Shooting Star, 2 Tips, Bag, Tube, 8 Ft. 6 In., 2 Piece	385.00
Rod, Orvis, Trout, Model 1882, 2 Tips, Bag, Tube, Wood Tube, Ferrule Plugs, 9 Ft., 3 Piece	1430.00
Rod, Payne, Trout, Model 98, 2 Tips, Bag, Tube, Ferrule Plug, 7 Ft., 2 Piece	3630.00
Rod, Winchester, Steel, No. 5710, Black Paint, Varnished Walnut Grip, 6 Ft., 3 Piece	90.00
Rod, Winston, Steelhead, Montana, 2 Tip, 9 Ft., 2 Piece	935.00
Rod, Winston, Trout, 2 Tips, Bag, Tube, 8 Ft. 6 In., 2 Piece	1100.00
Rod Case, Bamboo, Leather Cap & Bottom, 40 x 1 3/4 In.	250.00
Rod Case, Turner Brothers, Delight, Cord Wrapped, Leather Strap, 42 x 2 3/4 In.	85.00
Sign, Bristol Steel Fishing Rods, Steel, Flanged, 1920s, 27 1/2 x 17 1/2 In.	1965.00
Tin, Diamond Brand Lead Sinkers, Celluloid Top, Contents, St. Louis, Mo., 1 5/8 In.	110.00

FLAGS are included in the Textile category.

FLASH GORDON appeared in the Sunday comics in 1934. The daily strip started in 1940. The hero was also in comic books from 1930 to 1970, in books from 1936, in movies from 1938, on the radio in the 1930s and 1940s, and on television from 1953 to 1954. All sorts of memorabilia are collected, but the ray guns and rocket ships are the most popular.

Button, Buster Crabbe As Flash Gordon, England, 1990s, 1 In.	15.00
Comic Book, 10 Cents, No. 10, 4-Color, Dell, 1943, 68 Pages	276.00
Figure, Wood, Composition, Multi Products, 1944, 4 3/4 In.	400.00

Pin, Adventure Club, Red Border, Picture Of Flash, 1930s, 1 1/4 In. 1905.00
Pistol, Click Ray, Tin, Marx, Box, 10 In. 1356.00
Poster, Rocket Ship, Buster Crabbe, 1 Sheet, Filmcraft, c.1938, 41 x 27 In. 335.00
Press Book, Flash Gordon's Trip To Mars, Australia, 1938, 17 x 11 In., 4 Pages 475.00
Ring, Post Toasties Corn Flakes, 1949, 2 1/4 In. 80.00
Toy, Gun, Cap, Lone Star, England, Box, 1981, 10 x 11 In. 170.00
Toy, Rocket Fighter, No. 5, Tin Lithograph, Windup, 12 In. 415.00
Toy, The Martian, Plastic, Graphic Art Box, Revel, Original Box, 9 In. 75.00
Toy Set, Cast Metal, Plastic, Tootsietoy, Box, c.1978, 17 1/2 x 11 1/2 In., 9 Piece 50.00
Water Pistol, Plastic, Blue, Marx, Box, 7 In. 770.00

FLORENCE CERAMICS

FLORENCE CERAMICS were made in Pasadena, California, from World War II to 1977. Florence Ward created many colorful figurines, boxes, candleholders, and other items for the gift shop trade. Each piece was marked with an ink stamp that included the name *Florence Ceramics Co.* The company was sold in 1964, and although the name remained the same the products were very different. Mugs, cups, and trays were made.

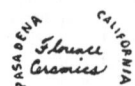

Dish, Applied Bow, Yellow, Gold Trim, Handles, 8 1/2 In. 60.00
Figurine, Annabel, Woman With Basket, Pink Gown & Hat, 8 1/4 In. 125.00
Figurine, Bird, Pouter Pigeon, Betty Davenport, 9 In. 65.00
Figurine, Cinderella & Prince Charming, White Clothes, 11 In. 710.00
Figurine, Fair Lady, Deep Rose Gown, Lace Down Center, Auburn Hair, 12 In. 800.00
Figurine, Grandmother & I, Women Having Tea, 12 In. 910.00
Figurine, Melanie, Pink Tiered Dress, Bonnet, 7 1/2 In. .... *Illus* 95.00
Figurine, Pinkie, Blue Boy, Children From Paintings, 12 In., Pair 250.00
Figurine, Princess, Blue Gown, Blue & White Flowers & Bow, 11 In. 430.00
Figurine, Victoria, Woman In Bonnet, On Settee, Blue Gown, 8 In. 210.00

FLOW BLUE

FLOW BLUE was made in England and other countries about 1830 to 1900. The dishes were printed with designs using a cobalt blue coloring. The color flowed from the design to the white body so that the finished piece has a smeared blue design. The dishes were usually made of ironstone china. More Flow Blue may be found under the name of the manufacturer.

Bowl, Arcadia, Chariots, Octagonal Paneled Body, England, 19th Century, 7 1/2 In. 115.00
Bowl, Nonpariel, Scalloped Rim, Burgess & Leigh, 8 1/2 In., 8 Piece 288.00
Bowl, Rose Pattern, W.H. Grindley & Co., 9 In. 85.00
Bowl, Vegetable, Cover, Normandy, Oval, Johnson Brothers, 9 In. 325.00
Casserole, Cover, Holland Onion, Handles, c.1900-30, 5 1/2 x 10 In. 155.00
Casserole, Cover, Water Lily, F & R Pratt, 11 3/4 In. 495.00
Cup & Saucer, Chapoo, John Wedgwood 350.00
Cup & Saucer, Temple, Podmore & Walker 325.00
Pitcher, Camels & Elephants, Relief Molded, Lustered, 5 1/2 In. 375.00
Pitcher, Flowers, Gold, 7 1/2 In. 165.00
Pitcher, St. Regis, New Wharf, 6 3/4 In. 295.00
Pitcher, Syrian, Hindley, 13 1/2 In. 375.00

Florence Ceramics, Figurine, Melanie, Pink Tiered Dress, Bonnet, 7 1/2 In.

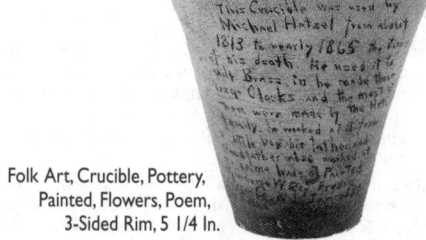

Folk Art, Crucible, Pottery, Painted, Flowers, Poem, 3-Sided Rim, 5 1/4 In.

Pitcher, Water, Normandy, Johnson Brothers, 8 In. 350.00
Pitcher & Basin, Indian Jar, 12-Sided, J. & T. Furnival, Staffordshire, 11 In. 588.00
Pitcher & Basin, Savoy, Woods & Son, 18-In. Bowl 2395.00
Plate, Amoy, Davenport, 10 1/4 In. 145.00
Plate, Conway, New Wharf, 9 In. 145.00
Plate, Gothic, Davenport, 10 1/4 In. 125.00
Plate, Manila, Podmore & Walker, 7 3/4 In. 275.00
Plate, Touraine, Stanley Pottery Co., 7 In. 75.00
Plate, Watteau, Doulton, 10 1/2 In. 75.00
Platter, Beaufort, Oval, W.H. Grindley & Co., 18 In. 350.00
Platter, Canterbury, Oval, Booths, 17 In. 495.00
Platter, Colandine, Oval, 15 1/4 In. 750.00
Platter, Fairy Villas, Oval, William Adam & Sons, 15 1/2 In. 1150.00
Platter, Oregon, Oval, Johnson Brothers, 16 In. 325.00
Soup, Dish, Kyber, W. Adams, 9 In. 140.00
Tureen, Cover, Osborne, Oval, Thos. Rathbone & Co., 8 1/4 In. 250.00
Tureen, Cover, Underplate, Ladle, Landscape, Copeland Spode, 8 1/2 x 14 In. 1595.00
Tureen, Cover, Underplate, Ladle, Macao, Thomas Goodwin, 12 In. 850.00

FLYING PHOENIX, see Phoenix Bird category.

FOLK ART is also listed in many categories of this book under the
actual name of the object. See categories such as Box, Cigar Store Figure, Paper, Weather Vane, Wooden, etc.

    Airplane, Carved, 4-Engine, Tin Tail, Red, White, Wooden, 44-In. Wing Span, 30 In. 200.00
    Bald Eagle, Stylized, Stippled Paint, Glass Eyes, Carved Pine Base, Ohio, 26 In. 4995.00
    Bird On Pedestal, Pine, Multicolored, Glass Bead Eyes, Virginville Carver, 9 1/4 x 9 In. .. 6325.00
    Bird Wheel, Carved Wood, Tin, Wire, Titled, Signed, Öof Spring, D. Noyes, 21 x 24 In. 1610.00
    Birdhouse, Stand, Wood, Metal, Church Shape, Red, Green, Early 1900s, 74 x 12 x 12 In. . 200.00
    Boat, Side-Wheeler, Metal American Flag, Iron Stand, Curved Legs, 18 x 36 In. 575.00
    Book Box, Inlaid Stars, Geometric Borders, Sliding Panel, c.1900, 3 1/2 x 2 1/2 In. 500.00
    Brick, Red Clay, Don't Spit On Sidewalk, Kansas, 20th Century, 8 3/4 In. 115.00
    Building, Meeting House, 10 Windows, Hinged Door, White Wash Paint, 8 x 11 x 8 In. ... 50.00
    Bust, Native American Indian, Carved, Laminated Wood, Painted, 9 1/2 In. 290.00
    Carousel, Model, Wood, Paper Lithograph, Multicolored, Early 1900s, 29 1/2 x 29 In. 235.00
    Church, Model, Wood, Metal, Stain Glass Construction, Spires, 33 1/2 x 23 1/2 x 17 In. 980.00
    Coconut, Indian Chief & Princess, Carved, Painted, New York, 1920s, 10 In., Pair 275.00
    Collage, Postage Stamps, Flower Basket, Bowknot, Silver & Gold Painted Frame, 14 In. .. 200.00
    Cow, Sheet Metal, Silhouette, Cutout, Painted, Black, White, Early 1900s, 26 x 30 3/4 In. . 1530.00
    Crucible, Pottery, Painted, Flowers, Poem, 3-Sided Rim, 5 1/4 In. .... *Illus* 200.00
    Diorama, Dutch Port, Semicircular, Windmill, Church, 20 x 33 1/2 x 15 In. 345.00
    Diorama, Farm, Plywood, Pine, Celluloid Animals, Frank Wheelahan, Aged 94, 25 x 9 In. . 175.00
    Display, Filmup Tavern, Policeman, Drunk Man, Lamp Post, 24 x 24 In. 210.00
    Duck, Carved, White & Yellow Paint, Metal Legs In Base, Webbed Feet, 3 3/4 In. 430.00
    Eagle, Black, Red, Green, Yellow, Wood Carving, Wilhelm Schimmel, 1800s, 8 In. 6325.00
    Eagle, Iron, Late 1800s, 5 x 11 In. 105.00
    Egg, Ostrich, Inscribed, American Great Seal, Man Dancing, Sunburst, Stand, 6 1/4 In. 1150.00
    Fish, Carved, Line For Scales, Gold Paint, Mary Thornton, 7 In. 175.00
    Giraffe, Calf, Carved, Painted, Brown, Off-White, 66 In. 5175.00
    Head, Carved Ears, Applied Nose, Relief Eyes, Painted, Pennsylvania, 6 In. 3450.00
    Horse, Carved, Saddle, Wire Bit, Carved Signature, 1931, 8 3/4 In. 546.00
    Horse, Leather Ears, Rope Mane, Tail, Black Paint, White Hooves, 23 In. 635.00
    Horse Race, 20 Jockeys & Horses, Carved, Multicolored, 1930s-40s, 35 x 46 In. 5290.00
    House, Wood, Blue & Yellow, Orange Trim, Porches, Divided Rooms, 21 x 20 x 18 In. ... 2415.00
    Indian Chief, Seated, Folded Arms, E. Reed, 29 x 10 3/4 In. 3740.00
    Judge, Black Robe, Articulated Arms, Base, 6 In. 775.00
    Lion, Running, Carved, Gray Paint, Stand, 27 x 36 In. 1380.00
    Lion, Turned Head, Striding, Curved Tail, Carved, 25 x 36 In. 2070.00
    Man, Cane, Top Hat, Wood, Carved, Painted Red & Green, Black Base, 1938, 14 In. 193.00
    Man, Wearing Coat & Hat, Short Arms & Legs, Pine, Black Painted Accents, 5 x 2 1/2 In. . 385.00
    Medicine Man, Plaid Coat, Beaver Hat, Black Bag, Carved, Painted, 60 In. 1265.00
    Owl, Standing, Gold, Black Eyes, White Face, Breast, Wood, Carved, Painted, 25 In. 58.00
    Owl, Wood, Chip Carved, Rectangular Wood Stand, 15 In. 633.00

Pig, Wood, Black Paint, JB, Tenn., 8 x 16 In. 720.00
Raven, Sheet Iron, Black Paint, 19 In. 144.00
Retablo, El Nino De Atocha, Oil On Tin, Mexico, 19th Century, 14 x 10 In. 288.00
Riverboat, 3 Steam Stacks, Masts, Decks, Lifeboats, Flowers, 33 1/2 x 40 1/2 In. 575.00
Rooster, Pa., 5 1/4 In. 430.00
Rooster, Pine, Painted, Wilhelm Schimmel, Pa., c.1885, 7 1/2 x 5 In. 8400.00
Rooster, Polychrome, Paint, Wilhelm Schimmel, 6 1/2 In. 660.00
Root Man, Carved, Painted, Extended Arm, Burnished Spots, Maine, c.1900, 37 1/2 In. ... 5750.00
Sculpture, Sea Gull, Wood, Tin, Painted, Wooden Ice Fishing Decoy, Related Items, 35 In. 403.00
Shadowbox, Seed Flowers, Velvet Birds, Cloth Leaves, Octagonal, 23 x 5 3/4 In. 330.00
Shore Bird, Standing On Driftwood, Wood Carved, 12 In. 115.00
Snake, Wood Carving, Red, Yellow Polka Dots, Blue Eyes, Early 1900s, 25 1/2 In. 575.00
Squirrel, Eating Nut, Painted, Pine, Wilhelm Schimmel, Pa., c.1875, 7 1/2 x 5 In. 8400.00
Squirrel Cage, Pine, 2 Wooden Figures Turn Crank, Wire Wheel, Feed Trough, 20 x 17 In. 7762.00
Stool, Salmon Paint, Flowers, Pennsylvania, c.1850, 12 x 7 x 7 In. 600.00
Stool, Scene On Top, Farm For Sale, White House, Tree, Early 1800s, 4 5/8 x 6 3/4 In. ... 1495.00
Swallows, Nest, Wood, Carved, Blue & White, Red Throats, Wire Legs, 8 x 10 In. 1035.00
Toy, Cat, Mouse In Mouth, Movable Tail, Wheels On Feet, White, Gray, 14 In. 660.00
Train Car, Cigar Box, Pressed Tin, 1800s Coin Wheels, 7 x 3 In. 248.00
Tree With Birds, Stick Tree, Carved & Painted Birds, Red, Yellow, Black, Blue, 34 In. ... 2090.00
Uncle Sam, High Top Hat, Pine Base, Edgar Tolson, 26 3/4 In. 4315.00
Velocipede, Farm Equipment Parts, 52 x 48 In. 575.00
Whirligig, Man Cutting Wood With Saw, Wood, c.1930, 25 In. 250.00
Whirligig, On Barrel, Windmill Turns, 2 Men Pumping 715.00
Whirligig, Sailor, Dewey Boy, Holding Paddles, Wood, Painted, Anchor Line Ltd., 15 In. .. 265.00
Whirligig, Soldier, Carved, Painted, 19th Century, 13 3/4 In. 881.00
Whirligig, Windmill, Shingled, Blue, White, Figure Turning Crank, 38 In. 374.00
Windmill Model, White Paint, Red Highlights, 1930-40, 53 In. 230.00
Woman, Green Dress, Head Scarf, Wood, Carved, Marked, Hannigan, 11 1/4 x 5 In. 105.00

FOOTBALL collectibles may be found in the Card and the Sports categories.

FOSTORIA glass was made in Fostoria, Ohio, from 1887 to 1891. The factory was moved to Moundsville, West Virginia, and most of the glass seen in shops today is a twentieth-century product. The company was sold in 1983; new items will be easily identifiable, according to the new owner, Lancaster Colony Corporation. Additional Fostoria items may be listed in the Milk Glass category.

American, Bonbon, Blue, 6 3/4 In. 250.00
American, Bowl, Salad Dressing, Sections, 6 1/4 In. 35.00
American, Bowl, Vegetable, Sections, Oval, 10 In. 25.00
American, Box, Handkerchief, Cover, Blue,.2 1/2 x 4 x 4 5/8 In. 830.00
American, Butter, Cover, 1/4 Lb. .... .35.00 to 50.00
American, Butter, Cover, Round, 6 x 7 1/4 In. 145.00
American, Cake Plate, 3-Footed, 12 In. 50.00
American, Cake Stand, Square, 7 x 10 In. 220.00
American, Candlestick, Octagonal Foot, 6 1/4 In., Pair 50.00
American, Candy Dish, Cover, Footed, 9 In. 55.00
American, Candy Dish, Cover, Round, 5 x 5 1/8 In. 20.00
American, Cracker Jar, Cover, 8 5/8 x 6 1/4 In. 325.00
American, Cup & Saucer 18.00
American, Goblet, Hexagonal Foot, 6 3/4 In. 15.00
American, Ice Tub, Tab Handles, 5 3/4 In. 70.00
American, Jar, Pickle, Cover, 5 3/4 x 3 In. 1000.00
American, Nappy, Tricornered, Handle, 6 In. 10.00
American, Oyster Cocktail, Footed, 3 1/2 In. 20.00
American, Pitcher, Ice Lip, 1/2 Gal. 120.00
American, Plate, Dinner, 9 1/2 In. 40.00
American, Plate, Salad, 8 3/8 In. 25.00
American, Relish, Footed, 8 In. 35.00
American, Salt & Pepper, Tray, 2 1/2 In. 70.00
American, Soup, Cream, Handles, 4 3/4 In. 95.00
American, Straw Jar, Cover 695.00

American, Sugar & Creamer, Tray, 3 In. 150.00
American, Tray, 4 Sections, Square, 11 In. 295.00
American, Tumbler, Footed, 9 Oz., 5 1/2 In. 15.00
American, Tumbler, Footed, Flared, 7 Oz., 5 3/8 In. 12.00
American, Tumbler, Iced Tea, 6 In. 18.00
American, Tumbler, Iced Tea, Pink, 6 In. 12.00
American, Tumbler, Juice, 4 3/4 In. 25.00
American, Vase, Flip, Cupped Rim, 10 In. 290.00
American Lady, Cocktail, Amethyst Bowl, Clear Stem & Foot, 3 1/2 Oz., 4 In. 45.00
American Lady, Tumbler, Iced Tea, Footed, Amethyst, 5 1/2 In. 25.00
Baroque, Bowl, Topaz, 11 In. 75.00
Baroque, Candlestick, 6 In., Pair 45.00
Baroque, Cup, Azure 30.00
Baroque, Relish, Topaz, 3 Sections, Oblong, 10 In. 60.00
Baroque, Vase, Azure, Handles, 7 In. 200.00
Brocaded Acorns, Vase, Pink, 8 1/4 In. 295.00
Brocaded Palm Trees, Bowl, Pink, Scroll Handles, 10 In. 350.00
Century, Candlestick, 3-Light, Pair 100.00
Century, Relish, Sections, Oval, 7 3/8 In. 23.00
Century, Sandwich Server, Center Handle, 11 In. 45.00
Coin, Creamer, Olive 40.00
Coin, Plate, 8 In. 50.00
Coin, Urn, Cover, Amber, 12 3/4 In. 75.00
Coin, Urn, Cover, Emerald Green, 12 3/4 In. 295.00
Coin, Vase, Bud, Emerald Green, Footed, 8 In. 95.00
Coin, Wedding Bowl, Cover, Ruby, 8 1/2 In. 85.00
Colony, Candlestick, 2-Light, 6 1/2 In. 35.00
Colony, Cheese & Cracker Set, 2 Piece 75.00
Colony, Pitcher, Ice Lip, 3 Pt., 8 1/2 In. 310.00
Colony, Sandwich Server, Center Handle, 11 1/2 In. 45.00
Colony, Sugar & Creamer, Tray, Individual 35.00
Colony, Tumbler, Iced Tea, Footed, 12 Oz., 5 3/4 In. 22.00
Eagle, Bookends, 7 1/2 In. 230.00
Fairfax, Bowl, Grapefruit, Ice Liner, Topaz, 2 Piece 40.00
Fairfax, Cake Plate, Ebony, Handles, 10 In. 60.00
Fairfax, Candlestick, Topaz, 4 1/2 In., Pair 65.00
Fairfax, Cup & Saucer, Azure 25.00
Fairfax, Pitcher, Clear Body, Amber Foot, 9 3/4 In. 95.00
Fairfax, Plate, Bread & Butter, Azure, 6 1/4 In. 13.00
Fairfax, Plate, Bread & Butter, Topaz, 6 1/4 In. 10.00
Fairfax, Plate, Luncheon, Rose, 8 1/4 In. 10.00
Fairfax, Plate, Luncheon, Topaz, 8 1/4 In. 16.00
Fairfax, Plate, Salad, Topaz, 7 1/2 In. 12.00
Fairfax, Relish, Green, Sections, Oval, 8 1/2 In. 35.00
Fairfax, Sugar & Creamer, Rose, 2 1/2 In. 65.00
Figurine, Colt, Standing, Blue, 3 7/8 In. 50.00
Figurine, Madonna, Satin Mist, 10 In. 70.00
Figurine, Pelican, Clear To Purple, 1910, 4 x 4 x 3 In. 88.00
Heirloom, Bowl, Blue Opalescent, 6 x 9 In. 275.00
Heirloom, Epergne, 1-Lily, Pink Opalescent, 9 x 14 1/2 In. 290.00
Horizon, Bowl, Cereal, Cinnamon, 6 In. 26.00
Horizon, Candy Dish, Cover, Spruce Green, 5 In. 50.00
Horizon, Console, Spruce Green, 12 In. 50.00
Horizon, Cup & Saucer, Cinnamon 24.00
Horizon, Plate, Dinner, Cinnamon, 10 In. 32.00
Iris Ware, Vase, Blue Iridescent Loopings, Cylindrical, Folded Rim Handles, 10 In. 1175.00
Iris Ware, Vase, Cylindrical Body, Fold Over Rim, Green & Gold Vines, 11 In. 1800.00
Iris Ware, Vase, Cylindrical, Square Mouth, Fold Over Rim, Emerald Green, 11 In. 2975.00
Iris Ware, Vase, Gold & Green Pulled Leaf & Vine, Cylindrical, Square Mouth, 11 In. 1750.00
Iris Ware, Vase, Green, Iridescent Pulled Leaf & Vine, Round, Square Mouth, 11 3/4 In. .. 3330.00
Iris Ware, Vase, Opal, Gold & Green Lily Pad & Vine, Round, Square, Folded Rim, 11 In. 1960.00
June, Candleholder, Topaz, 3-Footed, 4 3/8 In. 40.00
June, Console, Rose, 11 3/4 In. 125.00

June, Pail, Whipped Cream, Blue 225.00
June, Tumbler, Iced Tea, Footed, 12 Oz., 6 In. 35.00
June, Wine, 3 Oz., 5 3/8 In. 32.00
Mayflower, Bowl, Fruit, 13 In. 60.00
Mayflower, Goblet, 7 1/4 In. 35.00
Mayflower, Relish, 3 Sections, Oblong, 12 1/2 In. 45.00
Morning Glory, Console Set, 3 Piece 110.00
Navarre, Bell, Dinner, 4 7/8 In. 45.00
Navarre, Claret, Azure Bowl, Clear Stem & Foot, 6 1/2 Oz., 6 3/8 In. 85.00
Navarre, Nappy, Handle, 5 1/8 In. 32.00
Navarre, Plate, Cracker, 10 1/2 In. 50.00
Navarre, Tumbler, Juice, Footed, 4 1/2 In. 32.00
Trojan, Bouillon, Topaz, Handles 32.00
Trojan, Console, Topaz, 3-Footed, 12 In. 90.00
Trojan, Sherbet, Topaz Bowl, Clear Stem & Foot, 4 1/2 In. 45.00
Tut, Vase, Handles, Ebony, 6 1/2 In. 125.00

FOVAL, see Fry category.

FRAMES are included in the Furniture category under Frame.

FRANCISCAN is a trademark that appears on pottery. Gladding, McBean and Company started in 1875. The company grew and acquired other potteries. They made sewer pipes, floor tiles, dinnerwares, and art pottery with a variety of trademarks. In 1934, dinnerware and art pottery were sold under the name Franciscan Ware. They made china and cream-colored, decorated earthenware. Desert Rose, Apple, El Patio, and Coronado were best-sellers. The company became Interpace Corporation and in 1979 was purchased by Josiah Wedgwood & Sons. The plant was closed in 1984 but a few of the patterns are still being made. For more information, see *Kovels' Depression Glass & Dinnerware Price List.*

Antique Green, Cup & Saucer 36.00
Apple, Chop Plate, 14 In. 195.00
Apple, Cookie Jar, Cover, 9 1/4 In. 345.00
Apple, Cup & Saucer ....13.00 to 16.00
Apple, Gravy Boat, Underplate, 8 In. 35.00
Apple, Jam Jar, Cover, 4 1/4 In. 600.00
Apple, Pitcher, Milk, 6 1/4 In. 75.00
Apple, Plate, Dinner, 10 1/2 In. 24.00
Apple, Plate, Salad, 8 In. 14.00
Apple, Plate, Snack, Round, 10 1/2 In. 295.00
Apple, Platter, Oval, 13 3/4 In. 190.00
Apple, Platter, Oval, 19 In. 295.00
Apple, Saucer, 5 3/4 In. 24.00
Apple, Tray, Square, 8 3/8 In. 190.00
Arcadia, Cup & Saucer, Gold 38.00
Arcadia, Cup & Saucer, Green 38.00
Arcadia, Plate, Bread & Butter, Gold, 6 1/2 In. 12.50
Arcadia, Plate, Dinner, Gold, 10 1/2 In. 24.00
Autumn, Bowl, Fruit, 5 1/8 In. 13.00
Autumn, Bowl, Vegetable, Lug Handles, 9 In. 38.00
Autumn, Creamer 13.00
Cafe Royale, Plate, Bread & Butter, 6 1/2 In. 14.00
Cafe Royale, Platter, Oval, 14 1/4 In. 38.00
Cloud Nine, Creamer 14.00
Corinthian, Cup & Saucer 38.00
Coronado, Bowl, Vegetable, Round, Yellow, 7 1/2 In. 12.50
Coronado, Chop Plate, Coral, 13 3/4 In. 38.00
Coronado, Creamer, Turquoise 23.00
Coronado, Gravy Boat, Underplate, Ivory 23.00
Coronado, Gravy Boat, Underplate, Maroon 35.00
Coronado, Plate, Dinner, Coral, 10 1/2 In. 12.00

Coronado, Plate, Luncheon, Turquoise, 9 1/4 In. 14.00
Coronado, Plate, Orange, 6 3/8 In. 9.00
Coronado, Sherbet, Coral 165.00
Coronado, Soup, Cream, Underplate, Maroon 23.00
Coronado, Soup, Dish, Coral 24.00
Coronado, Soup, Dish, Ivory 24.00
Coronado, Soup, Dish, Turquoise 24.00
Coronado, Soup, Dish, Yellow 24.00
Coronado, Sugar & Creamer, Cover, Coral ....24.00 to 38.00
Coronado, Sugar, Cover, Coral 14.00
Coronado, Vase, Coral, 6 In. 750.00
Daisy, Relish, 12 In. 35.00
Del Rio, Plate, Dinner, Platinum Trim, 10 1/2 In. 15.00
Desert Rose, Ashtray, 9 In. 90.00
Desert Rose, Baking Dish, 13 1/2 x 8 1/2 In. 200.00
Desert Rose, Bowl, Cereal, 6 In. ....12.50 to 15.00
Desert Rose, Bowl, Vegetable, 2 Sections, 10 7/8 In. 39.00
Desert Rose, Bowl, Vegetable, 9 In. 35.00
Desert Rose, Butter, Cover, 1/4 Lb. 45.00
Desert Rose, Candy Dish, Cover, 6 In. 500.00
Desert Rose, Canister, Cover, Tea, 5 3/4 In. 330.00
Desert Rose, Casserole, Cover, 2 1/2 Qt. 400.00
Desert Rose, Compote, Footed, 4 x 8 In. 80.00
Desert Rose, Cookie Jar, Cover, 10 1/2 x 6 1/2 In. 300.00
Desert Rose, Cover, Toast, 3 x 7 In. 230.00
Desert Rose, Cream & Sugar 49.00
Desert Rose, Cup & Saucer ....13.00 to 24.00
Desert Rose, Ginger Jar, Cover, Insert, 4 3/4 x 3 1/4 In. 430.00
Desert Rose, Jam Jar, Cover, Squat, 3 1/2 x 5 In. 350.00
Desert Rose, Mixing Bowl Set, 3 Piece 430.00
Desert Rose, Napkin Ring, 1 1/2 In., 4 Piece 200.00
Desert Rose, Pitcher, Milk, 6 1/4 In. 90.00
Desert Rose, Plate, Dinner, 10 1/2 In. ....14.00 to 17.00
Desert Rose, Plate, Luncheon, 9 1/2 In. 22.00
Desert Rose, Plate, Salad, 8 In. 12.00
Desert Rose, Platter, Oval, 14 In. 37.00
Desert Rose, Salt & Pepper, 2 1/4 In. ....24.00 to 38.00
Desert Rose, Sugar & Creamer, Cover 35.00
El Dorado, Plate, Dinner, 10 1/2 In. 24.00
El Patio, Bowl, Vegetable, Coral, 8 1/4 In. 14.00
El Patio, Sugar, Cover, Coral 25.00
Floral, Plate, Salad, 8 1/2 In. 13.00
Floral, Salt & Pepper, 3 In. 12.00
Forget-Me-Not, Bowl, Cereal, 7 In. 23.00
Forget-Me-Not, Plate, Dinner, 10 1/2 In. 39.00
Forget-Me-Not, Tray, Snack, 8 1/2 In. 145.00
Fremont, Cup & Saucer 38.00
Fremont, Plate, Dinner, 10 1/2 In. 46.00
Fremont, Plate, Salad, 8 1/2 In. 23.00
Fremont, Platter, Oval, 12 1/2 In. 173.00
Glenfield, Sugar & Creamer, Cover 36.00
Gold Band, Cup & Saucer 36.00
Greenhouse, Bowl, Vegetable, Round, 9 1/2 In. 24.00
Greenhouse, Sugar, Cover 24.00
Hacienda Gold, Bowl, Cereal 14.00
Hacienda Gold, Pitcher, Pitcher, Milk, 6 In. 15.00
Hacienda Gold, Plate, Dinner, 10 1/2 In. 13.00
Hacienda Gold, Salt & Pepper 23.00
Hacienda Gold, Sugar, Cover 23.00
Hacienda Green, Bowl, Vegetable, 7 1/2 In. 14.00
Hacienda Green, Butter, Cover, 1/4 Lb. 38.00
Hacienda Green, Cup & Saucer 22.00

Hacienda Green, Plate, Bread & Butter, 6 1/2 In. 8.00
Hacienda Green, Plate, Dinner, 10 1/2 In. 22.00
Hacienda Green, Plate, Salad, 8 1/2 In. 10.00
Hacienda Green, Soup, Dish 18.00
Hacienda Green, Sugar, Cover 38.00
Huntington, Cup & Saucer 36.00
Indian Summer, Creamer 12.00
Indian Summer, Platter, 13 In. 24.00
Ivy, Bowl, Fruit, 5 1/2 In. 35.00
Ivy, Bowl, Salad, 11 In. 195.00
Ivy, Bowl, Vegetable, 8 In. 38.00
Ivy, Chop Plate, 11 3/4 In. 95.00
Ivy, Cup & Saucer 95.00
Ivy, Teapot, Cover, 6 1/2 In. 290.00
Madeira, Creamer 17.00
Madeira, Salt & Pepper 22.00
Martinique, Cup & Saucer 36.00
Meadow Rose, Coffeepot, Cover 185.00
Meadow Rose, Sugar, Cover 38.00
Meadow Rose, Teapot, Cover 200.00
Melrose, Bowl, Vegetable, Oval, 8 3/4 In. 38.00
Melrose, Creamer 38.00
Melrose, Platter, 12 1/2 In. 36.00
Merry-Go-Round, Sugar, Cover 38.00
Mesa, Cup & Saucer 22.00
Mesa, Plate, Dinner, 10 1/2 In. ....22.00 to 36.00
Moondance, Plate, Dinner, 10 1/2 In. 24.00
Moondance, Platter, Oval, 13 1/2 In. 22.00
Oasis, Cup & Saucer 25.00
October, Baker, Square, 9 1/2 In. 200.00
October, Casserole, Cover, 1 1/2 Qt. 170.00
October, Pitcher, 6 1/2 In. 170.00
Olympic, Ashtray 38.00
Olympic, Cup & Saucer 36.00
Pebble Beach, Bowl, Vegetable, Round, 9 In. 23.00
Pebble Beach, Gravy Boat, Underplate, Cover 23.00
Pebble Beach, Plate, Dinner, 10 1/2 In. 13.00
Pebble Beach, Plate, Salad, 8 1/2 In. 13.00
Platinum Band, Plate, Dinner, 10 1/2 In. 38.00
Reflections, Plate, Dinner, Silver Gray, 10 1/2 In. 24.00
Renaissance Gold, Bowl, Vegetable, Oval, 9 In. 250.00
Renaissance Gray, Cup & Saucer 36.00
Rosette, Plate, Dinner, 10 1/2 In. 24.00
Sea Sculptures, Casserole, Cover, 3 Qt. 165.00
Sea Sculptures, Plate, Dinner, 10 3/4 In. 12.00
Silver Lining, Plate, Dinner, 10 1/2 In. 36.00
Silver Pine, Cup 14.00
Spring Song, Gravy Boat, Underplate, 6 In. 35.00
St. Louis, Cup & Saucer 23.00
Starburst, Gravy Boat, Underplate 55.00
Starburst, Mug, 7 Oz. 60.00
Starburst, Plate, Bread & Butter, 6 1/2 In. ....14.00 to 22.00
Starburst, Plate, Dinner, 10 1/2 In. 26.00
Starburst, Relish, 3 Sections, 7 In. 22.00
Sundance, Bowl, Vegetable, 7 3/4 In. 35.00
Sundance, Creamer 22.00
Sundance, Cup & Saucer 15.00
Sundance, Plate, Dinner, 10 1/2 In. 16.00
Sundance, Plate, Salad, 8 1/2 In. 9.00
Sundance, Platter, 13 1/2 In. 42.00
Sundance, Soup, Dish 12.00
Sundance, Sugar 27.00

Sycamore, Plate, Bread & Butter, 6 1/4 In.	13.00
Tahiti, Sugar, Cover	38.00
Tara, Gravy Boat, 6 In.	35.00
Tiempo, Ashtray, Mustard, Square, 3 In.	14.00
Tiempo, Bowl, Vegetable, Divided, Sprout, 11 In.	40.00
Tiempo, Cup & Saucer, Leaf	14.00
Tiempo, Cup & Saucer, Mustard	14.00
Tiempo, Gravy Pitcher, Coral, 7 In.	13.00
Tiempo, Nut Dish, Chocolate, Square, 3 In.	14.00
Tiempo, Platter, Mustard, Rectangular, 13 In.	36.00
Trianon, Cup & Saucer	23.00
Tulip Time, Bowl, Fruit, 5 1/4 In.	13.00
Tulip Time, Bowl, Vegetable, 7 3/4 In.	26.95
Tulip Time, Plate, Bread & Butter, 6 3/4 In.	6.00
Winsome, Bowl, Vegetable, 2 Sections, 10 7/8 In.	38.00
Woodside, Cup & Saucer, After Dinner	36.00

FRANKART, Inc., New York, New York, mass-produced nude *dancing lady* lamps, ashtrays, and other decorative Art Deco items in the 1920s and 1930s. They were made of white lead composition and spray-painted. *Frankart Inc.* and the patent number and year were stamped on the base.

Lamp, Woman, Holding Glass Globe, Seated On Pillar, Cast Metal, Green Paint, 8 1/2 In.	520.00
Lamp, Woman, Nude, Kneeling, Holding Tray, Black, Brown, 9 x 8 x 6 In.	230.00

FRANKOMA POTTERY was originally known as The Frank Potteries when John F. Frank opened shop in 1933. The factory is now working in Sapulpa, Oklahoma. Early wares were made from a light cream-colored clay from Ada, Oklahoma, but in 1956 the company switched to a red burning clay from Sapulpa. The firm makes dinnerwares, utilitarian and decorative kitchenwares, figurines, flowerpots, and limited edition and commemorative pieces. John Frank died in 1973 and his daughter, Joniece, inherited the business. Frankoma went bankrupt in 1990. It was bought by Richard Bernstein in 1991 and is still in business.

Ashtray, Dog, Sleeping, Prairie Green	85.00
Ashtray, Oklahoma On Interior, John B. Baumert, Supreme Counselor, 1968-69	9.00
Baker, Cover, Aztec, Green & Brown Glaze, Ada Clay	10.00
Bowl, Blue, Green, 3 1/2 x 11 x 5 In.	95.00
Bowl, Gray, 7 1/2 In.	10.00
Bowl, Leaf Form, Brown, 4 1/2 In.	24.00
Bowl, Mint, Prairie Green, 3 3/4 In.	70.00
Bowl, Oval, White, 3 1/4 x 10 In.	20.00
Butter, Cover, Lazybones, Robin Egg Blue	25.00
Candleholder, Oral Roberts, Christ The Light Of The World, Desert Gold, 1971	50.00
Candleholder, Paddle Cactus, Desert Gold, Pair	30.00
Candy Dish, Foam Green, Swirled Brown, 9 x 5 In.	22.00
Candy Dish, Leaf Form, Desert Gold	65.00
Canister, Cover, Desert Gold	100.00
Casserole, Cover, Horseshoe Handles, 6 x 10 In.	59.00
Casserole, Cover, Prairie Green, 6 x 9 In.	22.00
Centerpiece, Horn Of Plenty, Desert Gold, No. 222, 12 In.	60.00
Cookie Jar, Barrel, Prairie Green	50.00
Creamer, Wagon Wheel, Desert Gold	25.00
Crock, Cover, Warmer	55.00
Cup, Footed, Flame	12.00
Cup, Wagon Wheel, Desert Gold	12.00
Cup, Wagon Wheel, Light Green	12.00
Cup, Wagon Wheel, Prairie Green	12.00
Cup & Saucer, Plainsman, Mossy Green, Sapulpa Clay, 7 Oz.	9.00
Decanter, Aztec, Peach Glow	30.00
Dish, Honey, Straw Bee Skep, Sapulpa Clay, Desert Gold	10.00

Figurine, Bird, Flame Red, Sapulpa Clay, Pair 60.00
Figurine, Bowl Maker, Prairie Green 55.00
Figurine, Buffalo, White 95.00
Figurine, Cowboy Boot, Pink 10.00
Figurine, Fan Dancer, Under Platter, Prairie Green 375.00
Figurine, Flower Girl, Prairie Green 165.00
Figurine, Garden Girl, Prairie Green, 6 In. 165.00
Figurine, Irish Setter, Desert Gold 45.00
Figurine, Trojan Horse, Prairie Green 65.00
Hot Plate, Cattle Brands, 6 In. 70.00
Jar, Ball, Beige, Brown 50.00
Jardiniere, Prairie Green, 4 1/2 x 4 1/4 In. 10.00
Jug, Cork, Desert Gold, 8 1/4 In. 25.00
Juice Set, Gurnsey, Pitcher, Cover, 6 Glasses 95.00
Mug, Barrel, 5 1/2 x 4 1/2 In. 10.00
Mug, Desert Gold 10.00
Mug, Lazybones, Prairie Green, 18 Oz. 9.00
Mug, Mayan-Aztec, White Sand Glaze, Sapulpa Clay, 8 Oz. 9.00
Mug, Pilot International, Desert Gold 25.00
Mug, Political, Donkey, Carter, Mondale, 1977 .... 23.00
Mug, Political, Donkey, Democrat, 1976 .... 23.00
Mug, Political, Elephant, Nixon Agnew GOP, 3 7/8 x 5 1/4 In. 85.00
Mug, Toby, Uncle Sam, White, 1977 .... 23.00
Pitcher, Aztec, Desert Gold, 2 Qt. 57.00
Pitcher, Aztec, Prairie Green 25.00
Pitcher, Barrel, Prairie Green, 2 Qt. 60.00
Pitcher, Blue High Glaze, 2 1/4 In. 17.00
Pitcher, Flame Red, No. 8, 7 1/4 In. 115.00
Pitcher, Guernsey, Prairie Green 20.00
Pitcher, Prairie Green, 6 In., 32 Oz. 50.00
Pitcher, Prairie Green, 8 In. 65.00
Pitcher, Waffle Batter, Osage Brown, No. 91, 7 x 8 1/4 In. 85.00
Planter, Cactus, Ada Clay, 7 x 5 3/4 In. 65.00
Planter, Cornucopia, Flame, 5 x 6 3/8 In. 20.00
Planter, Cowboy Boot, Mauve, 1981 .... 25.00
Planter, Crescent, Desert Gold, No. 211 .... 50.00
Planter, Crescent, Satin Brown, No. 211 .... 50.00
Planter, Paneled, Red Clay, 4 x 4 3/4 In. 10.00
Planter, Rectangular, No. 14, Prairie Green Glaze, 3 1/2 x 8 1/4 x 4 1/4 In. 20.00
Plaque, Jesus The Carpenter, Desert Gold 24.00
Plate, Bread & Butter, Plainsman, Desert Gold, 6 In. 9.00
Plate, Christmas, 1965, Good Will Toward Men 35.00
Plate, Christmas, 1968, Flight Into Egypt, Della Robbia White, 8 1/2 In. 60.00
Plate, Christmas, 1969, Laid In A Manger, 8 1/4 In. 50.00
Plate, Christmas, 1970, King Of Kings, 8 1/4 In. 50.00
Plate, Dinner, Plainsman, Brown Satin Rutile, Sapulpa Clay, 10 In. 10.00
Plate, Dinner, Plainsman, Desert Gold, 10 1/4 In. 22.00
Plate, Easter, 1972, Jesus Is Not Here, He Has Risen 10.00
Plate, Texas, White Glaze, 8 1/4 In. 25.00
Platter, Aztec, White, Sapulpa Clay 10.00
Platter, Prairie Green, 11 3/4 x 7 In. 10.00
Salt & Pepper, Handles, Green & Olive Glaze, Red Clay, Rubber Stoppers, 5 In. 22.00
Salt & Pepper, Shocks, Prairie Green 20.00
Saucer, Lazy Bones, Robin Egg Blue, 5 In. 10.00
Saucer, Wagon Wheel, Prairie Green, 5 In. 12.00
Sign, Prairie Green, 3rd In Series 25.00
Spoon Rest, Lazy Bones, Robin Egg Blue, 6 x 3 1/2 In. 25.00
Statue, Medicine Man, Black Matte 75.00
Stein, Prairie Green, 6 In. 10.00
Sugar, Wagon Wheel, Prairie Green, Miniature 10.00
Sugar & Creamer, Desert Gold 10.00
Sugar & Creamer, Prairie Brown 10.00
Sugar & Creamer, Prairie Green ....10.00 to 22.00

Teapot, Warmer, Westwind, Brown Satin, 6 Cup	55.00
Toothpick, 2 3/8 In.	9.00
Tray, Brown Glaze, 7 x 11 1/2 In.	10.00
Trivet, American Flag, Prairie Green Glaze	25.00
Trivet, Butterfly, Beige, Round, 6 1/2 In.	24.00
Trivet, Niroga, Elephant & Donkey Sneezing At Same Time, Eggshell White, 1980	25.00
Trivet, Oklahoma Diamond Jubilee	20.00
Trivet, Owl, Light Blue	25.00
Trivet, Rooster, Round, 6 1/4 In.	53.00
Trivet, Sequoyah Cherokee Alphabet, 6 1/4 In. Diam.	65.00
Trivet, Whooooo Owl, Have A Hootin' Good Day, 6 1/4 In.	10.00
Tumbler, Wagon Wheel, Prairie Green	25.00
Vase, Bud, Crocus, Brown Satin, No. 43	60.00
Vase, Bud, Pink, 3 1/2 In.	5.00
Vase, Bulbous, Flared, Handles, Desert Gold, 10 1/2 In.	80.00
Vase, Carved Stylized, Green, Brown Glaze, 8 In.	294.00
Vase, Crocus, Ada Clay, 8 In.	63.00
Vase, Flame Red, Incised Rings, 12 In.	89.00
Vase, Free-Form, Brown, Ada Clay, 5 1/2 x 6 In.	24.00
Vase, Musical Note, Blue Flecks, 5 In.	23.00
Vase, Prairie Green, Black Base, John Frank, 15 In.	100.00
Vase, Prairie Green, Flared, Footed, 6 x 6 3/4 In.	25.00
Vase, Snail, Black, Ada Clay, 6 In.	10.00
Vase, Wagon Wheel, Prairie Green, Ada White Clay	60.00
Wall Pocket, Peter Pan, Prairie Green	45.00
Wall Pocket, Phoebe, Woman's Face, 1948-49, 7 x 5 In.	245.00

FRATERNAL objects that are related to the many different fraternal organizations in the United States are listed in this category. The Elks, Masons, Odd Fellows, and others are included. Also included are service organizations, like the American Legion, Kiwanis, and Lions Club. Furniture is listed in the Furniture category. Shaving mugs decorated with fraternal crests are included in the Shaving Mug category.

Knights Of Pythias, Hall Bench, Oak, Carved, Limed, 3 Lollipop Backs, 66 In.	690.00
Knights Of Pythias, Program, 93rd Convention, 1960	7.00
Masonic, Chair, Upholstered Arms, Seat, Back, Carved, Scroll Crest, 85 x 37 x 24 In.	575.00
Masonic, Clock, Ingraham, Ionic Wall, Masonic Design, Walnut, Round, c.1890, 10 In.	700.00
Masonic, Clock, Tall Case, Silas Hoadley, Federal, Brass Balls, Conn., 1825-40, 90 In.	6038.00
Masonic, Document Box, Hinged Lid, Symbol, Geometric Inlay, 1800s, 6 3/4 x 14 x 8 In.	1880.00
Masonic, Jug, Memento Mori, World Is In Pain, Liverpool, c.1800, 6 1/2 x 12 In.	1610.00
Masonic, Sword, Etched, Brass Hilt, Wood Grip, c.1845, 32 1/2-In. Blade	215.00
Masonic, Tracing Board, Oil On Canvas, Frame, 53 x 42 1/2 In.	6463.00
Masonic, Tracing Board, Oil, On Canvas, Frame, 19th Century, 53 x 42 1/2 In.	6465.00
Odd Fellows, Apron, Deer Skin, Painted, Eye, Scales, Ax, Sword, July 4, 1829, 13 x 21 In.	385.00
Odd Fellows, Ax, Carved, Black Handle, Gold Painted Blade, Red FLT, 33 In.	264.00
Odd Fellows, Finial, Star & Crescent On Baluster Stem, Copper, Verdigris, 31 In., Pair	3525.00

FRY GLASS was made by the H. C. Fry Glass Company of Rochester, Pennsylvania. The company, founded in 1901, first made cut glass and other types of fine glasswares. In 1922, they patented a heat-resistant glass called *Pearl Ovenglass*. For two years, 1926–1927, the company made Fry Foval, an opal ware decorated with colored trim. Reproductions of this glass have been made. Depression glass patterns made by Fry may be listed in the Depression Glass category. Some pieces of cut glass may also be included in the Cut Glass category.

FRY, Atomizer, Opalescent With Classical Pattern On Blue Base, Pump, 7 1/2 In.	545.00
Bowl, Elsie Cutting, Scalloped Edge, 8 1/2 In.	90.00
Celery Dish, Hobstar, Vesica, Fan Cutting, Oval, 12 In.	175.00
Pitcher, Amber, Crackle, Clear Handle, 1904-31, 10 In.	105.00
Pitcher, Lemonade, Cover, 9 1/2 In.	50.00
FRY FOVAL, Casserole, Cover, Square, 8 1/2 In.	65.00
Grill Plate, Heat Resistant, 10 1/2 In., 8 Piece	250.00
Muffin Pan, 6 Sections, Heat Resistant, 9 1/2 x 6 1/2 In.	80.00

FULPER Pottery Company was incorporated in 1899 in Flemington, New Jersey. They made art pottery from 1910 to 1929. The firm had been making bottles, jugs, and housewares from 1805. Doll heads were made about 1928. The firm became Stangl Pottery in 1929. Fulper art pottery is admired for its attractive glazes and simple shapes.

Bookends, White, Frothy Blue Green Glaze, Pair, 5 x 5 In.	176.00
Bowl, Beige Glaze Exterior, Turquoise Glaze Interior, 2 Handles, 9 In.	150.00
Bowl, Blue Mottled Matte Finish, Ink Stamped, 10 In.	15.00
Bowl, Blue, Brown Flambe Glaze, Square Handles, 3 1/2 x 6 1/4 In.	175.00
Bowl, Brown To Light Blue Flambe Glaze, 4 In.	265.00
Bowl, Crystalline Green Glaze, Over Brown, 2 1/4 x 9 In.	150.00
Bowl, Effigy, 3 Creatures Holding Bowl, Blue Flambe, Blue Matte Glaze, 7 x 10 In.	575.00
Bowl, Effigy, Copper Dust Crystalline Interior, Mirror Black Exterior, 7 x 10 1/4 In.	1645.00
Bowl, Effigy, Mahogany & Amber Glazed Top, Blue & Beige Bottom, 7 1/2 x 10 1/2 In.	825.00
Bowl, Gray Blue Crystalline Glaze, Over Sea Green Glaze, 3 x 11 In.	374.00
Bowl, Ibis, 3 Birds, Blue Matte Glaze, Green Flambe Interior, 5 1/2 x 11 In.	1528.00
Bowl, Low, Green, 2 Handles, 2 x 7 1/2 In.	265.00
Bowl, Mottled Blue Matte, 10 In.	170.00
Bowl, Swirled Blue & Ivory Glaze, 10 1/2 In.	230.00
Bowl, Variegated Glaze, Embossed Rim, 9 In.	46.00
Candlestick, Blue, Tan, Brown, Flambe, 10 3/4 In.	90.00
Chamberstick, Brown Flambe Glaze, Broad Form, 5 In.	30.00
Console, Lotus, Green Crystalline Leopard Skin Glaze, 4 x 11 1/2 In.	345.00
Dish, Rose, Green Blue Crystalline Glaze, Footed, 2 In.	150.00
Doorstop, Bulldog, Amber, Blue, Purple Crystalline Glaze, 8 x 10 In.	705.00
Doorstop, Bulldog, Mustard Matte Glaze, Elephant's Flambe, 8 x 11 In.	1410.00
Doorstop, Siamese Cat, Sleeping, Ivory To Brown Flambe, Black, c.1910, 5 x 9 1/2 In.	2300.00
Flower Frog, Scarab Beetle, Green, Brown Glaze, 1 1/4 x 3 In.	80.00
Jug, Copper Dust Crystalline Glaze, Tall Handle, 11 3/4 x 7 3/4 In.	3819.00
Lamp Base, Earth Tone Browns, Ink Stamped, 11 In.	125.00
Lemonade Service, Cream, Rose Matte Glaze, c.1915, 11 1/4-In. Pitcher, 6 Piece	635.00
Placecard Holder Set, Turquoise & Gunmetal Flambe Glaze, Box, 2 1/4 In., 12 Piece	1880.00
Plate, Salad, Cream, Rose Matte Glaze, c.1915, 8 1/2 In., 6 Piece	345.00
Urn, Frothy Mirror Black Glaze, 2 Handles, 9 x 9 In.	1645.00
Urn, Moss To Rose Flambe Glaze, 11 3/4 In.	325.00
Vase, Amber To Turquoise Glaze, Baluster Shape, 13 In.	350.00
Vase, Black Crystalline Glaze, 2 Handles, 6 1/2 In.	825.00
Vase, Blue & Green Flambe Drip, Shouldered, Square Cutout Handles, 10 In.	1058.00
Vase, Blue Flame Over Green Glaze, Incised Mark, 8 In.	259.00
Vase, Blue Snowflake, Vertical Oak Ink Stamp, 11 7/8 In.	1380.00
Vase, Blue Wisteria & Mahogany Glaze, Bottle Shape, 8 1/4 In.	325.00
Vase, Blue, Gray Flambe Glaze Over Cream, Incised Mark, 7 In.	460.00
Vase, Blue, Green Flambe Glaze, Squat, 3 3/4 In.	230.00
Vase, Blue, Green, Yellow, Purple Crystalline Glaze, Bulbous, 5 1/2 In.	355.00
Vase, Blue, Ivory Drip, Mustard, Shouldered, 9 In.	440.00
Vase, Blue, Lavender Flambe Glaze, 7 1/4 In.	230.00
Vase, Blue, Pink, Tapered, 5 1/2 In.	210.00
Vase, Brown, Green, Mustard Drip Glaze, Bulbous, 2 Handles, 5 1/2 In.	264.00
Vase, Bud, Flemington Green Glaze, Dripped, 5 1/2 In.	176.00
Vase, Bud, Green Ground, Brown, White Crystals, 8 1/2 In.	80.00
Vase, Bud, Sheer Ivory Drip, Mustard Matte Glaze, Baluster, 9 In.	410.00
Vase, Butterscotch, Blue Flambe Glaze, 12 1/2 In.	1725.00
Vase, Cat's-Eye Flambe Glaze, 6 3/4 x 9 1/2 In.	120.00
Vase, Cat's-Eye Flambe Glaze, Baluster, 16 1/2 x 9 In.	1880.00
Vase, Chinese Blue Flambe Glaze, Cylindrical, 13 x 3 1/2 In.	646.00
Vase, Copper Dust Crystalline Glaze, Pinched Waist, 11 1/2 x 8 1/2 In.	9400.00
Vase, Copper Dust Crystalline, Caramel Flambe Glaze, Squat, Angular Handles, 4 3/4 In.	265.00
Vase, Crystalline Glaze, Tan, Cream, Brown, Blue, Egg Shape, c.1915, 8 In.	375.00
Vase, Crystalline Green Glaze, Hexagonal Baluster Shape, 10 1/2 In.	520.00
Vase, Crystalline, Cucumber Green, Black Striations, Ink Stamp, 12 1/2 In.	345.00
Vase, Crystalline, Green, 2 Handles, 7 1/2 In.	355.00
Vase, Cucumber Green Crystalline Glaze, Melon Shape, 14 x 12 In.	5581.00

Vase, Frothy Blue Crystalline Glaze Over Green Matte, Incised, 7 In. 460.00
Vase, Frothy Blue, Moss To Rose Flambe Glaze, Bulbous, 7 1/2 In. 529.00
Vase, Frothy Flemington Green Flambe Glaze, Closed-In Rim, Spherical, 5 1/2 In. 705.00
Vase, Frothy Moss To Rose Flambe Glaze, 2 Buttressed Handles, 6 1/4 x 7 1/2 In. 470.00
Vase, Frothy Moss To Rose Flambe Glaze, Bulbous, Banded Neck, 9 3/4 x 8 1/4 In. 470.00
Vase, Frothy Moss To Rose Flambe Glaze, Faceted, 11 In. 325.00
Vase, Frothy Moss To Rose Flambe Glaze, Gourd Shape, 2 Handles, 7 1/2 In. 265.00
Vase, Gray, Purple Flambe Glaze, Baluster, 12 In. 206.00
Vase, Green & Gunmetal Glaze, Speckled, Buttressed Collar Rim, Spherical, 1915, 5 In. . . . 206.00
Vase, Green & Turquoise Crystalline Glaze, Ink Stamp, Oval, 7 3/4 In. 205.00
Vase, Green Crystalline Glaze, Closed-In Rim, Egg Shape, 8 x 5 1/4 In. 470.00
Vase, Green Crystalline Glaze, Green Matte, Flat Shoulder, Squat, 7 3/4 x 7 3/4 In. 1295.00
Vase, Green Glaze, Bulbous, 10 In. 129.00
Vase, Green Matte Glaze, Charcoaling, 6-Sided, 10 3/4 In. 545.00
Vase, Green Matte Glaze, Copper Dust Crystalline Glaze Interior, 2 Handles, 3 1/2 In. 430.00
Vase, Green, 2 Handles, 6 In. 325.00
Vase, Green, Pink, Flared, 7 In. 165.00
Vase, Green, Turquoise Glaze, 11 7/8 In. 259.00
Vase, Gunmetal To Copper Dust Crystalline Flambe Glaze, Tear Shape, 13 x 7 1/2 In. 2235.00
Vase, Gunmetal, Amber, Blue, Mottled Flambe Glaze, Bulbous, 5 In. 175.00
Vase, Leopard Skin Crystalline Glaze, Buttressed, 8 1/4 x 6 In. 590.00
Vase, Lime Green Matte Glaze, Egg Shape, 9 1/2 In. 323.00
Vase, Mirror Black Crystalline Glaze, Egg Shape, 6 3/4 In. 325.00
Vase, Mirror Black Glaze, Baluster, Curled Handles, 8 3/4 x 5 1/2 In. 235.00
Vase, Mirror Black Glaze, Egg Shape, 6 1/2 In. 175.00
Vase, Mirror Black Glaze, Silver, Marked, 16 5/8 In. 978.00
Vase, Mirror Black, Copper Dust Crystalline Flambe Glaze, Bottle Shape, 8 x 6 In. 470.00
Vase, Mirror Crystalline Flambe Glaze, Hammered, Bulbous, 12 x 11 1/2 In. 2585.00
Vase, Mission Matte Glaze, Bulbous, Double Ribbon Handles, 8 3/4 x 9 In. 1295.00
Vase, Mission Verde & Gunmetal Flambe, Vasekraft Faceted, 4-Sided, 8 1/4 In. 590.00
Vase, Moss To Rose Flambe Glaze, Baluster, 11 3/4 In. 440.00
Vase, Moss To Rose Flambe Glaze, Beehive Shape, 2 Handles, 8 3/4 In. 295.00
Vase, Moss To Rose Flambe Glaze, Bulbous, 2 Handles, 7 x 6 1/2 In. 295.00
Vase, Moss To Rose Flambe Glaze, Bullet Shape, Ring Handles, 12 3/4 In. 380.00
Vase, Mottled Gray & Amber Flambe Glaze, Bulbous, 2 Handles, 7 x 6 3/4 In. 558.00
Vase, Mottled Green, Blue Glaze, Footed, Bulbous, 5 1/2 In. 410.00
Vase, Multitone Blue, Crystalline Glaze, Handles, 8 In. 1000.00
Vase, Multitone Green Flambe Glaze, 5 1/2 In. 295.00
Vase, Mustard Yellow Matte Glaze, Squat, Cylindrical, 6 In. 405.00
Vase, Pink Glaze, Flared Body, Ring Handle, Vertical Mark, 12 3/4 In. 705.00
Vase, Pink, Green, 2 Handles, 7 1/2 In. 529.00
Vase, Pink, Red Crystalline Glaze, Tapered, 5 1/2 In. 410.00
Vase, Tan, Blue, Brown Crystalline Glaze, Handles, 12 In. 646.00
Vase, Turquoise, Green, Crystalline Glaze, Paneled, 13 1/2 In. 265.00
Vase, Urn, Blue Crystalline Glaze, 2 Scrolled Handles, 9 In. 529.00
Vase, Wisteria Matte Flambe Glaze, Egg Shape, 9 1/4 x 6 In. 325.00
Vase, Wisteria Over Green Crystalline Glaze, Ink Stamped, 11 3/8 In. 460.00
Vase, Yellow, Green, Blue, 2 Handles, 14 1/2 In. 4115.00
Wall Pocket, Chinese Blue Flambe Glaze, Embossed, Art Deco, 8 x 4 1/2 In. 410.00
Wall Pocket, Mottled Brown Matte Glaze, Acorn Shape, 7 In. 520.00

FURNITURE of all types is listed in this category. Examples dating from the seventeenth century to the 1970s are included. Prices for furniture vary in different parts of the country. Oak furniture is most expensive in the West; large pieces over eight feet high are sold for the most money in the South, where high ceilings are found in the old homes. Condition is very important when determining prices. These are NOT average prices but rather reports of unique sales. If the description includes the word *style*, the piece resembles the old furniture style but was made at a later time. It is not a period piece. Garden furniture is listed in the Garden Furnishings category. Related items may be found in the Architectural, Brass, and Store categories.

Altar, Cabinet, Brasses, Side Flanges, Dragons, Chinese, 1700s, 34 x 36 x 22 In. 2235.00

Armchairs are listed under Chair in this category.
Armoire, A. Sornay, Rosewood, Brass Inlay, 2 Doors, 6 Shelves, c.1935, 65 x 53 In. 9560.00
Armoire, Anglo-Colonial, Rosewood, 4 Doors, Breakfront, Cornice, c.1850, 79 x 98 In. 6040.00
Armoire, Art Deco, Sycamore, Fruitwood, Shelves, Lollipop Key, 71 x 51 In. 1645.00
Armoire, Art Deco, Walnut, Shelves, Drawers, c.1940, 69 x 36 x 22 1/4 In. 115.00
Armoire, Burl Walnut, 2 Doors, 2 Drawers, Block Feet, 95 x 64 x 24 1/2 In. 2820.00
Armoire, Directoire, Fruitwood, 2 Doors, Early 1800s, 82 x 49 x 22 In. 1725.00
Armoire, Edwardian, Brass Mounted, Leather Clad, Double Doors, 68 x 40 In. 2990.00
Armoire, French Provincial, Fruitwood, 2 Inset Panel Doors, Scroll Feet, 84 x 56 In. 2990.00
Armoire, French Provincial, Oak, Carved Cornice, Early 1800s, 86 1/4 x 62 In. 3680.00
Armoire, French Provincial, Oak, Molded Cornice, Panel Doors, 1800s, 92 x 68 x 24 In. ... 1269.00
Armoire, French Provincial, Walnut, 2 Full-Length Doors, Late 1700s, 86 x 57 In. 1710.00
Armoire, French Provincial, Walnut, Carved, Mirror Doors, 104 x 56 x 20 In. 1725.00
Armoire, Louis XV Style, Fruitwood, Late 19th Century, 92 x 55 x 23 In. 4600.00
Armoire, Louis XV Style, Fruitwood, Late 19th Century, 94 x 51 x 22 In. 2990.00
Armoire, Louis XV Style, Mahogany, Walnut, 2 Doors, Early 1800s, 100 x 64 In. 2530.00
Armoire, Louis XV Style, Oak, 2 Doors, Flowers, c.1850, 100 x 55 x 23 In. 6325.00
Armoire, Louis XV, Walnut, 2-Paneled Doors, 84 1/2 x 52 x 22 1/2 In. 2530.00
Armoire, Mahogany, Carved Shell Crest, Beveled Mirror, Drawers, 59 x 22 x 94 In. 1265.00
Armoire, Maple, Scrolled Leaf Crest, Continental, 84 x 26 x 114 In. 270.00
Armoire, Neoclassical, Mahogany, 2 Doors, Projecting Cornice, c.1835, 93 x 67 In. 2530.00
Armoire, Oak, Carved Crest, Bow, Urns, 2 Drawers, Fluted Pilasters, 60 x 25 x 96 In. 575.00
Armoire, Pine, France, Mid 19th Century, 78 x 43 x 19 In. 1765.00
Armoire, Renaissance Revival, Walnut, Door, Mirror, Ohio, c.1865, 112 x 53 x 25 In. 2990.00
Armoire, Rococo Revival, Mahogany, 2 Doors, c.1850, 118 x 66 In. 5520.00
Armoire, Rococo Revival, Mahogany, Bonnet, Carved Doors, 103 x 66 x 24 In. 5290.00
Armoire, Victorian, Oak, 19th Century, 2 Piece 235.00
Armoire, Walnut, Arched Top, 3 Mirrored Doors, 3 Drawers, 100 x 94 In. 1380.00
Bar, C. Malmsten, Rosewood, Elm, Birch, Fruitwood Marquetry, c.1928, 46 x 33 In. 4500.00
Bar, Pop Art, Lacquered, Stereo Components, c.1965, 28 x 16 x 60 In. 120.00
Bed, American Restauration, Mahogany, Figured Head & Footboards, 42 x 77 In. 1955.00
Bed, Arts & Crafts, Mahogany, Spindles, Tapered Posts, Through Tenon, 85 x 84 In. 825.00
Bed, Baroque Style, Carved, Painted, Piazza San Marco, Italy 4025.00
Bed, Biedermeier, Fruitwood, Ebonized, Scrolled, 41 x 37 1/2 x 81 1/2 In. 2300.00
Bed, Brass, 4 Capped Posts, Applied Brass Scroll, Victorian, 69 x 57 x 78 In. 1840.00
Bed, Brass, Cast Iron, Scalloped, White Paint, Acanthus Leaf Accents, 61 x 62 In. 720.00
Bed, Brass, Cast Iron, Shells, Flowers, White Paint, Ball, Beehive Accents, 54 x 78 In. 489.00
Bed, Brass, Curved, Turned Accents, 56 x 54 In. 460.00
Bed, Cannonball, Cherry, Turned Posts, Rope, 52 x 45 x 70 In. 175.00
Bed, Cherry, Rope, American, 36 x 55 x 74 In. 240.00
Bed, Cherry, Turned Posts, Paneled Headboard, Blanket Roll, 47 x 72 x 52 In. 115.00
Bed, Curly Maple, Cherry, Urn Finials, Scroll Headboard, Rope, 51 1/2 x 47 In. 115.00
Bed, Directoire Style, Beech, Green & Gray, Early 20th Century, 45 x 77 In. 1150.00
Bed, Federal Style, Mahogany, Acorn Finials, 20th Century, 48 x 64 In. 130.00
Bed, Federal Style, Mahogany, Carved, Broken Arch Headboard, 89 x 64 x 90 In. 920.00
Bed, Federal Style, Pale Blue Paint, 32 x 54 x 77 In. 120.00
Bed, Federal, Mahogany, Carved, Inlaid, 1795-1810, 87 x 60 x 73 In. 10150.00
Bed, Four-Poster, American Restauration, Mahogany, Mid 1800s, 106 x 60 x 78 In. 7765.00
Bed, Four-Poster, Birch, Lamb's Tongue Chamfers, Urn Carved, Rope, 80 x 56 x 81 In. ... 546.00
Bed, Four-Poster, Birch, Pine, Carved, Graining, Ring Turned, 55 x 71 1/2 In. 5175.00
Bed, Four-Poster, Cherry, Flat Canopy, Early 20th Century, 82 x 56 x 84 In. 3105.00
Bed, Four-Poster, Chippendale Style, Mahogany, Canopy, c.1820, 90 x 46 x 70 In. 1610.00
Bed, Four-Poster, Chippendale, Maple, Turned, New England, Late 18th Century 3290.00
Bed, Four-Poster, Ethan Allen, Maple, Spiral Carved Posts, 84 x 67 x 88 In. 980.00
Bed, Four-Poster, Federal Style, Mahogany, Carved, Rice Pattern, 89 x 64 x 90 In. 750.00
Bed, Four-Poster, Federal Style, Mahogany, Early 20th Century, 62 x 56 x 83 In. 115.00
Bed, Four-Poster, Federal, Birch, Maple, Pine, New England, c.1820 .... 750.00
Bed, Four-Poster, Federal, Cherry, Arched Canopy, Headboard, 83 x 49 x 72 In. 9400.00
Bed, Four-Poster, Federal, Curly Maple, Red Wash, Trundle, c.1815, 54 1/2 In. 920.00
Bed, Four-Poster, Federal, Mahogany, Maple, Canopy, c.1820, 90 x 49 x 71 3/4 In. 7050.00
Bed, Four-Poster, Federal, Maple, Arched Canopy, Headboard, 80 x 51 In. 4995.00
Bed, Four-Poster, Georgian Style, Arched Full Canopy, 93 In. 1150.00
Bed, Four-Poster, Gothic Revival, Bird's-Eye Maple, Walnut, 3 Arches, 79 x 73 x 54 In. ... 4315.00

Bed, Four-Poster, Mahogany, 8 Recessed Panels, 20th Century, 80 x 64 In. 470.00
Bed, Four-Poster, Mahogany, Carved, Scrolled Headboard, c.1930, 49 x 40 x 81 1/2 In. ... 230.00
Bed, Four-Poster, Mahogany, Early 20th Century, 72 1/2 x 43 x 81 In., Pair 635.00
Bed, Four-Poster, Mahogany, Turned Posts, England, Late 1800s, 82 x 67 In. 1725.00
Bed, Four-Poster, Maple, Acorn Finials, Scrolled Head, Footboard, 80 x 53 x 69 In. 345.00
Bed, Four-Poster, Maple, Pine, Tapered Posts, Legs, 87 x 54 1/2 x 78 1/2 In. 345.00
Bed, Four-Poster, Serpentine, Carved Crest, Panels, 19th Century, 112 x 67 x 83 In. 3680.00
Bed, Four-Poster, Sheraton, Cherry, Birch, Vase Posts, 55 x 66 x 73 In. 1035.00
Bed, Four-Poster, Sheraton, Cherry, Ring Turnings, Miss. Valley, 92 x 58 x 81 In. 5520.00
Bed, Four-Poster, Sheraton, Maple, Pine, Acorn Finials, 1800s, 92 x 60 In. 2185.00
Bed, Four-Poster, Sheraton, Maple, Rope, Early 19th Century, 47 x 55 x 85 In. 1265.00
Bed, Four-Poster, Sheraton, Maple, Scrolling Headboard, Rope, 46 x 54 In. 1265.00
Bed, Four-Poster, Softwood, Red & Black Paint, Rope, Pennsylvania, 34 x 72 x 50 In. 660.00
Bed, G. Nakashima, Black Walnut, Platform, Grass Mats, 84 x 63 1/2 x 11 In. 4700.00
Bed, G. Nelson, Thin Edge, Birch, Steel, Herman Miller, 36 x 78 x 39 In., Pair 4400.00
Bed, G. Stickley, No. 912, Peaked Top Rail, Paneled Head, Footboard, 58 x 79 x 51 In. ... 3819.00
Bed, G. Stickley, No. 922, Horizontal Boards, Short Headboard, 47 x 79 x 45 In. 1645.00
Bed, G. Stickley, No. 923, 5 Wide Head & Foot Slats, Tapered Posts, 50 x 80 x 60 In. 4995.00
Bed, G. Stickley, Paneled Head & Footboard, V Crest Rails, 50 x 58 x 78 In. 5300.00
Bed, George III Style, Mahogany, Turned & Reeded Posts, Garlands, 84 x 78 In. 6000.00
Bed, Georgian Style, Mahogany, Canopy, Scrolled Boards, 93 1/2 x 58 In. 1150.00
Bed, Gothic Revival, Mahogany, Trilobe Boards, c.1840, 42 1/2 x 60 x 86 In. 440.00
Bed, Louis XV Style, Mahogany, Carved Crest, Padded Back, 52 x 45 x 78 In., Pair 805.00
Bed, Louis XVI Style, Beech, Carved, Stained, 3/4 Size, 56 x 43 x 81 In. 1840.00
Bed, Louis XVI Style, Painted, Canopy, Early 1800s, 93 x 75 x 45 In. 5290.00
Bed, Mahogany, Acorn Finials, 20th Century, 46 1/2 x 57 In. 265.00
Bed, Mahogany, Bell Posts, Rolling-Pin Head & Footboards, 1835, 50 x 80 In. 800.00
Bed, Mahogany, Outscrolled Crest, Paneled Back, 42 1/2 x 48 x 80 In. 1725.00
Bed, Maple, Cherry, Double Cannonball, 43 1/2 x 52 1/2 In. 690.00
Bed, Maple, Low-Post, Scrolling Ends, Ball Finials, c.1930, 39 x 54 x 78 In. 230.00
Bed, Maple, Turned Bamboo Design, Ball Feet, Late 19th Century, 49 x 81 In. 825.00
Bed, Napoleon III, Cast Iron, Steel, Scroll End, 44 x 74 x 45 In. 7190.00
Bed, Neoclassical, Mahogany, Carved, Figured, Veneered, N.Y., c.1810, 49 x 54 In. 7200.00
Bed, Painted, Scalloped, Paneled Headboard, Rope, c.1820 .... 690.00
Bed, Poplar, Pine, Black Ink Graining, Canvas Ticking, Rope, 58 x 44 In. 115.00
Bed, Poplar, Scrolled Headboard, Heart Cutout, Rope, c.1820, 51 x 83 In. 1610.00
Bed, Rococo Revival, Mahogany, Shell, Cabochon Crest, 1800s, 74 x 73 x 78 In. 6615.00
Bed, Rococo Revival, Rosewood, Canopy, Double, c.1825 .... 3910.00
Bed, Rococo Revival, Rosewood, Half-Tester, Beaded Serpentine, 104 x 68 x 87 In. 13800.00
Bed, Rococo Revival, Walnut, Half-Tester, c.1865, 112 x 67 x 94 In. 3680.00
Bed, Shaker, Cherry, Pine, Red Stain, New Lebanon, N.Y., c.1850, 34 x 36 x 76 In. 1840.00
Bed, Sheraton, Canopy, Red Paint, Carved Fruit, Rosettes, Rope, Pa., 92 x 54 In. 7150.00
Bed, Sheraton, Pine, Shaped Rails, Late 19th Century, 39 x 45 x 76 In. 460.00
Bed, Sheraton, Swelled Legs, Reverse Bell Finials, Rope, 1800s, 41 x 80 x 54 In. 1725.00
Bed, Sleigh, American Restauration, Mahogany, Trefoils, c.1835, 43 1/2 x 37 In. 920.00
Bed, Sleigh, Empire, Mahogany, Scrolled, Paneled, c.1830, 37 1/2 x 60 x 79 In. 825.00
Bed, Sleigh, Flame Mahogany, Scrolled Boards, c.1835, 44 x 60 x 85 In. 1880.00
Bed, Sleigh, Mahogany, Neoclassical, Leaves, Swan, Urn, 41 1/2 x 45 x 64 In. 1955.00

**Brown or black felt-tip markers can
be used to camouflage a small nick
in furniture. You can use several
markers and blend the color.**

Furniture, Bed Steps,
Mahogany, Leather
Treads, Sliding Steps,
Victorian, 27 In.

Bed, Sleigh, Rococo Revival, Mahogany, Serpentine Top, Carved, 58 x 60 x 86 In. 865.00
Bed, Stickley Bros., Paneled Head & Footboard, Tapered Posts, 48 x 57 x 80 In. 5300.00
Bed, Trundle, Poplar, Mushroom Finials, Ball Feet, Casters, 60 In. 375.00
Bed, Victorian, Rosewood, Canopy, Double, 101 x 71 3/4 In. 3910.00
Bed, Victorian, Walnut, Carved Flowers, Footboard, 53 x 54 x 68 In. 403.00
Bed, Victorian, Walnut, Carved, Veneered Panels, c.1900, 55 x 61 x 84 1/2 In. 230.00
Bed, Victorian, Walnut, Leaf & Shell Crest, Burl Veneer Panels, 59 x 84 In. 600.00
Bed, Wegner, Cane Headboards, Teak Legs, Getama, Pair 1095.00
Bed Steps, Mahogany, 3 Steps, Early 19th Century, 28 1/2 x 31 In. x 19 1/2 In. 420.00
Bed Steps, Mahogany, Commode, 1780, 25 In. 2400.00
Bed Steps, Mahogany, Leather Treads, Sliding Steps, Victorian, 27 In. . . . . *Illus* 1410.00
Bed Steps, Shaker, Pine, Painted, 3 Steps, 1-Board Ends, Lollipop Finial, 36 x 15 In. 4485.00
Bedroom Set, Eastlake, High-Back Bed, Chest, 5 Drawers, Marble Top, Mirror, 3 Piece . . 8100.00
Bedroom Set, Galle, Art Nouveau, Satinwood, France, c.1890, 3 Piece 3740.00
Bedroom Set, Jacobean Style, Mahogany, Mahogany Veneer, 4 Piece 550.00
Bedroom Set, Mahogany, Crotch Mahogany Veneer, 3 Piece 1955.00
Bedroom Set, Oak, Bed, Dresser, Mirror, Aulsbrook & Sturges, 3 Piece 1610.00
Bedroom Set, Victorian, Dresser, Marble Top, 19th Century, 3 Piece 825.00
Bedroom Set, Woodard, Oak, Leaf Carving, Commode, Bed, Dresser, 3 Piece 1670.00
Bench, Blue Green Over Red Paint, Cutout Legs 29 1/2 x 80 x 18 In. 2750.00
Bench, Bucket, Blue Paint, Gothic Arch Cutout Feet, 29 1/2 x 16 x 13 In. 920.00
Bench, Bucket, Pine, Cherry, Shelf, Backsplash, Scalloped, Doors, c.1810, 44 x 44 In. 3450.00
Bench, Bucket, Pine, Green Paint, Shaped Legs, Metal Strap Edges, 20 x 10 x 27 In. 250.00
Bench, Bucket, Pine, Painted, Dovetailed Sides, Early 1800s, 36 x 37 In. 940.00
Bench, Bucket, Pine, Shelves, Scrolled, Bootjack Feet, 42 x 23 1/2 x 13 In. 495.00
Bench, Bucket, Walnut, Shaped Ends, 2 Mortised Shelves, 39 x 12 x 6 In. 1670.00
Bench, Charles X Style, Mahogany, X-Brace Legs, c.1860, 19 x 19 x 14 In. 1095.00
Bench, Chinese Chippendale, Mahogany, Upholstered, 26 x 48 x 21 In. 80.00
Bench, Chippendale Style, Needlework Upholstery, c.1925, 40 x 18 x 19 In. 259.00
Bench, Church, Gothic, Oak, Carved, 3 Seats, Late 1800s, 35 x 83 x 24 In. 650.00
Bench, Church, Pine, 19th Century, 30 x 10 In., Pair 650.00
Bench, Deacon's, 3 Chairbacks, Grapes, New England, 1835-45, 75 In. 1150.00
Bench, Egyptian Style, Teak, Cane Seat, Paneled Back, Animals, 32 1/2 x 16 In. 2850.00
Bench, Empire Style, Mahogany, Ormolu Mounted, c.1900, 18 x 32 In. 1095.00
Bench, Fireside, Pine, Pumpkin Color, Barrel Back, 69 x 15 x 68 In. 4025.00
Bench, French Provincial, Walnut, Open Back, Plank Seat, 32 x 47 x 16 In. 210.00
Bench, G. Nakashima, Walnut, 2 Seat Cushions, c.1960, 10 x 96 x 26 In., Pair 5975.00
Bench, G. Nelson, Enameled Metal, 2 Cushions, Central Table, Herman Miller, 73 In. 705.00
Bench, G. Nelson, Platform, Birch, Herman Miller, 1950s, 68 x 18 1/2 x 14 In. 1380.00
Bench, G. Nelson, Slat, Birch, Ebonized Legs, 68 x 18 1/2 x 14 1/4 In. 765.00
Bench, G. Nelson, Slat, Birch, Ebonized Legs, Herman Miller, 1950s, 14 x 72 In. 1410.00
Bench, G. Nelson, Slat, Birch, Ebonized, Herman Miller, 1960s, 14 x 48 x 19 In. 1000.00
Bench, G. Stickley, No. 217, Piano, Slab Sides, Cutout Top, 22 x 36 x 13 In. 4115.00
Bench, George III Style, Mahogany, Upholstered, Brass Tacks, 19 x 46 x 20 In. 805.00
Bench, George III, Mahogany, High Padded Sides, Carved, Fluted Legs, 36 In. 2530.00
Bench, Georgian Style, Mahogany, Needlepoint Slip Seat, Late 1800s, 18 x 38 In. 635.00
Bench, Georgian Style, Mahogany, Upholstered, Scroll Armrests, 26 x 51 x 19 In. 230.00
Bench, Gilt, Seminude Women On Arms, Padded, 47 x 103 x 20 In. 8915.00
Bench, Hall, Limbert, Slatted Back, Curved Crest Rail, Branded, 42 x 18 In. . . . . *Illus* 2938.00
Bench, J. Hoffmann, Bentwood, Black, Upholstered, 48 x 20 x 28 In. 355.00
Bench, Johan Borgersen, Oak, c.1900, 31 x 42 1/2 x 13 In. 9000.00
Bench, L. & J.G. Stickley, No. 209, Left Seat, Gothic Slats, 37 x 42 x 18 In. 5290.00
Bench, Leather, Steel, Tufted Cushions, 6 Legs, International, 17 x 72 x 18 In. 2760.00
Bench, Limbert, Left Seat, Slatted Back, Curved Crest Rail, 42 x 42 x 18 In. 2940.00
Bench, Louis XV Style, Fruitwood, Aubusson Upholstery, 20 x 36 x 15 In. 1795.00
Bench, Louis XV Style, Gilt, Upholstered, France, 1800s, 30 In. 760.00
Bench, Louis XV Style, Walnut, Caned, 29 x 20 x 51 In. 3450.00
Bench, Louis XVI Style, Beech, Carved, Parcel Gilt, Pier, 20 x 80 x 17 In. 2990.00
Bench, Louis XVI Style, Ivory Paint, Gilt, Upholstered, 19 x 19 x 17 In., Pair 1795.00
Bench, Louis XVI Style, Polychrome, Oval Top, Cushion, Fluted Legs, 20 x 35 x 14 In. 978.00
Bench, M. Dufrene, Gilt, 1930, 19 1/2 x 32 x 19 1/2 In. 5380.00
Bench, Neoclassical, Mahogany, Curule, Needlepoint Upholstery, c.1820 . . . . 980.00
Bench, Nutting, No. 162, Maple, 4 Legs, 72 x 14 x 18 In. 715.00

Furniture, Bench, Hall, Limbert, Slatted Back,
Curved Crest Rail, Branded, 42 x 18 In.

Furniture, Bench, Peter Hunt Style,
Painted, 38 In.

Bench, Oak, Lift Seat, 40 x 16 x 39 In. 719.00
Bench, Oak, Scrolled Arms, 55 x 36 In. 230.00
Bench, Peter Hunt Style, Painted, 38 In. .... *Illus* 431.00
Bench, Pierced Frame, Entwined Serpents & Birds, 6 Cabriole Legs, Chinese, 57 In. 2875.00
Bench, Pine, 2 Shelves, Handhold, 23 x 36 In. 105.00
Bench, Pine, Backsplash, V-Cut Legs, Snow Hill Society Meeting House, 123 In. 305.00
Bench, Pine, Crest Rail, Tapered Spindles, 19th Century, 32 x 96 x 18 In. 380.00
Bench, Pine, Painted, Early 20th Century, 18 x 13 x 96 In. 200.00
Bench, Plank Seat, Spindled Back, Bentwood Crest, 37 x 84 In. 460.00
Bench, Poplar, Red Combed, 1-Board, 2-Slat Back, 78 x 16 x 33 In. 1323.00
Bench, Regency Style, Faux Rosewood, Gilt, Curule, 25 x 45 x 18 In., Pair 4140.00
Bench, Regency Style, Mahogany, Klismos, Lion's-Head Finials, 27 x 29 x 17 In. 1840.00
Bench, Rosewood, Steel, 19 x 72 x 16 In. 160.00
Bench, Shaker, Hardwood, Arched Ends, Shirley, Mass., c.1850, 18 3/4 x 34 x 10 In. 1495.00
Bench, Shaker, Pine, Red Stain, 1-Board Top, Hancock, Mass., 15 1/2 x 96 In. 2415.00
Bench, Shaker, Work, Pine, Blue Paint, 1-Board Top, Shelf, c.1850, 20 x 23 3/4 In. 1380.00
Bench, Sleigh, Maple, 34 x 15 1/2 x 8 In. 127.00
Bench, Softwood, Double Skirt, Cutout Legs, Orange Paint, Pa., 16 x 36 x 14 In. 3520.00
Bench, Softwood, Grain Painted, 2 Interior Compartments, 28 x 69 x 20 In. 3575.00
Bench, Softwood, Shaped Cutout Legs, Painted Base, 20 x 38 x 12 In. 3300.00
Bench, Victorian, Pine, Carved, Frame & Panel Back, 40 x 51 x 20 In. 489.00
Bench, Vienna Secession, Bentwood, Circle & Scroll Base, Padded Seat, 17 x 31 In. 1910.00
Bench, William IV, Rosewood, Upholstered, Carved Legs, c.1850, 16 x 54 x 24 In. 2070.00
Bench, Window, French Provincial, Upholstered Arms, 29 x 47 x 16 1/2 In., Pair 411.00
Bench, Window, Louis XVI Style, Painted, Parcel Gilt, Cushions, 28 x 18 x 41 In. 3360.00
Bench, Window, Mahogany, Turned Legs, 20th Century, Pair 190.00
Bench, Window, Regency, Beech, Ebonized, Gilt Trim, 2 Bolster Cushions, 51 In. 1380.00
Bench, Window, Victorian, Rosewood, Needlework Top, 1930s, 18 x 36 In. 529.00
Bench, Window, William & Mary Style, Oak, Turned, Cane Side Panels, 37 In. 345.00
Bench, Windsor, Bamboo, Mustard Paint, Stenciled Flowers, 76 x 27 x 34 In. 1725.00
Bench, Windsor, Single Plank, Shaped Arms, Spindle Gallery, 30 x 96 x 18 In. 1150.00
Bench, Wood, Painted, Upholstered, Loose Cushion, 19th Century, Pair 660.00
Bench-Table, Mennonite, Meetinghouse, Pine, Pennsylvania, 1800s, 120 In. 2300.00
Book Table, L. & J.G. Stickley, Vertical Slats, Overhanging Top, 29 x 27 x 27 In. 5290.00
Book Trough, G. Stickley, Lower Shelf, Cutouts, 32 x 10 x 31 In. 920.00
Book Trough, Stickley Bros., Mahogany, 2 Shelves, 30 x 30 x 12 In. 650.00
Bookcase, 3 Glazed Doors, 3 Drawers, Turned Columns, c.1875, 74 1/2 x 58 x 14 In. 1840.00
Bookcase, American Restauration, Mahogany, Ogee Cornice, 2 Doors, 87 x 64 In. 5750.00
Bookcase, American Restauration, Mahogany, Stepped Top, 4 Doors, 67 x 82 In. 5520.00
Bookcase, Arts & Crafts, Door, Shelves, Front Cutout, 33 x 13 x 48 In. 880.00
Bookcase, Arts & Crafts, Oak, Galleried Top, 4 Shelves, 78 x 39 x 15 In. 1058.00
Bookcase, Arts & Crafts, Oak, Glass Door, 1900s, 52 x 29 x 15 In., Pair 700.00
Bookcase, Baltic, Ebonized, 2 Glazed Doors, Paneled, Drawers, 72 x 47 x 14 In. 2990.00
Bookcase, Circassian Walnut, Adjustable Shelves, Early 1800s, 46 x 42 In. 1995.00
Bookcase, Edwardian, Burl Walnut, Bookmatched Top, 38 x 51 In. 805.00
Bookcase, Empire Revival, Mahogany, Stepped, 2 Doors, Shelves, 35 x 28 In. 1058.00

Bookcase, Empire Style, Mahogany, 3 Doors, 56 x 72 x 19 In. 655.00
Bookcase, Federal Style, Pine, Double, 20th Century, 87 x 97 x 19 In. 264.00
Bookcase, G. Stickley, 2 Doors, Mullion, Harvey Ellis, 42 x 14 x 64 In. 11500.00
Bookcase, G. Stickley, 2 Doors, Through Tenon, 16 Panes, 56 x 46 x 13 In. 4995.00
Bookcase, G. Stickley, No. 542, 2 Doors, 56 x 36 x 13 In. 6463.00
Bookcase, G. Stickley, No. 716, 2 Doors, Through Tenon, 16 Panes, 56 x 43 In. 11165.00
Bookcase, George III Style, Mahogany, 2 Astragal Glazed Doors, 84 x 50 x 16 In. 3450.00
Bookcase, George III Style, Mahogany, 2-Panel Doors, Splayed Feet, 77 x 27 In. 1610.00
Bookcase, George III Style, Mahogany, Astragal Glazed Doors, 68 x 44 x 13 In. 1725.00
Bookcase, George III Style, Mahogany, Step Back, Drawers, 49 x 18 x 11 In. 690.00
Bookcase, George III, Faux Bois, Cornice, Astragal Glazed Doors, 54 x 20 In. 1725.00
Bookcase, George III, Mahogany, Astragal Glazed, 1800s, 80 x 43 x 18 In. 3910.00
Bookcase, George III, Mahogany, Cornice, Fret Carved Frieze, 86 x 47 x 16 In. 3450.00
Bookcase, Globe-Wernicke, Oak, Stack, Cornice, 34 x 12 x 72 In. 1095.00
Bookcase, Gothic Revival, Mahogany, 49 x 56 x 18 In. 657.00
Bookcase, Gothic Revival, Oak, Timepiece, 3 Over 3 Doors, 1800s, 98 In. 6170.00
Bookcase, Heart Pine, 5 Adjustable Shelves, Beadboard Back, S.C., 84 x 56 x 13 In. 1380.00
Bookcase, L. & J.G. Stickley, No. 637, 2 Doors, 8 Panes, 36 x 13 x 56 In. 4994.00
Bookcase, L. & J.G. Stickley, No. 647, 3 12-Pane Doors, Gallery Top, 55 x 73 In. 11750.00
Bookcase, L. & J.G. Stickley, Oak, Gallery Top, Through Tenon, c.1912, 55 x 30 In. 1293.00
Bookcase, Lifetime Puritan, Glass Doors, Paper Label, 51 1/2 x 45 In. .... *Illus* 3055.00
Bookcase, Lifetime, Door, Overlaid Mullions, 28 x 13 x 56 In. 1175.00
Bookcase, Limbert, 1 Door, Leaded Glass, Through Tenon, Paper Label, 55 In. 4755.00
Bookcase, Limbert, Ash, 2 Doors, Iron Hardware, Slab Sides, 44 x 14 x 56 In. 1765.00
Bookcase, Limbert, Ebon-Oak, 2 Doors, 6 Shelves, Copper, 60 x 48 x 14 In. 4115.00
Bookcase, Limbert, No. 321, 2 Leaded Glass Doors, 7 Shelves, 54 x 43 In. 5580.00
Bookcase, Limbert, No. 359, Overhanging Top, 3 Glazed Doors, 57 x 66 In. 4065.00
Bookcase, Limbert, No. 372, 2 Arched Doors, 6 Shelves, Copper, 60 x 48 In. 5300.00
Bookcase, Louis Philippe, Cuban Mahogany, Overhanging Cornice, 71 x 40 x 13 In. 2300.00
Bookcase, Louis XVI Style, Mahogany, 2 Glazed Doors, c.1885, 74 x 59 In. 1610.00
Bookcase, Mahogany, 3 Doors, Carved Posts, Claw Feet, 1910, 58 x 77 x 20 In. 1610.00
Bookcase, Mahogany, Adjustable Shelves, Reeded Half Columns, 45 x 30 x 10 In. 300.00
Bookcase, Mahogany, Glass Doors, c.1920, 36 x 24 x 11 In., Pair 430.00
Bookcase, Mahogany, Raised Corner Blocks, Incised Rosettes, 46 x 13 x 46 In. 115.00
Bookcase, Mahogany, Step Back, 2 Sections, Double Doors, 68 x 19 x 93 In. 1440.00
Bookcase, Mahogany, Waterfall, 4 Shelves, 2 Drawers, England, 49 x 26 x 12 In. 805.00
Bookcase, Maple, Brass, Decorative Wood Inlays, 1950s, 29 x 36 x 13 In. 60.00
Bookcase, Oak, 3 Glazed Doors, Continental, Late 1800s, 64 1/2 x 78 In. 2850.00
Bookcase, Oak, Carved, Turned Columns, Drawers, 19th Century, 86 x 73 x 19 In. 355.00
Bookcase, Oak, Stack, 5 Sections, Cornice Base, 34 x 12 x 66 In. 1035.00
Bookcase, Oak, Stack, 5 Sections, Gallery Top, Paneled Ends, 32 x 12 x 67 In. 750.00
Bookcase, Onondaga Shops, No. 519, Gallery Top, 2 Doors, 56 1/2 x 52 In. 7640.00
Bookcase, Oriental, Elm, High Legs, 9 Sections, 3 Drawers, 63 x 20 x 76 In. 1265.00
Bookcase, Regency Style, Mahogany, Gallery, Cock-Beaded Edges, 44 x 39 In., Pair 4600.00
Bookcase, Regency Style, Mahogany, Graduated Shelves, 44 x 39 In. 3680.00
Bookcase, Regency Style, Mahogany, Waterfall, 4 Tiers, 43 x 39 x 11 In. 635.00
Bookcase, Regency, Mahogany, 3 Shelves, Early 1800s, 36 1/2 x 54 x 13 In. 1265.00
Bookcase, Regency, Mahogany, 3 Shelves, Maidens' Heads, 37 x 31 In., Pair 4600.00
Bookcase, Regency, Mahogany, Pediment, Paneled Doors, 89 x 38 x 16 In. 2300.00
Bookcase, Renaissance Revival, Walnut, 3 Doors, Shelves, 90 x 74 x 20 1/2 In. 3820.00
Bookcase, Renaissance Revival, Walnut, Carved, 2 Doors, 57 x 54 x 16 In. 1528.00
Bookcase, Revolving, Danners, Mahogany, Canton, Ohio, 20 x 21 x 43 In. 1265.00
Bookcase, Revolving, Edwardian Style, Mahogany, Burl Walnut, 31 x 18 In. 635.00
Bookcase, Revolving, Edwardian, Inlaid Elm, Square Top, Crossbar, 31 x 18 In. 345.00
Bookcase, Revolving, Edwardian, Mahogany, Crossbanded, Marquetry, 34 x 18 In. 266.00
Bookcase, Revolving, Oak, Glass Door, Molded Panel, 16 x 36 In. 575.00
Bookcase, Rohde, Herman Miller, c.1939, 25 x 36 x 13 In., Pair 2938.00
Bookcase, Tiger Maple, 2 Sections, 4 Doors, New England, c.1835, 92 x 94 In. 11165.00
Bookcase, Udell, Oak, Stack, 6 Sections, 33 3/4 x 12 x 82 1/4 In. 1150.00
Bookcase, Victorian, Mahogany Inlay, Ogee Cornice, 58 x 48 x 14 In. 1265.00
Bookcase, Victorian, Mahogany, Urn Crest Finial, Glass Doors, 53 x 16 x 77 In. 1380.00
Bookcase, Victorian, Walnut, Carved, 3 Sections, 3 Drawers, 79 x 19 x 96 In. 3105.00
Bookcase, Victorian, Walnut, Cornice, 2 Glass Doors, Over Drawer, 43 x 79 In. 690.00

Bookcase, Victorian, Walnut, Gallery, Rosette & Line Carving, 54 x 15 x 71 In. 1550.00
Bookcase, Victorian, Walnut, Rosewood, Cornice, Glass Doors, 49 x 19 x 92 In. 2990.00
Bookcase, Victorian, Walnut, Step Back, 2 Sections, 89 1/2 x 52 x 18 In. 2015.00
Bookcase, Walnut, Crossbanded, 3 Doors, Bracket Feet, 42 1/2 x 60 In. 905.00
Bookcase, Walnut, Rope-Carved Border, Drawer, Lion's-Paw Feet, 69 x 52 In. 2015.00
Bookcase, Weis Furniture, Oak, Stack, 8 Sections, Drawer, 34 x 11 x 95 In. 690.00
Bookcase, William IV, Mahogany, 3 Shelves, Turned Pilasters, 44 x 53 In. 2070.00
Bookcase, William IV, Mahogany, Astragal Glazed Doors, 91 x 54 x 17 In. 4370.00
Bookcase, William IV, Mahogany, Molded Cornice, Glazed Doors, 80 x 57 x 18 In. 1495.00
Bookcase-Cabinet, Empire, Mahogany, Glazed Doors, c.1835, 86 x 42 x 22 In. 1175.00
Bookcase-Cabinet, Oak, Carved, Continental, 19th Century, 96 x 55 x 22 In. 765.00
Bookcase-Cabinet, Regency, Black Lacquer, Early 1800s, 68 x 32 x 18 In. 2760.00
Bookrack, Victorian, Mahogany, Block & Ring-Turned Legs, 9 x 16 x 10 In. 290.00
Bookstand, 18th-Century Style, Mahogany, X-Stretcher, 33 x 36 x 15 In. 265.00
Bookstand, Arts & Crafts, Oak, 4 Shelves, Cutout Sides, Through Tenon, 46 In. 499.00
Bookstand, Brass, Folding, Openwork Arrow Design, 9 x 8 x 8 In., Pair 60.00
Bookstand, Burl Elm, Rosewood, Continental, 30 x 21 In. 1035.00
Bookstand, G. Stickley, 3 Shelves, Slab Sides, Cutouts, c.1904, 30 x 38 In. 4995.00
Bookstand, Georgian Style, Mahogany, 2 Bookrests, Drawer, 4 Shelves, 56 x 23 In. 1095.00
Bookstand, Gilt, Framed Leaves, Flowers, Beaded, Italy, 11 x 15 x 12 In. 1495.00
Boot Rack, William IV, Mahogany, Shaped Shelf Posts, Pegs, c.1840, 42 x 32 In. 635.00
Bottle Case, George III, Mahogany, Inlaid, Stand, 25 x 18 x 16 In. 1135.00
Bracket, Wall, Chinese Chippendale, Gilt, 13 x 8 In., Pair 1840.00
Breakfront, Federal Style, Mahogany, Veneer, Glass Doors, Sides, 87 x 53 x 17 In. 1150.00
Breakfront, Frank Lloyd Wright, Open Shelves, Heritage Henredon, 62 x 20 x 79 In. 4600.00
Breakfront, George III Style, Mahogany, Glazed Doors, 5 Drawers, 82 x 21 x 87 In. 4370.00
Breakfront, George III Style, Mahogany, Mesh Lower Cupboards, Marble, 68 In. 575.00
Breakfront, George III, Crossbanded Top, 5 Drawers, c.1830, 41 x 43 x 21 In. 2185.00
Breakfront, Thomasville, Georgian Style, Mahogany, 83 x 65 x 19 In. 748.00
Breakfront, Walnut, 3 Domed Cabinets, 4 Glass Doors, England, 85 x 92 In. 2875.00
Breakfront-Bookcase, Edwardian Style, Mahogany, Pediment, 80 x 61 x 16 In. 748.00
Breakfront-Bookcase, Empire, Mahogany, c.1835, 89 x 94 x 26 In. 7640.00
Breakfront-Bookcase, George III Style, Mahogany, 81 x 82 x 19 1/2 In. 3220.00
Breakfront-Bookcase, George III Style, Mahogany, 87 1/4 x 89 1/2 x 16 In. 6325.00
Breakfront-Bookcase, George III Style, Mahogany, 95 x 102 x 22 In. 8915.00
Breakfront-Bookcase, George III Style, Mahogany, Glazed Doors, 93 x 76 In. 1679.00
Breakfront-Bookcase, George III, Mahogany, Early 1800s 5175.00
Breakfront-Bookcase, Georgian Style, Chinoiserie, Lacquer, c.1915, 82 x 74 In. 5290.00
Breakfront-Bookcase, Georgian Style, Mahogany, 4 13-Pane Doors, 101 x 94 In. 8625.00
Breakfront-Bookcase, Gothic Revival, England, c.1885, 102 x 110 In. 4600.00
Breakfront-Bookcase, Mahogany, Broken Arch Pediment, 1900s, 88 x 56 x 16 In. 865.00
Breakfront-Bookcase, Renaissance Revival, Walnut, c.1865, 112 x 67 In. 4140.00
Buffet, American Restauration, Fruitwood, Frieze Drawer, 38 x 53 x 22 In. 3450.00
Buffet, Art Deco, Rosewood, Brass Moldings, Marble Top, 38 x 19 1/2 x 57 In. 1640.00
Buffet, Art Deco, Rosewood, France, c.1930 . . . . 2185.00
Buffet, Art Nouveau, Walnut, Carved, 2 Sections, Paneled, 106 x 56 In. 2530.00
Buffet, Axel Einar Hjort, Birch, Stained, 30 3/4 x 61 x 19 3/4 In. 1080.00
Buffet, Empire Style, Mahogany, Gilt Bronze, 3 Drawers, 40 x 71 x 23 In. 9200.00

Furniture, Bookcase,
Lifetime Puritan,
Glass Doors, Paper
Label, 51 1/2 x 45 In.

Furniture, Bureau,
Ralph Cahoon Jr., Floral
Bouquet, 1930s-40s, 32 In.

Buffet, Empire, Fruitwood, 3 Drawers, 2 Doors, c.1815, 43 x 62 x 22 In. 3450.00
Buffet, Louis Philippe Style, Fruitwood, 38 x 51 1/2 x 23 In. 2070.00
Buffet, Louis XV Style, Marble Top, 4 Drawers, Doors, Inset Panels, 40 x 103 In. 4370.00
Buffet, Louis XV Style, Oak, Mid 19th Century, 40 x 53 x 23 In. 2760.00
Buffet, Louis XV Style, Oak, Parquetry, 2 Drawers, Doors, Early 1900s, 43 x 82 In. 3220.00
Buffet, Louis XV, Walnut, Mid 18th Century, 51 x 60 x 19 In. 2990.00
Buffet, Louis XVI Style, Oak, 19th Century, 42 x 66 x 21 1/2 In. 5060.00
Buffet, Stickley Bros., Oak, Carved Backsplash, 2 Drawers, 2 Doors, 42 x 67 In. 360.00
Bureau, Dutch Rococo, Walnut, Bombe, Marquetry, 19th Century, 45 x 51 In. 4600.00
Bureau, Federal, Cherry, Bird's-Eye Maple, Backsplash, 7 Drawers, c.1825, 58 x 45 In. . . . 4600.00
Bureau, Federal, Mahogany, Cherry, 4 Drawers, New England, c.1810, 34 x 38 In. 2940.00
Bureau, George II Style, Burl Walnut, Slant Front, 4 Drawers, 40 x 28 x 19 In. 1150.00
Bureau, George II Style, Burl Walnut, Slant Front, 5 Drawers, 40 x 38 In. 1840.00
Bureau, George III Style, Mahogany, Slant Front, 5 Drawers, 43 x 37 x 21 In. 3220.00
Bureau, George III, Chinoiserie, Lacquer, Drop Front, 4 Drawers, c.1800, 38 x 36 In. 4370.00
Bureau, George III, Mahogany, Drop Front, 5 Drawers, c.1790, 40 x 40 In. 1840.00
Bureau, George III, Mahogany, Slant Front, 4 Drawers, c.1785, 41 x 36 x 20 In. 1380.00
Bureau, George III, Oak, Mahogany, Slant Front, Inset Leather, 43 x 39 x 20 In. 2990.00
Bureau, Gibbings, Maple, 6 Drawers, Lip Pulls, 31 x 68 1/4 x 20 1/4 In. 295.00
Bureau, Louis XVI Style, Satin & Olive Wood, Inlay, Marble Top, 35 x 44 In. 2415.00
Bureau, Louis XVI, Mahogany, Brass, Marble Top, Mirror, 51 x 26 x 18 In. 2115.00
Bureau, Mahogany, Bombe, Serpentine Drop Front, Dutch, 43 x 46 x 24 In. 1610.00
Bureau, Mahogany, Veneer, Columns, 4 Drawers, Paw Feet, 43 x 45 x 21 In. 865.00
Bureau, Neoclassical, Mahogany, 2 Over 3 Drawers, Cheval Mirror, 70 x 45 In. 635.00
Bureau, Neoclassical, Mahogany, 5 Drawers, Carved Posts, Paw Feet, 56 x 37 In. 545.00
Bureau, Queen Anne, Japanned Chinoiserie, Slant Front, 4 Drawers, 34 x 30 In. 2390.00
Bureau, Queen Anne, Walnut Burl, Feathered, Banded, c.1780, 40 x 37 x 22 In. 3105.00
Bureau, Queen Anne, Walnut, Crossbanded, Slant Front, 40 x 36 x 23 In. 5875.00
Bureau, Ralph Cahoon Jr., Floral Bouquet, 1930s-40s, 32 In. . . . . *Illus* 690.00
Bureau, Renaissance Revival, Rosewood, 92 x 44 In. 3680.00
Bureau, Sheraton, Mahogany, Bowfront, Columns, Drawers, 36 x 43 1/2 In. 920.00
Bureau, William & Mary, Oak, Elm, Ivory, Mother-Of-Pearl, 39 x 36 x 21 In. 865.00
Bureau-Bookcase, George III Style, Mahogany, Astragal Doors, 4 Drawers, 89 In. 3680.00
Bureau-Bookcase, George III, Mahogany, 2 Glazed Doors, 4 Drawers, 91 x 42 In. 4780.00
Bureau-Bookcase, George III, Mahogany, Swan's-Neck Pediment, 89 x 46 In. 8050.00
Bureau-Bookcase, George III, Satinwood, Inlaid Mahogany, 91 x 48 x 23 In. 4600.00
Bureau-Bookcase, Georgian Style, Mahogany, Broken Pediment, 84 x 38 x 23 In. 520.00
Bureau-Bookcase, Georgian Style, Mahogany, Drop Front, c.1840, 87 3/4 x 45 In. 4830.00
Bureau-Bookcase, Georgian Style, Mahogany, Drop Front, c.1850, 95 In. 5750.00
Bureau-Bookcase, Georgian, Walnut, Inlay, Doors, Early 1700s, 89 x 44 x 22 In. 10575.00
Bureau-Bookcase, Rococo Revival, Figured Walnut, 3 Sections, 82 x 42 In. 3450.00
Bureau-Bookcase, Walnut, Kneehole, Glazed Doors, Drop Front, 4 Drawers, 87 x 39 In. . . . 633.00
Cabinet, Aesthetic Revival, Mahogany, Mirror, Griffins, Late 1800s, 72 x 46 In. 2070.00
Cabinet, American Restauration, Mahogany, Drawer, Panel Door, 54 x 31 In., Pair 1840.00
Cabinet, Art Deco, Burled Veneer, Bakelite, Chrome, England, c.1930, 40 x 29 x 17 In. 940.00
Cabinet, Art Deco, Frieze Drawer, Doors, Dutch, 34 x 22 x 14 In. 94.00
Cabinet, Art Deco, Satinwood, Amboyna, Marble Top, Early 1900s, 46 x 53 x 21 In. 7765.00
Cabinet, Arts & Crafts, 2 Doors, Brass Hardware, Overhanging Top, 50 x 58 In. 1265.00
Cabinet, Arts & Crafts, Brass, Marble, Early 1900s, 25 x 15 x 16 1/2 In., Pair 190.00
Cabinet, Arts & Crafts, Drawers, Mirrored Back, Brass Hardware, 60 x 22 x 58 In. 2585.00
Cabinet, Arts & Crafts, Glasgow Roses, England, 32 x 16 x 15 In. 2115.00
Cabinet, Arts & Crafts, Oak, Glazed Door, Early 20th Century, 52 x 28 x 14 In. 489.00
Cabinet, Axel Einar Hjort, Birch, Stained, 63 3/4 x 54 x 18 In. 1680.00
Cabinet, Axel Einar Hjort, Macassar Ebony, Birch, c.1925, 56 x 26 x 17 In. 3900.00
Cabinet, Baroque Revival, Walnut, Inlaid, Carved Paneled Door, 61 x 41 x 21 In. 470.00
Cabinet, Biedermeier, Drawers, Door, Early 1800s, 32 x 21 In. 475.00
Cabinet, Biedermeier, Fruitwood, 2 Doors, Continental, Mid 1800s, 38 x 38 x 19 In. 1840.00
Cabinet, Biedermeier, Mahogany, Columns, Gilt Swans, 35 x 34 x 20 In. 3910.00
Cabinet, Biedermeier, Walnut, 3 Glazed Doors, 71 x 76 x 20 In. 3220.00
Cabinet, Black Lacquer, 2 Drawers, Doors, Chinese, 24 x 16 x 13 In., Pair 489.00
Cabinet, Black Lacquer, Gilt, River Landscape, Pagodas, Chinese Export, 69 x 60 In. 2475.00
Cabinet, Bombe, Painted Flowers, 3 Drawers, 26 x 22 x 12 In., Pair 530.00
Cabinet, Bugatti, Ebonized Wood, Copper, Pewter, Bone, c.1902, 80 x 35 x 26 In. 59750.00

Cabinet, C. Malmsten, Birch, Ebony, Rosewood, Fruitwood, 55 x 64 x 18 In. 1560.00
Cabinet, Carved, Lacquer, Relief-Carved Doors, Chinese, 68 x 43 x 21 In. 460.00
Cabinet, China, 1 Door, 3 Panes, Side Shelves, 59 x 45 x 15 1/2 In. 4700.00
Cabinet, China, Art Deco, Walnut, Early 20th Century, 72 x 46 x 19 In. 100.00
Cabinet, China, Arts & Crafts, 2 Doors, Plate Rack, Shelves, 42 x 15 x 58 In. 705.00
Cabinet, China, Cherry, c.1900, 58 x 43 x 16 In. 85.00
Cabinet, China, Drexel, Chippendale, Black Lacquer, Gold Accents, 84 x 54 In. 375.00
Cabinet, China, G. Stickley, 1 Door, Gallery Top, 58 x 36 x 13 In. 5875.00
Cabinet, China, G. Stickley, 2 8-Pane Doors, Copper Hardware, 63 x 42 x 15 In. 5875.00
Cabinet, China, G. Stickley, 2 Doors, Gallery Top, Copper V Pulls, 64 x 39 1/2 In. 10000.00
Cabinet, China, G. Stickley, No. 820, 12-Pane Door, 63 x 36 x 15 In. 5580.00
Cabinet, China, L. & J.G. Stickley, No. 761, Arched Door, Glass Sides, 60 x 36 In. 6465.00
Cabinet, China, Limbert, No. 452, Quartersawn Oak, 3 Windows, 45 x 17 x 59 In. 7000.00
Cabinet, China, Limbert, Oak, Arched Double Doors, 1910, 58 In. 3450.00
Cabinet, China, Mahogany, 2 Sections, 20th Century, 66 x 49 x 50 In. 118.00
Cabinet, China, Mahogany, 3 Glass Doors, 20th Century, 50 1/2 x 55 x 16 In. 530.00
Cabinet, China, Oak, 3 Shelves, Mirror, Curved Glass, 63 x 40 In. 375.00
Cabinet, China, Oak, Carved, Beveled Glass Panels, Gold Leaf, 55 x 21 x 74 In. 1035.00
Cabinet, China, Oak, Carved, Scroll, Bellflowers, Glass Shelves, 47 x 19 x 65 In. 1955.00
Cabinet, China, Oak, Curved Front, Pilasters, Glass Shelves, Paw Feet, 23 x 64 In. 1670.00
Cabinet, China, Oak, Curved, Ogee Scrolls, S Feet, 37 x 15 x 63 In. 575.00
Cabinet, China, Oak, Curved, Round Pilasters, Shelves, Paw Feet, 38 x 15 x 32 In. 805.00
Cabinet, China, Oak, Glass Door, Curved, Paw Feet, 45 x 15 x 72 In. 1380.00
Cabinet, China, Oak, Mirrored Gallery, Arched Door, Drawers, 47 x 16 x 76 In. 1380.00
Cabinet, China, Oak, Serpentine Front, Beveled Mirror, Paw Feet, 37 x 16 x 69 In. 1120.00
Cabinet, China, Pine, Mansard Top, Paneled Doors, 89 x 57 x 21 In. 650.00
Cabinet, China, Prairie School, 2 Doors, 3 Shelves, Shoefoot Base, 44 x 56 In. 1410.00
Cabinet, China, Rohde, No. 3321, Formal, Herman Miller, c.1940, 52 x 36 In. 4995.00
Cabinet, China, Rohde, No. 3979, Walnut, Herman Miller, c.1940, 50 x 36 In. 1175.00
Cabinet, Chinese, Lacquer, Recessed Panel, c.1880, 48 x 39 x 20 3/4 In. 460.00
Cabinet, Chippendale Style, Mahogany, Glazed Doors, Stepped, c.1865, 97 x 49 In. 2300.00
Cabinet, Christian Krass, Burl, Ivory, c.1930, 53 x 23 3/4 x 14 In. 4500.00
Cabinet, Circassian Walnut, Glazed Doors, Bracket Feet, 1800s, 41 x 21 x 50 In. 2375.00
Cabinet, Corner, Arts & Crafts, Chamfered Doors, Copper Hardware, 27 x 19 x 33 In. 940.00
Cabinet, Corner, Biedermeier, Flower Marquetry, Glazed Door, 68 x 40 In. 1710.00
Cabinet, Corner, Cherry, Top Door, 2 Bottom Doors, c.1825, 86 In. 3800.00
Cabinet, Corner, Chestnut, Painted, Arch Opening, 3 Shelves, 2 Doors, 87 x 49 In. 1725.00
Cabinet, Corner, Eastern White Pine, c.1830, 79 In. 3800.00
Cabinet, Corner, Empire Style, Mahogany, Half Columns, 87 x 37 x 22 In. 978.00
Cabinet, Corner, George III Style, Mahogany, Bowfront, 2 Doors, 72 x 26 x 16 In. 575.00
Cabinet, Corner, George III, Mahogany, Bowfront, Veneered, Inlay, 84 x 30 In. 9600.00
Cabinet, Corner, Hanging, George II, Pine, Polychrome, 51 x 20 x 12 In., Pair 4830.00
Cabinet, Corner, Hanging, Oak, 1790-1820, 37 3/8 x 19 1/2 In. 1995.00
Cabinet, Corner, Hanging, Queen Anne, Black Lacquer, Bowfront, 44 x 23 x 15 In. 3680.00
Cabinet, Corner, Mahogany, 2 Parts, 4 Doors, Bracket Feet, c.1800, 93 x 41 In. 3055.00
Cabinet, Corner, Mahogany, Molded Cornice, 20th Century, 72 x 35 In. 235.00
Cabinet, Corner, Mahogany, Molded Crown, c.1900, 81 x 65 1/2 x 31 In. 2300.00
Cabinet, Corner, Oak, Paneled Door, Shelf, England, 38 1/2 x 26 x 18 In. 575.00
Cabinet, Corner, Pine, Red Paint, Molded Top, 19th Century, 49 x 24 1/2 In. 200.00
Cabinet, Corner, Walnut, Carved, Scrolled Cresting, c.1790, 88 x 42 1/2 x 20 In. 3820.00
Cabinet, Corner, Walnut, Gilt, Bowfront, Continental, Early 1900s, 41 x 34 x 23 In. 345.00
Cabinet, Corner, Walnut, Glazed Upper Doors, 81 1/4 x 43 x 28 In., Pair 750.00
Cabinet, Corner, Yellow Pine, Molded Bracket Feet, Blue Interior, 90 In. 8900.00
Cabinet, Coromandel Lacquer, Pietra Dura, 4 Doors, 2 Drawers, c.1900, 52 x 36 In. 690.00
Cabinet, Dinesen, Teak, Birch, Drawers, Drop Front, Denmark, 40 x 34 In. 2938.00
Cabinet, Display, American Oak, Arched Crown, c.1900, 74 x 47 1/2 x 16 In. 2185.00
Cabinet, Display, Baker, Mahogany, Astragal Glazed Doors, 92 x 41 x 18 In. ....2990.00 to 3335.00
Cabinet, Display, Baroque, Oak, 2 Doors Over 3 Doors, Gallery Edge, 90 x 66 In. 5288.00
Cabinet, Display, Corner, Mahogany, Step Back, 5 Tiers, Drawer, 59 x 25 In. 115.00
Cabinet, Display, Dutch Pine, Arched Top, 20th Century, 87 x 69 x 15 In. 1000.00
Cabinet, Display, Eastlake, Gilt, Beaded Frames, c.1875, 26 x 19 x 19 In. 200.00
Cabinet, Display, George III Style, Inlaid Mahogany, Glass Door, 72 x 44 1/2 In. 1035.00
Cabinet, Display, Georgian Style, Mahogany, Parcel Gilt, Glass, 84 x 26 In., Pair 2185.00

Cabinet, Display, Glass, Illuminated, 20th Century, 80 x 20 x 20 In. 355.00
Cabinet, Display, Hardwood, Birds, Animals, Leaves, Chinese, c.1885, 28 x 22 5/8 In. 1495.00
Cabinet, Display, Hardwood, Carved, Glass Panels, Chinese, c.1890, 65 x 41 In. 230.00
Cabinet, Display, Italianate, Drawer, Ormolu, Painted Scene, Couple, 68 In., Pair 865.00
Cabinet, Display, Louis XV Style, Kingwood, Ormolu Mounted, 66 x 37 x 18 In. 865.00
Cabinet, Display, Louis XVI Style, Brass, Beveled Glass, Lift Top, Lacquer, 30 x 17 In. . . 1045.00
Cabinet, Display, Mahogany, Ormolu Trim, Glass Shelves, 28 x 13 x 48 In. 345.00
Cabinet, Display, Marble Top, Gold Paint, Ormolu Trim, 26 x 13 x 55 In. 750.00
Cabinet, Display, Oak, Curved Glass Door, c.1890, 66 x 44 x 17 In. 748.00
Cabinet, Display, Oak, Glass, Paneled Ends, Mirrored Doors, 31 x 24 1/2 x 42 In. 175.00
Cabinet, Display, Painted, Ormolu, Gallery, Bowed Glass Sides, Door, 27 x 15 x 57 In. . . . 460.00
Cabinet, Display, Rosewood, Oak, Bows, Flowers, England, c.1860, 65 x 62 In. 1725.00
Cabinet, Display, Shibayama, Inlaid, Figural Landscape, Japan, 46 x 33 In. 920.00
Cabinet, Donald Deskey, Art Deco, Mahogany, 5 Drawers, 35 x 19 x 39 In., Pair 2185.00
Cabinet, Ebonized, Slate Top, Boulle Frieze, 44 x 41 x 17 In. 3220.00
Cabinet, Ebony, Bone Inlay, Slots, Pen Rest, Inkwell Holes, Drawers, 20 x 14 In. 470.00
Cabinet, Edwardian, Marquetry, 4 Glazed Doors, 4 Drawers, 83 1/2 x 71 In. 2950.00
Cabinet, Edwardian, Satinwood, Painted, Bowfront, Doors, 30 x 27 x 19 In. 3585.00
Cabinet, Empire Style, Rosewood, Brass Mounted, 40 x 39 3/4 x 15 7/8 In. 1265.00
Cabinet, Folio, Aesthetic Revival, Ebonized, Mirror, Porcelain Mount, c.1875, 46 In. 3600.00
Cabinet, French Provincial, Fruitwood, 3 Drawers, Doors, Late 1700s, 46 x 56 In. 1330.00
Cabinet, French Provincial, Oak, Carved, Early 19th Century, 36 x 31 1/2 x 17 In. 1840.00
Cabinet, French Provincial, Walnut, Gallery, Early 19th Century, 29 x 16 x 13 In. 430.00
Cabinet, G. Nakashima, Walnut, Vertical Slab Supports, c.1970, 48 x 12 x 50 In. 10925.00
Cabinet, G. Nelson, Oak, Grained, Hairpin Legs, Herman Miller, 34 x 19 x 30 In. 430.00
Cabinet, G. Nelson, Primavera, Walnut, 2 Doors, Herman Miller, 30 x 34 In. 440.00
Cabinet, G. Nelson, Primavera, Walnut, 3 Drawers, Door, Herman Miller, 24 x 56 In. 470.00
Cabinet, G. Nelson, Primavera, Walnut, 5 Drawers, Door, Herman Miller, 34 x 56 In. 881.00
Cabinet, G. Nelson, Rosewood, 3 Drawers, Herman Miller, 1956, 34 x 18 x 30 In. 3645.00
Cabinet, G. Nelson, Steel, Glass, Laminate, Herman Miller, 34 x 17 x 30 In. 805.00
Cabinet, G. Nelson, Thin Edge, Rosewood, Herman Miller, c.1956, 31 x 34 x 19 In. 3640.00
Cabinet, George III Style, Mahogany, Glazed Doors, Paneled Door, 73 In., Pair 4370.00
Cabinet, George III, Mahogany, Doors, Paneled, 1800s, 77 x 49 x 24 In. 4370.00
Cabinet, George III, Mahogany, Inlaid, Wine Coaster Holders, 34 x 37 x 21 In. 345.00
Cabinet, Gio Ponti, Mahogany, 3 Doors, Singer, U.S.A., 72 x 20 x 30 In. 10925.00
Cabinet, Gothic Revival, Doors, Decoupage Medieval Scenes, 32 x 26 x 20 In. 115.00
Cabinet, Grosfeld, Black Lacquered Wood, 8 Drawers, Brass Pulls, 34 x 58 In. 1265.00
Cabinet, Gustav Bergstrom, Elm, Sycamore, Birch, Mahogany, c.1928, 51 x 34 In. 2700.00
Cabinet, Gustave Eiffel, Pierced Steel, Wrought Iron, c.1889, 83 x 43 x 14 In., Pair 6038.00
Cabinet, Hanging, Arts & Crafts, 2 Doors, Shepherd, Fisherman, 26 1/2 x 24 x 7 In. 1765.00
Cabinet, Hanging, G. Nakashima, Walnut, Drawers, Slide Doors, c.1960, 20 x 106 In. 16730.00
Cabinet, Hanging, Glazed Doors, Interior Shelf, Dutch, 33 x 33 In. 430.00
Cabinet, Hanging, Gothic Revival, Pine, Mahogany Flame Veneer, 10 x 10 x 22 In. 750.00
Cabinet, Hanging, Pine, Raised Panel Door, Shelf, 1700s, 34 x 23 1/2 x 12 1/2 In. 1645.00
Cabinet, Hanging, Rohlfs, Mahogany, Leaded Glass Panels, c.1907, 45 x 31 In. 2350.00
Cabinet, Hanging, Walnut, Molded Crest, Pa., 18th Century, 24 x 28 x 18 In. 18800.00
Cabinet, Hardwood, Drawers, Sliding Panels, Chinese, Early 1900s, 73 x 45 x 22 In. 489.00
Cabinet, Herter Bros., Aesthetic Revival, Walnut, Parquetry, c.1870, 48 In., Pair 9000.00
Cabinet, Hung Mu, 6 Doors, Chinese, 19th Century, 24 x 62 In. 690.00
Cabinet, Hung Mu, Shelves, Drawer, Sliding & Hinged Doors, Chinese, 51 x 41 In. 345.00
Cabinet, Italian Renaissance Revival Style, Walnut, 1800s, 60 x 43 x 18 In. 1610.00
Cabinet, Jewelry, Black Lacquer, Chinoiserie, Gilt, England, 13 x 13 x 7 In. 1495.00
Cabinet, Jewelry, Lacquer, Drawers Over Doors, Gilt, Scenic, 18 x 15 1/2 x 7 1/2 In. 345.00
Cabinet, Jewelry, Victorian, Rosewood, Inlaid Mother-Of-Pearl Berries, Vines, 16 In. 895.00
Cabinet, Jewelry, Victorian, Rosewood, Mother-Of-Pearl Inlay, 17 x 17 x 11 In. 1208.00
Cabinet, Johnson Brothers, Mahogany, Burl, 4 Doors, 70 x 20 x 33 In. 4900.00
Cabinet, Kingwood, 3 Drawers, Galleried Top, 29 x 20 x 10 In., Pair 130.00
Cabinet, Limbert, Somnoe, Square Top, Drawer, Lower Shelf, 16 x 16 x 29 In. 2990.00
Cabinet, Liquor, Queen Anne Style, Burl Walnut, Bonnet Top, c.1900, 50 x 24 1/2 In. 865.00
Cabinet, Louis XV Style, Chinoiserie, Black Lacquer, 61 x 34 1/2 x 14 1/2 In. 3107.00
Cabinet, Louis XV Style, Gilt Bronze Mounted, 4 Doors, 37 x 98 x 23 In. 3285.00
Cabinet, Louis XV Style, Mahogany, Domed Cornice, Carved, 70 x 26 In. 2300.00
Cabinet, Louis XVI Style, Kingwood, Gilt Bronze Mounted, c.1900, 54 x 24 In. 1495.00

Cabinet, Louis XVI Style, Mahogany, Gilt Brass, Lacquer, Drawers, 41 x 83 x 18 In. 5520.00
Cabinet, Louis XVI Style, Oak, Walnut, Marquetry, Bowfront, 19 x 14 x 33 In. 575.00
Cabinet, Louis XVI, Mahogany, Marquetry, Oval, Bronze Mounted, 34 x 35 x 23 In. 390.00
Cabinet, Louis XVI, Painted, Faux Marble, Doors, Shelves, c.1800, 33 x 40 x 24 In. 6613.00
Cabinet, Mahogany, 12 Drawers, Late 19th Century, 33 x 20 x 13 In. 1265.00
Cabinet, Mahogany, Beveled Crown, Glass Doors, American, 1850 .... 1840.00
Cabinet, Mahogany, Faux Stack Of Books, England, 25 x 15 x 12 In., Pair 546.00
Cabinet, Mahogany, Sycamore, Gilt, Door, Shelves, 39 x 50 x 17 In. 8365.00
Cabinet, Majorelle, Walnut, Wrought Iron, Macassar Ebony, c.1900, 68 x 38 In. 31070.00
Cabinet, Marquetry, Marble Top, France, c.1850, 44 x 34 In. 3140.00
Cabinet, Marquetry, Ormolu Mounted, Glazed Doors, Mid 1800s, 43 x 16 x 45 In. 1259.00
Cabinet, Marquetry, Spice Chest Shape, Strap-Hinged Door, 14 x 16 x 8 In. 1150.00
Cabinet, McCobb, Mahogany, Bifold Doors, Drawers, Shelf, 48 x 19 x 35 In. 560.00
Cabinet, McCobb, Maple, Grasscloth Sliding Doors, Drawers, 60 x 19 x 32 In. 529.00
Cabinet, Molded Cornice, 2 Shelves, Doors, Stile Feet, 76 x 54 x 17 In. 4670.00
Cabinet, Music, G. Stickley, Mahogany, Inlaid Top Over Panel Door, 48 x 20 In. 9400.00
Cabinet, Music, G. Stickley, No. 70, Amber Glass Panes, 48 x 20 In. 10575.00
Cabinet, Napoleon III, Ebonized Wood, Marquetry, 44 x 50 x 16 In. 1495.00
Cabinet, Napoleon III, Ebonized, Marble Top, Door, Ormolu, Late 1800s, 42 x 32 In. 4370.00
Cabinet, Napoleon III, Gilt Brass Mounted, Paris Porcelain Inset, 47 x 70 x 18 In. 8625.00
Cabinet, Napoleon III, Kingwood, Rosewood, Marble Top, Drawer, 40 x 40 x 18 In. 3680.00
Cabinet, Napoleon III, Mahogany, Kingwood, Marble Top, 1870s, 48 x 32 x 17 In. 2530.00
Cabinet, Neoclassical, Mahogany, Late 19th Century, 34 3/8 x 19 3/4 x 19 In. 575.00
Cabinet, Neoclassical, Mahogany, Stepped Cornice, c.1850, 67 x 48 x 18 In. 1840.00
Cabinet, Neoclassical, Maple, Gilt, Marble, Continental, 34 x 48 In. 6900.00
Cabinet, Oak, 12 Drawers, Glass Slides, Keystone View Co., 20 x 21 x 17 In. 345.00
Cabinet, Oak, Carved Cornice, Continental, Early 1800s, 52 x 34 x 24 In. 1840.00
Cabinet, Oak, Curved Front, Lion's Head, Claw Feet, c.1910, 39 x 30 x 19 In. 750.00
Cabinet, Oak, Inlaid, 2 Sections, 2 Glazed Over 2 Paneled Doors, 87 x 49 In. 5600.00
Cabinet, Oak, Mahogany Veneer, Boulle, Ormolu, 33 x 16 x 44 In. 980.00
Cabinet, Oak, Painted, England, Late 19th Century, 79 x 32 x 19 In. 260.00
Cabinet, Oriental, Hardwood, Metal Mounted, Double Doors, 57 1/2 x 40 x 28 In. 290.00
Cabinet, P. Evans, Bronze, Bifold Doors, Shelf, Slate Inserts, 84 x 21 x 31 In. 4115.00
Cabinet, Phipps & Wynn, Harbor Scene, Drawers, Arched Doors, 57 x 21 In. .... *Illus* 3335.00
Cabinet, Pietra Dura Inlay, Women In Garden, 2 Doors, 1900s, 30 1/2 x 22 In. 230.00
Cabinet, Pine, 2 Doors, 3 Shelves, Drawer, 19th Century, 44 x 28 In. 219.00
Cabinet, Pine, 3 Drawers, Raised, Door, Continental, 45 x 33 x 18 In. 224.00
Cabinet, Pine, Painted, 3 Drawers, Doors, Continental, 1800s, 38 x 36 x 22 In. 380.00
Cabinet, Queen Anne Style, Mahogany, Veneer, Tombstone Doors, 39 x 16 x 74 In. 545.00
Cabinet, Regency, Japanned, Lacquered, Drawer, Gilt Birds, 36 x 33 x 18 In. 1610.00
Cabinet, Regency, Mahogany, 4 Grilled Doors, Paw Feet, 1800s, 37 x 60 x 13 In. 3220.00
Cabinet, Regency, Mahogany, Pedestal, Ormolu Mounted Frieze, 38 x 19 x 16 In. 2185.00
Cabinet, Regency, Rosewood, Brass Mounted, Early 1800s, 34 x 35 1/4 x 12 In. 6610.00
Cabinet, Renaissance Revival, Marquetry, c.1875, 55 x 66 x 21 In. 9400.00
Cabinet, Renaissance Revival, Rosewood, Marquetry, Ebonized, 52 x 31x 18 In. 3680.00
Cabinet, Rohde, Mahogany, 2 Doors, Wooden Knobs, Shelf, 40 x 17 x 42 In. 1765.00
Cabinet, Rohde, No. 3624, Bedroom Group, Herman Miller, 43 x 18 x 36 In., Pair 4600.00

Furniture, Cabinet,
Phipps & Wynn,
Harbor Scene,
Drawers, Arched
Doors, 57 x 21 In.

Furniture, Cabinet,
Southern Heart Pine,
Molded Crown, 4 Doors,
1850s, 81 In.

Cabinet, Rohde, No. 4140, Herman Miller, 1940s, 45 x 18 In., Pair 5175.00
Cabinet, Russel Wright, 6 Drawers, Conant & Ball, c.1950, 32 1/2 x 48 x 20 In. 825.00
Cabinet, Sheraton Style, Satinwood Veneer, Paneled, 29 x 13 1/2 x 14 In., Pair 1115.00
Cabinet, Sheraton Style, Satinwood, Painted, 20th Century, 35 x 52 x 22 In. 2940.00
Cabinet, Smoking, G. Stickley, No. 89, Drawer, Iron Hardware, 20 x 14 x 29 In. 5875.00
Cabinet, Southern Heart Pine, Molded Crown, 4 Doors, 1850s, 81 In. .... *Illus* 2530.00
Cabinet, Spanish Style, Pine, Fir, Dentil Molding, 78 x 53 x 27 In. 400.00
Cabinet, Spice, Hanging, Oak, 6 Drawers, Rolling Pin Drawer, 14 x 18 In. 495.00
Cabinet, Spice, Pine, 5 Drawers, Square Pulls, 11 x 10 x 5 In. 190.00
Cabinet, Stereo, G. Nakashima, Walnut, Hinged Top, c.1960, 18 x 62 x 20 In. 2629.00
Cabinet, Teak, Drawers, Fold-Up Glass Doors, Wicker Baskets, 40 x 53 x 17 In. 375.00
Cabinet, Teak, Ivory & Ebony Inlay, Lift Top, Drawer, 2 Doors, c.1900, 26 x 24 In. 400.00
Cabinet, Teak, Molded Top, 3 Doors, 2 Shelves, Early 1900s, 67 x 50 x 17 In. 235.00
Cabinet, Teak, Molded Top, Door, Shelves, Base, 51 x 24 x 17 In. 411.00
Cabinet, Teak, Stepped, Glass Doors, Drawers, Wicker, 83 x 49 x 19 In. 460.00
Cabinet, Victorian, Ormolu, Jasperware, Gilt, Burl Inlay, Mirror, 41 x 65 x 17 In. 2300.00
Cabinet, Walnut, 3 Shelves, Drawers, Molded Crown, Continental, 1800s, 73 x 49 In. 2185.00
Cabinet, Walnut, Carved, 2 Doors, Bottom Drawer, Bracket Feet, Italy, 36 x 27 In. 750.00
Cabinet, Walnut, Parquetry, Triangular Pediment, Glazed Door, Ball Feet, 21 x 14 In. 510.00
Cabinet, Walter Teague, Lacquered Wood, Metal, Hastings, c.1939, 37 x 16 In. 3300.00
Cabinet, William IV, Mahogany, Doors, Shelves, Ogee Frieze Drawers, 75 x 30 In. 1645.00
Cabinet, Wood, Red Lacquer, 2 Drawers, Chinese, 73 x 36 x 22 In., Pair 2185.00
Cabinet, Wormley, Walnut, Bifold Doors, 2 Shelves, Dunbar, 32 x 20 x 29 In. 920.00
Cabinet-On-Stand, Burl Walnut, Inlaid, 24 Drawers, Thumbnail Edge, 41 x 46 In. 1725.00
Cabinet-On-Stand, Chinoiserie, Lacquer, Figures, Landscape, 75 x 45 In. 2570.00
Cabinet-On-Stand, Georgian Style, Mahogany, Glass Doors, 92 x 36 x 21 In. 635.00
Cabinet-On-Stand, Georgian Style, Mahogany, Sliding Doors, 48 x 53 x 20 3/4 In. 550.00
Cabinet-On-Stand, Mahogany, 2 Glazed Panel Doors, Claw & Ball Feet, 81 x 54 In. 1265.00
Cabinet-On-Stand, Mjolby Intarsia, 2 Doors, Folk Figures Inlay, c.1940, 57 x 47 In. 2870.00
Cabinet-On-Stand, Queen Anne, Mahogany, 2 Doors, Drawer, 63 x 36 In. 920.00
Cabinet-On-Stand, Renaissance Revival, Rosewood, Ivory Inlay, 56 x 34 x 15 In. 4585.00
Cabinet-On-Stand, Victorian, Mahogany, 10 Shallow Drawers, 41 x 19 In. 980.00
Cabinet-On-Stand, Walnut, Ebony, 2 Doors, Drawers, 17th Century, 17 In. 2350.00
Cabinet-On-Stand, William & Mary, Ash, Burl Walnut Inlay, Doors, Drawers, 54 In. 1955.00
Caddy, Flatware, Cherry, Carved Handle, Casket Shape, Early 1800s, 10 x 13 x 9 In. 375.00
Candlestand, Arts & Crafts, Brass, Hammered, 4 Strap Legs, 13 x 42 In. 1115.00
Candlestand, Birch, Square Top, Red Paint, Early 1800s, 29 x 17 1/2 x 18 In. 2015.00
Candlestand, Butternut, Maple, Octagonal Top, Tripod Base, 28 x 17 In. 1530.00
Candlestand, Cherry, Birch, Square, Ring Turned, Snake Feet, 25 x 14 In. 430.00
Candlestand, Cherry, Drawer, Round Top, Birdcage, Early 1800s, 28 x 19 In. 1880.00
Candlestand, Cherry, Red Wash, Turned Column, Tripod, 14 x 14 x 28 In. 230.00
Candlestand, Cherry, Round Top, Ball & Urn Post, Arched Legs, 1800s, 26 x 19 1/4 In. ... 235.00
Candlestand, Cherry, Tilt Top, Square, Bulbous Shaft, 3 Arched Feet, 28 x 19 x 20 In. 805.00
Candlestand, Cherry, Urn Pedestal, Square, Snake Head Feet, 27 x 16 x 16 1/2 In. 529.00
Candlestand, Chippendale Style, Curly Maple, Dish Top, Tilt Top, 25 3/4 x 29 1/2 In. 155.00
Candlestand, Chippendale, Cherry, Cabriole Legs, Snake Feet, Urn Shape Column, 26 In. . 750.00
Candlestand, Chippendale, Cherry, Poplar, Ring-Turned Column, 16 x 26 In. 375.00
Candlestand, Chippendale, Mahogany, Hexagonal Top, 3-Part Column, 42 In., Pair 2090.00
Candlestand, Chippendale, Mahogany, Serpentine Tilt Top, Tripod Base, 29 x 28 In. 4115.00
Candlestand, Chippendale, Maple, Octagonal Top, Urn Column, Snake Feet, 28 In. 690.00
Candlestand, Chippendale, Tilt Top, Mahogany, Vase Shape Column, 26 x 29 In. 575.00
Candlestand, Chippendale, Walnut, Dish Tilt Top, Cabriole Legs, 27 In. 920.00
Candlestand, Federal, Birch, Inlaid, Tilt Top, Tripod Base, 29 In. 5758.00
Candlestand, Federal, Birch, Red Stain, Round Tilt Top, c.1810, 29 x 14 x 22 In. 3820.00
Candlestand, Federal, Birch, Tripod, Arched Legs, N.H., 1800-20, 27 x 14 In. 4888.00
Candlestand, Federal, Brown Paint, Round Top, Tapered Legs, Early 1800s, 30 x 20 In. ... 1410.00
Candlestand, Federal, Cherry, Cabriole Legs, Snake Feet, c.1810, 26 1/2 x 14 3/4 In. 800.00
Candlestand, Federal, Cherry, Conn. River Valley, c.1800, 26 3/4 x 14 In. 1200.00
Candlestand, Federal, Cherry, Dish Top, Birdcage, Spider Legs, 27 x 17 3/4 In. 4830.00
Candlestand, Federal, Cherry, Dish Top, Tapered Urn Shaft, Snake Legs, 28 x 16 In. 690.00
Candlestand, Federal, Cherry, Inlaid Border, Ring-Turned Post, Tripod, 27 x 15 In. 1115.00
Candlestand, Federal, Cherry, Oval Corners, New England, c.1800, 27 x 17 x 17 In. 1058.00
Candlestand, Federal, Cherry, Oval Tilt Top, Early 19th Century, 28 In. 380.00

Candlestand, Federal, Cherry, Rosehead Nails, Iron Spider, Tripod, 27 x 2 3/8 In. 545.00
Candlestand, Federal, Cherry, Shaped Top, Turned Shaft, 28 3/4 x 23 x 17 1/2 In. 240.00
Candlestand, Federal, Cherry, Square Top, Drawer, Tripod, c.1800, 29 1/2 x 17 In. 430.00
Candlestand, Federal, Cherry, Tilt Top, New England, c.1810, 27 x 15 x 20 3/4 In. 558.00
Candlestand, Federal, Cherry, Wavy Edges, Tripod, Cabriole Legs, 26 x 18 In. 2940.00
Candlestand, Federal, Flowers, Black Over Red Paint, Tripod, c.1800, 26 x 16 In. 2115.00
Candlestand, Federal, Mahogany, 3 Tiers, Urn Shaft, Cabriole Legs, Tripod Base, 43 In. . . 7640.00
Candlestand, Federal, Mahogany, Cabriole Legs, Carved Knees, c.1800, 28 x 18 In. 1725.00
Candlestand, Federal, Mahogany, Oval Tilt Top, Ring-Turned Post, 28 In. 8815.00
Candlestand, Federal, Mahogany, Rectangular, New England, c.1800, 27 x 18 x 20 In. . . . 940.00
Candlestand, Federal, Mahogany, Tilt Top, Tripod Base, c.1790, 28 x 16 x 22 In. 3820.00
Candlestand, Federal, Mahogany, Tilt Top, Turned Post, Tripod, 1700s, 28 x 17 In. 8815.00
Candlestand, Federal, Maple, Cherry, Birch, Square, New England, c.1810, 28 x 15 In. . . . 1440.00
Candlestand, Federal, Maple, Oval Top, New England, Early 1800s, 27 x 16 1/2 In. 7800.00
Candlestand, Federal, Maple, Round Top, Tripod, New England, c.1790, 24 In. 175.00
Candlestand, Federal, Maple, Square Top, New England, c.1775, 25 1/2 x 16 x 17 In. 1440.00
Candlestand, Federal, Tiger Maple, Inlaid, Octagonal, 29 x 14 x 19 In. 3290.00
Candlestand, Federal, Tilt Top, Oval, 3 Snake Feet, 27 3/4 In. 660.00
Candlestand, Federal, Walnut, Adjustable, Late 18th Century, 32 In. 777.00
Candlestand, Federal, Walnut, Oval, Tilt Top, Vase Standard, 3 Legs, 30 x 24 x 14 In. 978.00
Candlestand, Federal, Walnut, Tilt Top, Tripod Pedestal, 28 x 18 x 16 In. 978.00
Candlestand, Federal, Yellow Paint, Square Top, Scalloped Skirt, 29 x 12 x 12 In. 805.00
Candlestand, George III Style, Mahogany, Octagonal Top, Tripod Base, 16 In. 168.00
Candlestand, George III, Mahogany, Piecrust Top, Cabriole Legs, c.1800, 29 x 17 In. 518.00
Candlestand, Gilt Wood, Carved, 19th Century, 27 In., Pair 805.00
Candlestand, Hepplewhite, Birch, Cherry, Cabriole Legs, 20 x 18 x 26 In. 145.00
Candlestand, Hepplewhite, Birch, Red Wash, Tapered Legs, 18 x 19 x 30 In. 690.00
Candlestand, Hepplewhite, Cherry, Banded Mahogany, Tilt Top, 28 x 21 x 16 In. 1325.00
Candlestand, Hepplewhite, Curly Maple, New England, 1800-10, 28 In. 3500.00
Candlestand, Hepplewhite, Curly Maple, Paint, Gold Trim, Octagonal, 21 x 27 In. 3335.00
Candlestand, Hepplewhite, Mahogany, Oval Tilt Top, c.1800, 29 x 24 x 16 In. 1035.00
Candlestand, Hepplewhite, Maple, Octagonal Top, Tripod Base, 29 x 20 x 14 1/2 In. 260.00
Candlestand, Hepplewhite, Maple, Spider Base, Urn Column, 16 x 17 x 29 In. 400.00
Candlestand, Laminated Hardwood, Square Top, Shaped Legs, 16 x 15 1/2 x 30 In. 375.00
Candlestand, Mahogany, 1-Board Top, Urn Shaft, 3 Arched Legs, 27 x 18 In. 1840.00
Candlestand, Mahogany, Dish Tilt & Turn Top, Baluster Shaft, Philadelphia 2600.00
Candlestand, Mahogany, Dish Top, Urn Support, Tripod, 20th Century, 21 x 16 In. 80.00
Candlestand, Mahogany, Tilt Top, Snake Legs, 1700s, 27 x 21 In. 1000.00
Candlestand, Mahogany, Tilt Top, Tripod Base, N.Y., c.1820, 30 x 18 x 23 In. 705.00
Candlestand, Maple, Cherry, Dish Top, Round Platform Base, 14 x 27 In. 345.00
Candlestand, Maple, Green Paint, Spider Base, Vase-Shape Column, 28 In. 2990.00
Candlestand, Maple, Pine, Octagonal, Red Paint, New England, Late 1700s, 27 x 17 In. . . 645.00
Candlestand, Maple, Square Top, Shaped Corners, Snake Feet, 27 x 16 x 17 In. 605.00
Candlestand, Maple, Tilt Top, Early 19th Century, 19 x 16 3/4 x 28 In. 325.00
Candlestand, Neoclassical, Mahogany, Tilt Top, Tripod Base, c.1825, 28 x 20 In. 325.00
Candlestand, Neoclassical, Rectangular Top, Ring-Turned Standard, 1800s 410.00
Candlestand, Nutting, No. 21, Maple, Whirling, Block Brand 1405.00
Candlestand, Oak, Pine, Round Top, Shelf, Tripod, Splayed Legs, 27 x 15 1/2 In. 920.00
Candlestand, Oriental, Cast Metal, Lily Pad Dish Top, Lion's Heads, 35 x 16 In., Pair 460.00
Candlestand, Pine, Beveled Corners, Octagonal Top, 15 x 12 x 25 In. 575.00
Candlestand, Pine, Stained, Round Top, Dish Molded, Tripod, c.1800, 27 x 14 1/2 In. 325.00
Candlestand, Prairie School, 4 Mid-Body Spindles, Square Base & Top, 30 In. 265.00
Candlestand, Queen Anne Style, Mahogany, Dish Top, Tripod, 29 1/2 x 18 1/2 In. 575.00
Candlestand, Queen Anne Style, Mahogany, Tilt Top, 20th Century, 26 1/2 In. 130.00
Candlestand, Queen Anne Style, Pine, Scroll Feet, Turned Column, 13 x 24 In. 460.00
Candlestand, Queen Anne, Birch, Cherry, Snake Feet, 15 x 15 x 26 In. 315.00
Candlestand, Queen Anne, Cherry, Square Top, Tripod Base, c.1775, 28 x 17 x 16 In. 940.00
Candlestand, Queen Anne, Cherry, Tilt Top, Cabriole Legs, c.1770, 27 1/2 x 18 In. 1095.00
Candlestand, Queen Anne, Cherry, Tilt Top, Pedestal Base, Pad Feet, 29 x 24 In. 880.00
Candlestand, Queen Anne, Cherry, Tilt Top, Ring-Turned Pedestal, Cabriole Legs, 27 In. . 1410.00
Candlestand, Queen Anne, Grain Painted, New England, c.1775, 27 x 17 x 17 In. 590.00
Candlestand, Queen Anne, Mahogany, Dish Top, Birdcage, c.1760, 29 x 23 In. 8050.00
Candlestand, Queen Anne, Mahogany, Dish Top, Birdcage, c.1790, 28 x 19 In. 6900.00

Candlestand, Queen Anne, Mahogany, Tilt Top, 20 1/8 x 19 x 28 In. 2415.00
Candlestand, Queen Anne, Mahogany, Tilt Top, Birdcage, Pa., c.1760, 28 x 21 In. 2400.00
Candlestand, Queen Anne, Round Top, Tripod Legs, New England, c.1795, 27 x 17 In. . . . 1840.00
Candlestand, Queen Anne, Walnut, Dish Top, Birdcage, Pennsylvania, 28 3/4 x 19 In. 7475.00
Candlestand, Queen Anne, Walnut, Dish Top, Tripod Legs, c.1760, 27 1/2 x 23 In. 11350.00
Candlestand, Queen Anne, Walnut, Tilt Top, Round, c.1775, 28 x 20 In. 940.00
Candlestand, Shaker, Cherry, Round Top, Snake Legs, c.1840, 26 x 18 1/2 In. 1150.00
Candlestand, Tiger Maple, Oblong Tilt Top, Tripod Base, Early 1800s, 28 In. 1530.00
Candlestand, Walnut, Mahogany, Tilt Top, Urn-Turned Pedestal, 26 x 18 x 18 In. 60.00
Candlestand, Walnut, Marquetry, Tripod, Cabriole Legs, Italy, 28 1/2 x 19 3/4 In. 230.00
Candlestand, Walnut, Oblong Top, Tripod Base, Arched Legs, 1800s, 25 1/2 In. 265.00
Candlestand, Walnut, Tilt Top, Round, Dish Molded, 18th Century, 28 In. 1880.00
Candlestand, Walnut, Tilt Top, Vase Pedestal, New England, 1800s, 27 x 19 In. 705.00
Candlestand, Windsor, Hickory, Red Paint, Candle Socket, 3 Turned Legs, 36 In. 2990.00
Candlestand, Windsor, Pine, Birch, Green Paint, Platform Base, 12 x 24 In. 230.00
Candlestand, Wrought Iron, 31 Holders, Miraculous Medal Plaque, 113 In. 1725.00
Canterbury, Eastlake, Walnut, Bird's-Eye Maple, Carved, 22 x 14 1/2 In. 230.00
Canterbury, George III, Mahogany, Drawer Base, Castors, 19 In. 3565.00
Canterbury, George III, Mahogany, Late 18th Century, 15 x 19 x 13 In. 600.00
Canterbury, Mahogany, Marquetry, Rose Stencil, Bellflowers, 18 x 11 x 29 In. 65.00
Canterbury, Neoclassical, Mahogany, Carved, c.1830, 19 x 22 x 15 In. 720.00
Canterbury, Regency Style, Mahogany, 4 Compartments, Drawer, 24 x 19 In. 430.00
Canterbury, Victorian, Mahogany, Pierced Scrolled Panels, 17 x 18 x 13 In. 125.00
Canterbury, Victorian, Rosewood, Fretwork, Drawer, Lyre Support, 36 x 20 x 14 In. 430.00
Cart, Bar, Johnson Co., Flip Top, Laminate, Doors, Drawer, 42 x 30 In. 1410.00
Cart, Sewing, Wegner, Teak, Birch, Lift Top, Rattan Basket, Denmark, 23 x 16 x 23 In. . . . 530.00
Cassone Chest, Walnut, Women In Relief, Iron Strap Hinges, Lid, 24 x 66 x 21 In. 430.00
Cellarette, Arts & Crafts, Pullout Copper Shelf, 2 Doors, 24 x 16 x 42 In. 805.00
Cellarette, George III, Mahogany, Handles, Stand, Molded Legs, 28 x 17 x 12 In. 1530.00
Cellarette, George III, Mahogany, Lozenge, Brass Bound, 24 In. 6845.00
Cellarette, George III, Mahogany, Satinwood, Stand, Hinged Lid, 26 x 25 x 15 In. 1380.00
Cellarette, Mahogany, Ebonized, Pictorial Pottery Plaque, 31 x 18 x 15 In. 8965.00
Cellarette, Mahogany, Stand, Hinged Top, Late 1800s, 42 x 22 x 17 In. 1035.00
Cellarette, Pine, Applied Molding, 12 Bottles, Strap Hinges, Lift Top, 29 x 19 x 15 In. 400.00
Cellarette, Regency, Mahogany, Gilt Bronze, Egyptian Details, c.1805, 20 x 29 In. 7200.00
Cellarette, Regency, Mahogany, Paneled, Tapered Sides, Casters, 24 x 27 x 19 In. 4370.00
Cellarette, Walnut, Inlay, Butt Hinges, Kite Escutcheon, Shoebox Lid, 42 x 18 In. 8250.00
Chair, Aalto, Birch, Bentwood, Wool Upholstery, Label, ICF, 40 In. . . . . *Illus* 380.00
Chair, Aalto, Tank, Birch Sides, Original Tiger Skin Upholstery, 28 x 30 In. . . . . *Illus* 3055.00
Chair, Aesthetic Revival, Mahogany, Carved, Marquetry, c.1900, 37 x 26 x 24 In. 145.00
Chair, Aluminum, Wood Base, Upholstered, 1960s, 25 x 30 x 28 In., Pair 1035.00
Chair, American Restauration, Gondola, Mahogany, Padded Back, Seat, 31 In., Pair 1035.00
Chair, Architect's, Molded Plywood, Steel, Adjustable, c.1965 . . . . 100.00
Chair, Arne Jacobsen, Egg, Fiberglass, Aluminum, Fritz Hansen, Denmark, 40 In. 2000.00
Chair, Arne Jacobsen, No. 3105, Fritz Hansen, c.1955, 30 1/2 x 16 x 19 In., Pair 400.00
Chair, Arne Jacobsen, Teak, Molded Plywood, Chrome Bent Tubular Steel, 1955 . . . . 120.00
Chair, Art Deco, Beech, Leather Upholstery, France, c.1930, 32 In., Pair 6000.00
Chair, Art Nouveau, Mahogany, Carved, Throne, Arms, c.1905, 46 In. 7768.00
Chair, Art Nouveau, Walnut, Carved, Square Back, Arched Crest, France, Pair 329.00
Chair, Art Nouveau, Walnut, Leather Upholstery, Arms, Austria, c.1900, 31 1/4 In. 600.00
Chair, Arts & Crafts, Oak, Leather, Brass, England, 1900s, 39 x 17 1/2 x 20 In., Pair 210.00
Chair, B. Mathsson, Eva, Birch, Fiber Webbing, Dux International, 24 x 27 x 33 In. 690.00
Chair, Baker Furniture, Regency Style, Painted, Black Lacquer, Gilt, Arms, 33 In., Pair . . . 1150.00
Chair, Bamboo, Fretwork Splat, Chinese, 19th Century, 38 x 22 x 21 In., Pair 635.00
Chair, Banister Back, Arms, New England, Child's 3675.00
Chair, Banister Back, Black Paint, Rush Seat, Arms, 18th Century 825.00
Chair, Banister Back, Black Paint, Splint Seat, Ring & Baluster Legs, 41 In. 489.00
Chair, Banister Back, Black Paint, Woven Rush Seat, Scalloped Crest, 43 In. 805.00
Chair, Banister Back, Black Paint, Woven Splint Seat, Arched Crest, 42 In., Pair 1322.00
Chair, Banister Back, Turned Legs, Scalloped Crest, Rush Seat, Arms, 44 1/2 In. 690.00
Chair, Baroque Style, Upholstered, Carved Arms, Scrolled Legs, Arms, Pair 1175.00
Chair, Baroque, Walnut, Carved, Needlework Upholstery, Open Arms, 43 In., Pair 8625.00
Chair, Bergere, Beidermeier Style, Maple, Sweden, Pair 720.00

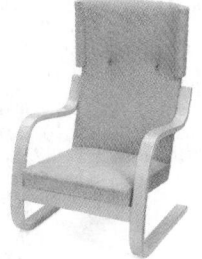

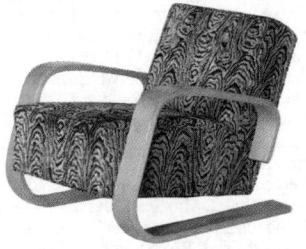

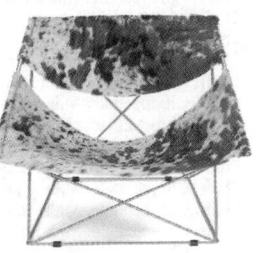

Furniture, Chair, Aalto, Birch,
Bentwood, Wool Upholstery,
Label, ICF, 40 In.

Furniture, Chair, Aalto, Tank,
Birch Sides, Original Tiger Skin
Upholstery, 28 x 30 In.

Furniture, Chair, Lounge, Paulin,
No. 675, Cowhide, Rod Base,
Artifort, 30 x 26 In.

Chair, Bergere, Louis Philippe, Walnut, Bowed Seat, 1800s, 40 In. 2760.00
Chair, Bergere, Louis XV Style, Fruitwood, Green Paint, Upholstered, Pair 2030.00
Chair, Bergere, Louis XV Style, Upholstered, 1900s, 40 x 27 In. 325.00
Chair, Bergere, Louis XV Style, Walnut, Needlework, 45 x 27 x 31 In. 1610.00
Chair, Bergere, Louis XV, Painted, Carved Crest Rail, Early 1800s, 37 In. 2760.00
Chair, Bergere, Louis XV, Painted, Scrolling, Crewel Work, 43 In., Pair 3335.00
Chair, Bergere, Louis XV, Walnut, Padded, Early 1800s, 48 In. 2185.00
Chair, Bergere, Louis XVI Style, Gilt, Upholstered, 1800s 805.00
Chair, Bergere, Louis XVI Style, Painted, Gilt, Square Back, Pair 5975.00
Chair, Bergere, Louis XVI Style, Painted, Ivory, Gilt, 39 x 27 In., Pair 1035.00
Chair, Bergere, Louis XVI Style, Upholstered, Painted, Padded Arms, Pair 2270.00
Chair, Bergere, Louis XVI, Beech, Carved, Padded Back, 31 In., Child's 920.00
Chair, Bergere, Louis XVI, Gilt, Aubusson Upholstery, Pair 4185.00
Chair, Bergere, Louis XVI, Gilt, Cushioned Cane Seat, Pair 4830.00
Chair, Bergere, Regency, Mahogany, Mid 1800s, 23 In., Child's 800.00
Chair, Bergere, Wood, Venice, Italy, Late 1800s, 30 1/4 In., Pair 4370.00
Chair, Biedermeier, Ash, Padded Back, Seat, Arms, Early 1800s, 39 In., Pair 2760.00
Chair, Biedermeier, Birch, Gilt, Ebony Accents, Arms, 36 In., Pair 2530.00
Chair, Biedermeier, Fruitwood, Concave Crest, Scalloped Edge, Overupholstered, Pair 940.00
Chair, Biedermeier, Fruitwood, Concave, Carved Rail, 19th Century, 35 In., Pair 1035.00
Chair, Biedermeier, Fruitwood, Ebonized, Fan Splat, Open Arms, Padded Seat, Pair 1075.00
Chair, Biedermeier, Mahogany, Upholstered, Arms, 34 x 26 x 27 In., Pair 765.00
Chair, Biedermeier, Walnut, Crescent Back, Round Seat, c.1820 . . . . 520.00
Chair, Biedermeier, Walnut, Landscape Needlepoint Upholstery, Scrolling, 37 In. 230.00
Chair, Biedermeier, Walnut, Leaf-Carved Crest, Cane Seat, Arms, c.1815, 34 In., Pair 1380.00
Chair, Birch, Old Red Paint, Woven Splint Seat, 3 Arched Slats, 37 In. 86.00
Chair, Black Paint, 4 Arched Back Slats, Arms, Delaware Valley, 43 In. 4313.00
Chair, Black Paint, Banister Back, Arms, N.Y., c.1875, 46 In. 9000.00
Chair, Brown, 5 Arched Back Slats, Ball Turnings, Arms, Delaware Valley, 45 In. 5175.00
Chair, Bugatti, Vellum Cover, Pewter Inlays, Copper Banding, c.1900 . . . . 7475.00
Chair, Bugatti, Wood, Vellum Covered, Inlaid, c.1902, 66 x 29 x 25 In. 9560.00
Chair, C. Malmsten, Mahogany, Ebonized Birch, Upholstered, c.1924, 32 In., Pair 4200.00
Chair, Carved Crest Rail, Upholstered, Arms, 19th Century, 40 x 27 x 36 In. 70.00
Chair, Cast Iron, Brass, Square Seat, Arms, 21 x 16 In. 430.00
Chair, Cesare Leonardi, CL 9, Ribbon, Fiberglass, Chromed Metal, c.1961, 23 In., Pair . . . 4780.00
Chair, Charles II, Oak, Carved Crest Rail, Flowers, c.1660, 36 1/2 In. 5400.00
Chair, Cherry, Rush Seat, Serpentine Crest Rail, Late 18th Century, 39 1/4 In., Pair 825.00
Chair, Chinoiserie, Decorated Leather, Continental, 18 In., Child's 777.00
Chair, Chippendale Style, Leather Upholstery, Open Arms, Pair 460.00
Chair, Chippendale Style, Mahogany, Cabriole Legs, Ball, Claw Feet, 41 In., Pair 920.00
Chair, Chippendale Style, Mahogany, Carved, 33 In. 90.00
Chair, Chippendale Style, Mahogany, Pierced, Carved Splat, Arms, 38 In., Pair 805.00
Chair, Chippendale Style, Mahogany, Ribbonback, Leather Seat, Tacks, 37 x 18 In. 230.00
Chair, Chippendale Style, Mixed Hardwood, Scroll Splat, Spanish Feet, 40 In. 430.00
Chair, Chippendale Style, Shaped Back, Arms, 20th Century, 40 x 28 x 32 In. 590.00

Chair, Chippendale, Black Paint, Rush Seat, Square Legs, Mass., 1700s, 36 3/4 In., Pair . . . 590.00
Chair, Chippendale, Cherry, Fan Carved, Mass., Late 1700s, 38 In., Pair 1765.00
Chair, Chippendale, Curved Crest, Arms, Delaware River Valley, 1700s, 41 In. 5875.00
Chair, Chippendale, Mahogany, Carved, New York, c.1790, Pair 1410.00
Chair, Chippendale, Mahogany, Curved Crest, Carved, Owl Splats, 38 In., Pair 4115.00
Chair, Chippendale, Mahogany, Curved Crest, Gothic Splat, c.1775 . . . . .865.00 to 1150.00
Chair, Chippendale, Mahogany, Eared Crest, Vase-Shape Splat, Ireland, 38 In., Pair 10925.00
Chair, Chippendale, Mahogany, Leaf-Carved Crest, Padded, Arms, 40 In., Pair 1725.00
Chair, Chippendale, Mahogany, Pierced Splat, Cabriole Legs, c.1770 . . . . 2070.00
Chair, Chippendale, Mahogany, Pierced Splat, Serpentine Arms, c.1790 . . . . 3680.00
Chair, Chippendale, Mahogany, Pierced Splat, Slip Seat, Mass., 1760-90, 37 In. 825.00
Chair, Chippendale, Mahogany, Ribbonback, Shaped Crest Rail, Mid 1700s 5875.00
Chair, Chippendale, Mahogany, Scrolled Crest, Box Stretcher, 37 In. 115.00
Chair, Chippendale, Mahogany, Serpentine Crest Rail, Cabriole Legs, c.1785, Pair 8050.00
Chair, Chippendale, Mahogany, Serpentine Crest Rail, Open Arms, 18th Century 1765.00
Chair, Chippendale, Mahogany, Serpentine Crest, Boston, c.1765, 38 x 17 1/2 In. 4995.00
Chair, Chippendale, Mahogany, Slip Seat, Curved Crest, Rhode Island, 1700s, 39 In. 590.00
Chair, Chippendale, Mahogany, Slip Seat, Needlepoint Tapestry Upholstery, c.1770 . . . . . . 1495.00
Chair, Chippendale, Mahogany, Yellow Pine Slip Seat, Pa., c.1780, 38 In., Pair 2100.00
Chair, Chippendale, Maple, Shaped Crest, Slip Seat, Square Legs, Mass., c.1780, 39 In. . . . 175.00
Chair, Chippendale, Ribbonback, Plank Seat, Saddle Carved, Arms, 36 1/2 In. 520.00
Chair, Chippendale, Serpentine Crest, Upholstered, Late 1700s, 45 x 32 x 18 In. 3055.00
Chair, Chippendale, Walnut, Philadelphia, c.1760, 38 1/2 In. 4800.00
Chair, Chippendale, Yew, Chamfered Back, Stretcher Base, 38 In., Pair 430.00
Chair, Christopher Maier, Egyptian Style, Mahogany, Gilt, Carved, 34 In. 690.00
Chair, Club, Art Deco, Leather Upholstery, Arms, Early 20th Century, 29 In., Pair 2530.00
Chair, Club, Art Deco, Leather Upholstery, Arms, Early 20th Century, 33 In. 1095.00
Chair, Club, Art Deco, Leather Upholstery, Arms, Early 20th Century, 34 In., Pair 1840.00
Chair, Club, Art Deco, Leather, Distressed Buff, Dark Piping, Early 1900s, 31 In., Pair 2990.00
Chair, Club, Frank Lloyd Wright, Taliesin, Upholstered, Heritage Henredon 1265.00
Chair, Club, Knoll, Wood, Steel, 24 x 32 x 32 In., Pair 225.00
Chair, Club, Leather Upholstery, France, c.1930, Pair 260.00
Chair, Club, Leather, Brass Tacks, Scalloped Back, Bun Feet, 28 x 40 x 33 In., Pair 4025.00
Chair, Colombo, ABS, Black, Kartell, c.1965, 28 1/2 x 17 In., Pair 175.00
Chair, Colonial Revival, Rosewood, Ivory Mounted, Reclining, Arms, 35 x 20 x 23 In. 2760.00
Chair, Contemporary, Iron, Leather Seat, Arms, 36 x 20 x 18 In., Pair 295.00
Chair, Corner, Bamboo, Latticework, Woven Seat, Painted Geometrics, 32 In. 259.00
Chair, Corner, Chinese Chippendale, Mahogany 69.00
Chair, Corner, Chippendale Style, Mahogany, Carved, 33 In. 175.00
Chair, Corner, Chippendale Style, Mahogany, Claw & Ball Feet, 33 In. 259.00
Chair, Corner, Chippendale Style, Mahogany, Solid Splats, Drop Seat, c.1875 . . . . 880.00
Chair, Corner, George III Style, Mahogany, Padded Seat, Mid 1800s, 34 In. 635.00
Chair, Corner, Hardwood, Pierced, Carved Backrest, Chinese, Late 1800s, 37 In. 200.00
Chair, Corner, Mahogany, Carved, Slip Seat, Upholstered, Paw Feet, 18 x 33 In. 230.00
Chair, Corner, Mahogany, Slip Seat, Continuous Arms, Late 18th Century 645.00
Chair, Corner, Maple, Rush Seat, Turned Legs, 31 In. 345.00
Chair, Corner, Queen Anne, Black & Gold, Shaped Rail, Rush Seat, 28 In. 520.00
Chair, Corner, Queen Anne, Maple, Early 18th Century 2270.00
Chair, Corner, Walnut, Carved, 20th Century, 33 x 23 In. 130.00
Chair, Curly Maple, 2 Arched Slats, Turned Posts, Splint Seat, 35 In. 259.00
Chair, E. Gaillard, Rosewood, Carved, Upholstered, c.1910, 37 In., Pair . . . . . . .5020.00 to 6575.00
Chair, Eames, Aluminum, Tufted Leather, Wool, Swivel Base, 27 x 35 In. 470.00
Chair, Eames, DCM, Herman Miller, c.1945, 29 1/2 x 19 1/4 x 21 In. 190.00
Chair, Eames, DCM, Herman Miller, c.1945, 29 1/2 x 19 1/4 x 21 In., Pair 410.00
Chair, Eames, DCW, Plywood 235.00
Chair, Eames, DKR-1, Herman Miller, 31 x 21 x 19 In. 235.00
Chair, Eames, LCM, Walnut, Herman Miller, c.1945 . . . . 325.00
Chair, Eames, LCW, Evans Products, c.1946, 25 1/2 x 22 x 23 In. 1295.00
Chair, Eames, PKW, Wire Seat, Herman Miller, 1949, 19 x 21 x 31 In. 1440.00
Chair, Eames, PKW-1, Postman's Bag Leather, Herman Miller, c.1951 . . . . 1000.00
Chair, Eames, PKW-2, Dowel Legs, Herman Miller, c.1952 . . . . 1115.00
Chair, Eames, Plywood, Black Aniline, Shock Mounts, c.1950, 22 x 25 x 27 In. 875.00
Chair, Eames, Time-Life, Aluminum, Upholstered, Herman Miller, 29 x 27 x 33 In. 2415.00

Chair, Eames, Walnut, Plywood, Molded, Shock Mounts, 22 x 25 x 26 1/2 In. 1060.00
Chair, Eastlake, Walnut, Adjustable Back Support, Cane Seat, 33 1/2 In. 92.00
Chair, Eastlake, Walnut, Brown Leather, Arms, 36 3/4 x 22 1/4 x 19 In. 35.00
Chair, Eastlake, Walnut, Cane Back, Arms, c.1880, 37 In., Pair 175.00
Chair, Edwardian, Green, Leather Upholstery, Lobed Backrest, Child's 1175.00
Chair, Edwardian, Satinwood, Banded Crest, X-Shape Splat, Arms, c.1900, 31 In. 1150.00
Chair, Edwardian, Satinwood, Shield Back, Cane Seat, Arms, c.1900, 37 In., Pair 2760.00
Chair, Eero Saarinen, Grasshopper, Upholstered, Knoll, 1950s, 26 In., Pair 2300.00
Chair, Eero Saarinen, No. 72, Knoll, 1948, 22 x 20 x 32 In., Pair 235.00
Chair, Eero Saarinen, Tulip, Fiberglass, Aluminum, Wood, Knoll, 32 x 25 x 25 In. 150.00
Chair, Eero Saarinen, Womb, Fiberglass, Tubular Steel, Upholstered, c.1947 . . . . 605.00
Chair, Eileen Gray, Bibendum, Arms, Classicon, c.1929, 28 1/2 x 38 x 33 In. 1060.00
Chair, Elephant, Tropical Wood, Carved, 43 x 24 In., Pair 250.00
Chair, Empire Style, Mahogany, Carved, Scrolls, Acanthus, 1890s, 39 x 28 x 27 In. 430.00
Chair, Empire Style, Mahogany, Eared Crest, Round Back, Leather, Arms, 38 In., Pair 1150.00
Chair, Empire Style, Mahogany, Ebonized, Gilt, Upholstered, Arms, Pair 360.00
Chair, Empire Style, Mahogany, Ormolu Mounted, Padded, c.1850, 36 In. 345.00
Chair, Empire Style, Mahogany, Upholstered Seat, Swan-Form Arms, c.1875 . . . . 805.00
Chair, Empire, Polychrome, Backswept Leaf-Carved Crest, Early 1800s, 35 In. 1725.00
Chair, Esherick, Walnut, Arms, 1959, 32 In., Pair 5020.00
Chair, European Birch, Curved Back, Ebonized Swan Head, 27 In. 1090.00
Chair, Federal, Mahogany, Carved, c.1800, 35 1/2 In. 480.00
Chair, Federal, Mahogany, Carved, New York, Early 19th Century, Pair 7170.00
Chair, Federal, Mahogany, Maple, Arched Crest, Upholstered, c.1820, 47 x 17 In. 4115.00
Chair, Federal, Mahogany, Maple, Birch, Upholstered, Open Arms, Mass., c.1800, 44 In. . . . 5750.00
Chair, Federal, Mahogany, Maryland, 1790-1810, 33 1/2 In., Pair 2870.00
Chair, Federal, Mahogany, Plume-Carved Center Panel, Early 19th Century 590.00
Chair, Federal, Mahogany, Scrolled Arms, Tapered Legs, c.1830, Pair 750.00
Chair, Federal, Mahogany, Shieldback, Massachusetts, c.1805 . . . . 460.00
Chair, Federal, Mahogany, Shieldback, Philadelphia, c.1800, Pair 825.00
Chair, Federal, Mahogany, Square Back, Rosette Corners, New York, c.1805, 36 In. 2115.00
Chair, Federal, Mahogany, Turned, Striped Upholstery, New England, c.1810, 41 In. 3000.00
Chair, Federal, Mahogany, Upholstered, Arms, New York, 1810-20 . . . . 3585.00
Chair, Federal, Mahogany, Upholstered, c.1800, 44 In. 5975.00
Chair, Federal, Maple, Ebony, Flat Crest Rail, Arms, c.1820, 32 1/2 In. 2940.00
Chair, Federal, Maple, Upholstered, c.1790, 43 x 28 x 30 In. 5875.00
Chair, Federal, Red Paint, Instrument & Ribbon Backrest, Rush Seat, 35 In., Pair 3910.00
Chair, Federal, Walnut, Carved, Shieldback, Wheatear Splats, c.1800, 39 In. 185.00
Chair, Finn Juhl, Chieftain, Teak, Leather, Baker Furniture, 40 x 35 x 38 In. 8050.00
Chair, Fledermaus, Beech, Leather Upholstery, Austria, c.1906, 28 3/4 In., Pair 4800.00
Chair, Florence Knoll, Chocolate Leather, Arms, c.1948, 29 x 30 x 30 In., Pair 2645.00
Chair, Folding, Marco Zanuso, 1951, 29 1/2 In. 1435.00
Chair, French Provincial, Fruitwood, Open Back, Padded Seat, 36 In. 230.00
Chair, French Provincial, Oak, 3-Slat Back, Rush Seat, 16 1/2 x 32 5/8 In. 115.00
Chair, French Provincial, Walnut, Cane, Mortise & Peg, Stretcher, 17 x 37 In. 375.00
Chair, French Provincial, Walnut, Carved, Cane Back, Arms, 1800s, 36 x 24 x 19 In. 1035.00
Chair, French Provincial, Walnut, Upholstered, Open Arms, c.1885, 48 x 30 x 29 In. 2300.00
Chair, Fruitwood, Woven Reeded Seats, Italy, Mid 20th Century, Pair 300.00
Chair, G. Nakashima, High, Walnut, 4 Legs, Arms, c.1969, 32 3/8 In., Pair 4185.00
Chair, G. Nakashima, Walnut, Arms, c.1959, 30 1/2 In. 4185.00
Chair, G. Nakashima, Walnut, Hickory, Cushion, Arms, Widdicomb, 36 x 26 In., Pair 3525.00
Chair, G. Nelson, DAF, Herman Miller, c.1958, 28 x 28 1/2 x 21 In. 825.00
Chair, G. Nelson, No. 5569, Coconut, Herman Miller, 1955, 40 x 33 x 32 In. 2940.00
Chair, G. Nelson, Perch, Aluminum, Flat Steel, Herman Miller, c.1964 . . . . 345.00
Chair, G. Stickley, Drop-In Cushions, Through Tenon, Arms, 42 x 29 x 30 In. 940.00
Chair, G. Stickley, H-Back, Leather Seat, 17 x 16 x 30 In. 325.00
Chair, G. Stickley, Morris, 5 Vertical Side Slats, Rope Seat, 36 In. 3500.00
Chair, G. Stickley, Morris, Als I Kan Decal, 32 1/2 x 30 In. 1295.00
Chair, G. Stickley, Morris, Mahogany Spindles, Sling Seat, 39 x 30 1/2 x 36 In. 4115.00
Chair, G. Stickley, No. 310, Ladder Back, 3 Slats, 25 x 22 x 34 In. 150.00
Chair, G. Stickley, No. 312, V-Back, 5 Back Slats, Leather Seat, Arms, 36 x 26 x 21 In. . . . 880.00
Chair, G. Stickley, No. 324, Mahogany, Slats, Arms, 29 x 30 x 39 In. 1115.00
Chair, G. Stickley, No. 330, Wide Arm Slats, Cushion, 29 x 30 x 39 In. 1725.00

Chair, G. Stickley, No. 335, Cube, Even Arms, 18 Slats, Leatherette Cushions 7050.00
Chair, G. Stickley, No. 344, 3 Slats, Leather Seat, Arms, 18 x 14 x 26 In., Child's 59.00
Chair, G. Stickley, No. 354 1/2, 5 Slats, Recovered Seat, 19 x 17 x 36 In. 1295.00
Chair, G. Stickley, No. 356, Leather Seat, 36 1/2 x 19 x 18 1/2 In. 1410.00
Chair, G. Stickley, No. 362, Leather Seat, Back, Swivel Base, 18 x 26 x 33 In. 2350.00
Chair, G. Stickley, No. 369, Morris, 6 Side Slats, 38 x 33 x 37 1/2 In. . . . . .5875.00 to 7050.00
Chair, G. Stickley, No. 384, Oak, Spindles, c.1907, 46 In. 3585.00
Chair, G. Stickley, No. 386, 29 Vertical Spindles, 28 x 23 x 49 In. 4410.00
Chair, G. Stickley, No. 390, 24 Vertical Arm Spindles, 38 x 29 x 30 In. 5875.00
Chair, G. Stickley, No. 819, 3 Horizontal Back Slats, Leather Seat, Arms 1530.00
Chair, G. Stickley, No. 1292, U-Back, 4 Vertical Slats, Cushion, 24 x 23 x 35 In. 1000.00
Chair, G. Stickley, No. 1295, Leather Seat & Back, 33 x 19 1/2 x 17 In. 1295.00
Chair, G. Stickley, No. 2582, Mahogany, Arms, c.1901, 39 x 29 x 24 In. 590.00
Chair, G. Stickley, No. 2604, Ladder Back, 3 Slats, Arms, 25 x 27 x 36 In. 645.00
Chair, G. Stickley, Tall, V-Back, 26 x 21 x 54 In. 7480.00
Chair, G. Stickley, V-Back, Leather Seat, Arms, 36 x 26 x 20 1/2 In. 940.00
Chair, G. Stickley, Vertical Slats, Arms, 25 x 23 x 39 In. 295.00
Chair, G. Summers, Curved Back, Padded Seat, Arms, c.1934, 26 x 18 x 18 In. 7640.00
Chair, George I, Gilt, Upholstered, Lenygon & Co., Pair 5400.00
Chair, George II Style, Burl Walnut, Arched Back, Leather Slip Seat, 42 3/4 In., Pair 805.00
Chair, George II Style, Mahogany, Padded Back, Seat, Carved Arms, 38 In. 1035.00
Chair, George II, Walnut, Inlaid, Trapezoid Seat, Italy, c.1740, Pair 750.00
Chair, George III Style, Mahogany, Carved, Leather Slip Seat, Late 1800s, 41 In., Pair 635.00
Chair, George III Style, Mahogany, Leather, Open Arms, c.1900, 38 1/4 x 25 1/4 In. 175.00
Chair, George III Style, Mahogany, Padded & Domed Back, Late 1800s, 40 In., Pair 1035.00
Chair, George III Style, Marlborough, Mahogany, Padded Back, Early 1900s, 38 In. 175.00
Chair, George III Style, Oval Back, Upholstered, Carved Open Arms, 1900s 345.00
Chair, George III, Mahogany, Arched Top, Pierced Splat, Upholstered, c.1790 . . . . 260.00
Chair, George III, Mahogany, Carved & Pierced Back, c.1765 . . . . 9600.00
Chair, George III, Mahogany, Coat Of Arms, Fluted Legs, 36 x 18 1/4 x 20 In. 920.00
Chair, George III, Mahogany, Leaf-Carved Crest, Owl-Eye Splat, Pair 2350.00
Chair, George III, Mahogany, Pierced Ladder Back, Late 1700s, 36 In. 520.00
Chair, George III, Mahogany, Shieldback, Arms, c.1790 . . . . 800.00
Chair, Georgian Style, Beech, Shaped Top Rail, Upholstered, Arms, 35 In., Pair 345.00
Chair, Georgian Style, Mahogany, Carved, Eagle Heads, Arms, Pair 1175.00
Chair, Georgian Style, Mahogany, Elm, Carved, Strapwork Splat, Arms, 39 In. 690.00
Chair, Georgian Style, Mahogany, Slip Seat, Pierced Splat, Arms, 40 3/4 In., Pair 1955.00
Chair, Georgian Style, Mahogany, Waved Crest Rail, Upholstered Seat, Pair 315.00
Chair, Gilt, Flower-Carved Crest Rail, Arms, Italy, Late 1800s, Pair 865.00
Chair, Gilt, Painted, Carved, Continental, 38 In., Pair 635.00
Chair, Gilt, Upholstered, Scroll, Floral Crest Rail, Arms, 37 x 72 x 32 In., Pair 259.00
Chair, Gothic Revival, Cast Iron, Openwork Back, Shaped Seat, 36 In., Pair 1265.00
Chair, Gothic Revival, Mahogany, Arms, Early 20th Century, 44 In. 230.00
Chair, Gothic Revival, Rosewood, Shaped Crest, Mid 19th Century, 44 In., Pair 4370.00
Chair, Gothic Revival, Walnut, Openwork, Hinged Plank Seat, Victorian, Pair 175.00
Chair, Gothic Revival, Walnut, Trefoil Cutouts, Beaded Seat Rail, 49 In., Pair 1035.00
Chair, Gothic Revival, Walnut, Upholstered, Trefoils, c.1865, 44 In. 460.00
Chair, Grain Painted, Freehand Decorations, Vase Splat, Conn., c.1775, 39 In., Pair 1295.00
Chair, H. Bertoia, Diamond, Chromium, Wool, Knoll, c.1975, 30 1/2 x 33 x 29 In. 325.00
Chair, H. Bertoia, Diamond, Enameled Steel, 30 1/2 x 33 x 28 In. 180.00
Chair, Hans & Wassili Luckhardt, Arms, Thonet, c.1933, 29 x 24 x 21 In. 1175.00
Chair, Hardwood, Carved, Mother-Of-Pearl Inlay, Open Arms, Chinese, Pair 375.00
Chair, Hendrik Van Kepple & Taylor Green, Arms, c.1948, 30 x 20 1/2 In. 645.00
Chair, Hepplewhite Style, Mahogany, Shieldback, Upholstered, 37 In., Pair 290.00
Chair, Hepplewhite Style, Satinwood, Painted, Arms, Pair 800.00
Chair, Hepplewhite, Birch, Red Finish, Stretcher Base, 37 In. 290.00
Chair, Hepplewhite, Mahogany, Shieldback, Fan Inlay, 37 x 21 In. 400.00
Chair, Hepplewhite, Martha Washington, Mahogany, Brocade, Arms, 45 In. 3395.00
Chair, Heywood-Wakefield, Wicker, Cushion Seat, Continuous Arms, 43 In., Pair 1035.00
Chair, Hickory, Banister Back, Tulip & Scallop Crest, Rush Seat, 45 In. 520.00
Chair, Hitchcock Style, Plank Seat, Painted, Pin Striping, Stenciled, Pair 90.00
Chair, Huali Wood, Plain Ogee Splats, Straight Stiles, 39 In., Pair 1510.00
Chair, Hung Mu, Medallion Carved Bird, Prunus Back, Arms, Pair 690.00

Chair, Hunting, Oak, Leather, Sweden, c.1960, 21 x 31 x 30 In. 1295.00
Chair, Indian Red, 4 Arched Back Slats, Ball Feet, Arms, Delaware Valley, 44 In. 2015.00
Chair, Indian Red, 5 Arched Back Slats, Ball Feet, Arms, Delaware Valley, 44 In. .1725.00 to 5750.00
Chair, J.M. Young, Morris, 4 Vertical Arm Slats, Flat Arms, 37 x 30 1/2 x 36 1/2 In. 1530.00
Chair, J.M. Young, Morris, 5 Vertical Arm Slats, Through Tenon, 46 x 36 In. 940.00
Chair, J.M. Young, Morris, No. 186, 5 Vertical Slats, Flat Arms, 38 x 37 x 38 In. 3820.00
Chair, Jacobean Style, Mahogany, Padded Back, Seat, Arms, 53 1/2 x 26 x 23 In. 1035.00
Chair, Jacobean Style, Painted, Cane, Scroll Crest, Stretcher, Spanish Feet, 49 In. 60.00
Chair, Kem Weber, Airline, Walt Disney Label, c.1935, 31 x 25 x 32 In. 11750.00
Chair, Knoll, Chocolate Leather, 1948, 30 x 30 x 29 In., Pair 2645.00
Chair, Knoll, Steel, Leather, Arms, 32 x 23 1/2 x 21 In., Pair 2185.00
Chair, Kofod Larsen, Beech, Metal Frame, Leather, 29 x 21 x 24 In., Pair 529.00
Chair, Koloman Moser, Beech, Leather, Arms, c.1901, 38 x 21 x 19 In. 3900.00
Chair, L. & J.G. Stickley, Ladder Back, 3 Slats, Leather Seat, Arms, 39 x 26 In., Pair 2820.00
Chair, L. & J.G. Stickley, No. 408, Prairie, Slatted, Leather Seat, Arms, 32 x 27 In. 4400.00
Chair, L. & J.G. Stickley, No. 452, 3 Vertical Slats, Spring Seat, Flat Arms, 40 x 29 In. 1530.00
Chair, L. & J.G. Stickley, No. 471, Morris, Leather Seat, Flat Arms, 40 x 35 In. 3525.00
Chair, L. & J.G. Stickley, No. 471, Morris, Spring Seat, Flat Arms, 41 x 32 In. 4115.00
Chair, L. & J.G. Stickley, No. 750, 5 Slats, Leather Cushion, Arms, 28 x 22 x 39 In. 1145.00
Chair, Ladder Back, Arched Slats, Turned Posts, Stretchers, Bowed Arms, 42 In. 375.00
Chair, Ladder Back, Ball Finials, Rush Seat, Arms, 18th Century, 45 In. 60.00
Chair, Ladder Back, Birch, Hickory, Green Paint, Gold Flower Stenciling, 39 In. 60.00
Chair, Ladder Back, Brown Paint, Delaware Valley, 1700s, 44 1/4 In., Pair 7170.00
Chair, Ladder Back, Brown Paint, Rush Seat, Arms, N.J., c.1800s, 24 In., Child's 480.00
Chair, Ladder Back, Brown Paint, Turned Posts, Rush Seat, 45 In. 430.00
Chair, Ladder Back, Maple, 4 Arched Slats, Ball Finials, Rush Seat, Stretcher, 41 In. 230.00
Chair, Ladder Back, Maple, 5 Slats, Ball Finials, 51 1/2 In. 115.00
Chair, Ladder Back, Maple, Ash, Arms, New England, Late 1700s, 44 1/2 In. 1560.00
Chair, Ladder Back, Maple, Ash, Red Paint, Rush Seat, Arms, c.1725, 44 In. 2400.00
Chair, Ladder Back, Nutting, No. 390, S-Back, Pair 235.00
Chair, Ladder Back, Oak, Hickory, 3 Slats, Turned Posts, Rush Seat, 43 In. 400.00
Chair, Ladder Back, Oak, Maple, Rush Seat 130.00
Chair, Ladder Back, Paint Scraped To Sage Green, Reed Seat, Child's 7250.00
Chair, Ladder Back, Red Paint, 4 Arched Slats, Tapered Posts, Rush Seat, 42 In. 100.00
Chair, Ladder Back, Red Paint, Woven Splint Seat, Turned Finials, Arms, 13 x 42 In. 138.00
Chair, Ladder Back, Rush Seat, Turned Legs, Spindles, Arms, Pair 80.00
Chair, Ladder Back, Rush Seat, Turned Stretcher, Bun Feet, Arms, 16 x 45 1/2 In. 575.00
Chair, Ladder Back, Salmon Paint, 3 Slats, Rabbit-Ear Posts, Tape Seat, 36 In., Pair 1610.00
Chair, Ladder Back, Walnut, Ice Cream Cone Finials, Split Seat, 46 1/2 In., Pair 316.00
Chair, Leather, Brass Tacks, Shaped Skirts, 19th Century, 29 x 27 x 33 In. 3105.00
Chair, Leather, Steel, Chrome Plated, Tubular, Bent, 29 x 32 x 25 1/2 In. 1955.00
Chair, Lifetime, No. 129, T-Back, Leather Seat, Paper Label, 17 x 17 x 37 In. 235.00
Chair, Limbert, 3 Vertical Back Slats, Spring Cushion, Arms, 37 x 27 x 23 In. 530.00
Chair, Limbert, Morris, Spring Seat, Back Pillow, Flat Open Arms, 36 x 29 x 36 In. 3820.00
Chair, Limbert, No. 8201, 4 Vertical Back Slats, Drop-In Seat, 37 x 19 x 19 In. 2235.00
Chair, Lolling, Federal, Mahogany, Upholstered, Arms, c.1800 . . . . 1765.00
Chair, Lolling, George III, Mahogany, Brocade Upholstery, c.1800, 38 In. 1150.00
Chair, Lolling, Mahogany, Curved Flat Arms, Upholstered, 37 1/2 x 24 In. 2300.00
Chair, Louis Philippe, Marquetry, Arms, 37 In. 4830.00
Chair, Louis XIII, Walnut, Padded Back, Seat, Stretcher, Mid 1600s, 41 In., Pair 980.00
Chair, Louis XV Style, Beech, Needlepoint Tapestry, Arms, France, c.1920, Pair 750.00
Chair, Louis XV Style, Curved Top Rail, Scrolling Skirt, Downswept Arms, 45 In., Pair . . . 2070.00
Chair, Louis XV Style, Medallion Back, Victorian 185.00
Chair, Louis XV Style, Needlepoint Upholstery, Arms, 37 In., Pair 230.00
Chair, Louis XV Style, Polychrome, Scrolling Crest, Upholstered, 36 x 32 In. 2530.00
Chair, Louis XV Style, Upholstered, Arms, 20th Century, 35 x 26 x 22 In. 95.00
Chair, Louis XV Style, Walnut, Balloon Back, Arms, Victorian 220.00
Chair, Louis XV Style, Walnut, Cabriole Legs, Upholstered, Arms, 17 x 35 In. 345.00
Chair, Louis XVI Style, Arched Bow & Ribbon Crest Rail, c.1900, Pair 200.00
Chair, Louis XVI Style, Beech, Carved, Padded Seat, Back, Silk Upholstery 200.00
Chair, Louis XVI Style, Beech, Oval Backrest, Serpentine Seat, Upholstered 500.00
Chair, Louis XVI Style, Brown Paint, Carved, Fluted, Silk Upholstery, 44 In. 259.00
Chair, Louis XVI Style, Carved, Reeded Legs, Upholstered, Arms, 37 1/2 In. 750.00

Chair, Louis XVI Style, Gilt, Arched Top Rail, Upholstered, Arms, 43 In. 460.00
Chair, Louis XVI Style, Gilt, Medallion, Upholstered, Arms, c.1900, 40 In., Pair 1610.00
Chair, Louis XVI Style, Gilt, Padded Back, Arms, c.1900, 40 In., Pair 635.00
Chair, Louis XVI Style, Mahogany, Parcel Gilt, Upholstered, Arms, Late 1800s, 40 In. 4600.00
Chair, Louis XVI Style, Medallion Back, Gold Leaf, Upholstered, Arms, Pair 1035.00
Chair, Louis XVI Style, Polychrome, Arms, Mid 19th Century, 39 3/4 In., Pair 5290.00
Chair, Louis XVI Style, Polychrome, Padded, Arms, 36 1/4 In. 2760.00
Chair, Louis XVI, Cream Paint, Gilt, Carved, Silk Upholstery, 1 With Arms, Pair 750.00
Chair, Louis XVI, Padded, Scrolling Arms, Late 18th Century, 35 1/2 In., Pair 3680.00
Chair, Lounge, Aalto, No. 41, Paimio, Artek, c.1931, 26 x 32 In. 1880.00
Chair, Lounge, B. Mathsson, Canvas, Leather, Chromed Steel, Swivel, 22 x 39 In. 825.00
Chair, Lounge, Baker Furniture, Far East Collection, Upholstered, 1950s, 28 x 27 In. 1265.00
Chair, Lounge, Bartolucci & Waldeheim, Barwa, c.1946, 42 x 52 x 20 In., Pair 590.00
Chair, Lounge, Eames, Aluminum Group, High Back, Herman Miller, 35 x 30 In., Pair 765.00
Chair, Lounge, Eames, Mahogany, Plywood Seats, Legs, c.1949, 26 x 22 In. 1880.00
Chair, Lounge, Eames, No. 670, Herman Miller, 32 x 35 x 32 In. 1955.00
Chair, Lounge, Eames, Rosewood Plywood, Leather Cushions, 32 x 35 x 32 In. 1530.00
Chair, Lounge, Florence Knoll, Walnut, Tufted Wool Upholstery, 24 x 30 1/2 In. 150.00
Chair, Lounge, France & Son, Teak, Flared Arms, Upholstered, 1960, 27 x 30 In., Pair 825.00
Chair, Lounge, G. Nakashima, Walnut, 1 Arm, c.1962, 32 1/2 In. ....3100.00 to 5020.00
Chair, Lounge, Marco Zanuso, Regent, Arflex, Italy, c.1958, 32 x 35 In. 4400.00
Chair, Lounge, McCobb, Directional, Upholstered, Calvin, 26 x 30 x 37 In. 805.00
Chair, Lounge, McCobb, Mahogany, Upholstered, Calvin, 27 x 35 In. 1175.00
Chair, Lounge, McCobb, Tubular Brass, Mahogany, 27 x 25 x 21 In., Pair 1380.00
Chair, Lounge, Painted, Welded, Wire, Loose Leather Cushion, Swivel, c.1980 .... 225.00
Chair, Lounge, Paulin, No. 675, Cowhide, Rod Base, Artifort, 30 x 26 In. ....*Illus* 7640.00
Chair, Lounge, Plycraft, Bent Plywood, Steel, Leather, Tag, 27 x 26 1/2 x 26 In. 350.00
Chair, Lounge, Risom, Knoll, 1946, 24 x 27 x 29 1/2 In. 700.00
Chair, Lounge, Rosewood, Chromed Metal, Suede, Quistgaard, c.1965, 29 In., Pair 9560.00
Chair, Lounge, Victorian, Mahogany, Leather, Tufted Back, 41 x 26 x 30 In. 1150.00
Chair, Lounge, W. McArthur, Leather, Aluminum, Rolled Arms, 26 x 32 In. 1645.00
Chair, Lounge, W. Platner, No. 1725, Knoll, c.1966, 39 1/2 x 41 x 36 In. 1410.00
Chair, Lounge, Walter Lamb, Brown Jordan, c.1950, 30 x 24 x 28 In., Pair 3820.00
Chair, Lounge, Wegner, Wood, Cushion, c.1958, 28 1/2 x 26 1/2 x 29 In., Pair 1295.00
Chair, Lounge, Wormley, Mahogany, Sculpted Arms, Cane Sides, 26 x 28 In. 2000.00
Chair, Mahogany, Balloon Back, Late 19th Century, 35 In., Pair 145.00
Chair, Mahogany, Carved, Cane Splat, Continental, c.1900, 45 x 25 x 20 In. 175.00
Chair, Mahogany, Carved, Leaves, Eagle On Crest, Upholstered, Pair 940.00
Chair, Mahogany, Carved, Relief-Carved Leaves, Cabriole Legs, Pad Feet, 38 In. 400.00
Chair, Mahogany, Carved, Scrolled Leaf Carving, c.1880, 37 1/4 In. 405.00
Chair, Mahogany, Carved, Serpentine Seat, c.1900, 39 x 30 x 32 In. 290.00
Chair, Mahogany, Crest, Serpentine Seat, c.1880, 33 In. 105.00
Chair, Mahogany, Line Inlay, Satinwood Banding, Arms, c.1885, 37 In., Pair 3600.00
Chair, Mahogany, Open Back, Leaf, Flower, Silk Upholstery, 35 In., Pair 200.00
Chair, Mahogany, Pedestal Back, Horsehair Seat, c.1790, 38 1/4 In., Pair 590.00
Chair, Mahogany, Shaped Crest, Scrolling Arms, Hinged Cane Seat, 35 x 23 x 21 In. 750.00
Chair, Mahogany, Upholstered Back, Open Arms, 18th Century, 41 x 27 In. 2115.00
Chair, Majorelle, Aux Clematites, Mahogany, Carved, Arms, c.1905, 41 In., Pair 8965.00
Chair, Maple, 5 Arched Slats, Turned Posts & Legs, Rush Seat, 45 In. 4115.00
Chair, Maple, Ash, 5 Arched Back Slats, Arms, Delaware Valley, 47 In. 10350.00
Chair, Maple, Ash, Banister Back, Arms, New England, 1700s, 48 1/2 In. 1175.00
Chair, Maple, Ash, Slat Back, Connecticut, 1700s, 43 In. 705.00
Chair, Maple, Ash, Spindle Back, 19th Century, Pair 45.00
Chair, Maple, Banister Back, Yoked Crest, Splint Seat, Turned Stretchers, 43 In. 1175.00
Chair, Maple, Cane Seat, Harp-Shape Splats, Saber Legs, 33 In., Pair 575.00
Chair, Maple, Cane Seat, New York, c.1820, Pair 1380.00
Chair, Maple, Ladder Back, 4 Arched Slats, Arms, Delaware Valley, 44 1/2 In. 5175.00
Chair, Maple, Slat Back, Painted, Turned Stiles, Arms, Late 1700s, 21 In., Child's 2000.00
Chair, Marcel Breuer, Wassily, Chromed Steel, Leather, Italy, c.1925, Pair ....460.00 to 565.00
Chair, Marcel Breuer, Wassily, Knoll, c.1968, 29 x 31 In., Pair 765.00
Chair, Meeks, Rosewood, Laminated, Henry Ford Pattern, 43 x 17 x 18 In. 1900.00
Chair, Michel Dufet, Limed Oak, Cotton Upholstery, Arms, 32 x 23 In., 1930s, Pair 2390.00
Chair, Mies Van Der Rohe, Barcelona, Chromium, Leatherette, 1960s, 29 x 32 In. 700.00

Furniture, Chair, Paulin, No.
577, Tongue, Original Larsen
Stretch Jersey, 25 In.

Furniture, Chair,
Onondaga Shops, Morris,
Mahogany, 7 Slats,
38 1/2 x 31 1/2 In.

Chair, Mies Van Der Rohe, Barcelona, Knoll International, 30 x 30 In., Pair 4900.00
Chair, Mies Van Der Rohe, Barcelona, Leather, Steel, 1968, 30 x 30 In. 2350.00
Chair, Mies Van Der Rohe, Brno, Black, Knoll, c.1930, 31 x 23 x 24 In., Pair 1410.00
Chair, Mies Van Der Rohe, MR, Knoll, c.1926, 32 x 32 x 22 In., Pair 2115.00
Chair, Mies Van Der Rohe, MR20, Steel, Cane Seat, Stendig, c.1960, 32 In., Pair 1765.00
Chair, Mixed Wood, Plank Seat, Medallion Back, Pencil-Post Legs, 33 x 35 In. 260.00
Chair, Moravian, Pierced Heart, Splayed Legs, 18th Century, 34 x 16 x 13 In. 230.00
Chair, Moravian, Walnut, Plank Seat, Scrolled Edge, Cutout Heart, Tapered Legs, 35 In. .. 1870.00
Chair, Napoleon III, Rosewood, Medallion Back, Upholstered, Arms, 39 1/2 In., Pair 800.00
Chair, Neoclassical, Birch, Scrolled Crest, Padded Seat, Arms, Sweden, 33 In., Pair 4140.00
Chair, Neoclassical, Cane Seat, Shaped Crest Rail, Turned Legs, 1800s, 32 In., Pair 35.00
Chair, Neoclassical, Carved Flower Crest, Oval Back, Arms, Italy, Pair 5500.00
Chair, Neoclassical, Mahogany, Curved Crest & Splat, Gadroon Trim, 33 In., Pair 1175.00
Chair, Neoclassical, Painted, Gilt, Ivory, Versace Velvet, Arms, Russia, Pair 1554.00
Chair, Neoclassical, Painted, Tapestry Upholstery, 19th Century, Pair 4670.00
Chair, Neoclassical, Tiger Maple, Paw Feet, New York, Early 19th Century 3585.00
Chair, Niedecken, Solid Seat, Diagonal Support, c.1912, 33 x 20 In. 2000.00
Chair, Nielsen, Laminex, Beech, 2 Sections, 21 1/4 x 30 x 27 1/2 In. 650.00
Chair, Nutting, No. 473, Martha Washington, Chippendale, Upholstered, Arms 935.00
Chair, Nutting, No. 493, Maple, Rush Seat, Arms, 25 x 47 In. ....700.00 to 850.00
Chair, Oak, Architectural Detailing, Flat Seat, England, c.1885, 36 5/8 In., Pair 345.00
Chair, Oak, Ash, High Back, c.1900, 41 In. 230.00
Chair, Oak, Bentwood, 2 Tiers Of Spindles, Arms, 45 1/2 x 20 1/2 x 32 1/2 In. 520.00
Chair, Oak, Carved, 19th Century, 40 x 27 x 25 In. 705.00
Chair, Oak, Carved, Arms, France, c.1800, 34 In. 635.00
Chair, Oak, Carved, Wainscot, Arms, England, Late 1800s, 59 x 23 x 26 In. 545.00
Chair, Oak, Northwind Crest, Scroll Arms, 50 1/2 In. 80.00
Chair, Onondaga Shops, Morris, Mahogany, 7 Slats, 38 1/2 x 31 1/2 In. ....*Illus* 2115.00
Chair, Papier-Mache, Black Lacquer, Mother-Of-Pearl Inlay, Cane Seat, c.1865, 33 In. 920.00
Chair, Papier-Mache, Black Lacquer, Multicolored, Girls, Dog, Cane Seat, Pair 295.00
Chair, Papier-Mache, Black Lacquer, Spoon Back, Sleeping Girl, Dog, Cane Seat 120.00
Chair, Papier-Mache, Ebonized Finish, Gilt, Shell Inlay, 31 x 17 x 17 In. 265.00
Chair, Paulin, No. 577, Tongue, Original Larsen Stretch Jersey, 25 In. ....*Illus* 4750.00
Chair, Pesce, Pratt, Urethane, Molded, N.Y., 1984, 36 In. 7200.00
Chair, Plail Bros., Barrel Back, Drop-In Spring Seat, Arms, 32 In. 2470.00
Chair, Plank, Yellow, Fruit Basket, 31 In., Pair 750.00
Chair, Poul Kjaerholm, Leather, Steel, Arms, 1958, 27 In. 1435.00
Chair, Prairie School, 9 Spindles, Tall Back, Leather, 48 In. 1725.00
Chair, Pretzel Back, Philadelphia, 1770-80, Pair 5875.00
Chair, Pugin, Gothic Revival, Leather Upholstery, Arms, c.1840 .... 765.00
Chair, Queen Anne Style, Fruitwood, Crest Rail, Arms, Continental, c.1900, 45 In., Pair ... 978.00
Chair, Queen Anne Style, Maple, Baluster Arms, Rush Seat, Block Legs, 44 In. 375.00
Chair, Queen Anne Style, Maple, Vase-Shape Splat, Arms, 26 In., Child's 230.00
Chair, Queen Anne Style, Painted Trim, Flowers, Upholstered Seat, 41 In., Pair 145.00
Chair, Queen Anne Style, Walnut, Padded Back, Pad Feet, 43 x 26 In., Pair 1265.00
Chair, Queen Anne Style, Walnut, Scrolled Knees, Slip Seat, 42 In., Pair 575.00
Chair, Queen Anne Style, Walnut, Shaped Back, Crook Arms, Cushion Seat, 36 In. 489.00
Chair, Queen Anne, Black Japanned, Chinoiserie, Cane Panels, Seat 1475.00
Chair, Queen Anne, Black Paint, Splint Seat, Sausage-Turned Legs, Arms, 47 3/4 In. 290.00

Chair, Queen Anne, Burl Walnut, Cresting, Baluster Splat, Pad Feet, Pair 4400.00
Chair, Queen Anne, Cherry, Carved Shaped Crest, Rush Seat, c.1775, 42 In. 1175.00
Chair, Queen Anne, Mahogany, Inlaid, Vase-Form Back, Upholstered Seat, Dutch 800.00
Chair, Queen Anne, Mahogany, Pierced Splat, Mid-Atlantic, c.1770, 39 In. 3900.00
Chair, Queen Anne, Maple, Ash, Red Wash, Banister Back, c.1740, Pair 570.00
Chair, Queen Anne, Maple, Fussell Slavery School, Philadelphia, 1700s, 41 In. 5020.00
Chair, Queen Anne, Maple, Hickory, Banister Back, Rush Seat, Arms, 43 In. 290.00
Chair, Queen Anne, Maple, New England, c.1760, 41 In., Pair 9000.00
Chair, Queen Anne, Maple, Poplar, Sausage-Turned Legs, Stretcher, 39 In. 259.00
Chair, Queen Anne, Maple, Rush Seat, Turned Stretchers, c.1730, 40 x 36 x 20 In. 800.00
Chair, Queen Anne, Maple, Slip Seat, Boston, c.1760, 39 In. 4700.00
Chair, Queen Anne, Maple, Turned Vase Back, New England, c.1775, 40 x 17 In. 560.00
Chair, Queen Anne, Pumpkin Paint, Splint Seat, Serpentine Arms, 19 x 46 In. 520.00
Chair, Queen Anne, Square Back, Upholstered, Hoof Feet, Arms, 39 In. 3795.00
Chair, Queen Anne, Stretchers, Rush Seat, Sausage-Turned Legs, Arms, 46 In. 1035.00
Chair, Queen Anne, Vase-Form Splat, 18th Century, 37 x 17 1/2 In. 460.00
Chair, Queen Anne, Walnut, Baluster-Turned Legs, Upholstered Seat & Back, 41 In. 175.00
Chair, Queen Anne, Walnut, Brown, Pennsylvania, c.1750, 40 1/2 In. 5700.00
Chair, Queen Anne, Walnut, Carved, Pennsylvania, c.1750, 40 In.   9000.00
Chair, Queen Anne, Walnut, Serpentine Crest Rail, Cabriole Front Legs, c.1760 . . . .   4600.00
Chair, Queen Anne, Walnut, Serpentine Crest, Slip Seat, Mass., c.1750, 37 3/8 In. 825.00
Chair, Queen Anne, Walnut, Shell-Carved Crest, Knees, Trifid Feet, c.1765 . . . .   4140.00
Chair, Queen Anne, Walnut, Vase-Shape Back, Cabriole Legs, Pad Feet, 19 In. 2010.00
Chair, Queen Anne, Walnut, Yoked Crest, Upholstered Seat, Boston, c.1760, 40 In. 590.00
Chair, Regency Style, Cane Sides & Back, Damask Upholstery, England 460.00
Chair, Regency Style, Carved, Gilt, Upholstered, Pair 3820.00
Chair, Regency Style, Ebonized, Lyre Back, Upholstered, Open Arms, Pair 2185.00
Chair, Regency Style, Fruitwood, Flat Back, Upholstered, Arms, c.1850, 45 In. 1725.00
Chair, Regency Style, Mahogany, Upholstered, Early 1900s, 36 1/2 x 31 x 29 In. 405.00
Chair, Regency, Faux Rosewood, Applied Uprights, 19th Century, 34 1/2 In., Pair 3450.00
Chair, Regency, Mahogany, Square Back, Canted Corners, Cartouche, Plank Seat, Pair 1910.00
Chair, Regency, Mahogany, Turned Stiles, Reeded Outstretched Arms 200.00
Chair, Renaissance Revival, Oak, Upholstered, Arms, Pair 330.00
Chair, Renaissance Revival, Rosewood, Marquetry, N.Y., c.1865, 37 3/4 In. 865.00
Chair, Renaissance Revival, Walnut, Carved Masques, Upholstered, Italy, 48 In., Pair 2300.00
Chair, Renaissance Revival, Walnut, Scrolled, Carved, Plank Seat, Pair 500.00
Chair, Richard Riemerschmid, Beech, Arms, c.1900, 33 x 23 5/8 x 18 1/2 In. 2700.00
Chair, Risom, Walnut, Leather Upholstery, Closed Arms, 31 x 23 In., Pair . . . . *Illus*   500.00
Chair, Rocker, is listed under Rocker in this category.
Chair, Rococo Revival, Rosewood, Laminated, Carved, Upholstered, 1800s, 36 In. 635.00
Chair, Rococo Revival, Rosewood, Laminated, Upholstered, c.1850, 44 In. 5520.00
Chair, Rococo Revival, Walnut, Balloon Back, Upholstered Seat, 19th Century, Pair 60.00
Chair, Rococo Revival, Walnut, Carved, Upholstered, Arms, 1860-75 . . . .   239.00
Chair, Rod Back, Bamboo Turned, 32 In., Child's 129.00
Chair, Rosewood, Carved, Chinese, 19th Century 200.00
Chair, Rosewood, Gilt, Carved Crest, Tapestry Upholstery, 38 In., Pair 2015.00
Chair, Roycroft, Morris, Leather, 4 Arm Slats, 40 x 30 x 38 In. 3820.00
Chair, Roycroft, Straddle, Leather Seat, 34 1/4 x 24 x 22 In. 2000.00

Furniture, Chair, Risom, Walnut, Leather
Upholstery, Closed Arms, 31 x 23 In., Pair

Push your antique sofa against a
wall if the back is slightly loose.
Large friends won't be able to sit
down with a thud against the
weak back.

Chair, Rush Seat, 4 Arched Back Slats, Spire Feet, Arms, Delaware Valley, 45 In. 1725.00
Chair, Rush Seat, Arms, Continental, 19th Century, Child's 140.00
Chair, Scalloped Crest Rail, 2-Panel Back, Plank Seat, Arms, c.1670, 43 1/2 In. 3000.00
Chair, Shaker, Birch, Splint Seat, Tilters, Enfield, N.H., c.1835, 41 In. 2530.00
Chair, Shaker, Cherry, 3 Slats, Rush Seat, Tilters, Watervliet, N.Y., c.1840, 41 In. 1610.00
Chair, Shaker, Maple, 2 Slats, Cane Seat, Harvard, Mass., c.1840, 29 1/2 In., Child's 1035.00
Chair, Shaker, Maple, Birch, Pine, Revolving, Mt. Lebanon, c.1865, 28 x 19 In. 8225.00
Chair, Shaker, No. 3, Maple, Shawl Bar, Tape Seat, Mt. Lebanon, N.Y., c.1880, 33 In. 800.00
Chair, Shaker, No. 6, 4 Arched Slats, Tape Seat, Mt. Lebanon, 40 1/2 In. 1725.00
Chair, Shaker, Weaver's, Maple, Oak, 2 Slats, Tape Seat, Mt. Lebanon, c.1835, 42 In. 1035.00
Chair, Sheraton Style, Mahogany, Cane Seat, Silk Cushion, Pair 3525.00
Chair, Sheraton Style, Mahogany, Faux Leather Upholstery, Scrolled Arms, 34 In. 430.00
Chair, Sheraton Style, Plank Seat, 5-Spindle Back, Shaped Crest, 10 1/2 x 23 In. 60.00
Chair, Sheraton, Mahogany, Scrolled Arms, 32 1/2 In., Pair 400.00
Chair, Sleigh, All Metal Frame, Seat, Victorian, 31 x 41 In. 50.00
Chair, Slipper, Aesthetic Revival, V-Shape Crest, Openwork, Carved Legs 470.00
Chair, Slipper, Victorian, Faux Bamboo, Gilt Paint, Upholstered 720.00
Chair, Slipper, Victorian, Scrolled Back, Upholstered, Tapered Square Legs, Pair 500.00
Chair, Stickley & Brandt Co., Cutout Back Slats, Spring Seat, Arms, 37 x 30 In. 2820.00
Chair, Stickley Bros., No. 405 1/2, Oak, 5 Back Slats, Black Stencil 230.00
Chair, Teak, Mahogany, Carved, Pierced, Elephant Crest, Cushion, 33 In., Pair 290.00
Chair, Tete-A-Tete, Louis XVI Style, Gilt, Aubusson Needlepoint, c.1890, 42 x 43 In. 2300.00
Chair, Troubadour Style, Fruitwood, Inlaid, Russia, Late 1800s, 38 In., Pair 1840.00
Chair, Tub, Louis Philippe, Mahogany, Back Scroll Crest, Mid 1800s, 32 In. 750.00
Chair, Tub, Louis Philippe, Mahogany, Molded, Padded Back, 1800s, 31 In. 1265.00
Chair, Tub, Regency Style, Faux Rosewood, Upholstered, Arms, 34 In., Pair 2185.00
Chair, Tub, William IV Style, Mahogany, Curved Back, Scrolled Legs, 35 1/2 In. 1955.00
Chair, V. Panton, Baydur, Molded, Vitra, c.1968, 31 x 18 1/2 x 24 In., Pair 1765.00
Chair, V. Panton, Painted Wood, Steamed, Steel, Paper Label, 31 x 23 x 19 In. 1500.00
Chair, Victorian, Carved Back, Needlepoint Seat, 40 In. 25.00
Chair, Victorian, Copper Paint, Turned Spindles, 35 In., Pair 115.00
Chair, Victorian, Ebonized, Wedgwood Mounted, Lacquered, Cane Seat, Pair 1410.00
Chair, Victorian, Hardwood, Ebonized, Painted Flowers, Balloon Back 179.00
Chair, Victorian, Mahogany, Shell, Leaf-Carved Backrest, Hinged Seat, Pair 1060.00
Chair, Victorian, Rosewood, Upholstered, Casters, Arms, 36 5/8 x 24 x 22 In. 200.00
Chair, Victorian, Walnut, Balloon Back, Arms 210.00
Chair, Victorian, Walnut, Carved, c.1890, 42 1/2 x 23 3/4 x 31 1/4 In. 58.00
Chair, Victorian, Walnut, Carved, Turned Finials, 44 In. 430.00
Chair, W. McArthur, Aluminum, Vinyl Upholstery, 15 x 20 x 31 In., Pair 235.00
Chair, W. McArthur, Anodized Aluminum, Tubular, Upholstered, 32 In., Pair 2474.00
Chair, W. McArthur, Folding, Aluminum, c.1950, 33 x 21 In., Pair ....120.00 to 175.00
Chair, W. Platner, Nickel-Plated Steel, Rubber Upholstery, Knoll, c.1966 .... 450.00
Chair, Walnut, Carved, Upholstered, Arms, Mid 19th Century 1435.00
Chair, Walnut, Carved, Upholstered, Scrolled Arms, Late 19th Century, 42 In. 145.00
Chair, Walnut, Marquetry, Scroll Crest Rail, Continental, c.1900, 35 In. 259.00
Chair, Walnut, Needlework Seat, Open Back, Scrolled Hip Rest, 38 In. 115.00
Chair, Walnut, Scrolled, Cane Back, Padded, Late 19th Century, 44 1/2 In., Pair 1495.00
Chair, Walnut, Shaped Back, X-Stretcher, Early 1900s, 50 In., Pair 235.00
Chair, Walnut, Urn & Ring-Turned Posts, Mushroom-Turned Finials, 33 x 16 In. 690.00
Chair, Wanscher, Rosewood, Cane, Leather, Jeppesen, Denmark, 33 x 25 x 27 In. 3250.00
Chair, Wegner, Chinese, Cherrywood Design, Arms, Fritz Hansen 1495.00
Chair, Wegner, Cow Horn, Teak, Cane, 30 x 25 x 21 In. 425.00
Chair, Wegner, No. JH513, Arms, Johannes Hansen, c.1952, 35 1/2 x 27 x 19 In. 823.00
Chair, Wegner, Oak, Molded Plywood, Denmark, c.1960, Pair 240.00
Chair, Wegner, Oak, Velvet, 30 x 25 x 21 In., Pair 550.00
Chair, Wegner, Teak, Leather, Branded, 28 1/2 x 22 x 18 In. 160.00
Chair, Wegner, Valet, Oak, Brass, Leather, Branded, 37 x 19 3/4 x 20 In. 4250.00
Chair, Wegner, Y, Oak Frame, Woven Paper Cord Seat, c.1950 .... 240.00
Chair, Wendell Castle, Padouk, Leather, Gilt Metal, c.1988, 31 In., Pair 11355.00
Chair, Wilhelm Schmidt, Beech, Black Lacquer, Leather, c.1902, Arm, 34 In. 7200.00
Chair, William & Mary Style, Hardwood, Painted, Upholstered, Arms, 1800s, 24 In....... 259.00
Chair, William & Mary Style, Mahogany, Cane Back, Needlepoint Upholstery 55.00
Chair, William & Mary, Black Paint, Carved Crest, Rush Seat, Early 1700s, 44 In. 2000.00

Chair, William & Mary, Black Paint, Gilt Decoration, Boston, c.1715, 44 In. 6000.00
Chair, William & Mary, Black Paint, Slat Back, Arms, 18th Century 1435.00
Chair, William IV Style, Mahogany, Carved Shell Back, Curved Seat, 38 In., Pair 1380.00
Chair, William IV Style, Mahogany, Carved, Late 19th Century, 33 1/2 In., Pair 115.00
Chair, William IV, Gondola, Rosewood, Carved Scroll, 35 1/2 In., Pair 6325.00
Chair, William IV, Mahogany, Cane Back & Arms, c.1835, 38 In., Pair 6040.00
Chair, William IV, Mahogany, Carved, Padded, Barrel Back, Padded Seat, 33 In. 1495.00
Chair, William IV, Mahogany, Crest Over Shaped Back, Saddle Seat, 40 In., Pair 805.00
Chair, William IV, Mahogany, Curved Crest, Padded Seat, c.1835, 35 In., Pair 980.00
Chair, William IV, Mahogany, Shieldback, Top-Shaped Feet, 1800s, 35 In. 1725.00
Chair, William IV, Oak, Arched Padded Back, Upholstered, c.1835, 43 In. 1380.00
Chair, William Long, Mahogany, Upholstered Seat, Branded, c.1805, 38 In., Pair 2400.00
Chair, Windsor, Arrow Back, Black Paint, Eagle, New England, c.1820, 35 In., Pair 7800.00
Chair, Windsor, Arrow Back, Green Paint, Writing Arm, Drawer Under Seat, 31 In. 690.00
Chair, Windsor, Arrow Back, Yellow Paint, Vermont, c.1825, 33 1/2 In., Pair 5700.00
Chair, Windsor, Black Paint, 7 Spindles, Bamboo Turnings, Continuous Arm, 34 In. 1495.00
Chair, Windsor, Black Paint, 7 Spindles, Birdcage, Bamboo Turnings, 34 1/2 In. 865.00
Chair, Windsor, Black Paint, Low Back, Turned, Arms, Pennsylvania, c.1785, 28 1/2 In. . . . 3600.00
Chair, Windsor, Bow Back, 6 Spindles, Shield Seat, Bamboo Legs, c.1795 . . . . 6325.00
Chair, Windsor, Bow Back, 7 Spindles, Crest, Saddle Seat, Arms, c.1780, 35 In. 1645.00
Chair, Windsor, Bow Back, 7 Spindles, Painted, Bamboo-Turned Legs, c.1810, 39 In. 645.00
Chair, Windsor, Bow Back, 9 Spindles, Saddle Seat, Early 1800s, 37 1/2 In., Pair 980.00
Chair, Windsor, Bow Back, Brace Back, Green Paint, R.I., c.1785, 38 In., Pair 720.00
Chair, Windsor, Bow Back, Continuous Arm, Conn., c.1790, 37 1/2 x 18 In. 2235.00
Chair, Windsor, Bow Back, Green Paint, 9 Spindles, 35 x 17 1/2 In. 200.00
Chair, Windsor, Bow Back, Green Stain, Turned Legs, Arms 660.00
Chair, Windsor, Bow Back, Potty Seat, 19th Century 125.00
Chair, Windsor, Bow Back, Vase-Turned Legs, Arms, 39 1/2 x 21 1/2 x 16 In. 825.00
Chair, Windsor, Brace Back, 6 Spindles, Saddle Seat, Continuous Arm, 37 In. 940.00
Chair, Windsor, Brace Back, Blue White Paint, Philadelphia, c.1810 . . . . 1035.00
Chair, Windsor, Brace Back, Brown Paint, Continuous Arm, 35 In., Pair 3450.00
Chair, Windsor, Brace Back, Green Paint, 9 Spindles, Continuous Arm, 37 In. 1840.00
Chair, Windsor, Brace Back, Green Paint, Plank Seat, New England, c.1780, 37 In., Pair . . 1555.00
Chair, Windsor, Brace Back, Incised Crest, Shaped Seat, Arms, R.I., 1775-1800, 38 In. 410.00
Chair, Windsor, Brace Back, Red Paint, New York, Late 18th Century 1076.00
Chair, Windsor, Brace Back, Shaped Seat, Vase & Ring-Turned Legs, c.1795 . . . . 575.00
Chair, Windsor, Comb Back, 15 Spindles, Scrolled Ears & Arms, 45 x 28 In. 1430.00
Chair, Windsor, Comb Back, Black Paint, 8 Spindles, Bentwood Arms, 41 In. 2760.00
Chair, Windsor, Comb Back, Carved, Turned, Arms, Philadelphia, c.1770, 44 In. 9560.00
Chair, Windsor, Comb Back, Painted, 7 Spindles, Shield Seat, Relief Carved, 44 In. 2300.00
Chair, Windsor, Comb Back, Red Paint, Arms, Pennsylvania, 18th Century, 40 In. 7050.00
Chair, Windsor, Comb Back, Red Paint, Turned, Arms, c.1775, 42 In. 6000.00
Chair, Windsor, Comb Back, Serpentine Crest, Arms, c.1800 . . . . 2470.00
Chair, Windsor, Comb Back, Serpentine Crest, Philadelphia, Mid 1900s, 39 In. 3820.00
Chair, Windsor, Comb Back, Shaped Crest, Carved Volute Ears, Philadelphia, c.1770 . . . . . 6465.00
Chair, Windsor, Curved Crest, Tapered Spindles, E. Tracy, Lisbon, Conn., c.1780, 35 In. . . 2700.00
Chair, Windsor, Elm, Solid Seat, Turned Supports, Arms, Early 19th Century, 40 In. 420.00
Chair, Windsor, Fanback, 7 Spindles, Arched Crest, Bamboo-Turned Legs, 37 In. 400.00
Chair, Windsor, Fanback, 7 Spindles, Flared Crest, H-Stretcher, Turned Legs, 36 In. 980.00
Chair, Windsor, Fanback, 7 Spindles, Saddle Seat, H-Stretcher, 36 In. 920.00
Chair, Windsor, Fanback, 7 Spindles, Shield Seat, Bamboo Turnings, 35 In. 520.00
Chair, Windsor, Fanback, Multicolored, New England, c.1875, 36 In. 1080.00
Chair, Windsor, Fanback, Painted, Tapered Spindles, New England, Late 1700s, 38 In. 175.00
Chair, Windsor, Fanback, Pine, Oak, Arched Crest, Early 19th Century, 35 In. 315.00
Chair, Windsor, G. Gammon, Grain Painted, Black, Red, Flowers, Halifax, Nova Scotia . . . 2630.00
Chair, Windsor, Green Paint, 7 Spindles, Baluster & Ring-Turned Legs, Arms, 37 In. 750.00
Chair, Windsor, Hoop Back, 7 Spindles, Bamboo Turnings, 36 1/2 In. 445.00
Chair, Windsor, Hoop Back, Elm, Yew, Pierced Splat, Plank Seat, Turned Legs 510.00
Chair, Windsor, L. Stickley, Classical Revival, Mixed Wood, c.1935, 44 In., Pair 2070.00
Chair, Windsor, Leather Upholstered Seat, Continuous Arm, S. Tracy 1980.00
Chair, Windsor, Loop Back, 9 Spindles, Bamboo Turnings, Arms, Pa., c.1800, Pair 1880.00
Chair, Windsor, Loop Back, Curved Crest Rail, H-Stretcher, Arms, c.1800 . . . . 560.00
Chair, Windsor, Low Back, Saddle Seat, Scrolling Arms, c.1770 . . . . 1035.00

Chair, Windsor, Low Back, Turned, Arms, Pennsylvania, c.1785, 28 1/2 In. 3300.00
Chair, Windsor, Maple, Hickory, 9 Spindles, Bamboo Turnings, 37 In. 345.00
Chair, Windsor, Nutting, No. 301, Brace Back, 39 In. 360.00
Chair, Windsor, Nutting, No. 306, Bamboo Turnings, Straight Stretcher, c.1930 . . . . 760.00
Chair, Windsor, Nutting, No. 410, Comb Back, c.1918, 39 In. 995.00
Chair, Windsor, Nutting, No. 451, Writing Arm 3395.00
Chair, Windsor, Painted, Bamboo Turnings, New England, c.1810, 36 In., Pair 4115.00
Chair, Windsor, Painted, Stenciled Fruit Crest, Plank Seat, 31 1/2 In. 40.00
Chair, Windsor, Red Paint, Concave Crest, 3 Spindles, Flared Arms, c.1820, 35 In. 940.00
Chair, Windsor, Rod Back, Bamboo Turnings, c.1800 . . . . 2070.00
Chair, Windsor, Sack Back, 7 Spindles, Incised Oval Seat, 37 1/2 In. 1840.00
Chair, Windsor, Sack Back, Black Paint, Baluster & Ring-Turned Legs, Arms, 34 In. 1095.00
Chair, Windsor, Sack Back, Black Paint, Thomas Blackford, Phila., c.1785, 37 In. 2400.00
Chair, Windsor, Sack Back, Brown Paint, Arms, c.1785, 37 In. 1320.00
Chair, Windsor, Sack Back, Green Paint Over Red, Baluster-Turned Legs, 38 In. 2300.00
Chair, Windsor, Sack Back, Green Paint, Carved Knuckles, Potty Seat, Arms, 1800s 1725.00
Chair, Windsor, Sack Back, Green Paint, New York, 19th Century 600.00
Chair, Windsor, Sack Back, Maple, Ash, 7 Spindles, Plank Seat, 39 3/4 In. 2235.00
Chair, Windsor, Sack Back, Maple, Ash, Painted, New England, c.1780, 37 In. 1175.00
Chair, Windsor, Sack Back, Maple, Pine, Hickory, Arms, Pennsylvania, c.1900 . . . . 1265.00
Chair, Windsor, Sack Back, Painted, 7 Spindles, Turned Legs & Stretcher, Arms, 37 In. . . . 4900.00
Chair, Windsor, Sack Back, Turned, Arms, New England, c.1780, 36 1/2 In. 2280.00
Chair, Windsor, Sack Back, Worn Paint, 7 Spindles, Turned Legs, Arms, 37 In. 1955.00
Chair, Windsor, Serpentine Crest, Carved Ears, Lancaster County, Pa., c.1800 . . . . 2235.00
Chair, Windsor, Tan Paint, H-Stretcher, 36 1/2 In. 30.00
Chair, Wing, Chippendale Style, Southwood Furniture Co., Rhode Island 115.00
Chair, Wing, Chippendale, Mahogany, Curved Crest, New England, c.1800, 48 In. 9200.00
Chair, Wing, Chippendale, Mahogany, Square Legs, Rolled Arms, Upholstered, 44 In. 4600.00
Chair, Wing, Chippendale, Mahogany, Upholstered, Late 18th Century 3585.00
Chair, Wing, George III Style, Mahogany, Leather, Lexterten, 1900s, 38 x 31 In. 635.00
Chair, Wing, George III Style, Walnut, Upholstered, Scrolled Arms, 27 1/2 x 27 In. 2160.00
Chair, Wing, George III, Mahogany, Upholstered, Tapered Legs, 45 In. 2160.00
Chair, Wing, George III, Oak, Elm, Arched Crest, Arms, c.1780, 44 1/2 In. 5100.00
Chair, Wing, George III, Walnut, Crewelwork Upholstery, c.1780 . . . . 1725.00
Chair, Wing, Georgian Style, Mahogany, Black Leather, Carved Seat Rail, Molded Arms . . 2000.00
Chair, Wing, Georgian Style, Mahogany, Leather, 43 In. 635.00
Chair, Wing, Georgian Style, Oak, Leather, Tall Backrest, High Sides 1410.00
Chair, Wing, Hepplewhite Style, Mahogany, Upholstered, 1900s, 29 In., Child's 600.00
Chair, Wing, Mahogany, Serpentine Crest Rail, Late 1700s 1295.00
Chair, Wing, Mahogany, Striped Velvet Upholstery, H-Stretcher, 37 1/2 x 10 In. 325.00
Chair, Wing, Mahogany, Upholstered, Cabriole Legs, Walker Furniture, 50 In. 575.00
Chair, Wing, McCobb, Tapered Mahogany Legs, 24 x 31 x 31 In. 295.00
Chair, Wing, Oak, Carved, Brocade Upholstery, Tapered Legs, 43 1/2 x 32 x 30 In. 175.00
Chair, Wing, Queen Anne Style, Mahogany, Crewel Upholstery, 44 In. 375.00
Chair, Wing, Queen Anne Style, Mahogany, Floral Upholstery, Early 1900s, 43 In. 200.00
Chair, Wing, Queen Anne Style, Walnut, Domed Back, 19th Century, 47 In. 635.00
Chair, Wing, Queen Anne Style, Walnut, Double Domed Crest, Upholstered, 45 In. 2185.00
Chair, Wing, Queen Anne Style, Walnut, Plaid Upholstery, 22 x 46 In. 980.00
Chair, Wing, Queen Anne, Maple, Arch Back, Turned Stretchers, New England 825.00
Chair, Wing, Sheraton, Mahogany, Boston, 1800-15 . . . . 3450.00
Chair, Wing, Sheraton, Mahogany, Cyma-Curved Crest, Rolled Arms 3450.00
Chair, Wormley, Mahogany, Naugahyde, Arms, Dunbar, 21 x 23 x 29 In. 690.00
Chair, Yoke Back, Shaped Spindle Arms, Back, 19th Century, 40 x 22 x 18 In., Pair 805.00
Chair & Footstool, Horn, Black Leather Upholstery, Arms, Late 1800s, 40 x 39 In. 3450.00
Chair & Ottoman, Arne Jacobsen, Leather, Aluminum, 35 x 43 & 22 x 16 x 17 In. 2940.00
Chair & Ottoman, Arne Norell, Leather, Chromed Steel, Sweden, c.1970 . . . . 1080.00
Chair & Ottoman, Club, Leather, 31 1/2 x 40 x 36 In. & 13 x 36 x 27 In. 400.00
Chair & Ottoman, Eames Style, Molded Plywood, Leather, Cast Aluminum, Swivel 175.00
Chair & Ottoman, Eames, No. 670 & No. 671, Plywood, Leather, Herman Miller, 33 In. . . 3819.00
Chair & Ottoman, G. Nakashima, Walnut, c.1975, 30 1/2 x 31 x 33 1/2 In. 4700.00
Chair & Ottoman, G. Nakashima, Walnut, Grass Seat, 26 2/3 & 12 1/2 In. 2630.00
Chair & Ottoman, G. Nelson, Coconut, Wool Upholstery, Herman Miller 5750.00
Chair & Ottoman, Hans Olsen, Dansk, Leather, C.S. Mobler 185.00

Chair & Ottoman, Jorge Ferrari-Hardoy, Butterfly, Black Leather, 1950s 345.00
Chair & Ottoman, Paulin, No. 582, Ribbon, Artifort, c.1965 .... 4700.00
Chair & Ottoman, Saarinen, Womb, Steel, Fiberglass, Foam, Wool, Knoll 500.00
Chair & Ottoman, Wegner, Teak, Upholstered, c.1960, 34 x 29 x 48 In. ....4115.00 to 4700.00
Chair & Ottoman, Wormley, Mahogany, Upholstered, Dunbar, 28-In. Chair 1000.00
Chair Set, Andre Arbus Style, Art Deco, Mahogany, Padded Back, Arms, 41 In., 4 .... 8625.00
Chair Set, Andre Arbus, Sycamore, Cherry, Bronze, Upholstered, 1936, 41 In., 6 .... 7800.00
Chair Set, Andre Arbus, Sycamore, c.1940, 34 1/4 In., 6 .... 4200.00
Chair Set, Art Deco, Mahogany, Bentwood, Sleigh Back, France, 4 .... 400.00
Chair Set, Art Deco, Mahogany, Continental, 36 x 18 x 20 In., 4 .... 225.00
Chair Set, Bartoll, Sheraton, Hitchcock Style, Painted Scenes, 35 x 18 In., 6 .... 9200.00
Chair Set, Biedermeier, Walnut, Lions Inlay On Crest, 35 In., 6 .... 1610.00
Chair Set, Brown Graining, Red & White Flowers, Morning Glories, Pa., 32 In., 4 .... 660.00
Chair Set, Brown Paint, Flowers, Half-Spindle Back, Turned Legs, 32 1/4 In., 6 .... 690.00
Chair Set, Brown Paint, Stenciled, Balloon Back, Plank Seat, 34 In., 6 .... 660.00
Chair Set, Cane, Parcel Gilt, Painted, Ebonized, c.1825, 4 .... 750.00
Chair Set, Chinese Chippendale, Faux Bamboo, Latticework Back, 36 3/4 In., 4 .... 635.00
Chair Set, Chinese Chippendale, Mahogany, Carved, 39 In., 10 .... 1495.00
Chair Set, Chinese Chippendale, Mahogany, Ribbonback, 2 Armchairs, 40 In., 10 .... 4600.00
Chair Set, Chippendale Style, Mahogany, Carved, 8 .... 865.00
Chair Set, Chippendale Style, Mahogany, England, Early 1900s, 2 Armchairs, 8 .... 4830.00
Chair Set, Chippendale Style, Mahogany, Ladder Back, Upholstered Seat, 8 .... 1430.00
Chair Set, Chippendale Style, Mahogany, Upholstered, 10 .... 1150.00
Chair Set, Chippendale Style, Rose-Carved Crest, 44 In., 12 .... 5060.00
Chair Set, Chippendale, Interlacing Arch Back, 42 In., 12 .... 4600.00
Chair Set, Chippendale, Mahogany, 1780-90, 2 Armchairs, 6 .... 3910.00
Chair Set, Chippendale, Mahogany, Relief-Carved Splat, 37 In., 6 .... 2875.00
Chair Set, Chippendale, Mahogany, Ribbonback, Upholstered Seat, 6 .... 3680.00
Chair Set, Chippendale, Mahogany, Upholstered, Square Legs, c.1925, 40 In., 4 .... 805.00
Chair Set, Chippendale, Walnut, Slip Seat, Vase-Shape Splat, 39 1/4 In., 4 .... 8050.00
Chair Set, Chippendale, Walnut, Virginia, 1760-80, 3 .... 2300.00
Chair Set, Chippendale, Wavy Ladder Back, Carved, Pierced, Upholstered Seat, 8 .... 3450.00
Chair Set, Club, Rosewood, Leather, Cotton Webbing, Denmark, 24 x 26 x 24 In., 5 ...... 1600.00
Chair Set, Colombo, ABS, Black, Kartell, Italy, c.1965, 28 1/2 x 17 x 18 In., 4 .... 140.00
Chair Set, Eames, DKR, Eiffel Tower, Wire, Vinyl, Herman Miller, 32 In., 4 .... 880.00
Chair Set, Eames, La Fonda, Fiberglass, Vinyl, Chrome, Herman Miller, 28 x 25 In., 4 .... 650.00
Chair Set, Eames, Plywood, Molded, Aniline Red, Shock Mounts, 20 x 21 x 30 In., 4 .... 3525.00
Chair Set, Eames, Shell, Zinc Base, Vinyl Upholstery, Nylon Glides, 26 x 31 1/2 In., 4 ... 700.00
Chair Set, Eames, Walnut, Molded, Chromed Steel, Nylon Glides, 20 x 30 In., 4 .... 764.00
Chair Set, Empire, Mahogany, Needlepoint Seat, Pierced Carved Crests, 33 In., 4 .... 360.00
Chair Set, Empire, Mahogany, Parcel Gilt, Flowers, Paneled Crest, Padded, 33 In., 6 ..... 3220.00
Chair Set, Empire, Mahogany, Vase-Form Splat, Shaped Crest, 33 In., 11 .... 1610.00
Chair Set, Faux Rosewood, Padded Seat, Scrolled Crest, Ormolu, c.1815, 33 In., 6 .... 4370.00
Chair Set, Federal, Carved, Black Paint, Stenciled, Early 19th Century, 3 .... 120.00
Chair Set, Federal, Mahogany, Square Back, 3 Pierced Splats, Upholstered, 36 In., 4 ..... 1175.00
Chair Set, Federal, Mahogany, Upholstered, Shield Back, c.1795, 6 .... 4700.00
Chair Set, Finn Juhl, Bovirke, Copenhagen, Denmark, c.1953, 29 x 23 x 20 In., 4 .... 4115.00
Chair Set, Frank Lloyd Wright, Upholstered, Heritage Henredon, 20 x 22 In., 4 .... 1095.00
Chair Set, French Provincial, Beech, Carved, Upholstered Seat, Back, 4 .... 350.00
Chair Set, French Provincial, Oak, Ladder Back, Arched Slats, Rush Seat, 12 .... 2629.00
Chair Set, French Provincial, Scroll & Shell Crest, 39 x 24 x 24 In., 6 .... 2115.00
Chair Set, G. Nelson, Tubular, Zinc Plated, Upholstered, 20 x 20 1/2 x 32 In., 5 .... 590.00
Chair Set, G. Stickley, No. 306 1/2, Ladder Back, Rush Seat, 36 x 17 x 18 In., 8 .... 2585.00
Chair Set, G. Stickley, No. 353, 4-Rung Ladder Back, Leather Upholstery, 6 .... 3335.00
Chair Set, G. Stickley, V-Back, 5 Vertical Slats, Leather Seat, 36 x 18 3/4 In., 6 .... 7640.00
Chair Set, George II Style, Mahogany, Leather Seat, c.1900, 2 Armchairs, 40 In., 10 ..... 5750.00
Chair Set, George II Style, Mahogany, Upholstered, 2 Armchairs, 6 .... 1725.00
Chair Set, George II, Walnut, Painted, Carved Splat, 39 In., 12 .... 2875.00
Chair Set, George III Style, Mahogany, Carved, Padded Seat, Arms, 39 In., 10 .... 4900.00
Chair Set, George III Style, Mahogany, Curved Crest, Pierced Splat, 38 In., 6 .... 2300.00
Chair Set, George III Style, Mahogany, H-Stretcher, 39 In., 12 .... 3220.00
Chair Set, George III Style, Mahogany, Oval Back, Padded Seat, 2 Armchairs, 39 In., 6 ... 2530.00
Chair Set, George III Style, Mahogany, Serpentine Rail, Pierced Splat, Square Legs, 8 .... 3350.00

Chair Set, George III Style, Mahogany, Shaped Crest, Stretcher, 40 In., 12 .... 3450.00
Chair Set, George III Style, Satinwood, Painted, Upholstered Arms, 4 .... 4480.00
Chair Set, George III, Mahogany, Carved, Shieldback, Early 1900s, 38 In., 4 .... 1035.00
Chair Set, George III, Mahogany, Upholstered Seat, 36 In., 8 .... 3450.00
Chair Set, Georgian Style, Mahogany, Carved, 2 Armchairs, 10 .... 2689.00
Chair Set, Georgian Style, Mahogany, Carved, Scrolling Crest, 1900s, 38 In., 4 .... 1265.00
Chair Set, Georgian, Walnut, Leaf-Carved Waved Crest, Pierced Splat, 38 In., 8 .... 3100.00
Chair Set, Green, Gold & Black Stenciled Cornucopia, 17 1/2 x 35 1/2 In., 6 .... 1150.00
Chair Set, Green, Yellow Paint, Black Stripes, Plank Seat, 17 x 33 In., 6 .... 1035.00
Chair Set, H. Bertoia, Diamond, Chromium, Wool, Knoll, 30 x 21 x 22 In., 6 .... 750.00
Chair Set, Henry II Style, Mahogany, Leather, Spindle Back, Late 1800s, 39 In., 8 .... 1380.00
Chair Set, Hepplewhite Style, Mahogany Inlay, Overupholstered, Spade Feet, 10 .... 4995.00
Chair Set, Hepplewhite Style, Mahogany, Backrest, Foliage, 2 Armchairs, 8 .... 4110.00
Chair Set, Hepplewhite Style, Mahogany, Overupholstered, 2 Armchairs, 10 .... 880.00
Chair Set, Hepplewhite Style, Mahogany, Serpentine Crest, 2 Armchairs, 8 .... 1175.00
Chair Set, Hepplewhite, Shieldback, Upholstered, 36 x 17 x 21 In., 7 .... 1440.00
Chair Set, Hepplewhite, Transitional, Carved, Late 1800s, 17-In. Seat, 36 In., 6 .... 1800.00
Chair Set, Hitchcock, Black Ground, Stenciled, Pillow Back, Turned Legs, 5 .... 300.00
Chair Set, Hitchcock, Grain Painted, Gold Leaf, c.1850, 33 In., 4 .... 705.00
Chair Set, Hudson River Valley Style, Black, Rush Seat, Vase Splat, 18 In., 8 .... 2185.00
Chair Set, Italian Rococo Style, Fruitwood, Painted, Arms, 6 .... 3585.00
Chair Set, L. & J.G. Stickley, Ladder Back, Saddle Seat, 36 x 18 x 16 1/2 In., 4 .... 1115.00
Chair Set, Ladder Back, Red Paint, 4 Arched Slats, Rush Seat, 47 In., 8 .... 7765.00
Chair Set, Lollipop Public Seating Group, Robin Bush, c.1960, 106 In., 4 .... 865.00
Chair Set, Louis XV Style, Bronze Mounted, 2 Armchairs, 14 .... 2630.00
Chair Set, Louis XV Style, Gilt, Aubusson Upholstery, Arms, Early 1900s, 4 .... 2530.00
Chair Set, Louis XV Style, Oak, Shell-Carved Crest, 35 In., 8 .... 1495.00
Chair Set, Louis XVI Style, Medallion Back, Upholstered Seat, Back, 4 .... 550.00
Chair Set, Mahogany, Cross-Framed Back, Upholstered, Saber Legs, c.1820, 7 .... 4485.00
Chair Set, Mahogany, Interlacing Splat, Padded, Dutch, c.1785, 36 1/2 In., 6 .... 5520.00
Chair Set, Mahogany, Ladder Back, Rush Seat, England, 42 In., 10 .... 2530.00
Chair Set, Maple, Birch, Ladder Back, Turned Rungs, Scalloped Slats, 36 3/4 In., 4 ...... 345.00
Chair Set, Maple, Ladder Back, Red Stain, Rush Seat, Early 1800s, 41 In., 6 .... 18000.00
Chair Set, McCobb, Stacking, Fiberglass, Steel, St. John Seating Co., 1950s, 32 In., 6 .... 765.00
Chair Set, Michael Taylor, Baker Furniture, c.1970, 21 1/4 x 22 x 33 In., 8 .... 3525.00
Chair Set, Napoleon III, Beech, Polychrome, 37 1/4 In., 4 .... 750.00
Chair Set, Neoclassical, Gondola, Mahogany, N.Y., 1820-40, 31 In., 6 .... 720.00
Chair Set, Neoclassical, Mahogany, Carved Crest, Upholstered Seat, c.1820, 8 .... 3055.00
Chair Set, Neoclassical, Mahogany, Carved, Early 1900s, 33 In., 6 .... 705.00
Chair Set, Neoclassical, Mahogany, Continuous Crest & Rail, Shaped Splat, 31 In., 6 ..... 4350.00
Chair Set, Neoclassical, Mahogany, Late 19th Century, 33 In., 5 .... 635.00
Chair Set, Neoclassical, Mahogany, Lyre Back, 2 Armchairs, Dutch, 34 1/2 In., 8 .... 3680.00
Chair Set, Neoclassical, Mahogany, Parcel Gilt, Leather Seat, Russia, 37 In., 4 .... 2760.00
Chair Set, Neoclassical, Painted Backs, 4 Landscapes, 1820-30, 35 In., 4 .... 9560.00
Chair Set, Neoclassical, Painted, Stenciled, Pennsylvania, c.1850, 5 .... 705.00
Chair Set, Oak, 3 Arched Slats, Rush Seat, 38 In., 6 .... 2070.00
Chair Set, Oak, Carved, Dome Crest Rail, Scrolled Leaves, c.1900, 37 In., 6 .... 259.00
Chair Set, Oda, Teak, Upholstered, Denmark, c.1960, 2 Armchairs, 31 In., 6 .... 1530.00
Chair Set, P. Evans, Bronze, Upholstered, 2 Armchairs, 27 1/2 x 32 1/2 In., 6 .... 2115.00
Chair Set, Painted, 5-Spindle Back, Stenciled Fruit, Pennsylvania, 6 .... 2800.00
Chair Set, Pennsylvania Dutch, Red Brown, Flowers, Stretchers, 32 In., 5 .... 520.00
Chair Set, Prairie School, Shaped Slat, Splayed Legs, Shoefoot, 1 Armchair, 6 .... 2350.00
Chair Set, Queen Anne Style, 20th Century, 39 x 24 In., 4 .... 325.00
Chair Set, Queen Anne Style, Walnut Inlay, Marquetry Splat, 41 In., 8 .... 1840.00
Chair Set, Queen Anne Style, Yew, Scrolled, Shell-Carved Back, Upholstered, Arms, 8 ... 2390.00
Chair Set, Queen Anne, Walnut, Shaped Crest Rail, 18th Century, 4 .... 3050.00
Chair Set, Queen Anne, Walnut, Vase-Form Splats, 2 Armchairs, 8 .... 3020.00
Chair Set, Red Paint, Ladder Back, Turned Posts, Rungs, Splint Seats, 39 1/2 In., 4 ...... 605.00
Chair Set, Regency Style, Fruitwood, 8 .... 3585.00
Chair Set, Regency Style, Mahogany, Shell-Carved Splat, 34 In., 8 .... 1725.00
Chair Set, Regency, Mahogany, Carved Scroll, Leaves, Slip Seat, Saber Legs, 6 .... 1645.00
Chair Set, Regency, Mahogany, Curved Crest, Rope-Twist Crest, 33 In., 10 .... 4140.00
Chair Set, Regency, Mahogany, Leaf-Carved Back, Brass-Inlaid Splat, 6 .... 1259.00

Chair Set, Robert Thompson, Oak, Carved, Leather, 34 x 17 1/4 x 15 1/2 In., 6 . . . . 3750.00
Chair Set, Rohde, Birch, Vinyl, Herman Miller, c.1940, 1 Armchair, 32 1/2 In., 6 . . . . 2350.00
Chair Set, Ruhlmann, Art Deco, Black Lacquer, 32 In., 6 . . . . 4600.00
Chair Set, Sheraton Style, Mahogany, Fluted Splats, Upholstered Seat, 8 . . . . 2685.00
Chair Set, Sheraton Style, Mahogany, Shieldback, 38 In., 6 . . . . 635.00
Chair Set, Sheraton Style, Walnut, Medallion Crest, Ring-Turned Legs, 33 In., 6 . . . . 720.00
Chair Set, Sheraton, Tiger Maple, Ring-Turned Crest Rail, Cane Seat, 5 . . . . 4140.00
Chair Set, Stacking, Molded Plastic, c.1970, 4 . . . . 224.00
Chair Set, Stacking, Muller & Stewart, Molded Plywood, Canada, 1968, 4 . . . . 345.00
Chair Set, Stickley Bros., No. 479 1/2, 3 Vertical Back Slats, Drop-In Seat, 37 In., 6 . . . . . . 3819.00
Chair Set, Stickley Bros., No. 715, Rush Seat, Wide Slat, 19 x 16 x 34 In., 4 . . . . 1265.00
Chair Set, Teak, Plywood, Molded, Denmark, c.1960, 4 . . . . 430.00
Chair Set, Thayer Coggin, Chrome, Tubular, Velour Upholstery, 24 x 31 In., 6 . . . . 1175.00
Chair Set, Tiger & Bird's-Eye Maple, Pierced Crest, Cane Seat, c.1850, 32 In., 6 . . . . 1293.00
Chair Set, Tiger Maple, 1 Armchair, 19th Century, 6 . . . . 4050.00
Chair Set, Victorian, Upholstered, Carved Crest Rail, Late 19th Century, 40 In., 3 . . . . 200.00
Chair Set, Victorian, Walnut, Balloon Back, Upholstered Seats, Turned Legs, 4 . . . . 600.00
Chair Set, W. McArthur, Aluminum, Leather Seats, 24 x 19 x 31 1/2 In., 4 . . . . 1295.00
Chair Set, W. Platner, Knoll, c.1966, 29 x 24 x 21 In., 4 . . . . 1410.00
Chair Set, Wegner, No. 4103, Stacking, Fritz Hansen, c.1958, 28 3/4 x 20 In., 4 . . . . 1765.00
Chair Set, Wegner, Oak, Velvet, Branded, 30 x 21 3/4 x 17 In., 6 . . . . 1600.00
Chair Set, Wegner, Wishbone, Ebonized Wood, Papercord, 28 1/2 x 22 In., 4 . . . . 650.00
Chair Set, William & Mary, Black Paint, Turned, Carved, 18th Century, 4 . . . . 2235.00
Chair Set, William IV, Mahogany, Curved Crest, Leather Seat, c.1850, 35 In., 6 . . . . 4140.00
Chair Set, William IV, Mahogany, Shaped Crest, Padded Seat, Arms, c.1850, 35 In., 6 . . . . 690.00
Chair Set, Windsor, Apple Green Paint, 4 Arrow Spindles, Pa., c.1825, 34 In., 6 . . . . 3408.00
Chair Set, Windsor, Bow Back, Black, 9 Spindles, 37 In., 8 . . . . 5290.00
Chair Set, Windsor, Bow Back, Green Paint, 8 Spindles, New England, c.1810, 38 In., 4 . . 4113.00
Chair Set, Windsor, Brace Back, Shield Seat, Baluster-Turned Legs, c.1790, 3 . . . . 1150.00
Chair Set, Windsor, Firehouse, Cane & Solid Seat, 6 . . . . 138.00
Chair Set, Windsor, Grain Painted, Plank Seat, New England, c.1830, 35 In., 6 . . . . 1880.00
Chair Set, Windsor, Medallion Back, Double Bar Crest, Early 19th Century, 11 . . . . 4113.00
Chair Set, Windsor, Mustard Paint, Decorated, New England, 33 x 17 In., 8 . . . . 2013.00
Chair Set, Windsor, Painted, Birdcage, 2 Horizontal & 7 Vertical Spindles, 35 In., 5 . . . . . . 3290.00
Chair Set, Windsor, Plank Seat, Mustard Paint, Flowers, Rod Back, 35 In., 6 . . . . 489.00
Chair Set, Windsor, Rod Back, Yellow Paint, Baltimore, Early 1800s, 33 In., 4 . . . . 764.00
Chair Set, Windsor, Salmon Paint, 7 Spindles, New England, Early 1800s, 37 In., 4 . . . . . . 1175.00
Chair Set, Windsor, Sproson & Marsh, Black Paint, Bow Back, N.Y., c.1798, 3 . . . . 5945.00
Chair Set, Wormley, Mahogany, Upholstered Seat, Dunbar, 33 In., 6 . . . . 2468.00
Chair Set, Wrought Iron, Square Seat, Cloth Insert, Arched Legs, 46 1/2 In., 6 . . . . 690.00
Chair-Table, Birch, Pine, Scrubbed, Pegged Construction, Stretcher Base, 50 x 29 In. 2070.00
Chair-Table, Maple, Pine, Round, Box Base, Shoe Feet, c.1830, 29 x 54 In. 5750.00
Chair-Table, Pine, 3-Board Tongue & Groove Top, Hinged, Plank Seat, 38 x 26 1/2 In. 360.00
Chair-Table, Pine, American, 60 x 41 1/2 In. 5800.00
Chair-Table, Pine, Compartment, Turned Legs, Pennsylvania, 59 1/2 x 40 In. 920.00
Chair-Table, Pine, Maple, Red Paint, Drawer, Late 1700s, 27 x 48 In. 5580.00
Chair-Table, Pine, Red Paint, Checkerboard, Drawer, Turned Pull, 53 x 28 In. 3565.00
Chair-Table, Red Paint, Curved Rails, Square Legs, Pa., 28 x 29 x 44 In. 2185.00
Chair-Table, Round, Red Paint, 4-Board Top, Scrub Top, 2 Sections, 50 x 29 In. 4485.00
Chaise Longue, B. Mathsson, Pernilla 3, Birch, Sheepskin, Leather, 36 x 68 In. 3055.00
Chaise Longue, Le Corbusier, LC4, Cowhide, Cassina, c.1970, 22 x 63 x 28 In. 2875.00
Chaise Longue, Le Corbusier, LC4, Leather, Tubular Steel, c.1928, 64 In. 635.00
Chaise Longue, Le Corbusier, LC4, Original Cowhide Upholstery, 63 In. . . . . *Illus* 3525.00
Chaise Longue, Louis XV Style, Beech, Carved, 31 x 64 In. 1725.00
Chaise Longue, Louis XV Style, Fruitwood, Painted, Upholstered Sides, 34 x 80 In. 3680.00
Chaise Longue, Louis XV Style, Gilt, Shell-Carved, Curved Arms, Cushion, 64 In. 2990.00
Chaise Longue, Louis XV Style, Padded, Cushions, Flower Crest, 33 x 57 x 27 In. 1380.00
Chaise Longue, Louis XV Style, Painted, FRC Reuze, c.1800, 33 1/2 In., Pair 1840.00
Chaise Longue, Louis XV, Painted, Upholstered, 1700s, 37 1/2 In., Pair 1955.00
Chaise Longue, Louis XVI Style, Cane, Gilt, Cushion, Late 1800s, 39 x 72 In. 4140.00
Chaise Longue, Mahogany, Cane, Shell Carved, Continental, 35 x 22 x 71 In. 1725.00
Chaise Longue, Mahogany, Carved, Upholstered, 40 1/2 x 27 x 81 In. 290.00
Chaise Longue, Oak, Wrought Iron, Rope, 64 In. 2630.00

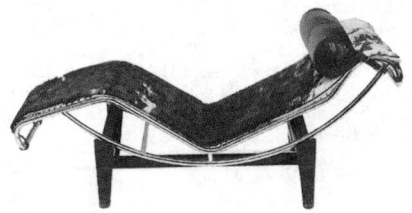

Furniture, Chaise Longue, Le Corbusier, LC4,
Original Cowhide Upholstery, 63 In.

Furniture, Chest, Blanket, Pennsylvania Dutch
Design, Ralph Cahoon Jr., 1940s, 47 In.

Chaise Longue, T. Heine, Steel, Black Rubber, c.1975, 35 1/2 x 19 1/2 x 64 In. 7770.00
Chaise Longue, V. Kagan, Tri-Symmetric, Kagan & Assoc., c.1958, 34 x 26 x 59 In. 9400.00
Chest, Art Deco, Rosewood, 3 Drawers, Cyma Platform, c.1920, 34 x 37 x 18 In. 1955.00
Chest, Bachelor's, Georgian, Mahogany, Folding Top, 2 Over 3 Drawers, 30 x 29 In. 1495.00
Chest, Bachelor's, Walnut, Mahogany, Serpentine Top, Figured Veneer, 32 x 40 In. 1380.00
Chest, Baker Furniture, George III Style, Mahogany, 1900s, 34 x 44 x 22 In. 705.00
Chest, Baker Furniture, Louis XVI Style, 2 Drawers, 1900s, 33 1/2 x 47 x 19 In. 560.00
Chest, Biedermeier, Burl, Ebonized, Drawers, Column Pilasters, 31 x 21 In. 4370.00
Chest, Biedermeier, Fruitwood, Molded Top, 3 Drawers, c.1820, 35 1/2 x 44 In. 1880.00
Chest, Birch, Reeded Front, Pilasters, 4 Drawers, Maine, 32 x 40 1/2 x 16 1/2 In. 575.00
Chest, Black Lacquer, 2 Over 4 Drawers, Marble Top, France, c.1915, 48 x 38 In. 2530.00
Chest, Blanket, 6-Board, Painted, Ship In Oval, Hinged Lid, 21 x 48 In. 590.00
Chest, Blanket, 6-Board, Painted, Smoke Decorated, Till, New England, 25 x 45 In. 1610.00
Chest, Blanket, 6-Board, Quarter Fans, New England, Early 1800s, 28 x 41 x 20 In. 1765.00
Chest, Blanket, Amish, Applied Molding, Drawers, Turned Feet, 31 x 47 x 21 In. 1495.00
Chest, Blanket, Amish, Poplar, Hickory, Red Vinegar Decoration, Ohio, 50 x 25 In. 520.00
Chest, Blanket, Arts & Crafts, Lift Top, Strap Hinges, Slab Sides, 38 x 21 x 18 In. 2115.00
Chest, Blanket, Blue Paint, Till, Secret Compartment, Late 1700s, 26 x 42 In. 840.00
Chest, Blanket, Blue Putty Decoration, Sunburst, 15 1/2 x 17 1/2 x 37 1/2 In. 230.00
Chest, Blanket, Bull's-Eye Decoration, Lehigh County, c.1840, 17 x 15 x 10 In. 3740.00
Chest, Blanket, Camphorwood, Pietra Dura, Lift Top, c.1875, 23 x 40 In. 115.00
Chest, Blanket, Carved Rosette Lid, Spain, 20 x 35 x 17 In. 380.00
Chest, Blanket, Carved, Lift Top, 24 x 38 In. 430.00
Chest, Blanket, Cherry, 6-Board, Bootjack Ends, Hinge Rail, 60 x 18 x 21 In. 430.00
Chest, Blanket, Cherry, Cedar Lined, Lane, 21 x 47 1/2 x 16 1/2 In. 69.00
Chest, Blanket, Chinese Red Lacquer, Hinged Lid, c.1880, 39 x 37 x 25 In. 200.00
Chest, Blanket, Chippendale, 2 Drawers, Iron Strap Hinges, 50 x 23 x 29 In. 1035.00
Chest, Blanket, Chippendale, 2 Drawers, Lift Top, 42 x 46 x 19 In.   480.00
Chest, Blanket, Chippendale, Birch, Pine, 2 Drawers, 36 x 17 x 41 1/2 In. 690.00
Chest, Blanket, Chippendale, Birch, Pine, Red Wash, 18 x 10 x 11 In. 1150.00
Chest, Blanket, Chippendale, Lift Top, 2 Drawers, 42 x 46 x 19 In. 480.00
Chest, Blanket, Chippendale, Pine, Maple Drawer Front, Lift Top, 49 x 37 x 19 In. 920.00
Chest, Blanket, Chippendale, Pine, Painted, Blue, Lift Top, Late 1700s, 52 x 39 x 21 In. . .   3825.00
Chest, Blanket, Chippendale, Walnut, Drawer, Lift Top, Pa., c.1785, 27 x 43 1/2 In. 6600.00
Chest, Blanket, Chippendale, Walnut, Hinged Top, Side Till, c.1790, 26 x 44 In. 980.00
Chest, Blanket, Chippendale, Walnut, Iron Strap Hinges, Ky., 45 x 25 In. 1725.00
Chest, Blanket, Drawer, Hinged Lid, New England, 1800s, 32 x 41 x 16 In. 1530.00
Chest, Blanket, Federal, Softwood, Black Paint, 2 Drawers, Bracket Feet, 28 x 49 In. 2090.00
Chest, Blanket, French Provincial, Walnut, Mid 19th Century, 26 x 63 x 24 In. 575.00
Chest, Blanket, George II, Oak, Elm, Lift Top, 2 Drawers, Oval Panels, c.1740, 22 x 26 In.   2160.00
Chest, Blanket, George III, Mahogany, Lift Top, Scalloped Gallery, 1700s, 41 x 66 In. 3450.00
Chest, Blanket, Gothic Panel, Hinged Plank Top, Early 1700s, 25 x 16 x 26 In. 1175.00
Chest, Blanket, Grain Painted, 19th Century, 24 x 38 x 18 In. 7170.00
Chest, Blanket, Grain Painted, 2 Drawers, Hinged Lid, c.1825, 23 x 32 x 17 In. 500.00
Chest, Blanket, Grain Painted, Black, Red, Drawer, Bracket Feet, 30 x 39 x 18 In. 2750.00
Chest, Blanket, Grain Painted, Hinged Lid, Early 1800s, 6 x 13 1/2 x 6 1/2 In. 355.00
Chest, Blanket, Grain Painted, Ocher, Burnt Umber, 2 Drawers, Hinged Lid, 40 x 40 In. . .   2350.00
Chest, Blanket, Grain Painted, Panels, 19th Century 8050.00

Chest, Blanket, Mahogany, 5-Board Base, Cutout Skirt, Lift-Off Lid, 5 x 12 x 6 In. 120.00
Chest, Blanket, Maple, Dome Top, Black Paint, Flowers, D.O.D., c.1835, 12 x 27 In. 3000.00
Chest, Blanket, Maple, Multicolored, Lift Top, New England, c.1840, 19 x 40 x 20 In. 1200.00
Chest, Blanket, Molded Edge, Brass Hardware, 2 Drawers, Lift Top, 36 x 43 x 16 In. 420.00
Chest, Blanket, Oak, Carved, Paneled Front, Hinged Top, Candle Box, 27 x 21 x 51 In. ... 670.00
Chest, Blanket, Oak, Paneled, Molding, Tang Hinges, England, 25 x 54 In. 805.00
Chest, Blanket, Painted, Tan & Brown Brush & Finger, Black Feet, 25 x 49 In. 1265.00
Chest, Blanket, Paneled, 2 Drawers, Hinged Top, Mass., c.1735, 43 x 39 x 18 In. 8815.00
Chest, Blanket, Pennsylvania Dutch Design, Ralph Cahoon Jr., 1940s, 47 In. .... *Illus* 575.00
Chest, Blanket, Pine, 2 Drawers, Bracket Feet, 34 1/2 x 40 In. 865.00
Chest, Blanket, Pine, 2 Drawers, Hinged Lid, Bracket Feet, 25 x 46 x 20 In. 235.00
Chest, Blanket, Pine, 2 Drawers, Lift Top, Chippendale Bracket Base 950.00
Chest, Blanket, Pine, 2 Drawers, Shaped Apron, Lift Top, 40 x 42 x 18 1/2 In. 460.00
Chest, Blanket, Pine, 4 Drawers, Lift Top, Bracket Feet, c.1800, 42 x 44 In. 1610.00
Chest, Blanket, Pine, 6-Board, Hinged, Dovetailed, Applied Molded, 18 x 17 1/2 x 44 In. . 440.00
Chest, Blanket, Pine, 6-Board, Painted, Hinged Lid, c.1825, 25 5/8 x 12 5/8 In., Child's ... 1293.00
Chest, Blanket, Pine, 6-Board, Snipe Hinges, 24 1/2 x 45 x 18 In. 520.00
Chest, Blanket, Pine, Black Smoke Grained, Curved Bootjack, 43 x 18 x 23 In. 1035.00
Chest, Blanket, Pine, Blue Paint, 6-Board, Hinged Lid, 9 5/8 x 20 3/4 x 10 3/8 In. 530.00
Chest, Blanket, Pine, Bottom Drawer, c.1890, 35 x 39 3/4 In. 920.00
Chest, Blanket, Pine, Dome Top, Multicolor Paint, T. Matteson, c.1835, 10 x 21 In. 6000.00
Chest, Blanket, Pine, Dovetailed, Grain Painted Over Blue, 12 3/4 x 6 x 8 In. 720.00
Chest, Blanket, Pine, Early 19th Century, 18 1/2 x 50 1/4 x 19 1/2 In. 210.00
Chest, Blanket, Pine, Ebonized, Sponge Painted, Hinged Lid, c.1820-30, 24 In. 2185.00
Chest, Blanket, Pine, Fluted Pilasters, Bootjack Ends, Switzerland, 1800s, 16 x 25 x 12 In. 590.00
Chest, Blanket, Pine, Grain Painted, 2 Drawers, Lift Top, c.1830, 40 x 42 In. 3600.00
Chest, Blanket, Pine, Grain Painted, Drawer, Lift Top, New England, c.1840, 24 x 18 In. .. 1380.00
Chest, Blanket, Pine, Grain Painted, Hinged Lid, Early 1800s, 30 x 50 x 23 In. 1060.00
Chest, Blanket, Pine, Grain Painted, Hinged Lid, Mass., c.1850, 36 x 71 In. 411.00
Chest, Blanket, Pine, Grain Painted, Yellow, Brown, Iron Hinges, Ball Feet, 25 x 44 In. ... 660.00
Chest, Blanket, Pine, Lift Top, Bun Feet, Inscription, Pennsylvania, 1857, 15 x 20 x 13 In. . 8400.00
Chest, Blanket, Pine, Multicolored, 3 Drawers, Lift Top, New England, c.1820, 29 In. 9600.00
Chest, Blanket, Pine, Painted, 2 Drawers, Lift Top, c.1820, 37 3/4 x 39 1/2 In. 9000.00
Chest, Blanket, Pine, Painted, 3 Locks, Mohawk Valley, N.Y., c.1780, 19 x 51 x 19 In. 2400.00
Chest, Blanket, Pine, Painted, 6-Board, Lift Top, New England, c.1800, 16 x 37 x 17 In. ... 5290.00
Chest, Blanket, Pine, Painted, Drawer, Bracket Feet, c.1820, 25 x 45 In. 805.00
Chest, Blanket, Pine, Painted, Drawer, Hinged Top, Early 1800s, 30 x 41 x 17 In. 3055.00
Chest, Blanket, Pine, Painted, Drawer, Hinged Top, New England, c.1810, 32 x 42 In. 3820.00
Chest, Blanket, Pine, Painted, Drawer, New England, Early 1800s, 35 1/2 x 42 x 19 In. 2940.00
Chest, Blanket, Pine, Painted, Lift Top, Bracket Feet, c.1800, 23 x 49 In. 805.00
Chest, Blanket, Pine, Peg & Nail, Brushwork Graining, New England, 39 In. .... *Illus* 2750.00
Chest, Blanket, Pine, Poplar, 2 Drawers, Hinged Top, New England, c.1815, 43 x 40 In. ... 3055.00
Chest, Blanket, Pine, Poplar, Painted, Lift Top, Glass Pulls, c.1820, 31 x 49 3/4 In. 4600.00
Chest, Blanket, Pine, Red Paint, 6-Board, Hinged Lid, 1800s, 12 x 16 1/4 In., Child's 1175.00
Chest, Blanket, Pine, Red Paint, Drawer, Rosehead & Square-Cut Nails, 42 x 28 In. 1090.00
Chest, Blanket, Pine, Red Panels, Brown Wash, Tulips, Roses, 49 x 23 x 26 In. 345.00
Chest, Blanket, Pine, Scalloped Ends, Wrought Iron Staple Hinges, 35 x 21 In. 230.00
Chest, Blanket, Pine, Sponge Painted, Lift Top, New England, c.1835, 18 x 38 x 16 In. ... 5400.00
Chest, Blanket, Pine, Walnut, Red Wash, Pennsylvania, 1833, 48 x 22 x 30 In. 690.00

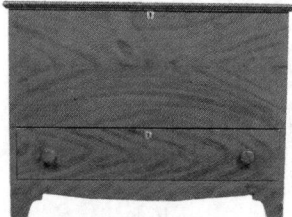

Furniture, Chest, Blanket, Pine, Peg & Nail,
Brushwork Graining, New England, 39 In.

Furniture, Chest, Blanket, Poplar, Grain Painted,
Dovetailed, Interior Till, 30 x 51 In.

Chest, Blanket, Poplar, Bittersweet, Sponged Brown, Pennsylvania, 21 x 49 x 22 1/2 In. ... 2300.00
Chest, Blanket, Poplar, Brown Over Yellow, Grain Painted, 21 x 9 x 9 3/8 In. 1265.00
Chest, Blanket, Poplar, Decoupage, Lift Lid, Soap Hollow, 1901, 22 x 41 In. 2300.00
Chest, Blanket, Poplar, Grain Painted Brown Over Salmon, 3 Drawers, 30 x 51 In. 3850.00
Chest, Blanket, Poplar, Grain Painted, Covered Interior Till, 44 x 21 x 22 In. 400.00
Chest, Blanket, Poplar, Grain Painted, Dovetailed, Interior Till, 30 x 51 In. .... *Illus* 3850.00
Chest, Blanket, Poplar, Inlaid Walnut, Chestnut, 2 Drawers, Hinged Top, 1835, 27 x 42 In. 6465.00
Chest, Blanket, Poplar, Ocher Paint, 2 Drawers, Lift Top, Turned Feet, 29 x 49 In. 2070.00
Chest, Blanket, Poplar, Painted, Orange, Ocher, Drawers, c.1820, 27 x 46 In. 1610.00
Chest, Blanket, Poplar, Red & Black Paint, Stencil, c.1872, 22 x 42 x 17 In. 5750.00
Chest, Blanket, Poplar, Red Paint, Dovetailed, Shoe Feet, 30 x 16 x 19 In. 290.00
Chest, Blanket, Poplar, Sponged, 3 Drawers, Hinged Top, Side Till, c.1825, 40 In. 980.00
Chest, Blanket, Poplar, Vinegar Design, Fan Corners, Drawer, 41 x 30 In. 2530.00
Chest, Blanket, Poplar, Walnut Panels, Compass Star In Circle, Ohio, 43 x 23 In. 630.00
Chest, Blanket, Queen Anne, Gumwood, Butterfly Hinges, N.Y., c.1740, 39 x 43 In. 5400.00
Chest, Blanket, Queen Anne, Pine, Drawers, Teardrop Pulls, Lift Top, 40 x 38 x 20 In. 495.00
Chest, Blanket, Red Wash, Yellow Script, 2 Drawers, Pennsylvania, 1833, 48 In. 690.00
Chest, Blanket, Salmon Paint, Bracket Feet, N.J., c.1840, 38 x 16 x 19 In. 520.00
Chest, Blanket, Salmon Swirl, Inscribed, c.1820, 28 1/2 x 62 In. 2300.00
Chest, Blanket, Shaker, Pine, 2 Faux Over 3 Real Drawers, Lift Top, 45 x 35 x 18 In. 4025.00
Chest, Blanket, Shaker, Pine, Red Paint, Molded Top, 1790, 24 x 43 x 17 In. 920.00
Chest, Blanket, Shaker, Poplar, Cherry, Drawers, Lift Top, Watervliet, N.Y., c.1850, 43 In. . 2300.00
Chest, Blanket, Sheraton, Cherry, Paneled, Turned Feet, 45 3/4 x 18 x 30 In. 290.00
Chest, Blanket, Sheraton, Walnut, Iron Hinges, Pegged Joints, 21 x 32 x 16 In. 3450.00
Chest, Blanket, Sponge Design, Till, Turned Feet, Painted, Pa., 1800s, 23 x 43 x 21 In. ... 1410.00
Chest, Blanket, Walnut, 6-Board, Dovetailed, c.1865, 17 x 30 x 20 In. 115.00
Chest, Blanket, Walnut, Dovetailed, Drawers, Bracket Feet, 25 x 41 x 16 In. 375.00
Chest, Blanket, Walnut, Drawer, Lift Lid, Ogee Bracket Feet, c.1790, 12 1/2 x 16 In. 750.00
Chest, Blanket, Walnut, Hinged Lid, Interior Till, Pennsylvania, 1804, 16 x 42 x 18 In. ... 6756.00
Chest, Blanket, Walnut, Till, Strap Hinges, Lancaster County, Pa., c.1750, 20 x 52 In. 6600.00
Chest, Blanket, White Pine, Blue Paint, 6-Board, New England, 1700s, 16 x 41 x 17 In. ... 1295.00
Chest, Blanket, White Pine, Blue Paint, 6-Board, New England, 1700s, 24 x 48 In. 1115.00
Chest, Blanket, William & Mary, Walnut, Applied Molded Sides, 13 3/4 x 26 In. 4140.00
Chest, Blanket, Yellow Pine, Painted, Lid, Iron Butt Hinges, Bracket Feet, 25 x 50 In. 1955.00
Chest, Blue Paint, 2 Over 4 Drawers, New England, Early 1800s, 54 x 40 x 17 1/2 In. 6230.00
Chest, Blue Paint, Interior Document Box, Sweden, 1796, 17 x 37 x 24 In. 250.00
Chest, Bodafon, 4 Drawers, Sweden, c.1950, 37 1/2 x 43 1/2 x 19 In. 120.00
Chest, Broyhill, Queen Anne Style, Mahogany, 36 1/2 x 25 x 16 In. 375.00
Chest, Burl Walnut, Bombe, 3 Graduated Drawers, Paw Feet, 40 x 40 In. 3580.00
Chest, Burl, Graduated Drawers, Marble Top, 19th Century, 36 x 51 x 24 In. 1725.00
Chest, Butler's, Cherry, 6 Drawers, Side Lock, Victorian, 39 x 21 x 57 In. 920.00
Chest, Butler's, Mahogany, 4 Drawers, Drop Front, Brass Pulls, England, 37 x 37 In. 310.00
Chest, Butler's, Napoleon IV, Rosewood, Marble Top, c.1865, 39 x 54 In. 4600.00
Chest, Campaign, Mahogany, Paduk, Fold-Out Surface, 3 Drawers, 1800s, 40 x 38 In. 4485.00
Chest, Campaign, Victorian, Oak, Mahogany, Brass, 5 Drawers, 40 x 42 In. 1035.00
Chest, Captain's, Pine, Dome Top, Iron Handles, 1800s, 18 x 48 x 20 In. 460.00
Chest, Cherry, 4 Drawers, c.1830, 44 x 44 x 19 In. 1350.00
Chest, Cherry, 4 Graduated Drawers, Overhanging Top, Flared Feet, 36 x 45 In. 1410.00
Chest, Cherry, 6 Graduated Drawers, Bracket Base, 41 x 18 3/4 In. 4255.00
Chest, Cherry, Poplar, 4 Dovetailed Drawers, Stamped Brass Pulls, 14 x 10 In. 3795.00
Chest, Chippendale Style, Mahogany, Block Front, 29 x 27 x 16 In., Pair 290.00
Chest, Chippendale Style, Mahogany, Block Front, Thomasville, 34 x 38 x 19 In. 430.00
Chest, Chippendale Style, Mahogany, Columns, Ogee Feet, 23 x 20 In. 2645.00
Chest, Chippendale Style, Mahogany, Triple Block Front, 32 x 64 x 18 In. ....175.00 to 259.00
Chest, Chippendale, 5 Drawers, Bracket Feet, 1809, 54 x 40 x 19 In. 4300.00
Chest, Chippendale, 10 Drawers, Reeded Columns, Bracket Feet 9775.00
Chest, Chippendale, Birch, 4 Drawers, Reverse Serpentine, N.E., c.1780, 31 x 41 In. 3350.00
Chest, Chippendale, Birch, Pine, 4 Drawers, 39 x 19 1/2 x 36 In. 690.00
Chest, Chippendale, Cherry, 4 Dovetailed Drawers, Bracket Feet, 38 x 20 x 33 In. 3335.00
Chest, Chippendale, Cherry, 4 Dovetailed Drawers, Reeded Columns, 36 x 39 In. 7760.00
Chest, Chippendale, Cherry, 4 Drawers, Reverse Serpentine, c.1775, 35 x 39 x 17 In. 7170.00
Chest, Chippendale, Cherry, 4 Graduated Drawers, Gadroon Base, 37 x 36 In. 4400.00
Chest, Chippendale, Cherry, 5 Drawers, Painted, Cock-Beaded, 47 x 36 x 19 In. 4700.00

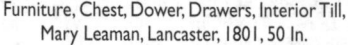

Furniture, Chest, Dower, Drawers, Interior Till,   Furniture, Chest, Dower, Floral, Interior Till,
Mary Leaman, Lancaster, 1801, 50 In.   Lancaster County, 1780s, 50 In.

Chest, Chippendale, Cherry, 6 Drawers, New England, Early 1800s, 50 x 36 In. 1645.00
Chest, Chippendale, Cherry, 6 Drawers, Sutton, Mass., c.1800, 41 x 53 In. 17250.00
Chest, Chippendale, Cherry, Pennsylvania, c.1780, 41 x 42 x 22 In. 1725.00
Chest, Chippendale, Curly Maple, 5 Graduated Drawers, 36 x 49 In. 3450.00
Chest, Chippendale, Mahogany, 4 Drawers, 18th Century, 34 1/2 x 40 x 22 In. 14100.00
Chest, Chippendale, Mahogany, 4 Drawers, Claw & Ball Feet, 34 x 41 In. 3525.00
Chest, Chippendale, Mahogany, Line Inlay, Bracket Feet, 33 x 35 x 19 In. 6050.00
Chest, Chippendale, Maple, 2 Short Over 4 Graduated Drawers, 42 x 36 In. 4115.00
Chest, Chippendale, Maple, 2 Short Over 6 Graduated Drawers, 57 x 36 In. 8815.00
Chest, Chippendale, Maple, 4 Drawers, New England, Late 1700s, 34 x 40 x 19 In. 3290.00
Chest, Chippendale, Maple, 5 Graduated Dovetailed Drawers, 47 x 35 In. 3565.00
Chest, Chippendale, Maple, 5 Graduated Drawers, Overhanging Top, 47 x 35 In. 3055.00
Chest, Chippendale, Maple, 5 Graduated Drawers, Painted, c.1775, 45 x 36 In. 3525.00
Chest, Chippendale, Tiger Maple, 7 Drawers, New England, c.1790, 36 x 19 x 38 In. 10350.00
Chest, Chippendale, Walnut, 4 Drawers, Ogee Bracket Feet, 42 In. 4400.00
Chest, Chippendale, Walnut, 4 Drawers, Pennsylvania, c.1770, 33 x 37 x 21 1/2 In. 9600.00
Chest, Chippendale, Walnut, 8 Over 5 Drawers, Late 1700s, 68 x 47 x 23 In. 7640.00
Chest, Chippendale, Walnut, 9 Drawers, c.1780, 60 x 43 In. 3220.00
Chest, Chippendale, Walnut, Reeded Frieze, Late 1700s, 89 x 43 x 23 In. 8815.00
Chest, Dower, Carved, Painted, Wheels, Early 20th Century, 40 x 49 x 20 In. 750.00
Chest, Dower, Cedar, 2 Drawers, Cabriole Legs, 42 x 43 1/2 x 21 In. 290.00
Chest, Dower, Drawers, Interior Till, Mary Leaman, Lancaster, 1801, 50 In. .... *Illus* 13200.00
Chest, Dower, Floral, Interior Till, Lancaster County, 1780s, 50 In. .... *Illus* 10450.00
Chest, Dower, Iron Hinges, Till, Pennsylvania German, c.1800, 18 x 52 x 20 In. 6500.00
Chest, Dower, Pennsylvania Dutch, Hand Painted, Snipe Hinges, 21 x 48 x 23 In. 925.00
Chest, Dower, Poplar, Lift Top, Clover-Shaped Panels, c.1790, 23 x 47 In. 2530.00
Chest, Eastlake Style, Marble Top, Teardrop Pulls, Victorian, 33 x 40 x 19 In. 160.00
Chest, Eastlake, Chestnut, Marble, c.1890, 33 3/4 x 38 x 17 In. 60.00
Chest, Eastlake, Mahogany, Burl Walnut, Beaded, 2 Over 5 Drawers, 64 In. 865.00
Chest, Elm, Dentillated Frieze, 3 Drawers, Denmark, Early 1800s, 35 x 30 x 19 In. 1495.00
Chest, Empire Style, Fruitwood, Boxwood Inlay, Herringbone, 37 x 39 x 20 In. 1295.00
Chest, Empire, 2 Over 3 Drawers, Cutout Base, Early 1800s, 43 x 43 In. 275.00
Chest, Empire, Cherry, Black, Yellow Paint, 4 Dovetailed Drawers, 40 x 20 x 47 In. 1035.00
Chest, Empire, Cherry, Rectangular Top, 4 Drawers, 1800s, 49 1/2 x 41 3/4 x 22 In. 353.00
Chest, Empire, Mahogany, 2 Over 2 Drawers, Ivory Knobs, 9 x 4 1/2 x 9 In. 690.00
Chest, Empire, Mahogany, 3 Dovetailed Drawers, Columns, 14 x 14 x 9 In. 575.00
Chest, Empire, Mahogany, 3 Over 4 Drawers, Mirror, 79 x 42 x 20 In. 460.00
Chest, Empire, Mahogany, 4 Drawers, Turned Columns, 1855, 17 In., Child's 2970.00
Chest, Empire, Mahogany, 6 Drawers, Backsplash, c.1835, 54 x 50 x 21 In. 530.00
Chest, Empire, Pine, Poplar, Sponged, 3 Long, 2 Short Drawers, 42 x 46 In. 4600.00
Chest, English Oak, 4 Graduated Drawers, Cutout Feet, 42 x 38 1/2 x 17 In. 520.00
Chest, Faux Marble Painted Top, 3 Drawers, 19th Century, 33 x 36 x 18 In. 1610.00
Chest, Federal, 4 Drawers, Bracket Feet, c.1800, 32 x 38 x 15 In. 2115.00
Chest, Federal, 4 Drawers, Cornucopia Carved Corners, 44 x 41 x 21 In. 1165.00
Chest, Federal, Birch, Maple, Red Stain, 6 Drawers, c.1810, 60 x 39 x 19 In. 45000.00
Chest, Federal, Bowfront, 4 Drawers, Bracket Feet, c.1800, 37 x 38 x 19 In. 2585.00
Chest, Federal, Cherry, 4 Drawers, New England, 1790-1800, 34 x 36 x 18 In. 2115.00
Chest, Federal, Cherry, 4 Graduated Drawers, Overhanging Top, 35 x 40 x 21 In. 2705.00

Chest, Federal, Cherry, 5 Drawers, Late 1700s, 39 x 37 x 21 In. 2470.00
Chest, Federal, Cherry, Barber Pole Inlay, Graduated Drawers, 41 x 37 x 19 In. 6900.00
Chest, Federal, Cherry, Bird's-Eye Maple, 8 Drawers, c.1795, 65 x 44 x 22 In. 2990.00
Chest, Federal, Cherry, Bowfront, 33 x 39 1/2 x 25 1/8 In. 4600.00
Chest, Federal, Cherry, Inlaid Fans, 4 Drawers, Shaped Skirt, 37 x 43 In. 3055.00
Chest, Federal, Cherry, Mahogany Veneer, French Bracket Feet, c.1810 .... 16100.00
Chest, Federal, Mahogany, 4 Drawers, Bracket Feet, c.1790, 36 x 40 x 23 In. 4400.00
Chest, Federal, Mahogany, 4 Drawers, New England, Early 1800s, 44 x 42 x 20 In. 1150.00
Chest, Federal, Mahogany, 4 Graduated Drawers, c.1810, 37 x 41 x 21 In. 1380.00
Chest, Federal, Mahogany, Bowfront, 4 Crossbanded Drawers, 35 x 41 In. 4115.00
Chest, Federal, Mahogany, Bowfront, 4 Drawers, c.1800, 38 x 41 x 23 In. 1410.00
Chest, Federal, Mahogany, Bowfront, 4 Drawers, c.1805, 39 x 43 x 23 In. 1840.00
Chest, Federal, Mahogany, Bowfront, 4 Drawers, Mass., c.1820, 35 x 41 x 23 In. 1765.00
Chest, Federal, Mahogany, Bowfront, Brass Pulls, Mass., c.1820, 40 x 41 x 20 In. 1115.00
Chest, Federal, Mahogany, Carved, 4 Drawers, Salem, c.1800, 44 x 42 x 21 In. 11165.00
Chest, Federal, Mahogany, Inlaid, 4 Graduated Drawers, c.1800, 37 x 39 x 19 In. 2470.00
Chest, Federal, Mahogany, Inlaid, Bowfront, 4 Drawers, c.1810, 38 x 42 In. 2530.00
Chest, Federal, Mahogany, Molded Top, 4 Drawers, c.1800, 36 x 42 x 21 In. 1060.00
Chest, Federal, Mahogany, Molded Top, 4 Drawers, c.1800, 38 x 42 1/2 x 20 In. 1410.00
Chest, Federal, Mahogany, Satinwood Inlay, 5 Drawers, 33 x 38 x 21 In. 1955.00
Chest, Federal, Mahogany, Satinwood Inlay, Bowfront, c.1800, 36 x 39 x 23 In. 4370.00
Chest, Federal, Mahogany, Scalloped, Stenciled Acorn, Oak Leaf, c.1840, 47 x 43 In. 1095.00
Chest, Federal, Mahogany, Swelled Front, 4 Drawers, c.1795, 38 x 41 x 22 In. 2230.00
Chest, Federal, Maple, Mahogany, 4 Drawers, 44 x 42 x 21 In. 805.00
Chest, Federal, Maple, Painted, 4 Drawers, New England, Early 1800s, 37 x 44 In. 5975.00
Chest, Federal, Pine, Grain Painted, 4 Drawers, c.1830, 48 x 42 1/2 In. 3600.00
Chest, Federal, Satinwood, Mahogany Inlay, 2 Drawers, Mirror, c.1815, 38 x 25 In. 420.00
Chest, Federal, Satinwood, Mahogany, Bowfront, c.1810, 41 x 43 x 23 In. 1610.00
Chest, Federal, Tiger Maple, 4 Drawers, Mass., Early 1800s, 40 x 39 x 17 In. 6465.00
Chest, Federal, Tiger Maple, Mahogany, 2 Over 4 Drawers, 47 1/2 x 43 x 20 In. 865.00
Chest, Federal, Walnut, 4 Drawers, Applied Molding, c.1820, 41 x 41 x 21 In. 635.00
Chest, Federal, Walnut, Bowfront, 4 Drawers, c.1815, 43 1/2 x 39 In. 2760.00
Chest, Federal, Walnut, Bowfront, 4 Drawers, New England, c.1800, 36 x 39 In. 5290.00
Chest, Federal, Walnut, Inlay, 4 Graduated Drawers, c.1820, 46 x 40 In. 865.00
Chest, Federal, Walnut, Satinwood, c.1805, 40 1/2 x 38 x 21 In. 1380.00
Chest, Federal, Walnut, Tulip, Fan Inlays, Flared Feet, 69 3/4 x 41 In. 7475.00
Chest, French Empire, Oak, Pine, Gold, Black Enamel, 4 Drawers, 38 x 17 x 36 In. 1095.00
Chest, French Provincial, Mahogany, 4 Drawers, 34 x 31 x 17 In., Pair 1495.00
Chest, G. Nakashima, Walnut, c.1965, 31 3/4 x 36 x 20 In. ....7170.00 to 7770.00
Chest, G. Nelson, Rosewood, Porcelain Pulls, c.1955, 31 x 46 x 18 1/2 In. 4185.00
Chest, G. Stickley, 2 Over 2 Drawers, Swivel Mirror, Paneled Sides, 68 x 54 In. 10000.00
Chest, G. Stickley, 2 Over 3 Drawers, Paneled Sides, Chamfered Back, 42 x 27 In. 9985.00
Chest, G. Stickley, Chestnut, 2 Over 3 Drawers, Wood Knobs, 45 x 36 x 21 In. 2000.00
Chest, G. Stickley, No. 909, 2 Half Drawers, 3 Full Drawers, 37 x 20 x 42 In. 2650.00
Chest, G. Stickley, No. 913, Curly Maple, Ellis, 51 x 36 x 20 In. ....4185.00 to 5290.00
Chest, George I, Satinwood, Inlaid, Crossbanded, c.1710, 41 x 39 x 21 In. 1495.00
Chest, George II Style, Burl Walnut, Inlaid, 5 Drawers, c.1850, 41 1/2 x 42 In. 2300.00
Chest, George II Style, Burl Walnut, Sunburst Inlay, 5 Drawers, 38 x 41 x 21 In. 1955.00
Chest, George II, Burl Walnut, 5 Drawers, Splayed Feet, 1800s, 40 x 41 x 19 In. 1840.00
Chest, George II, Burl Walnut, Crossbanded, 5 Drawers, 1700s, 35 x 38 x 22 In. 3910.00
Chest, George III Style, Chinoiserie, 2 Short Over 3 Long Drawers, 38 x 40 In. 2990.00
Chest, George III Style, Mahogany, 4 Drawers, Late 19th Century, 43 x 47 x 22 In. 2300.00
Chest, George III Style, Mahogany, 4 Graduated Drawers, 32 x 23 x 36 In. 410.00
Chest, George III Style, Mahogany, 5 Drawers, Bowed Top, 43 x 42 x 22 In. 2760.00
Chest, George III Style, Mahogany, 5 Drawers, c.1825, 34 x 36 x 20 In. 1900.00
Chest, George III Style, Mahogany, 5 Drawers, c.1860, 38 3/4 x 42 x 19 3/4 In. 1265.00
Chest, George III Style, Mahogany, Bowfront, 5 Drawers, 1880s, 40 x 42 x 19 In. 1150.00
Chest, George III Style, Mahogany, Bowfront, 5 Drawers, c.1860, 46 x 44 x 21 In. 1840.00
Chest, George III Style, Mahogany, Bowfront, c.1840, 56 x 43 x 23 In. 2300.00
Chest, George III Style, Mahogany, Bowfront, c.1875, 41 x 42 x 21 In. 805.00
Chest, George III Style, Mahogany, Bowfront, Late 19th Century, 42 x 42 x 22 In. 2185.00
Chest, George III Style, Mahogany, Inlaid, Bowfront, 39 12 x 43 5/8 x 22 In. 1035.00
Chest, George III Style, Mahogany, Inlaid, Bowfront, c.1825, 38 x 46 x 21 In. 2645.00

Chest, George III Style, Mahogany, Mid 19th Century, 32 1/2 x 35 x 17 3/4 In. 1035.00
Chest, George III, Mahogany, 2 Over 3 Drawers, Bracket Feet, 37 1/2 In. 950.00
Chest, George III, Mahogany, 2 Over 3 Graduated Drawers, 40 x 41 x 22 In. 1150.00
Chest, George III, Mahogany, 3 Drawers, Bracket Feet, 31 1/2 x 19 x 32 In. 1615.00
Chest, George III, Mahogany, 4 Dovetailed Drawers, Beaded Edge, 39 x 43 In. 2070.00
Chest, George III, Mahogany, 4 Drawers, Sliding Shelf, Bracket Feet, 35 x 37 In. 3680.00
Chest, George III, Mahogany, 4 Graduated Drawers, Bracket Feet, 31 x 37 x 20 In. 940.00
Chest, George III, Mahogany, 4 Graduated Drawers, Shaped Feet, 33 In. 4140.00
Chest, George III, Mahogany, 5 Drawers, Bracket Feet, 36 x 20 x 36 In. 2690.00
Chest, George III, Mahogany, 5 Drawers, Bracket Feet, c.1800, 37 x 39 x 17 In. 1725.00
Chest, George III, Mahogany, 5 Drawers, c.1800, 41 1/2 x 45 1/4 x 21 In. 1265.00
Chest, George III, Mahogany, 5 Graduated Drawers, c.1800, 39 x 40 x 22 In. 1610.00
Chest, George III, Mahogany, Bowed Top, Banded, 39 x 42 x 21 3/4 In. 1725.00
Chest, George III, Mahogany, Bowfront, 2 Over 3 Drawers, 39 x 41 x 20 In. 2300.00
Chest, George III, Mahogany, Bowfront, 2 Over 3 Drawers, c.1785, 41 x 41 1/2 In. 1610.00
Chest, George III, Mahogany, Bowfront, 5 Drawers, 40 x 40 x 22 In. 2530.00
Chest, George III, Mahogany, Bowfront, 5 Drawers, c.1800, 40 x 40 x 20 In. 2185.00
Chest, George III, Mahogany, Bowfront, 5 Drawers, Late 1700s, 43 x 42 x 21 In. 2530.00
Chest, George III, Mahogany, Bowfront, Banded Top, 3 Drawers, c.1815, 39 x 42 In. 1725.00
Chest, George III, Mahogany, Bowfront, Banded Top, c.1800, 34 x 43 x 21 In. 2185.00
Chest, George III, Mahogany, Bowfront, c.1800, 39 x 41 x 20 In. 1955.00
Chest, George III, Mahogany, Bowfront, Late 18th Century, 44 x 41 x 21 In. 2185.00
Chest, George III, Mahogany, Bowfront, Reeded Edge, c.1800, 42 x 42 x 20 In. 1610.00
Chest, George III, Mahogany, Inlaid, 19th Century, 40 1/4 x 41 1/2 x 18 In. 635.00
Chest, George III, Mahogany, Inlaid, 4 Graduated Drawers, 34 x 37 In. 1495.00
Chest, George III, Mahogany, Molded Top, 3 Drawers, 37 x 42 x 21 In. 1150.00
Chest, George III, Mahogany, Satinwood, Inlaid, 4 Drawers, 31 x 41 x 20 In. 1955.00
Chest, George III, Mahogany, Serpentine Front, 4 Drawers, Mirror, 43 In. 7600.00
Chest, George III, Mahogany, Serpentine Front, 4 Graduated Drawers, 42 In. 4830.00
Chest, George III, Mahogany, Walnut, c.1775, 37 3/4 x 38 x 20 In. 1380.00
Chest, George III, Oak, Stained, 2 Short Over 3 Long Drawers, 38 x 41 x 21 In. 1495.00
Chest, George III, Walnut, Mahogany, 5 Drawers, Bracket Feet, c.1885, 41 x 42 In. 1955.00
Chest, George IV, Mahogany Inlay, Ebony Stringing, 5 Drawers, 43 x 42 x 21 In. 1265.00
Chest, George IV, Mahogany Inlay, Holly & Ebony Stringing, 40 x 42 x 19 In. 1840.00
Chest, George IV, Mahogany, 2 Short Over 3 Long Drawers, 42 x 43 x 22 In. 2530.00
Chest, George IV, Mahogany, 3 Drawers, Brass Mounted, c.1835, 21 x 21 In. 460.00
Chest, George IV, Mahogany, Inlay, Bowfront, 5 Drawers, 43 x 42 x 21 In. 2530.00
Chest, George IV, Mahogany, Serpentine, Crossbanded, c.1840, 34 x 39 x 23 In. 1725.00
Chest, George IV, Satinwood, Mahogany Inlay, Bowfront, 45 1/2 x 41 x 20 In. 1610.00
Chest, Georgian Style, Mahogany Inlay, Bowfront, 3 Drawers, 41 x 39 In. 1840.00
Chest, Georgian Style, Mahogany, 6 Drawers, Splayed Feet, c.1825, 40 x 44 x 20 In. 635.00
Chest, Georgian Style, Mahogany, Bowfront, 5 Drawers, c.1880, 41 x 41 x 21 In. 2185.00
Chest, Georgian Style, Mahogany, Bowfront, c.1860, 35 x 41 x 21 In. 1495.00
Chest, Georgian Style, Mahogany, Inlaid, 5 Drawers, Bracket Feet, 33 x 39 x 19 In. 750.00
Chest, Georgian Style, Satinwood Inlay, 5 Drawers, Late 1800s, 43 x 43 x 23 In. 1265.00
Chest, Georgian, Bowfront, 5 Drawers, Scalloped Base, c.1880, 44 x 43 x 21 In. 1495.00
Chest, Georgian, Mahogany Inlay, Bowfront, 1800s, 41 x 40 x 21 In. 1840.00
Chest, Georgian, Mahogany, 2 Short & 3 Graduated Drawers, 41 x 39 x 20 In. 2070.00
Chest, Georgian, Mahogany, 6 Drawers, Dentil Cornice, c.1775, 65 x 38 In. 2700.00
Chest, Golden Oak, Serpentine Front, Mirror, 37 x 20 x 74 In. 520.00
Chest, Grain Painted, 4 Drawers, Pennsylvania, 11 1/2 x 5 1/2 x 10 In. 990.00
Chest, Grain Painted, Brown, Circles, Dovetailed, Nails, Iron Key Latch, 13 x 33 x 17 In. . . 358.00
Chest, Grain Painted, Fan-Carved Drawer Over 4 Long Drawers, 49 x 41 In. 4400.00
Chest, Grain Painted, Salmon, Feathered Brown, Dovetailed, Turned Feet, 13 x 21 In. 1760.00
Chest, Hardwood, Painted, Dragons, Drawers, Chinese, Early 1900s, 67 x 39 In. 920.00
Chest, Hepplewhite, 4 Beaded Drawers, French Bracket Feet, 38 x 38 In. 990.00
Chest, Hepplewhite, Birch, Mahogany Veneer, Bowfront, 4 Drawers, 42 x 22 In. 575.00
Chest, Hepplewhite, Bird's-Eye Maple, Mahogany Banding, 4 Drawers 4600.00
Chest, Hepplewhite, Cherry, Satinwood, Bowfront, 4 Drawers, 42 x 21 x 40 In. 690.00
Chest, Hepplewhite, Cherry, Veneer, Poplar, Bowfront, 4 Drawers, 41 x 22 x 37 In. 7475.00
Chest, Hepplewhite, Inlaid Reeded Columns, Sunburst, 4 Drawers, 38 x 41 In. 2200.00
Chest, Hepplewhite, Mahogany, Bowfront, 4 Drawers, 40 x 39 1/2 x 23 In. 2475.00
Chest, Hepplewhite, Mahogany, Demilune Inlay, Bowfront 3105.00

Chest, Hepplewhite, Mahogany, Inlaid, 4 Drawers, 38 1/2 x 40 x 17 In. 2300.00
Chest, Hepplewhite, Maple, Wavy Birch, Flame Birch, Bowfront, N.H. 9200.00
Chest, Hepplewhite, Poplar, Painted, Bowfront, 4 Dovetailed Drawers, 41 x 37 In. 4315.00
Chest, Hepplewhite, Walnut, Fan, Line Inlaid Corners, c.1810, 36 x 33 3/4 In. 4140.00
Chest, Italian Baroque, Walnut, 2 Sections, 13 Small Drawers, 86 In. 8625.00
Chest, L. & J.G. Stickley, 2 Over 4 Drawers, Brass Hardware, 57 x 40 x 22 In. 5290.00
Chest, L. & J.G. Stickley, No. 77, 2 Half Drawers, 3 Drawers, Apron, 36 x 18 x 39 In. 1175.00
Chest, Limbert, 5 Drawers, Backsplash, Loop Hardware, 49 3/4 x 36 x 20 In. 3400.00
Chest, Limbert, 5 Drawers, Copper Hardware, Arched Toe Board, 36 x 20 x 50 In. 4090.00
Chest, Louis Philippe Style, Mahogany, Marble, Continental, c.1900, 31 x 19 In. 3450.00
Chest, Louis XV, Silver, Gilt, 1900s, 35 1/2 x 55 x 22 In. 235.00
Chest, Mahogany Veneer, 4 Drawers, Chamfered Feet, Mid-Atlantic, c.1805 . . . . 4900.00
Chest, Mahogany, 2 Short Over 3 Long Drawers, c.1880, 39 x 41 x 31 In. 575.00
Chest, Mahogany, 2 Short Over 6 Graduated Drawers, England, 68 x 46 x 23 In. 3450.00
Chest, Mahogany, 3 Drawers, Bail Handles, Bracket Base, 39 x 41 1/2 x 21 In. 520.00
Chest, Mahogany, 3 Drawers, Bracket Feet, Continental, 18 1/2 x 12 3/4 x 16 In. 260.00
Chest, Mahogany, 3 Drawers, Bracket Feet, England, Late 1800s, 33 1/4 x 43 1/2 In. 635.00
Chest, Mahogany, 3 Drawers, Brass Bail Handles, 39 x 41 1/2 x 19 1/2 In. 800.00
Chest, Mahogany, 3 Drawers, Rounded Front Corners, 1800s, 31 x 36 In. 489.00
Chest, Mahogany, 3 Graduated Drawers, Early 19th Century, 12 x 12 In. 530.00
Chest, Mahogany, 3 Graduated Drawers, Scotland, c.1860, 58 1/2 x 51 x 21 In. 1295.00
Chest, Mahogany, 5 Drawers, Shaped Splayed Feet, c.1860, 42 x 41 x 20 In. 1610.00
Chest, Mahogany, 6 Drawers, Scroll Supports, Scotland, 1900s, 58 x 47 x 21 In. 1060.00
Chest, Mahogany, Beaded Edge, 5 Drawers, Late 1800s, 42 x 43 x 22 In. 550.00
Chest, Mahogany, Bowfront, 2 Over 3 Drawers, Scotland, 48 x 49 In. 1495.00
Chest, Mahogany, Bowfront, 2 Short, 3 Long Drawers, c.1860, 43 x 44 x 22 In. 1840.00
Chest, Mahogany, Bowfront, 4 Drawers, Molded Top, 1800s, 12 x 12 1/2 In. 800.00
Chest, Mahogany, Bowfront, 4 Drawers, New England, c.1800, 38 1/2 x 41 In. 7200.00
Chest, Mahogany, Bowfront, 4 Drawers, Turned Feet, c.1830, 36 x 41 x 19 In. 1725.00
Chest, Mahogany, Bowfront, 5 Graduated Drawers, England, 46 x 41 x 21 In. 1610.00
Chest, Mahogany, Crossbanded, Straight Front, 4 Drawers, Turned Supports, 22 In. 810.00
Chest, Mahogany, Inlaid, Bowfront, 5 Drawers, England, c.1875, 42 x 38 x 19 In. 1495.00
Chest, Mahogany, Pine, 4 Drawers, Brass Pulls, Turned Feet, 10 x 7 x 13 In. 175.00
Chest, Mahogany, Satinwood Inlay, 8 Drawers, England, c.1900, 75 x 43 x 14 In. 12500.00
Chest, Mahogany, Scrolling, 4 Drawers, Brass Rosette Hardware, 49 x 39 x 17 In. 520.00
Chest, Mahogany, Serpentine Front, 4 Drawers, Carved Center Drop, 36 1/2 In. 14500.00
Chest, Mahogany, Walnut Inlay, Scotland, Mid 19th Century, 37 x 51 x 24 In. 1035.00
Chest, Maple, 4 Drawers, Bracket Feet, c.1780, 37 x 37 x 19 In. 4850.00
Chest, Maple, 6 Drawers, Molded Edge, Dovetailed, Bracket Feet, c.1785, 42 x 38 In. 3680.00
Chest, Maple, 6 Graduated Drawers, Shaped Apron, Bracket Feet, 51 x 40 In. 2870.00
Chest, Maple, Painted, 5 Drawers, Ring-Turned Legs, c.1825, 54 x 36 x 18 In. 4115.00
Chest, Maple, Pine, 3 Drawers, Dovetailed, Flame Graining, 26 x 19 x 29 In., Child's 2590.00
Chest, Mixed Woods, 5 Drawers, Continental, Late 1700s, 38 x 37 x 23 In. 1725.00
Chest, Moravian, Walnut, 19th Century, 43 x 41 1/2 x 21 In. 705.00
Chest, Mother-Of-Pearl Inlay, Ivory, 3 Drawers, 1600s, 23 x 14 x 20 In. 380.00
Chest, Mule, Brown Sponging Over Yellow, Vinegar Decoration, 38 x 16 x 28 In. 2875.00
Chest, Mule, Chippendale, Pine, 3 Drawers, 3 Fake Drawers, Lift Top, 53 x 38 In. 1550.00
Chest, Mule, Chippendale, Pine, 3 Drawers, False Fronts, D. Bratten, 54 x 35 In. 4485.00
Chest, Mule, Oak, Crossbanded, 5 Drawers, 3 Fake Drawers, Lift Top, c.1750, 58 1/2 In. . . 1425.00
Chest, Mule, Oak, Incised, 2 Bottom Drawers, Lift Top, England, 51 In. 430.00
Chest, Mule, Pine, Chestnut, Red Paint, 2 Drawers, Painted Borders, 40 x 18 x 39 In. 1955.00
Chest, Mule, Pine, Grain Painted, Brown, 2 Drawers, 2 Fake Drawers, 41 x 41 In. 635.00
Chest, Mule, Pine, Red Over Yellow Flame Graining, Drawer, 42 x 19 x 37 In. 1495.00
Chest, Mule, Poplar, Pine, Walnut, Blue Paint, 2 Drawers, 39 x 18 x 40 In. 1840.00
Chest, Mule, Poplar, Red Wash, 2 Drawers, Serpentine Bracket Feet, 46 x 21 x 44 In. 805.00
Chest, Mule, William & Mary, Painted, 2 Drawers, 4 Fake Fronts, Bulb Feet 2070.00
Chest, Neoclassical, Bird's-Eye Maple, Stained, Vermont, c.1830, 41 x 43 3/4 In. 880.00
Chest, Neoclassical, Cherry, Mahogany, Mid 19th Century, 47 x 46 x 24 In. 1840.00
Chest, Neoclassical, Mahogany, Beaded, 4 Drawers, Bun Feet, 47 x 47 In. 920.00
Chest, Niedecken, Walnut, 2 Over 2 Drawers, Prairie School Details, 27 x 56 In. 8225.00
Chest, Oak, 5 Drawers, Bail Handles, Backsplash, 59 1/2 x 33 1/2 x 19 In. 200.00
Chest, Oak, Fruitwood, 4 Drawers, Paneled Sides, Bracket Feet, 1600s, 40 In. 5060.00
Chest, Oak, Marquetry, Marble Top, 2 Drawers, 39 x 18 x 35 In. 1265.00

Chest, Oak, Oxbow Front, 4 Drawers, Fluted Columns, Bracket Feet, 30 x 28 x 17 In.	140.00
Chest, Oak, Pine, Inlaid, 6 Dovetailed Drawers, Bracket Feet, 45 x 19 x 51 In.	400.00
Chest, Oak, Scrolling Inlay, 5 Drawers, Channel Isles, c.1840, 48 x 49 x 23 In.	1840.00
Chest, Oak, Serpentine Front, S Supports, 33 x 20 x 71 In.	375.00
Chest, Oak, Straight Front, 3 Drawers, Bracket Feet, 33 1/2 x 18 x 36 In.	810.00
Chest, Painted, Bulgaria, c.1850, 13 1/2 x 33 x 16 In.	385.00
Chest, Painted, Serpentine Front, 3 Drawers, 38 x 45 x 23 In.	3738.00
Chest, Painted, Stenciled, Early 20th Century, 42 x 28 x 17 In.	60.00
Chest, Pine, 2 Over 3 Drawers, Shaped Backsplash, 16 x 11 1/2 x 5 1/2 In.	290.00
Chest, Pine, 6-Board, Wire-Hinged Lid, Early 1800s, 10 1/4 x 14 x 8 In., Child's	705.00
Chest, Pine, Blue Paint, 3 Dovetailed Drawers, Brass Pulls, 14 1/2 x 7 1/2 In.	1870.00
Chest, Pine, c.1890, 30 x 43 1/2 x 18 In.	175.00
Chest, Pine, Dovetailed, Dome Top, Painted, Comb Graining, 13 x 27 x 18 In.	220.00
Chest, Pine, Grain Painted, Polychrome, 3 Drawers, c.1840, 11 x 12 x 6 In.	15600.00
Chest, Pine, Hand Painted Flowers, Germany, 1800s, 13 x 20 x 12 In.	450.00
Chest, Pine, Maple, Grain Painted, 2 Drawers, Hinged Top, Mass., 1720s, 45 x 39 In.	2585.00
Chest, Pine, Painted, Iron Handles, James Selkrig, c.1773, 16 x 40 x 22 In.	700.00
Chest, Pine, Painted, Serpentine Top, Molded Edge, 1800s, 34 x 43 x 22 In.	5980.00
Chest, Pine, Red Ocher Paint, Wavy Lines, 5 Drawers, 18 5/8 x 24 3/4 In.	1430.00
Chest, Poplar, Red Ocher Paint, 4 Large Over 3 Small Drawers, 49 x 42 In.	4620.00
Chest, Queen Anne Style, Burl Walnut, 2 Over 3 Drawers, Bun Feet, 39 x 42 In.	2185.00
Chest, Queen Anne Style, Burl Walnut, 4 Drawers, c.1790, 36 x 37 3/4 x 22 In.	1610.00
Chest, Queen Anne Style, Burl Walnut, 7 Drawers, Early 1800s, 32 x 38 x 20 In.	3910.00
Chest, Queen Anne Style, Oyster Walnut, Line Stringing, c.1800, 38 x 40 In.	1840.00
Chest, Queen Anne Style, Painted, 4 Drawers, 85 x 39 1/2 x 21 3/4 In.	7050.00
Chest, Queen Anne Style, Walnut, 2 Over 3 Drawers, 34 x 42 x 20 In.	2185.00
Chest, Queen Anne Style, Walnut, 2 Short Over 3 Long Drawers, 36 x 41 x 20 In.	2760.00
Chest, Queen Anne Style, Walnut, Inlaid, Banded Top, c.1800, 36 x 42 x 21 In.	3220.00
Chest, Queen Anne, Burl Walnut, 5 Drawers, 18th Century, 39 x 38 x 22 In.	2185.00
Chest, Queen Anne, Cherry, 5 Drawers, New England, c.1775, 74 1/2 In.	5875.00
Chest, Queen Anne, Cherry, 11 Drawers, Mass., c.1755, 69 1/2 x 38 3/4 In.	9400.00
Chest, Queen Anne, Cherry, 11 Drawers, Pinwheel, Fan, Conn., 1700s, 79 x 38 In.	10575.00
Chest, Queen Anne, Cherry, Mixed Woods, Bonnet Top, Conn., c.1755, 82 In.	8365.00
Chest, Queen Anne, Maple, 6 Drawers, New England, c.1760, 60 x 36 In.	9990.00
Chest, Queen Anne, Maple, N.H., c.1760, 79 1/2 x 38 In.	9560.00
Chest, Queen Anne, Maple, Pine, 8 Drawers, New England, c.1775, 73 x 38 In.	9400.00
Chest, Queen Anne, Walnut, Crossbanded Top, 5 Drawers, 34 x 38 x 22 In.	3910.00
Chest, Queen Anne, Walnut, Inlaid, 2 Over 3 Drawers, Bracket Feet, 33 x 38 x 20 In.	1610.00
Chest, Queen Anne, Walnut, Oyster Veneer, 3 Drawers, 30 x 35 x 18 In.	1150.00
Chest, Queen Anne, Walnut, Veneer Top, 6 Drawers, Early 1700s, 35 x 40 x 21 In.	3450.00
Chest, Red Paint, 2 False Drawers, 2 Drawers, Turned Pulls, Bracket Feet, 45 x 38 In.	8815.00
Chest, Red Paint, 5 Drawers, Bracket Base, New England, 1700s, 52 x 39 x 18 In.	3820.00
Chest, Regency Style, Mahogany, 19th Century, 12 1/2 x 10 1/4 x 6 1/2 In.	800.00
Chest, Regency Style, Mahogany, 7 Drawers, England, c.1860, 54 x 50 x 24 In.	1380.00
Chest, Regency Style, Mahogany, Bowed, Banded, 6 Drawers, 40 x 17 In.	1955.00
Chest, Regency, Mahogany, 5 Drawers, Plinth Base, 42 x 42 x 22 In.	750.00
Chest, Regency, Mahogany, Bowfront, 2 Over 3 Drawers, c.1815, 38 1/2 x 41 1/2 In.	1265.00
Chest, Regency, Mahogany, Bowfront, 2 Over 3 Drawers, c.1815, 44 x 42 x 21 In.	1495.00
Chest, Regency, Mahogany, Bowfront, 2 Over 3 Drawers, c.1815, 45 1/2 x 47 In.	1955.00
Chest, Regency, Mahogany, Bowfront, 2 Short & 3 Long Drawers, 42 x 42 x 21 In.	1380.00
Chest, Regency, Mahogany, Bowfront, 5 Drawers, D-Shape Top, 41 x 21 x 44 In.	1330.00
Chest, Regency, Mahogany, Bowfront, 5 Drawers, Scotland, 45 x 46 x 23 In.	2070.00
Chest, Regency, Mahogany, Bowfront, 6 Drawers, 51 x 43 x 20 In.	2990.00
Chest, Regency, Mahogany, Bowfront, Reeded Edge, 5 Drawers, 41 x 39 x 18 In.	1725.00
Chest, Regency, Mahogany, Bowfront, Reeded Edge, 5 Drawers, 44 x 43 x 23 In. 1100.00 to	1150.00
Chest, Regency, Mahogany, Frieze Drawer, 5 Drawers, Scotland, 47 x 50 x 24 In.	1265.00
Chest, Regency, Mahogany, Inlaid, Bowfront, 5 Drawers, 44 x 42 x 21 In.	2070.00
Chest, Regency, Mahogany, Inlaid, Bowfront, Bracket Feet, 43 x 40 x 21 In.	1955.00
Chest, Rococo Revival, Walnut, Marble Top, 4 Drawers, c.1865, 35 x 43 x 22 In.	635.00
Chest, Rohde, 8 Drawers, Brown Saltman, 1939, 60 x 19 x 32 In.	1115.00
Chest, Rosewood, 3 Crossbanded Drawers, Square Fluted Legs, Denmark, 41 In.	1955.00
Chest, Rosewood, Carved, Brass Inlay Top, 6 Drawers, 20th Century, 18 x 24 x 12 In.	85.00
Chest, Shaker, Birch, Pine, 6 Drawers, Bracket Base, 51 x 36 1/2 x 17 In.	9200.00

Chest, Shaker, Pine, Ocher Stain, 6 Drawers, Edward Johnson, 44 x 24 x 20 In. 2530.00
Chest, Shaker, Pine, Red Paint, 6 Drawers, Enfield, Conn., c.1840, 15 x 15 x 10 In. 2645.00
Chest, Shaker, Tailor's, Counter, Maple, Pine, Mt. Lebanon, N.Y., 1840s, 32 x 105 In. 9400.00
Chest, Sheraton Style, Mahogany, 5 Drawers, c.1830, 42 x 46 1/2 x 21 In. 1265.00
Chest, Sheraton, Bird's-Eye Maple, Shaped Top, 4 Drawers, 41 x 42 x 19 In. 10925.00
Chest, Sheraton, Cherry, 4 Drawers, c.1830, 42 x 41 x 21 In. 980.00
Chest, Sheraton, Cherry, 4 Graduated Drawers, 39 x 41 1/4 x 19 3/4 In. 980.00
Chest, Sheraton, Cherry, Bird's-Eye Maple, Scrolled Backboard, 55 x 46 x 21 In. 920.00
Chest, Sheraton, Cherry, Pine, Inlay, Bowfront, 4 Drawers, 41 x 21 x 42 In. 750.00
Chest, Sheraton, Cherry, Red Wash, 4 Drawers, Brass Pulls, 42 x 51 1/4 In. 980.00
Chest, Sheraton, Mahogany, Backsplash, 2 Glove Drawers, 4 Drawers, 49 x 45 In. 3450.00
Chest, Sheraton, Mahogany, Bowfront, 4 Drawers, Ball Feet, c.1815, 40 x 43 In. 1060.00
Chest, Sheraton, Mahogany, Bowfront, 4 Drawers, c.1830, 42 x 45 x 24 In. 1380.00
Chest, Sheraton, Mahogany, Inlaid, 20th Century, 31 x 37 x 21 In. 705.00
Chest, Sheraton, Mahogany, Inlaid, 4 Drawers, 41 x 19 x 39 In. 1265.00
Chest, Sheraton, Mahogany, String Inlay, Bowfront, Cookie Corners, Boston 3740.00
Chest, Sheraton, Swell Front, New England, c.1920, 40 x 43 x 23 In. 2950.00
Chest, Sheraton, Walnut, Bowfront, 4 Drawers, 1800s, 42 3/4 x 22 1/2 In. 1200.00
Chest, Sheraton, Walnut, c.1830, 45 1/2 x 42 x 20 1/2 In. 635.00
Chest, Sheraton, Walnut, Ring-Turned Legs, c.1830, 41 x 41 x 20 In. 375.00
Chest, Spice, Cherry, 15 Drawers, Lid Rises When Drawer Pulled, 21 x 10 x 18 In. 3680.00
Chest, Spice, Cherry, Inlaid, Late 18th Century, 14 x 12 In. 3525.00
Chest, Spice, Federal, Walnut, Star, Line Inlay, Door, 8 Drawers, 1800s, 15 x 13 In. 10925.00
Chest, Storage, Poplar, Dovetailed Corners, Mid 19th Century, 22 x 42 x 25 In. 175.00
Chest, Storage, Shaker, Pine, Gray, Iron Handles, Molded Lid, 19 x 72 x 24 In. 690.00
Chest, Sugar, Amish, Pine, Turned Legs, 26 x 34 1/2 x 17 In. 1295.00
Chest, Sugar, Cherry, Diamond Inlay, Lower Drawer, Kentucky, c.1830, 33 In. 6040.00
Chest, Sugar, Cherry, Dovetailed Corners, Drawer, Turned Legs, 27 x 27 x 18 In. 8950.00
Chest, Sugar, Cherry, Drawer, Hinged Plank Top, Tennessee, 1800s, 33 x 25 x 18 In. 4370.00
Chest, Sugar, Cherry, String Inlay, Drawer, Hinged Lid, 35 x 32 x 16 1/2 In. 12925.00
Chest, Sugar, Sheraton Style, Cherry, Poplar, Hinged Lid, 48 x 20 x 35 In. 865.00
Chest, Tansu, Red Lacquer, Iron Mounts, Sendai Style, Japan, c.1910, 42 x 18 x 33 In. 705.00
Chest, Tiger Maple, 4 Drawers, Rhode Island, 40 3/4 x 40 In. 13500.00
Chest, Tiger Maple, Pillared Front, 4 Drawers, Glass Pulls, 45 x 42 In. 345.00
Chest, Victorian, Feathered Veneer, 4 Drawers, 38 x 43 x 18 In. 115.00
Chest, Victorian, Mahogany, 6 Drawers, Square Top, 53 x 43 x 21 In. 650.00
Chest, Victorian, Mahogany, Burl Veneer Panels, Sunflower Crest, 43 x 21 x 65 In. 920.00
Chest, Victorian, Mahogany, c.1860, 45 x 38 x 18 In. 115.00
Chest, Victorian, Mahogany, Serpentine, 20th Century, 47 3/4 x 40 x 21 In. 490.00
Chest, Victorian, Mahogany, Straight Front, 2 Over 4 Long Drawers, 51 x 47 x 22 In. 1495.00
Chest, Victorian, Rosewood, Serpentine Front, Marble Top, 4 Drawers, 33 x 41 In. 345.00
Chest, Victorian, Walnut, 3 Drawers, 30 x 32 In. 230.00
Chest, Victorian, Walnut, 3 Drawers, Backsplash, Candlestands, 40 x 28 1/2 In. 185.00
Chest, Victorian, Walnut, Applied Turnings, Carved Handles, 35 x 39 x 19 In. 200.00
Chest, Victorian, Walnut, Drop Center, Mirror, 6 Drawers, 51 x 18 1/2 In. 575.00
Chest, Victorian, Walnut, Marble Top, Carved Beehive Crest, 111 x 51 x 18 In. 2015.00
Chest, Victorian, Walnut, Raised Veneered Panels, 4 Drawers, 40 x 41 x 17 In. 260.00
Chest, Victorian, Walnut, Scalloped Gallery, 2 Glove Drawers, 39 x 19 x 48 In. 315.00
Chest, Victorian, Walnut, Scalloped Gallery, Glove Drawers, 41 x 18 x 51 In. 490.00
Chest, Victorian, Yellow, Ocher, Brown, Flowers, Carved Wood Pulls, 33 x 42 In. 230.00
Chest, Walnut, 3-Board Top, 4 Drawers, Chamfered Backboard, 46 x 43 1/2 x 18 In. 545.00
Chest, Walnut, Drop Center, Marble Top, Oval Mirror, 65 x 38 x 17 In. 400.00
Chest, Walnut, Gallery, 6 Drawers, 36 x 20 x 55 In. 490.00
Chest, Walnut, Maple, 2 Short Over 3 Long Drawers, 1800s, 16 x 17 In. 2415.00
Chest, Walnut, Molded Cornice, 3 Over 6 Graduated Drawers, 65 x 44 x 25 In. 2185.00
Chest, Walnut, Pine, Panel Doors, Iron Latches, Continental, c.1690, 36 x 51 In. 2415.00
Chest, Wellington, Edwardian Style, Mahogany, Painted, 6 Drawers, 43 x 19 In. 635.00
Chest, Wellington, Edwardian Style, Sheet Music, Instrument Cartouches, 42 x 18 In. 1035.00
Chest, William & Mary, Burl Walnut, Inlaid Top, 4 Drawers, Bun Feet, 31 x 40 In. 1725.00
Chest, William & Mary, Oak, Burl Walnut, 4 Graduated Drawers, 38 x 38 In. 3350.00
Chest, William & Mary, Walnut, Mulberry, Split Case, Bracket Feet, 36 x 41 x 20 In. 1295.00
Chest, William & Mary, Walnut, Oyster Veneer, 8 Drawers, Bun Feet, 47 x 47 In. 4600.00
Chest, William IV, Mahogany, 5 Drawers, Brass Lion's-Head Pulls, 43 x 48 In. 1840.00

Chest, Wood, Flowers, Iron Hasp & Lock, Gypsy-Made, Bulgaria, 13 x 23 x 15 In. 425.00
Chest, Yellow Paint, Blue Paint, Shenandoah Valley 3900.00
Chest-On-Chest, Chippendale Style, Mahogany, Carved Shell, 83 x 39 x 20 In. 4600.00
Chest-On-Chest, Chippendale, Walnut, 6 Drawers, Pa., 18th Century, 84 In. 25850.00
Chest-On-Chest, Federal, Mahogany, New England, c.1800, 60 x 40 x 22 In. 1880.00
Chest-On-Chest, Federal, Mahogany, Veneer, 4 Drawers, c.1800, 78 x 49 x 23 In. 4400.00
Chest-On-Chest, George I, Walnut, c.1715, 62 x 39 x 21 In. 6325.00
Chest-On-Chest, George III, Mahogany, 2 Short, 3 Long Graduated Drawers, 73 x 44 In. ... 5060.00
Chest-On-Chest, George III, Mahogany, 7 Drawers, Cabriole Legs, 71 x 39 x 19 In. 1410.00
Chest-On-Chest, George III, Mahogany, 8 Drawers, Bracket Feet, c.1785, 72 x 42 In. 2760.00
Chest-On-Chest, George III, Walnut, Mahogany, Oak, Dentil Cornice, 70 x 42 In. 4140.00
Chest-On-Chest, Georgian, Mahogany, Dentil Molded, c.1830, 75 x 47 x 23 In. 4600.00
Chest-On-Frame, Chippendale, Cherry, 4 Drawers, 40 x 37 x 19 In. 520.00
Chest-On-Frame, Gilt, Red Lacquer, Drawers, Batwing Pulls, Japan, 63 x 35 In. 1380.00
Chest-On-Frame, Lacquer, Flowers, Birds, Japan, c.1900, 14 1/2 x 11 1/2 In. 430.00
Chest-On-Frame, Queen Anne Style, Walnut, 8 Drawers, 66 x 43 x 24 In. 2070.00
Chiffonnier, Louis XV Style, Mahogany, Ormolu, Marble Top, c.1900, 30 x 19 In. 550.00
Clothespress, George III, Mahogany, 2-Paneled Doors, 3 Drawers, 56 x 50 In. 475.00
Clothespress, George III, Mahogany, Paneled Doors, 4 Drawers, 85 x 15 In. 2470.00
Coat Rack, 4 Animal Heads, Sheep, Horse, Dog, Rooster, New England, c.1890, 23 In. ... 4800.00
Coat Rack, Arts & Crafts, Cruciform Base, 17 x 19 x 71 In. 440.00
Coat Rack, Cast Iron, Bronze Finish, 2 Arms, Tassel Finial, Round Base, 71 In. 69.00
Coat Rack, Costumer, G. Stickley, No. 53, 2 Tapered Posts, 72 x 13 x 22 In. .....3740.00 to 3820.00
Coat Rack, Hanging, Black Forest, Mountain Goat, Flowers, Vines, c.1880 .... 1100.00
Coat Rack, Lazy S Ranch, Gun Rack, Wood, Metal, 1950s, 20 x 22 In. 46.00
Coat Rack, Oak, Bentwood, Beehive Finial, 75 In. 145.00
Coat Rack, Thonet, Beech, Bentwood, 80 x 30 In. 1295.00
Coat Rack, Victorian, Metal, Round, Early 20th Century, 76 x 31 In. 230.00
Coffer, Baroque Style, Oak, Heavily Carved, Turned-Leg Stand, 32 x 32 x 18 In. 980.00
Coffer, Chinese Lacquer, Hinged Lid, Bail Handles, 14 1/2 x 30 x 21 In. 200.00
Coffer, Oak, Guilloche Panels, Leaf Carved, Hinged Lid, 1700s, 29 x 56 x 24 In. 1380.00
Coffer, Oak, Leaf Decoration, Hinged Lid, England, Late 1700s, 22 x 40 x 19 In. 1380.00
Coffer, Rosewood, Carved, Mother-Of-Pearl Inlay, Hip Roof, England, 13 1/2 x 12 In. ... 1100.00
Coffer, Walnut, Carved, Figural Pilasters & Panels, c.1825, 26 x 60 In. 2070.00
Commode, Adam Style, Satinwood, Painted, Drawer, Cupboard, 35 x 30 x 15 In. 1495.00
Commode, American Restauration, Mahogany, 3 Drawers, c.1810, 33 x 35 In. 2990.00
Commode, American Restauration, Walnut, Marble, 4 Drawers, c.1810, 36 x 43 In. 2530.00
Commode, Art Deco, Mahogany, Nickel Mounted, 4 Drawers, 37 x 41 x 19 In. 4830.00
Commode, Art Deco, Mirror, 36 x 28 x 18 In., Pair 7770.00
Commode, Art Deco, Walnut, 4 Drawers, 34 x 39 x 18 1/2 In. 980.00
Commode, Baker Furniture, Regency Style, Marble Top, 34 x 42 x 22 In. 1725.00
Commode, Biedermeier, Mahogany, 3 Drawers, Stepped Top, c.1815, 34 x 38 In. 1840.00
Commode, Biedermeier, Maple, Mahogany, Marble Top, Cylindrical, 32 In. 1610.00
Commode, Biedermeier, Walnut, Step Top, 4 Drawers, c.1850, 39 x 37 x 18 In. 1955.00
Commode, Blue Ground, Painted, Flower Sprigs, 2 Drawers, 18th Century, 37 In. 420.00
Commode, Burl Walnut, Continental, 22 In., Pair 12650.00
Commode, Chinoiserie, Japanned, Marble Top, Bombe, 3 Drawers, 32 x 42 In. 3350.00
Commode, Directoire Style, Mahogany, France, 19th Century, 46 1/2 In. 1595.00
Commode, Empire Style, Gilt Bronze, Marble Top, 3 Drawers, 33 x 51 x 23 In. 470.00
Commode, Faux-Bois Top, Laurel Wreaths, 2 Drawers, 33 x 48 x 20 In. 3450.00
Commode, French Provincial, Oak, Serpentine Front, c.1800, 33 x 49 x 24 In. 4600.00
Commode, French Provincial, Walnut, 2 Drawers, Pierced Apron, c.1750, 48 In. 6655.00
Commode, George III Style, Burl Elm, c.1900, 27 x 21 x 16 In., Pair 2300.00
Commode, George III Style, Mahogany, Serpentine Front, 3 Drawers, 48 In. 2375.00
Commode, George III, Mahogany, Drawer, 2 Doors, 3/4 Gallery, c.1785, 33 x 22 In. 1840.00
Commode, George III, Mahogany, Square Top, 18th Century, 30 3/4 x 19 x 17 In. 805.00
Commode, George III, Mahogany, Square Top, Doors, c.1800, 29 x 21 x 19 In. 750.00
Commode, Italian Neoclassical, Rosewood, Walnut Inlay, 50 In. 4900.00
Commode, Louis Philippe, Mahogany, D-Shape, 3 Drawers, Gilt Metal, 33 x 34 In. 7140.00
Commode, Louis Philippe, Walnut, Marble Top, 4 Drawers, 36 x 50 x 22 In. 1150.00
Commode, Louis XV Style, Gilt Bronze, Marble Top, c.1865, 36 x 57 x 25 In. 14400.00
Commode, Louis XV Style, Kingwood, Ormolu Mounted, c.1890, 34 x 48 x 21 In. 1265.00
Commode, Louis XV Style, Marquetry, Gilt Metal Mounted, 34 x 37 x 17 In. 956.00

Commode, Louis XV Style, Marquetry, Marble Top, Bombe, 35 x 38 In. 3800.00
Commode, Louis XV Style, Marquetry, Marble Top, Late 1800s, 33 x 22 x 14 In. 1265.00
Commode, Louis XV Style, Tulipwood, Bombe, 4 Drawers, Marble Top, 45 1/2 In. 1260.00
Commode, Louis XV, Chinoiserie, Black Lacquer, Gilt Bronze, 34 x 45 x 23 In. 4780.00
Commode, Louis XV, Fruitwood, 3 Drawers, France, 1700s 8340.00
Commode, Louis XV/XVI Style, Tulipwood, Marquetry, Parquetry, 35 x 41 x 20 In. 825.00
Commode, Louis XV/XVI, Marquetry, Ormolu Mounted, 32 x 36 x 20 In. 1410.00
Commode, Louis XVI Style, Fruitwood, c.1800, 35 x 49 x 24 In. 6325.00
Commode, Louis XVI Style, Fruitwood, Marble Top, 36 x 50 x 23 In. 1955.00
Commode, Louis XVI Style, Rosewood, Crossbanded, Marble Top, Late 1800s, 31 In. 2375.00
Commode, Louis XVI, Fruitwood, Marble Top, Late 1700s, 30 x 16 x 12 In. 1495.00
Commode, Louis XVI, Mahogany, Marquetry, 48 In. 4025.00
Commode, Louis XVI, Parquetry, Mahogany Inlay, Marble Top, 36 x 48 x 23 In. 895.00
Commode, Mahogany, Bowfront, 4 Drawers, Denmark, 31 x 36 x 17 In. 1095.00
Commode, Mahogany, Inlaid, Carved, Sweden, 35 x 39 1/2 x 23 In. 2760.00
Commode, Mahogany, Marble Top, 3 Drawers, Late 1800s, 24 In. 715.00
Commode, Mahogany, Marble Top, 3 Drawers, Sweden, Early 1800s, 35 In. 3990.00
Commode, Mahogany, Reeded Frieze, Greek Key Carved, 32 x 30 x 20 In. 1955.00
Commode, Mahogany, Scandinavia, Mid 19th Century, 34 x 32 x 18 In. 1265.00
Commode, Marble Top, Canted Corners, 2 Drawers, Sweden, Early 1800s, 43 In. 5895.00
Commode, Marble Top, Straight Front, 3 Drawers, Italy, Late 1700s, 48 In. 3420.00
Commode, Napoleon III, Walnut, Marble Top, Mid 1800s, 37 x 50 1/2 x 22 In. 1725.00
Commode, Neoclassical, Cherry Inlay, Italy, Late 18th Century, 35 x 39 x 17 In. 2300.00
Commode, Neoclassical, Mahogany, Bowfront, 34 3/4 x 43 x 22 In. 1610.00
Commode, Neoclassical, Parquetry, Mahogany Inlay, Italy, 36 x 43 x 23 In. 1675.00
Commode, Neoclassical, Pine, Antique Yellow, Parcel Silver, 31 x 51 x 25 In. 2990.00
Commode, Neoclassical, Rosewood, Graduated Drawers, 34 x 53 x 25 In. 4830.00
Commode, Oak, Serpentine Front, Wishbone Towel Rack, 32 x 20 In. 345.00
Commode, Oak, Towel Bar, Applied Leaf Carving, 38 x 18 x 61 In. 360.00
Commode, Pine, 3 Drawers, Painted Flowers, Leaves, Switzerland, 1800s, 30 x 38 In. 560.00
Commode, Pine, Blue & Sienna Paint, 2 Drawers, Late 1700s, 30 x 29 x 17 In., Pair 6120.00
Commode, Pine, Oak, Polychrome, c.1800, 36 1/2 x 41 1/2 x 20 1/2 In. 4370.00
Commode, Regency, Kingwood, Parquetry, Bronze, Brass, Marble, 31 x 30 x 18 In. 4585.00
Commode, Rosewood, Marble Top, Drawer, Cupboard Door, 32 x 20 x 19 In. 1210.00
Commode, Victorian, Brass, Aluminum Mounts & Pulls, 24 x 16 x 34 In. 185.00
Commode, Victorian, Cherry, Teardrop Pulls, 29 x 15 x 33 In. 160.00
Commode, Victorian, Walnut, Marble Top, Beveled Edge, 29 x 15 x 37 3/4 In. 259.00
Commode, Victorian, Walnut, Marble Top, Candlestands, 29 x 36 1/2 x 16 In. 259.00
Commode, Victorian, Walnut, Raised Drawer Panels, 30 x 16 x 35 In. 290.00
Commode, Walnut, Ebonized, Burl Inlay, 3 Drawers, Cabriole, 37 x 48 x 19 In. 4830.00
Commode, Walnut, Gameboard Inlay, Drawers, Early 1800s, 34 x 47 x 26 In. 4140.00
Commode, Walnut, Serpentine Front, 3 Drawers, Cabriole Legs, 34 x 49 In. 2300.00
Cradle, Mahogany, Carved Feet, 44 In. 375.00
Cradle, Maple, 24 1/2 x 38 1/4 x 25 In. 100.00
Cradle, Maple, Oval Turned Finials, Double Arch, 1700s, 41 In. 1410.00
Cradle, Pine, Painted, Cutout Scallops, Stenciled Birds, Fruit, 15 x 23 In. 45.00
Cradle, Pine, Unpainted, England, c.1860, 14 x 37 In. 200.00
Cradle, Red Paint, Dovetailed Corners, Deep Rockers, Side Scrolls, 41 x 16 x 19 In. 110.00
Cradle, Red Paint, Raised Gallery, Cutout Handles, Peg Sides, 1800s, 19 x 37 In. 575.00
Cradle, Regency Style, Turned Spindles, c.1890, 27 x 36 1/4 x 20 In. 115.00
Cradle, Softwood, Pegged, Dovetailed, Scalloped Hood, 27 x 41 In. 385.00
Cradle, Splint, Oak, Green Paint, Cheese Cutter Rockers, 15 x 30 In. 440.00
Cradle, Swing, Painted, Ribbed, Turned Supports, Sleigh Rails, 29 x 47 x 22 In. 94.00
Cradle, Victorian, Mahogany, Turned Spindles, Trestle Frame, 44 In. 1035.00
Cradle, Victorian, Painted, Cast Iron, Wire, Scrolled Trestle Base, 40 x 37 In. 940.00
Cradle, Victorian, Swing, Cast Iron, Wrought Iron, Tall Finials, 1840 . . . . 850.00
Cradle, Windsor, 24 Turned Spindles, Scalloped Rockers, Oval, 40 x 17 x 22 In. 520.00
Cradle, Windsor, Bamboo, Poplar, Hickory, Square Nails, 39 x 20 In. 400.00
Cradle, Windsor, Salmon Paint, 16 1/2 x 37 In. 450.00
Credenza, Burl, Marble Top, Drawers Beveled Glass, Doors, c.1930, 82 x 61 In. 590.00
Credenza, Circassian Walnut, Breakfront, Mid 19th Century, 59 In. 2520.00
Credenza, Florence Knoll, No. 2542, Teak, Marble, c.1951, 25 1/2 x 37 x 18 In. 2115.00
Credenza, G. Nelson, No. 64800, Executive Office, Herman Miller, c.1958, 26 x 70 In. 1645.00

Credenza, Italian Baroque, Walnut, 2 Drawers Over 2 Doors, Bun Feet, 36 x 49 In. 1725.00
Credenza, Mahogany, 3 Glass Panel Doors, 1900s, 30 x 64 x 18 In., Pair 590.00
Credenza, Renaissance Revival, Walnut, 5 Drawers, 2 Doors, Paneled, Italy, 51 x 68 In. 6465.00
Credenza, Rosewood, Serpentine Front, Fretwork Doors, Mirrored Back, 79 In. 1725.00
Credenza, Second Empire, Pietra Dura, Gilt Metal Mounts, France, c.1870, 77 x 67 In. ... 4600.00
Credenza, Teak, Sliding Doors, Shelves, Drawers, Lip Pulls, c.1960, 33 x 93 x 20 In. 2470.00
Credenza, Victorian, Burl Inlay, Marble Top, Shaped Front, 60 x 18 x 35 In. 2245.00
Credenza, Walnut, Marquetry, Stringing, Glazed Door, Shelves, 40 x 33 In. 920.00
Crib, Brass, Cannon Ball Finials, 48 1/2 x 29 x 45 In. 259.00
Cupboard, Adirondack Style, Birch Bark Trim, Step Back, 72 x 37 x 19 In. 345.00
Cupboard, Arts & Crafts, Oak, Step Back, 86 x 53 x 22 In. 960.00
Cupboard, Biedermeier, Fruitwood, Ebonized Top, Marble Inset, Door, 29 x 16 In. 1075.00
Cupboard, Charles I, Oak, Projecting Leaf-Carved Frieze, 1673, 39 x 39 x 19 In. 4200.00
Cupboard, Chippendale, Pine, Paneled Door, Pennsylvania, Late 18th Century, 89 In. 2470.00
Cupboard, Chippendale, Pine, Step Back, Pennsylvania, Early 1800s, 54 x 24 In. 4780.00
Cupboard, Chippendale, Walnut, Step Back, 92 x 68 x 21 In. 9560.00
Cupboard, Corner, 2 Parts, 2 Drawers, 3 Doors, New England, 88 x 45 x 23 In. 3220.00
Cupboard, Corner, Built-In, Open Top, 2 Drawers, 2 Doors, New England, 84 In. 2090.00
Cupboard, Corner, Cherry, 2 Drawers, 4 Doors, 12 Glass Panes, Ohio, 79 x 53 x 27 In. ... 4025.00
Cupboard, Corner, Cherry, 2 Glass Doors, 2 Panel Doors, 53 x 23 x 87 In. 2590.00
Cupboard, Corner, Cherry, 6-Pane Doors, Drawer, Panel Doors, 48 x 27 x 85 In. 2185.00
Cupboard, Corner, Cherry, 12-Pane Upper Door, 2 Blind Doors, Pennsylvania, 83 In. 8030.00
Cupboard, Corner, Cherry, Glazed Doors, Shelves, Panel Doors, 96 x 49 x 25 In. 1380.00
Cupboard, Corner, Chippendale Style, Cherry, Mahogany, 2 Sections 1610.00
Cupboard, Corner, Chippendale, 2 Parts, 2 Drawers, 3 Doors, 88 x 44 x 23 In. 10350.00
Cupboard, Corner, Chippendale, Walnut, 2 Doors, 2 Inside Shelves, 75 x 35 In. 3740.00
Cupboard, Corner, Edwardian, Mahogany, Inlaid, Glazed Door, Shelf, 48 x 22 In. 690.00
Cupboard, Corner, Elm, Burl, Astragal Glazed Doors, 76 x 33 x 21 In. 635.00
Cupboard, Corner, Empire, 2 Doors, Faux Grained, New England, 82 x 44 x 25 In. 1380.00
Cupboard, Corner, English Elm, Burl, Crown, Canted Corners, Glazed Doors 635.00
Cupboard, Corner, Federal Style, Satinwood, Mahogany Inlay, 92 x 46 x 23 In. 5750.00
Cupboard, Corner, Federal, Cherry, 1 Over 2 Doors, New England, c.1815, 88 x 42 In. ... 10200.00
Cupboard, Corner, Federal, Pine, 2 Over 2 Doors, Shelves, 81 x 52 x 27 3/4 In. 8915.00
Cupboard, Corner, Federal, Pine, 2 Sections, Panel Doors, c.1830, 86 x 44 In. 2760.00
Cupboard, Corner, Federal, Salmon Paint, Pennsylvania, 68 1/2 x 47 1/2 x 26 In. 5975.00
Cupboard, Corner, Federal, Walnut, Inlaid, Swan's-Neck Pediment, c.1790, 81 In. 2350.00
Cupboard, Corner, Federal, Walnut, Paneled Doors, c.1810, 81 x 41 x 18 In. 2235.00
Cupboard, Corner, George III, Mahogany, Astragal Glazed Door, 65 x 31 In. 525.00
Cupboard, Corner, George III, Mahogany, c.1780, 42 1/2 x 25 1/4 x 15 In. 529.00
Cupboard, Corner, Georgian, Oak, Mahogany, Panel Doors, c.1800, 46 x 37 In. 865.00
Cupboard, Corner, Green Paint, Paneled Doors, 3 Shelves, 2 Doors, 84 x 40 In. 2585.00
Cupboard, Corner, Hickory, Wallpaper Lining, 4 Doors, 5 Shelves, 23 In. 350.00
Cupboard, Corner, Italian Rococo Style, Green Paint, Single Door, 39 x 24 x 17 In. 480.00
Cupboard, Corner, Late Georgian Style, Mahogany, Paneled, 76 x 30 In. 760.00
Cupboard, Corner, Maple, Pitched Pediment, 2 Tin Doors, Nailed Drawer, 74 x 40 In. 460.00
Cupboard, Corner, Northern European Pine, 19th Century, 60 x 33 x 20 1/2 In. 1000.00
Cupboard, Corner, Oak, Molded Cornice, c.1800, 39 1/2 x 30 1/2 x 16 In. 260.00
Cupboard, Corner, Pine, Blue Paint, 12 Panes Upper, Blind Lower Door, Pa., 83 In. 12100.00
Cupboard, Corner, Pine, Blue Paint, Mid-Atlantic States, c.1840, 48 x 23 In. 4800.00
Cupboard, Corner, Pine, Double-Barrel Doors, 19th Century, 85 1/2 x 52 In. 1265.00
Cupboard, Corner, Pine, Drawer, 2 Doors, New England, 78 x 39 x 22 In. 1840.00
Cupboard, Corner, Pine, Fluted & Reeded Upper, Paneled Doors, N.J., 72 x 48 In. 1380.00
Cupboard, Corner, Pine, Glazed Door, Porcelain Pull, Shelves, Crest Rail, 32 x 15 In. 460.00
Cupboard, Corner, Pine, Grain Painted, 4 Doors, Late 1700s, 99 x 58 1/2 In. 1440.00
Cupboard, Corner, Pine, Painted Interior, 2 Over 2 Doors, 84 x 47 In. 489.00
Cupboard, Corner, Pine, Poplar, 2 Parts, Plate Grooves, Slots, Drawer, 38 x 76 In. 6800.00
Cupboard, Corner, Pine, Red Wash, Dry Scraped, 44 x 19 x 84 In. 1095.00
Cupboard, Corner, Pine, Single Door, 4 Shelves, 19th Century, 52 x 28 1/2 In. 405.00
Cupboard, Corner, Poplar, Door, Inset Panels, Bracket Feet, 37 x 20 x 74 In. 8050.00
Cupboard, Corner, Poplar, Grain Painted, Polychrome, c.1840, 83 x 49 x 23 In. 12000.00
Cupboard, Corner, Poplar, Pine, Red Flame Graining, 2 Parts, 53 x 26 x 85 In. 2300.00
Cupboard, Corner, Poplar, Red Wash, 2 Parts, Paned Glass Door Top, 49 x 25 In. 2645.00
Cupboard, Corner, Softwood, Painted, 16-Pane Door, 2-Paneled Doors, 88 x 43 In. 4950.00

Cupboard, Corner, Victorian, Oak, Molded Cornice, 2 Glass Doors, 51 x 87 In. 1840.00
Cupboard, Corner, Walnut, 2 8-Pane Doors, Over 2 Doors, Kentucky, c.1825, 90 In. 4900.00
Cupboard, Corner, Walnut, 4-Paneled Doors, Brass Hinges, Pennsylvania, 79 x 48 In. 2070.00
Cupboard, Corner, Walnut, 6-Pane Panel Doors, Ogee Drawers, 60 x 25 x 81 In. 1610.00
Cupboard, Corner, Walnut, Panel Doors, Molding, 84 x 56 x 17 In. 2070.00
Cupboard, Corner, Yew, Bowfront, 2 Glazed Doors Over 2 Panel Doors, 86 In. 1150.00
Cupboard, Edwardian, Mahogany, Crossbanded, 4 Glazed Doors, 75 x 28 In. 1240.00
Cupboard, Elizabethan Style, Oak, Inlaid, Carved, 71 x 76 1/2 x 20 In. 2530.00
Cupboard, Elm, House Form, 2 Doors, Pierced Panels, Chinese, 46 x 34 In. 375.00
Cupboard, Empire, Pine, Step Back, Arched Doors, Paneled Lower Doors, 85 x 62 In. 4950.00
Cupboard, Federal, Cherry, Glazed Door, Pennsylvania, c.1800, 88 x 46 x 24 In. 5580.00
Cupboard, Federal, Cherry, Step Back, Pennsylvania, 85 x 45 1/4 x 19 In. 4115.00
Cupboard, French Provincial, Painted, Molded Cornice, Slatted Doors, 64 x 52 In. 1150.00
Cupboard, Fruitwood, Painted, Continental, 80 x 80 x 17 In. 1725.00
Cupboard, George IV, Mahogany, Paneled Doors, 32 x 47 x 19 In., Pair 2760.00
Cupboard, Georgian Style, Mahogany, Mid 19th Century, 31 x 23 x 15 In. 200.00
Cupboard, Green, Step Back, Glass Doors, 81 x 48 In. 1350.00
Cupboard, Hanging, Chestnut, Drawer, 19th Century, 39 x 27 x 11 In. 495.00
Cupboard, Hanging, Corner, Bowfront, Mahogany, 2 Doors, 4 Shelves, 41 x 29 In. 1035.00
Cupboard, Hanging, Corner, George III, Mahogany, c.1800, 44 x 27 1/2 x 15 In. 980.00
Cupboard, Hanging, Corner, George III, Mahogany, Glazed Doors, 39 x 34 In. 315.00
Cupboard, Hanging, Corner, Mahogany, Panel Doors, Shells & Stars Inlay, 44 In. 1955.00
Cupboard, Hanging, Corner, Pine, Red Paint, Green Interior, Panel Door, 29 x 28 In. 1265.00
Cupboard, Hanging, Corner, Poplar, Red Paint, Raised Cornice, 30 x 13 x 21 In. 1265.00
Cupboard, Hanging, Corner, Walnut, 2 Full-Length Doors, c.1750, 38 1/2 x 35 In. 585.00
Cupboard, Hanging, Dovetailed, 2 Drawers, Doors, c.1855, 29 x 11 x 30 In. 750.00
Cupboard, Hanging, Oak, Mahogany, Glazed Door, Drawer, Mirrors, c.1890, 26 In. 380.00
Cupboard, Hanging, Phipps & Wynn, Painted, Inlet Through Window, 27 In. .... *Illus* 1380.00
Cupboard, Hanging, Pine, Grain Painted, Red Flame, 12 Sections, 24 x 11 x 34 In. 230.00
Cupboard, Hanging, Pine, Green Paint, Board Door, Beaded Trim, 26 x 9 x 20 In. 1610.00
Cupboard, Hanging, Pine, Red Paint, T-Head Nails, Door, 2 Shelves, 18 x 24 In. 3105.00
Cupboard, Hanging, Poplar, Green, Yellow Line Border, Shelves, 28 x 9 x 22 In. 1150.00
Cupboard, Hanging, Yellow, Raised Panel Door, Iron Rattail Hinges, 46 x 31 In. 1320.00
Cupboard, Jelly, Ash, Walnut, 2-Door Base, 3 Shelves, 2 Drawers, 45 x 19 x 54 In. 920.00
Cupboard, Jelly, Pine, Brown, Yellow Graining, 4 Shelves, Cornice, 73 x 42 In. 460.00
Cupboard, Jelly, Pine, Doors, Shelves, Crescent Apron, 43 x 44 x 15 In. 990.00
Cupboard, Jelly, Poplar, Painted, Drawers Over Doors, 49 x 48 In. 2990.00
Cupboard, Jelly, Poplar, Salmon Paint, 2 Doors, 43 3/4 x 18 1/2 x 54 In. 1380.00
Cupboard, Jelly, Red Paint, 2 Drawers, 2 Doors, Pennsylvania, 55 x 48 In. 4180.00
Cupboard, Jelly, Rosewood Grain Painted, 2 Drawers, Doors, 45 x 42 3/4 In. 590.00
Cupboard, Jelly, Southern Pine, Punched Tin Panels, 1800-50, 77 In. .... *Illus* 1610.00
Cupboard, Louis Philippe, Mahogany, Round Marble Top, Mid 1800s, 31 x 16 In. 1095.00
Cupboard, Louis XV Style, Cherry, Steel, 83 x 39 x 83 In. 3450.00
Cupboard, Louis XVI Style, Mahogany, Marble Top, 28 x 17 x 12 In. 865.00
Cupboard, Mahogany, Green Man Crest, Urn Quarter Column, 40 x 22 x 73 In. 1265.00
Cupboard, Maple, Step Back, 4 Doors, 2 Drawers, New England, c.1780, 81 x 48 In. 9000.00
Cupboard, Oak, 2 Doors, Shelf, L'Ange De France, 1800s, 51 x 54 x 23 In. 2000.00

Furniture, Cupboard,
Hanging, Phipps & Wynn,
Painted, Inlet Through
Window, 27 In.

Furniture, Cupboard, Jelly,
Southern Pine, Punched Tin
Panels, 1800-50, 77 In.

Cupboard, Oak, Carved, 2 Parts, Drawers, Spindles, Wheel Designs, 48 x 88 In. 2300.00
Cupboard, Oak, Harness, 2 Panel Doors, 3 Faux Drawers, 2 Drawers, 77 x 52 In. 3910.00
Cupboard, Oak, Panel Doors, 6 Drawers, Pilaster, Bracket Feet, c.1750, 77 x 63 In. 2375.00
Cupboard, Pennsylvania Dutch, Pine, 3 Drawers, 4 Doors, Red Paint, 84 In. 9625.00
Cupboard, Pine, 2 Glazed Doors, 3 Shelves, 21 1/2 x 16 x 8 In. 475.00
Cupboard, Pine, 2 Half Drawers, 2 Doors, 46 x 51 x 20 In. 805.00
Cupboard, Pine, Brown Paint, Step Back, 3 Shelves, c.1825, 74 x 43 x 19 In. 1530.00
Cupboard, Pine, Distressed, Step Back, Late 19th Century, 88 x 59 x 22 In. 1150.00
Cupboard, Pine, Glazed, Wrought-Iron Hinges, 1700s, 9 1/2 x 8 3/4 x 5 In. 1765.00
Cupboard, Pine, Grain Painted, 4 Doors, 2 Drawers, Pa., 1825, 74 x 46 x 17 In. 2350.00
Cupboard, Pine, Painted, Panel Doors, 2 Drawers, Bun Feet, 56 x 79 In. 6040.00
Cupboard, Pine, Plain Edge Top, 2 Doors, Mid 1800s, 24 x 30 x 12 In. 405.00
Cupboard, Pine, Polychrome, Cornice, 3 Drawers, Continental, 76 x 48 x 26 In. 1955.00
Cupboard, Pine, Poplar, Grain Painted, Step Back, Early 1800s, 80 x 51 x 19 In. 15600.00
Cupboard, Pine, Raised Panel Door, 82 x 41 1/2 x 13 1/2 In. 360.00
Cupboard, Pine, Red Brown, Over Yellow Vinegar Decoration, 36 x 11 x 31 In. 575.00
Cupboard, Pine, Red Paint, 19th Century, 57 x 34 1/4 x 20 1/2 In.   4540.00
Cupboard, Pine, Red Paint, 3 Shelves, Door Base, 73 x 35 1/2 x 14 In. 935.00
Cupboard, Pine, Step Back, 2 Shelves, 47 x 19 x 76 In. 4600.00
Cupboard, Pine, Step Back, 4 Doors, 2 Drawers, Porcelain Pulls, 1800s, 83 x 44 In. 980.00
Cupboard, Pine, Step Back, Shelves, Doors, 19th Century, 81 x 42 x 16 1/2 In. 1955.00
Cupboard, Pine, White, Sawtooth Crown, c.1910, 72 x 38 In. 750.00
Cupboard, Poplar, Red Paint, Step Back, 2 Parts, Pennsylvania, 53 x 24 x 87 In. 2590.00
Cupboard, Poplar, Red, Step Back, Panel Doors, Bracket Feet, 25 x 16 x 80 In. 4315.00
Cupboard, Poplar, Walnut, Step Back, 2 Parts, 2 Dovetailed Drawers, 42 x 19 In. 2530.00
Cupboard, Poplar, Walnut, Step Back, Door Top, 9 Panes, 42 x 20 x 89 In. 2530.00
Cupboard, Poplar, Yellow Paint, Gallery Top, Door, 46 In. 920.00
Cupboard, Red Paint, 2 Sections, 3 Drawers Over 2-Paneled Doors, 85 x 57 In. 6465.00
Cupboard, Red Paint, Square Nails, Carved Cornice, Screen Door, c.1860, 61 In. 695.00
Cupboard, Red Paint, Step Back, 2 Parts, Hudson Valley, N.Y., c.1820 . . . .   3525.00
Cupboard, Red Paint, Step Back, 2-Paneled Doors, Plate Shelf, 68 x 47 x 21 In. 1210.00
Cupboard, Regency Style, Bronze, Porcelain Mount, Druce & Co., London, 73 In., Pair   . .   6040.00
Cupboard, Regency Style, Mahogany, Gallery Top, Late 1800s, 33 x 14 x 16 In. 550.00
Cupboard, Regency, Mahogany, Stepped Cornice, Astragal Doors, 78 x 45 x 21 In. 1840.00
Cupboard, Shaker, Pine, Door, 5 Shelves, Mt. Lebanon, N.Y., c.1840, 60 x 20 In. 2760.00
Cupboard, Shaker, Pine, Door, 6 Inset Panels, Enfield, N.H., c.1850, 93 x 42 x 15 In. 2300.00
Cupboard, Shaker, Poplar, 2 Sections, 2 Doors, Mt. Lebanon, N.Y., c.1871, 81 In. 4600.00
Cupboard, Shanxi Province, Red, Gold, Black Chinoiserie, Drawers, Chinese, 37 x 49 In. . .   315.00
Cupboard, Southern Pine, New England, 18th Century, 76 x 55 In. . . . . *Illus*   5580.00
Cupboard, Victorian, Oak, Ogee Cornice, Glass & Panel Doors, 44 x 18 x 85 In. 1035.00
Cupboard, Victorian, Walnut, Ogee Cornice, Glass Doors, 71 x 18 x 90 In. 2990.00
Cupboard, Walnut, Fruitwood, Fluted Columns, Broken Arch Crest, 63 x 101 In. 1380.00
Cupboard, Walnut, Open Shelves, Plate Lips, Panel Doors, 78 x 43 x 17 In. 1265.00
Cupboard, Walnut, Pine, Poplar, Cut Nails, Panel Doors, Drawers, 47 x 54 x 19 In. 2070.00
Cupboard, Walnut, Pine, Poplar, Step Back, Glass, 2 Parts, Pennsylvania, c.1800 . . . . 12500.00
Cupboard, Walnut, Plank Door, Battens, Cut Nails, Shelves, 74 x 36 x 14 In. 805.00
Cupboard, William IV, Rosewood, 2 Grilled Doors, c.1850, 39 3/4 x 49 In. 2300.00
Cupboard, Yellow Pine, 4-Pane Doors, 2 Drawers, Punched Tin Panels, 72 x 50 In. 1035.00
Cupboard, Yellow Pine, Poplar, Scrolled Arch Pediment, 4-Pane Door, 30 x 24 In. 375.00
Daybed, American Restauration, Mahogany, Bronze Wreath, Ormolu, 43 x 77 In. 2185.00
Daybed, B. Mathsson, Berlin, Platform, Sweden, 18 x 78 1/2 x 61 1/2 In. 2350.00
Daybed, Birch, Red Paint, Upholstered, 74 x 26 x 27 In. 175.00
Daybed, Cherry, Rope, Turned Posts, c.1790, 19 x 35 x 73 In. 260.00
Daybed, French Provincial, Beech, Upholstered Cushions, 34 x 30 x 76 In. 1680.00
Daybed, G. Nelson, Birch, Dowel Legs, Zinc-Plated Steel Supports, 75 x 34 x 24 In. 825.00
Daybed, G. Stickley, No. 216, Oak, Slatted Head & Footboard, Decal, 31 x 80 In. 1955.00
Daybed, Maison Jansen, Maple, Ebony Inlay, Upholstered, c.1940, 32 x 77 x 35 In. 4800.00
Daybed, Peter Hvidt, Teak Frame, Floating Backrest, 1960s, 76 x 30 x 28 In. 1725.00
Daybed, Sheraton, Maple, Cylindrical Rails, Turnip Feet, Pennsylvania, 26 x 72 In. 4600.00
Daybed, Sheraton, Pine, Ring-Turned Tapered Legs, Ball Feet, 20 x 71 x 36 In. 890.00
Daybed, Walnut, Carved Rosettes, Bud Finials, Velvet Cover, France, c.1900, 77 In. 1150.00
Daybed, Wegner, Teak, Upholstered, Woven Backrest, Folding, 29 x 78 x 34 In. 2700.00
Desk, Anders Lundberg, Sycamore, Cherry, 29 1/2 x 55 x 27 3/4 In. 3600.00

Furniture, Cupboard, Southern
Pine, New England, 18th Century,
76 x 55 In.

Furniture, Desk, G. Stickley,
Pewter Pulls, Metal Inlay,
Harvey Ellis, 29 3/4 In.

Furniture, Desk, Shaker,
Ash, Oak, Pine, Alfred, Me.,
c.1886, 48 x 38 In.

Desk, Art Deco, Black Lacquer, Pedestal, 20th Century, 31 x 48 x 28 In.	115.00
Desk, Art Nouveau, Slant Front, Mahogany, 3 Pigeonholes, 41 x 32 x 18 In.	175.00
Desk, Art Nouveau, Walnut, Pierced Gallery, Stained Glass, Kneehole, Germany, 50 In.	550.00
Desk, Arts & Crafts, Lift-Up Writing Board, 2 Doors, Inset Leather, 31 x 49 In.	1000.00
Desk, Arts & Crafts, Oak, 2 Doors, Drawers, Arched End Panels, c.1925, 28 x 43 In.	375.00
Desk, Arts & Crafts, Oak, Copper, Leaf-Carved Corners, 31 x 48 x 29 1/2 In.	380.00
Desk, Arts & Crafts, Oak, Drawer, Bail Handles, Bookcase Sides, 30 x 43 x 27 In.	650.00
Desk, Arts & Crafts, Slant Front, Drawer, Copper Hardware, 32 x 18 x 40 In.	290.00
Desk, Arts & Crafts, Slant Front, Oak, 20th Century, 43 x 32 x 15 In.	120.00
Desk, Biedermeier, Inlaid Walnut Veneer, Tooled Leather, c.1940, 31 x 40 x 22 In.	2070.00
Desk, Butler's, Drop Front, Mahogany, Scotland, c.1830, 49 x 47 x 24 In.	1610.00
Desk, Butler's, Federal, Mahogany, Fold-Out Panel, Maryland, c.1810, 43 x 40 x 21 In.	1150.00
Desk, Butler's, George III Style, Mahogany, Fold-Down, Drawers, 46 x 49 x 23 In.	2875.00
Desk, Butler's, Mahogany, Felt Surface, 3 Drawers, 1800s, 48 x 45 1/2 x 20 In.	645.00
Desk, Campaign, George IV, Rosewood, Brass, Drawers, c.1825, 20 x 20 x 13 In.	1265.00
Desk, Campaign, Mahogany, 2 Sections, Fitted Interior, Stand, 31 x 21 1/2 In.	205.00
Desk, Campaign, Mahogany, Hinged Flip Top, England, 1800s, 29 x 36 x 18 In.	805.00
Desk, Campaign, Regency, Slant Front, Mahogany, Brass Bound, 22 x 20 x 10 In.	865.00
Desk, Charlton House, Edwardian, Mahogany, Kidney Top, 38 x 43 In.	1840.00
Desk, Cherry, 2-Pane Doors, Vertical Files, 2 Parts, 60 x 30 x 22 In.	1380.00
Desk, Chinoiserie Lacquer, Black, Green Leather, Collapsible Stand, 22 x 37 In.	500.00
Desk, Chippendale Style, Mahogany, Carved, Pedestal, 30 x 72 x 42 In.	3680.00
Desk, Chippendale Style, Slant Front, Mixed Wood, c.1900, 41 x 30 x 16 In.	230.00
Desk, Chippendale, Drop Front, Mahogany, 4 Drawers, Late 1700s, 43 x 40 In.	3820.00
Desk, Chippendale, Drop Front, Maple, Ogee Feet, 38 x 34 x 19 In.	1815.00
Desk, Chippendale, Oxbow Front, Cherry, Ogee Bracket Feet, 44 x 43 x 25 In.	3740.00
Desk, Chippendale, Slant Front, Birch, 4 Drawers, 43 x 37 1/2 x 18 1/2 In.	2300.00
Desk, Chippendale, Slant Front, Cherry, 4 Drawers, Compartments, 41 x 38 In.	2470.00
Desk, Chippendale, Slant Front, Cherry, 4 Drawers, Dovetailed, 40 x 38 In.	1325.00
Desk, Chippendale, Slant Front, Cherry, 4 Drawers, Dovetailed, 40 x 42 In.	4900.00
Desk, Chippendale, Slant Front, Cherry, Pennsylvania, 1760-90, 46 x 41 x 22 In.	6575.00
Desk, Chippendale, Slant Front, Mahogany, 4 Drawers, c.1780, 42 x 39 x 20 In.	3525.00
Desk, Chippendale, Slant Front, Mahogany, 4 Drawers, Pigeonholes, 31 x 41 In.	2070.00
Desk, Chippendale, Slant Front, Mahogany, Philadelphia, c.1785, 44 x 42 x 23 In.	10575.00
Desk, Chippendale, Slant Front, Maple, Pine, New England, 36 x 17 x 41 In.	4900.00
Desk, Chippendale, Slant Front, Red Wash, Pigeonholes, 36 x 19 x 41 In.	2300.00
Desk, Chippendale, Slant Front, Tiger Maple, 4 Drawers, Late 1700s, 43 x 39 x 20 In.	4995.00
Desk, Chippendale, Slant Front, Tiger Maple, New England, Late 1700s, 41 x 36 In.	5875.00
Desk, Chippendale, Slant Front, Walnut, 4 Drawers, Late 1700s, 41 x 39 x 20 In.	1469.00
Desk, Chippendale, Slant Front, Walnut, 4 Drawers, Pennsylvania, c.1785, 44 x 40 In.	2115.00
Desk, Chippendale, Slant Front, Walnut, 4 Drawers, Pinwheel Carving, 42 x 40 In.	3820.00
Desk, Chippendale, Slant Front, Walnut, Mahogany, 24 x 24 1/2 In.	3000.00
Desk, Colonial Revival, Figured Walnut, 3 Leather Panels, 5 Drawers, 50 x 26 In.	1800.00

Desk, Davenport, Mahogany, Harlequin, Late 1800s, 38 x 23 x 22 In. 1610.00
Desk, Davenport, Victorian, Drop Front, Walnut, Leather, c.1860, 30 x 21 x 22 In. 920.00
Desk, Davenport, Victorian, Mahogany, Veneer, 4 Drawers, 23 x 23 x 37 In. 690.00
Desk, Davenport, Victorian, Slant Front, Walnut, Yew Inlay, Inset Leather, 21 In. 1265.00
Desk, Directoire Style, Mahogany, Brass Inlay, Lid, Hinges, 35 x 37 x 16 In. 560.00
Desk, Drop Front, Fan-Carved Door, 20th Century, 41 x 30 x 20 In. 560.00
Desk, Drop Front, Mahogany, Brass Gallery, 20th Century, 45 x 29 x 18 In. 560.00
Desk, Drop Front, Walnut, Crossbanded, 4 Drawers, Fitted Interior, c.1750, 36 In. 2090.00
Desk, Edwardian, Mahogany, Banded, 5 Drawers, Tapered Legs, Spade Feet, 48 In. 1955.00
Desk, Edwardian, Marquetry, Satinwood Inlay, Leather Top, Pedestal, 60 x 30 In. 3885.00
Desk, Edwardian, Rosewood, Marquetry, 2 Columns, 4 Drawers, 40 x 20 x 36 In. 905.00
Desk, Empire, Drop Front, Mahogany, Drawers, c.1845, 54 x 47 x 22 In. 2235.00
Desk, English Oak, Pigeonholes, Leather Inlaid Top, c.1890, 44 x 66 x 38 In. 2185.00
Desk, English Yew, Molded Top, Tooled Brown Leather, Pedestal, 31 x 48 x 24 In. 460.00
Desk, Escritoire, Brass Detail, Leather Top, Stand, 20th Century, 26 x 17 x 10 In. 35.00
Desk, Escritoire, Mother-Of-Pearl Inlay, Hinged Lid, Leather, Stand, 22 x 16 In. 95.00
Desk, Federal, Slant Front, Cherry, Drawers, Niches, c.1800, 40 x 43 x 18 In. 2530.00
Desk, Federal, Slant Front, Mahogany, Cherry, Diamond Inlay, 4 Drawers, 44 x 39 In. 4400.00
Desk, Flat Top, Oak, Center Drawer, 3 Side Drawers, 41 x 30 x 31 In. 98.00
Desk, French Provincial, 5 Drawers, 30 1/2 x 47 1/2 x 25 1/2 In. 440.00
Desk, G. Nelson, Drop Front, Dividers, Drawers, Wood Pulls, 40 x 40 In. 940.00
Desk, G. Nelson, Middle Management, Herman Miller, c.1958, 30 x 66 x 30 In. 470.00
Desk, G. Nelson, No. 4658, Home Office, Walnut, Herman Miller, 41 x 54 x 28 In. 5875.00
Desk, G. Nelson, Rosewood, Herman Miller, c.1955, 72 x 36 x 28 3/4 In. 2350.00
Desk, G. Stickley, 2 Drawers, Copper Hardware, Arched Rail, Gallery, 38 x 23 x 37 In. ... 700.00
Desk, G. Stickley, Drop Front, Chestnut, Plank Sides, Cutout Handles, 38 x 29 In. 1410.00
Desk, G. Stickley, No. 363, Roll Top, Drawers, Writing Boards, 60 x 32 x 43 In. 4415.00
Desk, G. Stickley, No. 710, Rectangular Top, Kneehole, Half Drawers, 42 x 24 x 29 In. ... 880.00
Desk, G. Stickley, No. 728, Drop Front, Oak, c.1906, 43 x 30 x 13 In. 2630.00
Desk, G. Stickley, Pewter Pulls, Metal Inlay, Harvey Ellis, 29 3/4 In. .... *Illus* 58750.00
Desk, George I, Slant Front, Burl, 4 Drawers, Bracket Feet, 42 x 36 In. 1840.00
Desk, George II Style, Burl Walnut, Tooled Leather Inset, 31 x 60 3/8 x 36 In. 920.00
Desk, George II, Drop Front I, Mahogany, 3 Drawers, Fitted Interior, 38 In. 1995.00
Desk, George II, Walnut, Kneehole, Crossbanded, 9 Drawers, 1800s, 31 x 41 x 21 In. 980.00
Desk, George III Style, Mahogany, Carved, Leather, Pedestals, 32 x 71 x 42 In. 6040.00
Desk, George III Style, Mahogany, Double Pedestal, Leather, 5 Drawers, 30 x 60 In. 920.00
Desk, George III Style, Walnut, Pedestal, Leather Top, 30 x 65 x 35 In. 2585.00
Desk, George III, Drop Front, Mahogany, 2 Over 3 Drawers, Bracket Feet, 37 In. 475.00
Desk, George III, Mahogany, Double Pedestal, Leather, 7 Drawers, 31 In. 2660.00
Desk, George III, Mahogany, Kneehole, 18th Century, 31 3/4 x 36 x 20 In. 805.00
Desk, George III, Mahogany, Kneehole, 7 Drawers, Bracket Feet, c.1785, 30 x 34 In. 3450.00
Desk, George III, Mahogany, Oak, Kneehole, Dovetailed Drawers, 40 x 21 x 33 In. 2645.00
Desk, George IV, Architect's, Mahogany, Lift Top, c.1830, 31 x 32 1/4 In. 2760.00
Desk, Georgian Style, Leather Top, 9 Drawers, Plinth Base, Pedestal, 37 x 36 In. 1495.00
Desk, Georgian Style, Slant Front, Mahogany, Cabriole Legs, 41 x 34 x 19 In. 260.00
Desk, Georgian Style, Slant Front, Mahogany, Pigeonholes, 42 x 36 x 20 In. 260.00
Desk, Georgian, Mahogany, Carved, Tooled Leather, 3 Drawers, 30 x 48 In. 1150.00
Desk, Hepplewhite Style, Roll Top, Mahogany, Veneer, Maddox, 36 x 19 x 42 In. 520.00
Desk, Hepplewhite, Roll Top, Mahogany, Maple Panels, 5 Drawers, 42 x 40 In. 1840.00
Desk, Hepplewhite, Walnut, Dovetailed, 3 Drawers & 3 Hidden, 17 x 13 In. 1850.00
Desk, Italian Rococo Style, Slant Front, Painted, 3 Drawers, 40 x 35 x 17 In. 4465.00
Desk, Leopold Bauer, Maple, Black Stain, Marble Top, 31 x 56 x 33 In. 600.00
Desk, Lifetime, Drawer Over Kneehole, Half Drawers, Copper Hardware, 50 x 28 In. 1530.00
Desk, Limbert, No. 736, Letter Slots, Arched Drawer, 38 x 30 x 21 In. 1530.00
Desk, Louis XV Style, Tulipwood, Gilt Bronze Mounted, 29 x 27 x 17 In. 3000.00
Desk, Louis XV Style, Walnut, U-Shape, Drawers, Cabriole Legs, 29 x 45 x 20 In. 500.00
Desk, Louis XVI Style, Kingwood, Marquetry, 20th Century, 34 x 38 x 24 In. 635.00
Desk, Louis XVI Style, Mahogany, Bronze Mounted, Cylinder, 62 x 35 x 21 In. 1195.00
Desk, Louis XVI Style, Mahogany, Gilt Bronze, E. Poteau, c.1890, 40 x 41 In. 4800.00
Desk, Louis XVI Style, Mahogany, Kingwood, Marquetry, 43 x 37 x 20 In. 2990.00
Desk, Mahogany, 9 Drawers, Double Pedestal, Leather, 1800s, 30 x 28 x 48 In. 1615.00
Desk, Mahogany, 9 Drawers, Double Pedestal, Plinth Bases, c.1850, 48 In. 595.00
Desk, Mahogany, Brass Mounts, Double Pedestal, 30 x 26 x 48 In. 800.00

Desk, Mahogany, Carved, 2 Sections, Slots, Doors, Urn Supports, 53 x 31 x 70 In. 1265.00
Desk, Mahogany, Inlaid, Sloping Lift Top, 19th Century, 39 x 43 x 19 In. 2940.00
Desk, Mahogany, Mitered Corners, Drawer, Tapered Legs, 29 x 40 1/2 x 23 In. 2070.00
Desk, Mahogany, Serpentine, Dovetailed Drawers, Brass Gallery, 44 x 42 In. 1200.00
Desk, Napoleon II, Ebonized, Boulle, 1900s, 36 1/2 x 30 x 18 1/2 In. 200.00
Desk, Napoleon III, Kingwood, Rosewood, Pierced Brass Gallery, 49 x 30 In. 2070.00
Desk, Napoleon III, Mahogany, Leather Surface, Mid 1800s, 29 x 54 x 31 In. 1955.00
Desk, Napoleon III, Slant Front, Ebonized, Boulle, Brass Gallery, c.1865, 36 x 26 In. 1725.00
Desk, Napoleon III, Slant Front, Kingwood, Flower Medallion Inlay, 37 x 28 In. 2070.00
Desk, Oak, Carved, Green Leather Top, Lion's-Head Pulls, 49 x 60 x 30 In. 1980.00
Desk, Oak, Ebonized, Limed, Leather, Brass, Austria, c.1910, 31 x 55 x 29 In. 9000.00
Desk, Oak, Folding Chair, 27 x 27 In., Child's 69.00
Desk, Oak, Lift Top, 3 Drawers, Doors, Dutch, 1800s, 25 In. 325.00
Desk, Oriental, Lacquer, Gold Japanned, 32 x 55 x 19 In. 690.00
Desk, Osvaldo Borsani, Executive, Rosewood, 3 Drawers, Tecno, c.1958, 30 x 87 In. 5580.00
Desk, Partners, Chippendale Style, Mahogany, Double Pedestal, 6 Drawers, 32 x 71 In. ... 4830.00
Desk, Partners, Chippendale, Mahogany, Swags & Ovals, Paw Feet, 31 x 72 In. 4255.00
Desk, Partners, Chippendale, Painted, Early 20th Century, 29 x 54 x 34 In. 940.00
Desk, Partners, George III Style, Mahogany, Brass Mounted, 31 x 53 x 43 In. 5290.00
Desk, Partners, George III Style, Mahogany, Gilt Tooled Leather, 31 x 75 x 48 In. 4370.00
Desk, Partners, L. & J.G. Stickley, Slant Front, Letter Rack, Inkwell, 36 x 46 x 40 In. 2350.00
Desk, Partners, Louis Philippe, Mahogany, Inset Leather, Drawers, 31 x 57 x 31 In. 3450.00
Desk, Partners, Neoclassical, Mahogany, 4 Over 2 Drawers, 29 x 50 In. 1265.00
Desk, Partners, Renaissance Revival, Oak, Ebonized Accents, 56 x 36 x 30 In. 1265.00
Desk, Partners, William IV, Mahogany, Leather Surface, 20 x 54 x 41 In. 3450.00
Desk, Pine, Maple, Lift Top, Beaded, Early 1800s, 35 1/2 x 36 In. 765.00
Desk, Pine, Sloping Lift Top, Drawers, Cubbyholes, 49 x 37 x 28 In. 460.00
Desk, Plantation, Drop Front, Walnut, Cubby Holes, Victorian, 89 x 39 In. 865.00
Desk, Plantation, Mahogany, Poplar, 4 Doors, Turned Feet, 54 x 56 In. 2185.00
Desk, Queen Anne Style, Burl Walnut, Crossbanded, 7 Drawers, 31 x 32 x 18 In. 2645.00
Desk, Queen Anne Style, Drop Front, Cherry, Early 1900s, 13 x 10 In. 750.00
Desk, Queen Anne, Maple, New England, 1730-50, 38 x 34 In. 9560.00
Desk, Queen Anne, Slant Front, Walnut, 4 Drawers, Bracket, 1700s, 40 x 37 In. 2600.00
Desk, Queen Anne, Slant Front, Walnut, Inlaid, Pigeonholes, c.1740, 42 x 36 In. 4830.00
Desk, Renaissance Revival, Drop Front, Oak, Fitted Interior, c.1880, 43 x 47 In. 705.00
Desk, Renaissance Revival, Drop Front, Spindle Crest, Trestle Base, 53 x 27 In. 825.00
Desk, Risom, Walnut, 5 Drawers, 2 Pullout Writing Surfaces, 81 x 28 In. 705.00
Desk, Rohde, Mahogany, Drop Front, Drawer, 40 x 17 x 42 In. 1290.00
Desk, Roll Top, C Roll, Walnut, Wood Gallery Top, 6 Drawers, Cubbies, 49 x 60 x 30 In. .. 1265.00
Desk, Roll Top, S Roll, Mahogany, Raised Panel, 9 Drawers, 45 x 50 x 36 In. 345.00
Desk, Roll Top, S Roll, Oak, Drawers, Stationery Slots, 66 x 38 x 51 In. 3335.00
Desk, Roll Top, S Roll, Oak, Fitted Interior, 9 Bowfront Drawers, 50 x 34 x 50 In. 2358.00
Desk, Roll Top, S Roll, Oak, Raised Panel, 51 x 50 x 34 In. 2500.00
Desk, Roll Top, S Roll, Oak, Veneer, Paneled Ends, Back, 49 x 30 x 50 In. 430.00
Desk, Rosewood, 3 Sections, Pedestal, Chinese, 19th Century, 34 x 54 x 23 In. 880.00
Desk, Rosewood, Ivory, Mother-Of-Pearl, Copper, Brass, Germany, 66 x 42 In. 3450.00
Desk, Rosewood, Parquetry, Doors, Drawers, Brass 3/4 Gallery, 41 x 14 x 27 In. 2185.00
Desk, School, Mahogany, Leather Insert, Inkwell, c.1880, 31 x 30 x 24 In. 290.00
Desk, School, Pine, Painted, Lift Top, Backsplash, Stencils, 34 x 28 x 19 In. 980.00
Desk, Schoolmaster's, Pine, Slant Lid, Breadboard Ends, Backsplash, Shelf, 34 x 18 In. ... 230.00
Desk, Schoolmaster's, Pine, Stenciled Cartouche, Turned Legs, 1854, 45 x 26 In. 9200.00
Desk, Schoolmaster's, Red Wash, Dovetailed Drawers, Tapered Legs, 33 x 29 x 24 In. 895.00
Desk, Schoolmaster's, Sheraton, Painted, Scrolling Backboard, 1835, 45 x 39 In. 690.00
Desk, Serpentine, Painted Flowers, 7 Drawers, Venice, Early 1900s, 31 x 49 In. 865.00
Desk, Shaker, Ash, Oak, Pine, Alfred, Me., c.1886, 48 x 38 In. .... *Illus* 11500.00
Desk, Sheraton, Slant Front, Walnut, Dovetailed Drawer, 93 x 39 In. 2645.00
Desk, Shop Of The Crafters, No. 338, Drop Front, Cutouts, 32 x 20 x 42 In. 1765.00
Desk, Slant Front, 4 Drawers, Bracket Feet, Conn., c.1760, 42 x 38 x 18 In. 3500.00
Desk, Slant Front, 8 Interior Compartments, Conn., 1700s, 43 x 40 x 18 In. 3175.00
Desk, Slant Front, Birch, Bracket Feet, New England, 1700s, 37 In. 3500.00
Desk, Slant Front, Cherry, 18th Century, 34 1/2 x 43 x 19 In. 5875.00
Desk, Slant Front, Cherry, 4 Drawers, Bracket Feet, c.1800, 43 x 43 In. 1150.00
Desk, Slant Front, Cherry, Dovetailed, Drawer, Spindle Gallery, 40 x 30 x 59 In. 460.00

Desk, Slant Front, Mahogany, 4 Drawers, 20th Century, 39 x 33 3/4 x 19 In. 1175.00
Desk, Slant Front, Mahogany, Pigeonholes, 4 Drawers, c.1800, 39 x 46 x 22 In. 1725.00
Desk, Slant Front, Maple, 6 Cubbies, Shell-Carved Drawer, 1700s, 31 x 39 x 16 In. 3175.00
Desk, Slant Front, Maple, Dark Stain, 3 Drawers, 1730-50, 15 x 14 x 10 In. 3760.00
Desk, Slant Front, Maple, Dovetailed, Breadboard, Drawers, Cubbies, 41 x 34 In. 4140.00
Desk, Slant Front, Maple, New England, 24 x 18 x 11 In., Child's 2645.00
Desk, Slant Front, Maple, White Pine, New England, c.1770, 39 x 35 x 18 In. 3500.00
Desk, Slant Front, Oak, Gallery Top, Tapered Legs, England, Late 1800s, 61 x 37 In. 1035.00
Desk, Slant Front, Pine, Brown Stain, Gallery, Drawer, 1800s, 36 x 21 x 22 In. 265.00
Desk, Slant Front, Tiger Maple, 4 Drawers, Rhode Island, 1700s, 40 x 36 In. 5760.00
Desk, Slant Front, Walnut, Pigeonholes, Drawers, c.1790, 41 x 41 x 22 In. 1725.00
Desk, Stickley Bros., Drop Front, Oak, Copper Hardware, 1904 .... 3800.00
Desk, Stickley Bros., Gallery Top, Drawer, Slatted Base, 36 x 36 x 23 In. 1175.00
Desk, Tiger Maple, 4 Drawers, R.I., c.1780, 42 x 36 x 18 In. 7640.00
Desk, Victorian, Mahogany, Carved, Twin Pedestal, 47 In. 590.00
Desk, Victorian, Slant Front, c.1860, 51 x 42 x 31 In. 440.00
Desk, Victorian, Walnut, Inkwell, Drawer, c.1878, 31 x 34 1/2 In. 290.00
Desk, Walnut, Carved Roman Soldiers, Horses, Hercules Holding Top, 67 x 32 In. 2300.00
Desk, Walnut, Flame, Burl Veneer, Shell Knees, 31 x 19 x 39 In. 800.00
Desk, Walnut, Green Surface, American Of Martinsville, 30 x 49 x 26 In. 145.00
Desk, Walnut, Kidney Shape, Carved, Chair, Mid 1900s, 30 x 43 x 21 In. 315.00
Desk, Walnut, Open Shelf, 6 Cubbyholes, 2 Drawers, 78 x 36 3/8 x 16 In. 590.00
Desk, Walnut, Poplar, 7 Cubbyholes, Fallboard, Hinges, 40 x 37 x 26 In. 460.00
Desk, Wicker, White, 36 x 31 x 22 In. 450.00
Desk, William & Mary Style, Slant Front, Walnut Inlay, Seaweed Marquetry 2350.00
Desk, William & Mary, Slant Front, Maple, Dovetailed, 41 x 35 In. 4310.00
Desk, Wood, Glass, Illuminated, 5 Drawers, France, 1930, 30 x 44 x 24 In. 3110.00
Desk, Wormley, Walnut, Inset Leather, 6 Drawers, Rosewood Handles, 72 x 29 In. 1765.00
Desk-Bookcase, Federal, Mahogany, Inlaid, c.1800, 51 x 40 x 20 In. 2115.00
Desk-Bookcase, Federal, Mahogany, Mass., c.1800, 85 x 37 x 22 In. 6465.00
Desk-Bookcase, Side-By-Side, Double Mirror Crest, Leaf Carving, 39 x 75 In. 520.00
Desk-Bookcase, Side-By-Side, Slant Front, Oak, Leaf Carving, 46 x 19 x 81 In. 2645.00
Dining Set, Art Deco, Walnut, Pedestal Table, France, c.1935, 30 x 40 In., 7 Piece 455.00
Dining Set, Drexel, Federal Style, New Travis Court Collection, c.1950, 9 Piece 690.00
Dining Set, Federal Style, Bleached Mahogany, 20th Century, 10 Piece 1530.00
Dining Set, Hans Olsen, Teak, Denmark, c.1965, 41 In., 5 Piece 455.00
Dining Set, Hepplewhite, Mahogany, Inlaid, Round Table, Sideboard, 11 Piece 3220.00
Dining Set, Jacobean Revival, Oak, Draw-Leaf Table, 10 Piece 1910.00
Dining Set, Mahogany, Bubinga, Primavera, Chrome Plated, c.1930, 7 Piece 3825.00
Dining Set, Mastercraft, Italian Style, Burl Walnut, Brass, 83 x 46 In., 11 Piece 865.00
Dining Set, Neoclassical, White Paint, Broken Pediment, c.1930, 8 Piece 880.00
Dining Set, Oak, Carved, Parquetry Top, Rococo Scrolls, 5 Piece 575.00
Dining Set, Sheraton Style, Mahogany, 20th Century, 71 x 45 x 15 In., 9 Piece 499.00
Dining Set, W. Platner, Welded Steel Rods, Beveled Glass Top, 1966, 4 Piece 1645.00
Dining Set, Widdicomb, Ebonized Table, 6 Upholstered Chairs, Leaves, 9 Piece 865.00
Dresser, Art Deco, Mirror, Curved Top, Drawers, France, c.1925, 67 x 69 x 20 In. 1060.00
Dresser, Dinesen, Teak, Tapered Birch Legs, 8 Drawers, Denmark, 59 x 18 x 34 In. 4415.00
Dresser, Donald Deskey, No. 217, 8 Drawers, c.1935, 32 x 44 In., Pair 2585.00
Dresser, Dunbar, Mahogany, Curved Front, 8 Drawers, Brass Pulls, 56 x 29 In. 295.00
Dresser, Faux Bamboo, Drop Well, 19th Century, 88 x 63 x 19 In. 4600.00
Dresser, Faux Bamboo, Side Lock, 19th Century, 74 x 31 x 18 In. 4900.00
Dresser, Frank Lloyd Wright, Heritage Henredon, 28 x 61 In. 1380.00
Dresser, French Provincial, Pine, Ireland, Early 1800s, 79 1/2 x 56 1/2 x 20 In. 1495.00
Dresser, Fruitwood, Mirror, Early 20th Century, 69 x 46 1/2 x 18 In. 145.00
Dresser, G. Nelson, Steel Frame, Birch-Front Drawers, Enameled, 34 x 52 In. 1645.00
Dresser, G. Stickley, No. 911, Half Over Full Drawers, 48 x 20 x 42 In. 1765.00
Dresser, George III Style, Mahogany, Serpentine, Mirror, c.1900, 69 x 47 x 23 In. 200.00
Dresser, George III, Walnut, Crossbanded Oak, Wales, 18th Century, 33 x 99 x 20 In. 6325.00
Dresser, Gothic Revival, Mahogany, c.1880, 76 x 43 x 20 In. 200.00
Dresser, Gothic Revival, Mahogany, Marble Top, Mirror, c.1865, 75 x 43 In. 1380.00
Dresser, Mahogany, 3 Drawers, 20th Century, 37 x 47 1/2 x 20 In. 265.00
Dresser, Mahogany, Fitted Interior, 4 Drawers, c.1910, 39 x 44 x 22 In. 175.00
Dresser, Mahogany, Oval Mirror, 2 Short Over 3 Long Drawers, 71 x 50 x 26 In. 545.00

Dresser, Mahogany, Rosewood, Shell Crest, Mirror, Urn Finials, 54 x 25 x 98 In. 1900.00
Dresser, McCobb, Maple, 8 Drawers, Brass Pulls, 60 x 18 x 33 3/4 In. 175.00
Dresser, McCobb, Planner Group, Maple, 6 Drawers, 29 x 48 x 18 In. 175.00
Dresser, Nutting, No. 942, Pine, 75 x 50 x 18 1/2 In. 5500.00
Dresser, Oak, Applied Leaf Carving, Oval Mirror, 40 x 18 x 51 In. 115.00
Dresser, Oak, Leaf, Scroll Carving, Serpentine, Mirror, 45 x 21 x 72 In. 430.00
Dresser, Oak, Molded Top, 4 Drawers, Brass Pulls, England, c.1600, 34 x 86 x 18 In. 5290.00
Dresser, Rococo Revival, Rosewood, Mirror, Mid 1800s, 100 x 48 x 24 In. 2530.00
Dresser, Victorian, Mahogany, Late 1800s, 34 x 39 x 17 In., Pair 235.00
Dresser, Victorian, Mahogany, Marble Topped, Bowed Front, 34 x 44 x 22 In. 230.00
Dresser, Victorian, Oak, Dumbbell Drawer Pulls, 39 x 18 x 39 In. 195.00
Dresser, Victorian, Walnut, 19th Century, 33 x 45 x 21 In. 360.00
Dresser, Victorian, Walnut, 3 Drawers, 19th Century, 32 1/2 x 45 x 21 In. 360.00
Dresser, Victorian, Walnut, 4 Drawers, c.1830, 36 1/2 x 40 3/4 x 20 In. 540.00
Dresser, Victorian, Walnut, Burl Veneer, Marble Top, Mirror, 45 x 20 x 89 In. 750.00
Dresser, Victorian, Walnut, Mirror, Glove Box, 21 x 38 In. 185.00
Dry Sink, 2-Paneled Lower Doors, Shelf, 36 x 47 x 21 In. 575.00
Dry Sink, Amish, Softwood, Grain Painted, Pennsylvania, 34 x 45 x 18 In. . . . . *Illus* 990.00
Dry Sink, Ash, Poplar, Blue Paint, Center Drawers, Paneled Door, 62 x 19 x 36 In. 1840.00
Dry Sink, Cherry, Hinged Cover Over Well, Interior Shelves, 1850s, 33 3/4 In. . . . . . . *Illus* 690.00
Dry Sink, Cherry, Recessed Panel Doors, Pennsylvania, 19th Century, 70 x 36 x 19 In. 764.00
Dry Sink, High Top, 4 Doors, Drawer, Grain Painted, c.1875, 45 x 20 In., Child's 999.00
Dry Sink, Pine, Drawer, Door Below, 19th Century, 20 1/2 x 28 1/2 In. 345.00
Dry Sink, Pine, High Back, 2 Drawers, Scalloped Shelf, 2 Doors, 48 x 47 In. 3630.00
Dry Sink, Pine, Walnut, Red, Yellow Paint, 2 Doors, 4 Drawers, 56 x 22 x 53 In. 2185.00
Dry Sink, Poplar, Painted, 2 Drawers, 2 Doors, Zinc-Lined Well, 34 x 46 In. 2530.00
Dry Sink, Poplar, Painted, Step Back, Zinc Liner, Blind Doors, 82 x 46 In. 6600.00
Dry Sink, Red Paint, 2 Drawers, Paneled Doors, 60 In. 4950.00
Dumbwaiter, Edwardian, Mahogany, 3 Plate Supports, Tripod, 31 1/2 In. 315.00
Dumbwaiter, George III, Mahogany, 3 Circular Trays, Tripod Base, 43 In. 2376.00
Dumbwaiter, George III, Mahogany, 3 Tiers, Tripod, c.1815, 49 x 29 In. 750.00
Dumbwaiter, George III, Mahogany, Circular Tiers, Cabriole Legs, 49 x 23 In. 665.00
Dumbwaiter, Mahogany, 2 Tiers, Paw Caps, 20th Century 59.00
Dumbwaiter, Mahogany, 3 Drop Leaf Tiers, Brass Cuffs, Casters, 48 x 24 x 18 In. 1380.00
Easel, Bamboo, 23 1/2 x 67 In. 115.00
Easel, Cincinnati Art-Carved, Leaf Carved, Gold, 21 In. 590.00
Easel, Renaissance Revival, Rosewood, Bull's-Eye Crest, Reeded Legs, 68 1/2 In. 558.00
Etagere, Art Nouveau, Mahogany 430.00
Etagere, Bamboo, Galleried Top, 20th Century, 50 x 27 1/4 x 13 In., Pair 130.00
Etagere, Corner, Mahogany, Gilt, Shaped Back, 56 x 19 x 17 In. 550.00
Etagere, Edwardian, Satinwood, Crossbanded Mahogany, 4 Tiers, c.1920, 36 x 20 In. 765.00
Etagere, Galle, Mahogany, Marquetry, Poppy Motif, c.1900, 55 x 24 x 16 In. 3110.00
Etagere, Heywood Bros. & Co., Oak Rattan, 4 Tiers, 43 x 26 x 13 In. 896.00
Etagere, Mahogany, 4 Tiers, Drawer, Turned Feet, Brass Casters, 50 x 20 x 20 In. 920.00
Etagere, Mahogany, Green Face On Door, Mirror, 36 x 11 1/2 x 61 1/4 In. 460.00
Etagere, Mahogany, Pagoda Shape, Pierced Gallery, 4 Tiers, 70 x 20 1/2 In., Pair 4140.00

Furniture, Dry Sink, Amish, Softwood, Grain
Painted, Pennsylvania, 34 x 45 x 18 In.

Furniture, Dry Sink, Cherry, Hinged Cover
Over Well, Interior Shelves, 1850s, 33 3/4 In.

Etagere, Mahogany, Telescoping, 3 Tiers, Stretcher Base, England, 54 x 45 x 22 In. 345.00
Etagere, Regency, Rosewood, 3 Tiers, Bulbous Uprights, c.1815, 38 x 30 In. 865.00
Etagere, Rococo Revival, Rosewood, Cabinet Base, American, c.1865, 74 x 50 In. 8050.00
Etagere, Victorian, Calamander, Gilt Metal, 1800s, 28 1/2 x 21 1/4 x 15 1/4 In. 6600.00
Etagere, Victorian, Carved Grapes, Flowers, Marble, 6 Tiers, 49 x 20 x 91 In. 2875.00
Etagere, Victorian, Mahogany, Divided Tiers, Mirrors, Early 1900s, 51 x 21 x 9 In. 86.00
Etagere, Victorian, Mahogany, Shield & Leaf Crest, Mirror, 46 x 14 x 90 In. 2990.00
Etagere, Victorian, Rosewood, 4 Tiers, Casters, Mid 1800s, 43 x 18 x 14 In. 750.00
Etagere, Victorian, Rosewood, Leaves, Flowers, Branch Pulls, 55 x 19 x 90 In. 2300.00
Etagere, Victorian, Walnut, 3 Tiers, Turned Columns, 49 x 24 x 15 In. 895.00
Etagere, Victorian, Walnut, Pierced, Carved Leaves, Mirror, 50 x 18 x 82 In. 1265.00
Footstool, Arts & Crafts, Oak, Arched Side Rails, Pinned Legs, 15 x 17 x 12 In. 150.00
Footstool, Brass, Lion Decoration, Flat Top, Claw & Ball Feet, 4 x 10 x 6 In. 60.00
Footstool, Cherry, Curly Maple, Figured Walnut, 14 x 8 x 9 In. 290.00
Footstool, Chinese Style, Carved, 20 & 20 In., Pair 260.00
Footstool, Empire Style, Mahogany Veneer, Upholstered, 16 x 22 x 18 In. 60.00
Footstool, French Provincial, Walnut, Carved, Upholstered Top, 7 x 10 x 20 In. 295.00
Footstool, G. Stickley, No. 300, Leather, Straight Rail, 15 x 20 x 16 In. 765.00
Footstool, G. Stickley, No. 302, Oak, Replaced Seat, Red Decal, 4 1/2 x 12 In. 259.00
Footstool, G. Stickley, No. 395, Oak, Leather, 7 Side Spindles, c.1907, 15 x 20 x 16 In. 1795.00
Footstool, George I Style, Walnut, Upholstered, Cabriole Legs, Pad Feet, 21 x 16 In. 620.00
Footstool, George II Style, Walnut, Scroll Skirt, Slip Seat, 1800s, 19 x 22 x 16 In. 375.00
Footstool, Georgian, Walnut, Scalloped Skirt, Shell-Carved, Needlepoint, 20 In. 2760.00
Footstool, Harden, Drop-In Leather Cushion, Slatted Sides, 16 x 20 x 14 In. 1175.00
Footstool, Harden, Slatted Sides, Loose Pillow, 15 x 17 3/4 x 14 In. 590.00
Footstool, Limbert, Cricket, Cutout, Flared Slab Legs, 18 x 10 x 6 In. 290.00
Footstool, Louis XV Style, Beech, Oval, Damask Upholstery, 1800s, 10 x 16 In. 315.00
Footstool, Louis XV Style, Carved, Gray Lacquer, Upholstered, 17 x 31 In. 235.00
Footstool, Louis XV Style, Gilt, Padded Oval Top, 11 x 22 1/2 x 17 In. 201.00
Footstool, Louis XV Style, Walnut, 19th Century, 7 x 13 x 9 In., Pair 920.00
Footstool, Mahogany, Dome Top, Whalebone, Ebony, Hearts, Diamonds, 12 x 9 In. 1725.00
Footstool, Mahogany, Leather, Scrolled Legs, Mid-Victorian, 29 x 24 In. 620.00
Footstool, Mahogany, Needlework, Spray Of Roses, 6 x 13 x 11 In. 75.00
Footstool, Neoclassical, Mahogany, Curule Shape, c.1820 .... 4185.00
Footstool, Painted, Flowers, Gold, Yellow Borders, Oval, Tapered Legs, 12 x 7 In. 805.00
Footstool, Pine, Grain Painted, Red Ground, White Stripes, 5 1/2 x 16 x 5 5/8 In. 460.00
Footstool, Pine, Yellow Paint, Applied Leaves & Stars, Square Nails, 14 x 7 In. 1035.00
Footstool, Queen Anne, Walnut, Carved, Leather, c.1850, 19 x 22 x 17 In. 460.00
Footstool, Regency, Mahogany, Early 19th Century, 7 x 12 1/2 x 9 In., Pair 920.00
Footstool, Regency, Mahogany, Padded, Paw Feet, c.1900, 9 x 12 x 12 In., Pair 2185.00
Footstool, Shaker, Cherry, Mortise & Peg, Enfield, Conn., c.1840, 4 x 15 In. 520.00
Footstool, Shaker, Maple, Dark Walnut Finish, Mt. Lebanon, c.1890, 6 1/2 x 12 In. 430.00
Footstool, Shaker, Tiger Maple, Red Stain, Splayed Peg Legs, Mt. Lebanon, 8 x 13 In. 1840.00
Footstool, Victorian, Mahogany, Needlework Cover, c.1880, 19 x 24 x 20 In. 315.00
Footstool, Victorian, Wood, Leaf Shields, Needlework, Cabriole Legs, 15 In. 69.00
Footstool, Walnut, Star Inlay, Union Shields, Serpentine Top, c.1875, 8 x 18 x 9 In. 1530.00
Footstool, White Metal, Painted, Upholstered, 20th Century, 9 x 14 x 10 In., Pair 165.00
Footstool, Windsor, Bamboo, Poplar, Red Wash, Oval Top, 12 x 7 x 8 In. 115.00
Footstool, Windsor, Brown Paint, Mortised Legs, 7 1/4 x 13 1/2 x 9 In. 550.00
Footstool, Windsor, Pine, Painted, Upholstered, New England, c.1820, 7 x 11 x 8 In. 59.00
Footstool, Wood, 2 Bears, Glass Eyes, Center Panel, Switzerland, c.1900, 7 x 17 x 6 In. .. 2175.00
Footstool, Wood, Inlaid Heart, Rectangular, Canted Sides, Early 1800s, 7 x 7 x 13 In. 765.00
Frame, Art Deco, Chalcedony, Champleve, 14K Gold Fittings 2235.00
Frame, Art Deco, Wood, 12 In. 590.00
Frame, Art Nouveau, Repousse Copper, Patina, 13 In. 529.00
Frame, Arts & Crafts, Brass, Hammered, Raised Leaves, 10 1/2 In. 355.00
Frame, Arts & Crafts, Bronze, Hammered & Cutout Designs, Austria, 5 1/2 In. 325.00
Frame, Arts & Crafts, Bronze, Tooled Flowers, Austria, 5 1/2 In. 235.00
Frame, Arts & Crafts, Faux Alligator Skin, 11 1/2 x 14 In. 295.00
Frame, Arts & Crafts, Silver, Hammered, England, 6 x 6 1/2 In. 323.00
Frame, Arts & Crafts, Wood, Carved, Applied Metal Lizard, 14 In. 460.00
Frame, Cream & Rust Paint, 14 3/8 x 10 In. 405.00
Frame, Faberge, Bird's-Eye Maple, Silver Mounted, 1896-1903, 13 x 9 In. 8295.00

Frame, Federal, Tiger Maple, Mahogany, Block Corners, c.1810, 14 x 17 In. 805.00
Frame, Polychrome, Sausage-Turned Edges, 10 1/2 x 12 3/4 In., Pair 1245.00
Frame, Red & Black Paint Decorated, 8 x 13 In. 200.00
Frame, Tabernacle, Brass, Gothic Design, Inset Paper Icon, 19 1/2 x 12 1/2 In. 165.00
Frame, Tabernacle, Giltwood, Carved, Columns, Pediment Panel, 34 x 23 In. 980.00
Frame, Tiger Maple, 12 x 15 In. 430.00
Frame, Walnut, Black Paint, Raised Corner Blocks, Turned Rosettes, 15 1/4 x 13 1/4 In. . . 230.00
Frame, Wood, Gesso, Carved, Late 20th Century, 32 1/2 x 44 1/2 In. 30.00
Hall Stand, Beech, Stained, J. & J. Kohn, c.1905, 78 x 17 In. 4500.00
Hall Stand, Cast Metal, Figural, William Wallace, Scotland, 30 x 18 x 9 In. 210.00
Hall Stand, Chinese, Red Lacquer, Gilt, Shelf, Drawers, c.1890, 65 x 18 3/8 x 19 In. 200.00
Hall Stand, G. Stickley, No. 224, Paneled Back, Slab Sides, Seat, 42 x 48 In. 9400.00
Hall Stand, Iron, Tree, Cannons, Mirror, Corneau Freres Charleville, 75 In. 1650.00
Hall Stand, Neogothic, Mahogany, Mirror, Pegs, Cane Well, 84 x 25 x 13 In. 705.00
Hall Stand, Oak, Arched Top, Mirror, Bench, Early 20th Century, 70 x 32 x 20 In. 645.00
Hall Stand, Oak, Curved Crest, Mirror, Lyre Hooks, Lift Seat, 36 x 18 x 78 In. 1440.00
Hall Stand, Renaissance Revival, Walnut, Mirror, Pegs, Drawer, c.1880, 92 In. 880.00
Hall Stand, Victorian, Mahogany, Mirror, Spool Crest, Iron, Lift Seat, 44 x 18 x 84 In. 950.00
Hall Stand, Victorian, Walnut, Mirror, Umbrella Stand, 78 In. 259.00
Hall Tree, Art Deco, Mahogany, Iron, 96 x 36 In. 660.00
Hall Tree, Arts & Crafts, Double Posts, 3 Slats, Brass Hardware, 20 x 18 x 73 In. 235.00
Hall Tree, Bavarian, Carved, Mountain Goat, Branches, Ferns, c.1910 . . . . 2235.00
Hall Tree, Mahogany, Acanthus Carved Standard, Brass Eagle, c.1890, 88 In. 2990.00
Hall Tree, Neogothic, Yellow Pine, 19 Pegs, Umbrella Racks, 93 x 67 x 19 In. 690.00
Hall Tree, Regency Style, Mahogany Inlay, Urn Finial, 20th Century, 69 x 22 In. 190.00
Hall Tree, Victorian, Bamboo, Pediment-Shape Back, 80 x 44 x 12 In. 1495.00
Hall Tree, Victorian, Walnut, Spade Leaf Crest, Marble Top, 91 x 41 x 12 In. 1670.00
Hall Tree, Victorian, Walnut, Spindle Crown, c.1875, 99 x 62 1/2 x 17 In. 1495.00
Hat Rack, Oak, Quatrefoil, Mirror, 33 1/2 x 23 In. 290.00
Hat Rack, Oak, Shield Shape, Mirror, 6 Double Hooks, 34 x 29 In. 230.00
Headboard, 18th-Century Style, Mahogany, Floral Marquetry, France, 64 In. 335.00
Headboard, Carved, Painted, Mexico, 20th Century, 51 x 60 x 8 In. 880.00
Headboard, G. Nelson, Oak, Padded Backrests, Hairpin Legs, 56 x 12 x 40 In. 345.00
High Chair, Art Deco, Wood, Chrome, Upholstered, Adjustable, 15 x 22 x 35 In. 805.00
High Chair, Ladder Back, 2 Slats, Hardwoods, Turned Arms, 19 1/2 x 34 In. 145.00
High Chair, Ladder Back, Rush Seat, Turned Legs 290.00
High Chair, Maple, 3 Arched Slats, Tape Seat, Birch Footrest, c.1870, 21 In. 3450.00
High Chair, Maple, Birch, 3 Arched Slats, Shaped Arms, Splayed Legs, 40 In. 1060.00
High Chair, Oak, Ash, Hickory, Turned Posts, Ball Finials, 34 x 16 x 16 In. 430.00
High Chair, Queen Anne, Ladder Back, 3 Slats, Maple, Hickory, 21 x 39 In. 575.00
High Chair, Shaker, Maple, 3 Arched Slats, Tape Seat, Mt. Lebanon, c.1870, 36 In. 3450.00
High Chair, Sheraton Style, Early 19th Century, 33 In. 300.00
High Chair, Wicker, Natural Finish, Oak Tray, Footrest, Tooled Leather Seat, 40 In. 290.00
High Chair, Windsor, Bow Back, Bamboo Turnings, Footrest, 37 1/2 In. 9490.00
High Chair, Windsor, Sack Back, Black Paint, 7 Spindles, Oval Seat, 32 In. 8625.00
Highboy, Chippendale Style, Mahogany, Broken-Arch Bonnet Top, 86 x 37 x 17 In. 290.00
Highboy, Chippendale Style, Mahogany, Broken-Arch Pediment, 80 x 40 x 16 In. 460.00
Highboy, George III Style, Mahogany, 5 Drawers, Mid 1800s, 66 x 38 x 19 In. 2990.00
Highboy, Mahogany, Bonnet Top, Rosettes, Drawers, Cabriole Legs, 81 x 45 x 20 In. 2185.00
Highboy, Queen Anne Style, Poplar, Black Over Red, Sewickley, 63 x 39 x 23 In. 2300.00
Highboy, Queen Anne, 2 Parts, 9 Drawers, Cutout Apron, Slipper Feet, 44 x 65 In. 3500.00
Highboy, Queen Anne, Cherry, 8 Drawers, Cabriole Legs, c.1745, 65 x 38 In. 6600.00
Highboy, Queen Anne, Mahogany, 79 x 39 1/2 x 18 In. 375.00
Highboy, Queen Anne, Mahogany, Broken-Arch Pediment, Carved Fan, 80 x 38 In. 2630.00
Highboy, Queen Anne, Maple, 2 Short Over 4 Drawers, 2 Drop Pendants, 62 In. 5020.00
Highboy, Queen Anne, Maple, Molded Cornice, Secret Drawer, 4 Drawers, 68 x 38 In. 4400.00
Highboy, Queen Anne, Maple, Tulip, Early 19th Century, 74 x 40 x 20 In. 11165.00
Highboy, Walnut Inlay, 2 Sections, Cornice, 7 Drawers, 18th Century, 75 x 44 In. 3820.00
Hoosier Cabinet, Painted, White, Double Doors, Metal Top, 68 3/4 x 40 3/8 x 23 In. 175.00
Huntboard, French Provincial, Pearwood, Tilt Top, Mid 19th Century, 29 x 59 In. 1380.00
Huntboard, Mahogany, 4 Drawers, Tapered Legs, 19th Century, 40 x 47 x 21 In. 2300.00
Huntboard, Mahogany, Inlaid, 2 Center Drawers, Bowed Front, 54 x 20 x 41 In. 2415.00
Huntboard, Oak, Plank Top, 2 Drawers, Column Legs, 28 x 12 x 28 In. 635.00

Huntboard, Sheraton, Mahogany, 3 Drawers, 4 Doors, c.1800, 40 x 61 x 21 In. 3450.00
Hutch, Pine, 3 Shelves, 2 Drawers, 2-Paneled Doors, 84 x 53 1/2 x 19 In. 1495.00
Hutch, Pine, Molded Top, 3 Shelves, Paneled Doors, 77 x 47 In. 1210.00
Hutch, Walnut, Sliding Doors, 3 Drawers, Pennsylvania, 80 x 63 x 22 In. 8812.00
Kas, Softwood, 4-Paneled Doors, 3 Drawers, H-Shape Iron Hinges, 79 x 79 x 27 In. 4950.00
Kennel, Travel, Base Document Drawer, Australia, c.1900, 24 In. 1500.00
Kneeler, Prie Dieu, Red Paint, Black Line Border, Ackerman, 37 1/2 x 6 5/8 In. 630.00
Kneeler, Prie Dieu, Rosewood, Velvet Upholstery, c.1875 .... 1150.00
Kneeler, Wrought Iron, 1920s, 32 x 25 In., Pair 145.00
Lap Desk, Flame Mahogany, Brass Mounted, Leather, 8 x 20 x 10 In. 490.00
Lap Desk, George IV, Brass Bound, Slant Front, Mid 19th Century, 22 x 12 x 10 In. 1035.00
Lap Desk, George IV, Rosewood, Brass Inlay, Mid 19th Century, 22 x 15 x 11 In. 1035.00
Lap Desk, Mahogany, Brass Bound, 6 1/2 x 18 3/4 x 9 1/2 In. 193.00
Lap Desk, Mahogany, Brass Bound, Hinged Cover, England, 1800s, 6 x 14 x 9 In. 345.00
Lap Desk, Mahogany, Brass Bound, Lift Top, 6 1/2 x 20 x 10 In. 140.00
Lap Desk, Mahogany, Brass Mounts, Blue Felt Interior, Late 1800s, 7 x 23 x 12 In. 105.00
Lap Desk, Mahogany, Dovetailed, Brass Handles, Diamond Key Plate, 17 x 10 x 7 In. 520.00
Lap Desk, Regency, Mahogany, Brass Bound, Early 19th Century, 22 x 17 x 10 In. 635.00
Lap Desk, Rosewood, Brass Bound, 6 x 11 1/2 x 9 In. 140.00
Lap Desk, Rosewood, Ebonized, Brass Inlay, England, 19th Century, 8 x 15 x 12 In. 290.00
Lap Desk, Rosewood, James G. Blake, Boston, 20 1/2 x 11 x 7 In. 130.00
Lap Desk, Shaker, Butternut, Pine, Slant Front, Drawer, 6 x 20 3/4 x 14 In. 12075.00
Lap Desk, Victorian, Papier-Mache, Mother-Of-Pearl Inlay, 1890, 12 x 9 x 4 In. 325.00
Lectern, Carved, Drawer, 39 x 32 In. 375.00
Lectern, Mahogany, Top Swivels, Tilting, Top, Tripod Base, 1800s, 30 x 24 x 19 In. 1175.00
Lectern, William IV Style, Rosewood, Slant Front, 2 Doors, 1800s, 54 x 41 x 24 In. 1150.00
Library Ladder, George III Style, Mahogany, Leather, Brass Nail, England, 102 In. 1495.00
Library Ladder, Georgian Style, Pole, Mahogany, Brass, 110 In. 4540.00
Library Ladder, Regency Style, Mahogany, 5 Rungs, 56 x 20 x 39 In. 635.00
Library Ladder, Regency Style, Mahogany, Folding, 4 Rungs, Brass Tread, 48 x 18 In. ... 805.00
Library Steps, George III Style, Mahogany, Brass Casters, 69 1/2 x 23 1/2 In. 865.00
Library Steps, Georgian Style, Mahogany, Turned Spindles, 7 Steps, 68 x 27 x 39 In. 1650.00
Library Steps, Regency Style, Mahogany, 4 Steps, Curved Base, 75 x 22 In. 345.00
Library Steps-Chair, Neogothic, Oak, Fabric Treads .... *Illus* 558.00
Library Steps-Chair, Regency Style, Curved Top, Leather Seat, Scrolled Arms, 35 In. 920.00
Library Steps-Chair, Victorian, Walnut, Carved, Boston, 1880, 21 In. 2900.00
Linen Press, Cherry, Circle Inlay, Pennsylvania, c.1812, 79 x 40 x 21 3/4 In. 21150.00
Linen Press, Chippendale, Cherry, 2 Doors Over 3 Drawers, c.1790, 77 x 47 In. 14375.00
Linen Press, Chippendale, Mahogany, c.1800, 84 x 46 x 21 In. 2530.00
Linen Press, Federal, Cherry Inlay, Pennsylvania, Early 1800s, 79 x 43 1/2 x 20 In. 7640.00
Linen Press, George III Style, Mahogany, 2 Doors, 4 Drawers, c.1860, 87 x 56 In. 3680.00
Linen Press, George III Style, Mahogany, 2 Doors, 4 Drawers, c.1885, 80 x 53 In. 3680.00
Linen Press, George III Style, Mahogany, 2 Doors, Drawers, 79 x 48 x 22 In. 2990.00
Linen Press, George III, Mahogany, 2 Doors, 4 Drawers, c.1785, 87 x 48 In. 4600.00
Linen Press, George III, Mahogany, 2 Recessed Panel Doors, 5 Drawers, 82 In. 4600.00
Linen Press, George III, Mahogany, 2-Panel Doors, c.1785, 80 x 48 In. 2990.00
Linen Press, George III, Mahogany, 2-Panel Doors, 4 Drawers, 81 x 49 In. 4830.00
Linen Press, George III, Mahogany, Late 18th Century, 78 1/2 x 50 x 23 In. 4600.00

Furniture, Library
Steps-Chair,
Neogothic, Oak,
Fabric Treads

Keep a leather sofa or chair clean by dusting regularly. When necessary, wipe with a damp cloth dipped in detergent-free soapy water. If someone spills food on the leather, wipe it off immediately and wipe the entire sofa to avoid a spot.

Linen Press, George III, Mahogany, Slide-Out Trays, 4 Drawers, 1820 .... 4000.00
Linen Press, Georgian Style, Mahogany, Inlaid Doors, Shelves, Bracket Feet, 78 x 73 In. ... 1840.00
Linen Press, Grain Painted, 2 Doors, Shaped Panels, 2 Drawers, 81 x 47 In. 5290.00
Linen Press, Mahogany, Arched Panel Doors, Leaf Carved, 3 Drawers, 75 x 51 In. 2070.00
Linen Press, Mahogany, Step Back, Glass Doors, 4 Drawers, 84 x 40 x 17 In. 720.00
Linen Press, Regency, Mahogany, Domed Cornice, Paneled Doors, 86 x 48 In. 2530.00
Linen Press, Regency, Mahogany, Molded Cornice, Inlaid Frieze, 84 x 52 In. 3450.00
Linen Press, Sheraton Style, Mahogany, 4 Drawers, Doors, c.1830, 86 x 55 In. 3335.00
Linen Press, William IV, Mahogany, Cornice, Doors, Inset Panel, 84 x 48 In. 3220.00
Love Seat, Eastlake, Walnut, Carved, c.1875, 39 x 60 In. 173.00
Love Seat, Edwardian, Beech, Cane, Painted, Cushion, c.1900, 40 x 60 x 29 In. 2070.00
Love Seat, Florence Knoll, Walnut Frame, Tufted Wool, 56 x 31 x 30 In. 530.00
Love Seat, Georgian Style, Mahogany, Double Chair, Carved, Upholstered, 39 x 46 In. ... 315.00
Love Seat, Hepplewhite Style, Mahogany, 20th Century, 39 x 53 x 30 In. 750.00
Love Seat, L. & J.G. Stickley, No. 214, Slatted, Leather Seat, Arms, 32 x 62 In. 7638.00
Love Seat, Queen Anne Style, Walnut, Camelback, Upholstered, 40 x 48 In. 375.00
Love Seat, Sheraton Style, Mahogany Inlay, Damask Upholstery, 34 x 42 x 22 In. 575.00
Love Seat, Victorian, Fruitwood, c.1900, 39 x 33 1/2 x 21 In. 90.00
Love Seat, Victorian, Mahogany, Gooseneck Arm, c.1890, 36 x 57 x 32 In. 230.00
Love Seat, Victorian, Walnut, Carved, Serpentine Front, Upholstered, c.1865, 67 In. 175.00
Love Seat, Wormley, Mahogany, Down-Filled Cushions, 55 x 33 x 27 In. 1060.00
Lowboy, Bowfront, Mirror, Cabriole Legs, 42 x 22 x 75 In. 375.00
Lowboy, Chippendale Style, Mahogany, Carved, Link-Taylor, 32 x 36 x 21 In. 345.00
Lowboy, Chippendale Style, Scroll Supports, 3 Drawers, 1900s, 30 x 34 x 19 In. 880.00
Lowboy, Chippendale, Mahogany, Open Claw & Ball, c.1770, 36 x 39 x 19 In. 4830.00
Lowboy, Chippendale, Walnut, 1 Long Over 3 Dovetailed Drawers, 33 x 19 In. 2590.00
Lowboy, George III, Mahogany, 1 Over 3 Drawers, Ireland, c.1865, 32 1/4 x 37 In. 10350.00
Lowboy, George III, Walnut, Drawer, Scalloped Skirt, Late 1700s, 29 x 33 x 21 In. 2530.00
Lowboy, Georgian Style, Mahogany, Carved, Faux Drawers, 31 x 45 x 20 In. 290.00
Lowboy, Nutting, No. 691, Mahogany, 4 Drawers, c.1928, 20 x 39 x 30 In. 7700.00
Lowboy, Queen Anne Style, Mahogany, 3 Drawers, Continental, 29 x 24 In. 345.00
Lowboy, Queen Anne Style, Mahogany, Shell, 4 Drawers, Cabriole Legs, 41 x 40 In. 480.00
Lowboy, Queen Anne Style, Walnut, Shell Carved, 2 Drawers, c.1890, 31 x 42 In. 2185.00
Lowboy, Queen Anne, Cherry, Late 18th Century, 34 x 38 x 20 In. 805.00
Lowboy, Queen Anne, Dovetailed Drawers, Beaded Edges, England, 32 x 20 x 28 In. 2415.00
Lowboy, Queen Anne, Oak, 4-Board Top, 3 Beaded Drawers, 1800s, 33 x 28 In. 1610.00
Lowboy, Queen Anne, Walnut, Leather Writing Surface, Drawer, 31 x 43 x 21 In. 1265.00
Lowboy, Queen Anne, Walnut, Mahogany, c.1780, 28 x 32 x 19 In. 4830.00
Lowboy, Queen Anne, Walnut, Veneers, 3 Drawers, Cabriole Legs, 30 x 29 x 18 In. 2875.00
Lowboy, Walnut, 4 Drawers, Scalloped Apron, 18th Century, 34 x 20 x 29 In. 9900.00
Lowboy, William & Mary Style, Oak, 3 Drawers, Late 1800s, 26 x 28 In. 1060.00
Luggage Rack, Stickley Bros., Slatted, 3 Spindles, 28 x 15 x 19 In. 805.00
Mirror, 16th-Century Style, Black Chinoiserie Lacquer Frame, 19 x 15 In. 210.00
Mirror, 16th-Century Style, Giltwood, Carved, Strapwork, Beveled, 73 x 52 In. 4200.00
Mirror, 18th-Century Venetian Style, Giltwood, Cartouche, 33 x 14 In. 690.00
Mirror, Adam Style, Giltwood, Carved, Shield Shape, 1800s, 41 x 30 In., Pair 3220.00
Mirror, Adam Style, Giltwood, Festooned Leafy Scrolls, 48 x 26 In. 3450.00
Mirror, Adam Style, Giltwood, Relief Molded Gesso, Urn & Feather Crest, Oval, 42 x 24 In. 460.00
Mirror, Aesthetic Revival Style, Giltwood, Ebonized, c.1900, 36 x 29 In. 635.00
Mirror, Applied & Etched Glass, Venetian, Rosette & Wheel Cut, 20 x 24 In. 115.00
Mirror, Art Deco, American Indian On Horseback, Blue Tint, Round, 25 In. 570.00
Mirror, Art Deco, Beveled Glass, Wrought Iron, Oval, France, c.1928, 36 3/4 In. 1645.00
Mirror, Art Deco, Rosewood, Ivory Inlay, Arched Top, France, c.1925, 71 x 29 x 15 In. ... 1528.00
Mirror, Art Deco, Walnut, 1930s, 18 1/2 x 17 In. 90.00
Mirror, Art Nouveau, Bronze, Standing Female Support, Oval, Late 1800s, 16 In. 105.00
Mirror, Arts & Crafts, Arched Frame, 28 x 20 In. 150.00
Mirror, Arts & Crafts, Copper, Hammered, Raised Over Wood, 21 x 26 In. 1295.00
Mirror, Arts & Crafts, Painted Wood, Pewter, Enamel, Brass, England, 20 x 10 In. 2990.00
Mirror, Arts & Crafts, Wood, Pewter Overlay, Leaves, Flowers, England, 13 In. 470.00
Mirror, Arts & Crafts, Wrought Iron, Applied Designs, 28 x 14 1/2 In. 765.00
Mirror, Baroque Style, Florentine Scroll, Giltwood, Carved, 54 x 35 1/2 In. 1610.00
Mirror, Baroque Style, Florentine, Giltwood, Convex, 18 x 15 In. 920.00
Mirror, Baroque Style, Giltwood, Italy, Late 1800s, 32 x 42 In. 635.00

Mirror, Baroque, Walnut, Gilt Gesso, Continental, Late 1700s, 29 x 12 3/4 In. 355.00
Mirror, Biedermeier, Mahogany, Swag, Silvered Bronze Crest, 43 1/2 x 20 In. 978.00
Mirror, Bird's-Eye Maple, 24 1/2 x 17 1/2 In. 270.00
Mirror, Bradley & Hubbard, Cast Iron, Brass Finish, Scrolls, 14 x 18 In. 175.00
Mirror, Brass, Beveled Glass, Scrolled Leaves, Torches, Relief Face, 16 x 11 In. 175.00
Mirror, Bugatti, Wood, Vellum Covered, Inlaid, c.1902, 39 x 33 In. 11950.00
Mirror, Bull's-Eye, Giltwood, Eagle Crest, Philadelphia, c.1795, 47 In. 15950.00
Mirror, Carved Wood, Gilt, Anthemia, Wheat, Chinoiserie, 47 x 24 In. 805.00
Mirror, Carved Wood, Scroll, Leaves, Gesso, Gilt, 3 x 43 In. 1150.00
Mirror, Carved, Gilt, Openwork Shells, Scrolls, Crest Rail, Tendrils, 48 x 30 In. 805.00
Mirror, Cheval, Chippendale Style, Mahogany, Leaves, Claw & Ball Feet, 27 x 83 In. 4800.00
Mirror, Cheval, George III, Mahogany, Trestle Support, c.1790, 75 x 30 x 22 In. 4800.00
Mirror, Cheval, Georgian, Mahogany, Rope & Ring-Turned Trestle, 62 x 30 In. 980.00
Mirror, Cheval, Limbert, No. 496, Adjustable, Arched Top, Posts, 30 x 18 x 68 In. 2585.00
Mirror, Cheval, Mahogany, Carved, Ormolu, Saber Legs, Paw Feet, c.1900, 84 In. 1380.00
Mirror, Cheval, Neoclassical, Mahogany, Baltic, 80 3/4 x 43 1/2 x 31 1/2 In. 2530.00
Mirror, Cheval, Regency, Mahogany, Domed, Shaped Plate, Casters, 33 x 31 In. 1380.00
Mirror, Cheval, Victorian, Mahogany, 65 x 26 1/2 In. 1095.00
Mirror, Cheval, Victorian, Mahogany, Satinwood Inlaid, 70 x 36 x 26 In. 805.00
Mirror, Cheval, Walnut, Mahogany, Fan Crest, 35 x 75 In. 405.00
Mirror, Chinoiserie, Landscape, Beveled Glass, 20th Century, 41 x 21 In. 106.00
Mirror, Chinoiserie, Pavilion Top, Multicolored, Gilt, England, c.1900, 35 x 25 In. 1090.00
Mirror, Chippendale Style, Chinoiserie, Wood, Lacquer, c.1750, 29 x 20 In. 1150.00
Mirror, Chippendale Style, Fret Carved, Gilt Molding, 1900s, 36 1/2 x 20 In. 106.00
Mirror, Chippendale Style, Mahogany, Carved, 54 x 41 1/2 In. 230.00
Mirror, Chippendale Style, Mahogany, Giltwood, 36 x 19 In. 748.00
Mirror, Chippendale Style, Mahogany, Inlay, Carved, Urn Finial, 48 x 28 In. 230.00
Mirror, Chippendale Style, Mahogany, Parcel Gilt, 19th Century, 51 In. 978.00
Mirror, Chippendale Style, Mahogany, Scrolling, c.1890, 41 x 22 In. 80.00
Mirror, Chippendale, Mahogany, Carved, Gilt Phoenix Crest, 39 1/2 In. 1035.00
Mirror, Chippendale, Mahogany, Fret Carved, Late 18th Century, 28 1/2 In. 235.00
Mirror, Chippendale, Mahogany, Gilt Gesso, Shaped, Scrolled, 44 x 22 In. 3055.00
Mirror, Chippendale, Mahogany, Gilt Spread-Wing Birds, 39 x 21 In. 2590.00
Mirror, Chippendale, Mahogany, Gilt Spread-Wing Eagle, 36 x 19 In. 575.00
Mirror, Chippendale, Mahogany, Parcel Gilt, Inlaid, Fret Carved, 47 1/4 In. 590.00
Mirror, Chippendale, Mahogany, Parcel Gilt, Shell Crest, 1800s, 53 x 28 In. 1530.00
Mirror, Chippendale, Mahogany, Phoenix Crest, Pierced, Gilt, Oval, 42 x 22 In. 1550.00
Mirror, Chippendale, Mahogany, Pine, Scrolls, Scallop, 28 1/2 x 15 1/4 In. 259.00
Mirror, Chippendale, Mahogany, Pine, Veneer, Arched, Scrolled Crest, 15 x 10 In. 175.00
Mirror, Chippendale, Mahogany, Scroll Cut, 33 1/2 x 17 In. 880.00
Mirror, Chippendale, Mahogany, Scroll, Scalloped, Bird-Head Finials, 19 x 11 1/4 In. 290.00
Mirror, Chippendale, Mahogany, Scrolled Pediment, Late 18th Century, 33 In. 355.00
Mirror, Chippendale, Mahogany, Scrolled, New England, c.1800, 21 x 12 1/2 In. 325.00
Mirror, Chippendale, Walnut, Giltwood, Shaped Crest, Scrolls, 27 1/2 x 15 1/2 In. 230.00
Mirror, Chippendale, Walnut, Parcel Gilt, c.1775, 37 1/2 x 20 In. 3055.00
Mirror, Courting, Etched Scrolls, Reverse Painted Panel, Late 1700s, 17 x 11 In. 920.00
Mirror, Courting, Pine, Reverse Painted, 17 1/4 x 12 1/2 In. 690.00
Mirror, Curly Maple, Poplar, Stepped Border, 30 x 21 3/4 In. 690.00
Mirror, Curly Maple, Shaped Crest, 12 1/2 In. 345.00
Mirror, Directoire Style, Sunburst, Carved, Giltwood, Convex, Italy, 28 In. 1725.00
Mirror, Divided, Colored Lithograph At Top, 55 x 16 In. 175.00
Mirror, Dressing, Federal, Mahogany, Bowfront, 3 Drawers, New England, c.1810, 22 In. . . 2040.00
Mirror, Dressing, Federal, Mahogany, Scrolls, c.1820, 35 x 32 x 11 In. 2820.00
Mirror, Dressing, Mahogany, 2 Drawers, Square, 23 x 26 x 29 In. 59.00
Mirror, Dressing, Oak, Serpentine Front, Applied Carving, 44 x 22 x 71 In. 290.00
Mirror, Dressing, Oak, Serpentine Front, Double Towel Rack, 42 x 21 x 64 In. 430.00
Mirror, Dressing, Renaissance Revival, Gilt Brass, Scrolls, Continental, c.1885, 21 In. 2300.00
Mirror, Dressing, Rope Twist Surround, Oval, Austro-Hungarian, 21 x 16 In. 1430.00
Mirror, Dressing, Stylized Hands Holding Glass, Franz Hagenauer, 15 x 26 In. 3450.00
Mirror, Dressing, William IV, Mahogany, Mid 1800s, 32 x 35 1/2 x 13 In. 575.00
Mirror, Eastlake, Black, Gold Paint, Urn Finials, Rope Twist Pilasters, 27 x 56 In. 290.00
Mirror, Eastlake, Walnut, c.1880, 59 x 29 In. 225.00
Mirror, Eastlake, Walnut, Gilt, Ebony, c.1880, 45 x 24 1/2 In. 85.00

Mirror, Eastlake, Walnut, Gold Accents, Line Carving, 26 3/4 x 52 1/2 In. 230.00
Mirror, Eastlake, Walnut, Shadowbox Frame, Gilt, Oval, c.1880, 28 1/2 x 24 1/2 In. 230.00
Mirror, Ebonized, Gilt, Silvered Wood, Continental, 21 x 18 In., Pair 690.00
Mirror, Embossed Silver, Lotus, Middle Eastern, Early 20th Century, 11 1/2 In. 490.00
Mirror, Empire, Ebonized, Giltwood, 87 x 40 In. 19550.00
Mirror, Empire, Mahogany, Ogee, 32 x 22 In. 85.00
Mirror, Engraved, Molded, Amber Glass, Monogram, Mid 1800s, 58 x 34 In. 3680.00
Mirror, Federal Style, Eagle Crest, Convex, Early 20th Century, 24 x 16 In. 690.00
Mirror, Federal Style, Giltwood, Eagle Pediment, Convex, c.1860, 36 x 22 In. 1495.00
Mirror, Federal Style, Mahogany, Parcel Gilt, Early 1900s, 39 x 25 In. 430.00
Mirror, Federal, Gesso Roses, Reverse Painted, Country Scene, 2 Parts, 34 x 19 In. 115.00
Mirror, Federal, Gilt, Gesso, Cottage, Pond, c.1820, 24 1/2 x 15 1/2 In. 560.00
Mirror, Federal, Gilt, Gesso, Paneled Frieze, New England, c.1820, 37 x 25 In. 1175.00
Mirror, Federal, Gilt, Gesso, Reverse Painted Tablet, Flowers, Urn, c.1815, 39 x 21 In. 1765.00
Mirror, Federal, Gilt, Gesso, Reverse Painted Tablet, Girl, Woods, c.1810, 37 x 21 In. 765.00
Mirror, Federal, Giltwood, Carved Flowers, Oval, 49 In., Pair 9490.00
Mirror, Federal, Giltwood, Eagle Crest, Oak Leaves, Acorns, 2 Sconces, Convex, 34 x 21 In. 8280.00
Mirror, Federal, Giltwood, Flat Crest Rail, 2 Sections, 19th Century, 40 In. 470.00
Mirror, Federal, Giltwood, Flat Crest Rail, Early 19th Century, 39 5/8 In. 645.00
Mirror, Federal, Giltwood, Flat Crest, 2 Sections, Early 19th Century, 31 In. 355.00
Mirror, Federal, Giltwood, Landscape, Half Columns, 31 x 18 1/2 In. 200.00
Mirror, Federal, Giltwood, Oval, c.1800, 42 x 40 In. 9560.00
Mirror, Federal, Giltwood, Reverse Painted, Cornice, 60 x 47 x 22 In. 489.00
Mirror, Federal, Giltwood, Reverse Painted, John Doggett Boxbury, 28 x 16 In. 405.00
Mirror, Federal, Giltwood, Reverse Painted, Mount Vernon, c.1815, 48 x 28 In. 4200.00
Mirror, Federal, Giltwood, Round, Early 19th Century, 40 In. 3290.00
Mirror, Federal, Giltwood, Spheres, Reverse Painted Panel, Child, Fruit, 33 x 20 In. 1495.00
Mirror, Federal, Giltwood, Woman On Shore, Sailing Ship, c.1820, 30 x 14 In. 920.00
Mirror, Federal, Gold Leaf, Eagle Crest, Enamel, Convex, 40 x 23 1/2 In. 1955.00
Mirror, Federal, Mahogany, Gilt, Reverse Painted, Lady Liberty, Shield, Ships, 33 x 17 In. 990.00
Mirror, Federal, Mahogany, Parcel Gilt, Carved, Early 1800s, 57 x 26 In. 4140.00
Mirror, Federal, Mahogany, Pennsylvania, c.1830, 23 x 35 1/2 In. 405.00
Mirror, Federal, Mahogany, Reverse Painted Panel, 2 Parts, 34 x 18 In. 375.00
Mirror, Federal, Pine, Red, Yellow Graining, Reverse Stenciled, 21 x 13 In. 2420.00
Mirror, Federal, Pine, Reverse Painted, Man Fishing, Columns, 21 x 13 In. 2530.00
Mirror, Federal, Reverse Painted Panel, White Panel, Gold Base, 29 x 16 In. 460.00
Mirror, Federal, Reverse Painted Upper Pane, Cottage, Lake, Sailboats, 23 x 13 In. 190.00
Mirror, Federal, Reverse Painted, 2 Parts, Early 1800s, 38 x 25 In. 650.00
Mirror, Federal, Tiger Maple, c.1800, 27 x 25 In. 2350.00
Mirror, Florentine Baroque Style, Giltwood, Carved, 59 x 41 In. 1840.00
Mirror, Florentine, Giltwood, Leaf Scrolls, Beaded Edge, Oval, c.1865, 41 x 39 In. 863.00
Mirror, French Provincial, Giltwood, Eros' Arrows, c.1815, 24 x 13 In. 489.00
Mirror, G. Nakashima, Walnut, Widdicomb, 46 1/4 x 37 1/2 In. 2470.00
Mirror, G. Stickley, 4 Coat Hooks, Crest Rail, 28 x 36 In. 2350.00
Mirror, G. Stickley, No. 66, Peaked Top, 4 Iron Hooks, 28 x 36 In. 3820.00
Mirror, G. Stickley, No. 910, Arched Top, Hooks, Chains, 28 x 23 In. 650.00
Mirror, G. Stickley, Shaving, Pivoting, Shoe Feet, 21 1/2 x 26 x 6 3/4 In. 2235.00
Mirror, George I, Gilt, Gesso, Carved, Arched, Beveled, c.1720, 48 x 25 In. 4200.00
Mirror, George I, Giltwood, Partition Plate, c.1715, 68 x 29 In., Pair 6615.00
Mirror, George II Style, Burl Walnut, Parcel Gilt, Scrolled, 47 x 24 1/2 In. 295.00
Mirror, George II Style, Walnut, Parcel Gilt, Early 20th Century, 45 x 22 In., Pair 690.00
Mirror, George II, Mahogany, Giltwood, Carved, Parcel Gilt, 32 x 17 In. 1265.00
Mirror, George III Style, Giltwood, Thomas Johnson, 70 x 41 In., Pair 9775.00
Mirror, George III Style, Mahogany, Prince Of Wales Plumes, 41 x 25 In. 190.00
Mirror, George III Style, Pine, Carved, 20th Century, 54 x 26 1/2 In. 1060.00
Mirror, George III, Gilt, Gesso, Convex, England, c.1815, 45 In. 6900.00
Mirror, George III, Giltwood, Chinoiserie, Late 18th Century, 37 x 18 In., Pair 4600.00
Mirror, George III, Giltwood, Crest, Hoho Bird, C-Scrolls, Late 1700s, 52 x 27 In. 3055.00
Mirror, George III, Mahogany, Carved, Pierced, Beveled Plate, 41 x 22 In. 1805.00
Mirror, George III, Mahogany, Giltwood, 18th Century, 42 x 22 12 In. 1035.00
Mirror, George III, Mahogany, Giltwood, c.1765, 55 x 29 In. 7190.00
Mirror, George V, Giltwood, Carved, Convex, 19 In. 490.00
Mirror, Georgian Style, Mahogany, Giltwood Carved, Broken Pediment, 61 x 73 x 10 In. . . . 2760.00

Mirror, Georgian Style, Walnut, Stand, 62 x 34 In. 315.00
Mirror, Georgian, Carved, Faux Rosewood Grain, Parcel Gilt, Ireland, 29 x 23 In. 690.00
Mirror, Georgian, Giltwood, Carved, Convex, Early 19th Century, 23 In. 980.00
Mirror, Georgian, Giltwood, Carved, Parcel Ebonized, Convex, 25 In. 980.00
Mirror, Georgian, Giltwood, Silvered, Ireland, Late 18th Century, 24 x 20 1/2 In. 1955.00
Mirror, Georgian, Regency, Giltwood, Carved, Ebonized, Convex, 35 x 25 In. 2300.00
Mirror, Gilt Bronze, Scrolling, Masque, Lion's Heads, c.1900, 22 x 15 In. 175.00
Mirror, Gilt Gesso, Beveled, 20th Century, 56 x 46 In. 345.00
Mirror, Gilt Metal, Etched, Continental, 24 1/4 x 22 In. 7410.00
Mirror, Giltwood, 2 Radiating Leaf Borders, Convex, Italy, c.1900, 24 In. 750.00
Mirror, Giltwood, Bowknot Crest, Oval, Dutch, c.1915, 25 x 12 In. 260.00
Mirror, Giltwood, Cartouche Shape, Scrolling Leaves, Shells, 16 x 9 In. 380.00
Mirror, Giltwood, Carved Leaves & Flowers, Pediment, Ruins, 36 x 25 In. 1495.00
Mirror, Giltwood, Carved, Arched Plate, Leafy Columns, 64 x 47 In. 2185.00
Mirror, Giltwood, Carved, Continental, Early 19th Century, 36 x 23 In. 4140.00
Mirror, Giltwood, Carved, Continental, Late 19th Century, 72 x 48 1/2 In. 980.00
Mirror, Giltwood, Carved, Half Columns, Fleur-De-Lis, 53 x 28 In. 1150.00
Mirror, Giltwood, Carved, Reeded, Leaf Molded, 20th Century, 41 x 26 In. 575.00
Mirror, Giltwood, Carved, Scrolling, Pierced Frame, Continental, 48 x 26 In. 2530.00
Mirror, Giltwood, Carved, Waisted Shield Shape, Late 1800s, 28 x 22 In. 315.00
Mirror, Giltwood, Domed, Molded, Carved Ship, Mid 1800s, 69 x 44 In. 3910.00
Mirror, Giltwood, Eagle, Convex, Early 1800s, 39 x 25 In. 1235.00
Mirror, Giltwood, Flower Basket Crest, Scrolling, 19th Century 765.00
Mirror, Giltwood, Flower Basket Crest, Scrolls, Florence, 39 x 22 In. 315.00
Mirror, Giltwood, Flowers, Painted Panel, Town, Dutch, c.1850, 24 In., Pair 690.00
Mirror, Giltwood, Mahogany, Ogee, Fillet, Gilt Border, Early 1900s, 45 x 23 In. 230.00
Mirror, Giltwood, Mirrored Bevels, Arabesque, c.1850, 67 x 39 In. 3450.00
Mirror, Giltwood, Molded, Bead Decoration, 20th Century, 38 x 36 In. 80.00
Mirror, Giltwood, Octagonal, 20th Century, 78 x 48 In. 470.00
Mirror, Giltwood, Openwork, Shell, Flowers, Scrolls, Beveled Glass, Oval, 39 x 26 In. . . . 1495.00
Mirror, Giltwood, Pierced & Carved Scrolling Leaves, Oval, England, 24 x 30 In. 69.00
Mirror, Giltwood, Plaster, Ribbon & Scale Carved, Scrolls, Oval, c.1865, 65 x 45 In. 1380.00
Mirror, Giltwood, Quatrefoil Shape, 3 Candle Sconces, Late 1800s, 40 x 20 In. 950.00
Mirror, Giltwood, Reticulated Scrolls, Shells, Oval, Late 1800s, 51 x 41 In. 1610.00
Mirror, Giltwood, Rope Twist, Beveled, Late 1800s, 48 x 35 In. 1150.00
Mirror, Giltwood, Rounded Corners, Wavy Molded Edge, Late 1800s, 68 x 41 In. 1955.00
Mirror, Giltwood, Scroll & Ribbon Border, 20th Century, 24 x 23 1/2 In. 80.00
Mirror, Giltwood, Shell Carved, Divided, 1800s, 54 x 28 In. 315.00
Mirror, Giltwood, Shell Molded, Ogee, Beveled Glass, c.1890, 36 x 41 In. 460.00
Mirror, Giltwood, Split Spindle, Reverse Painted, Girl, New England, c.1830, 34 x 15 In. . . 2760.00
Mirror, Girandole, Louis XVI Style, Napoleon III, Giltwood, Carved, 27 x 15 In. 690.00
Mirror, Gold Paint, Shell & Flower Crest, 40 x 34 In. 115.00
Mirror, Gothic Revival, Gilt Bronze, Cloisonne, Jewels, 14 1/4 x 11 3/4 In. 1435.00
Mirror, Grand Rapids Chair Co., Copper Hooks, Beveled Glass, 77 x 44 x 15 In. 1765.00
Mirror, Half Columns, Panel, Sailing Vessel, American Flag, 30 1/4 x 14 In. 260.00
Mirror, Hepplewhite Style, Mahogany, Giltwood, Broken Arch, 55 x 27 In. 400.00
Mirror, James Todd, Split Spindle, Reverse Painted, Boat, Maine, c.1815, 29 x 14 In. 2185.00
Mirror, Japanese Style, Giltwood, Carved, Bamboo, England, 30 x 18 In. 690.00
Mirror, Lacquered, Mother-Of-Pearl Inlay, Stand, Japan, 19th Century, 22 x 21 In. 295.00
Mirror, Leaf Carved, Ribbon, Flowers, 20th Century, 46 x 21 In. 325.00
Mirror, Louis XIV Style, Giltwood, Carved, Napoleon III, 64 x 46 In. 2300.00
Mirror, Louis XIV Style, Giltwood, Octagonal, 52 x 35 In. 1150.00
Mirror, Louis XV Style, Giltwood, Girandole, 30 x 18 1/2 In. 460.00
Mirror, Louis XVI Style, Giltwood, Bead Carved, Oval, France, 18 x 14 In., Pair 635.00
Mirror, Louis XVI Style, Giltwood, Flower Basket, c.1815, 37 x 21 In. 865.00
Mirror, Louis XVI Style, Giltwood, Notched Spine Rays, Convex, 24 1/2 In. 405.00
Mirror, Louis XVI Style, Giltwood, Scroll, Mask, Birds, Leaf Swags, 42 In. 645.00
Mirror, Louis XVI Style, Giltwood, Segmented Rays, Convex, 27 1/2 In. 1150.00
Mirror, Louis XVI, Giltwood, Sunburst, 69 In. 17250.00
Mirror, Mahogany, Egg & Swag Gilt Cornice, 20th Century, 33 x 17 In. 140.00
Mirror, Mahogany, Fret Carved, Scrolled, Giltwood, Late 1700s, 30 In. 560.00
Mirror, Mahogany, Fret Carved, Scrolled, Late 1700s, 33 1/2 x 18 1/4 In. 295.00
Mirror, Mahogany, Giltwood, Carved, Oval, 19th Century, 48 x 40 In. 9775.00

Mirror, Mahogany, Molded Top, c.1890, 38 x 24 In. 60.00
Mirror, Mahogany, Scrolled Crest, 20th Century, 40 x 25 1/2 In. 35.00
Mirror, Mahogany, Shell Crest, Leaf Scroll Accents, 39 x 59 In. 520.00
Mirror, Mahogany, Yew Rondels, Inlaid Pilasters, Dutch, c.1835, 45 x 30 In. 1265.00
Mirror, Molded Cornice, Gilt Beveled Edge, Reverse Painted, 2 Sections, 24 In. 460.00
Mirror, Napoleon III, Giltwood, Carved, Cenotaph Shape, Beaded, 61 x 32 In. 2070.00
Mirror, Napoleon III, Giltwood, Carved, Plaster, Oval, Convex, 18 x 15 In. 345.00
Mirror, Napoleon III, Giltwood, Cenotaph Shape, Mid 1800s, 39 x 28 In. 1095.00
Mirror, Napoleon III, Giltwood, Domed, Ogee Molded, 52 x 38 In. 2185.00
Mirror, Napoleon III, Giltwood, Leaf Scrolled Crest, Oval, c.1865, 34 x 25 In. 460.00
Mirror, Napoleon III, Giltwood, Plaster, Ribbons, Flowers, Oval, c.1865, 60 x 38 In. 4600.00
Mirror, Napoleon III, Giltwood, Rope Twist, 59 x 25 In. 920.00
Mirror, Neoclassical, Cherry, Mahogany Veneer, New England, c.1825, 47 x 26 In. 355.00
Mirror, Neoclassical, Faux Marble, Sphinx Capitals, 52 3/4 x 35 1/2 In. 375.00
Mirror, Neoclassical, Gilt Gesso, Split Baluster, Cornucopia, c.1825, 29 x 14 In. 410.00
Mirror, Neoclassical, Gilt, Gesso, Reverse Painted, Boy, c.1815, 37 x 21 In. 880.00
Mirror, Neoclassical, Giltwood, Ebonized, Split Baluster, c.1820, 38 x 18 In. 705.00
Mirror, Neoclassical, Giltwood, Pilasters, Acanthus Molding, c.1825, 31 x 68 In. 880.00
Mirror, Neoclassical, Giltwood, Pineapple Pilasters, c.1815, 37 x 25 In. 529.00
Mirror, Neoclassical, Giltwood, Reverse Painted, Building, c.1820, 54 1/2 x 31 In. 6000.00
Mirror, Neoclassical, Giltwood, Reverse Painted, Early 1800s, 70 x 33 In. 1840.00
Mirror, Neoclassical, Giltwood, Ring & Urn Pilasters, c.1840, 47 x 28 1/2 In. 295.00
Mirror, Neoclassical, Giltwood, Rosettes, Leaf Carved, 42 x 30 In. 2750.00
Mirror, Neoclassical, Giltwood, Urn Top, Shell & Laurel, Oval, 27 x 26 In. 590.00
Mirror, Neoclassical, Parcel Ebonized, Gilt, Carved, 53 x 23 In., Pair 1955.00
Mirror, Neoclassical, Parcel Gilt, Continental, 48 x 25 1/2 In. 3220.00
Mirror, Neoclassical, Polychrome, Parcel Gilt, 1800s, 37 x 17 1/2 In. 1150.00
Mirror, Neogothic, Empire, Mahogany, 40 1/2 x 25 In. 115.00
Mirror, Oak, 4 Brass Coat Hooks, 29 x 49 In. 80.00
Mirror, Pier, American Restauration, Carved, Giltwood, Fleurettes, 66 x 31 In. 865.00
Mirror, Pier, Biedermeier, Mahogany, Square & Diamond Inlay, 61 x 29 In. 980.00
Mirror, Pier, Cherry, Burl Veneer, Stick & Ball Crest, 12 Drawers, 43 x 14 x 97 In. 1095.00
Mirror, Pier, Gesso, Fruit, Vegetables, 3 Sections, 87 x 7 In. 345.00
Mirror, Pier, Louis XVI Style, Giltwood, Ivory Paint, 59 x 21 In., Pair 720.00
Mirror, Pier, Napoleon III, Giltwood, Carved, Mid 1800s, 71 x 36 In. 1725.00
Mirror, Pier, Neoclassical, Giltwood, Isaac Platt Attribution, c.1825, 62 x 37 In. 6575.00
Mirror, Pier, Neoclassical, Giltwood, Turned Pilasters, 3 Sections, 76 In. 290.00
Mirror, Pier, Neoclassical, Mahogany, Acorns, Turned Pilasters, c.1815, 53 x 31 In. 880.00
Mirror, Pier, Neoclassical, Mahogany, Carved, Inlaid, 84 x 38 In., Pair 2760.00
Mirror, Pier, Palladian Style, Silvered Wood, Christopher Maier, 81 x 30 In. 1265.00
Mirror, Pier, Rococo Revival, Giltwood, 19th Century, 86 x 47 In. 420.00
Mirror, Pier, Victorian, Mahogany, Burl Veneer, Leaf Crown, 36 x 16 x 123 In. 2185.00
Mirror, Pier, Victorian, Mahogany, Burl Veneer, Marble Top, 36 x 14 x 99 In. 1035.00
Mirror, Pier, Walnut, Fluted Pilasters, Marble, 2 Sections, 50 x 19 x 113 In. 1725.00
Mirror, Pine, Carved, 28 x 15 In. 80.00
Mirror, Pine, Poplar, Mahogany Flame Veneer, 2 Parts, 44 x 23 1/2 In. 230.00
Mirror, Queen Anne Style, Chinoiserie, Arch Top, 57 1/2 x 25 In. 400.00
Mirror, Queen Anne Style, Red Japanned, Parcel Gilt, 1900s, 54 x 24 In., Pair 2115.00
Mirror, Queen Anne Style, Walnut, Turned Supports, 3 Drawers, 29 x 8 x 18 In. 336.00
Mirror, Queen Anne, Mahogany, Gilt Liner, Engraved Brass Plate, c.1750, 42 In. 2820.00
Mirror, Queen Anne, Mahogany, Pine, Eagle Crest, Scalloped Base, Ears, 42 x 24 In. 1090.00
Mirror, Queen Anne, Mahogany, Pine, Scroll & Arch Top, 22 3/4 x 11 3/4 In. 635.00
Mirror, Queen Anne, Mahogany, Scalloped Crest, Gilt Shell, 42 1/2 x 17 In. 2070.00
Mirror, Queen Anne, Mahogany, Veneer, Molded, 16 1/2 x 10 In. 375.00
Mirror, Queen Anne, Pine, Rose-Head Nails, 11 1/2 x 7 In. 2645.00
Mirror, Queen Anne, Walnut, Pine, Beveled Glass, Scrolled Crest, 23 x 12 In. 635.00
Mirror, Queen Anne, Walnut, Serpentine Crest, Ogee Border, Beveled, 37 x 17 In. 880.00
Mirror, Red Stained, Brown Sponging, 9 1/2 x 6 In. 200.00
Mirror, Regency Style, Brown Paint, Parcel Gilt, Convex, c.1915, 13 In., Pair 545.00
Mirror, Regency Style, Giltwood, Bull's Eye, Eagle Crest, Ebony Slip, 28 x 18 In. 260.00
Mirror, Regency Style, Giltwood, Carved, Napoleon III, 57 x 46 In. 1840.00
Mirror, Regency Style, Giltwood, Carved, Oval, 35 x 26 In. 865.00
Mirror, Regency Style, Giltwood, Convex, c.1900, 23 In. 1150.00

Mirror, Regency Style, Giltwood, Eagle, Oval, 45 x 21 In., Pair 4830.00
Mirror, Regency Style, Giltwood, Late 19th Century, 36 x 32 In. 1380.00
Mirror, Regency Style, Urn & Flower Crest, 20th Century, 63 x 35 In. 700.00
Mirror, Regency, Gilt, Parcel Ebonized Wood, Gilt, Convex, 1800s, 24 In. 1265.00
Mirror, Regency, Giltwood, Acanthus Carved, Reed Pilasters, 67 x 45 In. 4600.00
Mirror, Regency, Giltwood, Carved, Parcel Ebonized, Convex, 1800s, 42 x 25 In. 4140.00
Mirror, Regency, Giltwood, Ebonized, Wreaths, Convex, England, c.1915, 23 In. 1095.00
Mirror, Renaissance Revival, Charcoal Paint, Gilt, c.1900, 30 x 27 In. 1035.00
Mirror, Renaissance Revival, Giltwood, Carved, Napoleon III, 60 x 40 In. 2990.00
Mirror, Renaissance Revival, Walnut, Parcel Gilt, Marble, 100 x 27 x 12 In. 470.00
Mirror, Reverse Painted Surround, Flowers, Engraved Eagle, Basket, 44 x 20 In. 2030.00
Mirror, Reverse Painted, House, Fence, Half Columns, 2 Parts, 20 1/2 x 11 In. 290.00
Mirror, Reverse Painted, Stone Tower, Sailboat, Ball Drops, 30 x 19 In. 105.00
Mirror, Rococo Style, Giltwood, Cartouche Shape, Italy, 55 x 29 In., Pair 2990.00
Mirror, Rococo, Molded Composition, Gilt, Beveled Glass, 34 x 38 In. 230.00
Mirror, Rococo, Walnut, Gilt Gesso, Shaped Crest, Reverse Painted Man, 31 In. 940.00
Mirror, Shaving, Georgian, Mahogany, Serpentine, Holly Band, 23 x 17 x 8 In. 405.00
Mirror, Shaving, Pine, Drawer, Arched Top, Lollipop Crest, Wire Nails, 18 x 9 In. 230.00
Mirror, Shaving, Portable, Folding, c.1860, 8 x 11 x 3 In. 225.00
Mirror, Shaving, Queen Anne Style, Burl Walnut, Giltwood Scrolls, 25 1/2 In. 529.00
Mirror, Shaving, Queen Anne, Burl Veneer, 3 Drawers, c.1730, 24 x 16 In. 1035.00
Mirror, Shaving, Sheraton Style, Mahogany, Bowfront, Georgian, 17 x 21 In. 520.00
Mirror, Shaving, William IV, Mahogany, Serpentine, Swing, c.1835, 25 x 23 In. 375.00
Mirror, Sheraton, Mahogany, Column Sides, Applied Leaves, 2 Sections, 33 x 17 In. 200.00
Mirror, Sheraton, Split Column, Reverse Painted, Woman On Stage, 29 1/2 x 14 In. 690.00
Mirror, Silver On Copper Frame, Continuous Vine, Woman's Head, Art Nouveau, 14 1/2 In. 430.00
Mirror, Silver, Adjustable Support, Austria-Hungary, c.1856, 20 x 18 In. 920.00
Mirror, Stickley Bros., Horizontal Rails, Mortised Sides, 7 Hooks, 32 x 43 In. 1645.00
Mirror, Tabernacle, Federal, Giltwood, Reverse Painted Panel, c.1805, 39 x 22 In. 1265.00
Mirror, Trumeau, Louis XVI Style, Giltwood, Gris-De-Trianon, c.1915, 63 x 35 In. 805.00
Mirror, Trumeau, Louis XVI Style, Parcel Gilt, Green Paint, c.1900, 75 x 52 In. 1150.00
Mirror, Trumeau, Regency Style, Carved, Polychrome, Parcel Gilt, 73 x 46 x 3 In. 2760.00
Mirror, Venetian Rococo Style, Etched Amber Glass, 1900s, 46 x 35 1/2 In. 2070.00
Mirror, Venetian Rococo Style, Etched, Applied Detail, Oval, Mid 1800s, 36 In. 3335.00
Mirror, Venetian Rococo, Silverwood, Carved, 43 x 33 In. 1265.00
Mirror, Venetian Style, Cut Glass, Frosted, Mid 20th Century, 53 1/2 x 30 In. 3220.00
Mirror, Venetian Style, Etched, 20 1/2 x 11 3/4 In., Pair 145.00
Mirror, Venetian, Reverse Etched, Elongated Octagonal, 52 x 33 In. 5060.00
Mirror, Venetian, Scrolled Pediment, Ribbon Crest, 56 x 30 In. 3285.00
Mirror, Victorian, Walnut, Grape Crest, Giltwood Liner, Tombstone, 27 x 63 In. 290.00
Mirror, Walnut Veneer, Scrolled Crest, Heart, Early 1700s, 35 3/4 x 18 In. 1175.00
Mirror, William IV, Gilt Brass Clad, Mid 1800s, 48 x 34 In. 575.00
Mirror, William IV, Giltwood, Convex, Mid 19th Century, 25 1/2 In. 1265.00
Mirror, William IV, Mahogany, Boxes In Base, Oval, c.1835, 35 x 30 In. 430.00
Mirror, William IV, Mahogany, Cushion Shape, Mid 19th Century, 18 x 16 In. 635.00
Mirror, Wood, Gilt Gesso, Reverse Painted Panel, Acorns, Mass., c.1815, 25 x 15 In. 410.00
Mirror, Wrought Iron, Rose, Leaf, Octagonal, France, 1930, 24 x 36 In. 235.00
Mirror, Wrought Iron, Sunburst, Mid 20th Century, 19 In. 460.00
Ottoman, Edwardian Style, Mahogany, Leather, Stamped Ritz, 18 x 43 In. 6035.00
Ottoman, Empire, Mahogany, Brocade Upholstery, Slip Seat, 4 Bracket Feet 230.00
Ottoman, Empire, Mahogany, Lift Top, Upholstered, Cartouche, c.1840, 20 x 16 In. 380.00
Ottoman, Empire, Mahogany, Upholstered, c.1830, 17 x 36 x 22 In. 1175.00
Ottoman, Faux Bamboo, Gilt, Octagonal, Continental, 1880s, 15 x 18 x 18 In. 980.00
Ottoman, Mahogany, Leather, Concave Case, Squat Feet, c.1850, 18 x 45 In. 3220.00
Ottoman, Victorian, Leather, Padded Top, Tapered Case, c.1850, 16 x 35 In. 1840.00
Ottoman, Victorian, Mahogany, Leather, 18 x 26 x 19 In. 920.00
Ottoman, Victorian, Mahogany, Leather, Mid 19th Century, 22 x 49 x 21 In. 4140.00
Ottoman, Victorian, Mahogany, Leather, Tufted Top, 17 x 32 x 23 In. 2300.00
Ottoman, Victorian, Walnut, Padded Top, Applied Leaf Apron, 7 x 12 x 17 In. 1425.00
Ottoman, William IV Style, Mahogany, Leather, Tufted Top, 17 x 31 In. 1150.00
Overmantel Mirror, see Architectural category.
Parlor Set, Aesthetic Revival, Mahogany, Walnut, Carved, Settee, 2 Chairs 660.00
Parlor Set, Heywood-Wakefield, Wicker, Leather, Rolled Arms, 2 Piece 1380.00

Parlor Set, Louis XV Style, Gilt, c.1880, 2 Armchairs, 44-In. Settee 9000.00
Parlor Set, Louis XVI Style, Fruitwood, Painted, Upholstered, c.1925, 4 Piece 1265.00
Parlor Set, Louis XVI Style, Walnut, Ormolu Mounted, Early 1900s, 8 Piece 5750.00
Parlor Set, Mahogany, Carved, Cane Seat & Back, 3 Piece 690.00
Parlor Set, Mahogany, Carved, Marquetry, Settee, Chairs, c.1900, 3 Piece 8965.00
Parlor Set, Victorian, Walnut, Burl Veneer, Spool Turnings, Leaf Design, 3 Piece 375.00
Pedestal, Aalto, Bird's-Eye Maple, Painted Base, Octagonal, 24 3/4 x 22 In. 530.00
Pedestal, Adam Style, Mahogany, Carved, Tripod, c.1900, 58 In., Pair 1840.00
Pedestal, Aesthetic Revival, Walnut, Gilt, 37 1/2 x 12 In. 705.00
Pedestal, Arts & Crafts Style, Oak, 42 1/2 x 12 In. 90.00
Pedestal, Arts & Crafts, Oak, Early 20th Century, 33 3/4 x 10 x 10 In. 69.00
Pedestal, Baroque Style, Walnut, Spiral Column, Continental, c.1820, 47 In. 1080.00
Pedestal, Black Onyx, Rouge Marble, 44 In. 840.00
Pedestal, Blackamoor Standard, Scrolled Skirt Top, Tripod, Continental, 47 In., Pair 2990.00
Pedestal, Bronze, Inlaid Marble, Square Top, Bronze Inset, c.1950, 29 x 11 In. 590.00
Pedestal, Carved, Painted, Continental, 20th Century, 58 x 34 x 13 In., Pair 3680.00
Pedestal, Ebonized, Gilt, Ringed Eagle's Head, 3 Legs, c.1890, 33 x 14 In. 920.00
Pedestal, Edwardian, Mahogany, Round, Acanthus, Tripod Base, England, 33 x 17 In. 175.00
Pedestal, Edwardian, Walnut, Round Top, Turned Pedestal, Acanthus, 46 In., Pair 3990.00
Pedestal, Elm, Parcel Gilt, Continental, Mid 19th Century, 49 x 16 x 16 In. 805.00
Pedestal, Faux Marble, Plaster, Fluted, Square Base, 20th Century, 28 x 9 In., Pair 230.00
Pedestal, Green Marble, Round Top, Octagonal Base, Late 1800s, 17 x 15 In. 155.00
Pedestal, Limbert, No. 238, Round Top, Cutout Shelf, 15 1/2 x 26 In. 1880.00
Pedestal, Louis XVI Style, Faux Marble Base, Italy, 45 In., Pair 2300.00
Pedestal, Louis XVI Style, Flute Carved, Violet Marble, France, c.1900, 47 In. 2530.00
Pedestal, Lucite, 4 Sections, 20th Century, 10 1/2 x 28 x 14 In., Pair 35.00
Pedestal, Mahogany, Carved, Molded Round Top, Carved Fluted Column, 54 In. 1150.00
Pedestal, Mahogany, Round Top, Carved Support, 20th Century, 41 x 13 In. 176.00
Pedestal, Marble Top, Ormolu Mounted, 32 x 12 x 12 In. 230.00
Pedestal, Marble, Brass Flower Mounts, Brown, Square Top, 1900s, 40 x 8 In. 490.00
Pedestal, Marble, Brass Mounted, Baluster Column, 47 1/2 x 13 In., Pair 1380.00
Pedestal, Marble, Green, White Striations, Ormolu Detail, Brass Wire, 39 1/2 In. 175.00
Pedestal, Marble, White & Brown, Square Top, Octagonal Support, 51 x 12 In. 235.00
Pedestal, Napoleon III, Ebonized, Ormolu Mounted, Marble Top, 39 x 16 In. 290.00
Pedestal, Napoleon III, Ebonized, Parcel Gilt, Marble Top, c.1865, 42 In., Pair 3910.00
Pedestal, Neoclassical, Alabaster, Turned, Carved, 42 In. 420.00
Pedestal, Neoclassical, Faux Marble, Mottled Black, 44 In. 455.00
Pedestal, Neoclassical, Gilt Brass, Marble, Reeded, Scrolling Handles, 55 In., Pair 635.00
Pedestal, Neoclassical, Green Marble, Square Top, Base, 44 x 10 In. 200.00
Pedestal, Neoclassical, Mahogany, Barley-Twist Standard, c.1900, 34 x 16 In. 980.00
Pedestal, Neoclassical, Mahogany, Black Marble Top, Tapered, 41 x 15 In, Pair 1035.00
Pedestal, Neoclassical, Onyx, Brass, Continental, c.1900, 33 In., Pair 1265.00
Pedestal, Oak, Round Base, Scroll Feet, 13 x 35 1/2 In. 320.00
Pedestal, Oak, Tapered Column, Fluted Urn, Paw Feet, 13 1/2 x 36 In. 155.00
Pedestal, Renaissance Revival, Walnut, Ebonized, Sawtooth Frieze, 34 x 18 x 12 In. 440.00
Pedestal, Round Top, Twist Support, 20th Century, 35 x 20 In. 155.00
Pedestal, Round Top, Twist Support, Paw Feet, 20th Century, 58 x 19 In. 190.00
Pedestal, Variegated Marble, Octagonal, Square Top, 20th Century, 34 x 11 In. 235.00
Pedestal, Victorian, Cast Iron, Marble Top, 29 In. 315.00
Pedestal, Walnut, Carved Figural, Classical Man, Turned, Beaded, 1910s, 28 In. 355.00
Pedestal, White Marble, Victorian, 35 1/2 x 14 In. 200.00
Pedestal, Wood, Carved, Pierced Sides, Italy, 20th Century, 42 x 39 In. 575.00
Pedestal, Wood, Carved, Round Top, Twist Column, 3 Squat Ball Feet, 42 In. 345.00
Pedestal, Wood, Marble Top, Octagonal, Claw & Ball Feet, Chinese, c.1900, 33 x 15 In. .. 345.00
Pedestal, Yellow Sienna, Black Scagliola, Continental, 49 x 16 x 16 In. 1840.00
Pew, Oak, Quartersawn, Shaped Side Panels, Curved Seat, 37 x 39 x 25 In. 460.00
Pie Safe, Board Top, Drawers, Doors, Mid 1800s, 60 x 41 x 19 In. 2070.00
Pie Safe, Cherry, Poplar, Pine, Punched Tin, Baskets, 3 Shelves, 40 x 44 In. 1670.00
Pie Safe, Mixed Wood, 2 Drawers, Punched Tin Panels, Cottage, Clock, 54 1/2 In. .... *Illus* 1430.00
Pie Safe, Painted, Stenciled, Screened Doors, Rotating, Octagonal, 1870 Patent, 72 In. 2420.00
Pie Safe, Pierced Tin Panels, Tennessee, c.1850 .... 3500.00
Pie Safe, Pine, Board Top, 2 Drawers, Punched Tin Inserts, Turned Legs, 60 In. ..... *Illus* 2070.00
Pie Safe, Poplar, 12 Pierced Tin Panels, Tapered Legs, 64 x 42 x 19 In. 2760.00

Furniture, Pie Safe, Mixed Wood, 2 Drawers, Punched Tin Panels, Cottage, Clock, 54 1/2 In.

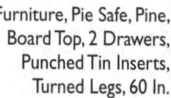

Furniture, Pie Safe, Pine, Board Top, 2 Drawers, Punched Tin Inserts, Turned Legs, 60 In.

Pie Safe, Poplar, Cherry, Drawer, 2 Doors, Punched Tin Panels, 46 x 45 In. 1380.00
Pie Safe, Walnut, Drawers, Doors, Shelves, Pierced Tin, 48 x 4 1/2 x 16 1/2 In. 825.00
Pie Safe, Walnut, Poplar, 2 Drawers, Chamfered Panels, Turned Feet, 49 x 54 x 19 In. 2645.00
Planter, Cast Cement, Log Shape, Dionisio Rodriguez, 1930s 350.00
Planter, Rohlfs, Oak, Openwork Base, Buttons, Scrolls 28000.00
Podium, Williams Lodge, No. 556, Walnut, Butternut, Rope-Twist Posts, c.1940, 36 In. . . . 403.00
Pulpit, Gothic Revival, Grain Painted, 8 Arched Pillars, 1800s, 38 x 49 x 26 In. 480.00
Rack, Bartender's, Mahogany, Scrolling Metalwork, 88 x 58 x 18 In. 870.00
Rack, Clothes, Cast Iron, Black Paint, 2 Rods, Tassel & Brass Ball Finial, 23 x 74 In. 175.00
Rack, Clothes, Painted, 3 Tiers, 12 Wood Spindles, Pease Clothes, Plaque, 69 In. 210.00
Rack, Drying, Pine, Mortised Construction, 29 1/2 x 48 1/2 In. 115.00
Rack, Drying, Shaker, Pine, 3 Sections, Hinged, Canterbury, N.H., c.1855, 64 In. 920.00
Rack, Drying, Shaker, Walnut, Folding, Mortise Construction, 36 x 43 x 21 In. 635.00
Rack, Magazine, Hanging, Victorian, Carved, God Bless Our Home, 28 1/2 x 17 1/2 In. . . . 90.00
Rack, Magazine, Robsjohn-Gibbings, Mahogany, Widdicomb, 29 x 23 x 23 In. 750.00
Rack, Magazine, Thonet, Steam-Bent Beech, c.1900, 16 1/2 x 21 x 20 In. 940.00
Rack, Magazine, Walnut, Slats, Turned Feet, Artisans' Shop, 18 x 18 x 12 In. 430.00
Rack, Plate, G. Stickley, No. 903, Chamfered Board Back, 24 1/2 x 45 In. 5290.00
Rack, Quilt, Renaissance Revival, Walnut, Trestle Base, 35 x 27 & 32 x 23 In. 295.00
Rack, Quilt, Thonet, Beech, Horizontal Rails, Curled Legs, 26 x 16 x 35 In. 295.00
Rack, Quilt, Victorian, Mahogany, 29 1/2 In. 1435.00
Rack, Spoon, Hanging, Butternut, Black, Green Graining, Arch Crest, 20 x 10 In. 290.00
Rack, Spoon, Nutting, No. 903, Dark Finish, Carved, 24 3/4 In. 935.00
Rack, Towel, Wood, Multicolor, Moor, Holding Snake, 1800s, 12 x 22 In. 940.00
Recamier, Empire Style, Mahogany, Swan's Neck, Ormolu, c.1890, 36 x 27 In. 2990.00
Recamier, Reform Movement, Mahogany, Oak, England, c.1885, 30 x 76 x 35 In. 2070.00
Recamier, Regency, Japanned, Black, Brass Mounted, Parcel Gilt, Early 1800s, 63 In. 1150.00
Recamier, Regency, Mahogany, 19th Century, 32 x 75 In. 1955.00
Recamier, Regency, Padded, Outscrolled End, Splayed Legs, c.1815, 35 x 78 In. 6325.00
Recamier, Rococo Revival, Rosewood, Carved Backrest, 39 x 65 In., Pair 5290.00
Rocker, Amish, Bentwood, Lancaster County, Pennsylvania, c.1910, 42 x 24 In. 405.00
Rocker, Bentwood, Hickory, Pine, 37 1/2 In. 200.00
Rocker, Boston, Painted, Flower Stencils, Cane Seat, c.1880, 24 x 16 x 20 In., Child's 230.00
Rocker, Boston, Shaped Crest, Landscape, Rolled Seat, c.1825, 42 In. 645.00
Rocker, Eames, Fiberglass Shell, Birch Runners, Zinc Struts, 25 x 27 x 26 In. 1175.00
Rocker, Eames, RAR, Herman Miller, 1960s, 25 x 25 x 27 In. 805.00
Rocker, Eames, RKR, Wire, Vinyl, Hopsack Seat, Herman Miller, c.1952, 29 In. 705.00
Rocker, Eastlake, Platform, Victorian, 40 In. 69.00
Rocker, Eastlake, Upholstered, Folding, c.1875 . . . . 140.00
Rocker, G. Nakashima, Walnut, 1 Arm, c.1961, 33 1/4 In. 4780.00
Rocker, G. Stickley, High Back, Spindles, Tapered Corbels, Leather Seat 6800.00
Rocker, G. Stickley, No. 232, Rope Foundation, Cushion, 5 Arm Slats, 38 x 32 In. 3525.00
Rocker, G. Stickley, No. 305 1/2, Ladder Back, 3 Slats, 17 x 24 x 31 In. 529.00
Rocker, G. Stickley, No. 323, 5 Slats, Split To Top, Stretcher, 42 x 28 3/4 x 30 In. 2940.00
Rocker, G. Stickley, No. 337, 3 Vertical Slats, Leather Seat, 18 x 24 x 33 In. 529.00
Rocker, G. Stickley, No. 343, Horizontal Slats, Leatherette Seat, 18 x 19 x 25 In. 375.00
Rocker, G. Stickley, No. 375, High Back, 11 Vertical Slats, 44 x 28 x 28 In. 5580.00

Rocker, G. Stickley, No. 2607, Oak, 4 Back Slats, Leather Cushion, c.1902, 34 In. 6875.00
Rocker, G. Stickley, V-Back, Rush Seat, 33 3/4 x 26 x 27 1/2 In. 470.00
Rocker, G. Stickley, V-Back, Upholstered, 34 x 26 x 20 1/2 In. 1175.00
Rocker, George III, Oak, Chestnut, Shaped Crest, Arms, c.1780, 50 In. 8400.00
Rocker, Green Paint, Shaped Crest, Pierced Splat, Scrolled Arms, Pa., c.1850, 44 In. 440.00
Rocker, Harden, Slatted Sides, Through Tenon, Drop-In Cushion, 32 x 20 In. 529.00
Rocker, J. Adnet, Leather Upholstery, 1950s, 35 x 28 1/2 x 30 In., Pair 4780.00
Rocker, Jacobean Style, Mahogany, Twist Sides, 20th Century, 39 x 18 x 29 In. 24.00
Rocker, L. & J.G. Stickley, Morris, Leather Drop-In Cushion, 5-Slat Back, 39 In. 1380.00
Rocker, L. & J.G. Stickley, No. 409, Slatted, Leather Seat, Arms, 32 x 27 In. 3525.00
Rocker, L. & J.G. Stickley, Slatted Sides, Back, Drop-In Cushion, 31 x 27 x 25 In. 3290.00
Rocker, L. & J.G. Stickley, Spring Seat, Flat Paddle Arms, 37 x 31 x 35 In. 3819.00
Rocker, Ladder Back, 3 Horizontal Slats, Double Box Stretcher, 41 x 15 In. 75.00
Rocker, Ladder Back, 4 Horizontal Slats, Turned Posts, Splint Seat, Arms, 46 x 18 In. 75.00
Rocker, Ladder Back, Curly Maple, Woven Splint Seat, Arms, Birch Stretchers, 42 In. 175.00
Rocker, Ladder Back, Mixed Hardwoods, Turned Posts, Splint Seat, Arms, 41 In. 58.00
Rocker, Ladder Back, Painted, 5 Arched Slats, Cane Seat, Turned Posts, 48 In. 990.00
Rocker, Limbert, 3 Slats, Leather Seat, 26 x 28 x 34 In. 118.00
Rocker, Limbert, 3 Vertical Back Slats, Through Tenon Arms, 43 x 27 x 23 In. 1116.00
Rocker, Lincoln Style, Cane Seat, Back, 26 In., Child's 150.00
Rocker, Maple, Pine, Cane Seat, Back, 34 In. 80.00
Rocker, Oak, Woven Split Seat, 19th Century, 40 3/4 In. 105.00
Rocker, Old Red Paint, Wooden Peg Construction, Turned Posts, Finials, 30 In. 230.00
Rocker, Painted, Banister Back, 3 Slats, Spindle Arms, Rush Seat, 25 In., Child's 575.00
Rocker, Painted, Cat Sides, c.1900, 25 1/2 In., Child's 765.00
Rocker, Painted, Horse Silhouette Sides, Upholstered Seat, 18 x 34 In. 58.00
Rocker, Painted, Pierced & Shaped Splat, Scrolled Arms, Pennsylvania, c.1850, 43 In. 410.00
Rocker, Shaker, 4 Slats, Splint Seat, Arms, Mt. Lebanon, N.Y., c.1835, 42 In. 2300.00
Rocker, Shaker, Ladder Back, Tan Tape Seat, Shawl Bar, Mt. Lebanon, N.Y., 41 In. 750.00
Rocker, Shaker, Maple, 3-Slat Back, Rush Seat, Arms, Watervliet, N.Y., c.1840, 38 In. 460.00
Rocker, Shaker, Maple, Birch, Woven Tape Seat, Acorn Finials, Mt. Lebanon, N.Y., 42 In. . 489.00
Rocker, Shaker, Maple, Cherry Arms, Rush Seat, Mt. Lebanon, N.Y., c.1850, 43 In. 2015.00
Rocker, Shaker, Maple, Tape Seat & Back, Arms, Mt. Lebanon, N.Y., c.1875, 23 In. 1265.00
Rocker, Shaker, Maple, Tape Seat & Back, Arms, Mt. Lebanon, N.Y., c.1880, 29 In. 1035.00
Rocker, Shaker, No. 0, Maple, Tape Seat, Back, Mt. Lebanon, c.1880, 24 In. . . . . .835.00 to 2415.00
Rocker, Shaker, No. 0, Tape Seat, Mt. Lebanon, New York, Decal, 24 In., Child's 3290.00
Rocker, Shaker, No. 1, Maple, Walnut Stain, Tape Seat, Back, Mt. Lebanon, N.Y. 1725.00
Rocker, Shaker, No. 3, Dark Finish, 3 Arched Slats, Rush Seat, Mt. Lebanon, N.Y., 35 In. . . 435.00
Rocker, Shaker, No. 3, Maple, Tape Seat & Back, Arms, Mt. Lebanon, N.Y., c.1880, 34 In.   800.00
Rocker, Shaker, No. 3, Maple, Tape Seat, Arms, Mt. Lebanon, N.Y., c.1885, 35 In. 460.00
Rocker, Shaker, No. 3, Maple, Tape Seat, Red Stain, Mt. Lebanon, N.Y., 35 In. 460.00
Rocker, Shaker, No. 3, Maple, Tape Seat, Red, Mt. Lebanon, N.Y., c.1880, 34 1/2 In. 690.00
Rocker, Shaker, No. 3, Maple, Walnut Stain, Tape Seat, Mt. Lebanon, N.Y., 35 In. . . . *Illus* 460.00
Rocker, Shaker, No. 4, 3 Back Slats, Tape Seat, Shawl Bar 173.00
Rocker, Shaker, No. 5, Maple, Stained, Tape Seat, Mt. Lebanon, N.Y., c.1885, 38 In. . *Illus* 1265.00
Rocker, Shaker, No. 6, Ladder Back, Tape Seat, Turned Supports, Acorn Finials, 42 In. . . . 315.00
Rocker, Shaker, No. 7, 4 Arched Slats, Tape Seat, Arms, Mt. Lebanon, N.Y., c.1900, 41 In.   645.00
Rocker, Shaker, No. 7, 4 Slats, Tape Seat, Shawl Bar, Mt. Lebanon, N.Y., c.1880, 41 In. . . . 1725.00
Rocker, Shaker, Walnut, Red, 4 Slats, Tape Seat, New Lebanon, N.Y., c.1840, 45 In. 3450.00

Furniture, Rocker, Shaker, No. 3, Maple, Walnut Stain, Tape Seat, Mt. Lebanon, N.Y., 35 In.

Furniture, Rocker, Shaker, No. 5, Maple, Stained, Tape Seat, Mt. Lebanon, N.Y., c.1885, 38 In.

Rocker, Sheraton, Salmon, Strawberry Decoration, Rush Seat, N.J., c.1830, 18 In. 575.00
Rocker, Splint Seat, Turned Arms, Finials, Child's 130.00
Rocker, Stickley Bros., Mahogany, Vertical Slats, Cushions, c.1912, 32 In. 2235.00
Rocker, Stickley Bros., No. 405, 5 Back Slats, 3 Arm Slats, Cushions, 27 x 28 x 33 In. 645.00
Rocker, Stickley Bros., No. 515, 4 Slats, Leatherette Seat, Arms, 27 x 23 x 35 In. 825.00
Rocker, Twig, Arched Back, Heart, Geometric Designs, Arms, c.1850 .... 6325.00
Rocker, Victorian, Carved, Padded Open Arms, Tufted Upholstered Back, 40 In. 345.00
Rocker, Wicker, Rattan, Natural Finish, Late 1800s, 42 x 14 1/2 In. 350.00
Rocker, Windsor, Bamboo, Green Paint, 5 Spindles, Stenciled Crest, 14 x 31 In. 750.00
Rocker, Windsor, Comb Back, Black Paint, Scroll Arms, 45 In. 144.00
Rocker, Windsor, Comb Back, Black Paint, Stenciled Rose, Bamboo Turnings, 41 In. 175.00
Rocker, Windsor, Comb Back, Stencil Decorated, 5 Spindles, Arms, c.1825 .... 940.00
Rocker, Windsor, High Comb Back, Multicolored, New England, c.1820, 45 In. 9000.00
Rocker, Windsor, Oak, Carved Flower Crest, Upholstered, Platform, 47 In., Pair 259.00
Rocker, Windsor, Oak, Spindle Back, 37 In. 69.00
Rocker, Windsor, Rod Back, Faux Bamboo, Shaped Arm Supports, 32 x 20 x 20 In. 635.00
Screen, 2-Panel, Lacquer Frame, Gilt, Carved Border, Figures, Japan, 65 In. 1955.00
Screen, 2-Panel, Rosewood Frame, Needlework, 20th Century, 66 x 51 In. 235.00
Screen, 3-Panel, Arts & Crafts, Poppies, Motto, House Well Fill'd, Hinged, 48 x 18 In. ... 1058.00
Screen, 3-Panel, Egyptian Style, Wood, Ebonized, Parcel Gilt, c.1900, 64 x 54 In. 10638.00
Screen, 3-Panel, Louis XVI, Gilt, Carved, Mirror, Flowers, 67 x 48 In. 1495.00
Screen, 3-Panel, Oak, Carved, Hunting Scenes, Brass Hinges, 78 x 30 In. 635.00
Screen, 3-Panel, Painted Arch, 20th Century, 74 1/2 x 80 In. 295.00
Screen, 4-Panel, Birch, Carved, Empire Wreath, Gabled, Christopher Maier, 84 In. 865.00
Screen, 4-Panel, Black Lacquer, Eggshell, 1930, 72 x 72 In. 7770.00
Screen, 4-Panel, Gilt, Brown Lacquer, Jeweled, Chinese, c.1900, 72 x 72 In. 978.00
Screen, 4-Panel, Hardwood, Gilt, Polychrome, Chinese, 19th Century, 71 x 74 In. 805.00
Screen, 4-Panel, Leather, Fox Hunt, Hand Painted, Hinged, 78 x 92 In. 1140.00
Screen, 4-Panel, Napoleon III, Leather, Oriental Figures, c.1840, 84 x 90 In. 3220.00
Screen, 4-Panel, Needlework, Figures, Landscape, Japan, c.1850, 63 x 45 In. 3738.00
Screen, 4-Panel, Painted, Lithograph, Acrobats, Columns, Obelisks, 53 x 14 In. 3345.00
Screen, 4-Panel, Pine Trees, Flowering Plants, 19th Century, 7 x 25 In. 2185.00
Screen, 4-Panel, Table, Cloisonne, Bird, Flower, Japan, 6 x 10 3/4 In. 520.00
Screen, 5-Panel, Gothic Revival, Arched Top, Medallion, England, 72 x 19 In. 235.00
Screen, 6-Panel, Arts & Crafts, Wood, Wire Flowers, Dragonflies, 70 x 16 In. 2585.00
Screen, 6-Panel, Painted, Gilt, Silk, Tranquil Home-Life Settings, 72 x 151 In. 1295.00
Screen, 6-Panel, Serpentine, Birds, Flowers, Lotus, Fretwork, 12 In. 1510.00
Screen, 7-Panel, Blue Cut Velvet Floral Fabric, Continental, 124 x 147 In. 546.00
Screen, 8-Panel, Mythological Figures, Landscape, Korea, 1800s, 65 x 168 In. 1150.00
Screen, American Restauration, Rosewood, Needlepoint, Stand, c.1865, 49 x 29 In. 1725.00
Screen, Bamboo, Carved, Landscape, Pavilions, Mountains, River, Japan, c.1910, 29 In. .. 480.00
Screen, Bamboo, Hung Mu Wood, Tsuitate, Mt. Fuji, 1800s, 39 x 45 In. 635.00
Screen, Black Lacquer, Gilt, River Landscape, Stand, Chinese, 1900s, 21 x 21 x 16 In. 600.00
Screen, Dreamstone Panels, 9 Mountains, Japan, 1700s, 20 1/2 x 19 1/2 In. 4025.00
Screen, Eames, FSW-6, Walnut, Herman Miller, 60 x 68 In. 1955.00
Screen, Elm, Latticework Panel, Interlocking Slats, Chinese, c.1890, 42 x 40 In. 200.00
Screen, Empire, Mahogany, Acorn Finials, Mirror, France, 40 x 27 x 14 In. 345.00
Screen, Francois Boucher Style, Painted, France, 18th Century, 91 x 54 In. 1725.00
Screen, Juan Carlos III, Polychrome, Parcel Gilt, Cordoban, 87 x 23 In., Pair ....2530.00 to 2760.00
Screen, Lacquer, Gilt, Inset Soapstone Figures, Painted, Chinese, 50 x 24 In. 115.00
Screen, Louis XVI Style, Upholstered, Gilt, 40 x 43 In. 840.00
Screen, M. & F. Higgins, Rondelay, 48 Fused Glass Disks, c.1960, 35 x 48 In. 4600.00
Screen, Mahogany, Needlework, Romantic Scene, Oval, Stepped Base, 55 In., Pair 545.00
Screen, Needlework, Mahogany, Trestle Base, 1700s, 57 x 25 x 23 In. 920.00
Screen, Shaker, Infirmary, Pine, Red Paint, Slats, Canterbury, N.H., 74 In. .... *Illus* 27600.00
Screen, Shell Carved, Figures, Gardens, Wood Stand, Japan, 1800s, 14 x 10 3/4 In. 1093.00
Screen, Turned Stands, Needlepoint & Beaded Insert, Late Victorian, 43 x 32 In. 405.00
Secretary, Art Deco, Drop Front, Fruitwood, Diamond Parquetry, France, 53 x 31 In. 3585.00
Secretary, Biedermeier, Drop Front, Birch, 14 Drawers, 60 x 45 In. 3910.00
Secretary, Biedermeier, Drop Front, Birch, 76 x 44 x 23 In. 6615.00
Secretary, Birch, Painted, Drop Front, Maine, Early 1800s, 71 x 33 In. 2470.00
Secretary, Butler's, Empire, Curly Maple, Cherry, Walnut, 43 x 22 x 46 In. 1035.00
Secretary, Butler's, Mahogany, 3 Sections, Lower Doors, 84 x 41 x 20 In. 2015.00

Furniture, Screen,
Shaker, Infirmary,
Pine, Red Paint,
Slats, Canterbury,
N.H., 74 In.

Furniture,
Secretary,
Povl Dinesen,
Teak, Drawers,
Birch Interiors,
Denmark, 34 x 19 In.

Secretary, Chippendale Style, Mid 20th Century, 80 x 31 x 17 In. 290.00
Secretary, Chippendale, Walnut, Inlaid, Pierced Crest, 4 Drawers, 95 In. 7640.00
Secretary, Drop Front, Burl Walnut, Drawers, Bun Feet, Continental, 66 x 21 x 40 In. 800.00
Secretary, Drop Front, Mahogany, Marble Top, Boston, c.1834, 60 1/2 x 39 In. 8225.00
Secretary, Drop Front, Veneer, Marble Top, Drawers, Doors, 1920, 44 x 25 x 12 In. 2100.00
Secretary, Eastlake, 2 Sections, c.1880, 82 x 38 x 21 In. 940.00
Secretary, Edwardian, Drop Front, Burl Walnut, c.1900, 60 x 43 x 22 In. 3680.00
Secretary, Empire, Drop Front, Mahogany, 3 Drawers, c.1860, 48 x 43 In. 1150.00
Secretary, Federal Style, Drop Front, Mahogany, Glazed Doors, Drawers, 78 x 42 In. 805.00
Secretary, Federal, Mahogany Inlay, Molded Cornice, 1800s, 69 x 36 x 18 In. 3820.00
Secretary, Federal, Mahogany, Hinged Desk, c.1807, 92 x 47 x 22 In. 3220.00
Secretary, Federal, Mahogany, Inlaid, Mass., c.1800, 71 x 38 In. 5465.00
Secretary, Federal, Slant Front, Mahogany, Drawers, Glazed Doors, 78 x 38 In. 2875.00
Secretary, George III Style, Mahogany, Glazed Doors, 92 x 21 x 44 In. 1425.00
Secretary, George III, Mahogany, 2 Doors, 6 Drawers, c.1785, 89 x 49 In. 5520.00
Secretary, George III, Mahogany, 2 Doors, c.1785, 91 x 44 x 23 In. 10350.00
Secretary, George III, Mahogany, Drawers, Late 1700s, 84 x 36 x 20 In. 6040.00
Secretary, George III, Mahogany, Glazed Doors, 3 Drawers, 18th Century 1645.00
Secretary, George III, Mahogany, Glazed Doors, 4 Drawers, 35 x 9 In. 3420.00
Secretary, George III, Mahogany, Glazed Doors, Pediment, 92 x 43 x 21 In. 6615.00
Secretary, George III, Slant Front, Mahogany, Glazed Doors, 85 x 43 x 22 In. 5750.00
Secretary, George III, Slant Front, Mahogany, Glazed Doors, 87 x 42 In. 9200.00
Secretary, George IV, Mahogany, c.1850, 84 x 47 x 23 In. 5520.00
Secretary, Georgian Style, Mahogany, c.1850, 104 x 51 x 23 In. 4830.00
Secretary, Georgian Style, Mahogany, Shelves, Drawers, 82 x 38 x 21 In. 690.00
Secretary, Georgian, Slant Front, Mahogany, Brass, 93 x 42 x 21 In. 4140.00
Secretary, Gilt, Polychrome, 3 Drawers, Mid 19th Century, 43 x 42 x 23 In. 2185.00
Secretary, Gothic Revival, Mahogany, Glass Doors, Inlaid Tympanum, Mass., 78 In. 8000.00
Secretary, Gothic Revival, Mahogany, Veneers, Cornice, Doors, 76 x 45 x 21 In. 920.00
Secretary, Gothic Revival, Satinwood, Mahogany, Victorian, 103 x 49 x 18 In. 8050.00
Secretary, Gustav Bergstrom, Mahogany, Sycamore Inlay, c.1925, 47 x 25 In. 5400.00
Secretary, Hepplewhite, Mahogany, Doors, 6 Drawers, 46 1/2 x 41 In. 1035.00
Secretary, John Widdicomb, Walnut, Double Dome Top, 86 x 41 x 20 In. 2300.00
Secretary, Louis Philippe, Boulle, Ebonized, Mirrored Cupboards, 46 x 24 x 44 In. 1426.00
Secretary, Louis XV Style, Burl Walnut, Marquetry, 56 x 21 x 32 In. 2090.00
Secretary, Louis XV/XVI Style, Mahogany, Gilt Metal Mounts, 41 x 30 x 19 In. 2390.00
Secretary, Louis XVI Style, Brass Inlay, Marble Top, 56 x 41 x 16 3/4 In. 590.00
Secretary, Louis XVI Style, Mahogany, Marquetry, Gilt Metal Mounts, 51 In. 4900.00
Secretary, Mahogany, Marble Top, Frieze Drawer, Inset Leather, 56 x 39 x 17 In. 2300.00
Secretary, McCobb, Drop Front, 4 Drawers, Glass Shelf, 60 x 18 x 45 In. 1175.00
Secretary, Napoleon III, Drop Front, Rosewood, Marble Top, 37 x 50 In. 2760.00
Secretary, Napoleon III, Kingwood, Marquetry, Marble Top, c.1865, 42 x 25 In. 1380.00
Secretary, Neoclassical, Arched Glass Doors, 1830-40, 92 x 52 x 22 In. 1075.00
Secretary, Oak, Roll Top, Cornice, Carved Shell, 3 Drawers, 37 x 22 x 85 In. 1555.00
Secretary, Povl Dinesen, Teak, Drawers, Birch Interiors, Denmark, 34 x 19 In. ...... *Illus* 2940.00
Secretary, Queen Anne Style, Double Bonnet, 85 x 34 x 18 In. 3220.00
Secretary, Rococo Revival, Rosewood, Satinwood, c.1855, 79 x 34 In. 7475.00

Secretary, Rococo Revival, Walnut, 2 Drawers, 4 Doors, c.1865, 103 x 45 In. 3450.00
Secretary, Sheraton, Drop Front, Cherry, 12-Pane Top, Ohio, c.1830, 80 In. 5750.00
Secretary, Sheraton, Mahogany, 2 Sections, Glazed Doors, 77 x 44 x 21 In. 1725.00
Secretary, Slant Front, Cornice, Interior Compartments, 1800s, 65 x 38 x 25 In. 500.00
Secretary, Thomas Day, 2 Glass Doors, North Carolina, c.1850, 93 x 47 In. 7975.00
Secretary, Victorian, Mahogany, Cylinder, 83 x 33 x 20 In. 2030.00
Secretary, Victorian, Slant Front, Walnut, Carved Cornice, 44 x 20 x 90 In. 800.00
Secretary, Victorian, Walnut, Burl Veneer, 4 Drawers, Iron Pulls, 40 x 26 x 95 In. 750.00
Secretary, Victorian, Walnut, Burl Veneer, Roll Top, 46 x 24 x 94 In. 2300.00
Secretary, Victorian, Walnut, Burl Veneer, Roll Top, Glass Doors, 40 x 23 x 87 In. 1610.00
Secretary, Walnut, 2 Sections, Ogee Bracket Feet, 88 x 41 In. 3525.00
Secretary, William IV Style, Walnut, 2 Drawers, c.1840, 52 x 41 x 22 In. 1725.00
Secretary, William IV, Mahogany, Leather, Glazed Doors, Drawer, 89 x 48 In. 2300.00
Semainier, Louis XV Style, Cherry, 19th Century, 55 x 20 x 13 In. 1035.00
Semainier, Louis XV Style, Kingwood, Rosewood Parquetry, Gilt Bronze, 48 x 26 In. 1435.00
Semainier, William IV, Mahogany, Reeded Pilasters, c.1850, 60 x 54 x 22 In. 2070.00
Server, Arts & Crafts, Shelf, 2 Drawers, Brass Hardware, 34 x 44 x 20 In. 1175.00
Server, Black, Carved, 2 Doors, Medallions, Shelves, Drawers, 44 x 15 x 36 In. 290.00
Server, Chippendale Style, Burl Walnut, Mahogany, Carved, Ireland, 35 x 80 In. 2070.00
Server, Edwardian, Mahogany, 3 Drawers, c.1900, 36 1/2 x 37 1/2 x 19 In. 2530.00
Server, French Provincial, Walnut, Carved, c.1900, 40 3/8 x 49 1/2 x 18 In. 460.00
Server, G. Stickley, 3 Drawers, Chamfered Sides, Red Decal, 38 x 19 In. . . . . *Illus* 29375.00
Server, G. Stickley, 3 Drawers, Wood Knobs, Through Tenon, 38 x 60 x 16 In. 11165.00
Server, G. Stickley, No. 802, Oak, Harvey Ellis, c.1903, 40 x 42 x 16 In. 4185.00
Server, G. Stickley, No. 818, Backsplash, 3 Drawers, Iron Pulls, Shelf, 39 x 48 In. 2000.00
Server, George III Style, Mahogany, Brass Gallery, Mid 1800s, 49 x 42 In. 2645.00
Server, George III Style, Mahogany, Frieze, Drawers, Early 1900s, 37 x 65 In. 1495.00
Server, Georgian, Mahogany, Demilune Top, 2 Drawers, Faux Drawers, 34 x 47 In. 4370.00
Server, L. & J.G. Stickley, Oak, Rectangular Top, Drawer, c.1916, 33 x 32 x 16 In. 1410.00
Server, Mahogany, 3 Tiers, Marble Insets, Rope-Carved Columns, 33 x 24 In. 635.00
Server, Mahogany, Bowfront, 2 Short & 3 Long Drawers, 2 Doors, 34 x 59 In. 175.00
Server, Mahogany, Carved, Cabriole Legs, Claw & Ball Feet, 33 x 52 x 17 In. 115.00
Server, Mahogany, Concave Front, 2 Drawers, Late 1700s, 33 x 23 x 54 In. 3040.00
Server, Mahogany, Marble, Gallery, Continental, Late 19th Century, 37 x 58 x 20 In. 2185.00
Server, Mahogany, Rectangular Top, 4 Drawers, Shaped Apron, 34 x 16 x 72 In. . . .490.00 to 520.00
Server, McCobb, Mahogany, Brass Frame, 2 Drawers, 36 1/2 x 28 1/2 In. 500.00
Server, Poplar, Brown Finish, Panel Doors, Wooden Pulls, 43 x 20 x 38 In. 920.00
Server, Prairie School, Rectangular Top, Drawer, Open Shelf, Splayed Legs, 44 x 56 In. . . . 1645.00
Server, Queen Anne Style, Cherry, 3 Drawers, Cabriole Legs, 35 x 66 x 19 In. 545.00
Server, Rectangular Top, Curved Ends, Fitted Doors, England, c.1930, 36 x 55 x 20 In. . . . 1880.00
Server, Regency, Mahogany, 3 Frieze Drawers, 1800s, 28 x 37 x 20 In. 355.00
Server, Regency, Mahogany, 3 Tiers, Shell Carvings, c.1815, 57 x 50 x 28 In. 2185.00
Server, Walnut, Shell Crest, Marble Top, 2 Drawers, Shelves, 47 x 21 x 79 In. 520.00
Settee, American Restauration, Mahogany, Padded Back, 37 x 71 In. 2530.00
Settee, Arne Jacobsen, Swan, Tan Leather, Fritz Hansen, c.1960, 57 In. 2585.00
Settee, Arts & Crafts, Ladder Back, Through Tenon, Leather, 35 x 44 1/2 In. 880.00
Settee, Brazilian Colonial, Ironwood, Openwork Backrest, Mid 1800s, 82 In. 825.00
Settee, Chippendale Style, Double Chairback, 38 x 46 x 20 In., Pair 1035.00
Settee, Chippendale Style, Mahogany, Triple Chairback, England, c.1875, 71 In. 2185.00
Settee, Chippendale Style, Mahogany, Upholstered, Claw & Ball Feet, 76 In. 4750.00
Settee, Curved, High Back, Faux Grain Painted, England, 60 x 72 In. 5250.00
Settee, Directoire, Mahogany, Padded, Closed Arms, Swan's Neck, c.1810, 41 x 53 In. . . . 2070.00
Settee, Double Chairback, Twin Arched Crest, Mid 1800s, 22 x 26 In., Child's 380.00
Settee, Eastlake, Walnut, Tufted Velvet Upholstery, 51 x 43 In. 300.00
Settee, Empire Style, Faux Rosewood & Giltwood, Cushion, c.1880, 32 x 90 In. 4830.00
Settee, George III Style, Mahogany, Double Chairback, 39 x 48 In., Pair 1150.00
Settee, George III Style, Mahogany, Padded, Domed Back, Cushion, 39 x 80 x 28 In. 1840.00
Settee, George III Style, Multicolored, Caned, Scrolled Crest, c.1890, 39 x 56 In. 1150.00
Settee, George III Style, Oak, Double Chairback, Carved Arms, 41 x 55 In. 690.00
Settee, George III Style, Oak, Double Chairback, Pierced Splat, 41 x 55 In. 260.00
Settee, George III, Mahogany, Upholstered, 8 Spade Feet, 75 In. 3450.00
Settee, George III, Mahogany, Upholstered, Bead-Carved Arms, c.1780, 76 In. 4500.00
Settee, Georgian Style, Mahogany, Carved, Triple Chairback, 40 1/2 x 65 1/2 In. 200.00

Settee, Grain Painted, Serpentine Crest, Plank Seat, Upholstered, c.1850, 34 x 84 In. 2350.00
Settee, J. Hoffmann, No. 675/C, Beech, Upholstered, c.1910, 30 x 55 x 27 In. 8400.00
Settee, Limbert, 8 Vertical Back Slats, Spring Cushion, 37 x 47 x 25 In. 1175.00
Settee, Louis XV Style, Double Cushioned Back, Cabriole Legs, 32 x 55 In., Pair 6615.00
Settee, Louis XV Style, Gilt, Padded Back, Flower Crest, Late 1800s, 34 x 52 In. 920.00
Settee, Louis XV Style, Walnut, Mid 19th Century, 32 x 36 x 18 In. 1495.00
Settee, Louis XVI Style, Painted, Gilt, Ivory, Upholstered, 84 In. 420.00
Settee, Louis XVI Style, Polychrome, Cane, Late 19th Century, 37 x 43 x 21 In. 1495.00
Settee, Louis XVI Style, Polychrome, Padded Back, Ribbon Crest, 34 x 50 x 25 In. 575.00
Settee, Louis XVI Style, Walnut, Inset Panels, Upholstered, Reeded Legs, 1800s 575.00
Settee, Louis XVI, Beech, Padded Seat, Back & Arms, Upholstered, 54 In. 690.00
Settee, Louis XVI, Beech, Silk Upholstery, Fluted Circular Legs, c.1790, 64 In. 6465.00
Settee, Louis XVI, Gilt, Concave Crest, Wreath, Torchere, 37 x 48 x 25 In. 1610.00
Settee, Louis XVI, Mahogany, Padded, Domed Back, 38 x 68 x 26 In. 3450.00
Settee, Mahogany, Bow Back, Dolphin & Lyre Splats, Italy, c.1810, 79 In. 3230.00
Settee, Marcel Kammerer, Beech, Stained, Vienna, c.1905, 30 x 48 x 28 In. 9000.00
Settee, Modern Design, Upholstered, Rolled Arms, Tufted Back, 30 x 62 x 35 In. 129.00
Settee, Neoclassical, Walnut, Lyre Back, 27 x 39 x 20 In. 2390.00
Settee, Old Hickory, 1930s, 54 In. 1295.00
Settee, Ole Wanscher, 3 Seats, Green Cushions, Paoul Jeppesen, c.1955 .... 825.00
Settee, Painted, Stencils, Scrolled Crest, Pa., c.1830, 34 x 69 In. 1410.00
Settee, Paolo Deganello, Torso, Cassina, c.1982, 42 x 68 x 28 In. 999.00
Settee, Pine, Half-Spindle Back, Cutout Crest Rail, Pennsylvania, Mid 1800s, 75 3/4 In. ... 590.00
Settee, Plail Bros., Barrel Design, Vertical Spindles, Leather Cushion, 46 x 20 x 31 In. ... 2300.00
Settee, Queen Anne, Mahogany, Carved Shells, Needlepoint, Slip Seat, 42 x 48 In. 3740.00
Settee, Queen Anne, Mahogany, Carved, Inlaid, Crest, c.1900, 38 x 40 x 20 In. 690.00
Settee, Queen Anne, Mahogany, Upholstered, Scroll Arms, 6 Legs, 41 x 52 In. 4025.00
Settee, Regency Style, Beechwood, Aubusson Tapestry, Late 1800s, 45 x 50 x 24 In. 4830.00
Settee, Regency Style, Fruitwood, Needlework Upholstery, 1800s, 45 x 55 x 27 In. 4830.00
Settee, Renaissance Revival, Burl Walnut, Triple Chairback, Reclining Cupids 3190.00
Settee, Risom, Knoll, c.1946, 29 1/2 x 44 1/2 x 28 In. 700.00
Settee, Rococo, Fruitwood, Ivory Inlay, 3 Splats, Putti, Upholstered, Italy, 54 In. 1175.00
Settee, Sheraton Style, Walnut, Upholstered, Fluted Column-Turned Legs, 48 In. 605.00
Settee, Sheraton, Mahogany, Double Shieldback, Watered Silk Upholstery, 37 In. 1035.00
Settee, Sheraton, Mahogany, Upholstered, Early 19th Century, 57 x 36 In. 3410.00
Settee, Sheraton, Painted, Compote & Flower Decorations, 72 In. 1095.00
Settee, Stickley & Brandt, Cutout Slats, Spring Seat Cushion, 38 x 62 x 25 In. 3175.00
Settee, Stickley Bros., No. 349, Oak, Black Stencil, Back Slats, 54 1/2 In. 260.00
Settee, Stickley Bros., Slatted & Upholstered Back, Upholstered Seat 1895.00
Settee, Turkish Revival, Upholstered, Fringed Apron, c.1880, 32 x 58 x 31 In. 1150.00
Settee, Victorian, Double Chairback, Rosewood, 32 x 30 x 32 In. 315.00
Settee, Victorian, Mahogany, Needlepoint Upholstery, Open Arms, 35 x 43 x 23 In. 200.00
Settee, Victorian, Mahogany, Tufted Back, c.1880, 36 x 56 x 28 In. 155.00
Settee, Victorian, Walnut, Burl Veneer, Tufted Red Velvet Upholstery, 42 x 33 In. 520.00
Settee, Walnut Inlay, Upholstered Back, Seat, Continental, Late 1800s, 36 x 57 In. 805.00
Settee, Walnut, Marquetry, Parquetry Panels, Mid 19th Century, 70 In. 1259.00
Settee, William & Mary Style, High Back, Upholstered, c.1900, 52 x 58 In. 865.00
Settee, Windsor, 15 Spindles, Straight Crest, Bamboo-Turned Arms, 36 x 44 In. 2600.00

Furniture, Sideboard,
Arts & Crafts, Drawers,
Doors, Mirror,
Repousse, England, 73 In.

Furniture, Server, G. Stickley, 3 Drawers,
Chamfered Sides, Red Decal, 38 x 19 In.

Settee, Windsor, Arrow Back, Flat Crest Rail, Plank Seat, 1800, 77 In. 1000.00
Settee, Windsor, Arrow Back, Painted, Stenciled, Early 19th Century, 77 1/2 In. 999.00
Settee, Windsor, Painted, Paneled Crest, Cornucopia, c.1810, 34 x 76 x 22 In. 2700.00
Settee, Windsor, Rod Back, 14 Bamboo Spindles, Splayed Legs, c.1815, 35 x 41 In. 4370.00
Settle, Black Over Red Paint, Stenciled Baskets, Backrest, Arms, 76 x 34 In. 865.00
Settle, Franch Provincial, Wood, Polychrome, Trestle Foot, 39 x 52 x 32 In. 1150.00
Settle, G. Stickley, No. 171, Double Horizontal Rails, 6 Legs, 78 x 33 x 28 In. 5750.00
Settle, G. Stickley, No. 222, 19 Back Slats, 8 Arm Slats, 72 x 33 x 36 In. 16415.00
Settle, G. Stickley, Vertical Slats, Split Cane Seat, Cushions, 30 x 55 x 22 In. 3525.00
Settle, J.M. Young, Drop Arm, Drop-In Spring Seat, 34 x 72 x 31 In. 2115.00
Settle, Knotty Pine, 55 x 82 In. 210.00
Settle, L. & J.G. Stickley, No. 216, Vertical Slats, Leatherette Seat, 36 x 72 x 26 In. 2115.00
Settle, L. & J.G. Stickley, No. 222, 20 Slats, Even Arms, 76 x 31 x 39 In. 10000.00
Settle, L. & J.G. Stickley, No. 232, 5 Slats, Spring Cushion, Even Arms, 72 x 27 x 28 In. ... 2350.00
Settle, Panel Back, Half-Moon Cutouts, Plank Seat, Shaped Arms, 59 x 65 In. 345.00
Settle, Pine, 2-Board Seat, Shaped Arms, Rosehead Nails, 5 x 20 x 48 In. 145.00
Settle, Pine, Bonnet Top, Folding Writing Surface, 65 x 75 x 16 In. 8800.00
Settle, Pine, Cutout Base, Shaped Sides, Square Back, 47 x 48 x 15 In. 175.00
Settle, Pine, Red Paint, Curved Back, 53 x 36 In. 8970.00
Settle, Poplar, Red & Black Graining, Plank Seat, Fruit Baskets, Arms, 34 x 70 In. 635.00
Settle, Prairie School, Spindles, Cushion, Even Arms, 81 x 31 x 34 In. 3525.00
Settle, Windsor, Poplar, Maple, Spindle Back, Scrolled Arms, 38 x 77 1/2 In. 5460.00
Shelf, Arts & Crafts, Oak, Square Top, Pierced, Miller Cabinet Co., 44 x 14 In. 705.00
Shelf, Baroque Style, Carved Gilt, Bowfront, Raphael Cherubs, Bracket, 12 In. 920.00
Shelf, Beech, Satyr Masque, Bracket, c.1900, 27 x 29 In. 1495.00
Shelf, Biedermeier, Fruitwood, Plaster, Demilune, Bracket, 2 x 16 x 8 In. 290.00
Shelf, Black Forest, Oak Leaves, Acorn, Goat Head, 1890s, 9 1/2 x 10 In. 690.00
Shelf, Carved, Leaf Pendant, Gilt, Demilune, Bracket, c.1900, 12 x 12 x 6 In. 546.00
Shelf, Faux Bamboo, Gilt Bronze, Glass Shelves, Late 1800s, 38 x 30 x 12 In. 1095.00
Shelf, G. Nakashima, Walnut, c.1961, 16 x 15 1/2 x 43 3/4 In. 8365.00
Shelf, Hanging, Cherry, 6 Tiers, Graduated, Scalloped Sides, 50 x 36 x 10 In. 1840.00
Shelf, Hanging, Chinoiserie, 2 Colors, Parcel Gilt, Black Lacquer, 20 x 12 x 4 In. 575.00
Shelf, Hanging, Dutch Rosewood, Marquetry, Glaze Inlay, 39 1/2 x 38 x 8 In. 920.00
Shelf, Hanging, Edwardian, Mahogany, Boxwood, Harewood Inlay, 28 x 34 In. 955.00
Shelf, Hanging, Grain Painted, 5 Shelves, New England, Early 1800s, 45 x 19 x 6 In. 2585.00
Shelf, Hanging, Louis XV, Fruitwood, Graduated Tiers, Serpentine Sides, 31 In., Pair 530.00
Shelf, Hanging, Pine, 2 Tiers, 24 x 37 1/2 x 9 In. 265.00
Shelf, Hanging, Pine, Mahogany, Line Carved, Turned Supports, 25 x 7 x 12 In. 105.00
Shelf, Hanging, Shaker, Poplar, Red Paint, Document Well, c.1860, 16 x 22 In. 3450.00
Shelf, Hanging, Softwood, Painted, Scalloped, Scrolled Cutouts, 27 x 22 x 8 In. 1650.00
Shelf, Hanging, Victorian, Walnut, Pierced Gallery, 3 Shelves, 39 x 18 In. 145.00
Shelf, Hanging, Victorian, Walnut, Tulip Supports, Line Carved, 24 x 8 x 12 In. 105.00
Shelf, Hanging, Walnut, 2 Drawers, New England, Early 1800s, 367 x 25 x 8 1/2 In. 1175.00
Shelf, Hanging, Walnut, Bowfront, Rounded Top, 3 Shelves, 20 x 9 x 28 In. 865.00
Shelf, Hanging, Walnut, Graduated Shelves, 29 1/2 x 22 x 6 3/4 In. 990.00
Shelf, Louis XVI Style, Bracket, Carved, Gilt, Bowfront, 19 x 12 x 8 In. 2760.00
Shelf, Pine, Painted, Bowed, 3 Graduated Shelves, Curved Scallops, 15 x 22 In. 7130.00
Shelf, Regency Style, Carved, Gilt, Openwork Scallop Shell, Bracket, 12 In. 460.00
Shelf, Regency, Mahogany, Marble Top, Mirrored Back, Inset Pilasters, 32 x 36 In. 2530.00
Sideboard, Adam Style, Mahogany, Crossbanded, 2 Pedestals, 37 x 80 x 22 In. 4830.00
Sideboard, Art Deco, Burl Walnut, Bakelite Pulls, France, c.1928, 51 x 76 x 20 In. 705.00
Sideboard, Art Deco, Rosewood, Dominique, France, c.1930, 38 x 93 x 20 In. 5700.00
Sideboard, Arts & Crafts, Drawers, Doors, Mirror, Repousse, England, 73 In. .... *Illus* 1765.00
Sideboard, Chippendale Style, Mahogany, 36 x 72 x 21 In. 865.00
Sideboard, Chippendale Style, Mahogany, Pedestals, c.1870, 47 x 90 x 26 In. 2070.00
Sideboard, Classical Revival, Mahogany, Scroll Supports, 51 x 57 x 24 In. 1095.00
Sideboard, Eastlake, Burl Walnut, Incised, Marble Top, c.1885, 85 x 56 x 23 In. 980.00
Sideboard, Edwardian, Mahogany, Inlaid, Carved, c.1890, 38 x 84 x 28 In. 2070.00
Sideboard, Edwardian, Mahogany, Inlaid, Serpentine Front, Drawers, Spade Feet, 46 In. ... 3335.00
Sideboard, Empire Revival, Mahogany, Drawers, Doors, c.1890, 41 x 60 x 24 In. 575.00
Sideboard, Empire Revival, Walnut, Mirrored Back, c.1890, 53 x 54 x 21 In. 200.00
Sideboard, Empire Style, Walnut, Mahogany, Columns, c.1890, 54 x 73 x 24 In. 2070.00
Sideboard, Empire, Mahogany, Drawers, Doors, Backsplash, c.1860, 51 x 68 x 25 In. 375.00

Sideboard, Federal Style, Mahogany, Serpentine, Doors, Drawers, 42 x 73 x 26 In. 4370.00
Sideboard, Federal, Mahogany, 5 Drawers, 6 Legs, Early 1800s, 36 x 70 x 33 In. 8815.00
Sideboard, Federal, Mahogany, Block Front, Baltimore, c.1810, 40 x 69 In. 1725.00
Sideboard, Federal, Mahogany, Crossbanded, Center Doors, 5 Drawers, 41 x 43 In. 4995.00
Sideboard, Federal, Mahogany, Flat Front, 3 Drawers, 4 Doors, 40 x 64 In. 3450.00
Sideboard, Federal, Mahogany, Inlaid, Mid Atlantic States, c.1800, 39 x 72 In. 9000.00
Sideboard, Federal, Satinwood, Inlay, 3 Drawers, 4 Doors, c.1915, 65 x 41 In. 1380.00
Sideboard, Federal, Tiger Maple, Mahogany, Columns, Paw Feet, 1800s 2300.00
Sideboard, G. Stickley, No. 814, Plate Rail, 4 Drawers, 2 Doors, 49 x 66 x 24 In. 7640.00
Sideboard, G. Stickley, No. 814 1/2, 3 Drawers, 2 Doors, 49 x 56 x 22 In. 5875.00
Sideboard, George III Style, Mahogany, Bowfront, Banded, Spade Feet, 65 In. 5290.00
Sideboard, George III Style, Mahogany, Serpentine Front, Drawer, Doors, 36 x 72 In. 2950.00
Sideboard, George III, Mahogany, Bowed Top, 5 Drawers, c.1785, 37 x 64 x 30 In. 5750.00
Sideboard, George III, Mahogany, c.1930, 36 x 72 x 22 In. 2470.00
Sideboard, George III, Mahogany, Serpentine Front, Drawers, Square Legs, 50 In. 9979.00
Sideboard, George III, Satinwood, Inlaid, Crossbanded Mahogany, c.1790, 39 x 75 In. 2300.00
Sideboard, George III, Satinwood, Mahogany, Bowfront, c.1770, 37 x 78 x 31 In. 4600.00
Sideboard, George IV, Mahogany, Inlaid, Drawer, 2 Doors, c.1825, 34 x 50 In. 3680.00
Sideboard, Georgian Style, Mahogany, 5 Drawers, c.1830, 38 x 64 x 29 In. 1150.00
Sideboard, Georgian Style, Mahogany, Ireland, Mid 19th Century, 46 x 81 x 23 In. 2530.00
Sideboard, Georgian Style, Mahogany, Serpentine Front, 36 x 60 x 21 In. 550.00
Sideboard, Georgian Style, Mahogany, Thomasville, 37 x 62 x 22 In. 635.00
Sideboard, Georgian, Mahogany, Bowfront, Arched Backboard, 47 x 69 In. 4140.00
Sideboard, Hepplewhite Style, Mahogany Inlay, 20th Century, 35 x 61 x 20 In. 1265.00
Sideboard, Hepplewhite Style, Mahogany, Bowfront, Drawer, Kittinger, 72 x 26 In. 2300.00
Sideboard, Hepplewhite, Mahogany, Inlaid, Bowed Top, Arched Skirt, 39 x 79 In. 9775.00
Sideboard, Hepplewhite, Mahogany, Robt. W. Irwin Co., c.1950, 38 x 72 x 24 In. 1150.00
Sideboard, Jules Leleu Style, Cherry, Drawers, Doors, France, 35 x 71 In. 6600.00
Sideboard, L. & J.G. Stickley, No. 709, Plate Rack, 6 Drawers, 2 Doors, 48 x 54 In. 4115.00
Sideboard, L. & J.G. Stickley, Oak, Plate Rack, 3 Drawers, 2 Doors, 1916, 44 x 47 In. 5285.00
Sideboard, Late Georgian, Mahogany, 2 Drawers, Cellarette, Cupboard, 75 In. 2376.00
Sideboard, Limbert, Plate Rack, 3 Drawers, 2 Doors, Copper Hardware, 43 x 45 In. 3525.00
Sideboard, Mahogany Veneer, Carved, Classical, 4 Doors, c.1820, 46 x 67 x 24 In. 6465.00
Sideboard, Mahogany, 3 Doors, Claw Feet, New York, 1815, 45 x 60 3/4 x 25 In. 840.00
Sideboard, Mahogany, 3 Drawers Over 4 Doors, Columns, Scrolled Feet, 44 x 69 In. 1210.00
Sideboard, Mahogany, Cherry, False Door, 2 Panel Doors, c.1815, 59 x 50 x 21 In. 1495.00
Sideboard, Mahogany, Drawer, Cupboard, Cellarette, c.1850, 36 x 70 In. 4600.00
Sideboard, Mahogany, Early 20th Century, 40 1/2 x 66 x 26 In. 400.00
Sideboard, Mahogany, Molded Drawers, Doors, Bowed Fronts, 59 x 65 x 25 In. 805.00
Sideboard, Mahogany, Recessed Flame Veneered Front, 29 x 67 x 21 In. 60.00
Sideboard, Maple, Dovetailed Drawers Over 4 Doors, Backboard, 41 x 66 x 21 In. 2990.00
Sideboard, Maple, Yellow Pine, 10 Drawers, Door, Cut Details, 49 x 60 x 21 In. 1725.00
Sideboard, Neoclassical, Cherry, Brass Pulls, c.1825, 60 x 45 3/4 x 23 In. 705.00
Sideboard, Neoclassical, Mahogany, 12 Drawers, c.1815, 40 x 67 x 26 In. 3820.00
Sideboard, Neoclassical, Mahogany, Marble, Mirror, Pedestal Ends, 61 x 74 x 24 In. 2070.00
Sideboard, Oak, Carved, Mirror, Shelves, Scroll Supports, 73 x 47 x 22 In. 345.00
Sideboard, Oak, Columns, c.1890, 77 1/2 x 50 x 25 5/8 In. 345.00
Sideboard, Oak, Dragonfly Door, Drawer, Flowers, Herrmann, 71 x 42 In. 7775.00
Sideboard, Oak, Marble Top, Beveled Mirrors, American, c.1895, 104 x 70 In. 3220.00
Sideboard, Oak, Mirror Back, Broken Arch Crest, Scrolls, Medallions, 75 x 93 In. 1785.00
Sideboard, Oak, Veneer, Dolphin, Leaded Glass, Pilaster Supports, 47 x 19 x 69 In. 2760.00
Sideboard, Regency Style, Mahogany Inlay, Mirror, c.1890, 66 x 60 x 23 In. 1035.00
Sideboard, Regency, Mahogany, Paneled Back, Pedestal, 49 x 90 x 24 In. 5750.00
Sideboard, Regency, Mahogany, Rosewood, Bowed Top, 37 x 71 3/4 x 24 In. 2300.00
Sideboard, Renaissance Revival, Burl Walnut, Marble Top, 85 x 63 x 24 In. 4600.00
Sideboard, Rohde, Mahogany, Curved Front, 4 Doors, Rosewood Base, 71 x 33 In. 5290.00
Sideboard, Rohde, No. 3321, Formal Group, Walnut, Herman Miller, c.1940, 35 x 66 In. .. 7050.00
Sideboard, Rohde, No. 3979, Walnut, Herman Miller, c.1940, 32 x 60 In. 3290.00
Sideboard, Sheraton Style, Mahogany, 7 Drawers, 2 Doors, Reeded Legs, 50 x 77 In. 460.00
Sideboard, Sheraton, Mahogany, 3 Drawers, 4 Doors, Reeded Feet, 41 x 62 In. 1210.00
Sideboard, Sheraton, Mahogany, 4 Drawers, Gallery, Fluted Legs, 72 In. 920.00
Sideboard, Stickley & Brandt Co., 3 Half & Full Drawers, Doors, Brasses, 48 x 51 In. 1530.00
Sideboard, Stickley Bros., 2 Drawers, 2 Doors, Paneled Plate Rack, 44 x 50 x 22 In. 2350.00

Sideboard, Stickley Bros., 4 Drawers, 2 Doors, Paneled Plate Rack, 44 x 55 x 22 In. 7640.00
Sideboard, Stickley Bros., No. 8604, 2 Doors, Strap Hinges, Drawers, 70 x 22 x 64 In. ... 3290.00
Sideboard, Stickley Bros., No. 8837, Drawers, Doors, 50 x 22 x 50 In. 1600.00
Sideboard, Stickley Bros., No. 8840, Plate Rack, 2 Drawers, 2 Doors, 45 x 50 In. 2820.00
Sideboard, Victorian, Mahogany, Carved Gallery, 2 Drawers, 48 x 27 x 82 In. 670.00
Sideboard, Victorian, Walnut, Leaf-Carved Backsplash, 2 Drawers, 59 x 21 x 54 In. 630.00
Sideboard, William & Mary Style, Walnut, Feather, Crossband, 35 x 60 x 21 In. 2990.00
Sideboard, William IV, Flame Mahogany, Drawer, 2 Doors, c.1835, 50 x 89 In. 3220.00
Sideboard, William IV, Mahogany, 2 Tapered Pedestals, 1850s, 38 x 83 x 29 In. 2760.00
Sideboard, William IV, Mahogany, 3 Drawers, 2 Pedestals, c.1835, 37 x 84 x 24 In. 2070.00
Sideboard, William IV, Mahogany, Splashboard, 4 Drawers, 35 x 54 x 24 In. 1765.00
Sideboard, Wormley, 3 Drawers, 3 Sliding Doors, Burlap, Dunbar, 1950 .... 2820.00
Sideboard & Hutch, G. Nakashima, Walnut, Widdicomb, 66 1/4 x 84 x 22 In. 4700.00
Sofa, Art Deco, Mahogany, Upholstered, Continental, 43 x 80 x 29 In. 325.00
Sofa, Art Nouveau, Scroll Arm, 20th Century, 35 x 73 x 27 1/2 In. 355.00
Sofa, Biedermeier, Ash, Shaped Top Rail, Scrolled Arms, Splayed Feet, 80 In. 6570.00
Sofa, Biedermeier, Ebonized Birch, Upholstered, c.1820, 39 x 76 In. 2300.00
Sofa, Biedermeier, Satinwood, Blond, Paneled Crest, Shaped Arms, 41 x 83 x 29 In. 3450.00
Sofa, C.A. France & Son, Teak, Upholstered, Flared Armrests, 69 x 30 x 30 In. 2115.00
Sofa, Chesterfield, Leather Upholstery, Tufted, Rounded Back, 28 x 74 x 32 In. 2760.00
Sofa, Chinese Chippendale, Mahogany, Upholstered, Southwood, 35 x 77 In. 690.00
Sofa, Chippendale, Camelback, Mahogany, Floral Tapestry, 1800, 69 In. 2990.00
Sofa, Chippendale, Camelback, Mahogany, Upholstered, Late 18th Century, 88 In. 5020.00
Sofa, Chippendale, Mahogany, Upholstered, Scroll Arms, Late 1700s, 37 x 79 In. 1530.00
Sofa, Curly Maple, Turned Frame, Arms, Rolled Crest, 32 x 71 x 21 1/2 In. 2010.00
Sofa, Eames, A. Girard, Vinyl, Herman Miller, c.1954, 72 x 29 x 35 In. 2585.00
Sofa, Eames, Compact, Black, White, Herman Miller, c.1954, 35 x 72 x 29 In. 2585.00
Sofa, Eastlake, Walnut, 2 Square Back Panels, Spoon Carved, Victorian, 55 x 41 In. 315.00
Sofa, Edwardian Style, Chesterfield, Tufted Brown Leather, 81 In. 4995.00
Sofa, Edwardian, Chesterfield, Leather, Padded, Tufted, c.1900, 26 1/2 x 76 x 34 In. 3680.00
Sofa, Empire, Mahogany, Carved, Scrolled Ends, S-Curve Arms, c.1830, 33 x 89 In. 1035.00
Sofa, Empire, Mahogany, Scroll Arms, Upholstered, 39 x 90 x 24 In. 1265.00
Sofa, Empire, Mahogany, Shaped Crest Rail, Eagles, Flared Arms, 1800s, 40 x 104 In. 2235.00
Sofa, Federal Style, Humpback, Scroll Arms, Upholstered, 1900s, 36 x 82 x 27 In. 500.00
Sofa, Federal, Mahogany, Carved, New York, c.1810 .... 6615.00
Sofa, Federal, Mahogany, Cornucopia, Scroll Arms, c.1830, 84 In. 1150.00
Sofa, Federal, Mahogany, Curved Back, Early 19th Century, 39 x 81 In. 2235.00
Sofa, Federal, Mahogany, Flat Crest Rail, Curved Molded Arms, Phila., c.1815, 71 In. 1295.00
Sofa, Federal, Mahogany, Maple, Upholstered, New England, c.1815, 36 x 72 In. 3165.00
Sofa, Federal, Mahogany, Upholstered, Mass., c.1800, 72 In. 2400.00
Sofa, Finn Juhl, Poet, Beech, Upholstered, Niels Vodder, c.1950, 33 x 56 In. 9600.00
Sofa, Florence Knoll, No. 53, Parallel Bar, Upholstered, c.1960, 86 In. .... *Illus* 1292.00
Sofa, Francesco Soro, Leather, Tubular Steel, Italy, c.1879 .... 865.00
Sofa, Frank Lloyd Wright, Cantilever, Robie House, c.1909, 95 x 39 x 25 In. 2300.00
Sofa, French Empire Style, Birch, Bundled Reed Carved, Late 1800s, 35 x 74 In. 920.00
Sofa, French Provincial, Mahogany, Rosette Crest, Cushion, Arms, 64 In. 855.00
Sofa, G. Nelson, 2 Seats, Bench, Cushions, Herman Miller, c.1956, 28 x 72 x 26 In. 880.00
Sofa, G. Nelson, 2 Seats, Table End, Herman Miller, c.1956, 28 x 72 x 26 In. 590.00
Sofa, G. Nelson, No. 4678, Birch, Upholstered, Herman Miller, c.1955, 32 x 80 In. 765.00
Sofa, G. Nelson, Sleeper, Girard Hexagons Upholstery, 81 In. .... *Illus* 3835.00
Sofa, G. Nelson, Steel, 2 Seats, Bench, Herman Miller, c.1956, 72 x 26 x 28 In. 880.00
Sofa, George III Style, Upholstered, Serpentine Back, 20th Century, 37 x 88 x 34 In. 1410.00
Sofa, Hepplewhite, Camelback, Mahogany, Upholstered, 8 Legs, 36 x 84 In. 605.00
Sofa, Hepplewhite, Mahogany Stretcher, Velvet Upholstery, 73 x 25 x 32 In. 2530.00
Sofa, Hickory, Upholstered, 69 x 26 x 30 In. 865.00
Sofa, Kittinger, Camelback, Mahogany, 8 Legs, Stretchers, Crewelwork, 78 x 31 In. 978.00
Sofa, Kittinger, Camelback, Scroll Ends, Silk Upholstery, 36 1/2 x 65 In. 865.00
Sofa, Leather, Steel, 2 Seats, 27 x 53 3/4 x 27 In. 2870.00
Sofa, Louis XV Style, Beech, Upholstered, Late 1800s, 39 x 81 In. 780.00
Sofa, Louis XV Style, Walnut, Victorian, 64 x 34 In. 315.00
Sofa, Louis XVI Style, Gilt, c.1900, 39 x 62 3/4 In. 690.00
Sofa, Louis XVI Style, Gilt, Oval, Padded Back & Arms 855.00
Sofa, Mahogany, Leather Upholstery, Padded Back, Outscrolled Arms 3450.00

Furniture, Sofa,
Florence Knoll, No. 53,
Parallel Bar, Upholstered,
c.1960, 86 In.

Furniture, Sofa, G. Nelson, Sleeper,
Girard Hexagons Upholstery, 81 In.

Sofa, Mahogany, Neoclassical, Carved, Upholstered, Boston, c.1815, 36 x 41 In. 5580.00
Sofa, Mahogany, Serpentine Ends, Spinneybeck Leather, Italy, 82 x 31 x 31 In. 690.00
Sofa, Mahogany, Upholstered, Slatted Splayed Supports, 31 x 78 x 33 In. 470.00
Sofa, Neoclassical, Mahogany, Carved, Roll Pillows, N.Y., c.1830, 73 In. 3100.00
Sofa, Neoclassical, Mahogany, Carved, Shaped Rail, Upholstered, c.1825, 85 In. 705.00
Sofa, Neoclassical, Mahogany, Rounded Rail, Scrolled Ends, c.1825, 33 x 77 In. 1295.00
Sofa, Neoclassical, Mahogany, Scrolled Crest & Arms, Paw Feet, 38 x 84 In. 1150.00
Sofa, Neoclassical, Mahogany, Scrolled Crest, Lovebirds, Dolphins, 1800s, 58 In. 1530.00
Sofa, Poplar, Scrolled Head, High Legs, Angled Feet, Zoar, c.1898, 71 x 24 In. 575.00
Sofa, Regency Style, Black Lacquer, Shaped, Padded Back, Arms, 34 x 30 x 83 In. 490.00
Sofa, Regency Style, Carved Crest & Frame, 38 x 73 1/2 In. 345.00
Sofa, Regency Style, Carved, Acanthus Leaves, Claw Feet, 31 1/2 x 89 In. 260.00
Sofa, Renaissance Revival, Walnut, Open Arms, c.1865, 35 x 62 x 27 In. 1265.00
Sofa, Rococo Revival, Mahogany, Upholstered, Casters, Victorian, 42 x 68 In. 538.00
Sofa, Rococo Revival, Rosewood, 3-Part Back, American, c.1865, 43 x 68 In. 1380.00
Sofa, Sectional, Vinyl, Scrolling Flowers, Leaves, Casters, 31 x 48 x 34 In. 470.00
Sofa, Sheraton Style, Mahogany, Oak, Upholstered, Arms, c.1900, 33 x 66 In. 920.00
Sofa, Sheraton Style, Mahogany, Silk Upholstery, Pillows, 80 x 32 x 32 In. 1495.00
Sofa, Sheraton Style, Mahogany, Upholstered, Early 1900s, 53 x 29 x 34 In. 575.00
Sofa, Upholstered, 3 Cushions, Clayton Marcus, 85 In. 750.00
Sofa, Upholstered, Straight Back, Ball Feet, 33 x 74 x 27 In. 175.00
Sofa, Victorian, Hardwood, Carved Crest, Padded Back, 36 x 72 x 32 In. 2185.00
Sofa, Victorian, Mahogany, Scrolls, Shells, Serpentine, 43 In., Pair 1840.00
Sofa, Victorian, Walnut, Crest, Medallion Back, 38 x 61 1/2 In. 145.00
Sofa, Victorian, Walnut, Medallion Back, Carved Grape Crest, 72 x 43 1/2 In. 660.00
Sofa, Victorian, Walnut, Upholstered, Round Pillow Arms, 48 3/4 x 75 x 26 In. 805.00
Sofa, Walnut, Upholstered, Dutch, 1940, 30 x 76 x 31 In. 1555.00
Sofa, Wormley, Angled, Upholstered, Black Base, Dunbar, 29 x 79 In. 1725.00
Sofa, Wormley, Mahogany, Down-Filled Cushions, Dunbar, 91 x 33 x 27 In. 2235.00
Sofa, Wormley, Straight Sides, Upholstered, 6 Black Legs, Dunbar, 29 x 91 In. 980.00
Sofa, Yellow Ground, Gold Grained, Upholstered, Greek Key Decoration, 26 x 32 In. 1208.00
Sofa & Armchair, Slimline, Walnut, Frame, Robin Bush, Canada, c.1953 . . . . 605.00
Stand, Adirondack, Square, 3-Stick Base, Cross Stretchers, 28 1/2 x 13 1/2 In. 29.00
Stand, Amboyna, Fruitwood, Mother-Of-Pearl, Stylized Flowers, 30 x 15 x 18 In. 2235.00
Stand, American Restauration, Mahogany, Marble Top, Mid 1800s, 32 x 19 x 17 In. 1150.00
Stand, Art Deco, Bird's-Eye Maple Veneer, Marble Top, France, c.1930, 31 x 16 In. 205.00
Stand, Arts & Crafts, Rectangular Top, 2 Shelves, Tapered Legs, 24 x 18 x 29 In. 705.00
Stand, Baker Furniture, Mahogany, Drawer, Lower Shelf, 20 x 20 x 23 In., Pair 575.00
Stand, Biedermeier, Walnut Veneer Inlay, 2 Drawers, c.1930, 31 x 24 x 14 In. 315.00
Stand, Bird's-Eye Maple, Marble Shelf, Bamboo Turnings, Slide, Drawer, 33 x 15 In. 405.00
Stand, Bugatti, Pewter Arabic Inlays, Copper Banding, 1900 . . . . 3910.00
Stand, Cherry, Bird's-Eye Maple, New England, c.1820, 32 In. 4250.00
Stand, Corner, Federal, Mahogany, Shaped Backsplash, Skirt, Shelf, Reeded Legs, 43 In. . 1295.00
Stand, Dinesen, Teak, Birch-Lined Drawers, Open Storage, Denmark, 18 x 24 In. 825.00
Stand, Federal Style, Mahogany, Drawer, Reeded Legs, 28 1/4 x 17 x 15 In. 145.00
Stand, Federal, Birch, Maple Drawer, Red Stain, Tapered Legs, c.1810, 29 x 20 x 16 In. . . 1115.00
Stand, Federal, Black Paint, Scalloped Shelf, Square Legs, N.H., 28 x 16 In. 2185.00
Stand, Federal, Cherry, 2 Drawers, Turned Legs, c.1830, 29 In. 120.00

Stand, Federal, Cherry, Drawer, Square Legs, New England, Early 1800s, 29 x 21 In. 1295.00
Stand, Federal, Cherry, Inlaid, Drawer, New England, c.1800, 29 x 18 x 17 1/2 In. 1060.00
Stand, Federal, Cherry, Tiger Maple Oval Inlay, Tilt Top, 27 x 19 x 18 1/2 In. 635.00
Stand, Federal, Mahogany, 2 Drawers, Glass Knobs, 30 x 19 1/2 x 16 In. 520.00
Stand, Federal, Mahogany, Carved, 2 Drawers, c.1815, 30 1/2 x 22 x 16 In. 720.00
Stand, Federal, Maple, Figured, Drawer, New England, c.1800, 30 In. 3819.00
Stand, Federal, Painted, Faux Grain, Drawer, Tapered Square Legs, 29 x 17 1/4 In. 5750.00
Stand, Federal, Pin, Painted E, Drawer, Starflower, Pa., 1800s, 30 x 25 x 25 In. 6900.00
Stand, Federal, Pine, c.1800, 16 1/2 x 17 x 28 1/2 In. 705.00
Stand, Federal, Poplar, Painted, Drawer, Rectangular, c.1850, 29 x 24 x 19 In. 2115.00
Stand, Federal, Walnut, Drawer, Shaped Top, Pa., c.1825, 28 x 20 x 21 In. 1840.00
Stand, Federal, Walnut, Inlaid, Drawer, Early 19th Century, 29 x 27 x 16 In. 240.00
Stand, Fern, Gold Paint, Onyx, Cast Iron, Leafy Scroll Design, 23 x 15 x 38 In. 460.00
Stand, Fern, Pine, Tan, Rose, Gold & Brown Paint, Carved Petals, 32 In., Pair 635.00
Stand, Folio, Regency, Rosewood, c.1825, 49 x 45 x 27 In. 9000.00
Stand, G. Nakashima, Drawer, Widdicomb, c.1959, 21 x 22 x 21 In., Pair 3995.00
Stand, G. Nelson, Walnut, Door, Drawer, 18 x 18 1/2 x 24 In. 1765.00
Stand, G. Stickley, Inset Grueby Tile, Turned Legs, 21 x 18 1/4 In. 295.00
Stand, George III Style, Mahogany, 3/4 Gallery, Pad Feet, 30 x 22 In., Pair 1150.00
Stand, Gothic Revival, Walnut, Ring-Turned Posts, Drop Finials, 28 x 25 x 16 In. 260.00
Stand, Hardwood, Shelves, Pierced Fret-Carved Base, Chinese, Early 1900s, 21 x 20 In. .. 219.00
Stand, Hepplewhite Style, Satinwood, Oval Top, Inlaid Reserve, 29 x 18 x 12 In. 805.00
Stand, Hepplewhite, Birch, Pine, 2 Drawers, Wooden Pulls, 23 x 18 x 30 In. 1035.00
Stand, Hepplewhite, Cherry, Divided Drawer, Tapered Legs, 19 x 17 x 28 In. 2760.00
Stand, Hepplewhite, Cherry, Drawer, Glass Pull, Tapered Legs, 29 x 18 In. 575.00
Stand, Hepplewhite, Cherry, Drawer, Tapered Legs, Pegged Joints, 28 x 19 In. 1780.00
Stand, Hepplewhite, Cherry, Pine, 2 Drawers, Brass Pulls, 14 x 17 x 29 In. 1035.00
Stand, Hepplewhite, Cherry, Walnut, Dovetailed Drawers, Brass Pulls, 22 x 16 In. 1150.00
Stand, Hepplewhite, Curly Maple, 2-Board Top, Drawer, 18 x 16 x 29 In. 980.00
Stand, Hepplewhite, Curly Maple, Poplar, Drawer, 19 x 16 x 29 In. 635.00
Stand, Hepplewhite, Mahogany, Pine, Eagle Brass Pulls, Square Legs, 28 1/2 x 16 In. 460.00
Stand, Hepplewhite, Pine, Drawer, Mortise & Peg, Tapered Legs, 20 x 20 x 30 In. 805.00
Stand, Hepplewhite, Pine, Mustard, Black Flowers, Scroll Stencil, 17 x 18 x 29 In. 345.00
Stand, Hepplewhite, Pine, Painted, Drawer, Square Nails, Tapered Legs, 24 x 30 In. 1670.00
Stand, Hepplewhite, Walnut, 2-Board Top, Pegged, Splay Legs, 29 x 20 In. 2820.00
Stand, Hung Mu, Carved, Pierced Apron, Chinese, 19th Century, 15 x 36 1/2 In. 210.00
Stand, L. & J.G. Stickley, Chafing Dish, Shelf, Arched Apron, 28 x 18 x 12 In. 2700.00
Stand, L. & J.G. Stickley, No. 22, Round Top, Splayed Legs, 18 x 29 In. 3525.00
Stand, L. & J.G. Stickley, No. 105, 2 Drawers, 20 x 14 x 29 In. 2000.00
Stand, L. & J.G. Stickley, No. 542, Round Top, Through Tenon, Shelf, 29 x 36 In. 1116.00
Stand, Louis XV Style, Bird's-Eye Maple, Mahogany, 3 Drawers, c.1890, 29 In., Pair 690.00
Stand, Louis XV Style, Carved, Blue, Antique White, 30 x 25 x 18 In., Pair 2530.00
Stand, Louis XV Style, Carved, Gilt, Inset Marble Top, 16 x 39 In. 635.00
Stand, Magazine, Arts & Crafts, 3 Shelves, Cut Corner, Splayed, 17 x 13 x 40 In. 175.00
Stand, Magazine, Arts & Crafts, 4 Shelves, 3 Vertical Spindles, 19 x 13 x 46 In. 823.00
Stand, Magazine, G. Stickley, No. 69, 4 Shelves, D-Shape Handles, 40 x 14 In. 2350.00
Stand, Magazine, G. Stickley, No. 72, Overhanging Top, Arch Sides, 42 x 22 x 13 In. 3525.00
Stand, Magazine, G. Stickley, No. 79, 6 Shelves, D-Shape Handles, 40 x 14 In. 1528.00
Stand, Magazine, G. Stickley, No. 547, 3 Shelves, Paneled Sides, 35 x 15 In. 4700.00
Stand, Magazine, G. Stickley, Rectangular Top, Apron, Shelves, 22 x 13 x 42 In. 2585.00
Stand, Magazine, Grand Rapids Furniture, 4 Shelves, Square Top, 33 In. 1998.00
Stand, Magazine, Jacques Guillon, Plywood, Woven Cord, c.1955, 18 x 12 x 17 In. 105.00
Stand, Magazine, Mahogany, Slatted Back & Sides, 46 x 15 x 12 1/2 In. 1115.00
Stand, Magazine, Michigan Chair Co., 4 Shelves, Through Tenon, 33 x 17 x 17 In. 1645.00
Stand, Magazine, Pierced Gallery, 2 Shelves, Turned Reeded Legs, 22 x 18 x 12 In. 60.00
Stand, Magazine, Roycroft, 3 Shelves, Arched Sides, 37 x 18 x 15 In. 6465.00
Stand, Magazine, Roycroft, Canted Sides, Overhanging Top, Pedestal, 64 x 22 In. 7050.00
Stand, Magazine, Roycroft, No. 80, 5 Shelves, Slab Sides, Key & Tenon, 64 x 21 In. 8225.00
Stand, Magazine, Roycroft, No. 80, Oak, c.1906, 63 x 18 x 20 In. 16730.00
Stand, Magazine, Stickley Bros., No. 4706, 4 Shelves, 26 x 13 x 40 In. 1765.00
Stand, Magazine, Stickley Bros., Slat Back, Sides, Cutouts, 49 x 14 x 12 In. 2115.00
Stand, Mahogany, Brass Inlay, Serpentine Drawer, Mounts, 34 x 19 x 12 In. 345.00
Stand, Mahogany, Crotch Mahogany Veneer, 28 x 15 x 31 In., Pair 575.00

Stand, Mahogany, Fruitwood, Drawer, Incised Monogram, 17 x 16 x 28 In. 430.00
Stand, Mahogany, Kingwood, Marble Top, 3 Drawers, France, 29 In. 1150.00
Stand, Mahogany, Ormolu Decoration, Lift Top, France, Late 1800s, 24 x 15 In. 145.00
Stand, Mahogany, Satinwood, Drawer, Drop Leaf, 15 x 19 x 29 In. 230.00
Stand, Mahogany, Tambour Front, Pierced Hearts, Gallery, 16 x 11 x 28 In. 405.00
Stand, Mahogany, Veneer Inlay, Fluted Columns, Slipper Feet, 36 x 21 x 29 In. 145.00
Stand, Maple, Drawer, Mortise & Peg, Turned Legs, Ball Feet, Ohio, 24 x 23 In. 860.00
Stand, Maple, Square Top, Tapered Legs, 1800s, 12-In. Top 670.00
Stand, Marble 4-Lobed Top, Rouge, Chinese, Mid 1800s, 23 x 15 In. 460.00
Stand, Marble 8-Lobed Top, Rouge, Chinese, Mid 1800s, 36 x 17 In. 575.00
Stand, Marble Top, Dragonfly, Lotus Carving, Chinese, Mid 1700s, 18 x 16 In. 259.00
Stand, Marble Top, Rouge, Bamboo Design, Chinese, Mid 1800s, 32 x 15 In. 345.00
Stand, Marble Top, Rouge, Chinese, Mid 1800s, 32 x 16 1/2 In. 635.00
Stand, Music, 4 Shelves, Stick & Ball, 38 x 18 In. 195.00
Stand, Music, Art Nouveau, Walnut, Gilt Bronze, Iron, Organic Shape, 51 x 19 x 20 In. ... 2868.00
Stand, Music, Classical, Mahogany, Brass Inlay, Adjustable, c.1820, 54 1/2 In. 1195.00
Stand, Music, Duet, Mahogany, England, 1870-80, 55 In. 3100.00
Stand, Music, George III Style, Mahogany, Column Standard, 40 x 24 In. 489.00
Stand, Music, Louis XV Style, Painted, 39 x 22 In. 1440.00
Stand, Music, Victorian, Walnut, Stamped, 36 1/2 In. 1090.00
Stand, Napoleon III Style, Black Lacquer, 3 Drawers, Early 1900s, 29 x 17 In. 1035.00
Stand, Napoleon III, Ebonized, Faux Marble, Drawer, c.1865, 31 x 17 In. 980.00
Stand, Neoclassical, Mahogany, Cherry, Maple, Drop Leaf, c.1840, 31 x 30 In. 920.00
Stand, Oriental, Rosewood, Marble Top, Carved Skirt, Legs, 32 x 12 In. 115.00
Stand, Parquetry Decoration, Marble Top, 2 Drawers, Late 1800s, 27 x 24 In. 690.00
Stand, Parquetry, Drawer, France, 29 1/2 x 24 In., Pair 1035.00
Stand, Pine, Painted, Drawer, 1800s, 29 1/2 x 24 x 19 1/2 In. 120.00
Stand, Pine, Paneled Sides, Square Top, Drawer, Chinese, 19th Century, 33 x 18 In. 315.00
Stand, Plant, 3 Scrolled Feet, Hook, Iron, 55 1/2 x 15 1/2 x 13 In. 230.00
Stand, Plant, Arts & Crafts, Oak, 24 x 17 x 12 In. 105.00
Stand, Plant, Brass, Mahogany Top, Shelf, Claw & Ball Feet, 14 x 35 In. 115.00
Stand, Plant, Brass, Marble Top, 2 Tiers, 20th Century, 39 x 12 In. 188.00
Stand, Plant, Brass, Marble, Reeded Handles, Onyx Medallions, 23 x 15 x 32 In. 290.00
Stand, Plant, Chiparus, Louis XV Style, Bronze, Figural Pedestal, c.1875, 29 In. 7050.00
Stand, Plant, French Provincial, 32 x 28 In. 550.00
Stand, Plant, G. Stickley, Square Top, Arched Aprons, Through Tenon, 22 x 14 In. 1175.00
Stand, Plant, G. Stickley, Square Top, Flared Legs, Wide Apron, 18 x 18 x 20 In. 999.00
Stand, Plant, Lacquered, Rectangular Top, Chinese, Late 1800s, 31 x 20 x 13 In. 145.00
Stand, Plant, Limbert, Round Top, Arched Apron, Shelf, 33 x 12 In. 1060.00
Stand, Plant, Limbert, Round Top, Shelf, Curved Legs, 30 x 13 In. 4400.00
Stand, Plant, Louis XV, Rosewood, Parquetry, Gilt Bronze Mounts, 30 x 25 x 17 In. 1320.00
Stand, Plant, Mahogany, Beaded Molded Top, 20th Century, 43 x 20 In. 129.00
Stand, Plant, Mahogany, Carved Top, Urn Support, Early 1900s, 55 x 24 In. 380.00
Stand, Plant, Marble Scalloped Top, Shelf, Carved Frieze, 5 Legs, Chinese, 32 x 21 In. ... 805.00
Stand, Plant, Marble, Pink & White, Square Top, Octagonal Base, 29 x 12 In. 165.00
Stand, Plant, Neoclassical, Mahogany, Round, Reed Support, 1900s, 77 x 24 In. 105.00
Stand, Plant, Oak, Hexagonal Top, Stick & Ball, 21 In. 335.00
Stand, Plant, Ormolu, Onyx Top, Brass Gallery, 4 Tapered Legs, Stretcher, 34 x 15 In. 2935.00
Stand, Plant, Poplar, Red Paint, Scalloped Supports, 3 Shelves, 40 x 20 x 35 In. 259.00
Stand, Plant, Rosewood, Marble Inset Top, Chinese, 19th Century, 32 x 22 In. 1095.00
Stand, Plant, Stickley Bros., Vertical Slats, Cutouts, 16 x 16 x 20 In. 825.00
Stand, Plant, Teak, Carved Chinese Decoration, 20th Century, 36 In., 3 Piece 155.00
Stand, Plant, Victorian, Walnut, Oval Top, Turned Column, 4 Legs, 27 x 21 x 16 In. 240.00
Stand, Plant, Victorian, Walnut, Pine, 3 Tiers, Scalloped Aprons, Turned Legs, 31 x 38 In. .. 405.00
Stand, Plant, Wrought Iron, Applied Flowers, 20th Century, 39 In. 129.00
Stand, Plate, Limbert, Round Top, Corbel, Shelf, Cutout Flared Sides, 30 x 20 x 20 In. ... 2705.00
Stand, Reading, William IV, Mahogany, Bookrests, 31 x 33 1/2 x 17 1/2 In. 1645.00
Stand, Red Lacquer, Drawer, 2 Doors, Chinese, 29 1/2 x 20 x 18 In., Pair 460.00
Stand, Red Lacquer, Scallop Top, Carved Feet, Chinese, 44 x 22 In., Pair 431.00
Stand, Red Paint, Drawer, Dovetailed, Tapered Legs, Maine, 29 x 17 x 18 In. 2300.00
Stand, Regency Style, Metal, Round Top, 3 Supports, c.1815, 42 x 19 In., Pair 1840.00
Stand, Regency, Mahogany, Telescopic, 3 Tiers, Flat Ball Feet, 40 x 29 x 24 In. 1058.00
Stand, Renaissance Revival, Burl Walnut, Marble Top, c.1865, 28 x 25 In. 1265.00

Stand, Rosewood, Carved, Round Top, Flower Inlay, Mid 1800s, 28 x 20 In. 1035.00
Stand, Rosewood, Trestle Base, Tin Lining Under Top, 28 x 20 In. . . . . *Illus* 235.00
Stand, Shaker, Cherry, Pine, Square Top, Drawer, c.1850, 29 x 15 x 14 3/4 In. 1150.00
Stand, Shaving, Georgian Style, Mahogany, Round Top, 2 Drawers, Tripod, 34 In. 145.00
Stand, Shaving, Mahogany, 26 In. 150.00
Stand, Sheraton, Basin, Yellow, Red Sponge, Multicolored Flowers, Shelf, 37 x 17 In. 880.00
Stand, Sheraton, Birch, Bird's-Eye Maple, Drop Leaf, 17 x 19 x 30 In. 980.00
Stand, Sheraton, Black Paint, Gold Stencils, Drawer, Wood Knob, 29 x 18 x 16 In. 100.00
Stand, Sheraton, Cherry, 2 Dovetailed Drawers, Mortise, Peg, Turned Legs, 22 x 28 In. . . . 720.00
Stand, Sheraton, Cherry, Drawer, 18 1/2 x 18 1/4 x 28 In., Pair 430.00
Stand, Sheraton, Cherry, Drawer, 20 x 1 x 29 In. 230.00
Stand, Sheraton, Cherry, Poplar, 2 Drawers, 29 1/4 x 22 x 19 In. 1840.00
Stand, Sheraton, Cherry, Poplar, Drawer, Turned Legs, 19 x 17 x 29 1/2 In. 660.00
Stand, Sheraton, Cherry, Walnut, Drawer, Ball Feet, 20 x 18 x 29 In. 520.00
Stand, Sheraton, Curly & Straight-Grain Maple, 2 Drawers, 22 1/2 x 22 x 30 In. 980.00
Stand, Sheraton, Curly Maple, Cherry, Drawer, Pegged Joints, 27 x 21 In. 690.00
Stand, Sheraton, Mahogany, Bird's-Eye Maple, 2 Graduated Drawers, 20 x 19 x 29 In. . . . 345.00
Stand, Sheraton, Maple, Grain Painted, Black, Red, Drawer, 28 x 19 x 16 In. 780.00
Stand, Sheraton, Maple, Mahogany, Drawer, Wood Pull, 29 x 20 x 17 In. 290.00
Stand, Sheraton, Salmon Paint, Pennsylvania, c.1840, 21 x 22 x 30 In. 978.00
Stand, Sheraton, Tiger Maple, Cherry, Drawer, Pennsylvania, 1830-50 . . . . 1265.00
Stand, Sheraton, Walnut, Drawer, Brass Knobs, 26 1/2 x 24 x 17 In. 690.00
Stand, Smoking, Art Deco, Aluminum, Glass, 26 x 20 1/2 In. 275.00
Stand, Smoking, Bear Pedestal, Glass Eyes, 2 Compartments, Switzerland, 35 x 18 x 14 In. 3745.00
Stand, Smoking, Brass Finish, Onyx, Openwork Leaf Scroll, Cast Iron, 12 x 29 In. 60.00
Stand, Stickley Bros., No. 2569, Drop Leaf, 2 Half Drawers Over Drawer, 18 x 29 In. 1115.00
Stand, Stickley Bros., No. 2615, Round Copper Top, Splayed Legs, 18 x 28 In. 1175.00
Stand, Teak, Chinoiserie Design, 20th Century, 36 x 15 In., Pair 118.00
Stand, Teakettle, George III, Mahogany, Serpentine Top, Gallery, 27 1/2 x 12 In. 6715.00
Stand, Teakettle, Georgian Style, Mahogany, Oval Top, 1900s, 24 x 14 x 10 1/2 In. 265.00
Stand, Telephone, Arts & Crafts, Oak, Half-Gallery Top, Square Legs, 30 x 18 x 16 In. . . . 390.00
Stand, Telephone, Marble Top, Demilune, Chair, Early 1900s, 40 x 29 1/2 In. 1410.00
Stand, Victorian, Carved Head, Turned Post, 35 1/2 In. 230.00
Stand, Victorian, Mahogany, Carved, Scrolling Frieze, Columns, 29 x 19 x 16 In. 145.00
Stand, Victorian, Rosewood, Lift Top, Tin Lining, Trestle, 29 x 20 x 14 In. 235.00
Stand, Victorian, Round Footed Base, 33 1/2 x 19 In. 220.00
Stand, Victorian, Walnut, Marble, Serpentine Top, Stretchers, 37 x 27 x 32 In. 546.00
Stand, Victorian, Wicker, Oak, Ornate Decoration, 20 x 16 x 28 In. 865.00
Stand, Walnut, Gilt, Metal, c.1900, 31 1/2 x 16 x 11 3/4 In. 2868.00
Stand, Walnut, Inlaid, Drawer, Rounded Corners, Tapered Legs, 29 x 27 x 20 In. 3190.00
Stand, Walnut, Marquetry Top, 3 Legs, 28 1/2 In. 105.00
Stand, Walnut, Wooden Pegs, Lipped Drawer, Tapered Legs, 28 x 22 x 18 In. 1725.00
Stool, Arne Jacobsen, Round Orange Top, 3 Legs, Fritz Hansen, c.1958, 17 x 13 In. 235.00
Stool, Arts & Crafts, 18 x 14 In., Pair 325.00
Stool, Baroque, Mahogany, Padded Seat, Frieze, Cabriole Legs, 21 x 24 x 19 In. 690.00
Stool, Bauhaus, 3 Legs, c.1930, 13 x 20 1/2 In. 3230.00
Stool, Charles II, Oak, Rectangular, Baluster Legs, c.1660, 22 In. 2160.00
Stool, Cherry, Scroll, Star Inlays, Pinwheel, 5 1/2 x 11 1/2 x 5 In. 660.00
Stool, Eames, Birch Plywood, Molded, P. Evans, c.1945, 8 x 12 x 10 In., Child's 1765.00
Stool, Eames, No. 412, Time Life, Herman Miller, c.1960, 15 x 13 In. 1645.00
Stool, Egyptian, Camel Shape, Bench Base, Vinyl Upholstery, 19 x 33 x 15 In. 188.00
Stool, Empire Style, Gilt, Padded Seat, Square, Winged Lion's Heads, 18 x 22 In., Pair . . . 2760.00
Stool, Empire Style, Mahogany, Gilt, Padded Seat, c.1900, 17 x 15 x 14 In. 1265.00
Stool, English Oak, Rope Carving, 1700s, 14 1/2 x 17 x 10 In. 950.00
Stool, Esherick, Hickory, Cottonwood, 3 Legs, 1960, 25 In. 5875.00
Stool, Esherick, Walnut, Ash, 1953, 25 1/2 In. 4185.00
Stool, G. Stickley, Gout, Leather Seat, 4 Flaring Feet, 4 1/2 x 12 x 12 In. 2820.00
Stool, George I Style, Walnut, Oval, Upholstered Seat, 18 x 24 x 17 In. 460.00
Stool, George II Style, Gilt, Padded Seat, c.1850, 20 x 21 x 17 In. 1610.00
Stool, George II Style, Mahogany, Padded Seat, Cabriole Legs, 20 x 23 1/2 In. 290.00
Stool, George III Style, Mahogany, Leather Seat, Cabriole Legs, c.1910, 18 x 38 In. 920.00
Stool, George III Style, Mahogany, Needlepoint Slip Seat, c.1890, 18 x 38 In. 1095.00
Stool, Italian Style, Gilt, Padded Square Seat, 20 x 17 x 17 In., Pair 1610.00

Stool, Italian Style, Gilt, Padded, Rectangular Seat, Block Feet, 14 x 24 In., Pair 2070.00
Stool, Italian Style, Gilt, Tufted Rectangular Seat, 15 x 42 x 21 In. 2070.00
Stool, Karl Springer, Brass, Bamboo, Upholstered, 1970s, 18 x 20 x 17 In., Pair 956.00
Stool, Louis XV Style, Gilt, Celery Paint, Upholstered, 19 x 19 x 17 In., Pair 718.00
Stool, Louis XVI, Gilt, Padded Seat, Medallion Frieze, 18 x 23 x 17 In., Pair 1495.00
Stool, Mahogany, Floral Needlepoint, England, 18th Century, 15 x 21 x 21 In. 1265.00
Stool, Mahogany, Upholstered, Acanthus Carved X-Form Ends, c.1830, 17 1/2 In. 765.00
Stool, Needlework Cushion, Ogee Feet, 6 x 16 x 12 In. 85.00
Stool, Nutting, No. 127, Windsor, Ogee, New England 293.00
Stool, Perriand, Pine, 3 Legs, c.1967, 18 In. 1800.00
Stool, Piano, Adjusting Knobs, c.1900, 24 x 15 3/4 In. . . . . .45.00 to 60.00
Stool, Piano, Carved, Back Support, Swivel Seat, Claw & Ball Feet, 36 x 15 x 15 In. 80.00
Stool, Piano, Mahogany, Brass, Swivel Seat, 4 Lady's Boot Legs, 19 x 15 In. 2760.00
Stool, Piano, Mahogany, Carved Edge, Column Legs, 20th Century, 19 x 17 In. 235.00
Stool, Piano, Oak, Brass, Swivel Seat, Glass Ball Feet, 1800s, 19 x 18 1/2 In. 106.00
Stool, Piano, Oak, Brass, Swivel Seat, Glass Claw & Ball Feet, c.1880 . . . . 80.00
Stool, Piano, Oak, Glass Claw & Ball Feet, 19 In. 150.00
Stool, Piano, Oak, Painted Metal & Glass Claw & Ball Feet, 19 1/2 x 18 1/2 In. 120.00
Stool, Piano, Oak, Screw Shaft Seat, Fluted Leg Supports, 19th Century, 17 x 17 In. 80.00
Stool, Piano, Victorian, Mahogany, Padded Square Top, c.1850, 20 x 14 x 14 In. 460.00
Stool, Pine, Grain Painted, Hearts, Scrolls On Legs, 6 x 12 x 7 In. 550.00
Stool, Pine, Inlaid Shields, Compass Wheels, Stars, Diamonds, Hearts, 7 x 15 x 8 In. 360.00
Stool, Pine, Painted, Red, Yellow & Blue Stars & Dots, 4 Legs, 5 x 8 5/8 In. 558.00
Stool, Queen Anne Style, Poplar, Flame-Stitched Seat, Stretcher, 18 x 18 x 19 In. 460.00
Stool, Queen Anne Style, Walnut, Brocade Seat, Cabriole Legs, c.1850, 15 x 18 1/2 In. . . . 805.00
Stool, Queen Anne, Mahogany, Slip Seat, Pad Feet, 18 x 21 x 16 In. 1725.00
Stool, Red Paint, Round Seat, Turned Rungs, Splayed Legs, 30 In. 345.00
Stool, Regency, Curule Shape, Painted, Parcel Gilt, c.1810, 30 x 35 x 19 In. 5100.00
Stool, Renaissance Revival, Walnut, Hinged Seat, Trestle, 19 x 23 x 11 In. 265.00
Stool, Rush, Maple, 4 Legs, c.1930, 18 In. 550.00
Stool, Shaker, Maple, Pine, 2 Steps, Dowel Legs, Watervliet, N.Y., 21 x 17 x 14 In. 2300.00
Stool, Shaker, Maple, Tape Seat, 8 Stretchers, Mt. Lebanon, N.Y., c.1880, 16 x 13 In. 805.00
Stool, Shaker, Maple, Tape Seat, Mt. Lebanon, N.Y., 16 x 14 In. 1035.00
Stool, Shaker, Pine, 3 Steps, Yellow, New Lebanon, N.Y., c.1850, 24 x 15 1/2 In. 1840.00
Stool, Shaker, Pine, Revolving, Flared Legs, 29 1/2 x 12 1/2 In. 460.00
Stool, Sori Yanagi, Butterfly, Laminated Rosewood, 1960s, Pair 2645.00
Stool, Upholstered, Flowers, Gold, Blue, Gray, Melon, Reeded Legs, 13 x 23 In. 294.00
Stool, Victorian, Mahogany, Needlepoint, Ogee Bracket Feet, 16 x 21 x 17 In. 345.00
Stool, Victorian, Walnut, Carved, Needlework Cushion, 16 x 20 x 16 In. 135.00
Stool, Windsor, Birch, Pine, Round Seat, Bamboo-Turned Legs, 11 x 10 In. 375.00
Stool, Windsor, Black Stain, Round Seat, Turned Legs, Rungs, 12 x 15 In. 230.00
Stool, Windsor, Pine, Triangular Hooked-Rug Seat, 3 Turned Legs, 12 x 13 In. 1090.00
Stool, Windsor, Red Repaint, Round Dish Seat, Turned Legs, Rungs, 18 In. 460.00
Stool, Windsor, Red, Dish Seat, Upholstered, Turned Legs, Rungs, 18 In. 175.00
Stool, Windsor, Walnut, Dish Seat, Tapered Legs, 29 x 12 In. 315.00
Stool Set, Bar, B. Mathsson, Oak, Bent, Leather Seat, 14 x 14 x 26 In., 3 . . . . 705.00
Stool Set, G. Nakashima, Walnut, c.1960, 11 x 18 In., 4 . . . . 5736.00
Stool Set, Habitat, Round Black Top, c.1965, 17 x 12 In., 3 . . . . 410.00
Stool Set, Stacking, Molded Plywood, Teak, Tubular Steel, Denmark, c.1960, 3 . . . . 86.00
Table, Aalto, Birch, Plywood, Celluloid, 22 x 16 x 23 1/2 In. 200.00
Table, Adirondack, Bent Twig, Birch Bark, Heart Designs, 29 1/2 x 21 1/2 In. 288.00
Table, Aldo Tura, Walnut, Fluted Edge, 3 Legs, Italy, 1950s, 17 1/2 x 22 In. 2350.00
Table, Altar, Hardwood, Painted, Scalloped Legs, 34 x 64 x 17 3/4 In. 518.00
Table, Altar, Hung Mu, Carved Censers, Fret Design, Chinese, 1900s, 96 x 43 In. 1840.00
Table, Altar, Hung Mu, Pierced Apron, Knot Design, Chinese, 1900s, 33 x 45 In. 460.00
Table, Altar, Hung Mu, Pierced Dragon Apron, 33 x 48 In. 805.00
Table, Altar, Queen Anne Style, Rosewood, Marble, Chinese, c.1875, 33 x 30 In. 1725.00
Table, Altar, Rosewood, Fretwork Apron, Inlaid Panels, Chinese, 33 x 46 x 16 In. 920.00
Table, Anthony Quervelle, Neoclassical, Mahogany, c.1820, 29 x 42 In. 2868.00
Table, Art Deco, Burl, Ebony, Ash Inlay, Canted Legs, Leaves, c.1930, 29 x 79 x 40 In. . . . 1175.00
Table, Art Deco, Mahogany, Continental, 29 3/4 x 35 In. 200.00
Table, Art Deco, Mahogany, Round, 4 Scrolled Brackets, 23 x 27 1/2 In. 2300.00
Table, Art Deco, Rosewood, Veneer, Double Lyre Base, 30 x 61 x 38 1/2 In. 7188.00

Table, Art Deco, Walnut, Oyster Veneer, Round Top, Stepped Base, France, 31 x 23 In. ... 1840.00
Table, Art Nouveau, Marquetry, Mahogany Inlay, Shelf Stretcher, 29 x 26 x 16 In. 329.00
Table, Art Nouveau, Marquetry, Mahogany, Shelf Stretcher, 29 x 19 In. 269.00
Table, Arts & Crafts, Ebonized, Carved Flowers, Through Tenon, 96 x 54 x 29 In. 2938.00
Table, Arts & Crafts, Pine, Poplar, Black Paint, Cutouts, 32 x 25 In. 385.00
Table, Arts & Crafts, Rectangular Top, Slab Sides, Stretcher, 60 x 36 x 29 In. 529.00
Table, Arts & Crafts, Round Leather Top, Chessboard, Pedestal Base, 32 x 29 In. 646.00
Table, Arts & Crafts, Round Top, 4 Flared Legs, 24 x 29 In. 60.00
Table, Arts & Crafts, Round Top, Ebonized Front, Dutch, 35 x 22 In. 2415.00
Table, Arts & Crafts, Round Top, Shelf, 18 x 27 In. 205.00
Table, Arts & Crafts, Square, 20th Century, 18 x 16 In. 120.00
Table, Arts & Crafts, Thick Round Top, Notched Cross Stretcher, Shelf, 34 x 29 In. 382.00
Table, Arts & Crafts, Tile Top, 4 Majolica Tiles, Flowers, England, 30 x 15 In. 500.00
Table, B. Mathsson, Folding, 1936, 110 x 35 1/2 x 28 1/2 In. 2940.00
Table, Baker Furniture, Mahogany, 2 Drawers, Lower Shelf, 26 x 26 x 23 In. 175.00
Table, Baker's, Napoleon III, Wrought Iron, Marble, Cast Stone, 31 x 28 In. 3220.00
Table, Bamboo Carving, Square, Chinese, 20th Century, 33 x 15 In. 259.00
Table, Bamboo Carving, Stepped Aprons, Mortised, 63 x 17 x 34 In. 405.00
Table, Baroque, Mahogany, 20th Century, 30 x 20 x 66 In. 175.00
Table, Baroque, Mahogany, Plank Top, Iron Stretcher, 29 x 36 x 80 In. 920.00
Table, Baroque, Walnut, Vine Legs, X-Stretcher, Continental, 31 x 50 x 24 In. 590.00
Table, Baroque, Walnut, Wrought-Iron Stretcher, Bobbin-Turned Legs, 49 In. 3824.00
Table, Basswood, Pine, Yellow Paint, Red & Blue Flowers, 34 x 19 x 30 In. 575.00
Table, Biedermeier, Ash, Round, Baluster Support, 3 Hipped Legs, 30 x 42 In. 1315.00
Table, Biedermeier, Birch, Cyma-Molded Apron, Cheval Base, 18 x 23 In. 518.00
Table, Biedermeier, Birch, Granite Top, Cheval Base, Drop Finials, 17 x 23 In. 535.00
Table, Biedermeier, Burl Walnut, Pedestal, 4 Feet, c.1850, 29 x 23 x 18 In. 1610.00
Table, Biedermeier, Burl, Banded Round Top, Mid 1800s, 31 x 24 In. 3680.00
Table, Biedermeier, Elm, Round, Frieze Drawer, Paw Feet, 1800s, 30 x 50 x 35 In. 4140.00
Table, Biedermeier, Fruitwood, Parquetry, Oak Inlay, 28 x 35 In. 5520.00
Table, Biedermeier, Mahogany, Oval, Lyre Pedestal, 28 x 23 x 19 In., Pair 840.00
Table, Biedermeier, Mahogany, Rectangular, Column Supports, 31 x 26 x 16 In. 1495.00
Table, Biedermeier, Maple, Frieze Drawer, Scrolling Legs, 27 x 32 x 16 In., Pair 920.00
Table, Biedermeier, Walnut, Maple, Stringing, Baluster Pedestal, 29 x 42 In. 5020.00
Table, Bijouterie, Edwardian, Mahogany, Inlaid, Kidney Shape, Lift Top, 21 In. 1150.00
Table, Birch, Macassar Ebony, Rosewood, Fruitwood, c.1927, 24 x 29 1/2 In. 4200.00
Table, Black Lacquer, 3 Intertwining Horns, 29 1/2 x 46 1/2 x 26 In. 3680.00
Table, Black Lacquer, Papier-Mache, Chinese Landscape, Scalloped, 30 x 16 In. 1095.00
Table, Blond Wood, Parchment, Glass Top, c.1930, 16 1/2 x 41 3/4 x 19 3/4 In. 3825.00
Table, Brass, 2 Tiers, France, Mid 19th Century, 22 x 25 x 11 In., Pair 3450.00
Table, Bugatti, Wood, Vellum Covered, Inlaid, c.1902, 29 x 25 In. 11355.00
Table, Burl Walnut Veneer, Scalloped Edge, Tripod, 20th Century, 27 x 24 In. 105.00
Table, Burl Walnut, Marquetry Medallion, Round, Tripod Base, 20 In. 440.00
Table, Burl Walnut, Scalloped Edge, Alabaster Pedestal, c.1850, 29 x 21 x 26 In. 715.00
Table, C. Malmsten, Burl Elm, Birch, Ash, 1917, 27 3/4 x 34 x 22 In. 1920.00
Table, C. Malmsten, Mahogany, Birch, c.1926, 24 1/2 x 35 1/2 In. 1200.00
Table, California Mission, 4-Tile Top, Butterflies, Wood Base, 18 x 17 3/4 In. 235.00
Table, Card, Apple Wood, Inlaid, Springfield, Mass., 36 1/4 In. 12500.00
Table, Card, Empire, Flip Top, Pedestal, 19th Century, 30 x 34 x 17 In. 130.00
Table, Card, Empire, Mahogany, Carved, Platform Base, Paw Feet, 36 x 17 x 30 In. 460.00
Table, Card, Empire, Mahogany, Flip Top, Lyre Base, 29 x 35 3/4 x 17 3/4 In. 345.00
Table, Card, Empire, Mahogany, Rectangular Top, Pedestal, c.1835, 31 x 36 x 18 In. 500.00
Table, Card, Empire, Mahogany, Rectangular, Pedestal, c.1835, 25 x 36 x 18 In. 880.00
Table, Card, Empire, U-Shape Base, Scroll Feet, 28 1/2 x 34 x 16 1/2 In. 115.00
Table, Card, Federal, Birch, Inlaid, Hinged Top, Bowed Ends, N.H., 30 x 36 x 17 In. 1265.00
Table, Card, Federal, Mahogany, Bird's-Eye Maple Veneer, Mass., c.1800, 29 x 36 In. 2700.00
Table, Card, Federal, Mahogany, c.1820, 27 x 35 3/4 x 34 In. 480.00
Table, Card, Federal, Mahogany, Carved, Flip Top, William Hook, c.1810, 36 x 18 In. 3055.00
Table, Card, Federal, Mahogany, Demilune Top, String Inlay, c.1795, 29 x 36 In. 1295.00
Table, Card, Federal, Mahogany, Demilune, 3-Panel Skirt, 30 x 36 In. 2468.00
Table, Card, Federal, Mahogany, Flame Veneer, Rope Twist, 36 x 18 x 30 In. 575.00
Table, Card, Federal, Mahogany, Inlaid, c.1800, 29 1/2 x 36 x 17 1/2 In. 2270.00
Table, Card, Federal, Mahogany, Inlaid, Flip Top, Mass., c.1795, 29 x 35 x 16 In. 2468.00

Furniture, Stand, Rosewood, Trestle Base, Tin Lining Under Top, 28 x 20 In.

Furniture, Table, Charles X, Burl Elm, Troubadour, Scalloped Apron, c.1810, 27 In.

Furniture, Table, Coffee, Kindt-Larsen, Teak, Inlay, Raised Lip, 16 x 72 In.

Table, Card, Federal, Mahogany, Inlaid, New England, c.1800, 29 x 16 x 34 In. 2390.00
Table, Card, Federal, Mahogany, Inlay, Tapered Legs, c.1800, 30 x 36 In. 3055.00
Table, Card, Federal, Mahogany, Maple Veneer, Boston, c.1800, 31 x 35 1/2 In. 5580.00
Table, Card, Federal, Mahogany, Shaped Top, Philadelphia, c.1815, 29 x 36 In. 940.00
Table, Card, George III, Mahogany, Oak, Drawer, 36 x 17 x 29 In. 575.00
Table, Card, George III, Rosewood, Ebonized Wood Inlay, c.1800, 29 x 37 x 18 In. 2530.00
Table, Card, Hepplewhite Style, Mahogany, Inlay, Serpentine Apron, 36 x 17 x 31 In. 460.00
Table, Card, Hepplewhite, Mahogany, Diamonds, New England, c.1800, 28 x 36 In. 1700.00
Table, Card, Hepplewhite, Mahogany, Inlay, Demilune Top, c.1810, 29 x 35 In. 1035.00
Table, Card, Hepplewhite, Mahogany, New England, Early 1800s, 28 x 35 In. 1400.00
Table, Card, Hepplewhite, Mahogany, Serpentine, Mass., 1790-1810, 29 x 35 In. 2100.00
Table, Card, Hepplewhite, Mahogany, Veneer, Oval Corners, 29 1/2 x 35 In. 1840.00
Table, Card, Mahogany Inlay, Bellflowers, 20th Century, 30 x 36 x 18 In., Pair 2235.00
Table, Card, Mahogany, Bowfront, Flip Top, N.H., c.1810, 29 x 36 x 18 In. 2585.00
Table, Card, Mahogany, Demilune, Flip Top, 20th Century, 30 x 47 x 23 In. 440.00
Table, Card, Mahogany, Inlaid, Pencil-Line Inlay, c.1790, 36 x 29 x 18 In. 1645.00
Table, Card, Mahogany, Inlaid, Rectangular, Rounded Corners, 29 x 36 In. 2235.00
Table, Card, Mahogany, Inlaid, Swelled Front, Flip Top, 5 Legs, c.1810, 36 x 29 1/2 In. . . . 700.00
Table, Card, Mahogany, Veneers, Concave Apron, Scrolled Legs, 30 x 35 x 17 1/2 In. 2415.00
Table, Card, Neoclassical, Black, Gold, Scrolls, Geese, Phila., 29 x 36 x 18 In. 7475.00
Table, Card, Neoclassical, Mahogany, Flip Top, Maryland, c.1815, 29 x 44 x 21 In. 765.00
Table, Card, Neoclassical, Mahogany, Rectangular Top, c.1820, 30 x 40 In. 1410.00
Table, Card, Neoclassical, Mahogany, Swivel Top, N.Y., c.1820, 30 x 37 x 19 In., Pair 2235.00
Table, Card, Neoclassical, Mahogany, Veneer, c.1825, 28 x 36 x 16 In. 470.00
Table, Card, Queen Anne Style, Demilune, Flip Top, Curved Skirt, 30 x 30 x 16 In. 865.00
Table, Card, Sheraton, Flip Top, Swing Leg, 30 x 41 1/2 x 33 1/2 In. 175.00
Table, Card, Sheraton, Mahogany Inlay, Fluted Legs, 29 x 38 x 18 In. 1380.00
Table, Card, Sheraton, Mahogany, Banded Inlay, Black Paint, 35 x 17 x 29 In. 660.00
Table, Card, Sheraton, Mahogany, Bird's-Eye Maple, Serpentine, 31 x 36 In. 750.00
Table, Card, Sheraton, Mahogany, Flip Top, Phila., c.1810, 35 3/4 x 29 x 17 In. 1115.00
Table, Card, Sheraton, Mahogany, Inlaid Top, Ring-Turned Legs, England, 29 x 36 In. 489.00
Table, Card, Sheraton, Serpentine, Hinged Top, 5 Reeded Legs, 1800s, 29 x 37 In. 1725.00
Table, Card, Victorian, Walnut, Oval, Bands, Splayed Legs, Mid 1800s, 16 x 48 In. 1265.00
Table, Cast Iron, Art Deco, Flowers, 1920s, 19 x 21 In. 127.00
Table, Cast Iron, Bellflower & Shell Design, Glass Top, 24 x 14 x 22 In. 60.00
Table, Cast Iron, Painted, Marble Top, Scrolling Base, Continental, 37 x 27 x 26 In. 805.00
Table, Center, Aesthetic Revival, Marble, Turret Corners, 31 x 47 x 31 In. 3995.00
Table, Center, Aesthetic Revival, Walnut, Carved Discs, Turned Legs, 30 In. 750.00
Table, Center, Aesthetic Revival, Walnut, Marquetry, 28 In. 200.00
Table, Center, Biedermeier, Satinwood, Ebony Band, Round, c.1900, 31 x 29 In. 3220.00
Table, Center, Eastlake, Walnut, Turned Center Post, Flat Cut Legs, 32 In. 145.00
Table, Center, Eastlake, Walnut, Turned Pedestal, c.1875, 26 x 28 x 20 In. 80.00
Table, Center, Elm, Square Top, Openwork Apron, Chinese, c.1880, 32 x 36 3/8 In. 345.00
Table, Center, Empire Style, Iron, Marble Top, Hexagonal Base, 32 x 50 In. 6615.00

Table, Center, Empire, Mahogany, Marble Top, 1800s, 30 x 43 3/8 In. 2415.00
Table, Center, Empire, Rosewood, Marble Top, Gothic Arches, c.1830, 29 x 26 In. 2940.00
Table, Center, George III Style, Mahogany, Tilt Top, Round, 4 Legs, c.1900, 30 x 44 In. ... 575.00
Table, Center, Gilt, Porcelain Top, Sleeping Scene, 31 x 19 In. 4370.00
Table, Center, Louis Philippe, Mahogany, Marble Top, c.1835, 31 x 37 1/2 In. 6900.00
Table, Center, Mahogany, Burl, Starburst, Continental, c.1850, 29 x 25 1/2 In. 1840.00
Table, Center, Neoclassical, Mahogany, Marble Top, Tripod, Russia, c.1815, 33 x 33 In. ... 9775.00
Table, Center, Neoclassical, Walnut, Carved Shell, S-Shape Feet, American, 32 x 50 In. ... 1555.00
Table, Center, Oak, Octagonal, 8 Turned Legs, c.1910, 27 x 18 In. 460.00
Table, Center, Regency, Mahogany, Round, Rosewood Banding, c.1815, 30 x 54 In. 7765.00
Table, Center, Regency, Mahogany, Tilt Top, Round, Ireland, c.1815, 30 x 57 In. 3220.00
Table, Center, Regency, Rosewood, Tilt Top, Round, c.1815, 29 x 50 In. 2990.00
Table, Center, Renaissance Revival, George Washington, Centennial, 27 x 45 In. 20900.00
Table, Center, Renaissance Revival, Walnut, Marble Top, 18 x 24 x 34 In. 750.00
Table, Center, Rococo Revival, Rosewood, Marble Top, American, c.1865, 29 x 51 In. 8050.00
Table, Center, Rococo Revival, Rosewood, Marble, Turtle Top, c.1850, 31 x 48 x 31 In. ... 5875.00
Table, Center, Rosewood, Round Top, Tapered Column, c.1880, 30 x 50 1/2 In. 1495.00
Table, Center, Victorian, Oval Marble Top, Flat Carved & Turned Center Post, 34 x 30 In. . 375.00
Table, Center, Victorian, Walnut, Beveled Edge, Carved Frame, 33 x 24 x 30 In. 315.00
Table, Center, Walnut, Beveled Top, Turned Center Post, 29 x 32 In. 259.00
Table, Center, Walnut, Octagonal, Turned Pedestal Base, 19th Century, 30 x 29 In. 58.00
Table, Center, William IV Style, Mahogany, Rosewood Band, Splayed Legs, 65 In. 3680.00
Table, Center, William IV, Mahogany, Round, Tilt Top, 3-Footed, c.1835, 29 x 52 In. 2300.00
Table, Charles X, Bird's-Eye Maple, Marquetry, String Inlay, 28 x 22 In. 2760.00
Table, Charles X, Burl Elm, Troubadour, Scalloped Apron, c.1810, 27 In. .... *Illus* 2900.00
Table, Charles X, Mahogany, Marble Top, Mid 19th Century, 28 1/2 x 38 In. 1610.00
Table, Chinese Chippendale, Mahogany, Heart-Shape Top, 3 Pierced Legs, 29 x 36 In. 2990.00
Table, Chinese Rosewood, Scrolled Apron, Shelf, Beaded Legs, 28 x 16 x 12 In., Pair 690.00
Table, Chippendale Style, Mahogany, Carved Skirt, Pedestal, 32 x 16 x 16 In. 115.00
Table, Chippendale, Mahogany, Square Legs, 28 x 36 x 16 1/2 In. 1150.00
Table, Coffee, Art Deco, Mahogany, Round, Shelf, 22 x 23 1/2 In. 2070.00
Table, Coffee, Art Deco, Rosewood, Mother-Of-Pearl, Brass, c.1928, 31 x 17 x 13 In. 2760.00
Table, Coffee, Chinese Red Crackle Lacquer, c.1900, 33 x 37 x 37 In. 315.00
Table, Coffee, Chinese, Lacquered, Red, Strapwork Skirt, Early 1900s, 20 x 38 x 38 In. ... 633.00
Table, Coffee, Eero Saarinen, No. 166MW, Pedestal Group, Knoll, c.1956, 15 x 36 In. 1115.00
Table, Coffee, Eero Saarinen, No. 167MC, Pedestal Group, Knoll, c.1956, 15 In. 999.00
Table, Coffee, Faux Marble, Silver, Scalloped Edge, Drop Leaf, Italy, 21 x 42 In. 1150.00
Table, Coffee, Felix Davin, Ebonized Wood, Glass, c.1930, 17 x 53 x 15 In. 1080.00
Table, Coffee, Frankl, Cork Top, Round, Mahogany Legs, Brass Caps, 36 x 14 In. 325.00
Table, Coffee, French Provincial, Marble Top, 18 x 43 In. 375.00
Table, Coffee, G. Nakashima, English Walnut, 1963, 12 3/4 x 46 1/2 In. 7000.00
Table, Coffee, G. Nakashima, Persian Walnut, c.1973, 16 x 59 x 22 In. 15535.00
Table, Coffee, G. Nakashima, Slab, Black Walnut, c.1952, 12 x 100 x 20 In. 11750.00
Table, Coffee, G. Nakashima, Slab, Black Walnut, c.1952, 14 x 89 1/4 x 20 In. 8815.00
Table, Coffee, G. Nelson, Wrought Iron, Glass Top, Arbuck, 1950s, 36 x 21 x 15 In. 345.00
Table, Coffee, George III Style, Yew, Crossbanded, Splayed Legs, 48 In. 1150.00
Table, Coffee, Gilt, Glass Turtle Top, Scrolled Legs, 17 x 47 x 39 In. 4600.00
Table, Coffee, Jules Wabbes, Hardwood, Glass, c.1960, 15 x 60 In. 4780.00
Table, Coffee, Karl Springer, Wood Patchwork Top, Brass Trim, 51 x 26 x 17 In. 635.00
Table, Coffee, Kindt-Larsen, Teak, Inlay, Raised Lip, 16 x 72 In. .... *Illus* 470.00
Table, Coffee, Lift Glass Tray, Oval, Carved Nude Figure In Well, 27 x 19 In. 220.00
Table, Coffee, Louis Sognot, Oak, Chromed Metal Mount, c.1930, 25 x 33 1/2 In. 3585.00
Table, Coffee, Louis XV Style, Beech, Marble Top, Early 1900s, 17 x 44 x 21 In. 115.00
Table, Coffee, Louis XVI Style, Multicolor, Marble Top, Brass, Oval, 26 x 38 x 32 In. 1380.00
Table, Coffee, Mahogany, Ship Door, Brass Porthole, 16 x 57 1/2 x 27 3/4 In. 375.00
Table, Coffee, Mahogany, Tooled Leather, Faux Bamboo, Round, England, 19 x 40 In. 520.00
Table, Coffee, Marquetry, 20th Century, 19 x 33 x 23 In. 410.00
Table, Coffee, Metal, Rectangular Glass Top, Brass Finish, Knoll, 17 x 42 x 20 In. 235.00
Table, Coffee, Mirror Top, Oval, Brass Gallery, Fluted Legs, 1900s, 21 x 51 In. 115.00
Table, Coffee, Moredo, Walnut, Dowel Legs, Raised Lip, Denmark, 73 x 22 x 18 In. 470.00
Table, Coffee, Painted, Mirrored Glass, c.1940, France, 17 x 54 3/4 x 19 5/8 In. 300.00
Table, Coffee, Paul Mayen, Pink Granite, Chromed Steel, 36 x 14 In. 1410.00
Table, Coffee, Philip & Kelvin LaVerne, Pewter, Bronze, c.1950, 17 x 42 In. 4830.00

Table, Coffee, Plywood, Steel, 10 1/2 x 89 1/2 x 29 3/4 In. 5378.00
Table, Coffee, Poul Kjaerholm, Stainless Steel, Glass, 12 3/4 x 37 1/2 In. 850.00
Table, Coffee, Ramsay, Gilt Bronze, Glass, Ram's Head Legs, c.1940, 18 x 43 In. 7800.00
Table, Coffee, Ramsay, Gilt Bronze, Marble, c.1940, 15 x 26 3/4 In. 2400.00
Table, Coffee, Rohde, Low, Wood, Herman Miller, c.1938, 15 x 44 x 22 In. 1175.00
Table, Coffee, Rosewood, Chromium Steel, Glazed Tile, 16 3/4 x 48 x 18 In. 400.00
Table, Coffee, Sheraton Style, Mahogany, Oval, 17 x 46 x 26 In. 92.00
Table, Coffee, Teak Inlay, India, Early 20th Century, 18 1/2 x 40 x 19 3/4 In. 230.00
Table, Coffee, Teak, Elliptical Glass Top, 59 x 19 x 18 In. 1175.00
Table, Coffee, Teak, Round, Denmark, c.1965, 48 In. 120.00
Table, Coffee, Victorian, Walnut, Marble Top, 20th Century, 19 1/2 x 37 x 27 In. 85.00
Table, Coffee, W. Platner, Chrome, Glass Top, Knoll, c.1966, 15 x 42 In. 865.00
Table, Coffee, Wegner, Wood, Round, Denmark, 16 1/2 x 49 In. 765.00
Table, Coffee, Wegner, Wood, Shelf, Andreas Tuck, c.1950, 20 x 51 1/2 x 20 In. 825.00
Table, Coffee, William Alexander, Laminated, c.1955, 13 3/4 x 70 In. 855.00
Table, Coffee, Wormley, Mahogany, Brass Stretchers, 48 x 28 x 22 In. 380.00
Table, Coffee, Wormley, Mahogany, Swagged Apron, 1940, 34 x 13 In. 325.00
Table, Console, Adam Style, Mixed Wood, Painted, Inlaid, Elliptical, 32 x 64 In. 1610.00
Table, Console, Art Deco, Pierced Iron Frieze, Marble Top, 30 x 51 x 24 In. 2760.00
Table, Console, Baroque Style, Mahogany, Marble Top, 3 Drawers, 36 x 88 In. 3220.00
Table, Console, Beaux Arts Style, Wrought Iron, Marble Top, 39 x 58 x 12 In. 2760.00
Table, Console, Biedermeier, Mahogany, Demilune, c.1900, 33 x 37 1/2 x 19 In. 2990.00
Table, Console, Cherry, D-Shape, Skirt, 19th Century, 29 x 42 x 21 In. 1035.00
Table, Console, Demilune, Serpentine Top, Late 20th Century, 30 x 40 x 21 In. 70.00
Table, Console, Directoire, Mahogany, Marble Top, c.1800, 31 x 41 x 19 In. 1150.00
Table, Console, Directoire, Mahogany, Marble Top, Frieze Drawer, 35 x 40 x 20 In. 3220.00
Table, Console, Ebonized, Gilt, Faux Marble, Painted Contortionist, 37 x 44 x 18 In. 956.00
Table, Console, Elm, Half-Round Top, Shaped Legs, Chinese, c.1890, 33 x 37 x 19 In. 259.00
Table, Console, Empire Style, Mahogany, Black Marble Top, 34 x 49 x 21 In. 4600.00
Table, Console, Empire, Cuban Mahogany, Marble Top, c.1800, 35 x 51 x 19 In. 2070.00
Table, Console, Empire, Mahogany, Marble Top, c.1800, 37 x 43 x 17 In. 2530.00
Table, Console, English Yew, Mahogany, Oyster Veneer, 31 x 45 x 19 In. 750.00
Table, Console, Federal, Mahogany, Batten Edge, c.1810, 35 x 13 x 30 In. 1645.00
Table, Console, Federal, Ribbed Legs, Stretcher, Brass Feet, Casters, 29 x 36 x 19 In. 2875.00
Table, Console, French Provincial, Kingwood Veneer, Demilune, 30 x 25 x 13 1/2 In. 380.00
Table, Console, G. Poillerat, Wrought Iron, Onyx, 1900s, 35 x 35 x 9 In. 8550.00
Table, Console, George II Style, Gilt, Marble Top, 36 1/2 x 50 In., Pair 3335.00
Table, Console, George III Style, Mahogany, Gilt, c.1900, 33 x 44 1/2 In., Pair 9775.00
Table, Console, George III Style, Mahogany, Gilt, c.1900, 33 x 56 In. 4370.00
Table, Console, George III Style, Walnut, Mahogany, Demilune, 33 x 45 x 19 In., Pair 2300.00
Table, Console, George III Style, Walnut, Scalloped Apron, 31 x 54 x 19 In. 920.00
Table, Console, George III, Pine, Mahogany, c.1785, 35 x 40 x 18 In., Pair 7475.00
Table, Console, Gilt Iron, Marble Top, Early 20th Century, 36 x 24 x 14 In. 460.00
Table, Console, Gilt Wrought Metal, Black Marble Top, 68 In. 1520.00
Table, Console, Gilt, Marble Top, 2 Dolphins, Italy, 37 x 49 x 23 In., Pair 5060.00
Table, Console, Hepplewhite Style, Mahogany, Demilune, 33 x 45 x 20 In., Pair 2185.00
Table, Console, Hepplewhite, Mahogany, Drawers, Doors, 29 x 17 1/2 x 26 In. 1725.00
Table, Console, L. & J.G. Stickley, 2 Drawers, 28 3/4 x 40 x 19 In. 2115.00
Table, Console, Leaf-Carved Frieze, Gilt, Marble Top, 12 x 8 x 15 In. 2015.00
Table, Console, Lifetime Furniture, 2 Drawers, Mich., c.1916, 32 x 60 In. 2800.00
Table, Console, Lifetime Puritan, Drawer, Corbels, Paine Furn. Co., 31 x 67 In. . . . . . *Illus* 5288.00
Table, Console, Limbert, Rectangular, Shelf, 30 x 36 x 17 In. 940.00
Table, Console, Louis XIV Style, Ivory, Gilt, Yellow Marble Top, 34 x 60 x 22 In. 2690.00
Table, Console, Louis XIV Style, Mahogany, Lift Top, 31 x 60 x 19 In. 780.00
Table, Console, Louis XV Style, Gilt, White Marble Top, 1900s, 32 x 40 x 13 In. 265.00
Table, Console, Louis XV Style, Gilt, White Marble Top, 39 x 48 x 18 In. 780.00
Table, Console, Louis XV Style, Iron, Marble, c.1950, 35 x 42 x 18 In. 635.00
Table, Console, Louis XV Style, Ivory, Teal Paint, Smoky Mirror, 34 x 44 x 14 In., Pair . . . 1315.00
Table, Console, Louis XV Style, Mahogany, Cabriole Legs, 32 x 16 x 31 In., Pair 375.00
Table, Console, Louis XV Style, Marble, Carved Frieze, 33 x 77 x 23 In. 2990.00
Table, Console, Louis XV Style, Serpentine, Marble Top, 52 x 18 In. 575.00
Table, Console, Louis XVI Style, Brass, Wrought Iron, 18 x 53 x 35 1/2 In. 2070.00
Table, Console, Louis XVI Style, Gilt, Marble Top, c.1790, 34 x 47 x 23 In. 3680.00

Table, Console, Louis XVI Style, Mahogany, Marble, Demilune, 33 x 39 x 20 In.	1380.00
Table, Console, Louis XVI Style, Multicolor, Marble Top, Reeded Legs, 33 x 93 In.	635.00
Table, Console, Louis XVI Style, Oak, Marble Top, 28 x 30 x 20 In.	1265.00
Table, Console, Louis XVI Style, Painted, Marble Top, 32 1/2 x 22 1/2 x 46 In.	950.00
Table, Console, Louis XVI Style, White Marble Top, 1900s, 34 x 43 x 22 In.	940.00
Table, Console, Louis XVI, Gilt, Marble Top, Late 18th Century, 30 x 30 x 16 In.	4140.00
Table, Console, Mahogany, Carved Apron, Claw & Ball Feet, 33 x 43 x 18 In.	530.00
Table, Console, Mahogany, Fluted Frieze, Square Tapered Legs, 33 x 69 In.	3100.00
Table, Console, Mahogany, Inlaid, Burl Panel, D-Shape Top, 32 x 46 x 16 In.	2415.00
Table, Console, Mahogany, Rosewood Veneer, 20th Century, 31 x 34 x 16 In.	200.00
Table, Console, Napoleon III, Beech, Polychrome, White Wash, 33 x 45 x 21 In.	3450.00
Table, Console, Neoclassical, Beech, Lapis Blue, Parcel Gilt, 36 x 30 x 15 In., Pair	2530.00
Table, Console, Neoclassical, Mahogany, Carved, Marble, 1800s, 36 x 46 x 20 In.	10060.00
Table, Console, Neoclassical, Mahogany, Marble Top, Demilune, 40 x 33 x 16 1/2 In.	1095.00
Table, Console, Neoclassical, Mahogany, Serpentine Marble Top, 29 x 35 x 21 In.	490.00
Table, Console, Neoclassical, Mahogany, Serpentine Top, c.1850, 28 x 34 x 14 In.	805.00
Table, Console, Neoclassical, Polychrome, Marble Top, Stretcher, 33 x 38 x 18 In.	4140.00
Table, Console, Oak, Carved Apron, Lion's Mask, Mid 19th Century, 65 In.	880.00
Table, Console, Oriental, Hardwood, Carved, Demilune, 34 x 52 x 26 In., Pair	1380.00
Table, Console, P. Evans, Burl Veneer, Patchwork, Brass, 72 x 20 x 27 In.	1060.00
Table, Console, Paneled Frieze, Gilt, Faux Marble, 1800s, 35 x 27 x 15 In., Pair	5290.00
Table, Console, Paul Laszlo, Folding, Brown Saltman, c.1939, 29 x 60 x 36 In.	999.00
Table, Console, Polychrome, Marble Top, c.1900, 34 1/2 x 53 x 25 1/2 In.	3450.00
Table, Console, Regency Style, Carved, Gilt, France, c.1880, 33 x 80 x 48 In.	12650.00
Table, Console, Regency, Burl Walnut, Ebonized Paw Feet, c.1835, 38 x 48 In., Pair	5520.00
Table, Console, Regency, Mahogany, Marble Top, Early 1800s, 36 x 37 x 18 In.	1725.00
Table, Console, Regency, Mahogany, Marble Top, Inset, Figures, 45 x 42 x 23 In.	978.00
Table, Console, Regency, Rosewood, Ogee-Molded Frieze, 40 x 62 x 20 In.	2300.00
Table, Console, Robsjohn-Gibbings, Wood, White Paint, Marble, 30 x 44 x 13 In.	10755.00
Table, Console, Rococo, Painted, Green Marble Top, 34 x 45 x 23 In.	5220.00
Table, Console, Sheraton Style, Mahogany, Demilune, Spade Feet, c.1850, 29 x 54 In.	800.00
Table, Console, Victorian, Mahogany, Carved, c.1875, 32 x 56 1/2 x 19 In.	750.00
Table, Console, Walnut, Marble Top, Gilt Lion's Heads, c.1815, 35 x 38 In., Pair	6325.00
Table, Console, Wrought Iron, Mottled Red Marble Top, France, 49 x 38 In.	3200.00
Table, Console, Wrought Iron, Shells & Leaves, Green Marble Top, 35 x 60 In.	2760.00
Table, Corner, Drop Leaf, Gateleg, England, 20th Century, 25 x 19 1/2 In.	190.00
Table, Corner, Mahogany, Bowed Front, Millwork, Continental, 32 x 20 x 28 In., Pair	1840.00
Table, Dinette, Arne Jacobsen, Pedestal, Fritz Hansen, c.1958, 28 3/4 x 35 1/2 In.	999.00
Table, Dinette, I. Noguchi, No. 311, Knoll, c.1954, 28 3/4 x 35 3/4 In.	1175.00
Table, Dining, Art Deco, Oval, Geometric Inlay, Medallion, c.1930, 30 x 72 x 44 In.	1410.00
Table, Dining, Arts & Crafts, Rectangular, Shelf, Cutout Sides, c.1912, x 84 x 35 In.	3175.00
Table, Dining, B. Mathsson, Folding, K. Mathsson, c.1936, 28 1/2 x 35 1/2 x 110 In.	2940.00
Table, Dining, Baroque Style, Mahogany, Gilt, Double Pedestal, 30 x 70 x 42 In.	478.00
Table, Dining, Biedermeier, Walnut, Ebonized, Hexagonal Pedestal, 31 x 52 In.	3680.00
Table, Dining, Borge Mogensen, Wood, 2 Leaves, c.1955, 29 x 55 x 35 1/2 In.	1410.00
Table, Dining, Carlo Scarpa, Glass Top, Steel Legs, Rectangular, 28 x 36 x 86 In.	1195.00
Table, Dining, Cast Iron, Painted, White, Round, Lower Shelf, 27 x 39 In.	720.00

Furniture, Table, Console, Lifetime Puritan, Drawer, Corbels, Paine Furn. Co., 31 x 67 In.

Furniture, Table, Dining, Ejner Larsen, A. Bender Madsen, Denmark, 1950s, 28 x 51 In.

Table, Dining, Drop Leaf, Chippendale, Tiger Maple, New England, 28 x 43 x 15 In. 520.00
Table, Dining, Drop Leaf, Federal, 2 Pedestals, c.1810, 29 x 50 1/2 x 93 1/2 In. 5520.00
Table, Dining, Drop Leaf, Federal, Maple, Birch, New England, 1800s, 28 x 36 In. 720.00
Table, Dining, Drop Leaf, Federal, Tiger Maple, New England, c.1805, 28 x 16 In. 5300.00
Table, Dining, Drop Leaf, Mahogany, Oval, 6 Tapered Legs, Pad Feet, 58 x 20 In. 3680.00
Table, Dining, Drop Leaf, Mahogany, Reeded Edge, 20th Century, 30 x 65 x 48 In. 295.00
Table, Dining, Drop Leaf, Mahogany, Straight Skirt, Tapered Legs, 29 x 48 In. 1528.00
Table, Dining, Drop Leaf, Neoclassical, Mahogany, Veneer, c.1830, 28 x 39 In. 1315.00
Table, Dining, Drop Leaf, Pine, Red Paint, 19th Century, 29 x 43 x 61 In. 2030.00
Table, Dining, Drop Leaf, Queen Anne, Walnut, Late 1700s, 28 x 50 In. 765.00
Table, Dining, Drop Leaf, Queen Anne, Walnut, Mid 1700s, 40 x 43 x 27 In. 1528.00
Table, Dining, Drop Leaf, Sheraton Style, 19th Century, 29 x 42 x 60 In. 230.00
Table, Dining, Drop Leaf, Sheraton Style, Mahogany, 19th Century, 30 x 51 x 72 In. 175.00
Table, Dining, Drop Leaf, Sheraton Style, Mahogany, 3 Pedestals, 30 x 41 x 62 In. 315.00
Table, Dining, Drop Leaf, Sheraton, Cherry, c.1825, 62 x 46 x 29 In. 355.00
Table, Dining, Drop Leaf, Walnut, Stringing, Bellflowers, 30 x 44 x 113 In. 4140.00
Table, Dining, Eero Saarinen, No. 164MC, Pedestal Group, Knoll, c.1956, 26 x 54 In. 518.00
Table, Dining, Eero Saarinen, Tulip, Aluminum, Laminate, Knoll, 29 x 54 In. 900.00
Table, Dining, Ejner Larsen, A. Bender Madsen, Denmark, 1950s, 28 x 51 In. . . . . *Illus* 1410.00
Table, Dining, Empire Style, Mahogany, Oval, Pedestal, Scroll Feet, 30 x 54 x 65 In. 1440.00
Table, Dining, Empire Style, Mahogany, Twist-Turned Legs, c.1890, 31 x 54 x 83 In. 978.00
Table, Dining, Federal Style, Mahogany, Satinwood, Leaves, 29 1/2 x 44 x 65 In. 1725.00
Table, Dining, Federal, Mahogany, 3 Sections, Silas Cheney, c.1790, 54 x 27 In. 8815.00
Table, Dining, Federal, Mahogany, Extension, Mass., 1810-20, 30 x 51 x 48 In. 3585.00
Table, Dining, Federal, Mahogany, Inlaid, D-Shape Sections, 29 x 80 1/2 In. 2300.00
Table, Dining, Federal, Walnut, Inlaid, 2 Sections, c.1795, 75 x 42 x 29 1/2 In. 1528.00
Table, Dining, G. Nakashima, Walnut, c.1960, 28 x 38 x 37 In. 2150.00
Table, Dining, G. Nelson, Walnut Top, H-Frame, Herman Miller, 1960, 30 x 96 In. 2940.00
Table, Dining, G. Stickley, No. 631, Oak, Clipped Corner, c.1903, 29 x 96 x 47 In. 23900.00
Table, Dining, G. Stickley, No. 634, Split Pedestal, 6 Leaves, 30 x 54 In. 8225.00
Table, Dining, G. Stickley, No. 656, Pedestal, 4 Shoe Feet, 29 x 54 In. 7640.00
Table, Dining, George III Style, Banding, 3 Pedestals, Splayed Legs, 30 x 52 In. 4600.00
Table, Dining, George III Style, Mahogany, 2 Pedestals, 29 x 65 x 40 In. 200.00
Table, Dining, George III Style, Mahogany, 2 Pedestals, 3 Leaves, 29 x 44 x 93 In. 950.00
Table, Dining, George III Style, Mahogany, 2 Pedestals, 41 x 46 In. 1240.00
Table, Dining, George III Style, Mahogany, 3 Pedestals, 2 Leaves, 29 x 150 In. 5325.00
Table, Dining, George III Style, Mahogany, 3 Pedestals, 20 1/2 x 35 3/4 In. 2520.00
Table, Dining, George III Style, Mahogany, 3 Pedestals, Fluted Supports, 23 x 36 In. 2350.00
Table, Dining, George III Style, Mahogany, Crossbanded, 3 Pedestals, 96 In. 3825.00
Table, Dining, George III Style, Mahogany, Inlaid, 2 Pedestals, 29 x 62 x 43 In. 980.00
Table, Dining, George III Style, Mahogany, Pedestal, Bulbous Standard, 30 x 104 In. 2530.00
Table, Dining, George III, Mahogany, Inlaid, Oval, 2 Pedestals, 43 x 66 In. 4600.00
Table, Dining, Georgian Style, Mahogany, 2 Pedestals, Leaf, c.1900s, 29 x 51 In. 2760.00
Table, Dining, Georgian Style, Mahogany, Pedestal, c.1840, 30 x 49 In. 2415.00
Table, Dining, Georgian Style, Mahogany, Turned Pedestal, 30 x 39 x 60 In. 575.00
Table, Dining, Georgian, Mahogany, Egg & Dart Edge, 2 Pedestals, Saber Legs, 48 In. 2875.00
Table, Dining, Horseshoe, George III, Mahogany, 32 x 63 x 88 In. 2300.00
Table, Dining, Horseshoe, Regency Style, Mahogany, 5 Extension Leaves, 62 In. 4370.00
Table, Dining, Horseshoe, Regency Style, Mahogany, 5 Leaves, 32 x 89 In. 2185.00
Table, Dining, I. Noguchi, Birch, Iron, Steel Wire, Laminate, Knoll, 29 x 36 In. 1645.00
Table, Dining, Josef Frank, Cherry, Leaves, 1941, 27 1/2 x 51 In. 1920.00
Table, Dining, Keiser, Enameled Steel, Glass, 30 x 35 x 70 In. 160.00
Table, Dining, L. & J.G. Stickley, No. 717, Round Top, Pedestal, 6 Leaves, 54 x 30 In. 5875.00
Table, Dining, L. & J.G. Stickley, Round Top, 5 Legs, 2 Leaves, 30 1/2 x 54 In. 1530.00
Table, Dining, Louis XV Style, Walnut, Carved, c.1900, 28 x 46 1/2 x 41 In. 230.00
Table, Dining, Mahogany, 2 Pedestals, Paw Feet, 31 x 41 x 72 1/2 In. 345.00
Table, Dining, Mahogany, Anglo-Indian, 1830-50, 60 x 47 In. 2750.00
Table, Dining, Mahogany, Carved, Folding Top, 3 Leaves, 30 x 40 x 74 In. 405.00
Table, Dining, Mahogany, Oval, Cabriole Legs, 2 Leaves, 1900s, 30 x 65 x 18 In. 165.00
Table, Dining, Mahogany, Oval, Painted Landscapes, Flowers, 61 x 44 In. 900.00
Table, Dining, Mahogany, Oval, Reeded Edges, 20th Century, 30 x 62 x 39 In. 265.00
Table, Dining, Mahogany, Round, Pedestal, 2 Leaves, c.1835, 29 x 53 x 153 In. 4025.00
Table, Dining, Meeks, Neoclassical, Mahogany, Accordion, N.Y.C., 1830, 30 x 56 In. 4780.00

Table, Dining, Mixed Wood, Late 19th Century, 30 x 36 x 72 In. 200.00
Table, Dining, Neoclassical, Mahogany, 2 Pedestals, Splayed Feet, 28 x 46 In. 3410.00
Table, Dining, Neoclassical, Mahogany, Round, 4 Leaves, Late 1800s, 30 x 54 x 106 In. ... 2530.00
Table, Dining, Oak, Round, Carved Claw Feet, 3-In. Apron, 48 x 23 In. 635.00
Table, Dining, P. Evans, Bronze, Glass, Serpentine Stalagmite Base, 96 x 48 x 29 In. 1880.00
Table, Dining, Paolo Buffa, Mahogany, Inlaid Glass Top, 32 x 79 x 39 In. 7770.00
Table, Dining, Poul Kjaerholm, Steel Oak, Green Marble, 27 x 80 x 40 In. 2200.00
Table, Dining, Prairie School, Round Top, Cutout Base, Shoefoot, 4 Leaves, 50 x 30 In. ... 3055.00
Table, Dining, Queen Anne Style, Mahogany, 2 Pedestals, Leaves, 29 x 58 x 44 In. 1555.00
Table, Dining, Queen Anne, Mahogany, Crossband Top, 2 Leaves, 30 x 106 x 44 In. 405.00
Table, Dining, Queen Anne, Walnut, Demilune, Straight Skirt, 29 x 50 x 19 In. 5580.00
Table, Dining, Regency Style, Mahogany, Pedestals, 2 Leaves, 29 x 49 x 124 In. 5520.00
Table, Dining, Regency Style, Mahogany, Rosewood Band, Extension, 30 x 52 In. 10350.00
Table, Dining, Rohde, All Walnut, Patchwork, Herman Miller, c.1940, 29 x 70 In. 2350.00
Table, Dining, Rohde, No. 3321, Formal Group, Herman Miller, c.1940, 29 x 60 In. 4115.00
Table, Dining, Rohde, Paldao, 2 Leaves, Herman Miller, 1939, 68 x 40 x 29 In. 3230.00
Table, Dining, Shaker, Black Walnut, 3-Board Top, 30 x 64 x 35 1/2 In. 4900.00
Table, Dining, Sheraton, Cherry, Mid 20th Century, 30 1/2 x 48 x 20 1/2 In. 100.00
Table, Dining, Sheraton, Spiral Carved, Gateleg, Caster Feet, 29 x 44 x 20 In. 805.00
Table, Dining, Shop Of The Crafters, No. 322, Round, Inlaid Flowers, 5 Legs, 29 x 50 In. . 2235.00
Table, Dining, Spanish Style, Pecan, Parquetry, 3 Leaves, 28 1/2 x 44 x 135 In. 489.00
Table, Dining, Stickley Bros., Circular Top, 4 Shoe Feet, 2 Leaves, 30 x 48 In. 2468.00
Table, Dining, Stickley Bros., No. 2638, Round Top, 5 Legs, 54 x 29 In. 1035.00
Table, Dining, Stickley Bros., Pedestal, Round Top, 12-In. Leaf, 30 x 48 In. 880.00
Table, Dining, Teak, Denmark, c.1960, 35 x 30 x 75 In. 175.00
Table, Dining, Victorian, Mahogany, Baluster Legs, Brass Casters, 29 x 48 x 91 In. 1000.00
Table, Dining, Victorian, Walnut, Raised Burl Panels, Incised, 48 x 29 In. 635.00
Table, Dining, Walnut, Cherry, D-Shape Ends, 4 Sections, c.1900, 30 x 42 x 84 In. 1035.00
Table, Dining, Walnut, Marquetry, Oval, Cabriole Legs, Continental, 30 x 43 x 69 In. 315.00
Table, Dining, Wegner, Round, Metal Mounts, Cross Stretcher, c.1960, 61 In. 1880.00
Table, Dining, William IV Style, Mahogany, 3 Pedestals, 30 x 52 x 102 In. 3220.00
Table, Dining, William IV, Mahogany, Round, Mid 19th Century, 29 1/2 x 49 In. 545.00
Table, Dining, Wormley, No. 4576, Mahogany, Dunbar, 28 x 42 x 30 In. 690.00
Table, Dining, Wormley, Walnut, Mahogany, Hexagonal, 2 Leaves, Dunbar, 29 x 52 In. ... 1410.00
Table, Directoire Style, Painted, Gilt Brass Mounts, Round, France, 30 x 19 In. 1035.00
Table, Directoire, Mahogany, Marble Dish Top, c.1800, 29 1/2 x 40 1/2 In. 1265.00
Table, Donald Deskey, Low, Black, Green, Silver, c.1930, 13 x 54 x 28 In. 1410.00
Table, Drafting, Directoire, Mahogany, Tulipwood, Early 1800s, 29 x 37 x 21 In. 8625.00
Table, Dressing, Beau Brummel, George III Style, Mahogany, c.1890, 32 x 22 In. 1265.00
Table, Dressing, Chippendale, Mahogany, 2 Drawers, Cabriole Legs, 29 In. 5875.00
Table, Dressing, Directoire, Mahogany, Stretcher, c.1800, 28 x 26 x 16 In. 690.00
Table, Dressing, Edwardian, Mahogany, Satinwood, Beveled Mirror, Drawers, 39 In. 420.00
Table, Dressing, Empire Style, Mahogany, Marble, Shaped Mirror, 63 x 19 x 13 In. 1035.00
Table, Dressing, Federal, Cherry, Frieze Drawer, Turned Legs, c.1820, 29 x 30 In. 546.00
Table, Dressing, Federal, Painted, Stencils, New England, c.1820, 36 x 33 In. 10200.00
Table, Dressing, G. Stickley, No. 914, Maple Veneer, Inlays, Tilt Mirror 27500.00
Table, Dressing, George III, Mahogany, Ebony, Brass Casters, 31 x 39 x 20 In. 150.00
Table, Dressing, George V, Mahogany, Inlaid, 3 Folding Sections, Silver Gilt 6900.00
Table, Dressing, Georgian Style, Mahogany, Mirror, Early 1900s, 57 x 39 x 17 In. 575.00
Table, Dressing, Georgian, Walnut, Drawer, Kneehole, 1700s, 29 x 32 x 19 In. 1880.00
Table, Dressing, Hepplewhite Style, Mahogany, 5 Drawers, c.1935, 31 x 43 In. 690.00
Table, Dressing, Kingwood, Gilt Metal Mounts, Continental, 76 x 40 x 17 In. 345.00
Table, Dressing, Louis XV Style, Parquetry, 4 Drawers, 29 x 13 x 32 In. 1330.00
Table, Dressing, Louis XV Style, Walnut Marquetry, Hinged Lid, 29 x 23 x 15 In. 355.00
Table, Dressing, Louis XV Style, Walnut, Carved, c.1900, 29 x 34 3/4 x 20 In. 200.00
Table, Dressing, Louis XV, Mahogany, Marquetry, Mirror, c.1900, 28 x 20 x 15 In. 175.00
Table, Dressing, Mahogany, Marble Top, c.1849, 72 1/2 x 38 x 20 In. 1725.00
Table, Dressing, Napoleon III, Kingwood, Sevres Style Plaque, 29 x 21 x 15 In. 1955.00
Table, Dressing, Neoclassical, Mahogany, Birch, New England, c.1820, 32 x 33 In. 1880.00
Table, Dressing, Painted Fruit Basket, Turned Legs, c.1830, 37 x 33 x 18 1/2 In. 765.00
Table, Dressing, Poplar, c.1820, 35 x 34 x 18 In. 695.00
Table, Dressing, Queen Anne Style, Walnut, 20th Century, 29 1/2 x 40 x 19 In. 225.00
Table, Dressing, Queen Anne Style, Walnut, Beveled Mirror, c.1900, 62 x 48 x 23 In. 290.00

Table, Dressing, Queen Anne, Walnut, New England, c.1755, 31 x 36 x 20 In. 11950.00
Table, Dressing, Queen Anne, Walnut, Pennsylvania, c.1750, 30 x 36 x 23 1/2 In. 16730.00
Table, Dressing, Satinwood, Inlaid, 4 Drawers, c.1900, 58 x 40 x 21 In. 460.00
Table, Dressing, Sheraton, Pine, Red & Yellow Paint, New England, 34 x 15 x 31 In. 2990.00
Table, Dressing, William IV, Mahogany, Marble Top, Cheval Mirror, 58 x 31 x 16 In. 518.00
Table, Drop Leaf, 2-Board Top, Drawer, Tapered Legs, 28 x 19 x 33 In. 315.00
Table, Drop Leaf, Butterfly Supports, Turned Legs, Box Stretcher, 23 x 25 x 20 In. 60.00
Table, Drop Leaf, Chestnut, Maple, Gateleg, 28 x 40 3/4 x 17 1/2 In. 635.00
Table, Drop Leaf, Chippendale Style, Rope Carved, Chinese, c.1880, 29 x 42 In. 865.00
Table, Drop Leaf, Chippendale, Curly Maple, Birch, Pine, 42 x 16 x 28 In. 1325.00
Table, Drop Leaf, Chippendale, Mahogany, Scalloped, 1700s, 29 x 17 x 48 In. 2300.00
Table, Drop Leaf, Chippendale, Walnut, c.1770, 29 x 45 3/4 x 20 In. 4800.00
Table, Drop Leaf, Country Pine, Rounded Leaves, Square Tapered Legs, 29 x 36 x 36 In. . . 173.00
Table, Drop Leaf, Edwardian, Satinwood, Painted, 2 Drawers, c.1900, 28 x 18 In. 3525.00
Table, Drop Leaf, Empire, Curly Maple, Bird's-Eye Veneer, 43 x 19 x 29 In. 315.00
Table, Drop Leaf, Empire, Mahogany Veneer, 2 Drawers, 29 x 15 x 19 In. 405.00
Table, Drop Leaf, Empire, Mahogany, Round Pedestal, 28 x 42 In. 144.00
Table, Drop Leaf, Empire, Pine, Drawers, Pedestal, Scroll Feet, 28 x 17 x 18 In. 115.00
Table, Drop Leaf, English Oak, Oval, Block-Turned Legs, c.1720, 29 x 45 x 54 In. 690.00
Table, Drop Leaf, Federal, Mahogany, 19th Century, 30 1/4 In. 235.00
Table, Drop Leaf, Federal, Mahogany, 2 Drawers, 29 x 29 3/4 x 26 In. 865.00
Table, Drop Leaf, Federal, Mahogany, 6 Legs, c.1820, 29 x 56 1/2 x 46 In. 575.00
Table, Drop Leaf, Federal, Mahogany, Breakfast, c.1825, 39 x 51 In. 2000.00
Table, Drop Leaf, Federal, Mahogany, Center Pedestal, Casters, 31 x 41 x 20 In. 2245.00
Table, Drop Leaf, Federal, Mahogany, Early 19th Century, 29 x 46 x 42 In. 900.00
Table, Drop Leaf, Federal, Maple, New England, c.1790, 22 x 35 x 27 1/2 In. 235.00
Table, Drop Leaf, Federal, Maple, New England, c.1800, 28 x 18 x 33 In. 1060.00
Table, Drop Leaf, Federal, Walnut, Rectangular Top, 1800s, 36 x 35 In. 235.00
Table, Drop Leaf, G. Nelson, Oak, Birch, c.1950, 40 x 18 1/2 x 30 In. 1060.00
Table, Drop Leaf, G. Nelson, Walnut Veneer, Gateleg, Herman Miller, 1948, 30 x 60 In. . . . 1765.00
Table, Drop Leaf, G. Stickley, Narrow Bottom Stretcher, Shoe Feet, 28 x 41 In. 2470.00
Table, Drop Leaf, George III, Mahogany, 1790, 24 In. 3200.00
Table, Drop Leaf, George III, Mahogany, Drawer, Pedestal, 25 x 36 In. 675.00
Table, Drop Leaf, George III, Mahogany, Ebony, 2 Drawers, Splayed Feet, 36 x 22 In. 3450.00
Table, Drop Leaf, Handkerchief, Georgian Style, Mahogany, 28 x 32 x 32 In. 1150.00
Table, Drop Leaf, Handkerchief, Queen Anne Style, Mahogany, Pad Feet, 33 x 17 In. 345.00
Table, Drop Leaf, Hepplewhite, Birch, Dovetailed Drawer, Tapered Legs, 15 x 36 In. 520.00
Table, Drop Leaf, Hepplewhite, Birch, Maple, Scrubbed Top, 28 x 41 In. 1208.00
Table, Drop Leaf, Hepplewhite, Cherry, Reeded-End Aprons, 19 x 39 x 28 In. 1095.00
Table, Drop Leaf, Hepplewhite, Cherry, Tapered Legs, 26 x 33 x 16 In. 315.00
Table, Drop Leaf, Hepplewhite, Cherry, Tapered Legs, 27 3/4 x 25 x 16 In. 635.00
Table, Drop Leaf, Hepplewhite, Cherry, Tiger Maple Inlay, Tapered Legs, 29 x 48 In. 9350.00
Table, Drop Leaf, Hepplewhite, Curly Maple, Pine, 40 x 16 In. 635.00
Table, Drop Leaf, Hepplewhite, Maple, Black Over Red Paint, 48 x 18 x 29 In. 115.00
Table, Drop Leaf, L. & J.G. Stickley, Rectangular Cutout Sides, 24 x 8 x 24 In. 440.00
Table, Drop Leaf, Mahogany, c.1825, 28 1/2 x 50 x 41 3/4 In. 805.00
Table, Drop Leaf, Mahogany, Cherry, Bird's-Eye Maple, c.1840, 31 x 17 1/2 x 30 In. 920.00
Table, Drop Leaf, Mahogany, Late 19th Century, 29 x 50 1/2 x 42 In. 225.00
Table, Drop Leaf, Mahogany, Turned Tapered Supports, c.1850, 14 x 8 In. 760.00
Table, Drop Leaf, Maple, Butterfly, Ring-Turned Legs, 1700s, 26 x 42 x 35 1/2 In. 5580.00
Table, Drop Leaf, Maple, Drawer, Gateleg, 26 x 40 x 15 1/2 In. 750.00
Table, Drop Leaf, McCobb, Walnut, Aluminum Stretchers, 25 1/2 x 54 In. 500.00
Table, Drop Leaf, Napoleon III, Ebonized Burl, Ormolu Mount, 30 x 28 x 44 In. 1265.00
Table, Drop Leaf, Napoleon III, Rosewood, Drawer, c.1865, 28 x 34 In. 1035.00
Table, Drop Leaf, Neoclassical, Early 19th Century, 47 1/2 x 38 x 28 In. 1058.00
Table, Drop Leaf, Neoclassical, Mahogany, Carved, Rectangular, c.1815, 29 x 42 In. 880.00
Table, Drop Leaf, Neoclassical, Marquetry, 20th Century, 27 x 35 x 18 In. 190.00
Table, Drop Leaf, Oak, Box Stretcher, Turned Legs, 17 x 20 x 30 In. 90.00
Table, Drop Leaf, Oak, Drawer, Tapered Legs, Pad Feet, 18th Century, 48 x 18 In. 635.00
Table, Drop Leaf, Oak, Hinged Oval Top, 29 x 51 x 46 In. 2015.00
Table, Drop Leaf, Oak, Splayed Base, Bamboo Stretchers, 24 x 10 x 10 In. 575.00
Table, Drop Leaf, Oak, Turned Legs, Extension Leaf, 42 x 24 x 28 In. 201.00
Table, Drop Leaf, Pine, Early 19th Century, 28 1/2 x 36 x 39 In. 115.00

Table, Drop Leaf, Pine, Mahogany Finish, 2 Drawers, Turned Legs, 29 x 16 x 17 In. 375.00
Table, Drop Leaf, Pine, Turned Legs, 28 x 39 In. 160.00
Table, Drop Leaf, Queen Anne Style, Cherry, Trifid Feet, 43 x 15 x 28 In. 115.00
Table, Drop Leaf, Queen Anne Style, Mahogany, Column Legs, 29 x 56 x 42 In. 579.00
Table, Drop Leaf, Queen Anne, Curly Maple, Pad Feet, Early 1700s, 45 In. 17250.00
Table, Drop Leaf, Queen Anne, Gateleg, c.1780, 54 x 41 In. 750.00
Table, Drop Leaf, Queen Anne, Mahogany, Early 1700s, 28 x 49 x 54 In. 1765.00
Table, Drop Leaf, Queen Anne, Mahogany, Oak, Pad Feet, 42 x 14 x 28 In. 290.00
Table, Drop Leaf, Queen Anne, Mahogany, Pad Feet, 27 x 42 x 12 In. 920.00
Table, Drop Leaf, Queen Anne, Mahogany, Pine, Drawer, 15 x 43 x 17 In. 575.00
Table, Drop Leaf, Queen Anne, Mahogany, Rectangular, Pad Feet, 27 x 52 In. 3525.00
Table, Drop Leaf, Queen Anne, Maple, Birch, Cabriole Legs, 15 x 48 x 27 In. 4600.00
Table, Drop Leaf, Queen Anne, Maple, Cabriole Legs, 28 x 15 x 46 In. 2070.00
Table, Drop Leaf, Queen Anne, Maple, Oval Top, Cabriole Legs, 29 x 48 x 17 In. 2130.00
Table, Drop Leaf, Queen Anne, Maple, Yellow Pine, 42 x 13 x 29 In. 865.00
Table, Drop Leaf, Queen Anne, Walnut, Pennsylvania, c.1750, 28 x 48 x 22 1/2 In. 7200.00
Table, Drop Leaf, Regency Style, Mahogany, Spider Gateleg, 28 x 27 x 34 In. 429.00
Table, Drop Leaf, Regency, Mahogany, Carved, Ebony Inlay, 28 x 21 x 32 In. 2820.00
Table, Drop Leaf, Regency, Mahogany, D-Shape Flaps, Trestle Supports, 27 x 36 x 26 In. . . 865.00
Table, Drop Leaf, Regency, Mahogany, Pedestal, Early 1800s, 28 x 27 x 50 In. 460.00
Table, Drop Leaf, Sheraton Style, Mahogany, 29 1/2 x 36 x 45 In. 35.00
Table, Drop Leaf, Sheraton Style, Mahogany, Gateleg, Late 1800s, 30 x 46 x 66 In. 345.00
Table, Drop Leaf, Sheraton, Gateleg, Brass Casters, 30 3/8 x 45 x 26 1/8 In. 748.00
Table, Drop Leaf, Sheraton, Mahogany, 2 Drawers, Rope-Turned Legs, 29 x 18 In. 690.00
Table, Drop Leaf, Sheraton, Mahogany, 2 Drawers, Turned Legs, 29 x 19 In. 400.00
Table, Drop Leaf, Sheraton, Mahogany, c.1815, 43 1/4 x 38 x 28 3/4 In. 265.00
Table, Drop Leaf, Sheraton, Mahogany, Drawer, Reeded Legs, 29 x 48 x 19 In. 460.00
Table, Drop Leaf, Sheraton, Mahogany, Drawer, Spiral Legs, 29 x 42 x 46 In. 575.00
Table, Drop Leaf, Sheraton, Mahogany, Rope-Turned Legs, 29 x 38 x 19 In. 400.00
Table, Drop Leaf, Sheraton, Mahogany, X-Brace Supports, 1800s, 29 x 42 x 43 In. 805.00
Table, Drop Leaf, Sheraton, Pine, Hardwood Base, 28 x 42 x 43 In. 120.00
Table, Drop Leaf, Sheraton, Pine, Turned Legs, c.1850, 29 x 38 1/2 x 42 1/2 In. 545.00
Table, Drop Leaf, Sheraton, Walnut, Gateleg, 42 x 21 x 29 In. 360.00
Table, Drop Leaf, Sheraton, Walnut, Gateleg, 48 x 24 x 27 In. 195.00
Table, Drop Leaf, Stickley Bros., 4 Slab Legs, 30 x 30 In. 940.00
Table, Drop Leaf, Victorian, Mahogany, Folding Base, 37 In. 630.00
Table, Drop Leaf, Walnut, Oval, Gateleg, Turned Legs & Stretchers, 30 x 42 x 41 In. 475.00
Table, Drop Leaf, Wicker, Wood Top, c.1910, 30 1/2 x 42 x 53 In. 290.00
Table, Drop Leaf, William IV, Mahogany, Crossbanded, c.1835, 28 x 22 In. 940.00
Table, Drum, Georgian Style, Mahogany, Leather Insert, Brass Feet, 22 x 20 In. 635.00
Table, Drum, Regency, Oak, Leather Surface, Early 1800s, 29 x 45 In. 3680.00
Table, Dunand, Black Lacquer, Crushed Eggshells, c.1925, 13 x 18 x 14 In. 41825.00
Table, Eames, ETR, Surfboard, Herman Miller, c.1951, 10 x 89 x 30 In. 2700.00
Table, Eames, La Fonda, Marble Top, Chrome Base, Herman Miller, 1960s, 18 x 30 In. . . . 529.00
Table, Eames, OTW, Herman Miller, 1940s, 35 x 24 x 15 1/2 In. 2300.00
Table, Eastlake Style, Drawer, 30 x 46 x 25 In. 80.00
Table, Eastlake, Mahogany, Marble Top, c.1875, 30 x 27 x 20 In. 200.00
Table, Eastlake, Spoon Carved, Stick & Ball, Square, 29 x 20 In. 345.00
Table, Eastlake, Walnut, Burl Veneer Panel, Marble Top, 26 x 18 x 30 1/2 In. 375.00
Table, Ebonized Wood, Bone Inlay, Drawer, Austria-Germany, c.1885, 32 x 39 In. 2070.00
Table, Ebony, Ivory, Teak Inlay, Leaves, Flowers, India, Early 1900s, 18 x 24 In. 105.00
Table, Edwardian Style, Oak, Leather, Octagonal Top, 27 x 16 In., Pair 2300.00
Table, Edwardian, Mahogany, Boxwood Banding, Square Legs, 20 x 15 In. 285.00
Table, Edwardian, Satinwood, Inlaid, Crossbanded, Turned Stretchers, 30 x 13 In. 2645.00
Table, Eero Saarinen, No. 160F, Pedestal Group, 1963, 16 x 20 1/2 In., Pair 880.00
Table, Eero Saarinen, No. 161F, Pedestal Group, Oval, Knoll, c.1956, 21 x 23 x 15 In. 1880.00
Table, Elizabethan Style, Mahogany, Green Marble Hexagonal Top, 31 x 27 In. 1912.00
Table, Empire Style, 3 Black Glass Insets, Frieze, Tapered Legs, 25 x 30 x 11 In. 145.00
Table, Empire Style, Mahogany, Leather Top, Ormolu Heads, 1900s, 30 x 17 x 18 In. 690.00
Table, Empire Style, Mahogany, Scalloped Edge, Pedestal, c.1850, 28 x 36 In. 115.00
Table, Empire Style, Marble Top, Round, 20th Century, 27 x 24 In. 500.00
Table, Empire, Gilt, Marble Top, Winged Maidens, 28 x 21 In. 2300.00
Table, Empire, Lacquer, Round, Pierced Brass Gallery, 30 x 22 In., Pair 2760.00

Table, Empire, Mahogany, Marble Top, Carved Paw Feet, Casters, 30 x 35 In. 1725.00
Table, Empire, Mahogany, Marble Top, Rectangular, c.1830, 29 x 46 x 21 In. 4405.00
Table, Ethan Allen, Mahogany, Shallow Drawers, Cane Insert, 28 x 28 x 16 In., Pair 575.00
Table, Federal Style, Mahogany, Leather Inset, 1900s, 31 x 40 x 21 In. 430.00
Table, Federal Style, Walnut Inlay, Stringing, Tapered Legs, 22 x 18 x 16 In., Pair 400.00
Table, Federal, Satinwood, Inlaid Mahogany, Mass., c.1810, 32 x 20 x 19 In. 980.00
Table, Finn Juhl, Teak, Cane Lower Shelf, Metal Tag, France & Son, 27 1/2 In. . . . . . . *Illus* 235.00
Table, Florentine, Ebonized, Multicolored, Blackamoor, Early 1800s, 30 In. 1725.00
Table, French Empire, Satinwood, Carved, Gilt, Round, Scrolled Acanthus, 46 x 30 In. . . . 1150.00
Table, French Provincial, Fruitwood, c.1900, 30 1/2 x 78 x 39 In. 1955.00
Table, French Provincial, Fruitwood, Plank Top, Drawer, Mid 1800s, 29 x 29 x 22 In. 259.00
Table, French Provincial, Mahogany, Marble, Hoof Feet, Mid 1800s, 29 x 22 x 14 In. 635.00
Table, French Provincial, Oak, Mid 19th Century, 31 1/2 x 78 1/2 x 36 In. 1840.00
Table, French Provincial, Polychrome, Drawer, Mid 1700s, 30 x 44 x 24 In. 460.00
Table, French Provincial, Walnut, Carved, c.1800, 20 x 29 1/2 x 26 1/2 In. 145.00
Table, French Provincial, Walnut, Drawer, France, 30 x 61 x 31 In. 1265.00
Table, French, Iron, Peach Marble Top, Round, Mid 19th Century, 19 1/2 x 27 1/2 In. 316.00
Table, Fruitwood, Parquetry, Hexagonal, Bone, Mother-Of-Pearl, 23 x 15 In. 100.00
Table, G. Nelson, Drawer, Shelf, Herman Miller, c.1956, 18 1/2 x 17 x 24 In. 675.00
Table, G. Nelson, Rosewood, Crossed Legs, Herman Miller, c.1955, 29 x 72 x 36 In. 2350.00
Table, G. Nelson, Walnut, Steel Base, Herman Miller, c.1955, 17 x 18 In. 825.00
Table, G. Stickley, Mortised, Round, Arched Stretchers, 29 x 36 In. 2705.00
Table, G. Stickley, No. 18, Round, Wide Apron, Spool Legs, 30 x 30 x 30 In. 880.00
Table, G. Stickley, No. 603, Oak, c.1910, 20 x 18 In. 840.00
Table, G. Stickley, No. 644, Round, Faceted, Arched Cross Stretcher, 30 x 29 In. 2115.00
Table, G. Stickley, No. 647, Leather, Vertical Stretcher, 39 x 27 x 30 In. 1765.00
Table, G. Stickley, No. 663, Shelf, Vertical Leg Cutouts, 29 x 27 In. 2350.00
Table, G. Stickley, No. 668, Round, Notched Cross Stretcher, 44 x 29 In. 1175.00
Table, G. Stickley, Round, Arched Cross Stretchers, 26 x 20 In. 1295.00
Table, G. Stickley, Round, Arched Cross Stretchers, 30 x 35 3/4 In. 2705.00
Table, Galle, Mahogany, Marquetry, 2 Tiers, c.1900, 30 x 31 x 17 In. 2390.00
Table, Galle, Marquetry, Flower Inlay, Shelf, Tapered Legs, 21 x 15 1/2 x 29 In. 880.00
Table, Galle, Marquetry, Flowers, Tilt Top, 30 x 21 x 9 In. 1000.00
Table, Galle, Nesting, Marquetry, c.1900, 28 1/2 In. 9560.00
Table, Game, Arts & Crafts, Circular Top, Leatherette Covers, 6 Chairs, 48 x 30 In. 350.00
Table, Game, Biedermeier, Flip Top, Tapered Square Supports, Early 1800s, 31 In. 715.00
Table, Game, Chippendale Style, Mahogany, Lift Top, Ireland, c.1860, 29 x 26 In. 1035.00
Table, Game, Chippendale, Cherry, Connecticut, c.1785, 29 x 34 In. 17250.00
Table, Game, Chippendale, Mahogany, Cabriole Legs, Paw Feet, Ireland, 29 x 36 In. 1840.00
Table, Game, Chippendale, Mahogany, Carved, Flip Top, c.1800, 29 x 32 x 16 In. 1058.00
Table, Game, Chippendale, Mahogany, Molded Lower Edge, c.1770, 33 x 34 In. 2235.00
Table, Game, Chippendale, Mahogany, Overhanging Top, Square Legs, 29 x 34 In. 2820.00
Table, Game, Circassian Walnut, Flip Top, Serpentine, Splayed Legs, 36 In. 1380.00
Table, Game, Empire Style, Mahogany, Swivel Top, Pedestal, c.1840, 27 x 36 x 17 In. 230.00
Table, Game, Empire, Mahogany, Dolphin Support, Phila., c.1835, 29 x 34 x 17 In. 705.00
Table, Game, Empire, Mahogany, Molded Top, Apron, Pedestal, 1800s, 31 x 37 In. 210.00
Table, Game, English Oak, Octagonal Top, Chessboard, Pedestal, 28 x 20 In. 175.00
Table, Game, Federal, Mahogany, Birch, Rosewood, Mass., c.1795, 30 x 39 In. 6000.00
Table, Game, Federal, Mahogany, Hinged Top, Compartments, c.1820, 28 x 16 x 13 In. . . . 260.00
Table, Game, Federal, Maple, Mahogany, Serpentine, Mass., c.1805, 26 x 17 In. 4800.00
Table, Game, Fruitwood, Mahogany Veneer, Backgammon, Checkerboard, 34 In. 230.00
Table, Game, George II Style, Walnut, Carved, Inlaid Flip Top, 31 x 38 x 20 In. 1495.00
Table, Game, George II, Walnut, Lobed Corners, Drawer, 31 x 35 In. 3450.00
Table, Game, George III Style, Mahogany, Demilune, Flip Top, 31 x 42 x 21 In. 2070.00
Table, Game, George III Style, Mahogany, Serpentine Top, Drawer, 28 x 34 In. 865.00
Table, Game, George III Style, Rosewood, Inlaid, Tapered Legs, 37 In. 1150.00
Table, Game, George III, Mahogany Inlay, Ankle Collars, c.1870, 28 x 36 x 18 In. 1840.00
Table, Game, George III, Mahogany, Accordion, Flip Top, c.1815, 30 x 34 x 17 In. 3105.00
Table, Game, George III, Mahogany, Carved Pedestal, Splayed Legs, 36 In. 4600.00
Table, Game, George III, Mahogany, Hinged Serpentine Top, c.1780, 29 x 36 In. 4800.00
Table, Game, George III, Mahogany, Reeded Edge & Legs, c.1800, 29 x 36 In. 2530.00
Table, Game, George III, Mahogany, Serpentine Top, Molded Edges, 29 x 36 In. 1495.00
Table, Game, George III, Satinwood, Demilune, Flip Top, c.1790, 29 x 39 x 19 In. 4140.00

Furniture, Table,
Finn Juhl, Teak,
Cane Lower Shelf,
Metal Tag, France
& Son, 27 1/2 In.

Furniture, Table,
George III Style,
Mahogany,
Drawers, c.1900,
28 In., Pair

Table, Game, Georgian Style, Mahogany, Frieze Drawer, Square Legs, 28 x 22 In. 540.00
Table, Game, Georgian, Mahogany, D-Shape, Pad Feet, 32 In. 3900.00
Table, Game, Georgian, Mahogany, Demilune, Flip Top, Flared Pedestal, 36 In. 865.00
Table, Game, Karl Springer, Brass Inlay, Embossed Leather, 1986, 29 x 36 In. 2390.00
Table, Game, L. & J.G. Stickley, Cut Corner Top, Cross Stretcher, 30 x 30 x 29 In. 560.00
Table, Game, Mahogany, Drawer, Straight Legs, 29 x 36 x 18 In. 2070.00
Table, Game, Mahogany, Drawer, Turret Corners, Claw & Ball Feet, England, 29 x 36 In. . . 5500.00
Table, Game, Mahogany, Flip Top, 28 1/2 x 21 1/2 x 16 In. 1910.00
Table, Game, Marquetry, Ebonized, Ormolu, France, 19th Century, 29 x 16 In. 1495.00
Table, Game, Neoclassical, Mahogany, Flip Top, 29 x 22 x 16 In. 1910.00
Table, Game, Neoclassical, Mahogany, Marquetry, Flip Top, c.1800, 31 x 15 In. 3450.00
Table, Game, Queen Anne Style, Mahogany, Flip Top, Late 1800s, 29 x 29 x 15 In. 1150.00
Table, Game, Regency, Mahogany, Burl, Early 1800s, 29 x 32 x 16 In. 3220.00
Table, Game, Regency, Mahogany, Rosewood Beaded Top, c.1820, 28 x 36 In. 2070.00
Table, Game, Regency, Rosewood, Baize Lined, Splayed Legs, c.1815, 29 x 36 In. 1380.00
Table, Game, Regency, Rosewood, Brass Marquetry, Flip Top, c.1815, 29 x 36 In. 2875.00
Table, Game, Regency, Rosewood, Platform Base, Pedestal, Paw Feet, 24 In. 2185.00
Table, Game, Satinwood, Demilune, Flip Top, Woman, Flowers, 29 x 36 x 18 In. 3680.00
Table, Game, Victorian, Satinwood, Burl Walnut, Marquetry, Flip Top, 30 x 24 In. 2530.00
Table, Gateleg, Jacobean Style, Oak, 19th Century, 18 1/2 x 22 1/2 In. 230.00
Table, Gateleg, Mahogany, Turned Stretchers, Bulbous Feet, 35 x 54 x 22 In. 635.00
Table, Gateleg, Oak Base, 1-Board Walnut Top, Drawer, 44 x 15 x 18 In. 9200.00
Table, Gateleg, Walnut, Block & Ring-Turned Supports, 28 x 44 x 48 In. 7050.00
Table, Gateleg, William & Mary Style, Turned Legs, Stretchers, Flat Ball Feet, 48 In. 330.00
Table, George II Style, Walnut, Marquetry, 28 x 26 x 16 In. 489.00
Table, George III Style, Burl Elm, Fruitwood, 33 x 45 x 19 In., Pair 3220.00
Table, George III Style, Mahogany, 2 Drawers, 36 x 44 x 16 In. 489.00
Table, George III Style, Mahogany, Carved, Cabriole Legs, 29 1/2 x 18 x 18 In. 69.00
Table, George III Style, Mahogany, D-Shape Top, Green Felt, c.1870, 28 x 36 x 18 In. 1610.00
Table, George III Style, Mahogany, Demilune, Rosewood, 33 x 45 x 19 In., Pair 1725.00
Table, George III Style, Mahogany, Drawers, c.1900, 28 In., Pair . . . . *Illus* 920.00
Table, George III Style, Mahogany, Inlaid, Late 1800s, 28 x 48 x 35 In. 1150.00
Table, George III Style, Mahogany, Oval, 28 x 22 5/8 x 17 5/8 In., Pair 1495.00
Table, George III Style, Mahogany, Parquetry, Tripod, Late 1800s, 22 In. 1035.00
Table, George III Style, Mahogany, Round, 3 Pedestals, 27 x 52 In. 6900.00
Table, George III Style, Mahogany, Round, Cabriole Legs, Pad Feet, 25 x 11 In. 489.00
Table, George III Style, Mahogany, Rounded Rectangular, 3 Pedestals, 30 x 52 In. 5060.00
Table, George III Style, Mahogany, Serpentine Top, Fretwork, 28 x 19 x 19 In., Pair 1840.00
Table, George III Style, Mahogany, Tripod, Mid 19th Century, 28 x 24 In. 1285.00
Table, George III Style, Rectangular, Frieze Drawer, Square Legs, 28 x 26 x 18 In. 825.00
Table, George III Style, Satinwood, Mahogany, Oval, 30 x 32 x 23 In. 1435.00
Table, George III, Chinese Chippendale, Mahogany, Fretwork, 31 x 30 x 19 In. 6900.00
Table, George III, Mahogany, 3 Drawers, Tapered Legs, c.1800, 36 x 42 x 18 In. 1725.00
Table, George III, Mahogany, Bowfront, Drawer, Turned Supports, 39 In. 805.00
Table, George III, Mahogany, Demilune, Spade Feet, 32 1/2 x 51 x 25 In., Pair 2990.00
Table, George III, Mahogany, Ebonized, 3 Drawers, Early 1800s, 36 x 44 x 14 In. 1725.00
Table, George III, Mahogany, Leather Top, Cannon Barrel Pedestal, 28 x 20 In. 460.00
Table, George III, Mahogany, Octagonal, Turned Pedestal, Tripod, 19 x 19 In. 530.00

Table, George III, Mahogany, Oval, Frieze, Hinged Top, c.1770, 28 x 38 x 41 In.	1725.00
Table, George III, Mahogany, Round, Baluster-Turned Pedestal, Tripod, 31 In.	855.00
Table, George III, Mahogany, String Inlay, c.1800, 36 x 62 x 20 In.	3450.00
Table, George III, Sycamore, Demilune, Gilt, Polychrome, 1790s, 35 x 56 x 22 In.	8050.00
Table, George IV, Burl Elm, Ebonized, Parcel Gilt Brass, c.1820, 29 x 54 In.	4830.00
Table, Georgian Style, Mahogany, 2 Tiers, Turned Legs, Brass Casters, 29 x 18 In.	1208.00
Table, Georgian Style, Mahogany, Dish Top, Shaped Skirt, 1800s, 28 x 31 x 21 In.	2300.00
Table, Georgian Style, Mahogany, Flip Top, Pad Feet, 22 In., Pair	1711.00
Table, Georgian Style, Mahogany, Frieze Drawer, 3 Sections, Leaves, 29 x 54 In.	1175.00
Table, Georgian Style, Mahogany, Piecrust Top, 27 x 23 1/2 In.	58.00
Table, Georgian Style, Mahogany, Silver Plated Mount, Tripod, 1900s, 22 x 15 In., Pair	441.00
Table, Georgian, Mahogany, Inlaid, Frieze Drawer, Tapered Legs, 30 x 18 x 15 In.	940.00
Table, Georgian, Mahogany, Leaf, Shell & Rosette Carving, Tripod, 29 x 39 In.	3220.00
Table, Giancarlo Piretti, Platone, Chrome, Fiberglass, Folding, c.1970, 27 x 25 x 32 In.	295.00
Table, Gilt Metal, Glass, Oval, Italy, 17 x 42 x 20 In.	240.00
Table, Gilt, Pierced Frame, Marble Top, France, c.1880, 33 x 46 1/2 In.	1265.00
Table, Gueridon, American Restauration, Mahogany, Marble Top, Ormolu, 31 x 38 In.	5060.00
Table, Gueridon, Charles X Style, Gilt Bronze, Marble, 29 x 26 In.	2629.00
Table, Gueridon, Empire Style, Gilt Bronze, Marble Top, 28 x 27 In., Pair	3910.00
Table, Gueridon, Empire Style, Gilt Bronze, Marble Top, Eagle Heads, 29 x 29 In.	3910.00
Table, Gueridon, Empire Style, Gilt Bronze, Marble Top, Round, 29 x 27 In., Pair	2070.00
Table, Gueridon, Gilt Bronze, Rouge Marble, Continental, 29 x 24 In.	3220.00
Table, Gueridon, Regency Style, Brass, Marble Top, Bamboo Turnings, 32 x 18 In., Pair	3450.00
Table, Gueridon, Regency Style, Gilt Brass, Marble Top, Tripod, 31 x 21 In., Pair	4830.00
Table, Hardwood, Flower-Carved Apron, Demilune, Chinese, 1800s, 33 x 37 x 19 In.	200.00
Table, Harvest, Shaker, Tiger Maple, Red Stain, Breadboard Top, Drawers, 57 In. *Illus*	5750.00
Table, Harvest, White Paint, Wood Peg Construction, Maine, 72 In.	3850.00
Table, Hepplewhite, Pine, Red Paint, Drawer, Brass Pull, 18 x 24 x 27 3/4 In.	460.00
Table, Hepplewhite, Walnut, 2 Drawers, Tapered Legs, 30 x 23 x 29 In.	978.00
Table, Hepplewhite, Walnut, 3-Board Top, Flame Grain, Drawer, 35 x 29 In.	3105.00
Table, Hispano-Moresque Design, Tile Top, 4 Tiles, 4 Iron Legs, 18 x 12 In.	645.00
Table, Horseshoe, George III Style, Mahogany, Carved, Brass Mounted, 32 x 63 In.	2300.00
Table, Hung Mu, Rectangular, Shelf, Drawer, 24 x 20 & 20 In., Pair	375.00
Table, Ice Cream, Cast Iron, Cabriole Legs, Late 19th Century, 32 x 30 In.	265.00
Table, Ice Cream, Cast Iron, Round White Marble Top, 24 x 30 In., 4 Chairs	230.00
Table, Indo-Persian, Bronze, Cobra-Head Legs, 20th Century, 24 x 15 In.	575.00
Table, Iron, Marble Top, Pierced Frieze, Early 20th Century, 21 1/2 x 28 1/2 In.	690.00
Table, Iron, Marble Top, Scrolled Iron Base, Early 19th Century, 16 x 41 x 19 In.	1035.00
Table, Italian Rococo Walnut, Serpentine Top, 2 Drawers, 1800s, 34 x 36 x 18 In.	1765.00
Table, J. Adnet, Nickel, Mirror Glass, France, c.1930, 22 x 21 x 15 In.	5378.00
Table, J. Hoffmann, Beech, Glass, Leather, Brass, c.1905, 30 x 27 1/2 In.	2700.00
Table, J. Hoffmann, No. 915/1P, Beech, Glass, Fabric, c.1905, 28 x 23 1/2 In.	3000.00
Table, J. Van Den Bosch, Oak, Round Top, 4 Flared Legs, 20 x 19 In.	825.00
Table, Jacobean Style, Elm, Sliding Panel, Turned Legs, 26 x 21 x 29 1/2 In.	2000.00
Table, Jules Leleu, Mahogany, Patinated, Gilt Bronze, c.1958, 21 x 21 5/8 x 14 In.	7768.00
Table, Jules Leleu, Rosewood, Marquetry, Brass, Round, 1940, 18 x 34 In.	5019.00
Table, Kittinger, Mahogany, Drawers, 19 x 18 x 26 In.	200.00
Table, L. & J.G. Stickley, Hexagonal, Wagon Wheel, Lift Apron, 29 x 48 In.	3525.00
Table, L. & J.G. Stickley, No. 560, Round Top, Lower Shelf, 18 x 29 In.	705.00
Table, L. & J.G. Stickley, No. 561, Cut-Corner Top, Shelf, 29 x 18 x 18 In.	825.00
Table, L. & J.G. Stickley, No. 575, Round Top, Shelf, Arched Stretchers, 24 x 30 In.	1265.00
Table, L. & J.G. Stickley, No. 720, Round Top, 5 Tapered Legs, 48 x 29 In.	1295.00
Table, Library, Aesthetic Revival, Marquetry, Ebonized, 30 x 40 x 24 In.	750.00
Table, Library, American Restauration, Fruitwood, Drawer, 1850s, 31 x 54 In.	1610.00
Table, Library, Arts & Crafts, 2 Drawers, Copper Hardware, Spindles, 50 x 24 x 30 In.	765.00
Table, Library, Arts & Crafts, Oak, Drawer, Square Legs, Early 1900s, 29 x 39 x 23 In.	290.00
Table, Library, G. Stickley, Ebonized Finish, 2 Drawers, 29 x 54 In.	6465.00
Table, Library, G. Stickley, No. 652, Oak, c.1907, 29 x 36 x 24 In.	2629.00
Table, Library, G. Stickley, No. 653, Drawers, Copper Pull, 48 x 30 x 30 In.	1645.00
Table, Library, G. Stickley, No. 653, Drawers, Iron Hardware, 48 x 30 x 30 In.	1380.00
Table, Library, G. Stickley, No. 655, 13 Vertical Side Spindles, 28 x 36 x 24 In.	1410.00
Table, Library, G. Stickley, No. 659, Spindles, 3 Drawers, Copper Pulls, 29 x 54 In.	4405.00
Table, Library, George III, Mahogany, Green Leather Top, Gilt Trim, 32 x 38 In.	1795.00

Table, Library, George IV, Mahogany, Leather Top, 4 Drawers, c.1825, 30 x 49 In. 9600.00
Table, Library, Jacobean Revival, Oak, Leaf, Drawer, Trestle Base, 32 x 51 x 35 1/2 In. . . . 2300.00
Table, Library, Jacobean Style, Mahogany, Veneer, 60 x 24 x 30 1/2 In. 345.00
Table, Library, L. & J.G. Stickley, Drawer, Mortised Lower Shelf, 29 x 42 x 28 In. 1175.00
Table, Library, L. & J.G. Stickley, Round Top, Arched Cross Stretchers, 29 x 42 In. 1530.00
Table, Library, Lifetime, Shelf, Drawer, Copper Hardware, 36 x 24 x 29 In. 825.00
Table, Library, Limbert, Drawer, Mortised Shelf, Arched Apron, 29 x 48 x 28 In. 1115.00
Table, Library, Limbert, Turtle Top, Blind Drawer, Plank Sides, 29 x 48 x 30 In. 3055.00
Table, Library, Mahogany, 2 Dovetailed Drawers, 50 x 33 x 29 In. 345.00
Table, Library, Mahogany, 2 Drawers, Masques, Continental, c.1890, 31 x 50 In. 2300.00
Table, Library, Mahogany, Carved, Female Masques, Acanthus, 31 x 50 x 30 In. 1955.00
Table, Library, Neoclassical, Mahogany, 2 Carved Supports, 30 x 54 In. 4400.00
Table, Library, Neoclassical, Mahogany, Carved, c.1820, 29 x 26 x 39 In. 4540.00
Table, Library, Oak, 2 Drawers, Bun Feet, 48 x 28 x 31 In. 720.00
Table, Library, Oak, 4 Hinged Leather Surfaces, Square Legs, 30 x 84 In. 1265.00
Table, Library, Oak, Center Drawer, 2 Urn Pedestals, 42 x 26 x 30 1/2 In. 259.00
Table, Library, Oak, Lyre Ends, Drawer, Knoxville Tables, 42 x 26 x 29 In. 345.00
Table, Library, Oak, Oval, Drawer, Scroll Supports, Feet, Shelf, 48 x 28 x 29 In. 259.00
Table, Library, Regency Style, Satinwood Veneer, Inlay, 60 x 36 x 32 In. 1095.00
Table, Library, Regency, Mahogany, Square Top, Leather, Drawers, 29 x 49 x 49 In. 3230.00
Table, Library, Renaissance Revival, Walnut, Oval, 1880, 29 x 95 x 47 In. 3175.00
Table, Library, Roycroft, Chestnut, Overhanging Top, Macmurdo Feet, 28 x 30 In. 1765.00
Table, Library, Stickley Bros., No. 189, Drawer, Double Stretchers, 45 x 26 x 29 In. 530.00
Table, Library, Victorian, Walnut, Drawer, Flat Stretcher, 30 x 44 In. 315.00
Table, Library, William & Mary Style, Oak, 2 Drawers, 48 x 30 x 30 1/2 In. 175.00
Table, Library, William IV, Mahogany, Leather, Rectangular, 31 x 59 x 39 In. 3910.00
Table, Limbert, 4 Spindles, Stretcher, 30 x 22 x 29 In. 940.00
Table, Limbert, No. 105, Bookrack, Drawer, 6 Legs, Corbel Supports, 42 x 28 x 29 In. 880.00
Table, Limbert, No. 141, Pullout & Lift Writing Surface, Inkwell, 29 x 24 x 20 In. 940.00
Table, Limbert, No. 240, Oak, Pedestal 4495.00
Table, Limbert, Oval, Slab Sides, Cutouts, 45 x 30 x 30 In. 2470.00
Table, Limbert, Round, Oilcloth, Cross-Shape Base, 29 1/2 x 28 1/2 In. 4700.00
Table, Louis XV Style, Bronze Mounted, 33 x 78 x 40 In. 1910.00
Table, Louis XV Style, Ebonized Wood, Ormolu Mounted, 29 x 40 x 25 In. 1380.00
Table, Louis XV Style, Fruitwood, Glass Top, Drawer, 2 Shelves, 28 x 26 In. 290.00
Table, Louis XV Style, Gilt, Gray & White Marble Top, Oval, 20 x 31 x 24 In. 1435.00
Table, Louis XV Style, Mahogany, Carved Frieze, c.1900, 31 x 44 x 28 In. 489.00
Table, Louis XV Style, Mahogany, Ormolu Swags, Marble Top, 27 x 21 In. 290.00
Table, Louis XV Style, Mahogany, Parquetry, 30 x 23 x 17 In. 600.00
Table, Louis XV Style, Mahogany, Parquetry, Bronze Mounted, 34 x 30 x 21 In. 2640.00
Table, Louis XV Style, Parquetry, Gilt Bronze, 3 Drawers, Late 1800s, 29 x 46 In. 6000.00
Table, Louis XV Style, Tulipwood, Parquetry, Ormolu Mounted, 29 x 23 x 17 In. 1495.00
Table, Louis XV, Black Lacquer, Gilt Bronze Mount, 1800s, 30 x 63 x 31 In. 4480.00
Table, Louis XV, Mahogany, Bronze Mount, Marble Top, 21 x 42 x 22 In. 598.00
Table, Louis XV, Mahogany, Bronze Mount, Oval, Brass Gallery, 29 x 23 x 17 In. 2150.00
Table, Louis XV, Marquetry, Rouge Marble Top, 3 Drawers, 28 x 12 x 10 In. 1795.00
Table, Louis XVI Style, Carved, Gilt, Faux Marble Inset, Garland, 27 In. . . . . *Illus* 1265.00
Table, Louis XVI Style, Cream Paint, Oval, 20th Century, 30 x 32 x 22 In. 129.00

Furniture, Table, Harvest, Shaker, Tiger Maple,
Red Stain, Breadboard Top, Drawers, 57 In.

Furniture, Table,
Louis XVI Style,
Carved, Gilt, Faux
Marble Inset,
Garland, 27 In.

Table, Louis XVI Style, Ivory Lacquer, Marble Top, 23 x 17 In. 530.00
Table, Louis XVI Style, Kingwood, Round Top, Central Bouquet Inlay, 28 x 27 In. 895.00
Table, Louis XVI Style, Mahogany, Bronze Mount, White Marble Top, 29 x 32 In. 1315.00
Table, Louis XVI Style, Mahogany, Leather, Drawer, Early 1900s, 27 x 26 In., Pair 1035.00
Table, Louis XVI Style, Marquetry, Rosewood Inlay, Continental, 28 x 21 In. 1955.00
Table, Louis XVI Style, Walnut, Fluted Legs, Marble Top, Gallery, 20 x 20 In. 460.00
Table, Louis XVI Style, Wrought Iron, Specimen Marble, France, 32 x 72 x 32 In. 2185.00
Table, Louis XVI, Mahogany, Gallery, Marble Top, Mirror Back, 36 x 60 x 22 In. 1795.00
Table, Louis XVI, Mahogany, Marble Top, Brass Gallery, 1700s, 10 In. 1955.00
Table, Mahogany, Acanthus Carved, Vase-Form Pedestal, 156 x 28 x 60 In. 2900.00
Table, Mahogany, Black Marble Top, Carved Swans, Triangle Column, 30 x 39 In. 2990.00
Table, Mahogany, Boxwood Inlay, Serpentine Front, 3 Apron Drawers, 78 In. 5520.00
Table, Mahogany, Drum, Tooled Leather, Drawer, Paw Feet, 20th Century 235.00
Table, Mahogany, Gadrooned Edge, Reeded Apron, 3 Supports, 30 x 43 In. 1035.00
Table, Mahogany, Half-Round, Square Supports, 38 In., Pair 1511.00
Table, Mahogany, Inlay, Shelf Stretcher, 20th Century 175.00
Table, Mahogany, Lozenge Parquetry, Dutch, Early 1800s, 30 x 35 x 35 In. 715.00
Table, Mahogany, Marble Turtle Top, Carved Flowers, Urn Pedestal, 39 x 27 x 30 In. 835.00
Table, Mahogany, Marble Turtle Top, Carved Leaf Medallions, 34 x 26 x 30 In. 805.00
Table, Mahogany, Oval Top, Scroll Inlay, c.1850, 20 x 34 x 29 In. 575.00
Table, Mahogany, Piecrust Top, Pedestal, Tripod, Claw & Ball Feet, 26 In. 715.00
Table, Mahogany, Reeded Edges, 2 Parts, 1800s, 28 3/4 x 46 x 46 In. 355.00
Table, Mahogany, Satinwood Inlay, Round, Turned Pedestal, Platform, 52 In. 1610.00
Table, Mahogany, Wood Banding, String Inlay, Brass Casters, 35 x 25 x 21 In. 520.00
Table, Maison Jansen, Painted, Marble, c.1940, 16 1/2 x 23 3/4 x 19 In. 5400.00
Table, Maple, Cherry Finish, Cabriole Legs, 20 x 29 In. 115.00
Table, Maple, Pine, Painted, Drawer, Stretcher, 1700s, 26 x 43 x 25 3/4 In. 7638.00
Table, Maple, Walnut, Black Paint, Stretcher, Early 1700s, 28 x 68 x 30 In. 2350.00
Table, Marcel Breuer, No. B10, Board, Tubular Steel, Thonet, c.1931, 26 x 29 In. 3600.00
Table, Massimo Morozzi, Karonte, Maple, Mahogany, Marble, Italy, 30 x 50 In. 1880.00
Table, McCobb, Glass Top, Tubular Brass, 20 x 15 1/2 In. 825.00
Table, McCobb, Maple, Brass Stretchers, Dowel Legs, 54 x 36 x 29 In. 410.00
Table, McCobb, Walnut, Shelf, Drawer, Aluminum, Signed, 21 x 21 x 24 In. 1765.00
Table, Mies Van Der Rohe, Chrome, X Frame, Primary Colors, 22 In., 4 Piece 440.00
Table, Minton Tile Inset, Old Hancock House, Parquetry Borders, 18 x 16 x 9 In. 176.00
Table, Mustard Paint, Stenciled, Drawer, Backsplash, 34 x 31 1/2 x 15 1/2 In. 748.00
Table, Napoleon II, Mahogany, Marquetry, Pierced Brass Gallery, 33 x 16 x 12 In. 690.00
Table, Napoleon III Style, Beech, Ebonized, Gilt Bronze, Porcelain, 30 x 32 In. 24150.00
Table, Napoleon III, Ebonized, Boulle, Ormolu, Chariot, 31 x 53 x 34 In. 3220.00
Table, Napoleon III, Fruitwood, Ebonized, Gilt Brass, Boulle, Round, 30 x 33 In. 2990.00
Table, Napoleon III, Kingwood, Marble, Brass Gallery, Drawer, c.1860, 28 In. ...... *Illus* 1265.00
Table, Napoleon III, Rosewood, Ivory Inlay, Mid 1800s, 29 x 52 x 29 In. 4600.00
Table, Neoclassical, Brass, Glass Inset, Putti, Scrolling Leaves, 40 x 62 x 39 In. 8545.00
Table, Neoclassical, Faux Ebony, Grained, Continental, 28 x 22 In., Pair 3450.00
Table, Neoclassical, Fruitwood, Concave Top, Sweden, 1800s, 33 x 26 x 16 In. 2990.00
Table, Neoclassical, Mahogany, Carved, Arched Legs, c.1830, 30 1/2 x 40 x 26 In. 880.00
Table, Neoclassical, Maple, Mahogany Inlay, Lacquer, Dutch, 31 x 30 In. 4830.00
Table, Neoclassical, Marquetry, Satinwood, Banded, Dutch, 30 x 33 In. 1380.00
Table, Neoclassical, Metal, Brass, Round Top, 20th Century, 22 x 17 In. 235.00
Table, Neoclassical, Multicolored Wood, Brass, Wrought Iron, 32 x 74 x 34 In. 3680.00
Table, Neoclassical, Walnut, Parquetry, Drawer, Italy, c.1800, 29 x 45 x 34 In. 1840.00
Table, Nesting, Denmark, c.1955, 24 x 16 1/2 x 22 In., 4 Piece 380.00
Table, Nesting, Fan Inlay, 20th Century, 29 1/2 x 38 x 18 In., 4 Piece 235.00
Table, Nesting, Gehry, Easy Edge, Cardboard, Fiberboard, 1972, 22 x 26 In., 3 Piece 10200.00
Table, Nesting, Hung Mu, Fret Carved Apron, Chinese, 1900s, 28 x 22 In., 3 Piece 460.00
Table, Nesting, J. Hoffmann, Beech, Stained, 29 1/2 x 22 1/2 x 17 In. 7800.00
Table, Nesting, Laminated Wood, Tubular Steel, 21 x 15 x 18 In., 3 Piece 173.00
Table, Nesting, Regency Style, Mahogany, Thumb-Molded Edge, 27 x 20 x 13 1/2 In. 470.00
Table, Nesting, Regency Style, Mahogany, Trestle Base, England, 29 In., 3 Piece .... *Illus* 646.00
Table, Nesting, Rosewood, Denmark, 18 1/2 x 23 3/4 In., 3 Piece 230.00
Table, Nesting, Teak, Tile Inset, Scandinavia, 1958, 23 x 15 3/4 x 19 3/4 In. 590.00
Table, Niedecken, Square Top, Column Base, 30 x 24 1/2 In. 7050.00
Table, Oak, Bamboo, Quatrefoil, Shelf, 24 x 29 In. 236.00

Table, Oak, Lobed Top, Shelf, Cabriole Legs, 24 x 24 x 30 1/2 In. 175.00
Table, Oak, Round, Pedestal, Paw Feet, 2 Leaves, 47 x 31 In. 315.00
Table, Oak, Square, Shelf, Splayed Fluted Legs, Fremont Furniture Co., 28 x 30 In. 155.00
Table, Oak, Tapered, Fluted Legs, 2 Leaves, 48 x 47 x 30 In. 430.00
Table, Oak, Turned Legs, Flat Stretchers, Square Feet, 72 x 20 x 30 In. 460.00
Table, Oriental, Mahogany, Lion's-Head Legs, Claw & Ball Feet, 51 x 34 x 30 In. 489.00
Table, Otto Prutscher, Beech, Leather, Brass, Glass, c.1910, 30 x 23 3/4 In. 4800.00
Table, Painted, Blue Over Red & White, 2-Board Top, 49 x 21 x 21 In. 430.00
Table, Papier-Mache, Black, Gilt, Mother-Of-Pearl, Hinged Lid, 32 x 24 x 15 In. 2875.00
Table, Papier-Mache, Ebonized, 3-Part Base, c.1865, 25 x 17 x 14 In. 1495.00
Table, Paul Laszlo, Brown Saltman, c.1950, 16 x 20 x 20 In., ... 560.00
Table, Pedestal, Oak, Round, Scroll Legs, Kershan Bros. Brandts Co., Ohio, 46 x 29 In. ... 230.00
Table, Pembroke, Chinese Chippendale, Mahogany, Link-Taylor, 28 x 52 x 16 In. 175.00
Table, Pembroke, Chippendale, Mahogany, Conn., c.1770, 30 x 32 x 19 In. 7050.00
Table, Pembroke, Federal, Cherry, Apron Drawer, c.1800, 36 x 32 x 28 1/2 In. 1058.00
Table, Pembroke, Federal, Cherry, Inlaid, Drawer & Faux Drawer, 29 x 37 In. 2350.00
Table, Pembroke, Federal, Cherry, X-Stretcher, c.1800, 36 1/2 x 30 x 29 In. 705.00
Table, Pembroke, Federal, Mahogany, 28 3/4 x 20 1/2 x 41 3/4 In. 518.00
Table, Pembroke, Federal, Mahogany, c.1790, 30 x 36 x 27 1/2 In. 4406.00
Table, Pembroke, Federal, Mahogany, Half-Round Leaves, Tapered Legs, 29 In. 4994.00
Table, Pembroke, Federal, Mahogany, Inlaid, Bellflower, c.1800, 29 x 32 x 21 In. 1265.00
Table, Pembroke, Federal, Mahogany, New England, c.1805, 28 x 20 In. 3600.00
Table, Pembroke, Federal, Mahogany, Stiles, c.1810, 29 x 45 x 36 In. 1725.00
Table, Pembroke, Federal, Mahogany, Tapered Legs, c.1800, 29 x 21 x 30 In. 2070.00
Table, Pembroke, Federal, Mahogany, X-Stretcher, 27 x 21 x 30 In. 3680.00
Table, Pembroke, Federal, Rectangular, Rounded Leaves, c.1805, 28 x 32 In. 646.00
Table, Pembroke, Federal, Satinwood, Mahogany Inlay, c.1800, 29 x 43 x 36 In. 2300.00
Table, Pembroke, Federal, Satinwood, Mahogany Inlay, c.1805, 29 x 40 x 34 In. 2990.00
Table, Pembroke, George III, Mahogany, 27 x 20 1/2 x 29 3/4 In. 6600.00
Table, Pembroke, George III, Mahogany, Banded, 2 Leaves, 29 x 38 x 43 In. 635.00
Table, Pembroke, George III, Mahogany, c.1760, 28 x 24 x 25 In. 6600.00
Table, Pembroke, George III, Mahogany, Crossband, String Inlay, c.1790, 27 x 30 In. 1175.00
Table, Pembroke, George III, Mahogany, Inlay, Flip Top, 28 x 19 x 33 In. 1725.00
Table, Pembroke, George III, Mahogany, Satinwood Inlay, Oval, Leaves, 29 In. 5750.00
Table, Pembroke, George III, Rosewood, Satinwood Inlay, 27 x 36 x 20 In. 1530.00
Table, Pembroke, George III, Satinwood, Emboyna Wood Panels, Banded, 28 x 20 In. 4315.00
Table, Pembroke, George III, Satinwood, Inlaid, Banded, c.1790, 27 x 43 x 33 In. 825.00
Table, Pembroke, Hepplewhite Style, Mahogany Inlay, Hammary, 28 x 20 x 28 In. 345.00
Table, Pembroke, Hepplewhite Style, Mahogany, Crossbanded, 27 x 30 x 27 In. 200.00
Table, Pembroke, Hepplewhite, Mahogany, Birch, Pine, Inlaid, 36 x 21 x 28 In. 345.00
Table, Pembroke, Hepplewhite, Maple, Drawer, Glass Knob, 28 x 36 x 18 In. 175.00
Table, Pembroke, Mahogany, Continental, Early 1800s, 31 x 40 x 28 In. 1265.00
Table, Pembroke, Mahogany, D-Shape Leaves, Frieze, c.1850, 29 x 22 x 41 In. 690.00
Table, Pembroke, Mahogany, Putti In Clouds, Flowers, Leaves, 29 x 42 x 32 In. 3680.00
Table, Pembroke, Mahogany, Reeded Edges, Drawer, Faux Drawer, 29 x 36 In. 1265.00
Table, Pembroke, Mahogany, Satinwood, Brass Cuffs, Casters, 28 x 22 x 31 In. 2300.00
Table, Pembroke, Mahogany, Scalloped Leaves, Paw Feet, c.1835, 29 x 40 In. 2300.00
Table, Pembroke, Reeded, Drawer, Turned Legs, Casters, 29 x 39 x 27 In. 2760.00
Table, Pembroke, Regency Style, Walnut, D-Shape Flaps, 28 5/8 x 55 x 42 In. 145.00
Table, Pembroke, Regency, Mahogany, Baluster Standard, c.1865, 28 x 42 In. 1610.00
Table, Pembroke, Regency, Mahogany, Early 1800s, 29 x 19 x 34 In. 1265.00
Table, Pembroke, Regency, Mahogany, Rectangular, 2 Drawers, c.1820, 28 x 29 In. 2160.00
Table, Pembroke, Regency, Mahogany, Saber Legs, 28 x 48 In. 1035.00
Table, Pembroke, Sheraton, Mahogany, Boxwood Inlay, D-Shape Leaves, 28 In. 1725.00
Table, Pembroke, Sheraton, Mahogany, Inlaid, Shaped Leaf, 30 x 36 x 21 In. 690.00
Table, Pembroke, Sheraton, Rosewood, Reeded Legs, c.1825, 40 x 23 In. 1095.00
Table, Philip Laverne, Chinoiserie, Hardwood, Brass Mounted, 24 x 38 In. 3285.00
Table, Pier, Mahogany, Figured Veneer, Marble Top, Gilt Griffins, 35 x 50 In. 7050.00
Table, Pier, Mahogany, Marble Top, N.Y., Early 19th Century, 37 x 43 x 17 In. 5019.00
Table, Pier, Neoclassical, Mahogany, Carved, Marble, c.1840, 35 x 41 x 18 In. 2468.00
Table, Pine Plank Top, X-Shape Legs, Snow Hill Cloister, Pa., 31 x 137 x 24 In. 715.00
Table, Pine, Oval, Drawer, 19th Century, 26 x 30 1/2 x 19 In. 80.00
Table, Pine, Rectangular, Baluster Turned Legs, 1800s, 30 x 119 x 31 In. 2468.00

Furniture, Table, Napoleon III,
Kingwood, Marble, Brass
Gallery, Drawer, c.1860, 28 In.

Furniture, Table, Nesting,
Regency Style, Mahogany, Trestle
Base, England, 29 In., 3 Piece

Furniture, Table, Roycroft,
Corseted Legs, Carved Orb
Signature, 29 1/2 x 30 In.

Table, Pine, Red Paint, Mortised & Pegged, Drawer, Turned Legs, 30 x 48 x 32 In. 3300.00
Table, Pine, Tile Top, Flowers, Scalloped Apron, Early 1800s, 32 x 35 x 25 In. 3450.00
Table, Pine, Tile Top, Landscape, Denmark, Early 19th Century, 32 x 35 x 25 In. 3910.00
Table, Poplar, Dark Stain, 2 Drawers, Turned Legs, 1850-60, 39 x 36 x 20 In. 795.00
Table, Poul Kjaerholm, PK55, E. Kold Christensen, c.1957, 27 x 80 1/2 x 40 In. 3820.00
Table, Prairie School, Flared Cutout, Shoefoot, 4 Leaves, 50 x 30 In. 2700.00
Table, Queen Anne Style, Mahogany, Early 1900s, 28 1/2 x 36 x 26 In. 1095.00
Table, Queen Anne Style, Mahogany, Shaped Apron, 27 1/4 x 32 x 20 3/4 In. 750.00
Table, Queen Anne Style, Maple, Pine, Gateleg, Turned Legs, 44 x 19 In. 200.00
Table, Queen Anne Style, Oak, Drawer, Open Shelf, 1800s, 26 x 20 1/2 In. 705.00
Table, Queen Anne Style, Walnut, Herringbone Band, c.1800, 30 x 41 x 21 In. 2530.00
Table, Queen Anne, Chinoiserie, Painted Landscape, Scalloped Edge, 18 x 26 In. 545.00
Table, Queen Anne, Flip Top, Demilune, Gateleg, 29 x 27 x 27 In. 1840.00
Table, Queen Anne, Fruitwood, Mahogany, Shell Knees, 41 x 14 x 14 In. 460.00
Table, Queen Anne, Maple, 2-Board Top, Serpentine Skirt, 25 x 29 In. 2585.00
Table, Queen Anne, Walnut, Yellow Pine, Poplar, Pad Feet, 48 x 31 x 29 In. 1150.00
Table, Reeded Legs, Bundled Bamboo, Chinese, Early 1900s, 33 x 38 x 19 In., Pair 1150.00
Table, Refectory, American Restauration, Cherry, 19th Century, 30 x 69 x 32 In. 1840.00
Table, Refectory, Louis XVI Style, Checkerboard, 30 x 145 x 49 In. 705.00
Table, Refectory, Oak, Block & Turned Legs, Box Stretcher, 31 x 78 x 32 In. 6900.00
Table, Refectory, Oak, Carved Apron, Turned Supports, Draw Leaves, 78 x 36 In. 3680.00
Table, Refectory, Oak, Plank Top, Box Stretcher, England, c.1900, 30 x 72 x 34 In. 1265.00
Table, Refectory, Roycroft, Chestnut, Curved Ends, 5 Legs, 30 x 132 x 42 In. 2470.00
Table, Regency Style, Black Lacquer, Pedestal, 25 x 17 x 17 In. 478.00
Table, Regency Style, Burl, Round, Scalloped Edge, Brass Paw Feet, 27 x 28 In. 960.00
Table, Regency Style, Ebonized, Lyre Supports, 29 x 17 x 15 In., Pair 5290.00
Table, Regency Style, Mahogany, Bowed Top, Backboard, Drawers, 30 x 48 x 24 In. 2070.00
Table, Regency Style, Mahogany, Rosewood, Satinwood Band, Round, 29 x 96 In. 4315.00
Table, Regency Style, Mahogany, Round, Beaded Edge, Leather Insert, 30 x 48 In. 5060.00
Table, Regency Style, Mahogany, Stone Top, Late 19th Century, 29 x 21 x 20 In. 405.00
Table, Regency Style, Mahogany, String Inlay, Ebonized, Round, 29 x 69 In. 2990.00
Table, Regency, Gilt, Ebonized, Chinoiserie Penwork Stencil, 29 x 36 x 28 In. 8625.00
Table, Regency, Gilt, Marble Top, Octagonal, c.1815, 28 x 20 In., Pair 5290.00
Table, Regency, Mahogany, 2 Drawers, Turned Pedestal, Mid 1800s, 54 x 27 In. 470.00
Table, Regency, Mahogany, Rosewood Band, Melon Feet, Casters, 29 x 39 x 52 In. 2300.00
Table, Regency, Satinwood, Mahogany Inlay, Oval, Casters, 27 1/2 x 58 x 43 In. 1765.00
Table, Renaissance Revival, Mahogany, Burl Veneer, Octagonal, 29 x 31 In. 230.00
Table, Renaissance Revival, Walnut, Carved, Mottled Black Marble Top, 22 x 36 In. 575.00
Table, Renaissance Revival, Walnut, Marble Top, Carved Roundels, 30 x 36 x 26 In. 1495.00
Table, Robsjohn-Gibbings, Widdicomb, 23 1/2 x 20 x 21 In., Pair 2645.00
Table, Rococo Style, Fruitwood, Crossbanded, 3 Drawers, 1800s, 29 x 13 x 11 In. 441.00
Table, Rococo Style, Gilt, Glass, 17 x 42 x 24 In. 1315.00
Table, Rococo Style, Russet Paint, Gilt, Leather Surface, Italy, c.1885, 30 x 36 In. 3450.00
Table, Rouge Marble, Double Inlay, Pierced Apron, Asia, 1800s, 21 x 35 x 21 In. 1840.00

Table, Rounded Corners, 2 Drawers, Brass Pulls, Tapered Legs, 28 x 38 x 25 In. 5520.00
Table, Roycroft, Corseted Legs, Carved Orb Signature, 29 1/2 x 30 In. . . . . *Illus*   4115.00
Table, Ruhlmann, Rosewood, Extension, c.1929, 29 x 41 x 41 In. 71700.00
Table, Russel Wright, Conant & Ball, c.1935, 16 x 14 x 26 In. 120.00
Table, Satin Birch, Tulipwood, Oval, Continental, Late 18th Century, 30 In. 1765.00
Table, Sawbuck, Hickory, Pine, 3-Board Top, 42 x 33 1/2 x 29 In.   230.00
Table, Sawbuck, Pine, Ash, Rectangular Top, 3-Part Base, 1800s, 27 1/2 x 69 In. 590.00
Table, Sawbuck, Pine, Chamfered Corners, Square Legs, 35 x 48 1/2 x 28 In. 805.00
Table, Sawbuck, Pine, Green Paint, 71 x 36 x 28 In. 1840.00
Table, Sawbuck, William & Mary, Pine, Pennsylvania, 1700s, 33 x 80 x 30 In. 9560.00
Table, Sewing, Biedermeier, Walnut, Mahogany, Serpentine Legs, 24 x 17 x 31 In. 660.00
Table, Sewing, Cherry, Poplar, Blue Paint, Drawer, Zoar, c.1898, 36 x 24 x 30 In. 105.00
Table, Sewing, Empire Style, Walnut, Bird's-Eye Maple, Drawers, 21 x 16 x 30 In. 460.00
Table, Sewing, Empire, Mahogany, 2 Drawers, Pedestal, c.1835, 29 x 21 1/2 x 18 In. 380.00
Table, Sewing, Empire, Mahogany, 2-Part Top, 3 Drawers, 1800s, 28 x 23 x 20 In. 235.00
Table, Sewing, Empire, Mahogany, Hinged Lid, 2 Drawers, 1800s, 29 x 22 x 17 In. 705.00
Table, Sewing, Empire, Mahogany, Rectangular, 2 Drawers, c.1830, 28 x 23 x 15 In. 325.00
Table, Sewing, Federal, Bird's-Eye Maple, Oak, Drawers, Curved Legs, 28 In. 2705.00
Table, Sewing, Federal, Mahogany, 2 Drawers, 1800s, 29 x 23 x 16 In. 235.00
Table, Sewing, Federal, Mahogany, 2 Drawers, Mass., c.1800, 28 3/4 x 21 In. 9000.00
Table, Sewing, Federal, Mahogany, 2 Drawers, Mass., c.1810, 30 x 20 In. 8400.00
Table, Sewing, Federal, Mahogany, 2 Drawers, New England, c.1815, 28 x 21 In. 1765.00
Table, Sewing, Federal, Mahogany, 3 Drawers, c.1820, 28 x 20 x 16 In. 3175.00
Table, Sewing, Federal, Mahogany, Brass Pulls, Mass., c.1800, 30 x 20 x 16 In. 10158.00
Table, Sewing, Federal, Mahogany, Drop Leaf, 2 Drawers, c.1825, 30 x 17 x 28 In. 410.00
Table, Sewing, Federal, Mahogany, Drop Leaf, 3 Drawers, c.1820, 29 x 22 x 18 In. 1645.00
Table, Sewing, Federal, Mahogany, Veneer, Square Top, c.1810, 29 x 17 In. 1410.00
Table, Sewing, Federal, Maple, Birch, Drawer, New England, c.1815, 29 x 20 In. 1920.00
Table, Sewing, Federal, Maple, Grain Painted, Mid-Atlantic, c.1810, 28 x 25 In. 1920.00
Table, Sewing, Federal, Maple, Pine, 2 Drawers, c.1810, 27 x 18 x 17 In. 470.00
Table, Sewing, Federal, Marble Top, Drawer, Philadelphia, c.1805, 28 x 20 In. 9000.00
Table, Sewing, Federal, Tiger Maple, Multicolor, Stencil, Mass., c.1810, 29 x 20 In. 6600.00
Table, Sewing, Federal, Tiger Maple, Shaped Hinged Top, Pedestal, 32 x 22 In. 2820.00
Table, Sewing, Fruitwood, Scalloped Apron, Beaded Legs, 36 x 26 x 30 In. 520.00
Table, Sewing, G. Stickley, No. 630, 2 Drawers, Drop Leaf, 18 x 18 x 28 In. . . . . .590.00 to 1765.00
Table, Sewing, Heywood Bros. & Co., Wicker, Dome Lid, Mass., c.1890, 30 x 12 In. 558.00
Table, Sewing, Mahogany Veneer, 2 Drawers, Phila., c.1825, 31 x 22 x 18 In. 3290.00
Table, Sewing, Mahogany, 2 Drawers, 1800s, 30 x 23 x 17 In. 410.00
Table, Sewing, Mahogany, 2 Drawers, Glass Pulls, Dolphin Feet, c.1810, 28 x 21 In. 3450.00
Table, Sewing, Mahogany, Drop Leaf, 2 Drawers, Flared Column, Bun Feet, 28 x 18 In. . .   490.00
Table, Sewing, Mahogany, Hinged Top, Upholstered Sides, c.1890, 29 x 23 In. 1265.00
Table, Sewing, Mahogany, Rosewood Cross Banding, Pedestal, c.1850, 20 In. 380.00
Table, Sewing, Maple, Pine, 2-Board Top, Drawer, 13 x 26 3/4 x 56 In. 1265.00
Table, Sewing, Multicolored, Flowers, Dome Top, Italy, c.1850, 28 In. 1495.00
Table, Sewing, Neoclassical, Mahogany, 2 Drawers, Shelf, c.1825, 29 x 22 x 17 In. 1058.00
Table, Sewing, Neoclassical, Mahogany, Carved, Inlaid, c.1815, 30 x 20 In. 2160.00
Table, Sewing, Neoclassical, Mahogany, Drop Leaf, Drawers, Boston, c.1820, 30 x 21 In. . .   1765.00
Table, Sewing, Pine, Apron Drawer, Early 19th Century, 15 x 21 x 28 In. 225.00

Furniture, Table, Sewing, Shaker, Pine, Cherry,
Butternut, New Lebanon, N.Y., 37 In.

Furniture, Table, Sewing, Southern Heart Pine,
Plank Top, Square, c.1790, 32 x 48 In.

Table, Sewing, Poplar, Drawer, Blue Gray Paint, Turned Legs, 28 x 25 x 26 In. 660.00
Table, Sewing, Regency, Mahogany, Pullout Bin, Early 1800s, 29 x 19 x 15 In. 805.00
Table, Sewing, Rosewood, Mahogany, Drawer, Pedestal, Bun Feet, 21 x 18 In. 575.00
Table, Sewing, Shaker, Maple, Walnut, Tilt Top, Oval, Harvard, Mass., 1860, 23 x 42 In. . . . 2015.00
Table, Sewing, Shaker, Pine, Cherry, Butternut, New Lebanon, N.Y., 37 In. . . . . *Illus* 18400.00
Table, Sewing, Shaker, Pine, Cherry, Lift Top, Drawer, 26 3/4 x 24 3/4 x 21 In. 7475.00
Table, Sewing, Shaker, Pine, Red, Drop Leaf, Hancock, Mass., 1825, 28 x 31 x 15 In. 6900.00
Table, Sewing, Shaker, Poplar, Pine, 1-Board Top, Drawer, c.1850, 31 x 29 x 16 In. 2015.00
Table, Sewing, Shaker, Tiger Maple, Cherry, Pine, 2 Drawers, 3 Legs, 24 x 22 x 20 In. 10925.00
Table, Sewing, Southern Heart Pine, Plank Top, Square, c.1790, 32 x 48 In. . . . . *Illus* 1093.00
Table, Sewing, Walnut, Turned Posts, 35 x 22 1/2 In. 104.00
Table, Sewing, William IV, Rosewood, Lift Top, Scotland, 28 x 18 In. 1610.00
Table, Shaker, Starch, Pine, Maple, Red Paint, New Lebanon, N.Y., 28 x 27 In. . . . . . . *Illus* 4025.00
Table, Sheraton Style, Cherry, Gateleg, Rope-Turned Legs, 44 x 28 x 30 In. 185.00
Table, Sheraton Style, Maple, Turned Legs, c.1860, 30 x 22 x 18 In. 345.00
Table, Sheraton, Mahogany, 3 Drawers, Rope-Turned Legs, 28 x 18 In. 690.00
Table, Sheraton, Mahogany, Bird's-Eye Maple Drawers, 29 x 21 x 17 In. 546.00
Table, Sheraton, Mahogany, Cherry, 2 Half Drawers, Turned Legs, 31 x 33 x 18 In. 1265.00
Table, Sheraton, Pine, Round Top, Square-Edge Skirt, Turned Legs, 29 In. 635.00
Table, Side, Biedermeier, Crossbanded, Drawer, Square Supports, c.1825, 19 In. 455.00
Table, Side, Biedermeier, Lift Top, Platform Base, Early 1800s, 36 x 30 In. 1758.00
Table, Side, Edwardian, Mahogany, Crossbanded, 3/4 Gallery, 33 x 12 x 14 In. 285.00
Table, Side, Edwardian, Mahogany, Marquetry, Door, 30 x 13 x 16 In. 340.00
Table, Side, Eero Saarinen, No. 160F, Pedestal Group, Knoll, c.1963, 20 x 16 In., Pair 880.00
Table, Side, Flemish Baroque, Fruitwood, Walnut, Inlay, Drawer, 30 x 41 In. 4700.00
Table, Side, France & Son, Teak, Cane, Metal Tag, Denmark, 23 x 28 x 19 In. 350.00
Table, Side, French Provincial, Chestnut, Cabriole Legs, c.1800, 26 x 27 x 18 In. 805.00
Table, Side, Fruitwood, 3 Drawers, 3/4 Gallery, Italy, 1800s, 30 x 17 In. 1645.00
Table, Side, George I Style, Gilt Gesso, 33 x 52 x 29 In. 7800.00
Table, Side, George III Style, Mahogany, 3 Drawers, Spade Feet, 36 x 33 x 17 In. 865.00
Table, Side, George III, Mahogany, 3 Drawers, Square, Tapered Legs, 34 In. 1000.00
Table, Side, George III, Mahogany, Boxwood Stringing, Fluted, Legs, 54 In. 1805.00
Table, Side, George III, Mahogany, Crossbanded, Drawer, 36 In. 855.00
Table, Side, George III, Mahogany, Drawer, Square, Tapered Supports, 27 In. 1045.00
Table, Side, George III, Mahogany, Oblong, Dish Top, c.1800, 30 x 36 In. 1380.00
Table, Side, George III, Walnut, Rectangular Top, Trestle Supports, 36 In. 760.00
Table, Side, Georgian Style, Mahogany, Oval, Fluted Legs, 22 x 23 x 18 In., Pair 575.00
Table, Side, Georgian Style, Walnut, Apron Drawer, Open Shelf, 28 x 19 In. 470.00
Table, Side, Huang Huali Wood, Chinese, Early 1900s, 32 x 48 x 11 1/2 In. 745.00
Table, Side, Italian Baroque, Walnut, Overhanging Top, Drawer, 25 x 32 In. 4025.00
Table, Side, Italian Neoclassical, Demilune, Marble Top, Secret Drawer, 29 x 43 In. 863.00
Table, Side, Louis XV Style, Parquetry, Brass Gallery, 3 Drawers, 28 x 16 In. 589.00
Table, Side, Louis XV Style, Parquetry, Marble Top, Drawer, Oval, 27 x 10 x 14 In. 808.00
Table, Side, Louis XV, Rectangular Top, Drawer, Hoof Feet, c.1790, 25 x 31 x 25 In. 920.00
Table, Side, Louis XVI Style, Gilt Bronze, Ebonized, Marble Top, 30 x 26 x 17 In. 8400.00
Table, Side, Louis XVI Style, Parquetry, Gilt Bronze, c.1865, 28 x 25 x 17 In. 7200.00
Table, Side, Mahogany, D-Shape, Tambour Doors, Dutch, Early 1800s, 27 In. 950.00
Table, Side, Mahogany, Marble Top, Tapered Supports, Pad Feet, c.1750, 40 In. 5700.00
Table, Side, Neoclassical, Fruitwood, Inlay, Tambour Door, c.1825, 30 x 19 In. 295.00
Table, Side, Queen Anne, Oak, Drawer, c.1725, 28 x 31 x 18 1/2 In. 825.00
Table, Side, Stickley Bros., Oval Top, Through Tenon, 28 x 25 1/2 x 15 In. 1998.00
Table, Side, W. Platner, Nickel-Plated Wire, Glass Top, Knoll, 16 x 18 In., Pair 3450.00
Table, Side, William & Mary, Oak, Drawer, 30 1/2 x 34 x 23 In. 1175.00
Table, Side, Wood, Hand Carved, Camel Shape, 26 x 29 In. 605.00
Table, Slate Top, Gilt, Leaf-Carved Frieze, 20th Century, 33 x 35 x 13 In. 1095.00
Table, Stickley Bros., Overhanging Top, Lower Shelf, 29 x 26 x 20 In. 1295.00
Table, Stickley Bros., Round Top, Shaped Cross Stretchers, 29 x 40 In. 645.00
Table, Tavern, Black Walnut, 2 Apron Drawers, 52 x 33 x 30 1/2 In. 3290.00
Table, Tavern, Breadboard Top, New England, c.1740, 25 1/2 x 34 In. 4600.00
Table, Tavern, Chestnut, Board Top, Scalloped Skirt, 1600, 29 x 31 x 21 In. 1955.00
Table, Tavern, Curly Maple, Birch, Pine Top, 29 x 23 1/2 x 27 1/2 In. 920.00
Table, Tavern, Fruitwood, Drawer, H-Stretcher, 1700s, 25 x 47 x 21 In. 210.00
Table, Tavern, Hepplewhite, Pine, Red Paint, Wrought Iron, 42 x 29 x 26 In. 805.00

Furniture, Table, Shaker, Starch, Pine, Maple, Red Paint, New Lebanon, N.Y., 28 x 27 In.

Furniture, Table, Tavern, Pine, Maple, Red Stain, Drawers, Late 1700s, 27 x 43 In.

Table, Tavern, Maple, Breadboard Ends, New England, 25 x 39 x 22 1/2 In. 2070.00
Table, Tavern, Maple, Pine, Red Wash, New England, c.1750, 25 x 36 In. 1560.00
Table, Tavern, Moravian, Walnut, Drawer, Turned Legs, 1900s, 30 x 61 x 34 In. 6050.00
Table, Tavern, Paint, Apron, Pad Feet, R.I., 1700s, 26 x 33 x 24 In. 6575.00
Table, Tavern, Pine, Birch, Red Stain, Drawer, New England, 29 x 42 In. 2700.00
Table, Tavern, Pine, Maple, Red Stain, Drawers, Late 1700s, 27 x 43 In. . . . .*Illus* 1410.00
Table, Tavern, Queen Anne, Cherry, Walnut, New England, c.1770, 27 x 42 x 30 In. 9000.00
Table, Tavern, Queen Anne, Maple, New England, c.1750, 25 x 43 x 27 In. 7200.00
Table, Tavern, Queen Anne, Maple, Pine, Dovetailed Drawer, Pegged, 36 x 23 In. 1610.00
Table, Tavern, Queen Anne, Maple, Pine, Straight Skirt, 25 x 35 x 26 In. 1035.00
Table, Tavern, Red Paint, Shelf, Tripod Base, Pennsylvania, 1800s, 30 x 45 In. 5175.00
Table, Tavern, Scrubbed, Scalloped Skirt, Red Base, New England, 26 x 30 x 47 In. 10925.00
Table, Tavern, Walnut, English Stretcher, Turned Ball Feet, 24 x 18 x 27 In. 575.00
Table, Tavern, Walnut, Pine, Black Paint, 40 x 28 x 26 In. 430.00
Table, Tavern, William & Mary, Pine, Maple, New England, 25 x 35 x 24 In. 3740.00
Table, Tavern, William & Mary, Red Paint, Oval, Trestle Base, 25 x 22 x 32 In. 2990.00
Table, Tavern, William & Mary, Walnut, 28 x 48 x 32 In. 5975.00
Table, Tavern, William & Mary, Walnut, Drawer, c.1750, 28 x 20 x 35 In. 2300.00
Table, Tavern, Wood, Painted, American, c.1790, 27 x 38 x 28 In. 5019.00
Table, Tavern, Yellow Pine, Poplar, Box Stretcher, 27 x 46 x 35 In. 1380.00
Table, Taylor Of California, 4-Tile Round Top, Bird Of Paradise, Wood Base, 18 x 19 In. . . 2000.00
Table, Tea, Art Deco, Walnut, Rectangular, Swivel, France, c.1928, 28 x 35 x 44 In. 1880.00
Table, Tea, Cherry, Rectangular, Cabriole Legs, New England, 27 x 22 x 33 In. 1610.00
Table, Tea, Chinese Chippendale, Mahogany, Fret Carving, 27 x 24 In., Pair 1725.00
Table, Tea, Chippendale Style, Scalloped Piecrust Edge, 1900s, 28 1/2 x 29 In. 529.00
Table, Tea, Chippendale, Maple, Dish Top, Birdcage, 3 Cabriole Legs, 28 x 38 In. 1115.00
Table, Tea, Drop Leaf, Turned Legs, 18 x 21 In. 210.00
Table, Tea, Eastlake, Square Top, 4 Flat Spoon Carved Legs, Victorian, 31 x 14 In. 130.00
Table, Tea, Federal, Mahogany, Inlaid, 33 x 34 x 23 In. 2870.00
Table, Tea, Federal, Maple, New England, c.1800, 27 x 32 x 25 1/2 In. 825.00
Table, Tea, G. Stickley, Round Top, Shelf, Cross Stretcher, 24 x 26 In. 1528.00
Table, Tea, George III Style, Chinese Chippendale, Mahogany, 27 In., Pair . . . . *Illus* 863.00
Table, Tea, George III Style, Mahogany, Pierced Gallery, 28 x 33 x 19 In. 460.00
Table, Tea, George III, Chinese Chippendale, Mahogany, 1800-25, 30 In. . . . . *Illus* 6900.00
Table, Tea, George III, Mahogany, Shell Medallion, Oval, Silver Handles, 29 In. 2875.00
Table, Tea, Queen Anne Style, Mahogany, Drawer, 31 x 33 x 22 In., Pair 5290.00
Table, Tea, Queen Anne Style, Walnut, Drawer, c.1900, 26 x 37 x 20 In. 2530.00
Table, Tea, Queen Anne, Mahogany, Dish Top, Birdcage, c.1760, 28 x 33 In. 4600.00
Table, Tea, Queen Anne, Mahogany, England, 1700s, 27 x 28 1/2 In. 3900.00
Table, Tea, Queen Anne, Mahogany, Scalloped Apron, 26 x 19 x 28 In. 2940.00
Table, Tea, Queen Anne, Maple, Beech, Red Paint, N.H., c.1770, 26 x 32 x 28 In. 7765.00
Table, Tea, Queen Anne, Maple, Birch, Cabriole Legs, Pad Feet, 28 x 21 In. 8915.00
Table, Tea, Queen Anne, Maple, Oval Top, Rhode Island, 1700s, 28 x 29 x 37 In. 4500.00
Table, Tea, Queen Anne, Maple, Round Top, Pedestal, Mass., 24 x 26 In. 1150.00
Table, Tea, Regency, Rosewood, Quatrefoil Base, Bun Feet, 12 1/2 x 17 In. 1235.00

Table, Tea, Tilt Top, Cherry, Birdcage Mechanism, Early 1800s, 29 x 34 In. 855.00
Table, Tea, Tilt Top, Cherry, Birdcage, Tripod, Cabriole Legs, 28 3/4 x 36 1/2 In. 3055.00
Table, Tea, Tilt Top, Chippendale Style, Mahogany, 20th Century, 29 x 30 In. 325.00
Table, Tea, Tilt Top, Chippendale, Birch, Snake Feet, Wrought-Iron Latch, 27 In. 1265.00
Table, Tea, Tilt Top, Chippendale, Mahogany, 3-Footed, Pa., Late 1700s, 28 x 32 In. 26290.00
Table, Tea, Tilt Top, Chippendale, Mahogany, Birdcage, c.1775, 27 x 33 In. 2645.00
Table, Tea, Tilt Top, Chippendale, Mahogany, Birdcage, c.1790, 28 x 33 In. 4700.00
Table, Tea, Tilt Top, Chippendale, Mahogany, Cabriole Legs, Snake Feet, 28 x 26 In. 575.00
Table, Tea, Tilt Top, Chippendale, Mahogany, Tripod Base, 26 x 26 In. 865.00
Table, Tea, Tilt Top, Chippendale, Walnut, Dish Top, Philadelphia, c.1790, 36 In. 4600.00
Table, Tea, Tilt Top, English Mahogany, Cabriole Legs, Pad Feet, 28 x 28 In. 290.00
Table, Tea, Tilt Top, George II, Mahogany, Carved, Cabriole Legs, c.1775, 28 x 29 In. 1095.00
Table, Tea, Tilt Top, George III, Mahogany, c.1760, 29 x 27 x 14 In. 1840.00
Table, Tea, Tilt Top, George III, Mahogany, Tripod, c.1770, 27 x 34 In. 575.00
Table, Tea, Tilt Top, Georgian Style, Fruitwood, Square Tapered Legs, 36 In. 865.00
Table, Tea, Tilt Top, Georgian, Mahogany, Inset Candle Wells, Tapered Feet, 32 In. 2760.00
Table, Tea, Tilt Top, Mahogany, Round, New England, Late 1700s, 28 x 29 In. 1530.00
Table, Tea, Tilt Top, Mahogany, Round, Tripod Cabriole Legs, c.1765, 28 x 26 In. 4700.00
Table, Tea, Tilt Top, Queen Anne, Mahogany, England, 33 x 30 In. 520.00
Table, Tea, Tilt Top, Queen Anne, Maple, Cherry, New England, 1700s, 28 x 28 In. 590.00
Table, Tea, Tilt Top, Queen Anne, Walnut, Ebonized Birdcage, R.I., c.1770, 28 x 32 In. ... 8050.00
Table, Tea, Tilt Top, Walnut, Round, Turned Pedestal, 33 x 28 1/2 In. 315.00
Table, Tea, Walnut, Oval, 4 Turned Legs, 29 x 19 In. 140.00
Table, Tea, Walnut, Vase-Turned Pedestal, 30 x 29 In. 145.00
Table, Tilt Top, Black Lacquer, Mother-Of-Pearl Inlay, c.1890, 28 x 20 In. 230.00
Table, Tilt Top, Cherry, Birdcage, Early 1800s, 28 x 31 In. 865.00
Table, Tilt Top, Cherry, Round, Baluster Pedestal, Saber Legs, c.1800, 28 x 35 In. 750.00
Table, Tilt Top, Chippendale, Cherry, Cabriole Legs, Snake Feet, 25 x 35 3/4 In. 575.00
Table, Tilt Top, Chippendale, Mahogany, Carved, Piecrust Top, c.1890, 32 x 28 In. 520.00
Table, Tilt Top, Chippendale, Mahogany, Piecrust, Claw & Ball Feet, 27 x 23 In. 1035.00
Table, Tilt Top, Chippendale, Piecrust, Birdcage, Tripod, Claw & Ball Feet, 28 In. 1195.00
Table, Tilt Top, Federal, Butternut, Inlaid, Octagonal, Mass., Early 1800s, 28 x 21 In. 600.00
Table, Tilt Top, Federal, Cherry, Urn Standard, c.1800, 28 x 7 1/2 x 26 In. 400.00
Table, Tilt Top, Fruitwood, Dutch Marquetry, Gallery, 30 x 35 x 12 In. 1555.00
Table, Tilt Top, George III, Chippendale, Mahogany, Piecrust, Tripod, 28 x 27 In. 2468.00
Table, Tilt Top, George III, Mahogany, Brass Stringing, 22 x 25 1/2 In. 445.00
Table, Tilt Top, George III, Mahogany, Curved Legs, Brass Casters, c.1800, 28 x 53 In. 2760.00
Table, Tilt Top, George III, Mahogany, Pedestal, Tripod, 31 x 28 In. 950.00
Table, Tilt Top, George III, Mahogany, Piecrust, Fluted Stem, Cabriole Legs, 28 x 29 In. .. 3210.00
Table, Tilt Top, George III, Mahogany, Rectangular, Rounded Corners, 27 x 21 In. 1265.00
Table, Tilt Top, George III, Mahogany, Turned Pedestal, Tripod, 25 1/2 In. 1520.00
Table, Tilt Top, George III, Oak, Vase-Form Pedestal, Cabriole Legs, 28 x 31 In. 920.00
Table, Tilt Top, George IV, Mahogany, Square, Tripod, Reeded Legs, 28 x 21 x 19 In. 635.00
Table, Tilt Top, Georgian Style, Mahogany, c.1900 .... 201.00
Table, Tilt Top, Georgian Style, Mahogany, Rectangular, c.1875, 31 x 54 In. 1035.00
Table, Tilt Top, Georgian, Mahogany, Early 1800s, 28 x 39 x 60 In. 2070.00
Table, Tilt Top, Mahogany, Dark Stain, New England, 1700s, 28 x 19 In. 825.00

Furniture, Table, Tea, George III Style, Chinese Chippendale, Mahogany, 27 In., Pair

Furniture, Table, Tea, George III, Chinese Chippendale, Mahogany, 1800-25, 30 In.

Table, Tilt Top, Mahogany, Dish Top, Birdcage Support, Phila., 23 1/2 In.	2750.00
Table, Tilt Top, Mahogany, Inlay, Pedestal, 4 Spider Legs, England, 1800s, 48 x 35 In.	2300.00
Table, Tilt Top, Mahogany, Oval, Turned Post, 29 x 50 x 37 In.	1680.00
Table, Tilt Top, Mahogany, Round, 20th Century, 28 x 29 In.	235.00
Table, Tilt Top, Mahogany, Tripod, Cabriole Legs, England, c.1825, 38 x 24 In.	1380.00
Table, Tilt Top, Papier-Mache, Black Lacquer, Chinese Figures, 1860, 30 x 29 In.	1090.00
Table, Tilt Top, Queen Anne, Maple, Cherry, Square, New England, c.1775, 28 x 29 In.	558.00
Table, Tilt Top, Regency Style, Mahogany, Reeded Shaft, c.1920, 29 1/2 x 20 In.	175.00
Table, Tilt Top, Regency, Mahogany, Brass Paw Feet, Early 1800s, 28 x 37 x 25 In.	374.00
Table, Tilt Top, Regency, Mahogany, Oval, Pedestal, 4-Footed, 29 x 52 x 30 In.	1330.00
Table, Tilt Top, Regency, Mahogany, Oval, Pedestal, c.1815, 27 x 39 x 51 In.	3910.00
Table, Tilt Top, Regency, Mahogany, Oval, Reeded Edge, c.1815, 27 x 39 x 51 In.	2070.00
Table, Tilt Top, Regency, Mahogany, Round, 3-Part Base, c.1880, 29 x 47 In.	3450.00
Table, Tilt Top, Regency, Mahogany, Round, Ireland, 1800s, 30 x 57 In.	1725.00
Table, Tilt Top, Regency, Mahogany, Spiral Reeded, Brass Casters, 28 x 60 x 33 In.	590.00
Table, Tilt Top, Regency, Rosewood, Round, 3-Part Plinth, Early 1800s, 29 x 50 In.	2990.00
Table, Tilt Top, Regency, Rosewood, Round, Plinth, Paw Feet, 28 x 53 1/2 In.	9200.00
Table, Tilt Top, Rosewood, Baluster Pedestal, Mid-Victorian, 30 x 51 In.	2000.00
Table, Tilt Top, Sheraton Style, Round, Pedestal, 1900s, 28 x 44 In.	690.00
Table, Tilt Top, Victorian, Chinoiserie, Painted, Black, Polychrome, Round, 29 x 27 In.	540.00
Table, Tilt Top, Victorian, Walnut, Demilune, c.1850, 29 x 41 x 20 In.	920.00
Table, Tilt Top, Walnut, Baluster Column, Round, Cabriole Legs, 28 x 32 In.	660.00
Table, Tilt Top, William IV, Mahogany, Rectangular, c.1835, 27 x 27 x 21 In.	633.00
Table, Tilt Top, William IV, Oak, Marquetry, Stars, c.1835, 31 x 53 In.	2760.00
Table, Tray, Chinese Chippendale, Mahogany, 18 1/2 x 37 x 24 In.	115.00
Table, Tray, English Oak, Turned Legs, Folding, Leather Straps, 31 x 19 x 24 In.	230.00
Table, Tray, G. Nelson, No. 4950, Herman Miller, c.1948, 15 x 15 x 19 In.	1765.00
Table, Tray, George III, Mahogany, Oval, 4 Hinged Leaves, c.1800, 24 In.	1035.00
Table, Tray, George III, Mahogany, Stand, Early 19th Century, 32 x 31 x 17 In.	239.00
Table, Tray, Mahogany, Brass-Bound Corners, 1800s, 24 x 14 x 21 In.	718.00
Table, Tray, Mahogany, Scalloped Sides, Folding, England, 31 x 29 x 19 In.	635.00
Table, Tray, Oak, Full Gallery, Cutout Handles, 39 x 30 In.	748.00
Table, Tray, Papier-Mache, Lacquer, Gilt, Spindle Legs, 1800s, 24 x 18 In.	865.00
Table, Tray, Papier-Mache, Lacquer, Mother-Of-Pearl, Greek Key, 29 In.	2415.00
Table, Tray, Papier-Mache, Mother-Of-Pearl Inlay, Oriental Landscape, 27 In.	2070.00
Table, Tray, Stand, Regency, Papier-Mache, Parcel Gilt, c.1820, 21 x 33 x 24 In.	3450.00
Table, Tray, Tole, Chinoiserie, Octagonal, Bamboo-Turned Stand, 32 x 22 x 19 In.	3290.00
Table, Tray, Victorian, Fruitwood, X-Form Stand, 2 Handles, 34 x 28 x 30 In.	2235.00
Table, Tray, Victorian, Mahogany, Oval, Shaped Gallery, 23 x 25 x 17 In.	375.00
Table, Tray, Walnut, Flip-Up Sides, Bamboo-Turned Legs, 27 x 41 x 31 In.	460.00
Table, Trestle, English Oak, 2-Board Top, Ring, Block Supports, 1800s, 29 x 48 x 20 In.	290.00
Table, Trestle, G. Stickley, No. 593, Shelf, Keyed Through Tenon, 30 x 48 In.	2235.00
Table, Trestle, Jacobean Style, Oak, Rounded Ends, H-Stretcher, 30 x 48 In.	2415.00
Table, Trestle, L. & J.G. Stickley, No. 594, Keyed Through Tenon, 72 x 45 x 29 In.	4995.00
Table, Trestle, L. & J.G. Stickley, No. 596, Shelf, 30 x 60 x 29 In.	2585.00
Table, Trestle, L. & J.G. Stickley, Original Finish, 29 x 60 x 34 In.	2115.00
Table, Trestle, Nutting, No. 615, Maple, 30 x 60 In.	2500.00
Table, Trestle, Oak, 2-Board Plank Top, 28 x 31 x 71 In.	1140.00
Table, Trestle, Oak, Apron Drawer, 43 In.	550.00
Table, Trestle, Pine, Baluster Uprights, 19th Century, 29 x 92 In.	6465.00
Table, Trestle, Pine, Painted, 18th-Century Couple, Drawer, Germany, 29 x 29 In.	355.00
Table, Trestle, Shaker, Walnut, Tiger Maple, Arched Legs, 1900s, 24 x 59 In.	805.00
Table, Trestle, Walnut, Balusters, Continental, 18th Century, 27 x 66 x 24 In.	2070.00
Table, Victorian, Black Lacquer, Gilt, Japanese Style, 28 1/2 x 26 x 17 In.	1265.00
Table, Victorian, Burl Walnut, Marble Top, Bull's Eye, Hoof Feet, 33 x 22 x 31 In.	660.00
Table, Victorian, Mahogany, Brass Mountings, 31 x 27 In., Pair	210.00
Table, Victorian, Mahogany, Burl Veneer Accents, Round, Pedestal, 46 x 29 In.	460.00
Table, Victorian, Mahogany, Oval Top, Late 19th Century, 30 x 29 x 21 1/2 In.	120.00
Table, Victorian, Mahogany, Round, Urn Finial, 3 Flat Legs, 33 x 31 In.	316.00
Table, Victorian, Mahogany, Square Top, 19th Century, 30 x 39 1/2 x 25 In.	190.00
Table, Victorian, Mahogany, Trestle Base, Shelf Stretcher, 35 x 45 x 22 In.	840.00
Table, Victorian, Mahogany, Veneers, Aesop's Fable Scene Inlay, 29 x 51 x 27 In.	4600.00
Table, Victorian, Marble Top, Oval, Urn Finial, 25 x 18 x 29 In.	550.00

Table, Victorian, Marble Turtle Top, Walnut, Urn Finial On Shelf, 29 x 18 x 27 In. 489.00
Table, Victorian, Rosewood Veneer, Marble Turtle Top, 34 x 26 x 29 In. 1380.00
Table, Victorian, Rosewood, Divided Well, Folding, Late 1800s, 31 x 24 x 14 In. 290.00
Table, Victorian, Walnut Inlay, Oval Top, Casters, c.1860, 29 x 39 x 22 In. 345.00
Table, Victorian, Walnut, Bull's Eyes, Marble Top, Oval, 36 x 26 x 31 In. 865.00
Table, Victorian, Walnut, Burl Veneer, Marble Top, Beveled Edge, 33 x 24 x 29 In. 489.00
Table, Victorian, Walnut, Burl Veneer, Round, Ring-Turned Pedestal, 30 x 29 In. 200.00
Table, Victorian, Walnut, Leaf & Bull's Eye, Green Marble Top, 30 x 22 x 30 In. 575.00
Table, Victorian, Walnut, Marble Top, Apron, 30 x 20 x 30 In. 290.00
Table, Victorian, Walnut, Marble Top, Beveled Edge, 29 x 21 x 29 In. 290.00
Table, Victorian, Walnut, Marble Top, Beveled Edge, Hoof Feet, 35 x 26 x 32 In. 575.00
Table, Victorian, Walnut, Marble Top, c.1870, 30 x 30 x 24 In. 260.00
Table, Victorian, Walnut, Marble Top, Oval, 29 x 22 x 28 In. 460.00
Table, Victorian, Walnut, Marble Top, Oval, Bevel Edge, Urn Pedestal, 36 x 26 x 31 In. . . . 575.00
Table, Victorian, Walnut, Marble Turtle Top, 27 x 21 x 28 1/2 In. 200.00
Table, Victorian, Walnut, Marble Turtle Top, 36 x 25 In. 1025.00
Table, Victorian, Walnut, Oval Top, Turned Stem, c.1870, 27 x 26 x 18 In. 230.00
Table, Victorian, Walnut, Oval, Turned Column, Late 1800s, 29 x 29 x 21 In. 80.00
Table, Victorian, Walnut, White Marble Top, Beveled, 29 x 30 1/2 In. 200.00
Table, Victorian, Walnut, White Marble, Beveled Edge, Turtle Top, 36 x 23 x 29 In. 690.00
Table, Victorian, Wood, Cast Iron, Pierced, Round Top, c.1900, 28 x 20 In. 403.00
Table, W. McArthur, Melamine Top, Aluminum, Rubber Feet, 30 x 29 In. 530.00
Table, Wally Rizzo, Chrome, Brass, Glass, 2 Tiers, 1970s, 16 x 20 x 32 In., Pair 2390.00
Table, Walnut, Carved, Inlaid, Scrolling Leaves, Flowers, Continental, 32 x 43 x 69 In. . . . 1265.00
Table, Walnut, End Drawer, Fluted Tapered Legs, 21 x 31 1/2 x 29 1/2 In. 200.00
Table, Walnut, Marquetry, Parquetry, Star, Feather Band, Italy, 31 1/2 x 24 x 16 In. 2749.00
Table, Walnut, Rosewood Veneer, Marquetry, Ink Graining, 39 x 24 x 29 In. 1325.00
Table, Wegner, No. 302L, 3 Leaves, Hansen & Son, c.1955, 28 1/2 x 47 In. 940.00
Table, Wegner, No. GE225, Flagline, Getama, c.1950, 31 x 48 x 41 In. 4820.00
Table, Wegner, Teak, Raised Lip, Oak Base, 3 Legs, 35 1/2 x 17 In. 325.00
Table, Wendell Castle, Maple, Stack, Laminated, 1973, 27 1/8 In. 7170.00
Table, William & Mary, Oval Top, Gateleg, Mass., c.1740, 30 x 44 x 40 In. 765.00
Table, William & Mary, Walnut, Rectangular, Drawer, Turned Legs, 28 x 31 In. 4800.00
Table, William IV, Mahogany, Scroll Carving, Runner Feet, 31 x 39 x 28 In. 2185.00
Table, William IV, Rosewood, Mahogany, Round, Leather Inset, c.1850, 29 x 23 In. 2070.00
Table, William IV, Rosewood, Round, Panel Standard, Gilt Feet, 29 x 52 In. 2070.00
Table, Wormley, Bleached Mahogany, Laminate, 60 x 18 & 42 x 15 In., 2 Piece 580.00
Table, Wormley, Cherry, Brass, Stone Top, c.1958, 20 x 17 In. 2235.00
Table, Wormley, Mahogany, Inset Travertine Top, 24 x 24 x 16 In., Pair 1765.00
Table, Wormley, Mahogany, Trapezoid, Dunbar, 1940s, 21 x 22 In. 825.00
Table, Wormley, Sheaf Of Wheat, Marble Top, Dunbar, 1950s, 21 x 21 In. 1410.00
Table, Wormley, Stone Top, Round, Dunbar, c.1958, 16 3/4 x 20 In. 2235.00
Table, Wormley, Walnut, Faux Leather, Laminate Top, Shelf, 29 x 19 x 24 In., Pair 880.00
Table, Writing, 1750s Style, Mahogany, Leather, Cabriole Legs, 42 x 26 In. 1615.00
Table, Writing, Aesthetic Revival, Walnut, Felt Top, Frieze Drawers, 29 x 37 x 22 In. 355.00
Table, Writing, Art Nouveau, Walnut, Leather, Tapered Legs, 32 x 35 In. 1175.00
Table, Writing, Boulle, Lift Top, Mirror, Drawer, England, 31 x 30 x 19 In. 6000.00
Table, Writing, Edwardian, Mahogany, c.1910, 30 x 54 x 32 In. 2185.00
Table, Writing, Edwardian, Rosewood, Marquetry, Drawers, 34 x 20 x 37 In. 620.00
Table, Writing, Empire, Fruitwood, Inset Leather Top, Apron Drawer, 50 In. 865.00
Table, Writing, G. Stickley, No. 417, Drawer, Drop-Down Cabinets, 48 x 39 In. 4995.00
Table, Writing, George III Style, Mahogany, Leather Surface, 3 Drawers, 31 x 64 In. 1610.00
Table, Writing, George III Style, Satinwood, Mid 1800s, 29 x 36 x 21 In. 1840.00
Table, Writing, George III, Mahogany, 3-Sided Gallery, 2 Drawers, 34 x 64 In. 4140.00
Table, Writing, George III, Mahogany, Kidney Top, Frieze, 29 x 39 x 24 In. 2990.00
Table, Writing, George III, Mahogany, Lift Top, Tapered Supports, 17 x 29 In. 1765.00
Table, Writing, Leather, 4 Drawers, Gilt Metal, Early 1800s, 31 In. 855.00
Table, Writing, Louis XV Style, Mahogany, Ormolu Mounted, 32 x 50 x 30 In. 2300.00
Table, Writing, Louis XV, Black Leather, Drawer, Cabriole Legs, 28 x 33 In. 3110.00
Table, Writing, Neoclassical, Mahogany, Russia, Early 1800s, 30 x 42 x 22 In. 3450.00
Table, Writing, Regency Style, Leather Top, Drawers, England, 29 x 40 x 21 In. 470.00
Table, Writing, Regency Style, Mahogany, Leather Top, Drawers, Stepped, 29 x 42 In. 765.00
Table, Writing, Regency, Mahogany, Leather, 3 Drawers, Pullout Sides, 35 In. 6655.00

Table, Writing, Regency, Pollard, Oak, 3/4 Gallery, Splayed Legs, 29 x 28 x 18 In. 1610.00
Table, Writing, Rosewood, Ebony Inlay, Lift Top, Drawer, 1800s, 28 x 23 x 15 In. 230.00
Table, Writing, William IV, Blond Oak, Leather Insert, 1800s, 30 x 53 x 41 In. 1725.00
Table, Writing, William IV, Mahogany, Gilt Leather, 1800s, 30 x 48 x 30 In. 6615.00
Table, Wrought Iron, Glass Top, X-Supports, Scroll & Rosette, 30 x 32 x 56 In. 1060.00
Table, Wrought Iron, Green Marble Top, 28 x 29 In. 290.00
Table Set, Enameled Tiles, Painted Peacocks, Brass Frame, 21 x 15 x 16 In., 3 Piece 880.00
Tabouret, G. Stickley, No. 602, Round Top, Cross Stretcher, 16 x 18 In. . . . . .355.00 to 410.00
Tabouret, L. & J.G. Stickley, 8-Sided, Legs Mortised Through Top, 17 x 15 In. 765.00
Tabouret, L. & J.G. Stickley, Clip Corner, Arched Stretchers, 18 x 16 x 16 In. 1175.00
Tabouret, L. & J.G. Stickley, No. 559, Octagonal Top, 20 x 18 x 18 In. 2235.00
Tabouret, Limbert, No. 206, Octagonal Top, Splayed Legs, Cutout, 15 x 15 x 18 In. 470.00
Tabouret, Louis XVI Style, Gilt, Aubusson Tapestry, c.1820, 22 In. 750.00
Tabouret, Marble Top, Round Beaded Inset, Pierced Apron, 18 x 21 In. 190.00
Tabouret, Prairie School, Square, 11 Vertical Side Spindles, 22 x 15 x 15 In. 1175.00
Tabouret, Roycroft, No. 49, Mahogany, Square, Through Tenon, 20 x 14 x 14 In. 2115.00
Tabouret, Roycroft, Square, 4 Plank Sides, Keyhole Cutouts, 20 3/4 x 15 In. 4115.00
Tabouret, Stickley Bros., No. 138, Through Post, Mackmurdo Feet, 18 x 14 x 14 In. 355.00
Tea Cart, Mahogany, Removable Tray, Handles, c.1900, 29 x 28 x 18 In. 259.00
Tea Cart, Stickley Bros., Slatted Sides, Removable Tray, 2 Wheels, 33 x 32 x 19 In. 765.00
Terrarium, Victorian, Walnut, Zinc Lined, Glass Case, Turned Finials, 29 x 29 x 21 In. . . . 520.00
Trolley, Walnut, 3 Tiers, Brass Cupped Caster Feet, 36 x 27 x 15 In. 980.00
Umbrella Stand, Arts & Crafts, 2 End Slats, 4 Side Slats, Drip Pan, 24 x 16 x 11 In. 705.00
Umbrella Stand, Arts & Crafts, 40 Slots, 32 x 21 x 26 In. 470.00
Umbrella Stand, Arts & Crafts, Copper, Hammered, Tapered, Ring Handles, 25 1/2 In. . . . 2585.00
Umbrella Stand, Arts & Crafts, Cylindrical, Green Matte Glaze, 10 x 20 1/2 In. 235.00
Umbrella Stand, Fornasetti, Triangular, Musical Instruments, Italy, 22 In. 765.00
Umbrella Stand, G. Stickley, No. 33, 3 Slots, Tapered Legs, 21 x 11 x 34 In. 1115.00
Umbrella Stand, G. Stickley, No. 54, 4 Posts, Copper Drip Pan, 12 x 34 In. 1116.00
Umbrella Stand, G. Stickley, No. 80, Wood, Tapered, Copper Bands, 27 x 13 In. 7050.00
Umbrella Stand, G. Stickley, No. 100, Slatted, Copper Drip Pan, 24 x 12 In. 2235.00
Umbrella Stand, G. Stickley, No. 382, Copper, Hammered, Repousse, 25 x 13 In. 2115.00
Umbrella Stand, Perspex, Spring Shape, Round Base, 1960s, 23 In. 86.00
Vanity, Tabletop, Hardwood, 3 Mirrors, 2 Tiers, Drawers, Japan, 42 x 12 x 46 In. 1116.00
Vitrine, Biedermeier, Ebonized, Triangular Pediment, 67 x 47x 21 In. 5220.00
Vitrine, Black Lacquer, Hinged Top, Glazed Panels, France, 1800s, 20 x 30 x 20 In. 805.00
Vitrine, Edwardian, Chinese Style, c.1900, 76 x 45 x 18 In. 920.00
Vitrine, Empire Style, Mahogany, Metal Mounted, 29 1/2 x 32 x 17 In. 1095.00
Vitrine, George III Style, Mahogany, Glazed Top, Drawer, 14 In. 430.00
Vitrine, Inlaid Mahogany, Round, Inset Green Marble, Paw Feet, 45 x 24 In., Pair 1265.00
Vitrine, Louis XV Style, Kingwood, Early 1900s, 29 1/2 x 101 x 24 In. 355.00
Vitrine, Louis XV Style, Mahogany, Gilt Metal Mounted, 54 x 26 x 15 In. 598.00
Vitrine, Louis XV Style, Mahogany, Gilt Metal Mounted, 55 x 28 x 13 In. 660.00
Vitrine, Louis XV Style, Painted, Vernis Martin Style, 75 x 34 x 19 In. 540.00
Vitrine, Louis XV, Mahogany, Serpentine Top, Glass Door & Sides, 59 x 27 In. 805.00
Vitrine, Louis XVI Style, Mahogany, Gilt Bronze, Early 1900s, 30 x 30 x 19 In. 3600.00
Vitrine, Louis XVI Style, Mahogany, Marble, Gilt Bronze, 43 x 50 x 17 In. 8965.00
Vitrine, Mahogany, Bowfront, 20th Century, 72 x 28 x 17 In. 765.00
Vitrine, Mahogany, Line Border Inlay, Silhouettes, 24 x 16 x 31 In. 175.00
Vitrine, Mahogany, Satinwood Inlay, Lift Top, 2 Drawers, 19 x 24 x 16 In. 1380.00
Vitrine, Mahogany, Ship Model, Wheels, 70 x 128 x 124 In. 85.00
Vitrine, Napoleon III, Ebonized, Marble Top, c.1865, 55 x 26 In. 1035.00
Vitrine, Napoleon III, Mahogany, Ormolu, Pierced Brass Gallery, 66 x 35 x 19 In. 3680.00
Vitrine, Oak, Molded, 4 Slide Doors, 96 x 26 1/2 x 15 In. 160.00
Vitrine, Paint Decorated, Gilt Bronze Mounted, 20th Century, 55 x 26 x 13 In. 880.00
Vitrine, Walnut, 2 Drawers, Paneled Ends, Green Marble Base, 36 x 18 x 32 In. 288.00
Vitrine, Walnut, Ebonized Top & Lower Case, Felt Lined, 29 x 23 x 16 In. 345.00
Wall Unit, Eames, 400 Series, Storage, Herman Miller, c.1950, 59 x 47 In. 15535.00
Wall Unit, Eames, ESU-200, Birch, Drawers, Shelves, Herman Miller, 1950s, 33 x 47 In. . . 4115.00
Wall Unit, G. Nelson, CSS, 13 Shelves, 4 Lights, Cabinets, Herman Miller, c.1958 . . . . 4995.00
Wall Unit, Teak, Modular, Metal Framework, c.1960, 69 x 35 x 17 In. 2350.00
Wardrobe, Chippendale Style, Mahogany, Pine, Bracket Feet, 54 x 24 x 78 In. 1495.00
Wardrobe, G. Stickley, No. 920, 2 Doors, Shelves, Drawers, 60 x 34 x 16 In. 7640.00

Wardrobe, George III Style, Mahogany, 2 Doors, Drawers, 81 x 47 x 22 In. 920.00
Wardrobe, Mahogany, Burl Veneer, 2-Paneled Doors, Drawers, 54 x 19 x 85 In. 775.00
Wardrobe, Mahogany, Line Inlay, Step Back Drawers, 1900s, 50 x 38 x 23 In. 325.00
Wardrobe, Mahogany, Veneer, Dome Top, Cabriole Legs, 32 x 20 x 71 In. 489.00
Wardrobe, Neoclassical, Mahogany, Acanthus Pilasters, Claw Feet, 1840, 71 x 54 In. 3175.00
Wardrobe, Neoclassical, Mahogany, Doric Column Sides, 2 Doors, 87 x 86 In. 2990.00
Wardrobe, Oak, Carved, 2 Doors, Side-By-Side Drawers, 88 x 52 x 20 In. 635.00
Wardrobe, Oak, Copper, Ruskin Cabochons, Glasgow School Of Art, c.1900 . . . . 9500.00
Wardrobe, Pine, Gray Blue Paint, Maine, 19th Century, 74 x 47 x 15 In. 960.00
Wardrobe, Rattan, Split Bamboo, Drawer, Long Door, 68 x 34 x 19 In. 201.00
Wardrobe, Tiger Maple, Grain Painted, c.1830, 74 x 48 x 20 In. 3055.00
Wardrobe, Victorian, Walnut, Cornice, Paneled Doors, Drawers, 50 x 20 x 88 In. 920.00
Wardrobe, Victorian, Walnut, Double Panel Doors, Ogee Cornice, 67 x 26 x 86 In. 1325.00
Wardrobe, Victorian, Walnut, Paneled Doors, 2 Drawers, 56 x 20 x 89 In. 635.00
Wardrobe, Victorian, Walnut, Shield Crest, Medallions, Paneled, 54 x 23 x 101 In. 1495.00
Wardrobe, Walnut Veneer, 2 Doors, Mirrors, France, Late 1800s, 98 x 50 In. 978.00
Wardrobe, Walnut, Carved Cornice, Mirrored Doors, Drawer, Scroll Legs, 97 x 50 In. 1265.00
Wardrobe, Walnut, Panel Door, Cornice, 86 x 64 x 21 In. 1075.00
Washstand, Corner, George III, Mahogany, Rising Gallery, Drawer, 27 In. 420.00
Washstand, Corner, Victorian, Mahogany, Backsplash, Shelf, Drawer, 33 x 22 In. 118.00
Washstand, Corner, Walnut, Backsplash, 45 1/2 x 18 In. 315.00
Washstand, G. Stickley, No. 628, 2 Drawers, 2 Doors, 45 x 40 x 21 In. 3525.00
Washstand, George III, Mahogany, Pitted Slat Top, 2 Drawers, 18th Century, 45 x 20 In. . . 2235.00
Washstand, Georgian Style, Inlaid Mahogany, c.1825, 36 x 22 x 18 In. 1610.00
Washstand, Hepplewhite, Pine, Drawer, Pegged Joints, 32 x 16 1/2 In. 460.00
Washstand, Lindenwood, Carved, Fruit, Mid 19th Century, 83 x 26 x 15 In. 1095.00
Washstand, Louis XV Style, Mahogany, Bronze, 36 In. 269.00
Washstand, Mahogany, Bowfront, Drawer, Brass Mounts, 40 x 18 x 18 In. 230.00
Washstand, Mahogany, Marble Top, Arched Backsplash, Drawer, c.1875, 39 x 28 In. 1380.00
Washstand, Mahogany, Marble Top, Brass Towel Bar, Late 1800s, 35 x 39 x 21 In. 315.00
Washstand, Neoclassical, Mahogany, c.1820, 34 x 23 x 18 In. 1115.00
Washstand, Oak, c.1900, 30 1/2 x 34 x 19 In. 145.00
Washstand, Pine, Yellow Paint, Stenciled Fruit, Drawer, 17 x 14 x 38 In. 345.00
Washstand, Rococo Revival, Rosewood, Marble, Cupboard Doors, 36 x 39 x 24 In. 1035.00
Washstand, Shaker, Walnut, Poplar, Door, Union Village, c.1830, 33 x 30 In. 1150.00
Washstand, Sheraton, Basswood, Birch, Red Wash, Drawer, 18 x 15 x 35 In. 175.00
Washstand, Sheraton, Basswood, Drawer, Leaves, Berries, 36 1/2 x 17 x 17 In. 1610.00
Washstand, Sheraton, Grain Painted, Stencils, Drawer, 38 x 17 x 14 In. 980.00
Washstand, Sheraton, Tiger Maple, Backsplash, Drawer, Turned Legs, 34 x 19 In. 460.00
Washstand, Tiger Maple, Shaped Gallery, American, 1800-10 . . . . 650.00
Wastebasket, Fornasetti, Paperboard, Brass Rim, Italy, 1950s, 10 x 11 In. 259.00
Wastebasket, G. Stickley, No. 94, Slats, Hammered Iron Hoops, 14 x 12 In. 2940.00
Wastebasket, Lakeside Craftshop, Slats, Straps, Copper Tacks, 12 x 12 x 16 In. 355.00
Wastebasket, Stickley Bros., Slats, Cutout Handles, 18 x 14 1/4 x 14 1/4 In. 1295.00
Whatnot Shelf, George III, Pine, 4 Tiers, Column Supports, 50 x 18 In. 1075.00
Whatnot Shelf, Georgian Style, Mahogany, 5 Tiers, Drawer, c.1885, 62 x 16 x 14 In. 1725.00
Whatnot Shelf, Regency Style, Mahogany, 5 Tiers, Columns, Drawer, 62 In. 2070.00
Whatnot Shelf, Regency, Mahogany, Telescopic, Ball Feet, 1825-50, 40 In. . . . . *Illus* 1060.00
Whatnot Shelf, William IV, Rosewood, 3 Tiers, Drawer, c.1825, 45 x 18 In. 1645.00

Don't put too much in old furniture drawers. Weight will loosen the drawer bottom and wear out the bottom of the drawer's sides. Put candle wax on the drawer runners to help them open easily.

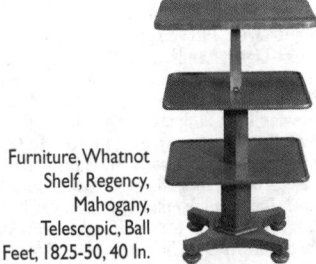

Furniture, Whatnot Shelf, Regency, Mahogany, Telescopic, Ball Feet, 1825-50, 40 In.

Window Seat, Biedermeier, Mahogany, Finials, Mortise & Tenon Joints, 23 x 24 In.	550.00
Window Seat, Biedermeier, Wood, Padded Seat, Armrest, 24 x 21 x 16 In., Pair	980.00
Window Seat, Louis XVI Style, Multicolored, Padded, Outscrolled, 30 x 60 x 21 In.	4370.00
Window Seat, Regency Style, Mahogany, Outscrolled Arms, Ball Feet, 48 In.	1435.00
Window Seat, Regency Style, Mahogany, Ribbon-Carved Frieze, 20 x 39 x 17 In.	345.00
Wine Cooler, Mahogany, Coffin Shape, Beveled Edges, Bun Feet, 22 x 29 In.	1840.00

G. ARGY-ROUSSEAU is the impressed mark used on a variety of objects in the Art Deco style. Gabriel Argy-Rousseau, born in 1885, was a French glass artist. In 1921, he formed a partnership that made pate-de-verre and other glass. He worked until 1952 and died in 1953.

G-ARGY-ROUSSEAU

Box, Rose, Signed, 3 In.	4320.00
Lamp, Radio, Panels, Stylized Flowers, Pate-De-Verre, 9 1/4 x 7 3/4 In.	10925.00
Paperweight, 2 Moths, Mottled Amber, Square, Pate-De-Verre, 2 1/2 In.	5290.00
Paperweight, Cube, 2 Butterflies, Amber, Brown, Signed, 2 1/4 x 1 3/4 In.	3000.00
Pendant, Black Insect, Amber Translucent Wings, Pate-De-Verre, 2 1/2 In.	1020.00
Pendant, Rose, Green Accents, Signed, 2 1/4 In.	1550.00
Vase, 3 Butterflies, Green, Orange, Brown, Mottled Green, Pate-De-Verre, 3 In.	11750.00
Vase, Amber, Tapered, Ribbed Corners, Cone Foot, Signed, 8 1/4 In.	3345.00
Vase, Amethyst, Black Wolves, Mottled, Lavender, Frosted, 9 1/2 In.	44850.00
Vase, Dancing Men, Women, Brown, Amethyst, Signed, 6 1/4 In.	12075.00
Vase, Girl Atop Stone Wall, Picking Apples, Pate-De-Verre, Signed, 9 1/2 In.	9480.00
Vase, Mottled Pink, Amethyst, Frosted, Signed, 6 1/4 In.	6463.00
Vase, Peonies, Amethyst Ground, Pate-De-Verre, 5 3/4 In.	10000.00
Vase, Raised Thistle, Red, Green Leaves, Mottled Purple, Green Ground, 4 In.	3525.00
Vase, Repeating Thistles, Mottled Frosted Ground, Pate-De-Verre, 6 In.	3525.00
Vase, Thistles, Orange, Amethyst, Black, Orange Ground, Pate-De-Verre, 3 7/8 In.	4115.00
Vase, Women Picking Apples, Stylized Stone Wall, Pate-De-Verre, 9 1/2 In.	7475.00

GALLE was a designer who made glass, pottery, furniture, and other Art Nouveau items. Emile Galle founded his factory in France in 1874. After Galle's death in 1904, the firm continued to make glass and furniture until 1931. The name *Galle* was used as a mark, but it was often hidden in the design of the object. Galle glass is listed here. Pottery is in the next section. His furniture is listed in the Furniture category.

Galle

Atomizer, Red Flowers, Leaves, Amber Field, Oval, Marked, 8 1/2 In.	690.00
Bowl, Fougeres, Canoe Shape, Clear, Green, Hematite Enamel, Cameo, c.1885, 2 x 4 In.	805.00
Bowl, Thistle, Leaves, Pink, Burgundy, Black, Cream, Smoky, Pinched Rim, 6 1/4 In.	1645.00
Box, Cover, Grape Design, Gray, Amber Overlay, Amethyst, Cameo, c.1900, 6 3/4 In.	1610.00
Box, Cover, Scenic, Gray, Pink Overlay, Green, Brown, Cameo, c.1900, 6 In.	1150.00
Carafe, Enameled, Rampant Lion, Leaves, Footed, Stopper, c.1890, 10 In.	1115.00
Decanter, Clear, Ribbed, Blue & White Enameled Monogram, 12 In.	1200.00
Decanter, Women Playing Instruments, Grapes, Masks, Donut Shape, Stopper, 11 In.	430.00
Dish, Cover, Cherry Blossoms, Yellow Ground, Bulbous, 4-Sided, Cameo, 5 In.	2300.00
Fire Screen, Inlaid Wood, Lilies, Carved Frame, c.1895, 41 x 22 1/4 In.	4400.00
Jardiniere, Foliage, Green, Amethyst, Blue, Amber Ground, Cameo, 11 In.	3055.00
Jardiniere, Wisteria, Purple, Lemon Ground, Cameo, 9 5/8 In.	1295.00
Lamp, Clematis, Flowers, Purple, Frost Ground, Signed, 21 In.	9300.00
Lamp, Flower, Vine, Burgundy, Green, Caramel Ground, Cylindrical, c.1925, 14 1/4 In.	470.00
Lamp, Hanging, Hydrangeas, Frosted Yellow, Cream, Crown Shape, Cameo, 11 1/2 In.	4315.00
Lamp, Light Blue, Lavender Flowers, Green Leaves, Yellow, Cameo, Signed, 17 In.	6900.00
Lamp, Perfume, Red Flowers, Camphor, Cameo, Brasswork, Signed, 6 In.	2160.00
Night-Light, Flowers, Butterfly, Cameo, Iron, c.1910, 4 1/2 In.	805.00
Night-Light, Landscape, Blue, Purple, Green, Yellow Ground, Cameo, Metal, 7 In.	1765.00
Perfume Bottle, Cameo, Landscape, Green, Pink Ground, 5 In.	880.00
Pitcher, Insects, Flowers, Egyptian Bird Handle, Aesthetic Movement, 12 1/4 In.	2235.00
Powder Box, Poppies, Amber, Rose, Cushion Shape, Dome Cover, c.1885, 2 x 4 In.	1035.00
Tray, Oak Leaves, Acorns, Frosted To Orange, Triangular, Rim, Cameo, Signed, 9 In.	805.00
Vase, Amethyst Flowers, Blue Frosted Ground, Cameo, Signed, 8 1/4 In.	690.00
Vase, Amethyst, Lavender, Leaves, Flowers, Cameo, Signed, 5 In.	750.00
Vase, Banjo, Flowers, Leaves, Violet-Brown, Frosted, Cameo, Signed, 5 1/2 In.	850.00
Vase, Blown-Out Cherry Branches, Frosted Amber Ground, 11 1/8 In.	8225.00
Vase, Blown-Out Clematis, Blue, Purple, Signed, 9 1/2 In.	8340.00

Vase, Blue Clematis, Leaves, Yellow Ground, Bulbous, Cameo, 7 1/2 In. 2530.00
Vase, Branches, Blossoms, Lilac, Green, Pink, White Frosted Ground, Cameo, 6 In. 765.00
Vase, Bud, Lotus Blossoms, Striated Clear To Red, Cameo, Silver Rim, c.1900, 8 7/8 In. . . 1495.00
Vase, Burgundy Fuchsia, Shaded Citron, Oval, Flared Rim, Footed, Cameo, 6 In. 1265.00
Vase, Butterfly, Leaves, Bulbous Base, Frosted, Cylindrical Neck, Cameo, 6 In. 1075.00
Vase, Camellias, Red, Orange, Cameo, 8 In. 1530.00
Vase, Camphor, Green Blown-Out Plums, Yellow Ground, Signed, 15 1/2 In. 5465.00
Vase, Catkins, White, Citron Green, Olive Overshaded Peach, Cameo, c.1885, 6 In. 750.00
Vase, Cherry Blossoms, Citron Ground, Flattened Disc, Cameo, 6 In. 2300.00
Vase, Cherry Blossoms, Green, Apricot, Cameo Signature, 14 In. 4113.00
Vase, Cherry Branches, Leaves, Citron Ground, Oval, Peaked Rim, Cameo Signed, 8 In. . . 2185.00
Vase, Cluster Of Cherries, Branches, Leaves, Citron Ground, Flattened Disc, Cameo, 8 In. . 1900.00
Vase, Daisies, Green, Cameo, 11 In. 3055.00
Vase, Double Seed Pods, Vine, Apricot, Lime, Olive Green, Cameo, Signed, 6 5/8 In. 1150.00
Vase, Figural Entwined Fish, Open Mouths, Gold, Lilac Iridescent, Enameled, Signed, 6 In. 900.00
Vase, Flowers, Amethyst Over Shaded Yellow Ground, Cameo, Signed, 3 7/8 In. 325.00
Vase, Flowers, Gray, Yellow, Amethyst, Cameo, c.1900, 4 1/2 In. 820.00
Vase, Flowers, Leaves, Peach, Frosted Ground, Cameo, Signed, 6 In. 805.00
Vase, Flowers, Peach, Garnet, Oil Jar Shape, Cameo, c.1885, 4 In. 750.00
Vase, Flowers, Red, Frosted Ground, Cameo, Signed, 15 In. 1410.00
Vase, Flowers, Shaded Purple To Frosted White, Bottle Shape, Cameo, 6 In. 540.00
Vase, Flowers, Vines, Leaves, Lavender, Frosted Ground, Signed, 7 In. 115.00
Vase, Freesias, White, Amber, Ruby, Baluster, Cameo, c.1885, 8 In. 1265.00
Vase, Fuchsia, Rum On Yellow, Frosted Ground, Cameo, Signed, 20 In. 4315.00
Vase, Garden Flowers & Leaves, Citron Over Deep Maroon, Cameo, 1900, 6 In. 2130.00
Vase, Gingko Leaves, Amethyst, Frosted Green, Pink Ground, Rolled Rim, Cameo, 9 In. . . 865.00
Vase, Gooseberries, Red, Clear, Frosted Ground, Cameo, Signed, 8 1/4 In. 825.00
Vase, Grapes, Leaves, Vines, Amethyst, Green Frosted Ground, Baluster, Cameo, 7 1/2 In. . 1555.00
Vase, Grapevines, Leaves, Clusters, Blue, Gray, Amber, Salmon, Cameo, Signed, 15 In. . . . 8340.00
Vase, Gray, Yellow, Amethyst, Flowers, Shouldered Oval, Cameo, c.1900, 7 1/2 In. 950.00
Vase, Green, Brown Trees, Blue Mountains, Yellow, Flattened, Cameo, Signed, 5 In. 1645.00
Vase, Honeysuckle Branch, Red On Lemon Ground, Cameo, 4 1/2 In. 705.00
Vase, Hydrangeas, Lavender, Green, Mottled Peach, Cameo, 18 In. . . . . .2875.00 to 3840.00
Vase, Iris, Leaves, Cream, Maroon Ground, Cameo, Signed, 13 3/4 In. 1840.00
Vase, Irises, Amethyst, Frosted, Fire Polished, Cameo, 7 1/2 In. 1880.00
Vase, Lake Scene, Leaves, Trees, Pillow, Enameled, Cameo, 13 In. 5520.00
Vase, Landscape, Amethyst, Blue, Baluster, Cameo, 14 1/2 In. 4480.00
Vase, Landscape, Brown, Frosted, Yellow Ground, Bulbous Foot, Cameo, Signed, 6 In. . . . 990.00
Vase, Landscape, Green, Brown, Frosted, Pink Ground, Cameo, 7 In. 940.00
Vase, Landscape, Mountains, Lake, Pine Trees, Blue, Gray, Peach, Cameo, Signed, 17 In. . 10945.00
Vase, Leaf, Green, Pink, Yellow, Signed, 19th Century, 14 In. 3220.00
Vase, Leaves, Berries, Gray Shaded With Orange, Red, Cameo, 3 In. 200.00
Vase, Leaves, Branches, Seedpods, Frosted Mauve Ground, Cameo, 7 3/4 In. 635.00
Vase, Leaves, Gray, Yellow, Moss Green, Cameo, c.1900, 3 3/4 In. 520.00
Vase, Leaves, Green, Frosted, Pink Ground, Cameo, Signed, 4 In. 470.00
Vase, Lilacs, Stylized, Purple, Green, Cameo Signature, 14 In. 1765.00
Vase, Lotus Blossom, Pond, Citron, Frosted, Flattened Oval, Boat Shaped Mouth, 8 3/4 In. 2590.00
Vase, Lotus Blossoms, Lily Pads, Frosted Colorless, Blue, Oval, Cameo, 3 x 11 In. 1795.00
Vase, Orange, Yellow Chrysanthemums, Cylindrical, Cushion Foot, 30 In. 3220.00
Vase, Phlox, Lavender & Green, Frosted Apricot Ground, Flared Base, Cameo, 13 3/4 In. . 1440.00
Vase, Pilgrim, Flowers, Frosted, Green, Lavender, Cameo, 1900-20, 5 1/8 In. 1265.00
Vase, Purple Hyacinths, Leaves, Frosted Ground, Blue To Yellow, Signed, 12 In. 8625.00
Vase, Purple Poppies, Frosted Ground, Fire Polished, Cameo, Signed, 13 1/2 In. 1500.00
Vase, Red Poppies, Yellow, Frosted Ground, Cameo, 8 In. 2875.00
Vase, Red, Clear Ground, Art Nouveau Leaves, Iridescent, Cameo, Signed, 7 1/4 In. 4890.00
Vase, Sailboats, Seagulls, Slender, Flaring Foot, Cameo, 21 In. 3335.00
Vase, Stick, Flowers, Leaves, Gray, Amethyst, Bulbous Base, Cameo, c.1900 . . . . 1840.00
Vase, Stick, Green To Frost Ground, Art Nouveau Leaf, Flowers, Cameo, Signed, 23 In. . . . 2015.00
Vase, Thistle, Gray, Burgundy, Etched, Cameo, c.1910, 12 In. 1725.00
Vase, Thistle, Green, Pink To Cream Ground, Cameo, Signed, 16 1/4 In. 1140.00
Vase, Trees, Lake, Shaded Citron, Frosted, Tapered, Flattened, Peaked Rim, Cameo, 8 In. . 1610.00
Vase, Trees, Leaves, Mountains, Tapering, Oval, Circular Neck, Flared Base, Signed, 6 In. . 750.00
Vase, Violets, Purple, Lemon Ground, Cameo, Signed, 5 In. 1000.00

Vase, Wisteria, Leaves, Gray, Amethyst, Cameo, c.1900, 12 1/2 In. 775.00

GALLE POTTERY was made by Emile Galle, the famous French designer, after 1874. The pieces were marked with the initials *E. G.* impressed, *Em. Galle Faiencerie de Nancy*, or a version of his signature. Galle is best known for his glass, listed above.

Figurine, Cat, Yellow, Blue Heart, Applied Glass Eyes, Signed, 14 1/2 In. 2350.00
Jug, Embossed Dragonfly, Underglaze, Parcel Gilt Ground, 7 In. 5520.00
Tray, Gray, Cranberry Enamel, Quill, Shell Shape, Faience, Signed, 15 In. 400.00
Vase, Blown-Out Flowers, Teal, Multicolored Enamel, Parcel Gilt, c.1885, 8 1/2 In. 1725.00
Vase, Crimson Seaweed, Green To Pink Glaze, Faience, 5 In. 345.00
Vase, Insect, Stylized Wings, Enamel, Gold Leaf, Aesthetic Movement, 3-Footed, 5 1/2 In.   353.00
Vase, Lion Of Lorraine, Enameled, Parcel Gilt, 3-Footed, Applied Accents, Signed, 12 In. .   2590.00
Vase, Scene, Laroche, Chicken, Rooster, Oval, Footed, Pillow Shape, 7 x 12 x 5 In. 520.00

GAME collectors like all types of games. Of special interest are any board games or card games. Transogram and other company names are included in the description when known. Other games may be found listed under Card, Toy, or the name of the character or celebrity featured in the game.

$10,000 Pyramid, Milton Bradley, Board, 1974 . . . .   10.00
$20,000 Pyramid 4th Ed., Milton Bradley, Board, 1977 . . . .   10.00
Adventures Of Robin Hood, Milton Bradley, 1938, 9 1/2 x 19 x 1 3/4 In. 133.00
All Star Basketball, Gardner, Accessories, Board, Box, 1950s, 13 In. 80.00
Alpha Football Game, Replica, Board, Box, 1940s, 12 1/2 x 19 x 1 In. 85.00
Arcade, Speedway, Chicago Spin, Pedal Accelerator, Steering Wheel, c.1965, 69 In. 345.00
Babe Ruth's Baseball Game, Milton Bradley, Board, Box, 20 In. 935.00
Bambino, Baseball, Wooden Ball, Metallic Playing Surface, Box, 19 x 12 1/2 In. 115.00
Baseball Strategy, Avalon Hill Co., Board, Box, 1974, 11 x 14 x 1 1/2 In. 58.00
Battle Game, Soldiers, Paper Lithograph, Guns, Wood Bullets, Parker Bros., Box, 15 In. . . .   180.00
Beetle Bailey, Hilarious New Army, Jaymar, Board, 1950 . . . .   40.00
Beginner's Bridge, Milton Bradley, 1965 . . . .   4.00
Bent Out Of Shape, Gabriel, 1971 . . . .   10.00
Bike Race, 4 Laps To The Mile, 2 Person, Amusement Park, Narragansett Machine Co. 16500.00
Billy Bumps Visits Boston, Parker Brothers, Card, 1888, 6 1/2 x 5 In. 77.00
Bingo, Milton Bradley, Board 10.00
Blastoff Space, Rocket Ships, Tin, Replogle Globe, Box, 1953, 11 In. 760.00
Bliss Mama Katz Comic Ladder, 32 In. 165.00
Bliss Marble, 19 In. 495.00
Blondie Goes To Leisureland, No. 3, Westinghouse, Board, 29 x 20 1/2 In. 35.00
Board, Backgammon, Red, Mustard, Black, 1 1/2 x 10 x 12 3/4 In. 1380.00
Board, Checkers & Compass Design, 2-Sided, Black, Wood, Varnished, Patina, 13 1/2 In. .   550.00
Board, Checkers & Parcheesi, Rectangular, 1800s, 18 1/2 x 27 3/4 In. 410.00
Board, Checkers, 2-Sided, Painted Red, Yellow, Black, 17 x 17 3/4 In. 605.00
Board, Checkers, 2-Sided, Red, Black, Yellow, Ouija Symbols, 21 x 21 1/2 In. 470.00
Board, Checkers, 9 Man Morris, 2-Sided, Painted, 15 1/2 x 27 3/4 In. 805.00
Board, Checkers, Black, Natural Wood, Varnished, 8 3/8 In. 440.00
Board, Checkers, Black, Natural Wood, Varnished, 18 3/4 In. 250.00
Board, Checkers, Curled Ash & Rosewood Veneer, Walnut Moldings, 28 1/2 x 28 1/4 In. . .   115.00
Board, Checkers, Inlaid Mixed Woods, Natural, Varnished, 10 In.   165.00
Board, Checkers, Maple, Walnut Inlay, Mustard Paint, Cutout Handle, 19 1/2 x 29 3/4 In. .   345.00
Board, Checkers, Red & Ocher, Divided Compartments, Edge Molding, 18 x 28 In. 690.00
Board, Checkers, Stars, Inlaid, Clubs, Diamonds, Spades, Hearts, Varnished, 22 In. 1045.00
Board, Checkers, Walnut, Inlaid, Natural Finish, Varnished, Molded Edges, 15 1/2 In. 495.00
Board, Checkers, Wood, Black Frame, c.1900, 10 3/4 x 10 3/4 In.   106.00
Board, Checkers, Wood, Red & Black, Yellow Accents, 2 Tin Trays, 16 x 19 In. 1760.00
Board, Chess, Onyx, Marble, Stone Pedestal, 30 1/2 x 21 x 21 In. 179.00
Board, Combination, Combinola, 2-Sided, Literature, Leonard, c.1900, 29 1/4 In. 115.00
Board, Combination, Flag Border, Pieces, Book, Archarena Co., Peoria, Il., c.1900, 28 In. .   810.00
Board, Combination, National Combination Game Board Co., c.1901, 28 1/2 In. 255.00
Board, Combination, Universal, 2-Sided, South Bend Toy Co., Indiana, c.1900, 28 3/4 In. .   375.00
Board, Cribbage, Scrolled, Turned Feet, Brass Pegs, England, c.1760 . . . .   295.00
Board, Crokinole, Checkerboard, A.E. Hourd & Co., Round, Ontario, 1897, 27 1/4 In. 115.00

Board, Crokinole, Combination, Fiberboard, Wood Frame, Milton Bradley, c.1920, 24 In. .   511.00
Board, Crokinole, Combination, Red, Wire Arches, Archarena Co., Peoria, Il., c.1900, 24 In.   115.00
Board, Crokinole, Octagonal, Disks, Rule Book, M.B. Ross, N.Y., 1880, 31 1/2 In. 620.00
Board, Game Of The States, Milton Bradley, c.1940-50 . . . .   10.00
Board, Inlaid, Black Walnut, Mahogany, Birch, Variegated Bands, Diamonds, 24 x 24 In. . .   430.00
Board, Owl, Combination, 4 Owls, Rule Book, Edw. Mikkelsen, Chicago, c.1901, 28 In. . .   316.00
Board, Owl, Combination, Rule Book, Edw. Mikkelsen, Chicago, c.1901, 28 1/2 In. 175.00
Board, Painted, Alternate Squares, Yellow, Black, Frame, 19th Century, 21 x 32 In. 588.00
Board, Painted, Poplar, Gold, Black Blocks, Red Borders, Black Ground, 25 x 15 In. 805.00
Board, Papier-Mache, Abalone Inlay, Gilt, Bone Pieces, England, 1800s, 17 3/4 x 20 In. . .   520.00
Board, Parcheesi, 2-Piece, Folding, Red Green Yellow, Blue Paint, 19 1/2 x 19 1/2 In. 575.00
Board, Parcheesi, Blue, Pink, Yellow, White Ground, 24 In. 315.00
Board, Parcheesi, Brown, White, Black, Molded Edge, Wide Side Trays, 30 1/2 x 18 In. . .   259.00
Board, Parcheesi, Multicolored Paint, 19 In. 3163.00
Board, Parcheesi, Pine, Beveled Edges, Brown Ground, Green, Gold, 22 x 21 1/2 In. 2185.00
Board, Parcheesi, Pine, Painted, Black, White, 1800s, 23 1/4 x 18 In. 500.00
Board, Parcheesi, Wood, Multicolored, c.1900, 19 x 19 3/8 In. 5975.00
Board, Pine, Breadboard Ends, Red & Black Checkerboard, 17 1/2 x 24 In. 144.00
Booby Trap, Parker Brothers, Board, 1965 . . . .   15.00
Box, Pine, Checkerboard Paint, Wooden Chessmen, Folding, 1800s, 10 x 9 3/4 In. 1175.00
Box, Rosewood, Dovetailed, Printed Cards, Counters, G. Williams, N.Y., 10 x 12 In. 690.00
Bridge For Juniors, Selchow & Righter Co., 1965 . . . .   5.00
Bridgette, Game Of Games, Card, 1959 . . . .   5.00
Brownie Motor Race, Tin Lithograph Board, 4 Cars, Box, 12 x 12 In. 165.00
Bullwinkle Ring Toss, Unopened, Whitman, Box, 1972, 8 x 15 1/2 In. 30.00
Bullwinkle's Magnetic Crazy Maze, Standard Toycrafts, Box, 1962, 10 x 15 x 3 In. 106.00
Candid Camera, Lowell, Allen Funt, Board, 1963 . . . .   80.00
Capping The Clown, Eclipse Co., England 55.00
Captain Kidd Junior Walking The Plank, Parker Bros., Board, c.1920, 12 x 11 In. 80.00
Cardino, Milton Bradley, Board, 1970 . . . .   7.00
Catching Mice, McLoughlin, Paper Lithograph, Cardboard, 7 3/4 x 15 1/2 In. 825.00
Champion Game, Base Ball, D. Brouthers & J. Clarkson, Board, Spinners, 1889 . . . .   2185.00
Championship Base Ball Parlor Game, Round Board, Dice, 1914, 9 1/2 x 22 In. 460.00
Chess Set, Ivory, Carved, White & Red Stain, Chinese, Mid 20th Century, 1 1/2 To 3 1/2 In.   635.00
Chess Set, Ivory, Leaves, Beadwork, Red & White, Early 20th Century, 4 In. 420.00
Chit Chat, Hugh Downs Game Of Conversation, Milton Bradley, Board, 1963 . . . .   11.00
Cinderella, Put The Shoe On The Foot, Printed Linen, 17 x 30 In.   415.00
Clown Game, POP Manufacturing Co., 16 x 14 In. 85.00
Common Sense Card Lizard Sleeve Holder, Cheating Device, Nickel Plated, c.1885, 2 In. .   28.00
Course A Anes, Donkey Game, Box, France, 1800s, 24 In. 193.00
Crazy Ball, Parker Bros., 14 x 14 In. 55.00
Cribbage, Game Pieces, Dice Shaker, Painted, Oval, 1800s, 7 1/8 x 2 3/4 In. 411.00
Cribbage Board, Ivory, Chrysanthemum, Japan, 7 In. 69.00
Cross Up, Pictures Lucille Ball, Milton Bradley, Board, 1974 . . . .   10.00
Crossword Lexicon, Parker Brothers, 1938 . . . .   35.00
Crow Hunt, Guns, Crows, Box, Parker Brothers, 18 In. 33.00
Dating Game, Card, Money, Hasbro, Board, 1968 . . . .   30.00
Dexterity Puzzle, Felix The Cat, Round, 2 In. 28.00
Dice Tumbler, Carnival, Steel Cage, Brass Columns, Wood, Early 1900s, 19 x 18 In. 118.00
Dominoes, Cased, Bird's-Eye Maple, Black Dots, Sliding Top, 10 In., 55 Pieces 210.00
Dr. Fusby, McLaughlin Bros., Card, c.1890, 4 1/2 x 6 1/4 In. 175.00
Dragonmaster, Lowe, Card, 1981 . . . .   10.00
Fantasy Island, View Of Island On Box, Columbia Pictures, Ideal, Board, 1978 . . . .   30.00
Faro Casekeeper, Hinged, B.C. Wills Co., Detroit 968.00
Fast Mail, Milton Bradley, Board, c.1920 . . . .   250.00
Felix The Cat, Hand Game, Round, 2 1/4 In. 165.00
Fibber McGee & Wistful Vista Mystery, Milton Bradley, Board, 1940 . . . .   65.00
Figure, 6-Cat Game, Canvas, Stuffed, Oblong, Painted, 1900s, 21 x 9 1/2 In., 6 Piece 441.00
Fox Hunting, Figures, Board, Box, 20 In. 165.00
Frank Cavanaugh's American Football Game, Board, c.1955, 15 x 12 x 1 1/4 In. 95.00
French Parlor, Jeux, Hinged Box, Glass Front Compartments, c.1890, 17 x 12 In. 335.00
Funny Bones, Parker Brothers, Card, 1968 . . . .   5.00
Game Of Golf, Clark's, 1890s 545.00

Game Of On Guard, McLoughlin Bros., 1899 .... 750.00
Garrison, Game Of Merit, Knight, Shield, Castle, 13 x 13 In. 39.00
Gee Wiz, Racing Game Sensation, Tin, Wolverine, Box, 16 In. 110.00
Golf, Indoor, Schoenhut Manufacturing Co., c.1922 .... 2820.00
Golfing, Great Indoor Golf Game, England, c.1910 .... 495.00
Goren's Beginners' Bridge, Milton Bradley, 1967 .... 5.00
Grand Steeple Chase, Tin Board & Horses, JEP, Box, France, 11 x 28 In. 88.00
Green Ghost, Transogram, Board, 1965 .... 80.00
Gunsmoke, Lowell, Board, Box, 1958 .... 250.00
Gypsy Fortune Teller, Milton Bradley No. 4003, 14 x 8 In. 69.00
Hands Down, Ideal, 1964 .... 15.00
Happy Hooligan, Bowling, Milton Bradley, Board, 1925, 11 x 15 In. 660.00
Hit The Dodger, Black, Knock Him Out, Target, Bell Rings, Wooden, Tethered Ball, 1910 . 545.00
Honey West, Girl Private Eye, Ideal, Board, c.1965, 9 3/4 x 18 1/2 In. 190.00
Horse Race, Mechanical, Felt Board, JDP, France, Box, 13 x 13 In. 250.00
How Silas Popped The Question, Parker Brothers, Card, 1915, 6 1/2 x 5 In. 17.00
Humpty Dumpty Marble Game, Reed & Co., 25 1/2 In. 550.00
Humpty Dumpty Marble Game, Reed & Co., c.1900, 18 In. 330.00
I'm Gary Moore & I've Got A Secret, Lowell Toy Co., Board, 1956 .... 55.00
In The Dark, Parker Brothers, 1969 .... 5.00
Indoor Golf, Tommy Green & Cassy Lofter Clubs, Schoenhut Mfg., Pat. 1922 .... 2850.00
Jackie Robinson's Pocket Baseball Game, c.1950, 9 x 6 1/2 In. 315.00
Jetsons Out Of This World, Hanna Barbera, Transogram, Board, Box, c.1963, 10 x 19 In. . 160.00
Jeu De Course Rond, Tin, Lead Horses, Spins, France, Box, 6 3/4 In. 330.00
Jigsaw Puzzle, American Fire Department, Insert, Milton Bradley, Box, 1882 .... 549.00
Jigsaw Puzzle, Annie Oakley, 3 Puzzles, Gail Davis, Milton Bradley, Box, 6 3/4 x 10 In. ... 44.00
Jigsaw Puzzle, Borax, Hauling 20 Mule Team Borax Out Of Death Valley, 1933, 10 x 8 In. 35.00
Jigsaw Puzzle, Carrot Farm, Gabby Hayes, 14 1/2 x 10 1/2 In. 16.00
Jigsaw Puzzle, Fire Engine, Wood Box, McLaughlin, 1887, 24 3/4 x 17 3/4 In. 605.00
Jigsaw Puzzle, Gunsmoke, Matt Dillon, 14 1/2 x 11 1/2 In. 22.00
Jigsaw Puzzle, Gunsmoke, Matt Dillon, Kitty, 14 1/2 x 11 1/2 In. 28.00
Jigsaw Puzzle, Little Black Sambo, 3 Puzzles, Saalfield, Hays, Box, 1942, 9 1/2 x 9 In. ... 650.00
Jigsaw Puzzle, Munsters, Kayro Vue Productions, Whitman, Box, c.1965, 11 x 8 1/2 In. ... 65.00
Jigsaw Puzzle, Night Before Christmas, Milton Bradley, Boxed Set Of 3 .... 355.00
Jigsaw Puzzle, Old American Airline, A Greeting From The Air, c.1940, 13 x 9 1/2 In. 35.00
Jigsaw Puzzle, Outer Limits, Sea Creatures, Daystar, Milton Bradley, Box, c.1964, 8 x 13 In. 75.00
Jigsaw Puzzle, Sohio Standard Oil, In Dutch, No. 2, Box, 1933, 11 x 14 1/2 In. 30.00
Jigsaw Puzzle, The Prince, Maxfield Parrish, 1920s, 12 x 9 1/2 In. 90.00
Jungle Ball, Box, 21 In. 45.00
Junior Auto Race, Board, c.1930, 11 1/2 x 11 1/2 In. 70.00
Keyword, Parker Brothers, Board, 1953 .... 18.00
Kitty Kat Cup Ball, Rosebud Art Co., U.S.A., 10 x 15 In. 110.00
Lex-O-Grams, Whitman, 1949 .... 20.00
Lookout, Board, Box, 14 In. 415.00
Loteria Board, Hand Printed, Mexico 150.00
Mad Magazine, Parker Brothers, Card, 1979 .... 20.00
Magnetic Fish Pond, Box, 1800s, 12 x 12 In. 130.00
Major League Indoor Baseball, Philadelphia Game Co., 1910, 19 x 13 In. 4025.00
Man From U.N.C.L.E., Card, Milton Bradley, Box, 1965, 6 x 10 In. 30.00
Marble, Cast Iron, Figure Shoots Marble, Gold Paint, Table Top, J. & E. Stevens, 9 3/4 In. . 525.00
Marble, Clowns, Wooden, 15 In. 330.00
Mickey Mantle Action, Baseball Plastic Figure, Kohner Brothers, Board, 1960s 805.00
Mickey Mantle's Big League Baseball, Board, Gardner, Box, 1958, 7 3/4 x 15 x 1 1/2 In. .. 190.00
Mikado Juggler, Box, Germany, Late 1800s, 23 x 10 In. 495.00
Mr. Ree, Selchow & Righter, Board, Box, 1937, 19 In. 22.00
NFL Franchise, Rohrwood, Inc., Board, 1989 .... 7.00
Parlor Tether Ball, Parker Brothers., 13 x 13 In. 85.00
Pathfinder, Milton Bradley, Board, 1977 .... 10.00
Piggeries, Latest Craze, Spears Patent, Accessories, Box, 10 x 10 In. 165.00
Pigskin, Parker Brothers, Board, Box, 18 In. 35.00
Pinhead, Hide & Seek, Remco, Board, 1959 .... 9.00
Play Football, Whitman, Board, Box, 1934 .... 70.00
Poosh-M-Up Jr., 4 Games, Northwestern Products, Box, 11 x 17 In. 115.00

Pop The Bird, Target Game, Miniature Bagatelle, Wood, Metal, 12 In. 55.00
Price Is Right, Lowell Toy, 1958 . . . .   30.00
Pro Hockey Game, Rod Gilbert, Unopened, Box, 1974, 11 x 5 1/2 x 4 1/2 In. 45.00
Punch & Judy, Parker Brothers, 11 x 13 In. 165.00
Puzzle, Blocks, Girl Holding Rabbit, Paper, Lithograph, Box, 1890s 165.00
Puzzle, Pussy Cat, Milton Bradley, 3 Puzzles, Box, 18 1/2 x 13 In.   330.00
Puzzle, Shredded Wheat, Sgt. Biff O'Hara, Round, Metal, 3 Balls, Premium, Nabisco 15.00
Puzzle, Victorian Parlor Scene, Child Assembling Puzzle, Paper On Wood, 14 In. 44.00
Rifleman, Milton Bradley, Four Star Sussex, Board, 1959 . . . .   111.00
Ring Toss, Goat, Bear Bean Bag, Molded Cardboard, Papier-Mache, 13 In. 550.00
Roadway Race, Tin, Paper Lithograph Board, Northwestern Products, 8 x 18 In. 55.00
Rose Bowl, Pressed Fiber Game Board, Lowe, Box, c.1940, 12 x 15 x 1 In. 314.00
Rube Bressler's Baseball Game, Board, 1936 . . . .   338.00
Santa Claus, Parker Brothers, Box, 15 In. 550.00
Scrabble Crossword, Pocket Edition, Selchow & Righter Co., 1976 . . . .   10.00
Scrabble Crossword Cubes, Selchow & Righter Co., 1964 . . . .   10.00
Scrabble Crossword Dominoes, Selchow & Righter Co., 1975 . . . .   7.00
Scribbage, Lowe, Board, 1963 . . . .   6.00
Sergeant Preston, Milton Bradley, Box, 1956, 8 1/2 x 16 1/2 In. 40.00
Shenanigans, Milton Bradley, Board, 1964 . . . .   17.00
Shoot The Works, Popgun, Monkey Clown, Ducks, Box, 17 In. 65.00
Skill It, Milton Bradley, 1966 . . . .   7.00
Slap Trap, Ideal, Board, 1967 . . . .   20.00
Snap Judgment, Simon & Schuster, 1933 . . . .   498.00
Snapshot, Parker Brothers, 1972 . . . .   10.00
Spill & Spell, Parker Brothers, 1957 . . . .   15.00
Stagecoach West Adventure, Transogram Board, Box, c.1961, 9 x 17 1/2 In. 90.00
Sub Attack, Milton Bradley, Board, 1965 . . . .   15.00
Swamp Fox, Parker Brothers, 1960, 9 3/4 x 19 x 1 1/4 In. 85.00
T.H.E. Cat, Ideal, c.1966, 10 x 19 3/4 In. 2000.00
Target, Air Defense, Wolverine, Shoots At 5 Airplanes, Tin, Spring Loaded, 18 In. 310.00
Target, Fast Draw, Out Draw The Outlaw, Plastic, Mattel, Box, 1959, 18 1/2 x 9 In. 116.00
Target, Jolly Darkie Game, Milton Bradley, 19 x 11 In. 660.00
Target, Untouchables, Mechanical Arcade, Plastic, Tin, Marbled, Box 165.00
Telegraph Messenger Boy, 1910, 6 3/4 x 5 1/4 In. 176.00
Texas 28 Shooting, Wood, Tin, Leather, 5 Corks, 2 Indian Targets, SN, Japan, Box, 29 In. .   70.00
Tiddly Winks, Hop Scotch Tiddly Winks, Parker Brothers, 1891, 6 3/4 x 10 1/2 In. 110.00
Tiddly Winks, McLoughlin, Combo, Wood Game Cup, Chips, Mats, Box, 9 x 13 In. 330.00
Time Tunnel, Ideal Toy Corp., Board, Box, 1966, 10 x 19 1/2 In. 170.00
Tivoli, Spear's Games, Box, 11 x 8 In. 275.00
Tom Corbett Space Cadet, Peerless Playthings Co., c.1953, 10 1/4 x 21 In. 403.00
Top Pro Football Quiz, Ed-U-Card, Board, 1970 . . . .   9.00
Touche Turtle, Garbriel, Board, 1977 . . . .   10.00
Toy Village, Milton Bradley, No. 4420, 11 1/2 x 8 1/2 In. 69.00
Uncle Sam's Mail, Mailman With Pouch On Cover, Milton Bradley, Board, 16 x 15 In. 2300.00
Uncle Wiggily, Milton Bradley, Board, 8 x 17 In. 22.00
Uncle Wiggily, Parker Brothers, Board, 1979 . . . .   10.00
Wheel, Playing Cards, Square 48 In. 495.00
Wheel, White Band, Black Numerals, Orange Center, Rim, 6 Iron Spokes, 19 In. 405.00
Wheel Of Chance, Carnival, 2-Sided, White Ground, Early 1900s, 42 In. 59.00
Wheel Of Chance, Carnival, Pine, Painted, Mustard Ground, c.1900, 32 1/4 In. 1175.00
Who's Afraid Of The Big Bad Wolf, Parker Brothers, Board, 1933 . . . .   190.00
Willie Mays Say Hey, Baseball Game, Box, 1950s, 9 x 14 1/2 In. 340.00
Wiry Dan's Electric Baseball Game, Harett-Gilmar, Board, 1950s, 8 1/2 x 11 x 2 In. 115.00
Wizard Of Oz, Instructions, Box, England, 1939, 2 3/8 x 3 5/8 x 3/4 In., 44 Cards 404.00
Word Nerd, Hasbro, 1979 . . . .   15.00
You Don't Say, Milton Bradley, Board, 1963 . . . .   10.00

GAME PLATES

GAME PLATES are plates of any make decorated with pictures of birds, animals, or fish. The game plates usually came in sets consisting of twelve dishes and a serving platter. These sets were most popular during the 1880s.

Bird, Cobalt Blue & Gold Border, Marked, STW Bavaria Germany, 10 1/2 In. 125.00

Ducks, Red & Gold Border, Scalloped Rim, Theodore Haviland, c.1903, 9 In. 175.00
Fish Set, Different Freshwater Fish, Green Borders, Gold Trim, Bavaria, 9 In., 6 Piece 90.00
Partridges, Transfer Border, Ironstone, Marked, Mason's, 1970s, 10 1/2 In. 75.00
Quail, Green & Gold Border, Signed, RK Beck, 8 1/2 In. 55.00
Snipe, Red & Gold Border, Scalloped Irm, Theodore Haviland, c.1903, 9 In. 175.00

GARDEN FURNISHINGS have been popular for centuries. The
stone or metal statues, wire, iron, or rustic furniture, urns and fountains, sundials, and small figurines are included in this category. Many
of the metal pieces have been made continuously for years.

Basin, Tripod Legs, Animal Heads, Shallow, Stone, 18th Century, 16 x 21 In. 575.00
Bench, Curved, White, Iron, England, c.1870 . . . .   4200.00
Bench, Double Chairback, Arched Panels, Cast Iron, 39 x 42 x 17 1/2 In. 748.00
Bench, Ferns, Cast Iron, Coalbrookdale, England, 19th Century, 34 x 55 x 22 In. 690.00
Bench, Gothic Revival, Cast Iron, 36 x 47 x 20 In. 1955.00
Bench, Grape & Vine Pattern, Painted White, Cast Iron, 2 Settees, 2 Chairs, Table 1495.00
Bench, Reeded Crest Rail, Diamond, Scroll Splat, Cast Iron, 38 x 60 x 22 In. . . . .2185.00 to 2990.00
Bench, Serpentine Horseshoe Backrest, Pierced Seat, Scrolls, Cast Iron, 37 x 62 In. 1380.00
Bench, Victorian Style, Ferns, Closed Arms, Wood Seat, Cast Iron, 35 x 58 In., Pair 1955.00
Bench, Victorian Style, Serpentine Crest Rail, Twig Legs, Cast Iron, 34 x 71 x 22 In., Pair .   805.00
Birdbath, Cherub Head, Acanthus, Black, Cast Iron, 35 x 29 1/2 In. 200.00
Birdbath, Fluted Basin, Tapered Pedestal Base, Cast Iron, White, Victorian, 27 In. 1035.00
Birdbath, No. 300, Terra-Cotta, Greek Eye, Diamond, Teco, 28 x 38 In. 1998.00
Birdbath, Shell Shape, Basin, Birds Around Edge, Cast Iron, 22 x 19 1/2 x 12 In. 207.00
Birdhouse, 16 Round Entrances, Hand Cut Shingles, 15 x 12 In. 160.00
Birdhouse, Metal Architectural Details, Church Shape, Early 1900s, 40 x 21 x 30 In. 690.00
Birdhouse, Stand, Metal Architectural Details, Church Shape, 1900s, 94 x 13 In. 460.00
Bootscraper, 2 Posts, Flattened & Scrolled Ends, Iron Patina, 13 1/2 x 12 In. 184.00
Bootscraper, Black, Conjoined Eagle, Oval Base, 19th Century, 14 1/2 In. 382.00
Chair, Black, Bent Steel, Lalance & Grosjean, N.Y., 1866, 35 x 27 In. 470.00
Chair, Curled & Twisted, White, Wrought Iron, c.1895, Pair 489.00
Chair Set, Gothic Revival, Cabriole Legs, Cast Iron, 36 x 27 x 19 In., 5 Piece 2875.00
Chair Set, Lyre, Flower Back, Openwork, Cabriole Legs, Iron, 32 In., 4 Piece 1035.00
Figure, Dog, Seated, Cast Zinc, J.L. Mott Iron Works, N.Y., 1870, 17 x 22 In. 6038.00
Figure, Duck, Pottery, 13 In. 2390.00
Figure, Putti, Holding Heart In Left Hand, Bow In Right, Lead, 30 x 16 x 12 In. 1265.00
Figure, Rabbit, Cast Stone, c.1900, 10 In. 59.00
Figure, Woman, Classical, Carrying Bundle, Cast Iron, 45 1/2 In. 172.00
Figure, Woman, Nude, Classical, Draped Toga, Marble, 62 In. 2070.00
Fountain, Boy, Classical, Shell Bowl, Cement, 33 x 24 x 24 In. 411.00
Fountain, Bronze, Art Deco, 3 Maidens, Octagonal Marble Top, Continental, 40 In. 7050.00
Fountain, Classical Style, Children, Women, Flared Basin, Bronze, Continental, 98 x 42 In.   5750.00
Fountain, Figure, Pan, Flutes Emit Water, Bronze, Late 20th Century, 33 In. 546.00
Fountain, Victorian Style, 3 Tiers, Tazza Shape Bowls, Dolphin Base, Cast Iron, 96 x 46 In.   1610.00
Gazing Ball Set, Victorian, Graduated Sizes, 10 To 14 In., 4 Piece 863.00
Hitching Post, Black Boy, Holding Chain, Hook, Square Base, Cast Iron, Fiske, 46 In. . . .   805.00
Hitching Post, Black Man's Head, Iron, Wood Base, c.1900, 9 In.   5700.00
Hitching Post, Black, Reeded Column, Preening Swan Head Finial, Iron, 64 In. 860.00
Hitching Post, Clenched Fist, Fluted Column, Urn Base, 41 In. 1380.00
Hitching Post, Clenched Hand, Retractable Chain, Iron Shaft, Square Base, 1800s, 62 1/2 In.   1175.00
Hitching Post, Figural, Jockey, Blue, White & Black Paint, Pedestal Base, Iron, 37 1/2 In. .   400.00
Hitching Post, Horse Head, Trunk Base, Brown Finish, Iron, 52 1/2 In. 1840.00
Hitching Post, Jockey, Extended Arm, Black Boy, Square Base, Cast Iron, 44 In. 1093.00
Hitching Post, Jockey, Orange, Cast Iron, 35 In. 1265.00
Hitching Post, Jockey, Yellow Pants, Red Coat, Black Boots, Cast Iron, 45 In. 1045.00
Hitching Post, Swan Finial, Preening, Reeded Column, Black, Cast Iron, 63 In. 805.00
Hitching Post Finial, Black Boy, 3/4 Length Figure, Yellow, Iron, 11 1/4 In. 2875.00
Lawn Cannon, Wooden Support, Cast Iron, 41 x 22 In. 538.00
Lawn Sprinkler, Brass Head, Cast Iron Base, Winchester, 11 3/4 x 7 3/4 In. 1068.00
Lawn Sprinkler, Rocket, Red, Cast Iron, 13 In. 275.00
Lawn Sprinkler, Turtle, Cast Iron, 9 In. 220.00
Ornament, Koi Head, Interior Container, Ceramic, 19 In. 115.00

Pedestal, Neoclassical Style, 4 Masques, Acanthus, Cast Iron, 32 x 19 In., Pair 575.00
Pedestal, Neoclassical Style, Urn Shape Standard, Cast Iron, England, 34 x 15 In., Pair ... 518.00
Plant Stand, see Furniture, Stand, Plant
Seat, Blue & White Flowers, Scroll Band, Arched Cutout Handles, Pottery, 20 1/2 In. 230.00
Seat, Flowers, Leaves, 3 Key Fret Feet, Minton, c.1870, 18 In. 2400.00
Seat, Porcelain, Canton Waterfront Scene, Blue & White, c.1840, 17 1/2 In. 4600.00
Seat, Rose Medallion, Panel Decoration, Birds, Flowers, People, Buildings, 19 x 13 In. ... 2128.00
Seat, Urn Shape, Yellow, Hexagon, Chinese, 20th Century, 21 In. 179.00
Sundial, Diptych, France, Engraved Roman Numerals, String Gnomon, Ivory Case 265.00
Sundial, Diptych, Germany, Paper Scales, String Gnomon, Fruitwood Case, 4 In. 295.00
Table & Chairs, Textured Glass, Wrought Iron, 29 x 48 x 30 In., 5 Piece 264.00
Urn, Black Paint, Leaf Handles, Square Base, Cast Iron, 34 x 31 1/2 In. 115.00
Urn, Classical Figures, Multicolored, Handles, England, Cast Iron, 76 In., Pair 4600.00
Urn, Flared Rim, Masque Heads, Laurel Wreaths, Lion Head Handles, Iron, 29 x 22 In., Pair 316.00
Urn, Neoclassical Style, Campana Shape, Fluted Base, Marble, 26 x 21 In., Pair 1610.00
Urn, Neoclassical Style, Flared Rim, Griffins, Masques, Cast Iron, 36 x 32 In., Pair 748.00
Urn, Raised Wreath, Leaves, Scrolled Leaf Feet, Cast Iron, 28 x 15 x 14 In. 862.00
Urn, Scrolled Leaves, Flying Swallows, Flowers, Square Base, Cast Iron, 33 In, Pair 460.00

GAUDY DUTCH pottery was made in England for America from
about 1810 to 1820. It is a white earthenware with Imari-style decorations of red, blue, green, yellow, and black. Only sixteen patterns of
Gaudy Dutch were made: Butterfly, Carnation, Dahlia, Double Rose,
Dove, Grape, Leaf, Oyster, Primrose, Single Rose, Strawflower, Sunflower, Urn, War Bonnet, Zinnia, and No Name. Other similar wares
are called *Gaudy Ironstone* and *Gaudy Welsh.*

Bowl, Footed, Cobalt Blue Heart Shape Leaves, Pink Luster Stem, 10 x 6 In. 230.00
Creamer, Butterfly, 4 1/2 In. 3190.00
Creamer, Sunflower, 4 1/2 In. 360.00
Creamer, War Bonnet, Helmet Form, 4 1/2 In. 415.00
Cup & Saucer, Butterfly, Handleless 1375.00
Cup & Saucer, Sunflower, Handleless 305.00
Cup & Saucer, Urn, Handleless 910.00
Pitcher, War Bonnet, Bulbous, 6 In. 1045.00
Plate, Butterfly, 6 1/2 In. 1650.00
Plate, Butterfly, 10 In. 2090.00
Plate, Carnation, 8 1/4 In. 715.00
Plate, Carnation, 9 3/4 In. 1155.00
Plate, Double Rose, 10 In. 2420.00
Plate, Dove, 8 1/4 In. 1540.00
Plate, Dove, 10 In. ....2938.00 to 2990.00
Plate, Grape, 7 In. 575.00
Plate, Oyster, 10 In. 2255.00
Plate, Single Rose, 8 1/4 In. 1075.00
Plate, Single Rose, Pink Flowers, Impressed H, 8 1/2 In. 1780.00
Plate, Soup, Double Rose, 8 In. 330.00
Plate, Soup, Single Rose, 9 3/4 In. 360.00
Plate, Strawflower, 8 1/2 In. 2640.00
Plate, Sunflower, 9 3/4 In. 2090.00
Plate, Urn, 5 In. 690.00
Plate, Urn, 7 1/2 In. 105.00
Plate, Urn, Flowers, Leaves, 7 3/8 In. 525.00
Plate, War Bonnet, 9 3/4 In. 1375.00
Sugar, Cover, Single Rose, Drop Ring, Shell Handles, Bulbous 2860.00
Teapot, Butterfly, 6 1/2 In. 1155.00
Toddy Plate, War Bonnet, 5 1/4 In. 290.00
Waste Bowl, Butterfly, 3 x 5 3/4 In. 580.00
Waste Bowl, Carnation, 3 x 5 3/4 In. 195.00
Waste Bowl, Double Rose, 2 3/4 x 5 1/2 In. 275.00
Waste Bowl, Single Rose, 3 x 5 1/2 In. 1430.00
Waste Bowl, Urn, 2 3/4 x 5 1/2 In. 305.00

GAUDY IRONSTONE is the collector's name for the ironstone wares with the bright patterns similar to Gaudy Dutch. It was made in England for the American market after 1850. There may be other examples found in the listing for Ironstone or under the name of the ceramic factory.

Charger, 5-Color, Flowers, Leaves, Mann & Co., 17 In.	145.00
Charger, Stylized Urn, Cobalt, Orange Flowers, Leaves, Copper Luster, 11 In., Pair	430.00
Charger, Yellow Daisy, Tornado Shaped Blooms, Cobalt Blue Leaves, 12 In.	345.00
Cup, Strawberry, Handleless	22.00
Cup & Saucer, Carnation, Handleless	195.00
Cup & Saucer, Floral, Blue Leaves, Luster	50.00
Cup & Saucer, Single Rose, Handleless	660.00
Cup & Saucer, Sprig Style, Handleless	28.00
Pitcher, Cobalt & Medium Blue Leaves, Band Along Rim & Spout, 8 1/2 In.	604.00
Pitcher, Milk, Grape, 7 1/4 In.	690.00
Plate, 4 Flowers, Blue Leaves, Luster, 6 5/8 In.	18.00
Plate, 6 Flowers, Blue Leaves, Luster, 9 1/2 In.	22.00
Plate, Grapevine & Blossoms, Blue Rim, 8 1/2 In.	138.00
Plate, Green & Red Flowers, Flow Blue Leaves, Luster Highlights, 8 1/4 In., Pair	220.00
Plate, Rabbit, Frog, In Center Medallion, Cobalt Blue Sponged Flowers, 9 In.	175.00
Plate, Scalloped Edge, Black Flowers, Purple & Green Leaves, Staffordshire, 9 3/4 In. ...	115.00
Plate, Seeing Eye, 8 5/8 In.	55.00
Plate, Seeing Eye, 9 5/8 In.	60.00
Plate, Sprig Style, 8 1/4 In.	50.00
Plate, Strawberry & Flowers, Signed, Thos. Walker, 6 1/2 In.	30.00
Plate, Strawberry & Flowers, Signed, Thos. Walker, 8 1/2 In.	100.00
Plate, Strawberry, Blue Rim, 6 5/8 In.	175.00
Plate, War Bonnet, 8 1/4 In.	550.00
Teapot, Grape, 7 In.	1980.00
Teapot, Single Rose	525.00
Teapot, Strawberry & Flowers, Paneled, 9 1/4 In.	770.00
Toddy Plate, Seeing Eye, 5 1/8 In.	110.00
Toddy Plate, Zinnia, 4 3/4 In.	303.00
Washbowl, Flowers, Blue Leaf, Luster, 13 In.	250.00
Waste Bowl, Double Rose, 2 3/4 x 5 1/2 In.	105.00
Waste Bowl, Seeing Eye	28.00

GAUDY WELSH is an Imari-decorated earthenware with red, blue, green, and gold decorations. Most Gaudy Welsh was made in England for the American market. It was made from 1820 to about 1860.

Bowl, Oyster, 3 x 6 In.	175.00
Cake Plate, Sunflower, 7 3/4 In.	195.00
Cup & Saucer, Angel's Trumpet	195.00
Cup & Saucer, Marigold	155.00
Cup & Saucer, Oyster	95.00
Jug, Conwys, 9 In.	750.00
Jug, Grape, 7 1/4 In.	375.00
Pitcher, Bethesda, Paneled, Scalloped Rims, Dragon Handle, 6 3/8 In., Pair	288.00
Pitcher, Grape Variant, Molded Flower Rim, Foot, 10 1/4 In.	201.00
Plate, Flower Basket II, Scalloped Rim, 9 In.	175.00
Plate, Grape, Reverse Scalloped Rim, Square, 8 1/2 In.	175.00
Plate, Tulip, Scalloped Rim, Square, 8 1/2 In.	175.00
Teapot, Drape	675.00

GEISHA GIRL porcelain was made for export in the late nineteenth century in Japan. It was an inexpensive porcelain often sold in dime stores or used as free premiums. Pieces are sometimes marked with the name of a store. Japanese ladies in kimonos are pictured on the dishes. There are over 125 recorded patterns. Borders of red, blue, green, gold, brown, or several of these colors were used. Modern reproductions are being made.

Bowl, Orange Trim, Scalloped Edge, Finger Hole, 7 1/2 In.	15.00
Chocolate Set, Girls In Garden, Cobalt Blue Trim, 11 Piece	85.00
Sugar Shaker, Orange Trim, 4 1/2 In.	25.00

Tea Set, Pot, Cups, Saucers, Sugar, Creamer, 15 Piece 60.00

GENE AUTRY was born in 1907. He began his career as the *Singing Cowboy* in 1928. His first movie appearance was in 1934, his last in 1958. His likeness and that of the Wonder Horse, Champion, were used on toys, books, lunch boxes, and advertisements.

Badge, Sheriff's Posse, Flying A Symbol, Star Shape, Brass, Embossed, 1950s, 2 5/8 In. ... 605.00
Book, Guitar Folio, No. 1, 1942, 12 x 9 In., 24 Pages 52.00
Book, Guitar Folio, No. 2, 5 Songs, 1942, 12 x 9 In., 12 Pages 69.00
Button, Fan Club Member, Blue Tone Photo, Red Ground, Early 1950s, 1 1/4 In. 299.00
Button, Gene Autry Club Badge, Round, 1940s, 1 1/4 In. 45.00
Button, Guitar Club, Gene On Champ, Holding Guitar, Australia, c.1950, 1 In. 120.00
Button, Portrait, Late 1930s, 1 3/4 In. 40.00
Cap Gun, 44, Metal, Plastic, Marked L-H On Handle 220.00
Cap Gun, Black, Cast Iron, Mother-Of-Pearl Grips, Signature, Kenton, 8 1/2 In. 159.00
Cap Gun, Bull's-Eye, White Handles, Cast Iron, Kenton 85.00
Cap Gun, Buzz Henry, 7 3/4 In. 70.00
Cap Gun, Cast Iron, Kenton Hardware, Box, 7 In. 385.00
Cap Gun, Engraved, White, Horse Head Grips, Leslie-Henry 44, 11 In. 160.00
Cap Gun, Hats & Spurs On Red Handles, Marked Dummy, Cast Iron, Kenton 160.00
Cap Gun, Junior Model, Repeating, Cast Iron, Mother-Of-Pearl, Dummy, Kenton, Box ... 215.00
Cap Gun, Red Handles, Gene Autry On Both Sides, Cast Iron, Kenton 145.00
Cap Gun, Repeater, Nickel Plated, Horsehead Grips, Leslie-Henry, Box, 8 In. 311.00
Cap Gun, Repeating, Cast Iron, Kenton, Box, c.1950, 8 In. 1111.00
Cap Gun, Repeating, Jr. Model, Cast Iron, Kenton, Box, 1940s, 6 In. 250.00
Cap Gun, Revolving Cylinder, Engraved, White, Horse Head Grips, L-H 44, Large Frame . 152.00
Cap Gun, White Handles, Engraved DP, Cast Iron, Kenton ....105.00 to 145.00
Cap Gun, White Handles, Gene Autry On Both Sides, Cast Iron, Kenton 130.00
Card, Fortune Telling, Republic Pictures, J.J. Newberry Co., Peerless, 1 1/8 x 2 1/8 In. 25.00
Card, Gene Autry Champions Membership, c.1950, 2 1/2 x 4 In. 100.00
Comic, Mailer, Premium, Quaker Puffed Wheat & Rice, 1950s, 5 Piece 510.00
Comic Book, No. 100, Dell, 1955 .... 15.00
Cuffs, Light Tan, 4 Blue Jewels, Metal Steer Head Medallion, Gene Autry Brand 127.00
Daybill, Sioux City Sue, Gene Autry & Champion, 1953, 14 x 36 In. 110.00
Figurine, Ceramic, Glazed, 1940s, 7 3/4 x 3 In. 635.00
Game, Dude Ranch, Built-Rite, Board, 1956 .... 55.00
Guitar, Instructions, Cord Selector, Cardboard Carry Case, Emenee, 32 In., Child's 205.00
Guitar, Plastic, Embossed Western Scene, Emenee, 1950s, 32 In. 135.00
Guitar, Plastic, Emenee Musical Toys, Box, 1950s, 33 In. 165.00
Gun & Holster Set, 2 Cap Guns, Leslie-Henry, Box, 12 x 14 In. 715.00
Gun & Holster Set, Double, Leather, Red Grips, Cap Guns, Kenton, Box, 1941 .... 955.00
Gun & Holster Set, Single, Flying A Ranch, Leslie-Henry, Box, 9-In. Gun 347.00
Holster Set, Double, Black Leather Belt, Gold Metal Holsters, 1 Gun, Leslie-Henry 405.00
Lobby Card, Melody Ranch, Jimmy Durante, Ann Miller, 1940, 11 x 40 In. 86.00
Lobby Card, Twilight On Rio Grande, No. 7, 11 x 14 In. 25.00
Magazine, Champions, First Issue, December 1950, 9 x 6 In., 16 Pages 159.00
Medal, Champ Crack Shot, On Card, 1940, 4 1/4 x 3-In. Card, 1 1/4 In. 950.00
Paper Doll Book, Melody Ranch, Whitman, 1950, 13 x 10 1/2 In., 12 Pages 75.00
Pennant, Red, White, 28 x 11 In. 75.00
Poster, Gene Autry & Mounties, 27 x 41 In. 111.00
Poster, Old Monterey, 27 x 41 In. 163.00
Poster, Sunset In Wyoming, Republic Picture, 1941, 27 x 41 In. 230.00
Rug, Gene Autry & Champ, Champ's Head, Embroidered, Fringe, 26 x 38 In. 90.00
Wallet, Always Your Pal, Box 55.00

GIBSON GIRL black-and-blue decorated plates were made in the early 1900s. Twenty-four different 10 1/2-inch plates were made by the Royal Doulton pottery at Lambeth, England. These pictured scenes from the book *A Widow and Her Friends* by Charles Dana Gibson. Another set of twelve 9-inch plates featuring pictures of the heads of Gibson Girls had all-blue decoration. Many other items also pictured the famous Gibson Girl.

Drawing, Charles Dana Gibson, Pen & Ink, Gilt Frame, 15 Piece 1610.00

Pillow, Girl In Blue, Printed Silk, Cord Trim, Down Filled, Square, 1908, 23 In. 205.00
Plate, Day After Arriving At Her Journey's End, Blue Border, 10 1/2 In. 200.00
Plate, Miss Babbles Brings A Copy, Blue Border, 10 1/2 In. 140.00
Plate, Mrs. Diggs Is Alarmed, Blue Border, 10 1/2 In. 140.00
Plate, She Finds Exercise Does Not Improve Her Spirits, 10 1/2 In. 180.00
Plate, Some Think She Has Remained In Retirement, 1900, 10 In. 295.00

GIRL SCOUT collectors search for anything pertaining to the Girl
Scouts, including uniforms, publications, and old cookie boxes. The
Girl Scout movement started in 1912, two years after the Boy Scouts.
It began under Juliette Gordon Low of Savannah, Georgia. The first
Girl Scout cookies were sold in 1928.

Badge, Cook, Square, 1920s 6.00
Book, How Girls Can Help Their Country, Handbook For Girl Scouts, 1916 .... 110.00
Book, Proficiency Badge Requirements And Special Awards, 1934, 7 In., 88 Pages 10.00
Bracelet, Bangle, Gold Metal Band, Green Trefoils, 1943 .... 25.00
Button, Wave Recruiting Aide, Senior Girl Scout, Wish I Were A Wave, 1 In. 100.00
Compact, Wooden, Metal Emblem, 1940s-50s, 3 x 3 In. 95.00
Cookie Jar, Brownie, Blond Hair, Metlox, 9 In. 415.00
Doll, Brownie, Effanbee, Box, 1965 .... 65.00
Doll, Muslin, Oil Painted Face, Yarn Braids, Green Dress, Cap, c.1938, 14 In. 520.00
Handbook, 1947 .... 10.00
Knife, Pocket, Remington 105.00
Pin, Badge Of Merit, Brass, Ribbon, 1919, 2 1/2 In. 320.00
Pin, Trefoil, Eaglet, 1919, 3/4 In. 160.00
Postcard, Greetings From Camp, Orange, 1969-73 .... 15.00
Shoes, Brown Leather, Box, Size 10 B/AA 90.00
Uniform, Brownies, Dress, Bloomers, Cap, Tan, 1920s 500.00
Uniform, Senior, Dress, Socks, Green, 1950s 55.00

GLASS-ART. Art glass means any of the many forms of glassware
made during the late nineteenth or early twentieth century. These
wares were expensive and production was limited. Art glass is not the
typical commercial glass that was made in large quantities, and most of
the art glass was produced by hand methods. Later twentieth-century
glass is listed under Glass-Contemporary, Glass-Midcentury, or Glass-
Venetian. Even more art glass may be found in categories such as
Burmese, Cameo Glass, Tiffany, and other factory names.

Bowl, Crimson Shaded To Pink To Cream, Crimped Amber Tipped Rim, 8 1/4 In. 115.00
Bowl, Fruit, Berries, Leaves, Yellow Ground, Black Stand, 2 1/8 x 4 1/4 In. 290.00
Bowl, Gilt Oriental Landscape, Applied Fish Handles & Feet, Oval, Auguste Jean, 13 In. .. 635.00
Bowl, Opalescent, Blue, 6 x 4 In. 40.00
Bowl, Paisley, Flower, Acid, Applied Pedestal, 13 In. 145.00
Bowl, Rose, Caramel, Spattered, Flared Rim, France, 7 3/4 x 13 3/4 In. 880.00
Bowl, White Crackle, Yellow Rim, Green Bands, WMF, Ikora, c.1929, 13 In. 242.00
Claret Jug, Gourd Shape, Silver Mount, Alphonse Debain, c.1900, 7 1/2 x 6 1/2 In., Pair .. 2990.00
Compote, Threaded Amethyst Rim, Hollow Stem, c.1920, 7 In. 90.00
Pitcher, Cranberry Swirl, Ruffled Square Rim, Applied Clear Handle, Bulbous, 9 In. 316.00
Pitcher, Frances Ware, Hobnail Base, Amber Neck, Hobbs, Brockunier, 5 1/4 In. 170.00
Pitcher, Onyxware, Enameled, Opalescent Glass, Variegated Pink, Amber, 7 1/2 In. 160.00
Pitcher, Serpentine Ribs, Silver Vines, Cascading Flowers, 6 In. 230.00
Shade, Blue Hooked Feathers, White Opalescent, Gold Trim, Bell Form, 2 1/4 x 5 In. 230.00
Shade, Blue Pulled Feathers, Iridescent Gold Ground, Corseted, 2 1/4 x 5 1/2 In., 3 Piece . 230.00
Shade, Gold Ground, Vertical Stripes, Purple Hearts, Ruffled Edge, 4 1/2 x 4 1/2 In. 60.00
Shade, Iridescent Gold, Ribbed, Fishscale, Threading, 5 3/4 In. 115.00
Shade, Iridescent Opal, Green, Gold Pulled Feather, 5 1/2 In. 230.00
Shade, Iridescent, Pulled Gold Thread, Green, Gold, Opaque Ground, 1920s, 5 In. 310.00
Vase, Black, Jean Luce, c.1930, 11 1/4 In. 7770.00
Vase, Bottle Shape, Iridescent Green, Amethyst, Pewter, Art Nouveau, Austria, 6 In. 560.00
Vase, Butterscotch, Multicolored Flowers, Leaves, Stems, Bulbous, 8 1/2 In. 190.00
Vase, Classical Figures, Embossed, Frosted, De Feure, France, c.1910, 5 1/2 In. 175.00
Vase, Cobalt Blue, Faceted, Footed, Josef Hoffman, Wiener Werkstatte, 6 In. 2585.00

Vase, Enameled Flowers, Bees, Butterflies, Beetles, Gold, Fluted, France, 6 1/8 In. 230.00
Vase, Enameled, Green, Applied Rim, Feet, Auguste Jean, c.1885, 10 1/2 In. 545.00
Vase, Florentine Cameo, Cranberry, Enameled Apple Blossoms, 1900s, 10 In., Pair 230.00
Vase, Ikora, Yellow Crackle, Oval, Rolled Rim, WMF, 1930s, 8 In. 85.00
Vase, Iridescent Green, Hour Glass Shape, Applied Handles, 7 1/4 x 4 3/8 In. 275.00
Vase, Iridescent Purple, Applied Cabochon, Gold Enameled Corset, 7 In. 660.00
Vase, Iridescent Ruby, Onion Skin, WMF, Germany, Early 1900s, 6 1/2 In. 345.00
Vase, Pink To White, Gold Flowers, Signed, Kimball & Durand, 6 7/8 In. 780.00
Vase, Stick, Pink, Satin, Footed, Bulbous Base, 10 In. 30.00
Vase, Vine, Leaf, Art Deco, France, c.1930, 10 1/4 In. 175.00
Vase, White Shaded To Pink, Gold Enameled, Vines, Flowers, 19th Century, 10 1/4 In. 410.00

GLASS-BLOWN was formed by forcing air through a rod into molten
glass. Early glass and some forms of art glass were hand blown. Other
types of glass were molded or pressed.

Bird Feeder, Clear, Tapered Cylinder, Cobalt Blue Finial, England, 6 In. . . . . .33.00 to 55.00
Bowl, 16 Ribs, Puce, Mold Blown, Footed, 4 1/2 In. 1035.00
Bowl, 20 Ribs, Rolled Rim, Amethyst, 3 x 4 In. 660.00
Bowl, Amber, Flared, Rolled Rim, 2 1/2 x 5 1/2 In. 1595.00
Bowl, Aqua, Flared Rim, 4 3/4 x 9 1/2 In. 715.00
Bowl, Aqua, Wide Rolled Rim, New York, Mid 19th Century, 5 x 13 In. 880.00
Bowl, Black Amber, Pinched Sides, Rolled Rim, 4 x 7 In. 1980.00
Bowl, Blue, Violet Striations, Flared Rim, Footed, 5 1/4 x 11 In. 1870.00
Bowl, Cover, Amethyst, Swirled Interior, Early 1800s, 3 1/4 x 3 3/8 In. 500.00
Bowl, Deep, Aqua, Flared, Rolled Rim, 6 3/4 x 9 1/2 In. 715.00
Bowl, Emerald Green, Slightly Flared, 3 5/8 x 6 7/8 In. 1870.00
Bowl, Fish Shape, Globular Top, Flared Base, 19th Century, 16 1/2 In. 1293.00
Bowl, Sapphire Blue, Lily Pad, Flared Rim, Domed Base, 4 In. 176.00
Canister, Aqua, Tin Lid, 2 3/4 x 6 In. 290.00
Canister, Cover, 2 Applied Cobalt Blue Rings, Hollow Finial, Pittsburgh, 5 1/2 x 10 In. . . . 575.00
Celery Vase, Pillar Mold, 8 Ribs, Notches, Flared Scalloped Rim, Clear, 10 1/2 In. 200.00
Compote, Blue & White Looping, Clear, Footed, c.1860, 10 x 5 In. 140.00
Compote, Blue Threading, Reverse Baluster Stem, Domed Foot, Rolled Rim, 4 In. 1155.00
Compote, Overshot, Scalloped Rim, Ruby Serpent On Stem, 7 3/8 x 7 1/2 In. 415.00
Compote, Pillar Mold, Plain Stem, Round Base, 9 x 7 1/2 In. 545.00
Cordial, Red Amber, Sheared Rim, Pontil, 3 1/8 In. 650.00
Creamer, Amethyst, Flared Rim, Tooled Lip, Handle, Pontil, 3 3/4 In. 2100.00
Creamer, Amethyst, Medial Ribbed Band, Strap Handle, 4 1/2 In. 9900.00
Creamer, Aqua, Tooled Rim, Circular Foot, Applied Handle, 5 In. 770.00
Creamer, Cobalt Blue, Bulbous, Pour Spout, Tooled Mouth, 1820-50, 4 3/8 In. 550.00
Creamer, Cobalt Blue, Expanded Diamond, 4 Rows Of 12, Kick-Up Base, 3 1/8 In. 360.00
Creamer, Cobalt Blue, Rolled Rim, Funnel Foot, Applied Shaped Handle, 6 In. 880.00
Creamer, Cobalt Blue, Tooled Flared Mouth & Lip, 3-Piece Mold, 3 7/8 In. 3000.00
Creamer, Olive Amber, White Flecks, Strap Handle, Footed, 5 In. 1100.00
Darner, Cobalt Blue, Knop Handle, 7 1/4 x 2 1/2 In. 230.00
Decanter, Barrel Shape, Yellow Olive, 3-Piece Mold, c.1830, Pt. 600.00
Decanter, Barrel, Diamond Diaper, Ribbed, Yellow Green, Applied Mouth, Pontil, Pt. 1200.00
Decanter, Square, Pressed Flower Stopper, 7 3/4 In. 50.00
Decanter, Sunburst & Diamond Diaper Band, Olive Green, Flared Lip, Rayed Base, 7 In. . . 825.00
Decanter, Sunburst & Diamond Diaper Band, Olive Yellow, Sheared Mouth, Pontil, Pt. . . . 700.00
Dish, Dome Cover, Round Notched Knop, Funnel Foot, 1800s, 12 x 10 1/2 In. 825.00
Globe, Fish, Light Amethyst, Folded Rim, 5 x 5 3/4 In. 45.00
Goblet, Amethyst, Ribbed Bowl, Knopped Stem, Cone Shape Foot, 3 1/2 In. 300.00
Goblet, Blue Green, Ogee Bowl, Cut Stem, 5 In. 155.00
Goblet, Corseted Bowl, Spiral Air Twist Stem, Cone Shape Foot, 6 3/4 In. 495.00
Goblet, Flared Bowl, Molded Base, Wide Twist Stem, Stepped Foot, 3 3/4 In. 990.00
Goblet, Green, Funnel Bowl, Button Stem, Square Foot, Pinched Corners, 4 5/8 In. 1760.00
Goblet, Opaque White Mercury Air Twist Stem, Cone Shape Foot, 6 1/2 In. 1840.00
Goblet, Opaque White Spiral Twist Stem, Cone Shape Foot, 5 3/4 In. 520.00
Goblet, Opaque White Spiral Twist Stem, Funnel Bowl, Cone Shape Foot, 5 3/4 In. 1035.00
Goblet, Spiral Molded Funnel Bowl & Stem, Cone Shape Foot, 6 3/4 In. 660.00
Goblet, Syllabub, Corseted Bowl, Heavy Ribbed Foot, 3 7/8 In. 230.00

Goblet, White Enamel Twist Stem, Cone Shape Foot, 5 3/4 In. 470.00
Hat, Cobalt Blue, Rough Pontil, 2 1/4 x 3 x 4 3/8 In. 80.00
Hat, Deep Smoky Green, Tooled Rim, Rough Pontil, 2 1/8 x 4 1/2 x 5 In. 265.00
Hat, Olive Yellow, Green, Rolled Rim, Pontil, 3 1/2 In. 2500.00
Hat, Puce, Pinched Rim, Rough Pontil, 1 3/4 x 3 1/4 x 4 In. 120.00
Hourglass, Turned Wood Stand, 1800s, 6 1/2 In. 881.00
Hurricane Shade, Grape Cluster & Vine, Engraved, Rolled Rim, c.1835, 22 1/2 In. 1035.00
Milk Pan, Aqua, Flared & Rolled Rim, Pour Spout, Domed Base, 6 x 23 In. 2310.00
Milk Pan, Sapphire Blue, Flared, Folded Rim, 4 x 10 3/4 In. 1760.00
Milk Pan, Teal Green, Flared & Rolled Rim, Rough Pontil, 2 1/4 x 7 1/2 In. 470.00
Mug, Blue, 16 Vertical Ribs, Swirled To Right, Crimped & Curled Handle, 3 In. 1980.00
Mug, Cobalt Blue, Cylindrical, Applied Handle, 4 In. 230.00
Pitcher, 2 Engraved Chain Bands, Gray Tint, Applied Handle, 7 In. 4950.00
Pitcher, Amber, Bulbous, Flared Rim, Crimped Foot, Shaped Handle, 7 In. 4400.00
Pitcher, Aqua, Bulbous, Threaded Neck, Applied Strap Handle, New York, 8 In. 3300.00
Pitcher, Aqua, Lily Pad Decoration, c.1835, 8 7/8 In. 7050.00
Pitcher, Aqua, Lily Pad, Footed, Applied Solid Handle, 5 7/8 In. 4125.00
Pitcher, Cobalt Blue, Pinched, Applied Handle, Polished Pontil, 6 1/4 In. 100.00
Pitcher, Olive Green, Straight Sides, Applied Neck Threads & Handle, 6 1/4 In. 1210.00
Pitcher, Overshot, Bulbous, Rope Twist Handle, 12 In. 230.00
Plate, 12 Swirled Ribs, Pattern Molded, Pale Amber, Inward Folded Rim, 4 In. 110.00
Punch Bowl, Cover, Underplate, Clambroth, Rayed Base, Stylized Acorn Finial, 15 In. . . . 210.00
Rolling Pin, Cobalt Blue, Knob Ends, Open Rough Pontil, 14 1/2 x 2 In. 100.00
Rolling Pin, Deep Red Amber, Open End, Pontil, 15 x 2 1/4 In. 100.00
Salt, 2 Rows Of Diamonds Over Pointed Flutes, Cobalt Blue, Bulbous Top, Footed, 3 In. . . 413.00
Salt, 12 Ribs, Swirled To Left, Ribbed Stem, Footed, Cobalt Blue, 3 In. . . . . .250.00 to 360.00
Salt, Basket Shape, Fiery Opalescent Blue, Ribbed Gold, 3 1/2 x 3 3/8 In. 110.00
Salver, Ribbed Teardrop Stem, Galleried Rim, Domed Folded Foot, 6 x 13 In. 523.00
Stein, Enameled, Topaz, Carved Horn Medallion Of Running Stag, c.1900, 9 In. 290.00
Sugar, Cover, Amber, Folded Rim, Footed, Hollow Ball Finial, 6 In. 1265.00
Sugar, Cover, Bottom Swirled To Right, Funnel Foot, Pressed Knop Finial 1430.00
Sugar, Cover, Bulbous, Cobalt Blue, 1820-50, 5 3/4 x 4 1/8 In. 784.00
Sugar, Cover, Green, Flared Rim, Foot, Hollow Ball Finial, 6 3/4 In. 2310.00
Sugar, Cover, Swag Sides, Loop Handles, Crimped Foot, Blue Bird Finial, 6 In. 2090.00
Sugar, Dome Cover, Cylindrical, Pontil, 6 x 4 7/8 In. 450.00
Sugar, Expanded Diamond, 10 Rows Of 15, Cobalt Blue, Footed, 3 1/2 In. 525.00
Sugar, Swirled Dome Cover, Blood Red, Bulbous, Compressed, 8 1/4 In. 880.00
Syrup, Sunburst, Rosette Base, Applied Handle, Clear, Tin Lid, 7 In. 175.00
Tumbler, Ale, Overlapping Spirals, Cone Shape, Ribbed Knop, Footed, 4 5/8 In. 240.00
Tumbler, Flip, 4 Flower Panels, Engraved, 6 1/2 In. 460.00
Tumbler, Flip, Engraved, American, Early 19th Century, 6 In. 70.00
Tumbler, Flip, Three-Quarter Ribbing, Engraved Border, Crosshatched Ovals, 6 1/4 In. . . . 375.00
Tumbler, Flip, Tulip In Basket, Engraved, 4 1/4 In. 345.00
Vase, Aqua, Amber Lily Pad, Flared, Crimped Foot, 8 1/2 In. 220.00
Vase, Hyacinth, Amethyst, Cone Shape, Flared Base, 8 In. 120.00
Vase, Hyacinth, Cobalt Blue, Cone Shape, Flared Base, 8 7/8 In. 155.00
Vase, Hyacinth, Deep Cobalt Blue, Baluster Shape, Indented Base, 8 1/4 In. 240.00
Vase, Trumpet, Amethyst, Blue, Cupped Mouth, 7 1/8 In. 896.00
Vase, Trumpet, Amethyst, Waist Ring, Footed, 11 1/2 In. 220.00
Vase, Trumpet, Opaque White, Flattened Dome Foot, 18 In. 275.00
Whimsy, Bellows, Cranberry, Clear Rigaree Edges & Handles, 3 x 11 In. 155.00
Whimsy, Cane, Aqua Green, Twisted Ribs, 56 In. 110.00
Whimsy, Pipe, Amber, Tulip Bowl, Twisted Stem, Pig Tail Curled End, 61 1/2 In. 120.00
Whimsy, Pipe, Opaque Pearl White, Bulbous Bowl, Electric Blue Rim, 15 In. 255.00
Whimsy, Pipe, Saxophone Shape, Multicolored Stripes, Flared Rim Bowl, 28 In. 100.00
Wine, Blue Green, Cupped Bowl, Bladed Knop Stem, 5 In. 190.00
Wine, Emerald Tinted, Anglo-Irish, Mid 1800s, 5 x 2 1/2 In., 12 Piece 545.00
Wine, Saucer-Top Bowl, Spiral Air Twist Stem, Footed, 6 In. 250.00
Witch's Ball, Aqua, Applied Threading, Stand, 10 1/4 In. 440.00
Witch's Ball, Aqua, Translucent Red & Blue Swirls, 4 In. 200.00
Witch's Ball, Cobalt Blue, Baluster Stand, Knopped Stem, Funnel Foot, 13 In. 1650.00
Witch's Ball, Cobalt Blue, Open Pontil, 5 1/2 In. 175.00
Witch's Ball, Ruby, Rough Open Pontil, 7 3/4 In. 715.00

GLASS-BOHEMIAN Bohemian glass is an ornate overlay or flashed glass made during the Victorian era. It has been reproduced in Bohemia, which is now a part of the Czech Republic. Glass made from 1875 to 1900 is preferred by collectors.

Basket, Iridescent Green, Gold Dragonfly, Fern, Ruffled Edge, Reeded Handle, 6 1/2 In. ...	200.00
Beaker, Viking Warriors, Double Wall, Zwischengoldglas, 1800s, 3 3/4 In.	1790.00
Biscuit Jar, Green, Applied Glass Trailings, Pallme-Koenig, 7 In.	230.00
Bowl, Flowers, Blossoms, Vines, Blue, Orange, Yellow, Green, 8 1/2 In.	575.00
Bowl, Optic Ribbed, Blue, Enameled Roses, Fish Feet, Jeweled Eyes, Harrach, 8 1/2 In.	1725.00
Bowl, Optic Ribbed, Cobalt Blue, Applied Ruffled Edge, Harrach, 5 In.	127.00
Bowl, Silverina, Cranberry Shaded To Green, Squat, Pinched, Ruffled Edge, 5 In.	605.00
Candlestick, Blue Cut To Clear, Round Base, Tapered Shaft, 8 3/4 In., Pair	345.00
Decanter, Amber Flashed, Cut Optic Pattern, c.1900, 16 In., Pair	175.00
Decanter Set, Ruby Cut To Clear, Grapevine Design, Decanter, 6 Cordials	260.00
Dresser Box, Green With Gilt Bronze Frame, 1900, 4 1/2 In.	290.00
Epergne, 1-Lily, Green Shaded To Maroon, Footed, Ruffled Edges, 18 In.	690.00
Goblet, Blue, Applied Jewels, Gold Tracery, Early 20th Century, 13 In.	145.00
Goblet, Cartouche, Figures, Intaglio Gold Scrolling, 4-Lobed Bowl, Lobmeyr, 6 In., Pair ..	230.00
Goblet, Enameled, Cut, Couple, Gold Leaf Scrolls, Lobmeyr, 6 In., 4 Piece	750.00
Goblet, Engraved Architectural View Of Blue-Cut-To-Clear Ground, Gilt Trim, 5 In.	345.00
Goblet, Jacobite Bucket Bowl, Engraved Deer & Leaves, Silesian Stem, 6 1/4 In.	415.00
Jar, Cover, Amber Stain, Engraved, Woodland Scene, 9 1/4 In., Pair	450.00
Liqueur Set, Ball Shape, Black, Orange Feet, Handle & Spout, 5 Piece	460.00
Liqueur Set, Ruby Cut To Clear, Grapevines, c.1910, 7 Piece	260.00
Pitcher, Wine, Grapes & Vines Design, Jaeger & Co., 1902, 14 In.	795.00
Ramekin, Enameled, Paneled Rims, Enameled Scrolled Leaves, c.1910, 4 Piece	316.00
Tumbler, Cobalt Enameled Gold, c.1865	140.00
Tumbler, Flashed, Cut Glass, Flower Decoration, c.1900, 6 1/2 In.	431.00
Tumbler, Ruby Stain, American Views, Footed, 6 In.	4125.00
Urn, Cranberry, Coat Of Arms, Multicolored Flower, Applied Jewels, 11 In.	201.00
Vase, Amethyst, Iridescent Blue Oil Spot, Bulbous, Stick, 8 1/4 In.	140.00
Vase, Azure Blue, Cut, Parcel Gilt, Early 20th Century, 12 In.	235.00
Vase, Blue Zigzag Ribbon, Mottled Red, Ivory Ground, c.1925, 11 1/2 In.	145.00
Vase, Blue, Gilt, Classical Figures, Dancing, Landscape, Gold Enameled, c.1900, 14 In.	340.00
Vase, Enameled, Young Woman, Cartouche, Pink Opaque, 14 In.	430.00
Vase, Fan, Amber, Blue Iridescent Waves, Faceted, Rindskopf, 13 In.	460.00
Vase, Flower Form, Clear Shaded To Cranberry, Gold Ruffled Edge, Scrolling, 14 1/2 In. ..	230.00
Vase, Garniture, Cased Blue Over Opal, Late 19th Century, 9 1/2 In., Pair	200.00
Vase, Gold, Cased, Swirled, Red, Black, Ivory, Pulled, Austria, c.1900, 6 In.	1095.00
Vase, Green Iridescent, Gold, Green, Purple, Dimples, Ruffled Edge, Austria, 7 In.	175.00
Vase, Green Malachite, Molded Grecian Scene, Schlevoght, c.1935, 9 1/2 In.	400.00
Vase, Iridescent Purple, Applied Threads, Pinched Sides, Ruffled Edge, Austria, 6 1/2 In. ..	520.00
Vase, Iridescent, Amber Green To Rose, Cylindrical, Rindskopf, 10 In.	200.00
Vase, Orange, Black Oil Spots, Applied Handles, c.1925, 6 1/2 In.	200.00
Vase, Pepita, Green Shaded To Iridescent Amethyst, Waves, Tricornered, 13 In.	345.00
Vase, Random Spots, Crimson & Burgundy, Spherical, Flared Edge, 7 1/2 In.	140.00
Vase, Red Pulled Loops, Yellow Ground, c.1925, 9 1/2 In.	85.00
Vase, Red, Applied Black Handle, c.1925, 8 1/2 In.	230.00
Vase, Red, Iridescent Gold Crackle, Bulbous Cylindrical, Pinched Rim, 13 In.	805.00
Vase, Shaded Caramel, Cased, Enameled, c.1900, 13 In.	140.00
Vase, Stick, Cranberry Iridescent, Applied Amber Snake Handle, 10 In.	115.00
Vase, Stick, Cranberry, Gold Oil Spot, Threading, Bulbous Base, 8 1/4 In.	175.00
Vase, Stick, Grenada Pattern, Applied Snake, Rindskopf, 8 1/4 In.	175.00
Vase, Trumpet, Iridescent Purple, Pulled Loops, Tricornered, 13 In.	260.00
Vase, White Cut To Blue, Vermicelli Pattern, c.1885, 8 In., Pair	975.00
Vase, White Cut To Cranberry, Enameled, Portrait, 17 In.	510.00

Valuable glass should not be washed in a dishwasher.

Products that are used to remove lime buildup in showers will also work on glass vases.

Glass-Contemporary,
Figurine, Lady's Slipper,
Jadite, L.E. Smith,
2 3/4 x 6 In.

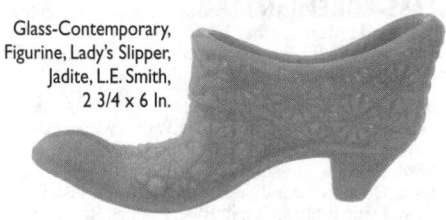

Water Set, Cobalt Blue, Gold Enameled, Gilt Bands, Pink Flowers, 11 In., 6 Piece 145.00
Wine, Cranberry Cut To Clear, Gold Enameled, 7 3/4 In., 8 Piece 1910.00

GLASS-CONTEMPORARY includes pieces by glass artists working
after 1975. Many of these pieces are free-form, one-of-a-kind sculptures. Paperweights by contemporary artists are listed in the Paperweight category. Earlier studio glass may be found in Glass-Venetian.

Bowl, Insert, Sea Form, Red, Black Undulating, Lip Wrap, Oval, Chihuly, 12 In. 4025.00
Charger, Arabesque Pattern, Higgins Art Glass, Signed, 12 In. 179.00
Compote, Opal, Green & Gold Loopings, Gold Inside, Footed, C. Lotton, 7 In. 280.00
Figurine, Lady's Slipper, Jadite, L.E. Smith, 2 3/4 x 6 In. . . . . *Illus*   18.00
Plaque, Summer Framie, Fused, Landscape, Frances Higgins, Frame, 20 x 10 In. 4025.00
Sculpture, Cactus, Green, Pink Flowers, Clear Flowerpot, Elio Raffaeli, 1980s, 24 3/4 In. .   735.00
Sculpture, Macchia, Dale Chihuly, c.1984, 17 In. 16730.00
Scupture, Spiraling Amethyst Bubbles, Studio Ahus, 1990, 10 In. 86.00
Vase, Amber, Yellow Pull-Up, Inscribed, Labino, 1982, 5 In. 575.00
Vase, Amethyst, Iridescent Flecks, Flaring, Cased, Carina, c.1990, 11 In. 120.00
Vase, Applied Flowers, Vines, Mottled Ground, Signed, John Nygren, 1988, 7 1/2 In. 630.00
Vase, Blue Iridescent, Pink Flowers, Footed, 9 In. 235.00
Vase, Blue, Pulled & Iridized Finish, Lundberg Studios, 1977, 7 In. 460.00
Vase, Cherries, Leaves, Branches, Frosted, Concave Shape, Kisslinger, 7 In. 35.00
Vase, Cherry Blossom, Blue Iridescent, Cylindrical, Carl Radke, 13 In. 365.00
Vase, Crazy Quilt, Banded Cylindrical, Richard Marquis, c.1979, 13 In. 8965.00
Vase, Iridescent Blue, Combed, Hooked Feathers, Signed, Orient & Flume, 1975, 7 In. 205.00
Vase, Iridescent, Pulled Thread, Karl Schantz, 1975, 5 1/2 In. 120.00
Vase, Multicolored Plumes, On White, Inscribed, Labino, 1982, 5 In. 460.00
Vase, Nacreous Opaque White, Yellow, Stylized Leaves, Karl Schantz, c.1975, 3 3/4 In. . . .   110.00
Vase, Opal, Turquoise Pulled Wisteria & Rim, Egg Shape, Flared Rim, C. Lotton, 6 1/2 In.   395.00
Vase, Opalescent, Applied Drooping Trees, Footed, Signed, Nygren, 1987, 10 3/4 In. 1265.00
Vase, Opalescent, Gold, Green Hooked, Pulled, 9 In. 120.00
Vase, Paperweight, Blue, Yellow, Red Pulled Flame, Signed, Labino, 1974, 5 1/4 In. 690.00
Vase, Spiral Opaque White Ribbons, Oval, Carina, 1990, 9 1/2 In. 430.00
Vase, Water Sprinkler Form, Red Iridescent, Blue Pulled Feathers, C. Lotton, 1980, 13 In. .   615.00

GLASS-CUT, see Cut Glass category.

GLASS-DEPRESSION, see Depression Glass category.

GLASS-MIDCENTURY refers to art glass made from the 1950s to
the 1980s. Some glass factories, such as Baccarat or Orrefors, are listed under their own categories. Earlier glass may be listed in the Glass-Art and Glass-Contemporary categories. Italian glass may be found in Glass-Venetian.

Bowl, Green, Cupped Rim, Per Lutken, Holmegaard, c.1960, 17 1/4 In. 240.00
Bowl, Tapio Wirkkala, Engraved Signature, 1970s, 6 1/4 In. 400.00
Box, Lid, Layered Blue Strips, Teak Base, Denmark, c.1960, 8 In. 196.00
Mobile, Dingle-Dangle, Colored Strips, Higgins, 1970s, 22 x 3 x 22 In. 1840.00
Vase, Blue, Orange, Red, Blue, Green Ribbons, Internal Decoration, 1950s, 16 In. 240.00
Vase, Gold, Swirling, 4 Tooled Petals, Dominic Labino, 1967, 9 1/2 In. 200.00
Vase, Hourglass Shape, Amethyst, No. 9591, Whitefriars, 5 1/2 In. 135.00
Vase, Orange, Opaque White, Kastrup Holmegaard Carnaby, 1960s, 10 In. 85.00

Vase, Oval, Amber, Bubbles, Gunnel Nyman, Nuutajarvi Perkband, Late 1940s, 10 In. 345.00
Vase, Savoy, Amber, Alvar Aalto, Iittala, 1936, 5 1/2 x 6 In. ....130.00 to 240.00
Vase, Square, Embossed Greek Key, Amber, Whitefriars, 7 In. 180.00
Vase, Trumpet, Michael Bang, Kastrup Holmegaard Carnaby, 1960s, 12 1/4 In. 90.00

GLASS-VENETIAN. Venetian glass has been made near Venice,
Italy, since the thirteenth century. Thin, colored glass with applied decoration is favored, although many other types have been made. Collectors have recently become interested in the Art Deco and 1950s
designs. Glass was made on the Venetian island of Murano from 1291.
The output dwindled in the late seventeenth century but began to flour-
ish again in the 1850s. Some of the old techniques of glassmaking
were revived, and firms today make traditional designs and original
modern glass. Since 1981, the name *Murano* may only be used on
glass made on Murano Island. Other pieces of Italian glass may be
found in the Glass-Contemporary and Glass-Midcentury categories of
this book.

Aquarium Block, Underwater Scene, Fish, Sea Grass, Cenedese, 1960s, 6 x 5 In., Pair 315.00
Basket, Green Iridescent, Blue Trailings, Red Ruffled Edge, Strini, 12 In. 785.00
Bird, Coroso, Tyra Lundgren, Iridescent, Venini, Italy, 8 x 7 In. 1725.00
Bottle, Stopper, Fasce Verticale, Fulvio Bianconi, Venini, Orange Bands, 12 In. 980.00
Bowl, Green & Gray Interior Decoration, Barbini, 1950s, 15 In. 4315.00
Bowl, Oval, Bands, Red, Green, Amethyst, Blue, Shallow, Footed, Italy, 13 In. 90.00
Bowl, Pierre Cardin, Square, Blue, Opaque Yellow, Engraved, Venini, 3 In., 5 Piece 375.00
Candleholder, Drum Shape, Applied Black Design, Red, Blue, Venini, 4 In., Pair 2070.00
Clown, Standing, White Outfit, 3 Red Ball Buttons, Black Tie, Hat, Italy, 14 In. 520.00
Compote, Latticinio Bowl, White, Clear Spangled Pedestal, Murano, 8 x 8 3/4 In. 175.00
Ewer, Cordonato-Oro Series, Ercole, Barovier & Toso, c.1950, 17 In. 865.00
Figurine, Bird, White, Red, Green, Silver Leaf, Murano, Italy, 3 Piece 175.00
Figurine, Christ, Archimede Seguso, 1950s, 9 1/2 In. 345.00
Figurine, Turtle, Blue, White, Murano, 9 1/2 In. 190.00
Fish, Brown, Silver Metallic Body, Gold Metallic Fins, Clear Cased, 12 In. 60.00
Jar, Lid, Murrine, Cenedese, Transparent Green, Multicolored Medial Band, 12 In. 460.00
Tazza, Smokey Topaz, Cobalt Blue, Applied Chain Link, 9 x 8 In. 240.00
Vase, Amethyst, Bubbles, Gold Metallic Inclusions, Ribbed, Raised Foot, 10 3/4 In. 355.00
Vase, Murano, 9 1/2 In. 478.00
Vase, Opaque Red & White, Tapered, Slender, AVEM, 1950s, 17 3/4 In. 105.00
Vase, Oval, Ribbed, Gold Spangle, Scalloped Rim, Murano, 12 1/4 In. 1115.00
Vase, Sommerso, Fishtail, Red, Blue, Green, Murano, 1950s, 13 1/2 In. 1294.00
Wine, Twisted Stem, Applied Decoration, Gold Scrolls, c.1900, 6 In., Pair 70.00

GLASSES for the eyes, or spectacles, were mentioned in a manuscript
in 1289 and have been used ever since. The first eyeglasses with rigid
side pieces were made in London in 1727. Bifocals were invented by
Benjamin Franklin in 1785. Lorgnettes were popular in late Victorian
times. Opera Glasses are listed in their own category.

Bakelite, Men's, Round Lenses, 1920-30, 5 1/4 In. 100.00
Cat's-Eye, Women's, Black & Clear Lucite, Carved Edge, France, 1950s, 5 1/4 In. 60.00
Cat's-Eye, Women's, Flame Ends, Aurora Rhinestones, Sergio, Italy 70.00
Cat's-Eye, Women's, White Pearlescent Plastic, France, 5 1/4 In. 25.00
Horn Rimmed, Men's, Apolo, Black, Featherweight Dupont Nylon, 5 3/4 In. 95.00
Horn Rimmed, Men's, Imitation Tortoiseshell, Diplomat, Late 1950s, 5 1/4 In. 150.00
Horn Rimmed, Men's, Imitation Tortoiseshell, Foremost Optical, Early 1960s, 6 In. 200.00
Lorgnette, Diamonds, Platinum, Hand Engraved, Bar, Chain, c.1920 .... 2300.00
Lorgnette, Engraved, Filigree, 12K Gold, Leather Case 90.00
Lorgnette, Floral Repousse, Brass, Gold Filled Handle Case, Late 1800s 310.00
Lorgnette, Flowers, Birds, Gold, Pierced, Engraved, Continental, Late 1800s, 3 In. 245.00
Lorgnette, Tortoiseshell Celluloid, Dragon Handle Case, 5 1/2 In. 55.00
Magnifying, Carved Bone Dog Head, Glass Eyes, Carved Whistle, 12 In. 50.00
Pince-Nez, Chain, 14K White Gold, Case, 1917 .... 55.00
Sewing, Brass, Adjustable, Fred Von Santen Fancy Good, Leather Case, 1890s 55.00
Sun, Brass Frames, Green Lenses, Paper Case, Mounted In Wood Case, Late 1700s 235.00

Sun, Ray-Ban, Aviator, Shooter Model, Gold Filled, Glass Lenses, 5 5/8 In.	80.00
Sun, Women's, Square, Pink & White Rims, Cazal, Germany, Late 1970s . .	65.00

GLIDDEN Pottery worked in Alfred, New York, from 1940 to 1957. The pottery made stoneware, dinnerware, and art objects.

Bowl, Mottled Turquoise, 4 x 7 In.	40.00
Casserole, Cover, Fish Shape, Blue, Green Lines, 3 1/2 x 16 x 4 1/2 In.	39.00
Dish, White, Incised Design, Square, Marked, 8 1/4 x 8 1/4 In.	38.00
Planter, Mustard Color, Marked, 4 7/8 x 6 3/4 In.	20.00
Snack Set, 3 Cream Colored & 3 Green Rectangular Bowls, Adjustable Iron Stand	250.00
Sugar & Creamer, White, Incised Design	83.00
Tray, Poodle In Center, Cream Background, Yellow Rim, Square, 5 1/2 x 5 1/2 In.	15.00

GOEBEL is the mark used by W. Goebel Porzellanfabrik of Oeslau, Germany, now Rodental, Germany. Many types of figurines and dishes have been made. The firm is still working. The pieces marked *Goebel Hummel* are listed under Hummel in this book.

Bank, Owl, Brown, Cream, Yellow Beak, 3 Felt Disks On Bottom, 5 In.	28.00
Figurine, Cat, White, Green Eyes, 1 1/2 x 2 1/2 In.	32.00
Figurine, Chick In Half Of Eggshell, 2 3/4 x 2 x 2 In.	28.00
Figurine, Flower Madonna, Stylized Bee Mark, 8 In.	138.00
Figurine, Girl, Ruffled Skirt, With Dog On Leash, 8 1/4 In.	62.00
Figurine, Rabbit Peeking Out Of Yellow Basket, Foil Label, 3 1/4 x 3 x 2 1/2 In.	20.00
Lamp, Dachshund, Brown & White, Orange Polka Dot Scarf, 7 In.	90.00

GOLDSCHEIDER has made porcelains in three places. The family left Vienna in 1938 and started factories in England and in Trenton, New Jersey. The New Jersey factory started in 1940 as Goldscheider-U.S.A. In 1941 it became Goldscheider-Everlast Corporation. From 1947 to 1953 it was Goldcrest Ceramics Corporation. In 1950 the Vienna plant was returned to Mr. Goldscheider, and the company continues in business. The Trenton, New Jersey, business, now called *Goldscheider of Vienna*, imports all of the pieces.

Figurine, 2 Scottie Dogs, White, 8 3/4 In.	535.00
Figurine, Easter Parade, Tiered Dress, Flowers, Peggy Porcher, 6 1/2 In. . . . . *Illus*	50.00
Figurine, Grandfather With Violin, Dancing With Little Girl, 12 In.	400.00
Figurine, Marie Antoinette, Peggy Porcher, 6 1/2 In.	35.00
Figurine, Pekinese Dog, 4 In.	75.00
Figurine, Woman, Dancing, Blue Dress, Multicolored, Vienna, 19 x 16 1/2 In.	1710.00
Figurine, Woman, Dancing, Burgundy Strapless Gown, Signed, 1931, 15 In.	1135.00
Figurine, Woman, Dancing, Clingy Dress With Short Cape, Katzhutte, 10 In.	275.00
Plaque, Angel Fish, Art Deco, 6 In.	75.00
Wall Mask, Woman, Holding Lemon, Red Curly Hair, Terra-Cotta, 1930s, 8 In.	600.00
Wall Mask, Woman, Short Blond Hair, West Germany, 8 1/2 In.	165.00

GOLF, see Sports category.

GONDER Ceramic Arts, Inc., was opened by Lawton Gonder in 1941 in Zanesville, Ohio. Gonder made high-grade pottery decorated with flambe, drip, gold crackle, and Chinese crackle glazes. The factory closed in 1957. From 1946 to 1954, Gonder also operated the Elgee Pottery, which made ceramic lamp bases.

Figurine, Hawaiian Woman, Shoulder Yoke, Dangling Baskets, Green Glaze, 12 3/4 In. . . .	300.00
Figurine, Our Lady Of Fatima, Ivory Glaze, Box, 9 In.	65.00
Planter, Nautilus Shell, Red Flambe Glaze, No. 216, 6 1/4 x 19 In.	225.00
Vase, 4 Rounded Columns, Mottled White & Burgundy Glaze, 8 5/8 In.	35.00
Vase, Baluster, Flared Rim, Marbleized Black & White Glaze, 7 3/4 In.	40.00
Vase, Baluster, Wavy Triple Handles, Red Flambe Glaze, 9 1/2 In.	50.00

GOOFUS GLASS was made from about 1900 to 1920 by many American factories. It was originally painted gold, red, green, bronze, pink, purple, or other bright colors. Many pieces are found today with flaking paint, and this lowers the value.

Pickle Jar, Embossed Flowers, Aqua, Gold, Green Paint, Sheared & Ground Lip, 12 3/4 In.	150.00

Goldscheider, Figurine, Easter Parade, Tiered Dress, Flowers, Peggy Porcher, 6 1/2 In.

Goss, Bust, Man's Head, Scarf With Buckle Around Shoulders, Footed, Bisque, 5 1/4 In.

Gummed tags can be removed by heating the tag with a hairdryer, then loosening it with a flat knife.

Pickle Jar, Milk Glass, Embossed Flowers, Sheared & Ground Lip, 15 1/8 In.	290.00
Pickle Jar, Parrot, Branch, Fruit, Gold, Red, Blue Gray Paint, Ground Lip, c.1905, 12 1/2 In.	380.00

GOSS china has been made since 1858. English potter William Henry Goss first made it at the Falcon Pottery in Stoke-on-Trent. The factory name was changed to Goss China Company in 1934 when it was taken over by Cauldon Potteries. Production ceased in 1940. Goss china resembles Irish Belleek in both body and glaze. The company also made popular souvenir china, usually marked with local crests and names.

W. H. COSS

Bell, Southern Belle, Yellow Dress, Black Bonnet, 4 In.	150.00
Building, Glastonbury Abbey, Abbot's Kitchen, Brown, Green Moss, 2 3/4 In.	505.00
Building, Manx Cottage, Yellow, Green, 1 3/4 x 2 1/2 In.	115.00
Bust, Man's Head, Scarf With Buckle Around Shoulders, Footed, Bisque, 5 1/4 In. . . . *Illus*	95.00
Bust, Peeping Tom Of Coventry, Square Plinth, 4 1/2 In.	230.00
Candlestick, Manor Of Minchinhampton Crest, 1862-91, 5 In., Pair	135.00
Cup, Royal Pump Rooms Spa, Celtic Shape, 3 In.	200.00
Mug, Lincoln Jack, Worcestershire Regiment Crest, 3 In.	140.00
Vase, Oyserth Falls Near Rhyl, Cirencester Shape, 3 In.	230.00
Vase, St. Neots, Orange Poppy, 2 3/4 In.	300.00
Wall Pocket, Hatfield Hall Crest, Durham, 2 1/4 In.	35.00

GOUDA, Holland, has been a pottery center since the seventeenth century. Two firms, the Zenith pottery, established in the eighteenth century, and the Zuid-Hollandsche pottery made the brightly colored art pottery marked *Gouda* from 1898 to about 1964. Other factories followed. Many pieces featured Art Nouveau or Art Deco designs. Pattern names in Dutch, listed here, seem strange to English speaking collectors.

PLAZUID
GOUDA
HOLLAND

Bowl, Beek, Abstracts, Rust, Green, Yellow Dot, Blue Swirl, 1922, 3 1/2 x 7 3/4 In.	375.00
Candlestick, 4 Handles, Blossom, Blue & Green Glaze, Signed, A.L., 11 x 4 1/2 In.	405.00
Candlestick, Autumn, Leaves, Teal & Brown Ground, Ribs, 8 x 3 3/4 In., Pair	105.00
Candlestick, Egyptian, Phoenix Birds, Aqua, Cobalt, Chartreuse, 1923, 13 x 8 In.	200.00
Candlestick, Merapi, Crystalline Blossoms, Blue, Chartreuse, Double Neck, 18 x 6 In.	430.00
Candlestick, Rhodian, Green Abstracts, Rust, Brown, Double Neck, 1924, 15 x 5 In.	175.00
Inkwell Tray, Dome Cover, Anjer, Blossoms, Peach, Burgundy, Cobalt, 1927, 3 3/4 x 8 In. .	145.00
Jar, Cover, Dorian, Teardrops, Stripes, Arches, Embossed, Prins, 1924, 6 1/2 x 5 1/2 In. . . .	95.00
Jug, Addoe, Mushrooms, Brown, Yellow, Aqua Panel, 1931, 6 1/2 x 5 1/4 In.	145.00
Jug, Cobalt Blue Dots, Rust Swirls, Aqua Matte, Green, 1920, 9 1/2 x 5 In.	1150.00
Jug, Damascus, Cobalt Blue, Yellow Swirls, Tapered, Raised Bands, 7 x 4 1/2 In.	115.00
Jug, Futura, Poppy, White, Sage Green Ground, Metallic Sheen Finish, 10 x 6 1/2 In.	145.00
Jug, Mary, Blossoms, Blue, Yellow, Golden Abstracts, Gray Matte Ground, 1923, 9 x 6 In. .	230.00
Jug, Massa, Cobalt Blue Swirls, Dots, Teardrop Band, Sage, Rust, Cobalt, 10 x 6 1/2 In. . .	200.00
Lamp, Ada, Abstracts, Rust, White, Cobalt, Green Matte, Tapered, Spherical, 25 In.	520.00
Lamp, Tekla, Vine, Rust Blossoms, Band, White & Sage Ground, Cloth Shade, Signed, 16 In.	490.00

Lantern, Massa, Flowers, Open Chimney, Pierced Flowers, Green, Blue, Yellow, 10 x 6 In. 145.00
Pitcher, Pansy, Purple, Magenta, Tulips, Green & Sage Ground, Signed, 6 x 4 In. 345.00
Pitcher, Quola, Rust, Yellow, Cobalt Abstracts, White & Green Fields, 9 3/4 x 6 In. 145.00
Planter, Henley, Burgundy, Orange Circles, Gray, Aqua, Brown, Handles, 1925, 4 x 12 In. 115.00
Planter, Serma, Multicolored Abstracts, White Ground, Looped Handles, 3 x 10 In. 175.00
Plaque, Peacock, Stylized Sun, Cobalt, Yellow, Purple, Jo Bennis, 1923, 19 In. Diam. 1725.00
Plaque, White Buds, Blossoms, Yellow Abstract, Teal, Blue, Caramel, 11 1/2 In. Diam. . . . 400.00
Plate, Rosario, Stylized Blossom, Rust, Cobalt, Aqua, Yellow, Black, Ivory Ground, 8 In. . 35.00
Tazza, Bochara, Flowers, Rust, Cobalt, Green Abstracts, Scalloped, 1922, 5 3/4 x 10 In. . . . 200.00
Tea Set, Teapot, Creamer, 6 Cups, Saucers, Marantha, Tan, Cobalt, Green, Ivory Ground . . 260.00
Tray, Bianca, Yellow, Cobalt Blue, Rust, Ivory Ground, 1930, 11 1/2 In. Diam. 115.00
Vase, Anjer, Blossoms, Burgundy, Yellow Stamen, Vines, Ivory Ground, 1926, 12 x 5 In. . . 290.00
Vase, Baluster, Yellow Flowers, Dots, Green Abstracts, Stars, Black Ground, 12 x 7 1/2 In. 1265.00
Vase, Beek, Raised Dot, Yellow, Rust, Green Abstracts, Cobalt Swirls, Oval, 8 1/4 x 5 In. . 260.00
Vase, Blue, Purple Flowers, Pink Dots On Ivory Ground, 1925, 12 In. 455.00
Vase, Boat, Windmill, Lake, Village, Green To Cerulean Grass Line, Signed, 10 1/2 x 5 In. 375.00
Vase, Bud, Appel, Brown & Yellow Apples, Dot Abstracts, 1922, Signed, 8 1/2 In. 70.00
Vase, Candia, Bulbous, Flared, Circles, Blue Swirl Band, Rust, Cobalt Handles 14 x 5 In. . 230.00
Vase, Cira, Blossoms, Yellow, Blue Ground, Globular, Handles, Brown, 1922, 5 3/4 x 6 In. 175.00
Vase, Clouda, Blossom, Blue, Swirl Stamen, Gray, Brown Ground, 1926, 4 1/2 x 5 In. 175.00
Vase, Cobo, Stylized Flower, Blue, Orange, Gray Ground, Broad, Signed, 5 x 6 1/2 In. 145.00
Vase, Dam III, Flower Buds, Mint, Mauve, Cobalt Trim, Blue & White Band, 5 x 5 In. 200.00
Vase, Flowers, Purple, Turquoise, Rust, Yellow, Gloss, Double Gourd Shape, 4 3/4 In. 69.00
Vase, Gelria, Pansies, Blue Stamen, Orange Dot, Teal, Cobalt, Brown, Black, 6 x 2 3/4 In. . 200.00
Vase, Geometric Designs, Curved Handles, Johannes Van Schaick, 5 3/4 x 5 1/2 In. 520.00
Vase, Goldeele, Bird, Branch, Yellow Feathers, Leg Under Breast, Flowers, 1920, 6 x 4 In. 1610.00
Vase, Grotius, Abstract Design, Rust, Purple, Cobalt, Yellow, Oval, Handles, 14 x 5 1/2 In. 405.00
Vase, Hurh, Rust, Blue, Butterscotch Matte, Broad, Ribbed, Tapered, Signed, 11 x 6 In. . . 315.00
Vase, Ivora, Pansies, Purple, Magenta, Foliage, Blue, Brown, Black, Bulbous, 12 x 5 In. . . 405.00
Vase, Laristan, Bulbous, Recessed Panels, Multicolored, Signed, c.1910, 10 3/4 x 5 In. 290.00
Vase, Lely, Abstract Design, Flower, Brown, Green, Cobalt, Swirls, 1922, 10 1/2 x 6 In. . . . 290.00
Vase, Mary, Blossoms, Blue, Yellow, Gray Matte Ground, Red Bead, Handles, 11 x 7 In. . . 245.00
Vase, Massa, Green Matte, Yellow Abstracts, Bands, Cobalt, Rust, Oval, Flared, 10 x 7 In. . 245.00
Vase, Muller, Brown Flambe, Tan Lines, Ivory Ground, Bulbous, Spattered, 11 1/2 In. 175.00
Vase, Rhodesia, Rust, Green, Caramel, Yellow Accents, c.1904-10, 7 1/4 x 4 1/4 In. 175.00

GRANITEWARE is an enameled tinware that has been used in the
kitchen from the late nineteenth century to the present. Earlier graniteware was green or turquoise blue, with white spatters. The later ware
was gray with white spatters. Reproductions are being made in all
colors.

Cake Pan, Round, Tube 8.00
Can, Cream, Boston, Tin Lid, 5 In. 100.00
Can, Cream, Seamed, Tin Lid, 10 In. 30.00
Can, Cream, Tin Lid, L&G Paper Label, 10 1/2 In. 45.00
Candlestick, Metal Insert 40.00
Coffeepot, 9 In. 18.00
Coffeepot, Granite Lid, Paper Label, Greystone, 9 In. 50.00
Creamer, Fluted, Pewter Trim 200.00
Creamer, Pewter Trim, Scalloped Edge 55.00
Cuspidor, Blue Belle, Large, 2 Piece 60.00
Fish Cooker, Oval, Gray, Mottled 15.00
Flask 55.00
Frypan, Egg, 12 In. 50.00
Funnel, Fruit Jar 7.00
Gravy Strainer 10.00
Grinder, Vegetable, Small 28.00
Kettle, Cover, Granite Lid, Bail Handle, 5 In. 30.00
Kettle, Preserve, Lipped, Large 13.00
Ladle, Cocoa, Wooden Handle 235.00
Ladle, Side Snipe 70.00
Ladle, Skimmer 9.00
Ladle, Strainer 15.00

Ladle, Wooden Handle	55.00
Lunch Pail, Rectangular, Tin Cup, 4 Piece	65.00
Measure, Dry, Graduated, Qt.	15.00
Measure, Gill, Seamed, Strap Handle	95.00
Measure, Liquid, Qt.	20.00
Measure, Seamless, 2 3/4 In.	110.00
Measuring Cup, 2 1/2 In.	55.00
Mixing Bowl, Paper Label, Greystone, 11 In.	35.00
Mold, Tube, Scalloped	15.00
Muffin Pan, 6 Hole	15.00
Mug, Blue Belle, 2 3/4 In.	25.00
Pail, Batter, Tin Lid, Spout Cover	85.00
Pan, Egg, Mottled, Child's	1.00
Pan, Wash, Paper Label	10.00
Pie Plate	5.00
Pitcher, Syrup, Blue Belle	135.00
Pitcher, Water, 11 1/2 In.	60.00
Pitcher, Water, Ice Lip, 7 1/2 In.	250.00
Pitcher & Washbasin	60.00
Plate, Dinner, 7 1/4 In.	5.00
Plate, Painted, War Scene, 9 1/2 In.	25.00
Plate, Soup, 6 1/4 In.	23.00
Platter, Vegetable, Oval, L&G Stamp	25.00
Pot Scraper, Nesco Boy	300.00
Roaster, Oval, Nesco, 16 In.	10.00
Saucepan, Handle	5.00
Saucepan, Toy	70.00
Scoop, Spice	110.00
Scoop, Strap Handle	40.00
Scoop, Thumb	40.00
Skillet, 7 In.	10.00
Skillet, Chef-Ette Enameled Ware Paper Label, 10 In.	13.00
Soap Dish, Hanging Shell	35.00
Stove, Iron Gray, Mottled, Round, 3 Burners	15.00
Strainer, Handle, Pierced Bottom	5.00
Teapot, Gooseneck, Blue Belle	65.00
Teapot, Pewter Trim, Enameled Bottom	75.00
Teapot, Squat, End Of Day, 4 1/2 In.	145.00
Teapot, Tin Lid, Granite Tube Handle, 7 1/2 In.	50.00
Teapot, Tin Lid, Greystone Paper Label, 6 1/2 In.	75.00
Teapot, White, Violets, Pewter Spout, Lid & Rim, 1900, 7 1/2 In.	325.00
Tumbler, 3 1/4 In.	75.00
Tumbler, 3 3/4 In.	40.00
Urn, Coffee, Tin Lid, Brass Spigot	45.00

GRUEBY Faience Company of Boston, Massachusetts, was incorporated in 1897 by William H. Grueby. Garden statuary, art pottery, and architectural tiles were made until 1920. The company developed a green matte glaze that was so popular it was copied by many other factories making a less expensive type of pottery. This eventually led to the financial problems of the pottery.

Bookends, Ceramic Tile, Brown Glaze, Hammered Copper Frame, 6 1/2 In.	920.00
Bowl, Cucumber Matte Ground, Flaring, Ruth Erickson, 5 1/2 x 9 In.	2235.00
Bowl, Green Matte Glaze, Textured, Marked, 9 1/2 In.	645.00
Bowl, Leaves, Feathered Green Matte Glaze, 4-Sided, 3 1/4 x 6 In.	1060.00
Jardiniere, Tan Matte, Impressed Tulip Mark, 3 1/4 x 5 In.	750.00
Paperweight, Scarab, Green Matte Glaze, Leathery, Impressed Mark, 1 1/2 x 3 In.	635.00
Paperweight, Scarab, Indigo Matte Glaze, 4 x 2 1/2 In., Pair	1116.00
Paperweight, Scarab, Oatmeal Blue Green Glaze, 4 x 2 3/4 In.	499.00
Paperweight, Scarab, Pale Green Glaze, On Deep Green Ground, Impressed, 2 1/4 In.	490.00
Paperweight, Scarab, Tan Matte Glaze, Impressed Tulip Mark, 1 3/8 x 4 In.	400.00
Planter, Cucumber Matte Glaze, Leaves, Flaring, Edith R. Felton, 4 1/2 x 12 In.	1290.00
Tile, 2 Children, Fruit Basket, 12 x 24 In.	1880.00

Tile, Bird Flying Over Water, Bronze Frame, Square, 4 1/2 In. 1410.00
Tile, Blue Glaze, Geometric, Marked, Square 3 In. 90.00
Tile, Brown Clay, Geometric Design, Blue, Square, 3 In. 355.00
Tile, Carved Stylized Flower, Tan, Black Glaze Ground, Frame, Square, 13 In. 1175.00
Tile, Chamberstick, Green, Yellow, Square, 6 In. 3819.00
Tile, Fountain, Fish, Red, Oak Frame 3500.00
Tile, Geometric Design, Cruciform Pattern, Blue, Green, Yellow, Orange, 8 In. 645.00
Tile, Green Matte, Marked, 6 x 3 In. 80.00
Tile, Green, Brown, Blue Matte Glazes, Dog In Flower Garden, 6 x 6 In. 2990.00
Tile, Landscape, Trees, Mountains, Square 6 In. 4700.00
Tile, Leaves, Green, Ivory Matte, 6 In., 4 Piece 530.00
Tile, Lion, Rampant, Laurel Wreath, Brown Matte, Raised Outline, Diamond Shape, 8 In. . 3525.00
Tile, Pan & Flute, Greek God, Half Human Torso, Tan & Aqua Matte, Frame, 9 1/2 In. 750.00
Tile, Putto, Playing Cymbals, Ivory Matte Glaze, Blue Ground, 6 In. 470.00
Tile, Ship At Sea, Square 6 In. 1765.00
Tile, Stylized Leaf, Brown Clay, Square, 4 In. 175.00
Tile, Stylized Leaf, Ivory, Green Ground, Square, 4 In. 235.00
Tile, Tortoise, Leaves, Matte Glaze, Square, 6 In. 5580.00
Tile, Tree, Hillside, Cloud, 8 x 8 In. 7850.00
Tile, Tulip, Carved, Ivory, Green, Blue, 4 1/2 In. 1175.00
Tile, Tulip, Golden, Green Leaves, Dark Green Ground, Raised Outline, 6 x 6 In. 4115.00
Tile, Tulip, Green Matte Glaze, 6 x 6 In. 2760.00
Tile, Tulip, Green, Yellow, Bronze Frame, Square, 6 1/2 In. 2820.00
Tile, Yellow Horses, Green Ground, 6 x 6 In. 7900.00
Tile Frieze, Water Lilies, Lily Pad, Raised Outline, 3 6-In. Tiles 4115.00
Vase, 7 Molded Leaf Panels, 5-Petal Yellow Flower, Green Glaze, 10 3/4 x 7 In. 9315.00
Vase, Applied Ivory Quatrefoils, Feathered Mustard Matte Ground, Squat, 4 3/4 x 5 In. ... 4115.00
Vase, Applied Leaves, 3 Curled Handles, Bulbous, Green Matte Glaze, 9 3/4 x 7 1/2 In. ... 3525.00
Vase, Applied Leaves, Feathery Green Matte, 7 1/2 x 4 In. 3290.00
Vase, Applied Leaves, Frothy Green Matte, Oval, 8 1/4 x 4 3/4 In. 2000.00
Vase, Applied Leaves, Green Matte Crystalline Glaze, Bulbous, 11 x 8 In. 6465.00
Vase, Applied Narrow, Wide Leaves, Green Matte Glaze, Barrel Shape, 9 1/4 x 7 In. 3290.00
Vase, Arts & Crafts, Cylindrical, Leaves, Blades, Green Matte Glaze, c.1905, 12 x 10 In. .. 3525.00
Vase, Blue Matte Glaze, Impressed Mark, 3 1/8 In. 405.00
Vase, Blue Matte Glaze, Impressed Tulip Mark, 8 In. 1150.00
Vase, Blue Suspended Matte Glaze, Flared, Impressed, 2 1/2 In. 380.00
Vase, Bottle Shape, Leaves, Green Matte Glaze, Gertrude Priest, 6 3/4 x 4 1/2 In. 1295.00
Vase, Brown Matte, 5-Sided Neck, Ivory Buds, Leaves, Wilhelmina Post, 11 1/4 x 5 1/2 In. 10000.00
Vase, Bulbous, Feathered Green Matte Glaze, 6 In. 940.00
Vase, Bulbous, Feathered Green Matte Glaze, 11 x 9 In. 3290.00
Vase, Bulbous, Rounded Leaves, Feathered Green Matte Glaze, 7 In. 1410.00
Vase, Carved, Applied Leaves, Green Matte Glaze, Marked, 7 1/2 In. 2940.00
Vase, Cream Suspended Matte Glaze, Gourd Shape, Impressed, 7 In. 530.00
Vase, Cucumber Matte Glaze, Spade Shape Leaves, Marie Seaman, 11 1/2 x 5 3/4 In. 4115.00
Vase, Cucumber Matte, Barrel Shape, Irises, Leaves, Wilhelmina Post, 9 x 7 1/2 In. 4995.00
Vase, Cucumber Matte, Squat, Bulbous, Flared Rim, Spade Shape Leaves, 5 x 4 In. 4995.00
Vase, Cylindrical, Vertical Ribs, Green Matte Glaze, ER, 6 1/2 In. 940.00
Vase, Feathered Green Matte Glaze, Flat Shoulder, 9 1/2 In. 2350.00
Vase, Green Glaze, Squat, Rolled Rim, 3 1/2 In. 805.00
Vase, Green Matte Glaze, Bud, Stem, Leaf, 7 1/4 In. 2530.00
Vase, Green Matte Glaze, Carved Leaves, Impressed Mark, 10 1/2 In. 2300.00
Vase, Green Matte Glaze, Egg Shape, Stylized Leaves, 7 1/4 x 5 1/2 In. 1765.00
Vase, Green Matte Glaze, Flaring, Yellow Buds, Green Leaves, Marie Seaman, 13 x 9 In. .. 7050.00
Vase, Green Matte Glaze, Flat Shoulder, 7 1/2 x 6 1/2 In. 3055.00
Vase, Green Matte Glaze, Flat Shoulder, Leaves, 3 1/2 x 3 In. 3055.00
Vase, Green Matte Glaze, Leathery, Impressed Tulip Mark, 10 1/2 In. 1610.00
Vase, Green Matte Glaze, Leaves, Bulbous, 9 1/2 x 6 In. 2700.00
Vase, Green Matte Glaze, Shouldered, Vertical Lines, Signed, 7 1/2 In. 1645.00
Vase, Green Matte, Carved, Applied Leaves, 7 1/2 In. 2938.00
Vase, Green Matte, Squat, Bulbous, Rolled Rim, Yellow Buds, Broad Leaves, 4 x 4 1/4 In. . 3410.00
Vase, Green, Gray, Glaze, Boston, 1899, 3 In. 590.00
Vase, Indigo Glaze, Egg Shape, 8 x 4 In. 1410.00
Vase, Leaves On Base, Squat, Green Matte Glaze, Oatmealed, 4 1/2 x 5 1/2 In. 1528.00

Vase, Leaves, Baluster, Green Matte Glaze, Wilhelmina Post, 9 x 8 1/2 In. 4400.00
Vase, Leaves, Black Green Drip Glaze, Bulbous, Elongated Neck, Marked, 8 x 5 In. 5750.00
Vase, Leaves, Buds, Green Matte, Closed-In Rim, Florence Liley, 10 3/4 x 5 1/4 In. 8225.00
Vase, Leaves, Sculpted, Vertical, Tapered, Green Matte Glaze, 7 1/2 In. 3055.00
Vase, Leaves, Short, Rounded, Buds, Full-Length, Bulbous, Feathered Green Matte, 7 In. . . 2350.00
Vase, Leaves, Yellow Buds, Leathery Green Matte Glaze, Wilhelmina Post, 8 x 4 In. 4700.00
Vase, Modeled Tulips, Circular Impressed, Incised Initials, 6 7/8 x 9 In. 1610.00
Vase, Mottled Brown, Suspended Matte Glaze, Impressed, 6 1/2 In. 529.00
Vase, Mustard Glaze, Impressed Tulip Mark, 4 1/2 In. 460.00
Vase, Ribbed, Impressed, 7 5/8 In. 750.00
Vase, Tapered, Carved, Applied Vertical Leaves, Buds, Green Matte Glaze, 8 In. 2415.00
Vase, Tapered, Ocher Matte Glaze, Broad, Flat Leaves, 7 1/4 x 4 1/2 In. 5300.00
Vase, Tile, Purple Grapes, Leaves, Vines, Tan Matte Ground, Impressed, Square 6 In. 460.00

GUNDERSEN glass was made at the Gundersen-Pairpoint Glass
Works of New Bedford, Massachusetts, from 1952 to 1957. Gundersen
Peachblow is especially famous.

Creamer, Burmese, Diamond-Quilted, Applied Reeded Handle, 4 In. 145.00
Vase, Bud, Peachblow, Glossy, Tapered, Footed, 7 In. 63.00
Vase, Jack-In-The-Pulpit, Peachblow, 9 3/4 In. 635.00

GUNS that may be classed as toys, such as BB guns, air rifles, and cap guns, are
listed in the Toy category.

GUSTAVSBERG ceramics factory was founded in 1827 near Stockholm, Sweden. It is best known to collectors for its twentieth-century
artwares, especially a green stoneware with silver inlay called *Argenta*.

Gustafsberg

Charger, Dolphin, Argenta, No. 1035, Label, 17 1/2 In. 717.00
Figure, Hippopotamus, 3 White Seagulls, Mottled Brown Glaze, 1960s, 6 3/4 In. 86.00
Figure, Nude Woman, On Pedestal, Parian, P. Hasselberg, 19 In. 410.00
Vase, Carved, Blue Stylized Leaves, Matte Glaze, 1930s, 7 In. . . . . *Illus* 200.00
Vase, Geometric Designs, Blue Matte Glaze, Berndt Friberg, c.1962, 5 In. 1175.00
Vase, Plant, Grid, Turquoise Glaze, Rectangular, 2 Handles, Argenta, 6 In. 265.00
Vase, Silver Fish, Green Glaze, Straight Sides, Footed, Argenta, 7 In. . . . . *Illus* 100.00

GUTTA-PERCHA was one of the first plastic materials. It was made
from a mixture of resins from Malaysian trees. It was molded and used
for daguerreotype cases, toilet articles, and picture frames in the nineteenth century.

Buckle, Floral, Art Nouveau, 1/2 In. 20.00
Earrings, Pierced, Linked Hoops, Victorian, 3/4 In. 55.00
Frame, Columns, Floral Arches, Engraving Of Napoleon, France 250.00
Inkwell, Cylinder, 2 Wells, L. Bandau & Co., 3 1/8 x 4 In. 165.00
Locket, Applied Rose, Engraved Interior, Mourning, 1850s, 1 3/4 In. 50.00
Match Holder, Engraved Advertisement, J.K. Rishel Furniture, 2 3/4 In. 50.00
Mirror, Asymmetrical C-Scrolling, 11 x 7 3/4 In. 200.00
Union Case, Lion In Love, Wadlams Manufacturing Co., 3 15/16 x 3 7/16 In. 940.00

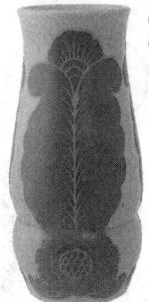

Gustavsberg, Vase,
Carved, Blue Stylized
Leaves, Matte Glaze,
1930s, 7 In.

Gustavsberg, Vase,
Silver Fish, Green
Glaze, Straight Sides,
Footed, Argenta, 7 In.

Haeger, Vase, Bud,
Green Drip Glaze,
Bulbous Bottom,
7 1/4 In.

Union Case, Scrolled Medallion, 5 3/8 x 4 7/16 In. 450.00

HAEGER Potteries, Inc., Dundee, Illinois, started making commercial
artwares in 1914. Early pieces were marked with the name *Haeger* written over an *H*. About 1938, the mark *Royal Haeger* was used in honor
of Royal Hickman, a designer at the factory. The firm is still making
florist wares and lamp bases. See also the Royal Hickman category.

Bank, Winking Puppy, Orange Glaze, 8 1/2 In. 25.00
Console Set, Shell, Angel Fish Flower Frog, Leaf Candleholders, Mottled Pink, 4 Piece ... 40.00
Dish, Cover, Stylized Triangle, Turquoise Interior, Sanded White Exterior, Brass Finial ... 35.00
Figurine, Gray Mermaid On Green Swordfish, High Gloss Glaze, Royal Haeger, 20 In. ... 175.00
Figurine, Hen, Rooster, Red & Black Glaze, c.1960, 12 In., Pair 85.00
Lamp, Bucking Bronco, Tan & Yellow Glaze, Royal Haeger, 15 1/2 In., Pair 230.00
Lamp, TV, Deer, In Cutout Disc, Black Glaze, Fiberglass Screen, 11 In. 85.00
Planter, Figural Elephant, Light Green Matte Glaze, 6 1/2 In. 15.00
Vase, Bottle Shape, Sunset Glaze, 15 In. 50.00
Vase, Bud, Green Drip Glaze, Bulbous Bottom, 7 1/4 In. .... *Illus* 10.00
Vase, Flying Saucer Body, Flared Neck, Blue Green Mottled Glaze, 7 x 12 1/2 In. 65.00
Vase, Gazelle, Cone Shaped Flower Holder, Black Glaze, 7 In., Pair 70.00
Vase, Rectangular Shape, White & Tan Glaze, 6 1/2 In. 6.00
Vase, Squat, Wide Rim, Orange Peel Glaze, 7 1/2 x 8 1/2 In. 74.00
Vase, Trojan Horse, Light Blue Glaze, 9 In. 40.00

HALF-DOLL, see Pincushion Doll category.

HALL CHINA Company started in East Liverpool, Ohio, in 1903. The
firm made many types of wares. Collectors search for the Hall teapots
made from the 1920s to the 1950s. The dinnerwares of the same
period, especially Autumn Leaf pattern, are also popular. The Hall
China Company is still working. For more information, see *Kovels'
Depression Glass & Dinnerware Price List*. Autumn Leaf pattern
dishes are listed in their own category in this book.

Blue Blossom, Bean Pot, Cover, Handle, 6 x 8 In. 390.00
Blue Blossom, Jug, Donut, 7 1/2 In. 390.00
Chinese Red, Bowl, 5 1/2 In. 40.00
Chinese Red, Tureen, Cover, Tab Handles, 10 x 9 1/2 In. 380.00
G.E., Leftover, Cover, Addison Gray & Daffodil Yellow, c.1938 .... 12.00
Game Bird, Tea Set, 3 Piece 175.00
Montgomery Ward, Bowl, Delphinium, 7 In. ....30.00 to 35.00
Montgomery Ward, Water Server, Delphinium, 1940s 50.00
Poppy, Coffeepot, Cover, Bellevue, 2 Cup 2900.00
Poppy, Teapot, Bellevue, 2 Cup 2800.00
Poppy, Teapot, Donut 530.00
Quartermasters, Sauceboat, White, 1940s, 10 In. 25.00
Refrigerator Ware, Water Server, Plaza, Red 390.00
Rhythm, Teapot, Cobalt Blue, 6 In. 370.00
Thorley, Teapot, Apple, Black, Gold Trim, 6 1/4 x 9 1/2 In. 480.00
Westinghouse, Leftover, Refrigerator Ware, Yellow, 8 1/2 x 5 In. 45.00
Wild Poppy, Teapot, Radiance 390.00

HALLOWEEN is an ancient holiday that has changed in the last 200
years. The jack-o'-lantern, witches on broomsticks, and orange decorations seem to be twentieth-century creations. Collectors started to
become serious about collecting Halloween-related items in the late
1970s. The papier-mache decorations, now replaced by plastic, and old
costumes are in demand.

Button, Monmouth Annual Halloween, Witch, Cats, Pumpkin, 1914, 1 1/4 In. 310.00
Candy Container, Black Cat, With Rider, Glass Eyes 1695.00
Candy Container, Jack-O'-Lantern, Orange Painted Glass, Metal Bail, Cover, 1930s, 5 In. .. 460.00
Candy Container, Jack-O'-Lantern, Paper Leaf Slide, Hand Pressed, c.1910 .... 495.00
Candy Container, Veggie Head Girl, Papier-Mache, Hand Pressed, c.1915 .... 495.00
Candy Container, Witch, In Rocket, Plastic, Black & Orange, Contents, 8 In. 995.00
Candy Container, Witch, On Broom, Plastic, Black & Orange, 5 1/4 In. 475.00

 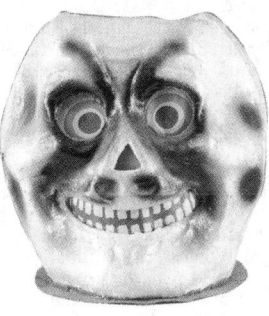 

Halloween, Figure, Pumpkin
Head, Watermelon Mouth,
Papier-Mache, Bells, 10 In.

Halloween, Jack-O'-Lantern,
Smiling Skull, Papier-Mache,
Paper Insert, 5 In.

Halloween, Nodder, Witch
On Cat, Papier-Mache, Felt,
Sticker, Made in Germany, 6 In.

Candy Container, Witch, On Motorcycle, Plastic, Black & Orange, 7 In.	695.00
Costume, Bewitched, Samantha, Ben Cooper, Box, 1965, 8 1/2 x 11 In.	100.00
Costume, Evel Knievel, Ben Cooper, Box, 1974	145.00
Costume, Land Of Lost, Ben Cooper, Box, c.1975, Size Medium	100.00
Costume, Shari Lewis Charlie Horse, Plastic, Halco, 1961	55.00
Devil, Head, Horns, Composition, Hand Painted, Facial Expression, 5 In.	80.00
Figure, Pumpkin Head, Watermelon Mouth, Papier-Mache, Bells, 10 In. .... *Illus*	920.00
Jack-O'-Lantern, Black Cat Head, c.1920, 5 1/2 In.	750.00
Jack-O'-Lantern, Black Cat, 2-Sided, Cardboard, 7 1/2 x 3 In.	165.00
Jack-O'-Lantern, Cardboard, 2-Sided, Inserts, Candle, 5 1/2 In.	40.00
Jack-O'-Lantern, Cardboard, Tissue Insert, Candleholder, Germany, 1930s, 2 1/2 In. .88.00 to 165.00
Jack-O'-Lantern, Composition, Paper Insert, Orange, Green Base, Wire Handle, 4 1/2 In. ...	55.00
Jack-O'-Lantern, Original Paper Insert, 8 In.	220.00
Jack-O'-Lantern, Papier-Mache, Original Insert, Germany, 2 In.	140.00
Jack-O'-Lantern, Pressed Cardboard, 2-Sided, Wide Mouth, Eyes, Metal Handle, 8 In.	65.00
Jack-O'-Lantern, Pressed Cardboard, Orange, Green, Tissue Insert, Metal Handle, 6 In.	80.00
Jack-O'-Lantern, Pressed Cardboard, Orange, Green, Tissue Insert, Side Glancing, 6 In.	65.00
Jack-O'-Lantern, Pressed Cardboard, Orange, Tissue Insert, 5 In.	65.00
Jack-O'-Lantern, Pressed Cardboard, Paper Insert, Handle, Oval Mouth, 5 In.	90.00
Jack-O'-Lantern, Pressed Cardboard, Tissue Insert, Handle, 5 In.	55.00
Jack-O'-Lantern, Smiling Skull, Papier-Mache, Paper Insert, 5 In. .... *Illus*	920.00
Jack-O'-Lantern, Steel, Pierced Features, Carrying Stick, Candleholder Inside, 44 In.	575.00
Jack-O'-Lantern, Witch Head, Composition, c.1925, 7 In.	795.00
Lantern, Black Cat, Original Insert, Papier-Mache, Germany, 2 In.	195.00
Lantern, Cat, Cardboard, Lithograph, 2-Sided, Tissue Insert, 7 In.	35.00
Lantern, Cat, Pressed Cardboard, Tissue Insert, Handle, 5 1/2 In.	90.00
Lantern, Witch Head, Papier-Mache, Parade Scale, Germany, 18 x 13 In.	4980.00
Mask, Gray Ghost, Hat, Mustache, Goatee	25.00
Nodder, Pumpkin Head Man, Papier-Mache, Multicolored Paint, Germany, 8 1/2 In.	1955.00
Nodder, Witch, On Cat, Papier-Mache, Felt, Sticker, Made In Germany, 6 In. .... *Illus*	1035.00
Noisemaker, Frying Pan, Tin Lithograph, Chein, 1930s	35.00
Postcard, Black Cat, On Jack-O'-Lantern, 1909, Unused, 3 1/2 x 5 1/2 In.	55.00
Postcard, Black Cat, On Jack-O'-Lantern, 1910, 3 1/2 x 5 1/2 In.	70.00
Ratchet, Veggie Man, Composition, Crepe Collar, Wood, Hand Painted, Germany	90.00
Skeleton, Embossed, Die Cut, Jointed, Marked Germany, 1920s, 27 In.	225.00
Skull In Coffin, Papier-Mache, Stage Prop, 19th Century, Half Life Size	495.00
Toy, Black Clown, Pull String, Germany	895.00
Toy, Clown, Devil Pops Out Of Top Of Head, Pull String, Germany, c.1900	695.00
Toy, Pirate's Auto, Jack-O'-Lantern On Hood, Plastic, Blue, Black, Orange, 5 In.	1430.00
Toy, Squeak, Black Cat, On Stick, Composition, Germany, c.1900	475.00
Toy, Squeak, Devil Head, On Stick, Composition, Germany, c.1900	395.00
Toy, Witch, Driving Rocket Car, Plastic, Black, Orange Wheels & Hat, 5 In.	220.00
Toy, Witch, Driving Rocket Car, Plastic, Black, Orange Wheels, 8 In.	1650.00
Toy, Witch, Driving Rocket Car, Plastic, Orange Car, Yellow Wheels, Black Hat, 5 In.	1430.00

Toy, Witch, Pushing Pumpkin, Black Cat, Plastic, Wheels, Black, Orange, 9 In. 1540.00
Toy, Witch, Riding Broomstick, Plastic, Black, Orange, 5 In. 1430.00
Toy, Witch, Riding Motorcycle, Plastic, Blue Wheels, Orange, Black, 7 In. 1540.00
Toy, Witch, Riding Rocket, Wheels, Plastic, Black, Orange, 6 In.   2090.00
Wall Decoration, Cat, Black, Mouth Open, Embossed, 15 x 7 In. 135.00
Wall Decoration, Witch, On Broom, Orange, Black, White, Cardboard, Embossed, 7 In. . .   70.00
Whirligig, Witch, Cutout, Weathered Paint, Tin Arms & Broom, c.1935 . . . .   385.00
Whistle, Plastic, E. Rosen, 1950s, 4 3/4 In. 110.00

HAMPSHIRE pottery was made in Keene, New Hampshire, between
1871 and 1923. Hampshire developed a line of colored glazed wares as
early as 1883, including a Royal Worcester-type pink, olive green,
blue, and mahogany. Pieces are marked with the printed mark or the
impressed name *Hampshire Pottery* or *J.S.T. & Co., Keene, N.H.* Many
pieces were marked with city names and sold as souvenirs.

Bowl, Treescape Relief At Shoulder, Green Matte Glaze, M In Circle, 2 3/4 x 5 In. 176.00
Bowl, Water Lily, Water, Embossed, Green Matte Glaze, Marked, 2 1/4 x 5 1/2 In. 690.00
Lamp, Green Matte Glaze, Incised, Ribbed, Beehive Style, 12 x 8 1/2 In. 865.00
Lamp, Oval Panels, Green Matte Glaze, Incised, Globular, Long Neck, 21 x 7 1/2 In. 1265.00
Lamp Base, Leaves, Flowers, Green Matte Glaze, Electrified, 15 x 9-In. Pot 1998.00
Vase, Blue Green & Pink Mottled Matte Glaze, 7 1/2 In. 470.00
Vase, Broad Leaf Design, Green Matte Glaze, Marked M In Circle, 7 1/4 In. 529.00
Vase, Cocoa Brown Glaze, Oval, Rolled Lip, Incised, 7 1/4 x 4 1/2 In. 400.00
Vase, Dandelions, Feathered Cobalt Blue Matte Glaze, Barrel Shape, 6 x 5 1/4 In. 1116.00
Vase, Double Gourd, Geometric Designs, Green Matte Glaze, 8 In. 825.00
Vase, Embossed Flowers & Leaves, Green Matte Glaze, Incised, 4 1/2 x 5 In. 575.00
Vase, Green Matte Glaze, Molded Vertical Ribs, 4 1/2 In. 235.00
Vase, Green Matte Glaze, Squat, Ridge Along Neck, 4 x 4 1/2 In.   230.00
Vase, Leaves, Buds, Brownish Pink Mottled Glaze, 6 1/2 In. 529.00
Vase, Leaves, Feathered Green Glaze, Bottle Shape, 9 1/4 x 6 1/2 In. 1175.00
Vase, Leaves, Frothy Blue Green Matte Glaze, Egg Shape, 7 x 4 1/2 In. 825.00
Vase, Leaves, Gourd, Green Matte Glaze, Marked, 3 3/4 x 3 1/2 In. 345.00
Vase, Leaves, Raised Edge, Aqua Cerulean Glaze, Black Charcoaling, 7 x 4 1/2 In. 1150.00
Vase, Mottled Green Matte, Bulbous, Protruding Lobes, 5 1/2 In.   1060.00
Vase, Red Earthen Glaze Over Yellow, Experimental, Copper Dust, Signed, 3 x 3 In. 1380.00
Vase, Water Lily, Embossed, Buds, Leaves, Green Matte Glaze, Marked, 7 1/2 x 5 1/2 In. . .   1035.00

HANDEL glass was made by Philip Handel working in Meriden, Connecticut, from 1885 and in New York City from 1893 to 1933. The firm
made art glass and other types of lamps. Handel shades were made not
only of leaded glass in a style reminiscent of Tiffany but also of reverse
painted glass. Handel also made vases and other glass objects.

Chamberstick, Hammered Copper, Removable Inserts, Pair, 6 1/4 x 6 1/4 In. 470.00
Chandelier, 8 Caramel Slag Glass Panes, Roses, 3 Sockets, Chain, 9 1/2 x 24 In. 1645.00
Humidor, Burnish Bulbous Body, Horse, Dog, Bronze Lid With Pipe, 7 In. 500.00
Humidor, Cover, Monk, Earth Tone Colors, Cylindrical, 5 3/4 In.   500.00
Humidor, Horse & Dog, Bulbous, Bronze Cover, Pipe, 7 In. 560.00
Lamp, 3-Light, Bronze Tone, 4-Footed, Square, Urn Shape, Acorn Pulls, 25 In. 635.00
Lamp, 3-Light, Hanging, 8 Panels, Hawaiian Sunset, Signed, 24 In. 7475.00
Lamp, 3-Light, Stylized Leaf Border, 3-Footed, Urn Shape, 23 1/4 In. 480.00
Lamp, 4-Sided Lantern Shade, Leaves, Berries, Caramel Ground, 1/2 Harp, 48 x 7 In. 2235.00
Lamp, 8 Panels, Metal Overlay, Cattails, Green & Caramel Slag, 3 Sockets, 23 In. 40250.00
Lamp, 9 Panels, Hawaiian Tropic, Filigree Overlay, Palm Tree, Sunset, Acorn Pulls, 24 In.   5750.00
Lamp, Aurene Glass Domed Shade, Bronzed Metal, Harp, Plain Foot, 58 x 10 In. 3525.00
Lamp, Bronzed Metal Base, Adjustable Arm, 6-Sided Glass Shade, 6 In. 4025.00
Lamp, Caramel Leaded Glass Shade, Bronzed Metal Base, 24 x 17 In. 2940.00
Lamp, Chipped Glass Shade, Forest, Moon, Arts & Crafts Base, 3 Sockets, 25 x 18 In. 7050.00
Lamp, Chipped Glass Shade, Palm Trees, Ship, Bronze Base, John Bailey, 24 x 18 In. 9400.00
Lamp, Chipped Glass Shade, Palm Trees, Ship, Moon, 1 Socket, 56 1/2 x 14 In. 8225.00
Lamp, Chipped Glass Shade, Wild Roses, Butterflies, 2 Sockets, 23 x 18 In. 10575.00
Lamp, Cutout, Paneled, Bronze, Caramel Colored Glass, 18 x 24 In. 2875.00
Lamp, Daffodils Filigree Overlay, Slag Panel, Striated Ground, 3-Socket Base, 21 In. 5175.00
Lamp, Desk, Painted, Green, Yellow, Brown, Geometric, Early 20th Century, 14 In. 1208.00

Lamp, Domed Chipped Ice Shade, Landscape, 5 In. 1200.00
Lamp, Domed Shade, Band Of Scrolling Flowers, c.1920, 25 x 18 In. 2990.00
Lamp, Domed Shade, Red Flowers, Green Leaves, Slag Glass, Sawtooth Border, 16 In. ... 1840.00
Lamp, Evergreen Trees, Mountains, Bronzed Metal Base, 19 3/4 x 14 In. 8813.00
Lamp, Hanging, Carriage, Amber & Red Glass, Bronze Brickwork, 6 1/2 In., Pair 1898.00
Lamp, Jungle Bird, Macaws Resting On Branch, Flying, Leaves, Pierced Foot, 23 In. 17825.00
Lamp, Jungle Bird, Tropical Leaves, 3 Sockets, Painted Base, 23 In. 13225.00
Lamp, Leaded & Stained Glass Shade, Flowers, Early 1900s, 23-In. Shade 3190.00
Lamp, Leaded Glass, Metal, Patinated, c.1915, 64 3/4 x 24 In. 7768.00
Lamp, Leaded Glass, Robins & Flowers, Signed Base, 18-In. Shade, 25 In. 550.00
Lamp, Lobed Harp Base, Swiveling Socket, Green Slag Glass Shade, 18 1/2 x 10 1/2 In. .. 2585.00
Lamp, Mosserine Glass Shade, Harp Armature, 56 1/2 x 14 x 9 3/4 In. 5875.00
Lamp, Mt. Fuji, Bamboo Trees, Ship, Dock, Bamboo Base, Signed, 23 In. 7475.00
Lamp, Reverse Shade, Embossed Trees, 3 Sockets, Bronze, 23 1/2 x 16 In. 6463.00
Lamp, Ribbed Glass, Tall Ships, Acanthus Leaf Base, 3 Sockets, 23 1/4 x 15 In. 6463.00
Lamp, Roses, Mottled Yellow Ground, Bronzed Metal Base, 20 1/2 x 14 In. 3173.00
Lamp, Sailboats, Windmills, Bronzed Metal Base, 25 x 18 In. 5581.00
Lamp, Student, 2 Shades, Pine Needle, Green Glass, Bronzed Metal, 22 x 6 x 21 In. 1998.00
Lamp, Trees, Leaves, Sunset Ground, 13 In. 2300.00
Lamp, Water Lily, 16 Glass Panes, Slag, Opalescent, Bronze Patinated, c.1915, 18 1/2 In. . 1840.00
Shade, Parrots, Flowers, Orange, Pink, Purple, Yellow Crackle, Egg Shape, 6 1/2 In. 403.00
Shade, Teroma, Daffodils, Frosted Ground, Vertical Ribbing, 5 1/4 x 4 1/2 In., Pair 1175.00
Vase, Scalloped Rim, Landscape, Iridescent Gold, Amber, 7 x 5 1/4 x 5 1/4 In. 345.00
Vase, Teroma, Tropical Leaf Scene, Pedestal Foot, Fluted Top, Signed, 10 1/2 In. 1783.00

HARDWARE, see Architectural category.

HARKER Pottery Company was incorporated in 1890 in East Liverpool, Ohio. The Harker family had been making pottery in the area since 1840. The company made many types of pottery but by the Civil War was making quantities of yellowware from native clays. They also made Rockingham-type brown-glazed pottery and whiteware. The plant was moved to Chester, West Virginia, in 1931. Dinnerwares were made and sold nationally. In 1971 the company was sold to Jeannette Glass Company and all operations ceased in 1972. For more information, see *Kovels' Depression Glass & Dinnerware Price List.*

Advertising, Ashtray, Abe Lincoln, Compliments Of Were's Variety Store, 5 1/2 In. 18.00
Advertising, Ashtray, Doral Hotels, Miami, Miami Beach, Fla., Ivory, Round 10.00
Alpine, Salt & Pepper, Intaglio, Cameoware 18.00
Alpine, Soup, Dish, Intaglio, Cameoware 9.00
Amy, Pie Server, 9 1/4 In. 18.00
Amy, Plate, Salad, 7 1/4 In. 9.00
Bakerite, Pie Plate, c.1930 .... 8.00
Bakerite, Platter, c.1930, 12 In. 20.00
Bakerite, Salt & Pepper, c.1930, 3 In. 10.00
Bakerite, Sugar & Creamer, c.1930 .... 10.00
Bamboo, Platter, Beige, Cameoware, 11 1/2 In. 20.00
Blue & White, Rolling Pin, Blue, White Handles 75.00
Blue Basket, Creamer, 3 In. 16.00
Cameo Rose, Spoon, Salad, Cameoware 16.00
Cameoware, Bowl, Yellow, 5 In. 10.00
Cameoware, Cup 10.00
Chesterton, Cup & Saucer 9.00
Chesterton, Plate, Dinner, 1950s, 9 1/2 In. 8.00
Chesterton, Plate, Gray, 7 1/4 In. 8.00
Chesterton, Platter, 13 1/2 In. 20.00
Chesterton, Platter, Gray, Oval, 1950s, 12 In. 20.00
Chesterton, Soup, Dish, Gray, 1950s, 8 1/2 In. 9.00
Colonial Lady, Pie Baker, 9 In. 28.00
Dogwood, Cup & Saucer, Intaglio, Cameoware 9.00
Dogwood, Platter, Parchment Beige 10.00
Dogwood, Soup, Dish, 7 1/2 In. 8.00
Embassy, Sugar, Cover, Handles, Gold Trim 20.00
Godey, Plate, Gadroon Rim, 22K Gold 18.00

Golden Dawn, Platter, 13 In.	20.00
Ivy, Platter, Intaglio, Cameoware, Oval, 13 x 11 1/2 In.	18.00
Ivy Vine, Gravy Boat	16.00 to 19.00
Ivy Vine, Plate, Square, 8 1/2 In.	8.00
Ivy Vine, Saltshaker	18.00
Ivy Vine, Sugar, Cover, Handles	18.00
Laurelton, Bowl, Sage Green, White, 6 3/4 In.	4.00 to 5.00
Laurelton, Plate, Dinner, Aqua	8.00
Laurelton, Plate, Dinner, Parchment Beige	9.00
Laurelton, Platter, Gray, 13 3/4 In.	16.00
Mallow, Bowl, Handles, 6 1/4 In.	10.00
Mallow, Plate, 8 In.	22.00
Modern Tulip, Bowl, Cereal, 6 1/8 In.	9.00
Modern Tulip, Bowl, Vegetable, 8 1/4 In.	20.00
Modern Tulip, Cake Plate, Metal Handle	20.00
Modern Tulip, Pie Dish, 10 In.	22.00
Modern Tulip, Plate, Dinner, 9 1/2 In.	9.00
Modern Tulip, Plate, Square, 6 5/8 In.	8.00
Modern Tulip, Water Jug, Cover, 1939, 8 In.	28.00
Monterey, Custard, Hot Oven Kitchenware, 2 In.	20.00
Petit Point, Cheese Plate, 11 In.	40.00
Petit Point, Creamer, Cover	28.00
Petit Point, Creamer, Silver Trim	28.00
Petit Point, Pie Baker, 10 1/4 In.	28.00
Petit Point, Plate, 10 In.	25.00
Pine Cone, Soup, Dish, 1 1/2 x 8 In.	8.00
Rosebud, Cup & Saucer, Gold Trim, Heritance Form	16.00
Shellridge, Cup & Saucer	9.00
Shellridge, Plate, Bread & Butter, 6 1/8 In.	8.00
Skyscraper, Salt & Pepper, 3 Flowers, Daisy, Rose, Morning Glory	44.00
Tulip Bouquet, Plate, Bread & Butter, Square, 6 3/4 In.	4.00
Wheat, Cup & Saucer, Parchment Beige	9.00
Wheat, Pie Server, 9 7/16 In.	19.00
Wheat, Plate, Dinner, Parchment Beige	9.00
White Rose, Teapot, Blue, Cameoware, 1940s	56.00
Wild Rose, Pie Server, Gold Trim, 1940s, 9 1/4 In.	28.00

HARLEQUIN dinnerware was produced by the Homer Laughlin Company from 1938 to 1964, and sold without trademark by the F. W. Woolworth Co. It has a concentric ring design like Fiesta, but the rings are separated from the rim by a plain margin. Cup handles are triangular in shape. Seven different novelty animal figurines were introduced in 1939. For more information on Harlequin dinnerware, see *Kovels' Depression Glass & Dinnerware Price List.*

Chartreuse, Bowl, Fruit	30.00
Chartreuse, Creamer	20.00
Green, Tumbler, Water, Car Decal	80.00
Light Green, Cup	15.00
Light Green, Plate, Salad, Individual	15.00
Mauve Blue, Eggcup, Single	14.00
Medium Green, Cup & Saucer	8.50
Red, Bowl, Nappy, 9 In.	11.00
Red, Pitcher, 22 Oz.	95.00
Rose, Tumbler, Water	80.00
Turquoise, Bowl, Salad, Individual	20.00
Turquoise, Cup	15.00
Yellow, Ashtray, Basketweave	45.00
Yellow, Bowl, 36s	20.00
Yellow, Bowl, Fruit	32.00
Yellow, Bowl, Salad, Individual	24.00
Yellow, Pitcher, Ball	11.00
Yellow, Platter, 13 In.	35.00
Yellow, Sauceboat	17.00

HATPIN collectors search for pins popular from 1860 to 1920. The long pin, often over four inches, was used to hold the hat in place on the hair. The tops of the pins were made of all materials, from solid gold and real gemstones to ceramics and glass. Be careful to buy original hatpins and not recent pieces made by altering old buttons.

Art Nouveau, Twisted Wire Heart, Gold Metal, 9 In.	90.00
Enamel, Suffragette Purple, Silver Metal Band, 1910, 10 1/2 In.	120.00
Enamel, University Of Michigan, 8 In.	15.00
Glass, Faceted Amethyst, 8-Sided Cone, 6 In.	15.00
Glass, Faceted Red Flower Blossoms, Brass Bouquet Holder, 11 1/4 In.	75.00
Rhinestone, Inverted Pear Shape, 5 In.	85.00
Satsuma, Birds In Trees, 8 In.	460.00
Simulated Gold Nugget, Bennett's Jewelry Store, Cripple Creek, Colo., Pat. 1904, 6 In.	96.00
Sterling Silver, Kewpie Doll, 6 1/8 In.	120.00
Sterling Silver, Openwork Bow, Victorian, 9 In.	90.00
Sterling Silver, Poodle, Hoop, Rhinestone Eye, Birmingham, England, 1907, 8 1/4 In.	350.00

HATPIN HOLDERS were needed when hatpins were fashionable from 1860 to 1920. The large, heavy hat required special long-shanked pins to hold it in place. The hatpin holder resembles a large saltshaker, but it often has no opening at the bottom as a shaker does. Hatpin holders were made of all types of ceramics and metal. Look for other pieces under the names of specific manufacturers.

Carnival Glass, Grape & Cable, Amethyst, 7 In.	225.00
Hull, Little Red Riding Hood, Holder In Basket	100.00
Nippon, Satsuma Style, Flowers, Swags, Gold Beading, 4 5/8 In.	12.00
Porcelain, Peacock, Standing On Stump, 10 1/4 In.	65.00
Porcelain, Queen Louise, Egg Shape, Gold Paint, 10 In.	380.00
Porcelain, Tree Stump, Black Cat, Attached Pin Tray, 1890s, 4 1/4 In.	280.00
Royal Bayreuth, Floral Decal, Green, Attached Pin Tray, Gold Trim, 4 1/2 In.	165.00
Transferware, Classical Scene, Lovers Embracing, Black, 1880, 5 In.	130.00

HAVILAND china has been made in Limoges, France, since 1842. The factory was started by the Haviland Brothers of New York City. Pieces are marked *H & Co., Haviland & Co.,* or *Theodore Haviland.* It is possible to match existing sets of dishes through dealers who specialize in Haviland china. Other factories worked in the town of Limoges making a similar chinaware. These porcelains are listed in this book under Limoges.

HAVILAND & CO.

Bowl, Vegetable, Cover, Juliet Pattern, Pink Floral Sprays, 8 1/4 In.	145.00
Butter, Cover, Strainer, Scrolled Handles, Gold Trim, 8 1/4 In.	135.00
Casserole, Cover, Glenbrook Pattern, Oval, Theodore Haviland, 8 3/4 In.	100.00
Coffeepot, Blue Garland Pattern, Johann Haviland, 11 In.	110.00

Haviland, Pitcher, Duck,
Green & White, Head Stopper,
Sandoz, Reissue, 6 1/4 In.

Head Vase, Siamese Woman,
Iridescent Headdress, Pink,
Green, Blue Collar, Japan, 6 In.

Head Vase, Woman, Blond Hair,
Black Hat, White Bow, Pearls,
Inarco, 1961, 4 3/4 In.

Creamer, Royal Lace, Platinum Trim 50.00
Finger Bowl, Underplate, Violets, Light Green Ground, 4 3/4 In. 120.00
Gravy Boat, Attached Underplate, Green Border With Gold Animals, Flowers, 8 x 5 In. ... 150.00
Lobster Dish, Shell Shape, 2 Sections, Birds, Duck, Iris, Hand Painted, Label, 11 3/4 In. .. 345.00
Pitcher, Duck, Green & White, Head Stopper, Sandoz, Reissue, 6 1/4 In. .... *Illus* 100.00
Pitcher, Gold Trimmed Flowers, Fluted Cylinder, Scalloped Base, H & C, 9 In. 95.00
Plate, Dinner, Royal Lace, Platinum Trim 35.00
Plate, Egyptian Scene, Square, C.H. Field, 8 1/4 In., 6 Piece 2450.00
Plate, Hand Painted, Roses, 11 In. 65.00
Plate, Pink, Art Nouveau Flower In Center, 12 1/2 In. 128.00
Plate Set, Dessert, Gilt Scalloped Rim, Fruit Scenes, Early 1900s, 7 3/4 In., 8 Piece 115.00
Platter, Petite Rose Spray, Scalloped Oval, Haviland & Co., 15 1/4 In. 125.00
Urn, Barbotine, Roses, Indigo Ground, 10 1/4 In. 1530.00

HAWKES cut glass was made by T. G. Hawkes & Company of Corning, New York, founded in 1880. The firm cut glass blanks made at other glassworks until 1962. Many pieces are marked with the trademark, a trefoil ring enclosing a fleur-de-lis and two hawks. Cut glass by other manufacturers is listed under either the factory name or in the general Cut Glass category.

Bowl, Hobstars, Diamonds, Fans, Signed In Base, Early 20th Century, 8 In. 160.00
Bowl, Thistle Cutting, 2 x 10 In. 385.00
Goblet, Wine, Verre-De-Soie, Engraved Bowl, Teardrop Stem, Signed, 6 3/4 In., 3 Piece .. 430.00
Tray, North Star, Signed, 15 In. 2645.00
Vase, Amethyst, Carved Flowers, Paneled, Ribbed, Sterling Repousse Band, 9 1/4 In...... 345.00
Vase, Flared Top, Alternating Brilliant & Flower Engraved Panels, 14 In., Pair 500.00
Vase, Sterling, Irises, Fluted Lip Border, Signed, 8 3/4 In. 635.00

HEAD VASES, generally showing a woman from the shoulders up, were used by florists primarily in the 1950s and 1960s. Made in a variety of sizes and often decorated with imitation jewelry and other lifelike accessories, the vases were manufactured in Japan and the U.S.A. Less elaborate examples were made as early as the 1930s. Religious themes, babies, and animals are also common subjects. Other head vases are listed under manufacturers' names and can be located through the index at the back of this book.

Candy, Brunette, Green Striped Dress, Straw Hat, Necklace, Betty Lou Nichols, 6 In. 620.00
Doris Day, Blue Bow, White Ruffled Collar, Inarco, 7 1/4 In. 550.00
Jackie Onassis, White Veil, Black Dress, Gloves, Inarco, 6 In. 600.00
Nellie, Brunette Braids, Pink Dotted Swiss Hat & Dress, Betty Lou Nichols, 8 1/2 In. 380.00
Siamese Girl, Black Hair, Ivory Headdress, Mandarin Collar, Japan, 6 In. 35.00
Siamese Woman, Iridescent Headdress, Pink, Green, Blue Collar, Japan, 6 In. ...... *Illus* 45.00
Teen, Ash Blond Ponytail, Green Patterned Dress, Pearl Earrings, Relpo, 7 In. 285.00
Teen, Ash Blond, Red Bow & Dress, White Collar, Pearls, Earrings, Relpo, 7 In. 265.00
Teen, Blond Braids, Green Hat & Dress, Pink Bows, Lego, 7 In. 280.00
Woman, Ash Blond, Bonnet, Pink Daisies, Turquoise Ring, Royal Crown, 7 1/2 In. 1800.00
Woman, Ash Blond, Flowers In Hair, Green Dress, Pearls, Earrings, Relpo, 7 In. 370.00
Woman, Ash Blond, White Jacket, Hood, Pearl Earrings, Rubens, 6 1/2 In. 330.00
Woman, Ash Brunette, Upswept Hair, Green Draped Dress, Pearls, Napco, 9 In. 90.00
Woman, Blond Hair, Black Hat, White Bow, Pearls, Inarco, 1961, 4 3/4 In. .... *Illus* 85.00
Woman, Blond, Bristle Eyelashes, Green Cape, White Flowers, Ucagco, 5 1/2 In. 70.00

HEINTZ ART Metal Shop used the letters *HAMS* in a diamond as a mark. Otto Heintz took over the Arts & Crafts Company in Buffalo, New York, in 1903. By 1906 it had become the Heintz Art Metal Shop. It remained in business until 1930. The company made ashtrays, bookends, boxes, bowls, desk sets, vases, trophies, and smoking sets. The best-known pieces are made of patinated bronze with silver overlay. Similar pieces were made by Smith Metal Arts and were marked *Silver Crest.* Some pieces by both companies are unmarked.

Lamp, Bulbous Base, Sterling On Bronze, Poppies, Apricot Lining, 10 x 8 1/2 In. 1880.00
Lamp, Domed Shade, Sterling Over Bronze, Panels, Silk Liner, Signed, 12 x 18 In. 4113.00
Lamp, Helmet Shade, Harp Base, Sterling On Bronze, Flower Overlay, Verdigris, 13 In. 1645.00

Lamp, Mushroom Shade, Sterling Silver Overlay, Flared Base, Bronze, 15 x 13 In.	1880.00
Trophy, Revolver Score, Sterling Silver Overlay, Handles, Bronze, 1920, 12 In.	411.00
Vase, Sterling On Bronze, Poppies, 10 x 3 1/2 In.	1175.00

HEISEY glass was made from 1896 to 1957 in Newark, Ohio, by A. H. Heisey and Co., Inc. The Imperial Glass Company of Bellaire, Ohio, bought some of the molds and the rights to the trademark. Some Heisey patterns have been made by Imperial since 1960. After 1968, they stopped using the *H* trademark. Heisey used romantic names for colors, such as *Sahara*. Do not confuse color and pattern names. The Custard Glass and Ruby Glass categories may also include some Heisey pieces.

Admiralty, Sherry, 2 Oz.	5.00
African, Goblet, Moongleam Foot, Stem, 10 Oz.	75.00
Animal, Airedale	600.00
Animal, Clydesdale	175.00 to 180.00
Animal, Colt, Balking	65.00
Animal, Colt, Kicking	100.00
Animal, Elephant	130.00 to 400.00
Animal, Filly, Head Back	1000.00
Animal, Filly, Head Forward	1200.00
Animal, Fish, Match Holder	160.00
Animal, Flying Mare	3000.00
Animal, Giraffe, Head Back	100.00
Animal, Goose, Wings Down	210.00
Animal, Goose, Wings Half	30.00
Animal, Hen	200.00
Animal, Mallard, Wings Half	90.00
Animal, Pig, Mama	275.00 to 500.00
Animal, Rabbit, Paperweight	55.00
Animal, Rooster	300.00
Animal, Scottie Dog	65.00
Animal, Show Horse	400.00
Animal, Wood Duck	575.00
Arch, Tumbler, Tangerine, 4-Toed	925.00
Aristocrat, Candlestick, 7 1/2 In., Pair	55.00
Aristocrat, Candlestick, 11 In.	90.00
Aristocrat, Candlestick, 15 In., Pair	325.00
Aristocrat, Candy Jar, Cover, Footed, Cobalt Blue	950.00
Athena, Candlestick, 2-Light, Pair	20.00 to 40.00
Athena, Cocktail	50.00
Athena, Sugar & Creamer, Tray	15.00 to 45.00
Banded Flute, Cruet, Stopper, 4 Oz.	40.00
Banded Flute, Horseradish Jar, Cover	45.00
Banded Flute, Tray, 13 In.	15.00
Barbara Fritchie, Goblet, 10 Oz.	10.00
Barbara Fritchie, Goblet, Del Monte Cutting, 10 Oz.	30.00
Beaded Panel & Sunburst, Nappy, Handle, 5 In.	25.00
Beaded Swag, Nappy, Enameled Poppy, 8 In.	55.00
Beaded Swag, Toothpick, Opal	20.00
Beaded Swag, Toothpick, Ruby Stain, Engraved Name Charlie, 1903	20.00
Bonnet, Basket, 7 In.	90.00
Brazil, Nut Dish, Moongleam	45.00
Cabochon, Candelette, Pair	10.00
Carcassone, Goblet, Cobalt Blue, 10 Oz.	55.00
Carcassone, Tumbler, Soda, Cobalt Blue, Footed, 5 Oz.	45.00
Carcassone, Tumbler, Wine, Alexandrite, 2 1/2 Oz.	25.00
Cascade, Candlestick, 3-Light, Pair	35.00
Caswell, Creamer, Moongleam, Footed	15.00
Coarse Rib, Finger Bowl	10.00
Coarse Rib, Mustard, Cover	15.00
Cobel, Cocktail Shaker, Enameled Waterbirds	160.00
Cobel, Cocktail Shaker, Tally Ho Etch, Qt.	75.00

Colonial, Basket, Daisy Cutting, 7 In.	85.00
Colonial, Dish, Jelly, Footed	20.00
Colonial, Sugar & Creamer	25.00
Continental, Goblet, Westchester Cutting, 10 Oz.	30.00
Continental, Sherbet	5.00
Continental, Toothpick	55.00
Corby, Sugar & Creamer	85.00
Coventry, Goblet, Belvedere Etch, 10 Oz.	25.00
Creole, Cocktail, Alexandrite, 3 1/2 Oz.	50.00
Creole, Tumbler, Soda, Alexandrite, Footed, 8 Oz.	75.00
Crystolite, Bottle, Oil, Stopper	15.00
Crystolite, Bowl, Floral, Oval, 13 In.	15.00
Crystolite, Candleblock, Pair	5.00
Crystolite, Candlestick, 2-Light	10.00
Crystolite, Candlestick, 3-Light, Pair	15.00
Crystolite, Candy Dish, Shell, 7 In.	25.00
Crystolite, Cheese Dish, Footed	5.00
Crystolite, Cigarette Box, Cover, 4 In.	5.00
Crystolite, Cruet	15.00
Crystolite, Dish, Jelly, Tricornered, Handle, Spider Web Base	10.00
Crystolite, Dish, Mayonnaise, Shell Shape	10.00
Crystolite, Ice Bucket	25.00
Crystolite, Nappy, 4 In.	5.00
Crystolite, Nappy, 8 In.	25.00
Crystolite, Nut Dish, Swan, Master	20.00
Crystolite, Punch Set, 15 Piece	90.00
Crystolite, Relish, 5 Sections, Round, 10 In.	15.00
Crystolite, Relish, Leaf, 4 Sections	20.00
Crystolite, Salt & Pepper	25.00
Crystolite, Sugar & Creamer	5.00
Crystolite, Tray, Oval, 13 In.	50.00
Crystolite, Tumbler, Juice, Footed, 6 Oz.	30.00
Diamond Point, Ashtray	10.00
Dolphin, Candlestick, Flamingo, 10 In, Pair	550.00
Double Rib & Panel, Basket, Flamingo	110.00
Double Rib & Panel, Goblet, 10 Oz.	15.00
Duquesne, Goblet, Pompeii Etch, 9 Oz.	5.00
Duquesne, Saucer, Champagne, Chintz Etch	5.00
Empress, Candlestick, Alexandrite, Dolphin-Footed, 6 In., Pair	800.00
Empress, Candlestick, Sahara, Dolphin-Footed, 6 In., Pair	250.00
Empress, Celery Dish, Arctic Etch, 13 In.	25.00
Empress, Celery Dish, Moongleam, 13 In.	30.00
Empress, Cruet, Sahara	85.00
Empress, Dish, Mayonnaise, Sahara, 5 In.	65.00
Empress, Nappy, Alexandrite, 6 In.	65.00
Empress, Nappy, Sahara, Footed, 7 1/2 In.	35.00
Empress, Plate, Sahara, 6 In.	40.00
Empress, Relish, 3 Sections, Sahara, 7 In.	45.00
Empress, Sandwich Server, Center Handle, Sahara, Lotus Etch, 12 In.	95.00
Empress, Tumbler, Sahara, 10 Oz.	160.00
Ernshaw, Syrup, 12 Oz.	30.00
Fancy Loop, Celery Dish	50.00
Fancy Loop, Cruet	20.00
Fancy Loop, Punch Cup, Footed	20.00
Fancy Loop, Toothpick	70.00
Fancy Loop, Toothpick, Emerald, Gold Trim	170.00
Fandango, Bottle, Water	80.00
Fandango, Dish, Jelly, Tricornered, Handle	10.00
Fandango, Nappy, Tricornered, 6 In.	5.00
Fandango, Spooner	5.00
Fandango, Toothpick	10.00
Flamingo, Salt	10.00

Flat Panel, Bowl, Floral, 8-Sided, 12 In. 10.00
Flat Panel, Horseradish Jar, Cover 35.00
Flat Panel, Knife Rest ....10.00 to 40.00
Flat Panel, Nut Dish 5.00
Flat Panel, Nut Dish, Flamingo 20.00
Flat Panel, Relish, 5 Sections, Oval, 13 1/2 In. 35.00
Flat Panel, Spooner & Sugar, Cover 15.00
Flat Panel, Straw Holder 80.00
Flat Panel, Syrup, 7 Oz. 30.00
Flat Panel, Toothpick 45.00
Flat Panel, Tray, Ice Cream, 12 In. 75.00
Flat Panel, Tumbler, Soda, Amber, 10 Oz. 40.00
Flat Panel, Vase, Trumpet, 12 In. 150.00
Gascony, Goblet, Sahara, Ambassador Etch, 11 Oz. 30.00
Gascony, Tumbler, Soda, Footed, Tangerine, 10 Oz. 165.00
Gascony, Wine, Ambassador Etch, 2 1/2 Oz. 15.00
Gascony, Wine, Tangerine, 2 1/2 Oz. 160.00
Georgian, Candlestick, 9 In., Pair ....50.00 to 65.00
Georgian, Candlestick, 11 In., Pair 180.00
Greek Key, Butter, Cover 60.00
Greek Key, Claret, 3 Oz. 130.00
Greek Key, Compote, Jelly, 5 1/2 In. 60.00
Greek Key, Jug, Star Base, 1/2 Gal. 50.00
Greek Key, Tray, French Roll, 12 1/2 In. 160.00
Hanover, Goblet, 10 Oz. 30.00
Hanover, Tumbler, Juice, Hermitage Etch, 4 Oz. 5.00
Horsehead, Bookends, Pair 40.00
Horsehead, Cocktail, 3 Oz. 330.00
Jack-Be-Nimble, Candlestick, Pair 25.00
Jamestown, Goblet, Palmetto Cutting, 9 Oz. 10.00
Kalonyal, Bonbon 25.00
Kalonyal, Bottle, Water 400.00
Kalonyal, Bowl, Footed, 10 1/2 In. 85.00
Kalonyal, Dish, Jelly, Crimped, Handle, 5 1/2 In. 35.00
Kalonyal, Eggcup... 30.00
Kalonyal, Plate, 8 In. 25.00
Kalonyal, Plate, 10 In. 25.00
Kalonyal, Spoon Tray 25.00
Kimberly, Goblet, Krall Cutting, 10 Oz. 160.00
King Arthur, Goblet, Flamingo, 10 Oz. 40.00
King Arthur, Goblet, Snowflake Cutting, 10 Oz. 45.00
Kohinoor, Goblet, Churchill Cutting, 10 Oz. 40.00
Lady Leg, Goblet, Zodiac Etch, 8 Oz. 30.00
Lariat, Bowl, Floral, Crimped, 13 In. 30.00
Lariat, Candlestick, 3-Light, Pair 30.00
Lariat, Candy Dish, Cover, 5 In. 30.00
Lariat, Egg Plate 95.00
Lariat, Mayonnaise Set, 3 Piece 20.00
Lariat, Vase, Fan, 8 In. 25.00
Leaf, Candlestick, 6 3/4 In., Pair 50.00
Little King, Pitcher, 8 Oz. 55.00
Lobe, Dish, Pickle, Moongleam, 8 In. 25.00
Locket On Chain, Cake Salver 85.00
McGrady, Syrup, Cover, Flamingo, 7 Oz. 55.00
McGrady, Syrup, Cover, Sahara, 7 Oz. 60.00
McGrady, Syrup, Flamingo, 5 Oz. 45.00
Midcentury, Cordial, 1 Oz. 50.00
Monte Cristo, Goblet, Olympiad Etch, 9 Oz. 10.00
Monte Cristo, Goblet, Waikiki Cutting, 9 Oz. 28.00
Narrow Flute, Dish, Jelly, Handles, 5 In. 35.00
Narrow Flute, Eggcup, Souvenir, Boston 5.00
Narrow Flute, Mustard, Cover ....10.00 to 20.00

Narrow Flute, Tray, Biscuit, 8 In. 110.00
New Era, Cordial, 1 Oz. 25.00
Oakwood, Tumbler, Soda, Tally Ho Etch, 7 Oz. 35.00
Octagon, Cheese Dish, Handle, Moongleam, 6 1/2 In. 10.00
Octagon, Cheese Plate, Flamingo, Handle, 6 1/2 In. 15.00
Octagon, Dish, Dessert, Flamingo, Footed 5.00
Octagon, Dish, Mayonnaise, Flamingo, Footed 20.00
Octagon, Tray, 4 Sections, Fuchsia Etch 70.00
Old Dominion, Cordial, Sahara, 1 Oz. 45.00
Old Dominion, Goblet, Alexandrite, 10 Oz. 80.00
Old Glory, Goblet, 8 Oz. 15.00
Old Sandwich, Ashtray, Sahara 20.00
Old Sandwich, Bowl, Oval, Sahara, 12 In. 210.00
Old Sandwich, Cruet, Cross Stopper 30.00
Old Sandwich, Decanter, Sherry, Sahara, Oval 550.00
Old Sandwich, Mug, 10 Oz. 25.00
Old Sandwich, Tumbler, Bar, Sahara, 2 Oz. 90.00
Old Williamsburg, Candelabrum, 5-Light, 25 In., Pair 700.00
Old Williamsburg, Candlestick, 9 In. 25.00
Old Williamsburg, Candlestick, 11 In., Pair 210.00
Orchid Etch, Bowl, Floral, Waverly 25.00
Orchid Etch, Candlestick, Mercury, Pair 30.00
Orchid Etch, Dish, Jelly, Footed, Waverly 20.00
Orchid Etch, Dish, Mayonnaise, Footed, Waverly 20.00
Orchid Etch, Goblet, Graceful, 10 Oz. 30.00
Orchid Etch, Shrimp Server, Liner, Universal 100.00
Paneled Cane, Toothpick 5.00
Park Avenue, Cordial, 1 Oz. 45.00
Patrician, Candlestick, 7 1/2 In. 5.00
Peerless, Decanter, Stopper, Pt. 5.00
Peerless, Pitcher, 3 Pt. 45.00
Peerless, Toothpick 20.00
Penguin, Decanter, Sherry, Stopper, Pt. 300.00
Petal, Sugar & Creamer, Moongleam 60.00
Phyllis, Sugar & Creamer, Moongleam 60.00
Pillows, Spooner 30.00
Pillows, Table Set, 3 Piece 90.00
Pineapple & Fan, Mug, Emerald 30.00
Pineapple & Fan, Toothpick 65.00
Pineapple & Fan, Vase, 8 In. 30.00
Pinwheel & Fan, Nappy, 8 In. 25.00
Pinwheel & Fan, Nappy, Vaseline, 4 3/4 In. 290.00
Plantation, Bowl, Floral, 12 In. 50.00
Plantation, Bowl, Gardenia, 12 1/2 In. 25.00
Plantation, Bowl, Gardenia, Footed, 11 1/2 In. ....150.00 to 200.00
Plantation, Cake Salver 200.00
Plantation, Candleblock, Pair 60.00
Plantation, Candlestick, Pair 220.00
Plantation, Claret, 4 Oz. 50.00
Plantation, Coaster 20.00
Plantation, Cruet 140.00
Plantation, Dish, Mayonnaise, Underplate 35.00
Plantation, Goblet, 10 Oz. 20.00
Plantation, Goblet, Ivy Etch, 10 Oz. 15.00
Plantation, Plate, Buffet, 18 In. 200.00
Plantation, Relish, 3 Sections, Oval, 11 In. 15.00
Plantation, Sherbet 15.00
Plantation, Tray, Condiment, 9 In. 70.00
Plantation, Tumbler, Iced Tea, Ivy Etch, Footed, 12 Oz. 100.00
Pleat & Panel, Cruet, Flamingo, 3 Oz. ....40.00 to 50.00
Pleat & Panel, Plate, Flamingo, 6 In. 45.00
Pluto, Candlestick, Flamingo, Pair 35.00

Polonaise, Goblet, Cameo Necklace Etch, 10 Oz. 10.00
Prince Of Wales, Punch Bowl, Base, 10 In. 100.00
Prince Of Wales, Toothpick 240.00
Priscilla, Butter Chip 10.00
Priscilla, Punch Set, 12 Piece 295.00
Priscilla, Toothpick ....15.00 to 40.00
Prison Stripe, Sugar & Creamer, Hotel 45.00
Provincial, Cruet 20.00
Punty Band, Mug, Opal 5.00
Puritan, Ashtray, Horsehead 55.00
Puritan, Candy Jar, Cover, Floral Cutting, 1 Lb. 90.00
Puritan, Champagne, 6 1/2 Oz. 15.00
Puritan, Jar, Pickle, Cover 55.00
Puritan, Plate, 8 In. 10.00
Puritan, Toothpick, Footed 150.00
Quator Hotel, Sugar & Creamer 10.00
Queen Ann, Candleholder, Saucer Base, 3 In., Pair 20.00
Queen Ann, Candlestick, Prisms, 7 1/2 In., Pair 75.00
Queen Ann, Dish, Mint, Orchid Etch, 5 1/2 In. 25.00
Queen Ann, Goblet, Belle-Le-Rose Etch, 10 Oz. 5.00
Queen Ann, Goblet, Everglade Cutting, 10 Oz. 10.00
Queen Ann, Relish, 3 Sections, Orchid Etch 10.00
Raindrop, Bowl, Floral, Moongleam, 12 1/2 In. 35.00
Ramshorn, Goblet, 10 Oz. 70.00
Ramshorn, Goblet, Sea Nymph Etch, 10 Oz. 75.00
Recessed Panel, Basket, 7 In. 65.00
Recessed Panel, Candy Jar, Cover, 1/2 Lb. 20.00
Recessed Panel, Vase, Flared, 9 In. 30.00
Renaissance, Water Set, 5 Piece 230.00
Revere, Honey, Cover, Flower Cutting 80.00
Revere, Lemon Dish, Cover, Butterfly Cutting 10.00
Revere, Plate, Vaseline, 9 In. 85.00
Ridgeleigh, Ashtray, Huntington Etch, 6 In. 15.00
Ridgeleigh, Bowl, Centerpiece, 11 1/2 In. 15.00
Ridgeleigh, Candelabrum, 7 In. 10.00
Ridgeleigh, Candle Vase 20.00
Ridgeleigh, Candle Vase, Zircon, 5 In. 190.00
Ridgeleigh, Celery Dish, 12 In. 20.00
Ridgeleigh, Cruet 5.00
Ridgeleigh, Relish, 5 Sections, Star, 10 In. 20.00
Ridgeleigh, Relish, Sections, Oblong, 10 1/2 In. 10.00
Ridgeleigh, Sugar & Creamer, Tray ....20.00 to 35.00
Ridgeleigh, Tumbler, Iced Tea, Footed, 12 Oz. 140.00
Rooster, Cocktail Shaker, 4 1/4 In., Pair 196.00
Saturn, Tidbit, Zircon 60.00
Saturn, Vase, Optic, Zircon, 10 1/2 In. 260.00
Shasta, Goblet, 10 Oz. 130.00
Skirted Panel, Candlestick, Toy, Pair 50.00
Spanish, Champagne, Cobalt Blue, 6 Oz. 40.00
Spanish, Goblet, 10 Oz. 35.00
Spanish, Goblet, Cobalt Blue, 10 Oz. 95.00
Stanhope, Goblet, Saturn Optic, 10 Oz. 10.00
Steele, Rose Bowl, Moongleam 50.00
Suez, Cordial, Midwest Cutting, 1 Oz. 55.00
Suez, Goblet, Belvedere Cutting, 9 Oz. 20.00
Suez, Goblet, Florida Cutting, 10 Oz. 75.00
Sunburst, Candlestick 5.00
Sunburst, Punch Bowl, 14 In. 110.00
Sunflower, Candlestick, 3 1/2 In., Pair 10.00
Sweet Ad-O-Line, Goblet, 14 Oz. 5.00
Symphone, Champagne, Krall Rose Cutting, 6 Oz. 50.00
Taper, Cologne, Moongleam, Dauber, 1/4 Oz. 130.00

Toujours, Sugar & Creamer 25.00
Town & Country, Dish, Mayonnaise, Underplate, Dawn 55.00
Town & Country, Tumbler, Dawn, 8 Oz. 60.00
Tricorn, Candlestick, 3-Light, Flamingo 85.00
Trident, Bowl, Floral, Oval, 12 In. 35.00
Trident, Candlestick, 2-Light, Sahara 40.00
Triplex, Candlestick, 3-Light, Sahara, Pair 240.00
Trojan, Cordial, 1 Oz. 35.00
Tudor, Bowl, Footed, Cone Shaped, Rolled Edge, 9 In. 10.00
Tudor, Candy Box, Cover, Oval 50.00
Tudor, Cruet, Stopper, 6 Oz. 10.00
Tudor, Goblet, 10 Oz. 15.00
Twist, Bowl, Nasturtium 70.00
Twist, Cruet, Stopper, 4 Oz. 20.00
Twist, Cruet, Stopper, Flamingo, 4 Oz. 20.00
Twist, Cruet, Stopper, Moongleam, 4 Oz. 90.00
Twist, Nut Dish, Flamingo 20.00
Twist, Nut Dish, Marigold 35.00
Universal, Champagne, Hollow Stem, 6 Oz. 5.00
Universal, Cordial, 1 Oz. 15.00
Victorian, Bottle, Stopper, French Dressing 10.00
Victorian, Cruet, Stopper 10.00
Wabash, Candy Box, Cover, Flamingo 110.00
Wabash, Wine, Frontenec Etch, 2 1/2 Oz. 5.00
Warwick, Candlestick, 2-Light, Pair 260.00
Warwick, Candlestick, Cobalt Blue ....75.00 to 100.00
Warwick, Vase, 5 In. 10.00
Waverly, Epergnette 5.00
Waverly, Relish, 2 Sections 5.00
Waverly, Salt & Pepper, Flower Cutting 15.00
Waverly, Sugar & Creamer, Pair 10.00
Windsor, Candlestick, 9 1/2 In., Pair 60.00
Wine, Puritan, 2 1/2 Oz. 25.00
Winged Scroll, Spooner, Emerald 40.00
Winged Scroll, Spooner, Ivorina Verde ....15.00 to 30.00
Winged Scroll, Tray, Oblong, Emerald, 10 In. 250.00
Winged Scroll, Trinket Box, Emerald 45.00
Yeoman, Cruet, Stopper, 2 Oz. 20.00
Yeoman, Cruet, Stopper, Sahara, 2 Oz. 60.00

HEREND, see Fischer category.

HEUBACH is the collector's name for Gebruder Heubach, a firm
working in Lichten, Germany, from 1840 to 1925. It is best known for
bisque dolls and doll heads, their principal products. They also manufactured bisque figurines, including piano babies, beginning in the
1880s, and glazed figurines in the 1900s. Piano Babies are listed in their
own category. Dolls are included in the Doll category under *Gebruder
Heubach* and *Heubach*. Another factory, Ernst Heubach, working in
Koppelsdorf, Germany, also made porcelain and dolls. These will also
be found in the Doll category under Heubach Koppelsdorf.

Figurine, Baseball Batter, Red Stripes, Wooden Bat, 1880s, 9 3/4 In. 1200.00
Figurine, Baseball Pitcher, Blue Striped Shirt & Hat, 1880s, 14 In. 2195.00
Figurine, Bicycle, Bisque, Separate Bikes, 14 In. 2700.00
Figurine, Boy In Bunny Costume, White, Mask On Head, Easter Egg, 1910, 9 In. 2910.00
Figurine, Dog, Pointer, Ready To Play Position, 9 In. 165.00
Figurine, Dutch Boy & Girl, Bisque, High Gloss Glaze, 7 In. 40.00
Figurine, Dutch Girl, Red Skirt, Green Top, White Hat, 7 In. 140.00
Figurine, Lady & Cherubs, 8 1/2 x 9 In. 15.00
Figurine, Young Man, Woman, Holding Metal Bicycles, Bisque, Painted, 14 In., Pair 1175.00

HISTORIC BLUE, see factory names, such as Adams, Clews, Ridgway, and
Staffordshire.

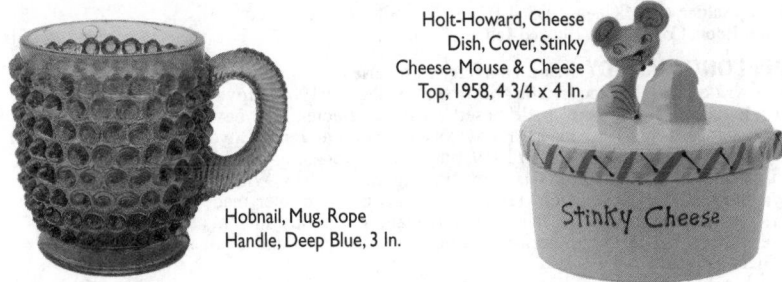

Hobnail, Mug, Rope
Handle, Deep Blue, 3 In.

Holt-Howard, Cheese
Dish, Cover, Stinky
Cheese, Mouse & Cheese
Top, 1958, 4 3/4 x 4 In.

HOBNAIL glass is a style of glass with bumps all over. Dozens of hobnail patterns and variants have been made. Clear, colored, and opalescent hobnail have been made and are being reproduced. Other pieces of hobnail may also be listed in the Duncan & Miller, Fenton, and Francisware categories.

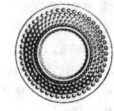

Bowl, Blue, Square, Ruffled Edge, 9 In.		30.00
Mug, Rope Handle, Deep Blue, 3 In.	*Illus*	20.00

HOLLY AMBER, or golden agate, glass was made by the Indiana Tumbler and Goblet Company of Greentown, Indiana, from January 1, 1903, to June 13, 1903. It is a pressed glass pattern featuring holly leaves in the amber-shaded glass. The glass was made with shadings that range from creamy opalescent to brown-amber.

Butter, Cover, 6 x 7 1/2 In.	1495.00
Creamer, 4 In.	835.00
Dish, Pickle, 9 In.	450.00
Pitcher, Straight Sides, 9 1/8 In.	3750.00
Tumbler, 4 In., Pair	835.00 to 1325.00

HOLT-HOWARD was an importer who started working in 1949 in Stamford, Connecticut. The company sold many types of table accessories, such as condiment jars, decanters, spoon holders, and saltshakers. The figures shown on some of his pieces had a cartoon-like quality. The company was bought out by General Housewares Corporation in 1969. Holt-Howard pieces are often marked with the name and the year or *HH* and the year stamped in black. The HH mark was used until 1974. There was also a black and silver label. Production of Holt-Howard ceased in 1990. Similar pieces by the same Holt-Howard designer are being made today and are marked GHA.

Beverage Set, Winking Santa, Pitcher, Mugs, 1960, 7 Piece		25.00
Candle Ring, Blue Bird, 1958, Pair		10.00
Candleholder, 2-Light, Bride & Groom, 1958, 4 1/4 x 4 In.		20.00
Candleholder Set, Noel Angels, One Red Letter On Each, 1958		185.00
Candy Jar, Cover, Cozy Kitten Popup, Kitty Pops Up When Opened, 1961, 6 1/2 In.		200.00
Cheese Dish, Cover, Stinky Cheese, Mouse & Cheese Top, 1958, 4 3/4 x 4 In.	*Illus*	65.00
Chili Sauce Jar, Pixie Ware, Red Stripes & Cheeks, Black Hair, 1959		380.00
Cookie Jar, Cozy Kitten, 2 Kittens Cuddling, 10 1/2 In.		90.00
Cruet, Pixie Ware, Russian Dressing, Beard, Cossack Hat, 1959, 6 1/2 In.		110.00
Decanter, Party Gremlin, 300 Proof, Blue Base & Hair, Red Nose, 1958		955.00
Dish, Cottage Cheese, Cover, Cozy Kitten, Plaid Border, 1958, 4 3/4 In.		65.00
Eggcup, Coq Rouge, Rooster, 4 Piece		20.00
Figurine Set, Pink Spaghetti Poodles, Mama & Babies, Gold Chain, 3 Piece		25.00
Hot Stuff, Jar, Cover, Orange Stripes, Square, Handle, 1960, 2 1/2 In.		510.00
Instant Coffee Jar, Pixie Ware, Blue Stripes, Blond, 1958		175.00
Ketchup Jar, Pixie Ware, Tomato Face, Green Hair, 1958		80.00
Napkin Holder, Christmas Tree, Painted Bell, 1961, 5 In.		25.00
Salt & Pepper, Coq Rouge, Figural Rooster		19.00
Salt & Pepper, Santa, 1960, 4 3/4 In.		80.00

String Holder, Cozy Kitten, 1958, 4 1/2 In. 25.00
Towel Hook, Cozy Kitten, Hooked Tail, 6 1/2 In. 75.00

HOPALONG CASSIDY was a character in a series of twenty-eight books written by Clarence E. Milford, first published in 1907. Movies and television shows were made based on the character. The best-known actor playing Hopalong Cassidy was William Lawrence Boyd. His first movie appearance was in 1919, but the first Hopalong Cassidy film was not until 1934. Sixty-six films were made. In 1948, William Boyd purchased the television rights to the movies, then later made fifty-two new programs. In the 1950s, Hopalong Cassidy and his horse, named *Topper*, were seen in comics, records, toys, and other products. Boyd died in 1972.

Badge, Suspender, Silver Luster, 6-Point Star, Photograph, c.1950, 1 In. 50.00
Bank, Removable Hat, Bronze Color, First National, Meadville, Pa., 4 1/2 In. 54.00
Bank, Save Along With Hopalong, Hoppy's Savings Club, Plastic, Box, 4 x 3 In. 304.00
Bedspread, Hopalong Cassidy, Bar 20, Chenille, 102 x 84 In. 125.00
Belt, Switch A Buckle, Leather, Frontier Trophy Buckle, Card, Yale, 1950s, 25 In. 208.00
Book, Hopalong & Lucky At Double X Ranch, Pop-Up, 1950, 11 In., 12 Pages 46.00
Book, Hopalong Cassidy & Stampede, No. 511-5, Samuel Lowe Co., c.1950 . . . .   12.00
Book, Jump-Up, 5 Pop-Up Pictures, England, 1950s, 10 1/2 x 8 1/2 In., 16 Pages 570.00
Box, Chocolate Coconut Candy, 5 Cents, 1950, 3 x 9 x 5 1/4 In. 380.00
Box, Official Hopalong Cassidy Holster Set, Box Only, 12 x 7 1/2 In. 365.00
Bunkhouse Clothes Corral, Wood, Garden Farm Milk, 24 x 4 3/4 In. 110.00
Button, Green, Black, Red, White, Blue, Ribbon, Boot, 1950s, 1 x 1 In. 26.00
Button, Hoppy's Favorite, Hawthorne-Mellody, Silver Luster, 1950, 1 3/8 In. 45.00
Button, Jensen Foods, Lithograph, Black On Yellow Ground, c.1950, 1 1/8 In. 75.00
Button, Lithograph, Black Image, Yellow Ground, c.1950, 1 1/8 In. 40.00
Button, Member Knockout Hopalong Cassidy Club, c.1950, 1 1/4 In. 150.00
Button, Puritan Dairy, Lithograph, Black On Yellow Ground, c.1950, 1 1/8 In. 56.00
Camera & Flash Reflector, Plastic, Aluminum, Galter, Box, 1940, 5 3/4-In. Box 200.00
Can, Grape Juice, Betsy Ross, Unopened, 3 3/4 In. 125.00
Can, Potato Chips, 2 Hoppy Images, Wm. Boyd, 1950, 11 x 7 1/2 In. 200.00
Cap Gun, Buck'n Bronc, Black Grips, Busts, Nickel Finish, G. Schmidt, 10 In. 260.00
Cap Gun, Engraved, Black Grips, Hoppy Bust, George Schmidt, 9 In., Pair 445.00
Cap Gun, Piston, Single Shot, Rope Script, White Grips 90.00
Card, Birthday, Hoppy On Topper, Mechanical, Buzza Cardozo, 6 1/4 x 5 1/4 In. 50.00
Chair, Official Bar 20 TV, Wood, Folding, 1950s, Child's, 22 x 15 In. 320.00
Charm, Glossy Photograph, 1950, 1 In. 17.00
Clock, Alarm, Hoppy, Topper, Black Metal, U.S. Time, 5 1/2 In. 395.00
Clock, Royal Crest Dairy Products, Double Bubble 1980.00
Cookie Jar, Cookie Corral, Bar 20 Brand, Ceramic, 1950s, 6 x 8 In. 500.00
Cowboy Outfit, Gun, Holster, Chaps, Shirt, Box, 11 x 14 In. 385.00
Cuffs, Silver Beads, Tumbleweed Togs, Viral Mfg., Los Angeles, Box, Pair 300.00
Cup & Saucer, Bowl, Marked, W.S. George, c.1950 . . . .   175.00
Decal, Dairylea, Hoppy's Brand, Reflective, Square, Early 1950s, 2 1/4 In. 75.00
Dish Set, Chuck Wagon, W.S. George, Box, 1950s, 9 1/2 x 10 1/2 In., 3 Piece 340.00
Doll, Gold Gun, Die Cast, Badge, Holster Set, 1950s, 22 1/2 In. 546.00
Doll, Plastic, Leather Outfit, Felt Chaps, Hat, Rattle, 1950s, 7 In.   28.00
Dominoes, Instructions, Milton Bradley, Box, 1950 . . . .   90.00
Figurine, White Horse, Black & Silver Saddle, Guns, Hat, Hartland, 13 In. 232.00
Film Viewer, Television Shape, Plastic, Green, Key Chain, c.1950, 1 1/4 In. 50.00
Fishing Pole, Nylon Rod, Hoppy Decal On Handle, 5 In. 480.00
Game, Board, Insert, Milton Bradley, Box, 1950 . . . .   44.00
Game, Hopalong Cassidy Canasta, Pacific Playing Card Co., Box, c.1950 . . . . .110.00 to 115.00
Game, Lasso, Transogram, Box, 1950, 2 x 12 1/4 x 19 1/4 In. 175.00
Game, Official Pony Express Toss, Transogram, Box, 1950, 12 x 18 1/2 In. 165.00
Guitar, Bar 20 Ranch, Hopalong, Topper, Wood, Cardboard Laminate, 28 In. 60.00
Guitar, Hopalong & Topper, Gut Strings, Wood, Painted, 28 In. 59.00
Gun, Zoomerang, Tigrett Enterprises, Box, 1950, 9 In. 150.00
Gym Set, Official, Dyer Products, Box, 9 1/2 x 12 1/4 In., 5 Piece 1445.00
Holster Set, Cap Gun, Pearl Grips, Box, 7 x 12 In. 825.00
Label, Butter-Nut Bread 25.00

Label, Langendorf Enriched Bread 50.00
Lamp, Motion, 2 Scenes, Red, Rotovue Lamp Jr., Econolite, Box, c.1949, 9 x 6 In. 653.00
Lamp, Motion, 2 Scenes, Yellow, Rotovue Lamp Jr., Econolite, c.1949, 9 x 6 In. ...489.00 to 550.00
Lobby Card, Leather Burners, No. 43, 1943, 11 x 14 In. 40.00
Lunch Box, Hoppy On Horse, Metal, Aladdin, 1954 .... 255.00
Lunch Box, Hoppy Sticker, Chuck Wagon Sticker, Aladdin, c.1952 ....138.00 to 275.00
Lunch Box, Metal, Aladdin, c.1954 .... 295.00
Lunch Box Thermos, Yellow, Red Top, Rubber Stopper, Aladdin, 6 1/2 In. 55.00
Marionette, Rubber Head, Stringless, Stand, 15 In. 200.00
Night-Light, Bullet Shape, Hoppy Decal, Aladdin 515.00
Pajamas, Hopalong On Front Pocket, Blue, Red, Flannel, Kaufmanns Price Tag 85.00
Pen, Ballpoint, Official, Parker, Box, 6 In. 100.00
Picture Gun & Theater, Stevens Products, Box, 1950, 8 x 12 1/2-In. Box ....175.00 to 449.00
Pillow, Fringe, 9 x 14 In. 39.00
Pin, Bar 20 Ranch, Secret Gun, On Card, c.1950, 3 1/4 x 3 In. 50.00
Poster, Movie, Texas Trail, Paper Lithograph, 41 x 27 In. 150.00
Radio, Electric, Red, Steel, Plastic Trim, Model 441T, Arvin, 1950, 5 x 8 In. ....340.00 to 395.00
Record, My Horse Topper, Picture Sleeve, 78 RPM 28.00
Record Reader, Hopalong Cassidy & Singing Bandit, Capitol ....28.00 to 35.00
Record Reader, Square Dance Holdup, Capitol, 1950, 36 Pages, 2 Records 50.00
Rocking Chair, Black & White Vinyl, Chrome Frame, 22 In. 89.00
Saddle, Pony, Leather, 1950 .... 800.00
School Bag, Leather, Black, White, Briefcase Style, Western Buckles, 10 x 14 In. 100.00
Scrapbook, Embossed Picture, 10 x 13 1/2 In. 45.00
Sign, Hopalong In Sunday News, Gun Shape, Cardboard, 2-Sided, 4 x 9 In. 87.00
Soap, Pure Castile, Daggett & Ramsdell, Box, 1950s, 4 1/2 x 6 1/2 In. 139.00
Sparkler, Plastic, Metal Plunger, 1950s, 2 3/4 In. 120.00
Spurs, Leather Straps, Gold Color Rowels, George Schmidt, Box 175.00
Statue, Chalk, Painted, c.1950, 16 In. 96.00
Tie Rack, Composition, Glick, 3 1/2 x 11 1/2 In. 125.00
Tie Slide, Bar 20 Ranch, Metal, On Card, William Boyd, c.1950, 3 3/4 x 3 In. 50.00
Toothpick, Milk Glass, Embossed Face 22.00
Toy, Hopalong & Topper, Ideal, Box, 4 3/4 x 5 1/2 In. 330.00
Toy, Range Rider, Tin, Windup, Marx, 1940s 375.00
Toy, Shaving Kit, Razor, Shaving Brush, Soap, Box, Merry Mfg. Co., 1950 .... 220.00
Tumbler, Western Series, Indian Tribes, 1950s, 4 3/4 x 2 1/2 In. 60.00
Tumbler, Western Series, Western Wagons, 1950s, 4 3/4 x 2 1/2 In. 60.00
Utensils, Knife, Fork, Spoon, Stainless Steel, Engraved, 3 Piece ....33.00 to 55.00
Wallpaper, Roll, 12 Images, c.1950, 18 Ft. x 19 In. 135.00
Watch, Pocket, Chrome Case, U.S. Time, c.1948, 2 In. 800.00
Watch, Pocket, U.S. Time, c.1948, Box, 2 In. 670.00
Wood Burning Set, American Toy & Furniture Co., Chicago, 2 x 13 x 17 In. 55.00
Wristwatch, Black Plastic Case, Decorated Band, U.S. Time, Box, 1955 ....525.00 to 595.00

HORN was used to make many types of boxes, furniture inlays, jewelry, and whimsies.

Cup, Libation, Rhinoceros, High Relief, Figures, Pavilions, Mountain Landscape, 6 In. ... 7975.00
Figure, Carved, Peacock Resting, Rock Formation, Wood Base, Early 1900s, 12 In. 175.00

HOWARD PIERCE began working in Southern California in 1936. In 1945, he opened a pottery in Claremont. He moved to Joshua Tree in 1968 and continued making pottery until 1991. His contemporary-looking figurines are popular with collectors. Though most pieces are marked with his name, smaller items from his sets often were not marked.

Howard Pierce

Figurine, Cat, Cream Shaded To Brown, 10 1/4 In. ....*Illus* 95.00
Figurine, Goose, Yellow, Brown Beak & Base, No. 250P, 8 1/2 In. ....*Illus* 50.00

HOWDY DOODY and Buffalo Bob were the main characters in a children's series televised from 1947 to 1960. Howdy was a redheaded puppet. The series became popular with college students in the late 1970s when Buffalo Bob began to lecture on campuses.

Bank, Bob Smith, Embossed, Pottery, Glazed, Early 1950s, 7 x 3 x 5 In. 250.00

Howard Pierce, Figurine, Cat, Cream Shaded To Brown, 10 1/4 In.

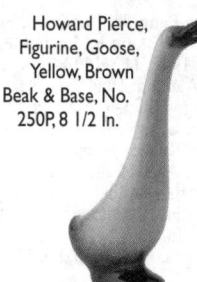

Howard Pierce, Figurine, Goose, Yellow, Brown Beak & Base, No. 250P, 8 1/2 In.

Put a piece of chalk in your silver drawer or chest to absorb moisture.

Bank, Shawnee Pottery, 7 In.	675.00
Bottle, Welch's Grape Juice, Paper Label, 1946, 9 1/4 In.	74.00
Button, Howdy Doody For President, Celluloid, Round, 1952, 1 3/4 In.	219.00
Button, It's Howdy Doody Time, Celluloid, 1 3/4 In.	15.00
Button, Sunday's News, New Color Comic, Red Border, Lithograph, 1 7/8 In.	175.00
Button, Yellow Star, Blue Ground, Cardboard, Early 1950s, 2 In.	202.00
Clock, Alarm, Janex, Box, 1974, 6 3/4 x 7 In.	86.00
Decorated Tumbler, Welch's Grape Juice, 4 Characters, 1953, 4 In.	20.00
Decorated Tumbler, Welch's Jelly, Howdy Doody Shoots Apple Off Clarabell's Head	85.00
Doll, Howdy Doody, Plastic, Jointed Arms, 1950s, 7 1/2 In.	75.00
Doll, Stuffed, Plastic Head, 12 In.	16.50
Dominoes, Ed-U-Cards, Kagran Corp., Box, 1950s, 10 3/4 x 16 In.	75.00 to 199.00
Figurine, Buffalo Bob, Danbury Mint, 21 In.	44.00
Figurine, Howdy Doody, Danbury Mint, 16 In.	33.00
Game, Doodyville, Premium, Welch's Grape Juice, 1953, 11 x 8 1/2 In.	200.00
Handkerchief, 1954, 9 In.	22.00 to 30.00
Light, Howdy Doody & Santa, Plastic, Royal Electric, Box, 14 x 10 In.	110.00
Lunch Box, Pals, Plastic, King Sealey Thermos Co., 1977, 8 1/2 In.	50.00
Marionette, Clarabell	99.00
Marionette, Composition Head, Peter Puppet Playthings, Box, 1950s, 16 In.	220.00 to 277.00
Marionette, Composition, Blue Painted Eyes, Molded Red Hair, Lid, 17 In.	176.00
Marionette, Dilly-Dally, Kagran, Peter Puppet Playthings, Box, 1950s, 14 1/2 In.	670.00
Marionette, Flub-A-Dub, Kagran, Peter Puppet Playthings, Box, 1950s, 14 1/2 In.	670.00
Mug, Ovaltine, Plastic, c.1950, 4 In.	25.00
Mug, Shake-Up, Plastic, Ovaltine, Box, c.1950, 4 3/4 In.	365.00
Night-Light, Howdy Doody On Pig, Ceramic, 9 In.	60.00
Painting Kit, Plaster Figures, Paints, Instruction, Card, Hadley	250.00
Pencil Holder, Howdy Doody Head, 6 1/2 In.	30.00
Puppet, Clarabell, Mitten, Blue, Original Package, 1950	50.00
Puppet, Composition Head, Hands, Feet, Cloth Covered, 16 In.	143.00
Puzzle, Dexterity, Poll Parrot Says Vote For Howdy, Cardboard, 1952, 2 x 2 In.	50.00
Puzzle Set, Milton Bradley, Box, 1950s, 3 Piece	60.00
Record Player, Shura-Tone, Kagran, 1950s, 7 x 10 3/4 x 12 In.	154.00
Sand Forms, Plastic, Ideal, On Card, 5 x 8 1/4-In. Shovel	83.00
Sign, Howdy Doody, NBC-TV Saturday, Cardboard, Die Cut, 1950s, 20 x 13 In.	2015.00
Spurs, Badge, Shrinkwrap Package	49.00
Swim Ring, Vinyl, Ideal, 1955, 20 In.	11.00 to 40.00
Tie, Brown, Child's	11.00
Tool Box, Official Ranchhouse, Liberty Steel Chest, Kagran, 1950s, 6 x 14 x 3 In.	205.00
Towel, It's Howdy Doody Time, Characters, Cannon, 1950s, 37 x 20 In.	50.00
Toy, Band, Bob Smith Plays Piano, Tin, Unique Art, Box, 1950s, 8 1/2 In.	715.00 to 825.00
Toy, Band, Clarabell, Plays Piano, Howdy, Dances, Tin, Linemar, 1950s, 5 3/4 In.	1653.00
Toy, Howdy Doody, Cowboy Costume, Squeaks, Vinyl, 1950s, 13 x 4 In.	100.00
Toy, Pump Mobile, Tin Lithograph, Painted, Windup, Nylint, 8 1/2 In.	280.00
Toy, Time Teacher, Unopened, Schwab, 1950s, 18 x 10 In.	28.00
Watch, Vinyl Over Leather Band, Patent Watch Co., c.1950, 1 1/8 In.	219.00
Wristwatch, Chrome, Blue Vinyl Band, Eyes Move, Patent Watch Co., 1954	1610.00

Wristwatch, Chrome, Red Plastic Band, Ideal Watch Co., Box, 1950s . . . . .735.00 to 1425.00

HULL pottery was made in Crooksville, Ohio, from 1905. Addis E. Hull bought the Acme Pottery Company and started making ceramic wares. In 1917, A. E. Hull Pottery began making art pottery as well as the commercial wares. For a short time, 1921 to 1929, the firm also sold pottery imported from Europe. The dinnerwares of the 1940s, including the Little Red Riding Hood line, the high gloss artwares of the 1950s, and the matte wares of the 1940s, are all popular with collectors. The firm officially closed in March 1986.

Hull U.S.A.

Blossom Flite, Basket, 6 In.	35.00
Blue Belle, Washbowl, Pitcher, 12 In. & 8 1/2 In., 2 Piece	100.00
Bow Knot, Basket, 12 In.	1000.00
Bow Knot, Basket, Pink, Blue, 6 1/2 x 5 1/2 In.	290.00
Bow Knot, Cornucopia, 7 1/2 In., Pair	595.00
Bow Knot, Cup & Saucer Wall Pocket, Blue, 6 1/2 In.	295.00
Bow Knot, Jardiniere, Bow Handles, 9 3/8 In.	300.00
Bow Knot, Plaque, 10 In.	910.00
Bow Knot, Sugar, Cover	180.00
Bow Knot, Vase, 12 1/2 In.	550.00
Bow Knot, Vase, c.1949, 6 1/2 In.	295.00
Bow Knot, Vase, Double Cornucopia, 13 In.	225.00 to 255.00
Bow Knot, Vase, Pink, Blue, 6 3/4 x 5 1/2 In.	250.00
Butterfly, Pitcher, 13 1/2 In.	80.00
Continental, Vase, Persimmon, Yellow Stripes, Tapered, 15 In.	40.00
Cookie Jar, Gingerbread Man, Mirror Brown, 10 1/4 In.	125.00 to 160.00
Cookie Jar, Green Drip Glaze, Embossed Cookies, 7 1/2 In.	70.00
Cookie Jar, Yellowware, Embossed Alpine Scene, 9 1/4 In.	50.00
Floral, Bowl, White, Rust & Green, Scalloped Sides, Leafy Base, 10 x 4 In.	20.00
House & Garden, Bean Pot, Mirror Brown, 2 Qt.	15.00
House & Garden, Casserole, Hen On Nest Cover, Butterscotch, 11 In.	80.00
House & Garden, Casserole, Hen On Nest Cover, Mirror Brown, 11 In.	20.00
House & Garden, Egg Plate, Mirror Brown, 12 Wells, 9 1/2 In.	50.00
House & Garden, Gravy Boat, Underplate, Mirror Brown	15.00
House & Garden, Ice Jug, Mirror Brown, 1960, 2 Qt.	25.00
House & Garden, Mixing Bowl, Mirror Brown, 6 In.	15.00
House & Garden, Pitcher, Mirror Brown, 9 In.	15.00
House & Garden, Platter, Figural, Fish, Mirror Brown, 11 x 8 In., Pair	75.00
House & Garden, Spoon Rest, Mirror Brown, Embossed Words Spoon Rest, 6 3/4 In.	25.00
House & Garden, Stein, Mirror Brown, 16 Oz., 4 Piece	25.00
House & Garden, Tray, Gingerbread Man, Mirror Brown, 10 In.	18.00
Little Red Riding Hood, Canister Set, Flour, Sugar, Coffee, Tea, 4 Piece	60.00
Little Red Riding Hood, Cookie Jar, Closed Basket, 13 In.	155.00 to 550.00
Little Red Riding Hood, Creamer, Poppies & Daises, 5 1/4 In.	135.00
Little Red Riding Hood, Drip Jar, Basketweave, Cover, Applied Flowers, 4 3/4 In.	3300.00
Little Red Riding Hood, Pitcher, 8 In.	350.00
Little Red Riding Hood, Salt & Pepper, 3 In.	175.00
Little Red Riding Hood, Salt & Pepper, Poppies & Daisies, 5 1/4 In.	175.00
Little Red Riding Hood, Sugar, Side Pour, 5 1/8 x 4 3/8 In.	185.00
Little Red Riding Hood, Teapot, Roses	125.00
Little Red Riding Hood, Wall Pocket, 1940-50, 9 1/2 In.	200.00
Magnolia, Teapot, 6 1/2 In.	275.00
Magnolia, Vase, Footed, Flared & Scalloped Rim, Handles, 15 In.	235.00
Magnolia, Vase, Footed, Flared, Handles, Marked, 10 1/2 In.	195.00
Open Rose, Console Set, Doves, Bowl, 2 Candlesticks, 3 Piece	295.00
Open Rose, Creamer, 5 In.	100.00
Orchid, Ewer, 13 In.	265.00
Parchment & Pinecone, Console Set, Bowl, Candleholders, 3 Piece	40.00
Piggy Bank, Corky, Bull's-Eye Back, Green & Pink, 1957, 5 1/2 In.	110.00
Piggy Bank, Corky, Mirror Brown, Nose Ring Stopper, 1957, 5 1/2 In.	80.00
Piggy Bank, Corky, Yellow, Blue Trim, 1957, 5 1/2 In.	115.00
Planter, Bamboo, Oval, 7 1/2 In.	25.00
Planter, Brown Drip Glaze, Oval, Fluted, Footed, 8 In.	40.00

Planter, Goose, Pink, Green, Yellow, 12 1/4 In. 50.00
Planter, Horse, Tan, 1950s, 14 In. 8.00
Planter, Kitten, Pink, 1940s, 5 x 8 In. 15.00
Planter, Kitten, White, Pink Bow, 7 x 7 1/4 In. 46.00
Planter, Lamb, 1940s, 8 1/2 In. 45.00
Planter, Llama & Cart, Green, 9 1/4 x 11 1/2 In. 80.00
Planter, Pig, Blue, Pink Bow, 6 In. 60.00
Planter, Swan, Green, Coronet, No. 213, 1960s, 7 x 10 In. 35.00
Tokay Tuscany, Basket, Branch Handle, 8 In. 35.00
Tokay Tuscany, Basket, Moon, 10 1/2 In. 35.00
Tokay Tuscany, Vase, Cornucopia, Square Foot, 6 1/2 In. 15.00
Tulip, Pitcher, 13 1/2 In. 335.00
Water Lily, Vase, 9 & 12 1/2 In., Pair 115.00
Wheat, Canister, Cover, Sugar, Yellowware, 6 In. 210.00
Wildflower, Teapot, 8 In. 750.00
Woodland, Lazy Susan, Turquoise, Gray Edges, 5 Sections, Holder 70.00
Woodland, Tea Set, 2-Tone, 11 In., 3 Piece 161.00
Woodland, Tea Set, Pot, Sugar, Creamer, 3 Piece 175.00
Woodland, Wall Pocket, 7 1/2 In. 35.00

HUMMEL figurines, based on the drawings of the nun M.I. Hummel
(Berta Hummel), are made by the W. Goebel Porzellanfabrik of Oeslau, Germany, now Rodenthal, Germany. They were first made in
1935. The *Crown* mark was used from 1935 to 1949. The company
added the *bee* marks in 1950. The *full bee* with variations, was used
from 1950 to 1959; *stylized bee*, 1957 to 1972; *three line mark*, 1964 to
1972; *last bee*, sometimes called *vee over gee*, 1972 to 1979. In 1979
the V bee symbol was removed from the mark. *U.S. Zone* was part of
the mark from 1946 to 1948; *W. Germany,* was part of the mark from
1960 to 1990; The *Goebel, W. Germany* mark, called the *missing bee*
mark, was used from 1979 to 1990; *Goebel, Germany* with the crown
and WG, originally called the *new mark,* was used from 1991 through
part of 1999. The newest version of the bee mark with the word
Goebel, the *current mark* or *Goebel with full bee,* was adopted in 2000.
A special *Year 2000* backstamp was also introduced. Porcelain figures
inspired by Berta Hummel's drawings were introduced in 1997. These
are marked BH followed by a number. They are made in the Far East,
not Germany. Other decorative items and plates that feature Hummel
drawings have been made by Schmid Brothers, Inc., since 1971.

Ashtray, No. 62, Happy Pastime, 3 1/2 x 6 1/2 In. 35.00
Ashtray, No. 166, Boy With Bird, 3 1/4 x 6 1/4 In. 35.00
Figurine, No. 1, Puppy Love, Vee Over Gee .... .225.00 to 330.00
Figurine, No. 10/1, Flower Madonna, Vee Over Gee 148.00
Figurine, No. 11/0, Merry Wanderer, Double Mark 110.00
Figurine, No. 12/2/0, Chimney Sweep, Missing Bee .... 90.00 to 130.00
Figurine, No. 13/0, Meditation, Three Line Mark .... *Illus* 175.00
Figurine, No. 16/2/0, Little Hiker, Vee Over Gee 170.00
Figurine, No. 21/0/1/2, Heavenly Angel, Full Bee 440.00
Figurine, No. 32/0, Little Gabriel, Missing Bee 90.00
Figurine, No. 43, March Winds, Full Bee 311.00
Figurine, No. 49/3/0, To Market, Stylized Bee 230.00
Figurine, No. 56, Culprits, Stylized Bee 136.00
Figurine, No. 56/A, Culprits, Full Bee 385.00
Figurine, No. 56/B, Out Of Danger, New Mark 150.00
Figurine, No. 58/0, Playmates, Vee Over Gee 100.00
Figurine, No. 66, Farm Boy, Full Bee 114.00
Figurine, No. 66, Farm Boy, Three Line Mark 325.00
Figurine, No. 67, Doll Mother, Stylized Bee 350.00
Figurine, No. 67, Doll Mother, Vee Over Gee 125.00
Figurine, No. 69, Happy Pastime, Stylized Bee 225.00
Figurine, No. 71/2/0, Stormy Weather, Missing Bee 259.00
Figurine, No. 79, Globe Trotter, New Mark 140.00
Figurine, No. 79, Globe Trotter, Vee Over Gee 220.00

Figurine, No. 80, Little Scholar, Full Bee 460.00
Figurine, No. 81, School Girl, Full Bee 225.00
Figurine, No. 81/0, School Girl, Missing Bee 125.00
Figurine, No. 81/2/0, School Girl, Vee Over Gee 200.00
Figurine, No. 82, School Boy, Crown Mark 500.00
Figurine, No. 82/2/0, School Boy, New Mark 110.00
Figurine, No. 85/0, Serenade, Missing Bee 150.00
Figurine, No. 86, Happiness, Stylized Bee 210.00
Figurine, No. 89/1, Little Cellist, Three Line Mark 100.00
Figurine, No. 94/1, Surprise, Full Bee 136.00
Figurine, No. 94/3/0, Surprise, Full Bee 275.00
Figurine, No. 95, Brother, Stylized Bee 320.00
Figurine, No. 98, Sister, Full Bee 125.00
Figurine, No. 98, Sister, Stylized Bee 350.00
Figurine, No. 110/1, Lets Sing, Stylized Bee 280.00
Figurine, No. 111/1, Wayside Harmony, New Mark 225.00
Figurine, No. 112/1, Just Resting, Full Bee 425.00
Figurine, No. 112/3/0, Just Resting, Stylized Bee 225.00
Figurine, No. 117, Advent Candlestick Boy With Horse 40.00
Figurine, No. 118, Little Thrifty, Full Bee 450.00
Figurine, No. 119, Postman, Stylized Bee 125.00
Figurine, No. 123, Max & Moritz, Missing Bee 120.00
Figurine, No. 127, Doctor, New Mark 100.00
Figurine, No. 129, Band Leader, Full Bee .... 100.00 to 320.00
Figurine, No. 131, Street Singer, New Mark 100.00
Figurine, No. 132, Star Gazer, Stylized Bee 350.00
Figurine, No. 135, Soloist, Stylized Bee .... 100.00 to 180.00
Figurine, No. 141/3/0, Apple Tree Girl, Vee Over Gee .... *Illus* 200.00
Figurine, No. 150/2/0, Happy Days, Stylized Bee 120.00
Figurine, No. 152/3/2/0, Umbrella Girl, New Mark .... *Illus* 375.00
Figurine, No. 152/A/2/0, Umbrella Boy, New Mark 345.00
Figurine, No. 174, She Loves Me, She Loves Me Not, Three Line Mark 80.00
Figurine, No. 175, Mother's Darling, Full Bee 440.00
Figurine, No. 179, Coquettes, Vee Over Gee 114.00
Figurine, No. 182, Good Friends, Full Bee 360.00
Figurine, No. 184, Latest News, Stylized Bee 420.00
Figurine, No. 194, Watchful Angel, Stylized Bee 490.00
Figurine, No. 195, Barnyard Hero, Stylized Bee 114.00
Figurine, No. 195/1, Barnyard Hero, New Mark 100.00
Figurine, No. 199/0, Feeding Time, New Mark 100.00
Figurine, No. 199/1, Feeding Time, Vee Over Gee 320.00
Figurine, No. 200/0, Little Goat Herder, Full Bee 136.00
Figurine, No. 204, Weary Wanderer, Stylized Bee 310.00
Figurine, No. 217, Boy With Toothache, Three Line Mark .... *Illus* 320.00
Figurine, No. 218/2/0, Birthday Serenade, Stylized Bee 400.00

Hummel, Figurine, No. 13/0,
Meditation, Three Line Mark

Hummel, Figurine, No. 141/3/0,
Apple Tree Girl, Vee Over Gee

Hummel, Figurine, No. 152/3/2/0,
Umbrella Girl, New Mark

To test whether or not a bracelet is real Bakelite, hold it under hot water. It should smell like varnish, formaldehyde, or carbolic acid.

Hummel, Figurine, No. 217, Boy With Toothache, Three Line Mark

Hutschenreuther, Figurine, Cherub, Standing, Playing Flute, No. 2405, Marked, 4 3/4 In.

Figurine, No. 224/1, Wayside Harmony, Stylized Bee	227.00
Figurine, No. 257/0, For Mother, New Mark	70.00
Figurine, No. 300, Bird Watcher, Vee Over Gee	130.00
Figurine, No. 306, Little Bookkeeper, Vee Over Gee	125.00
Figurine, No. 317, Not For You, Stylized Bee	600.00
Figurine, No. 317, Not For You, Three Line Mark	295.00
Figurine, No. 332, Soldier Boy, Three Line Mark	225.00
Figurine, No. 333, Blessed Event, Missing Bee	170.00
Figurine, No. 333, Blessed Event, Three Line Mark	295.00
Figurine, No. 336, Close Harmony, Three Line Mark	500.00
Figurine, No. 337, Cinderella, Stylized Bee	1150.00
Figurine, No. 337, Cinderella, Vee Over Gee	125.00
Figurine, No. 340, Letter To Santa Claus, New Mark	144.00
Figurine, No. 345, A Fair Measure, Stylized Bee	780.00
Figurine, No. 347, Adventure Bound	920.00
Figurine, No. 373, Just Fishing, Missing Bee	114.00
Figurine, No. 381, Flower Vendor, New Mark	130.00
Figurine, No. 406, Pleasant Journey, Missing Bee	650.00
Figurine, No. 422, What's New?, Missing Bee	175.00
Figurine, No. 429, Hello World, New Mark	150.00
Figurine, No. 440, Candleholder, Birthday Candle, Missing Bee	175.00
Figurine, No. 441, Clock, Call To Worship, Missing Bee	489.00
Figurine, No. 442, Clock, Chapel Time, Missing Bee	635.00
Figurine, No. 447, Morning Concert, Missing Bee	100.00
Figurine, No. 449, Little Pair, New Mark	140.00
Figurine, No. 471, Harmony In Four Parts, Missing Bee	690.00
Figurine, No. 485, Gift From A Friend, New Mark	90.00
Figurine, No. 487, Let's Tell The World, Missing Bee	633.00
Figurine, No. 493, Two Hands, One Treat, New Mark	50.00
Figurine, No. 530, Land In Sight, New Mark	748.00
Figurine, No. 600, We Wish You The Best, New Mark	635.00
Figurine, No. 635, Welcome Spring, New Mark	460.00
Figurine, No. 662/1, Friends Together, New Mark	420.00
Figurine, No. 751, Loves Bounty, New Mark	633.00
Figurine, No. 837, Bumblebee Friend, Millennium Bee	195.00
Plaque, No. 187/A, Authorized Dealer, New Mark	80.00
Plaque, No. 310, Searching Angel, Missing Bee	150.00
Plaque, No. 323, Merry Christmas, Missing Bee	150.00
Plaque, No. 690, Smiling Through, Vee Over Gee	40.00
Plate, Annual, 1971, Heavenly Angel	150.00 to 600.00
Plate, Annual, 1972, Hear Ye, Hear Ye	125.00
Plate, Annual, 1973, Globe Trotter	125.00
Plate, Annual, 1976, Apple Tree Girl	85.00
Plate, Annual, 1980, School Girl	70.00

Plate, Annual, 1981, Umbrella Boy	40.00
Plate, Annual, 1982, Umbrella Girl	115.00
Plate, Christmas, 1972, Angel Blowing Horn, Schmid Brothers	20.00
Plate, Christmas, 1975, Christmas Child	10.00 to 25.00
Plate, Christmas, 1976, Sacred Journey, Schmid Brothers	22.00 to 30.00
Plate, Christmas, 1980, Parade Into Toyland, Schmid Brothers, 7 1/2 In., Box	41.00 to 44.00
Plate, Christmas, 1981, Angelic Procession, Schmid Brothers, 4 In.	25.00
Plate, Christmas, 1982, Angelic Procession, Schmid Brothers, 7 1/2 In.	65.00
Plate, Mother's Day, 1972, Boy With Toys	65.00
Plate, Mother's Day, 1973, Little Fisherman, 7 3/4 In.	30.00 to 35.00
Plate, Mother's Day, 1982, Flower Basket, Schmid Brothers, Box, 7 3/4 In.	35.00
Plate, Mother's Day, 1986, Home From School, Schmid Brothers	56.00 to 65.00

HUTSCHENREUTHER Porcelain Company of Selb, Germany, was established in 1814 and is still working. The company makes fine quality porcelain dinnerwares and figurines. The mark has changed through the years, but the name and the lion insignia appear in most versions.

Dinner Set, Bavarian, Ivory, Gilt Scroll Banding, 20th Century, 63 Piece	265.00
Figurine, Cherub, Standing, Playing Flute, No. 2405, Marked, 4 3/4 In. .... *Illus*	75.00
Figurine, Dancer, Biscuit Glaze, Germany, 11 In.	410.00
Plaque, Cinderella, Girl Beside Fire Feeding Birds, L.R. Wagner, 6 x 4 In.	2000.00
Plate, Christmas, 1978, Mother & Child, Ole Winther, 12 1/4 In.	225.00
Plate Set, Instrumenti Musicali, Fornasetti, 1960s, 10 1/2 In., 3 Piece	140.00
Plate Set, Service, Intaglio Gilt Rim, Green Inner Rim, 11 In., 12 Piece	540.00

ICONS, special, revered pictures of Jesus, Mary, or a saint, are usually Russian or Byzantine. The small icons collected today are made of wood and tin or precious metals. Many modern copies have been made in the old style and are being sold to tourists in Russia and Europe and at shops in the United States. Rare, old icons have sold for over $50,000.

All-Seeing Eye Of God, Russia, 19th Century, 10 1/2 x 12 1/4 In.	173.00
Apostle, Greece, 18th Century, 11 x 14 In.	403.00
Archangel Michael, Holding Sword & Shield, Clouds, Russia, 11 x 8 1/2 In.	230.00
Archangel Michael, Prophet Elijah, Baptism Dedication, 18th Century, 11 x 9 In.	776.00
Archangel Michael, Russia, 18th Century, 14 x 12 In.	1380.00
Baptism Of Christ, Russia, 19th Century, 13 1/2 x 12 In.	518.00
Crucifixion, Bronze, Enamel, Russia, 19th Century, 33 x 23 In.	690.00
Entry Into Jerusalem, Russia, 19th Century, 20 x 15 3/4 In.	460.00
Guardian Angel & Venerable Maria, Russia, 19th Century, 7 3/4 x 8 3/4 In.	288.00
Holy Water Font, Jesus On Cross, Angel, Horn, Glass, Pat. July 22, 1913, 6 In., 2 Piece	80.00
Iverskaya Mother Of God, Gilded Silver Riza Overlay, Moscow, c.1900, 7 x 6 In.	518.00
Kazan Mother Of God, Old Style, Riza, Russian, 19th Century, 10 x 12 In.	288.00
Lord Almighty, Engraved Silver Riza, Gospel Text, Moscow, c.1900, 10 x 9 In.	920.00
Man, Woman, Child, Dove, Metal, Black Wood Frame, 1800s, 13 1/2 x 9 1/2 In.	201.00
Mother Of God, Joy To All Who Suffer, Angels, Russia, 19th Century, 12 x 11 In.	1035.00
Mother Of God, Joy To All Who Suffer, Russia, 19th Century, 7 x 6 In.	259.00
Mother Of God Of Perpetual Help, Triptych, Painted, Greece, 20th Century, 18 x 16 In.	1840.00
Pokrov Mother Of God, Russia, 19th Century, 12 x 10 In.	575.00
Resurrection & Descent Into Hades, Russia, 19th Century, 12 1/4 x 10 1/2 In.	604.00
Resurrection Scene In Center, 12 Feasts Surrounding, 19th Century, 12 x 14 In.	690.00
Retablo, Saint, Cross & Skull, Tempera, Gesso, Wood, New Mexico, 1800s, 12 x 8 In.	4406.00
Scenes From Life Of Christ, Multicolored, Parcel Gilt, Early 20th Century, 8 1/2 x 6 In.	201.00
Smolensk Hodigetria Mother Of God, Russia, 19th Century, 14 1/2 x 12 1/2 In.	259.00
Smolensk Mother Of God, Engraved Silver Riza, Suspension Loop, Russia, c.1874, 3 In.	489.00
St. George, On Horseback, Slaying Dragon, Female Saint, Greek, 18th Century, 5 x 4 In.	295.00
St. John The Theologian, Greece, Early 19th Century, 9 x 7 In.	635.00
St. Nicholas, Engraved Metal Riza, Russia, 19th Century, 12 1/4 x 14 In.	345.00
St. Nicholas, On Throne, Delivers Blessing, Holds Gospels, Greece, c.1700, 16 x 11 In.	1265.00
St. Peter, Moscow School, Bas-Relief Silvered Brass Riza, Late 19th Century, 9 x 7 In.	259.00
St. Peter & St. Paul, 19th Century, 13 x 11 In.	690.00
St. Seraphim, Benediction, Multicolored, Brass Riza, Wooden, Russia, c.1765, 9 x 7 In.	865.00

Tikhvin Mother Of God, Russia, 18th Century, 20 1/2 x 24 In. 575.00
Triptych, Mother Of God, Ivory, Angel Placing Crown, Gothic Frame, 1800s, 17 1/2 In. . . .   2519.00
Virgin & Child, Wooden, Multicolored, Chased Brass Repousse Riza, Mid 1800s, 9 x 7 In. .   405.00
Virgin Mary, Wooden, Articulated, 1800s, 24 In. 1900.00
Vladimir Mother Of God, Triptych, Painted, Greece, 20th Century, 13 x 11 In. 175.00

IMARI porcelain was made in Japan and China beginning in the 17th
century. In the 18th century and later, it was copied by porcelain factories in Germany, France, England, and the United States. It was especially popular in the 19th century and is still being made. Imari is
characteristically decorated with stylized bamboo, floral, and geometric designs in orange, red, green, and blue. The name comes from the
Japanese port of Imari, which exported the ware made nearby in a factory at Arita. *Imari* is now a general term for any pattern of this type.

Bowl, 3 Friends, Flower Center, c.1850, 11 1/2 In., Pair 490.00
Bowl, Bell Shape, Bird, Prunus Tree, Phoenix, Paulownia Flowers, Early 1800s, 7 1/2 In. . .   190.00
Bowl, Bell Shape, Clamshell, Bird, Flower Garden, Landscape, 19th Century, 6 3/4 In. 240.00
Bowl, Bell Shape, Sages, Bamboo Grove, Brocade, Early 1800s, 9 In. 345.00
Bowl, Birds, Rabbits, Blue, White, Paneled Sides, c.1740, 5 3/4 In.   1920.00
Bowl, Chrysanthemum Shape, Crest, Brocade, Late 1800s, 5 In. 130.00
Bowl, Chrysanthemum Shape, Phoenix, Flowers, Early 1800s, 5 In.   130.00
Bowl, Chrysanthemum, Multicolored, Concentric Double Foot, c.1912, 13 1/2 In. 805.00
Bowl, Cover, Phoenix Interior, Bird & Flower Exterior, c.1820, 10 1/2 In. 690.00
Bowl, Cover, Women, Pomegranates, c.1840, 4 1/2 In., Pair 130.00
Bowl, Cylinder Shape, Flared Rim, Landscape, Crane, Mythical Beast, Grass, 1700s, 7 In. .   630.00
Bowl, Dome Lid, Flowers, Multicolored Enamels, Applied Handle, c.1900, 10 In. 460.00
Bowl, Dragon, Landscape, Birds, Flowers, c.1850, 8 1/2 In. 259.00
Bowl, Floral, Urn Of Flowers Center, Scalloped Rim, Footed, Signed, 9 1/2 In. 80.00
Bowl, Flower Shape, Crane, Pine Tree, c.1850, 7 1/2 In. 160.00
Bowl, Flower, Landscape, Early 19th Century, 8 3/4 In. 220.00
Bowl, Geese, Marsh Grass, Flower Gardens, c.1800, 13 1/2 In. 690.00
Bowl, Landscape, Phoenix, Flowers, Early 1800s, 10 3/4 In. 375.00
Bowl, Oval, Leaf Shape Feet, c.1770, 3 x 12 x 10 In. 1095.00
Bowl, Samurai Helmet Shape, Dragon, Lion, Flowers, Stylized Vines, c.1760, 11 In. 690.00
Bowl, Scalloped Rim, Reeded Body, Red, Green, Gold, c.1880, 5 x 12 In. 575.00
Bowl, Scroll Cartouche, Leaves, Banner, c.1830, 9 1/2 In. 840.00
Bowl, Tassels, Flowers, Birds & Flower Lattice Exterior, 19th Century, 6 1/2 In. 290.00
Bowl Set, Dragons, Auspicious Emblems, 19th Century, 6 In., 12 Bowls 380.00
Bowl Set, Pine, Bamboo, Prunus Tree, Bird, Wave, Early 1800s, 6 1/4 In., 4 Bowls 330.00
Box, Passion Flower, Medallions, Karakusa Ground, 2 Parts, Cylindrical, Early 1800s, 3 In.   130.00
Charger, 100 Flowers, Blue Flower Border, 19th Century, 18 In. 660.00
Charger, 100 Flowers, Red & Blue Flower Border, 19th Century, 18 In. 720.00
Charger, Birds, Snails, Butterflies, On Red, White Scrolls, Cobalt Blue Boat Center, 12 In.   115.00
Charger, Blue, Rust, Fan, Bird, Dragon, Flowers, Hanging Cross Strap, 22 In. 978.00
Charger, Central Flower Basket, Foo Dogs, Brocade Balls, 17 3/4 In. 345.00
Charger, Cranes, Tortoises On Border, Scalloped Rim, c.1860, 12 3/4 In. 259.00
Charger, Drunken Sprite, Wine Barrel, Brocade Border, Flower, Vine, 1800s, 24 In., Pair . .   1265.00
Charger, Flower Medallion, Hearts, Foo Dogs, Peacocks, Lotus Blossoms, 16 In. 690.00
Charger, Flowering Plants, Central Medallion, Red, Blue, Gilt, Circles, 1 3/4 x 15 1/2 In. . .   690.00
Charger, Landscape, Boy, Fruit, Flowers, c.1750, 17 3/4 In. 600.00
Charger, Open Books, Figures, Landscapes, Dragons, Flowers, 1700s, 18 In. 2880.00
Cup, Prunus Branches, Bamboo, Peony, c.1860, 3 In., 10 Piece 489.00
Cup & Saucer, England, Early 19th Century, 3 1/4 x 5 1/4 In. 115.00
Dish, Butterfly, Flower, Lozenge Shape, 7 1/4 In., 5 Piece 290.00
Dish, Figures, Bird, Flower, c.1850, 9 1/2 In., 9 Piece 660.00
Dish, Figures, Birds, Flowers, Rectangular, c.1850, 7 1/2 In., 5 Piece 360.00
Dish, Ginko Leaf, Bird, Flower, Book, 7 1/4 In. 400.00
Dish, Landscape, Rectangular, 8 3/4 In. 69.00
Dish, Mount Fuji, Blue, Gold, Early 1800s, 6 1/4 In. 60.00
Dish, Scallop Shell Shape, Lake, Landscape, c.1880, 6 1/2 In., 10 Piece 1150.00
Dish Set, Bird, Flowers, Clamshell Shape, Blue, White, 1690-1730, 3 1/4 In., 6 Piece 575.00
Figurine, Beautiful Woman, Court Costume, 13 1/2 In. 600.00
Figurine, Beautiful Woman, Kimono, Dragons, Late 19th Century, 19 1/4 In. 2040.00

Figurine, Beautiful Woman, Kimono, Morning Glories, 19th Century, 17 In.	1800.00
Figurine, Geisha Wearing Kimono, Cat, 11 1/2 In.	145.00
Jar, Brocade Ground, Inverted Pear Shape, 8 In.	460.00
Jar, Cover, 19th Century, 10 In.	206.00
Jar, Lid, Birds, Flowers, Urn Shape, Fluted, Finial, Blue & Gold Ground, c.1870, 17 In.	920.00
Jar, Mounted As Lamp, Late 19th Century, 12 1/4 x 26 In.	800.00
Jardiniere, Dragon, Samurai, 19th Century, 16 In.	660.00
Plate, Bird, Flower, Fan Shape, c.1750, 6 1/2 In., Pair	460.00
Plate, Bird, Flower, Fan Shape, c.1750, 7 3/4 In., Pair	375.00
Plate, Bird, Flower, Fan Shape, c.1750, 8 1/2 In., Pair	375.00
Plate, Chrysanthemum, Phoenix, Brocade Work, Early 1900s, 9 3/4 In.	127.00
Plate, Figures, Birds, Flowers, c.1850, 8 1/2 In., 8 Piece	450.00
Plate, Flower Basket Center Design, Scalloped Edge, Square, 19th Century, 17 In.	1765.00
Plate, Flowers, Scalloped Border, Cobalt Blue, Red, Vase, Square 13 In.	750.00
Plate, Octagonal, Cartouche Border, Center Figures In Garden Scene, c.1875, 12 1/2 In.	105.00
Plate, Prunus Tree, Cloud, 9 1/2 In.	105.00
Platter, Oval, Multicolored, Pierced, c.1900, 15 3/8 In.	805.00
Sake Cup, Figures, Landscape, Flowers, c.1800, 2 In.	96.00
Sauce, Passion Flower, Figures, Birds, Flowers, c.1850, 4 3/4 In., 9 Piece	270.00
Serving Dish, Grape Vines, Oblong, Scalloped Rim, Blue, Iron Red, 10 & 12 In., 2 Piece	200.00
Temple Jar, Cover, Flower Basket, Inverted Pear Shape, Sunputei, Mark, c.1800, 27 In.	1800.00
Temple Jar, Orange, Cobalt, Foo Dog Finial, 11 1/2 In.	750.00
Umbrella Stand, Birds In Garden, Enameled, Multicolored, 19th Century, 23 1/2 In.	1610.00
Umbrella Stand, Vase, Flowers, Pheasant, 19th Century, 24 x 9 1/2 In.	690.00
Vase, Birds, Trees, Floral Neck, Swirling Base Bands, 4 Round Reserves, 25 In.	690.00
Vase, Chrysanthemum, Teardrop Shape, 11 In.	1955.00
Vase, Egg Shape, Flared Rim, Red Over Blue Design, c.1860, 12 In.	375.00
Vase, Exotic Birds, Leaves, Painted Panels, 20th Century, 17 x 4 In.	129.00
Vase, Flowers, Trees, Gilded Accents, c.1870, 14 1/2 In.	345.00
Vase, Flowers, Trees, Oval, Ribbed, Scalloped, Flared Rim, 1800s, 12 5/8 In., Pair	765.00
Vase, Landscapes, Birds, Flared Neck, Egg Shape Body, c.1850, 30 1/2 In., Pair	1265.00
Vase, Mounted As Fluid Lamp, Electrified, 15 In., Pair	2030.00
Vase, Ribbed Body, Floral Panels, Gilt Detail, 14 1/2 In., Pair	2070.00

IMPERIAL GLASS Corporation was founded in Bellaire, Ohio, in 1901. It became a subsidiary of Lenox, Inc., in 1973 and was sold to Arthur R. Lorch in 1981. It was sold again in 1982, and went bankrupt in 1984. In 1985, the molds and some assets were sold. The Imperial glass preferred by the collector is freehand art glass, carnival glass, slag glass, stretch glass, and other top-quality tablewares. Tablewares and animals are listed here. The others may be found in the appropriate sections.

Animal, Giraffe, Light Blue	60.00
Animal, Mother Rabbit, Ultra Blue, 5 In.	250.00
Animal, Scottie Dog, Black	150.00
Art Glass, Vase, Blue & Orange Iridescent, Loops, Tricornered Rim, Footed, 11 In.	1445.00
Art Glass, Vase, Blue Iridescent, Azure & White Marbleized Swirl, Flared Neck, 10 In.	460.00
Art Glass, Vase, Opal & Yellow, Pulled Loops, Flared Neck, 9 7/8 In.	230.00
Art Glass, Vase, Opal Iridescent, Green Trailing Hearts & Vines, Baluster, 10 In.	1288.00
Art Glass, Vase, Orange Iridescent, Blue Gold Pulled Leaves & Vines, Tapered, 11 3/4 In.	675.00
Art Glass, Vase, Orange Iridescent, Blue Looping, Cylindrical, Flared Rim, 8 1/2 In.	200.00
Art Glass, Vase, Orange, Blue Pulled Design, Bulbous Base, Flared Neck, 9 3/4 In.	335.00
Art Glass, Vase, Sea Gulls Flying, Silhouetted, Midnight Blue Sky, Marked, 19 1/2 In.	430.00
Beaded Block, Celery Dish, Marigold, 8 1/2 In.	85.00
Beaded Block, Dish, Jelly, Blue Opal, Handles, 2 1/8 x 6 1/4 In.	35.00
Beaded Block, Dish, Pickle, Marigold, Handles, Oval, 6 1/2 In.	60.00
Beaded Block, Plate, Amber, Square, 7 3/4 In.	20.00 to 80.00
Beaded Block, Plate, Blue, Square, 7 3/4 In.	20.00
Beaded Block, Plate, Canary, Square, 7 3/4 In.	60.00
Beaded Block, Plate, Green, Square, 7 3/4 In.	50.00
Beaded Block, Plate, Pink, Square, 7 3/4 In.	45.00
Beaded Block, Syrup, 6 1/4 In.	30.00
Beaded Block, Vase, Bud, Cobalt Blue, 5 1/8 In.	25.00 to 45.00

Black lights can detect repairs
to antiques that are invisible
to the eye, but be sure you use
a longwave black light. A short-
wave black light could injure
your eyes or skin.

Imperial, Caramel Slag, Dish, Pie Wagon, Marked

Candlewick, Ashtray, Ruby, 5 In.	16.00
Candlewick, Cake Plate, Birthday, 13 In.	500.00
Candlewick, Cocktail, 4 Oz., 5 In.	17.50
Candlewick, Console, Mallard, Engraving, 13 In.	156.00
Candlewick, Cup & Saucer, Coffee	25.00
Candlewick, Plate, Salad, Floral Engraving, 8 In.	19.00
Candlewick, Plate, Upturned Edge, Handles, 10 In.	24.00
Candlewick, Powder Jar, Star Engraving, 4 3/4 x 4 In.	190.00
Candlewick, Relish, 2 Sections, 6 1/2 In.	25.00
Candlewick, Relish, 2 Sections, Handles, 7 In.	20.00
Candlewick, Relish, 4 Sections, 4 Handles, 8 1/2 In.	32.00
Candlewick, Salt & Pepper	18.00 to 20.00
Candlewick, Sugar & Creamer, Individual	19.00 to 25.00
Cape Cod, Candy Dish, Cover, Footed, 10 In.	75.00
Cape Cod, Jam Jar, Cover	45.00
Cape Cod, Pitcher, Crystal, Footed, Ice Lip, 40 Oz.	100.00
Cape Cod, Plate, 17 In.	50.00
Cape Cod, Relish, 4 Sections, 9 1/2 In.	48.00
Caramel Slag, Dish, Pie Wagon, Marked .... *Illus*	150.00
Cut Glass, Vase, Marigold Iridescent, Blue & Gold Leaves, Tapered, 11 3/4 In.	600.00
Cut Glass, Vase, Marigold Iridescent, Blue Heart, Vine, Bulbous, 10 In.	633.00
Cut Glass, Vase, Orange Iridescent, Blue Draped Loops, Tricornered Rim, 11 In.	1325.00
Cut Glass, Vase, Yellow, Orange Iridescent Interior, Bulbous, No. 1690, 6 1/2 In.	115.00
Green Slag, Owl Jar	55.00
No. 612, Toothpick, Handles, Pink	14.78
Twisted Optic, Bowl, Vegetable, Pink, Handles, 2 1/2 x 9 In.	35.00
Twisted Optic, Candlestick, Amber, 3 In., Pair	50.00
Twisted Optic, Candlestick, Ice Blue, 3 In., Pair	55.00
Twisted Optic, Candy Dish, Cover, Green	38.00
Twisted Optic, Cup, Pink	8.50
Twisted Optic, Dresser Set, Pink, Perfume Bottle, Powder Jar, Tray, 3 Piece	330.00
Twisted Optic, Sandwich Server, Canary Yellow, Center Handle, 4 1/2 x 10 1/8 In.	50.00
Twisted Optic, Sandwich Server, Green, Handles, 10 In.	33.00
Twisted Optic, Sherbet, Amber	7.00
Twisted Optic, Soup, Cream, Pink, Handles, 4 3/4 In.	23.50
Twisted Optic, Vase, Pink, Handles, 8 In.	45.00
Windmill, Pitcher, Marigold	100.00

INDIAN art from North America has attracted the collector for many
years. Each tribe has its own distinctive designs and techniques. Baskets, jewelry, pottery, and leatherwork are of greatest collector interest.
Eskimo art is listed in another category in this book.

Amulet, Tlingit, Carved Ivory, Raven, Human, Alaska, 1900s, 1 1/2 x 6 1/2 In.	127.00
Armband, Cheyenne, Beadwork, Buffalo Hide, Sinew Sewn, Early 1900s, 2 x 8 In., Pair	290.00
Awl Bag, Plains, Beaded, Tufted Cones, c.1880, 14 In.	303.00
Awl Case, Apache, Beaded, Chevron, Sliding Cover, Leather Fringe, 7 In.	575.00
Awl Case, Apache, Buckskin, Beaded Flaps, Yellow Ocher Tip, c.1950, 16 In.	633.00
Awl Case, Apache, Chevron, Scallop, Beaded, Tassels, 9 1/2 In.	1150.00

Awl Case, Crow, Wrapped Beading, White Hearts, Trim, Dangles, Late 1800s, 8 In. 630.00
Awl Case, Sioux, Beaded Allover, Blue, Red, Cream, Fringe, c.1920, 9 In. 520.00
Badge, Territory Police, Metal Circle, 5-Point Star Cutout, Safety Pin Catch, c.1900, 2 In. .   470.00
Bag, Apache, American Flags, Beaded, Fringe, Early 1900s, 6 1/2 In. 190.00
Bag, Apache, Hide, Beaded Star, Fringe, Drawstring, c.1900, 15 x 8 1/2 In. 160.00
Bag, Apache, Peyote, Buckskin, Beaded, Sun Design, c.1950, 6 x 8 In. 460.00
Bag, Arapaho, Dispatch, Beaded, Geometric Design, Southern Cross, c.1890, 18 x 10 In. . .   3450.00
Bag, Athabascan, Moose Foot, Flowers, Leaves, Beadwork, c.1920, 9 x 11 1/2 In. 230.00
Bag, Cheyenne, Pipe Bag, c.1880, 17 3/4 In. 965.00
Bag, Cheyenne, Pipe Bag, Lazy Stitch, Beaded, Horse, Fringe, 1900-50, 18 1/4 x 8 1/4 In. .   3165.00
Bag, Chippewa, Bandolier, Flowers, Beaded Allover, Wide Strap, Early 1900s, 20 x 14 In. .   2300.00
Bag, Cree, Buckskin, Beaded Leaves, Fringe, Drawstring, Early 1900s, 4 x 5 1/2 In. 489.00
Bag, Crow, Teepee, Beaded, Buffalo Hide, Early 19th Century, 8 x 12 In. 2300.00
Bag, Crow, Women's, Tobacco, Beaded, Star, Cross, c.1910, 10 In. 690.00
Bag, Eastern Woodlands, Child's, Bandolier, Flags, Stroud Backing, Beadwork, 7 x 9 In. . .   635.00
Bag, Great Lakes, Bandolier, Loom Beaded, Multicolored, Geometric, Late 1800s, 32 In. . .   3819.00
Bag, Iroquois, 2-Sided, Flap, Beaded Leaves, Cotton Lining, Late 1800s, 6 x 6 In. 115.00
Bag, Nez Perce, Beaded, Horse, Flowers, c.1910, 9 x 11 In. 748.00
Bag, Nez Perce, Cornhusk, Chevron, Arrow, Hand Woven, 1900-50, 13 1/2 x 17 1/2 In. . . .   1495.00
Bag, Nez Perce, Seed, Buckskin, Woven Cornhusk, Strawberries, Early 1900s, 10 x 8 In. . .   1095.00
Bag, Northern Plains, Crow, Trapezoid, Fringe, Beaded Strap, 19th Century, 18 In. 2468.00
Bag, Ojibwa, 2-Sided, Flap, Beaded Flowers, Red Cotton Edge, Late 1800s, 7 x 7 In. 175.00
Bag, Ojibwa, Bandolier, Cloth, Pouch, Shoulder Strap, Bugle Bead Swags, c.1900, 35 In. .   1410.00
Bag, Plains, Beaded, Flowers, Fringe, 1880s, 13 1/2 In. 385.00
Bag, Plains, Tobacco, Beaded, Lazy Stitch, Quilled Panel, Fringe, Late 1800s, 30 x 7 In. . .   2415.00
Bag, Plateau, Beaded, Cloth, Pictorial, Hide Carrying Straps, Early 1900s, 12 x 10 In. 999.00
Bag, Plateau, Buckskin Flag, Beaded Bird, Tepee, Strap, 8 x 11 x 23 In. 290.00
Bag, Plateau, Buckskin, Beaded Allover, Leaves, Trapezoid, Early 1900s, 6 x 5 1/4 In. 175.00
Bag, Plateau, Cornhusk, Multicolored, 18 1/2 In. 705.00
Bag, Plateau, Cornhusk, Multicolored, Embroidered, Geometric, Hide Strap, c.1900, 7 In. .   411.00
Bag, Plateau, Cornhusk, Multicolored, Geometric, Yarn, c.1900, 22 x 15 In. 940.00
Bag, Plateau, Cornhusk, Multicolored, Yarn Band, 22 In. 881.00
Bag, Plateau, Tanned White Buckskin, Mother, Child, Flowers, 15 1/4 x 12 In. 635.00
Bag, Sauk Fox, Bandolier, Geometric, Red Tassels, Late 1800s, 13 x 9 In. 290.00
Bag, Shoshone, Mystery, Buckskin, Sinew Sewn, Lazy Stitch Beaded, c.1885, 3 x 8 In. . . .   138.00
Bag, Sioux, Leather, Blue, Tan, Red, Canvas Back, c.1880, 21 x 11 In. 1980.00
Bag, Sioux, Parfleche, Buckskin, Beaded, Fringe, 12 x 3 1/4 In. 160.00
Bag, Sioux, Sinew Sewn, Lazy Stitch, Beaded, Fringe, Drawstring, Early 1900s, 5 x 6 In. .   115.00
Bag, Winnebago, Bandolier, Cloth, Strap, Beaded Geometric, Hearts, Silk Ribbons, 33 In. .   3055.00
Bag, Yakima, Beadwork, Panel, 14 x 12 In. 210.00
Ball, Cheyenne, Beaded, Bars, Carrying Strap, Late 1800s, 6 1/2 In. 880.00
Basket, Apache, Bowl, Banded Geometric, Reverse Star, c.1940, 14 x 3 In. 575.00
Basket, Apache, Bowl, Martynia, Lighting Bands, 3 x 9 In. 978.00
Basket, Apache, Bowl, Pictorial, Deer, Martynia Band, Stepped Diamonds, 4 x 9 In. 375.00
Basket, Apache, Butterflies, Star, Blossom, c.1970, 16 x 1 In. 546.00
Basket, Apache, Plate, Radiating Geometric, 4-Point Star, 14 In. 978.00
Basket, Athabascan, Tray, Handles, Red, Green, 1900s, 14 1/2 x 1 1/2 In. 189.00
Basket, California Mission, Black & Orange Triangle Bands, Early 1900s, 4 1/2 x 8 In. . . .   375.00
Basket, California Mission, Boat Shape, Geometric, Early 1900s, 2 1/2 x 8 x 5 In. 805.00
Basket, California Mission, Bowl, Pedestal, Central Star, Early 1900s, 2 1/2 x 9 In. 575.00
Basket, California Mission, Bowl, Stepped Band, Martynia, c.1910, 4 x 8 In. 400.00
Basket, California Mission, Bowl, Yellow, Black, Geometric, c.1940, 7 x 4 In. 290.00
Basket, California Mission, Single Rod, Beaded Allover, Geometric, 6 x 8 In. 980.00
Basket, Cherokee, River Cane, Double Woven, Geometric, Walnut, Bloodroot, 4 x 7 In. . . .   518.00
Basket, Cherokee, River Cane, Oak, Hickory Bark Rim, Brown, Orange, 12 x 10 In. 489.00
Basket, Cherokee, River Cane, Square-To-Round, Butternut, Bloodroot, 4 x 9 In. 978.00
Basket, Cherokee, Splint, Square Bottom, High Round Shoulder, Flared Rim, 14 x 13 In. .   500.00
Basket, Cherokee, Twilled, Multicolored, Round, Square Bottom, Mid 1900s, 15 x 14 In. .   529.00
Basket, Chitimacha, Twilled, Squares, Rectangles, Diagonal Ground, Lid, 5 In. 2350.00
Basket, Hopi, Plaque, Second Mesa, Geometric, Hanging Strap, c.1950, 13 In. 375.00
Basket, Hopi, Second Mesa, 5 Kachina Faces, Geometric, c.1950, 6 x 12 In. 575.00
Basket, Hupa, Black, White, Pedestal, Geometric, Open Weave Base, 8 3/4 x 2 1/2 In. 315.00
Basket, Hupa, Gambling Tray, c.1900, 9 1/2 In. 750.00

Basket, Hupa, Geometric, Hanging Wall Pocket, 9 1/2 x 11 x 4 1/4 In. 290.00
Basket, Jicarilla Apache, Snake, Multicolored, Lid, Early 1900s, 6 1/2 x 9 In. 489.00
Basket, Karok, Red, White Geometric, 13 In. 920.00
Basket, Klickitat, Berry, Early 1900s, 7 x 7 In. 489.00
Basket, Maine, 2 Painted Blue Bands, 21 x 11 x 13 In. 400.00
Basket, Navajo, Central Star, Geometric, c.1950, 3 x 18 In. 375.00
Basket, Navajo, Wedding, Black, Red, Spirit Release, c.1940, 14 x 3 In. 290.00
Basket, Nootka, Round, Ducks, Boat, Men, Lid, 2 x 3 1/2 In. 175.00
Basket, Northeast, Splint, Fishing Creel, Leather Straps, Late 1800s, 8 1/2 x 11 In. 265.00
Basket, Papago, Jar, Diagonal Stepped Terrace Lid, c.1970, 4 x 5 1/4 In. 90.00
Basket, Papago, Mountain, Step, c.1950, 6 x 14 In. 550.00
Basket, Papago, Oval, People, Animals, Early 1900s, 9 x 18 x 12 In. 920.00
Basket, Passamaquaddy, Splint, Ribbon Curl Work, Swing Handle, c.1900, 13 x 10 In. . . . 489.00
Basket, Pima, Bowl, Flat Bottom, Geometric, Squash Blossom Figure, c.1940, 7 x 3 In. . . . 575.00
Basket, Pima, Coiled, Flared Rim, Triangle Designs, 4 1/2 x 9 1/4 In. 259.00
Basket, Pima, Horses, Contrasting Rim, Early 1900s, 5 x 5 3/4 In. 375.00
Basket, Pima, Modified Key Design, Black Center, Early 1900s, 5 1/2 In. 375.00
Basket, Pima, Olla, Geometric, Early 1900s, 7 1/2 x 10 In. 220.00
Basket, Pima, Oval, Flat Bottom, Flared, Geometric, c.1950, 2 7/8 x 2 1/2 In. 140.00
Basket, Pomo, Gift, Coiled, Stepped Grid, Red Tuft Feathers, c.1900, 7 3/8 In. 2585.00
Basket, Pomo, Serpent, Geometric, 2 Colors, Early 1900s, 1 1/2 x 3 1/2 In. 805.00
Basket, Salishan, Multicolored, Coiled, Imbricated, Lid, Late 19th Century, 10 x 17 1/2 In. 295.00
Basket, Skokomish, Bowl, Dog Figures, Scalloped Open Rim, Geometric, 8 x 7 In. 690.00
Basket, Skokomish, Imbricated Designs, Rim Loops, Early 1900s, 14 1/2 x 12 In. 2070.00
Basket, Tlingit, Twined, Multicolored, Fret Design, Rattle Top, c.1900, 4 1/2 x 5 In. 1725.00
Basket, Tohono O'odham, Papago, Yucca Fiber Body, 7 x 5 1/2 In. 200.00
Basket, Tsimshian, Cedar, Brown, Arrow Center Band, Early 1900s, 4 x 8 In. 518.00
Basket, Washo, Bowl, Checkerboard, Arrow, Early 1900s, 4 x 8 In. 1265.00
Basket, Washo, Bowl, Spiral, c.1950, 6 x 4 In. 575.00
Basket, Washo, Single Rod, Diamonds, Lid, c.1920, 4 x 6 1/2 In. 259.00
Basket, Winnebago, Split Ash, Vegetal Dyed, c.1920, 11 x 14 In. 69.00
Basket, Yurok, Quails, Early 1900s, 9 In. 865.00
Belt, 10 Conchas, Silver, Turquoise, Stamped, Sterling Buckle, 38 1/2 In. 575.00
Belt, Cheyenne, Beaded Hide, Multicolored, Dog, Thunderbird, Morning Star, 25 1/2 In. . . 355.00
Belt, Chippewa, Beaded, Flowers, Hide, Cloth Edge, c.1910, 44 x 4 In. 160.00
Belt, Dance, Sioux, Bells, Harness Leather, 1900s, 34 1/2 In. 100.00
Belt, Navajo, 6 Conchas, Stamped, Repousse, Winged Buckle, Silver, 20th Century, 4 In. . 880.00
Belt, Navajo, Butterfly Conchas, Silver, Turquoise, Buckle, Stamped, Repousse, 50 In. . . . 645.00
Belt, Navajo, Child's, 12 Conchas, Silver, Stamped, Repousse, Buckle, 25 In. 470.00
Belt, Plateau, Beaded, Flower, Butterflies, Leaves, Vines, Beaded Ground, 40 In. 145.00
Belt Pouch, Northern Plains, Hide, Morning Star, Ribbon Binding, 1800s, 6 x 3 1/4 In. . . . 115.00
Blanket, Cree, Buckskin, Flowers, Leaves, Beaded, Embroidered, c.1950, 58 x 47 In. 575.00
Blanket, Dance, Tlinglit, Chilkat, Woven, Mountain Goat Wool, Cedar Bark, 44 x 25 In. . . 18800.00
Blanket, Navajo, Diamond, Blue, White, Red, Black Border, 32 x 32 In. 460.00
Blanket, Navajo, Saddle, Double, c.1940, 30 x 44 In. 345.00
Blanket, Navajo, Saddle, Tree Of Life Variant, Pictorial, Double, c.1940, 24 x 48 In. 460.00
Blanket, Plains, Saddle, Rawhide, 2 Horns, Harness, Leather Straps, 18 x 13 In. 633.00
Blanket Strip, Blackfoot, Muslin Strip, Geometric, Binding, 61 x 5 In. 2000.00
Blanket Strip, Lakota, Hide, Metallic, Glass Beads, Geometric, c.1900, 58 In. 1645.00
Blanket Strip, Lakota, Maltese Cross Rondels, Geometric, Beads, 64 x 3 In. 2350.00
Bolo, Zuni, Turquoise Cluster, Silver Mounting, c.1962, 4 x 2 3/4 In. 315.00
Bonnet, Sioux, Child's, Beaded, Cap Style, Sinew Sewn, Calico, Geometric, 5 1/2 In. 2070.00
Boots, Athabascan, High Top, Sealskin, Drawstring Top, c.1950, 11 x 18 In. 140.00
Boots, Chippewa, Moose Hide, Beaded Flower Panels, c.1920, 9 x 14 In. 259.00
Boots, Chippewa, Smoked Moose Hide, Flower Beadwork, Early 1900s, 9 x 14 In. 545.00
Bow, Plains, Red Wool Tufts, Painted On Back, c.1880, 49 In. 1045.00
Bow Case, Quiver, Plains, Buffalo Hide, Red Pigment Trace, Mid 19th Century, 41 In. 940.00
Bowl, Acoma, Pottery, Multicolored, Shouldered, Brown, Orange Geometric, 7 x 10 In. . . . 1116.00
Bowl, Apache, Basket, Coiled, Modified Pinwheel Design, 19th Century, 4 x 13 1/4 In. . . . 410.00
Bowl, Apache, Basket, Coiled, Shallow, Radiating Pattern, c.1900, 2 1/2 x 10 In. 1410.00
Bowl, Apache, Basket, Morning Star Design, Willow, Martynia, 2 3/8 x 10 In. 489.00
Bowl, Apache, Pictorial, Coiled, 5-Petal Pattern, Animals, 4 1/2 x 17 In. 2470.00
Bowl, Hopi, Pottery, Multicolored Hopi Designs, Early 1900s, 2 1/4 x 5 1/2 In. 315.00

Bowl, Hopi, Pottery, Multicolored, Abstract Feathers, Signed, Ampeyo, Fannie, 3 x 6 In. .. 825.00
Bowl, Hopi, Pottery, Multicolored, Rounded, Flat Bottom, Step Designs, 4 1/2 x 6 3/4 In. ... 410.00
Bowl, Hopi, Pottery, Multicolored, Umber Design, Red Ocher Accents, Slip Body, 5 x 7 In. 345.00
Bowl, Hopi, Seed Jar Shape, Bear Paw, Hatch Marks, Red, Brown Slip, 4 1/2 x 7 1/2 In. .. 765.00
Bowl, Maidu, Basket, Coiled, Flared, Red Diagonals, Late 1800s, 6 x 11 In. 1585.00
Bowl, Maidu, Basket, Coiled, Flared, Red, Brown Diagonals, 1800s, 16 x 24 In. 3175.00
Bowl, Nampeyo, Pottery, Flattened, Stylized Birds, c.1950, 2 3/4 x 7 1/2 In. 290.00
Bowl, Northwest Coast, Effigy, Wood, Bone Inlay, Stylized Animal Heads, 16 In. 400.00
Bowl, Paiute, Beaded, Basket, Zigzag & Concentric Geometric, c.1930, 2 x 3 1/2 In. 529.00
Bowl, Papago, Basket, Coiled, Petal Center, Fret Pattern, Early 1900s, 3 x 15 In. 235.00
Bowl, Pima, Basket, Coiled, Convex Bottom, Pinwheels, c.1900, 5 x 16 In. 1410.00
Bowl, Pima, Basket, Coiled, Flaring Sides, 4-Panel Pattern, Late 19th Century, 6 x 20 In. .. 1410.00
Bowl, Pima, Basket, Multicolored, Coiled, Bulbous, Flat Bottom, Mazes, 11 x 12 In. 1295.00
Bowl, San Ildefonso, Blackware, Mountain, Stepped Cloud, Marie & Santana, 3 x 4 In. ... 865.00
Bowl, San Ildefonso, Multicolored, Flared Scalloped Rim, 2 Handles, 5 x 10 In. 295.00
Bowl, San Ildefonso, Pottery, Blackware, Fret Pattern, Marie & Julian, 2 5/8 x 4 1/8 In. ... 999.00
Bowl, Santo Domingo, Pottery, Dough, Game Animals, c.1950, 17 In. 980.00
Bowl, Santo Domingo, Pottery, Leaves, Pinched Top, Handle, Early 1900s, 5 3/4 x 8 In. ... 405.00
Bowl, Tesuque Pueblo, Pottery, Black Paint On Cream, 1870s, 4 3/4 x 7 In. 520.00
Bowl, Tsimshian, Basket, Multicolored, Twined, Cylindrical, Bird, Flags, c.1900, 4 x 6 In. . 645.00
Bowl, Yokuts, Basket, Multicolored, Coiled, Rattlesnake Pattern, Late 1800s, 6 x 15 In. ... 825.00
Bowl, Zuni, Pottery, Frogs, Leaves, Red, Black Geometric, Cream, Globe Shape, 4 x 7 In. . 325.00
Bowl, Zuni, Pottery, Globe Shape, Splayed Frogs, Red Orange Leaves, c.1885, 5 x 8 In. ... 880.00
Box, Algonquin, Birch Bark, Round, Lid, Hand Sewn, Cloverleaf, 5 x 4 In. 230.00
Box, Micmac, Quilled Bark, Oval, Decorated, Geometric, Lid, 3 x 5 1/2 In. 440.00
Box, Navajo, Sterling, Hand Stamped, Flowers, Geometric, c.1950, 3 1/4 x 1 1/2 In. 405.00
Bracelet, Navajo, 5 Lander, Spider Web Turquoise, Silver, 1900, 5 3/8 x 1 In. 690.00
Bracelet, Navajo, 25 Turquoise & Silver Clusters, 1960s, 2 x 5 3/4 In. 185.00
Bracelet, Navajo, 45 Turquoise & Silver Clusters, 2 x 6 In. 178.00
Bracelet, Navajo, Cuff, Silver, 2 Turquoise, 5 1/4 x 1 1/4 x 3 1/4 In. 545.00
Bracelet, Navajo, Cuff, Silver, 5 Green Turquoise, 1900s, 5 3/8 x 1 1/2 x 3/4 In. 115.00
Bracelet, Navajo, Cuff, Spider Web Turquoise, Sterling, c.1970, 1 1/4 x 5 3/4 In. 375.00
Bracelet, Navajo, Cuff, Stamped, Silver, Arrow, Thunderbird, 1 1/4 x 6 1/2 In. 80.00
Bracelet, Navajo, Cuff, Turquoise, Shaped Matrix, 1900s, 5 5/8 x 1 1/8 In. 175.00
Bracelet, Navajo, Cuff, Turquoise, Silver, 6 In. 690.00
Bracelet, Navajo, Silver, 2 Oval Turquoise, 3 Bands, 1 Square, 2 3/4 In. 2585.00
Bracelet, Navajo, Silver, 3 Turquoise Cabochons, c.1950, 2 1/2 In. 138.00
Bracelet, Navajo, Silver, 23 Turquoise, Cluster, 1900s, 3 x 1 3/4 In. 138.00
Bracelet, Navajo, Silver, Turquoise, 5 Bands, 2 Stones, Mid 1900s, 3 1/2 In. 440.00
Bracelet, Navajo, Silver, Turquoise, Coral, Water Bird Design, Signed, 1980, 7 x 1 In. 190.00
Bracelet, Navajo, Turquoise, Raised Engraved Designs, c.1920 .... 145.00
Bracelet, Zuni, Inlaid Turquoise, 2 Rows, c.1960, 2 1/4 In. 315.00
Bracelet, Zuni, Silver, Inlaid Stone, Sand Cast, Knife Wing Man, 1950s, 2 3/8 x 2 In. 560.00
Breastplate, Plains, Bone Hair-Pipes, Brass Beads, Shell Discs, Late 1800s, 18 In. 2785.00
Breastplate, Plains, Hair-Pipes, Hide Strung Bone, Leather Spacers, 21 1/2 In. 1645.00
Breastplate, Plains, Hair-Pipes, Hide Strung Bone, Leather Strips, Beads, Pendant, 19 In. . 1060.00
Breastplate, Plains, Hair-Pipes, Mink, Trade Cloth, Copper Gorgets, Cross, 12 x 24 In. ... 445.00
Breastplate, Sioux, Warrior's, Hair-Pipes, c.1950, 11 x 16 In. 315.00
Buckle, Navajo, 3-Piece Ranger, Clasp, Tip, Signed, Sterling, c.1980, 2 3/4 x 2 1/2 In. 220.00
Canoe Model, Chippewa, Birch Bark, Incised, c.1900, 12 In. 175.00
Canteen, Acoma, Pottery, Multicolored, 2 Lugs, Abstract Bird, Cream Ground, 4 3/4 In. ... 265.00
Canteen, Santo Domingo, Pottery, Hand Painted, Red Back, Early 1900s, 9 x 10 x 6 In. ... 865.00
Case, Jewelry, Iroquois, Beaded, Velvet & Silk Interior, c.1900, 4 1/2 x 3 In. 138.00
Choker, Crow, Beaded, Orange, White, Shell, c.1900, 12 In. 150.00
Club, Iroquois, Ball, Slender Shaft, c.1860, 18 In. 520.00
Club, Plains, Stone Head, Rawhide Wrapped, Sinew Sewn, Handle, 5 1/2 x 2 1/2 x 15 In. ... 127.00
Club, Plains, Stone, Flat Side, Soft Point, Pre-1800s, 6 3/4 x 5 In. 345.00
Club, Sioux, Rawhide Wrapped, Sinew Sewn, Beater, Buckskin, 1800s, 2 x 1 x 11 1/4 In. .. 345.00
Club, Sioux, War, Seed Beaded, Sinew Wrapped, Stone Head, Horsehair Drop, 51 In. 640.00
Cradle, Apache, Doll's, Beaded, c.1880, 5 x 12 In. 1610.00
Cradle, Apache, Doll's, Calico Padding, Rickrack, 17 x 7 In. 69.00
Cradle, Cheyenne, Beaded, Geometric, Rawhide Tab, Muslin, Cotton, 34 In. 3819.00
Cradle, Cheyenne, Doll's, Beaded Hide, Cloth, Wood, 19th Century, 8 In. 2235.00

Cradle, Crow, Doll's, Beaded Hide, Cloth, Hide Doll, Geometric, Fringe, Late 1800s, 8 In.   3055.00
Cradle, Mono, Doll's, Toy, Basket, Sunshade, Chevron, Wood Doll, c.1950, 19 x 6 x 8 In. .   316.00
Cradle, Navajo, Wooden, Buckskin Boot, Sunshade, 16 x 7 1/2 x 9 1/2 In. 80.00
Cradle, Ojibwa, Carved Wood, Bentwood Sunshade, 1900, 23 x 9 In. 920.00
Cradle, Paiute, Beaded, Buckskin, c.1940, 15 x 38 In. 690.00
Cradle, Southern Plains, Comanche, Doll's, Muslin, Net Beaded, Lines, Diamond, 8 In. . . .   4350.00
Cradle, Umatilla, Doll's, Wood Board, Beads, Bells, Wooden Doll, c.1920, 27 x 10 In. 375.00
Cradle, Ute, Doll's, Wood, Buckskin, Beaded, Geometric, Fringe, 21 In. 2350.00
Cradleboard, Chippewa, Beaded Cover, Heart Cutout, Anemones, c.1860, 14 x 6 In. 1440.00
Cradleboard, Lakota Sioux, Hide, Beaded, Lazy Stitch, c.1885, 29 1/4 In. 9200.00
Cradleboard, Sioux, Quills, Beadwork, Red Wool, Hawk Bells, 1900-50, 15 x 39 In. 5175.00
Cradleboard, Ute, Girl's, Great Basin, Ocher Leather, Wicker Frame, c.1890, 21 x 8 In. . . .   1150.00
Cradleboard, Ute, Girl's, Ocher, Loom Beaded, Initials, 1880-95, 31 In. 4600.00
Cuffs, Chippewa, Flowers, Beaded Allover, c.1950, 8 x 7 In. 160.00
Cuffs, Cree, Beaded, Multicolored, Saskatchewan, c.1920 . . . .   470.00
Cuffs, Sioux, Quilled, Beaded, Fringed, Star Center, c.1900, 14 x 8 In. 870.00
Dance Ball, Arapaho, Grass, Beaded Allover, c.1900, 2 1/2 In. 690.00
Dance Roach, Crow, Cloth Base, Dyed Horsehair, Porcupine Hair, Early 1900s, 13 1/2 In. .   115.00
Dance Wand, Hopi, Zigzag End, Early 1900s, 24 In. 635.00
Doll, Cree, Hide, Beaded Face, Gloves, Moccasins, 13 x 6 In. 375.00
Doll, Iroquois, Corn Husk, Mother, Child, Bead Dress, Leggings, 1900s, 17 x 5 In. 970.00
Doll, Navajo, Cloth, Male & Female, Metal Buttons, Beaded Necklace, 1940s, 13 In., Pair .   165.00
Doll, Navajo, Red Velvet Blouse, Satin Skirt, Seed Bead, Sequin Jewelry, c.1970, 17 x 6 In.   80.00
Doll, Osage, Buckskin, Moccasins, Dress, Quill Breastplate, Horsehair, 1900s, 10 In. 403.00
Doll, Pima, Girl, Beaded Necklace, Moccasins, Earrings, c.1960, 12 1/2 In. 35.00
Doll, Skookum, Chief, Bully Good Indian, Composition, Side-Glancing Eyes, c.1935, 27 In.   1345.00
Doll, Skookum, Composition Face, Human Hair, Bead Necklace, 17 In. 410.00
Doll, Skookum, Composition Face, Synthetic Fiber Wig, Eyes To Right, Baby, 13 In. 120.00
Doll, Skookum, Squaw With Papoose, Composition Head, Wool Blanket, 11 In. 145.00
Dress, Blackfoot, Buckskin, Beaded Yoke, Pony Bead Fringe, c.1930, 48 x 21 In. 980.00
Dress, Cheyenne, Buckskin, Beaded Shoulders, Fringe, c.1950, 52 x 23 In. 1150.00
Dress, Crow, Dance, Tanned Doeskin, Lazy Stitch Beadwork, Fringe, 1900s, 36 x 18 In. . .   375.00
Dress, Lakota, Beaded Cloth, Yoke, Multicolored Geometric, Fringe, Girl's 3820.00
Dress, Nez Perce, Buckskin, Pony Bead Yoke, Fringe, c.1910, 44 x 24 In. 2185.00
Drum, Blackfoot, Rawhide, Painted, Wooden Hoop, Mid 1900s, 17 In. 40.00
Drum, Crow, Rawhide, 1900s, 4 1/2 x 15 In. 865.00
Drum, Hopi, Cottonwood, Rawhide, Handle, 13 1/2 x 10 x 12 In. 460.00
Drum, Kwakiutl, 2-Sided, Whale, Raven, Late 1900s, 23 x 5 In. 690.00
Drum, Pueblo, Cottonwood, Rawhide, Beater, Red, White, Blue, 1960s, 12 x 10 In. 430.00
Drum, Pueblo, Taos, Cottonwood, Rawhide, c.1950, 7 1/4 x 7 In.   185.00
Drum, Sioux, Cedar Hoop, Rawhide, Warrior, c.1970, 12 1/4 In. 35.00
Drum, Sioux, Rawhide, Steel Barrel Section, c.1940, 18 1/2 In. 185.00
Drum, Taos, Turned Wood, Rawhide, 1900s, 6 1/2 x 5 3/4 In. 40.00
Earrings, Navajo, Oval Coral Cabochons, Silver, 2 3/4 In. 130.00
Earrings, Zuni, Coral Inlay, Clip-On, c.1960, 2 1/4 In. 259.00
Earrings, Zuni, Knife Wing Dancer, Sterling Hoops, c.1950, 1 1/2 In. 489.00
Fetish, Plains, Lizard, Umbilical, Beaded Hide, Late 1800s, 6 1/2 In. 3400.00
Fetish, Plains, Turtle, Umbilical, Buckskin, Beaded Top, c.1950, 3 1/2 In. 345.00
Fetish, Sioux, Turtle, Umbilical, Beaded Allover, Geometric, Crosses, c.1910, 3 x 5 In. . . .   520.00
Gauntlets, Blackfoot, Beaded, Buckskin, Fringe, Early 1900s, 16 1/2 In. 460.00
Gauntlets, Plains, Geometric, White Ground, Fringe, c.1900, 11 1/2 In. 590.00
Gauntlets, Plains, Hide, Beaded, Suie Slow Bull, Wild West Show, 14 3/4 In. 2530.00
Gauntlets, Plateau, Cuff, Beaded, Flowers, Fringe, 8 1/2 In. 230.00
Gloves, Cree, Silk, Flowers, Embroidered, c.1900 . . . .   415.00
Hand Drum, Northwest Coast, Salish, Rawhide, Otters, Snakes, Birds, c.1890, 22 In. 2415.00
Hat, Chehalis, Basket, c.1890, 6 x 8 In. 375.00
Hat, Nez Perce, Cornhusk, Trade Yarn, Chevron, Quail, 1920s, 7 x 8 In. 1095.00
Headdress, Plains, Deer, Porcupine Hair Roach, 17 1/2 In. 195.00
Jacket, Cree, Moose Hide, Beadwork, Fringe, c.1930, 15 x 24 In.   80.00
Jar, Acoma, Pottery, Black, Orange Geometric, Feathers, Cream, 9 x 11 In. 940.00
Jar, Acoma, Pottery, High Shoulder, Handles, Black, Yellow Geometric, c.1920, 10 x 9 In. .   705.00
Jar, Acoma, Seed, Pottery, Mimbres Rabbit, Flowers, R. Lucario, c.1960, 4 1/4 x 2 1/2 In. .   185.00
Jar, Laguna, Black On Red, Geometric, Fingernail Trim, c.1970, 6 x 7 In. 140.00

Jar, Maricopa, Curvilinear Design, Black On Red, Amble Sunn, c.1971, 5 1/2 x 4 1/2 In. ..   100.00
Jar, Paiute, Diamond Beaded, Cylindrical, c.1960, 6 1/4 x 3 1/4 In. 80.00
Jar, Panamint, Basket, Multicolored, Coiled, High Shoulders, Black Bands, 3 1/2 x 6 In. ...   3820.00
Jar, Pima, Coiled, High Shoulder, Flared Rim, 14 x 13 In. 880.00
Jar, Pueblo, Gray Slip, Black Geometric Figures, Rag Polished, c.1900, 5 x 5 1/2 In. 145.00
Jar, San Ildefonso, Blackware, Feathers, Signed, Tonita, 7 x 4 1/4 In. 460.00
Jar, San Ildefonso, Globe Shape, High Neck, Polished Black, 9 x 7 1/2 In. 3645.00
Jar, Santa Clara, Pottery, Multicolored, Margaret Luther, Globular, Painted, 8 1/2 x 6 In. ...   1645.00
Jar, Santo Domingo, Black Design, Tan Slip, Red Concave Bottom, 7 x 9 In. 375.00
Jar, Santo Domingo, Pottery, 4 Red Frogs, Early 1900s, 6 1/2 x 10 In. 750.00
Jar, Yokuts, Basket, Coiled, High Shoulders, Flared Neck, c.1900, 4 x 5 In. 3525.00
Jar, Yokuts, Basket, Rattlesnake, Coiled, Zigzag, Topknot Feathers, 1800s, 5 1/2 x 9 In. ...   5875.00
Jar, Zia, Pottery, Multicolored Birds, Geometric, Red Base, c.1950, 6 x 7 1/2 In. 489.00
Jar, Zia, Pottery, Multicolored, Geometric, Bird, Slip Ground, 3 x 3 1/2 In. 115.00
Kachina, Hopi, 2 Kokopelli, 1 Hoop Dancer, R. Largo, 20th Century, 10 In., 3 Piece 115.00
Kachina, Hopi, Blue Painted, Holds Rattle, Stick, 20th Century, 17 In. 90.00
Kachina, Hopi, Cottonwood Root, Pigment Paint, Early 1900s, 8 1/2 In. 2300.00
Kachina, Hopi, Cow, Cottonwood Root, c.1950, 14 1/2 In. 259.00
Kachina, Hopi, Multicolored, Depicting Mudhead, 20th Century, 17 In. 1528.00
Kachina, Hopi, Owl, Cottonwood Root, 1960s 315.00
Kachina, Hopi, Rainbow Dancer, Route 66, c.1950, 12 In. 92.00
Kachina, Hopi, Witch, Carved, Painted, Yarn, Fur, P. Smith, 20th Century, 18 In. 150.00
Kachina, Hopi, Wolf-Like Mouth, Ears, 14 1/2 In. 115.00
Kachina, Hopi, Wood, Olive Green Mask, 5 In. 95.00
Kachina, Hopi, Wood, Painted Mouth, Horned, Antennae, Yellow Mask, 5 In. 60.00
Kachina, Hopi, Wood, Painted Mouth, Rust Mask, 4 In. 70.00
Kachina, Hopi, Wood, Snout Mouth, Black Mask, 3 1/4 In. 50.00
Kachina, Hopi, Wood, Snout Mouth, Blue Mask, 5 1/4 In. 90.00
Kachina, Hopi, Wood, Tubed Mouth, Dark Green Mask, 7 In. 154.00
Kachina, Hopi, Wood, Tubed Mouth, Turquoise Mask, 7 In. 120.00
Keton, Navajo, Silver, Leather, Hourglass, Border Pattern, Leather Strap, c.1900, 3 3/4 In. ..   2700.00
Knife Sheath, Arapaho, Sinew Sewn, Lazy Stitch Beading, Early 1900s, 12 1/2 In. 920.00
Knife Sheath, Blackfoot, Tacked Leather, Knife, Wood Handle, Mid 1900s, 12 1/2 In. 160.00
Knife Sheath, Cheyenne, Beaded Hide, Stiff Rawhide Liner, Late 19th Century, 8 3/4 In. ...   5290.00
Knife Sheath, Plains, Sinew Sewn, Morning Star, Quilled, 10 In. 430.00
Knife Sheath, Sioux, Plains, Beading, Tin Cone & Horsehair Dangles, 4 1/2 In. 145.00
Lacrosse Stick, Algonquin, Round Head, Heart Point, 1870-80, 35 1/4 In. 345.00
Lacrosse Stick, Winnebago, Bentwood, c.1900, 24 In., Pair 185.00
Legging Strip, Sioux, Lazy Stitch, Sinew Sewn, Geometric, Early 1900s, 30 x 2 1/2 In. ...   290.00
Leggings, Blackfoot, Blue Trade Cloth, Geometric Beaded Strip, c.1880, 40 1/2 x 14 In. ...   1380.00
Leggings, Crow, Beaded Panel, Trim, Navy, Red, Trade Cloth, c.1880, 29 In. 750.00
Leggings, Crow, Flowers, Horseshoe, Fringe, 1900s, 22 1/2 In. 2000.00
Leggings, Lakota, Women's, Beaded Hide, Geometric, Canvas, Late 1800s, 12 1/2 In., Pair   940.00
Leggings, Pawnee, Hide, Fringe, c.1900, 27 In. 290.00
Leggings, Ute, Elk Hide, Muslin, Beaded Panel, Geometric, 19th Century, 18 In. 500.00
Mask, Forehead, Kwakiutl, Wood, Carved, Painted, Cedar Bark, Cloth, 1950s, 13 1/2 In. ..   590.00
Mitts, Cree, Moose Hide, Flower Beadwork, Rabbit Trim, Fringe, 13 1/2 In. 69.00
Moccasins, Apache, High Top, Painted Hide, Rawhide Soles, Cactus Kicker Toes, 41 In. ..   5300.00
Moccasins, Arapaho, Crosses, Morning Star, Green Vamp, Blue Border, 10 1/2 In. 1880.00
Moccasins, Blackfoot, Lazy Stitch, Beaded, Sinew Sewn, Hard Sole, 1900s, 10 1/2 In. 115.00
Moccasins, Cheyenne, Beaded Allover, Blue, Yellow, White Glass Beads, 9 1/2 In. 1495.00
Moccasins, Cheyenne, Beaded Hide, Hard Sole, Geometric, 8 1/2 In. 118.00
Moccasins, Cheyenne, Geometric, Buffalo Tracks, Hard Sole, 10 1/2 In. 1765.00
Moccasins, Cheyenne, Men's, Beaded, Target-Like Design, 1880s, 10 1/4 In. 1210.00
Moccasins, Cheyenne, Men's, White, Red & Green Beads, Buffalo Hide, 1870s, 10 3/4 In. ..   1705.00
Moccasins, Cheyenne, Southern Plains, Yellow Ocher Stained Hide, Beading, 9 In. 460.00
Moccasins, Cree, Buckskin Boots, Fur, Beaded Toes, c.1940, 10 In. 69.00
Moccasins, Cree, Child's, Red Trade Cloth, Buckskin, Beaded, Canada, 1930s, 5 In. 315.00
Moccasins, Crow, Beaded Buffalo Hide, Maltese Crosses, c.1880, 8 1/2 In. 750.00
Moccasins, Crow, Women's, Buffalo Hide, Blue Stylized Flowers, 9 1/2 x 9 1/4 In. 150.00
Moccasins, Eastern Woodlands, Moose Hide, Fur Trim, Flower Beaded, 10 In. 198.00
Moccasins, Iroquois, Men's, Tan, Black, c.1920, 10 1/2 In. 210.00
Moccasins, Lakota, Beaded Soles & Uppers, Late 19th Century, 3 1/4 In. 705.00

Moccasins, Lakota, Child's, Buffalo Hide, Multicolored Geometric, Buffalo Tracks, 6 In. . .	1295.00
Moccasins, Navajo, Hide, Silver & Turquoise Buttons, c.1950, 9 1/2 In.	345.00
Moccasins, Navajo, Turquoise, Silver Buckles, 10 In.	120.00
Moccasins, Osage, Men's, Slipper Type, c.1880, 9 3/4 In.	550.00
Moccasins, Plains, Tanned Buckskin, Hard Soles, Sinew Sewn, Beaded, 1900s, 9 1/2 In. . .	230.00
Moccasins, Seneca, Moose Hair Embroidered, Pony Bead Trim, Late 1800s, 10 In.	460.00
Moccasins, Sioux, Beaded, Buffalo, 1880s, 9 1/4 In.	660.00
Moccasins, Sioux, Beaded, Green, Blue, Red, White, Parfleche Soles, 10 1/2 In., Pair	980.00
Moccasins, Sioux, Ceremonial, Blue, Green, Red, White Beads, 1800s, 10 1/4 In.	1725.00
Moccasins, Sioux, Child's, Beaded Allover, Sinew Sewn, Buffalo Hide, Early 1900s, 8 In. .	635.00
Moccasins, Sioux, Child's, Beaded Sole, Ceremonial, White Hearts, 5 In.	865.00
Moccasins, Sioux, Child's, c.1880, 5 1/4 In.	715.00
Moccasins, Sioux, Men's, Beaded, Tin Cone Danglers, c.1880, 10 1/2 In.	880.00
Moccasins, Southern Plains, Sinew Sewn, Buffalo, Red & White Hearts, Fringe, 7 In.	720.00
Moccasins, Western Apache, White River Area, Conchas, Beaded, 9 x 16 In.	575.00
Moccasins, Woodlands, Beaded Cloth, Hide, Red Trade Cloth, Flowers, 10 In., Pair	150.00
Moose Call, Eastern Woodlands, Bark Shape, Ash Ring, Sewn Lengthwise, 20 In.	230.00
Necklace, Crow, Trade Beads, Russian Blues, Millefiori, Late 1800s, 28 In.	80.00
Necklace, Navajo, 6 Strands, Red Coral, Silver, 1900s, 18 In.	230.00
Necklace, Navajo, 66 Silver Beads, Stamped, c.1980, 24 In.	230.00
Necklace, Navajo, Graduating Squash Blossom, Silver, Turquoise, Pendant, Naja, 15 In. . .	355.00
Necklace, Navajo, Squash Blossom, Naja, Blue Turquoise, 1900s, 25 In.	290.00
Necklace, Navajo, Squash Blossom, Silver, Turquoise, 15 In.	290.00
Necklace, Navajo, Squash Blossom, Silver, Turquoise, Serrated Bezel, c.1900, 13 1/2 In. . .	2350.00
Necklace, Navajo, Turquoise Bead, 3 Sets Jocla, c.1970, 18 x 4 In.	220.00
Necklace, Pueblo, 3 Strands, Turquoise, Heishi, Agate, Shell, Hematite, Bone, 28 In.	140.00
Necklace, Pueblo, 10 Strands, Red Coral, Sterling Silver, 1900s, 21 In.	160.00
Necklace, Santa Fe, 3 Strands, Coins, Trade Beads, 1900s, 30 In.	105.00
Necklace, Santo Domingo, 2 Strands, Turquoise Roundels, Gold Cones, c.1974, 18 In.	185.00
Necklace, Santo Domingo, 9 Strands, Olive Shell Heishi, c.1974, 26 In.	80.00
Necklace, Santo Domingo, Rolled Turquoise Heishi, c.1974, 21 In.	105.00
Necklace, Southwest, Copper, Squash Blossom, Beads, Turquoise, Naja, 16 1/2 In.	325.00
Necklace, Squash Blossom, Silver & Coral, Rope Twist Detail, 25 In.	520.00
Necklace, Zuni, Silver, Turquoise, Squash Blossom, Needlepoint Settings, 1900s, 15 In. . . .	325.00
Necklace & Earrings, Navajo, Silver, Squash Blossom, Beads, Curled Top, 26 In.	290.00
Olla, Acoma, Pottery, Geometric Designs, Early 1900s, 10 x 13 In.	2875.00
Olla, Acoma, Pottery, Red, Brown, Black Geometric, On Cream, c.1930, 10 1/2 x 13 In. . .	4100.00
Olla, Pima, Basket, Flat Bottom, Modified Key, c.1970, 1 1/4 In.	115.00
Olla, Pueblo, Acoma, Pottery, Parrot, 8 x 9 In.	150.00
Olla, Pueblo, Santo Domingo, Pottery, Multicolored, Flowers, Bird, Concave Base, 7 x 6 In.	860.00
Olla, Santo Domingo, Pottery, Game Animals, c.1950, 12 x 13 In.	1150.00
Olla, Santo Domingo, Pottery, Leaves, Geometric, Black Rim, Early 1900s, 10 x 9 1/2 In. .	3450.00
Olla, Santo Domingo, Pottery, Multicolored, Early 1900s, 9 1/4 x 9 1/2 In.	920.00
Olla, Zuni, Pottery, Multicolored, Black, Red, Brown Rainbird, Round, 9 1/2 x 12 In.	3819.00
Owl, Zuni, Pottery, Nellie Bica, c.1920, 4 In.	403.00
Paddle, Kwakuitl, Ceremonial, Caved, Painted, 5 x 24 In.	69.00
Parfleche, Nez Perce, Mineral Painted, c.1950, 13 x 27 In.	2185.00
Pillow, Cheyenne, Teepee, Beaded, Canvas, Yarn Tufts, c.1950, 20 x 28 In.	920.00
Pillow, Chippewa, Glass Beads, c.1900, 14 x 17 In., Pair	1800.00
Pillow, Iroquois, Beaded, Niagara Falls, American Flag, 1890s, 8 x 10 In.	345.00
Pin, Navajo, Silver, 21 Turquoise, c.1940, 3 x 1 In.	80.00
Pipe, Eastern Woodlands, Burl, Carved, Free-Form Bowl, 1830s, 4 x 3 In.	290.00
Pipe, Plains, Wood, Stone, Lead Turtle, Buffalo Hoof Inlay, 24 1/2 In.	2350.00
Pipe, Plateau, Incised Eagle, c.1960, 4 1/4 x 2 3/4 In.	69.00
Pipe & Stem, Sioux, Catlinite L Bowl, Hardwood Stem, Frame, 1880s, 25 x 11 1/2 In.	1035.00
Pipe Bag, Cree, Hide, Beaded Flowers, Fringe, Braided Drawstring, c.1940, 22 x 7 In.	259.00
Pipe Bag, Crow, Leather, Beaded, Cones, c.1900, 29 In.	545.00
Pipe Bag, Lakota, Beaded, Geometric, Fringe, 20th Century, 37 In.	1530.00
Pipe Bag, Lakota, Beaded, Quilled Hide, Fringe, Late 19th Century, 39 In.	2940.00
Pipe Bag, Lakota, Beaded, Quilled Hide, Geometric, Rawhide Slats, Fringe, 39 In.	1175.00
Pipe Bowl, Plains, Catlinite, 7 1/4 In.	92.00
Plaque, Hopi, Coiled, Muted Red, Black, Yellow, c.1910, 7 x 5 In.	345.00
Pouch, Apache, Buckskin, Beaded Fringe, Drawstring, Early 1900s, 6 x 4 1/2 In.	290.00

Indian, Rug, Navajo, Crystal,
Feathers, Leaves, Figures,
Mid 1900s, 74 x 55 In.

Indian, Rug, Navajo,
Germantown, Early 20th
Century, 49 x 32 In.

Indian, Rug, Navajo,
Klagetoh, 1930s,
75 1/2 x 45 3/4 In.

Pouch, Apache, Round, Beaded, Sunburst, Fringe, Tin Cone Danglers, 6 In. 1410.00
Pouch, Cheyenne, Beaded, Hide, Geometric, White Ground, Fringe, 9 1/2 In. 529.00
Pouch, Chippewa, Eagle, Shield, Black Velvet, Initials, Metallic Beads, 7 x 6 In. 345.00
Pouch, Iroquois, Leaf Beadwork, Flap, 2-Sided, Early 1900s, 4 1/4 x 4 1/4 In. 230.00
Pouch, Iroquois, Niagara Falls, Crossed Flags, Holly, Berries, White Edging, 5 x 5 In. 230.00
Pouch, Lakota, Beaded, Geometric, White Ground, Fringe, 19th Century, 11 In. 380.00
Pouch, Sioux, Antelope Hide, Geometric, Handle, Fringe, Early 1900s, 4 x 4 In. 290.00
Purse, Iroquois, Seed Beads, Leaves, 13 x 3 3/4 In. 230.00
Purse, Nez Perce, Beaded, Zipper, 1900s, 9 x 5 1/2 In. 185.00
Purse, Sioux, Allover Beaded, Sinew Sewn, Lazy Stitches, c.1950, 5 x 6 In. 140.00
Quirt, Plains, Elk Horn, Buffalo Hide Wrist Strap, Lashes, Cloth, 1800s, 11 1/2 In. 4995.00
Rattle, Hopi, Gourd, Cottonwood Root Handle, Carved, Painted, c.1930, 5 x 10 1/2 In. . . . 127.00
Rattle, Kwakiutl, Painted, Raven, Whale, 16 x 5 In. 150.00
Rattle, Kwakiutl, Sea Hawk, Carved, Late 1900s, 18 In. 220.00
Rattle, Northwest Coast, Carved Wood, Whale, Animal Face, 20th Century, 10 1/2 In. 265.00
Rattle, Plains, Buffalo Dew Claw, Late 1800s, 12 In. 978.00
Reins, Ogalala, Horsehair, Twisted, Halter, 1900s, 13 x 3 1/2 In. 230.00
Ring, Zuni, Phoenix Bird, Turquoise Inlay, Jet, Mother-Of-Pearl, 1 3/4 In. 127.00
Ring, Zuni, Rainbow God, Turquoise, Silver, c.1976, 1 1/4 In. 140.00
Rug, Chimayo, Multicolored, Geometric, Gray Ground, 20th Century, 75 x 53 In. 235.00
Rug, Chimayo, Wool, Eagle, Striped Ends, c.1920, 84 x 52 In. 315.00
Rug, Navajo, 2 Diamonds, Black, Gray, Red, Serrated Edge, Black Border, 78 x 39 In. 575.00
Rug, Navajo, 2 Gray Hills Style, Intertwining Hook, Diamonds, 26 x 39 In. 345.00
Rug, Navajo, 2 Gray Hills, Yellow, Gray, Black, Cream, 84 x 52 In. 605.00
Rug, Navajo, 4 Yei Dancers, Cornstalks, Heather Ground, Frame, 1920s, 41 x 33 In. 805.00
Rug, Navajo, 5 Yei Dancers, Multicolored, Black Ground, 38 1/2 x 29 1/2 In. 355.00
Rug, Navajo, 8 Yei Dancers, Frame, 1900s, 10 1/4 x 15 1/4 In. 375.00
Rug, Navajo, 12 Figures, Teec Nos Pos Style, 39 x 74 In. 1495.00
Rug, Navajo, Banded Crystal, Green, Rust, Yellow, Irene Clark, 1900s, 36 x 48 In. 575.00
Rug, Navajo, Bright West Reservation Area, Eye Dazzler, Arrow Heads, 92 x 61 In. 3795.00
Rug, Navajo, Brown, Cream, Black, c.1920, 95 x 67 In. 825.00
Rug, Navajo, Central Panel, Horses, Stepped Border, 49 1/2 x 37 1/2 In. 9400.00
Rug, Navajo, Checkered, Geometric Medallion, Brown, Black, Ivory, 47 x 28 In. 470.00
Rug, Navajo, Classic Serape Pattern, Red Ground, 71 x 44 In. 3645.00
Rug, Navajo, Concentric Diamond, Red Ground, 57 x 38 In. 1645.00
Rug, Navajo, Cornstalk, Cows, Lizards, Horses, Multicolored Ground, Border, 81 x 47 In. . 9400.00
Rug, Navajo, Cream, Brown Serrated Diamonds, 64 1/2 x 38 In. 470.00
Rug, Navajo, Cream, Red, Brown, Homespun Wool, Woven, Bird, Feathers, 80 x 39 In. . . . 1140.00
Rug, Navajo, Crosses, Triangles, Diamonds, c.1930, 60 x 84 In. 865.00
Rug, Navajo, Crystal, Feathers, Leaves, Figures, Mid 1900s, 74 x 55 In. . . . . *Illus* 2588.00
Rug, Navajo, Crystal, Tan, Black, Gray, c.1940, 53 x 82 In. 1955.00
Rug, Navajo, Diamonds, Black, Gray, Cream Field, c.1940, 26 x 44 In. 520.00
Rug, Navajo, Diamonds, Brown, Red, Black, Orange, c.1930, 48 x 54 In. 2585.00

Rug, Navajo, Diamonds, Central, Gray, Red, Black, Cream Field, c.1920, 71 x 114 In. 4700.00
Rug, Navajo, Diamonds, Red, Black, Green, Orange, Cream Field, c.1930, 61 x 71 In. 3820.00
Rug, Navajo, Early Klagetoh, Storm, 60 x 108 In. 3220.00
Rug, Navajo, Eye Dazzler, Brown Center, Diamond Columns, Black, Red, White, 71 x 48 In. 900.00
Rug, Navajo, Ganado, Red, Valero Stars, 32 x 42 In. 1150.00
Rug, Navajo, Ganado, Serrated Diamonds, c.1950, 61 x 33 In. 403.00
Rug, Navajo, Geometric & Feather Designs, 1900s, 83 x 53 In. 999.00
Rug, Navajo, Geometric Designs, Serrated Border, c.1950, 35 x 50 In. 290.00
Rug, Navajo, Geometric, Brown, White, Gray Field, 44 x 66 In. 259.00
Rug, Navajo, Geometric, Red, Beige Ground, Brown Border, 31 x 66 In. 355.00
Rug, Navajo, Germantown, 4 Ply, Fringe, c.1920, 22 x 36 In. 405.00
Rug, Navajo, Germantown, Black, Purple, White, Crosses, 19th Century, 56 x 79 In. 4400.00
Rug, Navajo, Germantown, Early 20th Century, 49 x 32 In. ....*Illus* 2600.00
Rug, Navajo, Germantown, Zigzags, Green, White, Red, c.1950, 48 x 29 In. 690.00
Rug, Navajo, Gray, Black, White, Red, Storm, 1900s, 26 1/4 x 40 1/2 In. 375.00
Rug, Navajo, Klagetoh, 1930s, 75 1/2 x 45 3/4 In. ....*Illus* 2588.00
Rug, Navajo, Multi Pattern, Red, Cream, Brown, Late 19th Century, 75 x 60 In. 12650.00
Rug, Navajo, Multicolored Yei Dancers, Cream Ground, 34 1/2 x 55 In. 705.00
Rug, Navajo, Multicolored, Storm, Gray Ground, 3-Color Border, 69 1/2 x 47 In. 529.00
Rug, Navajo, Red, Black, Cream, c.1930, 67 x 44 In. 275.00
Rug, Navajo, Red, White, Black, Burnt Orange, Gray, Brown Ground, c.1930, 36 x 55 In. . 940.00
Rug, Navajo, Red, White, Black, Gray, Storm, 1900s, 28 3/4 x 38 1/4 In. 374.00
Rug, Navajo, Serrated Bands, Brown, Red, Tan, Gray, White, c.1920, 50 x 81 In. 520.00
Rug, Navajo, Shiprock, Cattle, Sheep, Trees, Figures, 1900s, 16 1/2 x 29 In. 230.00
Rug, Navajo, Stepped Crosses, Multicolored, Feather, Gray Ground, 66 x 44 In. 650.00
Rug, Navajo, Transformation, Snakes, c.1950, 48 x 39 In. 460.00
Rug, Navajo, Transition, Carded Gray Ground, Bands Of Serrated Diamonds, 42 x 71 In. .. 805.00
Rug, Navajo, Transitional, Red, Orange Ground, Serrated Diamonds, 30 x 48 In. 2070.00
Rug, Navajo, White, Brown, Geometric, 20th Century, 70 x 48 In. 440.00
Rug, Navajo, X-Pattern, Feather, Lightning, Multicolored Ground, 66 x 39 In. 1175.00
Rug, Navajo, Yei Dancers, Feather Headdress, Border, c.1920, 58 x 28 In. 1645.00
Rug, Navajo, Yei Dancers, Red Ground, Triangles At Base, 50 x 144 In. 4025.00
Rug, Navajo, Yei Figures, Arrows, Vegetal Dye, West Reservation Border, 44 x 65 In. 345.00
Saddle Blanket, Navajo, Storm Variant, Spiderwoman Corner Crosses, c.1930 .... 432.00
Sash, Hopi, Germantown, Virginia Mary, c.1920, 90 x 3 3/4 In. 185.00
Sash, Menominee, Beaded, Leaves, Geometric, Early 1900s, 44 1/2 x 3 1/2 In. 315.00
Scoop, Iroquois, Maple, Curved Handle, Beaver Finial, Niagara Falls Area, 4 1/4 In. 9200.00
Shirt, Lakota, Boy's, Beaded Hide, Cloth Lining, Metallic Geometric, 18 1/2 In. 2115.00
Shirt, Lakota, Ghost Dance, Cloth, Fringe, Black Elk, Iowa, c.1950, 21 x 25 In. 345.00
Shirt, Lakota, Men's, Beaded Hide, Calico Lining, Multicolored Geometric, 20 In. 3525.00
Shirt, Sioux, War, Beaded Crosses, Horsehair Drops, Leather Fringe, 51 x 34 In. 4015.00
Shirt, Sioux, War, Buckskin, Quilled, Horsehair Drops, 1970s, 34 x 24 In. 4900.00
Shirt, Winnebago, Calico, Wool Tape Ribbons, Beaded Panels, Leaves, 1900s, 29 In. 2235.00
Skirt, Iroquois, Beaded Cloth, Black Wool Ribbon, Buttons, 29 In. 380.00
Snowshoes, Cree, Red Tufts, c.1870, 42 1/2 In., Pair 220.00
Spoon, Navajo, Whirling Log, Bow, Arrow, Warrior, Feather Bonnet, Spear, 5 3/8 In. 120.00
Spoon, Sioux, Horn, Beaded Leather Handle Wrap, White Heart, Feather, Danglers, 7 In. .. 315.00
Tomahawk, Woodlands, Wood, Metal, Cutout Diamond, Brass Head, Flowers, 20 1/4 In. .. 940.00
Totem, Argillite, Eagle, Bear, Fish, 1930s, 4 In. 520.00
Totem Pole, Northwest Coast, 7 Figures, Eagle Top, c.1950, 17 In. 150.00
Totem Pole, Northwest Coast, Cedar, 3 Figures, Early 1900s, 20 1/2 In. 550.00
Totem Pole, Northwest Coast, Cedar, 4 Figures, L.V.F., c.1950, 16 1/2 In. 375.00
Toy, Horse, Plains, Hide, Sewn, Wool Mane, Horsehair Tail, Painted, Early 1900s, 7 In. ... 1058.00
Trade Beads, Columbia River, 3 Strings, Oregon, Late 1800s, 30 In. 140.00
Tray, Hopi, Basket, Whirlwind Design, 1950s, 15 In. 185.00
Tray, Navajo, Basket, Ceremonial, Geometric, c.1950, 15 1/2 In. 260.00
Tray, Salish, Basket, Round, Imbricated Star, Diamond Border, Handles, 16 In. 175.00
Trousers, Cree, Buckskin, Moccasins, Beaded Bird, Flowers, Leaves, 1900s, 19 x 42 In. .. 690.00
Trousers, Santee Sioux, Hide, Beaded, Flowers, Bird, Heart, Fringe, Late 1800s, 39 In. ... 1035.00
Vase, Acoma, Pottery, Wedding, Multicolored, Early 1900s, 9 x 7 In. 400.00
Vase, Acoma, Wedding, Multicolored, Early 20th Century, Signed, 8 3/4 In. 185.00
Vest, Chippewa, Beaded Edge Band, c.1890, 32 1/2 x 29 1/2 In. 550.00
Vest, Flathead, Beaded, Flowers, Stars, Elk Hide Back, Early 1900s, 19 1/2 x 20 1/2 In. 1610.00

Inkstand, Porcelain,
Beehive Shape,
Applied Flowers,
Jacob Petit, Darte
Freres, 8 In.

Do not display glass inkwells in a
window or sunny location. The
glass may turn slightly purple.

Small nicks and scratches in iron
can be covered with black crayon.
Wipe off the excess with paper.

Vest, Oklahoma, American Flags, Loom Beaded Strips, c.1910, 16 x 15 In. 489.00
Vest, Sioux, Child's, Hide, Flags, Geometric, Sinew, Calico Binding, c.1890, 10 x 12 In. . . 3450.00
Vest, Sioux, Yellow Ocher Hide, Beaded, Flowers, Cloth Lining, 23 In. 1725.00
Wampum, Nez Perce, Clamshell, On String, 1900-50, 48 In. 160.00
War Club, Comanche, Beaded, Flop Top, Early 1900s, 20 In. 115.00
War Club, Sioux, Horse Head, Bead Wrapped Handle, Buffalo Hide, Late 1800s, 18 In. . . . 635.00
War Club, Sioux, Rawhide Wrapped Handle, c.1910, 17 In. 219.00
War Shirt, Plains, Bead Decoration, Tanned Leather, Sinew Sewn, c.1900 . . . . 16500.00

INKSTANDS were made to be placed on a desk. They held some type
of container for ink, and possibly a sander, a pen tray, a pen, a holder
for pounce, and even a candle to melt the sealing wax. Inkstands date
to the eighteenth century and have been made of silver, copper, ceramics, and glass. Additional inkstands may be found in these and other
related categories.

Calamander Wood, Drawer, Cut Glass Jars, Silver Mounts, Handle, Bun Feet, 13 In. 2070.00
Ceramic, Bronze, Figural, Lady, Flowers, Hinged Lid, France 375.00
Ceramic, Snail, White, Red, Black, Gold, Brass Quill Holder, 3 1/2 In. 286.00
Figural, Man & Woman, In Rowboat, Eagle Figurehead, Flag, Porcelain, 9 x 9 In. 2588.00
Gilt Bronze, Oriental Black Lacquer, Napoleon III, Louis XIV Style, 6 x 14 In. 1380.00
Gilt Bronze, Urn, Enameled, Jewels, Oval Tray, Viennese Style, c.1850, 7 1/4 In. 690.00
Mahogany, Banded Inlay, Drawer, Ebonized Finish, 1800s, 9 x 5 x 5 In. 200.00
Porcelain, Beehive Shape, Applied Flowers, Jacob Petit, Darte Freres, 8 In. . . . . Illus 11500.00
Pottery, King George, Head, Gaping Mouth, Brown, Tan, Salt Glaze, 3 In. 920.00
Redware, 3 Wells, Sander, 2 Compartments, Manganese Glaze, Pa., 4 x 3 1/2 x 8 In. 605.00
Salt Glaze, Tan, Brown, Quill Holes, Daniel Lambert, 2 3/4 In. 3069.00
Silver, Edwardian, Cut Glass Wells, Rectangular, Messrs. Carrington, 1914, 12 1/4 In. . . . 1037.00
Silver, George IV, Drawer, Cut Glass Bottles, Joseph Angel, London, 1822, 11 In. 4500.00
Silver, Rectangular, 2 Cut Glass Wells, Edward & John Barnard, 1856, 7 3/4 In. 848.00

INKWELLS, of course, held ink. Ready-made ink was first made
about 1836 and was sold in bottles. The desk inkwell had a narrow
hole so the pen would not slip inside. Inkwells were made of many
materials, such as pottery, glass, pewter, and silver. Look in these categories for more listings of inkwells.

Bakelite, Pen Receptacle, Carved Wooden Soldier Holding Pick, France, 12 1/2 In. 230.00
Brass, Owl Shape, Outstretched Wings, Tilting Head, 20th Century, 4 x 9 1/2 In. 48.00
Bronze, 4 Winged Gargoyles, Raised On Claw Feet, Hinged Cover, Eagle Finial, 9 x 7 In. . 345.00
Bronze, Book Form, Post Office London Directory 1902, Austria 600.00
Bronze, Grand Tour, Baroque Style, Melon-Ribbed Well, Winged Sea Monsters, 6 In. 259.00
Bronze, Louis XVI Style, Puttie, Scrolling Waves, Shells, Bird, c.1860, 7 x 15 x 11 In. 345.00
Bronze, Pen Rest, Combination, 7 1/2 In. 140.00
Bronze, Scarab, Gold Favrile, c.1910, 4 1/8 In. 9560.00
Cast Aluminum, Crab, Well Inside Body, Black, Pan American, 1901, 6 x 6 In. 355.00
Cast Iron, Figural, Pick Up Pen & Inkwell Opens, Newton, 5 x 4 x 8 1/2 In. 935.00
Cast Metal, Embossed, Stylized Pattern, Arts & Crafts, 3 3/4 x 6 1/2 In. 265.00
Cast Metal, Girl, Dog, Bronzed, c.1900, 8 1/2 x 12 In. 750.00

Cast Metal, Owl, Glass Eyes, Original Paint, 4 In. 675.00
Ceramic, Flowers, White Center, Pink Top, Base, Gold Highlights, Perry & Co., 3 In. 39.00
Copper, Applied Gorham Silver, Glass Inserts, Monogram, Spaulding & Co., 12 1/2 In. ... 325.00
Copper, Tray, Arts & Crafts, 10 In. 90.00
Cube, Vicar Of Stow Pattern, Matte Glaze, Copper Cover, Moravian, 4 3/4 x 3 3/4 In. 235.00
Cut Glass, Amber, Square 275.00
Cut Glass, Cobalt Blue, Painted Flowers, Birds 525.00
Glass, Amber Olive, 3-Mold, 2 1/4 In. 115.00
Glass, Blown, Deep Amber, Keene, N.H., c.1830, 1 1/2 x 2 1/4 In. 220.00
Glass, Blown, Olive Amber, 14-Diamond Base, 2 x 2 5/8 In. 155.00
Glass, Bottle Form, Johann Hoff Berlin, Austria 300.00
Glass, Bronze Ram's Head Lid, Rindskopf, c.1890, 5 In. 575.00
Glass, Millefiori, Paperweight Type, Bottle Form, Stopper, Red, Pink, White, England, 6 In. 400.00
Glass, Woman Holding Wells, Metal Covers, Ink Pen, Alabaster Handle, Art Nouveau 430.00
Hammered Copper, Bell Form, Arts & Crafts 70.00
Leather, 2 Inkwells, Pen Brush, Ink Printed On Top 300.00
Leather, Doctor's Bag, Alligator Patterned Leather 525.00
Metal, Camel, Figural, Painted, Glass Insert, 4 x 6 In. 176.00
Patinated Bronze, Military, Drum & Bayonet Rifles, Pad Feet, Russia, 13 x 7 In. 1195.00
Porcelain, Famille Rose, Gold Washed Silver, Jade Top, Finial, Chinese, 4 In. 3910.00
Porcelain, Fox Head, Wood Carving, 19th Century, 5 In. 365.00
Porcelain, Isobath, Reservoir Gum Pot, Green Glaze, Doulton Lambeth, 4 3/4 In. 127.00
Pottery, Circular, Tan, 4 Quill Holes, Cornelies Nitingale, 1847, 2 x 3 In. 470.00
Pottery, Fat Man, Tan, Brown, Salt Glaze, Daniel Lambert, England, 2 1/2 In. 979.00
Pottery, Figural, Baseball, Ball Atop Home Plate, Catcher's Mitt Vessel, c.1910 .... 770.00
Pottery, Lord Brougham, Head, Shoulders, Brown, Salt Glaze, 2 Quill Holes, 3 In. 820.00
Pottery, Lord Brougham, Shells, Improve The Mind, 2-Sided, Quill Holes, Salt Glaze, 3 In. 1705.00
Pottery, Monk, Holding Basket, Brown, Salt Glaze, Harrison, 422 Strand, 3 3/4 In. 685.00
Pottery, Monk, Holding Basket, Quill Hole, Brown, Salt Glaze, 3 3/4 In. 2660.00
Pottery, Mr. Punch, Seated, Tan, Brown, Salt Glaze, Gardners Ink Works, London, 5 In. .. 880.00
Pottery, Reclining Lion, Brown Glaze, Rockingham, 4 3/4 In. 259.00
Pottery, Tree Trunk, Bird's Nest, Tan, Brown, Salt Glaze, England, 3 1/2 In. 295.00
Pressed Glass, 10-Panel Scalloped Dome, 8-Sided Base & Finial, 4 1/4 x 3 1/2 In. 120.00
Redware, Dog, Seated, Raised Paw, Penholder, Brown Glaze, 5 x 7 1/4 x 4 3/4 In. 880.00
Satin Glass, Blue, Quilted, Square 275.00
Silver, Dome Lid, Cut Glass, Swirled, Zipper Design, Flower Repousse Foot, 4 1/2 In. 405.00
Sterling Silver, Flowers, Hammered Background, Hinged Lid, Glass Insert, Square 2 In. .. 575.00
Stoneware, 1/2 Barrel, Salt Glaze, Tyzack & Co., England, 1 3/4 x 3 1/2 x 3 In. 294.00
Stoneware, Brown Glaze, 2 In. 55.00
Stoneware, Pillar Box Shape, White Glaze, Perry & Co., London, 3 1/2 In. 90.00
Tan Salt Glaze, 1/2 Barrel, 2 x 4 x 3 1/2 In. 59.00
Ugly Woman, Bonnet, Projecting Bottom Jaw, Tan Matte Glaze, England, 2 1/2 In. 69.00

INSULATORS of glass or pottery have been made for use on telegraph
or telephone poles since 1844. Thousands of different styles of insulators have been made. Most common are those of clear or aqua glass;
most desirable are the threadless types made from 1850 to 1870.

Brookfield, No. 31, Side Wire Groove, Single Petticoat, Aqua 1.00
Brookfield, No. 38, Side Wire Groove, Double Petticoat, Green Aqua 10.00
Canadian Pacific Ry. Co., Side Wire Groove, Single Petticoat, Slug Embossing, Green 7.50
Chicago Insulating Company, No. 135, Blue 80.00
Diamond, Side Wire Groove, Single Petticoat, Smooth Base, Wrinkly, Yellow Green 14.50
Gaynor, No. 90, Side Wire Groove, Single Petticoat, Sharp Drip Points, Blue Aqua 5.00
Hemingray, No. 8, Side Wire Groove, Single Petticoat, Ice Green 100.00
Hemingray, No. 60, Saddle Wire Grooves, Ice Blue 25.00
Hemingray, No. 63, Saddle Wire Grooves, Hemingray Blue 365.00
McLaughlin, No. 16, Side Wire Groove, Single Petticoat, Dark Green 20.00
Mershon, Umbrella, Side Wire Groove, Triple Petticoat, Dark Aqua 75.00
New Eng. Tel. & Tel. Co., Side Wire Groove, Single Petticoat, Aqua 5.00
Pyrex, No. 401, Embossed Skirt, 1 Piece, Power Style, Carnival To Clear 50.00
Pyrex, No. 453, 1 Piece, Power Style, Light Yellow 30.00
Star, Side Wire Groove, Single Petticoat, Smooth Base, Aqua 9.50

Sterling, Side Wire Groove, Single Petticoat, Smooth Base, Aqua 15.00
W.F.G. Co., No. 16, Side Wire Groove, Single Petticoat, Light Purple 75.00
Whitall Tatum, No. 14, Side Wire Groove, Double Petticoat, Pink 8.00
Willington Glass, 8-Sided, Olive Yellow, Hollow Cone, Bulbous, 5 7/8 x 2 5/8 In. 1100.00

IRISH BELLEEK, see Belleek category.

IRON is a metal that has been used by man since prehistoric times. It is a popular metal for tools and decorative items like doorstops that need as much weight as possible. Items are listed here or under other appropriate headings, such as Bookends, Doorstop, Kitchen, Match Holder, or Tool. The tool that is used for ironing clothes, an iron, is listed in the Kitchen category under Iron and Sadiron.

Aquarium, Victorian, Molded Decoration, 4 Glazed Panels, Cast, 30 x 14 1/2 In. 420.00
Bootjack, Naughty Nellie, Cast, 10 1/2 In. ....165.00 to 198.00
Bootjack, Pistol Shape, Eagle, Wings Spread, Cast Iron, c.1880, 9 1/4 In. 94.00
Bust, Beethoven, Cast, Early 20th Century, 22 In. 316.00
Candleholder, Rush Light, Tripod Base, Adjustable, 30 1/2 To 51 3/4 In. 863.00
Cannon, Signal, Winchester, Cast, Black Paint, W.R.A. Co., 17 x 7 In. 431.00
Censer, Cottage Shape, Thatched Roof, 6-Footed Base, 19th Century, 4 1/2 In. 127.00
Cigar Cutter, Figural, Put Cigar Tip In Man's Mouth, June 16, 1886, 4 x 8 In. 330.00
Cigar Cutter, Pig, Gold Paint, 8 In. 110.00
Cigarette Box, Inlaid Komai Bamboo, Square, Japan, 3 In. 215.00
Cuspidor, Turtle, Bronze Washed Tin Shell, Cast, Chicago, 1890s, 4 x 14 In. 990.00
Door Mat, Heart Designs, Linked, Pa., c.1900, 22 1/2 x 29 1/2 In. 2700.00
Figure, Deer, Painted Brown, Yellow Antlers, Glass Eyes, 16 1/2 x 19 In., Pair 880.00
Figure, Dog, St. Bernard, With Pack, Brown, Gold Trim, A.C. Williams, 5 1/2 x 7 3/4 In. .. 66.00
Figure, Eagle, Wings Spread, Gold Paint, Wood Base, 10 1/2 x 31 x 14 In. 275.00
Figure, Hand, Open, Resting On Molded Base, Wrought, 4 3/4 x 5 x 7 In., Pair 374.00
Figure, Monkey, Seated, Brown, Black, Cast, 8 In., Pair 175.00
Figure, Salamander, Spotted, Cast, Paint Decoration, Black Ground, Gold Spots, 7 x 2 In. . 220.00
Figure, Stable Boy, Wood Base, White, Black, Teal Paint, J.W. Fiske, 31 x 18 x 18 In. 330.00
Hook, Spike Ends, Decorative Scroll Fronts, Wrought Iron, 6 1/2 x 8 x 6 In., Pair 120.00
Plaque, American Eagle, Shield Shape, E Pluribus Unum Banner, Late 1800s, 16 In. 764.00
Safe, Cast, Black, American Eagle & Shield Stencil, 15 1/2 x 16 x 22 In. 374.00
Safe, Cast, Black, Landscape, Owner's Name, Security Safe Co., Chicago, Ill., 22 In. 345.00
Safe, Cast, Black, Landscape, Owner's Name, Vulcan Safe & Lock Co., 16 x 18 x 26 In. .. 489.00
Safe, Cast, Black, Landscape, Reliable Safe & Lock Co. Inc., 19 x 19 x 30 In. 115.00
Safe, Embossed Dog, Family Safe, Patented June 20, 1856, 12 x 14 x 12 In. 2640.00
Shackles, Slave, 2 Hand-Forged Ankle Bands, Joined By 7 Links, 31 In. 600.00
Stove Plate, Peaceable Kingdom Theme, Man, Violin, Animals, Pa., 13 x 17 1/4 In. 2300.00
Windmill Weight, Bull Shape, Raised Letters, Wood Stand, Fairbury, Neb., 19 1/2 x 24 In. 460.00
Windmill Weight, Bull, 2-Piece Cast Body, Simpson Windmill & Machine Co., 14 In. 2185.00
Windmill Weight, Bull, Flat, Brown & White Paint, Fairbury Windmill Co., c.1915, 24 In. 1135.00
Windmill Weight, Rooster, No. 2, Elgin, 17 3/4 In. 575.00
Windmill Weight, Rooster, Painted, White, Red, Yellow, No. 2, 12 x 17 In. 1045.00
Windmill Weight, Rooster, Raised Lettering, 12 x 17 In. 1495.00

IRONSTONE china was first made in 1813. It gained its greatest popularity during the mid-nineteenth century. The heavy, durable, off-white pottery was made in white or was decorated with any of hundreds of patterns. Much flow blue pottery was made of ironstone. Some of the decorations were raised. Many pieces of ironstone are unmarked, but some English and American factories included the word *Ironstone* in their marks. Additional pieces may be listed in other categories, such as Chelsea Grape, Chelsea Sprig, Flow Blue, Gaudy Ironstone, Mason's Ironstone, Moss Rose, Staffordshire, and Tea Leaf Ironstone.

Basket, Stand, Brown Transfer, Pink Luster, Pierced, Birds, Fruit, England, 12 1/4 In. 575.00
Charger, 5-Color, Red Stick Spatter Borders, Flowers, Red Swags, Cobalt Blue, 17 In. 115.00
Charger, Blue Sponge Design, 10 1/8 In. 175.00
Charger, Bordeaux Blue, Flowers, David Johnston, c.1840, 19 In. 189.00
Dish Set, Red Transfer, Teapot, Sugars, Creamers, Cups, Saucers, 16 Piece 130.00

Pitcher, Blue Sponge, 6 1/2 In. 200.00
Pitcher, Paneled Body, Imari Colors, Late 19th Century, 8 1/2 In. 115.00
Plate, Dinner, Ashworth Brothers, Gilt, Multicolored, Imari Style, 11 In., 8 Piece 1380.00
Platter, Cut Corner, Imari Colors, Trees, Flowers, 17 x 12 3/4 In. 259.00
Platter, Flowers, White Glaze, Oval, England, Late 1800s, 17 1/2 In. 60.00
Platter, Meat, Blue Transfer, Flowers, Over Enameled, Pink, Yellow, Red, c.1875, 21 In. . . 235.00
Platter, Simlay, Oval, Multicolored, Green, Yellow, Rose, Gold, 16 x 19 In. 360.00
Platter, Well & Tree, Leaves, Flowers, Scalloped Rim, England, c.1850, 17 x 20 3/4 In. . . 115.00
Syrup, Bennetts, Embossed Flowers, 7 3/4 In. 92.00
Tureen, Cover, Red Cliff, Paneled Pedestal, Underplate, Early 20th Century, 12 In. 175.00
Tureen, Dome Lid, Oval Fluted Finial, Twig Handles, Pedestal, c.1900, 11 x 14 In........ 200.00

IVORY from the tusk of an elephant is thought by many to be the only
true ivory. To most collectors, the term *ivory* also includes such natural
materials as walrus, hippopotamus, or whale teeth or tusks, and some
of the vegetable materials that are of similar texture and density. Other
ivory items may be found in the Scrimshaw and Netsuke categories.
Collectors should be aware of the recent laws limiting the buying and
selling of elephant ivory and scrimshaw.

Box, Figures In Boat, Birds, Flowers, Butterflies, Multicolored, Late 1800s, 3 3/4 In. 405.00
Box, Makeup, Travelers Beneath Mt. Fuji, Japan, 2 3/4 In. 175.00
Brushpot, Dragons, Pierced Ground, 4 3/4 In. 260.00
Brushpot, Landscape, Cylinder, Engraved, Calligraphy, Stand, Chinese, 18th Century, 5 In. 575.00
Brushpot, Maidens, Engraved, Calligraphy, 5 3/4 In. 570.00
Buckle, Belt, Relief Carved, Flower Of Bacchus, Silver Mounted, Canada, 2 3/4 In. 275.00
Button, Figural, Seal, Inuit, c.1900, 3 Piece 450.00
Candleholder, Silver, 2 Sockets, Column, Arabesques, India, 19th Century, 21 1/2 In...... 335.00
Card Case, Figures, Landscape, Rectangular, Chinese, Early 19th Century, 4 1/2 In. 690.00
Card Case, Figures, Southern Landscape, Chinese, 1800s, 4 1/4 In. 340.00
Card Case, Ornate Figures, Landscape, 4 1/2 In. 690.00
Cricket Cage, Gourd, Pierced Cover, Dragon, Lattice, Chinese, 19th Century, 4 In. 295.00
Cup, Coconut Shell, Figures, Silver Mounted, Ivory Finial, 3-Footed, c.1810, 6 In. 1265.00
Cup, Scene, Courting Couple, Putti, Landscape, Stream, Continental, c.1885, 5 In. 705.00
Elephant Tusk, African Figures, 38 In. 750.00
Elephant Tusk, Pagodas, Figures, Boats, Trees, Teak Stand, 30 1/2 In. 978.00
Figurine, 2 Asian Women With Lotus Branches, Mid 20th Century, 12 In. 575.00
Figurine, Actor Holding Fan, Mask, Multicolored, Signed, Japan, 6 1/2 In. 520.00
Figurine, Armored Woman Warrior On Horse, Sword, Bow, Spear, 19th Century, 9 In. 690.00
Figurine, Armorer Fashioning Kendo Helmet, Signed, 2 1/2 In. 210.00
Figurine, Bearded Mandarin Seated On Throne, 19th Century, 5 1/4 In. 1956.00
Figurine, Bearded Wise Man, Caramel Patina, Asian, Early 20th Century, 14 In. 805.00
Figurine, Carved, Buddhist Lion, Puzzle Ball, Chinese, 13 In., Pair 1015.00
Figurine, Carved, Meiren, Holding Ruyi Scepter & Peony, Chinese, 15 In. 2270.00
Figurine, Carved, Phoenix, Perched On Peony Blossoms, Chinese, 14 In., Pair 1795.00
Figurine, Carved, Warrior, Dressed In Armor, Chinese, 8 In. 720.00
Figurine, Carved, Warrior, On Chariot, Tilework Base, Chinese, 12 In., Pair 2150.00
Figurine, Carved, Warrior, Sword Raised, Chinese, 8 3/4 In. 658.00
Figurine, Carved, Women Playing Instruments, Clouds, Chinese, 11 1/2 In. 1195.00
Figurine, Cherub, Feathered Cap, Kneeling By Rose Bush, c.1875, 3 5/8 In. 470.00
Figurine, Cherub, Nude, Standing, Continental, c.1975, 8 3/8 In. 2000.00
Figurine, Doctor's Lady, Woman Holding Fan, Wearing Shoes, Sofa Stand, c.1900, 21 In. . 4025.00
Figurine, Doctor's Lady, Woman Lying On Palm Leaf, 5 3/4 In. 900.00
Figurine, Doctor's Lady, Woman Wearing Shoes, Bracelets, 10 1/4 In. 345.00
Figurine, Doll Maker, Shoki Doll, Youth, 3 In. 1785.00
Figurine, Elephant Tusk, Oriental Figures, Landscape, 19th Century, 4 x 3 In. 230.00
Figurine, Elephant, Raised Trunk, 1900s, 3 1/2 In. 259.00
Figurine, Elephant, Rampant, Standing On Ball, 8 1/2 In. 390.00
Figurine, Elephant, Walking, Trunk Down, Japan, 3 1/4 In. 315.00
Figurine, Emperor, Empress Seated On Thrones, Coral, Turquoise, Chinese, 6 In., Pair 1035.00
Figurine, Fisherman, Standing, Casting Net Into Waves, Japan, 6 1/4 In. 290.00
Figurine, Flute Player, Exotic Wood Base, 8 3/4 In. 180.00
Figurine, Jovial Nobleman, Incised, Multicolored, Asia, 20th Century, 8 In. 345.00
Figurine, Lobster, Articulated, Japan, c.1900, 8 1/2 In. 355.00

Figurine, Man, Fruit, Vegetables, Signed, Japan, 5 In. 1150.00
Figurine, Man, Straw Apron, Holding Basket Of Fish, Signed, Shunzan, Japan, 7 1/4 In. ... 750.00
Figurine, Man, Woman Carrying Peony Blossom, Basket, Chinese, 20 In. 1925.00
Figurine, Peasant Carrying 2 Sticks, Signed, Japan, 6 3/4 In. 750.00
Figurine, Phallus, Carved, 4 Japanese Figures, Kimono Designs, 3 3/8 In. 750.00
Figurine, Putto, Grasping Wheat, Grapes, Inscribed, Early 19th Century, 4 1/4 In. 550.00
Figurine, Sennin Standing By Tree Stump, Ringing Bells, Japan, 4 In. 460.00
Figurine, Virgin, Carved, Round, Glass Eyes, Goanese, 18th Century, 5 In. 1725.00
Figurine, Woman, Carrying Purse, Umbrella, Chinese, 8 3/8 In. 375.00
Figurine, Woman, Holding Basket, Flowers, Chinese, 12 1/2 In. 590.00
Figurine, Woman, Holding Branch, Man, Holding Staff, Japan, c.1850, 9 3/4 In., Pair 5175.00
Figurine, Woman, With Child Holding Lute, Japan, 19th Century, 4 1/4 In. 325.00
Group, 3 Graces, Oval Socket, Continental, 8 In. 1850.00
Group, Boy Feeding Cranes, Signed, Japan, 3 1/2 In. 660.00
Group, Buddhist Monks Holding Duck, Prunus, Lotus, Chrysanthemums, Chinese, 10 In. . 25.00
Group, Crab Trap, Woven, Crabs Among Water Weeds, Wood Stand, Japan, 6 1/2 In. 1000.00
Group, Figures Climbing Mountain, 1736-95, 13 1/2 In. 1090.00
Group, Lilies Of The Valley, Oval Jardiniere, Early 1900s, 5 1/2 In. 259.00
Group, Man, Woman, Raised On Hardwood Pedestal, 7 In., Pair 3885.00
Group, Mary Queen Of Scots, Round, Hinged Dress, France, 1800s, 8 In. 6325.00
Group, Nativity, Manger, Multicolored, Gilding, Wood Base, 12 x 7 In. 6325.00
Group, Oriental, Floating Palace, Attendants, Stylized Wave Wood Stand, 9 In. 920.00
Group, Red Lilies, Oval Jardiniere, Wood Stand, Early 1900s, 3 3/4 In. 160.00
Group, Tiger Lilies, Oval Jardiniere, Wood Stand, Early 1900s, 4 1/4 In. 230.00
Group, Virgin & Child, Round, Multicolored, Baroque, Flemish, 18th Century, 4 In. 805.00
Group, Virgin & Child, Round, Spanish Colonial, 18th Century, 3 In. 750.00
Group, Woman, Attendant, Wearing Fan, Robe, Tree Peony, Early 1900s, 17 1/2 In. 335.00
Group, Woman, Holding Parasol, Bucket, Boy, Japan, 7 In. 980.00
Hippo Tusk, Carved, Men, Women, European Clothing, 12 In. 1000.00
Incense Burner, Carved Dragon, Phoenix Panels, Coral, Turquoise, Stand, Chinese, 7 In. . 89.00
Jar, Carved, Dragon Handle, Phoenix Spout, Pierced Cover, Dragon, Chinese, 14 In. 1075.00
Knife, Silver Handle, Chased, Embossed, Boy Blowing Horn, Birds, Scrolls, House, 16 In. 295.00
Letter Opener, Bust, Military Man, Acanthus Over Blade, Continental, c.1880, 13 In. 470.00
Luck Gods Set, Wood Stand, Japan, Early 20th Century 430.00
Miniature, Portrait, Young Girl, White Dress, Necklace, Case, Frame, 4 x 3 3/4 In. 1006.00
Necklace, 11 Stylized Heads, Black Glass Bead Spacers, Africa 1000.00
Needle Case, Dragon & Cloud, Carved, Chinese, c.1830, 6 In. 230.00
Okimono, Basket Seller, Signed, Japan, 1900s, 6 1/4 In. 575.00
Okimono, Emma, Tea Stained, Parcel Gilt, Signed, 1912-25, 11 In. 1955.00
Okimono, Farmer, Baggy Pants, Jacket, Lantern, Japan, c.1900, 12 1/2 In. 1495.00
Okimono, Father & Child, Smiling, Basket At Waist, Holding Boy, Japan, c.1900, 7 In. ... 545.00
Okimono, Fisherman, Bronze, Wood Stand, Signed, Japan, 19th Century, 14 In. 1840.00
Okimono, Fisherman, Japan, 19th Century, 9 3/4 In. 3680.00
Okimono, Horned Demon, Holding Rat, Japan, 2 1/2 In. 1495.00
Okimono, Hunter, Flintlock Rifle, Patterned Jacket, Monkey, Goose, Japan, c.1900, 20 In. . 5037.00
Okimono, Immortal, Man, Beard, Holding Staff, Signed, Japan, 1900s, 3 1/2 In. 260.00
Okimono, Immortals, Rock, Dragon, Clouds, Tiger, 2 Monkeys, Japan, c.1900 .... 840.00
Okimono, Man, Gamecock, Signed, Japan, 1900s, 6 In. 345.00
Okimono, Man, Net Of Fish, Signed, Japan, 1900s, 6 In. 230.00
Okimono, Mice, Signed Masamitsu, Japan, Early 20th Century 1060.00
Okimono, Monkeys, Rocks, Chounsai & Gyokumin, Japan, c.1900, 8 1/4 In. 795.00
Okimono, Wood Cutter, Wife, Child, Hardstone, 3 1/2 In. 240.00
Okimono, Wood Cutter, Wood, Japan, 19th Century, 12 1/2 In. 1840.00
Paginator, Spatulate Blade, Carved, Oni, With Bag, Fan, On Rock, c.1893, 13 1/2 In. 840.00
Panel, Figures, Flower Border, Velvet Mounted, Chinese, 1800s, 6 x 12 In. 1610.00
Paper Knife, Ray Skin Design, Turquoise Inlay, 19th Century, 13 1/4 In. 400.00
Pendant, 3 Figures, Wrestling Fish, Chinese, c.1950, 2 1/2 x 1 1/2 In. 140.00
Pie Crimper, Bone, Shell Inlay, 2 Diamond Shapes, Heart Shape, 6 1/4 In. 185.00
Plaque, Nativity, Adoration Of The Angels, Deep Relief, 19th Century, 7 x 5 In. 1265.00
Sculpture, Girl, Alabaster Tray, D. Chiparus, 5 In. 2115.00
Shoehorn, Horse-Hoof Handle, Brass Shoe Nails, Leather Loop, France, 1930s, 21 In. 175.00
Spectacles Case, Nickel Mounted, Carved, Double Compartment, 1800s, 1 x 6 x 3 In. 520.00
Trumpet, Warrior Figures, Curved Tapered Form, Scroll, Dark Patina, Africa, 28 In. 5875.00

Vase, Cover, Lion Mask & Ring Handles, Early 20th Century, 13 In., Pair 1380.00
Watch Case, Jasperware Mounted, Medallion, Female Silhouettes, c.1900, 1 x 2 x 3 In. 260.00
Wrist Rest, Tree Branch, Plum Blossoms, Insects, Chinese, c.1800, 9 In. 1840.00

JACK ARMSTRONG, the all-American boy, was the hero of a radio serial from 1933 to 1951. Premiums were offered to the listeners until the mid-1940s. Jack Armstrong's best-known endorsement is for Wheaties.

Advertisement, Wheaties, Box Panel, Cardboard, 8 1/4 x 6 1/8 In. 190.00
Airplane, Tru-Flite, Spitfire, FW-190, Paper, Uncut, 1944 .... 35.00
Big Little Book, Ivory Treasure, General Mills, 1937 .... 16.00
Game, Adventures With Dragon Talisman, Wheaties, Envelope, 1936, 7 x 11 In. 1185.00
Pedometer, Hike-O-Meter, Wheaties Premium, 1938, 2 5/8 In. 35.00
Pre-Flight Training Kit, Wheaties, Envelope, 1945, 6 1/2 x 10 1/2 In. 200.00
Ring, Dragon's Eye, Glow-In-The-Dark, Green Center, 1940 .... 150.00
Ring, Dragon's Eye, Wheaties, Mailer, 1940, 2 1/4 x 3 In. 900.00
Telescope, Explorer, Metal, Black Paper, Premium, 6 3/4 In. Closed 20.00

JACK-IN-THE-PULPIT vases, oddly shaped like trumpets, resemble the wild plant called jack-in-the-pulpit. The design originated in the late Victorian years. Vases in the jack-in-the-pulpit shape were made of ceramic or glass, and the complete list of page references can be found in the index.

Vase, Gold Ground, Pulled Feather, 12 In. 920.00
Vase, Iridescent Gold, Crackle Face, Signed, Lundberg, 10 3/4 In. 259.00
Vase, Ivrene, 6 1/2 In., Pair 805.00

JADE is the name for two different minerals, nephrite and jadeite. Nephrite is the mineral used for most early Oriental carvings. Jade is a very tough stone that is found in many colors from dark green to pale lavender. Jade carvings are still being made in the old styles, so collectors must be careful not to be fooled by recent pieces. Jade jewelry is found in this book under Jewelry.

Bowl, Allover Scales, Flower Handle Rings, Cover, Ball Finial, Mythological Figures, 6 In. 635.00
Bowl, Double, Relief Carving, 4 Children, White, c.1800, 10 1/4 In. 6325.00
Bowl, Lion's Head, Loose Ring Handles, Gourd, Vines, Leaves, Insect, Inverted Rim, 7 In. 3450.00
Brush, Black Mounts, Wooden Case, Sliding Cover, White, 8 3/4 In., Pair 460.00
Brush Handle Set, Nephrite, Various Stones, Chinese, 19th Century, 3 In., 5 Piece 170.00
Brush Rest, Mountain, Deer Carving, Celadon, 19th Century, 4 1/4 In. 360.00
Censer, Cover, Dragon Handles, Leaves, Peony Finial, Green, Stand, Chinese, 11 In. 9600.00
Cup, Chrysanthemum Form, Flower Handles, White, 5 1/2 In., Pair 70.00
Dish, Chrysanthemum Blossom, White, Translucent, Mogul Style, c.1800, 7 1/4 In. 2415.00
Dish, Lotus Form, Transparent, Spinach Green, 4 In. 630.00
Figurine, Buddhist Lion, Detachable Heads, Jadeite, Chinese, Early 1800s, 6 3/4 In., Pair . 1400.00
Figurine, Dog, Lying Down, Snarling, Pale Green, Nephrite, Chinese, 1800s, 2 In. 170.00
Figurine, Horse, Drinking In River, Patterned Saddle Blanket, Nephrite, Green Stone, 7 In. 1345.00
Figurine, Hound, Reclining, Translucent, 5 In. 705.00
Figurine, Lion, Reclining, Black, White, 2 1/2 In. 185.00
Figurine, Meijin, Holding Scroll, Wood Stand, 7 In. 185.00
Figurine, Meijin, With Brazier, Wood Stand, 6 1/2 In. 115.00
Figurine, Meiren, Apple Green, Wooden Base, Mounted As Lamp, Chinese, 5 3/4 In. 980.00
Figurine, Rooster, Holding Jui Fungus, White, 20th Century, 3 In. 2160.00
Figurine, Woman, Holding Peony, Nephrite, Fly Whisk, Openwork Wood Base, 15 In. 2940.00
Figurine, Woman, Lavender, Green, Tan, 6 1/4 In. 355.00
Hairpin, Ju-I Form, Off-White, 5 1/4 In. 69.00
Jar, White, Speckled, Urn Shape, Lion's Head Handles, Domed Cover, Lion, 3-Footed, 6 In. 805.00
Kueh, Dragon Handle, Phoenix Spout, Spinach Green, 20th Century, 5 In. 920.00
Mirror, Hand, Metal Mounted, Gourd & Vine Pattern, Nephrite, Dragon, Hydra, 10 In. 756.00
Paper Knife, Spatulate Blade, Archaic Characters, Gray, Green, Chinese, 1900s, 12 1/2 In. . 1215.00
Pendant, Gray, 2 Squirrels, 1 3/4 In. 115.00
Pendant, Monkey, Nephrite, Playing On Rock, Flowers, Chinese, 19th Century, 2 1/2 In. .. 210.00
Snuff Bottle, Green Stone, Chinese, 19th Century 295.00
Snuff Bottle, Green, Red, White Jade Top, Gilt Engraved Metal Mounts, Early 1900s 530.00

Tray, Oriental, Carved, Leaf Shape, Figural Frog, Snails, 19th Century, 3 1/2 In. 370.00
Vase, Cover, Celadon, Carved Lyres, Leaves, Urn Shape, Mythological Animals, 7 In. 520.00
Vase, Cover, Leaves, Dragon Finial, Handles, Animal Foot, White, 20th Century, 6 In. 570.00
Vase, Hu Shape, Celadon Color, White Striations, Brown Markings, Chinese, 7 In. 1295.00
Vase, Oriental, Mutton Fat Nephrite, Cover, Dragon Handles, Rings, Wood Base, 7 1/2 In. .   230.00
Water Coupe, Green, Mughal Style Carving, Peach, Leaves, 5 x 4 In. 2940.00

JAPANESE WOODBLOCK PRINTS are listed in this book in the Print category under
Japanese.

JASPERWARE can be made in different ways. Some pieces are made
from a solid colored clay with applied raised designs of a contrasting
colored clay. Other pieces are made entirely of one color clay with
raised decorations that are glazed with a contrasting color. Additional
pieces of jasperware may also be listed in the Wedgwood category or
under various art potteries.

Bowl, Indian Hunting 2 Mountain Lions, Green, White, Marked, c.1900, 6 1/2 x 5 In. 270.00
Flask, Eagle, Banner, Stars, Glass Lined, 4 1/4 x 3 In. 210.00
Pin Tray, Indian Chief On Horse, Rifle, Blue, White, 6 In. 275.00
Pin Tray, Indian Drawing Bow, Green, White, Marked, c.1900, 6 x 5 1/4 In. 225.00
Plaque, Cherubs, Fan Shape, Blue, Germany, 15 In. 200.00
Plaque, Light Blue, Oval, Applied White Relief, 3 Putti, Frame, 19th Century, 4 1/2 In. . . .   590.00

JEWELRY, whether made from gold and precious gems or plastic and
colored glass, is popular with collectors. Values are determined by the
intrinsic value of the stones and metal and by the skill of the craftsmen
and designers. Victorian and older jewelry have been collected since
the 1950s. More recent interests are Art Deco and Edwardian styles,
Mexican and Danish silver jewelry, and beads of all kinds. Copies of
almost all styles are being made. American Indian jewelry is listed in
the Indian category. Tiffany jewelry is listed here.

Belt, Celestial, Crystal Stars, Moons, Tiger's-Eye, Carnelian, Onyx Beads, Judith Leiber . .   1265.00
Belt, Diamond Shaped Buckle, 8 Blue Glass Cabochons, Gold Metal, 1980s, 39 In. . . *Illus*   75.00
Bracelet, 3 Diamonds, 14K Gold Bar Links, Art Deco, c.1935, 7 In. 764.00
Bracelet, 5 Square Cut Blue Sapphires, 32 Diamonds, 14K Gold, David Yurman 2070.00
Bracelet, 29 Old Mine Diamonds, Emerald, 18K Gold, Art Deco, 6 3/4 In. 1528.00
Bracelet, 44 Old Mine Diamonds, Platinum, Scrolled, Art Deco, 6 3/4 In. 3525.00
Bracelet, 58 Full Cut Diamonds, Sapphire, Platinum, Art Deco, Box 6169.00
Bracelet, 59 French Cut Sapphires, Engraved Edges, 18K White Gold, c.1935, 7 In. 2468.00
Bracelet, 120 Diamonds, Baroque Pearls, White Gold, Art Deco, 7 In. 1610.00
Bracelet, 405 Round Diamonds, Platinum Open Links, Art Deco, 7 In. 7480.00
Bracelet, Asymmetrical, Signed, Nancy Linkin, 18K, 7 1/4 In. 765.00
Bracelet, Bakelite, Bangle, Apple Juice, Rhinestone, Hinged, 6 1/4 In. 560.00
Bracelet, Bakelite, Bangle, Licorice, Acorns, Oak Leaves, Carved, Wide, 7 3/4 In. 265.00
Bracelet, Bakelite, Bangle, Swirl, Green, Yellow, 8 In. 129.00
Bracelet, Bakelite, Butterscotch, Hinged, Triangles, Multicolor, Philadelphia, 6 1/2 In. 3525.00
Bracelet, Bakelite, Red & 2 Cream Inlays, Bar & Circle, 3 1/4 In.   230.00
Bracelet, Bangle, 3 Square Cut Peridots, 14K Gold, Art Nouveau 499.00
Bracelet, Bangle, 14K Yellow Gold, 11 Round Cut Diamonds, c.1950 . . . .   865.00
Bracelet, Bangle, 120 Diamonds, Emeralds, Platinum, 14K White Gold, T.B. Starr 4115.00
Bracelet, Bangle, Child's, Wood, Flowers, Leaves, 18K Gold, China, 1910 . . . .   235.00

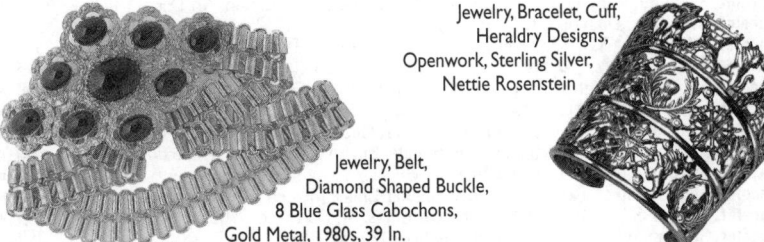

Jewelry, Bracelet, Cuff,
Heraldry Designs,
Openwork, Sterling Silver,
Nettie Rosenstein

Jewelry, Belt,
Diamond Shaped Buckle,
8 Blue Glass Cabochons,
Gold Metal, 1980s, 39 In.

Jewelry, Bracelet, Link, Morpho Butterfly Wings,
Reverse Painted Glass, Silver, 1970s, 7 1/2 In.

Jewelry, Necklace,
Hammered Sterling
Silver, Glass Cabochon,
Rafael Alfandary, c.1975

Bracelet, Bangle, Diamond, Enamel, Inscription, Tiffany, Box, c.1866, 5 3/8 In. 2468.00
Bracelet, Bangle, Diamonds, 14K Gold, c.1885 . . . . 1495.00
Bracelet, Bangle, Hinged, Bicolor Gold, Wirework, Etruscan Revival, 14K Gold 590.00
Bracelet, Bangle, Hinged, Flowers, Black Enamel, 14K Gold, Victorian 470.00
Bracelet, Bangle, Hinged, Quatrefoil Wirework, 14K Gold, Etruscan Revival 558.00
Bracelet, Bangle, Hinged, Ruby, Emerald, Sapphire, 14K Gold, c.1950 . . . . 529.00
Bracelet, Bangle, Leaf, 14K Gold, Etruscan Revival, Pair 1763.00
Bracelet, Bangle, Sterling Silver, Polished Cube, Rutilated Quartz, G. Jensen, Denmark . . . 466.00
Bracelet, Bangle, Stylized Lotus Blossoms, Turquoise, Art Nouveau, 1887 . . . . 1058.00
Bracelet, Bead Set, 119 Diamonds, Platinum, Art Deco, 6 7/8 In. 5581.00
Bracelet, Beadwork, Engraved, 18K Gold, Etruscan Revival, c.1880, Pair 1495.00
Bracelet, Box Set, Full Cut Diamond Melee, Bar Links, Engraved Flowers, Art Deco, 7 In. 2468.00
Bracelet, Braided Cuff, Applied Bead, Wirework, 18K Gold, Victorian 646.00
Bracelet, Cabochon Green Quartz Ovals, Pearls, 14K Gold Rope Twist, c.1960, 7 In. 316.00
Bracelet, Charm, 14K Yellow Gold Links, Mesh Band, 8 Charms, c.1960, 7 In. 1725.00
Bracelet, Charm, Sterling, 11 Current Affair Figures, c.1920, 7 In. 69.00
Bracelet, Crystal, Scottie, Reverse, Links, 14K Gold, Enos Richardson, 7 3/8 In. 1410.00
Bracelet, Cuff, Heraldry Designs, Openwork, Sterling Silver, Nettie Rosenstein . . . . . *Illus* 86.00
Bracelet, Cuff, Ram's Head, Coiled Wirework, 18K Gold, Etruscan Revival 1528.00
Bracelet, Earrings, 4 Enameled Ladybugs, 18K Gold, Cartier, 7 1/4 In. 2940.00
Bracelet, Earrings, Quatrefoil Links, 18K Gold, Van Cleef & Arpels, 7 1/2-In. Bracelet . . . 2585.00
Bracelet, Figure 8, Diamond Melee, 18K Bicolor Gold, Paloma Picasso, Tiffany, 7 In. 1295.00
Bracelet, Flexible, 14K Gold, Tiffany & Co., c.1940, 7 1/2 x 1 In. 865.00
Bracelet, Flexible, 14K Yellow & Rose Gold, Austria, c.1940, 7 1/4 x 1 1/4 In. 800.00
Bracelet, Flexible, 31 Garnets, Flower Clasp, 14K Gold, c.1950, 7 1/4 x 1 In. 690.00
Bracelet, Flexible, Arched & Straight Links, Retro, 18K Gold, c.1940, 7 3/4 In. 750.00
Bracelet, Flexible, Citrine, Retro, 14K Gold, c.1940, 6 1/2 In. 460.00
Bracelet, Flexible, Diamond, Blue Sapphire, 14K White Gold, Art Deco, c.1930, 7 In. 1035.00
Bracelet, Flowers, Sterling Silver, Agate, Laurence Foss, 7 1/4 In. 500.00
Bracelet, Garnet, 9 Links, 14K Gold, Art Deco, c.1920, 6 3/4 In. 575.00
Bracelet, Link, Morpho Butterfly Wings, Reverse Painted Glass, Silver, 1970s, 7 1/2 In. *Illus* 25.00
Bracelet, Lion Mask, Diamond, Ruby, 10K Gold, Late 1800s, 7 1/2 In. 546.00
Bracelet, Onyx, Diamonds, Mesh, 14K Gold, Edwardian, c.1915, 7 In. 635.00
Bracelet, Pearl, Diamond, Crossover, Enamel, 18K Gold, Victorian, c.1880 . . . . 1095.00
Bracelet, Platinum, Diamonds, Rectangular, Full Cut, c.1950, 7 1/2 In. 8815.00
Bracelet, Platinum, Marquise, Baguette, Full & Single-Cut Diamonds, 1940s, 6 3/4 In. . . . 7050.00
Bracelet, Ruby, Diamond, 18K Gold, Art Deco 750.00
Bracelet, Sapphire, Ruby Leaves, Diamonds, Diamond Links, Platinum, Art Deco, 7 In. . . 7050.00
Bracelet, Sapphires, Diamond, 15K Gold, c.1890 . . . . 515.00
Bracelet, Silver Gilt, Claw Set, Oval Cut Amethysts, William IV, 6 1/2 In. 530.00
Bracelet, Smoky Quartz, 7 Links, 18K Gold, Edwardian, c.1910, 7 In. 1095.00
Bracelet, Square Links, Frosted Crystal, Round Brilliant Cut Diamond, Art Deco, c.1940 . 690.00
Bracelet, Sterling Silver, Abalone, Pearls, Signed, Rebajes 355.00
Bracelet, Sterling Silver, Agate, Leaf Links, No. 11, Georg Jensen, 1933-44, 7 1/2 In. 470.00
Bracelet, Sterling Silver, Carnelian, Round Florets, Engraved Clasp, Laurence Foss, 8 In. . 500.00
Bracelet, Sterling Silver, Cobalt Blue Enamel, Gucci 295.00
Bracelet, Sterling Silver, Double Edge Rectangular Links, Mexico 310.00
Bracelet, Sterling Silver, Enamel, Flower, Leaf Links, M. De Taxco, 7 1/2 In. 235.00
Bracelet, Sterling Silver, Hand Wrought, Applied Designs, Bjarne, 7 In. 382.00

Bracelet, Sterling Silver, Overlapping Square Links, Niels Erik, Denmark 310.00
Cigarette Case, Bird, Trellising Vine, 14K Gold, c.1885, 4 x 3 In. 1095.00
Cigarette Case, Black Onyx, Enamel, Diamond, Carnelain, France, Art Deco, c.1925, 3 In. 2070.00
Cigarette Case, Enamel, Branches, Engraved Flowers, Green, 18K Gold, Art Deco 1530.00
Cigarette Case, Florentine, Flowers, Vine, 14K Gold, Art Deco, c.1885, 3 1/2 x 3 In. 690.00
Cigarette Case, Gold, Basket Weave, Herringbone, Rectangular, Continental, 1900s, 4 In. . 1037.00
Cigarette Case, Gold, Rectangular, Hinged Lid, Continental, 1900s, 3 1/2 In. 1980.00
Cigarette Case, Horizontal Bands, Initials, 14K Gold, c.1950, 2 7/8 In. 550.00
Cuff Links, 2 Engraved Circles, Gold Bar, 14K Yellow Gold, Onyx Cabochon, Pair 230.00
Cuff Links, Coin, Helmeted Roman, 18K Gold, Signed, Wiese 2000.00
Cuff Links, Double Link, Leaves, Oval, 14K Gold, Art Nouveau 380.00
Cuff Links, Double Link, Roaring Lion, 14K Gold, Art Nouveau 470.00
Cuff Links, Greek Key, Diamond, 14K Gold, Art Nouveau, Durand & Co. 765.00
Cuff Links, Romanoff Crown, Silver, Diamond, Enamel, 14K Gold, 1900s, 3/4 In. 748.00
Cuff Links, Romanoff Crown, Silver, Diamond, Enamel, Garnet, 14K Gold, 1900s 805.00
Cuff Links, Round, Chased, Diamonds, 14K White Gold, 20th Century, Pair 50.00
Cuff Links, Sterling Silver, Oval 18K Gold Floral Inserts, Georg Jensen 390.00
Cuff Links, Sterling Silver, Tortoiseshell, William Spratling 294.00
Cuff Links, Tragedy & Comedy Masks, 18K Gold, Art Nouveau 940.00
Earrings, Blossom Spray, Diamond, 18K Gold, Clip-On, Mario Buccellati, Box 4994.00
Earrings, Citrine, Ruby, 14K Gold, Clip-On, c.1940, 1 In. 460.00
Earrings, Diamond, Blue Chalcedony, Ribbed, Half Loop, Silver, Gold, D. Yurman 765.00
Earrings, Diamonds, Ribbed Clusters, 18K Gold, H. Stern, 1 In. 2300.00
Earrings, Gold, Cultured Pearls, Flattened Ribbon, 18K Gold, Signed, Janiye 360.00
Earrings, Mabe Pearls, Basket Weave Border, 18K Gold, Diana Kim, England 558.00
Earrings, Malachite Cabochon, 18K Gold Frame, Signed, Schlumberger 940.00
Earrings, Oval Garnet, Diamond Melee, Platinum, Cathy Waterman 1880.00
Earrings, Pendant, Chalcedony, Coral Beads, Marcasite, Onyx, Pagoda, Fahrner 2940.00
Earrings, Pendant, Drop, Coral, Pearls, 14K Gold, c.1890 . . . . 920.00
Earrings, Platinum, Diamond, 14K Gold, Clip-On, Art Deco, c.1930, 1 x 1/2 In. 575.00
Earrings, Round Wirework, Silver Ball, Beads, Sterling Silver, Kalo Shop, 5/8 In. 195.00
Earrings, Shell, Turquoise, Banded 14K Gold, Signed, Seaman Schepps 1060.00
Earrings, Silver, Ruby, Diamond, 14K Gold, Russian Style, 1900s, 1 In. 570.00
Earrings, Single Leaf, Domed, Chased Veins, Screwback, Kalo Shop, 7/8 In. 235.00
Earrings, Sterling Silver, Wire Frame, Leaf & Bead, Screwback, Gilbert Oakes, 5/8 In. . . . 900.00
Earrings, Turquoise Beads, Tassels, 14K Yellow Gold, Victorian, 1 3/4 In. 235.00
Hatpins are listed in this book in the Hatpin category.
Lavaliere, Bow, Oval Garland, Platinum, Diamond, Edwardian, Tiffany, Box, 16 1/2 In. . . . 6170.00
Lavaliere, Platinum, Diamond, Trace Link Chain, Edwardian, 15 1/2 In. 3290.00
Lavaliere Pin, Platinum, Diamond, Pearls, Bog Oak, Art Deco, c.1925, 2 x 2 x 1 In. 2300.00
Locket, Blond Girl, Enamel, Diamond, Seed Pearls, Platinum, Edwardian, 15K Gold 880.00
Locket, Blossoms, Multicolored Enamel, 18K Gold, Openwork, Victorian 999.00
Locket, Blue Enamel, Seed Pearl Drop, Open Face, c.1910 . . . . 400.00
Locket, Cabochon Sapphire, Oval, Mirror, 14K Gold, Edwardian, 25 In. 325.00
Locket, Diamond, Bicolor, Pierced Flowers, 18K Gold, Victorian 500.00
Locket, Gold, Chased Border, Seed Pearls, Woman's Portrait, 20th Century, 1 1/2 In. 294.00
Locket, Heart Shape, Lion's Head, Diamond In Mouth, 14K Gold, Victorian, 1 1/2 In. 200.00
Locket, Round, Winged Lion Holding Tablet, Rubies, 18K Gold, Signed, Nardi 529.00
Locket, Sunburst, Diamond, Pearls, Cobalt Blue Enamel, Oval, 14K Gold, Victorian 1265.00
Necklace, 58 Cultured Pearls, Silver Box Clasp, Silk Pouch, Mikimoto, 16 1/2 In. 705.00
Necklace, 86 Cultured Pearls, Platinum, Diamond, 2 Strands, Box Clasp, Tiffany, 16 In. . . . 1410.00
Necklace, 95 Round Brilliant Cut Diamonds, 14K Gold, Riviera Style, 16 In. 4600.00
Necklace, Aluminum, Graduated Discs, Embossed Trees, Wendell August Forge, 17 In. . . . 50.00
Necklace, Bakelite, 6 Fruits, Trace Link Chain, 16 1/2 In. 500.00
Necklace, Bakelite, Long-Stemmed Cherries, Trace Link Chain, 16 In. 325.00
Necklace, Beads, Plastic, Lavender, Tubular, Graduated, Signed, c.1970, 16 1/2 In. 440.00
Necklace, Book Link, Leaf Shape Links, Gold, Gold Filled, Victorian, 19 1/2 In. 490.00
Necklace, Bracelet, Ring, Silver, Enamel, Snake Grasping Tail, Margot De Taxco 1293.00
Necklace, Chain, Openwork Navette Links, 18K Gold, Art Nouveau 765.00
Necklace, Choker, 52 Pearls, Diamonds, c.1850, 16 In. 1380.00
Necklace, Choker, 160 Pearls, England, c.1910 . . . . 690.00
Necklace, Choker, Silver, Turquoise, Latticework Links, c.1900, 13 In. 1175.00
Necklace, Choker, Sterling Silver, Double Chain Link, Half Spheres, Mexico, 17 In. 345.00

Necklace, Choker, Turquoise, Trace Link Chain, 14K Gold, c.1900, 13 In. 765.00
Necklace, Diamond, 18K Gold, 3 Strands, Tassels, Mayors, France, c.1960, 15 In. 4140.00
Necklace, Fan Shape Links, Quails, Flowers, Gold Clasp, Shakudo, c.1900, 18 In. 3055.00
Necklace, Flowers, Cartouches, Baton Shape Links, 18K Gold, Art Nouveau, 16 In. 999.00
Necklace, Hammered Sterling Silver, Glass Cabochon, Rafael Alfandary, c.1975 . . . . *Illus* 310.00
Necklace, Heart Shape Pendant, 18K Gold, Paloma Picasso, Tiffany, 16 1/4 In. 295.00
Necklace, Heart Shape, Trace Link Chain, 18K Gold, Signed, Elsa Peretti, 25 In. 700.00
Necklace, Heart, Diamonds, Herringbone Links, 18K Gold, Cartier, 14 3/4 In. 4700.00
Necklace, Heart, Full Cut Diamonds, 18K Gold, Elsa Peretti, Tiffany, Box, 16 In. 645.00
Necklace, Ivory, Nantucket Basket Pendant, Ebonized Wood, Whale On Lid, 15 1/2 In. . . . 630.00
Necklace, Keshi Pearl, Silver Gray, 3 Strands, 14K Gold, Gump's, 36 In. 1058.00
Necklace, Links, 18K Gold, Signed, Cartier, 18 1/2 In. 1998.00
Necklace, Mexican Sterling Silver, Swirl Links, Cabochon Amethysts, 16 In. 188.00
Necklace, Pearls, 2 Strands, Platinum Leaf Clasp, Diamonds, Van Cleef & Arpels 9200.00
Necklace, Pearls, Cultured, 12K White Gold Clasp, c.1930 . . . . 58.00
Necklace, Pearls, Cultured, 2 Strands, 14K White Gold, Pearl Clasp, 20th Century, 16 In. . . 95.00
Necklace, Pearls, Cultured, Full Cut Diamond, Trace Link Chain, Tiffany, Box, 16 In. 560.00
Necklace, Pendant, Amethyst, Diamonds, Link Chain, Platinum, Edwardian, 28 1/4 In. . . . 4348.00
Necklace, Pendant, Contemporary Design, 5 Round Opals, 14K Yellow Gold, 17 In. 82.00
Necklace, Pendant, Fan, Oval Locket, Mt. Fuji, Flowers, Birds, 14K, Shakudo, 24 In. 1765.00
Necklace, Pendant, Leaves, Brown Stone, Silver, Arts & Crafts, 9 In. 560.00
Necklace, Pendant, Link, Diamond, 18K Gold, Cartier, c.1960, 27 In. 940.00
Necklace, Pendant, Silver, Ebony, Ivory, Claude Jensen, c.1960, 30 In. 235.00
Necklace, Pendant, Silver, Mythological Winged Beast, Wesley Emmons, 19 In. 47.00
Necklace, Platinum, 29 Natural Pearls, Diamond, c.1910, 16 In. 10000.00
Necklace, Platinum, Sapphire, Diamond, 18K Gold, Hemmerle, Munich, 15 In. 7050.00
Necklace, Rhinestone, Bib Shape, c.1920 . . . . 25.00
Necklace, Round & Elongated Links, 14K Pink Gold, c.1900, 20 In. 105.00
Necklace, Sand-Cast Sterling Silver, Turquoise Beads, Rainbow Dancer, Zuni, 27 In. 430.00
Necklace, Silver, Pendant, 4 Amethysts, 3 Abalone Shells, Germany, 12 In. 325.00
Necklace, Silver, Star Links, Pendant Beads, Victorian, 17 1/2 In. 295.00
Necklace, Sterling Silver, Enamel, Leaves, Link Chain, Arts & Crafts, Liberty & Co., 19 In. 355.00
Necklace, Sterling Silver, Enamel, Trace Link Chain, Arts & Crafts, Liberty & Co., 22 In. . 295.00
Necklace, Sterling Silver, Fringe Of Overlapping Panels, Georg Jensen, No. 113 . . . . 805.00
Necklace, Sterling, Flower Shape Pendant, 3 Pearls, 4 Diamonds, c.1910 . . . . 920.00
Pearls, Continuous Strand, Baroque, 26 In. 1380.00
Pendant, 47 Old Mine Diamonds, Removable Pinback, 14K Gold, c.1890 . . . . 6900.00
Pendant, Abstract Mount, Carved & Pierced Jadeite, Diamonds, 18K Gold, Birks, 23 In. . . 520.00
Pendant, Aquamarine, Emerald Cut, Diamond Bow On Top, Platinum Chain, c.1950 . . . . . 3220.00
Pendant, Buddha, Coral, Seed Pearls, Wirework, 18K Gold, Tiffany & Co., c.1910 . . . . . . 1998.00
Pendant, Chain, Sterling Silver, Agate Cabochon, Rafael Alfandary, c.1975 . . . . 225.00
Pendant, Chain, Sterling Silver, Navette Shape Amethyst Cabochon, 14K Gold, c.1985 . . . 260.00
Pendant, Coin, $10, Indian Head, Rope Twist Bezel, Chain, 14K Yellow Gold, 1932 . . . . . 2185.00
Pendant, Cross, Silver, Diamond, Blue Enamel, 14K Gold, Russian Style, 2 3/4 In. 690.00
Pendant, Cross, Silver, Diamond, Enamel, 14K Gold, Russian, 1900s, 3 x 1 1/2 In. .375.00 to 460.00
Pendant, Draped Ram, 18K Yellow Gold, 14K Yellow Gold Rope Chain, Cartier, 34 In. . . 705.00
Pendant, Draped Ram, 18K Yellow Gold, Sterling Silver, Hematite Beads, Cartier 670.00
Pendant, Empress Elizabeth, Diamond, Sapphire, Enamel, Russian Style, 1900s, 3 In. 1380.00
Pendant, Filigree, Yellow Sapphire, 14K Gold, Art Deco, c.1930, 2 x 1 In. 800.00
Pendant, Fish, 22K Gold, 1972, Wooden Box 9400.00
Pendant, Pin, 52 Diamonds, Cultured Pearl Tassel, 14K Gold, c.1900, 2 x 1 In. 865.00
Pendant, Pin, Diamond, 14K Filigree White Gold Flower, Victorian, c.1900, 3/4 In. 5290.00
Pendant, Pin, Sunburst, Diamond, Seed Pearls, 14K Gold, c.1910, 2 In. 201.00
Pendant, Pin, Sunburst, Seed Pearls, Diamonds, Gold, c.1900, 1 1/4 In. 316.00
Pendant, Platinum, 59 Rose Cut Diamonds, Chain, 18K Gold, Edwardian 2199.00
Pendant, Rainbow Moonstone, Full Cut Diamond, Silk Cord, 18K Gold, Zaffiro, 16 In. . . . 940.00
Pendant, Sterling Silver, Enamel, Coral, Black, Faceted Stone Panels, Art Deco, Fahrner . . 1880.00
Pendant, Sterling Silver, Pear Shape, Inset Etched Glass Panels, Janna Thomas, Mexico . . 95.00
Pendant, Sterling Silver, Pierced, Blue Mottled Agate, Chain, Art Silver Shop, 1 1/2 In. . . . 550.00
Pill Box, Diamond, Gem Stones, Carnelian, Platinum, Gold, Russian Style, 1900s, 2 In. . . . 2185.00
Pin, 2 Flowers, Leaves, Diamond, Ruby, Gem Set, 18K Gold, Buccellati 1880.00
Pin, 2 Horses, 14K Gold, American Hallmark 411.00
Pin, 4 Circular Cut Sapphires, Prong Set, Signed, Retro, 18K Gold 2291.00

Pin, 18K Yellow Gold, Golden Topaz, Anchor Link Frame, Retro Moderne, c.1945 ...... 750.00
Pin, 29 Oval Emeralds, Full Cut Diamonds, Platinum, 18K Gold, Signed, Gazdar, Box 9400.00
Pin, Abstract Flower, Pear Shape, Oval Cut Amethysts, 14K Gold, c.1950 .... 1116.00
Pin, Amethyst, Enamel, Seed Pearls, 14K Gold Mount, Edwardian 1765.00
Pin, Amethyst, Seed Pearls, White Enamel, 14K Gold, Victorian 265.00
Pin, Bakelite, Butterscotch Giraffe, Brown Spots, Leather Spots, 4 In. 2550.00
Pin, Bakelite, Giraffe, Swirled Yellow, Inset Eye, Leather Ears, Martha Sleeper 120.00
Pin, Bakelite, Saturn, Yellow, Black Star Set, 4 1/2 In. 645.00
Pin, Bar, 3 Mice, Sterling Silver, Pierced, Chased, Rectangular, Potter Studio, 2 In. 325.00
Pin, Bar, 6 Pink Star Sapphire Cabochon, Diamonds, Platinum, Art Deco 1528.00
Pin, Bar, 23 Old Mine Cut Diamonds, Platinum Topped, 18K Gold Mount, Art Deco 1058.00
Pin, Bar, Diamond, Platinum, Filigree, 14K Gold, Art Deco, 2 1/2 In. 259.00
Pin, Bar, Filigree, 5 Diamonds, 14K White Gold, Art Deco, c.1920 .... 290.00
Pin, Bar, Jade, Carved, 14K Gold Mount, Art Deco, Tiffany & Co., c.1930, 2 1/2 x 3/4 In. . 805.00
Pin, Bar, Platinum, Diamonds, Bezel Set, Gold, Art Deco 1000.00
Pin, Bar, Platinum, Old Mine Cut Diamond, Enameled, Spider Web, Art Deco, c.1920 .... 1610.00
Pin, Basket, Tourmaline, Citrines, Garnets, 14K Gold, Lucien Piccard 295.00
Pin, Beast Eating Tail, Bead Color, Pendant Bead, 15K Gold, Castellani 2938.00
Pin, Bluebell Spray, Sapphire Melee, 18K Gold, Tiffany & Co. 500.00
Pin, Bow, 35 Old Mine Cut Diamonds, Platinum, Sapphire, Art Deco 1645.00
Pin, Bow, Filigree, 17 Diamonds, Platinum, 18K White Gold, Garrard & Co., Box 1790.00
Pin, Bow, Old Mine Cut Diamonds, Platinum, Pierced Mount, Art Deco 1880.00
Pin, Bowknot, Diamond, Sapphire, 3-Color Gold, Larter & Sons, N.J., 2 x 2 1/2 In. 1035.00
Pin, Bowknot, Platinum, Diamond, Blue Sapphire, Art Deco, 1920-30, 2 1/4 In. 1840.00
Pin, Brass, Handwrought, Acid-Etched Stylized Flowers, Carence Crafters, 2 x 3 In. 365.00
Pin, Buckle, Relief Vine, Inscribed, 14K Gold, Art Nouveau 558.00
Pin, Butterfly, Diamond, Opals, Sapphires, Emerald, Rubies, 14K Gold, c.1910 .... 1765.00
Pin, Butterfly, Silver Filigree Body, Gold, Blue & Purple Enamel Wings, Art Nouveau 315.00
Pin, Calla Lily, Full Cut Diamond Melee, Enamel, 18K Gold, Art Nouveau Style 1115.00
Pin, Cameo, 3 Baroque Pearls, Coral Branch, 18K Gold, Arthur King 1000.00
Pin, Cameo, 3 Muses, Oval, Sterling Silver Frame, 19th Century, 2 1/2 In. 129.00
Pin, Cameo, Classical Woman, Carved Shell, 10K Gold, Early 1900s, 2 1/2 x 2 In. 144.00
Pin, Cameo, Classical Woman, Seed Pearl Border, 10K Gold, Early 1900s, 2 1/4 In. 115.00
Pin, Cameo, Roman Figure, Horse, Castle, Gold Plated Frame, Oval, Victorian 315.00
Pin, Cameo, Roman Soldier, Oval, Carved, Silver Frame, 19th Century, 2 In. 140.00
Pin, Cameo, Woman's Profile, Coral, Seed Pearl Frame, 14K Gold, Victorian 294.00
Pin, Cameo, Woman, Seed Pearls, White Enamel Greek Frame, 14K Gold, Riker Brothers . 441.00
Pin, Chameleon, Silver, Diamond, Ruby, Opal, Rose Gold, Russian Style, 1900s, 3 x 2 In. . 1035.00
Pin, Christmas Tree, Natural Style, Blue & Green Stones, Hedy, 1940-60, 2 1/4 In. 65.00
Pin, Christmas Tree, Rhinestones, Weiss, 2 x 1 3/8 In. 250.00
Pin, Christmas, Multicolored, Gold Cast Alloy, Hollycraft, 2 1/2 x 1 3/4 In. 50.00
Pin, Circle, Platinum, Bead Set Diamonds, Pearl, Art Deco 2115.00
Pin, Circle, Swan, Pearls, Blue, White Enamel Head, Neck, 14K Gold, Edwardian 645.00
Pin, Classical Figure, Mother-Of-Pearl, Sunburst, Intaglio Pendant, Elizabeth Locke 3450.00
Pin, Coin, 2 Rectangular Shapes, Wavy Bars, 24K & 18K Gold, Signed, Janiye 499.00
Pin, Coral, Cameo, Openwork Frame, 14K Gold, Italy, c.1880 .... 316.00
Pin, Coral, Round, Hellenistic, 18K Gold, Victorian, c.1860 .... 1090.00
Pin, Cornucopia, Ruby, Sapphire, Emerald, 18K Gold, Tiffany & Co. 1290.00
Pin, Crescent Shape, 15 European Cut Diamonds, Sapphires, c.1910, 1 In. 345.00
Pin, Crescent, Opals, Diamonds, Edwardian 1116.00
Pin, Crescent, Persian Turquoise Beads, Diamonds, Black, Starr & Frost, 1880s, 3 In. 2200.00
Pin, Crescent, Sapphire, Seed Pearls, 14K Gold, Bippart, Bennet & Co., Edwardian 265.00
Pin, Cruise Ship With Suspended Suitcase & Fish, Bakelite, 2 1/2 In. 600.00
Pin, Deer, Branches, Jadeite, Diamond, 18K Gold, Arthur King 560.00
Pin, Diamond Melee, Pearls, Triangular, Scrolled Frame, 14K Gold, Art Nouveau 560.00
Pin, Diamond, 14K White Gold Filigree, Art Deco, c.1920, 1 3/8 x 2 In. 748.00
Pin, Diamond, 1927 Gold Coin, Platinum Frame 978.00
Pin, Diamond, Platinum, 95 European, Single Cut & Baguettes, 3-Sided, Art Deco 2990.00
Pin, Diamond, Sapphire, Filigree, Platinum, Art Nouveau, c.1910, 3/4 x 1 1/8 In. 2875.00
Pin, Dragonfly, Plique-A-Jour, Sapphire, Diamonds, 18K Gold, Art Deco 1725.00
Pin, Dragonfly, Silver, Seed Pearl Wings, Tiger's-Eye Body, Ruby Eyes, Art Nouveau 460.00
Pin, Duck, Coral, Lapis, Labradorite, Diamond Collar, Tail, 18K, Van Cleef & Arpels 6465.00
Pin, Earrings, Bird In Heart Shape Frame, Sterling Silver, Geog Jensen, Denmark 380.00

Pin, Eiffel Tower, Platinum, Diamond, Art Deco, 1920-30, 1 3/4 x 1/2 In. 1095.00
Pin, Eye Miniature, Brown, Oval, Brown Hair Lock, Encircling Gold Serpent, 1/2 In. 2990.00
Pin, Eye Miniature, Pale Blue, Cloud Puffs, Oval, Gold Plated Frame, c.1795, 1 In. 3680.00
Pin, Feather, 14K Gold, Tiffany & Co., 3 In. 520.00
Pin, Fish, Bezel Set, Table Cut Diamonds, Pink, Green, White Enamel, India, 14K, Pair . . . 645.00
Pin, Fleur-De-Lis, Bead Set, Rose Cut Diamonds, Silver Topped, 18K Gold Mount 705.00
Pin, Floral Wreath, Round, 30 Rubies, Sapphires, Diamonds, 18K White Gold, Birks 840.00
Pin, Flower Bouquet Shape, Sapphires, Diamonds, 18K Gold, Raymond Yard 3210.00
Pin, Flower Petals, Diamond Cluster, 18K Gold, Hammerman Brothers 705.00
Pin, Flower Spray, Doves, Blond Hair Over Shell, Ivory, 15K Gold, Victorian 235.00
Pin, Flower Spray, European Cut, Rose Cut Diamond, Pearl Buds, Pearl Drop, 18K Gold . . 3525.00
Pin, Flower Spray, Old Mine, Rose Cut Diamonds, Silver Top, 18K Gold Mount 4113.00
Pin, Flower Spray, Pear Shape Smoky Quartz, Rose Cut Diamonds, 14K Gold 1175.00
Pin, Flower, Leaves, Diamond, Amethyst, 14K Gold, c.1880, 4 1/4 In. 1840.00
Pin, Flower, Silver Topped, Red Spinel, Diamond, 14K Gold, 1800s, 2 3/4 x 2 1/2 In. 2185.00
Pin, Frog, Green Beryl Eyes, 14K Gold, Signed, Kurt Wayne 705.00
Pin, Frog, Silver, Diamond, Ruby, 14K Rose Gold, Russian Style, 1900s, 1 x 1 1/2 In. 518.00
Pin, Frog, Silver, Diamond, Ruby, 14K Rose Gold, Russian Style, 1900s, 1/2 x 1 3/4 In. 575.00
Pin, Garlands, Circles, Bezel Set Diamonds, Platinum, Pearls, Edwardian, Box 5525.00
Pin, Gold, Abstract, Array of Twigs, Ed Weiner, 1 3/4 In. . . . . *Illus* 800.00
Pin, Grasshopper, Ruby Eyes, 18K Gold, Signed, Kurt Wayne, 1969 . . . . 1410.00
Pin, Greek Temple, Black Onyx, Micro Mosaic, Scalloped, 14K Gold, Victorian, 2 In. 980.00
Pin, Green Enamel Clover, European Cut Diamonds, 14K Gold, Tiffany, Box 323.00
Pin, Green Tourmaline, Seed Pearls, 15K Gold, Edwardian 764.00
Pin, Heart Shape, Citrine, Diamond Ribbon Surround & Tassel Drop, c.1910 . . . . 7480.00
Pin, Horseshoe, 37 Old Mine Cut Diamonds, Platinum Topped, 14K Gold, Edwardian 1175.00
Pin, Large Pearls, 7 Diamonds, 18K Gold, Abstract Design, Stittgen 518.00
Pin, Leafy Openwork, Rectangular, Sterling Silver, Georg Jensen . . . . *Illus* 362.00
Pin, Liberty Bell, Diamond Melee, Platinum, 18K Gold, Coopers Of Philadelphia 1058.00
Pin, Lizard, Demantoid Garnets, Old Mine Cut Diamonds, Ruby Eyes, 14K Gold, c.1910 . 6169.00
Pin, Lizard, Diamond, Demantoid Garnet, 18K Gold Mount, c.1920 . . . . 8519.00
Pin, Maltese Cross, Diamond, Silver Top, 10K Gold, c.1850, 1 1/4 x 1 1/4 In. 3450.00
Pin, Man In Garden, Flower Blossoms, Green Glass, 18K Gold, India 382.00
Pin, Moonstone, Cushion, Circular Cut Sapphires, 14K Gold, Arts & Crafts 1410.00
Pin, Moonstone, Seed Pearls, Platinum-Topped 14K Gold Mount, Allsopp & Allsopp 1293.00
Pin, Mourning, Pietra Dura, 14K Gold, Inscription, c.1885, 2 In. 518.00
Pin, Old Mine Cut Diamonds, Ribbons, Rubies, Flowerhead Mounts, 14K Gold, c.1840 . . . 881.00
Pin, Onyx, 38 Old Mine Cut Diamonds, Platinum, Art Deco 4700.00
Pin, Oval Amethyst, Bezel Set, Grapevine, 14K Gold, Signed J.W. Shaw, Arts & Crafts . . . 3408.00
Pin, Oval, Chased Grape Leaf Cluster, Domed Leaves, Kalo Shop, 1 1/4 x 1 3/4 In. 350.00
Pin, Owl's Face, Sterling Silver, Moonstone, Sapphire, Signed, D.R. Longh 235.00
Pin, Oyster Shape, Enamel, Seed Pearls, 14K Gold, A.J. Hedges, Edwardian 1528.00
Pin, Pearl Center, 128 Smaller Pearls In Rays, Round, 14K Gold Mount, c.1960, 2 In. 690.00
Pin, Pearl, Intaglio, Classical Scene, Openwork Hinged Bail, 18K Gold, Signed Locke 1998.00
Pin, Pearls, White, Pink, Black, Gold, Flower Setting, Ed Wiener, 1950s, 1 1/2 In. . . . *Illus* 500.00
Pin, Platinum, 7 Diamonds, Black Enamel, 14K White Gold, Art Deco, 2 1/2 In. 575.00

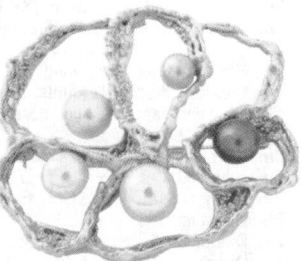

Jewelry, Pin, Gold, Abstract,
Array of Twigs,
Ed Weiner, 1 3/4 In.

Jewelry, Pin, Leafy
Openwork, Rectangular,
Sterling Silver,
Georg Jensen

Jewelry, Pin, Pearls, White, Pink,
Black, Gold, Flower Setting, Ed
Wiener, 1950s, 1 1/2 In.

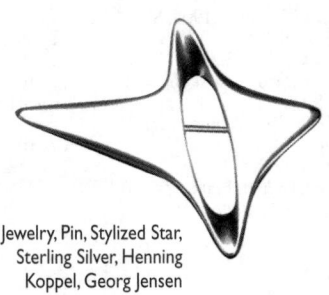

Jewelry, Pin, Stylized Star,
Sterling Silver, Henning
Koppel, Georg Jensen

Jewelry, Pin, Table, Black & White
Check, Red Chair, Memphis,
Acme Studios, 1 1/8 In., 2 Piece

Pin, Platinum, 32 Full-Cut Diamonds, Prong Set, Shreve, Crump & Low 2350.00
Pin, Platinum, 76 Diamonds, Art Deco, Box, 2 x 1 In. 1610.00
Pin, Portrait Bust Of Female, Gold Plated, Engraved Loop Trim, Victorian, 1880 .... 255.00
Pin, Prong Set, 14 Baguette & 60 Full Cut Diamonds, c.1950 .... 4465.00
Pin, Rectangular, Acid Etched Flowers, German Silver, Carence Crafters, 2 1/2 In. 300.00
Pin, Riding Crop, Star Sapphire, Diamond, Platinum, 14K Gold, Tiffany & Co. 355.00
Pin, Rose Cut Diamond, Oval Cut Pink Topaz, 18K Gold, Edwardian 7050.00
Pin, Round, Pierced, Chased Oak Leaf, Sterling Silver, Kalo Shop, 2 1/4 In. 375.00
Pin, Sapphire, 33 Marquise Diamonds, Platinum, Art Deco 1058.00
Pin, Scarecrow, Lapis Head, Gem Set, 18K Gold, Signed, J. Rossi 530.00
Pin, Schnauzer, Beaded Collar, Sterling Silver, Signed, Mary Gage 355.00
Pin, Schooner, Sterling Silver, Domed & Hammered Surface, Franklin Porter, 1 1/2 In. 95.00
Pin, Sculpted Bow, 45 Single Cut Diamonds, Calibre Cut Sapphire, Platinum, Art Deco ... 3525.00
Pin, Serpent Shape, Bezel Set Diamond, Red Spinel Pendant, 14K Gold, Birks 200.00
Pin, Serpent, Turquoise Stone On Head, 14K Gold, Late 1800s, 2 1/2 In. 175.00
Pin, Silver, Geometric Pattern, Green, Orange, Paste Stones, Art Deco 190.00
Pin, Silver, Hardstone, Scottish Dirk Shape, Citrine, Agate, Jasper, Late 19th Century 520.00
Pin, Spider, Garnet, Pearls, Diamond, 14K Gold Mount, c.1920 .... 590.00
Pin, Spiky Cluster, Full Cut Diamonds, 18K Gold, Signed, Tiffany & Co. 825.00
Pin, Sporting, Enamel Skis, Poles, Golf Club, Larter & Sons, 14K Gold 150.00
Pin, Stars & Stripes, Suspended From Bar, Bakelite, Cream & Black, 3 In. 910.00
Pin, Step Cut Sapphire, Full Cut Diamond Melee, 18K White Gold, Art Deco 1116.00
Pin, Sterling Silver, 3-Sided Abstract Shape, Brown Enamel, Georg Jensen 400.00
Pin, Sterling Silver, 4 Discs, Bezel Set Opal Cabochon, Marcasites, Fahrner, Germany 175.00
Pin, Sterling Silver, 5 Cabochon Garnets, Georg Jensen, 1915-30 .... 1050.00
Pin, Sterling Silver, Cluster Center, Pearl, Flowers, Leaves, Rokesley Shop, 2 1/4 In. 1200.00
Pin, Sterling Silver, Key & Heart, Set Paste Stones, Kramer 26.00
Pin, Sterling Silver, Rectangular, Open Leaf Design, Georg Jensen, Denmark 360.00
Pin, Sterling Silver, Round, Chased Thistle, Hand Wrought, Panis Gallery, 1 5/8 In. 165.00
Pin, Stick, Dart Shape, Pear Cut Sapphire, Diamonds, Diamond Point, Art Deco 3220.00
Pin, Stylized Fern, Coiled Fronds, Emeralds, 18K Gold, Tiffany & Co. 590.00
Pin, Stylized Star, Sterling Silver, Henning Koppel, Georg Jensen .... *Illus* 360.00
Pin, Sunburst Shape, Moonstone Cameo, Bezel Set Rubellites, Pearls, Elizabeth Locke ... 2070.00
Pin, Swirls, 7 Diamonds, 14K Gold, Edwardian, 1 In. 375.00
Pin, Table, Black & White Check, Red Chair, Memphis, Acme Studios, 1 1/8 In., 2 Piece *Illus* 200.00
Pin, Triangle, Silver Vines, Iron Background, Jern/Solv, Georg Jensen, Denmark 311.00
Pin, Triangular Star Burst, Open Oval, Sterling Silver, Henning Koppel, G. Jensen, 3 In. .. 365.00
Pin, Turquoise, 6 Pearls, Old Mine Cut Diamonds, 14K Gold, Edwardian 1765.00
Pin, Twigs, Citrine, 18K Gold, Tiffany & Co., c.1940 .... 5750.00
Pin, Watch, Dragon Clutching Arrow, 14K Gold, Art Nouveau 940.00
Pin, White Gold, Diamond, Pearl, Ribbon Top, Leaf Designs, 2 x 1 In. 690.00
Pin, White Pearl, 24 Old Mine Cut Diamonds, 18K Gold 1645.00
Pin, Wire Frame, 3 Applied Stylized Leaves, Sterling Silver, Handwrought, J. Leslie, 1 In. .. 95.00
Pin, Woman Profile, Rose Cut Diamond, 18K Gold, Art Nouveau, Signed 323.00
Pin, Wreath, Dove Center, Handwrought, Sterling Silver, Georg Jensen, 1 5/8 In. 350.00
Pin & Earrings, Orange Coral Cameo, Seed Pearls, 14K Gold, Victorian, 1 1/2-In. Pin 431.00
Pin & Earrings, Sterling Silver, Moonstone, Lily Pad, Bezel Set, Mary Gage 1058.00
Ring, 2 Brilliant Cut Round Diamonds, 10 Round Diamonds, 14K Gold, c.1940, Size 4 ... 345.00

Ring, 2 Old Mine Cut Diamonds, 24 Rose Cut Diamonds, 18K Gold, c.1900, Size 4 1/2 ...   575.00
Ring, 3 Old Mine Cut Diamonds, 18K Gold, Art Deco, Size 10 1/2 ....   3643.00
Ring, 3 Old Mine Cut Diamonds, Sapphires, 14K Gold, Edwardian, Size 9 3/4 ....   1058.00
Ring, 3 Round, Old European Cut Diamonds, Platinum, Art Deco, c.1930, Size 4 1/4 .....   1093.00
Ring, Amethyst, Citrine, 18K Gold, Maria Cassetti, Size 8 1/2 ....   410.00
Ring, Arabesque Design, Emerald, Seed Pearls, Dome, Gold, 20th Century, Size 7 ....   71.00
Ring, Bead Set Diamonds, Platinum, Art Deco, Size 6 1/4 ....   1058.00
Ring, Bead Set Diamonds, Platinum, Navette Mount, Art Deco, Size 11 ....   1528.00
Ring, Bead Set, Full Cut Diamond Knot, 18K Gold, Signed, Cartier, France, Size 6 1/2 ...   2350.00
Ring, Belt Shape, Green Enamel, Diamond Buckle, 18K Gold, Corletto, Italy 489.00
Ring, Bezel Set Emerald, Platinum, Art Deco, Size 8 1/2 ....   1550.00
Ring, Bezel Set, Jadeite Cabochon, 14K Gold, Birks 690.00
Ring, Blue Sapphire, 2 Diamonds, 14K Gold, c.1915, Size 6 3/4 ....   920.00
Ring, Blue Topaz, Diamond, Platinum Mount, Georg Jensen, Box 345.00
Ring, Bypass, 7 Full Cut Diamonds, 4 Rubies, 18K White Gold, Retro, Size 8 1/4 ....   470.00
Ring, Cameo, Blue, Green, Beryl, Bearded Solider Profile, Gold, Victorian 710.00
Ring, Cat's Eye Chrysoberyl, 11 Old Mine Cut Diamonds, Edwardian, Size 5 ....   6169.00
Ring, Cluster, 21 Diamonds, 14K White Gold, Art Deco, c.1930, Size 4 1/4 ....   345.00
Ring, Cocktail, Blue Diamond, 14 K Yellow Gold, c.1970, Size 6 ....   6900.00
Ring, Crossed Ribbons, Black Enamel, 13 Diamonds, 18K Gold, Georgian, Size 5 1/2 ....   2585.00
Ring, Diamond, 8 Blue Sapphires, 18K White Gold, Art Deco, c.1930, Size 6 3/4 ....   1725.00
Ring, Diamond, 14K Gold, Art Deco, c.1930, Size 4 3/4 ....   375.00
Ring, Diamond, 14K Gold, c.1950, Size 5 1/2 ....   115.00
Ring, Diamond, 18K Pink, White, Yellow Gold, Cartier, Size 5 1/2 ....   1295.00
Ring, Diamond, Platinum, Art Deco, 1920s, Size 7 ....   1380.00
Ring, Diamond, Raised Marquise Cut, 14 Round, 14K White Gold, c.1950, Size 6 ....   460.00
Ring, Diamond, Synthetic Sapphires, 18K White Gold, Art Deco, 1920-30, Size 4 1/2 ....   980.00
Ring, Diamonds, 14K Gold, Vienna Hallmarks KM, c.1930, Size 6 ....   825.00
Ring, Diamonds, 14K White Gold, Art Deco, c.1930, Size 7 1/4 ....   230.00
Ring, Diamonds, Coral, Ribbed Shank, 18K Gold, Van Cleef & Arpels, Pouch, Size 5 .....   645.00
Ring, Diamonds, Geometric, Platinum, Red Stones, 14K Gold, Retro, Size 4 ....   529.00
Ring, Diamonds, Marquise Cut Ruby Florets, 18K Gold, Tiffany, Size 4 1/2 ....   1295.00
Ring, Diamonds, Platinum, 18K Gold, G. Seifert & Sons, Quebec, c.1915, Size 5 3/4 .....   980.00
Ring, Diamonds, Platinum, Art Deco Carved Band, c.1925, Size 6 1/2 In. 2990.00
Ring, Diamonds, Platinum, Open Gallery, Art Deco, Size 3 1/2 ....   705.00
Ring, Diamonds, Sapphire, 18K Gold, G. Seifert & Sons, Quebec, c.1910, Size 6 ....   430.00
Ring, Diamonds, Turquoise Cabochon, 14K Gold, Edwardian, Size 2 3/4 ....   646.00
Ring, Dinner, Elliptical Shape, Diamonds, Emeralds, 18K White Gold, Art Deco, Size 7 ...   430.00
Ring, Emerald, 2 Baguette Diamonds, Cartier, Size 6 1/4 ....   1610.00
Ring, Eternity Band, Platinum, 27 Diamonds, Tiffany & Co., c.1930, Size 6 ....   1495.00
Ring, Eternity Band, Platinum, 78 Single Cut Diamonds, Art Deco, c.1930, Size 6 3/4 ....   865.00
Ring, Eternity Band, Yellow Gold, Pearl, Channel Set, 18 Pearls, 20th Century, Size 7 ....   105.00
Ring, Flip, Platinum, Diamond, Sapphires, Rubies, Art Deco, Size 7 ....   940.00
Ring, Gold, Aquamarine, 18K White Gold Filigree, Art Deco, c.1920, Size 4 1/2 In. 290.00
Ring, Hardstone Cameo, Woman, 24 Diamonds, Art Deco, c.1930, Size 5 3/4 ....   748.00
Ring, Jade, Carved, 14K Yellow Gold, 20th Century, Size 5 1/4 ....   35.00
Ring, Jadeite Cabochon, Prong Set, 24K &18K Gold, Signed, Miye 2350.00
Ring, Jadeite, Emerald, 14K White Gold, Art Deco, c.1930, Size 7 ....   900.00
Ring, Mourning, Strap & Buckle Shape, Hair Panel, 18K Yellow Gold, Victorian 275.00
Ring, Octagonal Illusion Mount, Solitaire Diamond, 14K Gold, c.1930, Size 6 3/4 ....   1610.00
Ring, Old Mine Cut Diamond, Channel Set Ruby, Platinum, Signed Cartier, Size 5 3/4 ...   2235.00
Ring, Opal, Openwork Table, Central Diamond, 20th Century, Size 7 1/4 ....   95.00
Ring, Oval Faceted Aquamarine, 22 Diamonds, 18K Gold, Van Cleef & Arpels, Size 6 ....   1495.00
Ring, Palladium Topped Diamond, Ruby, 14K Gold, Michaelson, c.1885, Size 4 3/4 ......   300.00
Ring, Pearl, 2 Old Mine-Cut Diamonds, 14K Gold, c.1900, Size 7 ....   1150.00
Ring, Pearl, Prong Set, Lotus Blossoms, 18K Gold, Tiffany, Art Nouveau, Size 3 1/4 .....   2820.00
Ring, Pink Step Cut Tourmalines, 1/2 Channel Set, 18K Gold, Tiffany, Size 6 1/4 ....   590.00
Ring, Platinum Topped, Diamond, 14K Gold, Art Deco, 1920s, Size 5 1/4 ....   400.00
Ring, Platinum, 3 Diamonds, Art Deco, c.1920, Size 6 3/4 ....   2760.00
Ring, Platinum, Blue Sapphire, Diamond, Art Deco, 1920-30, Size 6 1/2 ....   3680.00
Ring, Platinum, Blue Star Sapphire, Diamond, Art Deco, 1920-30, Size 4 1/4 ....   1380.00
Ring, Platinum, Diamond Solitaire, Bead Set Diamonds, Pierced, c.1935, Size 7 1/4 ......   4406.00

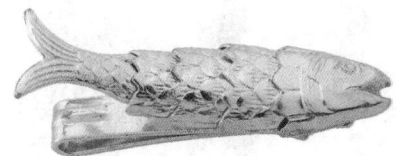

Jewelry, Tie Bar, Fish, Flexible Scales,
Gold, 1 3/4 In.

Jewelry, Tie Bar, Pretzel, Brown Enamel, White Spots,
Mounted On Gold Clip, 1 3/4 In.

Ring, Platinum, Diamond, 2 Blue Sapphires, Art Deco, c.1930, Size 9 1/4 . . . . 920.00
Ring, Platinum, Diamond, Emerald, c.1930 . . . . 1495.00
Ring, Platinum, Diamonds, Art Deco, 1920s, Size 7 1/2 . . . . 750.00
Ring, Platinum, Emerald, Diamond, Twin Stone, Oscar Heyman, 1930s, Size 6 . . . . 4818.00
Ring, Platinum, Old European Cut Diamond, 14K Gold, Art Deco, c.1930, Size 6 1/4 . . . . . 630.00
Ring, Platinum, Old European Cut Diamonds, Art Deco, 1920-30, Size 6 1/2 . . . . 1380.00
Ring, Platinum, Old European Cut Diamonds, Art Deco, 1920-30, Size 9 . . . . 3220.00
Ring, Red Spinel, Old Mine Cut Diamond Melee, 14K Gold, c.1910, Size 7 . . . . 2700.00
Ring, Ruby, Diamond, 14K Gold, Edwardian, c.1915, Size 5 1/4 . . . . 1150.00
Ring, Sapphire, Diamonds, Openwork Navette, 18K Gold, Art Deco 880.00
Ring, Sapphire, Pink Star, Oval Cabochon, Platinum, Art Deco, Size 3 1/4 . . . . 940.00
Ring, Sculpted Maiden, Sapphire, Diamond, Emerald Headdress, Gold Mount, c.1900 . . . . 4183.00
Ring, Serpent, Flower, White Opal, Diamond, Ruby, 18K Gold, Late 1800s, Size 6 1/2 . . . . 1035.00
Ring, Shield, Amethyst, Bezel Set, Drop, Matte Finish, 14K Gold, Kalo, Size 4 1/2 . . . . 2415.00
Ring, Silver, 19 Diamonds, 14K Gold, Russian Style, 1900s, Size 9 1/2 . . . . 575.00
Ring, Silver, Diamond, 14K Gold, Russian Style, 1900s, Size 8 1/2 . . . . 805.00
Ring, Silver, Diamond, Sapphire, Garnet, Enamel, 14K Gold, Russian Style, 1900s 575.00
Ring, Solitaire Diamond, 20 Small Diamonds, Platinum, Art Deco, c.1930, Size 5 3/4 . . . . . 2760.00
Ring, South Sea Pearl, 29 Baguette Diamonds, 18K Gold, Van Cleef & Arpels, Size 5 . . . . . 2875.00
Ring, Sterling Silver, Dome, W. Spratling 80.00
Ring, Stylized Leaf, Turquoise, Sterling Silver, 14K Gold Accents, Frank Hale, Size 6 . . . . 3100.00
Ring, Swirling Leaves, Vines, Pearls, Pink Sapphire, 14K Gold, Arts & Crafts, Size 7 3/4 . . 1175.00
Ring, Turquoise, Diamond, Leaf Shoulders, Black, Starr & Frost, Art Deco, Size 5 1/4 . . . . 4110.00
Ring, Turquoise, Rope Twist Mount, 18K Yellow Gold, Early 20th Century 200.00
Ring, Wedding Band, 5 Diamonds, Platinum, 14K Gold, Art Deco, Size 6 3/4 . . . . 460.00
Ring, Wedding Band, Plain, Polished, 18K Yellow Gold, Tiffany & Co. 200.00
Ring, White Opal, 4 Coral Cabochons, 14K Gold, Arts & Crafts, Size 5 1/2 . . . . 323.00
Ring, Yellow Sapphire, 18K White Gold, Art Deco, c.1930, Size 7 1/4 . . . . 805.00
Slide Chains, Gold Filled, Opals, Victorian, Pair 69.00
Stickpin, Spaniel's Head, Amethyst, Diamond, Enamel, 18K Gold, Cabrelli, France 2350.00
Stud Set, Double Cuff Links, 4 Studs, Opal, 18K Gold, Edwardian, Marcus & Co. 2115.00
Stud Set, Sterling Silver, Flowers, Cufflinks, Tie Bar & Tack, Georg Jensen, 4 Piece 310.00
Tie Bar, Fish, Flexible Scales, Gold, 1 3/4 In. . . . . *Illus* 10.00
Tie Bar, Pretzel, Brown Enamel, White Spots, Mounted On Gold Clip, 1 3/4 In. . . . . . *Illus* 8.00
Watches are listed in their own category.
Watch Chain, Trace Link, 9 Opals, 14K Gold, Carter, Howe & Co., 32 In. 823.00
Wristwatches are listed in their own category.

JOHN ROGERS statues were made from 1859 to 1892. The originals

were bronze, but the thousands of copies made by the Rogers factory
were of painted plaster. Eighty different figures were created. Similar
painted plaster figures were produced by some other factories. Rights
to the figures were sold in 1893 and they were manufactured for several
more years by the Rogers Statuette Co. Never repaint a Rogers figure
because this lowers the value to collectors.

Group, Council Of War, Abraham Lincoln, 1868, 24 In. 1750.00
Group, Neighboring Pews, Women In Church, 1883-84, 18 1/2 In. 450.00
Group, Town Pump, Soldier & Girl, Type B, 1862, 12 In. 515.00
Group, Wounded Scout, 1864 . . . . 715.00

Josef Originals, Figurine, Girl,
Holding Cat, Raised Cats & Flowers
On Dress, Brown Ponytail, 5 In.

Kay Finch, Figurine, Godey
Man & Woman, Flowers,
Muff, Pink, 7 1/2 In., Pair

Kay Finch, Figurine, Pig, Smiley,
Violets, Green Leaves, Curly
Tail, Pink, 6 1/2 x 8 In.

JOSEF ORIGINALS ceramics were designed by Muriel Joseph George. The first pieces were made in California from 1945 to 1962. They were then manufactured in Japan. The company was sold to George Good in 1982 and he continued to make Josef Originals until 1985. The company was then sold to Southland Corporation. The name is now owned by Applause, and the Birthday Girl series is still being made.

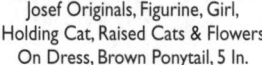

Egg Timer, Woman In Cap, Composition	40.00
Figurine, Adelaide, Colonial Days, White Dress, Pink & Gold, 9 1/2 In.	145.00
Figurine, Girl, Holding Cat, Raised Cats & Flowers On Dress, Brown Ponytail, 5 In. . *Illus*	85.00
Figurine, Girl, White Dress, Pink Kitten Border, Holding Gray Kitten, 5 In.	95.00
Figurine, Horse, Palomino, Tan, 7 In.	75.00
Figurine, Louise, Colonial Days, White Dress, Pink & Gold, 9 1/2 In.	150.00
Figurine, Maria, Colonial Days, Turquoise Dress, Lute, 9 1/2 In.	85.00
Figurine, Nurse, Woman & Child, 7 In.	200.00
Figurine, Poodles, Mama, Papa, Puppy, 2 1/4 & 1 3/4 In., 3 Piece	30.00
Figurine, Snowflake, My Favorite Things, Girl, Red Dress, 6 1/2 In.	110.00
Music Box, Doggie For Sale, House, Dog In Window, 5 1/2 In.	25.00
Music Box, Humoresque, Girl Playing Piano, Pink Dress, 6 1/4 In.	25.00

JUGTOWN Pottery refers to pottery made in North Carolina as far back as the 1750s. In 1915, Juliana and Jacques Busbee set up a training and sales organization for what they named *Jugtown Pottery*. In 1921, they built a shop at Jugtown, North Carolina, and hired Ben Owen as a potter in 1923. The Busbees moved the village store where the pottery was sold to New York City. Juliana Busbee sold the New York store in 1926 and moved into a log cabin near the Jugtown Pottery. The pottery closed in 1959. It reopened in 1960 and is still working near Seagrove, North Carolina.

Bottle, Salt Glazed Base, Chinese White Flambe Top, 1920s-30s	70.00
Bowl, Cone Shape, Footed, High Gloss Black Glaze, Ben Owens III, 1985, 6 In.	80.00
Bowl, Slip Painted Chicken Center, Orange Glaze, 10 In.	200.00
Candlestick, Brown Glaze, Painted Pussywillow, 11 3/4 In.	45.00
Jar, Cover, Applied Handles, Redware, Mottled Orange & Green Glaze, Stamped, 9 1/4 In.	374.00
Vase, Dogwood, Chinese White Glaze, 7 1/8 In.	155.00
Vase, Finger Groves, Bulbous, Orange & Green Lead Glaze, 6 1/4 In.	160.00
Vase, Red Clay, Salt Glaze, Charles Moore, 4 1/4 In.	45.00
Vase, Tapered, Blue Glaze, 5 In.	294.00
Vase, Tapered, Chinese Ware Glaze, Impressed Die, 4 In.	299.00
Vase, Urn Shape, Handles, Blue Flambe Glaze, 7 In.	1250.00

JUKEBOXES play records. The first coin-operated phonograph was demonstrated in 1889. In 1906 the *Automatic Entertainer* appeared, the first coin-operated phonograph to offer several different selections of music. The first electrically powered jukebox was introduced in 1927. Collectors search for jukeboxes of all ages, especially those with flashing lights and unusual design and graphics.

Capehart, Model 4, 78 RPM, Countertop, 1930s, 21 x 20 In. 2530.00
Mills, Empress, Catalin, Wood, Chrome, 20 Selections, 78 RPM, 1941, 58 x 34 In. 8052.00
Rock-Ola, Model 1426, 20 Selections, 78 RPM, 57 3/4 x 30 In., 1947 .... 5500.00
Rock-Ola, Model A, Walnut, Wurlitzer Amplifier, 12 Selections, 78 RPM, 1935, 50 In. 1425.00
Seeburg, Model 147M, Trashcan, Red, White, Blue Mirrored Tile, c.1947, 57 In. 1495.00
Seeburg, Model 8800, Wood, Catalin, Chrome, 20 Selections, 78 RPM, 1941, 61 x 36 In. . 7320.00
Seeburg, Select-O-Matic, Chrome Case, Curved Glass Finish, c.1940, 12 1/2 In. 290.00
Seeburg, Select-O-Matic, Plastic Case, Button Selections, c.1940, 13 In. 125.00
Seeburg, Wall-O-Matic, Selector, Key, Table Top, 1940-67, 16 x 12 x 5 In. 165.00
Wurlitzer, Model 61, Wood, Catalin, Chrome, 12 Selections, 78 RPM, 1938, 23 x 22 In. .. 4099.00
Wurlitzer, Model 800, Wood, Catalin, Chrome, 24 Selections, 78 RPM, 1940, 60 x 37 In. . 12654.00
Wurlitzer, Model 1015, Bubbler, 24 Selections, 78 RPM, c.1947, 61 x 33 x 25 In. 6600.00
Wurlitzer, Wall Mount Selector, Insert 5 Cents, 10 Cents, 25 Cents, 13 x 9 In 132.00

KATE GREENAWAY, who was a famous illustrator of children's books, drew pictures of children in high-waisted Empire dresses. She lived from 1846 to 1901. Her designs appear on china, glass, and other pieces.

Book, Almanack For 1885, Color Printing, Hardbound 45.00
Napkin Ring, Boy & Girl On Teeter-Totter, Simpson, Hall, Miller Co. 1440.00
Pincushion, Spool Holder, Girl At Table, Silver Plate, James Tufts, 5 In. 165.00

KAY FINCH Ceramics were made in Corona Del Mar, California, from 1935 to 1963. The hand-decorated pieces often depicted whimsical animals and people. Pastel colors were used.

Bowl, Rooster & Hen, White, Square, 11 3/4 In. 50.00
Figurine, Cat, Pink, Flowered Paws, Curly Whiskers, 8 1/2 In. 170.00
Figurine, Dog, Airedale Welsh Terrier, Tan, Black, 5 1/2 In. 80.00
Figurine, Dog, Maltese, White With Gray, 11 In. 245.00
Figurine, Dog, Wire Hair Fox Terrier, White, Black, Tan, 5 1/2 In. 80.00
Figurine, Godey Man & Woman, Flowers, Muff, Pink, 7 1/2 In., Pair .... Illus 300.00
Figurine, Pig, Smiley, Strawberries, 8 In. 75.00
Figurine, Pig, Smiley, Violets, Green Leaves, Curly Tail, Pink, 6 1/2 x 8 In. .... Illus 100.00
Figurine, Rooster, Blue, Yellow, Green, Red, 11 In. 115.00

KAYSERZINN, see Pewter category.

KELVA glassware was made by the C. F. Monroe Company of Meriden, Connecticut, about 1904. It is a pale, pastel-painted glass decorated with flowers, designs, or scenes. Kelva resembles Nakara and Wave Crest, two other glasswares made by the same company.

Box, Cover, Flowers, Crown Mold, Green, 6 1/2 In. 650.00
Box, Cover, Flowers, Lavender, Footed, 5-Sided 500.00
Box, Hinged Cover, Blue Mottled Ground, Wild Pink Roses, Round, Signed, 2 x 4 1/2 In. . . 400.00
Vase, Pink Flowers, Gold Scrolls, Mottled Blue & White Ground, Footed, 8 In. 805.00

KEMPLE glass was made by John Kemple of East Palestine, Ohio, and Kenova, West Virginia, from 1945 to 1970. The glass was made from old molds. Many designs and colors were made. Kemple pieces are usually marked with a *K* on the bottom. Many milk glass pieces were made with or without the mark.

Candy Dish, Cover, Jewel & Dewdrop, Milk Glass, 8 1/2 In. 14.00
Dish, Hen On Nest Cover, Milk Glass, Brown, Red, Green Paint, 7 In. 45.00
Dish, Rooster On Basket Cover, Milk Glass, Red Comb & Eye, 7 In. 50.00
Figurine, Jumping Horse, Amber, 9 1/2 In. 55.00
Pitcher, Lace & Dewdrop, Milk Glass, 7 1/2 In. 55.00
Sugar & Creamer, Large Lace & Dewdrop, Milk Glass 13.00
Sugar & Creamer, Yutec, Amber 12.00

KENTON HILLS Pottery in Erlanger, Kentucky, made artwares, including vases and figurines that resembled Rookwood, probably because so many of the original artists and workmen had worked at the Rookwood plant. Kenton Hills opened in 1939 and closed during World War II.

Bowl, Green High Glaze, Marked, Seyler, 6 In. 60.00

Candlestick, Goldstone Matte Glaze, Marked, Seyler, 4 In. 175.00
Candlestick, Rooster, Turquoise High Glaze, Marked, 9 1/2 In. 245.00
Dish, Cover, Green High Glaze, Marked, 7 In. 75.00
Figurine, Lamb, Blue, Marked, Seyler, 5 x 4 1/4 In. 265.00
Figurine, Mother & Child, Brown High Glaze, Marked, Seyler, 14 In. 590.00
Figurine, Nude, Holding Star, Leaves, Ivory Glaze, Marked, Arthur Conant, 10 In. 440.00
Figurine, Woman's Head, Brown Hair, Eyes, Marked, Seyler, 6 1/4 In. 530.00
Lamp, Horses, Ivory Ground, Stripes, Metal Base, Signed, 10 In. 825.00
Paperweight, Woman's Head, Goldstone Glaze, Marked, 4 1/4 In. 175.00
Vase, Blue Matte Glaze, Footed, 7 In. 175.00
Vase, Broad Leaves, Geometric Design, Butterfat Glaze, 12 In. 590.00
Vase, Brown Drip Glaze, Yellow Ground, Bulbous, David Seyler, 6 In. 350.00
Vase, Flower Form, Pink Matte Glaze, Marked, Hentschel, 6 3/4 In. 235.00
Vase, Flower Form, Turquoise High Glaze, Marked, Hentschel, 6 3/4 In. 175.00
Vase, Goldstone Glaze, Bulbous, Marked, 7 In. 295.00
Vase, Green High Glaze, Bulbous, Flared, Handles, Marked, Conant, 6 In. 175.00
Vase, Green High Glaze, Bulbous, Marked, 7 In. 175.00
Vase, Green High Glaze, Marked, David Seyler, 4 In. 60.00
Vase, Green High Glaze, Raised Design, Bulbous, Tapered, Marked, 4 1/4 In. 380.00
Vase, Green Matte Glaze, Bulbous, Flared, Handles, Marked, Conant, 6 In. 115.00
Vase, Green Matte Glaze, Marked, 5 1/4 In. 410.00
Vase, Molded Vertical Leaves, Green Matte Glaze, Flared, Conant, 3 1/2 In. 145.00
Vase, Molded Vertical Leaves, Yellow Matte Glaze, Marked, Conant, 1/2 In. 175.00
Vase, Mottled Brown & Tan High Glaze, Flared, Marked, 6 1/2 In. 205.00
Vase, Pink Matte Glaze, Raised Dots, Lines, Hentschel, 6 1/2 In. 325.00
Vase, Purple Matte Glaze, Bulbous, Tapered, 4 1/4 In. 120.00
Vase, Raised Leaves, Dark Blue High Glaze, Bulbous, Marked, Hentschel, 6 1/4 In. 295.00
Vase, Raised Leaves, Green Matte Glaze, Bulbous, Marked, W. Hentschel, 6 1/4 In. 590.00
Vase, Rose Drip Over Ivory Glaze, Bulbous, Tapered, Marked, 4 1/4 In. 120.00
Vase, Stylized Flowers, Black, Ivory Ground, Brown Rim, Flared, Hentschel, 12 In. 825.00
Vase, Stylized Flowers, Cream Ground, Bulbous, Flared Rim, Signed, 12 1/2 In. 590.00
Vase, Stylized Flowers, Gourd Form, Marked, Charlotte Haupt, 6 1/4 In. 825.00
Vase, Stylized Flowers, Leaves, Pink, Green, Ivory, Tapered, Hentschel, 12 1/2 In. 1000.00
Vase, Stylized Flowers, Shoulder Form, Signed, Hentschel, 12 In. 1115.00
Vase, Stylized Flowers, Stem, Pink, Blue Center, Marked, Rosemary Dickman, 8 In. 765.00
Vase, Stylized Leaves, Berries, Brown High Glaze, Signed, Hentschel, 4 In. 60.00
Vase, Stylized Leaves, Berries, Flared, Marked, Hentschel, 12 1/2 In. 765.00
Vase, Stylized Leaves, Turquoise High Glaze, Footed, Marked, Hentschel, 7 In. 410.00
Vase, Stylized Rose, High Glaze, Bulbous, Hentschel, 7 In. 705.00
Vase, Turquoise Matte Glaze, Raised Leaves, Marked, W. Hentschel, 5 1/4 In. 410.00
Vase, Yellow High Glaze, Raised Dots, Lines, Marked, Hentschel, 5 1/2 In. 705.00
Vase, Yellow High Glaze, Raised Lines, Marked, Hentschel, 5 1/4 In. 590.00

KEW BLAS is the name used by the Union Glass Company of Somerville, Massachusetts. The name refers to an iridescent golden glass made from the 1890s to 1924. The iridescent glass was reminiscent of the Tiffany glass of the period.

Vase, Gold Iridescent, Pulled Feathers, Cream Ground, Gold Rigaree, Signed, 7 3/4 In. ... 1325.00
Vase, Gold Pulled Feathers, Ivory Ground, Applied Lip, Gold Interior, 9 In. 705.00
Vase, Green Feathers, Gold, Ivory Ground, Gold Interior, Bulbous, Signed, 5 3/8 In. 1785.00
Vase, Opal, Green & Gold Pulled Feathers, Gold Interior, Reverse Trumpet, 9 In. 1150.00

KEWPIES, designed by Rose O'Neill, were first pictured in the *Ladies' Home Journal.* The figures, which are similar to pixies, were a success, and Kewpie dolls and figurines started appearing in 1911. Kewpie pictures and other items soon followed. Collectors search for all items that picture the little winged people.

Bisque, 1-Piece Head, Loop-Jointed Arms, Legs, O'Neill, Box, Germany, c.1912, 5 In. ... 550.00
Bisque, 1-Piece Head, Loop-Jointed Arms, O'Neill, Germany, c.1910, 12 In. 770.00
Bisque, Blunderboo, Crawling Baby, Blue Wings, Rose O'Neill, c.1912, 4 1/4 In. 1456.00
Bisque, Blunderboo, On Stomach, Doodle Dog, On Back, O'Neill, Germany, c.1910, 3 In. 2860.00
Bisque, Doodle Dog, Umbrella, 1 Piece, O'Neill, Germany, c.1910, 2 1/2 In. 880.00

A RECORD-SETTING YEAR

The media love to report record prices, amazing auctions, and high-priced discoveries that have little to do with the antiques and collectibles market of the average collector. It is news when a 240-year-old table sells for over $8 million or an 1899 ice cream dipper attracts a bid topping $17,000. Television's *Antiques Roadshow* likes to save a high-priced find for the dramatic ending, never mentioning that perhaps 10,000 appraisals were given before that one great treasure was found. EBay sends out publicity about high-priced sales on its Internet auctions, but little is said about the numerous collectibles offered on the website that did not sell.

Record prices are entertaining, but they're not a true measure of the general market or the possible finds in Grandma's attic. The fine arts market—paintings and sculptures—saw many record-setting sales this year. Several important painting collections were auctioned, perhaps because investments in the stock market were iffy and tangible assets were attractive. The surprise this year is that collectors of fine arts who feel prices are getting too high are turning to the decorative arts—chairs, art pottery, silver, or pieces by important twentieth-century industrial designers. This has raised prices for the best of the best. At the same time, prices for everyday vintage pieces, like head vases or toys, are going up, too, as serious collectors get older, wiser, and richer.

Wise collectors of any age and with a budget of any size know that buying the rarest pieces of the highest quality will almost always be good investments. Some are just much more expensive than others. Here are some of the past year's most interesting sales and record prices.

The Badminton cabinet was not named for the game, but for Badminton House, an historic estate in Gloucestershire, England, owned by the duke of Beaufort. (The game was also named for the estate.) The cabinet, commissioned by the third duke of Beaufort in 1726, has been called the last great work of art made in Florence, Italy, under the Medici family. It is now the most expensive piece of furniture ever sold at auction. Price: $36.7 million. The cabinet, bought for the Liechtenstein Museum in Vienna, is made of ebony, ormolu, lapis lazuli, agate, Sicilian red and green jasper, chalcedony, amethysts, and other hardstones.

Colored Victorian glass sold well at a January auction, setting several records. The surprise of the show was this 3½-inch-high Holly Amber tumbler with a beaded rim. The tumbler had been described but never pictured in books about Greentown glass, made by the Indiana Tumbler and Glass Company of Greentown, Indiana. There was some discussion of how the "tumbler" was meant to be used, because the rim made it hard to use as a drinking glass. It sold for a record $8,810.

Keep old toys away from children. Miss Liberty, an iron bell-ringing toy, sold for a high price at a toy auction in Maine because it was rare and in good condition. The toy, made by Kyser & Rex, had a repainted arm but still set a world record at $14,950. The auction of a famous toy collection was so successful, thirty-five new records were set.

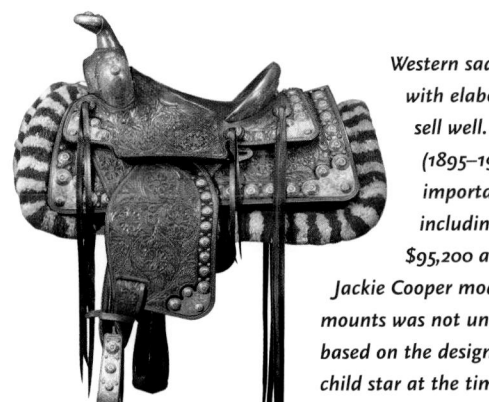

Western saddles made of tooled leather with elaborate silver mounts always sell well. Edward H. Bohlin (1895–1980) was one of the most important makers of western gear, including saddles and belts. So the $95,200 auction price of Bohlin's 1930s Jackie Cooper model saddle with sterling silver mounts was not unexpected. The saddle was based on the design of one made for Cooper, a child star at the time, for the film Lone Cowboy. The Cooper model available to the public with all accessories sold for $700 in the 1930s.

The Nicholas Brown tea table sold for a record $8.42 million at auction this year. The table, attributed to the famous cabinetmaker John Goddard of Newport, Rhode Island, was made about 1760. The mahogany Chippendale table, 26 3/4 inches high by 33 inches long by 19 1/2 inches deep, had descended through members of the Brown family.

Age alone does not determine value. This 33-inch-high Kangourou armchair was manufactured by the workshops of Jean Prouvé about 1951. The oak chair frame has legs and a "cushion" made of lacquered sheet and tubular metal. It brought a record $136,800.

The French Vincennes Porcelain Manufactory made pieces marked in blue with the entwined initials LL and a letter date. This oval bowl is marked with the letter A for 1753 and the marks of a decorator, Louis Denis Armand, who is known for decorations that include birds. The bowl sold for a Vincennes record $481,450 in March, only to be surpassed in May by a Vincennes cistern at $1.8 million.

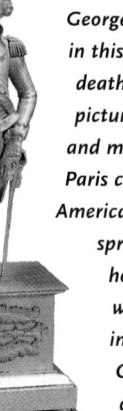

George Washington has always been an icon in this country. For many years after his death, his image was used on clocks, fabrics, pictures, and even furniture. A cast-brass and mercury-gilded mantel clock by Dubuc, a Paris clockmaker, was made about 1810 for American buyers. The clock has an eight-day spring-powered clockwork that strikes the hour and the half hour. The familiar words, "Washington, First in War, First in Peace, First in the Hearts of His Countrymen" and "E Pluribus Unum," are on the front of the clock. The eagle with an olive branch and shield and the sword held by Washington are all symbols of his life. The 19½-inch-high clock sold at auction for a record $314,000.

An auction house sometimes publicizes a top price as a record for its own sales, whether or not it's also a world record. An auction in Ohio sold a Toulouse-Lautrec poster, Le Divan Japonais, after the auctioneer tried out his best pun: "Everyone should bid. After all, what do you have Toulouse?" The crowd may have groaned, but bidders reacted by pushing the price up to $32,200 and setting a record for the auction house.

Every collector dreams of finding a piece of Fabergé that has been ignored because the owner could not translate the Russian alphabet. The hardstone figures Carl Fabergé made in the early 1900s are small and were once fairly inexpensive. This figure, made about 1910, is only 6 inches high and represents a boyar, a Russian nobleman. It was not inexpensive. The figure sold for a record $1.8 million.

Grueby pottery, made in Boston from 1897 to 1920, has been among the highest-priced American art pottery since the 1970s. This 14⅝-inch-high green matte vase decorated with yellow irises auctioned for a record $136,800. The vase is impressed Grueby Faience Co., Boston USA. The letter N in a circle on the bottom of the vase is the mark used by the modeler Lillian Newman.

The first gold coin made in America was the famous doubloon designed by Ephraim Brasher in 1787. It was made before there was a working United States Mint. Fewer than ten examples of the legendary Brasher doubloon still exist. The coin is known outside the numismatic world because of a 1947 mystery movie titled The Brasher Doubloon. The coin dealer in the movie said the doubloon was worth $10,000 or more. A doubloon that sold at auction in 1981 for $625,000 was auctioned again this year for $2.99 million.

Sometimes a record price is set by a cleverly designed piece that was made to solve a problem inexpensively. In 1949 Jean Prouvé and his brother designed inexpensive houses and buildings to be constructed in France's African colonies. Some of the prefabricated building parts were never packed and shipped. This pair of perforated metal doors auctioned for $680,000 to tie the world auction record for a postwar design. Prouvé had previously designed several prefab houses for working-class families that included built-in beds and a complete bathroom and kitchen.

A few rare baseball cards in mint condition have set records in the past. This 1915 Cracker Jack card is rare and graded "mint 9," the highest possible designation. Ty Cobb is the pictured player. The card's quality and rarity led to a record auction price of $82,356.

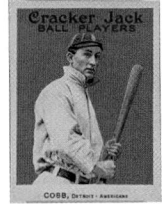

Figurines of owls are not common. These 9-inch-high Bow porcelain tawny owls were made about 1755. The pair sold for $228,000, a world auction record for Bow porcelain.

Honus Wagner is probably the most famous baseball player there ever was, if you ask baseball card collectors. Fewer than ten Sweet Caporal Cigarettes T206 Wagner cards in good or better condition are known to exist. Owners of a Wagner card have elite status among collectors. This card, in fabulous condition, did not set a new record, but it sold for $205,831. The highest price ever paid for the T206 Wagner card is $1.27 million.

Furniture with a black enamel or lacquered finish called japanning was the height of elegance in eighteenth-century America. Few pieces were signed by the artist. This Queen Anne maple and pine high chest of drawers made about 1735 is signed "Rob Davis," the name of a well-known japanner working in Boston. The extraordinary value of the high chest is the result of its well-preserved decoration. The auction price was a record $1.88 million.

Russia's Grand Duke Constantin Nicholaevich owned this thirty-piece gilded silver tea and coffee set. It was made by Sazikov of Moscow in 1848. A telephone bidder bought it at auction for a record $1.8 million.

Delft is a tin-glazed pottery made since the seventeenth century. Today the name is associated with the blue and white pottery manufactured in the Netherlands and other countries. This Dutch Delft plaque picturing a river landscape was made in the late seventeenth century. The 22³/₄-by-16³/₄-inch plaque sold for the world record price of $162,688.

Any collectible that moves or makes noise has added value. In 1879 a Canadian gold mine owner took a trip to Switzerland and ordered this music box. The B. A. Bremond orchestral music box with twelve interchangeable 19¹/₄-inch cylinders sold this year for a surprising $82,500, a record price and more than twice the presale estimate. The box, with organ and flute attachments, was on a matching three-drawer stand.

Sometimes a toy is so rare, it is the only one known to exist. But that doesn't mean a new record is set every time that one toy is sold. The only known Mego Man robot, a 10-inch Japanese-made toy, is probably the rarest of toy robots. It was in the well-known F. H. Griffith collection. The colorful lithographed toy auctioned for $23,100 last fall, but it sold for $37,500 five years ago.

It is probably not a surprise that the auction record for a music or concert poster belongs to a Beatles sign. The 1966 Shea Stadium concert poster by Murray Poster Printing Company, 23½ by 18½ inches, sold for $132,737 at an absentee auction. The poster was in good condition, with a few minor creases and wrinkles.

Advertising items have been popular with collectors since the 1980s. Art pottery is the most searched-for subject on our website and other Internet sites for collectors. So when a "double-dash" Pepsi syrup dispenser, designed by Frederick Hurten Rhead about 1902 and marked "Avon Co.," was offered for sale on eBay, the record price of $34,925 was not totally unexpected. The previous record for the dispenser, set in March 2004, was $27,000.

Hires Root Beer is almost as popular with advertising collectors as Pepsi-Cola. This syrup dispenser, showing the Hires boy in a bib, has brown trim, one of a few trim colors originally used. The 19-inch-high urn sold for $67,100 even though the lid had been restored. It is a record price for this version of the dispenser.

The tall-case clock, often called a grandfather clock, was an important timepiece in the eighteenth century. The case was large enough to hold the swinging pendulum that powered the movement of the hands. This carved mahogany Queen Anne clock by Peter Stretch shows the phases of the moon and the date, as well as the time. It was a record at $1.69 million.

Provenance (ownership) is important.
If a member of John F. Kennedy's family owned a chair, table, or even a wastebasket, it will sell for a high price at auction. When some furniture from the Kennedy family homes was auctioned, the prices were interesting. A rocking chair, probably used by the president and made by the P. and P. Chair Company of Asheboro, North Carolina, brought $96,000. A similar chair without the Kennedy association would sell for less than $350.

Even an inexperienced collector can recognize the skill and workmanship required to create this reticulated vase. The Royal Worcester porcelain vase, made about 1900, is 6³/₄ inches high. Its body is solid, with an added layer of porcelain hand-cut in an open honeycomb pattern. The vase, with serpent-shaped handles, raised gilt dots, and subtle blue and buff glaze, auctioned for a record-setting $31,725.

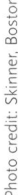

A yellow pine hanging cupboard sat undisturbed in a dark closet for 150 years. Before that, it was used as a medicine cabinet. The cupboard, it turned out, had been painted and decorated about 1800 by Johannes Spitler, a well-known Virginia folk artist. The paint was in excellent original condition; the porcelain knobs were nineteenth-century replacements. The cupboard, 35 inches high by 18½ inches wide by 12 inches deep, sold for the record price of $962,500.

Art critics were shocked when a pair (only one is shown) of "kitschy" dog paintings by Cassius Marcellus Coolidge sold for a record $590,400. The dogs playing poker are a part of our American "vocabulary," and copies were made for calendars, art prints, and even TV commercials. These original oil paintings, part of a group of sixteen made for the advertising firm of Brown & Bigelow, were painted in 1903.

Ice cream dippers bring surprisingly high prices at flea markets and shows, and rarities sell for thousands. Veeder Manufacturing Company of Hartford, Connecticut, made this scoop with an automatic counting mechanism in the handle. The scoop, made of nickel-plated brass, was patented in 1899. It sold for the record price of $17,325.

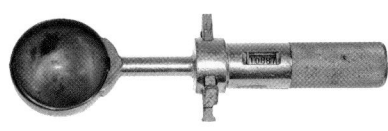

A pair of ormolu-mounted Höchst figurines of parrots sold for a world auction record of $156,000. The ormolu-mounted German birds date from about 1752.

This unusual appliquéd cotton Civil War–era quilt shows buildings, figures, animals, and more. It is made of printed cotton with embroidered details. The buildings were all important to the maker, Margaret Hazzard of Berrien County, Michigan. She made it for her husband to take to the war. The 1864 quilt sold for $82,250.

The Jazz Bowl is probably the most important example of Art Deco design made in America. The 16-inch-diameter punch bowl was made by the Cowan Pottery Studio of Rocky River, Ohio, in 1931. The designer and potter was Viktor Schreckengost, who is well-known for both his pottery and his industrial designs for items like children's pedal cars, bicycles, printing presses, electric fans, and dinnerware. The bowl was a special order from Eleanor Roosevelt, who ordered a "New Yorkish" design. She later ordered two more to give to her husband when he won the 1932 presidential election. Eventually, about one hundred examples of the Jazz Bowl were made. Some were produced with slight variations in color, size, or style of rim. This bowl, dating from about 1931, brought a record $254,400 at auction.

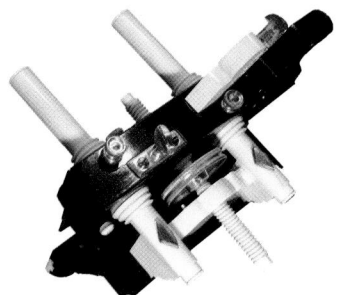

Tools are rarely as beautiful as this record-setting center-wheel plow plane. It was made by the Sandusky Tool Company of Sandusky, Ohio, for a show, possibly the 1876 Centennial Exhibition, and was never intended for use. The plane is made of ebony and ivory with nickel-plated metal parts. It brought $114,400 at a tool auction.

Southern-made antique furniture was often mistakenly identified as English until the 1950s. Examination of the wood types, records of known furniture makers, and other information have made it possible to attribute this Chippendale table to Virginia. The mahogany and cherry table made between 1760 and 1775 has a maple top. Its style is now recognized as a distinctly eastern Virginia version of English Chippendale. The table sold for the high price of $124,750.

A collection of lacy glass open salt dishes, most made by the Boston & Sandwich Glass Works, was auctioned in the fall. Top salt was an emerald green Basket of Flowers design in exceptional condition. The buyers had flown to Virginia from Chicago to bid on the glass. The price: a record $10,450.

Steamboat-shaped open salts are popular with collectors. A blue opaque salt purchased in 1974 for $500 sold this year for $7,425, setting a new record for the shape. The salt is embossed with the name "Lafayet" and has two four-pane windows on the stern. The record price for a steamboat salt was broken four times at the auction.

As early as the 1940s, folk art collectors recognized the quality of the wood carvings of Wilhelm Schimmel, a Pennsylvania carver. His carved figures, especially eagles, were often bought for museums and important collections. This late nineteenth-century painted pine eagle, 28 inches wide, sold for the record price of $254,400.

This wool quilt has been called the finest American embroidered quilt known. It was made in South Solon, Maine, about 1830–35. It was probably designed by the maker. Included in the design are embroidered soldiers on horseback or carrying flags, portraits of men, women, and children probably related to the quilter, a cat on a cushion, a tree filled with turkeys, a large bird on a building, and other unusual designs. Many different types of stitches were used to make outlines, hair, or tufts. Bidders agreed with the experts and the amazing quilt brought $97,750.

Enameled silver or copper was popular during the Arts and Crafts period. Elizabeth Copeland studied enameling in England, then returned to Boston to work at the Handicraft Shop. Her work was admired and nationally recognized. Her intricate handmade silver and enamel pieces required hours of work and are rare. This 1915 silver box with cloisonné enamel set a record for her work when it sold for $66,000. It measures $3^{3}/_{4}$ by $7^{1}/_{2}$ by $5^{1}/_{4}$ inches.

Sometimes a record is set because of great interest in the style or maker, new information about rarity, or auction fever. Last year a table (a Janus-line side table, Model 5633) designed in 1957 by Edward Wormley for Dunbar sold for $8,280 at auction. The tabletop was set with old Tiffany Studios Favrile glass tiles. An almost identical table sold this year for a record $27,600. The table must have pleased the designer. There's a period photo of a similar table in Wormley's living room.

Who wouldn't want a poster for the 1959 cult movie Attack of the 50 Ft. Woman? *The record price of $13,800 was paid for the three-sheet poster, 81 by 41 inches. The poster, mounted on linen, had minor damage and restoration. More than five other movie posters set records at the same sale.*

Sometimes a vintage collectible that was originally inexpensive has nostalgic appeal that ups the resale price. There are many collectors of head vases, the inexpensive florist ware popular in the 1960s and 1970s. A never-seen-before 7-inch vase sold at the Head Vase Convention auction for the highest price ever paid for a head vase, $6,100. At the same auction, a Marilyn (Monroe) vase brought $4,400. Before this auction, the highest price ever paid for a head vase was $4,000.

Soap Hollow is a valley near Johnstown, Pennsylvania. Amish and Mennonite craftsmen made stencil-decorated furniture there from 1836 to 1924. A 40½-inch-high cherry and poplar chest with original red and green paint, gold stenciled decorations, and porcelain pulls was sold at an Ohio auction. The chest was signed "Manufactured by Jeremiah Stahl" and had "S.M. 1867" on a side panel. It set a record at $132,250, more than ten times the estimated price.

Russian porcelains, especially those from the Imperial Porcelain Manufactory of St. Petersburg, are among the finest in the world. These 54-inch-high palace vases have an 1825 mark. Each vase is skillfully decorated with an Italian landscape. The pair brought the record price of $3.94 million.

Who can resist the chubby, googly-eyed cherub with topknot and blue wings known as a Kewpie? The elfin creatures first appeared in the Ladies Home Journal in 1909. They were the creations of Rose O'Neill, an American illustrator. There soon were Kewpie dolls, figures, paper dolls, vases, and other items. A huge collection of Kewpie memorabilia brought record prices this year. This bisque Kewpie riding a mountain goat, made in Germany about 1912, auctioned for the record price of $6,325.

Kewpie, Print,
Kewpie In Baseball
Cap, Eating Ice
Cream, No. 836,
11 1/2 x 8 1/2 In.

Kewpie, Print, Kewpie
On Moon, Eating Ice
Cream, No. 2531,
14 1/2 x 10 1/2 In.

Bisque, Football Player, Side-Glancing Eyes, c.1915, 4 3/4 In. 420.00
Bisque, Glass Sleep Eyes, Looking Down, Jointed Shoulders, Mohair, Dressed, 6 In. 220.00
Bisque, Green Chair, Book, Head Turned, Blue Wings, Rose O'Neill, c.1912, 5 1/2 In. 3025.00
Bisque, Hottentot, Brown, Standing, Outstretched Arms, O'Neill, Germany, 1910, 4 1/2 In. . 1320.00
Bisque, Huggers, Boy & Girl, Painted Features, Original Clothes, 2 1/4 In. 60.00
Bisque, Huggers, Unjointed, Smiling, Looking At Each Other, Blue Wings, 3 1/2 In. 127.00
Bisque, Jointed Arms, Blue Overalls, Garden Hat, O'Neill, Germany, c.1910, 4 1/2 In. 2090.00
Bisque, Jointed Arms, Romper, Stocking Cap, O'Neill, Germany, c.1910, 4 1/2 In. 1430.00
Bisque, Jointed Arms, Side-Glancing Eyes, Bow Around Neck, Box, 5 1/2 In. 310.00
Bisque, Jointed Shoulders, Looking Left, Blue Wings, Dress, O'Neill, 6 In. 165.00
Bisque, Loop-Jointed Arms, Blue Wings, Side-Glancing Eyes, c.1910, 10 1/2 In. 1100.00
Bisque, Loop-Jointed Arms, Blue Wings, Side-Glancing Eyes, Rose O'Neill, c.1910, 9 In. . 530.00
Bisque, Loop-Jointed Limbs, Blue Wings, Side-Glancing Eyes, c.1910, 8 In. 660.00
Bisque, Loop-Jointed, Starfish Shaped Hands, Blond Topknot, Side-Glancing Eyes, 5 In. . . 825.00
Bisque, On Yellow Sled, Germany, c.1910, 2 In. 1045.00
Bisque, Painted Features, Molded, Painted Hair, Wings, Jointed Arms, O'Neill, 5 1/4 In. . . 50.00
Bisque, Painted Features, Molded, Painted Hair, Wings, Jointed Arms, O'Neill, 5 3/4 In. . . 105.00
Bisque, Painted Features, Side-Glancing Eyes, Reclining, O'Neill, 4 In. 305.00
Bisque, Policeman, Painted Socks & Blacks Hose, Brass Buttons, O'Neill, 1910, 4 In. 530.00
Bisque, Seated, On Pillow, Ball, No. 5496, Germany, c.1910, 3 1/2 In. 1430.00
Bisque, Seated, Outstretched Arms, Black Cat, Germany, c.1910, 3 In. 550.00
Bisque, Shoulder Head, Painted Eyes To Left, Smiling, Alt, Beck & Gottschalck, 5 In. 715.00
Bisque, Side-Glancing Eyes, Blond Topknot, Standing Inside Egg, 4 1/2 & 5 In., Pair 715.00
Bisque, Soldier, Tall Helmet, Belt, Rifle, Sword, Germany, c.1910, 5 In. 1870.00
Bisque, Traveler, Unjointed, Looking Right, Molded Hair, Umbrella, Satchel, 3 1/2 In. 149.00
Bisque, Unjointed, Molded Hair, Wings, Holding Shamrock, 2 In. 360.00
Candy Container, Barrel Bank, Glass, Tin Lid, Coin Slot, Painted, c.1919, 3 1/8 In. 80.00
Celluloid, Jointed Arms, Molded & Painted Hair, O'Neill, 4 In. 10.00
Celluloid, Tree Light, Violin, Japan, 6 1/8 In. 45.00
Composition, Elastic Jointed Arms, 1913 Patent, 8 1/2 In. 200.00
Composition, Jointed, Tag, Cameo, Box, 12 In. 395.00
Pin, Bisque, Painted, Paper Label, 2 In. 45.00
Postcard, Preparing Yule Log, Christmas Tree Seen Through Windowpane Scene, 1913 . . . 39.00
Print, Kewpie In Baseball Cap, Eating Ice Cream, No. 836, 11 1/2 x 8 1/2 In. . . . . *Illus* 184.00
Print, Kewpie On Moon, Eating Ice Cream, No. 2531, 14 1/2 x 10 1/2 In. . . . . *Illus* 201.00
Salt & Pepper, Porcelain, Seated, Looking To Left, Chick, Egg, Bunny, 2 In. 330.00
Scootles, Composition, Painted Features, Cameo Doll Co., 12 In. 190.00
Seated Feeding Bottle To Doodle Dog, 3 1/2 In. 2750.00
Soap, Votes For Women Tag, Box, c.1917 . . . . 560.00
Tea Service, Porcelain, Royal Rudolstadt, Germany, c.1915, 5 1/2-In. Pot, 15 Piece 880.00
Vase, Holding Teddy Bear, Square Column, Germany, c.1910, 5 1/4 In. 990.00

KIMBALL, see Cluthra category.

KING'S ROSE, see Soft Paste category.

KITCHEN utensils of all types, from eggbeaters to bowls, are collected today. Handmade wooden and metal items, like ladles and apple peelers, were made in the early nineteenth century. Mass-produced pieces, like iron apple peelers and graniteware, were made in the nineteenth century. Also included in this category are utensils used for other household chores, such as laundry and cleaning. Other kitchen wares are listed under manufacturers' names or under Advertising, Iron, Tool, or Wooden.

Apple Corer, Silver Mounted, George III, Ivory Handle, Phipps & Robinson, 1805, 5 In. . .	424.00
Bed Smoother, Wood, Painted Flowers, Inset Handle, Curved Edge, 1838, 20 In. . . . . *Illus*	80.00
Beef Shaver, Enterprise Improved Rotary, Wood Base, Drawer, Phila., 1901, 22 x 26 In. . . .	415.00
Board, Cutting, Pine, Breadboard Ends, 24 x 17 1/2 In.	90.00
Board, Slaw, Maple, Hand Forged Blade, Cutout Heart, 22 x 7 1/2 In.	330.00
Board, Slaw, Maple, Sawtooth Blade, Circular Cutout Top, Hole, 23 x 7 1/2 In.	275.00
Board, Slaw, Maple, Steel Blade, Cutout Handle, 24 1/2 x 8 In.	385.00
Board, Slaw, Oak, Steel Blade, 2 Cutouts, Half-Circle, 18 x 7 1/2 In.	140.00
Board, Slaw, Oak, Steel Blade, Lollipop Cutout Handle, 20 3/4 x 6 1/2 In.	330.00
Board, Slaw, Pine, Metal Blades, Lollipop Top, Pennsylvania German, 52 x 12 1/2 In.	115.00
Board, Slaw, Walnut, Hand Forged Blade, Cutout Heart Shape Handle, 20 1/4 x 8 1/4 In. . .	385.00
Board, Slaw, Walnut, Round Cutout Handle, Hole, 22 1/2 x 9 1/4 In.	300.00
Board, Slaw, Walnut, Steel Blade, 2 Cutout Hearts, Scrolled Top, 19 1/4 x 6 3/4 In.	440.00
Board, Slaw, Walnut, Stylized Heart Cutout, Germanic Stars, 1887, 16 1/2 x 7 In.	2090.00
Broom, Cornstalk, Woven, Tied, Wooden Handle, 47 In.	66.00
Broom, Hearth, Turned Wood Handle, Stenciled Fruit, 2-Color Horsehair Bristles, 30 In. . .	200.00
Butter Mold, look under Mold, Butter in this category.	
Butter Paddle, Carved, Horse Head Handle, 12 In.	345.00
Butter Paddle, Maple, Carved, Exotic Bird Handle, Patina, 8 1/4 In.	2070.00
Butter Paddle, Oak, Inscribed Ann Besson, Feb. 12th, 1860, 7 1/4 x 3 3/4 In.	50.00
Butter Paddle, Wood, Carved, Heart, Crosshatched, Reeded, 9 x 2 5/8 In.	220.00
Butter Scoop, Curly Maple, Hook Handle, Incised Tulip, 1850, 5 1/2 In.	920.00
Butter Stamp, Acorn, 1-Piece Handle, Round, 4 In.	400.00
Butter Stamp, Bird, Serrated Edge, Carved, Turned, Poplar, 2 x 3 In.	105.00
Butter Stamp, Bull & Fence, Leaves, Scalloped Coggle Wheel Border, Pine, 5 In.	190.00
Butter Stamp, Chip, Gouge Carved, Eagle, Spread Wings, Tulip, 1800s, 5 & 3 1/4 In.	3290.00
Butter Stamp, Compass Star, Hearts, 1-Piece Handle, Scrubbed Surface, 4 1/4 In.	489.00
Butter Stamp, Cow Over Cow, Softwood, 4-Sided, 3 3/4 x 2 3/8 In.	50.00
Butter Stamp, Cow, Leaf, Cogwheel Border, Carved, Poplar, 2 x 4 3/8 In.	200.00
Butter Stamp, Diamond, Stylized Flowers, Serrated Edges, Wood, 8 3/8 x 3 1/4 In.	165.00
Butter Stamp, Eagle, Leaves, Serrated Border, Pine, 2 1/2 x 4 3/4 In.	1210.00
Butter Stamp, Eagle, Leaves, Star, Coggle Wheel Band, Pine, 2 1/2 x 4 1/2 In.	798.00
Butter Stamp, Eagle, Leaves, Star, Serrated Border, Pine, 3 x 4 1/2 In.	550.00
Butter Stamp, Eagle, Shield, Flowers, Incised Band, Softwood, 2 1/2 x 4 In.	55.00
Butter Stamp, Eagle, Spread Wings, Shield, Branch, Handle, 2 5/8 In.	230.00
Butter Stamp, Flowers, 2 Fern Leaves, Poplar, Carved, 4 3/8 In.	11.00
Butter Stamp, Flowers, Geometric Design, Handle, Carved, Poplar, 6 x 3 5/8 In.	120.00
Butter Stamp, Geometric Flowers, Carved, Softwood, 4 x 3 1/8 In.	44.00
Butter Stamp, Lollipop, 2-Sided, Hearts, Starflower, Dark Patina, 11 3/8 In.	775.00
Butter Stamp, Lollipop, Carved, 6-Point Star, Flower, Rope Border, Pine, 9 x 4 In.	3300.00
Butter Stamp, Lollipop, Compass Wheel, Serrated Chip Carved Edge, Pine, 7 x 4 In.	165.00

Kitchen, Bed Smoother, Wood, Painted
Flowers, Inset Handle, Curved Edge,
1838, 20 In.

Kitchen, Dough
Box, Mixed
Wood, Sliding
Top, Coffin
Shape, 1800-25,
29 x 37 In.

Butter Stamp, Oak Leaves, Acorns, Incised, Peg Handle, Poplar, 3 1/2 x 4 1/2 In. 45.00
Butter Stamp, Pineapple, Cased, Pewter Straps, Plunger, 4 3/4 x 4 1/2 In. 85.00
Butter Stamp, Pineapple, Stars, Coggle Wheel Band, Carved, Poplar, 2 5/8 x 3 5/8 In. 60.00
Butter Stamp, Pinwheel, Coggle Wheel Border, Round, Poplar, 2 1/2 x 3 3/4 In. 300.00
Butter Stamp, Sheaf Of Wheat, 1776 Centennial, 1876, Coggled Border, Poplar, 3 x 4 In. . 770.00
Butter Stamp, Sheaf Of Wheat, Flower Band, Handle, Case, Softwood, 5 x 3 1/2 In. 17.00
Butter Stamp, Sheaf Of Wheat, Flowers, Serrated Border, Carved, Pine, 4 x 7 x 3 1/2 In. . 300.00
Butter Stamp, Strawberry, Screw-On Handle, Poplar, 3 x 3 In. 165.00
Butter Stamp, Swan, Flowers, Serrated Border, Turned Case, Poplar, 5 1/2 x 4 1/2 In. 66.00
Butter Stamp, Swan, On Water, Coggle Wheel Band, Poplar, 2 1/2 x 4 3/8 In. 39.00
Butter Stamp, Thistle, Scalloped Bands, Round, Turned, Poplar, 2 1/2 x 4 1/4 In. 45.00
Butter Stamp, Tulip, Chip Carved, Poplar, 3 3/4 x 2 In. 2090.00
Butter Stamp, Tulip, Heart, Compass Wheel, Oval, Pine, 3 3/4 x 6 3/4 In. 2860.00
Cabbage Cutter, 2 Tiers, Pierced Detail, Brass Fittings, Hickory, Ash, 13 x 7 x 7 In. 85.00
Cabbage Cutter, 3 Steel Blades, Indianapolis Sanitary, Patent April 18, 1905 .... 110.00
Cabbage Cutter, Cutout Heart Crest, 2 Blades, Oak Panel, 49 In. 200.00
Cabbage Cutter, Heart Cutout Handle, Iron Cutting Base, Poplar, 23 x 7 3/4 In. 175.00
Cake Board, Carved, Basket Of Fruit Flowers, Bird, J. Conger, 10 3/4 x 11 1/4 In. 2070.00
Cake Board, Carved, Horse, Rider, Swan, Ship, Adam & Eve, Rooster, 21 1/2 x 3 In. 359.00
Cake Board, Flower Basket, Wreath, Yellow Ground, Handle, 1831, 31 1/2 In. 1295.00
Cake Board, Indian Brave, Mahogany, J. Conger, N.Y., c.1800, 11 3/4 x 5 1/2 In. 2040.00
Cake Board, Indian Princess, Walnut, 2-Sided, Paladin & Palmer, N.Y., c.1740, 7 x 14 In. . 2400.00
Cake Board, Man On Horse, Relief Carved, Poplar, 3 1/4 x 14 In. 240.00
Cake Board, War Of 1812, Officers, Ship, Mahogany, M. Hall, N.Y., c.1815, 12 x 12 In. ... 7800.00
Cake Board, Woman, 10 Men, Articulated, Tin Outlines, 11 1/2 x 9 3/4 In. 358.00
Candy Roller Machine, 4 Pair Of Pattern Rollers, Early 1900s 440.00
Canister, Cover, Metal, Mexicana, Homer Laughlin, 7 In. 30.00
Canister, Tin, Cylindrical, 2 Handles, Cone Shaped Lid, Curved Handle, 12 x 9 In. 20.00
Carpet Sweeper, Winchester, Sanitary, Store Version, Rope Bumper, 48 x 14 In. 1135.00
Carpet Sweeper, Winchester, Sanitary, Wood Handle, 14 x 4-In. Head 460.00
Cauldron, Brass, Iron, Painted, American, 19th Century, 17 In. 60.00
Cherry Pitter, Tin, Removes Pits From 8 Cherries, Marshall Mfg., 1920, 12 In. 135.00
Cherry Stoner, Cast Iron, No. 1, Enterprise, Philadelphia, 1809 .... 89.00
Churn, Oak, Steel Bands, Broom Handle Dasher, 19th Century, 19 1/2 In. 288.00
Churn, Wood, Gray Paint, Stave, Iron Hoop, Early 1800s, 34 1/2 In. 410.00
Churn, Wood, Side Crank Handle, Metal Straps, Provence, 17 x 12 In. 500.00
Coffee Grinders are listed in the Coffee Mill category.
Coffee Maker, Mr. Coffee, Joe DiMaggio, Box 40.00
Coffeepot, Tin, Painted, Black, Yellow Flowers, Red, Yellow Bands, Hooked Spout, 11 In. 1528.00
Colander, Tin, Round, Punched Flowers, Bands, 2 Reeded Strap Handles, 4 x 12 In. 1870.00
Cookie Board, Carved, Steam Engine, Engineer, 7 3/4 x 11 In. 345.00
Cookie Board, Man On Horse, Carved Wood, Watkins, Conger, Late 1800s, 10 3/4 In. 645.00
Cookie Cutter, Bird, Crested, Flat Back, Tin, 4 1/2 In. 39.00
Cookie Cutter, Bird, Fantail, Flat Back, Tin, 4 1/2 x 5 In. 28.00
Cookie Cutter, Bird, Fantail, Flat Back, Tin, 4 x 2 1/2 In. 25.00
Cookie Cutter, Bird, Fantail, Folk Art Style, Flat Back, 6 1/2 x 5 1/2 In. 230.00
Cookie Cutter, Bird, Flat Back, Hole, C-Shape Handle, 3 1/2 x 3 3/4 In. 35.00
Cookie Cutter, Bird, Flat Back, Hole, Tin, 2 1/2 x 2 5/8 In. 25.00
Cookie Cutter, Bird, Flat Back, Hole, Tin, 2 7/8 x 4 5/8 In. 25.00
Cookie Cutter, Bird, Flying, Flat Back, Tin, Hole, Strap Handle, 3 x 4 In. 25.00
Cookie Cutter, Bird, On Pedestal, V-Shaped Tail, Flat Back, Tin, 4 1/2 x 3 1/4 In. 50.00
Cookie Cutter, Bird, Standing, Flat Back, 3 Holes, Strap Handle, Tin, 3 x 2 In. ......25.00 to 55.00
Cookie Cutter, Bird, Standing, Large Tail, Flat Back, Hole, Tin, 3 1/2 x 4 3/4 In. 35.00
Cookie Cutter, Birds, On Nest, Kissing, Square Back, Applied Handle, Tin, 6 x 3 In. 745.00
Cookie Cutter, Cavalryman, On Horseback, Tin, 10 x 8 3/4 In. 489.00
Cookie Cutter, Chimney Sweep, Tinned Sheet Iron, 1800s, 8 x 6 In. 645.00
Cookie Cutter, Deer, Tinned Sheet Iron, 1800s, 6 1/8 x 6 1/2 In. 175.00
Cookie Cutter, Dog, Flat Back, Hole, Tin, 3 1/2 x 5 In. 22.00
Cookie Cutter, Dove, Flying, Flat Back, 3 Holes, Tin, 4 1/2 x 6 1/4 In. 95.00
Cookie Cutter, Eagle, Flat Back, Strap Handle, Tin, 7 x 7 7/8 In. 195.00
Cookie Cutter, Eagle, Sheet Iron, 1800s, 3 7/8 x 4 5/8 In. 120.00
Cookie Cutter, Eagle, Stylized, Flat Back, Applied Strap Handle, 4 1/2 x 4 In. 65.00
Cookie Cutter, Elephant, Flat, Tin, 4 1/2 x 3 1/2 In. 45.00

Kitchen, Flue Cover, Agate Ware, Stands The Racket, Children Banging Pots, Cardboard, 9 In.

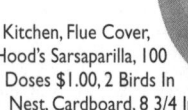

Kitchen, Flue Cover, Hood's Sarsaparilla, 100 Doses $1.00, 2 Birds In Nest, Cardboard, 8 3/4 In.

Cookie Cutter, Gentleman, Galvanized Sheet Metal, c.1900, 5 x 12 1/2 In. 120.00
Cookie Cutter, Goose, Flying, Flat Back, Hole, Tin, 2 x 2 3/4 In. 25.00
Cookie Cutter, Heart, Flat Back, Tin, 4 x 4 1/4 In. 95.00
Cookie Cutter, Heart, In Hand, Flat Back, Strap Handle, Tin, 3 1/8 x 3 In. 935.00
Cookie Cutter, Heart, In Hand, Flat Back, Tin, 3 1/4 x 3 In. 800.00
Cookie Cutter, Horse, Flat Back, 2 Holes, Tin, 4 x 5 7/8 In. 75.00
Cookie Cutter, Horse, Flat Back, Crimped Edges, 2 Holes, Tin, 5 x 8 1/4 In. 110.00
Cookie Cutter, Horse, Prancing, Galvanized Sheet Metal, 1900s, 8 x 9 1/8 In. 90.00
Cookie Cutter, Parrot, Perched, Flat Back, 2 Holes, Tin, 8 1/2 x 3 3/4 In. 135.00
Cookie Cutter, Peacock, Flat Back, 2 Holes, Tin, 3 1/4 x 5 In. 35.00
Cookie Cutter, Peacock, Tail, Flat Back, Hole, Tin, 3 1/4 x 4 3/4 In. 55.00
Cookie Cutter, Pig, Tinned Sheet Iron, 1800s, 3 3/8 x 6 1/8 In. 145.00
Cookie Cutter, Pitcher, Flat Back, Hole, Tin, 4 1/4 x 3 3/4 In. 30.00
Cookie Cutter, Rabbit, Seated, Tin, 10 1/2 In. 200.00
Cookie Cutter, Rooster, Crowing, Crimped Edges, Flat Back Plate, Tin, 6 x 3 x 1 In. 330.00
Cookie Cutter, Rooster, Tinned Sheet Iron, Late 1800s, 6 1/4 x 6 1/8 In. 120.00
Cookie Cutter, Whale, Flat Back, Strap Handle, Tin, 1 5/8 x 3 7/8 In. 40.00
Cream Separator, Clam Shell Shape, Wooden, Patinated, N.Y., 1800s, 7 1/2 x 4 1/2 In. ... 345.00
Cream Separator, DeLaval, Table Top, Junior No. 2, Art Deco Design, 22 In. 259.00
Crock, Cake, Tanware, Brown Glaze, Tulips, Leaves, New Geneva, 9 x 7 1/4 In. 1150.00
Crock Stand, Yellow Pine, Poplar, Green Paint, 2 Shelves, 37 x 14 x 44 In. 400.00
Dipper, Open Handle, Carved, Scratch Carved Date, Patina, Wood, 1744, 3 7/8 In. 718.00
Dipper, Scalloped, Carved, Burl Bowl, Wooden Handle, Dark Patina, 12 3/4 In. 1380.00
Dough Box, Mixed Wood, Sliding Top, Coffin Shape, 1800-25, 29 x 37 In. .... *Illus* 633.00
Dough Box, Pine, On Frame, Turned Legs, Late 1800s, 25 1/2 x 33 x 17 In. 595.00
Dough Box, Pine, Vinegar Decorated, Canted, Cutout Handles, c.1840, 9 x 14 x 21 In. 2530.00
Dough Box, Red Paint, Turned & Raked Legs, 27 1/2 x 23 x 40 1/2 In. 1150.00
Dough Scraper, 3-Sided Blade, Wrought Iron, Brass Handle, Marked, 1853, 4 In. 1870.00
Dough Scraper, 3-Sided Blade, Wrought Iron, Cutout Heart, 3 1/2 x 4 In. 385.00
Dough Scraper, Bell Blade, Wrought Iron, Wriggle Work Tassels, 1854, 3 3/4 In. 1430.00
Dough Scraper, Bell Shaped Blade, Wrought Iron, Wriggle Work, 4 In. 3300.00
Dough Scraper, Brass Handle, Wrought Iron, 1843, 3 1/2 x 2 1/2 In. 1485.00
Dough Scraper, Brass, Iron, Peter Derr, 1856, 3 1/2 In. 1350.00
Dough Scraper, Heart Shaped Cutout On Blade, Wrought Iron, 3 1/2 x 3 1/4 In. 415.00
Dough Scraper, Triangular Blade, Wrought Iron, c.1900, 3 1/2 x 4 1/2 In. 310.00
Dough Scraper, Tulip Wriggle Work, Wrought Iron, Jonestown, 3 1/2 In. 1375.00
Duster, Peacock Feather, Cloth Weave, Turned Wood Handle, Wire Hanging Loop, 38 In. .. 70.00
Egg Carrier, 12 Milk Glass Eggs, Star Co., 8 1/2 x 6 1/2 In. 230.00
Egg Poacher, Pan, Copper, 2 Handles, 1870s, 10 1/2 In. 355.00
Egg Timer, Flip The Frog, Ceramic, 3 In. 275.00
Egg Timer, Prayer Lady, Ceramic, Pink & White, Enesco 95.00
Egg Timer, Rabbits, Ceramic, Double-Type, Goebel, Germany, 4 In. 75.00
Egg Timer, Telephone, Black Glaze On Clay, Japan, 2 In. 25.00
Egg Timer, Timothy Timer, Upraised Arms, Ceramic, Conley Liley, Cape May 65.00
Egg Timer, Windmill, Dog On Base, Ceramic, Japan, 3 3/4 In. 85.00
Egg Timer, Windmill, Pigs On Base, Ceramic, Japan, 3 3/4 In. 85.00
Egg Timer, Windmill, Yellow, Bird On Top, Ceramic, 4 In. 75.00
Eggbeater, Rotary, Wooden Handle, 1916 .... 10.00

Flour Sifter, Androck, 3 Screens, Hand-I-Sift, Red & White, Pantry Pattern, 1950s 30.00
Flue Cover, Agate Ware, Stands The Racket, Children Banging Pots, Cardboard, 9 In. *Illus*   65.00
Flue Cover, Girl, Flowers, Embossed, Cast Iron, Bradley Hubbard, 1911, 8 In. 280.00
Flue Cover, Hood's Sarsaparilla, 100 Doses $1.00, 2 Birds In Nest, Cardboard, 8 3/4 In. *Illus*   60.00
Flue Cover, Lady Gypsy, 7 1/4 In. 55.00
Flue Cover, Little Girl, Flowers, Ostrich Plumes On Hat, Brass Frame, 14 1/2 In. 259.00
Food Chopper, Horse Shape Swivel, Iron Blade, Wood Base & Handle, 14 x 6 1/2 In. 220.00
Fork, 2 Tines, Heart Handle, Incised Lines, Iron, 19 In. 98.00
Fork, Flesh, Iron, Punched Rosettes, Flat Handle, Hook, H. R. Fetter, 12 3/4 In. 415.00
Fork, Hearts, Arrow Finial, Diamond Shape Handle, Wrought Iron, 19 In. 800.00
Fork, Iron, 2 Tines, Flattened Handle, Stamped Decoration, 10 3/4 In. 305.00
Fork, Iron, Round To Flat Handle, Punch Design, Scrolled Hook, 15 3/4 In. 165.00
Fork, Roasting, 2 Tines, Baluster Handle, Cutout Heart, Hook, 15 x 2 In. 2970.00
Fork, Roasting, Iron, 2 Tines, Baluster Shaft, Stamped Panel, 1815, 17 x 2 In. 745.00
Grater, Nutmeg, Rectangular, Casket Shape, Silver, Canada, A.G. Wiseman, c.1865, 2 In. .   1885.00
Grater, Vegetable, Schroeter No. 10, Tin Hopper, Wood Plunger, Paint, c.1915, 13 1/2 In. .   70.00
Grater, Wooden, Metal Blade, Hanger Hole, 10 1/4 x 4 In. 85.00
Griddle, Hanging, Curved Arm, Iron, 15 x 15 x 14 In. 403.00
Griddle, Iron, Heart Shape, Flat Handle, Hanging Hole, 21 3/4 x 11 1/2 In. 140.00
Griddle, Revolving, Tripod Base, Scroll Feet, Handle, Wrought Iron, 13 x 4 1/2 In. 316.00
Griddle, Round, Revolving Plate, 3-Footed Frame, Tapered Handle, Iron, 4 x 16 x 37 In. . . .   316.00
Hot Dog Steamer, Stadium, Copper, Glass Panes, Condiment Cups On Lip, c.1925, 26 In.   1870.00
Hot Plate, Safety, Cast Iron, Round, Freidag, Freeport, Ill., 7 In. 55.00
Ice Crusher, Alaska, No. 1, Cast Iron, Alaska Freezer Co., 1880-1930, 13 x 11 In. 99.00
Ice Crusher, North Brothers, No. 100, Cast Iron, Philadelphia, 1930s, 13 x 10 In. 210.00
Ice Shaver, Crank Handle, Cast Iron, Snow King, Clawson, 20 x 18 x 11 In. 120.00
Ice Shaver, D.L. Bates & Brother, Cast Iron, Brass, Dayton, Ohio, 36 x 8 x 14 In. 3500.00
Icebox, Herrick, Oak, 5 Doors, Brass Hardware, Iowa, c.1905, 58 x 48 x 25 In. 430.00
Icebox, Oak Cabinet, 4 Paneled Doors, 6 Wire Shelves, Salesman's Sample, 16 In. 3175.00
Icebox, Oak, White Clad, Tin Liners, Simmons Hardware Co., 25 x 18 x 48 In. 460.00
Iron, Alcohol, Traveling, Omega, Trivet, Pad, Bottle, Case, Germany 125.00
Iron, Alcohol, Trivet, Fish In Hoop Trademark, Carl Kaltschmid, Germany 140.00
Iron, Charcoal, 2 Chimneys, 6 Dampers, Lift-Off Top, Electro, c.1913, 7 1/2 In. 160.00
Iron, Charcoal, Marvel, 3 Dampers, Trivet, c.1924, 6 5/8 In. 100.00
Iron, Combination, Embosser, Fluter, Brass Fluter Plates, Myers, 1871 Patent 270.00
Iron, Combination, Magic Fluter & Polisher, N.R. Streeter, 1876 Patent 400.00
Iron, Combination, Revolving, Victor, Laundry Iron Co., Racine, Wis., c.1890, 6 1/2 In. . . .   900.00
Iron, Combination, Sensible, Fluter, Rocker Plate, Box, N.R. Streeter, Pat'd 1876, 7 In. . . .   1000.00
Iron, Electric, Atlas, 220V, 400W, Porcelain, Cream Color, Germany, c.1850, 9 In. 90.00
Iron, Electric, Casco, Model N 101, Chrome, Hinged Bakelite Handle 20.00
Iron, Electric, Flat Work, Round, Chrome, Bakelite Handle, Knapp Monarch, c.1935, 6 In.   140.00
Iron, Electric, No. W100, Nickel Plated Body, Wood Handle, Winchester, c.1935, 6 3/4 In.   190.00
Iron, Electric, Saunders, Silver Streak, Blue, Pyrex, Art Deco, Mid 1900s, 7 1/2 In. 3100.00
Iron, Electric, Saunders, Silver Streak, Clear, Pyrex, Art Deco, Mid 1900s, 7 1/2 In. 2500.00
Iron, Fluter, Climax, Machine, Crank, Henry B. Adams, c.1869, 6 3/4 In. 300.00
Iron, Fluter, Crank, Mary Kenney Royal, No. 77, Pedestal, Red, Gold Trim 310.00
Iron, Fluter, Crank, Sliding Counter Weight, Cole Prize Medal, 1866 Patent 775.00
Iron, Fluter, Hand, Rolling, Slug, Sheet Brass, Henry A Doty, Wisconsin, 1872 Patent 400.00
Iron, Gas, Clarks, Fairy Prince, Trivet, Porcelain, Blue Enamel, England, Mid 1900s, 6 In.   275.00
Iron, Gas, Curved Side Chimney, Single Post Handle, Brass Plate, Beetall, England, 1896 .   375.00
Iron, Goffering, Cast Iron, Center Well, 2 Side Barrels, 2 Heaters, Tripod Base, c.1824 . . . .   2500.00
Iron, Goffering, Snake Head On Clamp, Handmade, Clamp-On, 1700s 225.00
Iron, Hat, Brim, Kenrick, No. 1, Wood Handle, c.1900, 15 In. 200.00
Iron, Hat, Brim, Tolliker, G.T. Brim, Toledo, O., 10-12-31 . . . .   225.00
Iron, Hat, Shell, J.B. Mast Co., No. 2, Heated With Hot Rocks, N.Y., 1868 . . . .   90.00
Iron, Kerosene, Kerosafe, Embossed Letters, Thomas Mfg. Co., Dayton, c.1930, 8 3/8 In. .   40.00
Iron, Kerosene, Paraffin, Tilley Paraffin Iron, Ivory Enamel, England, 1950, 7 1/2 In. 75.00
Iron, Lace, No. 1, Double Point, Trivet, Detachable Handle, Kenrick, Box, 4 1/8 In. 250.00
Iron, Natural Gas, Revolving, Trent, Hose, 5 3/8 In. 450.00
Iron, Pelouze Universal, Electric, Slate-Based Trivet, c.1909 . . . .   65.00
Iron, Petroleum, Coleman 4A, Instant Lite, Pump, Stand, Wrench, 1940, 10 1/2 In. 70.00
Iron, Petroleum, Coleman Magic, No. 10, Green Tank & Handle, Can 140.00
Iron, Petroleum, Coleman, Model 4A, Blue Porcelain, Trivet, Tools, Box, 1940, 10 1/2 In. .   180.00

Iron, Polisher, Marry Ann B. Cook, Rounded Edges, 1848 Patent, 5 1/4 In. 100.00
Iron, Pressing, Brass, Cast Iron Slug, England, 1870-80 . . . .   200.00
Iron, Sleeve, Double Point, Red Handle, Base, Dover USA 10.00
Iron, Sleeve, Sweeney, No. 8, 1899 Patent 120.00
Iron, Smoothing Board, Horse Shape Handle, Starflowers, Denmark, 1828, 7 x 27 x 6 In. .   1840.00
Iron, Smoothing Board, Stylized Horse Handle, Painted, Flowers, Continental, 30 x 6 In. . .   895.00
Iron, Traveling, Alcohol, Feldmeyer's Patent, Trivet, Board, Case, Germany, c.1900 . . . . . .   175.00
Iron, Victor No. 10, Wood Grip, J. & E. Stevens, c.1900, 3 In. 475.00
Juicer, Osborne Newark, N.J., Meat & Juice Press, Cast Iron, Pat. Mar. 1884 . . . .   50.00
Kettle, Cast Iron, 3-Footed, Wrought Iron Handle, 8 1/4 x 11 5/8 In. 120.00
Kettle, Cast Iron, Gooseneck Spout, Swivel Handle, Tin Lid, 6 1/4 x 8 1/2 In. 30.00
Kettle, Copper, Iron Bale Handle, Round, 8 1/2 x 13 In. 35.00
Kettle, Copper, Rolled Rim, Swing Handle, Straight Sides, 10 x 14 In. 120.00
Kettle, Doughnut, Copper, 2 Iron Handles, Rounded Bottom, 7 x 18 In. 175.00
Kettle Stand, Brass, Iron, 2 Cabriole Legs, 2 Rod Legs, Handles, 1800s, 19 x 12 In. 200.00
Kettle Stand, Wrought Iron, 3 Canted Uprights, 10 Shelves, Flared Feet, 78 In. 230.00
Knife Set, Steak, French Scroll, Hollow Handle, Alvin, c.1953, 8 Piece 145.00
Ladle, Brass Bowl, Beveled Handle, Hanging Hook, 15 In. 195.00
Ladle, Brass Bowl, Hammered, Flattened, Turned, Iron Handle, 18 x 5 In. 495.00
Ladle, Brass, Thistle, Fish, Tassel Wriggle Work, Iron Handle, 13 In. 2145.00
Ladle, Brass, Tulip, Fish, Tassel, Iron Handle, 13 In. 1980.00
Ladle, Copper Bowl, Flattened Handle, Marked PH, 1828, 24 x 6 1/2 In. 770.00
Ladle, Copper, Flat Handle, Ring, Signed, 1848, 12 1/2 In. 495.00
Ladle, Iron, Ring Turned, Heart, Wriggle Design, Flattened Handle, 13 1/2 In. 550.00
. **Ladle,** Iron, Stamped Stylized Leaves, Hook End, Marked AM, 1849, 7 x 2 In. 605.00
Ladle, Toddy, Long Handle, Wooden, England, c.1780 . . . .   250.00
Mangle Board, Carved, Blue Paint, c.1820, Child's Size, 12 In. 1700.00
Mangle Board, Chip Carved, Horse Handle, Scandinavia, 1773 . . . .   1000.00
Mangle Board, Horse Handle, Geometric Carving, Horsehair Tail, Painted 700.00
Match Holders can be found in their own category.
Match Safes can be found in their own category.
Meat Grinder, No. 12, Winchester, Cutting Blade, Wood Crank Handle 90.00
Meat Tenderizer, Mallet Shape, Tapered, Stoneware, Handle Hole, Cobalt Lines, 4 3/8 In. . .   3105.00
Mixer, Malt, Green Porcelain Base, Hamilton Beach Co., 6 x 18 In. 120.00
Mixer, Malt, Ivory Porcelain Base, Hamilton Beach Co., 6 x 18 In. 120.00
Mixer, Milk Shake, Porcelain, Myers Bullet Mixers, 19 x 6 In. 155.00
Mixer, Milk Shake, Stainless Steel, Mixall, Original Cup, 4 1/2 x 14 In. 39.00
Mixer, Milk Shake, Triple, Ceramic, Hamilton Beach, 19 x 13 In.   440.00
Mixing Bowl, Cattail, Universal, 8 In. 25.00
Mold, Ice Cream, see also Pewter category.
Molds may also be found in the Pewter and Tinware categories.
Mold, Bundt, Relief Spiral, Orange, Black Drip, Redware, John Bell, Pa., 5 x 8 In. 2200.00
Mold, Butter, Glass, Reclining Putti, Oval, Late 19th Century, 4 1/2 In. 35.00
Mold, Cake, Lamb, Cast Iron, 14 In. 100.00
Mold, Cake, Raised Spirals, Scalloped, Yellow, Black Mottled Glaze, Redware, 12 In. 825.00
Mold, Cake, Sheep, 2 Parts, Full-Bodied, Cast Iron, 14 x 8 In. 127.00
Mold, Cake, Swans Down Cake Flour, Pat. Dec. 18, 1923, Marked, E. Katzinger 85.00
Mold, Candle, see Tinware category.
Mold, Cheese, Cylindrical, Tin, Punched Circles, Diamonds, Strap Handles, 6 In. 195.00
Mold, Cheese, Heart Shape, Punched Tin, Conical Feet, Hanging Loop, 3 x 6 In. 580.00
Mold, Cheese, Heart Shape, Punched Tin, Footed, Hanging Loop, 3 x 4 In. . . . . .220.00 to 275.00
Mold, Cheese, Heart Shape, Tin, Punched Bands, Strap Handle, 3-Footed, 5 x 7 In. 495.00
Mold, Dimpled, Brown Glaze, Redware, 1 1/4 x 3 3/8 In. 415.00
Mold, Fish, Applied Feet, Scales, Eye, Tin Glaze, Redware, 14 x 7 In. 86.00
Mold, Food, Fluted, Brown Running Glaze, Redware, 8 3/4 x 2 1/2 In. 70.00
Mold, Food, Pinwheel Interior, Orange, Black Spattered Glaze, Footed, Redware, 2 x 4 In. .   350.00
Mold, Food, Raised Design, Orange, Black Mottled Glaze, Redware, 2 x 4 1/4 In. 275.00
Mold, Food, Scalloped Rim, Orange, Brown, Green Mottled Glaze, Redware, 2 x 4 1/2 In. . .   195.00
Mold, Food, Yellow Glaze, Swirl Base, Redware, Stamp, John Bell, Waynesboro, 10 x 7 In.   1725.00
Mold, Gelatin, Embossed, Scalloped Rim, Brown, Orange Glaze, Green Base, Redware, 7 In.   220.00
Mold, Gelatin, Raised Spirals, Orange & Manganese Black Glaze, Redware, 3 1/2 x 7 In. . . .   165.00
Mold, Glazed Interior, Molded Detail, Redware, 18 x 8 In. 115.00
Mold, Muffin, 12-Cup, Redware, Applied Scrolled Handle, Early 1800s, 2 x 9 x 12 3/4 In. . .   410.00

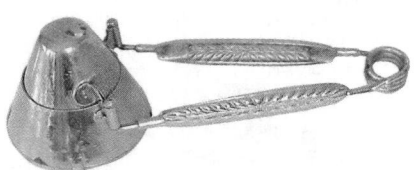

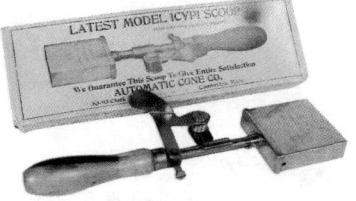

Kitchen, Scoop, Ice Cream, Cone, Nickel,
Kingery Manufacturing Co., No. 6, 1890s, 9 In.

Kitchen, Scoop, Ice Cream, Icypi, For
Sandwiches, Automatic Cone Co., 1920s, 10 In.

Mold, Muffin, 24 Hearts, Tin, Lockwood, 17 x 25 In. 605.00
Mold, Pudding, Corncob Shape, Oval Foot, Redware, 2 3/4 x 8 x 6 1/4 In. 145.00
Mortar, Pestle, Burl, Flame Graining, Incised Rings, 7 In. 375.00
Mortar & Pestle, Burl, 5 1/2 In. 259.00
Mortar & Pestle, Oval, Birch, Red Paint, Wide Band, 8 1/4 In. 230.00
Oven Mitt, Quilted, Wrap Around, Desert Rose Pattern, Franciscan, 30 x 7 In. 13.00
Oven Mitt, Quilted, Wrap Around, Ivy Pattern, Franciscan, 30 x 7 In. 13.00
Pants Press, Nu-Pantz Creaser, Meta Fuel, c.1920, 6 3/4 In. 25.00
Pastry Cutter, Multiple Blades, Quick Bun Cutter, Philadelphia, 24 x 8 In. 79.00
Pastry Stand, Mahogany, 5 Tiers, Top Handle, England, c.1925, 35 x 10 x 16 In. 115.00
Pea Sheller, Wood, Hand Cranked, c.1850 .... 495.00
Peel, Iron, Diamond Headed Handle, 18th Century, 43 x 8 In. 115.00
Pie Bird, Rooster, White, Red, Blue, Black, Cleminson, California, c.1940, 4 1/2 In. 60.00
Pie Bird, Song Bird, Blue, Yellow, 4 1/2 x 1 1/2 In. 80.00
Pie Board, Poplar, Handle, 26 1/2 x 19 In. 110.00
Pie Board, Round, Handle, Wooden, 26 x 18 In. 660.00
Pie Crimper, Early 19th Century, 8 1/2 In. 145.00
Pie Crimper, Wrought Iron, Baluster T-Shaped Handle, 6 x 2 1/2 In. 715.00
Pie Crimper, Wrought Iron, Banded, Brass Coggle Wheel, 6 x 1 1/4 In. 110.00
Pie Crimper, Wrought Iron, Coggle Wheel, Bent Hook Handle, 6 x 2 In. 965.00
Pie Crimper, Wrought Iron, Crescent Zigzag Stamp, Inscribed Eagle, Brass Wheel, 7 In. ... 1320.00
Pie Crimper, Wrought Iron, Incised Wheel & Handle, Rattail Hook, 8 In. 660.00
Pie Top Cutter, Crisscross Lattice, Unopened, Clough Products, Kansas, c.1952 .... 8.00
Pitcher, Wooden, Brass Bound, Spout, Handle, Continental, c.1900, 22 3/4 x 11 In. 230.00
Pot, Iron, Arched Swivel Hanger, Tapered Sides, 21 x 17 In. 300.00
Pot, Water, Mantis, Stone Tooled Ground, Iron, Motomura, Signed, 7 1/4 In. 334.00
Rack, Herb Drying, 2 Sections, Pine, Mortised, Green Paint, 36 1/2 x 24 In. 260.00
Rack, Herb Drying, 3 Sections, Folding, Green Paint, Tapered Legs, Ball Tops, 35 In. 260.00
Rack, Pine, Painted, Austria, 11 x 12 Ft., Pair 295.00
Rack, Utensil, Ring, 8 Hooks, Wrought Iron, 12 1/2 x 15 In. 115.00
Reamers are listed in their own category.
Refrigerator, General Electric, Top Mounted Condenser, Early 1900s, 64 x 29 x 23 In. 430.00
Roaster, Iron, Easel Type, Folding, 18th Century, 14 3/4 x 15 x 8 In. 660.00
Roaster, Revolving Grate, Tapered Handle, Wrought Iron, 11 3/4 x 22 1/2 In. 288.00
Rolling Pin, Turned Handles, Poplar, 10 x 2 In. 28.00
Rolling Pin, White With Cobalt Blue Bands, Stoneware, Trade With Us & Save, 7 3/4 In. ... 605.00
Sadiron, Ferris Cold Handle, Spiral Wire Handle, St. Louis, 1891, 6 1/4 In. 225.00
Sadiron, Monitor, No. 7, W. Shimer Sons & Co., 8 3/4 In. 120.00
Sadiron Heater, 3 Sadirons, J.F. Rathbone, Albany, c.1862, 24 In. 200.00
Sadiron Heater, Centennial Heater, Corn Cob Grip, John B. Christian, c.1876 .... 200.00
Sadiron Heater, Noxall, 3 Irons, Quincy Foundry & Novelty, Ill., Late 1800s, 9 1/4 In. ... 240.00
Sadiron Heater, Stove Top, Griddle Type, No. 2, A&W Co., Chicago, c.1883, 8 1/2 In. ... 90.00
Salt, Wooden, Violas, Salmon Ground, Footed, Initials LBL, Joseph Lehn, 2 1/2 x 3 In. ... 1322.00
Salt & Pepper Shakers are listed in their own category.
Scoop, Burl Walnut, Fish Hook Handle, 10 1/4 x 6 In. 300.00
Scoop, Ice Cream, Bronze, Metal, Gilcrest, No. 30, c.1914 .... 20.00
Scoop, Ice Cream, Cone, Nickel, Kingery Manufacturing Co., No. 6, 1890s, 9 In. ..... *Illus* 236.00
Scoop, Ice Cream, Gilcrest 31, Size 6 .... 80.00
Scoop, Ice Cream, Heart Shape, Manos Novelty Co., Toronto, Ohio, 1925, 11 In. 8740.00

Kitchen, Scoop, Ice Cream,
Pi-Alamoder, Aluminum,
Wood, c.1926, 10 In.

Kitchen, Toaster,
Bersted, Model No.
72, 2 Hinged Doors,
Sheaf Of Wheat
Decoration, 7 In.

Scoop, Ice Cream, Icypi, For Sandwiches, Automatic Cone Co., 1920s, 10 In. . . . . *Illus*   248.00
Scoop, Ice Cream, Pi-Alamoder, Aluminum, Wood, c.1926, 10 In. . . . . *Illus*   2645.00
Scoop, Iron, Bell Shaped Shovel, Baluster Handle, Marked MB, 15 1/2 In. 770.00
Scoop, Maple Butter, Carved, Eagle Handle, 19th Century, 11 x 5 In. 430.00
Scoop, Maple, Carved Horse Head Handle, 10 1/4 In. 920.00
Scoop, Medallion Butter Print Handle, Incised Milk Cow, Wooden, 12 x 6 3/4 In. 575.00
Scottish Broiler, 3 Hearts, Splayed Feet, Hinged, Wrought Iron, 15 x 16 In. 115.00
Sieve, Tin, Cone Shape, Punched, Embossed Lines, Rolled Wire Edges, Handle, 5 x 14 In. .   39.00
Sifter, Tin, Hunter, Salesman's Sample, Patented 1874, 3 1/2 x 2 In. 215.00
Skillet, Iron, Long Handle, 30 In. 60.00
Skimmer, Brass, Flattened Iron Handle, Scrolled Hanging Hook, 8 5/8 In. 580.00
Skimmer, Iron, Flat Handle, Hook, Signed, J. Schmidt, 1843, 20 1/4 In. 300.00
Slickenstone, Smoothing Stone, Green Glass, Mushroom Shape, Handle, 5 x 3 3/4 In. 200.00
Smoothing Board, Horse Handle, Wooden, Paint Traces, Marked, Norway, 1831, 24 In. . .   1200.00
Spatula, Fork, Iron, Heart Cutout, Flattened & Rounded Shaft, 18 In. 2530.00
Spatula, Heart Cutout, Signature, A. Nantz, Round Finial, Wrought Iron, 17 1/2 In. 259.00
Spatula, Iron, Bell-Shaped Blade, Round Shaft, Stamped Decoration, 17 x 3 In. 275.00
Spatula, Iron, Brass, Stars, Crescents, Curving Vines, 15 In. 1555.00
Spatula, Iron, Cutout Diamond, Circles, Flattened Handle, E. Sebastian, 20 In. 4620.00
Spatula, Iron, Flat Handle, Hook, Signed, P. E. Will, 15 In. 195.00
Spatula, Iron, Notched Flat Handle, Heart Cutout, Signed, H. R. Eby, 10 1/2 In. 155.00
Spatula, Iron, Shaped Blade, Round To Flat Handle, Punch Work, Hook, 20 In. 250.00
Spice Box, 9 Drawers, Dovetailed, 16 1/4 x 24 1/2 x 8 1/2 In. 320.00
Spice Box, Inlaid Mahogany, Flip Lid, Front Doors, Side Drawers, 1700s, 12 1/2 x 16 1/2 In.   1950.00
Spice Box, Nutmeg Grater, Punched Design, Fish, Cylindrical Grater, Ring Feet, 6 x 4 x 3 In.   489.00
Spice Box, Painted Flowers, Footed, Round, Cover, Continental, c.1850, 14 1/2 In. 325.00
Spice Box, Pine, Molded Top Edge, Sliding Lid, Interior Compartments, Penn., 9 x 6 x 2 In. .   430.00
Spice Box, Tin, 8-Point Star, Punched, Nutmeg Grater, Ring Feet, 3 x 6 x 3 3/4 In. 415.00
Spice Box, Wall, 9 Drawers, Ash Front, Porcelain Name Plates, 11 x 9 In. 195.00
Spice Box, Walnut, Maple, Hanging, 4 Drawers, Painted, Pa., 1800s, 13 1/2 x 6 5/8 In. . . .   4370.00
Spice Tower, 4 Tiers, Mace, Cloves, Nutmeg, Cinnamon, England, Early 1800s, 7 1/4 In. . .   520.00
Spoon, Curly Maple, Carved Heart Handle, Date & Initials, JTD, 1786, 5 3/4 In. 720.00
Spoon Rest, Clown, 6 In. 20.00
Sprinkler Bottle, Chinese Boy, Cholly, Say More Better Sprinkler Bottle Way 140.00
Sprinkler Bottle, Lady Bug, Plastic, Yellow 260.00
Strainer, Brown, Stoneware, Albany Glaze, Impressed, c.1870, 6 Qt., 17 In. 190.00
Stringholder, Beehive, Cast Iron, 6 1/2 In. 79.00
Stringholder, Dog's Head, Schnauzer, Ceramic, Japan 165.00
Sugar Nipper, Handle, Bronze Pedestal, Wood Base, Wrought Iron, Early 1800s, 14 In. . . .   260.00
Tea Warmer, Chrome Holder, Burner, Round Lithophane Insert, Family Scenes, Handle . .   138.00
Teakettle, Copper, Gooseneck Spout, Recessed Base, New York, 12 x 10 In. 110.00
Teakettle, Copper, Gooseneck Spout, Swing Handle, Pennsylvania, 12 1/2 x 13 In. 1320.00
Teakettle, Copper, Gooseneck Spout, Tapered Sides, Stamped J. Kidd, 11 x 12 In. 1100.00
Toast Rack, 3 Bars, Hinged, Shaped Handle, Iron, 6 x 13 x 20 In. 175.00
Toaster, Bersted, Model No. 72, 2 Hinged Doors, Sheaf Of Wheat Decoration, 7 In. . . *Illus*   25.00
Toaster, Kistler's Sandwiches, Chrome, 7 x 15 In. 366.00
Toaster, Torrid, Swing-Arm, Breadsley & Wolcott, Patented 1920, 7 x 8 In. 75.00
Toaster, White Porcelain, Flowers, High-Frame Wire Basket, G.E. Co., 1908 Patent, 8 In. .   480.00
Tongs, Iron, Geometric Relief Designs, Pineapple Pincher Ends, 23 3/4 In. 523.00
Tongs, Snake Handle, Scallop Shell Ends, 18th Century, 14 x 3 1/2 In. 403.00

Trivet, see Trivet category.

Utensil Rack, Iron, Scroll Heart, Punched Design, 2 1/2 x 12 In. 495.00
Utensil Rack, Iron, Wall Mount, Scroll Work, 6 x 14 In. 415.00
Utensil Set, Iron, Brass, Strainer, Ladle, Fork, Spatula, 14 x 15 In., 4 Piece 345.00
Wafer Press, Eagle Holding Branch, Olives, 16 Stars, Iron, 18th Century, 28 x 5 3/4 In. ... 1380.00
Wafer Press, Ecclesiastical Symbols, Hinged Handles, Iron, 19th Century, 36 1/4 In. 200.00
Waffle Iron, B&W Chatham, New England, Early 1800s 195.00
Waffle Iron, Chrome Plated, Round, Model W36, Winchester, 5 1/2 x 9 1/4 In. 259.00
Waffle Iron, Rectangular, Interior Heart, Cast Iron, 28 In. 200.00
Washboard, Brown, Stoneware, Wooden Frame, c.1880, 23 x 12 1/2 In. 550.00
Washboard, Redware Insert, Brown Daubed Glaze, Wooden Frame, 23 x 12 In. 230.00
Washboard, Redware, Pine, Common Sense Wash Board, Late 1800s, 23 1/2 x 12 In. 499.00
Washboard, Zinc & Pine, Ridged Front, R. Clark Co., Milwaukee, 1890 .... 95.00
Wee Washer & Dry Cleaner, Hand Crank, Wee Specialty Co., Detroit, Mich., 12 x 10 In. ... 88.00
Whiskbroom, Cornstalk, Wire & Cloth Bound, 16 1/2 In. 11.00
Whiskbroom, Horsehair, Pine Handle, 9 1/2 x 2 In. 11.00

KNIFE collectors usually specialize in a single type. In the 1960s, the United States government passed a law that required knife manufacturers to mark their knives with the country of origin. This seemed to encourage the collectors, and knife collecting became an interest of a large group of people. All types of knives are collected, from top quality twentieth-century examples to old bone- or pearl-handled knives in excellent condition.

Bowie, Clip Point, Stag Handles, Edward Barnes & Sons, 10 5/8 In. 220.00
Bowie, Sheffield Clip Point, 2 Piece Stag Handle, Alfred Williams, Pre 1900, 10 In. 83.00
Cattle, No. 4952, 4 Blades, Bone Handles, Bar Shield, Winchester, 3 5/8 In. 116.00
Civilian Survival, Leather Handle, Sheath, Sharpening Stone, No. 50S, 6-In. Blade 190.00
Curved, Bone Handle, Scabbard, No. 1005, Collins & Co., Hartford, Conn., 20 In. 250.00
Dagger, Double Edge, Queen Anne Brass Knuckle, Revolutionary War Era, 6 3/4-In. Blade . 400.00
Dagger, Hunting, Double Bevel Blade, Handmade, Scabbard, Germany, c.1900, 8 5/8 In. .. 90.00
Dagger, India, Acorn Finial Pommel, Jewel Inlaid, Elephant Head, 25 In. 485.00
Dagger, India, Hunting, Curved Blade, Pierced, Gilt, Figures, Animals, 15 1/2 In. 560.00
Dagger, Silver Cased, Engraved, Turquoise & Red Glass Inset, c.1900, 11 1/2 In. 69.00
Dagger, Turkey, Silver Mount, Jewel Inlay, Curved Blade, Inscriptions, Scabbard, 31 In. .. 1050.00
Dirk, American Defender, English Style, Sterling Silver Handle, Sheath, c.1880, 9 1/4 In. . 375.00
Dirk, Double Edge, Inscription, Silver Handle, Leather Sheath, c.1850, 9 1/4 In. 605.00
Dirk, Ivory Handle, Inscription, Sheath, Coin Silver Hilt, J. Lingard, Sheffield, 1800s, 11 In. 425.00
Dirk, Ivory Handle, Leaf Design, Steel Blade, Woman's, 8 1/4 In. 175.00
Hospital Corps, Model 1904, Leather Sheath, c.1911, 12-In. Blade 345.00
Hunting, Aluminum Pommel, Leather Washer Handle, Leather Sheath, Kinfolks, 7 In. 28.00
Hunting, Ideal, Leather Handle, Marbles, 6-In. Blade 46.00
Hunting, Ideal, No. 43, Marbles, 1892 Patent, 6-In. Blade, 10 3/8 In. 378.00
Hunting, Ideal, No. 46, Brass Hilt, Stag Handle, Leather Sheath, Marbles, 5 5/8-In. Blade . 230.00
Hunting, RH-4, Jigged Bone Handles, Leather Sheath, Remington, 4 1/4 In. 70.00
Hunting, RH-32, Leather Washer Handle, Aluminum Pommel, Sheath, Remington, 8 In. ... 55.00
Hunting, US Model 1880, Ribbed Wood Handle, Scabbard, US Springfield, 8-In. Blade ... 700.00
Kitchen, Remington, Kleanbore, No. K8607, Bakelite Handle, Paper Box, 7-In. Blade 28.00
Machete, Hospital Corp, Walnut Grip, Sheath, Springfield Armory, 1914, 12-In. Blade 345.00
Outdoor, No. 58, Leather Handle, Aluminum Pommel, Marbles, 4 1/2-In. Blade 45.00
Paper Knife, Brass, Bird, Flowers, Figures & Horse Handle, 19th Century, 10 1/2 In. 105.00
Paper Knife, Brass, Ivory, Dragon, Cloud, c.1900, 10 1/2 In. 138.00
Pocket, 2 Blades, Rosewood Handle, No. 2681, Winchester, 1930s, 3 3/4 In. 385.00
Pocket, Bulldog Brand, Stockman, Broken Chain Celluloid Handle, Germany, Box, 3 In. .. 40.00
Pocket, Case, Classic Whittler, Red Bone Handle, No. R6391, Box 89.00
Pocket, Fight'n Rooster, No. 10 Of 10, 100 Blades, Mother-Of-Pearl Scales, Box 2090.00
Pocket, No. 1936, Saber Clip Blade, Stag Handle, Winchester, 5 In. 70.00
Pocket, No. 2976, Jigged Bone Handle, Winchester, 3 In. 130.00
Pocket, No. 3005, Balloon, Sleeveboard, Black Celluloid Handles, Winchester, 3 5/8 In. ... 120.00
Pocket, No. 3948, Reverse Gunstock Pattern, Bone Handle, Winchester, 3 5/8 In. 135.00
Pocket, Simmons Hardware, Hornet, 3 Blades, Celluloid Handle, Germany, 1960s, 4 In. .. 58.00
Pocket, Space Ship Jack, Celluloid Handle, USA, 3 1/2 In. 11.00
Pocket, Winchester, No. 2317, Serpentine Jack, 2 Blades, Pearl Handle, 3 In. 90.00

Pocket, Winchester, No. 2928, 2 Blades, Stag Handle, 3 1/2 In. 127.00
Side, Pewter Pommel, Iron Hilt, Rosewood Handle, Will & Finck, 1800s, 10 1/2 In. 1040.00
Silver, Brass, Scroll, Vine Scabbard, Tibet, 8 1/2 In. 230.00
Skinning, RH-32, Leather Handle, Aluminum Pommel, Remington 46.00
Skinning, RH-32, Leather Sheath, RemUMC Logo, Remington, 8 1/4 In. 30.00

KNOWLES, TAYLOR & KNOWLES items may be found in the KTK and Lotus Ware categories.

KOREAN WARE, see Sumida.

KOSTA, the oldest Swedish glass factory, was founded in 1742. During the 1920s through the 1950s, many pieces of original design were made at the factory. In 1971, Kosta became part of the Afors Group. In 1976, the name *Kosta Boda* was adopted. The company merged with Orrefors in 1990 and is still working.

KOSTA

Shade, Mottled Sea Green & Turquoise, Bell Shape, Octagonal Rim, 5 1/4 In. 145.00
Vase, Blue Spiral Lines, Clear Glass Over Green, Optical Cross Weave, Signed, 8 1/4 In. ... 470.00

KPM refers to Berlin porcelain, but the same initials were used alone and in combination with other symbols by several German porcelain makers. They include the Konigliche Porzellan Manufaktur of Berlin, initials used in mark, 1823–1847; Meissen, 1723–1724 only; Krister Porzellan Manufaktur in Waldenburg, after 1831; Kranichfelder Porzellan Manufaktur in Kranichfeld, after 1903; and the Kister Porzellan Manufaktur in Scheibe, after 1838.

K.P.M

Dish, Floral Gilt, 2 Sections, Handles, Stamped, 12 In. 58.00
Jar, Cover, 4 Flower Reserves, Blue Ground, Gilt, c.1890, 11 1/2 In. 940.00
Lithophane, see also Lithophane category.
Plaque, Young Woman, Facing Right, Grenier, c.1900, 5 x 7 x 14 1/2 In. 2300.00
Plate, Scenic, Das Brandenburger Thor, Gilt Leaf Scrolls, Green Ground, c.1875, 9 3/4 In. 355.00
Urn, Campagna, Courting Couple Scene, Floral Bouquets, Gilt Enamel Edge, 16 In., Pair . 1175.00
Vase, 2 Handles, Decorated, Frolicking Putto, 24 In., Pair 5380.00

KTK are the initials of the Knowles, Taylor & Knowles Company of East Liverpool, Ohio, founded by Isaac W. Knowles in 1853. The company made many types of utilitarian wares, hotel china, and dinnerwares. They made the fine bone china known as Lotus Ware from 1891 to 1896. The company merged with American Ceramic Corporation in 1928. It closed in 1934. Lotus Ware is listed in its own category in this book.

K.T.&K.
CHINA

Butter Chip, Bluebird, 3 1/2 In. 12.00
Casserole, Cover, Bluebirds, Ivory, Cobalt Blue Band, 2 Handles, 1920s, 2 1/2 x 8 1/2 In. . 95.00
Cuspidor, White, Gold Filigree, Chintz, Woman's 149.00
Mug, Little Red Riding Hood, Decal, 1920s, 3 In. 40.00
Plate, Portrait, Napoleon, Josephine, Cobalt Blue Border, Gold Trim, 8 In., Pair 35.00
Syrup, White, Ironstone, Pewter Cover, Bird Finial, 1878-85 .... 30.00

KU KLUX KLAN items are now collected because of their historic importance. Literature, robes, and memorabilia are available. The Klan was outlawed in 1869 and reemerged in 1915. It is still in existence, so new material is found.

Button, Chas. Brumm Helms For State Secretary, Sepia Photo, c.1920, 1 1/4 In. 35.00
Button, Hiram Wesley Evans, KKK Wizard, Brown, White, Celluloid, 1920, 1 1/4 In. 335.00
Saber, Sheath, Plumed Knight, Cloaked Rider 495.00

KUTANI porcelain was made in Japan after the mid-seventeenth century. Most of the pieces found today are nineteenth-century. Collectors often use the term *Kutani* to refer to just the later, colorful pieces decorated with red, gold, and black pictures of warriors, animals, and birds.

Bowl, Bell Shape, Phoenix, Flower Ground, Blue Green, 1800s, 6 1/2 In. 345.00
Bowl, Cover, Flowers, Birds, Shishi Handles & Finial, Red Ground, Gilt, 9 1/2 x 14 In. ... 865.00
Bowl, Dome Cover, Crane & Pine Tree, Flower Finial, Early 1900s, 6 1/4 In. 127.00
Bowl, Dome Cover, Mount Fuji, Flower Finial, Early 1900s, 6 1/2 In. 205.00
Bowl, Warrior, Landscape, Egg Shell Porcelain, 6 In., Pair 690.00

L.G. Wright, Hen
With Eggs On
Nest, Dish, Cover,
Purple Mosaic,
1970s, 7 1/4 In.

Very dirty lacquer can be cleaned with a paste of flour and olive oil.

Bowl Set, Nesting, Signed, c.1912, Largest 9 1/8 In.	300.00
Censer, Cover, Boy-Shaped Legs, Elephant, Landscape, Rectangular, Late 1800s, 7 x 7 In.	690.00
Censer, Cover, Landscape, 4 Legs, Blue Green, Rectangular, 19th Century, 9 1/4 x 7 In.	575.00
Censer, Cylindrical, Pierced Sides, Dragon Handles, Flower Brocade, 1900s, 3 3/4 In.	120.00
Compote, Figures, Flowers, Landscape, Kozan, 19th Century, 3 x 9 In., Pair	259.00
Compote, Figures, Flowers, Landscape, Kozan, 19th Century, 5 1/2 x 9 In., Pair	345.00
Compote, Warrior, Landscape, Egg Shell Porcelain, 19th Century, 5 x 8 1/2 In., Pair	1020.00
Cup & Saucer, Demitasse, Warriors, Landscape, Egg Shell Porcelain, 1800s, 18 Piece	1150.00
Figure, Cat, Sleeping, Red Ribbon Collar, Gold Highlights, c.1920, 8 1/4 In.	489.00
Figure, Goddess Of Mercy, Lotus Base, Hazan, 19th Century, 17 1/2 In.	345.00
Figure, Red-Headed Sprite, Standing Beside Wine Barrel, Tortoise, 19th Century, 8 1/2 In.	575.00
Plate, Figures, Dragon Headed Boat, Signed, 7 1/2 In.	120.00
Plate, Figures, Flowers, Landscape, Kozan, 19th Century, 9 In., 12 Piece	345.00
Plate, Flower Shape, 1000 Flowers, Chrysanthemum, Tree Border, Late 1800s, 7 In.	140.00
Plate, Warrior, Landscape, Eggshell Porcelain, 19th Century, 7 In., 12 Piece	1265.00
Sake Cup, Boy, Flowers, 19th Century, 2 In.	110.00
Sake Cup, Cartoon Figures, Brown Ground, 19th Century, 2 In.	29.00
Sake Cup, Flowers, Calligraphy, Early 1900s, 1 1/2 In., Pair	60.00
Sake Cup, Horse Medallions, Early 1900s, 2 In.	29.00
Sake Cup, Landscape, Gold Enameled, Calligraphy, c.1900, 2 1/4 In.	96.00
Sake Cup, Noh Dancers, Marbleized Exterior, Kinshodo, 1800s, 2 In.	65.00
Sake Cup, Plum Blossom, Moon, Plum, Early 1800s, 2 1/4 In.	60.00
Tea Set, Warriors, Landscape, Egg Shell Porcelain, Early 1900s, 8 1/4-In. Pot, 5 Piece	1610.00
Teabowl, Boy, Flower Rondels, c.1850, 5 In.	175.00
Vase, Baluster Shape, Boy In Garden, 19th Century, 11 3/4 In., Pair	230.00
Vase, Baluster Shape, Figural Pierce Work Handles, Fan Designs, c.1900, 7 1/2 In., Pair	290.00
Vase, Bucket Shape, Geese, Grass, Watabaya, 19th Century, 8 In.	210.00
Vase, Elongated Neck, Spherical Body, Woman, Garden, Bird, Flowers, 1800s, 7 In., Pr.	545.00
Vase, Falcon, Butterfly, Peony, Yellow, Bronze Lamp Mounts, 19th Century, 13 In.	5400.00
Vase, Lion Handles, Scenic, Families In Spring Landscape, c.1880, 12 1/2 In., Pair	1150.00
Vase, Well Bucket Shape, Bird, Flower, Landscape, 19th Century, 5 3/4 In.	185.00
Vase, Well Bucket Shape, Flowers, Wood Stand, Watano, 1800s, 5 3/4 In.	195.00

L.G. WRIGHT Glass Company of New Martinsville, West Virginia, started selling glassware in 1937. Founder "Si" Wright contracted with Ohio and West Virginia glass factories to reproduce popular pressed glass patterns, like Rose & Snow, Baltimore Pear, and Three Face, and opalescent patterns, like Daisy & Fern and Swirl. Collectors can tell the difference between the original glasswares and L.G. Wright reproductions because of colors and differences in production techniques. Some L.G. Wright items are marked with an underlined W in a circle. Items that were made from old Northwood molds have an altered Northwood mark—an angled line was added to the N to make it look like a W. Collectors refer to this mark as "the wobbly W."

Cranberry Opalescent, Barber Bottle, Melon Ribbed, 8 In.	100.00
Daisy & Button, Pitcher, Ice Blue, 5 1/4 In.	25.00
Daisy & Fern, Tumbler, Cranberry Opalescent, 3 3/4 In.	30.00
Dolphin, Compote, Shell Bowl, Amberina, 4 1/2 In.	30.00
Embossed Rose, Fairy Lamp, Cobalt Blue, Clear Insert, 6 1/2 In.	45.00
Eye Winker, Spooner, Green Opalescent, 5 3/4 In.	15.00

Hen With Eggs On Nest, Dish, Cover, Purple Mosaic, 1970s, 7 1/4 In. . . . . *Illus*   25.00
Maple Leaf, Water Set, Cobalt Blue Carnival, 7 Piece 120.00
Moon & Star, Lamp, Kerosene, Milk Glass, 8 In. 95.00
Moon & Star, Toothpick, Green 7.00
Priscilla, Candy Dish, Cover, Green, Footed, 10 In. 20.00
Priscilla, Rose Bowl, Amber, 3 1/4 In. 15.00
Roman Pedestal, Lamp, Hand Painted Roses, Electric, 21 1/2 In. 255.00
Topaz Opalescent, Barber Bottle, Melon Ribbed, 8 In. 130.00
Wreath Of Roses, Fairy Lamp, Ice Blue, Satin, Clear Insert, 6 1/2 In. 40.00

LACQUER is a type of varnish. Collectors are most interested in the
Chinese and Japanese lacquer wares made from the Japanese varnish
tree. Lacquer wares are made from wood with many coats of lacquer.
Sometimes the piece is carved or decorated with ivory or metal inlay.

Box, Black, Gold, Daikoku Standing On Rice Bales, Japan, 3 1/4 In. 865.00
Box, Flowers, Rectangular, Burmese, 13 1/2 x 17 1/2 In. 120.00
Box, Red, Waved Top, Mirror, 4 Drawers, Gold Birds, Butterflies, Handles, Chinese, 11 In.   210.00
Box, Shou Design, Red Flower Ground, Round, Japan, 1900s, 13 In. 60.00
Cabinet, 5 Claws, Dragon, Black Ground, 4 Doors, 2 Drawers, 44 1/2 x 45 In. 1850.00
Comb Suite, Red, Gold, Flowers, Hairpin, Signed, Masanao, Japan 210.00
Figurine, Buddha Seated On Lotus Throne, Gold, Wood, Japan, 16 3/4 In. 1725.00
Figurine, Buddha, Wearing Long Robes, Octagonal Lotus Base, Gold, 41 In. 4302.00
Sake Cup, Red, Cherry Blossom, Japan, c.1950, 4 1/4 In. 45.00
Tray, Black, Gold, Oval, 2 Handles, Leaves, Gilt, 19th Century, 30 x 23 In. 265.00
Tray, Gold, Mountain, Pavilions, Rectangular, Lobed Corners, Japan, c.1890, 13 x 10 In. . . .   460.00
Tray, Maple Leaf Design, Black, Square, 1900s, 9 3/4 In. 115.00
Tray, Wajima, 2 Fish, 19th Century, 20 In. 259.00
Wall Plaque, Birds Of Prey, Mother-Of-Pearl, Japan, Early 1900s, 18 x 3 1/2 In., Pair 1840.00

LADY HEAD VASE, see Head Vase.

LALIQUE glass was made by Rene Lalique in Paris, France, between
the 1890s and his death in 1945. The glass was molded, pressed, and
engraved in Art Nouveau and Art Deco styles. Pieces were marked
with the signature *R. Lalique.* Lalique glass is still being made. Pieces
made after 1945 bear the mark *Lalique.* Jewelry made by Rene Lalique
is listed in the Jewelry category.

R.LALIQUE

Ashtray, Alice, 8 Figures, Clear, Frosted, Engraved R. Lalique, c.1924, 4 3/8 In. 823.00
Ashtray, Antheor, Siren, Clear, Frosted, Blue Patina, Engraved R. Lalique, c.1927, 5 In. . . .   764.00
Ashtray, Archers, Amber, Molded R. Lalique, c.1922, 4 1/2 In. 1058.00
Ashtray, Caravelle, Ship, Clear, Frosted, Blue Patina, Stenciled R. Lalique, c.1930, 2 In. . .   411.00
Ashtray, Dindon, Turkey, Topaz, Engraved R. Lalique, c.1925, 2 1/2 In. 235.00
Ashtray, Fauvettes, Warblers, Opalescent, Engraved R. Lalique, c.1924, 6 3/4 In. 294.00
Ashtray, Feuilles, Leaves, Blue, White Patina, Engraved R. Lalique, c.1934, 6 7/8 In. 1765.00
Ashtray, Jamaique, Amber, Wheel Cut, R. Lalique, c.1928, 5 1/2 In. 825.00
Ashtray, Medicis, 4 Figures, Opalescent, Engraved R. Lalique, c.1924, 5 7/8 In. 1295.00
Ashtray, Medicis, 4 Figures, Opalescent, Sepia, Molded R. Lalique, c.1924, 5 7/8 In. 1175.00
Ashtray, Muguet, Flowers, Frosted, Green Patina, Stenciled R. Lalique, c.1931, 3 In. 705.00
Atomizer, Epines, Throns, Intaglio, Frosted, Metal Collar, Spray, Marked, 3 3/4 In. 480.00
Blotter, Faune Et Nymphe, Fawn & Nymph, Clear, Frosted, Chrome Metal, c.1920, 6 In. .   2350.00
Bookends, Faucon, Falcon, Clear, Black Glass, Base, Signed R. Lalique, 7 In., Pair 4140.00
Bookends, Hirondelle, Swallow, Frosted, Inscribed, 1942, 6 x 4 In. 750.00
Bookends, Tete De Coq, Rooster Head, Clear, Frosted, Lalique, c.1928, 7 5/8 In. 1295.00
Bowl, Fleurville, Opalescent, Green Patina, Molded R. Lalique, c.1928, 11 1/2 In. 765.00
Bowl, Marguerites, Daisies, Overlapping, Brown Patina, Fluted, 2 3/4 x 14 1/2 In. 410.00
Bowl, Nemours, Flower Heads, Frosted, Black Enamel Centers, Post 1945, 9 3/4 In. 865.00
Bowl, Nemours, Flower Heads, Frosted, Black Enamel, R. Lalique, 1929, 10 In. . . .745.00 to 765.00
Bowl, Ondines, Water Nymphs, Opalescent, Wheel Cut R. Lalique, 8 1/8 In. 2115.00
Bowl, Perruches, Parakeets, Opalescent, 1931, 9 3/8 In. 5380.00
Bowl, Pinsons, Molded Birds, Center, Signed, 9 1/4 x 3 5/8 In. 145.00
Bowl, Plumes De Paon, Peacock Feathers, Opalescent, Stenciled, 12 1/8 In. 1060.00
Bowl, Poissons No. 1, Fish, Opalescent, Stenciled R. Lalique, c.1931, 11 3/4 In. 940.00
Bowl, Volubulis, 3 Morning Glories, Frosted, Cut R. Lalique, Engraved, c.1921, 8 1/2 In. . .   705.00
Bowl, Volubulis, 3 Morning Glories, Opalescent, Cut R. Lalique, c.1921, 8 1/2 In. 880.00

Bowl, Volutes, Spiraling Bubbles, Opalescent, Stenciled R. Lalique, c.1934, 8 In. 600.00
Box, Cover, Isabelle, 3 Peacocks, Leaves, Frosted, Reeded Collar, Round, 1 1/2 x 3 1/4 In. .   345.00
Box, Cover, Roger, Birds & Cabochons, Textured Cover, Round, Post 1945, 5 1/2 In. 600.00
Candleholder, Mesanges, Birds, Flower Wreaths, Frosted Stem, Hexagonal, 7 In., Pair 635.00
Decanter, Marienthal, Yellow, Engraved, 8 1/4 In. 705.00
Decanter, Six Figurines, Panels, Vines, Women In Gowns, Sepia, Crown Stopper, 14 In. . .   1380.00
Figurine, Colombe Charis, Dove, Clear, Frosted, Engraved Lalique, c.1970, 10 In. 645.00
Figurine, Colombe, Auxo, Dove, Spread Wings, Clear, Frosted, Lalique, c.1970, 9 1/2 In. .   600.00
Figurine, Coq De Jungle, Rooster, Clear, Frosted, Stenciled R. Lalique, c.1936, 17 In. 4115.00
Figurine, Deux Poissons, Double Fish, Clear, Frosted, Lalique, c.1970, 11 In. 1410.00
Figurine, Gros Poisson Algues, Fish, Clear, Bronze Base, Light Filter, c.1922, 15 1/2 In. . .   5875.00
Figurine, Louisiane, Bird, Clear, Frosted, Engraved Lalique, 13 3/4 In. 825.00
Figurine, Miroir Cygnes, Swans On Mirror, Clear, Frosted, Lalique, c.1970, 33 In. 5875.00
Figurine, St. Therese, Clear & Frosted, Saint Holding Rosary, 1945, 13 In. 460.00
Figurine, St. Therese, Clear & Frosted, Saint Holding Rosary, Post 1945, 13 In. 345.00
Figurine, Vierge A L'enfant, Virgin & Child, Clear, Frosted, Wood Base, 1934, 13 1/4 In. . .   5380.00
Glass, Marienthal, Amber, Frosted, Clear, Ribbed & Raised Roundels, Signed, 4 1/2 In. . . .   150.00
Glass Set, Liqueur, Enfants, Frosted, Seated Children, Grapes, Post 1945, 2 In., 6 Piece . . .   345.00
Goblet, Champagne, Anges, Clear, Frosted, Engraved, c.1980, 8 In., 4 Piece 500.00
Goblet, Champagne, Saint-Nabor, Clear, Black Enamel, Engraved, 3 7/8 In., Pair 530.00
Goblet, Water, Ricquewihr, Clear, Frosted, Sepia, Engraved, c.1925, Pair 530.00
Hood Ornament, Chrysis, Nude, Clear, Frosted, Grey Patina, R. Lalique, c.1931, 5 1/4 In.   5580.00
Hood Ornament, Coq Houdan, Rooster, Frosted, Chrome Collar, R. Lalique, 8 In. 8225.00
Hood Ornament, Faucon, Falcon, Clear, Frosted, Molded R. Lalique, 6 1/4 In. 4700.00
Hood Ornament, Grenouille, Frog, Frosted Glass, 2 1/2 In. 15432.00
Hood Ornament, Longchamp A., Clear, Frosted, Chrome Collar, Marble Base, 4 7/8 In. . .   10000.00
Hood Ornament, Longchamp B., Clear, Frosted, Molded R. Lalique, 5 In. 8225.00
Hood Ornament, Sirene, Clear, Frosted, Sepia Patina, R. Lalique, c.1920, 3 7/8 In. 2950.00
Hood Ornament, Tete De Belier, Clear, Frosted, Amethyst, R. Lalique, 3 3/4 In. 7640.00
Ice Bucket, Ganymede, Clear, Frosted, Engraved, c.1970, 9 In. 1116.00
Ice Cream Cup, Ormeaux, Elm Leaves, Clear, Frosted, Stenciled, R. Lalique, c.1931, 4 In.   175.00
Inkwell, Biches Does, Clear, Frosted, Grey Patina, Wheel Cut R. Lalique, c.1912, 6 x 6 In.   645.00
Inkwell, Cover, Nenuphar, Water Lily, Clear, Frosted, Engraved R. Lalique, c.1910, 3 In. . .   880.00
Inkwell, Trois Papillons, Clear, Frosted, Molded R. Lalique, c.1912 . . . .   2550.00
Jardiniere, Mesanges, Birds, Clear, Frosted, Sepia, Wheel Cut, Engraved, c.1927, 21 In. . .   5580.00
Menu Holder, Faune, Clear, Frosted, Grey Patina, Engraved, c.1928, 5 3/8 In. 1765.00
Paperweight, Antilope, Topaz, Engraved R. Lalique, c.1929, 3 1/2 In. 1295.00
Paperweight, Tete D'Aigle, Eagle Head, Frosted, 4 1/2 In. 345.00
Perfume Bottle, Coty, Ambre Antique, Clear, Frosted, Sepia Patina, c.1910, 6 In. 2115.00
Perfume Bottle, Coty, L'Origan, Clear, Frosted, Label, Box, c.1920, 2 1/2 In. 295.00
Perfume Bottle, Coty, Lilas Pourpre, Clear, Frosted, Leather Box, c.1911, 2 5/8 In. 590.00
Perfume Bottle, Coty, Styx, Clear, Frosted, Sepia Patina, Wasp, Stopper, c.1912, 4 3/4 In. .   1410.00
Perfume Bottle, D'Orsay, Le Lys, Clear, Frosted, Sepia Patina, R. Lalique, c.1922, 7 In. . .   1293.00
Perfume Bottle, D'Orsay, Le Lys, Clear, Frosted, Sepia Patina, R. Lalique, c.1922, 10 In. .   823.00
Perfume Bottle, Dahlia, Frosted, Molded Flower Head, Stopper, Post 1945, 7 In. 210.00
Perfume Bottle, Deux Fleurs, Frosted, 2 Flower Heads, Post 1945, 3 1/2 In. . . . . . .104.00 to 155.00
Perfume Bottle, Gabilla, La Violette, Clear, Frosted, Violet Enamel, c.1925, 3 1/4 In. 3525.00
Perfume Bottle, Houbigant, La Belle Saison, Clear, Frosted, Sepia, Box, c.1925, 4 1/4 In. .   3055.00
Perfume Bottle, Jay Thorpe, Jaytho, Clear, Frosted, Ocher, R. Lalique, c.1927, 4 In. 470.00
Perfume Bottle, L'Aimant, Coty, Molded & Frosted, Duncan Flacon No. 2, 7 1/2 In. 865.00
Perfume Bottle, Marquita, Frosted, Stopper, Overlapping Leaves, Signed, 3 1/2 In. 1610.00
Perfume Bottle, Roger Et Gallet, Cigalia, Cicadas, Wood, Paper, Box, c.1924, 3 In. 705.00
Perfume Bottle, Sirene, Frosted, Mottled Figures, Spherical, Flattened, c.1920, 9 3/4 In. . .   7480.00
Perfume Bottle, Worth, Imprudence, Clear, Label, Box, c.1938, 2 1/2 In. 355.00
Perfume Bottle, Worth, Vers Le Jour, Clear, Frosted Amberina, c.1927, 4 1/4 In. 765.00
Plate, Asters No. 2, Opalescent, Stenciled R. Lalique, c.1935, 11 In. 560.00
Plate, Center, Cote D'Or, 3 Figurines & Grapes, Clear, Frosted, Lalique, 1943, 15 3/4 In. .   1765.00
Plate, Chasse, Chiens, Hunting Dogs, Clear, Frosted, Sepia, R. Lalique, c.1914, 8 In. 441.00
Plate, Chasse, Chiens, Hunting Dogs, Embossed, Blue Patina, c.1914, 8 1/2 In. 690.00
Plate, Marienthal, Frosted, Stylized Waves, Pebbles, 1930s, 7 1/4 In. 155.00
Plate, Poissons No. 1, Fish, Opalescent, Molded R. Lalique, c.1931, 10 3/4 In. 600.00
Plate Set, Dessert, Muguet, Lily Of The Valley, Green, R. Lalique, 8 1/2 In., 12 Piece 1530.00
Seal, Deux Colombes, 2 Doves, Clear, Frosted, Sepia Patina, R. Lalique, c.1931, 1 3/4 In. .   2468.00

Seal, Poisson, Fish, Teal Blue, Molded Lalique, c.1955, 1 7/8 In. 235.00
Seal, Sauterelle, Grasshoppers, Blue, Molded Lalique, c.1913, 1 5/8 In. 825.00
Seal, Statuette Drapee, Frosted, Green Patina, c.1913, 2 1/2 In. 3525.00
Shade, Hanging, Frosted Leaves, Blown-Out Dahlias, Clear Ground, 12 In. 1920.00
Sign, Trade, Clear, Frosted, c.1960, 5 In. 325.00
Sign, Trade, Clear, Frosted, c.1970, 4 1/4 In. 210.00
Sign, Trade, Frosted, Gilt, c.1950, 3 7/8 x 3 7/8 In. 295.00
Vase, Bacchantes, Nudes, Frosted, Signed, 9 5/8 In. 1554.00
Vase, Bagatelle, Fledglings, Leaves, Frosted, Signed, Lalique, 7 In. 1100.00
Vase, Biches, Deer, Fruit Trees, Leaves, Silver Rim, Ovoid, Etched R. Lalique, 6 3/4 In. . .   3450.00
Vase, Boutons D'Or, Buttercups, Opalescent, Flaring, Flowers, Long Stems, 5 1/2 In. 1210.00
Vase, Branches Fleurs, Couvercle Branches, Cover, Cire Perdue, c.1921, 4 1/2 In. 38188.00
Vase, Canards, Ducks, Frosted, c.1935, 5 1/4 In. 345.00
Vase, Chardons, Thistles, Opalescent, Blue, Signed, 8 1/2 In. 3120.00
Vase, Dahlias, Clear, Black Center, Bulbous, 1923, 5 In. 1410.00
Vase, Domremy, Thistles, White Opalescent, Oval, R. Lalique, 8 3/4 In. 2300.00
Vase, Fontaines, Cascading Water, Gray Patina, Oval Form, Inscribed, 6 In. 1150.00
Vase, Fougeres, Peacock Feathers, Blue, c.1930, 6 In. 5350.00
Vase, Perruches, Parakeets, Blue, c.1919, 10 1/8 In. 11950.00
Vase, Quatre Groups De Lezards, Lizards, Frosted, Gray Patina, c.1912, 12 3/8 In. 21150.00
Vase, Renocules, Flowers, Blue Wash, Flared, Signed, No. 1044, 5 3/4 x 5 In. 1500.00
Vase, Saint-Marc, Birds Perched On Wavy Tiers, Frosted, Clear, Engraved, 6 5/8 In. 405.00
Vase, Soudan, Oval, 3 Bands Running Stags, Flower, Signed, 1928, 6 1/2 In. 1115.00
Vase, Thibet, Ibex Handles, Etched R. Lalique, France, 8 In. 2870.00
Vase, Vichy, Leaves, Flowers, Frosted, Post 1945, 6 3/4 In. . . . . .345.00 to 605.00
Wine, Hagueneau, Tulip Form, Signed R. Lalique, 7 1/4 In. 150.00
Wine, Saverne, Frosted, Clear, Signed R. Lalique, 5 1/2 In. 150.00

LAMPS of every type, from the early oil-burning Betty and Phoebe
lamps to the recent electric lamps with glass or beaded shades, interest
collectors. Fuels used in lamps changed through the years; whale oil
(1800–40), camphene (1828), Argand (1830), lard (1833–63), tur-
pentine and alcohol (1840s), gas (1850–79), kerosene (1860), and
electricity (1879) are the most common. Other lamps are listed by
manufacturer or type of material.

Advertising, AC Spark Plug, Ceramic, Brass Base, 1960s, 28 In. 80.00
Advertising, Budweiser, Hand Holding Beer Can, Gooseneck, Box, 1990, 14 1/2 In. 32.00
Aladdin, B-75, Tall Lincoln Drape, Alacite 92.00
Argand, 2-Light, Gilt Bronze, Patinated, Pair 7475.00
Argand, Gilt Brass Mounts, Cut Glass, Electrified, Johnston Brooke & Co., c.1815, 22 In. .   3910.00
Argand, Regency, Bronze, Dolphin, Flower & Vine Shade, Electrified, c.1835, 17 x 12 In. .   5060.00
Argand, Van Bunschoten, Patent, 1856 . . . .   900.00
Astral, American Empire, Brass, Glass, Marble, Electrified, 19th Century, 23 1/2 In. 360.00
Astral, Brass, Frosted Glass Shade, Marble, Electrified, Early 1800s, 21 In. 1293.00
Astral, Chimney, W.F. Shaw, Boston 1100.00
Astral, Empire, Gilt Metal, Marble, Cut Glass, 19th Century, 23 1/2 In. 359.00
Astral, Etched Satin Glass Shade, Brass Burner, Column, Prisms, c.1845, 28 In. 1035.00
Astral, Etched Satin Glass Shade, Brass Font, Column, Cornelius & Co., c.1843, 31 In. . . .   863.00
Astral, Tin, Chimney, Brass Reflector 200.00
Astral, Tin, W.F. Shaw, Patent, 1840s-50s 550.00
Banquet, Pink Embossed Globe, Quatrefoil Medallions, Dutch Scenes, Cast Iron, 32 In. . .   633.00
Betty, Tin Standard, Ipswich, 1680-1700 . . . .   475.00
Betty, Tin, Oval, Cone Base, Oval Handle, Hinged Lid, Wick Holder, Chain Wick Pick, 5 In.   413.00
Bouillotte, 2-Light, Restauration Style, Gilt Brass, Painted, c.1900, 22 In. 3680.00
Bouillotte, 3-Light, Gilt Brass, Painted, Laurel Leaf Band, France, Late 1800s, 25 1/2 In. .   1093.00
Bouillotte, 3-Light, Louis XVI Style, Gilt Brass, Arms From Central Sphere, 19 In. 1610.00
Bouillotte, 3-Light, Louis XVI Style, Silver Plate, Black Tole, Quiver, Horn, 33 In. 1725.00
Bouillotte, Neoclassical, Silver Plate, Tapering Standard, c.1900, 27 In., Pair 3680.00
Bradley & Hubbard lamps are included in the Bradley & Hubbard category.
Chandelier, 2-Light, Brass, Satin Bowl Shades, Wreath & Torch Design, Gas, 26 x 45 In. . .   374.00
Chandelier, 2-Light, George III Style, Cut Glass, 20th Century, 19 In., Pair 748.00
Chandelier, 2-Light, Gilt Bronze, Quiver Shape, Round Base, Early 1900s, 28 x 3 In. 2300.00
Chandelier, 3 Light, Prairie School, Bronze, Slag Glass, Hanging Lanterns, 36 x 30 In. . . .   4100.00

Chandelier, 3-Light, Antlers, Intertwined, Tin Drip Pans, Wrought Iron, 35 x 40 In. 2875.00
Chandelier, 3-Light, Brass, Center Pendant, Opalescent Swirl Flame Shade, 19 x 37 In. . . . 460.00
Chandelier, 3-Light, Brass, Dome, Pendant Shades, Painted Winter Scene, 19 x 32 In. 288.00
Chandelier, 3-Light, Burnished Copper, Amber Pressed Glass Bowls, Gas, 28 x 31 In. 81.00
Chandelier, 3-Light, Carved Oak, Owl, Germany, 16 x 22 In. 835.00
Chandelier, 3-Light, Cast Iron, Bowl Shades, Satin Flowers, Victorian, Gas, 38 x 31 In. . . . 374.00
Chandelier, 3-Light, Cast Iron, Torch & Swags, Victorian, Kerosene Font, 32 x 41 In. 374.00
Chandelier, 3-Light, Copper, Satin Glass Ruffled Shades, Flower, Gas, 24 x 34 In. 230.00
Chandelier, 3-Light, Silver Metal, Etched Glass Shades, France, c.1925, 29 In. 705.00
Chandelier, 4-Light, Art Deco, Brass, Satin Opalescent Shades, Tulips, 19 x 35 In. 374.00
Chandelier, 4-Light, Brass, Crown Center, Leaf Arms, Kerosene Fonts, 38 x 43 In. 690.00
Chandelier, 4-Light, Brass, Pressed Glass Shades, Starbursts, Stippled Ground, 28 x 34 In. 403.00
Chandelier, 4-Light, Brass, Pressed Glass, Satin Cut To Clear, Pendant Globes, 17 x 35 In. 259.00
Chandelier, 4-Light, Brass, Satin Glass Dome, Flowers, Shades, Ribbed, 26 x 31 In. 230.00
Chandelier, 4-Light, Caramel Slag Glass, Wreath, Wheat Design, Iron Chain, 21 x 38 In. . . 230.00
Chandelier, 4-Light, Cast Aluminum, Round, Satin Glass Bell Shaped Shades, 17 x 36 In. . 104.00
Chandelier, 4-Light, Copper Patina, Etched Frosted Globes, Leaf Scroll, Gas, 19 x 34 In. . . 173.00
Chandelier, 4-Light, Copper, Brass Patina, Metal Fonts, Embossed, Kerosene, 33 x 39 In. . 661.00
Chandelier, 4-Light, Frosted Cut To Clear Glass Dome, Pendant Globes, 22 x 30 In. 173.00
Chandelier, 4-Light, Frosted Glass Grape Shades, Burnished Copper, Gas, 23 x 38 In. 374.00
Chandelier, 4-Light, Gilt Bronze, Glass, Continental, Late 19th Century, 28 x 24 In. 1150.00
Chandelier, 4-Light, Gold Aurene Shades, Brass Pendant, Marked Steuben, 16 x 22 In. . . . 403.00
Chandelier, 4-Light, Louis XV Style, Gilt Metal, Multicolored, Cast Leaves, 20 x 15 In. . . . 2151.00
Chandelier, 4-Light, Muller Freres, Wrought Iron, Pink Frosted Glass Globes, 36 x 22 In. . 1554.00
Chandelier, 4-Light, Neoclassical, Bust, Woman, Frosted Bowl Shades, Gas, 28 x 35 In. . . 2070.00
Chandelier, 4-Light, Ruffled Shade, Sunflower Design, Gas, 25 1/2 x 34 In. 431.00
Chandelier, 5-Light, Art Nouveau, Bronze, Iron, Leaf, Flower, Continental, c.1900, 31 In. . 1175.00
Chandelier, 5-Light, Arts & Crafts, Aurene Glass Shades, Brass, 13 In. 1680.00
Chandelier, 5-Light, Aurene Glass, Bell Shape, Gold, Ribbed, Bronze Holder, 17 x 40 In. . 1438.00
Chandelier, 5-Light, Brass, White Satin Quatrefoil Shade, Painted Birds, 32 x 35 In. 575.00
Chandelier, 5-Light, Bronze Patina, Pendant Shades, Scroll Design, Gas, 32 x 55 In. 3450.00
Chandelier, 5-Light, Cut Glass, Urn Shape, Free-Form Leaves, 20th Century, 21 x 28 In. . . 188.00
Chandelier, 5-Light, Opalescent Swirl Ball Globes, Pendant, 22 x 31 In. 546.00
Chandelier, 5-Light, Prisms, Frosted Cut To Clear Dome, 24 x 29 In. 546.00
Chandelier, 5-Light, Satin Shades, Hand Painted Maroon Roses, Pendant, 20 x 29 In. 173.00
Chandelier, 5-Light, Venetian Glass, White, Amber, Swirl Molded Arms, 17 1/2 In. 633.00
Chandelier, 5-Light, Wrought Iron, Candle Cups, Twisted Arms, Chain, 1700s, 47 In. 1293.00
Chandelier, 6-Light, 18th Century Style, Cut Glass, Molded, Button Chains, 38 x 29 In. . . . 546.00
Chandelier, 6-Light, Baccarat Crystal, Bobeches, France, 19th Century, 30 x 23 In. 3220.00
Chandelier, 6-Light, Barbedienne, Gilt Bronze, Glass, Champleve Enamel, c.1890, 31 In. . . 5400.00
Chandelier, 6-Light, Brass, Leaves, Vine, Geese, Opal Glass, Gold Iridescent, 25 x 26 In. . 1560.00
Chandelier, 6-Light, Cast Iron, Kerosene Fonts, Torch & Wreath, Victorian, 37 x 39 In. . . . 719.00
Chandelier, 6-Light, George III, Cut Glass, Baluster Stem, Beads, Drops, 48 x 30 In. 2160.00
Chandelier, 6-Light, Gilt Brass, Glass, Leaf-Shape Covered Cage, 44 x 24 In. 1093.00
Chandelier, 6-Light, Gilt Wrought Iron, Cut Glass, France, c.1900, 31 x 19 In. 2990.00
Chandelier, 6-Light, Iron, White, Cage Form, Blue Opaline Glass Beads, 27 x 20 In. 489.00
Chandelier, 6-Light, Louis XIV Style, Carved, Silvered Beechwood, 18 x 21 In. 3450.00
Chandelier, 6-Light, Louis XV Style, Bronze, Patinated, Wrought Iron, 32 x 17 In. 2530.00
Chandelier, 6-Light, Louis XV Style, Wrought Iron, 42 x 22 In. 978.00
Chandelier, 6-Light, Louis XVI Style, Brass, Cut Glass, Cage, 25 x 17 In. 863.00
Chandelier, 6-Light, Louis XVI Style, Gilded Brass, Cage Form, Glass Drops, 30 x 19 In. . 1380.00
Chandelier, 6-Light, Louis XVI Style, Gilt Brass, Cut Glass, Cage Shape, Mid 1800s, 32 In. 863.00
Chandelier, 6-Light, Maple Hub, Wire Arms, New England, 1700s, 13 1/2 x 14 In. 4406.00
Chandelier, 6-Light, Neoclassical, Gilt, Crown, Scrolled Arms, 32 In. 418.00
Chandelier, 6-Light, Oak Column, Serpentine Wrought Iron Arms, Dutch, 23 x 32 In. 1265.00
Chandelier, 6-Light, Parcel Gilt Beechwood, Carved, Green Painted, France, 36 x 26 In. . . 2760.00
Chandelier, 6-Light, Pressed Glass, Diamond, Cut Glass Bead Chains, 40 x 21 In. 1610.00
Chandelier, 6-Light, Red Paint, S-Scrolled Arms, Crimped Edge, 1800-20, 12 1/2 In. 2530.00
Chandelier, 6-Light, Restauration Style, Gilt Brass, Black Paint, Electrified, 32 x 26 In. . . . 1955.00
Chandelier, 6-Light, Scrolls, Silvered Metal Mounts, c.1935, 27 1/2 In. 588.00
Chandelier, 7-Light, Louis XIV Style, Bronze Argente, Baluster, 22 1/2 x 28 1/2 In. 1955.00
Chandelier, 8-Light, Antiqued Brass, Openwork Cage Shape, 24 x 28 In. 1610.00
Chandelier, 8-Light, Brass, Etched Globes, Trumpet Shades, Green, Gas, 25 x 70 In. 4140.00

Chandelier, 8-Light, Empire Style, Gilt Brass, Glass Spires, France, c.1900, 34 x 35 In. ... 1495.00
Chandelier, 8-Light, Flemish Design, Brass, Ball-Turned, 20th Century, 25 x 32 In. 53.00
Chandelier, 8-Light, Glass Bead Roping, Prisms, Scroll Frame, 1900s, 25 x 31 In. 411.00
Chandelier, 8-Light, Louis XV Style, Gilt Bronze, Glass 777.00
Chandelier, 8-Light, Louis XV Style, Gilt Metal, Caryatids, Cornucopia, 30 x 20 In. 705.00
Chandelier, 8-Light, Louis XV Style, Gilt Metal, Prisms, 29 x 22 In. 1195.00
Chandelier, 8-Light, Maria Theresa Style, Gilt Brass, Cage Shape, Austria, 30 x 26 In. 1725.00
Chandelier, 8-Light, Neoclassical, Gilt Brass, Cut Glass, Sweden, c.1885, 40 x 27 In. 1725.00
Chandelier, 8-Light, Pressed Glass Bobeches, Prisms, 27 x 37 In. 316.00
Chandelier, 8-Light, Regency Style, Gilt Bronze, Scroll Arms, Shells, Leaves, 38 x 30 In. . 3346.00
Chandelier, 8-Light, Regency Style, Wrought Iron, Glass Prisms, 30 x 22 In. 2689.00
Chandelier, 8-Light, Rococo Style, Giltwood, Carved, Mid 19th Century, 37 x 29 In. 2300.00
Chandelier, 8-Light, Scrolling Arms, Prince Of Wales Plumes, Early 1800s, 37 x 33 In. ... 7223.00
Chandelier, 8-Light, Tin, Painted, Candle Sockets Around Center Column, 27 x 43 In. 86.00
Chandelier, 9-Light, Louis XVI, Gilt Metal, 3 Seated Female Herm Figures, 43 x 22 In. ... 7768.00
Chandelier, 9-Light, Silvered Brass, Cut Glass, Triangular, c.1915, 42 x 21 In. 1265.00
Chandelier, 9-Light, Wood, Gilded, Silvered, Carved, Wrought Iron, 36 x 33 In. 4830.00
Chandelier, 10-Light, Brass, Central Globe, Scroll & Rosette Arms, 1900s, 35 x 26 In. 353.00
Chandelier, 10-Light, Louis XV Style, Cut Glass, Ormolu, c.1900, 52 In. 4600.00
Chandelier, 10-Light, Venetian Style Glass, Raindrop Prisms, Roping, 1900s, 36 x 28 In. .. 470.00
Chandelier, 12-Light, 1700s Style, Cut Glass, Glass Balusters, Electrified, 38 x 28 In. 3220.00
Chandelier, 12-Light, Brass, 2 Tiers, 18th Century Dutch Style, 27 x 27 In. 420.00
Chandelier, 12-Light, French Style, Bronze, Leaves, S-Shape Arms, 28 x 28 In. 1438.00
Chandelier, 12-Light, Gilt Brass, Opalescent White Glass, France, c.1835, 32 x 28 In. 1840.00
Chandelier, 12-Light, Gilt Metal, Beads, Pendants, Stylized Flower Heads, 36 In. 1150.00
Chandelier, 12-Light, Louis XVI Style, Gilt Bronze, Electrified, 33 x 24 In. 5400.00
Chandelier, 12-Light, Louis XVI Style, Gilt Bronze, Electrified, 44 x 18 In. 5400.00
Chandelier, 12-Light, Maria Theresa Style, Brass, Cut Glass, Continental, 32 x 32 In. 1840.00
Chandelier, 12-Light, Venetian Style Glass, Multilevel Prisms, Scrollwork, 20th Century .. 441.00
Chandelier, 15-Light, Cut Glass Chains, Spears, Pendants, 2 Tiers, 30 x 32 In. 2500.00
Chandelier, 18-Light, 18th Century Style, Gilt Metal, Cut Glass, Scrolling Mounts, 42 In. . 3992.00
Chandelier, 18-Light, Baroque Style, Bronze, Cartouche Shaped Drops, 2 Tiers, c.1925 .. 1998.00
Chandelier, 18-Light, Brass, Shell, Bow Motif, Pink Metal Candle Tubes, Gas, 34 x 61 In. 5060.00
Chandelier, 18-Light, Louis XV Style, Gilt Bronze, Electrified, 32 x 30 1/2 In. 3600.00
Chandelier, 24-Light, 18th Century Style, Gilt Metal Frame, Scrolling, Leaves, 41 x 33 In. 2661.00
Chandelier, 36-Light, Georgian Style, Bronze, 55 x 38 In. 3286.00
Chandelier, Art Deco, Cast Aluminum Frame, Glass Dome Pendant, Prisms, 17 x 38 In. .. 144.00
Chandelier, Art Deco, Cast Aluminum, 5 Amber Scoop Shades, Flowers, 16 x 40 In., Pair . 690.00
Chandelier, Art Deco, Cast Iron, Frosted Scoop Shades, Embossed Flowers, 20 x 24 In. ... 288.00
Chandelier, Art Deco, Cast Iron, Satin Scalloped Bowl Shades, Embossed, 19 x 36 In. 316.00
Chandelier, Arts & Crafts, Leaded Glass, Acorn Shape, Geometric Design, 10 x 7 In. 2151.00
Chandelier, Brass, Cut Glass Center Column, Pressed Glass Leaves, Prisms, Swags, 27 In. 460.00
Chandelier, Frosted Glass Ground, Embossed Designs, Shaded Panels, Trees, 14 x 35 In. .. 184.00
Chandelier, Glass, Beaded, Elongated Opalescent Teardrops, White Beads, 17 x 20 In. ... 920.00
Chandelier, Opaque White Glass Dome, Green Bands, Painted Vining Roses, 16 x 31 In. .. 144.00
Chandelier, White Satin Glass Dome, Embossed Acanthus Leaves, 14 x 30 In. 173.00
Electric, 2-Light, Antler, Wrought Iron, Brass, Patinated, c.1900, 14 In. 2760.00
Electric, 2-Light, Brass, Green Pulled Feather Shades, 26 In. 259.00
Electric, 2-Light, Daum Shades, Wrought Iron, Mottled Glass, 16 3/4 In. 956.00
Electric, 3-Light, Brass, Painted Shade, 20th Century, 23 In., Pair 600.00
Electric, 6 Caramel Slag Panels, Metal, Reticulated Leaf Frame, c.1915, 21 In. 460.00
Electric, 6 Slag Glass Panels, Caramel, Metal Overlay, Ribbed Standard, 15 3/4 In. 176.00
Electric, 6-Light, White Metal, Figural Fairy, Grass, Reeds, Patina, Libelle, c.1920, 49 In. . 1293.00
Electric, Acid Cut Black Glass, Black Cut With Flowers, Early 20th Century, 24 In. 259.00
Electric, Agrafee, Black Lacquered Aluminum, Serge Mouille, 1950s, 26 x 11 In. 8864.00
Electric, Albert Cheuret, Bronze, Silvered, Alabaster Shades, c.1925, 15 1/4 In. 3585.00
Electric, American Machine Age, Aluminum, Lucite, c.1935, 6 1/2 In., Pair 223.00
Electric, Aquarium, Dunhill, Painted Fishes, Seahorses, Brass Mechanism, c.1930, 3 In. .. 949.00
Electric, Arredoluce Monza, Italy, c.1955, 14 In. 1410.00
Electric, Arredoluce, Ceiling, Brass, 12 Cascading Arms, Colored Enamel, 30 x 30 In. 1380.00
Electric, Art Deco, Domed Shade, Wrought Iron Frame, Metal Base, France, 1930, 68 In. . 3290.00
Electric, Art Deco, Frosted Glass, Embossed Flowers, Czech, 10 1/2 In. 259.00
Electric, Art Deco, Gilt Bronze, Faux Bamboo, Tripod, Footed, Mid 20th Century, 55 In. .. 1725.00

Electric, Art Glass, Mottled Orange, Magenta, Disk Shape, Baluster Base, 23 x 14 In. 1434.00
Electric, Art Nouveau, Bronze, Jeweled, 2-Tone Embossed Bronze Base, c.1900, 22 In. ... 3450.00
Electric, Art Nouveau, Gilt Bronze, Loie Fuller, Figural, Outstretched Arms, 13 1/2 In. ... 5079.00
Electric, Art Nouveau, Glass, Gilt Bronze, Mermaid, Whelk Shell, Inkstand, 1910s, 15 In. . 4348.00
Electric, Art Nouveau, Gold Iridescent Lotus, Pulled Feathers, Bronze Woman, 11 In. 1610.00
Electric, Art Nouveau, Hammered Brass Shade, Jewels, Bronzed Serpent, 11 x 19 In. 881.00
Electric, Art Nouveau, Leaded Glass, Wisteria, Bronze Baluster Base, 26 x 22 1/2 In. 896.00
Electric, Art Nouveau, Metal, Long-Stem Flower Sockets, Crane, Lily Pad Base, 62 In. ... 823.00
Electric, Art Nouveau, Reverse Painted Parrot, 14 In. 480.00
Electric, Art Nouveau, Woman, Holding Shell Shade, Bronzed Metal, Marble Base, 13 In. . 3231.00
Electric, Arts & Crafts, Bronze, Glass, 3 Sockets, Acorn Pulls, Bulbous, 22 x 16 1/2 In. ... 1058.00
Electric, Arts & Crafts, Green Slag Glass, Hand Hammered, 8 Panels, 24 x 14 In. 201.00
Electric, Arts & Crafts, Green, Opaque White Slag Glass, Square Shade, c.1910, 19 In. ... 207.00
Electric, Arts & Crafts, Hand Hammered, Tooled, Raised Designs, Fringe, 12 x 20 In. 1150.00
Electric, Arts & Crafts, Leaded Glass Shade, Leaves, Berries, Bronzed Metal Base, 22 In. . 1175.00
Electric, Arts & Crafts, Leaded Slag Glass, 3 Sockets, Egg Shape Base, 33 x 22 In. 1175.00
Electric, Arts & Crafts, Mica Shade, Bulbous, Hammered Copper, 17 x 21 In. 3408.00
Electric, Arts & Crafts, Mica Shade, Iron, Painted, Leaves, Marble Base, 28 In. 242.00
Electric, Arts & Crafts, Overlaid Metal, Geometric, Amber Glass, Wood Base, 14 x 14 In. . 881.00
Electric, Arts & Crafts, Painted Leaves, Acorn Shade, Bronze Tree Trunk, Meyer, 17 In. .. 2233.00
Electric, Arts & Crafts, Paneled Slag Glass, Trees, Bulbous Base, Acanthus Leaves, 22 In. . 2585.00
Electric, Arts & Crafts, Slag Shade, Light Base, Cutout, Green Glass Inserts, 15 x 15 In. .. 529.00
Electric, Barovier & Toso, Opaque White Glass, Silver Aventurine, Vase, 1950s, 36 In. ... 86.00
Electric, Black Forest Style, Carved Wood, Squirrel, Basket, Feather Shade, 18 In. 1323.00
Electric, Black, Brushed Metal Shafts, Square Base, 20th Century, 54 In., Pair 47.00
Electric, Brass, Acanthus Leaf, Lion's Head Accents, Ribbed White Glass Shade, 19 In. ... 98.00
Electric, Brass, Double Branch, Bird & Leaf Supports, 20th Century, 24 x 12 In. 529.00
Electric, Bronze, Argente, Louis XVI Style, Silk Shade, Carrara Marble Base, 20 In. 431.00
Electric, Bronze, Birds, Flowers, High Relief, Japan, c.1900, 68 In. 1763.00
Electric, Bronze, Cold Painted, Cast As Mosque, Austria, 30 In. 3585.00
Electric, Bronze, Harlequin, Frosted Glass, Marble Base, c.1925, 10 1/2 x 16 3/8 In. 2629.00
Electric, Bronze, Urn Shape, 2 Winged Lions Support, Handles, Chain, 28 In., Pair 460.00
Electric, Caramel Slag, Overlay Grill, Bronze Coated, Flowers, Lattice Work, 17 x 22 In. . 288.00
Electric, Cast Iron, Sundial Base, White, Green Slag Glass Petal Shade, 18 In. 173.00
Electric, Cast Iron, Wood, Opaque Satin Shade, Hand Painted Violets, 60 In............. 104.00
Electric, Ceiling, Bat, Pallme-Konig Shade, Green, Black, 21 1/2 x 20 3/4 In. 2585.00
Electric, Ceiling, G. Stickley, 4-Light, Copper, Glass, Oak Mount, c.1909, 26 x 26 In. 7170.00
Electric, Champleve, Tapered, Raised Enamel Bands, Flowers, Figures, 36 In. 82.00
Electric, Cherubs, Bulbous Vase, Gold Background, Brass Fittings, Mid 1900s, 35 In. 29.00
Electric, Chrome, American, 1930s, 16 3/4 In. 121.00
Electric, Clement Massier, Art Nouveau, Iridescent, Ceramic, Gilt Bronze, 24 In. 1016.00
Electric, Cloisonne, Brass Claw Feet, 33 In. 250.00
Electric, Corinthian Column, Putti, Silver Plate, England, c.1950, 19 1/2 x 6 In., Pair 978.00
Electric, Cranberry, Coin Spot, Melon Shape Globe, 9 x 27 In. 316.00
Electric, Curved Caramel Slag Panels, Overlay Metal Grill, Ribbed Base, 22 x 14 In. 374.00
Electric, Cut Glass, Bound Wheat Pattern Stem, 24 In., Pair 69.00
Electric, Cut Glass, Mushroom Shape, Cut Flowers, Pendant Prisms, Early 1900s, 23 In. .. 460.00
Electric, Decorated Opal Shade, Font, Electrified, Victorian, 13 1/2 In. 345.00
Electric, Decorated Opal Shade, Font, Electrified, Victorian, 14 In. 219.00
Electric, Desk, Brass, Frosted Blue Satin Shade, Tadpoles, 25 In. 230.00
Electric, Desk, Cowboy, Figural, Raised Leg, Porcelain, Marble Base, 1930s, 15 In. 350.00
Electric, Desny, Chromed Metal, c.1930, 7 In. 8365.00
Electric, Desny, Metal, Nickel Plated, Glass, Myrbor, c.1935, 6 1/2 x 4 3/4 In. 3824.00
Electric, Edwardian, Black Lacquer, Bulbous Standard, Molded Base, c.1900, 52 In. 863.00
Electric, Edwardian, Black Lacquer, Bulbous Standard, Molded Base, c.1900, 59 In. 920.00
Electric, Edwardian, Brass, Natural Shaped Leafy Standard, 3 Splayed Feet, c.1900, 61 In. 1495.00
Electric, Emeralite, Green Cased Glass Shade, Tapered Brass Base, 9 x 8 x 17 In. 382.00
Electric, Emeralite, Movable Arm, Clamp Style, Green Shade, 23 In. 201.00
Electric, Enameled Satin Glass Shade, 14 1/2 In. ....195.00 to 285.00
Electric, Ernesto Gismondi, Cantilevered, Artemide, 1980s, 24 In., Pair 105.00
Electric, Floor, Adnet Style, Enameled Faux Bamboo Standard, Brass, Italy, 1950s, 54 In. . 1840.00
Electric, Frosted Glass Shade, Wrought Iron, Tooled, Applied Design, 15 In............. 558.00
Electric, Fruit Basket Form, Colored Glass Fruit, 6 3/4 In. 380.00

Electric, G. Stickley, No. 233, Candlestick Shape, Copper, Hammered, Straps, 16 x 5 In. . . . 2820.00
Electric, G. Stickley, No. 506, Copper Shade, Amber Glass Panels, 16 x 12 In. 8225.00
Electric, Gilt Spelter, Brass, Murano Spiral Goldstone Striped, Latticinio Glass, 18 In. 115.00
Electric, Gino Valenti, Glass, Vistosi, c.1968, 20 1/2 x 19 In. 705.00
Electric, Gorham Co., Leaded Glass, Bronze, c.1910, 29 x 23 In. 7170.00
Electric, Gorham, Copper, Metal, Foo Dog Heads, Socket Set In Oil Font, 1885, 14 In. . . . 1645.00
Electric, Green Slag Glass, Stylized Shade, Brass Cast Support, 16 x 6 In. 212.00
Electric, Hanging, 2-Light, Iridescent Gold Shades, 12 x 8 In. 173.00
Electric, Hanging, 3-Light, Brass, Calcite Shades, Steuben, 22 In. 345.00
Electric, Hanging, 3-Light, Brass, Carved Lorene Shades, 35 In. 460.00
Electric, Hanging, 24-Light, Sputnik, Radiating Candelabra Lights, 24 In. 316.00
Electric, Hanging, Angel, Figural, Gilt Metal, France, 13 In. 633.00
Electric, Hanging, Art Deco, Opalescent, Leaf & Bar Pattern, 10 x 10 x 33 1/2 In. 86.00
Electric, Hanging, Arte & Ingrand, Saucer Shape, Glass, Gilt, Brass, 20 x 27 1/2 In., Pair . . 9330.00
Electric, Hanging, Billiard Table, 3-Light, Brass, Urn, Scroll, Tole, 41 x 18 x 54 In., Pair . . 470.00
Electric, Hanging, Blue, Hobnail Shade, 14 1/4 In. 1150.00
Electric, Hanging, Le Verre Francais, Dragonflies, Cameo, Rose, Orange, 15 x 27 In. 2350.00
Electric, Hanging, Leaded Glass, Panels & Flowers, c.1925, 22 In. 219.00
Electric, Hanging, Leaded Glass, Scrolls & Flowers, c.1925, 24 1/2 In. 316.00
Electric, Hanging, Leaded Glass, Textured Ice Ground, Geometric, 3 Chains, 16 In., Pair . . 8400.00
Electric, Hanging, Olive Hobnail Shade, Pressed Font, Jeweled Frame, 14 x 36 In. 575.00
Electric, Hanging, Opaque Shade, Rose Transfer, Jeweled Frame, 14 x 40 In. 259.00
Electric, Hanging, Peach Shaded Opaque Shade, Hand Painted, White Lilies, 14 x 47 In. . . 230.00
Electric, Hanging, Reverse Painted, Birds, Branches, Blue, Gold, Mushroom Shade, 11 In. 3290.00
Electric, Hanging, Swirled Cranberry Shade, 7 1/2 x 29 In. 316.00
Electric, Hanging, Swirled Ruby Cylinder Shade, 7 x 37 In. 230.00
Electric, Hanging, Swirled, Tomato Red, Bell Shape Shade, 7 1/2 x 19 In. 345.00
Electric, Hanging, Tiffany Style, Tulip Shade, Blue & Green Floral Glass, 19 x 18 In. 176.00
Electric, Hubley, Geisha Girl, Kimono, Cast Iron, 12 In. 330.00
Electric, Imari Vase, Flowers, 2 Floral Fans, Wood Base, 9 1/2 In. 201.00
Electric, Iron, Dome, Opaque Satin Shade, Painted, Openworked Base, Painted, 59 In. 201.00
Electric, Jacques-Emile Ruhlmann, Gilt Bronze, Alabaster, c.1925, 7 1/8 In., Pair 26290.00
Electric, Jefferson, Reverse Painted Flowers, Mottled Green Glass, 2 Sockets, 23 x 16 In. . 1175.00
Electric, Jefferson, Reverse Painted, Autumn Scene, Copper Color, 24 In. 2300.00
Electric, Juno, Embossed Brass Font, Copper Accents, 20 x 47 In. 207.00
Electric, Kite, Pierre Guariche, Disderot, c.1953, 58 1/4 In. 6463.00
Electric, Lampadaire, Modernist, Chromed Metal, France, c.1930, 69 In. 9560.00
Electric, Leaded Glass, Graduated Green Slag Rows, Yellow Band, Brass Base, 23 1/2 In. . 1150.00
Electric, Leaded Glass, Slag Glass, Green, Pink, Bronze Standard, Tripod, Pad Feet, 48 In. 441.00
Electric, Levior, Helmet, Red Plastic Body, Tinted Visor, 1980s, 10 In. 35.00
Electric, Marble, Green, Ormolu Mounts, Oval, Branch Handles, Square Base, 31 In., Pair 2990.00
Electric, Marble, Onyx, Eagle & Globe, Pedestal, Round Column, Stepped Base, 60 In. . . . 1150.00
Electric, Marcel Bergue, Art Deco, Wrought Iron, Stylized Leaves, 58 In. 1315.00
Electric, Mary Gregory Style, Enameling, 2 Blue Glass Sections, Mid 1900s, 40 In. 489.00
Electric, Metal, Pierced, Tubular, Painted, Yellow, c.1950, 15 1/4 In. 3346.00
Electric, Mosque, Mamluk Revival, Cairo Pierced Copper, Silver & Brass, 1900, 54 In. . . . 2040.00
Electric, Nakashima, Rag Paper Shade, Walnut Base, 1976, 59 x 16 1/2 In. 10575.00
Electric, Neoclassical, Patinated Bronze, Stylized Ironic Column, 21 3/4 In., Pair 633.00
Electric, Nessen, Brushed Steel, Adjustable Enameled Cylinder Shades, 12 x 20 In., Pair . . 748.00
Electric, Night-Light, Tin, Courteen & Burgess, Patent, 1920 . . . . 65.00
Electric, Oscar Bach, Fish Design, 7 x 36 In. 530.00
Electric, Oscar Bach, Hammered Bronze, Carved, Reticulated, 8 x 30 In. 1528.00
Electric, P. Sarchi, Alabaster, Marble, Classical, Girl, Chariot, Soldier, Italy, 21 x 9 In. 805.00
Electric, Painted Flower Shade & Base, Electrified, Victorian, 20 In. 144.00
Electric, Palmetto Tree Shape, Cast Metal, 36 In., Pair 259.00
Electric, Patinated Brass, Enamel, Skeletal Shape, Enameled, 1960s, 28 In., Pair 224.00
Electric, Paul McCobb, c.1958, 22 1/4 In. 1645.00
Electric, Permaflector, Aluminum, Pittsburgh Reflector Co., 1930s, 18 In. 210.00
Electric, Piano, Art Deco, Iron, France, c.1930, 16 In. 160.00
Electric, Pierre D'Avesn, Molded Glass, Silvered Metal, c.1925, 25 x 16 In. 736.00
Electric, Pittsburgh, House In Meadow, Bronzed Base, P.L.B. & G. Co., 22 In. . . . . . . *Illus* 1150.00
Electric, Pole, Chinoiserie, Black, Gold, Garden, Rocks, Plants, Japanned, 63 In. 1955.00
Electric, Pole, Chinoiserie, Black, Gold, Oriental Figures, Landscape, Japanned, 61 In. . . . 1955.00

Electric, Pole, George V, Gold Japanned, Black, c.1900, 60 In.	431.00
Electric, Pop Art, Molded Plastic, Orange Shade, Tubular Steel, c.1960, 65 In.	180.00
Electric, Porcelain, Canister Shape, Chinese, Early 20th Century, 30 x 4 1/2 In.	188.00
Electric, Porcelain, Dancing Couple, 20th Century, 14 In., Pair	165.00
Electric, Porcelain, Kneeling Woman, Roses, Painted, Continental, 1930s, 8 1/2 In.	224.00
Electric, Porcelain, Man, Woman, Tree, Potschappel, Germany, 20th Century, 7 In., Pair	575.00
Electric, Porcelain, Painted, Floral Putti, Maiden, Gilt, 20th Century, 33 x 20 In., 2 Piece	223.00
Electric, Prairie School, 4-Panel Shade, Wood Frame, Slag Glass, 2 Sockets, 18 x 20 In.	2820.00
Electric, Prairie School, Faceted Leaded Glass Shade, 4 Sockets, 21 x 18 1/2 In.	2585.00
Electric, Regency Style, Bronze, Basalt, Egyptian Maidens, Vase On Heads, 35 In., Pair	1610.00
Electric, Restauration Style, Green Paint, Gilt Brass, 21 1/2 In.	345.00
Electric, Restauration Style, Steel, Brass Mounted, Octagonal Base, France, 23 In., Pair	345.00
Electric, Reverse Painted Shade, Lake, Sailboats, Bronzed Metal Base, 16 x 22 In.	1058.00
Electric, Reverse Painted, Pink Apple Blossom, Green Ground, Blue Gray Border, 24 In.	3819.00
Electric, Reverse Painted, Trees, Hills, Water, Orange, Yellow, Paw Feet, 24 In.	294.00
Electric, Reverse Painted, Windmill Scene, Orange, 12 1/2 In.	175.00
Electric, Rock Crystal, Giltwood, 36 In., Pair	7200.00
Electric, Rooster, Figural, Crystal, Paden City, 11 1/8 x 6 1/2 In.	230.00
Electric, Ruby Satin Glass, Openwork Metal Foot, Bowl, Brass Font, 21 1/2 In.	690.00
Electric, Sailboat, Bakelite, Patinated Metal, 1930s	207.00
Electric, Samuel Yellen, Iron, Isinglass, Stamped, 1924, 24 1/2 In.	8000.00
Electric, Samuel Yellin, Iron, 2 Sockets, Twisted Tripod Base, 61 1/2 x 17 1/2 In.	4700.00
Electric, Silver Plate, Urn, Column, Ram's-Head Supports, Early 1900s, 37 x 8 In., Pair	764.00
Electric, Silvercrest, Candlestick Shape, Sterling On Bronze, Mica Shade, 15 In., Pair	294.00
Electric, Skyscraper, Cylindrical, Steel, Frosted Glass Shade, c.1931, 75 In.	7768.00
Electric, Soapstone, Chinese, Birds, Flowers, Figural, Wooden Base, 1900s, 27 x 7 In.	294.00
Electric, Spelter, Balloon Shape, White Globe, Swags, Winged Animal Base, 24 In.	50.00
Electric, Spelter, Flowers & Vines, Stained & Leaded Glass, Molded Base, 24 x 12 In.	30.00
Electric, Spelter, Oriental Sailboats, Reverse Painted, Dome, 19 x 13 In.	60.00
Electric, Spelter, Pink Roses, Leaves, Reverse Painted, Dome, Molded Base, 19 x 17 In.	30.00
Electric, Spelter, Stained & Leaded Glass, Dragonflies, 30 x 22 In.	250.00
Electric, Spelter, Stained & Leaded Glass, Water Lilies, Fluted Support, Vine Base, 68 In.	160.00
Electric, Spotlight, Bronze Case, Guide Motor Lamp Co., Cleveland, 22 x 10 In.	395.00
Electric, Stickley Bros., Slag Glass Shade, Hammered Copper Base, 23 x 19 In.	1998.00
Electric, Student, Art Nouveau, Brass, Scrolling, Flame Finial, 2 Iridescent Shades, 28 In.	1093.00
Electric, Student, Brass, 2 Fixtures, Faux Reservoir, 26 In.	58.00
Electric, Student, Brass, Faux Reservoir, Glass Shade, 28 1/2 In.	108.00
Electric, Student, Silver Plated, Glass Shade, Chimney, Belgium Co., 1870-80	575.00
Electric, Table, Art Nouveau, Leaf-Shape Shade, Stylized Harp, Column Shaft, 1900s, 26 In.	188.00
Electric, Table, Slag Glass Panel Shade, Green, Blue, Trees, Buildings, 16 x 27 1/2 In.	920.00
Electric, Teak, Brass, Shade, Denmark, 1950s, 36 x 58 In.	411.00
Electric, Tiffany Style, Stained Glass, Marble, Corinthian Column Support, 36 In., Pair	106.00
Electric, Tubular Steel, Leather, c.1970, 36 In.	155.00
Electric, Turkish Style, Copper, Glass, Crescent-Moon Cutouts, 32 x 32 In.	269.00
Electric, TV, Deer, Leaping, Chestnut, Style No. 160, Phil-Mar Corp., Ohio	80.00
Electric, Vase, Bronze, Melon-Ribbed Body, Elephant-Trunk Handles, Oriental, 16 In.	86.00
Electric, Vase, Cloisonne, Flowers, 3 Dragon Rings, Wood Base, 24 In.	58.00
Electric, Walnut, Square Tubular Brass, Opaque Diffuser, 1960, 55 1/2 In.	88.00
Electric, Warrior, Running, Figural, Flame Shape, 41 In.	3910.00
Electric, Wilkerson, Leaded Glass, 23 In.	5500.00
Fairy, 3 Scrolled Arms, 4 Clarke's Cricklites, Embossed, Center Piece, Brass Base, 18 In.	230.00
Fairy, Clarke's Patent, Blue Glass, 1883	45.00
Fairy, Clarke's Patent, Clear Glass, 1883	30.00
Fat, Brass Reservoir, Hinged Lid, Iron Hanger, Wick Pick, Marked P.D. 1851, 6 In.	3300.00
Fat, Iron, Gimbal, c.1800s	275.00
Fluid, Bells, Patent, 1854, Pair	950.00
Fluid, Blown Glass, Brass Collar & Burner, Pewter Snuffer, Quatrefoil Base, 13 In., Pair	1150.00
Fluid, Brass Reflector, 6 Wicks, Cornelius & Wilhelm, Patent, 1849	500.00
Fluid, Brass, Dyott & Kent, Philadelphia	100.00
Fluid, Brass, Iron, Candleholder, Adjustable, Early 1800s, 16 x 7 1/4 In.	1265.00
Fluid, Brass, Jennings, 1831	35.00
Fluid, Brass, Tin, Engraved, Leaf Scrolls, Round Base, Adjustable, France, c.1850, 23 In.	920.00
Fluid, Bronze, 3 Elephant Masks, Supporting Neoclassical Bowl, Chinese, 58 In.	2151.00

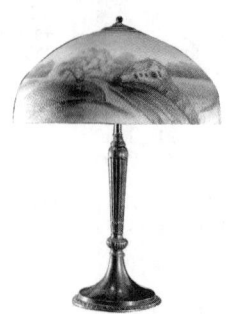

Lamp, Electric, Pittsburgh, House
In Meadow, Bronzed Base, P.L.B.
& G. Co., 22 In.

Lamp, Kerosene, Gone With The
Wind, Daylilies, Green Ground,
Metal Base, Handles

Lamp, Kerosene, Gone With
The Wind, Pansies, Openwork
Base, Duplex Burner

Fluid, Double Cut Overlay Glass, Quatrefoil Cuts, Brass, Late 1800s, 10 1/8 In. 529.00
Fluid, Flint Glass, Giant Sawtooth Pattern, 10 In. 85.00
Fluid, Jennings, Patent, 1847 .... 50.00
Fluid, Marble, Gilt Bronze, Leaf Collar, Lavender Marble Body, Continental, 17 In., Pair .. 748.00
Fluid, Miner's, 3 Tubes, Symonds, Patent, 1865 .... 275.00
Fluid, Miner's, Horsford's, Patent, 1855 .... 125.00
Fluid, Pigeon, Patent, 1885 .... 35.00
Fluid, Pinkham, Patent, 1862 .... 250.00
Fluid, Pratt, Patent, 1863 .... 145.00
Fluid, Reflector, Silver, Dietz Brother 1500.00
Fluid, Silver Plate, Electrified, Victorian, c.1880, 34 In. 575.00
Fluid, Skater's, Brass, Green Globe, 7 In. 546.00
Fluid, Skater's, Tin, Amethyst Globe, Marked Jewel, 7 In. 1093.00
Fluid, Stewart, Patent, 1850 .... 15.00
Fluid, Tin Tole, S. Rust, Patent, 1844 .... 500.00
Fluid, Tin, Improved Lamps, Cornelius, Patent, 1843 .... 50.00
Fluid, Tin, Kinnear, Patent, 1851 .... 130.00
Fluid, Tin, Marcy, Patent, 1866 .... 45.00
Fluid, Tin, Tomilinson, Patent, 1843 .... 75.00
Fluid, Van Bunschoten, Patent, 1856 .... 1300.00
Franciscan, Desert Rose, Hurricane Candle, 9 In. 440.00
Gas, 2-Light, Ribbed, Frosted Center Globe, Rose Swags, Leaves, Candles, 14 x 33 In. ... 460.00
Gas, Hanging, 12-Light, Etched & Frosted Shades, Electrified, Victorian, 44 In. 8625.00
Gas, Hanging, Etched Ruffle Shade, Blue Threading, Burnished Copper, 41 x 32 In. 374.00
Handel lamps are included in the Handel category.
Hanging, Opalescent Swirl, Ball Globe, Domed Shade, Brass Frame, 8 x 35 In. 115.00
Hanging, Opaque Shade, Vanilla Cream Bands, Painted Flowers, Butterfly, 13 x 40 In. 201.00
Kerosene, Amethyst Glass, Gilt Bronze Mounted, Continental, 28 3/4 In., Pair 6000.00
Kerosene, Banquet, Blown Glass Shade, Base, Molded Drape, Brass Mount, Foot, 22 In. ... 719.00
Kerosene, Banquet, Embossed Brass, Rope Twist Stems, Cast Iron Base, 25 1/2 In., Pair .. 546.00
Kerosene, Banquet, Glass, Frosted Ball Shade, Brass Font, Pierced Brass Frame, 31 In. ... 288.00
Kerosene, Banquet, Opaque Font, Column, Flower & Fern Transfer, Cast Iron Base, 27 In. 109.00
Kerosene, Blown Glass, Cranberry, White Threading, Brass Stem, Marble Base, 7 1/2 In. . 1980.00
Kerosene, Blue Opaque, Vertical Ribs, Greek Key Design, 15 In., Pair 230.00
Kerosene, Brass, Wire Base, Font Frame, Brass Burner, P & A Mfg. Co., Bannes, 12 1/2 In. 180.00
Kerosene, Bronze, Censer Shape, Handles, Round Base, 3 Legs, Footed, 16 x 11 In. 748.00
Kerosene, Cast Iron, Eagle Head, Old Red Paint, 8 In. 635.00
Kerosene, Cast Iron, Opaque Shade, Winter Scene, Crackle Font, 9 1/2 x 37 In. 173.00
Kerosene, Cast Iron, Transfer Print, Lion's Head, Brass Mounted, Opaline, c.1885, 14 In. . 575.00
Kerosene, Ceiling, Ice Cream, Copper, Round Beveled Glass, Jewels, 21 x 8 1/2 In. 880.00
Kerosene, Classical Style, Bronze Mounted, Polished Travertine Marble, 1800s, 26 In. 2990.00
Kerosene, Coach, Brass, Beveled Glass, Elongated Shield-Shape Windows, 31 In., Pair .. 4140.00
Kerosene, Cranberry Glass Oval Reeded Font, Square Black Base, 8 In. 880.00
Kerosene, Cranberry Thumbprint Shade, 7 x 24 In. 316.00

Kerosene, Cranberry, Embossed Frame, Victorian, 13 In. 316.00
Kerosene, Cranberry, Kerosene, Electrified, Victorian, 12 In. 316.00
Kerosene, Cranberry, Opalescent Hobnail Cylinder Shade, 8 1/2 x 27 In. 1150.00
Kerosene, Embossed Amber Shade, Brass Mounts, Victorian, Germany, 10 In. 184.00
Kerosene, Finger, Glass, Blue Amethyst, Bulbous Font, Pulled Foot, Applied Handle, 3 In. 2860.00
Kerosene, Gilt Spelter, Copper Mounts, White Opaline Glass, c.1885, 17 1/2 In., Pair 1265.00
Kerosene, Gone With The Wind, Daylilies, Green Ground, Metal Base, Handles ..... *Illus* 303.00
Kerosene, Gone With The Wind, Embossed, Decorated Tiger Lilies, Brass Font, 21 In. 115.00
Kerosene, Gone With The Wind, Green, Yellow Bands, Dragon, Newt, Iron, 24 In. 431.00
Kerosene, Gone With The Wind, Onyx, Garlands, Leafy Scrolls, Roses, Metal Base, 34 In. 403.00
Kerosene, Gone With The Wind, Pansies, Openwork Base, Duplex Burner .... *Illus* 121.00
Kerosene, Gone With The Wind, Red, Frosted, Raised Design, Brass Font, Foot, 26 In. ... 374.00
Kerosene, Hanging, Cranberry Hobnail Shade, Brass Font, 14 x 46 In. 805.00
Kerosene, Hanging, Cranberry Hobnail Shade, Clear Font, 14 x 36 In. 604.00
Kerosene, Hanging, Cranberry Hobnail Shade, Pressed Glass Font, 13 x 44 In. 690.00
Kerosene, Hanging, Cranberry Hobnail Shade, Satin Font, Diamonds, Jeweled, 15 x 48 In. 805.00
Kerosene, Hanging, Green Opaque Shade, Pressed Glass Font, Smoke Bell, 13 x 36 In. ... 259.00
Kerosene, Hanging, Green Shade, Transfer, Lilacs, Embossed Brass Font, 14 x 43 In. 431.00
Kerosene, Hanging, Green, Demi Shade, Pressed Glass Font, Smoke Bell, 13 x 32 In. 144.00
Kerosene, Hanging, Hobnail Shade, Pigeon Blood, Brass, Pressed Glass Font, 14 x 44 In. . 1093.00
Kerosene, Hanging, Milk Glass Shade, Flower Decoration, Brass Frame, 14 In. 98.00
Kerosene, Hanging, Opalescent Hobnail Shade, Brass, Opaque Smoke Bell, 14 x 43 In. ... 863.00
Kerosene, Hanging, Opalescent Swirl, Brass, 7 x 33 1/2 In. 230.00
Kerosene, Hanging, Opalescent, Ribbed, Peachblow, Bell Shape Shade, 7 x 26 In. 201.00
Kerosene, Hanging, Opaque Ribbed Shade, Pansies, Ribbed Sheath, 14 x 41 In. 86.00
Kerosene, Hanging, Opaque Robin's-Egg Blue Shade, Pressed Font, 13 x 36 In. 345.00
Kerosene, Hanging, Opaque Satin Shade, Yellow Blush, Mum Transfer, 14 x 38 In. 316.00
Kerosene, Hanging, Opaque Shade, Blue & Cream, Apple Blossom Transfer, 14 x 40 In. ... 230.00
Kerosene, Hanging, Opaque Shade, Blue Honeysuckle, Green, Rust Leaves, 14 x 36 In. ... 201.00
Kerosene, Hanging, Opaque Shade, Blue, Yellow, Landscape, Flower Transfer, 14 x 42 In. 345.00
Kerosene, Hanging, Opaque Shade, Carnation Transfer, Daisy & Bar Font, 13 1/2 x 44 In. . 201.00
Kerosene, Hanging, Opaque Shade, Dogwood, Mountains, Amber Font, 14 x 35 In. 259.00
Kerosene, Hanging, Opaque Shade, Green Blush, Roses, Pressed Glass Font, 14 x 47 In. .. 863.00
Kerosene, Hanging, Opaque Shade, Green, Painted, White, Rust Mums, 14 x 36 In. 518.00
Kerosene, Hanging, Opaque Shade, Green, Red Morning Glories, Brass Font, 14 x 44 In. . 374.00
Kerosene, Hanging, Opaque Shade, Hand Printed Pansies, Pressed Glass Font, 14 x 32 In. . 230.00
Kerosene, Hanging, Opaque Shade, Ivy, Brown, Rust, Pressed Glass Diamond, 14 x 40 In. 173.00
Kerosene, Hanging, Opaque Shade, Morning Glories, Satin Smoke Bell, 14 x 39 In. 259.00
Kerosene, Hanging, Opaque Shade, Painted, Yellow Rose, Pressed Glass Font, 14 x 48 In. . 173.00
Kerosene, Hanging, Opaque Shade, Red Flowers, Aqua Pressed Glass Font, 14 x 41 In. ... 316.00
Kerosene, Hanging, Opaque Shade, Ribbed Band, Painted, Forget-Me-Nots, 14 x 39 In. ... 201.00
Kerosene, Hanging, Opaque Shade, Transfer, Daisies, Pressed Glass Font, 14 x 36 In. 230.00
Kerosene, Hanging, Opaque Shade, Winter Scene, Pressed Glass Font, 13 x 45 In. 288.00
Kerosene, Hanging, Opaque Shade, Yellow, Courting Couple, Brass Font, 14 x 39 In. 460.00
Kerosene, Hanging, Opaque, Transfer, Morning Glories, Peacock Feather, 14 x 37 In. 374.00
Kerosene, Hanging, Pattern Molded, Grape & Lattice Shade, Grape Pendants, 29 In. 920.00
Kerosene, Hanging, Peachblow Opalescent Swirl, Hourglass Shade, 8 1/2 x 11 1/2 In. 431.00
Kerosene, Hanging, Rochester, Opaque Shade, Roses, Embossed Brass Font, 14 x 39 In. .. 374.00
Kerosene, Hanging, Ruby Hobnail, Bell Shape Shade, 8 x 36 In. 345.00
Kerosene, Hanging, Ruffled Opaque Shade, White Font, Smoke Bell, 16 1/2 x 42 In. 230.00
Kerosene, Hanging, Satin Opaque Shade, Font, Painted, Forget-Me-Nots, 14 x 44 In. 374.00
Kerosene, Hanging, Yellow To Brown Blush Shade, Pink & Rust Mums, 14 x 36 In. 201.00
Kerosene, Hearse, Brass, Beveled Glass, Etched Scene, Woman, Memorial Marker, 27 In. . 58.00
Kerosene, Kitchen, Cast Iron, Opaque White Shade, Pressed Glass Font, 13 x 35 In. 173.00
Kerosene, Napoleon III, Bronze, Handles, Vase Shape, Electrified, c.1865, 31 In., Pair 1150.00
Kerosene, Napoleon III, Engine-Turned Brass, 2 Handles, Electrified, c.1865, 31 In., Pair . 518.00
Kerosene, Peacock, Carnival Glass, Red 325.00
Kerosene, Pink Opalescent Glass, Daisy Spray, Ruffled Shade, Milk Glass Pedestal, 17 In. 1725.00
Kerosene, Pink Satin Glass, Urn Shape Shade, 8 x 29 1/2 In. 403.00
Kerosene, Porcelain, Courting Couple, Figural, Brass Base, Germany, 1800s, 14 In., Pair .. 230.00
Kerosene, Pressed Glass, 3 Face Pattern, G. Duncan & Son, 9 In. 4400.00
Kerosene, Pressed Glass, Wright, Patent, 1863 .... 175.00
Kerosene, Shaded Rainbow Shade, Hand Painted Dogwood, 19 In. 86.00

Kerosene, Student, Tin, Conical Shade, Glass Font, Camphene Burners, c.1850, 10 1/2 In. .   764.00
Kerosene, Wall, Brass Holder, Baldwin, Patent, 1867 ....   75.00
Lard, Brass, Terry, Patent, 1843 ....   300.00
Lard, Canting, Chamberlain, Patent, 1854 ....   250.00
Lard, Center Draft, Tomlinson, Patent, 1843 ....   85.00
Lard, Houghton & Wallace, Patent, 1843 ....   400.00
Lard, Kinnear, Patent, 1851 ....50.00 to 150.00
Lard, Maltby & Neal, Patent, 1842 ....   600.00
Lard, Perry, Patent, 1842 ....100.00 to 300.00
Lard, Southworth, Patent, 1842 ....300.00 to 525.00
Lard, Swope, Patent, 1860 ....   300.00
Lard, Tilting, Howard, Patent, 1843 ....   150.00
Lard, Tin, Cornelius, Patent, 1843 ....   700.00
Lard, Tin, Hassenpflug, Patent, 1861 ....   325.00
Lard, Tin, Swope, Patent, 1860 ....   105.00
Lard, Tin, Terrel Patent, 1866 ....   600.00
Lard, Tomlinson, Patent, 1843 ....   150.00
Lard, Valspar Can, c.1920 ....   20.00
Oil, 3-Light, Brass, Bouillotte, Squat Oval Font, Ogee Rim, Black Tin Frame, 19 1/2 In. ...   411.00
Oil, Blown Glass Font, Pressed Glass Lacy Base, 6 1/2 In. 259.00
Oil, Blown Glass, Brass Column, Marble Base, 12 x 5 x 5 In. 138.00
Oil, Blown Glass, Bulbous Font, Bladed Wafer, Pressed Glass Paw Foot, Pewter, 10 In. ...   880.00
Oil, Blown Glass, Bulbous Font, Ringed Wafer, Pressed Glass 5-Step Base, 11 In. 110.00
Oil, Blown Glass, Solid Stem, Round Base, Pewter Collar, 6 In. 144.00
Oil, Blown Glass, Squat Ball-Shaped Font, Plain Stem, Circular Foot, 5 3/4 In. 121.00
Oil, Blown Glass, Urn Shape Font, Ball Knop, Pressed Glass Base, c.1845, 10 1/2 In. 660.00
Oil, Brass, Incised Bands, Swivel Hinge, Iron Stand, Baluster, Patent, 1856, 10 x 5 In. 8250.00
Oil, Brass, Satin Glass, Milk Glass Shade, Gilt Metal, Electrified, 19th Century, 24 In. 104.00
Oil, Bulbous Shade, Paneled Stem, Gilt Metal, Late 19th Century, 25 In. 81.00
Oil, Cranberry Opalescent Glass, Fern & Daisy, Metal Spread Foot, 21 In. 86.00
Oil, Cut Glass, Brass, Column Standard, Marble Base, Late 1800s, 23 In. 345.00
Oil, Finger, Cone-Shape Font, Applied Angular Handle, Thumb Rest, Footed, 3 1/2 In. 242.00
Oil, Finger, Pressed Glass, Lyre, Applied Handle, Brass Collar, 3 3/4 In. 303.00
Oil, Finger, Pressed Glass, Moon & Star, Applied Handle, Cable Base, 4 1/2 In. 468.00
Oil, Hanging, Opaque White Shade, Red Roses, Mums On Font, 14 x 35 In. 431.00
Oil, Iron, Stand, Swivel Hook, Rooster Finial, Wrought Iron, 20 1/2 x 5 1/4 In. 330.00
Oil, Lucerna, Brass, 4 Spouts, Reflector 35.00
Oil, Milk Glass, Amber, Stepped Base, Light Bulb Shape, Brass Fittings, 12 1/2 In. 60.00
Oil, Miner's, Carbide, Nickel Plated Reflector, Flint Lighter, Early 1900s, 7 In. 95.00
Oil, Miner's, Folding, 1865 Patent 55.00
Oil, Miner's, Hearts, Early 19th Century, 9 x 3 1/4 In. 173.00
Oil, Miner's, Tin, Dunlap, Patent, 1899 ....   30.00
Oil, Miner's, Tin, Murray, Patent, 1908 ....   35.00
Oil, Mother-Of-Pearl, Blue Diamond Quilt, Bronze, J.L. Paris Burner, 1800s, 21 In. 431.00
Oil, Open Saucer, Red Clay, Mennonite, Indiana 125.00
Oil, Painted Shade, Lilies, Tropical Flowers, c.1880, 25 In. 316.00
Oil, Pallme-Konig, Green, Oil Spot, Random Threading, Burner Knob, 20 In. 489.00
Oil, Peg, Ball Shape, 12 Panels, Brass Collar, c.1830, 4 1/4 In. 165.00
Oil, Peg, Blown Glass, Ball Shape, Cork Double-Tube Burner, 1825-45, 4 1/4 In. 275.00
Oil, Peg, Brass, Cut Cane Pattern, 9 1/4 In., Pair 288.00
Oil, Petticoat, Clark, Patent, 1839 ....   50.00
Oil, Porcelain, Heart Medallions, Oriental, 5 In., Pair 173.00
Oil, Pressed Glass, Cable With Ring Stand, Double Burner, Hexagonal Base, 10 In. 330.00
Oil, Pressed Glass, Hearts, Hexagonal Base, Brass Collar, 10 In. 132.00
Oil, Pressed Glass, Loop Fonts, Paneled Hexagonal Base, 11 In., Pair 173.00
Oil, Pressed Glass, Moorish Arch, Hexagonal Base, 1840-60, 9 1/2 In. 99.00
Oil, Pressed Glass, Octagonal Font, Disk Wafer, Monument Base, 10 1/4 In. 77.00
Oil, Red Glass Font, Brass Stem, Marble Base, 21 In. 100.00
Oil, Renaissance Revival, Cut Glass, Ormolu, 1884, 40 In. 920.00
Oil, Satin Glass, Painted, Flowers, 17 1/2 In. 35.00
Oil, Tin, Maltby & Neal's, Patent, 1842 ....   150.00
Oil, Vaseline Glass, Thumbprint Pattern, Paneled, Spread Foot, 10 In. 259.00
Pairpoint lamps are in the Pairpoint category.

Perfume, Art Glass, Bronze, Brass, Signed, 14 1/2 In. 250.00
Rush, Cast Iron, Round, Stepped Base, Counterweight, 8 In. 173.00
Rush, Iron, Arched Tripod Base, Penny Feet, Scroll Push-Up, 12 In. 690.00
Rush, Iron, New England, c.1800, 7 In. 518.00
Rush, Wrought Iron, Stand, Swivel Top, Spring Action, Tripod Base, 22 1/2 x 9 In. 990.00
Rush, Wrought Iron, Tripod Base, Trefoil Feet, Clamp, Counterweight, 11 In. 489.00
Safety Valve, Dreyfus, Patent, 1869 .... 100.00
Safety Valve, Lewars & Klaitz, Patent, 1877 .... 100.00
Sconce, 2-Light, 20 Radiating Mirror Plates, 1700s, 13 3/4 In., Pair 9775.00
Sconce, 2-Light, Brass, Rearing Hippocampus, Electrified, c.1900, 10 In., Pair 805.00
Sconce, 2-Light, Bronze, 10-Point Deer Head, 16 1/2 x 13 In., 4 Piece 805.00
Sconce, 2-Light, Bronze, Incised, Molded, Drip Pans, Electrified, 21 x 12 In. 60.00
Sconce, 2-Light, Bronze, Mirror, Ribbon & Bow Pediment, 32 x 12 1/2 In., Pair 920.00
Sconce, 2-Light, Empire Style, Bronze, Rope & Tassel, Electrified, France, c.1880, 16 In. . 863.00
Sconce, 2-Light, Gilt Plaster, Molded Cornucopia, 19th Century, 10 x 9 x 6 In. 633.00
Sconce, 2-Light, Gilt, Scrolling Leaves, Flowers, C-Scroll Arms, 19 x 11 1/4 x 6 In., Pair .. 460.00
Sconce, 2-Light, Gilt, Wrought Iron, Cord & Tassel, Mid 1900s, 15 x 15 x 5 In., Pair 518.00
Sconce, 2-Light, Italian Baroque Style, Parcel Gilt, Green Painted, Mirrored, 24 In., Pair .. 1610.00
Sconce, 2-Light, Louis XIV Style, Bronze, Diana The Huntress Plate, 17 1/2 In., Pair 2070.00
Sconce, 2-Light, Louis XV Style, Glass Lustres, 20th Century, 11 7/8 In., Pair 120.00
Sconce, 2-Light, Louis XVI Style, Gilt Bronze, Black Painted, Metal, 26 In., Pair 3286.00
Sconce, 2-Light, Louis XVI Style, Gilt Bronze, Caduceus, c.1900, 16 x 11 x 5 In., Pair 2185.00
Sconce, 2-Light, Louis XVI Style, Giltwood, Musical Instruments, Italy, 40 x 15 In., Pair .. 1150.00
Sconce, 2-Light, Restauration Style, Gilt Bronze, Lyre Shape, Late 1800s, 16 x 10 In., Pair 2300.00
Sconce, 2-Light, Rock Crystal, 40 1/4 In., Pair 13200.00
Sconce, 2-Light, Silver Plate, Urn & Torch Shape Backplate, 13 1/2 x 9 1/2 In., Pair 144.00
Sconce, 2-Light, Urn Finial, Crown Shades, Diamond Point, Gas, 21 x 19 In. 431.00
Sconce, 3-Light, Bird, Flowers, Cut Glass, Gilt Brass, c.1935, 21 1/2 In., Pair 5290.00
Sconce, 3-Light, Candle, Scroll Arms, Drip Pan, 20th Century, 13 x 13 In. 58.00
Sconce, 3-Light, Gilt Bronze, Ribbon Tied Scrolling Vine, 25 In., Pair 1427.00
Sconce, 3-Light, Gilt, Scrolling Leaf Backplate, 27 x 13 x 7 In., Pair 575.00
Sconce, 3-Light, Leaf & Flower Backplate, Gilt Metal, France, 1900s, 26 3/4 In., Pair 1885.00
Sconce, 3-Light, Louis XVI Style, Bronze, Hunting Horn, Late 1800s, 19 x 10 x 6 In. 1150.00
Sconce, 3-Light, Louis XVI Style, Bronze, Jasperware Oval Portrait Plaque Inset, 34 In. .. 1076.00
Sconce, 3-Light, Louis XVI Style, Gilt Bronze, Flaming Garland Vase, 16 1/2 In., Pair 1955.00
Sconce, 3-Light, Louis XVI Style, Gilt Bronze, Late 19th Century, 20 x 14 x 9 In., Pair ... 1150.00
Sconce, 4-Light, Louis XV Style, Gilt Bronze, Leafy Cast Arm, Cherub, 29 In., Pair 5975.00
Sconce, 5-Light, Brass, Gilt Lacquer, Bearded Mask Front, c.1865, 17 1/2 In., Pair 805.00
Sconce, 5-Light, Crystal, Metal, c.1900, 20 x 16 In. 316.00
Sconce, 5-Light, Louis XV Style, Bronze, 18 In., Pair 508.00
Sconce, 5-Light, Louis XV Style, Gilt Brass, Electrified, France, 16 1/2 x 15 In., Pair 2530.00
Sconce, 5-Light, Louis XVI Style, Brass, Quiver, France, 26 In., Pair 2300.00
Sconce, 6-Light, Gilt Bronze, 22 In., Pair 2390.00
Sconce, Arne Jacobsen, Louis Poulsen, c.1956, 13 1/2 In., Pair 823.00
Sconce, Art Deco, Frosted Glass, Flower Molded Shade, Patinated Brass, 14 In., Pair 819.00
Sconce, Arts & Crafts, Leaded Glass Panels, Flowers, Wood Frame, 6 x 6 x 12 In., Pair ... 1495.00
Sconce, Brass, France, c.1930, 16 1/2 x 8 In. 144.00
Sconce, Bronze, Silvered, Alabaster Shades, Ruhlmann, c.1929, 13 x 19 In., Pair 28680.00
Sconce, Christophe Gevers, Brass, c.1955, 4 x 16 In., Pair 499.00
Sconce, Forged Iron, Etched Glass Shades, Electrified, 1893 Patent, Pair 790.00
Sconce, Frank Lloyd Wright, Geneva Inn, Glass Pivot Shade, c.1911, 7 x 7 x 9 In., Pair ... 4888.00
Sconce, Jean Perzel, Frosted Glass, Chrome Plated Metal, No. 324C, c.1930, 20 1/4 In. ... 8963.00
Sconce, Jean Perzel, Glass, Chrome Plated Metal, No. 650, c.1930, 21 In., Pair 8963.00
Sconce, Jules Leleu, Bronze, Alabaster, 1900s, 15 x 6 In., Pair 4821.00
Sconce, Nessen, Flared Shade, White Enameled Metal, 11 x 14 x 15 In. 115.00
Sconce, Otto-Mueller, Glass, Nickel Plated Fittings, Sistrah, c.1932, 12 3/4 x 12 1/2 In. ... 1763.00
Sconce, Pendant, Acanthus Leaf, Leaf Scroll Design, Bellflower Swags, Kerosene, 26 In. . 575.00
Sconce, Pistillo, Valenti, Silver Balls, c.1969, 12 In., Pair 1175.00
Sconce, Prairie School, Mahogany Frame, Leaded Panes, Geometric, 18 x 8 1/2 In., Pair .. 8813.00
Sconce, Saturne, Serge Mouille, Black Lacquered Aluminum, 1900s, 11 x 14 In., Pair 8864.00
Sconce, Tapered Rope-Twist Column Supports, Scalloped Bowl Shade, Gas, 18 x 21 In. .. 230.00
Sconce, Tin, Half Circle Base, Crimped Reflector, Green Paint, Kerosene, 14 x 4 In., Pair . 385.00
Sconce, Tin, Round Base, Reeded & Scalloped Reflector, Kerosene, 19 x 5 In., Pair 358.00

Sconce, Wrought Iron, Brass, Copper, Alabaster, France, 1930s, 25 x 14 x 14 1/2 In., Pr. ..   8553.00
Sconce, Wrought Iron, Stamped, Samuel Yellen, 16 x 12 In. 2000.00
Tiffany lamps are listed in the Tiffany category.
Torchere, 5-Light, Bronze, Young Woman, Figural, Mideastern Dress, 84 In., Pair 1035.00
Torchere, Ercole Barovier, Glass Shade, Gold Leaf, Tripod Base, Italy, c.1940, 23 x 71 In. .   9200.00
Torchere, Giltwood, Tripartite Base, Scroll Feet, Italy, Mid 19th Century, 64 In. 920.00
Torchere, Mahogany, Round, Dish Top, Turned Shaft, Claw & Ball Feet, 40 x 10 In., Pair .   230.00
Torchere, Oak, Carved, Trumpet Shape Top, Carved Stem, 1920s, 60 1/2 In. 259.00
Torchere, Victorian, Walnut, Twist-Carved Column, 3 Legs, 1900s, 69 In. 400.00
Torchere, William IV, Mahogany, Carved, Reeded Column, Late 19th Century, 59 x 18 In. .   173.00
Torchere, Wood, Carved, Painted, Reeded Stem, 62 In. 173.00
Whale Oil, Adjustable, Dearborn, 1804 . . . .   50.00
Whale Oil, Baluster Shape, New England, c.1830, 11 In., Pair 460.00
Whale Oil, Brass, Cone Shape Font, Double Burners, Turned Shaft, 8 1/2 In., Pair 748.00
Whale Oil, Brass, Dyott, Philadelphia 75.00
Whale Oil, Brass, Tubular Wick, Glass Globe, 1840-50, 23 1/2 In.   595.00
Whale Oil, Cast Iron, Gold Gilded 325.00
Whale Oil, Copper, Lead Soldering, Flat Bottom, Rolled Edges, 1860s, 5 In. 173.00
Whale Oil, Etched Glass Shade, Prisms, Marble Base, c.1850, 22 In. 230.00
Whale Oil, Flint Glass Font, Oval Decoration, Marble Square Base, Brass Stem, 23 1/2 In.   920.00
Whale Oil, Frosted Glass, Bulbous Font, Bladed Wafer, Pressed Lotus Base, 8 1/4 In. 605.00
Whale Oil, Glass, Benson, Patent, 1843 . . . .   500.00
Whale Oil, Glass, Onion, Tin, Ring Handle, c.1835, 14 1/2 In. 940.00
Whale Oil, Glass, Triple Wick, 10 In. 325.00
Whale Oil, Pierced Tin, Blown Glass, Bull's-Eye, New England, c.1825 . . . .   1320.00
Whale Oil, Pressed Glass, Block & Mirror 250.00
Whale Oil, Pressed Glass, Waisted Loop, Clambroth, Hexagonal Base, Brass Collar, 10 In.   275.00
Whale Oil, Round, Etched Glass Shade, Prisms, Cut Glass, Brass Font, Mid 1900s, 22 In. .   978.00
Whale Oil, Surgeon's, Silver, England, c.1850 . . . .   60.00
Whale Oil, Tin, Baker's 110.00
Whale Oil, Tin, Glass, Tin Bail, Star & Diamond Perforations, 1800s, 17 In. 411.00
LAMPSHADE, Hanging, Caramel Slag Glass, Urn & Vining Berry Leaf Design, 23 x 12 In. . . .   460.00
    Petal Crown, Slag Glass, Green, White, Brown, Flowers, Metalwork, 24 x 10 In., Pair 316.00
    Slag, Caramel, Bead Fringe, Embossed Roses, 23 1/2 x 28 In. & 25 x 12 In., 2 Piece 219.00
    Western, Man, Woman, Buckboard, Mail Stagecoach, Red, Brown, Green, 8 In. 29.00

LANTERNS are a special type of lighting device. They have a light
source, usually a candle, totally hidden inside the walls of the lantern.
Light is seen through holes or glass sections.

Art Deco, Wrought Steel, Brass, Cut Glass Shade, 30 x 8 In. 863.00
Bronze, Cut Glass Bowl, Prism Cut, Neoclassical Style, c.1900, 24 In., Pair 1495.00
Carriage, 4 Beveled Glass Panels, Silver Plated Brass, Metal, Electrified, 38 In., Pair 2185.00
Ceiling, Gilt Brass Frame, Shaped Glass Panels, 18th-Century Style, 27 x 15 In. 1679.00
Copper, Glass, Colonial Shape, 2-Light, Scroll Bracket, Mid 20th Century, 26 1/2 In., Pair .   115.00
Copper, Moravian Star, 12 Points, 5 Textured Glass Panels, Electric, 17 In. 546.00
Figural, Embossed, Satin Glass, Cottage Shape, 19th Century, 7 1/2 In. 58.00
G. Stickley, Ceiling, Copper, Hammered, Heart Cutout, Globe, 6 1/2 x 12 In. 1410.00
G. Stickley, Ceiling, Copper, Hammered, Hearts, Spades, Glass Liner, 9 1/2 x 25 1/2 In. . . .   2530.00
G. Stickley, Wall, Copper, Hammered, Hearts, Spades, Glass Liner, 9 1/2 x 8 1/4 In., Pair . .   7050.00
Gas, Burnished Copper Finish, Clear Globe, Tin Shade, 32 In. 173.00
Globe, Onion, Brass, Hinged, Fluted Peak, Blown Glass, Wire Guards, Tin Font, 15 In. . . .   230.00
Globe, Onion, Copper Base, Wire Protectors, Bail Handle, Electrified, 18 In. 374.00
Hall, Wrought Iron, 3-Light, Cut Metal, Continental, c.1900, 80 x 26 In. 4830.00
Hanging, Frosted, Cut Glass, Brass, 19th Century, 30 In. 1016.00
Portico, Louis XVI Style, Gilt Brass, Cylindrical, 4 Faux Candles, Electrified, 25 1/2 In. . . .   1725.00
Portico, Louis XVI Style, Gilt Brass, Glass, 6 Faux Candles, Electrified, France, 35 In. . . .   1380.00
Sheet Iron, Glass, Strap Ring Handle, Conical Top, Pa., c.1800, 21 x 11 1/2 In. 764.00
Tin, 3 Panes, Ring Handle, Sliding Panel, 10 5/8 In. 259.00
Tin, 6 Panes, Vented Cone Roof, Latch Door, Black Paint, 18 x 8 In., Pair 165.00
Tin, Cylindrical, Removable Glass Window, Wood Top & Side Handles, 15 x 9 In. 303.00
Tin, Glass Sided, Spring Top, Folk Art, c.1840, 16 x 10 1/2 x 9 In. 460.00
Tin, Glass, Applied Ring, 13 x 17 In. 115.00
Tin, Peaked, Dormer Window Vents, Ring Handle, Black Paint, 12 In. 403.00

Tin, Pierced Stars, Diamonds, Glass Globe, New England, 12 In.	196.00
Tin, Pyramid Shape, 4 Beveled Glass Panels, Latch, Oil Font, Waterbury, Conn., 11 1/4 In.	546.00
Tin, Wire Pane Guards, Ruffled Chimney, 3-Sided, Latch Door, Ring Handle, 15 x 8 In.	55.00
Walnut, Carved, Glass Sides, Twist Columns, Rectangular, Brass Handle, 1800, 12 In.	1763.00
Winchester, No. 4811, Red Case, Nickel Plated, Box	134.00
Winchester, Olin, No. 4801, Red Body, Chrome Trim, Handle, Utility, Portable, Box	88.00
Wood, Glass Inserts, Bail Handle, 19th Century, 11 In.	161.00
Wood, Glass Panels, Rectangular, 15 1/2 In.	230.00

LE VERRE FRANCAIS is one of the many types of cameo glass made in France. The glass was made by the C. Schneider factory in Epinay-sur-Seine from 1918 to 1933. It is a mottled glass, usually decorated with floral designs, and bears the incised signature *Le Verre Francais*.

Compote, Yellow, Orange & Blue Overlaid Art Nouveau Flowers, 6 1/2 In.	920.00
Lamp, Decor Azurette, Flowers, Etched, Mottled, c.1924, 13 1/2 In.	4370.00
Lamp, Ginkgo Leaf, Red, Mottled Yellow Ground, Wrought Iron, 20 In.	9775.00
Lamp, Leaf Shade, Red Ground, Bronzed Metal Base, Electric, 6 In.	940.00
Pitcher, Amethyst & Red Orchids, Blue Shaded To Yellow, Mottled, 13 In.	1840.00
Vase, Blue, Rust Fuchsia, Mottled Turquoise & Yellow Ground, 10 In.	1035.00
Vase, Clear, Enameled Yellow Stripes, Bulbous Foot, 20 In.	150.00
Vase, Etched, 1920s, 19 In.	3585.00 to 4540.00
Vase, Flowers, Mottled Yellow, Orange, Blue, c.1925, 17 1/2 In.	2300.00
Vase, Mottled Orange, Amethyst, Orange Overlay, 7 In.	460.00
Vase, Mottled Orange, Yellow, Etched, Handles, c.1925, 12 In.	2070.00
Vase, Orange, Carved & Overlaid Blue Art Deco Flowers, Signed, 10 In.	1035.00
Vase, Orange, Mottled Green, Yellow, 12 1/2 In.	1115.00
Vase, Roses, Mottled Amber Ground, Bulbous, Flared Neck, 4 1/2 In.	1495.00
Vase, Stylized Flowers, Russet, Mottled Citron Ground, Bulbous, 9 1/2 In.	2935.00
Vase, Stylized Foxglove, Mottled Red, Pink Ground, 18 3/4 In.	1880.00
Vase, Trumpet Flower, Yellow, Pink, Orange, Signed, 14 3/4 In.	2070.00

LEATHER is tanned animal hide and it has been used to make decorative and useful objects for centuries. Leather objects must be carefully preserved with proper humidity and oiling or the leather will deteriorate and crack. This damage cannot be repaired.

Bucket, Portrait, Man With Tie, Gilt Wreath, Borders, Maroon Ground, 18 1/2 x 9 In.	635.00
Chaps, Attach To Saddle, Adjustable, 29 x 58 In.	220.00
Chaps, Porter, Batwing, Pockets, Metal Medallions, LK Monogram, Phoenix, Arizona	330.00
Coat Hooks, J. Adnet, 1950s, 11 x 19 x 4 In., Pair	2870.00
Flagon, Blackjack, Brass Rim, 1640-1720	550.00
Holster, Belt, Back & Shoulder Harnesses, 4 Pockets, Stamped, Wells Fargo, U.S., 4 In.	115.00
Holster, Belt, Colt, Right Hand, Cartridge Loops, Nickel Silver Buckle, c.1940, Size 40	115.00
Mail Bag, Wells Fargo Express	220.00
Pouch, Brown, Wells Fargo, S.D. Myers, Sweetwater, Texas, c.1899, 15 1/2 x 7 In.	173.00
Saddle, Stirrups, McClellan, 12 In.	305.00
Scabbard, Saddle, Carbine, Connolly Bros., Billings, Mont., c.1894, 30 1/2 In.	405.00

LEEDS pottery was made at Leeds, Yorkshire, England, from 1774 to 1878. Most Leeds ware was not marked. Early Leeds pieces had distinctive twisted handles with a greenish glaze on part of the creamy ware. Later ware often had blue borders on the creamy pottery. A Chicago company named Leeds made many Disney-inspired figurines. They are listed in the Disneyana category.

LEEDS POTTERY.

Bowl, Creamware, Multicolored Sides, Flowers, Geometric Reserves, Late 1700s, 3 x 7 In.	765.00
Bowl, Multicolored Flowers & Leaves, Green Rim, 4 1/2 x 9 In.	715.00
Bowl, Multicolored Flowers & Leaves, Yellow, Blue, Green, 4 x 9 In.	330.00
Chop Plate, Cobalt Blue Flowers In Yellow & Brown Urn, Leaves, Soft Paste, 14 3/8 In.	2990.00
Creamer, Basket, Blue Flowers Under Spout, 5 Colors, 3 3/4 In.	345.00
Creamer, Peafowl, Orange, Gold, Blue, Branches, Green Leaves, 3 7/8 In.	1155.00
Cup & Saucer, Blue 6-Petal Flower, Yellow Center, Green Leaves, Handleless	105.00
Cup & Saucer, Blue Flower, Green Leaves, Orange Sprays, Handleless	155.00
Pitcher, Bulbous, Floral, Leaves, 5 Colors, Applied Handle, 8 1/4 In.	403.00
Pitcher, Exotic Peafowl, Green Sponge Tree, 5 Colors, 6 In.	460.00

Pitcher, Farmer's Arms, Sheaf Of Wheat, 5 Colors, 7 In. 2300.00
Plate, American Eagle, Blue Feather Edge, Scalloped Rim, 4 Colors, 7 1/4 In. 1380.00
Plate, Bird, Leaves, Flower Border, Multicolored, Octagonal, c.1800, 6 In. 646.00
Plate, Bird, Tree, Blue Feather Edge, 6 1/4 In. 715.00
Plate, Bird, Yellow, Black, Green Foliage, Embossed, Scalloped, 9 1/2 In. 550.00
Plate, Brown Feather Edge, Peafowl, Yellow & Brown Highlights, 8 1/8 In. 330.00
Plate, Dahlia Center, Acorns, Green Feather Scalloped Edge, Leaves, Fish Scales, 8 In. ... 546.00
Plate, Multicolored Flowers, Blue Feather Edge, 8 1/4 In. 300.00
Plate, Peafowl Center, Blue Crest, Green Tree, Scalloped Feather Edge, 8 1/8 In. 834.00
Plate, Peafowl On Branch, Green Feather Edge, 6 1/4 In. 605.00
Plate, Peafowl, Blue & Yellow Highlights, Blue Feather, Scalloped Edge, 8 3/8 In. 495.00
Plate, Peafowl, Blue & Yellow Highlights, Green Feather Edge, 7 7/8 In. 250.00
Plate, Peafowl, Blue Feather Edge, 8 1/8 In. 330.00
Plate, Peafowl, Gold, Black, Branches, Green Leaves, 8 7/8 In. 365.00
Sugar, Cover, Birds & Flowers, 4 1/4 In. 660.00
Teapot, Flowers, 4 Colors, 4 1/8 In. 430.00
Teapot, Flowers, Blue, White, Dome Lid, 11 1/4 In. 195.00
Toddy, Peafowl, Wing Detail, Orange Pompadour, Green Feather Edge, 4 Colors, 5 In. 1095.00
Washbowl, Blue Flowers & Leaves, 13 3/8 In. 275.00
Waste Bowl, Peafowl, 4 Colors 305.00

LEFTON is a mark found on pottery, porcelain, glass, and other wares
imported by the Geo. Zoltan Lefton Company. The company began in
1941 and is still in business. It was restructured in 2002 and is now
called the Lefton Company. The company mark has changed through
the years; but because marks have been used for long periods of time,
they are of little help in dating an object.

Ashtray, White Holly, 7 1/4 In. 30.00
Bank, Billiken, Tan & Brown, Billiken Label, 7 1/2 In. 25.00
Bell, Candy Cane Girl, Red & Green Striped Dress, Muff, 4 In. 175.00
Bell Set, Noel Angels, Each Holding A Letter, Holly Trim, 3 1/2 In., 4 Piece 210.00
Butter, Cover, Rose Chintz, 1/4 Lb. 70.00
Cake Topper, Bride & Groom Children, Gray Tuxedo, Pink Flower In Veil, 1987, 5 In. 20.00
Candleholder, Evergreen, Elf Wearing Christmas Tree, Holding Stocking, 4 In., Pair 215.00
Candy Box, Cover, White Holly, Red Bow, No. 6073, 6 x 4 In. 8.00
Candy Box, Holly Leaves Overall, Berries, Bow Finial, 6 In. 75.00
Candy Dish, Cover, White Holly, Christmas, 6 x 4 In. 40.00
Cheese Dish, Dome Cover, Bluebird, Figural, 4 3/4 In. 225.00
Coffee Set, Heavenly Rose, Pot, Sugar, Creamer, 3 Piece 75.00
Coffeepot, Brown Heritage Floral, Gold Handle & Trim, 9 In. 50.00
Cookie Jar, Miss Priss, Cat's Head, Blue & Pink, Floral Cover, 7 1/2 In. 170.00
Cookie Jar, Pixie's Head, Red Hair, Green Collar, Leaf Hat, 8 In. 105.00
Cruet, Fruit, Leaves, Flowers, 6 In., Pair 5.00
Figurine, Candy Cane Kids, Red & White Stripes, 4 In. 40.00
Figurine, Cat, Siamese, Tan, Chocolate Points, 10 In. 20.00
Figurine, Dog, Collie, Tan, White, 5 x 7 1/2 In. 40.00
Figurine, Lady In Rose Chintz, Blond, Sun Hat, 6 In. 150.00
Jam Jar, Cover, Underplate, Spoon, Brown Floral Heritage, 4 1/4 In., 3 Piece 30.00
Night-Light, Woman In Peachy Floral Gown, Blond, Bisque, 6 3/4 In. 50.00
Planter, Valentine Girl, Dog, Heart Background, 7 x 6 In. 35.00
Plaque, Mermaids, Blue & Turquoise Iridescent Tails, 6 In., Pair 70.00
Sugar & Creamer, Dainty Miss, Floral Bonnet, Blue Collar 25.00
Teapot, Dainty Miss, Girl In Bonnet, 6 x 8 1/2 In. 75.00
Teapot, Miss Priss, Cat's Head, Blue & Pink, Floral Cover, 1950s, 4 Cup 260.00
Toothpick, Salt & Pepper, Christmas Tree Shape, 7 1/4-In. Toothpick, 3 Piece 60.00
Tray, Dresser, Hand Holding Open Fan, Applied Flowers, Gold Trim, 6 In. 25.00
Wall Pocket, Bluebird, Boy In Top Hat, Girl In Pink Bonnet, 6 In. 155.00
Wall Pocket, Straw Hat, Flowers Around Rim, 7 3/4 In. 15.00

LEGRAS was founded in 1864 by Auguste Legras at St. Denis, France.
It is best known for cameo glass and enamel-decorated glass with Art
Nouveau designs. Legras merged with Pantin in 1920 and became the
Verreries et Cristalleries de St. Denis et de Pantin Reunies.

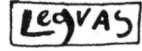

Bowl, Stylized Flower, Mottled Overshot, Bulbous, 4-Fold Rim, Signed, 3 3/4 In. 290.00

Bowl, Winter Landscape, Enameled, Signed, 10 1/4 In. 650.00
Lamp Base, Enameled, Blue, Green & Black Butterflies, Pink & Green Striations, 9 In. ... 690.00
Vase, Art Nouveau Flowers, Yellow Ground, Cylindrical, Swollen Mouth, Cameo, 14 In. . . 4255.00
Vase, Burgundy Leaves & Berries, Frosted Ground, Flared Rim, Cameo, Signed, 6 3/4 In. . 201.00
Vase, Carnelian, Nasturtiums On Vine, Enameled, Beige, Pink, Cameo, 5 In. 259.00
Vase, Enameled, Gray, Etched, Painted, Amethyst, Maple Keys, Leaves, Cameo, 7 1/2 In. . 155.00
Vase, Enameled, Gray, Etched, Painted, Violet, Leaves, Flowers, Cameo, c.1900, 8 In. 310.00
Vase, Geometric, White, Green, Squat, 20th Century, 3 3/4 In. 460.00
Vase, Gray, Opaque White, Mottled Orange, White, Green, Red, Cameo, c.1900, 4 1/2 In. . 520.00
Vase, Leaves, Berries, Maroon Stain, Peach Ground, Flared Rim, Cameo, 10 3/4 In. 635.00
Vase, Pink Satin Glass, Flowers, Enameled, c.1920, 12 In. 175.00
Vase, Red Leaves, Translucent Ground, Oval, Cameo, 5 3/4 In. 450.00
Vase, Reed, Seashell, Cameo, 23 In. 1410.00
Vase, Swollen Cylindrical, Purple Cut To Pink Grapevine, Cameo, 15 In. 540.00

LENOX is the name of a porcelain maker. Walter Scott Lenox and
Jonathan Cox founded the Ceramic Art Company in Trenton, New Jersey, in 1889. In 1906, Lenox left and started his own company called
Lenox. The company makes a porcelain that is similar to Irish Belleek.
The marks used by the firm have changed through the years and collectors prefer the earlier examples. Related pieces may also be listed in
the Ceramic Art Co. category.

Bowl, Vegetable, Tuscany, Gold Trim, Coupe Shape, Oval 205.00
Cup & Saucer Set, Demitasse, Leaf Design, 2 3/4 In., 24 Piece 60.00
Pitcher, Paneled, Silver Swags & Wreaths, Shaped Handle, 8 1/2 In. 150.00
Pitcher, Water, Leaf Design, Off-White Glaze, 6 1/2 In. 50.00
Stein, Minstrel Cellist, Straight Tapered Sides, Black Handle, Belleek, 5 1/2 In. 90.00
Stein, Monk In Cellar, Silver & Copper Lid, 1 Liter 1065.00
Sugar, Cover, Windsong, Coupe Shape, Platinum Trim 110.00
Tankard, Artist Decorated, Signed, Belleek, 13 In. 196.00
Tea Set, Brown Glaze, Floral Sterling Overlay, Art Nouveau, Monogram, c.1925, 3 Piece . 410.00

LETTER OPENERS have been used since the eighteenth century.
Ivory and silver were favored by the well-to-do. In the late nineteenth
century, the letter opener was popular as an advertising giveaway and
many were made of metal or celluloid. Brass openers with figural handles were also popular.

Art Nouveau, Tortoiseshell Blade, Gold Bird-Claw Handle 375.00
Buffalo, Glass Eyes, Ivory, France, 10 x 1 1/2 In. 95.00
Butte, Montana, Embossed Mining Scene, Brass, 9 1/4 In. 30.00
Dagger Style, Bone, Engraved Handle, Cartouche, Initials, 12 3/4 In. 75.00
Devil, Holding Victim, Wings Are Blade, Seal-Stamp Finial, Vienna, Bronze, 9 In. 550.00
Faberge, Jade Blade, Gold Guilloche Handle, Ruby Insets, 9 3/4 In. 1950.00
Georg Jensen, Sterling Silver, Grapevine Handle, Jorgen Jensen, 4 In. 120.00
Miami Beach, Alligator Handle, Bronze, 1930s 15.00
Napoleon, Bronze Blade & Bust, Ivory Face, C. Villain, 9 In. 235.00
Portrait, Rococo Gentleman, Celluloid, Engraved, France, 8 In. 25.00
Russian Style, Enamel, Diamond, Silver, 14K Gold, 9 x 1 In. 2185.00
Sleepy Hollow Bridge, 200th Anniversary, Original Bridge, Sterling, 1897 .... 2450.00
Totem, Ivory, Alaska, 4-In. Blade, 6 In. 25.00
William Spratling, Tortoiseshell Blade, Sterling Silver Handle, 4 1/2 In. 985.00
Yosemite National Park, Bronze, 7 1/2 In. 18.00

LIBBEY Glass Company has made many types of glass since 1888,
including the cut glass and tablewares that are collected today. The
stemware of the 1930s and 1940s are once again in style. The Toledo,
Ohio, firm was purchased by Owens-Illinois in 1935 and is still working
under the name *Libbey Incorporated.* Maize is listed in its own category.

Bonbon, Amberina, Optic Ribbed, Flared & Ruffled Rim, 7 In. 520.00
Bottle, Amberina, Inverted Thumbprint, 8 In. 430.00
Bowl, Amberina, Oval, Flared & Scalloped Rim, 3 Amber Feet, 4 In. 460.00
Bowl, Center, Green Feather, White, Pedestal, 4 1/4 x 12 In. 210.00
Bowl, Centerpiece, Geometric Cutting, Etched Mark, c.1900, 3 3/4 x 9 In. 115.00

Bowl, Cut Diamond Point Bands, Etched Flowers, c.1910, 9 In. 260.00
Bowl, Hobstar Cutting, Signed, Early 20th Century, 8 In. 115.00
Bowl, Serving, Gloria Cutting, 3 1/2 x 9 In. 325.00
Celery, Ellsmere Cutting Variant, Rolled Rim, 2 3/4 x 11 3/4 x 5 1/2 In. 490.00
Compote, Amberina, Flared Fuchsia Rim, Honey Amber Foot, 7 1/2 In. 520.00
Compote, Amberina, Optic Ribbed, Flared & Flattened Rim, Disc Foot, 4 In. 575.00
Creamer, Peachblow, Ribbed, Applied Opal Handle, 3 In. 430.00
Custard Cup, Underplate, Amberina, 6 Sets 900.00
Jug, Wedgemere Cutting, Stopper, 8 In. 2875.00
Jug, Whiskey, Corona Cutting, Stopper, 7 In. 895.00
Pitcher, Water, Amberina, Ribbed, Flared, Reeded Handle, 2 1/2 In. 1380.00
Relish, Lovebirds Etch, 11 1/2 In. 425.00
Toothpick, Amberina, Diamond-Quilted, Barrel Shape, 2 1/2 In. ....145.00 to 290.00
Toothpick, Opal, Pink, Blue Cascading Vines, Lobed Bottom, 2 1/2 In. 290.00
Vase, Amberina, Optic Ribbed, Footed, Acid Stamped, 8 In. ....400.00 to 575.00
Vase, Bud, Amberina, Optic Ribbed, Signed, 1917, 9 In. 900.00
Vase, Bud, Amberina, Tapered, Shouldered, Elongated Neck, Amber Foot, 9 In. 1035.00
Vase, Lily, Amberina, Ribbed, Petal Rim, 10 In. 520.00

LIGHTERS for cigarettes and cigars are collectible. Cigarettes became popular in the late nineteenth century, and with the cigarette
came matches and cigarette lighters. All types of lighters are collected,
from solid gold to the first of the recent disposable lighters. Most
examples found were made after 1940. Some lighters may be found in
the Jewelry category in this book.

Amico, Petty Pinup Girls, Chrome Finish, Box, 1950s, 1 3/4 x 2 x 1/2 In. 20.00
Aurora, Super Lighter, Flashlight, Cellophane Wrap, Box, 2 5/8 x 3 1/8 x 1 In. 27.00
Cigar, Cinco Cigars, Black Smith Figure, Anvil, Cast Aluminum, 19 x 6 In. 1650.00
Cigar, Lamp Post, Metal, Pull Chain, 9 1/2 x 3 In. 175.00
Cigar, Midland Jump Spark, Davenport Manf., Countertop, 15 x 7 x 7 In. 415.00
Cigar, Paul Jones, Cast Iron, 9 x 7 1/2 In. 2640.00
Cigar, Piedmont, Metal, Glass, Wood, Ruby Globe, Cigar Cutter, 13 x 8 1/2 In. 1100.00
Cigar, Woman, Under Glass, Wood Case, Tall Arched Pipe, 9 1/2 x 10 1/2 In. 415.00
Comet, Wristwatch, Japan, Box, 1950s, 1 1/2 x 3 3/4 x 1 In. 305.00
E.B. Pool Drug Co., Merry Christmas, Smoke Here, Not Hereafter, Texas, 2 1/2 In. .... *Illus* 110.00
K.K.W., Photo Flash, Camera, On Tripod, Japan, Box, 1940s, 3 x 4 1/4 x 3/4 In. 135.00
Kem, Royal Crown Cola, Bottle, Detroit, 2 5/8 In. 35.00
Leader, Radio, Perpetual Calendar, Chrome, Occupied Japan, 1 1/2 x 2 3/4 In. 175.00
Miller Lite, Beer Can, Miniature, 2 3/4 x 1 In. 10.00
Pabst Blue Ribbon, Beer Can, 12 Fl. Oz. 22.00
Penquin, Atlantic, Imperial Gasoline, No. 18250, Enameled, 2 1/2 x 2 x 3/8 In. 18.00
President Kennedy, European Trip, Presidential Seal, June, 1963 .... 890.00
Ronson, Deco, Chrome, Laminated, 2 Cigarette Boxes, 3 x 20 x 10 1/2 In. 295.00
Ronson, Playboy, Rabbit, Stainless Steel, Inscription, Case, Bag, 1970s, 2 1/2 x 2 3/4 In. .. 20.00
Ronson, Princess, Pink, Poodle, Box, 1950s, 1 1/2 x 1 3/4 x 5 In. 60.00
Zippo, Ace Of Spades, Brushed Chrome 17.00
Zippo, American Flag, No. 250, Silver Metal Case, Paper Instructions, Box 50.00
Zippo, Covered In Textured Black Leather, 1953 .... 100.00
Zippo, Piece Of Pie On Front, Says By Fasano, 1950s 43.00
Zippo, USS Emblem, 1966 .... 19.00

Lighter, E.B. Pool Drug
Co., Merry Christmas,
Smoke Here, Not
Hereafter, Texas, 2 1/2 In.

LIGHTNING ROD and lightning rod balls are collected. The glass balls were at the center of the rod that was attached to the roof of a house or barn to avoid lightning damage.

Cast Iron & Copper, Robin's-Egg Blue Ball, 5 1/2-Ft. Rod	50.00
Electra, Embossed Sun Colored Amethyst Ball, Signed Stand, 32 In.	78.00
Purple Glass Ball, Wrought Iron B, 3 Legs, 36-In. Rod	56.00
Weathervane, Amber Glass Ball, Tripod Mount	42.00
LIGHTNING ROD BALL, 10-Sided, D & S, Marked, 5 x 3 1/2 In.	20.00
Amber Glass, Doorknob	60.00
Amber Grape, Silver Mercury Lined, 18-Ball Center Band, 5 In.	13499.00
Blue Milk Glass, 4 1/2 In.	25.00
Blue Milk Glass, Moon & Stars	26.00
Frosted Ear Of Corn, 4 1/4 In.	61.00
Milk Glass	55.00
Milk Glass, Quilted Diamond	12.00
Ruby Red	72.00

LIMOGES porcelain has been made in Limoges, France, since the mid-nineteenth century. Fine porcelains were made by many factories, including Haviland, Ahrenfeldt, Guerin, Pouyat, Elite, and others. Modern porcelains are being made at Limoges and the word *Limoges* as part of the mark is not an indication of age. Haviland, one of the Limoges factories, is listed as a separate category in this book.

Biscuit Jar, Hand Painted, Acorns, Oak Leaves, T & V, 1907-19, 5 x 8 1/2 x 6 1/2 In.	325.00
Bowl, Condiments, Double Compartment, Rococo Style, c.1900, 3 1/2 x 9 In.	230.00
Bowl, Underliner, Roses, Paneled Sided, Gold Trim, 9 1/2-In. Bowl, 11-In. Underliner	50.00
Box, Portrait, Hand Painted, 4 1/2 In.	95.00
Bust, Queen Charlotte-Amelie, Biscuit, Late 19th Century, 8 1/2 In.	86.00
Cachepot, Poppy, Hand Painted, 8 1/2 x 7 3/4 In.	375.00
Coffee Set, Swirled Mold, Gilt Decoration, Londe Limoges, 9 1/2 In., 11 Piece	150.00
Compote, Presidential Eagle, National Remembrance Shop, 9 1/2 In.	450.00
Dish, Leaf Form, Plum, Hand Painted, Marked, A. Rich, June 27, 1906, 12 3/4 In.	105.00
Eyecup, Pedestal, Fluted Bowl & Stem, White, 2 1/2 In.	176.00
Fish Set, Fish, Scrolls, Green Border, Gilt Trim, Signed, Muville, 23-In. Platter, 12 Plates	865.00
Fish Set, Flower Borders, Game Fish Center, Square, c.1885, 9 In., 12 Piece	200.00
Fish Set, Gutierrez, Japanese Style, Scallop Shell Border, 13 Piece	1035.00
Game Plate, Fowl & Game Birds, Landscapes, J. Barbarin, Platter, 12 Plates	2115.00
Game Plate Set, Dulac, Puisonyes & Collderl, Game Birds, 4 Piece	405.00
Game Plate Set, Game Birds, T & V Blanks, c.1900, 18 In., Platter, 8 Plates	635.00
Pitcher, Lemonade, Hand Painted, Pink, Gold, Red Berries, White Ground, 10 In.	145.00
Pitcher, Lemonade, Red, Green Grapes, Yellow, Green Ground, 11 In.	173.00
Pitcher, Tankard, Hand Painted, Iris, France, 15 1/2 In.	400.00
Plaque, Enameled, Village In Winter, Signed Betourne, 13 x 10 In.	635.00
Plaque, Game, Coronet, Fowl, Artist Signed, France, 11 1/2 In.	160.00
Plaque, Game, Coronet, Quail, France, Artist Signed, 10 In.	175.00
Plaque, Game, Quail, France, 10 In.	25.00
Plaque, Man Tickling Sleeping Woman, Late 19th Century, 5 x 3 1/4 In.	575.00
Plaque, Myrta Louise Bennett Wieland, Gilt Wood Frame, c.1899, 12 In.	1095.00
Plaque, Pheasants, Artist Signed Baptiste, France, 16 In.	550.00
Plate, Louis XVI Style, Tressemann & Vogt, Gilt, c.1885, 10 1/2 In., 10 Piece	2185.00
Plate, Romantic Couple, Landscape, Late 1800s, 9 3/4 In.	115.00
Serving Set, Asparagus, Tray, John Gauches, c.1885, 14-In. Tray, 9 1/4-In. Plate, 9 Piece	345.00
Tankard, Artist Decorated, Figural Dragon Handle, 14 1/2 In.	520.00
Tray, French Seaside, Chalk Cliffs, Hand Painted, Signed, 1920s, 11 1/2 x 8 1/4 In.	595.00
Vase, Artist Decorated, Signed, Mueller, 13 In.	489.00
Vase, Bust Portrait, Gentleman, 2 Handles, Marked, Hersey Rich, 1908, 7 3/4 In.	145.00
Vase, Cranes, Flowers, Enamel, Camille Faure, 4 1/4 In.	1530.00
Vase, Enamel, Stags In Forest, Castle, c.1900, 7 1/2 In.	805.00
Vase, Gourd Shape, Enamel, Geometric, Blue, Black, White, Camille Faure, 10 In.	5875.00
Vase, Poppy Flower, France, c.1890, 7 x 8 In.	350.00
Vase, Raised Flower, Enamel, Metal Foot, Rim, Signed, France, 4 1/2 In.	1765.00
Vase, Shell Shape, Nautilus, White, Early 20th Century, 7 1/2 In., Pair	35.00
Vase, Slip Glazed, Stenciled, Art Nouveau, Edward Colonna, c.1901, 12 In.	8365.00

LINDBERGH was a national hero. In 1927, Charles Lindbergh, the aviator, became the first man to make a nonstop solo flight across the Atlantic Ocean. In 1932, his son was kidnapped and murdered, and Lindbergh was again the center of public interest. He died in 1974. All types of Lindbergh memorabilia are collected.

Ashtray, Ceramic, Our National Hero Co. Ceramic, Yellow	45.00
Bank, Bust, Fly Suit, N. Tregor, 1928, 6 1/2 In.	175.00
Button, Hero Of 1927, Spirit Of St. Louis, Celluloid, 1 1/4 In.	125.00
Button, Lindbergh, Sled, 2 Great Fliers, Plucky Lindy & Flexible, Late 1920s	29.00
Button, Plucky Lindy, Horseshoe, 1 3/4 In.	35.00
Button, Pride Of U.S.A., Metal Plane, 1927, 7/8 In.	245.00
Button, Propeller, Welcome Lindbergh, Paper, Tab, Red, White, Blue, 5 In.	55.00
Button, Welcome Home, Slim Lindy, Capt. Chas. Lindbergh, Blue, Silver, 1 3/8 In.	105.00
Button, Welcome Our Hero, Capt. Charles A. Lindbergh, 1 1/4 In.	175.00
Calendar, Plane, Thos. D. Murphy Co., Sample, Jan., 1929, 22 1/2 x 14 1/2 In.	259.00
Candy Container, Spirit Of St. Louis Airplane, Glass Body, Tin Wings, Contents, 4 1/2 In.	545.00
Display Card, Button, Every Boy's Idol, Plucky Lindy, Celluloid, 10 1-In. Buttons	405.00
Doll, Composition Shoulder Head, Painted Features, Cloth Body, Stitch Joints, 29 In.	1375.00
Poster, Post Office Reward, Charles A. Lindbergh, Jr. Kidnapping, 1932, 21 1/2 x 15 In.	1610.00
Program, Official Banquet, Buffalo, N.Y., July 29, 1927, 12 1/4 x 9 1/4 In.	420.00
Toy, Airplane, Lindy, Spirit Of St. Louis, Cast Iron, Hubley, 13-In. Wingspan	3575.00
Toy, Airplane, Lindy, Wyandotte, c.1927	275.00
Toy, Airplane, Lockheed Cirrus, Lindy, WR 211, Cast Iron, Hubley, 11-In. Wingspan	9900.00
Toy, Airplane, Spirit Of St. Louis, Cast Metal, Wood, Rubber, 4 x 11 x 13 In.	415.00
Toy, Airplane, Spirit Of St. Louis, Pressed Steel, Push Handle, 24-In. Wingspan	5225.00
Toy, Airplane, Spirit Of St. Louis, Single Engine, Hubley, 13-In. Wingspan	3575.00
Watch Fob, Compass, New York To Paris, Eiffel Tower, Statue Of Liberty, Metal, 2 In.	69.00

LIVERPOOL, England, has been the site of many pottery and porcelain factories since the eighteenth century. Color-decorated porcelains, transfer-printed earthenware, stoneware, basalt, figurines, and other wares were made. Sadler and Green made print-decorated wares from 1756. Many of the pieces were made for the American market and feature patriotic emblems, such as eagles, flags, and other special-interest motifs. Liverpool pitchers are always called Liverpool jugs by collectors.

Jug, Apotheosis, Washington's Death, c.1800, 8 x 4 1/2 In.	3165.00
Jug, Arms Of United States, Eagle, Shield, Poem, Creamware, 5 1/2 In.	2050.00
Jug, Behold Our Support, 2 Transfers, c.1800, 7 x 4 1/4 x 7 1/2 In.	650.00
Jug, Emblem Of America, Black Transfer Printed, c.1800, 11 1/4 In.	3410.00
Jug, George Washington Memorial, America In Tears, Creamware, c.1800, 9 In.	2780.00
Jug, George Washington Memorial, Early 1800s, 10 1/4 x 9 1/8 In.	1930.00
Jug, Guillotining Of King Louis XVI, French Liberty, Creamware, 7 1/4 In.	3175.00
Jug, Map Of Planned New Capital At Washington, Creamware, c.1798, 9 1/4 In.	4230.00
Jug, Masonic Symbols, Black Transfers, Gilding, 11 In.	3450.00
Jug, Putting Off, 3-Masted Ship, Transfer, Enamel, Early 1800s, 10 1/2 In.	1060.00
Jug, Ship Caroline, James Leech, Shipwright's Arms, Second Period, 8 3/4 In.	865.00
Jug, Ship Decoration, On Green Ocean, Medallion In Latin, 8 1/2 In.	1725.00
Jug, Shipwright's Arms, 3-Masted Ship, Transfer, Enamel, Early 1800s, 8 1/2 In.	825.00
Jug, Washington, Crowned With Laurel By Liberty, Creamware, 8 1/2 In.	3306.00
Mug, Cupid, 3 Graces, Black Transfer, Creamware, England, Late 1700s, 6 In.	190.00
Plate, Prince William Henry Commder, c.1810, 9 3/4 In.	330.00
Punch Bowl, Ben Franklin, General Washington, Creamware, 4 1/2 x 10 1/4 In.	4760.00
Tankard, World In Planisphere, Sun, 4 Figures, Map, Creamware, 6 In.	1590.00

LLADRO is a Spanish porcelain. Juan, Jose, and Vicente Lladro opened a ceramics workshop in Almacera in 1951. They soon began making figurines in a distinctive, elongated style. In 1958 the factory moved to Tabernes Blanques, Spain. The company makes stoneware and porcelain figurines and vases in limited and unlimited editions.

LLADRÓ

Figurine, Archangel Michael, Fiery Sword, Defeating Satan, 37 In.	3680.00
Figurine, Girl, Holding Goose, 10 In.	95.00
Figurine, Girl, With Basket & Dogs, 8 In.	75.00
Figurine, Mother & Child, 14 In.	316.00

Figurine, Mother & Child, No. 2429, 18 1/4 In.	259.00
Figurine, Perfect Drive, Woman Golfer, No. 6689, 14 1/2 In.	115.00

LOCKE ART is a trademark found on glass of the early twentieth century. Joseph Locke worked at many English and American firms. He designed and etched his own glass in Pittsburgh, Pennsylvania, starting in the 1880s. Some pieces were marked *Joe Locke*, but most were marked with the words *Locke Art*. The mark is hidden in the pattern on the glass.

Sherbet, Interlocking Daisies, Saucer Foot, 3 1/2 In.	100.00
Tumbler, Lemonade, Poppies, Handle, 5 1/4 In.	150.00
Vase, Chrysanthemums, Ruffled Edge, Footed, 12 In.	2250.00

LOETZ glass was made in many varieties. Johann Loetz bought a glassworks in Austria in 1840. He died in 1848 and his widow ran the company; then in 1879, his grandson took over. Most collectors recognize the iridescent gold glass similar to Tiffany, but many other types were made. The firm closed during World War II.

Basket, Iridescent, Square, Folded-In Rim, Bronze Art Nouveau Holder, 7 x 7 3/4 In.	460.00
Bowl, Blue, Crimped Rim, Pewter Base, Stylized Trees, Pinecones, 9 1/2 & 12 In.	355.00
Bowl, Green Iridescent, 3 Applied Tadpoles, Rolled 4-Fold Rim, Squat, 5 In.	85.00
Bowl, Green Iridescent, Amber, Blue, Oval, 5 1/2 In.	2185.00
Bowl, Oil Spot, Blue, Gold Iridescent, Fold Down Rim, 8 1/2 In.	290.00
Bowl, Opal Iridescent, Footed, Pinched Rim, Maria Kirschner, 8 1/2 x 7 In.	4480.00
Bowl, Papillon, Undulating Green, c.1900, 9 1/2 In.	690.00
Bowl, Red Iridescent, Ruffled Edge, Dimpled Shoulder, 20th Century, 7 1/2 x 13 1/2 In.	825.00
Candlestick, Clear, Textured, Applied Iridescent Spirals, Cabochons & Edges, 15 In.	460.00
Compote, Gold Iridescent, Blue Cabochons & Rim, Blue Iridescent Foot, 7 In.	835.00
Compote, Trumpet, Amber, Gold Iridescent, c.1900, 6 3/4 In.	184.00
Lamp, Oil Spot, Green, Blue, Flying Gargoyles, Dolphin Heads, Cat's-Paw Feet, 18 In.	2645.00
Lamp, Oil Spot, Pink, Brass Base, Shade, Art Deco, 7 x 14 In.	705.00
Lamp, Platinum Iridescent, Citrine Ground, Entwined Leaves, Gilt Metal Base, 17 In.	3335.00
Pitcher, Green Iridescent, Internal Stems, Applied Handle, 6 In.	115.00
Urn, Oil Spot, Blue Iridescent, Gold Iridescent Rim & Ribbed Handles, Footed, 9 In.	1495.00
Vase, Aeolus, Amber, Iridescent Threading, Dimpled, c.1902, 10 In.	825.00
Vase, Amber To Green Iridescent, Threading, Applied Gold Pussy Willows, 8 1/2 In.	4255.00
Vase, Amber, Blue Iridescent Waves, Pink Tadpoles, Flared Rim, 4 1/4 In.	3220.00
Vase, Apples, Leaves, Red, Green, Pink Ground, 4-Fold Rim, Footed, Cameo, Signed, 9 In.	865.00
Vase, Astraa, Gold Iridescent, 4 Handles, 10 In.	4700.00
Vase, Blue Iridescent, 3 Indentations, Gourd Form, Signed, 12 In.	530.00
Vase, Blue Iridescent, Dimpled Green Ground, Flared Rim, 7 In.	460.00
Vase, Blue Iridescent, Green, Purple, Blue, 10 1/2 In.	520.00
Vase, Blue, Green Iridescent, Pulled, Silver Overlay Flowers, Leaves, Vines, Flared, 5 In.	2070.00
Vase, Blue, Purple Iridescent, Molded Swirls, Repeating Petals, 6 1/2 In.	690.00
Vase, Candia Papillon, Blue, Purple, Organic Form, Looping Feet, Austria, 9 1/2 x 4 In.	4090.00
Vase, Citron, Maroon & Orange Lilies, Reverse Trumpet, Oval Base, Cameo, 12 1/2 In.	980.00
Vase, Clear, Cobalt Blue Threads, Folded Rim, Pontil, 8 In.	1380.00
Vase, Clear, Iridescent, Applied Medallion, 2 In.	265.00
Vase, Clear, Satin, Applied Pussy Willows & Leaves, Blue Iridescent Ruffled Foot, 9 In.	1035.00
Vase, Cobalt Blue Iridescent, Iridescent Gold Sculptured Foot, Entwining Leaves, 6 In.	1150.00
Vase, Crackle, 2 Applied Amber Glass Buttresses, Flared, 8 In.	588.00
Vase, Cranberry, Green, Gold Iridescent, Quilted, Threaded, Flattened Base, 13 In.	520.00
Vase, Enameled Bird On Grape, Iridescent, Urn Shape, Scroll Handles, Signed, 5 1/2 In.	230.00
Vase, Federzeichnung, Cased Satin, Gold, Octopus, 10 In.	1210.00
Vase, Federzeichnung, Gold Enameled, Octopus, Butterscotch, Signed, 10 1/4 In.	4600.00
Vase, Federzeichnung, Green To Opal, Flowers, Leaves, Bulbous, Ruffled Edge, 5 1/2 In.	1035.00
Vase, Figural, Fish, Gold Iridescent, Purple Threading, Eyes, Scales, Gills, 5 1/2 In.	1100.00
Vase, Gold Iridescent, Art Nouveau Floral, Silver Overlay, Tricornered, 3 1/2 In.	460.00
Vase, Gold Iridescent, Gold Art Nouveau Medallions, Turquoise & Jade Jewels, 4 In.	345.00
Vase, Gold Iridescent, Silver Blue Iridescent, Swirls, Pinched, Ruffled Edge, 6 3/4 In.	2475.00
Vase, Green Iridescent Blue & Green Drapes, c.1900, 8 In.	690.00
Vase, Green Iridescent, Blue Dimples, Bulbous, Squat, Pinched Sides, Folded Rim, 4 In.	200.00
Vase, Green Iridescent, Gold Enameled Butterflies, Jeweled Wings, Bulbous, 7 1/2 In.	720.00

Vase, Green, Blue Iridescent, Internal Stems, Cylindrical, Pinched Sides, 8 In. 290.00
Vase, Green, Blue Iridescent, Stems, Leaves, Tricornered, Cameo, 3 3/4 In. 805.00
Vase, Green, Diamond-Quilted Mother-Of-Pearl, Silver Overlay, c.1890, 7 1/4 In. 1840.00
Vase, Iridescent, Ruffled, Crystallized Leafy Foot, Vining Branch, Flower Form, 8 1/2 In. . . 1150.00
Vase, Jack-In-The-Pulpit, Green, Blue, c.1900, 9 In. 310.00
Vase, Marmorierte, Enameled, Pastel Interior, Fluted Rim, Tapered, 7 In. 375.00
Vase, Medici, Silver, Blue, Oil Spots, Salmon Iridescent, Engraved, 5 3/4 In. 1100.00
Vase, Oil Spot, Amber & Pink, Yellow Over Purple, Folded Edge, 7 1/2 In. 2185.00
Vase, Oil Spot, Aqua, Applied Gold Iridescent Flowering Stems, 11 5/8 In. 175.00
Vase, Oil Spot, Blue, Green Iridescent Over Cinnamon, 4-Pinch Rim, Oval, 8 In. 1380.00
Vase, Oil Spot, Blue, Green Iridescent, Melon Ribbed, Flared Rim, Vertical Lines, 5 In. . . . 575.00
Vase, Oil Spot, Blue, Yellow, Shouldered, Squat, 4 1/2 In. 325.00
Vase, Oil Spot, Green Iridescent, Gourd Form, Twisted Top, Austria, 10 1/2 In. 530.00
Vase, Oil Spot, Green, Melon Rib Shape, Silvery Blue Ribbons, c.1900, 8 In. 460.00
Vase, Oil Spot, Platinum, Yellow, Green To Blue Feathers, Silver Orchid Overlay, 5 1/4 In. 3450.00
Vase, Oil Spot, Red Threading, Satin Handles, 7 In. 120.00
Vase, Oil Spot, Yellow, Blue, Green Pulled, Platinum, Gourd Form, 3 1/4 In. 880.00
Vase, Olive Green, Blue Iridescent Stripes, c.1890, 5 1/4 In. 1150.00
Vase, Olive Green, Burgundy Threading, Pinched, Sheared Collar, 3 3/4 In. 315.00
Vase, Opal Iridescent, Applied Branch, Cylindrical, 8 In. 125.00
Vase, Opal Iridescent, Green Applied Handles, Marie Kirschner, Signed, 10 x 3 In. 1000.00
Vase, Orpheus, Green Iridescent, Turquoise Medallions, 11 1/4 In. 200.00
Vase, Pampas, Amber Iridescent, Flared Bottom, Flattened Top, Pulled, 11 1/2 In. 2875.00
Vase, Pampas, Cobalt Blue, Paris World Exposition, Undulating Baluster, c.1900 . . . . 3795.00
Vase, Pampas, Purple Iridescent, Gourd Form, Flared Rim, 9 1/2 In. 1035.00
Vase, Papillon, Applied Butterflies Fluttering, Midnight Blue, 7 5/8 In. 575.00
Vase, Papillon, Cobalt Blue, Applied Tendrils, 8 1/2 In. 2040.00
Vase, Papillon, Figural, Stork, Gold, Applied Wings, Beak, Eyes, Purple Iridescent, 9 In. . . 4700.00
Vase, Papillon, Gold Iridescent, Applied Handles, 4 Medallions, 9 1/2 In. 825.00
Vase, Papillon, Gold Iridescent, Seashell, Applied Green Feet, c.1900, 7 In. 690.00
Vase, Papillon, Golden, Iridized Frosted, 5 7/8 In. 175.00
Vase, Phanomen Pulled, Gold Iridescent, 3 Handles, 7 In. 4115.00
Vase, Phanomen, Cobalt Blue, Clear Stem, Bulbous, Footed, 1900, Signed, 12 1/4 In. 3525.00
Vase, Phanomen, Iridescent Blue, Almond Threading, Flared Rim, Ribbed, 4 3/4 In. 2300.00
Vase, Phanomen, Opal, Indented Shoulder, Black Base, Gourd Form, Signed, 6 1/2 In. 9400.00
Vase, Phanomen, Yellow, Swirls, Green, Gold, Silver Iridescent Oil Spots, 4 1/2 In. 1725.00
Vase, Platinum Astaglas, Seashell Shape, Iridescent Gold, Red, Green, c.1895, 11 In. 765.00
Vase, Platinum Pulled Feather, Orange Ground, Signed, 5 In. 1780.00
Vase, Platinum Pulled Hearts, Salmon, Gold, Shouldered, Flared, Signed, 6 In. 2000.00
Vase, Platinum Pulled Loops, Orange, Applied Pods, Blue, Platinum, Signed, 6 1/2 In. 4600.00
Vase, Purple, Blue Pulled, Opaque Yellow Ground, 7 In. 1060.00
Vase, Purple, Blue Spots, Stripes, Gourd Form, Controlled Bubbles, For Rindskopf, 6 In. . . 940.00
Vase, Rubin Phanomen, Red, Blue Iridescent, c.1890, 12 3/4 In. 3450.00
Vase, Ruby To Shaded Emerald, 5 In. 2530.00
Vase, Rust To Yellow, Applied Iridescent Silver Overlay, 8 1/2 In. 4140.00
Vase, Rusticana, Green Iridescent, 6 1/4 In. 115.00
Vase, Rusticana, Transparent Green, 5 3/4 In. 175.00
Vase, Stick, Amber Iridescent, Blue Pulled Loops, Bulbous, 8 1/2 In. 1495.00
Vase, Stick, Green, Bubbles, Gold Scrolls, White Dots, Hearts, Bulbous Base, 10 In. 5980.00
Vase, Tango, Blue, 4 Yellow Windows, Applied Black Tendrils, 1918-25, 4 1/2 In. 825.00
Vase, Tango, Lavender, Applied Red Tendrils, 4 1/4 In. 705.00
Vase, Tango, Opaque Orange, Applied Blue Tendrils, Blue Rim, 4 In. 325.00
Vase, Texas, Amber To Green Iridescent, Vertical Threads, Pussy Willows, 8 In. 3700.00
Vase, Titania, Pinched Rim, Signed, Austria, 3 1/2 In. 2000.00
Vase, Titanium, Green, Cranberry, Silver Overlay, Marked, 8 1/4 In. 4945.00
Vase, Titanium, Green, Platinum Over Orange, Cylindrical, 8 1/4 In. 1725.00

LONE RANGER, a fictional character, was introduced on the radio in
1932. Over three thousand shows were produced before the series
ended in 1954. In 1938, the first Lone Ranger movie was made. Television shows were started in 1949 and are still seen on some stations.
The Lone Ranger appears on many products and was even the name of
a restaurant chain for several years.

Badge, Merita Safety Club, Brass, Star Shape, Die Cut, c.1938, 1 1/2 In. 115.00
Basketball, Bantam, Sun Rubber Co., Barberton, Oh., 1938, 7 In. 55.00
Belt, Plastic, Metal Buckle, Kix Cereal, Mailer, 1941, 2 x 2 x 2 1/2 In. 140.00
Billfold, Vinyl, Zipper, Hidecraft, Box, c.1948, 4 x 5 x 1 In. 200.00
Binocular, 3 Power, Plastic, Red, Black, Box, 1950s, 5 x 6 x 2 1/4 In. 175.00
Button, Buchanan's Buttermilk Bread, Tonto, 7/8 In. 40.00
Button, Buchanan's Enriched Bread, 7/8 In. 60.00
Button, Buchanan's Lone Ranger Community Safety Club, Captain, 1940s, 1 1/4 In. 350.00
Button, Lone Ranger Every Week, Sunday Advertiser, Yellow, Red, c.1938, 1 In. . . .60.00 to 100.00
Button, Lone Ranger Magazine Club, Brass, Enamel, Trojan, 1937, 7/8 In. 1525.00
Button, Lone Ranger, On Silver, Plastic Saddle Charm, Ribbon, 1 1/4 In. 28.00
Button, Lone Ranger, Silver's Lucky Horseshoe, c.1938, 1 3/8 In. 190.00
Button, Sunday Herald & Examiner, 1 In. 15.00
Button, Tab, Lone Ranger Victory Corps, 10 Cents, On Card, 1942, 2 1/2-In. Card 115.00
Button, WFIL Daily News Safety Club, Red, Black, White, Celluloid, 1 In. 100.00
Calendar, Merita Bread, 1950, 15 x 8 1/4 In. 375.00
Calendar, Merita Bread, Join Safety Club, Paper, Starts March, 1940, 26 x 13 In. 600.00
Chaps, Lone Ranger, Tonto, Silver, Denim, Felt, Lasso Writing 110.00
Clock, Alarm, Lone Ranger, Silver, Bullets, Windup, Bradley, 1980, 6 x 4 x 2 In. 120.00
Comic Book, Heigh-Yo Silver, No. 3, Dell, 1938, 11 1/2 x 8 1/2 In., 72 Pages 166.00
Cryptograph Decoder, Weber's Bread, 1943, 2 3/4 x 3 3/4 In. . . . . .200.00 to 225.00
Display, Lone Ranger Badges, 10 x 11 In., 12 Badges 154.00
Display Card, Lone Ranger Ring, Cardboard, 12 x 8 3/4 In. 325.00
Doll, Composition Head, Stuffed Body, Dollcraft Novelty, 1938, 15 1/2 In. 820.00
Doll, Tonto, Outfit, Accessories, Captain Action, Ideal, 1960s 225.00
Figure, Lone Ranger, On Silver, Chalk, Rose Gold, I.A.S. Co., 1935, 11 x 7 1/2 In. . .75.00 to 132.00
Figure, Lone Ranger, On Silver, Hartland, 1950s, 5 x 5 In. . . . . .75.00 to 138.00
Figure, Tonto, On Horse, Plastic, Hartland, Box, 9 In. 155.00
First Aid Kit, American White Cross Labs, 1938, 4 x 4 In. 155.00
Game, Assorted Puzzles, Tin, Box, 1944, 5 1/2 x 15 In. 165.00
Game, Kix Air Base, General Mills, Mailer, 1945, 10 1/2 x 7 In. 195.00
Game, Lone Ranger & Tonto, Warren Paper Products, Box, c.1978, 9 1/2 x 17 In. 69.00
Game, Ring Toss, Rosebud Art Co., Box, 1946, 10 x 12 1/2 In. 250.00
Game, Target, Original Gun & Dart, Marx, Box, 1946, 17 In. 550.00
Guitar, Wood, Paper Laminate, Stencils, Ranger, Tonto, Silver, Jefferson, 1960s, 30 In. . . . 85.00
Gum Wrapper, Hi-Yo Silver, 1 Cent, Bowman, 1940s, 4 1/2 x 6 In. 170.00
Gun, Clicker, Hi-Yo Silver, Louis Marx, Box, c.1938, 7 1/2 In. 565.00
Gun, Rubber Band, Paper, Morton's Salt, Frame, c.1938, 4 3/4 x 8 1/2 In. 55.00
Gun, Smoker Pistol, Plastic, Marx, Box, c.1955, 9-In. Gun 305.00
Gun & Holster, Belt, Spurs, Box, 1950s 635.00
Gun & Holster, Clicker, Hi-Yo Silver, Silver Color, Leather Holster, Marx, 1938 . . . . 110.00
Hat, Cook's, Pirate, Hi-Yo Silver, Orange, T.L.R. Inc., 1939 . . . . 28.00
Hat, Lone Ranger, Hi-Yo Silver, Cloth, Blue Letters, White, 1942, 2 x 22 In. 175.00
Hat, Lone Ranger, Hi-Yo Silver, Cloth, White Letters, Blue, Orange, 1930s, 2 x 22 In. 150.00
Holster, Double, Fringe, 4 Bronco Buster Medallions, Leather, Steer Head Buckle 289.00
Holster, Single, Deluxe, Horse Head Medallions, 10 Bullets 90.00
Horseshoe Set, Rubber, Gardner Games, Chicago, Box, 1950, 6 x 12 In. 90.00
Instructions, Atomic Bomb Ring, Kix Cereal, 4 x 4 In. 75.00
Lantern, Chuck Wagon, Dietz, Box, c.1945, 8 x 5 3/4 In. 320.00
Lunch Box, Legend Of Lone Ranger, Aladdin, 1980 . . . . .69.00 to 88.00
Lunch Box, Legend Of Lone Ranger, No Thermos Bottle, Aladdin, 1980 . . . . 20.00
Lunch Box, No Thermos, Adco Liberty, 1954, 3 3/4 x 6 1/2 x 9 In. 1250.00
Mask Set, Wheaties, 1950s, 8 Piece 735.00
Model Kit, Lone Ranger, Aurora, Box, Unopened, 1974, 4 1/2 x 7 x 10 1/2 In. 115.00
Model Kit, Tonto, Aurora, Box, Unopened, 1974, 4 1/2 x 7 x 10 1/2 In. 70.00
Movie Viewer, Lone Ranger Rides Again, 3 Films, Acme Product Co., Box, 1946 . . . . 449.00
Pencil Bag, Lone Ranger, Tonto, Hi-Yo Silver, Vinyl, Zipper, 1959, 8 x 3 3/4 In. 135.00
Photograph, Lone Ranger & Tonto, Autographed, Frame, Certificate, 15 x 12 In. 39.00
Radio, Hi-Yo Silver, Lone Ranger, Plastic, White, Electric, Pilot, 1938, 9 x 14 x 7 In. 1140.00
Record Player, Wood Case, Record, Decca, c.1950, 12 1/2 x 10 x 6 In. 890.00
Rifle & Holster Set, Legend Of Lone Ranger, Gabriel, Box, 1980, 13 x 28 x 4 1/2 In. 184.00
Ring, Atomic Bomb, Brass, Kix Cereal, 1947 . . . . 175.00

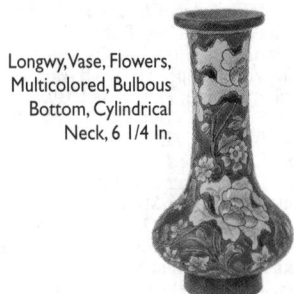

Longwy, Vase, Flowers, Multicolored, Bulbous Bottom, Cylindrical Neck, 6 1/4 In.

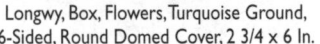

Longwy, Box, Flowers, Turquoise Ground, 6-Sided, Round Domed Cover, 2 3/4 x 6 In.

Ring, Flicker, Ranger & Captain Action, Silver Plastic, Hong Kong, 1960s 35.00
Ring, Flicker, Tonto & Captain Action, Silver Plastic, Hong Kong, 1960s 20.00
Ring, Meteorite, Brass, Kix Cereal, 1942 .... 2000.00
Siren, National Defenders, Warning, Plastic, Wood, Kix Cereal, Mailer, 1941, 7 In. 529.00
Toy, Bat-O-Ball, Cardboard, Pure Oil Co., 1939, 9 3/4 x 4 3/4 In. 335.00
Toy, Hi-Yo Silver, Lone Ranger, On Silver, Tin, Windup, Marx, Box, c.1940, 9 In. . .330.00 to 385.00
Toy, Punch-Out Set, Lone Ranger Rides Again, Silver, Tonto, Scout, Fence, Box, 1947 .... 139.00
View-Master, 3 Reels, No. 4651-4652-4653, 1956 .... 20.00
Watch, Pocket, Chrome, Gun & Holster Fob, New Haven, 1939 .... 593.00
Wristwatch, Leather Band, 3-Color Watch Face, c.1950s 55.00
Wristwatch, Riding Silver, Chrome, Tan Leather Band, New Haven, Box, 1939 .... 3630.00

LONGWY Workshop of Longwy, France, first made ceramic wares in 1798. The workshop is still in business. Most of the ceramic pieces found today are glazed with many colors to resemble cloisonne or other enameled metal. Many pieces were made with stylized figures and Art Deco designs. The factory used a variety of marks.

Box, Flowers, Turquoise Ground, 6-Sided, Round Domed Cover, 2 3/4 x 6 In. .... *Illus* 375.00
Vase, Flowers, Multicolored, Bulbous Bottom, Cylindrical Neck, 6 1/4 In. .... *Illus* 400.00
Vase, Incised, Painted, Flowers, Leaves, 1880s, 8 1/2 In. 475.00
Vase, Primavera, Black Art Deco Design, Blue Ground, 12 1/2 In. 940.00
Vase, Trees, Painted, Incised, 7 In. 645.00

LONHUDA Pottery Company of Steubenville, Ohio, was organized in 1892 by William Long, W. H. Hunter, and Alfred Day. Brown underglaze slip-decorated pottery was made. The firm closed in 1896. The company used many marks; the earliest included the letters *LPCO*.

Pitcher, Honeysuckle, Black Glaze, Tricornered Rim, Handle, 7 In. 200.00
Vase, Jug Shape, Blackberries & Leaves, Black & Brown Glaze, 5 1/2 In. 300.00
Vase, Leaf & Berry Design, 9 In. 375.00

LOTUS WARE was made by the Knowles, Taylor & Knowles Company of East Liverpool, Ohio, from 1890 to 1900. Lotus Ware, a thin porcelain that resembles Belleek, was sometimes decorated outside the factory. Other types of ceramics that were made by the Knowles, Taylor & Knowles Company are listed under KTK.

Finger Bowl, Water Lily, 2 x 5 1/4 In. 275.00
Rose Bowl, Olive Green Matte, Applied Gold Leaves, Berries, 3-Footed, 4 1/2 In. 600.00
Rose Bowl, Raised Dots, Blue, Gold, Red, Gold Washed Ruffled Rim, 4 1/2 In. 748.00
Teapot, White, Bamboo Handle, 7 1/2 In. 560.00

LOW art tiles were made by the J. and J. G. Low Art Tile Works of Chelsea, Massachusetts, from 1877 to 1902. A variety of art and other tiles were made. Some of the tiles were made by a process called *natural,* some were hand modeled, and some were made mechanically.

Tile, Grecian Woman, Embossed Portrait, Flower Border, Green High Glaze, Round, 6 In. . 230.00

LOY-NEL-ART, see McCoy category.

LUNCH BOXES and lunch pails have been used to carry lunches to school or work since the nineteenth century. Today, most collectors want either early tobacco advertising boxes or children's lunch boxes made since the 1930s. These boxes are made of metal or plastic. Boxes listed here include the original Thermos bottle inside the box unless otherwise indicated. Movie, television, and cartoon characters may be found in their own categories. Tobacco tin pails and lunch boxes are listed in the Advertising category.

LUNCH BOX, Addams Family, Metal, King Seeley Thermos Co., 1974	69.00
Archies, Metal, No Thermos, Aladdin, 1969	69.00
Barbie & Midge, Vinyl, King Seeley Thermos Co., 1960s	115.00
Bread Loaf, Dome, Metal, Aladdin, 1968	410.00
Canada, Map, Coat Of Arms Of Canada, Metal, General Steel Wares, c.1960, 7 x 9 In.	213.00
Cheerleaders, Football Stadium, Vinyl, Pink, Travel Toy, Early 1960s, 7 x 9 x 4 In.	40.00
College Pennants, Oval, 2 Swing Handles, Cover, Ohio Art, 1950-54	25.00
Cowboy In Africa, Chuck Connors, King Seeley Thermos Co., 1968	87.00
Cowboy In Africa, Chuck Connors, No Thermos, King Seeley Thermos Co., 1968	40.00
Denim Diner, Dome, Metal, Aladdin, 1975	49.00
Donny & Marie, Vinyl, Aladdin, 1976	39.00
Double Deckers, Metal, Aladdin, 1970	99.00
E.T., Metal, Aladdin, 1982, 7 x 8 x 4 In. . . . . .59.00 to 65.00
Evel Knievel, Metal, Aladdin, 1974	28.00
Football Scene, Vinyl, Blue, Abema Industries, 1960s, 7 x 8 x 4 In.	40.00
Guns Of Will Sonnett, Metal, King Seeley Thermos Co., 1968 . . . . .49.00 to 58.00
Gunsmoke, Double LL, Metal, Aladdin, 1959	199.00
Gunsmoke, Metal, Aladdin, 1972	100.00
Gunsmoke, Metal, No Thermos, Aladdin, 1973	59.00
Holly Hobby, Metal, No Thermos, Aladdin, 1981	39.00
Home Town Airport, Dome, Metal, King Seeley Products Co., 1960, 7 x 9 In.	750.00
How The West Was Won, King Seeley Thermos Co., 1979	110.00
Incredible Hulk, Metal, Aladdin, 1978	42.00
Joe Palooka, Swing Handles, Cover, Han Fisher, Continental Can, c.1948, 5 x 7 x 4 In. . . .	65.00
Kewtie Pie, Vinyl, Aladdin, 1967	120.00
Knight Rider, Metal, King Seeley Thermos Co., 1984	49.00
Lawman, Metal, No Thermos, King Seeley Thermos Co., 1961	99.00
Little House On The Prairie, Metal, No Thermos, King Seeley Thermos Co., 1978	48.00
Lost In Space, Dome, Metal, King Seeley Thermos Co., 1967, 7 x 9 x 4 1/2 In.	400.00
Magic Of Lassie, Metal, King Seeley Thermos Co., 1978	69.00
Merry Christmas, Old Woman In Shoe, Tin, Lithograph, Tindeco, c.1930, 5 1/2 x 5 In. . . .	165.00
Mod Tulips, Dome, Metal, No Thermos, Ohio Art, 1962	89.00
Mork & Mindy, Metal, American Thermos Co., 1979	69.00
Muppets, Kermit, King Seeley Thermos Co., 1979	39.00
NFL, Yellow Border, Metal, King Seeley Thermos Co., 1975	49.00
Night Before Christmas, Santa Scenes, Tin, Tindeco, 1920-36	80.00
Partridge Family, No Thermos, King Seeley Thermos Co.	79.00
Peter Pan Peanut Butter, Plastic, Derby Foods, 1964, 7 x 10 In.	46.00
Pussycats, Brunch Bag, Vinyl, Red, Black Handle, Aladdin, 1968	130.00
Red Barn, Open Doors, Dome, Metal, No Thermos, American Thermos Co.	89.00
Rifleman, Metal, Aladdin, 1961, 7 x 8 x 4 In.	295.00
Scooby Doo, No Thermos, King Seeley Thermos Co.	69.00
Six Million Dollar Man, No Thermos, Aladdin, 1978	45.00
Smoky The Bear, Forest, Vinyl, King Seeley Thermos Co., c.1965, 9 x 7 x 3 3/4 In.	332.00
Snack Sack, 2 Girls Sharing Soda, Brown, Vinyl, 1960s, 6 1/2 x 8 1/2 In.	150.00
Sports, Tennis, Soccer, Baseball, Metal, King Seeley Thermos Co., 1968, 7 x 9 x 4 In. . .	670.00
Strawberry Shortcake, Picket Fence, Swing Handles, Cover, No Thermos, 1980s	20.00
Tina Teen, Girl Placing Photos In Scrapbook, Blue, Vinyl, 1960s, 6 1/2 x 8 In.	200.00
Tom Corbett, Red, No Thermos, Aladdin, 1952	99.00
U.S. Mail, Dome, Metal, No Thermos, Aladdin, 1969	59.00
Waltons, Metal, Aladdin, 1973	69.00
Wild Bill Hickock & Jingles, Metal, Aladdin, 1955	80.00
World Of Barbie, Vinyl, Blue, King Seeley Thermos Co., 1971	59.00
World Of Barbie, Vinyl, Pink, King Seeley Themos Co., 1971	49.00

LUNCH BOX THERMOS, Annie Oakley & Tagg, Stopper, No Lid, Aladdin, c.1950s 45.00
    Barbie, Midge, Skipper, King Seeley Thermos Co., 1965 . . . .   27.00
    G.I. Joe, Metal, King Seeley Thermos Co., 6 1/2 In. 50.00

LUNEVILLE, a French faience factory, was established about 1730 by
Jacques Chambrette. It is best known for its fine biscuit figures and
groups and for large faience dogs and lions. The early pieces were
unmarked. The firm was acquired by Keller and Guerin and is still
working.

    Bowl, Centerpiece, Roses, Square, Canted Corners, Hand Painted, 10 In. 50.00
    Pitcher, Pansies, Green Border, Majolica, Keller & Guerin, 9 In. 75.00
    Plaque, Working Man In Relief, Tan, Brown Matte Glaze, 4 1/4 x 7 3/4 In. 295.00
    Plate, Asparagus, Embossed, Well, Majolica, Keller & Guerin, 8 In. 80.00
    Plate, Oranges, Pink Ground, Keller & Guerin, 9 In. 50.00
    Sugar Shaker, Roses, Hand Painted, Footed, 8 In. 45.00

LUSTER glaze was meant to resemble copper, silver, or gold. The
term *luster* includes any piece with some luster trim. It has been used
since the sixteenth century. Some of the luster found today was made
during the nineteenth century. The metallic glazes are applied on pottery. The finished color depends on the combination of the clay color
and the glaze. Blue, orange, gold, and pearlized luster decorations
were used by Japanese and German firms in the early 1900s. Tea Leaf
pieces have their own category.

    Copper, Cachepot, Liner, Lion's Mask Ringed Handles, Figural Groups, 5 1/2 In., Pair 345.00
    Copper, Creamer, 2 Blue Bands, Raised Flower, 5 1/4 In. 45.00
    Copper, Creamer, Blue Banded Waist, Raised Girl & Animals, 5 In. 35.00
    Copper, Creamer, Green Banded Waist, Flowers, 5 In. 29.00
    Copper, Mug, Handle, Blue Banded Waist, Leaves, 3 1/2 In. 60.00
    Copper, Mug, Handle, Blue Banded Waist, Raised Flowers, 3 1/4 In. 60.00
    Copper, Mug, Handle, Green Banded, 3 Raised Multicolored Panels, Figures, 4 1/4 In. . . .   60.00
    Copper, Mug, Handle, Pink Luster Band, Flowers, 3 3/4 In. 75.00
    Copper, Mug, Handle, Raised Flowers, 3 1/4 In. 60.00
    Copper, Pitcher, Dancing Figures, 7 3/4 In. 45.00
    Copper, Pitcher, Green, Raised Flowers, Phoenix, Phoenix Form Handle, 7 1/4 In. 150.00
    Copper, Pitcher, Pink, House, 6 In. 127.00
    Fairyland luster is included in the Wedgwood category.
    Peach, Blue, Candy Dish, Felix The Cat Stands At Back, Japan, 4 3/4 x 4 x 5 In. 55.00
    Pink, Cup & Saucer Set, Demitasse 374.00
    Pink, Figurine, Cupid, Wood & Caldwell, 1810-15, 17 1/2 In. 1725.00
    Pink, Pitcher, Black Transfers, Military Heroes, Perry, Pike, 7 In.   405.00
    Pink, Pitcher, Hunt Scene, England, 6 1/2 In. 191.00
    Pink, Pitcher, Hunters, Dogs, Multicolored, England, Early 1800s, 6 5/8 In. 323.00
    Pink, Pitcher, Putti, Landscape, Highlighted, Molded, Multicolored, England, 6 1/2 In. 690.00
    Pink, Plate, Andrew Jackson, Hero Of New Orleans, c.1824, 8 3/4 In. 1455.00
    Pink, Teapot, Flamingo, Japan, 7 3/4 In. 29.00
    Pink Splash, Vase, Classical Shape, Footed, England, 8 In., Pair 865.00
    Purple, Pitcher, Children Playing, Blue Glaze, Wood & Caldwell, 6 1/2 In. 299.00
    Rainbow, Jam Jar, Bulldog, 5-Color, Spoon Tongue, Japan, 5 1/2 x 3 1/2 In. 98.00
    Rainbow, Tea Set, Orange, White, Black Trim, Czechoslovakia, c.1930s, 3 Piece . . . . *Illus*   60.00
    Silver, Mantel, Green Glass, Scalloped Rim, Flower Embossed Bowl, 1900s, 15 x 8 In., Pair   294.00
    Sunderland luster pieces are listed in the Sunderland category.
    Tea Leaf luster pieces are listed in the Tea Leaf Ironstone category.

Luster, Rainbow, Tea Set,
Orange, White, Black Trim,
Czechoslovakia,
c.1930s, 3 Piece

LUSTRE ART GLASS Company was founded in Long Island, New York, in 1920 by Conrad Vahlsing and Paul Frank. The company made lampshades and globes that are almost indistinguishable from those made by Quezal. Most of the shades made by the company were unmarked.

Shade, Opal, Gold, Ribbon, 5 In. 115.00
Shade, White Pulled Feathers, Gold, Trumpet Shaped, Signed, 2 1/4 x 5 In. 85.00

LUSTRES are mantel decorations or pedestal vases with many hanging glass prisms. The name really refers to the prisms, and it is proper to refer to a single glass prism as a lustre. Either spelling, luster or lustre, is correct.

Clambroth, Translucent, Round Pedestal Base, Ruffled Rim, 7 Prisms, 10 3/4 In., Pair 130.00
White & Red Opaque, Painted Floral Panels, Buttons, Prisms, Gilt, Bohemian, 11 In., Pair 2185.00

MAASTRICHT, Holland, was the city where Petrus Regout established the De Sphinx pottery in 1836. The firm was noted for its transfer-printed earthenware. Many factories in Maastricht are still making ceramics.

Bowl, Rooster, Red & Rust Transfer, 5 3/4 In. 55.00
Bowl, Sana Pattern, Asian Scene, Caramel Luster, 6 In. 20.00
Plate, KLM, 1924, First Flight, Amsterdam To Bavaria, Hand Painted, Delft, 9 3/4 In. 200.00
Plate, Timor Pattern, Asian Scene, Handles, 14 In. 45.00

MACINTYRE, see Moorcroft category.

MAIZE glass was made by W.L. Libbey & Son Company of Toledo, Ohio, after 1889. The glass resembled an ear of corn. The leaves were usually green, but some pieces were made with blue or red leaves. The kernels of corn were light yellow, white, or light green.

Bowl, Centerpiece, Amber Corn, Blue Leaves, John Locke, 9 In. 288.00
Bowl, Green Husks, 8 In. 375.00
Celery Vase, Green Husks, 6 1/2 In. 50.00
Sugar, Blue Husks, 5 1/2 In. 125.00
Sugar Shaker, Barrel Form, Mauve Corn, Custard Husks, 5 3/4 In. . . . . .300.00 to 345.00
Sugar Shaker, Gold-Tipped Blue Husks, 5 1/2 In. 485.00
Syrup, Green Husks, Pewter Lid, 7 1/4 In. 785.00
Tumbler, Green & Gold Trim, 4 In. 90.00

MAJOLICA is a general term for any pottery glazed with an opaque tin enamel that conceals the color of the clay body. It has been made since the fourteenth century. Today's collector is most likely to find Victorian majolica. The heavy, colorful ware is rarely marked. Some famous makers include Wedgwood; Minton; Griffen, Smith and Hill (marked *Etruscan*); and Chesapeake Pottery (marked *Avalon* or *Clifton*). Majolica made by Wedgwood is listed in the Wedgwood category.

Apothecary Jar, Blue, White, Cover, Printed, Valeriana Off., Syr. Pom. Dule, 13 In., Pair . . 2530.00
Basket, Brown, Violet Interior, 8 In. 45.00
Basket, Frogs, Strawberries, 2 1/2 x 7 1/2 In. 175.00
Bowl, Centerpiece, Eichwald, Figural, Dolphin, Clamshell Bowl, Pedestal, 1800s, 23 In. . . 460.00
Bowl, Centerpiece, Lions, Eagles, Scrolling Vines, Dragon Shaped Handles, 8 x 18 In. 40.00
Bust, Young Boy, Brothers Urbach, 19th Century, 19 In. 750.00
Butter, Cover, Underplate, Bird Knop, Water Lily Design, c.1875, 4 1/2 In. 260.00
Cake Stand, Maple Leaf Pattern, Etruscan, Impressed, c.1880, 9 1/2 In. Diam. 350.00
Candlestick, Figurine Form, Brownie Policeman, Late 19th Century, 9 In. 460.00
Cheese Stand, Cover, Apple Blossoms, Basket Design, c.1875, 12 1/2 In. 2760.00
Cigar Holder, Turkey & Rabbit 450.00
Coffeepot, Bamboo Pattern, Etruscan, c.1880, 6 1/2 In. 260.00
Dish, Begonia Leaf, Variegated Coloration, c.1900, 9 1/2 x 12 In., 2 Piece 175.00
Dish, Sweetmeat, Shell, Man, Woman, Reptiles, Snails, Minton, 1863, 7 In., Pair 7890.00
Figurine, Multicolored, Man, Woman, c.1860-80, 17 In., Pair 3800.00
Humidor, Moorsman, Embossed, Painted, Austria, 9 In. 230.00
Jardinere, Triangular Form, Bird & Flower, 6 1/4 In. 130.00

Majolica, Planter, Putti, Basket, Grand Ducal
Majolica Manufactory, Germany, 14 In.

**Most old majolica pieces have a
colored bottom. The newer pieces
have white bottoms.
Old majolica pitchers have a glazed
interior. Many reproduction majolica
pitchers have bisque interiors.**

Jardiniere, Applied Roses, Sprigged Decoration, c.1900, 9 In.	70.00
Jardiniere, Art Nouveau, Molded Exotic Birds, 12 1/2 x 17 In.	600.00
Jardiniere, Flower Swags, Minerva Head Handles, Joseph Holdcroft, c.1875, 8 1/4 In.	750.00
Jardiniere, Pedestal, Art Nouveau, England, 38 1/2 In.	1675.00
Jardiniere, Undertray, Square, Relief Leaves, Bellflowers, c.1870, 7 1/4 In.	2940.00
Jug, Hinged Lid, Corn Syrup, Sunflower Pattern, Pewter, Etruscan, c.1880, 8 1/4 In.	230.00
Jug, Stork & Bamboo, c.1875, 8 1/4 In.	750.00
Lamp, Carcel, Napoleon III, Brass Mounted, Black Ground, c.1865, 15 In., Pair	1495.00
Oyster Plate, Seashells, Coral, Impressed, 1873, 9 In.	635.00
Pedestal, Figural, Mottled Brown, Seated Winged Sphinx, Late 1800s, 41 In.	2070.00
Pedestal, Square Top, Tapering Standard, Panels, Scrolling Leaves, 43 x 12 In.	1675.00
Pitcher, Cockatiel, 9 In., Pair	405.00
Pitcher, Embossed Bird's Nest Decoration, 19th Century, 10 In.	175.00
Pitcher, Embossed, Painted, Irises, France, c.1900, 6 In.	230.00
Pitcher, Fish Design, 19th Century, 8 In.	290.00
Pitcher, Flower & Basket Design, 7 1/4 In.	145.00
Pitcher, Flower Panels, Striped Blue Ground, 6 x 7 1/2 In.	315.00
Pitcher, Leaping Fish, 19th Century, 9 In.	175.00
Pitcher, Tree Blossoms, Basketry Base, Turquoise Ground, Pink Interior, 9 In.	480.00
Planter, Putti, Basket, Grand Ducal Majolica Manufactory, Germany, 14 In. _Illus_	700.00
Plaque, Last Supper, France, 12 In.	127.00
Plate, 7 Leaves, Impressed, George Jones, 9 In.	290.00
Plate, Fish, Flowers, Joseph Holdcraft, Impressed, 8 1/4 In.	230.00
Sardine Dish, Cover, Fish On Cover, c.1875, 8 1/2 In.	750.00
Sauceboat, Molded & Overlapping Lettuce Leaves, Pink Veins, Stalk Handle, 8 In.	3450.00
Server, Asparagus, Relief, Curved, 4 Twig Style Feet, Brown Border, 3 x 15 x 8 In.	315.00
Server, Grapes, Piecrust Border, Handles, 3 1/2 x 9 3/4 In.	80.00
Smoking Stand, Black Concertina Player, Continental, c.1900, 7 1/4 In.	405.00
Soup, Dish, Molded Strawberries, Flower Sprigs, Butterfly, Tendril Edge, 9 In.	1380.00
Strawberry Server, Stand, Sugar, Creamer, Mark, George Jones, c.1875, 14 In.	1840.00
Sugar, Cover, Raised Flowers, Basketry Ground, 3 3/4 In.	60.00
Tazza, Lily Pads, Flared Foot, Griffin, Smith & Hill, Pa., 9 5/8 In.	190.00
Teapot, Quail & Chick, Moore Brothers, c.1905, 6 In.	3220.00
Tobacco Jar, Black Man's Head, Majolica, c.1900, 4 1/2 In.	145.00
Tobacco Jar, Cat Playing With Ball, Continental, c.1900, 5 In.	345.00
Tobacco Jar, Elephant, Wearing Smoking Jacket, Continental, c.1900, 6 3/4 In.	460.00
Tobacco Jar, Mother Goose, c.1900, 8 1/2 In.	345.00
Urn, Blue Interior, Brown, Gray & Red Exterior, Footed, Signed, WS&S, c.1880, 10 In.	595.00
Urn, Wedding, Cover, Classical Shape, Square Pedestal, Cherub Finial, 1800s, 19 In.	430.00
Vase, Figural, Tree Trunk, Supported By Bear, Bretby, 13 1/2 In.	1435.00

MALACHITE is a green stone with unusual layers or rings of darker
green shades. It is often polished and used for decorative objects. Most
malachite comes from Siberia or Australia.

Desk Set, Porcelain Lined Inkwell, Marked Asprey, London, 1904, 4 To 6 In., 5 Piece	950.00

MAP 477 MAP, South Carolina

MAPS of all types have been collected for centuries. The earliest known printed maps were made in 1478. The first printed street map showed London in 1559. The first road maps for use by drivers of automobiles were made in 1901. Collectors buy maps that were pages of old books, as well as the multifolded road maps popular in this century.

American Oil, Amoco Map Of Space Mysteries, Window Of Universe, 1958, 18 x 25 In. ...	25.00
Azores, Nautical, Islands, Anchorages, Sayer, Laurie, Whittle, 1794, 24 x 18 In.	310.00
Bermuda, Tribes, Shares Divisions, Engraved, Speed, c.1626, 21 x 13 1/2 In.	7840.00
British Possessions In North America, Matthew Carey, Philadelphia, c.1814, 15 x 17 In. .	290.00
California, San Francisco Bay, Los Angeles, Parke, 1854-1855, 35 x 28 1/2 In.	170.00
Carolinas, Colonial, May River To Albermarle Sound, 1700, 5 x 5 In.	280.00
Carte Des Isle Tonga, France, 1834, 13 1/2 x 9 In.	95.00
Colorado, Continental Divide, Gilpin, 1873, 21 x 20 In.	530.00
Colorado, Utah, Pacific Railroad Surveys, Gunnison, 1855, 23 x 31 1/2 In.	85.00
District Of Columbia, Buildings, Railroad Tracks, 1882, 20 x 13 1/2 In.	100.00
Dutch, Black, White, Engraved, O. Lindeman, Hand Colored, Frame, 13 1/2 x 17 1/2 In. ...	200.00
England, Embroidered, Silk, Round, Leaf Surround, Giltwood Frame, 18 x 22 1/4 In.	175.00
Georgetown, City Of Washington, Johnson & Ward, c.1863, 13 3/4 x 16 1/2 In.	300.00
Globe, Celestial, Constellations, Zodiac, Months, Walnut Stand, 1800, 9 x 16 x 24 In.	1725.00
Globe, Celestial, Mahogany, Bronze Mounted, Stand, Woodward, London, 51 x 32 In.	4830.00
Globe, Celestial, Parchment, 12 Gores, 2 Polar Calottes, Hand Drawn, Eng., 1800s, 6 In. ...	565.00
Globe, Celestial, Turned Wood Base, Cary Of London, 12 In.	1380.00
Globe, Table, Fruitwood Stand, G. Thomas Paris, 4 & 11 In.	385.00
Globe, Table, Terrestrial, Italian, Baroque Style, Multicolored Wooden Base, 25 x 22 In. ..	1093.00
Globe, Terrestrial, Arts & Crafts, Oak Stand, Peerless Co., 12 x 20 In.	315.00
Globe, Terrestrial, Gilman Joslin, Wood Stand, Boston, c.1840, 9 In.	1075.00
Globe, Terrestrial, Gilt Brass Meridian, Bronze Atlas, England, 12 x 23 In.	1150.00
Globe, Terrestrial, Kittenger Co., 1920s, 33 x 17 In.	995.00
Globe, Terrestrial, Louis XV Style, Oak Stand, Cabriole Legs, Replogle, 16 In., Stand	315.00
Globe, Terrestrial, Mahogany Stand, Compass, George & John Cary, 1824, 15 x 40 In.	10200.00
Globe, Terrestrial, On Stand, Late 19th Century, 23 In.	2870.00
Globe, Terrestrial, Turned Wood Base, Cary's New Terrestrial Globe, London, 1829, 15 In.	3335.00
Globe, Wooden Tripod Base, Replogle 10-In. Reference Globe Legend, 10 x 32 1/2 In. ...	1735.00
Hawaiian Islands, Kealakekua Bay, Hogg, c.1784, 13 x 8 1/2 In.	420.00
Illinois, Roads, Railroads, Towns, Villages, Johnson & Ward, 1864, 17 x 23 In.	135.00
Maine State Atlas, J.H. Stuart & Co., Red Bound, Town Views, 1902-1903, 19 x 15 In. ...	430.00
Mississippi & Ohio Rivers, Indian Nations, 1784, 14 x 20 In., 2 Pages	1780.00
Moon, Copper, Engraved, Moon Phases, Mortar Piece, c.1788, 18 x 13 1/4 In.	225.00
Moon, Craters, Engraved, Kircher, c.1664, 13 x 14 1/4 In.	728.00
Natick, Massachusetts, Lithograph, Pendleton's, Boston, 1829, 15 x 13 In.	295.00
Nevada, Humboldt Mountains, Mud Lakes, Beckwith, 1855, 18 x 20 1/2 In.	85.00
Nevada, Utah, Great Salt Lake, Humboldt Range, Beckwith, 1855, 19 x 20 1/2 In.	50.00
North & South Carolina, Towns, Railroads, Johnson & Ward, 1863, 24 x 17 In.	95.00
North America, Color, Time Period, Caribbean, Panama, Burgess, 1853, 8 1/4 x 11 In.	85.00
North America, Engraved, Hand Colored, C. Brightly, Suffolk, Frame, c.1806, 9 x 11 In. ...	345.00
North America, Northwest Passage, Sea Of West, Janvier, 1762, 17 1/2 x 12 In.	476.00
North Carolina, South Carolina, Engraved, Frame, Al Johnson, c.1865, 17 x 24 In.	575.00
North Riding Of Yorkeshire, Willem & Joan Blaeu, Frame, c.1648, 15 x 19 In.	144.00
Northeastern U.S., Canada, Florida & Carolinas Inset, Chambon, 1756, 23 x 32 In.	2300.00
Ohio, Ohio River Bridge, Waterfront, Industrial, Business, T.R. Davis, 1872, 20 x 13 In. ...	170.00
Ohio, Wall, 9 Sheets, 11 Counties, 1807, 23 x 22 1/2 In.	1232.00
Palestine, Hand Drawn, American Sunday School Union, Phila., Early 1900s, 58 x 36 In. .	155.00
Scotland, Herman Moll, North Part Of Britain Called Scotland, Frame, 1714, 25 x 42 In. ..	460.00
Scotland, Northern, Shetland Islands, Pinkerton, c.1811, 28 x 20 In.	365.00
Scotland, Orkney Islands, Compass Rose, 4 Distance Scales, Tirion, c.1780, 14 x 12 In. ...	215.00
South Atlantic, South America, Africa, Islands, Imray, 1881, 49 x 40 In.	110.00
South Carolina, Abbeville District, Engraved, Frame, Robert Mills, c.1820, 19 x 24 In. ...	748.00
South Carolina, Kershaw District, Robert Mills, c.1825, 18 1/2 x 22 3/4 In.	604.00
South Carolina, Lexington District, Engraved, Frame, Robert Mills, c.1820, 20 x 24 In. ...	518.00
South Carolina, Newberry District, Engraved, Frame, Robert Mills, 1820, 19 x 26 In.	345.00
South Carolina, Newberry District, Engraved, Frame, Robert Mills, c.1820, 20 x 27 In. ...	345.00
South Carolina, Newberry District, Engraved, Frame, Robert Mills, c.1825, 19 x 19 In. ...	405.00

South Carolina, Print, Colored, Frame, GW & CB Colton, c.1855, 14 x 17 In. 1150.00
South Carolina, Sumter District, Robert Mills, Boykin, Ta˜nner, c.1821, 21 x 16 In. 375.00
United States, Central, Pacific Railroad Surveys, Stevens, 1853-1854, 36 1/2 x 24 1/2 In. . 85.00
United States, Inset Of Gold Region California, Matted, Frame, 1852, 18 x 24 In. 56.00
United States, Midwest, Great Lakes, Rivers, Towns, Forts, c.1812, 9 1/2 x 7 1/2 In. 280.00
United States, Midwest, Mid Atlantic, Early Settlements, Russell, 1794, 18 x 14 1/4 In. .. 670.00
United States, Northeast, Color, Virginia, Maine, VonBergmann, c.1830, 7 x 5 In. 56.00
United States, Oregon Territory, Rivers, Mountains, Indian Areas, 1846, 8 x 10 In. 310.00
United States, Southeast, Villages, Tribes, Rivers, D'Anville, Santini, c.1784, 22 x 19 In. . 896.00
United States, Southern, Color, Railroads, Mitchell, 1871, 13 1/2 x 21 In. 56.00
United States, Western, Pacific Railroad Surveys, Gunnieson, 1855, 23 1/2 x 31 In. 70.00
Wales, Hand Colored, Engraving, Verso With Text, John Speed, c.1676, 15 x 20 In. 750.00
Washington D.C., Delaware, Maryland, Virginia, U.S. Coastal Survey, 1852, 30 x 21 In. .. 220.00
World, 2 Hemispheres, Dutch East India Company, Ships, Crest, c.1705, 18 x 13 1/4 In. .. 615.00
World, 2 Hemispheres, Northwest Passage, Chiquet, 1729, 8 1/2 x 6 1/2 In. 340.00
World, 6 Hemispheres, Australia, New Guinea, New Zealand, DeLeth, c.1739, 26 x 17 In. . 1120.00
World, Mariner, Landmasses, Divided Continents, Ruscelli, 1564, 9 1/2 x 7 In. 728.00
World, Oval, California As Island, Australia, New Zealand, Scherer, c.1700, 13 1/2 x 9 In. . 1790.00

MARBLE collectors pay highest prices for glass and sulphide marbles.
The game of marbles has been popular since the days of the ancient
Romans. American children were able to buy marbles by the mid-
eighteenth century. Dutch glazed clay marbles were least expensive.
Glazed pottery marbles, attributed to the Bennington potteries in Vermont, were of a better quality. Marbles made of pink marble were also
available by the 1830s. Glass marbles seem to have been made later.
By 1880, Samuel C. Dyke of South Akron, Ohio, was making clay
marbles and The National Onyx Marble Company was making marbles of onyx. The Navarre Glass Marble Company of Navarre, Ohio,
and M. B. Mishler of Ravenna, Ohio, made the glass marbles. Ohio
remained the center of the marble industry, and the Akron-made Akro
Agate brand became nationally known. Other pieces made by Akro
Agate are listed in this book in the Akro Agate category. Sulphides are
glass marbles with frosted white figures in the center.

Agate, Flame, Black, Orange, Yellow, Christensen, 3/4 In. 770.00
Agate, Set, Assorted, No. 10, Christensen, Box, 1 1/2 In., 5 Piece 770.00
Akro Agate, Set, Shoot Straight As A Kro Flies, Box, 6 In., 100 Piece 165.00
Bennington, White Base, Green, Blue, Brown, 1 In. 22.00
Blue Base, Coreless, Wide Dark Blue Stripes, Thin White, Green, Blue Stripes, 7/8 In. 110.00
Clambroth, White, Green, Pink, Purple, 7/8 In. 275.00
Clay, Brown, Blue, Unglazed, Various Sizes, Bag, 70 Piece 35.00
English Style Ribbon Swirl, Yellow, Green, Red Inside, Yellow & White Outer, 1 1/2 In. ... 385.00
Golden Rebel, Yellow, Orange, Brown, Machine Made, Peltier Co., 7/8 In. 2200.00
Joseph Swirl, Alternating Colors, Red, Yellow, Orange, Green, 1/2 In. 165.00
Joseph Swirl, Yellow, Orange, Blue, White, Red, Aventurine, 1 1/4 In. 220.00
Latticinio Core Swirl, Green, White Outer Bands, 7/8 In. 440.00
Latticinio Core Swirl, White Core, Red, Green, Blue Bands, White Strands, 2 1/4 In. 155.00
Latticinio Ribbon Swirl, Red & White Ribbon, Yellow Outer Bands, 1 1/2 In. 1540.00
Latticinio Swirl, 3-Stage, White Core, Red & Blue Middle Bands, Yellow Outer, 2 In. 190.00
Latticinio Swirl, White Core, Green, Red, Blue Bands, Ghost Core, 1 7/8 In. 70.00
Latticinio Swirl, White Inside Swirl, Multicolored Stripes, Germany, 1 2/3 In. 55.00
Latticinio Swirl, Yellow Latticinio Core, Green, Red, Blue, White Bands, 2 In. 190.00
Lutz, Black Base Opaque, Blue Lines, 3/4 In. 220.00
Lutz, Cherry Red, Baby Blue, Ribbon, Twist, 1 In. 1870.00
Lutz, Double Cherry Red Ribbon, 1 In. 935.00
Lutz, Green Transparent 3300.00
Lutz, Orange Ribbon, Twist, 1 In. 880.00
Lutz, Type 1, Yellow Bands, 1 3/8 In. 495.00
Lutz, Type I, Orange Band, 7/8 In. 220.00
Lutz, Type II, Green, Transparent, Yellow Bands, 1 1/4 In. 3300.00
Mica, Yellow, Transparent, 7/8 In. 110.00
Mocha Ware, Light Brown, Dark Brown & White Swirls, Early 1800s, 1 In. 77.00
Onion Swirl, Panels Of Blue, White & Orange Yellow, 2 5/16 In. 300.00

Onionskin, 3 Lobes, Mica, White Base, Yellow Overlay, Multicolored Splotches, 1 1/2 In. . 1760.00
Onionskin, 16 Lobes, Red, Yellow, Blue, White, 2 1/4 In. 605.00
Onionskin, Blue & White Spots, Mica, 1 7/8 In. 220.00
Onionskin, Blue, White, Yellow, Orange, Green, 1 1/2 In. 80.00
Onionskin, Clown Style, Multicolored, 1 1/4 In. 495.00
Onionskin, End Of Day, Single Pontil, 2 In. 2970.00
Onionskin, Green Base, White & Lavender Striping, 1 1/2 In. 110.00
Onionskin, Green, Orange, 1 In. 110.00
Onionskin, Mica, Red, White, Blue, 2 1/4 In. 1100.00
Onionskin, Pontil 4400.00
Onionskin Lutz, Yellow, Red, 3/4 In. 220.00
Onionskin With Mica, Pink, Blue & Yellow Spots, 1 27/32 In. 330.00
Peppermint Swirl, Blue, Red, White, 1 1/2 In. 470.00
Ribbon Swirl, Multiple Color Combinations, 2 1/2 In. 635.00
Sulphide, Baby In Basket, Pink Tint, 2 In. 385.00
Sulphide, Duck, 1 1/4 In. 165.00
Sulphide, Eagle, Flying, 1 3/4 In. 220.00
Sulphide, Eagle, Standing, Green, 1 1/2 In. 2860.00
Sulphide, Gnome, Tasseled Cap, 1 3/4 In. 715.00
Sulphide, Grazing Cow, 2 In. . . . . .88.00 to 90.00
Sulphide, Indian Head Penny, c.1859, 1 1/2 In. 2310.00
Sulphide, Lion, 1 1/2 In. 90.00
Sulphide, Monkey Holding Stringed Instrument, 1 1/2 In. 385.00
Sulphide, Seated Dog, 1 9/16 In. 110.00
Sulphide, Seated Rabbit, 1 1/2 In. 104.00
Sulphide, Squatting Boy On Potty, 1 3/4 In. 302.00
Sulphide, Squirrel Eating Nut, Clear, 2 1/2 In. 220.00
Sulphide, Squirrel, c.1880-90, 1 3/4 In. 44.00
Superman, Blue, Orange, Yellow, Peltier Co., 7/8 In. 990.00
Swirl, Divided Center, 1 1/2 In. 58.00
Swirl, Double Ribbon, Yellow & White Outer Strands, Pink, Green, Yellow, 1 3/4 In. 195.00
Transitional, Purple Brown, White Horizontal Swirl, Navarre, 1/4 In. 1210.00

MARBLE CARVINGS, such as large or small figurines, groups of people or animals, and architectural decorations, have been a special art form since the time of the ancient Greeks. Reproductions, especially of large Victorian groups, are being made of a mixture using marble dust. These are very difficult to detect and collectors should be careful. Other carvings are listed under Alabaster.

Altar Crucifix, Gilt Bronze, 3-Sided Base, Busts, Jesus, Joseph, Mary, 19th Century, 44 In. 865.00
Baluster, Alabaster, Late Renaissance Style, Carved, Vase Shape, 25 In., Pair 3450.00
Baptismal Font, 19th Century, 44 In. 635.00
Bowl, Italian Marble, Green, Sergio Asti, c.1972, 4 3/8 x 10 In. 1920.00
Bowl, Italian Marble, Rose, Sergio Asti, Knoll, c.1972, 10 x 17 In. 2700.00
Bust, George Washington, 6 1/2 In. 520.00
Bust, Girl, Grapes & Dove, Carrera White, 19 In. 1380.00
Bust, Marie Antoinette, Inscribed Base, Soc E Faise, France, Late 1800s, 32 In. 2530.00
Bust, Shunammite Woman, Ferdinando Vichi, c.1900, 23 1/2 In. 4200.00
Bust, Woman, Elaborate Dress, Egyptian Revival Style, 1900s, 10 In. 175.00
Bust, Woman, Upswept Hair, Draped Shoulders, Round Base, 25 1/2 In. 430.00
Bust, Young Man, Robe Draped Shoulders, Round Base, 22 In. 115.00
Bust, Young Woman, Continental, G. Herrmann, c.1919, 23 In. 1610.00
Column, Gilt Bronze Mounted, Red, Languedoc Marble Base, 17 x 5 x 5 In. 290.00
Column, Roman Patrician, Tour, Siena, Commemorative, Bronze, 20 x 8 x 8 In. 2300.00
Garniture, Ormolu, Woman On Marble Case, Marked, A. Bureau, 25 In., 3 Piece 750.00
Group, Woman, Dog, Alfredo Morelli, Early 1900s, 27 1/2 In. 3900.00
Obelisk, Figured, Torquay, Louis XVI Style, 10 1/2 In. 259.00
Onyx, Double S-Scroll Handle, Griffin Shape, Pedestal Base, 19th Century 645.00
Pedestal, Alabaster, Column, 38 In., Pair 540.00
Pedestal, Column, Green, 42 In. . . . . .510.00 to 960.00
Pedestal, Green, Continental, 34 1/2 In. 150.00
Pedestal, Mottled Brown, Continental, 38 1/2 In. 345.00
Picture, Abstract Still Life, Fruit, Marble Frame, Italy, 20th Century, 8 x 10 In. 130.00

Plaque, Young Woman, Relief Carved, c.1890, 8 1/4 In. 145.00
Statue, Athlete, White, Italy, 37 In. 1920.00
Statue, Civil War Soldier, Kepi, Cape, Sword, 3/4 Length, 6 In. 1035.00
Statue, Dancing Girl, Chinese, Early 20th Century, 30 In. 4400.00
Statue, Dove, Standing, Folding Wings, Wood Base, 10 1/2 x 10 1/2 x 5 In. 5100.00
Statue, Girl Reading Book, Italy, c.1900, 16 1/2 In. 690.00
Statue, Girl With A Basket, Carrara, 31 In. 5060.00
Statue, Indian Woman In Dugout Canoe, 1800s, 17 In. 7800.00
Statue, Lady Reclining, Holding Beads, 23 x 20 In. 4115.00
Statue, Lorenzo De' Medici, After Michelangelo, Continental, 1900s, 20 In. 865.00
Statue, Male Torso, Tuscany, 19th Century, 13 x 8 x 4 In. 1895.00
Statue, Priest Saint, Holding Monstrance, Full Round, Italy, c.1920, 72 In. 1840.00
Statue, Venus Italica, After Antonio Canova, Italy, 44 In. 8365.00
Statue, Woman, Nude, Seaside, Turquoise Belt, Bracelets, Italy, c.1900, 19 In. 2530.00
Statue, Young Girl, Tree Stump, Frederick John Williamson, c.1875, 41 In. 5100.00
Tray, Italian Marble, Gray, Sergio Asti, Knoll, c.1972, 2 x 13 3/4 In. 2280.00
Urn, Bronze Mounted, Flared Rim, Scroll Handle, Continental, 15 1/2 In. 230.00
Urn, Cover, Louis XVI Style, Gilt Bronze Mounts, c.1900, 18 In., Pair 3600.00
Urn, Cover, Louis XVI Style, Gilt Bronze Mounts, c.1900, 19 3/4 In., Pair 4800.00
Urn, Mantle, Gray, White Striations, Ormolu, Gilded Spelter, 17 1/2 In., Pair 489.00
Urn, Ormolu Mounted, Mottled, Red, Flower Rim, Scrolling Leaves, 14 x 11 In. 403.00
Urn, Oval, Flared Brass Rim, Scroll Base, Ormolu Mounted, 15 In. 375.00
Urn, Turned, Satin Polished, 20 1/2 In. 403.00
Vase, Alabaster, Urn Shape, Scalloped Rim, Neoclassical, Late 1800s, 28 In. 323.00

MARBLEHEAD Pottery was founded in 1905 by Dr. J. Hall as a reha-
bilitative program for the patients of a Marblehead, Massachusetts,
sanitarium. Two years later it was separated from the sanitarium and it
continued operations until 1936. Many of the pieces were decorated
with marine motifs.

Basket, Hanging, Blue Matte Glaze, Cylindrical, Paper Label, Impressed Mark, 6 In. 205.00
Basket, Hanging, Lavender Matte Glaze, 4 1/2 In. 4700.00
Bookends, Ship, Molded, Blue Matte Glaze, Paper Label, Impressed, 6 In., Pair 1295.00
Bowl, Blue Matte Glaze, 6 In. 205.00
Bowl, Blue Matte Glaze, Flared, 7 1/2 In. 294.00
Bowl, Blue Matte Glaze, Flared, Impressed Mark, 4 In. 325.00
Bowl, Blue Matte Glaze, Paper Label, Impressed Mark, 3 In. 325.00
Bowl, Gray & Blue Matte Glaze, Impressed Mark, 6 1/4 In. 206.00
Bowl, Gray Matte Glaze, Blue Speckles, Light Gray Interior, Ship Mark, 3 x 6 3/4 In. 200.00
Bowl, Gray Matte Glaze, Low Form, Impressed Mark, 6 In. 205.00
Bowl, Green Matte Glaze, 2 1/8 x 4 1/8 In. 240.00
Bowl, Green Matte Glaze, Impressed Mark, 4 1/4 In. 235.00
Bowl, Lavender Matte Glaze, Low Form, Impressed Mark, 6 In. 205.00
Bowl, Mustard Yellow Matte Glaze, Low Form, Impressed Mark, 6 In. 265.00
Bowl, Yellow Matte Glaze, Impressed Mark, 4 1/2 In., Pair 350.00
Bowl, Yellow Matte Glaze, Tapered, Impressed Mark, 9 In. 355.00
Candlestick, Scrolled Handles, 4 In. 81.00
Chamberstick, Green Matte Glaze, Low, 6 In. 470.00
Jar, Cover, Blue Matte Glaze, Broad Form, Impressed Mark, 5 In. 295.00
Tile, Ship, Blue, White, Matte Glaze, Arts & Crafts Oak Frame, Square, 5 3/4 In. 2235.00
Tile, Tall Ship, Blue, Green, Unglazed Outline, Round, 6 In. 1410.00
Tile, Trees, Potted, Green, Brown, Blue, Square, 6 1/4 In. 2705.00
Vase, Blue & Charcoal Matte Glaze, Textured, Waisted, Flared, Impressed, 10 In. 470.00
Vase, Blue Matte Glaze, Chicory Blue Interior, Squat, Ship Mark, 3 1/4 x 5 1/4 In. 300.00
Vase, Blue Matte Glaze, Cylindrical, Impressed Mark, 3 In. 265.00
Vase, Blue Matte Glaze, Cylindrical, Paper Label, Impressed Mark, 3 1/2 In. 295.00
Vase, Blue Matte Glaze, Fan Form, Impressed Mark, 5 3/4 In. 205.00
Vase, Blue Matte Glaze, Flared, Impressed Mark, 2 1/2 In. 265.00
Vase, Blue Matte Glaze, Flattened, Flared, Impressed Mark, 6 In. 205.00
Vase, Blue Matte Glaze, Insert, Impressed Mark, 4 In. 380.00
Vase, Blue Matte Glaze, Low Form, Impressed Mark, 1 3/4 In. 295.00
Vase, Blue Matte Glaze, Marked, 3 In. 265.00

Vase, Blue Matte Glaze, Ribbed Panels, Flared, Impressed Mark, 6 In. 410.00
Vase, Blue Matte Glaze, Shouldered, Impressed Mark, 9 In. 765.00
Vase, Blue Matte Glaze, Slender Form, Impressed Mark, 4 1/2 In. 355.00
Vase, Blue Matte Glaze, Slender Form, Impressed Mark, 6 In. 410.00
Vase, Blue Matte Glaze, Tapered, Broad Base, Impressed Mark, 6 1/4 In. 410.00
Vase, Blue Matte Glaze, Tapered, Impressed Mark, 3 1/2 In. 325.00
Vase, Blue Matte Glaze, Tapered, Impressed Mark, 5 In. 295.00
Vase, Blue Matte Glaze, Tapered, Impressed Mark, 9 1/2 In. 765.00
Vase, Brown Matte Glaze, Tapered, Cylindrical, Impressed Mark, 5 In. 350.00
Vase, Brown Matte Glaze, Tapered, Impressed Mark, 3 1/2 In. 325.00
Vase, Cobalt Blue Matte Glaze, Speckled, Teal Interior, Oval, Ship Mark, 6 x 5 In. 500.00
Vase, Dark Blue Matte Glaze, Tapered, Impressed Mark, 4 1/2 In. 355.00
Vase, Dark Gray Matte Glaze, Tapered, Impressed Mark, 3 3/4 In. 295.00
Vase, Flowers, Leaves, Lavender Ground, Bulbous, 3 3/4 x 4 1/2 In. 2000.00
Vase, Flowers, Leaves, Speckled Gray Ground, Barrel, Hannah Tutt, 4 1/4 x 4 In. 3820.00
Vase, Grape Vines, Stylized, Egg Shape, 7 x 4 In. 4113.00
Vase, Gray Matte Glaze, Candleholder, Bulbous, 4 1/2 In. 881.00
Vase, Gray Matte Glaze, Cylindrical, Squat, Impressed Mark, 4 In. 353.00
Vase, Gray Matte Glaze, Flared, Impressed Mark, 3 3/4 In. 265.00
Vase, Gray Matte Glaze, Slender Form, Impressed Mark, 4 1/2 In. 325.00
Vase, Gray Matte Glaze, Slender Form, Impressed Mark, 6 In. 530.00
Vase, Gray Matte Glaze, Tear Shape, 6 In. 705.00
Vase, Gray Matte, Purple Glaze, Cylindrical, 10 In. 1293.00
Vase, Gray, Purple Matte Glaze, Broad Shape, 5 1/2 In. 1495.00
Vase, Green & Brown Matte, Tapered, 5 In. 345.00
Vase, Green Glaze, Swollen Cylindrical Form, Ship Cipher On Base, 5 3/8 In. 470.00
Vase, Green Leaves, Blue Matte Ground, Egg Shape, Arthur Baggs, 6 3/4 x 4 In. 1528.00
Vase, Green Matte Glaze, Bulbous, Impressed Mark, 3 1/4 In. 355.00
Vase, Green Matte Glaze, Cylindrical, Impressed Mark, 3 1/2 In. 440.00
Vase, Green Matte Glaze, Handles, Impressed Mark, 2 In. 825.00
Vase, Green Matte Glaze, Impressed Mark, 5 In. 350.00
Vase, Green Matte Glaze, Impressed Mark, 7 1/2 In. 3760.00
Vase, Green Matte Glaze, Low Form, Impressed Mark, 9 In. Diam. 235.00
Vase, Green Matte Glaze, Petals, Incised, Vine Tendril, Carmel, Ship Mark, 4 x 3 In. 3000.00
Vase, Green Matte Glaze, Shouldered, Flared Rim, Impressed Mark, 4 1/2 In. 410.00
Vase, Green Matte Glaze, Slender, Impressed Mark, 4 1/2 In. 380.00
Vase, Green Matte Glaze, Tapered, Impressed Mark, 3 1/2 In. 410.00
Vase, Green Matte Glaze, Tapered, Impressed Mark, 4 1/2 In. 355.00
Vase, Green Matte Glaze, Tapered, Impressed Mark, 5 1/4 In. 650.00
Vase, Green Matte Glaze, Tapered, Impressed Mark, 6 In. .325.00 to 560.00
Vase, Indigo Matte Glaze, Bulbous, 3 3/4 In. 450.00
Vase, Lavender Matte Glaze, Bulbous, Impressed Mark, 3 1/2 In. 265.00
Vase, Lavender Matte Glaze, Tapered, Broad Base, Impressed Mark, 6 1/4 In. 440.00
Vase, Lemon Trees, Gray Matte Glaze, Tapered, 4 1/2 In. 2940.00
Vase, Metallic Glaze, Tapered, Slender Form, Impressed Mark, 5 In. 470.00
Vase, Mottled Brown & Orange Matte Glaze, Tapered, Impressed Mark, 5 In. 355.00
Vase, Mottled Gray Green, Dark Gray, Signed, Hannah Tutt, c.1910, 4 x 2 In. 2875.00
Vase, Mottled Gray Matte Glaze, Slender Form, Impressed Mark, 9 In. 295.00
Vase, Mottled Green Glaze, Broad, Impressed Mark, 4 In. 470.00
Vase, Mottled Orange & Tan Matte Glaze, Impressed Mark, 4 In. 325.00
Vase, Parrots, Gray Matte Glaze, Blue, White, Marked, 1911, 12 In. 4400.00
Vase, Purple Matte Glaze, 5 1/4 In. 645.00
Vase, Purple Matte Glaze, Bulbous, 6 1/2 In. 410.00
Vase, Purple Matte Glaze, Slender, Impressed Mark, 6 In. 380.00
Vase, Purple, Blue, Mottled, Matte Glaze, Egg Shape, 6 1/4 In. 560.00
Vase, Rose Matte Glaze, Speckled, Pinched Waist, White Interior, Ship Mark, 7 x 3 In. 450.00
Vase, Roses, Yellow, Blue Ground, Impressed Mark, 5 1/2 In. 3175.00
Vase, Stylized Grape Leaves, Tall Stems, Berries, Impressed Ship Cipher, 4 3/4 In. 5875.00
Vase, Stylized Pattern, Squat, Green, MT, 2 1/4 x 4 1/2 In. 4405.00
Vase, Textured Gray Matte Glaze, Flared, Impressed Mark, 5 In. 410.00
Vase, Turquoise High Glaze, Flared, Impressed Mark, 4 1/2 In. 205.00
Vase, Yellow Matte Glaze, Broad Form, Impressed Mark, 4 1/4 In. 355.00

Vase, Yellow Matte Glaze, Bulbous, Impressed Mark, 3 1/4 In.	470.00
Vase, Yellow Matte Glaze, Tapered, Broad Base, Impressed Mark, 6 1/4 In.	765.00
Wall Pocket, Blue Matte Glaze, Broad Form, Impressed Mark, 5 In.	205.00
Wall Pocket, Blue Matte Glaze, Paper Label, 6 In.	175.00
Wall Pocket, Brown Matte Glaze, Ribs, Impressed Mark, 5 1/4 In.	230.00

MARTIN BROTHERS of Middlesex, England, made Martinware, a salt-glazed stoneware, between 1873 and 1915. Many figural jugs and vases were made by the three brothers. Of special interest are the fanciful birds, usually made with removable heads.

Figure, Bird, Stoneware, c.1913, 9 In.	28680.00
Grotesque Creature, Crouching, London, 1898, 8 In.	9600.00
Jar, Cover, Bird, Stoneware, 1890	4445.00
Jug, Smiling Faces, Wavy Manes, Mottled Glaze, Brown, c.1890, 11 In.	1900.00
Pitcher, Face In Relief On Both Sides, Handles, Incised Mark, 8 In.	7050.00
Vase, Flowers, Mottled Tan, Brown Glaze, 2 Handles, 9 In.	825.00
Vase, Stoneware, 1892	12225.00

MARY GREGORY is the name used for a type of glass that is easily identified. White figures were painted on clear or colored glass as the decoration. The figures chosen were usually children at play. The first glass known as Mary Gregory was made about 1870. Similar glass is made even today. The traditional story has been that the glass was made at the Sandwich Glass works in Boston by a woman named Mary Gregory. Recent research suggests that it is possible that none was made at Sandwich. In general, all-white figures were used in the United States, tinted faces were probably used in Bohemia, France, Italy, Germany, Switzerland, and England. Children standing, not playing, were pictured after the 1950s.

Box, Hinged Cover, Baby Thumbprint Pattern, Cranberry, Enameled, 3 In.	115.00
Cologne Bottle, Boy Carrying Balloon, Blue, 6 In.	205.00
Decanter, Stopper, Boy Holding Stick, 9 In.	105.00
Jewelry Box, Children Fishing, Blue, Brass Mounts, 4 1/2 x 3 x 5 In.	450.00
Mug, Girl Holding Flower, Cranberry, 3 1/4 In.	135.00
Pill Box, Girl Holding Flower, Cobalt Blue, 2 In.	235.00
Pitcher, Boy Sitting In Tree, Green, 10 In.	195.00
Pitcher, Girl Walking Along Country Road, Amber, 10 1/4 In.	220.00
Pitcher, Woman Holding Staff, Lime Green, 10 In.	185.00
Scent Bottle, Dancing Fairy, Amethyst, Ball Stopper, 4 1/2 & 5 1/2 In., Pair	50.00
Tumbler, Boy With Hands In Pockets, Cranberry, 3 1/2 In.	75.00
Tumbler, Girl With Sprinkling Can, Cranberry	85.00
Tumbler, Gnome & Butterfly, Amber, 6 1/2 In.	70.00
Vase, Boy Blowing Dandelion Seeds, Cobalt Blue, Brass Base, 3 3/4 In.	265.00
Vase, Boy Holding Flower, Cranberry, 5 In.	155.00
Vase, Garniture, Cobalt Blue, 13 1/2 In.	400.00

MASON'S IRONSTONE was made by the English pottery of Charles J. Mason after 1813. Mason, of Lane Delph, was given a patent for this improved earthenware. He usually called it "Mason's Patent Ironstone China." It resisted chipping and breaking so it became popular for dinnerwares and other table service dishes. Vases and other decorative pieces were also made. The ironstone was decorated with orange, blue, gold, and other colors, often in Japanese inspired designs. The firm had financial difficulties but the molds and the name Mason were used by many owners through the years, including Francis Morley, Taylor Ashworth, George L. Ashworth, and John Shaw. Mason's joined the Wedgwood group in 1973 and the name is still found on dinnerwares.

Jug, Octagonal, Dragon Handle, Japanese Style Flowers & Leaves, c.1850, 8 In.	471.00
Mug, Cylindrical, Printed, Painted, Blue Underglaze, Iron Red, Green, 5 In.	200.00
Platter, Meat, Flowers, 18 x 14 1/2 In.	230.00

MASONIC, see Fraternal category.

MASSIER, a French art pottery, was made by brothers Jerome, Delphin, and Clement Massier in Vallauris and Golfe-Juan, France, in the late nineteenth and early twentieth centuries. It has an iridescent metallic luster glaze that resembles the Weller Sicardo pottery glaze. Most pieces are marked *J. Massier*.

J.Massier fils

Tile, 3 Insects, Iridescent, 3 1/2 x 4 In.	235.00
Vase, 3 Twisted Women, Green To Mauve, Art Nouveau, 19 In.	2350.00
Vase, Brown & Tan Drip Over Ivory & Blue Matte Ground, Tapered, Marked, 8 In.	175.00
Vase, Brown, Tan Drip, Ivory, Blue Matte, Tapered, 8 In.	150.00
Vase, Bulbous, Gourd Shape, Handles, Butterflies, Green, Pink Ground, 7 In.	345.00
Vase, Iridescent, Classic Baluster Shape, Flared Rim, 5 In.	450.00
Vase, Luster Glazed, Earthenware, Figural, c.1900, 8 1/4 x 15 1/2 In.	2390.00
Vase, Organic Form, 4 Handles, Iridescent Green, Red Glaze, Signed, 2 1/2 In.	295.00
Vase, Parakeets, Budding Branches, Early 1900s, 12 1/2 In., Pair	460.00
Vase, Silver Overlaid, Luster Glazed, Earthenware, c.1900, 8 1/2 In.	1675.00

MATCH HOLDERS were made to hold the large wooden matches that were used in the nineteenth and twentieth centuries for a variety of purposes. The kitchen stove and the fireplace or furnace had to be lit regularly. One type of match holder was made to hang on the wall, another was designed to be kept on a tabletop. Of special interest today are match holders that have advertisements as part of the design.

Adriance Farm Machinery, Corn Binder Machine, Tin Lithograph, 5 x 3 3/8 In.	300.00
Atlantic Ale Beer, Full Of Good Cheer, Black Waiter, Matchbook	20.00
Blue Flowers, Cone Shape, Rope Twist Striking Surface, Stoneware, 2 5/8 x 4 In.	90.00
Box, Skull, E. Bohne & Sohne, Porcelain, 3 1/4 In.	300.00
Brass, Boot, Ladies', Easel Back, 6 1/2 x 6 1/2 In., Pair	40.00
Burl, 2 Cup-Shaped Holders On Plaque, Incised Rings, Cutout Crest, 8 3/8 In.	115.00
Burl, Upside Down Heart Shape Hole, 2 Receptacles, 1800s, 5 x 4 In.	530.00
C. Parker, Cast Iron, 1869, 6 In.	95.00
Dead Game, Shotgun, Cast Iron, 11 In.	220.00
Devil's Head, Germany, Porcelain, 2 In.	115.00
Dockash Stove Factory, Tin Lithograph, 5 In.	45.00
Dr Pepper, 10-2-4 Logo, Green, Tin, 1940s, 6 x 3 1/4 In.	185.00
Dr Pepper, Wall, Drink A Bite Today, Green, Tin, 1940s, 6 x 3 1/4 In.	185.00
Dr. Shoop's Health Coffee, Tin Lithograph, 5 In.	460.00
Dr. Shoop's Lax-Ets, Candy Bowel Laxative, Tin, 4 3/4 x 3 1/4 In.	360.00
Dutch Boy Kid Shape, Die Cut, Tin Lithograph, 6 1/2 x 4 In.	330.00
Log Cabin, Cast Iron, 4 x 2 1/2 In.	120.00
Pioneers, Man Standing With Gun, Cast Iron, 4 x 4 1/2 In.	66.00
Wrigley, Juicy Fruit, Man, Red, White, Black, Tin Lithograph, 5 In.	445.00

MATCH SAFES were designed to be carried in the pocket. Early matches were made with phosphorus and could ignite unexpectedly. The matches were safely stored in the tightly closed container. Match safes were made in sterling silver, plated silver, or other metals. The English call these *vesta boxes*.

Anheuser-Busch, Eagle, Silver Plate, 2-Sided, 3 x 1 1/2 In.	300.00
Automobile Design, Art Nouveau Border	1650.00
Bowling, Smoking Man, Silver, Striker, Germany, 2 1/2 x 1 1/2 In.	295.00
Flowers, Repousse, Sterling Silver, c.1900	165.00
Luden's Cough Drops, Menthol, 1 1/2 x 2 3/4 In.	300.00
Man In The Moon, Glass Eyes, Brass, 2 x 1 In.	210.00
Owl, Figural, Brass	110.00
Ridges & Cartouche, German 800 Silver, c.1895	55.00
Salt Glaze, Diamond, Blue Band, Impressed, Stoneware, 3 In.	175.00
Salt Glaze, Matches, 3 Blue Bands, Stoneware, 4 3/4 In.	385.00
Snake, Figural, Brass, Glass Eyes	660.00
Trojan Explosives & Chemicals, Tin, Bronze Finish, 1 1/2 x 2 1/4 In.	600.00
Violin, Silver Plate Over Brass, Striker, 2 3/4 x 1 In.	200.00
Woman, Scrolling Flowers, Sterling Silver, Art Nouveau, c.1900	660.00

MATT MORGAN, an English artist, was making pottery in Cincinnati, Ohio, by 1883. His pieces were decorated to resemble Moorish wares. Incised designs and colors were applied to raised panels on the pottery. Shiny or matte glazes were used. The company lasted less than two years.

Vase, Swallows, Bamboo Sheets, Green, Orange, Gilt, 7 3/4 In. 460.00

MCCOY pottery was made in Roseville, Ohio. Nelson McCoy and J.W. McCoy established the Nelson McCoy Sanitary and Stoneware Company in Roseville, Ohio, in 1910. The firm made art pottery after 1926. In 1933 it became the Nelson McCoy Pottery Company. Pieces marked *McCoy* were made by the Nelson McCoy Pottery Company. Cookie jars were made from about 1940 until December 1990, when the McCoy factory closed. Since 1991 pottery with the McCoy mark has been made by firms unrelated to the original company. Because there was a company named Brush-McCoy, there is great confusion between Brush and Nelson McCoy pieces. See Brush category for more information.

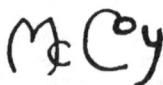

Bowl, Flower Frog, 2 x 4 1/2 In.	264.00
Bowl, Molded Fern, Green Matte, Footed, 4 x 7 1/4 In.	161.00
Cookie Jar, Bananas	125.00
Cookie Jar, Barnum's Animals	325.00
Cookie Jar, Bear, Cookie In Vest	10.00 to 15.00
Cookie Jar, Boy On Baseball	175.00
Cookie Jar, Chipmunk	135.00
Cookie Jar, Christmas Tree	300.00
Cookie Jar, Circus Horse	65.00
Cookie Jar, Clown Bust	45.00 to 55.00
Cookie Jar, Coalby Cat	155.00
Cookie Jar, Coffee Grinder	20.00
Cookie Jar, Cook Stove, White	15.00
Cookie Jar, Cookie Bank	65.00
Cookie Jar, Cookie House	85.00
Cookie Jar, Cookie Jug, Green	15.00
Cookie Jar, Cookie Safe	25.00
Cookie Jar, Covered Wagon	75.00
Cookie Jar, Dutch Boy	25.00
Cookie Jar, Dutch Girl	70.00
Cookie Jar, Dutch Treat Barn	40.00
Cookie Jar, Ear Of Corn	20.00
Cookie Jar, Early American Frontier Family	10.00
Cookie Jar, Engine, Black	35.00
Cookie Jar, Engine, Yellow	50.00
Cookie Jar, Fortune Cookie	20.00
Cookie Jar, Fox Squirrel	4000.00
Cookie Jar, Globe	95.00
Cookie Jar, Hobby Horse	125.00
Cookie Jar, Indian Head	633.00
Cookie Jar, Kangaroo, Blue	35.00
Cookie Jar, Kangaroo, Tan	55.00
Cookie Jar, Kissing Penguins	25.00
Cookie Jar, Kittens On Ball Of Yarn	75.00

Never try to dry a piece of marble with a hair dryer.

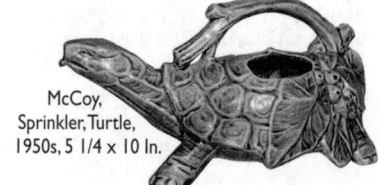

McCoy,
Sprinkler, Turtle,
1950s, 5 1/4 x 10 In.

Cookie Jar, Koala Bear	30.00
Cookie Jar, Lemon	25.00
Cookie Jar, Leprechaun, Brown	2400.00
Cookie Jar, Mac, Dog	95.00
Cookie Jar, Mammy With Cauliflower	295.00
Cookie Jar, Monk	50.00
Cookie Jar, Monkey On Stump	45.00
Cookie Jar, Orange	25.00
Cookie Jar, Pears On Basketweave	25.00
Cookie Jar, Pirates Chest, Gold	30.00
Cookie Jar, Pontiac Indian	425.00
Cookie Jar, Raggedy Ann	65.00
Cookie Jar, Sad Clown	25.00 to 95.00
Cookie Jar, Spaceship, Friendship 7	35.00 to 45.00
Cookie Jar, Stove, Black	5.00
Cookie Jar, Strawberrry, White	30.00
Cookie Jar, Teepee	185.00 to 403.00
Cookie Jar, Touring Car	30.00 to 35.00
Cookie Jar, Traffic Light	35.00
Cookie Jar, Turkey, Green & Brown	565.00
Cookie Jar, Windmill, Blue	35.00
Cookie Jar, Woodsy Owl	105.00
Cookie Jar, Yellow Mouse	10.00
Flowerpot, Zebra, 1956, 9 In.	392.00
Food Warmer, Chuck Wagon, Brass Frame, El Rancho, 1960s	248.00
Pitcher, Buccaneer	10.00
Planter, Monkey Face, 5 1/4 In.	40.00
Planter, Scottie, 8 In.	25.00
Sprinkler, Turtle, 1950s, 5 1/4 x 10 In.	*Illus* 60.00
Umbrella Stand, Brown Glaze, Painted, Water Lilies, 21 1/2 In.	206.00
Vase, Cabinet, Majolica, Flowers, Brown Ground, 4 1/4 In.	69.00
Vase, Green Matte, Tapered, Vertical Bands, Raised Edge, 8 1/4 In.	115.00

MCKEE is a name associated with various glass enterprises in the United States since 1836, including J. & F. McKee (1850), Bryce, McKee & Co. (1850 to 1854), McKee and Brothers (1865), and National Glass Co. (1899). In 1903, the McKee Glass Company was formed in Jeannette, Pennsylvania. It became McKee Division of the Thatcher Glass Co. in 1951 and was bought out by the Jeannette Corporation in 1961. Pressed glass, kitchenwares, and tablewares were produced. Jeannette Corporation closed in the early 1980s. Additional pieces may be included in the Custard Glass category.

Canister, Tea, Jadite, 48 Oz., 5 3/4 In.	220.00
Ink Blotter, Scottie, Jadite, 3 1/2 x 2 In.	105.00
Refrigerator Dish, Jadite, 3 x 10 x 5 In.	95.00

MECHANICAL BANKS are listed in the Bank category.

MEDICAL office furniture, operating tools, microscopes, thermometers, and other paraphernalia used by doctors are included in this category. Veterinary collectibles are also included here. Medicine bottles are listed in the Bottle category. There are related collectibles listed under Dental.

Bleeding Bowl, Pewter, Tapered Sides, Pierced Handle, 5 1/4 In.	2468.00
Blood Coagulator, Campbell, Type CA, No. 2738, 4 Bakelite Terminals, 45 In.	588.00
Bottle, Radam's Microbe Killer, Germ Bacteria, Red, Amber, Man, Skeleton, 11 In.	614.00
Brace, Trepanation, Surgeon's, C.P. Pilling & Son, Philadelphia, Case, 10 In.	660.00
Cabinet, Apothecary, 6 Drawers, Black, Ring Pulls, Chinese, 16 1/2 x 18 x 26 In.	230.00
Cabinet, Apothecary, 6 Drawers, Poplar, Gray Painted, 21 x 6 x 12 In.	865.00
Cabinet, Apothecary, 12 Drawers, Hung Mu, Brass, Paneled Front, Chinese, 17 x 14 In.	980.00
Cabinet, Apothecary, 14 Drawers, Mahogany, England, 19th Century, 29 x 25 In.	2070.00
Cabinet, Apothecary, 15 Drawers, Walnut, Cove Molded, Square Nails, 39 x 32 In.	2645.00
Cabinet, Apothecary, 21 Drawers, Pine, 3 Shelves, 68 x 38 In.	2590.00

Cabinet, Apothecary, 25 Drawers, Salmon, Mustard Over Red Paint, 41 x 72 1/4 In. 15950.00
Cabinet, Apothecary, 25 Short & 9 Large Drawers, 3 Bins, Pine, 79 x 57 x 20 In. 1150.00
Cabinet, Apothecary, 27 Drawers, Red Paint, 1800s, 45 x 48 In. 2300.00
Cabinet, Apothecary, Black Paint, American, c.1750, 71 x 40 x 16 In. 7170.00
Cabinet, Apothecary, Curly Maple, Asia, Mid 1800s, 46 x 30 x 22 In. 1035.00
Cabinet, Apothecary, Pine, 2 Piece, Open Top, 9 Drawers, 1800s, 84 x 79 x 21 In. 7500.00
Cabinet, Apothecary, Pine, Green Paint, 30 Drawers, 87 x 44 In. 3175.00
Cabinet, Doctor's Office, Glass Doors, 4 Sides, 6 Drawers, 1894 .... 4990.00
Cabinet, Metal, Gallery, Drawers, Mediterranean, 37 x 27 x 18 In. 59.00
Cabinet, Pharmacist's, Oak, Cast Iron Sides, 3 Drawers 585.00
Cabinet, Specimen, Pine, 7 Drawers, 21 x 19 x 14 In. 230.00
Cabinet, Sterilizer, Glazed Oak, Wire Trays, Plaque, Erie City Mfg. Co., 13 In. 206.00
Carboy, Pharmacy, Blown Glass, Clear, Oval, 2 Tiers, 19th Century, 25 In. 380.00
Chair, Birthing, Elm, Early 20th Century, 28 1/2 In.... .... 80.00
Chair, Invalid's, 3 Wheels, Grain Painted, Stencil, Mass., c.1845, 37 x 14 In. 3055.00
Chest, Apothecary, 12 Drawers, New England 3800.00
Chest, Apothecary, Box, Pine, Blue Green, 13 Bottles, 1800s, 8 1/2 x 17 x 10 1/2 In. 1410.00
Eyebath, Silver Plate, Pedestal, Detachable Bowl, 2 In. 335.00
Eyecup, Clear Glass Bowl, Rubber Bulb, England, 3 In. 80.00
Eyecup, Cobalt Blue, Molded Pedestal, Curved Ribs, 2 1/4 In. 245.00
Eyecup, Free-Blown Glass, Upturned Corners, Circular Foot, Emerald Green, 2 3/4 In. ... 49.00
Eyecup, Free-Blown, Clear Glass, Stubby Stem, England, 2 1/4 In. 100.00
Eyecup, Free-Blown, Cobalt Blue, Pontil Base, 3 3/4 In. 410.00
Eyecup, Free-Blown, Emerald Green, Pedestal, 2 1/2 In. 90.00
Eyecup, Free-Blown, Short Stem, Circular Foot, Ground Pontil Base, Amber, 1 3/4 In. 215.00
Eyecup, Free-Blown, Straight Stem, Circular Foot, Cobalt Blue, England, 2 3/4 In. 40.00
Eyecup, Free-Blown, Turquoise Blue, Upturned Corners, Knopped Stem, 2 3/4 In. 285.00
Eyecup, Free-Blown, Turquoise, Turned-In Rim, Knopped Stem, Circular Foot, 2 1/2 In. .. 450.00
Eyecup, Free-Blown, Upturned Corners, Knopped Stem, Circular Foot, Cobalt Blue, 3 In. .. 35.00
Eyecup, Glass, Ground Rim, Short Stem, Circular Foot, Amber, England, 2 1/4 In. 90.00
Eyecup, Glass, Petits, Eye Water, Howard Bros., Chemical Co., Buffalo, N.Y., 1 1/4 In. ... 39.00
Eyecup, Red, Rubber, Box, 1 1/2 In. 859.00
Eyecup, Rubber, Red, Unstemmed, W, Raised Letters, 1 1/2 In. 90.00
Inhaler, Maws, Earthenware, Double Valve, Flowers, No Mouthpiece, 8 3/4 In. 29.00
Leech Jar, Baluster Form, Acorn Finial, Black Lettering, Pierced Lid, Creamware, 17 In. .. 7640.00
Leech Jar, Creamware, Baluster Shape, Black Letters, Pierced Lid, Acorn Finial, 17 In. .. 7640.00
Leech Jar, White, Blue, Applied Handles, Perforated Lid, 7 1/2 In. 4690.00
Map Of The Human System, Smith's, American Manikin Company, c.1888, 44 x 40 In. 748.00
Model Eye, Wood, Biological Model Of Eye, Welch Scientific, 12 In. 470.00
Model Heart, Wood, Biological Parts, Southwestern Indiana Heart Association, 15 In. 300.00
Mortician Bench, Oak, Metal Trim, Collapsible, Portable, 37 x 19 In. Folded Up 40.00
Nasal Douche, Iglodine, Patented, White Glaze, Black Print, England, 2 1/4 In. 49.00
Ointment Pot, Good Samaritan, Samuel Morecroft, Armitage, Stafford, 1 1/2 In. 765.00
Saw, Amputation, Iron Frame, Tooled Side, Arnould A. Namur, 19 In. 600.00
Sign, Drugs, Painted, Gilded, Turned Shaft, Rectangular, 1800s, 26 x 67 1/2 In. 999.00
Sign, Mortar & Pestle, RX, Porcelain Over Steel, 2-Sided, 3 Piece, 23 x 12 In. 1050.00
Specie Jar, Peruv Bark, Coat Of Arms, Green, Gold Lid, Royal Pharmaceutical, 13 In. 70.00
Stethoscope, Wood, Turned, 7 In. 530.00
Universal Inhaler, Tin, Instructions Under Lid, Bullock & Co., London, Wooden Box 550.00
Vampire Killing Kit, Stake, Crucifix, Pistol, Walnut Box, c.1900, 11 3/4 In. 26400.00
Wheelchair, Wood, Wire Wheels, Reilly Bros. & Raub, Lancaster, Pennsylvania, 46 In. ... 280.00

MEISSEN is a town in Germany where porcelain has been made since
1710. Any china made in the town can be called Meissen, although the
famous Meissen factory made the finest porcelains of the area. The
crossed swords mark of the great Meissen factory has been copied by
many other firms in Germany and other parts of the world. Pieces of
Meissen dinnerware in the Onion pattern are listed in their own category in this book.

Basket, Applied Flowers, Leaf Shape, Branch Handle, c.1847, 15 1/2 In. 1725.00
Basket, Fruit, Latticework Body, Oval, Twig Handles, Gilt Trim, 1800s, 12 3/4 In. 355.00
Bowl, Fruit Design, Blue & White, Gilt, 3 Panels, Crossed Swords, 11 1/2 In. 115.00
Cabaret Service, Saxonia Shape, Art Nouveau, Early 1900s, 18 1/2-In. Tray, 8 Piece 5400.00

Candelabrum, 4-Light, Fruit Pickers, Flower Encrusted Candle Arms, 20 In., Pair 2530.00
Candelabrum, 4-Light, Seasons, Putti, Allegorical, Flower Encrusted, 16 In., Pair 3000.00
Canister, Tea, Cover, Painted, Gilt, Puce, Flowering Leaves, Butterflies, 1800s, 4 1/2 In. ... 320.00
Clock, Mantel, 4 Seasons, 4 Putti, Rocaille Form Case, Marked, 18 1/2 In. 5040.00
Clock, Mantel, Stand, 3 Winged Putto, Flowers, Lovers, Impressed, 21 In. 4025.00
Clock, Parcel Gilt, Putto, Scroll Feet, c.1900, 19 x 15 In. 1725.00
Coffee Set, Deutsche Blumen, Blue Crossed Swords Mark, 9 3/4-In. Pot, 13 Piece 345.00
Compote, Basket, Stemmed, Multicolored Flowers, 2 Handles, 2 Cherubs, 12 In. 890.00
Cup & Saucer, Cover, Painted, Gilt, Wreath, Putti, Garlands, Late 1800s, 5 In. 355.00
Cup & Saucer, Flowers, Orange, Green, Silk-Lined Case, 1900s, 6 Sets 405.00
Cup & Saucer, Pigeons & Cockerel Cup, Duck & Heron Plate, Early 1800s, 5 1/4 In. 285.00
Cup & Saucer, Swan, Painted, Gilt, Herons, Architectural Waterscape, Late 1800s, 6 In. ... 420.00
Figurine, Bread Seller, Man Carrying Large Basket Over Loves On Back, 7 1/2 In. 585.00
Figurine, Cherub, Holding 2 Birds, Standing Beside Cage, Crossed Swords Mark, 5 In. ... 635.00
Figurine, Cherub, Kneeling Holding Fish, Lobster Sack, Crossed Swords Mark, 4 3/8 In. .. 635.00
Figurine, Cherub, Seated, Making Hot Chocolate, Crossed Swords Mark, 4 1/2 In. 635.00
Figurine, Cherub, Tilling The Earth, Potted Trees, Crossed Swords Mark, 4 1/2 In. 750.00
Figurine, Children, With Jewelry Chest, 6 In. 3285.00
Figurine, Couple, Stroll, Flowers In Hand, Gilt Trim, Crossed Swords, 18 1/2 In., Pair 5175.00
Figurine, Elephant With Male Figure At Top, Crossed Swords Mark, 9 x 10 In. 3080.00
Figurine, Girl With Grapes, Boy With Flowers, Blue Crossed Swords, 5 1/2 In., Pair 1035.00
Figurine, Girl, Costume, Holding Apron, Flower Basket, Gilt, Late 19th Century, 5 In. 505.00
Figurine, Jackdaw, On Stump, 1700s Style, c.1865, 20 1/2 In. 575.00
Figurine, Jay, On Tree Stump, Acorns, Leaves, 1900s, 15 1/2 & 15 1/4 In., Pair 2700.00
Figurine, Man, Woman, 5 1/2 In., Pair 660.00
Figurine, Monkey, Violinist, Tree Trunk, Green Coat, Gold Trim, 5 1/4 In. 705.00
Figurine, Nodding Pagoda, Seated, Crossed Leg, Moving Hands, Tongue, 7 1/8 In. 6310.00
Figurine, Nude Woman, Seated, Knee Raised, White Glaze, Robert Ullman, 1939, 13 In. .. 945.00
Figurine, Polar Bear, Striding, White, Otto Jarl, Blue Crossed Swords, 20 1/2 In. 3220.00
Figurine, Woman, Costume, Holding Tray, Tumbler, Cup & Saucer, 19th Century, 7 In. ... 756.00
Figurine, Woman, Reading Letter, Holding Muff, Shaped Base, 7 1/2 In. 1610.00
Figurine Set, Monkey Band, 18th Century Dress, 5 Piece 5290.00
Flask, Perfume, Enamel, Parrot, Songbird, Gilt, Conforming Stopper, c.1875, 4 In. 705.00
Fruit Tray, White, Gilt Designs, Reticulated Edge, Blue Crossed Swords, 12 3/4 In. 35.00
Group, 2 Cherubs, Goat, Multicolored, Enamel, Gilt, Scrolled Rococo Base, 9 1/4 In. 2350.00
Group, 2 Women, Decisive Choice, c.1875, 12 3/4 In. 3900.00
Group, 4 Children Playing Ring Around The Rosie, 6 In. 865.00
Group, 5 Figures Around Mound & Tree Trunk, Impressed, Mark, 10 In. 1495.00
Group, Aphrodite, Reclining, Leaning On Urn, 2 Cherubs, Shells, c.1920, 5 x 6 In. 1645.00
Group, Children At Play, Dog, Lambs, Hand Painted, Gilt Trim, 5 3/4 x 7 In. 1610.00
Group, Courting Couple, Giving Rose Plant To Maiden, c.1875, 6 3/8 In. 1410.00
Group, Elegant Lady, Draped In Floral Chain By Gentleman, 2 Cherubs, 10 1/4 In. 2820.00
Group, Elephant & Soldiers, c.1875, 14 5/8 In. 6600.00
Group, Goddess, Upraised Arm, Flower Cornucopia, 2 Cupids, Late 1800s, 20 3/8 In. 5100.00
Group, Mandarin Family, 7 In. 1435.00
Group, Mother Earth, Cherubs, Cornucopia, Lion, Late 1800s, 9 In. 1415.00
Group, Mythological Ladies, Cherub, 19th Century, 10 In. 3200.00
Group, Venus, Holding Bow, Chariot, 2 Doves, Swans, Cupid, Clouds, c.1875, 17 1/2 In. .. 6000.00
Group, Woman, 18th Century Dress, Standing, Cherub, Reading, 2 Girls, 12 In. 6465.00
Group, Woman, Fox, Playing Harpsichord, No. 122, Late 1800s, 7 1/2 x 11 In. 3680.00
Group, Woman, Man, Tree Form Standard, Flower Encrusted, Pierced, 19 1/4 In. 3450.00
Group, Woman, Playing Guitar, Man Holding Hat, Boy Hold Wreath, 10 In. 1150.00
Mirror, Rococo Style, Arched, 54 x 35 In. 8050.00
Plate, Cobalt Blue, Embossed Gold Fruit & Scrolls, 9 In. 130.00
Plate, Embossed Lion Head Medallions, Vines, Leaves, Gold Trim, 11 In. 130.00
Plate, Tiger, Bamboo, Iron Red, Blue, Black, Gilt, c.1800, 9 1/4 In. 95.00
Platter, Courting Scenes, Flowers, Purple & White Panels, Gold Trim, Oval, 16 In. 220.00
Platter, Flower Sprays, Shaped Edge, Brown Rim, Octagonal, 16 1/2 In. 1265.00
Platter, Flowers, Lemon, Grapevine, Scalloped, Oval, Early 1900s, 22 1/4 x 17 In. 1265.00
Potpourri, Dome Top, Raised Flowers, Pierced Border, 15 x 14 1/2 x 10 In., Pair 1495.00
Salt, Shell Form, Flowers, Gilt, Footed, 3 In., Pair 195.00
Server, 2 Tiers, Graduated Plates, Cobalt Rim, Woman Gathering Flowers, 18 In. 1645.00
Stein, Harbor Scene, Inlaid Lid, C.G. Muller, 1764, 1/3 Liter, 5 1/2 In. 3380.00

Teapot, Stand, Deutsche Blumen, Marked, c.1750, 4 1/4 In. 1495.00
Tete-A-Tete, Continental, Teapot, Creamer, Sugar, Cup, Saucer, Tray 800.00
Tray, Gilt, Painted, Molded Scrolling Rim, Handles, Royal Blue, 4 x 22 1/2 x 14 In. 175.00
Tray, Harbor Scene, Floral Sprays, Crossed Swords Mark, Late 1800s, 14 3/4 In. 865.00
Tureen, Cover, Floral Pattern, Handles, 10 x 14 In. 230.00
Tureen, Cover, Purple Indian Flower, Undertray, Crossed Swords Mark, 9 x 17 In. 865.00
Urn, Cover, Rococo Style, Urn Shape Body, Flowers, Cherub, Stand, Late 1800s, 30 In. ... 9200.00
Urn, Grapevine Pattern, Blue Pommel Sword Crossed Mark, 11 3/4 In. 375.00
Urn, Neptune, 3 Figures, 2 Fish, 4 Horses, Marine Scene, 6 In. 5600.00
Vase, Cover, Stand, Flower Encrusted, Lovers, Landscape, c.1875, 34 3/4 In. 8400.00
Vase, Flowers, Face Shaped Handles, Acanthus Brackets, Dome Lid, c.1800, 13 1/2 In. 1380.00
Vase, Pate-Sur-Pate, 2 Cupids, Flower Garland, Cobalt Blue Ground, c.1900, 8 5/8 In. 6000.00
Vase, Spill, Figural, Man, Stepping Over Tree Trunk, Hounds, Late 1800s, 14 1/2 In. 840.00
Vegetable, Cover, Iris, Tulip, Hand Painted, Gilt, Unglazed Base, 6 1/2 x 12 In. 430.00

MERRIMAC POTTERY
Company was founded by Thomas Nickerson in Newburyport, Massachusetts, in 1902. The company made art pottery, garden pottery, and reproductions of Roman pottery. The pottery burned to the ground in 1908.

Jardiniere, Squat, Green & Gunmetal Frothy Glaze, 5 1/2 x 9 In. 1295.00
Lamp, Oil, Leaves, Stems, Green Matte, Tiffany Favrile Glass Shade, 12 1/2 x 5 1/4 In. ... 5300.00

METLOX POTTERIES
was founded in 1927 in Manhattan Beach, California. Dinnerware was made beginning in 1931. Evan K. Shaw purchased the company in 1946 and expanded the number of patterns. Poppytrail (1946-1989) and Vernonware (1958-1980) were divisions of Metlox under E.K. Shaw's direction. The factory closed in 1989.

Antigua, Coffeepot, Cover, 8 Cup 95.00
Antiqua, Bowl, Cereal, 7 1/8 In. 8.00
Antique Grape, Bowl, Vegetable, Cover, 2 Qt. 104.00
Autumn Leaves, Platter, Oval, 12 3/8 In. 55.00
Bouquet, Teapot, Cover, 4 1/2 Cup 90.00
Calico, Platter, Oval, 11 In. 55.00
California Ivy, Bowl, Vegetable, 9 In. 15.00
California Ivy, Creamer 25.00
California Peach Blossom, Gravy Boat, Underplate 80.00
California Povincial, Dish, Hen On Nest, 6 1/2 In. 120.00
California Provincial, Pitcher, Milk, Green Handle, Qt. 75.00
California Strawberry, Bowl, Cereal, 5 5/8 In. 18.00
California Strawberry, Plate, 10 1/4 In. 10.00
Cinnamon, Plate, 10 3/4 In. 15.00
Colonial Heritage, Clock, Steeple, 7 3/4 x 5 In. 65.00
Cookie Jar, Beau Bear, Cranberry Bow, 11 1/2 In. 75.00
Cookie Jar, Daisy Topiary, 11 In. 55.00
Cookie Jar, Humpty Dumpty, 11 In. 350.00
Cookie Jar, Lion, 12 In. 150.00
Cookie Jar, Mammy Cook, Yellow 550.00
Cookie Jar, Pig, Slenderella, 13 In. 200.00
Cookie Jar, Squirrel On Pinecone, 12 In. 160.00
Cookie Jar, Teddy Bear, Blue Sweater, 11 1/2 In. ....38.00 to 65.00
Cookie Jar, Topsy, 9 1/2 In. 595.00
Country Cousins, Teapot, Cover, 5 1/4 In. 60.00
Del Rey, Plate, Bread & Butter, 6 1/4 In. 8.00
Del Rey, Plate, Dinner, 10 1/8 In. 18.00
Della Robbia, Bowl, Fruit, 6 1/2 In. 12.00
Della Robbia, Bowl, Vegetable, Oval, Divided, 12 1/8 In. 55.00
Della Robbia, Bowl, Vegetable, Round, 10 5/8 In. 15.00
Della Robbia, Butter, Cover 38.00
Della Robbia, Casserole, Cover, 2 Qt. 104.00
Della Robbia, Gravy Boat 55.00
Della Robbia, Plate, 6 1/2 In. 9.00
Della Robbia, Platter, Oval, 11 1/8 In. 57.00
Della Robbia, Saucer, 6 1/2 In. 8.00

Della Robbia, Sugar, Cover	16.00
Figurine, Bear, Reclining, 5 1/2 In.	80.00
Heavenly Days, Tidbit, 3 Tiers, Vernonware	60.00
Homestead Provincial, Bean Pot, Handle, 7 3/4 In.	150.00
Homestead Provincial, Bowl, Vegetable, Divided, 12 In.	55.00
Homestead Provincial, Jam Jar, Handle, 4 3/4 In.	60.00
Marigold, Platter, Oval, 14 1/4 In.	55.00
Navajo, Gravy Boat, Underplate, Ladle	75.00
Navajo, Plate, 7 1/2 In.	14.00
Navajo, Teapot, Rattan Handle, 7 Cup	130.00
Oh Susanna, Bowl, Vegetable, Divided, Round, Tab Handles, 7 In.	26.00
Pepper Tree, Gravy Boat	56.00
Pepper Tree, Platter, Rectangular, 11 In.	55.00
Planter, Fire Wagon, Brass Wheels & Ladders, 8 5/8 x 14 In.	80.00
Provincial Blue, Coffeepot, Cover, 7 Cup, 10 7/8 In.	90.00
Provincial Fruit, Bowl, Cereal, 7 1/4 In.	9.99
Provincial Fruit, Canister Set, Covers, 3 Qt., 2 Qt., 1 1/2 Qt., 1 Qt., 4 Piece	165.00
Provincial Fruit, Platter, Oval, 16 In.	70.00
Red Rooster, Bowl, Salad, 11 1/8 In.	85.00 to 95.00
Red Rooster, Bowl, Vegetable, Cover, 10 In., 1 Qt.	100.00
Red Rooster, Bowl, Vegetable, Rectangular, Divided, Handle, 12 In.	60.00
Red Rooster, Bowl, Vegetable, Round, Handles, 8 In.	65.00
Red Rooster, Bread Server, 9 1/2 In.	100.00
Red Rooster, Butter, Cover	65.00
Red Rooster, Canister Set, Covers, 4 Piece	250.00
Red Rooster, Canister, Cover, Flour	80.00
Red Rooster, Carafe, Warmer, 6 Cup	140.00
Red Rooster, Casserole, Cover, 6 x 10 In.	85.00
Red Rooster, Plate, 6 3/8 In.	8.00
Red Rooster, Plate, 7 1/2 In.	10.00
Red Rooster, Plate, 10 In.	15.00
Red Rooster, Soup, Dish, 8 In.	18.00
Red Rooster, Sugar & Creamer	68.00
Rose-A-Day, Tidbit, 3 Tiers, 10 In.	60.00
San Fernando, Teapot, 6 Cup	90.00
Sculptured Daisy, Bowl, Salad, 12 1/8 In.	75.00
Sculptured Daisy, Chop Plate, 12 In.	60.00
Sculptured Daisy, Gravy Boat	58.00
Sculptured Daisy, Platter, Oval, 11 In.	64.00
Sculptured Daisy, Platter, Oval, 14 1/4 In.	85.00
Sculptured Grape, Bowl, Vegetable, Cover, 1 Qt.	68.00
Sculptured Grape, Bowl, Vegetable, Divided	55.00
Sherwood, Butter, Cover	25.00
Sorrento, Platter, Oval, 11 3/4 In.	55.00
Tickled Pink, Plate, 10 In.	9.00
Tickled Pink, Salt & Pepper, Wooden Stoppers	40.00
Tom & Jerry, Punch Set, Bowl, Cover, 6 Cups, 8 Piece	80.00
True Blue, Coffeepot, 8 Cup	67.00
Vase, Chartreuse, Flared, Scalloped Rim, 12 x 7 5/8 In.	125.00
Vase, Old Rose Glaze, Bulbous, Flared, Handles, 7 3/4 In.	85.00
Woodland Gold, Gravy Boat	56.00
Woodland Gold, Platter, Oval, 11 In.	55.00
Yorkshire, Candleholder, Poppy Orange, Handle, Footed, 4 3/4 In., Pair	70.00
Yorkshire, Teapot, Turquoise Blue, 2 Cup	100.00

METTLACH, Germany, is a city where the Villeroy and Boch factories worked. Steins from the firm are marked with the word *Mettlach*
or the castle mark. They date from about 1842. Pieces marked *Mettlach* are still being made. *PUG* means painted under glaze. The steins
can be dated from the marks on the bottom, which include a date-num-
ber code. Other pieces may be listed in the Villeroy & Boch category.

Beaker, No. 2327-1051, 1/4 Liter, Girl With Pitcher, PUG	70.00
Beaker, No. 2327-1137, 1/4 Liter, Couple At Festival, PUG	169.00

Beaker, No. 2327-1179, 1/4 Liter, Song, PUG 82.00
Beaker, No. 2327-1200, 1/4 Liter, Stadt Wiesbaden, PUG 500.00
Beaker, No. 2327-1290f, 1/4 Liter, State Crest Of Baden, PUG 135.00
Beaker, No. 2368-1032, 1/4 Liter, Gnomes Drinking, PUG 99.00
Beaker, No. 2775-1014, 1/2 Liter, Pilsner, Munich Child, H. Schlitt 230.00
Beaker, No. 2775-1130, 1 Liter, Gasthaus Scene, PUG 120.00
Bowl, No. 1215, Flowers, Leaves, Repeating Design, Mosaic, 5 In. 255.00
Candlestick, No. 3339, Art Deco, Red, White, Black, Etched, 8 1/4 In. 365.00
Charger, Painted, Art Nouveau Scene, Woman Near Lake, R. Thevenin, 15 1/2 In. 2875.00
Cigar Holder, No. 464, Tree Stump, Man Holding Match, 6 In. 302.00
Cookie Jar, No. 1347, Mosaic, Silver Plated Top Rim Handle, Lid, 8 In. 320.00
Desk Set, H. Taxis Baustoffe Sanitar, Letter Holder, Pen Rest, Ashtray, Glazed Relief 266.00
Jar, No. 2870, Mustard, Stoneware Lid, PUG, 3 3/4 In. 80.00
Jardiniere, No. 2427, Fish, Flowers, Bulbous, 16 x 12 In. 1265.00
Pitcher, No. 2486, Trees, Indigo Blossoms, Brown Accents, 7 In. 520.00
Planter, No. 2732, Flowers, Glazed Relief, Hein, 5 x 12 1/2 In. 485.00
Plaque, No. 1044, Birds & Flowers, PUG, 10 In. 420.00
Plaque, No. 1044-92, Stadthaus In Berncastel, PUG, 14 In. 205.00
Plaque, No. 1044-94, Altes Stadtthor Cochem., PUG, 12 In. 230.00
Plaque, No. 1044-128, Nurnberg Schloss, PUG, 12 In. 190.00
Plaque, No. 1044-129, Nurnberg Henkersteg, PUG, 12 In. 220.00
Plaque, No. 1044-147, Lichtenstein, PUG, 14 In. 365.00
Plaque, No. 1044-153, Deer, PUG, 12 In. 266.00
Plaque, No. 1044-157, Koln, PUG, 14 In. 360.00
Plaque, No. 1044-162, Niederwaldden Kmal, PUG, 14 In. 240.00
Plaque, No. 1044-168, Dresden, Buhlsche Terrasse, PUG, 12 In. 240.00
Plaque, No. 1044-176, Zugspitze U. Rissersee, PUG, 12 In. 255.00
Plaque, No. 1044-992, Dwarfs Carrying Grapes, PUG, H. Schlitt, 8 1/2 In. 420.00
Plaque, No. 1044-1099, Children, PUG, F. Reiss, 17 In. 965.00
Plaque, No. 1044-9031, Pheasants, PUG, 14 In. 129.00
Plaque, No. 1044-9033, Birds, PUG, 14 In. 129.00
Plaque, No. 1388, Knight, Etched, 10 1/2 In. 245.00
Plaque, No. 1651, Woman, Etched, 12 In. 420.00
Plaque, No. 1653, Snow White & 7 Dwarfs, PUG, 8 In. 300.00
Plaque, No. 1696, Winged Woman, Relief, 16 In. 755.00
Plaque, No. 1769, Arnold Von Winkelried, Etched, 14 1/2 In. 1150.00
Plaque, No. 2081, Military Hussar, Etched, Stocke, 15 In. 1450.00
Plaque, No. 2288, Knight & Lady, Etched, F. Quidenus, 17 In. 795.00
Plaque, No. 2507, Mermaid Woman & Child, Etched, Hein, 17 In. 1210.00
Plaque, No. 2517, Konigstein Town, Etched, 17 1/2 In. 920.00
Plaque, No. 2624, Cavalier Smoking Pipe, Etched, Quidenus, 7 1/2 In. 69.00
Plaque, No. 2712, Black Forest Girl, Etched, 9 1/4 In. 230.00
Plaque, No. 3161, Cavaliers, Drinking, Etched, 17 In. 845.00
Plaque, No. 3272, Ladies Dancing, Cameo, Stahl, 6 1/2 In. 270.00
Plaque, No. 7067, Woman, Children, Phanolith, Wood Frame, Stahl, 6 x 4 In. 280.00
Punch Bowl, No. 2226-989, 1 3/4 Liter, Gnomes Dancing, PUG 242.00
Punch Bowl, No. 2339-1028, 7 1/2 Liter, Gnomes At Wine Press, PUG 1630.00
Stein, No. 24, 1/2 Liter, Panels, With People, Inlaid Lid 360.00
Stein, No. 24, 1 Liter, Panels, With People, Inlaid Lid 360.00
Stein, No. 368, 1/2 Liter, Vines, Leaves, Relief, Inlaid Lid 135.00
Stein, No. 468, 1/4 Liter, Barrel Shape, Relief, Inlaid Lid 246.00
Stein, No. 485, 1 Liter, Musicians, Dancers, Relief, Inlaid Lid, 9 5/8 In. 426.00
Stein, No. 485, Band Playing, Couples Dancing, Grapevines, Pewter Lid, 10 1/2 In. 405.00
Stein, No. 812, 1/2 Liter, Hunting Scenes, Relief, Inlaid Lid 129.00
Stein, No. 1005, 1 Liter, Tavern Scenes, Relief, Inlaid Lid ....256.00 to 360.00
Stein, No. 1028, 1/2 Liter, Man, Woman, With Harvest, Relief, Inlaid Lid 135.00
Stein, No. 1104, 3 1/4 Liter, Gemetric, Mosaic, Inlaid Lid 360.00
Stein, No. 1132, 1/2 Liter, Man, Playing Violin, Pyramids, Crocodile, Etched, Inlaid Lid .. 439.00
Stein, No. 1146, 1/2 Liter, Students Drinking, Etched, Inlaid Lid, C. Warth 430.00
Stein, No. 1154, 1 Liter, Hunters, Etched, Inlaid Lid 336.00
Stein, No. 1162, 1/2 Liter, People Dancing, Etched, Inlaid Lid, C. Warth ....230.00 to 362.00
Stein, No. 1163, 1/2 Liter, Musician, Etched, Inlaid Lid, C. Warth 250.00
Stein, No. 1164, 1/2 Liter, Musician & Girl, Etched, Inlaid Lid 325.00

Stein, No. 1169, 2 1/2 Liter, Nurnberg Artists, Relief, Inlaid Lid 740.00
Stein, No. 1208, 1/2 Liter, Military, Military Thumblift, Etched 1210.00
Stein, No. 1266, 1/2 Liter, Men Drinking, Relief, Inlaid Lid 190.00
Stein, No. 1395, 1/2 Liter, French Card Design, Etched, Inlaid Lid 375.00
Stein, No. 1397, 1/2 Liter, Man With Hat, Etched, Inlaid Lid 175.00
Stein, No. 1403, 1/2 Liter, Bowling, Etched, Inlaid Lid, C. Warth . . . . .144.00 to 410.00
Stein, No. 1454, 1/2 Liter, White Horse, Etched, Inlaid Lid 276.00
Stein, No. 1467, 1/2 Liter, Relief, 4 Harvest Scenes, Relief, Inlaid Lid 180.00
Stein, No. 1475, 1/2 Liter, Dwarfs, Etched, Inlaid Lid 365.00
Stein, No. 1508, 1/2 Liter, Tavern Scene, Etched, Inlaid Lid 375.00
Stein, No. 1519, 1/2 Liter, Scull Racing, Etched, Inlaid Lid 605.00
Stein, No. 1520, 1/2 Liter, Cavaliers & Eagle, Etched, Inlaid Lid, Gorig 485.00
Stein, No. 1526, 1/2 Liter, Berlin, Brandenburg Gate, Flat Metal Lid 135.00
Stein, No. 1526, 1/2 Liter, Eagle, Hand Painted, Pewter Lid 1150.00
Stein, No. 1526, 1/2 Liter, Man, Verse, Transfer, Enameled, Pewter Lid 120.00
Stein, No. 1526, 1/2 Liter, Monkey Smoking Cigarette, PUG, Inlaid Lid 185.00
Stein, No. 1526, 1/2 Liter, Student Society, Ripauria Sei's Panier, Pewter Lid 240.00
Stein, No. 1526, 1/2 Liter, Student Society, Wallhalla Sei's Panier, Painted, Pewter Lid . . . 155.00
Stein, No. 1526-596, 1 Liter, Cavalier Drinking, PUG, Pewter Lid 375.00
Stein, No. 1526-607, 1/4 Liter, Boy Playing Violin, PUG, Pewter Lid 169.00
Stein, No. 1526-624, 1 Liter, Man & Woman, PUG, Pewter Lid 410.00
Stein, No. 1526-625, 1 Liter, People & Verse, PUG, Pewter Lid 375.00
Stein, No. 1526-1108, 1/2 Liter, Festive Scene, PUG, Pewter Lid, H. Schlitt 275.00
Stein, No. 1526-1110, 1/2 Liter, Man Sitting At Table, Transfer, Enameled, Pewter Lid 115.00
Stein, No. 1526-1502, 1/3 Liter, Military, PUG, Inlaid Lid 360.00
Stein, No. 1527, 1/2 Liter, Drinking Scene, Etched, Inlaid Lid, C. Warth 375.00
Stein, No. 1527, 1 Liter, Drinking Scene, Etched, Inlaid Lid, C. Warth . . . . .320.00 to 625.00
Stein, No. 1536, 1/2 Liter, Man With Pipe, Tapestry, Pewter Lid 205.00
Stein, No. 1562, 5 1/4 Liter, Trumpeter Of Sackingen, Etched, Pewter Lid 1335.00
Stein, No. 1655, 1/2 Liter, Young People Dancing, Etched, Inlaid Lid 440.00
Stein, No. 1656, 1/2 Liter, Old People Dancing, Etched, Inlaid Lid 605.00
Stein, No. 1675, 1/2 Liter, Heidelberg, Etched, Inlaid Lid .420.00 to 485.00
Stein, No. 1695, 1/2 Liter, 4 Scenes Of Hunters, Etched, Inlaid Lid 605.00
Stein, No. 1727, 1/2 Liter, Leaves & Scrolls, Relief, Inlaid Lid 125.00
Stein, No. 1732, 1/2 Liter, Prussian Eagle & 2 Soldiers, Etched, Inlaid Lid, C. Warth 500.00
Stein, No. 1733, 1/2 Liter, Jockeys, Horses, Etched, Inlaid Jockey Cap Lid, C. Warth 1289.00
Stein, No. 1745, 1/4 Liter, Leaves & Scrolls, Relief, Inlaid Lid . . . . .115.00 to 147.00
Stein, No. 1786, 1/2 Liter, St. Florian Extinguishing Fire, Etched, Pewter Lid 490.00
Stein, No. 1786, 1 Liter, St. Florian Extinguishing Fire, Etched, Pewter Lid 660.00
Stein, No. 1791, 2 3/5 Liter, Flower, Inlaid Lid 175.00
Stein, No. 1794, 1/2 Liter, Bismarck, Etched, Pewter Lid, C. Warth . . . . .200.00 to 275.00
Stein, No. 1819, 1/2 Liter, Masonic, Etched, Inlaid Lid, C. Warth 692.00
Stein, No. 1890, 1/2 Liter, 3 Kaisers, Etched, PUG, Inlaid Lid 120.00
Stein, No. 1909-702, 1/2 Liter, Beer Parade, PUG, Pewter Lid 190.00
Stein, No. 1909-726, 1/2 Liter, 3 Beer Steins To Be Filled, PUG, Pewter Lid, H. Schlitt . . . 470.00
Stein, No. 1909-727, 1/2 Liter, Dwarfs Bowling, PUG, Pewter Lid, H. Schlitt 390.00
Stein, No. 1909-980, 1/2 Liter, Miner, PUG, Pewter Lid, H. Schlitt 405.00
Stein, No. 1909-1009, 1/2 Liter, Dwarfs At Grape Press, PUG, Pewter Lid, H. Schlitt 305.00
Stein, No. 1909-1042, 1/2 Liter, Man & Woman Holding Key, PUG, Pewter Lid 381.00
Stein, No. 1909-1178, 1/2 Liter, Bier, PUG, Pewter Lid 391.00
Stein, No. 1909-1339, 1/2 Liter, Animals, Dwarf Playing Instruments, PUG, Pewter Lid . . 360.00
Stein, No. 1914, 1/2 Liter, 4F Stein, Etched, Inlaid Lid 430.00
Stein, No. 1934, 1/2 Liter, Military Uniform Evolution, 1689-1889, Etched, Inlaid Lid 1090.00
Stein, No. 1972, 1/2 Liter, 4 Seasons, Etched, Inlaid Lid 420.00
Stein, No. 1995, 1/2 Liter, Man Drinking, Etched, Inlaid Lid 330.00
Stein, No. 1997, 1/2 Liter, George Ehret, N.Y. Brewer, PUG, Etched, Inlaid Lid, Hein 210.00
Stein, No. 1998, 1/2 Liter, Trumpeter Of Sackingen, Etched, Inlaid Lid 415.00
Stein, No. 2001A, 1/2 Liter, Law, Etched, Relief, Inlaid Lid 315.00
Stein, No. 2001B, 1/2 Liter, Medicine, Glazed, Inlaid Lid 485.00
Stein, No. 2001C, 1/2 Liter, Scholar, Glazed, Inlaid Lid 635.00
Stein, No. 2001G, 1/2 Liter, Engineering, Etched, Relief, Inlaid Lid 1210.00
Stein, No. 2001K, 1/2 Liter, Commerce, Glazed, Inlaid Lid 425.00
Stein, No. 2002, 1/2 Liter, Munchen, German Verse, Etched, Inlaid Lid 289.00

Stein, No. 2007, 1/2 Liter, Black Cat, Etched, Inlaid Lid, F. Stuck 480.00
Stein, No. 2008, 1/2 Liter, Trumpeter On Horse, Etched, Inlaid Lid, F. Stuck 605.00
Stein, No. 2018, 1/2 Liter, Dog, PUG, Inlaid Lid 1027.00
Stein, No. 2024, 1/2 Liter, Berlin, Etched, Glazed, Inlaid Lid 605.00
Stein, No. 2025, 1/3 Liter, Festive Scene With Cherubs, Etched, Inlaid Lid 240.00
Stein, No. 2029, 1/2 Liter, Military, Etched, Inlaid Lid ....650.00 to 776.00
Stein, No. 2035, 1/2 Liter, Festive Scene, Etched, Inlaid Lid 155.00
Stein, No. 2035, 1/3 Liter, Festive Scene, Etched, Inlaid Lid 165.00
Stein, No. 2038, 3 4/5 Liter, Rodentstein, Inlaid Lid, Relief 3365.00
Stein, No. 2040, 4 Liter, Military Scene, Etched, Pewter Lid ....6280.00 to 7245.00
Stein, No. 2051, 1/2 Liter, Students Drinking, Etched, Inlaid Lid 385.00
Stein, No. 2052, 1/4 Liter, Munich Child With Children, Etched, Inlaid Lid 100.00
Stein, No. 2075, 1/2 Liter, Telegraph, Black Eagle, Etched, Glazed, Inlaid Lid ...1435.00 to 1932.00
Stein, No. 2077, 1/3 Liter, Coat Of Arms, Relief, Inlaid Lid 105.00
Stein, No. 2082, 1/2 Liter, William Tell, Son, Apple, Etched, Inlaid Lid ....740.00 to 920.00
Stein, No. 2090, 1/3 Liter, Man Drinking, Inlaid Lid, H. Schlitt 195.00
Stein, No. 2091, 1/2 Liter, St. Florian, Etched, Inlaid Lid, H. Schlitt ....546.00 to 750.00
Stein, No. 2092, 1/2 Liter, Dwarf Adjusting Clock, Etched, Inlaid Lid, H. Schlitt 530.00
Stein, No. 2094, 1/2 Liter, Music Scene, Etched, Inlaid Lid 385.00
Stein, No. 2097, 1/2 Liter, Music, Etched, Inlaid Lid 405.00
Stein, No. 2099, 1/3 Liter, Flowers, Art Nouveau, Mosaic, Inlaid Lid ....275.00 to 330.00
Stein, No. 2100, 1/2 Liter, Germans Meeting Romans, Etched, Inlaid Lid, H. Schlitt 362.00 to 730.00
Stein, No. 2107, 1 1/2 Liter, Gambrinus, Etched, Inlaid Lid, H. Schlitt 1090.00
Stein, No. 2118, 2 Liter, John C. White, White & Crafts Maltsters, PUG, Pewter Lid 604.00
Stein, No. 2126, 5 1/2 Liter, Symphonia, Etched, Pewter Lid, Schultz 6640.00
Stein, No. 2133, 1/3 Liter, Dwarf In Nest, Etched, Inlaid Lid, Schlitt 1495.00
Stein, No. 2134, 1/2 Liter, Dwarf In Nest, Etched, Inlaid Lid, Schlitt 2175.00
Stein, No. 2140-747, 1/2 Liter, 3 Gardte Regt Zu Fuss, Pewter Lid, PUG 720.00
Stein, No. 2140-790, 1/2 Liter, 2 Garde Field Artillerie, PUG, Relief Pewter Lid 640.00
Stein, No. 2140-801, 1/2 Liter, Garde Train Battalion, PUG, Relief Pewter Lid 690.00
Stein, No. 2140-807, 1/2 Liter, Magdeburg Husaren Regt. Nr 10, Pewter Lid, PUG 660.00
Stein, No. 2140-952, Man, Riding Standard Bicycle, PUG, Inlaid Lid 290.00
Stein, No. 2140-1047, 1/2 Liter, Dwarfs Smoking, PUG, Pewter Lid 425.00
Stein, No. 2184-967, 1/3 Liter, Dwarfs, PUG, Inlaid Lid 255.00
Stein, No. 2204, 1/2 Liter, Prussian Eagle, Etched, Relief, Inlaid Lid ....575.00 to 605.00
Stein, No. 2204, 1 Liter, Prussian Eagle, Etched, Relief, Inlaid Lid ....395.00 to 1090.00
Stein, No. 2205, 5 1/4 Liter, Hunters & Diana, Etched, Inlaid Lid, Boar Thumblift 2560.00
Stein, No. 2230, 1/2 Liter, Man & Woman, Etched, Inlaid Lid, H. Schlitt 415.00
Stein, No. 2271-1020, 1/2 Liter, Barmaid Speaking With Crowd, PUG, Pewter Lid 230.00
Stein, No. 2271-1055, 1/2 Liter, Drunken Cavaliers, PUG, Pewter Lid 260.00
Stein, No. 2282, 1/2 Liter, Man Caught In Cellar, Etched, Inlaid Lid ....190.00 to 485.00
Stein, No. 2285, 1/2 Liter, Man, Woman, Musician, Etched, Inlaid Lid 405.00
Stein, No. 2324, 1/2 Liter, Rugby Game, Etched, Pewter Lid ....970.00 to 1725.00
Stein, No. 2333-1033, 1/3 Liter, Dwarfs, PUG, Pewter Lid ....115.00 to 145.00
Stein, No. 2349-1024, 1/4 Liter, Man Playing Flute, PUG, Pewter Lid 115.00
Stein, No. 2373, 1/2 Liter, St. Augustine, Florida, Alligator Handle, Etched, Inlaid Lid ... 1090.00
Stein, No. 2382, 1/2 Liter, Thirsty Rider, Etched, Inlaid Lid, H. Schlitt ....605.00 to 638.00
Stein, No. 2382, 1 Liter, Thirsty Rider, Etched, Inlaid Lid, H. Schlitt 805.00
Stein, No. 2401, 1 Liter, Tannhauser In Venusberg, Etched, Inlaid Lid 1045.00
Stein, No. 2430, 3 Liter, Cavalier, Etched, Inlaid Lid 955.00
Stein, No. 2441, 1/2 Liter, Gambling Scene, Etched, Inlaid Lid 635.00
Stein, No. 2500, 1 Liter, Drunken Cavaliers, Etched, Inlaid Lid 690.00
Stein, No. 2501, 1/2 Liter, Drinking Scene, Etched, Inlaid Lid, F. Quidenus 400.00
Stein, No. 2520, 1 Liter, Man, Drinking, Barmaid, Etched, Inlaid Lid, H. Schlitt 445.00
Stein, No. 2530, 1 Liter, Boar Hunting, Cameo, Inlaid Lid, Stahl 645.00
Stein, No. 2532, 1/2 Liter, Gasthaus Scene, F. Quidenus, Etched, Inlaid Lid 440.00
Stein, No. 2585, 1/2 Liter, Munchen, Etched, Inlaid Lid 475.00
Stein, No. 2608, 1/3 Liter, Cameo, 3 Scenes Of Men, Woman Cameo, Inlaid Lid, Stahl ... 300.00
Stein, No. 2625, 1/2 Liter, Scenes From Gasthaus, Rodenstein, Cameo, Inlaid Lid 759.00
Stein, No. 2639, 1/2 Liter, Blacksmith & Cavelier, Etched, Inlaid Lid 385.00
Stein, No. 2640, 1/2 Liter, Cavalier & Barmaid, Etched, Inlaid Lid 415.00
Stein, No. 2662, 1/2 Liter, Drunk Student Counting Mice, Etched, Inlaid Lid 965.00
Stein, No. 2682, 2 Liter, Woman, Picking Grapes, Etched, Inlaid Lid, F. Quidenus 1495.00

Stein, No. 2693, 1/2 Liter, Gasthaus Scene, Etched, Inlaid Lid 400.00
Stein, No. 2716, 1/2 Liter, Waitress, Men, Etched, Inlaid Lid, F. Quidenus 385.00
Stein, No. 2716, 1 Liter, Waitress, Men, Etched, Inlaid Lid, F. Quidenus 535.00
Stein, No. 2718, 1/2 Liter, David & Goliath, Etched, Glazed, Inlaid Lid 1725.00
Stein, No. 2751, 2 1/2 Liter, Men At Table, Etched, Inlaid Lid, H. Schlitt 1289.00
Stein, No. 2752, 1/2 Liter, Men Drinking, At Table, Etched, Inlaid Lid, H. Schlitt 545.00
Stein, No. 2765, 1/2 Liter, Knights Riding White Horse, Etched, Inlaid Lid, H. Schlitt 835.00
Stein, No. 2767, 1/2 Liter, Munich Child, Etched, Inlaid Lid ....443.00 to 725.00
Stein, No. 2776, 1/2 Liter, Man In Cellar, Etched, Inlaid Lid ....470.00 to 645.00
Stein, No. 2778, 1/4 Liter, Carnival Scene, Etched, Inlaid Lid, H. Schlitt 2050.00
Stein, No. 2780, 1 Liter, Lovers, Etched, Inlaid Lid 840.00
Stein, No. 2796, 3 Liter, Heidelberg, Etched, Inlaid Lid ....1120.00 to 1780.00
Stein, No. 2797, 4 Liter, Richard Wagner, Etched, Inlaid Lid 2305.00
Stein, No. 2807, 1/2 Liter, Couple At Table, Inlaid Lid, Etched 60.00
Stein, No. 2808, 1/2 Liter, Bowling, Etched, Inlaid Lid 420.00
Stein, No. 2833C, 1/2 Liter, Rier Scene, Etched, Inlaid Lid 470.00
Stein, No. 2833E, 1/2 Liter, Soldiers, Etched, Inlaid Lid 485.00
Stein, No. 2844, 1/2 Liter, Farming, Hunting, Fishing, Inlaid Lid 890.00
Stein, No. 2871, 1 Liter, Cornell University, Etched, Inlaid Lid 1085.00
Stein, No. 2880, 1 Liter, Tavern Scene, Etched, Inlaid Lid 520.00
Stein, No. 2889, 1/2 Liter, Man On Horse, Etched, Inlaid Lid 385.00
Stein, No. 2900, 1/2 Liter, Quilmes, Argentina, Etched, Inlaid Lid 375.00
Stein, No. 2903, 1/2 Liter, Art Nouveau, Etched, Inlaid Lid 230.00
Stein, No. 2921, 2 4/5 Liter, Hunters At Campfire, Etched, Inlaid Lid 690.00
Stein, No. 2922, 1 Liter, Men, Around Campfire, Etched, Inlaid Lid 665.00
Stein, No. 2938, 1/2 Liter, Hunter, Etched, Inlaid Lid 575.00
Stein, No. 2951, 1 Liter, Prussian Eagle, Cameo, Pewter Lid 580.00
Stein, No. 2959, 1 Liter, Bowling, Etched, Inlaid Lid 420.00
Stein, No. 3003, 1/2 Liter, Man, Reading Paper, Pewter Lid 420.00
Stein, No. 3079-539, 1 Liter, Man Shooting With Child, Bavaria, Pewter Lid 800.00
Stein, No. 3087, 1/2 Liter, Tapestry, Woman, Pewter Lid 430.00
Stein, No. 3089, 1 Liter, Diogenes, Etched, Inlaid Lid, H. Schlitt 700.00
Stein, No. 3091, 1/2 Liter, Knight Drinking, Etched, Inlaid Lid, H. Schlitt ....725.00 to 800.00
Stein, No. 3091, 1 Liter, Knight Drinking, Etched, Inlaid Lid, H. Schlitt ....469.00 to 580.00
Stein, No. 3099, 1/3 Liter, Diogenes, Etched, Inlaid Lid, H. Schlitt 2900.00
Stein, No. 3135, 1/2 Liter, Eagle With American Flags, Etched, Inlaid Lid ......1810.00 to 2059.00
Stein, No. 3219, 1/2 Liter, Men Drinking, Etched, Inlaid Lid 440.00
Stein, No. 3221, 1/2 Liter, 2 Men, Toasting, Etched, Inlaid Lid, F. Quidenus 755.00
Stein, No. 3328-544, 1/2 Liter, Man Drinking, Bavaria, Inlaid Lid 345.00
Stein, No. 3329, 1 Liter, Card Game, Devil, Lady Luck, Etched, Relief, Inlaid Lid 2415.00
Stein, No. 3342, 1/3 Liter, 4-Sided, Bavaria, Inlaid Lid 875.00
Stein, No. 5005-5188, 1/2 Liter, Man Smoking, Faience, Pewter Lid 190.00
Stein, No. 5013-965, 1/2 Liter, Crest, Faience, Pewter Lid 485.00
Stein, No. 5019, 1 Liter, Flower, Faience, Pewter Lid 485.00
Stein, No. 5022, 1 Liter, Ships, Building, Faience, Pewter Lid 865.00
Stein, No. 5192, 5 Liter, Man Drinking, Delft, Pewter Lid 1050.00
Trivet, No. 3330, Art Nouveau, Round, Etched, 8 In. 240.00
Vase, No. 1336, Floral, Tan, Brown, Red, White, Mosaic, 10 1/2 In. 165.00
Vase, No. 1661, Flowers, Relief, 5 1/4 In. 195.00
Vase, No. 1829, Geometric, Brown, Gray, Mosaic, Relief, 7 In. 140.00
Vase, No. 2209, Lohengrin, Winged Helmet, Woman Handles, Etched, 17 In. 2300.00
Vase, No. 2731, Art Nouveau Flowers, Relief, 16 In. 280.00
Vase, No. 3270, Cameo, Girl, 3 1/4 In. 240.00
Vessel, Lid, Stylized Flowers, Marked, 7 1/2 In. 635.00

**Put felt pads on the bottom corners behind a
hanging picture frame to protect the wall
and to let air circulate.**

Milk Glass, Bank,
Figural Schoolhouse,
Roof Cover, Gold
Paint, 4 x 3 1/2 In.

Milk Glass, Box, Figural Uncle Sam Sitting
On USS Maine, 4 1/2 x 6 1/2 In.

MILK GLASS was named for its milky white color. It was first made
in England during the 1700s. The height of its popularity in the United
States was from 1870 to 1880. It is now correct to refer to some colored glass as blue milk glass, black milk glass, etc. Reproductions of
milk glass are being made and sold in many stores. Related pieces may
be listed in the Cosmos and Westmoreland categories.

Bank, Figural Schoolhouse, Roof Cover, Gold Paint, 4 x 3 1/2 In.	*Illus*	75.00
Box, Figural Uncle Sam Sitting On USS Maine, 4 1/2 x 6 1/2 In.	*Illus*	75.00
Compote, Swirls, Scalloped Rim, Powder Blue, 1830-50, 7 1/2 x 8 1/4 In.		385.00
Dish, Cover, Figural Melon, Green, Signed, Vallerysthal		65.00
Dish, Deer Cover, Fallen Tree Base, E.W. Flaccus Co., Wheeling, 7 In.		545.00
Dish, Dog On Rug Cover, Wicker Basket Base, Caramel, Painted, Vallerysthal	*Illus*	1050.00
Dish, Figural Turtle, Snail Cover, Blue, Vallerysthal		470.00
Dish, Figural Walking Bear, Co-Operative Flint	*Illus*	2500.00
Dish, Figural Walking Fish, Cover, Glass Eyes, Challinor Taylor		175.00
Dish, Hen On Basket Cover, Painted, Challinor Taylor, 7 In.		165.00
Dish, Hen On Nest Cover, Blue Head, Cased, Lacy Base, Atterbury		100.00
Dish, Hen With Chick On Nest Cover, Split Ribbed Base, McKee		165.00
Match Holder, Figural Hunter, Green, Portieux, Marked	*Illus*	175.00
Mug, Romeo & Juliet, Blue, Scenes In Relief, 4 1/2 In.	*Illus*	30.00
Pitcher, Grape & Leaves, Water, Pink & Green Leaves, 9 1/4 In.		100.00
Relish, Figural Bird, Head & Tail Handles, c.1870, 1 3/4 x 10 1/2 In.	*Illus*	40.00
Rolling Pin, Advertising, Nebraska Fuel Co., Pekin Coal, Best For Cooking		495.00
Tree Of Life, Syrup, Blue, Tin Cover, 7 In.		55.00
Vase, Bird, Red, White, Green, Yellow, Black, On Branch, Signed, 10 x 6 In.		240.00
Vase, Held By Hand, Pink Cased, Enameled Flowers, Cuff Base, 8 In.	*Illus*	125.00
Vase, Young Girl, Hand Painted, Portrait, Oval, 12 In., Pair		400.00

MILLEFIORI means, literally, a thousand flowers. Many small pieces
of glass resembling flowers are grouped together to form a design. It is
a type of glasswork popular in paperweights and some are listed in that
category.

Milk Glass, Dish, Dog On Rug
Cover, Wicker Basket Base,
Caramel, Painted,
Vallerysthal

Milk Glass, Dish, Figural Walking Bear,
Co-Operative Flint

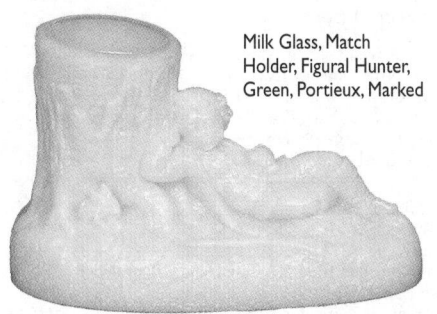

Milk Glass, Match
Holder, Figural Hunter,
Green, Portieux, Marked

Milk Glass, Mug,
Romeo & Juliet,
Blue, Scenes In
Relief, 4 1/2 In.

Perfume, Stopper, Rows Of Turquoise, Pink & White Canes, Globular, 6 In. 360.00
Shade, Green Matte, White, Pinched Waist, Scalloped Border, 2 3/8 x 5 3/4 In. 85.00
Vase, Sapphire Blue, Black, Brown, Cream, Canes, Signed, 4 3/4 In. 115.00

MINTON china has been made in the Staffordshire region of England
from 1793 to the present. The firm became part of the Royal Doulton
Tableware Group in 1968, but the wares continued to be marked
Minton. The word *England* was added in 1891. Minton majolica is
listed in this book in the Majolica category.

    Ashtray & Matchbox Holder, Guinness, Good For You, Center Barrel, 3 3/4 x 5 1/2 In. . . .   75.00
    Candlestick, Monkey, Olive Green Glaze, Majolica, Impressed, c.1890, 9 In. 290.00
    Charger, Winged Mythological Man Outing In Brown, Blue Ground, 1872, 11 In. 500.00
    Cup & Saucer, Pate-Sur-Pate, Classical Women, Putti, Alboin Birks, 1890s, 4 3/4 In. 2590.00
    Dessert Set, Floral Spray Decoration, Footed Cake Stand, 14 Plates, 9 In. 3286.00
    Figurine, Diana, Seated, Holding Dead Bird, Parian, England, Marked, c.1863, 13 1/2 In. .   1295.00
    Figurine, Jason, Classical Male, Draped, Seated, Walking Stick, Parian, c.1860, 16 In. . . .   705.00
    Figurine, Nude Female, Bather, Disrobing, By Tree Stump, 1867, 13 In. 610.00
    Figurine, Travelers Tales, Seated Man, Bronze Head, Hands, 7 In. 92.00
    Plate, Dinner, Aesthetic, Multicolored Design, 10 1/4 In., 10 Piece 260.00
    Plate, Dinner, Cream Ground, Green Band, 3 Gold Border Bands, 10 1/2 In., 6 Piece 430.00
    Plate, Dinner, Neoclassical Style, Garland Turquoise Borders, 10 In., 12 Piece 1725.00
    Plate, Dog Portrait, Spaniel, Terrier, 1872-76, 9 3/4 In., Pair 1700.00
    Plate, Green Laurel Wreath Center, Scattered Rosebuds, c.1925, 8 5/8 In., 12 Piece 380.00
    Plate, Minton Rose, Pink Rose Pendants, Aqua Fishscale Rim, c.1925, 10 In., 12 Piece . . .   265.00
    Plate, Service, Central Flower Spray, Fluted Rim, 20th Century, 10 1/2 In., 12 Piece 635.00
    Plate, Service, Ivory Center, Cobalt Blue, Embossed Gold Border, 10 In., 13 Piece 115.00
    Plate, Service, Magenta Rim, 11 3/4 In., 12 Piece 570.00
    Plate, Tower Of London From Across The Thames, Green Band, A. Holland, 15 In. 275.00
    Platter, Earthenware, Scalloped Rim, Flower Border, Blooming Tree Scene, 20 x 16 In. . .   375.00
    Vase, Pate-Sur-Pate, Cherub, Maiden, Mounted As Lamp, A. Birks, c.1905, 14 1/4 In. 3600.00
    Vase, Peacock Feathers, Swags, 2 Handles, Squeezebag, Art Nouveau, 12 x 5 1/2 In. 1060.00

Milk glass will yellow with repeated washings in a dishwasher.

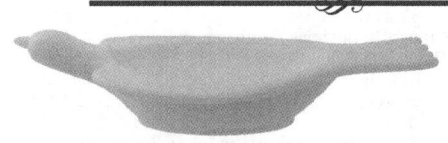

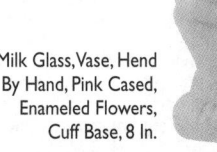

Milk Glass, Relish, Figural Bird, Head & Tail
Handles, c.1870, 1 3/4 x 10 1/2 In.

Milk Glass, Vase, Hend
By Hand, Pink Cased,
Enameled Flowers,
Cuff Base, 8 In.

MIRRORS are listed in the Furniture category under Mirror.

MOCHA pottery is an English-made product that was sold in America during the early 1800s. It is a heavy pottery with pale coffee-and-cream coloring. Designs of blue, brown, green, orange, black, or white were added to the pottery and given fanciful names, such as *Tree, Snail Trail,* or *Moss.* Mocha designs are sometimes found in pearlware. A few pieces of mocha ware were made in France, the United States, and other countries.

Bowl, Blue, White, Olive Banding, Dotted, c.1850, 5 1/2 x 3 In.	290.00
Bowl, Cat's-Eye, Parallel Wavy Trailings, Pearlware, 5 3/4 In.	1035.00
Bowl, Earthworm, Looping, London Shape, Pearlware, 5 1/2 In.	575.00
Bowl, Earthworm, Tricolored, Tooled Green Band, Striped Blue & White Band, 10 x 4 In.	375.00
Bowl, Seaweed, Hemispherical, Taupe & Brown Bands, Green Glaze, Leaf Handles, 11 In.	440.00
Box, Portrait, Napoleon III, Empress Eugenie, Transfer, Painted, c.1850, 5 In.	115.00
Canister, Brown Bands, Blue Seaweed, Lid, 8 In.	220.00
Chamber Pot, Earthworm, Taupe Ground, Dotted Rim, Pearlware, 8 In.	405.00
Coffeepot, Cover, Vertical Stripes, Acorn & Leaf Knop, Baluster, Pearlware, 10 1/4 In.	10925.00
Dish, Cover, Decorated Bands, England, c.1850, 4 1/2 In.	240.00
Goblet, Tobacco Leaf, Brown & White Tones, Chocolate Ground, Striped Foot, 4 In.	5750.00
Mixing Bowl, White Band, Blue Seaweed Design, Brown Lines, 13 x 6 In.	345.00
Mug, A. Davies, Black Horse, Banded, Dendritic Trees, Leaf Terminal Handle, Qt., 6 In.	3335.00
Mug, Black Seaweed Decoration, Extruded Handle, c.1880, 3 1/4 x 3 1/2 In.	575.00
Mug, Cat's-Eye, Black & Incised Green Bands, Blue, Black & Tan Wavy Lines	2760.00
Mug, Checkered, Brown, Early 1800s, 3 In.	259.00
Mug, Cover, Seaweed, Blue, White Band, 3 3/4 In.	345.00
Mug, Earthworm, Cat's-Eye, Banded, Pearlware, Qt., 6 In.	1150.00
Mug, Earthworm, Cat's-Eye, Blue Bands, Pearlware, Qt., 5 1/2 In.	3680.00
Mug, Earthworm, Rust Ground, Leafy Terminal Handle, 5 3/4 In.	575.00
Mug, Engine Turned Geometric Pattern, Banded, Pearlware, 5 1/2 In.	1095.00
Mug, Engine Turned, Zigzag Border, Rouletted Reeded Bands, Pearlware, 5 3/4 In.	4370.00
Mug, Geometrics, Engine Turned, Dendritic Borders, Pearlware, Qt., 5 3/4 In.	9200.00
Mug, Interlocking Circles, White Slip, Brown Ground, Pearlware, 5 3/4 In.	2530.00
Mug, Marbleized, Blue Border, Pearlware, Qt., 6 In.	3220.00
Mug, Marbleized, Leaf Terminal Handle, Herringbone Border, Pearlware, Qt., 6 In.	1840.00
Mug, Marbleized, Rouletted & Reeded Border, Qt., 5 3/4 In.	920.00
Mug, Seaweed, Blue Ground, 2 Black Bands Top & Bottom, Straight Sides, 5 1/8 In.	110.00
Mug, Seaweed, Gray & Blue Bands, Black Stripes, Applied Handle, 5 7/8 In.	1035.00
Mug, Slip Bands, Combed, Leaf Terminal Handle, Pearlware, Qt., 5 3/4 In.	3910.00
Mug, Slip Bands, Combed, Rouletted & Reeded Borders, Pearlware, Qt., 6 1/4 In.	4830.00
Mug, Slip Bands, Engine Turned, Pearlware, Wood & Caldwell, 1790-1818, 4 1/2 In.	8340.00
Mug, Slip Flowers, Rouletted & Reeded Borders, Pearlware, 7 3/4 In.	5520.00
Mug, Tobacco Leaf, Caramel Ground, Applied Handle, Molded Leaf Ends, 6 In.	5980.00
Mug, Tooled Blue Band, Dark Chocolate Ground, Painted Grapes & Flowers, 2 3/4 In.	660.00
Mug, Tulip, Seaweed, Blue Decoration	1920.00
Mug, Wavy Black Trailings, Rouletted & Reeded Bands, Pearlware, 3 1/2 In.	4315.00
Mustard, Stripes In Black, Blue & Brown, 2 1/4 In.	345.00
Pepper Pot, Bands, Combed, Blue Borders, Baluster, Pearlware, 4 1/2 In.	1265.00
Pepper Pot, Cover, Black Dendritic, Rust Ground, Baluster, 4 1/4 In.	405.00
Pepper Pot, Cover, Earthworm, Looping, Urn Shape, Pearlware, 4 3/4 In.	3335.00
Pepper Pot, Dendritic, Brown Ground, Baluster, Pearlware, 4 1/2 In.	575.00
Pepper Pot, Dendritic, Rouletted Reeded Border, Baluster, Brown, Pearlware, 4 1/4 In.	630.00
Pepper Pot, Marbleized, Black, Brown, Cream, Blue Border, Urn Shape, 5 In.	2875.00
Pepper Pot, Seaweed, Tan Ground, 5 1/4 In.	2300.00
Pitcher, Bands, Brown & White Lines, Baluster, Pearlware, 7 3/4 In.	16100.00
Pitcher, Bands, Wavy Parallel Trailings, Rouletting, Herringbone, Pearlware, 6 3/4 In.	6610.00
Pitcher, Blue & Black Stripes, Tooled Green Band, Polka Dots, Applied Handle, 7 3/8 In.	1035.00
Pitcher, Cat's-Eye, Banded, Brown, Rust, Blue, Buff, Barrel Shape, Pearlware, 7 In.	1150.00
Pitcher, Earthworm, Cat's-Eye, Barrel Shape, Pearlware, 6 1/2 In.	4900.00
Pitcher, Earthworm, Looping, Barrel Shape, Pearlware, 5 In.	978.00
Pitcher, Earthworm, Looping, Rouletted & Reeded Border, Spherical, Pearlware, 8 In.	1955.00
Pitcher, Earthworm, Looping, Taupe Ground, Baluster, Pearlware, 5 In.	865.00
Pitcher, Marbleized Splotches, Rouletting, Herringbone, Barrel Shape, Pearlware, 5 In.	1840.00

Pitcher, Orange & Blue Slip Twigs, Barrel Shape, Pearlware, 7 1/2 In. 1035.00
Pitcher, Seaweed, Beaded Diamonds, Chevron Bands, Early 1800s, 8 1/2 In. 1725.00
Pitcher, Seaweed, Blue, Brown Bands, 7 In. 495.00
Pitcher, Seaweed, Blue, White Band, 5 1/2 In. 220.00
Pitcher, Seaweed, Blue, Wide White Bands, 6 1/2 In. 375.00
Pitcher, Seaweed, Green, Blue, White Bands, 7 1/2 In. 978.00
Pitcher, Zigzags, Stylized Leaf Tip Swags, Barrel Shape, Pearlware, 7 3/4 In. 3450.00
Salt, Footed, Bands, Chocolate Brown Band, Black Seaweed Band, 3 x 2 In. 520.00
Sugar, Cover, Earthworm, Light Blue Stripes, 5 x 5 In. 805.00
Sugar, Cover, Marbelized, Brown, Burnt Orange, Cream, 4 3/4 In. 195.00
Sugar, Cover, Seaweed, Blue, White Ground, 4 3/8 x 3 1/2 In. 1380.00
Teapot, Black & White Stripes, Blue Seaweed, Applied Handle, 5 In. 489.00
Washbasin, Earthworm, Spiral, Rouletted & Reeded Rim, Pearlware, 10 3/4 In. 3100.00

MONMOUTH Pottery Company started working in Monmouth, Illinois, in 1892. The pottery made a variety of utilitarian wares. It became part of Western Stoneware Company in 1906. The maple leaf mark was used until 1930. If *Co.* appears as part of the mark, the piece was made before 1906.

Crock, Stamped Logo, 2 Gal. 45.00
Jug, Brown Top, 5 Gal. 50.00
Pitcher, Deep Blue, Embossed Shell Base, 6 In. 40.00
Umbrella Stand, Elk In The Forest, 15 1/2 x 12 1/2 In. 105.00
Vase, Blue Matte Glaze, Lily Pad Border Around Neck, 1920s, 14 In. 390.00

MONT JOYE, see Mt. Joye category.

MOORCROFT pottery was first made in Burslem, England, in 1913. William Moorcroft had managed the art pottery department for James Macintyre & Company of England from 1898 to 1913. The Moorcroft pottery continues today, although William Moorcroft died in 1945. The earlier wares are similar to the modern ones, but color and marking will help indicate the age.

Biscuit Box, Flamminian, Green, c.1914, 5 1/4 In. 259.00
Biscuit Jar, Rose Garlands, Silver Plated Rim, Signed, Macintyre, c.1910, 6 3/8 In. 590.00
Bottle, Pansy, c.1925, 4 3/4 In. 235.00
Bowl, Anemone, Black Ground, Footed, c.1970, 6 1/4 In. 235.00
Bowl, Caribbean, c.1963, 3 3/4 In. 250.00
Bowl, Claremont, Cut, Engraved Silver Mount, Macintyre, c.1905, 10 1/4 In. 3450.00
Bowl, Claremont, Macintyre, c.1905 .... 4600.00
Bowl, Cornflower, Green Ground, Blue, Red, Macintyre, c.1905, 3 1/2 In. 560.00
Bowl, Dura Ware, Green Ground, Red, Orange, Handles, Macintyre, c.1902, 3 1/2 In. 295.00
Bowl, Fish Interior, Inscription On Border, Signed, c.1935, 8 1/2 In. 825.00
Bowl, Freesia, c.1949, 10 In. 210.00
Bowl, Freesia, Washed Blue, Impressed Mark, Signed, c.1935, 12 In. 765.00
Bowl, Hibiscus, c.1975, 9 3/4 In. 190.00
Bowl, Moonlit Blue, Electroplate Mounted Rim, c.1925, 8 1/2 In. 1900.00
Bowl, Orange Luster, Footed, Marked, 11 In. 90.00
Bowl, Pansy, Blue Ground, 1930s, 8 1/4 In. 475.00
Bowl, Pomegranate, Blue, Orange, 2 Handles, c.1916, 12 3/4 In. 540.00
Bowl, Roses, Tulips, Loop Handles, Round Foot, Macintyre, c.1907, 5 In. 1410.00
Bowl, Spring Flowers, Red, Blue, Green Ground, Impressed Mark, c.1945, 5 3/4 In. 530.00
Candlestick, Burslem Orange Luster, Marked, c.1915, 6 In. 325.00
Candlestick, Pomegranate, Impressed Mark, Signed, c.1925, 3 1/4 In. 765.00
Candlestick, Poppy, Dark Blue Ground, Marked, Signed, c.1925, 8 In., Pair 1175.00
Coffeepot, Pomegranate, Green, Red, Dated 1913, 6 1/2 In. 2600.00
Compote, Pansies, Blue, Purple, Ivory, Green Ground, Footed, Handles, 1914, 6 In. 5600.00
Cup, Florian Violet, 2 Handles, White Ground, Inscribed, Macintyre, c.1900, 2 In. 690.00
Cup & Saucer, 18th Century, Gold Ground, Pink, Blue, Macintyre, c.1908, 4 1/2 In. 865.00
Cup & Saucer, 18th Century, White Ground, Pink, Green, Macintyre, c.1908, 4 1/2 In. 380.00
Cup & Saucer, Florian Poppy, Green, Macintyre, For Tiffany & Co., c.1905, 5 1/2 In. 520.00
Cup & Saucer, Pansy, c.1914, 4 1/2 In. 1900.00
Cup & Saucer, Pansy, c.1930, 5 1/2 In., Pair 690.00

Cup & Saucer, Pomegranate, Red, Green, Signed, c.1925 .... 645.00
Dish, Clematis, Impressed Mark, 1953, 7 1/4 In. 295.00
Dish, Freesia, Flambe, Impressed Mark, c.1930, 4 3/4 In. 32.00
Ginger Jar, Cover, Anemone, Blue Ground, c.1982, 8 1/4 In. 430.00
Ginger Jar, Cover, Hibiscus, Green Ground, c.1975, 8 In. 310.00
Inkstand, Florian Poppy, White Ground, Blue Flowers, Macintyre, c.1904, 8 3/4 In. 1640.00
Inkwell, Cover, Landscape, Moonlit Blue, Signed, Impressed Mark, c.1920, 2 1/2 In. 1880.00
Jar, Cover, 18th Century, White Ground, Pink Flowers, Macintyre, c.1908, 3 In. 225.00
Jar, Cover, Anemone, c.1955, 4 1/2 In. 145.00
Jar, Cover, Aurelian, Impressed Mark, Macintyre, c.1900, 5 1/2 In. 175.00
Jar, Cover, Flowers, Persian, Impressed Mark, Macintyre, 5 3/4 In. 2350.00
Jar, Cover, Orchid, c.1949, 3 3/4 In. 295.00
Jar, Cover, Potpourri, Cream Ground, Center Flower Band, Macintyre, 1912, 3 1/2 In. 560.00
Jug, Band Of Flowers, Entwined Ribbon, White Ground, Signed, c.1912, 5 1/2 In. 235.00
Jug, Florian Poppy, Blue Flower, Handle, Macintyre, 1902, 2 1/2 In. 1555.00
Jug, Florian, Peacock Feather, Blue, Green, Faience, Macintyre, 1900-02, 8 In. 1035.00
Jug, Florian, Peacock Feather, Macintyre, 1900-02 .... 1380.00
Lamp, Clematis, Flambe, c.1953, 28 1/4 In. 735.00
Lamp, Eventide, c.1930, 23 1/4 In. 2846.00
Lighter, Freesia, Multicolored, Paper Label, Impressed Mark, c.1930, 2 3/4 In. 265.00
Match Holder, Inscribed, Macintyre, c.1897, 2 1/2 In. 175.00
Mug, Caribbean, c.1963, 3 1/2 In. 380.00
Mug, Clematis, Black Ground, Red Flowers, 1960s, 2 1/4 In. 120.00
Mug, Flamminian, Green, c.1914, 3 3/4 In. 560.00
Pepper Castor, Florian Poppy, Faience, Blue, Macintyre, c.1900, 2 1/2 In., Pair 328.00
Pepper Castor, Florian Poppy, White Ground, Blue, Macintyre, 1903-04, 2 1/2 In. 520.00
Pitcher, Cover, Powder Blue, Impressed Mark, c.1930, 6 1/4 In. 90.00
Pitcher, Flowers, Red, Blue, Bulbous, Wide Rim, Spout, 8 In. 175.00
Pitcher, Metal Cover, Washington Faience, Macintyre, c.1894, 7 1/2 In. 440.00
Pitcher, Roses, Blue, Red, Burslem, Impressed Mark, c.1915, 6 1/4 In. 1410.00
Pitcher, Seaweed, Green, Blue, White Ground, Marked, Macintyre, 1915, 7 In. 705.00
Pitcher, Stand, Gesso, Faience, Green Matte, Macintyre, Harry Barnard, c.1897, 7 In. 155.00
Planter, Fruit & Vine, Green Ground, c.1986, 6 3/4 In. 295.00
Plate, Claremont, Mushrooms, Impressed Mark, c.1930, 4 3/4 In. 1000.00
Plate, Grapes & Leaves, Flambe, Impressed Mark, Signed, c.1930, 10 In. 825.00
Plate, Moonlit Blue, Landscape, Impressed Mark, c.1925, 7 1/4 In. 1175.00
Plate, Toadstools, Green, Silver Overlay, Signed, c.1914, 9 1/2 In. 5600.00
Shaker, Claremont, Mushrooms, Brown, Green Ground, Signed, 2 3/4 In. 2470.00
Tea Set, Florian, c.1913, 3 Piece 8050.00
Teapot, Pomegranate, Green Ground, Pink Flowers, Macintyre, 1910-13, 6 In. 2760.00
Tobacco Jar, Cover, Moonlit Blue, Pewter Mounted Rim, c.1925, 5 1/2 In. 1350.00
Tray, Advertising, Moorcroft Pottery, Green, Ivory Ground, Impressed Mark, 8 1/4 In. 300.00
Tray, Advertising, White Ground, 1980s, 8 1/4 In. 155.00
Tray, Flamminian, Green, 1913 & 1914, 5 In., Pair 330.00
Vase, 18th Century, White, Pink Flower Garland, Macintyre, c.1908, 3 1/2 In., Pair 1208.00
Vase, 18th Century, White, Pink Flowers, 3 Handles, Macintyre, c.1908, 2 1/2 In. 865.00
Vase, Alhambra, Gold Ground, Flower, Macintyre, c.1903, 4 In. 1555.00
Vase, Alhambra, Gold, Red, Blue, Miniature, Macintyre, c.1903, 3 In. ....1725.00 to 1900.00
Vase, Alhambra, Tan Ground, Blue, Red Flower, Macintyre, c.1903, 2 In. 1639.00
Vase, Anemone, Aqua Ground, 1960s, 4 1/2 In. 250.00
Vase, Anemone, Blue Ground, c.1989, 5 1/2 In. 120.00
Vase, Anemone, Flambe, 1930s, 4 In. 865.00
Vase, Anemone, Flambe, c.1955, 2 1/4 In. 330.00
Vase, Aurelian, Macintyre, c.1898 .... 550.00
Vase, Aurelian, White Ground, Blue, Macintyre, c.1898, 5 In. 325.00
Vase, Aurelian, White Ground, Blue, Miniature, Macintyre, c.1898, 3 In. 276.00
Vase, Baluster Shape, Flowers, 7 1/4 In. 510.00
Vase, Banded Honesty, c.1930, 10 In. 1080.00
Vase, Berries & Leaves, Flambe, Impressed Mark, c.1930, 3 1/4 In. 590.00
Vase, Burslem Persian, Flowers, Blue, Green, Red, White Ground, Signed, c.1918, 4 In. 5000.00
Vase, Claremont Toadstool, Washed Blue, Impressed Mark, Signed, c.1915, 7 1/4 In. 3055.00
Vase, Claremont, c.1925, 7 1/4 In. 4315.00
Vase, Claremont, Mushrooms, Bottle Shape, 16 1/2 x 6 1/2 In. 4400.00

Vase, Claremont, Mushrooms, Green, Signed, c.1920, 5 In. 4400.00
Vase, Claremont, Ruby Lustre, Macintyre, c.1910, 7 1/4 In. 2590.00
Vase, Clematis, c.1955, 4 1/4 In. 345.00
Vase, Clematis, Yellow Ground, c.1960, 5 In. 210.00
Vase, Columbine, Aqua Ground, c.1955, 4 1/4 In. 210.00
Vase, Columbine, Flambe, Black Ground, Red Glaze, 1947-49, 3 1/2 In. 949.00
Vase, Cornflower, Powder Blue, c.1928, 12 1/4 In. 1530.00
Vase, Dawn, Luster, White, Blue, Violet, c.1928, 3 1/2 In. 2760.00
Vase, Dianthus, Green Ground, Yellow & Red Flower, c.1955, 4 In. 560.00
Vase, Eventide, Tan, Red, c.1925, 3 1/2 In. 3795.00
Vase, Fairy Rings, c.1989, 7 In. 290.00
Vase, Flamminian, Green, 2 Handles, c.1916, 6 3/4 In. 1295.00
Vase, Flamminian, Green, 2 Handles, c.1916, 10 In. 415.00
Vase, Flamminian, Red, Macintyre, For Liberty & Co., 1906-13, 5 1/2 In. 360.00
Vase, Floral Panels, Blue Ground, Pink Flowers, c.1918, 9 3/4 In. 475.00
Vase, Florian Lilac, Purple, Blue Ground, Macintyre, Signed, c.1920, 8 1/2 In. 4400.00
Vase, Florian Lilac, White Ground, Green, Blue Flowers, Macintyre, c.1905, 2 1/2 In. 1725.00
Vase, Florian Poppy, Blue Flower, Miniature, Macintyre, c.1902, 2 1/2 In. 1725.00
Vase, Florian Poppy, White, Blue, Green Flowers, Macintyre, 1904, 2 3/4 In. 1640.00
Vase, Florian Poppy, Yellow, Green, Ivory, Blue Ground, Macintyre, c.1910, 4 In. 880.00
Vase, Florian Tulip, White Ground, Green, Miniature, Macintyre, c.1902, 2 1/2 In. 4140.00
Vase, Florian Violet, Tan Ground, Violet, Miniature, Macintyre, c.1900, 3 In. 3623.00
Vase, Florian Violet, White, Blue Flowers, Miniature, Macintyre, 1900, 3 In. . . . .1295.00 to 1465.00
Vase, Florian Violets & Butterflies, Macintyre, Signed, c.1915, 8 3/4 In. 2235.00
Vase, Florian, Blue Green Ground, Blue Flower, 1914-16, 3 3/4 In. 1725.00
Vase, Florian, Faience, Blue, Macintyre, c.1900, 3 1/2 In. 765.00
Vase, Florian, Gray Ground, Blue, Yellow, Macintyre, 1900-02, 5 In. 1380.00
Vase, Florian, Lilac, White Ground, Macintyre, 8 3/4 In. 1060.00
Vase, Florian, White Ground, Blue, Macintyre, c.1899, 3 1/2 In. 605.00
Vase, Florian, White, Green, Blue, Pink Flowers, Macintyre, c.1907, 4 In. 1725.00
Vase, Foxglove, Green, Pink, Black, 1994, 4 In. 235.00
Vase, Freesia, Blue Ground, Yellow Green Leaves, Orange, c.1960, 3 In. 310.00
Vase, Fruit & Flowers, Red, Blue Ground, Signed, Impressed Mark, c.1918, 5 1/2 In. 560.00
Vase, Grape & Leaf, c.1949, 7 In. 475.00
Vase, Grape & Leaf, Flambe, c.1935, 3 1/2 In. . . . . .475.00 to 560.00
Vase, Grape & Leaf, Flambe, c.1935, 12 1/2 In., Pair 4830.00
Vase, Grapes, Metal Rim, Signed, c.1910, 10 1/2 In. 1175.00
Vase, Green Poppies, Green Ground, Narrow Neck, Bulbous, 1918, 12 In. 1410.00
Vase, Hazledene, Green Ground, Green, Miniature, Macintyre, c.1913, 3 In. . . . . .3105.00 to 4830.00
Vase, Hibiscus, Brown Ground, Orange Flowers, c.1982, 10 In. 345.00
Vase, Hibiscus, Washed Blue, Impressed Mark, Signed, Mid 20th Century, 10 In. 645.00
Vase, Late Florian, Flambe, Squat, c.1920, 3 In. 2590.00
Vase, Lily, Yellow & Red Flowers, Cobalt Blue Ground, 4 3/4 In. 265.00
Vase, Moonlit Blue, c.1925, 9 In. 3625.00
Vase, Moonlit Blue, c.1925, 12 1/2 In. 4140.00
Vase, Moonlit Blue, Landscape, Signed, c.1925, 3 3/4 In. 1765.00
Vase, Orchid, Black Ground, c.1955, 8 1/2 In. 435.00
Vase, Orchid, Blue, Yellow, Red, Signed, Marked, c.1938, 6 In. 325.00
Vase, Orchid, Flambe, c.1940, 5 In. 690.00
Vase, Orchid, Flambe, Impressed Mark, Signed, c.1940, 3 1/4 In. 530.00
Vase, Orchid, Red Ground, Bulbous, 17 1/2 x 10 1/2 In. 4115.00
Vase, Pansy, Black Ground, Green Leaves, Purple Flower, 1930s, 3 3/4 In. 225.00
Vase, Pansy, Black Ground, Green Leaves, Red Flower, c.1925, 4 In. 605.00
Vase, Pansy, Black Ground, Pink, Yellow, Purple, c.1925, 9 In. 560.00
Vase, Pansy, Cream Ground, Yellow, Purple Flowers, 1914-16, 3 1/2 In. 1725.00
Vase, Pansy, Dark Blue Glaze, Impressed Mark, Signed, c.1930, 7 1/4 In. 500.00
Vase, Pansy, Dark Blue Ground, Impressed Mark, Signed, c.1925, 7 3/4 In. 500.00
Vase, Persian, Yellow Ground, Red Flower, 1914-16, 2 1/2 In. 5695.00
Vase, Pomegranate, Black Ground, Red Flowers, 1920-25, 3 1/4 In. 430.00
Vase, Pomegranate, Black Ground, Red Flowers, Miniature, c.1920, 2 3/4 In. 1555.00
Vase, Pomegranate, Bottle Shape, Washed Blue, Impressed Mark, Signed, c.1930, 6 In. . . . 590.00
Vase, Pomegranate, Bulbous, 8 In. 235.00
Vase, Pomegranate, Flared, Pewter Base, 7 1/2 In. 940.00

Vase, Pomegranate, Yellow Ground, Red, Miniature, 1913-20, 2 In. 2415.00
Vase, Poppy, Black Ground, Red Flower, c.1925, 3 1/2 In. 735.00
Vase, Red Tulips, Blue Flowers, Flared, Marked, Signed, Macintyre, c.1910, 9 In. 3410.00
Vase, Spring Flowers, Aqua Ground, c.1955, 3 1/2 In. 210.00
Vase, Spring Flowers, c.1935, 9 1/2 In. 1800.00
Vase, Spring Flowers, c.1949, 6 In. 630.00
Vase, Spring Flowers, Flambe, Signed, Impressed Mark, c.1930, 9 1/2 In. 1060.00
Vase, Waving Corn, Matte Finish, c.1935, 3 1/2 In. 560.00
Vase, Weeping Willow, c.1935, 5 In. 735.00
Vase, Wisteria, Black, Green Leaves, Red Flowers, 1914-16, 3 3/4 In. 735.00
Vase, Wisteria, Fruit, Flowers, Dark Blue, Impressed Mark, Signed, c.1930, 10 In. 646.00
Vase, Wisteria, Plated Mount, c.1925, 3 3/4 In. 240.00

MORIAGE is a special type of raised decoration used on some Japanese pottery. Sometimes pieces of clay were shaped by hand and applied to the item; sometimes the clay was squeezed from a tube in the way we apply cake frosting. One type of moriage is called *Dragonware* and is listed under that name.

Basket, Handle, 8 1/2 In. 375.00
Cup & Saucer, Dragonware, Geisha Girl Lithophane Base 60.00
Humidor, Imperial Nippon, 7 1/2 In. 316.00
Jug, Whiskey, Christmas Deer, Wicker Basket, M In Wreath, 8 In. 2100.00
Urn, 2 Handles, 8 1/2 In. 145.00
Vase, 3 Birds In Flight, 12 In. 161.00
Vase, Birds In Flight, Twisted Handles, 4-Footed, 12 In. 69.00
Vase, Blue Ground, Handles, Rs Japan Mark, 10 In. 165.00
Vase, Flowers, Pinched Waist, 16 In. 500.00
Vase, Miyako, 12 In. 115.00
Vase, Nile River Foliage, Handles, Green M In Wreath, 9 In. 345.00
Vase, Trees, Buildings, Raised Enamel, Green M In Wreath, 7 1/2 In. 140.00
Vase, White & Pink Roses, Gold, Cylinder, 15 1/2 In. 375.00

MOSAIC TILE COMPANY of Zanesville, Ohio, was started by Karl Langerbeck and Herman Mueller in 1894. Many types of plain and ornamental tiles were made until 1959. The company closed in 1967. The company also made some ashtrays, bookends, and related giftwares. Most pieces are marked with the entwined *MTC* monogram.

Coaster, Flower, Yellow, Blue, 1940-67, 3 1/2 In., 4 Piece 7.00
Plaque, Bluebird Sitting On Branch, Italy, 19th Century, 13 In. 85.00
Tile, Duck, Flying, Gray, White, Burgundy, Brown Black, Aqua Sky, Frame, 11 In. 50.00
Tile, Scrolls & Fleur-De-Lis, Yellow, Blue, Green, Black, 1920s, 4 1/4 x 6 In. 20.00
Tile, Vine, Heart Shape Leaves, Berries, White On Blue Background, 4 x 6 3/4 In. 45.00

MOSER glass is made by Ludwig Moser und Sohne, a Bohemian (Czech) glasshouse founded in 1857. Art Nouveau-type glassware and iridescent glassware were made. The most famous Moser glass is decorated with heavy enameling in gold and bright colors. The firm, Moser Glassworks, is still working in Karlsbad, West Czech Republic. Few pieces of Moser glass are marked.

Bowl, Amber, Engraved Bull Elk, Forest Scene, Oblong, Paneled, 9 x 3 3/4 In. 1150.00
Bowl, Amethyst, Raised Pheasants & Ducks In Pasture, Translucent, Signed, Oval, 7 In. . . 1955.00
Bowl & Stand, Scrolled Leaves, Enameled, c.1900, 7 In. 1035.00
Box, Cover, Amethyst, Amazon Warriors Band, Spanish Galleon Medallion, 5 1/4 In. 400.00
Candy Dish, Cover, Green Cut To Clear, Acid Stamped, 7 1/2 In. 175.00
Claret, Amethyst Cut To Clear, Intaglio, Stems, Leaves, Flowers, Handle, 11 1/2 In. 600.00
Cruet, Glass, Enameled, Fern, Berry, Insects, Topaz Colored Glass, c.1890, 6 1/2 In. 865.00
Decanter, 4 Colors, Spiral Cut Finial, Cranberry Base, 13 x 5 In. 1980.00
Decanter, Cranberry, Enameled Yellow Daffodils, Clear Handle & Stopper, 10 In. 200.00
Decanter, Translucent Green, Gilt Collar, Gold Flower Scrolling, Flat Sided, 8 3/4 In. 375.00
Dresser, Box, Cranberry, Gold Band, Multicolored Flowers, Hinged Cover, 3 1/2 In. 315.00
Dresser Box, Blue, Multicolored Fans, Leaves, 4 x 11 In. 430.00
Dresser Box, Green, Autumn Oak Leaves, Branches, Acorn Jewels, Translucent, 5 In. 550.00
Eggcup, Clear, Thumbprint, Red, Green, Blue & Yellow Leaves & Branches, 4 In. 520.00

Eggcup, Red, Blue, Yellow, Green Leaves, Vines, Translucent, 4 1/4 In. 265.00
Finger Bowl, Underplate, Cobalt Shaded To Clear, Gold Encrusted Leaves, 5 In. 750.00
Finger Bowl, Underplate, Cranberry, Gold Scrolling, Leaves, 6 x 3 In. 290.00
Finger Bowl, Underplate, Green, Gold Flowers, Scrolling, 6 x 3 In. 200.00
Finger Bowl, Underplate, Green, Gold Gilt Bands, Scrolls, Flowers, Translucent, 3 x 7 In. . 690.00
Goblet, Blue, Shamrock Shape, Silver Scrolling, Translucent, 6 1/4 In., Pair 775.00
Goblet, Cranberry, Flower, Verse, Clear Baluster Stem, Raspberry Prunt, 7 In., 6 Piece 750.00
Goblet, Cranberry, Gold Flowers, Scrolls, Stalactite Panels, 4-Lobed Bowl, 6 In., Pair 1035.00
Goblet, Painted, Flowers, Gilt Bands, 7 In. 545.00
Goblet, Scrolled Leaves, Green Rim, Enameled, Allover Gold, c.1900, 6 3/4 In., Pair 1265.00
Liqueur Set, Alexandrite, Gold Encrusted Design, Decanter, Tray, Cordials, 12 Piece 2100.00
Liqueur Set, Gold Encrusted Branches, Bulbous Decanter, Tray, Cordials, 12 Piece 2415.00
Liqueur Set, Green Medallions, Scrolling, Decanter, Cordials, Tray, 8 Piece 863.00
Perfume Bottle, Cranberry Glass, Enameled Flowers, Applied Fish, Gilt Finial, 6 In. 175.00
Perfume Bottle, Cranberry, Gold Encrusted Paneled Designs, Shouldered, 3 1/2 In. 490.00
Pitcher, Cranberry Crackle, Flower Sprays, Reeded Gold Handle, Pinched Sides, 9 In. 1265.00
Pitcher, Cranberry, Allover Enameled Leaves, Yellow, Blue, Red, Opal Handle, 8 In. 1610.00
Pitcher, Pink, Amethyst, Clear To Green, Enameled Poppies, Ice Lip, Ribbed, 8 1/2 In. . . . 345.00
Pitcher, Vertical Bands, White, Blue, Amethyst Flowers, Translucent, 6 3/4 In. 805.00
Sherbet, Cranberry, Multicolored Flowers, Gold Bands, Translucent, 4 1/2 In. 575.00
Sherbet, Scrolled Leaves, Enameled, Cranberry Shaded Rim, 4 1/2 In., Pair 1093.00
Tumbler, Cranberry, Multicolored Oak Leaves, Insects, 6 Applied Acorns, 3 3/4 In. 720.00
Vase, Amber Crackle, Enameled Fish, Applied Shell & Tadpole Trailings, 6 1/2 In. 920.00
Vase, Amber, Oak Leaves, Applied Acorns, Egg Shape, 4 Amber Feet, 4 In. 1150.00
Vase, Amethyst, Fish, Seaweed, Applied Teardrops, Enameled, 6 In. 1065.00
Vase, Art Deco, Topaz, Etched Stylized Flowers, Cameo, c.1925, 9 1/2 In. 575.00
Vase, Box Shape, Enameled, Green, 4 Toed Feet, c.1900, 7 In. 750.00
Vase, Chased Gold Frieze, Classical Warriors, Cobalt, Panel Cut, Beaker Shape, 14 In. 345.00
Vase, Cinnamon, Intaglio, Marquetry, Ribbed, Bulbous Top, Tapered Base, 13 In. 4900.00
Vase, Clear Shaded To Purple, Intaglio Flowers, Translucent, 3-Sided, 4 In. 489.00
Vase, Clear To Green, Gold, Engraved Medallion, Faceted, Cylindrical, Translucent, 6 In. . . 175.00
Vase, Crackle, Applied Fish, Seaweed, Conical, 10 In. 1035.00
Vase, Cranberry, Applied Blue Flowers, Green Stems, Enameled Ferns, Insects, 3 1/2 In. . . . 1150.00
Vase, Green To Clear, Enameled Stylized Oak Leaves, Limbs, Acorns, 12 1/2 x 5 1/2 In. . . . 4085.00
Vase, Red, Green, African Safari, Giraffes, Rhinoceros, Buffalo, Trees, Cameo, Signed . . . 5520.00
Vase, Ruby Red, Faceted, Tapering Octagonal, 8 3/4 In. 130.00
Vase, Smoky Gray, Faceted, Octagonal, 4 3/4 In. 35.00
Vase, Smoky Gray, Faceted, Trapezoidal, Footed, 8 In. 80.00
Vase, Stick, Cranberry, Gold, Silver, Multicolored Scrolling, Bulbous, Flared Rim, 9 In. . . . 345.00
Vase, Trumpet, Optic Ribbed, Clear To Pumpkin, Blue, Yellow Flowers, Footed, 16 1/4 In. . 575.00
Wine, Green, Gold Scrolling, 4-Lobed Bowl, Trumpet Foot, Translucent, 7 In., Pair 145.00
Wine Set, Diplomat, Alexandrite, Sapphire Blue, Pink, Amethyst, 5 1/4 In., 10 Piece 1035.00

MOSS ROSE

MOSS ROSE china was made by many firms from 1808 to 1900. It
has a typical moss rose pictured as the design. The plant is not as popular now as it was in Victorian gardens, so the fuzz-covered bud is
unfamiliar to most collectors. The dishes were usually decorated with
pink and green flowers.

Bowl, Oval, Gold Trim, Japan, 10 In. 85.00
Bowl, Vegetable, Cover, Pompadour Shape, Handle, Rosenthal, 10 1/2 In. 75.00
Cake Set, Server, Plates, Fluted & Scalloped Border, Royal Albert, 7 Piece 115.00

**Use paper plates between
your stored china plates to
help prevent chipping.**

Moss Rose,
Cup & Saucer,
Turquoise Rim

Coffeepot, Pompadour Shape, Rosenthal, 10 1/2 In.	80.00
Creamer, Royal Albert	15.00
Cup & Saucer, Gold Trim, Napco	22.00
Cup & Saucer, Turquoise Rim .... *Illus*	15.00
Mustard, Cover, Underplate, Petal Edges, Gold Trim	25.00
Platter, Oval, Scalloped Edge, Johann Haviland, 13 In.	15.00
Salt & Pepper, Japan, 3 In.	8.00
Sugar, Cover, Handles, Gold Trim, Germany, 1880s, 7 In.	25.00

MOTHER-OF-PEARL GLASS, or pearl satin glass, was first made in the 1850s in England and in Massachusetts. It was a special type of mold-blown satin glass with air bubbles in the glass, giving it a pearlized color. It has been reproduced. Mother-of-pearl shell objects are listed under Pearl.

Biscuit Jar, White, Moire, Square, Gold Flowers, Metal Collar & Lid, 5 In.	345.00
Bowl, Centerpiece, Rainbow, Diamond-Quilted, 3 Yellow Feet, 10 1/2 In.	4600.00
Bowl, Diamond-Quilted, Footed, Alternating Bands, Thorn Handles, 9 1/2 x 10 In.	5350.00
Bowl, Pink, Moire, Crimped & Folded Rim, 6 1/4 In.	400.00
Bowl, Rainbow, Diamond-Quilted, 4 Vaseline Feet, Ruffled Edge, 4 x 8 1/2 In.	920.00
Bowl, Rose Shaded To Pearl, Diamond-Quilted, Crimped Edges, 2 3/4 x 4 1/2 In.	173.00
Compote, Fuchsia Shaded To Pearl, Diamond-Quilted, Clear Stem, Foot, Rigaree, 5 In.	805.00
Creamer, Amber Shaded To Pearl, Raindrop, Camphor Handle, 3 1/4 In.	520.00
Ewer, Rainbow, Herringbone, Applied Handle, Ruffled Edge, 8 1/4 In.	1265.00
Ewer, Rainbow, Herringbone, Tricornered Rim, Clear Handle, 9 1/4 In.	865.00
Figural Scene, Pagoda Landscape, Chinese, 8 1/4 In.	269.00
Muffineer, Rainbow, Diamond-Quilted, 5 1/2 In.	4890.00
Opera Glasses, Audemair, Faceted Barrels, Gilt Metal Frame, Engraved, Paris, 3 In.	60.00
Pitcher, Pink, Diamond-Quilted, Frosted Thorny Handle, Crimped Rim, 4 1/2 In.	400.00
Pitcher, Rainbow, Diamond-Quilted, Bulbous, Flared Neck & Spout, 8 In.	1150.00
Pitcher, Rainbow, Diamond-Quilted, Clear Handle, 5 3/4 In.	1095.00
Pitcher, Red Shaded To Pearl, Diamond-Quilted, Ruffled Edge, Reeded Handle, 9 In.	70.00
Pitcher, Rose To Clear, Floral, Dragonfly, Thorn Handle, 8 In.	510.00
Rose Bowl, Pink, Diamond-Quilted, Crimped & Folded Rim, 5 1/2 In.	173.00
Rose Bowl, Rainbow & Clear Panels, Diamond-Quilted, 2 3/4 In.	2590.00
Rose Bowl, Rainbow, Diamond-Quilted, Crimped Rim, 3 1/4 In.	1495.00
Scent Bottle Coffer, Papier-Mache, Parcel Gilt, Black Lacquered, 6 x 6 x 6 In.	920.00
Sugar, Cover, Amber To Pearl, Honeycomb, Spherical, Camphor Loop Handle, 4 In.	1150.00
Tumbler, Rainbow, Pincushion Pattern, Gold Trim, 3 3/4 In.	345.00
Vase, Amethyst, Diamond-Quilted, Petaled Mouth, 3 Frosted Feet, 7 In.	1670.00
Vase, Crimson Shaded To Butterscotch, Diamond-Quilted, Bulbous, Long Neck, 11 In.	175.00
Vase, Frosted Apricot, Herringbone, Ruffled Edge, Footed, 5 1/4 In.	40.00
Vase, Green Shaded To Yellow To Pearl, Diamond-Quilted, Ruffled Edge, 7 In.	690.00
Vase, Pink, Herringbone, Bulbous Rim, Ruffled Edge, Thorny Camphor Handle, 10 In.	315.00
Vase, Rainbow, Herringbone, Egg Shape, Tapered, Trifold Rim, 8 In.	1035.00
Vase, Satin Blue To Pearl, Swirled Diamond-Quilted, Gourd Shape, 10 In.	200.00
Vase, White, Pink Inside, Herringbone, Ginko, Butterfly, Heart Shape, Rolled Rim, 6 In.	400.00
Vase, Yellow, Diamond-Quilted, Frosted Pearl, Flowers, Butterfly, Beaded, 6 In.	980.00

MOUNT WASHINGTON, see Mt. Washington category.

MOVIE memorabilia of all types is collected. Animation Art, Games, Sheet Music, Toys, and some celebrity items are listed in their own sections. A lobby card is 11 by 14 inches. A set of lobby cards includes seven scene cards and one title card. A one sheet, the standard movie poster, is 27 by 41 inches. A three sheet is 81 by 40 inches. A half sheet is 22 by 28 inches. A window card, made of cardboard, is 14 by 22 inches. An insert is 14 by 36 inches. A herald is a promotional item handed out to patrons. Press books, which contain many ad slicks, are sent to film exhibitors to aid in advertising the film. Press books and/or press kits (with photos) are sent to the media to promote a movie.

Banner, Drive-In, House Of Dracula, Lon Chaney, Jr., 1945, 24 x 82 In.	435.00
Display, Tobacco Road, Grapewin, Rambeau, Tierney, Tracy, Die Cut, c.1941, 36 x 20 In.	86.00
Display, Western Union, Young, Scott, Die Cut, Theatre Sticker, c.1941, 35 x 20 In.	115.00

Herald, Animal Crackers, Marx Brothers, 1930, 8 1/2 x 7 In., 4 Pages 275.00
Herald, Freshman, Harold Lloyd, Cardboard, Megaphone, 1925, 11 1/2 x 9 In. 60.00
Lobby Card, Forbidden Planet, Robby The Robot, 1956 .... 345.00
Lobby Card, Gun Crazy, Peggy Cummings, John Dall, 1950 .... 405.00
Lobby Card, Gunfight At Comanche Creek, Audie Murphy, 1963 .... 28.00
Lobby Card, House Of Horrors, 1946 .... 405.00
Lobby Card, Jamaica Inn, Hitchcock, Charles Laughton, 1939 .... 460.00
Lobby Card, Lost World, Willis H. O'Brien, Special Effects, 1925 .... 430.00
Lobby Card, Love Happy, Marx Brothers, 1949 .... 110.00
Lobby Card, Man Who Would Be King, Connery, Caine, 1975 .... 11.00
Lobby Card, Saturday Night Kid, Clara Bow, 1929 .... 290.00
Lobby Card, Speedy, Harold Lloyd, c.1928 .... 2346.00
Lobby Card Set, Spellbound, Bergman, Peck, 1945, 8 Piece 805.00
Lobby Card Set, Taxi Driver, Robert De Niro, Jodie Foster, 1976, 8 Piece 230.00
Lobby Card Set, The Terror From Space, 1958, 8 Piece 345.00
Photograph, James Dean, Signed To Susan, 9 1/2 x 8 In. 7475.00
Photograph, King Kong, Fay Wray, 8 x 10 In., 1933, 3 Piece 748.00
Poster, A Clockwork Orange, Malcom McDowell, 1971, 3 Sheet 290.00
Poster, American In Paris, Gene Kelly, Leslie Caron, 1951, 1 Sheet 460.00
Poster, Andy Warhol's Frankenstein, France, 1983, 47 x 63 In. 145.00
Poster, Arsenic & Old Lace, Cary Grant, 1944, 1 Sheet 1760.00
Poster, Babe Ruth Story, William Bendix, Claire Trevor, 1948, 6 Sheet 3450.00
Poster, Baby Puss, Tom & Jerry, Cartoon, 1943, 1 Sheet 1840.00
Poster, Barbarella, Jane Fonda, Linen Back, 1968, 1 Sheet 259.00
Poster, Bedlam, Boris Karloff, 1946, 1 Sheet 920.00
Poster, Belle Of New York, Fred Astaire, 1952, 1 Sheet 175.00
Poster, Best Years Of Our Lives, March, Loy, Linen Back, 1947, 1 Sheet 750.00
Poster, Big Parade, John Gilbert, 1925, 1 Sheet 6325.00
Poster, Black Cat, Lugosi, Rathbone, Sweden, 1941, 28 x 39 In. 489.00
Poster, Breakfast At Tiffany's, Audrey Hepburn, Linen Back, 1961, 1 Sheet 1150.00
Poster, Chicken Feed, Our Gang, 1927, 3 Sheet 2300.00
Poster, Chinatown, Jack Nicholson, 1974, 1 Sheet 259.00
Poster, Dangerous Years & Invisible Wall, Marilyn Monroe, 1948, Half Sheet 2875.00
Poster, Dark Victory, Bette Davis, Linen Back, 1939, 1 Sheet 11500.00
Poster, Desire, Marlene Dietrich, Gary Cooper, 1935, Insert 1150.00
Poster, Dial M For Murder, Grace Kelly, 1954, 1 Sheet 1380.00
Poster, Evil Of Frankenstein, Peter Cushing, France, 1964, 47 x 63 In. 201.00
Poster, Fighting Marine, Serial, Gene Tunney, 1926, 1 Sheet 1938.00
Poster, Fistful Of Dollars, Clint Eastwood, 1967, 1 Sheet 575.00
Poster, Five Easy Pieces, Jack Nicholson, 1970, 6 Sheet 175.00
Poster, Forbidden Planet, Robby The Robot, 1956, Insert 2185.00
Poster, Frankenstein Meets The Wolf Man, Lugosi, Chaney, 1943, Half Sheet 4025.00
Poster, From Russia With Love, Sean Connery, 1964, 1 Sheet 316.00
Poster, Giant, James Dean, Elizabeth Taylor, Rock Hudson, 1956, 6 Sheet 2300.00
Poster, Godzilla, Raymond Burr, 1956, 1/2 Sheet 1495.00
Poster, Gold Diggers Of 1937, Joan Blondell, 1936, Insert 375.00
Poster, Goldfinger, Connery, Linen Back, Argentina, 1964, 29 x 43 In. 290.00
Poster, Harvey, James Stewart, 1950, Half Sheet 690.00
Poster, How To Marry A Millionaire, Marilyn Monroe, 1953, Window Card 345.00
Poster, Indian Territory, Gene Autry, His Horse Champion, 1950, 31 x 45 In. 175.00
Poster, Invisible Ghost, Bela Lugosi, 1941, Insert 489.00
Poster, Jackie Robinson Story, Jackie Robinson, 1950, 1 Sheet 2070.00
Poster, Knute Rockne All American, Ronald Reagan, Pat O'Brien, 1940, Insert 1210.00
Poster, Let's Make Love, Marilyn Monroe, Yves Montand, 1960, 1 Sheet 230.00
Poster, Little Women, Katharine Hepburn, Linen Back, 1933, 1 Sheet 1495.00
Poster, Mean Streets, Robert De Niro, 1973, Insert 175.00
Poster, Mummy's Curse, Lon Chaney, Linen Back, 1944, 1 Sheet 2875.00
Poster, Niagara, Marilyn Monroe, 1953, 1 Sheet 1265.00
Poster, Personal Property, Jean Harlow, Robert Taylor, 1937, 1 Sheet 865.00
Poster, Prince & The Showgirl, Marilyn Monroe, Laurence Olivier, 1957, 1 Sheet 690.00
Poster, Rear Window, James Stewart, Grace Kelly, 1954, Half Sheet 1095.00
Poster, Safe At Home, Mickey Mantle, Roger Maris, 1962, 3 Sheet 1090.00
Poster, Seven Year Itch, Marilyn Monroe, 1955, 1/2 Sheet 920.00

Poster, Silken Affair, David Niven, Genevieve Page, Frame, 21 1/2 x 27 1/2 In. 50.00
Poster, Terry-Toon Cartoon Characters, Mighty Mouse, 1955, 1 Sheet 460.00
Poster, The Thin Man, William Powell & Myrna Loy, 1934, Window Card 990.00
Poster, To Catch A Thief, Grace Kelly, Cary Grant, 1955, Half Sheet 863.00
Poster, White Heat, James Cagney, 1949, Half Sheet 259.00
Press Book, I Am A Fugitive From A Chain Gang, Paul Muni, 1932 .... 175.00
Press Kit, The Champ, Voight, Schroder, 1979 .... 23.00
Program, Gone With The Wind, 1939 .... 95.00
Sheet Music, Funny Thing Happened On Way To Forum, Zero Mostel, 1962 .... 27.50

MT. JOYE is an enameled cameo glass made in the late nineteenth and twentieth centuries by Saint-Hilaire Touvier de Varraux and Co. of Pantin, France. This same company made De Vez glass. Pieces were usually decorated with enameling. Most pieces are not marked.

Compote, Cranberry Flowers, Green Leaves, Clover Shape, Metal Foot, 8 1/2 In. 316.00
Jar, Cover, Ruby & Gilt Decorations, Art Nouveau, Tapered Square, 3 1/2 In. 560.00
Letter Holder, Yellow & Purple Irises, Frosted, Gilt Icicle Trim, Round, Folded Sides, 10 In. 375.00
Rose Bowl, Relief Cameo Flower, Frosted, Textured, Gilt Trim, 2 In. 460.00
Tankard, Green Over Clear, Enameled, Metal Mount, c.1900, 13 In. 375.00
Vase, Gold Mums, Green Translucent Ground, Cameo, 12 1/2 In. 259.00

MT. WASHINGTON Glass Works started in 1837 in South Boston, Massachusetts. In 1870 the company moved to New Bedford, Massachusetts. Many types of art glass were made there until 1894, when the company merged with Pairpoint Manufacturing Co. Amberina, Burmese, Crown Milano, Cut Glass, Peachblow, and Royal Flemish are each listed in their own category.

Biscuit Jar, Albertine, Blue Blossoms, Branches, Painted, 10 In. 835.00
Bottle, Barber, Opal, Blue, Purple Pansies, Squat, 7 In. 115.00
Bowl, Peach To White, Leafy Branches, Raised Flowers, Ruffled Edge, 3 In. 115.00
Cruet, Ribbed, Yellow & White Mums, Green Vines, Stopper, 1890, 6 1/2 In. 4760.00
Dresser Box, Blue & Pink Daisies, Squat Melon Shape, Flip Lid, 4 1/2 In. 290.00
Jar, Cover, Colonial Ware, Raised Enameled Gold Scrolls, Silver Plated, 6 1/2 In. 405.00
Jar, Garden Of Allah, Desert Scene Of Bedouins, Camels, Blue Sky, 1890, 8 In. 1680.00
Lamp, Opaline, Raised Gold Scrolls, Flowers, Metal Base, Colonial Ware, 22 In. 805.00
Mustard Pot, Forget-Me-Nots, Fig Shape, Metal Cover, Shaped Handle, 3 In. 430.00
Pin Holder, Mushroom Shape, Raised Blue, White Flowers, Brown Stems, 3 1/2 In. 546.00
Pitcher, Cream, Pink Shaded To Pearl Blue Satin, 3 5/8 In. 2990.00
Pitcher, Green Ivy, Dickens Verse, Creeping Where No Life Is Seen, 1890, 7 In. 6160.00
Pitcher, Water, Orange, Red Flower Spray, Applied Thorny Handle, Signed, 9 In. 230.00
Rose Bowl, Blue Daisies, Beige Leaves, Crimped Rim, 5 In. 175.00
Rose Bowl, Cream Shaded To Pink, Purple & Amethyst Violets, No. 618, 4 In. 290.00
Salt & Pepper, Flowers, Egg Shape, 2 1/2 In. 50.00
Salt & Pepper, Pink, Blue Daisies, Red Mums, Egg Shape, 2 1/2 In. 140.00
Sugar & Creamer, Herringbone, Mother-Of-Pearl, Pearl Shaded To Blue, Crimped Rim ... 2875.00
Sugar Shaker, Blue To Cream, Enameled Daisy, 4 1/4 In. 345.00
Sugar Shaker, Blue To White, Enameled Flowers, Metal Caddy, 7 In. 690.00
Sugar Shaker, Chick's Head, Pink, Yellow & White Flowers, 3 3/4 x 4 In. 5465.00
Sugar Shaker, Chrysanthemums, Yellow, Blue, Amethyst, Egg Shape, 4 1/4 In. 415.00
Sugar Shaker, Enameled Daisies, Peach Ground, Fig Shape, 4 x 3 1/2 In. 1095.00
Sugar Shaker, Enameled Flowers, Tomato Shape, 2 1/4 x 4 In. 480.00
Sugar Shaker, Enameled Spider Mums, Fig Shape, Cover, 4 In. 1550.00
Sugar Shaker, Opal, Pansies, Melon Ribbed, 2 1/2 In. 290.00
Sugar Shaker, Opalescent, Pansy, Fig Shape, 3 1/4 x 4 In. 1380.00
Sugar Shaker, Rose, Blue, Rust Berries, Melon Ribbed, Embossed Metal Lid, 4 In. 345.00
Sugar Shaker, Spider Mums, Yellow, Fig Shape, 4 In. 1780.00
Sugar Shaker, White Blue Raised Flowers, Cream Ground, Tomato Shape, 2 3/4 In. 400.00
Sugar Shaker, Yellow & Green Daisies, Melon Ribbed, 3 1/2 In. 130.00
Syrup, Enameled Pink Daises, Hinged Cover, c.1890, 8 In. 90.00
Syrup, Gold Stem Flowers, Lobed Body, Metal Cover, 6 In. 460.00
Toothpick, Amethyst & Blue Stemmed Flowers, Barrel Shape, 2 1/2 In. 315.00
Toothpick, Crimson, Blue Flowers, 10 Lobed Body, 2 1/4 In. 259.00
Toothpick, Square Mouth, Ribbed, Blue Flowers, Leafy Stems, 2 3/4 In. 200.00

Vase, Burmese, Gourd Shape, 12 In. 315.00
Vase, Double Gourd, Multicolored Pansy, 6 3/4 In. 635.00
Vase, Flowers, Pink, Gold, Ivory Ground, 10 In. 355.00
Vase, Jack-In-The-Pulpit, Leaves, Flowers, Crimped Rim, Footed, 10 In. 1035.00
Vase, Lava Glass, Black, Bulbous, Circular Neck, Rolled Rim, 5 In. 1610.00
Vase, Pansies, 2 Indented & Curled Handles, Bulbous, 9 In. 1150.00

MULLER FRERES, French for Muller Brothers, made cameo and other glass from about 1895 to 1933. Their factory was first located in Luneville, then in nearby Croismare, France. Pieces were usually marked with the company name.

Chandelier, Roses, Frosted Ground, 3 Chains, Bronze Brackets, Cameo, 15 In. 805.00
Charger, Butterflies, Burgundy, Pink, Camphor, Cameo, Signed, 14 In. 4600.00
Ewer, Enameled, Nocturnal Shepherd Scene, Applied Handle, Cameo, Signed, 5 In. 3740.00
Lamp, Mottled Blue, Yellow, Orange, Art Deco, 12 In. 460.00
Lamp, Pheasant, Amber, Foil Inclusions, Art Deco, Open Metal Work, 17 x 20 In. 7475.00
Lamp, Red, Frosted, Wrought Iron, Round Base, Domed Shade, 13 x 14 In. 1410.00
Pitcher, Leaves, Applied Gold Enameled Bug, Handle, Cameo, 7 1/2 In. 3100.00
Vase, Apple Trees, Mottled Orange, Cherub, Sunset, Butterfly Band, Cameo, 12 In. 2760.00
Vase, Blackberry Brambles, Brown, Green, Opal Ground, Pillow, Cameo, 7 1/2 In. 2300.00
Vase, Blossoms, Leaves, Opalescent, Cameo, c.1910, 6 1/4 In. 2070.00
Vase, Flowers, Blue, Cream, Cameo, Signed, 9 3/8 In. 2530.00
Vase, Gray, Flowers, Silver Foil Inclusions, Cameo, c.1910, 11 1/2 In. 2760.00
Vase, Gray, Shaded With Orange, Yellow, Cameo, c.1900, 9 1/4 In. 1035.00
Vase, Green & Blue Forest, Dancing Ladies, Frosted Pink Ground, Cameo, 4 In. 520.00
Vase, Lake Scene At Sunset, Oval, Tall, Squared Mouth, Cameo, 8 1/2 In. 1075.00
Vase, Lake Scene, Peach & Green Over Opal, Cameo, c.1910, 5 1/2 In. 1035.00
Vase, Landscape, Trees, Lake, Almond, Tangerine, Brown, Cameo, Signed, 9 3/4 In. 1100.00
Vase, Landscape, Yellow Amber, Blue, Pink, Enameled, Cameo, c.1905, 10 3/4 In. 1410.00
Vase, Nautical Scene, Ships In Harbor, Blue Ground, Bulbous, Cameo, 13 In. 2590.00
Vase, Pomegranates, Cinnamon Over Citron Yellow, Cameo, Clear, c.1885, 5 1/2 In. 518.00
Vase, Red Roses, Brown Leaves, Stems, Cameo, Signed, 16 1/2 In. 2990.00
Vase, Trumpet, Scarlet Red, Blue, Black Leaves, Signed, 13 1/4 In. 375.00

MUNCIE Clay Products Company was established by Charles Benham in Muncie, Indiana, in 1922. The company made pottery for the florist and giftshop trade. The company closed by 1939. Pieces are marked with the name *Muncie* or just with a system of numbers and letters, like *1A*.

Bookends, Owls, Blue Matte Over Rose, 5 In. 440.00
Bowl, Blue Matte Over Rose, 7 1/2 In. 175.00
Bowl, Blue Matte Over Rose, 9 In. 60.00
Bowl, Green Matte Over Lilac, 10 1/2 In. 118.00
Bowl, Peachskin Glaze, Black Drip Over Orange, Tan, Swirls, Marked, 3 1/4 x 7 1/2 In. ... 230.00
Candlestick, Flambe, Peachskin Glaze, Black Flambe Drip, Marked, 9 x 4 1/2 In., Pair ... 200.00
Candlestick, Green Matte Over Lilac, 3 In., Pair 205.00
Candlestick, Green Matte Over Rose, 6 In., Pair 120.00
Flower Frog, Canoe Shape, Green Matte Over Rose, 11 1/2 In. 120.00
Lamp, Green Matte Over Pumpkin, 8 In. 145.00
Lamp Base, Love Birds, Yellow High Glaze, 8 In. 381.00
Pitcher, Bittersweet Glaze, Marked, 6 1/2 In. 175.00
Pitcher, Blue Matte Over Green, Hand Thrown, 5 In. 60.00
Pitcher, Green Matte Drip, 5 1/2 In. 235.00
Pitcher, Ruba Rombic, 5 In. 645.00
Vase, Art Pottery, Green Gray Drip Glaze, Mauve Ground, 8 1/4 In. 105.00
Vase, Blue Matte Over Green, Marked, 7 In. 175.00
Vase, Blue Matte Over Rose, 8 3/4 In. 115.00
Vase, Blue Matte Over Rose, Handles, 9 In. 120.00
Vase, Bulbous, Flared Neck, Glaze, Mint Green To Dark Rose, 6 In. 90.00
Vase, Curdled White Over Rose Matte, Hand Thrown, Marked, 5 In. 285.00
Vase, Glossy Black, Marked, 7 1/4 In. 60.00
Vase, Glossy Green, Hand Thrown, 5 In. 175.00
Vase, Glossy Sea Green, Impressed Backwards, 8 1/2 In. 60.00

Vase, Green Matte Over Lilac, 5 1/2 In.	120.00
Vase, Green Matte Over Lilac, Bottle Shape, Marked, 5 1/2 In.	145.00
Vase, Green Matte Over Lilac, Hand Thrown, 7 In.	120.00
Vase, Green Matte Over Lilac, Hand Thrown, Marked, 4 In.	175.00
Vase, Green Matte Over Lilac, Handles, Marked, 5 In.	60.00
Vase, Green Matte Over Lilac, Marked, 8 In.	120.00
Vase, Green Matte Over Pumpkin, Handles, Hand Thrown, 6 In.	325.00
Vase, Green Matte Over Rose, 5 1/2 In.	90.00 to 145.00
Vase, Green Matte Over Rose, 11 In.	355.00
Vase, Green Matte Over Rose, Hand Thrown, 6 In.	145.00
Vase, Green Matte Over Rose, Hand Thrown, 9 In.	325.00
Vase, Green Matte Over Rose, Marked, 8 In.	120.00
Vase, Green Matte Over White, 7 In.	60.00
Vase, Green Matte, 8 In.	265.00
Vase, Light Blue Glaze, 6 In.	35.00
Vase, Light Blue Over White, 9 In.	205.00
Vase, Ruba Rombic, Blue Matte Over Green, Marked, 5 In.	325.00
Vase, Ruba Rombic, Blue Matte Over Green, Marked, 7 In.	705.00
Vase, Ruba Rombic, Green Matte Over Lilac, Marked, 6 In.	1058.00
Vase, Ruba Rombic, Green Matte Over Pumpkin, Marked, 5 In.	825.00
Vase, Ruba Rombic, Green Matte Over Rose, 5 In.	325.00
Vase, White Curdling Over Rose, Marked, 6 In.	175.00
Vase, White Matte Over Blue, Marked, 5 In.	120.00
Vase, White Over Rose, Marked, 6 In.	120.00

MURANO, see Glass-Venetian category.

MUSIC boxes and musical instruments are listed here. Phonograph
records, jukeboxes, phonographs, and sheet music are listed in other
categories in this book.

Accordion, Hohner, Original Case, c.1900, 14 In.	60.00
Accordion, Lachenal & Co., Blind Fretwork, Mahogany Case, Late 1800s, 7 x 8 x 7 In.	489.00
Accordion, Organetto, Miland, c.1910, 11 In.	69.00
Autoharp, William Teubeur, Rosewood, Mother-Of-Pearl, Ivory Feet, Case, 22 x 16 In.	1295.00
Banjo, 5 Strings, W.A. Cole, Eclipse, Mahogany Neck, Ebony Fingerboard, c.1895	4400.00
Banjo, 8 Strings, Rettberg & Lange, Orheum, No. 1, Inlaid, c.1930, 23 1/2 In.	200.00
Bow, Viola, A. Lamy, Round Stick, Silver Mounted, Paris	1060.00
Bow, Viola, J.F. Raffin, Silver Mounted, Round Stick, Ebony Frog, France	1645.00
Bow, Viola, O. Blanchette, Silver Mounted, Baleen Wrap, Montreal	1530.00
Bow, Violin, Albert Nurnberger, Octagonal Stick, Silver Mounted, Ebony Frog, Germany	3175.00
Bow, Violin, Bernard Ouchard, Gold & Ivory Mounted, Ivory Frog, France	4465.00
Bow, Violin, G. Cone & Fils, Silver Mounted, Round Stick, Ebony Frog, France	3290.00
Bow, Violin, H.R. Pfretzschner, Gold, Octagonal Stick, Tortoiseshell Frog, Germany	2820.00
Bow, Violin, James Tubbs, Round Stick, Gold Mounted, Ebony Frog, England	1175.00
Bow, Violin, Jerome Thibouville Lamy Cie., Silver Mounted, Round Stick, France	265.00
Bow, Violin, Morizot Pere, Round Stick, Silver Mounted, Ebony Frog, France	2115.00
Bow, Violin, Pecatte School, Nickel Mounted, Round Stick, Ebony Frog, Pearl Eye	2235.00
Bow, Violin, W.E. Hill & Sons, Silver Mounted, Round Stick, Ebony Frog, England	2470.00
Bow, Violoncello, C. Bazin, Silver Mounted, Round Stick, Ebony Frog, Pearl Eye, France	4700.00
Bow, Violoncello, Dodd, Silver Mounted, Round Stick, Ebony Frog	3820.00
Bow, Violoncello, E. Herrmann, Silver Mounted, Round Stick, Germany	645.00
Bow, Violoncello, Eugene Sartory, Round Stick, Silver Mounted, Ebony Frog, France	14100.00
Bow, Violoncello, Gustav Schmidt, Round Stick, Nickel Mounted	325.00
Bow, Violoncello, W.R. Wild, Silver Mounted, Round Stick	470.00
Box, 9 Bells, 4 Bees, Inlaid Case, Tune Sheet In Lid, Swiss, 1880, 26 In.	6600.00
Box, Allard & Sandoz, Hand Carved Table, 5 18-In. Cylinders	7700.00
Box, Baker Troll, Rosewood Case, 2 Zithers, Swiss, 8 16 1/4-In. Cylinders, 48 In.	38500.00
Box, Bremond, Burl Walnut Veneer Case, 6 Tunes, 20 1/2 In.	2350.00
Box, Bremond, Visible Bells, Rosewood Case, 12 Tunes, 17-In. Cylinder, 28 In.	3400.00
Box, Capital, Mahogany Case, 25 Cuffs, 21 In.	4295.00
Box, Columbia, Sublime Harmony, Interchangeable Cylinder, Rosewood, Swiss, 50 In.	11550.00
Box, Cylinder, 2 Bisque Ballerinas, Walnut Banded Case, 10 Tunes, Swiss, 15 1/2 In.	2600.00
Box, Cylinder, 4 Tunes, Swiss, 3 1/2-In. Cylinder, c.1880, 14 1/2 In.	560.00

Box, Cylinder, Automaton, 2 Oriental Men, Dancing Bisque Figure, 8 Tunes, 23 1/2 In. ... 6050.00
Box, Cylinder, Burl Walnut, Veneer, Brass Handles, 6 Tunes, 31 x 16 x 16 In. 6900.00
Box, Cylinder, Drocourt, Oak Case, 6 Airs, 16 In. 1195.00
Box, Cylinder, Inlaid Rose Wood Case, Swiss, 13-In. Cylinder, 19th Century, 23 In. 489.00
Box, Cylinder, Interchangeable, 6 Bells, Bees, Zither, 1-Drawer Table, 35 In. 12650.00
Box, Cylinder, Interchangeable, Burl Case, Swiss, 4 17 1/4-In. Cylinders, 42 In. 22000.00
Box, Cylinder, Ornate Case, Inlaid Top, Front, 25 x 13 1/2 In. 1980.00
Box, Cylinder, Rosewood Case, 6 Bells, Bees, Drum, Swiss, 25 5/8-In. Cylinder, 44 In. ... 20900.00
Box, Cylinder, Rosewood, Marquetry, Glass, 8 Tunes, 8 x 20 x 9 In. 1495.00
Box, Cylinder, Sublime Harmony, Interchangeable, Burl Case, Table, 42 In. 22000.00
Box, Cylinder, Walnut Case, Swiss, 19th Century, 18 In. 750.00
Box, Drums, Bells, Castanets, Painted & Inlaid Case, 10 Tunes, Swiss, 24 In. 3220.00
Box, Ducommon Girod, Mahogany Case, Urn Inlay, 14-In. Cylinder, 25 In. 20350.00
Box, Empress, Concert Grand, Mahogany, Double Comb, 18 1/2-In. Disc, 42 In. 9900.00
Box, Langdorff, Grained Case, Key Wind, 6 Tunes, 11-In. Cylinder, 18 In. 1645.00
Box, Mahogany, Stand, Storage Slots, For 15 1/2-In. Discs, 1895 .... 880.00
Box, Mahogany, Trophy Inlays, Ebonized Feet, 6 Tunes, 7 x 26 x 10 In. 1035.00
Box, Mandoline Piccolo, Veneer Case, Ebonized, Inlaid, 12 Tunes, 33 In. 3055.00
Box, Mechanical Picture, Shoemaker's Shop, Lithograph, 10 1/2 x 13 3/4 In. 2300.00
Box, Mermod Freres, Grained Case, External Crank, 10 Tunes, 20 In. 825.00
Box, Mermod Freres, Inlaid Rosewood Case, 6 Cylinders, 6 Tunes Each, 28 In. 5170.00
Box, Mermod Freres, Mahogany Case, Interchangeable Cylinder, Zither, Table, 48 In. 49500.00
Box, Mira, Mahogany Case, 17 Discs, 12 1/2 x 27 x 20 In. 3285.00
Box, Mira, Mahogany Case, Double Comb, Upright, 18 1/2-In. Disc 6600.00
Box, Mira, Mahogany Case, Figured, Double Comb, 80 15 1/2-In. Discs, 25 In. 5875.00
Box, Mira, Walnut Case, Wind, Zither, Disc, Landscape Lid, 13 1/2 x 11 3/4 x 7 1/4 In. ... 690.00
Box, Nicole Freres, Cylinder, Aesthetic Design, Wood Case, 12 Airs, Swiss, 28 In. 1675.00
Box, Paillard, Grained Case, 12 Tunes, 8-In. Cylinder, 18 In. 825.00
Box, Paillard, Piccolo-Zither, Rosewood, Inlaid, 6 Tunes, 8-In. Cylinder, 17 In. 590.00
Box, Polyphon, Style 41, Grained Case, Ratchet Wind, Single Comb, 8 1/4-In. Disc, 12 In. 645.00
Box, Regina, Mahogany Case, Double Comb, 26 15 1/2-In. Discs, c.1895 .... 4730.00
Box, Regina, Mahogany, Stepped Lid, Single Comb, 35 15 1/2-In. Discs, 21 In. 2585.00
Box, Regina, Mahogany, Upright, Single Play, Alternating Combs, 12 Discs, c.1895, 25 In. 9625.00
Box, Regina, Orchestral Corona, No. 33, Mahogany, Serpents, 12 27-In. Discs, 66 In. 22000.00
Box, Regina, Sublima Corona, Self Changers, 15 1/2-In. Disc 18150.00
Box, Reuge, Double Comb, Drum, Brass Movement, Chopin, Swiss, 3 x 14 In. 900.00
Box, Rivenc, Zither Attachment, Inlaid Rosewood Case, 8 Airs, 24 In. 2000.00
Box, Singing Bird, 2 Feathered Birds, Gilt Bronze Cage, France, Early 1900s, 21 x 11 In. ... 865.00
Box, Singing Bird, 3 Birds, Brass Cage, 23 In. 6600.00
Box, Singing Bird, Birdcage, France, 10 1/2 In. 775.00
Box, Singing Bird, Birdcage, Jeweled Decoration, Germany 65.00
Box, Singing Bird, Cage, Feathers, Animated, Reuge, Swiss, c.1950, 12 In. 810.00
Box, Singing Bird, Cylinder, Ebony Case, Banded Inlay, 6 Tunes, 30 In. 30250.00
Box, Singing Bird, Silver Cage, Enamel, 3 Women, Swiss, c.1950, 1 1/2 x 4 In. 2575.00
Box, Singing Bird, Silver Gilt, Filigree, Gems, Austria-Hungary, c.1900, 3 1/4 x 4 1/2 In. .. 3015.00
Box, Stella, Carved Mahogany Case, Double Comb, Stand, 75 17-In. Discs, 45 In. 4400.00
Box, Stella, Orchestral Grand, Oak, Floor Model, 21 26-In. Discs, 41 In. 25300.00
Box, Symphonion, Eroica, Hall Clock, Walnut, Glass Door, 25 3-Disc Sets, 104 In. 46750.00
Box, Symphonion, Lithographed Animation, 5 Pigs, 16 Discs, 12 x 7 1/2 In. 7150.00
Box, Symphonion, Mahogany Case, Disc, Single Comb, 4 7 1/2-In. Discs, 10 1/2 In. 650.00
Box, Symphonion, Oak Case, Crank, 14 8 1/4-In. Discs, 14 In. 1115.00
Box, Symphonion, Riverboat, Walnut, Double Comb, c.1888, 12 17 1/2-In. Discs 12650.00
Bugle, Lanyard, Replaced Mouthpiece, England, Late 1870s, 12 x 8 1/2 In. 205.00
Bugle, Original Mouthpiece, 1850s, 18 x 7 In. 180.00
Bugle, Original Mouthpiece, Late 1860s, 17 1/4 x 6 1/2 In. 145.00
Case, Violin, Painted, Stencil, Salmon, Tan Ground, c.1860, 31 x 9 1/2 x 5 In. 630.00
Cello, Carved Scroll Neck, 4 Keys, Iron Hardware, 48 In. 345.00
Concertina, Tanzbar, Black Lacquered Case, 15 Rolls 2200.00
Cornet, Boston Musical Instrument, Plated Horn, Case 470.00
Drum, Parade, Bird's-Eye Maple, Maple, c.1900, 10 3/4 x 15 In. 440.00
Flute, G.L. Penzel & Mueller, Blackwood, Nickel Keys, Case, New York 530.00
Flute, Jerome Thibouville Lamy, Blackwood, Nickel Keys & Fittings 265.00
Flute, Meacham & Pond, Boxwood, Ivory Fittings, Brass Key, Albany, 1800s 765.00

Guitar, Buck Jones & Silver Guitar, Leather Case, Instructions, Child's, 36 In. 200.00
Guitar, C F. Martin, Model D-21, Rosewood, Celluloid, Mahogany, 1966, 20 x 15 3/4 In. . .   3400.00
Guitar, C F. Martin, Model D-28, Rosewood, Celluloid, Mahogany, 20 x 15 11/16 In. 3290.00
Guitar, C.F. Martin, Model 2-17, Mahogany, Rosewood, Black, Case, 1930, 18 In. 825.00 to 1060.00
Guitar, C.F. Martin, Model O-21, Rosewood, Mahogany, Ebony Fingerboard, 19 x 13 In. .   1880.00
Guitar, Electric, Fender, Stratocaster, Maple Neck, Rosewood, Pearl, 1965, 15 x 11 In. 6465.00
Guitar, Gibson, Model B-25-12, Mahogany, Rosewood Fingerboard, 1964, 18 In. 380.00
Guitar, Gibson, Model L-00, Mahogany, Rosewood Fingerboard, Pearl Dot Inlay, 1934 . . .   3055.00
Guitar, Gibson, Model L-5, Maple, Pearl Inlay, Ebony Fingerboard, 1935, 21 x 17 In. 4405.00
Guitar, Gibson, Model SJ, Mahogany Body, Rosewood Fingerboard, 1953 . . . .   2938.00
Guitar, Gibson, Model Super 400, Archtop, Sunburst Finish, Case, 1936 . . . .   5580.00
Guitar, Larson Brothers, Model A, Walnut Stained, Mahogany, Ebony, Pearl, 1928, 18 In. .   765.00
Guitar, National String, Resonator, Style 0, Nickel Plated Body, Ebony Fingerboard, 1932 .   1528.00
Guitar, Resonator, Mahogany Body, Sunburst Finish, c.1935, 9 1/2-In. Back 1058.00
Harmonica, Hohner, Marine Band, 2 Bells, 7 3/4 In. 155.00
Harmonica, Hohner, Trumpet Call, 5 Gold Trumpets, Germany, 3 x 5 In. 345.00
Harp, P.F. Browne & Co., Gilt Decorated, Paw Front Feet, Fluted, Victorian, 68 x 33 In. . .   4545.00
Harp, T. Dodd & Son, Paw Front Feet, Fluted Front, Winged Woman, 1890, 67 x 32 In. . . .   3680.00
Hawaiian Violin, 32 Strings, c.1920 . . . .   475.00
Mandola, Vivi Tone, Mahogany, Silkscreen, Ebony, Pearl, 1933, 13 7/8 In. 4700.00
Mandolin, A.C. Fairbanks, Model Regent, Case, c.1910 . . . .   560.00
Mandolin, C.F. Martin, Style 2, Case, c.1920 . . . .   765.00
Mandolin, Gibson, Model A, Cedar, Veneered Peghead, Earl, Ebony, Spruce, 1925, 14 In. .   2350.00
Mandolin, Gibson, Model A1, Cedar, Veneered, Pearl Inlay, Ebony, 1916, 13 3/4 In. 1295.00
Mandolin, Gibson, Model A4, Cedar, Pearl, Ebony, Spruce, 1924, 13 3/4 In. 4700.00
Mandolin, Gibson, Model A40, Mahogany, Rosewood Fingerboard, c.1935 . . . .   1295.00
Mandolin, Gibson, Model H1, Cedar, Laminated, Pearl, Ebony, Spruce, 1923, 15 In. 2350.00
Mandolin, Gibson, Model H4, Maple, Cedar, Ebony, Pearl Inlay, 1928, 14 5/8 In. 8815.00
Mandolin, Gibson, Model K1, Cedar, Laminated Peghead, Pearl Inlay, Ebony, 16 1/2 In. . .   3175.00
Melodeon, Mahogany Case, Circle & Arch Design, 48 x 20 x 41 In. 230.00
Melodeon, Mahogany, 1800s, 30 x 36 In. 69.00
One-Man Band, Washboard, Whistle, Bells, Noisemakers, Phily Police Pastimers, 1930s . .   875.00
Organ, Arburo, Dance, Jazz, 5 Instruments, Paper Rolls, 104 x 103 In. 17600.00
Organ, Barrel, A. Wagner, Rosewood Case, Portable Stand, Levian, Mexico, c.1910 . . . . . .   7700.00
Organ, Concert Roller, 10 Cobs, c.1886, 12 1/2 In. 756.00
Organ, Grand Roller, Ed Wing, Oak Case, Wood Rollers, Christmas, 1895, 23 1/2 In. 7150.00
Organ, Pump, Edna, Oak Stick & Ball, Vining Flowers, Leaves, 58 x 27 x 56 In. 405.00
Organ, Pump, Shoninger, Walnut, Mahogany, New Haven, Victorian, 45 x 25 x 49 In. 230.00
Organ, Roller, Gem, Walnut Case, Stenciling, 14 In. 310.00
Organ, Roller, Gockel, Bacigalupo, Mahogany Case, Metal Cart, 14 Rolls, 26 x 24 In. 905.00
Organ, Wurlitzer, No. 103, Military Band, Snow Scene, Oak Case, 15 6-In. Rolls, 44 In. . . 18700.00
Piano, Baby Grand, Julius Bluthner, Ebonized Finish, 1906-10, 70 In. 5290.00
Piano, Baby Grand, Steinway, Model T, Ebonized Mahogany, Bench, 1802, 72 In. 8365.00
Piano, Grand, Hagspiel & Co., Walnut, Burl Walnut, Dresden, c.1885, 35 x 55 x 70 In. . . .   2760.00
Piano, Grand, Steinway & Sons, Style VII, Rosewood, Carved, c.1879, 41 x 81 In. 1380.00
Piano, Grand, Weber, Mahogany Case, No. 66248, 64 In. 175.00
Piano, Grand, Wurlitzer, Removable, Tapered Legs, 1930s, 37 x 30 x 27 In., Child's 400.00
Piano, Player, Kreiter, Mahogany Case, Bench, Repeating, Honky Tonk, France, 56 x 63 In.   140.00
Pianoforte, E.N. Sheer, Mahogany, Gilt, Carved, Inscribed, 1800s, 35 1/2 x 67 1/2 In. 1265.00
Pianoforte, John Broadwood & Sons, Mahogany, London, 1820s, 66 In. 1500.00
Pianoforte, Loud & Brothers, Mahogany, Gilt, Carved Appliques, 1800s, 37 x 68 In. 1725.00
Pianoforte, Mahogany, Square Case, Carved Cabriole Legs, Late 1900s, 37 x 70 x 33 In. .   380.00
Piccolo, Granadilla Wood, Ivory Head Joint, Hanover, Germany, c.1870 . . . .   195.00
Saxophone, Alto, Conn, Brass Plated Horn, Case, 1955 . . . .   588.00
Saxophone, Alto, Martin Band, Case, 1920 . . . .   205.00
Saxophone, Tenor, Selmer & Co., Super Balanced Action, Brass, Flowers, Case, 1950 . . . .   7640.00
Sitar, Stand, Mideastern, 42 In. 375.00
Ukulele, C.F. Martin, Soprano, Style 1, Mahogany Body, Rosewood Fingerboard, c.1918 . .   295.00
Ukulele, C.F. Martin, Soprano, Style 3K, Koa Body, Mahogany, Rosewood, Case, c.1930 .   5580.00
Ukulele, C.F. Martin, Style O, Mahogany, Rosewood, Pearl, Case, 1930, 9 3/8 In. 590.00
Viola, Jacques LeClerc, 2-Piece Back, 1915, 15 3/4-In. Back 1880.00
Violin, Antonio Gastano, 2-Piece Back, Case, Messina, Italy, 1890, 14-In. Back 3055.00
Violin, Arthur E. Johnson, 2-Piece Back, Boston, 1960, 14-In. Back 1175.00

Violin, Bernardus Calcanius, 2-Piece Back, Golden Orange, Case, 14 In. 2115.00
Violin, Borhi Pietro Lugo, 1-Piece Back, Red, Brown, 13 15/16 In. 8815.00
Violin, E.H. Roth, 1-Piece Back, Germany, 1927, 14 1/16 In. 3055.00
Violin, Enrico Marchetti Mediolanensis, 1-Piece Back, 1921, 14-In. Back 4700.00
Violin, Fendt Family, 2-Piece Back, Brown Varnish, England, c.1830, 14-In. Back 8815.00
Violin, George Daniels, 2-Piece Back, Bow, Case, Waltham, 14-In. Back 1765.00
Violin, Giovanni Maria Ceruti, 2-Piece Back, Red, 1923, 14 1/8 In. 5580.00
Violin, J.B. Colin, 2-Piece Back, France, 1890, 14 1/8-In. Back 2820.00
Violin, James R. Carlisle, 2-Piece Back, Brown Varnish, Cincinnati, 1926, 14-In. Back 4115.00
Violin, Joseph Pineau, 1-Piece Back, Paris, 1926, 14-In. Back 7050.00
Violin, Max Renz, 2-Piece Back, Amber Varnish, Germany, 1949, 14 1/16 In. 3170.00
Violin, Michael Stadlmann, 1-Piece Back, c.1790, 14-In. Back 9400.00
Violin, Thomas Ranik, Lautern & Eigenmacher, Maple, Lupot Bow, Case, Label, 1731 . . . .   575.00
Violin, Tyrolian, 2-Piece Back, Case, c.1780, 14-In. Back 3525.00
Violoncello, Banks School, 2-Piece Back, Golden Varnish, Case, England, 29-In. Back 15275.00
Violoncello, J.H. Rockwell & Son, 2-Piece Back, Case, Providence, 1912, 29 1/4-In. Back .   350.00

NAILSEA glass was made in the Bristol district in England from 1788
to 1873. It was made by many different factories, not just the Nailsea
Glass House. Many pieces were made with loopings of either white or
colored glass as decoration.

Bottle, Gemel, Pink, White Loopings, 10 In. 115.00
Flask, Pink & White Ribs, Flat, 9 In. 230.00
Powder Horn, White Marbrie Loopings, Applied Lip & Neck Ring, 12 In. 145.00
Vase, Cranberry, Opal Loopings, Double Gourd, 3 In. 69.00
Vase, Emerald Green, Translucent, Opal Loopings, Rolled Rim, Squat, 5 x 2 1/2 In. 115.00
Vase, Grass Green, Opal Marbrie Loopings, Baluster Shape, Circular Foot, 7 1/2 In. 550.00
Vase, Opal Marbrie Loopings, 3 Shoulder Rings, Rolled Rim, Circular Foot, 11 In. 1155.00
Whimsy, Pipe Shape, Cranberry, Opal Loopings, c.1860, 16 In. 144.00
Witch's Ball, Clear, Amethyst Loopings, 3 1/2 In. 55.00
Witch's Ball, Clear, Blue Green Marbrie Loopings, 4 1/2 In. 210.00

NAKARA is a trade name for a white glassware made about 1900 by
the C. F. Monroe Company of Meriden, Connecticut. It was decorated
in pastel colors. The glass was very similar to another glass made by   **NAKARA**
the company called *Wave Crest*. The company closed in 1916. Boxes
for use on a dressing table are the most commonly found Nakara
pieces. The mark is not found on every piece.

Box, Beaded Enameling, Blue, 6-Sided, c.1890, 4 In. 230.00
Box, Bishop's Hat, Flowers, Blue Ground, 4 1/4 In. 375.00
Box, Bishop's Hat, Flowers, Blue, 7 In. 800.00
Box, Bishop's Hat, Portrait, Queen Louise, Blue, 7 In. 1200.00
Box, Cherubs In Haystack, Blue, Round, 6 In. 750.00
Box, Crown Mold, Peach, Flowers, 8 In. 1500.00
Box, Crown Mold, Pink, Flowers, 8 In. 2100.00
Box, Flowers, Blue Ground, c.1890, 8 In. 890.00
Box, Flowers, Green Ground, 7 1/2 In. 800.00
Box, Glove, Blue Daisy, Flowers, 6 x 10 In. 2000.00
Box, Hinged Cover, Blue, Enameled Beaded Trim, 6-Sided, Marked, 3 1/4 x 3 1/2 In. 431.00
Box, Hinged Cover, Gray, Embossed Flowers, 6-Sided, Marked, 4 x 3 In. 625.00
Box, Hinged Cover, Gray, Pink & White Flowers, Marked, 3 x 4 In. 719.00
Box, Pink, Flowers, Mirror In Cover, 8-Sided, 6 In. 725.00
Humidor, Cover, Flowers, Blue 875.00
Toothpick, Mauve, Beaded Flowers, Scrolls, 2 In. 489.00

NANKING is a type of blue-and-white porcelain made in Canton,
China, since the late eighteenth century. It is very similar to Canton,
which is listed under its own name in this book. Both Nanking and
Canton are part of a larger group now called *Chinese export* porcelain.
Nanking has a spear-and-post border and may have gold decoration.

Bowl, Tea Dusk Exterior, Landscape Interior, c.1750, 6 In. 170.00
Platter, Octagonal, 10 x 13 In. 575.00
Platter, Oval, Chinese, 1800s, 14 3/4 In. 411.00

Platter, Oval, Several Borders, 7 1/2 x 9 1/2 In. 201.00
Platter, Riverscape, 13 In., Pair 1265.00

NAPKIN RINGS were in fashion from 1869 to about 1900. They were made of silver, porcelain, wood, and other materials. They are still being made today. The most popular rings with collectors are the silver plated figural examples. Small, realistic figures were made to hold the ring. Good and poor reproductions of the more expensive rings are now being made and collectors must be very careful.

Bakelite, Bird, Butterscotch, Green Beak, 1940s, 2 1/2 x 2 1/2 In. 145.00
Bakelite, Dog, Airedale, Green, 1940s, 3 1/4 x 2 1/2 In. 140.00
Bakelite, Octagonal, Swirling From Taupe To Apple Green, 1 1/2 x 3/4 In. 40.00
Bakelite, Orange, Convex Intaglio Glass Dome, Relief Anchor, 1930s, 1 7/8 In. Diam. 35.00
Bakelite, Popeye, Transfer On Both Sides, 1940s, 2 3/4 x 2 In. 225.00
Bakelite, Rabbit, Mottled Greenish Color, Red Rodded Eye, 1940s, 3 x 2 In. 60.00
Bakelite, Rocking Horse, Butterscotch, Red Rodded Eye, 1940s, 1 3/4 x 2 1/2 In. 165.00
Figural, 2 Eagles, Silver Plate, Meriden 165.00
Figural, 2 Lions, Silver Plate, Toronto 155.00
Figural, 2 Rabbits, Reclining, Sitting, Square Base, Silver Plate 625.00
Figural, 2 Squirrels Holding Up Ring, Silver Plate, Hartford 325.00
Figural, 4 Figures Reading Books, Holding Ring, Silver Plate 300.00
Figural, Baby Bird On Branch, Silver Plate, Triple Plate, Rogers & Bro., 3 In. 60.00
Figural, Baby Bird, Silver Plate, Quadruple Plate, Meriden, 3 In. 25.00
Figural, Baby, Sitting On Rock, Leaf Base, Van Bergh Silver Co. 215.00
Figural, Barrel, On Branches & Leaves, Silver Plate .... 45.00 to 85.00
Figural, Bear, Round Fancy Base, Silver Plate, Queen City Silver Co. 275.00
Figural, Bee, Leaf Base, Silver Plate 385.00
Figural, Begging Dog, Silver Plate, Rogers 185.00
Figural, Bird On Holly Branch, Engraved JAD, Silver Plate, 5 In. 160.00
Figural, Bird On Wishbone, Engraved, Best Wishes, Silver Plate, 3 In. 28.00
Figural, Birds On Platform, Silver Plate, Meriden, 3 In. 79.00
Figural, Boy & Dog, Silver Plate, Rogers Smith & Co., 4 In. 135.00
Figural, Boy, Crawling, Silver Plate, Meriden, 4 In. 135.00
Figural, Boy, Leaning On Ring, Rectangular Base, Silver Plate, Middletown Plate Co. 375.00
Figural, Boy, Reading Book, Square, Engraved, Silver Plate, Aurora, 3 In. 370.00
Figural, Boy, Sitting, Silver Plate, 3 In. 79.00
Figural, Boy, Standing, Silver Plate, 3 In. 11.00
Figural, Boy, Standing, Silver Plate, Meriden, 3 In. 102.00
Figural, Bulldog, Silver Plate 105.00
Figural, Butterfly Feet, Silver Plate, Quadruple Plate, Wm. Rogers, 4 In. 57.00
Figural, Butterfly, Fans, Silver Plate, Meriden 400.00
Figural, Cat & Ball Of String, Silver Plate, 3 In. 310.00
Figural, Cat, Sitting, Ring Body, Silver Plate 575.00
Figural, Cat, Sitting, Silver Plate, 3 In. 339.00
Figural, Chair, Slat Back, Silver Plate 265.00
Figural, Cherub & Wishbone, Silver Plate, Quadruple Plate, Derby, 3 In. 35.00
Figural, Cherub, Holding Grapes, Silver Plate, Van Bergh, 3 In. 125.00
Figural, Cherub, Sitting, Silver Plate, Pairpoint, 5 In. 395.00
Figural, Cherub, Standing, Silver Plate, James W. Tufts, 4 In. 100.00
Figural, Cherubs, Holding Ring, Silver Plate, Meriden Britannia, c.1878, 4 In. 96.00
Figural, Cherubs, On Seesaw Barrel, Silver Plate, Quadruple Plate, Racine, 4 In. 125.00
Figural, Cherubs, Silver Plate, Quadruple Plate, Simpson, Hall, Miller & Co., 3 In. 150.00
Figural, Child, Standing, 3 In. 68.00
Figural, Children On Seesaw, Silver Plate, Simpson, Hall, Miller & Co., c.1880 .... 2500.00
Figural, Children Reading, Quadruple Plate, Simpson, Hall, Miller & Co., 4 In. 565.00
Figural, Cow, Standing, Silver Plate, Meriden, 3 In. 90.00
Figural, Dog & Pheasant, Silver Plate, Toronto Silver Plate Co., 3 In. 225.00
Figural, Dog Chasing Cat, Silver Plate, Rogers, c.1883, 4 In. 339.00
Figural, Egyptian Figures, Lion, Bud Vase Top, Silver Plate, Taunton 350.00
Figural, Fawn, Cymbals, Silver Plate, Roger Smith Co., Meriden, 3 In. 255.00
Figural, Girl, Feeding Begging Dog, Silver Plate, Meriden 350.00
Figural, Goat, Pulling Cart, Engraved, Quadruple Plate, Meriden, 5 In. 170.00
Figural, Grapes On Barrel, Silver Plate, Standard Silver, Toronto, 3 In. 70.00

Figural, Horse, Rearing, Silver Plate, Acme Silver Co., 4 In. 240.00
Figural, Kangaroo, Silver Plate, EPNS, 3 1/4 In. 35.00
Figural, Lily Pad Base, Engraved, Silver Plate, Triple Plate, Rogers & Bro., 3 1/2 In. 40.00
Figural, Lily Pad Base, Silver Plate, Meriden, 4 In. 79.00
Figural, Lion, Engraved, Silver Plate, Meriden, 3 In. 60.00
Figural, Lion, On Leaf Base, Ring Back, Silver Plate 155.00
Figural, Man, Military Uniform, Silver Plate 340.00
Figural, Monkey, Dressed, Standing, Silver Plate, James W. Tufts, 4 In. 160.00
Figural, Owl, On Fence, Ring Is Body Of Owl, Silver Plate 325.00
Figural, Parakeet, Large Leaf Base, Silver Plate, Toronto 375.00
Figural, Parrot, On Perch, Engraved, Silver Plate, Meriden, 4 In. 285.00
Figural, Parrot, On Ring, Leaf Base, Silver Plate 175.00
Figural, Rabbit, Easter Basket, Wishbone Base, Silver Plate, Victor, 3 In. 125.00
Figural, Ring On Chair, Silver Plate, 4 In. 40.00
Figural, Ring On Cross Buck, Silver Plate, 3 In. 17.00
Figural, Ring On Horseshoe Base, Silver Plate 375.00
Figural, Ring On Triangular Stand, Engraved BHD, Silver Plate, Meriden, 3 In. 28.00
Figural, Rooster, Standing, Silver Plate, Quadruple Plate, Wm. Rogers, 3 In. 370.00
Figural, Rose, Silver Plate, Quadruple Plate, Wm. Rogers, 3 In. 68.00
Figural, Sheet Music & Violin, Silver Plate, Wilcox Silver, 3 In. 150.00
Figural, Squirrel, Acorns, Oak Leaves, Silver Plate, Reed & Barton, 4 In. 147.00
Figural, Squirrel, Eating Nut, Quadruple Plate, S.P. Southington, 3 In. 125.00
Figural, Squirrel, With Nut, Silver Plate, Rogers Smith, Meriden, 3 In. 100.00
Figural, Squirrel, With Nut, Sitting On Rectangular Base, Silver Plate, Rogers 285.00
Figural, Swallow, On Leaf, Silver Plate, Meriden, 3 In. 68.00
Figural, Tennis Rackets, Silver Plate, MB, 4 In. 237.00
Glass, Fostoria, American Pattern, 2 x 3/4 In. 48.00
Pottery, Rooster, Red, Green, Yellow, Black & Apricot Luster Glaze, 3 x 3 1/2 In. 17.00
Pottery, Teapot, Spout, Handle, Blue Willow, 4 Piece 17.00
Red Rooster, Blue Tread On Wheels, Bakelite, 3 In. 175.00
Set, Silver Plate, Wallace, 20th Century, 8 Piece 259.00
Silver, Top Flourishes, Stamped.800 Grade, Marked Tezler, 1 3/4 x 1 3/8 In. 35.00
Sterling Silver, Engraved Florentine Finish, Rope Twist Border, Gorham, Oval, 1950s 50.00
Sterling Silver, Pierced Conjoined Ivy Leaves, Shield, Engraved, Boomerang Logo 125.00

NASH glass was made in Corona, New York, from about 1928 to 1931. A. Douglas Nash bought the Corona glassworks from Louis C. Tiffany in 1928 and founded the A. Douglas Nash Corporation with support from his father, Arthur J. Nash. Arthur had worked at the Webb factory in England and for the Tiffany Glassworks in Corona.

NASH

Bowl, Centerpiece, Chintz, Translucent, Alternating Green & Pink, 12 In. 345.00
Bowl, Centerpiece, Iridescent Gold, Ribbed, Flared Rim, Footed, 4 1/2 x 11 In. 374.00
Bowl, Iridescent Gold, Scalloped Panels, Flared Rim, Pedestal Base, 2 5/8 x 8 In. 690.00
Candlestick, Iridescent Gold, Baluster Stem, Signed, 4 In. 403.00
Candlestick, Iridescent Gold, Green, Blue, Purple, Veining, Signed, 3 3/4 In., Pair 588.00
Compote, Iridescent Gold, Trumpet Shape, Ribbed, Scalloped Rim, Footed, 4 1/2 In. 345.00
Plate, Flattened Shape, Etched, Pulled Zipper Design, Iridescent, Signed, 9 In. 290.00
Tumbler, Chintz, Striped Green & Amethyst, Signed, c.1930, 6 1/2 In. 161.00

NAUTICAL antiques are listed in this category. Any of the many objects that were made or used by the seafaring trade, including ship parts, models, and tools, are included. Other pieces may be found listed under Scrimshaw.

Artificial Horizon, Keuffel & Esser, Metal Trough, Glazed Cover, Mahogany Case, 9 In. . . 264.00
Bell, Ship's, Brass, Hanging Bracket, Iron Clapper 200.00
Bell, Ship's, Bronze, Cast, Iron Clapper, S-Shape Arm, Wall Bracket, 10 x 10 In. 405.00
Bell, Ship's, Trinity House 1945, Raised Lettering, Metal, 10 1/2 In. 345.00
Bell Clock & Barometer, Ship's Wheel Style, Brass, Bronze Base, 8 1/2 x 14 In 750.00
Binnacle, American Yacht, Copper, Brass, Hexagonal Top, 3-Footed, c.1890, 33 In. 1840.00
Binnacle, Floor, Brass, Wood, Cone Top, Round Window, 51 In. 360.00
Binnacle, Nickeled, Domed Lid, Gimbaled Compass, E.J. Willis Co., N.Y., 10 1/2 x 9 In. . . 430.00
Binnacle, Wood & Copper, Kelvin & Hughes, Ltd., Glasgow & London 1495.00
Binnacle, Yacht, Copper, Brass, Hexagonal Viewing Port, c.1890, 33 In. 1840.00

Binnacle, Yacht, Wood, Copper, Kelvin & Hughes, 49 In. 1495.00
Box, Razor, Cherry, Heart Shape Handle, Swivel Top, Incised Ship, 2 x 2 x 10 In. 325.00
Box, Sailor's, Cover, Chip Carved, Fingers, Iron Tacks, BM 1841, 81Y OLD, 4 1/2 In. 1785.00
Box, Sailor's, Walnut, 3 Carved Ivory Ring Handles, Hinged Lid, 8 5/8 x 17 3/4 x 9 In. . . . 1765.00
Cannon, Cast Iron, 18 3/4 In. 405.00
Cannon, Signal, Brass, Mahogany Base, 21 1/2 In. 3450.00
Cannon, Signal, Cast Iron, Wood Base, 19 1/2 In. 405.00
Canoe, Collapsible, Rubber Bottom, Camo Canvas Top, Flobot, 1950s, 16 x 3 1/2 Ft. 110.00
Chest, Campaign, Camphorwood, 4 Drawers, Drop Front, 39 x 32 In. 1895.00
Chest, Campaign, Mahogany, 4 Drawers, Drop Front, Pigeonholes, 40 x 38 In. 4485.00
Chest, Camphorwood, Lift Top, Brass Bound, Eagle, Iron Bail Handles, 20 x 38 In. 375.00
Chest, Man's, Pine, Painted, Ship, Hinged Lid, Rope Handles, 1800s, 18 x 38 x 17 In. 1880.00
Chest, Man's, Red Paint, Vines, Cartouches, Dome Top, Iron Handles, 24 x 42 In. 300.00
Chest, Man's, Walnut, Canted Sides, Dovetailed, 17 x 35 x 16 1/2 In. 865.00
Chest, Seaman's, Green Paint, Heart & Diamond Shaped Cleats, 15 x 41 x 17 In. 575.00
Chest, Seaman's, Painted, Stars, Fouled Anchor, Ship, Strap Hinges, 15 x 45 In. 430.00
Chest, Seaman's, Teak, Inlay, Tulip, Star, Lid, Till, Handles, 15 x 31 x 15 In. 805.00
Chest, Seaman's, Teak, Star & String Inlay, Dovetailed, Late 1800s, 19 x 37 x 17 In. 575.00
Chest, Teak, 6-Board, Geometric Inlay, 16 1/2 x 30 x 14 3/4 In. 805.00
Chronometer, A. Johannsen & Co., London, No. 4635, 56-Hour, Octagonal Case, 10 In. . . 825.00
Chronometer, Elgin, Double Case, Mahogany, Leather Strap, 7 x 7 In. 805.00
Chronometer, H. Hughes & Son Ltd., No. 7719, 2-Day, Mahogany Case, London, 7 In. . . . 1765.00
Chronometer, Hamilton, Felt Interior, Mahogany, Case, 7 1/4 x 8 1/4 x 5 1/4 In. 1325.00
Chronometer, Henry Robert, Paris, Double Case, 8 1/2 x 9 In. 2530.00
Chronometer, London, Thomas Mercer, No. 18078, 2-Day, 7 In. 1116.00
Chronometer, Parkinson & Frodsham, 2 Day, No. 596, Mahogany Box, c.1860, 6 3/4 In. . . 3920.00
Clock, Chelsea, Mariner, Ship's Bell, Brass, 8-Day, Mahogany, Bronze, c.1970, 10 1/4 In. . 615.00
Clock, Deck, Mark I, U.S. Navy, Wood Plaque, Round, 6 In. 865.00
Clock, Engine Room, 8-Day, Brass Case, France, c.1925, 9 In. 195.00
Clock, Engine Room, Mercer, Iver C. Weilbach, 8-Day, Brass, England, c.1930, 8 1/2 In. . . 390.00
Clock, Engine Room, Seth Thomas, 8-Day, Brass Case, Round, c.1936, 7 In. 196.00
Clock, Mark 1 Deck, Seth Thomas, U.S. Navy, Chrome Case, Black Dial, 1939 . . . . 225.00
Clock, Radio Room, Chelsea, 8-Day, 24-Hour Dial, Brass Case, c.1967, 7 1/4 In. 560.00
Clock, Ship's Bell, Chelsea, 8-Day, Brass Case, Hinged Bezel, c.1955, 6-In. Dial, 7 1/2 In. . 616.00
Clock, Ship's Bell, Chelsea, 8-Day, Brass Case, Silvered Brass Dial, c.1977, 4 3/4 In. 420.00
Clock, Ship's Bell, Chelsea, 8-Day, Tambour No. 4, Bronze Case, c.1915, 10 1/2 In. 785.00
Clock, Ship's Bell, Chelsea, Brass Case, 7 3/4 In. 1610.00
Clock, Ship's Bell, Chelsea, Hinged Bezel, Ball Feet, c.1920, 8 1/2-In. Dial 2520.00
Clock, Ship's Bell, Chelsea, Shreve Crump & Low, Bronze Finish, Ball Feet, c.1939, 7 In. . 670.00
Clock, Ship's, Deck, Waltham, 3 Piece Case, Gimbals, c.1940, 5 In. 616.00
Clock, Ship's, Enamel Dial, Brass Case, England, c.1920, 13 In. 476.00
Clock, Ship's, Seth Thomas, Bakelite Case, Hand Wind, 1930s, 6 In. 225.00
Clock & Barometer, Chelsea, Mahogany Base, Round, 4 In. 520.00
Clock & Barometer, Ship's Wheel Shape, Brass, Bronze Base, 8 1/2 x 14 In. 800.00
Compass, Andrew T. Lloyd Co., Boston, Brass, Pocket, Marked, 2 1/2 In. 70.00
Compass, D. Baker, Boston, No. 3874, Brass Gimbal Mount, Mahogany Frame, 12 In. 380.00
Compass, G.E. Pittenweem, Brass, Dry Card, 2 1/2 In. 130.00
Compass, Robert Merrill, N.Y., Dry Card, Gimbal Mount, Wood Case, 1851, 9 In. 520.00
Compass, Ship's, Richie, No. 119458, Round Copper Case, 9 In. 355.00
Deadeye, Wooden, Carved, Base, 9 In. 200.00
Depth Finder, Thomas Walker & Son, Birmingham, No. S2794, 25-Fathom Dial 765.00
Diorama, 3-Masted Ship, Carved, Painted, Full Sails, White Hull, 16 1/2 x 27 1/2 x 8 In. . . 575.00
Figurehead, Eagle, Shield Crest Pediment, Giltwood, Carved, Inscribed, 9 In. 1610.00
Figurehead, Lord Percy, Painted, Hardwood Stand, 19th Century, 28 In. 1150.00
Figurehead, Ship, Lady, Flowing Hair, Blue Coat, Red Dress, Wooden, 42 In. 1670.00
Figurehead, Woman, Arm Aloft, Flowing Dress, Painted, Multicolored, England, 38 In. . . . 11500.00
Fog Horn, Ship's, E.A. Gill, Gloucester, Mass. 140.00
Half-Model, Hull, Rappahannock, A. Sewall & Co., Bath, Maine, Mounted, 1890, 86 x 21 In. 3565.00
Half-Model, Yacht, America, 1851, 8 3/4 x 24 In. 185.00
Half-Model, Yacht, Valkyrie III, Planked Deck, Fittings, Mahogany, 7 1/2 x 30 In. 375.00
Harpoon Head, Spring Barb, Hand Forged Socket, 4-In. Barb, 22 In. 805.00
Helmet, Open-Diving, Snead Co., Jersey City, Cast Iron, Painted, Gilt Letters, 22 In. 1116.00
Lamp, Anchor, Copper, 360 Degrees, 18 In., Pair 315.00

Lamp, Brass, Stick Gimbal, Frosted Glass Globe, 15 3/4 In. 69.00
Lamp, Bulkhead, Ship's, Brass, Cage Shields, Pair 260.00
Lamp, Lake Erie Ship, Oil, Hanging, Gimbal Mount, Brass, Milk Glass Shade, 30 In. 230.00
Lamp, Masthead, Brass, Loop Handle, Cylindrical Glass Cover, 14 In. 265.00
Lamp, Port, Starboard, 8 1/4 In., Pair 345.00
Lamp, Ship's, Convoy, Brass, Red, Blue Glass Lens, Pair 259.00
Lantern, Masthead, Brass, 10 1/2 In. 430.00
Lantern, Ship's, 360 Degrees, Copper, Ribbed Glass Lens, Oil Burner, 19 1/2 In. 230.00
Life Preserver, Enclosed Center, Wood Panel, Nantucket Light Ship No. 85 . . . . 335.00
Mirror, Ship's Wheel, Mahogany Finish, Porcelain Hook & Knobs, 23 x 30 In. 120.00
Model, Adirondack Guide Boat, Cane Seat, 2 Benches, Ribs, 2 Oars, 7 1/2 x 37 In. 920.00
Model, Bark, Wanderer, Painted, Fully Rigged, Sailor Made, Case, 25 x 34 x 11 1/2 In. . . . 2530.00
Model, Catboat, Cape Cod, Sail Down, Case, 28 x 12 x 23 In. 920.00
Model, Clipper Ship, Flying Cloud, Black, White, 34 x 21 In. 345.00
Model, Clipper Ship, Sovereign Of The Seas, Black, Green, Sailor Made, 18 x 25 In. 460.00
Model, English Man-Of-War, Victory, Sails, Case, 29 x 29 x 13 In. 1610.00
Model, Ferryboat, Chinese Style, Side Wheel Paddle Boat, Cart, Man, 29 x 11 x 8 In. 115.00
Model, Lightship, Nantucket, Rigged, Finely Detailed, Case, 33 x 53 x 13 In. 2990.00
Model, Merchant Ship, Nailsea Court, Wood, Case, 1900s, 19 1/4 x 57 x 11 3/4 In. 4406.00
Model, Oil Tanker, Sheaf Royal, Wood, Case, Late 1900s, 15 3/8 x 46 x 14 In. 1410.00
Model, Puritan, America's Cup Defender 1885, G. Lawley, Boston, Case, 26 x 43 x 13 In. . . 1955.00
Model, Racer, 3-Masted Ship, Dog Figurehead, On Cradle, Sailor Made, 19 x 29 In. 635.00
Model, Sailboat, Pine Hull, Weighted Keel, Red, Black, 20th Century, 35 x 24 x 5 In. 415.00
Model, Schooner, 2-Masted, Shadowbox Frame, 22 x 26 In. 518.00
Model, Schooner, Laura, Painted Metal Sails, Figures, Carved Water, 16 x 12 x 23 In. 1528.00
Model, Ship, 3-Masted, Argo, Painted Red & Black, Tan Decks, On Cradle, 36 x 52 In. . . . 460.00
Model, Ship, 3-Masted, Fully Rigged, Back Hull, Lifeboat, Wooden, 17 x 27 In. 180.00
Model, Ship, British, Wood, Sea Mount, Case, Sailor Made, 12 1/2 x 18 1/2 x 9 In. 805.00
Model, Ship, English, Man-O-War, Lion Figurehead, 32 x 33 1/2 In. 1035.00
Model, Ship, Fully Rigged, Paul Jones, Sailor Made, 27 x 36 In. 546.00
Model, Ship, Santa Maria, 3-Masted, Leather Sails, Wooden, 16 x 21 In. 29.00
Model, Ship, Waterline, Grace Lee, Fully Rigged, Stormy Sea, 30 x 16 In. 460.00
Model, Steamboat, Aurora, Wood, Painted, 6 Decks, Wood Base, 22 x 46 In. 430.00
Model, Trawler, Green & Red Hull, Original Rigging, French Flag, 22 x 23 1/2 In. 259.00
Model, USS Constitution, Mahogany Frame, Case 4025.00
Model, Whaling Ship, Blue, Black, Sailor Made, 26 x 33 1/2 In. 460.00
Model, Whaling Ship, Lacoda, 3-Masted, Wood, 33 1/2 x 39 In. 4025.00
Model, Whaling Ship, Ocean Eagle, Rockport, Mass., Sailor Made, 41 x 55 In. 865.00
Octant, Spencer, Browning & Co., London, Brass Arm, Ivory Arc, Oak Case, 12 In. 470.00
Octant, Spencer, Browning & Co., London, Ebony, Brass, Engraved, John Kehew, 11 In. . 940.00
Octant, Wm. Harris & Co., London & Hamburg, Ebony, Ivory, Brass, Shaped Case, 15 In. 880.00
Pond Boat, 3-Masted, Canvas Sails, Stained Brown Hull, Red Paint On Keel, 37 x 28 In. . 259.00
Pond Boat, Yacht, Mast, Painted, Rigging, Brown, White, Green Hull, Wood, 67 x 50 In. . 403.00
Quadrant, Spencer & Co., Ebony, Brass, Ivory Scales, Case 750.00
Rope, Campanionway, Sailor Made, 61 In. 255.00
Rule, C. Smith Ltd., Rolling, Navigational, Brass, 18 x 3 In. 29.00
Rule, Parallel, Navigational, Engraved, E.J. Willis & Co., New York, 24 In. 345.00
Rule, Rolling, Chart Plotting, Brass, Fitted Mahogany Case, 24 In. 145.00
Sailboat, Pond, Marlboro, 1920s, 75 x 66 In. 4700.00
Sailor's Valentine, Box, Geometric Designs, Shells, Rectangular, 1800s, 14 x 10 1/2 In. . . . 1116.00
Sailor's Valentine, Shellwork, Octagonal, Flower, Concentric Rings, c.1850, 10 In. 1610.00
Sextant, Box, Elliot Brothers, London, Brass, Leather Pocket Case, 2 1/2 In. 380.00
Sextant, Cornelius Knudsen, Copenhagen, Brass, Case 750.00
Sextant, H. Hughes & Son Ltd., London, No. 22249, Frame, Teak Case, Engraved, 8 In. . . 235.00
Sextant, Lorieux, Lepetit & Poulin, No. 9776, Black Crackle Frame, Case, 7 1/2 In. 150.00
Sextant, Troughton & Simms, London, Brass, Fitted Mahogany Case, 5 In. 3175.00
Sextant, U.S. Navy, Mark II, No. 3126, Mahogany Case, 1940, 7 1/2 In. 118.00
Shadowbox, Schooner, Fully Rigged, Lighthouse, Waves, Carved Wood, 47 x 27 1/2 In. . . 2300.00
Ship Model, see Nautical, Model.
Ship's Log, Whaling, Calumet Of Stonington, World Map, 1846-49, 13 x 8 In. 2705.00
Ship's Stand, Oval Tilt Top, Bird's-Eye Maple, 7 Stars, 1800s, 28 x 23 1/2 x 14 3/4 In. . . . 940.00
Ship's Wheel, Mahogany, 8 Spokes, Boxwood Stringing, 42 In. 235.00
Ship's Wheel, Mahogany, Brass, 8 Spokes, 36 1/2 In. 375.00

Ship's Wheel, Oak, Carved, Turned, Early 20th Century, 37 In. 315.00
Ship's Wheel, Painted, Brown, 50 1/2 In. 460.00
Speaking Trumpet, Brass, 15 In. 160.00
Speaking Trumpet, Captain's, Brass, 13 1/2 In. 130.00
Spyglass, U.S Navy, Engraved, Kollmorgen, 16-Power, Vulcanite Cover, 1942, 31 In. 265.00
Stadimeter, Schick Inc., Sextant Type. 95.00
Storage Drum, Oval, Wood, Painted, Capt. J.B. Atkins, 1800s, 14 1/4 x 33 1/2 In. 1410.00
Telegraph, A. Robinson Co. Ltd., Brass, Retrofitted, Interior Light, 48 x 17 1/2 In. 500.00
Telegraph, Engine Room, Trident Telegraph, Thomas Walker & Son, Ltd., Birmingham . . .   1150.00
Telegraph, Ship's, Brass, Chadburn, Ltd., Liverpool, 48 In. 1495.00
Telescope, Spencer, Browning & Rust, London, Single Draw, Mahogany Body, 25 In. 590.00
Telescope, Tele-Vue, Hard Case 880.00

NETSUKES are small ivory, wood, metal, or porcelain pieces used as toggles on the end of the cord that held a Japanese money pouch or inro. The earliest date from the sixteenth century. Many are miniature, carved works of art. This category also includes the ojime, the slide or string fastener that was used on the inro cord.

Bamboo, Man, Woman Combing Man's Hair, Pine Forest, 18th Century 1840.00
Inro, 4 Compartments, Black, Gold Lacquer, Dragon, Cloud 402.00
Inro, 4 Compartments, Gold Lacquer, Bridge, Fish Trap 403.00
Ivory, 2 Boys With Puppy, Abalone Shell, Signed 863.00
Ivory, 2 Rams, Standing Side By Side, 20th Century, 2 In. 101.00
Ivory, Boy Resting On Sticks, Reading Book, 19th Century 575.00
Ivory, Cat Resting On Rice Bale, Movable Rat, 19th Century 660.00
Ivory, Chinese Lion, Guarding Brocade Ball, c.1800 . . . .   405.00
Ivory, Farmer With Hoe, Dog Finding Stash Of Coins, Signed, 19th Century 1150.00
Ivory, Fruit, Fungus In Basket, Signed, 19th Century 1725.00
Ivory, God Of Happiness With Boy, Multicolored, 2 1/2 In. 70.00
Ivory, God Of Wind With Windbag, Fish, Inlaid Eye, Mid 19th Century 1150.00
Ivory, Goddess Of Mirth Climbing From Grain Measure, 19th Century 805.00
Ivory, Gods Of Good Fortune With Goat, Signed 1840.00
Ivory, Grazing Horse, Signed, 1 3/4 In. 300.00
Ivory, Man Accosting Woman Bending Over Wash Bucket, 19th Century 750.00
Ivory, Monkey Holding Fish, Inlaid Eyes, Signed 1035.00
Ivory, Puppy Dog, 19th Century 1035.00
Ivory, Samurai Standing, Folded Fan, Man Kneeling At Feet, 18th Century 575.00
Ivory, Skeleton, Crouched 1725.00
Ivory, Sleeping Geisha, Signed 69.00
Ivory, Woman Holding Teapot, Gift, Child On Back, 19th Century 805.00
Ojime, Ivory, Chinese God, Signed, Calligraphy 58.00
Wood, 12 Zodiac Animals, Mountain 8625.00
Wood, Boy With Chinese Lion Mask, 19th Century 1495.00
Wood, Chinese God Holding Beggar's Bowl, Dragon, 18th Century 1725.00
Wood, Chinese God, Frog On Back, Belly, 18th Century 805.00
Wood, Fisherman, Seated, Mending Net, Signed 4025.00
Wood, Fox Cradling Baby, Signed, 19th Century 2875.00
Wood, Hen On Circular Drum, Inlaid Eyes 2300.00
Wood, Herd Boy On Reclining Water Buffalo 315.00
Wood, Man With Broken Sandal, Signed, Late 19th Century 1150.00

NEW HALL Porcelain Manufactory was started at Newhall, Shelton, Staffordshire, England, in 1782. Simple decorated wares were made. Between 1810 and 1825, the factory made a glassy bone porcelain sometimes marked with the factory name. Do not confuse New Hall porcelain with the pieces made by the New Hall Pottery Company, Ltd., a twentieth-century firm.

New Hall

Dish, Tobacco Pattern, Gilt Highlights, Painted Red Mark, 8 1/2 In., Pair 595.00

NEW MARTINSVILLE Glass Manufacturing Company was established in 1901 in New Martinsville, West Virginia. It was bought and renamed the Viking Glass Company in 1944. In 1987 Kenneth Dalzell, former president of Fostoria Glass Company, purchased the factory and renamed it Dalzell-Viking. Production ceased in 1998.

Moondrops, Ashtray, Ruby, 1 x 4 In. 30.00
Moondrops, Bowl, Amber, Ruffled Edge, 3 Legs, 9 1/2 In. 48.00
Moondrops, Candlestick, 3-Light, 5 1/2 x 7 In. 50.00
Moondrops, Candlestick, Pink, 5 1/8 x 4 1/2 In., Pair .... 125.00 to 185.00
Moondrops, Candlestick, Ruby, Ruffled Edge, 2 x 5 In., Pair 90.00
Moondrops, Cordial, Ruby, 3/4 Oz., 2 7/8 In. 58.00
Moondrops, Creamer, Ruby, 2 3/4 In. 18.00
Moondrops, Creamer, Ruby, 3 3/4 In. 17.00
Moondrops, Cup & Saucer, Ruby 30.00
Moondrops, Cup, Green 9.00
Moondrops, Cup, Ruby 16.00
Moondrops, Decanter, Green, Beehive Stopper, 10 1/2 In. 150.00
Moondrops, Dish, Mayonnaise, Cobalt Blue, 3-Footed, 2 7/8 x 5 1/2 In. 90.00
Moondrops, Goblet, Ruby, 3 3/4 In. 15.00
Moondrops, Plate, Dinner, Ruby, 9 1/2 In. 23.00
Moondrops, Relish, 3 Sections, 3-Footed, Ruby, 2 x 8 1/4 In. 60.00
Moondrops, Salt & Pepper, Green, 3 1/2 In. 45.00
Moondrops, Saucer, Green 6.00
Moondrops, Saucer, Ruby 6.00
Moondrops, Sherbet, Ruby, 2 5/8 In. 18.00
Moondrops, Soup, Dish, Ruby, 1 7/8 x 6 3/4 In. 78.00
Moondrops, Sugar, Cobalt Blue 18.00
Moondrops, Sugar, Ruby 18.00
Moondrops, Tumbler, Whiskey, 2 Oz., 2 3/4 In. 10.00
Moondrops, Tumbler, Whiskey, Amber, 2 Oz. 15.00
Moondrops, Tumbler, Whiskey, Amber, Handle, 2 Oz., 2 3/4 In. 12.00
Moondrops, Tumbler, Whiskey, Ruby, 2 Oz., 2 3/4 In. 22.00
Moondrops, Tumbler, Whiskey, Ruby, Handle, 2 Oz., 2 3/4 In. 20.00
Moondrops, Vase, Rocket, Tricornered, Ruby, 7 1/2 x 6 1/2 In. 130.00
Moondrops, Wine, Ruby, Metal Stem, 3 Oz., 5 1/8 In. 18.00

NEWCOMB Pottery was founded by Ellsworth and William Woodward at Sophie Newcomb College, New Orleans, Louisiana, in 1895.
The work continued through the 1940s. Pieces of this art pottery are
marked with the printed letters *NC* and often have the incised initials of
the artist as well. Most pieces have a matte glaze and incised decoration.

Bookends, Cypress, Palmettos, Anna Francis Simpson, 6 In. 2000.00
Bowl, Jonquil, Blue Matte Glaze, 3 1/8 x 5 3/4 In. 1840.00
Bowl, Jonquil, Broad, Anna Francis Simpson, 8 3/4 In. 2350.00
Bowl, Nasturtium, Blue, Yellow, Blue Matte Glaze, Sadie Irvine, 3 1/4 x 5 1/2 In. 1725.00
Pitcher, Milk, Cow & Tree Band, Blue, Green, Marie De Hoa LeBlanc, 1902, 8 x 6 In. ... 8225.00
Tile, Bayou Landscape, Cypress Trees, Arts & Crafts Frame, 6 x 10 In. 14900.00
Tile, Cat, 2 Rabbits, Aqua, Purple, White, Burgundy, Leona Nicholson, Frame, 9 In. 1400.00
Tile, Sailboats, Henrietta Bailey, Square, 3 In. 2940.00
Tyge, Jasmine, Motto, Drink To Me Only, Mazie T. Ryan, 1916, 8 1/2 x 8 1/2 In. 4115.00
Vase, 2 Handles, Blue Poppies, Life & Love, Harriet Joor, 1901, 6 1/2 x 9 1/2 In. 4115.00
Vase, Band Of Pin Irises, Squat Form, Blue, Pink & Green, 1924, 2 7/8 In. 635.00
Vase, Blue & Green Spanish Moss, Pink & Yellow Sky, Egg Shape, Sadie Irvine, 6 In. 5290.00
Vase, Blue Daffodils, Green Leaves, Cylindrical, Flared Rim, 10 In. 3525.00
Vase, Chrysanthemums, Egg Shape, A.F. Simpson, 1912, 9 x 3 1/2 In. 6465.00
Vase, Cypress Trees, Moss Laden, Carved & Painted, Henrietta Bailey, 6 1/4 x 3 In. 5875.00
Vase, Cypress Trees, Moss Laden, Carved & Painted, Sadie Irvine, 4 x 2 In. 2235.00
Vase, Daffodils, Blue Ground, No. 190, A.F. Connor-Simpson, 1917, 6 5/8 In. 1955.00
Vase, Daffodils, Flared, Sadie Irvine, 8 x 3 1/2 In. 940.00
Vase, Daisies, Blue Ground, Flared, Aurelia Arbo, c.1937, 3 1/2 x 3 1/4 In. 1060.00
Vase, Dogwood, Blue Ground, Sadie Irvine, 1932, 8 1/4 x 3 1/2 In. 1765.00
Vase, Double Gourd, Purple Matte Glaze, 5 1/4 x 3 1/2 In. 646.00
Vase, Dripping Green Over Light Green, Pinched Waist, Joseph Meyer, 12 1/2 In. 880.00
Vase, Flowers, Anna Francis Simpson, 3 1/2 In. 880.00
Vase, Flowers, Blue, Green Matte Glaze, Handles, 5 1/2 In. 1175.00
Vase, Flowers, Blue, Tapering, Bulbous, Sadie Irvine, 6 1/4 In. 2470.00
Vase, Flowers, Ivory, Green Stems, Blue, High Glaze, Sadie Irvine, 6 x 3 1/2 In. 1840.00
Vase, Flowers, Matte Glaze, Bulbous, Alma Mason, 5 In. 1410.00

Vase, Glossy Green Glaze, Egg Shape, Puce Ground, 7 In. 590.00
Vase, Gold Flowers, Leaves, Black Lines, Cream Glaze, Bulbous, Marked, 2 3/4 In. 4405.00
Vase, Green Matte Glaze, 3 1/4 In. 335.00
Vase, Green Scarabs, Pinched Waist, Stand, Leona Nicholson, 1906, 6 1/4 x 2 1/2 In. 11165.00
Vase, Irises, Bulbous, Anna Francis Simpson, 6 1/2 In. 4115.00
Vase, Landscape, Tree, Marie De Hoa LeBlanc, 5 1/2 In. 8815.00
Vase, Leaves, Berries, Sadie Irvine, 3 1/2 x 2 1/4 In. 1058.00
Vase, Moon & Moss, Vellum Glazed, Sadie Irvine, 8 1/4 In. 5290.00
Vase, Moon & Spanish Moss, Egg Shape, Blue & Green, 1932, 6 In. 3680.00
Vase, Moss Laden Trees, Dripping In Blue Green Glaze, Oval, Signed, 1930, 5 In. 3850.00
Vase, Narcissus, Green Ground, Transitional Bulbous, Sadie Irvine, 1913, 7 1/4 In. 2115.00
Vase, Nicotina Flowers, Tapering, Leona Nicholson, 1909, 12 x 4 1/4 In. 7050.00
Vase, Oak Trees, Spanish Moss, Full Moon, Egg Shape, Sadie Irvine, 1927, 6 1/2 x 3 In. . . 2700.00
Vase, Oak Trees, Spanish Moss, Landscape, Bulbous, A.F. Simpson, 1920, 5 x 5 1/4 In. . . . 3410.00
Vase, Oak Trees, Spanish Moss, Pink Sky, Sadie Irvine, 1919, 3 3/4 x 3 3/4 In. 3410.00
Vase, Oak Trees, Spanish Moss, Squat, Sadie Irvine, 1917, 3 1/2 x 3 In. 2820.00
Vase, Palm Trees, Moon, Blue, Green, Sadie Irvine, 10 x 6 3/4 In. 18400.00
Vase, Patchwork, Carved, Painted, Matte Glaze, Sadie Irvine, 3 1/2 x 3 1/2 In. 1410.00
Vase, Pine Trees, Spanish Moss, Full Moon, Egg Shape, A.F. Simpson, 1921, 6 x 3 In. 3055.00
Vase, Pinecone, Purple, Green, Carved, Blue Ground, Bailey, No. K147, 8 In. 6465.00
Vase, Pink Irises, Green Leaves, A.F. Simpson, 1919, 9 x 6 3/4 In. 10000.00
Vase, Pink Roses, Green Leaves, Blue Ground, Bulbous, Henrietta Bailey, 1927, 6 x 7 In. . . 4600.00
Vase, Round, Decorated, Blue Trees, Pink Ground, 3 1/4 In. 2990.00
Vase, Sailboats, Lake Pontchartrain, Trees, Henrietta Bailey, 1929, 6 x 4 3/4 In. 4115.00
Vase, Shouldered, Green Crystalline Glaze, Jules Gabry, 7 1/2 x 8 1/2 In. 1410.00
Vase, Spanish Moss On Trees, Blue, Magenta, Oval, A.F. Simpson, 2 3/4 x 3 In. 2415.00
Vase, Tea Roses, Cobalt Blue Ground, Bulbous, Henrietta Bailey, 1927, 6 1/2 x 7 In. 4400.00
Vase, Trees, Moss Laden, Carved, Painted, Matte Glaze, Sadie Irvine, 6 x 4 In. 3055.00
Vase, Trees, Spanish Moss, Full Moon, Cylindrical, A.F. Simpson, 1925, 10 x 4 In. 5875.00
Vase, Trees, Waving, Matte Glaze, Sadie Irvine, 3 1/2 In. 2938.00
Vase, Yellow Cinquefoils, Bulbous, May Louise Dunn, 1912, 9 x 3 1/4 In. 3820.00
Vase, Yellow Daffodils, Alma Mason, 1914, 8 In. 3100.00
Vase, Yellow Flowers, Green Stems, Bulbous, Sara Levy, c.1903, 5 1/2 x 3 1/2 In. 7640.00

NILOAK Pottery (Kaolin spelled backward) was made at the Hyten
Brothers Pottery in Benton, Arkansas, between 1909 and 1947.
Although the factory did make cast and molded wares, collectors are
most interested in the marbleized art pottery line made of colored
swirls of clay. It was called *Mission Ware*. By 1931 the company made
castware, and many of these pieces were marked with the name
Hywood.

Vase, Cabinet, Hexagonal, Rose, Green Accents, 3 1/2 In. 12.00
Vase, Marbleized, Blue, Brown, Black, Tan, Swollen Shape, 12 In. 645.00
Vase, Marbleized, Blue, Brown, Red, Cream, Shouldered, 10 1/2 In. 645.00
Vase, Marbleized, Blue, Red, Brown, Ivory, Flat Sides, 2 1/2 In. 90.00
Vase, Marbleized, Blue, Red, Brown, Ivory, Shouldered, Marked, 6 In. 120.00
Vase, Marbleized, Brown, Blue, Tan, Marked, 10 1/2 In. 150.00
Vase, Marbleized, Classical Shape, 12 1/2 In. 530.00
Vase, Marbleized, Cylinder Shape, Rust, Tan, Blue, Cream, 5 1/2 In. 230.00
Vase, Marbleized, Flared Lip, Brown, Blue, Cream, Tan, 4 5/8 In. 175.00
Vase, Marbleized, Rolled Rim, Tan, Blue, White, 5 1/2 In. 185.00
Vase, Marbleized, Rolled Rim, Tan, Rust, Brown, Blue, 6 1/4 In. 255.00
Vase, Marbleized, Shouldered, Brown, Red, 10 1/2 In. 375.00
Vase, Marbleized, Squat Shape, Rolled Rim, Brown, Rusts, Blue, 3 3/4 In. 127.00

NIPPON porcelain was made in Japan from 1891 to 1921. *Nippon* is
the Japanese word for *Japan.* A few firms continued to use the word
Nippon on ceramics after 1921 as a part of the company name more
than as an identification of the country of origin. More pieces marked
Nippon will be found in the Dragonware, Moriage, and Noritake
categories.

Basket, Roses, Stippled Gilt Ground, Handle, 7 1/2 In. 85.00

Bowl, Dragon, Melon Shape, Ribbed, Beaded Top, 6 1/4 In. 175.00
Bowl, Flowers, Gold Design, Royal Nippon Mark, 10 In. 125.00
Bowl, Poppies, Lavender, Gold, Handles, Mark, 10 In. 135.00
Bowl, Ruffled, Light Blue, Gold, Rose, Maple Leaf Mark, 10 1/2 In. 155.00
Box, Cover, Flowers, Green Maple Leaf Mark, 4 1/2 In. 100.00
Candlestick, Rose, Cobalt Decoration, Handle, Mark 55.00
Charger, Roses, Jeweled Gilt Rim, Blue Maple Leaf Mark, 11 1/2 In. 405.00
Chocolate Pot, Flowers, Gold, Royal Nippon Mark, 10 In. 245.00
Chocolate Pot Set, Gilt Raised Flowers, Green RC Mark, 10-In. Pot, 11 Piece 635.00
Chocolate Pot Set, Pink Wild Roses, Leaves, Gold Bands, Cups, Saucers, 8 In., 7 Piece .. 149.00
Chop Plate, Heavy Gold, Rose Medallions, Maple Leaf Mark, 13 In. 300.00
Cracker Jar, Gold Decoration, Mark, 5 In. 75.00
Cracker Jar, Roses, Cobalt, Gold, 7 In. 215.00
Humidor, 6-Panel Sides, Blue Maple Leaf Mark, 5 1/2 In. 115.00
Humidor, Lake, Mark, 6 1/2 In. 115.00
Humidor, Scene, Raised Enamel Decoration, 6 1/2 In. 230.00
Humidor, Trees, Water's Edge, Mark No. 27, 7 In. 130.00
Jug, Wine, Woodland, Blue Maple Leaf Mark, 9 1/2 In. 1610.00
Mustard, Flowers, 2 Handles, Sunrise Mark 8.00
Pitcher, Figural Handle, Blue Maple Leaf Mark, 8 In. 185.00
Plaque, Pheasants, Embossed Gilt Rim, Blue Maple Leaf Mark, 11 In. 460.00
Plate, Fleur-De-Lis, Gold, Handle, Mark, 11 In. 75.00
Plate, Flowers, Cobalt Blue, Pierced Edge, 10 In. 85.00
Plate, Flowers, Fruit, Green Background, Gold, 10 In. 205.00
Plate, Flowers, Gold, Pierced Edge, 11 In. 105.00
Plate, Gold, Flowers, Royal Nippon Mark, 9 In. 75.00
Plate, Rose, Gold, Maple Leaf Mark, 10 In. 265.00
Plate, Woman, Portrait, Gilt, Enameled, Jeweled Border, Blue Maple Leaf Mark, 9 In. 835.00
Powder Box, Cover, Pink Flowers, Gold Scrolls & Swags, Green Maple Leaf Mark, 6 In. . 140.00
Sugar & Creamer, Cobalt, Rose, Gold 95.00
Sugar Shaker, Handle, Flowers, Beading, Sunrise Mark, 4 In. 20.00
Tray, Rectangular, Cobalt, Gold, Flowers, 14 In. 145.00
Urn, Flowers, Red, Lavender, Gold, Handles, Bolted, 22 In. 500.00
Vase, Bud, Iris, Coralene, Blue Ground, Handles, Marked, 5 1/2 In. 375.00
Vase, Cartoon Scene, Raised Enameled Scrolling, Blue Maple Leaf Mark, 8 In. 127.00
Vase, Flowers, Cobalt Blue Ground, 2 Handles, 6 1/2 In. 80.00
Vase, Flowers, Coralene, 6-Footed, 4 3/4 In. 230.00
Vase, Flowers, Coralene, Gold Trim, Gold Handles, Peaked Rim, 1909, 7 In. 460.00
Vase, Flowers, Coralene, Green Ground, 9 In. 800.00
Vase, Flowers, Gilt Wreath, Handles, 9 3/4 In. 230.00
Vase, Flowers, Gold & Beaded Design, Handles, 2 3/4 In. 50.00
Vase, Flowers, Satin Ground, 2 Handles, Blue Maple Leaf Mark, 9 1/2 In. 575.00
Vase, Gilt Grapes, Over Painted Roses, 2 Handles, 10 In. 105.00
Vase, Halloween Or Cartoon Style Scenes, Blue Maple Leaf Mark, 8 In., Pair 1035.00
Vase, Lilies, Coralene, Yellow, Orange, Shaded Ground, c.1909, 8 3/4 x 4 3/4 In. 1058.00
Vase, Painted, Urn Shape, Applied Decoration, Scroll Handles, Early 1900s, 10 1/2 In. 130.00
Vase, Pastoral Scenes, Panels, Gold Filigree Neck, Foot, Petal Rim, 2 Gold Handles, 8 In. .. 190.00
Vase, Peonies, Coralene, Pink, Russet, Shaded Ground, c.1909, 8 1/4 x 5 In. 999.00
Vase, Portrait, Woman, Pink Dress, Lacy Gilt Ground, Blue Maple Leaf Mark, 7 In. 430.00
Vase, Roses In Medallions, 2 Handles, Blue Maple Leaf Mark, 7 1/4 In. 200.00
Vase, Roses, Gold Lattice, 2 Handles, Blue Maple Leaf Mark, 8 1/4 In. 115.00
Vase, Roses, Handles, Mark No. 38, Imperial Nippon, 11 In. 200.00
Vase, Roses, Pink, Gold Liner, Rope, Jewels, Maple Leaf Mark, 9 In. 170.00
Vase, Scene, Cherry Blossoms, Flowers, 12 1/2 In. 259.00
Vase, Stylized & Jeweled Flowers, 4 Scrolled Handles, 10 3/4 In. 195.00
Vase, Stylized Roses, Handles, Blue Maple Leaf Mark, 10 In. 315.00
Vase, Swan, Lake, Bridge, Trees, Tapestry, Sharkskin Finish, 5 1/2 In. 115.00
Vase, Tapestry, Sponge, 2 Handles, Purple Wisteria Blossoms, Leaves, Signed, 7 1/4 In. ... 405.00
Vase, Trees, Stream, Square, Blue Imperial Nippon Mark, No. 38, 8 In. 69.00
Vase, Western Mountain, Fir Tree, 3 Handles, Imperial Nippon, Mark No. 38, 11 1/4 In. ... 175.00
Vase, Windmill, Gold Bands, Pink, Blue, Red Beads, Signed, 6 In. 115.00

NODDERS, also called nodding figures or pagodas, are figures with heads and hands that are attached to wires. Any slight movement causes the parts to move up and down. They were made in many countries during the eighteenth, nineteenth, and twentieth centuries. A few Art Deco designs are also known. Copies are being made. A more recent type of nodder is made of papier-mache or plastic. These often represent sports figures or comic characters. Sports nodders are listed as bobbin' heads in the Sports category.

Andy Gump, Bisque, Germany, 4 1/4 x 1 In.	80.00
Cat, Papier-Mache, Glass Eyes, 1800s, Life Size	750.00
Hula Girl, Grass Skirt, K.N., Japan, c.1950-60, 6 In.	49.00
Man Playing Saxophone, Green Suit, 2 1/2 x 1 3/4 In.	30.00
Moon Mullins, 3 3/4 x 1 1/2 In.	75.00
Newsboy, Green, Red Hat, 3 In.	50.00
Oriental Man, Woman Seated, Holding Teacup, Fan, Bisque, 16 In., Pair	1265.00
Salt & Pepper shakers are listed in the Salt & Pepper category.	
Woman, Chinoiserie, Peacock, Butterfly Robe, Movable Head, Hands, 15 x 9 In.	529.00

NORITAKE porcelain was made in Japan after 1904 by Nippon Toki Kaisha. The best-known Noritake pieces are marked with the M in a wreath for the Morimura Brothers, a New York City distributing company. This mark was used until the early 1950s. There may be some helpful price information in the Nippon category, since prices are comparable. Noritake Azalea is listed in the Azalea category in this book.

Bowl, Cereal, Cafe Du Jour, No. 9094	13.00
Bowl, Fruit, Rosales, No. 5790	7.00
Bowl, Sailing Ship, Footed, M In Wreath, 6 1/2 In.	10.00
Bowl, Scene, 2 Handles, M In Wreath, 8 In.	55.00
Bowl, Vegetable, Cover, Blue Haven, 3 1/2 x 8 3/4 In.	45.00
Bowl, Vegetable, Oval, Altadena	44.00
Bowl, Vegetable, Oval, Dignatio	39.00
Bowl, Vegetable, Oval, Homecoming	39.00
Bowl, Vegetable, Round, Belmont	44.00
Bowl, Vegetable, Round, Berries 'n Such	39.00
Bowl, Vegetable, Round, Fantasia	45.00
Butter, Bernice	38.00
Butter, Cover, Simone	38.00
Butter, Marguerite	38.00
Cake Plate, Azalea, Handles	45.00
Casserole, Cover, Rosewood, 2 3/4 x 11 3/4 In.	75.00
Creamer, Asian Song	38.00
Creamer, Essay, 3 3/4 In.	12.00
Creamer, Segovia, No. 2216	26.00
Creamer, Westview	12.00
Cup & Saucer, Inverness	12.00
Cup & Saucer, Southern Lace	12.00
Cup & Saucer, Wedding Veil	12.00
Fernery, Trees, Water, Mountains, Gilt Handles, 4-Footed, Green M In Wreath, 9 In.	185.00
Gravy Boat, Attached Underplate, Japan Waltz, No. 2027, 3 x 8 1/2 In.	24.99
Gravy Boat, Berries 'n Such	44.00
Gravy Boat, Flower Time, No. 9072	58.00
Gravy Boat, Underplate, Leslie, 9 In.	39.00
Humidor, Blown Out, Camel, Jeweled Saddle, Green M In Wreath, 6 1/2 In.	2300.00
Humidor, Cover, Owl Sitting On Branch, Leaves, Acorns, Signed, 6 3/4 In.	633.00
Humidor, Lake, Medallions, M In Wreath, 4 1/2 In.	135.00
Humidor, Owl Relief, Hand Painted, 7 In.	748.00
Humidor, Sailing Ship Scene, M In Wreath, 5 1/2 In.	225.00
Humidor, Scene, M In Wreath, 6 In.	400.00
Jug, Hunt Scene, Blue Maple Leaf, Green Nippon Mark	345.00
Jug, Whiskey, Scenic Panels, Oriental Design, M In Wreath, 7 1/2 In.	450.00
Nut Bowl, Blown Out, Embossed Basket Weave, Green M In Wreath, 9 1/4 In.	200.00
Nut Set, Acorn, 7 Piece	75.00

Nut Set, Master Bowl, Footed, 6 Individual Dishes, Acorn, M In Wreath, 7 In. 95.00
Pitcher, Milk, Sailing Ships, Handles, M In Wreath, 5 In. 55.00
Plaque, Bellowing Elk, Relief Molded, Round, Green M In Wreath, 11 In. 345.00
Plaque, Fall Scene, Trees In Foreground, Round, Green M In Wreath, 10 In. 69.00
Plaque, Geese In Lake, White Rose Border, Round, Blue M In Wreath, 10 In. 316.00
Plaque, Lion & Lioness, Relief Molded, Round, Green M In Wreath, 10 1/2 In. 489.00
Plaque, Wooded Pasture, River, Purple Trees, Round, Blue M In Wreath, 10 1/2 In. 80.00
Plate, Bread & Butter, Laureate, 6 1/4 In. 12.00
Plate, Bread & Butter, Margot, No. 5605 .... 7.00
Plate, Bread & Butter, Victorian Lace, No. 9744 .... 9.00
Plate, Dinner, Daryl, 10 1/2 In. 12.00
Plate, Dinner, Harvesting 38.00
Plate, Dinner, Macon, 10 1/2 In. 12.00
Plate, Salad, Mardi Gras, No. 9019, 8 1/4 In. 9.00
Plate, Salad, Rosemary, c.1930, 7 1/2 In. 12.00
Platter, Bessie, Small 45.00
Platter, Casablanca, Small 45.00
Platter, Silver Key, Small 45.00
Platter, Sunny Side, 1975, 13 3/4 x 9 1/2 In. 45.00
Salt & Pepper, Platinum Trim, Fremont 38.00
Sugar, Cover, Eternal Blush 38.00
Sugar, Cover, Montblanc 38.00
Sugar, Cover, Palos Verde 11.00
Tea Set, River, Bridge, House, Bronzed Embossed Borders, Green M In Wreath, 14 Piece . 748.00
Tea Set, Scenic Medallions, Gilt Garland, Green M In Wreath, 8 1/2 In., 9 Piece 520.00
Teapot, Bowls Of Fruit, Child's, c.1920, 4 3/8 In. 11.00
Toothpick, Woodland, White, Green M In Wreath, 2 In. 160.00
Tray, Nile River, Sunset, Green M In Wreath, 9 3/4 In. 69.00
Vase, 4 Scenic Panels, Blown-Out Medallions, Bolted, Green M In Wreath, 14 1/2 In. 1325.00
Vase, Art Deco Flowers, 4 Paw Feet, Blue M In Wreath, 8 1/4 In. 230.00
Vase, Blackberries, Satin Ground, Green M In Wreath, 10 In. 145.00
Vase, Cottage, 4 Panels, Concave Shoulders, Green M In Wreath, 13 In. 690.00
Vase, Dutch Scene, Dragon Handles, Blue M In Wreath, 5 1/2 In. 575.00
Vase, Flowers, Jeweled Beads, 6 Panels, Green M In Wreath, 9 1/2 In. 219.00
Vase, House In Meadow, Green M In Wreath, 6 In., Pair 90.00
Vase, Hunt Scene, Enamel Banding, Blue M In Wreath, 8 3/4 In. 690.00
Vase, Mountain, Woman In Road, Trees, Jeweled Ring Handles, Green M In Wreath, 7 In. . 200.00
Vase, Nile River Scene, Handles, Green M In Wreath, 10 1/4 In. 200.00
Vase, Nile River, Winged Lions Base, Green M In Wreath, 8 3/4 In. 230.00
Vase, Roses, Gilt, 2 Handles, Blue M In Wreath, 7 1/2 In. 160.00
Vase, Ruins, Enameled Flowers, Green M In Wreath, 11 1/2 In. 290.00
Vase, Scene, Gold, Ring Pretzel Handles, M In Wreath, 9 1/2 In. 850.00
Vase, Snow Scene, 2 Handles, M In Wreath, 5 In. 259.00
Vase, Stylized Flowers, 2 Handles, Green M In Wreath, 10 1/2 In. 219.00
Wine Jug, Christmas Elk, Moriage Decoration, M In Wreath, 9 1/2 In. 2300.00

NORSE Pottery Company started in Edgerton, Wisconsin, in 1903. In
1904 the company moved to Rockford, Illinois. The company made a
black pottery, which resembled early bronze relics of the Scandinavian
countries. The firm went out of business in 1913.

Bowl, Copper Glaze, 2 Animal Head Handles, 8 In. 325.00
Vase, Salamander, Verdigris & Bronze Glaze, Norse 25, 11 1/2 x 7 In. 1000.00

NORTH DAKOTA SCHOOL OF MINES was established in 1892 at
the University of North Dakota. A ceramic course was included and
pieces were made from the clays found in the region. Students at the
university made pieces from 1909 to 1949. Although very early pieces
were marked *U.N.D.*, most pieces were stamped with the full name of
the university.

Bowl, Dots, Peaks, Recessed Neck, Frothy Blue Glaze, Marked, 3 x 4 In. 375.00
Bowl, Flowers, Leaves, Mocha Brown Matte, Green Speckled Interior, Marked, 3 x 4 In. .. 460.00
Charger, Flowers, Terra-Cotta Ground, Margaret Cable, 8 1/4 In. 530.00
Vase, Green Semimatte Glaze, Woodward, 6 In. 205.00

Avoid spray-on dusting products labeled "no wax." They may contain silicone oil that doesn't protect furniture from water damage and can interfere with refinishing.

Nutcracker, Dog, Painted Orange, Cast Iron, 5 1/2 x 12 In.

Vase, Periwinkle Blue High Glaze, Bulbous, Elongated Neck, Stamped, 5 1/2 x 4 In. 260.00
Vase, Roses, Brown Matte, Tapering, D. Dorchardt, 5 1/4 In. 1295.00
Vase, Tulips, Brown Matte Glaze, 8 x 5 3/4 In. 2585.00

NORTHWOOD Glass Company was founded by Harry Northwood, a glassmaker who worked for Hobbs, Brockunier and Company, La Belle Glass Company, and Buckeye Glass Company before founding his own firm. He opened one factory in Indiana, Pennsylvania, in 1896, and another in Wheeling, West Virginia, in 1902. Northwood closed when Mr. Northwood died in 1923. Many types of glass were made, including carnival, custard, goofus, and pressed. The underlined N mark was used on some pieces.

Pompeian, Vase, Mother-Of-Pearl, Maroon Shaded To Citron, Bulbous, Squat, 5 1/2 In. 1150.00
Royal Ivy, Toothpick, Parian Swirl, Rainbow Spatter, 2 1/2 In. 200.00
Vase, Yellow & Red, Glossy Pink Ground, Trifold Rim, 3 Claw Feet, 14 In. 2645.00

NU-ART see Imperial category.

NUTCRACKERS of many types have been used through the centuries. At first the nutcracker was probably strong teeth or a hammer. But by the nineteenth century, many elaborate and ingenious types were made. Levers, screws, and hammer adaptations were the most popular. Because nutcrackers are still useful, they are still being made, some in the old styles.

Dog, Cast Iron, Harker Supply Co., Chicago, 13 In. 335.00
Dog, Painted Orange, Cast Iron, 5 1/2 x 12 In. .... *Illus* 85.00
Squirrel, Press Down On Tail, Cast Iron, 10 x 4 x 9 In. 358.00

NYMPHENBURG, see Royal Nymphenburg.

OCCUPIED JAPAN was printed on pottery, porcelain, toys, and other goods made during the American occupation of Japan after World War II, from 1945 to 1952. Collectors now search for these pieces. The items were made for export.

Cup & Saucer, Flowers, Gold Rim, Marked LB, S.G.K. 16.00
Dessert Set, Cup & Saucer, Plate, Strawberries, 8-In. Plate 65.00
Figurine, Ballerina, Green & White Lace Skirt Trimmed With Pink Rose, 4 In. 17.00
Figurine, Boy & Girl, Carrying Basket, Red Mark, 5 In., Pair 35.00
Figurine, Bride & Groom, Celluloid, Original Box, 3 1/ 8 In. 110.00
Figurine, Woman Feeding Deer, 5 x 3 3/4 In. 16.00
Lemon Dish, Rose, Yellow, Pink, Green HP Elephant Mark, 5 1/2 In. 15.00
Planter, Boy & Girl, Red Paulux Mark, 5 x 4 1/4 In., Pair 40.00
Salt & Pepper, 4 1/4 In. 45.00
Toby Mug, Old Man Holding Pipe, 2 Dogs Beside Him, 8 x 5 1/2 In. 26.00
Toothpick, Geisha Girl, Vase Shape 20.00
Tray, Papier-Mache, Floral Center, Beige, Red, Scalloped Edge, 12 x 14 In. 63.00
Wall Pocket, Duck In Flight, 5 x 10 In. 17.00

OFFICE TECHNOLOGY includes office equipment and related products, such as adding machines, calculators, and check-writing machines. Typewriters are in their own category in this book.

Adding Machine, Alpina Universal, No. 004677, 19 Digit Display, Case, 6 In. 1410.00
Dictaphone, Ediphone, Thomas Edison Co., 36 x 14 x 12 In. 39.00
File, 16 Drawers, Oak, Reeded Columns, 24 x 17 x 42 1/2 In. 460.00
File, 17 Drawers, Oak, 30 x 21 x 75 In. 1035.00
File, Bank Check, 8 Drawers, Oak, Levey's, 12 1/2 x 24 1/2 x 51 In. 490.00
File, Drawers, Footed Base, US PO Dept., Globe-Wernicke, 33 x 17 x 71 In. 980.00
Filing System, Total Account System, Cast Iron, Walnut, 22 x 23 x 53 In. 175.00
Stock Ticker, No. 2403, Brass, Cast Iron Base, Glass Dome, New York Quotation Co. 7050.00

OHR pottery was made in Biloxi, Mississippi, from 1883 to 1906 by
George E. Ohr, a true eccentric. The pottery was made of very thin clay
that was twisted, folded, and dented into odd, graceful shapes. Some
pieces were lifelike models of hats, animal heads, or even a potato.
Others were decorated with folded clay *snakes*. Reproductions and
reworked pieces are appearing on the market. These have been
reglazed, or snakes and other embellishments have been added.

Bowl, Crumpled, Green Mirror Glaze, 3 In. 2938.00
Bowl, Flaring, Closed-In Rim, Gunmetal Drips Over Amber Ground, 3 x 6 1/2 In. 1528.00
Bowl, Flaring, Ruffled, Buff Bisque Clay, 3 x 5 1/2 In. 2468.00
Bowl, Green, Pink, Semimatte, 2 3/4 x 4 1/2 In. 7475.00
Bowl, High Glaze, 2-Tone, Green, Black, Tan, Brown Swirls, Marked, 2 3/4 x 3 1/2 In. . . . 1415.00
Bowl, Ruffled, Collapsed, Green Flambe Top, Pink Bottom, 2 3/4 x 4 1/2 In. 7050.00
Cup, Ear Shaped Handle, Gunmetal Over Mottled & Speckled Green Glaze, 6 3/4 In. 4400.00
Hat, Mottled Brown Glaze, 4 In. 1175.00
Inkwell, Bungalow Shape, Yellow On Brown Ground, Marked, 3 x 7 x 5 In. . . . . .2200.00 to 2530.00
Inkwell, Jefferson Davis House, Green, High Glaze, 1896, Marked, 2 3/4 x 7 In. 4025.00
Inkwell, Log Cabin, Green & Gunmetal Glaze, 2 In. 1058.00
Inkwell, Mule Head, Black & Olive Brown Glaze, Grooved Stand, Stamped, 2 x 5 3/8 In. . . 3890.00
Jug, Commemorative, President On Side, Ohr's Wife On Other, Star, Flowers, 7 1/2 In. . . . 3820.00
Jug, Cylindrical, Flared, Pinched Spout, Bulbous, Brown Matte Glaze, 4 3/4 In. 4348.00
Mug, Brown, Yellow, Purple, Triangular Handle, 4 3/4 x 5 3/4 In. 3738.00
Mug, Carved Animal Head, Handle, Drink Holes, c.1900, 3 1/2 In. 1765.00
Mug, Cylindrical, Waisted, Black Mirror Glaze, Signed, 4 3/4 In. 1175.00
Mug, Ear Shaped Handle, Gunmetal & Green Glaze, 4 In. 1530.00
Mug, Here's To Your Good Health, Family, Cylindrical, Handle, Green, Yellow Glaze, 6 In. 2820.00
Mug, Looping Handle, Blue Gunmetal Glaze, 6 x 6 In. 3290.00
Pitcher, Bisque, Folded, Pinched, Collapsed, Red, Beige, Marbleized, 4 1/4 x 6 In. 7475.00
Pitcher, Body Twist, Squat Base, Olive Green Glaze, 3 1/4 x 3 1/4 In. 3175.00
Pitcher, Lobed Rim, Ear Handle, Gunmetal Brown Drips, Khaki Ground, 3 x 5 1/2 In. 2705.00
Pitcher, Pinched & Cutout Handle, Cobalt & Green Glossy Glaze, 3 x 4 In. 3525.00
Vase, Beaker Shape, Green, Black, Brown Sponge Bands, Orange Ground, 5 x 4 1/2 In. . . . 4115.00
Vase, Bisque, Squat, 2 Handles, 4 1/4 In. 1998.00
Vase, Bottle Shape, Folded Rim, Red, White, Blue & Amber Sponge, 4 3/4 x 2 3/4 In. 8225.00
Vase, Buff Bisque Clay, Squat, Body Twist, Flaring Rim, 2 1/4 In. 2115.00
Vase, Bulbous, Closed-In Rim, Dimpled Band, Green, Purple, Mottled Glaze, 4 x 4 3/4 In. . 5875.00
Vase, Bulbous, Flared Top, Volcanic Multitoned, Brown, Red, Green Matte Glaze, 3 In. . . . 1610.00
Vase, Bulbous, Folded Rim, Brown, Black Speckled Glaze, Stamped, 7 3/4 x 4 1/2 In. 9400.00
Vase, Bulbous, Folded Rim, Green Gunmetal Glaze, 3 1/4 x 4 In. 3335.00
Vase, Bulbous, Footed, Folded Rim, Mottled Glaze, Green, Raspberry, 5 x 5 In. 5580.00
Vase, Bulbous, Green, Gun Metal, Indigo, Raspberry Sponge Glaze, 5 1/2 x 2 3/4 In. 9988.00
Vase, Bulbous, Lobed & Dimpled Shoulder, Amber & Green Speckled Glaze, 3 1/2 x 4 In. . 3820.00
Vase, Bulbous, Lobed Rim, Sponged-On Glaze, 3 x 3 1/2 In. 8225.00
Vase, Bulbous, Twisted, Folded Rim, Brown Gunmetal, Green Speckled Glaze, 6 x 4 In. . . 7637.00
Vase, Closed-In Rim, Marbleized Clay, Green Sheer Mottled Glaze, 3 1/2 In. 1410.00
Vase, Closed-In Rim, Sponged On Gunmetal Glaze, Mottled Base, 4 x 3 3/4 In. 6530.00
Vase, Coupe Shape, Folded Rim, Dimpled Band, Mottled Glaze, 4 3/4 x 4 In. 7640.00
Vase, Crimped, Flat Mouth, Raspberry, Green, Orange Speckles, Streaks, Marked, 3 x 4 In. 9200.00
Vase, Crumpled, Flaring, Brown Glaze, Glossy & Gunmetal Glaze, 3 1/2 x 4 1/2 In. 3525.00
Vase, Cupped Rim, Deep Body Twist, Brown, Green, Amber, Speckled, 3 1/4 x 3 3/4 In. . . 7475.00
Vase, Dimpled, Folded Rim, Brown, 3 1/2 x 4 1/2 In. 4315.00
Vase, Double Gourd, Brown Ground, Ivory, Green, Raspberry & Blue Sponge, 4 x 2 In. . . . 3525.00
Vase, Face, Gunmetal Glaze, Green Ground, 4 1/2 x 4 1/2 In. 3820.00
Vase, Flaring Top, Mottled Blue, Green, White, Glaze, 5 1/2 In. 280.00

Vase, Handles, Volcanic Black Glaze, 3 1/4 In. 2875.00
Vase, Pinched Waist, Folded Rim, Blue Green, Mottled Raspberry Base, 4 x 4 3/4 In. 7640.00
Vase, Red Bisque Clay, Folded Middle, Oxidized Side Pattern, 3 3/4 x 4 3/4 In. 2300.00
Vase, Sake Bottle Shape, 3 Brown Stripes, Ocher Ground, Speckled, 6 1/2 x 3 1/2 In. 1880.00
Vase, Squat, Dimpled & Folded Rim, Blue, Green, Mottled, Sponged, 3 3/4 x 4 1/4 In. 9775.00
Vase, Tapered, Folded Rim, Body Twist, White & Raspberry Sponge, 3 1/4 x 3 In. 10000.00

OLD PARIS, see Paris category.

OLD SLEEPY EYE, see Sleepy Eye category.

OLYMPIC, see Souvenir category.

ONION PATTERN, originally named *bulb pattern*, is a white ware decorated with cobalt blue or pink. Although it is commonly associated with Meissen, other companies made the pattern in the late nineteenth and the twentieth centuries. A rare type is called *red bud* because there are added red accents on the blue-and-white dishes.

Bowl, Blue Onion, Meissen, Oval, 15 1/2 In. 145.00
Mallet, Blue, Wood Handle 50.00
Plate, Tree Center, Reticulated, Scalloped, Meissen, 20th Century, 8 1/4 In., 10 Piece 500.00
Platter, Blue, Meissen, Crossed Swords, Waechtersburg Mark, 24 x 12 In. 290.00
Rolling Pin, Wooden Handle, A.H. Annaburg, 7 In. 180.00
Stein, Blue, Porcelain Lid, Hand Painted, Meissen, 1 Liter 145.00
Teapot, Blue, Marked TK 69.00
Tray, Rococo Style Border, Openwork Handles, Meissen, 16 1/2 In. 575.00

OPALESCENT GLASS is translucent glass that has the tones of the opal gemstone. It originated in England in the 1870s and is often found in pressed glassware made in Victorian times. Opalescent glass was first made in America in 1897 at the Northwood glassworks in Indiana, Pennsylvania. Some dealers use the terms *opaline* and *opalescent* for any of these translucent wares. More opalescent pieces may be listed in Hobnail, Northwood, Pressed Glass, Spanish Lace, and other glass categories.

Alaska, Berry Bowl, Vaseline, Master 100.00
Beaded Cable, Rose Bowl, Blue, 3-Footed, 4 In. 125.00
Beaded Shell, Sauce, Blue, 4-Footed 82.00
Daisy & Fern, Sugar Shaker, Cranberry, 4 3/8 In. 490.00
Dewdrop, Pitcher, Blue, 8 In. 400.00
Drapery, Berry Set, Blue, 7 Piece 195.00
Fine Ribbed Coinspot, Tumbler, Cranberry . . . . *Illus* 880.00
Herringbone, Syrup, Cranberry 3690.00
Hobnail, Bottle, Barber, Cranberry, Hobbs, 8 In. 200.00
Hobnail, Cruet, Cranberry, Clear Applied Handle, Clear Faceted Stopper, 7 In. 280.00
Hobnail, Dresser Set, Cranberry, 3 Piece 135.00
Holly With Cord & Tassel, Butter, Cover, 6 x 4 3/4 In. 300.00
Inverted Fan & Feather, Card Tray, White, 3-Footed, 6 5/8 In. 105.00

Opalescent Glass, Fine Ribbed
Coinspot, Tumbler, Cranberry

Opalescent Glass, Opaline
Brocade, Syrup, Cranberry

Opalescent Glass, Stars & Stripes,
Pitcher, Blue Opalescent

Lattice Medallions, Syrup, Cranberry	1045.00
Meander, Bowl, Green, 3-Footed, 9 In.	75.00
Opaline Brocade, Celery Vase, White, Crimped & Ruffled Edge, 5 1/2 In.	100.00
Opaline Brocade, Rose Bowl, Vaseline	140.00
Opaline Brocade, Syrup, Cranberry .... *Illus*	2200.00
Polka Dot Swirl, Water Set, White, 7 Piece	650.00
Seaweed, Cruet, Cranberry, 6 3/4 In.	850.00
Stars & Stripes, Pitcher, Blue Opalescent .... *Illus*	4510.00
Swag With Brackets, Berry Set, Vaseline, 5 Piece	250.00
Swag With Brackets, Butter, Cover, Blue	285.00
Swirl, Muffineer, Cranberry, Silvered Top, 4 1/4 In.	105.00
Swirl, Pitcher, Water, Cranberry, 8 1/2 In.	2000.00
Toothpicks are listed in the Toothpick category.	
Wishbone & Drapery, Plate, Blue, Footed, 8 In.	90.00

OPALINE, or opal glass, was made in white, green, and other colors. The glass had a matte surface and a lack of transparency. It was often gilded or painted. It was a popular mid-nineteenth-century European glassware.

Garniture, White, Restoration Style, Gilt Brass Mount, c.1900, 23 In.	1610.00
Vase, Blue, Floral Swags, Greek Key Band, Parcel Gilt, Ruffled Edge, 20 In., Pair	329.00
Vase, Enameled Classical Figures, Gold Trim, Bulbous, Flared, Pedestal Base, 17 In., Pair	120.00

OPERA GLASSES are needed because the stage is a long way from some of the seats at a play or an opera. Mother-of-pearl was a popular decoration on many French glasses.

Gilt Metal Body, Mother-Of-Pearl, Adjustable, Lemarie, France, c.1900, 6 x 4 In.	396.00

ORPHAN ANNIE first appeared in the comics in 1924. The red-headed girl and her friends have been on the radio and are still on the comic pages. A Broadway musical show and a movie in the 1980s made Annie popular again and many toys, dishes, and other memorabilia are being made.

Badge, Decoder, Brass, Ovaltine, ROA, 1936, 1 3/4 In.	46.00
Badge, Decoder, Brass, Round, Ovaltine, ROA, 1940, 1 1/2 In.	85.00
Bank, Save A Dime A Day, Tin Lithograph, 1936, 3 x 2 3/4 In.	300.00
Book, Big Little Book, 1933, 4 x 4 1/2 x 1 1/2 In., 316 Pages	95.00
Book, Little Orphan Annie In Cosmic City, Cupples & Leon, 8 3/4 In., 88 Pages	90.00
Book, Little Orphan Annie In Hollywood, Whitman, c.1937, 3 3/4 In., 64 Pages	200.00
Book, Orphan Annie & The Big Town Gunmen, Whitman, 64 Pages	60.00
Button, Annie & Joe Corntassel Voter's Button, 1931, 16 3/4 x 10 1/4 In.	465.00
Button, Contest, Los Angeles Evening Express, Celluloid, 1930s	50.00
Button, Little Orphan Annie Loves Red Cross Macaroni, Celluloid, c.1930, 1 1/4 In.	40.00
Button, Some Swell Sweater, Parisian Novelty, 1928, 1 1/4 In.	60.00
Dress Clip, Heart's Desire, Bird, Roses, Brass, Die Cut, Hinged, Ovaltine, 1930s, 2 In.	90.00
Game, Little Orphan Annie Shooting Game, Milton Bradley, Box, 1930s, 11 3/4 In.	290.00
Game, Treasure Hunt, 3 Ships, Premium, Original Mailer	85.00
Glosstone Colorettes, Annie In Florida, Envelope, 1940s, 8 x 11 In., 12 Sheets	200.00
Lunch Box, Metal, Thermos Bottle, Aladdin, 1982	39.00
Mug, Annie, Sandy, Ovaltine, Orange, Beetleware, 1933, 3 In.	870.00
Mug, Ovaltine, Annie, Holding Mug, Sandy, Ceramic, Wander Co., c.1932, 3 In. ....65.00 to 115.00	
Mug, Ovaltine, Shake-Up, Annie, Sandy, Lid, Beetleware, Late 1930s, 5 In. ....50.00 to 110.00	
Plate, Daddy Warbucks, 2nd Issue, William Chambers, E.M. Knowles, 1982, 8 1/2 In.	18.00
Ring, Post Raisin Bran, 1948, 2 1/2 In.	27.00
Ring, Silver Star, Triple Mystery, Secret Compartment, Ovaltine, 1938	800.00
Sheet Music, Ovaltine, Wander Company, 1931	24.00
Toothbrush Holder, Annie, Sandy, Souvenir, Spirit Lake, Iowa, Japan, 3 1/2 In.	260.00
Toy, Annie & Pluto, Tin Lithograph, Windup, 5 In.	468.00
Toy, Annie & Sandy, Celluloid, Windup, Kuramochi, Japan, Box, 6 1/2 x 2 3/4 In.	1150.00
Toy, Annie, Jumping Rope, Marx, Reproduction Box, 1 1/2 x 3 1/4 x 5 1/4 In.	660.00
Toy, Stove, Marx, 1930s, 8 1/2 x 10 In.	39.00
Wristwatch, Chrome, Tan Leather Band, New Haven, Box, 1948	508.00
Wristwatch, Sport, Chrome, Leather Band, New Haven, Harold Gray, 1935	1450.00

Ott & Brewer, Sardine Box, Cover, Underplate,
Cobalt Blue, Gold, Bamboo Handle, 5 x 6 In.

**Heat can affect a piano's sound.
Do not put an antique or new
piano in direct sunlight or near
a heat or air-conditioning vent.
An interior wall is best.**

ORREFORS Glassworks, located in the Swedish province of Smaaland, was established in 1898. The company is still making glass for use on the table or as decorations. There is renewed interest in the glass made in the modern styles of the 1940s and 1950s. In 1990, the company merged with Kosta Boda. Most vases and decorative pieces are signed with the etched name *Orrefors.*

Orrefors

Bottle, Cologne, Melon Form, Elongated Stopper, Signed, Sweden, c.1965, 8 1/2 In.	140.00
Lamp, Blown Glass, Engraved, Brass Cap, Stamped, 14 1/2 In., Pair	500.00
Punch Bowl Set, Blue Tint, Rolled Rim Bowl, Ribbed Stand, 15 Piece	173.00
Vase, Ariel, Blue, Amber, Woman, Troubadour, Gondola, Flowers, Cylindrical, 6 In.	3450.00
Vase, Etched Nude Dancer, Veiled, Signed, 13 In.	880.00
Vase, Funnel Shape, Amber, Ingeborg Lundin, 1950s, 6 1/2 In.	260.00
Vase, Graal, Fish Swimming, Seaweed, Signed, E. Hald, 4 3/4 In.	950.00
Vase, Graal, Fish, Paperweight Technique, 5 1/2 In.	540.00

OTT & BREWER Company operated the Etruria Pottery at Trenton, New Jersey, from 1863 to 1893. They started making belleek in 1882. The firm used a variety of marks that incorporated the initials *O & B.*

Sardine Box, Cover, Underplate, Cobalt Blue, Gold, Bamboo Handle, 5 x 6 In.	*Illus*	300.00
Vase, Belleek, Squat, Herons, Bamboo, 10 x 7 In.		2350.00

OVERBECK pottery was made by four sisters named Overbeck at a pottery in Cambridge City, Indiana. They started in 1911. They made all types of vases, each one-of-a-kind. Small, hand-modeled figurines are the most popular pieces with today's collectors. The factory continued until 1955, when the last of the four sisters died.

Bowl, Aqua High Glaze, Marked, Signed, 6 In.	645.00
Bowl, Mauve High Glaze, Impressed Mark, 3 1/2 In.	410.00
Bowl, Stylized Flowers, Brown, Green, Mauve Matte Ground, Footed, E. Francis, 3 In.	4115.00
Bowl, Village Scene, Blue High Glaze, Incised Mark, 3 In.	2590.00
Candlestick, Green & Blue Glaze, Impressed, 11 In., Pair	880.00
Candlestick, Stylized Design, Light Blue Matte Glaze, E. Francis, 9 1/2 In.	2350.00
Chamberstick, Blue Matte Glaze, Impressed Mark, 5 In.	825.00
Figurine, Bird Eating Corn, Impressed, 3 In.	350.00
Figurine, Bird, Impressed, 2 In.	295.00 to 410.00
Figurine, Bird, Stylized, Impressed, 3 1/2 In.	560.00
Figurine, Black Man, Pipe, Can, Impressed, 4 1/2 In.	646.00
Figurine, Bluebird, Impressed, 2 In.	500.00
Figurine, Boy Playing Cello, Impressed, 4 In.	590.00
Figurine, Brer Fox, 3 In.	900.00
Figurine, Brer Rabbit, 3 In.	900.00
Figurine, Choir Boy, Black Hair, Impressed, 4 1/2 In.	530.00
Figurine, Choir Boy, Yellow Hair, Impressed, 4 1/2 In.	530.00
Figurine, Cowboy, Impressed, 4 1/2 In.	530.00
Figurine, Dog, Blue, Tongue Out, Impressed, 2 1/2 In.	590.00
Figurine, Dog, Dachshund, Impressed, 3 In.	440.00
Figurine, Dog, Lying Down, Impressed, 4 1/2 In.	350.00

Figurine, Dog, Sitting, Pink, Blue, Black, White, 4 1/2 In. 470.00
Figurine, Donkey, Wearing Saddle, Impressed, 4 1/4 In. 500.00
Figurine, Farmer, Carrying Corn, 5 1/2 In. 295.00
Figurine, Farmer, Wheelbarrow, Impressed, 4 x 5 In. 560.00
Figurine, Goose, Wearing Tutu, Impressed, 4 In. 650.00
Figurine, Lady, Holding Basket, Impressed, 4 1/2 In. 410.00
Figurine, Lewis & Clark, American Flag, Nov. 21, 1946, 5 x 5 1/2 In. 3500.00
Figurine, Man, Bearded, Eating Watermelon, Impressed, 5 In. 725.00
Figurine, Old Lady In Bonnet, Impressed, 2 1/2 In. 350.00
Figurine, Rabbit, Impressed, 2 In. 705.00
Figurine, Rooster, Impressed, 5 In. 470.00
Figurine, Rooster, Large Feet, Impressed, 4 In. 470.00
Figurine, Southern Belle, Blue & Yellow Striped Dress, Impressed, 4 In. 440.00
Figurine, Southern Belle, Holding Hat, Impressed, 5 In. 410.00
Figurine, Southern Belle, Wearing Shawl, Impressed, 4 1/2 In. 440.00
Figurine, Squirrel, 2 x 2 1/2 In. 705.00
Figurine, Turtle, Smoking Pipe, Impressed, 2 1/2 In. 765.00
Figurine, Woodpecker, Impressed, 6 In. 380.00
Jar, Cover, Flower, Blue, Gray & Brown Matte Glaze, Tapered, Marked, 4 In. 1645.00
Mug, Yellow, Pink Interior, Applied Flower, Handle, Impressed Mark, 2 1/2 In. 650.00
Tile, Flower Bowl, Blue, Brown, Yellow, Semimatte Glaze, 5 1/2 x 5 1/2 In. 3175.00
Vase, Blue & Green Glaze, Tapered, Impressed Mark, 5 In. 560.00
Vase, Carved Figures, Medallions, Red Matte Glaze, Impressed Mark, 4 1/2 In. 6460.00
Vase, Carved Flower Panels, Tan Matte Glaze, Marked, 6 1/2 In. 6460.00
Vase, Carved Women, Blue Matte Glaze, Shouldered, Marked, 6 1/2 In. 6460.00
Vase, Carved, Painted, Red Stylized Fuchsia, Marked, 14 1/2 In. 19550.00
Vase, Green & Blue High Glaze, Shouldered, Tapered, Impressed Mark, 4 In. 295.00
Vase, Stylized Birds, Green High Glaze, Marked, 7 In. 2000.00
Vase, Stylized Flower, Painted, Tan, Mauve Glaze, Incised, 2 1/2 In. 1530.00
Vase, Stylized Flowers, Tan & Mauve Glaze, Impressed Mark, Signed, 2 1/2 In. 3780.00
Vase, Stylized Pinecones, Blue & Tan Matte Glaze, Marked, 5 3/4 In. 7640.00
Vase, Stylized Tulips, Bulbous, Impressed Mark, Signed, 5 1/2 In. 2585.00

OWENS Pottery was made in Zanesville, Ohio, from 1891 to 1928.
The first art pottery was made after 1896. Utopian Ware, Cyrano,
Navarre, Feroza, and Henri Deux were made. Pieces were usually
marked with a form of the name *Owens*. About 1907, the firm began to
make tile and discontinued the art pottery wares.

Jug, Faces, Bearded, Burnt Sienna Glaze, Billy Ray Hussey, 11 In. 1645.00
Mug, Lightweight, Indian, Incised, 7 5/8 In. 430.00
Pitcher, Utopian, Ear Of Corn, Impressed, 7 1/2 In. 260.00
Tile, Flowers, Arts & Crafts, Matte Glaze, Oak Frame, Owens, 12 x 6 In. 1765.00
Tile, Green, Mottled, White, Pink High Glaze, 3 x 6 In. 35.00
Vase, Gourd Shape, 2 Handles, Yellow Daisies, 7 1/2 x 6 1/2 In. 150.00
Vase, Henri Deux, 2 Maidens, Flowing Hair, Chocolate Ground, Handles, Squat, 9 x 7 In. . . 525.00
Vase, Lotus, Pansies, White, Blue Ground, 14 In. 460.00
Vase, Painted, Tot Steele, Roses, 15 x 4 1/2 In. 355.00
Vase, Painted, White Carnation, Shaded Gray To Brown, Handles, 14 In. 265.00
Vase, Utopian, Daisy Decoration, 7 1/2 In. 255.00
Vase, Utopian, Nasturtium, Monogrammed, 10 1/4 In. 260.00
Vase, Utopian, Red Woman, Indian, Tapered, Flattened, Signed, Marked, 10 1/2 In. 1060.00
Vase, Utopian, Yellow Roses, Impressed, 11 In. 460.00
Vase, Utopian, Yellow Wild Roses, Gourd Shape, Signed, 11 7/8 In. 80.00
Vase, Utopian, Yellow, Orange Pansies, 4 1/8 In. 160.00
Vase, Utopian, Young Woman, 11 In. 635.00

PADEN CITY Glass Manufacturing Company was established in
1916 at Paden City, West Virginia. The company made more than seventy different colors of glass. The firm closed in 1951. Paden City Pottery is not listed here.

Ardith, Candy Dish, Cover, 3 Sections, Cheriglo 90.00
Ardith, Ice Bucket, Cover, Black, Wicker Handle, 6 3/4 x 7 In. 290.00
Ardith, Tray, Center Handle, Yellow, Square, 4 1/2 x 10 In. 75.00

Bunny, Cotton Holder, Pink, Frosted, 5 x 4 1/2 In. 170.00
Chaucer, Cheese & Cracker Plate, Cover, 4 x 11 3/4 In. 200.00
Crow's Foot, Bowl, Cobalt Blue, Handles, 3 1/4 x 11 1/2 In. 90.00
Crow's Foot, Bowl, Oval, Ruby, 1 7/8 x 10 3/4 In. 55.00
Crow's Foot, Candlestick, Mushroom, Black, 2 1/2 x 4 1/2 In. 79.00
Crow's Foot, Candy Dish, Cover, Cobalt Blue, 3 3/4 x 7 In. 115.00
Crow's Foot, Compote, Cobalt Blue, 3 3/4 x 7 3/8 In. 70.00
Crow's Foot, Compote, Ruby, 3 7/8 x 6 1/2 In. 60.00
Crow's Foot, Gravy Boat, Ruby, Footed, 4 1/2 x 7 5/16 In. 140.00
Crow's Foot, Vase, Ruby, 9 3/4 x 6 5/8 In. 150.00
Cupid, Cake Stand, Pink, 2 x 11 1/4 In. 300.00
Cupid, Candy Dish, Cover, Ruby, 3 3/4 x 7 In. 190.00
Delilah Bird, Candlestick, 5 x 4 3/4 In. 115.00
Emerald Glo, Oil & Vinegar, Tray, 9 1/4 x 6 1/2 In. 90.00
Figurine, Pouter, Pigeon, 5 7/8 In. 79.00
Frost Etch, Candlestick, 2-Light, Gadroon, Pair 110.00
Frost Etch, Vase, 8 In. 195.00
Gazebo, Punch Set, Bowl, Underplate, Cups, 14 Piece 390.00
Gothic Garden, Champagne, Yellow, 5 3/4 x 4 In., 7 Oz. 75.00
Gothic Garden, Cheese & Cracker Plate, Pink, 11 3/4 In. 135.00
Gothic Garden, Dish, Mayonnaise, Rolled Edge, Footed, 3 5/8 x 5 3/4 In. 90.00
Jonquil, Bowl, Vegetable, Regina Shape, 1930s 20.00
Largo, Candlestick, Cobalt Blue, 4 3/4 x 4 3/4 In., Pair 300.00
Maya, Console Set, Bowl, Candlesticks, Silver Overlay, 3 Piece 165.00
No. 115, Candlestick, Amber, 7 x 4 In., Pair 70.00
No. 701, Candlestick, Amber, 4 3/4 x 2 1/2 In. 15.00
No. 701, Compote, Cheriglo, 3 1/4 x 7 1/2 In. 48.00
Orchid, Candlestick, 5 x 4 1/2 In. 240.00
Oriental Garden, Ice Bucket, Handles 95.00
Party Line, Bowl, Cheriglo, 9 In. 35.00
Party Line, Ice Bucket, Ruby, 4 3/8 x 7 7/8 In. 130.00
Peacock & Wild Rose, Bowl, Rolled Edge, Footed, Green, 2 3/4 x 11 In. 375.00
Peacock & Wild Rose, Vase, Black, Oval, 8 1/4 x 5 1/4 In. 490.00
Penny, Cup & Saucer, Amethyst Color 15.00
Penny, Tumbler, Ruby, Footed, 5 3/8 In. 22.00
Petit Point Bouquet, Platter, 12 In. 25.00
Shell Crest, Plate, Tab Handle, 10 1/2 In. 20.00
Spire, Cheese & Cracker Plate, Gold Encrusted 65.00
Spring Rose, Vase, Cheriglow, Fan, Gold Encrusted Rim, Footed, 8 1/2 In. 85.00

PAINTINGS listed in this book are not works by major artists but rather decorative paintings on ivory, board, or glass that would be of interest to the average collector. Watercolors on paper are listed under Picture. To learn the value of an oil painting by a listed artist you must contact an expert in that area.

Oil On Board, Arch, Allegory Of Peace, Gustav E.R. Michelson, c.1924, 30 x 21 In. 2390.00
Oil On Board, Boats At Dock, Henry Rodman Kenyon, c.1925, 10 x 12 In. 588.00
Oil On Board, California Landscape, Anna M. Valentien, c.1920, 16 x 20 In. 1725.00
Oil On Board, Cave Hideaway, Thomas Leitner, 1905, 35 1/2 x 24 1/4 In. 805.00
Oil On Board, Coastal Scene, Franklin Van Court, c.1948, 18 x 24 In. 470.00
Oil On Board, Guardian Of Banks, Fred Nelson Vance, c.1923, 20 x 16 In. 558.00
Oil On Board, Maine Landscape, Lake, Mountains, Tristam Richards, Frame, 7 x 9 In. 81.00
Oil On Board, Mexican Girl, Helen Hyde, c.1912, 20 x 10 In. 2350.00
Oil On Board, Pennsylvania Farmyard, A.M. Lindermuth, Burl Frame, 1800s, 12 x 15 In. .. 300.00
Oil On Board, Pueblo, Albert Looking Elk, c.1920, 9 x 12 In. 2875.00
Oil On Board, Rocky Coast, William B. Baird, c.1880, 8 x 6 In. 748.00
Oil On Board, Street Scene Normandy, Alfred Montague, c.1870, 14 x 10 In. 575.00
Oil On Board, Tall Ships On Rough Seas, H.L. Severance, Early 1900s, 18 x 22 In. 345.00
Oil On Board, Venice, Donald Shaw Maclaughin, c.1910, 8 1/2 x 10 In. 1150.00
Oil On Board, Woodland Nymphs, William C. Emerson, c.1910, 21 1/2 x 29 1/2 In. 1610.00
Oil On Canvas, 2 Geese, 4 x 7 1/2 In. 1150.00
Oil On Canvas, 2 Sisters, Classical Painting Reproduction, Gilt Frame, 38 x 32 In. 176.00
Oil On Canvas, Angling Amongst The Lily Pads, J.H. Boel, 1892, 30 x 20 In. 2415.00

Oil On Canvas, Autumn Clouds, Charles W. Dahlgreen, c.1915, 18 x 22 In. 3525.00
Oil On Canvas, Autumn In Connecticut, Guy Wiggins, c.1930, 8 x 10 In. 3055.00
Oil On Canvas, British Warship, H.M.S. 1839, Queen 110, Full Sail, Frame, 28 x 37 In. . . . 1437.00
Oil On Canvas, Elegant Ladies At Rest Beside Pond, Louis E. Adan, 1901, 15 x 22 In. 1793.00
Oil On Canvas, Embarking On A Crusade, P.A. Brunet-Houard, 1914, 27 1/2 x 63 In. 2415.00
Oil On Canvas, Farm Ducks, Howard Hill, c.1860, 7 1/4 x 9 1/4 In. 1058.00
Oil On Canvas, Figures Beside A Stream In A Forest Landscape, 13 x 18 In. 489.00
Oil On Canvas, Grinnell Mountain, Lake McDermott, Montana, Grover, 1924, 30 x 24 In. . . 3450.00
Oil On Canvas, Hudson River School, Landscape, Mountains, 19th Century, 14 x 22 In. . . . 460.00
Oil On Canvas, Laid To Board, Head Of Woman, J.C. Miller, Early 1900s, 7 3/8 x 6 In. . . . 90.00
Oil On Canvas, Landscape, River, Boy Fishing Off Rock, Oval, 10 x 12 In. 239.00
Oil On Canvas, Liberty Hill, c.1915, 16 x 20 In. 1880.00
Oil On Canvas, Mountain Bridge & Telephone Pole, Edgar Hewitt Nye, 28 x 33 In. 575.00
Oil On Canvas, Paris Street Scene, Woman, White Evening Dress, c.1963, 30 x 18 In. 235.00
Oil On Canvas, Path At Outskirts Of Taos Pueblo, Laura Hoernig, c.1940, 16 x 20 In. 460.00
Oil On Canvas, Portrait, Cleric Sitting Before Window, 37 x 30 In. 1150.00
Oil On Canvas, Portrait, Gentleman, Black Coat, High White Collar, Frame, 34 x 27 In. . . . 748.00
Oil On Canvas, Portrait, Gentleman, Brown Hair, Brown & Green Coat, 24 x 20 In. 660.00
Oil On Canvas, Portrait, Girl, Curly Light Brown Hair, Fancy Dress, 1800s, 30 x 25 In. . . . 3450.00
Oil On Canvas, Portrait, Girl, Red Dress, Hinkson, 19 Mos., Frame, 1868, 26 x 22 In. 920.00
Oil On Canvas, Seascape With Boats, American School, 25 x 37 In. 1150.00
Oil On Canvas, Shepard Returning Home, Robert Robin Fenson, 1912, 16 x 24 In. 1725.00
Oil On Canvas, Still Life With Trout, American School, Frame, 1800s, 18 x 27 In. 1116.00
Oil On Canvas, Wooded Landscape, W.A. Myers, Frame, 1896, 22 x 36 In. 374.00
Oil On Canvas Board, Hayama No Kiyoka, Yamagata, Sato Morihiro, Frame, 1951 . . . . . . 90.00
Oil On Celluloid, White Swans In Pond, Water Lilies, Gilt Frame, Ohio, 9 x 7 In. 230.00
Oil On Copper, Our Lady Of Guadalupe, Mexican School, 18th Century, 18 x 27 In. 2760.00
Oil On Onyx Stone, Snipe, Nesting On Grass, Round Corners, Monogram, 4 1/2 x 3/4 In. . . 145.00
On Ivory, Portrait, Young Man, Black Curly Hair, Ruffled Shirt, Frame, 6 In. 345.00
Scroll On Paper, Hanging, Figure In Boat, Mountain Landscape, Chinese, 44 x 9 1/2 In. . . 540.00
Scroll On Paper, Hanging, Ink, Color, Paper, Mountain Landscape, Chinese, 68 x 23 In. . . 970.00
Scroll On Paper, Hanging, Ink, Man In Boat, Mountain Landscape, Chinese, 38 x 19 In. . . 449.00
Scroll On Paper, Hanging, Lotus Blossoms, Chinese, 26 x 13 1/2 In. 179.00
Scroll On Silk, Geisha, Spring Landscape, Damask, Japanese, c.1900s, 67 x 25 In. 115.00
Scroll On Silk, Hanging, Ink, Color, 2 Deer, Next To River, Chinese, 26 1/2 x 41 1/4 In. . . . 1925.00
Scroll On Silk, Hanging, Ink, Scholar In Boat, River Landscape, Chinese, 49 x 25 3/4 In. . . 675.00

PAIRPOINT Manufacturing Company started in 1880 in New Bedford, Massachusetts. It soon joined with the glassworks nearby and
made glass, silver-plated pieces, and lamps. Reverse-painted glass
shades and molded shades known as *puffies* were part of the production until the 1930s. The company reorganized and changed its name
several times but is still working today. Items listed here are glass or
glass and metal. Silver-plated pieces are listed under Silver Plate.

Biscuit Jar, Enameled Red & White Flowers, Paneled Body, 9 In. 175.00
Biscuit Jar, Opal, Faceted, Enameled Sailboat Scene, Mauve Waves, 6 In. 750.00
Bowl, Centerpiece, Ambero, Enameled Red & Yellow Water Lilies, Signed, 13 In. 805.00
Bowl, Centerpiece, Diamonds & Printies, Mask Design Legs, c.1900, 14 1/2 In. 1035.00
Compote, Amethyst, Vintage Engraving, c.1900, 7 x 8 3/4 In. 145.00
Compote, Opal, Enameled Red Roses, Metal Cherub Stem, 5 1/2 x 6 In. 315.00
Ice Bucket, Engraved Ship, Silver Plated Handle & Rim, 6 In. 115.00
Lamp, Bird, Flowers, Silver Plated 3-Legged Base, Signed, 22 In. 2875.00
Lamp, Exeter Shade, Wind Decoration, Autumn Trees, No. D3070, 21 In. 2875.00
Lamp, Hurricane, Ambero, Citron, Reverse Painted Green, Rust Leaves, Wood Base, 9 In. . . 1035.00
Lamp, Jungle Bird, Diamond, Signed, 22 x 17 1/2 In. 2500.00
Lamp, Olympic Torch, Laurel Wreath, Domed Shade, Mottled Okra, 24 In. 575.00
Lamp, Pisa Shade, Ribbed, Garden Of Allah, Arabic Scenes, 15 In. 5465.00
Lamp, Puffy, Apple Tree, Blossoms, Butterflies, Bees, Leaves, Tree Trunk Base, 12 In. . . . 28750.00
Lamp, Puffy, Butterfly, Rose, Blossoms, Brass Base, 14 In. 3450.00
Lamp, Puffy, Flower Garlands, Green Leaves, Vines, Cream Ground, 21 3/4 In. 9300.00
Lamp, Puffy, Grape, Purple, Silver Plated Grapes, Lamp Base, 20 In. 1560.00
Lamp, Puffy, Orange Tree, Blossoms, Butterflies, Tree Trunk Base, 24 In. 46000.00
Lamp, Puffy, Pink & Yellow Roses, Bronze Base, No. 889, 15 In. 2990.00

Lamp, Puffy, Rose Bonnet, Red, Pink, Yellow, Green Ground, Tree Trunk Base, 11 In. 2875.00
Lamp, Puffy, Rose Bonnet, Roses, Red, Yellow, Green, Blue, White Lattice, 10 1/2 In. 6000.00
Lamp, Puffy, Roses, Butterflies, Green Ground, Gold Trim, Bronze Base, 13 1/2 In. 9890.00
Lamp, Puffy, Roses, Gilt Metal Base, 1907, 22 1/2 x 14 In. 2700.00
Lamp, Reverse Painted, Farm Scene, House, Trees, Birds, Frosted Ground, 21 In. 1680.00
Lamp, Reverse Painted, Grapes, c.1915, 19 x 15 In. 11355.00
Lamp, Reverse Painted, Meadow Scene, Trees, Horse Drawn Cart, Village, 24 In. 2360.00
Lamp, Reverse Painted, Seagulls, Ships, Blue, Purple, Green, Orange, H. Fisher, 25 In. ... 4600.00
Lamp, Reverse Painted, Trees, Buildings, Fields, Early 1900s 3410.00
Lamp, Reverse Painted, Windmills, Cows, People, Houses, Wood, Bronzed Metal, 18 In. ... 4700.00
Mustard Pot, Spoon, Coastal Scene, Lobed Body, Hinged Silver Plated Lid, 2 3/4 In. 805.00
Tray, Berwick Cutting, 17 In. 1800.00
Tumbler, Tavern Pattern, Enameled Whale, 4 In. 275.00
Vase, Tavern Pattern, Enameled Galleon, 8 In. 500.00

PALMER COX, BROWNIES, see Brownies category.

PAPER collectibles, including almanacs, catalogs, children's books, some greeting cards, stock certificates, and other paper ephemera, are listed here. Paper calendars are listed separately in the Calendar category. Paper items may be found in many other sections, such as Christmas and Movie.

Admission Pass, Bruno Hauptmann Trial, Flemington, N.J., February 12, 1935, 3 x 4 In. ... 160.00
Baby Announcement, Embossed, Wax Baby, Netting, Silver Trim, 1910, 4 1/2 In. ... *Illus* 30.00
Bond, New Jersey Southern Gas Electric Co., 1903 .... 150.00
Bond, North & South Carolina Railway, 1914 .... 200.00
Bond, Peoria & Eastern Railway, 1890 .... 125.00
Bond, Tallahassee, Perry & Southeastern Railway, 1906 .... 275.00
Bond, Texas Sabine Valley & Northwestern Railway, 1888 .... 150.00
Book, Family Record, An Age Book Made By John Barnard Mary 1805, 30 Pages 5750.00
Book, Little Golden Book, Cheyenne, Clint Walker, Gold Spine, Simon & Schuster, 1958 . 14.00
Booklet, Malt Nutrine, Greatest Of Tonics, Shows Uses, Calvert, 12 Pages 50.00
Booklet, Remington Firearms, Black Ground, Yellow Sun, 7 Geese Flying, 1930s, 32 Pgs . 45.00
Booklet, Studebaker Wagons, Mental Nuts, 100 Puzzles, Brain Twisters, 32 Pages 20.00
Bookplate, Watercolor, Tulips, Red, Yellow, Green, Maria Fesaud, c.1796, 8 x 7 In. 315.00
Catalog, Browning Sporting Arms, 1966, 8 1/2 x 11 In., 60 Pages 28.00
Catalog, Columbia Bicycles, Pope Manufacturing Co., 1888 .... 230.00
Catalog, Dent Toys, No. 10, 1910, Dent Hardware, Fullerton, Pa. 29.00
Catalog, Edwards Miller & Co., 1881, Lamps & Cigar Lighters 15.00
Catalog, Folsom Arms Sporting Goods, c.1928, 144 Pages 70.00
Catalog, Green Nursery Co., 1910, Syracuse New Hardy Raspberry, 68 Pages 66.00
Catalog, Henry N. Hooper & Co., 1858, Chandeliers, Girandoles, Candelabra & Lamps ... 10.00
Catalog, Hubley Kiddie Toys, Glossy, Folder, 1950s, 11 x 8 1/2 In., 4 Pages 50.00
Catalog, J. & E. Stevens, Cap Pistols, Banks, Early 1900s, 5 1/2 x 10 3/4 In., 24 Pages 135.00
Catalog, Kingsbury Toys, Motor Driven, c.1920, 24 Pages 275.00
Catalog, Kingsbury, 1927, Airplane Inserts, 12 Pages 605.00
Catalog, LC Smith, 1934, Hunting Dog Cover, Price List, 8 x 6 In., 24 Pages 95.00
Catalog, Ohio Tool Co., No. 23, 84 Pages 120.00
Catalog, Old Town Canoe Co., 1930, Fishing, Color, 37 Pages 135.00
Catalog, Real Texan Outfit, Betty Leach, Smart Style, Ridgefield, N.J., 12 Pages .....14.00 to 17.00
Catalog, Revell, 1957, Authentic Kits, Christmas, Full Color, 23 Pages 55.00
Catalog, Savage Arms, No. 61, Screaming Indian Cover 462.00
Catalog, Spalding, 1939, Babe Ruth, Bobby Jones, 10 x 6 3/4 In., 56 Pages 95.00
Catalog, Sun Rubber Toys, 1961, Price Sheets, Letter, Full Color 17.00
Catalog, Thomas Manufacturing Co., 1895, Farm Implements, 28 Pages 99.00
Catalog, Western Auto, 1929, Order Black & Envelope, 128 Pages 50.00
Catalog, Winchester Repeating Rifles, No. 64, 1899, Shotgun & Ammunition, 158 Pages .. 365.00
Catalog, Winchester, 1887, Black Moroccan Bound, Gold Letters On Spine, 80 Pages 750.00
Catalog, Winchester, No. 64, 1899, 158 Pages 215.00
Certificate, Civil War Service, Lady Liberty, Soldier, Children, 1861, 26 x 20 In. 920.00
Consul Appointment, G. O'Hara Taaffe, Signed, James Buchanan, Frame, 1859 .... 920.00
Family Record, Cyrus Wheeler, Elmira Goodemore, Tree, Watercolor, 1800s, 14 x 10 In. ... 690.00
Family Register, George & Susannah Albert, Huntington, Pa., 1834, 15 1/4 x 12 In. 10000.00

Paper, Baby
Announcement,
Embossed, Wax
Baby, Netting, Silver
Trim, 1910, 4 1/2 In.

Paper, Placecard, Woman, 1910 Dress, Parasol, Painted,
Stand-Up Base, 3 1/2 In., 7 Piece

Family Register, Mourning Scene, Woman, Urn, Willow, Spears Family, c.1800, 22 x 17 In.   165.00
Family Tree, Mary Eddie Family, Paint, On Oilcloth, 1800s, 17 1/2 x 17 1/2 In. 1840.00
Fraktur, A. Vorshrift, Ink, Watercolor, Wave Paper, c.1806, 12 x 7 3/4 In. 500.00
Fraktur, Angels, Eagle, Birds, Peters, Harrisburg, Frame, 1846, 19 x 17 In. 145.00
Fraktur, Baptism Certificate, Angels, Phillip Williams, Berks Co., Pa., 1822, 16 x 13 In. . .   140.00
Fraktur, Baptism Certificate, Parrots, Schmelzer, Berks, Co., Pa., 1809, 15 x 12 In. 5775.00
Fraktur, Baptism Certificate, Soldier, Flowers, Meyer, York Co., Pa., 1793, 20 x 16 In. . . .   11500.00
Fraktur, Baptism Certificate, Tulips, Vines, Johan Miller, Berks Co., Pa., 1786, 13 x 8 In. .   3575.00
Fraktur, Bird, On Tulip Branch, Urn, Red, Blue, Yellow, Brown, Inscribed Leith, 4 x 3 In. .   2300.00
Fraktur, Bird, On Urn, Branches, Red, Blue, Yellow, Brown, Watercolor, Ink, 4 x 3 3/4 In.   2990.00
Fraktur, Birds, Tree, German Text, Oley Township School Of Artists, Frame, 6 x 4 1/2 In. .   5225.00
Fraktur, Birth & Baptism, 2 Angels, Dauphin County, Pa., Frame, 1837, 19 x 17 In. 630.00
Fraktur, Birth & Baptism, Flowers, Birds, Henrich Otto, 1766, 13 1/4 x 16 1/2 In. 3819.00
Fraktur, Birth & Baptism, Parrots, Suns, Flowers, Johannes Albert, 1794, 13 x 16 In. 3175.00
Fraktur, Birth Record, Pandora, Ohio, Ink, Watercolor, German Text, 1852, 14 x 11 In. . . .   6670.00
Fraktur, Birth, Jacob Biern, Watercolor, Northampton County, Pa., 1773, 12 x 16 In. 2875.00
Fraktur, Block Printed, Heinrich Otto, York County, Pa., 1785, 13 x 16 In. 1760.00
Fraktur, Bookmark, Potted Flowering Vine, Face, Ink, Paper, Early 1800s, 4 x 2 1/2 In. . . .   1295.00
Fraktur, Bookplate, Red Ocher Frame, Jacob Witmeyer's Book, c.1835, 4 x 7 In. 385.00
Fraktur, Bookplate, Valentine, Watercolor, On Paper, Pa., 19th Century, 4 In. 210.00
Fraktur, Drawings, Maria & Aaron Spengler, Watercolor, Frame, c.1844, 6 x 8 In., Pair . . .   1765.00
Fraktur, Eagle, Heart Shaped Body, Holding Flowers In Talons, Inscribed Leith, 3 x 4 In. .   2070.00
Fraktur, Flowers, Bird, Face, Urn, Red, Yellow, Blue, Watercolor, Ink, 5 1/2 x 3 1/4 In. . . .   7475.00
Fraktur, Geometric, Tulips, Compass Stars, 6 1/4 x 8 1/2 In. 865.00
Fraktur, George Marsh, By Reverend Henry Young, Frame, Early 1800s, 9 1/2 x 7 In. 9600.00
Fraktur, Hand Drawn, Decorated, Birds, Flowers, Frederich Kuster, 7 3/4 x 12 1/2 In. 1610.00
Fraktur, Hand Drawn, Tulips, 7 1/2 x 12 1/2 In. 635.00
Fraktur, Lord's Prayer, Border, Henry Emletz, Conewago Twp., March 16, 1841, 3 x 3 In. .   990.00
Fraktur, Maria Salome, Confirmation, Marriage, Westmoreland Co., Pa., 18 x 15 In. 2645.00
Fraktur, Philip, Adam Glauss, Elisabeth, Linn Township, Pa., c.1811, 13 1/2 x 15 1/2 In. . .   1265.00
Fraktur, Potted Flowers, Compass Wheels, Tulips, Parrots, Pa., Frame, 10 x 8 In. 6600.00
Fraktur, Red, Brown, Tulip Border, Parrots, People, February 1721, Pen & Ink, 15 x 18 In.   2355.00
Fraktur, Tulips, Pot, Red, Yellow, Black, Green, Fly On Dogwood, 6 x 4 1/2 In. 460.00
Fraktur, Tulips, Red, Yellow, Gray Watercolor, J. Bauman, Ephrata, Pa., Frame, 18 x 21 In.   920.00
Fraktur, Watercolor, Berks Co., Pa., 1827, 16 x 12 In. 375.00
Fraktur, Watercolor, Ink, Wove Paper, Taufschein, A. Hoevelmann, c.1800, 6 1/2 x 8 In. . .   765.00
Fraktur, Watercolor, On Paper, Kuster, Blue Frame, c.1814, 12 3/4 x 15 1/2 In. 635.00
Fraktur, Watercolor, Rebecca Gerber, Geometric, Pinwheel, Flowers, 1797, 5 x 7 1/2 In. . .   805.00
Fraktur, Woman In Dress, Black Shoes, High Hair, Frame, 4 1/4 x 2 In. 635.00
Handbook, Harley-Davidson Service, Repair, Fourth Edition, 1977, 183 Pages 9.00
House Blessing, Angels, German Text, Grater & Blumer, Allentown, Pa., 14 x 12 In. 385.00
House Blessing, Blocks, Cherubs, Fruit, Vegetables, Gabriel Miesse, Reading, 16 x 13 In. .   165.00
House Blessing, Cherubs, Birds, German Text, Frame, Johann Ritter & Co., 15 x 13 In. . . .   415.00
House Blessing, Heart, 12 Small Hearts, 2 Bows, Orange, Blue, Yellow, 15 x 12 In. 550.00
House Blessing, Isaac Palm, Brecknock Twp., Lancaster County, 1860, 13 3/4 x 16 1/2 In. .   2420.00
Lottery Ticket, New Haven, For Building A Bridge Over East River, $10, Winner, 1780 . .   345.00
Magazine, American Agriculturalist, Vol. XXX, 1862 . . . .   15.00

Magazine, Life, December, 1921, Women, Polka Dot Dresses, Serving Food, 11 x 8 In. ...   145.00
Magazine, Life, October 13, 1921, Evening Image Cover, 11 1/8 x 8 1/4 In. 120.00
Magazine, Newsweek, Duke & Duchess Of Windsor, Aug. 12, 1940 ....   11.00
Magazine, Winchester Herald, January, 1923, Hockey Players, 12 1/8 x 9 1/4 In., 50 Pages   135.00
Magazine Cover, Scribner's, December 1897, Holiday Food, Silver Platters, 9 3/4 x 7 In. ..   300.00
Magazine Cover, Scribner's, December 1900, Shepherd, Wise Men, 9 3/4 x 6 5/8 In. 275.00
Military Appointment, Louis Vase, Signed, John Hancock, Frame, 1790 ....   4025.00
Naval Appointment, Joseph Wilson Jr., Signed, U.S. Grant, Frame, 1871, 19 x 15 In. 1265.00
Newspaper Page, Nantucket Journal, October 14, 1878, Extra, Hurricane, 21 x 15 In. 748.00
Placecard, Woman, 1910 Dress, Parasol, Painted, Stand-Up Base, 3 1/2 In., 7 Piece .. *Illus*   38.00
Poster, Eagles' Victory Celebration In Fireworks, Lady Liberty, Eagle, Frame, 43 x 29 In. .   468.00
Press Pass, Championship Boxing Match, John L. Sullivan, & Gentleman Jim, 1892 .....   1100.00
Program, Buffalo Bill Bids You Good Bye, c.1911, 10 x 7 In., 32 Pages 405.00
Program, Buffalo Bill's Wild West & Pawnee Bill's Far East, c.1909, 9 x 7 In., 32 Pages ..   748.00
Program, Follies Bergere, First Performance, California Auditorium, San Francisco, 1939 .   125.00
Program, Knights Of Pythias, 93rd Convention, 1960 ....   7.00
Program, Miss America Pageant, Phyllis George, 1971, 66 Pages 25.00
Push-Out Book, Tom Corbett, Unpunched, 1952, 14 x 10 In. 75.00
Revenue Tag, Cotton Bale, Union, c.1865, 5 1/4 x 2 In. 144.00
Scrapbook, Victorian, Die Cut Cards, Birds, Flowers, Greetings, Trade, 15 x 12 1/2 In. ...   115.00
Stock Certificate, Bank Of Pennsylvania, 1852 ....   475.00
Stock Certificate, California Improvement Co. Of Illinois, 1905 ....   65.00
Stock Certificate, Cleveland, Cincinnati, Chicago & St. Louis Railway, 1949-63 ....   50.00
Stock Certificate, Delling Motors Co., 1925-26, Signed By Pres. Of Co. 100.00
Stock Certificate, First National Bank Of Cooperstown, 1866 ....   150.00
Stock Certificate, Georgia Rail Road & Banking Co., Ga., 1846-59 ....   125.00
Stock Certificate, Hudson & Manhattan Railroad, 1934-35 ....   85.00
Stock Certificate, Iowa Falls & Sioux City Railroad, 1884-85 ....   85.00
Stock Certificate, Joliet & Chicago Railroad, 1879, Printed By Henry Seibert & Bros. 85.00
Stock Certificate, Madison & Kedzie State Bank, 1921 ....   50.00
Stock Certificate, Medical & Dental Building Corp, 1927 ....   50.00
Stock Certificate, Medical, Maryland Medical College Of Baltimore, 1901-05 ....   85.00
Stock Certificate, Milwaukee & St. Paul Railway, Russell Sage, c.1866, 6 x 10 In. 140.00
Stock Certificate, New York, Ontario & Western Railway, 1940s 60.00
Stock Certificate, Old Mesa Gold Company, Miner On Both Sides, 100 Shares, 1903 ....   145.00
Stock Certificate, Old Mesa Gold Company, Miner On Sides, 1903, 10 Shares 145.00
Stock Certificate, Peoria & Eastern Rwy., $1,000 Bond, American Bank Note, 1890 .....   125.00
Stock Certificate, Pharmaceutical, Parke, Davis & Co., 1951 ....   45.00
Stock Certificate, Pharmaceutical, Rexall Drug Co., 1955-60 ....   35.00
Stock Certificate, Pharmaceutical, Van Natta Drug Co., 1907 ....   125.00
Stock Certificate, Saint Joseph Union Depot Co., Mo., 1888, St. Joseph Stream Print Co. .   150.00
Stock Certificate, St. Louis, Alton & Terre Haute Railroad, 1897 ....   90.00
Stock Certificate, White Water Railroad, 1878 ....   65.00
Taufschein, Illuminated, Joseph Rudy, Dauphin County, Pa., 1818, 12 1/2 x 14 1/2 In. 605.00
Ticket, Woodstock Music & Art Fair, Unused, Globe Ticket, August, 16, 1969, 2 x 5 In. ...   290.00
Tourist Guide, Yosemite, Photo By Ansel Adams, 1936 ....   45.00

PAPER DOLLS

PAPER DOLLS were probably inspired by the pantins, or jumping jacks, made in eighteenth-century Europe. By the 1880s, sheets of printed paper dolls and clothes were being made. The first paper doll books were made in the 1920s. Collectors prefer uncut sheets or books or boxed sets of paper dolls. Prices are about half as much if the pages have been cut.

Archies Comic Strip, Archie, Betty, Veronica, Jughead, Whitman, 1969, 6 Pages, Uncut ...   30.00
Barbie Design-A-Fashion, Mix 'n' Match Patterns, Whitman, 1979 ....   16.00
Bewitched, Samantha, By Magic Wand, Box, 1965, 14 1/2 In., Uncut 250.00
Charlie's Angels, All 3 Angels, Box, 1977, Uncut 140.00
Eskimo Twins, Ladies Home Journal, 1922, Uncut 15.00
Hal Roach's Our Gang, Babo Cleanser, 12 x 19 1/2 In., Uncut Sheet 95.00
Janet Leigh, Dresses By Janet, 2 Dolls, Leigh-Mor, 1958, 12 1/4 x 9 In., 6 Pages, Uncut ..   65.00
John Wayne, Movie Roles, Book, Tom Tierney, 1981, 16 Pages, Uncut 12.00
Mary Poppins, Paper Doll Activity Book, 4 Dolls, Golden Press, 1964, 16 Pages 35.00
Meine Lieblingspuppe, Box, 13 1/2 In. 120.00

Rock Hudson, 2 Dolls, Universal, Whitman, 1957, 12 1/2 x 10 1/2 In., 8 Pages, Uncut	193.00
That Girl, Activity Set, Saalfield, Box, 1969, 5 1/2 x 14 1/4 In.	50.00
That Girl, Book, Card Stock, 3 Dolls, Saalfield, 1967, 8 1/4 x 12 1/4 In.	115.00
The Waltons, 7 Children, Outfits, Whitman, 1975, 8 Pages	55.00
Twiggy, Fashion Dresses, Cardboard Punch-Out, Whitman, Minnow Co., 1967	55.00

PAPERWEIGHTS must have first appeared along with paper in ancient Egypt. Today's collectors search for every type, from the very expensive French weights of the nineteenth century to the modern artist weights or advertising pieces. The glass tops of the paperweights sometimes have been nicked or scratched, and this type of damage can be removed by polishing. Some serious collectors think this type of repair is an alteration and will not buy a repolished weight; others think it is an acceptable technique of restoration that does not change the value. Baccarat paperweights are listed separately under Baccarat.

Advertising, A.P. Smith Mfg. Co., Fire Hydrant, East Orange, N.J., 6 1/4 In.	165.00
Advertising, Aikens Tile & Fireplaces, 2 1/2 x 4 x 1 In.	70.00
Advertising, American Brake Shoe Co., Lion, On Base, Cast Iron, Gold Color, 5 In.	66.00
Advertising, Hershey Bar, Gold Plate, Felt Back, 4 1/2 x 1 1/2 In.	13.00
Advertising, L. Rose Iron, Simonson Tailors Trim'gs, Los Angeles, 2 3/4 x 3 1/4 In.	40.00
Advertising, National Maxipress 2000, Press Shape, Die Cast, Side Pulley, 5 In.	88.00
Advertising, Powell, R.M. Stationer, Aldersgate St., Ceramic, England, 2 1/2 x 4 In.	63.00
Apple Shape, Deep Rose To Yellow, Glass, Clear Circular Base, 2 1/2 x 3 In.	990.00
Bacchus, Millefiori Pastel Canes, Cogwheels, Blue & White, 1850, 3 1/4 In.	6900.00
Blown Glass, Turtle, Opaque Black, Pulled Petal Feet, Tail & Head, 4 1/2 In.	66.00
Bouquet Of Fruit & Flowers, White Lattice Ground, 2 1/2 In.	269.00
Canes, Multicolored, Starburst Pattern, Blue Ground, 3 In.	80.00
Crystal, Golfer, 7 3/4 In.	46.00
Figurine, Green Rodent, Blue Eyes, Mottled Pink Disk, DeCorchemont, 4 In.	2590.00
Flower & Leaf Center, Clear, Faceted, 3 In.	70.00
Gas Pump, Cast Iron, Brass, Embossed, Blue, Yellow, Gold, Hayes, Wichita, 6 In.	605.00
Joe St. Clair, Crimped Rose, Pink, 4 Leaves, Signed, 3 1/2 In.	720.00
Latticinio Center, 2 Red Pears, Cranberry Cut To Clear, Faceted, 3 In.	105.00
Locomotive, Berkshire Steam No. 726, Lionel, Musical, 5 x 10 In.	125.00
Locomotive, New York Central, Lionel No. 2333, Musical, Windup, 10 In.	125.00
Lundberg, Peacock Feathers, Blue, Green Flowers, White Ground, Signed, 2 1/4 x 3 In.	150.00
Lundberg, Platinum Wave, Blue Flower, Signed, 1 x 2 3/4 In.	98.00
Millefiori, Blown Glass, 2 3/4 x 3 1/4 In.	230.00
Millefiori, Center Garnet Cane, Multicolored Pastry Mold, Star Canes, 1 3/4 In.	170.00
Millefiori, Green, Pink, Purple Canes, Alternating White Stars, Clichy, 1 7/8 In.	448.00
Millefiori, Pink Cane, Blue Pastry Mold, White & Green Canes, Clichy, 1 5/8 In.	270.00
N.Y. Sulfide, Compliments Of The Citizens To State Teachers Assn., Albany, 4 In.	49.00
National Lead Co., Dutch Boy, Solder, 3 2/3 In.	39.00
New England Glass Co., Pink Poinsettia, Green Petals, c.1880, 3 x 1 1/2 In.	375.00
Nygren, Amber, Mottled, Blue, Green, Applied Frog, Flowers, Signed, 1988, 3 1/2 In.	345.00
Nygren, Mottled Iridescent, Applied Frog, Yellow Feet, Signed, 1984, 2 1/2 In.	345.00

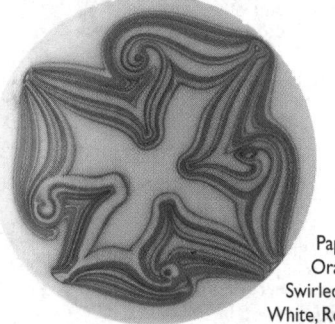

Paperweight,
Orange & Yellow
Swirled Design, Opaque
White, Round, 2 x 3 In.

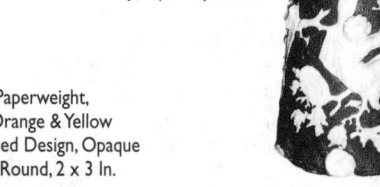

Parian, Pitcher, Bird
Nesting, Boy Climbing To
Get Nest, Thomas, John,
Joseph Mayer, 9 In.

Orange & Yellow Swirled Design, Opaque White, Round, 2 x 3 In. . . . . *Illus*   5.00
Parker, Davis, Glass, Scalloped Edge, 1904, 3 3/8 In. 794.00
Red Rose, Green Leaves, Diamond Point Panel Base, Glass, Bryden Pairpoint, 2 1/4 In. . . . 209.00
Sandwich Glass, Blue 10-Petal Flower, Green Leaves, Concave Base, 2 x 3 In. 550.00
Sandwich Glass, Poinsettia, Pink, Leaves, Blue Jasper Ground, Lutz Rose, 2 1/2 In. 403.00
Snowdome, Florida, 2 Boats, Palm Trees, Red Back, Blue Base, Hong Kong, 2 1/2 x 3 In. .   12.00
Spatter Glass, Lily, Bubbles, Multicolored, 3 1/2 In. 115.00
St. Clair, Bell Shape, Flower Interior, Yellow, Green, c.1975, 4 In. 25.00
St. Louis, Fuchsia Flower On Latticinio Ground, 2 15/16 In. 2415.00
Star Shape, Sepia Picture & Our Hero, Admiral Dewey, 6 1/4 In.   75.00
Sulphide, Dog Walking, Silvery White, Polished Base, 1 3/8 x 2 1/8 In. 110.00
Sulphide, Eagle, Crossed Cannons, Crossed Flags, c.1880-90, 1 3/4 In. 230.00
Venini, Dome, Radiating Opaque White Canes To The Base, 1970s, 4 In. 78.00
Verlys, Fish, Embossed, Frosted, 2 3/4 In. 58.00
Villeroy & Boch, Dresden, Character Dwarf, Glazed Finish, 3 1/2 x 6 3/4 In. 302.00
Yellow, Red & Green Fruit, Leaves, White Latticinio, Glass, 1 1/2 x 2 1/4 In. 385.00
Zellique, Iridescent Amethyst, Hawthorn Trailings, White Millefiori, 3 1/2 In. 56.00

PAPIER-MACHE is made from paper mixed with glue, chalk, and

other ingredients, then molded and baked. It becomes very hard and
can be painted. Boxes, trays, and furniture were made of papier-mache.
Some of the nineteenth-century pieces were decorated with mother-of-
pearl. Papier-mache is still being used to make small toys, figures,
candy containers, boxes, and other giftwares. Furniture made of
papier-mache is listed in the Furniture category.

Decanter Set, Double, Victorian, Mother-Of-Pearl Feet, Handle, 11 1/4 x 14 1/2 In. 880.00
Tray, Black Lacquer, Abalone, Mother-Of-Pearl Inlay, Parcel Gilt, 21 x 30 In. 748.00
Tray, Faux Bamboo Stand, Multicolored, Mother-Of-Pearl, 22 x 24 x 32 In. 1380.00
Tray, Flower Bouquet Center & Sprays, Moths, Painted, c.1875, 24 In. 880.00
Tray, Hoho Birds, Green, Gold, Floral Trees, Scrolls, Red Paint, c.1885, 30 In. 1880.00
Tray, Lily Stems, Flower Sprigs, Gilt Grapevine, Black Ground, c.1875, 31 In. 1058.00
Tray, Mother-Of-Pearl Inlay, Lacquer, Pheasant, Fountain, Oval, Stand, 19 x 29 In. 690.00
Tray, Mother-Of-Pearl Inlay, Scrolling Leaves, Flowers, England, c.1850, 25 In. 520.00
Tray, Oriental Scene, Clay, London, Victorian, 1800s, 22 1/2 x 28 1/2 In. 4800.00
Tray, Painted, Black, Oval, Ogee Rim, Scotland, Victorian, 32 x 25 In. 1765.00
Tray, Painted, Gilt Vines, Green Leaves, Blue Flowers, Ogee Rim, c.1875, 24 In. 1000.00
Tray, Pastry, Matte Gilt, Brass Handle, Multicolored, Jennens & Bettridge, 10 In. 316.00
Tray, Regency, Black Lacquer, Oval, Tortoiseshell, Early 1800s, 21 x 31 x 24 In. 2530.00
Tray, Stand, George IV, Gilt, Black Japanned, Ebonized Wood, 1820, 23 x 30 In. 2760.00
Tray, Stand, Mother-Of-Pearl Inlay, Moorish Temple, Victorian, 21 x 31 In. 1840.00
Tray, Stand, Regency Style, Black Lacquer, Walton, Birmingham, c.1865, 22 x 32 In. 1265.00
Tray, Stand, Regency, Black Lacquer, Rectangular, c.1815, 22 x 25 x 20 In. 1955.00
Tray, Tea, Black Star, Red Ground, Mid 19th Century, 24 1/2 x 19 In. 590.00

PARASOL, see Umbrella category.

PARIAN is a fine-grained, hard-paste porcelain named for the marble

it resembles. It was first made in England in 1846 and gained in favor
in the United States about 1860. Figures, tea sets, vases, and other
items were made of Parian at many English and American factories.

Bust, Abraham Lincoln, c.1863, 9 In. 660.00
Bust, Charles Sumner, Take Care Of My Civil Rights Bill, 11 In. 345.00
Bust, Classical Maidens, Clytie, After The Antique, Girl In Circlet, Late 1800s, 9 In., Pair . 325.00
Bust, Classical, Apollo, Maiden In Ivy Circlet, Late 1800s, 9 3/8 & 8 3/4 In., Pair 295.00
Bust, Napoleon Bonaparte, Composition, Socle Base, 17 In. 518.00
Bust, Young Woman, Iron Base, c.1900, 12 1/2 In. 405.00
Figurine, Woman, Classical, Draped In Robe, Greek Key Border, Braided Hair, 14 In. 115.00
Figurine, Woman, Draped, With Lyre, On Rocky Base, c.1870, 18 In. 765.00
Figurine, Woman, Seated, Draped Gown, Holding Knee, c.1870, 15 1/2 In. 410.00
Jug, Hinged Pewter Lid, Embossed Basket Weave Pattern, England, 1800s, 7 In. 127.00
Pitcher, Bird Nesting, Boy Climbing To Get Nest, Thomas, John, Joseph Mayer, 9 In. *Illus* 300.00
Pitcher, Relief Vignette, 3 Grieving Women, Classical Dress, 19th Century, 9 In. 115.00
Salt, Figural, 2 Putti, Playing With Scallop Shell, Late 19th Century, 5 In. 145.00

PARIS, Vieux Paris, or Old Paris, is porcelain ware that is known to have been made in Paris in the eighteenth or early nineteenth century. These porcelains have no identifying mark but can be recognized by the whiteness of the porcelain and the lines and decorations. Gold decoration is often used.

Basin, 2 Handles, 19 In.	359.00
Basket, Fruit, Reticulated, Gold & White, Navette Shape, Mid 1800s, 8 x 10 1/4 In.	980.00
Basket, Reticulated, Footed, Fruit, Round, Gold & White, Mid 19th Century, 9 x 8 1/2 In.	865.00
Basket, Reticulated, Footed, Porcelain, White & Gold, Early 1800s, 9 x 8 3/4 In.	1725.00
Basket, Reticulated, Footed, Porcelain, White & Gold, Mid 1800s, 10 x 11 In.	1095.00
Basket, Reticulated, Pierced, Gilded Basket, Pedestal Base, 19th Century, 8 x 10 In., Pair	575.00
Basket, White & Gold, Reticulated, Footed, Mid 19th Century, 8 x 8 1/2 In.	575.00
Bottle, Figural, Porcelain, Seated Turkish Man, 10 In.	540.00
Cachepot, Drain Bowl, Flared, Italianate Landscape Frieze, 9 1/2 x 9 1/2 In.	1610.00
Cachepot, Feuillet, Footed, Gilt, Blue Matte Ground, Flower Reserve, 8 1/8 x 7 3/4 In.	980.00
Cachepot, Mirror Black Ground, Bird & Butterfly Designs, 2-Piece, 8 x 7 1/4 In.	980.00
Cachepot, Rose Du Barry, Ground Footed, 2 Handles, Mid 19th Century, 7 5/8 x 8 3/4 In.	690.00
Cann, Cup, Saucer, Landscape, Figures, Ruins, Puce, Blue, Gilt Border, 1800s, 5 In.	189.00
Centerpiece, Parcel Gilt, Bronzed, 3 Women, Supporting Basket, c.1810, 12 1/2 In.	6600.00
Clock Group, Stand, Saracen, Horse, Lion, Flowers, Landscape, 25 1/2 In.	2700.00
Figurine, Gentleman, Colonial Dress, Red Coat, Green Pants, 9 3/4 In.	90.00
Lamp, From Sweetmeat Basket, Reticulated, White Biscuit Kneeling Angels, 23 In., Pair	1610.00
Lamp Base, Brass Mounted Beau Bleu Ground, Brass, Blown Glass Shade, 21 In., Pair	920.00
Plate, Dessert, Armorial, Parcel Gilt, R. Poisson, Honore, c.1835, 9 1/2 In., Pair	520.00
Punch Bowl, Upswept Rim, Green, Gilt Vine, Flowers, Medallion, 1800s, 5 3/4 x 13 In.	80.00
Tea Service, Decorated, Military Subjects, 9 1/2-In. Teapot, 6 Cups & Saucers	2689.00
Tea Service, Doll's, Rosewood Box, 8 1/4 In.	840.00
Tea Set, Dome Lid, Squat Body, Teapot, Cup & Saucer, Jacob Petit, 19th Century, 5 In.	200.00
Tray, Dresser, Quatrefoil, Flower Bouquet, Gilt Borders, Pink Ground, c.1920, 13 5/8 In.	120.00
Tureen, Sauce, Dome Lid, Classical Shape, Fruit Finial, Leaf Handles, 1800s, 8 x 10 In.	175.00
Urn, Painted, Bird, Flowers, Rose Ground, Late 19th Century, 13 1/4 In.	145.00
Vase, Campana Form, Blue Ground, Flower Basket, Flowers, c.1815, 10 1/2 In., Pair	1150.00
Vase, Cartouches, Woman's Face, Peach, Urn Shape, Flared Rim, Footed, 15 In., Pair	145.00
Vase, Classical Urn On Pedestal, Painted, Countryside Landscape, 8 In., Pair	489.00
Vase, Elliptical Rim, Urn Shape, Painted, Landscape, Footed, 19th Century, 11 3/4 In., Pr.	978.00
Vase, Farewell Scene, Bulbous, Scroll Stem Handles, 15 In.	375.00
Vase, Flattened Baluster Shape, Amorous Couple, Painted, Mounted As Lamp, 13 In., Pair	1795.00
Vase, Flowers, Fuchsia, Cobalt Blue & Gilt Trim, Tapered, Shaped Rim, 14 1/2 In.	230.00
Vase, Garniture, 2 Handles, Rococo Style, Fruit & Flower Reserves, Mid 1800s, 13 In.	345.00
Vase, Garniture, Bleu Du Roi Ground, 2 Handles, Rococo Style, 14 1/2 In.	489.00
Vase, Garniture, Italian Landscape, Gilt Ground, 2 Handles, c.1815, 9 1/2 In., Pair	920.00
Vase, Gilt Tracery, Hand Painted, 14 In.	105.00
Vase, Hand Painted, Scrolled Leaf Handles, 14 1/2 In.	345.00
Vase, Jeweled Lips, Jacob Petit Style, 4 Scroll Feet, Parcel Gilt Footed Base, 8 In., Pair	690.00
Vase, Painted, Leaves, Blossoms, Pink Ground, 19th Century, 13 In., Pair	345.00
Vase, Red Classical Scene, White, Bottle Shape, Jacob Petit, 6 1/2 In., Pair *Illus*	1955.00
Vase, Urn Shape, Petal Shaped Rim, Gilt Scrolling Vine, Leaf Handles, 15 1/2 In., Pair	175.00

PATE-DE-VERRE is an ancient technique in which glass is made by blending and refining powdered glass of different colors into molds. The process was revived by French glassmakers, especially Galle, around the end of the nineteenth century.

Paperweight, Francois-Emile Decorchement, 2 1/4 x 5 1/4 In.	4185.00
Pendant, Parakeet, Gabriel Argy-Rousseau, c.1923, 2 1/2 In.	1910.00
Tray, Swimming Fish, Green To Yellow, 6 In.	1670.00

PATE-SUR-PATE means paste on paste. The design was made by painting layers of slip on the ceramic piece until a relief decoration was formed. The method was developed at the Sevres factory in France about 1850. It became even more famous at the English Minton factory about 1870. It has since been used by many potters to make both pottery and porcelain wares.

Lamp, Classical Maiden, Etched Glass Globe, Glass Chimney, 16 1/4 In., Pair	5700.00

Lamp, Flowers, Leaves, Brass, Wood, Silk Shade, France, 1900s, 29 In., Pair 2640.00
Lamp, Green, White Classical Figures, Urns, Bronze Mounts, 16 1/2 In., Pair 1840.00
Stein, Diana The Huntress, Fox, Swan, Figural Relief, Pewter Lid, 3/4 Liter 355.00

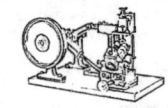

PATENT MODELS were required as part of a patent application for a
United States patent until 1880. In 1926 the stored patent models were
sold as a group by the U.S. patent office and individual models are now
appearing in the marketplace.

Bolt Action Magazine Rifle, No. 86520, Wood, Papers, V. Fogerty, 1869 .... 2070.00
Combination Reversible Sadiron Fluter, Young, Hewitt & Mooney, 1873 .... 8500.00
Combination Sad Embossing Iron, No. 136613, F. Meyers, c.1873 .... 6000.00
Crank Fluter, Crank Tension Adjuster, Papers, W.D. Corrister, 1868 .... 1000.00
Daniel's Improved Bolt Cutter, Patent Office Tag, May 17, 1870 .... 210.00
False Muzzle, Hinged, For Easy Muzzle Loading, No. 6124, Daniel Smith, 1849 .... 1495.00
Fuel Heated Sadiron, No. 191908, Tag, Papers, H.L. Wells, 1877 .... 800.00
Hat Shell Iron, No. 34848, John P. Ketrell, 1862 .... 450.00
Hewitt Sadiron, Wood, No. 135335, Patent Papers, 1880 .... 1000.00
Horse Halter, On Horse Head, Carved, Painted, T. Gingras, 1876, 8 1/4 In. 590.00
Ironing Board, No. 226548, G.H. Pearel, Papers, 1880 .... 350.00
Ironing Table, No. 160901, Removable Side Panels, S.C. Hamlin, 1875 .... 275.00
Ironing Table, No. 170366, Papers, J.S. Hays, 1875 .... 550.00
Ironing Table, Portable, No. 204-550, Papers, J.A. Eno, 1878 .... 350.00
Pressing Iron, Heated Over Kerosene Lamp, No. 222741, E.A. Russell, 1879 .... 5000.00
Sadiron Heater, No. 194284, Papers, J.B. Woolsey, 1877 .... 500.00
Sadiron Stand, Combination Iron & Stand, No. 123120, Frederick Meyers, 1872 .... 300.00
Washing Machine, No. 50621, Parsons & Dane, 1865 .... 600.00
Washing Machine, No. 101714, Red Paint, Roses, Tag, Papers, William A. Cox, 1870 .... 3000.00

PAUL REVERE POTTERY was made at several locations in and
around Boston, Massachusetts, between 1906 and 1942. The pottery
was operated as a settlement house program for teenage girls. Many
pieces were signed *S.E.G.* for Saturday Evening Girls. The artists concentrated on children's dishes and tiles. Decorations were outlined in
black and filled with color.

Bowl, Blue, Running Rabbit Band, Incised, Marked, AM, Numbered, 8 1/2 In. 1000.00
Bowl, Cereal, Swans, Water, 2 1/2 x 5 1/2 In. 1175.00
Bowl, Daffodils, Grass, A.M., 10 In. 3290.00
Bowl, Stylized Blue Blossoms, Brown Leaves, Green Ground, 3 x 8 In. 2940.00
Bowl, White Irises, Yellow Ground, 2 1/2 x 8 1/2 In. 1060.00
Breakfast Set, Cup, Plate, Bowl, White Goose, Mustard Matte Ground, 3 Piece 940.00
Creamer, 3 Chicks, Blue Band, Ivory Ground, SEG, Rose Bachini, 1913 .... 700.00
Creamer, Chick, Haystack, Yellow Band, Ivory Ground, Lines, 1913, 3 x 4 In. 175.00
Cup & Saucer, Landscape, Yellow, Blue, Green 400.00
Cup & Saucer, Yellow, White Band, Black Band, Fannie Levine 125.00
Mug, 3 Fishing Boats, CRS Monogram, 4 3/4 x 6 In. 2705.00
Pitcher, Cottage, Landscape, Teal Green, White Band, 6 3/4 x 7 1/2 In. 880.00

Paris, Vase, Red Classical Scene, White, Bottle
Shape, Jacob Petit, 6 1/2 In., Pair

Don't put a vase on your wooden
table if it is in sunlight. Eventually
the finish on the table will fade
around the vase and leave a
shadow on the wood.

Pitcher, Milk, Band Of Trees, Sky, EG, Marked, 4 1/4 In. 206.00
Plate, Geese, Water Lilies, Blue, White, Green Ground, 1917, 8 In. 1440.00
Plate, House & Trees Center, Incised, EW, Marked, 7 3/4 In. 705.00
Plate, Landscape Medallion, Blue, Gray Ground, 12 In. 2820.00
Sconce, Mountains, Trees, Irises, 7 3/4 x 4 1/4 In. 4995.00
Tile, Midnight Rider, Blue, Brown, Green, Circular, Edith Brown, 1926, 4 1/2 In. 650.00
Tile, Stylized Tree, Octagonal, 2 1/2 In. 635.00
Tumbler, White Lotus, Yellow Ground, 3 3/4 In. 999.00
Vase, 3 Swans, Ivory, Green, Blue Bands, Handle, 4 1/4 In. 940.00
Vase, Bulbous, Green, Brown Trees, Blue, White Sky, 4 1/4 x 4 In. 2585.00
Vase, Green Trees, Blue Sky, Gunmetal Ground, Egg Shape, 4 1/4 x 4 In. 2820.00
Vase, Tulip & Leaf Band, Blue Green Ground, 1925, 3 3/4 x 2 1/2 In. 1645.00
Wall Pocket, Bullet Shaped, Poppies, White, Green Ground, 6 x 4 1/4 In. 4700.00

PEACHBLOW glass was made by several factories beginning in the 1880s. New England peachblow is a one-layer glass shading from red to white. Mt. Washington peachblow shades from pink to bluish-white. Hobbs, Brockunier and Company of Wheeling, West Virginia, made coral glass that they marketed as Peach Blow. It shades from yellow to peach and is lined with white glass. Reproductions of all types of peachblow have been made. Related pieces may be listed under Gunderson and Webb Peachblow.

Bowl, Enameled Shasta Daisies, Mt. Washington, 3 1/2 In. 3450.00
Bowl, Satin, Hobbs, Brockunier, 2 1/2 x 4 1/2 In. 430.00
Bowl, Trefoil Rim, Ribbed, 3-Footed, Mt. Washington, 8 x 7 1/2 In. 13440.00
Bowl, Tricornered, Mt. Washington, 5 In. 1210.00
Bowl, Vaseline, Matsu-No-Ke, Ruffled Edge, 9 In. 575.00
Celery Vase, Hobbs, Brockunier, 4 1/4 x 3 1/8 In. 420.00
Creamer, Square Mouth, Amber Handle, Hobbs, Brockunier, 4 In. . . . . .750.00 to 980.00
Creamer, Wild Rose, Glossy, Low Looped Handle, New England, 4 1/2 In. 920.00
Cruet, Amber Faceted Stopper, Hobbs, Brockunier, 7 1/4 In. . . . . .920.00 to 980.00
Cruet, Amber Handle & Stopper, Glossy, Hobbs, Brockunier, 6 1/4 In. 2070.00
Cruet, Amber Reeded Handle, Faceted Amber Stopper, Glossy, Hobbs, Brockunier, 7 In. . . 1840.00
Cruet, Wild Rose, Pear Shape, Reeded Handle, Faceted Stopper, Glossy, New England, 7 In. 690.00
Decanter, Amber Twist Handle & Faceted Stopper, Hobbs, Brockunier, 9 1/2 In. 1035.00
Decanter, Reverse Trumpet, Tapered Collar, Flared Neck, 8 1/4 In. 835.00
Finger Bowl, Oval, Hobbs, Brockunier, 4 1/2 x 2 3/4 In. 315.00
Finger Bowl, Pink, Pinched Ruffled Rim, 5 1/2 In. 2070.00
Jug, Claret, Reeded Handle, Rigaree At Neck, Conical, Hobbs, Brockunier, 10 In. 1955.00
Jug, Flowers, Enameled, Victorian, 7 In. 201.00
Jug, Pelican Mouth, Amber Loop Handle, No. 324, Hobbs, Brockunier, 6 1/2 In. 7360.00
Jug, Square Mouth, Amber Handle, Glossy, Hobbs, Brockunier, 4 1/2 In. 460.00
Mustard, Hobbs, Brockunier, 3 In. 480.00
Mustard Pot, Glossy, Metal Collar & Handle, 2 1/2 In. 520.00
Pitcher, Applied Amber Handle, Bulbous, Hobbs, Brockunier, 5 3/4 In. 1380.00
Pitcher, Milk, Hobbs, Brockunier, 5 In. . . . . .805.00 to 920.00
Pitcher, Milk, Wild Rose, Reeded Scroll Handle, New England, 5 1/2 In. 1725.00
Pitcher, Water, Applied Amber Handle, Square Mouth, Hobbs, Brockunier, 7 In. 1210.00
Pitcher, Wheeling Drape, Clear Reeded Handle, Hobbs, Brockunier, 5 1/2 In. 405.00
Pitcher, Wheeling Drape, Clear Reeded Handle, Hobbs, Brockunier, 6 In. 865.00
Pitcher, Wild Rose, Glossy, Square Mouth, Cream Handle, New England, 7 1/4 In. 1150.00
Salt & Pepper, Hobbs, Brockunier, 2 1/2 In. 750.00
Sugar, Pinched Sides, Loop Handles, 2 1/2 x 5 In. 2015.00
Sugar Shaker, Hobbs, Brockunier, 5 1/4 In. 3105.00
Toothpick, Queen's Design Gold Rim, Square Mouth, Mt. Washington, 2 1/2 In. 16415.00
Tumbler, Hobbs, Brockunier, 3 1/2 In. . . . . .200.00 to 290.00
Tumbler, Wild Rose, Glossy, New England, 3 3/4 In. 260.00
Vase, Bulbous Base, Tapered Neck, Hobbs, Brockunier, 6 1/2 In. 1265.00
Vase, Bulbous, Overlaid, Gold Crosshatching, Satin Herringbone, c.1890, 7 In. 173.00
Vase, Double Gourd, 7 1/2 In. 690.00
Vase, Double Gourd, Glossy, Hobbs, Brockunier, 7 1/4 In. 4025.00
Vase, Lily, Wild Rose, Flared Tricornored Rim, New England, 8 In. 805.00
Vase, Lily, Wild Rose, New England, 11 1/2 In. 920.00

Join with your neighbors to keep informed about workmen who might be using a ladder or trying to get into a garage. Call the police if you are suspicious.

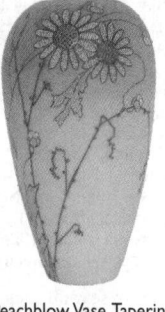

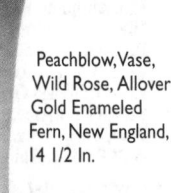

Peachblow, Vase, Wild Rose, Allover Gold Enameled Fern, New England, 14 1/2 In.

Peachblow, Vase, Tapering Oval, Queen's Design, Mt. Washington, 9 1/4 In.

Vase, Morgan, Flared Rim, Hobbs, Brockunier, 8 In.	1380.00
Vase, Morgan, Griffin Holder, Hobbs, Brockunier, 10 In.	1610.00 to 3450.00
Vase, Square Mouth, Hobbs, Brockunier, 4 In.	575.00 to 635.00
Vase, Stick, Bulbous Base, Glossy, 6 In.	1725.00
Vase, Stick, Fuchsia Shaded To Yellow, Hobbs, Brockunier, 8 In.	1668.00
Vase, Stick, Glossy, Rigaree Collar, Bulbous Base, Hobbs, Brockunier, 8 In.	575.00
Vase, Tapering Oval, Queen's Design, Mt. Washington, 9 1/4 In.	*Illus* 22400.00
Vase, Wild Rose, Allover Gold Enameled Fern, New England, 14 1/2 In.	*Illus* 5040.00

PEANUTS is the title of a comic strip created by cartoonist Charles M. Schulz (1922-2000). The strip, drawn by Schulz from 1950 to 2000, features a group of children, including Charlie Brown and his sister Sally, Lucy Van Pelt and her brother Linus, Peppermint Patty, and Pig Pen, and an imaginative and independent beagle named Snoopy. The Peanuts gang has also been featured in books, television shows, and a Broadway musical.

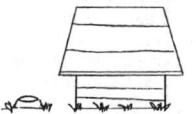

Book, Dear President Johnson, Bill Adler, Charles Schulz, Hardcover, 1964	30.00
Cookie Jar, Snoopy On Doghouse, McCoy	65.00
Figure, Snoopy, Vinyl, United Features, c.1958, 7 1/2 x 4 1/2 x 3 In.	120.00
Lunch Box, Baseball, Vinyl, Red, No Thermos	89.00
Lunch Box, Charlie Brown, Throwing Ball, Square Plastic Thermos	39.00
Lunch Box, Charlie, Lucy, Snoopy, Peppermint Patty, Under Tree, Metal, No Thermos	49.00
Lunch Box, Have Lunch With Snoopy, Doghouse, Dome, No Thermos	79.00
Mug, Snoopy, I Think I'm Allergic To Mornings, White, Fire-King, 10 Oz.	35.00
Wristwatch, Snoopy Time, White Band, United Features, Box, 1968, 1 1/4 x 9 1/4 In.	67.00

PEARL items listed here are made of the natural mother-of-pearl from shells. Such natural pearl has been used to decorate furniture and small utilitarian objects for centuries. The glassware known as mother-of-pearl is listed by that name. Opera glasses made with natural pearl shell are listed under Opera Glasses.

Card Case, Carved, Abalone Inset, 4 x 3 In.	155.00
Caviar Set, 6 Dishes, 6 Knives, Scimitar Blades, c.1900, 7 1/2 & 6 In.	575.00

PEARLWARE is an earthenware made by Josiah Wedgwood in 1779. It was copied by other potters in England. Pearlware is only slightly different in color from creamware and for many years collectors have confused the terms. Wedgwood pieces are listed in the Wedgwood category in this book. Most pearlware with mocha designs is listed under Mocha.

Pearl

Bowl, Peacock Pattern, Ocher, Blue, Yellow, Brown Bird, 7 1/8 In.	1880.00
Cup, Feeding, Shell Shaped Handles, Dog's Head Finial, Shorthose, 2 x 7 1/2 x 8 In.	215.00
Figurine, Cleopatra, Anthony, Reclining, Rocky Outcrop, Continental, 6 3/4 In., Pair	1697.00
Figurine, Lion, Green & Orange Highlights, Miniature, 2 1/4 In., Pair	403.00
Figurine, Lion, Lying Down, Orange, Green, Brown, Yellow, 4 1/4 In.	1265.00
Jug & Bowl, Cover, Mask Heads, Arched Panels, Urns, Classical Figures, c.1800, 13 In.	2350.00

Pitcher, Animal Trainer & Animal, Figural Lion Handle, 1840, 7 In.	1125.00
Pitcher, Cabbage Rose, England, 19th Century, 7 In.	500.00
Plaque, 2 Lions In Landscape, Molded, Oval, Blue, Orange, Brown, Green, 11 1/4 In.	3163.00
Plate, Cobalt Blue Dahlia Center, Green & Black Leaves, Brown Line Edge, 10 In.	402.00
Plate, Flower, Scalloped Feather Edge, England, Early 1800s, 14 1/8 In.	646.00
Plate, Peacock Pattern, Ocher, Blue, Yellow, Brown Bird, 9 3/4 In.	1293.00
Punch Bowl, Chinese House Pattern, Leaf Swag Border, England, Late 1700s, 5 x 11 In.	1175.00
Tea Set, Cabbage Rose, Baluster Shape Teapot, 26 Piece	825.00
Tea Set, Child's, c.1810, 11 Piece	1600.00
Teapot, Hand Painted Decoration, England, Early 19th Century, 11 1/2 In.	288.00

PEKING GLASS is a Chinese cameo glass first made popular in the eighteenth century. The Chinese have continued to make this layered glass in the old manner, and many new pieces are now available that could confuse the average buyer.

Bowl, Cobalt Blue, 6 In.	4540.00
Bowl, Cranberry, Lobed, 2 1/4 x 7 1/2 In.	1135.00
Candlestick, Cobalt Blue, Circular Foot Ring, 4 3/4 In., Pair	184.00
Jar, Cover, Globular Shape, Snowflake Bodies, Reserve Panels, 8 In., Pair	2300.00
Jar, Green, White Cameo Ducks, Water Lilies, Frosted Ground, 4 In.	145.00
Plate, Woman, 2 Children In Garden, Fruit, Flower Border, 9 In.	865.00
Vase, Bottle, Red Peking, Opaque Blue, 11 1/4 In.	970.00
Vase, Cobalt Blue, Oval, 4 1/4 In.	58.00

PENS replaced hand-cut quills as writing instruments in 1780 when the first steel pen point was made in England. But it was 100 years before the commercial pen was a common item. The fountain pen was invented in the 1830s but was not made in quantity until the 1880s. All types of old pens are collected. Float pens that feature small objects floating in a liquid as part of the handle are popular with collectors. Advertising pens are listed in the Advertising section of this book.

PEN, Float, PMS Liquid Feed Supplement, On/Off Valve, Brown Liquid, Ritepoint	15.00
Fountain, Shaffer Classic Lifetime Triumph, Plunger Filler, 5 1/4 In.	58.00
Rice-Stix Dry Goods, Lee T. Meyer, Dizzy, Paul Dean Shirts, Pearlescent, Celluloid, 5 In.	410.00
PEN & PENCIL, Sheaffer, Lifetime Lever Filling, Radite-Black & Pearl, Box, c.1925	35.00

PENCILS were invented, so it is said, in 1565. The eraser was not added to the pencil until 1858. The automatic pencil was invented in 1863. Collectors today want advertising pencils or automatic pencils of unusual design. Boxes and sharpeners for pencils are also collected. Pencil boxes are listed in the Box category. .

PENCIL, Carpenter's, Yellow, Winchester, Made In U.S.A., 7 In.	43.00
Commonwealth Edison, Light Bulb	5.00
Dixel Gas, Drive Safely, C.A. Norman Tank Wagon Service, Warrensburg, Mo.	25.00
Mechanical, Bomber Bowl, Bowling Pin, Odessa, Tex., 3 7/8 In.	30.00
Mechanical, Chevron Gas Not A Substitute, Truck, Logan, N.M.	25.00
Mechanical, Marathon Oil & Gas, Rogers Marathon Service, Carmi, Ill.	22.00
Mechanical, Merle A. Frey General Hauling, 18 Wheeler, R.D. 3, Chambersburg, Pa.	25.00
Mechanical, Mountain Iron & Supply Co., Autopoint	9.00
Mechanical, Oil Topper, Oil From Falls City Oil Fields, Falls City, Neb.	33.00
Mechanical, Red Goose Shoes, L.C. Porter, Princeton, W. Va.	24.00
Philco, High Fidelity Television	15.00
Poth's Beer, Christmas Colors, 1930s	12.00
Shell Oil Gas, Red, Yellow, Gold Clip	22.00
Swift, Premium Ham, Metal, Dark Maroon, 5 1/2 In.	7.50
PENCIL SHARPENER, Alligator, On Base, Souvenir Of Florida, 1 1/4 x 3 In.	15.00
Cast Iron, American Model	195.00
Cast Iron, Jupiter Model	675.00
Cast Iron, Planetary Model	650.00
Climax, Auto Feed, Crank Type, Brass Tag, Drawer	33.00
Dandy, Cast Metal, 8 In.	45.00
Handy, Oxidized Copper Finish, Instructions, Box	1925.00
Johann Faber, No. 5060, Cast Iron Base, Hand Crank, Adjustable Jaws	3630.00

Jupiter Pencil Pointer, Gear Mechanism, Iron Tray 310.00
Little Shaver 2750.00
Majestic, Spaceship Design, Battery Powered 495.00
New Era Pencil Sharpener, Plunger Type, Patent Pending 121.00
Peerless 1925.00
Pressed Steel, Large Wheel, Wood Handle, Automatic Pencil Sharpener Co., 5 In. 110.00
Queen Stove, Bronze Finish, Die Cast, 2 3/4 In. 66.00
Rapid Pencil Sharpener, Cast Iron Base, Adjustable, Rotate Top To Sharpen 1210.00
Reneo, Desk Clamp Type, Automatic Feeder, Shavings Drawer 240.00
Sewing Machine, Moving Wheel & Needle, Plastic, Germany, 1970s, 2 x 2 In. 30.00

PEPSI-COLA, the drink and the name, was invented in 1898 but was
not trademarked until 1903. The logo was changed from an elaborate
script to the modern block letters in 1963. Several different logos have
been used. Until 1951, the words *Pepsi* and *Cola* were separated by 2
dashes. These bottles are called *double dash.* In 1951 the modern logo
with a single hyphen was introduced. All types of advertising memorabilia are collected, and reproductions are being made.

Carrier, Wooden, 6-Bottle, 11 x 8 In. 77.00
Clock, Drink Pepsi-Cola Ice Cold, Double Bubble, Red, White, Blue, 15 In. Diam. 1430.00
Clock, Illusion Neon, Pepsi Decal Over R.C. Original, 8-Sided, 18 x 18 In. 930.00
Crate, 4 Sections, 18 x 6 x 12 In. 50.00
Door Push, Have A Pepsi, Yellow, Red, White, Blue, 32 x 3 In. 165.00
Glass, Hits The Spot, Syrup & Fill Lines, Anchor Hocking, 1930s, 4 1/4 In. 65.00
Hat, Soda Jerk, Say Pepsi Please, Cellucap Mfg. Co., Phila., Pa., 1950s 12.00
Menu Board, Drink Pepsi-Cola, Bigger-Better, Tin, 30 x 20 In. 440.00
Pin, Red, White, Blue, Celluloid, Japan, 1 In. 16.00
Record Set, Cardboard Jacket, 1960s, 6 Piece 100.00
Sign, Bottle, Pepsi, Die Cut, Wood, 7 In. 136.00
Sign, Bottle, Refreshing, Healthful, Die Cut, 5 Cents, Tin, 44 x 12 In. 220.00
Sign, Drink Iced Pepsi-Cola, Double Dash, Winter Scene, Cardboard, c.1940, 11 x 42 In. ... 338.00
Sign, Drink Pepsi-Cola Ice Cold, Light-Up, Bottle Cap, 15 In. Diam. 770.00
Sign, Drink Pepsi-Cola Iced, Canada Double Dash, Tin, Embossed, 1940, 18 x 53 In. 440.00
Sign, Drink Pepsi-Cola, America's Biggest Nickel's Worth, Tin, Embossed, 10 x 30 In. 247.00
Sign, Drink Pepsi-Cola, Blue & White Stripes, Red, Masonite, 18 x 32 In. 71.00
Sign, Enjoy A Pepsi, Red, White, Blue, Yellow, Porcelain, Bottle Cap, 9 1/2 x 29 1/2 In. ... 247.00
Sign, More Bounce To The Ounce, Tin, Embossed, 14 x 36 In. 220.00
Sign, Santa Claus, Holding Bottle, Cardboard, Die Cut, Stand-Up, 31 x 23 In. 110.00
Sign, Say Pepsi Please, Bottle, Embossed, Tin Lithograph, Self-Framed, 46 x 16 3/4 In. ... 385.00
Sign, Say Pepsi Please, Red, White, Blue, Yellow, Tin, Embossed, 18 x 54 In. 165.00
Sign, Say Pepsi Please, Yellow, Brown, Red, White, Blue, Tin, 47 x 10 In. 165.00
Sign, Sold Here, Die Cut, Tin, Flange, 2-Sided, 1940, 10 x 14 1/2 In. 715.00
Sign, Take Home A Carton, Refreshing, 6-Pack Carrier, Double Dash, Tin, 13 x 24 In. 275.00
Sign, Take Home Several Cartons, Pepsi-Cola Cap, 2-Sided, Light-Up, 17 x 27 x 4 In. 770.00
Sign, Tin, Embossed, Buvez, Yellow, Red, White, Blue, Brown, Bottle Cap, 19 x 27 In. ... 136.00
Thermometer, Have A Pepsi, Bottle Cap, Yellow Ground, 27 x 7 1/4 In. 55.00
Thermometer, More Bounce To The Ounce, Tin Lithograph, 1950s, 27 In. 203.00
Thermometer, Red, White, Blue, 18 In. Diam. 110.00
Thermometer, Say Pepsi Please, Tin Lithograph, Embossed Bottle Cap, 1960s, 27 In. 90.00
Toy, Truck, Box, 1965 .... 275.00
Toy, Truck, Nylint, 1960 .... 193.00
Tray, Bigger & Better, Tin Lithograph, 13 1/2 In. 283.00
Tray, Enjoy Pepsi-Cola, Hits The Spot, Tin Lithograph, 14 In. 90.00
Waxboard, Say Pepsi Please, Distance From Charlotte, N.C., 1955 .... 220.00

PERFUME BOTTLES are made of cut glass, pressed glass, art glass,
silver, metal, enamel, and even plastic or porcelain. Although the small
bottle to hold perfume was first made before the time of ancient Egypt,
it is the nineteenth- and twentieth-century examples that interest today's
collector. DeVilbiss Company has made atomizers of all types since
1888 but no longer makes the perfume bottle tops so popular with collectors. These were made from 1920 to 1968. The glass bottle may be by
any of many manufacturers even if the atomizer is marked *DeVilbiss.*

The word *factice*, which often appears in ads, refers to store display bottles. Glass or porcelain examples may be found under the appropriate name such as Lalique, Czechoslovakia, Glass-Bohemian, etc.

8-Sided Foot, Intaglio Glass Roses, Stopper, Signed, Czechoslovakia, 5 In.	140.00
Alvin, Silver Overlay, Irises, 1886-1928, 3 1/4 x 3 In.	350.00
Amethyst Glass, Clear, Czechoslovakia, c.1920, 5 1/4 In.	95.00
Atomizer, Crystal, Flowers, 4-Sided, DeVilbiss, 7 1/4 In.	69.00
Atomizer, Glass, 4 Corners, Stylized Flowers, 2 1/2 In.	150.00
Atomizer, Glass, Frosted, Metal, 3-Sided, Geometric, Gold Lining, 7 1/2 In.	160.00
Atomizer, Glass, Metal, Enameled Black, Gold, Pink Ball, Tassel, 9 1/2 In.	219.00
Atomizer, Glass, Nude Cupids, Enameled Internally, Tassel, 6 3/4 In.	90.00
Atomizer, Glass, Pink, Geometric, Metal Stand, 4 3/4 In.	138.00
Atomizer, Glass, Pink, Gold Enamel, 7 In.	185.00
Babani, Ambre De Delhi, Clear, Enamel, Gilt, Depinoix, c.1920, 5 1/4 In.	646.00
Balenciaga, Quadrille, Clear, Hang Tag, Box, c.1956, 6 In.	588.00
Blown Glass, Scrolling, White Stripes, Rigaree, Pewter Stopper, 3 1/2 In.	105.00
Blue, Brass Metal Overcap, Inner Stopper, 4 3/4 In.	130.00
Blue Glass, Clear, Dabber, Jeweled Metalwork, Czechoslovakia, c.1920	1410.00
Blue Glass, Filigree, Porcelain Plaque, Czechoslovakia, c.1920, 6 In.	529.00
Blue Glass, Lady With Flowers, Cutout Stopper, Dabber, Czechoslovakia, 8 3/4 In.	575.00
Blue Glass, Molded Flower Stopper, Signed, Czechoslovakia, 6 In.	230.00
Blue Glass, Star Cutting, Stopper, Signed, Czechoslovakia, 5 In.	175.00
Blue Iridescent, Gold Draping, Ball Stopper, Shouldered, Abelman, 1985, 4 In.	110.00
Bob Mackie, Mackie, Clear, Box, c.1970, 4 3/4 In.	95.00
Bonzo, Oolo, Black Glass, Hand Painted, 3 In.	385.00
Bryenne, Chu Chin Chow, Blue Glass, Pagoda Box, c.1918, 2 1/2 In. *Illus*	7638.00
Cadolle, Clear, Frosted, Flower Blossom, Leaves, Ocher Patina, c.1920, 2 1/2 In.	940.00
Cameo Glass, Citron, Flowers, Butterfly, Oval, Flattened, 3 1/4 In.	748.00
Cameo Glass, Frosted & Blue, Amber Flower, Chased Sterling Silver Cap, 4 In.	431.00
Carrere, Vent Fou, Green, White, Opaline Crystal, Ribbon Label, c.1945, 4 1/4 In.	294.00
Charles Of The Ritz, Directoire, Clear, Gilt Labels, Box, c.1946, 3 3/4 In.	411.00
Christian Dior, Miss Dior, Stopper, Box, 3 1/2 In.	69.00
Ciro, Maskee, Clear, Opaque Black, White Stopper, 4 Labels, Box, c.1923, 3 5/8 In.	2115.00
Clear, Stopper, Dabber, Enameled, Jeweled Hinged Metal Cover, Austria, 1920, 9 In.	940.00
Clear Glass, Black Threads & Stopper, Oval, Tapered, Signed, Libbey, 9 In.	260.00
Clear Glass, Frosted, Wreath Shaped Stopper, Dabber, Signed, Czechoslovakia, 5 1/4 In.	105.00
Clear Glass, Molded Bluebells Stopper, Dabber, Signed, Czechoslovakia, 10 1/2 In.	575.00
Clear Glass, Red Stopper, 2 Flowers, Dabber, Signed, Czechoslovakia, 4 1/2 In.	275.00
Clear Glass, Stopper Cut In Rows, Dabber, Signed, Czechoslovakia, 5 1/2 In.	230.00
Coeur De Feu, Frosted Red Glass, Wooden Base, c.1920, 4 In. *Illus*	825.00
Cologne, 12-Sided, Alternate Panels, Horizontal Ribs, Tooled, 1860-80, 5 1/2 In. *Illus*	504.00
Cologne, Dorothy Gray, Floral Fantasy, Ribbed, Turquoise Plastic Cap, 1940s	40.00
Cologne, Etched Glass, Sterling Collar, 10 Faceted Sides, Stopper, 6 1/4 In.	60.00
Cologne, Flower, Cranberry, Satin, Faceted Stopper, Val St. Lambert, 4 3/8 In.	200.00

Perfume Bottle, Bryenne, Chu Chin Chow, Blue Glass, Pagoda Box, c.1918, 2 1/2 In.

Perfume Bottle, Coeur De Feu, Frosted Red Glass, Wooden Base, c.1920, 4 In.

Perfume Bottle, Cologne, 12-Sided, Alternate Panels, Horizontal Ribs, Tooled, 1860-80, 5 1/2 In.

Cologne, Glass, Ribbons, White Looping, Sapphire Rimmed Mouth, Hourglass, 6 1/8 In. . .	1345.00
Cologne, Rococo, Applied Peasants, Porcelain, Jacob Petit, 10 In., Pair . . . . *Illus*	2070.00
Cologne, Sabino, Bathing Nudes, Signed	185.00
Cologne, Toilet Water, 8 Ribs, Swirled To Right, Canary, Pontil, 12 1/4 In.	750.00
Coty, A Suma, Clear, Frosted, Hang Tag, Box, c.1934, 2 1/2 In.	529.00
Coty, Imprevu, Stopper, Label, 9 1/2 In.	90.00
Coty, L'Aimant, Clear, Frosted, Label, Box, c.1928, 3 1/4 In.	206.00
Crystal, Black, Green, Pointed Stopper, 6 1/2 In.	150.00
Crystal, Dark Green, Inner Glass Stopper, Metal Overcap, 2 1/2 In.	90.00
Crystal, Flower Stoppers, 5 In., Pair	115.00
Crystal, Frosted, Woman Holding Flowers, Cutout Stopper, Dabber, 10 In.	805.00
Crystal, Glass, Yellow, Inner Glass Stopper, Silver Overcap, Flowers, 3 1/2 In.	196.00
Crystal, Peach Crystal Stopper, Cube, 4 1/4 In.	127.00
Crystal, Stopper, Metal Neck, Chain, Oval, 3 In.	115.00
Cut Glass, Cranberry Shaded, Stamped Hallmarks, Birmingham 1897, 3 In.	200.00
Cut Glass, Prism Stopper, 4 Stars On Sides, 4 1/2 In.	69.00
Cut Glass, Stopper, Faceted, 5 1/2 In.	58.00
Cut Glass, Vaseline, Sterling Silver Top, England, c.1897, 8 In.	345.00
D'Orsay, Divine, Clear, Hang Tag, Box, c.1947, 3 3/4 In.	176.00
D'Orsay, Divine, Clear, Hang Tag, Box, c.1947, 7 1/4 In.	295.00
De Marcy, L'Orange, 8 Enameled Orange Parts, Ceramic Holder, 1925, 2 1/2 In.	1410.00
Delettrez, Inalda, Stopper, Indented Rows With Dots, Cone Shape Stopper, 3 1/2 In.	1095.00
Delettrez, Parfum XXIII, String Of Pearls, Box, c.1923, 11 3/8 In. . . . . *Illus*	3819.00
Dorothy Gray, Indigo, Clear, Frosted, Label, c.1948, 3 3/4 In.	440.00
Dorothy Gray, Lady In The Dark, Clear, Gold, Label, c.1941, 3 In.	120.00
Dorothy Gray, Savoir Faire, Clear, Gilt, Enamel, Metallic Screw Cap, c.1947, 4 In.	470.00
Elizabeth Arden, Blue Grass, Cork Stopper, Label, 12 1/2 In.	105.00
Elizabeth Taylor, Passion For Men, Purple Glass, Wood Cap, 11 1/2 In.	12.00
Faberge, Aphrodisia, Clear, Gilded, Label, Holder, Box, c.1936, 3 1/2 In.	175.00
Felix The Cat, Glass, Germany, 5 In.	165.00
Felix The Cat, Mohair, Tin Lithograph Face, Jointed, Schuco, Germany, 4 3/4 In.	1100.00
Frosted, Man Caressing Woman's Hand, Lovebirds, Cutout Frosted Stopper, 7 In.	185.00
Glass, Rectangular, Angel's Head, Sterling Cover, Hinged, Glass Stopper, 3 1/4 In.	298.00
Globular, Tall Honeycomb Neck, Sterling Top, La Pierre, 1890-1920, 6 1/2 x 3 In.	369.00
Globular, Tall Neck, Cut Diamond Point, Sterling Top, England, 3 3/4 x 2 In.	236.00
Green Glass, Leaf Shaped Stopper, Signed, Czechoslovakia, 6 1/4 In.	115.00
Green Glass, Pink, Enameled Bronze Holder, Czechoslovakia, 1920, 4 In.	1765.00
Guerlain, Eau De Cologne Imperial, Stopper, Apothecary Shape, Label, 6 1/4 In.	46.00
Guerlain, La Mouchoir De Monsieur, Stopper, Triangular, Label, 5 In.	400.00
Guerlain, Ode, Clear, Plastic Screw Cap, Box, Wrapper, c.1950, 4 1/2 In.	200.00
Hattie Carnegie, Hypnotic, Woman's Head & Shoulder, Stopper, Gold Enamel, 4 In.	575.00
Houbigant, Chantilly, White Cap, Chair, Cushion, Flowers, Box, 2 In.	58.00
Houbigant, Le Parfum Ideal, Stopper, Gold Label, Box, 3 1/2 In.	69.00
Inner Glass Stopper, Metal Overcap, Enamel Flowers, Leaves, 2 3/4 In.	175.00
Inner Stopper, Sterling Silver Neck, Overcap, Enameled, 3 In.	90.00
Intaglio Glass, Dancer, Flowers, Stopper, Signed, Czechoslovakia, 4 3/4 In.	80.00
Intaglio Glass, Nude, Blue, Clear Stopper, Signed, Czechoslovakia, 5 1/2 In.	150.00

Perfume Bottle, Cologne,
Rococo, Applied Peasants,
Porcelain, Jacob Petit,
10 In., Pair

Perfume
Bottle, Delettrez,
Parfum XXIII, String Of Pearls,
Box, c.1923, 11 3/8 In.

Perfume
Bottle, Parfums
De Marcy, L'Orange,
8 Enameled Glass
Sections, Ceramic Case, c.1925

Iridescent Blue, Clear Teardrop Stopper, S. Fellerman, 1973, 4 7/8 In. 118.00
Jacques Griffe, Mistgri, Clear, Enameled Label, Box, c.1950, 6 1/2 In. 529.00
Jay Thorpe & Co., Jaytho, Clear, Frosted, Bud Stopper, Molded Bouquet Of Tulips, 4 In. . . . 6900.00
Jean d'Albret, Ecusson, Clear, Frosted, Gilt, Velvet Jewel Box, c.1950, 7 1/2 In. 3055.00
Jean Desprez, Votre Main, Porcelain, Applied Roses, Sevres, c.1939, 10 In. 3900.00
Jean Laporte, La Parfum Qui Vous Metamorphose, Clear, Opal, c.1970, 6 3/4 In. 176.00
Jean Patou, Moment Supreme, Stopper, Label, 6 1/2 In. 69.00
Jeanne Lanvin, Arpege, Gold Encased Stopper, Box, 2 In. 400.00
Lagerfeld, Chloe, 2 Flowers, Frosted Glass Stopper 35.00
Lander, Jasmin, Woman, Frosted Glass, Cork Tip Stopper, 4 In. 175.00
Lanvin, My Sin, Black Crystal, Gold, c.1930, 7 In. 206.00
Lanvin, My Sin, Black Crystal, Gold, Label, Box, c.1920, 2 1/2 In. 235.00
Lanvin, My Sin, Gilded Black Crystal, c.1920, 5 1/4 In. 880.00
Lanvin, Pretext, Clear, Gold, Label, Box, c.1937, 2 1/4 In. 147.00
Lentheric, Miracle, Blue Cased, Clear, Stopper, Cover, Val St. Lambert, c.1920, 3 1/2 In. . . . 206.00
Lentheric, Shanghai, Gold Stopper, Box, 1 1/2 In. 46.00
Lilly Dache, Dachelle, Clear, Labels, Hang Tag, Box, c.1960, 6 3/4 In. 200.00
Lilly Dache, Dashing, Poodle Sitting, Sash, Roses, Label, 3 1/4 In. 374.00
Liz Claiborne, Vivid, Stopper, Blue Liquid, 14 In. 12.00
Lucien Lelong, Opening Night, Clear, Box, c.1934, 2 1/2 In. 440.00
Lucien Lelong, Taglio, Clear, Label, Plastic Box, c.1945, 1 1/2 In. 95.00
Lucien Lelong, Tailspin, Razzle Dazzle, Clear, Screw Cap, Gyroscope, Box, c.1940, 3 In. . . 470.00
Lucien Lelong, Tailspin, Stopper, Molded Logo, Label, 2 3/4 In. 69.00
Luxor, Lybis, Blue Glass Stopper, Impressed Violets, Frosted, 5 1/2 In. 375.00
Mary Chess, Souvenir D'Un Soir, Clear, Frosted, Hang Tag, Box, c.1956, 3 1/2 In. 2938.00
Mary Chess, Souvenir D'Un Soir, Clear, Frosted, Label, Box, c.1956, 4 1/2 In. 8813.00
Molinard, Le Provencale, Frosted Glass Atomizer, Oval Frieze, Nude Women, 5 1/4 In. . . . 489.00
Morlee, Crystal, Diamond Shaped Peach Stoppers, 3 1/2 In. 115.00
Nina Ricci, Coeur-Joie, 2 Hearts, Gold Cap, Plastic Case, 2 1/4 In. 375.00
Nina Ricci, L'Air Du Temps, Frosted Glass, Metal Cap, Sunburst, 2 In. 207.00
Nude Sitting On Ball, Ball Shaped Base, Frosted Stopper, 7 1/2 In. 460.00
Nygren, Mottled, Applied Frog On Mushroom Stopper, Signed, 1987, 10 In. 1035.00
Odeon, Pour Amour, Frosted, Pinecone Stopper, Pine Branches, Cones, Patina, 3 1/2 In. . . 1745.00
Ota, Chypre, Pearl, Cork Closures, Silk Tassel, Box, c.1920, 4 In. 1295.00
Palmer, May Bloom, Stopper, Tax Stamp March 1, 1899, Box 160.00
Papillon, Cobalt Blue, Silver Overlay, Art Nouveau, Loetz, 4 In. 4320.00
Parfums De Marcy, L'Orange, 8 Enameled Glass Sections, Ceramic Case, c.1925 . . . . *Illus* 1410.00
Peach Glass, Fan Shape Stopper & Bottle, Red Coral Flower Shaped Medallion, Pair 460.00
Peggy Hoyt, Flowers, Iridescent, Verre De Soir, Blue Stopper, Steuben, c.1913, 3 1/2 In. . . 470.00
Perez Guerra, Muntaj, Glazed Ceramic, Gilt, Cork Closure, Stand, c.1940, 7 In. 235.00
Pink Glass, Clear, Basket Cut Stopper, Dabber, Signed, Czechoslovakia, 7 3/4 In. 635.00
Piver, Mascarade, Opaque Red, Gilt, Depinoix, Box, 1928, 2 In. 1293.00
Porcelain, Silver Top, Flowers, 1893, 3 In. 130.00
Porcelain, Stopper, Dabber, Painted Roses, 3 In. 105.00
Prince Matchabelli, Added Attraction, Gold Screw Cap, Enameled Label, Box, 1 1/2 In. . . 120.00
Prince Matchabelli, Stradivari, Frosted Glass, Stopper, Crown Shape, Signed, 4 In. 150.00
Red, Silver Neck, Chain, 1850-60, 3 3/4 In. 575.00
Red Glass Stopper, Leaf Shaped, Faceted, Signed, 4 In. 196.00
Renaud, Sur Deux Notes, Clear, Frosted, Oval, Spire Stopper, Leaves, Label, 5 1/2 In. 1380.00
Richard Hudnut, Pour Vous, Clear, Frosted, Green Patina, c.1923, 5 3/8 In. 3819.00
Rosine, Coup De Foudre, Clear, 4 1/4 In. 764.00
Rosine, Nuit De Chine, Clear, Blue, Plastic Ring Handle, Box, c.1913, 3 1/4 In. 1058.00
Schiaparelli, S, White Cap, Box, 1 In. 69.00
Schiaparelli, Zut, Stopper, Woman's Body, 5 1/2 In. 460.00
Schuco, Monkey, Red Mohair, 1920s 975.00
Shalimar, Glass, Frosted, Rosebud Stopper, 4 1/2 In. 58.00
Stopper, Etched, Silver Encased, 5 In. 140.00
Stork Club, Metal Encased, Metal Cap, 1 3/4 In. 46.00
Suzy, Golden Laughter, Clear, Green Enamel, Stand, c.1941, 4 3/8 In. 1645.00
Victoria's Secret, Encounter, Ball Stopper, 11 3/4 In. 35.00
Worth, Dans La Nuit, Stopper, Stars, Plastic Tip Stopper, 4 1/2 In. 92.00
Yardley, Enchantress, Clear, Box, c.1912, 4 1/4 In. 382.00
Yellow, Amber, Inner Glass Stopper, Meal Overcap, 4 In. 115.00

Yellow Glass, Dabber, Czechoslovakia, 6 1/2 In. 325.00
Ysianne, Saturnale, Clear, Frosted, Depinoix, c.1927, 6 1/2 In. 1175.00

PETERS & REED Pottery Company of Zanesville, Ohio, was founded by John D. Peters and Adam Reed in 1897. Chromal, Landsun, Montene, Pereco, and Persian are some of the art lines that were made. The company, which became Zane Pottery in 1920 and Gonder Pottery in 1941, closed in 1957. Peters & Reed pottery was unmarked.

Bowl, Moss Aztec, Carved, Dragonfly, 2 1/4 x 4 In. 104.00
Jug, Cherry Medallions, Brown Glaze, Bulbous, 9 1/2 In. 104.00
Jug, Demijohn, Applied Grape Clusters, Brown Glaze, 6 1/2 x 5 In. 92.00
Pedestal, Moss Aztec, Embossed, Roses, 17 In. 147.00
Planter, Nudes, 4-Sided, 7 In. 290.00
Tankard, Grapevine, Embossed, Painted, 11 3/4 In. 173.00
Tankard, Grapevine, Embossed, Painted, 13 1/2 In. 219.00
Vase, Bust Of Lincoln, Oak Branches, Tan Drip Glaze, 12 x 8 In. 150.00
Vase, Flared Rim, Raised Leaf, Cylindrical, 12 1/4 In. 353.00
Vase, Flower Garlands, Brown Glaze, Shouldered, High Shaped Handles, 13 In. 127.00
Vase, Flower Swags, Brown Glaze, Aladdin's Lamp Shape, Ruffled Rim, 4 x 9 In. 115.00
Vase, Green Matte, Waisted, Arts & Crafts Ivy Design, 8 In. 81.00
Vase, Lion's Head Medallions, Rose Garlands, Bulbous, Tapered Neck, Flared Rim, 14 In. .. 173.00
Vase, Mirror, Black, Green Drips, 8 1/2 In. 173.00
Vase, Mirror, Green, Green Drips, 4 1/2 In. 196.00
Vase, Mirror, Green, Green Drips, 7 In. 161.00
Vase, Moss Aztec, Embossed Roses, Pinched Waist, 14 In. 345.00
Vase, Mountainous Landscape, Sailboat, 8 1/2 x 5 1/2 In. 1955.00
Vase, Oval, Blue, Black, Brown Drip Glaze, Brown Ground, 12 1/2 In. 598.00
Vase, Shadow Ware, Flaring, Streaks, Yellow, Black, Green Glaze, 8 x 5 1/2 In. 106.00
Vase, Wreath Design, Embossed, Painted, 13 1/2 In., Pair 230.00

PETRUS REGOUT, see Maastricht category.

PEWABIC POTTERY was founded by Mary Chase Perry Stratton in 1903 in Detroit, Michigan. The company made many types of art pottery, including pieces with green matte glaze and an iridescent crystalline glaze. The company continued working until the death of Mary Stratton in 1961. It was reactivated by Michigan State University in 1968.

Plaque, Virgin Mary, Snake, Arched, White, Turquoise, 4 3/4 x 3 1/4 In. 295.00
Plate, Dragonflies, Blue, White Ground, 10 3/4 In. 2235.00
Tile, Blue, c.1985, 4 1/4 x 3 3/4 In. 69.00
Tile, Factory, Pewabic, Detroit, Burgundy Iridescence, Signed, Ira, Ella, Frame, 7 In. 175.00
Tile, Pottery, Urn, Molded 2 Handles, Green Glaze, 2 1/2 x 2 1/2 In. 46.00
Tile, Ship, Burgundy, Gold Iridescence, Frame, 7 In. 60.00
Vase, Blue, Gold Iridescent Glaze, 3 1/4 In. 276.00
Vase, Bulbous, Crackle Blue Glaze, Over Lustered Celadon, 4 3/4 x 4 In. 295.00
Vase, Flambe Glaze, Blue, Green, White, 2 1/2 x 2 3/4 In. 410.00
Vase, Orange Matte Glaze, Bulbous, Marked, 5 1/2 In. 410.00

PEWTER is a metal alloy of tin and lead. Some of the pewter made after 1840 has a slightly different composition and is called *Britannia metal*. This later type of pewter was worked by machine; the earlier pieces were made by hand. In the 1920s pewter came back into fashion and pieces were often marked *Genuine Pewter.* Eighteenth-, nineteenth-, and twentieth-century examples are listed here.

Basin, David Melville, DM Touchmark, Qt., 8 In. 1050.00
Basin, Jacob Whitmore, Middletown, Conn., Flared Sides, Single Reed Rim, 9 In. 1060.00
Basin, John Andrew Brunstrom, Philadelphia, Pa., Flared, Love, 1781-93, 6 11/16 In. 645.00
Basin, John Andrew Brunstrom, Philadelphia, Pa., Flared, Love, 1781-93, 9 1/8 In. 530.00
Basin, John Andrew Brunstrom, Philadelphia, Pa., Flared, Love, 1781-93, 12 5/8 In. 2820.00
Basin, John Watts, England, 1700s, 11 1/2 In. 200.00
Basin, Richard Austin, Boston, Single Reed Rim, c.1790-1810, Qt., 8 In. 645.00
Beaker, Boardman & Hart, Hartford, Conn., Flared Rim, Incised Bands, 3 1/8 In. 175.00
Beaker, Boardman & Hart, Hartford, Conn., Flared Rim, Touchmark, 3 1/2 In., Pair 345.00

Beaker, Samuel Danforth, Hartford, Conn., Flared Rim, Incised Rings At Rim, 5 In. 1765.00
Beaker, Timothy Boardman, New York, Tapered, Cylindrical, Incised Band, c.1823, 5 In. . 885.00
Bedpan, Hale & Sons, Screw-On Handle 100.00
Bowl, Baptismal, Thomas D. & Sherman Boardman, Conn., 1810-30, 3 3/4 x 8 1/4 In. 5250.00
Bowl, Kayserzinn, 2 Handles, Art Nouveau, 21 1/2 In. 600.00
Bowl, Liberty & Co., Hammered, 3 Applied Feet, 7 1/2 In. 441.00
Bowl, Monteith, Round, Bust & Scroll Borders, 19th Century, 9 1/2 In. 999.00
Box, Hammered, Frosted Glass, Grapevine, Moth, Jewels Inset, Art Nouveau, 8 1/2 x 4 In. 323.00
Box, Liberty & Co., Hammered, Arts & Crafts Design, 6 In. 1495.00
Box, Tobacco, Oval, Line Engraved Border, c.1796, 3 In. 499.00
Cake Decorator Applicator, Wood Shaft, Leather, 12 1/2 x 1 1/2 In. 10.49
Candlestick, Baluster, England, 4 1/8 In., Pair 375.00
Candlestick, Crane, 14 In., Pair 85.00
Candlestick, Freeman Porter, Westbrook, Maine, Baluster Stem, Round Foot, 6 In., Pair .. 765.00
Candlestick, Mathias Norling, 1828-52, Pair 395.00
Candlestick, Tapering Cylindrical Cup, Baluster Shape, 8 In., 4 Piece 382.00
Candlestick, Tudric, 3 Buttresses, Enameled Medallions On Base, 9 In. 2115.00
Charger, Engraved, Portrait, Eugene, Germany, 1700, 18 In. 173.00
Charger, Germany, 16 1/2 In. 600.00
Charger, IF Touchmark, England, 20 1/4 In. 1100.00
Charger, Robert Baldwin, Molded Rim, Wigan, England, c.1700, 20 1/2 In. 566.00
Charger, Roses, Stamped Initials, London, 15 In. 173.00
Charger, Samuel Duncombe, Initials, 18 In. 450.00
Charger, Samuel Ellis, Monogram, Touchmarks, 16 3/8 In. 345.00
Charger, Stephen Maxwell, Arms Of Marquis Of Zetland, Scotland, 18 In. 275.00
Charger, Thomas Alderson, Oval, London, 16 In. 375.00
Charger, Townsend & Compton, London, 14 3/4 In. 413.00
Cigarette Box, Tudric, Enameled Medallion, Cedar Lining, Liberty, England, 3 x 3 1/2 In. . 1058.00
Coffee & Tea Service, Royal Holland, 3 Piece 175.00
Coffeepot, Allen Porter, Ring-Turned Baluster Shape, Westbrook, Me., c.1830, 11 5/8 In. . 565.00
Coffeepot, Boardman & Co., Baluster Shape, Curved Handle, Conn., c.1825, 11 3/4 In. ... 294.00
Coffeepot, Boardman & Hart, N.Y., 11 In. 400.00
Coffeepot, Dome Lid, Sellew & Co., Cincinnati, City On Base, Serpentine Sides, 12 In. ... 115.00
Coffeepot, Eben Smith, 8 In. 175.00
Coffeepot, F. Porter No. 1, Westbrook, Maine, c.1840, 12 In. 750.00
Coffeepot, Glennore Co., G. Richardson, Eagle, A, Cranston, Rhode Island, 8 In. 130.00
Coffeepot, Griswold, Incised Horizontal Bands, 1800s, 10 1/2 In. 256.00
Coffeepot, I. Trask, Etched Design, 11 In. 375.00
Coffeepot, Lighthouse, Eagle, I. Trask, Beverly, Mass., c.1835, 11 1/2 In. 4800.00
Coffeepot, Oval, Tooled Center Ring, Flared Foot & Rim, Dome Lid, Wafer Finial, 11 In. . 316.00
Coffeepot, Rufus Dunham, Westbrook, Maine, Black Scroll Handle, Cone Lid, 7 1/4 In. .. 500.00
Coffeepot, Savage, No. 3, Scroll Handle, Middelton, Conn. 235.00
Coffeepot, Tooled Base, Rim Rings, Black Paint, Scrolled Ear Handle, 11 In. 259.00
Coffeepot, Tooled Rings, Dome Lid, Wooden Finial, Scrolled Ear Handle, c.1840, 12 In. ... 105.00
Communion Set, H. Yale & Co., 4 Chalices, 2 Plates, Flagon, Wallingford 4600.00
Cream Pot, Tudric, Cane, Enameled, Tapered, Cylindrical, Pouring Spout, 5 In. 359.00
Cup, Boardman & Hart, Round, Slightly Flared Rim, Early 19th Century, 3 In. 353.00
Dish, Deep, John Andrew Brunstrom, Philadelphia, Pa., Love, 1781-93, 8 3/4 In. 410.00
Dish, Deep, John Skinner, Boston, Hammered Bouge, Single Reed Rim, 8 In. 825.00
Dish, Deep, Thomas Danforth III, Phila., 11 1/2 In. 875.00
Dish, Deep, Thomas Danforth III, Stepney, Conn., c.1790, 6 1/8 In. 1645.00
Dish, John Andrew Brunstrom, Philadelphia, Pa., Love, London, 1790, 13 In. 500.00
Flagon, Boardman & Hart, Hinged Dome Lid, Hartford, Conn., Scroll Handle, c.1825, 13 In. 3055.00
Flagon, Cover, Normandy, Twin Acorn Thumbpiece, Fleur-De-Lis, 7 1/4 x 4 1/4 In. 120.00
Flagon, D. & Boardman, Disc Finial, Chairback Thumbpiece, Scroll Handle, c.1815, 9 In. . 4700.00
Flagon, Hunter, Dog, Relief, Pewter Lid, 1 1/2 Liter, 13 In. 405.00
Flagon, Lid, Jersey, Pot Capacity, Initials, 1700s, 10 1/2 In. 1000.00
Flagon, Sellew & Co., Cast Scroll Handle, Touchmark, Cincinnati, c.1860, 11 1/4 In. 405.00
Flagon, Spire, Boardman & Co., N.Y., 1800s, c.1825, 11 In. 2950.00
Flagon, T. Boardman, Hinged Lid, Chairback Thumbpiece, Double Scroll Handle, 14 In. .. 3820.00
Flagon, Thomas D. & Sherman Boardman, Hinged Lid, Scroll Handle, c.1815, 14 In. 3820.00
Inkwell, Art Nouveau, Bun Shape, Circular Stand, Bee Decoration, 9 In. 235.00
Jug, Ale, Bulbous, 2 Overlapping Cs Handle, 1700s, Qt., 7 1/4 In. 420.00

Jug, Ale, Grated Spout, Open Chairback Thumbpiece, 2 C-Scroll Handle, 1700s, 8 1/2 In. .   378.00
Ladle, D. Curtiss, Touchmark, 13 1/4 In. 145.00
Lamp, Chamber, Saucer Base, Finger Ring, 7 In. 374.00
Lamp, Oil, Acorn-Shape Font, Circular Base, Double-Tube Burner, 8 In., Pair 413.00
Lamp, Oil, S. Rust, Patent, 1844 ....   350.00
Lamp, Whale Oil, 3 On Bottom, American, 6 1/4 In. 295.00
Lamp, Whale Oil, Acorn Font, Saucer Base, Finger Ring, 4 1/4 In. 173.00
Lamp, Whale Oil, Comet Pattern, Baluster Shape, New England, 1850, 12 & 14 In., Pair . .   259.00
Lamp, Whale Oil, Freeman Porter, Westbrook, Maine, 7 1/8 x 4 5/8 In. 250.00
Lamp, Whale Oil, R. Gleason, 6 In. 275.00
Lavabo, Hanging, Family Crest, Free Standing Basin, 13 x 14 In. 161.00
Measure, Baluster, Double Volute, 1700s, Qt., 7 3/4 In. 1553.00
Measure, Barrel Form, Double C Handle, WR, Hallmarks, England, c.1800, 6 1/2 In. 850.00
Measure, Boardman & Hart, Baluster, N.Y., c.1847, Pt., 5 In. 1180.00
Meat Plate, Armorial Device To Rim, Crown X Mark, Oval Rim, Late 1700s, 24 In. 275.00
Mold, Candle, 7-Stick, Signed VB, Mid 19th Century, 15 x 15 In. 1695.00
Mold, Ice Cream, E & Co., Rabbit, Sitting On Grass, 4 Part, N.Y., 10 x 10 1/2 x 6 1/2 In. . .   865.00
Mold, Ice Cream, E & Co., Santa Shape, Pint, 11 x 6 1/2 In. 165.00
Mold, Ice Cream, Fr. Krauss & Sons, Apple, 3 Pt. 179.00
Mold, Ice Cream, Fruit Design, Touchmark, 7 x 3 1/2 In., 3 Piece 77.00
Mold, Ice Cream, Krauss, Pineapple, No. 14, Banquet Size, 3 Pt., 3 Piece 330.00
Mold, Spoon, Dognose Rattail Shape, 8 In. 228.00
Mug, Boardman & Hart, Hartford, Conn., S-Scroll Handle, Bud Terminal, Pt., 4 In. 1880.00
Mug, Jacob Whitmore, Middletown, Conn., 1757-90, 5 7/8 In. 4000.00
Mug, Jacob Whitmore, Middletown, Conn., Cylindrical, Scroll Handle, c.1760, 6 In. 9400.00
Mug, Joseph Danforth, Sr., Middletown, Conn., Scroll Handle, Bud Terminal, c.1780, 6 In.   4700.00
Mug, Samuel Hamlin, Hartford, Conn., Tapered, S-Scroll Handle, Bud Terminal, Qt., 6 In. .   3820.00
Mug, T. & S. Boardman, Hartford, Conn., Scroll Handle, Bud Terminal, c.1815, Pt., 4 In. . .   1530.00
Mug, T. & S. Boardman, S-Scroll Handle, Bud Terminal, c.1815, Qt., 6 In. 7050.00
Ornament, 2 Men Standing Before Blossoms, 6-Sided Base, Chinese, 18 1/4 In., Pair 920.00
Pen, Inkstand, Twin Center Hinged Lids, Early 19th Century, 6 1/2 In. 3525.00
Pitcher, Bulbous, Flared Rim, 7 1/2 In. 290.00
Pitcher, Communion, Cover, Handle, Incised Bands, Footed Base, Qt., 8 x 4 1/2 In. 110.00
Pitcher, F. Porter, Westbrook, Maine, c.1835, 6 1/2 In. 840.00
Pitcher, John Warne, Ye Olde Cheshire Cheese, 4 1/2 In. 250.00
Pitcher, Water, Hinged Top, Cast Iron Handle, Pour Spout, Footed Base, 10 x 6 In. 138.00
Plate, David Melville, Newport, R.I., 1755-93, 8 1/8 In. 550.00
Plate, Fredrick Bassett, 8 3/8 In. 985.00
Plate, Gershom Jones, Providence, R.I., 2 Lions In Gateway Mark, 1774-1809, 8 1/4 In. . .   1115.00
Plate, Harbeson, Philadelphia, 1765-1800, 5 7/8 In. 230.00
Plate, Henry Will, Single Reeded, Hammered Bouge, Crown Marks, Rose, 8 3/4 In. 365.00
Plate, Jacob Whitmore, Tudor Rose Touchmark, 1700s, 8 In. 366.00
Plate, James Taudin, Coat Of Arms, 10 In. 550.00
Plate, L. Boardman Warranted, Eagle & Shield In Circle, 8 5/8 In. 195.00
Plate, M. L. Schram, Engraved, Angel Touchmarks, Ohrdruf Stamp, 1861, 8 3/8 In., Pair . .   115.00
Plate, Richard Austin, Boston, Oval Touchmark, Dove, Lamb, 1792-1817, 7 7/8 In. 235.00
Plate, Semper Eadem, Boston, Late 1700s, 8 1/2 In. 975.00
Plate, Thomas Danforth Boardman, Conn., Touchmark, 10 3/4 In. 518.00
Plate, Thomas Danforth II, Middletown, Conn., Hammered, 2 Lions, Gateway, c.1765, 9 In.   3175.00
Plate, Townsend & Compton, 8 1/4 In. 125.00
Porringer, Bleeding Bowl, Inscribed Lines Marking 2 To 16 Oz., 5 1/4 In. 2468.00
Porringer, Continental, Footed, Handle, Relief Carving, Fisherman, Windmill, 3 x 4 In. ...   35.00
Porringer, Crown Shape Handle, Cast Touchmark, RG, 4 1/4 In. 200.00
Porringer, Flower Handle, c.1800 ....   385.00
Porringer, G. Jones, Providence, R.I., Flower Handle, Boss Bottom, Lion Mark, c.1800, 4 In.   2350.00
Porringer, Geometric Handle, England, Herringbone Twill Linen Mark, c.1750, 5 3/8 In. . .   925.00
Porringer, Pierced Handle, Touchmark, Rhode Island, 19th Century, 5 1/4 In. 765.00
Porringer, Richard Lee, Springfield, Vt., Openwork Handle, Crescents, Hearts, c.1800, 3 In.   590.00
Porringer, S. Hamlin, Jr., Providence, R.I., Flower Handle, Eagle, Anchor, 1820, 5 3/8 In. . .   1530.00
Porringer, S. Hamlin, Jr., Providence, R.I., Flower Handle, Eagle, Anchor, c.1825, 4 1/2 In.   1060.00
Porringer, Solid Handle, Pennsylvania, c.1781, 5 1/4 In. 1035.00
Porringer, T. & S. Boardman, Hartford, Conn., Crown Handle, c.1820, 5 In. 590.00

Porringer, T. & S. Boardman, Hartford, Conn., Old English Form Handle, c.1820, 4 In.	480.00
Slop Bowl, Crossman, West & Leonard, 4 1/2 In.	225.00
Snuffbox, Book Shape, Teissiere, Fres, c.1850, 2 1/2 x 1 1/2 x 3/8 In.	175.00
Soap Dish, Round, Ring Engraved, Hinged Lid, c.1825, 4 3/8 In.	470.00
Sugar, Ashbil Griswold, Meriden, Conn., 1808-30, 6 1/2 In.	550.00
Sugar & Creamer, Liberty, Hammered, 5 1/2 In.	294.00
Syrup, Cover, Hall & Cotton, 6 1/4 In.	175.00
Tankard, Cylindrical, Flowers, Leaves, Initials, Continental, c.1796, 9 1/4 In.	285.00
Tankard, Ingram & Hunt, Tulip, Bewdley, England, 1780-1806, Qt., 8 1/2 In.	2950.00
Tankard, Robert Isles, London, 1713-35, 6 1/2 In.	3950.00
Tankard, U-Shape, Tulip Variation, Pt., 5 3/4 In.	2250.00
Tappit Hen, Lid, Mutchkin Capacity, Shouldered, Scotland, c.1800, 6 1/2 In.	1890.00
Tea Set, Solitaire, Rectangular Body, Flat Cover, Loop Handles, Early 1900s, 3 Piece	70.00
Tea Set, Stieff, Williamsburg, 3 Piece	360.00
Tea Set, Tray, Kayserzinn, Tulip Motif, Leaf Decoration, Germany, c.1900, 17 1/4 In.	120.00
Tea Set, Tudric, Teapot, Creamer, Sugar, Hammered, Plate, 7 1/4, 10 In.	470.00
Teapot, Bachelor's, Dixon & Son, Ivory Finial, Black Wood Handle, 4 1/2 x 7 1/4 In.	280.00
Teapot, Bachelor's, Sheffield, Ebonized Wood Handle	100.00
Teapot, John Townsend, Queen Anne Style, 6 1/2 In.	3750.00
Teapot, L. Vickers, Wood Handle, 6 x 10 1/4 In.	710.00
Teapot, L.J. Curtiss, Relief Body Rings, Flared Base, Coned Lid, Ear Handle, 8 In.	259.00
Teapot, Pear Shape, Lovebird Touchmark, Pennsylvania, c.1800, 7 In.	8963.00
Teapot, Queen Anne, Pear Shape, Scrolled Handle, Paneled Spout, 7 1/2 In.	460.00
Teapot, R. Gleason, Black Painted Handle, 9 1/2 In.	350.00
Teapot, Scrolling Handle, Paneled Body, Pedestal Base, c.1900, 10 In.	60.00
Tobacco Jar, Blackamoor Finial, Tobacco Press, England, 1700s	350.00
Tray, Liberty & Co., Hand Hammered, Mark, Archibald Knox, 18 In.	315.00
Tray, Tudric, Hammered, Inset Turquoise Enamel, 10 In.	1060.00
Tray, W & CS, Hand Hammered, Riveted, 10 1/2 In.	60.00
Tureen, Arms Of Marquis Of Zetland, 10 1/2 x 14 In.	850.00
Urn, Coffee, Baluster Shape, Raised Pedestal, Ring Handles, 17 x 9 In.	35.00
Urn, Hot Water, Boardman & Hart, N.Y., 15 In.	475.00
Urn, Hot Water, Smith & Feltman, 19 In.	350.00
Vase, Cover, Kayserzinn, Raised Flower, Cut Glass Insert, 5 In.	295.00
Vase, Kayserzinn, Hammered, Flowers, 3 Applied Handles, 12 1/2 In.	530.00
Vase, Liberty & Co., Flaring, 3 Applied Looping Handles, 3 Agate Stones, 7 In.	650.00
Vase, Pierre Du Mont, Hammered, Geometric Designs, Paris, c.1930, 7 1/2 In.	999.00
Vase, Tudric, Flower Form, 2 Whiplash Handles, Footed, Marked, Liberty & Co., 10 In. ..	480.00
Vase, Tudric, Hammered, 3 Buttresses, Leaf & Vine, England, 11 1/2 In.	1058.00
Vase, Tudric, Liberty & Co., Hammered, Handles, Tray, 8 In.	765.00
Wall Pocket, Cartouche Shaped Backplate, Demilune Well, c.1800, 9 3/4 In., Pair	470.00
Warming Dish, Cover, Thomas Compton, Handles, Marked, London, 16 In.	690.00

PHOENIX BIRD, or Flying Phoenix, is the name given to a blue-and-white kitchenware popular between 1900 and World War II. A variant is known as Flying Turkey. Most of this dinnerware was made in Japan for sale in the dime stores in America. It is still being made.

Butter Chip, Blue, Japan, 3 3/8 In., 4 Piece	75.00
Cup & Saucer, Japan, 4 Sets	20.00
Teapot, 7 In.	55.00

PHOENIX GLASS Company was founded in 1880 in Pennsylvania. The firm made commercial products, such as lampshades, bottles, and glassware. Collectors today are interested in the "Sculptured Artware" made by the company from the 1930s until the mid-1950s. Some pieces of Phoenix glass are very similar to those made by the Consolidated Lamp and Glass Company. Phoenix made Reuben Blue, lavender, and yellow pieces. These colors were not used by Consolidated. In 1970 Phoenix became a division of Anchor Hocking, then was sold to the Newell Group in 1987. The company is still working.

Umbrella Stand, Thistles, Opal To Mauve Ground, Cylindrical, 17 1/4 In.	288.00
Vase, Tan Relief Vines & Fruit Clusters, Cream Ground, Lobed, Cameo, 8 1/2 In.	175.00

PHONOGRAPHS, invented by Thomas Edison in 1877, have been made by many firms. This category also includes other items associated with the phonograph. Jukeboxes and Records are listed in their own categories.

Berliner, Gram-O-Phone, Clarophonic, Mahogany, Painted, 1900s, 34 x 32 x 20 In.	489.00
Columbia, Grafanola Deluxe, Windup, 1920s, 48 1/2 In.	8800.00
Columbia, Graphophone, Coin-Operated, Oak Case, Clarion, 16 x 11 x 12 In.	4400.00
Columbia, Graphophone, Coin-Operated, Type BS, Nickel Plated Horn, c.1898	7700.00
Edison, Amberola 1A, Upright, Mahogany, 100 Cylinders, c.1909, 42 In.	6050.00
Edison, Amberola 30, Cylinder, Oak Case, c.1912, 16 x 12 1/2 x 13 In.	470.00
Edison, Diamond Disc, C-250, Mahogany Case, Gilt Trim, 50 In.	295.00
Edison, Fireside A, Cylinder, Oak Case, c.1910, 11 1/2 In.	265.00
Edison, Home, Nickel Plate, 10 Cylinders, 23-In. Morning Glory Horn	635.00
Edison, Standard B, Cylinder, Oak Case, Red Lacquered Flower Horn, 13 In.	940.00
Edison, Standard, Cylinder, C Reproducer, Oak Case, 12 x 12 In.	283.00 to 316.00
Edison, Triumph A, 2-Minute Cylinder, C Reproducer, 33-In. Flower Horn	3300.00
Edison, Triumph G, Cylinder, Diamond B Reproducer, Oak Case, c.1912	11500.00
Emerson, Wondergram, World's Smallest, Instructions, Box, c.1960, 9 In.	180.00
Horn, Morning Glory, Blue Ground, 22 In.	330.00
Peter Pan, Portable, Folding Turntable, Brown Leather-Covered Case, Horn In Lid	205.00
RCA Victor, Special Portable, Aluminum, Plastic, J. Vassos, c.1935, 15 x 8 x 17 In.	4000.00
Starr, Partners Desk, Mahogany, Electric, 1920s, 60 In.	2090.00
Victor, Monarch Junior, Type E, Oak Case, Belled Horn, c.1905, 18 In.	1790.00
Victor IV, Exhibition Reproducer, Mahogany Case, 10-In. Turntable	1870.00
Victor V, Exhibition Reproducer, Oak Case, 12-In. Turntable	1320.00
Victor Victrola 50, Mahogany Case, Portable, 17 In.	180.00
Zon-O-Phone, Disc, Magnetic Dancers, Oak Case, Horn, 18 x 54 In.	1100.00
Zon-O-Phone, Grand Opera, Disc, Oak, Glass, Brass Horn, Tabletop, 30 In.	8250.00

PHONOGRAPH NEEDLE CASES of tin are collected today by music and phonograph enthusiasts and advertising addicts. The tins are very small, about 2 inches across, and often have attractive graphic designs lithographed on the top and sides.

Marschall, 1 5/8 x 1 1/2 In.	36.00 to 44.00
Pegasus Nadeln, 1 7/8 x 1 3/8 In.	38.00
Regal Loud Tone, 1 3/4 x 1 3/8 In.	36.00
Rojar, 1 7/8 x 1 3/8 In.	40.00
Verona Needles, Nude Woman, 1 3/4 In.	80.00

PHOTOGRAPHY items are listed here. The first photograph was a view from a window in France taken in 1826. The commercially successful photograph started with the daguerreotype introduced in 1839. Today all sorts of photographs and photographic equipment are collected. Albums were popular in Victorian times. Cartes de visite, popular after 1854, were mounted on 2 1/2-by-4-inch cardboard. Cabinet cards were introduced in 1866. These were mounted on 4 1/4-by-6 1/2-inch cards. Stereo views are listed under Stereo Card. The cases for daguerreotypes are listed in the Gutta-Percha category. Stereoscopes are listed in their own section.

Album, Miniature, Leatherette Cover, General Tom Thumb, 1 1/2 In.	440.00
Albumen, Civil War Soldier, 39 ILL, Tinted, Mat, 12 x 9 In.	210.00
Albumen, Oklahoma Bank, Interior, Card Mount, c.1890, 8 x 10 In.	259.00
Albumen, Samuel Arnold, 1865, 6 1/4 x 5 In.	1380.00
Albumen, Sitting Bull, Arrapaho Prophet, Leader Of Ghost Dance, H.P. Robinson	1200.00
Albumen, Union Soldiers From Andersonville Prison, c.1865, 4 x 5 1/4 In.	2600.00
Ambrotype, 2 Boys, Looking At Departed Mother, Lying On Pillow, 1/2 Plate	4100.00
Ambrotype, Black Girl, Yellow Blouse, Constitution & Laws Case, 1/9 Plate	600.00
Ambrotype, Civil War Officer, Frame, 1/6 Plate	400.00
Ambrotype, Confederate Soldier & Wife, Full Case, 1/4 Plate	5300.00
Ambrotype, Julia White, Full Case, 1/6 Plate	60.00
Ambrotype, Maine Woman, Geometric Case, J. Bryant, Lewiston, Me., 1/9 Plate	155.00
Ambrotype, Man Seated With Bible, 1/2 Plate	50.00
Ambrotype, Man, Dog, Case, 1/6 Plate	175.00

Ambrotype, Outdoor Scene, 2 Horse Drawn Carts, Dog, 1/6 Plate 200.00
Ambrotype, Soldier, Albany Burgess Corp, 1/2 Plate 1200.00
Ambrotype, Union Soldier With Bayonet, Full Uniform, Leather Case, 1/6 Plate 690.00
Ambrotype, Violist, On Ruby Glass, Full Case, 1/6 Plate 400.00
Cabinet Card, 2 Schoolmarms, I.E. Scruby, Mazeppa, Minn. 75.00
Cabinet Card, Advertising Woman, State Bank Of Northwood, N.D., Pierce & Potter 250.00
Cabinet Card, Bicycle Club, High Wheel Bicycles, On Steps Of Building 335.00
Cabinet Card, Brooklyn Nationals Baseball Team, 4 1/4 x 6 1/2 In. 6900.00
Cabinet Card, Cleveland Ball Club, 1888, Joseph Hall, 4 1/4 x 6 1/2 In. 6325.00
Cabinet Card, Commanche, Mother, Children, Baby In Cradle, c.1900, 5 1/2 x 4 In. 235.00
Cabinet Card, Cor. John McDonald, Troop D 9th Cav USA, Holding Watch 780.00
Cabinet Card, Doctor Writing Prescription, Nurse, Tomlinson, Detroit 180.00
Cabinet Card, Emmett Bowman, Philadelphia Giants, 1903, 6 x 9 In. 1380.00
Cabinet Card, Franz Hacker, Strength Athlete, Grunberger, Prague, c.1898 . . . . 125.00
Cabinet Card, Girl, Dog, Puppies, Gus Jackson, Waco, Texas 95.00
Cabinet Card, Indian Policeman, Western Canada, Jones & Co., Victoria, B.C. 400.00
Cabinet Card, Louisville Ball Club, 1888, Joseph Hall, 4 1/4 x 6 1/2 In. 7475.00
Cabinet Card, Pawnee Chief, Charles Milton Bell, 12 x 9 In. 460.00
Cabinet Card, Rushing Bear, Charles Milton Bell, Washington, 1880 . . . . 900.00
Cabinet Card, Sow & Piglets, McLeod, Happy Hollow 95.00
Cabinet Card, Spanish American War Soldier, Parade Torch, Kauffman, York, Pa. 228.00
Cabinet Card, Survivors Of Greely Arctic Expedition, c.1883 . . . . 245.00
Cabinet Card, Victoria Claflin Woodhull, Female Candidate, President . . . . *Illus* 863.00
Cabinet Card, Waterspout Off Oak Bluffs, J.N. Chamberlain, Cottage City, Mass. 350.00
Cabinet Card, Yuma Indians, 3 Men, E.A. Bonine, 7 x 4 5/8 In. 530.00
Camera, Bolex, 16 mm Model 4, Lenses, 25 mm Switar, 16 mm & 75 mm Schneider 150.00
Camera, Brownie, No. 2, Eastman Kodak, Box, 6 In. 90.00
Camera, Eastman Kodak, 8 x 10 In. View, Model 2-D 115.00
Camera, Graflex 3Z Folmer & Schwing, Cooke F 4/5 Lens, c.1910 . . . . 45.00
Camera, Graflex Series B 2 1/4 x 3 1/4 In., Reflex, 5 1/2 In. Kodak F 4 1/2 Lens 69.00
Camera, Graflex, Wollensak Single Lens, Plane Shutter, c.1915, 5 x 7 In. 165.00
Camera, Kodak, Ektar, No. 3741, Black Leather-Covered, 2 Ektar Lenses, c.1945 . . . . 700.00
Camera, Kodak, Medalist I, 100 mm Ektar Lens, Camera Case 90.00
Camera, Kodak, Medalist II, 100 mm Ektar Lens, Camera Case 127.00
Camera, Kodak, Medalist II, Black Leather-Covered Body, Ektar 100 mm Lens, Case 100.00
Camera, Kodak, Target Six-20, Black Metal Box, 1946-52, 2 1/4 x 3 1/4 In. 30.00
Camera, Leica III, No. 164393, Chrome, Cristar F3.5 Lens, Case 200.00
Camera, Leica M2, No. 939667, Chrome, Leitz Summicron F2.5 Lens 590.00
Camera, Leica M5, 1:2/50 Lens, Black Body, Leather Case, Serial No. 1359368 . . . . 1840.00
Camera, Leica, 111c, Lenses, 90 mm Elmar, 35 mm Summaron, 135 mm Hektor 489.00
Camera, Leica, 111f, 50 mm F2 Summitar Lens, Leitz CAV00 Flash, Meter, Case 410.00
Camera, Leica, Reporter 250GG, No. 150129 . . . . 7265.00
Camera, Leitz, Super-Angulon F4 21 mm Lens 645.00
Camera, Multiscan Al-Vista 5B Panoramic, c.1905 . . . . 315.00
Camera, Nikon F2, Motor Drive, 3 Nikkor Lenses 645.00
Camera, Nikon N70 Outfit, 85 mm Nikon Lens, Filters, Converter, Bag, Flash 175.00
Camera, Nikon S, No. 60945161, Chrome, Red Dot, Nikkor S.C F1.5 5 Cm Lens 2705.00
Camera, Nikon S4, No. 6182355, Chrome, Red Dot, Nikkor C F3.5 Lens 705.00
Camera Case, Leitz, 5 Filters, 2 Film Cartridges 60.00
Carte De Visite, 2 Dogs, 1 Seated On Other, R.A. Miller, Boston 215.00
Carte De Visite, 2 Girls Seated By American Flag, c.1875 . . . . 65.00
Carte De Visite, 2 Men, 1 Pushing Wheelbarrow With Puppies 70.00
Carte De Visite, Abraham Lincoln & Son Thomas, c.1863 . . . . 75.00
Carte De Visite, Abraham Lincoln, The Martyr President, c.1865 . . . . 95.00
Carte De Visite, Andrew Johnson, Cabinet Members, c.1865 . . . . 75.00
Carte De Visite, Andrew Johnson, Seated In Brady Chair, c.1865 . . . . 135.00
Carte De Visite, Buffalo Bill, Wearing Coat With Fur Collar, 4 x 2 3/8 In. 230.00
Carte De Visite, Cemetery, Carbutt, Chicago 50.00
Carte De Visite, General Robert E. Lee, Without Beard, Union Case 345.00
Carte De Visite, General Ulysses Grant, Wearing Black Armband, c.1865 . . . . 125.00
Carte De Visite, Great Anaconda, Creature Of The Woods, McAllister & Bro. 75.00
Carte De Visite, Horace Greeley, c.1872 . . . . 70.00
Carte De Visite, John Wilkes Booth, c.1865 . . . . 125.00

Carte De Visite, John Wilkes Booth, Seated, Holding Cane, Tomlinson, Boston 240.00
Carte De Visite, Lincoln Mourning, Draped Public Building, Stein's, Ravenna, Ohio 250.00
Carte De Visite, Maggie Mitchell, c.1863 .... 65.00
Carte De Visite, Major General George A. Custer, 1865, 3 1/2 x 2 1/4 In. 920.00
Carte De Visite, Post Mortem, Baby, Mrs. Dr. J. Hitchcock, Canton, N.Y. 75.00
Carte De Visite, Ulysses Grant, Schuyler Colfax, 1868 .... 75.00
Carte De Visite, Young George A. Custer, Matthew B. Brady, 1864, 3 1/2 x 2 1/4 In. 1265.00
Daguerreotype, 2 Children, Hoop, S. Broadbent, Oval Mat, Full Case, 1/2 Plate 4100.00
Daguerreotype, 2 Scoundrels Getting Ready To Pour Another, Half Case, 1/6 Plate 90.00
Daguerreotype, 3 Surveyors With Level On Tripod, Leather Case, 1/4 Plate 1880.00
Daguerreotype, 3 Women Beside Ornate Column, Half Case, 1840s, 1/2 Plate 150.00
Daguerreotype, Australian Gentleman, 3/4 Profile, Mat, Case, 1/4 Plate 500.00
Daguerreotype, Boy Wearing Plaid Tunic, Lace Collar, 1/4 Plate 150.00
Daguerreotype, Child Seated, 1/6 Plate 160.00
Daguerreotype, Chilean Woman, Fancy Dress, Gilt, Leather Case, 1/4 Plate 1610.00
Daguerreotype, Dogs, One Playing Violin, Hand Colored, c.1850, 1/6 Plate, Pair 2530.00
Daguerreotype, Elderly Lady, Leather & Gilt Case, 1/6 Plate 40.00
Daguerreotype, Elderly Man, 1840, 1/6 Plate 20.00
Daguerreotype, Father & 2 Sons, Half Case, 1/4 Plate 90.00
Daguerreotype, French Girl, Hoop & Stick, Millet, Oval Frame, 1/2 Plate 650.00
Daguerreotype, Girl, Fur Hat, Winter Coat, 1/9 Plate 350.00
Daguerreotype, Husband & Wife, Embossed Gilt Case, Velvet, 1/2 Plate 259.00
Daguerreotype, Man, Bearded, Wearing Vest, Cravat, 1/6 Plate 40.00
Daguerreotype, Man, Holding Interesting Roll Of Paper, 1/6 Plate 150.00
Daguerreotype, Man, Top Hat, J. Gurney, 1/6 Plate............................... 485.00
Daguerreotype, Man, Top Hat, Seated, Littlefield Parsons Case, 1850s, 1/6 Plate 230.00
Daguerreotype, Man, Turned Eyes, Hand In Vest, Case, E. Jacobs, 1846, 1/6 Plate 1200.00
Daguerreotype, Man, With Cocked Hat, 1/6 Plate 130.00
Daguerreotype, Military, Lt. F. Wright, Hand Colored, Velvet Case, 1/4 Plate 315.00
Daguerreotype, Mother & 3 Well Dressed Daughters, 1/4 Plate 175.00
Daguerreotype, Mother & Daughter, Strong Lighting, Half Case, 1/6 Plate 75.00
Daguerreotype, Mother & Son, Tinted, Leather Case, c.1858, 1/4 Plate 2070.00
Daguerreotype, Mother, 2 Children, Leather Case, 1850s, 1/4 Plate 520.00
Daguerreotype, Mother, Child In Lap, Violet Background, Case, 1/4 Plate 1200.00
Daguerreotype, Newport Harbor, Fishing Boats, 1/2 Plate 1500.00
Daguerreotype, Post Mortem, Baby, With Rattle, Tinted, 1850s, Case, 1/6 Plate 400.00
Daguerreotype, Post Mortem, Woman, Half Case, 1850s, 1/6 Plate 375.00
Daguerreotype, Woman, Fancy Bonnet, 1/6 Plate 440.00
Daguerreotype, Woman, Fancy Cuffs, Ring, Earrings, Flower Vase Case, 1/6 Plate 225.00
Daguerreotype, Woman, In Dotted Dress, Drop Earrings, Brooch, 1/6 Plate 80.00
Daguerreotype, Woman, Wearing Day Cap, 1/6 Plate 150.00
Daguerreotype, Woman, Wearing Gilded, Pricked Jewelry, Half Case, 1/6 Plate 1200.00
Daguerreotype, Woman, With Braids Held By Comb, Case, 1/6 Plate 30.00
Daguerreotype, Young Woman, In Cap, Holding Book, Floral Case, 1/6 Plate 100.00
Daguerreotype, Young Woman, With Tinted Cheeks, 1/6 Plate 35.00
Glass Negative, Floral Scene, Distinction, Wallace Nutting, c.1930, 8 x 10 In. 225.00
Ivorytype, Boy, Blue Shirt, Red Curtain, B.F. Ferguson, Gilted Frame, Full Plate 1200.00
Ivorytype, Philadelphia Pioneer, McClees, Full Plate 2600.00
Magic Lantern, Brass, Tin, Pine Trunk, Wood Base, 17 1/2 x 14 3/4 In. 165.00
Magic Lantern, Ernst Plank, Brass Lens, Cylindrical Support, Slides, Box 380.00
Magic Lantern, Ernst Plank, Child's, Tinplate Body, Brass Lens, 12 Slides, Box, 11 In. ... 265.00
Magic Lantern, Kerosene Fired, Slides, Box, 9 x 12 In. 55.00
Magic Lantern, Tin Plate, Instructions, 11 In. 66.00
Mounting Iron, Better Pkgs Inc. Body Welder, Electric, Accessories, Box 55.00
Photograph, 1937 New York Black Yankees Team, 11 x 18 In. 1380.00
Photograph, 4 Military Drummers, Eagle Sword Belts, Frame, 13 x 16 In. 750.00
Photograph, Aloha, Washington, Lee Friedlander, Frame, 1967, 6 x 9 1/4 In. 4600.00
Photograph, Aspen, Colorado, Hand Colored, H.L. Standley, Frame, c.1925, 12 x 15 In. .. 45.00
Photograph, Baltimore Black Sox, Jud Wilson, 1923, 3 1/2 x 5 In. 1265.00
Photograph, Bermuda, H. Marshall Gardiner, c.1930, 9 x 7 In. 29.00
Photograph, Bermuda, House, Gated Entrance, c.1925, 9 x 7 In. 140.00
Photograph, Bikini Atoll Atomic Bomb Test, c.1946, 25 1/2 x 32 In. 95.00
Photograph, Birch Road, Hand Colored, Fred Thompson, Frame, c.1920, 12 x 10 In. 50.00

Photograph, Buckwood Inn, Shawnee On The Delaware, F. Radel, c.1920, 14 x 11 In. 80.00
Photograph, By The River, New England, David Davidson, Frame, c.1920, 12 x 10 In. . . .   22.00
Photograph, Calendar, Interior Scene, Frame, c.1931, 4 x 3 In. 190.00
Photograph, Canadian Rockies, Hand Colored, Byron Harmon, c.1920, 11 x 8 In. 35.00
Photograph, Canopied Road, Berkshire, Hand Colored, c.1935, 12 x 10 In. 70.00
Photograph, Chalet, Interior Scene, David Davidson, Mat, Frame, c.1935 . . . .   60.00
Photograph, Chapel San Juan, Calif., Charles Sawyer, Mat, Frame, 15 x 13 In. 140.00
Photograph, Charming Reflection, Girl, Garden Scene, Moran, c.1930, 10 x 12 In. 25.00
Photograph, Cinderella, Pretty Girl, Gene Pressler, c.1925 . . . .   24.00
Photograph, Covered Bridge, Hand Colored, Pedro Cacciola, c.1940, 8 x 10 In. 50.00
Photograph, Dante's Dream, After Dante Gabriel Rossetti, Black & White, 7 x 10 In. 45.00
Photograph, Decked As A Bride, Hand Colored, c.1925, 20 x 16 In. 59.00
Photograph, Dog Scene, New England, David Davidson, Frame, c.1935 . . . .   350.00
Photograph, Echo Lake, Hand Colored, Charles Sawyer, Frame, c.1920, 9 x 8 In. 55.00
Photograph, Elm & Bridge, Exterior Scene, c.1925 . . . .   210.00
Photograph, Ernest Brower's Sloop, Tammy, c.1910, 16 x 18 In. 90.00
Photograph, Evening Sunset, Florida, Hand Colored, E.G. Barnhill, c.1915, 10 x 8 In. 28.00
Photograph, Fireside Dreams, Interior, Fred Thompson, Frame, c.1925, 11 x 9 In. 80.00
Photograph, Florida Palm Scene, Hand Colored, James Harris, c.1930, 6 In. 55.00
Photograph, Florida Sunset Scene No. 3, Hand Colored, E.G. Barnhill, c.1920 . . . .   40.00
Photograph, Florida, Moss Covered Palm Tree, Heron, E.G. Barnhill, c.1920 . . . .   50.00
Photograph, Florida, Palm Trees, Water, Hand Colored, E.G. Barnhill, 3 1/2 x 10 In. 29.00
Photograph, Frosted Banks, Snow, Hand Colored, David Davidson, c.1925, 5 x 4 In. 120.00
Photograph, Fruit Luncheon, Mirror, Hand Colored, c.1925, 12 x 41 In. 190.00
Photograph, Girl, By House, Fred Thompson, c.1915, 5 x 9 In. 29.00
Photograph, Great Wayside Oak, Wayside Inn, Exterior, c.1935, 12 x 10 In. 140.00
Photograph, Heart Of Maine, New England Scene, Mat, Frame, c.1925, 7 In. 40.00
Photograph, Interior Scene, At The Fender, c.1935 . . . .   55.00
Photograph, Interior Scene, Hand Colored, Portsmouth N.H., c.1925, 9 x 7 In. 50.00
Photograph, James Joyce, Seated, Cane, Striped Tie, Jacket, Hat, c.1928, 14 x 11 In. 4485.00
Photograph, Josh Gibson, Josh The Basher, Sept. 3, 1943, Wright & Riley, 8 x 5 In. 4315.00
Photograph, Kent Fall, Conn., Hand Colored, Charles Sawyer, Mat, c.1920, 7 x 9 In. 88.00
Photograph, Lakota War Dance, Card Stock, D.F. Barry, 9 x 6 1/4 In. 1880.00
Photograph, Litchfield Minster, England, Mat, Frame, c.1925, 8 x 10 In. 59.00
Photograph, Living Emblem Of United States Marines, 1919, 13 x 10 In. 920.00
Photograph, Long's Peak, Colorado, Hand Colored, c.1925, 9 x 14 In. 25.00
Photograph, Margaier Valley, Wallace Macaskill, Nova Scotia, c.1925, 12 x 10 In. 29.00
Photograph, Midst The Flowers, Garden Scene, Moran, Frame, c.1935, 16 x 14 In. 94.00
Photograph, Mountain, Marmot Point, Mt. Rainier Natl. Park, Hand Colored, c.1925 . . . .   35.00
Photograph, Mt. Washington & Saco River, Charles Sawyer, N.H., c.1910, 9 x 6 In. 40.00
Photograph, Navajo Indian, Colored Frame, Signed Ford, 10 x 8 In. 46.00
Photograph, Norway, Maine, Charles Sawyer, Hand Colored, c.1970, 13 x 10 In. 35.00
Photograph, Pikes Peak, Colorado, From Palmer Park, c.1925, 11 x 9 In. 25.00
Photograph, Pilgrim Daughter, Massachusetts Interior Scene, c.1925, 15 x 12 In. 95.00
Photograph, Playing Cat's Cradle, David Davidson, Frame, c.1925, 13 x 16 In. 150.00
Photograph, Portland Head Light, Seascape, Arthur Ward, c.1925, 11 x 14 In. 129.00
Photograph, Puento Cabrill, Bridge, City Scene, M.L. Oakes, c.1925, 14 x 8 In. 40.00
Photograph, Rockbound Coast, Nova Scotia, Macaskill, Frame, c.1925, 20 x 16 In. 44.00
Photograph, Rodeo, 1st Annual Round-Up, Wichita, Kan., Frame, c.1920, 10 x 36 In. 546.00
Photograph, Saga Of The Sea, Lighthouse, Wallace Macaskill, c.1925, 11 x 14 In. 105.00
Photograph, Sailing Among Windmills, Holland, Frame, c.1925, 16 x 10 In. 556.00
Photograph, San Juan Capistrano Mission, Charles Sawyer, Frame, c.1925, 7 x 9 In. 55.00
Photograph, Satchel Paige, Kansas City Monarchs, 1942, 9 1/2 x 8 In. 1265.00
Photograph, Seascape, Charles Sawyer, New England, Frame, 6 x 4 In. 70.00
Photograph, Seashore, Breaking Waves, Sand Dune, c.1925 . . . .   25.00
Photograph, Sheep Scene, Fred Thompson, Frame, c.1925, 4 x 3 In. 105.00
Photograph, Shimmering Gold, Exterior Scene, Mat, c.1925, 15 In. 70.00
Photograph, Sir Wm. Johnson Parlor, Man, Red Jacket, Frame, c.1925, 16 x 13 In. 295.00
Photograph, Snow Basin, Canadian Rockies, David Davidson, c.1925, 5 x 7 In. 120.00
Photograph, Snow Scene, Massachusetts, c.1935, 11 x 9 In. 527.00
Photograph, Soldier's Farewell, American Flag, Fred Thompson, c.1915 . . . .   375.00
Photograph, South Grain Canon, Colorado, Hand Colored, c.1925, 12 x 15 In. 95.00
Photograph, Stagecoach, Longfellow's Home In 1820, LeBusch, Frame, 16 x 13 In. 105.00

Photography, Cabinet
Card, Victoria Claflin
Woodhull, Female
Candidate, President

Picture, Needlework, Cottage, Garden, Painted
Sky, Silk, Linen, England, 1931, 12 x 9 In.

Photograph, Stately Pines, Hand Colored, Willis A. Deane, c.1925, 13 x 11 In.	29.00
Photograph, Street Border, England, Hand Colored, c.1925, 1 x 12 In.	190.00
Photograph, Sunny Bower, California, Garden, c.1910, 11 x 14 In.	222.00
Photograph, Sunset Point, Signed, David Davidson, Mat, Frame, c.1935, 5 x 4 In.	40.00
Photograph, Surf At Pinnacle Rock, Seascape, Charles Sawyer, Frame, c.1925	150.00
Photograph, Swirling Seas, Seascape, Mat, Frame, c.1935, 20 x 16 In.	700.00
Photograph, Uncle Sam, Sunday Afternoon In The Old Home, c.1910, 16 x 12 In.	320.00
Photograph, Upper Winooski, Vermont, Frame, c.1925, 16 x 10 In.	199.00
Photograph, Veil Of Tighnnock, Charles Sawyer, Mat, c.1925, 13 x 16 In.	95.00
Photograph, Village Prattlers, David Davidson, c.1920, 13 x 16 In.	29.00
Photograph, Woodstock, Vt., Ivy Covered Porch, Girls, Frame, c.1925, 5 x 7 In.	40.00
Photograph, Wreck Of USS Maine, On Cardboard, c.1899, 10 x 8 In.	115.00
Photograph, Ye Olde Tyme Rose, Interior Scene, Fred Thompson, c.1915, 7 x 11 In.	59.00
Photograph, Yellowstone, Hand Colored, F. Jay Haynes, Frame, c.1925, 12 x 10 In.	45.00
Photograph, Young Child, Hand Colored, Isa Waugh, Frame, c.1900, 10 x 12 In.	35.00
Tintype, 4 Union Soldiers, 1/4 Plate	220.00
Tintype, African-American Woman With Flag, Hand Colored, 1/6 Plate, 1860s	11500.00
Tintype, American Indian Dignitary, Suit, 1/9 Plate	500.00
Tintype, Black Dog, Bowler Hat, Smoking Pipe, 1/16 Plate	106.00
Tintype, Cat, White, Lying Down, Mat, 1/8 Plate	115.00
Tintype, Early Currency, 3 Increments Of Paper Money, 1/4 Plate	562.00
Tintype, Elmwood Hotel, Waterville, Maine, 2 3/4 x 3 1/4 In.	374.00
Tintype, Man, Fishing Pole, Oval Frame, Full Plate	288.00
Tintype, Pennellograph, Soldier With Pistol & Musket, Frame, 1860, Whole Plate	2070.00
Tintype, Sisters, Sitting In Chairs, Griswold Patent Plate, Full Case, 1/6 Plate	160.00

PIANO BABY is a collector's term. About 1880, the well-decorated
home had a shawl on the piano. Bisque figures of babies were designed
to help hold the shawl in place. They range in size from 6 to 18 inches.
Most of the figures were made in Germany. Reproductions are being
made. Other piano babies may be listed under manufacturers' names.

Baby Sucking Toe, Naked, Lying On Back, Gebruder Heubach, c.1915, 7 In.	1008.00
Crawling, Bisque, Gebruder Heubach, Germany, 9 In.	400.00
Crawling, Gebruder Heubach, 6 1/2 In.	200.00
Lying Down, Bisque, Gebruder Heubach, Germany, 8 In.	400.00
Lying On Tummy, Painted Eyes, 17 In.	270.00
One Shoe Off, One Shoe On, Germany, c.1910, 12 In., Pair	560.00

PICKARD China Company was started in 1898 by Wilder Pickard.
Hand-painted designs were used on china purchased from other
sources. In the 1930s, the company began to make its own china wares
in Chicago, Illinois. The company now makes many types of porcelains, including a successful line of limited edition collector plates.

Chocolate Set, New Iris Conventional, Frederick Lindner, c.1903, 4 Piece	1495.00
Plate, Roses, Mark 7, Challinor, 8 5/8 In.	390.00
Punch Bowl, Grape, Coufall, T&V Limoges, c.1905, 11 In.	865.00
Sugar & Creamer, Grape Design, Yellow Ground, Louise	75.00

Tankard, Purple Grapes, Erhardt Seidel, Chicago, c.1905, 15 In. 1150.00
Tankard, Red Poppies, T&V Limoges, c.1905, 10 1/4 In. 1150.00
Vase, Carmen, Red Poppies, Jacob Kiefus, D&C, France, c.1905, 13 1/2 In. 575.00

PICTURE FRAMES are listed in this book in the Furniture category under Frame.

PICTURES, silhouettes, and other small decorative objects framed to
hang on the wall are listed here. Sandpaper pictures are black and
white charcoal drawings done on a special sanded paper. Some other
types of pictures are listed in the Print and Painting categories.

Charcoal, Sandpaper, Tomb & Residence, Washington, Mandaw Griffith, 14 x 18 In. 1955.00
Charcoal, Sandpaper, Washington's Tomb At Mount Vernon, M. Belknap, 17 x 22 In. 1035.00
Chromolithograph, Battle Of Princeton, Louis Kurz, Mat, Frame, c.1911, 26 x 33 In. 230.00
Diorama, 18th Century English Bookseller Shop, N. Thorne, Shadowbox, 11 x 15 In. 960.00
Diorama, Day At The Races, Narcissa Thorne, Shadowbox Frame, 15 x 11 1/2 In. 720.00
Diorama, Japanese Interior, Narcissa Thorne, Shadowbox Frame, 14 1/2 x 17 1/2 In. 359.00
Diorama, Paper Seascape Background, Shell Frame, 19th Century, 10 In. 225.00
Diorama, Ship, 2-Masted, Black Hull, Full Sail, Shadowbox Frame, 13 x 21 In. 920.00
Drawing, For Stained Glass Window, Angel, Charcoal, Ink, On Paper, 1920s, 42 x 30 In. .. 460.00
Drawing, Pencil, Farm Scene, House, Barns, Picket Fence, Hills, Trees, Frame, 17 x 21 In. 980.00
Eglomise, Landscape, Continental, 48 x 10 In. 239.00
Embroidery, Crewel, Bird On Branch, Flowers, Pa., Frame, Late 1700s, 15 x 15 1/2 In. ... 1725.00
Embroidery, Jacob, Leah, Rachel, Silk, Amy Ann Tillinghast, R.I., c.1810, 16 x 21 In. ... 9775.00
Embroidery, Woman, In Boat, Swordsman, Helen Cuthbert, Frame, 1816, 22 x 28 In. 2070.00
Etched Glass, Folk Landscape, Horse, Tree, House, Placed On Velvet, Frame, 13 x 13 In. . 1380.00
Etching, Broadstreet, N.Y., Leon Louis Dolice, Frame, c.1935, 9 x 13 In. 47.00
Etching, St. Paul's From Ludgate Hill, Alphege Brewer, Frame, c.1935, 11 x 18 In. 55.00
Gouache, On Board, Encampment Along The Nile, Paul Pascal, 1901, 12 x 17 1/2 In. 2760.00
Gouache, On Paper, Dancer, Warren B. Davis, Signed, c.1910, 5 1/2 x 4 In. 690.00
Gouache, On Paper, Ship Portrait, Alfrata, Hermaphrodite Brig, Funno, 16 x 24 In. 3565.00
Gouache, On Silk, Chinese Ancestor, Noblewoman, Tiger Skin, 54 x 37 In. 175.00
Graphite, On Paper, Young Man, Frame, 19th Century, 5 x 3 In. 18.00
Ink, Watercolor On Paper, Construction Site, Frank Perri, c.1940, 14 x 20 In. 235.00
Needlework, 3-Masted Ship, British Colonial Flag, Frame, 19th Century, 17 x 20 In. 865.00
Needlework, 10 Noble Figures, Pavilion, Frame, Japan, 1700s, 24 1/2 x 58 1/2 In. 980.00
Needlework, Achsah, Marriage To Othniel, Silk, Mass., 1805, 16 3/4 x 22 In. 9775.00
Needlework, Appliqued, Linen, E Pluribus Unum, Eagle, Flag, Banner, Frame, 29 x 5 In. . 1155.00
Needlework, Cottage, Garden, Painted Sky, Silk, Linen, England, 1931, 12 x 9 In. ... *Illus* 200.00
Needlework, Embroidered, Painted Silk, Wool, Late 19th Century, 17 1/2 x 14 1/4 In. 353.00
Needlework, Embroidered, Silk, Maiden, Giltwood Frame, c.1775, 14 x 11 In. 500.00
Needlework, Flowers, Fruit, Cattails, Ink Label, Columbus, O., Gilt Frame, 11 x 9 In. 630.00
Needlework, Kneeling Woman, Silk, Reverse Painted Glass Frame, Chinese, 16 x 14 In. .. 1035.00
Needlework, Map, England, Wales, Flower Border, Linen Ground, Signed Kensit, 27 In. .. 840.00
Needlework, Memorial, Maria Davis, Mass., c.1827, 18 x 17 In. 3335.00
Needlework, Panel, Silk, Embroidered, Woman, Sheep, Landscape, Oval, 24 x 19 In. 980.00
Needlework, Rose Vine Border, Weeping Willows, Chester County, Pa., c.1828 .... 3760.00
Needlework, Silk Threads, Native American, Eglomise Mat, Frame, c.1800, 11 x 8 In. 880.00
Needlework, Silk, 9 Noble Figures, Outdoors, Circular, Frame, Japan, 1800s, 21 1/2 In. .. 690.00
Needlework, Silk, American Eagle, Banner, Inscribed, Frame, Japan, c.1900, 24 x 18 In. .. 375.00
Needlework, Silk, Bird, Lotus, Frame, c.1900, 42 x 10 In. 230.00
Needlework, Silk, Ink, Architectural Ruins, Maple Frame, 9 In., Pair 345.00
Needlework, Silk, Woven, Toilet Of Venus, France, 19th Century, 7 x 5 1/2 In. 105.00
Needlework & Watercolor, Woman, Children, A. Bradford, Mass., 1813, 22 1/4 x 24 In. .. 6573.00
Pastel, Camping, 2 Men, Campfire, Lake, Andrew Gunderson, Frame, c.1900, 28 x 10 In. . 120.00
Pastel, Cottage, Oval, Late 19th Century, 6 3/4 x 5 In. 200.00
Pastel, Cows, Tree Lined Stream, William Henry Chandler, Frame, c.1900, 26 x 16 In. ... 275.00
Pastel, Lake & Mountains, Harry Linder, Frame, 1886-1931, 17 1/2 x 23 1/2 In. 605.00
Pastel, Landscape, Boats, Tree Lined Lake, William H. Chandler, c.1900, 20 x 10 In. 105.00
Pastel, Landscape, Evening, House On Lake, William H. Chandler, Frame, 20 x 16 In. 80.00
Pastel, Landscape, Lakeside, Trees, Boulders, W.H. Chandler, c.1900, 7 x 18 In. 129.00
Pastel, Landscape, Path, Lake, House, William H. Chandler, Frame, c.1900, 24 x 12 In. ... 110.00
Pastel, Portrait, Miss Myra Paine, Young Girl, White Print Dress, Frame, 18 x 14 In. 115.00
Pastel, Seascape, Crashing Waves, Shoreline, William H. Chandler, c.1900, 20 x 16 In. ... 190.00
Pastel, Still Life, Fruit, Decorated Jar, William H. Chandler, c.1900, 20 x 16 In. 199.00

Pen & Ink, Horse, Black Horse, Ornate Saddle, Black Molded Frame, 9 In. 1035.00
Pencil, On Paper, Baling Cotton, Black Men, Waiting For Riverboat, 20 x 16 In. 240.00
Pinprick, Watercolor, African American, Colonial Clothing, Dancing, Frame, 10 x 7 In. . . . 400.00
Portrait, Ancestral, Seated Male, Female, Chinese, Giltwood Frame, Pair, 67 x 44 In. 2530.00
Portrait, Ancestral, Watercolor, Chinese, Frame, 20th Century, 33 x 40 In., Pair 375.00
Reverse Painted, On Glass, Mount Vernon, River, Boat, Trees, Frame, 6 x 8 In. 550.00
Reverse Painted, On Glass, Woman, Yellow Dress, Coral Necklace, 9 x 7 In. 315.00
Sandpaper, Landscape, Hudson River Style, 21 x 31 In. 690.00
Sandpaper, Train, Landscape, Trestle Bridge, Train, Billowing Smoke, Frame, 10 x 14 In. . 173.00
Scroll, Official Seated On Throne, Ink & Color, On Silk, 19th Century, 55 x 33 In. 748.00
Scroll, Scene, 2 Monkeys Gathering Honey, Ink, On Silk, Chinese, 32 x 19 In. 1528.00
Silhouette, Dr. & Mrs. Gallupe, 2 Children, W.H. Brown, Frame, 1845, 17 x 15 In. 3105.00
Silhouette, Full-Length, Sea Captain, Red & Gold Telescope, Samuel Metford, 12 x 8 In. . 2760.00
Silhouette, Gentleman, Holding Letters, Herve, Maple Veneer Frame, 14 x 10 3/4 In. 805.00
Silhouette, Girl By Birdbath, W. Nutting, E.J. Donnelly, New Frame, c.1927, 4 x 4 In. 45.00
Silhouette, Girl On Bench, W. Nutting, E.J. Donnelly, Oval Frame, c.1927, 3 x 4 In. 22.00
Silhouette, Man & Woman, Portrait, India Ink, Gilt Frame, 5 3/4 x 4 7/8 In., Pair 430.00
Silhouette, Miniature, Hollow Cut, Ziba Westcott Kellum, Frame, 10 x 6 In. 460.00
Silhouette, Portrait, Full-Length, Double, Cutout, Rebecca Greening, c.1857, 13 In. 520.00
Silhouette, Portrait, Hollow Cut, Edward Brook, Aged 16, Mat, Gilt Frame, 6 x 5 1/4 In. . . 431.00
Silhouette, Portrait, Hollow Cut, Girl, Doll, Signed, Edouart, 1842, 10 x 8 In. 4715.00
Silhouette, Portrait, Hollow Cut, Girl, Parasol, Cat, Edouart, 1842, 10 x 10 In. 6210.00
Silhouette, Portrait, Hollow Cut, Man, Gilt Frame, 7 1/2 x 6 1/2 In. 115.00
Silhouette, Portrait, Hollow Cut, Man, Inked Hair, Scarf, Lapels, Gilt Frame, 5 5/8 x 5 In. . 430.00
Silhouette, Sea Captain, Telescope, Rhode Island, 1843, 11 x 8 In. 2760.00
Silhouette, Young Man, Holding Top Hat, Hubard, Rosewood Frame, 1800s, 16 x 12 In. . . 805.00
Theorem, Basket Of Fruit, Watercolor, Velvet, Eglomise Mat, Frame, 1800s, 13 x 21 In. . . 705.00
Theorem, Bird On Basket Of Fruit, Corner Blocks, Frame, D. Ellinger, 24 x 27 In. 4950.00
Theorem, Bowl With Fruit & Blue Bird, D. Ellinger, Grain Painted Frame, 22 x 24 In. 6050.00
Theorem, Compote Of Fruit, Bird, Painted Frame, W. Rank, Velvet, 1900s, 26 x 26 In. . . . 1150.00
Theorem, Eagle, Stars, Banner, B. Rank, Red & Black Sponged Frame, 14 x 12 In. 580.00
Theorem, Flower Basket, Adelia Howes, Velvet, Frame, 1823, 15 x 17 1/2 In. 2185.00
Theorem, Fruit Basket, Bird, Brown Grained Frame, Velvet, 18 x 22 In. 2645.00
Theorem, Great Horned Owl, Oak Tree, Sponge Painted Frame, B. Rank, 13 3/8 x 11 In. . . 715.00
Theorem, Hen On Nest, Bill Rank, Red & Black Sponged Frame, 14 3/4 x 12 3/4 In. 220.00
Theorem, Rooster, On Mound, D. Ellinger, Brown Grain Painted Frame, 10 x 8 In. 3300.00
Theorem, Spray Of Flowers, Watercolor, Velvet, Frame, 19th Century, 20 x 19 In. 705.00
Theorem, Still Life, Grapes, Peaches, Gold Velvet, Sophia Sewall, Gilt Frame, 14 x 17 In. . 575.00
Theorem, Vase, Blue Rings, Butterflies, Birds, J.W. Zook, Frame, 1864, 20 x 17 In. 460.00
Theorem, Velvet, Floral Bouquet, Signed, Laura Taylor, 15 x 13 In., Pair 405.00
Theorem, Watercolor, Basket, Stenciled Grapes, Peaches, Walnuts, Frame, 15 x 19 In. 920.00
Theorem, Watercolor, Fruit Basket On Table, Paper, Frame, 1800s, 16 x 18 In. 1880.00
Theorem, Watercolor, On Paper, Flower Basket, Yellow, Red, Blue, Green, 10 x 13 In. 375.00
Theorem, Watercolor, Pen, Ink, Velvet, Fruit Basket, Bird, Butterfly, 1800s, 15 x 17 In. . . . 3525.00
Theorem, Watercolor, Still Life, Fruit, Frame, 13 1/2 x 18 3/4 In. 6780.00
Theorem, Watercolor, Yellow & White Roses, Blue Tulips, Molded Frame, 8 x 6 1/4 In. . . . 776.00
Tray, Needlework, Oak, Blue & White, Birds & Flowers, Frame, 12 x 22 In. 12.00
Wall Hanging, Aluminum, Etched, Painted, Olivier Seguin, c.1971, 47 3/8 x 63 In. 4185.00
Watercolor, Battery View, Houses, Edith Francis Marsden, Frame, 19 x 24 In. 290.00
Watercolor, British Warship, Frederick Schiller Cozzens, 1800s 1380.00
Watercolor, Church, Graveyard, Signed, H. Matlack, Feb. 18 1845, 7 1/4 x 9 In. 1035.00
Watercolor, Ciscoe, Great Lakes Steamship, Lorian, Ohio, 25 1/2 x 38 1/2 In. 920.00
Watercolor, Ink, Alligator, With Seal, Paper, Frame, 1800s, 6 1/2 x 7 1/2 In. 940.00
Watercolor, Logging Camp, A. Bailey & Co. Camp Rifle River, Mich., 1873, 10 x 15 In. . . 2185.00
Watercolor, Near The Foothills, Pasture, Hills, Phillip A. Butler, Frame, 17 x 22 In. 259.00
Watercolor, Pulling Anchor, Moray Firth, Michael Brown, 11 x 16 1/4 In. 1955.00
Watercolor, Zebra In Colored Land, Juliet Kepes, c.1943, 19 x 22 In. 825.00
Watercolor & Gouache On Board, Happy Family, Clara Elsene Peck, c.1930, 21 x 9 In. . . 345.00
Watercolor & Gouache On Paper, David Street, Jerusalem, Lucien W. Powell, 25 x 19 In. 1955.00
Watercolor & Ink, True Lover's Knot, Lines, Written Sentiments, Frame, 12 x 11 In. 805.00
Watercolor On Ivory, Joseph De Beauharnais, Frame, 7 x 5 In. 575.00
Watercolor On Ivory, Velazquez & His Troops, Frame, 3 1/4 x 4 In. 660.00
Watercolor On Lined Paper, Birds, Tulip, Primary Colors, Painted Frame, 6 x 8 In. 1265.00

Watercolor on Silk, Floral, Chinese School, Signed, Artist's Seal, 1900s, 10 x 12 In. 52.00
Wax, Silhouette, Portrait, Officer & Lady, Georgian, Oval, 7 x 6 In., Pair 865.00
Wood, Inlaid, Woman, Holding Cigarette, Art Nouveau, France, Frame, 18 x 13 In. 940.00
Wood Engraving, Net Mending, Toulon, Clare Leighton, 1926, 9 1/4 x 7 1/2 In. 390.00

PIERCE, see Howard Pierce category.

PIGEON FORGE Pottery was started in Pigeon Forge, Tennessee, in 1946. Red clay found near the pottery was used to make the pieces. Molded or thrown pottery with matte glaze and slip decoration was made. The pottery closed in 2000.

Bowl, Orange Red High Glaze, Marked E. Wilson, 2 3/4 In. 35.00
Bowl, Volcanic Glaze, Red, Green, Curdling, Douglas Ferguson, 3 x 12 1/2 In. 184.00
Vase, Black Scratched To White, Marked, 5 1/4 In. 35.00

PILKINGTON Tile and Pottery Company was established in 1892 in England. The company made small pottery wares, like buttons and hatpins, but soon started decorating vases purchased from other potteries. By 1903, the company had discovered an opalescent glaze that became popular on the Lancastrian pottery line. The manufacture of pottery ended in 1937. Pilkington's Tiles Ltd. has worked from 1938 to the present.

Chalice, Royal Lancastrian Luster, 2 Handles, Painted Motto, c.1910, 9 1/2 In. 3625.00
Charger, Lancastrian, Ship, Earthenware, Richard Joyce, 1907, 10 In. 1440.00
Vase, Lancastrian, Sea Maidens, Walter Crane, Richard Joyce, c.1906, 10 3/8 In. 6600.00
Vase, Royal Lancastrian Luster, Mouse In Leaves, W.S. Mycock, c.1914, 6 3/4 In. 1639.00
Vase, Royal Lancastrian, Gold Luster, Red Flowers, Monogram, c.1915, 4 1/2 In. 940.00
Vase, Royal Lancastrian, Luster, Lavender Flowers, Red Coiled Ground, 5 7/8 In. 320.00

PINCUSHION DOLLS are not really dolls and often were not even pincushions. Some collectors use the term *half-doll*. The top half of each doll was made of porcelain. The edge of the half-doll was made with several small holes for thread, and the doll was stitched to a fabric body with a voluminous skirt. The finished figure was used to cover a hot pot of tea, powder box, pincushion, whisk broom, or lamp. They were made in sizes from less than an inch to over 9 inches high. Most date from the early 1900s to the 1950s. Collectors often find just the porcelain doll without the fabric skirt.

Arm Extended, Holding Flower, Stroked Hair, Hat, Bow, Bodice, 5 In. 224.00
Arms Close, Holding Tennis Racket, Head Band, No. 14508, 4 1/4 In. 22.00
Arms Extended, Art Deco, Gold Hair & Trim, 3 In. 105.00
Arms Extended, Holding Letter, Long Curls, Dressel & Kister, 4 1/2 In. 225.00
Arms Extended, Stroked Hair, Long Curls, Large Bonnet, Dressel & Kister, 4 3/4 In. 280.00
Arms Extended, Stroked Hair, Ruffled Hat, Dressel & Kister, 3 3/4 In. 280.00
Arms Extended & Crossed, Headdress, Karl Schneider, 5 In. 365.00
Blue Blouse, Gray Hair, Germany, c.1910, 4 1/2 In. 530.00
Brown Hair, Green Gown, Germany, c.1910, 6 In. 450.00
Carmen, Open & Returning Arm, Lace Mantilla, 6 In. 336.00
Chocolate Lady, Holding Tray, Cups, Hat, Bodice, 5 1/2 In. 560.00
Chocolate Lady, Holding Tray, Open & Returning Arms, Goebel, 3 1/2 In. 336.00
Closed Arms, Folded Hands, Black, Gold Trim, 2 In. 45.00
Egyptian, Nude, Arms Extended, Red Hat, Karl Schneider, 3 3/4 In. 225.00
Flapper, Arms Extended, Hat, Finger Ring, 3 1/2 In. 225.00
Flowing Hair, Pink Bonnet, Germany, c.1910, 4 1/2 In. 530.00
Gazing Into Mirror, Gray Hair, Flowers, Germany, c.1900, 7 In. 925.00
Gloves, Yellow Bonnet, Germany, c.1910, 5 In. 250.00
Holding Mirror, Flower, Bodice, Volkstedt Rudolstadt, 5 In. 280.00
Josephine Baker, Nude, Arms Extended, Jewelry, 3 1/2 In. 140.00
Miss Columbia, Extended Arms, Flowing Hair, 8 In. 106.00
Nightclub Entertainer, Karl Schneider, 4 1/2 In. 505.00
Nude, Arms Extended, Hair In Bun, Yellow Comb, 4 3/4 In. 125.00
Nude, Arms Extended, Holding Apple, Bonnet, Dressel & Kister, 3 1/4 In. 179.00
Nude, Arms Extended, Holding Flowers, Goebel, 3 1/2 In. 110.00
Nude, Arms Extended, Long Curls, Flowers, Ribbon, Goebel Jenny Lind, 6 In. 336.00

Nude, Arms Extended, Stroked Hair, Bow, Gold Comb, Dressel & Kister, 5 1/2 In. 310.00
Nude, Arms Extended, Stroked Hair, Dressel & Kister, 3 1/2 In. . . . . .84.00 to 280.00
Nude, Arms Extended, Stroked Hair, Hat With Flowers, Dressel & Kister, 3 In. 56.00
Nude, Arms Extended, Stroked Hair, Headband, Dressel & Kister, 4 1/2 In. 280.00
Nude, Open & Returning Arm, Gold Hairband, Blue Beads, Dressel & Kister, 4 In. 224.00
Nude, Open & Returning Arm, Holding Letter, 3 In. 34.00
Nude, Open & Returning Arms, Flower, 4 1/2 In. 84.00
Nude, Purple Turban, Germany, c.1910, 4 1/4 In. 390.00
Open & Returning Arm, Cloth Flowers, Hat, Plumes, Bodice, 5 3/4 In. 280.00
Open & Returning Arm, Fan, Hair Comb, Dressel & Kister, 5 3/4 In. 560.00
Open & Returning Arm, Flower, Rose Bodice, Goebel Jenny Lind, 5 1/2 In. 420.00
Open & Returning Arm, Holding Puppy, 3 3/4 In. 56.00
Pierrette, Folded Hands, Black Cap, Nude, 3 1/2 In. 20.00
Purple Turban, Tray, Germany, c.1910, 5 1/4 In. 670.00
Serving Tea, Goebel, Germany, c.1910, 6 In. 840.00
With Tray Of Fruit, Germany, c.1910, 5 In. 590.00
Woman, Holds Arms Out, Painted Hair, 3 1/2 In. 138.00
Woman, Madame Pompadour Style, Bisque, Germany 45.00
Woman, Medieval, Parrot, Pointed Hat, Germany, c.1910, 4 1/2 In. 505.00
Woman, Molded Hair, Painted Corset, Goebel, c.1926, 5 1/4 In. 104.00
Woman, Unjointed Arms Extended, Hat, Ribbon & Bow Trim, 3 1/2 In. 286.00
Woman, Wide Brim Hat, Striped Bodice, Germany, c.1910, 6 In. 448.00

PINK SLAG pieces are listed in this book in the Slag Glass category.

PIPES have been popular since tobacco was introduced to Europe by
Sir Walter Raleigh. Carved wooden, porcelain, ivory, and glass pipes
may be listed here.

Clay, Aly Sloper's Head, Red Nose, 5 1/2 In. 33.00
Clay, Bear, Sitting On Branch, 5 1/2 In. 140.00
Clay, Child Sitting On Potty, Mon Quin Petit Quin, 3 3/4 In. 50.00
Clay, Crystal Palace, Embossed, 7 1/2 In. 35.00
Clay, Dick Whittington, Leaning On Bowl, Black, John Palmer, England, 4 1/2 In. 45.00
Clay, Eagle's Claw Holding Bowl, Metal Mount, No Stem, 3 In. 20.00
Clay, Greyhound Head On Hunting Horn, No Stem, A. Stomer, 3 In. 55.00
Clay, Hand Holding Face Jug, No Stem, 2 1/2 In. 20.00
Clay, Nun's Head Shape Bowl, No Stem, Gambier, Paris, 2 1/4 In. 127.00
Clay, Santa Claus Head, Merry Christmas, Happy New Year, 8 In. 35.00
Clay, Skull Shape Bowl, No Stem, Gambier, Paris, 2 1/4 In. 110.00
Clay, Whole Dam Family, 5 Figures On Stem, Red, 5 1/2 In. 20.00
Glass, Free-Blown, Looping, Marbries, Red & White, 13 In. 365.00
Meerschaum, Rampaging Buffalo, 2 Indian Chiefs, Tomahawks, Amber, 9 1/2 In. 745.00
Porcelain, Character, Barmaid, Wood Stem, 10 In. 300.00
Porcelain, Regimental, 1 Artillery, 3 Company, Artillery Scene, c.1885, 84 In. 405.00
Porcelain, White Bowl, Hand Painted Ship, Realen, Full Sail, Inscription, c.1852, 5 In. . . . 175.00
Stoneware, Serpent, Coiled, Salt Glazed, Brown, England, c.1800, 6 1/2 In. 720.00
Wood, Bear, Seated, Legs Crossed, Smoking Pipe, Switzerland, c.1900, 2 x 6 1/2 In. 240.00
Wood, Bearded Man's Head, Deer's Head, Dog's Head, Stand, American, 1800s, 8 In. 765.00
Wood, Natural Branch, Carved, Man Riding Alligator, Brass Wire Reins, 10 1/2 In. 400.00

PISGAH FOREST pottery was made in North Carolina beginning in
1926. The pottery was started by Walter B. Stephen, who had been
making pottery in that location since 1914. The pottery continued in
operation after his death in 1961. The most famous kinds of Pisgah
Forest ware are the cameo type with designs made of raised glaze and
the turquoise crackle glaze wares.

Jar, Blue Crackle Glaze, Handles, 1940, 6 x 6 1/2 x 6 In. 200.00
Mug, Rooster, Blue Matte Glaze, Cameo, 1950, 3 3/4 In. 460.00
Vase, Aunt Nancy, 3 Handles, Turquoise Runny Glaze, 5 1/2 In. 288.00
Vase, Blue, White, Yellow Crystalline Glaze, Flared Rim, 9 1/2 In. 1880.00
Vase, Cameo, Wagon Train, Blue Background, Turquoise, 11 1/2 In. 825.00
Vase, Cameo, Wagon Train, Brown Background, Turquoise, Swollen Form, 6 1/2 In. 825.00
Vase, Crystalline Glaze, 6 In. 115.00
Vase, Green, Pink Matte Glaze, Bulbous, 6 1/2 In. 235.00

Vase, Green, Yellow Crystalline Glaze, Marked, Shouldered, 7 In.	705.00
Vase, White, Yellow, Crystalline Glaze, Bulbous, 5 1/2 In.	470.00

PLANTERS PEANUTS memorabilia is collected. Planters Nut and Chocolate Company was started in Wilkes-Barre, Pennsylvania, in 1906. The Mr. Peanut figure was adopted as a trademark in 1916. National advertising for Planters Peanuts started in 1918. The company was acquired by Standard Brands, Inc., in 1961. Standard Brands merged with Nabisco in 1981. Some of the Mr. Peanut jars and other memorabilia have been reproduced and, of course, new items are being made.

Ashtray, Mr. Peanut, Gold Tone, 50th Anniversary, 1906-1956, 5 1/2 x 5 In.	100.00
Bank, Hat Reads Mr. Peanut, Turn Hat To Open, Plastic, 1950s, 8 1/2 x 3 1/2 In.	75.00
Bank, Mr. Peanut, Figural, Plastic, c.1990, 8 1/2 In.	45.00
Book, Happy Time Paint, Story Of Planters Peanuts, Photographs	20.00
Bracelet, 5 Charms, Metal, Plastic, 1960s	30.00
Charms, Mr. Peanut, Plastic, 1950s, 2 1/8 In.	15.00
Coloring Book, Mr. Peanut's 12 Month, c.1970, 8 1/2 x 5 In.	12.00
Cup, Mr. Peanut Face, Top Hat, Pink, 1950s	30.00
Decals, Mr. Peanut, Nylon, Stick-On, 2 1/2 In., 40 Piece	25.00
Display, Stand-Up, c.1970, 4 Ft.	39.00
Display Stand, Chocolate Peanuts, Tin Lithograph, 14 x 8 1/2 x 4 1/2 In.	880.00
Jar, 1940 Leap Year Commemorative, Rectangular, 9 In.	52.00
Jar, 75th Anniversary Edition, 1981, 8 In.	18.00
Jar, Barrel Shape, 12 In.	384.00
Jar, Cover, Football, Peanut Handle, 9 x 8 x 7 In.	297.00
Jar, Embossed Peanut Corners, 13 In.	181.00
Jar, Octagonal, Glass, Embossed Lettering & Figures On All Sides, 8 x 12 In. . . . . . .66.00 to 154.00
Knife, Mr. Peanut, Red, Plastic, 1950-60, 6 3/4 In.	9.00
Measuring Cup, Pennant Salted Peanuts, Mr. Peanut, Tin, 2 3/4 x 1 3/4 In.	290.00
Patch, Mr. Peanut, Cloth, 1970s, 2 1/2 In.	8.00
Pen, Mr. Peanut On Barrel, Blue, Bic, 1970-80, 6 In.	10.00
Pen, Mr. Peanut, Planters Snacks, Metal, Retractable, Ballpoint, c.1970, 5 1/4 In.	20.00
Pin, Mr. Peanut, 75th Anniversary, 1906-1981, Gold Tone, 1 In.	22.00
Pin, Mr. Peanut, Red, Plastic, Stickpin, 1 In.	14.00
Razor, Mr. Peanut On Handle, Bic, 1970s	8.00
Salt & Pepper, Mr. Peanut, Pink, Plastic, 3 In.	28.00
Salt & Pepper, Red, Box, Mailing Label From Planters Nut & Chocolate Co.	20.00
Salt & Pepper, Tan, Black, Plastic, 4 In.	25.00
Serving Set, Serving Bowl, 6 Bowls, 6 & 3 In., 7 Piece	45.00
Sign, 5 Cents A Bag, Red, White, Reverse-Painted Glass, Frame, 22 1/2 x 20 1/2 In.	170.00
Spoon, Mr. Peanut, Green, Plastic, 1950s	8.00
Straw, Mr. Peanut, Plastic, 1970, 8 In.	13.00
Tennis Ball, Mr. Peanut, Dunlop, 1970-80	10.00
Tin, Jumbo, Blanched, Salted, Oval Brand, 10 Lb.	136.00
Tin, Mr. Peanut Center, 3 1/2 In. Diam.	7.00
Tin, Pennant, 10 Lb., 10 In.	33.00
Tin, Salted Peanuts, 11 In.	125.00
Transfer, Mr. Peanut, Iron On, 1970s, 9 In.	12.00
Whistle, Mr. Peanut, Blue, Plastic, Figural, 1970s	6.00

PLASTIC objects of all types are being collected. Some pieces are listed in other categories; gutta-percha cases are listed in photography, celluloid in its own category.

Plate Set, Gray, Turquoise, Green, Yellow, Boonton, Melmac, Child's, 2 In., 6 Piece . *Illus*	15.00
Switch Plate Cover, Steve McQueen On Motorcycle, 1968, 2 x 7 In.	55.00

PLATED AMBERINA was patented June 15, 1886, by Joseph Locke and made by the New England Glass Company. It is similar in color to amberina, but is characterized by a cream colored or chartreuse lining (never white) and small ridges or ribs on the outside.

Bowl, Amber Ribs, 5 In.	3450.00
Creamer, Applied Amber Handle, 2 1/2 In.	8625.00

<table>
</table>

Plastic, Plate Set, Gray, Turquoise, Green, Yellow,
Boonton, Melmac, Child's, 2 In., 6 Piece

Political, Button, Anderson, Breaking Away,
Independent, Badge-A-Minit, 1980

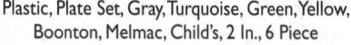

Finger Bowl, Ruffled Edge, Crimped Rim, 5 1/2 In.	6615.00
Lemonade, Amber Handle, 5 In.	4313.00
Pitcher, Amber Handle, 8 In.	38525.00
Pitcher, Water, 12 Protruding Amber Ribs, Amber Handle, Ruffled Rim, 6 1/2 In.	9775.00
Punch Cup, Barrel Shape, Amber Loop Handle, Folded-In Rim, 2 1/2 In.	3220.00
Sugar, 12 Mahogany Protruding Ribs, Amber Handles, 2 1/4 x 6 1/4 In.	9775.00
Toothpick, 2 1/4 In.	16100.00
Toothpick, Barrel Shape, 9 Ribs, 2 3/8 In.	8050.00
Tumbler, 3 3/4 In.	1840.00 to 3335.00
Vase, Lily, Amber Foot, 8 1/8 In.	4600.00
Vase, Lily, Amber Raised Disc Foot, 9 5/8 In.	6900.00

POLITICAL memorabilia of all types, from buttons to banners, is collected. Items related to presidential candidates are the most popular, but collectors also search for material related to state and local offices. Memorabilia related to social causes, minor political parties, and protest movements are also included here. Many reproductions have been made. A jugate is a button with photographs of both the presidential and vice presidential candidates. In this list a button is round, usually with a straight pin or metal tab to secure it to a shirt. A pin is brass, often figural, sometimes attached to a ribbon.

Ashtray, FDR Bust, Metal, Heart, Spade, Diamond, Club Cigarette Rests, 6 x 4 1/2 In.	50.00
Ashtray, U.S. Presidents To Johnson, 1966, 8 In.	19.00
Autograph, John F. Kennedy, Testimonial Dinner Program, April 19 1958, 10 x 7 In.	98.00
Badge, Benjamin Harrison, Levi Morton, Brass Shell, 1888	275.00
Badge, Democratic National Convention Alternate, San Francisco, 1920, 3 3/4 x 1 3/4 In.	48.00
Badge, Harrison, Morton, 1860, 3 In.	2132.00
Badge, LBJ In Garbage Can, Dump Johnson In 68, 2 1/2 x 2 1/4 In.	50.00
Badge, Truman, Philadelphia, 3 1/2 In.	152.00
Ballot, Buchanan, Black, White, Paper, 7 In.	424.00
Ballot, Election, South Africa, Independent Electoral Commission, April 27, 1994	10.00
Ballot, Grover Cleveland, Thomas Hendricks, Presidential Election, 1884, 3 x 7 3/4 In.	36.00
Ballot, Hayes, Black, White, Paper, 4 1/2 In.	55.00
Ballot, James Blaine, John Logan, Presidential Election, 1884, 6 1/2 x 13 In.	65.00
Ballot, O'Connor, J.Q. Adams, Third Party, Paper, 6 In.	75.00
Ballot, Rutherford Hayes, William Wheeler, Presidential Election, 1876, 10 1/2 x 3 3/4 In.	135.00
Ballot, Sample, Help President Kennedy, 1963, 8 1/4 x 11 In.	40.00
Ballot, Winfield Hancock, William English, Presidential Election, 1880, 3 1/2 x 8 1/2 In.	90.00
Bandanna, Blaine, Logan, Eagle, Red Border, Cloth, 1884, 19 1/2 x 18 In.	335.00
Bandanna, Cleveland, Thurman, Cloth, Red Ground, 1888	152.00
Bandanna, Dwight Eisenhower, 1952, 26 x 26 In.	50.00
Bandanna, Garfield, Arthur, Red, Black, White, Portraits, 1880, 19 x 22 In.	480.00
Bandanna, Gen. Ben. Harrison, 1888, 21 1/2 x 25 In.	1389.00
Bandanna, Harrison, Morton, Flags, Stars, Blue Ground, 1888, 22 x 21 In.	493.00
Bandanna, Nixon, Inaugural, 1969, By Frankie Welsh, Alexandria, Va., 11 x 8 1/2 In.	30.00
Bandanna, Theodore Roosevelt, Battle Flag, Cotton, 1912, 24 x 21 In.	375.00

Banner, Cleveland, 3 Stars, Blue, White, Red, Cloth, 24 x 18 In. 259.00
Banner, Hoover, Curtis, Vote Every Eagle, 4 More Years, Cloth, 30 x 115 In. 3174.00
Banner, McKinley, Patriotism, Protection, Prosperity, Frame, 1897, 12 3/4 x 19 1/2 In. 863.00
Banner, U.S. Grant, Schuyler Colfax, 1868, 12 1/2 x 16 1/2 In. 1191.00
Banner, Wendell Willkie, God Bless America, 1940, 5 x 6 1/4 In. 118.00
Banner, Win With Willkie, Square Deal, Rayon, 6 In. 15.00
Banner, Winfield Scott, William Graham, Preservation Of Union, 1852, 14 1/2 x 19 In. ... 4400.00
Bell, Porcelain, Old & Young Woman, Votes For Women, Arcadian China, 4 In. 2050.00
Bobbin' Head, Donkey, Kennedy For President, Japan, 7 1/2 x 2 1/2 x 3 1/4 In. 512.00
Book, Democratic National Convention, Philadelphia, 1936, 14 x 11 In., 396 Pages 41.00
Book, Republican National Convention, Cleveland, 1936, 14 x 11 1/2 In., 236 Pages 41.00
Booklet, LaFollette, Wheeler, Why People Cannot Support Davis, Coolidge, 5 x 8 1/2 In. . 40.00
Booklet, Meet Mr. Landon, Black, Green, 1936, 40 Pages 18.00
Booklet, Sweep The Country, Fireside Election Battle, 50 Cents, 1936, 11 x 8 1/2 In. 25.00
Bottle, Bryan, Sewall, Amber, Silver Dollar, Portrait, In Silver We Trust, 1896 .... 1340.00
Box, Notions, Lincoln, Lithograph Under Glass, 4 x 1 In. 4934.00
Bracelet, Charm, Goldwater, Bottle 10.00
Brush, William Henry Harrison, Wood, 1840, 13 3/4 In. 5096.00
Bumper Sticker, I'm The Watergate Bug, Bug Picture, c.1974, 12 In. 1.95
Bumper Sticker, Ike & Dick, I'm A Tennessee Democrat, Red, White, Blue, 4 x 9 In. 15.00
Bumper Sticker, McGovern, Shriver, 1972, 12 In. 1.95
Button, Adlai Stevenson, Our Next President, 1 1/4 In. 10.95
Button, Adlai Stevenson, Red, Cream, Blue, Black, Easel, Hanger Back, 1950s, 9 In. 51.00
Button, Adlai Stevenson, Red, White, Blue, 3 1/2 In. 49.00
Button, Al Smith, Donkey, Derby, Blue, Brown, Enamel, Brass, 1 In. 45.00
Button, Alfred E. Smith, For President, 1928, 7/8 In. 39.00
Button, Alice Roosevelt, Multicolored, Celluloid, 1 1/4 In. 45.00
Button, Anderson, Breaking Away, Independent, Badge-A-Minit, 1980 .... *Illus* 106.00
Button, Anderson, For President, 1980, 1 3/4 In. 4.95
Button, Anti-Nixonites For Nixon, Lithograph, 1 3/4 In. 3.95
Button, Bill Clinton, 1990 Governor, Red, White, Blue Celluloid, 3 In. 116.00
Button, Bill Clinton, Lover Of Cheeseburgers, Multicolored, Celluloid, 2 x 3 In. 150.00
Button, Bryan, Clean Sweep For Democracy, Bryan, Kern, 1908, 1 1/4 In. 645.00
Button, Bryan, Kern, Jugate, Celluloid, Patriotic Shield, Stars, Torch, 1908, 1 3/4 In. 4620.00
Button, Bryan, Lind, Stevenson, Trigate, Sepia, Celluloid, 1900, 1 1/4 In. 581.00
Button, Bryan, Sewall, Jugate, Washington, D.C., Celluloid, 1 3/4 In. 75.00
Button, Bryan, Stevenson Cornucopia, Photo, Color, 1 3/4 In. 1595.00
Button, Bryan, Stevenson, My Choice, Sepia, 1 3/4 In. 1219.00
Button, Bury Goldwater In 1964, 3 1/2 In. 15.00
Button, Charles E. Hughes, For Governor, 1906, 7/8 In. 29.00
Button, Chester Bowles For President, Red, White, Blue, Black, Celluloid, 3 In. 200.00
Button, Cleveland Needs Ness For Mayor, Red & White, Celluloid, 1947, 7/8 In. 160.00
Button, Clinton, Gore, Jugate, Multicolored, Celluloid, 1992, 2 1/4 In. 249.00
Button, Clinton, Man On Moon, Multicolored, Celluloid, No. 6, 2 1/4 In. 666.00
Button, Clinton, Vote Democratic Punch 10, Multicolored, Celluloid, 3 In. 85.00
Button, Clinton, Whistle Stop Tour, Blue, White, 2 1/2 In. 20.00
Button, Clinton-Gore Oval Office, Red, White, Blue, Yellow, Celluloid, 2 3/4 In. 110.00
Button, Coolidge & Dawes, 1924, 7/8 In. 80.00
Button, CORE, NAACP, Desegregation Of Schools, c.1960, 1 1/4 In. 65.00
Button, De Berry For President, 1964, 1 1/4 In. 8.00
Button, Deadheads For Dukakis, Red, White, Blue, Celluloid, 1988, 2 3/8 In. 325.00
Button, Debs, Harriman, Jugate, Red Ground, Celluloid, 1900, 1 1/4 In. 3872.00
Button, Debs, Harriman, Jugate, Shield, Celluloid, 1900, 1 1/4 In. 2795.00
Button, Dewey For President, Blue, White, 3 1/2 In. 23.00
Button, Dewey, Bricker, Labor, Red, White, Blue, 3 1/2 In. 55.00
Button, Dewey, Bricker, Red, White, Blue 7.00
Button, Dewey, Warren, Jugate, Red, White, Blue, 3 1/2 In. 45.00
Button, Dewey, Wren, 1948, Jugate, Photo Of Both, Red, White & Blue, 3 1/2 In. 550.00
Button, Dr. Silas C. Swallow, For President, Sepia, Celluloid, 1904, 1 3/4 In. 342.00
Button, Dukakis, Bentsen, Jugate, Red, White, Blue, Black, Celluloid, 1988, 3 In. 215.00
Button, Dukakis, Bentsen, Party Of Inclusion, Nov. 8, 1988, Jugate, 1 1/4 In. .... *Illus* 85.00
Button, E.V. Debs, B. Hanford, Jugate, 1908, 7/8 In. 725.00
Button, Eugene Debs, Convict, For President, Red, Black, White, Celluloid, 1920, 1 In. .. 880.00

Political, Button, Dukakis,
Bentsen, Party Of Inclusion, Nov.
8, 1988, Jugate, 1 1/4 In.

Political, Button, Johnson,
Humphrey, Vote Democratic,
Cord, Easel Back, 1964, 9 In.

Political, Button, Let Them Eat
Jellybeans, Anti-Ronald Reagan,
1981, 1 1/2 In.

Button, Eugene Debs, We Want Debs, Red, White, Celluloid, 7/8 In.	535.00
Button, Eugene McCarthy Staff, Blue, White, Celluloid, 1968, 2 1/2 In.	20.00
Button, FDR, Cardboard, War Medal, 1944 Convention, Chicago, Ribbon	52.00
Button, FDR, Inauguration Picture, 1933, 1 1/4 In.	284.00
Button, FDR, Sepia, Celluloid, Red, White, Blue, Gold, Ribbon, 1944	67.00
Button, FDR, Vote The New Deal, 1936, 3 1/2 In.	798.00
Button, Flying High With George Bush, Red, White, Blue, Yellow, Celluloid, 3 In.	60.00
Button, Franklin D. Roosevelt, For President, V, 1944, 1 1/4 In.	38.00
Button, Franklin Roosevelt, Gold, Black, Celluloid, 6 In.	470.00
Button, Gen. Dwight D. Eisenhower, Red, White, Blue, 1 1/4 In.	14.00
Button, George Ryan For Governor, Blue, Black, White, Celluloid, 1 3/4 x 2 3/4 In.	88.00
Button, George W. Bush, Rick Perry, Inauguration, Red, White, Blue, Black, 3 1/2 In.	85.00
Button, George Wallace, Lurleen Wallace, Celluloid, 2 1/4 In.	455.00
Button, Goldwater For Nixon Lodge, Celluloid, 1960, 1 3/4 In.	150.00
Button, Goldwater For President, William Miller, Rectangular, 2 3/4 x 1 3/4 In.	8.00
Button, Goldwater In 64, 1 1/4 In.	15.00
Button, Goldwater, Hotwater, Bread 'n Water, 3 1/2 In.	13.00
Button, Goldwater, Vote In '64, 1 1/4 In.	5.00
Button, Grant, Colfax, Jugate, Ferrotype, Brass Rim, Round, 1868, 1/2 In.	595.00
Button, Greeley, Acts Not Words, Ferrotype, Brass Shell Frame, 1872, 1 1/2 In.	4959.00
Button, Greeley, Brown, Ferrotype, Round, 1872, 3/4 In.	5950.00
Button, Harry S. Truman For President, Celluloid, 1948, 7/8 In.	605.00
Button, Harry S. Truman, Inauguration, 1949, 1 3/4 In.	70.00
Button, Harry Truman, 1948, 1 1/2 In.	110.00
Button, Harry Truman, Red, White, Blue, Gold, Black, Celluloid, 9 In.	347.00
Button, Hearst For President, Black, White, Celluloid, 1932, 7/8 In.	368.00
Button, Henry Wallace, Coattail, African-American Candidate, 1948, 1 1/2 In.	506.00
Button, Herbert Clark Hoover, For President, 1928, 7/8 In.	69.00
Button, Herbert Hoover For President, Celluloid, 4 In.	736.00
Button, Herbert Hoover, Celluloid Ribbon Backing, 1928, 3/4 In.	70.00
Button, Hoover For President, Black, White, Celluloid, 2 1/4 In.	25.00
Button, Hoover, Curtis For All Of U.S., Celluloid, 1928, 1 1/4 In.	639.00
Button, Hoover, Picture, 1 3/4 In.	220.00
Button, Hoover, Pull First Lever, Vote Republican, Celluloid, 1932, 3 1/2 In.	60.00
Button, Hughes & Fairbanks, Pictured Together, Celluloid, 1916, 1 3/4 In.	650.00
Button, Hughes Notification, Celluloid, September 16, 1908, 1 1/4 In.	880.00
Button, Hughes, Photograph, Red, White, Blue Border, 1916, 7/8 In.	170.00
Button, Humphrey For President, 1960, 2 1/4 In.	9.00
Button, Humphrey Wobble Eyes, Nixon, Red, White, Blue, Black, Celluloid, 3 1/2 In.	200.00
Button, Humphrey, Muskie To Make Needed Change, Dark, Light Blue, Celluloid, 1 In.	220.00
Button, I Don't Want Eleanor Either, 7/8 In.	13.00
Button, I Like Ike, Celluloid, 1952, 2 1/8 In.	605.00
Button, I Would Row Wilson & Marshall To Victory, 1 1/4 In.	3736.00
Button, I'm For Hubert In 68, LBJ, Red, White, Blue, Celluloid, 2 1/4 In.	495.00
Button, I'm Gone For John, Black, White Celluloid, 1960, 3 1/2 In.	4590.00
Button, If I Were 21, I'd Vote For Kennedy, Lithograph, 4 In.	9.00

Button, Ike, Nixon, Red, White, Blue, 3 1/2 In. 50.00
Button, Ike, Red, Blue, Black, Celluloid, America's Dairyland, Ribbon, 1953, 3 1/2 In. ... 120.00
Button, Ike, Red, White, Blue, 3 1/2 In. 7.00
Button, Ike, Remember 1912, Blue & White, Celluloid, 1952, 3 1/2 In. 249.00
Button, Ikke I Kvell, Yiddish, Blue & Cream, 2 1/4 In. 330.00
Button, It's Bobdolzilla, Bob Dole As Godzilla Wrecking Hollywood, 2 x 3 In. 179.00
Button, It's Magic, Magic Johnson For Clinton, Gore, Red, Black, Celluloid, 3 1/2 In. 334.00
Button, Jack Once More In 64, Red, White & Blue, Celluloid, Photo Of Kennedy, 4 In. ... 4690.00
Button, James M. Cox For President, Celluloid, 1 1/4 In. 605.00
Button, James M. Cox, Right Man, Wrong Time, Celluloid, 1920, 1 3/4 In. 635.00
Button, James M. Cox, Round, 1920, 1 1/4 In. 628.00
Button, JFK, Man For The 60s, Black, White, 3 In. 15.00
Button, Jimmy Carter, Mr. Peanut On Roller Skates, Hat, Monocle, Black, White, 2 In. ... 177.00
Button, Jimmy, Peanut In Background, 1 3/4 In. 6.00
Button, Joe & I For Willkie, Joe Louis, 1 1/4 In. 557.00
Button, John Garner, Lithograph, 1940, 1/2 In. 23.00
Button, John Nance Garner, Cactus Jack, Rider, Horse, Blue, White, Celluloid, 1941, 2 In. ... 296.00
Button, John W. Davis, For President, 1924, 4 In. 4927.00
Button, John William Davis, For President, 1924, 1 1/4 In. 1455.00
Button, Johnson, Humphrey, Eagle, Rectanglular, Star Border, 2 1/2 In. 9.00
Button, Johnson, Humphrey, Kennedy, N.Y. Senate Coattail, Celluloid, 1964, 3 1/2 In. ... 30.00
Button, Johnson, Humphrey, Vote Democratic, Cord, Easel Back, 1964, 9 In. .... *Illus* 25.00
Button, K For Kennedy, Robert Kennedy Staff, Enamel, Red, White, Blue, Silver, 7/8 In. . 60.00
Button, Keep Coolidge, Keystone Shape Around Picture, 1924, 7/8 In. 69.00
Button, Keep Coolidge, Red, White, Blue, Celluloid, 4 In. 1080.00
Button, Keep Coolidge, Round, 1924, 3 1/2 In. 5026.00
Button, Kennedy For President, 2 In. 29.00
Button, Kennedy In 1980, 1 1/4 In. 2.00
Button, Kennedy, America Needs Kennedy, 1960, 3 1/2 In. 666.00
Button, Kennedy, Vote For, AFL, Essex County C.O.P.E., 1960, 3 1/2 In. 6869.00
Button, LaFollette Committee '48, Blue, White, Celluloid, 1 1/4 In. 164.00
Button, Landon, Knox, Sunflower, Jugate, 2 1/8 In. 4926.00
Button, LBJ Go Away, 1 1/4 In. 4.00
Button, LBJ In 64, 7/8 In. 7.00
Button, LBJ, Support Johnson & Civil Rights, Portrait, Flag, 1964, 3 In. 1495.00
Button, Let Them Eat Jellybeans, Anti-Ronald Reagan, 1981, 1 1/2 In. .... *Illus* 50.00
Button, March On Washington, Jobs & Freedom, 1963, 2 1/4 In. 80.00
Button, McGovern, Shriver, Vote Democratic, Jugate, 1972, 1 3/4 In. .... *Illus* 14.00
Button, McKinley & Roosevelt, Ribbon Ground, Celluloid, 1900, 7/8 In. 50.00
Button, McKinley Eclipsing Bryan, Celluloid, May 1900, 1 1/4 In. 3146.00
Button, McKinley For President, 1896, 3 1/2 In. 1984.00
Button, McKinley, 7/8 In. ....15.00 to 28.00
Button, McKinley, Roosevelt, Jugate, 1900, 1 1/4 In. 2245.00
Button, McKinley, Roosevelt, Jugate, Red & White Stripes, Blue, 1900, 1 1/2 In. 364.00
Button, McKinley, Teddy Roosevelt Riding Elephant, 1900, 1 3/4 x 2 1/2 In. 1122.00
Button, McKinley, Teddy Roosevelt, Horseback, Celluloid, 1 3/4 In. 314.00

Political, Button, McGovern,
Shriver, Vote Democratic, Jugate,
1972, 1 3/4 In.

Political, Button, Nixon's The
One, 1968, 1 1/2 In.

Political, Button, Nixon, Lodge,
Experience Counts For A Better
America, Jugate, 2 1/2 In.

Political, Button, Students For
Kennedy, Tin Lithograph, 1960

Political, Button, Suffrage
Means Prohibition, Blue,
Gold, 5/8 In.

Political, Button, Votes For
Women, Green, Black, White,
Gold, 1 In.

Button, Move Over For Kefauver, Blue, White, Celluloid, 2 1/2 In. 128.00
Button, National Urban League, Racial Equality, Civil Rights, 1960, 1 1/4 In. 40.00
Button, Nebraska Traveling Men's Bryan Club, Photo, Celluloid, 1 1/4 In. 370.00
Button, Nixon Scranton In '64, Red, White, Blue, 1964, 7 In. 35.00
Button, Nixon's The One, 1968, 1 1/2 In. ....*Illus* 55.00
Button, Nixon, Agnew, Uncle Sam, 1972, 1 In. 5.00
Button, Nixon, Lodge, Cooper, Dickey, Coattail, 1 In. 365.00
Button, Nixon, Lodge, Experience Counts For A Better America, Jugate, 2 1/2 In. .... *Illus* 52.00
Button, Nixon, Peace, Prosperity, Blue, White, 1972, 1 1/4 In. 5.50
Button, Nixon, Potesta, Red, White, Blue, Celluloid, Coattail, 1972, 3 In. 327.00
Button, Nixon, Reagan, V.P. Hopeful, Red, White, Blue, Celluloid, 3 1/2 In. 41.00
Button, Nixon, Why Relish It, 1 1/4 In. 6.00
Button, No Man Is Good Three Times, 1940, 1 1/4 In. 12.95
Button, No Third Term, Blue, White, 1 In. 6.00
Button, Our Next President, Roosevelt, 1912, 7/8 In. 79.00
Button, Pat For First Lady, Lithograph, 1960, 2 1/4 In. 8.00
Button, Phooey On Dewey, Celluloid, 1948, 1 1/4 In. 50.00
Button, Poor People's Campaign, March On Washington, 1968, 3 1/2 In. 65.00
Button, Reagan California Delegation, 1980 GOP Convention, Multicolored, 4 In. 1185.00
Button, Republicans For McCarthy, Lithograph, 1 3/4 In. 1.00
Button, Right On, Right On, Black Panther, c.1968, 1 1/4 In. 10.00
Button, Robert F. Kennedy For President, Red, Blue, Black, 1968, 1 3/4 In. 5.00
Button, Roosevelt Bull Moose, Progressive Party, Celluloid, 1912, 1 1/2 In. 480.00
Button, Roosevelt, Curley, Economic Security, Mass., 2 1/4 In. 345.00
Button, Roosevelt, Garner, 7/8 In. 40.00
Button, Ross Perot, Knocking Down Republican, Democrat Pillars, Multicolored, 2 x 3 In. 95.00
Button, Say No To Monopolies, Vote Communist Twigg & Berlin, 1970s, 1 3/4 In. 115.00
Button, Score Against Hitler, Ban On Negro Players, Red, White, Blue, 1 1/4 In. 3050.00
Button, Seymour, Ferrotype, Scalloped Frame, 1868, 1/2 In. 345.00
Button, Smith, Robinson, Brown Derby, Round, 4 In. 7690.00
Button, SNCC, Racial Harmony, Civil Rights, c.1963, 2 1/4 In. 75.00
Button, Sock It To 'Em Spiro, 1 3/4 In. 7.00
Button, Stephen A. Douglas, Ferrotype, Oval, 1860, 1 1/2 x 1 In. 7935.00
Button, Stevenson, Straight Democratic, Red, White & Blue, 4 In. 485.00
Button, Stevenson, Vote Straight Democratic, Red, White, Blue & Black, 1952, 3 1/2 In. .. 445.00
Button, Strom Thurmond, Save The Constitution, 1968, 1 In. 13.00
Button, Students For Kennedy, Tin Lithograph, 1960 ....*Illus* 12.00
Button, Suffrage Means Prohibition, Blue, Gold, 5/8 In. ....*Illus* 748.00
Button, Taft, Sepia, Celluloid, 2 1/4 In. 68.00
Button, Taft, Sherman, Lady Liberty, Jugate, 1 3/4 In. 872.00
Button, Taft, Sherman, Roscoe Conklin, Jugate, Unconditionals, 1 1/4 In. 877.00
Button, Teddy Roosevelt, America Demands Him, Celluloid, 1912, 2 In. 2258.00
Button, Teddy Roosevelt, Buffalo League, Sepia, 2 1/8 In. 516.00
Button, Teddy Roosevelt, Fairbanks, Eagle, Jugate, Celluloid, F.F. Pulver Co., 1904, 1 In. .. 1645.00
Button, Teddy Roosevelt, Fairbanks, Shield, Jugate, Celluloid, 1 1/4 In. 1598.00
Button, Teddy Roosevelt, First Voters Club, 1904, 1 In. 79.00

Button, Teddy Roosevelt, Flag Ribbon, Whitehead & Hoag Back Paper, 3 1/4 In. 140.00
Button, Teddy Roosevelt, Georgia Day, Celluloid, 1907, 2 1/8 In. 1150.00
Button, Teddy Roosevelt, Hat In The Ring, Celluloid, Frame, Rosette, Ribbons, 1 1/4 In. . . 935.00
Button, Teddy Roosevelt, Hat Is In The Ring, Celluloid, 1912, 1 In. 1936.00
Button, Teddy Roosevelt, Remember San Juan Hill, Celluloid, 1 3/4 In. 2146.00
Button, Teddy Roosevelt, Rough Rider Uniform, Sepia, 1 1/4 In. 560.00
Button, Teddy Roosevelt, Square Deal, Black, Blue, White, Celluloid, 7/8 In. 130.00
Button, Teddy Roosevelt, Sunrise, Uncle Sam Tips Hat, Rising Sun, 1 1/4 In. 270.00
Button, Teddy Roosevelt, The People's Choice, Black, White, Celluloid, 7/8 In. 180.00
Button, Teddy Roosevelt, Uncle Sam, 3 1/2 In. 159.00
Button, Theodore Roosevelt For President, San Juan Hill, 1904, 1 1/4 In. 865.00
Button, Theodore Roosevelt, Charles Fairbanks, 1904, 1 1/4 In. 175.00
Button, Theodore Roosevelt, Flags & Eagle, Celluloid, 1904, 1 1/4 In. 930.00
Button, Theodore Roosevelt, Rough Rider L.A. Times, Celluloid, 1 1/4 In. 1145.00
Button, To Hell With Wallace, 1968, 3 1/2 In. 7.00
Button, Truman, Barkley, 3/4 In. 39.00
Button, Truman, Crossed Flags, Celluloid, 3 1/2 In. 259.00
Button, Virginia Citizens Love The Reagans In '80, 2 1/4 In. 8.00
Button, Vote For America First, Wilson, Marshall, Jugate, 7/8 In. 70.00
Button, Vote For Women's Suffrage, Black, Yellow, Celluloid, 1 1/4 In. 248.00
Button, Vote Nixon Lodge, Blue, White, 1960, 1 In. 20.00
Button, Vote Truman For President, Celluloid, Red, White, Blue, Black, 9 In. 1430.00
Button, Votes For Women, Green, Black, White, Gold, 1 In. . . . . *Illus* 345.00
Button, Walter Johnson For Congress, Red, White, Blue, Celluloid, 7/8 In. 297.00
Button, Warren G. Harding, For President, 1920, 1 1/4 In. 827.00
Button, Warren G. Harding, For President, Blue Ground, 1920, 7/8 In. 39.00
Button, Washington Sweepstakes, Wendell, Franklin, Eleanor, 1 1/4 In. 13.00
Button, We Want Mamie, 1 1/4 In. 25.00
Button, Welcome Charles Lindbergh, Black, White, Celluloid, Ribbon, 1 3/4 In. 296.00
Button, William H. Taft, For President, 1912, 7/8 In. 59.00
Button, William H. Taft, I'm For Playgrounds, Black, White, Celluloid, 7/8 In. 212.00
Button, William Howard Taft Trumpeter, 1 3/4 In. 605.00
Button, William Howard Taft, James Sherman, 1908, 7/8 In. 80.00
Button, William Jennings Bryan, 1896, 7/8 In. 49.00
Button, William Jennings Bryan, 1908, 7/8 In. 69.00
Button, William Jennings Bryan, Adlai Stevenson, Constitution & Flag, 1900, 1 1/4 In. . . . 90.00
Button, William Jennings Bryan, Arthur Sewall, 16 To 1, 1896, 7/8 In. 80.00
Button, William McKinley, 1896, 7/8 In. 39.00
Button, William Randolph Hearst, For Governor, 1906, 7/8 In. 39.00
Button, Win With Wilson, 1912, 7/8 In. 59.00
Calendar, Franklin & Eleanor Roosevelt, 1937, 23 1/2 x 15 In. 205.00
Calendar, Send John Ashbrook To Congress, 4 Panels, 4 Years, 1960-67 . . . . 22.00
Candle, Nixon Caricature, Unused 20.00
Cane, William McKinley, Eagle, Streamer, Protection Prosperity, 1896, 35 In. 222.00
Card, Female Suffragist For Warden, c.1905, 3 3/4 x 2 1/4 In. 45.00
Card, Henry Ford, America Needs This Man In The U.S. Senate, 4 In. 352.00
Card, Hold To Hoover, He's Leading Us Out Of The Depression, 1932, 5 1/2 x 4 1/2 In. . . . 12.95
Card, John F. Kennedy, Appearance, San Francisco, 1960 . . . . 45.00
Card, Senator John F. Kennedy, Gold Embossed Senate Seal, c.1958 . . . . 65.00
Certificate, Poll Watcher, Kennedy, Johnson, 1960, 11 x 14 In. 30.00
Chamber Pot, Lincoln Bedroom, Maddocks Lamberton Works, 9 In. . . . . *Illus* 1530.00
Charm, Blaine, Logan, Openwork Frame, 1884, 1 x 1 In. 198.00
Charm, Blaine, Logan, Portraits 68.00
Charm, Cleveland, Hendricks, Eagle Hanger 53.00
Charm, Harrison, Morton 69.00
Cigar Band, American Citizen Cigars, George Washington, c.1900, 6 In. 5.00
Cigarette Pack, Stevenson For President, Red, White, Blue . . . . .30.00 to 55.00
Clicker, Click With Dick, Red, White 12.00
Clock, Alarm, McKinley, Roosevelt, Spanish American War Heroes, 5 In. 1107.00
Coaster, Willkie, Metal, Red, White, Blue, 1940, 3 In. 30.00
Coin, Flipping, Roosevelt, Parker, 1904, 1 1/4 In. 25.00
Coin Holder, Humphrey, Muskie, Plastic, Coin-A-Reddy, Hillsdale, N.J., 1968, 3 x 4 In. . . 9.75
Dart Board, Stick Dick, Nixon Caricature, Administration Failures, Red, Blue, Cork 22.00

Political, Hat, Fedora,
Franklin Roosevelt,
Felt, Stamped FDR
In Sweatband

Political,
Chamber Pot,
Lincoln Bedroom,
Maddocks Lamberton
Works, 9 In.

Decal, Windshield, Truman, Black, Yellow, 7 1/2 In. 60.00
Door Hanger, Ronald Reagan, George Bush, Prouder, Stronger, Better, 1980, 12 In. 3.00
Eyeglasses, Goldwater, Die Cut, Cardboard, 1964, 2 In. 17.00
Fan, I Am A Landon & Bricker Fan, Save America, Paper, 14 In. 65.00
Fan, I'm An Ike, Jenner & Craig Fan, Wooden Stick, 12 1/2 In. 18.00
Fan, Washington To Coolidge Panels, 14 1/2 In. 40.00
Ferrotype, Douglas, Johnson, Portrait Each Side, Brass Frame, 1860, 1 In. 503.00
Ferrotype, Lincoln, Hamlin, Gilt Brass Frame, Pierced For Ribbon Hanger, 1860, 1 In. ... 1093.00
Ferrotype, Lincoln, Hamlin, Portrait Each Side, Brass Frame, Round, 1860, 1 In. 2248.00
Ferrotype, Lincoln, Hamlin, Portrait Each Side, Red Composition Frame, 1860, 1 1/4 In. . 2645.00
Figure, Elephant, Cast Iron, Red Blanket, G.O.P., Willkie, 1940, 6 In. 136.00
Figure, Elephant, Nixon, Agnew On Sides, Frankoma Pottery, 1969 .... 22.00
Flag, Car, Kennedy, Johnson, Plastic, 2-Sided, 1960, 10 In. 17.00
Flag, Lincoln, Hamlin, Red, White, Blue, Anchors, 1909, 1 1/2 x 2 3/4 In. 518.00
Flag, McKinley For President, Prosperity For All, Accordion Fold, 66 x 19 In. 330.00
Flasher, I Like Ike, 2 1/2 In. 13.00
Flasher, I'm For Nixon, 1960, 2 1/2 In. 9.00
Flasher, Kennedy For President, He Will Win, 2 1/4 In. 33.00
Gallery Pass, Congress Session To Decide 1876 Presidential Election 225.00
Game, Spinner, White House McKinley, Bryan, TR, Dewey, Croaker, 4 1/2 x 4 1/2 In. ... 23.00
Goblet, Greeley, Brown, Glass, 1872, 6 1/2 In. 2777.00
Handkerchief, Benjamin Harrison, Red, White, Blue, Silk, Flag, Stars, 15 1/2 In. 230.00
Handkerchief, Theodore Roosevelt, Charles Fairbanks, Cotton Muslin, 1904, 18 x 18 In. .. 65.00
Handkerchief, Wm. McKinley, G. Hobart, Sound Money, Square, 1896, 17 In. 89.00
Hanger, Wall, FDR, Eagle, USA, Raised, Metal, 11 In. 110.00
Hat, Convention, Kennedy, Johnson, 1960 .... 25.00
Hat, Convention, Nixon, Lodge, 1960 .... 20.00
Hat, Fedora, Franklin Roosevelt, Felt, Stamped FDR In Sweatband .... *Illus* 8526.00
Hat Band, Votes For Women, Black On Yellow, 1 1/2 x 23 In. 145.00
Hat Pin, Crowing Rooster, Promoting Democratic Candidates, c.1880 .... 65.00
Invitation, Inaugural Ball, Ronald Reagan, George Bush, 1981, 5 1/2 x 7 1/2 In. 25.00
Invitation, Inauguration, Eisenhower, Nixon, 1953 .... 100.00
Invitation, Inauguration, Governor John Connally, Preston Smith, Austin Texas, 1963 .... 45.00
Invitation, Inauguration, Kennedy, Johnson, 1961 .... 140.00
Invitation, Inauguration, Truman, Barkley, 1949 .... 150.00
Invitation, Official Kickoff Of Nixon For Governor, Engraved Card, Embossed, 1961 .... 100.00
Invitation, William Clinton, Albert Gore, Inauguration, 1993, 8 1/2 x 11 In. 30.00
Keychain, Ike, January 20, 1953 .... 5.00
Label, Cigar Box, American Citizen Cigars, George Washington, c.1900, 4 1/4 x 4 1/4 In. . 13.00
Label, Cigar Box, American Citizen Cigars, George Washington, c.1900, 9 x 6 1/4 In. 25.00
Label, Cigar Box, Commander Cigars, General John Pershing, c.1918, 9 x 7 In. 39.00
Label, Cigar Box, Mark Twain Cigars, Scenes From Youth, c.1910, 9 x 7 In. 37.00
Label, Cigar Box, Old Hickory Cigars, Andrew Jackson, c.1900, 9 x 6 1/2 In. 25.00
Lantern, Clay Forever, Punched Tin, 12 1/2 In. 3368.00
Lapel Stud, Harrison, Blue Ground, Enamel, Scalloped Border 60.00
Letter, Alton Parker, Portrait, Signed, 1907, 8 1/2 x 11 In. 136.00
Letter, Teddy Roosevelt, N.Y. Governor Letterhead, Signed, 1900, 8 x 6 In. 369.00
License Plate Attachment, Alf Landon, Aluminum, Aluminum Spec. Co., Ks., 1936 ..... 520.00
License Plate Attachment, Dewey, Warren, 4 5/8 In. 152.00

License Plate Attachment, Drive Ahead With Roosevelt, Uncle Sam, FDR, 11 In. 410.00
License Plate Attachment, Franklin Roosevelt, Wendell Willkie 345.00
License Plate Attachment, Hoover, Black, Yellow Cream, 5 x 12 1/2 In. 29.00
License Plate Attachment, Keep Rosy With Roosevelt, Roses, Stars, Metal, 9 1/2 In. 2536.00
License Plate Attachment, LaFollette For President, Green Ground, 1924, 11 3/4 In. 805.00
License Plate Attachment, Landon For President, Man Of People, Photograph, 6 1/4 In. . .   225.00
License Plate Attachment, Landon, Knox, Sunflower, c.1936, 4 3/4 In. 175.00
License Plate Attachment, Let's Go Places, Elephant, 1948, 5 3/4 In. 53.00
License Plate Attachment, Roosevelt & Garner, Beer Mug, 9 1/2 In. 4927.00
License Plate Attachment, Roosevelt, Wallace, Shield Shape, Red, White, Blue, 5 In. 136.00
License Plate Attachment, Smith For President, Photograph, Round, 4 In. 193.00
License Plate Attachment, Stevenson, Portrait, Metal 665.00
License Plate Attachment, Truman Reflector, 1948, 10 In. 654.00
License Plate Attachment, We Want Willkie, Oval Top, 6 1/4 In. 228.00
License Plate Attachment, We Want Willkie, Red, White, Blue, 1940, 4 7/8 In. 65.00
License Plate Attachment, Willkie, Me Too, Donkey, 8 1/2 In. 106.00
License Plate Attachment, Win With Willkie Reflector, Red, Silver, Blue, Black, 12 In. . .   83.00
Magazine Cover, Time, Sec. Of State Henry Kissinger, March 10, 1975 . . . .   30.00
Matchbook, Betty For First Lady, 76, 1976 . . . .   6.00
Matchbook Cover, Goldwater For President, Blue, White, 1964 . . . .   8.00
Matchbook Cover, Rockefeller For President, 1964 . . . .   7.50
Matchbook Cover, Salute To Eisenhower Dinner, Man Of Peace, 1956 . . . .   20.00
Mirror, FDR Photograph, Birthstones Border, 2 1/4 In. 2018.00
Mirror, McKinley, Memorial, Pocket, Color Tinted, Oval, 3 1/2 In. 83.00
Mirror, Pocket, Bobby Kennedy, Destined To Become President, 1968, 3 1/2 In. 33.00
Mug, Beer, Franklin Roosevelt, New Deal, Repeal Of Prohibition, c.1932, 5 In. 65.00
Mug, Gerald Ford, Caricature, Brown, White, Baltimore, Md., 4 1/4 In. 35.00
Mug, Milk Glass, Plains, Ga., Home Of Jimmy Carter, Cartoon, 1976, 6 In. 20.00
Necktie, Harry Truman, Blue, White 132.00
Necktie, Landon For President, White, Black Letters & Image, 1936 . . . .   47.00
Necktie, Teddy Roosevelt, Our Teddy, Red, White, Blue 549.00
Paddles, Ping-Pong, Nixon, Mao, Paper Images, Wood, Rubber, c.1972, 10 x 6 In., 2 Piece   20.00
Parade Hat, McKinley, White Top, Black Brim, 9 In. 668.00
Parade Horn, McKinley As Napoleon, Papier-Mache, Painted, 1896, 9 1/2 x 15 In. 2478.00
Pencil, FDR, Garner, Celluloid, Bullet Shape, 1936 . . . .   85.00
Pencil, Goldwater, In Your Heart, You Know He Is Right 4.00
Pencil, Stevenson, Sparkman, Portraits, Mechanical 23.00
Penknife, Carter, Mondale, Gray, White, Barlow Co., 1976 . . . .   25.00
Penknife, Wallace, Lemay, American & Confederate Flag, 1972, 3 1/2 In. 25.00
Pennant, Bobby Kennedy, Destined To Become President, 1968, 14 In. 40.00
Pennant, Campaign, William Howard Taft, 1908, 34 In. 1320.00
Pennant, Eisenhower Inauguration, Blue Ground, 1953, 17 In. 15.00
Pennant, For Our Next President, Hoover, Blue & White, 24 In. 110.00
Pennant, I Like Ike, White Letters, Black Ground, Gettysburg, Pa., 26 In. 24.00
Pennant, Keep Cool-Idge, Felt, 1924, 19 1/2 In. 164.00
Pennant, McGovern For President, Red, White, Blue, 17 In. 8.00
Pennant, Nixon's The One, Color Picture, 26 In. 10.00
Pennant, Our 35th President, John F. Kennedy, 1961, 17 1/2 In. 23.00

**Never store an old textile in a
plastic bag, cardboard box, or
wooden trunk. A possible reaction
between the textile and the
container will weaken the fabric.**

Political, Pennant, Pennsylvania Bicentennial,
William Penn, Star Border, 1882, 33 x 24 In.

Pennant, Pennsylvania Bicentennial, William Penn, Star Border, 1882, 33 x 24 In. . . . *Illus*   200.00
Pennant, Votes For Women, Felt, Purple, Green, White, 7 x 15 In.   1091.00
Pennant, Wallace, Stand Up For America, 1968, 29 In. 15.00
Pin, Alfred Smith Brown Derby, 1928, Happy Warrior, Celluloid, 1 1/4 In. 780.00
Pin, Bug, Bryan, 16 To 1 Slogan, Silver, Mechanical, 1896, 1 1/4 In. 250.00
Pin, Dustpan, Harrison, Cardboard Portrait, 1888, 3/4 x 1 In. 150.00
Pin, Elephant, McKinley, Hobart, GOP, Mechanical, Red, Gold, Black, White, 1 1/4 In. . . .   185.00
Pin, McKinley Railroad Men's Club, Ft. Wayne, Engine & Coal Tender Top, Brass, 2 In. . .   305.00
Pin, Presidential Chair, Who Shall Occupy It, Cleveland, Brass, 1888, 1 x 2 In. 240.00
Pin, Rooster, Cleveland Banner, Enamel, 1888, 1/2 In. 105.00
Pin, Sulfide, Harrison & Reform, Log Cabin, Black, White, Rectangular, 1840, 3/4 x 1 In. .   895.00
Pin, Sulfide, Harrison & Reform, Log Cabin, White On Salmon, 1840, 1 1/8 x 1 In. 2248.00
Pin, Teddy Roosevelt, Rough Rider, Sword, Brass, 1904, 3 x 1 3/4 In. 2515.00
Pin Tray, Taft, Iroquois China, Syracuse, N.Y., 3 1/2 x 5 1/2 In. 45.00
Pipe Bowl, George Washington, Terra-Cotta, c.1850, 1 1/2 In. 75.00
Pipe Bowl, Henry Clay, Terra-Cotta, 1844, 2 3/4 In. 135.00
Pipe Bowl, Michigan Senator, Democratic Presidential Candidates, c.1850, 1 1/2 In. 575.00
Pipe Bowl, President Franklin Pierce, c.1850, 1 1/2 In. 175.00
Placard, Promoting USO, President John F. Kennedy, c.1962, 28 x 11 In. 50.00
Placard, Radio, Television Broadcasts Of Inauguration Ceremonies, 1953, 11 x 14 In. 65.00
Placard, Thanksgiving Fast For African-Americans, Racial Equality, 1960, 11 x 14 In. 65.00
Plate, Eisenhower, Military Uniform, Gold On Green Border, 7 In. 28.00
Plate, Lee & Jackson At Chancellorsville, Last Meeting, May 1, 1863, 1920, 7 In. 50.00
Plate, McKinley, Protection & Plenty, Clear Glass, Frosted, 9 1/4 In. 35.00
Plate, President & Mrs. Eisenhower, Fine China, Gold Highlights, 1950s, 11 In. 28.00
Plate, Presidents Through Nixon, Kettlesprings Kilns, Alliance, Ohio, 11 In. 40.00
Plate, Teddy Roosevelt, Flowers, Blue, White, Syracuse, N.Y., 1903, 9 1/4 In. 60.00
Playing Card, Teddy Roosevelt Leading San Juan Hill Charge 17.00
Poker Set, Harry Truman, Holder, Chips, Cards, Marked HST, 11 1/2 In. . . . . *Illus*   3537.00
Postcard, Bryan, Kern, Multicolored, 1908 . . . .   40.00
Postcard, Fan, Harrison To Cleveland Panels 45.00
Postcard, Give Our People Eisenhower, Postmark, 3 x 4 In., 1952 . . . .   17.00
Postcard, Richard Nixon, Henry Cabot Lodge, Civil Rights Rally, 1960 . . . .   39.00
Postcard, Roosevelt, Johnson Progressive Party, 1912, 7 1/2 x 4 1/2 In. 575.00
Postcard, Taft, Brown, Black, White, 1908 . . . .   13.00
Postcard, Teddy Roosevelt, Admiral Evans, Unfolds, Warships, Mechanical 75.00
Postcard, Thurmond, Wright, Black, White, 1948 . . . .   170.00
Postcard, Willkie, Cross Roads Of America, To White House, Canceled, 1940 . . . .   65.00
Postcard, Woodrow Wilson On Horseback, Visiting Army Encampment, c.1918 . . . .   45.00
Poster, Agnew Oops, Day-Glo, 1970, 35 x 23 In. 25.00
Poster, American Red Cross Drive, Woodrow Wilson, 1918, 20 x 28 In. 65.00
Poster, Anti-Vietnam War Demonstration, 1971, 12 1/2 x 40 In. 65.00
Poster, Bill Clinton Speaking To Children & Youth, 1992, 17 x 22 In. 15.00
Poster, Bill Clinton, Al Gore, 52nd Presidential Inaugural, 1993, 18 x 24 In. 19.00
Poster, Charles E. Hughes, Roto Ravure Portrait, 1916, 11 x 8 In.   18.95
Poster, Charles Hughes, Republican Presidential, 1916, 16 1/2 x 20 1/2 In. 165.00
Poster, Davis, Bryan, Democracy Offers You, 1924, 16 x 20 In. 794.00
Poster, FDR, Churchill, Frame, 9 x 12 In. 48.00
Poster, FDR, Uncle Sam, I Want You, Stay, Finish The Job!, J.M. Flagg, 1944, 21 x 16 In. . .   805.00
Poster, Franklin D. Roosevelt For President, 1932, 12 1/2 x 17 1/2 In. 69.00
Poster, Franklin D. Roosevelt For President, Sweeney Litho Co., Belville, N.J., 17 x 12 In.   50.00
Poster, Franklin Roosevelt, Promoting Candidacy, Slogan, 1936, 12 1/2 x 19 In. 69.00
Poster, General Douglas McArthur, Opposing Draft, Vietnam War, 1968, 21 x 29 1/2 In. . .   19.00
Poster, Goldwater, Space Age Candidate, 17 x 10 In. 56.00
Poster, Harding, Coolidge, Sepia, America Always First, 11 x 16 In. 302.00
Poster, Herbert Hoover, Presidential Candidate, 1928, 12 1/2 x 19 In. 85.00
Poster, Hubert Hubie Humphrey, Caricature, Donkey, 1968, 24 x 18 In. 25.00
Poster, James Blaine, John Logan, 1884, 15 11 1/2 In. 275.00
Poster, JFK, LBJ, Black, White, Red, White, Blue Letters, Frame, 17 1/2 x 24 1/2 In. 158.00
Poster, Jimmy Carter, Walter Mondale, Spanish Language, 1976, 13 x 21 In. 19.00
Poster, Lyndon Johnson, Opposing Vietnam War, 1968, 21 x 29 1/2 In. 19.00
Poster, March To End The War, New York, Los Angeles, 1969, 22 x 17 In. 45.00
Poster, Nelson A. Rockefeller, Elephant, Money Bags, Caricature, 1968, 24 x 18 In. 25.00

Political, Poker Set, Harry Truman, Holder, Chips, Cards, Marked HST, 11 1/2 In.

Political, Ribbon, Michigan Equal Suffrage Association, Port Huron, 1905, 6 x 2 In.

Political, Seal, Presidential, Richard Nixon, Republican Convention, 1972, 30 In.

Poster, Nixon, Agnew, Uneasy Riders, 1970, 35 x 23 In.	50.00
Poster, Nixon, In Nashua, New Hampshire, Open House, 1968, 22 x 14 In.	80.00
Poster, Nixon, Raising Arm, This Time, 1968, 66 x 42 In.	49.00
Poster, Re-Elect Carter, Best President Panama Ever Had, 1978, 36 x 24 In.	29.00
Poster, Robert Kennedy, Princeton, N.J., 1968, 19 x 25 In.	79.00
Poster, Ronald Reagan In Cowboy Hat, Reagan Country Slogan, 1980, 22 x 28 In.	95.00
Poster, Ronald Reagan, George Bush, 1984, 25 x 19 In.	75.00
Poster, Uncle Sam, I Want You For U.S. Army, James M. Flagg, 1917, 40 x 30 In.	2875.00
Poster, W.J. Bryan, Liberty, Justice, Humanity, Paper, 1900, 30 x 20 In.	1650.00
Poster, Wallace, It Takes Courage, Stand Up For America, 1968, 40 x 56 In.	100.00
Poster, Walter Mondale, Geraldine Ferraro, Presidential Candidates, 1984, 14 x 22 In.	25.00
Poster, We Fought For Your Right To Vote, Now Use It, Cardboard, VFW, 18 x 12 In.	60.00
Poster, William McKinley, Theodore Roosevelt, Candidates, 1900, 28 x 18 In.	2675.00
Poster, You Win, When You Vote For Ike & Dick, 1952, 13 3/4 x 10 1/4 In.	70.00
Print, Taylor & Fillmore, Lithograph, Nathaniel Currier, 1848, 10 x 14 In.	550.00
Program, Harding, Red, White, Blue, 1918	108.00
Program, Inauguration Ceremonies, 1965, 6 1/4 x 9 In.	20.00
Program, Inauguration Ceremonies, U.S. Govt. Printing Office, 1949, 6 1/4 x 9 In.	40.00
Program, Indiana Banquet, Truman, Kartke, 1958	55.00
Program, John F. Kennedy, Reception, Dinner, 1961	50.00
Ribbon, Abraham Lincoln, Union, Liberty, Paper, 1864, 7 1/2 x 3 In.	1955.00
Ribbon, Abraham Lincoln, We Mourn, Father Slain, Black, Brown Linen, c.1865	300.00
Ribbon, Badge, FDR, Fob, 1934	110.00
Ribbon, Blaine, Logan, October 24, 1884, Illinois, 10 1/2 In.	230.00
Ribbon, Bryan, Washington Reception, Black, Cream, Celluloid, 1907, 7 In.	80.00
Ribbon, Buchanan, Poem, Polk-Ed, Pierce-D, Buck 'Em, Red, Black, 5 In.	485.00
Ribbon, Cleveland, Thurman, Golden Yellow, 11 In.	235.00
Ribbon, Delegate, Whig National Convention, 1856, 7 1/4 x 2 In.	280.00
Ribbon, Eisenhower, Red, White Blue, Paper, Pin, Clip, 10 In.	50.00
Ribbon, Fillmore, Silk, Pink, Beige, 1856	315.00
Ribbon, Fremont, Dayton, Free Speech, Free Men, Free Kansas, 1856, 7 3/4 x 2 1/4 In.	1650.00
Ribbon, Garfield Campaign, Red, Blue, Paper Photograph, 1880, 8 1/2 x 1 3/4 In.	496.00
Ribbon, Garfield, Arthur, Soldier, Top Star, Bottom Fringe, 1880, 7 1/2 x 2 In.	990.00
Ribbon, Gen. J.A. Garfield, For President, Silk, Blue, 5 1/2 x 2 1/2 In.	136.00
Ribbon, Gen. W. H. Harrison, Silk, 1840, 7 3/4 x 3 In.	357.00
Ribbon, General W. Scott, Hero Of Many Battles, Silk, Green, 1852, 7 x 3 1/4 In.	1455.00
Ribbon, Goldwater, Red, White, Blue, Plastic, Gold, San Francisco Convention	39.00
Ribbon, GOP Presidents, Sepia, Gold, 1906 Jubilee, Philadelphia, 1 3/4 In.	580.00
Ribbon, Greenback Labor, Harrisburg, 1882, 6 x 3 1/2 In.	275.00
Ribbon, Grover Cleveland, Red, White & Blue Flags, Shield, Woven, 4 3/4 x 2 1/2 In.	198.00
Ribbon, Grover Cleveland, Thomas Hendricks, 1884, 6 In.	125.00
Ribbon, Harrison, Morton, Club, Blue, Rockton, Pa., 1888, 6 1/2 x 2 1/4 In.	430.00
Ribbon, Harrison, Tippecanoe Club, Our Country's Hope, Cabin, 1840, 2 1/2 x 5 3/4 In.	218.00
Ribbon, Hayes, Wheeler, Red, White, Blue Stripes, Brass Top Bar, 1876, 5 x 1 7/8 In.	795.00
Ribbon, Hayes, Wheeler, Republican Nomination, Woven, 1876, 5 3/4 x 1 3/4 In.	560.00

Ribbon, Henry Clay, Boston, Young Men's Whig Club, Convention, 1844, 7 3/4 x 2 3/4 In.	370.00
Ribbon, Henry Clay, Frelinghuysen, Silk, 1844, 7 3/4 x 3 In.	860.00
Ribbon, James K. Polk, Young Hickory Of Tennessee, 1844, 5 1/2 In.	1695.00
Ribbon, John C. Fremont, 1856, 7 In.	180.00
Ribbon, Lincoln Support, 1863, 6 1/2 In.	145.00
Ribbon, Lincoln, Brady, Portrait, 1860	2470.00
Ribbon, Lincoln, Funeral, Silk, Black Borders, Whatever Shall Appear To Be God's Will	375.00
Ribbon, Lincoln, Hamlin, Silk, Red, 1860, 6 1/2 x 2 3/8 In.	11240.00
Ribbon, Lincoln, Johnson, Pink, Silk, 1864	1855.00
Ribbon, Lincoln, Mourning, Silk, 1865	285.00
Ribbon, Martin Van Buren, 1839, 8 3/4 In.	1695.00
Ribbon, Martin Van Buren, Independent Treasury Bill, Silk, 1840, 7 3/4 x 2 1/2 In.	2250.00
Ribbon, McKinley, Hobart, Red, White, Blue, Black, 1896, 6 1/2 In.	80.00
Ribbon, McKinley, Hobart, Red, White, Blue, Black, Woven, 1896, 8 1/2 In.	325.00
Ribbon, McKinley, Republican Club, Red, White, 1892, 7 1/2 In.	45.00
Ribbon, McKinley, Sound Money, No Repudiation, Celluloid Disc, Flag, 1900, 7 In.	2545.00
Ribbon, Michigan Equal Suffrage Association, Port Huron, 1905, 6 x 2 In. .... *Illus*	835.00
Ribbon, Nixon Rally, Special Guest, 1960, 6 In.	19.00
Ribbon, Our Glorious Union For Ever, Shield, Laurel, Civil War, Silk, 11 x 2 1/4 In.	270.00
Ribbon, Polk, Dallas, Democratic, National Badge, Woman, Flag, Silk, 1844, 7 1/4 x 3 In.	2515.00
Ribbon, Seymour, Blair, Woven, Tassel, Red & Blue Letters, 1868, 7 x 1 3/4 In.	990.00
Ribbon, Stephen Douglas, Silk, 1860, 6 3/4 In.	1236.00
Ribbon, Teddy Roosevelt, Fremont, California Republican Clubs, Delegate, 1906, 7 x 2 In.	235.00
Ribbon, Teddy Roosevelt, GOP Presidents, Sepia, Rosette, Ribbons, 1 3/4 In.	96.00
Ribbon, Teddy Roosevelt, Rough Rider, Governor, Red, Blue, Black, Celluloid, 1 3/4 In.	240.00
Ribbon, Theodore Roosevelt, 1904, 5 1/2 In.	195.00
Ribbon, W.H. Harrison, Silk, Sanding Portrait, 1840	45.00
Ribbon, Weaver Green Party, 1881, 6 In.	575.00
Ribbon, Welcome Keynoter Judd, Satin, Cello, October 10, 1960, 2 x 7 In.	27.00
Ribbon, William Henry Harrison, Harrison Jubilee, 1840, 2 1/2 x 5 1/4 In.	275.00
Ribbon, William Howard Taft, 1908, 5 1/2 In.	50.00
Ribbon, Wilson, Marshall, Democratic Club, Red, Tan, November 5, 1912, 7 1/2 In.	140.00
Ribbon, Wisconsin People's Party, National Convention, Omaha, Flag, 1892, 6 x 2 In.	170.00
Ruler, Ike & Mamie, We Like Ike, Every Inch Of The Way, Heavy Paper, 6 In.	24.00
Scarf, I Like Ike, Eisenhower In Corners, Silk, Red, White, Blue, Square, 1952, 16 In.	40.00
Seal, Presidential, Richard Nixon, Republican Convention, 1972, 30 In. .... *Illus*	9183.00
Sheet Music, Bryan By Acclamation, Crockett, Cook, 1900, 14 x 10 In.	105.00
Sheet Music, Elliott, I Want To Be A Cap'n Too, 8 1/2 x 11 In.	36.00
Sheet Music, Grover Cleveland's March To Victory, 1884	65.00
Sheet Music, Let's Re-Re-Re-Elect Roosevelt, 1944	15.00
Sheet Music, On Right Road With Roosevelt, 1932, 9 1/4 x 12 In., 6 Pages	60.00
Sheet Music, Our Franklin D, 1942	28.00
Sheet Music, President George Bush March, 1988	15.00
Sheet Music, President Lyndon Baines Johnson March, 1964	14.00
Sheet Music, President Richard M. Nixon March, 1968	16.00
Sheet Music, Thomas Dewey, Dewey-We Do, 1944	40.00
Sheet Music, Win With Roosevelt, 1940	28.00
Shirt Front, Parade, McKinley, Hobart, Flags, Linen, 1896, 14 x 8 In.	560.00
Sign, Cleveland vs. Harrison, Butter & Sugar Price Comparison, 22 x 74 In.	2875.00
Sign, Harrison, Morton, Reverse On Glass, Frame, 1888, 12 x 16 In.	1850.00
Sign, LBJ Himself, For Remco Doll, 8 1/2 x 22 In.	25.00
Sign, Window, Re-Elect Roosevelt, 1936, 8 x 11 In.	25.00
Song Sheet, Prosperity, U.S.A. Recovery Song, FDR, 1934, 12 1/4 x 9 In., 6 Pages	80.00
Spinner, Stickpin, Teddy Roosevelt, McKinley, Rough Rider Hat	225.00
Spoon, National Woman Suffrage Convention, Silver, Demitasse, 1912, 4 In.	1058.00
Stickpin, Anti-Bryan, Skeleton, Mechanical, Shield Pops Open	1200.00
Stickpin, Benjamin Harrison, Copper Bust, c.1888	35.00
Stickpin, Bryan, Skeleton, Mechanical, Pops Open	1497.00
Stickpin, Bull Moose, Teddy Roosevelt, 7/8 In.	20.00
Stickpin, Cleveland, Whiskbroom, Brass, Albumen Portrait, 1 1/8 x 3/4 In.	90.00
Stickpin, Elephant, Smiling, Wearing Glasses, 3/4 In.	3.00
Stickpin, Teddy Roosevelt, Multicolored, 10 In.	140.00
Stickpin, Teddy Roosevelt, Rough Rider, Hat, Throw This Hat In The Ring, Brass, 7/8 In.	120.00

Stopper, Bottle, JFK, Figural, Wooden, 1962, 4 In. 55.00
Stud, Cleveland, Celluloid Covered Lithograph, Round, 1892, 3/4 In. 45.00
Stud, Donkey Shape, Roosevelt, Enamel, Blue, White, Silver, 7/8 In. 20.00
Stud, Elephant Shape, Hughes, 7/8 In. 17.00
Stud, Harrison & Morton, Raccoon, Log Cabin, Brass, Copper, 1888, 3/4 In. 55.00
Stud, Harrison, Star, Brass, On Card, 1888, 3/4 In., 4 Piece 170.00
Stud, Landon, Liberty Bell, Red, White, Blue, Gold, Enamel 55.00
Stud, Peoples Party, Shield Shape, 1892, 1/2 In. 118.00
Stud, Rooster Shape, Cox, 7/8 In. 20.00
Stud, Shield Shape, Hughes, Enamel, Red, White, Blue, Gold, 3/8 In. 28.00
Sugar & Creamer, Franklin D. Roosevelt, Gold Trim, Royal Winton, England 75.00
Table Cover, Teddy Roosevelt, Rough Rider Uniform, c.1888, 17 x 17 In. 342.00
Telegram, Grover Cleveland, To Isadore Rayner, Balto, Oct. 27, 1898, 6 x 8 1/2 In. 40.00
Textile, Declaration Of Independence, Brown Ink, Linen, c.1826, 33 x 27 In. 4370.00
Textile, Harrison & Reid, Printed Cotton, Red, White, Blue, Frame, 1892-1896, 23 1/2 In. .. 330.00
Ticket, Democratic National Convention, Chicago Stadium, 3rd Session, 1944 .... 17.00
Ticket, Democratic National Convention, St. Louis, 1904 .... 49.00
Ticket, Dewey, Warren Rally, Madison Square Garden, Gold, Black, October, 1948, 6 In. . 50.00
Ticket, Impeachment, Andrew Johnson, U.S. Senate, Cardboard, April 21, 1868 .... 390.00 to 800.00
Ticket, Inauguration Ceremonies, Rotunda Photographers Stand, 1965 .... 15.00
Ticket, Landon, Bleakley Rally, Madison Square Garden, N.Y., 1936 .... 12.50
Ticket, McKinley Inaugural Dinner, Admit One, One Dollar, 1897, 4 x 1 1/2 In. 480.00
Ticket, Truman, Ike, Army Day, Soldier Field, Chicago, April 6, 1946 .... 63.00
Tie, I Like Ike, Blue, White, 1950s 22.00
Tie Clasp, Adlai Stevenson, Hole In Shoe, Sterling, 1956 .... 23.00
Tie Clasp, Elephant With Eyeglasses, Goldwater 11.00
Tie Clip, Kennedy For President, 1 1/2 In. 23.00
Tip Tray, Grand Old Party 1908, Howard Taft, GOP Presidents 1856-1908, 4 In. 180.00
Tip Tray, Taft & Sherman, Grand Old Party, White House, Tin Lithograph 192.00
Toilet Tissue Roll, McGovern, Red, White, Blue, Unopened 12.50
Token, Cleveland, Diamond Shape, 1888 .... 15.00
Toothpick, Teddy, Bear, Tree Trunk, Rough Rider Hat, Ceramic, Germany, 3 1/2 In. 125.00
Toy, Dancing Nixon, Convict Outfit, Windup, 6 1/2 In. 90.00
Toy, Nixon, Dancing Can-Can, Dances, Hands On Hips, Windup, c.1972, 7 x 6 1/2 In. 75.00
Tray, McKinley, Roosevelt, Tin Lithograph, Oval, 1900, 13 x 17 In. 1256.00
Trigate, Harding, Cox, Coolidge, Channing Cox, Celluloid, 1 1/2 In. 4026.00
Tumbler, Eisenhower, Military Uniform, Clear Glass 20.00
Tumbler, Glass, Gold, Black Image Of Goldwater With Elephant On Back, 1964 On Sides . 15.00
Tumbler, Goldwater, Lincoln Day Dinner, United Republican Fund, Clear Glass, 1964 .... 25.00
Umbrella, McKinley, Hobart, Protection, Sound Money, Cloth, 1896, Full Size 495.00
Watch Fob, Cox, Roosevelt, High Relief Busts, Original Strap, 1920 .... 215.00
Watch Fob, Cox, Roosevelt, Pewter, 1 1/4 In. 105.00
Watch Fob, Harding, Brass, 1920, 1 1/4 In. 140.00
Watch Fob, Harding, Coolidge, Gold, 1920 .... 70.00
Watch Fob, Woodrow Wilson, Celluloid, 1 1/2 In. 550.00
Window Sign, Johnson For President, Vote Democratic, 9 x 12 In. 13.00
Window Sticker, Landon & Knox, Sunflower, 5 In. 2.95

POMONA glass is a clear glass with a soft amber border decorated with pale blue or rose-colored flowers and leaves. The colors are very, very pale. The background of the glass is covered with a network of fine lines. It was made from 1885 to 1888 by the New England Glass Company. First grind was made from April 1885 to June 1886. It was made by cutting a wax surface on the glass, then dipping it in acid. Second grind was a less expensive method of acid etching that was developed later.

Berry Bowl, Band Of Cornflowers, Ruffled Rim, 2nd Grind, 8 1/2 In. 144.00
Card Holder, Fan Shape, Ruffled Amber Edge, Petaled Foot, 1st Grind, 2 x 4 In. ... 345.00 to 403.00
Celery Vase, Cornflowers, Ruffled Edge, Petaled Foot, 2nd Grind, 6 1/4 In. 201.00
Finger Bowl, Blue Cornflower, Pleated Rims, c.1870, 5 1/4 x 2 1/2 In., 6 Piece 550.00
Finger Bowl, Underplate, Ruffled Edge, 2nd Grind, 3 x 6 1/2 In. 115.00
Lemonade, Cornflower, 1st Grind, 5 5/8 In. 403.00
Pitcher, Tankard, Cornflower, Gold Stain, 6 3/4 In. 863.00

Punch Cup, 1st Grind, 2 1/2 In., Pair 173.00
Sugar & Creamer, Cornflowers, Ruffled Edge, Petaled Foot, 2nd Grind 230.00
Sugar & Creamer, Oval, 3 Applied Feet, 1st Grind, 5 In. ....400.00 to 460.00
Sugar & Creamer, Ruffled Edge, Applied Amber Handle, 2nd Grind 115.00
Toothpick, Inverted Trifold Rim, 1st Grind, 2 In. 316.00
Tumbler, 2nd Grind, 3 3/4 In., 6 Piece 115.00
Tumbler, Amber, Cornflower Decoration, New England Glass, 1st Grind, 3 3/4 In. 42.00
Tumbler, Lemonade, Cornflowers, Clear Handle, 1st Grind, 5 5/8 In. 546.00
Tumbler, Lemonade, Cylindrical, 1st Grind, 5 1/2 In. 230.00
Vase, Rigaree Collar, Crimped Ruffled Top, 5 3/4 In. 259.00
Water Set, Tankard Pitcher, Diamond-Quilted, Tumblers, 8 1/2 & 3 3/4 In., 13 Piece 863.00

PONTYPOOL, see Tole category.

POOLE POTTERY was started by Jesse Carter in 1873 in Poole, England. The company specialized in architectural ceramics. In 1908 the company was incorporated as Carter and Company. In 1920 it became Carter & Co. The name Poole Pottery Ltd. was taken in 1963. The company is still in business.

Basin, Tiny Purple Flowers, Pink Rim, Flared, Truda Carter, 1921, 15 In. 545.00
Bookends, Knight On Horseback, Stepped Base, H. Brownsword, c.1929, 8 In. 831.00
Bookends, Springbok, Leaping, Tan, Rectangular Base, John Adams, c.1930, 8 In. 393.00
Boot Scraper, Scroll Design, Brown Glaze, Owen Carter, c.1900, 6 3/4 In., Pair 284.00
Bowl, Band Of Blue Birds, Flowers, Multicolored, Hilda Hampton, c.1940, 9 1/2 In. 118.00
Candelabrum, 3-Light, Grapevine, Light Blue Glaze, John Adams, c.1948, 10 In. 313.00
Candlestick, Caramel Glaze, Luster, 4-Sided, Tapered, Owen Carter, 1905, 16 In., Pair 655.00
Charger, Iridescent Red Luster, 3 Curved Depressions, Owen Carter, 1903, 17 In. 2080.00
Charger, Landscape, Bridge, Blue, Bloomsbury Style, J.R. Young, c.1918, 16 In. 4155.00
Dish, Stylized Owl, Robert Jefferson, 1962-63, 16 1/4 In. ....·.. *Illus* 16366.00
Figurine, Bull, Cherubs & Flowers Atop, Phoebe Stabler, c.1922, 12 1/2 In. 5466.00
Figurine, Fighting Gamecock, Tan Glaze, Harold Stabler, Marked, 1924, 7 1/2 In. 1095.00
Figurine, Girl In Bath Towel, Blue, White, Phoebe Stabler, c.1922, 7 1/2 In. 765.00
Figurine, Harpy Eagle, Marked, Harold Sabler, 1916, 25 1/2 In. 6998.00
Figurine, Lavender Woman, Phoebe Stabler, 1911, 7 3/4 In. 925.00
Figurine, Picardy Peasant Man, Blue, White, Phoebe Stabler, c.1922, 10 In. 1530.00
Figurine, Picardy Peasant Woman, Blue, White, Phoebe Stabler, 1922, 10 1/2 In. 2405.00
Figurine, Potter Seated At Wheel, Guy Sydenham, c.1970, 16 In. 6125.00
Ginger Jar, Cover, Chinese Blue Glaze, Marked, John Adams, c.1930, 7 1/4 In. 1857.00
Plaque, Yellow, White & Purple Flowers, Oval, Faience, Harold Stabler, c.1921, 14 In. ... 1750.00
Plate, Persian Deer, Lavender, Green, T. Adams & G. Warren, c.1925, 14 In. 2625.00
Plate Set, Calendar, Medieval, Tony Morris, 1970s, 12 3/4 In., 12 Piece 650.00
Tile, Frieze, Cow & Sheep In Pasture, Painted, J.R. Young, 1926, 23 x 15 In. 3060.00
Tile, Frieze, Turkey, Multicolored, Square, Frame, E.E. Strickland, c.1925, 11 3/4 In. 1049.00
Vase, Allover Flowers, Truda Carter, Ann Hatchard, CSA Mark, 15 1/4 In. ....*Illus* 13095.00

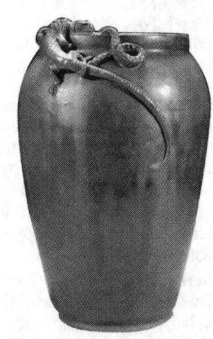

Poole, Dish, Stylized Owl,
Robert Jefferson,
1962-63, 16 1/4 In.

Poole, Vase, Allover Flowers,
Truda Carter, Ann Hatchard,
CSA Mark, 15 1/4 In.

Poole, Vase, Applied Lizard,
Carter's Luster, Lily Gilham,
Owen Carter, 1915-18, 12 1/2 In.

Vase, Applied Lizard, Carter's Luster, Lily Gilham, Owen Carter, 1915-18, 12 1/2 In. . *Illus*   2836.00
Vase, Bird, Stylized Flowers, Multicolored, Bulbous, 2 Handles, T. Carter, 5 In. 875.00
Vase, Dark Red Luster, Applied Lizard On Rim, Lily Graham, c.1916, 12 In. 2840.00
Vase, Flowers, Green Zigzag At Rim, Wide Mouth, 2 Shaped Handles, Marked, 7 In. 1857.00
Vase, Green Glaze, Blue Accent, Luster, Melon Ribbed, Bulbous, Tapered, 12 In. 1310.00
Vase, Peacock, Stripes, Swirls, Dots, Green, Purple, T. Adams, 1924, 19 In. 3060.00
Vase, Red & Brown Decoration, Luster, Flared, Waisted, Ruffled Rim, Owen Carter, 6 In. . .   1420.00
Vase, Sponged Design, Multicolored, Enamel, Marked, c.1970, 9 1/2 In. 90.00
Vase, Stylized Multicolored Flowers, Dotted Rim, Truda Carter, 1930, 8 1/2 In. 1530.00

POPEYE was introduced to the Thimble Theatre comic strip in 1929. The character became a favorite of readers. In 1932, an animated cartoon featuring Popeye was made by Paramount Studios. The cartoon series continued and became even more popular when it was shown on television starting in the 1950s. The full-length movie with Robin Williams as Popeye was made in 1980. KFS stands for King Features Syndicate, the distributor of the comic strip.

Badge, Admiral, Popeye Navy, Brass, 1930s, 1 1/2 In. 290.00
Bank, Daily Quarter Register, Tin Lithograph, Kalon, Box, 1950s, 4 3/4 x 3 x 4 In. 230.00
Bank, Knockout, Tin, Straits Manufacturing, Box 990.00
Book, Among White Savages, Pop-Up, Blue Ribbon Press, KFS, 1934, 5 x 4 In., 60 Pages   220.00
Book, Popeye Meets His Rival, 9 x 11 In. 17.00
Book, Popeye Sees The Sea, Big Little Book, No. 1163, 1936 . . . .   45.00
Button, Popeye The Sailor Man, Red, White, Blue, c.1970, 1 3/4 In. 23.00
Button, Popeye, Cap'n Jim, Channel 11, Lithograph, 1970s, 1 1/2 In. 35.00
Button, Popeye, Pep 15.00
Button, Wimpy & Hamburger, Brass, Enamel, 1970s, 1 1/4 In. 15.00
Button, Wimpy & Hamburger, Enamel, 1930s, 1 1/4 In. 50.00
Button, Wimpy, Pep 27.00
Card, Get Well, Anchor Around Popeye's Neck, Hallmark, KFS, 1936, 5 x 4 In. 56.00
Christmas Tree Light Shade, Marked, KFS, 1929, Set Of 8 . . . .   325.00
Coaster, Popeye Smoking Pipe, Wood, 6 1/2 In. 28.00
Doorstop, Cast Iron, King Features, Hubley, c.1929, 9 In. 3300.00
Figure, Carousel, Popeye Riding Rocket, 43 In. 605.00
Figure, Eugene, Wooden, Segmented, 1935, 12 In. 1300.00
Figure, Olive Oyl, Wood Composition, Syroco, 1944, 4 3/4 In. 169.00
Figure, Popeye, Celluloid, Windup, Head Goes Up & Down, 1930s, 8 In. . . . . .495.00 to 950.00
Figure, Popeye, Jointed, Wood, J. Chein, 1932, 8 In. 230.00
Figure, Popeye, Rubber, King Features, 12 In. 35.00
Figure, Popeye, Rubber, Schavoir Rubber Co., KFS Inc., 1935, 7 x 2 x 3 In. 165.00
Figure, Popeye, Wood, Composition, Jointed, KFS, 1935, 12 x 3 x 5 In. 310.00
Figure, Wood, Arms Move, Hat, Brim, Pipe, 1930s, 2 1/2 In. 115.00
Flashlight, Battery Operated, Bantam Lite, On Card, 1950s, 8 x 2 1/2 In. 75.00
Game, Dexterity, Tin Lithograph, Bar-Zim Toys, 3 1/2 x 5 In. 99.00
Game, Pipe Toss, Wood, Cardboard, Lithograph, Rosebud Art Co., 1935, 10 In. . . . . .66.00 to 115.00
Game, Popeye Pipe Toss, Box, 9 In. 66.00
Game, Roly Poly Popeye Target, Cork Gun, Plastic, Paper Lithograph, Box, 9 1/2 x 20 In. .   175.00
Lamp, Boat, Original Paint & Cord, Popeye Inside, Aerolux, 1930s, 6 1/2 In. 685.00
Marble Set, Akro Agate, Box, 1929, 49 Piece 2225.00
Membership Card, Movie Theater, Liberty Theater, 1930s, 2 1/2 x 3 1/2 In. 75.00
Night-Light, Popeye, Carrying Ice Cream Cone, 1930s 106.00
Pail, Beach Scene, Popeye, Olive Oyl, Swee'pea, Bluto, Jeep, Tin, Cohn, 1936, 4 In. 190.00
Pail, Popeye & Wimpy, Tin Lithograph, 6 x 9 In. 275.00
Pail, Popeye The Sailor, Tin Lithograph, Handle, T. Cohn, KFS, 1933, 3 3/4 x 4 In. 465.00
Paint Set, No. 1935, American Crayon, Box, c.1933, 10 1/4 In. 295.00
Pencil, Eagle Pencil Co., Box, 10 1/2 In. 28.00
Pencil Box, Popeye, Paper-Covered Cardboard, Snap, KFS, 1934, 6 x 10 3/4 In. 87.00
Pencil Sharpener, Popeye, Catalin Plastic, Rectangular, c.1929, 1 In. 90.00
Pencil Sharpener, Tin Lithograph, Tin Shavings Tray, Irwin, 1929, 2 3/4 In. 225.00
Pocket Knife, 3 Blades, Imperial, Providence, R.I., 1930s, 3 3/4 In. 177.00
Toy, Brutus, Horse Drawn Cart, Tin Lithograph, Windup, Celluloid, Marx, Box, 7 In. 1100.00
Toy, Gun Set, Gilgour Cast Iron Guns, Paper Lithograph Backdrop, Halco, 12 In. 305.00
Toy, Olive Oyl, Pop-Up, Squeaker, Umbrella, Cloth, Composition, Linemar, Box, 7 In. 660.00

Popeye, Toy, Popeye, Walker, Clenched Fist, Tin Lithograph, c.1935, Box, 6 In.

Popeye, Toy, Popeye, Sparkler, Tin Lithograph, No. 251, Chein, Box, 1930s, 6 In.

Toy, Popeye & Brutus, Funny Fire Fighters, Tin Truck, Celluloid, Marx, Box, 10 In. 3575.00
Toy, Popeye & Olive Oyl, Dancing On Roof, Playing Accordion, Marx, 9 1/2 In. . .905.00 to 1150.00
Toy, Popeye & Olive Oyl, Dancing On Roof, Playing Accordion, Marx, Box, 9 1/2 In. 2310.00
Toy, Popeye & Olive Oyl, Handcar, Slinky, Pull, Linemar, 7 In. 770.00
Toy, Popeye & Olive Oyl, Juggling, Tin Lithograph, Linemar, Box, 9 In. 2970.00
Toy, Popeye & Wimpy, Walker, Plastic, Nodding Heads, Marx, Box, 5 In. 120.00
Toy, Popeye & Wimpy, Walking, Plastic, King Features Syndicate, 1964 . . . . 225.00
Toy, Popeye Express, Train, Bridges, Flying Airplane, Windup, Marx, 1930s, 9 In. Diam. . . 750.00
Toy, Popeye Express, Train, Bridges, Tunnels, Flying Airplane, Marx, Box, 9 In. Diam. . . . 3080.00
Toy, Popeye Playing Xylophone, Wood, Pull, KFS, Fisher Price, 11 x 10 In. 468.00
Toy, Popeye Tank, Rollover, Tin Lithograph, Windup, Linemar, 4 In. . . . . .300.00 to 1150.00
Toy, Popeye, Bag Puncher, Floor Bag, Tin Lithograph, Chein, Box, 7 In. 1870.00
Toy, Popeye, Bag Puncher, No. 257, Tin, Windup, Brown Bag, Chein, Box, 7 1/2 In. 3850.00
Toy, Popeye, Bag Puncher, Overhead Bag, Tin, Celluloid, Chein, Box, 9 In. . . . .4675.00 to 12100.00
Toy, Popeye, Barrel Walker, Tin Lithograph, Windup, Chein, 1932, 7 In. . . . . .330.00 to 625.00
Toy, Popeye, Basketball Player, Bounces Ball, Lithograph, Windup, Linemar, 9 In. 930.00
Toy, Popeye, Basketball Player, Bounces Ball, Lithograph, Windup, Linemar, Box, 9 1/2 In. 2860.00
Toy, Popeye, Boom Boom, Lithograph, Fisher-Price, Pull, 10 In. 1870.00
Toy, Popeye, Boxer, Shadow, Tin, Windup, Chein, Box, 7 In. 2750.00
Toy, Popeye, Champ, Big Fight, Tin, Celluloid Clockwork, Marx, Box, 7 In. 2970.00
Toy, Popeye, Champ, Boxing Ring, Tin, Celluloid Clockwork, Marx, 7 In. 1210.00
Toy, Popeye, Dancing On Roof, Tin Lithograph, Marx, Box, 10 In. 1760.00
Toy, Popeye, Dancing On Roof, Windup, Marx, 1930s, 10 In. 685.00
Toy, Popeye, Drummer, Tin, Chein, Box, 7 In. 7150.00
Toy, Popeye, Heavy Hitter, Tin, Windup, Chein, Original Box, 1930s, 11 1/2 In. .7150.00 to 14300.00
Toy, Popeye, Horse Drawn Cart, Tin, Celluloid, Marx, Box, 7 1/2 In. 1540.00
Toy, Popeye, Ladder, Flip-Flops, Wood, 1930s, 20 x 6 In. 127.00
Toy, Popeye, Parrot Cages, Carrying, Chein, 8 In. . . . . .375.00 to 650.00
Toy, Popeye, Parrot Cages, Carrying, Tin Lithograph, Windup, Marx, Box, 8 In. 605.00
Toy, Popeye, Parrot Cages, Carrying, Tin, 8 1/2 In. 275.00
Toy, Popeye, Parrot On Wheelbarrow, Tin, Celluloid, Windup, Marx, Box, 9 In. 1870.00
Toy, Popeye, Pilot, Eccentric Plane, Tin Lithograph, Marx, Box, 1930s, 8 In. 1540.00
Toy, Popeye, Ringing Bell, Celluloid, Metal Bell, Rubber, Wood, 1929, 5 1/2 In. 90.00
Toy, Popeye, Skater, Holding Platter Of Spinach, Windup, Linemar, 1950s, 7 In. . . . .595.00 to 750.00
Toy, Popeye, Skater, Tin Lithograph, Windup, Linemar, Japan, Box, 6 In. 1320.00
Toy, Popeye, Smoking, On Spinach Can, Battery Operated, Linemar, Japan, Box, 9 In. 1650.00
Toy, Popeye, Sparkler, Round, Tin Lithograph, Spring Loader, Chein, Box, 5 1/2 In. 250.00
Toy, Popeye, Sparkler, Tin Lithograph, No. 251, Chein, Box, 1930s, 6 In. . . . .*Illus* 7700.00
Toy, Popeye, Spinach Eater, Movable Arms, Pull, Fisher-Price, 9 In. 660.00
Toy, Popeye, Walker, Clenched Fist, Tin Lithograph, c.1935, Box, 6 In. . . . .*Illus* 770.00
Toy, Popeye, Walker, Tin Lithograph, Windup, Chein, 6 1/2 In. 360.00
Toy, Thimble Theatre, Mystery Playhouse, Box, 12 x 10 In. 1045.00
Toy, Wimpy, Walker, Celluloid, Japan, 7 In. 220.00
Toy, Wimpy, Walker, Celluloid, Japan, Box, 7 In. 495.00
Tumbler, Popeye, Eugene The Jeep, Swee'pea, Canada, 1950, 4 3/4 In. 75.00
Wristwatch, Animated Hands, Popeye, Olive Oyl, Wimpy, New Haven, Box, 1935 . . . . . . 4577.00
Wristwatch, Popeye, Wimpy, Olive Oyl, Swee'pea, Box, c.1948 . . . . 1830.00

PORCELAIN factories that are well known are listed in this book under the factory name. This category and the two following list pieces made by the less well-known factories. Porcelain-Contemporary lists pieces made by artists working after 1975. Porcelain-Midcentury includes pieces made from the 1940s to the 1980s.

Apothecary Jar, Blue & White, Mounted As Lamp, Printed, V. Rosatrum, 17 1/2 In.	460.00
Basin, Vertical Sides, Mottled Blue Ground Set, Flowers, 1800s, 11 1/2 In.	460.00
Basket, 6-Sided, Hand Painted Flowers, Scrolled Feet, 12 x 13 3/4 x 6 1/2 In.	805.00
Basket, Reticulated, 2 Tiers, Chinaman Support, Mottahedeh, 26 In.	1725.00
Biscuit Jar, Gaudy Decorated, Rococo Mold, F.J. Emery, Burslem, England, c.1890, 7 1/2 In.	173.00
Bottle, Blue & White, Globular, Narrow Neck, Dragon, Pearl, Chinese, 16 3/4 In., Pair	805.00
Bottle Vase, Yellow Ground, Green Branch, Purple Flowers, 12 1/2 In.	410.00
Bowl, 8-Sided, Kirin, Dragon, Phoenix, Late 1800s, 6 In.	204.00
Bowl, Blue & White, Painted, Dragon Roundels, 19th Century, 8 1/2 In., Pair	200.00
Bowl, Chrysanthemum, Kakiemon, Japan, 5 1/2 In.	518.00
Bowl, Copper Red, Early 20th Century, 6 1/2 In.	505.00
Bowl, Dragon, Blue & White, 8 1/4 In.	58.00
Bowl, Dragon, Cloud, Salmon Red, Blue, Enamel, 15 1/2 In.	405.00
Bowl, Embossed Flowers, Roses, Germany, 10 1/4 In.	140.00
Bowl, Flower, Peach Center, Flower Border, Kakiemon, Japan, 7 3/4 In.	345.00
Bowl, Flower-Form Rim, Birds, Flowers, Kakiemon, Japan, 4 3/4 In.	1955.00
Bowl, Phoenix, Red-Gold Border, Crane, Cloud, c.1850, 8 1/4 In.	345.00
Bowl, Planter Shape, Flat Rim, Flower Decoration, 4 Painted Goldfish, 10 x 12 In.	75.00
Bowl, Serpentine, Lotus Shape, Lotus & Scroll Clusters, Pale Green, 1900s, 5 1/2 In.	500.00
Bowl, Silver Dragon, Red Ground, Early 1900s, 9 1/2 In.	90.00
Box, Chrysanthemum Shape, Flower Petals, 19th Century, 3 1/4 In.	260.00
Bust, Maiden, Blue Water Lilies In Her Hair, Art Nouveau, 15 In.	657.00
Butter, Cover, Pink Roses, Austrian Blank, Signed, R.O. Briggs, Austin, Tex. *Illus*	150.00
Cachepot, Art Nouveau Style, Daffodil Design, 9 1/2 x 12 1/4 In.	259.00
Cachepot, Sevres Style, Gilt Bronze, Cobalt Blue, Napoleonic Crest, 9 x 13 In.	1910.00
Cake Plate, Embossed Flower Mold, Germany, 10 3/4 In.	85.00
Candelabrum, Putti, Fruit Garlands, Marked, Schierholz, Germany, 22 In., Pair	345.00
Candy Dish, Felix The Cat, Square, Germany, Late 1920s, 5 In.	88.00
Centerpiece, Sevres Style, Cobalt Blue, Oval, 2 Handles, Medallions, 10 x 14 3/4 In.	690.00
Centerpiece, Sevres Style, Ormolu Mount, Cobalt Blue, Figures, 17 1/4 x 20 3/4 In.	8625.00
Centerpiece, Sevres Style, Ormolu Mount, Paw Feet, Lovers, c.1900, 7 1/4 x 16 1/2 In.	920.00
Centerpiece, Sevres Style, Yellow Ground, Oval, Figures, Ormolu Mount, 15 1/2 In.	575.00
Charger, Blue & White, Landscape, Scholar On Horseback, On Bridge, Japan, 19 In.	765.00
Charger, Embossed, Stork, Putto, Center Relief Panel, Cherubs, Austria, 1800s, 19 In.	115.00
Charger, Faience, Molded Ring, Stylized Flowers, White Glaze, 13 1/2 In.	405.00
Charger, Oriental Decoration, Birds, Carnations, Butterfly, Gold, Cobalt Blue, Red, 20 In.	345.00
Charger, Oriental Style, Painted, Arab Soldier, With Sword, Gilt Wood Frame, 20 In.	1095.00
Charger, Peacock Eye Flowers, Blue, Rust, Band Of Horses, 18 1/4 In.	405.00
Chocolate Pot Set, Geisha Girl Scene, Gold, Oriental, 5 Cups	170.00
Coffeepot, Crested Pheasant, Chinese Flowers, Gilt Brass, Germany, c.1765, 10 1/2 In.	1095.00
Compote, 3 Women On Pedestal, Reticulated Basket, Germany, c.1900, 21 In.	460.00
Compote, Applied Figures, Flowers, Scrolled Base, Germany, 14 1/2 In.	375.00
Compote, Basket, Latticework, Ruffled Border, Pedestal, Rocaille, 11 1/4 x 17 In.	1495.00

Porcelain, Butter, Cover, Pink Roses, Austrian
Blank, Signed, R.O. Briggs, Austin, Tex.

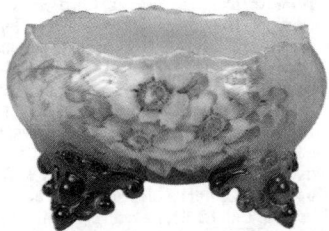

Porcelain, Fernery, Pink Roses, Limoges Blank,
Signed, B.E. Mehling '99, American, 8 In.

Compote, Brass Mounted, Pierced, Brass Cherubs, 9 1/2 x 12 x 7 3/4 In., Pair 1150.00
Cup, Stem, Landscape, Blue, White, Late 1800s, 3 1/4 In. 69.00
Cup & Saucer, Nyon, Puce Panels, Putti, Gilt, Black Bands, Garlands, 19th Century, 5 In. . 85.00
Dish, Arita, Square, 5 Geese, Ogee Rim, Lotus Reserves, c.1900, 13 1/2 In. 120.00
Dish, Blue & White, Leafy Shape Rim, Japanese, 20th Century, 18 1/4 In. 518.00
Dish, Continental, Leaf Shape, Mark, c.1900, 7 1/2 x 7 1/2 In. 25.00
Dish, Entree, Cover, Flowers, Gilt, Scroll Handles, England, 1825-30, 11 1/2 In. 615.00
Dish, Lozenge Shaped, Exotic Birds, Flowers, Molded Rim, Mennecy, Late 1700s, 12 In. . 1415.00
Dish, Painted, Iron Red Dragons, Blue Clouds, China, Early 20th Century, 7 1/2 In. 70.00
Dog, Spaniel, Carrying Flower Basket, c.1920, 21 In. 975.00
Dresser Box, Hand Painted Gilt, Court Scenes, France, 7 In. 150.00
Dresser Tray, Porcelain, Roses, 12 In. 30.00
Ewer, Gilt Griffin Shape Handle, Pirkenhammer, Early 20th Century, 10 In. 140.00
Fernery, Pink Roses, Limoges Blank, Signed, B.E. Mehling '99, American, 8 In. ..... *Illus* 184.00
Figurine, Blanc De Chine, Quan Yin Holding Child, 8 In. 69.00
Figurine, Boy, Dog Seated, 19th Century, 7 x 7 x 3 3/4 In. 316.00
Figurine, Courtier, Standing, Dragon Decorated Robe, 19th Century, 13 In. 259.00
Figurine, Dog, Greyhound, Resting Position, Austria, 10 1/4 In. 145.00
Figurine, Female Musician, Chinoiserie, Frankenthal, Late 1800s, 10 In. 566.00
Figurine, Flower Seller, Black Bonnet, Red Cape, 2 Barrels, c.1890, 4 In. 225.00
Figurine, Gamecocks, Apple Green, Yellow, Gray Glaze, Chinese, 20th Century, 18 In. ... 375.00
Figurine, Geisha, In Black Kimono, Multiolor, Gilded Flowers, c.1890, 15 In. 200.00
Figurine, Geisha, Poised, Green Floral Kimono, Japan, c.1890, 10 3/4 In. 200.00
Figurine, Girl Dancing, Tambourine, Swirling Skirt, Bisque, Germany, 16 1/2 In. 235.00
Figurine, Lion, Buddhistic, Multicolored Enamel, Chinese, 6 x 7 1/2 In. 259.00
Figurine, Nude Maiden, Seated On Closed Book, Art Nouveau, 5 1/2 In. 600.00
Figurine, Our Lady Of Lourdes, Hand Painted, France, 19th Century, 16 In. 144.00
Figurine, Pug, Gray, Terra-Cotta, Glass Eyes, 12 1/2 x 14 1/2 In. 2115.00
Figurine, Romantic Musical Scene, Figures Playing Harps, Germany, 9 1/2 In. 430.00
Figurine, Seated Maiden, Art Nouveau, Austria, 7 1/2 x 10 3/4 In. 956.00
Figurine, Tree Stump, Entwined Serpent & Ivy, Palissy Style, Mid 1800s, 21 In. 1095.00
Figurine, Tree Trunk, Bird Top, Sitzendorf, Germany, c.1920, 8 In. .... *Illus* 95.00
Figurine, Young Boy & Girl, Sitzendorf, 19th Century, 10 In., Pair 185.00
Foo Dog, Chinese, Famille Verte Enamels, Yellow Ground, 13 In., Pair 405.00
Foo Dog, Seated, Plinth Base, Green, Yellow, 17 In., Pair 865.00
Ginger Jar, Bulbous Style, Dragon, Goldfish, Green Yellow Ground, China, 8 1/2 In. 35.00
Ginger Jar, Cover, Squat, Figure Riding Chi-Lin, Blue, White, Chinese, Late 1800s, 8 In. . 145.00
Group, Bear & Bull Fighting, Germany, 15 1/4 In. 260.00
Group, Blanc De Chine, 8 Immortals On Curling Waves, 11 3/4 x 11 3/4 In. 430.00
Group, Courting Couple, Marked Germany, 5 1/2 In. 23.00
Group, Dresden Style, Mother & 2 Children, 11 1/2 In. 105.00
Group, Dutch Girl With Geese, Germany, 9 1/2 In. 127.00
Group, Figures At Table Drinking, Germany, Early 1900s, 11 x 20 x 11 In. 865.00
Jar, Cylinder, Cover, Painted, Bamboo, Peonies, Peach Finial, Early 1900s, 10 In. 250.00
Jar, Leaves, Flowers, Double Happiness Characters, Blue, White, Chinese, 1900s, 17 In. ... 200.00
Jar, Leeches, Applied Knobs At Side, Applied Letters, 7 1/2 In. 4675.00
Jardiniere, Birds, Bamboo, Blue, White, 1800s, 11 1/2 x 14 In. 575.00
Jardiniere, Blue & White, Painted, Lotus, Yellow Ground, 20th Century, 6 In., Pair 670.00
Jardiniere, Butterfly, Flowers, Blue & White, 10 In. 115.00
Jardiniere, Dragon, Phoenix, Carp, Sea Grass, Japan, Early 1900s, 16 x 18 1/2 In., Pair ... 2415.00
Jardiniere, Egg Shape, Birds, Flowers, Japan, Early 1900s, 17 x 21 1/2 In. 980.00
Jardiniere, Flowers, Landscapes, Octagonal, Blue, White, Chinese, 8 x 11 In., Pair 290.00
Jardiniere, Lattice Design, Blue, White, 3-Footed, c.1720, 16 1/2 x 24 In. 1140.00
Jardiniere, On Stand, Gilt Metal, Cobalt Blue Bowl, Flared Rim, Continental, 33 x 24 In. . 750.00
Jardiniere, Painted, Bamboo Reserve, 20th Century, 8 In. 75.00
Jardiniere, Tapered, Crosshatched Rows, Leaf Design, Gold, Blue Stripes, 12 x 15 In. 865.00
Medicine Jar, Flowers, Vine, 6-Sided, Zoshuntei, 1840-1860, 4 In. 630.00
Mug, Figural, Floral Reserves, Peony & Butterfly Field, Loop Handle, 4 1/2 In. 160.00
Mug, Leaf Scroll Handle, Flowers, Leaves, Waisted Body, England, c.1830, 3 In. 189.00
Mustard, Lid, Ladle, Lavender Floral Decoration, Made In Japan, 3 In. 20.00
Night-Light, Owl, Germany, 7 In. 80.00
Pitcher, Cider, Stylized Apples, Gilt Ground, 8 In. .... *Illus* 90.00
Pitcher, Gilt Decoration, Continental, 13 In. 90.00

Porcelain, Figurine, Tree Trunk,
Bird Top, Sitzendorf, Germany,
c.1920, 8 In.

Porcelain, Pitcher, Cider,
Stylized Apples, Gilt
Ground, 8 In.

Porcelain, Vase, Dragon Head,
Jacob Petit Style, Mid 19th
Century, 13 1/4 In., Pair

Pitcher, Sevres Style, 3 Portraits, Louis XIV, Jewels, Cobalt Blue Ground, 7 In. 780.00
Plaque, 2 Dogs At Chase, Three Crown, Germany, 12 In. 75.00
Plaque, Children, Dog, Cart, Cow, 2-Sided, Cameo, Taxile Doat, Sevres, 1907, 6 x 6 1/2 In. 2350.00
Plaque, Children, Street Scenes, Eating Fruit, Continental, 1800s, 11 1/2 x 8 In., Pair 325.00
Plaque, Depicting Ruth, Signed Meyer, Continental, 9 x 6 In. 1555.00
Plaque, Exterior Scene, Couple Holding Hands, Frame, 20th Century, 21 x 16 In. 115.00
Plaque, Man Playing Zither, Woman Knitting, Frame, c.1890, 15 1/4 x 12 1/4 In. 4226.00
Plaque, Mater Delorosa, Hand Painted, After Carlo Dolci, Wood Bezel Mount, 3 In. 160.00
Plaque, Old Man, Cane, Sleeping Boy, Germany, 9 x 7 In. 840.00
Plaque, Poets Lounging By Censer, Dragon Pattern Hardwood Frame, Stand, 39 In. 800.00
Plaque, Portrait, Hand Painted, Victoria Austria, Cherub Scene, 12 In. 45.00
Plaque, Young Woman, Hand Painted, Walnut Frame, c.1890, 7 1/2 In. 90.00
Plate, Flowers, Hand Painted, Handles, Germany, 10 1/2 In. 30.00
Plate, Flowers, Multicolored, Yellow Ground, 9 3/4 In., Pair 140.00
Plate, Hibiscus, Wave Border, Hirado, 19th Century, 7 1/2 In., Pair 270.00
Plate, Hirado, Kirin, Carved Flowers, 1800s, 8 3/4 In., Pair 375.00
Plate, Lobed, Basket Weave Rim, Flowers, Fly, Chantilly, Late 1700s, 9 1/2 In. 566.00
Plate, Red Chili Peppers, Flowers, Leaf Border, Secessionist, c.1910, 9 1/2 In. 168.00
Plate, Shaped Rim, Gilt Edges, Flowers, Leaf Scrolls, Insects, Nantgarw, 10 In. 1595.00
Plate, Square, Grapevine, Basket Weave, Crown Devon, 8 1/2 In., 2 Piece 29.00
Plate, Stylized Flowers, Blue & White, 9 In., 2 Piece 104.00
Plate Set, Multicolored, Gilt, Black Knight, Royal Bavarian, c.1950, 8 1/2 In., 12 Piece . . 1150.00
Plate Set, Soup, Multicolored, Parcel Gilt, Black Knight, Royal Bavarian, 10 Piece 635.00
Platter Set, Blue & White, Willow Pattern, Chinese, 10 x 11 1/2 In., 3 Piece 460.00
Punch Bowl, Cabbage & Moth, Wood Stand, Chinese, 20th Century, 15 1/2 In. 999.00
Punch Bowl, Seated Scholars, Deities, Dragon Center, Japan, Late 1800s, 5 1/2 x 12 In. . . . 805.00
Rose Bowl, Red, Pink, Yellow Roses, Gold Rim, Hand Painted, Wiltelsbach, 5 x 4 In. 45.00
Tea Caddy, Figure Landscape, Blue & White, 8 In. 175.00
Tea Urn, Dome Lid, Egg Shape Body, Birds, Figural Legs, Japan, 1800s, 18 In. 1380.00
Teapot, Blue & White, Bird, Flower, 8 1/2 In. 127.00
Teapot, Cover, Fluted Globular Body, Multicolored Enamel, 1700s, 5 1/4 In. 4115.00
Tray, Oriental Style, Parrot, Fish, Turquoise Ground, Cast Bronze Frame, 13 x 18 In. 575.00
Trinket Box, Mating Chickens, Flower, Insects, France, 20th Century, 2 1/2 x 3 1/2 In. 85.00
Tumbler, Gilt Eagle In Wreath, Green Ground, Bell Foot, Continental, 5 In. 70.00
Tureen, Blue & White, Cover, Boar Head Handles, Flower Finial, Chinese, 7 In., Pair 865.00
Urn, Cover, Sevres Style, Ormolu Mount, Woman With Quiver, 3 Putti, 42 In. 8625.00
Urn, Cover, Sevres Style, Tapered, Paneled, Men Drinking, Landscape, 12 3/4 In., Pair . . . 3450.00
Urn, Cover, Underglaze Blue, Bird Scene, Flowering Plants, Lion Head Handles, 24 In. . . . 3220.00
Urn, Covered, Puce Landscape Reserves, Yellow Ground, Continental, 9 In., Pair 570.00
Urn, Oriental, Cartouches, Dragons, 20th Century, 36 In. 145.00
Urn, Sevres Style, Ormolu Mount, Putto Reserve, Flower Spray, c.1900, 14 In., Pair 1095.00
Urn, Stand, Ormolu Mount, Cobalt Blue, Flaring Rim, 13 1/2 x 10 In. 546.00
Vase, 4 Cartouches, Scenes Of Everyday Life, Japan, Late 1800s, 12 1/4 In. 259.00

Vase, Baluster, Antiques, Buddhist Symbols, Foo Dog Finials, Chinese, 23 In., Pair 1150.00
Vase, Baluster, Landscape, Pavilions, Figures, Boats, Blue, White, Chinese, 12 1/2 In. 345.00
Vase, Baluster, Waterscape, Figures, Houses, Blue, Foo Dog Handles, Chinese, 25 In. 230.00
Vase, Birds, Iris, Bronze Handles, Base, F.A. Mehlem, Germany, c.1900, 13 1/2 In., Pair .. 1380.00
Vase, Blue & White, Pear Shape, Fretwork Band, Tendrils, Korea, 1800s, 84 1/2 In. 1309.00
Vase, Blue Dragon, Yellow Ground, Trumpet Shape, 7 1/2 In. 2185.00
Vase, Bottle, Globular, Slender Neck, Dragons, Clouds, Blue, White, Chinese, 17 In., Pair . 748.00
Vase, Bulbous, Ivory & Green Drip Glaze, Taxile Doat, 6 1/2 In. 940.00
Vase, Cover, Raised Dog, Serpents, Flower Panels, Chinese, 9 x 3 1/2 In., Pair 411.00
Vase, Double Gourd Shape, Kingfisher, Flowers, 19th Century, 5 3/4 In. 600.00
Vase, Double Gourd, Brand, Flower, Blue, 7 1/4 In. 29.00
Vase, Dragon Head, Jacob Petit Style, Mid 19th Century, 13 1/4 In., Pair .... *Illus* 12075.00
Vase, Egg Shape, Dragon In Clouds, Blue, White, Early 1800s, 16 3/4 In. 1380.00
Vase, Painted, Birds, Butterflies, Dragonflies, Dogwood, 15 x 11 x 7 1/2 In., Pair 590.00
Vase, Peachbloom, Squat, Baluster Shape, Tall Neck, Lotus Lappet Base, 6 1/2 In. 1679.00
Vase, Pear Shape, Lacquer, Flared Rims, Birds, Peonies, Geese, 1800s, 15 1/4 In., Pair 575.00
Vase, Portrait, Squat Shape, Elongated Neck, Amphora, 5 1/2 In. 1795.00
Vase, Sevres Style, Engraved, Enameled, Gilt Brass, Flowers, France, c.1885, 9 1/4 In. ... 1035.00
Vase, Sevres Style, Tambourine Shape, Painted Scenes, Couple, Lake, C. Gernier, 10 In. .. 375.00
Vase, Slender, Ivory Matte & High Glaze, Enamel, Cameo Profiles, Taxile Doat, 10 1/2 In. 2700.00
Vase, Teadust, Globular, Tall Neck, Orange Peel Texture Glaze, Olive On Brown, 12 In. ... 360.00
Vase, Trumpet Mouth, Dragon Handles, Enameled Flowers, Japan, Early 1900s, 25 In. 235.00
Vase, Urn Shape Body, Painted Landscape, Yellow, Green, Oriental, 15 In. 58.00
Vase, White Crystalline Glaze, Dalpayrat, 9 x 2 3/4 In. 705.00
Vase, Wisteria, Lavender, White, Moss Rose Ground, Trumpet Shape, 14 In. 7475.00
Water Dropper, Frog, Robin's-Egg Blue, 3 3/4 In. 230.00
Water Vessel, Blue & White, Octagonal Flared Rim, Landscape Scene, 10 x 5 In. 82.00

PORCELAIN-CONTEMPORARY lists pieces made by artists working after 1975.

Figurine, Accordion Player, Dahl Jensen, 8 1/2 In. 725.00
Figurine, Bali Woman, In Turban, Dahl Jensen, 8 1/2 In. 900.00
Figurine, Bird, Goldfinch, Dahl Jensen, 4 In. 190.00
Figurine, Dog, German Shepherd, Dahl Jensen, 7 1/4 In. 725.00
Figurine, Dog, Wire Haired Fox Terrier, Standing, Dahl Jensen, 7 In. 346.00
Figurine, Girl, In Nightdress, Dahl Jensen, 7 1/4 In. 450.00
Figurine, Girl, Selling Pearls, Dahl Jensen, 5 1/8 In. 450.00
Figurine, Polar Bear, Dahl Jensen, 4 3/4 In. 139.00

POSTCARDS were first legally permitted in Austria on October 1,
1869. The United States passed postal regulations allowing the card in
1872. Most of the picture postcards collected today date after 1910.
The amount of postage can help to date a card. The rates are: 1872 (1
cent), 1917 (2 cents), 1919 (1 cent), 1925 (2 cents), 1928 (1 cent), 1952
(2 cents), 1959 (3 cents), 1963 (4 cents), 1968 (5 cents), 1973 (8 cents),
1975 (7 cents), 1976 (9 cents), 1978 (10 cents), 1981 (12 cents), 1981
(13 cents), 1985 (14 cents), 1988 (15 cents), 1991 (19 cents), 1995 (20
cents).

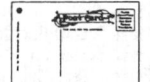

Broadmoor Hotel, Colorado, Parrish Illustration, Color, 3 1/2 x 5 1/2 In. 55.00
Covered Wagon, Old Oregon Trail Monument Expedition, Real Photo, 1906 .... 196.00

Postcard, Dutch Scene, Applied
Metal Windmill, Horseshoe,
Remember Me, 1910

Postcard, Easter, Chick, Broken Egg, Wreath, Applied Metal Egg Cart, Tuck's

Postcard, House & Fountain, Framed By Gate, Applied Gold Metal Turkey

Postcard, Valentine, Hearts, Flowers, Applied Silver Foil Cupid, For My Valentine, Frame

Dame, Stoddard & Co., Addressed, Postmarked, 1906, 3 1/2 x 5 1/2 In.	16.50
Derryfield Gun Club, Club Shoot, Men Shooting In Field, Manchester, N.H.	28.00
Dutch Scene, Applied Metal Windmill, Horseshoe, Remember Me, 1910 ....*Illus*	10.00
Easter, Chick, Broken Egg, Wreath, Applied Metal Egg Cart, Tuck's ....*Illus*	12.00
Glacier National Park, Fold-Out, 18 Color Views, 1930, 3 1/2 x 5 In.	10.00
Grand Canyon National Park, Shows Guests Arriving, 1912	10.00
House & Fountain, Framed By Gate, Applied Gold Metal Turkey ....*Illus*	20.00
Kentucky Lake State Park, Photo Of Bathhouse, 1952	9.00
Kukla, Fran & Ollie, Hello, We're Back From Vacation, 1949 Postmark, 3 1/4 x 5 1/2 In.	35.00
Matches Sir?, Young Child, Selling Matches, Real Photo	80.00
Post Cereal Club House, Battle Creek, Michigan, 3 1/2 x 5 1/2 In.	9.00
Red Pig Household Knives, Shur Edge, Robeson Cutlery Co., Rochester, N.Y.	80.00
Schultze Powders, Best In World, 5 Woman, Water Proof, Hard Grained, c.1895	85.00
US Cartridge, Smiling Man, I Want Some, Black Shells, c.1910, 6 x 3 1/2 In.	110.00
Valentine, Hearts, Flowers, Applied Silver Foil Cupid, For My Valentine, Frame ....*Illus*	25.00
White Star Liner Titanic, Real Photo	185.00

POSTERS have informed the public about news and entertainment events since ancient times. Nineteenth-century advertising or theatrical posters and twentieth-century movie and war posters are of special interest today. The price is determined by the artist, the condition, and the rarity. Other posters may be listed under Movie, Political, and World War I and II.

2nd Liberty Loan Bond Of 1917, Uncle Sam, 30 x 20 In.	440.00
American Negro Exposition, Chicago Coliseum, 1940, 21 1/2 x 13 3/4 In.	705.00
Americans All, Victory Liberty Loan, Lady Liberty, Honor Roll, Cardboard, 40 x 27 In.	165.00
Bill Graham Concert, Hand, Holding Flower, Eyes, David Singer, 1970, 22 x 14 In.	55.00
Circus, Christy Bros. Wild Animal Show, Riverside Print Co., Chicago, Frame, 30 x 44 In.	978.00
Clyde Beatty, Cole Bros., Combine Circus, Paper Lithograph, 1958, 36 x 42 In.	25.00
Dailey Bros. Circus, Animals & Trainer, Paper Lithograph, Frame, 12 3/4 x 15 3/4 In.	175.00
Family Dog Concert, Multiple Bands, Avalon Ballroom, November, 1967, 20 x 14 In.	40.00
Golden Girl Of The West, Girl, Sitting On Table, 1906, 30 x 20 In.	1430.00
Harlem Globetrotters, Wilt Chamberlain Holding Suitcase, Jan. 6, 1959, 28 x 41 In.	900.00
Hippie, Holding Flower, Guitar On Ground, Rick Reinert, c.1970, 30 3/4 x 16 1/4 In.	85.00
Inter-Tribal Indian Ceremonial, Gallup, New Mexico, 1936, 22 x 14 In.	345.00
Jim Salzer, Jimi Hendrix, Psychedelic, Santa Barbara, Aug. 9, 1967, 23 1/4 x 17 1/4 In.	183.00
Jules Cheret, Maitres Issue 25, December 1897, Frame, Chaix, Paris, 11 x 15 In.	750.00
Kar-Mi, Buried Alive For 32 Days, Paper Lithograph, Linen Back, 81 x 40 In.	425.00
Mistinguett, Silkscreen, Daniel De Losues, c.1911, 75 In.	550.00
Thomas Wildey, First Lodge At Baltimore, Lithograph Paper, Frame, c.1819, 31 x 25 In.	165.00
Tournoi De Lutte, Wrestlers, Armand Rassenfosse, A. Bernard, Frame, 1900, 14 x 11 In.	355.00

POTLIDS are just that, lids for pots. Transfer-printed potlids had their heyday from the 1840s to the early 1900s. The English Staffordshire potteries made ceramic containers with decorative lids for bear's grease, shrimp or meat paste, cold cream, and toothpaste. Printed advertising and pictures of historical events, portraits of famous people, or scenic views were designed in black and white or color. Reproductions have been made.

2 Men In Courtyard, Eating, Drinking, Dog, Base, Pratt, 4 1/2 In.	28.00
Alas Poor Bruin, Multicolored, Line & Dot Border, Pratt, Base, 3 In.	127.00
Albarose Toothpaste, Woman With Headscarf, Black Transfer, 3 1/2 In.	2455.00
Alexandra Toothpaste, Dr. Diemer's, 2 3/4 In.	137.00 to 147.00
Anthracoline, Pink Ground, Black, 3 1/4 In.	145.00
Areca Nut Cherry, Bristol Toothpaste, False Teeth, 3 1/2 In.	2046.00
Areca Nut Toothpaste, Chauvin Et Cie, Paris Et Londres, Cherries, Men, Boat, 2 1/2 In.	215.00
Areca Nut Toothpaste, Mosque, Palm Trees, Thompson & Hillard, 2 1/2 In.	140.00
Bear Pit, Multicolored, Dome, Line & Dot Border, Pratt, 2 3/4 In.	140.00
Bears At School, Multicolored, Line & Dot Border, Pratt, 3 In.	112.00 to 165.00
Burgoyne Burbidges & Co., Girl With Long Hair, Smiling, 2 3/4 In.	4910.00
Charing Cross, Base, Pratt, 4 1/4 In.	50.00
Cherry Toothpaste, 4 Cherries, 2 3/4 In.	80.00
Cherry Toothpaste, Bird, Pink Ground, Black Transfer, 3 1/2 In.	920.00
Cherry Toothpaste, For Preserving Teeth & Gums, O G & Co., 2 3/4 In.	55.00
Cherry Toothpaste, Preserving, Beautifying, Sailboat, F. Newberry & Sons, 2 1/2 In.	215.00
Cold Cream, Pictorial Scene, Flower Border, 2 3/4 In.	100.00
Cold Cream, Snowdrops, 2 1/2 In.	80.00
Country Quarters, Horse, Dog, Multicolored, Title & 2-Line Border, Pratt, Base, 4 3/4 In.	100.00
Dr. Dosteels, Cherry Toothpaste, Queen Victoria, 3 1/4 In.	2660.00
Dr. Johnson, Men Seated In Room, Multicolored, Pratt, 1860s, 4 In.	80.00
Dr. Leslies Toothpaste, Hygienic, Base, 3 3/4 In.	1025.00
Fishbarrow, Multicolored, Lace Design Border, Pratt, 4 In.	65.00
Fisherboy, Multicolored, Line & Dot Border, Pratt Factory, 3 In.	100.00
G.H. Bayley Saltaire Toothpaste, Buildings, Figures, 4 1/4 In.	1640.00
Harbour Margate, Multicolored, Chain Border, Cauldon, 4 3/4 In.	160.00
High Life, Multicolored, Line & Dot Border, Pratt, 4 In.	120.00
Holloway's Ointment, Classical Woman, Seated, 3 1/4 In.	59.00
J.J. Matthias Unrivalled Cherry Toothpaste, Prince Of Wales, 3 In.	1230.00
Lady Reading Book, Multicolored, Pratt, 3 In.	235.00
Landing The Fare, Begwell Bay, Pratt, 4 In.	50.00
Letter From The Diggings, Base, Pratt, 4 1/2 In.	29.00
Low Life, Multicolored, Line & Dot Border, Pratt, 4 In.	82.00
Ning Po River, Multicolored, 2-Line Border, Pratt, 4 In.	130.00
Osox Toothpaste, Black Transfer, Square, 2 1/2 In.	325.00
Patrician Tooth Powder, Woman In Dress, Headdress, Oval, 3 3/4 In.	705.00
Preparing For The Ride, Multicolored, Pearl Dot Border, Pratt, 4 In.	80.00
Rimmels Coral Toothpaste, Seashells, 3 In.	615.00
Room In Which Shakespeare Was Born, Stratford On Avon, 1564, Base, Pratt, 4 1/2 In.	25.00
Savage's Celebrated, Peruvian Balm, Restoring Hair, Flower Vase, 2 3/4 In.	127.00
Shepherd Boy, Multicolored, Cauldon, 4 In.	80.00
Shepherdess, Multicolored, Cauldon, 4 In.	78.00
Shooting Bears, Multicolored, Pratt, Base, 3 In.	160.00
Shrimpers, Multicolored, Pratt, 4 In.	69.00
Thames Embankment, Base, Pratt, 4 1/4 In.	59.00
The Times, English Man Enjoying Newspaper, Base, Pratt, 4 1/4 In.	28.00
Toothpaste, Men, In Boat, Shooting Ducks, Trees, 2 3/4 In.	80.00 to 90.00
Village Wedding, Multicolored, Pratt, 4 1/4 In.	63.00 to 72.00

POTTERY and porcelain are different. Pottery is opaque; you can't see through it. Porcelain is translucent. If you hold a porcelain dish in front of a strong light, you will see the light through the dish. Porcelain is colder to the touch. Pottery is softer and easier to break and will stain more easily because it is porous. Porcelain is thinner, lighter, and more durable. Majolica, faience, and stoneware are all pottery. Additional pieces of pottery are listed in this book in the categories Pottery-Art,

Pottery-Contemporary, Pottery-Midcentury, and under the factory
name. For information about pottery makers and marks, see *Kovels'*
Dictionary of Marks—Pottery & Porcelain: 1650–1850 and *Kovels'*
New Dictionary of Marks—Pottery & Porcelain: 1850 to the Present.

Baby Feeder, Ceramic, Flowers, Blue & White, England, 6 3/4 In.	685.00
Baby Feeder, Ceramic, Leaves, Blue & White, England, 7 In.	785.00
Bowl, Green & Brown Matte Glaze, Mottled, Turned Rim, Broad, Arts & Crafts, 9 In.	150.00
Bowl, Pewter Leaf Shape, Woman Profile, c.1900, 14 1/2 In.	480.00
Cachepot, Molded, Flowers, Bulbous Body, Variegated, Brown & Green, 8 x 11 In.	600.00
Censer, Hunters In Forest, Green Glaze, Acorn Shape, Chinese, 9 In.	390.00
Compote, Flowers, Mauve, White, Yellow, Green, Blue Ground, France, c.1930, 6 x 12 In.	705.00
Creamer, Character, Blue & White, Germany, 3 3/4 In.	127.00
Crock, Molded, Yellow Clay, American Eagle, 2 Stars, Amber Glaze, Kent, Ohio, 5 x 4 In.	80.00
Cup, Slip, Frog, Female Characteristics, Tan, Green Glaze, 2 3/4 In.	60.00
Figurine, Bird, White Clay, Gold, Green & Black, Glossy Glaze, 3 3/8 In.	200.00
Figurine, Cat, Seated, White Clay, Brown Glaze, Slip Stripes, Hollow Molded, 6 In., Pair	750.00
Figurine, Dancing Drummer, Green Glaze, Chinese, 8 1/2 In.	605.00
Figurine, Dog, Seated Spaniel, White Bristol Glaze, Atwater, Summit County, Ohio, 8 In.	920.00
Figurine, Dog, Seated, Molded White Clay, Running Amber Brown Glaze, Ohio, 8 1/2 In.	316.00
Figurine, Dog, Spaniel, Seated, Blue Glaze, Ohio, c.1850, 11 1/2 In.	3165.00
Figurine, Dog, Spaniel, Seated, White Clay, Dark Brown Glaze, Oval, c.1897, 7 In.	230.00
Figurine, Dog, Spaniel, Seated, Yellow Clay, Running Blue, Brown Glaze, 11 1/2 In.	7130.00
Figurine, Dog, Spaniel, White Clay, Cream, Brown Sponging, Dog, Deer, Ohio, 10 In.	920.00
Figurine, Dog, Yellow Clay, Blue, Green Flint Enamel Glaze, Seated Spaniel, 11 1/2 In.	8165.00
Figurine, Kneeling Man Wearing Court Hat, Multicolored, Chinese, 5 1/2 In.	140.00
Figurine, Owl Shape, Perched On Log, Drilled As Lamp, 13 1/4 In.	140.00
Figurine, Puffin, Celadon Crystalline Glaze, H.W. Hunsicker, 1931, 7 3/4 x 8 1/2 In.	350.00
Figurine, Seated Lokopala, Curved Horn, Flower, Straw Glaze, Chinese, 13 3/4 In.	748.00
Figurine, Woman In Long Dress, Hair In Bun, Red Stoneware, Green Ash Glaze, 7 1/2 In.	230.00
Figurine, Woman, Nayarit, Hands To Belly, Spread Legs, Black Pigment Trace, 17 In.	250.00
Figurine, Woman, Nayarit, Kneeling, Holding Cup To Shoulder, Painted, 12 In.	25.00
Flask, Figural, Queen Alexandrina Victoria, Leaf Decorated Dress, Beaded Jewelry, 8 In.	345.00
Jar, Mottled Green, Blue, Burgundy Glaze, Lion Faces, Burley & Winter, Ohio, 18 In.	230.00
Jar, Salt Glazed, Oval, Marked Charleston, Impressed Double Hearts, 14 x 9 In.	1208.00
Jug, Applied Vines, Leaves, Grapes, John Meaders, Cleveland, Ga., 26/7, 9 In.	259.00
Jug, Clay, Albany Slip, Inscribed Shoo Fly, Applied Woman Chasing Fly, 5 1/4 In.	2415.00
Jug, Hans Wewerka, Gray Glaze, Applied Medallions, Blue, c.1908, 8 1/2 In.	230.00
Jug, Harvest, Running Brown Glaze, Handle Rings, Cuyahoga Falls, Ohio, 8 3/4 In.	575.00
Jug, Marbleized Vine, Hinged Pewter Cover, Dixon & Sons, c.1875, 12 In. .... *Illus*	250.00
Mug, Princeton Football Player, Christy Illustration, Maddocks & Sons, 1905, 5 In.	610.00
Mug, Slipware, Brown Glaze, Yellow Decoration, England, Late 1700s	495.00
Mug, White Clay, Albany Slip, Cut Away Designs, Yale Forever '95, 6 In.	545.00
Pitcher, Dutch Children, Blue & White, 7 In.	58.00 to 115.00

Pottery, Jug, Marbleized Vine, Hinged Pewter Cover, Dixon & Sons, c.1875, 12 In.	Pottery, Vase, Applied Hydrangea & Branches, Limoges-Style Glaze, France, 13 In.	Pottery-Art, Vase, Applied Gilt Dragon, Christopher Dresser, Marked, Old Hall, 14 In.

Pitcher, Irises, Chevrons, Gray Matte Glaze, Jervis, 5 x 6 1/2 In. 650.00
Pitcher, Shenandoah, Peter Bell, Mottled Green, Brown, Cream Glaze, 5 3/4 In. 1555.00
Pitcher, Wash, Calla Lily, Blue & White, 10 1/2 In. 140.00
Plate, Blue Feather Edge, Oriental Pagoda Design, Scalloped, 9 1/2 In. 175.00
Plate, Felix The Cat, Keep On Walking, Lithograph, Oval, Empire Ware, England, 7 x 6 In.   250.00
Plate, Slipware, Sunflower Design, 19th Century, 3 1/2 x 3/4 In. 230.00
Platter, Seashells, Blue Transfer, Longport, c.1935, 20 1/2 In. 1955.00
Pot, Squat, Spout, Hollow Handle, Mottled Amber To Brown, Zoar, 5 1/2 x 3 In. 775.00
Sake Cup, Eiraku, Crane, Silver Interior, Ikoma Kiln, 19th Century, 2 In. 35.00
Umbrella Stand, Embossed Flowers, Variegated Glaze, Early 1900s, 19 3/4 In. 219.00
Vase, 2 Handles, Horizontal Ribs, Hand Turned, 1930s, 26 In. 600.00
Vase, Applied Hydrangea & Branches, Limoges-Style Glaze, France, 13 In. . . . . *Illus*   400.00
Vase, Cattails, Green, Brown, Glaze, Gesetze Gesch, 12 1/2 In. 300.00
Vase, Corset Shape, Luster Mauve, Green Gloss, Matte Glaze, Rambervillers, 12 In. 210.00
Vase, Cylindrical, Brown, Bronze Frame, Art Nouveau Design, Lenormanch, 7 In. 765.00
Vase, Embossed Flowers, Green Matte Gaze, 8 1/2 In. 150.00
Vase, Floor, Crystalline Brown, Blue Glaze, Green & Tan Ground, 22 In. 375.00
Vase, Floor, Speckled Green To Blue Semimatte Glaze, 26 In. 355.00
Vase, Gold Flowers, Cabochon Hearts, Green Ground, Marigold, Teren, Austria, 14 In. . . .   295.00
Vase, Green Matte, Molded Leaf, 8 1/4 In. 140.00
Vase, Impressed Dimple Pattern, Monogram, Scandinavian, 1900s, 11 In. 230.00
Vase, Mobach Holland, Rust, Light Blue Glaze, Signed, Chantal, 8 3/4 In. 130.00
Vase, Nasturtium Pods, Flowers, Mottled, Flambe, Moore Brothers, 10 1/2 x 8 In. 4110.00
Vase, Organic Shape, 4 Swirling Handles, Green, Red, Wilhelm Schiller & Son, 12 1/2 In. .   999.00
Vase, Pine Needles, Pinecones, Banded Shoulder, Fremington, 5 1/2 x 5 In. 160.00
Vase, Ram's-Head Applied Designs, Mottled Green-Brown Glaze, Early 1900s, 6 In. 90.00
Vase, Spill, Bulbous, 5 Spouts, 4 Twisted Branch Handles, Brown To Black, 9 In. 175.00
Vase, Stylized Leaves, Blue Vellum Glaze, Lachenal, 6 In. 705.00
Vase, Stylized Plumes, Mid 20th Century, 13 1/2 In. 260.00
Vase, Tulips, Windblown, Blue Ground, Hubert Krumeich-Remmy, Germany, 11 In. 470.00
Vase, Wiener Werkstatte, Leaves, 3 Handles, Opaque Glaze, c.1930, 7 1/2 In., Pair 475.00
Vase, Winter, Orange, Green, Burley, 6 1/2 In. 128.00
Wall Pocket, Crab Shape, Green, Hollow, Vase Top, Hanging Hole, 8 x 11 In., Pair 290.00
Wash Set, Earthenware, Pitcher, Bowl, Brush Holder, 2 Soap Dishes, c.1900 . . . .   60.00
Water Dispenser, Salt Glazed, Brush Blue Flowers, Mid Atlantic, 12 1/2 x 7 3/4 In. 835.00

POTTERY-ART

POTTERY-ART Art pottery was first made in America in Cincinnati, Ohio, during the 1870s. The pieces were hand thrown and hand decorated. The art pottery tradition continued until the 1930s when studio potters began making the more artistic wares. American, English, and Continental art pottery by less well-known makers is listed here. Most makers listed in *Kovels' American Art Pottery,* such as Arequipa, Ohr, Rookwood, Roseville, and Weller, are listed in their own categories in this book. More recent pottery is listed under the name of the maker or in the Pottery category.

Bowl, Amphora, Riessner Stellmacher & Kessel, Dragon, Painted, c.1900, 10 1/2 In. 949.00
Bowl, Black, Tan Design, Charles Vyse, 2 x 4 1/4 In. 230.00
Bowl, Matt Morgan, Pumpkin Ground, Black Painted Oriental Scene, 5 1/2 In. 345.00
Bowl, Nicodemus, Swirl Interior, Blue Over Brown, Footed, 2 In. 25.00
Bowl, North State, Flared Shape, Red Crystalline Glaze, 11 In. 400.00
Box, Oval, Applied Beetle, Blue, Green, Brown Glaze, Signed, Denbac, 4 1/4 In. 118.00
Cake Plate, Flowers, Enamel, Transfer, 4-Sided, Hampden, C. Dresser, 2 3/4 x 9 In., Pair .   500.00
Charger, Bird, Ruby & Gold Luster, Cattail Ground, Signed C.P., DeMorgan, 14 In. 4715.00
Charger, Exotic Bird, Geometric Border, Louis Leon Parvillee, 1870s, 21 In. 475.00
Ewer, Dragon Handles, Bulbous, Oriental Blossoms, Old Hall, C. Dresser, 12 1/4 In., Pr. . . .   1175.00
Figurine, Cat, Bisque, Signed, C. Masson, France, 2 1/2 In. 650.00
Figurine, Pierrefonds, Lizard, Green, Blue Crystalline Glaze, 5 1/2 In. 750.00
Flask, Pilgrim, Apple Blossoms, Louise McLaughlin, c.1880, 11 x 9 1/2 In. 2468.00
Jardiniere, Peacock, Garden, Green, Blue, No. 2115, Burmantofts, England, 42 In. 3824.00
Jardiniere, Pedestal, Squeezebag Decoration, Rhead Style, Vance Avon, Early 1900s 13200.00
Pitcher, Hound Handle, Bennington Mold, Parian Biscuit, Green To Amber Glaze, 10 In. .   3565.00
Pitcher, Hound Handle, Hunting Scene, Grapes, Vance Faience, Ohio, c.1900, 9 5/8 In. . . .   590.00

Plaque, Socrates, Green & Ivory Glaze, Moravian, 15 1/2 x 10 1/4 In. 2940.00
Plate, White Slip, Ducks Flying Over Pond, Blue Ground, Maling, 1920s, 11 In. 5175.00
Soap Dish, Frog, Shell, Teal Green Matte Glaze, Mueller Mosaic, 3 1/2 x 5 1/2 In. 590.00
Tazza, Dragon, Grapevine Border, Ruby, Silver & Green, Blue Ground, DeMorgan, 9 In. . . 3450.00
Tea Set, Butterfly Handles, Finials, Painted, Raoul Lachenal, 1920s, 15 Piece 600.00
Tray, Nude Figure, Gray, Blue, Pink Matte Glaze, Signed, Mougin, 6 In. 480.00
Tumbler, Enamel Decoration, Green & White Mistletoe, Blue Ground, Jervis, 4 x 3 In. . . . 2350.00
Vase, 2 Handles, Blue Crystalline Glaze, Green Gray Ground, Pierrefonds, 10 In. 345.00
Vase, 2 Handles, Organic Designs, Crystalline Drip, Blue, Green, Brown, Denbac, 10 In. . . 645.00
Vase, 4 Handles, Crystalline Glaze, Purple, Brown, Green, Denbac, 10 In. 529.00
Vase, Albion, Squirrels, Stone Wall, Pine Limb, Edwin Bennett, 1895, 8 x 8 1/2 In. 2820.00
Vase, Applied Gilt Dragon, Christopher Dresser, Marked, Old Hall, 14 In. . . . . *Illus* 1880.00
Vase, Blue Crystalline Glaze, Gray, Tan, Hi-Glaze, Pierrefonds, 8 1/2 In. 185.00
Vase, Blue, Black, Green, Cream Hi-Glaze, Flowers, Thomas J. Wheatley, c.1879, 7 In. . . . 745.00
Vase, Blue, Gilt, Carnations, Gray Ground, Charlotte Rhead, c.1954, 9 1/4 In. 205.00
Vase, Bud, Bulbous, Frothy Green & Amber, Chicago Crucible, 8 In. 645.00
Vase, Bud, Pitcher Form, Moss Green Glaze, Marked, North State, 4 1/4 x 3 1/4 In. 80.00
Vase, Bulbous, Blue, Pierre Fonds, 9 In. 155.00
Vase, Bulbous, Brown, Gray Crystalline Glaze, 10 1/2 In. 520.00
Vase, Bulbous, Embossed, Mermaids, Fish In The Sea, Vance Avon, 12 1/2 x 10 In. 206.00
Vase, Bulbous, Flame Painted, Luster, Amber, Brouwer, 8 x 6 In. 2820.00
Vase, Bulbous, Long Neck, Green & Black Drip Glaze, Wannopee, 8 1/4 In. 29.00
Vase, Bulbous, Long Neck, Mottled White, Oxblood Red Hi-Glaze, Bretby, 12 1/2 In. 185.00
Vase, Bulbous, Mirror Black Glaze, W.J. Walley, 7 1/2 In. 705.00
Vase, Bulbous, Multitoned, Brown, Red, Tan Drip Glaze, Delaherche, 8 1/2 In. 2645.00
Vase, Bulbous, Turquoise Band, Rust, Cream Ground, 9 In. 160.00
Vase, Bulbous, Turquoise Hi-Glaze, Over Brown, Clement Masier, 7 1/4 In. 230.00
Vase, Cafe Au Lait & Verdigris Crystalline Glaze, Adelaide Robineau, 3 x 4 1/4 In. 2940.00
Vase, Crystalline Glaze, Amber Drip, No. 433, Pierrefonds, Early 1900s, 9 1/4 In. 460.00
Vase, Cylindrical, Prunt, Gunmetal Glaze, Roblin, 4 In. 646.00
Vase, Fan Shape, Painted, Flowers, Leaves, Pink Ground, Maling, 1930s, 7 In. 120.00
Vase, Flared, Peacock Feather, Green, Purple, Brown Matte Glaze, Denbac, 7 1/2 In. 635.00
Vase, Flaring, Pink Flowers, Green Matte Ground, Chicago Crucible, 8 3/4 In. 705.00
Vase, Flattened Shape, White To Black Glaze, Kahler, 7 3/4 In. 25.00
Vase, Glazed Earthenware, Jean Luce, c.1925, 9 3/8 x 7 1/4 In. 1910.00
Vase, Gourd Shape, Animal, Mustard & Burgundy Glaze, Dalpayrat, 9 x 5 1/2 In. 7640.00
Vase, Hammered Texture, Bronze, 3 Handles, 3 Tear Shaped Cabochons, Bretby, 9 In. 705.00
Vase, Limoges Style, Blue, Green, Brown Glaze, Ivory Flowers, Coultry Pottery, 9 In. 175.00
Vase, Organic Shape, 4 Open Handles, Mottled, Green, Brown, Blue, Denbac, 8 1/2 In. . . . 590.00
Vase, Organic Shape, Red, Turquoise, Blue, Eugene Baudin, 7 In. 590.00
Vase, Oriental, Gilded Dragon, Bulbous Base, Flowers, Old Hall, C. Dresser, 14 x 9 In. . . . 1880.00
Vase, Polygonal, Buttresses, Green, Purple, Tan Glaze, Signed, Denbac, 7 In. 175.00
Vase, Purple, Blue Crystalline Glaze, Charles Byse, 3 3/4 In. 115.00
Vase, Round, Mottled Brown Matte Glaze, Crimped Rim, Walley, 4 1/2 In. 175.00
Vase, Slender, Tapered, Purple Metallic Glaze, Orange & Red Drip, Pierrefonds, 16 In. 880.00
Vase, Squat Shape, Abstract Design, Blue, Brown, Green, Tan Field, Kahler, 3 1/4 In. 46.00

Pottery-Contemporary, Bowl, Silver Lizards,
Dragonflies, Emilia Castillo, Mexico, 1991, 9 1/2 In.

Pottery-Contemporary, Bowl, Turquoise, Black
Engobe, Diamonds, Flowers, Walters, 10 In.

Vase, Squat, Rolled Rim, Green, Brown Flambe Glaze, 3-Footed, W.J. Walley, 5 x 7 1/2 In. 1765.00
Vase, Striped Glaze, Blue Green Over Tan, Pierrefonds, 7 In. 46.00
Vase, Underplate, Squat, Denby, 8 x 12 1/4 In. 106.00
Vase, Watcombe, Birds, Flowers, Torquay, Enameled, Bottle Shape, c.1885, 10 In. 345.00
Vase, Zanesville, LaMoro, Glazed, Flowers, Albert Radford, 11 In. 865.00

POTTERY-CONTEMPORARY lists pieces made by artists working after 1975.

Bowl, Ladies, Brown & Cream Ground, Square, Pillin, 4 In. 400.00
Bowl, Luster Glazed, Footed, Beatrice Wood, 4 1/4 In. 2870.00
Bowl, Silver Lizards, Dragonflies, Emilia Castillo, Mexico, 1991, 9 1/2 In. 450.00
Bowl, Turquoise, Black Engobe, Diamonds, Flowers, Walters, 10 In. . . . . *Illus* 800.00
Dish, Black & White Stripes, 6 1/2 In. 46.00
Figurine, Giraffe, Wire Connectors, Accolay, France, 1960s, 11 In. . . . . *Illus* 95.00
Pitcher, Luster Glaze, Beatrice Wood, 4 1/2 In. 1435.00
Pitcher, Woman's Head, Wearing Hat, Bjorn Wiinblad, c.1967, 6 1/2 In. 86.00
Plate, Horses, Cream Ground, Pillin, 5 1/2 In. 175.00
Plate, Women & Birds, Blue Ground, Pillin, 5 1/2 In. 260.00
Tray, Horses, Blue Gray Ground, Black Border, 3-Sided, Pillin, 6 In. 300.00
Tray, Woman Holding Bird, Pillin, 7 In. 375.00
Vase, 2 Running Horses, Tumbler Form, Pillin, 3 In. 315.00
Vase, 4 Fish, Blue Ground, Tumbler Shape, Pillin, 3 1/4 In. 230.00
Vase, Birds, Pink Ground, Pillin, 3 3/4 In. 400.00
Vase, Blue Horses On Cream Ground, 3-Sided, Pillin, 8 In. 850.00
Vase, Bud, 3 Roosters, Cream & Brown Ground, Bulbous, Pillin, 5 3/4 In. 600.00
Vase, Bud, 4 Birds, Pillin, 7 In. 400.00
Vase, Chickens & Birds, Green Ground, Bottle Form, Pillin, 6 1/2 In. 105.00
Vase, Chickens, Brown Ground, Pillin, 4 In. 350.00
Vase, Globular, Aqua, Black Drip Glaze, Rose Cabat, 2 3/4 x 2 1/8 In. 175.00
Vase, Globular, Buttermilk, Golden Yellow Glaze, R. Cabat, Marked, 3 x 2 1/2 In. 115.00
Vase, Globular, Jade Green, Lime Glaze, Black Enamel Drip, R. Cabat, Marked, 3 x 2 1/4 In. 230.00
Vase, Horses, Gray Ground, Cylindrical, Pillin, 7 1/2 In. 115.00
Vase, Horses, Turquoise Ground, Bulbous, Pillin, 5 In. 450.00
Vase, Lady, Birds, Rainbow Ground, Tumbler Form, Pillin, 3 In. 375.00
Vase, Mottled Glaze, Pillin, 8 In. 275.00
Vase, Onion, Frothy Brown, Speckles, Yellow On Neck, R. Cabat, Marked, 2 1/2 x 2 1/4 In. 175.00
Vase, Oval, Speckles, Gray Brown, Lavender, Ocher Band, R. Cabat, 6 1/2 x 3 1/2 In. 920.00
Vase, Oval, Tan, Brown, Speckles, Black Streaks, R. Cabat, Marked, 3 1/2 x 1 3/4 In. 175.00
Vase, Oval, Teal, Purple Crystalline, Olive Flecks, R. Cabat, Marked, 3 1/2 x 2 1/8 In. 230.00
Vase, Rust, Tans, White Gray, Marked, 7 In. 25.00
Vase, School Of Fish, Light Blue Ground, Pillin, 6 1/2 In. 650.00
Vase, Slender, Chartreuse, Olive Glaze, Black Drip, Speckles, R. Cabat, 3 3/4 x 2 In. 175.00
Vase, Stick, 4 Fish, Aqua & Gray Ground, Pillin, 7 In. 450.00
Vase, Stick, Horses, Multicolored Ground, Pillin, 6 In. 550.00
Vase, Teardrop, Hunter Green, Black Feathered Glaze, R. Cabat, Marked, 3 3/4 x 2 1/4 In. . 290.00
Vase, Teardrop, Lavender Streaks, White Glaze, Black, R. Cabat, Marked, 3 1/4 x 2 1/4 In. . 175.00
Vase, Tooled Shoulder Design, Signed, 8 3/4 In. 58.00
Vase, Twisting Oraganic Form, Metallic Glaze, Signed, Gaziello, 6 In. 265.00

Pottery-Contemporary,
Figurine, Giraffe, Wire
Connectors, Accolay,
France, 1960s, 11 In.

Pottery-Midcentury, Chip & Dip Set, Celadon Glaze,
Footed, Ruffled Edge, 1940s, 2 Piece

Pottery-Midcentury, Figurine, Girl
Sitting On Chair,
Thelma Winter,
1950s, 4 3/4 In.

Pottery-Midcentury, Egg Plate, Rooster Salt &
Pepper, A. Price, Japan, 9 In., 3 Piece

Pottery-Midcentury,
Figurine, Rooster, Gray, Blue,
Thelma Winter, 1950s, 11 In.

Vase, Woman & Birds, Gray Ground, Oval, Pillin, 6 In. 475.00
Vase, Women & Birds, Blue Ground, Square Base, Pillin, 6 In. 500.00

POTTERY-MIDCENTURY includes pieces made from the 1940s to the 1980s.
Bowl, Berndt Friberg, Glazed Ceramic, c.1965, 3 x 5 3/4 In. 410.00
Bowl, Earthenware, Swan, Outstretched Wings, Wiinblad, Nymolle, c.1950, 7 In. 121.00
Bowl, Flaring, Brown Glaze, Crackle Glaze Interior, Natzler, 4 In. 355.00
Bowl, Incised Fish, Turquoise Interior, Black Outside, Roseland, 13 1/4 In. 30.00
Bowl, Stylized Snowflake, Citron Yellow, Sage Green, Roseland, 11 In. 16.00
Charger, Abstract Pattern, Brooklin, Theo & Susan Harlander, 1950s, 14 3/4 In. 259.00
Charger, La Pique, Glazed Terre De Faience, Painted, Pablo Picasso, 15 1/4 In. 3880.00
Chip & Dip Set, Celadon Glaze, Footed, Ruffled Edge, 1940s, 2 Piece . . . . *Illus* 150.00
Egg Plate, Rooster Salt & Pepper, A. Price, Japan, 9 In., 3 Piece . . . . *Illus* 30.00
Figurine, Bird Of Paradise, Off-White, Brown & Yellow Highlights, 7 In. 10.00
Figurine, Giraffe, Gray, Marked, Roseland, 7 In. 4.00
Figurine, Girl Sitting On Chair, Thelma Winter, 1950s, 4 3/4 In. . . . . *Illus* 300.00
Figurine, Peacock, Turquoise, Pink, Yellow & White, Marked Roseland, 12 In. 25.00
Figurine, Roadrunner, Green & Yellow, Marked Roseland, 4 x 9 In. 30.00
Figurine, Rooster, Gray, Blue, Thelma Winter, 1950s, 11 In. . . . . *Illus* 600.00
Jar, Cover, Dark Red Drip Glaze, Desiree, Stentoj, Denmark, 1970s, 6 1/2 In. . . . . *Illus* 175.00
Jar, Cover, Incised, Painted, Brooklin, Theo & Susan Harlander, 1950s, 7 In. 259.00
Vase, Black Matte Glaze, Free-Form Figures, W. Germany, 6 1/4 In. . . . . *Illus* 55.00
Vase, Blue, Band Of Figures, Straight Sides, Scheier, 7 1/2 x 7 In. . . . . *Illus* 875.00
Vase, Cylindrical, Geometric Designs, Rachel Koopmans, 1960s, 19 3/4 In. 94.00
Vase, Delicate Shape, Turquoise Glaze, Natzler, 7 In. 1295.00
Vase, Mirrored Glaze, Amber, Ocher, Brown, Egg Shape, Charles F. Binns, 1931, 7 x 5 In. . 3820.00
Vase, Organic Shape, Yellow, Brown, Red Clay, Natzler, 7 In. 1060.00
Vase, Oval, Red, Turquoise Glaze, Natzler, 6 1/2 In. 2235.00
Wall Sconce, Harlequin, Playing Lute, Holding Bottle, 1950s, 9 3/4 In., Pair 330.00

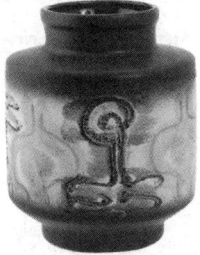

Pottery-Midcentury, Jar, Cover,
Dark Red Drip Glaze, Desiree,
Stentoj, Denmark, 1970s, 6 1/2 In.

Pottery-Midcentury, Vase,
Black Matte Glaze, Free-
Form Figures, W. Germany, 6
1/4 In.

Pottery-Midcentury, Vase, Blue,
Band Of Figures, Straight Sides,
Scheier, 7 1/2 x 7 In.

POWDER FLASKS AND POWDER HORNS were made to hold the gunpowder used in antique firearms. The early examples were made of horn or wood; later ones were of copper or brass.

POWDER FLASK, Ames, Peace, Copper, 4-Position Spout, Eagle, Olive Branch, Arrows, 7 In.	460.00
Ames, U.S.N. Fouled Anchor, Copper, Initials, c.1843, 9 1/4 In.	575.00
Colt 1st Model Dragoon, Brass, Repousse, Patterson Rifles, Revolvers, 9 In.	2760.00
Copper, Brass, Embossed, Liberty Or Death, State Of Texas, Alamo, c.1836, 7 3/4 In.	1060.00
Copper, Eagle, Head Turned Left, Brass Top & Spout, Pocket Size	1725.00
Horn & Copper, Engraved, J.E. Scheid 1767, 6 1/4 x 3 x 1 1/2 In.	350.00
POWDER HORN, 12-Masted Ship, Free Trade, Sailor's Rights, A. Thomas, 1810-30, 12 1/2 In.	1150.00
Black Painted Ground, Flowers, 13 In.	175.00
Boston Map, Ships, Animals, Nathan Worden, Revolutionary War, c.1775, 12 In.	5750.00
Carved, Engraved, Eagle, Geometric, 11 In.	210.00
Carved, Engraved, Sailing Ships, Village Scenes, Geometric, 15 In.	230.00
Carved, Engraved, Sailors, Anchor, Figures, Liberty & Justice, 17 1/4 In.	460.00
Carved, Engraved, Ship's Figurehead, Sailor, Octant, Belle Of Oregon, 17 1/2 In.	405.00
Carved, Engraved, Whales, Sea Life, Lighthouse, 13 In.	185.00
Carved, Engraved, Whaling Scenes, Greasy Luck To Whalers, 19 In.	575.00
Carved, Ships, Mermaid, Sea Serpents, Marked, JT, c.1815, 15 1/4 In.	1150.00
Engraved, 3-Masted Ship, Rt. Williams, Walnut Plug, Late 1700s, 15 1/4 In.	4025.00
Engraved, Animals, Scallop & Line Border, AM, 1823, 10 1/2 In.	440.00
Engraved, Compass Stars, Waves, Sun, Horse & Carriage, John Goddard, 16 In.	1175.00
Engraved, Dome Pine Plug, Flared End, Carrying Strap, 1840, 16 1/2 In.	230.00
Engraved, Inscribed, Whaling, Walnut Plug, Late 1800s, 18 1/4 In.	646.00
Engraved, Job Waterman, Feb The 10 AD 758, Providence, Lobed, 14 In.	880.00
Engraved, Peleg E. Bryant, 3-Masted Ship, Woman, Early 1800s, 10 3/8 In.	440.00
Fish, Scrolling Leaves, Sun Face, A.W. Tunengburg, G. Hutt, c.1759, 19 In.	7200.00
Incised, Animals, Compass Designs, T.F., 1791 & 1807, 10 1/4 x 2 3/4 In.	195.00
Map, Coat Of Arms, North River Route, Fort Stanwix, Jacob Cuyler, 1761, 11 In.	2445.00
Maps, Inscriptions, Coat Of Arms, Banner, Paul Warren Meay, N.Y., 1763, 10 3/4 In.	11165.00
Masted Ship, American Flag, AAB, 6 In.	518.00
New York Map, British Coat Of Arms, Thos. Arrowsmith, c.1759, 12 3/4 In.	3165.00
Sunburst, Flower, House, Inscription, Made For John Douglas, Lake Abeneki, 9 In.	1795.00
Whale's Tooth, Scrimshaw, Balloons, Shapes, French Indian War, c.1723, 16 In.	3740.00
Whale's Tooth, Scrimshaw, British & Napoleonic War Designs, 1800s, 18 In.	1840.00
Whale's Tooth, Scrimshaw, Fish Scales, Silver Plated Dolphin's Head, 16 In.	2875.00
Whale's Tooth, Scrimshaw, Houses, Windmill, Unicorn, Wood Plug, British & Canadian	2070.00
Whale's Tooth, Scrimshaw, Joseph Parmenter, Ship, Brass Spout, c.1800, 17 In.	1035.00

PRATT ware means two different things. It was an early Staffordshire pottery, cream-colored with colored decorations, made by Felix Pratt during the late eighteenth century. There was also Pratt ware made with transfer designs during the mid-nineteenth century in Fenton, England. Reproductions of the transfer-printed Pratt are being made. More Pratt may be listed in Potlid.

PRATT FENTON

Cachepot, Landscapes, 3 Panels, Semicircular, Soft Paste, Pearlware, 8 x 4 1/2 x 6 In.	2070.00
Creamer, Cow, Milkmaid Dressed In Yellow, Sponge Decorated, 7 In.	345.00
Figurine, Eagle, Molded, Soft Paste, 5 Colors, 3 1/4 In.	1495.00
Mug, Molded Design, Man Counting Money, Arches, Leaves, Frog Inside, 4 Colors, 4 In.	862.00
Plaque, 2 Lions, Lying Down, Oval, Pearlware, England, 10 3/4 In.	1725.00
Plaque, 2 Lions, Lying Down, Oval, Sam Till, Pearlware, England, 9 3/4 In.	2185.00
Stirrup Cup, Pope & Devil Images	1650.00
Teapot, Leaves, Flowers, Feathering, Chain Links, Child Finial, 7 3/4 In.	632.00
Toby Jug, Man, Green Coat, Ocher Breeches, Holding Jug, 8 In.	920.00
Tray, Blind Fiddler, Pink Band, Gilt Border, Oval, 2 Handles, Oval Foot, 14 In., Pair	575.00

PRESSED GLASS was first made in the United States in the 1820s after the invention of glass pressing machines. Hundreds of patterns of pressed glass were made in complete table settings. Although the Boston and Sandwich Works was the most famous of the pressed glass factories, there were about sixteen other factories making pressed glass from 1830 to 1850, and still more from 1850 to 1900, when pressed glass reached its greatest popularity. It is now being widely repro-

duced. The pattern names used in this listing are based on the information in the book *Pressed Glass in America* by John and Elizabeth
Welker. There may be pieces of pressed glass listed in this book in
other categories, such as Lamp, Ruby, Sandwich, and Souvenir.

1000-Eye pattern is listed here as Thousand Eye.
Acanthus pattern is listed here as Ribbed Palm.
Actress, Compote, Cover, 7 x 11 In. 55.00
Actress, Goblet, Lotta Portrait, 6 1/2 In. 88.00
Amberette, Berry Set, Amber Stain, Satin, 7 Piece 275.00
Amberette, Sauce, Amber Stain, Footed, 1 3/4 x 4 In. .... *Illus* 20.00
Amberette, Tumbler, Amber Stain, Frosted, 4 In. 80.00
Arched Leaf, Goblet, 6 1/8 In. 65.00
Argus, Goblet, 5 Row, 6 In. 90.00
Argus, Salt, Cover, 5 Row, Acorn Finial, 5 In., Pair 165.00
Argus, Tumbler, 3 3/4 In. 39.00
Ashburton, Bowl, Footed, 3 1/4 x 8 1/8 In. 35.00
Ashburton, Celery Vase, Scalloped Rim, 10 1/2 In. 176.00
Ashburton, Eggcup, Clear, Footed, c.1860, 3 1/2 In. .... *Illus* 25.00
Ashburton, Tumbler, Ale, Long Tom, 6 1/4 In. 110.00
Ashburton, Tumbler, Ship's, Flared Rim, Hexagonal Foot, 4 1/4 x 3 3/4 In. 110.00
Ashburton With Sawtooth, Tumbler, Handle, 3 3/4 In. 90.00
Atlanta, Creamer, 5 In. 45.00
Atlanta, Goblet, 5 3/4 In. 121.00
Baby Thumbprint pattern is listed here as Dakota.
Bakewell Block, Celery Vase, Scalloped Rim, 9 In. 120.00
Balder pattern is listed here as Pennsylvania.
Baltimore Pear, Cake Plate, 6 1/2 x 9 In. 110.00
Banded Portland, Bowl, Oval, Maiden's Blush, Gold Trim, 8 3/4 x 12 In. 165.00
Banded Portland, Goblet, Maiden's Blush, 6 In. 50.00
Barrel Honeycomb, see the related pattern Honeycomb.
Beaded Acorn With Leaf Band, Goblet, 5 7/8 In. 165.00
Bearded Head pattern is listed here as Viking.
Beaver Band, Goblet, 5 1/2 In. 1045.00
Bellflower, Bowl, Left Facing Vine, Footed, 4 1/4 In. 550.00
Bellflower, Butter, Cover, Right Facing Vine On Cover, Left On Base 80.00
Bellflower, Champagne, Left Facing Vine, 5 In. 175.00
Bellflower, Compote, Left Facing Vine, 7 5/8 x 8 1/4 In. 605.00
Bellflower, Compote, Left Facing Vine, Double Flower, 8 x 8 In. 770.00
Bellflower, Creamer, Left Facing Vine 198.00
Bellflower, Creamer, Left Facing Vine, 3 1/4 In. 660.00
Bellflower, Spooner, Left Facing Vine, 5 1/2 In. 39.00
Bellflower, Spooner, Left Facing Vine, Cobalt Blue, Scallop & Point Rim, 5 5/8 In. 9900.00
Bellflower, Wine, Left Facing Vine, Straight Sides, Rayed Foot, 4 In. 120.00
Bellflower, Wine, Right Facing Vine, Barrel Shape, Knop Stem, 4 In. 50.00
Bellflower Double Vine, Decanter, Left & Right Facing Vines, Qt., 9 1/2 In. 468.00
Bellflower Double Vine, Decanter, Right Facing Vines, Pewter Stopper, Pt., 9 5/8 In. 1760.00

Pressed Glass, Amberette,
Sauce, Amber Stain, Footed,
1 3/4 x 4 In.

Pressed Glass,
Ashburton, Eggcup, Clear,
Footed, c.1860, 3 1/2 In.

Pressed Glass, Deer & Pine Tree,
Mug, Amber Stain,
Footed, 3 1/4 In.

Bellflower Double Vine, Tumbler, Right Facing Vines, Footed, 4 3/4 In. 230.00
Bellflower With Loops, Goblet, 5 7/8 In. 198.00
Bigler, Tumbler, Lemonade, Handle, 3 In. 145.00
Bird & Strawberry, Tumbler, Ruby Stain, 4 3/8 In. 132.00
Blaze, Sugar, Cover, Octagonal Stem, Circular Foot, 7 1/2 In. 33.00
Bleeding Heart, Cake Stand, Octagonal Stem, 5 x 10 In. 185.00
Bleeding Heart, Spooner, Scalloped Rim, 5 1/2 In. 55.00
Block & Fine Cut pattern is listed here as Fine Cut & Block.
Bluebird pattern is listed here as Bird & Strawberry.
Bradford Blackberry, Tumbler, 3 3/4 In. 55.00
Bradford Grape pattern is listed here as Bradford Blackberry.
Brilliant, Goblet, 6 1/8 In. 35.00
Bull's-Eye, Creamer 286.00
Bull's-Eye, Goblet, Knob Stem, 6 In. 55.00
Bull's-Eye, Goblet, Low Knob Stem, 6 1/2 In. 65.00
Bull's-Eye & Rosette, Whiskey, 3 In. 275.00
Bull's-Eye & Wishbone, Goblet, 6 In. 190.00
Bull's-Eye With Diamond Point, Goblet, 6 3/4 In. ....120.00 to 165.00
Bull's-Eye With Diamond Point, Whiskey, 3 1/4 In. 198.00
Bull's-Eye With Fleur-De-Lis, Goblet, 6 1/4 In. 99.00
Bungalo, Water Set, 9 7/8-In. Pitcher, 7 Piece 935.00
Button Arches, Butter, Cover, Ruby Stain, 5 1/2 In. 80.00
Button Arches, Salt & Pepper, Ruby Stain, 3 In. 39.00
Cabbage Leaf, Butter, Cover, Frosted, 5 x 6 In. 630.00
Cable, Compote, 7 1/4 x 8 In. 55.00
Cable, Decanter, Bar, Qt., 10 1/4 In. 190.00
Cable, Goblet, 5 1/2 In. 120.00
Cable, Goblet, 6 3/8 In. 88.00
Cable, Tumbler, 3 7/8 In. 145.00
Cable With Ring, Sugar & Creamer, Cover 198.00
Candlewick as a pressed glass pattern is properly named *Banded Raindrop*. There is also a pattern called *Candlewick*, which has been made by Imperial Glass Corporation since 1936. It is listed in this book in the Imperial Glass category.
Cape Cod, Goblet, 5 1/2 In. 45.00
Centennial, see the related patterns Liberty Bell.
Chandelier, Goblet, 6 1/8 In. 65.00
Chilson, Goblet, 6 5/8 In. 385.00
Church Windows pattern is listed here as Columbia.
Circle & Ellipse, Vase, Amethyst, Octagonal, 7 1/2 In., Pair 660.00
Classic, Creamer, Log Feet, 5 1/2 In. 100.00
Coin Spot pattern is listed in this book in its own category.
Colonial, Creamer 230.00
Colonial, Goblet, 6 1/4 In. 99.00
Columbia, Compote, 7 5/8 x 8 1/2 In. 35.00
Comet, Goblet, 6 In. 90.00
Comet, Tumbler, 3 1/2 In. 176.00
Comet, Tumbler, Lemonade, Handle, 3 In. 1210.00
Corona, Pitcher, Water, Ruby Stain, 8 3/4 In. 100.00
Cosmos pattern is listed in this book as its own category.
Croesus, Creamer, Amethyst, Gold Trim, 3 In. 154.00
Croesus, Creamer, Emerald Green, Gold Trim 17.00
Crown Jewels is a name used for a different pattern listed here as Chandelier.
Crystal Wedding, Goblet, Amber, 5 3/4 In. 210.00
Crystal Wedding, Sugar, Ruby Stain 44.00
Cube With Fan pattern is listed here as Pineapple & Fan.
Curling Heartless, Compote, Pagoda Style Cover, 10 1/4 In. 231.00
Cut Bellflower, Goblet, 6 In. 770.00
Dahlia pattern is listed here as Square Fuchsia.
Dakota, Pitcher, Milk, Engraved Fern & Berry, Qt., 9 1/4 In. 80.00
Deer & Doe With Lily Of The Valley, Goblet, 6 In. 275.00
Deer & Dog, Goblet, Claret, 4 3/4 In. 50.00
Deer & Dog, Pitcher, Milk, Tankard Shape, Reeded Handle, 7 In. 330.00
Deer & Dog, Sugar, Cover 190.00

Deer & Pine Tree, Bread Tray, Apple Green, 9 1/2 x 13 In. 99.00
Deer & Pine Tree, Mug, Amber Stain, Footed, 3 1/4 In. .... *Illus* 20.00
Diamond Point, Compote, Paneled Baluster Stem, Round Base, Flint, 10 x 10 In. 345.00
Diamond Point, Pitcher, Water, 9 3/8 In. 415.00
Diamond Point, Sugar & Creamer, Cover 176.00
Diamond Point With Panels, Champagne, 5 1/8 In. 55.00
Diamond Point With Panels, Goblet, 6 1/4 In. 65.00
Diamond Point With Panels, Tumbler, Lemonade, Handle, Footed, 3 5/8 In. 209.00
Diamond Thumbprint, Compote, 6 x 8 3/8 In. 99.00
Diamond Thumbprint, Compote, 7 1/2 x 10 1/4 In. 120.00
Diamond Thumbprint, Goblet, 6 1/2 In. 209.00
Diamond Thumbprint, Tumbler, 3 1/2 In. 45.00
Diamonds In Ovals, Goblet, 6 In. 55.00
Diamonds With Double Fans, Spooner, Ruby Stain, 4 3/8 In. 39.00
Divided Heart, Goblet, Variant, 6 1/4 In. 145.00
Dolphin, Compote, Frosted Stem & Foot, 7 1/4 x 8 1/2 In. 80.00
Double Vine pattern is listed here as Bellflower Double Vine.
Double Wedding Ring pattern is listed here as Wedding Ring.
Dragon, Goblet, 5 5/8 In. 2860.00
Early Moon & Star, Tumbler, Footed, 4 1/4 In. 190.00
Early Thumbprint, Compote, 7 Rows, 32-Scallop Rim, 9 1/8 x 11 1/2 In. 1045.00
Early Thumbprint, Cordial, 3 1/4 In. 35.00
Early Thumbprint, Decanter, Bar, Qt., 10 7/8 In. 130.00
Early Thumbprint, Goblet, 5 3/4 In. 45.00
Early Thumbprint, Goblet, 6 1/2 In. 39.00
Early Thumbprint, Pitcher, Water, 9 1/8 In. 605.00
Early Thumbprint, Tumbler, 3 5/8 In. 65.00
Early Thumbprint, Tumbler, Footed, 5 In. 20.00
English Hobnail Cross pattern is listed here as Amberette.
Esther, Jelly Compote, Green, Gold Trim, 5 x 4 In. 50.00
Etched Alligator, Goblet, 6 1/4 In. 55.00
Etched Camel Caravan, Goblet, 6 1/4 In. 33.00
Etched Dakota pattern is listed here as Dakota.
Etched Feeding Swan, Goblet, 5 3/4 In. 45.00
Etched Giraffe, Goblet, 6 In. 80.00
Etched Ibex, Goblet, 6 1/4 In. 65.00
Etched Monkey Climber, Goblet, 6 In. 28.00
Etched Stork, Goblet, 6 1/4 In. 18.00
Etched Two Tigers, Goblet, 6 In. 99.00
Eureka, Creamer, Octagonal Stem, Round Foot 55.00
Excelsior, Creamer 580.00
Festoon & Grape pattern is listed here as Grape & Festoon.
Fine Cut, Goblet, Amber Stain, 6 Panels, 6 In. 66.00
Fine Cut & Block, Sugar, Cover, Pink Stain 165.00
Fine Cut & Panel, Cake Plate, Blue, 10 1/4 In. 99.00
Fine Diamond Point, Goblet, 6 1/8 In. 20.00
Fine Rib, Champagne, 5 1/4 In. 55.00
Fine Rib, Compote, 7 3/4 x 9 In. 45.00
Fine Rib, Goblet, 6 1/4 In. 20.00
Fine Rib, Tumbler, Lemonade, Handle, 3 In. 165.00
Fine Rib, Wine, 4 In. 17.00
Fine Rib With Cut Ovals, Bowl, 3 Row, 8 1/8 In. 55.00
Fine Rib With Cut Ovals, Compote, 7 x 8 1/4 In. 90.00
Fine Rib With Cut Ovals, Goblet, 2 Row, 6 1/4 In. 990.00
Fine Rib With Cut Ovals, Tumbler, 3 Rows, 3 1/2 In. 305.00
Fine Rib With Cut Ovals, Wine, 3 Row, 4 In. 110.00
Flamingo, Goblet, 6 1/4 In. 110.00
Flat Diamond & Panel, Decanter, Stopper, Qt., 10 3/4 In. 28.00
Flat Diamond & Panel, Goblet, 6 1/4 In. 165.00
Florida, Spooner, Ruby & Amber Stain, 4 1/2 In. 66.00
Flower Medallion, Goblet, 6 1/8 In. 99.00
Flute With Bull's Eye Variant, Goblet, 6 In. 45.00
Four Petal, Sugar & Creamer, Cover ....110.00 to 220.00

Four Ring, Pitcher, Water, 9 In. 55.00
Frosted patterns may also be listed under the name of the main pattern.
Frosted Eagle, Compote, Cover, 10 3/4 In. 65.00
Frosted Flower Band, Butter, Cover, 7 x 6 In. 44.00
Frosted Flower Band, Pitcher, Water, 9 1/4 In. 99.00
Frosted Leaf, Champagne, 4 7/8 In. 110.00
Frosted Leaf, Decanter, Stopper, Pt., 11 1/2 In. 150.00
Frosted Leaf, Goblet, 5 3/4 In. 100.00
Frosted Leaf, Goblet, 6 1/2 In. 28.00
Frosted Leaf, Wine, 3 3/4 In. 145.00
Garden Of Eden, see also the related pattern Lotus & Serpent.
Garfield Drape, Pitcher, Milk, Inverted Feather Above Handle, 8 1/2 In. 154.00
Giant Prism With Thumbprint Band, Celery Vase, 9 In. 120.00
Giant Prism With Thumbprint Band, Tumbler, Ale, 6 3/4 In. 190.00
Giant Prism With Thumbprint Band, Tumbler, Ship's, Concave Sides, 4 1/2 In. 100.00
Giant Prism With Thumbprint Band, Tumbler, Whiskey, 3 3/8 In. ....65.00 to 110.00
Girl With Fan, Goblet, Straight Stem, 5 7/8 In. 50.00
Gothic, Champagne, Plain Foot, 5 1/8 In. 132.00
Gothic, Wine, 3 7/8 In. 80.00
Gothic Arch, Celery Vase, Flared Scalloped Rim, 10 In. 165.00
Gothic Arch & Plume, Plate, Oval, Lacy, Midwestern, 6 1/4 x 9 1/4 In. 230.00
Grape, see also the related pattern Magnet & Grape with Frosted Leaf.
Grape & Cable pattern is listed in this book in the Northwood category.
Grape & Festoon, Buttermilk, Footed, 4 1/2 x 3 3/4 In. .... *Illus* 32.00
Hamilton With Clear Leaf pattern is listed here as Hamilton With Leaf.
Hamilton With Leaf, Tumbler, Lemonade, Handle, 2 7/8 In. 550.00
Hand, Cake Plate, Blue, Ribbed Domed Foot, 11 1/8 In. 88.00
Harp, Goblet, 6 1/8 In. 2420.00
Hawaiian Pineapple, Tumbler, 3 5/8 In. 120.00
Hinoto pattern is listed here as Diamond Point with Panels.
Hobnail pattern is in this book as its own category.
Holly, Cake Plate, 6 1/4 x 10 3/4 In. 143.00
Holly, Goblet, 5 7/8 In. 209.00
Honeycomb, Celery Vase, 9 3/4 In. 210.00
Horn Of Plenty, Bowl, Domed Foot, 3 1/2 x 7 In. 80.00
Horn Of Plenty, Butter, Cover, Washington's Head, 5 x 6 In. 1100.00
Horn Of Plenty, Celery Vase, 8 3/4 In. ....190.00 to 198.00
Horn Of Plenty, Champagne, 5 1/4 In. 65.00
Horn Of Plenty, Compote, 6 1/2 x 8 In. 77.00
Horn Of Plenty, Compote, 8 1/2 In. 210.00
Horn Of Plenty, Creamer, 8-Lobed Foot, 6 1/2 In. 470.00
Horn Of Plenty, Decanter, Diamond Point Stopper, 11 1/2 In. 230.00
Horn Of Plenty, Goblet, 6 1/4 In. 80.00
Horn Of Plenty, Tumbler, 3 3/4 In. ....39.00 to 44.00
Horn Of Plenty, Tumbler, Lemonade, Handle, 3 In. 120.00
Horn Of Plenty, Whiskey, 3 In. 120.00
Horn Of Plenty, Wine, 4 1/2 In. 50.00
Horse, Cat & Rabbit, Goblet, 6 3/8 In. 605.00
Inverted Fern, Champagne, 4 7/8 In. 90.00
Inverted Fern, Tumbler, 3 1/2 In. 120.00
Inverted Strawberry, Tumbler, Ruby Stain, 3 3/4 In. 35.00
Ivy In Snow, Cake Plate, Amber Stain, Square, 6 x 10 In. 468.00
Jersey Variant, Creamer, 7-Sided, Strap Handle, 4 1/4 In. 66.00
Jeweled Moon & Star pattern is listed here as Moon & Star Variant or Moon & Star.
Jumbo, Goblet, 6 1/8 In. 523.00
Jumbo, Spooner, 5 In. 33.00
Kamoni pattern is listed here as Pennsylvania.
King's Crown, Celery Vase, Ruby Stain, 6 In. 55.00
King's Crown, Goblet, Ruby Stain, 5 3/4 In. .... *Illus* 10.00
Klondike pattern is listed here as Amberette.
Lattice & Oval Panels pattern is listed here as Flat Diamond & Panel.
Leaf & Flower, Celery Vase, Amber Stain, Frosted, 6 5/8 In. 39.00
Leaf & Scroll, Spooner, 4 7/8 In. 66.00

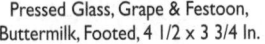

Pressed Glass, Grape & Festoon,
Buttermilk, Footed, 4 1/2 x 3 3/4 In.

Pressed Glass, King's Crown,
Goblet, Ruby Stain, 5 3/4 In.

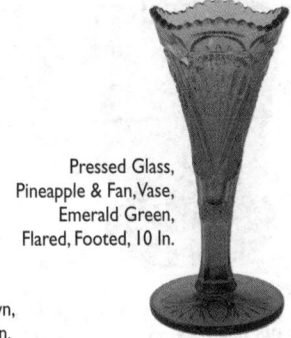

Pressed Glass,
Pineapple & Fan, Vase,
Emerald Green,
Flared, Footed, 10 In.

Liberty Bell, Creamer, 6 3/4 In.	44.00
Liberty Bell, Pitcher, Water, 9 In.	525.00
Liberty Bell, Salt & Pepper, Embossed 1776 Liberty 1876, Metal Lid, 3 In.	475.00
Liberty Bell, Sugar, Cover, 8 7/8 In.	65.00
Lincoln Drape, Compote, 5 x 7 In.	55.00
Lincoln Drape, Goblet, 6 In.	130.00 to 155.00
Lincoln Drape, Molasses Jug, Handle, Metal Cover, 6 3/4 In.	145.00
Lincoln Drape With Tassel, Goblet, 5 7/8 In.	255.00 to 340.00
Lion, Butter, Cover, Frosted, 7 3/4 In.	70.00
Lion, Compote, Cover, Frosted, 10 In.	175.00
Lion, Compote, Cover, Frosted, 13 In.	144.00
Lion, Compote, Cover, Frosted, Lion & Tree Trunk Finial, 11 1/4 x 7 In.	209.00
Lion, Creamer, Frosted, 7 In.	60.00
Lion, Dish, Cover, Frosted, Oval, 6 1/2 In.	90.00
Lion, Goblet, Frosted, 6 5/8 In.	65.00
Lion, Marmalade, Cover, Frosted, 7 In.	115.00
Lion, Pitcher, Milk, Frosted, Applied Handle, Pressed Fan On Crimp, 6 3/4 In.	715.00
Lion, Plate, Frosted, 12 1/4 In.	45.00
Lion, Platter, Frosted, Oval, 13 In.	45.00
Lion, Spooner, Frosted, 5 1/2 In.	45.00
Lion, Sugar, Cover, Frosted, 8 1/2 In.	85.00
Lion, Syrup, Frosted, Britannia Cover, 7 In.	525.00
Little Red Riding Hood, Punch Set, Girl, Wolf, Grandmother, Child's, 1890, 7 Piece	255.00
Log Cabin, Compote, Cover, 10 1/4 x 7 In.	935.00
Log Cabin, Pitcher, Water, 8 1/4 In.	1045.00
Lotus & Serpent, Goblet, 6 In.	130.00
Magnet & Grape With Frosted Leaf, Champagne, 5 In.	255.00
Magnet & Grape With Frosted Leaf, Compote, Domed Foot, 7 7/8 In.	65.00
Magnet & Grape With Frosted Leaf, Goblet, 6 1/2 In.	66.00 to 88.00
Magnet & Grape With Frosted Leaf, Tumbler, 3 1/2 In.	77.00
Magnet & Grape With Frosted Leaf, Tumbler, Footed, 5 3/4 In.	90.00
Millard, Sugar, Cover, Ruby Stain	50.00
Mirror, Champagne, 4 3/4 In.	22.00
Mirror, Creamer, 5 3/4 In.	90.00
Monkey, Butter, Cover, Rayed Base, 6 In.	515.00
Monkey, Celery Vase, 6 3/4 In.	715.00
Monkey, Pitcher, Water, Rayed Base, 8 3/4 x 4 1/2 In.	1265.00
Moon & Star, Cake Plate, 7 1/4 x 10 In.	55.00
Moon & Star, Molasses Jug, Tin Cover, 6 3/4 In.	187.00
Moon & Star, Spill Holder, Canary, Footed, Flint, 4 1/2 In.	230.00
Morning Glory, Compote, 6 1/8 In.	242.00
Morning Glory, Goblet, 6 In.	1210.00 to 1375.00
Nail, Champagne, Etched Leaves, 5 In.	28.00
New England Pineapple, Goblet, 6 1/8 In.	80.00
New England Pineapple, Sugar, Cover, Footed	198.00

Pressed Glass, Rabbit, Mug,
Cobalt Blue, 3 3/8 In.

Pressed Glass, Rose In Snow, Relish,
Blue, Handles, 8 1/4 In.

New England Pineapple, Tumbler, 3 3/4 In. 110.00
Old Abe pattern is listed here as Frosted Eagle.
One-Thousand Eye pattern is listed here as Thousand Eye.
Oregon, see the related pattern Skilton.
Ovals With Long Bars, Goblet, 6 5/8 In. 55.00
Owl pattern is listed here as Bull's-Eye with Diamond Point.
Owl & Possum, Goblet, 6 In. 99.00
Owl & Pussycat, Cheese Dish, Cover, 6 1/4 x 8 In. 350.00
Paneled Flattened Sawtooth, Goblet, 6 5/8 In. 65.00
Paneled Forget-Me-Not, Wine, 4 1/4 In. 50.00
Paneled Ribbed Shell With Daisy & Button, Pitcher, Water, Vaseline, 8 7/8 In. 176.00
Paneled Wheat, Sugar, Cover 360.00
Pavonia, Waste Bowl, Ruby Stain, 3 x 4 In. 50.00
Pennsylvania, see also the related pattern Hand.
Pennsylvania, Goblet, Ruby Stain, 6 In. 330.00
Pigs In Corn, Goblet, Left Husk Bent, 5 7/8 In. 525.00
Pillar, Jam Jar, 6 In. 45.00
Pinafore pattern is listed here as Actress.
Pineapple & Fan, Vase, Emerald Green, Flared, Footed, 10 In. . . . . *Illus* 200.00
Plain Tulip, Tumbler, Lemonade, Handle, 2 7/8 In. 66.00
Polar Bear, Goblet, Frosted, 6 In. 176.00
Portland With Diamond Point Band pattern is listed here as Banded Portland.
Primrose, Cup, Shelley 55.00
Prism, Cruet, Handle, Footed, 10 In. 120.00
Prism, Giant, Pitcher, Water, 9 1/2 In. 198.00
Prism With Diamond Points, Tumbler, 3 3/8 In. 45.00
Rabbit, Mug, Cobalt Blue, 3 3/8 In. . . . . *Illus* 30.00
Ribbed Clover, Tumbler, 3 1/2 In. 28.00
Ribbed Ivy, Salt, Cover, Flower Finial, 4 1/2 In. 120.00
Ribbed Ivy, Tumbler, 3 1/4 In. 66.00
Ribbed Ivy, Whiskey, Handle, 2 3/4 In. 132.00
Ribbed Palm, Bowl, Footed, 4 1/4 x 7 In. 35.00
Ribbed Palm, Pitcher, Water, 9 In. 468.00
Ribbed Palm, Tumbler, 2 1/2 In. 39.00
Ribbed Palm, Tumbler, 3 1/2 In. 90.00
Ringed Framed Ovals, Tumbler, Blue Green, Footed, 4 3/8 In. 440.00
Roanoke, Berry Set, Ruby Stain, 9-In. Master, 5 Piece 132.00
Roman Key, Champagne, Frosted, 4 7/8 In. 55.00
Roman Key, Goblet, Frosted, 5 7/8 In. 55.00
Roman Key, Tumbler, 3 1/2 In. 44.00
Roman Key, Tumbler, Frosted, 3 1/2 In. 77.00
Roman Key, Tumbler, Frosted, Footed, 5 In. 28.00
Roman Key With Broken Petals, Tumbler, 3 1/2 In. 45.00
Roman Key With Petals, Goblet, Frosted, 6 In. 110.00
Rose In Snow, Relish, Blue, Handles, 8 1/4 In. . . . . *Illus* 95.00
Rose Sprig, Compote, Blue, 6 x 8 1/2 In. 50.00
Ruby Thumbprint, see the related pattern King's Crown.
Rustic, Compote, Cover, Tree Stump Finial, 9 3/4 x 7 1/2 In. . . . . *Illus* 50.00
Sandwich Flute, Goblet, 6 1/2 In. 45.00

Saxon, Spooner, Ruby Stain, 6 In.	55.00
Scalloped Swirl, Saltshaker, Ruby Stain, 3 In.	28.00
Scarab, Goblet, Rayed Foot, 6 3/8 In.	77.00
Scarab, Wine, Rayed Foot, 4 3/8 In.	77.00
Shell & Tassel, Bowl, Amber, Oval, 9 3/4 In.	35.00
Shell & Tassel, Cake Plate, Square, 10 In.	110.00
Shell & Tassel, Sugar, Cover, Round, Dog Finial	120.00
Shield & Anchor, Goblet, 6 1/4 In.	55.00
Sitting Swan, Goblet, 6 1/8 In.	825.00
Skilton, Compote, Ruby Stain, 4 1/2 x 7 In.	45.00
Skilton, Tumbler, Ruby Stain, 3 5/8 In.	35.00
Square Fuchsia, Goblet, Canary, 5 5/8 In.	90.00
Square Fuchsia, Goblet, Wine, Canary, 4 In.	80.00
Square Fuchsia, Pitcher, Water, Blue, 8 3/4 In.	90.00
Square Fuchsia, Pitcher, Water, Canary, 8 3/4 In.	99.00
Squirrel, Goblet, 6 In.	468.00
Squirrel, Pitcher, Water, 8 3/4 In.	468.00
St. Bernard, Compote, Cover, 9 1/2 x 7 1/4 In.	176.00
Star & Punty pattern is listed here as Moon & Star.	
Swag Block, Goblet, Ruby Stain, 6 1/4 In.	55.00
Swan, Butter, Cover, 6 1/2 x 7 In.	55.00
Swan With Fish, Goblet, 5 1/2 In.	635.00
Thousand Eye, Goblet, Blue, 6 In. *Illus*	30.00
Three Birds, Pitcher, Water, 9 In.	230.00
Three Face, Cake Plate, 8 1/4 x 10 1/2 In.	220.00
Three Face, Compote, Cover, 9 1/4 In.	660.00
Three Face, Goblet, 6 1/4 In.	90.00
Three Graces, see the related pattern Three Face.	
Three Sisters pattern is listed here as Three Face.	
Three-Printie Block, Goblet, 5 3/4 In.	715.00
Tidy pattern is listed here as Rustic.	
Tree Of Life, Champagne, 6 1/8 In.	90.00
Tree Of Life, Claret, 5 1/4 In.	100.00
Tree Of Life, Cordial, 4 3/8 In.	99.00
Tree Of Life, Epergne, Scalloped Rim, 6-Petal Top, 19 x 8 In.	710.00
Tree Of Life, Mug, Amethyst, 3 5/8 In.	275.00
Tree Of Life, Pitcher, Water, 9 In.	358.00
Tree Of Life, Wine, 4 3/4 In.	110.00
Tree Of Life With Hand, Butter, Cover, Frosted Finial & Foot, 6 In.	110.00
Tree Of Life With Hand, Compote, 8 3/4 x 8 In.	80.00
Trilby, Goblet, 5 3/4 In.	190.00
Tulip With Sawtooth, Compote, 10 x 9 In.	66.00
Tulip With Sawtooth, Decanter, Stopper, Qt., 12 In.	155.00
Tulip With Sawtooth, Tumbler, 3 5/8 In.	65.00
Tulip With Sawtooth, Tumbler, 3 5/8 In., Pair	145.00
U.S. Coin, Compote, Cover, 10 1/2 In.	715.00
Valentine pattern is listed here as Trilby.	
Victoria, Compote, 10 1/2 x 10 1/4 In.	176.00

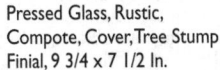

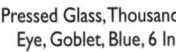

Pressed glass banana stands are being used today to hold rolled hand towels in a bathroom.

Pressed Glass, Rustic, Compote, Cover, Tree Stump Finial, 9 3/4 x 7 1/2 In.

Pressed Glass, Thousand Eye, Goblet, Blue, 6 In.

Viking, Eggcup, 3 1/2 In. 55.00
Waffle, Creamer, Allover Pattern, 5 In. 65.00
Waffle, Tumbler, 3 5/8 In. 39.00
Waffle & Thumbprint, Champagne, 5 1/2 In. 110.00
Waffle & Thumbprint, Decanter, 1/2 Pt., 7 In. 265.00
Waffle & Thumbprint, Goblet, 6 1/8 In. 110.00
Waffle & Thumbprint, Sugar, Cover, 9 1/2 In. 300.00
Waffle & Thumbprint, Tumbler, 3 1/2 In. 44.00
Waffle & Thumbprint, Wine, 4 5/8 In. 80.00
Washington, Celery Vase, 8 1/2 In. 39.00
Washington, Goblet, 5 1/2 In. 50.00
Washington, Salt, Master, 2 3/4 x 2 3/4 In. 17.00
Wedding Ring, Tumbler, 3 1/2 In. 99.00
Westward Ho, Celery Vase, 8 1/2 In. 155.00
Westward Ho, Compote, Cover, Oval, 9 1/8 In. 175.00
Westward Ho, Creamer, 7 In. 110.00
Westward Ho, Spooner, 6 1/2 In. 65.00
Wildflower, Syrup, Light Blue, Britannia Cover, 8 In. 190.00
Wyoming, Cake Plate, 4 x 9 In. 55.00
Yoke Band, Goblet, Ruby Stain, 5 1/2 In. 275.00

PRINT, in this listing, means any of many printed images produced on paper by one of the more common methods, such as lithography. The prints listed here are of interest primarily to the antiques collector, not the fine arts collector. Many of these prints were originally part of books. Other prints will be found in the Advertising, Currier & Ives, Movie, and Poster categories.

Audubon bird prints were originally issued as part of books printed from 1826 to 1854. They were issued in two sizes, 26 1/2 inches by 39 1/2 inches and 11 inches by 7 inches. The quadrupeds were issued in 28-by-22-inch prints. Later editions of the Audubon books were done in many sizes, and reprints of the books in the original size were also made. The bird pictures have been so popular they have been copied in myriad sizes by both old and new printing methods. This list includes originals and later copies because Audubon prints of all ages are sold in antiques shops.

Audubon, American Oystercatcher, 1834, 26 5/8 x 39 1/2 In. 4541.00
Audubon, Belted Kingfisher, 1829, 39 1/2 x 26 3/8 In. 11950.00
Audubon, Black Vulture, Lithograph, Frame, Marked, J. Bien, 1860, 25 x 38 In. 863.00
Audubon, Blue-Winged Teal, 1836, 26 1/2 x 39 1/2 In. 8963.00
Audubon, Blue-Winged Yellow Warbler, R. Havell, 1827, 39 1/4 x 26 In. 7170.00
Audubon, Bonaparte Flycatcher, W. H. Lizars, 1826, 39 1/2 x 26 1/2 In. 3107.00
Audubon, Cedar Wax-Wing, R. Havell, 1828, 39 1/4 x 26 1/4 In. 9560.00
Audubon, Cerulean Warbler, R. Havell, 1828, 39 1/2 x 26 7/8 In. 3585.00
Audubon, Common Nighthawk, 1832, 39 1/4 x 26 5/8 In. 9560.00
Audubon, Downy Woodpecker, 1831, 39 3/8 x 26 3/8 In. 8963.00
Audubon, Great Carolina Wren, 1829, 39 1/4 x 28 1/8 In. 5975.00
Audubon, Indigo Bunting, R. Havell, 1829, 39 1/4 x 26 1/2 In. 5019.00
Audubon, Kentucky Warbler, R. Havell, 1828, 39 x 26 1/4 In. 4541.00
Audubon, Painted Bunting, R. Havell, 1829, 39 5/8 x 26 1/2 In. 14340.00
Audubon, Piping Plover, 1834, 26 1/2 x 39 3/4 In. 3107.00
Audubon, Red-Headed Woodpecker, R. Havell, 1827, 39 1/4 x 26 In. 7170.00
Audubon, Turkey Vulture, 1832, 39 5/8 x 26 5/8 In. 5019.00
Battle Of Spottsylvania, Color Lithograph, Frame, c.1887, 15 x 21 In. 374.00
Boileau, Philip, Pretty Girl, Cover, Sunday Magazine, Sunday Star, c.1914, 14 x 20 In. ... 12.00
Buzza, Motto, Happiness & Home, Art Deco Style, Verse, Frame, c.1926, 10 x 7 In. 35.00
Cheffetz, Asa, Wood Engraving, Landscape, Vermont, Church, Frame, c.1935, 9 x 6 In. ... 90.00
Christy, Howard Chandler, Soldier, Frame, c.1900, 15 x 22 In. .... 40.00 to 90.00
Daniell, William, London, Looking Across River, Colored, Frame, 17 x 25 In. 58.00
Denton, Sherman Foote, Spanish Mackerel, Fish, Frame, c.1905, 11 x 6 In. 25.00
Denton, Sherman Foote, Steelhead, Salmon Trout, Lithograph, Frame, c.1905, 11 x 8 In. ... 55.00
Denton, Sherman Foote, Tautog, Fish, Frame, c.1949, 14 x 21 In. 30.00

Erte, Enchanted Melody, Silkscreen, Embossed, 242/300, c.1983, 38 x 27 In.	992.00
Fox, R. Atkinson, Battle Of The Wild, Animals, Frame, c.1925, 9 x 7 In.	35.00
Fox, R. Atkinson, Dreamland, Garden, c.1925, 12 x 8 In.	41.00
Fox, R. Atkinson, Dreamland, Garden, c.1925, 14 x 22 In.	47.00
Fox, R. Atkinson, Garden Of Contentment, Frame, c.1925, 10 x 14 In.	29.00
Fox, R. Atkinson, Garden Of Happiness, Garden, c.1925, 14 x 10 In.	41.00
Fox, R. Atkinson, Garden Of Romance, Frame, 1920-25, 12 x 8 In.	40.00
Fox, R. Atkinson, Indian Summer, Landscape, Frame, c.1925, 14 x 20 In.	30.00
Fox, R. Atkinson, June Morn, Frame, c.1925, 16 x 11 In.	110.00
Fox, R. Atkinson, Love Birds, Garden, Frame, 10 x 8 In.	25.00
Fox, R. Atkinson, Midsummer Magic, c.1925, 22 x 14 In.	70.00
Fox, R. Atkinson, Peaceful Summer Day, Cows, Frame, c.1925, 8 x 10 In.	29.00
Fox, R. Atkinson, Poppies, Still Life, Frame, c.1925	29.00
Fox, R. Atkinson, Promenade, Frame, c.1925, 14 x 22 In.	50.00
Fox, R. Atkinson, Romance Canyon, Frame, c.1925, 12 x 10 In.	100.00
Fox, R. Atkinson, Romance Canyon, Metal Frame, c.1925, 10 x 8 In.	29.00
Fox, R. Atkinson, Sunny South, Garden, Blue & Gold Frame, c.1925, 15 x 10 In.	35.00
Fox, R. Atkinson, Twilight, Frame, c.1925, 12 x 16 In.	140.00
Fox, R. Atkinson, Wanetah, Indian Maiden, c.1925, 10 x 8 In.	188.00
Garavaglia, Giovita, Virgin, Child, St. John, Engraving, Cotton Rag Paper, 15 x 19 In.	345.00
Grasset, Eugene, Women, Flowers, Mat, Frame, 20 x 15 1/2 In.	353.00
Grimball, Meta M., A Lap Full, Colonial Child Scene, Frame, 14 x 11 In.	225.00
Grimball, Meta M., Candle Making, Colonial, Frame, c.1916, 7 x 9 In.	45.00
Grimball, Meta M., End Of The Trail, Frame, c.1919, 17 x 13 In.	350.00
Grimball, Meta M., Faith Hope & Charity, Frame, c.1918, 13 x 20 In.	600.00
Grimball, Meta M., Gossip, Child, Sepia, Frame, 9 x 12 In.	94.00
Grimball, Meta M., Loving Cup, Adult, Frame, 8 x 10 In.	152.00
Grimball, Meta M., Old Friends, Frame, c.1920, 19 x 14 In.	250.00
Gutmann, Bessie Pease, Awakening, Child, Scalloped Frame, c.1918, 12 x 12 In.	59.00
Gutmann, Bessie Pease, Blossoms, Frame, c.1914, 15 1/2 x 19 In.	220.00
Gutmann, Bessie Pease, Falling Out, Frame, c.1905, 15 x 12 In.	170.00
Gutmann, Bessie Pease, Friendly Enemies, Child, Frame, c.1937, 14 x 11 In.	82.00
Gutmann, Bessie Pease, Hearing Child, c.1909, 9 x 12 In.	152.00
Gutmann, Bessie Pease, Home Builders, Frame, c.1917, 18 x 14 In.	70.00
Gutmann, Bessie Pease, In The Library, Frame, c.1916, 7 x 9 In.	350.00
Gutmann, Bessie Pease, Love Is Blind, Child, Frame, 21 x 14 In.	117.00
Gutmann, Bessie Pease, Love's Message, Cupid, Frame, 18 x 14 In.	94.00
Gutmann, Bessie Pease, Making Up, Childen, Frame, c.1905, 17 x 12 In.	152.00
Gutmann, Bessie Pease, Oh Oh A Bunny, Frame, c.1909, 12 x 9 In.	180.00
Gutmann, Bessie Pease, On Dreamland's Border, Child, Frame, c.1921, 18 x 14 In.	53.00
Gutmann, Bessie Pease, Poverty & Riches, Pretty Girls, c.1915, 20 x 14 In.	234.00
Gutmann, Bessie Pease, Priceless Necklace, Child, Woman, Oval Frame, c.1925, 18 x 14 In.	410.00
Gutmann, Bessie Pease, Smile Smile Smile, Child & Dog, Frame, c.1918, 20 x 14 In.	199.00
Gutmann, Bessie Pease, Tasting, Child, Frame, c.1909, 12 x 9 In.	117.00
Gutmann, Bessie Pease, To Have And To Hold, Bride & Groom, Frame, c.1912, 18 x 14 In.	176.00
Gutmann, Bessie Pease, To Love & Cherish, Bride, Frame, c.1911, 18 x 14 In.	94.00

Icart prints were made by Louis Icart, who worked in Paris from 1907 as an employee of a postcard company. He then started printing magazines and fashion brochures. About 1910 he created a series of etchings of fashionably dressed women and he continued to make similar etchings until he died in 1950. He is well known as a printmaker, painter, and illustrator. Original etchings are much more expensive than the later photographic copies.

Icart, Speed, Etching, Drypoint, c.1927, 14 1/2 x 24 3/4 In.	1912.00

Jacoulet prints were designed by Paul Jacoulet (1902-1960), a Frenchman who spent most of his life in Japan. He was a master of Japanese woodblock print technique. Subjects included life in Japan, the South Seas, Korea, and China. His prints were sold by subscription and issued in series. Each series had a distinctive seal, such as a sparrow or butterfly. Most Jacoulet prints are approximately 15 x 10 inches.

Jacoulet, Butterflies, Tropics, 1939	2300.00

Jacoulet, Cactus, South Seas, 1941 .... 3105.00
Jacoulet, Chinese Mask Seller, 1940, 15 x 11 In. .... .402.00 to 575.00
Jacoulet, Dance Of Okesa, Sado, Japan, 1952 .... 720.00
Jacoulet, Dead Parakeet, 1948 .... 1610.00
Jacoulet, Green Caterpillar, Korea, 1936 .... 978.00
Jacoulet, Homage To The Ancestors, Shinto Priest, Japan, 1956 .... 316.00
Jacoulet, Korean Baby In Ceremonial Costume, Seoul, 1934 .... 978.00
Jacoulet, Lady In Red, 1935 .... 14950.00
Jacoulet, Laundress, Korea, 1955 .... 920.00
Jacoulet, Living God, Nagano, Japan, 1952 .... 575.00
Jacoulet, Master Potter, Korea, Mat, Frame, 15 1/4 x 11 1/2 In. 705.00
Jacoulet, My Friend Francisco Ogarto, Marianas, 1935 .... 920.00
Jacoulet, Old Ainu Lady, Chikabumi, Hokkaido, Japan, 1950 .... 978.00
Jacoulet, On The Island Of Tinian, Mariana, 1960 .... 3220.00
Jacoulet, Pearls, Manchuria, 1950 .... 920.00
Jacoulet, Portrait Of Ramon, Watercolor, Pencil, 1940 .... 5750.00
Jacoulet, Snowflakes, Beng-Yong, Korea, 1956 .... 1800.00
Jacoulet, Substitute, Mongol, 1955 .... 1680.00
Jacoulet, Sunset In Menado, Celebes, 1938 .... 920.00
Jacoulet, Treasure, Korea, 1940 .... 635.00
Jacoulet, Under The Banana Trees Tomil, Yap, 1948 .... 1265.00
Jacoulet, Yap Man, West Carolines, 1935 .... 1265.00

Japanese woodblock prints are listed as follows: Print, Japanese, name
of artist, title or description, type, and size. Dealers use the following
terms: Tate-e is a vertical composition. Yoko-e is a horizontal composition. The words Aiban (13 by 9 inches), Chuban (10 by 7 1/2 inches),
Hosoban (13 by 6 inches), Koban (7 by 4 inches), Nagaban (20 x 9
inches), Oban (15 by 10 inches), Shikishiban (8 x 9 inches), Tanzaku
(15 x 5 inches) denote approximate size. Modern versions of some of
these prints have been made. Other woodblock prints that are not
Japanese are listed under Print, Woodblock.

Japanese, Bamboo With Cherry Blossoms, Poem, Beni-E, Frame, Tate-e, 30 1/2 x 14 In. ... 77.00
Japanese, Chikanobu, Girl In Festive Dress, Oban, Tate-e 377.00
Japanese, Chikanobu, Girl Practicing Calligraphy, Oban, Tate-e 377.00
Japanese, Chikanobu, Young Woman Holding Fan, Oban, Tate-e 507.00
Japanese, Eizan, Young Woman With Child, Oban, Tate-e 2145.00
Japanese, Gakutei, Minamoto No Yoritomo Freeing 2 Cranes, Shikishiban 2925.00
Japanese, Gekko, Ogata, Cherry Blossoms At Azumadai, Triptych, Oban 1274.00
Japanese, Gekko, Ogata, Rainbow Over Temple, c.1890, Shikishiban, 8 3/8 x 9 In. 325.00
Japanese, Hasui, Kawase, Early Summer Showers At Sanno Shrine, 1919, 15 x 10 In. 2990.00
Japanese, Hasui, Kawase, Morning Of Onegashi, 1927, 15 x 10 In. 2535.00
Japanese, Hasui, Kawase, Myohonji Temple At Kamakura, Oban, Tate-e, c.1931 .... 101.00
Japanese, Hasui, Kawase, Pink Clouds At Tega Marsh, 1930, 15 x 10 In. 1950.00
Japanese, Hasui, Kawase, Spring Evening At Kintai Bridge, c.1947, 14 x 10 In. 345.00
Japanese, Hasui, Kawase, Yufuku Hotsprings In Iwami, 1924, 15 x 10 In. 3120.00
Japanese, Hiromitsu, Awabi Diver, 11 x 18 In., Tate-e 637.00
Japanese, Hiroshige II, Fuji Seen From Inume Pass, Oban, Tate-e 4940.00
Japanese, Hiroshige II, Night Fishing In Oki, Oban, Tate-e 1755.00
Japanese, Hiroshige, Eijiri, Landscape Of Bay And Peninsula Of Miho, Oban, Yoko-e 2405.00
Japanese, Hiroshige, Great Bridge At Okazaki, Chuban, Yoko-e 637.00
Japanese, Hiroshige, Kannon Temple In Tajima, Oban, Tate-e 2080.00
Japanese, Hiroshige, Kinryuzan Temple In Asakusa, 17 x 21 In. 403.00
Japanese, Hiroshige, Night Rain At Karasaki, c.1900, 13 1/2 x 16 In. 173.00
Japanese, Hiroshige, Okazaki, Daimyo's Procession Over Trestle Bridge, Oban, Yoko-e ... 2145.00
Japanese, Hiroshige, Shinagawa, Procession In The Village, Sailboats, Oban, Yoko-e 2405.00
Japanese, Hiroshige, Snowy View Of Nihon Bashi, 12 x 15 In. 575.00
Japanese, Hiroshige, Sudden Shower At Shono, 1890s, 18 x 22 In. 230.00
Japanese, Hokusai, Mount Fuji In Clear Weather, 12 x 15 In. 405.00
Japanese, Kasamatsu, Shiro, Pagoda In Evening Rain, Yanaka, 15 x 10 In., Tate-e 1287.00
Japanese, Koitsu, Benkei Bridge, Oban, Tate-e, c.1933 .... 185.00
Japanese, Koitsu, Tsuchiya, Winter At Miyajima, 10 x 15 In., Yoko-e 1495.00
Japanese, Koitsu, Tsuchiya, Yotsuya, Teahouse, Color, Artist Stamp, c.1935, 14 x 9 1/2 In. 430.00

Japanese, Koson, Ohara, Eagle On Tree, Nagaban 1274.00
Japanese, Koson, Ohara, Magpie, Tanzaku 715.00
Japanese, Kunisada, Standing Beauty, c.1842, Vertical Oban Diptych 1895.00
Japanese, Kunisada, Utagawa, Parody Of Actors As Summer Vendors, Oban, Tate-e 1105.00
Japanese, Kunisada, Woman Holding Tray, 1862, Oban 1820.00
Japanese, Kuniyoshi, Woman Showing An Open Book, Oban, Tate-e 1495.00
Japanese, Saito Kiyoshi, Winter In Aizu, 10 x 15 In. 805.00
Japanese, Seien, Shima, Departed Spirit Of A Courtesan, 1923, 18 x 12 In., Tate-e 767.00
Japanese, Shodo, Yukawa, Female Student Practicing Violin, 17 x 11 In. 507.00
Japanese, Shunsen, Natori, Woman Before The Mirror, 1928, 17 x 11 In. 2860.00
Japanese, Sosen, Mori, 2 Monkeys, 7 1/4 x 6 5/8 In. 1690.00
Japanese, Toyokuni II, Beauties Of Edo & 12 Signs Of The Zodiac, Oban, Tate-e 2860.00
Japanese, Utamaro, 3 Courtesans Resting In Hallway, Oban, Tate-e 5070.00
Japanese, Utamaro, Tsukioka Of Hyogoya As Poetess Ono No Komachi, Oban, Tate-e 6370.00
Japanese, Yoshida, Hiroshi, Chionin Temple Gate, Oban, Yoko-e, c.1935 .... 252.00
Japanese, Yoshida, Hiroshi, Glittering Sea, Color, c.1926, 14 5/8 x 9 3/4 In. 1265.00
Japanese, Yoshida, Hiroshi, Morning Of Abuto, Signed, 10 x 15 In. 920.00
Japanese, Yoshida, Hiroshi, Sulphur-Crested Cockatoo, 16 x 11 In., Tate-e 3835.00
Japanese, Yoshida, Toshi, Benkei Bridge, 1941, Chuban, Tate-e 507.00
Japanese, Yoshimori, Ikkosai, Kyoto, Censor's Seal, 13 x 8 1/2 In. 46.00
Japanese, Yoshitoshi, Kyoto Waitress, Looking Capable, 1888, 14 x 9 3/8 In. 1690.00
Japanese, Yoshitoshi, Town Geisha, Looking As If She Wants A Drink, 14 3/4 x 10 In. 2340.00
Japanese, Zeshin, Shibata, Vegetables & Kitchen Utensils, Large Surimono, 16 x 22 In. ... 1105.00
Kenyon, Zula, Pretty Girl, Lakeside Evening, Frame, c.1930, 16 x 8 In. 70.00
Kurz & Allison, Battle Of Bunker Hill, Chromolithograph, Mat, Frame, 27 x 37 In. 230.00
Lithograph, Always Tomorrow, Aldolph Dehn, c.1935, 16 x 11 In. 115.00
Lithograph, Andersonville Prison, Fort Sumter, Ga., Oak Frame, 49 x 68 3/4 In. 2070.00
Lithograph, Carnival In New Orleans, John McGrady, c.1942, 11 1/2 x 16 In. 805.00
Lithograph, Declaration Of Independence, Silk, Wm. Woodruff Engraving, 28 x 20 In. ... 1035.00
Lithograph, Dove, Doris Lee, 1952, 16 x 12 In. 405.00
Lithograph, Femme A La Marguerite, Femme Au Livre, Jane Atche, 14 x 14 In. 1435.00
Lithograph, Hydrangea, Queen Wilhelmina, Paul Berthon, 15 x 14 In. 240.00
Lithograph, Le Arlequins, Gino Severini, 1954, 15 x 11 1/4 In. 1610.00
Lithograph, Madonna & Child, Grand Tour, Hand Colored, Late 1800s, 16 x 12 In. 460.00
Lithograph, Marine, Kate, Ocean City, N.J., Herbert Pullinger, c.1930, 14 x 11 In. 105.00
Lithograph, New York Waterfront, Charles Locke, 8 3/4 x 12 In. 625.00
Lithograph, Reverie Du Soir, Repose De La Nuit, Alphonse Mucha, c.1899, 16 x 6 In. 896.00
Lithograph, Swampland, Signed, Henry Pitz, Mat, Frame, 1900s, 10 5/8 x 12 3/4 In. 145.00
Lucioni, Luigi, Sunlit Patterns, Landscape, Etching, Frame, c.1938, 14 x 20 In. 29.00
Magnus, Charles, Battles Of The Rebellion, New York, 1863, 23 x 20 3/4 In. 1035.00
Memorial, Confederate, Our Lost Cause, Color Lithograph, Frame, c.1896, 20 x 16 In. ... 115.00

Nutting prints are now popular with collectors. Wallace Nutting is
known for his pictures, furniture, and books. Nutting *prints* are actually hand-colored photographs issued from 1900 to 1941. There are   *Wallace Nutting*
over 10,000 different titles. Wallace Nutting furniture is listed in the
Furniture category.

Nutting, A Fruit Luncheon, Frame, c.1925 .... 120.00
Nutting, A Pilgrim Daughter, Hand Colored, c.1925 .... 129.00
Nutting, An English Doorway, Frame, c.1925, 10 x 12 In. 165.00
Nutting, Apple Over The Brook, Hand Colored, Frame, 17 x 11 In. 50.00
Nutting, April Birches, 1915-25, 16 x 13 In. 80.00
Nutting, Autumn Grotto, Conn., c.1925, 20 x 16 In. 80.00
Nutting, Awaiting The Hostess, c.1910, 14 x 11 In. 175.00
Nutting, Blossom At The Lake, c.1925, 14 x 11 In. 70.00
Nutting, Blossom Point, Exterior, Frame, c.1925, 11 x 9 In. 105.00
Nutting, Braiding A Rag Rug, Hand Colored, Frame, c.1925, 12 x 8 In. 50.00
Nutting, California Garden, c.1925, 9 x 7 In. 129.00
Nutting, Candle, Silhouette, Frame, c.1927, 4 x 4 In. 140.00
Nutting, Choosing A Bonnet, c.1910, 16 x 13 In. 120.00
Nutting, Coming Out Of Rosa, Hand Colored, c.1925 .... 150.00
Nutting, Cow Scene, New England, Frame, c.1925, 11 x 7 In. 175.00
Nutting, Cutting A Silhouette, c.1925, 16 x 12 In. 120.00

Nutting, Dell Dale Road, Mystic Conn., Mat, Frame, c.1925, 14 x 12 In. 70.00
Nutting, Dell Of Blossoms, Hand Colored, c.1925, 17 x 14 In. 90.00
Nutting, Desk, Silhouette, c.1927, Frame, 4 x 4 In. 50.00
Nutting, Domestic Scene, Untitled, Hand Tinted, 6 x 8 In. 90.00
Nutting, Dutch Knitting Lesson, Mother, Child, c.1935, 3 x 4 In. 140.00
Nutting, Embroidering, Hand Tinted, Signed, 4 x 6 In. 138.00
Nutting, Exterior Scene, New England, c.1925, 10 x 8 In. 50.00
Nutting, Exterior Wetlands Scene, Untitled, Hand Tinted, Signed, 19 x 36 In. 207.00
Nutting, Floral Scene, Mass., Frame, c.1935, 4 x 6 In. 129.00
Nutting, Flowering Time, Exterior Scene, c.1925, 16 x 12 In. 95.00
Nutting, Foreign Bridge Scene, Hand Colored, c.1925, 9 x 7 In. 80.00
Nutting, Foreign Scene, Dog, Lying Down, c.1925, 8 x 12 In. 199.00
Nutting, Garden Enclosed, Frame, c.1910, 12 x 16 In. 295.00
Nutting, Garden Of Larkspur, England, Frame, c.1925, 10 x 12 In. 80.00
Nutting, Garden Of Larkspur, Mat, Frame, c.1925, 20 x 20 In. 150.00
Nutting, Garden, Paradise Portal, c.1935, 4 x 6 In. 35.00
Nutting, Girl By Spider, Silhouette, c.1927, 4 x 4 In. 29.00
Nutting, Girl By Statue, Silhouette, c.1927, 4 x 4 In. 25.00
Nutting, Girl On Fence, Silhouette, Frame, c.1927, 4 x 4 In. 18.00
Nutting, Girl Snipping, Silhouette, Frame, c.1927 . . . . 20.00
Nutting, Girl With Necklace, Silhouette, Frame, c.1927, 5 x 6 In. 18.00
Nutting, Grafton Windings, Hand Tinted, Signed, 7 x 13 In. 104.00
Nutting, Hollyhock Cottage, c.1925, 20 x 16 In. . . . . .105.00 to 130.00
Nutting, Honeymoon Drive, Massachusetts, c.1925, 16 x 14 In. 80.00
Nutting, Honeymoon Stroll, Hand Colored, Mat, c.1925, 14 x 12 In. 59.00
Nutting, In The Brave Days Of Old, c.1925, 16 x 13 In. 59.00
Nutting, In Upland New England, Wallace Frame, c.1910 . . . . 95.00
Nutting, Interior Bedroom Scene, Untitled, Hand Tinted, Signed, 3 x 4 In. 90.00
Nutting, Interior Hearth Scene, Untitled, Hand Tinted, Signed, 3 x 6 1/2 In. 90.00
Nutting, Interior Parlor Scene, Untitled, Hand Tinted, Signed, 3 x 7 In. 90.00
Nutting, Interior Scene, A Bit Of Sewing, c.1925 . . . . 105.00
Nutting, Interior Scene, Stitch In Time, Frame, c.1925, 13 x 10 In. 120.00
Nutting, Interior, New England, Frame, c.1925, 10 x 8 In. 29.00
Nutting, Investigating An Heirloom, Hand Tinted, Signed, 10 x 8 In. 69.00
Nutting, Joy Path, Hand Tinted, 9 x 6 1/2 In. 80.00
Nutting, Justifiable Vanity, c.1935, 9 x 11 In. 70.00
Nutting, Langdon Door, Architectural Scene, c.1910, 11 x 14 In. 80.00
Nutting, Life Of The Golden Age, Sheep Scene, c.1925, 16 x 13 In. 150.00
Nutting, Little River, New Hampshire, Hand Colored, c.1935 . . . . 55.00
Nutting, Maple Sugar Cupboard, Frame, c.1910 . . . . 140.00
Nutting, Marina, Capri, c.1910, 15 x 9 In. 700.00
Nutting, Mary's Lamb, Silhouette, Frame, c.1925, 7 x 8 In. 70.00
Nutting, Morning Among Birches, R.I., c.1905, 19 x 16 In. 70.00
Nutting, Morning Duties, Interior, Nantucket, Mass., c.1925, 14 x 9 In. 50.00
Nutting, Mother's Day Card, c.1940, 3 1/2 x 5 1/2 In. 50.00
Nutting, Neath The Blossoms, Sheep, c.1915, 11 x 7 In. 210.00
Nutting, Nova Scotia Idyll, c.1935, 20 x 16 In. 295.00
Nutting, Old Back Door, Hand Colored, Frame, c.1925 . . . . 140.00
Nutting, Old Four Poster, Interior Scene, c.1925, 11 x 14 In. 350.00
Nutting, Old Wentworth Days, Interior Scene, c.1925, 17 x 14 In. 120.00
Nutting, Patti's Favorite Walk, England, Frame, c.1925, 12 x 10 In. 95.00
Nutting, Pergola, Amalfi, Italy, Hand Colored, c.1925, 14 x 12 In. 150.00
Nutting, Quiet Life, Hand Colored, Frame, 1915-25, 15 x 9 In. 220.00
Nutting, Scotland Forever, Frame, c.1925, 15 x 12 In. 129.00
Nutting, Silhouette Card, Small Format, c.1927 . . . . 29.00
Nutting, Sleeping Canal, Hand Tinted, Signed, 5 x 7 In. 374.00
Nutting, Springfield Curve, Vermont, Frame, 9 x 7 In. 25.00
Nutting, Stair Of Stone, Penn., c.1925, 16 x 13 In. 645.00
Nutting, Stepping Heavenward, Garden, Frame, c.1935 . . . . 700.00
Nutting, Stony Brook Bridge, Hand Colored, Frame, c.1920, 15 x 13 In. 145.00
Nutting, Swimming Pool, Vermont, c.1925, 17 x 14 In. 40.00
Nutting, Tap At The Squire's Door, Frame, c.1920, 11 x 14 In. 25.00
Nutting, Tea At Yorktown Parlor, Webb House, c.1925, 16 x 10 In. 120.00

Nutting, Tufted Shore, Exterior Scene, c.1925, 15 x 12 In. 50.00
Nutting, Vermont Road, Hand Colored, c.1925, 13 x 15 In. 95.00
Nutting, Virginia Reel Interior, c.1925 .... 105.00
Nutting, Warm Spring Day, Sheep, c.1925, 16 x 10 In. 150.00
Nutting, Wayside Inn Garden, Wallace Frame, c.1925 .... 80.00
Nutting, Wissahickon Blossoms, c.1925, 15 x 13 In. 439.00

Parrish prints are wanted by collectors. Maxfield Frederick Parrish was an illustrator who lived from 1870 to 1966. He is best known as a designer of magazine covers, posters, calendars, and advertisements.

Parrish, Contentment, Enchanted, 13 x 10 In. 29.00
Parrish, Daybreak, Blue & Gold Frame, c.1923, 18 x 10 In. 275.00
Parrish, Dinkey Bird, Enchanted, c.1915, 7 x 5 In. 47.00
Parrish, Garden Of Allah, Blue & Gold Frame, c.1918, 9 x 18 In. 200.00
Parrish, Garden Of Allah, Enchanted, Frame, 15 x 30 In. 199.00
Parrish, Knave Of Hearts, Blue Hose & Yellow Hose, c.1925, 9 x 12 In. 47.00
Parrish, Knave Of Hearts, c.1925, 12 x 9 In. ....59.00 to 117.00
Parrish, Village Brook, Landscape, Period Frame, c.1940, 20 x 16 In. 164.00
Smith Brothers & Co., Portland, Me., Bird's-Eye View, Lithograph, 1800s, 28 x 43 In. ... 460.00
Van De Velde, Henry, Tropon, Art Nouveau Design, Lithograph, Mat, Frame, 14 x 11 In. .. 1175.00
Vasarely, Optic Image, Silkscreen, Signed, 19/30, 14 x 11 1/2 In. 207.00

Woodblock prints that are not in the Japanese tradition are listed here. Most were made in England and the United States during the Arts and Crafts period. Japanese woodblock prints are listed under Print, Japanese.

Woodblock, Baumann, Gustav, Eagle Ceremony, Mat, Frame, Square, 6 1/2 In. 411.00
Woodblock, Baumann, Gustav, Malapai, Frame, 9 1/2 x 11 In. 7638.00
Woodblock, Bixler, David, Eagle With Shield, Frame, 3 1/2 x 2 3/4 In. 6050.00
Woodblock, Bixler, David, Father & Son, Frame, 3 3/4 x 2 3/4 In. 1925.00
Woodblock, Bixler, David, Horse, Signed, Frame, 4 x 3 1/8 In. 6050.00
Woodblock, Gearhart, Frances, Sierra Sky Scrapers, Mat, Frame, 12 1/2 x 10 3/4 In. 4994.00
Woodblock, Hyde, Helen, 3 Asian Girls, Signed 3 Times, Mat, Frame, 1914, 13 x 5 In. ... 411.00
Woodblock, Hyde, Helen, Mirror, Mat, Frame, 1904, 14 1/4 x 4 1/4 In. 823.00
Woodblock, Jacques, Bertha, Irises, Mat, Frame, 15 x 6 In. 353.00
Woodblock, Kaufman, Ester, 2 Birds, Flower, 1825, Frame, 4 x 6 1/4 In. 6895.00
Woodblock, Lum, Bertha, Building, Trees, Gates, Raised Line, Mat, Frame, 15 1/2 x 9 In. . 588.00
Woodblock, Lum, Bertha, Chinese Fishing Boats, Mat, Frame, 1924, 8 1/2 x 4 1/4 In. 470.00
Woodblock, Lum, Bertha, Fox Woman, Signed, 1916, 16 1/2 x 10 In. 558.00
Woodblock, Lum, Bertha, Rain, Mat, Frame, 10 3/4 x 6 1/4 In. 3525.00
Woodblock, Lum, Peter, Middle East Scene, Buildings, Arts & Crafts Frame, 11 x 8 In. ... 400.00
Woodblock, Millbourn, Melville Vaughn, Columbine, c.1940, 7 1/4 x 6 In. 440.00
Woodblock, Miller, Lillian, East Mountain, Kyoto, Sunrise, 9 3/4 x 10 3/4 In. 765.00
Woodblock, Miller, Lillian, Japanese Dwarf Berry Tree, Signed, 1928, 11 1/2 x 8 1/2 In. .. 323.00
Woodblock, Miller, Lillian, Pagoda At Dusk, Signed, 6 x 13 3/4 In. 353.00
Woodblock, Miller, Lillian, Rain Blossoms, Japan, Frame, 1928, 9 1/2 x 14 In. 940.00
Woodblock, Miller, Lillian, Toyko Coolie Boy, 1920, 10 3/4 x 4 3/4 In. 705.00
Woodblock, Norton, Elizabeth, 2 Lions, Black, White, Mat, 1926, 8 x 9 3/4 In. 118.00
Woodblock, Novak, Louis, Autumn Vista, Mat, Frame, 8 x 9 3/4 In. 940.00
Woodblock, Richert, Charles, Horse Barn, Black, White, Frame, 8 x 10 In. 411.00
Woodblock, Richert, Charles, Windmill, Mat, New Frame, 3 3/4 x 5 In. 499.00

PURINTON POTTERY COMPANY was incorporated in Wellsville, Ohio, in 1936. The company moved to Shippenville, Pennsylvania, in 1941 and made a variety of hand-painted ceramic wares. By the 1950s Purinton was making dinnerware, souvenirs, cookie jars, and florist wares. The pottery closed in 1959.

Apple, Baker, 7 In. 11.00
Apple, Bean Pot, Cover, 3 3/4 In. 20.00
Apple, Bowl, Cereal, 5 1/4 In. 8.00
Apple, Bowl, Dessert, 4 In. 11.00
Apple, Bowl, Salad, 11 In. 20.00
Apple, Bowl, Spaghetti, 14 1/2 In. 75.00

Apple, Bowl, Vegetable, Divided, 10 1/2 In. 25.00
Apple, Bread Tray, 11 In. ....5.00 to 25.00
Apple, Candleholder, Star Shape, 2 x 6 In. 255.00
Apple, Candy Dish, Handle, 6 1/4 In. 45.00
Apple, Canister Set, Oval, 4 Piece 40.00
Apple, Canister Set, Wooden Lids, Lazy Susan, 5 Piece 1100.00
Apple, Chop Plate, Plain Border, 12 In. 35.00
Apple, Coffeepot, 8 Cup 60.00
Apple, Cookie Jar, Oval, 9 1/2 In. 70.00
Apple, Cup & Saucer 5.00
Apple, Dish, Cover, Oval, 9 In. 20.00
Apple, Dish, Pickle, 6 In. 23.00
Apple, Grease Jar, Cover, 5 1/2 In. 35.00
Apple, Jam Dish, 5 1/2 In. 45.00
Apple, Jam Jar, 4 1/2 In. 15.00
Apple, Jug, Dutch, 2 Pt. 25.00
Apple, Jug, Dutch, 5 Pt. 30.00
Apple, Jug, Honey, 6 1/4 In. 310.00
Apple, Jug, Kent, 4 1/2 In. 30.00
Apple, Jug, Kent, 6 1/4 In. 325.00
Apple, Mug, 8 Oz., 4 In. 7.00
Apple, Mug, Beer, 16 Oz., 4 3/4 In. 35.00
Apple, Oil & Vinegar, 9 1/2 In., 2 Piece 40.00
Apple, Oil & Vinegar, Square, 5 In., 2 Piece 55.00
Apple, Plate, Breakfast, 8 In. 7.00
Apple, Plate, Dinner, 9 3/4 In. 5.00
Apple, Plate, Salad, 6 3/4 In. 4.00
Apple, Platter, 12 In. ....13.00 to 25.00
Apple, Salt & Pepper, Range, 4 1/2 In. 30.00
Apple, Salt & Pepper, Stacking, 2 1/4 In. 50.00
Apple, Sugar & Creamer 11.00
Apple, Tumbler, 5 In. 5.00
Apple, Wall Pocket, 3 1/2 In. 65.00
Chartreuse, Bowl, Cereal, 5 1/4 In. 8.00
Chartreuse, Bowl, Vegetable, 8 1/2 In. 35.00
Chartreuse, Chop Plate, 12 In. 45.00
Fruit, Oil & Vinegar, Square, Blue Trim, 5 In. 35.00
Fruit, Salt & Pepper, Blue Trim, Range, 4 In. 35.00
Heather Plaid, Plate, Dinner, 9 3/4 In. ....5.00 to 20.00
Heather Plaid, Saltshaker, Jug, Cork, 2 1/2 In. 20.00
Ivy, Chop Plate, Red Blossom, 12 In. 145.00
Ming Tree, Chop Plate, 12 In. 600.00
Mountain Rose, Chop Plate, 12 In. 275.00
Mountain Rose, Planter, Rum, Jug, 6 1/2 In. 10.00
Normandy Plaid, Chop Plate, 12 In. 25.00
Normandy Plaid, Juice, 6 Oz. 10.00
Normandy Plaid, Plate, Dinner, 9 3/4 In. 6.00
Normandy Plaid, Plate, Salad, 6 3/4 In. 3.00
Normandy Plaid, Salt & Pepper, Range 35.00
Normandy Plaid, Teapot, 4 Cup 20.00
Normandy Plaid, Teapot, 6 Cup 10.00
Normandy Plaid, Tumbler, 12 Oz., 5 In. 3.00
Pennsylvania Dutch, Beer Mug, 16 Oz., 4 3/4 In. 75.00
Pennsylvania Dutch, Bowl, Dessert, 4 In. 15.00
Pennsylvania Dutch, Bowl, Fruit, 12 In. ....105.00 to 150.00
Pennsylvania Dutch, Bowl, Spaghetti, 14 1/2 In. 425.00
Pennsylvania Dutch, Bowl, Vegetable, Divided, 10 1/2 In. 25.00
Pennsylvania Dutch, Candleholder, Star Shape, 2 x 6 In. 160.00
Pennsylvania Dutch, Chop Plate, 12 In. 110.00
Pennsylvania Dutch, Cookie Jar, Square, Wood Cover, 9 1/2 In. 50.00
Pennsylvania Dutch, Cup & Saucer 6.00
Pennsylvania Dutch, Jug, Honey, 6 1/4 In. 50.00
Pennsylvania Dutch, Mug, 8 Oz. 110.00

Pennsylvania Dutch, Planter, Basket, 6 1/4 In.	80.00
Pennsylvania Dutch, Planter, Rum, Jug, 6 1/2 In.	225.00
Pennsylvania Dutch, Plate, Dinner, 9 3/4 In.	10.00
Pennsylvania Dutch, Plate, Dinner, Blue Scalloped Rim, 9 3/4 In.	245.00
Pennsylvania Dutch, Plate, Salad, 6 3/4 In.	5.00
Pennsylvania Dutch, Platter, Oval, 12 In.	55.00
Pennsylvania Dutch, Relish, 3 Sections	95.00
Pennsylvania Dutch, Tumbler, 12 Oz., 5 In.	35.00
Red Ivy, Jug, Kent, Honey, 6 1/4 In.	20.00
Rooster, Cookie Jar	95.00
Turquoise, Chop Plate, 12 In.	40.00

PURSES have been recognizable since the eighteenth century, when leather and needlework purses were preferred. Beaded purses became popular in the nineteenth century, went out of style, but are again in use. Mesh purses date from the 1880s and are still being made. How to carry a handkerchief and lipstick is a problem today for every woman, including the Queen of England.

Alligator, Constance, Goldtone Hardware, Magnetic Closure, Shoulder Strap, Hermes	3525.00
Alligator, Gilt, Tiger Applique, Envelope Clutch, Shoulder Strap, Judith Leiber	1150.00
Beaded, Brass Plated Frame, Green & Black Beads, 6 x 6 In.	60.00
Beaded, Cut Steel Beads, Frame, Chain Handle, Beth Sheba Morrow, Penn., 5 x 3 In.	60.00
Beaded, Fish Scale Design, Cast Frame, Fine Chain Handle, France, 6 1/2 x 5 In.	60.00
Beaded, Flower, Braided Drawstring, 7 x 5 In.	80.00
Beaded, Gold Plated Frame, Red Stones, Flower Design, 6 x 5 In.	69.00
Beaded, Heart Shape, Plated Cast Frame, Chain Handle, Brown, Red, Black, 9 x 7 In.	69.00
Beaded, White & Gray Beads, Made In Belgium, 7 1/2 x 6 In.	46.00
Crocodile, Brown, Rectangular, Goldtone Fittings, 3 Pockets, Hermes	4115.00
Crocodile, Burgundy, Clasp Closure, 9 x 3 1/4 x 11 1/2 In.	380.00
Crocodile, Burgundy, Flap Closure, Italy, 13 3/4 x 3 1/4 x 10 1/4 In.	605.00
Crocodile, Rectangular, Goldtone Fittings, 3 Interior Pockets, Exterior Pocket, Hermes	999.00
Crystal, Obi Fabric, Clutch, Toggle Clasp, Shoulder Strap, Judith Leiber	980.00
Crystal, Pave, Nautilus Shell, Gilt Lined, Toggle Clasp, Shoulder Strap, Judith Leiber	3910.00
Embroidered Silk, Enameled Frame, Marcasite, Carnelian Thumbpiece, Art Deco	1115.00
Fabric, Faux, Gilt Metal Frame, Leather Lined, Shoulder Strap, Judith Leiber	1035.00
Gold Metal, Gold Dollar Sign On Front, Rhinestones, Chain Handle, 3 x 4 In.	120.00
Leather, Black, Goldtone Fittings, Detachable Shoulder Strap, 3 Pockets, Hermes, Box	3055.00
Leather, Brass, Enamel, Lion's Head, Drawstring, Wine Color, Gucci, Shoulder Bag	175.00
Leather, Burgundy, Shoulder Strap, Goldtone Metal Fittings, Hermes, 9 x 7 x 2 1/2 In.	355.00
Leather, Cabana, Silvertone Hardware, 2 Shoulder Straps, 4 Pockets, Blue, Hermes	1765.00
Leather, Canvas, Kelly, Goldtone Fittings, Initials, 3 Pockets, Hermes, 11 1/4 In.	1410.00
Leather, Crystal, Yellow, Envelope Clutch, Flannel Bag, Box, Judith Leiber	980.00
Leather, Kelly, Goldtone Hardware, Detachable Shoulder Strap, 3 Pockets, Black, Hermes	2350.00
Leather, Kelly, Goldtone Hardware, Shoulder Strap, 3 Pockets, Brown, Hermes	4820.00
Leather, Ostrich, Yellow, Shoulder, Tiger's-Eye Terminals, Grosgrain Lined, Judith Leiber	1840.00
Leather, Piano, Oblong, Rigid, Goldtone Fittings, Sleeves, Pockets, Black, Hermes, c.1950	705.00
Leather, Shirred, Brown, Clutch, Semiprecious Cabochons, Satin Lined, Judith Leiber	575.00
Leather, Suede, Canvas, Dog Carrier, Zipper, Pocket, Hermes, 16 x 14 x 6 In.	1060.00
Lizard, Brown, Clutch, Gilt Brass Turtles In Relief, Shoulder Strap, Judith Leiber	1380.00
Lizard, Ivory, Clutch, Pearl, Leopard's Head Clasp, Shoulder Strap, Judith Leiber	920.00
Lizard, Shirred, Scarlet, Clutch, Shoulder Strap, Gilt Brass Frame, Judith Leiber	865.00
Lizard, Taupe, Box, Gilt Brass Handle, Satin Lined, Coin Purse, Mirror, Judith Leiber	1035.00
Lizard, White, Glazed, Gilt Brass Frame, Gathered, Quartz Cabochons, Judith Leiber	1150.00
Lizard, Yellow, Envelope Clutch, Judith Leiber	620.00
Mesh, 14K Gold, Leaf Engraved Frame, Paper Clip Chain, Sapphire Thumbpiece	1175.00
Mesh, 14K Gold, Mirror & Compact Lid, Flower, Leaves, Durand & Co., c.1914	765.00
Mesh, 18K Gold, Diamond, Pearl, Scrolling Frame, Gold Ball Fringe	825.00
Mesh, Art Deco, 14K Tricolor Gold, Blue Cabochon Sapphires, c.1930, 12 1/2 x 3 3/4 In.	805.00
Mesh, Chain Handle, Hinged Top, Whiting & Davis, c.1920, 9 1/2 In.	46.00
Mesh, Enameled, Red, White, Blue, Cast Frame, Whiting & Davis, 6 x 3 1/2 In.	115.00
Mesh, Openwork Frame, Turquoise Cabochons, Diamond, Garnet, 14K Gold	1765.00
Mesh, Red, White, Blue, Orange, Pink, Cast Frame, Whiting & Davis, 6 1/2 x 3 1/2 In.	160.00
Mesh, Silver Colored, Jeweled Latch, Original Box, Whiting & Davis	127.00

Mesh, Soldered, Gold Washed, Chain Handle, German Silver, c.1900, 5 x 4 In. 140.00
Minaudiere, Moth, Silver, Black, Red Pave Crystal, Cabochon Onyx Clasp, Judith Leiber .   2185.00
Pearl, Crystal Set, Recumbent Horse, Gilt Leather Lined, Flannel Bag, Box, Judith Leiber .   3220.00
Pigskin, Tote, Drawstring, Grosgrain, Leather Lined, Chanel 1725.00
Satin, Black, Clutch, Shoulder Strap, Coin Purse, Comb, Mirror, Judith Leiber 1265.00
Satin, Embroidered, Tiger's-Eye Set, Gilt Brass Frame, Shoulder Strap, Judith Leiber 1610.00
Silver, Cast Frame, Chased, Embossed Putto, Woven Wire, Marked, Alpagoa, 7 x 7 In. 160.00
Silver, Chased Frame, Chain Link Handle, Woven Wire, Teardrops, Germany, 5 1/2 x 5 In. .   175.00
Silver, Enamel, Evening, Japanese Inro Shape, Tassel, Continental, c.1920, 9 1/2 In. 345.00
Silver, Kid Leather Lining, Cast Fame, Repeat Designs, Germany, 4 1/2 x 4 In. 80.00
Snakeskin, Camel Color, Brown Piping, Shoulder Strap, Judith Leiber, 1970s, 15 x 14 In. .   530.00
Snakeskin, Tote, Red, Embroidered, Grosgrain Lined, Gilt Brass Frame, Judith Leiber 1095.00
Snakeskin, Yellow, Clutch, Tiger's-Eye Cabochon, Lined, Strap, Flannel Bag, Judith Leiber 920.00
Wool, Needlework, Crewel Embroidery, Fish Scale Pattern, 1700s, 5 1/4 x 8 3/8 In. 2938.00
Wool, Needlework, Flame Stitch, Pocketbook, 18th Century, 7 x 4 In. 645.00
Wool, Needlework, Irish Stitch, Diamond Pattern, Benjamin Pierce, 1790, 4 5/8 x 9 In. . . .   2468.00

QUEZAL glass was made from 1901 to 1924 by Martin Bach, Sr., in Queens, New York. Other glassware by other firms, such as Loetz, Steuben, and Tiffany, resembles this gold-colored iridescent glass. Martin Bach died in 1921. His son-in-law, Conrad Vahlsing, Jr., went to work at the Lustre Art Company about 1920 and his son, Martin Bach, Jr., worked at the Durand Art Glass division of the Vineland Flint Glass Works after 1924.

Quezal

Bowl, Gold Iridescent, Ribbed, 4 In. 440.00
Chandelier, 4-Light, Gold Iridescent Shades, Acanthus Leaf Fixtures, Bronze 3450.00
Compote, Flower Shape, Gold Iridescent, Green Loopings, Wide Ruffled Edge, 5 In. 4485.00
Lamp, 2-Light, Gold Iridescent, Curved Brass Arms, Onyx Base, 3 Paw Feet, 20 In. 750.00
Lamp, Art Nouveau, Woman With Arm Spread, 17 x 2 1/4 x 5 In. 900.00
Lamp, Boudoir, Gold Iridescent, Leaf Shape, Brass, c.1915, 8 3/4 In. 575.00
Lamp, Electric, Brass, 3-Light, Signed, 21 In. 1093.00
Lamp, Iridescent Glass, Vase Shape, Opaque White Glass, Leaves, c.1920, 31 In. 604.00
Lamp, White, Green, Pulled Feather, Ribbed, Gold, Brass Base, Signed, 16 In., Pair 1955.00
Salt, Shouldered, Applied Ribs, Signed, 2 1/2 x 1 1/4 In. 230.00
Shade, Bell Shape, Gold Iridescent, Ribbed, 6 In., Pair 530.00
Shade, Bell Shape, Gold Iridescent, White Coils, 6 In. 1035.00
Shade, Bell Shape, Gold Iridescent, Zipper, 5 1/2 In. 170.00
Shade, Blue Iridescent, Gold Pulled Feathers, Ribbed, Caramel Inside, 5 1/4 In., 4 Piece . .   9200.00
Shade, Blue Iridescent, Pulled Feather, Gold Tipped, Opal Ground, 5 In. 345.00
Shade, Blue Iridescent, Pulled Feathers, Opal Panels, Gold Trim, 5 In. 460.00
Shade, Blue, Pulled Feathers, Gold Iridescent, Raspberry, Gold Interior, 6 x 5 In. .1325.00 to 1440.00
Shade, Blue, Pulled Feathers, Gold Trim, Ivory Ground, Signed, 2 1/4 x 5 In. 805.00
Shade, Bullet Shape, Opal, Gold, Yellow Pulled Zipper, Signed, 5 1/8 x 4 1/8 In. 605.00
Shade, Chartreuse, Color, Gold, Green, Reverse Drape, Ribbed, 5 In. 660.00
Shade, Clambroth, Ribbed, Gold Wave, Signed, 2 1/4 x 5 In. 480.00
Shade, Cone Shape, Opal, Gold Iridescent Interior, Signed, 10 In.   590.00
Shade, Egg Shape, Green, Gold, Pulled Feather, 4 1/2 In. 230.00
Shade, Gold Iridescent Zipper, Lime Green Ground, Mushroom Shape, 5 In. 518.00
Shade, Gold Iridescent, Fishnet Threading, Signed, 3 1/4 x 7 In. 635.00
Shade, Gold Iridescent, Green, Pulled Feathers, Light Green Ground, 6 1/4 x 4 3/4 In. 520.00
Shade, Gold Iridescent, Lattice Threading, Opal Ground, Gold Interior, 4 3/8 x 2 1/4 In. . . .   200.00
Shade, Gold Iridescent, Pulled Feather, Opaque Yellow Ground, Signed, 4 1/2 x 3 1/2 In. . .   115.00
Shade, Gold Iridescent, Snakeskin, 4 3/4 In. 195.00
Shade, Gold Iridescent, White Fish Scale, Flared Iridescent Green Rim, 5 1/4 In. 260.00
Shade, Green & Gold Pulled Feather, Ivory Ground, Gold Interior, 5 1/4 In., 4 Piece 880.00
Shade, Green Flower, Gold Lily Pads, Vines, Opal Ground, Signed, 2 3/4 x 3 In. 2935.00
Shade, Green Hooked Feathers, Gold Borders, White Ground, 6 x 5 1/2 In., Pair 1725.00
Shade, Green, Gold, Pulled Feathers, White Ground, Scalloped, Gold Interior, 3 1/2 In. . . .   900.00
Shade, Green, Gold, Pulled Leaf, Gold Threading, 4 3/4 In. 175.00
Shade, Green, Pulled Feather, Gold Trim, Ivory Ground, 1 1/2 x 3 1/2 In. 345.00
Shade, King Tut, Green Iridescent, Blue, Purple Iridescent, Ribbed, 6 1/2 x 4 5/8 In. 1495.00
Shade, King Tut, Opal, Gold, Zipper, Lavender Iridescent, Harp, 4 1/2 x 6 1/8 In. 1265.00
Shade, Lily, Fishnet Threading, Gold, Opal, Ribbed, Swirled Rim, 5 5/8 x 3 1/4 In. 1440.00

Shade, Marigold Iridescent, Ribbed, 5 1/4 In., Pair 230.00
Shade, Opal Iridescent, Gold Pulled Feathers, 5 In. 85.00
Shade, Trumpet, Gold Iridescent, Ruffled Edge, 6 1/2 x 5 In., 4 Piece 1585.00
Shade, Tulip Shape, White Pulled Feathers, Green Trim, Gold Ground, 2 1/4 x 5 In. 270.00
Sherbet, Gold Iridescent, Stemmed, Blue Coiled Threading, Signed, 4 In. 805.00
Urn, Cover, Marigold, Green Swirl, Gold Iridescent Foot, Shouldered, Signed, 13 1/2 In. ... 6325.00
Vase, Blue Green Iridescent, Tapered, Stand-Up Rim, Signed, 4 1/2 In. 375.00
Vase, Blue Iridescent, Oval, Shouldered, Signed, 6 In. 920.00
Vase, Blue Iridescent, Silver Floral Overlay, Spherical, Short Neck, Signed, 4 x 4 3/4 In. ... 1610.00
Vase, Flower Shape, Gold Iridescent Pulls, Wintergreen Loops, Tricornered, Signed, 5 In. . 2015.00
Vase, Flower Shape, Green, Gold Iridescent, Pulled Designs, Ruffled Edge, 9 3/4 In. 6465.00
Vase, Gold Iridescent, Pinched Sides, Flared Rim, Signed, 3 3/4 In. 175.00
Vase, Gold Iridescent, Squat Base, Flared Neck, Wide Ruffled Edge, Signed, 8 1/2 In. 805.00
Vase, Gold Iridescent, Swirls, Hooked Feathers, White Ground, Signed, 12 In. 3565.00
Vase, Jack-In-The-Pulpit, Bronze Base, Serpents, Leaves, 1910, 18 1/2 x 5 In. 2700.00
Vase, Jack-In-The-Pulpit, Flower Face, Iridescence Gold, Opal Body, Wintergreen, 12 In. . 1100.00
Vase, Jack-In-The-Pulpit, Gold Iridescent Top, Green Pulled Feather Border, 6 1/2 In. 3795.00
Vase, Jack-In-The-Pulpit, Gold Iridescent, Green Pulled Feather, Alabaster, 6 1/2 In. 2588.00
Vase, Jack-In-The-Pulpit, Gold Iridescent, Pink, Lavender, Feathers, Bulbous Base, 12 In. . 1150.00
Vase, Jack-In-The-Pulpit, Gold Iridescent, Wintergreen Stem, Pulled Feathers, 12 In. 1265.00
Vase, Jack-In-The-Pulpit, Green Pulled Feather, Gold Iridescent Tipped, Signed, 6 In. 1840.00
Vase, King Tut, Gold Iridescent, Cream Ground, Gold Interior, Signed, 12 1/2 In. 2645.00
Vase, Lily Shape, Gold Interior, Pulled Feathers, 5 In. 2235.00
Vase, Lily Shape, Gold, Amber, Iridescent, 15 In. 2350.00
Vase, Lily Shape, Opal, Green & Gold Pulled Feathers, Gold Iridescent Inside, 10 1/4 In. .. 2300.00
Vase, Marigold Iridescent, Green, Gold Pulled Hearts, Vines, Baluster, Flared Rim, 8 In. .. 978.00
Vase, Opal Iridescent, Gold Lappets, Flared Rim, Gold Iridescent Liner, Signed, 3 5/8 In. .. 1035.00
Vase, Opal, Pink & Gold Lappets, Green, Pink & Gold Swirls, Ovoid, Flared Rim, 10 1/2 In. 7360.00

QUILTS have been made since the seventeenth century. Early textiles were very precious and every scrap was saved to be reused. A quilt is a combination of fabrics joined to a filler and a backing by small stitched designs known as quilting. An appliqued quilt has pieces stitched to the top of a large piece of background fabric. A patchwork, or pieced, quilt is made of many small pieces stitched together. Embroidery can be added to either type.

Amish, Center Diamond, Heart, Leaf Edges, Lancaster County, Penn., Crib, 40 x 41 In. ... 4676.00
Amish, Diamond In The Square, Corner Blocks, Mulberry, Green Diamonds, 1940, 76 In. . 805.00
Amish, Patchwork, Diamond In Square, Mulberry Border, Greens, 76 x 76 In. 805.00
Amish, Patchwork, Hired Hands, Shoo-Fly, Green, Blue, Holmes County, 72 x 43 In. 115.00
Appliqued, 4 Flowerpots, Long Stem Flowers, Border, Green, Rose, Tan, 78 x 78 In. 470.00
Appliqued, 5 Roses, Buds, Surrounded By Green Leaves, 80 x 75 In. 360.00
Appliqued, 12 Blocks, 4 Flowers, Off-White Ground, Swag Borders, 103 x 84 In. 520.00
Appliqued, 16 Blocks, Vine & Blackberries, White Ground, Aqua Grid Border, 82 x 86 In. 4000.00
Appliqued, 20 Medallion Blocks, Flowers, Berries, c.1849, 82 x 88 In. 1380.00
Appliqued, Album, Baltimore, Carroll Family, 17 Signatures, 1914 & 1917, 80 x 77 In. ... 11500.00
Appliqued, Album, Dated 1850 To 1885, 90 In. .... *Illus* 3150.00
Appliqued, American Eagle, Green Wings, Union County, Pa., c.1875, 80 x 85 In. 5400.00
Appliqued, Baskets, Red, Yellow, Green, White, Vining Flower Border, 81 x 82 In. 195.00
Appliqued, Bird & Urn, Stuffed, 3 Dimensional Cherries, N.Y., 71 x 73 In. 3450.00
Appliqued, Birds, Flowering Branches, Blue Ground, Stuffed Flowers, c.1934, 79 x 88 In. . 6555.00
Appliqued, Carolina Lily, Rust Red, Green Calico, White, Black Triangles, 78 x 82 In. 430.00
Appliqued, Comforter, Children, Cherry Branches, Blue & White Scotty Dogs, 88 x 65 In. 320.00
Appliqued, Cornucopias, Flowers, Red, Green, Yellow, On White, Calico, 74 x 93 In. 520.00
Appliqued, Eagle With Baton, Orange Ground, Green, Pink, Yellow, 1800s, 80 x 80 In. ... 940.00
Appliqued, Embroidered, Album, Elizabeth McCrea, c.1847, 106 x 106 In. 9560.00
Appliqued, Floral Wreath & Diamond, Vine Border, Yellow, Red & Blue, 86 x 86 In. 1650.00
Appliqued, Flower Basket, Green Ground, Colored Flowers, c.1930, 76 x 86 In. 695.00
Appliqued, Flowers, Birds, White, Red & Green, White Ground, 76 x 74 In. 1980.00
Appliqued, Flowers, Red, Blue, Goldenrod, Sawtooth Edge, Vining Borders, 72 x 78 In. .. 575.00
Appliqued, Friendship, Eagle Center, Ink Autographs, 68 x 91 In. .... *Illus* 15000.00
Appliqued, Friendship, Van Houten Blauvelt, Thomas Families, N.Y., c.1860, 88 x 86 In. . . 11400.00
Appliqued, Lady Of The Lake, Tester Bedpost Cut, 1848, 69 x 77 In. 580.00

Appliqued, Patriotic, Flowers, Cotton, Muslin, C.C. Shufelt, 1853, 77 x 97 In.	8225.00
Appliqued, Pillows, Tulips, Roses, Oak Leaves, 77 x 77 In.	635.00
Appliqued, Scalloped, Flower Center, Corners, 75 x 88 In.	220.00
Appliqued, Tree, Sawtooth, Hearts, Bird, Band Border, Ida Corl, 1930, 80 x 104 In.	1072.00
Appliqued, Tulip Basket, Rainbow Colors, c.1880, 84 x 94 In.	750.00
Appliqued, Tulips, Vines, 88 x 76 In.	150.00
Appliqued, Wedding, Feathered Heart, Collingwood, N.J., 90 x 76 In.	1725.00
Crazy, Embroidered, Silk, Velvet, Leaves, Roses, Black Field, Crib, 1882, 35 x 52 In.	2070.00
Crazy, Embroidered, Silk, Velvet, Prints, Black, Burgundy Border, 60 x 65 In.	115.00
Crazy, Multicolored, 20 Blocks, Flowers, Jockey Hat, Corncob, 1880, 71 x 71 In.	405.00
Crazy, Multicolored, Decorative Stitching, Mass., 1880, 71 x 71 In.	405.00
Crazy, Multicolored, Silk, Velvet, Wool, Cotton, Ohio, 1880s, 79 x 81 In.	150.00
Crazy, Red, Blue, Black, Brown & Beige, Wool & Cotton, c.1920, 84 x 64 In.	750.00
Crazy, Stars, Pinwheels, Spiders, Flowers, Birds, Perry County, 80 x 80 In.	175.00
Crazy, Trapunto Flowers, Silk, 19th Century, 71 x 71 In.	315.00
Embroidered, Animal Motif, Blue, White, Crib, 38 x 27 In.	115.00
Embroidered, Friendship, Painted Flowers, Silk, Violet Stokes Family, N.J., 76 x 92 In.	690.00
Honeycomb, Green, Red, Blue, Yellow, c.1930, 68 x 84 In.	385.00
Patchwork, 9-Patch Variation, Double Red Borders, Crib, 37 x 37 In.	345.00
Patchwork, Appliqued, Star Of Bethlehem, Red Ground, 72 x 72 In.	1725.00
Patchwork, Baskets, Green, On White, Green Border, Diamond Quilting, 76 x 80 In.	315.00
Patchwork, Baskets, Yellow Triangles, Border, White Ground, Feather Stitching, 79 x 79 In.	1530.00
Patchwork, Box Pattern, White & Red Gingham, 67 x 72 In.	210.00
Patchwork, Bride's Basket, Rose, White, Cotton, 35 Panels, 75 x 93 In.	550.00
Patchwork, Carolina Lily, Calicos, Montgomery County, Penn., c.1880, 77 x 77 In.	2300.00
Patchwork, Center Medallion, Silk, Chintz, Cotton, Ribbon, R.I., c.1830, 91 x 91 In.	6900.00
Patchwork, Chain, White Diamonds, Blue & Black Stepped Design, 81 x 94 In.	920.00
Patchwork, Chintz, Flowers, Diamond Flower Border, Early 1800s, Crib, 56 x 51 In.	380.00
Patchwork, Cotton, Center Sunburst, 25 Blocks, c.1850, 88 x 89 In.	1116.00
Patchwork, Dazzle, Orange, Indigo, Blue, Salmon, Diamonds, Hearts, 1930s, 78 x 78 In.	410.00
Patchwork, Diamond, Periwinkle & Blue Diamonds, White Ground, c.1890, 79 x 79 In.	290.00
Patchwork, Double Wedding Ring, Blue & White, 97 x 77 In.	259.00
Patchwork, Double Wedding Ring, Scalloped Edge, 75 x 84 In.	207.00
Patchwork, Double Wedding Ring, White, Blue Border, Gingham, 61 x 79 In.	489.00
Patchwork, Dresden Plate, Gingham, 89 x 74 In.	210.00
Patchwork, Drunkard's Path, Red, On White, Scalloped Edge, N.Y., c.1940, 73 x 81 In.	316.00
Patchwork, Flower Basket, Blue, Vines, Draped Window, Urns, Garden, Pond, 86 x 90 In.	980.00
Patchwork, Flying Geese, Blue & White, Hand Sewn, 70 x 70 In.	315.00
Patchwork, Friendship, Green Calico Stars On White, Name On Each Star, 75 x 81 In.	545.00
Patchwork, Friendship, Multicolored, Stenciled Names In Block, c.1900, 84 x 86 In.	220.00
Patchwork, Geometric, Red, Brown, Pink, c.1920, 75 x 80 In.	220.00
Patchwork, Geometrics, Blue, Yellow, Black, c.1900, 73 x 75 In.	220.00
Patchwork, Grandma's Flower Garden, Late 20th Century, 103 x 60 In.	185.00
Patchwork, Green, Red, Yellow, Applied Tulip, Chain Vine Border, c.1900, 81 x 83 In.	220.00
Patchwork, Irish Chain, Blue & Salmon Calico, Hand Sewn, 78 x 78 In.	220.00
Patchwork, Lily, Cotton, Flowers, Pink, Green, Red, Yellow, c.1900, 88 x 84 In.	705.00

Quilt, Appliqued,
Dated 1850 & 1885,
90 In.

Quilt, Appliqued, Friendship,
Eagle Center, Ink
Autographs, 68 x 91 In.

Quilt, Patchwork, Lone Star,
Satelite Stars, Green, Red, Beige,
Calicos, c.1835-40, 96 In.

Patchwork, Log Cabin, 20 Blocks, Hand, Machine Stitched, Silk, Satin, Velvet, 58 x 74 In.   315.00
Patchwork, Log Cabin, Barn Raising, Solids, Prints, Flour Bag Backing, 76 x 76 In. 115.00
Patchwork, Log Cabin, Red, White Blue Border, Stars, c.1900, 87 x 87 In. 230.00
Patchwork, Lone Star, Multicolored, 75 x 68 In. 160.00
Patchwork, Lone Star, Orange, Yellow, White, 76 x 81 In. 220.00
Patchwork, Lone Star, Satellite Stars, Green, Red, Beige Calicos, c.1835-40, 96 In. . . *Illus*   875.00
Patchwork, Martha Washington's Flower Garden, Calico, 66 x 86 In. 230.00
Patchwork, Multiblock Diamond, Red, Brown, Blue, White, c.1900, 63 x 73 In. 305.00
Patchwork, Northern Star, Red, Blue, White, Beige Corners, Borders, Doll, 13 x 18 In. . . .   115.00
Patchwork, Oak Leaf, Blue & White, 68 x 76 In. 260.00
Patchwork, Pineapple, Light & Dark, Pink, White, Red, Black, Tan, 65 x 65 In. 230.00
Patchwork, Pinwheel, Light Blue, White, Hand Stitched, Pennsylvania, 56 x 69 In. 230.00
Patchwork, Pinwheel, Red, White, Cotton, c.1910, 70 x 80 In. 360.00
Patchwork, Pinwheel, Star, Gingham, 55 x 93 In. 140.00
Patchwork, Robbing Peter To Pay Paul, Red, Black, White Dots, 70 x 81 In. 575.00
Patchwork, Squares, Yellow & White, Embroidered Tree In White Squares, 68 x 72 In. . . .   430.00
Patchwork, Star Flower, Black, Red, Cotton, c.1890, 68 x 79 In. 110.00
Patchwork, Star Of Bethlehem, Cotton, Yellow, Red, Green, Late 1800s, 96 x 80 In. 1000.00
Patchwork, Star Of Bethlehem, Cotton, Yellow, Red, Green, Pa., c.1900, 74 x 72 In. 1760.00
Patchwork, Starburst, Red, White, Blue, Waldoboro, Maine, c.1900, 80 x 80 In. 1155.00
Patchwork, Stars, White, Blue, Brown Prints, White Ground, New York State, 64 x 82 In. . .   110.00
Patchwork, Strawberry, Trapunto Center, Swag Border, Penn., c.1850, 84 x 84 In. 10735.00
Patchwork, Striped Star, Yellow, Red, Green Ground, c.1900, 80 x 80 In. 440.00
Patchwork, Sunbonnet Sue, Flowers, Animals, Fish, Wool, 1889, 70 x 70 In. 110.00
Patchwork, Trapunto, Flowers, Baskets, Calico, Flower & Sawtooth Borders, 84 x 86 In. .   950.00
Patchwork, Trapunto, Pieced Flowers, Blue, Pink Calico, Basket Of Feathers, 84 x 88 In. .   345.00
Patchwork, Trapunto, Stars, Green, Pink, Brown Print, Red, Green Swag Border, 82 x 90 In.   546.00
Patchwork, Tree Pattern, Solid, Prints, Hand Sewn, Feather Quilting, 3 Borders, 66 x 78 In.   400.00
Patchwork, Turkey Tracks, Sawtooth Border, Pink, Green, Ind., c.1890, 73 x 69 In. 120.00
Patchwork & Appliqued, Album, Cotton, 48 Blocks, Flowers, N.J., c.1850, 88 x 100 In. . .   2115.00
Patchwork & Appliqued, Baltimore Flower Basket, E. Livingston, Pa., 1807, 84 x 86 In. .   1000.00
Patchwork & Appliqued, Flowering Plant, Large Squares, Sawtooth Border, 81 x 78 In. . .   500.00
Patchwork & Appliqued, Friendship, 16 Squares, Oak Leaves, c.1850, 90 x 90 In. 765.00
Patchwork & Appliqued, Friendship, Embroidered, Squares, Flowers, 1800s, 94 x 92 In. . . .   2235.00
Patchwork & Appliqued, Nine Patch, Leaf Border, 1800s, 110 x 106 In. 500.00
Patchwork & Appliqued, Potted Tulip, Red, Blue, Orange, Late 19th Century, 88 x 88 In. .   1800.00
Patchwork & Appliqued, Snowball Design, Beige Ground, White Balls, 1890, 89 x 78 In. .   1835.00
Patchwork & Appliqued, Wild Cucumber, Teal, Brown, Pink, Family History, 73 x 84 In. .   750.00
Square, Red, White Cross, Maudie Maritt, 12 x 12 In. 12.00
Squares, Sawtooth Border, Floral Green, Pink Printed, Ida Corl, 1935, 90 x 87 In. 410.00
Stenciled, Signed, Cabot, Vermont, c.1890 . . . . 12500.00
Whole-Cloth, 3 Lengths Together, Green, Diamond, Pinwheel, Wool, 111 x 102 In. 1058.00

QUIMPER pottery has a long history. Tin-glazed, hand-painted pottery has been made in Quimper, France, since the late seventeenth century. The earliest firm, founded in 1685 by Jean Baptiste Bousquet, was known as HB Quimper. Another firm, founded in 1772 by Francois Eloury, was known as Porquier. The third firm, founded by Guillaume Dumaine in 1778, was known as HR or Henriot Quimper. All three firms made similar pottery decorated with designs of Breton peasants and sea and flower motifs. The Eloury (Porquier) and Dumaine (Henriot) firms merged in 1913. Bousquet (HB) merged with the others in 1968. The group was sold to a United States family in 1984. The American holding company is Quimper Faience Inc., located in Stonington, Connecticut. The French firm has been called Societe Nouvelle des Faienceries de Quimper HB Henriot since March 1984.

HR
Quimper

Casserole, Cover, Standing Woman, Loop Handles, Flower Border, 7 1/2 x 3 1/2 In. 116.00
Clock, Triangular, Breton Landscape, Family, Ermine Crest, HB, 6 1/2 x 7 In. 1950.00
Dish, Fish Shape, Woman Peasant, c.1930, 10 1/2 x 4 1/2 In. 195.00
Inkwell, Trefoil Shape, Insert, c.1930, 4 x 4 x 3 1/4 In. 295.00
Jardiniere, Fan Shape, Flowers, Croisille Borders, Dragons On Base, 9 1/2 x 15 1/4 In. . . .   2500.00
Jardiniere, Star Shape, Brittany Coat Of Arms, Flowers, HB, c.1895, 12 x 12 1/2 In. 1950.00
Plate, Woman Spinning, Rocking Cradle, Pig Feeds From Trough, Signed HB, 8 1/8 In. . .   1500.00

Platter, Woman Knitting, Man Serenading Outdoor, HB Quimper, 10 x 7 1/4 In. 1250.00
Salt, Double, Woman Seated Beside 2 Baskets Form, 4 3/4 In. 80.00
Snuff Bottle, Bagpipe Shape, Henriot, 1920s, 3 In. 495.00
Snuff Bottle, Book Shape, Rooster, Motto, My Love Will Last Until, 2 1/8 In. 395.00
Snuff Bottle, Peasant Woman, 19th Century, 3 1/4 In. 450.00
Tazza, Man, Woman, In Work Clothes, Delft Borders, Signed, 2 x 9 1/4 In., Pair 1500.00
Vase, Flower, Seated Man Playing Instrument, 5 Flared Spouts, Oval, 6 1/2 x 4 1/2 In. 105.00

RADIO broadcast receiving sets were first sold in New York City in 1910. They were used to pick up the experimental broadcasts of the day. The first commercial radios were made by Westinghouse Company for listeners of the experimental shows on KDKA Pittsburgh in 1920. Collectors today are interested in all early radios, especially those made of Bakelite plastic or decorated with blue mirrors. Figural advertising radios and transistor radios are also collected.

Addison, Bakelite, Brown, Ivory Buttons & Wraparound Grill, 1950, 7 1/2 x 12 x 8 5/8 In.   265.00
Addison, Model 5, Catalin, Yellow, Maroon Grill & Knobs, 1940, 8 3/4 x 12 In. 2200.00
Advertising, Charlie The Tuna, Star Kist Foods, Box, 1970, 5 In. 75.00
Air King, Model 52, Plastic, Lavender, Skyscraper Style, Art Deco, 1933, 12 x 9 In. 13180.00
Amico, Spiderman's Head, Plastic, Red, AM Solid State, Box, 1978, 4 x 4 1/4 x 5 3/4 In. .. 351.00
Arvin, Model 440T, Midget, Red, Metal, 1950s, Table 60.00
Arvin, Model 532, Catalin, Maroon, Orange, Vertical Grill, 2 Knobs, 1938, 5 1/2 x 9 In. ... 1905.00
Arvin, Model 532, Catalin, Yellow, Tortoise Trim, Vertical Grill, 2 Knobs, 1938, 5 x 9 In. .. 2195.00
Automatic Radio Co., Model 933, Tom Thumb, Catalin, Yellow, Stripes, 1939, 5 x 7 In. .. 5125.00
Automatic Radio Co., Model 955, Tom Thumb, Catalin, Green, Oval Dial, 1938, 5 x 7 In. . 9515.00
Automatic Radio Co., Model 955, Tom Thumb, Catalin, Red, Oval Dial, 1938, 5 x 7 In. .. 10980.00
Bendix, Model 526C, Catalin, Marbleized Green, Black Grill, 1946, 7 x 11 In. 1170.00
Bush, Model DAC90A, Bakelite, Brown, c.1950, 9 x 12 x 7 In. 280.00
Crosley, Center Bull's-Eye, Bakelite, Black, 3 1/2 x 9 1/2 x 4 3/8 In. 160.00
Crosley, Clock, Pewter Plastic Case, Bronzed Dials, Table, c.1955, 13 In. 260.00
Crosley, Gray Plastic, Bronzed Dials & Turners, 1955, 13 In. 310.00
Detrola, Model 281, Catalin, Yellow, Marbleized Green Split Grill, Knobs, 1939, 6 x 9 In. . 8785.00
Dewald, Model 561, Jewel, Catalin, Alabaster, Red Bezel, Handle, Knobs, 1941, 6 x 10 In. 2196.00
Emerson, Model 53, Bakelite, Yellow, Red Grill, 2 Knobs, 1947, 5 1/2 x 11 x 6 5/8 In. 615.00
Emerson, Model 400, Aristocrat, Catalin, Blue, Red, Star Knobs, 1940, 7 x 11 In. 3660.00 to 4980.00
Emerson, Model 400, Aristocrat, Catalin, Yellow, Red, White, Blue Trim, 1940, 7 x 11 In. . 2195.00
Emerson, Model 564, Catalin, Red Marble, 1940, 5 x 5 x 4 In. 4390.00
Emerson, Model AX-235, Little Miracle, Catalin, Black, Orange, 1938, 5 1/4 x 8 7/8 In. .. 10248.00
Emerson, Model AX-235, Little Miracle, Catalin, Maroon, Ivory, 1938, 5 1/4 x 8 7/8 In. .. 2340.00
Emerson, Model AX-235, Little Miracle, Catalin, Red, Ivory, 1938, 5 1/4 x 8 7/8 In. 3800.00
Emerson, Model BM-258, Big Miracle, Maroon, Brown Grill, 2 Knobs, 1937, 7 x 9 In. ... 4390.00
Emerson, Model BT-245, Tombstone, Catalin, Blue Marble, White, 1938, 10 In. 8050.00
Emerson, Model BT-245, Tombstone, Catalin, Green Marble, White, 1938, 10 In. 5270.00
Emerson, Model BT-245, Tombstone, Catalin, Red Marble, White, 1938, 10 In. 4100.00
Emerson, Model EP-375, Catalin, Marbleized Blue, Tan, 1941, 5 x 9 1/2 In. 5856.00
Emerson, Model EP-375, Catalin, Marbleized Red, Green, Vertical Grill, Knobs, 5 x 9 In. . 2635.00
Fada, Model 52, Catalin, Green, Yellow Wraparound Grill, Knobs, 1938, 5 1/2 x 9 In. 7030.00
Fada, Model 53, Catalin, Yellow, Curved Top, Shaped Footed Base, 1938, 5 5/8 x 9 In. ... 3220.00
Fada, Model 115, Bullet, Streamlined, Catalin, Blue, Orange Trim, 1941, 6 x 10 3/8 In. ... 2490.00
Fada, Model 115, Bullet, Streamlined, Catalin, Marbleized Green, Yellow, 1941, 6 x 10 In. 5860.00
Fada, Model 115, Bullet, Streamlined, Catalin, Marbleized Orange, Red, 1941, 6 x 10 In. .. 2345.00
Fada, Model 252, Temple, Catalin, Marbleized Blue, Yellow, Split Dial, 1941, 6 x 11 In. .. 4980.00
Fada, Model 700, Catalin, Yellow, Red Handle, Knobs, 1946, 6 1/4 x 10 1/2 In. . .1390.00 to 1465.00
Fada, Model 711, Catalin, Yellow, Red Handle, Knobs, 1946, 5 3/4 x 9 3/4 In. 730.00
Fada, Model 1000, Bullet, Maroon, Yellow Bezel, Handle, 2 Knobs, 1946, 10 1/2 x 6 In. .. 1900.00
Fada, Model 5F60, Catalin, Yellow, Yellow Insert Grill, c.1939, 8 x 5 1/2 In. 2635.00
Fada, Model L56 Bell, Catalin, Orange, Red Grill, 1939, 9 x 6 In. 13180.00
Fada, Model L56, Bell, Catalin, Marbleized Green, Yellow Grill, Knobs, 1939, 6 x 9 In. 11710.00
Garod, Model 1450, Arched Top, Maroon, Yellow Trim, 1940, 8 x 10 1/2 In. 2635.00
Garod, Model 6AU1, Commander, Yellow, Red Wraparound Grill, 1946, 6 3/4 x 11 In. ... 1465.00
General Electric, Model F40, Bakelite Panel, Blue, Gold, Brass Pointer, 1937, 8 x 7 In. 745.00
General Electric, Model L570, Catalin, Yellow, 1941, 6 1/4 x 9 1/2 x 6 In. 1245.00

General Electric, Model L622, Jewel Box Style, Catalin, Brown, Yellow, Lift Lid, c.1940 .   3660.00
Globe, Bakelite, Black, Wraparound Grill, c.1940, 5 x 9 3/4 In. 732.00
Illfelder Toy, Space 1999, Chest Pack, Solid State Transistor, Box, 1976, 8 x 10 x 3 1/2 In. . .   40.00
Kadette, Model K25, Clockette, Marbleized Green, Brass Trim, 1937, 8 x 8 x 5 In. 3220.00
Motorola, Model 50XC, Catalin, Marbleized Green, Yellow Trim, 6 x 9 5/8 In. 6590.00
Motorola, Model 50XC, Catalin, Marbleized Red, Amber, Hexagonal Knobs, 1940, 6 x 9 In. 11000.00
Motorola, Model 51X16, Catalin, Black, Red Handle, S-Shape Grill, 1941, 6 x 10 In. 6150.00
Motorola, Model 51X16, Catalin, Yellow, Green S-Shape Grill, 1941, 6 x 9 3/4 In. 2635.00
Oxford Tartak, Catalin, Marbleized Orange, 1940, 5 x 6 5/8 4 1/4 In. 3220.00
Philco, Model 40-190, Console, Slide Rule Dial, Push Buttons, Wood, 1940, 41 x 29 In. . .   140.00
Philco, Model 49-501, Transitone, Turquoise, Cream, Glowing Dial, 1949, 11 x 6 1/2 In. . .   815.00
Quick Quaker Oats Container, Paper Cover, Transistor, 5 In. 30.00
Sentinel, Model 195 Ulta, Catalin, Yellow, Tortoise, Push Button, 1939, 10 x 6 3/4 In. 3660.00
Sentinel, Model 284NI, Catalin, Marbleized Yellow, 1945, 7 1/2 x 11 x 6 In. 1610.00
Silvertone, Model 6110, Rocket, Plastic, Black, Fins, Top Push Buttons, 1938, 6 x 12 In. . . 2930.00
Sonora, Model KM, Coronet, Catalin, Alabaster, Green Trim, 1941, 5 1/2 x 9 In. 2780.00
Sparton, Model 500, Cloisonne, Catalin, Yellow, Blue Enamel, Chrome, 1939, 6 x 8 In. . . 9080.00
Sparton, Model 500, Cloisonne, Catalin, Yellow, Maroon Enamel, Chrome, 1939, 5 x 8 In. 4390.00
Sparton, Model 517, Sled, Mirrored Blue, Chrome Fins, 3 Sled Feet, 1936, 9 x 15 3/8 In. . 4099.00
Stewart Warner, Model 07-511, 1939, 4 3/4 x 9 3/8 In. 293.00
Stewart Warner, Model 62T36, Catalin, Tortoise, Yellow, 1946, 8 x 13 In. 615.00
Tesla, Talisman, 306U, Bakelite, Brown, Ivory Grill & Knobs, 1951, 6 5/8 x 11 3/4 In. 1025.00

RAILROAD enthusiasts collect any train memorabilia. Everything
is wanted, from oilcans to whole train cars. The Chessie system has
a store that sells many reproductions of their old dinnerware and
uniforms.

Ashtray, Pullman Company, Bakelite, 2 Cigar & 2 Cigarette Holders, 5 1/2 In. 65.00
Badge, Police, Shield, Star, Special Officer, Great Northern Railroad, 1920s, 3 3/4 In. 400.00
Badge, Santa Fe, Baggage Handler, No. 5 Station, Hat, 4 1/4 In. 645.00
Bell, Cast Iron Frame, 24 In. 509.00
Bench, Shoeshine, Oak, Walnut, Drawers, 3 Seats, P.P. Lagomarsine & Co., 1880, 86 In. . . 3975.00
Brochure, Pullman Progress, Railroad Cars, Full Color, 1929, 48 x 12 In., 8 Panels 29.00
Button, Brotherhood Of Railroad Employees, Crew, Train, Orange, 1950s, 1 1/4 In. 20.00
Button, Chattanooga Choo Choo, General Engine, Blue, White, c.1927, 1 1/2 In. 35.00
Button, Pennsylvania Railroad Safety Eastern Division, That's For Me, 1 1/4 In. 29.00
Calendar, Great Northern, Indian Man, Roll Down, Partial Pad, 1943, 33 1/2 x 16 In. 145.00
Calendar, Great Northern, Indian Woman, Roll Down, Partial Pad, 1943, 33 1/2 x 16 In. . .   145.00
Celery Dish, Milwaukee Road Traveler, Syracuse China, c.1947, 9 3/4 x 4 5/8 In. 165.00
Gravy Boat, SAL, Green Stripes, China, 10 1/2 x 3 3/4 x 4 3/4 In. 30.00
Lantern, Canadian Pacific, Clear Globe 55.00
Lantern, Canadian Pacific, Ruby Red Globe, Wire Base, Metal Bottom, Adlake Kero 160.00
Lantern, Chicago Milwaukee St. Paul, Wire Ring Bottom, Adams & Westlake Co., 5 In. . .   250.00
Lantern, Dressel, Arlington, N.J., Marked, 19th Century, 18 In. 144.00
Lantern, Hartford, New York, New Haven, Caboose, 14 In. 138.00
Lantern, New York Central, Ruby Glass Globe, Vulcan, Dietz U.S.A., N.Y. 150.00
Lantern, New York Central, Switching, 15 In. 150.00
Lock, C B & Q, Brass Body, Steel Shackle, Yale, Pin Tumbler, Push Key, 2 In. 250.00
Lock, Erie Railroad Co., Brass, 2 1/2 In. 115.00
Lock, Great Central, Brass, 2 3/8 In. 550.00
Lock, GTP, Grand Trunk Pacific, Steel Body, Brass Shackle, Pin Tumbler, Yale, 2 1/2 In. . .   680.00
Lock, Wabash Signal Dept., Brass, Yale, 3 In. 35.00
Lock, WM Signal, Brass, Yale, 3 In. 50.00
Postcard, Florida East Coast Railway, Train, Key West Extension, Harris, c.1912 . . . .   45.00
Postcard, Hotel De China, Central Pacific, Worker's Hut, Master Photographers, No. 28 . .   2.00
Postcard, West End Of Great Northern Railway Yards, Breckenridge, Minn., 1908 . . . .   35.00
Poster, Brotherhood Of Railroad Union, Paper, Frame, 32 1/2 x 25 1/2 In. 360.00
Poster, Orient Express, Victoria Station, London, Linen Back, 1985, 12 x 19 In. 260.00
Poster, Societe Nationale Des Chemins De Fer Francais, France, 1938, 40 x 25 In. 1160.00
Sign, Railway, Express, Porcelain, 6 x 20 In., 2 Piece 110.00
Statue, Conductor, Holding Suitcase, No. 27, True Builder 135.00
Stove Plate, Northwest Train Line, Cast Iron, Locomotive, c.1875, 17 1/4 x 23 1/2 In. 3300.00

Telegraph Voltaic Cell, Chloride Model, Glass, Zinc, Carbon, Fitch Perfect Battery, c.1897	65.00
Ticket Envelope, Pennsylvania Railroad, 6 1/4 x 3 5/8 In.	6.00
Timetable, Chicago To Milwaukee, 1962, 4 x 2 1/2 In.	2.00
Timetable, Nickel Plate Road Of New York, Chicago, St. Louis, Oct. 30, 1955, 9 x 4 In.	6.00
Timetable, Penn Central, Laminated, 1973	15.00
Towel, Pullman Train Car, Linen, Property Of Pullman Company, 24 x 16 1/4 In.	18.00

RAZORS were used in ancient Egypt and subsequently wherever shaving was in fashion. The metal razor used in America until about 1870 was made in Sheffield, England. After 1870, machine-made hollow-ground razors were made in Germany or America. Plastic or bone handles were popular. The razor was often sold in a set of seven, one for each day of the week. The set was often kept by the barber who shaved the well-to-do man each day in the shop.

Box, Gillette Tech Razor, World Series Special, 5 Ballplayers, 3 3/4 x 2 x 1 In.	95.00
Keen Kutter, Logo On Head, Wood Handle, Black	16.50
Keen Kutter, Logo On Head, Wood Handle, Green	16.50
Keen Kutter, Logo On Head, Wood Handle, Red	16.50
Remington, Electric, DeLuxe 60, Bakelite, Plastic	9.00
Strap, Winchester, No. 8370, Leather, Padded Handle, Metal Hook, Radium Finish, 25 In.	220.00
Strap, Winchester, No. 8375, 2 Handles, Canvas, Leather	347.00
W.R. Case & Sons, Straight, Real Blue Point, Leatherette Box, 1910-20	179.00
Winchester, Safety, Blades, Instructions, Box, Unopened	201.00
Winchester, Safety, Shaves, Satisfies, As Good As The Gun, Box	58.00

REAMERS, or juice squeezers, have been known since 1767, although most of those collected today date from the twentieth century. Figural reamers are among the most prized.

Glass, Clear, Tab Handle, Hazel Atlas, 6 In.	14.00
Glass, Flowers, Pink, Paden City, 4 Cup, 8 1/4 x 7 1/2 In.	170.00

RECORDS have changed size and shape through the years. The cylinder-shaped phonograph record for use with the early Edison models was made about 1889. Disc records were first made by 1894, the double-sided disc by 1904. High-fidelity records were first issued in 1944, the first vinyl disc in 1946, the first stereo record in 1958. The 78 RPM became the standard in 1926 but was discontinued in 1957. In 1932, the first 33 1/3 RPM was made but was not sold commercially until 1948. In 1949, the 45 RPM was introduced. Compact discs became available in the U.S. in 1982 and many companies began phasing out the production of phonograph records.

Barbie, Sings, 6 Terrific Teenage Tunes, 45 RPM	38.00
Deanna Durbin, Trifold Cover, Decca, 78 RPM, 1940s, 10 1/2 x 10 1/4 In., 3 Records	40.00
Jayne Mansfield, Music For Bachelors, RCA Victor, 33 1/3 RPM, 1956, 12 x 12 1/2 In.	40.00
Johnny Mathis, Right From The Heart, Columbia, 45 RPM, c.1985	8.00
Yogi Bear & Huckleberry Hound, Fairy Tales, 33 1/3 RPM, 1977	7.00

RED WING Pottery of Red Wing, Minnesota, was a firm started in 1878. The company first made utilitarian pottery, including stoneware jugs and canning jars. In the 1920s art pottery was made. Many dinner sets and vases were made before the company closed in 1967. Rumrill pottery made by the Red Wing Pottery for George Rumrill is listed in its own category. For more information, see *Kovels' Depression Glass & Dinnerware Price List.*

Advertising, Bean Pot, Cover, From Country Kitchen Of The Farmer's Wife Magazine	600.00
Advertising, Bean Pot, It Pays To Trade With Shors & Alexander, Pocahontas, Ia.	65.00
Advertising, Bean Pot, Shop & Save With Emmons Merc. Co., Jack Sprat Store, Minn.	155.00
Advertising, Beater Jar, Call Again, Nielsen Groc., 3 Blue Bands	550.00
Advertising, Beater Jar, It Pays To Mix With Albrecht, Anamoose, N.D., Spongeware	1050.00
Advertising, Bowl, Merry Christmas From Weigolb & Nordby, Gray Line, 8 In.	105.00
Advertising, Casserole, Cover, Gray Line, Christmas, Hokah Co-Op Creamery, 8 In.	165.00
Advertising, Crock, Butter, Goodhue County Co-Operative, 5 Lb.	85.00
Advertising, Crock, Enjoy Lakeside Dairy Products, Jackson, Mich., 1 Lb.	45.00

Advertising, Crock, North American Creameries Inc., Meadowbrook Butter, 3 Lb. 115.00
Advertising, Crock, O'Donnell's Baked Beans, 1 Lb. 145.00
Advertising, Flowerpot, Hans Rosacker Co. For Flowers, Blue Band, Handle 475.00
Advertising, Jar, Lard, Cover, Compliments Of Dan's, Store State Center, Iowa, Western .. 300.00
Advertising, Jug, Fargo Creamery Supply House, St. Paul, Minn., Gal. 125.00
Advertising, Jug, John P. Gagan Wholesale Liquors, Lafayette, Ind., Brown, 2 Gal. 165.00
Advertising, Jug, Mason House & Mineral Springs, Shield & Oval, Shoulder, 5 Gal. 700.00
Advertising, Mug, Good Luck Malt Syrup, Blue Band 125.00
Advertising, Mug, I Came From Atlas Malt Products, Blue Band 95.00
Advertising, Mug, Liberty Home Beverage Co., Detroit, Mich., Blue & White 165.00
Advertising, Mug, Souvenir, West End Commercial Club, St. Paul, June 21-26, 1909 ..... 155.00
Advertising, Pitcher, Compliments Of A.L. Bailey, Dows, Ia., Scroll Handle 95.00
Advertising, Pitcher, Compliments Of Mangus Johnson, Jewel, Iowa, Scroll Handle 900.00
Advertising, Pitcher, Compliments Of Max Bros., Kaylor, S. Dakota, Cherry Band 170.00
Art Pottery, Box, Cover, Pink Matte Glaze, Applied Leaf, 4 1/2 x 3 1/2 In. 120.00
Art Pottery, Cake Plate, Pink Fleck Zephyr, Fluted, Pedestal, 3 1/2 x 11 1/4 In. 100.00
Art Pottery, Cornucopia, Fleck Nile Blue, Colonial Bluff, Interior, 9 x 15 In. 95.00
Art Pottery, Figurine, Bird On Stump, 6 In. 90.00
Art Pottery, Pitcher, Ball, Orange, 7 1/2 In. 45.00
Art Pottery, Planter, Boy, Eggshell Ivory Glaze, 6 1/4 In. 100.00
Art Pottery, Planter, Cart, Butterscotch, 8 1/2 In. 75.00
Art Pottery, Planter, Deer, Green Glaze, 6 x 6 In. 100.00
Art Pottery, Planter, Giraffe, Brown, Tan Fleck, 11 In. 385.00
Art Pottery, Planter, Lamb, Eggshell Ivory Glaze 80.00
Art Pottery, Planter, Lion, Green Glaze, Stamped, 11 In. ....265.00 to 353.00
Art Pottery, Planter, Lion, Greenglaze, Stamped, 7 1/2 In. 235.00
Art Pottery, Prismatique, Planter, Lemon Yellow, White Interior, 3 1/8 x 8 1/4 In. 80.00
Art Pottery, Prismatique, Planter, Mandarin Orange, Celadon Interior, 3 3/4 x 10 In. 100.00
Art Pottery, Vase, Adobe, Apricot Interior, Ruffled Edge, Terra-Craft, No. 954, 6 In. 125.00
Art Pottery, Vase, Bud, Long Handle, Green Glaze, 7 In. 10.00
Art Pottery, Vase, Fan, White, Gypsy Trail, 4 1/2 In. 90.00
Art Pottery, Vase, Flower Form, Bulbous, Blue-Gray, Pink Interior, 6 1/2 x 7 In. 95.00
Art Pottery, Vase, Leaf Form, Gray Cluster, Brown Interior, 10 In. 90.00
Bake & Serve, Ramekin, Round, 1963, 2 3/4 x 8 In. 35.00
Blossom Time, Cup & Saucer, Tea, Stoneware 15.00
Bob White, Bowl, Vegetable, Divided V-Shape, 14 In. 75.00
Bob White, Pitcher, 112 Oz., 15 In. 350.00
Bob White, Pitcher, Water, 60 Oz., 10 In. 45.00
Bob White, Platter, 13 In. 45.00
Bob White, Salt & Pepper, 6 In. 35.00
Butterfly, Pitcher, Blue & White 325.00
Capistrano, Casserole, Cover 48.00
Capistrano, Saucer 4.00
Cherry Band, Pitcher, Large 155.00
Cherry Band, Pitcher, Small, 6 In. ....170.00 to 225.00
Churn, Cover, Elephant Ear Handles, Union Oval, 5 Gal. 650.00
Churn, Elephant Ear Handles, Lid, 3 Gal. 325.00
Coffee Dripolator, Leaves, 4 Cup 50.00
Cookie Jar, Baker, Blue 105.00
Cookie Jar, Baker, Yellow 95.00
Cookie Jar, Basket Weave & Morning Glory, Put Your Fist In, 8 In. 710.00
Cookie Jar, Jack Frost, Pumpkin, 8 1/2 In. 1500.00
Cookie Jar, Katrina, Dutch Girl, Blue, 11 In. 75.00
Cookie Jar, Katrina, Dutch Girl, Yellow, 11 In. 90.00
Gray Line, Bowl, Spongeband, 9 In. 135.00
Gray Line, Bowl, Spongeband, 10 In. 80.00
Gray Line, Casserole 115.00
Gray Line, Casserole, Cover Only, Spongeband, 6 1/2 In. 100.00
Gray Line, Casserole, Spongeband, Medium 90.00
Gray Line, Cookie Jar, Cover, Cookies, Sponge Band 1000.00
Gray Line, Pitcher, Spongeband, 7 1/2 In. 395.00
Gray Line, Saltshaker, Spongeband 105.00
Greek Key, Bowl, 6 In. 95.00

Gypsy Trail, Casserole, French, Green, 1930s, 8 In. 15.00
Koverwate, 3 Gal. 450.00
Koverwate, 15 Gal. 375.00
Magnolia, Teapot 28.00
Normandy, Plate, Dinner, 1941, 10 In. 20.00
Oomph, Teapot, Brown & Green Glaze, 6 In. 125.00
Pepe, Plate, Salad, 6 In. 16.95
Pepe, Sugar & Creamer 50.00
Random Harvest, Sugar & Creamer 50.00
Stoneware, Beater Jar, Spongeware 55.00
Stoneware, Bowl, Brown, Marked, 1/2 Pt., 6 In. 20.00
Stoneware, Butter Jar, Wing, 20 Lb. 275.00
Stoneware, Churn, Birch Leaves, Union Oval, 3 Gal. ....225.00 to 250.00
Stoneware, Churn, Birch Leaves, Union Oval, 4 Gal. 225.00
Stoneware, Churn, Birch Leaves, Union Oval, 6 Gal. 400.00
Stoneware, Churn, Cover, Birch Leaves, Union Oval, 8 Gal. 1100.00
Stoneware, Churn, Cover, Wing & Union Oval, 6 Gal. 400.00
Stoneware, Churn, Wing & Union Oval, 4 Gal. 185.00
Stoneware, Churn, Wing & Union Oval, 5 Gal. 195.00
Stoneware, Churn, Wing & Union Oval, 10 Gal. 2100.00
Stoneware, Crock, 2 Sets Of Birch Leaves, Union Oval, Molded Handles, 40 Gal. 2200.00
Stoneware, Crock, Birch Leaf, Salt Glaze, 20 Gal. 170.00
Stoneware, Crock, Birch Leaves, Salt Glaze, 20 Gal. 850.00
Stoneware, Crock, Birch Leaves, Ski Oval, 15 Gal. 275.00
Stoneware, Crock, Birch Leaves, Union Oval, 4 Gal. 45.00
Stoneware, Crock, Birch Leaves, Union Oval, Molded Handles, 5 Gal. 65.00
Stoneware, Crock, Birch Leaves, Union Oval, Molded Handles, 8 Gal. 195.00
Stoneware, Crock, Cobalt Blue Leaf, Salt Glaze, 15 Gal. 1430.00
Stoneware, Crock, Large Wing & Union Oval, 8 Gal. 75.00
Stoneware, Crock, Large Wing & Union Oval, 20 Gal. 115.00
Stoneware, Crock, Leaf, Salt Glaze, Stamped, Minnesota Stoneware, 10 Gal. 235.00
Stoneware, Crock, Salt Glaze, Target, 2 Gal. 60.00
Stoneware, Crock, Union Oval, Rolled Rim, 2 Gal., 9 In. 58.00
Stoneware, Custard, Spongeware 80.00
Stoneware, Jar, Applesauce, 4-In. Wing, Weir Lid, 3 Gal 135.00
Stoneware, Jar, Applesauce, Ball Lock Lid, Wing & Union Oval, 5 Gal. 155.00
Stoneware, Jar, Canning, 1/2 Gal. 265.00
Stoneware, Jug, Beehive, Birch Leaf, Union Oval, 4 Gal. 1000.00
Stoneware, Jug, Beehive, Rib Cage & Target, Salt Glaze, 6 Gal. 450.00
Stoneware, Jug, Beehive, Threshing, Wing & Union Oval, Spigot Hole, 5 Gal. 1500.00
Stoneware, Jug, Beehive, Wing & Oval, 3 Gal. 325.00
Stoneware, Jug, Beehive, Wing & Oval, 4 Gal. 500.00
Stoneware, Jug, Beehive, Wing & Oval, 5 Gal. 300.00
Stoneware, Jug, Brown Shoulder, Wing, 1/2 Gal. 215.00
Stoneware, Jug, Brown Shoulder, Wing, Gal. 175.00
Stoneware, Jug, Brown, Marked, 1/2 Pt. 95.00
Stoneware, Jug, Shoulder, Wing & Union Oval, 5 Gal. ....65.00 to 70.00
Stoneware, Jug, Union Oval, 5 Gal., 18 In. 175.00
Stoneware, Pitcher, Cherry Band, Large 155.00
Stoneware, Pitcher, Dutch Blue, 1938, 5 1/2 In. 325.00
Stoneware, Snuff Jar, Albany Slip, North Star Stoneware Company 115.00
Stoneware, Water Cooler, 6 Gal. 605.00
Stoneware, Water Cooler, Blue Bands, 3 Gal., 15 In. 288.00
Stoneware, Water Cooler, Lid, 4 In. Wing & Union Oval, Hand Turned, 2 Gal. 1600.00
Stoneware, Water Cooler, Lid, 4 In. Wing & Union Oval, Hand Turned, 4 Gal. 300.00
Stoneware, Water Cooler, Lid, 4 In. Wing & Union Oval, Hand Turned, 6 Gal. 500.00
Stoneware, Water Cooler, Lid, 6 In. Wing & Union Oval, Hand Turned, 8 Gal. 1600.00
Tampico, Gravy Boat, Underplate 25.00
Town & Country, Pitcher, Dusk Blue, Eva Zeisel, 1940s, 3 Pt. 95.00
Town & Country, Plate, Dinner, Dusk Blue, Eva Zeisel 35.00
Town & Country, Relish, Dusk Blue, Eva Zeisel, 1947, 7 x 5 In. 35.00
Washbowl, Pitcher, Spongeware, Blue Band, 12 In. 635.00

REDWARE is a hard, red stoneware that originated in the late 1600s and continues to be made. The term is also used to describe any common clay pottery that is reddish in color.

Bank, Acorn Form, Molded, Coin Slot, Yellow Slip, 4 x 3 7/8 In.	165.00
Bank, Apple, Coin Slot Top, Red, Yellow Highlights, 2 1/2 x 3 3/4 In.	825.00
Bank, Bird & Baby Sitting On Nest, Incised Details, Orange Glaze, 5 x 7 In.	1100.00
Bank, Bird, Perched On Arched Base, Yellow & Green Slip, Pennsylvania, 7 In.	2875.00
Bank, Bulbous, Cream, Brown & Blue Drip, Knob Finial, 4 1/4 x 3 1/4 In.	440.00
Bank, Lion, Applied Coleslaw Mane, Yellow, Brown Slip, Coin Slot In Base, 7 x 3 x 4 In.	3300.00
Bank, Orange, Green, Brown Mottled Glaze, Round, Finial, Inscribed, 1860, 4 1/4 x 4 In.	2200.00
Bank, Oval, Brown Sponging, Tooled Line, 3 3/4 In.	290.00
Bank, Sgraffito, 3-Ring Finial, Incised, William Mountjoy, 29 May 1839, 6 In.	4890.00
Basket, Tan, Brown Mottled Glaze, Applied Handle, 2 3/8 x 3 1/8 In.	1100.00
Batter Bowl, Coggled Band, Brown Sponge, Tapered Sides, Pour Spout, Handle	440.00
Bean Pot, Cover, Incised Flowers, Bird, Bands, Black Glaze, Strap Handles, 11 x 13 In.	9900.00
Bean Pot, Cover, Red Brown Glaze, 2 Ear Handles, Pointed Finial, 7 1/2 x 6 1/2 In.	250.00
Betty Lamp Stand, Incised Decoration, Clear Glaze, 19th Century, 4 1/4 x 3 3/4 In.	460.00
Bird Whistle, Bird With 4 Smaller Ones, Tree Trunk, 10 In.	690.00
Bowl, 8-Point Starflower, Cream, Green, Wavy Bands, Snow Hill, 1800s, 12 In. 7765.00 to	8625.00
Bowl, Concave Sides, Pinched Flattened Handles, Running Glaze, 6 1/2 x 3 In.	460.00
Bowl, Crimped Rim, Pumpkin & Brown Spattered Glaze, 1 1/8 x 3 1/8 In.	330.00
Bowl, Flat Rim, Brown, Black Mottled Glaze Interior, 1 1/4 x 3 3/8 In.	330.00
Bowl, Glazed, 3 Rows Of Cream Slip Double Lines, Shallow, 7 7/8 In., Pair	690.00
Bowl, Glazed, Slip Decorated, Concave Rim, Undulating Yellow Line, 8 3/8 In.	3820.00
Bowl, Man Smoking Pipe, Hat, Dots, Rectangular, Yellow Slip, 13 x 9 5/8 In.	85.00
Bowl, Manganese, Sponged, 19th Century, 8 1/4 x 4 In.	430.00
Bowl, Milk, Sponge, Mid 19th Century, 11 In.	290.00
Bowl, Mottled, Orange Glaze, Miller Pottery, 1 1/2 x 6 3/8 In.	440.00
Bowl, Orange Glaze, 2 Applied Handles, 2 1/4 x 3 3/4 In.	605.00
Bowl, Pennsylvania Dutch, Flared Sides, Inward Turned Rim, 19th Century, 5 x 13 In.	430.00
Bowl, Pierced Bottom, Twisted Handle, Footed, Brown, Orange Mottled Glaze, 3 x 5 3/8 In.	3850.00
Bowl, Porridge, Bulbous, Flared Rim, Yellow & Brown Glaze, 3 1/2 x 4 3/4 In.	415.00
Bowl, Porridge, Green Ground, Black Spatter, Handle, 4 3/8 x 4 7/8 In.	195.00
Bowl, Pumpkin, Band Of Green, 2 x 4 In.	525.00
Bowl, Sloped Sides, Scalloped Rim, Berry & Vine, Chain Decoration, 3 1/4 x 12 In.	175.00
Bowl, Sunflowers, Black Glaze, Incised & Banded Rim, Strap Handles, 5 x 12 In.	165.00
Bowl, Unglazed Exterior, Yellow & Green Slip Interior, Moravian, 12 x 4 In.	375.00
Bowl, Yellow & Black Slip, Pumpkin Glaze, 3 1/4 x 12 In.	1430.00
Bowl, Yellow & Green Slip, Orange Glaze, Stamped, W. Smith, Womelsdorf, 1 1/4 x 7 In.	4620.00
Bowl, Yellow Slip, Brown Glaze, c.1870, 3 In.	1073.00
Bowl, Yellow Slip, Orange, Stamped, W. Smith, Womelsdorf, 1 1/2 x 8 1/8 In.	2310.00
Bulb Planter, Underplate, Salmon Glaze, Manganese, 9 3/4 x 8 In.	920.00
Candleholder, Jug Form, C-Shape Handle, Green Brown Interior, J.S. Stahl, 1939, 6 x 5 In.	468.00
Candleholder, Light Brown Glaze, Applied Handle, 1 1/2 x 4 3/4 In., Pair	275.00
Candleholder, Mottled Brown & Orange Glaze, Cutouts, Cone Shape, Handle, 7 In.	6600.00
Candlestick, Brown, Cream, c.1830, 8 In.	578.00
Charger, Coggled Rim, 3-Line Yellow Slip, 13 3/8 In.	375.00
Charger, Serrated Rim, 3-Line Yellow Slip, 13 In.	360.00
Charger, Serrated Rim, 5-Line Yellow Dot Slip, Lead Glaze, 13 3/4 In.	625.00
Creamer, Bulbous, Manganese Black, Applied Handle, 3 1/8 x 2 1/2 In.	275.00
Creamer, Cover, Bulbous, Orange Glaze, Black Dripping, 4 x 3 In.	770.00
Creamer, Orange Lead Glaze, Incised Band, Applied Handle, 2 5/8 x 3 1/4 In.	250.00
Crock, Bulbous, Mottled Tan, Black, Brown Glaze, Incised Bands, Applied Handle, 6 x 5 In.	495.00
Crock, Egg Shape, Wide Mouth, Red Orange Glaze, Brush Marks, Lug Handles, 9 In.	385.00
Crock, Rim, Brown & Manganese Glaze, 2 In.	80.00
Crock, Rim, Pumpkin Glaze, Stamped, John W. Bell, Waynesboro, 4 3/4 x 5 1/2 In.	415.00
Cup, Manganese Black Glaze, Applied Handle, 1 5/8 x 2 1/2 In.	360.00
Cup, Manganese, 2 x 2 1/4 In.	105.00
Cuspidor, Ladies', Pumpkin Orange, Brown Daubs, 3 3/4 x 2 In.	230.00
Custard Cup, Coggled Rim, Incised, Brown Glaze, 1 7/8 x 3 1/4 In.	50.00
Custard Cup, Coggled Rim, Incised, Orange & Brown Glaze, 1 7/8 x 3 1/2 In.	220.00

Dish, Glazed Slip, Sgraffito Decorated, German Inscription, Penn., c.1855, 10 1/2 In. 470.00
Dish, Glazed, Slip Decorated, Stylized Flowers, Early 1900s, 12 1/2 In. 1175.00
Dish, Oblong, Brown Daubed Glaze, 9 1/2 x 11 1/2 x 3 In. 175.00
Dish, Sweetmeat, Orange Glaze, Yellow Drip, 4 Conjoined Cups, Arched Handle, 5 x 7 In. 580.00
Door Knob, Brown Glaze, Black Accent, 8 Piece 165.00
Dough Tray, Slip Decorated, Trailings, Oblong, Coggled Rim, 1800s, 12 x 15 In. 17625.00
Figurine, Bear, Hand Formed, Incised, Oval Base, Stamped Flowers, John Bell, 4 x 9 In. . . 1760.00
Figurine, Cat, Glazed, Black Stripes, Oval Base, Penn., 5 3/4 In. 17625.00
Figurine, Dog, Coleslaw Fur, Floppy Ears, Freestanding, Manganese Glaze, 5 1/4 In. 1265.00
Figurine, Dog, Fruit Basket In Mouth, Glazed, Penn., 7 1/4 In. 15275.00
Figurine, Dog, King Charles Spaniel, Brown & Yellow Slip, Galena, Ill., c.1860, 9 In. 1560.00
Figurine, Dog, Setter, Seated, Stamped Triangles, Molded Rose, Tulip, Inscribed Tess, 6 In. 3105.00
Figurine, Dog, Spaniel, White Paint, Black Dots, Hollow, Molded Details, 13 In. 800.00
Figurine, Dog, Tooled, Basket In Mouth, Freestanding, Manganese Glaze, Pa., 4 1/2 In. . . . 5980.00
Figurine, Goose, Incised Wings, Eyes, Brown, Black Glaze, Rattle, 2 1/2 x 1 1/2 x 3 1/4 In. 660.00
Figurine, Goose, Incised Wings, Eyes, Red, Brown Glaze, Rattle, 2 1/2 x 1 5/8 x 3 1/2 In. . 2310.00
Figurine, Lion, Crouching, Coleslaw Mane, Tail, Oval Base, Jacob Fritz, 2 3/8 x 4 In. 175.00
Figurine, Pelican, Circular Base, 1797, 7 In. 1645.00
Figurine, Rooster, Orange Manganese Glaze, Red, Over Painted Comb, 10 3/4 x 6 In., Pair 2200.00
Figurine, Squirrel, Eating Nut, Glazed, c.1880, 5 x 3 3/4 In. 5100.00
Flowerpot, Bisque, Applied Decoration, Painted, Glazed, 5 x 5 1/2 In. 345.00
Flowerpot, Coggled Rim, Orange, Black Splotches, Saucer Base, Stamped LKT, 6 x 7 In. . . 770.00
Flowerpot, Incised Bands, Orange, Black Sponge Decoration, Crimped Rim, 7 x 8 In. 910.00
Flowerpot, Manganese & Pinched Decoration, Hanging, Chester County, Pa., 1800s 2260.00
Flowerpot, Mottled Brown & Yellow Glaze, Base, 4 3/8 x 5 In. 220.00
Flowerpot, Orange, Black, Yellow Mottled Glaze, Incised Band, Attached Base, 3 x 4 In. . . 635.00
Flowerpot, Red, Black, Yellow Mottled Glaze, Incised Band, 3 3/8 x 5 3/8 In. 495.00
Flowerpot, Undertray, Shenandoah, Slip Wash, Solomon Bell, Strasburg, Va., 8 In. 2415.00
Flowerpot, Yellow & Green Glaze, Bangor Stoneware Co., 12 x 12 In. 265.00
Hotplate, Black Glaze Crosses, 8 Ball Feet, 6 1/2 In. 275.00
Jar, Apple Butter, Orange, Brown Spattered Glaze, W. Smith, Womelsdorf, 5 x 5 In. 360.00
Jar, Apple Butter, Oval, Flared Rim, Daubed Glaze, 5 3/4 In. 345.00
Jar, Brick Glaze, Brushed Manganese Design At Top, Applied Handles, 8 3/4 In. 430.00
Jar, Bulbous Oval, Green Slip Squiggles, Yellow Dots, Initials S.G., Moravian, 1784 . . . . . 7150.00
Jar, Bulbous, 2 Incised Bands, Brown & Black Mottled Glaze, 5 3/4 x 5 In. . . . . . . .165.00 to 195.00
Jar, Bulbous, 2 Incised Bands, Brown & Black Mottled Glaze, 7 1/4 x 5 1/4 In. 495.00
Jar, Bulbous, 2 Incised Bands, Brown & Black Mottled Glaze, 7 1/4 x 6 In. 690.00
Jar, Bulbous, Coggle Wheel Bands, Brown, Mottled Drip Glaze, Applied Handles, 6 x 7 In. 1540.00
Jar, Bulbous, Turned, Rim, Brown & Black Spattered Glaze, Stamped, W. Smith, 5 x 5 In. . 275.00
Jar, Bulbous, Turned, Rim, Incised Band, Brown Glaze, Stamped, W. Smith, 5 1/2 x 5 1/8 In. 250.00
Jar, Coggle Wheel Bands, Brown, Tan, Green Mottled Drip, Strap Handles, 11 x 9 In. 1100.00
Jar, Coggled Bands, Cylindrical, Rolled Rim, Manganese Glaze, 10 x 6 3/4 In. 495.00
Jar, Cover, Round, Strap Handle, Tapering, Egg Shaped Base, 12 1/2 x 14 1/2 In. 265.00
Jar, Cream Glaze, Mottled Green, Brown Spots, S. Bell & Sons, Shenandoah, 8 3/4 In. 3335.00
Jar, Cylindrical, Fluted Rim, 2 Incised Bands, Brown, Manganese Black Spots, 12 x 7 In. . 525.00
Jar, Cylindrical, Rolled Rim, Orange Ground, Black Spatter Trim, 6 3/4 x 5 1/2 In. 195.00
Jar, Flared Rim, Flowers, Squiggle Lines, Egg Shape, Lug Handles, 1841, 10 1/2 In. 5875.00
Jar, Flared Rim, Sloped Shoulder, Brown Green Glaze, Dark Brown Streaks, 7 In. 350.00
Jar, Flowers, Molded, Brown Mottled Glaze, Stamped, Henry Swopes Pottery, 11 x 6 In. . . 3025.00
Jar, Incised & Wavy Bands, Egg Shape, Manganese Slip Glaze, c.1885, 12 In. 3600.00
Jar, Manganese Black, Rim, 4 1/8 x 3 1/4 In. 230.00
Jar, Mottled Green, Amber, Orange Glaze, Galena, 8 1/8 In. 430.00
Jar, Orange, Brown, Sponge Design, Square Incised Banding, 3 3/4 x 2 3/4 In. 1925.00
Jar, Oval, Incised Band, Pumpkin Colored Glaze, Manganese Sponging, Handles, 9 In. 259.00
Jar, Oval, Incised Neck Rings, Double Handles, Brown Manganese Brushed Daubs, 8 In. . . 489.00
Jar, Oval, Raised Rim, Lug Handles, Brown Streak, Conn., Early 19th Century, 11 In. 1530.00
Jar, Pear Shape, Cover, Button Finial Lid, Orange Brown Glaze, 7 5/8 x 6 In. 1045.00
Jar, Raised Rim, Egg Shape, Lug Handles, Early 1800s, 9 5/8 In. 355.00
Jar, Running Yellow, Cream, Green, Brown Manganese Glaze Applied Handles, 8 In. 489.00
Jar, Slip Decorated, Cover, 2 Handles, Penn., 19th Century, 7 In. 325.00
Jar, Storage, Pumpkin Colored Glaze, Brown Floral Decoration, 9 5/8 In. 1495.00
Jar, Tulips, Egg Shape, Handle, Flared Mouth, 1800s, 8 1/2 In. 380.00
Jar, Yellow Slip, Tree, Flowers, Orange Ground, Black Trim, Cylindrical, 11 x 5 1/2 In. . . . 2750.00

Jug, Applied Handle, Brown Manganese Glaze, 8 1/4 x 7 1/4 In.	209.00
Jug, Applied Handle, Brown, Black Mottled Glaze, York County, Penn., 3 x 2 1/2 In.	110.00
Jug, Brown Glaze, Strap Handle, 4 x 2 3/4 In.	195.00
Jug, Bulbous, Applied Handle, Incised Bands, Manganese Glaze, 6 1/2 x 5 1/2 In.	440.00
Jug, Cobalt Blue Decoration, Olive Glaze, Whittem S.P., Sept. 12, 1934, 5 In.	200.00
Jug, Green Yellow Glaze, Red, Brown, Lines, Tooled Lip, Applied Handle, 7 1/2 In.	115.00
Jug, Grotesque, Bulging Eyes, Open Mouth, Shard Teeth, Albany Slip, N.C., 6 1/2 In.	920.00
Jug, Incised Bands, Egg Shape, Brown Mottled Drip Glaze, Strap Handle, 9 1/2 In.	935.00
Jug, Incised Lines, Egg Shape, Brown Speckled Glaze, Strap Handle, c.1900, 7 1/4 In.	355.00
Jug, Incised Shoulder Lines, Pumpkin Orange Glaze, 8 1/2 In.	405.00
Jug, Oval, Incised Rings, Green, Orange In Glaze, Brown Daubs, Applied Handle, 6 In.	635.00
Jug, Oval, Incised Rings, Mottled Glaze, Manganese Specks, Applied Handle, 8 In.	375.00
Jug, Oval, Manganese Glaze, Applied Strap Handle, 6 In.	175.00
Jug, Salmon, Pale Yellow Glaze, Applied Strap Handle, 7 1/2 In.	200.00
Mixing Bowl, Incised Bands, Orange Glaze, Turned, Applied Handles, 6 x 13 1/2 In.	1045.00
Mold, Candle, Redware Tubes, Bootjack Ends, 18 x 6 1/4 x 15 In.	200.00
Mug, Dark Brown Spot, Streaks, Reddish Ground, Oval, C-Shape Handle, 6 In.	405.00
Mug, Incised Bands, Flared Rim, Green, Brown Spatter, Applied Handle, 4 1/4 x 4 1/2 In.	495.00
Mug, Manganese, 19th Century, Penn., 3 1/4 x 3 In.	400.00
Pan, Loaf, Coggled Rim, 3-Line Yellow Slip, 10 x 13 1/4 In.	920.00
Pan, Loaf, Coggled Rim, 4-Line Yellow Slip, Tapered Sides, 16 x 10 1/2 In.	635.00
Pan, Loaf, Coggled Rim, White Glazed Interior, Brown Slip Feather Design, 11 x 14 In.	1320.00
Pan, Loaf, Combware, White Slip, Coggled Rim, 17 1/2 x 14 x 3 In.	1840.00
Pan, Loaf, Shallow, Coggled Rim, Yellow Slip Wavy Line, 7 1/2 x 11 In.	690.00
Pan, Loaf, Slip Decorated, Coggled Edge, Penn., Mid 1800s, 11 1/2 x 11 1/4 In.	4115.00
Pan, Loaf, Yellow Slip Decoration, Wavy Lines, Pa., 1820-40, 16 x 12 In.	4800.00
Pie Plate, Coggled Rim, 3-Line Yellow Slip, 8 In.	430.00
Pie Plate, Coggled Rim, 3-Line Yellow Slip, 10 1/4 In.	400.00
Pie Plate, Coggled Rim, Yellow Slip, Wavy Lines, 5 3/4 In.	400.00
Pie Plate, Coggled Rim, Yellow Slip, Wavy Lines, 10 1/4 In.	316.00
Pie Plate, Coggled Rim, Yellow Slip, Wavy Lines, Dots, 9 3/4 In.	605.00
Pie Plate, Coggled Rim, Yellow, Green Slip, Wavy Lines, 8 1/4 In.	630.00
Pie Plate, Slip Decorated, Orange Base Glaze, Squiggle Lines, 1 3/4 x 8 5/8 In.	1375.00
Pitcher, Black Drip, Incised Bands, Bulbous, Flared Rim, Orange Glaze, 6 x 5 1/2 In.	305.00
Pitcher, Bulbous, Brown, Mottled Black Manganese, 2 3/4 x 2 1/4 In.	440.00
Pitcher, Cover, Tan, Green, Brown Mottled Glaze, Finial, 3 3/4 x 2 1/2 In.	470.00
Pitcher, Cylindrical Collar, Oval, Strap Handle, 9 1/2 In.	265.00
Pitcher, Flared Rim, Egg Shape, 1800s, 8 3/4 In.	120.00
Pitcher, Incised Rings, Brown Manganese Daubs, Applied, Ribbed Strap Handle, 8 In.	316.00
Pitcher, Oval, Manganese Glaze, Extruded Handle, 10 x 7 1/2 In.	200.00
Pitcher, Oval, Raised Ring, Brown Manganese, Yellow Glaze, Applied Handle, 10 1/2 In.	315.00
Pitcher, Raised Flowers, Bulbous, Green Glaze, 5 1/4 x 5 In.	330.00
Pitcher, Salmon Glazed Interior, Manganese Exterior, 1800s, 6 1/2 x 4 3/4 In.	345.00
Pitcher, Salt Glaze Style Flowers, Incised Bands, Flared, 9 1/2 In.	1320.00
Planter, Collared Base, Ruffled Neck, 19th Century, 8 3/4 x 8 In.	635.00
Plate, Coggled Rim, 3-Line & Dot, Yellow Slip, 10 1/2 In.	550.00
Plate, Coggled Rim, 3-Line Yellow Slip, 4 In.	330.00
Plate, Coggled Rim, 5-Line Yellow Slip, 11 3/4 In.	7700.00
Plate, Coggled Rim, Orange Glaze, Double S Slip Design, C. Schutter, 6 5/8 In.	605.00
Plate, Coggled Rim, Pumpkin & Black Sponge, 1 1/4 x 11 In.	550.00
Plate, Coggled Rim, Wavy Line & Dot Slip, Yellow, Pa., Early 1800s, 10 In.	590.00
Plate, Coggled Rim, Yellow Slip, Flower, Orange Glaze, 13 1/4 In.	2090.00
Plate, Coggled Rim, Yellow Slip, Spiral Bands, 12 1/2 In.	770.00
Plate, Red & Yellow Slip Dots, Stamped, Willoughby Smith, Womelsdorf, 1 x 6 1/8 In.	1210.00
Plate, Red, Yellow Slip Swirls, Serrated Edges, 1 3/4 x 11 In.	110.00
Plate, Sgraffito, Tulips, Double Bird, Yellow, Orange, Incised Bands On Rim, 12 In.	4125.00
Platter, Coggled Rim, 3-Line Hash Marks, Yellow Slip, 12 3/4 x 9 3/8 In.	770.00
Porringer, Brushed Brown Design, Orange Lead Glaze, Applied Handle, 3 1/4 x 5 1/4 In.	1100.00
Pot, Herb, Flanged Mouth, Light Orange Slip Glaze, Strap Handle, Thumbprint, 3 In.	220.00
Pot, Olive Green Glaze, Orange Splashes, Handles, New England, 5 In.	230.00
Salt, Master, Incised Bands, Brown, Black Glaze, Adams Co., Penn., 1882, 2 x 3 3/4 In.	2310.00
Salt Dish, Mottled Brown Alkaline Glaze, c.1850, 2 1/4 In.	65.00
Sugar, Lid, Manganese, Decorated, 19th Century, 4 x 4 In.	1065.00

Sugar, Mocha Ferns, Brown Bands, Orange Glaze, Horizontal Loop Handles	935.00
Teapot, Blue Running Over Ivory Base, 5 1/2 In.	140.00
Teapot, Pinched Spout, Manganese Glaze, Applied Handle, 6 1/4 In.	2300.00
Vase, Bulbous, Flared Rim, Brown Glaze, Black Spatter, 9 x 7 1/2 In.	250.00
Vase, Cylinder, Tooled, Textured, Orange To Green, 10 x 6 1/2 In.	230.00
Vase, Incised Bamboo, Plant Decoration, Japan, 6 5/8 In.	23.00
Vase, Incised Straight & Wavy Lines, Bulbous, Flared Rim, Brown, Black Glaze, 6 3/4 In.	330.00
Vase, Oval, Coggled Shoulder, Amber, Brown, Applied Strap Handles, 10 3/4 In.	750.00
Whistle, Bird, Glazed, Penn., 3 In.	2600.00
Whistle, Bird, Orange Ground, Black & White Accents, 2 3/4 x 4 1/2 In.	660.00
Whistle, Bird, Rooster Form, Whistle In Tail, Brown Glaze, 4 x 2 x 5 1/2 In.	3080.00
Whistle, Rooster, Whistle In Tail, Brown Glaze, 4 3/8 x 2 3/4 x 5 1/2 In.	3080.00

REGOUT, see Maastricht category.

RICHARD was the mark used on acid-etched cameo glass vases, bowls, night-lights, and lamps made by the Austrian company Loetz after 1918. The pieces were very similar to the French cameo glasswares made by Daum, Galle, and others.

Vase, Coastal Buildings, Trees, Brown Over Orange Ground, Cameo, 11 3/4 In.	635.00
Vase, Dragonfly, Butterflies, Flowers, Blue, Orange, Long Flared Neck, 6 In.	575.00
Vase, Orchids, Spiked Leaves, Raspberry Shades, Creamy Ground, Cameo, 11 5/8 In.	635.00
Vase, Tudor Cottage, Lake, Trees, Salmon Ground, Tapered, Rolled Foot, Signed, 36 In.	1840.00

RIDGWAY pottery has been made in the Staffordshire district in England since 1808 by a series of companies with the name Ridgway. The transfer-design dinner sets are the most widely known product. They are still being made. Other pieces of Ridgway are listed under Flow Blue.

Bowl, Beauties Of America, Octagon Church, Reticulated, Blue, 12 1/2 In.	2070.00
Bowl, Vegetable, Library Of Trinity College, Cambridge, Blue, 9 1/2 In.	405.00
Dessert Service, Flowers, Blue Bands, Gilt Borders, c.1840, 17 Piece	1650.00
Plate, Beauties Of America, Athenaeum, Boston, 6 1/4 In.	230.00
Plate, Beauties Of America, Library, Philadelphia, 8 1/4 In.	230.00
Platter, Beauties Of America, Capitol, Washington, Blue, 20 3/4 In.	1725.00
Platter, Blue Willow, Ironstone, c.1930, 17 1/2 x 14 In.	175.00
Platter, Boston Scene, Castkill Moss Border, Transfer Print, 1831-48, 14 x 19 In.	430.00
Tureen, Soup, Beauties Of America, Almshouse, Boston, Cambridge College, 15 3/4 In.	1495.00

RIFLES that are firearms are not listed in this book. BB guns and air rifles are listed in the Toy category.

RIVIERA dinnerware was made by the Homer Laughlin Co. of Newell, West Virginia, from 1938 to 1950. The pattern was similar in coloring and in mood to Fiesta and Harlequin. The Riviera plates and cup handles were square. For more information, see *Kovels' Depression Glass & Dinnerware Price List.*

COLONIAL

Blue, Casserole, Cover	140.00
Blue, Teapot	105.00
Blue, Tumbler, Handle	75.00
Green, Batter Jug, Cover, 8 1/4 In.	190.00
Green, Soup, Plate, 8 In.	27.00
Ivory, Cup, Tea	13.00
Ivory, Platter, 13 1/2 x 11 In.	20.00
Ivory, Sauceboat, Attached Underplate	145.00
Mauve Blue, Plate, Bread & Butter, 6 In.	11.00
Red, Bowl, Dessert, 5 1/4 In.	14.00
Red, Bowl, Vegetable, 8 1/4 In.	30.00
Red, Casserole, Cover	90.00
Yellow, Butter, Cover, 1/2 Lb.	125.00
Yellow, Creamer	13.00
Yellow, Pitcher, Juice, 5 3/4 In.	195.00
Yellow, Plate, Salad, 7 In.	15.00

Yellow, Platter, 13 1/2 x 11 In. 25.00
Yellow, Teapot 185.00

ROCKINGHAM, in the United States, is a pottery with a brown glaze that resembles tortoiseshell. It was made from 1840 to 1900 by many American potteries. Mottled brown Rockingham wares were first made in England at the Rockingham factory. Other types of ceramics were also made by the English firm. Related pieces may be listed in the Bennington category.

Bottle, Flask, Gun, Flintlock Pistol, 8 3/4 In. 144.00
Cruet, Arch Design, Applied Handle, East Liverpool, Ohio, 9 1/4 In. 115.00
Figurine, Dog, Spaniel, Glaze, 7 1/2 In., Pair 150.00
Figurine, Dog, Spaniel, Seated, Free-Standing Front Legs, Flower, Shell Base, 9 1/2 In. 520.00
Foot Warmer, Glazed, c.1860, 10 x 7 In. 230.00
Inkwell, Standish, Candlestick, Covered Jar, Green & White, Flowers 720.00
Paperweight, Spaniel Top, Glazed, Lyman Fenton & Co., 1849-58, 3 x 4 1/2 In. 645.00
Pitcher, Anchor Design, c.1860, 9 In. 105.00
Pitcher, Horse Head Spout, Crane Design, c.1850, 7 In. 175.00
Pitcher, Hound Handle, c.1850, 6 1/2 In. 145.00
Pitcher, Hound Handle, Hunting Scenes, Grapevines, c.1852-62, 8 3/4 In. 440.00
Pitcher, Hound Handle, Spread Eagle, Pouring Lip, Greatbach, c.1850, 10 1/2 In. 150.00
Pitcher, Scrolled, Relief Figures, 19th Century, 9 1/2 In. 92.00
Pitcher, Tapered In Middle, Applied Handle, 6 In. 115.00
Strainer, Plate Shape, Punched Holes, 8 3/4 In. 290.00
Teapot, Cover, Acanthus Leaf Pattern, 1844-58, 5 In. 230.00
Teapot, Rebecca At The Well, Brown Drip Glaze, 8 1/2 In. .... *Illus* 85.00
Tobacco Jar, Cover, Paneled Gothic Arch, Leaf Handles, c.1858, 8 1/2 x 8 In. 250.00
Window Stop, Head Shape, Wavy Hair, 4 5/8 x 3 1/2 In., Pair 550.00

ROGERS, see John Rogers category.

ROOKWOOD pottery was made in Cincinnati, Ohio, from 1880 to 1960. All of this art pottery is marked, most with the famous flame mark. The R is reversed and placed back to back with the letter P. Flames surround the letters. After 1900, a Roman numeral was added to the mark to indicate the year. The name and some of the molds were purchased in 1984. A few new pieces were made, but these were glazed in colors not used by the original company.

Ashtray, 2 Fingers, V For Victory Sign, 1944, 3/4 x 5 1/2 In. 150.00
Ashtray, Alligator, Unglazed, 1922, 2 1/4 x 6 3/4 In. 920.00
Ashtray, Blue Matte Glaze, 1920, 1 x 5 In. 115.00
Ashtray, Dice, Green High Glaze, Square, 1940, 2 3/4 In. 69.00
Ashtray, Fish, Chinese Turquoise Glaze, 1945, 6 In. 150.00
Ashtray, Frog Perched, Ivory Matte Glaze, 1932, 1 1/4 x 6 In. 90.00
Ashtray, Jeep Willys Station Wagon, Dog Chasing, Wine Madder Glaze, 1 x 6 1/2 In. 259.00
Ashtray, Penguin, Ivory Matte Glaze, 1942, 5 x 5 3/4 In. 500.00
Ashtray, Yellow, White Glaze, Stylized Initials, Terrace Plaza Hotel, 1 x 5 3/4 In. 105.00

Rookwood, Tile, 2 Pink
Tulips, Green Leaves,
Frame, 6 x 6 In.

Rockingham, Teapot,
Rebecca At The Well,
Brown Drip Glaze, 8 1/2 In.

Basket, Flowers, Leaves, Silver Overlay, Standard Glaze, H. Wilcox, 1893, 7 x 10 In. 2185.00
Bookends, Basset Hound, Brown Matte, Louise Abel, 1930, 4 3/4 x 6 1/2 In. 500.00
Bookends, Beagle, Coromandel Glaze, Louise Abel, 1937, 4 7/8 In. 460.00
Bookends, Cardinal, Chartreuse Matte Glaze, 1937, 5 1/4 In. 265.00
Bookends, Cornucopia, Nubian Black Glaze, W. McDonald, 5 In. 175.00
Bookends, Dutch Boy & Girl, Behind Fence, Sallie Toohey, 1928, 6 In. 325.00
Bookends, Dutch Boy & Girl, Behind Fence, Sallie Toohey, 1946, 6 In. 380.00
Bookends, Eagle, William McDonald, 1928, 1930, 6 1/2 In. 460.00
Bookends, Elephant, Blue Glaze, 1920, 5 3/4 x 7 In. 920.00
Bookends, Elephant, Gunmetal Glaze, 1920, 1921, 5 1/2 In. 175.00
Bookends, Elephant, Ivory Matte Glaze, 1931, 6 1/2 x 6 1/2 In. 460.00
Bookends, Elephant, Ivory Matte Glaze, William McDonald, 1929 .... 315.00
Bookends, Elephants, Blue Matte Drip Glaze, 5 x 6 In. 210.00
Bookends, Giraffe, Mottled Cinnamon Brown Glaze, Louise Abel, 1940, 5 x 6 1/2 In. 2760.00
Bookends, Horse Head, Frogskin Glaze, 1928 .... 690.00
Bookends, Hound Dog, Ivory Matte, 5 In. 290.00
Bookends, Monk With Fox, Rose Color, 7 1/2 In. 165.00
Bookends, Owl, Ivory Matte Glaze, William McDonald, 5 1/2 In. 375.00
Bookends, Panther, Wine Madder Glaze, W.P. McDonald, 1944, 5 1/2 In. 175.00
Bookends, Peacock, Pink Matte Glaze, 4 1/2 In. 410.00
Bookends, Peacock, Yellow Matte Glaze, 1921, 4 3/4 x 5 In. 185.00
Bookends, Pelican, Shirayamadani, 1934 .... 865.00
Bookends, Penguins On Rocks, Shell Base, Dark Brown Matte Glaze, Marked, 1934 ..... 940.00
Bookends, Rook, Blue Matte Glaze, William McDonald, 1926, 5 1/2 In. 880.00
Bookends, Rook, Bronze Matte Glaze, 1925, 5 1/8 In. 520.00
Bookends, Rook, Brown, Blue, Crystalline Glaze, W. McDonald, 1925, 5 1/2 x 5 1/2 In. .. 558.00
Bookends, Rook, Celadon Glaze, W. McDonald, 1956, 5 In. 325.00
Bookends, Rook, Chartreuse Matte Glaze, William McDonald, 1930, 5 In. ....440.00 to 880.00
Bookends, Rook, Flowers, 7 In. 880.00
Bookends, Rook, Ivory Matte Glaze, William McDonald, 1929 .... 375.00
Bookends, Rook, Open Book, Midnight Blue, Red Flower, Yellow Pages, 6 1/4 In. 1210.00
Bookends, Scarlett O'Hara, Ivory Matte Glaze, 1937 .... 290.00
Bookends, Seal, Green, Shirayamadani, 1922, 6 1/2 In. 865.00
Bookends, Sphinx, Olive Green Matte Glaze, Louise Abel, 1921 .... 245.00
Bookends, St. Francis, Fox, Bird, 1945, 7 1/2 x 5 In. 235.00
Bookends, Water Lilies, 1940s, 6 In. 185.00
Bookends, Windmill, Sallie Toohey, 1930 .... 920.00
Bowl, 2 Elephants, Aventurine Glaze, William McDonald, 1925, 11 3/8 In. 520.00
Bowl, Arrowhead, Relief, Blue Green Glaze, 1917, 5 1/4 In. 260.00
Bowl, Butterfly, Dark Blue Over Light Blue Glaze, 1923, 5 1/2 In. 345.00
Bowl, Cover, Flowers, Leaves, Purple, Pink, Green, Ocher, Sarah Sax, 1929, 9 x 12 In..... 3335.00
Bowl, Dragonflies, Incised, Blue, Green, Olive Matte Glaze, Toohey, 1904, 5 1/4 In. 1150.00
Bowl, Flowers, Blue Matte Glaze, 1926, 3 1/2 x 9 In. 140.00
Bowl, Glaze, Purple Exterior, Maroon Interior, c.1919, 4 1/2 x 10 In. 175.00
Bowl, Green Vellum, Modified Greek Key Design, c.1909, 6 3/8 x 1 1/8 In. 575.00
Bowl, Red Brown Matte Glaze, Brown, Green, c.1901, 3 x 7 In. 175.00
Bowl, Robin's-Egg Blue Matte Glaze, White Clay, 9 In. 175.00
Bowl, Stylized Design, Pink Tinted Glaze, Lorinda Epply, 1925, 13 In. 705.00
Box, Cover, Scottie Dog, Nubian Black Glaze, Louise Abel, 1931, 6 In. 1150.00
Calendar Holder, Cerulean Blue Matte Glaze, Triangular, 1900, 7 In. 175.00
Candleholder, Fish, Nubian Black Glaze, Shirayamadani, 1928, 3 5/8 In. 345.00
Candleholder, Red Matte Glaze, 1906, 3 1/4 In. 295.00
Candlestick, Embossed Flowers, c.1921, 5 In., Pair 115.00
Candlestick, Nasturtium, Peach, Green Leaves, Anna Marie Valentien, 1894, 2 1/2 x 5 In. . 400.00
Candlestick, Water Lilies, Persian Red Glaze, Sara Sax, 1928, 3 3/4 In., Pair 325.00
Card Holder, Blue Green Drip Matte Glaze, 1927, 3 1/2 In. 70.00
Chamberstick, Poppy, Mustard, Brown, Production, 1903, 8 1/4 In. 325.00
Creamer, Cameo Glaze, Grace Young, 2 7/8 In. 160.00
Creamer, Cherries, Branches, Leaves, Yellow & Brown Glaze, 1892, 2 3/4 x 5 In. 375.00
Cup, Blue, Green, 1921, 2 3/4 In. 115.00
Cup & Saucer, Prunus Blossoms, Blue Glaze, White Clay, Taylor 127.00
Ewer, Cherry Blossoms, A.R. Valentien, 1890, 14 x 8 In. 1295.00
Ewer, Classical Figures, Blue High Glaze, 1945, 11 In. 115.00

Ewer, Clover, Blossoms, Silver Overlay, Standard Glaze, Valentien, 1894, 9 3/4 In. 4025.00
Ewer, Crabs Swimming Through Waves, Green, M.A. Daly, 1885, 8 1/4 x 4 3/4 In. 1955.00
Ewer, Leaves, Holly, Berries, Silver Overlay, Olga G. Reed, 1892, 9 x 4 1/2 In. 2875.00
Ewer, Maple Leaves, Falling, Standard Glaze, 1899, 7 In. 705.00
Ewer, Poppies, Yellow, Red, Standard Glaze, Albert Valentien, 1891, 16 7/8 In. 4140.00
Ewer, Roses, Silver Overlay, Standard Glaze, Shirayamadani, 1891, 12 3/4 x 9 In. 2300.00
Ewer, Wild Yellow Roses, 1899, 10 In. 440.00
Figurine, Cockatoo, Multicolored, 1953, 10 In. 295.00
Figurine, Fisherman, Jean Reich, 1942, 8 7/8 In. 1150.00
Figurine, Lioness, White Opal Glaze, 1946, 6 1/2 In. 350.00
Figurine, Pheasant, High Glaze, Ora King, 1949, 8 5/8 In. 690.00
Figurine, Rooster, Multicolored, William McDonald, 1945, 5 In. 470.00
Figurine, Woman, Art Deco, Louise Abel, 1930, 11 1/4 In. 1495.00
Flower Frog, 2 Nudes Kneeling, 1920, 6 In. 185.00
Flower Frog, Girl Kneeling On Lily Pad, Myrtle Green Glaze, 1930, 5 1/2 In. 235.00
Flower Frog, Gray Green Matte Glaze, 1919, 3 3/4 In. 70.00
Flower Frog, Plum Matte Glaze, 1916, 2 1/2 In. 35.00
Flower Frog, Spring Flowers, Glossy, Lorinda Epply, 1929, 6 1/2 x 13 In. 1645.00
Flowerpot, Terra-Cotta Like, Flared Form, Unglazed, 4 3/4 x 6 3/4 In. 80.00
Ginger Jar, Cover, Flowers, Multicolored, E.T. Hurley, 1922, 15 1/2 x 9 1/2 In. 5175.00
Humidor, Cover, Chief White Man, Kiowa, A.D. Sehon, 1901, 6 x 6 In. 1765.00
Humidor, Indian, Antonio Jose, Governor Of Nambe, Sadie Markland, 1898, 5 x 6 1/4 In. . 500.00
Humidor, Indians Dancing With Torches, H.E. Wilcox, 1893, 6 1/2 x 6 1/2 In. 1150.00
Incense Burner, Mask Shape, Large Mouth, Blue Crystalline, 1921, 3 3/4 x 5 1/2 In. 380.00
Inkwell, Cover, Blue Crystalline Matte Glaze, 1922, 6 1/2 In. 3105.00
Inkwell, Frog Lid, Z-Line, Green Matte Glaze, 1903, 2 3/4 In. 410.00
Inkwell, Pen Tray, Oak Leaf, Perched Rook, 1921, 2 3/4 x 9 1/4 In. 980.00
Inkwell, Standard Glaze, Sage Green, Ed Abel, c.1892, 2 1/4 In. 230.00
Jar, Cover, Blossoms, Violet, Leaves, Jens Jensen, 1928, 7 3/4 x 5 In. 1035.00
Jar, Cover, Double Vellum, Tischler & Jones, 1923, 5 In. 1410.00
Jar, Cover, Fish, Yellow, Swimming, Swirling Seaweed, Brown Ground, Daly, 1885, 5 In. . 460.00
Jar, Cover, Light Blue Turquoise Matte Glaze, 1926, 5 1/2 In. 175.00
Jar, Flower Blossom Band, Aqua, Azure, White Clay, Katherine Jones, 1926, 4 1/2 In. 600.00
Jardiniere, Geometric, Green Matte Glaze, 1904, 12 x 11 In. 1410.00
Jug, Barnyard, Chickens, Standard Glaze, Sturgis Laurence, 1897, 5 1/2 x 4 In. 1150.00
Jug, Birds, Flying, Reeds, Limoges Glaze, Valentien, 1882, 5 In. 700.00
Jug, Butterfly, Reeds, Limoges Glaze, Matt Daly, 1882, 4 1/2 In. 700.00
Jug, Corn Ears, Lenore Asbury, c.1898, 6 In. 635.00
Jug, Daisies, White, Blue Over Brown Ground, Limoges Glaze, Handle, 5 In. 325.00
Jug, Old Man Praying To Moon, Trees, H.E. Wilcox, 1893, 6 1/4 x 5 1/2 In. 1150.00
Jug, Virginia Creeper, Carved, Brown Clay, Limoges Glaze, 1883, 4 3/4 In. 265.00
Jug, Whiskey, Stopper, Standard Glaze, Sara Sax, 1898, 7 3/8 In. 800.00
Lamp Base, Magnolias, Buds, Branches, Brown, Cream Ground, Milky Glaze, 13 1/2 In. . 520.00
Lamp Base, Wheat, Ivory High Glaze, Margaret Helen McDonald, 1936, 26 x 6 In. 600.00
Medallion, Gates Of Rookwood, Earl Menzel, 5 3/4 x 3/4 In. 578.00
Mug, Black Man Smiling, Wearing Hat, Standard Glaze, Sturgis Laurence, 1896, 5 x 5 In. . 1610.00
Mug, Cavalier, Sturgis Laurence, 1895, 6 In. 560.00
Mug, Clover, Branch, Buds, Silver Overlay, Sallie E. Coyne, 1905, 5 1/2 x 5 In. 978.00
Mug, Frog Dressed As Waiter, Drinking, Tree, Silver Overlay, McDonald, 5 1/4 x 5 In. 2415.00
Mug, Goblin On Tree Branch, Wheat, Flowers, Silver Overlay, Wilcox, 1892, 4 1/2 x 5 In. . 3220.00
Mug, Gray High Glaze, 5 In. 80.00
Mug, Indian Holding Ceremonial Object, G. Young, 1899, 7 1/2 x 6 1/2 In. 4600.00
Mug, Indian, Standard Glaze, Sadie Markland, 1898, 5 1/4 In. 2185.00
Mug, Monk Portrait, 1900, 5 In. 650.00
Mug, Monkey, Mouth Open, Sitting In Tree, Harriet Wilcox, 1898, 5 In. 2235.00
Mug, Vellum Glaze, Applied Sterling Silver Handle, 1905, 5 3/8 In. 230.00
Paperweight, Book, Open, Clover Cover, Brown Matte Glaze, c.1924, 3 1/2 In. 200.00
Paperweight, Bulldog, Louise Abel, 1936, 4 1/2 In. 1035.00
Paperweight, Cocker Spaniel, Raised Paw, Gray Glaze, 1965, 5 In. 380.00
Paperweight, Dachshund, Nubian Black Glaze, Louise Abel, 1937, 3 1/8 x 5 1/2 In. 748.00
Paperweight, Dog, Blue Matte Glaze, 1927, 5 In. 430.00
Paperweight, Dog, Ivory Matte Glaze, 1926, 4 7/8 In. 259.00
Paperweight, Dog, Lying Down, Tan Glaze, Blue Highlights, 1934, 2 3/8 x 4 3/4 In. 690.00

Paperweight, Duck, Ivory Matte Glaze, 1965, 3 1/2 In.	90.00
Paperweight, Elephant, Celadon Glaze, 1944, 3 1/2 In.	175.00
Paperweight, Elephant, Seated, Ivory Matte Glaze, 1936, 3 3/4 In.	290.00
Paperweight, Elephant, Seated, White Opal Glaze, 1952, 4 In.	235.00
Paperweight, Elephant, Seated, Wine Madder Glaze, 1945, 3 3/4 In.	235.00
Paperweight, Fruit Basket, Multicolored, Sallie Toohey, 1928, 3 x 4 1/2 In.	460.00
Paperweight, Galleon, Chartreuse Green Matte Glaze, 1925, 4 In.	145.00
Paperweight, Galleon, Ivory Matte Glaze, 1930, 4 x 3 In.	185.00
Paperweight, Geese, Standing On Rock, Yellow Matte Glaze, 1927, 4 1/2 x 5 In.	350.00
Paperweight, Kitten, Ivory Matte Glaze, 1943, 3 1/2 In.	405.00
Paperweight, Lion, Green Matte Glaze, Abel, 1927, 6 In.	500.00
Paperweight, Monkey On Book, Blue, Tan Matte Glaze, 1927, 3 1/2 x 4 1/4 In.	520.00
Paperweight, Nude Woman Seated, Ivory Glaze, Louise Abel, 1928, 4 1/2 In.	345.00
Paperweight, Panther, Tan High Glaze, 1946, 3 x 6 In.	290.00
Paperweight, Pelican, Roosting, Gray Glaze, 1960, 6 In.	500.00
Paperweight, Penguin, Shirayamadani, 1926	805.00
Paperweight, Rabbit, Ivory Matte Glaze, 1933, 3 1/2 In.	325.00
Paperweight, Rabbit, Ivory Matte Glaze, 1937, 3 1/4 In.	430.00
Paperweight, Rabbit, Ivory Matte Glaze, 1954, 3 1/2 In.	235.00
Paperweight, Rook, Blue Matte Glaze, Sallie Toohey, 1921, 3 x 4 In.	405.00
Paperweight, Rook, Brown Matte Glaze, 1924, 4 1/2 In.	650.00
Paperweight, Rooster, Ivory Matte Glaze, William P. McDonald, 1928, 5 1/4 In.	259.00
Paperweight, Rose, Leaf, Stem, Yellow Matte Glaze, 1940, 3 1/2 In.	150.00
Paperweight, Tortoise, Emerald Green Matte Glaze, 1965, 4 In.	295.00
Pipe Rest, Boat, Celadon Glaze, 6 1/4 In.	90.00
Pipe Rest, Ship, Celadon Glaze, William McDonald, 2 1/2 x 6 1/2 In.	150.00
Pitcher, Berries & Branches, Brown & Green Ground, Wilcox, 1889, 6 1/2 In.	405.00
Pitcher, Berries, Brown To Yellow, Caroline Steinle, 1900, 4 3/4 x 6 1/2 In.	300.00
Pitcher, Blue-Gray Matte Glaze, 1921, 5 3/4 In.	130.00
Pitcher, Brownie Sitting On Moon, Silver Overlay, Tricornered, E. Felten, 8 3/4 x 7 In.	1380.00
Pitcher, Brownies Playing, Braided Silver Overlay, B. Horsfall, 1893, 6 1/4 x 5 1/2 In.	2875.00
Pitcher, Butterfly, Blue, Reeds, Limoges Glaze, Martin Rettig, 1885, 5 1/2 In.	470.00
Pitcher, Crabs, Brown, Red, Green Ground, Valentien, 1884, 8 1/4 x 6 3/4 In.	2300.00
Pitcher, Flowers, Blue, White Ground, Eliza Lawrence, 1906, 7 In.	375.00
Plaque, 2 Trees, Road, Vellum, Frame, Sara Sax, 1912, 7 1/2 x 6 In.	3820.00
Plaque, Creek, Trees, Snow, Vellum, Frame, F. Rothenbusch, 1916, 11 x 8 1/2 In.	9990.00
Plaque, Griffins, Dark Blue Matte Glaze, Sallie Toohey, 1922, 5 In.	530.00
Plaque, Landscape, Trees, Evergreens, Vellum, E. Diers, 1916, 14 3/4 x 9 In.	6325.00
Plaque, Mountain Landscape, Vellum Glaze, Sara Sax, 9 x 12 In.	7770.00
Plaque, Mountainous West Coast, Trees, Frame, Patti Conant, 1916, 5 1/4 x 8 1/4 In.	4700.00
Plaque, Orchids, Green Leaves, Brown Ground, Standard Glaze, 8 1/4 x 9 3/4 In.	9775.00
Plaque, Ravine, Vellum, Frame, Fred Rothenbusch, 1913, 8 x 4 In.	3175.00
Platter, Ship, Matte Glaze, John Dee Wareham, c.1900, 12 3/8 In.	2990.00
Potpourri Jar, 2 Covers, Rabbits, Flowers, Arthur Conant, 1919, 4 3/4 x 5 In.	4115.00
Ring Tray, Rook, Blue Matte Glaze, 1933, 4 1/2 x 7 In.	382.00
Shaker, Cover, Green High Glaze, Cork Insert, Spout Plug, 1951, 10 5/8 In.	175.00
Sign, Rookwood, Cincinnati, Cerulean Blue Matte Glaze, 1924, 13 In.	2940.00
Soap Dish, Cover, Cameo Glaze, Shirayamadani, 1888, 3 1/4 In.	489.00
Sugar & Creamer, Holly Berries, c.1898, 5 1/4 In.	220.00
Sugar & Creamer, Holly Berries, Marked, 1898, 5 1/4 In.	220.00
Sugar & Creamer, Ming Yellow Glaze, 1930	145.00
Tankard, Black Man Wearing Hat, Standard Glaze, Silver Overlay, G. Young, 6 3/4 x 6 In.	2990.00
Tankard, Fish, Green, Silver Overlay, Grape Cluster, Daly, 6 1/2 x 6 1/2 In.	3335.00
Tankard, Green Matte Glaze, William Hentschel, 1911, 9 In.	440.00
Teapot, Cover, Holly Leaves & Berries, 1892, 6 In.	470.00
Tile, 2 Pink Tulips, Green Leaves, Frame, 6 x 6 In. *Illus*	200.00
Tile, Acorn & Oak Leaf, Green, Brown, Blue, Faience, 6 In.	646.00
Tile, Acorns, Leaves, Red Ground, 8 x 8 In.	2400.00
Tile, Celtic Design, Green, Turquoise, Blue Matte Glaze, 6 x 6 In.	345.00
Tile, City Of Schenectady, Incorporated 1798, Haystack, Faience, Round, 14 In.	1000.00
Tile, Elephant, Molded, Green Matte Glaze, Square, 1921, 3 1/2 In.	460.00
Tile, Lamp, Turquoise Matte Glaze, Faience, 8 In.	440.00
Tile, Lion, Rampant, Molded, Faience, Brown, Amber, 12 In.	2115.00

Tile, Parrot, Flowering Branches, Blue, Mauve, Crimson, Red Matte Glazes, Frame, 6 In. .	920.00
Tile, Rook, Brown Glaze, 1993 .	145.00
Tile, Scrub Oak Tree, Embossed, Faience In Beige Medallion, Frame, 8 In.	2820.00
Tile, Seagulls Flying, Ivory, Tan, Blue Ground, Round, 1919, 5 1/2 In.	355.00
Tile, Ship, Faience, Frame, Square, 12 In.	2820.00
Tile, Stylized Grapes, Blue Matte Ground, Marked, 6 In.	440.00
Tile, Stylized Rose, Faience, Brown, Green, 6 In.	470.00
Tile, Swan, Faience, Ivory, Brown, Green, 6 In.	350.00
Tray, Bat, Emerald Green Matte Glaze, 1927, 6 In.	500.00
Tray, Bullfrog, 1922, 3 3/4 x 6 3/4 In.	405.00
Tray, Leaf & Berry, Cerulean Matte Glaze, 1920, 6 1/2 In.	235.00
Tray, Nude, Reclining, Ivory Matte Glaze, 1926, 4 1/2 In.	325.00
Tray, Rook, Blue & Black Matte Glaze, 1913, 4 x 7 In.	765.00
Tray, Seal, Orange, Brown Matte Glaze, Shirayamadani, 1930, 4 x 6 1/4 In.	430.00
Trivet, Cows, Windmill, Double Vellum, Square, 1942, 5 7/8 In.	1265.00
Trivet, Duck, Blue, Yellow, White, Double Vellum, Square, 1924, 5 5/8 In.	575.00
Trivet, Dutch Scene, Multicolored, 1927, 5 1/2 In.	205.00
Trivet, Geese, White, Double Vellum, Square, 1926, 5 5/8 In.	375.00
Trivet, Geometric, Blue High Glaze, 1954, 5 1/2 In.	175.00
Trivet, Goose, Ivory, Blue & Green Matte Glaze, 1929, 5 1/2 In.	350.00
Trivet, Ivy & Berries, Green & Blue Matte Glaze, Hexagonal, 1922, 5 1/2 In.	230.00
Trivet, Rook, Blue, Black, Square, 1945, 5 1/2 In.	375.00
Trivet, Ship, Carved, Blue & Ivory Matte Glaze, Frame, 1915, 6 In.	530.00
Trivet, Southern Belle, Multicolored Matte Glaze, Square, 1930, 5 1/2 In.	259.00
Trivet, Stylized Leaves, Cross, Yellow & Light Blue Matte Glaze, Carved, 1925, 5 1/2 In. .	265.00
Trivet, Woman, Child, Multicolored Matte Glaze, Square, 1943, 5 1/2 In.	230.00
Umbrella Stand, Acorns, Oak Leaves, Green Matte Glaze, Cut Designs, 23 1/2 In.	5580.00
Umbrella Stand, Fish, Crabs, Lily Pads, Blue Ground, Gold Highlights, 25 In.	4140.00
Urn, Flowers, Leaves, Red, Yellow Ground, Wax Mat, Jens Jensen, 1929, 8 1/2 In.	1295.00
Vase, 3 Buttresses, Amber Matte Glaze, 1920, 10 In.	590.00
Vase, 3 Panels, Stylized, Matte Glaze, Incised, Elizabeth Lincoln, 1919, 3 5/8 In.	750.00
Vase, 4 Lobes, Pomegranate Glaze, White Interior, 7 1/8 In.	150.00
Vase, 4 Panels, Green Matte Glaze Exterior, Pink Matte Glaze Interior, 1929, 11 1/2 In.	260.00
Vase, 6 Panels, Crimped Leaves, Baluster, Sallie Coyne, 1903, 8 1/2 x 5 1/2 In.	375.00
Vase, Aqua Matte, Embossed Lotus Petals, c.1931, 5 3/8 In.	255.00
Vase, Asian Figures, Cartouches, Flowers, Arabesque, W. Hentschel, 1922, 13 x 8 In.	4025.00
Vase, Baluster, Yellow Interior, Blue Exterior, 1921, 14 In.	410.00
Vase, Band Of Rooks, Matte Yellow, 1927, 5 3/4 In.	259.00
Vase, Bell Shaped Flowers, Squeezebag Decoration, Elizabeth Barrett, 1927, 8 In.	999.00
Vase, Berries, Baluster Shape, Standard Glaze, Bruce Horsfall, 1895, 11 1/2 x 5 1/2 In.	1058.00
Vase, Berries, Leaves, Baluster Shape, Vellum, Lenore Asbury, 1924, 9 1/2 x 5 In.	3820.00
Vase, Birds Among Daisies, Blue, White, Pink, Vellum, Hurley, 1931, 6 x 5 1/2 In.	4315.00
Vase, Birds Flying, Trees, Pond, Vellum, Shirayamadani, 1910, 16 In.	4485.00
Vase, Birds In Grass, Sea Green, Matthew A. Daly, 1894, 7 1/4 x 3 In.	4315.00
Vase, Birds On Branches, Cherry Blossoms, Albert R. Valentien, 1883, 23 1/2 x 11 In.	5750.00
Vase, Birds, Branches, Multicolored, 2 Handles, E. T. Hurley, 1924, 9 x 7 In.	4600.00
Vase, Birds, In Flight, Celadon Glaze, 1936, 8 1/2 In.	260.00
Vase, Birds, Outstretched Wings, Tree Branches, Yellow Matte Glaze, 1921, 9 5/8 In.	355.00
Vase, Bleeding Heart, Tapered, Double Vellum, L. Abel, 1921, 12 1/2 In.	2000.00
Vase, Blossoms, Branches, Buds, Charles J. McLaughlin, 1916, 6 x 3 1/2 In.	1265.00
Vase, Blossoms, Leaves, Branches, Brown, Yellow Ground, Vellum, Squat, 1924, 4 In.	1150.00
Vase, Blossoms, Purple, Blue Green, Bottle Shape, Carved Matte, 8 1/4 x 4 In.	765.00
Vase, Blossoms, Stylized, Black Opal, Squat, Cobalt Ground, Sara Sax, 4 3/4 x 6 3/4 In. .	2470.00
Vase, Blue Bell Flowers, Bottle Shape, Sea Green, Sally Toohey, 1899, 12 1/2 x 3 3/4 In. .	5875.00
Vase, Blue Ground, Handles, 1923, 6 In.	165.00
Vase, Blue, Art & Crafts Flowers, 1920, 10 In.	920.00
Vase, Blue, Green, Red Matte Glaze, Carved Shoulder, 1917, 5 In.	1000.00
Vase, Blue, Stylized Flower Band, 2 Handles, 14 1/4 In.	980.00
Vase, Blue, Turquoise, Magenta Glaze, Bulbous, Elizabeth Lincoln, 1921, 4 3/4 In.	600.00
Vase, Boats At Sea, Vellum, Seagulls, Blue, Green, C. Schmidt, 1925, 7 1/2 x 3 3/4 In.	7480.00
Vase, Boy With Wings On Catfish, Iris Glaze, Albert R. Valentien, 1891, 16 1/2 x 5 In.	9775.00
Vase, Branches, Buckeyes, Leaves, Standard Glaze, Matthew A. Daly, 1890, 18 x 7 In.	6325.00
Vase, Branches, Flowers, Yellow Ground, Bulbous, 1937, 4 1/2 In.	150.00

Vase, Branches, Leaves, Squeezebag, William Hentschel, 1927, 12 1/4 x 5 3/4 In. 940.00
Vase, Branches, Relief, Pink Matte Glaze, 1932, 4 3/4 In. 260.00
Vase, Bud, Birds, Burnt Orange, Brown, Gold Ground, Shirayamadani, 7 1/2 x 3 1/2 In. . . . 8050.00
Vase, Bud, Flowers, Blue, Red, Teal, E.T. Hurley, Square, 1922, 7 3/4 x 2 3/4 In. 3100.00
Vase, Buttercups, Madeline Nourse, 1891, 5 3/4 x 3 1/2 In. 375.00
Vase, Butterflies, Tan High Glaze, 1945, 4 7/8 In. 125.00
Vase, Cactus Flowers, Molded, Pomegranate Glaze, 1947, 11 3/4 In. 375.00
Vase, Carnation, Buds, Trailing Stems, Earthtone, Greens, Mauve, c.1904, 9 1/2 In. 1530.00
Vase, Cavalier, Grace Young, 1903, 9 1/2 In. 1410.00
Vase, Cherry Blossoms, Double Vellum, Squat, K. Jones, 1930, 4 In. 590.00
Vase, Cherry Blossoms, Iris Glaze, Closed-In Rim, Irene Bishop, 1906, 4 1/2 x 4 1/2 In. . . . 880.00
Vase, Cherry Blossoms, Lavender Ground, Iris Glaze, Rose Fechheimer, 1901, 3 In. 705.00
Vase, Cherry Blossoms, Vellum, E.T. Hurley, 1929, 5 In. 1295.00
Vase, Cherry Blossoms, Vellum, Fred Rothenbusch, 1931, 9 In. 1880.00
Vase, Cherry Blossoms, Vellum, Squat, E.T. Hurley, 1928, 3 1/2 x 6 In. 765.00
Vase, Cherry Blossoms, White, Red, Eggplant Ground, 5 x 4 In. 1175.00
Vase, Chicks, Yellow, Tiger Eye Glaze, Daniel Cook, 1894, 5 3/4 In. 2820.00
Vase, Chinese Turquoise Glaze, 1939, 6 In. 130.00
Vase, Chrysanthemum, Red, Leaves, Harriet E. Wilcox, 1903, 9 x 3 3/4 In. 9200.00
Vase, Chrysanthemums, Black, Gray, Green Ground, Shouldered, Conant, 1919, 7 In. 1880.00
Vase, Clover Blossoms, Yellow, 1893, 4 In. 410.00
Vase, Daffodils, Jewel Porcelain, K. Shirayamadani, 1946, 7 1/4 x 4 In. 1880.00
Vase, Daffodils, Standard Glaze, Tapered, Lenore Asbury, 1901, 8 1/2 In. 1060.00
Vase, Daisies, Blue Gray Ground, Banded Vellum, M.G. Denzler, 1915, 5 1/2 In. 560.00
Vase, Daisies, Narrow Neck, Bulbous, 1900, 9 In. 440.00
Vase, Daisies, Wax Mat, Bulbous, Elizabeth Lincoln, 1927, 7 1/4 x 3 3/4 In. 880.00
Vase, Deer, Leaves, Art Deco, William Hentschel, 1944, 11 5/8 In. 290.00
Vase, Dog Herding Sheep, Dull To High Glaze, White, Blue, Amelia Sprague, 6 1/2 In. 6900.00
Vase, Dogwood Flowers, Jewel Porcelain, Blue, White, Jens Jensen, 1944, 9 In. 1060.00
Vase, Dogwood, Jewel Porcelain, Blue, Ivory, Jens Jensen, 1948, 10 In. 2235.00
Vase, Donkey, Embossed, Mexican Village Scene, Green High Glaze, 1950, 5 3/4 x 4 In. . . 225.00
Vase, Dragon, Tiger Eye, Gold, Brown, 6 3/4 x 5 1/2 In. 2300.00
Vase, Fall Landscape, Vellum, Ed Diers, 1916, 8 3/4 x 3 3/4 In. 5290.00
Vase, Fish, Sea Green, Egg Shape, E.T. Hurley, 1902, 8 x 4 1/2 In. 3820.00
Vase, Fish, Sea Plants, Butterfat Ground, Squat, William Hentschel, 1911, 6 x 8 3/4 In. . . . 2235.00
Vase, Fish, Swimming, Sea Green, Celadon, E.T. Hurley, 1901, 8 x 3 3/4 In. . . . . .6325.00 to 8050.00
Vase, Fish, Swimming, Sea Green, Flared, Shirayamadani, 1894, 9 1/2 x 5 In. 2990.00
Vase, Fish, Swimming, Sea Green, Tan Ground, Hurley, 1903, 7 x 8 1/4 In. 5750.00
Vase, Fishing Boats, Venetian Harbor, Vellum, Carl Schmidt, 1921, 9 3/4 x 4 In. 5875.00
Vase, Flower Wreath, Wax Mat, Bulbous, Elizabeth Lincoln, 1922, 7 1/4 x 4 In. 825.00
Vase, Flower, Blue, Leaves, Wax Mat, Bulbous, Katherine Jones, 1927, 6 1/4 In. 529.00
Vase, Flower, Rust, Standard Glaze, Demarest, 1902, 9 3/4 In. 1610.00
Vase, Flower, Yellow, Green Leaves, Standard Glaze, 1902, 6 3/4 In. 690.00
Vase, Flowering Vine, Pink High Glaze, Harriet Wilcox, 1925 . . . . 635.00
Vase, Flowers, Blue, Burgundy, Green, Rose Matte, Blue Flecks, Klinger, 1925, 8 x 5 In. . . 1000.00
Vase, Flowers, Blue, Green, Beige Faded To Blue Ground, Rothenbusch, 1929, 4 1/4 In. . . . 750.00
Vase, Flowers, Blue, Purple, Bands, Green Leaves, Cream Ground, Epply, 1943, 6 1/2 In. . . 690.00
Vase, Flowers, Blue, White Ground, Oval, Edith Noonan, 1906, 7 In. 970.00
Vase, Flowers, Brown, Gold Ground, Bulbous, Clara Lindeman, 1903, 5 1/4 In. 450.00
Vase, Flowers, Brown, Gold Ground, Bulbous, Laura Lindeman, 5 1/4 In. 410.00
Vase, Flowers, Burgundy, Cobalt, Mottled Yellow, Pink Over Rose, Jensen, 1930, 7 x 7 In. . 600.00
Vase, Flowers, Burgundy, Green, Cobalt, Aqua, Oval, Sallie Coyne, 1924, 26 x 6 In. 1100.00
Vase, Flowers, Carved, Green, Purple, Green Matte, Handles, Todd, 1915, 14 1/2 In. 2705.00
Vase, Flowers, Daisies, Tan, Blue, Purple Ground, Indigo Flecks, Barrett, 1925, 7 x 3 In. . . 800.00
Vase, Flowers, Double Vellum, Charles Todd, 1921, 8 In. 2000.00
Vase, Flowers, Double Vellum, Elizabeth Lincoln, 1931, 4 1/2 In. 1300.00
Vase, Flowers, Double Vellum, Lobed Foot, Vera Tischler, 1923, 10 In. 1116.00
Vase, Flowers, Fish, Jewel Porcelain, Ivory, 1945, 8 1/2 In. 3800.00
Vase, Flowers, Golden, Amber Ground, K. Shirayamadani, 1890, 11 3/4 In. 650.00
Vase, Flowers, High Glaze, Cream, Brown Rim, Lorinda Epply, 1927, 6 1/4 In. 1265.00
Vase, Flowers, Jewel Porcelain, Ivory, Lorinda Epply, 1930, 10 1/2 In. 1645.00
Vase, Flowers, Leaves, Trailing Stem, Iris Glaze, Peach Underglaze, White, 1901, 10 In. . . 1530.00
Vase, Flowers, Mock Orange, C.J. McLaughlin, 1915, 11 In. 500.00

Vase, Flowers, Ocher Faded To Lavender, White Clay, 1919, 7 1/2 In. 980.00
Vase, Flowers, Peach, Cream, Gray, Iris Glaze, Cylindrical, L. Lindeman, 1906, 5 3/4 In. . . 980.00
Vase, Flowers, Pink, Red, Midnight Blue To Deep Blue, Harriet Wilcox, 1901, 5 1/4 In. . . . 3910.00
Vase, Flowers, Pink, Teal Leaves, Mocha, Vellum, C.C. Crabtree, 1927, 7 x 3 3/4 In. 550.00
Vase, Flowers, Purple, Black & Green Mottled Ground, Van Horne, 1917, 6 1/2 In. 2700.00
Vase, Flowers, Purple, Vellum, Fred Rothenbusch, 1911, 9 1/4 x 3 1/2 In. 1765.00
Vase, Flowers, Red, Blue Green, Yellow, Waisted, Double Vellum, Lincoln, 1922, 13 In. . . 3525.00
Vase, Flowers, Red, Wax Mat, Bottle Shape, C.S. Todd, 1921, 7 3/4 x 5 1/4 In. 1530.00
Vase, Flowers, Standard Glaze, 2 Handles, Anna Marie Valentien, 1891, 7 1/2 In. 430.00
Vase, Flowers, Stems, Leaves, Vellum Glaze, F. Rothenbusch, 1905, 8 3/8 In. 978.00
Vase, Flowers, Tree Branches, Jewel Porcelain, Taupe Ground, 7 1/4 x 4 1/4 In. 5750.00
Vase, Flowers, Wax Mat, Elizabeth N. Lincoln, 1926, 6 In. 690.00
Vase, Flowers, Wax Mat, Yellow Ground, Lenore Asbury, 1931, 8 x 6 In. 1530.00
Vase, Flowers, Yellow, Blue Ground, Harriet Wilcox, 1901, 2 1/2 x 4 3/4 In. 2645.00
Vase, Flowers, Yellow, Green Stems, Green & Brown Ground, Steinle, 1902, 7 In. 575.00
Vase, Flowers, Yellow, Incised Mat Closed-In Rim, Charles Todd, 1919, 5 1/2 In. 700.00
Vase, Forest, Stream, Mountains, Vellum, Carl Schmidt, 1916, 12 x 5 1/4 In. 4900.00
Vase, Forest, Vellum, Sallie Coyne, 1921, 8 1/2 In. 3800.00
Vase, Forsythia, Elongated Neck, Spherical Base, Edward Abel, 1895, 7 x 6 1/4 In. 550.00
Vase, Frog, Painted, Carved, Tiger Eye Glaze, Valentien, 1898, 6 In. 2000.00
Vase, Geese, Charcoal Ground, Vellum, A.M. Valentien, 1905, 7 1/2 x 3 1/2 In. 1175.00
Vase, Geese, Flying, Pink Green Sky, Vellum, E.T. Hurley, 1906, 6 1/4 x 3 1/4 In. 2350.00
Vase, Geometric, Carved, Blue, Yellow, Red Mottled Matte Glaze, 14 In. 1765.00
Vase, Geometric, Green Matte Glaze, 1901, 4 1/2 In. 325.00
Vase, Geometric, Incised, Light Blue Matte Glaze, 1940, 5 In. 260.00
Vase, Geometric, Multitone Green Matte Glaze, 1909, 7 In. 880.00
Vase, Gooseberries, Bulbous, Irene Bishop, 1901, 10 In. 700.00
Vase, Grapes, Leaves, Vines, Blue, White Ground, John D. Wareham, 5 1/2 x 2 In. 1610.00
Vase, Grapes, Leaves, Vines, Purple, White, Iris Glaze, Sara Sax, 1901, 6 1/2 x 4 In. 2760.00
Vase, Grapes, Purple, Hanging From Vines, Shirayamadani, 1888, 19 In. 5290.00
Vase, Grapes, Standard Glaze, Josephine Zettel, 1896, 7 5/8 In. 575.00
Vase, Green Matte Glaze, Turquoise High Glaze Interior, c.1921, 10 1/4 In. 255.00
Vase, Green Mottled With Dark Rose Glaze, 1906, 7 In. 200.00
Vase, Green Overspray, c.1920, 7 In. 260.00
Vase, Green Overspray, c.1930, 4 3/4 In. 150.00
Vase, Green Poppies, Egg Shape, Harriet Wilcox, 1929, 8 x 3 3/4 In. 3820.00
Vase, Hexagonal Panels, Blue, Green Glaze, 7 7/8 In. 140.00
Vase, Hollyhocks, Jewel Porcelain, Green Ground, 1924, 12 1/4 x 5 1/2 In. 5875.00
Vase, Hollyhocks, Wax Mat, Red, Butterfat Ground, Bulbous, 1928, 6 3/4 In. 1765.00
Vase, Honeysuckle, Yellow, Amelia Browne Sprague, 1889, 7 x 3 1/2 In. 500.00
Vase, Hummingbirds, Iris Glaze, Tapered, John D. Wareham, 1900, 12 3/4 x 5 In. 2705.00
Vase, Hyacinths, Leaves, Indigo, Iris Glaze, Matthew A. Daly, 1901, 8 x 5 1/2 In. 5175.00
Vase, Indian In Headdress, Grace Young, 10 x 5 In. 8625.00
Vase, Indian In Profile, Standard Glaze, Matthew A. Daly, 1900, 12 x 7 In. 2990.00
Vase, Irises, Lavender, Leaves, Iris Glaze, Carl Schmidt, 1907, 11 x 6 In. 9775.00
Vase, Irises, Pink, Blue, Vellum, Carl Schmidt, 1926, 8 1/4 x 4 In. 8225.00
Vase, Irises, Purple Ground, Vellum, Bulbous, Fred Rothenbusch, 1908, 11 1/4 x 5 In. 2115.00
Vase, Irises, Purple, Shaded Ground, Carl Schmidt, 1912, 15 1/2 x 8 In. 4700.00
Vase, Jonquil, Iris Glaze, Green To Cream Ground, Josephine Zettel, 1901, 6 5/8 In. 2645.00
Vase, Jonquils, Frothy Burgundy, Green Matte Glaze, 1910, 8 1/2 x 4 1/2 In. 825.00
Vase, Landscape, Blue, Purple, Mountain Lake, Vellum, 1916, 7 3/4 x 2 3/4 In. 1880.00
Vase, Landscape, Celadon, Black To Ivory Sky, Iris Glaze, Shirayamadani, 7 In. 3055.00
Vase, Landscape, Gray Sky, Vellum, Fred Rothenbusch, 1914, 12 3/4 x 5 In. 3055.00
Vase, Landscape, Green, Vellum, Elizabeth Lincoln, 1911, 6 x 2 1/2 In. 1880.00
Vase, Landscape, Lake, Trees, Snow, Pink, Blue Sky, Sallie Coyne, 1918, 7 3/4 In. 2070.00
Vase, Landscape, Lake, Trees, Vellum, E.T. Hurley, 1940, 6 7/8 In. 2990.00
Vase, Landscape, Oriental, Jewel Porcelain, Arthur Conant, 1919, 5 1/4 x 3 3/4 In. 5290.00
Vase, Landscape, River, Trees, Vellum, Ed Diers, 1919, 6 3/4 x 3 In. 2000.00
Vase, Landscape, River, Vellum, Bulbous, Sallie Coyne, 1915, 7 1/2 x 3 1/2 In. 2940.00
Vase, Landscape, River, Vellum, E.T. Hurley, 1931, 9 x 4 1/2 In. 3175.00
Vase, Landscape, Sunset, Green, Vellum, Sallie Coyne, 1912, 9 x 3 3/4 In. 4110.00
Vase, Landscape, Trees, Hills, Vellum, Fred Rothenbusch, 1937, 7 3/4 x 4 3/4 In. 4700.00
Vase, Landscape, Trees, Lake, Vellum, Lorinda Epply, 1917, 9 1/4 In. 2645.00

Vase, Landscape, Trees, River, Snow, Vellum, Sallie E. Coyne, 1920, 11 x 5 In. 3105.00
Vase, Landscape, Twilight, Green Vellum, Cylindrical, Lorinda Epply, 1911, 6 In. 3172.00
Vase, Landscape, Vellum, Carl Schmidt, 1918, 10 In. 7050.00
Vase, Landscape, Vellum, Lenore Asbury, 1916, 11 In. 2230.00
Vase, Landscape, Vellum, Lorinda Epply, 1914, 7 3/4 x 3 3/4 In. 2115.00
Vase, Leaves, Acanthus, Lavender, Gray, Iris Glaze, M.A. Daly, 1899, 8 1/2 x 3 3/4 In. 4025.00
Vase, Leaves, Berries, Brown, Gold Ground, Elizabeth Lincoln, 1903, 8 3/4 In. 450.00
Vase, Leaves, Berries, Silver Overlay, Handles, J. Zettel, 1892, 6 1/2 x 3 3/4 In. 2415.00
Vase, Leaves, Berries, Standard Glaze, Grace M. Hall, c.1904, 4 3/4 In. 185.00
Vase, Leaves, Green To Brown Ground, Standard Glaze, Sallie Coyne, 1903, 8 1/2 In. 690.00
Vase, Leaves, Holly, Berries, Sea Green, Sallie E. Coyne, 1901, 5 1/2 x 3 1/4 In. 2070.00
Vase, Leaves, Pods, Bulbous, Cream Glaze, Turquoise Rim, 1932, 6 1/2 In. 200.00
Vase, Leaves, Standard Glaze, Howard Altman, c.1903, 5 1/4 In. 160.00
Vase, Lilacs, Vellum, Rothenbusch, 1925, 9 1/2 In. 4400.00
Vase, Lily Pad, Floating Flowers, Coromandel, Lorinda Epply, 1920, 8 1/2 x 5 In. 2760.00
Vase, Lily, Molded, Ivory Matte, 3 3/4 In. 69.00
Vase, Man On Sled, Dogs, Aurora Borealis, Aerial Blue, Bruce Horsfall, 1895, 9 7/8 In. . . . 9775.00
Vase, Man, Portrait, Standard Glaze, Grace Young, 1902, 12 1/4 x 4 1/2 In. 1380.00
Vase, Maple Leaves, Standard Glaze, Elizabeth Lincoln, 1900, 6 3/4 x 3 1/4 In. 470.00
Vase, Maroon Matte Glaze, Molded Design At Shoulders, c.1914, 3 In. 210.00
Vase, Matte Glaze, Blue Green Mottled Glaze, 2 Handles, c.1929, 5 5/8 In. 160.00
Vase, Mermaid Caught In Fishing Net, Sea Green, Shirayamadani, 1896, 12 3/8 In. 2760.00
Vase, Morning Glories, Pink Ground, 1917, 7 In. 705.00
Vase, Morning Glories, Wax Mat, Amber Ground, 1923, 6 3/4 x 5 1/4 In. 1295.00
Vase, Mottled Brown, Purple Matte Glaze, Flared, 1916, 6 In. 325.00
Vase, Mottled Flowers, 2 Handles, Lincoln, 1918, 15 In. 580.00
Vase, Mottled Pink Matte Glaze, Handle, 1920, 7 3/4 In. 355.00
Vase, Mushrooms, Iris Glaze, 2 Handles, Carl Schmidt, 1902, 3 3/4 x 5 In. 1410.00
Vase, Mushrooms, Multicolored, Vellum, Carl Schmidt, 1906, 7 x 5 1/2 In. 9775.00
Vase, Mushrooms, Russet, Gray, Green, Iris Glaze, Carl Schmidt, 1909, 7 3/4 x 4 1/2 In. . . 4600.00
Vase, Nasturtium Blossoms, Yellow, Orange, Harriet E. Wilcox, 1901, 3 3/4 x 3 In. 3740.00
Vase, Nasturtiums, Bottle Shape, A.R. Valentien, 1897, 17 1/2 x 11 In. 1765.00
Vase, Nasturtiums, Double Vellum, Shouldered, 1929, 8 In. 1060.00
Vase, Nasturtiums, Orange, Russet, Standard Glaze, Silver Overlay, 5 3/4 x 4 3/4 In. 2070.00
Vase, Nightscape, Moon Reflecting Off Lake, Vellum, E.T. Hurley, 1910, 9 x 4 3/4 In. 5175.00
Vase, Nude Woman, Gray Ground, D.W. Seyler, 1937, 4 1/2 x 3 In. 1090.00
Vase, Nude Woman, Green Matte Glaze, Squat, A.M. Valentien, 1901, 3 x 3 1/4 In. 2415.00
Vase, Oak Leaves, Acorns, Brown Matte Glaze, 1922, 7 3/4 In. 410.00
Vase, Oak Leaves, Acorns, Egg Shape, Lenore Asbury, 1908, 7 x 5 1/4 In. 999.00
Vase, Orange Flowers, Leaves, Wax Mat, Egg Shape, Janet Harris, 1930, 5 In. 825.00
Vase, Orchids, Mauve, Charcoal To Mocha, Copper Dust, McDonald, 1929, 7 1/2 x 4 In. . . 1000.00
Vase, Orchids, Yellow, Standard Glaze, 2 Handles, E. Nourse, 1903, 5 3/4 In. 410.00
Vase, Palm Fronds, Seagulls, E.T. Hurley, 1907, 6 3/4 x 5 1/4 In. 1530.00
Vase, Pansies, Brown, Yellow Stamen, 6 1/2 x 4 1/2 In. 375.00
Vase, Pansies, Purple, Yellow, Iris Glaze, Sara Sax, 1902, 5 x 3 In. 1765.00
Vase, Peacock Feathers, Black Opal Glaze, Sara Sax, No. 966, 1926, 3 1/2 In. 1410.00
Vase, Peacock Feathers, Jewel Porcelain, Egg Shape, Jens Jensen, 1944, 7 In. 825.00
Vase, Peacock Feathers, Molded, Blue Matte Glaze, c.1922, 7 3/4 In. 290.00
Vase, Peacock Feathers, Pink Matte Glaze, 1920, 7 3/4 In. 325.00
Vase, Peacock Feathers, Vellum, Bulbous, Sara Sax, 1911, 7 1/2 In. 1060.00
Vase, Peasant, Oriental, Green, Brown, Blue, Flared, 1882, 11 1/2 x 6 1/2 In. 3105.00
Vase, Pepper Berry, Brown, Green Leaves, Lenore Asbury, 1896, 7 1/4 x 3 1/4 In. 900.00
Vase, Pinecone, Embossed, c.1927, 6 1/2 In. 230.00
Vase, Pink Matte Glaze, Transparent Green Drip, 2 Handles, 1926, 5 1/2 In. 130.00
Vase, Pink, Green Glaze, Oval, 1930, 3 In. 115.00
Vase, Poppies, Brown Ground, Clara Lindeman, 1903, 8 1/2 In. 650.00
Vase, Poppies, Brown, Yellow, Standard Glaze, Bottle Shape, 1900, 8 x 7 In. 1060.00
Vase, Poppies, Buds, Orange, Standard Glaze, Valentien, 10 3/4 x 5 1/2 In. 1380.00
Vase, Poppies, Carved, Blue, Pink, Red, Yellow Matte Glaze, Shirayamadani, 1929, 12 In. . 3410.00
Vase, Poppies, Dark Blue Matte Glaze, 1927, 11 In. 765.00
Vase, Poppies, Leaves, Cream Ground, Iris Glaze, Rose Fechheimer, 1904, 9 7/8 In. 1670.00
Vase, Poppies, Pink, Vellum, Ed Diers, 1912, 8 x 4 In. 1116.00
Vase, Poppies, Russet, Brown, Green, Gold Ground, Shirayamadani, 9 1/4 x 3 3/4 In. 5465.00

Vase, Poppies, Wax Mat, Sally Coyne, 1928, 7 3/4 x 3 1/2 In. 1645.00
Vase, Poppies, White, Gray & Lavender Ground, Iris Glaze, Rothenbusch, 1903, 10 In. . . . 3175.00
Vase, Poppies, White, Iris Glaze, Gray Ground, A.R. Valentien, 1902, 10 3/4 x 5 1/2 In. . . . 2468.00
Vase, Purple Over Brown Over Blue, 1932, 3 In. 265.00
Vase, Raven, Embossed, Blue Matte Glaze, 5-Sided, 1926, 4 3/4 x 2 3/4 In. 375.00
Vase, Red Flowers, Green Leaves, Wax Mat, Elizabeth Lincoln, 1929, 13 1/4 x 5 In. 3175.00
Vase, Red Flowers, Wax Mat, Lobed, Flaring, Elizabeth Lincoln, 1923, 7 x 3 In. 1645.00
Vase, Red Matte Glaze, Green Overspray, Vellum, 1910, 11 3/4 In. 375.00
Vase, Rook, Green High Glaze, 5-Sided, c.1930, 4 3/4 In. 430.00
Vase, Rooks Perched On Branch, Moon, H.E. Wilcox, 1919, 7 x 4 1/2 In. 4315.00
Vase, Rose, Leaves, Standard Glaze, Silver Overlay, Daly, 11 1/2 x 4 1/2 In. 1610.00
Vase, Roses, Branch, Standard Glaze, Silver Overlay, Coyne, 1894, 6 1/2 x 3 1/2 In. 2300.00
Vase, Roses, Iris Glaze, Pink, Ed Diers, 7 3/4 x 3 3/4 In. 1880.00
Vase, Roses, Iris Glaze, White, Bulbous, Clara Lindeman, 1904, 7 1/4 x 5 1/2 In. 1295.00
Vase, Roses, Leaves, Black Ground, Olga Geneva Reed, 1906, 12 1/4 In. 3220.00
Vase, Roses, White, Branches, Blossoms, Laura A. Fry, 1884, 6 x 3 In. 920.00
Vase, Sailboats At Dusk, C. Schmidt, 1926, 7 1/4 x 3 1/2 In. 2990.00
Vase, Ships, Vellum, Fred Rothenbusch, 1908, 10 3/4 x 4 1/2 In. 3055.00
Vase, Ships, Winter Landscape, Flaring, 1916, 5 1/2 x 5 3/4 In. 5175.00
Vase, Snowflakes, Blue Crystals, Striated Brown Glaze, 1929 . . . . 430.00
Vase, Spade Shape Leaves, Brown Flambe, Bulbous, W. Hentschel, 1911, 7 1/2 In. 2700.00
Vase, Spider Stalking Butterfly, Black, Sea Green, Valentien, 1893, 8 x 4 1/2 In. 6325.00
Vase, Stylized Flower, Mottled Brown Matte Glaze, Oval, 1911, 4 In. 580.00
Vase, Sunflowers, Standard Glaze, Silver Overlay, Shirayamadani, 1899, 13 x 5 In. 2415.00
Vase, Swans, Carved, Ombroso, William Hentschel, 1914, 6 7/8 In. 2875.00
Vase, Swans, Ombroso, 1913, 3 1/2 In. 560.00
Vase, Sweetpeas, Iris Glaze, Purple, Oval, 6 1/2 x 3 3/4 In. 1410.00
Vase, Teal Mottled Glaze, Flared Rim, 1924, 6 1/2 In. 175.00
Vase, Thistle, Gray, Celadon, White, Iris Glaze, Irene Bishop, 1899, 7 x 3 In. 2645.00
Vase, Thistle, Green Leaves, Iris Glaze, Gray Ground, O.G. Reed, 1903, 8 1/2 x 4 1/2 In. . . . 3290.00
Vase, Thistles, Curls, Standard Glaze, Silver Overlay, Humphreys, 1902, 8 1/4 x 3 1/2 In. . 2070.00
Vase, Thistles, Lavender Blossoms, Iris Glaze, Matthew A. Daly, 1899, 8 3/4 x 4 1/2 In. . . . 9775.00
Vase, Thrush Near Trees, Amber Sky, Shirayanadani, 1897, 9 In. 4140.00
Vase, Tiger, Standard Glaze, Brown Ground, Bruce Horsfall, 1895, 11 1/2 x 7 1/2 In. 2990.00
Vase, Tree, Pink Faded To Moss Green, Vellum, Hentschel, 1910, 8 1/2 In. 2415.00
Vase, Tree, Snow, Peach Sky, Vellum, Fred Rothenbusch, 1911, 11 3/4 In. 3795.00
Vase, Trees, Mottled Ground, Vellum, Fred Rothenbusch, 1916, 9 1/2 x 4 In. 2705.00
Vase, Trees, Stream, Purple To Pink, Cream Sky, Vellum, Shirayamadani, 1909, 10 1/4 In. . 2760.00
Vase, Trees, Twilight Sky, Snowy Grove, 1912, 8 1/8 In. 4830.00
Vase, Tropical Plants, Baluster, Shirayamadani, 1935, 7 1/2 x 3 3/4 In. 1175.00
Vase, Trumpet Vines, Iris Glaze, Egg Shape, Fred Rothenbusch, 1901, 6 1/2 x 3 1/4 In. 1645.00
Vase, Trumpet Vines, Vellum, Bulbous, M.H. McDonald, 1930, 6 x 4 In. 1175.00
Vase, Tulips, Green To Rose Butterfat Matte Ground, 1914, 11 3/4 In. 500.00
Vase, Tulips, Leaves, Purple Ground, Maroon Interior, Shirayamadani, 1924, 9 5/8 In. 6643.00
Vase, Tulips, Red, Leaves, Blue, Yellow Ground, Red Overspray, Trumpet Shape, 8 3/4 In. . 1725.00
Vase, Tulips, Standard Glaze, Red, Brown, Yellow, Silver Overlay, Bonsall, 7 3/4 In. 2530.00
Vase, Tulips, Tapered, Bulbous Top, Art Nouveau Silver Mount, E. Noonan, 7 1/2 In. 1955.00
Vase, Tulips, White, Fronds, Vellum Glaze, Ed Diers, 1906, 10 3/8 In. 2185.00
Vase, Tulips, White, Lacy, Iris Glaze, Asbury, 1907, 10 In. 3290.00
Vase, Tulips, Yellow, Open, Green, Sallie Toohey, 1902, 10 5/8 In. 1150.00
Vase, Tulips, Yellow, Stems, Matthew A. Daly, 1899, 14 1/2 x 5 1/2 In. 6325.00
Vase, Turquoise Glaze, Shouldered, Oval, 2 Handles, c.1928, 7 1/2 In. 85.00
Vase, Van Dyck, Portrait, Standard Glaze, Grace Young, 10 x 4 1/4 In. 1725.00
Vase, Violets, Blue, Iris Glaze, Egg Shape, Elizabeth Nourse, 1909, 7 x 3 1/2 In. 2820.00
Vase, Virginia Creeper, Elizabeth Lincoln, 1921, 5 7/8 In. 805.00
Vase, Virginia Creeper, Lavender, Leaves, Vines, Iris Glaze, F. Rothenbusch, 1903, 5 In. . . . 1495.00
Vase, Virginia Creeper, Wax Mat, Egg Shape, J.W. Pullman, 1929, 7 x 4 In. 1530.00
Vase, White High Glaze, Over Caramel, c.1950, 3 1/4 In. 130.00
Vase, Wild Roses, Green, Brown, Standard Glaze, Shirayamadani, 1887, 18 x 6 In. 6325.00
Vase, Wild Roses, Yellow, Standard Glaze, Bulbous, Irene Bishop, 1894, 7 In. 500.00
Vase, Woman's Portrait, Champagne Bottles, 3 Handles, A. Van Briggle, 1893, 8 x 10 In. . . . 2000.00
Vase, Women, Dancing, Silhouette, Blue Ground, E. Barrett, 1935, 11 3/4 x 7 In. 4025.00
Vase, Wreath, Blossoms, Carved, Multicolored, Yellow Ground, 3 3/4 x 5 In. 705.00

Vase, Yellow Matte Glaze, 1927, 6 3/4 In.	259.00
Vase, Yellow Matte Glaze, Fluted, Ribbed, 1923, 11 In.	259.00
Wall Pocket, Blue Matte Glaze, 1922, 10 In.	315.00
Wall Pocket, Pink Matte Glaze, 1930, 7 1/2 In.	205.00

RORSTRAND was established near Stockholm, Sweden, in 1726. By the nineteenth century they were making English-style earthenware, bone china, porcelain, ironstone china, and majolica. The company is still working. The three crown mark has been used since 1884.

Pitcher, Majolica, Embossed, Reticulated Medallions, 10 In.	140.00
Vase, Farina Design, Semi-Translucent Black High Glaze, 3-Sided, Nyland, 7 x 4 In.	80.00
Vase, Flambe, Flowers, Diamond Design, Gold Bands, Brown, Oval, Nyland, 4 x 3 In.	105.00
Vase, Owl Feather Glaze, Drip Design, Incised, Horizontal Bands, Nyland, 6 1/2 x 3 In.	175.00
Vase, Owl Feather Glaze, Vertical, Ribbed Body, Tan Glaze, Gray Drip, Incised, 3 x 3 In.	80.00

ROSALINE, see Steuben category.

ROSE CANTON china is similar to Rose Mandarin and Rose Medallion, except no people or birds are pictured in the decoration. It was made in China during the nineteenth and twentieth centuries in greens, pinks, and other colors.

Bowl, 8 In.	400.00
Plates, 10 In., 8 Piece	460.00
Spoon, 9 1/4 In.	90.00

ROSE MANDARIN china is similar to Rose Canton and Rose Medallion. If the panels in the design picture only people and not birds, it is called Rose Mandarin.

Bowl, Punch, Scholars, Greek Key Border, Floral Rim, 6 x 15 In.	1380.00
Charger, 14 3/4 In.	489.00
Plate, Courtyard Scene, Fish Pond, Armored Warrior, Copper Color, 10 In.	375.00
Platter, Court Scene, 16 Figures, Alternating, Oriental Calligraphy, Gilt, 15 x 17 In.	2070.00
Shrimp Dish, Butterfly Border, Fruit, Gilt Border, Gold Trim, 10 x 10 In.	805.00
Tray, Oval, Scalloped Edge, Gilt, Rose Border, 9 1/2 x 11 In.	230.00
Vase, Lion's Head, Handles, Baluster Form, 14 In.	750.00

ROSE MEDALLION china was made in China during the nineteenth and twentieth centuries. It is a distinctive design with four or more panels of decoration around a central medallion that includes a bird or a peony. The panels show birds and people. The background is a design of tree peonies and leaves. Pieces are colored in greens, pinks, and other colors. It is similar to Rose Canton and Rose Mandarin.

Basket, Fruit, Underplate, Oval, Reticulated Sides & Rim, c.1860, 10-In. Plate	1150.00
Bowl, Figures, Man At Window, Roses, Birds, 10 x 4 In.	259.00
Candlestick, Figures, Paneled Scenes, Cylindrical, Flared Base, c.1900, 7 In., Pair	690.00
Canister, Cover, Cylindrical, 1 3/4 In.	60.00
Charger, Pie Shape Panels, Mandarin Scenes, 16 In.	400.00
Creamer, 2 1/2 In.	160.00
Cup Set, Loop Handle, Figures, Flowers, 2 3/4 In.	230.00
Jar, Dome Cover, Temple, Frog, Inverted Pear Shape, Foo Dog Finial	145.00
Mug, Entwined Handle, 5 1/2 In.	315.00
Plate, Butter, 5 1/2 In., 5 Piece	140.00
Plate Set, Reticulated Edges, Gilding, 8 3/4 In., 4 Piece	315.00
Platter, Figures, Flowers, 14 x 11 In.	230.00
Platter, Oval, Butterflies, Flowers, 20th Century, 16 x 12 In.	90.00
Platter, Paneled, Well & Tree, 17 x 13 In.	1150.00
Platter, Well & Tree, 1800s, 18 7/8 In.	590.00
Punch Bowl, 1800s, 5 1/2 x 13 3/8 In.	880.00
Punch Bowl, 6 Cartouches, Bird & Flowers, Figures, 16 In.	1955.00
Punch Bowl, Famille Rose, Black, Gilt, 12 In.	1150.00
Punch Bowl, Hardwood Stand, c.1908, 7 x 16 In.	1495.00
Saucer, Gilt Details, 6 1/2 In., 8 Piece	259.00
Serving Dish, Cover, Scene, Figures, Red Flowers, 6 x 10 x 8 In., Pair	865.00

Serving Dish, Orange Peel Glaze, Figure, Bird Panels, Cover, 10 x 9 x 6 In.	145.00
Tea Set, Teapot, Creamer & Sugar, Early 20th Century, 23 Piece	375.00
Teapot, Basket Cased, Lid, Wire Handles, 19th Century, 4 1/2 In.	130.00
Teapot, Dome Cover, Scrolled Handle, FFE Monogram, 1800s, 8 1/4 In.	825.00
Teapot, Gilding, Double Wire Bail Handle, 5 1/4 In.	69.00
Tureen, Handles, Oval, 14 1/2 In.	140.00
Vase, 4 Panels, Birds, Butterflies, Rocks, Tree Peonies, 14 In.	315.00
Vase, Baluster, Applied Dragons & Foo Dogs, Late 1800s, 15 3/4 In., Pair	1840.00
Vase, Lobed Shape, Central Stem, 5 Extra Holes, 8 1/2 In.	1095.00
Vase, Mounted As A Lamp, 19th Century, 12 In.	380.00

ROSE O'NEILL, see Kewpie category.

ROSE TAPESTRY porcelain was made by the Royal Bayreuth factory of Tettau, Germany, during the late nineteenth century. The surface of the porcelain was pressed against a coarse fabric while it was still damp, and the impressions remained on the finished porcelain. It looks and feels like a textured cloth. Very skillful reproductions are being made that even include a variation of the Royal Bayreuth mark, so be careful when buying.

Box, Gilt Feet, Round, Marked, 2 1/2 x 4 1/4 In.	375.00
Creamer, Beaded Collar, Pinched Spout, Scroll Handle, 4 3/4 In.	98.00
Creamer, Pinched Spout, 3 1/4 In.	170.00
Creamer, Pinched Spout, Blue Mark, 3 1/4 In.	175.00
Dresser Set, 10-In. Tray, Hair Receiver, Blue Stamp	460.00
Hair Receiver, Blue Mark	175.00
Hatpin Holder, White, Yellow, Red Roses, 4 1/2 In.	260.00
Plate, 3 Roses, Open Handle, Blue Mark, 10 In.	275.00
Vase, Bud, 4 1/2 In.	240.00

ROSENTHAL porcelain was made at the factory established in Selb, Bavaria, in 1880. The factory is still making fine-quality tablewares and figurines. A series of Christmas plates was made from 1910. Other limited edition plates have been made since 1971.

Figurine, Commedia Del'arte Character, Reclining Figure, 1900s, 10 In.	880.00
Figurine, Fortuna, Woman, Partially Nude, Standing On Ball, Ernst Wenck	1100.00
Figurine, Nude Woman, Leaning, Sipping Water, Cupped Hands, 1900s, 7 1/4 In.	529.00
Figurine, Small Grumble, Outstretched Arm, Tilted Head, Grete Zschabtiz, c.1926, 6 In.	345.00
Figurine, Woman, Nude, Seated, Upswept Hair, Incised Initials LFG, 8 1/2 In.	235.00
Plaque, Der Mann Mit Dem Goldhelm, After Rembrandt, Giltwood Frame, 12 x 11 In.	489.00
Tea Service, TAC1, Walter Gropius, c.1968, 15 Piece	345.00
Vase, Flower Design, Gold Outline, White Ground, Signed, 7 In.	115.00

ROSEVILLE Pottery Company was organized in Roseville, Ohio, in 1890. Another plant was opened in Zanesville, Ohio, in 1898. Many types of pottery were made until 1954. Early wares include Sgraffito, Olympic, and Rozane. Later lines were often made with molded decorations, especially flowers and fruit. Most pieces are marked *Roseville*. Many reproductions made in China have been offered for sale the past few years.

Apple Blossom, Basket, Green, 8 In.	230.00
Apple Blossom, Bookends, Pink, 5 In., Pair	206.00
Apple Blossom, Cornucopia, Blue, 4 7/8 In.	70.00
Apple Blossom, Jardiniere, Pedestal, Blue, 20 In.	1295.00
Apple Blossom, Vase, Blue, 10 1/4 In.	185.00
Apple Blossom, Vase, Green, 6 1/8 In.	175.00
Apple Blossom, Vase, Green, 10 3/8 In.	185.00
Apple Blossom, Vase, Pink, 7 3/8 In., 3 Piece	195.00
Apple Blossom, Vase, Pink, Flared, Footed, Handles, Marked, 8 In.	150.00
Apple Blossom, Vase, Pink, Handles, Marked, 10 In.	235.00
Apple Blossom, Vase, Pink, Handles, Marked, 18 In.	560.00
Artcraft, Jardiniere, Brown, Green Glaze, 6 x 8 In.	150.00
Artwood, Planter, Green, Brown, 6 1/4 x 8 3/4 In.	60.00

Artwood, Planter, Green, Brown, Raised Marks, 9 x 12 1/2 In. 90.00
Aztec, Vase, Bulbous, Banded Squeezebag, Speckled Blue Ground, 8 1/2 x 4 1/2 In. 590.00
Aztec, Vase, Squeezebag, Ivory, Blue, Yellow Flowers, Green Ground, 10 1/2 x 3 In. 440.00
Aztec, Vase, Tapered, Squeezebag, White Flowers, 11 x 4 1/2 In. 410.00
Azurean, Vase, Painted, Wooded Trail, W. Myers, 15 x 4 In. 4405.00
Baneda, Bowl, Green, Handles, 3 x 8 1/2 In. 235.00
Baneda, Jardiniere, Green, 4 x 5 1/2 In. 355.00
Baneda, Jardiniere, Pedestal, Green, 10 x 15 In. 3175.00
Baneda, Urn, Pink, 6 1/2 x 4 In. 410.00
Baneda, Vase, Bud, Green, 6 x 3 1/2 In. 470.00
Baneda, Vase, Bud, Pink, Bulbous, 6 1/2 x 3 1/2 In. 355.00
Baneda, Vase, Green, 2 Handles, Crystalline Glaze, 8 In. 1095.00
Baneda, Vase, Green, 5 In. 690.00
Baneda, Vase, Green, 7 In. 765.00
Baneda, Vase, Green, Bulbous, 4 x 4 In. 355.00
Baneda, Vase, Green, Bulbous, 9 1/2 x 4 1/2 In. 825.00
Baneda, Vase, Green, Handles, 6 In. 489.00
Baneda, Vase, Green, Handles, 12 In. 2300.00
Baneda, Vase, Green, Tapered, Handle, Foil Label, 6 In. 500.00
Baneda, Vase, Pink, 2 Handles, 7 x 5 1/4 In. 520.00
Baneda, Vase, Pink, Bulbous, 8 1/2 x 7 1/2 In. 646.00
Baneda, Vase, Pink, Foil Label, 6 In. 430.00
Baneda, Vase, Pink, Handles, 7 1/4 In. 290.00
Baneda, Vase, Pink, Squat, 4 1/2 x 5 1/2 In. 325.00
Baneda, Vase, Pink, Squat, 7 x 7 In. 529.00
Bank, Pig Shape, Green & Yellow Spots, 2 1/2 x 5 In. 295.00
Bittersweet, Sugar & Creamer, Gray, Raised Marks, 3 x 2 1/2 In. 80.00
Bittersweet, Vase, Gray, Raised Marks, 6 3/8 x 5 1/2 In. 115.00
Bittersweet, Vase, Green, 14 In. 355.00
Bittersweet, Vase, Yellow, 5 1/8 In. 115.00
Blackberry, Basket, Hanging, 5 x 7 In. 825.00
Blackberry, Candlestick, 3 1/2 x 13 In., Pair 590.00
Blackberry, Jardiniere, 4 1/8 In. 375.00
Blackberry, Jardiniere, 6 x 8 1/2 In. 646.00
Blackberry, Jardiniere, 8 1/4 In. 375.00
Blackberry, Planter, Bulbous, 4 x 5 In. 355.00
Blackberry, Vase, 5 In. 440.00
Blackberry, Vase, 6 1/2 x 5 3/4 In. 650.00
Blackberry, Vase, 8 1/4 In. 635.00
Blackberry, Vase, Bulbous, 2 Handles, 4 x 4 1/2 In. 316.00
Blackberry, Vase, Bulbous, 2 Handles, 6 1/2 x 5 1/2 In. 440.00
Blackberry, Vase, Bulbous, 6 In. 705.00
Blackberry, Vase, Bulbous, 8 1/2 x 5 In. 500.00
Blackberry, Vase, Bulbous, Handles, 5 1/2 x 4 3/4 In. 705.00
Blackberry, Vase, Bulbous, Handles, 12 1/2 x 8 In. 1295.00
Blackberry, Vase, Green, Handles, 6 In. 489.00
Blackberry, Vase, Label, 8 1/4 In. 865.00
Blackberry, Vase, Squat, 4 x 6 In. 295.00
Blackberry, Wall Pocket, 8 1/4 In. 920.00
Bleeding Heart, Jardiniere, Pedestal, Pink 1058.00
Bleeding Heart, Vase, Blue, 12 In. 176.00
Bleeding Heart, Vase, Pink, 10 3/8 In. 259.00
Bowl, Flower Frog, Fish, Waves, Speckled Orange To Brown Glaze, 5 x 4 In. 325.00
Bushberry, Basket, Green, 8 1/2 In. 195.00
Bushberry, Basket, Hanging, Green, 5 1/4 In. 175.00
Bushberry, Bookends, Green, 5 1/4 In. 127.00
Bushberry, Compote, Green, 10 In. 205.00
Bushberry, Ewer, Brown, 15 In. 765.00
Bushberry, Jardiniere, Pedestal Set, Brown, 8 In. 705.00
Bushberry, Jardiniere, Pedestal, Brown, Marked, 25 x 12 In. 1060.00
Bushberry, Vase, Blue, 18 In. 295.00
Bushberry, Vase, Blue, Raised Marks, 18 1/4 In. 400.00
Bushberry, Vase, Brown, 14 In. 470.00

Bushberry, Vase, Green, 14 In. 355.00
Carnelian, Bowl, Blue, 12 In. 115.00
Carnelian, Wall Pocket, Green, Ink Stamp, 8 In. 175.00
Carnelian I, Plate, Broad Form, Yellow, Marked, 12 1/2 In. 380.00
Carnelian I, Vase, Bulbous, Burnt Yellow Drip Glaze, Yellow Ground, 9 1/2 x 9 In. 106.00
Carnelian I, Vase, Green, Handles, 18 x 6 1/2 In. 500.00
Carnelian I, Vase, Yellow Green Glaze, 2 Handles, 5 1/4 In. 69.00
Carnelian I, Vase, Yellow, Drip Glaze, Handles, 9 1/2 In. 235.00
Carnelian I, Wall Pocket, Beige, Green Dipping Glaze, 2 Handles, Marked, 8 x 5 In. 259.00
Carnelian I, Wall Pocket, Blue, 8 1/4 & 10 In., Pair 235.00
Carnelian II, Bowl, Ribbed, Red, Green, Ocher Drip Glaze, 4 x 10 In. 325.00
Carnelian II, Vase, Fan, Pink, Green, Ocher Glaze, 8 1/4 x 4 1/2 In. 295.00
Carnelian II, Vase, Green & Purple, Handles, 5 In. 350.00
Carnelian II, Vase, Mottled Pink & Brown Glaze, Green Drip, Handles, 6 In. 1000.00
Cherry Blossom, Jardiniere, Orange Background, 8 1/4 x 11 In. 175.00
Cherry Blossom, Jardiniere, Pink, 6 x 8 1/2 In. 560.00
Cherry Blossom, Vase, Brown, Squat, 2 Handles, 3 1/2 In. 290.00
Cherry Blossom, Vase, Pink, 7 In. 705.00
Cherry Blossom, Vase, Pink, Oval, 7 1/2 x 5 In. 380.00
Cherry Blossom, Vase, Pink, Squat, 4 1/4 x 5 1/2 In. 150.00
Chloron, Candleholder, Green, Fish Holding Candle Cup, Fish Handle, 7 In. 1035.00
Chloron, Pitcher, Green Matte Glaze, 6 x 5 In. 500.00
Chloron, Vase, Green Matte Glaze, Embossed, Blossoms, Tapered, 6 1/2 x 5 In. 500.00
Chloron, Vase, Green Matte Glaze, Twisted Leaves, Blossoms, Oval, 8 1/4 x 4 1/2 In. 375.00
Clemana, Vase, Blue, Bulbous, Handles, Marked, 6 In. 325.00
Clemana, Vase, Brown, Bulbous, Marked, 9 1/2 In. 440.00
Clematis, Bookends, Green Background, 5 In. 115.00
Clematis, Console, Blue, Raised Mark, 3 3/8 In. 46.00
Clematis, Cookie Jar, Cover, Brown, Raised Marks, 11 In. 259.00
Clematis, Cornucopia, Blue, 5 1/4 & 6 In., Pair 150.00
Clematis, Ewer, Blue, Raised Mark, 10 1/2 In. 130.00
Clematis, Ewer, Brown, Raised Marks, 10 1/2 In. 130.00
Clematis, Teapot, Brown, Raised Marks, 7 x 11 In. 46.00
Clematis, Vase, Blue, Handles, Raised Mark, 12 1/2 In. 130.00
Clematis, Vase, Brown, Raised Marks, 9 1/4 In. 69.00
Clematis, Vase, Cornucopia, Green Glaze, Pink Flower, 6 1/4 In. 80.00
Clematis, Vase, Green, Handles, Raised Mark, 8 3/8 In. 160.00
Colonial, Pitcher & Basin, Blue, 4 1/2 x 15 1/2 In. 120.00
Columbine, Bowl, Pink, Handles, 4 x 4 In. 127.00
Columbine, Vase, Blue, 16 In. 590.00
Cosmos, Basket, Brown, Footed, Marked, 10 In. 175.00
Cosmos, Vase, Blue, 8 3/8 In. 230.00
Cosmos, Vase, Blue, Flared, 10 In. 353.00
Cosmos, Vase, Blue, Flared, 18 In. 705.00
Cosmos, Vase, Blue, Handles, Marked, 12 In. 205.00
Cranes, Trees, Clouds, Suns, Umbrella Stand, 21 x 9 In. 1645.00
Cream Ware, Plate, Dog, 8 In. 176.00
Cream Ware, Smoking Set, Native American, Geometric Designs, 3 Piece 575.00
Cremona, Vase, Flat, Pedestal, Green Drip Over Berries, Leaves, Vines, 4 x 6 1/2 In. 130.00
Cremona, Vase, Pink Matte Glaze, Handles, 10 1/2 In. 350.00
Dahlrose, Candlestick, 3 1/2 In., Pair 206.00
Dahlrose, Planter, 6 1/2 x 11 In. 500.00
Dahlrose, Vase, Bulbous, 10 x 10 In. 635.00
Dahlrose, Vase, Bulbous, Handles, 4 In. 175.00
Della Robbia, Planter, White Irises, Stylized Leaves, 4-Sided, 3 1/4 x 4 1/2 In. 1380.00
Della Robbia, Vase, Bulbous, White Morning Glories, 8 1/2 x 6 In. 8225.00
Della Robbia, Vase, Poppies, Spade Shape Leaves, 11 x 4 In. 3645.00
Della Robbia, Vase, Squat, Flared Rim, Vines, Spade Shape Leaves, 6 1/2 x 7 1/2 In. 7640.00
Dogwood II, Jardiniere, 9 5/8 In. 175.00
Dogwood II, Jardiniere, Pedestal, 28 In. 825.00
Donatello, Basket, 12 x 6 1/2 In. 295.00
Donatello, Candlestick, 8 In., Pair 176.00
Donatello, Jardiniere, Pedestal, 32 3/4 In. 690.00

Donatello, Planter, Rectangular, 6 x 12 In. 265.00
Donatello, Powder Box, Lid, Embossed, Nudes, Playing Instruments, 2 x 4 1/2 In. 530.00
Donatello, Vase, Cupids, Ribs, c.1915, 8 In. 195.00
Dutch, Tobacco Jar, Boy, Girl, Boat, 6 In. 205.00
Egypto, Bowl, 3 Handles, 2 3/4 x 8 In. 520.00
Egypto, Vase, Bulbous, Embossed, Blossoms, Leaves, 10 1/2 x 6 In. 1645.00
Falline, Candlestick, Blue, Green Pea Pods, 4 1/2 In., Pair 318.00
Falline, Vase, Blue Green, Brown, 6 1/4 In. 546.00
Falline, Vase, Blue, Bulbous, Stepped Neck, Handles, 7 1/4 x 6 1/4 In. 2705.00
Falline, Vase, Blue, Flared, 8 x 6 In. 705.00
Falline, Vase, Brown, Bulbous, Handles, 6 In. 500.00
Falline, Vase, Brown, Green, Handles, 6 In. .... *Illus* 690.00
Falline, Vase, Brown, Low Handles, 12 1/2 In. 1645.00
Falline, Vase, Open Seedpod Design, 2 Handles, c.1933 .... 660.00
Ferella, Vase, Brown, 2 Handles, 9 1/2 x 6 1/4 In. 529.00
Ferella, Vase, Rose, Cutout Rim, Flared, Handles, 5 x 6 3/4 In. 980.00
Ferella, Vase, Rose, Cutouts, Green Rim, 2 Handles, 6 1/4 x 7 1/4 In. 978.00
Ferella, Vase, Rose, Flaring, 2 Handles, 9 1/2 x 6 In. 825.00
Ferella, Vase, Rose, Mottled, Handles, 9 1/4 In. .... *Illus* 770.00
Figure, Dog, Ivory Glaze, 2 x 6 In. 500.00
Fish, Umbrella Stand, Majolica Type Glaze, Green, Yellow Interior, 21 x 11 In. 1000.00
Florane, Bowl, Handles, 4 5/8 In. 127.00
Florentine, Bowl, Brown, 2 5/8 In. 35.00
Florentine, Compote, Brown, Ink Stamp, 3 7/8 In. 46.00
Florentine, Jardiniere, Brown, 6 1/8 In. 46.00
Florentine, Jardiniere, Brown, 10 In. 130.00
Florentine, Jardiniere, Pedestal, Brown, 28 1/4 In. 690.00
Florentine, Jardiniere, Pedestal, Ivory, 26 1/2 In. 470.00
Florentine, Umbrella Stand, Brown, 20 1/2 x 10 1/2 In. 530.00
Florentine, Umbrella Stand, Ivory, 20 1/2 x 10 1/2 In. 410.00
Florentine, Vase, Brown, 8 1/4 In. 45.00
Florentine, Wall Pocket, Brown, Ink Stamp, 7 1/8 In. 60.00
Foxglove, Basket, Blue, 10 In. 235.00
Foxglove, Basket, Blue, 12 In. 410.00
Foxglove, Vase, Blue, 16 In. 705.00
Foxglove, Vase, Blue, Raised Marks, 18 3/8 In. 690.00
Foxglove, Vase, Double Bud, Blue, 4 1/2 In. 115.00
Foxglove, Vase, Green, 14 In. 825.00
Foxglove, Vase, Green, 15 In. 529.00
Foxglove, Vase, Pink, Fan Shape, Handles, Marked, 8 In. 150.00
Freesia, Basket, Tangerine, Raised Marks, 7 1/8 In. 160.00
Freesia, Bookends, Green, 5 In., Pair 176.00
Freesia, Candlestick, Console, Blue, Raised Marks, 2 1/8 x 4 In. 150.00
Freesia, Ewer, Blue, Raised Marks, 6 1/4 In. 115.00
Freesia, Ewer, Brown, Raised Marks, 6 1/4 In. 69.00
Freesia, Jardiniere, Brown, Raised Marks, 6 1/8 In. 45.00
Freesia, Jardiniere, Pedestal, Blue, Marked, 25 x 12 In. 880.00
Freesia, Sugar & Creamer, Brown, Raised Marks 58.00
Freesia, Vase, Brown, Raised Mark, 8 3/8 In. 138.00
Fuchsia, Basket, Attached Flower Frog, Green, 8 1/2 In. 590.00
Fuchsia, Bowl, Blue, Handles, 4 In. 184.00
Fuchsia, Bowl, Flower Frog, Blue, 3 1/4 In. 175.00
Fuchsia, Bowl, Green, Marked, 12 In. 200.00
Fuchsia, Jardiniere, Pedestal, Blue, 10 In. 3290.00
Fuchsia, Planter, Brown, Handles, Marked, 5 In. 260.00
Fuchsia, Vase, Blue, 18 In. 880.00
Fuchsia, Vase, Blue, 2 Handles, 6 In. 196.00
Fuchsia, Vase, Blue, Handles, 4 In. 185.00
Fuchsia, Vase, Blue, Handles, Marked, 6 In. 295.00
Fuchsia, Vase, Brown, 12 In. 440.00
Fuchsia, Vase, Green, 6 1/8 In. 115.00
Fudjiyama, Vase, Flowers, Tan, Brown, Green Enamel, Ink Stamp, 11 1/4 In. 865.00
Futura, Candlestick, Brown, Flower, Handles, Paper Label, 6 1/2 In. 175.00

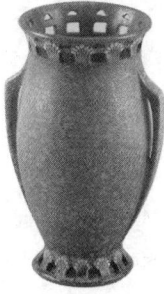

Roseville, Falline, Vase, Brown,   Roseville, Ferella, Vase, Rose,   Roseville, Jonquil, Vase,
Green, Handles, 6 In.   Mottled, Handles, 9 1/4 In.   Handles, 8 In.

Futura, Jardiniere, Orange, Leaves, 7 x 10 In. 175.00
Futura, Vase, Ball Bottle, Pink-Gray Green, Stepped Neck, 8 1/2 x 5 In. 430.00
Futura, Vase, Blue, Yellow Tulip, 12 In. 645.00
Futura, Vase, Green High Glaze, Graduated Rings, 12 In. 940.00
Futura, Vase, Green, 5 1/2 In. 590.00
Futura, Vase, Green, Emerald Urn, 9 In. 375.00
Futura, Vase, Green, Pink, Ball Bottle, 8 In. 405.00
Futura, Vase, Orange Shaded Ground, Thistle, Handles, Footed, 12 In. 690.00
Futura, Vase, Orange, Flared, Green Buttresses, Foot, 8 1/2 x 5 In. 705.00
Futura, Vase, Pink Twist, Blue, Green, Geometric, 8 In. 489.00
Futura, Vase, Pink, 4-Sided, Green Chevron Design, 7 In. 646.00
Futura, Vase, Pink, Green, Star Shape, 8 1/2 x 3 1/2 In. 150.00
Futura, Vase, Pink, Handle, 6 1/2 In. 325.00
Futura, Vase, Rocket Ship, Blue, Green, 8 x 5 In. 920.00
Futura, Vase, Turquoise, Blue, 4-Sided, Round Foot, 9 In. 630.00
Gardenia, Candleholder, Gray, Raised Marks, 1 3/4 In., Pair 80.00
Gardenia, Jardiniere, Pedestal, Gray & Purple, Marked, 30 1/2 x 13 In. 880.00
Hexagon, Vase, Green Matte Glaze, Stamp Marked, 4 In. 176.00
Hexagon, Vase, Green, 2 1/2 x 6 In. 175.00
Hexagon, Vase, Green, 5 x 3 1/2 In. 325.00
Imperial II, Ashtray, Blue & Yellow Mottled Glaze, 2 x 9 In. 1645.00
Imperial II, Bowl, Blue & Yellow Glaze, Flared, 5 x 12 1/2 In. 590.00
Imperial II, Bowl, Rib Bands, Mottled Green & Orange Glaze, 3 x 9 In. 175.00
Imperial II, Vase, Blue & Yellow Mottled Glaze, Ribbed Band, 11 1/2 x 5 1/2 In. 2235.00
Imperial II, Vase, Bulbous, Blue Tourmaline Glaze, 7 1/4 x 6 1/4 In. 205.00
Imperial II, Vase, Green Mottled Glaze, Squat, Ribbed, 4 1/2 x 8 In. 470.00
Imperial II, Vase, Lavender & Yellow Glaze, Tapered, Ribbed, 6 1/4 x 6 In. 440.00
Imperial II, Vase, Orange Drip Glaze, Burnt Orange Ground, Handles, 8 1/2 x 7 1/2 In. ... 470.00
Imperial II, Vase, Ribbed Bands, Green & Gray Mottled Glaze, 5 1/2 x 3 3/4 In. 325.00
Imperial II, Vase, Yellow & Green Glaze, Blue Gray Matte Ground, 5 1/2 x 8 1/4 In. 1645.00
Iris, Jardiniere, Turquoise, Handles, 7 In. 175.00
Iris, Vase, Mauve, White, Handles, Label, 5 In. 90.00
Iris, Vase, Orange Background, Handles, 3 1/2 In. 90.00
Jonquil, Basket, 8 3/4 x 5 1/4 In. 940.00
Jonquil, Basket, Hanging, 5 In. 500.00
Jonquil, Bowl, Handles, Oval, 3 3/4 x 12 In. 175.00
Jonquil, Jardiniere, Brown, Handles, 8 In. Diam. 205.00
Jonquil, Jardiniere, Pedestal, Pink, Green, 10 x 14 In. 2115.00
Jonquil, Planter, Strawberry, 6 1/2 x 7 1/2 In. 980.00
Jonquil, Vase, 2 Handles, 9 1/2 x 6 In. 355.00
Jonquil, Vase, 2 Low Handles, 7 x 5 In. 400.00
Jonquil, Vase, 6 In. 316.00
Jonquil, Vase, 7 1/2 In. 210.00
Jonquil, Vase, Black Label, 6 1/2 In. 375.00
Jonquil, Vase, Brown, Handles, 8 In. 235.00

Jonquil, Vase, Bulbous, Handles, 4 In. 175.00
Jonquil, Vase, Handles, 10 In. 545.00
Jonquil, Vase, Handles, 6 1/2 In. 290.00
Jonquil, Vase, Handles, 8 In. .... *Illus* 430.00
Juvenile, see Roseville, Cream Ware
Landscape, Jardiniere, 7 In. 460.00
Landscape, Pitcher, 7 1/4 In. 58.00
Luffa, Jardiniere, Pedestal, Green, 24 x 11 In. 1295.00
Luffa, Jardiniere, Pedestal, Green, 28 In. 1725.00
Luffa, Lamp, 12 In. 300.00
Luffa, Vase, Brown & Green, Handles, Marked, 15 1/2 In. 1290.00
Luffa, Vase, Brown, Bulbous, 6 1/2 x 6 1/2 In. 175.00
Luffa, Vase, Caramel, Green, White Blossoms, 2 Handles, 6 1/4 In. 575.00
Luffa, Vase, Green, 6 In. 265.00
Magnolia, Basket, 10 In. 230.00
Magnolia, Basket, 12 1/2 In. 230.00
Magnolia, Cider Pitcher, Blue, Raised Marks, 9 In. 259.00
Magnolia, Cookie Jar, Cover, Blue, Squared Handles, 10 In. 230.00
Magnolia, Cookie Jar, Cover, Brown, Raised Marks, 10 1/4 In. 185.00
Magnolia, Cookie Jar, Cover, Green, 8 In. 207.00
Magnolia, Cornucopia, Blue, 6 In. 80.00
Magnolia, Jardiniere, Pedestal, Blue, 30 1/4 In. 430.00
Magnolia, Vase, Blue, 9 1/8 In. 138.00
Magnolia, Vase, Brown, 9 In. 160.00
Magnolia, Vase, Brown, Handles, Marked, 12 In. 265.00
Magnolia, Vase, Green, 9 1/4 In. 140.00
Magnolia, Vase, Green, Handles, Marked, 12 In. 325.00
Magnolia, Vase, Green, Handles, Raised Marks, 18 5/8 In. 489.00
Matte Green, Vase, 2 Handles, 3 1/2 In. 210.00
Matte Green, Vase, Bud, Double, 4 1/2 x 8 In. 115.00
Matte Green, Wall Pocket, Flowers, 11 1/4 x 4 3/4 In. 405.00
Matte Green, Wall Pocket, Geometric, 10 1/4 x 5 In. 315.00
Ming Tree, Basket, Pink, Brown Trees, Raised Marks, 12 3/4 In. 80.00
Ming Tree, Console Set, Candleholders, White, 4 1/2 x 14 In., 3 Piece 105.00
Ming Tree, Planter, White, Blue, Raised Marks, 4 1/4 x 11 In. 69.00
Ming Tree, Vase, Blue, Raised Marks, 10 1/4 In. 69.00
Mock Orange, Vase, Brown, Yellow, Handle, 3-Footed, 8 x 9 In. 150.00
Moderne, Bowl, White, Footed, Marked, 6 In. 230.00
Moderne, Vase, Corseted, Green, 2 Handles, 10 In. 325.00
Moderne, Vase, Turquoise Matte Glaze, Handle, Footed, Flared, Marked, 8 1/2 In. 295.00
Monticello, Vase, Blue, 2 Handles, 5 1/4 In. 290.00
Monticello, Vase, Brown, 2 Handles, 4 x 5 In. 345.00
Monticello, Vase, Green, 2 Handles, 4 x 5 In. 200.00
Monticello, Vase, Green, Bulbous, 2 Handles, 7 1/2 In. 206.00
Monticello, Vase, Green, Bulbous, 5 x 5 1/2 In. 235.00
Monticello, Vase, Green, Squat, 4 1/2 x 5 In. 235.00
Morning Glory, Vase, Beige, Flowers, 5 1/4 In. 185.00
Morning Glory, Vase, Green, 2 Handles, 8 1/2 x 6 3/4 In. 920.00
Morning Glory, Vase, Green, Flared, Handles, 5 In. 325.00
Morning Glory, Vase, White, 2 Handles, Bulbous, 6 1/2 x 7 In. 460.00
Morning Glory, Vase, White, Flared, 8 In. 380.00
Moss, Vase, Blue, Flattened, Handles, Marked, 7 1/2 In. 205.00
Moss, Vase, Blue, Handles, Marked, 8 1/2 In. Diam. 325.00
Mostique, Jardiniere, 10 In. 225.00
Mostique, Jardiniere, Pedestal, 29 x 15 In. 529.00
Mostique, Jardiniere, Stomped On Base, 10 In. 200.00
Mostique, Vase, Bulbous, White & Green Flowers, 12 x 8 In. 294.00
Mostique, Vase, Flared, 2 Handles, White Flowers, 10 1/2 x 7 In. 410.00
Mostique, Vase, Flared, Gray, 12 In. 259.00
Mostique, Vase, Gray, 10 1/4 In. 160.00
Orian, Bowl, Red, Footed, 5 x 13 In. 265.00
Pauleo, Vase, Bulbous, Copper Over Fuchsia Glaze, 15 x 8 In. 1765.00
Pauleo, Vase, Bulbous, Red, 10 x 6 1/2 In. 765.00

Pauleo, Vase, Red, 19 x 7 1/2 In.	1175.00
Peony, Basket, Hanging, Green, 5 In.	80.00
Peony, Conch Shell, Yellow, Yellow, Raised Marks, 6 1/2 x 9 In.	58.00
Peony, Console, Yellow, 3 3/4 In.	45.00
Peony, Urn, Yellow, Handles, 9 In.	145.00
Peony, Vase, Green, Handles, 18 7/8 In.	460.00 to 489.00
Peony, Vase, Yellow, 2 Angular Handles, 15 In.	230.00
Peony, Vase, Yellow, Raised Marks, 12 3/8 In.	290.00
Persian, Basket, Hanging, 5 In.	355.00
Pine Cone, Ashtray, Brown, Impressed Marks, 4 3/4 In.	105.00
Pine Cone, Basket, Brown, 8 In.	295.00
Pine Cone, Basket, Brown, 10 In.	470.00
Pine Cone, Basket, Green, 10 In.	355.00
Pine Cone, Basket, Hanging, Brown, 5 1/2 x 7 1/2 In.	235.00
Pine Cone, Bookends, Brown, 5 In.	120.00 to 175.00
Pine Cone, Bowl, Blue, 12 In.	410.00
Pine Cone, Bowl, Brown, 9 In.	118.00
Pine Cone, Bowl, Brown, 15 In.	206.00
Pine Cone, Bowl, Brown, Raised Marks, 2 3/4 In.	259.00
Pine Cone, Bowl, Brown, Tan, Bulbous, Branch Handles, 7 In.	175.00
Pine Cone, Candlestick, Brown, Impressed Marks, 2 5/8 In., Pair	230.00
Pine Cone, Centerpiece, Blue, Flower Holder, 6 Candle Holders, 6 In.	705.00
Pine Cone, Centerpiece, Brown, Flower Holder, 6 Candle Holders, 6 In.	355.00
Pine Cone, Console Set, Blue, Bowl, Candlesticks	380.00
Pine Cone, Console Set, Brown, Bowl, Candlesticks	380.00
Pine Cone, Console, Blue, 15 In.	235.00
Pine Cone, Ewer, Brown, Duck Bill, Raised Marks, 10 3/8 In.	430.00
Pine Cone, Flowerpot, Brown, Silver Foil Label, Impressed, 5 1/8 In.	115.00
Pine Cone, Jar, Sand, Brown, Handles, Impressed, 15 In.	865.00
Pine Cone, Jardiniere, Blue, 4 In.	275.00
Pine Cone, Jardiniere, Blue, 7 In.	295.00
Pine Cone, Jardiniere, Blue, 8 In.	295.00 to 380.00
Pine Cone, Jardiniere, Brown, 8 In.	382.00
Pine Cone, Jardiniere, Brown, 10 In.	410.00 to 440.00
Pine Cone, Jardiniere, Green, 10 In.	440.00
Pine Cone, Jardiniere, Pedestal, Blue, 20 In.	4115.00
Pine Cone, Jardiniere, Pedestal, Brown, Marked, 25 x 12 In.	1175.00
Pine Cone, Pitcher, Bulbous, Blue, Branch Handle, Marked, 8 In.	765.00
Pine Cone, Pitcher, Bulbous, Green, Branch Handle, Marked, 7 1/2 In.	705.00
Pine Cone, Tray, Blue, 12 In.	235.00
Pine Cone, Tray, Double, Blue, 6 1/2 x 13 In.	764.00
Pine Cone, Vase, Blue, 7 In.	325.00
Pine Cone, Vase, Blue, 8 In.	382.00 to 410.00
Pine Cone, Vase, Blue, 10 In.	410.00
Pine Cone, Vase, Blue, 12 In.	355.00
Pine Cone, Vase, Blue, Bulbous, 2 Branch Handles, Square Base, 7 1/2 x 7 In.	748.00
Pine Cone, Vase, Blue, Footed, Branch Handles, Marked, 6 In.	380.00
Pine Cone, Vase, Blue, Handles, 10 1/2 In.	350.00
Pine Cone, Vase, Blue, Low, Bulbous, Branch Handles, Marked, 4 In.	205.00
Pine Cone, Vase, Blue, Spherical, 6 1/4 x 7 1/2 In.	410.00
Pine Cone, Vase, Brown, 7 1/4 In.	170.00
Pine Cone, Vase, Brown, 10 In.	440.00 to 560.00
Pine Cone, Vase, Brown, 12 In.	410.00
Pine Cone, Vase, Brown, Bulbous, 10 In.	529.00
Pine Cone, Vase, Brown, Footed, Buttressed Base, 10 In.	410.00
Pine Cone, Vase, Brown, Impressed, 8 1/8 In.	460.00
Pine Cone, Vase, Brown, Impressed, Pillow, 8 1/2 In.	635.00
Pine Cone, Vase, Bud, Triple, Blue, 8 In.	375.00
Pine Cone, Vase, Bulbous, Blue, 9 In.	705.00
Pine Cone, Vase, Bulbous, Blue, 12 In.	765.00
Pine Cone, Vase, Bulbous, Footed, 6 1/2 x 7 In.	355.00
Pine Cone, Vase, Green, Footed, Branch Handles, 14 1/2 In.	825.00
Pine Cone, Vase, Pillow, Blue, 8 In.	590.00

Pine Cone, Vase, Pillow, Brown, 8 In. 265.00
Pine Cone, Wall Plate, Blue, 7 1/2 In. 825.00
Pine Cone, Wall Plate, Brown, 8 In. 590.00
Pine Cone, Wall Plate, Green, 8 In. 470.00
Pine Cone, Wall Pocket, Green, 3 Holders, Marked, 8 1/2 In. 440.00
Pine Cone, Wall Pocket, Triple, Brown, 5 x 8 1/2 In. 235.00
Pine Cone, Wall Shelf, Brown, 8 1/2 x 5 In. 470.00
Pine Cone, Window Box, Brown 355.00
Poppy, Bowl, Green, Handles, Marked, 8 1/2 In. 90.00
Poppy, Jardiniere, Blue, 7 1/4 x 9 In. 160.00
Poppy, Vase, Blue, Handle, Footed, Marked, 12 In. 590.00
Poppy, Vase, Green, Impressed Marks, 5 3/4 In. 184.00
Poppy, Vase, Pink, Green, Yellow, Handle, 10 In. 235.00
Poppy, Vase, Pink, Handles, Marked, 8 In. 120.00
Primrose, Jar, Sand, Pink, 14 x 10 In. 295.00
Primrose, Teapot, Blue, Arched Handle White Flowers, Green Leaves, Lid, 7 In. 175.00
Rosecraft, Bowl, Azurine, 3 3/4 In. 12.00
Rosecraft, Jar, Cover, Blue, 11 1/2 In. 545.00
Rosecraft Hexagon, Bowl, Brown, 2 1/2 In. 138.00
Rosecraft Panel, Bowl, Low, Green, 1 1/2 x 5 In. 69.00
Rosecraft Panel, Vase, Brown, 8 1/2 In. 207.00
Rosecraft Panel, Vase, Green, Nudes, 11 1/2 x 5 1/2 In. 645.00
Rosecraft Panel, Wall Pocket, Brown, Pumpkins, 9 In. 206.00
Rozane, Basket, Clover, Wafer Seal, 7 1/2 x 10 In. 259.00
Rozane, Ewer, Painted, Adams, Corn Ears, 15 1/2 x 7 In. 176.00
Rozane, Ewer, Ruffled Rim, Painted, Myers, Berries, Leaves, 16 x 6 1/2 In. 120.00
Rozane, Tray, Acorns, Painted, Myers, 13 x 8 1/2 In. 590.00
Rozane, Vase, Bottle Shape, Painted, Nasturtium, 7 1/2 x 4 In. 235.00
Rozane, Vase, Carnation, Yellow, Orange, 20 1/2 In. 294.00
Rozane, Vase, Green, Bulbous, 8 In. 150.00
Rozane, Vase, Green, Handles, 9 1/2 In. 176.00
Rozane, Vase, Orange & Yellow Flowers, Squat, 2 Handles, 6 x 7 In. 150.00
Rozane, Vase, Orange Blossoms, Leaves, Bulbous, Painted, Gerwick, 8 x 5 In. 264.00
Rozane, Vase, Orange Rose, Pillow, Scroll Handles, Ruffled Rim, Painted, 7 1/2 x 9 In. ... 355.00
Rozane, Vase, Pansies, Green Glaze, Squat, Flared Rim, 5 1/2 x 6 1/2 In. 70.00
Rozane, Vase, Pillow, Painted, Elk, 21 x 12 In. 440.00
Rozane, Vase, Rose, Twisted Baluster Shape, Handles, Ruffled Rim, 5 1/4 In. 138.00
Rozane, Vase, Ruffled Rim, Dog With Bird In Mouth, Pillow, 9 x 11 In. 460.00
Rozane Fudji, Vase, Blue Flowers, Ocher Rim Band, 4-Sided, 8 1/2 x 3 1/2 In. 2820.00
Rozane Mongol, Red, Flared, Bulbous, Marked, 14 In. 2585.00
Rozane Mongol, Vase, Poppies, Blue Ground, Marked, 12 1/2 In. 1116.00
Rozane Royal, Vase, Yellow, Rose Blooms, Handles, Initialed, 10 In. 518.00
Rozane Royal Dark, Tankard, Terrier Wearing Green Ribbon, Impressed Marks, 14 In. 1150.00
Rozane Royal Dark, Vase, Handles, Blackberries On Bush, 12 3/4 In. 430.00
Rozane Royal Dark, Vase, Handles, Red Clover, Impressed, 6 x 6 7/8 In. 220.00
Rozane Royal Dark, Vase, Orange Flowers, Bee, Impressed, 18 1/2 In. 690.00
Rozane Royal Dark, Vase, Orange Iris, Buds, Greenery, Impressed, 11 5/8 In. 290.00
Rozane Royal Light, Vase, Bud, Pink, Lavender Pansies, Painted, Bulbous, 5 x 4 In. 705.00
Rozane Royal Light, Vase, Daffodil, Painted, Cylindrical, Timberlake, 10 1/2 In. 560.00
Rozane Royal Light, Vase, Irises, Ivory Squeezebag, 3 Handles At Rim, 14 x 5 1/2 In. 2700.00
Rozane Royal Light, Vase, Tapered, 3 Rim Handles, Painted, Sweet Peas, 19 x 6 In. 2585.00
Rozane Woodland, Vase, Bud, Yellow & Red Flowers, 6 x 2 1/2 In. 380.00
Rozane Woodland, Vase, Carved, Painted, Fish, Blue Waves, 8 x 4 1/2 In. 4406.00
Rozane Woodland, Vase, White Blossoms, Leaves, Cylindrical, 15 x 3 3/4 In. 1000.00
Russco, Vase, Bud, Double, Green, 8 3/4 In. 375.00
Silhouette, Basket, Orange, 10 In. 105.00
Silhouette, Ewer, Orange, 10 1/2 In. 35.00
Silhouette, Planter, Red Matte, 4 1/2 In., Pair 81.00
Silhouette, Vase, Double, 9 1/2 In. 290.00
Silhouette, Vase, Fan, Red, 7 In. 325.00
Silhouette, Vase, Fan, Tan, Brown, Scalloped Edge, 7 In. 490.00
Silhouette, Vase, Nude In White, Flattened, 7 1/2 In. 265.00

Silhouette, Vase, Orange, Brown, Nude, 8 1/4 In. 460.00
Silhouette, Vase, Pillow, Red, Leaves, 9 In. 120.00
Silhouette, Vase, Red, Nude In Forest, 10 In. 470.00
Snowberry, Basket, Hanging, Green 260.00
Snowberry, Basket, Pink, Marked, 10 In. 150.00
Snowberry, Bookends, Medium Blue, White Blossoms, 5 1/4 In. 150.00
Snowberry, Bowl, Green, 5 In. 138.00
Snowberry, Ewer, Green, Marked 175.00
Snowberry, Jardiniere, Blue, Raised Marks, 6 In. 58.00
Snowberry, Jardiniere, Pedestal, Pink, Marked, 25 x 12 In. 825.00
Snowberry, Tea Set, Green, Teapot, 7 1/2 In., 3 Piece 185.00
Snowberry, Vase, Blue, 18 In. 355.00
Snowberry, Vase, Green, Crescent, Raised Marks, 6 3/8 In. 115.00
Snowberry, Vase, Green, Raised Mark, 5 In. 105.00
Snowberry, Vase, Green, Raised Mark, 9 In. 69.00
Snowberry, Vase, Pink, Raised Mark, 12 1/2 In. 175.00
Sunflower, Bowl, Flaring, 4 x 7 In. 1820.00
Sunflower, Jardiniere, 8 1/4 x 11 In. 382.00
Sunflower, Vase, 2 Handles, 5 x 4 In. 546.00
Sunflower, Vase, Bulbous, 4 x 5 1/2 In. 470.00
Sunflower, Vase, Bulbous, 6 1/2 x 7 In. 325.00
Sunflower, Vase, Bulbous, Handles, 5 In. 825.00
Sunflower, Vase, Bulbous, Handles, Foil Label, 9 In. ....1400.00 to 1800.00
Sunflower, Vase, Flat Shoulder, 7 x 6 1/2 In. 1095.00
Sunflower, Vase, Green, 5 In. 865.00
Sunflower, Vase, Green, 6 7/8 In. 978.00
Sunflower, Vase, Green, 8 1/4 In. 865.00
Sunflower, Vase, Green, Handles, 6 1/4 In. 460.00
Sunflower, Vase, Green, Handles, 10 1/4 In. ....800.00 to 920.00
Sunflower, Vase, Green, Waisted, 8 1/4 In. 999.00
Sunflower, Vase, Oval, 10 1/4 x 6 In. 2950.00
Sunflower, Vase, Squat, 5 1/2 x 6 1/2 In. 646.00
Teasel, Ewer, Blue, 18 In. 529.00
Teasel, Vase, Blue, 12 In. 150.00
Thorn Apple, Bowl, Blue, Impressed Marks, 6 1/4 x 10 In. 175.00
Thorn Apple, Centerpiece, Candlesticks, Brown, Impressed Marks, 4 1/2 x 10 1/2 In. 140.00
Thorn Apple, Flower Frog, Pink, Raised Marks, Green Gardenia, 3 1/2 In. 115.00
Thorn Apple, Vase, Blue, 16 In. 560.00
Thorn Apple, Vase, Blue, Handles, Marked, 15 In. 375.00
Thorn Apple, Vase, Brown, Impressed Marks, 6 3/8 In. 69.00
Topeo, Vase, Blue, Bulbous, 6 x 7 In. 295.00
Topeo, Vase, Blue, Flared Rim, 10 1/2 x 6 In. 765.00
Topeo, Vase, Blue, Tapered, 8 x 6 In. 590.00
Topeo, Vase, Red, Bulbous, 7 x 4 1/2 In. 325.00
Topeo, Vase, Red, Round, Collared Rim, 6 x 7 1/4 In. 175.00
Tourmaline, Vase, Blue, Geometric Design Around Rim, Squat, 5 x 6 1/2 In. 290.00
Tourmaline, Vase, Blue, Handles, 6 In. 175.00
Tourmaline, Vase, Blue, Stepped, Flared, 8 1/4 x 6 In. 460.00
Tourmaline, Vase, Green, Blue, Brown, Yellow, Bulbous, Handles, 5 1/2 In. 235.00
Tuscany, Vase, Pink, Bulbous, 10 1/2 x 9 In. 180.00
Tuscany, Wall Pocket, Pink, Handles, 7 In. 265.00
Velmoss, Candlestick, Ocher, Scroll, 8 In. 196.00
Velmoss, Urn, Orange Glaze, 8 1/4 x 6 3/4 In. 560.00
Velmoss, Vase, Mottled Brown, Green Glaze, 6 In. 575.00
Velmoss, Vase, Pink, 12 In. 235.00
Vista, Jardiniere, 8 1/2 x 9 1/2 In. 410.00
Vista, Jardiniere, Pedestal, Green, 9 1/2 In. 1610.00
Vista, Vase, 18 x 8 In. 1725.00
Vista, Vase, Blue, Purple, Green, Cylinder Shape, Bulbous Bottom, 12 In. 920.00
Vista, Wall Pocket, 9 1/2 x 4 1/2 In. 1175.00
Water Lily, Basket, Hanging, Blue, Raised Marks, 5 1/2 x 8 In. 150.00
Water Lily, Basket, Hanging, Pink, 5 1/2 x 8 In. 175.00

Water Lily, Bookends, Pink, 5 1/2 In., Pair 205.00
Water Lily, Cookie Jar, Brown, 8 In. ....235.00 to 265.00
Water Lily, Cookie Jar, Cover, Pink, 8 In... 138.00
Water Lily, Ewer, Blue, 15 1/4 In.. 315.00
Water Lily, Ewer, Brown, 6 1/2 In. ....46.00 to 92.00
Water Lily, Ewer, Brown, 15 In. 295.00
Water Lily, Jardiniere, Blue, 4 In. 58.00
Water Lily, Vase, Blue, Raised Marks, 8 1/4 In. 127.00
Water Lily, Vase, Brown, 14 In. 147.00
Water Lily, Vase, Brown, 16 In. 441.00
Water Lily, Vase, Brown, 18 In. 294.00
Water Lily, Vase, Green, 15 1/2 In. 460.00
Water Lily, Vase, Pink To Green Background, Seashell Shape, 6 1/2 x 9 1/2 In. 120.00
Water Lily, Vase, Rose, 2 Angular Handles, 6 In. 127.00
Water Lily, Vase, Shading Turquoise To Salmon, 2 Handles, Signed, 6 1/4 In. 80.00
White Rose, Vase, Brown, Handles, 8 3/8 In. ....100.00 to 115.00
White Rose, Vase, Rust, Green, c.1940, 6 1/2 In. 115.00
Wincraft, Basket, Blue, 12 1/4 In.. 69.00
Wincraft, Basket, Tan, Orange, 8 1/2 In... 104.00
Wincraft, Bookends, Yellow, 6 1/4 In., 2 Pair...................................... 176.00
Wincraft, Flowerpot, Yellow, 5 In.. 92.00
Wincraft, Vase, Blue, 12 In. 205.00
Wincraft, Vase, Brown, 15 In... 235.00
Wincraft, Vase, Green, Brown, 12 1/2 In.. 127.00
Wincraft, Vase, Green, Yellow, 10 1/4 In.. 81.00
Wincraft, Vase, Tan, Orange, 6 1/8 In. 58.00
Windsor, Vase, Blue, 2 Handles, 6 1/2 x 4 In.. 206.00
Wisteria, Bowl, Blue, Handles, 4 In. 575.00
Wisteria, Bowl, Brown, 3 x 12 In. 470.00
Wisteria, Bowl, Brown, 3 x 7 1/2 In. 230.00
Wisteria, Bowl, Oblong, Tan, 9 3/8 In. 345.00
Wisteria, Jardiniere, Brown, 4 In. ....300.00 to 400.00
Wisteria, Jardiniere, Brown, 5 In. 288.00
Wisteria, Vase, Blue, 4 In.. 431.00
Wisteria, Vase, Blue, Bulbous, 5 1/2 x 7 In. 118.00
Wisteria, Vase, Blue, Bulbous, 7 In... 999.00
Wisteria, Vase, Blue, Gourd Shape, 6 1/2 x 4 1/2 In. 588.00
Wisteria, Vase, Blue, Gourd Shape, 8 In...............................940.00 to 1440.00
Wisteria, Vase, Blue, Squat, 4 1/2 x 6 In. 380.00
Wisteria, Vase, Blue, Squat, 4 In...................................400.00 to 470.00
Wisteria, Vase, Brown, 6 1/2 In. 558.00
Wisteria, Vase, Brown, 8 1/2 x 8 In. 1058.00
Wisteria, Vase, Brown, Bottle Shape, 9 1/2 x 5 1/2 In. ....470.00 to 500.00
Wisteria, Vase, Brown, Bulbous, 2 Handles, 8 1/2 x 7 1/2 In. 529.00
Wisteria, Vase, Brown, Gourd Shape, 8 In. 588.00
Wisteria, Vase, Brown, Handles, 10 1/2 In. 823.00
Wisteria, Vase, Brown, Purple, Handles, 8 In. 765.00
Wisteria, Vase, Tan, 5 In... 115.00
Zephyr Lily, Basket, Blue, 8 1/2 In.. 138.00
Zephyr Lily, Basket, Brown, 8 1/2 In.. 127.00
Zephyr Lily, Basket, Green, 10 In... 160.00
Zephyr Lily, Basket, Hanging, Blue 175.00
Zephyr Lily, Cookie Jar, Blue, 10 In.. 288.00
Zephyr Lily, Ewer, 15 1/2 In... 460.00
Zephyr Lily, Ewer, Blue, 10 1/2 In... 104.00
Zephyr Lily, Jardiniere, Pedestal, Blue, 24 1/2 In. 1035.00
Zephyr Lily, Sugar & Creamer, Brown 115.00
Zephyr Lily, Tea Set, Blue, Pot, Creamer, Sugar 290.00
Zephyr Lily, Vase, Blue, Raised Marks, 18 1/2 In. 315.00
Zephyr Lily, Vase, Green, 9 3/8 In. 160.00
Zephyr Lily, Vase, Green, 10 1/2 In. 80.00
Zephyr Lily, Vase, Green, Brown, Handle, Marked, 7 In. 120.00
Zephyr Lily, Vase, Green, Flared, Irregular Mouth, Handles, 9 In. 127.00

Rowland & Marsellus, Plate, Battle Of Bunker Hill, June 17th, 1775, Red Transfer, 10 In.

Rowland & Marsellus, Plate, Boston Massacre, Old State House, Red Transfer, 10 In.

ROWLAND & MARSELLUS Company is part of a mark that appears on historical Staffordshire dating from the late nineteenth and early twentieth centuries. Rowland & Marsellus is the mark used by an American importing company in New York City. The company worked from 1893 to about 1937. Some of the pieces may have been made by the British Anchor Pottery Co. of Longton, England, for export to a New York firm. Many American views were made. Of special interest to collectors are the plates with rolled edges, usually blue and white.

Cup & Saucer, Auld Lang Syne, c.1900, 3 1/2 In.		105.00
Plate, Battle Of Bunker Hill, June 17th, 1775, Red Transfer, 10 In.	*Illus*	50.00
Plate, Boston Massacre, Old State House, Red Transfer, 10 In.	*Illus*	50.00

ROY ROGERS was born in 1911 in Cincinnati, Ohio. In the 1930s, he made a living as a singer; in 1935, his group started work at a Los Angeles radio station. He appeared in his first movie in 1937. From 1952 to 1957, he made 101 television shows. The other stars in the show were his wife, Dale Evans, his horse, Trigger, and his dog, Bullet. Roy Rogers memorabilia is collected, including items from the Roy Rogers restaurants.

Advertisement, Roy Rogers Gun, No. 100, Toy Paper Cap Pistol, Disc Caps, Kilgore	16.50
Bandanna, Cloth, Roy Rogers, Trigger, Fossil Watch	12.00
Bandanna, Roy Rogers & Trigger, King Of The Cowboys, Black, White, Silk, 1950s, 25 In.	102.00
Bank & Lamp, Dale Evans, First Federal Savings & Loan, Ky., Plasto Toys Shade	896.00
Bottle, Molasses Barbecue Sauce, Montana Beef Council, Amber, Paper Label, 8 1/2 In.	150.00
Bracelet, Dale Evans, Thrift Novelty, On Card	66.00
Button, Dale Evans, Tab, Slot, Post Raisin Brand, 1953, 1 5/8 In.	25.00
Button, Member Of Roy Rogers Club, England, 1950s, 1 1/4 In.	255.00
Button, Portrait, Australia, 1940s, 3/4 In.	95.00
Button, Roy Rogers 100% For Democracy, Blue, Cream, 1 1/4 In.	877.00
Camera, Flash, Roy Rogers & Trigger, Herbert George Co., 1950s	117.00
Camping Equipment Set, Gabby Hayes, Sgt. Preston, Quaker Puffed Wheat & Rice	45.00
Cap Gun, Embossed Barrel, Double R Brand, 5 1/2 In.	55.00
Cap Gun, Revolving Cylinder, Horse Head Grips, Nickel Finish, Kilgore, c.1955, 10 In.	200.00
Chaps, Roy Rogers Standing Next To Trigger, Size 10	80.00
Christmas Card, Roy Rogers & Dale Evans Fan Club, Members Only, 1950s	75.00
Clock, Alarm, Roy, Trigger, Metal, Animated, Ingraham, Box, 1951, 2 1/2 x 4 1/2 x 5 In.	300.00
Cookie Jar, Golden Signature Edition	80.00
Cookie Jar, Roy Rogers & Trigger, 18 In.	95.00
Costume, Dale Evans Western Suit, Beaded Pockets, Fringe, Brown, Box, Size 8	110.00
Dish Set, Porcelain, Rodeo, Gold Leaf Edges, Universal, Box, 5 Piece	495.00
Doll, Bobble Head, Plaster, Japan, 1960s, 6 1/2 In.	87.00 to 110.00
Doll, Bullet, Stuffed, Rubber Face, 33 In.	70.00
Doll, Roy Rogers & Dale Evans, Western Outfits, Swivel Head, 1950s, 8 In., Pair	55.00 to 83.00

Figurine, Dale Evans, On Buttermilk, Hartland, Box, 1950s, 8 x 9 In. 147.00
Figurine, Roy Rogers On Trigger, Plastic, Hartland, Box, 1950s, 9 In. 154.00
Flashlight, Cowboy, Bantam Lite, Box, 1950, 2 1/2 In. 198.00
Flashlight, Signal Siren, Usalite, Box, 1954, 6 In. 187.00
Flyer, Schwinn Bicycles, I Like Riding Schwinn Bikes The Best, Fold-Out, 17 x 23 In. ... 65.00
Game, Puzzle, Roy Rogers, Fence, Frame Tray Inlay, Whitman, 11 1/4 x 14 1/2 In. 35.00
Gloves, Red Horseshoe, White, Suede, Fringes, Studs, Size 5 .... 75.00
Guitar, Cardboard, Range Rhythm, 30 x 11 In. 39.00
Guitar, Child's, 28 x 10 1/2 In. 135.00
Gun, BB, Roy Rogers & Dale Evans, Collector's Edition, No. 536, Daisy, Box 154.00
Gun, BB, Roy Rogers & Gabby Hayes, Collector's Edition, No. 1708, Daisy, Box 110.00
Gun, BB, Roy Rogers & Trigger, Collector's Edition, No. 618, Daisy, Box 209.00
Gun, Cork, Revolutionary War, Japan, c.1960 .... 165.00
Gun, Rifle, Winchester Carbine, Plastic, Marx, 1950s, 25 In. ....116.00 to 193.00
Gun & Holster Set, Dale Evans, Queen Of West, Box 715.00
Gun & Holster Set, Double, Flash Draw, Schmidt Guns, Classy Products, Box, 14 x 12 In. 1155.00
Gun & Holster Set, Double, Reversible Draw, Bullets, Copper Grips, Classy Products, Box 910.00
Gun & Holster Set, Double, Schmidt Guns, Classy Products, Box, c.1958, 12 x 13 In. ... 880.00
Harmonica, Roy Rogers Riders, 1950s, 4 1/2 In............................... .50.00 to 72.00
Hat, Quick Shooter, Secret Gun, Ideal, Box, 1961, 13 In. 468.00
Holster, Double, 8 Red Bullets, Leather, Flowers, Embossed RR, 38 3/8 In. 347.00
Horseshoe Set, Box ....77.00 to 110.00
Knife, Lock Blade, Novelty Knife Co., Box 25.00
Knife, Pocket, 3 Blades, Ulster Knife Co. 90.00
Knife, Sheath, Rubber, c.1955, 7 1/2 In. 70.00
Lamp, Dale Evans, Plaster, Painted, Paper Shade, Plasto Mfg., 1950s, 15 In. 317.00
Lamp, Roy Rogers & Trigger, Plaster, Painted, Paper Shade, Plasto Mfg., 1950s, 15 In. ... 320.00
Lunch Box, Chow Wagon, Dome Top, No Thermos, American Thermos Co. .... .79.00 to 157.00
Lunch Box, Dale Evans, Double R Bar Ranch, Trigger, Bullet, American Thermos Co., 1954 110.00
Lunch Box, Roy & Dale, Double R Bar Ranch, No Thermos ....47.00 to 73.00
Lunch Box, Saddlebag, Vinyl, No Thermos, King Seeley Thermos Co., 1960, 9 x 7 In. 198.00
Magazine, Life, Roy Rogers On Rearing Horse Cover, July 12, 1943, 11 x 14 In. 290.00
Moccasins, Box 176.00
Model Kit, Ranch, Punch-Out, Cardboard, Post Cereals, c.1950, 3 7/8 x 8 1/2 In. 115.00
Outfit, Cowboy, Official, Yank Boy Play Clothes, Box 175.00
Outfit, Dale Evans, Queen Of West, Yank Boy Play Clothes, Box 145.00
Outfit, Shirt, Chaps, Roy Rogers Rearing On Trigger, Large 55.00
Outfit, Western Suit, Vest, Chaps, Shirt, Holster, Gun, Belt, Lainard, Box 170.00
Paper Doll Set, Folder, Roy, Dale, Dusty, 24 Outfits, Whitman, 1957, 10 x 7 1/2 In. 125.00
Pen, Ball, Unopened, Tuckersharpe, On Card, Early 1950s 165.00
Pencil Box, Contents, Pledge Insert, Eagle Pencil Co., c.1955, 4 3/4 x 8 1/2 In. 99.00
Pencil Case, Gun, Holster, Plastic, 10 In. 187.00
Plate, Riders Club, 9 1/2 In. 28.00
Play Set, Rodeo Ranch, Marx, Box, 1950s 130.00
Program, Souvenir, Information On Roy & Dale's Lives, 1950s 87.00
Puppet, Hand 55.00
Raincoat, Dale Evans, Plastic 55.00
Raincoat, Duster, Leather, Metal Snaps, Yellow, Black, Child's 110.00
Raincoat, Vinyl, Hood, Original Tag 55.00
Record, King Of The Cowboys, 45 RPM 28.00
Ring, Branding, Quaker, 1958 .... 66.00
Ring, Hat, Facsimile Signature, Sterling Silver, Quaker, 1948 .... 425.00
Ring, Roy On Trigger, Crossed Branding Irons, R, Sterling Silver, 1940s 175.00
Rocking Horse, 26 x 35 In. 110.00
Saddle, Leather, Roy Rogers On Trigger Rearing, 1950, Child's ....368.00 to 550.00
Scarf, Silk, Green, Roy Rogers On Trigger, 4 x 36 In. 25.00
Scarf & Slide, Silk, Roy Rogers, Trigger, Bullet, Yellow, White Border, 24 x 24 In. 55.00
School Bag, Dale Evans, Tooled Leather, Briefcase Style, Roy On Pocket, 10 x 14 In. 83.00
Sewing Kit, Dale Evans, 1950s, 4 x 4 In. 90.00
Shirt, Blue & White Checkered, Roy Rogers & Trigger, Pearl Buttons, Size 10 .... 60.00
Shirt, Western, Green, Roy Rogers Frontier Shirts, Rob Roy, 1950s, Size 8 .... 85.00
Spurs, Silver, Leather Wraps, Silver Studs, Double R Brand 58.00

T-Shirt, Roy Rogers & Trigger, 1950s, Child's 95.00
Telephone, Western, Ideal, Box, 1950s, 9 In. . . . . .115.00 to 176.00
Thermos, Roy Rogers, Dale Evans, Trigger, Metal, American Thermos Co., c.1956 . . .44.00 to 77.00
Toy, Buckboard, Plastic, Ideal, Box, 1958 . . . . 610.00
Toy, Chuck Wagon, Fix-It, Do It Yourself, Plastic, Ideal, Box, 1950s, 24 In. . . . . . .358.00 to 440.00
Toy, Dress-Up Kit, Dale Evans, Colorforms, Box, c.1959 . . . . 70.00
Toy, Stage Coach Wagon Train, Marx, Box, 1950s 242.00
Toy, Stagecoach, Fix-It, Plastic, Ideal, Box, 1955, 15 In. . . . . .165.00 to 282.00
Toy, Target Board, Champion, Gabby Hayes, Masonite, 18 x 18 In. 110.00
View-Master Reels, Roy Rogers Adventure Roundup, Booklet, 3 Reels 50.00
Wallet, Vinyl 55.00
Wood Burning Set, Rapaport Bros., Box, Early 1950s, 15 1/2 x 9 1/2 x 2 1/2 In. . . .115.00 to 143.00
Wristwatch, Dale Evans, Buttermilk, Chrome, Leather Band, Bradley Time, Box, 1957 . . . 225.00
Wristwatch, Dale Evans, Queen Of West, Bradley Time, Box, c.1953 . . . . 173.00
Wristwatch, Roy Rogers, Green Face, Ingraham, 1950 . . . . 83.00

ROYAL BAYREUTH is the name of a factory that was founded in Tettau, Bavaria, in 1794. It has continued to modern times. The marks have changed through the years. A stylized crest, the name *Royal Bayreuth*, and the word *Bavaria* appear in slightly different forms from 1870 to about 1919. Later dishes may include the words *U.S. Zone*, the year of the issue, or the word *Germany* instead of *Bavaria*. Related pieces may be found listed in the Rose Tapestry, Sand Babies, Snow Babies, and Sunbonnet Babies categories.

Berry Set, Peasant Musicians, Blue Stamp, 9 3/4 x 5 In., 6 Piece . . . . .230.00 to 575.00
Bowl, Embossed Scallops, Satin Finish, 10 1/2 In. 115.00
Charger, Grape, Blue Stamp, 13 In. 90.00
Chocolate Pot, White Flowers, Ivory, Reticulated Base, 9 In. 130.00
Creamer, Devil & Cards, 4 In. 115.00
Creamer, Elk, Blue Stamp, 4 1/2 In. . . . . .70.00 to 140.00
Creamer, Fish Head, Blue Stamp, 4 1/2 In. 130.00
Creamer, Old Ivory, Tray, Blue Stamp, 8 In. 25.00
Creamer, Robin, Blue Stamp, 4 In. 127.00
Jug, Cows Watering, Blue Stamp, 5 In. 100.00
Jug, Spiky Shell, Green Stamp, 4 1/2 In. 80.00
Pitcher, Apple, Blue Stamp, 6 In. 290.00
Pitcher, Elk, Blue Stamp, 7 In. 259.00
Plaque, Fishermen, Green Stamp, 9 In. 69.00
Plate, Portrait, Arab & Camel, 9 In. 115.00
Plate, Portrait, Arab On Horse, Green Stamp, 9 1/4 In. 46.00
Salt & Pepper, Elk, 3 In. 90.00
Shoe, Cobalt Blue Glaze, 5 In. 69.00
Sugar & Creamer, Tomato, Blue Stamp, 4 In. 115.00
Tea Set, Hunt Scene, 7 In., 3 Piece 201.00
Tea Set, Tapestry, Violets, Teapot, Cream, Sugar, Blue Stamp, 7 In. 460.00
Vase, Cows Watering, Blue Stamp, 4 1/2 In. 92.00
Vase, Sirens Bathing Near Castle, Tapestry, 6 1/4 In. 200.00
Vase, Skiff With Sail, Blue Stamp, 7 In. 92.00
Vase, Tapestry, Ladies Dancing, Green Stamp, Germany, 9 1/4 In. 225.00
Vase, Ye Old Belle, 3 Handles, Blue Stamp, 9 In. 184.00

ROYAL BONN is the nineteenth- and twentieth-century trade name for the Bonn China Manufactory. It was established in 1755 in Bonn, Germany. A general line of porcelain was made. Many marks were used, most including the name *Bonn*, the initials *FM*, and a crown.

Clock, Ansonia, Hand Painted, Irises, 15 x 12 In. 750.00
Clock, Ansonia, La Capelle, 8-Day, Time & Strike, c.1895, 15 In. 590.00
Clock, Ansonia, La Chartres, 8-Day, Gong Strike, Flowers, Green, c.1910, 12 In. 390.00
Clock, Ansonia, La Layon, 8-Day, Time & Strike, c.1905, 12 In. 1065.00
Clock, Ansonia, La Mane, Flowers, Gold Highlights, Blue Accents, c.1901, 12 In. 784.00
Clock, Ansonia, La Rambla, 8-Day, Time & Strike, Aqua, Flowers, c.1914, 12 In. 505.00
Clock, Ansonia, La Somme, c.1910, 11 In. 700.00

Console Set, Tapestry, Gilt Metal, c.1900, 13 1/2 x 14 In., 3 Piece 2990.00
Vase, Classically Draped Woman, Flowers, Lake Scene, Ovoid, Gilt Handles, 11 In. 506.00
Vase, Portrait, Bust, Woman, Landscape, Transfer, 12 In. 430.00

ROYAL COPENHAGEN

porcelain and pottery have been made in Denmark since 1775. The Christmas plate series started in 1908. The figurines with pale blue and gray glazes have remained popular in this century and are still being made. Many other old and new style porcelains are made today.

Bowl, 2 Fish, 1923-30, 7 3/4 In. 275.00
Bowl, Geometric Design, Brown, Yellow Border, Brown Bands, Gerd Bogelund, 5 1/2 In. . . 200.00
Bowl, Rectangular, Fish, Brown Glaze, Nils Thorsson, Marselis, Alumina, 1930s, 12 In. 121.00
Bust, Francis Kedegaard, Mid 20th Century, 6 In. 130.00
Charger, Swan In Lake Landscape, Wave Mark, St. Ussing, 9271, 15 1/2 In. 600.00
Cup, Christmas, Choosing A Christmas Tree, 1979 .... 40.00
Cup, Snowman, 1985 .... 50.00
Dish, 3 Sparrows Perched On Rim, Oval, Signed, Theodor Madsen, 9 1/2 In. 260.00
Dish, Cover, Butterfly, Flowers, 1939, 4 1/4 In. 150.00
Dish, Cover, Flowers, Blackberries, Pre 1923, 5 In. 275.00
Dish, Flora Danica, Botanical, Early 20th Century, 13 In. 1095.00
Dish, Solbjerg, Toucan, On Branch, Leaves, Nils Thorsson, Alumina, 1950s, 10 1/4 In. 86.00
Dish Set, Nested, Flora Danica, Triangular, Marked, 10 1/2 In., 2 Piece 1840.00
Figurine, Dog, Dachshund, 13 In. 195.00
Figurine, Heron, Reeds, Signed, Theodor Madsen, Early 20th Century, 10 3/4 In. 130.00
Figurine, Mermaid, No. 1212, 3 x 7 1/2 In. ....*Illus* 250.00
Figurine, Nymph & Faun, Kissing, Oval Plinth Base, Garlands, 10 1/2 In. 575.00
Figurine, Pan, Holding Flute, Kneeling In Grass, 6 In. 604.00
Figurine, Satyr, Pulling Rabbit's Ear, Signed, Christian Thomsen, 5 1/4 In. 200.00
Figurine, Satyr, Seated On Columns, Stamped Wave Mark, 8 1/2 In., Pair 269.00
Group, Mother & Child, Stamped Wave Mark, 10 1/4 In. 191.00
Mug, Hans Andersen, 1971, 3 In. 30.00
Mug, Mogens Andersen, 1987, 3 In. 40.00
Mug, Niels Thorson, 1967, 3 In. 200.00
Mug, Silver Base Disk, Bodil Buch, 1974, 4 1/2 In. 40.00
Mug, Silver Base Disk, Ellen Malmer, 1968, 4 1/2 In. 60.00
Mug, Silver Base Disk, Ivan Weiss, 1984, 4 1/2 In. 40.00
Perfume Bottle, Stopper, Nude, Flying Goose, Label, 4 3/4 In. 140.00
Plate, Chop, Flora Danica, Botanical, 19th Century, 15 In. 1840.00
Plate, Christmas, 1908, Madonna & Child, 6 In. 6000.00
Plate, Christmas, 1909, Danish Landscape, 6 In. 220.00
Plate, Christmas, 1910, Magi, 6 In. 195.00
Plate, Christmas, 1911, Danish Landscape, 7 In. 165.00
Plate, Christmas, 1913, Spire Of Frederik's Church, Copenhagen, 7 In. 180.00
Plate, Christmas, 1914, Sparrows In Tree At Church, 7 In. 160.00
Plate, Christmas, 1915, Danish Landscape, 7 In. 160.00
Plate, Christmas, 1916, Shepherds In Field On Christmas Night, 7 In. 110.00
Plate, Christmas, 1919, In The Park, 7 In. 100.00
Plate, Christmas, 1920, Mary With Child Jesus, 7 In. 85.00
Plate, Christmas, 1922, 3 Singing Angels, 7 In. 75.00
Plate, Christmas, 1924, Christmas Star Over The Sea, 7 In. 115.00

Sculptures should be dusted with a clean, dry paintbrush. Never use water.

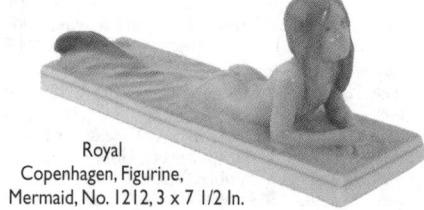

Royal Copenhagen, Figurine, Mermaid, No. 1212, 3 x 7 1/2 In.

Plate, Christmas, 1925, Street Scene From Christianshavn, 7 In.	90.00
Plate, Christmas, 1927, Ship's Boy At Tiller, 7 In.	125.00
Plate, Christmas, 1928, Vicar Family On Way To Church, 7 In.	90.00
Plate, Christmas, 1931, Mother & Child, 7 In.	120.00
Plate, Christmas, 1932, Statue Of King Frederik VI, 7 In.	120.00
Plate, Christmas, 1936, Roskilde Cathedral, 7 In.	220.00
Plate, Christmas, 1938, Round Church In Osterlars Bornholm, 7 In.	330.00
Plate, Christmas, 1939, Expedionary Ship In Pack-Ice Of Greenland, 7 In.	475.00
Plate, Christmas, 1940, Good Shepherd, 7 In.	550.00
Plate, Christmas, 1941, Danish Village Church, 7 In.	450.00
Plate, Christmas, 1942, Bell-Tower Of Old In Jutland, 7 In.	550.00
Plate, Christmas, 1943, Flight Of Holy Family To Egypt, 7 In.	680.00
Plate, Christmas, 1944, Typical Danish Winter Scene, 7 In.	350.00
Plate, Christmas, 1947, Good Shepherd, 7 In.	320.00
Plate, Christmas, 1950, Boeslunde Church, 7 In.	250.00
Plate, Christmas, 1951, Christmas Angel, Opening Door, 7 In.	450.00
Plate, Christmas, 1953, Frederiksborg Castle, Hillerod, 7 In.	130.00
Plate, Christmas, 1956, Rosenborg Castle, Copenhagen, 7 In.	150.00
Plate, Christmas, 1957, Good Shepherd, Herd, 7 In.	110.00
Plate, Christmas, 1960, Stag, In Forest, 7 In.	140.00
Plate, Christmas, 1962, Little Mermaid At Wintertime, 7 In.	180.00
Plate, Christmas, 1963, Hojsager Windmill, Snow Covered Landscape, 7 In.	60.00
Plate, Christmas, 1965, Little Skaters, 7 In.	55.00
Plate, Christmas, 1966, Blackbird At Christmas Time, 7 In.	45.00
Plate, Christmas, 1969, Old Farmyard, 7 In.	35.00
Plate, Christmas, 1971, Hare In Winter, 7 In.	32.00
Plate, Christmas, 1973, Going Home For Christmas, 7 In.	24.00
Plate, Christmas, 1974, Winter Twilight, 7 In.	35.00
Plate, Christmas, 1976, Vibaek Mill, 7 In.	35.00
Plate, Christmas, 1978, Greenland Scenery, 7 In.	35.00
Plate, Christmas, 1984, Jingle Bells, 7 In.	37.00
Plate, Christmas, 1985, Snowman, 7 In.	75.00
Plate, Christmas, 1987, Winter Birds, 7 In.	65.00
Plate, Mother & Child, 1982, Mother Robin & Her Young	40.00
Plate, Mother & Child, 1986, Mother Dog & Her Young	40.00
Plate, Mother's Day, 1971, American Mother	10.00
Plate, Mother's Day, 1979, A Loving Mother	30.00
Plate, Mother's Day, 1982, Children's Hour	40.00
Platter, Flora Danica, Botanical, 19th Century, 19 In.	2530.00
Platter, Flora Danica, Round, Reticulated, Marked, 13 In., Pair	3220.00
Tureen, Flora Danica, Oval, Gold Trim, Crabstock Handle, 15 5/8 In.	1530.00
Vase, 7 Bats, Landscape, Town, 7 1/2 In.	1000.00
Vase, Butterfly, Handle, Pre 1923, 7 In.	300.00
Vase, Carved Leaves, Brown, Signed, Melihe, Stamped, c.1960, 1 3/4 x 3 In., Pair	145.00
Vase, Ducks, 1923-30, 9 1/2 In.	300.00
Vase, Flowers, Art Nouveau, 1923-30, 8 In.	400.00
Vase, Nils Thorsson, Sea Life, Blue High Glaze, 7 In.	825.00
Vase, Nude Woman & Man, Black De Chine, H.H. Hansen, 1945, 9 In.	350.00
Vase, Stylized Eye Decoration, Blue, White, 7 In.	70.00

ROYAL COPLEY china was made by the Spaulding China Company of Sebring, Ohio, from 1939 to 1960. The figural planters and the small figurines, especially those with Art Deco designs, are of great collector interest.

Figurine, Duck, Tan, Blue, Brown, 5 x 6 In.	24.00
Head Vase, Wall Pocket, Oriental Girl, Large Hat, Maroon & Grey, 7 1/2 In.	50.00
Planter, Dog, At Mailbox, 8 1/2 In.	45.00
Planter, Duck, Eating Grass, 5 1/2 In.	19.00
Planter, Rooster, 7 1/4 x 7 3/4 In.	50.00
Vase, Cream, Rose Decal, 2 Handles, 6 In.	20.00
Vase, Philodendron Leaves, White Ground, High Glaze, 7 1/4 In.	36.00

ROYAL CROWN DERBY

ROYAL CROWN DERBY Company, Ltd., was established in England in 1890. There is a complex family tree that includes the Derby, Crown Derby, and Royal Crown Derby porcelains. The Royal Crown Derby mark includes the name and a crown. The words *Made in England* were used after 1921. The company is now a part of Royal Doulton Tableware Ltd.

Knife Set, Fruit, Decorated Handles, Marked, Fitted Case, 7 In., 6 Piece	230.00
Paperweight, Imperial Panda, Signed, Hugh Gibson, 4 In.	70.00
Plate, Service, Ivory Ground, Raised Fruit, Flowers, 1900, 10 In., 12 Piece	6900.00
Saucer, Coffee, After Dinner, Imari Design, Late 19th Century, 4 1/2 In., Pair	60.00
Tea & Coffee Service, Imari Pattern, Pattern 1128, 4 Piece	940.00
Vase, Cover, Flowers, Bronzed, Silvered, Gilded, c.1894, 14 1/2 In.	2115.00
Vase, Cover, Raised Gold & Enamel Fruit, Leaves, c.1891, 6 1/2 In.	645.00
Vase, Gilt, Cobalt Blue Ground, 2 Handles, C. Harris, 1899, 11 1/2 In.	2400.00
Vase, Painted Flowers, Gilt Decoration, Signed, Leroy, c.1904, 8 In.	6325.00
Vase, Pink Glazed Background, Gilt, Bottle Shape, 9 x 5 1/2 In.	60.00
Vase, Portrait, Baluster Form, Oval Cartouche, Ruby Ground, 13 In., Pair	3585.00

ROYAL DOULTON

ROYAL DOULTON is the name used on Doulton and Company pottery made from 1902 to the present. Doulton and Company of England was founded in 1853. Pieces made before 1902 are listed in this book under Doulton. Royal Doulton collectors search for the out-of-production figurines, character jugs, vases, and series wares. Some vases and animal figurines were made with a special red glaze called flambe. Sung and Chang glazed pieces are rare. The multicolored glaze is very thick and looks as if it were dropped on the clay.

Animal, Cat, Character Kitten, Licking Paw, HN 2580, 2 1/2 In.	105.00
Animal, Cat, Lucky, Black, White Face, K 12, 2 3/4 In.	130.00
Animal, Dog, Bulldog, HN 1044, 3 x 6 In.	250.00
Animal, Dog, Cocker Spaniel, Black, Lucky Star Of Ware, HN 1021, 3 1/2 In.	175.00
Animal, Dog, Cocker Spaniel, White & Brown, HN 1037, 5 In.	195.00
Animal, Dog, Dachshund, Smooth, K 17	95.00
Animal, Dog, Pekinese, HN 1012, 4 1/2 In.	215.00
Animal, Dog, Terrier, Yawnng, White & Brown, HN 1099, 4 1/2 In.	100.00
Animal, Elephant, Trunk Up, HN 2644, 4 x 6 In.	125.00
Animal, Horse, Shetland Pony, Brown, DA 47, 5 1/2 In.	110.00
Animal, Leaping Salmon, Flambe, HN 666, 1940-50, 12 1/2 In.	633.00

Royal Doulton character jugs depict the head and shoulders of the subject. They are made in four sizes: large, 5 1/4 to 7 inches; small, 3 1/4 to 4 inches; miniature, 2 1/4 to 2 1/2 inches; and tiny, 1 1/4 inches. Toby jugs portray a seated, full figure.

Character Jug, Aramis, D 6441, Large	80.00
Character Jug, Collector, D 6796, Large	149.00
Character Jug, Dick Whittington, D 6375, Large	55.00
Character Jug, Falstaff, D 6287, Large	49.00
Character Jug, George III & George Washington, D 6749, Large	138.00
Character Jug, Granny, D 5521, Large	49.00
Character Jug, Izaak Walton, D 6404, Large	63.00
Character Jug, Lord Nelson, D 6336, Large	138.00
Character Jug, Mephistopheles, D 5758, Small	604.00
Character Jug, North American Indian, D 6611, Large	130.00
Character Jug, Old King Cole, D 6871, Tiny	49.00
Character Jug, Sairey Gamp, D 5451, Large	49.00
Character Jug, Santa Claus, D 6705, Small	49.00
Character Jug, Snowman, Holly & Berry Handle, D 7062, Miniature	99.00
Character Jug, Snowman, Robin & Wreath Handle, D 7159, Miniature	99.00
Character Jug, St. George, D 6618, Large	199.00
Character Jug, Touchstone, D 5613, Large	199.00
Character Jug, Winston Churchill, D 6171, Large	193.00
Charger, Dickens, Tony Weller, 12 1/2 In.	127.00
Dinner Set, Canterbury, Grapevine, 48 Piece	374.00
Dinner Set, English Renaissance, 59 Piece	575.00

Dinner Set,	Rosell, 59 Piece	288.00
Dinner Set,	Selborne, Transfer Print, c.1896, 39 Piece	345.00
Ewer,	Birds, Flowers, 12 3/4 In.	588.00
Figurine,	4 O'Clock, HN 1760, 1936-49	1800.00
Figurine,	Ace, HN 3398, 1991-95	125.00
Figurine,	Adrienne, HN 2152, 1964-76	200.00
Figurine,	Alexandra, HN 2398, 1970-76	129.00
Figurine,	Alfred The Great, HN 3821, 1996-97	325.00
Figurine,	And So To Bed, HN 2966, 1982-85	250.00
Figurine,	Angela, HN 3419, 1992	300.00
Figurine,	Arnold Bennett, HN 4360	250.00
Figurine,	Balinese Dancer, HN 2808, 1982	825.00
Figurine,	Beachcomber, HN 2487, 1973-76	225.00
Figurine,	Beggar, HN 526, 1921-49	1200.00
Figurine,	Biddy Penny Farthing, HN 1843, 8 1/2 In.	150.00
Figurine,	Biddy, HN 1445, 1931-37	450.00
Figurine,	Bon Jour, HN 1888, 1938-49	1800.00
Figurine,	Boy From Williamsburg, HN 2183, 1969-83	225.00
Figurine,	Bride, HN 1600, 1933-49	1800.00
Figurine,	Bridesmaid, HN 2874, 1980-89	100.00
Figurine,	Bridesmaid, M11, 1932-38	550.00
Figurine,	Buddies, Matte, HN 2546, 1973-76	225.00
Figurine,	Bunnykins, Buntie Helping Mother, DB 2, 1972-93	65.00
Figurine,	Bunnykins, Caddie, DB 271	65.00
Figurine,	Bunnykins, Digger, DB 248	185.00
Figurine,	Bunnykins, Fireman, DB 75, 1989	40.00
Figurine,	Bunnykins, Henry VIII, DB 305	43.00
Figurine,	Bunnykins, Home Run, DB 43, 1986-93	75.00
Figurine,	Bunnykins, Jockey, DB 169, 1997	225.00
Figurine,	Bunnykins, Little Miss Muffet, DB 240	50.00
Figurine,	Bunnykins, Matador, DB 281	175.00
Figurine,	Bunnykins, Old Balloon Seller, DB 217	99.00
Figurine,	Bunnykins, Samurai, DB 280	175.00
Figurine,	Bunnykins, Uncle Sam, DB 175, 1997	200.00
Figurine,	Bunnykins, Wizard, DB 168, 1997	325.00
Figurine,	Buttercup, HN 2309, 1964-97	200.00
Figurine,	Catherine, HN 3451, 1993-99	100.00
Figurine,	Charity, HN 3087, 1987	450.00
Figurine,	Charley's Aunt, HN 35, 1913-36	1100.00
Figurine,	Chloe, M 9, 1932-45	500.00
Figurine,	Christmas Day, HN 3488, 1993-99	125.00
Figurine,	Clarissa, HN 2345, 1968-81	129.00
Figurine,	Cobbler, HN 1705, 1935-49	1300.00
Figurine,	Cobbler, HN 1706, 1935-69	350.00
Figurine,	Corinthian, HN 1973, 1941-49	1800.00
Figurine,	Corporal, 1st New Hampshire Regiment, 1778, HN 2780, 1975	1400.00
Figurine,	Cup Of Tea, HN 2322, 1964-83	250.00
Figurine,	Daddy's Girl, HN 3435, 1993-98	150.00
Figurine,	Damaris, HN 2079, 1951-52	2300.00
Figurine,	Darby, HN 1427, 1930-49	450.00
Figurine,	Daydreams, HN 1731, 1935-96	199.00
Figurine,	Deidre, HN 2020, 1949-55	600.00
Figurine,	Do You Wonder Where Fairies Are, HN 1544, 1933-49	1400.00
Figurine,	Dulcie, HN 2305, 1981-84	149.00
Figurine,	Eleanor Of Provence, HN 2009, 1948-53	825.00
Figurine,	Ellen Terry, HN 3826, 1996	550.00
Figurine,	Elsie Maynard, HN 639, 1924-49	1600.00
Figurine,	Ermine Coat, HN 1981, 1945-67	450.00
Figurine,	Evelyn, HN 1637, 1934-40	1800.00
Figurine,	Fair Maiden, HN 2211, 1967-94	99.00
Figurine,	Fat Boy, HN 555, 1923-39	725.00
Figurine,	Father Christmas, HN 3399, 1992-99	350.00
Figurine,	First Violin, HN 3704, 1995	550.00

Figurine, Fleur, HN 2368, 1968-95	200.00
Figurine, French Horn, HN 2795, 1976	1000.00
Figurine, Frodo, HN 2912, 1980-84	175.00
Figurine, Gardener, HN 3161, 1988-91	300.00
Figurine, Gay Morning, HN 2135, 1954-67	375.00
Figurine, Gentlewoman, HN 1632, 1934-49	1200.00
Figurine, Georgiana, HN 2093, 1952-55	2000.00
Figurine, Giselle, HN 2139, 1954-69	475.00
Figurine, Gollywog, HN 1979, 1945-59	195.00
Figurine, Good King Wenceslas, HN 2118, 1953-76	120.00
Figurine, Good King Wenceslas, HN 3262, 1989-92	125.00
Figurine, Grace, HN 2318, 1966-81	275.00
Figurine, Granny's Heritage, HN 2031, 1949-69	725.00
Figurine, Gretchen, HN 1562, 1933-40	1500.00
Figurine, Groucho Marx, HN 2777, 1991	475.00
Figurine, Hazel, HN 3167, 1988-91	325.00
Figurine, Heidi, HN 2975, 1983-85	200.00
Figurine, Helen, HN 2994, 1985-87	2994.00
Figurine, Henrietta Maria, HN 2005, 1948-53	825.00
Figurine, Herminia, HN 1644, 1934-38	2000.00
Figurine, Hilary, HN 2335, 1967-81	149.00
Figurine, Ibrahim, HN 2095, 1952-55	600.00
Figurine, In The Stocks, HN 2163, 1955-59	1000.00
Figurine, Jacqueline, HN 2333, 1982-91	225.00
Figurine, James, HN 3013, 1983-87	675.00
Figurine, Janet, M 69, 1936-49	825.00
Figurine, Jennifer, HN 2392, 1982-92	325.00
Figurine, Jester, HN 2016, 1949-97	120.00
Figurine, Jolly Sailor, HN 2172, 1956-65	1000.00
Figurine, Judith, HN 2089, 1952-59	425.00
Figurine, Julie, HN 2995, 1985-95	100.00
Figurine, June, M 65, 1935-49	900.00
Figurine, Karen, HN 1994, 1947-55	675.00
Figurine, Kate Hardcastle, HN 1719, 1935-49	1300.00
Figurine, Kate, HN 2789, 1978-87	225.00
Figurine, Lalla Rookh, HN 2910, 1981	675.00
Figurine, Lillie Langtry, HN 3820, 1996	500.00
Figurine, Linda, HN 4450, 2002	275.00
Figurine, Little Bo Peep, HN 3030, 1984-87	175.00
Figurine, Little Boy Blue, HN 2062, 1950-73	225.00
Figurine, Lobster Man, HN 2317, 1964-94	225.00
Figurine, Marguerite, HN 1946, 1940-49	2250.00
Figurine, Marianne, HN 2074, 1951-53	1600.00
Figurine, Marie Sisley, HN 3475, 1994	675.00
Figurine, Marjorie, HN 2788, 1980-84	325.00
Figurine, Mary Queen Of Scots, HN 3142, 1989	900.00
Figurine, Masquerade Man, HN 599, 1924-36	1400.00
Figurine, Mayor, HN 2280, 1963-71	425.00
Figurine, Memories, HN 2030, 1949-59	625.00
Figurine, Mirabell, M 68, 1936-49	900.00
Figurine, Miss Demure, HN 1402, 1930-75	300.00
Figurine, Moor, Flambe Glaze, HN 3642, 1994-95, 17 1/2 In.	2500.00
Figurine, Mr. Micawber, HN 557, 1923-39	725.00
Figurine, My Love, HN 2339, 1969-96	149.00
Figurine, Newsboy, HN 2244, 1959-65	600.00
Figurine, Old Balloon Seller, HN 1315, 1929-98	225.00
Figurine, Old King, HN 2134, 1954-92	300.00
Figurine, Olga, HN 2463, 1972-75	149.00
Figurine, Once Upon A Time, HN 2047, 1949-55	575.00
Figurine, Ophelia, HN 3674, 1995	450.00
Figurine, Organ Grinder, HN 2173, 1956-65	1300.00
Figurine, Owd Willum, HN 2042, 1949-73	325.00
Figurine, Paisley Shawl, M 4, 1932-45	375.00

Figurine, Pantalettes, M 15, 1932-45 .... 575.00
Figurine, Parisian, HN 2445, 1972-75... 225.00
Figurine, Past Glory, HN 2484, 1973-79.. 375.00
Figurine, Patricia, M 28, 1932-45 .... 575.00
Figurine, Patricia, M 7, 1932-45 .... 575.00
Figurine, Penny's Worth, HN 2408, 1986-90 .... 225.00
Figurine, Penny, HN 2338, 1968-95 .... 100.00
Figurine, Pillow Fight, HN 2270, 1965-69 .... 325.00
Figurine, Pocahontas, HN 2930, 1982 .... 1300.00
Figurine, Polly Peachum, HN 549, 1922-49 .... 850.00
Figurine, Pretty Polly, HN 2768, 1984-86 .... 225.00
Figurine, Prince Of Wales, HN 1217, 1926-38 .... 2200.00
Figurine, Priscilla, HN 1340, 1929-49 .... 600.00
Figurine, Priscilla, M 24, 1932-45 .... 550.00
Figurine, Private Rhode Island Regiment 1781, HN 2759, 1977 .... 1300.00
Figurine, Professor, HN 2281, 1965-81 .... 225.00
Figurine, Queen Anne, HN 3141, 1988 .... 550.00
Figurine, Queen Elizabeth The Queen Mother, HN 2882, 1980 .... 900.00
Figurine, Romany Sue, HN 1757, 1936-49 .... 2000.00
Figurine, Rosamund, M 33, 1932-45.. 1000.00
Figurine, Rose, HN 1368, 1930-95 .... 100.00
Figurine, Ruth, Kate Greenaway Series, Green Dress, HN 2799, 1976-81, 6 In. 235.00
Figurine, Santa Claus, HN 4175, 2000 .... 340.00
Figurine, Sara, HN 2265, 1981-2000 .... 300.00
Figurine, Sarah Bernhardt, HN 4023, 1998 .... 400.00
Figurine, Sea Harvest, HN 2257, 1969-76 .... 375.00
Figurine, Sergeant Virginia 1st Regiment 1777, HN 2844, 1978 .... 4500.00
Figurine, Sheikh, HN 3083, 1987-89 .... 225.00
Figurine, Sir Walter Raleigh, HN 1751, 1936-49 .... 1600.00
Figurine, Sleepyhead, HN 3761, 1996-98 .... 150.00
Figurine, Spanish Flamenco Dancer, HN 2831, 1977 .... 1400.00
Figurine, Springtime, HN 3033, 1983 .... 149.00
Figurine, Stitch In Time, HN 2352, 1966-81 .... 250.00
Figurine, Stop Press, HN 2683, 1977-81.. 225.00
Figurine, Susan, HN 2056, 1950-59 .... 525.00
Figurine, Suzette, HN 1487, 1931-50 .... 625.00
Figurine, Sweet Anne, M 5, 1932-45 .... 425.00
Figurine, Sweet Dreams, HN 2380, 1971-90 .... 149.00
Figurine, Teatime, HN 2255, 1972-95 .... 250.00
Figurine, Teresa, HN 1682, 1935-49 .... 2700.00
Figurine, Toinette, HN 1940, 1940-49 .... 2700.00
Figurine, Town Crier, HN 2119, 1953-76 .... 250.00
Figurine, Tuppence A Bag, HN 2320, 1968-95 .... 150.00
Figurine, Valerie, HN 2107, 1953-95 .... 125.00
Figurine, Vera, HN 1729, 1935-40 .... 1200.00
Figurine, Victorian Lady, M 1, 1932-45 .... 600.00
Figurine, Vivienne, HN 2073, 1951-67 .... 375.00
Figurine, Votes For Women, HN 2816, 1978-81 .... 300.00
Figurine, Wayfarer, HN 2362, 1970-76 .... 250.00
Figurine, Wee Willie Winkie, HN 2050, 1949-53 .... 400.00
Figurine, West Indian Dancer, HN 2384, 1981 .... 825.00
Figurine, Winsome, HN 2220, 1960-85 .... 129.00
Figurine, Wizard, HN 2877 .... 120.00
Figurine, Yeoman Of The Guard, HN 2122, 1954-59 .... 900.00
Figurine, Yum-Yum, HN 2899, 1980-85 .... 900.00
Figurine, Yvonne, HN 3038, 1987-92 .... 225.00
Garniture, Cobalt Blue, Gold, Longneck, Aesthetic Style, 16 In., Pair 2530.00
Humidor, Cover, Country Landscape, Mark, 5 3/4 In. 207.00
Jardiniere, Neoclassical Figures, Mustard Band, Ruby Ground, 10 1/4 In. 837.00
Match Striker, Dewar's, Brown & Green Mottled Glaze, c.1920, 4 1/2 In. 111.00
Pitcher, Old Bob Ye Guard, Coaching Party, Series Ware, 7 3/4 In. 173.00
Pitcher & Bowl, Transfer Prints, Blue, Gold, Art Nouveau, c.1910, 12 3/4 In. 460.00
Plate, Cobalt Blue, Gilt Scroll Border, RA 3454, 10 1/4 In., 12 Piece 1610.00

Plate, Flowering Tree, Art Deco, 1915, 10 In., 12 Piece 690.00
Plate, Hudson-Fulton Celebration, Zeppelins, Biplanes, Ships, Transfer, 1909, 10 In. 153.00
Plate, Shakespeare, Shylock, 8 1/2 In. 46.00
Pub Jug, Mr. Pickwick, Jim Beam, 3 3/4 In. 44.00
Teapot, Balloon Man & Woman, D 7171, 2002, 7 1/4 In. 175.00
Teapot, Cowboy & Indian, D 7176, 2002, 7 In. 175.00
Teapot, Gamekeeper & Poacher, D 7175, 2002, 6 1/2 In. 175.00
Teapot, Pirate & Captain, D 7182, 2003, 6 3/4 In. 175.00
Toby Jug, Falstaff, D 6062, Large ....71.00 to 97.00
Urn, Flowers In Ribbon-Tied Gilt Wreath, Ovoid, 2 Gilt Handles, Footed, 10 In. 460.00
Vase, Babes In The Woods, Child Picking Flowers, 6 In. 200.00
Vase, Babes In The Woods, Child With Basket, Cylindrical, 7 In. 350.00
Vase, Blue Crystalline Matte Glaze, Applied Peacock Feather Eyes, 2 In. 58.00
Vase, Cover, Cattle In Woods, Gilt, Handles, c.1910, 12 1/2 In. 2267.00
Vase, Flambe Sung, Blue, Black, Green, Yellow, c.1920, 6 3/4 In. 920.00
Vase, Flambe Sung, Mottled Purple & Blue Glaze, Red Ground, 1930s, 5 1/2 In. 1208.00
Vase, Flambe, Cows In Barnyard, Marked, 9 1/2 In. 431.00
Vase, Flambe, Dragon, Stylized Clouds, Oval, 1920s, 18 In. 9488.00
Vase, Flambe, Mottled White, Brown, Black Glaze, Black Ground, 1930s, 6 In. 259.00
Vase, Flambe, Mottled, Blue, Yellow, Green, Red Ground, 1930s, 6 In. 345.00
Vase, Flambe, Mottled, Yellow, Green, Blue, Brown, Red Ground, 1930s, 10 In. 311.00
Vase, Flowers, Raised, Blue, Purple, Green, No. 8218, 7 In., Pair 470.00
Vase, Midnight Blue Glaze, Oval, Pinched Sides, 5 In. 81.00
Vase, Sheep, Incised, Blue, Green, Brown & Ivory Design, 7 In. 529.00
Vase, Stylized Diamond & Leaf Design, Translucent Glaze, c.1925, 10 In. 264.00
Vase, Stylized Flowers, Mottled Gray Green Ground, 11 In. 150.00
Vase, Tailed Swirls, Squares, Mottled Gray Blue, Slip, 5 7/8 In. 127.00
Vase, Titanian, Bird On Bamboo Stalk, Cylindrical, 10 x 3 1/4 In. 764.00
Vase, Titanian, Herring Gulls, c.1925, 7 3/4 In. 1645.00

ROYAL DUX is the more common name for the Duxer Porzellanman-
ufaktur, which was founded by E. Eichler in Dux, Bohemia, in 1860.
By the turn of the century, the firm specialized in porcelain statuary
and busts of Art Nouveau–style maidens, large porcelain figures, and
ornate vases with three-dimensional figures climbing on the sides. The
firm is still in business.

Bowl, Figural, Sheep Herder, Holding Flute & Sheep, 13 x 13 In. 600.00
Bowl, Pedestal, Shepherd Boy, Mother, Sheep, Triangle Mark, 15 1/2 x 10 In. 900.00
Bust, Woman, Flowers In Hair, Smelling Flower, Art Nouveau, 10 1/2 x 9 In. 411.00
Figurine, Horses & Rider, 13 x 12 In. 800.00
Figurine, Hounds, Oval Base, Painted, 8 In., Pair 168.00
Figurine, Man, Moroccan Water Bearer, Wearing Robe, c.1920, 15 1/2 In. 382.00
Figurine, Man, Woman, Water Bearers, Landscaped Base, 24 In., Pair 1495.00
Figurine, Pheasant, 9 In., Pair 138.00
Group, Vide Poche, Man On Rocky Outcrop, Sea Nymph, Hempel, c.1900, 12 1/4 In. 1508.00

ROYAL FLEMISH glass was made during the late 1880s in New Bedford, Massachusetts, by the Mt. Washington Glass Works. It is a colored satin glass decorated with dark colors and raised gold designs.
The glass was patented in 1894. It was supposed to resemble stained
glass windows.

Sugar Shaker, Enameled Flowers, Fig Shape, Metal Shaker Cap, 3 3/4 In. 2590.00
Vase, Cover, Amethyst, Mauve, Silver & Gold Roses, Gold Finial, 11 1/2 In. 12650.00
Vase, Peacock, Gold Enamel, Applied Red Jewels On Branch, Gold Leaves, 13 In. 5463.00
Vase, Thistle Design, Gold Trim, Pulled Neck, 11 In. 1100.00
Vase, Thistle, Gold Tracery, Frosted, Squat Base, Long Neck, 11 In. 1265.00
Vase, Winged Dragon, Beast Head, 7 1/2 In. 4313.00

ROYAL HAEGER, see Haeger category.

ROYAL HICKMAN designed pottery, glass, silver, aluminum, furniture, lamps, and other items. From 1938 to 1944 and again from the
1950s to 1969, he worked for Haeger Potteries. Mr. Hickman operated
his own pottery in Tampa, Florida, during the 1940s. He moved to Cal-

ifornia and worked for Vernon Potteries. The last years of his life he livd in Guadalajara, Mexico, and continued designing for Royal Haeger. Pieces made in his pottery listed here are marked *Royal Hickman* or *Hickman*.

Vase, Pink, Green Crystalline Top, Petty Glaze, Mid 1940s, 11 In. 115.00

ROYAL IVY, see Northwood, Royal Ivy

ROYAL NYMPHENBURG is the modern name for the Nymphenburg porcelain factory, which was established at Neudeck-ob-der-Au, Germany, in 1753 and moved to Nymphenburg in 1761. The company is still in existence. Marks include a checkered shield topped by a crown, a crowned *CT* with the year, and a contemporary shield mark on reproductions of eighteenth-century porcelain.

Group, Playful Putti, Crown Blue Underglaze Mark, 14 In. 633.00

ROYAL OAK pieces are listed in the Pressed Glass category by that pattern name.

ROYAL RUDOLSTADT, see Rudolstadt category.

ROYAL VIENNA, see Beehive category.

ROYAL WORCESTER is a name used by collectors. Worcester porcelains were made in Worcester, England, from about 1751. The firm went through many different periods and name changes. It became the Worcester Royal Porcelain Company, Ltd., in 1862. Today collectors call the porcelains made after 1862 *Royal Worcester*. In 1976, the firm merged with W. T. Copeland to become Royal Worcester Spode. Some early products of the factory are listed under Worcester.

Bowl, Salad, Leaf Molded, 3 Handles, England, c.1899, 9 In. 560.00
Bust, Alexandra, Princess Of Wales, Circular Socle, Parian, c.1864, 12 1/2 In. 470.00
Creamer, Spouted, Flowers, 3 1/2 In. 10.00
Cup & Saucer, Cobalt Blue Band, Gilt Arabesques, 1938, 6 Sets 460.00
Demitasse Set, Cup, Saucer, Spoon, Gilt Lace, Leather Case, c.1880, 2 In., 6 Sets 1093.00
Dish, Boy & Girl Holding Large Basket, 9 1/2 In. 390.00
Ewer, Figural Ram's Head, Gilt Flowers, 9 In. 290.00
Ewer, Flowers, Raised Gold, Enamel, Scroll Handle, Marked, c.1899, 13 1/4 In. 380.00
Ewer, Flowers, RW Mark, 14 In. 100.00
Figurine, Bather Surprised, 1895, 24 3/4 In. 1415.00
Figurine, Bird, Thrush, Lady Slippers, Blue Iris, Dorothy Doughty, 9 1/2 In., Pair 2300.00
Figurine, Boy With Basket, Dancing Girl, 8 1/2 In., Pair 420.00
Figurine, Downy Woodpeckers, Dorothy Doughty, c.1967, 11 1/4 In. 805.00
Figurine, Kneeling Water Bearers, Man & Woman, 10 1/4 In., Pair 1135.00
Figurine, Robin, Dorothy Doughty, 1964, 6 3/4 In. .... *Illus* 748.00
Figurine, Water Baby, Young Child, Marked, F.G. Daughty, 6 In. 200.00
Figurine, Water Carriers, 31 1/2 In., Pair 3885.00
Flower Frog, Marked, 3 3/4 In. 30.00
Jardiniere, Decorated, Highland Cattle, Signed John Stinton, 8 x 10 1/2 In. 4185.00
Jug, Decorated, Flowers, Ivory Ground, 9 In. 180.00

Royal Worcester, Figurine, Robin, Dorothy Doughty, 1964, 6 3/4 In.

When buying postcards remember: the larger the city the lower the value of the card. The smaller the city the higher the value of the card because fewer cards were made.

Jug, Flower Handle Finial, Painted, Gilt, Wildflowers, c.1897, 8 In. 220.00
Oyster Plate, Shell Shape Dishes, 6 Piece 225.00
Pitcher, Applied Salamander, Marked, 6 In. 1100.00
Pitcher, Gold Flowers, Marked, 10 In. 185.00
Plate, Dessert, Fruits, Flower, Gilt Border, A Shuck, 1925, 9 In., 6 Piece 2160.00
Plate, Dinner, Cordova, 10 1/2 In., 12 Piece 520.00
Plate, Flowers, Gilt Rims, Hand Painted, A.H. Williamson, 9 1/4 In., 12 Piece 375.00
Plate, Painted, Gilt, Cream Ground, Swans, Marshland, c.1887, 8 1/2 In. 1845.00
Platter, Game, Pheasants, Pheasant Handles, Oval, c.1891, 17 3/4 In. 800.00
Rose Bowl, Flowers, Marked, 2 3/4 In. 75.00
Sugar & Creamer, Cover, Cream Background, Rose Decoration, 5 In. 80.00
Tazza, Blue Ribbon Border, Beaded Gilt Border, Late 19th Century, 5 1/2 In. 59.00
Tazza, Low, Leaf Molded, Gilt & Enamel Flower Design, c.1887, 10 In. 175.00
Urn, Cover, Embossed, Handle, Reticulated Neck, Bronzed Finish, 14 1/2 In. 750.00
Vase, 2 Handles, Decorated With Roses, 9 1/2 In. 780.00
Vase, Bamboo, Ivory, Gold & Red Enameling, 3 Branch Handles, 1883, 6 3/4 In. 500.00
Vase, Bud, Flowers, Handles, 6 1/2 In. 75.00
Vase, Finches, Gorse, Cream Ground, 2 Handles, 1901, 14 3/4 In. 10135.00
Vase, Flowers, Footed, Marked, 3 In. 85.00
Vase, Flowers, Vase, Flowers, Cobalt, Openwork On Neck, Handles, Marked, 14 In. 165.00
Vase, Gilt & Enamel Flowers, Elongated Neck, Pointed Handles, c.1891, 10 In. 295.00
Vase, Gilt Rural Scenes, Gilt Seeding, Pierced Outer Body, Egg Shape, 4 In. 2415.00
Vase, Landscape, Pheasants, Enamel, Dolphin Head Handles, c.1921, 12 In. 650.00
Vase, Majolica, Handles, Molded, Painted, Branches, Basket Weave, 7 1/2 In. 336.00
Vase, Posy, Birds, Enamel, Painted, Gilt Trim Borders, c.1883, 5 In. 265.00
Vase, Potpourri, Cover, Swans, 2 Handles, 1898, 9 1/4 In. 4800.00
Vase, Swans, Gilt Reeds, Sunset, Octagonal, Drilled, Late 1800s, 16 1/4 In. 2400.00
Vase, Swans, Persian Style, Raised Gilding, 2 Handles, 1889, 20 1/2 In. 3600.00

ROYCROFT products were made by the Roycrofter community of
East Aurora, New York, in the late nineteenth and early twentieth centuries. The community was founded by Elbert Hubbard, famous
philosopher, writer, and artist. The workshops owned by the community made furniture, metalware, leatherwork, embroidery, and jewelry.
A printshop produced many signs, books, and the magazines that promoted the sayings of Elbert Hubbard. Furniture by the Roycroft community is listed in the Furniture category.

Andirons, Curls, Rivets, Twisted Links, No. 069, 24 x 14 1/2 In. 2350.00
Bench, Ali Baba, Split Log, Intact Bark, 44 x 14 x 19 In. 16415.00
Bookends, Copper, Hammered, 5 In. 240.00
Bookends, Copper, Hammered, Curled Riveted Arch, 5 x 4 In. 410.00
Bookends, Copper, Hammered, Tooled Designs, 5 In. 325.00
Bookends, Hammered Copper, Impressed Mark, 8 1/2 In. 145.00
Bowl, Copper, Hammered, 3-Footed, Orb, Cross Mark, 10 1/4 In. 380.00
Bowl, Copper, Hammered, Squat, 10 3/4 In. 825.00
Box, Copper, Hammered, Hinged, Quatrefoil, Hinged, 1 3/4 x 7 x 3 1/2 In. 500.00
Box, Cover, Tooled Leather, Suede Lining, Poppy Medallion, 1 1/2 x 4 x 4 In. 560.00
Box, Pine, Hammered Copper Handles, Corner Brackets, 9 1/4 x 23 x 12 1/4 In. 590.00
Candlestick, 3-Socket, Copper, Hammered, Curled Bands, 3 x 8 1/4 In., Pair 590.00
Candlestick, Copper, Hammered, Brass Wash, Princess, Wood Grain Pattern, 8 In., Pair ... 1175.00
Candlestick, Copper, Hammered, Column Shaft, 6 1/4 In. 175.00
Candlestick, Copper, Hammered, Nickel Plated, 3 1/2 In., Pair 90.00
Candlestick, Copper, Hammered, Peasant, Wood Grain Pattern, 6 1/2 In. 2470.00
Candlestick, Princess, Brass Washed, Double Shaft, Faceted Base, 7 1/2 In., Pair 765.00
Crumber Set, Copper, Hammered, Tooled Flowers, 8 In., 2 Piece 175.00
Desk Set, Brass Washed, Stylized Flowers, 4 Piece 235.00
Desk Set, Brass Washed, Wood Grain Pattern, 5 Piece 380.00
Desk Set, Copper, Hammered, 6 Piece 410.00
Frame, Copper, Hammered, Flowers, 3 1/2 In. 410.00
Frame, Copper, Hammered, Quatrefoils, 8 x 5 3/4 In. 1295.00
Frame, Original Finish, 16 x 38 In. 430.00
Hook, Backplate, Copper, Hammered, Swiveling, 12 x 16 1/2 In. 880.00
Humidor, Copper, Cylindrical, 8 In. 120.00

Inkwell, Copper, Hammered, Beehive Shaped, Incised Flowers, 3 3/4 In.	265.00
Lamp, Copper, Hammered, Brass Wash, Mica Shade, 10 x 10 1/2 In.	410.00
Lamp, Copper, Hammered, Brass Washed, Helmet Shade, Red Glass, 13 1/2 x 10 In.	7638.00
Lamp, Copper, Hammered, Heraldic Shape, Mica Band, 15 x 10 In.	4115.00
Lamp, Copper, Hammered, Steuben Glass Shade, Zigzag Border, 16 1/2 x 10 In.	10000.00
Lamp, Hammered Copper Shade, Base, Amber Mica, Stylized Leaves, Signed, 14 In., Pair	8625.00
Mat, Leather, Circular, Embossed Grapes & Leaves, 20 In.	1645.00
Mat, Leather, Round, Tooled Designs, 21 In.	315.00
Sconce, Copper, Hammered, 8 In., Pair	645.00
Tray, Copper, Hammered, 2 Handles, 15 In.	325.00
Tray, Copper, Hammered, Hexagonal, Stitched Border, 2 Handles, 14 3/4 In.	560.00
Vase, American Beauty, Copper, Hammered, Brass Washed, 12 In.	1410.00
Vase, American Beauty, Hammered, Riveted, Squat Base, Tall Stovepipe Neck, 18 In.	2600.00
Vase, Bud, Copper, Hammered, Cylindrical, Wood Grain Pattern, 4 Buttresses, 8 x 4 In.	5875.00
Vase, Copper, Hammered, Cylindrical, Flared Base, Riveted, 10 1/2 x 6 1/4 In.	4410.00
Vase, Copper, Hammered, Cylindrical, Quatrefoil Band, 4 3/4 In.	500.00
Vase, Copper, Hammered, Cylindrical, Quatrefoil Band, 7 x 2 1/2 In.	1120.00 to 1880.00
Vase, Copper, Hammered, Glass Insert, 8 3/4 In.	2700.00
Vase, Copper, Hammered, Impressed Mark, 5 1/2 In.	440.00
Vase, Copper, Hammered, Impressed Mark, 22 In.	4100.00
Vase, Copper, Hammered, Quatrefoil, Verdigris Band, 5 In.	645.00
Vase, Copper, Hammered, Shell Casing Shape, Cylindrical Neck, 10 1/4 x 6 In.	3525.00
Vase, Cylindrical, Copper, Hammered, Tooled, Patina, 10 In.	2185.00
Wine Cooler, Copper, Hammered, Stovepipe Neck, Squat Base, 3 Footed, 11 x 11 In.	2940.00

ROZANE, see Roseville category.

ROZENBURG worked at The Hague, Holland, from 1890 to 1914.
The most important pieces were earthenware made in the early twentieth century with pale-colored Art Nouveau designs.

Charger, Rooster, Earth Tones, Marked, c.1900, 17 1/2 In.	6465.00
Cup & Saucer, Bird On Perch, Yellow, Orange, Brown, Signed, c.1911	646.00
Vase, Bellflower, Magenta, Trumpet Form, Blue & Green Ground, Signed, 9 3/4 x 4 In.	1265.00
Vase, Crested Pheasant, Brown, Gold, Black, Marked, 1896, 13 1/4 In.	1880.00
Vase, Dandelion, Handles, C. Van Bredbarodz, Bird Logo, c.1900, 8 3/4 In. .... *Illus*	920.00
Vase, Dandelion, Yellow, Green, Blue, Handles, C. Van Bredbarodz, c.1900, 9 x 5 In.	920.00
Vase, Flowers, Leaves, Red Ground, 1898, 22 1/4 In.	2400.00
Vase, Hyacinth, Purple, Green Stems, Brown, Baluster, Signed, c.1898, 9 1/2 x 6 In.	1095.00
Vase, Jonquil, Semi-Translucent Glaze, Bird Logo, 8 3/4 In. .... *Illus*	1095.00
Vase, Jonquil, Yellow, Green, Brown To Cobalt Blue Ground, Signed, NK, 9 x 4 1/2 In.	1095.00
Vase, Stylized Flower, Navy Blue, Gold, Purple, Ivory Ground, Marked, 1913, 12 In.	588.00
Vase, Stylized Leaf, Green, Brown, Gold, Burgundy, 1897, 11 1/2 In.	940.00
Vase, Stylized Tulip, Blue & Turquoise, Bulbous, Long Neck, Marked, 1895, 16 1/4 In.	825.00
Vase, Stylized Tulips, Gold, Green, Brown, Blue Ground, Baluster, Signed, 14 x 8 1/2 In.	1380.00

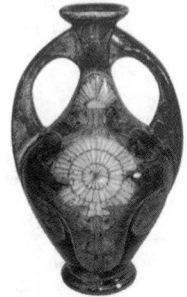

Rozenburg, Vase, Dandelion,
Handles, C. Van Bredbarodz,
Bird Logo, c.1900, 8 3/4 In.

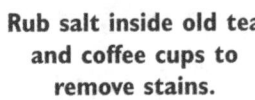

Rub salt inside old tea
and coffee cups to
remove stains.

Rozenburg, Vase, Jonquil,
Semi-Translucent Glaze,
Bird Logo, 8 3/4 In.

RRP or RRP, Roseville, is the mark used by the firm of Robinson-Ransbottom. It is not a mark of the more famous Roseville Pottery. The Ransbottom brothers started a pottery in 1900 in Ironspot, Ohio. In 1920, they merged with the Robinson Clay Product Company of Akron, Ohio, to become Robinson-Ransbottom. The factory is still working.

Jardiniere, Pedestal, Purple Glaze, Geometric Designs, Blue, Green, 33 In.	2703.00
Jug, Ear Handles, Sea Green, Ivory, Ocher Over Green Glaze, 15 x 12 In.	235.00
Vase, Floor, Bulbous, Frothy Green Over Matte Pink Glaze, 24 x 16 In.	705.00

RS GERMANY is part of the wording in marks used by the Tillowitz, Germany, factory of Reinhold Schlegelmilch from 1914 until about 1945. The porcelain was sold decorated and undecorated. The Schlegelmilch families made porcelains marked in many ways. See also ES Germany, RS Poland, RS Prussia, RS Silesia, RS Suhl, and RS Tillowitz.

Berry Bowl, Poppies, Brown, 5 1/4 In.	40.00
Berry Set, Pink Flowers, Green, 11 In., 7 Piece	200.00
Bowl, Lily Mold, 10 1/2 In.	150.00
Box, Cover, Snowball & Rose, Brown, 4 1/2 In.	60.00
Celery Tray, Handles, Blue Flowers, 12 In.	20.00
Creamer, Roses, Pink, White, Light Green	40.00
Ewer, Flowers, Green Mark, 4 3/4 In.	69.00
Mush Set, White Roses, Cream, Gold Border, 3 Piece	230.00
Mustard Pot, Spoon, Flowers, Signed	55.00
Pitcher, Cider, Flowers, 6 1/2 In.	115.00
Sugar & Creamer, Yellow Daffodils, Green, No. 505	50.00
Toothbrush Holder, Pink Roses, Green	170.00
Toothpick, Roses, White, Handles	50.00
Tray, Village & White Horse Scene, Oval, 10 In.	90.00

RS POLAND (German) is a mark used by the Reinhold Schlegelmilch factory at Tillowitz from about 1946 to 1956. After 1956, the factory made porcelain marked PT Poland. This is one of many of the RS marks used. See also ES Germany, RS Germany, RS Prussia, RS Silesia, RS Suhl, and RS Tillowitz.

Centerpiece, Pedestal, Rose Garlands	675.00
Hair Receiver, Roses, 1945-56	80.00
Mayonnaise Set, Hydrangeas, Hand Painted, Footed Bowl, Saucer	125.00 to 175.00
Plate Set, 3 Flower Sprigs, Scalloped, 6 1/2 In., 5 Piece	150.00
Vase, Pheasants, Woods, 11 In.	1295.00

RS PRUSSIA appears in several marks used on porcelain before 1917. Reinhold Schlegelmilch started his porcelain works in Suhl, Germany, in 1869. See also ES Germany, RS Germany, RS Poland, RS Silesia, RS Suhl, and RS Tillowitz.

Berry Bowl, Pink Roses, Multicolored Ground, 3-Footed, No. 25, 5 1/2 In.	30.00
Berry Bowl, Spring Portrait On Green Ground, 5 1/2 In.	120.00
Berry Set, Embossed Wavy Scalloped Rim, 8 3/4 In.	210.00
Berry Set, Gilt Decorated Rim, Master & 6 Individual Bowls, 10 In.	160.00
Berry Set, Pink Roses, Multicolored, Gold, 7 Piece	600.00
Berry Set, Scalloped Rim, Fruit Decoration, Master & 6 Individual Bowls	210.00
Biscuit Jar, Cover, Clematis Flowers, 9 In.	200.00
Biscuit Jar, Cover, Flowers, 5 1/2 In.	90.00
Bowl, Blown Out, Embossed Scallops, 10 1/2 In.	185.00
Bowl, Embossed Flower, 10 In.	175.00
Bowl, Embossed Grape, 10 1/2 In.	185.00
Bowl, Embossed Scrolled Scallops, 10 1/4 In.	210.00
Bowl, Embossed Wavy Scallops, Satin Finish, 10 1/4 In.	195.00 to 290.00
Bowl, Fleur-De-Lis, Roses, Green Ground, 10 In.	125.00
Bowl, Flowers, Cream, Blue, 10 1/2 In.	80.00
Bowl, Fruit, White, Green, Yellow Ground, 10 1/4 In.	110.00
Bowl, Hanging Basket Design, Yellow, Purple, 11 In.	125.00
Bowl, Ivy & Blossom, Green, Marbleized Green Border, 9 3/4 In.	110.00

Bowl, Lily Of The Valley, Pink Flowers, White & Green, 10 3/4 In.	175.00
Bowl, Lily, Footed, 10 1/2 In.	260.00
Bowl, Pink Poppy, Green Ground, 10 In.	100.00
Bowl, Portrait, Dice Player, 5 1/2 In.	260.00
Bowl, Reflected Flower Decoration, 11 In.	185.00
Bowl, Roses, Pink & White, Yellow & Green Ground, Shield, 10 3/4 In.	250.00
Bowl, Scalloped Rim, Lily Decoration, 11 In.	150.00
Bowl, Summer Portrait, Green Ground, 10 In.	400.00
Bowl, Summer Scene, Medallion Portraits, Recamier, Potocka, Lebrun, 10 1/2 In.	2700.00
Bowl, Swans & Evergreens, 10 In.	400.00
Bowl, White & Pink Roses, Green, 10 1/2 In.	130.00
Bowl, Yellow Roses, Light Green & Lavender, 10 3/4 In.	130.00
Cake Plate, Fleur-De-Lis, Fall Season, Violets, Peach Border, Handles, 9 1/2 In.	650.00
Cake Plate, Hanging Basket, Honeycomb, Green, Handles, 10 1/2 In.	70.00
Cake Plate, Pink Rose, White & Green Luster, Handles, 11 1/2 In.	30.00
Cake Plate, Pink Roses, Cream, Green Lavender, Handles, 11 In.	100.00
Cake Plate, Reflecting Lilies, Red Mark, 11 In.	150.00
Cake Plate, Winter Season, Green & Lavender, Handles, 9 1/2 In.	550.00
Celery Dish, Pink Roses, White, Tan, 12 1/4 In.	50.00
Celery Dish, Roses, 12 In.	85.00
Celery Tray, Dice Throwers, Pink Jewels, 13 1/2 x 7 In.	600.00
Chocolate Pot, Pink Rose, Light Green, 9 1/4 In.	80.00
Chocolate Pot, Pink Rose, White & Green, 10 In.	40.00
Chocolate Pot, Rose, 9 1/2 In.	145.00
Chocolate Pot, Snowberries, Poppies, Satin Finish, 10 In.	375.00
Coffeepot, Snowball & Rose, Green & Yellow, 9 In.	80.00
Compote, Water Lilies Reflecting, Teal Ground, 4 1/2 x 6 In.	225.00
Cracker Jar, Embossed Flower Mold, 9 In.	230.00
Cracker Jar, Fruit, Light Brown, Handles, 10 3/4 In.	60.00
Cracker Jar, Pink Roses, White, Green, Handles, 5 x 9 In.	100.00
Cracker Jar, Red Roses, 7 In.	290.00
Cracker Jar, Scrolled Handles, 6 In.	185.00
Cracker Jar, Scrolled Leaf Handles, Feet, 7 In.	259.00
Creamer, Flowers, 3 1/4 In.	40.00
Creamer & Sugar, Flower, Pedestal, 4 3/4 In., 2 Piece	175.00
Cup & Saucer, LeBrun Portrait, Cream Ground, Red & Gold Border	70.00
Cup & Saucer, Melon Eater, Green	200.00
Cup & Saucer, Sheep Herder Scene, Green	125.00
Cup & Saucer, Winter Scene	275.00
Dresser Tray, Flowers, 11 3/4 In.	160.00
Ewer, Swan & Evergreen, Handle, 8 1/4 In.	200.00
Hair Receiver, Cover, Pink Roses, White Pearl Luster, 2 1/2 x 3 1/2 In.	90.00
Hair Receiver, Surreal Dogwood, Green Finish, 4 x 2 1/2 In.	80.00
Muffineer, Roses & Daisies, 5 In.	150.00
Mustard, Cover, Rose, 3 1/4 In.	35.00
Mustard, Daisies, Pink, White	35.00
Mustard, Pink Flowers, White & Green	70.00
Pin Box, Bird Of Paradise, Brown, 2 3/4 In.	175.00
Pin Tray, Rose Garlands, Cream, Gold Trim, 5 1/2 x 3 1/2 In.	100.00
Plate, Cream, Pink, Green, 10 1/2 In.	110.00
Plate, Flower, Red Mark, 8 3/4 In.	104.00
Plate, Flowers, 10 In.	65.00
Plate, Handles, Flowers, 11 1/2 In.	55.00
Plate, Keyhole, Roses, Gold & Pink, Red Trim, 9 In.	500.00
Plate, Masted Schooner, 6 In.	70.00
Plate, Scenic, Swans On Lake, Red Mark, 9 In.	201.00
Relish Tray, Barnyard Animals, Swallows, 8 In.	175.00
Relish Tray, Pink Poppies, Green Ground, 9 1/2 In.	50.00
Relish Tray, Roses, Yellow, Pink, Cream, Green, Lavender, 9 1/2 In.	50.00
Salt & Pepper	100.00
Shaving Mug, Embossed Flowers, 3 3/4 In.	81.00
Shaving Mug, Flowers, Early Years, Handle	135.00
Shaving Mug, Hidden Image, Handle	750.00

Shaving Mug, Lilies, Molded, Handle	275.00
Shaving Mug, Mirror, Handle	750.00
Shaving Mug, Palm Leaves, Cobalt Blue, Gold, Handle	275.00
Shaving Mug, Roses, Light Green Ground, Stipple	70.00
Shaving Mug, Snowbird, Fancy Handle	275.00
Shaving Mug, Violets, Green Leaves, Green	110.00
Sugar & Creamer, Castle, Brown, Yellow	350.00
Sugar & Creamer, Hanging Basket, Light Blue & White Ground	90.00
Sugar & Creamer, Lily, White, Green	50.00
Sugar & Creamer, Man In Mountain, Green	130.00
Sugar & Creamer, Pheasants, Evergreens, Swallows	150.00
Sugar & Creamer, Roses, White & Light Green	100.00
Sugar & Creamer, Winter Portrait, Iris, 4 In., 2 Piece	259.00
Sugar & Creamer, Winter Scene, Green	200.00
Syrup, Flowers, 4 In.	40.00
Syrup, Underplate, Roses, Pink, Cream	160.00
Syrup, Underplate, Violets, Light Yellow, Green	40.00
Tankard, Footed, 10 3/4 In.	259.00
Teapot, Roses, Pink, White, Blossoms, Green, 5 1/2 In.	45.00
Tidbit, Flowers, 9 In.	55.00
Toothpick, Dogwood & Roses, 3 Handles	100.00
Toothpick, Pink Roses, Handles	150.00
Toothpick, Roses, Multicolored, Handles	90.00
Toothpick, Roses, Pink, White, Green & Cream Ground, Handle	80.00
Toothpick, Roses, Yellow, White, Handles	110.00
Toothpick, Snowball & Roses, Handles	60.00 to 100.00
Toothpick, White, Green, Glass Bowl, Handles	100.00
Tray, Dresser, Fleur-De-Lis, Mill Scene, Brown, 11 3/4 In.	550.00
Tray, Dresser, Melon Eater Scene, Green, Ribbon & Jewels, 11 3/4 In.	1000.00
Tray, Dresser, Spilled Basket, White, Medallion, 11 1/2 In.	

RUBINA is a glassware that shades from red to clear. It was first made
by George Duncan and Sons of Pittsburgh, Pennsylvania, about 1885.
This coloring was used on many types of glassware.

Pitcher, Tankard, Inverted Thumbprint, Reeded Handle, 10 3/4 In.	259.00
Water Set, Inverted Thumbprint, Straight Sides, 7-In. Pitcher, 4-In. Tumblers, 5 Piece	120.00

RUBINA VERDE is a Victorian glassware that was shaded from red
to green. It was first made by Hobbs, Brockunier and Company of
Wheeling, West Virginia, about 1890.

Celery Vase, Inverted Thumbprint, Corseted Bowl, 6 1/2 In.	288.00
Pitcher, Inverted Thumbprint, Square Mouth, Rope Twist Handle & Collar, 7 1/2 In.	230.00
Shade, Flared Ruffled Rim, 4 x 6 1/2 In., 4 Piece	662.00
Vase, Enameled, Flowers, Leaves, Branches, 4 1/2 In.	104.00

RUDOLSTADT was a faience factory in the Thuringia region of Germany from 1720 to about 1791. In 1854, Ernst Bohne began working
in the area. From about 1887 to 1918, the New York and Rudolstadt
Pottery made decorated porcelain marked with the RW and crown
familiar to collectors. This porcelain was imported by Lewis Straus
and Sons of New York, which later became Nathan Straus and Sons.
The word *Royal* was included in their import mark. Collectors often
call it *Royal Rudolstadt.* Most pieces found today were made in the late
nineteenth or early twentieth century. Additional pieces may be listed
in the Kewpie category.

Dish, Shell Shape, Pink & Purple Petaled Flowers, 5 1/4 x 5 In.	45.00
Ewer, Cascade Of Flowers, 10 1/2 In.	220.00
Kewpie, Transfer, Porcelain, Germany, 5 Piece	110.00
Plate, Hand Painted Cherries, Crown Above Anchor Mark, 8 1/2 In.	40.00
Plate, Pink Tulips, Gold Rim, 8 1/2 In.	30.00
Vase, Cherub, Flowers, Grapevines, Handle Wraps Around Neck, 12 3/4 In.	450.00
Vase, Woman, Purple, Blue, Green Crackle Ground, Bottle Shape, 9 x 4 In.	175.00

RUGS have been used in the American home since the seventeenth century. The oriental rug of that time was often used on a table, not on the floor. Rag rugs, hooked rugs, and braided rugs were made by housewives from scraps of material.

Afghan, Medallions, Red Field, Blue Border, c.1940, 5 Ft. 2 In. x 3 Ft. 10 In.	345.00
Afshar, Blue, Ivory Ground, Burgundy Borders, 3 Ft. 9 In. x 5 Ft. 4 In.	115.00
Afshar, Floral Lattice, Red, Blue, Ivory Field, Leaves, Meandering Borders, 5 x 4 Ft.	1610.00
Afshar, Seraband Pattern, Ivory Ground, Border, 4 Ft. 2 In. x 5 Ft. 4 In.	115.00
Akstafa, East Caucasus, Blue Field, Medallions, c.1885, 8 Ft. 4 In. x 4 Ft. 1 In.	4500.00
Anatolian, Pole Medallion, Red Ground, Flower Border, c.1900, 12 Ft. 4 In. x 3 Ft. 7 In.	4860.00
Anatolian, Prayer, Stepped Mirab, Flower Border, Red Ground, c.1910, 6 x 4 Ft.	467.00
Anatolian, Stepped Lozenge Medallion, Ivory, Gold, Gray, c.1920, 6 Ft. 9 In. x 3 Ft. 3 In.	100.00
Art Deco, Chinese, Cream, Blue, Stylized Peacock, 9 Ft. x 11 Ft. 5 In.	2350.00
Arts & Crafts, Drugget, Flowers, Wheat Field, Purple Border, 9 Ft. 2 In. x 3 Ft.	645.00
Arts & Crafts, Morris Style, Flowers, Blue Ground, Oakleaf Border, 6 Ft. 2 In. x 9 In.	646.00
Arts & Crafts, Vines, Flowers, Green, Brown, Ivory Ground, Olive Border, 19 x 2 Ft.	235.00
Aubusson, Beige Ground, Red Bouquet, Trellis Vine Guard Border, 13 x 8 Ft.	1840.00
Aubusson, Flower Lattice, Oval Medallion, Garlands, 1800s, 18 Ft. 5 In. x 16 Ft. 4 In.	6296.00
Aubusson, Fruit, Garlands, Beige Field, Ivory & Gold Border, 9 Ft. 7 In. x 6 Ft. 5 In.	2300.00
Aubusson, Louis XVI Style, 8 x 10 Ft.	575.00
Bagface, Turkish, Flat Weave, Geometric Designs, Burgundy, Tan, 2 Ft. 4 In. x 2 Ft. 6 In.	115.00
Bagshaish, North Persia, Red Field, Ivory & Blue Medallion, c.1870, 16 Ft. 9 In. x 10 Ft.	9000.00
Bakhtiari, Cruciform Oval Medallion, Vines, Red Ground, c.1935, 6 Ft. 8 In. x 4 Ft. 7 In.	500.00
Bakhtiari, Cypress Trees, Flowers, Blue, Red, Ivory, Red Border, c.1935, 13 Ft. x 12 In.	588.00
Bakhtiari, Flowers, Red, Blue, Ivory, Palmette, c.1910, 13 Ft. 6 In. x 10 Ft. 3 In.	7136.00
Bakhtiari, Garden, Roses, Cypress Trees, Flower & Bird Border, c.1940, 7 x 5 Ft.	1028.00
Bakhtiari, Garden, Square, Ivory, Blue, Stylized Flower Border, 5 Ft. 6 In. x 9 Ft. 4 In.	294.00
Baluchi, Diamond Lattice, Blue, Red, Camel Field, Early 1900, 3 Ft. 2 In. x 1 Ft. 10 In.	120.00
Baluchi, Northeast Persia, Epp Diamonds, Serrated Leaves, c.1900, 4 Ft. 2 In. x 2 Ft. 4 In.	470.00
Baluchi, Staggered Rows, Hooked Guls, Brown Ground, Ivory Border, c.1885, 5 x 3 Ft.	295.00
Bidjar, Herati, Blue, Rose, Ivory, Brown, Green, Ivory Border, c.1885, 7 Ft. x 4 Ft. 6 In.	529.00
Bidjar, Herati, Slant Leaf & 2 Flower Guard Borders, c.1920, 5 Ft. 2 In. x 3 Ft. 8 In.	610.00
Bidjar, Rows Of Palmettes, Rosettes, Red, Blue, Gold, Ivory, Turtle Border, 18 x 12 Ft.	9988.00
Bokhara, Red, Rust, White Medallions, Green Field, 6 Ft. 4 In. x 3 Ft. 9 In.	115.00
Braided, Hooked, Flower, Leaves, Rope Twist Border, Oval, 113 x 109 In.	1265.00
Braided, Oval, Multicolored, Pink, 28 1/2 x 23 In.	195.00
Braided, Round, Blue, Red, Green, 39 In.	190.00
Braided, Round, Multicolored, Hooked Center Star, 33 In.	660.00
Caucasian, 3 Red, Green Medallions, Navy Field, Multiple Borders, c.1940, 4 x 6 Ft.	805.00
Caucasian, Animal, Comb, Geometrics, Blue Ground, Rosette Guard Border, 4 x 3 Ft.	2185.00
Caucasian, Blue Field, Allover Pattern, Animals, 3 Borders, 5 Ft. x 3 Ft. 9 In.	1095.00
Caucasian, Boteh, Blue Field, Animal Border, 19th Century, 9 Ft. 6 In. x 5 Ft.	1150.00
Caucasian, Kilim, Center Field, 12 Blocks, White Border, 10 x 6 Ft.	2590.00
Caucasian, Medallions, Tan, Figures, Birds, Animals, Crab Borders, 3 x 13 Ft. 9 In.	1380.00
Caucasian, Prayer, Geometric, Serrated Diamonds, Pole Borders, 4 Ft. x 4 Ft. 9 In.	920.00
Caucasian, Red Ground, Rosette Field, Medallions, Multicolored Ground, 5 x 3 Ft.	260.00
Center Medallion, Red Field, Flowers, Navy, Ivory, Brown, Blue, 6 Ft. 7 In x 10 Ft. 4 In.	660.00
Central Medallion, Navy, Ivory, Red Field, Scroll, Flowers, Border, 9 Ft. 11 In. x 13 Ft.	1320.00
Chinese, Camel Field, Floral Roundel, Flowers, Butterflies, Lapis Blue, 9 Ft. 9 In. x 8 Ft.	1315.00
Chinese, Center Vase, Vines, Flowers, Birds, Beige, Greek Key, 11 Ft. 11 In. x 14 Ft. 4 In.	1380.00
Chinese, Flowering Branch, Birds, Butterfly, Blue Field, Mid 1900s, 15 Ft. 2 In. x 11 Ft.	325.00
Chinese, Flowers, Blue, Green, Gray, 8 Ft. 9 In. x 12 Ft.	2415.00
Chinese, Hand Woven, Sculpted, Flower Design, Aqua Ground, 9 Ft. x 12 Ft. 10 In.	345.00
Chinese, Imperial Gilt Metallic Thread, Embroidered, Silk, Mid 1800s, 9 Ft. 8 In. x 8 Ft.	8625.00
Chinese, Medallion, Pictorial Spheres, Blue, Green, Salmon Field, 15 Ft. 9 In. x 11 Ft.	690.00
Chinese, Multicolored Field, Open Flower Blue Ground, Mid 1900s, 6 Ft. 8 In. x 4 Ft.	150.00
Chinese, Round Pendant Medallion, Greek Key Border, c.1920, 5 Ft. 9 In. x 3 Ft.	190.00
Chinese, Scattered Flowers, Spandrels, Gray Field, Blue Border, 11 Ft. 8 In. x 9 Ft.	1095.00
Daghestan, Diamond Striped Field, Rosette Guard Border, 10 Ft. 8 In. x 3 Ft. 9 In.	400.00
Ersari, 4 8-Sided Medallions, Flower Borders, c.1930, 5 Ft. 8 In. x 3 Ft. 6 In.	280.00
Ersari, 6 Octagonal Turret Guls, West Turkestan, Early 1900s, 3 Ft. 8 In. x 3 Ft. 4 In.	560.00
Fereghan, North Persia, Blue Field, Herati, Palmette Border, c.1900, 19 Ft. 8 In. x 13 Ft.	3600.00

Rug, Hooked, Black Horses On Red, Floral Vines
On Orange, Mary Hull, 1897, 40 x 28 In.

Rug, Hooked, Dog, Butterflies, Stars, Vine,
Leaves, Flowers, Scalloped Edge, 41 x 33 In.

Fereghan, North Persia, Blue Field, Herati, Palmette Border, Late 1800s, 16 Ft. 4 In. x 6 Ft.　2160.00
Fereghan Sarouk, West Persia, Flowering Tree, Birds, Late 1800s, 7 Ft. 2 In. x 4 Ft. 7 In. . 10000.00
Grenfell, Eskimo, Rescue Workers, Sled Dogs, Hooked, 40 x 26 In. . . . .　1765.00
Hamadan, 4 Hooked Diamonds, Blue Floral Border, c.1930, 5 Ft. 11 In. x 3 Ft. 4 In. . . . . .　175.00
Hamadan, 5 Medallions, Latticework, Salmon Field, Guard Stripes, 15 Ft. x 2 Ft. 11 In. . . .　405.00
Hamadan, 7 Flowers, Birds, Leaves, Blue Ground, Red Guard Borders, 6 Ft. x 3 Ft. 8 In. . .　510.00
Hamadan, Blue Center Medallion, Rose Field, Allover Design, 6 Ft. 2 In. x 4 Ft. 3 In. . . . .　170.00
Hamadan, Boteh, Red Field, c.1920, Runner, 19 x 3 Ft. . . . .　1840.00
Hamadan, Flowering Branches, Leaves, Red Field, Vine Border, 6 Ft. x 2 Ft. 9 In. . . . .　230.00
Hamadan, Flowers, Red Field, Geometric Border, 2 Blue Vines, 11 Ft. 7 In. x 8 Ft. 10 In. .　1840.00
Hamadan, Herati, Gray Field, Ivory Rosette Border, Persia, 6 Ft. 6 In. x 3 Ft. 11 In. . . . . .　209.00
Hamadan, Herati, Palmette Border, 4 Flower Borders, c.1925, 4 Ft. 7 In. x 3 Ft. 3 In. . . . . .　280.00
Hamadan, Ivory, Blue, Tan Borders, Blue Spandrels, Ivory Ground, 4 Ft. x 5 Ft. 8 In. . . . . .　315.00
Hamadan, Medallion, Flower, Blue Ground, Ivory Border, c.1970, 4 Ft. 6 In. x 7 Ft. 3 In. . .　500.00
Hamadan, Mirror Flowers, 3 Flower Slant Leaf Borders, c.1910, 6 Ft. 5 In. x 3 Ft. 4 In. . . .　400.00
Hamadan, Pendant Medallion, Flowers, Blue Ground, c.1920, 6 Ft. 2 In. x 3 Ft. 6 In. . . . . .　187.00
Hamadan, Red Herati Ground, Blue Spandrels, Flower Border, c.1920, 5 Ft. x 3 Ft. 5 In. . . .　100.00
Hamadan, Stepped Medallions, Brown Field, Persia, c.1925, Runner, 10 Ft. 6 In. x 3 Ft. . .　570.00
Hamadan, West Persia, Mid 20th Century, 4 Ft. 9 In. x 3 Ft. 3 In. . . . .　120.00
Herati, Northwest Persian, Hand Woven, c.1910, 11 Ft. 2 In. x 15 Ft. 10 In. . . . .　550.00
Heriz, 2 Blue Geometric Medallions, Red Ground, Flower Border, c.1920, 4 x 3 Ft. . . . . . .　235.00
Heriz, 8-Pointed Medallion, Cinnabar Ground, Blue Border, 1970s, 8 Ft. x 11 Ft. 4 In. . . . .　940.00
Heriz, 8-Pointed Medallion, Ivory Spandrels, Red Ground, 1970s, 10 Ft. x 12 Ft. 8 In. . . . .　1645.00
Heriz, Center Medallion, Salmon, Blue, Olive Corner Work, 8 Ft. 7 In. x 10 Ft. 9 In. . . . . .　3910.00
Heriz, Central Medallion, Red, Blue, Ivory Field, 11 Ft. 3 In. x 9 Ft. 6 In. . . . .　5520.00
Heriz, Flowers, Red Ground, Palmette Border, Early 1900s, 11 x 8 Ft. . . . .　4110.00
Heriz, Gabled Square Medallion, Blue, Camel, Red Field, Serrated Leaf Border, 12 x 9 Ft. .　2585.00
Heriz, Geometric Flowers, Palmette Border, Red Ground, c.1910, 11 Ft. 2 In. x 8 Ft. . . . . .　1495.00
Heriz, Geometric Flowers, Serrated Plamettes, Blue Ground, c.1910, 4 Ft. 5 In. x 3 Ft. . . . .　300.00
Heriz, Herati Field, Vines, Blue Ground, Guard Border On Red, c.1940, 9 Ft. x 2 Ft. 6 In. .　690.00
Heriz, Medallion, Red Field, Navy Palmette Flowerhead Border, 12 Ft. 6 In. x 9 Ft. 9 In. . .　4140.00
Heriz, Palmette Medallion, Spandrels, Red Ground, Blue Border, c.1950, 18 x 12 Ft. . . . . .　5425.00
Heriz, Silk, Pole Medallion, Flower Vines, Flower Border, Early 1900s, 6 Ft. x 4 Ft. 7 In. .　4500.00
Heriz, Square Medallion, Flowers, Brown Border, c.1950, 13 Ft. 2 In. x 10 Ft. . . . .　880.00
Heriz, Star Medallion, Red Field, Indigo Spandrels, Rosette & Leaf Border, 10 x 8 Ft. . . . .　2868.00
Heriz Azerbejan, Blue Border, Rust Ground, Camel, Green Accents, 9 Ft. x 12 Ft. 6 In. . . .　6610.00
Hooked, 2 Flowers, Green Leaves, Stretcher, 33 x 64 In. . . . .　5175.00
Hooked, 2 Kissing Horses, Field Of Flowers, Horseshoe Corners, 1920s, 31 x 42 In. . . . . .　3855.00
Hooked, 2 Reindeer, Flowers, Oak Leaves, Red Border, Wool, Late 1800s, 31 x 64 1/2 In. .　1530.00
Hooked, 3 Houses, Trees, Wool, Linear Border, 1892, 39 1/4 x 69 In. . . . .　3175.00
Hooked, 3-Masted Ship, At Sea, 33 1/2 x 54 In. . . . .　350.00
Hooked, 4 Circles, Leaves, Geometric Border, Braided Edge, New England, 33 x 36 In. . . .　3450.00
Hooked, 8 Colored Hearts On Gray & White Striated, Navy Blue Edge, 29 x 40 In. . . . . . .　405.00
Hooked, Amish, Multicolored, Cat, Reclining, Blue, Black Cloth Border, 21 x 22 In. . . . . .　3300.00
Hooked, Angled Line Border, Green Corners, Horse's Head, Multicolored, 26 x 45 In. . . . .　259.00
Hooked, Basket Of Fruit, Yellow Scalloped Border, Mounted, 34 x 25 1/2 In. . . . .　440.00
Hooked, Basket, Flowers, Brown Border, Stretcher, Cape Cod, Mass., c.1850, 24 x 35 In. .　1150.00

Hooked, Bird Dogs, Landscape, Multiple Borders, 26 x 38 In. 175.00
Hooked, Black & White Cat With Blue Eyes, Tabby Kitten, Gray, 1930s, 18 x 20 In. 115.00
Hooked, Black Horse, Tan & Red Oak Leaf, Pale Blue Ground, 1900, 24 x 38 In. 1295.00
Hooked, Black Horses On Red, Floral Vines On Orange, Mary Hull, 1897, 40 x 28 In. *Illus* 7700.00
Hooked, Blossoms, Leaves, Scrolled Leaf Border, Wool, Late 1800s, 32 3/4 x 64 In. 325.00
Hooked, Blue Bellflower Center, Central Shaped Field, Blue Border, 60 x 40 In. 60.00
Hooked, Braided, Flowers, Rainbow, Linen, Wool, Maine, c.1870, 24 1/2 x 46 In. 1610.00
Hooked, Brown, Tan, Green Border, Dog Holding Leash, Walking Puppy, 25 x 40 In. 635.00
Hooked, Cat & 3 Kittens, Bright Colors, Mounted, 59 x 36 In. 2450.00
Hooked, Cat, Oval, Wool, 1940s, 30 x 20 In. 450.00
Hooked, Cheshire Cat, Blue Eyes, Gray Ground, 1948, 28 x 17 In. 525.00
Hooked, Conestoga Wagon, Horses, House, Water Pump, Sheep, Fish, 31 x 46 In. 715.00
Hooked, Diamonds, Squares, Multicolored, Cotton, Wool, c.1900, 77 3/4 x 35 3/4 In. 1435.00
Hooked, Dog, Butterflies, Stars, Vine, Leaves, Flowers, Scalloped Edge, 41 x 33 In. . *Illus* 2750.00
Hooked, Dog, Crazy Quilt Background, E.G.M., 39 x 30 In. .... *Illus* 7150.00
Hooked, Dog, Gray, Salmon Butterflies, Stars, Scalloped Border, 41 x 33 In. 2750.00
Hooked, Farm Scene, Homes, Animals, People, Red, Green, Purple, 1909, 38 x 53 In. 300.00
Hooked, Flower Bouquet Center, Flower & Chain Border, Wool, Late 1800s, 36 x 53 In. .. 206.00
Hooked, Flower Design, Pastel, Pink, Green, Ivory, Black Ground, 108 x 144 In. 115.00
Hooked, Flower Medallion, Leaf Scroll Border, Red, Pink, Gray Ground, 37 1/2 x 80 In. .. 575.00
Hooked, Flower Medallion, Pastel, Ivory Ground, Black Border, Burlap Back, 46 x 71 In. . 85.00
Hooked, Flower Urn, Diamonds, Stretcher, 1800s, 30 x 48 1/2 In. 5460.00
Hooked, Flowers, Lavender Border, Ivory Ground, Frame, 9 x 12 1/2 In. 400.00
Hooked, Flowers, Multicolored, N.Y., c.1930, 108 x 144 In. 4200.00
Hooked, Flowers, Oval Medallion, Wool, Wooden Frame, c.1900, 26 x 37 1/4 In. 265.00
Hooked, Flowers, Stars, Dec. 1901, 64 x 22 1/2 In. 1095.00
Hooked, Geometric, 4 Concentric Squares, Wool, Wooden Frame, c.1900, 29 x 52 In. 760.00
Hooked, Geometric, Log Cabin Pattern, c.1930, 43 x 72 In. 2070.00
Hooked, Geometric, Multicolored, Cloth, 36 x 22 In. 935.00
Hooked, Grass, Brown Beaver, Tan Ground, Leaves, 19 x 32 1/2 In. 145.00
Hooked, Gray Rabbit, Red Tulips, Scalloped Pink Border, Adams, Penn., 25 x 18 In. 690.00
Hooked, Grenfell, Island, Boats, Whale, Lighthouse, North Wind, 32 x 42 In. 275.00
Hooked, Hawaiian Quilt Design, Gold Loops, Abstract Border, 1800s, 42 x 51 In. 3450.00
Hooked, Heart Design, Green, Cream, Pink, Coral, Scalloped Border, 40 x 58 In. 1840.00
Hooked, Hearth, Horse, Yarn, Flower Border, Stretcher, March, 1852, 27 1/2 x 60 In. 9200.00
Hooked, Hearts, Red, Pink, On Gray & White Striated Ground, Stretcher, 29 x 40 In. 400.00
Hooked, Horse Pulling Sleigh, White Ground, Brown Black, Red & Green, 35 x 22 In. ... 1850.00
Hooked, Horse, Oval Border, Floral Ground, Mounted, 25 x 48 In. 305.00
Hooked, Horse, Trotting, Yellow, Tan, Black Tail, Mane, Stretcher, 26 x 41 In. 1840.00
Hooked, House, Airplane, Spirit Of St. Louis, Rectangular, Brown, Green, Beige, 39 x 63 In. 975.00
Hooked, Indian, Holding Tomahawk, Striped Border, c.1917, 36 x 20 In. 5775.00
Hooked, Ivory Medallion, Floral Sprays, Charcoal Ground, Garland Border, 105 x 84 In. .. 240.00
Hooked, Leaf Medallion, Flower Border, Burlap Ground, Early 20th Century, 80 x 78 In. . 3819.00
Hooked, Log Cabin, Light & Dark Variation, 36 Blocks, Black Border, 40 x 78 In. 1955.00
Hooked, Log Cabin, Red, Pink, Beige, Green, Blue, Black, Wool, Cotton, 24 x 37 In. 380.00
Hooked, Man, Beard, Top Hat, On Horseback, Red, Black Border, 33 x 40 In. 345.00

Rug, Hooked, Dog, Crazy Quilt Background,
E.G.M., 39 x 30 In.

**It is better for a rug to be
cleaned by a carpet sweeper than
a vacuum cleaner. If a vacuum
cleaner must be used, be sure it
is on low suction power.**

Hooked, Multicolored, Blue Elephant, Black Legs, Eye, Ear, Trunk, 35 x 20 In. 1320.00
Hooked, Multicolored, Cat, Whiskers, Border, Cloth Backing, 27 x 11 1/2 In. 1210.00
Hooked, Multicolored, Center Running Horse, Butterflies, Birds, 39 x 24 In. 1705.00
Hooked, Multicolored, Dog, Lying, Crazy Quilt Ground, Initials E.G.M., 39 x 30 In. 7150.00
Hooked, Multicolored, Geometric, Center Dog, Hearts, c.1921, 42 1/2 x 39 In. 2530.00
Hooked, Owl, On Leafy Branch, Cotton, Late 1800s, 32 1/2 x 62 In. 265.00
Hooked, Pot Of Red Tulips, Leaves, Multicolored Diamonds, Houses, 30 x 60 In. 20125.00
Hooked, Rabbit In Diamond, Scalloped, Geometric Decoration, Mounted, 38 x 19 In. 360.00
Hooked, Rag, Lined Tick Backing, c.1860, 45 1/2 x 25 In. 315.00
Hooked, Red, Tan Leaves, Gray Ground, Scroll Border Center, 48 x 28 In. 58.00
Hooked, Roses, Leaves, Scrolled Leaf Border, Wool, Late 1800s, 34 x 80 In. 999.00
Hooked, Saddle Pony, Leaf Border, Wool, Northeast, c.1885, 24 x 37 1/4 In. 3600.00
Hooked, Scottie Dog, Oval Cream Field, 2 Dogs, Purple Border, 38 x 23 In. 85.00
Hooked, Striated, America, 1800s, 111 x 114 In. 1700.00
Hooked, Theorem Style, Flower Basket, Black Ground, Red Scalloped Border, 32 x 20 In. 1155.00
Hooked, Tile Design, Green, Pink, Maroon, Tan, Black Border, 77 x 84 In. 5750.00
Hooked, Waldoboro Type, Flower Medallion, Late 1800s, 36 x 62 In. 750.00
Hooked, Welcome, Robin Holding Leaf, 4 Hearts, Xs, Wool, 1800s, 20 1/4 x 40 In. 530.00
Hooked, White Cat, Red Scrolls, 51 x 26 In. 60.00
Hooked, White, Brown, Wirehaired Terrier, Ivory Ground, Salmon Border, 13 x 14 1/2 In. . 200.00
Hooked, Winter Scene, Horse Drawn Sleigh, Farm House, 10 x 12 In. 170.00
Hooked, Winter Village, 18 x 34 In. 545.00
Hooked, Yellow, Red Tulip, Beige & Brown Ground, 17 x 17 In. 155.00
Indo-Persian, Geometric Flowers, Blue Ground, Ivory Border, 12 Ft. 3 In. x 18 Ft. 2 In. .. 2530.00
Indo-Sarouk, Tan Field, Ascending Pattern, Flowers, Vine, Plum Border, 12 x 9 Ft. 720.00
Isfahan, 2-Lobed Medallion, Blue, Ivory, Red Field, Palmette Border, 7 Ft. x 4 Ft. 4 In. ... 3910.00
Isfahan, 8-Pointed Rosette Medallion, Red Ground, c.1970, 10 Ft. 4 In. x 15 Ft. 3 In. 1880.00
Isfahan, Blue Field, Flowers, Palmettes, Red Ground, Mid 1900s, 7 Ft. x 4 Ft. 8 In. 840.00
Isfahan, Flowers, Star Medallion, Blue, Rose, Beige Ground, 5 Ft. 10 In. x 3 Ft. 10 In. 300.00
Isfahan, Multicolored Pendant Medallion, Flowers, Late 1800s, 6 Ft. 6 In. x 4 Ft. 1 In. 3930.00
Isfahan, Pendant Medallion, Flower Trellis, Serrated Leaf Border, 1800s, 4 Ft. x 3 Ft. 7 In. 1775.00
Isfahan, Pendant Medallion, Palmette Ground & Border, c.1950, 9 Ft. 5 In. x 5 Ft. 1 In. ... 6545.00
Isfahan, Red Field, Flowers, Blue, Ivory, Medallion, Borders, 13 Ft. 8 In. x 9 Ft. 8 In. 865.00
Kabistan, Stepped Diamond Medallions, Rosette & Vine Border, Blue Ground, 5 x 4 Ft. .. 865.00
Kandahar, Flowers, Blue Field, c.1950, 16 x 12 Ft. 4600.00
Karabagh, 4 Geometric Flower Medallions, Crab Border, c.1920, 8 Ft. 4 In. x 4 Ft. 5 In. .. 1400.00
Karabagh, Blue Border, Lightning Designs, Red & Black Ground, 3 Ft. 5 In. x 7 Ft. 10 In. . 460.00
Karabagh, Cross Shaped Medallions, Flower Border, c.1920, 9 Ft. x 3 Ft. 3 In. 1122.00
Karabagh, Dense Center Panel, Dragons, Blue Ground, c.1910, 3 Ft. x 5 Ft. 7 In. 470.00
Karabagh, Medallions, Brown, Blue, Ivory Crab Style Border, Runner, 3 Ft. 8 In. x 13 Ft. . 1840.00
Karabagh, Olive & Lavender Border, Blue Ground, 3 Ft. 3 In. x 5 Ft. 3 In. 345.00
Karaja, Blue & Ivory Borders, Persimmon Ground, 2 Ft. 2 In. x 3 Ft. 9 In. 175.00
Karaja, Hand Woven, Mid 20th Century, Runner, 2 Ft. 2 In. x 10 Ft. 230.00
Karaja, Medium Blue Border, Red Ground, Runner, 3 Ft. x 11 Ft. 3 In. 690.00
Karaja, Red Ground, 5 Medallions, Flower Border, c.1920, Runner, 10 Ft. x 2 Ft. 7 In. 610.00
Kashan, 4-Pointed Center Medallion, Red Ground, Blue Border, 1970s, 10 x 15 Ft. 1765.00
Kashan, Blue Ground, Lobed Medallion, Vine Guard Border, 6 Ft. 8 In. x 4 Ft. 5 In. 1725.00
Kashan, Blue Medallion, Rose Field, Flowers, Borders, Persia, 6 Ft. 8 In. x 4 Ft. 6 In. 2689.00
Kashan, Center Medallion, Salmon Field, 4 x 7 Ft. 920.00
Kashan, Center Panels, Blue, Red, Multicolored Flower Border, 4 Ft. 6 In. x 6 Ft. 10 In. .. 200.00
Kashan, Flowers, Blue Field, c.1920, Runner, 19 x 3 Ft. 1840.00
Kashan, Flowers, Leaves, Deer Border, Silk, Early 1900s, 6 Ft. 8 In. x 4 Ft. 4 In. 6465.00
Kashan, Flowers, Leaves, Ivory Field, Borders, Animals, c.1930, 10 Ft. 4 In. x 6 Ft. 11 In. .. 3300.00
Kashan, Flowers, Vines, Blue Ground, Red Border, c.1920, 6 Ft. 1 In. x 3 Ft. 795.00
Kashan, Flowers, Vines, Palmette Border, c.1920, 11 Ft. 8 In. x 9 Ft. 4 In. 3179.00
Kashan, Flowers, Wine Field, Palmette, Flower Border, Silk, c.1910, 6 x 4 Ft. 1680.00
Kashan, Lobed Pendant Medallion, Spandrels, Aubergine Field, 6 Ft. 11 In. x 4 Ft. 4 In. ... 1725.00
Kashan, Madder Field, Central Medallion, Palmettes, Vine Border, 8 Ft. 11 In. x 6 Ft. 960.00
Kashan, Medallion, Blue, Salmon Field, Ivory Flower Borders, Geometric, 4 Ft. 5 In. x 7 Ft. 1380.00
Kashan, Medallion, Ivory, Blue Field, Blue, Olive, Ivory Border, 4 Ft. 7 In. x 6 Ft. 8 In. ... 3910.00
Kashan, Pendant Medallion, Claret Field, Navy Spandrels, Vines, 14 Ft. 7 In. x 10 Ft. 6 In. 3100.00
Kashan, Pendant Medallion, Flowers, Red Ground, Palmette Border, c.1920, 19 x 12 Ft. ... 5236.00
Kashan, Pendant Medallion, Palmette & Flower Border, Silk, c.1920, 7 Ft. 3 In. x 4 Ft. ... 4490.00

Kashan, Pendant Medallion, Red Field, Blue Spandrels, Navy Palmette Border, 12 x 8 Ft. . 3110.00
Kashan, Prayer, Ivory Tree Of Life, Animals, Blue Mihrab, c.1920, 6 Ft. 10 In. x 4 Ft. 7 In. 1510.00
Kashan, Scalloped Diamond Medallion, Blue Borders, c.1960, 8 Ft. 2 In. x 12 Ft. 2 In. 2585.00
Kashmir Kashan, Central Medallion, Ivory Field, Flowers, Multicolored, 9 Ft. 10 In. x 13 Ft. 550.00
Kasvin, Diamond Medallion, Vines, Blue Field, Red Border, 20 Ft. 8 In. x 10 Ft. 8 In. 2700.00
Kayseri, Plum Field, Medallion, Palmette & Vine Border, 9 Ft. 7 In. x 6 Ft. 6 In. 720.00
Kazak, 2 Geometric Medallions, Slant Leaf Border, c.1910, 4 Ft. 10 In. x 3 Ft. 6 In. 680.00
Kazak, 2 Stepped Diamond Medallions, Blue Ground, Armenia, c.1898, 6 Ft. x 3 Ft. 2 In. . 645.00
Kazak, 3 Central Medallions, Blue Field, Multiple Borders, c.1900, 8 Ft. x 5 Ft. 2 In. 4025.00
Kazak, 3 Medallions, Red Field, Blue Border, c.1910, 4 Ft. 6 In. x 9 Ft. 2990.00
Kazak, 3 Medallions, Red Field, Camel, Navy, Blue, Fringe, 7 Ft. 4 In. x 9 Ft. 4 In. 880.00
Kazak, 3 Stepped Latch Hook Medallions, Herringbone Border, c.1910, 6 Ft. 7 In. x 4 Ft. . 280.00
Kazak, 6 Cruciform Medallions, Cinnabar Ground, 1930s, 3 Ft. 10 In. x 8 Ft. 11 In. 825.00
Kazak, Animals, Geometric Designs, c.1875, 5 Ft. 4 In. x 3 Ft. 4 In. 1765.00
Kazak, Hand Woven, Russia, Mid 20th Century, 3 Ft. 4 In. x 4 Ft. 10 In. 185.00
Kazak, Lambolo, 5 Flower Medallions, Pomegranate Border, c.1900, 7 Ft. 2 In. x 4 Ft. 3 In. 2245.00
Kazak, Medallion, Hooked Designs, Stars, Animals, Red, Ivory, Blue, 7 Ft. x 6 Ft. 9 In. . . . 1725.00
Kazak, Medallion, Horse, Flowers, Birds, Geometric Border, 1929, 9 Ft. x 5 Ft. 10 In. 3039.00
Kazak, Medallion, Red Ground, Green Accents, Blue Border, 4 Ft. 4 In. x 6 Ft. 6 In. 1035.00
Kazak, Prayer, Red, Flower Boteh, Blue, Lattice, Flower Border, Late 1800s, 4 x 3 Ft. 1175.00
Kazak, Repeating Medallions, Ivory Border, c.1900, 7 Ft. x 4 Ft. 10 In. 3220.00
Kazak, Stripes, Medallions, Geometric, Rosette Guard Border, 11 Ft. 2 In. x 5 Ft. 1 In. . . . 600.00
Kazak, Uzbek, Trellis Center, Cinnabar Ground, Ivory, Blue, 5 Ft. 8 In. x 8 Ft. 4 In. 999.00
Kerman, Allover Palmettes, Red Field, Ivory Vine Border, 17 Ft. 4 In. x 8 Ft. 10 In. 4780.00
Kerman, Aubergine & Ivory Medallions, Flower & Vine Border, 8 Ft. 9 In. x 2 Ft. 6 In. 800.00
Kerman, Blue Flower Ground, Flower Borders, c.1935, 16 x 10 Ft. 3365.00
Kerman, Blue Ground, Medallion, Flowers, Red Border, 14 Ft. 2 In. x 10 Ft. 2 In. 960.00
Kerman, Blue, Red Pendant, Medallion, Blue Flowers, c.1925, 12 Ft. 10 In. x 9 Ft. 1 In. . . 2350.00
Kerman, Ivory Field, Flowers, Vines, Palmette, Persia, Early 1900s, 11 Ft. x 8 Ft. 9 In. . . . 2270.00
Kerman, Medallions, Multicolored, Cochineal Field, Ivory Border, 21 Ft. x 10 Ft. 4 In. . . . 1645.00
Kerman, Oriental, Allover Flower Design, Pastel Colors, 6 Ft. 1 In. x 2 Ft. 9 In. 315.00
Kerman, Pendant Medallion, Flower Border, c.1940, 15 x 9 Ft. 1310.00
Kerman, Persian, 10 Ft. 1 In. x 13 Ft. 3 In. 805.00
Kerman, Tree Of Life, Birds, Flowers, Purple, Beige, Blue, Ivory, 6 Ft. 10 In. x 4 Ft. 7 In. . 1840.00
Khamseh, 3 Diamond Medallions, Geometrics, Blue Field, c.1900, 6 Ft. 3 In. x 4 Ft. 6 In. . 865.00
Kilim, Bessarabian, Tan Field, Flowers, Vining, Balkans, 1900s, 8 Ft. 8 In. x 5 Ft. 7 In. . . . 540.00
Kilim, Orange, Beige, Blue, Brown Border, c.1960, 6 Ft. 4 In. x 12 Ft. 5 In. 765.00
Kilim, Turkish, Ivory Field, Mauve & Brown, Early 1900s, 10 Ft. 3 In. x 4 Ft. 3 In. 149.00
Kilim, Veramin, North Persia, Eye Dazzler, Diamond Medallions, c.1910, 11 x 6 Ft. 705.00
Kuba, Blue Ground, Geometric Flower Lattice, Late 1800s, 4 Ft. 10 In. x 3 Ft. 8 In. 300.00
Kula, Leaf Shaped Medallion, Scarlet Field, Blue Leaf Border, 5 Ft. 3 In. x 3 Ft. 3 In. 359.00
Kurdish, 10 Hooked Octagonal Flowers, Blue Field, Red Geometric Border, 7 Ft. x 4 Ft. . . 518.00
Kurdish, Flower Medallions, Serrated Leaves, Runner, 16 Ft. 8 In. x 2 Ft. 6 In. 654.00
Kurdish, Geometric Flowers, Brown Field, Pole & Star Borders, 8 Ft. 9 In. x 4 Ft. 518.00
Kurdish, Herati, Multicolored, Blue Field, Red Border, c.1935, 7 Ft. 6 In. x 4 Ft. 470.00
Kurdish, Hexagonal Medallion, Flowers, Camel Field, Ivory Border, c.1910, 7 x 3 Ft. 470.00
Kurdish, Medallion, Flowers, Spandrels, Red, Green, Ivory, Brown, c.1935, 6 Ft. x 4 Ft. 2 In. 400.00
Kurdish, Multicolored, Flower Lattice, 3 Geometric Borders, c.1925, 9 Ft. x 3 Ft. 9 In. . . . 260.00
Laver Kerman, Flower Medallion, Palmette Border, c.1925, 9 Ft. 11 In. x 7 Ft. 9 In. 3740.00
Laver Kerman, Medallion, Blue & Yellow, Flowers, c.1910, 11 Ft. 2 In. x 8 Ft. 1 In. 1765.00
Laver Kerman, Pendant Medallions, Palmette Border, Early 1900s, 12 Ft. 8 In. x 10 Ft. . . . 840.00
Laver Kerman, Red Field, Medallion, Flowered Vines, Ivory Border, 15 Ft. 8 In. x 13 Ft. . . 896.00
Laver Kerman, Trees, Birds, Flowers, Deer, Southeast Persia, Late 1800s, 6 Ft. x 4 Ft. 8 In. 3819.00
Lillihan, Blossoms, Ivory, Indigo, Red Field, Flowerhead Border, 10 Ft. 8 In. x 7 Ft. 6 In. . . 2070.00
Lillihan, Central Flowers, 6 Vases, Blue, Red, Gold, Brown, Red Field, 6 Ft. x 4 Ft. 10 In. . . 999.00
Lillihan, Flower Heads, Floral Motifs, Blue Ground, Early 1900s, 4 Ft. 6 In. x 3 Ft. 4 In. . . 440.00
Lillihan, Flower Heads, Plants, Red Field, Dark Blue Border, 11 Ft. 6 In. x 8 Ft. 10 In. 2235.00
Lillihan, Flowers, Red Field, Blue Floral Border, Stripes, c.1930, 4 Ft. 6 In. x 3 Ft. 2 In. . . . 160.00
Lillihan, Flowers, Red Ground, Blue & Ivory Border, c.1940, Runner, 10 Ft. x 2 Ft. 11 In. . 320.00
Lillihan, Rosettes, Flowers, Vines, Red Field, Blue Vining, Runner, 3 Ft. x 23 Ft. 9 In. 780.00
Lori, Southwest Persia, 3 Gabled Medallions, Flowers, Birds, c.1910, 6 Ft. 8 In. x 4 Ft. . . . 1175.00
Mahal, Allover Design, Red Field, Multicolored Borders, 8 Ft. 4 In. x 11 Ft. 9 In. 1150.00
Mahal, Flowers, Blue Field, Ivory, Salmon Borders, 10 Ft. 7 In. x 13 Ft. 7 In. 3105.00

Mahal, Red Herati, Blue Palmette Border, 10 Ft. 10 In. x 7 Ft. 9 In. 795.00
Malayer, Allover Lattice Field, Salmon, Green, c.1915, 16 Ft. x 5 Ft. 1 In. 630.00
Malayer, Flower Ground & Border, Blue, Red, Orange, Ivory, c.1915, 16 Ft. x 3 Ft. 6 In. ... 935.00
Malayer, Flowering Lattice, Blue Spandrels, Red & Ivory Borders, 15 Ft. 10 In. x 3 Ft. ... 750.00
Mashad, Flower Vines, Serrated Leaves, Flower Border, c.1920, 10 Ft. x 6 Ft. 6 In. 490.00
Mashad, Flowers, Red Field, Blue Ground, 10 Guard Borders, 12 Ft. x 8 Ft. 11 In. 1265.00
Mashad, Red, Blue, Ivory, Center Medallion, Flowers, Mid 1900s, 12 Ft. 9 In. x 10 Ft. 690.00
Mazlaghan, Lozenge Center Medallion, Ivory Ground, Blue Border, 4 Ft. x 6 Ft. 9 In. 355.00
Meshed, Palmettes & Vines, Indigo Field, Turtle Palmette Border, 20 Ft. 9 In. x 12 Ft. .. 7170.00
Modern, Edward Fields, Typhoon Pattern, Orange, Yellow, Wool, 1967, 9 Ft. x 5 Ft. 10 In. 259.00
Modern, Paule Leleu, Wool, c.1950, 9ft. 5 In. x 7 Ft. 5 In. 1550.00
Modern, Shag, Flower, Sweden, c.1965, 58 x 87 In. 175.00
Modern, Verner Panton, Circles, Squares, Unika Vaev, Copenhagen, 1960, 7 x 7 Ft. 2350.00
Morris Style, Flowers, Green, Blue Ground, Ivy Border, Runner, 2 Ft. 6 In. x 12 Ft. 705.00
Needlepoint, Embroidered, Hearth, Wool, On Wool Ground, Fringe, c.1860, 72 x 36 In. .. 9500.00
Needlepoint, Louis Philippe, Aubusson Style, 6 x 9 Ft. 345.00
Northwest Persia, 3 Flowering Plants, Camel Field, Early 1900s, 6 Ft. x 3 Ft. 4 In. 500.00
Northwest Persia, Flowers, Navy Panel, Salmon, Ivory, Tan, Runner, 3 Ft. 4 In. x 14 Ft. ... 1650.00
Northwest Persia, Madder Field, Pole Medallions, Runner, c.1900, 17 Ft. x 3 Ft. 6 In. 600.00
Northwest Persia, Rows Of Geometric Designs, Animals, Early 1900s, 7 Ft. x 3 Ft. 6 In. . 880.00
Northwest Persia, Staggered Rows Of Hooked Diamonds, c.1935, 6 Ft. 8 In. x 3 Ft. 9 In. . 355.00
Oriental, Center Red Field, 6 Diamonds, Multiple Borders, 6 Ft. 10 In. x 3 Ft. 10 In. 345.00
Oriental, Geometric, Brown Field, Geometric Border, 4 Ft. 10 In. x 3 Ft. 240.00
Oriental, Red Medallions, Blue Abrash Ground, Ivory Border, 3 Ft. 6 In. x 5 Ft. 2 In. 1208.00
Oushak, Palmettes, Geometric Medallions, Flower Border, c.1890, 17 Ft. x 9 Ft. 7 In. .. 2057.00
Penny, 3 Blocks Of Hearts, Pieced, Appliqued, Red, Wool, 24 x 27 In. 345.00
Penny, 6-Sided, Appliqued Felt Circles, Yellow Birds, Berries, Leaves Flowers, 57 x 32 In. 2090.00
Penny, 6-Sided, Multicolored Bull's Eyes, Wool, Sateen, 22 3/4 x 37 In. 230.00
Penny, Appliqued, Runner, Table, Round Discs, Black, Yellow, Blue, Red, 37 x 24 In. 1210.00
Penny, Diamonds, Red, Blue, Green, Orange, Yellow, Black, 24 x 39 1/2 In. 633.00
Penny, Hexagonal, Concentric Circles Of Red, Yellow & Green Fabric, 31 x 39 In. 100.00
Penny, Layered Circles, Diamonds, Red, Blue, Green, 24 x 39 In. 635.00
Penny, Triple Layer, Wool Coat Scraps, c.1880, 80 x 39 In. 1495.00
Persian, 4 Medallions, Multicolored Flowers, Birds, Geometric Border, 4 Ft. x 9 Ft. 6 In. .. 206.00
Persian, Allover Flowers, Red, Ivory, Blue, 13 Ft. 5 In. x 10 Ft. 1150.00
Persian, Blue Pendant Medallion, Salmon Ground, c.1890, 11 Ft. 6 In. x 8 Ft. 1930.00
Persian, Blue, Flowers, Dark Red Field, 5 Ft. x 6 Ft. 3 In. 375.00
Persian, Central Diamond, Blue, Brown, Brown Field, 91 x 125 In. 1645.00
Persian, Flowers, Red, Dark Blue, 9 Ft. 7 In. x 12 Ft. 7 In. 1295.00
Persian, Geometric, Ivory, Blue, Maroon, 8 Ft. 2 In. x 10 Ft. 2 In. 558.00
Persian, Geometric, Red Blue, Light Blue, Brown, 9 Ft. 8 In. x 14 Ft. 2 In. 1528.00
Persian, Hamadan, Center Medallion, Red Field, 6 Ft. 8 In. x 3 Ft. 3 In. 201.00
Persian, Herati, Circular Medallion, Matching Spandrels, Multicolored, 6 Ft. 8 In. x 4 Ft. . 355.00
Persian, Heriz, Blue, Red, Ivory, 11 Ft. 3 In. x 7 Ft. 8 In. 748.00
Persian, Heriz, Center Medallion, Geometric, Red, Blue, Cream, 7 Ft. 3 In. x 9 Ft. 2 In. ... 1000.00
Persian, Heriz, Center Medallion, Red, Blue Border, 8 Ft. 5 In. x 11 Ft. 8 In. 1410.00
Persian, Heriz, Rust, Ivory, Blue, Natural Borders, 4 Ft. 5 In. x 3 Ft. 11 In. 450.00
Persian, Kashan, Flowers, Red, Dark Blue, Light Blue, 9 Ft. 8 In. x 12 Ft. 8 In. 1175.00
Persian, Medallion Center, 13 Borders, Blue Field, 13 Ft. x 10 Ft. 11 In. 4315.00
Persian, Red Field, 3 Geometric Medallions, 7 Ft. 8 In. x 5 Ft. 2 In. 315.00
Persian, Repeating Designs, Blue, Black, Geometric Borders, Runner, 3 Ft. x 15 Ft. 8 In. .. 633.00
Persian, Sarouk, Flowers, Red, Black, Tan, 3 Ft. 10 In. x 6 Ft. 441.00
Persian, Sarouk, Flowers, Red, Dark Blue, Light Blue, 9 Ft. 10 In. x 13 Ft. 1520.00
Persian, Tabriz, Flowers, Red, Dark Blue, Tan, 9 Ft. 10 In. x 13 Ft. 2 In. 1410.00
Qashqai, 3 Flower Lozenge Medallions, Diagonal Stripes, c.1910, 5 Ft. 11 In. x 4 Ft. 1 In. . 225.00
Qashqai, 3 Hooked Medallions, Red, Gold, Blue Field, Meandering Border, 10 x 6 Ft. 350.00
Qashqai, 3 Lozenge Medallions, Flowers, Birds, Animals, c.1920, 10 Ft. 6 In. x 7 Ft. 2 In. .. 1775.00
Qashqai, Medallion, Ivory, Flowers, Blue Field, Borders, c.1900, 9 Ft. 5 In. x 5 Ft. 5 In. ... 1090.00
Qashqai, Palmette Medallions, Birds, Geometric Borders, c.1900, 9 Ft. 2 In. x 5 Ft. 1 In. ... 1400.00
Qum, Allover, Flowers, Vines, Ivory Field, Blue Border, Silk, 10 Ft. 7 In. x 7 Ft. 6 In. 1435.00
Qum, Blue Mirab, Palmettes, Animals, Rust Palmette Border, 6 Ft. 9 In. x 4 Ft. 8 In. 2150.00
Qum, Flower Pendant Medallions, Palmette Borders, Silk, c.1975, 7 Ft. x 4 Ft. 6 In. 900.00
Sarouk, Allover Flower Sprays, Blue, Red, Camel, Gold, Red Field, 5 Ft. x 3 Ft. 7 In. 235.00

Sarouk, Blue Center Medallion, Red Field, Allover Flowers, 9 Ft. 5 In. x 6 Ft. 1035.00
Sarouk, Blue Field, Flower Medallion, Crimson Palmette, Vine Border, 8 Ft. 8 In. x 6 Ft. . . .   4185.00
Sarouk, Burgundy Ground, Midnight Blue Border, Fringe, 8 Ft. 7 In. x 11 Ft. 7 In. 460.00
Sarouk, Center Medallion, Blue, Ivory, Salmon Field, Geometric, Flower Border, 4 x 7 Ft. .   3220.00
Sarouk, Circular Medallion, Flower Sprays, Multicolored, Red Field, 6 Ft. 6 In. x 2 Ft. 705.00
Sarouk, Diamond Medallion, Spandrels, Vines, Dark Blue Field, 6 Ft. 7 In. x 4 Ft. 4 In. . . .   1060.00
Sarouk, Fereghan, Bird Of Paradise, Trellis Field, Blue Ground, 9 Ft. 8 In. x 7 Ft. 10 In. . .   9775.00
Sarouk, Fereghan, Blue Ground, Boteh, Palmette, Leaf, Vine, c.1910, 6 Ft. x 4 Ft. 8 In. 1800.00
Sarouk, Fereghan, Lobed Medallion, Red Field, Palmette Border, 4 Ft. 10 In. x 3 Ft. 3 In. .   1610.00
Sarouk, Fereghan, Sawtooth Pendant Medallion, Flower Border, c.1910, 6 Ft. 3 In. x 4 Ft. .   1589.00
Sarouk, Flower Bouquets, Red Field, Blue Palmette Border, 11 Ft. 4 In. x 7 Ft. 9 In. 1195.00
Sarouk, Flower Spandrels, Salmon Ground, Checked Border, 9 x 12 Ft. 2530.00
Sarouk, Flower Vines, Red Ground, Flower Border, 2 Guard Borders, c.1930, 5 x 3 Ft. . . .   840.00
Sarouk, Flowering Vase, Red Field, Blue Vine Border, 16 Ft. x 10 Ft. 7 In. 2390.00
Sarouk, Flowers, Red Field, Blue & Gold Border, 6 Ft. 2 In. x 5 Ft.   290.00
Sarouk, Flowers, Red Field, c.1940, 12 x 9 Ft. 1265.00
Sarouk, Flowers, Red Ground, Blue Ground, Vine Guard Border, c.1940, 12 x 9 Ft. 690.00
Sarouk, Flowers, Red Ground, Flower Border, c.1925, 9 Ft. x 7 Ft. 9 In. 2620.00
Sarouk, Flowers, Red Ground, Palmette Border, c.1920, 6 Ft. 6 In. x 4 Ft. 3 In. 1775.00
Sarouk, Flowers, Red Ground, Vines, Guard Border, c.1935, 11 Ft. 10 In. x 8 Ft. 10 In. . . .   840.00
Sarouk, Lobed Pendant, Red Field, Blue Flowerhead Border, 6 Ft. 4 In. x 4 Ft. 2 In. 3220.00
Sarouk, Medallion, Flowering Branches, Ivory, Green, Salmon, Blue Vine, 12 x 9 Ft. 3600.00
Sarouk, Pendant Medallions, Flowers, Red Ground, c.1930, 10 Ft. 6 In. x 8 Ft. 2 In. 1122.00
Sarouk, Pots Of Flowers, Red Field, Blue Flower Border, 11 Ft. 6 In. x 9 Ft. 1080.00
Sarouk, Rosettes, Vines, Blue, Red, Gold, Dark Blue Field, Red Border, 4 Ft. 6 In. x 3 Ft. .   705.00
Sarouk, Serrated Leaves, Flower Vines, Palmette Border, c.1920, 11 Ft. 11 In. x 9 Ft. 9 In. .   5800.00
Sarouk, Vines, Palmettes, Salmon, Red, Blue, Dark Blue Field, 8 Ft. 5 In. x 5 Ft. 3 In. 980.00
Savonnerie, Louis Philippe Style, 9 x 12 Ft. 3220.00
Seichur, 2 Central Medallions, Lime, Ivory, Blue, Dog Border, c.1900, 6 Ft. 9 In. x 4 Ft. . .   2530.00
Senneh, Kurd, Blue Herati Ground, Crab Palmette, Flowers, c.1910, 11 Ft. x 8 Ft. 11 In. . .   4200.00
Senneh, Persian, Hand Woven, Late 20th Century, 4 x 5 Ft. 219.00
Seraband, Flower Lattice, Red Ground, Flower Borders, c.1900, 9 Ft. 6 In. x 3 Ft. 5 In. . . .   980.00
Seraband, Staggered Rows Of Boech, Blue, Apricot, Ivory, Terra-Cotta, 19 Ft. x 7 Ft. 7 In.   2938.00
Serapi, Central Ivory Medallion, Red Ground, Ivory Corners, c.1900, 11 Ft. 9 In. x 12 Ft. .   8050.00
Shiraz, 3 Medallions, Rust, Blue, Ivory, 7 Ft. 7 In. x 4 Ft. 8 In. 345.00
Shiraz, Caucasian, Diagonals, Blue, Red, Ivory, Gold, Multiple Borders, 3 x 5 Ft. 460.00
Shiraz, Flowers, Rust Field, Navy Corners, 4 Ft. 2 In. x 2 Ft. 9 In. 748.00
Shiraz, Red Field, Center Medallion, Symbols, Black Corners, Border, 9 Ft. x 6 Ft. 5 In. . .   345.00
Shirvan, 3 Medallions, Red Field, Leaf Border, c.1910, 4 x 6 Ft. 1265.00
Shirvan, 3 Medallions, Red Field, Pole Borders, 7 Ft. 3 In. x 3 Ft. 10 In. 259.00
Shirvan, 4 Central Medallions, Navy Field, Kufic Script, Dog Border, 6 Ft. 10 In. x 4 Ft. . .   5520.00
Shirvan, Animals, Flowers, 3 Stepped Lozenge Medallions, c.1900, 6 Ft. x 3 Ft. 10 In. 1685.00
Shirvan, Double Keyhole Medallion, Navy Field, Red Kufic Script Border, 5 x 3 Ft. 1495.00
Shirvan, Flowers, Brown Field, Ivory Ground, Late 1800s, Runner, 13 Ft. 7 In. x 4 Ft. 3860.00
Shirvan, Multicolored Flower Lattice, Red Ground, c.1915, 5 Ft. 4 In. x 3 Ft. 10 In. 375.00
Shirvan, Multicolored Flowers, Hour Glass, Medallions, Late 1800s, 4 Ft. 5 In. x 3 Ft. 750.00
Shirvan, Stepped Lozenge Medallion, Flower Border, Late 1800s, 4 Ft. 11 In. x 4 Ft. 935.00
Sivas, Anatolia, Tan Field, Madder Star, Mountain, Columns, 1900s, 5 Ft. 9 In. x 4 Ft. 450.00
Soumak, Flatweave, 3 Blue Ground Flower Medallions, 1800s, 6 Ft. 4 In. x 4 Ft. 6 In. 800.00
Soumak, Saddle Bags, Birds, Northwest Persia, Late 1800s, 38 x 22 In. 940.00
Table, Appliqued, Brown Diamonds, Red, Berries, Sawtooth Borders, Wool, 25 x 42 In. . .   375.00
Tabriz, Center Medallion, Salmon, Ivory Field, Vine, Corner Flowers, 4 Ft. 11 In. x 7 Ft. . .   1150.00
Tabriz, Flowers, Blue Border, Camel Ground, 8 Ft. 7 In. x 11 Ft. 3 In. 4025.00
Tabriz, Ivory & Blue Medallion, Red Field, Ivory Corners, 10 Ft. 7 In. x 14 Ft. 865.00
Tabriz, Northwest Persia, Flower Urn, Camels, Birds, Silk, Late 1800s, 5 Ft. 7 In. x 4 Ft. . .   3290.00
Tabriz, Pendant Medallion, Rust Field, Brown Spandrels, Vine Border, 4 Ft. 9 In. x 3 Ft. . .   800.00
Tabriz, Red Field, Trellis, Palmettes, Ivory, Blue, Salmon, Late 1800s, 11 Ft. 8 In. x 9 Ft. . .   1765.00
Tabriz, Trellising Vine Field, 4 Center Medallions, Spandrels, Ivory Ground, 13 x 3 Ft. . . .   800.00
Tekke, 3 Columns, Black, Ivory, Apricot, Gray, Red Field, c.1925, 5 Ft. 8 In. x 4 Ft. 4 In. . .   470.00
Tekke, Chuval, 3 Tekke Gul Rows, Geometric Flower Border, c.1910, 4 Ft. x 3 Ft. 10 In. . .   245.00
Tekke, Chuval, Gul Rows, Diamonds, Flower Head Borders, c.1900, 4 Ft. x 3 Ft. 7 In. 195.00
Tekke, Gul Rows, Burgundy, Red Field, Stylized Flowers, c.1900, 9 Ft. x 6 Ft. 7 In. 925.00
Tekke, Guls, Serrated Hooked Flower Border, Red Ground, c.1920, 11 Ft. x 7 Ft. 8 In. 935.00

Tibetan, 2 Vines, 12 Lotus Flowers, Beige Ground, Early 1900s, 5 Ft. 1 In. x 2 Ft. 11 In. . .	560.00
Tibetan, 3 Multicolored Lotus Medallions, Cloud Border, Early 1900s, 5 Ft. 6 In. x 3 Ft. . .	700.00
Tibetan, Blue Bird Lattice, Ivory Star Border, Early 1900s, 5 Ft. 2 In. x 3 Ft. 1 In.	610.00
Tibetan, Multicolored Lotus Flowers, Clouds, Early 1900s, 4 Ft. 11 In. x 2 Ft. 10 In.	560.00
Tibetan, Red Coin Medallions, 8 Lucky Symbols, Early 1900s, 4 Ft. 6 In. x 2 Ft. 6 In.	700.00
Turkish, Geometric, Red, Dark Blue, Light Blue, 6 Ft. 10 In. x 5 Ft. 6 In.	470.00
Turkish, Medallions, Flowers, Blue, Purple, Ivory Field, Mid 1900s, 5 Ft. 10 In. x 3 Ft. . . .	252.00
Turkish, Prayer, Lantern, Gold Field, Flowers, Leaf Guard Borders, Silk, 6 x 4 Ft.	1150.00
Turkish, Prayer, Red, Medallions, Flower Border, Early 1900s, 5 Ft. 11 In. x 4 Ft. 3 In. . . .	1090.00
Turkoman, Medallions, Stars, Cinnabar Ground, c.1920, 6 Ft. 9 In. x 7 Ft. 3 In.	1410.00
Ushak, Medallion, Palmette Spandrels, Flower Borders, c.1900, 14 Ft. 8 In. x 10 Ft. 1 In. . .	2060.00
Ushak, Medallion, Spandrels, Vine Border, Late 1800s, 11 Ft. 10 In. x 8 Ft. 2 In.	940.00
Ushak, Stepped Medallion, Flowers, Palmette Border, c.1920, 11 Ft. 9 In. x 8 Ft. 7 In.	2620.00
Yomud, 36 Guls, Blue, Red, Ivory, Claret Field, Slant Leaf Border, 10 Ft. x 6 Ft. 7 In. . . .	4313.00
Yomud, Rows Of Kepse Guls, Ivory Ground, Pole Borders, 10 Ft. 6 In. x 8 Ft. 4 In.	2760.00

RUMRILL Pottery was designed by George Rumrill of Little Rock, Arkansas. From 1933 to 1938, it was produced by the Red Wing Pottery of Red Wing, Minnesota. In 1938, production was transferred to the Shawnee Pottery in Zanesville, Ohio. It was moved again in December of 1938 to Florence Pottery Company in Mt. Gilead, Ohio, where Rumrill ware continued to be manufactured until the pottery burned in 1941. It was then produced by Gouda Ceramic Arts in South Zanesville until early 1943.

RumRill

Candlestick, 2-Light, Sylvan, No. 397, 5 1/4 In., Pair	95.00
Vase, Aqua Matte Glaze, Art Deco, 10 x 7 In.	120.00
Vase, Athenia Nudes, Pink, No. 570, 10 In.	15.00
Vase, Blue, 3 Leaves, Red Wing, 7 In.	40.00
Vase, Blue, Bulbous, Cylindrical Neck, Footed, No. 725, 7 1/2 In.	10.00
Vase, Blue, Handles, No. 505, 7 3/4 In. . . . . .25.00 to 40.00
Vase, Blue, Indian Group, No. 309, 5 1/2 In.	30.00
Vase, Blue, Ribs, 6 In.	30.00
Vase, Square, Stepped Wing Decoration, No. 701, 9 In.	165.00

RUSKIN is a British art pottery of the twentieth century. The Ruskin Pottery was started by William Howson Taylor, and his name was used as the mark until about 1899. The factory, at West Smethwick, Birmingham, England, stopped making new pieces in 1933 but continued to glaze and sell the remaining wares until 1935. The art pottery is noted for its exceptional glazes.

RUSKIN POTTERY WEST SMETHWICK

Vase, Blue Matte Glaze, Dripping Over Orange High Glaze, 6 3/4 In.	161.00
Vase, Corseted, Purple, Green, Red, Crystalline Glaze, 1910, 9 1/2 x 5 In.	1880.00
Vase, Cylinder Shape, Blue Crystalline Glaze, Tan Ground, 9 1/4 In.	489.00

RUSSEL WRIGHT designed dinnerwares in modern shapes for many companies. Iroquois China Company, Harker China Company, Steubenville Pottery, and Justin Tharaud and Sons made dishes marked *Russel Wright.* The Steubenville wares, first made in 1938, are the most common today. Wright was a designer of domestic and industrial wares, including furniture, aluminum, radios, interiors, and glassware. Dinnerwares and other pieces by Wright are listed here. For more information, see *Kovels' Depression Glass & Dinnerware Price List.*

Russel Wright MFG. BY STEUBENVILLE

American Modern, Creamer, Steubenville, 3 x 7 1/2 In.	15.00
American Modern, Cup, White, Steubenville	25.00
American Modern, Ice Box, Cover, Steubenville, 3 x 5 1/2 In.	150.00
American Modern, Pickle, Liner, Coral, 10 1/2 In.	20.00
American Modern, Plate, Bread & Butter, Coral, Steubenville, 6 1/4 In.	4.00
American Modern, Plate, Bread & Butter, Seafoam, Steubenville, 6 1/4 In.	4.00
Iroquois Casual, Dinnerware Service For 8, 6 Serving Pieces, c.1946	1116.00
Iroquois Casual, Platter, Oval, Pink Sherbet, 12 3/4 In.	35.00
Tray, 2 Metal Tiers, Wood Supports, c.1935, 13 1/2 In.	140.00
Tray, Serving, Circular Handle, Ball In Center, Round, c.1935, 13 In.	118.00

SABINO glass was made in the 1920s and 1930s in Paris, France. Founded by Marius-Ernest Sabino (1878–1961), the firm was noted for Art Deco lamps, vases, figurines, and animals in clear, colored, and opalescent glass. Production stopped during World War II but resumed in the 1960s with the manufacture of nude figurines and small opalescent glass animals. The new pieces are a slightly different color and can be recognized.

Sabino
France

Bonbon, 3 Nude Mermaids, Oval, 20th Century, 6 1/2 In.	235.00
Figurine, Nude Woman, Opalescent, Paris, 20th Century, 9 1/2 In.	380.00
Perfume Bottle, Abstract Geometric, Stopper, Basket Of Flowers, France, 6 3/4 In.	105.00
Vase, Art Deco, Clear, Frosted, Octagonal Rim, Bulbous, c.1930, 9 1/2 In.	2645.00
Vase, Oval, Frosted, Sepia, Dragonflies, Stylized Foliage, 1920s, 5 1/2 In.	380.00

SALT AND PEPPER SHAKERS in matched sets were first used in the nineteenth century. Collectors are primarily interested in figural examples made after World War I. *Huggers* are pairs of shakers that appear to embrace each other. Many salt and pepper shakers are listed in other categories and can be located through the index at the back of this book.

Ballantine Ale, Cardboard, Metal Lids, Box, 2 3/8 In.	19.00
Barrels, Old MacDonald's Farm, Gold Trim, 4 In.	135.00
Blatz Pilsner, Bottle Shape, Amber Glass, Metal Lid, 3 In.	26.00
Boy & Girl, Old MacDonald's Farm, Regal China, 3 1/2 In.	120.00
Bunny, Hugger, Yellow, Russet, Signed, Van Tellingen, Regal China, c.1950, 3 1/2 In.	45.00
Churns, Old MacDonald's Farm, Regal China	90.00
Coney Island, N.Y., Sweethearts On Beach, Plastic, c.1950, 2 1/2 In.	29.00
Coney Island Rides, Parachute Jump, Cyclone, Wonder Wheel, Pottery, 1950s	75.00
Coors Beer Bottle, Amber, Plastic Cap, 4 In.	12.00
Cowboy & Cowgirl, Ceramic, Cork Stoppers, 1950s	17.00
Dutch Boy & Girl, Hugger, Signed, Van Tellingen, Regal China	32.00
Ken-L-Ration, Dog & Cat, Plastic, F & F, c.1960, 3 1/2 In.	18.00
Kool Cigarette Penguins, Ceramic, Black & White, 1940s	45.00
Old Smokey Bear, Pottery, Japan, 4 In.	55.00
Peerless Beer Co., Figural Gnome, Celluloid, 5 1/4 In.	28.00
Sears, Snowdome, America's Largest Selling Washers & Dryers, 1960s, 2 3/4 x 3 3/4 In.	95.00
Tuborg & Carlsberg Beer, Bottle Shape, Glass, Metal Lid, Wooden Stand, 2 1/2 In.	29.00

SALT GLAZE has a grayish white surface with a texture like an orange peel. It is a method of decoration that has been used since the eighteenth century. Salt-glazed pieces are still being made.

Flask, Barrel Shape, E. Lock Wine & Spirit Merchant, Oval, Tan, S. Green Lambeth, 5 In.	390.00
Jug, Bellarmine Type, Applied Handle, Brown, England, 12 In.	88.00
Jug, Bellarmine Type, Applied Handle, Brown, England, 14 1/2 In.	69.00

SAMPLERS were made in America from the early 1700s. The best examples were made from 1790 to 1840. Long, narrow samplers are usually older than square ones. Early samplers just had stitching or alphabets. The later examples had numerals, borders, and pictorial decorations. Those with mottoes are mid-Victorian. A revival of interest in the 1930s produced simpler samplers, usually with mottoes.

ABCDE

Alphabet, 5 Crown, Elizabeth Somerville, August 1797, 15 x 9 In.	955.00
Alphabet, 6 Birds, Pansies & Tulips, Maria Waller Aged 22, 1875, 35 x 33 In.	1100.00
Alphabet, Adam & Eve, Vine Border, Jane Stephenson, c.1833, 16 x 15 In.	50.00
Alphabet, Birds, Trees, Margaret Wilkie, 1832, Various Stitches, Frame, 19 x 10 In.	575.00
Alphabet, Eagle, Vine Border, Alice Nickerson, Chatham, 1853, Frame, 14 x 11 In.	2705.00
Alphabet, Elizabeth Martin, 9 Years, Providence, 1799, 11 3/8 x 10 5/8 In.	470.00
Alphabet, Floral Border, Amy Robbins, N.J., Silk, c.1820, 16 1/2 x 13 In.	1116.00
Alphabet, Floral Border, Phebe Lippencott, Monmouth, c.1806, 17 1/2 x 12 1/2 In.	2585.00
Alphabet, Flowering Vine, Mary N. Southwick, 9 Years, 1819, Frame, 17 1/2 x 14 3/4 In.	3525.00
Alphabet, Flowers, Religious Designs, 19th Century, 45 x 8 1/2 In.	489.00
Alphabet, Flowers, Trees, Martha G. Davis, Aged 8, Boston, 1816, Frame, 17 x 17 3/4 In.	4995.00
Alphabet, Guilelma Willetts, Silk, Linen, c.1849, 9 x 17 1/2 In.	560.00
Alphabet, House Scene, 1854, Grain Painted Frame, 20 x 17 1/2 In.	4620.00

Alphabet, House, Plants, Katherine Sawyer, Boston, 1834, Frame, 13 3/4 x 19 3/8 In. 2235.00
Alphabet, Numbers, 5 Lines, Border Bands, Cross, Silk, Linen, 1784, 9 x 8 In. 460.00
Alphabet, Numbers, 5 Lines, Verse, 10 Lines, Wool, 15 1/4 x 12 1/4 In. 115.00
Alphabet, Numbers, Birds, Elizabeth Niblock, Silk, Linen, Frame, c.1825, 15 x 14 In. 1035.00
Alphabet, Numbers, Elizabeth Steward, Aged 7, Frame, 14 x 14 In. 125.00
Alphabet, Numbers, Flowers, L. Palmire, c.1864, 17 x 12 3/4 In. 345.00
Alphabet, Numbers, Genealogy, Grace Hill, Age 8 Yrs, October, 1798, Linen, 5 x 12 In. . . 460.00
Alphabet, Numbers, Hannah Pargeter, Verse, 1823, Cotton On Linen, 13 x 12 In. 323.00
Alphabet, Numbers, House, Basket, Flowers, Martha Lane Wilson, Silk, 25 3/4 x 17 In. . . . 173.00
Alphabet, Numbers, Mary Dean, 1781, Age 9 Years, Silk, Linen, 15 x 8 In. 290.00
Alphabet, Numbers, Mary Roe, 8 Years, Ohio 1827, Wool, On Linen, Frame, 11 x 7 In. . . . 219.00
Alphabet, Numbers, Strawberries, Mary Ann Otty, Aged 11, 1824, Frame, 16 x 13 1/4 In. . 980.00
Alphabet, Numbers, Verse, Hannah E. Lakeman, Maine, Frame, c.1820, 17 x 17 In. 575.00
Alphabet, Panel, House, Trees, Wool Yarn On Linen, c.1835, 18 x 13 In. 646.00
Alphabet, Stylized Medallions, Mary Barrett, Silk, Frame, c.1824, 18 x 17 In. 881.00
Alphabet, Various Stitches, August 1817, Shadow Box Frame, Gilt Liner, 12 x 16 In. 115.00
Alphabet, Verse, Ann Billiat, 17th Century, 18 1/2 x 14 1/2 In. 489.00
Alphabet, Verse, Ann Dean Rich, Silk, Linen, c.1820, 14 1/2 x 12 1/2 In. 1880.00
Alphabet, Verse, Birds, Hannah Pearson, Born 1770, Giltwood Frame, 15 1/2 x 9 3/8 In. . . 2350.00
Alphabet, Verse, Flower Vine, House, Mary Tidy, England, Wool, 1838, 18 x 13 In. 1000.00
Alphabet, Verse, Flowers, Eliza W. Gale, M. Tufts School, Age 12, 1813, 22 x 19 In. 6453.00
Alphabet, Verse, Flowers, Geometric, Elizabeth Gorham, 1758, Frame, 16 1/4 x 8 In. 1060.00
Alphabet, Verse, Flowers, Michner Family, Silk & Wool, Linen, c.1835, 17 x 18 1/4 In. . . . 410.00
Alphabet, Verse, Sarah H. Dana Oxford, Aged 8, 1823, Frame, 14 1/4 x 13 1/8 In. 7640.00
Alphabet, Verse, Star, Birds, Tree, Lucenda Bingham, Aged 11 Years, 1809, 17 x 11 In. . . . 2703.00
Alphabet, Verse, Trees, Birds, Elizabeth Crandall, Frame, Late 1700s, 13 1/2 x 8 In. 1000.00
Alphabet, Verse, Trees, Mary B. Nath, Aged 11 Years, 1825, Frame, 19 1/2 x 18 3/4 In. . . . 6040.00
Alphabet, Verse, Urns, Flowers, Lucinda Swain, Age 10, New England, 19 x 16 1/2 In. . . . 690.00
Alphabet, Victorian, Frame, c.1868, 17 x 24 In. 300.00
Alphabet, Vine Border, Lavina R. Harman, c.1833, 17 1/4 x 13 1/2 In. 1765.00
Alphabet Panels, C. Kolls, 1829, Silk On Linen, 8 3/4 x 10 5/8 In. 176.00
Alphabets, Basket, Flowers, Strawberry Vine Border, G.F., 1834, Frame, 11 x 10 In. 330.00
Alphabets, Flowerpots, Lydia Ann Tyler, Silk On Linen, Frame, 14 x 17 1/4 In. 375.00
Alphabets, House, Tulip, Heart, Margaret Eddie, Aged 9, 1831, Silk, Frame, 18 x 10 In. . . . 920.00
Alphabets, Numbers, Margret Webster, Öyear Of Our Lord 1774, Frame, 12 x 10 In. 460.00
Alphabets, Numbers, People, Animals, Furniture, F.S.D. 1759, Frame, 32 x 11 In. 385.00
Alphabets, Numbers, Tan & Green, Hannah A. Holts, Silk On Linen, Frame, 13 x 9 In. . . . 345.00
Alphabets, Strawberry Border, Flowers, Isabella Henry, 1849, Mat, Frame, 18 x 16 In. 750.00
Alphabets, Strawberry Border, Gold, Green, Martha Hughes, September 7, 1819 . . . . 1840.00
Alphabets, Verse, Amey Cougill, L. Peck School, Frame, Late 1700s, 11 1/2 x 10 1/2 In. . . 646.00
Alphabets, Verse, Elizabeth Voorheis, Age 13, 1834, Frame, 15 1/2 x 16 1/2 In. 2300.00
Alphabets, Verse, Flowers, Mary Kickinbotham, 1821, Silk On Wool, 13 x 12 3/8 In. 999.00
Alphabets, Verse, Maria Smith, Aged 13, 1824, Silk & Cotton On Linen, 14 x 12 In. 499.00
Alphabets, Verses, Strawberry Border, Mary Anne Stuart, 1765, 8 x 11 In. 725.00
Biblical Verses, Trees, Flowers, Mary Ratcliff, 1803, Frame, 19 1/4 x 19 3/8 In. 777.00
Courting Scene, Sally Burrs, Decbr 2th 1802, 10th Year, Paper Label, Frame, 11 x 9 In. . . . 3680.00
Family Tree, Samuel & Grace Barnes, Watertown, Mass., Frame, c.1794, 17 x 15 In. 2990.00
Flower Urn, Red House, Flower Basket, Alphabet, Flowers, Elizabeth Davies, 14 x 14 In. . 460.00
Flower Vine, 3 Verse Poem, House, Elizabeth Martin 1899, 12 x 10 In. 230.00
Flowers, House, Elsabeth Swan, Silk On Linen, Frame, c.1810, 19 x 17 In. 575.00
Flowers, Levine Fisher, Harrisburg, Pa., 1835, Silk On Linen, 19 1/2 x 19 1/2 In. 598.00
Genealogy, Monument, Weeping Willow, Charlotte Perkins, 12 Years, 1819, 24 x 24 In. . . 2585.00
Life Of Happy Man, Flowers, Butterflies, Hannah Webb, Aged 12, 1818, 18 x 13 In. 410.00
Sarah A. Bunn Worked This Sampler At Eliza Rues School, 1828, Wool, 18 x 16 In. 9000.00
Signed Sicily Simonton, N.Y. State, Wool, Silk, c.1815, 13 1/2 x 17 In. 1380.00
Solomon's Temple, Flower Border, Verse, Silk, Wool, Linen, 24 1/2 x 23 3/4 In. 805.00
Solomon's Temple, Flowers, Windmill, Elizabeth Storey, 1843, Frame, 23 x 20 In. 1265.00
Star Spangled Banner, Alphabet, Margaret Emily Lukens, 1855, Frame, 18 x 17 1/2 In. . . . 9600.00
Strawberries, Pink, Green, Red, Ivory & Tan, Mary Ann Otty, Aged 11, 1824, 16 x 13 In. . 975.00
Strawberry Vine Border, Basket, Church, Birds, Sarah Knights, 1848 . . . . 940.00
Strawberry Vine Border, Flower, Church, Heart, Trees, Sarah Knight, 1848 . . . . 940.00
Stylized Flowering Vine, Flower Urns, Verse, Silk On Linen, 17 x 18 In. 764.00
Tree Of Knowledge, Building, Eliza Godly, Aged 9 Years, 1827, Frame, 19 x 15 In. 1293.00

Verse, 4 Lines, Bridge, Butterfly, Elizabeth Benson Wool, Linen, 21 x 17 In. 748.00
Verse, 4 Lines, House, Fence, Lamb, Birds, Boy, Girl, Dog, Emley Litchfield, 17 5/8 x 13 In.   633.00
Verse, 16 Lines, Caroline Victery, 1798, Frame, 14 x 11 In. 431.00
Verse, 16 Lines, Psalm 51, Elizabeth Humphries, Silk, Wool, 17 1/8 x 12 1/4 In. 748.00
Verse, 18 Lines, Animals, Fruits, Flowers, Maria Hodgkinson, 1822, 15 1/4 x 13 1/4 In. . . .   748.00
Verse, 18 Lines, Birds, Lions, Trees, Crowns, Elizabeth Marriot Bram, 1787, 21 x 12 In. . .   518.00
Verse, Animals, Flowers, Mary Butler, 1764, Silk, Linen, Frame, 21 x 16 1/4 In. 1673.00
Verse, Building, Fence, Flowers, Trees, Animals, Frame, Early 1800s, 25 x 25 In. 1410.00
Verse, Butterflies, Flowers, Mary Austin, 11 Years Of Age, 1814, Frame, 17 x 12 1/2 In. . . 10575.00
Verse, Eliza Conner, December 6 1844, 18 x 14 In. 345.00
Verse, Eliza Jane Mackerduff, 10th Year Of Her Age, Wool, c.1845, 20 x 21 In. 2115.00
Verse, Emily Pattinson, Aged 11, 1825, Silk On Linen, Frame, 17 x 15 In. 1610.00
Verse, Flower Basket, Vine Border, Sarah Knight, Penn., c.1848, 19 1/2 x 21 In. 940.00
Verse, House, Flower Border, Rachel Long, March 8, 1821, Wool, Linen, 18 x 17 In. 598.00
Verse, House, Tree, Bird, Sarah Bullock, Age 9, Silk, Homespun, Frame, 20 x 17 In. 1495.00
Verse, House, Trees, Martha Dudley, Aged 9 Years, 1827, Frame, 17 3/4 x 16 1/4 In. 1840.00
Verse, House, Trees, Susannah Smith, Aged 12, 1808, Silk On Linen, Frame, 20 x 15 In. . .   837.00
Verse, Man, Birds, Duck, Mary Green August 20, 1819, Silk On Linen, Frame, 14 x 14 In. .   1035.00
Verse, Trees, Flowers, Animals, Elisabeth Gowland, Aged 12, 1819, Frame, 30 x 27 In. . . .   1955.00
Verses, Girl, Roses, Flowers, Birds, Margaret Morse, Frame, 1800s, 20 x 15 1/2 In. 1380.00
Verses, Potted Flowers, Swags, Cherubs, Silk On Linen, Frame, 12 1/4 x 16 1/4 In. 430.00
White Dove, Mary Barnard, Great St., Deerfield, c.1793, 13 1/2 x 10 In. 12075.00

SAMSON and Company, a French firm specializing in the reproduction of collectible wares of many countries and periods, was founded
in Paris in the early nineteenth century. Chelsea, Meissen, Famille
Verte, and Chinese Export porcelain are some of the wares that have
been reproduced by the company. The firm uses a variety of marks on
the reproductions. It is still in operation.

Bowl, Cover, Chinese Export Style, Gilt Bronze Mounted, Late 1800s, 21 3/4 In. 6000.00
Figurine, Bird, Exotic, Circular Base, c.1900, 6 In. 300.00
Jug, Imari, Side Handle, Gilt Silver Top, Marked, Early 20th Century, 7 In. 430.00
Plate, Raised Vine, Flowers, Armorial, Imitating Chinese Export, 9 1/2 In. 150.00
Vase, Garniture, Louis XVI Style, Paris, c.1885, Pair 4140.00
Vase, Garniture, Multicolored, Masque-Handled, Stopper, 14 1/2 In., Pair 920.00

SANDWICH GLASS is any of the myriad types of glass made by the
Boston and Sandwich Glass Works in Sandwich, Massachusetts,
between 1825 and 1888. It is often very difficult to be sure whether a
piece was really made at the Sandwich factory because so many types
were made there and similar pieces were made at other glass factories.
Additional pieces may be listed under Pressed Glass and in related
categories.

Basket, Fruit, Openwork, 16 Vertical Staves, 8-Sided Knop & Foot, 8 1/2 In. 605.00
Bowl, Fruit, Oval, Overshot, Rolled Ruffled Rim, 4 1/2 x 7 x 10 1/2 In. 44.00
Candlestick, Column, Blue, Petal Socket, Square Base, 9 1/4 In., Pair 2760.00
Candlestick, Column, Blue, Petal Socket, Stepped Base, 9 1/4 In. 145.00
Candlestick, Column, Canary, Petal Socket, Stepped Base, 9 1/4 In. . . . . .115.00 to 590.00
Candlestick, Column, Clambroth, Petal Socket, Stepped Base, 9 1/4 In. 145.00
Candlestick, Dolphin, Clambroth, Lavender Tint, Petal Socket, 2-Step Base, 10 In., Pair . .   3300.00
Candlestick, Dolphin, Clambroth, Petal Socket, Starch Blue, 2-Step Base, 10 In. 375.00
Candlestick, Dolphin, Clambroth, Starch Blue Petal Socket, 10 In., Pair 1530.00
Candlestick, Faceted Stem, Petal Socket, Circular Base, Violet Blue, Swirls, 6 3/4 In. 1155.00
Candlestick, Hexagonal, Amber, 9 In. 865.00
Candlestick, Hexagonal, Cobalt Blue, 9 1/4 In. 575.00
Candlestick, Lacy, Stippled Socket, Waterfall Base, 6 3/4 In., Pair 660.00
Candlestick, Petal & Loop, Clambroth, 7 In. . . . . .200.00 to 495.00
Candlestick, Petal & Loop, Green, 7 In. 575.00
Candlestick, Petal & Loop, Circular Base, Canary, 6 3/4 In. 300.00
Celery Vase, Magnet & Grape With Frosted Leaf, Scalloped Rim, Lacy, 8 1/2 In. 255.00
Claret, Cranberry Cut To Clear, House & Trees, Grapevine, 5 In. 470.00
Claret, Emerald Pattern, Cranberry Cut To Clear, Bee & Wheat, 4 3/4 In. . . . . .230.00 to 305.00
Cologne, Covered Basket Shape, Pale Translucent Blue, Gold Trim, Stopper, 4 3/4 In. 1540.00

Cologne, Star & Punty, Canary, Stopper, 6 3/4 In. 315.00
Creamer, Acanthus Leaf & Shield, Scalloped Octagonal Foot, Lacy, 4 1/4 In. 305.00
Creamer, Gothic Arch, Palm & Chain, Lacy, 4 1/8 In. 130.00
Creamer, Heart & Scale, Lacy, 4 1/2 In. 220.00
Cruet, Ribbed, Cobalt Blue, Folded Lip, 3-Piece Mold, Tam-O'-Shanter Stopper, 6 1/4 In. . 275.00
Curtain Tieback, Flower, Fiery Opalescent, Pewter Hardware, 4 1/2 In., Pair 90.00
Decanter, Baroque, Neck Rings, Ribbed Base, 3-Piece Mold, Qt., 10 3/4 In. 415.00
Decanter, Peacock Tail, 3-Piece Mold, Pressed Wheel Stopper, Qt., 11 1/2 In. 605.00
Decanter, Ribbed Arches, 3-Piece Mold, Folded Lip, Swirled Rib Stopper, Pt., 8 3/4 In. ... 470.00
Decanter, Sunburst & Diamond, Rayed Base, 3-Piece Mold, Wheel Stopper, Pt., 7 1/2 In. . 175.00
Dish, Cover, Princess Feather & Diamond, Basket Of Flowers, 8 3/4 x 10 1/2 In. 230.00
Flowerpot, Opal, 1874-87, 7 1/4 In. 4500.00
Honey Dish, Stepped Cover, Gothic Arch & Heart, Blue, 5 x 6 1/2 In. 3105.00
Jar, Pomade, Figural Bear, Clambroth, 5 In. 470.00
Jug, Overshot, Bulbous, Applied Reeded Handle, 7 In. 65.00
Jug, Water, Peacock Tail, Neck Rings, Rayed Base, 3-Piece Mold, 8 1/4 In. 3080.00
Lamp, Cable With Ring, Brass Burner, Snuffer, 4 In. 495.00
Lamp, Fluid, Inverted Diamond With Thumbprint Font, 8-Sided Base, Pewter Collar, 9 In. . 110.00
Lamp, Fluid, Prism & Flattened Sawtooth Font, Wafer, Hexagonal Base, 10 In. 120.00
Lamp, Fluid, Star & Punty Font, Jade Green, Gold Branches, 10 In. 6900.00
Lamp, Kerosene, Star & Quatrefoil Font, White Cut To Clear, Clambroth Base, 14 In. 990.00
Lamp, Kerosene, Waisted Loop Font, Disk Wafer, Monument Base, 11 1/4 In. 155.00
Lamp, Kerosene, White Cut To Clear Font, Opalescent, 3-Dolphin Base, Gold Trim, 12 In. . 7150.00
Lamp, Oil, Fiery Opalescent, Triple Dolphin Base, Cut Overlay Font, Gilt 7150.00
Lamp, Safety, Inverted Diamond & Thumbprint Font, 6-Sided Base, 8 1/2 In. 115.00
Lamp, Whale Oil, Conical Font, Wheat Sheaf, Cup Plate Base, 6 7/8 In. 1980.00
Lamp, Whale Oil, Pewter Burner, c.1840, 3 1/4 In., Pair 350.00
Lamp, Whale Oil, Pressed Loop Font, Hexagonal Base, Sapphire Blue, 9 1/2 In. 1045.00
Lamp, Whale Oil, Star Pattern, 1840-60, 11 1/4 In. 431.00
Mustard, Underplate, Peacock Eye, Lacy 495.00
Nappy, Crossed Peacock Eye, Footed, Lacy, 4 1/8 x 7 1/2 In. 415.00
Nappy, Crossed Peacock Eye, Shaped & Scalloped Rim, Lacy, 9 1/4 In. 145.00
Nappy, Dahlia, Scalloped Rim, Lacy, 2 x 9 3/8 In. 385.00
Nappy, Rose & Thistle, Lacy, 8 1/4 In. 305.00
Nappy, Sunburst In Diamond Band, Folded Rim, Rayed Base, 3-Piece Mold, 5 In., Pair ... 130.00
Plate, Diamond Band, Folded Rim, Rayed Base, 3-Piece Mold, 5 In. 90.00
Plate, Double Peacock Eye, Octagonal, Canted Corners, Lacy, 9 1/8 x 12 In. 360.00
Plate, Hairpin, Square, Lacy, 7 3/8 x 7 3/4 In. 7700.00
Plate, Pipes Of Pan, Scalloped & Pointed Rim, Octagonal, Lacy, 6 1/4 x 8 1/4 In. 300.00
Plate, Plume & Acorn, Amber, 6 In. 115.00
Plate, Plume & Acorn, Amethyst, 5 1/4 In. 260.00
Plate, Strawberry Diamond, Sheaf Of Wheat, Oval, Lacy, 6 1/4 x 9 1/2 In. 715.00
Plate, Sunburst Diamond, Folded Rim, Rayed & Ringed Base, 3-Piece Mold, 4 In. 220.00
Salt, Basket Of Flowers, Opalescent Violet Blue, Crisscross Base, Lacy, 2 x 1 3/4 x 3 In. .. 1100.00
Salt, Beaded Strawberry-Diamond, Deep Purple Blue, Lacy, 1 3/4 x 3 1/2 In. 495.00
Salt, Boat, 16-Point Star On Stern, Cobalt Blue, 4 In. 1150.00
Salt, Chariot, Mottled Silvery Opaque Blue, Lacy, 1 3/4 x 2 1/8 x 2 7/8 In. 1265.00
Salt, Cover, Beaded Scroll & Basket Of Flowers, Lacy, 3 x 1 7/8 x 3 1/8 In. 1595.00
Salt, Eagle & Shield, Fiery Opalescent, Lacy, 2 1/8 x 2 1/8 x 3 1/4 In. 605.00
Salt, Eagle & Ship, Scalloped Edge, Round, Lacy, 1 7/8 x 3 In. 2530.00
Salt, Lafayet Steamboat, Scrolled Fleur-De-Lis Base, Lacy, 1 5/8 x 1 7/8 x 3 5/8 In. 415.00
Salt, Lafayet Steamboat, Star & Beaded Rim Base, Cobalt Blue, Lacy, 1 5/8 x 3 5/8 In. ... 2750.00
Salt, Lyre, Plain Wheat Sheaf Base, Lacy, 1 7/8 x 2 1/8 x 3 1/8 In. 330.00
Salt, Peacock Eye, Dark Blue, Oval, Rayed Base, 1 3/8 x 2 7/8 x 3 3/4 In. 2640.00
Salt, Scrolled Heart, Light Green, Lacy, 1 3/4 x 1 7/8 x 3 In. 880.00
Salt, Shell, Red Amethyst, Scroll Pedestal, Srawberry-Diamond Base, Lacy, 1 3/4 In. 645.00
Salt, Shell, Strawberry-Diamond Base, Scroll Pedestal, Lacy, 2 5/8 In. 705.00
Salt, Stag's Horn, Gray Blue, Violet Tinted 24-Ray Base, Lacy, 1 3/4 x 3 In. 1375.00
Salt, Strawberry-Diamond, Cobalt Blue, Fluted 20-Ray Base, Lacy, 2 x 2 3/4 In. 715.00
Salt, Strawberry-Diamond, Medium Amber, Fluted 16-Ray Base, Lacy, 2 x 2 7/8 In. 2310.00
Spoon Holder, Horn Of Plenty, Clambroth, 4 1/2 In. 175.00
Spoon Holder, Inverted Diamond & Thumbprint, Amethyst, 4 1/2 In. 575.00

Spoon Holder, Sandwich Star, 1/4 Diamond, Canary, 5 1/4 In. 315.00
Spoon Holder, Sandwich Star, 1/4 Diamond, Electric Blue, 5 1/4 In. 980.00
Spoon Holder, Star & Punty, Footed, Canary, 4 3/4 In. 490.00
Spoon Holder, Star & Punty, Footed, Jade Green, 4 3/4 In. 4025.00
Spooner, Sandwich Star, Translucent Electric Blue, Hexagonal Foot, 5 In. 1265.00
Sugar, Cover, Gothic Arch, Footed, Canary, Lacy, 5 1/4 In. 635.00
Sugar, Cover, Gothic Arch, Peacock Blue, 5 1/4 In. 520.00
Syrup, Embossed Leaf, Stippling, Green, c.1850 .... 1225.00
Toddy Plate, Grape Vine & Harp, Peacock Blue, 4 3/8 In. 120.00
Toothpick, Basket Weave, Translucent Starch Blue Base, Alabaster Cover 300.00
Tray, U.S.F. Constitution, Star & Heart Border, Lacy, 4 1/2 x 7 In. 2640.00
Tumbler, 9-Panel, Translucent Starch Blue, 1 5/8 x 1 5/8 In. 110.00
Tumbler, Flip, Diamond Band, Ribbed Bands, Rayed, Ringed Base, 3-Piece Mold, 5 In. 360.00
Tumbler, Pointed Oval, Teal Green, 10-Scallop Rayed Base, Lacy, 2 x 1 5/8 In. 525.00
Tumbler, Worcester, Amethyst, 4 1/4 In. 200.00
Vase, 3-Printie, Gauffered Rim, Hexagonal Base, Canary, 9 1/4 In. 260.00
Vase, Elongated Loop, Bisecting Lines, Amethyst, Octagonal Foot, 4 3/4 In. 990.00
Vase, Elongated Loop, Bisecting Lines, Fiery Opalescent, Octagonal Foot, 4 3/4 In. 1265.00
Vase, Hobnail, Clambroth, Gold Trim, Oval, Flared Neck, 6 5/8 In. 50.00
Vase, Sawtooth, Jade Green & Clambroth, Blown, Applied Snake, Footed, 9 In. 2090.00
Vase, Tulip, Amethyst, Paneled, Scalloped Rim, Octagonal Base, 10 In. 2115.00
Vase, Tulip, Dark Amethyst, Paneled, Scalloped Rim, Octagonal Base, 9 3/4 In. . .4700.00 to 4950.00
Wafer Dish, Blue & White Swirl, 2 1/4 In. 475.00
Whimsy, Pipe, Cranberry Loopings, Tulip Shape Bowl, Long Stem, Blown, 1890, 18 In. .. 575.00

SARREGUEMINES is the name of a French town that is used as part of a china mark. Utzschneider and Company, a porcelain factory, made ceramics in Sarreguemines, Lorraine, France, from about 1775. Transfer-printed wares and majolica were made in the nineteenth century. The nineteenth-century pieces, most often found today, usually have colorful transfer-printed decorations showing peasants in local costumes.

Character Mug, John Bull, 20th Century, 7 In. 70.00
Figure, Eagle, Haig Whisky, Great Scot!, France, 11 1/4 In. 1055.00
Vase, Brown, Purple, Silver, Gold, Crystalline Glaze, Gourd, 10 1/2 In. 705.00
Vase, Flared End, Folded Tricornered Rim, Green Crystalline Glossy Glaze, 6 x 7 In. 405.00

SASCHA BRASTOFF made decorative accessories, ceramics, enamels on copper, and plastics of his own design. He headed a factory, Sascha Brastoff of California, Inc., in West Los Angeles, from 1953 until about 1973. He died in 1993. Pieces signed with the signature *Sascha Brastoff* were his work and are the most expensive. Other pieces marked *Sascha B.* or with a stamped mark were made by others in his company.

Ashtray, Enamel, Orange, White Petaled Flowers, Signed, 7 1/2 x 4 5/8 In. 37.00
Ashtray, Star Steed, Mauve, Turquoise, White, 8 Cigarette Rests, Signed, 8 7/8 In. 40.00
Charger, Lime Green Fading To Black, Fruit Designs, Signed On Front, 14 In. 145.00
Cup & Saucer, Demitasse, Surf Ballet, Black & Gold 28.00
Decanter, Stopper, Rust & Blue Geometrics, Black Lines, White Glaze, 17 1/2 In. 23.00
Platter, Abstract Design, Browns & Golds, Glass Cabochons, Signed, 17 3/4 In. 165.00
Vase, Enamel, Green, White Flowers, 9 1/4 In. 485.00
Vase, Flattened Pillow, Gold On Gold Decoration, Rooster Mark, c.1960, 3/4 In. 85.00
Vase, Lava Glaze, Turquoise, 24K Gold Lines, Raw Umber Interior, 5 1/2 x 4 In. 38.00

SATIN GLASS is a late-nineteenth-century art glass. It has a dull finish that is caused by hydrofluoric acid vapor treatment. Satin glass was made in many colors and sometimes has applied decorations. Satin glass is also listed by factory name, such as Webb, or in the Mother-of-Pearl category in this book.

Bowl, Underplate, Diamond-Quilted, Blue To Fuchsia, Amber, Ruffled Rim, 5 3/4 In. 2130.00
Compote, Blue To Fuchsia, Amber, Applied Foot, Ruffled Edge, 5 1/2 In. 2070.00
Cracker Jar, Victorian, Enameled Flowers, Silvered Mounted Lid, 7 1/2 In. 150.00

Ewer, Blue To Pearl, Burgundy Leaves, Melon Ribbed, Ruffled Edge, Handles, 10 In. 110.00
Ewer, Lime Green Shaded To Green, Flowers, Ruffled Edge, Clear Handle, 9 3/4 In. 100.00
Ewer, Robin's-Egg Blue, Ruffled Edge, Applied Camphor Handles, 9 In. 95.00
Ewer, Salmon To Creamy White, Flowers, Elongated Neck, Camphor Handle, 9 3/4 In. . . .   170.00
Pitcher, Pink, Applied Handle, 6 3/8 In. 260.00
Rose Bowl, Pink Shaded To Green, Molded Shells, Crimped Edge, 3 1/2 In. 60.00
Vase, Blue Shaded To Pearl, Butterflies, Flowers, 3 Clear Looped Handles, 9 In., Pair 335.00
Vase, Blue, Swirl, White Interior, Polished Pontil, 5 1/4 In. 260.00
Vase, Medium Blue To Light, Bird Perched On Branches, Crimped Rim, Oval, 6 1/2 In. . . .   175.00
Vase, Robin's-Egg Blue, Silver Pearl, Swallows, Flowers, Melon Ribbed, 11 In. 50.00
Vase, Shaded Blue, Bird On Branch, Egg Shape, Crimped Rim, 6-Footed, 6 1/2 In. 195.00
Vase, Shaded Blue, Butterflies, Leaves, Gold Trim, Crimped Rim, Thorn Handles, 12 In. . .   195.00
Vase, Shaded Pink, Enameled Flowers, Victorian, 7 In. 315.00
Vase, Shades Of Blue, Butterflies, Green Leaves, Thorn Handles, Crimped Rim, 12 In. 175.00

SATSUMA is a Japanese pottery with a distinctive creamy beige crackled glaze. Most of the pieces were decorated with blue, red, green, orange, or gold. Almost all Satsuma found today was made after 1860, especially during the Meiji Period, 1868–1912. During World War I, Americans could not buy undecorated European porcelains. Women who liked to make hand painted porcelains at home began to decorate plain Satsuma. These pieces are known today as *American Satsuma.*

Bowl, 9 Gods, Wisteria Landscape, Shell Shape, Shell Shape Feet, 1800s, 17 In. 978.00
Bowl, Flower Shape, Figures, Landscape, Brocade Ground, 6 1/4 In. 460.00
Bowl, Flower, Figure Cartouche, Butterfly Brocade Ground, 5 Lobes, Signed, 5 In. 430.00
Bowl, Holy Man, Goddess Of Mercy, Dragons, Lobed Rim, Late 1800s, 10 In. 50.00
Bowl, Low Relief Holy Man, Painted, c.1900, 8 In. 400.00
Bowl, Seated Figures, Red Border, Gilt Flowers & Geometrics, Script, Lobed, 6 In. 575.00
Brush Jar, Bamboo Stalks, Bird, Branch, Enameled Gold, Green, Footed, 4 1/4 In. 170.00
Censer, Scrolls, Fans, Brocade Pattern, Blue Ground, Satsuma Mons Mark, 1800s, 11 In. . .   350.00
Censer, Temple Landscape, Oval, Kinkozan, 3 3/4 In. 3450.00
Charger, Allegorical, 3 Priests, Tiger, Bird 259.00
Cup & Saucer, Figures Under Weeping Cherry Tree 35.00
Cup & Saucer, Figures, Textile Pattern Ground, Gyokushu, Early 1900s, 5 1/2-In. Saucer . .   90.00
Cup & Saucer, Women In Garden, 8 1/4 In., 6 Piece 127.00
Figurine, Monkey Holding Red Pepper, 8 In. 1380.00
Figurine, Woman Adjusting Makeup, Mirror, 12 In. 1380.00
Jar, Cover, Brocade, 3 x 3 1/2 In. 29.00
Jar, Heroic, Mythological Figures, Sea, Eizan Of Kiyomizu, Kyoto, Japan, 40 In. 8625.00
Pitcher, Flowers, Figures, Gold, Cream Ground, Bamboo Handle, 6 In. . . . . *Illus*   145.00
Plate, 10 Figures, Flowers, Landscapes, Flower Ground, 7 1/2 In.   890.00
Plate, Dessert, Figures, Trees, Mt. Fuji, 7 1/2 In., 6 Piece 750.00
Plate, Scholars In A Garden, 8 1/4 In. 69.00

Satsuma, Pitcher, Flowers, Figures, Gold,
Cream Ground, Bamboo Handle, 6 In.

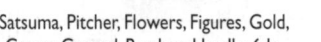

Ivory will darken if kept in the dark. Keep a piano open so the keys will be in natural light. Keep figurines, chess sets, scrimshaw, and other ivory in the open.

Restaurant Model, 2 Tiers, Paulownia Flowers, Kakimoto, Early 1800s, 6 3/4 x 10 1/2 In. . 2645.00
Tete-A-Tete, Tea Set, Teapot, Sugar, Cover, Creamer, Cover, 2 Cups & Saucers, 5 1/2 In. . . 210.00
Vase, Carp In Sea, Teardrop, Signed, 6 In. 375.00
Vase, Cover, Blue Flowers, Bamboo, Gilt, Earthenware, 19th Century, 8 1/2 In. 538.00
Vase, Dragon Cartouches, Ho-Ho Birds, Chrysanthemums, 10 1/2 In. 2990.00
Vase, Duck, Lotus, Gourd Form, Makazu Kozan, 13 In. 805.00
Vase, Emperor, Empress, Ormolu Mount, Griffin Handles, 34 In., Pair 3565.00
Vase, Family Near Red House, Trees, Gilt Feathers & Rim, Egg Shape, 7 1/4 In., Pair 750.00
Vase, Figure, Landscape, Inverted Pear Shape, 3 1/2 In. 230.00
Vase, Figures, Dragon Handles, Brocade Ground, 3 1/2 In. 290.00
Vase, Figures, Landscape Ground, Oval, 2 3/4 In. 489.00
Vase, Flower Garden, Fence, Inverted Pear Shape, Signed, 3 In. 210.00
Vase, Flowers, Butterflies, Birds, 6 Cylinders Form Row Of Bud Vases, 4 x 6 1/2 In. 290.00
Vase, Flowers, Butterfly, Urn Shape Body, Painted, Gilt Accents, c.1900, 19 In. 345.00
Vase, Landscape Cartouche, Flower Ground, Inverted Pear Shape, Signed, 16 3/4 In. 2070.00
Vase, Landscape, 3 1/2 In., Pair 80.00
Vase, Procession Of Scholars, Mountains, 2 Elephant Trunk Handles, Footed, 24 In. 239.00
Vase, Roosters, Hens, Chicks, Garden, Flowers, Birds, Squat, Candlestick Shape, 9 1/2 In. . 5463.00
Vase, Samurai & Garden Ladies, Baluster Shape, Flared Neck, c.1890, 12 In. 200.00

SATURDAY EVENING GIRLS, see Paul Revere Pottery category.

SCALES have been made to weigh everything from babies to gold.
Collectors search for all types. Most popular are small gold dust scales
and special grocery scales.

Apothecary, 2 Nickel Plated Pans, White Marble Platform, Mahogany Lid, 13 In. 88.00
Balance, Analytical Beam, Chainematic, C. Becker Inc., N. Y., Style 89C, Case, 18 In. 120.00
Balance, Analytical Beam, H. Troemner, Philadelphia, Brass Pillar, & Pans, Case, 14 In. . . 180.00
Balance, Analytical Beam, Volland & Sons, Brass Pillar, Nickel Plated Pans, Case, 14 In. . 15.00
Balance, Beam, Avery, Class B, Brass Tray, Pan, Finial, Mahogany Base, 7 Weights, 23 In. 200.00
Balance, Beam, H. Troemner, Philadelphia, Brass, Cast Iron Base, Paw Feet, 38 In. 325.00
Balance, Brass, Iron, Wood Stand, 2 Drawers, China, 19th Century, 43 x 13 x 26 In. 1380.00
Balance, Brass, Iron, Wooden Stand, 2 Drawers, Handles, China, 43 x 26 In. 1380.00
Balance, Coin, Steel Arm, 2 Brass Pans, 7 Weights, Mahogany Case, France 100.00
Balance, French-Balance Pendule, Walnut Case, Marble Top, 3 Weights, 10 x 25 In. 275.00
Balance, Henry Troemner, Black Rectangular Base, Dial, Marble Top, 2 Pans, 18 In. 115.00
Balance, Iron, Red, Mustard & Black Paint, Penn., 16 1/2 x 24 In. 750.00
Balance, Torsion Balance Co., Cast Iron, Chrome, Glass Case, 16 x 7 x 9 1/2 In. 81.00
Balance, Torsion Balance Co., Style 600, New York, Nickel Plated Beam, Case, 9 In. 90.00
Candy, Cast Iron, Hushallsvag, 14 x 9 In. 50.00
Character Readings, Your Future?, Metal, 48 In. 450.00
Computing, Countertop, Dayton, 15 x 13 In. 105.00
Drugstore, Old Fashioned, Porcelain, Cast Iron, Tile Foot Plate, Mirror, Peerless, 69 In. . . 660.00
Fortune Teller, 1 Cent, Cast Iron, Porcelain, Mirrored Front, Watling, 50 x 25 x 16 In. 440.00
Gold, Hand Held Balance, 2 Brass Hands, Weights, Wood Hinged Case, 5 1/2 x 2 1/2 In. . . 145.00
Gold, Hunt & Co., Brass, 7 Weights, Walnut, California Gold Rush, London, 23 x 20 In. . . 8250.00
Grain Tester, Fairbanks, St. Louis, Brass, Sliding Poise, Suspension Ring, 1877, 13 In. 205.00
Hanging, Purina, Feed Saver & Cow Culler, No Pan, 8 In. Diam. 190.00
Honest Weight, Cast Iron, Countertop, International Business Machine, 32 x 20 In. 470.00
Horoscope, Coin-Operated, Watling Co., 64 x 24 x 17 In. 440.00
Letter, Balance, Salter, No. 11, 8 In. 55.00
Penny, 1 Cent, Cast Iron, Porcelain, Mills Novelty, 46 x 23 x 12 In. 330.00
Penny, 1 Cent, Floor Model, Marion Machine Tool Co., Marion, Ohio, 40 x 22 x 10 In. . . . 195.00
Postage, Brass Beam, 2 Trays, Serpentine Rosewood Base, 5 Weights, 7 In. 265.00
Standing Pan, Brass, Iron, DeGrave Co., London, 1760-95 . . . . 1250.00
Tradesman's, 6 Graduated Brass Weights, Milk Glass, Swansea, England, Late 1800s 490.00
Weighing, Caille Bros., George Washington, 1 Cent, Floor Model 12100.00
Weighing, Coin-Operated, 1 Cent, Porcelain Dial, Cast Iron, National Novelty Co, 67 In. . . 990.00
Weighing, Coin-Operated, 1 Cent, Weigh Your Fate, American Scale Co., 51 In. 140.00
Weighing, Hanging, Tripod, Chair Hangs From Scale, Guesser 770.00
Weighing, No. 49, Cast Iron, Weighs To 20 Lbs., Cast Iron, 13 In. 240.00
Weighing, Turnbull's Family, Brass Dial, Metal Pan, Weighs Up To 8 Lbs., 11 x 12 In. 330.00
Weighing, Watling, Coin-Operated, 1 Cent, 67 x 12 In. 175.00

SCHAFER & VATER, makers of small ceramic items, are best known for their amusing figurals. The factory was located in Volkstedt-Rudolstadt, Germany, from 1890 to 1962. Some pieces are marked with the crown and R mark, but many are unmarked.

Egyptian Obelisk, Pink & White Matte, 5 In.	340.00
Vase, Cat, I Want My Vote, Rudoltstadt, Pre 1914, 5 In.	2513.00
Victorian Shoe, Green Cameo, White Matte, 4 In.	700.00
Wall Pocket, Tussy Mussy, Applied Pink Roses, Matte, 6 1/2 In.	400.00

SCHNEIDER Glassworks was founded in 1913 at Epinay-sur-Seine, France, by Charles and Ernest Schneider. Art glass was made between 1913 and 1930. The company still produces clear crystal glass. See also La Verres Français.

Dish, Sweetmeat, Orange, Mulberry, Cobalt Blue, Footed, Stamped, 2 3/4 In.	175.00
Ewer, Mottled Amber, Yellow, Blue, Applied Amethyst Handle, Etched Signature, 16 In.	1880.00
Lamp, Umber, Cobalt, Acid Etched, Flowers, Brass Mount, 16 In.	440.00
Vase, Mottled Amethyst, Yellow, Corseted, Art Nouveau, 8 In.	800.00
Vase, Mottled Blue, Purple, Pink, Orange, c.1915, 17 1/4 In.	1560.00
Vase, Yellow, Purple Variegated, Applied Amethyst Handles, Inscribed, c.1920, 8 1/2 In.	865.00

SCIENTIFIC INSTRUMENTS of all kinds are included in this category. Other categories such as Barometer, Binoculars, Dental, Nautical, Medical, and Thermometer may also price scientific apparatus.

Anemometer, A.E. Thornton, Manchester, Anodized Brass, 6 Dials	145.00
Anemometer, Biram, Short & Mason, No. 13396, 5 Registers, 10 Blades, 6 In.	120.00
Anemometer, No. 557, 8-Blade Fan, 3 Brass Legs, 3 1/4 In.	480.00
Arithmometer, Burkhardt, Black Enamel Plate, 16 Digit Display, 23 In.	1530.00
Barograph, Short & Mason, No. J362, Brass, Mahogany Case, 12 In.	355.00
Calculator, Keuffel & Esser, Model 4012, No. 5008, Rotating Cylinder, Case, 21 In.	499.00
Calculator, Thancher's, Deuffel & Esser, Model 4012, 23 x 6 In.	1150.00
Chain, Surveyor's, Helffrict, Philadelphia, 2 Poles, Brass Handles	275.00
Chain, Surveyor's, W. & L.E. Gurley, 1 Brass & 1 Steel Handle, 100 Ft.	165.00
Chronometer, Eggert & Son, No. 276, Mahogany & Brass Case, 8 In.	3175.00
Compass, Andrew T. Lloyd Co., Boston, Brass, 2 1/2 In.	69.00
Compass, Dobbie McInness Ltd., Glasgow, Serpentine Mahogany Stand, 16 In.	235.00
Compass, Prismatic, Stanley, No. 6258, Folding Sight, Prism, Shades, 3 In.	70.00
Compass, Surveyor's Railroad, W. & L.E. Gurley, Troy, New York	1540.00
Compass, Surveyor's, Brass, Spencer, Browning, & Rust, London, 14 1/2 In.	715.00
Compass, Surveyor's, Daniel King, Mass., 14 1/2 In.	3408.00
Compass, Surveyor's, Daniel King, Salem China, Birch, Fleur-De-Lis North, 14 In.	3410.00
Compass, Surveyor's, E. & G.W. Blunt, New York, 15 1/2 In.	990.00
Compass, Surveyor's, G.L. Whitehouse, Vernier, 2 Vanes, Painted Box, 14 In.	2350.00
Compass, Surveyor's, Grier Bluhm, Brass, Painted Metal, Case, Tripod	155.00
Compass, Surveyor's, Gurley, Troy, N.Y., Vernier, Mahogany Case, 15 1/2 In.	999.00
Compass, Surveyor's, Thaxter, Boston, Mahogany, Fleur-De-Lis, Scrolls, 15 In.	1880.00
Compass, Surveyor's, Thomas Greenough, Wood, Steel Needle, 2 Vanes, 15 In.	1528.00
Compass, Surveyor's, W. & L.E. Gurley, Vernier Transit, Case, 13 In.	1200.00 to 1760.00
Compass, Surveyor's, William J. Young, Fitted Wooden Case, Tripod, 1850	1450.00
Compass, Surveyor's, Wm. J. Young, Vernier, Brass, Wood Case, 15 1/2 In.	1870.00
Helio-Chronometer, P.F & Cie, Paris, Bronze Sight, Rotating Lens, Pivot Base, 8 In.	650.00
Hydrometer, Buss, London, Brass Bulb, Ivory Thermometer, Case, 8 In.	120.00
Hydrometer, Sikes, Weight Set, Cherry Box, Plush Lining, Book	480.00
Hydrometer Set, T. Armstrong, 6 Mercury-Filled Bulbs, Silk Lined Case, 13 In.	200.00
Level, H.L. Silver, Los Angeles, No. 7585, Brass, Tripod, Mahogany Case, 12 In.	235.00
Level, Starrett, No. 101-A, Nickel-Plated, Tripod Base, Case, 12 1/2 In.	29.00
Level, Surveyor's, Adie, England, Brass, Mahogany Case, Inscription, 17 In.	565.00
Magnifying Glass, Parrot Head Handle, England, Late 1800s	295.00
Microscope, Bausch & Lomb, Dissecting, No. 49995, Case, 7 In.	295.00
Microscope, Bausch & Lomb, No. 202709, Petrographical, Case, 14 In.	825.00
Microscope, Bausch & Lomb, Stereo, Binocular Eyepiece, Rotating Drum, 10 In.	205.00
Microscope, Bausch & Lomb, Student, Brass, Twin Pillar Mount, Y-Foot, Case, 12 In.	1410.00
Microscope, Leitz, No. 19513, Compound, Mahogany Case, 11 In.	440.00

Microscope, Nachet Et Fils, France, Compound, Brass, c.1870, 13 In.	945.00
Microscope, Physician, Black U-Foot, Fitted Case, 12 In.	1058.00
Microscope, Spencer, No. 13, Brass, Cast Iron Limb, Y-Foot, Case, 14 In.	1880.00
Microscope, Zeiss, No. 180012, Compound, Black Enameled, Roll-Front Case, 13 In.	295.00
Microscope, Zentmayer, Dissecting, Round Foot, Mahogany Case, 3 1/2 In.	106.00
Pantograph, C. Hearn, Montreal, Brass Frame, Engraved Indices, Ivory Wheels, 36 In.	206.00
Pantograph, W.L. Jones Holborn, London, No. 135, Brass, Pine Case, 15 In.	325.00
Parallel Rule, W.H. Harling Ltd., Boxwood, Brass Roll, Mahogany Case	45.00
Protractor, Price's Patent, No. 726615, Brass Sector Rule, 2 Arcs, 24 In.	295.00
Radiometer, Tube, J.D. Biddle, Philadelphia, 4-Blade Vane, Turned Wood Base, 12 In.	235.00
Refractometer, Spencer, No. 156, Prism, Eyepiece, Reflector, Scale, 11 In.	176.00
Ring Dial, Equinoctial, Le Maire, Paris, 2 Brass Rings, Sliding Steel Cursor	3410.00
Sextant, Brass, Cased, Rosewood, Spencer, Browning & Rust, 11 x 13 In.	575.00
Spectroscope, Bausch & Lomb, Black Crackle Finish, Tripod Base, 14 In.	235.00
Telescope, 3 Draw, Dollond, London, Day Or Night, Mahogany, Brass, 12 In.	440.00
Telescope, 4 Draw, Dollond, London, Ebonized Wood, Brass, Tripod, 9 1/2 In.	529.00
Telescope, 4 Draw, Rosewood Body, Brass Column, Tripod Feet, 10 1/4 In.	1175.00
Telescope, Astronomical, Refracting, W. Gardam & Sons, New York, 59 In.	3290.00
Telescope, Bardou & Son, Paris, Brass, Tabletop, 19th Century, 46 In.	1265.00
Telescope, Bardou & Son, Paris, Wooden Tripod, Open Legs, 37 In.	2070.00
Telescope, England, Leather, Brass Fitting, Mahogany Tripod, 65 x 37 In.	1765.00
Telescope, Navy Issue, Tripod, Brass Plaque, 23 In.	120.00
Telescope, Single Draw, Daniel & Jones, London, Day Or Night, Brass, 21 In.	118.00
Telescope, Single Draw, Osborne, London, Leather, Brass, 38 In.	175.00
Telescope, Single Draw, Spencer, Browning & Co., London, Day Or Night, 20 In.	410.00
Transit, Keuffel & Esser Co., Case, Tripod, 1900s, 17 x 14 x 9 In.	200.00 to 633.00
Transit, Surveyor's, Buff & Berger, Accessories, Brass, Case	690.00
Transit, Surveyor's, Buff & Berger, Boston, No. 952, Brass, Twin A-Frames, 12 In.	705.00
Transit, Surveyor's, Buff & Berger, No. 121, Bubble-Levels, 2 Vernier Scales, 12 In.	1115.00
Transit, Surveyor's, Stackpole & Bros., No. 1880, Brass, Vernier, Case, 12 In.	999.00
Transit, Surveyor's, T.F. Randolph, Cin., Ohio, Brass, Wood, Case, 11 In.	1045.00
Transit, Surveyor's, W. & L.E. Gurley, Troy, New York, Signed, c.1870, Case, 15 In.	1210.00
Tripod, Surveyor's Compass, Mahogany Legs, Brass Fittings, 48 In.	220.00
Wye Level, J.C. Ulmer & Co., Cleveland, No. 426, Brass, 4 Screw Base	120.00

SCRIMSHAW

SCRIMSHAW is bone or ivory or whale's teeth carved by sailors and others for entertainment during the sailing-ship days. Some scrimshaw was carved as early as 1800. There are modern scrimshanders making pieces today on bone, ivory, or plastic. Other pieces may be found in the Ivory and Nautical categories.

Busk, Bone, Curved Shape, Incised Eagle, 2 Sailing Ships, Star, Compass, 8 1/4 In.	345.00
Busk, Bone, Incised Diamond Border, Star, Tree, Basket, Duck, 14 1/2 In.	1265.00
Busk, Whalebone, 5 Panels, Sailor, Eagle, House, Ship, Girl, 13 3/4 In.	750.00
Busk, Whalebone, Geometric Pinwheels, Homestead Scene, 13 In.	910.00
Cane, Wood, Carved, Frog, White Ivory Eyes, Ivory Column, 37 1/2 In.	690.00
Pie Crimper, Whale Ivory, Star-Centered Wheel, Arched Shape, Fist Handle, 8 In.	2530.00
Walrus Tusk, Whales, Whale Ship, Signed, Charles A. Menghis, 18 In.	635.00
Watch, Walrus Ivory, Chain, 17 3/4 In.	1955.00
Whale Ear Bones, Shell Shape, 5 x 3 In., Pair	290.00
Whale's Tooth, 2 Sailing Ships, Rock Formation, Turbulent Sea, E.E., 1800s, 4 3/8 In.	1058.00
Whale's Tooth, 3-Masted Ships, American Flags, Early 1800s, 4 1/2 In.	1530.00
Whale's Tooth, Eagle's Head Form, Holding Banner, In God We Trust	240.00
Whale's Tooth, Engraved Woman, Whaling Ship, 8 1/4 In.	5750.00
Whale's Tooth, Fashionable Lady, Fountain, 1800s, 6 1/4 In.	825.00
Whale's Tooth, Lady, Fancy Dress, Hat, Red Wax Band, 5 1/8 In.	1530.00
Whale's Tooth, Seaport, Clock Towers, Ships, Fort, Flag, Manor, 19th Century, 6 1/2 In.	7475.00
Whale's Tooth, Ship, Erupting Volcano, Fort, Flag, Frigate, 19th Century, 6 1/2 In.	6900.00
Whale's Tooth, Whaling Ship, Boats, Whale, Burning Ship, Early 1800s, 6 In.	1765.00
Whale's Tooth, Whaling Ship, Sailing Near Iceberg, 7 In.	430.00
Whale's Tooth, Woman In Fashionable Dress, Bust Of Woman With Hat, 1800s, 5 In.	500.00
Whale's Tooth, Woman Reading Book, 6 1/2 In.	835.00
Whalebone, E Pluribus Unum, Patriotic, Eagle, Flat, Rounded Ends, 13 1/2 x 1 1/2 In.	1445.00

SEBASTIAN MINIATURES were first made by Prescott W. Baston in 1938 in Marblehead, Massachusetts. More than 400 different designs have been made, and collectors search for the out-of-production models. The mark may say *Copr. P. W. Baston U.S.A.*, or *P. W. Baston, U.S.A.*, or *Prescott W. Baston*. Sometimes a paper label was used.

Aunt Polly, P.W. Baston, 1948, 4 3/4 In.	30.00
Little Mother, No. SML213A, 3 1/2 In.	40.00
Old Salt, Fisherman, No. SML148A, 3 1/4 In.	30.00
Rub A Dub Dub, 3 Girls Hiding Cake From Goose In Tub, No. SML377, 4 In.	50.00
Weaver & Loom, No. SML174, 3 In.	50.00
Williamsburg Couple, No. SML285A, 3 In.	35.00

SEG, see Paul Revere Pottery category.

SEVRES porcelain has been made in Sevres, France, since 1769. Many copies of the famous ware have been made. The name originally referred to the works of the Royal Porcelain factory. The name now includes any of the wares made in the town of Sevres, France. The entwined lines with a center letter used as the mark is one of the most forged marks in antiques. Be very careful to identify Sevres by quality, not just by mark.

Cachepot, Portrait, Turquoise Ground, Flower Panels, Scroll Feet, c.1900, 5 1/2 In., Pair	565.00
Candelabrum, 5 Cups, Spiral Urn, Cobalt & White Flowers, Gilt, Marked, 17 7/8 In., Pair	2415.00
Compote, Hand Painted Scene, Couple Courting, Blue Ground, Mid 1800s, 12 In.	290.00
Dish, Bronze, Flowers, Lady, 2 Handles, Scrollwork, Garlands, Leaves, Grapes, 7 x 14 In.	2475.00
Dresser Box, Rectangular, Floral Garland Border, Gilt Enamel Swags, c.1900, 7 1/4 In.	120.00
Figurine, Elephant, Textured Glaze, France, c.1953, 12 x 19 In.	940.00
Figurine, Emperor Napoleon I, Standing, Biscuit, Porcelain, In Military Dress, 10 1/2 In.	550.00
Figurine, Street Urchin, Tattered Clothing, 18th Century, 5 In.	115.00
Jardiniere, Blue, Yellow, Green Crystalline Glaze, Cameo Rim Design, 9 3/4 x 9 1/2 In.	545.00
Lamp, Pedestal, Signed Henrion, 54 In.	4400.00
Plate, Chateau De Pau, Yellow Border, Gilt, 1844, 9 1/2 In.	450.00
Urn, Campana, Portraits, Napoleon, Josephine, Flowers, Green Ground, c.1900, 7 In., Pair	1000.00
Urn, Cover, Courting Couples, Blue Ground, Gilt Trim, 9 1/2 In., Pair	1725.00
Urn, Cover, Gilt White Metal Mounts, Base, Landscape, Courting Scenes, 17 x 6 In.	155.00
Urn, Dark Blue, Gold Enamel, Center Panel, Man, Woman On Bench, 17 1/2 In., Pair	1150.00
Urn, Napoleonic Scene, Green Ground, Plastic Base, 19 In.	1370.00
Vase, Cover, Gray, Glazed, Egg Shape, 14 x 12 1/2 In.	3600.00
Vase, Cover, Napoleon III, Gilt Bronze, Blue Celeste, Mid 1800s, 29 x 14 In., Pair	12650.00
Vase, Cover, Putti, Ormolu Mounted, Turquoise Ground, Ovoid, 11 1/2 In., Pair	2760.00
Vase, Cover, Seated Woman, Putto, Jeweled Gilt Border, Turquoise Ground, 7 In., Pair	2185.00
Vase, Egg Shape, Footed, Brown On Russet Ground, 1895, 32 3/4 In.	6000.00
Vase, Garniture, Cover, Napoleon III, Gilt Bronze, Bleu Celeste, 2 Handles, 28 In., Pair	17825.00
Vase, Garniture, Napoleon III, Gilt Bronze Mount, Bleu-Du-Roi, Handles, 31 In., Pair	13225.00

SEWER TILE figures were made by workers at the sewer tile and pipe factories in the Ohio area during the late nineteenth and early twentieth centuries. Figurines, small vases, and cemetery vases were favored. Often the finished vase was a piece of the original pipe with added decorations and markings. All types of sewer tile work are now considered folk art by collectors.

Bank, Child's Head, Smiling, 1920s, 4 1/2 In.	175.00
Bank, Pig, Seated, Hand Tooled Eyes, Red Brown Glaze, Incised 1926, 10 In.	1380.00
Birdhouse, Cone Shape Roof, Hand Tooled Bark Lines, 7 1/2 In.	200.00
Bowl, Insulator, Brown Glaze, Incised, Stella, Lisbon, Ohio, c.1904, 3 In.	230.00
Buffalo, Orange, Brown Glaze, Albany Slip, 9 x 15 In.	690.00
Bust, Man, Long Beard, Mustache, Curly Hair, Lapelled Coat, Mottled Glaze, 8 In.	345.00
Bust, Man, Mustache, Wearing Vest & Hat, Carrying Bundle, 11 In.	175.00
Bust, Woman, Short Hair, Initials, EOG, 7 1/4 In.	430.00
Chair, Tree Trunk, Combed Bark, Limb Arms, x Supports, Star, Moon, 37 In., Pair	6785.00
Figure, Camel, Orange Clay, Gray Brown Glaze, Metallic Specks, 10 x 8 In.	315.00
Figure, Cat, Incised Eyes, Nose & Paws, 4 1/2 x 11 In.	575.00
Figure, Child's Head, Tooled Hair & Face, Incised Signature RLW, 4 In.	690.00

Figure, Crow, On Stump, Brown Salt Glaze, Tuscarawas County, Ohio, 14 x 10 In. 3795.00
Figure, Dog, Cobalt Sponging, Violet Glaze Over Gray, Houghton & Co., 10 1/2 In. 2130.00
Figure, Dog, Flathead, Molded, Incised, Separate Front Paws, 11 In. 920.00
Figure, Dog, Mastiff, Bulging Eyes, Rectangular Base, Metallic Sparkles, 8 In. 230.00
Figure, Dog, Mastiff, Reclining, Curved Base, Gray Base, 9 1/2 In. 865.00
Figure, Dog, Seated, On Bucket, Red & Buff Glaze, Carved Initials, E.J.E., Ohio, 3 3/4 In. . 776.00
Figure, Dog, Spaniel, Seated, Freestanding Front Legs, 8 3/4 In. 345.00
Figure, Dog, Spaniel, Seated, Freestanding Front Legs, Sherman Monypenny, 10 In. 890.00
Figure, Football, Molded Lacing, 7 1/2 In. 430.00
Figure, Football, Unglazed, 10 1/2 In. 1550.00
Figure, Frog, Elongated, Brown Over Gray Glaze, 6 1/4 In. 720.00
Figure, Horse Head, Hand Molded, Tooled Mane, 6 In. 145.00
Figure, Lion Head, Mane, Hand Formed, Metallic Glaze, 8 1/2 In. 170.00
Figure, Lion, Full Mane, Smile, Unglazed, Hand Tooled, 10 1/8 x 7 In. 300.00
Figure, Lion, Lying Down, Mottled Brown Glaze, c.1850, 7 1/2 x 9 In. 198.00
Figure, Lion, Lying Down, Oval Base, 9 x 15 x 9 1/2 In. 720.00
Figure, Lion, Molded, Tooled, Camp & Thompson, Summit County, Ohio, 10 In. 635.00
Figure, Lion, Reclining, Base, Red Clay, Unglazed, Wadsworth, 4-22-34, 8 1/2 In. 400.00
Figure, Lion, Reclining, Crossed Paws, Rectangular Base, Hand Tooling, 8 1/2 In., Pair . . 690.00
Figure, Lion, Reclining, Hand Tooled Bark, Gray Glaze, Beatrice Sewer Pipe Co., 11 In. . . 835.00
Figure, Lion, Reclining, Metallic Glaze, Rectangular Base, 11 1/4 x 6 In. 460.00
Figure, Lion, Reclining, Rectangular Base, American Sewer Pipe Co., Akron, Ohio, 11 In. . 489.00
Figure, Lion, Reclining, Scalloped Base, Metallic Flecks, c.1889, 9 1/2 In. 345.00
Figure, Lion, Reclining, White Clay, Green Glaze, Brown Trim, Applied Coleslaw, 7 In. . . 575.00
Figure, Lion, Reclining, White Clay, Oval Base, White Bristol Glaze, 4 3/4 In. 115.00
Jug, Figural, Owl, Big Eyes, Hooked Beak, 2-Tone Brown Glaze, 10 1/4 In. 460.00
Planter, Incised Bark Design, Applied Vines, Raised Dots, 12 x 10 In. 115.00
Planter, Tree Trunk, Incised Bark, Molded Limbs, Red Brown Glaze, 14 In. 200.00
Planter, Tree Trunk, Limbs, Incised 1868, 27 In. 520.00
Plaque, Indian Head, Lion Head Above, Embossed Superior Clay Corp, Ohio, 17 In. 690.00
Smoking Set, Tree Stumps, Schoenbrunn, New Philadelphia, Ohio, 5 3/4 In. 69.00
Turtle, Bright Copper Metallic Glaze, Signed Gonda, 70 In. 80.00
Vase, Child's Head, Inset Eyes, White Clay Teeth, Incised W.R. Daum, 4 3/4 In. 259.00

SEWING equipment of all types is collected, from sewing birds that
held the cloth to tape measures, needle books, and old wooden spools.
Sewing machines are included here. Needlework pictures are listed in
the Picture category.

Basket, Coil, Lid, Carved Frog Finial 259.00
Basket, Rye Straw, Openwork, Applied Pincushion, Flared Rim, 7 x 8 x 13 In. 10725.00
Bird, Spring Clamp, Disk Thumbscrew, Wrought Steel, No Pincushion, 6 3/8 In. 230.00
Bird, Wrought Iron, Inlaid Brass Medallions, Marked 1868 & J.K., Pincushion, 7 3/4 In. . . 660.00
Box, Decorated, Mirrored Lift Top, Black, Red, c.1880, 10 1/2 x 7 x 10 In. 805.00
Box, Grain Painted, Flowers, Red Pinstriping, Mid 19th Century, 15 1/2 x 9 1/2 In. 595.00
Box, Hanging, Pine, Painted, Brass Hooks, 2 Drawers, 10 Posts, Pincushion, 17 x 8 In. . . . 632.00
Box, Octagonal, Figures, Landscape, Black Lacquer, Gilt, Chinese, 1800s, 6 x 12 In. 480.00
Box, Poplar, Painted, Green, Scrolls, Open Spool Holder On Side, Penn., 6 x 15 In. 1045.00
Box, Stand, Walnut, Inlaid Birds, Pincushion Lid, Porcelain Knobs, 27 1/2 x 15 x 11 In. . . 230.00
Box, Turned Maple, Pin Container Inside, Early 1800s 295.00
Box, Wood, Ivory, Pierced Scrolls, Fretwork, Hinged Sloping Flaps, Anglo-Indian, 9 In. . . 1380.00
Button Fastener, High Top Shoes, Walnut Base, Cast Iron Stand, 1895 Patent 495.00
Cabinet, Spool, see Advertising category under Cabinet, Spool.
Cabinet, Spool, Chestnut, Walnut Veneer, 6 Drawers, Labels, 17 1/2 x 18 In. 330.00
Cabinet, Spool, Victorian, Walnut, 6 Drawers, 4 Legs, 37 x 26 x 20 In. 430.00
Caddy, Poplar, Painted, Center Post, Bowl Base, Cloth Pincushion Top, 5 x 11 1/2 In. 865.00
Cart, Birch, Lift Top, Compartments, Rattan Basket, Denmark, 23 In. . . . . *Illus* 529.00
Chest, Wood, Chip Carved, Sweethearts, Initials, AJ, FJ, Hinged Lid, c.1924, 12 In. 145.00
Embroidery Frame, Poplar, Old Ink Graining, Unfinished Sampler, 1809, 21 x 18 In. 1495.00
Lacemaker's Lamp, Oil, Blown Glass, Ball Shape Font, Handle, Domed Foot, 9 3/4 In. . . . 231.00
Lacemaker's Lamp, Pink Satin Glass, Pattern Molded, Brass Oil Font, 2 Handles, 17 In. . . 949.00
Lacemaker's Lamp, Round Blown Font, Base, Hollow Stem, 7 3/4 In. 374.00
Machine, Climax, Tabletop, Black, Green, Gold, Art Deco, Geometric, 13 x 9 x 10 In. 115.00
Machine, Florence, No. 7839, Painted Flowers, Serpentine Mahogany Case, 30 x 34 In. . . . 499.00

Put fine lace in a jar with warm water and detergent. Shake the jar to clean. Empty the jar, refill with clean water to rinse. Dry the lace on thick terry cloth towels.

Sewing, Cart, Birch, Lift Top, Compartments, Rattan Basket, Denmark, 23 In.

Machine, Traveling, New Home, 10 1/2 x 6 x 10 In.	105.00
Needle Book, Food Fair Grocery Store, 6 Needle Packets, Threader	8.00
Needle Book, Grand Union Supermarkets, 6 Needle Packets, Threader	8.00
Needle Book, Liberty National Life Insurance Co., Statue Of Liberty, Birmingham, Ala.	5.00
Needle Book, New York World's Fair, 1939, 7 x 3 3/4 In.	14.00
Needle Book, Rexall Drugs, Make A Point Of Saving At Our Drug Store	15.00
Needle Book, Sears, A Gift To You From Kenmore, Japan	7.00
Needle Book, Virginia Slims, Men Would Needle Women, 1970s, 3 x 4 1/4 In.	10.00
Needle Holder, Prudential Insurance, Woman & Baby, Cardboard, 2 1/2 x 1 1/2 In.	10.00
Needle Threader, Prudential Insurance, Strength Of Gibraltar, 5 Needles, 2 3/4 In.	7.00
Niddy Noddy, Carved, Pegged, Initials S.K., 18 3/4 x 13 1/2 In.	690.00
Pinball, Glass Base, EB To Elizabeth Easton, 1831, 4 1/4 x 2 In.	1750.00
Pincushion, 8-Sided Star, Brown & Red, Blue & Purple On Reverse, Hang Loop, 4 In.	90.00
Pincushion, Bird Shape, Brown Cloth, Leaf Pattern, 4 x 1 1/2 In.	195.00
Pincushion, Carrot Man, Velvet, Face, Straw Top, 19th Century, 9 In.	1495.00
Pincushion, Cloth, Lace Bands, Box Base, Wallpapered, Blue, Red, Gold, 1889, 2 x 3 In.	1320.00
Pincushion, Doughnut Shape, Brown & Black, Light & Dark Blue On Reverse, 1 x 6 In.	85.00
Pincushion, Elephant, Solid Silver, English Hallmark, 1 In.	160.00
Pincushion, Iron Shape, Velvet, Compliments, Dover Mfg., Canal Dover, Ohio, 4 In.	150.00
Pincushion, Needlework, Flowers, Blue Band, Zigzag Stitches, Tan, Green, Yellow, 2 In.	525.00
Pincushion, Needlework, Printed Cloth, Blue Ribbon Band, Zigzag Stitches, 2 In.	495.00
Pincushion, Red Blown Glass Base, Red & Green Cloth, 6 In.	489.00
Pincushion, Strawberry, Make-Do Cushion, Felt, Yarn, Glass Pedestal, 9 1/2 In.	3080.00
Pincushion, Strawberry, Velvet, Red, Green Stem, Yellow Silk Embroidery, 8 1/2 In.	405.00
Pincushion, Wooden, Shoe Form, Carved, Painted, 7 x 10 1/4 In.	748.00
Pincushion, Wool, Black Edges, Multicolored, Checkerboard Pattern, 6 x 6 In.	165.00
Pincushion Dolls are listed in their own category.	
Sewing Bird, Wrought Iron, Cutout Thumb Screw, 4 1/4 In.	110.00
Spool Cabinets are in the Advertising category under Cabinet, Spool.	
Spool Stand, Mahantango Type, 3 Tiers, Heart Shaped Finial, Spiral Post, 1880, 18 x 6 In.	1725.00
Straight Pins, Warrior, Cardboard Box, 1 Lb., 4 1/4 x 2 3/4 In.	7.00
Swift, Walnut, Pine, Blue Green Paint, Squirrel Cage, Shoe Footed, 39 1/2 In.	173.00
Tape Loom, Pine, Incised Compass Star, Carved Letters, 21 x 6 1/2 In.	1093.00
Tape Loom, Tombstone Shape Upright, Wood Gears, Spool, Box, Early 1800s, 15 x 21 In.	118.00
Tape Measure, Elder Shirts Of Merit, Parisian Novelty, c.1919, 1 1/2 In.	25.00
Tape Measure, Gardner Trust Company, Man, Holding Saber, c.1930s, 1 1/2 In.	25.00
Tape Measure, Lee Cloth, Hard Cardboard, 60 In.	35.00
Tape Measure, Owosso Casket Co., Quality Caskets Since 1882, Celluloid, 1 1/2 In.	20.00
Tape Measure, Red Kap Uniforms, Every Way You Measure, 60 In.	9.00
Tape Measure, San Joaquin Valley Bank, Stockton, Ca., c.1904, 1 3/4 In.	46.00
Tape Measure, Stromberg Carburetor, Celluloid, J.H. McCullough & Son Co., 1 1/2 In.	75.00
Tape Measure, Warren Five Cent Saving Bank, Save Something, 1930s, 1 1/2 In.	20.00
Thimble, Luzianne Coffee, Aluminum	12.00
Tin, Singer, Sewing Machine Oil, 4 Oz., 5 1/4 x 2 1/4 x 1 1/8 In.	5.00
Wool Winder, Mahogany, Turned Base, Square Plinth, England, 1800s, 25 1/2 In.	358.00
Yarn Winder, Ash, Hickory, Red Finish, Rectangular Chamfered Base, Tapered, 38 In.	80.00

SHAKER items are characterized by simplicity, functionalism, and orderliness. There were many Shaker communities in America from the eighteenth century to the present day. The religious order made furniture, small wooden pieces, and packaged medicines, herbs, and jellies to sell to *outsiders*. Other useful objects were made for use by members of the community. Shaker furniture is listed in this book in the Furniture category.

Apple Peeler, Birch, Pine, Maple, Red Paint, 10 x 26 x 8 In.	460.00
Basket, Black Ash, Orange Varnish, Round, Spiral Weave, 2 x 3 1/2 In.	1150.00
Basket, Cheese, Black Ash, Blue Paint, 5 x 14 In.	1150.00
Basket, Drying, Black Ash, Open Weave Bottom, Single Wrapped Rim, 11 x 36 x 23 In.	575.00
Basket, Gathering, Black Ash, Hickory Handles, Enfield, N.H., c.1840, 11 1/2 x 21 In.	1725.00
Basket, Gathering, Cylindrical, Square Base, Hancock, Mass., c.1840, 13 x 18 In.	1725.00
Basket, Gathering, Oval, Black Ash, Shirley, Mass., c.1840, 17 1/2 x 21 1/2 In.	2990.00
Basket, Lid, Cane, Black Ash, Swing Handle, Mt. Lebanon, N.Y., 4 1/2 x 3 In.	5175.00
Basket, Sewing, Round, Rosewood, Maple, Silk, Enfield, Ct., c.1880, 3 1/2 x 7 1/2 In.	2300.00
Basket, Splint, Black Ash, Double Wrapped Rim, Hoop Handle, 11 x 14 x 9 3/4 In.	6900.00
Basket, Splint, Black Ash, Single Wrapped Rim, 2 Hickory Handles, 9 x 15 1/2 x 12 In.	1725.00
Basket, Splint, Round Body, Raised Center, Oval Rim, Upright Handle, 1800s, 14 In.	235.00
Basket, Split, Black Ash, Square, Lid, 5 x 7 In.	1495.00
Basket, Tatting, Lid, Black Ash, Swing Handle, New Lebanon, N.Y., c.1835, 6 x 3 3/4 In.	8625.00
Basket, Work, Splint, Black Ash, Double Wrapped Rim, 4 Handles, 14 1/2 x 24 In.	920.00
Bonnet, Poplarware, Gray, Beige, No. 8, 7 1/4 x 9 In.	175.00
Bonnet, Poplarware, Purple Silk Neck Flounce, Brown Silk Ribbon Tie, 7 In.	1035.00
Bonnet, Winter, Black Velvet, Fur, Silk Ribbon, 10 x 8 In.	405.00
Bottle Filler, Double, Cherry, Tin Funnels, Adjustable Height, 17 1/4 x 12 1/2 x 4 3/4 In.	635.00
Bottle Filler, Maple, Sheet Tin, 2 Candleholders, Bottle, 18 1/2 x 7 1/2 x 13 1/2 In.	1725.00
Box, 2-Finger, Oval, Copper Tacks, 6 In.	460.00
Box, 2-Finger, Oval, Natural Patina, Copper Tacks, 6 x 2 In.	546.00
Box, 2-Finger, Oval, Writing On Lid, Brown Ink, Copper Tacks, 3 3/4 In.	630.00
Box, 3-Finger, Maple, Pine, Mustard Yellow Paint, 2 x 5 1/4 x 3 1/4 In.	3105.00
Box, 3-Finger, Oval, Flowers, Sister Cora Helena Sarle, Canterbury, N.H., 1 1/2 x 3 In.	3450.00
Box, 3-Finger, Oval, Green Paint, Lid, 11 x 7 3/8 x 4 In.	1095.00
Box, 3-Finger, Oval, Maple, Burled Maple Lid, 2 x 5 In.	4140.00
Box, 3-Finger, Oval, Maple, Pine, Red Orange Paint, East Family, 2 5/8 x 7 3/4 In.	5465.00
Box, 3-Finger, Oval, Maple, Pine, Red Paint, 1 3/4 x 4 1/2 In.	3130.00
Box, 3-Finger, Oval, Maple, Pine, Red Paint, 2 1/2 x 6 1/4 x 4 In.	6325.00
Box, 3-Finger, Oval, Maple, Pine, Red, 3 x 7 1/4 In.	1150.00
Box, 3-Finger, Oval, Maple, Pine, Yellow Paint, 1 1/2 x 3 1/2 In.	1725.00
Box, 3-Finger, Oval, Maple, Pine, Yellow Paint, 2 1/8 x 5 1/4 x 3 1/4 In.	1150.00
Box, 3-Finger, Oval, Olive Gray Paint, Copper Tacks, 11 x 4 In.	575.00
Box, 3-Finger, Oval, Pine, Maple, Red, 2 3/4 x 5 3/4 x 3 3/4 In.	1440.00
Box, 3-Finger, Round, Maple, Poplar, Birch, Natural Varnish, 2 x 4 1/4 In.	2875.00
Box, 4-Finger, Oval, Maple, Pine, Green Paint, 3 3/8 x 9 1/8 x 6 3/4 In.	1095.00
Box, 4-Finger, Oval, Maple, Pine, Green Paint, Sabbathday Lake, Me., 3 x 8 3/4 x 6 In.	3450.00
Box, 4-Finger, Oval, Maple, Pine, Iron Tacks, 5 1/4 x 13 1/2 x 10 In.	460.00
Box, 4-Finger, Oval, Maple, Pine, Red Paint, 3 1/2 x 9 x 6 5/8 In.	10350.00
Box, 4-Finger, Oval, Maple, Pine, Red Paint, 4 x 10 1/8 x 7 In.	3450.00
Box, 4-Finger, Oval, Maple, Pine, Red Paint, Canterbury, N.H., 11 3/8 x 8 1/4 In.	6325.00
Box, 4-Finger, Oval, Maple, Pine, Red Paint, Canterbury, N.H., c.1835, 2 x 5 x 3 1/2 In.	6040.00
Box, 4-Finger, Oval, Maple, Pine, Yellow Paint, 5 x 11 3/4 x 8 1/8 In.	5175.00
Box, 4-Finger, Oval, Maple, Pine, Yellow Stain, Hancock, Mass., 3 3/4 x 9 1/4 x 6 1/8 In.	2300.00
Box, 4-Finger, Oval, Maple, Pine, Yellow, Iron Tacks, c.1820, 4 3/4 x 11 1/2 x 8 5/8 In.	575.00
Box, 5-Finger, Oval, Maple, Pine, Green Paint, 4 1/4 x 10 5/8 x 8 In.	5175.00
Box, 5-Finger, Oval, Maple, Pine, Natural Finish, 5 1/2 x 13 1/4 x 9 1/4 In.	1725.00
Box, 5-Finger, Oval, Maple, Pine, Natural Finish, Charlotte, 1829, 6 x 14 3/4 x 10 3/4 In.	4320.00
Box, 5-Finger, Oval, Maple, Pine, Yellow Paint, 5 3/4 x 13 1/4 x 9 In.	4025.00
Box, Bonnet, Pine, Dovetailed, Breadboard Lift Lid, 8 x 11 1/4 x 11 1/4 In.	575.00
Box, Hat, 2-Finger, Butternut, Poplar, Leather Strap, New Lebanon, c.1865, 14 x 22 In.	1380.00
Box, Pantry, 3-Finger, Oval, Brown Patina, Copper Tacks, 12 x 5 In.	635.00
Box, Pantry, 3-Finger, Oval, Natural Patina, 9 x 3 In.	460.00
Box, Rectangle, Pine, Yellow Varnish, Dovetailed, Leather Hinge, 2 1/2 x 7 3/4 In.	3165.00

Box, Round, Paper, On Cardboard, Orange Paint, 2 1/4 x 3 1/2 In. 4600.00
Box, Sewing, 3-Finger, Oval, Straw Needle Holder, Maine, 3 1/2 x 9 1/2 In. 230.00
Box, Sewing, 4-Finger, Oval, Maple, Cherry, Swing Handle, Contents, 6 x 7 In. 345.00
Box, Sewing, 5-Finger, Maple, Pine, Contents, R.W. Belfit, Watertown, Conn., 6 x 14 In. ... 920.00
Box, Sewing, Walnut, 5 Inside Compartments, Dovetailed, Enfield, Ct., c.1885, 7 x 12 In. .. 3680.00
Box, Slide Lid, Poplar, Dovetailed, Olive Stebbins, Enfield, Ct., c.1855, 4 1/2 x 8 3/4 In. ... 690.00
Bread Cutter, Iron, Swivel Blade, Cherry Handle, New Lebanon, N.Y., 28 In. 460.00
Bucket, Lid, Pine, Blue Paint, Iron Bands, Turned Handle, c.1850, 10 1/4 In. 940.00
Bucket, Pine, Blue Interior, Wire Bail, Birch Handle, Initials EA, 13 1/2 x 10 In. 3165.00
Bucket, Pine, Red Paint, Iron Bands, Wire & Birch Handle, Drain & Plates, 7 x 5 1/2 In. ... 2415.00
Bucket, Pine, Yellow Paint, Steel Bands, Swing Handle, Mt. Lebanon, N.Y., c.1850, 15 In. . 3335.00
Bucket, Pine, Yellow Paint, Wire Bail, Turned Wood Handle, 11 x 8 In. 2300.00
Bucket, Pine, Yellow, Iron Bands & Bail, Wood Handle, Canterbury, N.H., c.1850, 12 x 9 In. 1610.00
Bucket, Wood, 3 Bands, Staves, Bentwood Handle, Bottom Stenciled A.M., 11 3/4 In. 7200.00
Butter Churn, Tin, Blue Paint, Birch Dasher, Pine Lid, Mt. Lebanon, N.Y., c.1860, 41 In. .. 460.00
Carrier, 2-Finger, Maple, Pine, Fixed Handle, Mt. Lebanon, N.Y., c.1920, 8 x 14 x 11 In. .. 405.00
Carrier, 3-Finger, Oval, Maple, Pine, Hickory Handle, 7 1/2 x 11 x 8 In. 1725.00
Carrier, 3-Finger, Oval, Red Paint, N.H., c.1860, 6 1/2 x 11 x 3 In. 12000.00
Carrier, Candle, Tin, Wire Screen, Handle, Saucer Base, 10 x 4 1/2 In. 865.00
Carrier, Rectangle, Birch, Maple, Dovetailed, Swing Handle, Canterbury, N.H., 6 x 8 In. .. 2760.00
Carrier, Rectangle, Poplar, Fixed Ash Handle, Dovetailed, Inset Lift Lid, 14 1/2 x 17 In. .. 460.00
Carrier, Sewing, 3-Finger, Oval, Maple, Swing Handle, Sabbathday Lake, Me., 6 x 8 In. .. 290.00
Carrier, Sewing, 4-Finger, Birch, Cherry, Pine, Silk Lining, Contents, 6 1/2 x 8 3/8 In. 690.00
Carrier, Sewing, 4-Finger, Oval, Maple, Sabbathday Lake, Me., 1900s, 3 1/4 x 9 1/4 In. ... 235.00
Cheese Press, Pulley System, Octagon Shape Plate, Trestle Construction, 26 1/2 x 26 In. .. 60.00
Cloak, Wool, Purple, Silk Lining, Dorothy, Hart & Shepard, E. Canterbury, N.H., 48 In. ... 635.00
Cloak, Wool, Red, Silk Lining, Hood, Dorothy, Hart & Shepard, Canterbury, N.H., 50 In. .. 690.00
Crib, Oak, Pine Bottom, Octagonal Spindles, Mt. Lebanon, N.Y., c.1845, 36 x 51 x 25 In. . 1725.00
Crutches, Maple, Mt. Lebanon, N.Y., c.1860, 49 1/2 In. 115.00
Deed, Quit Claim, Caleb M. Dyer, Enfield, N.H., Society Of Shakers, c.1859, 14 x 8 In. 140.00
Dipper, Maple, Carved, Turned, 2 1/2 x 6 x 4 1/4 In. 1955.00
Doll, Porcelain, Gray Cloak, Hood, Silk Ribbons, Poplar Bonnet, Gray Dress, 13 In. 1265.00
Drying Rack, Birch, Red, 2 Bars, Canterbury, N.H., c.1840, 32 1/2 x 23 1/2 In. 1150.00
Drying Rack, Herb, Oak, Maple, 4 Tiers, Mortised, Pegged, Hancock, c.1855, 57 x 94 In. . 805.00
Drying Rack, Pine, 4 Sections, Mortised, Pegged, Canterbury, N.H., c.1850, 71 x 38 In. ... 805.00
Drying Rack, Pine, Mortised, Pegged, X-Shape, New Lebanon, N.Y., c.1845, 77 x 39 In. .. 1035.00
Drying Rack, Pine, Poplar, 3 Bars, Mortised, Pegged, Trestle Feet, 35 1/2 x 38 In. 60.00
Fret Saw, Cherry, Steel, Turned Handle, Mt. Lebanon, c.1845, 12 1/2 x 9 In., 5-In. Blade .. 635.00
Fruit Press, Maple, Iron Hinge, Shaped Handles, Canterbury, N.H., 15 1/2 In. 630.00
Label, Asthma Cure, Mt. Lebanon, N.Y., Frame, 6 x 3 1/2 In. 345.00
Letter Opener, Bird's Eye Maple, Peg Hole In Handle, 8 1/4 In. 3680.00
Pegboard, 9 Pegs, Red Wash, Molded Edge, 54 x 3 In. 175.00
Pegboard, Maple, 2-Sided, 4 Pegs On Each Side, c.1850, 94 In. 805.00
Pegboard, Pine, 9 Maple Pegs, Natural Finish, 160 In. 575.00
Postcard, Shakers Working In Bee Garden, North Family Shakers, Mt. Lebanon, N.Y. 425.00
Poster, Shakers' Dried Green Sweet Corn, Cardboard, Mt. Lebanon, N.Y., 14 x 11 In. 1840.00
Rake, Wood, Red Paint, Yellow Tines, 1800s, 72 x 25 1/2 In. 175.00
Rolling Pin, Double, Maple, 20 1/2 In. 1208.00
Rug, Knitted & Crocheted, Wool Yarn, Rectangles, New England, c.1885, 23 x 35 In. 7800.00
Rug Whip, Maple Handle, Twisted Wire Loop, Mt. Lebanon, N.Y., 31 1/2 In. 230.00
Seed Box, Pine, Red, Shakers Genuine Seeds, Mt. Lebanon, N.Y., 3 1/2 x 23 x 11 1/2 In. .. 6325.00
Seed Planter, Birch, New England, 29 x 3 1/4 x 5 3/4 In. 145.00
Spinning Wheel, Flax Wheel, Maple, Oak, Birch, Alfred, Me., c.1825, 34 x 34 1/2 In. 575.00
Spinning Wheel, Flax Wheel, Oak, Maple, Alfred, Me., c.1801, 51 1/2 x 31 In. 690.00
Spinning Wheel, Walking Wool Wheel, Birch, Maple, Mt. Lebanon, c.1840, 61 x 41 In. 1035.00
Spinning Wheel, Walking Wool Wheel, Birch, Oak, Maple, Alfred, 1800s, 59 x 46 In. 805.00
Spool, Maple, Hourglass Shape, Yellow Stain, 2 3/4 In. 290.00
Square, Carpenter's, Walnut, Mortised & Pinned, Harvard, Mass., 1834, 12 1/2 x 23 In. ... 290.00
Swift, Maple, Yellow Stain, Hancock, Mass., 24 1/2 In. 260.00
Tape Loom, Pine, Birch, Adjustable Drums, Foot Pedals, Mortised, Pegged, 36 x 23 In. ... 315.00
Towel Rack, Pine, 2 Rails, Mortised, Mt. Lebanon, N.Y., c.1860, 38 x 23 1/2 In. 690.00
Tray, Pine, Rectangle, Canted Sides, 2 Handles, 2 3/4 x 16 1/4 x 11 3/4 In. 805.00
Trivet, Elm, Carved, Chip Carved, Flower Petal Shape, Mt. Lebanon, N.Y., 11 In. 865.00

Tub, Pine, Blue Paint, Hickory Handle, 17 x 14 1/2 In. 2070.00
Tub, Pine, Red Exterior, 4 Bands, Canterbury, N.H., c.1835, 17 1/2 x 20 In. 805.00

SHAVING MUGS were popular from 1860 to 1900. Many types were
made, including occupational mugs featuring pictures of men's jobs.
There were scuttle mugs, silver-plated mugs, glass-lined mugs, and
others.

2 Monkeys Dressed In Hats & Suits, 2 Sections, 4 x 3 1/2 In. 100.00
3 Flower Panels, Scalloped Rim, Hand Painted, Porcelain, c.1900 .... 50.00
Berries & Birds, Flared Rim, Hand Painted, Handle 65.00
Church, Lake, Man In Rowboat, Henry Ebeling, V & D, Austria, 3 1/2 In. 55.00
Drape & Flower, Purple, Red, Gold Trim, H.C. Boyer, 4 In. 60.00
Fire Helmet 35.00
Flower, Transfer, Scalloped & Embossed Rim, 2 Sections 45.00
Flowers, Blue, Gold, Scalloped Rim, Handle 75.00
Flowers, Red, Yellow, Green, Mirror, 2 Sections, Germany, 4 x 3 1/2 In. 89.00
Fraternal, B.P.O.E., Elk's Head, Geo. Burns, E. Beringhaus Co., 3 3/4 In. 50.00
Fraternal, Independent Order Of Odd Fellows, J.P. Snodgrass 225.00
Frog, Sitting Under Mushroom, Nels, 3 3/4 In. 165.00
Hunter, Dog, Shooting Bird, W. Morris, Germany, 3 3/4 In. 55.00
Ladies In Continental Court Dress, 4 x 3 1/2 In. 145.00
Occupational, 2 Men On Horse Drawn Firehouse Wagon, M. F. Melter, 3 3/4 In. 825.00
Occupational, Architects Drafting Table & Tools, Will Kerr, c.1885-1925, 3 1/2 In. 280.00
Occupational, Back Half Of Dairy Cow, D. Wm. Schmid, 3 7/8 In. 360.00
Occupational, Baker, By Oven, F. Cook, 3 5/8 In. 715.00
Occupational, Bakery, 3 Men Making Bread, Claud Peters, 3 7/8 In. 300.00
Occupational, Bar Room, John J. Walsh, 3 3/4 In. 120.00
Occupational, Barber Shop, Clarence Wright, c.1885-1925, 4 In. 830.00
Occupational, Barber Shop, W.H. Smith, 3 3/4 In. 280.00
Occupational, Blacksmith, 3 Men Working On Anvil, Joe. Shear 170.00
Occupational, Blacksmith, Horse Looking At Man, D.G. Mabery, 3 5/8 In. 880.00
Occupational, Blacksmith, Shoeing Horse, H.E. Friddle, W.G. & Co., Limoges, 4 In. 240.00
Occupational, Blacksmith, Shoeing Horse, John Kidney, 3 3/8 In. 150.00
Occupational, Blacksmith, Working At Anvil, Joseph Glide, 3 3/4 In. 50.00
Occupational, Brick Layer, Working On Wall, J. Fitzgerald, T & V France, 3 1/2 In. 620.00
Occupational, Cabinetmaker, A.B. Dietz, 3 3/4 In. 180.00
Occupational, Carpenter, Tools, F. Ledur, T & V Limoges, France, 3 5/8 In. 155.00
Occupational, Cow, John F. Keller, c.1885-1925, 3 3/8 In. 300.00
Occupational, Farmer, Plow, E. Charnley, 4 In. 470.00
Occupational, Fire Chief Hat, E. Devine, c.1885-1925, 3 5/8 In. 1880.00
Occupational, Fire Engine, Horse Drawn, Steam, C. Halleck, 3 7/8 In. 830.00
Occupational, Furniture & Undertaking Store Front, Chas, S. Amerman, 4 In. 720.00
Occupational, Grocery Store, C.M. Glover, Koen Barbers Supply Co., 4 In. 395.00
Occupational, Grocery Store, F.B. Allen, c.1885-1925, 3 1/2 In. 420.00
Occupational, Hand Holding Printer's Block, E.T. Philbin, Leonard, Vienna Austria, 4 In. . 200.00
Occupational, Horse Drawn Baker's Wagon, B. Kramer, Lorenz Bakery Genessee, 4 In. .. 495.00
Occupational, Horse Drawn Delivery Wagon, Fred Smith, T & V Limoges, France, 4 In. .. 240.00
Occupational, Horse Drawn Livery Wagon, D.F. Lynch, Phl Vienna, 3 7/8 In. 450.00
Occupational, Horse Drawn Lumber Wagon, H. B. Slavin, c.1885-1925, 4 In. 1230.00
Occupational, Horse Drawn Stake Wagon, Dan Burnett, 3 1/2 In. 280.00
Occupational, Horse, Standing, Ralph Smith, 3 3/4 In. 70.00
Occupational, Koken Barber Supply Co., Man, Raven, On Tree Limb, 4 x 4 In. 66.00
Occupational, Livery Stable, Geo. H. Harlin, W.G. & Co. Limoges, France, 4 In. 340.00
Occupational, Livery Stable, Matthews Bros., c.1885-1925, 4 1/8 In. 415.00
Occupational, Locomotive & Tender, J. Dunham, CFH GDM France, 3 7/8 In. 265.00
Occupational, Man, Boxing Cigars, J. Polack, 3 1/4 In. 300.00
Occupational, Man, Driving Horse Drawn Hearse, R. Lee, c.1885-1925, 3 5/8 In. 450.00
Occupational, Man, Driving Horse Drawn Moving Wagon, L. Seinfeld, 3 7/8 In. 180.00
Occupational, Man, Driving Horse Drawn Sulky, 4 In. 100.00
Occupational, Man, Driving Horse Drawn Sulky, Sam Kennedy, c.1885-1925, 4 In. 610.00
Occupational, Man, Horse Drawn Delivery Wagon, Frank Minsky, T & V Limoges, 3 5/8 In. 170.00
Occupational, Man, Making Harness, C.E. Shumway, J.P.L. France, 3 5/8 In. 560.00
Occupational, Man, Operating Large Wood Planer, E.C. Knotts, c.1885-1925, 4 In. 780.00

Occupational, Man, Shovel On Shoulder, Edward Schmester, c.1885-1925, 3 7/8 In. 480.00
Occupational, Man, Standing Next To Horse & Buggy, Thos. Patchett, 3 1/2 In. 430.00
Occupational, Man, Standing Next To Steer, C.H.A. Padley, c.1885-1925, 3 7/8 In. 390.00
Occupational, Man, Stoking Furnace, Double Door, George Shaw, 3 5/8 In. 450.00
Occupational, Man, Training Horse, Thomas Boyle, c.1885-1925, 3 3/4 In. 280.00
Occupational, Milk Can, S. G. Smith, c.1885-1925, 3 5/8 In. 450.00
Occupational, Mortar & Pestle, Dr. E.F. May, T.U. 1911, 3 5/8 In. 330.00
Occupational, Mortar & Pestle, J.A. Maiers, V & D Austria, 3 5/8 In. 240.00
Occupational, Photographer, Taking Woman's Picture, W.K. Brown, 3 1/2 In. 230.00
Occupational, Photographer, Woman Sitting, J.J. Thurston, 3 5/8 In. 1110.00
Occupational, Steer's Head, Crossed Butchers Tools, E.R. Daniels, Vienna, 3 5/8 In. 50.00
Occupational, Tailor, Dave Rothe, CFH GDM France, 3 5/8 In. 300.00
Occupational, Tinsmith, John Clabrou, Koken B.S. Co. St. Louis, 3 7/8 In. 240.00
Occupational, Trolley, Driver, Passengers, W.A. Slauenewhite, T & V Limoges, 3 5/8 In. .. 285.00
Occupational, Typesetter, Press, J.R. Phillips, Aug. Kern Barber Supply Co., 3 5/8 In. 480.00
Occupational, Woman, Driving Horse Drawn Delivery Wagon, W.L. Bishop, 3 5/8 In. 240.00
Occupational, Woodworker, Planing A Board, J.A. Dubois, 3 1/8 In. 300.00
Pansies, Purple, Leaves, Green, W. F. Clark, 4 In. 35.00
Patriotic, Banner Across Stars & Stripes Shield, Jacob Bauer, 3 3/8 In. 82.00
Patriotic, Eagle, Crossed American Flags, William Parrilla, T & V Limoges, 3 7/8 In. 155.00
Porcelain, Gold Trim, Scalloped Rim, 2 Sections, Fancy Handle, 2 3/8 In. 55.00
Saloon Scene, Chas. Higgins, 3 3/4 In. 220.00
Seaman Smoking Pipe, Germany, 4 In. 148.00
Tin, Punched Decoration On Brush Holder, Strap Handle, Cup Holder, 4 1/2 x 6 In. 60.00
Use Tonique De Luxe, W.G. & Co. Limoges, France, 3 7/8 In. 190.00

SHAWNEE POTTERY was started in Zanesville, Ohio, in 1937. The
company made vases, novelty ware, flowerpots, planters, lamps, and
cookie jars. Three dinnerware lines were made: Corn, Lobster Ware,
and Valencia (a solid color line). White Corn pattern utility pieces were
made in 1945. Corn King was made from 1946 to 1954; Corn Queen,
with darker green leaves and lighter colored corn, from 1954 to 1961.
Shawnee produced pottery for George Rumrill during the late 1930s.
The company closed in 1961.

Ashtray Set, Card Suits, Speckled Blue, Yellow, Red, Green, 5 In., 4 Piece 49.00
Bank, Smiley Pig, 10 1/4 In. 475.00
Bowl, Corn King, No. 92, Oval, 6 In. 55.00
Bowl, Corn King, No. 94, Oval, 6 1/2 In. 60.00
Butter, Cover, Corn King, No. 72 .... 52.00
Candlestick, Ivory Matte, Gold Trim, 4-Lobed Rim, J. Mangus Book P. 92, 4 In., Pair 60.00
Casserole, Corn King, 11 In. 75.00
Console, Celadon Green Chartreuse, Speckled, Scalloped Rim, 5 x 14 1/2 In. 24.00
Console, Ivory Matte, Flower, 4 Lobes, Fluted, 4 Gold-Tipped Feet, 6 x 10 In. 65.00
Cookie Jar, Corn King, 10 1/2 In. 200.00
Cookie Jar, Drum Major, Robert Hickman, 1940s, 10 In. 300.00
Cookie Jar, Dutch Boy Jack 105.00
Cookie Jar, Dutch Boy, Holding Sailboat 55.00
Cookie Jar, Dutch Girl, Brown Hair & Eyes, Blue & White Dress, 10 In. 290.00
Cookie Jar, Fruit Basket, Yellow Basket, No. 83 .... 130.00
Cookie Jar, Jill Or Dutch Girl, Pink Tulip On Skirt, Blue Trim & Ribbons, 12 In. 235.00
Cookie Jar, Muggsy, Blue Scarf, 11 3/4 In. 600.00
Cookie Jar, Muggsy, Flowers, Gold Trim 795.00
Cookie Jar, Smiley Pig, All White 120.00
Cookie Jar, Smiley Pig, Chrysanthemums, 11 1/2 In. 350.00
Cookie Jar, Winking Owl, White, Gray & Peach Feathers, 11 1/2 In. 230.00
Cookie Jar, Winnie Pig, Blue Flowers, 11 1/2 In. 275.00
Corn Holder, Corn King, 8 1/2 In., Pair 80.00
Creamer, Elephant .... 65.00 to 75.00
Creamer, Puss-'n-Boots, Yellow, Green, Burgundy, Gold Trim, 4 3/4 In. 250.00
Creamer, Smiley Pig, 8 In. .... 165.00 to 300.00
Creamer, Smiley Pig, Peach Flowers, 4 1/2 In. 135.00
Figurine, Bear, Flax Blue, 3 In. 50.00
Figurine, Elephant, Pink, 2 3/4 In. 18.00

Figurine, Squirrel, 2 1/2 In.	65.00
Figurine, Tumbling Bear, c.1950, 3 In.	95.00
Flowerpot, Brown, Tulip Form, No. 1065, 5 1/2 x 6 In.	23.00
Flowerpot, Liner, Yellow Pot, Geometric, Black Liner	24.00
Flowerpot, Pink, Green, No. 534, 3 1/2 x 5 In.	20.00
Jardiniere, Bamboo, Burgundy, Pillow, 4-Sided, 5 In.	24.00
Lamp Base, Elephant With Ball, Cold Paint, 7 In.	50.00
Pie Bird, Chick, Blue, c.1939-60, 5 In.	75.00 to 85.00
Pitcher, Ball, Fern, 2 Qt.	65.00
Pitcher, Bo Peep, 8 In.	125.00 to 175.00
Pitcher, Chanticleer, Rooster, 7 1/2 In.	150.00 to 185.00
Pitcher, Little Boy Blue, 7 1/2 In.	225.00
Pitcher, Smiley Pig, Flowers, Gold Trim, 7 3/4 In.	225.00
Planter, 2 Fawns, 5 1/2 In.	20.00
Planter, 3-Button Shoe & Dog, 4 1/2 In.	19.00
Planter, Boy & Stump, No. 533, 6 x 4 In.	25.00
Planter, Coolies With Basket, 4 x 5 1/4 In.	25.00
Planter, Cornucopia, Blue Flower, White Matte, 6 In.	22.00
Planter, Doe & Fawn, 6 1/4 x 7 1/4 In.	55.00
Planter, Doe, Yellow, 7 In.	68.00
Planter, Duckling, 4 In.	10.00
Planter, Fawn & Log, 6 1/2 x 7 In.	55.00
Planter, Fawn & Stump, 5 3/4 In.	24.00
Planter, Glossy Green, 4-Sided, No. 450, 4 x 6 3/4 In.	20.00
Planter, Hound On Jug, 4 In.	25.00
Planter, Lavender, White, Ruffled Edge, 5 1/2 x 7 In.	20.00
Planter, Pixie Shoe, 4 x 5 3/4 In., Pair	25.00
Planter, Pixie, Aqua, Rose, 3 1/2 x 2 1/2 In.	25.00
Planter, Rocking Horse, Peach, 5 3/4 In.	22.00
Planter, Shell, Blue, 2 1/4 x 6 In.	23.00
Planter, Swan, 4 3/4 In.	20.00
Planter, Terrier & Dog House, 4 1/4 In.	25.00
Planter, Train Engine, Blue	24.00
Planter, Tropical Fish, 7 1/4 x 10 In.	70.00
Salt & Pepper, Bo Peep & Little Boy Blue	50.00 to 75.00
Salt & Pepper, Chanticleer, Gold Trim, 4 In.	150.00
Salt & Pepper, Chef, 3 1/4 In.	30.00
Salt & Pepper, Chef, Gold Trim, 3 1/4 In.	60.00
Salt & Pepper, Dutch Boy & Girl, Brown Hair, Blue Eyes & Trim, 5 In.	75.00 to 115.00
Salt & Pepper, Muggsy, 2 In.	110.00
Salt & Pepper, Muggsy, 3 1/4 In.	125.00
Salt & Pepper, Owls, 3 In.	25.00 to 35.00
Salt & Pepper, Smiley Pig, Green Neckerchief, 5 In.	175.00
Salt & Pepper, Watering Can, 1940s	30.00
Salt & Pepper, Winking Owl, Gold Trim, 3 In.	75.00
Sock Darner, Round Head, Flared Handle, 5 In.	99.00
Sugar, Cover, Corn King, 5 1/2 In.	50.00
Sugar, Cover, Sunflower, 3 3/4 In.	24.00
Teapot, Cover, Pink Rose, Embossed, 6 1/2 In.	23.00
Teapot, Embossed Rose, Cream Ground, Fluted, Rose Finial, 7 x 9 In.	49.00
Teapot, Granny Ann	150.00 to 165.00
Teapot, Tom The Piper's Son	110.00 to 225.00
Vase, Aqua, White Speckled, No. 1026, 7 1/2 x 6 1/2 In.	24.00
Vase, Bud, Light Gray, Embossed Flowers, Handles, 5 1/2 In.	20.00
Vase, Cornucopia, White Matte Glaze, 6 1/4 In., Pair	88.00
Vase, Doe In Shadowbox, Gray, 9 x 5 In.	69.00
Vase, Doe In Shadowbox, Green, 9 x 5 In.	59.00
Vase, Doves, Burgundy, Fluted Sides, Flared, 6 1/4 In.	95.00
Vase, Fawn In Shadowbox, 7 In.	80.00
Vase, Swan, Burgundy	20.00
Wall Pocket, Little Jack Horner, 5 In.	24.00
Window Box, Cameo, Platinum Gray, 4 x 14 In.	25.00

SHEARWATER pottery is a family business started by Mr. and Mrs. G. W. Anderson, Sr., and their three sons. The local Ocean Springs, Mississippi, clays were used to make the wares in the 1930s. The company is still in business.

Figurine, Bird, Light Blue High Glaze, 5 In.	235.00
Vase, Cabinet, Turquoise Glaze, 3 In.	29.00
Vase, Ducks, Tan, Green Glaze, Marked, 6 1/2 In.	4175.00
Vase, Green & Blue Matte Glaze, Ribbed, Impressed Mark, 8 In.	175.00
Vase, Mottled Blue, Gray, Brown Glaze, Low Form, 4 In.	59.00

SHEET MUSIC from the past centuries is now collected. The favorites are examples with covers featuring artistic or historic pictures. Early sheet music covers were lithographed, but by the 1900s photographic reproductions were used. The early music was larger than more recent sheets, and you must watch out for examples that were trimmed to fit in a twentieth-century piano bench.

Anchors Aweigh, Song Of The Navy, 1930	12.00
Bye Bye Blues, Fred Hamm, Dave Bennett, B. Lown, Blue & White, 1930	10.00
Chimes, Novelty Rag, As Played Nightly On Steamer Island, Homer Denney, 1910	10.00
Chocolate Brown, Art Cover, 1921	110.00
Corn Shucks Rag, Girl's Face, 1908	44.00
Dark Blue Blues, Man Pondering, 1923	62.00
Did I Remember, Featuring Jean Harlow, H. Adamson, W. Donaldson, 1936	6.00
Do I Worry, Ink Spots, Stanley Cowan, Bobby Worth, 1941	10.00
Drinking Again, No Art Cover, Johnny Mercer, 1962	12.00
Entertainers Rag, Jay Roberts, 1912	3.00
Firemen March, San Francisco Buildings Burning, 1906	51.00
Freshie, Fred Waring's Pennsylvanians, Jesse Greer, 1925	10.00
Friend & A Lover, Partridge Family, 1973	12.00
Hob-Gob-Gog-O-Lin-Man, T.B. Roberts, Lucien Denney, 1911	15.00
Hottest Gal In New Orleans	110.00
I'm Always Drunk In San Francisco, No Art Cover, T. Wolf, 1962	18.00
I'm Making Believe, Sweet & Low Down, Mack Gordon, James Monaco, 1944	3.00
I've Got My Love To Keep Me Warm, Dick Powell, Alice Faye, Irving Berlin, 1937	10.00
In Summer At Gay Seashore, Men & Women At Beach, 1913	55.00
Ivanhoe, Van Alstyne & Butler, 1908	8.00
Junkman Rag, Luokyth, Roberts, 1913	15.00
Just As Though You Were Here, Tommy Dorsey, Edgar De Lange, J.B. Brooks, 1942	16.00
Lady-Bug, Lady-Bug, Fly Away Home, Duncan J. Muir, 1900	10.00
My Love Song To You, Jackie Gleason & Bob Manning, 1954, 3 Pages	15.00
My One & Only Highland Fling, Fred Astaire & Ginger Rogers Cover, 1949	15.00
New Orleans Wiggle, Piron's New Orleans Orchestra, 1924	65.00
Oh Joe Get Your Fiddle & Your Bow, Louisiana Five, 1920	30.00
Oh Look At Me Now, Color Cover, John Devries, Joe Bushkin, 1941	18.00
Palmetto State Song, Booklet On Sheet Music, George O. Robinson, c.1860	750.00
Penthouse Romance, Piano, 1934	33.00
Pick Up Your Tears & Go Home, Four Freshmen, 1951	30.00
Pinochle Rag, Hand Of Cards, 1911	39.00
Poor Loulie Jean, Woman In Swamp, 1943	50.00
Pretty Mama Blues, Ivory Joe Hunter, 1948	28.00
Ragtime Soldier Man, Irving Berlin	18.00
Russian Rag, Photos, Will Rossiler, George L. Cobb, Rachmaninoff, 1918	8.00
Sad River Blues, 1934	28.00
Saint Louis Blues, Dorothy Lamour, W.C. Handy, 1914	4.00
Santa Claus Is Coming To Town, 1934	8.00
Satin Pillows, Bobby Vinton, 1965	28.00
Shim-Me-Sha-Wabble, Evil Looking Couple, Dancing, 1917	28.00
Shooting The Chutes, Water Ride, 1896	35.00
Slightly Out Of Tune, John Hendricks, Antonio C. Jobim, 1959	12.00
Soft As Spring, No Art Cover, Alec Wilder, 1941	28.00
Some Little Bird, Haven Gillespie, Lindsey McPhail, 1920	10.00
Spaghetti Rag, Jack Fina, Dick Rogers, George Lyons, 1950	3.00
Stairway To Stars, Glenn Miller, 1939	33.00

Stars, Hollywood, Charles Doug Travis, America's Youngest Composer, 1930 .... 3.00
Street Of Dreams, Bing Crosby, 1932 .... 33.00
String Of Pearls, Glenn Miller, 1942 .... 28.00
Surfin' U.S.A., Beach Boys, 1963 .... 55.00
Sweet Dreams, Patsy Cline, 1955 .... 28.00
Sweet Little Rock & Roller, Chuck Berry, 1958 .... 79.00
The Beetles Dance, Color Cover, Stitched Seam, Edward Holst, 1910 .... 15.00
The Music Goes Round & Round, Red Hodgson, Ed Farley, 1935 .... 12.00
Tie A Yellow Ribbon Round Ole Oak Tree, I. Levine & R. Brown, 1972 .... 11.00
Tillie The Toiler, Russ Westover, Comic Strip, 1931 .... 106.00
Western Life, Cowgirl, March, 2 Step, J.P. Sousa Band, Central Engraving, 1906 .... 17.00
Whatever Happened To Old Jack, Freddie Slack, Bob Russell, Carl Sigman, 1949 .... 11.00
Wizard Of Oz, Selection, Francis Day & Hunter, England, 1940, 11 x 8 1/2 In., 8 Pages ... 125.00

SHEFFIELD items are listed in the Silver Plate and Silver-English categories.

SHIRLEY TEMPLE, the famous movie star, was born in 1928. She made her first movie in 1932. Thousands of items picturing Shirley have been and still are being made. Shirley Temple dolls were first made in 1934 by Ideal Toy Company. Millions of Shirley Temple cobalt blue glass dishes were made by Hazel Atlas Glass Company and U.S. Glass Company from 1934 to 1942. They were given away as premiums for Wheaties and Bisquick. A bowl, mug, and pitcher were made as a breakfast set. Some pieces were decorated with the picture of a very young Shirley, others used a picture of Shirley in her 1936 *Captain January* costume. Although collectors refer to a cobalt creamer, it is actually the 4 1/2-inch-high milk pitcher from the breakfast set. Many of these items are being reproduced today.

Book, Real Little Girl & Her Own Honolulu Diary, Saalfield, 1938 .... 65.00
Bracelet, 4 Charms, Enamel, Brass, 1930s, 6 In. 200.00
Button, My Friend Shirley Temple, Red, Black, White, Celluloid, 1 1/4 In. 40.00
Dish Set, Juvenile, Cobalt Blue, 3 Piece, 3 1/4-In. Pitcher, 5 3/4-In. Bowl, 3-In. Mug 45.00
Doll, Composition Head & Body, Mohair Wig, Hazel Eyes, Music Dress, 13 In. 660.00
Doll, Dolls Dreams Love, Pink Dress, Leather Shoes, Stand, 1984, 36 In. 400.00
Doll, Green Sleep Eyes, Blond Ringlets, Trunk & Wardrobe, 1935, 18 In. 2350.00
Doll, Ideal, Composition Body, Jointed, Original Outfit & Wig, 20 In. 790.00
Doll, Ideal, Composition Head, Brown Eyes, Polka Dot Dress, Trunk, c.1935, 15 In. 3530.00
Doll, Ideal, Composition Head, Flirty Eyes, Multi-Tiered Gown, Hat, c.1936, 27 In. 3430.00
Doll, Ideal, Composition Swivel Head, Glassine Sleep Eyes, 15 In. 168.00
Doll, Ideal, Composition Swivel Head, Glassine Sleep Eyes, 21 In. 265.00
Doll, Ideal, Composition, Blue Organdy Dress, Pin, Box, 18 In. 820.00
Doll, Ideal, Composition, Music Dress & Pin, Box, 18 In. 1045.00
Doll, Ideal, Composition, Swivel Head, Sleep Eyes, Jointed, Little Colonel, 20 In. 505.00
Doll, Ideal, Hazel Sleep Eyes, Composition, c.1930, 18 In. 295.00
Doll, Ideal, Hazel Sleep Eyes, Open Mouth, Mohair, Composition, c.1930, 13. In. 440.00
Doll, Ideal, Mohair, Open Mouth, Hazel Flirty Eyes, 27 In. 206.00
Doll, Ideal, Open Mouth, Teeth, Blond Mohair, Composition, c.1930, 25 In. 265.00

Shirley Temple, Pitcher, Cobalt Blue Glass, Honeycomb Sides, Shaped Handle, 4 1/4 In.

Tell your neighbors when you will be away for a long time. Ask them to remove any newspapers or mail left in front of the house and to check on any trucks, especially unmarked trucks, that are in the driveway.

Doll, Ideal, ST-15, Vinyl, Hazel Sleep Eyes, Rooted Hair, 1957, 15 In. 305.00
Doll, Ideal, Stowaway Outfit, Box, 1982, 11 In. 75.00
Doll, Ideal, Vinyl Socket Head, Brown Sleep Eyes, Pink Dress, 1958-65, 17 In. 358.00
Doll, Ideal, Vinyl Socket Head, Brown Sleep Eyes, Poor Little Rich Girl, 1960, 15 In. 305.00
Doll, Ideal, Vinyl Socket Head, Brown Sleep Eyes, Striped Dress, c.1958, 12 In. 330.00
Doll, Ideal, Vinyl, Blue, Black Dress, 17 In. 305.00
Doll, Ideal, Vinyl, Flirty Eyes, 1957, 18 In. 50.00
Doll, Ideal, Vinyl, Hazel Sleep Eyes, Wee Willie Winkie, Box, 1957, 17 In. 330.00
Doll, Ideal, Vinyl, Red, White, Blue Dress, Purse, 12 In. 165.00
Doll, Pink Organdy Dress, Hair Bow, Black Shoes, Tag, 1957-58, 12 In. 350.00
Doll, Sleep Eyes, Open Mouth, Blond Wig, Jacket, 18 In. 69.00
Doll, Sleep Eyes, Sailor Suit, Hair Net, Tag, 1957-58, 12 In. 350.00
Mirror, Cream Ground, Celluloid, Pocket, Fox Film Corp., c.1935, 1 3/4 In. 44.00
Paper Doll, Uncut, 1 Doll, 4 Clothes Pages, Whitman, 1976 .... 55.00
Pitcher, Cobalt Blue Glass, Honeycomb Sides, Shaped Handle, 4 1/4 In. .... *Illus* 75.00
Sheet Music, Animal Crackers In My Soup, Curly Top, Sam Fox, 1935 .... 18.00
Statue, Dimples, Carnival Art Statuary, 1936, 16 1/2 x 3 3/4 x 5 3/4 In. 465.00
Stringholder, Chalk, 1940s-60s, 6 3/4 x 6 1/4 In. 395.00

SHRINER, see Fraternal category.

SILVER DEPOSIT glass was first made during the late nineteenth
century. Solid sterling silver is applied to the glass by a chemical
method so that a cutout design of silver metal appears against a clear or
colored glass. It is sometimes called silver overlay.

Bowl, Centerpiece, Black Amethyst Glass, Silver Scrolls & Leaves, 12 1/2 In. 80.00
Bowl, Centerpiece, Green Glass, Silver Flowers, 12 1/2 In. 245.00
Bowl, Fruit, Clear Glass, Art Deco Overlay, Footed, 12 1/2 In. 120.00
Liqueur Set, Bulbous Decanter, Cordials, Green Glass, Silver Daisies, 7 Piece 105.00
Liqueur Set, Slender Decanter, Cordials, Cobalt Blue Glass, Silver Rings, 7 Piece 385.00
Vase, Clear Glass, Art Nouveau Overlay, Baluster, 10 In. 50.00
Vase, Dark Red Color Glass, 12 In. 1150.00
Vase, Gourd Form, Green Glass, Leaf Overlay, Opalescent Jewel, 10 x 6 1/2 In. 1645.00
Vase, Stick, Flowers, Green Translucent Glass, Overlay Flowers, Bulbous, 8 In. 520.00

SILVER FLATWARE includes many of the current and out-of-production silver
and silver-plated flatware patterns made in the past eighty years. Other silver is
listed under Silver-American, Silver-English, etc. Most silver flatware sets that are
missing a few pieces can be completed through the help of one of the many silver
matching services that advertise in many of the national publications.

SILVER FLATWARE PLATED, Always, Tablespoon, Oneida, 1958 .... 8.00
Dessert Set, Forks & Knives, Wood Case, Mappin & Webb, 24 Piece 215.00
Fish Set, Bamboo, Ivory Handles, Walker & Hall, Victorian, 2 Piece 230.00
Fish Set, Forks & Knives, Wood Case, Mappin & Webb, 24 Piece 239.00
Fish Set, Pierced, Engraved, Acanthus, Arabesques, Leatherette Case, c.1880, 2 Piece 69.00
Floral, Punch Ladle, R. Wallace & Son, Wallingford, c.1902, 12 In. 90.00
Forever, Cake Server, Community, 1939 .... 25.00
French Thread, Fork, T.W. Freeman, Augusta, Ga., c.1850, 7 5/8 In. 345.00
Grape Scissors, Decorated Handles, 6 In., Pair 167.00
SILVER FLATWARE STERLING, Alhambra, Pickle Knife & Fork, Monogram, Gorham, c.1880 . 226.00
Arabesque, Serving Fork, Whiting, c.1875, 9 1/2 In. 145.00
Chantilly, Stuffing Spoon, Gorham, c.1895, 12 1/4 In. 431.00
Clematis, Punch Ladle, Gorham, c.1885, 12 1/4 In. 145.00
Diamond, Gio Ponti, Salad Set, Black Plastic, Reed & Barton, 13 In. 1035.00
Doric, Jelly Server, Manchester Silver Co., 1932, 6 1/8 In. 32.00
Francis I, Salad Serving Set, Reed & Barton, c.1907, 9 1/2 In. .... 800.00 to 805.00
Hepplewhite, Tea Strainer, Over The Cup, Reed & Barton, c.1920, 8 In. 230.00
Imperial Chrysanthemum, Shovel, Gold Washed Bowl, Monogram, Gorham 230.00
Jac Rose, Salt Spoon, Master, Gold Washed Bowl, Gorham, c.1885, Pair 138.00
Laureate, Serving Fork, Whiting, c.1890, 9 In. 145.00
Lotus, Coffee Spoon, George P. Blanchard, 5 1/2 In. 45.00
Lotus, Fish Fork, George P. Blanchard, 7 1/2 In. 165.00
Lotus, Teaspoon, Pointed Bowl, George P. Blanchard, 6 In. 55.00
Lotus, Tongs, George P. Blanchard, 2 3/4 In. 125.00

Louis XV, Serving Spoon, Whiting Division Of Gorham 69.00
Louis XV, Soup Ladle, Whiting Division Of Gorham 184.00
Love Disarmed, Fish Set, Reed & Barton, 2 Piece 600.00
Luxembourg, Claret Spoon, Twisted Stem, Shaped Bowl, Gorham, 13 In. 201.00
Marquis, Fish Set, F.M. Whiting, c.1889, 2 Piece 325.00
Medallion, Berry Spoon, Wood & Hughes, New York, c.1860, 9 In. 403.00
Medallion, Demitasse Set, Gorham, Case, 1885, 12 Piece 345.00
Medallion, Salt Spoon, Gorham, 3 5/8 In., Pair 268.00
Medallion, Sugar Sifter, Gorham, c.1864 .... 495.00
Mythologique, Egg Spoon, Gorham 130.00
Nightingale, Fish Set, Monogram, Gorham, c.1885, 2 Piece 695.00
Old Maryland, Serving Spoon, Engraved, Coquille Bowl, Kirk Steiff, c.1936, 9 1/2 In. 105.00
Puritan, Salt Spoon, Master, Stieff 38.00
Repousse, Bacon Fork, S. Kirk 195.00
Repousse, Chipped Beef Fork, S. Kirk 100.00
Repousse, Cream Soup Spoon, S. Kirk 40.00
Repousse, Ice Spoon, Pierced, S. Kirk 375.00
Repousse, Ice Tongs, S. Kirk 895.00
Rose, Ice Cream Fork, Stieff 65.00
Sovereign, Dinner Set, Forks, Knives, Spoons, Gorham, 158 Piece 3107.00
Trianon Pierced, Fork, Dominick & Haff, 7 In. 55.00
Trianon Pierced, Fork, Dominick & Haff, 8 In. 75.00
Trianon Pierced, Olive Spoon, Pierced, Dominick & Haff 99.00
Trianon Pierced, Serving Spoon, Monogram, Dominick & Haff 95.00
Tuileries, Serving Fork, Gorham, c.1906, 9 1/4 In. 175.00
Versailles, Asparagus Tongs, Pierced, Gorham 395.00
Versailles, Berry Fork, Monogram, Gorham 75.00
Versailles, Butter Spreader, Gorham 80.00
Versailles, Salad Serving Set, Gorham, c.1888, 8 1/2 In. 520.00

SILVER PLATE is not solid silver. It is a ware made of a metal, such as nickel or copper, that is covered with a thin coating of silver. The letters *EPNS* are often found on American and English silver-plated wares. Sheffield is a term with two meanings. Sometimes it refers to sterling silver made in the town of Sheffield, England. In this section, Sheffield refers to a type of silver plate, usually English.

Basket, Hinged Handle, Round Body, Pierced Base, Ruffled Rim, Late 1800s, 9 x 12 In. ... 58.00
Basket, Wirework, Handle, Sheffield, 12 x 8 1/2 x 5 In. 460.00
Basket, Wirework, Reeded Rim, Swing Handle, Oval, Sheffield, c.1800, 14 1/2 In. 380.00
Biscuit Box, Cut Crystal, Hinged Lid, Green, Silver Frame, Scroll Feet, 9 x 7 In. 175.00
Biscuit Box, Cut Crystal, Hinged Lid, Scroll Feet, 9 x 7 1/4 In. 259.00
Biscuit Box, Sheffield, Shell Shape, Hinged, Scroll Legs, 1900s, 10 x 8 1/2 x 6 In. 259.00
Biscuit Jar, Pierced, Ring Handles, Engraved Hinged Cover, Frosted Glass Insert, 7 In. ... 400.00

Silver Plate, Cocktail Shaker,
Penguin, Napier,
12 1/2 In.

Silver Plate, Cocktail Shaker,
Rooster, Hammered,
Wallace Brothers, 14 1/2 In.

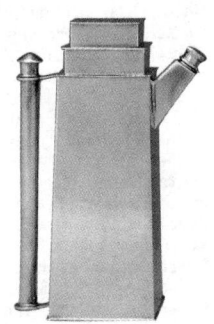

Silver Plate, Cocktail Shaker,
Skyscraper, Cap, Bernard Rice's
Sons Inc., 1930, 11 In.

Bowl, Stand, 25 1/2 x 11 1/2 In., Pair	375.00
Breakfast Set, 2 Covered Warming Dishes, Condiment Bowls, Stand, 9 x 10 In.	69.00
Candelabrum is listed in its own category.	
Candlesticks are listed in their own category.	
Cheese Scoop, Monogram, Victorian, James Dixon & Sons, c.1880, 8 In.	50.00
Claret Jug, Tapered Faceted Body, Angular Handle, Hinged Cover, 11 In., Pair	780.00
Cocktail Shaker, Dumbbell Shape, Asprey & Co., 10 In.	2629.00
Cocktail Shaker, Engraved, c.1932, 15 In.	6575.00
Cocktail Shaker, Hammered, Pairpoint	80.00
Cocktail Shaker, Penguin, Napier, 12 1/2 In. .... *Illus*	1076.00
Cocktail Shaker, Rooster, Hammered, Wallace Brothers, 14 1/2 In. .... *Illus*	3346.00
Cocktail Shaker, Skyscraper, Cap, Bernard Rice's Sons Inc., 1930, 11 In. .... *Illus*	2271.00
Coffee Urn, Amphora Shape, Leaf Handles, Acorn Finial, Engraved Bird, 13 1/2 In.	230.00
Cruet Frame, Shaped Handle, Reticulated Base, Paw Feet, 11 1/2 In.	80.00
Cruet Stand, Sheffield, Cut Glass, 6 Bottles, Late 19th Century, 12 In.	800.00
Crumber, Engraved Reserve, Leather Case, 11 1/2 In.	145.00
Decanter Stand, Putti, 4 Cut Glass Decanters, George R. Collins, London, c.1880, 9 In.	1955.00
Decanter Stand, Rounded, Convex, Triangular, 3 Decanters, Victorian, 11 x 9 In.	1610.00
Dish, Cover, Stand, Shell, Flower & Leaf Border, 4-Footed, T. & J. Creswick, 14 In., Pair	1265.00
Dish, Entree, Cover, Oval, J. Dixon & Sons, Sheffield, Edwardian, c.1910, 6 x 9 x 11 In.	145.00
Dish, Entree, Dome Cover, Sheffield, Oval, Hinged Top, 6 1/2 In.	230.00
Dish, Entree, Oval, U-Shape Handles, Acanthus, Dragon, 6 x 8 x 12 In., Pair	200.00
Dish, Entree, Revolving Top, Engraved, Elkington & Co., 20th Century, 16 3/4 In.	315.00
Dish, Entree, Warming Stand, Removable Handles, Sheffield, c.1800, 13 In., Pair	805.00
Dish, Savory, Serpentine Sides, Reeded Rim, Sheffield, George III, c.1800, 13 x 9 In.	375.00
Dish Stand, Wirework, Revolving, Sheffield, Early 1800s, 11 In.	265.00
Epergne, 5 Glass Baskets, Lion Paw Form Supports, England, 14 x 22 1/2 In.	1380.00
Epergne, Squirrel & Nut, Etched Glass Insert, No. 295, Meriden, 11 1/4 In.	550.00
Epergne, Vase Shape, 3 Swing Handle Baskets, 12 1/2 In.	160.00
Epergne, Wirework Cage, 6 Scrolling Arms, Supporting Baskets, Regency, 23 x 20 In.	2760.00
Frame, Bourbon Family Coat-Of-Arms, Flower Pressed Design, 1800s, 21 x 15 In.	546.00
Fruit Bowl, Flower & Fruit Repousse, Marked Made In England, 12 In.	80.00
Hamilton Bottle Stand, England, 4 1/4 In.	98.00
Hot Water Urn, Egg Shape, Matthew Boulton, Sheffield, George III, c.1790, 21 x 12 In.	1840.00
Hot Water Urn, Knop Stem, Reeded Handles, Spigot, Rocaille Panel Feet, Sheffield, 15 In.	575.00
Hot Water Urn, Vase Shape, Laurel Swags, Sheffield, George III, c.1790, 22 x 11 In.	865.00
Ice Bucket, Dome Lid, Handles, Poole Silver, Taunton, Mass., 9 1/4 x 7 1/4 In.	29.00
Ice Bucket, Tapered, 2 Lion Head Handles, Elkington, 8 x 7 1/2 In., Pair	430.00
Jardiniere, Bulbous Oval, Spiral Fluting, Scroll Feet, c.1900, 5 x 11 x 16 In.	1265.00
Jewelry Box, Removable Tray, Blue Velvet Interior, Late 1800s, 6 x 10 x 6 In.	58.00
Kettle, Hot Water, Bulbous, Dome Lid, Ring Handles, Pedestal, England, 16 x 9 In.	405.00
Kettle, Hot Water, Medallion, Grotesque Masque, Gorham, Early 1900s, 14 1/2 In.	575.00
Kettle, On Stand, Claw Feet, Wooden Handle & Finial, 18th Century Style, 12 1/2 In.	80.00
Meat Cover, Royal Sussex Light Infantry, England, 1800s, 10 1/2 x 17 x 12 In.	460.00
Mirror, Octagonal Frame, Beveled, Pressed Metal, 34 3/4 x 37 In., Pair	460.00
Monteith, Scalloped Rim, Spiral Flutes, Lion Mask Ring Handles, England, 9 x 12 In.	490.00
Mug, Cylindrical, Greek Key Rim, Foot, Engraved, Egg & Dart, c.1862, 3 x 4 x 3 In.	46.00
Mug, Wooden Handle, Engraved, Christopher Dresser, Hukin & Heath, 4 In.	440.00
Napkin Rings are listed in their own category.	
Pitcher, Ice Water, Embossed, Chased, Jaccard & Co., c.1870, 12 1/2 In.	200.00
Pitcher, Ice Water, Tilting, Stand, Goblet, Tumbler, Walrus Hunters, Rogers Smith, c.1872	550.00
Pitcher, Water, Victorian, Cover, Porcelain Liner, Etched, Late 19th Century	105.00
Platter, Dome, Oval, Leaf & Flower Border, Leaf Handle, Sheffield, c.1840, 24 1/2 In.	920.00
Punch Bowl, Scalloped Rim, Scrolling Vines, Grapes, 10 x 16 In.	175.00
Punch Set, Bowl, Tray, Ladle, 10 Cups & Saucers, Oneida, Sheridan, 23 Piece	145.00
Salt, Open, Molded, Scrolling Leaves, Flowers, Sheffield, c.1840, 3 3/4 In., 6 Piece	210.00
Salver, Outscrolled Handles, Sheffield, George V, c.1925, 12 x 8 In.	145.00
Salver, Shaped Scroll & Leaf Border, Sheffield, Circular, c.1835, 22 1/2 In.	840.00
Salver Set, Scalloped Rim, Scrolled Flowers, 6 1/2, 8 1/2, 9, & 12 1/2 In., 4 Piece	290.00
Spoon, Souvenir, see Souvenir category.	
Tea & Coffee Set, Classical Shape, Shell Design, 1900s, 10-In. Coffeepot, 5 Piece	375.00
Tea & Coffee Set, Coffeepot, Teapot, Covered Sugar, Round Tray, 10 1/2 In.	60.00
Tea & Coffee Set, Creamer, Sugar, Waste Bowl, Tray	150.00

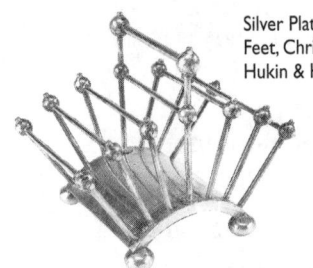

Silver Plate, Toast Rack, Ball
Feet, Christopher Dresser,
Hukin & Heath, 4 3/4 x 5 In.

Silver-American, Bowl,
Repousse Birds, Chinese
Scenes, Coin, Samuel
Kirk, 1830-46, 7 In.

Tea & Coffee Set, Egyptian Revival, Britannia Ware, Meriden Co., c.1870, 7 In.	259.00
Tea & Coffee Set, FB Rogers, Sugar & Cream, Footed Tray, 14 x 25 In.	69.00
Tea & Coffee Set, Georgian Style, Sheffield, c.1920, 11 1/2 In., 4 Piece	35.00
Tea & Coffee Set, Urn Shape, Coffeepot 12-In., Teapot 11-In., 5 Piece	145.00
Tea Set, Aesthetic Movement, Fern & Clover Design, c.1890, 4 Piece	105.00
Tea Set, Classical Design, Pairpoint, Early 20th Century, 5 1/2 In., 3 Piece	80.00
Tea Set, Flower Repousse Banding, Coffee & Tea Pots, Sugar & Creamer, Tray	120.00
Tea Set, Flowers, Beaded Rim, Teapot, Creamer, Sugar, Milk Pitcher, 1900s	60.00
Tea Set, Relief Panels, Chased, Engraved Flowers, Scrolls, Cast Handles, 4 Piece	230.00
Tea Urn, Flower Finial, S-Scroll Handles, Bun Feet, Victorian, 1800s, 16 1/2 In.	225.00
Toast Rack, Ball Feet, Christopher Dresser, Hukin & Heath, 4 3/4 x 5 In. .... *Illus*	588.00
Toothpick Holder, Man, High Wheel Bike, Barrel On Back, No. 2649, 7 In.	678.00
Tray, Eggcups, Spoons, 20th Century, 8 x 7 1/2 In., 6 Eggcups	59.00
Tray, Embossed, Ribbed, Sheffield, 30 In.	489.00
Tray, Gallery, Openwork Band, Embossed Bellflower, DR & Sons, 1900s, 24 In.	800.00
Tray, Leaf Design, Claw Form Feet, 2 Handles, 25 In.	127.00
Tray, Molded Serpentine Border, 2 Handles, 20th Century, 28 x 18 In.	25.00
Tray, Oval, Egg & Dart Rim, Rural Scenes, Rogers, Smith & Co., Conn., 23 x 36 In.	1035.00
Tray, Oval, Leaf & Flower Handles, Grape & Leaf Border, Reticulated, 28 x 18 In.	120.00
Tray, Oval, Pierced & Beaded Rim, Arabesques & Scrolls, Handles, Victorian, 30 In.	575.00
Tray, Scrolling Leafy Design, 28 1/2 In.	200.00
Tray, Serving, Acanthus Leaf Handles, Engraved Center, Rococo Style, 32 In.	460.00
Tray, Serving, Gallery Rim, Pierced Handles, Round Body, Crest, Motto, 2 x 24 In.	690.00
Tray, Serving, Oval Rim, Handles, Gorham, 1900s, 24 1/2 In.	315.00
Tray, Serving, Scrolling Flowers, Engraved Central Design, 27 x 15 3/4 In.	230.00
Tray, Serving, Sheffield, Horse Decorated Border, Steeplechase, 1900s, 20 In.	520.00
Tray, Sheffield, Handles, Chased Decoration, c.1823, 28 In.	575.00
Tureen, Cover, Ladle, Sheffield, George III, 1780, 15 In.	370.00
Tureen, Revolving, Chased, Etched, Dome Over Warming Tray, 10 x 15 x 10 In.	345.00
Urn, Cover, Vase Form, Sheffield, c.1791, 16 In.	290.00
Warming Dish, Gadroon Rim, Acanthus Loop Handles, Crestwick, 8 x 14 In., Pair	1675.00
Wine Coaster, Sheffield, Wood Turned Bases, Silver Plate Frame, England, 2 x 6 In., Pair .	90.00
Wine Cooler, Campana Form, Liner, Bulbous, Sheffield, c.1820, 9 In., Pair	1380.00
Wine Trolley, 2 Bottles, England, Late 19th Century, 13 1/2 In.	1150.00
Wine Trolley, 2 Circular Wine Coasters Form, Frame, Wheels, Loop Handle, 18 In.	430.00

SILVER, SHEFFIELD, see Silver Plate; Silver-English categories.

SILVER-AMERICAN. American silver is listed here. Coin and sterling silver are included. Most of the sterling silver listed in this book is
subdivided by country. There are also other pieces of silver and silver
plate listed under special categories, such as Candelabrum, Napkin
Ring, Silver Flatware, Silver Plate, Silver-Sterling, and Tiffany Silver.
For information about makers and marks, see *Kovels' American Silver
Marks: 1650 to the Present.*

SILVER-AMERICAN, Basket, Hinged Handle, Oval, Watson, Early 1900s, 10 1/2 x 10 3/4 x 8 In.	290.00
Basket, Hinged Handle, Reticulated Oval Body, Marked, 10 1/2 In.	288.00
Basket, Oval, Beaded, Hinged Handle, Seashells, Footed, J. Mood, Charleston, 10 In.	9200.00
Basting Spoon, Hanoverian, Oval Bowl, Charles Leroux, N.Y., c.1730, 15 In.	5400.00
Beaker, Cylindrical, Tapered, Arms, Monogram, W. Williams, c.1820, 3 In., Pair	3900.00

Beaker, Demi-Barrel Shape, Engraved, Bassett Nichols, c.1815, 4 Piece 6000.00
Bowl, 2 Handles, Flowering Urns, Lebkuecher & Co., Newark, N.J., c.1920, 13 1/2 In. 345.00
Bowl, 3 Formed Feet, Frans Gyllenberg, 1 7/8-In. High 395.00
Bowl, Beaded Edge, Dominick & Haff, 10 In. 145.00
Bowl, Center, Chased Flowers, Fans, Flared Rim, Frontenac, Gorham, c.1935, 10 In. 690.00
Bowl, Center, Frontenac Pattern, Raised Flowers, Gorham, 1935, 10 In. 690.00
Bowl, Center, Hammered, Flared Rim, Footed, Georg Jensen Style, 6 x 10 1/2 In. 978.00
Bowl, Chased Flowers, Birds, Whiting, c.1910, 4 1/4 In. 160.00
Bowl, Fluted Form, Pedestal Base, Frans Gyllenberg, 4 1/8 x 7 1/4 In. 875.00
Bowl, Footed, Francis I, Reed & Barton, c.1953, 2 1/4 x 8 In. 460.00
Bowl, Footed, Kylix Shape, Classical Maiden Head Handles, Gorham, 1870s, 10 In. 945.00
Bowl, Francis I, Reed & Barton, c.1953, 1 1/2 x 8 In. 460.00
Bowl, Gilt, Monogram, Round, Wavy Edge, Gorham, R.I., 2 1/2 x 8 1/2 In. 145.00
Bowl, Hammered, Flowers, Scalloped Foot, Chicago Art Silver Shop, 17 x 20 In. 825.00
Bowl, Hammered, Fluted Form, Flared Sides, Karl F. Leinonen, 5 3/8 In. 365.00
Bowl, Hammered, Lobed, Kalo Shop, Chicago, 2 x 7 In. 575.00
Bowl, Leafy Band Rim & Foot, Parcel Gilt Interior, Gorham, 1900, 13 In. 690.00
Bowl, Low, Leaf Handles, Randahl, 7 3/4 In. 230.00
Bowl, Low, Ring Foot, 2 Flared Tab Handles, Allan Adler, 15 In. 1750.00
Bowl, Monteith, Late 1600s Style, John Letelier, 12 In. 6000.00
Bowl, On Pedestal, Coin Silver, Geradus Boyce, N.Y., 6 x 7 In. 1265.00
Bowl, Oval, Chased Design, Gorham, 13 In. 690.00
Bowl, Pierced Scalloped Sides, Beaded Rim, Bigelow Kennard & Co., 13 In. 190.00
Bowl, Repousse Birds, Chinese Scenes, Coin, Samuel Kirk, 1830-46, 7 In. .... *Illus* 863.00
Bowl, Repousse, Buildings, Bridges, River, Animals, Footed, S. Kirk, c.1925, 11 In. 2590.00
Bowl, Round, Fluted, Turned In Rim, Pedestal, Engraved, Julius Randahl, 4 x 8 In. 795.00
Bowl, Round, Ring Foot, Chased, Repousse Panel, Arthur J. Stone, 9 1/2 In. 3800.00
Bowl, Vegetable, Narrow & Wide Flutes, Divided, Falick Novick, 12 x 3 In. 1000.00
Box, Cover, Cylindrical, Enameled Flower Top, Elizabeth Copeland, 2 1/4 x 2 1/2 In. 2820.00
Box, Cover, Stylized Star, 2 1/4 x 3 1/4 In. 80.00
Brandy Warmer, Cylindrical, Wood Handle, T. Hammersley, N.Y., c.1760, 7 1/2 In. 3600.00
Brandy Warmer, Nuremburg, Gorham 275.00
Brandy Warmer, Pear Shape, Sparrow Beak, Revere, 1900s, 2 3/8 x 3 1/2 In. 50.00
Bread & Butter Dish Set, Serpentine Scroll, Woodside Silver Co., 12 Piece 400.00
Bread Tray, Hammered, Oval, Broad Flared Rim, Gorham, 13 1/4 In. 495.00
Bread Tray, Oval, Pierced, Monogram, Reed & Barton, 14 1/2 In. 259.00
Cake Basket, Rococo Revival, Gold Washed, C-Scroll Cartouches, Towle, 14 1/4 In. 1175.00
Cake Stand, Pierced Rim, Applied Flowers, Redlich & Co., Early 1900s, 12 In. 690.00
Candelabrum is listed in its own category.
Candlesticks are listed in their own category.
Cann, Cup, Cover, T & A.E. Warner, Baltimore, c.1810, 7 1/4 In. 4200.00
Cann, Cup, Elongated Pear Shape, Scroll Handle, Benjamin Burt, c.1770, 5 1/2 In. 2700.00
Cann, Cup, Tapered Cylinder, 4 Hoof Feet, Benjamin Wynkoop, N.Y., c.1725, 5 In. 7200.00
Cann, Cup, Tapered Cylinder, Bombe Foot, Simeon Soumaine, N.Y., c.1730, 4 1/4 In. 6600.00
Card Case, Gilded, Engraved, Gilded, Gorham, Mid 19th Century, 3 1/2 In. 145.00
Castor, Baluster Shape, Daniel Henchman, Boston, c.1760, 5 1/2 In. 3900.00
Castor, Baluster Shape, Monogram, Zachariah Brigden, c.1780, 5 1/2 In. 2700.00

Silver-American, Cocktail
Pitcher, Braided, Beaded
Handle, Zimmerman,
1920, 10 In.

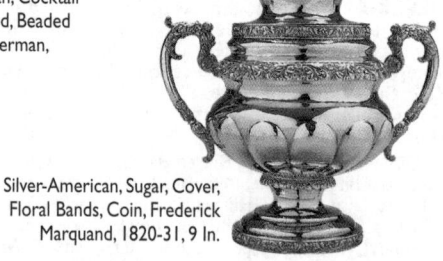

Silver-American, Sugar, Cover,
Floral Bands, Coin, Frederick
Marquand, 1820-31, 9 In.

Castor, Baluster Shape, Pierced & Engraved Cover, Joseph Richardson Sr., 4 In. 600.00
Cheese Scoop, Shovel Shape, Wood Handle, J. Letelier, Phila., c.1780, 9 3/8 In. 1920.00
Chest, Jewel, 3 Drawers, Hinged Doors, Temple, Mt. Fuji, Japan, 5 1/2 In. 1265.00
Chest, Jewel, 4 Drawers, Hinged Doors, Chrysanthemums, Peony, Bamboo, 8 In. 2185.00
Cocktail Pitcher, Braided, Beaded Handle, Zimmerman, 1920, 10 In. . . . . *Illus* 10755.00
Cocktail Shaker, Martini, Glass, 3 Piece 130.00
Coffee Set, Demitasse, Art Nouveau, Coffee Pot, Creamer, Open Sugar, Gorham 780.00
Coffee Set, Demitasse, Mauser, 10-In. Coffeepot, 3 Piece 375.00
Coffee Set, Demitasse, Persian Pattern, Durgin 960.00
Coffee Set, Nesting, Round, Angular Handles, Lebolt & Co., 5 1/2 In., 3 Piece 750.00
Coffeepot, Baluster, Scroll Handle, Inscription, John Jones, Boston, c.1821, 11 In. 945.00
Coffeepot, Elongated Shaped Spout & Handle, Watson, 7 1/4 In. 259.00
Coffeepot, Urn Form, Leaf Design, Pineapple Finial, Redlich & Co., c.1900, 11 In. 1400.00
Cold Meat Fork, Leaf & Bead Design, 2 Tines, David Carlson, 9 In. 195.00
Compote, Chrysanthemum Pattern, Chased Fruit, Black, Starr & Frost 410.00
Compote, Repousse Chased Rim, Footed, S. Kirk & Son, 3 x 5 In. 145.00
Cream Jug, Engraved, Script Initials, Saunders, Pitman, 7 In. 575.00
Cream Pot, Pear Shape, 3 Hoof Feet, Scroll Handle, HB Maker Mark, c.1740, 4 In. 2400.00
Cream Pot, Pear Shape, 3-Footed, William Homes, Sr., Boston, c.1750, 3 1/2 In. 4800.00
Cream Pot, Pear Shape, Waved Rim, Scroll Handle, Cary Dunn, c.1775, 4 In. 7200.00
Creamer, Coin, Helmet Shape, Beaded Rim, Handle, Chased, c.1815, 7 In. 315.00
Creamer, Cover, Hammered, Engraved, Arts & Crafts, Shreve & Co., 3 x 4 In. 230.00
Creamer, Federal Coin, Budding Vine Band, Baldwin Gardiner, c.1814, 7 1/8 In. 410.00
Creamer & Sugar Basket, Basket Weave, Eoff & Shepherd, N.Y., c.1855, 7 1/4 In. 1320.00
Cup, 2 Stylized Riveted Strapwork Handles, Barbour Silver Co., c.1910, 9 In. 85.00
Cup, 2 Twisted Handles, Gorham, 6 In. 50.00
Cup, Beaded Scroll Handle, Coat Of Arms, Peter Van Dyck, N.Y., c.1745, 3 In. 4200.00
Cup, Beaker Shape, S Scroll Handle, Benjamin Wynkoop, N.Y., c.1740, 3 1/2 In. 7200.00
Cup, Coin, Beadwork Rim, Floral Cartouche, John Veal, S.C., c.1857, 4 In. 1035.00
Cup, Cylindrical, Tapered, Scroll Strap Handle, Samuel Vernon, c.1725, 3 In. 4200.00
Cup, Flared, Cylindrical, Engraved B, Edward Breese, 2 3/4 In., 6 Piece 550.00
Dessert Spoon, Charleston Coin, Nathaniel Vernon, c.1835, 7 In. 200.00
Dish, Basket Shape, Pierced Rim, Intertwined Grapevine, Whiting, c.1907, 6 In. 175.00
Dish, Cover, Maiden, Old Man, Strapwork, Oval, Gorham, c.1865, 18 1/2 In. 6000.00
Dish, Entree, Cover, Oval, S. Kirk, Baltimore, c.1865, 12 1/4 In., Pair 7800.00
Dish, Leaf Shape, Shreve, Crump & Low, 3 Round Feet, 2 3/4 x 7 1/2 In. 60.00
Dish, Mayonnaise, Hammered, Flared, Pedestal, Monogram, Lebolt & Co., 5 1/4 In. 400.00
Dish, Oval, Flat Rim, Engraved Laurel Wreath, Porter Blanchard, c.1920, 2 x 12 In. 375.00
Dish, Oval, Ring Foot, Strap Handle, Looped Scrolls, Lona P. Schaeffer, 4 In. 245.00
Dish, Quatrefoil Form, Flower, Leaves, Kirk & Son, 13 In., Pair 2300.00
Dish, Shell Form, 4 Ball Form Feet, Red & Barton, 8 1/4 In. 50.00
Dish, Vegetable, Oval, Shaped Leaf Scroll Rim, W.W. Wattles & Sons, 12 In., Pair 489.00
Dresser Set, Repousse, Monogram, Dominick & Haff, 4 Piece 230.00
Ewer, Baluster Shape, Grapevine, Presentation, 16 1/4 In. 2100.00
Ewer, Coin, Egg Shaped Body, Jones, Shreve, Brown & Co., c.1860, 13 x 7 In. 1380.00
Ewer, Coin, Hallmark, Footed, Tall Handle, Repousse Flowers, 17 In. 2185.00
Fernery, Old Newbury Crafters, Pieced Brass Cover, c.1900 . . . .   375.00
Fork, Shell, Engraved Mimh, Hayden & Co., Charleston, c.1850, 7 3/8 In. 259.00
Fork Set, Coin, Plain Tipt Pattern, Monogram, c.1850, 12 Piece 345.00
Grape Shears, Vines, Fruit, Egyptian Designs, Gorham, Late 1800s, 6 1/2 In. 450.00
Gravy Boat, Meriden Britannia, Conn., c.1920, 4 x 7 In. 230.00
Ice Bucket, Baroque, Wallace, 11 In. 105.00
Julep Cup, Engraved, Fisher, N.J., 3 In. 45.00
Kettle, Hot Water, Coin Silver, Bulbous, Ball, Tompkins & Black, c.1845, 15 In. 1150.00
Kettle, Stand, Repousse, Chased, Oval, Hinged Scroll Handle, Gorham, 1898, 13 In. 1610.00
Ladle, Coin, Oval Bowl, Plain Handle, Engraved Initials, Early 1800s, 13 In. 375.00
Ladle, Double Swell, Fiddle Tip, Eugene Jaccard & Co., St. Louis, c.1870, 13 In. 105.00
Ladle, French Thread, Glaze & Radcliffe, Columbia, S.C., 1850, 12 5/8 In. 3200.00
Ladle, Oval Bowl, Bead Pattern, Platt & Bro., Coin, c.1825, 13 1/2 In. 485.00
Ladle, Oyster, Shaped Bowl, Peter Krider, Philadelphia, 8 3/4 In. 200.00
Ladle, Pierced Design, Richard Dimes, 5 1/2 In. 125.00
Matchbox Cover, Book Cover Form, Arthur J. Stone, 1 3/4 In., Pair 150.00
Mirror, Art Deco, 18 x 14 3/4 In. 1075.00

Moustache Brush, Towle, 4 1/2 In. 90.00
Mug, Coin, Chased Flowers, Marked, Gorham, c.1860, 3 3/8 In. 288.00
Mug, Cylindrical, Oak Leaf, Acanthus Leaf, Nathan Hobbs, c.1815, 3 3/4 In. 325.00
Napkin Rings are listed in their own category.
Nut Dish, Good Luck, Oval, 4-Leaf Clover, Reed & Barton, c.1970, 1/2 x 3 x 4 In. 50.00
Nut Dish, Oval, Shaped, Pierced, Scroll Rim, 4 Feet, Alvin Corp., 4 In., 12 Piece 375.00
Pepper Box, Tankard Shape, Scroll Handle, Dome Cover, c.1730, 3 1/2 In. 3000.00
Pipkin, Bulbous, Wooden Handle, Towle, c.1950, 3 In. 460.00
Pipkin, Chippendale, Piecrust Edge, Ebonized Handle, Gorham, c.1949, 2 x 8 In. 145.00
Pitcher, Bulbous, Hollow Handle, Wide Spout, Gorham, 7 3/4 In. 2100.00
Pitcher, Dome Lid, Whippet Finial, Repousse, S. Kirk & Son, c.1860, 8 In. 1840.00
Pitcher, Fluid Shape, Hollow Handle, Danish Style, Julius Randahl, 9 1/2 In. 950.00
Pitcher, Japanese Style, Repousse, Fish, Handle, Dragon, Gorham, 1882, 9 In. 17925.00
Pitcher, Male & Female Masks, Strapwork, God Mask, Gorham, c.1865, 12 In. 4800.00
Pitcher, Milk, Squat, Looped Hollow Handle, Arthur J. Stone, 4 1/4 In. 950.00
Pitcher, Oval Body, Cartouches, Acanthus, Graff Washbourne & Dunn, 11 In. 1955.00
Pitcher, Profile Medallions, Actors, Warriors, Gorham, c.1865, 11 1/2 In. 3600.00
Pitcher, Rosepoint Pattern, Wallace International, 10 1/2 In. 956.00
Pitcher, Royal Danish Pattern, International, 8 1/4 In. 359.00
Pitcher, Urn Shape, Scrolling Handle, Old Newbury Crafters, c.1915, 9 In. 800.00
Pitcher, Water, Baluster, Leaf Scroll, Presentation, Bailey & Co., 1857, 11 In. 3300.00
Pitcher, Water, Bulbous, Loop Handle, 3 Line Design, James T. Woolley, 7 In. 1700.00
Pitcher, Water, Engraved Initial, W.K. Vanderslice, Late 19th Century, 12 In. 1320.00
Pitcher, Water, Inscribed, Radnor Hunt, Wallace, c.1932, 20 Oz. 265.00
Pitcher, Water, Landscape Repousse, Schofield Co., c.1900, 10 x 29 1/2 In. 3290.00
Pitcher, Water, Leaf Scrolled Panels & Foot, Gorham, 1904, 10 In. 805.00
Pitcher, Water, Pantheon Pattern, International, 9 In. 520.00
Pitcher, Water, Repousse, House, Trees, Bird, Engraved, Gorham, 10 1/2 In. 1840.00
Pitcher, Water, Swirl-Form Body, Shell Designs, Gorham, 8 1/2 In. 1440.00
Plate, Chippendale Edge, Monogram, Howard & Co., 10 In. 185.00
Plate, Gadroon Border, John McMullin, Round, 5 3/4 In., Pair 2040.00
Plate Set, Dessert, Rocaille Shells, Black, Starr & Frost, 1891-1902, 9 1/4 In., 6 Piece 765.00
Plate Set, Hexagonal, Pierced Lattice, Engraved, c.1915, 10 In., 12 Piece 2300.00
Plate Set, Rocaille Shells, Black, Starr & Frost, 1891-1902, 11 In., 10 Piece 2705.00
Platter, Oval, Ring Foot, Kirk, 24 In. 5750.00
Platter, Oval, Shaped Leaf & Scroll Rim, Dominick & Haff, 1900, 18 1/2 In. 605.00
Porringer, 2-Arch Keyhole Handle, Deep Bowl, J. Dixwell, c.1720, 8 In. 4200.00
Porringer, 2-Arch Keyhole Handle, Moody Russell, Mass., c.1750, 7 In. 4200.00
Porringer, 2-Arch Keyhole Handle, Thomas Edwards, c.1740, 7 1/4 In. 3000.00
Porringer, 3-Hole Handle, Benjamin Wynkoop, 1700s, 7 In. 8400.00
Porringer, Bombe Bowl, Geometric Handle, S. Vernon, Newport, R.I., c.1730, 8 In. 4500.00
Porringer, Bombe Bowl, Tab Handle, W. Ghiselin, Philadelphia, c.1760, 7 In. 7800.00
Porringer, Bombe, Pierced Handle, Scrolls, Jacob Boelen, N.Y., c.1700, 8 In. 5100.00
Porringer, Geometric Handle, Heart, Jeremiah Dummer, Boston, c.1700, 7 1/8 In. 3300.00
Porringer, Keyhole Handle, B. Woodcock, Wilmington, De., c.1760, 7 3/8 In. 9600.00
Porringer, Keyhole Handle, Deep Bowl, Elias Pelletreau, N.Y., c.1785, 7 1/2 In. 7200.00
Porringer, Keyhole Handle, Elias Pelletreau, Long Island, c.1760, 7 5/8 In. 5100.00
Porringer, Keyhole Handle, Engraved, Jacob Hurd, Boston, c.1740, 7 3/8 In. 4200.00
Porringer, Keyhole Handle, Engraved, John Burt, Boston, c.1740, 8 In. .... 2700.00 to 3900.00
Porringer, Keyhole Handle, Engraved, Thomas Edwards, Boston, c.1740, 8 In. 5100.00
Porringer, Keyhole Handle, Engraved, William Burt, Boston, c.1750, 7 1/2 In. 3900.00
Porringer, Keyhole Handle, Engraved, William Homes Sr., Boston, c.1750, 8 In. 5400.00
Porringer, Keyhole Handle, Isaac Anthony, Newport, R.I., c.1730, 7 5/8 In. 6600.00
Porringer, Keyhole Handle, Jeremiah Elfreth Jr., Philadelphia, 1759, 7 1/2 In. 4800.00
Porringer, Keyhole Handle, Jonathan Otis, Newport, R.I., c.1760, 7 3/8 In. 3300.00
Porringer, Keyhole Handle, Wide Bowl, Samuel Burt, Boston, c.1745, 8 1/4 In. 3300.00
Punch Bowl, Pedestal Foot, Round, Molded Scroll Rims, c.1896, 11 In. 1595.00
Punch Bowl, Regimental, Leaf & Gadroon Rim, American Eagle, c.1825, 11 In. 8400.00
Punch Ladle, Double Swell Acanthus Mounts, R. Wallace & Son, c.1900, 11 In. 90.00
Punch Ladle, Medallion, Hotchkiss & Schreuder, c.1868, 14 1/2 In. 510.00
Punch Ladle, Triple Monogram, Bigelow, Kennard & Co., c.1889, 12 In. 60.00
Punch Strainer, 2 Handles, Samuel R. Richards Jr., Philadelphia, c.1800, 6 In. 2700.00
Punch Strainer, Punch Beaded Rim, Pierced, Handle, JD, c.1785, 5 3/4 In. 1200.00

Punch Strainer, Quatrefoil Pierced, 2 Handles, T. Hammersley, N.Y., c.1760, 10 In. 4500.00
Rose Bowl, Hammered, Undulating Molded Rim, 9 1/2 In. 520.00
Salad Set, Hammered, Leaf & Bead Design, David Carlson, 8 1/2 In. 425.00
Salt, Bombe, Circular, 3 Scroll & Hoof Feet, Jacob Hurd, c.1745, 2 1/2 In., Pair 4500.00
Salt & Pepper Set, Urn Shape, Reed & Barton, c.1900, 8 Piece 1495.00
Salt Spoon, Bead, T.W. Radcliffe, Columbia, S.C., c.1850, 3 3/4 In. 374.00
Salt Spoon, Coin, Engraved Initials TNS, Allen, c.1869, 3 3/4 In., Pair 175.00
Salver, Round, Molded Rim, Trumpet Foot, George Fielding, N.Y., c.1730, 5 1/2 In. 8400.00
Sauceboat, Molded Rim, Loop Handle, Oval Foot, Stebbins & Co., 1800s, 6 In. 425.00
Sauceboat, Oval, Double Scroll Handle, Thomas Hammersley, c.1760, 7 1/4 In. 3300.00
Server, Spade Form, Rounded End On Handle, Hammered, Porter Blanchard, 9 In. 235.00
Serving Spoon, Coin, Fancy Handle, Engraved Initials GAG, c.1848, 8 1/2 In. 635.00
Serving Spoon, Coin, Shell Shape Bowl, Fiddle Thread Handle, Galt, c.1879, 9 In. 489.00
Serving Spoon, Plain Tipt Pattern, Engraved, Calhoun, c.1845, 8 1/2 In. 345.00
Soup Ladle, Shell Bowl, Joseph & Nathaniel Richardson, Phil., c.1785, 15 In. 3600.00
Spoon, Lily Pattern, C-Scrolls, Acanthus, Unger Brothers, N.J., c.1900, 7 3/4 In. 105.00
Spoon, Pierced Stars, Trefoil Shape Bowl, Radcliffe & Guignard, c.1855, 7 3/4 In. 1380.00
Spoon, Trifid, Fluted Rat Tail Bowl, Johannis Nys, Philadelphia, c.1700, 7 3/4 In. 5100.00
Spoon, Trifid, Laceback, Samuel Vernon, Newport, R.I., c.1715, 7 1/2 In. 2700.00
Spoon Set, Coin, Pattern Back, Birds, Feathers, 1765-1830, 3 Piece 200.00
Spoon Set, Demitasse, Porcelain Handles, Woman, Man, Gold Trim, 12 Piece 345.00
Spoon Set, Fiddle Handles, Monogram, S. Hutchinson, 6 Piece 165.00
Spoon Set, Ice Cream, Medallion Pattern, Duhme & Co., c.1865, 6 In. 575.00
Spurs, Star Shape, Oak Leaf Pattern, Leather Fringe, 1940s-50s, Pair 55.00
Sugar, Baluster, Dome Lid, 2 Handles, John McMullin, Philadelphia, 9 1/2 In. 355.00
Sugar, Cover, Baluster, J. & N. Richardson, Philadelphia, c.1780, 6 1/8 In. 7800.00
Sugar, Cover, Floral Bands, Coin, Frederick Marquand, 1820-31, 9 In. .... *Illus* 1380.00
Sugar, Cover, Inverted Pear Shape, Pineapple, Leaf Finial, 7 1/2 x 4 3/4 In. 5290.00
Sugar, Cover, Square Finial, Domed Body, c.1840, 8 x 8 In. 430.00
Sugar, Domed Cover, Fluted Panels, Claw, Ball Feet, Handles, Coin, 9 x 8 1/2 x 6 1/4 In. ... 1100.00
Sugar, Melon Form, Handles, Flowers, Leaves, Handles, Coin, 9 1/2 x 9 x 6 In. 1380.00
Sugar, Ogee Body, Chased, Scrolls, Leaves, Footed, Domed Cover, Parisien & Son 3220.00
Sugar & Creamer, Chased, Punch Work, Mary C. Knight, 1905, 2 1/2 & 3 1/2 In. 2200.00
Sugar & Creamer, Hammered, Strap Handles, George Gebelein, 2 3/4 In. 425.00
Sugar & Creamer, Round, Hammered, Ring Feet, Handles, Marshall Field, 2 3/4 In. 385.00
Sugar & Creamer, Tray, Hammered, Loop Handle, Falick Novick, 3 1/2 In., 3 Piece 725.00
Sugar Nips, Shell Shape Grips, Jeremiah Elfreth Jr., Philadelphia, c.1760, 5 In. 9000.00
Sugar Tongs, Joseph Richardson Jr., Philadelphia, c.1795, 3 3/8 In. 2280.00
Tablespoon, Bright Cut Decoration, Daniel Van Voorhis & Schank, 12 In. 420.00
Tablespoon, Monogram, Stamped, Early 19th Century, 10 In. 1195.00
Tankard, Cover, Tapered Cylinder, Andrew Underhill, N.Y., c.1775, 7 1/2 In. 9000.00
Tankard, Jonathan Stickney, Jr., Mass, c.1790, 10 1/2 In. 4185.00
Tea & Coffee Set, Adam Design, Ball, Black & Co., c.1860, 7 Piece 4830.00
Tea & Coffee Set, Bulbous, Scrolling, Greek Key Band, M. Jacobs, c.1866, 4 Piece 8625.00
Tea & Coffee Set, Classical Urn Shape, Greek Key, Bailey & Co., c.1878 .... 2070.00
Tea & Coffee Set, Coin Silver, Bailey & Kitchen, Philadelphia, c.1846, 5 Piece 5520.00
Tea & Coffee Set, Engraved, Flowers, Octagonal, Bigelow, Kennard & Co., 6 Piece 1955.00
Tea & Coffee Set, Hampton Court, Reed & Barton, 1952, 5 Piece 1795.00
Tea & Coffee Set, Lobed Baluster, Dominick & Haff, 1902, 29-In. Tray, 6 Piece 7800.00
Tea & Coffee Set, Repousse, S. Kirk & Son Co., c.1924, 14 In., 6 Piece 9200.00
Tea & Coffee Set, Royal Danish, Gorham, 9-In. Coffeepot, 4 Piece 1015.00
Tea & Coffee Set, Royal Danish, International Silver Co., c.1950, 5 Piece 900.00
Tea & Coffee Set, Tray, 2 Handles, Gorham, c.1950, 8 Piece 6000.00
Tea Set, Acanthus, Intaglio Flowers, James W. Tufts, c.1880, 10 In., 4 Piece 316.00
Tea Set, Chased, Embossed, Hibiscus, Whiting, c.1903 .... 520.00
Tea Set, Flowers, Jacobi & Co., Baltimore, Late 19th Century 4405.00
Tea Set, Repousse, Gorham, 1891, 3 Piece 840.00
Tea Set, Ribbed Melon, Looped Handle, Chased Finial, Arthur J. Stone, 3 Piece 3000.00
Tea Set, Teapot, Coffee Pot, Creamer, Sugar, Cover, Waste Bowl, Towle 800.00
Teapot, Dome Lid, Oval, Beaded Borders, W.G. Forbes, N.Y., c.1790, 12 1/2 In. 2160.00
Teapot, Lid, Double-Handled Sugar, Cover, Open Creamer, Mid 1800s 1195.00
Teapot, Lid, Drum Shape, Thomas Shields, Philadelphia, c.1780, 9 1/2 In. 6000.00
Teapot, Lid, Drum Shape, William Hollingshead, Philadelphia, c.1775, 8 In. 4200.00

Silver-American, Tureen, Cover, Floral & Bird
Bands, Swallow Finial, Duhme & Co., 11 In.

If cleaning the inside of a silver coffeepot with silver polish does not remove all the stains, fill the pot with warm water and drop in a five-minute denture-cleaning tablet for every two cups of water. Let stand for at least 10 minutes, then rinse.

Teapot, Lid, Oval, Beaded, John Letelier, Philadelphia, c.1785, 10 3/8 In. 3900.00
Teapot, Lid, Urn Shape, Pedestal, John Myers, Philadelphia, c.1790, 11 1/4 In. 3600.00
Teapot, Repousse, Scroll Border, Loop Handle, A.G. Schultz, c.1920, 11 3/4 In. 1035.00
Teapot, Round, Hollow Handle, Ivory Insulators, Karl F. Leinonen, 9 1/4 In. 725.00
Teapot, Round, Tapered, Wood Insulators & Finial, Isadore Friedman, 9 1/4 In. 1650.00
Teapot, Squat Shape, Eagle Head Spout, S. R. Richards, Jr., c.1800, 9 1/4 In. 1645.00
Teapot, Straight-Sided, Oval, Beaded Border, Freeman Woods, N.Y., c.1790, 12 In. 7200.00
Teaspoon Set, Spiral Twist, Medallion Handle, Monogram, Coin, c.1870, 6 In., 9 Piece ... 104.00
Toast Rack, Stamped, J.B. Jones & Co., Boston, 19th Century, 7 x 7 In. 1910.00
Toddy Ladle, Oval Bowl, Twist Baleen Handle, Silver Tip, 1800s, 16 In. 230.00
Tray, Cordial Set, Randahl, 7 In., 7 Piece 175.00
Tray, Gadroon Rim, Stepped Center, Round, Gorham, c.1950, 14 In. 345.00
Tray, Hammered, Applied Strapwork Border, Round, John Bellis, 5 5/8 In. 375.00
Tray, Hammered, Circular, Monogram BMH, Falick Novick, 16 In. 1880.00
Tray, Handles, Gorham, Early 20th Century, 15 In., Pair 550.00
Tray, Rectangular, Round Corners, Raised Flange, Lebolt & Co., 18 x 12 3/4 In. 1500.00
Tray, Round, Turned Up Rim, Wide & Narrow Flutes, Julius Randahl, 14 3/4 In. 1400.00
Tray, Scalloped Rim, Etched Flowers, Initials, Old Newbury Crafters, 1900s, 15 In. 460.00
Tureen, Cover, Floral & Bird Bands, Swallow Finial, Duhme & Co., 11 In. .... *Illus* 6325.00
Tureen, Dome Cover, Lions, R.&w. Wilson, Philadelphia, 10 1/2 In., Pair 6000.00
Tureen, Soup, Shell, Flowers, Handles, Monogram, Gorham, 1894, 9 In. 980.00
Vase, Inverted Conical, Flower Swags, Black, Starr & Frost, c.1920, 19 3/4 x 5 In. 1265.00
Vase, Japanese Style, Spiral Flutes, Trumpet Shape, Gorham, R.I., 1879, 9 1/4 In. 6900.00
Vase, Paneled, Tapered, Urn Shape, Octagonal Base, V. Siedman, 12 1/2 In. 520.00
Vase, Trumpet Shape, Scalloped, Floral & Vines On Lower Stem, Domed, Alvin, 14 In. ... 1495.00
Vase, Trumpet Shape, Scalloped, Reeded Domed Foot, Alvin, 14 In. 1495.00
Waiter, Gadroon Border, Flower Swags, Thomas Shields, c.1770, 6 1/2 In. 3600.00
Waste Bowl, Pedestal Foot, Reeded Rims, John Vernon, N.Y., c.1790, 6 1/2 In. 1920.00
Wedding Beaker, Inscription, Reed & Barton, c.1958, 3 1/4 In. 240.00
SILVER-AUSTRIAN, Bowl, Oval, Raised Medallion Heads, Head-Form Handles, 16 In. 575.00
Salt, Oblong, Stepped Pedestal Base, c.1842, 4 In., Pair 220.00
Teapot, Globular, Compressed, Wooden Scroll Handle, Late 1800s, 4 In. 190.00
Tray, 2 Handles, Art Nouveau, WMF, 23 x 14 In. 1645.00
Tray, Repousse, Fruit, Figural, Dolphin Head Handles, 1800s, 11 In. 175.00
Vase, Baluster, 2 Swan Handles, Reeded Rims, Vienna, c.1820, 5 1/2 In. 265.00
Wine Decanter, Chased Cherub Design, 11 In. 345.00
SILVER-CANADIAN, Basket, Boat Shape, Pierced, Engraved, Birds, Birks & Sons, 1900s, 10 In. 330.00
Bowl, 2 Handles, Iretta, Mid 20th Century, 12 3/4 In. 140.00
Bowl, Footed, Trumpet Shape, Applied Berries, Leaf Handle, Poul Petersen, c.1953 ...... 259.00
Bowl, Gadroon Round Foot, c.1960, 9 1/2 In. 285.00
Claret Jug, Lion & Shield, Inverted Baluster Glass Body, Domed Lid, Birks, 13 In. 920.00
Coffee Set, Oval, Scroll Handles, C. Sullivan, c.1950, 10 1/2 In. 3105.00
Pepperettes, Urn Shape, Leaf, Beading, Round Base, Poul Petersen, c.1953, Pair 120.00
Platter, Oval, Engraved Scrolling Bands, Birks, Montreal, 1927, 14 In. 460.00
Reliquary Cross, Hearts, Inscriptions, A. Lafrance, Quebec, Late 1800s, 3 3/4 In. 435.00

Tea & Coffee Set, Lobed Melon Shape, Henry Birks & Sons, c.1943, 5 Piece 1600.00
Tray, Oval, 2 Handles, Shaped Rim, Flowering Leaf Band, c.1920, 26 In. 1000.00
Waiter, Round, Shaped Rims, Scrolling Leaves, c.1942, 12 & 14 In., Pair 500.00
Wine Ewer, Egg Shape, Slender, Circular Foot, H. Birks & Sons, 1899, 13 3/4 In. 470.00
SILVER-CHINESE, Cream Jug, Baluster, Punched Bead Rim, Scroll Handle, Late 1800s, 4 In. . 218.00
  Dish, Sweetmeat, 6-Footed, Mother-Of-Pearl, Double Shell, Ear Handle, 14 1/4 x 3 1/2 In. 588.00
  Punch Bowl, Chased, Embossed Band, Equestrian Scene, 5 1/4 x 13 In. 1150.00
  Serving Spoon, Hammered Bowl, Monogram, Late 19th Century, 10 In. 70.00
  Sugar Basket, Cover, Boat Shape, Swing Handle, Cumshing, Canton, c.1800, 7 1/2 In. ... 2700.00
  Umbrella Handle, L Shape, Tapered Stem, Chasing, Embossing, 20th Century, 7 In. 175.00
SILVER-CONTINENTAL, Box, Rectangular, Arched Lid, Greek Gods, c.1900, 7 1/2 x 6 x 11 In. 2530.00
  Casket, Jewel Encrusted, Biblical Scenes, Repousse, 5 1/2 In. 1135.00
  Charger, 5 Cabochon Agates, 21 1/2 In. 1315.00
  Coffee Set, Louis XV Style, Spiral Fluted Body, 1900s, 7-In. Pot, 3 Piece 380.00
  Coffee Set, Pot, Sugar, Creamer, 1900s, 9-In. Pot 400.00
  Coffeepot, Pear, Bud Finial, FB Maker's Mark, Late 1700s, 14 3/4 In. 4500.00
  Container, Figural, Pheasant, Standing, Hinged Wings, Head Is Cover, 6 x 9 In. 400.00
  Decanter, Silver Spout & Handle, Cut Glass Baluster Shape Body, 13 In. 405.00
  Figure, Rooster, Hen, Enamel, Rose Quartz Base, c.1900, 5 1/2 In., Pair 2260.00
  Pill Box, Blue & Yellow Enameled Lid, Gold Wash Interior, Marked, 1 3/4 In. 46.00
  Tankard, Ivory Body, Allegorical Scene, Hafner Thumbpiece, 1800s, 12 1/2 In. 3770.00
  Tray, Oval, 15 3/4 In. 330.00
SILVER-DANISH, Bowl, Centerpiece, Incurving Sides, Loop Handles, George Jensen, 13 3/4 In. 4400.00
  Bowl, Centerpiece, Leaf & Berry Stem, Stepped Foot, Georg Jensen, Post 1945, 11 In. 7200.00
  Box, Globular, Shaped, Chased Swags, Hinged Cover, A. Michelsen, c.1919, 3 1/2 In. 269.00
  Box, Oval, Dome Lid, Hinged, Chased Rose Design, Georg Jensen, 2 x 5 In. 925.00
  Castor, Oval, Bell Shape Dome Lid, Grape Clusters, Georg Jensen, 6 1/2 In. 1435.00
  Cheese Scoop, Cactus Pattern, Elongated Bowl, Georg Jensen, 7 In. 300.00
  Cigarette Box, Rectangular, Engraved House, Crest, Wood Lined, Michelsen 239.00
  Coffee Set, Demitasse, Hammered Surface, 2-Handled Tray, Jensen, 1915 .... 4600.00
  Coffee Set, Pear Shape, Ivory Handle, Georg Jensen, Post 1945, 6 1/4-In. Pot, 3 Piece 6600.00
  Cruet Set, Armorial Crest, Shell Feet, 5 Cobalt Blue Glass Bottles, 8 3/4 In. 956.00
  Dish, Beaded Rim, Footed, Evald Nielsen, c.1920, 4 3/8 In. 120.00
  Fish Server, Georg Jensen, Copenhagen, c.1944, Pair 865.00
  Fork & Spoon, Serving, Floral Engraved, Openwork, Georg Jensen, 1945 .... 1035.00
  Pepper Shaker, Paneled, Tapered, Acorn Finial, G. Jensen, 1 3/4 In., 6 Piece 635.00
  Presentation Set, Cup, Napkin Ring, Spoon, Knife, Fork, Box, A. Michelsen, 5 Piece 300.00
  Salad Servers, Acorn, Georg Jensen, 1945 .... 325.00
  Salt Set, Porringer Form, Cobalt Enamel, Spoons, Acanthus, G. Jensen, No. 180, 12 Piece . 800.00
  Salt Spoon Set, Acanthus Pattern, Georg Jensen, 3 1/4 In., 6 Piece 173.00
  Sauceboat, Brandy, Beaded Borders, Ebony Handles, Georg Jensen, c.1944, Pair 949.00
  Serving Spoon, Georg Jensen 220.00
  Sugar, Oval, Molded, Flowers, Buds, Leaves, Domed Base, Georg Jensen, c.1945 .... 605.00
  Sugar Castor, Chased, Embossed Flowers, Ribbons, Baluster, Footed, Copenhagen, 9 In. ... 230.00
  Tazza, Grape Pattern, Presentation, Georg Jensen, 12 1/4 In. 8120.00
  Tazza, Grapevine, Spiral Twist Stem, Georg Jensen, c.1925, 10 1/2 In. 7200.00
  Tea Set, Ivory Handles, Georg Jensen, c.1908, 6-In. Teapot, 3 Piece 3421.00
  Vase, Cylindrical, Tapered, Chased Rose Blossoms, A. Michelsen, 1908, 10 In. 1195.00
SILVER-DUTCH, Breadbasket, Boat Shape, Pierced, Leaves, Rosettes, Ring Handles, 13 In. .. 1315.00
  Creamer, Cow Shape, Red Glass Eyes, Hinged Cover, Fly Finial, c.1900, 5 1/2 In. 945.00
  Decanter, Square, Canted, Flowers, Pierced Band, Horse Finial, 8 In., Pair 575.00
  Peppermint Box, Hinged Lid, Figures, Rural Setting, Schoonhoven, 1889, 1 1/4 In. 150.00
  Tea Set, Tete-A-Tete, Husk Bands, Fruitwood Handles, 1909-23, 5 In. 355.00
  Teapot, Flower Finial, Bulbous Body, Early 20th Century, 8 In. 405.00
  Tureen, Soup, Dome Cover, Stand, Circular, Scroll Handles, VK, 1867, 11 1/4 In. 3580.00

SILVER-ENGLISH. English sterling silver is marked with a series of
four or five small hallmarks. The standing lion mark is the most commonly seen sterling quality mark. The other marks indicate the city of
origin, the maker, and the year of manufacture. These dates can be ver-
ified in many good books on silver.

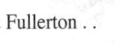

SILVER-ENGLISH, Asparagus Server, Cartouches, Flowers, Edwardian, Jackson & Fullerton .. 460.00
  Basket, Boat Shape, Beaded Rim, Solomon Hougham, George III, 5 1/2 In. 480.00

Basket, Oval, 2 Handles, Molded Scroll Rim, Pierced Scrollwork, c.1910, 10 In. 340.00
Basket, Oval, Gilt Bowl, Bail Handle, Reeded Borders, George III, 5 3/4 x 3 1/2 In. 400.00
Basket, Reticulated, Pierced, Swing Handle, England, 4 1/2 x 5 3/4 x 4 3/4 In. 865.00
Basket, Sugar, Scrolls, Leaves, Boat Shape, Reeded Swing Handle, Chawner, 3 In. 690.00
Basting Spoon, Old English Pattern, George III, c.1778 .... 168.00
Berry Spoon, Old English Pattern, Scalloped Bowl, Hester Bateman, Pair 370.00
Berry Spoon, Repousse, Chased Bowls, Gilt, George III, c.1805, 9 In., Pair 58.00
Biscuit Box, Spherical, Christopher Dresser, J. Dixon & Sons, Sheffield, 1880s, 6 3/4 In. ... 7800.00
Bodkin, Hatchwork Design, Early 16th To 17th Century 350.00
Bowl, Cartouches, Pierced Flowers, Shaped Foot, Ryrie, 1922, 9 In. 690.00
Bowl, Cover, Footed, Enamel Cover Design, Liberty & Co., 2 1/2 x 3 1/2 In. 1645.00
Bowl, Fruit, Circular, Repousse, Pedestal Foot, Edwardian, 1909, 9 1/4 In. 520.00
Bowl, Gadroon, Spiral Fluted Panels, Dome Foot, Dixon & Sons, 1898, 8 In. 380.00
Bowl, Hammered Finish, Round Foot, Scroll Feet, MH & Co., 1926, 10 1/4 In. 570.00
Bowl, Hammered, Green Stones, Omar Ramsden & Alwin Carr, 1912, 6 3/8 In. 4800.00
Bowl, Hemispherical Shape, Thread & Bead, George III, c.1760, 3 x 5 1/2 In. 1265.00
Bowl, Monteith, Cherubs, Lion's Masks, Shaped Rim, Footed, A. Fogelberg, 13 In. 4600.00
Bowl, Monteith, Molded Bands, Rim, Cast Scroll, Waisted, Edwardian, 8 1/2 x 12 In. 1725.00
Bowl, Oval, Pierced Lattice, Flower Border, 2 Handles, c.1934, 8 1/2 In. 420.00
Box, Candle, Cylindrical Drum Body, Reeded Border, E. Morley, George III, 1808, 3 In. ... 1600.00
Box, Enameled Lid, Castle, Landscape, Hinged Lid, Ramsden & Carr, 2 x 4 1/4 x 2 1/4 In. ... 2470.00
Caddy Spoon, I.A. Marks, London, George III, 1815, 3 3/4 In. 259.00
Caddy Spoon, Shell Form Bowl, S.A., London, George III, 1798, 3 3/4 In. 230.00
Cake Basket, Octagonal, Swing Handle, 4 Claw Feet, T.C., J.W.C., 1898, 10 1/2 In. 450.00
Cake Basket, Oval, Swing Handle, Barker Bros., Edwardian, 1904, 13 1/2 In. 570.00
Cake Basket, Repousse, Putti Masks, Flowers, Gadroon Border, Oval, Martin Hall, 13 In. . 1380.00
Cake Basket, Swivel Handle, William Plummer, George III, 13 1/2 In. 1955.00
Candelabrum is listed in its own category.
Candlesticks are listed in their own category.
Castor, Fluted Baluster Shape, Knop Finial, c.1910, 9 In. 378.00
Castor, Octagonal, Molded Borders, Pierced Leaf Cover, George I, 1715, 6 3/4 In. 1440.00
Centerpiece, 3 Tiers, Filigree, Polish Style, Insects, Flowers, Aaron Katz, 1897, 24 In. 3600.00
Chalice, Footed, Ribbed Pedestal, Edward VII, 4 In. 431.00
Cigar Box, Bracket Feet, Wood Lined, Goldsmiths & Silversmiths, c.1946, 7 In. 450.00
Cigar Box, Hammered, Wood Lined, William Comyns & Sons Ltd., 7 3/4 In. 450.00
Cigar Box, Rectangular, Engine Turned Surface, Asprey & Co., 1952, 5 3/8 In. 390.00
Cigarette Box, Rectangular, Wood Lined, Goldsmiths & Silversmiths, 7 In. 390.00
Cigarette Case, LHK Monogram, Engine Turned, c.1944, 4 1/2 In. 69.00
Claret Jug, Embossed Herons, Inscribed Banner, JW & JW, 1876, 12 In. 1150.00
Coaster Set, Wine, Sheffield, Turned Fruitwood Base, 19th Century, 6 In., Pair 375.00
Coffee Set, Islamic Style, Victorian, Elkington & Co., Birmingham, 1872, 3 Piece 2400.00
Coffee Set, Victorian, Coffeepot, Open Sugar, Cream Jug, 3 Piece 460.00
Coffee Urn, High Loop Handles, Urn Finial, George III, c.1798, 14 1/2 In. 1679.00
Coffeepot, Baluster, Dome Lid, Repousse, Flowers, C. Fox II, George III, 1824, 10 In. 1500.00
Coffeepot, Baluster, Reeded, Beaded, Repousse, F.B. McCrea, Victorian, 1887, 11 In. 520.00
Coffeepot, Dome Lid, Acorn Finial, Whipham & Wright, 1764, 10 1/2 In. 2350.00
Coffeepot, Dome Lid, Pear Shape, Egg Shape Finial, George III, 1762, 10 1/2 In. 700.00
Coffeepot, Fluted, Victorian, Frederick Bradford McCrea, 1889, 10 1/4 In. 380.00
Coffeepot, Lobed Body, Repousse, Flowers, R. Hennell III, William IV, 1836, 8 In. 380.00
Coffeepot, Lobed Body, Scroll Handle, Circular Foot, John Figg, 1836, 9 In. 565.00
Coffeepot, London, James Kidney Mark, George III, Late 18th Century, 10 In. 780.00
Coffeepot, Oblong, Large Ribs, Leaf-Capped Scroll Handle, D. Langlands, 1804, 9 In. ... 980.00
Coffeepot, Paneled Baluster, Repousse, DS, Sheffield, William IV, 1836, 9 1/2 In. 660.00
Coffeepot, Pear Shape, Dome Lid, Wooden Handle, W. Comyns, 1911, 9 1/2 In. 520.00
Coffeepot, Ribbed Body, Wood Handle, London Marks, 1896, 10 In. 375.00
Coffeepot, Tapered Body, Scroll Spout, Flowers, Leaves, George III, c.1750, 10 In. 1320.00
Coffeepot, Tapered Cylinder, Swan Neck, George I, c.1720, 8 7/8 In. 1920.00
Coffeepot, Urn Shape, Wooden Handle, Reeded Border, T. Watson, 1791, 13 1/2 In. 1885.00
Coffeepot, Walter & John Barnard, Victorian, c.1894, 9 1/2 In. 290.00
Condiment Set, Stepped Covers, Goldsmiths & Silversmiths Co., London, c.1936 .... 140.00
Cream Jug, Oval, Reeded Band, Rim, George III, c.1806, 3 1/2 In. 235.00
Cream Pail, Cylindrical, Flared, Reeded Bands, Swing Handle, T. Shepherd, 4 In. 1035.00
Creamer, Helmet Shape, Beaded Edge, Handle, Monogram, c.1800, 6 In. 140.00

Creamer, Helmet Shape, Reeded Handle, Hester Bateman, George III, 1790, 6 3/8 In. 1293.00
Creamer, Reeded Rim, Angular Handle, Laurel Wreaths, J. Emes, George III, 1800, 4 In. ... 264.00
Cruet Set, Canted Corners, Scroll Feet, 2 Glass Decanters, R. Hennell, George III, 9 In. .. 750.00
Crumber, Victorian, 3/4 Gallery, Engraved, Flowers, c.1880, 2 3/4 x 13 1/2 In. 115.00
Cup, 2 Long Looped Handles, Spread Foot, Elkington & Co., Edward VII, 9 In. 450.00
Cup, Birds, Fruit, Leaves, 2 Handles, Martin, Hall & Co., Victorian, 1889, 5 3/4 In. 470.00
Cup, Cover, Inverted Bell Shape, Arms, Busts, C. Hatfield, George II, 1732, 11 1/2 In. 9600.00
Cup, Reeded Border, Ovoid, 2 Scroll Handles, Footed, P. & A. Bateman, 6 1/4 In. 800.00
Cup, Urn Form, 2 Scroll Handles, Crichton Brothers, Edward VII, 8 1/4 In. 345.00
Decanter, Pierced Scrolls, Floral Stopper, Hourglass Shape, A. Clark, 10 In., Pair 520.00
Dish, Entree, Cover, Divider, London, Edward VII, c.1902, 14 1/2 In. 2689.00
Dish, Meat, William Burwash, Richard Sibley, London, George III, 1807, 16 3/4 In. 1040.00
Dish, Sweetmeat, Navette Shape, Beaded Rim, Oval Foot, Engraved, George III, 7 1/8 In. .. 235.00
Dish, Vegetable, Cover, Gadroon Rims, Helmet Finial, George III, 13 In., Pair 3450.00
Dish Cross, Beaded Rim, Monogram, Langlands & Roberts, George III, 13 3/8 In. 1410.00
Dish Cross, Burner Cover Engraved, London, George III, Late 1700s, 12 In. 960.00
Dish Ring, S-Scroll Supports, Shell Feet, Cooke & Gurney, George II, 1752, 8 1/4 In. 470.00
Egg, Surprise, Hippopotamus, Gilt, Stuart Devlin, London, c.1973, 2 3/4 In. 475.00
Egg Frame, Victorian, Round Base, 4 Egg Cups, Reeded Borders, c.1883, 7 In. 590.00
Ewer, Wine, Flask Shape, Goats On Lip, Scrolled Leaf Handle, George Storer, 9 In. 3680.00
Fish Server, Fiddle, George Adams, London, Victorian, 1856, Pair 377.00
Fish Server, Fiddle, John Emes, London, George III, 1806 .... 566.00
Fish Server, Ivory Handle, Navette Shape, Eley & Fearn, George III, 1799, 12 1/2 In. 588.00
Fish Set, Scrolls, Leaves, Mother-Of-Pearl Handle, Mappin & Webb, 13 In., 2 Piece 575.00
Fish Set, Sheffield, Artin Hall & Co., Pierced Leaves, Case, Victorian, 1862, 12 In. 400.00
Fish Slice, Old English Pattern, Pierced, Engraved, Fish, Stars, Victorian, c.1843 .... 235.00
Fish Slice, Stylized Shell Stem, Crest, William Kingdon, George IV, 1823, 12 In. 320.00
Fish Slice, Trowel Shape, Flower Basket, Pierced, Wooden Handle, c.1750, 13 In. 566.00
Fork, Old English, George Wintle, George III, 1807, 12 Piece 575.00
Goblet, Campana Shape Bowl, Flowers, C.T. & G. Fox, Victorian, 1848, 5 3/4 In. 280.00
Goblet, Gilt Lined Oval Bowl, Round Base, George III, c.1818, 6 1/2 In. 170.00
Grape Shears, King's Husk, William Chawner, London, George IV, 1825 .... 552.00
Hot Water Pot, Baluster, Scroll Handle, Whipham & Wright, George III, 1765, 11 In. 470.00
Hot Water Pot, Cylinder Shape, Fluted, Dome Lid, George III, c.1809, 9 In. 715.00
Hot Water Pot, Urn Shape, Wooden Handle, R. Morton, George III, 1777, 11 1/4 In. 210.00
Inkstand, 3 Cobalt Blue Glass Lined Holders, London Hallmark, 10 x 6 1/2 In. 750.00
Inkstand, Gadroon Rim, 2 Glass Wells, James Dixon & Sons, c.1928, 6 In. 480.00
Jug, Hot Water, Baluster Form, Gadroon Design, London, Georgian, 1764, 10 In. 1695.00
Jug, Hot Water, C-Scrolls, Flowers, Barrel Shape, Wood Handle, J. Eames, 1805, 8 In. 520.00
Jug, Hot Water, Fluted Lower Body, Horace Woodward & Co., 1894, 8 1/2 In. 285.00
Jug, Maker's Mark, Fuller White, Repousse, Chased Design, George II, 1754, 4 In. 400.00
Jug, Water, Egg Shape, Repousse, Shells, Cylinder, London, 1746, 8 3/4 In. 470.00
Jug, Water, Vase Form, Husk Frame, Henry Greenway, George III, 1778, 12 3/4 In. 1680.00
Kettle, Stand, Flower & Scroll Cartouches, Inverted Baluster, Crespel & Parker, 15 In. ... 1495.00
Kettle, Stand, Oval, Engraved Leaf Band, Ebonized Handle, Finial, Mapin & Webb, 14 In. 920.00
Knife & Fork, King Pattern, Gold Washed, Engraved Blade, P. Storr, George III, 8 1/2 In. .. 410.00
Lemon Strainer, Diamond Pierced, William Solomon, George II, c.1750, 9 1/2 In. 1080.00
Magnifying Glass, Pierced Bird, Insect, Cherub, London, 1819, 8 3/4 In. 230.00
Marrow Scoop, Crested, George I, c.1725 .... 300.00
Marrow Scoop, Double, Initials, Phoenix Bird, 9 In. 175.00
Mazarine, Oval, Pierced, Lattice Work, H. Chawner, George III, 1791, 15 3/4 In. 565.00
Mug, Baluster, Leaf Headed Scroll Handle, Foot, W. Neale & Sons, 1928, 5 In. 245.00
Mug, Baluster, Scroll Handle, Circular Foot, J. Gloster, 1933, 5 1/4 In. 300.00
Mug, Baluster, Scroll Handle, Initials, Edward Vincent, George II, 1735, 4 3/4 In. 700.00
Mug, Christening, Tapered Cylinder, 2 Reeded Bands, William Evans, 1871, 3 1/4 In. 265.00
Mug, Queen Anne, Leopard Marks, Late 17th Century, 5 In. 1150.00
Mug, Tapered, Cylindrical, Ribbed Bands, George III, 1809, 4 1/4 x 5 1/4 x 3 1/4 In. 575.00
Mug, Tapering Shape, Reeded Bands, Borders, George III, c.1814, 3 1/2 In. 320.00
Mustard Ladle, Jonathan Bateman, Tipt Back Handle, George III, 1790, 4 1/4 In. 980.00
Mustard Pot, Cylindrical, Gadroon Border, Glass Liner, London, 1810, 2 1/2 In. 340.00
Mustard Pot, Dome Lid, Urn Finial, Angular Handle, George III, 1811, 3 1/2 In. 150.00
Mustard Pot, Lid, Joseph & Albert Savory, London, 1836, 3 1/2 In. 345.00
Mustard Pot, Oval, Dome Lid, P. & A. Bateman, George III, 1796, 3 In. 360.00

Mustard Pot, Reeded Rim, Strap Handle, George V, 3 x 1 x 4 In., Pair 290.00
Mustard Pot, Spoon, Chased Figural Design, Glass Liner, Hallmarks, 1880 .... 115.00
Napkin Rings are listed in their own category.
Pepper Shaker, Baluster, Dome Pierced Top, Spiral Flame, 5 1/2 In. 145.00
Pepperette, Bird, Standing, Thomas Johnson, London, 1882, 4 In., Pair 570.00
Pitcher, Hester Bateman, Neoclassical Style, George III, 5 1/2 x 4 1/4 x 2 In. 800.00
Pitcher, Sheffield, Chased, Quatrefoil Medallions, c.1857, 7 1/4 In. 520.00
Pitcher, Water, Baluster Body, Scroll Handle, Footed, Wakely & Wheeler, 8 1/4 In. 1265.00
Placecard Holder, Enamel, Game Birds, Case, England, 1906, 1 1/2 x 2 In., 6 Piece 1495.00
Playing Card Box, Rectangular, Wood Interior, W.D. Barlow, 1906, 3 3/4 x 6 In. 265.00
Playing Card Case, Rectangular, Edward VII, Alexandra, 1901, 4 1/2 In. 300.00
Porringer, Beaded S-Scroll Handles, John Downes, Queen Anne, 1708, 4 1/4 In. 710.00
Punch Ladle, Bright Cut Feather Edge, Shell Shaped Bowl, London, 1777, 12 1/2 In. 325.00
Punch Ladle, Shell Form Bowl, London, George III, 1775, 11 In. 823.00
Salt, Beaded, Pierced Rim, Scrolls, Blue Glass Liner, Godbehere & Wigan, 3 In., Pair 345.00
Salt, Circular, Flowers, Leaves, David Mowden, George II, 1759, 2 3/4 In., Pair 285.00
Salt, Circular, Fluted Rims, Hoof Feet, Robert Hennell, George III, 1773, 2 3/4 In., Pair ... 245.00
Salt, Gadroon Border, Repousse, Robert Hennell II, George III, 1772, 2 3/4 In., Pair 265.00
Salt, Gadroon Rim, Glass Liner, 3 Hoof Feet, W. Cripps, George II, 1747, 3 In., Pair 1325.00
Salt, Shell Shape, Benoni Stephens, London, William IV, 1835, 3 1/2 In., 4 Piece 2830.00
Salt & Pepper, Cylindrical, Footed, Leaf Design, Chester Mark, 1900 .... 25.00
Salt Spoon, Peter, Anne & William Bateman, George III, Pair 80.00
Saltcellar Set, Engraved Crest, Monogram, George III, Early 1800s, 2 1/2 In. 300.00
Salver, Chased, Embossed, Flower Heads, Leaf Swags, J. Carter, 1768, 12 1/8 In. 2350.00
Salver, Circular, Molded Bead & Reeded Rim, John Huston, George III, 1788, 18 In. 2830.00
Salver, Circular, Molded Rim, Scroll Feet, Charles Stuart Harris, 1901, 16 In. 1885.00
Salver, Engraved Armorial, Footed, John Richardson, George II, 13 1/2 In. 1725.00
Salver, Engraved Flowers, Shell Rim, 4 Scroll Feet, J. Scofield, George III, 22 In. 6670.00
Salver, Engraved Stag Crest, Scrolling Leaves, George IV, c.1823, 8 3/4 In. 920.00
Salver, Flowers, Leaves, Scroll & Shell Rim, Emes, Barnard, George IV, 1825, 20 In. 1885.00
Salver, Galleried, Engraved Arms, Carter Smith & Sharp, George III, 1778, 20 In. 6000.00
Salver, Molded Edge, Gadroon Rim, Ebenezer Coker, 1772, 6 1/2 In. 765.00
Salver, Molded Gadroon Borders, Queen Anne, c.1702, 9 1/2 In. 2690.00
Salver, Molded Gadroon, Leaf & Shell Rim, 3 Feet, Atkin Bros., 1911, 15 In. 850.00
Salver, Molded Rim, Hoof Feet, J. Sanders, George II, 1740, 2 1/2 In., Pair 1265.00
Salver, Oval, 3 Scroll Feet, Engraved, Coat Of Arms, Thomas Parr, George II, 6 In. 999.00
Salver, Oval, Gadroon Border, Paul Storr, George III, Hallmarks, 1796, 11 In. 3335.00
Salver, Oval, Reeded Borders, Timothy Renou, George III, 1797, 12 1/4 In., Pair 7200.00
Salver, Round, Footed, Engraved Crest, Cartouche, George III, 13 In. 6575.00
Salver, Round, Gadroon Rim, Scroll Feet, George III, c.1766, 11 In. 1260.00
Salver, Shell & Scroll Border, 3 Hoof Feet, Joseph Sander, George II, 1742, 11 In. 1225.00
Salver, Shell & Scroll Border, 3 Scroll Feet, Barker Bros., 1898, 10 3/4 In. 320.00
Sauceboat, 3 Hoof Feet, Ogee Rim, John Pollock, London, George II, 1742, 7 3/4 In. 705.00
Sauceboat, Boat Shape, Lobed Rim, Serpentine Handle, John Seymoure, c.1810, 7 In. 2820.00
Sauceboat, Bulbous Oval, Shaped Rim, Domed Foot, George V, 4 x 71/2 In., Pair 1150.00
Sauceboat, Engraved, Flying Loop Handle, 3 Pad Feet, W. Shaw, George II, 6 1/4 In. 590.00
Sauceboat, Waved Rim, Eagle Head Handle, Oval, John Pollock, 1748, 6 5/8 In., Pair 5400.00
Serving Spoon, Hester Bateman, George III, 5 Piece 575.00
Serving Spoon, Old English, T. Wallis II, George III, 1808, 11 1/2 In. 132.00
Serving Spoon, Old English, William Robertson, Scotland, George III, 1790 .... 189.00
Serving Spoon, William Eley, W. Fearn & W. Chawner, Hallmark, 1809, 12 In. 145.00
Skewer, Meat, Ring Handle, George III, c.1811, 13 In. 220.00
Skewer, Meat, William Bateman II, William IV, 1832 .... 210.00
Skewer, Ring Handle, Stephen Adams II, London, George III, 1808, 11 1/4 In. 1508.00
Skewer, Ring Handle, Thomas Chawner, London, George III, 1783, 11 3/4 In. 210.00
Soup Ladle, Fiddle Shape Handle, Paul Storr, 1812, 12 3/4 In. 1035.00
Soup Ladle, Fiddle, R. Crossley & G. Smith, London, George III, 1809 .... 264.00
Soup Ladle, London, John Scofield, 1779 .... 200.00
Soup Ladle, Old English, Richard Crossley, George III, 1782 .... 322.00
Spirit Flask, Oblong, E.J. Greenberg, Birmingham, 1895, 6 3/4 In. 285.00
Spoon, Figural Tip, Oval Bowl Coin Insert, Charles II, c.1680, 8 In. 375.00
Spoon, Queen Anne, Hanoverian Pattern, Rattail Bowl, c.1709 .... 925.00
Spoon, Trifid, Beaded Rattail, Initials, William Scarlett, London, William III, 1700 ...... 570.00

Spoon, Trifid, Beaded Rattail, Thomas Foote, Queen Anne, 1707 . . . .   615.00
Spoon, Trifid, Scroll, Rattail, John King, London, Charles II, 1683 . . . .   800.00
Strawberry Dish, Oval, Repousse, Garlands, Martin Hall & Co., 1881, 10 1/4 In. 380.00
Stuffing Spoon, Molded Shell, R. Gosling, London, George II, 1750, 13 3/4 In. 650.00
Sugar, Bright Cut Engraved, Ribbon Tied Swags, Beaded Handles, George III, 8 1/4 In. 382.00
Sugar, Tongs, Kettle Shape, 3 Trifid Feet, Birmingham, c.1918, 2 x 3 3/4 In. 40.00
Sugar Nips, London, S. Adams, 1770 . . . .   210.00
Sugar Tongs, Bright Cut, Initials, Hester Bateman, George III, c.1785, Pair 230.00
Sugar Tongs, Bright Cut, Stephen Adams, London, Georgian, 5 1/4 In., Pair 175.00
Tablespoon, Fiddle, Channel Islands, Quesnell & De Gruchy, c.1825, Pair 189.00
Tablespoon, Old English, Hester Bateman, George III, Pair 275.00
Tankard, Baluster Shape, Domed Lid, Scrollwork, George II, c.1757, 7 1/2 In. 925.00
Tankard, Dome Lid, Gadroon, Leaf Thumbpiece, Acanthus Handle, 8 1/4 In. 1765.00
Tankard, Dome Lid, Lighthouse Form, London, George III, 1767, 8 1/4 In. 1645.00
Tankard, Dome Lid, Scroll Handle, Initials, George II, 1752, 7 In. 4500.00
Tankard, Dome Lid, Scroll Handle, T. Farren, George II, 1835, 7 3/4 In. 2075.00
Tankard, Tapered Cylindrical, Godbehere & Wigan, George III, 1789, 7 1/2 In. 3000.00
Tantalus, Victorian, Trefoil Shape, Central Handle, c.1849, 14 In. 715.00
Tea & Coffee Set, Chased, Embossed, Flowers, C-Scroll Handles, Roberts & Slater, 10 In. .   1765.00
Tea & Coffee Set, Engraved Garlands, Gadroon Border, Ivory Handle, C.T. Fox, 5 Piece . .   3680.00
Tea & Coffee Set, London, Victorian, 1866-67, 4 Piece 980.00
Tea & Coffee Set, Pierced Leaf Borders, Paw Feet, c.1913 . . . .   1680.00
Tea & Coffee Set, Ribbed Band, Ball Feet, Edward Barnard & Son, 1890, 3 Piece 1495.00
Tea & Coffee Set, Scrolling Bands, Globular, Footed, Mackay & Chisolm, 4 Piece 1725.00
Tea Caddy, Bombe Body, Hinged Lid, Elkington & Co., William IV, 5 In. 1035.00
Tea Caddy, Chased, Embossed, Inverted Pear Shape, Case, John Swift, George II 6169.00
Tea Caddy, Knife Box Shape, William Comyns & Sons Ltd., Edward VII, 8 In. 900.00
Tea Set, Bachelor's, Straight Sides, Oval, Leaves, R.T. Bowman, 1869, 4 In., 3 Piece 470.00
Tea Set, Bachelor's, Teapot, Lid, Open Creamer, Sugar, Tea Ball, George VI 300.00
Tea Set, Circular, Repousse, Flowers, W. Bateman I, William IV, 1832, 3 Piece 945.00
Tea Set, Engraved Panels, Flowers, Scrolls, Melon Fluted, W. Hunter, 1849, 3 Piece 1150.00
Tea Set, Melon Fluted, Chased, Engraved Flowers, Scrolls, Barker Bros., 6 Piece 3450.00
Tea Urn, Fluted Oval Body, Engraved, Scrolling, George III, 15 In.   805.00
Tea Urn, Vase Shape, Reeded Loop Handles, Urn Finial, Late 1800s, 22 1/2 In. 590.00
Teapot, Compressed Globular Shape, C. & J. Fry II, George IV, 1822, 4 1/2 In. 358.00
Teapot, Cover, Urn Shape, Pineapple Finial, Ivory Handle, J. Robins, 1786, 6 1/2 In. 3000.00
Teapot, Drum Shape, Wooden Handle, Fruit Finial, George III, c.1768, 4 In. 670.00
Teapot, Flat Lid, Fruitwood Finial, Ear Handle, Flower Swags, George III, 1790, 6 In. 410.00
Teapot, Lid, Oval Finial, Squat Oval, Ear Handle, Ball Feet, George IV, 1821, 11 1/4 In. . .   265.00
Teapot, Oval, Beaded Rim, Wood Finial & Handle, Hester Bateman, George III, 10 In. 1790.00
Teapot, Rectangular, Dome Lid, Wood Handle, P. & W. Bateman, George III, 1808, 6 In. . .   1600.00
Teapot, Repousse Florals, 19th Century, 8 In. 290.00
Teapot, Stand, Oval, Faceted, Wooden Handle, Pineapple Finial, Davenport, 6 1/2 In. 865.00
Teapot, Victorian, Bullet Shape, Scroll Handle, John Figg, 1852, 4 In. 380.00
Teapot, Victorian, Flower Garlands Pendant, Medallions, c.1875, 9 1/2 In. 430.00
Teaspoon, Spade Shape Leaves, Archibald Knox, Liberty & Co., 4 1/2 In. 588.00
Toast Rack, Arched Form, 5 Slice, Sheffield Hallmark, 1911-12, 4 x 5 In. 200.00
Toddy Ladle, Volute Whalebone Handle, George III, c.1801 . . . .   150.00
Tray, Engraved Leaves, Shells, Rounded Corners, Handles, Mappin & Webb, 1936, 27 In. .   2530.00
Tray, Flowers, Handles, Mappin & Webb, Sheffield, c.1925, 32 x 20 In. 4830.00
Tray, Gallery Rim, Pierced Handles, Crest & Motto, 24 In. 690.00
Tray, Handles, Gadroon, Acanthus Rim, Rectangular, Birmingham, 1925, 27 1/2 In. 2760.00
Tray, Oval, 2 Handles, Chased, Broad Flowering Leaf Band, c.1947, 27 1/2 In. 1595.00
Tray, Oval, Gadroon Rim, Molded Shell, Leaf Handles, c.1911, 26 1/2 In. 1259.00
Tray, Rectangular, Cusped Corners, Openwork Handles, 26 x 15 3/4 In. 2760.00
Tray, Rectangular, Flowers, Mappin & Webb, 1925, 32 x 2 In. 4830.00
Trinket Box, Hinged Cover, Chased & Hammered Scrolling Flowers, 1897, 3 x 7 In. 690.00
Trophy, Horse Race, Laurel Garland Rim, Gilt Inside, Elkington & Co., 1909, 14 In. 9000.00
Tumbler, EB, London, 1936, 2 3/4 In. 130.00
Tureen, Bulbous Oval, Acanthus Scroll, Handles, William IV, 11 x 9 1/2 x 16 In. 2990.00
Tureen, Cover, Eagle Finial, Oval, John Scofield, George III, 1795, 9 1/4 In., Pair 4800.00
Tureen, Cover, Flower, Loop Handles, Oval, Benjamin Laver, George III, 1782, 19 In. 9000.00
Tureen, Cover, Oval, Beaded Rim, Thomas Heming, George III, 1781, 11 In., Pair 3600.00

Do not store silver in cardboard boxes, newspapers, or any wrapping secured with rubber bands. They will all discolor the silver.

Silver-Sterling, Bowl, Cover, Hammered, Enamel Teardrops On Cover, Footed, 5 x 7 In.

Tureen, Gadroon Rim, Scroll Handles, Victorian, Robert Garrard, 1858, 13 3/4 In. 3580.00
Tureen, Sauce, Cover, Navette, Wakelin & Garrard I, George III, 1798, 5 1/2 In. 1415.00
Urn, Peaked Lid, Flat Leaf Serpentine Handles, London, George III, 1768, 15 In. 2470.00
Waiter, Circular, Leaf & Shell Gadroon Border, Henry Wilkinson, 1871, 8 In. 300.00
Waiter, Circular, Shell & Scroll Border, Ebenezer Coker, George III, 1765, 9 In. 1320.00
Waiter, Reticulated Rim, Chased Swags, Oak Leaf Bands, George III, 1 3/4 x 14 1/2 In. ... 1610.00
Waiter, Shell & Scroll Border, Alexander Clark, Sheffield, 1906, 7 3/4 In. 170.00
Water Urn, Laurel Swags, Rosettes, Wood Handles, George III, 21 x 9 x 10 In. 575.00
Wine Coaster, Cylinder Shape, Scrolled Handles, Walker & Hall, Sheffield, 8 In. 520.00
Wine Coaster, Turned Wood Base, Pierced Sides, George III, c.1787, 5 In., Pair 1930.00
Wine Coaster, Turned Wood Base, Pierced, Engraved, George III, 5 In., Pair 2015.00
Wine Coaster, Turned Wood Base, Robert Hennell, George III, 1774, 5 In., Pair 3016.00
Wine Cooler, Fluted, Leaf Form Handles, Liner, 8 1/2 In., Pair 800.00
Wine Funnel, Crested, R.P., London, George III, 1790, 5 1/2 In. 518.00
Wine Funnel, London Hallmarks, George III, 1786, 5 In. 315.00
Wine Funnel, Molded Gadroon Rim, Crested, George III, c.1810, 6 In. 629.00
Wine Funnel, Rebecca Emes, Edward Barnard, George III, c.1821, 5 In. 865.00
Wine Funnel, Reeded Borders, B. Mountigue, London, George III, 1790, 5 1/4 In. 615.00
Wine Jug, Victorian, Engraved Leaf Decoration, c.1818, 11 1/2 In. 715.00
SILVER-FRENCH, Berry Set, Hallmark, Strawberry Engraved Bowls, 6 x 9 In., 14 Piece 230.00
Canister, Figural, Rooster, 11 1/2 In. 1840.00
Compote, Vermeil Bowl, Decorative Band, Dolphin Stem, 1800s, 4 1/4 x 4 In. 230.00
Ice Cream Set, Art Nouveau, 10-In. Server, 12 Spoons, Chased, Gilt 260.00
Martini Set, Shaker, 6 Stems, Beaded Rim, Cartier, 1900s, 13 1/2-In. Shaker, 7 Piece 1955.00
Plateau, Serpentine Sided Mirror, Gustav Keller, c.1890, 2 x 15 1/2 In., Pair 3680.00
Platter, Oval, Molded Rim, Shells At Corners, Late 19th Century, 15 In. 380.00
Salt, Pierced Sides, Cherubs, Red Glass Liner, P. Fres., 1800s, 3 1/4 In., 4 Piece 700.00
Vase Holder, Scrolled Arms, 2 Clamps, Cyma Curve Edges, Cartier, 9 In. 115.00
Wine Taster, Circular, Ring Handle, c.1900, 5 In. 320.00
Wine Taster, Circular, Serpent Ring Handle, C. Sirdey, Late 1700s, 4 1/2 In. 755.00
SILVER-GERMAN, Basket, Swing Handle, Birds, Pedestal Foot, Schlingloff, c.1900, 13 In. ... 566.00
Basket, Oval, 2 Scroll Handles, Schleissner, c.1900, 16 In. 320.00
Basket, Pierced Figural Design, Swing Handle, Glass Lined, 1800s, 14 x 12 In. 2070.00
Bowl, Embossed Dismounted Cavalier, Lobed Rim, 19th Century, 9 3/4 In. 375.00
Castor, Inverted Pear Shape, Acanthus Scrolls, c.1900, 8 3/4 x 2 1/2 In., Pair 105.00
Chalice, Silver, Inscribed, H.L. Wenner, Arts & Crafts, 8 1/4 In. 355.00
Chalice, Silver, Inscribed, H.L. Wenner, Arts & Crafts, 14 1/2 In. 410.00
Ciborium, Cover, Waisted, Oak Leaves, c.1868, 12 1/2 x 4 In. 105.00
Claret Jug, Deco Style, Gilded Interior, 1930s, 10 1/2 In. 1050.00
Coffee Set, Oval Tray, Ebonized Handles, 5 Piece 1175.00
Coffeepot, Chased Design, Black Wood Handle, 8 1/2 In. 259.00
Fox, Detachable Head, Neresheiner, Hanau, c.1912, 13 3/4 In. 5100.00
Sugar Shaker, Chased Portrait Medallion, 8 In. 320.00
Tray, Art Deco, Treen Handles, Germany 1910.00
Tray, Oval, Gallery, Pierced, Cherubs, W.C. Hessenberg, c.1800, 23 3/4 In. 9000.00
Vase, Cover, Beaker Shape, Repousse, Engraved, Battle Scene, c.1900, 10 In. 590.00

Vase, Cover, Tapered Honeycomb Body, St. George & Dragon Finial, 8 In. 690.00
Vase, Flaring, Repousse, Soldier, Flowers, Schleissner, c.1900, 8 3/4 In. 226.00
Wine Goblet, Cast Grape & Leaf Band, Leaf Stem, Round Foot, c.1829, 5 In. 150.00
SILVER-HUNGARIAN, Beaker, Gilt, 3 Spread Wing Birds, G.H. Maker's Mark, c.1660, 7 In. . . 7800.00
SILVER-INDIAN, Casket, 10-Sided, Dome Cover, Repousse, Flowers, Leaves, c.1900, 10 In. . . 1791.00
   Saucepan, Circular, Dome Cover, Horn Handle, Hamilton & Co., c.1810, 6 In. 945.00
SILVER-IRISH, Beer Jug, Pear Shape, Scroll Handle, Pedestal Foot, Matthew West, 1777, 9 In. 3600.00
   Coffeepot, Oblong, Tongue & Dart Borders, J. Le Bas, George III, 1815, 10 1/2 In. 1885.00
   Coffeepot, Tapering Cylinder, Scroll Handle, Rococo Shell & Scroll, c.1800, 9 In. 1508.00
   Cream Jug, Oval, Reeded Border, Richard Sawyer, George III, 1806, 4 1/2 In. 360.00
   Cup, Chased Foliage, 2 Handles, Dublin Marks, George III, c.1760, 5 In., Pair 2875.00
   Cup, Flower Chased, Embossed, Oval, Handles, Trumpet Foot, Georgian, Dublin, 5 In. . . . 645.00
   Fish Slice, Fiddle, William Cummins, Victorian, 1844, 11 1/2 In. 566.00
   Goblet Set, Water, Bucket Shape, Flattened Knops, Elizabeth II, 4 1/2 In., 24 Piece 2115.00
   Ladle, Baleen Handle, Chased Floral, Scroll Designs, Phineas Garde, c.1815, 7 In. 315.00
   Marrow Scoop, Cut Decoration, Michael Keating, George III, 1801 . . . . 226.00
   Salver, Leaf, Scroll & Shell Rim, 4 Panel Feet, R. Breading, George III, 1810, 21 3/4 In. . . 3395.00
   Salver, Reeded Rims, Circular, 3-Footed, Swags, William Bond, c.1788, 8 3/8 In., Pair 3600.00
   Salver, Shell & Scroll Rim, Shell & Leaf Feet, M. Homer, George III, c.1785, 7 3/4 In. . . . 470.00
   Saucepan, Baluster, Engraved Crest, Wood Handle, AB Maker's Mark, 1725, 13 5/8 In. . . . 4800.00
   Spoon, Straining, Chased Coat Of Arms On Handle, c.1809, 12 In. 460.00
   Sugar Basin, Fluted, Oval, 2 Reeded Handles, Robert Breading, George III, 1803, 8 In. . . . 360.00
   Sugar Tongs, Openwork Arms, Flowers, Shell Grips, George III, Late 1700s 245.00
   Tea & Coffee Set, Chased, Rococo Style, Flowers, James Fray, 1823, 4 Piece 7200.00
   Teapot Stand, Oval, Reeded Rim, 4 Scroll Feet, John Stoyte, Dublin, 1802, 7 1/4 In. 850.00
   Urn, Cover, Shaped Body, Repousse Swags, Rosettes, George II, 15 x 13 In. 5290.00
   Wine Funnel, Strainer, Dublin, George IV, 1829, 6 x 3 In. 800.00
SILVER-ITALIAN, Dish, 3-Part, Buccellati, Leaf Shape, 17 In. 3885.00
   Sugar, Cover, Oval, Bombe, Beaded, Embossed Leaves On Cover, 4-Footed, Milan, 5 In. . 1380.00
   Tea & Coffee Set, Rococo Style, Marked, 800, c.1900, 4 Piece 865.00
SILVER-JAPANESE, Cordial, Gilt Bowl, Etched Flowers, Fitted Case, 20th Century, 3 In., Pair . 90.00
   Dessert Set, Plates, Bowls, Cordials, Flowers, Engraved, 36 Piece 1955.00
   Jewelry Cabinet, Flowers, Drawers, 1925-1997, 5 3/8 In. 690.00
   Punch Set, Footed Bowl, Stem Cups, Impressed, Miyata, Japan, 1900s, 27 Piece 2300.00
   Salt & Pepper, Lantern Shape, Tokugawa Mon Design, 1900s, 3 3/4 In. 290.00
   Salt & Pepper, Takarabune Shape, Treasure Ship, Gilt Leaf Highlights, 1900s, 2 3/4 In. . . . 255.00
   Salt Dish, Boat Shape, Wave Pattern Base, Early 1900s, 3 In. 115.00
   Teapot, Late 19th Century, 5 In. 485.00
SILVER-MEXICAN, Argyll, Gravy Warmer, Matching Sauce, Sanborns, Wood Handles, 6 In. . . 127.00
   Bowl, Plain, Straight Sides, William Spratling, 3 1/2 In. 235.00
   Bowl, Scalloped, Chased Rosettes, Handles, Sanborns, 7 1/4 In. 179.00
   Candlesnuffer, Chased Line, Braided Wire Border, Hector Aguilar, 13 In. 425.00
   Cigarette Case, Oval, Engraved, Gilt Rivets, c.1964, 3 1/2 In. 310.00
   Coffee Set, Sanborns, 10-In. Coffeepot, 3 Piece 478.00
   Cruet Stand, Shaped Oval, Scrolling Leaves, Flowers, 4-Footed, c.1780, 8 In. 230.00
   Dish, Entree, Cover, Ladle, Oval Lobed Body, Ball Feet, 1900s, 7 x 19 In. 1035.00
   Dish, Leaf Form, Sterling, 9 3/4 In. 69.00
   Goblet, Marked, LJR, 6 In., 12 Piece 598.00
   Jug, Water, Oval, Scooped Rim, Wooden Loop Handle, c.1950, 9 1/2 In. 505.00
   Ladle, Sterling, Oval Bowl, Curved, Tapered Handle, Flowers, Beaded End, 11 In. 400.00
   Pitcher, Ribbed Melon Shape, Stamped, Sanborns, Mid 1900s, 7 In. 259.00
   Salad Set, Fork, Spoon, Stamped, Hector Aguilar, 9 In. . . . . .425.00 to 950.00
   Salver, Chased Rosettes On Rim, Sanborns, 14 In. 239.00
   Spurs, Spanish Colonial Style, Figural, Jingle-Bobs, William Spratling, 1930s, 8 1/2 In. 11165.00
   Tea Set, Sterling, Coffeepot, Teapot, Beaker, Creamer, Tray, 26 In. 1790.00
   Tray, Plain, Round, 3 Scroll Carved Ebony Feet, William Spratling, 4 1/4 In. 410.00
SILVER-NORWEGIAN, Tankard, Peg, Embossed, Engraved, Trondhjem, Norway, 1749, 10 In. 5800.00
SILVER-ORIENTAL, Condiment Set, Street Merchant Pushing Cart, 1900s, 5 1/4 In. 175.00
   Tumbler Set, Oriental Characters, Dragon, 4 1/2 In., 8 Piece 460.00
SILVER-PERUVIAN, Mirror, Repousse, Dressing Table, Wood Back, 1900s, 24 In. 405.00
   Salver, Shaped Rim, Molded Swags, J. Porcile, 11 1/4 In. 95.00
SILVER-PORTUGUESE, Jug & Basin, Scrolled Flowers, Leaves, Fluted, 1853-62, 12 1/2 In. . . . 1885.00
   Tea & Coffee Set, Repousse, Flutes, Bird Finial, ESC, 1810-18, 4 Piece 2450.00

SILVER-RUSSIAN. Russian silver is marked with the Cyrillic, or Russian, alphabet. The numbers 84, 88, or 91 indicate the silver content. Russian silver may be higher or lower than sterling standard. Other marks indicate maker, assayer, or city of manufacture. Many pieces of silver made in Russia are decorated with enamel. Faberge pieces are listed in their own category.

SILVER-RUSSIAN, Bowl, 2 Handles, Engraved, Leaves, Shell Border, Late 1800s, 14 In.	269.00
Bowl & Spoon, Cloisonne, Jeweled Border, Signed, 3 1/2 x 4 5/8 In. . Cloisonne	2185.00
Box, Round, Shaded Enamel, Flowers, Leaves, Geometric, c.1912, 2 3/4 In.	565.00
Card Case, Plated, Cossack On Horseback, Gold, Garnet Clasp, 4 3/4 In.	300.00
Cigarette Box, Hinged Lid, Rectangular, Courting Couple By River, 4 1/2 In.	235.00
Cigarette Box, Hinged Lid, Rectangular, Hunter Visited By Winged Goddess, 4 3/8 In. . . .	470.00
Cigarette Case, Prince Ivan On Lid, Gilt Interior, Hallmark, 5 In.	460.00
Cup, Cover, Campana Shape, Engraved, Scroll Handle, Domed Base, Moscow, 6 In.	391.00
Cup, Loop Handle, Art Nouveau Flowers, Gilt Interior, 3 1/2 In.	345.00
Cup & Saucer, Tea, Enamel, Blue & Green Flowers, 5 In.	230.00
Kovsh, Gilt, Shaded Enamel, Stippled Ground, Feodor Ruckert, c.1910, 6 In.	4830.00
Purse, Change, Lady's Woven Handbag Shape, Garter & Chain Handle, 8 x 3 In.	235.00
Salt, Cauldron Form, 3 Ball Supports, Enamel, Flowers, Leaves, 1 1/4 In., Pair	160.00
Spoon, Enamel Decorated Bowl, Handle, 20th Century, 4 1/4 In.	120.00
Sugar Scoop, Cloisonne, Gustav Klingert, Moscow, 1892, 4 1/2 In.	300.00
Teapot, Band Of Anthemions, Fruit, Flowers, Wood Handle, Finial, Moscow, 1833, 5 In. . .	500.00
Teapot, Gilt Band, Relief Flowers, Fluted Bottom, Ebonized Handle, Moscow, 1827, 7 In. .	860.00
Teapot, Oval, Lobed, Ivory Finial & Handle, 4 Bun Feet, St. Petersburg, c.1826, 5 In.	460.00
Teaspoon Set, Zolotnik, Silver Gilt, Gustav Lingert, c.1895, 4 1/2 In., 12 Piece	1840.00
SILVER-SCANDINAVIAN, Beaker, Cylinder, Molded Rim, Inscription, Repousse, c.1750, 3 In. .	800.00
Beaker, Engraved Tulips, Cylindrical, 3 Ball Feet, C. Bolderus, 3 1/2 In.	920.00
Coffee Set, Bulbous, Black Shaped Handle, David Andersen, c.1950, 3 Piece	860.00
Tea Set, Bulbous, Loop Handles, David Andersen, c.1950, 5 1/4-In. Teapot	1610.00
SILVER-SCOTTISH, Cream Ladle, Horn Handle, Muirhead & Arthur, Glasgow, 1847, 9 1/4 In.	185.00
Salt, Circular, Gadroon Rim, 3 Paw Feet, John McDonald, George III, 1806, 3 In., Pair . . .	380.00
Tea Set, Oblong, Scroll Handles, J. McKay, George III, c.1814, 6 1/2-In. Pot, 3 Piece	1040.00
SILVER-SOUTH AMERICAN, Card Tray, Chased Swags, Buds On Rim, Camuso, Argentina, 9 In.	95.00
Ciborium, Knopped Stem, Round Foot, Domed Cover, Cross Finial, 9 3/4 In.	1725.00
SILVER-SPANISH, Stirrups, Colonial, Hand Chased, Repousse Scrolling Flowers, 8 1/2 In. . . .	575.00
Stirrups, Colonial, Hand Chased, Repousse Scrolls, Leaves, Flowers, 9 In.	635.00

SILVER-STERLING. Sterling silver is made with 925 parts silver out of 1,000 parts of metal. The word *sterling* is a quality guarantee used in the United States after about 1860. The word was used much earlier in England and Ireland. Pieces listed here are not identified by country. Other pieces of sterling quality silver are listed under Silver-American, Silver-English, etc.

SILVER-STERLING, Bottle, Dresser, Enamel, Faceted Cylinder Form, 2 3/4 In.	140.00
Bowl, Chased, Embossed, Flower Stems, S-Scrolls, S. Kirk & Son Co., 9 1/8 In.	650.00
Bowl, Cover, Hammered, Enamel Teardrops On Cover, Footed, 5 x 7 In. . . . . *Illus*	295.00
Bowl, Open Work Pedestal, Acanthus & Lion's Head, 6 x 10 1/2 In.	440.00
Bowl, Oval, Fluted, Dogwood Blossoms, Branches, 2 x 8 1/4 x 10 3/4 In.	230.00
Bowl, Round, Serpentine Scroll, Embossed, c.1890, 1 1/2 x 8 1/2 In.	230.00
Box, Hinged Cover, Engine Turned, Mahogany, c.1938, 1 1/4 x 3 1/2 x 8 3/4 In.	200.00
Cake Slice, Flowers, Morning Glory, Monogram, 20th Century, 10 1/2 In.	295.00
Candelabrum is listed in its own category.	
Candlesticks are listed in their own category.	
Cigarette Box, Teak Liner, Inscribed Signatures, 1 1/2 x 6 1/2 x 5 In.	35.00
Coffee Set, Demitasse, Art Deco, Creamer, Open Sugar, Pot	450.00
Coffeepot, Blossom Pattern, Oval Pot, Ivory Handle, Bun Feet, 1926, 8 1/2 In.	3290.00
Creamer, Repousse, Squat, Flowers & Leaves, Monogram, 3 1/4 In.	65.00
Cup, Loop Handle, Circular Foot, Child's, 3 1/4 In.	145.00
Dish, Chased Strawberry, Leaf Form, Ball Feet, 11 x 9 In.	260.00
Dish, Danish Modern, Embossed Spiral, Trilobe Handle, c.1945, 1 1/2 x 6 In.	633.00
Dresser Set, Arts & Crafts, Repousse Design, Stylized WD Monogram, c.1910	160.00
Dresser Set, Hammered Finish, WC Monogram, Mirror, Brushes, Jars, 1910	150.00
Dressing Table Set, Looking Glass, Hairbrush, Clothes Brush, Early 1900s	145.00

Ewer, Wine, Cover, Hinged, Grape, Vine, Art Nouveau, 15 In. 3740.00
Fish Serving Set, Orientalist Pattern, Spatulate Handles, Engraved, c.1800, 2 Piece 80.00
Fish Set, Sterling Mounts, Horn Handles, Monogram, 1844-94, 2 Piece 90.00
Frappe Glass Holders, Flared Inserts, 5 Piece 75.00
Ladle, Grecian Pattern, Engraved Initials, c.1860, 13 In. 290.00
Napkin Rings are listed in their own category.
Pen, Twist Design Handle, c.1920, 7 In. 45.00
Pitcher, Water, Bulbous, Cottage Landscape, Flowers, Scrolls, 1901, 10 1/2 In. 1840.00
Pitcher, Water, Helmet Form, Monogrammed, 9 In. 290.00
Pitcher, Water, Stag Handle, Scroll Rim, Bead Trim, 1900s, 7 1/2 x 9 x 6 In. 650.00
Platter, Chased Flower Repousse, Applied Leaves, Oval, Ring Foot, 24 In. 5750.00
Platter, Game, Shaped Rim, Well & Tree Center, 20th Century, 12 x 8 1/2 In. 290.00
Salad Server, Free-Form Twist Handles, Vermeil Bowls, 20th Century, 11 1/2 In. 155.00
Salad Serving Set, Spatulate Handles, Chased, Flowers, Scrolls, c.1900, 9 In. 259.00
Salt & Pepper, Gadroon Edge, Shell Carved Legs, 20th Century, 5 In. 95.00
Serving Spoon, Gilt, Iris Pattern, Durgin Company, N.H., c.1900, 9 3/4 In. 200.00
Spoon Set, Apostles, Engraved, Box, 5 1/2 In., 13 Piece 55.00
Spoon Set, Dessert, Byzantine Pattern, Wood & Hughes, c.1875, 5 In., 12 Piece 175.00
Spoon, Souvenir, see Souvenir category.
Strawberry Fork Set, Rococo Revival Style, R. Blackinton Co., c.1895, 12 Piece 230.00
Tea & Coffee Set, Coffeepot, Teapot, Creamer, Sugar, Waste Bowl, Waiter, 5 Piece 805.00
Tea & Coffee Set, Pear Shape Bodies, Greek Key Band, 8 Piece 6040.00
Tea & Coffee Set, Plymouth, Urn Form, Oval Foot, 4 Piece 1485.00
Tea Set, Teapot, Coffeepot, Creamer, Sugar, Tray, Flowers, Leaves, Paw Feet, 5 Piece 805.00
Tray, Oval, Gadroon Rim, Monogram K.G.C., Grogan, 12 In. 150.00
Tray, Rectangular, 2 Handles, Monogram, 1901, 29 1/2 In. 4900.00
Waste Bowl, Engraved, Cobalt Blue Glass Liner, 3 x 7 In. 200.00
Wine Coaster, 4-Footed, Jade Base, Carved Jade Handles, Grape Leaf Terminals, 10 In. .. 825.00
Wine Cooler, Cobalt Blue Liner, Urn Shape, Twig Handles, Grapes, 10 x 10 In., Pair 5375.00
SILVER-SWISS, Vase, Hammered, Waisted, Molded Girdle, J. K. Bossard, 8 3/4 In. 520.00
SILVER-TURKISH, Basin, Fluted, Impressed, 20th Century, 4 1/2 x 15 3/4 In. 520.00
     Salver, Circular, Strapwork, Flower, Leaves, Late 1800s, 16 1/4 In. 1130.00
     Tea & Coffee Set, Ribbon Borders, Late 1800s, 28-In. Tray, 5 Piece 2450.00
     Vase, Inverted Bell Shape, Reeded, Pedestal Base, Late 1800s, 5 In., Pair 895.00

SINCLAIRE cut glass was made by H.P. Sinclaire and Company of
Corning, New York, between 1905 and 1929. He cut glass made at
other factories until 1920. Pieces were made of crystal as well as
amber, blue, green, or ruby glass. Only a small percentage of Sinclaire
glass is marked with the S in a wreath.

     Candlestick, Blue Cup & Foot, Clear Stem, 10 In., Pair 535.00
     Decanter, Engraved Wheat Sheafs, 13 1/4 In. 200.00
     Decanter, Wheat, Facet Cut Stopper, Engraved Grape, Leaves, Donut Shape, 10 In. 173.00
     Saltshaker, Pressed Diamonds, Hoop Handle On Cover, 1 3/4 In. 25.00
     Vase, Fan, Pink, Footed, 7 In. 225.00
     Vase, Honey Amber, Globe Shape, Footed, 5 In. 130.00

SKIING, see Sports category.

SLEEPY EYE collectors look for anything bearing the image of the
nineteenth-century Indian chief with the drooping eyelid. The Sleepy
Eye Milling Co., Sleepy Eye, Minnesota, used his portrait in advertising from 1883 to 1921. It offered many premiums, including stoneware
and pottery steins, crocks, bowls, mugs, and pitchers, all decorated
with the famous profile of the Indian. The popular pottery was made
by Western Stoneware, Weir Pottery Company, and other companies
long after the flour mill went out of business in 1921. Reproductions of
the pitchers are being made today. The original pitchers came in only
five sizes: 4 inches, 5 1/4 inches, 6 1/2 inches, 8 inches, and 9 inches.
The Sleepy Eye image was also used by companies unrelated to the
flour mill.

     Butter Crock, Premium In 196 Lb. Flour Bag, 1903-04 .... 900.00
     Creamer, Indian In Medallion, Medium Blue, 2 3/4 In. 100.00
     Ink Blotter ....180.00 to 200.00

Letter Opener, Bronze, Figural Handle 775.00
Mug, Blue & White, 4 1/4 In. ....85.00 to 225.00
Mug, Blue Band, 4 1/4 In. ....240.00 to 290.00
Pitcher, Blue & White, Blue Rim, No. 1, 4 In. ....90.00 to 360.00
Pitcher, Blue & White, Blue Rim, No. 2, 5 1/4 In. ....425.00 to 510.00
Pitcher, Blue & White, Blue Rim, No. 4, 8 In. ....160.00 to 350.00
Pitcher, Blue & White, Blue Rim, No. 5, 9 In. ....75.00 to 105.00
Pitcher, Blue & White, No. 1, 4 In. ....77.00 to 120.00
Pitcher, Blue & White, No. 2, 5 1/4 In. ....90.00 to 105.00
Pitcher, Blue & White, No. 3, 6 1/2 In. 90.00
Pitcher, Blue & White, No. 4, 8 In. ....450.00 to 750.00
Pitcher, Blue & White, No. 5, 9 In. 675.00
Salt Bowl, Gray & Blue, Stoneware, 4 In. ....185.00 to 385.00
Stein, Blue & White, 7 1/2 In. ....170.00 to 900.00
Stein, Blue & White, Flemish, 8 In. ....150.00 to 400.00
Stein, Brown & Gold, 7 3/4 In. ....600.00 to 750.00
Stein, Brown & White, 7 3/4 In. ....550.00 to 1150.00
Stein, Brown, Tan, 7 3/4 In. 750.00
Stein, Dark Blue, 8 In. 1800.00
Stein, Green & White, 7 3/4 In. 1100.00
Stein, White, Brown Bands, 7 1/4 In. 1000.00
Stencil, Old Sleepy Eye, Frame, Original 775.00
Sugar Bowl 350.00
Trivet, Western Stoneware, Monmouth, Ill., 1910-30 .... 3000.00
Vase, Blue & White, 8 1/2 In. ....260.00 to 900.00
Vase, Cattail, Flemish, 9 In. ....325.00 to 460.00
Vase, Cattail, Green, White, 8 1/2 In. 2100.00
Vase, Cobalt Blue, 8 1/2 In. 1100.00
Vase, Green & White, 8 1/2 In. 2100.00

SLOT MACHINES are included in the Coin-Operated Machine category.

SMITH BROTHERS glass was made after 1878. Alfred and Harry
Smith had worked for the Mt. Washington Glass Company in New
Bedford, Massachusetts, for seven years before going into their own
shop. They made many pieces with enamel decoration.

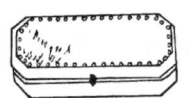

Biscuit Jar, Opal, Yellow & White Daisies, Metal Collar & Lid, 7 In. 315.00
Dresser Box, Earth Tone Ferns, Melon Ribbed, Signed, 3 1/2 In. 200.00
Sugar, Cover, Raised Earth Tone Flowers, Melon Ribbed, Metal Cover, 4 In. 230.00
Sugar & Creamer, Blue Pansies, Amber Stems, Embossed Metal Rim & Cover 175.00
Sugar & Creamer, Opal Shaded To Blue, Blue & White Daisies, 3 1/2 In. 230.00
Vase, Enameled Forget-Me-Nots, Beaded Rim, Swirled Ribs, Gold Rings, 7 In. 980.00
Vase, Ivy Vines, Opal, Gold Trim, Pinched Sides, Beaded Rim, 4 1/2 In. 230.00
Vase, Yellow To Pink, Swirled, Forget-Me-Nots, Beaded Rim, Signed, 7 In. 850.00

SNUFF BOTTLES are listed in the Bottle category.

SNUFFBOXES held snuff. Taking snuff was popular long before cigarettes became available. The gentleman or lady would take a small
pinch of the ground tobacco or snuff in the fingers, then sniff it and
sneeze. Snuffboxes were made of many materials, including gold, silver, enameled metal, and wood. Most snuffboxes date from the late
eighteenth or early nineteenth centuries.

Burl, Signed, George Sinclair Bonnington, England, 4 x 4 x 2 1/2 In. 595.00
Enamel, Hinged Lid, Boar's Head, Hunting Scene, France, 18th Century, 3 In. 470.00
Enamel, Robin On Grassy Ground, Staffordshire, Early 1800s, 2 1/2 x 2 1/2 In. 660.00
Gold, Enamel, Hinged Lid, Harbor, Rectangular, Continental, c.1900, 1 3/4 x 3 In. 5375.00
Horn, Hinged Wooden Lid With Horn, Brass Tacks, Incised, Initials MB, 3 1/2 In. 430.00
Porcelain, Hinged Lid, Birds, Flowers, Circular, Chinese Export, 1700s, 2 1/2 In. 445.00
Silver, Engine Turned Decoration, Leaf Borders, Oval, Germany, 1880, 2 3/4 In. 265.00
Silver, George I Style, Rectangular, Canted Corners, Engraved Scrolls, 1718, 2 1/2 In. 500.00
Silver, George III, Oblong, John Shaw, England, 1815, 2 1/2 In. 339.00
Silver, George III, Rectangular, Scrolling Flowers & Leaves, England, 1815, 2 3/4 In. 300.00
Silver, George IV, Rectangular, Turned Side Panels, 3 In. 715.00

Silver, Hinged Agate Lid, Scrollwork, Cartouche Shape, Continental, 3 In. 505.00
Silver, Hinged Lid, Flowers, Inscription, Rectangular, Canada, c.1850, 3 1/2 In. 1508.00
Silver, Hinged Lid, Flowers, Leaves, Rectangular, England, Edward Smith, 1856, 3 1/2 In. . 895.00
Silver, Hinged Lid, Flowers, Leaves, Shells, Rectangular, Continental, Early 1800s, 3 In. . . . 207.00
Silver, Nielloed, Hinged Lid, Figures, Leaves, Ribbed Sides, Russia, 1811, 3 1/4 In. 945.00
Silver, Scrollwork, Nathaniel Mills, Rectangular, Birmingham, England, 1845, 3 In. 320.00
Silver, Secretary Bookcase Shape, Chased, Engraved, Dutch, 2 3/4 In. 440.00
Silver Plate, Lion's Face Form, England, 1 3/4 In. 69.00
Tortoiseshell, Silver Mounted, Fluted Lid, Reeded Body, Oval, 3 1/2 In. 355.00

SOAPSTONE is a mineral that was used for foot warmers or griddles
because of its heat-retaining properties. Soapstone was carved into figurines and bowls in many countries in the nineteenth and twentieth
centuries. Most of the soapstone seen today is from China or Japan. It
is still being carved in the old styles.

Carving, Dragon, On Cloud, Japan, Early 1900s, 6 In. 374.00
Carving, Panel, Flower, Bird, Jade, Carnelian, Frame, Stand, 9 1/2 x 11 1/2 In. 115.00
Figurine, Man Offering Wine Cup To Woman, 6 In. 1680.00
Figurine, Quan Yin Seated, Chinese, 19th Century, 9 3/4 In. 900.00
Group, Carved, Pierced Sphere, Foo Dogs, Chinese, 20th Century, 16 In. 375.00
Group, Oriental Figures, Sages, Women, Scrolling Tree Shape Pedestal, 19 In. 80.00
Vase, 8 Relief Carved Monkeys & Birds, 11 In. 250.00
Vase, Relief Flowers & Leaves, 11 In. 200.00

SOFT PASTE is a name for a type of pottery. Although it looks very
much like porcelain, it is a chemically different material. Most of the
soft-paste wares were made in the early nineteenth century. Other
pieces may be listed under Gaudy Dutch or Leeds.

Bowl, King's Rose, Oyster Variant, Drape Border, 2 3/4 x 5 1/2 In. 415.00
Cup & Saucer, King's Rose, Oyster Variant, Drape Border, Handleless 275.00
Cup & Saucer, Queen's Rose, Vine Border 220.00
Pitcher, Horse & Gentleman Scene, Signed GB, 1792 . . . . 750.00
Pitcher, Vines, Flower Buds, Gaudy Cobalt Blue, Raised Panel Sides, Handle, 10 1/2 In. . . 345.00
Plate, King's Rose, Broken Border, 6 In. 195.00
Plate, King's Rose, Solid Border, 4 1/2 In. 605.00
Plate, King's Rose, Solid Border, 8 1/4 In. . . . . .220.00 to 250.00
Plate, Queen's Rose, Vine Border, Red Rim, 9 3/4 In. . . . . .305.00 to 330.00
Pot, Yellow Flowers, Blue Leaves, Ribbed Spout, Ear Handle, Beehive Finial, 12 In. 800.00
Sugar, Cover, Gaudy Blue Tulips, Applied Handles, 4 1/2 In. 800.00
Toddy Plate, King's Rose, Flowers, Pink Luster Accents, England, Early 1800s, 4 1/2 In. . 35.00

SOUVENIRS of a trip—what could be more fun? Our ancestors
enjoyed the same thing and souvenirs were made for almost every
location. Most of the souvenir pottery and porcelain pieces of the nineteenth century were made in England or Germany, even if the picture
showed a North American scene. In the twentieth century, the souvenir
china business seems to have gone to the manufacturers in Japan, Taiwan, Hong Kong, England, and America. Another popular souvenir
item is the souvenir spoon, made of sterling or silver plate. These are
usually made in the country pictured on the spoon. Related pieces may
be found in the Coronation and World's Fair categories.

Apron, Arizona Tourist, c.1950, 14 x 23 In. 30.00
Ashtray, Alaska, Land Of Midnight Sun, 49th State, Dog Sled, Metal, Japan, 7 x 5 In. 22.00
Ashtray, Blue Hole, Castalia, Ohio, Tin, 1950s 25.00
Ashtray, Horse Head, Figural, Chincoteague, Va., Japan, c.1950, 5 1/2 x 4 In. 26.00
Ashtray, Key City Diner, Phillipsburg, New Jersey, Glass, 4 1/4 In. 29.00
Bank, Deer, Mother & Baby, Aitkin, Minn., Pottery, Japan, 4 1/2 x 5 3/4 x 3 1/4 In. 30.00
Bowl, Atlantic City Steel Pier, Embossed Anchors, Fish, Wood, 9 In. 25.00
Button, Olympics, 1956, Melbourne, Kenya Team, Multicolored 300.00
Compact, Perfume, Florida Wiesner Of Miami, Beach Scene, Cloisonne, Bag 75.00
Creamer, Hotel McAlpin, Silver, 1939, 2 Oz., 2 1/2 x 3 3/4 In. 28.00
Creamer, Mt. Tom Railroad Co., Summit House, Holyoke, Mass., Porcelain, 2 In. 35.00
Creamer, Old Orchard Beach Maine, Yellow Frosted, Gold Trim, 1900-10, 2 1/2 In. 35.00

Clean old textiles before storing. Be sure to rinse fabrics until all soap residue is gone. Soap in the textile will scorch when you iron. Do not starch old fabrics. Folding a starched fabric causes the fibers to break.

Souvenir, Scarf, Olympics, Figures Playing
Sports, Olympic Rings On Border, 31 In.

Cup & Saucer, Bushkill Falls, The Niagara Of Pennsylvania, Porcelain	35.00
Dish, Olympics, 1936, Berlin, Asymmetrical Triangle, Weimler Porzellen, 5 In.	170.00
Menu, Knott's Berry Farm, Calico Ghost Town, Map, 1962, 8 x 5 1/4 In.	25.00
Menu, St. Clair Hotel, Illinois Room, Indian Design, 9 x 12 In.	45.00
Peep Egg, Niagara Falls & Bridge, Alabaster Body, Painted Flowers, 6 In.	206.00
Plaque, All God's Children, Embossed, Martha Holcombe, 1988, 6 1/2 x 8 1/2 In.	49.00
Plate, Field Museum Of Natural History, Chicago, Ill., Porcelain, Germany, 5 In.	40.00
Plate, First Congregational Church, Binghampton, N.Y., Germany, 6 1/4 In.	49.00
Plate, Old Miss America, Race Track, Pier, Atlantic City, N.J., Aristochrome, c.1950, 9 In.	39.00
Plate, Olympics, 1968, Mexico City, Staffordshire	295.00
Plate, Panama Canal, Lady Liberty, Nudes, Pacific Meets Atlantic, Austria, 7 1/2 In.	50.00
Plate, William Worrell Mayo Statue, Rochester, Minn., Porcelain, Germany, 6 3/4 In.	39.00
Postcard, Atlantic City, Bathing Beauty Gee, Postmarked 1923	8.00
Poster, Olympics, 1956, Stockholm, Equestrian Games, 39 1/4 x 24 1/2 In.	1330.00
Program, Olympics, 1924, Paris, Javelin Thrower On Cover, July 7, 9 x 11 In.	280.00
Program, Ringling Bros. & Barnum & Bailey Circus, 1937, 11 x 8 1/2 In., 10 Pages	38.00
Purse, Florida Orange, Flicker Eyes, Sailboat, Flamingo, Zipper, Vinyl, 1960s, 7 x 4 In.	24.00
Record Book, Olympics, 1936, Jim Thorpe Autograph	2090.00
Scarf, Olympics, Figures Playing Sports, Olympic Rings On Border, 31 In. .... *Illus*	20.00
Spoon, Sterling Silver, Figural Handle, Chinese Man With Umbrella, c.1900, 6 In.	345.00
Spoon, Sterling Silver, Ft. Meyers, Florida, Thomas Edison's Winter Home	16.00
Spoon, Sterling, Gold Wash Bowl, Beaded Handle, Ogdensbury, N.Y., 1900s, 5 3/4 In.	20.00
Tablecloth, Aloha Hawaii, Hawaiian Islands, Surfers, Volcanoes, Fringe, 36 x 36 In.	45.00
Tablecloth, Hula Girl, Aloha Hawaii, 29 x 29 In.	20.00
Tea Set, Atlantic City, Steel Pier, Pottery, Box, Japan, 1930s, 9 Piece	600.00
Thermometer, Porpoise, Florida, Ceramic, Japan, 5 1/2 In.	15.00
Ticket, Olympics, 1936, Berlin, Leichtathletik, Multicolored, 2 3/4 x 4 1/4 In.	90.00
Ticket Stub, Olympics, 1932, Lake Placid, Adult Bleacher, Feb. 12	105.00
Tin, Manhattan Island, Aeroplane View, 25 Scenes, 11 x 12 1/2 x 6 In.	156.00
Torch, Olympics, 1948, London, Inscription, E.M.J. Factories, 16 In.	4770.00
Torch, Olympics, 1976, Montreal, Queensway Machine Products, 26 In.	2925.00
Tray, Bermuda, Map, Woven, Wood, 12 1/2 In.	10.00
Tray, San Francisco, United States Shape, Metal, Japan, 1940-50, 4 x 2 1/2 In.	14.00
Tumbler, Collapsible, Shasta Springs, Cal., 2 5/8 In. Diam.	135.00
Tumbler, Lucky Casino, Mr. Lucky, 5 In.	18.00
Vase, Elmire Free Academy, New York, Porcelain, Germany, 5 In.	40.00
Vase, High School Bldg., Elkhart, Ind., Handles, Porcelain, Germany, 5 x 3 1/4 In.	39.00
Vase, Olympics, 1936, Berlin, Olympic Rings, BL Sandgemalsh Logo, China, 5 1/4 In.	280.00

SPATTERWARE is the creamware or soft paste dinnerware decorated with colored spatter designs. The earliest pieces were made in the late eighteenth century, but most of the spatterware found today was made from about 1800 to 1850, or it is a form of kitchen crockery with added spatter designs, made in the late nineteenth and twentieth centuries. The early spatterware was made in the Staffordshire district of England for sale in America. The later kitchen type is an American product.

Bowl, Bull's-Eye, Rainbow, Red, Green, Flared Edge, 9 In. 470.00
Bowl, Flower, Blue, Red Sprigs, Brown Border, Paneled, 5 1/4 In. 470.00
Bowl, Peafowl, Red, Yellow, Green, Blue Border, 5 1/4 In. 440.00
Bowl, Peafowl, Yellow, Blue, Green, Red Border, Paneled, 5 1/2 In. 195.00
Bowl, Rainbow, Alternating Bands, Green, Blue, Red, 10 In. 440.00
Child's Set, Tulip, Profile, Red, Teabowl, Saucer, Plate, c.1830, 7 3/8 In. 2468.00
Coffeepot, Rainbow, Red & Blue, Paneled, 8 1/2 In. 770.00
Creamer, Black, Purple, Embossed Shell Under Spout, Paneled 1925.00
Creamer, Blue, 2 Men In Raft, 4 1/4 In. 520.00
Creamer, Christmas Balls, Red, Green, Bulbous, Loop Handle, 3 1/2 In. 2750.00
Creamer, Cow, Milk Maid Form, Brown, Black, Green & Brown Base, 5 1/2 x 6 1/2 In. . . . 9350.00
Creamer, Dove, Blue, Yellow, On Branch, Blue, 5 In. 2200.00
Creamer, Fort, Tan, Brown, Green Trees, Blue Ground, 3 1/4 In. 745.00
Creamer, Peafowl, Blue, Yellow, Green, Red, 4 In. 495.00
Creamer, Peafowl, Blue, Yellow, Red, Blue Ground, Shaped Handle, 4 1/4 In. 770.00
Creamer, Peafowl, Purple, Green, Red, Green Ground, Loop Handle, 3 3/4 In. 440.00
Creamer, Peafowl, Red, Yellow, Green, Blue Ground, Applied Loop Handle, 3 1/2 In. 550.00
Creamer, Peafowl, Red, Yellow, Green, Blue, Bird, Bulbous, 4 1/4 In. 1100.00
Creamer, Purple, Red & Green Holly Berries, 4 In. 175.00
Creamer, Rainbow, 5-Color Vertical Pastel Bands, Scalloped Body, 6 1/2 In. 6600.00
Creamer, Rainbow, Blue, Red, Applied Loop Handles, 3 1/2 In. 600.00
Creamer, Rainbow, Brown, Yellow, Bulbous, Loop Handle, 3 3/4 In. 770.00
Creamer, Rainbow, Paneled, Blue & Burgundy Red Stripes, 4 5/8 In. 345.00
Creamer, Rainbow, Pink, Green, Paneled, Shaped Handle, 4 3/4 In. 220.00
Creamer, Red, 8-Point, Star, Blue, 4 1/2 In. 935.00
Creamer, Roses, Red, Green Leaves, Brown, Black, 4 In. 550.00
Creamer, Roses, Red, Green Leaves, Red & Blue Rainbow, 4 In. 4400.00
Creamer, Thistle, Red Flower, Green Leaves, Blue, Yellow, Bulbous, 3 1/4 In. 9900.00
Creamer, Thistle, Red, England, c.1840, 4 In. 235.00
Creamer, Tulip, Blue, Purple, Green Leaves, Blue Ground, Paneled, Shaped Handle, 6 In. . . 660.00
Cruet, Red, White, Yellow, Leaves, Applied Clear Handle, 8 In. 175.00
Cup & Saucer, 6-Point Star, Blue, Green, Red, Blue Border, Handleless 3300.00
Cup & Saucer, 6-Point Star, Red, Blue, Green, Red Border, Handleless 880.00
Cup & Saucer, Acorn, Brown, Teal Caps, Green Leaves, Handleless 2200.00
Cup & Saucer, Acorn, Yellow, Teal Caps, Green Leaves, Blue Border, Handleless 2310.00
Cup & Saucer, Blue Flower, Red 625.00
Cup & Saucer, Blue, Pink Bud Cluster, Handleless 175.00
Cup & Saucer, Bud Cluster, Red, Green Leaves, Blue, Handleless 415.00
Cup & Saucer, Buds, Red, Brown Ground, Handleless 165.00
Cup & Saucer, Bull's-Eye, Purple, Blue, Handleless, Child's 550.00
Cup & Saucer, Bull's-Eye, Rainbow, Red, Green, Handleless 1430.00
Cup & Saucer, Bull's-Eye, Rainbow, Red, Green, Handleless, Child's 660.00
Cup & Saucer, Bull's-Eye, Red, Blue, Handleless 495.00
Cup & Saucer, Bull's-Eye, Red, Green, Handleless 1430.00
Cup & Saucer, Castle, Brown, Handleless 225.00
Cup & Saucer, Castle, Red 250.00
Cup & Saucer, Christmas Balls, Red, Yellow, Green, Handleless 6050.00
Cup & Saucer, Cockscomb Center, Yellow, Red & Green, Handleless 1610.00
Cup & Saucer, Cockscomb, Blue, Green Leaves, Purple, Handleless 2750.00
Cup & Saucer, Dahlia, Red, Blue, Green Sprigs, Rainbow, Handleless 4510.00
Cup & Saucer, Deer, Red Border, Handleless 440.00
Cup & Saucer, Dove, Purple, Yellow, Blue, Green, Handleless 1006.00
Cup & Saucer, Festoon, Yellow, Red, Green, Handleless, Child's Size 11000.00
Cup & Saucer, Flower, Blue, Red, Green Leaves, Red Border, Handleless 660.00
Cup & Saucer, Fort, Tan, Brown, Red, Green Trees, Handleless 275.00
Cup & Saucer, Holly Berry, Blue Border, Loop Handle 495.00
Cup & Saucer, Holly Berry, Green Leaves, Blue Border, Loop Handle, Child's 495.00
Cup & Saucer, Peafowl, Blue, Black, Red, Green, Handleless 523.00
Cup & Saucer, Peafowl, Blue, Gray, Red, Red Border, Handleless 275.00
Cup & Saucer, Peafowl, Blue, Green, Red, Blue, Handleless 385.00
Cup & Saucer, Peafowl, Blue, Green, Red, Green Ground, Handleless . . . . .248.00 to 550.00
Cup & Saucer, Peafowl, Blue, Yellow, Black, Green, Handleless 165.00
Cup & Saucer, Peafowl, Blue, Yellow, Red, Blue Ground, Handleless 495.00

Cup & Saucer, Peafowl, Blue, Yellow, Red, Rainbow, Purple, Red, Handleless 2530.00
Cup & Saucer, Peafowl, Blue, Yellow, Red, Red Border, Handleless, Child's 1100.00
Cup & Saucer, Peafowl, Rainbow, Blue, Red, Purple 805.00
Cup & Saucer, Peafowl, Red, Green, Blue, Green Ground, Handleless 305.00
Cup & Saucer, Peafowl, Red, Yellow, Green, Blue Ground, Paneled, Child's, 5 1/4 In. 440.00
Cup & Saucer, Rainbow, Black, Purple, Handleless 1100.00
Cup & Saucer, Rainbow, Black, Purple, Handleless, Child's 1375.00
Cup & Saucer, Rainbow, Blue & Yellow Tulip, Purple Border, Handleless 2530.00
Cup & Saucer, Rainbow, Blue, Green, Center Dot, Handleless 2310.00
Cup & Saucer, Rainbow, Blue, Yellow, Handleless, Child's 1925.00
Cup & Saucer, Rainbow, Red & Blue, Handleless 550.00
Cup & Saucer, Rainbow, Red & Green 695.00
Cup & Saucer, Rainbow, Red, Blue, Center Dot, Handleless, Child's 770.00
Cup & Saucer, Rainbow, Red, Green, Handleless 470.00
Cup & Saucer, Rainbow, Red, Yellow, Handleless, Child's 1540.00
Cup & Saucer, Red, Light Blue, Mustard Yellow, Peafowl, Green, Handleless 145.00
Cup & Saucer, Red, Purple & Yellow Primrose Center, Handleless 776.00
Cup & Saucer, Rooster, Blue, Yellow, Red, Red Ground, Handleless 1155.00
Cup & Saucer, Rose Bud, Red Buds, Blue, Yellow Leaves, Handleless 4730.00
Cup & Saucer, Roses, Red, Black & Brown Ground, Handleless 210.00
Cup & Saucer, Roses, Red, Green Leaves, Black & Brown Border, Handleless 660.00
Cup & Saucer, Roses, Red, Green Leaves, Blue, Handleless, Child's 770.00
Cup & Saucer, Roses, Red, Green Leaves, Brown, Handleless 330.00
Cup & Saucer, Roses, Red, Green Leaves, Handleless 385.00
Cup & Saucer, School House, Blue, Yellow Roof, Green Tree, Red Border, Handleless 5720.00
Cup & Saucer, Star, Rainbow, Red, Blue, Green, Handleless 3300.00
Cup & Saucer, Star, Red, Green, Blue, Red Border, Handleless 715.00
Cup & Saucer, Thistle, Blue, Green Leaves, Red, Handleless 990.00
Cup & Saucer, Thistle, Flower, Red, Green Leaves, Purple Border, Handleless 440.00
Cup & Saucer, Thistle, Green & Black Stripes, Red, Green, Handleless 5630.00
Cup & Saucer, Thistle, Red Flower, Green Leaves, Black, Green Border, Handleless 5225.00
Cup & Saucer, Thistle, Red Flower, Green Leaves, Yellow, Handleless 4400.00
Cup & Saucer, Thistle, Red, Green Leaves, Red & Yellow Border, Handleless 1320.00
Cup & Saucer, Thistle, Red, Yellow, Handleless 2310.00
Cup & Saucer, Thistle, Yellow 3600.00
Cup & Saucer, Tulip, Blue 375.00
Cup & Saucer, Tulip, Blue, Red, Green Leaves, Handleless 440.00
Cup & Saucer, Tulip, Red, Green Leaves, Blue, Handleless, Child's 1650.00
Cup & Saucer, Tulip, Red, Green Leaves, Red Border, Handleless 1045.00
Cup & Saucer, Tulip, Red, Green Leaves, Yellow, Handleless 11000.00
Cup & Saucer, Vine & Berry, Red, Yellow, Green, Handleless 2310.00
Cup & Saucer, Windmill, Red, Blue Roof, Blue Border, Handleless, Child's 1320.00
Cup & Saucer, Yellow, Handleless 495.00
Figure, Clock, Tall Case, Red, Green, Yellow, 4 3/4 In. 220.00
Fort, Creamer, Brown, Gray, Green Trees, Red, 4 In. 2200.00
Master Salt, Green, Red, Footed, 2 x 3 In. 3850.00
Mug, Peafowl, Blue, Yellow, Red, Thomas, Green, Flared, 3 1/2 In. 1980.00
Pitcher, Cream, Peafowl, Purple, Green & Red, Green Ground, Barrel Shape, 3 3/4 In. 440.00
Pitcher, Fort, Gray, Red, Green Trees, Blue Border, Shaped Handle, 5 1/2 In. 1045.00
Pitcher, Rainbow, 5-Color Vertical Pastel Bands, Scalloped Body, 9 In. 11000.00
Pitcher, Rainbow, 5-Color, 10 In. 6670.00
Pitcher, Rainbow, Alternating Green, Yellow & Red Vertical Bands, Paneled, 6 In. 2750.00
Pitcher, Rainbow, Purple, Black, Loop Handle, 10 1/2 In. 1595.00
Pitcher, Roses, Red, Green Leaves, Blue Ground, Paneled, 12 1/4 In. 440.00
Plate, 6-Point Star, Red, Yellow, Green, Blue Border, 9 1/2 In. 990.00
Plate, 6-Point Star, Sunburst, Red, Green, Blue, Red Border, Paneled, 9 1/2 In. 2090.00
Plate, Acorn, Blue Border, 8 1/2 In. 305.00
Plate, Acorn, Brown, Teal Caps, Green Leaves, Purple Border, Paneled, 9 1/4 In. 1430.00 to 3300.00
Plate, Acorn, Brown, Teal Caps, Green Leaves, Red, Paneled, 9 1/4 In. 990.00
Plate, Acorn, Paneled, Blue, 8 1/2 In. 595.00
Plate, Acorn, Yellow, Green Leaves, Blue Border, Paneled, 8 1/2 In. 2750.00
Plate, Black Beauty, Black Flower Border, Red, Blue, Green Flowers, 9 1/8 In. 145.00
Plate, Blue & Purple Floral Center, Green Paneled Border, 8 1/2 In. 230.00

Plate, Blue Border, Pomegranate, Red, Green, Blue, Yellow, 10 In. 290.00
Plate, Bull's-Eye, Black, Purple, 5 In. 495.00
Plate, Bull's-Eye, Black, Purple, 9 1/2 In. 1760.00
Plate, Bull's-Eye, Brown, Purple, 8 1/4 In. 2750.00
Plate, Bull's-Eye, Green, Blue, 9 1/2 In. 4950.00
Plate, Bull's-Eye, Rainbow, Purple, Blue, 9 1/2 In. 880.00
Plate, Bull's-Eye, Rainbow, Red, Purple, 9 3/4 In. 495.00
Plate, Bull's-Eye, Red, Blue, 8 1/2 In. 2420.00
Plate, Bull's-Eye, Red, Green, 8 1/4 In. 770.00
Plate, Bull's-Eye, Red, Purple, 8 1/4 In. 1980.00
Plate, Bull's-Eye, Red, Purple, 9 1/2 In. 990.00
Plate, Castle, Red, White Ground, 8 1/2 In. 275.00
Plate, Cockscomb, Yellow, 8 1/2 In. 4370.00
Plate, Criss-Cross, Red, Blue, Paneled 935.00
Plate, Dahlia, Blue, Red, Green Sprigs, Blue Border, Paneled, 5 1/4 In. 660.00
Plate, Dahlia, Blue, Red, Green Sprigs, Purple, Paneled, 10 1/2 In. 2750.00
Plate, Dahlia, Purple, Staffordshire, c.1830, 9 In. 690.00
Plate, Dahlia, Red, Blue, Green Sprigs, Blue Border, 8 1/2 In. 440.00
Plate, Dahlia, Red, Blue, Green Sprigs, Rainbow, Paneled, 8 1/4 In. 1540.00
Plate, Dahlia, Red, Blue, Green Sprigs, Red & Blue Border, Paneled, 8 1/4 In. 1100.00
Plate, Eagle, Flying, Purple Border, Paneled, 8 1/2 In. 605.00
Plate, Flowers, Blue Edge, France, c.1860, 8 3/8 In. 290.00
Plate, Fort, Blue, Paneled, 9 1/2 In. 110.00
Plate, Fort, Gray, Brown, Green Trees, Blue Border, Paneled, 7 In. 660.00
Plate, Morning Glory, Blue, Green Leaves, Yellow Border, Paneled, 10 In. 1870.00
Plate, Open Tulip, Purple, England, c.1840, 8 1/8 In. 940.00
Plate, Pansy, Green Rosette Border, 8 3/4 In. 230.00
Plate, Peafowl, Blue, Green, Red, Green Tree, Red Border, Paneled, 9 1/2 In. 2475.00
Plate, Peafowl, Blue, Impressed Pearl Stoneware, 8 In. 295.00
Plate, Peafowl, Blue, Yellow, Green, Red Ground, 7 1/2 In. 715.00
Plate, Peafowl, Blue, Yellow, Green, Red Ground, 9 1/4 In. 440.00
Plate, Peafowl, Blue, Yellow, Red Bird, Green, Paneled, 9 1/4 In. 1210.00
Plate, Peafowl, Blue, Yellow, Red, Blue Ground, 8 1/4 In. 1870.00
Plate, Peafowl, Red, Impressed Adams, 8 1/2 In. 695.00
Plate, Peafowl, Red, Yellow, Green, Blue Border, Paneled, 9 3/4 In. 275.00
Plate, Peafowl, Yellow, Blue, Red, Green, Red Ground, 4 3/4 In. 1980.00
Plate, Pomegranate, Red, Blue Buds, Green Leaves, Blue, 9 1/2 In. 990.00
Plate, Primrose, Red, Yellow, Green Leaves, Blue Border, 8 3/4 In. 880.00
Plate, Profile Tulip, Blue, England, c.1830, 8 1/4 In. 999.00
Plate, Rainbow, Blue, Green, Red, 9 1/2 In. 4125.00
Plate, Rainbow, Bull's-Eye Center, Red & Green Stripes, 9 1/2 In. . . . . .575.00 to 690.00
Plate, Rainbow, Purple, Black, Bull's-Eye Center, 9 1/2 In. 1495.00
Plate, Rainbow, Red & Green, 9 1/2 In. 1195.00
Plate, Rainbow, Red, Green Christmas Colors, Bull's-Eye Center, 9 1/2 In. 750.00
Plate, Rainbow, Rose, Blue, Red, 8 1/2 In. . . . . .1265.00 to 1495.00
Plate, Rooster Peafowl, Blue, Yellow, Red, Blue, Paneled, 9 1/4 In. 1320.00
Plate, Rooster Peafowl, Blue, Yellow, Red, Red Border, Paneled, 8 1/4 In. 2750.00
Plate, Rooster, Blue, Yellow, Red, Blue Border, Paneled, 9 1/2 In. 3520.00
Plate, School House, Red & Yellow, Blue Spatter Rim, 8 In. 58.00
Plate, School House, Red, 8 1/2 In. 550.00
Plate, School House, Red, Brown, Green, 8 1/2 In. 3850.00
Plate, Soup, Peafowl, Green, Blue, Yellow, Red, 10 In. 633.00
Plate, Soup, Tulip, Dark Red Border, Red, White & Blue, Green Leaves, Mark, 10 In. 2185.00
Plate, Stars, Flowers, Black Rabbit & Green Frog Border, 9 1/4 In. 275.00
Plate, Stick, Rabbit & Frog Center Transfer, Gaudy Flower Border, 9 1/2 In. 500.00
Plate, Thistle, Paneled, Red Thistle & Ground, Green Leaves, 8 1/2 In. 165.00
Plate, Thistle, Red, Green Leaves, Red Border, 8 1/4 In. 1210.00
Plate, Toddy, Peafowl, Blue, Yellow, Green, Red Ground, 6 1/4 In. 440.00
Plate, Toddy, Peafowl, Red, England, c.1840, 4 7/8 In., 2 Piece 765.00
Plate, Toddy, School House, Blue, 5 3/4 In. 850.00
Plate, Toddy, School House, Cobalt Blue, Blue Roof, Tree, Red Border, 6 In. 2645.00
Plate, Toddy, Tulip, Open, Blue, Blue Paneled Border, Red, White, 5 In. 490.00
Plate, Tulip, Blue, Purple, Green Leaves, Green & Blue Border, Paneled, 9 1/4 In. 1430.00

Plate, Tulip, Blue, Red, Green Leaves, Blue Border, 9 1/2 In. 2530.00
Plate, Tulip, Blue, Red, Green Leaves, Red, Paneled, 8 1/2 In. 1100.00
Plate, Tulip, Red, Blue, Green Leaves, Black, Purple Border, Paneled, 8 1/4 In. 3025.00
Plate, Tulip, Red, Green Leaves, Green Border, Paneled, 8 In. 2310.00
Plate, Tulip, Yellow, Yellow, Blue, Red Sprigs, Green Leaves, Red Border, 8 1/4 In. 2750.00
Plate Set, Peafowl, Red, c.1860, 7 1/2 In., 4 Piece 1955.00
Platter, Bull's-Eye, Brown, Purple, Alternating Stripes, 10 1/4 x 13 1/2 In. 3680.00
Platter, Eagle, Shield, Blue, Cut Corners, 11 x 14 1/2 In. 385.00
Platter, Fort, Tan, Brown, Red, Green Trees, Blue Border, Cut Corners, 13 1/2 In. 1430.00
Platter, Fort, Trees, Blue Edge, Octagonal, 13 1/2 x 10 1/4 In. 489.00
Platter, Peafowl, Blue, Yellow, Green, Red Ground, Cut Corners, 8 x 10 1/2 In. 990.00
Platter, Rabbits, Playing Cricket, Flower Border, Brown Transfer, Oval, 10 x 15 In. 980.00
Platter, Rainbow, Blue & Purple, 10 x 13 1/2 In. 2200.00
Platter, Rainbow, Red & Green, Staffordshire, c.1830, 18 x 14 In. .... .4200.00 to 4830.00
Platter, Rooster Peafowl, Blue, Yellow, Green, Red, 6 3/4 x 9 1/4 In. 2310.00
Saucer, Rainbow, Yellow, Blue, Red & Green Thistle 1150.00
Saucer, School House, Red, Red Border, 5 3/4 In. 550.00
Soup, Dish, Peafowl, Blue, Yellow, Red, Purple, 10 1/2 In. 3960.00
Soup, Dish, Thistle, Red, Green Leaves, Blue Ground, 10 3/4 In. 1980.00
Sugar, Cover, Blue, Tepee, England, c.1840, 4 7/8 In. 705.00
Sugar, Cover, Peafowl, Blue, Yellow, Green, Red, 4 1/2 In. 495.00
Sugar, Cover, Peafowl, Blue, Yellow, Red, Blue Border, 2-Sided, 5 In. 440.00
Sugar, Cover, Peafowl, Purple, Green, Red Peafowl, 4 1/4 In. 385.00
Sugar, Cover, Purple, 2 Men In Raft, 4 1/2 In. 7475.00
Sugar, Cover, Rainbow, Black, Purple, Shell Form Handles, Paneled, 8 In. 3850.00
Sugar, Cover, Rainbow, Blue, Red, Open Handles, 4 1/4 In. 440.00
Sugar, Cover, Rainbow, Red, Blue, Bulbous 165.00
Sugar, Cover, Roses, Red, Green Leaves, Purple, Blue 605.00
Sugar, Cover, Thistle, Red Flower, Leaves, Black, Yellow Rainbow, Bulbous, 5 1/2 In. 13750.00
Sugar, Cover, Thistle, Red, Green Leaves, Black, Red, 5 1/2 In. 6050.00
Sugar, Cover, Thistle, Yellow 6900.00
Sugar, Cover, Tulip, Red & Yellow, Green Leaves, Blue & Purple, Child's, 3 1/4 In. 2200.00
Sugar, Red, Parrot, Green, Red, 4 1/2 In. 690.00
Tea Set, Peafowl, Red, Yellow, Blue, Purple & Blue Border, Teapot, Child's, 6 Piece 23100.00
Teapot, Peafowl, Blue, Yellow, Red, Purple, 5 1/2 In. 1650.00
Teapot, Rainbow, Christmas Colors, Red, Green, 7 In. 633.00
Teapot, Rainbow, Paneled, Red, Blue Vertical Stripes, Molded Handle, Spout, 9 In. 403.00
Teapot, Rainbow, Red, Blue, Bulbous, Loop Handle 605.00
Teapot, Rainbow, Red, Green, 5 3/4 In. 4400.00
Teapot, Rose Bud, Red, Green Leaves, Blue Ground, Child's, 4 In. 220.00
Teapot, Tulip, Blue, Red, Green Leaves, Red, Paneled, 9 In. 4620.00
Wash Set, Bowl, Pitcher, Fort, Tan, Brown, Red, Green Trees, Blue Border 2640.00
Waste Bowl, Bull's-Eye, Black, Purple, 3 1/4 x 5 3/4 In. 1870.00
Waste Bowl, Bull's-Eye, Red, Green, Flared, 3 x 5 1/2 In. 440.00
Waste Bowl, Flower, Purple, Yellow Center, Green Leaves, Red, 3 x 5 1/2 In. 1210.00
Waste Bowl, Peafowl, Blue, Green, Red, Red Ground, 3 x 5 3/4 In. 385.00
Waste Bowl, Peafowl, Blue, Yellow, Red, Green, 3 x 5 1/2 In. 935.00
Waste Bowl, Peafowl, Blue, Yellow, Red, Red Ground, 3 1/4 x 5 1/2 In. 440.00
Waste Bowl, Rainbow, 4 Colors, Alternating Bands, Flared, 2 1/2 x 2 7/8 In. 7150.00
Waste Bowl, Red, Primrose, Yellow Center, Purple Flower, Green Leaves, 5 1/2 In. 1210.00
Waste Bowl, Tulip, Red, Green Leaves, Blue, 2 3/4 x 4 3/4 In. 385.00

SPELTER is a synonym for a zinc alloy. Figurines, candlesticks, and
other pieces were made of spelter and given a bronze or painted finish.
The metal has been used since about the 1860s to make statues, tablewares, and lamps that resemble bronze. Spelter is soft and breaks easily. To test for spelter, scratch the base of the piece. Bronze is solid;
spelter will show a silvery scratch.

Ashtray, Roulette Wheel, Center Spins, 1960s, 6 In. 45.00
Candlestick, Figural, Medieval Craftsman, 11 1/2 In., Pair 900.00
Figurine, Dog, Scottish Terrier, 6 x 4 In. 85.00
Lamp, Art Nouveau, Woman, Grapevine Overhead, Glass Grapes, Bronze Leaves, 70 In. ... 7810.00
Statue, Medieval Troubadour, c.1890, 14 In. 450.00

Urn, Louis VX Style, Marble Base, Acanthus Leaf Legs, c.1860, 14 In., Pair 1190.00

SPINNING WHEELS in the corner have been symbols of earlier
times for the past 100 years. Although spinning wheels date back to
medieval days, the ones found today are rarely more than 200 years
old. Because the style of the spinning wheel changed very little, it is
often impossible to place an exact date on a wheel.

Flax, Fruitwood, Turned, Spindles, Carved, Switzerland, c.1900, 31 x 21 In. 118.00
Walking Wheel, Pulleys, Hand Turned, Mid 1800s 395.00

SPODE pottery, porcelain, and bone china were made by the Stoke-
on-Trent factory of England founded by Josiah Spode about 1770. The
firm became Copeland and Garrett from 1833 to 1847, then W.T.
Copeland or W.T. Copeland and Sons until 1976. It then became Royal
Worcester Spode Ltd. The word *Spode* appears on many pieces made
by the factories. Most collectors include all the wares under the more
familiar name of Spode. Porcelains may be listed in this book by the
name that appears on the piece. Related pieces may be listed under
Copeland, Copeland Spode, and Royal Worcester.

Cann, Cup & Saucer, Dollar Pattern, Leaves, Prunus, Kakiemon Style, c.1810, 5 In. 141.00
Cup & Saucer, Flowers, Gilt Ground, c.1810, 5 In. 141.00
Pitcher, Friendship Of Salem, Ships, 5 In., Pair 220.00
Pitcher, Ship, Friendship Of Salem China, 5 In., Pair 219.00
Plate Set, Green Ground, Oriental Flower Design, Mark, 8 In., 12 Piece 600.00
Platter, Earthenware, Flower Spray Border, Flowering Tree Center Scene, c.1815, 14 In. . . . 316.00

SPONGEWARE is very similar to spatterware in appearance. The
designs were applied to the ceramics by daubing the color on with a
sponge or cloth. Many collectors do not differentiate between spongeware and spatterware and use the names interchangeably. Modern pottery is being made to resemble the old spongeware, but careful
examination will show it is new.

Bowl, 2 Blue Bands, Blue, White, 3 1/2 x 8 3/4 In. 90.00
Bowl, Blue, White, Blue Bands, 4 1/2 x 14 In. 120.00
Bowl, Blue, White, c.1900, 7 1/4 x 2 1/2 In. 259.00
Bowl, Purple, Red Rose, Rectangular, Cut Corners, 5 x 6 3/4 In. 165.00
Bowl, Vegetable, Open, Blue, Octagonal, 19th Century, 16 x 13 x 3 1/4 In. 635.00
Canister, Lid, Blue, Cream, 7 In. 305.00
Charger, Peafowl, Yellow, Brown, Blue, Tree, Sponged Leaves, Scalloped, 13 In. 2070.00
Coffeepot, Lid, Blue, White, Salt Glaze, Petals, 10 In. 275.00
Creamer, Blue, Grape, Trellis, Glazed, 5 1/4 In. 145.00
Creamer, Blue, White, 3 3/4 In. 220.00
Creamer, Cow, Milkmaid, Black & Red Sponging, Green Base, Soft Paste, 7 In. 460.00
Creamer, Heron, Snake Relief, Blue, White, 5 1/2 In. 495.00
Crock, Butter, Blue, White, 4 1/4 x 6 1/4 In. 145.00
Cup & Saucer, Deer, Red Border, Handleless 1210.00
Cup & Saucer, Tulip, Red, Green Leaves, Blue Border, Handleless 360.00
Cuspidor, Blue, Gray, Basket Weave, 5 x 8 In. 65.00
Jug, Harvest, A. Noland, Blue, White, c.1860, 12 In. 690.00
Mug, Blue, White, Geometric, Handle, 3 In. 165.00
Pitcher, Blue Mottled Decoration, 9 In. . . . . .290.00 to 400.00
Pitcher, Blue, White, 9 In. . . . . .176.00 to 470.00
Pitcher, Blue, White, Bulbous, 9 In. 605.00
Pitcher, Blue, White, Cattail, 6 In. 22.00
Pitcher, Blue, White, Clay, Chicken Wire, 9 In. 220.00
Pitcher, Blue, White, Rose, 9 In. 190.00
Pitcher, Blue, White, Salt Glaze, Flying Birds, Blue Bands, 8 1/2 In. 300.00
Pitcher, Bulbous Base, Diamond Pattern, Blue, White, 9 In. 300.00
Pitcher, Bulbous, Blue, White, UHL Pottery Co., Huntingburg, Ind., 6 1/2 In. 300.00
Pitcher, Chicken Wire Design, Blue, White, 9 In. 165.00
Pitcher & Basin, Baluster Shape, Flared Rim, Blue, Late 1800s, 10 3/4 x 13 1/2 In. 140.00
Plate, Tulip, Red, Green Leaves, Blue Border, 8 3/4 In. 330.00
Plate Set, Soup, Whiteware, Geometric Band, Flowers, 1800s, 10 In., 6 Piece 350.00

Salt, Blue, White, Salt Glaze, Eagle, Shield, 4 x 6 In. 100.00
Salt, Footed, 2 1/2 x 2 1/4 In. 95.00
Salt & Pepper Combination, Blue, Brown, White, 3 In. 155.00
Syrup Jug, Bail Handle, Blue, White, Stencil, Grandmother's Syrup, N. Weeks, 5 1/4 In. .. 495.00
Tea Set, Red & Blue, Paneled, Child's, 3 Piece 880.00
Teapot, Blue, Red, Yellow, Green Tulips, 6 In. 230.00
Toothbrush Holder, 2 Blue Accent Bands, 5 In. 440.00

SPORTS equipment, sporting goods, brochures, and related items are
listed here. Items are listed by sport. Other categories of interest are
Bicycle, Card, Fishing, Sword, Toy, and Trap. Kentucky Derby glasses
are listed in the Decorated Tumblers category.

Auto Racing, Program, Indianapolis Motor Speedway 500 Mile Race, 1947, 92 Pages 28.00
Badminton, Birdie, Rubber Base, Feathers, Winchester 535.00
Baseball, Ashtray, Joe DiMaggio Model Bat, Hardwood, 29 In. 420.00
Baseball, Ball, Autographed, 500 Home Run Club, Mantle, Williams, Killebrew, Etc. 1375.00
Baseball, Ball, Autographed, Babe Ruth, 1927 .... 5963.00
Baseball, Ball, Autographed, Babe Ruth, Lou Gehrig, 20 Boston Red Sox, 1934 .... 8625.00
Baseball, Ball, Autographed, Baltimore Orioles, 38 Signatures, 1979 .... 355.00
Baseball, Ball, Autographed, Billy Martin 200.00
Baseball, Ball, Autographed, Bucky Harris 920.00
Baseball, Ball, Autographed, Cal Ripken Jr. ....55.00 to 75.00
Baseball, Ball, Autographed, Chicago Cubs, 26 Signatures, 1932 .... 825.00
Baseball, Ball, Autographed, Cleveland Indians, 31 Signatures, 1954 .... 1610.00
Baseball, Ball, Autographed, Detroit Tigers, 24 Signatures, 1968 .... 805.00
Baseball, Ball, Autographed, Dizzy Dean, c.1950 .... 2580.00
Baseball, Ball, Autographed, Jackie Robinson, c.1950 .... 10350.00
Baseball, Ball, Autographed, Joe DiMaggio, Rawlings American League 290.00
Baseball, Ball, Autographed, Lefty Grove 1380.00
Baseball, Ball, Autographed, Leo Gabby Hartnett, Red & Black Stitching 2580.00
Baseball, Ball, Autographed, Los Angeles Dodgers, World Champions, 25 Names, 1959 .. 3738.00
Baseball, Ball, Autographed, Lou Gehrig, 1935 .... 4887.00
Baseball, Ball, Autographed, Mickey Mantle, 1950s 9390.00
Baseball, Ball, Autographed, Mickey Mantle, Rawlings American League 220.00
Baseball, Ball, Autographed, New York Giants, World Champions, 29 Signatures, 1954 ... 3163.00
Baseball, Ball, Autographed, New York Giants, 25 Signatures, 1928 .... 1760.00
Baseball, Ball, Autographed, New York Yankees, 1955 .... 2300.00
Baseball, Ball, Autographed, New York Yankees, 23 Signatures, 1938 .... 4767.00
Baseball, Ball, Autographed, Pee Wee Reese, The Captain 125.00
Baseball, Ball, Autographed, Philadelphia Athletics, World Champions, 24 Names, 1930 .. 1454.00
Baseball, Ball, Autographed, Pittsburgh Pirates, 26 Signatures, 1972 .... 690.00
Baseball, Ball, Autographed, Roberto Clemente, 1960s 8625.00
Baseball, Ball, Autographed, Roberto Clemente, 1970 .... 2580.00
Baseball, Ball, Autographed, Roger Maris, 1961 .... 1840.00
Baseball, Ball, Autographed, Rogers Hornsby, 1955 .... 1320.00
Baseball, Ball, Autographed, Sandy Koufax ....437.00 to 1610.00
Baseball, Ball, Autographed, Satchel Paige 2095.00
Baseball, Ball, Autographed, Ted Williams 177.00
Baseball, Ball, Autographed, Willie McCovey, 521 HR 269.00
Baseball, Ball, Figure 8, c.1890-1910 .... 385.00
Baseball, Ball, Lemon Peel, c.1840 .... 1725.00
Baseball, Ball, Lemon Peel, Leather, c.1860, 1.4 Oz. 2195.00
Baseball, Ball, National League, John A. Heydler, Sealed, Spalding, Box, 1920s 1200.00
Baseball, Bambino Beans Sack, Babe Ruth, Burlap, Pinto Beans, Kansas, 100 Lb. 14.00
Baseball, Bat Rack, Adirondack, 40 Bat Capacity, Revolving, 3-Sided Sign, Late 1950s ... 2132.00
Baseball, Bat Rack, Hillerich & Bradsby, Metal, Late 1940s, 17 1/2 x 22 1/2 x 47 In. 2580.00
Baseball, Bat, Autographed, Barry Bonds, Game Used, 1993-97, 31 Oz., 34 In. 2580.00
Baseball, Bat, Autographed, Carl Yastrzemski, Game Used, 1978-79, 34 1/2 Oz., 36 In. ... 1320.00
Baseball, Bat, Autographed, Cincinnati Reds, 1975 .... 1938.00
Baseball, Bat, Autographed, Harmon Killebrew, Game Used, 1950s, 32 Oz., 35 In. 6980.00
Baseball, Bat, Autographed, Joe DiMaggio, Hillerich & Bradsby, 1941 .... 1840.00
Baseball, Bat, Autographed, National League All-Stars, 1966 .... 3436.00
Baseball, Bat, Autographed, Ted Williams, Boston Red Sox, Game Used, 1952-57 .... 5175.00

Baseball, Bat, Autographed, Tommy Henrich, Game Used, Rookie, 1930s, 31 Oz., 33 In. ... 1236.00
Baseball, Bat, Autographed, Willie Mays, New York Mets, Game Used, 1973 .... 4025.00
Baseball, Bat, Autographed, Willie McCovey, Game Used, 1974, 34 Oz., 36 In. 2790.00
Baseball, Bat, Babe Ruth Decal, Little League, Louisville Slugger, 29 In. 510.00
Baseball, Bat, Hank Aaron, Milwaukee Braves, Game Used, 1955-57 .... 13800.00
Baseball, Bat, Hank Aaron, Milwaukee Braves, Game Used, 1973-75 .... 3450.00
Baseball, Bat, Incised Handle Ring, c.1890-1910, 36 In. 1150.00
Baseball, Bat, Jim Delahanty, Game Used, 1910, 34 1/2 In. 1925.00
Baseball, Bat, Johnny Bench, Louisville Slugger, 1975, 35 1/2 In. 1210.00
Baseball, Bat, Kirby Puckett, Game Used, c.1985 .... 880.00
Baseball, Bat, Mickey Mantle Model, Louisville Slugger, c.1980, 16 In. 46.00
Baseball, Bat, Mickey Mantle, Game Used 20900.00
Baseball, Bat, New York Yankees World Champions, Black, Engraved Names, 1939 ..... 1265.00
Baseball, Bat, Roberto Clemente, Game Used, 1969-72 .... 7475.00
Baseball, Bat, Tim McCarver, Louisville Slugger, Game Used, 1965-68, 33 Oz., 35 In. 338.00
Baseball, Bat, Willie Mays Model, Adirondack, Leather Loop, Facsimile Signature, 18 In. .. 60.00
Baseball, Bat, Willie Stargell, Game Used, 1974 .... 1150.00
Baseball, Bobbin' Head Doll, Roberto Clemente, Pittsburgh Pirates, 1960s, 6 1/2 In. 3800.00
Baseball, Book, How To Throw Curves, Babe Ruth, Quaker Cereal, 1934, 5 x 3 In. 90.00
Baseball, Book, Jackie Robinson's Pocket Baseball Game, 1950, 6 1/2 x 4 3/4 In. 500.00
Baseball, Broadside, Campanella All-Stars vs. Black Barons, Cardboard, 1954, 14 x 22 In. 1072.00
Baseball, Broadside, Monarchs vs. Stars, Negro League, Tatum, Paige, 22 x 14 In. 415.00
Baseball, Button, 1897 Buffalo BB Club, Round, Portraits, Cameo Pepsin Gum 920.00
Baseball, Button, Babe Ruth Baseball Club, Babe's Face, Baseball Stitching, 1 In. 45.00
Baseball, Button, Babe Ruth Baseball Club, Quaker Oats, 1930s, 1 In. 136.00
Baseball, Button, Babe Ruth, Ask Me, Texaco, c.1935, Jumbo 305.00
Baseball, Button, Boston Rooters, Celluloid, Mat, Frame, 1903, 1 3/4 In. 6560.00
Baseball, Button, Cy Young, Cleveland Naps, 1 In. 130.00
Baseball, Button, I Love Mickey, Teresa Brewer, Mickey Mantle, Round, 1 3/4 In. 200.00
Baseball, Button, Keep The Dodgers In Brooklyn, Black, Yellow, Celluloid, 1957, 1 In. 1035.00
Baseball, Button, Mantle & Maris, 61 In '61 Or Bust, Celluloid, 1961, 3 1/2 In. 4600.00
Baseball, Button, New York Yankees, AL Champions, 1953, Blue Letters, 3 1/2 In. 345.00
Baseball, Button, Pittsburgh 1898, Shield Hanger, Crossed Bats, Ball 460.00
Baseball, Button, Roy Campanella, Celluloid, 2 1/4 In. 460.00
Baseball, Button, Walter Johnson, Washington Senators, 1 In. 120.00
Baseball, Cabinet Card, Kansas City Ball Club, Joseph Hall, 1888 .... 5700.00
Baseball, Cap, Johnny Lindell, New York Yankees, Game Used, c.1943 .... 1725.00
Baseball, Carte De Visite, Hartford Blue Stockings, 1875 .... 5700.00
Baseball, Catcher's Mask, Wire Cage, Square Mouth Hole, Leather, Winchester, No. 2203 . 1185.00
Baseball, Catcher's Mask, Wire Frame, Leather, Padded, Winchester, No. 2207, Boy's 605.00
Baseball, Catcher's Mitt, Tom Haller Model, Spalding, No. 42-7631, c.1970 .... 58.00
Baseball, Display, Leo Durocher Book, Sugar Crisp, Cardboard, 1955, 20 x 31 In. 700.00
Baseball, Display, Wiffle Bat & Ball, T. Williams, E. Mathews, W. Ford, $1.69, 1950s 305.00
Baseball, Fan, 16 Captains, Barton's Barber Shop, Paper, Wood Handle, c.1910, 9 x 10 In. .. 560.00
Baseball, Figure, Stan Musial, Hartland, No. 915, Box, Tag, Booklet 1730.00
Baseball, Figure, Ted Williams, Hartland, No. 914, Box, Tag, Booklet 1600.00
Baseball, Flag, Stadium, Baltimore Orioles, Black, Orange, 1960s 525.00
Baseball, Glove, Autographed, Lou Boudreau, 1940s 4710.00
Baseball, Glove, Babe Ruth Home Run Special, A.J. Reach Co., Box, 1920s, 8 1/2 In. 9775.00
Baseball, Glove, Big Leaguer, Draper, Maynard, Model DG935, Box, 1960s, 7 x 8 1/2 In. .. 187.00
Baseball, Glove, Billy Pierce Model, J.C. Higgins, Model 1686, 1950s 69.00
Baseball, Glove, Brooks Robinson Model, 1964 .... 145.00
Baseball, Glove, First Baseman's, Johnny Mize Model, c.1936 .... 46.00
Baseball, Glove, Horsehide Palm, Winchester, No. WB6 .... 352.00
Baseball, Glove, Leather, Wool Lining, Logo Button, Winchester, No. 2184, Boy's 606.00
Baseball, Glove, Tommy Henrich, Game Used, 1940s 1495.00
Baseball, Glove, White Buckskin, Webless, Crescent Style, c.1890 .... 2875.00
Baseball, Glove, Willie Mays Model, MacGregor, M17T, 1970s 115.00
Baseball, Glove, Winchester, No. 2118, Full Size 330.00
Baseball, Heel Spikes, 4 Spikes, Winchester, Box 867.00
Baseball, Inkwell, Figural, Home Plate, Catcher's Mitt, Pottery, 1910 .... 770.00
Baseball, Jersey, Autographed, Dave McNally, Baltimore Orioles, Game Used, 1965 ..... 3738.00
Baseball, Jersey, Autographed, Hoyt Wilhelm, Chicago White Sox, Game Used, 1968 .... 1840.00

Baseball, Jersey, Autographed, Pete Rose, Cincinnati Reds, Home, Game Used, 1986 . . . . . 4025.00
Baseball, Jersey, Autographed, Willie McCovey, S.F. Giants, Away, Game Used, 1970 . . . . 6900.00
Baseball, Jersey, Billy Moran, Indians, Home, Game Used, 1958 . . . . 1761.00
Baseball, Jersey, Eddie Murray, Baltimore Orioles, Away, Game Used, 1987 . . . . 3165.00
Baseball, Jersey, Garry Maddox, San Francisco Giants, Away, Game Used, 1972 . . . . 460.00
Baseball, Leather, Boston Braves, World Champions, Frame, 1914, 24 x 23 In. 1761.00
Baseball, Matchbook, Home Run In Fenway Park, United Service Motors, 1937, 4 x 3 In. . 101.00
Baseball, Milk Carton, Harmon Killebrew, Minnesota Twins, Franklin Milk, 1961 . . . . 1887.00
Baseball, Moviescope, Babe Ruth Hitting A Homer, Quaker Oats Co., 1934, 2 x 3 In. 301.00
Baseball, Pants, Sandy Koufax, Los Angeles Dodgers, 1964 . . . . 9185.00
Baseball, Pen & Pencil Set, New York Yankees, Bat Shape, 1943 . . . . 136.00
Baseball, Pencil Case, Jackie Robinson, Simulated Leather, W. Mullin, 3 x 8 In. 615.00
Baseball, Pencil, Chicago Cubs, Wooden, Mechanical, c.1950, 5 1/2 In. 20.00
Baseball, Pennant, 1929 World Series, Cubs vs. Athletics 1416.00
Baseball, Pennant, 1955 Worlds Series, Yankees vs. Dodgers, Fringe 1955.00
Baseball, Pennant, Baltimore Orioles, Orange & Black, 1971 . . . . 135.00
Baseball, Pennant, Chicago Cubs, 1932 World Series, Gold & Cream 1760.00
Baseball, Pennant, Chicago Cubs, Batting Bear, Cubs On White Bat, c.1910, 34 In. 2185.00
Baseball, Pennant, Cleveland Indians, American League, World Series, 1948, 26 In. 195.00
Baseball, Pennant, Cleveland Naps, 1905, 35 In. 3892.00
Baseball, Pennant, Jackie Robinson, 1st Base, Brooklyn Dodgers, 1947, 28 In. 1725.00
Baseball, Pennant, Joe DiMaggio, Yankee Slugger, Felt, 3 Streamers, 3 3/4 x 9 In. 75.00
Baseball, Pennant, Paul Waner, Pirates, Felt, Orange Ground, Black Print, 1937 . . . . 150.00
Baseball, Photograph, Autographed, Babe Ruth, Swinging Bat, Inscribed, 10 x 8 In. 5460.00
Baseball, Photograph, Autographed, Jimmie Foxx, At Bat, George Burke, 10 x 8 In. 4315.00
Baseball, Photograph, Autographed, Mantle & DiMaggio, Frame, Certificate, 8 x 10 In. . . . 305.00
Baseball, Photograph, Autographed, Mel Ott, George Burke, Frame, 1930s, 6 x 4 In. 3738.00
Baseball, Photograph, Autographed, Mel Ott, Mat, Frame, 4 3/4 x 6 1/4 In. 4280.00
Baseball, Photograph, Autographed, Roberto Clemente, 8 x 10 In. 2346.00
Baseball, Photograph, Autographed, Roger Maris, Record Breaking Home Run, 8 x 10 In. . 2305.00
Baseball, Photograph, Autographed, Ty Cobb, Black & White, 3 1/2 x 5 1/4 In. 6700.00
Baseball, Photograph, Cleveland Baseball Club, Mat, Frame, 1918, 13 x 37 In. 2580.00
Baseball, Photograph, Ty Cobb, 1930 . . . . 3630.00
Baseball, Pillow Top, Young Woman, Baseball Attire, Lithographed, 1907, 22 In. 1210.00
Baseball, Postcard, Cy Young, Boston, Rose Co., 1908, 3 1/2 x 5 1/2 In. 2536.00
Baseball, Postcard, Ty Cobb, Topping & Co., 1909, 5 1/2 x 3 1/2 In. 1265.00
Baseball, Poster, Home Run Cigarettes, Batter, Catcher, Uniform, 1910, 12 x 18 In. 3740.00
Baseball, Program, 1915 World Series, Boston Red Sox vs. Philadelphia, 10 Cents 1600.00
Baseball, Program, 1923 World Series, Yankees vs. Giants, Managers' Photographs 2094.00
Baseball, Program, Old Timer's Game, Cleveland, Ohio, August 9, 1975 . . . . 15.00
Baseball, Program, Yankees vs. Royals, 1976 . . . . 6.00
Baseball, Ring, Jim Rice, All-Star Game, Candlestick Park, 1984, Size 12 . . . . 2300.00
Baseball, Seat, Briggs Stadium, Double, Detroit, Nos. 1 & 2, Late 1930s 2415.00
Baseball, Seat, Ebbets Field, Brooklyn, No. 42, Blue Paint, 1913-57 . . . . 2920.00
Baseball, Seat, Polo Grounds, New York City, NY Figural Sides, Green Paint 7679.00
Baseball, Seat, Wrigley Field, Chicago, No. 3, Green Paint 665.00
Baseball, Seat, Yankee Stadium, Single, Plaque, Removed 1973, 20 1/2 x 17 x 32 In. 4158.00
Baseball, Sheet Music, Cubs On Parade, H.R. Hempel, 1907 . . . . 658.00
Baseball, Sheet Music, Milwaukee Braves Song, Blue Ground, 1953, 12 x 9 In. 78.00
Baseball, Shirt, Negro League, Autographed 2016.00
Baseball, Sign, Tuxedo Tobacco, Christy Mathewson, New York Giants, 1910, 14 x 18 In. . 3520.00
Baseball, Silk, 1911 New York Giants, Tobacco Premium, Beige, 30 In. 1100.00
Baseball, Silk, 1911 Philadelphia Athletics, Tobacco Premium, Purple, 30 In. 495.00
Baseball, Silk, 1912 Boston Red Sox, Tobacco Premium, Red, 30 In. 2420.00

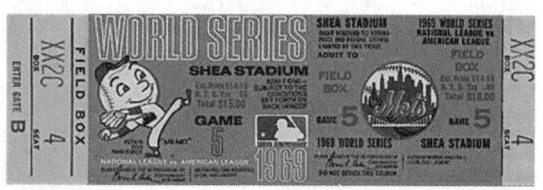

Sports, Baseball, Ticket, 1969
World Series, Baltimore
Orioles At N.Y. Mets, Game 5

Baseball, Silk, Johnny Evers, No. 109, Turkish Trophy, S81, 1912 .... 3125.00
Baseball, Silk, Nap Lajoie, No. 96, Turkish Trophy, S81, 1912, 6 7/8 x 8 7/8 In. 3540.00
Baseball, Sweater, New York Yankees, Steel Gray, Purple Trim, 2 Pockets, c.1921 .... 2875.00
Baseball, Ticket, 1912 World Series, Red Sox At Giants, Game 1, Polo Grounds 1570.00
Baseball, Ticket, 1921 World Series, Giants At Yankees, Polo Grounds, Game 2 .... 1070.00
Baseball, Ticket, 1935 World Series, Detroit At Chicago Cubs, Game 5, Wrigley Field 886.00
Baseball, Ticket, 1946 World Series, St. Louis At Boston, Game 3, Fenway Park 730.00
Baseball, Ticket, 1969 World Series, Baltimore Orioles At N.Y. Mets, Game 5 ...... *Illus* 900.00
Baseball, Ticket, All-Star Game, Cleveland, July 13, 1954 .... 605.00
Baseball, Ticket, All-Star Game, St. Louis, July 9, 1940 .... 1180.00
Baseball, Ticket, Brooklyn Dodgers, Ebbets Field, Opening Day, 1941 .... 510.00
Baseball, Ticket, Cincinnati vs. Cleveland, At Cincinnati, Opening Day, April 18, 1895 ... 3165.00
Baseball, Underwear Box, Babe Ruth Underwear, 1 Pair, Size 48, 9 3/4 x 12 1/2 In. 498.00
Basketball, Ball, Autographed, Boston Celtics, 13 Signatures, 1960-61 .... 1730.00
Basketball, Ball, Autographed, N.Y. Knicks, World Champions, 14 Signatures, 1972-73 .. 1428.00
Basketball, Ball, Autographed, North Carolina State, NCAA Champs, 17 Signatures, 1983 3069.00
Basketball, Ball, Autographed, Philadelphia Warriors, 12 Signatures, 1951-52 .... 2839.00
Basketball, Broadside, Harlem Globetrotters, Wilt Chamberlain, 1959, 13 1/2 x 21 1/2 In. . 2305.00
Basketball, Jacket, Cecil Hankins, St. Louis Bombers, 1946-47 .... 1815.00
Basketball, Jersey, Autographed, Maurice Cheeks, Philadelphia 76ers, Home, c.1980 ..... 1200.00
Basketball, Jersey, Bobby Jones, Philadelphia 76ers, Road, 1982-83 .... 1938.00
Basketball, Jersey, Wali Jones, No. 24, Philadelphia 76ers, Road, 1970-71 .... 615.00
Basketball, Mirror, Philadelphia Warriors, ABL, Schedule, Oval, c.1927, 1 3/4 x 2 3/4 In. . 1180.00
Basketball, Photograph, Autographed, Boston Celtics, 1956-57, 8 x 10 In. 1600.00
Basketball, Poster, Harlem Globetrotters, Jesse Owens, 1951, 42 x 28 In. 805.00
Basketball, Ring, Wilt Chamberlain, Philadelphia 76ers, World Champions, 1966-67 ..... 8348.00
Basketball, Tumbler Set, Portland Trailblazers Championship, 1977, 15 Piece 115.00
Billiards, Broadside, Wonders Of Billiard World, Lew & Nellie Shaw, c.1895, 18 x 12 In. . 575.00
Bowling, Button, Women's International Bowling Congress, 1930s, 1 1/8 In. 20.00
Boxing, Button, Ali-Spinks, ABC Sports, White, Brown, 1978, 2 1/4 In. 46.00
Boxing, Button, Be Lucky With Joe Louis, Photo, Black, Red, 15/16 In. 265.00
Boxing, Button, Henry Armstrong, Black, White, Late 1930s, 1 3/4 In. 35.00
Boxing, Button, Joe Louis, Good Luck Club, Horseshoe, 1 1/8 In. 237.00
Boxing, Glove, Autographed, Muhammad Ali 274.00
Boxing, Photograph, Autographed, Jack Dempsey, 1940s, 7 x 5 In. 145.00
Boxing, Photograph, Autographed, Muhammad Ali, Heart, Smiley Face, 10 x 8 In. 680.00
Boxing, Postcard, Jessie Willard vs. Jack Johnson, c.1916 .... 138.00
Boxing, Poster, Ali, Frazier, World Heavyweight Championship, 1971, 45 x 30 In. 95.00
Boxing, Poster, Graziano, Zale, Motion Pictures, Ruppert Stadium, c.1948, 43 x 32 In. 280.00
Boxing, Poster, Muhammad Ali, Farewell To Legend, Providence, R.I., 1979, 22 x 18 In. .. 95.00
Boxing, Poster, Pvt. Joe Louis Says We Are Going To Do Our Part, 1942, 7 1/4 x 10 In. ... 100.00
Boxing, Program, Frazier, Ali, Heavyweight Championship, Madison Sq. Garden, 1971 ... 465.00
Boxing, Program, J. Louis vs. T. Farr, Heavyweight Championship, Yankee Stadium, 1937 . 285.00
Boxing, Program, Liston vs. Clay, World Heavyweight Championship, 1964 .... 2580.00
Boxing, Program, Muhammad Ali vs. Trevor Berbick, Drama In Bahama, 1981 .... 818.00
Boxing, Shoes, 24 Eye Holes, Winchester, No. 4703, 11 1/2 x 3 1/2 x 6 In. 1215.00
Boxing, Speed Bag, Leather, Winchester, No. 3842 .... 1307.00
Boxing, Trunks, Autographed, Muhammad Ali, Satin 168.00
Boxing, Watch Fob, Dempsey, Gibbons, Shelby, Montana, 1923, 1 1/4 In. 314.00
Boxing, Watch Fob, Jeffries, Johnson, Reno, Nev., 1910, 1 3/4 In. 565.00
Dog Sledding, Trail Marker, Iditarod Trail, Alaska, 1985, 8 x 5 1/2 In. 77.00
Football, Ball, Autographed, Green Bay Packers, 46 Signatures, Wilson, 1963 .... 1200.00
Football, Ball, Autographed, Green Bay Packers, NFL Champions, 1962 .... 1995.00
Football, Ball, Autographed, Green Bay Packers, NFL Champions, 42 Signatures, 1965 ... 3215.00
Football, Ball, Autographed, Green Bay Packers, NFL Champions, 50 Signatures, 1966 ... 3450.00
Football, Ball, Autographed, Joe Montana, San Francisco, Wilson, Box 106.00
Football, Beer Can, Steelers Super Bowl, Aluminum, Pull Tab, Iron City, 1975, 12 Oz. ... 14.95
Football, Button, 16th Annual Homecoming, Ill. vs. Mich., 1925, 1 3/4 x 2 3/4 In. 403.00
Football, Button, Buddy Young, Baltimore Colts, 1950s, 1 3/4 In. 35.00
Football, Helmet, Leather, 6 Spokes, Stall & Dean, Model 5573, Early 1900s 506.00
Football, Helmet, Leather, Vented Dog Ears, Canvas Chin Strap, Goldsmith, 1920s 316.00
Football, Helmet, Super Bowl XXV, Commemorative, Riddell, 1991, 12 x 15 In. 209.00
Football, Jersey, Autographed, Jerry Rice, No. 80, 49ers, Red 193.00

Football, Jersey, Autographed, Walter Payton, No. 34, Bears 449.00
Football, Jersey, Dexter Manley, Washington Redskins, Road, 1980s 1200.00
Football, Jersey, Dick Gordon, Chicago Bears, Home, Late 1960s 1180.00
Football, Pennant, Philadelphia Eagles, 1944 .... 545.00
Football, Photograph, Autographed, Knute Rockne, 7 x 9 1/4 In. 6700.00
Football, Program, Chicago Bears vs. Green Bay Packers, 10 Cents, 1927, Blue Ground .. 1715.00
Football, Shoulder Pads, Leather, Fleece Lining, Buckle Strap, c.1890 .... 209.00
Football, Ticket, Cotton Bowl, Notre Dame vs. Houston, 1979 .... 250.00
Football, Ticket, Super Bowl XXVII, Cowboys vs. Bills, 1993 .... 187.00
Golf, Bag, Canvas, Leather Trim, Shoulder Strap, Metal Bottom, Winchester, 34 3/4 In. ... 980.00
Golf, Bag, Leather, Winchester, 35 x 6 1/2 In. 1155.00
Golf, Club Rack, Wood, Easel, 4 Club Capacity, Spalding, Lindsay Mfg., 54 In. 259.00
Golf, Club, Driver, Persimmon Head, Oak Shaft, Leather Grip, Left Handed, Winchester .. 200.00
Golf, Club, Jigger, Oak Shaft, Leather Grip, Winchester, No. 6627 .... 110.00
Golf, Club, Mid-Iron, Leather Handle, Wood, Winchester Pickwick Machie 110.00
Golf, Club, Putter, Oak Shaft, Leather Grip, Winchester, No. 6704 .... 182.00
Golf, Photograph, Autographed, Bobby Jones, Inscribed To Mary King, Frame, 10 x 8 In. . 3163.00
Golf, Photograph, Autographed, Bobby Jones, Inscription, 7 x 9 In. 2132.00
Golf, Scorecard, Matowac Golf Club, Paul Runyan, Unused, 1939, 5 1/4 x 6 In. 20.00
Hockey, Jersey, Autographed, Wayne Gretzky, Los Angeles Lakers 278.00
Hockey, Puck, Official, Composition Top & Bottom, Solid Core, Winchester, 3 x 1 In. 465.00
Hockey, Skates, Dit Clapper, Game Worn, 1929 .... 928.00
Hockey, Stick, Autographed, Wayne Gretzky 187.00
Hockey, Stick, Championship, Elm, Winchester, No. 4868, 48 x 11 1/2 x 2 1/2 In. 695.00
Hockey, Stick, Jim Craig, 1980 Olympics, Game Used 276.00
Hockey, Ticket, XIII Olympic Games, Series, Miracle On Ice Team, Frame, 1980, 8 Piece . 1380.00
Horse Racing, Horseshoe, Citation, Race Worn, 1948 .... 3123.00
Horse Racing, Riding Pants, Ron Turcotte, Secretariat's Jockey, 1973 .... 332.00
Horse Racing, Saddle Cloth, Seattle Slew, No. 8, Preakness, 1977 .... 4710.00
Horse Racing, Whip, Willie Shoemaker, Ferdinand, Kentucky Derby, 1986 .... 3215.00
Hunting, Award, Trap Shooting, Grand Central Palace, Brass, Gold Plated, 1915, 1 3/4 In. . 110.00
Hunting, Booklet, Clay Pigeon Shooting Rules, Ligowsky, 1883, 5 3/8 x 3 In., 15 Pages .. 200.00
Hunting, Bullet Sizing Tool, 45 Govt. Cal., Nickel Finish 41.00
Hunting, Button, Always Shoot Winchester, Bull's Eye, Multicolored, Round, 7/8 In. 65.00
Hunting, Button, Automatic Caliber 45, Sterling Silver, Handgun Shape, 1 In. 40.00
Hunting, Button, Ballistite & Empire, Best Smokeless Powders, Bastian Bros. 127.00
Hunting, Button, Daisy Cadet, Captain, Shield, Multicolored, Whitehead & Hoag, 1 In. ... 809.00
Hunting, Button, DuPont Smokeless Powder, Quail, Whitehead & Hoag, 1 1/4 In. 90.00
Hunting, Button, Experts Use Peters Cartridges, Bullet, Bastian Brothers 59.00
Hunting, Button, Laflin & Rand, Infallible, Smokeless, Wreath, 3-Stripe Flag, 1 1/4 In. ... 28.00
Hunting, Button, Peters Referee Shells, Multicolored, Bastian Bros., Round, 7/8 In. 90.00
Hunting, Button, Remington Autoloading, Rifle, Oval, Whitehead & Hoag, 1 In. 220.00
Hunting, Button, Shoot A Remington UMC 22 Repeater, 2 Bears, Bastian Bros., 7/8 In. ... 138.00
Hunting, Button, Shoot Peters Shells & Cartridges, Multicolored, Bastian Bros., 7/8 In. ... 92.00
Hunting, Button, Shoot Remington UMC Arrow, Nitro Club Shells, Phelps & Sons, 7/8 In. 140.00
Hunting, Button, Shoot Winchester Shotgun Shells & Shotguns, Red W Logo, 1 In. 62.00
Hunting, Button, UMC Arrow, No. 12, End Of Shotgun Shell, Brass, Early 1900s, 7/8 In. . 67.00
Hunting, Cartridge Box, Federal, Hi-Power, 16 Gauge, Flying Mallard Drake, Contents ... 35.00
Hunting, Cartridge Box, Peters, High Velocity, 20 Gauge, Flying Mallard Drake, Contents . 22.00
Hunting, Cartridge Box, Peters, Victor, Smokeless Shotgun Shells, 12 Gauge, Contents ... 20.00
Hunting, Cartridge Box, Remington Express, Long Range, 12 Gauge, Contents 24.00
Hunting, Cartridge Box, Remington UMC, Nitro Club, Loaded Shells, 24 Gauge, Full 700.00
Hunting, Cartridge Box, Winchester, Ranger W, Skeet Load, Staynless, 12 Gauge, Full ... 334.00
Hunting, Cartridge Box, Winchester, RS282, Super Speed Rifled Slugs, 20 Gauge, Full ... 16.00
Hunting, Crate, Western Super-X 12 Gauge Shotgun Shells, Wood, Nail Construction 139.00
Hunting, Crow Call, Herter's, World Famous, Walnut, Plastic Stopper, Box, 3 3/8 In. 75.00
Hunting, Display, Winchester, Gun, Ammunition, Window, Die Cut, 1914, 102 x 38 In. ... 2867.00
Hunting, Duck Call, Indian Glodo, Amber Stopper, Walnut Barrel, Herter, Box, 4 1/8 In. .. 40.00
Hunting, Duck Call, Vic Glodo, Wood, Metal Reed, Herter, 5 1/2 In. 32.00
Hunting, Envelope, National Sportsman, Blue Logo, Postmarked, 1914 .... 16.50
Hunting, Envelope, Peters, Duck Hunter, Loaded Shells Are Best, 3 3/4 x 6 1/4 In. 45.00
Hunting, Game Hook, Strap Crest, Hanging Ring, 5 Double Hooks, Iron, 17 x 14 In. 230.00
Hunting, Goose Call, Numara, Walnut Barrel, Bakelite Stopper, Herter, Box, 5 1/2 In. 87.00

Hunting, License, California, Hunters, Dogs, Birds, 1914, 2 5/8 x 4 1/4 In. 29.00
Hunting, License, Michigan, Resident, Small Game, 1931, Button, Celluloid, Bastian Bros. 117.00
Hunting, License, Michigan, Resident, Small Game, Round, 1928 . . . . 87.00
Hunting, License, Minnesota, Hunting & Trapping, 25 Cents, Paper, 1901 . . . . 65.00
Hunting, License, New York State, Citizen Resident, Special Deer, Celluloid, 1938, 2 In. . . 28.00
Hunting, License, New York State, Citizen Resident, Special Deer, Green, 1936, 1 3/4 In. . 38.00
Hunting, License, North Carolina, County Resident, 1927, Button, Celluloid, 1 3/4 In. 116.00
Hunting, License, North Carolina, County Resident, 1930-31, Button, Celluloid, 2 In. 138.00
Hunting, License, Ohio, White, Blue, Metal, 4 1/4 x 3 1/4 In. 20.00
Hunting, License, South Carolina, Quail, $3.10, Expires June 30, 1942, Button, 1 3/4 In. . . 325.00
Hunting, License, Tennessee, Hunting & Fishing, 1935-36, Button, Celluloid, 1 3/4 In. . . . 127.00
Hunting, License, Virginia County Resident, 1933-34, Button, Celluloid, 1 3/4 In. 90.00
Hunting, Loading Tool, 40-82 Cal., Winchester, Model 1894 . . . . 93.00
Hunting, Poster, Iver Johnson Revolvers, Shotguns, Woman, Fence, Dog, 23 x 31 1/2 In. . . 3152.00
Hunting, Predator Call, World Famous, Amber Stopper, Walnut Barrel, Herter, Box, 3 In. . 25.00
Hunting, Reloading Press, Lyman, Tru-Line Jr., Box 25.00
Hunting, Reloading Tool, 38-55 Cal., Winchester, 1891 Patent 165.00
Hunting, Rifle Cleaning Kit, Red, White, Contents, Ward's 30.00
Hunting, Sign, Hercules Powder Co., Infallible, Woman Walking, Gun, Dog, 15 x 10 In. . . 385.00
Hunting, Sign, Remington UMC, 3 Panels, 59 1/4 x 30 In. 1519.00
Hunting, Sign, Remington UMC, Teach Them To Shoot, Easel Back, 17 3/4 x 14 In. 565.00
Hunting, Sign, Stevens Arms Co., Self-Framed, 16 1/2 x 22 1/4 In. 790.00
Hunting, Sign, Stevens Buckhorn, 22 Rifle, Die Cut, Stand-Up, 21 7/8 x 13 3/4 In. 300.00
Hunting, Sign, Winchester, 2 Repeater Boxes, Powder Shells, 13 3/8 x 6 In. 300.00
Hunting, Skinning Board, White Pine, Winchester, 19 1/4 x 6 3/8 In. 440.00
Hunting, Turkey Call, M.L. Lynch, Model 102, Walnut, Box 20.00
Pool, Table, Brunswick, Oak, Rails, Slate, 1890, 4 x 8 Ft. 17000.00
Snowshoes, The Maine, Ash, Leather, Canvas, Rawhide, LL Bean, No. 1274, 48 x 14 In. . . 75.00
Tennis, Ball Tin, Tru-Flite Tennis Balls, Wright & Ditson, Unopened, 8 x 3 In. 20.00
Tennis, Racket, Ranger, Leather End Cap, Rawhide Strings, Winchester 365.00

STAFFORDSHIRE, England, has been a district making pottery and porcelain since the 1700s. Hundreds of kilns are still working in the area. Thousands of types of pottery and porcelain have been made in the many factories that worked and still work in the area. Some of the most famous factories have been listed separately, such as Adams, Davenport, Ridgway, Rowland & Marsellus, Royal Doulton, Royal Worcester, Spode, Wedgwood, and others. Some Staffordshire pieces are listed under categories like Fairing, Flow Blue, Mulberry, Shaving Mug, etc.

Bank, Cottage, Lattice Windows, Coleslaw Trim, Hand Painted, 5 In. 200.00
Basket, Stand, Salt Glaze, Stoneware, Reticulated, Pierced, c.1765, 9 1/2 In. 3000.00
Bowl, Bird, On Fence, Flowers, Salt Glaze, Stoneware, Enameled, c.1760, 6 1/2 In. 840.00
Bowl, Flow Blue, c.1890, 5 x 17 x 13 In. 175.00
Bowl, Lafayette At Franklin's Tomb, Blue, Enoch Wood & Sons, 9 1/2 In. 1610.00
Bowl, Lion In Pursuit Of Cow, Quadrupeds Series, Blue, John Hall, 11 In. 920.00
Bowl, The Shipwright's Arms, Outside, Republican Banner, Black Transfer, 9 1/2 In. 330.00
Bowl, Vegetable, Cover, Blue Transfer, Ship Of The Line In The Downs, 10 x 10 x 6 In. . . . 315.00
Bowl, Vegetable, Cover, Footed, Residence Of Late Richard Jordan, J.H. & Co., 6 x 13 In. . 980.00
Bowl, Vegetable, Cover, Square, Footed, Knop, Handles, Blue, 7 1/2 x 10 3/4 In. 1410.00
Bowl, Vegetable, Highlands, Catskills, Enoch Wood & Sons, 11 1/2 In. 2990.00
Box, Patch, Enamel, Oval, Butterflies, Flowers, Blue, Mirror, Early 1800s, 3 In. 245.00
Bust, George Washington, Born 1732, Died 1799, Enoch Wood, 1818, 8 1/2 In. 900.00
Chamber Pot, Blue Transfer, c.1900 . . . . 175.00
Charger, Boston State House, Blue, John Rogers & Sons, 14 3/4 In. 1035.00
Creamer, Boy & Cow, Girl & Cow, c.1860, 7 In., Pair 835.00
Creamer, Cabbage Rose, Handle, 4 1/2 In. 110.00
Cup & Saucer, Firm As Oak, Sobriety & Domestic Comfort, Green, 3 3/4 & 5 3/4 In. 175.00
Cup & Saucer, Handleless, Residence, Late Richard Jordan, J.H. & Co. 345.00
Dish, Cover, Animal, Duck On Nest, c.1840, 11 In. 520.00
Dish, Hen On Nest Cover, Marked S & S 4, White Feathers, 8 x 6 In. 475.00
Dish Set, Landing Of Lafayette, Blue, Nested, Staffordshire To Hartford, 4 Piece 3750.00
Figurine, 21st Lancers, Sailor, c.1890, 12 In. 315.00

Figurine, Admiral Nelson, Held Up By Naval Officers, Eyes Closed, 8 In. 255.00
Figurine, Boy & Pet, Girl & Pet, c.1860, 10 In., Pair 325.00
Figurine, Boy, Saying Prayers, c.1840, 4 In. 175.00
Figurine, Castle, 2 Towers, Drummer, Gilt Trim, Coleslaw Foliage, 7 1/4 In. 200.00
Figurine, Cat, 7 1/2 In., Pair 175.00
Figurine, Cat, Seated, Turned Heads, Striped Body, c.1760, 5 1/8 In. 2160.00
Figurine, Cockerels, Black Glazed, c.1880, 12 x 8 1/2 In., Pair 3200.00
Figurine, Cockerels, Standing, White Glaze, 11 3/4 In., Pair 2070.00
Figurine, Deer, Bocage, Overglaze Enamel, Rocky Base, c.1925, 6 3/4 In., Pair 880.00
Figurine, Dick Turpin On Horse, c.1850, 8 3/4 In. 380.00
Figurine, Dog, King Charles Spaniel, Seated, Black & White Spots, 6 In., Pair 590.00
Figurine, Dog, Poodle, c.1850, 6 In. 175.00
Figurine, Dog, Spaniel, Black Spotted Seated Figure, Gilt Collar, 7 1/2 In., 2 Pair 690.00
Figurine, Dog, Spaniel, Seated, Black, White, c.1850, 6 1/2 In., Pair 650.00
Figurine, Dog, Spaniel, Seated, c.1860, 12 In., Pair 475.00
Figurine, Dog, Spaniel, Seated, Copper Luster Accents, 10 In., Pair 200.00
Figurine, Dog, Spaniel, Seated, Free-Leg, c.1860, 14 In. 500.00
Figurine, Dog, Spaniel, Seated, Gilt Accents, Collars, 7 3/4 & 8 1/4 In., 2 Piece 175.00
Figurine, Dog, Spaniel, Seated, Gilt Spots, Collar With Chain, 19th Century, 13 In., Pair . . 490.00
Figurine, Dog, Spaniel, Seated, Glass Eyes, c.1880, 15 1/2 In., Pair 1395.00
Figurine, Dog, Spaniel, Seated, Red & White, Yellow Collar, 7 5/8 In., Pair 316.00
Figurine, Dog, Spaniel, Seated, Red Patches, Gold Lock, Chain, 13 In., Pair 230.00
Figurine, Dog, Spaniel, Seated, Red, White, c.1850, 7 1/2 In., Pair 595.00
Figurine, Dog, Spaniel, Seated, Red, White, c.1850, 10 1/2 In., Pair 620.00
Figurine, Dog, Spaniel, Seated, Red, White, c.1870, 8 1/2 In., Pair 545.00
Figurine, Dog, Spaniel, Silver Luster Highlights, 8 3/4 In., Pair 130.00
Figurine, Dog, Spaniel, Standing, Red Enamel, Oval Base, c.1825, 5 In., Pair 499.00
Figurine, Dog, Spaniel, White, Rust, Chain, Locket, Victorian, 8 5/8 & 8 3/4 In., Pair 695.00
Figurine, Dog, Whippet, Rabbit In Mouth, Enamel, Victorian, 10 3/4 In., Pair 410.00
Figurine, Fireman, Uniform Leaning By Water Pump, Horn, Badge On Hat, 9 In. 860.00
Figurine, Fish, c.1880, 10 In., Pair 740.00
Figurine, Garibaldi, Standing By Horse, c.1860, 9 In. 540.00
Figurine, Gin & Water, 2-Sided, Parr, c.1860, 9 In. . . . . *Illus* 350.00
Figurine, Girl, Standing, Parrot By Side, c.1860, 6 3/4 In. 115.00
Figurine, Group, Man, Woman, 13 In. 130.00
Figurine, Huntsman & Dog, c.1830, 7 In. 465.00
Figurine, Kitchener, Person, On Horseback, c.1865, 14 1/2 In. 260.00
Figurine, Lady & Goats, c.1840, 10 In. 250.00
Figurine, Lion Hunter, 16 1/2 In. 100.00
Figurine, Lion, Lamb, Molded, 19th Century, 8 3/4 In. 2470.00
Figurine, Lion, Lying Down, White, c.1900, 5 1/2 In., Pair 390.00
Figurine, Lion, Roaring, Forepaw Raised, c.1750, 6 1/4 In. 2280.00
Figurine, Madonna & Child, c.1860, 9 In. 250.00
Figurine, Man, On Horse, Orange Horse, Blue Coat, Green Cape, 14 x 10 In. 45.00
Figurine, Man, Stiff Jabot, Jacket, 2 Rows Of Buttons, c.1750, 4 1/2 In. 720.00
Figurine, Mr. & Mrs. Gladstone, 10 1/2 In. 130.00
Figurine, Multi-Storied House, Coleslaw Trim, Pierced Windows, 9 In. 316.00
Figurine, Prince With Pets, c.1850, 7 In. 340.00
Figurine, Reverend John Wesley, c.1840, 7 In. 275.00
Figurine, Robert Burns, c.1860, 5 1/2 In. 185.00
Figurine, Sankey & Moody, c.1870, 17 In., Pair 900.00
Figurine, Sheep, Standing Under Blossoming Tree, 19th Century, 5 In., Pair 380.00
Figurine, St. John, c.1860, 7 In. 145.00
Figurine, St. Mark, Multicolored, Walton, England, 7 1/8 In. 345.00
Figurine, St. Patrick, Standing, Hand To Heart, Enamel, Gilt, c.1860, 11 3/4 In. 205.00
Figurine, Topsy & Eva, c.1860, 5 1/4 In. 489.00
Figurine, Uncle Tom With Little Girl, 10 In. 220.00
Figurine, Victoria & Albert, c.1850, 9 1/2 In. 175.00
Figurine, Victoria, c.1865, 11 1/2 In. 230.00
Figurine, Virgin Mary & Jesus, c.1860, 14 In. 415.00
Figurine, Woman, Child Reading, Seated In Chair, 7 1/4 In. 80.00
Figurine, Woman, Mobcap, Revealing Petticoat, c.1750, 4 1/2 In. 720.00
Figurine, Woman, Seated, Playing Instrument, Dog, Bocage Type, c.1825, 6 3/4 In. 705.00

Staffordshire,
Figurine, Gin &
Water, 2-Sided,
Parr, c.1860,
9 In.

Staffordshire, Plate,
Mt. Vernon, Home Of
Washington, Red Transfer, 10 In.

Stangl, Fruit, Cup

Figurine, Zebra, Rein, 8 1/2 In., Pair	1265.00
Figurine, Zhong-Li Quan, Robed, Topknot, c.1750, 7 1/4 In.	9000.00
Flask, Salt Glaze, Square, Triangular Dot & Star Diaperwork, c.1750, 5 3/8 In.	1440.00
Flowerpot, Stand, Yellow Ground, Flower & Leaf Border, 4 1/4 In.	1035.00
Font, Holy Water, Angel Embracing 2 Girls, 14 1/4 In.	520.00
Goblet, Gilt, Eagle & Shield, Liberty Portrait, Stars, Beaded Border, 4 1/2 In.	230.00
Group, 2 Children, Naked, Tree Stump, Salt Glaze, Stoneware, c.1750, 3 1/2 In.	1200.00
Group, Children & Goat, Staffordshire, c.1860, 8 In.	230.00
Group, Man & Woman, Man Holds Basket, Woman Holds Umbrella, 7 In.	200.00
Group, Musician With Violin & Spaniel, 11 1/2 In.	60.00
Group, Prodigal's Return, Gilt Highlights, Enamel, Victorian, c.1880, 13 In.	355.00
Group, Scottish Couple, Feathered Caps, Green & Orange Tartan, 9 1/4 In.	115.00
Group, Tenderness, Male & Female, Lamb, Garland, Titled, c.1825, 6 In.	355.00
Group, Turkish Soldiers, Victorian, c.1860, 9 In.	465.00
Group, Uncle Tom & Eva, Oval Base, 8 1/4 In.	270.00
Group, Vicar & Moses, Creamware, 9 3/4 In.	300.00
Group, Victorian Gardening, Man, Woman, Wearing Hats, c.1860, 9 In.	175.00
Inkstand, Sheep & Tree Trunk, 19th Century	138.00
Inkwell, Figural, Whippet Shape, Spill Vase, Early 20th Century, 7 In., Pair	210.00
Inkwell, Girl, Puppy On Knee, c.1850, 6 1/2 In.	200.00
Jug, Chinoiserie Figure, Salt Glaze, Stoneware, Enameled, Baluster, c.1760, 7 In.	5400.00
Jug, Hearty Goodfellow, Man, Standing, Holding Jug & Pipe, c.1835, 10 1/2 In.	865.00
Jug, Portrait, Lafayette & Washington, Republicans, Black Transfer, 5 3/4 In.	575.00
Mug, Benjamin Franklin, Polychrome Transfer, American Eagles, Child's	405.00
Mug, Dr. Franklin's Poor Richard, Child's Motto, Black Transfer, 2 3/4 In.	170.00
Mug, Lafayette & Washington, Yellow Ground, Black Transfer, Child's, 2 1/2 In.	748.00
Mug, Love, Liberty, School, Transfer, Pearlware, Child's, 2 3/4 In.	690.00
Mug, Residence Of Late Richard Jordan, Flower Border, J.H. & Co., 7 3/4 In.	865.00
Mug, Tavern Scenes, Hand Painted Enamel, Full Bodied-Frog Inside, 4 3/4 In.	145.00
Mug, Washington, Patriot Of America, Purple Transfer, Child's, 2 1/4 In.	575.00
Pastille Burner, Cottage, Brick, Moss, Flowers, Rear Drawer, c.1820, 4 1/2 In.	660.00
Pitcher, Almshouse, Boston, Esplanade, Castle Garden, Stevenson, Williams, 9 In.	1610.00
Pitcher, Lord Nelson, Naval Uniform, Holding Horn, Cannon, Anchor, Rope, 11 In.	490.00
Pitcher, Swiss Cottage, Blue Transfer, J. & W. Pratt, 12 In.	58.00
Pitcher, Welcome Lafayette, Nation's Guest, James & Ralph Clews, 7 1/2 In.	3165.00
Pitcher & Basin, Lafayette At Franklin's Tomb, Flowers, Enoch Wood, 10 In.	1410.00
Plate, 1st Amendment, Blue Transfer, American Eagles, Scalloped Edge, 6 7/8 In.	259.00
Plate, Bagpiper, Fence, Horse, Salt Glaze, Stoneware, Enameled, c.1760, 9 1/4 In.	4800.00
Plate, Battery, N.Y., Blue, Ralph Stevenson & Williams, 7 In.	750.00
Plate, Beauties Of America, Blue Transfer, 9 7/8 In.	129.00
Plate, Boston Hospital, Blue Transfer, 9 1/4 In.	325.00
Plate, City Hall, New York, Blue, Joseph Stubbs, 6 3/4 In.	115.00
Plate, City Of Albany, Blue Transfer, c.1825, 10 In.	440.00
Plate, City Of Albany, N.Y., Shell Border, Enoch Wood & Sons, 10 1/4 In.	690.00
Plate, Commodore MacDonnough's Victory, Blue Transfer, Enoch Wood & Sons, 9 In.	560.00
Plate, Eagle Crest, Flowers, Salt Glaze, Enameled, c.1765, 13 1/4 In.	2160.00
Plate, Fair Mount, Near Philadelphia, Blue Transfer, J. Stubbs, Early 1800s, 10 In.	235.00 to 345.00

Plate, Falls Of Mont Morenci, Blue Transfer, c.1820, 9 In. 325.00
Plate, Ferry Bridge, River Schuylkill, Blue Transfer, J. Stubbs, Early 1800s, 8 3/4 In. 323.00
Plate, Gilpin's Mills, Brandywine, Shell Border, Enoch Wood & Sons, 9 1/4 In. 690.00
Plate, Hoboken In New Jersey, Blue, Joseph Stubbs, 7 1/4 In. . . . . .275.00 to 575.00
Plate, Hunting Scene, Scroll & Flower Border, Blue, Enoch Wood & Sons, 10 In. 248.00
Plate, Jim Along Josey, Flower Border, England, 1840-60, Child's, 7 1/4 In. 495.00
Plate, Landing Of Lafayette, Blue Transfer, Early 1900s, 9 In. 295.00
Plate, Leaves, Acorns, Salt Glaze, Leaf Molded, Lobed Rim, c.1760, 7 3/4 In. 1080.00
Plate, Mt. Vernon, Home Of Washington, Red Transfer, 10 In. *Illus*   50.00
Plate, Musician, Woman, Salt Glaze, Stoneware, Enamel, 8-Sided, c.1760, 8 1/2 In. 2760.00
Plate, Nahant Hotel, Near Boston, Blue, Joseph Stubbs, 8 3/4 In. 575.00
Plate, Park Theatre, N.Y., Acorn & Oak Leaves Border, Stevenson & Williams, 10 In. 230.00
Plate, Peony, Prunus Branches, Salt Glazed, Stoneware, Enameled, c.1765, 9 In. 1440.00
Plate, Plant, Butterfly, Salt Glaze, Stoneware, Enameled, Octagonal, c.1760, 8 1/2 In. 2700.00
Plate, Quadrupeds Series, Otter, Blue, John Hall, 8 3/4 In. 575.00
Plate, Quadrupeds Series, Running Antelope, Blue, John Hall, 8 In. 520.00
Plate, Salt Glazed, Stoneware, Leaf Molded, c.1760, 9 1/2 In. 1440.00
Plate, Seal Of Rhode Island, Blue Transfer, c.1829, 9 1/2 In. 529.00
Plate, Seal Of The United States, 13 Stars, Blue Shell Edge, 6 3/8 In. 575.00
Plate, Seal Of The United States, 15 Stars, Green Shell Edge, 8 In. 920.00
Plate, Shannondale Springs, Virginia, Red Transfer, Eagle & Cornucopia Mark, 8 In. 65.00
Plate, Soup, Chinese Musician, Salt Glaze, Stoneware, Enameled, c.1760, 9 1/2 In. 4200.00
Plate, Soup, Flower Vases, Salt Glaze, Stoneware, Enameled, c.1760, 9 1/4 In. 2400.00
Plate, Soup, Pine Orchard House, Catskills, Shell Border, Enoch Wood, 10 1/4 In. 575.00
Plate, Soup, The States, Blue Transfer, Early 1900s, 10 1/2 In. 382.00
Plate, Table Rock Niagara, Blue Transfer, c.1820, 10 In. 645.00
Plate, Toddy, Lafayette & Washington, Red Transfer, Import Mark, 4 5/8 In. 1495.00
Plate, Union Line, Blue Transfer, c.1825, 10 In. 705.00
Plate, Woodlands Near Phila., Blue Transfer, J. Stubbs, Early 1800s, 6 3/4 In. 225.00
Platter, 4 Cartouches, Salt Glaze, Stoneware, Enameled, Oval, c.1760, 16 1/2 In. 2700.00
Platter, Boston State House, Blue, John Rogers & Son, 18 3/4 In. 1035.00
Platter, Christianburg, Danish Settlement, Africa, Enoch Wood & Sons, 18 1/2 In. 4315.00
Platter, Couple, Garden, Salt Glaze, Stoneware, Enameled, Oval, c.1760, 12 1/4 In. 4500.00
Platter, Fair Mount Near Philadelphia, Blue, Joseph Stubbs, 20 3/4 In. 1265.00
Platter, Niagara Falls, American Side, Blue, Enoch Wood & Sons, 14 3/4 In. 3335.00
Platter, Quadrupeds Series, Moose & Hunters, Blue, John Hall, 15 In. 1955.00
Platter, Quadrupeds Series, Rhinoceros, Ship, Blue, John Hall, 18 In. 1380.00
Platter, Residence, Late Richard Jordan, Flowers, Transfer, J.H. & Co., 13 x 16 In. 750.00
Platter, Select Views, Church Of St. Charles, Ironstone, Ralph Hall, 14 3/4 x 19 In. 2300.00
Platter, Sheltered Peasants, Dark Blue Transfer, c.1835 . . . .   1095.00
Platter, Texian Campaigne Series, Battle Scene, Rose, Anthony Shaw, 13 1/4 In. 1610.00
Platter, Texian Campaigne Series, Battle Scene, Rose, Anthony Shaw, 15 In. 3200.00
Platter Set, Landing Of Lafayette, Blue, Nested, Staffordshire To Hartford, 4 Piece 6750.00
Sauceboat, Quadrupeds Series, Fox, Blue, John Hall, 7 1/4 In. 460.00
Scent Burner, Landscaped Castle Shape Base, Late 19th Century, 5 x 6 In. 105.00
Spill Holder, 2 Fawns At Stream, 5 In. 127.00
Spill Vase, Castle, 4 Towers, Stepped Base, c.1830, 5 In. 285.00
Spill Vase, Deer, Opposing, Running, Hounds, Tree Stump, 11 x 9 In., Pair 315.00
Spill Vase, Dog, Spaniel, Seated, c.1860, 13 In., Pair 650.00
Spill Vase, Dog, Spaniel, Seated, c.1870, 13 In., Pair 725.00
Spill Vase, Lion, Standing, Facing Left, c.1850, 7 1/2 In. 415.00
Spill Vase, Lion, Standing, Facing Right, c.1850, 7 1/2 In. 865.00
Spill Vase, Sheep, c.1880, 5 1/2 In., Pair 450.00
Table, Dolphin Shape, T.C. Brown, Moore & Co., 30 x 15 In. 39850.00
Teapot, Cover, Basket Work, c.1775, 4 1/2 In. 940.00
Teapot, Cover, Boston Harbor, Blue, John Rogers & Son, 7 1/2 In. 1495.00
Teapot, Cover, Flowers, Dolphins, Salt Glaze, Pecten Shell, Footed, c.1755, 4 In. 2160.00
Teapot, Cover, Salt Glaze, Stoneware, Enameled, Globular, c.1760, 3 3/4 In. 1200.00
Teapot, Cover, White, Lozenge Shape, Paneled Sides, Serpent, 6 In. 1175.00
Teapot, Cover, White, Octagonal, Arched Panels, Nude Figures, 3 3/4 In. 1410.00
Teapot, Multicolored Panels Of Urns & Bellflowers, 1795, 6 In. 2530.00
Teapot, Ye Old Cottage, Figural Cottage, Price Bros. 90.00
Toby Jugs are listed in their own category.

Toddy Plate, Residence Of Late Richard Jordan, Flower Border, J.H. & Co., 5 3/4 In.	290.00
Toddy Plate, Thatched Cottage, Hill, Castle Ruins, Sepia, Butterfly Border, 5 In.	88.00
Tureen, Belleville On The Passaic River, Blue, Enoch Wood & Sons, c.1825	14000.00
Tureen, Cover, Flowers, Transferware, Blue, White, Ford & Sons, Burslem, 15 In.	470.00
Tureen, Residence Of Late Richard Jordan, Flower Border, J.H. & Co., 5 3/4 In.	750.00
Tureen, Underplate, Passaic Falls, New Jersey, E. Wood & Sons, c.1835, 6 3/8 x 8 In.	1410.00
Wall Pocket, Cornucopia, Salt Glazed, Stoneware, c.1765, 7 3/4 In., Pair	5100.00
Wall Pocket, Flora Portrait, Salt Glazed, Stoneware, c.1765, 11 3/4 In., Pair	5100.00
Waste Bowl, Blue Transfer, Flowers, 2 Decorated Urns, 6 1/4 x 3 1/4 In.	290.00
Watch Holder, Tree, Flowers, Children, Plinth Base, c.1830, 9 1/2 In.	800.00

STANGL Pottery traces its history back to the Fulper Pottery of New Jersey. In 1910, Johann Martin Stangl started working at Fulper. He left to work at Haeger Pottery from 1915 to 1920. Stangl returned to Fulper Pottery in 1920, became president in 1926, and changed the company name to Stangl Pottery in 1929. Stangl acquired the firm in 1930. The pottery is known for dinnerware and a line of bird figurines. Martin Stangl died in 1972, and the pottery was sold to Frank Wheaton, Jr., of Wheaton Industries. Production continued until 1978, when Pfaltzgraff Pottery purchased the right to the Stangl trademark, and the remaining inventory was liquidated. A single bird figurine is identified by a number. Figurines made up of two birds are identified by a number followed by the letter "D" indicating "Double."

Antigua, Tidbit, Center Handle, 10 In.	20.00
Antique Gold, Ashtray, Square, 9 In.	18.00
Apple Delight, Bowl, Vegetable, Oval, Divided, 10 1/2 In.	20.00
Bird, Cardinal, No. 3444, Red, 7 In.	80.00
Bird, Cerulean Warbler, No. 3456, 4 1/4 In.	95.00
Bird, Chickadee, Triple, No. 3581	175.00
Bird, Fish Hawk, No. 3459, 9 1/2 In.	5656.00
Bird, Flying Duck, No. 3443, 9 In.	195.00
Bird, Goldfinch, Quadruple, No. 3635	230.00
Bird, Hen Pheasant, No. 3491, 11 In., Pair	259.00
Bird, Painted Bunting, No. 3452, 5 In.	125.00
Bird, Rooster, No. 3445, 9 In.	165.00
Bird, White Headed Pigeon, Double, No. 3518D	575.00
Bird, White Wing Crossbill, Double, No. 3754D, 9 x 8 In. .265.00 to 285.00
Bird, Wren, Double, No. 3401D, 6 In.	500.00
Bird, Yellow Warbler, No. 3447, 5 In.	80.00
Bittersweet, Plate, 8 In.	12.00
Bittersweet, Tidbit, 10 In.	45.00
Black Gold, Ashtray, 2 Sections, 4 x 6 In.	19.00
Black Gold, Bowl, Flower Shape, 7 In.	25.00
Blueberry, Cup & Saucer	16.00
Blueberry, Plate, 8 In.	12.00
Caughley, Bowl, Vegetable, Green, 8 In.	25.00
Clover, Plate, Bread & Butter, 5 In.	18.00
Country Garden, Bowl, Vegetable, 8 In.	25.00
Country Garden, Cup & Saucer . . . . .18.00 to 24.00
Country Garden, Snack Set, Cup, 10-In. Plate, 2 Piece	20.00
Fluted, Teapot	60.00
Fruit, Bowl, 11 1/4 In.	24.00
Fruit, Cup . . . . *Illus*	10.00
Fruit, Saucer	13.00
Fruit & Flowers, Plate, 6 In.	25.00
Garden Flower, Eggcup, 3 1/4 In.	20.00
Garland, Cup & Saucer	12.50
Golden Glo, Bowl, Square, Pink & Mottled Gold, 2 Gold Tab Handles, 6 3/8 In.	19.00
Golden Harvest, Bowl, Vegetable, 8 In.	30.00
Golden Harvest, Chop Plate, 12 In.	30.00
Golden Harvest, Plate, Bread & Butter, 6 1/4 In.	10.00
Golden Harvest, Platter, 13 3/4 In.	25.00
Granada Gold, Ashtray, 3-Sided, 3 Pairs Of Indentations	19.00

Granada Gold, Bowl, Centerpiece, Fruit, 4 x 9 1/2 In.	25.00
Granada Gold, Bowl, Flower, 8 1/2 In.	22.00
Granada Gold, Cigarette Lighter, Concave Sides, 4 In.	20.00
Granada Gold, Tidbit, 2 Tiers, Raised Flowers & Hearts, Center Handle, 6 & 10-In. Trays	25.00
Granada Gold, Vase, Concave Sides, 2 Squared Handles, 3 In.	23.00
Grape, Mug, 4 In.	6.00
Green Lustre, Ashtray, 2 3/4 x 10 In.	30.00
Green Lustre, Dish, Pear Shape, 8 In.	18.00
Indian Summer, Pitcher, White Earth, 5 In.	19.00
Jewelled, Christmas Tree, Plate, 8 In.	70.00
Kumquat, Plate, Salad, 8 In.	20.00
Magnolia, Bowl, Cereal, 6 In.	25.00
Magnolia, Chop Plate, 14 1/2 In.	37.00
Magnolia, Cup & Saucer	24.00
Orchard Song, Gravy Boat Liner	25.00
Orchard Song, Sugar & Creamer	25.00
Paisley, Chop Plate, 12 1/2 In.	25.00
Sculptured Fruit, Mug, 4 In.	25.00
Sculptured Fruit, Plate, Dinner, 10 In.	18.00
Sculptured Fruit, Plate, Salad, 8 In.	14.00
Sculptured Fruit, Soup, Dish, 7 3/4 In.	16.00
Terra Rose, Ashtray, Flower, Lavender, Blue, Yellow Center, 5 1/2 In., Pair	20.00
Thistle, Plate, 8 In.	18.00
Thistle, Plate, Dinner, 10 In.	22.00
Thistle, Tidbit, 10 In.	48.00
Town & Country, Plate, Salad, Blue, 8 In.	22.00
Town & Country, Salt & Pepper, Handle, 4 In.	19.00
Town & Country, Spoon Rest, Blue, 8 1/4 In.	22.00
Vase, Light Green, Gold Swirl, Bulbous Bottom, Flared Neck, Scalloped Edge, 7 1/2 In.	20.00
White Dogwood, Plate, Bread & Butter, 6 In.	6.00
Wild Rose, Bowl, Vegetable, Oval, Divided, 10 1/2 x 7 In.	35.00
Wild Rose, Plate, Dinner, 10 In.	9.00
Yellow Tulip, Bowl, Vegetable, 8 In.	20.00
Yellow Tulip, Sugar, Cover	25.00

STAR TREK AND STAR WARS collectibles are included here. The

original television series *Star Trek* ran from 1966 through 1969. The
series spawned an animated series, three sequels, and a prequel, which
is still in production. The first Star Trek movie was released in 1979
and 8 others followed, the most recent in 2002. The movie *Star Wars*
opened in 1977. Sequels were released in 1980 and 1983, prequels in
1999 and 2002, and 2005. Other science fiction and fantasy collectibles can be found under Batman, Buck Rogers, Captain Marvel,
Flash Gordon, Superman, Movie, and Toy.

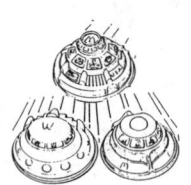

Bowl, Melmac, 1970s	14.00
Communicator, Inter-Space, 2 Handsets, Cord, Lone Star, England, Box, 1974, 6 x 9 In.	75.00
Figure, Keeper, Star Trek Aliens, Mego, On Card, 1975, 8 In.	180.00
Figure, Klingon, Paramount, Mego, On Card, 1975, 8 In.	200.00
Figure, Romulan, Star Trek Alien, Paramount, Mego, On Card, 1976, 8 In.	1575.00
Flashlight Ray Gun, Plastic, Battery Operated, Larami Corp., 1968, 6 In.	165.00
Game, Board, Star Fleet, McDonald's Meal Premium, 1979	35.00
Model Kit, USS Enterprise, Model S951, Paramount, AMT, Box, 1968, 8 1/2 x 10 In.	25.00
Toy, USS Enterprise, Motion Picture, Die Cast Metal, Card No. 803, Dinky, 1979, 4 In.	20.00
STAR WARS, Clock, 3-D, Electric, Quartz, Plastic, Battery, Bradley Time, Box, c.1982, 7 x 8 In.	65.00
Figure, Boba Fett, Empire Strikes Back, 41-Back Card, Kenner, c.1980, 3 3/4 In.	265.00
Figure, C-3PO, Kenner, Box, 1979, 12 In.	253.00
Figure, Emperor, Return Of Jedi, Lucasfilm, 79-Back Card, Kenner, 1984, 3 3/4 In.	48.00
Figure, Jawa, Accessories, 20th Century Fox, Kenner, Box, 1977, 8 In.	265.00
Figure, Power Droid, Return Of Jedi, Lucasfilm, 65-Back Card, Kenner, c.1983, 2 1/2 In.	95.00
Figure, R2-D2, Kenner, Box, 1979, 7 1/2 In.	400.00
Figure, Romba, Power Of Force, Coin, Blister Card, Kenner, 1985, 2 5/8 In.	50.00
Figure, Sand People, 20th Century Fox, 12-Back Card, Kenner, 3 3/4 In.	250.00
Figure, Urgah Lady Gorneesh, Ewoks, TV Series, On Card, Coin, Kenner, 1985, 3 1/4 In.	30.00

Figure, Warok, Power Of Force, Coin, Blister Card, Kenner, 1985, 2 5/8 In. 50.00
Game, Adventures Of R2-D2, Unopened, Kenner, Box, 1977, 8 1/2 x 16 1/2 In. 69.00
Game, Battle At Sarlacc's Pit, Parker Brothers, Box, 1983, 12 1/4 x 12 1/4 In. 40.00
Lunch Box, Empire Strikes Back, Spaceship, King Seeley Thermos Co., 1983 .... 40.00
Lunch Box, Empire Strikes Back, Swamp, No Thermos, King Seeley Thermos Co., 1980 .. 44.00
Lunch Box, Return Of Jedi, Jabba Hut, King Seeley Thermos Co., 1983, 7 x 8 1/2 In. .60.00 to 90.00
Playset, Death Star Space Station, Kenner, 1979, 22 x 14 x 6 In. 290.00
Playset, Droid Factory, Plastic, 20th Century Fox, Kenner, Box, 1979, 11 x 13 1/2 In. 135.00
Playset, Imperial Attack Base, Lucasfilm, Kenner, Box, 1980, 10 1/4 x 18 In. 125.00
Poster, Movie, Style A, 1st Printing, 20th Century Fox, 1 Sheet, 1977, 41 x 27 In. 515.00
Toy, Millennium Falcon, Die Cast, Metal, Plastic, Kenner, Box, 1977, 8 1/2 x 10 1/2 In. ... 85.00
Toy, Rebel Armored Snow Speeder, Empire Strikes Back, Kenner, Box, 1980, 11 x 13 In. ... 115.00
Toy, X-Wing Fighter, Die Cast, Metal, Plastic, Kenner, On Card, 1978, 4 1/2 In. 50.00

STEINS have been used by beer and ale drinkers for over 500 years.
They have been made of ivory, porcelain, stoneware, faience, silver,
pewter, wood, or glass in sizes up to nine gallons. Although some were
made by Mettlach, Meissen, Capo-di-Monte, and other famous factories, most were made by less important German potteries. The words
Geschutz or *Musterschutz* on a stein are the German words for
patented or *registered design,* not company names. Steins are still
being made in the old styles. Lithophane steins may be found in the
Lithophane category.

Blown Glass, Amber, Prunts, Enameled Barmaid Scene, Pewter Lid, 1 Liter 255.00
Blown Glass, Ribbed, White Enameled Mary Gregory Girl, Inlaid Lid, 1/2 Liter 130.00
Brewery, Augustinerbrau Munchen, Stoneware, Etched, Pewter Lid, 2/5 Liter 165.00
Brewery, Burgerliches Brauhaus Munchen, Pottery, Etched, Pewter Lid, 2/5 Liter 220.00
Brewery, Burgerliches Brauhaus Munchen, Stoneware, Pewter Lid, 1/2 Liter 105.00
Brewery, Domestic Beer Hotel Kaiserhof, Chicago, Glass, Porcelain Inlaid Lid, 1/2 Liter .. 250.00
Brewery, Eberlbrau Munchen, Glass, Pressed, Pewter Lid, Boar Thumblift, 1/2 Liter 145.00
Brewery, Edelweiss-Hofbrau 10 Cents, Glass, Porcelain Inlaid Lid, 1/2 Liter 235.00
Brewery, Gerevisiam Bibunt Homines, Glass, Relief, Pewter Lid, 1/2 Liter 180.00
Brewery, Independent Brewing Association Prima, Glass, Porcelain Inlaid Lid, 1/2 Liter .. 80.00
Brewery, Kloster-Brau Munchen, Pottery, Engraved, Pewter Lid, 2/5 Liter 220.00
Brewery, Kochelbrau, Ernst Erich, Munchen, Transfer, Enamel, Pewter Lid, 1/2 Liter 315.00
Brewery, Lowenbrau Munchen, Pottery, Pewter Lid, Transfer, Enameled, 1/2 Liter 110.00
Brewery, Munchener Burgerbrau, Transfer, Enameled, Pewter Lid, 1 Liter 290.00
Brewery, Munchener Kindl Keller, Stoneware, Pewter Lid, 1 Liter 315.00
Brewery, Paulaner Thomasbrau Muchen, Stoneware, Transfer, Pewter Lid, 1/2 Liter 210.00
Brewery, Pilsen Brewing Company, Olympia, Glass, Porcelain Inlaid Lid, 1/2 Liter 115.00
Brewery, Pschorr-Brau Munchen, Pottery, Transfer, Pewter Lid, 1/2 Liter ....145.00 to 240.00
Brewery, Spaten, Stoneware, Etched, Schultzmarke, Pewter Lid, 1 Liter 240.00
Character, Alligator, Porcelain, Inlaid Lid, E. Bohne & Sohne, 1/2 Liter 725.00
Character, Alpine Man, Porcelain, Inlaid Lid, 1/2 Liter 605.00
Character, Alpine Man, Porcelain, Porcelain Lid, Schierholz, 1/2 Liter 485.00
Character, Beehive, Pottery, Inlaid Lid, Reinhold Merkelbach, 1/2 Liter 350.00
Character, Bismarck, Porcelain, Lid, c.1960, 1/2 Liter 265.00
Character, Black Student, Majolica Glazed, Inlaid Lid, 1/2 Liter 210.00
Character, Bowling Pin, Porcelain, Lid, Bowling Ball Thumblift, Schierholz, 1/2 Liter 300.00
Character, Bowling Pin, Pottery, Inlaid Lid, 1/2 Liter 145.00
Character, Caroline, Porcelain, Lid, Schierholz, 1/2 Liter 605.00
Character, Cat Holding Fish, Porcelain, Inlaid Lid, 1/2 Liter 525.00
Character, Corona Jaguar, Limited Edition, 1/2 Liter 135.00
Character, Corona Parrot, Lid, Limited Edition, 1/2 Liter 75.00
Character, Corona Toucan, Limited Edition, 1/2 Liter 90.00
Character, Devil & Skull, Porcelain, Inlaid Lid, E. Bohne & Sohne, 1/4 Liter .....530.00 to 645.00
Character, Devil, Porcelain, Inlaid Lid, E. Bohne & Sohne, 1/2 Liter 645.00
Character, Drunken Monkey, Porcelain, Inlaid, Schierholz, 1/2 Liter ....360.00 to 550.00
Character, Father Jahn, Porcelain, Schierholz, 1 Liter 1600.00
Character, Fireman, Stoneware, Inlaid Lid, 1/2 Liter 250.00
Character, Frog, Porcelain, Inlaid Lid, E. Bohne & Sohne, 1/2 Liter 1690.00
Character, Hanswurst, Stoneware, Inlaid Lid, F. Ringer, 1/4 Liter, 6 In. 545.00
Character, High Wheel Bicycle, Porcelain, Lithophane, Inlaid Lid, Schierholz, 1/2 Liter .. 360.00

Character, Hobo, Pottery, Inlaid Lid, 1/2 Liter 375.00
Character, Hops Lady, Porcelain, Lid, Schierholz, 1/2 Liter . . . . .489.00 to 690.00
Character, Hot Air Balloon, Graf Zeppelin, Orville Wright, Pottery, Lid, 1 Liter 635.00
Character, Hot Air Balloon, Pottery, Pottery Lid, 3/4 Liter 350.00
Character, Hunter Rabbit, Porcelain, Inlaid Lid, 1/2 Liter 205.00
Character, Judge, Porcelain, Porcelain Lid, Schierholz, 1/2 Liter 780.00
Character, Lantern, Glass, Metal Lid, 1 Liter 175.00
Character, Man, Falling Off Bicycle, Porcelain, Inlaid Lid, Schierholz, 1/2 Liter 345.00
Character, Man, Holding Cat, Pottery, Inlaid Lid, Diesinger, No. 762, 1/2 Liter 936.00
Character, Martin Luther, Pottery Inlaid Lid, 1/2 Liter 395.00
Character, Military Frog, Pottery, Inlaid Lid, Dumler & Breiden, 1/2 Liter 485.00
Character, Monk, Goebel, Pewter Lid, Full Bee, c.1950, 1 Liter 300.00
Character, Monk, Inlaid Lid, Stoneware, No. 194, 1/4 Liter 145.00
Character, Monk, Stoneware, Inlaid Lid, 1/2 Liter 180.00
Character, Monkey, Pottery, Inlaid Lid, Diesinger, 1/2 Liter 790.00
Character, Munich Child On Barrel, Porcelain, Inlaid Lid, Schierholz, 1/2 Liter 420.00
Character, Munich Child, Lithophane, Transfer, Porcelain, Pewter Lid, 1/2 Liter 220.00
Character, Munich Child, Porcelain, Porcelain Lid, 1/2 Liter 240.00
Character, Munich Child, Pottery, Inlaid Lid, J. Reinemann, Munchen, 4 1/2 In., 1/8 Liter .   120.00
Character, Munich Child, Pottery, Inlaid Lid, Marked, J. Reinemann, 1/2 Liter 210.00
Character, Munich Child, Pottery, Pottery Lid, 1/8 Liter, 5 1/4 In.   185.00
Character, Munich Child, Transfer, Enameled, Pottery, Martin Pauson, 1/4 Liter, 5 1/4 In. .   195.00
Character, Munich Child, Transfer, Enameled, Pottery, Pewter Lid, 1/8 Liter, 4 3/4 In. 209.00
Character, Nun, Porcelain, Inlaid, Lid, 1/2 Liter 215.00
Character, Nurnberg Tower, Stoneware, Pewter Lid, 1/2 Liter 195.00
Character, Nurnberger Trichter, Porcelain, Funnel, Inlaid Lid, Schierholz, 1/2 Liter 325.00
Character, Old Woman, Newspaper, Porcelain, Lid, Schierholz, 1/2 Liter . . . . . . .1875.00 to 4490.00
Character, Old Woman, With Radishes, Porcelain, Porcelain Lid, Schierholz, 1/2 Liter 3900.00
Character, Owl, Pottery, Gerz No. 444, Inlaid Lid, 1/2 Liter 405.00
Character, Owl, Stoneware, Inlaid Lid, 1/2 Liter . . . . .230.00 to 360.00
Character, Pig, Singing, Porcelain, Inlaid Lid, Schierholz, 1/2 Liter 305.00
Character, Potato Head, Porcelain, Porcelain Lid, Schierholz, 1/2 Liter . . . . ⌐. 1075.00
Character, Rabbit, Porcelain, Schierholz, 1/2 Liter 2620.00
Character, Rich Man, Pottery, Inlaid Lid, No. 722, 1/2 Liter 218.00
Character, Scandinavian Woman, Pottery, Inlaid Lid, 1/2 Liter 1090.00
Character, Singing Pig, Porcelain, Inlaid Lid, Schierholz, 1/2 Liter 255.00
Character, Skull On Book, Porcelain, Inlaid Lid, E. Bohne & Sohne, 1/2 Liter 518.00
Character, Skull On Book, Pottery, Inlaid Lid, 1/2 Liter . . . . .120.00 to 185.00
Character, Skull, Porcelain, Inlaid Lid, E. Bohne & Sohne, 1/2 Liter 380.00
Character, Skull, Porcelain, Inlaid Lid, E. Bohne & Sohne, 1/3 Liter 345.00
Character, Snake Wrapped Around Apple, Monkey Lid, E. Bohne & Sohne, 1/2 Liter 1200.00
Character, Student Fox, Porcelain, Porcelain Inlaid Lid, 1/2 Liter 470.00
Character, Student Fox, Pottery, Inlaid Lid, 1/2 Liter 265.00
Character, Tyrolean Woman, Porcelain, Lid, M. Pauson, Munchen 1895, 1/2 Liter 3380.00
Character, Wilhelm I, Porcelain, Porcelain Lid, Schierholz, 1/2 Liter 1076.00
Clover, Pottery, Relief, Inlaid Lid, Hauber & Reuther, No. 611, 1/2 Liter 230.00
Faience, Building, Multicolored, Pewter Base Ring, Lid, Austria, c.1780, 1/2 Liter, 7 3/4 In.   489.00
Faience, Man Playing Flute, Hand Painted, Pewter Lid, c.1920, 1/2 Liter 90.00
Glass, Amber, Blown, White Enameled Cherub, Pewter Lid, 1/3 Liter 242.00
Glass, Amber, Cut Circle & Star, Pewter Base Ring & Lid, 1/2 Liter 245.00
Glass, Amber, Ribbed, Cast Brass Mounts, Torso On Handle, 10 In., 1/2 Liter 755.00
Glass, Blown, Blue, Horizontal Ribbing, Pewter Overlay, Pewter Lid, 14 In. 368.00
Glass, Blown, Clear, Engraved Deer In Forest, Engraved Dog, Inlaid Lid, c.1850, 1/2 Liter .   290.00
Glass, Blown, Clear, Flowers, Wedding Design, Hand Painted, Pewter Lid, c.1835, 1 Liter .   489.00
Glass, Blown, Clear, Fluted, Engraved Deer, Pewter Lid, 1/2 Liter 240.00
Glass, Blown, Clear, Fluted, Engraved Stag & Deer, Prism Inlaid Lid, 1/2 Liter 266.00
Glass, Blown, Clear, Lohengrin Scene, Enamel, Pewter Lid, 1 1/2 Liter 290.00
Glass, Blown, Clear, Man, Woman Dancing, Porcelain, Silver Inlaid Lid, 1/2 Liter 250.00
Glass, Blown, Clear, Nude Woman In Bed, Porcelain Inlaid Lid, 1/4 Liter 480.00
Glass, Blown, Cobalt Blue, Enameled Flower, Gold Verse, Red Glass Inlaid Lid, 1/3 Liter .   125.00
Glass, Blown, Cobalt Blue, Flowers, Enameled, Viel Gluck, Pewter Lid, c.1870, 1 Liter . . .   460.00
Glass, Blown, Cobalt Blue, Pewter Lid, Closed Hinge, c.1850, 2 1/4 In. 305.00
Glass, Blown, Cut, Gambrinus Scene, Hand Painted, Porcelain, Inlaid Lid, 1/2 Liter 170.00

Glass, Blown, Green Glass Swirl, Heidelberg Pewter Lid, Perkeo Thumblift, 2/5 Liter	110.00
Glass, Blown, Green, Enameled Man, Sword, Shield, Music Box, Inlaid Lid, 1/2 Liter	725.00
Glass, Blown, Milk, Enamel, Birds, Pewter Lid, Aus Freundschaft, c.1840, 1/2 Liter	360.00
Glass, Blown, Niagara Falls, Enameled Scenes, Applied Prunts, Pewter Lid, 1/2 Liter	240.00
Glass, Blown, Ribbed, Green, Enameled Flowers, Gold, Inlaid Lid, 1/3 Liter	110.00
Glass, Blown, Wasserfall In Harzburg, Engraved, Glass Inlaid Lid, 1/8 Liter, 3 3/4 In.	220.00
Glass, Blue, Pewter Lid, c.1850, 1/8 Liter, 3 3/4 In.	270.00
Glass, Boy With Ball, Pink Glass Inlaid Lid, 1/8 Liter, 4 3/4 In.	240.00
Glass, Clear, Card, Enameled, Crackle Style Surface, Inlaid Lid, 1/2 Liter	725.00
Glass, Clear, Deer Eating In Forest, Pewter Lid, Carved Horn Finial, Fluted, 1/2 Liter	730.00
Glass, Clear, Deer Scene, Engraved, Blue Stain, Fluted, Inlaid Lid, 1/2 Liter	340.00
Glass, Clear, Enameled White, Blue, Gold Design, Porcelain Inlaid Lid, 1/2 Liter	330.00
Glass, Clear, Engraved Circle, Stag, Metal Lid, Carved Horn Finial, Thumblift, 1/2 Liter ..	415.00
Glass, Clear, Hand Painted Princess, Porcelain Inlaid Lid, Dwarf Thumblift, 1/2 Liter	245.00
Glass, Clear, Red Stain, Gold Paint, Inlaid Lid, c.1850, 1/8 Liter, 4 1/4 In.	100.00
Glass, Clear, Red Stain, Schloss Pyrmont, Inlaid Lid, c.1850, 1/2 Liter	200.00
Glass, Clear, Young Girl, Green Glass Inlaid Lid, Fluted, 1/8 Liter, 4 1/4 In.	240.00
Glass, Enameled Crest, Green, Inlaid Lid, Eggermann, 1/2 Liter	290.00
Glass, Enameled Eagle With Crown, Green, Inlaid Lid, Eggermann, 1/2 Liter	375.00
Glass, Enameled Flowers, Cobalt Blue, Pewter Lid, 1 Liter	420.00
Glass, Engraved Hunter, Dogs, Forest, Pewter Lid, Carved Horn Finial, Fluted, 1/2 Liter ..	815.00
Glass, Engraved Scene, Deer Leaping, Flowers, Pewter Base Ring, Lid, c.1780, 1 Liter, 8 In.	965.00
Glass, Floral Wedding, Pewter Lid, c.1840, 1 Liter, 9 In.	475.00
Glass, Green, Thumbprint Design, 3 Children Playing Game, Blue Opaline Lid, 1/3 Liter ..	215.00
Glass, Wheat & Hops, Etched, Blown, Amber, Pewter Lid, 2 1/2 Liter, 16 1/2 In.	195.00
Jester & Verse, Pottery, Etched, Pewter Lid, Hauber & Reuther, No. 436, 1/2 Liter	400.00
Mettlach steins are listed in the Mettlach category.	
Military, 2nd AACS Sqdn. Mob. Hahn Airbase Group, Germany, Porcelain, Lid, 1/2 Liter .	170.00
Military, 4th Missile Bn. 6th Arty Spangdahlem, Porcelain, Pewter Lid, U.S.A., 1/2 Liter ..	195.00
Military, 601 St. Ord. Dep. Bn. Mainz Germany, Porcelain, Pewter Lid, U.S.A., 1/2 Liter ..	240.00
Military, 7100th Airbase Group, Wiesbaden Airbase Germany, Porcelain, Lid, 1/2 Liter ...	200.00
Military, Bavarian Soldiers, Battlefield, Glass, Pewter Lid, F. Ringer, 1914-15, 1/2 Liter ..	605.00
Military, Pferdelazarett 1 B 1 Ldw Div 1917, Stoneware, Pewter Lid, 1 Liter	590.00
Military, Soldiers Greeting One Another, Stoneware, Pewter Lid, 1914, 1/2 Liter	200.00
Milk Glass, Blown, Asian Man, Flowers, Painted, Pewter Lid, c.1740, 1 Liter, 9 1/2 In.	3500.00
Occupational, Blacksmith, Porcelain, Enameled, Pewter Lid, August Fischer, 1/2 Liter ...	320.00
Occupational, Coach Driver, Porcelain, Pewter Lid, Josef Prem, 1/2 Liter	460.00
Occupational, Construction, Porcelain, Pewter Lid, I. B. Braisch, 1/3 Liter	175.00
Occupational, Fireman, Porcelain, Pewter Lid, 1/2 Liter	195.00
Occupational, Fireman, Pottery, Pewter Lid, 1934, 1/2 Liter	165.00
Pewter, Flowers In Basket, Engraved, Silver Plated Finish, Pewter Lid, 1837, 1 Liter	235.00
Porcelain, Banquet Third Panel Sheriff's Jury, Ceramic Art Co., 1898, 1/2 Liter	485.00
Porcelain, Blue Onion Design, Hand Painted, Rauenstein, 1 Liter, 11 1/2 In.	670.00
Porcelain, Butterfly, Landing On Flowers, Hand Painted, Inlaid Lid, 1/2 Liter	215.00
Porcelain, Capo-Di-Monte, Children, Winged Woman Handle, 1 Liter	485.00
Porcelain, Flowers, Hand Painted, Inlaid Lyre & Sheet Music On Lid, 4F Turner, 1/2 Liter	145.00
Porcelain, Fruit, Hand Painted, Lithophane, Inlaid Lid, 1/3 Liter	140.00
Porcelain, Hand Painted, Royal Vienna Style, Inlaid Lid, Brass Finial, 1 Liter, 9 1/2 In. ...	3805.00
Porcelain, Kana Zucht & Vogelschutz Ver Koburg, Pewter Lid, Canary Club, 2/5 Liter	195.00
Porcelain, Socialist, Proletarier, Marx, Enameled, Lithophane, Pewter Lid, 1/2 Liter	680.00
Porcelain, Windmill, Blue Delft, Lithophane, Inlaid Lid, 1/2 Liter	190.00
Pottery, 4 Dwarfs, Etched, Dwarf Pottery Lid, Girmscheid, 2 Liter	409.00
Pottery, Bowling Scene, Etched, Inlaid Bowling Ball Lid, JWR, 1/2 Liter	240.00
Pottery, Cards, Etched, Pewter Lid, 1/2 Liter	195.00
Pottery, Cavalier On Horseback, Transfer, Enameled, Pewter Lid, 4 Liter, 20 In.	470.00
Pottery, Coblenz Rheinland, Etched, 1388, Inlaid Lid, 2/5 Liter	127.00
Pottery, Diesinger, Relief, Man On Horseback, Pewter Lid, 2 Liter	550.00
Pottery, Dom In Bamberg, Transfer, Enameled, Pewter Lid, 1/2 Liter	110.00
Pottery, Drinking Scene, Inlaid Lid, Coblenz Rheinland, No. 1358, 1/2 Liter	115.00
Pottery, Drunk People, Walking, Etched, Inlaid Lid, No. 1618, Marzi & Remy, 1 Liter	210.00
Pottery, Dwarfs Tapping Barrel, Etched, Pewter Lid, No. 1158, 3 Liter	360.00
Pottery, Etched, Dancing Scene, Hauber & Reuther, 1/2 Liter	240.00
Pottery, Etched, Family Scene, Gerz, No. 1326, Inlaid Lid, 1 Liter	362.00

Pottery, Etched, Gasthaus Scene, Inlaid Lid, Hauber & Reuther, No. 400, 1/2 Liter 349.00
Pottery, Etched, Jester, Pewter Lid, Hauber & Reuther, 1/2 Liter 435.00
Pottery, Etched, Pewter Lid, Girmscheid, Falstaff & Bardolph, No. 930, 1/2 Liter 140.00
Pottery, Etched, Tapestry, Metal Lid, Hauber & Reuther, 1/2 Liter 180.00
Pottery, Falstaff & Bardolf, Relief, Pewter Lid, Marzi & Remy, 1 Liter 175.00
Pottery, Festive Scene, Inlaid Lid, Etched, Hauber & Reuther, 1/2 Liter 205.00
Pottery, Gasthaus Scene, Relief, Pewter Lid, Diesinger, 1/2 Liter 169.00
Pottery, Greek Scene, Relief, Pewter Lid, Steinzeugwerke, 1/2 Liter 145.00
Pottery, Heidelberg, Etched, Pewter Lid, Hauber & Reuther, No. 424, 1/2 Liter 390.00
Pottery, Herman, Battle Scene, Relief, Pewter Lid, Marzi & Remy, 1 Liter 240.00
Pottery, Hunter, Dog, Women, Inlaid Lid, Etched, Marzi & Remy, 1/2 Liter 386.00
Pottery, Hunting Scene, Relief, Pewter Lid, Marzi & Remy, 1 Liter 254.00
Pottery, Innkeeper, Relief, Pewter Lid, 1 1/2 Liter 120.00
Pottery, Knights Drinking, Tower, Relief, Lid, 1/2 Liter 195.00
Pottery, Man's Face, Pan Flute, Hand Painted, Pewter Lid, 1/2 Liter 58.00
Pottery, Man, Barrel, Hand Painted, Pewter Lid, Hauber & Reuther, 1/2 Liter 515.00
Pottery, Man, Drinking, Tapestry, Etched, Pewter Lid, Hauber & Reuther, 1/2 Liter 145.00
Pottery, Monkeys, Multicolored, Pewter Lid, Dumler & Breiden, 1/2 Liter 180.00
Pottery, Musicians, Music Box Base, Transfer, Enameled, Pewter Lid, 1 Liter 120.00
Pottery, Musicians, Relief, Pewter Lid, Diesinger, 1/2 Liter 329.00
Pottery, N G P Veterans Corps, April 19 1907, Transfer, Enameled, Pewter Lid, 1/3 Liter .. 110.00
Pottery, People On Horses, Relief, Pewter Lid, Marzi & Remy, 1 Liter 185.00
Pottery, People Talking, Relief, Pewter Lid, Marzi & Remy, 1 Liter 175.00
Pottery, Postman On Horse, Relief, Pewter Lid, Post & Telegraph, 1/2 Liter 485.00
Pottery, Relief, Schneewittchen, Pewter Lid, 2 Liter 240.00
Pottery, Rookwood, George Wiedemann Brewing Co., Pewter Lid, 1/2 Liter 260.00
Pottery, Shooting Festival, 9 Deustches Bundes & Jubilaum, Pewter Lid, c.1912, 1/2 Liter 360.00
Pottery, Shooting Festival, IX D Bundesschiessen, Enameled, Pewter Lid, 1/2 Liter 360.00
Pottery, St. Louis, Eads Bridge Looking East, Transfer, Enameled, Pewter Lid, 1/2 Liter .. 120.00
Pottery, Teddy Roosevelt, African Hunting Scenes, Relief, Pewter Lid, 1 1/2 Liter 210.00
Pottery, Teddy Roosevelt, African Hunting Trip, Relief, Inlaid Leopard Lid, 1/3 Liter 240.00
Pottery, Trumpeter Of Sackingen, Relief, Pewter Lid, Thewalt, 1 Liter 90.00
Pottery, University Of Michigan, Siebentes Peninsular Sangerfest, 1886, 1/2 Liter 145.00
Pottery, University Of Michigan, Transfer, Enameled, Pewter Lid, 1/2 Liter 120.00
Pottery, Veste Coburg, Transfer, Enameled, Pewter Lid, 2 1/2 In. 100.00
Pottery, VII Deutsches Turnfest Munchen 1889, Pewter Lid, Transfer, Enameled, 1 Liter .. 310.00
Regimental, 1 Train B. San. Comp., Munchen, Cross, Porcelain, 1/2 Liter, 9 3/4 In. 1380.00
Regimental, 4 Comp. Infantry Reg. No. 161, Pottery, 1/2 Liter, 12 1/2 In. 320.00
Regimental, 15 Reserve Infantry, Xaver Scherer, 1/2 Liter, 12 1/4 In. 725.00
Regimental, Ansbach 1897-00, August Zoller, Saddle Thumblift, 1/2 Liter 965.00
Regimental, Armee Corp Ingolstadt 1914-15, Barbara Thumblift, 1/2 Liter 1869.00
Regimental, Cp. 6 Rhein. Infantry Regt. No. 68, Pottery, 1/2 Liter, 12 3/4 In. 605.00
Regimental, Darmstadt 1897-99, Porcelain, Lion Thumblift, 1/2 Liter, 11 In. 420.00
Regimental, Morchingen 1902-04, Inscription, Porcelain, 1/2 Liter, 11 In. 1087.00
Regimental, Munchen 1893-95, Porcelain, Flower Thumblift, 1/2 Liter, 9 In. 260.00
Regimental, Rastatt 1908-10, Porcelain, 1/2 Liter, 12 In. 695.00
Regimental, Rhein No. 8 Saarbrucken 1904-07, Pottery, Horse, Rider Thumblift, 1/2 Liter . 845.00
Regimental, Roster, 1 Batt. Kgl. Bayr., Lion Thumblift, 1906-1908, 1/2 Liter, 10 In. 390.00
Regimental, Roster, 1 Komp. Infantry 3, Res. Hackbeyl, 1/2 Liter, 13 1/4 In. 690.00
Regimental, Roster, 2 Foote Artillerie. Rgt. 10, Porcelain, 1/2 Liter, 10 1/4 In. 546.00
Regimental, Roster, 5 Ulannen Rgt. No. 1, Res. Kromer, Pottery, 1/2 Liter, 11 1/4 In. 2536.00
Regimental, Roster, 6 Komp. Infantry Rgt. 3, Pottery, c.1909, 1 Liter, 12 1/2 In. 725.00
Regimental, Roster, 8 Comp Infantry Regt., Res. Hulpert, 1 Liter, 12 3/4 In. 690.00
Regimental, Roster, 11 Komp Infantry Regt. 2, Pottery, c.1914, 1/2 Liter, 13 In. 440.00
Regimental, Roster, 15 Infantry 10 Comp Neuberg, 1905-07, 1/2 Liter, 11 1/2 In. 485.00
Regimental, Roster, Artillerie Rgt. No. 11, 1901-03, Porcelain, Eagle Thumblift, 1/2 Liter . 485.00
Regimental, Roster, Artillerie Rgt. No. 26, 1898-00, Porcelain, Eagle Thumblift, 1/2 Liter . 485.00
Regimental, Roster, Artillerie Rgt. No. 31, 1895-98, Porcelain, Eagle Thumblift, 1/2 Liter . 255.00
Regimental, Roster, Bekleidungs, 1898-00, Porcelain, Eagle Thumblift, 1/2 Liter, 11 In. .. 865.00
Regimental, Roster, Comp. Kurhess, 1903-05, Porcelain, Anchor Thumblift, 1/2 Liter 705.00
Regimental, Roster, Eisenbahn Regt., Gef. Herrlich, Pottery, 1/2 Liter, 10 1/2 In. 575.00
Regimental, Roster, Eisenbahn, 1901-03, Stoneware, Munich Child Thumblift, 1/2 Liter .. 725.00
Regimental, Roster, Esk. Hannov, 1907-10, Porcelain, Eagle Thumblift, 1/2 Liter 1150.00

Regimental, Roster, Feld Art Regt., 1900-02, Porcelain, Ball Thumblift, 1/2 Liter, 9 In. 865.00
Regimental, Roster, Garde Grenadier Regt. No. 2, Porcelain, c.1914, 1/2 Liter, 11 1/4 In. ..   665.00
Regimental, Roster, Kgl. Bayr. Infantry Regt. Comp. Regensburg, 1/2 Liter 245.00
Regimental, Roster, Kgl. Bayr., 1909-11, Stoneware, Lion Thumblift, 1/2 Liter, 11 In. 470.00
Regimental, Roster, Lothring, 1904-06, Porcelain, Anchor Thumblift, 1/2 Liter, 12 In. 840.00
Regimental, Roster, Porcelain, Lion Thumblift, 1/2 Liter, 11 3/4 In. 365.00
Regimental, Roster, Porcelain, Lion Thumblift, 1917, 1/2 Liter, 12 1/4 In. 665.00
Regimental, Roster, Porcelain, Wurttemberg Thumblift, 1/2 Liter, 11 3/4 In. 845.00
Regimental, Roster, Pottery, Eagle Thumblift, 1/2 Liter, 14 1/2 In. 1570.00
Regimental, Roster, S.M.S. Freya, 1908-11, Eagle Thumblift, 1 Liter, 14 1/2 In. 1610.00
Regimental, Roster, S.M.S. Weissenburg, Res. Gohner, 1/2 Liter, 11 1/2 In. 1449.00
Regimental, Roster, W Comp. Wurttb. Train Battl., Gef. Heim., 1/2 Liter, 13 In. 780.00
Regimental, S.M.S. Mecklenburg 1908-1911, Pottery, Eagle Thumblift, 1 Liter, 12 1/2 In. . 1117.00
Regimental, Tree Trunk, St. Hubert Thumblift, Porcelain, 1/2 Liter, 8 1/4 In. 1870.00
Shooting Festival, 15 Deutsches Bundesschiessen Munchen 1906, Pewter Lid, 1 Liter 725.00
Silver Plate, Munich Child, Engraved, Relief, Lid, 1 In. 215.00
Socialist, Relief, People Listening To Speech, Pottery, 1/2 Liter 424.00
Stoneware, 4 Horses, Pulling Post Coach, Pewter Lid, Ludwig Hohlwein, 1/2 Liter 1265.00
Stoneware, Art Nouveau, Pewter Lid, Reinhold Merkelbach Grenzhausen, 1/2 Liter 262.00
Stoneware, Barrel, Rope, Blue Glaze, Pewter Lid, No. 4, Whites, New York, 1 1/2 Liter ..   175.00
Stoneware, Bayrische Gewerbeschau Munchen, Transfer, Pewter Lid, 1/8 Liter, 4 1/2 In. ..   120.00
Stoneware, Blue Salt Glaze, Gerz, No. 623, Inlaid Lid, 1/2 Liter 75.00
Stoneware, Boy Carrying Flag, Transfer, Enameled, Pewter Lid, 1/8 Liter, 4 In. 175.00
Stoneware, Creussen, Chip Carved Pattern, Pewter Lid, c.1690, 1 Liter, 7 3/4 x 6 1/2 In. .. 3450.00
Stoneware, Dwarf, Cape, Transfer, Enamel, Pewter Lid, F. Ringer, Kochel, 1/8 Liter 230.00
Stoneware, Embossed Images, Pewter Lid, Germany, 4 x 7 In. 20.00
Stoneware, Etched, Gasthaus Scene, Pewter Lid, Girmscheid, No. 843, 1/2 Liter 145.00
Stoneware, Face On Both Sides, Relief, Pewter Lid, 1/8 Liter, 4 1/4 In. 55.00
Stoneware, Fight Scene, Etched, Inlaid Lid, Etched Monkey Finial, 1 Liter 130.00
Stoneware, Flower, Engraved, Pewter Lid, c.1800, 1/2 Liter, 8 1/2 In. 405.00
Stoneware, Flowers, Hand Engraved, Westerwald, c.1730, 1/2 Liter, 7 In. 1930.00
Stoneware, Horse, Combed Body, Pewter Lid, Westerwald, c.1800, 1 Liter, 10 3/4 In. 730.00
Stoneware, Kunst Exposition Munchen, Transfer, Enameled, Pewter Lid, 1 Liter 360.00
Stoneware, Little Red Riding Hood, Relief, Pewter Lid, 1/8 Liter, 4 3/4 In. 75.00
Stoneware, Men, Drinking, Relief, Pewter Lid, Whites Pottery, Utica, New York, 1/3 Liter   98.00
Stoneware, Monkeys, Multicolored, Pewter Lid, Dumler & Breiden, 1/2 Liter 240.00
Stoneware, Salt Glaze, Fort Edward Brew, Man, Woman Reading, Pewter Lid, 11 1/2 In. .. 1100.00
Stoneware, Salt Glaze, Man, Woman, Drinking At Table, Pewter Lid, 13 1/2 In. 155.00
Stoneware, Salt Glaze, Man, Woman, Drinking At Table, Vine, Pewter Lid, 11 1/2 In. 176.00
Stoneware, Salt Glaze, Tavern Scene, Vine & Acorn, Pewter Lid, 13 In. 468.00
Stoneware, Scrolled Leaves, Hand Engraved, Pewter Lid, Westerwald, c.1860, 1 Liter 200.00
Stoneware, Shooting Festival, 17 Deutsches Bundes, F. Ringer, c.1912, 1/2 Liter 360.00
Stoneware, Shooting Festival, Man, Holding Schutzen Rifle, Relief, Pewter Lid, 1/2 Liter .   240.00
Stoneware, Soldier Drinking, Woman, 4-Leaf Clover Pewter Lid, Franz Ringer, 1/2 Liter .   290.00
Stoneware, Threading, Clover Design, Art Nouveau Pewter Lid, 1 Liter 218.00
Student Society, Fecht Club Offenbach, Blown Glass, Germany, 1863-89, 1/2 Liter 240.00
Student Society, Glass, Grimensia Sei's Panier, Dresden, 1898, 1 1/2 Liter, 14 1/2 In. 1035.00
Student Society, Hortologia Sei's Panier, Pewter Lid, Art Nouveau, 1907-08, 1/2 Liter ...   380.00
Student Society, Pottery, Transfer, Enameled, Pewter Lid, Bonn 1925, 1/2 Liter 195.00
Third Reich, 11 Gebirgs Jager Komp. 19. I.R., Pottery, Pewter Helmet Lid, 1/2 Liter 545.00
Third Reich, Marineschule-Kiel, Naval School, Pottery, Pewter Anchor Lid, 1/2 Liter 575.00
Third Reich, Unteroffizier-Verein-Landsberg, Soldier, Mule, Machine Gun, 1/2 Liter 415.00

STEREO CARDS that were made for stereoscope viewers became
popular after 1840. Two almost identical pictures were mounted on a
stiff cardboard backing so that, when viewed through a stereoscope, a
three-dimensional picture could be seen. Value is determined by maker
and by subject. These cards were made in quantity through the 1930s.

Abe, Civil War Eagle, Cannon, Company C, Bennett, Wisconsin, Yellow Mount 139.00
Abe, Civil War Eagle, Company C, Wisconsin, Orange Backing, c.1876 ....   130.00
Alhambra Court Of The Crystal Palace, Negretti & Zambra, 6 3/4 x 3 1/4 In. 880.00
Behind The Greek Court, Crystal Palace, Negretti & Zambra, 6 3/4 x 3 1/4 In. 825.00
Bell's Gap From Point Lookout, Penn. Railroad Scenery, Gutekunst 75.00

Black Hills Photographer, Famous Black Hills Views, Coules & McBride, Deadwood 230.00
Blackberries, No. 2063, Gems Of Kentucky Scenery, J. Mullen 145.00
Boston Athenaeum, No. 1165, Series 2, Public Buildings 35.00
Chaudiere Falls, Ottawa, From Suspension Bridge, Notman, No. 231 ....   55.00
Cut At Alta, Looking East, No. 787, Muybridge, Helios Flying Studio 310.00
Deadwood, Street View, Ox, Wagon, Famous Black Hills Views, Coules & McBride 245.00
Dunlop's House, Petersburgh, Ruined Warehouse, Civil War Era 110.00
Flower Vendor In Street, Julius M. Wendt, Albany, N.Y. 35.00
Fort Tongass, View From The Fort, Alaska, Muybridge 250.00
Gardener, 2 Boys Gardening, Workshop Series, Series 1 ....   40.00
Harper's Building, Pearl St., N.Y., Yellow Mount, G.W. Thorne, Publisher 70.00
Haymakers' Consultation, Weather, Heywood, American Stereoscopic 50.00
Jamaica Pond, No. 645, D. Barnum 35.00
Jefferson & Pontoon Bridge On Shenandoah, No. 65, George Stacy 85.00
King Cotton At Yorktown, Virginia, Brady & Co., Civil War Era 120.00
Lincoln's Funeral, New York City, Anthony 85.00
Marshall House, Broughton Street, Savannah, Ga., Anthony 120.00
Parlor, Arched Entrance, Piano, Stuffed Birds, A.R. Newell, Conn. 45.00
Picket Guard On Alert, No. 2061, War Views, Anthony 245.00
Snake Chiefs, No. 579, A.J. Russell, Groups & Indians Series 270.00
Snow Sheds, Looking West From Summit, Russell, Rocky Mt. Scenery 65.00
St. Louis Fire Wagon, Tan Mount, Boehl Koenig 70.00
St. Louis World's Fair Scenes, Keystone Co., 1904, 49 Cards 95.00
Steamer, City Of Lawrence, E. Spaford, Norwich, Conn. 80.00
Train On Trestle, Famous Black Hills Views, Coules & McBride, Deadwood 225.00
Victoria Bridge, Raising Large Boulder, Notman, No. 25 ....   235.00
Western Hunting Party, Sepia, Underwood & Underwood, 25 Views 365.00
Where Prisoners Were Exchanged, Hartford, Conn., Civil War Era 180.00
White Mountain Views, Cascade In Crawford Notch, Notman, No. 254 ....   65.00
William Lloyd Garrison, No. 5471, Prominent Portraits, Anthony 150.00

STEREOSCOPES were used for viewing stereo cards. The hand

viewer was invented by Oliver Wendell Holmes, although more com-
plicated table models were used before his was produced in 1859. Do
not confuse the stereoscope with the stereopticon, a magic lantern that
used glass slides.

H.C. White, Wood, Brass, 1895-1905 ....   260.00
Monarch, Wood, Aluminum, 5 Cards, Keystone View Co., 1904 ....   70.00
Schneck, Walnut Lensboard, Fleur-De-Lis Mount, Velvet-Covered Hood, 17 In. 1116.00
Vitascope, Burlwood, Walnut, Stand, Griffith & Griffith, Philadelphia, c.1896 ....   395.00
Walnut & Rosewood, Box Shape, 5 Cards, German Views, 6 1/2 In. 395.00

STERLING SILVER, see Silver-Sterling category.

STEUBEN glass was made at the Steuben Glass Works of Corning,

New York. The factory, founded by Frederick Carder and T.G.
Hawkes, Sr., was purchased by the Corning Glass Company. They continued to make glass called *Steuben*. Many types of art glass were
made at Steuben. The firm is still making exceptional quality glass but
it is clear, modern-style glass. Additional pieces may be found in the
Aurene, Cluthra, and perfume bottle categories.

Ashtray, Selenium Red, Applied Clear Folded Leaf Handle, 5 1/4 In. 430.00
Bowl, Acid Cut, Flower, Green Jade Over Alabaster, Inward Rolled Sides, c.1928, 10 In. ..   805.00
Bowl, Amethyst, Optic Ribbed, 3 Applied Clear Feet, 8 In. 290.00
Bowl, Calcite, Gold Aurene Interior, c.1920, 10 In. ....290.00 to 315.00
Bowl, Centerpiece, 6-Footed Pedestal, Signed, 7 x 9 1/4 In. 240.00
Bowl, Centerpiece, Black Amethyst, Red Cabochons, Trim & Handles, 10 1/4 In. 4830.00
Bowl, Centerpiece, Grotesque, Signed, 6 1/2 x 13 In. 145.00
Bowl, Centerpiece, Rosaline, Inverted Rim, Ground Pontil, Early 20th Century, 10 In. 400.00
Bowl, Centerpiece, Rosaline, Wide Rolled Rim, 14 In. 345.00
Bowl, Cintra, Yellow, Amber, 4 3/4 In. 1100.00
Bowl, Cupped, Crystal, George Thompson, c.1946, 7 x 7 3/4 In. 920.00
Bowl, Flared Rim, Applied Horseshoes On Base, 6 1/2 x 8 1/2 In. 345.00
Bowl, Flared, White Opalescent, Undulating Rim, 5 x 9 In. 430.00

Bowl, Footed, Gold Colored, c.1925, 8 1/2 In. 219.00
Bowl, Footed, John Dreves, c.1949, 3 1/4 x 10 1/2 In. 750.00
Bowl, Green, Fleur-De-Lis Mark, Teakwood Stand, 5 3/4 x 7 3/4 In. 230.00
Bowl, Grotesque, Ivrene, Folded Rim, 4 In. 400.00
Bowl, Grotesque, Pomona Green Shaded To Crystal, Flared & Ruffled Rim, 5 In. 400.00
Bowl, Grotesque, Ruffled Green Rim, 6 In. 490.00
Bowl, Heritage Flare Pattern, Signed, Sidney Waugh, c.1935, 10 x 12 In. 490.00
Bowl, Oval, Lobed, Frederick Carder, c.1933, 3 1/2 x 8 In. 290.00
Bowl, Topaz, Reticulated Cover, Celeste Blue Decoration & Finial, 8 1/2 In. 1035.00
Bowl, Tulip Form, Paul Schulze, 1963, 3 1/4 x 7 1/2 In. 290.00
Bowl, Underplate, Calcite, Gold Aurene Interior, Ribbed, 5 In. 175.00
Bowl, Yellow, Jade, Rolled Rim, 10 x 1 3/4 In. 575.00
Candlestick, Cintra, Red, Black Center Disc, Wide Cone-Shaped Foot, 9 1/4 In. 5175.00
Candlestick, Crystal, Green, Etched Rim, 10 In. 175.00
Candlestick, Topaz, Baluster Stem, Raised Foot, 8 In., Pair 345.00
Candlestick, Topaz, Double Balled Stem, c.1925, 8 In., Pair 315.00
Chalice, Cover, Amber, Celeste Blue Cabochons & Crown Finial, 13 In. 865.00
Cocktail, Teardrop, Silver Base, Box, c.1939, 4 In., 12 Piece . . . . .950.00 to 1100.00
Compote, Blue Jade, Alabaster Foot, Wide Flattened Rim, 6 1/4 In. 460.00
Compote, Calcite, Blue Iridescent Folded Rim, 7 In. 1380.00
Compote, Flower Form, Calcite, Gold Aurene Interior, 5 1/2 In. 460.00
Compote, Ivrene, Swan Stem, Disc Foot, Shape, 5 In. 775.00
Compote, Pomona Green Bowl & Foot, Clear Twist Stem, 6 1/2 In. 345.00
Compote, Topaz, Celeste Blue, Venetian Style, Flared Bowl, Carder, 6 x 7 In., Pair 510.00
Console, Pink, Opal, Flared Rim, c.1920, 13 In. 290.00
Cordial Set, Spanish Green, Threading, Bubbles, Cabochon Stems, 7 1/2 In., 4 Piece 375.00
Cup & Saucer, Rosaline, Applied Opal Handle, c.1910, 4 1/2 In. 345.00
Figurine, Alligator, James Houston, 1968, 10 In. 2160.00
Figurine, Elephant, James Houston, 1964, 7 1/4 In. 635.00
Figurine, Koala Bear, 6 In. 450.00
Figurine, Love, Box, 1971, 4 1/4 In. 144.00
Figurine, Pigeon, Sitting, 6 In. 1265.00
Goblet, Blue, Corkscrew Stem, 8 In., 5 Piece 750.00
Goblet, Calcite, Gold Aurene Interior, c.1920, 4 In., Pair 295.00
Goblet, Cobalt Blue, Clear Stem, 6 1/4 In., Pair 60.00
Goblet, Pink, Opalescent, 5 3/4 In. 600.00
Goblet, Poppy, Opalescent Foot, 5 3/4 In. 375.00
Goblet, Spanish Green, Threaded, Bubbles, Stems, 7 1/2 In., 4 Piece 375.00
Jar, Cover, Cranberry, Swirled, Rectangular, Threaded Stopper, 5 In. 330.00
Lamp, Applied Pomona Green Handles, Feet, Hooked Ring, 10 In. 230.00
Lamp, Black Mirror, Corseted, 6 Applied Green Prunts, 26 1/2 In. 1100.00
Lamp, Blue To Yellow Jade, Acid Cut, Oval Shouldered, Metal Foot, Collar, 22 In. 2300.00
Lamp, Brown Aurene Dome, Intarsia Border, Harp Base, 56 In. 5880.00
Lamp, Chandelier, 4-Light, Gold Aurene Pendant Shades, 22 x 37 In. 805.00
Lamp, Cintra, Golden Yellow, Fruit Pods, Vine, Leaves, Tendrils, 30 1/2 In. 2415.00
Lamp, Opal, Pulled Feather, Green Loop, Gold Iridescent Border, 11 In. 1325.00
Lamp Base, Pink Shouldered, Threading, Acid Cut Acanthus Leaf, Club Footed, 8 1/2 In. . . 3450.00
Nut Dish, Calcite, Gold Aurene Interior, Ruffled Edge, 3 3/4 In. 400.00
Olive Dish, Crystal, John Dreves, c.1939, 3 x 5 In. 315.00
Pitcher, Water, Green Matsu-No-Ke Handle, Footed, Ovoid, 10 In. 330.00
Pitcher, Water, Translucent Clear, Amethyst Threading, Faceted Stopper, 10 In. 460.00
Sculpture, Adobe Mission, Windswept Sands, Maple Base, D. Dowler, 9 x 4 1/2 In. 2130.00
Sculpture, Night & Day, Sphere Slice, Standing, 9 3/4 In. 645.00
Shade, Alabaster, Iridescent Green, Gold Hooked Feather, Bell Form, 4 1/2 In., Pair 1380.00
Shade, Brown Ground, Gold Heart, Vine Border, Platinum Bands, 5 3/4 x 4 1/2 In. 3220.00
Shade, Brown, Calcite, Rose Iridescent, Blue Jade Drape, 5 1/8 x 4 3/8 In. 865.00
Shade, Calcite, Gold, Hooked Feather, Gold Interior, Signed, 2 1/4 x 5 1/8 In. 230.00
Shade, Calcite, Hooked Border, Gold Iridescent, Ruffled Edge, Signed, 5 1/4 x 4 1/4 In. . . . 430.00
Shade, Calcite, Ivy Etch, 5 1/2 In., 3 Piece 635.00
Shade, Calcite, Oak Leaf & Acorn, Etch, 4 3/4 In. 105.00
Shade, Calcite, Pulled Feathers, Flowers, Gold, Green, 4 x 5 1/4 In. 1610.00
Shade, Calcite, Ribbon Tied Garlands, Paterae, c.1910, 5 In., Pair 210.00
Shade, Calcite, Warwick Etch, 4 1/2 In. 110.00

Shade, Gold Hooked Pulled Feather, Zipper, Calcite Ground, Mushroom Form, 5 In.	425.00
Shade, Gold Transparent, Pulled Feather, Ivrene, Signed, 2 1/4 x 5 1/4 In.	200.00
Shade, Green, Gold, Drop Loop, Ruffled Rim, 5 In.	260.00
Shade, Green, Gold, Pulled Feathers, Tulip Form, 5 In.	75.00
Shade, Ivrene, Green, Hooked Feathers, Double Skirted Edge, Signed, 4 1/2 x 6 In.	460.00
Shade, Opal, Green, Gold, Pulled Loops, 3 1/2 In. . . . . .260.00 to 290.00
Shade, Opal, Marbellite, 4 3/4 In.	60.00
Sherbet, Calcite, Gold Aurene Interior, 3 3/4 In.	120.00
Sherbet, Spanish Green, Applied Stem, Threading, Bubbles, Acid Stamp, 4 In., 4 Piece . . .	260.00
Sherbet, Underplate, Calcite, Blue Aurene Interior, 6 In.	520.00
Sherbet, Underplate, Peach Etch, Signed, 5 1/2 In.	430.00
Sugar & Creamer, Amber, Swirls, Celeste Blue Handles, 4 1/2 In.	290.00
Torchere, Calcite, Cupped Bowl, Intaglio Design, Copper Base, c.1910, 62 In.	2185.00
Vase, Acid Cut, Bird, Leaves, Green Jade, Alabaster Foot, 9 In.	1150.00
Vase, Acid Cut, Blossoms, Branches, Rosaline, Spherical, Frosted, 6 1/2 In.	999.00
Vase, Acid Cut, Fir Cones, Green Jade Over Alabaster, c.1910, 12 In.	1035.00
Vase, Acid Cut, Lotus, Green Jade Over Alabaster, 1920s, 7 In.	1680.00
Vase, Acid Cut, Matzu, Rose & Alabaster, 7 x 8 In.	1265.00
Vase, Acid Cut, Ships, Seagulls, Green, Frosted Ground, 9 1/2 In.	2700.00
Vase, Acid Cut, Songbirds, Leafy Stems, Green Jade Over Alabaster, Shouldered, 9 1/2 In.	2300.00
Vase, Acid Cut, Stamford Pattern, Gazelles, Yellow Jade Ground, 9 1/2 In.	2270.00
Vase, Acid Cut, Stemmed Flowers, Branches, Peony, Green Jade, Shouldered, 10 In.	3740.00
Vase, Bristol Yellow, Swirls, Flared Rim, Footed, Signed, Fleur-De-Lis, 10 In.	290.00
Vase, Bubbles, Threaded Amber Rim, c.1930, 5 In., Pair	207.00
Vase, Cintra, Pink, Clear, c.1920, 6 1/4 In.	1020.00
Vase, Cornucopia, Optic Ribbed, Ruffled Edge, Flemish Blue Domed Foot, 8 1/4 In.	290.00
Vase, Crackle, Blue Moss Agate, Green, Purple, Amber Swirls, Acanthus Leaf Base, 29 In.	5750.00
Vase, Double Scroll Foot, George Thompason, c.1942, 8 5/8 In.	575.00
Vase, Fan, Engraved Ship, Optic Ribbed, Pomona Green Knop & Foot, 8 1/4 In.	575.00
Vase, Fan, Green, Engraved Galleon, Clear Ball Stem & Foot, 8 1/2 In.	345.00
Vase, Fan, Peach, Clear Knopped Stem & Disc Foot, 8 1/2 In.	230.00
Vase, Fan, Spanish Green, c.1928, 8 1/4 In.	173.00
Vase, French Blue, Optic Ribbed, Urn Shape, 7 In.	230.00
Vase, Green Jade, Alabaster, Fluted Neck, 1920s, 9 1/2 In.	1380.00
Vase, Grotesque, Amethyst Shaded To Clear, Clear Disc Foot, c.1932, 11 1/2 In.	575.00
Vase, Grotesque, Amethyst Shaded To Clear, Signed, 9 In.	316.00
Vase, Grotesque, Clear, Stamped, 6 1/2 x 12 1/2 In.	160.00
Vase, Iridescent Ivory, Blue Threaded Rim, Pink, Green, Frederick Carder, 12 1/2 In.	316.00
Vase, Ivrene, Flared Rim, Ribbed, 5 1/2 In.	259.00
Vase, Ivrene, Ribbed, Flared, Scalloped Rim, Footed, 9 In.	690.00
Vase, Lily, Calcite, Blue Aurene Interior, Gold Edge, 8 In.	1208.00
Vase, Millefiori, Gold Leaf, Vine, 5 3/4 In.	4315.00
Vase, Rose Quartz, Shouldered, Flared Rim, 8 3/4 In.	1440.00
Vase, Scroll Foot, Irene Benton, c.1946, 10 In.	635.00
Vase, Silverina, Translucent Green, Diamond-Quilted, Silver Flecks, Footed, 7 In.	374.00
Vase, Songbirds On Stems, Acid Cut, Green Jade Over Alabaster, Shouldered, 9 1/2 In. . . .	920.00
Vase, Topaz, Spiral Ribs, c.1930, 10 1/4 In.	230.00
Vase, Topaz, Swirled, Flared, 7 1/8 In.	115.00
Vase, Trumpet, Calcite, Blue Aurene Interior, Ruffled Edge, 6 In.	1380.00
Vase, Trumpet, Calcite, Round Base, Gold Aurene Interior, c.1910, 4 3/4 In.	275.00
Vase, Trumpet, Ivrene, 2 Lilies, Signed, 12 In.	1093.00
Vase, Trumpet, Selenium Red, Optic Ribbed, Round Foot, Signed, 6 In.	460.00
Wine, Oriental Poppy, Rose Color, Opalescent Bands, 5 3/4 In.	316.00

STEVENGRAPHS are woven pictures made like fancy ribbons. They were manufactured by Thomas Stevens of Coventry, England, and became popular in 1862. Most are marked *Woven in silk by Thomas Stevens* or were mounted on a cardboard that tells the story of the Stevengraph. Other similar ribbon pictures have been made in England and Germany.

Bookmark, The Ascension, Cross, Figure Of Christ, 8 x 2 In.	40.00
Bookmark, To One I Love, Hearts & Vines, Black Ground, 6 1/2 x 1 5/8 In.	35.00
Ribbon, Lincoln Mourning, Silk, Multicolored, 11 x 2 In.	335.00

STEVENS & WILLIAMS of Stourbridge, England, made many types of glass, including layered, etched, cameo, and art glass, between the 1830s and 1930s. Some pieces are signed *S & W*. Many pieces are decorated with flowers, leaves, and other designs based on nature.

Rose Bowl, Peach & Cranberry Swirls, Ruffled Edge, 4 1/2 In. 1150.00
Vase, Bud, 4-Prong, Free-Form, Cranberry, Entwining Tree Trunks, 8 In. ....300.00 to 345.00
Vase, Mother-Of-Pearl, Amber Shaded To Pink, Swirls, Bulbous, Cylindrical Neck, 4 In. .. 1495.00
Vase, Mother-Of-Pearl, Blue Shaded To Burgundy, Knopped Neck, 5 1/2 In. 1365.00
Vase, Mother-Of-Pearl, Osiris, Yellow, Rose Feathers, J. Northwood, 10 1/2 In. 2875.00
Vase, Mother-Of-Pearl, Peach & Cranberry Swirls, Cone Shape, 9 In. 1495.00
Vase, Mother-Of-Pearl, Pompeian Swirl, Cranberry To Apple Green, 6 In. 1400.00
Vase, Mother-Of-Pearl, Red Shaded To Green, Swirls, Folded Rim, 6 In. 1610.00
Vase, Mother-Of-Pearl, Yellow, Zipper Swirls, Bulbous, Flared Rim, 8 In. 520.00
Vase, Opal To Rose, Crimped Ruffled Top, Applied Amber Foot, 10 In. 430.00
Vase, Orange Cut To Pink, Applied Cherries, Ruffled Edge, 4 Amber Feet, 8 In. 575.00
Vase, Pink Satin, Flowers, Bulbous, Neck Ring, Cameo, 7 In., Pair 2185.00
Vase, Pink Shaded To Pearl, Applied Amber Branches, Ruffled Edge, 14 In. 920.00
Vase, Stick, Rainbow, Bulbous, Diamond-Quilted, Brass Base, Lion Mask, 14 In. 1800.00

STIEGEL TYPE glass is listed here. It is almost impossible to be sure a piece was actually made by Stiegel, so the knowing collector refers to this glass as *Stiegel type*. Henry William Stiegel, a colorful immigrant to the colonies, started his first factory in Pennsylvania in 1763. He remained in business until 1774. Glassware was made in a style popular in Europe at that time and was similar to the glass of many other makers. It was made of clear or colored glass and was decorated with enamel colors, mold blown designs, or etching.

Cologne, Bride's, Enameled Flowers, Pewter Collar, 4 3/4 In. 303.00
Creamer, Cobalt Blue, Diamonds, Applied Handle, Footed 415.00
Flip Glass, Tapered Body, Engraved Rim, 18th Century, 6 In. 345.00
Tankard, Bird, Foliage, Flared Foot, 7 x 3 3/4 In. 1210.00
Tumbler, Enameled Flowers & Leaves, 3 5/8 In. 110.00
Tumbler, Flip, Enameled, Bird On Blue Heart, Leaves, 3 1/2 In. 385.00

STONE includes those articles made of stones not listed elsewhere in this book. Micro mosaics (small decorative design, made by setting pieces of stone into a pattern), urns, vases, and other pieces made of natural stones are listed here. Alabaster, Jade, Malachite, Marble, and Soapstone are in their own categories. Stoneware is pottery and is listed in the Stoneware category.

Figure, Buddha, Bust, Tan Color, 12 1/4 x 8 x 16 1/4 In. 403.00
Figure, Indian Chief, E. Reed, Sandstone, 14 1/2 In. 1495.00
Figure, Owl, E. Reed, Sandstone, 7 3/4 In. 375.00
Figure, Rose Quartz, Buddha, Hands In Dhyana Mudra, Chinese, 6 In. 170.00
Figure, Sandstone, Head, Jeweled Crown, Asian Khmer, Stone Stand, 13 In. 2115.00
Head, Carved, Bodhisattva, Patinated, Wooden Base, Chinese, Tang Dynasty, 9 In. 1035.00
Opium Weight Set, Stylized Chickens, Burmese, 19th Century, 3/4 To 4 1/2 In., 8 Piece .. 230.00
Pietra Dura, Plaque, Inlaid Angel, Black Slate, Painted, Stones, Gothic Style, 18 In. 1438.00
Stele, Durga, Multi-Armed Goddess, With Weapons, Sandstone, East Indian, 1800s, 20 In. . 748.00

STONEWARE is a coarse, glazed, and fired potter's ceramic that is used to make crocks, jugs, bowls, etc. It is often decorated with cobalt blue decorations. In the nineteenth and early twentieth centuries, potters often decorated crocks with blue numbers indicating the size of the container. A "2" meant 2 gallons. Stoneware is still being made. American stoneware is listed here.

Batter Jar, Blue Highlights, W. Roberts, Binghamton, N.Y., c.1870, 4 Qt., 10 3/8 In. 355.00
Batter Jug, Cobalt Blue Leaves, Swing Handle, Cowden, Wilcox, 1869-87, 1 1/2 Gal. 1265.00
Batter Pail, Bail Handle, Blue Accents, N. White, Binghamton, c.1860, 4 Qt., 8 1/2 In. ... 415.00
Batter Pail, Bail Handle, Blue Accents, W. Roberts, Binghamton, c.1860, 6 Qt., 9 1/2 In. .. 305.00
Batter Pail, Bird, Bail Handle, N.A. White & Son, Utica, c.1875, Gal., 10 In. 1020.00
Batter Pail, Blue Flower, Bail Handle, Cowden & Wilcox, c.1850, 9 In. 880.00
Batter Pail, Blue, Tulip, Drooping, Bail Handle, c.1870, 6 Qt. 385.00

Batter Pail, Lid, Salt Glaze, Bail Handle, White's, Utica, 3 Qt., 8 In. 440.00
Bean Pot, Lid, Children Eating Beans, 6 1/2 In. 155.00
Bellarmine, Molded Face, Bearded Man, Egg Shape, Applied Handle, 11 1/8 In. 575.00
Bird Whistle, Cobalt Blue, Mulberry Wings & Beak, 2 1/2 In. 489.00
Bottle, Bristol Glaze, Blue Stencil, Down On Farm, Farmmato, c.1900, 6 1/2 In. 120.00
Bottle, Cobalt Blue Cone Top, Hiram V. Heaton, 1875, 10 In. 440.00
Bottle, M.C. Heald, Impressed, Blue Accent, 9 1/2 In. 165.00
Bottle, Mead, Dark Brown, Light Tan, Mottled, 8 In. 165.00
Bottle, Paneled Sides, Patent Pressed, W. Smith, N.Y., 6 1/2 In. 100.00
Bottle, Pig, Cobalt Blue Spots, Accents, 6 In. . . . . .980.00 to 4600.00
Bottle, R. Holloway, Impressed, Blue Accent, 10 In. 99.00
Bowl, 3 Cobalt Blue Lines, 7 1/4 x 4 1/4 In. 345.00
Bowl, Blue Flowers, Tapered Sides, Pour Spout, Gal., 5 1/4 x 11 In. 495.00
Bowl, Kirt Mangus, Hand Built, Crosshatch Design, 3 1/4 x 5 In. 45.00
Bowl, Milk, Cobalt Blue Design, Applied Handles, Impressed 1 . . . . 460.00
Brown, Flowerpot, Drain, Haxstun & Co., Ft. Edward, N.Y., c.1870, 2 Gal., 9 x 11 In. 305.00
Bulb Pot, Tapered Sides, Classical Medallions, Basalt, Turner, England, 8 3/4 In., Pair 2015.00
Bust, Mariner, Glazed, Polychrome, 19th Century, 16 1/2 In. 10000.00
Canister, Lid, Bristol Glaze, Flowers, Star Relief On Back, 7 In. 300.00
Canteen, Bardwell's Root Beer, White's, Utica, 14 In. 385.00
Canteen Jug, Bristol Glaze, Cambridge Springs, Pa., Brown, White, c.1900, 2 3/4 In. 22.00
Cheese Dish, Cover, Salt Glaze, White Relief Hunting Scene, Vine Borders, 12 In. 200.00
Churn, 3 Tooled Shoulder Bands, Ocher Wash, Boston, c.1805, 17 In. 2530.00
Churn, Base, Cobalt Blue, 4, Applied Handles, Flared Rim, Zanesville, 17 In. 375.00
Churn, Birch Leaf, Blue, Ear Handles, 3 Gal., 14 1/2 In. 69.00
Churn, Bird, Flower, Cobalt Blue, White & Wood, N.Y., c.1885, 5 Gal., 17 1/2 In. 8800.00
Churn, Bird, On Plume, Blue, New York Stoneware, c.1870, 6 Gal., 19 In. 635.00
Churn, Bird, On Tree Stump, Blue, West Troy, N.Y., c.1880, 6 Gal., 19 In. 1020.00
Churn, Bird, Paddletail, On Flowering Branch, Blue, N.A. White & Son., 3 Gal., 15 In. . . . 9900.00
Churn, Bull's-Eye Stylized Flower, New York Stoneware Co., c.1880, 5 Gal., 17 1/2 In. . . . 330.00
Churn, Dasher Guide, Iris, H.M. Whitman, Havana, N.Y., c.1860, 5 Gal., 18 In. 2200.00
Churn, Dotted Bird On Stump, J. Burger Jr., Rochester, N.Y., c.1885, 6 Gal., 20 In. 1210.00
Churn, Flower, Cobalt Blue, Cedar Falls, Iowa, c.1865, 17 1/4 In. 2875.00
Churn, Flowers, Raised Rim, Applied Handles, Ohio, 16 In., 4 Gal. 460.00
Churn, Initials AB, Cobalt Blue, Applied Handle, 3 1/8 In. 80.00
Churn, Leaf, Cobalt Blue, Frank B. Norton, Worcester, Mass., 4 Gal., c.1885, 17 In. 765.00
Churn, Lid, Dasher, Albany Glaze, c.1880, 6 3/4 In. 300.00
Churn, Maysville, Ky., 4 Gal. 1500.00
Churn, Paddletail Bird, N.A. White & Son, Utica, N.Y., c.1870, 3 Gal. 9900.00
Churn, Paddletail Bird, White & Wood, Binghamton, N.Y., 5 Gal., 17 In. . . . . *Illus* 8800.00
Churn, Ribbed Flower & Leaf, White's, Utica, c.1865, 6 Gal., 18 In. 300.00
Churn, Ribbed Orchid, Blue, N.A. White & Son, c.1865, 6 Gal., 18 In. 2640.00
Churn, Salt Glaze, Wood Cover, W. States, Stonington, c.1815, 3 Gal., 15 1/4 In. 690.00
Churn, Star Design, Cobalt Blue, Salt Glaze, Freehand Date 1856, 6 Gal. 4310.00
Churn, Swan, Blue, Gardiner, Me., c.1880, 3 Gal., 15 1/2 In. 495.00
Churn, Willow Tree, Cobalt Blue, N.Y. State, 15 3/4 x 9 1/4 In. 1725.00
Churn Base, Flower, Clouds, Cobalt Blue, Applied Handle, Raised Rim, 9 x 15 In. 633.00
Coffeepot, Tin Wire Straps, Handle, Spout, Lid, Bodine Pottery Co., c.1880, Qt., 9 In. 660.00
Cream Pot, Blue Flowers, N. Clark & Co., Rochester, N.Y., c.1850, 5 Gal., 15 1/2 In. 1100.00
Cream Pot, Blue Trumpet Flower, Harrington & Burger, Rochester, c.1853, 4 Gal., 14 In. . . 1540.00
Cream Pot, Butter & Dolly In Script, c.1840, 2 Gal., 10 1/2 In. 800.00
Cream Pot, Ribbed Flower, F. Stetzenmeyer, Rochester, N.Y., c.1860, 2 Gal., 11 In. 3300.00
Cream Pot, Tulip, Double, Cobalt Blue, Ballard & Bros., c.1860, 3 Gal., 10 1/2 In. 250.00
Cream Pot, Wreath, T. Harrington, c.1850, 2 Gal., 10 1/2 In. 330.00
Creamer, Mottled Olive Green Glaze, c.1930, 6 1/2 In. 22.00
Creamer, Wavy Lines, Cobalt Blue, Incised, Mottled Brown & Blue Rim, Handle, 3 In. . . . 460.00
Crock, 2 Flowers, Pail Shape, M. Woodruff, Cortland, c.1870, 3 Gal., 11 1/2 In. 220.00
Crock, 2 Stylized Hearts, Geddes, N.Y., 4 Gal. 1760.00
Crock, 3 Flowers, Single Stem, Cobalt Blue, Double Incised Shoulder Lines, Oval, 8 In. . . 908.00
Crock, 3 Leaves, Burger & Co., Rochester, N.Y., c.1869, 3 Gal., 10 1/2 In. 250.00
Crock, 4, Tulip, Wavy Lines, Cobalt Blue, 2 Handles, 10 1/2 x 12 1/4 In. 290.00
Crock, Apple Butter, Flower, Blue, L.H. Yeager & Co., Allentown, Pa., Handles, 7 x 9 In. . . 715.00
Crock, Apple Butter, Flowers, R.C.R., Phila., 6 1/4 x 5 In. 1210.00

Crock, Ark, A.O. Whittemore, Havana, N.Y., c.1870, 4 Gal., 11 In. 3080.00
Crock, Bird, Blue, Handles, Cowden & Wilcox, 2 Gal., 10 In. 4400.00
Crock, Bird, Branch, Fantail, White & Wood, Binghamton, N.Y., c.1885, 3 Gal., 8 In. 580.00
Crock, Bird, Cobalt Blue, West Troy, N.Y., 9 3/8 In. 200.00
Crock, Bird, Dotted Leaf, Ottman Bros & Co., Fort Edward, N.Y., c.1870, 3 Gal., 10 In. . . . 210.00
Crock, Bird, Fat, Blue, Ottman Bros. & Co., Ft. Edward, N.Y., c.1870, 3 Gal., 10 1/2 In. . . 550.00
Crock, Bird, Flower Brand, Harrington & Burger, 6 Gal. 7480.00
Crock, Bird, Flowering Branch, N.A. White & Son, c.1865, 3 Gal., 10 In. 910.00
Crock, Bird, Hiding In Brush, Cobalt Blue, c.1870, 3 Gal., 10 1/2 In. 3190.00
Crock, Bird, Leaves, Brown Slip, Wooden Lid, Stamped, Edmands & Co., 2, 11 3/4 In. . . . 980.00
Crock, Bird, On Flower, Blue, N.A. White & Son., c.1865, 3 Gal., 10 1/2 In. 330.00
Crock, Bird, On Twig, E. & N. Brownson, Troy, N.Y., c.1870, 2 Gal., 9 In. 605.00
Crock, Bird, Paddletail, Plume, White & Wood, Binghamton, N.Y., c.1885, 3 Gal., 10 In. . . 550.00
Crock, Bird, Pail Shape, E.S. Fox, Athens, c.1840, 2 Gal., 9 In. 575.00
Crock, Bird, Plume, Weston & Gregg, Ellenville, N.Y., c.1869, 6 Gal., 12 1/2 In. 1155.00
Crock, Bird, Singing, Blue, T.F. Connolly, New Brunswick, N.J., c.1870, 4 Gal., 11 In. 525.00
Crock, Brushed Decoration, Egg Shape, J. Clark & Co., Troy, c.1826, 9 1/2 In. 360.00
Crock, Butter, Blue & White, Embossed, 4 1/2 In., Pair 100.00
Crock, Butter, Clay, Flowers, Leaves, Richard Remmey, c.1850, 6 In. 470.00
Crock, Butter, Dome Lid, Brown Glaze, F.H. Cowden, Harrisburg, 8 1/2 x 9 1/2 In. 110.00
Crock, Butter, Lid, Bristol Glaze, Deer Hunt Scene, 3 1/2 x 6 3/4 In. 470.00
Crock, Butter, Lid, Trellis & Daisy, Salt Glaze, Blue, White, 5 x 7 In. 90.00
Crock, Butter, Western Dairy Co. Pasture Queen Butter, Chicago, Ill., 1 Lb. 80.00
Crock, Cake, Blue Decorated, Salt Glaze, Flared Rim, Banding, Tulip, 5 x 5 In. 3960.00
Crock, Cake, Flowers, Wm. Grange & Sons, Philadelphia, Ear Handles, 5 x 8 In. 330.00
Crock, Cake, Lid, Flowers & Leaves, Blue, c.1850, 7 x 11 In. 690.00
Crock, Cake, Plume, Blue, Dotted, J.A. & C.W. Underwood, c.1865, 2 Gal., 7 1/2 In. 175.00
Crock, Cake, Swag, Blue, Bristol Glaze, c.1880, Gal., 5 1/2 x 10 1/2 In. 300.00
Crock, Camel, Desert Scene, W.A. Macquoid, N.Y.C., c.1870, 1 1/2 Gal. 12650.00
Crock, Chicken Pecking Corn, Blue, c.1870, 2 Gal., 9 In. 690.00
Crock, Chicken Pecking Corn, F.B. Norton & Co., Mass., c.1870, 3 Gal., 10 1/2 In. 3850.00
Crock, Chicken Pecking, Cobalt Blue Slip, 4 Gal. 690.00
Crock, Clouds, Tree, Mountains, Tornados, Handles, Salt Glaze, c.1840, 11 In. 2090.00
Crock, Cover, Applied Ear Handles, Tooled Lines, c.1880, 3 1/2 In. 145.00
Crock, Cover, Flowers, Cobalt Blue, 2 C-Form Handles, 13 1/2 x 12 In. 345.00
Crock, Cow, Blue, Salt Glaze, Albany Slip Interior, Cylindrical, Lug Handles, 10 In. 880.00
Crock, Crossed Lovebirds, Blue, c.1870, 5 Gal., 12 In. 1100.00
Crock, Dotted Geometric, Orange Peel Oveglaze, c.1870, Gal., 7 1/2 In. 275.00
Crock, Double Bird, Cobalt Blue, Handles, Fort Edward, N.Y., 10 1/2 In. 1150.00
Crock, Dove, F.B. Norton Sons, Worcester, Mass., c.1886, 3 Gal., 10 In. 330.00
Crock, Eagle, Roses, Vines, Leaves, Stenciled, Freehand Stripes, c.1880, 5 Gal., 15 1/2 In. . 605.00
Crock, Eagle, Stenciled, Brown Brothers, c.1890, 2 Gal., 9 In. 470.00
Crock, Fern, Blue, Oval, c.1830, Gal., 8 1/2 In. 250.00
Crock, Fishing Lure, Midwest, c.1880, 2 Gal., 9 In. 385.00

Stoneware, Churn, Paddletail Bird, White & Wood, Binghamton, N.Y., 5 Gal., 17 In.

Stoneware, Crock, House, Tree, Steps, C.W. Braun, N.Y., c.1870, 4 Gal., 11 1/2 In.

Stoneware, Crock, Leaf Design, Haxstun Ottman & Co., Fort Edward, N.Y., c.1870, 3 Gal., 10 In.

Crock, Flower Sprigs, Cobalt Blue, Blue Bands, Pa., 1800s, 20 Gal., 22 1/2 x 13 1/2 In. ... 5465.00
Crock, Flower, 3 Angled Tulips, Leaves, Cobalt Blue, Flared Rim, 8 3/4 In. 290.00
Crock, Flower, Blue Freehand, Incised Rings, Stamped Label, Cortland, 9 In. 290.00
Crock, Flower, Blue, Cortland, c.1860, 2 Gal., 9 In. 690.00
Crock, Flower, Blue, N. Clark, Jr., Athens, N.Y., c.1850, 3 Gal., 10 In. 200.00
Crock, Flower, Blue, Smith & Brickner, c.1830, Gal., 9 In. 385.00
Crock, Flower, Double, Adam Caire, Poughkeepsie, c.1850, Gal., 7 1/4 In. 100.00
Crock, Flower, Leaves, Cobalt Blue, Double Handles, Wm. Moyer, 9 1/2 In. 980.00
Crock, Flower, Pinwheel, C.W. Braun, Buffalo, N.Y., c.1870, 3 Gal., 10 In. 220.00
Crock, Flower, Ribbed, C.W. Braun, Buffalo, N.Y., c.1870, 13 In. 330.00
Crock, Flowers & Heads, Blue, Salt Glaze, Ovoid, Handles, 13 x 10 In. 1155.00
Crock, Flowers In Compote, Cobalt Blue, Salt Glaze, Whites, Binghamton, 3 Gal., 11 In. ... 4500.00
Crock, Flowers, Blue, Banded Rim, Tab Handles, John Bell, Waynesboro, 4 Gal., 13 In. ... 4070.00
Crock, Flowers, Blue, Oval, S. Blair, Cortland, 1830, Gal., 8 1/2 In. 360.00
Crock, Flowers, Blue, Straight-Sided, Lid, Handles, No. 4, 18 x 11 In. 2420.00
Crock, Flowers, Brush, Slip, A.O. Whittemore, Havana, N.Y., c.1870, 5 Gal., 11 1/2 In. ... 275.00
Crock, Flowers, Butterfly, Bird, Slightly Rounded Sides & Rim, S.E. Bick, 6 x 6 In. 1045.00
Crock, Flowers, Cobalt Blue, Frye & Burrill, Orange, Mass., 4 Gal. 120.00
Crock, Flowers, Cobalt Blue, O.L. & A.K. Ballard, Burlington, Vt., 4 Gal. 120.00
Crock, Flowers, Cobalt Blue, O.L. & A.K. Ballard, Burlington, Vt., 5 Gal. 355.00
Crock, Flowers, Cobalt Blue, Salt Glaze, White's Pottery, Utica, N.Y., c.1880, 2 Gal., 10 In. 150.00
Crock, Flowers, Inscribed, 19th Century, 3 Gal., 14 In. 575.00
Crock, Flowers, Leaves, Handles, Incised Bands, Salt Glaze, 1860-80, 5 Gal., 13 In. 880.00
Crock, Flying Bird, Wreath, N.A. White & Son, Utica, N.Y., c.1870, 5 Gal., 12 1/2 In. 3960.00
Crock, Freehand Signature Harmell & Smyth, Tuscarawas County, Ohio, 15 In. 1495.00
Crock, Grocer's Name, Ed Berry, Cobalt Blue Freehand, Brittain, Ohio, 10 In. 315.00
Crock, Horse, Brushed & Sponge Blue, c.1870, 6 Qt., 8 In. 4400.00
Crock, House, Tree, Steps, C.W. Braun, N.Y., c.1870, 4 Gal., 11 1/2 In. . . . . *Illus* 7425.00
Crock, Incised Cartouche, John Remmey III, Leaves, Cobalt Blue Detail, Oval, 12 1/2 In. . 5175.00
Crock, Leaf & Seed Cluster, Cobalt Blue, Incised, c.1823, 12 In. 2760.00
Crock, Leaf Design, Haxstun Ottman & Co., Fort Edward, N.Y., c.1870, 3 Gal., 10 In. *Illus* 110.00
Crock, Leaf, Minnesota Stoneware Co., 3 Gal. 400.00
Crock, Leaves, Burger & Co., Rochester, N.Y., c.1870, 4 Gal., 9 In. 470.00
Crock, Leaves, Cobalt Blue Slip, Sheet Iron Cover, Baluster, c.1850, 4 Gal., 16 1/4 In. 4600.00
Crock, Leaves, Flowers, Cobalt Blue Freehand, 2 Handles, Impressed 3, 14 In. 750.00
Crock, Lid, Flowerpot, Cobalt Blue, 2 Gal. 325.00
Crock, Lovebirds, Blue, S. Hart, c.1875, 4 Gal., 11 In. 965.00
Crock, Name, Blue, No. 1, Tyler & Dillon, Albany, c.1825, Gal., 8 1/2 In. 250.00
Crock, Oak Leaf, N.A. White & Son, c.1865, Gal., 7 1/2 In. 305.00
Crock, Orchid Leaf, Dotted, White & Wood, Binghamton, N.Y., c.1885, 2 Gal., 9 In. 305.00
Crock, Orchid, Ribbed, Blue Washed Name, N.A. White & Co., Utica, N.Y., c.1870, 7 In. . 330.00
Crock, Paddletail Bird, N.A. White & Son, Utica, N.Y., c.1870, 4 Gal., 11 In. 700.00
Crock, Palm Tree, Dotted Stag, John Burger, Rochester, N.Y., c.1865, 6 Gal., 16 In. . . *Illus* 48950.00
Crock, Parrot, Double Plume, F.B. Norton & Co., Worcester, c.1870, 4 Gal., 11 1/2 In. 1210.00
Crock, Peacock, Incised Tree & Rim, Midwestern, c.1870, 10 Gal., 16 In. . . . . *Illus* 15950.00
Crock, Pecking Chicken, Cobalt Blue, Biedinger & C, Poughkeepsie, 11 x 10 In. 490.00
Crock, Pickle, H.J. Heinz & Co., Pittsburg, Tooled Bands, 5 1/2 In. 440.00
Crock, Pinwheel, Blue, Oval, Incised, c.1800, 2 Gal., 11 1/2 In. 880.00
Crock, Plume, Blue, Stylized, Satterlee & Mory, Ft. Edward, N.Y., c.1870, Gal., 7 1/2 In. ... 415.00
Crock, Plume, Dotted, Stylized, F.B. Norton & Co., Worcester, Mass., c.1870, 7 1/2 In. ... 275.00
Crock, Poppy, Blue, Double, Oval, Lid, N.A. White & Co., c.1860, 6 Gal., 13 1/2 In. 3410.00
Crock, Ribbed Leaves, Blue, No. 3, Geddes, N.Y., c.1870, 2 Gal., 9 1/2 In. 250.00
Crock, Robin On Plume, Haxstun & Co., Fort Edward, N.Y., c.1870, 3 Gal., 10 1/2 In. 1430.00
Crock, Rose, Blue, Petals, Dots, Squiggles, Oval, Haxstun & Co., c.1870, 4 Gal., 13 In. . . . 635.00
Crock, Squiggles, Blue, Open Handles, Oval, c.1850, Pt., 5 In. 145.00
Crock, Stag, Standing, Cobalt Blue, White's, Utica, c.1865, 3 Gal., 10 1/2 In. 3190.00
Crock, Stylized Blue Flower, Impressed Fair Heaven, Conn., 3 Gal., 10 1/4 x 11 In. 230.00
Crock, Stylized Flower, Dotted, Haxstun & Ottman, Fort Edward, c.1870, 4 Gal., 11 1/2 In. 110.00
Crock, Stylized Leaf, Haxstun Ottman & Co., Fort Edward, N.Y., c.1870, 3 Gal., 10 In. ... 110.00
Crock, Swag, Blue, Corlears Hook Commeraws, N.Y., Egg Shape, c.1805, 13 In. 5390.00
Crock, Swags, Blue, Open Handles, Oval, Incised Commeraws, c.1800, Gal. 908.00
Crock, Tan Surface Color, Cobalt Blue Flowers, 10 1/4 In. 86.00
Crock, Tornado, Blue, Geddes, N.Y., c.1870, 2 Gal., 9 In. 200.00

Crock, Trailing Tulips, Freehand, Cobalt Blue, Stamped 5, 15 1/4 In. 575.00
Crock, Tulip, Blue, Burger & Lang, Rochester, N.Y., c.1870, 2 Gal., 9 In. 745.00
Crock, Tulip, Blue, Oval, C. Hart & Co., c.1855, 2 Gal., 10 In. 415.00
Crock, Tulip, Cobalt Blue, Egg Shape, Wm. Farrar & Co., Geddes, N.Y., 4 Gal. 650.00
Crock, Tulip, Cobalt Blue, Oval, Handles, Signature, Tuscarawas County, Ohio, 12 In. 890.00
Crock, Tulip, Ribbed Lines, Burger Bros & Co., Rochester, N.Y., c.1869, 4 Gal., 11 1/2 In. 330.00
Crock, Tulips, Cobalt Blue, Oval, Double Handles, Impressed 4, 14 3/4 In. 315.00
Crock, Tulips, Vines, Borders, Cobalt Blue, Stenciled 10, Hand Decorated, 20 1/2 In. 6040.00
Crock, Turkey, In Tree, Cobalt Blue, Double Handles, 10, Akron, 14 x 18 In. 3740.00
Crock, Victorian Woman's Profile, c.1870, 7 In. 4620.00
Crock, Western In Maple Leaf, Cobalt Blue, Pointed Leaves, 10 Gal., 17 In. 80.00
Crock, Woman & Parasol, Bird On Sprig, Scenes, Thompson Pottery, 5 Gal. 16500.00
Crock, Wreath, Burger & Co., Rochester, N.Y., c.1877, 2 Gal., 9 In. 495.00
Cuspidor, Floral Band, Blue, Round, Cutout Handles, R.C.R., Philadelphia, 4 1/4 x 7 In. .. 660.00
Figurine, Dog, Spaniel, Cobalt Blue Lines, Salt Glaze, Riedinger & Caire, c.1865, 12 In. .. 7800.00
Figurine, Dog, Spaniel, Seated, Cobalt Blue Glaze, Ohio, Late 1800s, 10 1/4 In. 2235.00
Figurine, Dog, Spaniel, Seated, Mottled Brown Glaze, 9 1/2 In. 1035.00
Figurine, Dog, Spaniel, Seated, Octagonal Base, Buff Glaze, Akron, Ohio, 9 1/2 In. 1095.00
Figurine, Dog, Spaniel, Seated, Shiny Glaze, Hand Tooled, 1877, E.M. King Co., 1897, 7 In. 430.00
Figurine, Lion, Male, Lying Down, Crossed Paws, Cobalt Blue Decoration, 3 x 5 1/4 In. .. 3220.00
Figurine, Pig, Amber Gray Glaze, Incised Eyes & Mouth, Solid, 6 1/2 In. 575.00
Figurine, Rattlesnake, Coiled, Crocker, 5 1/2 x 12 1/2 In. 690.00
Figurine, Rooster, Brown, Tan Lead Glaze, 4 1/2 x 2 x 3 In. 990.00
Figurine, Rooster, Standing, Dark Brown Mottled Albany Glaze, c.1870, 4 In. 300.00
Flowerpot, Attached Drainage Dish, Tooled Rope, c.1880, 5 1/2 In. 90.00
Flowerpot, Undertray, Crimped Edges, Incised Lines, 9 In. 259.00
Foot Warmer, Molded Fruit & Leaves, Raised Handle, Cork Stopper, 12 x 6 x 9 In. 175.00
Frame, Picture, Molded Flowers, Leaves, Beading, Oval, Mogadore, Ohio, 5 3/4 In. 890.00
Humidor, Lid, Blue, Hunting Dog, Diamond, 6 1/2 In. 132.00
Humidor, Lid, Blue, Wave, Shell, Bristol Glaze, Diamond, 7 1/2 In. 176.00
Humidor, Lid, Bristol Glaze, Horse Head, Diamond Point Relief, 5 1/2 In. 248.00
Jar, Alkaline Glaze, Flared Rim, Handles, Catawba Valley, 17 In. 315.00
Jar, Alkaline Glaze, Loop Handle, Oval, D.F. Landrum, c.1870, 11 In. 750.00
Jar, Alkaline Glaze, Oval, Edgefield District, John Or Amos Landrum, 17 In. 920.00
Jar, Alkaline Glaze, Oval, Thomas Owenby, c.1860, 14 In. 575.00
Jar, Anchovy, Fish, Balloon, Impressed, Blue Accent, c.1810, 6 1/2 In. 745.00
Jar, Bird, On Branch, Cobalt Blue, Edmands & Co., Mass., c.1850, 2 Gal., 14 3/8 In. 530.00
Jar, Bird, Perched On Sprig, Salt Glaze, 10 1/4 In. 325.00
Jar, Brown, Green, Salt Glaze, Lug Handles, Solomon Loy, Stamped, 8 Gal. 5980.00
Jar, Canister, Lid, Dancing Daisy, Bristol Glaze, Bail Handle, 6 In. 468.00
Jar, Canning, 5 Blue Horizontal Stripes, c.1860, 8 1/2 In. 305.00
Jar, Canning, 5 Stripes, Hamilton & Jones, Greensboro, c.1870, 9 1/2 In. 578.00
Jar, Canning, Bird, Singing, Blue, Bristol Glaze, c.1880, 2 Gal., 12 In. 200.00
Jar, Canning, Blue Accents, Hamilton & Jones, Greensboro, c.1870, 8 1/4 In. 550.00
Jar, Canning, Brown Alkaline Glaze, Geo. Husher, Brazil, Ind., c.1860, 7 In. 250.00
Jar, Canning, Eagle, Cobalt Blue, Salt Glaze, A.P. Donaghho, Fredericktown, Pa., 9 1/2 In. 470.00
Jar, Canning, Fish, Swimming, H.M. Whitman, Havana, N.Y., c.1860, Gal. 7425.00
Jar, Canning, Flower, Double, Blue, Squiggles, Dots, Mantell & Thomas, c.1854, 2 Gal. .. 635.00
Jar, Canning, Flower, Haidle & Zipp, Union Pottery, Newark, c.1880, 4 Gal., 16 In. 165.00
Jar, Canning, Flower, Ribbed, John Burger, Rochester, c.1865, 3 Gal., 13 In. 330.00
Jar, Canning, Flower, Spitting, Cowden & Wilcox, Harrisburg, Pa., c.1870, 9 1/2 In. 525.00
Jar, Canning, Flower, Stenciled, Williams Reppert, Greensboro, c.1870, 3 Gal., 13 1/2 In. . 275.00
Jar, Canning, Flowers, Blue, Cowden & Wilcox, c.1870, 2 Gal., 12 In. 440.00
Jar, Canning, Horse Head, Cinnamon Clay, W. Hart, Ogdensburg, c.1860, 2 Gal., 10 In. 3300.00
Jar, Canning, Leaf, Slip & Dotted, C. Hart Sherburne, c.1858, 3 Gal., 13 In. 200.00
Jar, Canning, Lid, Leaf & Flower, Ribbed, F. Stetzenmeyer Goetzman, c.1857, 9 In. 910.00
Jar, Canning, Man In Moon, Cowden & Wilcox, Pa., c.1870, Gal., 9 1/4 In. 11550.00
Jar, Canning, Mottled Brown, Adams, Allison & Co., Middlebury, c.1890, 8 In. 130.00
Jar, Canning, Plume, Blue Slip, C. Hart & Son, Sherburne, c.1860, 2 Gal., 10 1/2 In. 190.00
Jar, Canning, Plume, Cobalt Blue, Black, N.A. White & Son, Utica, N.Y., 3 Gal., 14 In. ... 358.00
Jar, Canning, Rose, Dilliner & Eneix, New Geneva, Pa., c.1890, 2 Gal., 12 In. 825.00
Jar, Canning, Script, Blue, Cortland, c.1860, 2 Qt., 7 1/2 In. 305.00
Jar, Canning, Stencil & Brushstrokes, Hamilton & Jones, Pa., c.1870, Gal., 10 In. 385.00

Jar, Canning, Stenciled Label, Cobalt Blue, A. Conrad, New Geneva, Penn., 6 1/4 In. 980.00
Jar, Canning, Sunflower, Blue, F. Stetzenmeyer & Co., Rochester, c.1860, 2 Gal., 12 In. . . . 2090.00
Jar, Canning, Sunflower, John Burger, c.1865, 3 Gal., 13 In. 165.00
Jar, Canning, Texas Longhorn, Cowden & Wilcox, Pa., c.1870, 3 Gal., 12 1/2 In. 14300.00
Jar, Canning, Tulip, Drooping, Cinnamon, Cylinder, c.1860, 3 Gal., 15 In. 165.00
Jar, Canning, Tulip, W.A. Macquoid & Co., c.1870, 1 1/2 Gal.10 In. 360.00
Jar, Canning, Tulips, Cobalt Blue, Peter Hermann, c.1850, Gal., 10 In. 145.00
Jar, Canning, Vine & Flower, Double, J. Weaver, Pa., c.1850, 2 Gal., 11 In. 440.00
Jar, Circle Design, Stoneware Lid, Richard Riemerschmid, 3 1/2 In. 100.00
Jar, Confit, French Provincial, Ocher Glaze, 12 In. 290.00
Jar, Cover, Tulip, Straight-Sided, Rounded Shoulders & Rim, Knob Finial, 9 3/4 x 7 In. . . . 385.00
Jar, Dots, Swags, Cobalt Blue, Applied Double Handles, C. Crolius, c.1814, 12 3/4 In. 2645.00
Jar, Flattened Rim, Drip Glaze, Lug Handle, Salt Glaze, Solomon Loy, Stamped, 6 Gal. . . . 1725.00
Jar, Floral Band, Blue, Cylindrical, Rounded Shoulder & Rim, 11 x 7 In. 605.00
Jar, Flower, Blue, F. Stetzenmeyer & G. Goetzman, Rochester, c.1857, 2 Gal., 11 In. 1430.00
Jar, Flower, Blue, Oval, D. Roberts & Co., Utica, c.1838, Gal. 248.00
Jar, Flower, Cobalt Blue, Lug Handles, Herrmann Family, Wisc., c.1850, 13 3/4 In. 129.00
Jar, Flower, Egg Shape, S. Blair, c.1830, Gal., 9 In. 248.00
Jar, Flower, Egg Shape, Sipe & Sons, Williamsport, Pa., c.1870, 8 In. 176.00
Jar, Flower, Gray, Blue, Rounded Shoulder & Rim, 8 1/4 x 5 In. 330.00
Jar, Flower, Tan, Oval, Gilson & Co., c.1840, 2 Gal., 4 In. 440.00
Jar, Flowers, Blue, Oval, Sieve Bottom, Flared Rim, Ear Handles, 13 1/2 x 11 In. 2310.00
Jar, Flowers, Brown Slip, Lyman & Clark, Gardiner, Me., c.1840, 12 1/2 In. 1320.00
Jar, Freeform Design, Cobalt Blue, Applied Handles, Tapered Lid, Finial, 14 In. 860.00
Jar, Incised Line, Running Brick Brown & Green Glaze, Cylindrical, c.1811, 10 In. 3565.00
Jar, Leaves, Cobalt Blue, Impressed Taunton, Mass, Applied Handles, 16 In. 200.00
Jar, Lid, Birds, Singing On Twig, Riedinger & Caire, c.1870, 3 Gal., 13 In. 360.00
Jar, Lid, Brown, Ocher, Oval, Open Handle, F. Carpenter, c.1805, 2 Gal., 13 In. 470.00
Jar, Lid, Flower, Blue, Oval, N. Clark & Co., Lyons, c.1850, 10 1/2 In. 690.00
Jar, Lid, Flower, Cobalt Blue, Tapered Shoulder, Flared Rim, 10 In. 200.00
Jar, Lid, Flower, Oval, W. Smith, Greenwich, N.Y., c.1833, 2 Gal., 13 In. 690.00
Jar, Masonic Mark, Handles, Salt Glaze, T.W. Craven, Stamped, 13 x 11 In. 1265.00
Jar, Mottled Olive, Alkaline Glaze, Angled Shoulder, 10 1/2 In. 175.00
Jar, Oil, Alkaline Glaze, Squat Oval, Edgefield District, Miles Mill, c.1880, 5 1/2 In. 375.00
Jar, Olive Orange Glaze, Salt Glaze, Applied Strap Handles, Rounded Rim, Brown, 8 Gal. . 1265.00
Jar, Oyster, Handle, Bryant & Woodruf, Pittsfield, Me., c.1860, 7 1/2 In. 415.00
Jar, Oyster, Impressed, Blue Accent, Tode Bros., N.Y., c.1860, 4 In. 415.00
Jar, S & L Vickers, Dealers In Dry Goods, Cobalt Blue Stenciling, 10 In. 865.00
Jar, Signature, Stenciled Cobalt Blue, Tapered Sides, Penn., 10 1/8 In. 345.00
Jar, Snuff, C. Crolius, Manhattan Wells, New York, c.1848, 9 1/2 In. 1438.00
Jar, Stenciled Label, Cobalt Blue, Weyman & Bro. Pittsburgh, Pa., 9 1/4 In. 290.00
Jar, Swag & Leaf, Blue, J. Keister & Co., Strasburg, Va., c.1880, 2 Gal., 13 In. 2420.00
Jar, Swag, Blue, Oval, C. Croluis Mfg., N.Y., c.1800, 4 Gal., 13 In. 1925.00
Jar, T. Cunningham, Druggist & Grocery, Mohawk, Albany Glaze, c.1870, 7 1/2 In. 175.00
Jar, Tulip, Cobalt Blue Stencil, 2 Handles, T.F. Reppert, Greensboro, Pa., 15 3/4 In. 460.00
Jar, Tulip, Cobalt Blue, Tapered, Flared Rim, Molded Bands, Impressed 2, 10 3/4 In. 290.00
Jar, Tulip, Leaves, Cobalt Blue, Oval, Applied Handles, Ohio, 14 In. 2760.00
Jar, W.F. Hahn, Alkaline Glaze, Flared Rim, Ear Shape Handles, c.1880, 13 In. 690.00
Jar, Woman & Flower, Incised, Blue Accents, Cylindrical, 14 3/4 x 5 7/8 In. 1100.00
Jardiniere, Lid, Flowers, Vines, Blue, Impressed, c.1850, 3 Gal., 13 1/2 In. 495.00
Jug, 2 Flowers, Blue, J. Heiser, Buffalo, N.Y., c.1852, 2 Gal., 13 1/2 In. 305.00
Jug, 2 Tulips, Beehive Shape, E.A. Montell, Olean, N.Y., c.1870, 2 Gal., 13 1/2 In. 250.00
Jug, Albany Slip, Applied Decoration, Handle, 12 In. 1208.00
Jug, Albany Slip, Incised Name, B.J. Willits, 12 In. 86.00
Jug, Alkaline Glaze, Cylinder, W.F. Hahn, Trenton, S.C., c.1880, 8 In. 690.00
Jug, Allan Turner & Co., Chemists & Druggists, Brookville, Ontario, c.1870, 13 1/2 In. . . . 165.00
Jug, Animal Head, Stylized, Cobalt Blue, Salt Glaze, Egg Shape, Strap Handle, 14 In. 1060.00
Jug, Babcock Litner & Co., Druggist & Grocers, c.1880, 1/2 Gal., 9 1/2 In. 250.00
Jug, Bears, Blue Gray, Embossed, Pillow Shape, Wire Bail Handle, 11 In. 210.00
Jug, Bee Stinger Decoration, J. Fisher & Co., Lyons, c.1880, 2 Gal., 13 1/2 In. 175.00
Jug, Bird, Blue, Squat, Haxstun & Co., Ft. Edward, N.Y., c.1870, Gal., 11 1/2 In. 525.00
Jug, Bird, Fat, On Twig, Ottman Bro's & Co., Fort Edward, N.Y., c.1870, 2 Gal., 14 In. . . . 578.00
Jug, Bird, Long Tail, White's, Utica, c.1865, 11 1/2 In. 880.00

Stoneware, Crock, Palm Tree,
Dotted Stag, John Burger, Rochester,
N.Y., c.1865, 6 Gal., 16 In.

Stoneware, Crock, Peacock,
Incised Tree & Rim, Midwestern,
c.1870, 10 Gal., 16 In.

Stoneware, Jug, Plume Slip
Design, New York Stoneware
Co., 2 Gal., 13 1/2 In.

Jug, Bird, On Flower Branch, White's, Utica, c.1865, 3 Gal., 15 1/2 In.	715.00
Jug, Bird, On Mound, Flowers, Blue Slip, Salt Glaze, W.H. Farrar, c.1855, 2 Gal., 14 In.	6000.00
Jug, Bird, On Plume, Blue, Squat, West Troy, Pottery, 2 Gal., 15 In.	360.00
Jug, Bird, On Stylized Branch, Blue, Fort Edward Stoneware Co., c.1884, 3 Gal., 16 In.	550.00
Jug, Bird, Paddletail, Blue, Ribbed Wings, N.A. White & Son, Utica, 2 Gal., 11 1/2 In.	1595.00
Jug, Bird, Perched On Sprig, Salt Glaze, Binghampton, N.Y., 11 1/2 In.	316.00
Jug, Bird, Running On Flower Branch, N.A. White, Utica, N.Y., c.1865, 3 Gal., 16 In.	470.00
Jug, Bird, Running, N.A. White, Utica, N.Y., 2 Gal., 14 1/2 In.	495.00
Jug, Bird, Running, White's, Utica, c.1865, 2 Gal., 15 1/2 In.	495.00
Jug, Bird, West Troy, c.1880, 3 Gal., 16 In.	635.00
Jug, Boston, Stamped, Applied Handle, Albany Slip, c.1820, 9 3/8 In.	720.00
Jug, Brown, Blue & Black Daubs, Ring-Turned Top, Partial Stamp, Owen, 6 In.	175.00
Jug, Bull's-Eye Over Tornado, c.1865, 1 1/2 Gal., 12 In.	200.00
Jug, Butterfly, Cobalt Blue Slip, Double Incised 5, C. Hart & Son, Sherburne, N.Y., 5 Gal.	460.00
Jug, C. Person's Sons, Elm St., Buffalo, N.Y., Blue Script, Lyons, N.Y., c.1870, 11 In.	220.00
Jug, C.J. Sturcke & D. Bornman, Grocery & Liquor Stores, Dark Tan, c.1840, 8 1/2 In.	220.00
Jug, Charleston Grocer, 2 Klinck & Wickenberg, Flowers, Salt Glaze, 2 Gal., 14 In.	2300.00
Jug, Compliments Of D.J. Buckman, St. Louis, Mo., Albany Glaze, c.1890, 3 In.	175.00
Jug, Constine & Wolhow, W. Barre, Pa., James Ryan, Pittston, Pa., c.1890, 11 In.	175.00
Jug, D.J. Long & Co., Lincoln St., Boston, Ottman Bros., N.Y., c.1870, 12 1/2 In.	190.00
Jug, Dark Brown, Olive Alkaline Glaze, Rounded Shoulders, 13 1/2 In.	290.00
Jug, Dog, His Master's Breath, Brown, White, Bristol Glaze, c.1900, 5 In.	45.00
Jug, Dot & Leafy Stem, Cobalt Blue, West Troy Pottery, 5 Gal.	460.00
Jug, Dragonfly, Blue, Handle, Salt Glaze, Beehive, 1840-50, 10 In.	255.00
Jug, Dragonfly, Dotted, c.1880, Gal., 11 In.	210.00
Jug, Draping Flower, Blue, Handle, c.1850, 2 Gal., 14 In.	275.00
Jug, Feather, Cobalt Blue, 19th Century, 9 1/2 In.	150.00
Jug, Fish, Albany Slip Glaze, Applied Strap Handle, Brown, Green, Mottled Gray, 13 In.	81.00
Jug, Flower Scroll, Cobalt Blue Slip, West Troy, N.Y., 12 1/2 In.	460.00
Jug, Flower, Blue, Cylindrical, J.B. Magee, Ithaca, N.Y., c.1854, 10 1/2 In.	470.00
Jug, Flower, Blue, Egg Shape, D. Roberts & Co., Utica, c.1828, Gal., 10 1/2 In.	495.00
Jug, Flower, Blue, Handle, Salt Glaze, Oval, 1830-1850, 16 In.	600.00
Jug, Flower, Blue, John Burger, Rochester, c.1865, 2 Gal., 14 1/2 In.	470.00
Jug, Flower, Blue, N. Clark & Co., Rochester, N.Y., c.1850, 2 Gal., 14 1/2 In.	3520.00
Jug, Flower, Blue, Oval, N. & R. Seymour, c.1820, 2 Gal., 16 In.	440.00
Jug, Flower, Blue, Wm. Moyer, Harrisburg, Pa., c.1858, 11 In.	360.00
Jug, Flower, Cobalt Blue, Applied Strap Handle, J. Shepard, Jr., Geddes, N.Y., 10 1/2 In.	290.00
Jug, Flower, Cobalt Blue, Applied Strap Handle, Small Spout, Oval, 10 1/2 In.	230.00
Jug, Flower, Cobalt Blue, Freehand, Impressed J.B. Mayfield, Milwaukee, 15 In.	920.00
Jug, Flower, Cobalt Blue, Incised, Green Label, Paper Label, Geo. McKearin, 12 In.	1840.00
Jug, Flower, Cobalt Blue, Oval, Impressed, J.G. Ball & Co., Poughkeepsie, 16 In.	1035.00
Jug, Flower, Dots, Cobalt Blue, Applied Strap Handle, White's, Binghamton, 10 1/2 In.	230.00
Jug, Flower, Double, Blue, Dotted, C.E. Pharris & Co., c.1865, 2 Gal., 14 In.	800.00
Jug, Flower, Double, Cobalt Blue, N.A. White & Son, c.1865, 3 Gal., 17 In.	300.00

Jug, Flower, Edmands & Co., c.1870, 2 Gal., 13 In. 190.00
Jug, Flower, Egg Shape, Humiston & Stockwell, N.J., c.1830, 3 Gal., 15 In. 1870.00
Jug, Flower, Egg Shape, I. Seymour, Troy, c.1825, 3 Gal., 15 1/2 In. 300.00
Jug, Flower, Gray, Cobalt Blue, Oval, 19th Century, 11 In. 375.00
Jug, Flower, Orange Peel Glaze At Shoulder, Lyons, c.1860, 2 Gal., 14 In. 250.00
Jug, Flower, Stylized, Fenton & Hancock, St. Johnsbury, Vt., c.1852, 2 Gal., 14 1/2 In. 580.00
Jug, Flowerpot, On Table, Blue, P.V. Wiggins, Saratoga Springs, c.1870, 12 In. 523.00
Jug, Flowers & Scrolls, Cobalt Blue, F.B. Norton, Mass., 12 In. 460.00
Jug, Flowers, Blue, Dotted, Oval, J. Heiser, Buffalo, N.Y., 1852, Gal., 11 1/2 In. 330.00
Jug, Flowers, Dots, Cobalt Blue, Impressed C. Hart & Son, Sherburne 2, 12 1/2 In. 400.00
Jug, Flowers, Double Handle, N. Clark Jr., Athens, N.Y., c.1850, 2 Gal.18 1/2 In. 935.00
Jug, Flowers, Double, Blue, Beehive, Brown Brothers, c.1890, 2 Gal., 11 1/2 In. 440.00
Jug, Grape Cluster, Applied, Egg Shape, Brown Alkaline Glaze, c.1860, 7 1/2 In. 440.00
Jug, Label, Cobalt Blue, J. Kilmarton, Waterbury, Conn., Strap Handle, 9 In. 315.00
Jug, Leaf, Blue Accent, Lyons, c.1860, 2 Gal., 14 1/2 In. 220.00
Jug, Leaf, Blue, Raised Rings, Applied Arched Handle, Double Spouts, 14 In. 635.00
Jug, Leaf, Gray, Cobalt Blue, Oval, L. Norton & Co., 19th Century, 11 In. 316.00
Jug, Leaf, Stylized, N.Y. Stoneware Co., Fort Edward, c.1880, 2 Gal., 14 In. 190.00
Jug, Leaves, Cobalt Blue, Strap Handle, Impressed Label, R.W. Russell, 11 In. 375.00
Jug, Man, Long Hair, Beard, Incised, Blue, Egg Shape, c.1820, 2 Gal., 15 In. 3300.00
Jug, Mills & Co., Dealers In Stoneware, Cobalt Blue Stencil, Pittsburgh, Pa., 12 In. 230.00
Jug, Moore & Hubbard, Blue Script, Ottman Bros & Co., c.1870, 2 Gal., 14 1/2 In. 130.00
Jug, Morris Fischler, New Brunswick, N.J., Bristol Glaze, c.1890, Gal., 10 1/2 In. 220.00
Jug, Ocher Accents, 2-Tone Glaze, Egg Shape, Boston, c.1805, 11 In. 385.00
Jug, Orange Peel Glaze, Salt Glaze, 4 Bands, Incised Rings, Oval, Nicholas Fox, 13 In. ... 920.00
Jug, Orange Peel Glaze, Salt Glaze, Brown, Strap Handle, Oval, Stamped, 14 In. 575.00
Jug, Orchid, Drooping, Blue, N.A. White & Son., Utica, N.Y., c.1870, 3 Gal., 17 In. 440.00
Jug, Parrot On Stump, Blue, N.A. White & Son., c.1865, 2 Gal., 13 1/2 In. 495.00
Jug, Parrot, F.B. Norton & Co., Worcester, Mass., c.1870, 2 Gal., 13 1/2 In. 1485.00
Jug, Peacock, Haxstun & Co., Ft. Edward, N.Y., c.1870, 2 Gal., 14 1/2 In. 2090.00
Jug, Peafowl, Flower, Cobalt Blue, Impressed White's, Utica, 2, 14 In. 860.00
Jug, Phill. G. Kelly, Straight Whiskey, Richmond, Bristol Glaze, c.1900, 4 1/2 In. ..110.00 to 154.00
Jug, Pine Tree, Cobalt Blue, N.A. White & Son, Utica, N.Y., c.1870, Gal., 11 In. 330.00
Jug, Pine Tree, N.A. White & Son., Utica, N.Y., c.1870, Gal., 11 1/2 In. 305.00
Jug, Plant, Cobalt Blue, Impressed White's, Utica, 2, 15 In. 290.00
Jug, Plume Slip Design, New York Stoneware Co., 2 Gal., 13 1/2 In. .... *Illus* 275.00
Jug, Plume, Blue Accent, Egg Shape, c.1830, Gal., 11 In. 360.00
Jug, Plume, Blue, Lyons, c.1860, 2 Gal., 14 1/2 In. 360.00
Jug, Plume, Blue, Slip, New York Stoneware Co., c.1870, 2 Gal., 13 1/2 In. 275.00
Jug, Plume, Blue, T. Harrington, Lyons, c.1850, 2 Gal., 14 In. 330.00
Jug, Plume, Dotted, West Troy Pottery, c.1880, 12 In. 175.00
Jug, Plume, W.J. Seymour, Troy, N.Y., 2 Gal., 14 In. 99.00
Jug, Poppy, Blue Slip, N.A. White & Co., Binghamton, c.1860, Gal., 12 In. 415.00
Jug, Poppy, Dotted Double, White's, Binghamton, c.1860, 2 Gal., 12 1/2 In. 275.00
Jug, R.H. Gilgallon, Scranton, Cooperative Pottery, Lyons, N.Y., c.1890, 2 Gal., 12 1/2 In. .. 275.00
Jug, Roosters, Fighting, J.A. & C.W. Underwood, Fort Edward, c.1865, 4 Gal., 17 In. 8800.00
Jug, Runny Olive Alkaline Glaze, 2 Handles, Oval, 15 3/4 In. 69.00
Jug, Salt Glaze, Brown Glazed Bands, Boston, Egg Shape, 1800s, 3 Gal., 14 3/8 In. 355.00
Jug, Snake, Applied, Burlon Craig, Mottled Olive, Brown, Alkaline Glaze, 7 1/4 In. 316.00
Jug, Stamped Druggist Marks, Jacob Claire, Pokeepsie, N.Y., c.1852, 13 In. 805.00
Jug, Stamped Label, Cobalt Blue, Oval, Applied Handle, 13 In. 316.00
Jug, Stick Figure, Man, Walking Stick, J. Duntz, New Haven, Conn., c.1835, 9 In. 1100.00
Jug, Stick Figures, St. Johns, c.1870, Gal., 11 1/2 In. 1375.00
Jug, Storage, Alkaline Glaze, Loop Handle, Marked Swaine, c.1900, 13 In. 92.00
Jug, Storage, Edgefield District, Alkaline Glaze, B.F. Landrum Sr., c.1850, 5 1/2 In. 605.00
Jug, Storage, Edgefield District, Alkaline Glaze, Loop Handle, S.C., c.1870, 11 In. 490.00
Jug, Swags, Incised & Intertwined, Flowers, Commeraws Stoneware, 16 In. 4255.00
Jug, Tan, Rust, Marked, Armstrong & Wentworth, Norwich, 2 Gal., 14 1/2 In. 400.00
Jug, Tornado, Blue, D.W. Graves, Westmoreland, c.1860, 2 Gal., 13 In. 110.00
Jug, Tree, Egg Shape, Thomas D. Chollar Homer, c.1835, 2 Gal., 12 In. 910.00
Jug, Tulip, Blue, Double Handles, I.M. Mead, c.1840, 5 Gal., 18 1/2 In. 2750.00
Jug, Tulip, Blue, Lyons, c.1860, 2 Gal., 15 In. 210.00

Jug, Tulip, Serpentine Stem, T. Reed, 2, Tuscarawas County, Ohio, 13 1/2 In. 805.00
Jug, Vine Decoration, Double Handles, C L Williams, Pa., c.1897, 5 Gal., 19 In. 1265.00
Jug, Vine, Flower, Blue Slip, N.A. White & Son, c.1865, Gal., 11 In. 305.00
Jug, White, Gray, Dark Gray, Incised Circles, 1783-1800, 18 In. 315.00
Jug, Wine, Blue Salt Glaze, Pewter Lid, Hand Engraved, c.1860, 1 1/2 Liter 195.00
Keg, Brandy, Rowboat, Oars, Barrel Shape, Tyler & Dillon, Albany, N.Y., c.1825, 2 Gal. ... 5500.00
Lid, Band, Cobalt Blue, Finial, 5 1/4 In. 300.00
Lion, Buddhist, Crouching, Head Lowered, Iron Brown Glaze, 1900s, 12 1/2 In. 460.00
Milk Pail, Tapered Shape, Flared Rim, Georgia, c.1880, 8 x 10 In. 315.00
Milk Pan, 5 Brush Plumes, 3 Blue Dashes Under Spout, 1 1/2 Gal., 6 x 11 1/2 In. 330.00
Milk Pan, Flower, Drooping, Blue, c.1850, Gal., 5 x 11 1/2 In. 360.00
Milk Pan, Vines, Flowers, c.1850, 2 Gal., 6 x 12 In. 360.00
Mug, Dogs, Men On Horseback, Handle, Salt Glaze, 4 1/2 In. 55.00
Mug, Initials MB, Cobalt Blue, Crock Shaped, Applied Handle, 5 In. 50.00
Mug, Salt Glaze, Handle, Barrel Shape, 5 In. 175.00
Mustard Jar, Appetone More-Than-A-Mustard, Frank Tea & Spice, 5 In. 605.00
Pail, Butter, Bird, Cobalt Blue, Salt Glaze, Wire & Wood Handle, Gal., 9 1/2 x 8 In. 1320.00
Pitcher, 3 Tulips, Incised Bands, Cobalt Blue, Salt Glaze, Bulbous, 7 In. 4180.00
Pitcher, Apple Design, Cobalt Blue, Ohio, 3 Gal., 15 1/2 In. 3335.00
Pitcher, Bird, Blue Filled, Incised, Floral Sprig, Henry Remmey, Gal. 35200.00
Pitcher, Bird, On Branch, Blue, Ear Handles, Whites, Utica, 2 Gal., 9 1/2 x 10 In. 935.00
Pitcher, Brown Sponged Spots, Brown Glazed Interior, Bulbous, 8 x 6 1/2 In. 825.00
Pitcher, Buttermilk, Loop Handle, Southern, Catawba Crossroads, N.C., c.1920, 11 In. ... 175.00
Pitcher, Cherries, Blue, c.1850, 10 In. 990.00
Pitcher, Clover Design, Cobalt Blue, 8 1/2 In. 1440.00
Pitcher, Deer Hunt, Blue, German Verse, Deer Head Spout, Bristol Glaze, 6 In. 250.00
Pitcher, Deer Hunt, Blue, German Verse, Deer Head Spout, Bristol Glaze, 7 1/2 In. 145.00
Pitcher, Dotted Leaf, Squiggle On Spout, c.1870, Gal., 11 In. 495.00
Pitcher, Flower, Blue, N.A. White & Co., c.1860, Gal., 10 1/2 In. 440.00
Pitcher, Flower, Cobalt Blue, Handle, Impressed Burger & Lang, Rochester, N.Y., 11 In. ... 865.00
Pitcher, Flowering Stems, Leaves, Bands, Cobalt Blue, Oval, Flared Top, 10 1/2 In. 1725.00
Pitcher, Flowers, Blue, Incised Bands, Applied Handle, Gal., 10 1/4 x 7 1/2 In. 990.00
Pitcher, Flowers, Blue, Salt Glaze, Applied Handle, 7 1/2 x 5 1/2 In. 2200.00
Pitcher, Flowers, Cobalt Blue, Impressed, Cowden & Wilcox, 19th Century, 10 3/4 In. ... 460.00
Pitcher, Flowers, Cobalt Blue, Salt Glaze, 8 3/4 x 6 1/4 In. 1705.00
Pitcher, Flowers, Cobalt Blue, Salt Glaze, Decorated Rim, 7 1/4 In. 935.00
Pitcher, Flowers, Cobalt Blue, Salt Glaze, Incised Bands, Strap Handle, 12 3/4 x 9 In. 1045.00
Pitcher, Flowers, Leaves, Cobalt Blue, Penn., 7 1/2 In. 575.00
Pitcher, George Washington, Eagle, Shield, Flag, Brown, England, c.1807, 10 1/4 In. 1590.00
Pitcher, Grape, Bacchus' Head, Bacchus & Acanthus Leaf Handle, 10 1/2 In. 130.00
Pitcher, Paul Revere Scene, People At Table, Bristol Glaze, White's, Utica, 6 3/4 In. 210.00
Pitcher, Pouring, 2 Tulip, Blue Swags, RCR, Phila, c.1870, 1 1/2 Gal., 11 1/2 In. 1430.00
Pitcher, Remmey Type, Cobalt Blue Flowers, 19th Century, 10 1/2 In. 750.00
Pitcher, Stenciled Flower, Williams & Reppert, Greensboro, Pa., c.1880, 2 Gal., 13 In. ... 990.00
Pitcher, Swirled, Spout Guard, Applied Strap Handle, Incised Wavy Line, 8 1/2 In. 1380.00
Pitcher, Tanware, Cream, Brown Drape Design, Ribbed Flower, Western Pa., c.1870, 5 In. 1760.00
Pitcher, Tulip, Flowers, W.H. Lehew & Co., Strasburg, Va., c.1880, 2 Gal., 14 In. 3520.00
Pitcher, Tulips, Cobalt Blue, Glaze, Tall Neck, Strap Handle, Geneva, 6 1/2 In. 575.00
Pitcher, Valley, Blue Swag, Blue Accents At Spout & Handle, c.1870, 2 Gal., 13 1/2 In. ... 1045.00
Pitcher, Westerwald, Blue To Gray, c.1750, 6 In. 980.00
Pitcher, Yellow Clay, Albany Slip, Engraved Flowers, Handle, 1891, 10 1/2 In. 2415.00
Pitcher & Bowl, Cobalt Blue Rim, Leaves, Miniature, 3 x 1 1/2-In. Bowl 1210.00
Powder Jar, Lid, Salt Glaze, Beaded Bands, 3 1/2 x 5 In. 110.00
Punch Bowl & Pedestal, Jousting, Cobalt Blue, Salt Glaze, No. 750, 23 1/2 In. 260.00
Rolling Pin, Mix With Us & Save Dough, H.D. Byram & Son, Blue Band 450.00
Rooster, Cobalt Blue Highlights On Base, Tail & Comb, 4 In. 460.00
Shoe, Woman's, Blue & White Bristol Glaze, c.1880, 5 In. 250.00
Vase, Cobalt Blue, c.1860, 5 3/4 In. 155.00
Vase, Glazed, C.B. Masten, c.1930, 8 3/4 In. 1980.00
Vase, Thomas Balbo, Blue Glaze, 10 In. 160.00
Water Cooler, Bird On Plume, Double Handle, Satterlee & Mory, c.1870, 6 Gal., 2 In. 600.00
Water Cooler, Blue Birds & Accents, Somerset Potters, c.1870, 3 Gal., 15 In. 3960.00

Water Cooler, Blue Decorated, Loop Handles, 15 Gal., 21 In. 10170.00
Water Cooler, Blue Decoration, Straight Sided, Baltimore, c.1840, 7 Gal. 18700.00
Water Cooler, Blue, Bird, On Curlicue Plume, O.L. & A.K. Ballard, 6 Gal., 15 In. 2640.00
Water Cooler, Blue, Double Plume Flowers, Cylinder, c.1850, 4 Gal., 14 1/2 In. 495.00
Water Cooler, Blue, Flowers, Vines, Nickel Plated Tap, Bristol Glaze, 3 Gal., 13 1/2 In. . . . 275.00
Water Cooler, Blue, Flowers, Vines, Nickel Plated Tap, Bristol Glaze, 6 Gal., 16 In. 275.00
Water Cooler, Blue, Polar Bears, Flowers, Blue Glaze, 2 Gal., 12 In. 525.00
Water Cooler, Cobalt Blue Decoration, Westhafer & Lambright, Ohio, c.1866, 24 In. 23000.00
Water Cooler, Cobalt Blue Glaze, Relief Molded, Forest Scene, Spigot, Lid, 14 3/4 In. . . . 345.00
Water Cooler, Cobalt Blue Incised Bird, Wreath, Double Handle, c.1870, 19 1/2 In. 3960.00
Water Cooler, Oval, Cobalt Signature, J. Lambright, Newport, Ohio, 1873, 16 In. 7245.00
Water Cooler, Salt Glaze, Brown, Green, Blue, Columbus, Ships, Sun, 6 Gal., 15 In. 3960.00
Water Cooler, Tooled & Blue Bands, Kenton Cooler, 15 In. 415.00
Whistle, Bird Shape, Hand Formed, Rockingham Glaze, c.1870, 1 1/2 In. 90.00
Whistle, Owl, On Stump, Rockingham Glaze, c.1870, 3 1/2 In. 220.00
Whistle, Poodle, Seated, Rockingham Glaze, c.1870, 3 3/4 In. 350.00

STORE fixtures, cases, cutters, and other items that have no advertising as part of the decoration are listed here. Most items found in an old
store are listed in the Advertising category in this book.

Apothecary Show Globes, Hanging, Blown, Green, Red, Spiral Teardrop Shape, 22 In., Pr.   2300.00
Bag & String Holder, Cast Iron, Wood Stand, 13 Compartments, 36 In. 1130.00
Bin, Grain, 2 Doors, 4 Compartments, Canted, Original Paint, 72 x 16 x 20 In. 1400.00
Broom Holder, Metal, Wood, Brass Ball, 35 In. 226.00
Cabinet, Display, Roll-Up Glass Doors, 4 Glass Doors, 3 Paneled Doors, Marble Counter . 3105.00
Cabinet, Watchmaker's, Cherry, Dovetail Construction, 11 x 17 x 8 1/2 In. 330.00
Candy Jar, 6-Sided, Ground Cover, Puritan, Glass, 17 In. 550.00
Candy Jar, Cylindrical, Ground Cover, Dakota, Glass, 18 In. 275.00
Candy Jar, Cylindrical, Ground Cover, Sample, Columbia, Glass, 10 1/2 In. 110.00
Candy Jar, Cylindrical, Ground Cover, Sample, Columbia, Glass, 16 In. 220.00
Candy Jar, Globe, Ground Cover, Dakota, Glass, 15 1/2 In. 385.00
Case, Display, Curved Front, 2 Sliding Doors, Metal Frame, Tabletop, 35 x 22 x 14 In. 230.00
Case, Display, Maple, Slant Front, 2 Doors, Early 20th Century, 20 x 17 x 12 In. 230.00
Case, Display, Nickel Frame, Glass, Pyramid Shape, 5 Shelves, 34 1/2 x 25 In. 605.00
Case, Display, Oak, Glass Sides, Sliding Back Door, 17 x 31 x 28 In. 220.00
Case, Display, Oak, Glass Sides, Top, Beveled Front Glass, Floor Model, 42 x 66 x 29 In. . . 1320.00
Case, Display, Poplar, Pine, Cornice, Porcelain Pull, 2 Shelves, Tabletop, 14 x 15 x 27 In. . 290.00
Case, Display, Scissors, Oak Frame, Etched Glass Front, Revolving Rack, 16 x 32 In. 935.00
Case, Display, Triangular, Oak, Opening Rear Door, 41 In. 770.00
Cheese Cutter, Cast Iron, White Porcelain Base, 10 x 8 In. 20.00
Cigar Cutter, Bronze, Ram, Mechanical, Push Button, 1 1/4 x 2 1/4 In. 430.00
Cigar Cutter, Cast Iron, Enterprise Mfg. Co., Countertop, 7 x 19 In. 70.00
Cigar Cutter, Dog, Poodle, Tail Lever, Cast Iron, 7 x 4 x 5 In. 250.00
Cigar Cutter, Duck Head, Metal, Silver Plate, 5 1/2 x 1 In. 175.00
Cigar Cutter, Heads Or Tails, Donkey, Gambling Device, Cast Iron, 7 1/2 x 9 In. 1540.00
Cigar Cutter, Odd Or Even, Gambling Device, 5 1/2 x 4 In. 1210.00
Coffee Grinders are listed in their own category.
Counter, Oak Case, 8 Drawers, Glass Front, Beans, 34 x 72 x 30 In. 1430.00
Counter, Oak, Walnut, Arched Panels, Scrolled Supports, Molded Base, 49 x 22 x 36 In. . . 1440.00
Desk Top, Postal Clerk's, Walnut, Poplar, 2 Drawers, 44 Compartments, 35 x 47 In. 575.00
Egg Vending Machine, Zinc, Souvenir Vending Co., Chicago, Ill., c.1870 . . . . 8500.00
Hat Display, Woman's Head, Victorian, 16 In. 295.00
Hat Rack, Wood, 71 In. 850.00
Jar, Display, 12 Cylinder Jars, Brass Lids, Metal, 58 x 28 x 21 In. 360.00
Light, Brass, Embossed, Acanthus Leaf Detail, Tin Shade, 35 In. 200.00
Lollipop Holder, Puppy, Ceramic, Countertop, 7 1/2 x 5 1/2 In. 155.00
Mannequin, Bisque Head, Jointed Arms, Hands, France, c.1890, Life Size, 53 In. 8900.00
Mannequin, Child, Carved Hands, France, 1880s 1950.00
Rack, Display, Metal, 4 Legs, 16 Circular Holders, 8 x 8 x 10 In. 25.00
Sack Bin, Poplar, Brown Finish, Graduated Case, 10 Slots, 28 x 10 x 15 In. 400.00
Showcase, Rolling, Oak, Etched Glass Panels, Drawers, 74 1/2 x 36 x 15 1/2 In. 4400.00
Sign, Boot Maker, Wood, Tin, Painted, Black, White Letters, Applied Boot, 37 x 29 In. . . . 2530.00

Sign, Codfish, Copper Over Wood, 40 In. 6400.00
Sign, Cowboy Boot, Carved, Full Bodied, 1800s, 25 x 16 In. 1840.00
Sign, Cowboy Boot, Cast Iron, 1800s, 19 1/2 x 12 In. 1380.00
Sign, Cowboy Boot, Full-Bodied, Cast Iron, 19th Century, 19 x 12 In. 1200.00
Sign, Drug Store, Stained Glass, Early 1900s, 26 x 100 In. 330.00
Sign, Eyeglasses, Metal, Painted Eyes, 2-Sided, 5 x 23 In. 468.00
Sign, Horse, Running, Carved Wood, Bottle Cap Eyes, Weathered, 38 x 16 In. 1840.00
Sign, Key, Tin, Yellow Paint, 78 x 25 3/4 In. 3190.00
Sign, Locksmith, Skeleton Key Shape, Cast Iron, Silver & Red Paint, 26 1/2 In. 1150.00
Sign, Locksmith, Skeleton Key Shape, Sheet Metal, 2-Sided, 42 1/2 x 14 1/2 In. 690.00
Sign, Pig, Carved, Painted, Glass Eyes, Full-Bodied, Iron Loop, c.1900, 13 x 24 In. 1765.00
Sign, Pig, Curled Tail, Sheet Metal, Painted, 11 x 24 In. 230.00
Sign, Pocket Watch, Tin, Gray, Black & White Face, Roman Numerals, 31 x 23 In. 935.00
Sign, Shoes, Hand, Pointing Finger, Black Ground, 10 1/2 x 48 In. 1150.00
Strawholder, Clear Glass, Chrome Finished Base & Lid, Insert, Round, 10 x 5 1/2 In. 35.00
Strawholder, Clear Glass, Chrome Lid & Insert, 11 In. . . . . .75.00 to 110.00
Strawholder, Clear Glass, Metal Lid & Insert, Octagonal, 11 x 4 1/2 In. 28.00
Strawholder, Clear Glass, Metal Lid & Insert, Octagonal, 12 In. 90.00
Strawholder, Copper Finish Frame, Lid & Insert, Octagonal, 11 In. 300.00
Strawholder, Frosted Glass, Forest Scene, 11 x 4 In. 110.00
Strawholder, Green Glass, Metal Lid & Insert, Octagonal, 11 1/2 In. 176.00
Strawholder, Metal Lid & Insert, Octagonal, 11 1/2 In. . . . . .80.00 to 120.00
Tally Board, Walnut, 1700s 250.00
Tea Bin, Imperial, Metal, Country Store, 13 1/2 x 12 x 9 1/2 In. 110.00
Tobacco Cutter, Brighton 3, Cast Iron, 10 In. 60.00
Tobacco Cutter, Great Slice Plug, Cast Iron, 16 In. 176.00
Tobacco Cutter, Miller-DuBrul & Peters, Wood, Metal, 7 In. 95.00
Tobacco Cutter, Nude, Chamber Pot, Sterling Silver, 1 1/4 x 3/4 In. 295.00
Tobacco Cutter, Rex, S.C.W.W. Co., Iron, Lever Action, St. Louis, Mo. 65.00
Tobacco Cutter, Star, Cast Iron, 19 In. 165.00
Tobacco Leaf Cutter, Hand Forged, Kentucky, Late 1800s 45.00

STOVES have been used in America for heating since the eighteenth
century and for cooking since the nineteenth century. Most types of
wood, coal, gas, kerosene, and even some electric stoves are collected.

Cast Iron, 2 Burners, Ransom & Ransom Co., Toledo, Ohio, Patent 1918 . . . . 85.00
Franklin, Cast Iron, Inscribed, 18th Century 1035.00
Leaves, Cast Iron, North Lebanon Foundry, 19th Century, 25 x 42 In. 520.00
Phoenix, Man Holding Fish Above A Crown, Cast Iron, c.1766, 24 x 15 1/4 In. 805.00
Potbelly, Union Stove Works, New York 8600.00
Shaker, Cast Iron, Canted Sides, Peg Legs, Mt. Lebanon, N.Y., c.1840, 25 x 28 In. 460.00
Shaker, Cast Iron, Half Round Front Tray, Canted Sides, Penny Feet, 18 1/4 x 34 In. 920.00
Shaker, Cast Iron, Super Heater, New Lebanon, N.Y., c.1820, 25 x 34 x 10 In. 1325.00
Stove Plate, Arched Panels, Tulips, Hearts, Cast Iron, 18th Century, 24 x 26 In. . .1035.00 to 2185.00
Stove Plate, Conqueror, Cast Iron, 18th Century, 24 x 27 In. 345.00
Stove Plate, Horse, Leaf Cartouche, Cast Iron, 1758, 26 x 14 1/2 In. 290.00
Stove Plate, Horse, Leaf Cartouche, Cast Iron, 18th Century, 24 x 20 In. 175.00
Stove Plate, Hunter, Cast Iron, Germany, 18th Century, 24 1/2 x 14 1/4 In. 175.00
Stove Plate, Samson & Delilah, Cast Iron, Inscribed, 18th Century, 24 x 24 3/4 In. 3680.00
Stove Plate, Seated Woman, Leaf Cartouche, Inscribed, Pine Grove, Cast Iron, 22 x 29 In. . 920.00

SUMIDA is a Japanese pottery that was made from about 1870 to
1941. Pieces are usually everyday objects—vases, jardinieres, bowls,
teapots, and decorative tiles. Most pieces have a very heavy orange-
red, blue, brown, black, green, purple, or off-white glaze, with raised
three-dimensional figures as decorations. The unglazed part is painted
red, green, black, or orange. Sumida was sometimes mistakenly called
Korean Pottery or *Poo Ware* in the past.

Box, Tobacco, Silver Inlaid, Calligraphy, Korea, 19th Century, 4 1/4 In. 115.00
Brush Pot, Bamboo, Relief Carving, Birds, Prunus Tree, Brushes, 9 1/2 In. 115.00
Figurine, Daruma, Old Monk In Red Robe, Seated On Bell, 8 1/4 In. 720.00
Jar, Flowers, Blue & White, Oval, 3 In. 230.00

Jar, Peony, Blue & White, Yi Dynasty, 5 1/2 x 5 3/4 In. 575.00
Vase, Bottle, Double Gourd, Flower, Vine, Inlaid Celadon, 20th Century, 13 1/4 In. 345.00
Vase, Iris, Relief, Pear Shape, 9 1/2 In. 1495.00

SUNBONNET BABIES were first introduced in 1900 in the book
The Sunbonnet Babies. The stories were by Eulalie Osgood Grover,
illustrated by Bertha Corbett. The children's faces were completely
hidden by the sunbonnets. The children had been pictured in black and
white before this time, but the color pictures in the book were immediately successful. The Royal Bayreuth China Company made a full line
of children's dishes decorated with the Sunbonnet Babies. Some Sunbonnet Babies plates have been reproduced, but are clearly marked.

Bowl, Mending, 5 3/4 In. 135.00
Candlestick, Ironing, 4 1/4 In. 135.00
Candlestick, Mending, 5 1/2 In. 225.00
Candlestick, Mending, Pair, 4 In. 300.00
Candlestick, Shield, Fishing, 4 1/2 In. 400.00
Candlestick, Shield, Mopping, 5 In., Pair 275.00
Chocolate Pot, Cleaning Windows, 5 1/2 In. 450.00
Compote, Mending, 6 In. 250.00
Creamer, Cleaning Windows, 3 In. 135.00
Creamer, Fishing, 2 3/4 In. 115.00
Creamer, Fishing, 4 In. 155.00
Creamer, Ironing, 2 3/4 In. 145.00
Creamer, Mopping, Stick Handle, 2 1/2 In. 325.00
Creamer, Washing, 3 1/4 In. 125.00
Cup & Saucer, Demitasse 165.00
Cup & Saucer, Mopping 175.00
Dish, Feeding, Washing, 7 1/4 In. 350.00
Flowerpot, Mending, Handles, 3 In. 115.00
Hair Receiver, Mending 275.00
Hatpin Holder, Mending, 5 In. 650.00
Jar, Ironing, 3 x 3 1/2 In. 20.00
Milk Pitcher, Cleaning Windows, Pinched Spout, 4 In. 175.00
Milk Pitcher, Fishing, Pinched Spout, 5 1/4 In. 215.00
Mug, Cleaning Windows, 3 In. 125.00
Mug, Mending, 3 Handles, 3 1/4 In. 235.00
Mug, Mopping, 3 1/4 In. 185.00
Mug, Washing, 2 3/4 In. 195.00
Pin Box, Cover, Cleaning Windows, 2 1/2 In. 165.00
Pin Box, Cover, Fishing, 4 1/2 In. 255.00
Pitcher, Cleaning Windows, 3 1/2 In. 165.00
Pitcher, Cleaning Windows, 4 In. 85.00
Pitcher, Mopping, 4 In. 135.00
Pitcher, Mopping, 5 1/2 In. 195.00
Planter, Ironing, Insert, 3 3/4 In. 235.00
Plate, Ironing, 9 In. 195.00
Plate, Mending, 6 In. 145.00
Plate, Mopping, 6 In. 105.00
Plate, Washing, 7 1/2 In. 85.00
Plate, Washing, Handle, 10 1/2 In. 165.00
Powder Jar, Mending, 4 1/4 In. 225.00
Powder Jar, Mopping, Footed, 4 In. 285.00
Relish, Cleaning Windows, Handle, 7 3/4 In. 175.00
Salt & Pepper, Fishing 255.00
Sugar, Cover, Fishing, Handle, 3 In. 205.00
Sugar & Creamer, Fishing 275.00
Tray, Dresser, Ironing, 10 In. 225.00
Tray, Washing, Rectangular, 11 In. 245.00
Tumbler, Washing, 3 1/2 In. 145.00
Vase, Mending, 5 In. 275.00
Vase, Washing, 7 In. 175.00
Wall Pocket, Mopping, 4 1/2 In. 500.00

Wash Sumida ware carefully. The orange-red color is only lightly fired and will wash off.

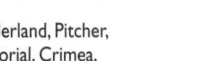

Sunderland, Pitcher,
Armorial, Crimea,
Verse, Sailors Farewell,
Pink Luster Trim, 7 In.

SUNDERLAND luster is a name given to a special type of pink luster made by Leeds, Newcastle, and other English firms during the nineteenth century. The luster glaze is metallic and glossy and appears to have bubbles in it. Other pieces of luster are listed in the Luster category.

Pitcher, Armorial, Crimea, Verse, Sailors Farewell, Pink Luster Trim, 7 In. . . . . *Illus*	650.00
Plaque, Luster, Polychrome Enamel Transfer, Verses, 8 x 9 In. & 9 x 10 In., Pair	405.00
Punch Bowl, Luster, Sailing Ship, 4 Paneled Scenes, 12 1/4 In.	805.00
Punch Bowl, Pink Luster, Central Transfer, View Of Cast Iron Bridge, 5 x 13 In.	105.00
Watch Holder, Tall Case Clock, 2 Children, Dixon Austin & Co., c.1820, 10 3/4 In.	850.00

SUPERMAN was created by two seventeen-year-olds in 1938. The first issue of *Action* comics had the strip. Superman remains popular and became the hero of a radio show in 1940, cartoons in the 1940s, a television series, and several major movies.

Action Figure, Krypto, Phantom Zone Protector, Rock, Captain Action, Ideal, 1960s	190.00
Bank, Dime Register, Tin Lithograph, Yellow Ground, 1940s, 2 1/2 x 2 1/2 In.	198.00
Birthday Card, 9th Birthday, Best Wishes, Quality Cards, 1940s, 5 3/4 x 4 3/4 In.	135.00
Box, Kellogg's Corn Flakes, Norman Rockwell Front, Flying Superman Offer On Back . . .	140.00
Box, Superman Candy & Toy, Perry White Card, Novel Package, 1950s, 3 x 7 In.	775.00
Box, Superman Cards, 5 Cents, Countertop Display, Topps, c.1965, 3 3/4 x 8 In.	310.00
Button, Read Superman Action Comics Magazine, Tin Lithograph, 1939, 7/8 In.	100.00
Button, Read Superman Daily, In Democrat, Round, c.1939	1000.00
Button, Supermen Of America, Yellow Edge, 1947, 1 1/4 In.	60.00
Card, Adventure, No. 5, Fighting A Tank, Pledge Stamp, 1941, 2 3/4 x 4 1/2 In.	1290.00
Card, Adventure, No. 17, Catches Spies, Pledge Stamp, 1941, 2 3/4 x 4 1/2 In.	1120.00
Coloring Set, Crayon By Numbers, National Comics, 1954, 9 1/2 x 11 1/2 In.	115.00
Comic Book, 3-Dimension Adventures, 3-D Glasses, National, 1953, 11 x 8 1/4 In.	345.00
Comic Book, No. 10, May-June, 1941	7500.00
Doll, Composition, Ideal, 13 In.	660.00
Figure, Wooden, Segmented, Painted, Ideal, 14 In.	370.00
Game, Adventures Of Superman, Milton Bradley, Board, c.1940, 9 3/4 x 19 1/4 In. . .250.00 to 625.00	
Game, Calling Superman, New Reporting, Transogram, Box, 1954, 9 x 17 1/2 In.	175.00
Game, Speed, Milton Bradley, Box, Early 1940s, 8 3/4 x 15 1/2 In.	100.00
Game, Superman Spin Cycle Series, Pressman Toy, Box, c.1967, 10 1/4 x 15 3/4 In.	75.00
Lobby Card, Electric Furnace, Chapter 7, Kirk Alyn, Columbia, c.1948, 11 x 14 In.	265.00
Lunch Box, Metal, Thermos Bottle	49.00
Membership Kit, Supermen Of America, 1961	465.00
Patch, Rectangular, 1940	2400.00
Poster, Amazing, Startling, Linen Mount, Fleischer, Paramount, 1941, 41 x 27 In.	11550.00
Ring, Flasher, Plastic, Leaping, Drifting Downward, Gold Color, 1966	125.00
Ring, Metal, Acrylic, Nestle, Envelope, Paperwork, c.1979, 4 1/4 In.	50.00
Ring, Tim, Superman Flying, Silver Luster, Solid Band, Non-Adjustable, 1930s	2000.00
Toy, Krypto Raygun, Flashes Picture Stories On The Wall, Box	385.00
Toy, Tank, Tin Lithograph, Windup, Marx, Box, 1940, 4 In.	440.00
Wrapper, Super Bubble Gum, Join Supermen Of America Club, c.1940, 4 1/2 x 6 In.	865.00
Wristwatch, Supertime, Chrome, Lightning Bolt Hands, Ingraham, No. 289, Box, 1948 . . .	4295.00

SUSIE COOPER began as a designer in 1925 working for the English firm A.E. Gray & Company. In 1932 she formed Susie Cooper Pottery, Ltd. In 1950 it became Susie Cooper China, Ltd., and the company made china and earthenware. In 1966 it was acquired by Josiah Wedgwood & Sons, Ltd. The name Susie Cooper appears with the company names on many pieces of ceramics.

Bowl, Cereal, Green Dresden, 9 In.	24.00
Bowl, Vegetable, Nosegay, 1932, 9 In.	65.00
Casserole, Lid, 2 Handles, Dresden Spray, Kestral Shape, Lid Is Another Bowl	100.00
Plate, Dinner, Cactus, 9 3/4 In.	27.00
Plate, Salad, Glen Mist, 8 3/8 In.	24.00
Soup, Coupe, 2 Handles Dresden Spray	30.00
Soup, Coupe, Parrot Tulip, 2 Handles	20.00
Sugar, Open, Glen Mist	38.00

SWANKYSWIGS are small drinking glasses. In 1933, the Kraft Food Company began to market cheese spreads in these decorated, reusable glass tumblers. They were discontinued from 1941 to 1946, then made again from 1947 to 1958. Then plain glasses were used for most of the cheese, although a few special decorated Swankyswigs have been made since that time. A complete list of prices can be found in *Kovels' Depression Glass & Dinnerware Price List*.

Blue Tulips, 5 Oz., 3 3/4 In., 4 Piece	15.00
Posy, Violets, 3 1/2 In.	8.00
Red Cornflower, 3 1/2 In., 2 Piece	16.00
White Diamonds, 3 5/8 In.	18.00

SWASTIKA KERAMOS is a line of art pottery made from 1906 to 1908 by the Owen China Company of Minerva, Ohio. Many pieces were made with an iridescent glaze.

Vase, Bulbous, Pink & Gold Irises, Bronze Ground, Stamped, 10 3/4 In.	490.00

SWORDS of all types that are of interest to collectors are listed here. The military dress sword with elaborate handle is probably the most wanted. Be sure to display swords in a safe way, out of reach of children.

Bayonet, 1872 Model, Marked, Frank DeCaro, New York, Scabbard, 1800s, 39 In.	490.00
Cutlass, Naval, Model 1862, Ames, Leather Grip, c.1864, 26-In. Blade	690.00
Dirk, Wood, Gilt Brass Mounts, Scabbard, Knife, Fork, Scotland, Late 1800s, 17 1/2 In.	707.00
Dress, Nicholas II, Engraved, Cyrillic, Partial Basket Hilt, Monogram, 38 1/4 In.	4110.00
European Court, Edeson, Ravenscroft, Etched, Triangular Blade, Scabbard, 31-In. Blade	200.00
Foot Officer's, Model 1850, Ames, Sharkskin Wrap, Leather Scabbard, 30 1/2-In. Blade	4600.00
Foot Officer's, Model 1850, Inscription, Brass Mounted Leather Scabbard, 31-In. Blade	2300.00
Infantry, England, Brass Hilt, Spiral Flute Grip, c.1750, 26-In. Blade	875.00
Infantry, Germany, Brass Hilt, Ribbed Grip, c.1820, 22 1/2-In. Blade	365.00
Infantry, Germany, Officer's, Non-Regulation, Scabbard, Post Civil War, 31 5/8-In. Blade	115.00
Jefferson Guard, St. Louis World's Fair, Louisiana Purchase Expo, Scabbard, 1904, 26 In.	1160.00
Katana, Mixed Metals, Japan, Shinto, 33 1/4 In.	650.00
Marked U.S. 1861, Brass Handle, Straight Blade, Scabbard, 34 1/2 In.	200.00
Militia, Ames, Bone Handle, Knight Head Pommel, Brass Scabbard, Etched, 31-In. Blade	575.00
Militia, Bone Grip, Blue & Gold Blade, Etched, Brass Scabbard, c.1830	1035.00
Militia, Eagle Head Pommel, Spiral Bone Grip, Stirrup Hilt, 31-In. Blade	550.00
Militia, Solingen, Blue & Gold Blade, Brass Scabbard, c.1830, 32 1/2-In. Blade	750.00
Musician's, Model 1840, Ames, 1862, 27 1/2-In. Blade	290.00
Napoleonic First Empire, Officer's, Ebony Grip, Curved Blade, Scabbard, 30-In. Blade	1900.00
Naval Officer's, England, Shark Skin Grip, Straight Blade, Engraved, c.1820, 25-In. Blade	565.00
Non-Commissioned Officer's, Model 1840, Ames, 1863, 32-In. Blade	290.00
Saber, Cavalry, British, Wilkinson, London, Iron Scabbard, Late 1800s, 34 1/2-In. Blade	115.00
Saber, Cavalry, C. Roby & Co., Brass Hilt, Leather & Wire Wrap, Scabbard, 1860, 42 In.	920.00
Saber, Cavalry, Model 1853, England, Leather Grip, Black Scabbard, 34 1/2-In.	400.00
Saber, Cavalry, Officer's, Model 1872, Ames, Scabbard, 31 1/2-In. Blade	400.00
Saber, Cavalry, US Model 1860, Wire Wrapped Leather Grip, Metal Scabbard, 34 1/2 In.	445.00
Saber, Enlisted Cavalry, Model 1840, Ames, c.1850, 35 1/2-In. Blade	750.00

Saber, Enlisted Cavalry, Model 1840, Emerson & Silver, Trenton, N.J.	345.00
Saber, Enlisted Cavalry, Model 1840, Scabbard, Horstmann, 35 1/2-In. Blade	489.00
Saber, Horseman's, Eagle Head Pommel, Blue, Gold Blade, Leather Scabbard, 32-In. Blade	5405.00
Saber, Indonesia, Carved Figures, Leaves, Script, Pommel, Wood Scabbard, 35 In.	375.00
Scabbard, Bound Handle, Lacquered, Japan, 20th Century, 19 In.	200.00
Silver, Kalishimare Blade, Silver Pommel & Guard, European, 29-In. Blade	1495.00
Staff & Field Officer's, Model 1850, Etched Flowers, Scabbard, 30 3/4 In.	555.00
Staff & Field Officer's, Model 1850, Steel Scabbard, Clauberg, Solingen, 31 1/2-In. Blade .	1064.00
Staff & Field Officer's, Model 1860, Eagle Hilt Design, Late 1800s, 28-In. Blade, 33 In. . . .	316.00
Staff & Field Officer's, Model 1860, Scabbard, Gaylord, Mass., 30-In. Blade	345.00
Tsuba, Bronze, Hokei Shape, Tokugawa Mon, Japan, Edo Period, 2 3/4 In.	345.00
Tsuba, Iron, Egg Shape, Da-Daiko, Bugaku Enclosure, Japan, Edo Period, 3 In.	655.00
Tsuba, Iron, Pearl Design, Shin No Maru Gata, Signed, 1700s, 3 In.	400.00
Tsuba, Shakudo, Egg Shape, Snowflake, Peony, Shigeyoshi, Japan, Edo Period, 2 3/4 In. . .	1215.00
Tsuba, Shakudo, Peony & Butterfly, Flowers, Japan, Edo Period, 2 3/4 In.	515.00
Tsuba, Soten School, Iron, Serpentine Rim, Openwork, Dragon, Japan, Edo Period, 3 In. . .	1028.00
Wakizashi, Japan, 19th Century, 20 In.	235.00

SYRACUSE is a trademark used by the Onondaga Pottery of Syracuse, New York. The company was established in 1871. It is still working. The name became the Syracuse China Company in 1966. It is known for fine dinnerware and restaurant china.

SYRACUSE China

Americana, Plate, Dinner, 10 In.	7.00
Appleton, Platter, Federal Shape, Gold Trim, 13 In.	24.00
Athena, Plate, Dinner, Virginia Shape, 10 In.	34.00
Belaire, Bowl, Vegetable, Oval, California Shape	62.00
Belmont, Plate, Dinner, Empire Shape, Platinum Trim	34.00
Blue Mist, Bowl, Vegetable, Round, Carefree Shape	35.00
Briarcliff, Platter, Federal Shape, Gold Trim, 13 3/4 x 10 1/4 In.	32.00
Briarcliff, Platter, Oval, Federal Shape, 12 x 9 In.	30.00
Bridal Rose, Bowl, Cereal, California Shape	30.00
Bridal Rose, Cup & Saucer, California Shape	32.00
Bridal Rose, Sugar & Creamer, California Shape	30.00
Castaways, Plate, Oriental Design, Gold Rim, Restaurant Ware, 7 1/2 In.	29.00
Celeste, Cup & Saucer	31.00
Champlain, Platter, Oval, Berkeley Shape, 12 3/4 x 8 3/4 In.	30.00
Coralbel, Cup & Saucer, Virginia Shape, Platinum Trim	33.00
Coralbel, Platter, Oval, Virginia Shape, 14 In.	35.00
Coralbel, Platter, Oval, Winchester Shape, 12 x 9 In.	30.00
Countess, Sugar, Cover, Carolina Shape	35.00
Finesse, Creamer, Carefree Shape, Ecru, Blue Flower	29.00
Flame Lily, Coffeepot, Carefree Shape, Copper Top, China Knob, 9 1/2 In.	38.00
Graymont, Sugar, Cover, Paul Revere Shape	30.00
Lilac Rose, Creamer, Berkeley Shape	30.00
Lilac Rose, Soup, Cream, Berkeley Shape, 4 7/8 In.	35.00
Lynnfield, Gravy Boat, Attached Underplate, Carefree Shape, 5 3/4 In.	29.00
Lyric, Cup & Saucer, Carolina Shape	31.00
Madame Butterfly, Sugar, Cover, Virginia Shape, Gold Trim	30.00 to 35.00
Mayflower, Creamer, Carefree Shape, Red	29.00
Meadow Breeze, Cup & Saucer, Carolina Shape	34.00
Meadow Breeze, Gravy Boat	140.00
Meadow Breeze, Plate, Salad, 8 In.	9.00
Monticello, Cup & Saucer, Winchester Shape	33.00
Monticello, Cup & Saucer, Winchester Shape, Gold Band	25.00
Nocturne, Creamer, California Shape	57.00
Nocturne, Cup & Saucer, California Shape	31.00
Old Ivory, Saucebote, Attached Underplate, Federal Shape, Red Trim	30.00
Plymouth, Platter, Oval, Blue Flower Swags, Gold Trim, 14 In.	30.00
Puritan, Bowl, Fruit, Scalloped Rim, Carefree XL Shape	6.00
Puritan, Gravy Boat, Green Flowers, Sponged Gold Trim	30.00
Raleigh, Bowl, Vegetable, Oval, Federal Shape, Pink, Gold Trim, 10 1/4 In.	35.00
Serene, Creamer, Carefree Shape	33.00
Sherwood, Cup & Saucer, Virginia Shape	33.00

Sherwood, Gravy Boat, Attached Underplate, Virginia Shape	35.00
Sherwood, Plate, Bread & Butter, 6 In.	14.00
Sherwood, Plate, Dinner, Virginia Shape, 10 In.	45.00
Sherwood, Soup, Cream, Underplate, Virginia Shape	48.00
Sherwood, Sugar, Cover, Virginia Shape	68.00
Sonata, Plate, Dinner, Silhouette Shape, 10 In.	45.00
Stansbury, Bowl, Vegetable, Oval, Federal Shape, 10 1/2 x 8 In.	35.00
Stansbury, Soup, Dish, Federal Shape	33.00
Suzanne, Bowl, Fruit, Federal Shape, Gold Trim	26.00
Suzanne, Soup, Cream, Federal Shape, Gold Trim	30.00
Victoria, Bowl, Vegetable, Oval, Federal Shape, 10 1/2 x 8 In.	35.00
Victoria, Cup & Saucer, Federal Shape	33.00
Windswept, Plate, Salad, Carefree Shape, 8 In.	8.00
Woodbine, Sugar, Cover, Carefree Shape	32.00

TAPESTRY, PORCELAIN, see Rose Tapestry category.

TEA CADDY is the name for a small box made to hold tea leaves. In the eighteenth century, tea was very expensive and it was stored under lock and key. The first tea caddies were made with locks. By the nineteenth century, tea was more plentiful and the tea caddy was larger. Often there were two sections, one for green tea, one for black tea.

Apple, Apple Shape, Hinged Lid, England, 19th Century, 4 1/2 In., Pair	14950.00
Apple, Carved, Painted, Red, Yellow, England, c.1790, 4 3/4 x 5 In.	3450.00
Beech, Oval Inlay, Tulipwood Chequer Banding, Octagonal, England, 5 1/2 In.	1610.00
Black Lacquer, Giltwood, 2 Compartments, Chinese Export, c.1835, 4 1/2 x 7 1/4 In.	489.00
Black Lacquer, Hinged Lid, Vignettes, Courting Scene, Chinese, c.1900, 9 In.	1410.00
Burl Walnut, Hinged Lid, Zinc Lined Compartments, England, 6 x 12 In.	340.00
Burl Walnut, Tunbridgeware, Dome Top, Parquetry Bands, Glass Bowl, 7 x 11 x 6 In.	780.00
Burl Walnut, Tunbridgeware, Parquetry, Geometric Shapes, c.1850, 6 x 9 x 6 In.	720.00
Burled Veneer, Satinwood Band, Claw & Ball Feet, Ring Handles, 13 x 7 x 8 In.	635.00
Copper, Silver, Spot Hammered, Butterfly, Frog, Plant, Gorham, 1883, 4 In.	2400.00
Fruitwood, Apple Shape, Domed & Hinged Lid, Stem, 5 x 4 In.	1150.00
Fruitwood, Brass, Gilt Pewter Mounted, Apple Shape, Georgian, 5 x 4 In.	290.00
Fruitwood, Pear Shape, Hinged Lid, 7 x 4 5/8 In.	550.00
Georgian, Burl, Rhomboid Shape, Bone Escutcheon, 5 1/2 x 6 1/2 x 5 5/8 In.	575.00
Gilt Brass Mounted, Chinoiserie, Black & Gold Penwork, Georgian, 7 x 13 In.	3220.00
Inlaid Burlwood, Cover, Ebonized, Quarter Column, Arched Panel, 6 1/2 x 6 x 6 In.	1610.00
Ivory, Tortoiseshell Inlaid, Hinged Lid, Coffin Shape, 6 x 7 1/2 x 4 3/4 In.	1725.00
Lacquer, 3 Compartments, Japanned, Chinoiserie Style, Georgian, c.1815, 5 x 8 x 6 In.	520.00
Lacquer, Hinged Lid, Gilded Garden, Red Ground, Chinese Export, 4 x 9 x 4 In.	690.00
Mahogany, Brass Mounted, Sarcophagus, Lion Mask Handles, 6 x 11 1/2 In.	750.00
Mahogany, Burl Veneer, Ivory, George III, c.1790, 6 3/4 x 11 1/2 In.	575.00
Mahogany, Coffin Shape, Dovetailed, England, Early 1800s, 5 1/4 x 8 1/2 In.	189.00
Mahogany, Coffin Shape, Fitted Interior, Glass Bowl, c.1840, 6 x 11 x 6 In.	230.00
Mahogany, Coffin Shape, Fitted Interior, Regency, Early 19th Century, 7 x 13 x 6 In.	460.00
Mahogany, Coffin Shape, Hinged Lid, Brass Handle, Regency Style, 7 x 12 x 6 In.	200.00
Mahogany, Crossbanded, Marquetry, Rectangular, England, Late 1700s, 5 1/2 In.	1500.00
Mahogany, Hinged Lid, Chamfered Corners, Fitted Interior, William IV, 6 x 12 In.	280.00
Mahogany, Hinged Lid, Dome Top, Coffin Shape, Regency, c.1825, 7 x 12 x 6 In.	200.00
Mahogany, Plated Mount, 3 Sections, Bone Grips, Ball Feet, 6 3/4 x 12 x 6 In.	259.00
Mahogany, Rectangular, Canted Corners, Kite Escutcheon, 5 1/2 x 9 3/4 x 5 1/2 In.	690.00
Mahogany Inlay, Hinged Lid, Divided Interior, England, 4 7/8 x 9 x 4 1/2 In.	345.00
Mahogany Inlay, Hinged Lid, Georgian, 5 x 4 x 4 In.	320.00
Mahogany Inlay, Star Design, Hinged Lid, Covered Interior, 6 x 5 x 5 In.	259.00
Mahogany Veneer, Inlaid Shells, 7 1/2 x 4 x 4 1/2 In.	260.00
Mahogany Veneer, Walnut, Brass Keyhole Escutcheon, Chippendale, 9 x 5 x 6 In.	345.00
Marble, Mottled Green, Gilt Bronze Dome Lid, Pineapple Finials, 8 x 17 In.	800.00
Marquetry, Inlaid Rosewood, Coffin Shape, Ogee Bracket Feet, 13 1/2 In.	550.00
Mother-Of-Pearl, Bone Feet, 19th Century, 4 x 5 x 3 1/2 In.	570.00
Mother-Of-Pearl, Rosewood, Carving, Coffin Shape, Regency, 1820, 6 x 8 x 5 In.	315.00
Oak Panels, Ebony & Sycamore Surround, Stepped Top, 2 Wells, 6 x 7 x 5 In.	329.00
Porcelain, Cover, Figures, Gilt Ground, Chinese, Mid 18th Century, 5 1/2 In.	300.00

Porcelain, Cover, Rectangular, 2 Interior Pewter Canisters, Chinese, c.1840, 11 In. 920.00
Red Lacquer, Rectangular, Cut Corners, 2 Pewter Canisters, Chinese, 11 In. 920.00
Rosewood, Brass Inlay, Coffin Shape, England, c.1820, 6 1/2 x 13 In. 660.00
Rosewood, Burlwood Band, Hinged, Thistle Engraved Glass Bowl, Scotland, 12 In. 715.00
Rosewood, Coffin Shape, Brass Stringing, Lion's Mask Ring Handles, Bun Feet, 14 In. . . .   1380.00
Rosewood, Coffin Shape, Hinged Lid, Regency, Early 1800s, 5 3/4 x 8 x 5 In. 520.00
Rosewood, Coffin Shape, Mirror, Lion's Mask Handles, 2 Wells, Bun Feet, 6 x 12 In. 300.00
Rosewood, Coffin Shape, Waisted, 3 Compartments, Hinged Lid, Squat Bun Feet, 14 In. . .   1150.00
Rosewood, Hinged Lid, Divided Interior, Regency, 19th Century, 6 x 12 x 6 In. 259.00
Rosewood, Mother-Of-Pearl Inlay, Coffin Shape, Regency Style, c.1850, 6 x 12 x 6 In. . . .   400.00
Rosewood, Rectangular, Hinged Lid, 2 Compartments, England, c.1850, 6 1/2 x 14 In. 330.00
Rosewood Veneer, Inlaid Mother-Of-Pearl Keyhole Escutcheon, 9 x 5 x 5 In. 175.00
Satinwood, Mahogany Strung, Coffin Shape, Oblong, Lion Masks, Early 1800s, 9 1/2 In. .   800.00
Satinwood, Mahogany, Banded, Shell, England, Late 1700s, 4 1/4 x 4 1/2 In. 1320.00
Satinwood, Mahogany, Coffin Shape, Regency, Early 1800s, 7 x 12 x 6 In. 259.00
Satinwood, Marquetry, Cornucopia, Flowers, George III Style, 6 x 11 1/2 x 5 3/4 In. 920.00
Satinwood Veneer, Inlaid Banding, Faux Ivory Keyhole, Foil Lined, 7 1/4 x 5 In. 345.00
Silver, Art Nouveau, Strapwork Handles, Oval, Birmingham, 1927, 3 x 4 1/4 In. 705.00
Silver, Copper, Japanese Style, Spot Hammered, Leaves, Berries, Whiting, c.1885, 4 In. . . .   3900.00
Silver, Hammered, Rectangular, Friction-Fit Cap, Engraved, Patterson & Co., 3 3/4 In. 300.00
Silver, Hinged Lid, Bud Finial, Flowers, Langland, Robertson, Newcastle, 1785, 5 In. 3600.00
Sorrento Ware, Marquetry, Book Shape, Peasant Scene, Italy, 1800s, 5 x 5 3/4 In. 425.00
Sterling Silver, Dome Lid, Urn Shape, Gorham, c.1892, 4 1/4 In.   320.00
Sterling Silver, Repousse, Chased & Embossed Flowers, Chinese, 5 In. 430.00
Tortoiseshell, 2 Compartments, Blockfront, Bone Edge, Regency, c.1835, 4 1/2 x 8 In. . . .   3450.00
Tortoiseshell, 2 Compartments, Dutch Style, England, Regency, c.1835, 4 x 6 3/4 In. 3450.00
Tortoiseshell, 2 Compartments, Metal Inlay, England, c.1835, 4 1/2 x 7 1/2 In. 1840.00
Tortoiseshell, Blond, 2 Compartments, Bone Edge, England, c.1835, 4 1/2 x 8 In. 2070.00
Tortoiseshell, Blond, 2 Compartments, Dome Lid, England, c.1835, 4 1/2 x 6 x 3 1/2 In. . .   3220.00
Tortoiseshell, Blond, 3 Compartments, Metal Inlay, England, c.1835, 5 1/4 x 12 In. 2185.00
Tortoiseshell, Canted Corners, Ivory Trim, Silver Fillets, Georgian, 5 x 5 x 4 In. 1495.00
Tortoiseshell, Canted Corners, Silver Fillets, Ivory Trim, Regency, 4 x 6 x 5 In. 1840.00
Tortoiseshell, Canted Corners, Silver, Ivory Trim, Georgian, 5 x 7 x 4 In. 1840.00
Tortoiseshell, Chocolate, George IV Style, 8-Sided, England, c.1900, 3 x 4 1/4 x 3 In. 2185.00
Tortoiseshell, Dome Lid, Rectangular, c.1810, 6 x 6 3/4 x 3 1/2 In. 1610.00
Tortoiseshell, Ivory Strung, Coffin Shape, Initials, England, c.1810, 4 1/4 x 5 3/4 In. 1700.00
Tortoiseshell, Ivory, 2 Compartments, William IV Style, c.1825, 4 3/8 x 6 x 4 1/4 In. 1840.00
Tortoiseshell, Mother-Of-Pearl Inlay, Silver Plate Feet, England, c.1825 . . . .   4800.00
Tortoiseshell, Silver Stringing, Coffin Shape, 2 Compartments, 1800s, 6 x 6 1/2 In. 1610.00
Walnut, Mahogany Panels, Bone Inlay, Raised, Molded Top, Regency, 6 x 9 x 6 In. 195.00
Walnut, Rectangular, Marquetry Figures In Panels, Flat Lid, 5 x 7 5/8 x 4 5/8 In. 1035.00
Walnut, Tunbridgeware, Feather & Barber Pole Bands, 2 Lidded Wells, 5 x 7 x 4 In. 329.00
Wood, 2 Sections, Inlay, England, c.1860, 9 x 5 In. 695.00
Wood, Bone Edge, Metal Inlay, 2 Compartments, Blockfront, England, c.1835, 4 1/2 x 7 In.   4370.00
Wood, Brass & Ivory Mounts, 2 Sections, England, c.1860, 8 3/4 x 5 In. 895.00
Wood, Painted, Oval Panel, House With River, Marked, 22 x 21 1/4 x 21 1/2 In. 3910.00
Wood, Pine, Thomas Wood & Co., Boston, 1800s, 8 3/8 x 19 1/2 x 18 In. 90.00

TEA LEAF IRONSTONE dishes are named for their decorations.

There was a superstition that it was lucky if a whole tea leaf unfolded
at the bottom of your cup. This idea was translated into the pattern of
dishes known as *tea leaf*. By 1850, at least twelve English factories
were making this pattern, and by the 1870s, it was a popular pattern in
many countries. The tea leaf was always a luster glaze on early wares,
although now some pieces are made with a brown tea leaf. There are
many variations of tea leaf designs, such as Teaberry, Pepper Leaf, and
Gold Leaf. The designs were used on many different white ironstone
shapes, such as Bamboo, Lily of the Valley, Empress, and Cumbow.

Bowl, Pitcher, Anthony Shaw, 14 x 14 In. 374.00
Bowl, Vegetable, Cover, Round, Handles, Shaw, 7 x 10 In. 193.00
Bowl, Vegetable, Gold Trim, Meakin, 9 5/8 In. 33.00
Brush Holder, Meakin 375.00
Butter, Cable, Shaw, 3 Piece 450.00

Cake Plate, Chelsea, Wedgwood	175.00
Cake Plate, Clementson Augusta, 10 1/4 In.	575.00
Eggcup, Adams Empress	200.00
Footbath, Gothic, Livesley & Powell	900.00
Gravy Boat, Lily Of The Valley, Shaw	325.00
Moustache Cup, Saucer, Shaw	475.00
Mug, Child's, Tobacco Leaf, Fanfare, Elsmore & Forster	425.00
Pitcher, Tulip, Cobalt Plumes, Elsmore & Forster, 7 1/2 In.	375.00
Relish, Gothic Shell, Luster Band, Walley	260.00
Relish, Lily Of The Valley, Shaw	400.00
Shaving Mug, Grindley Favorite	900.00
Sugar, Cover, Bell Flowers, Shaw	28.00
Teapot, Balanced Vine, Teaberry, Clementson	375.00
Teapot, Niagara Fan, Shaw, 9 1/2 In.	500.00
Teapot, Paneled, Bell Flowers, Gold Trim, Shaw	94.00
Waste Jar, Brocade, Meakin	2000.00
Waste Jar, Burgess Chrysanthemum, Gold Design	900.00
Waste Jar, Hexagon, Shaw	600.00
Waste Jar, Meakin Bamboo	570.00

TECO is the mark used on the art pottery line made by the American Terra Cotta and Ceramic Company of Terra Cotta and Chicago, Illinois. The company was an offshoot of the firm founded by William D. Gates in 1881. The Teco line was first made in 1885 but was not sold commercially until 1902. It continued in production until 1922. Over 500 designs were made in a variety of colors, shapes, and glazes. The company closed in 1930.

Bookends, Rebecca At Well, Maiden Carrying Jar, Green Pool, 6 3/4 x 5 1/2 In.	880.00
Chamberstick, Carved Leaf, Green Matte Glaze, 10 1/2 In.	1295.00
Jar, Cover, Green Matte Glaze, Charcoal Highlights, 3 1/2 In.	705.00
Jardiniere, Spherical, 4 Buttressed Feet, Green Matte Glaze, 8 1/2 In.	10000.00
Jardiniere, Squat, Corseted, 4 Whiplash Buttresses, Green Matte Glaze, 3 1/2 x 9 In.	1765.00
Pitcher, Bulbous, Handle, Green Matte Glaze, 4 In.	600.00
Pitcher, Green Matte Glaze, Handle, Gates, 3 1/4 In.	765.00
Pitcher, Smooth Matte Brown Glaze, 4 x 4 In.	440.00
Vase, 2 Handles, Brown Matte Glaze, 9 In.	705.00
Vase, 4 Buttressed Feet, 4 Lobed Rim, Yellow Marbleized Glaze, 13 1/2 x 6 In.	2115.00
Vase, 4 Buttresses, Pink Matte Glaze, 9 In.	2350.00
Vase, 4 Handles, Green Matte Glaze, Charcoal, 8 In.	4995.00
Vase, 4 Handles, Green Microcrystalline Glaze, Charcoal Handles, 11 x 4 1/2 In.	3819.00
Vase, 4 Lobes, Brown Matte Glaze, 9 In.	880.00
Vase, Barrel Shape, Ridged, Smooth Matte Green Glaze, Charcoal Base, 4 x 4 In.	880.00
Vase, Beaker Shape, 4 Angular Buttressed Handles, Green Matte Glaze, Charcoal, 8 x 6 In.	2115.00
Vase, Bottle Shape, Yellow Matte Glaze, 5 1/2 x 4 1/2 In.	558.00
Vase, Bud, 4 Arms, Sculptured, Green Matte Glaze, Charcoal, Marked, 8 3/4 x 4 In.	3105.00
Vase, Bulbous Base, 4-Sided, Flared Neck, Green Matte Glaze, 16 1/2 x 8 1/2 In.	9400.00
Vase, Bulbous, 4 Curled Handles, Green Matte Glaze, 6 3/4 In.	880.00
Vase, Bulbous, Green Glossy Glaze, 4 1/4 In.	470.00
Vase, Bulbous, Green Matte Glaze, 3 3/4 In.	590.00
Vase, Bulbous, Scalloped Rim, Green Matte Glaze, 5 In.	880.00
Vase, Buttressed Handles, Green Matte Glaze, 11 1/4 x 5 In.	1528.00
Vase, Corset Shape, Medium Brown Matte Glaze, 6 3/4 In.	550.00
Vase, Cylindrical, Buttressed Handles, Buff Matte Glaze, 10 3/4 x 3 1/2 In.	3525.00
Vase, Egg Shape, 2 Buttressed Handles, Green Matte Glaze, Charcoal, 5 1/2 x 3 In.	1175.00
Vase, Egg Shape, Brown Matte Glaze, 4 1/2 x 3 In.	825.00
Vase, Handle, Green Matte Glaze, 3 3/4 In.	765.00
Vase, Lobed, Rose Matte Glaze, 5 In.	590.00
Vase, Oval, 2 Buttressed Handles, Green, Crystalline Matte Glaze, Charcoal, 9 x 5 In.	1645.00
Vase, Oval, 3 Buttressed Feet, Green Matte Glaze, 11 In.	1095.00
Vase, Peacock Feather, 3 Handles, Blue, Yellow, Red, Brown, Albert Ponds, 1906, 8 In.	705.00
Vase, Pear Shape, Green Matte Glaze, 5 3/4 In.	880.00
Vase, Pinched Waist, Angular Buttressed Handles, Crystalline Green Matte, 7 x 4 In.	4400.00
Vase, Ribbed, 3 Handles, Green Matte Glaze, W.D. Gates, 6 1/2 In.	2470.00

Vase, Ribbed, Flaring Neck, Multiple Narrow Leaf Handles, Green Matte Glaze, 11 x 4 In.	5875.00
Vase, Ribbed, Green Matte Glaze, 5 1/2 In.	560.00
Vase, Squat, Flattened, 2 Angular Handles, Green Matte Glaze, Mark, 5 1/2 x 8 1/2 In.	1790.00
Vase, Swollen Lobed Shape, Green Matte Glaze, Charcoal Highlights, F. Albert, 10 1/4 In.	4115.00
Vase, Tankard, Curled Handle, Scalloped Feet, Green Matte Glaze, 15 1/4 x 6 In.	2470.00
Vase, Tulip Blossoms, Leaves, Squat, Green Matte Glaze, Charcoal, Stamped, 14 x 5 In. . .	2350.00

TEDDY BEARS were named for a president of the United States. The first teddy bear was a cuddly toy said to be inspired by a hunting trip made by Teddy Roosevelt in 1902. Morris and Rose Michtom started selling their stuffed bears as *teddy bears* and the name stayed. The Michtoms founded the Ideal Novelty and Toy Company. The German version of the teddy bear was made about the same time by the Steiff Company. There are many types of teddy bears and all are collected. The old ones are being reproduced. Other bears are listed in the Toy section.

Amber Golden, Jointed, Glass Eyes, Embroidered Nose, Velvet Pads, c.1935, 20 In.	605.00
Amish, Glass Eyes, Felt Clothing, Centre County, Pa., 22 In.	1980.00
Chenille, Plush, Cinnamon, Glass Eyes, Felt Pads, Squeaker, 22 In.	55.00
Chiltern, Mohair, Glass Eyes, Velveteen Pads, Shaved Nose, England, 1930s, 15 In. . . . *Illus*	935.00
Cinnamon, Collar, Tie, Fully Jointed, Cloth Pads, c.1940, 23 In.	99.00
Deans, Mohair, Golden, Glass Eyes, Brown Fabric Pads, Tag, Label, 16 In.	12.00
Growler, Plush, Golden, Glass Eyes, Muslin Pads, 21 In.	80.00
Hermann, Long Hair, Light Brown, Glass Eyes, Felt Pads, 16 In.	25.00
Ideal, Mohair, Golden, Glass Eyes, Swivel Head, Straw, Hump Back, 1910, 32 In.	1500.00
Knickerbocker, Mohair, Chocolate, Jointed, Glass Eyes, Velveteen Pads, c.1940, 16 In. . . .	275.00
Knickerbocker, Mohair, Cinnamon, Fully Jointed, Shoebutton Eyes, Felt Pads, 20 In.	275.00
Knickerbocker, Mohair, Cinnamon, Jointed, Glass Eyes, Velveteen Pads, c.1940, 14 In. . . .	180.00
Merry Thought, Mohair, Gray, Box, 17 In.	27.00
Mohair, Apricot, Fully Jointed, Glass Eyes, Felt Pads, 23 In.	300.00
Mohair, Apricot, Fully Jointed, Glass Eyes, Felt Pads, Straw Stuffed, England, 22 In.	175.00
Mohair, Apricot, Glass Eyes, Excelsior Stuffing, Glasses, Replaced Felt Pads, 18 In.	55.00
Mohair, Beige, Fully Jointed, Glass Eyes, Felt Pads, c.1910, 21 In.	385.00
Mohair, Beige, Fully Jointed, Glass Eyes, Mohair Pads, Germany, c.1950, 20 In.	385.00
Mohair, Beige, Fully Jointed, Shoebutton Eyes, Straw Stuffed, Germany, c.1920, 20 In. . . .	440.00
Mohair, Black, Swivel Head, Disc Jointed Limbs, Amber Glass Eyes, c.1930, 27 In.	935.00
Mohair, Blond, Fully Jointed, Shoebutton Eyes, Felt Pads, 15 In.	110.00
Mohair, Blond, Fully Jointed, Shoebutton Eyes, Wool Pads, Straw Stuffed, 20 In.	715.00
Mohair, Blond, Glass Eyes, Oilcloth Pads, 16 In.	55.00
Mohair, Blond, Shoebutton Eyes, Felt Pads, c.1910, 15 In.	1540.00
Mohair, Blond, Shoebutton Eyes, Felt Pads, Hump On Back, Germany, 14 In.	1100.00
Mohair, Brown, Fully Jointed, Plastic Eyes, Felt Pads, Growler, c.1950, 36 In.	190.00
Mohair, Brown, Short Hair, Glass Eyes, Felt Pads, 21 In.	520.00
Mohair, Brown, Short Hair, Glass Eyes, Felt Pads, 24 In.	155.00
Mohair, Champagne, Embroidered Nose, Jointed, Amber Eyes, Felt Pads, c.1940, 8 1/2 In.	165.00
Mohair, Cinnamon, Fully Jointed, Glass Eyes, Felt Pads, c.1920, 23 In.	300.00
Mohair, Cinnamon, Fully Jointed, Glass Eyes, Felt Pads, c.1940, 13 In.	330.00

Teddy Bear, Chiltern, Mohair, Glass Eyes, Velveteen Pads, Shaved Nose, England, 1930s, 15 In.

Teddy Bear, Mohair, Multicolored, Glass Eyes, Felt Pads, 14 In.

Mohair, Cinnamon, Fully Jointed, Glass Eyes, Felt Pads, Germany, c.1930, 16 In. 200.00
Mohair, Curly, Jointed, Glass Eyes, Wool Pads, 19 In. 70.00
Mohair, Dark Brown, Fully Jointed, Glass Eyes, Velvet Pads, c.1950, 30 In. 300.00
Mohair, Dark Gold, Fully Jointed, Shoebutton Eyes, Felt Pads, c.1910, 16 In. 330.00
Mohair, Gold, Curly, Glass Eyes, Velvet Pads, 24 In. 90.00
Mohair, Gold, Fully Jointed, Glass Eyes, Felt Pads, c.1920, 20 In. 175.00
Mohair, Gold, Fully Jointed, Glass Eyes, Felt Pads, c.1920, 28 In. 550.00
Mohair, Gold, Fully Jointed, Glass Eyes, Felt Pads, Straw Stuffed, c.1920, 24 In. 440.00
Mohair, Gold, Fully Jointed, Glass Eyes, Felt Pads, Tin Nose, England, c.1950 16 In. 250.00
Mohair, Gold, Fully Jointed, Shoebutton Eyes, Velvet Pads, c.1930, 20 In. 220.00
Mohair, Gold, Glass Eyes, Felt Pads, 14 In. 155.00
Mohair, Gold, Glass Eyes, Felt Pads, 23 In. 240.00
Mohair, Gold, Glass Eyes, Felt Pads, Excelsior Stuffing, American, 23 In. 210.00
Mohair, Gold, Glass Eyes, Replaced Felt Pads, American, 24 In. 100.00
Mohair, Gold, Jointed Head & Arms, Glass Eyes, Stuffed Straw, 25 In. 495.00
Mohair, Gold, Jointed, Round Face, Black Nose, Upturned, Amber Eyes, c.1945, 18 In. . . .   440.00
Mohair, Gold, Jointed, Shaved Snout, Shoebutton Eyes, Felt Tongue, Conn., c.1940, 11 In.   330.00
Mohair, Gold, Long Fur, Jointed, Swivel Head, Glass Eyes, Velvet Pads, c.1935, 25 In. . . .   990.00
Mohair, Gold, Shoebutton Eyes, Felt Pads, 18 In. 300.00
Mohair, Gold, Shoebutton Eyes, Felt Pads, Yellow Bow, 21 In. 120.00
Mohair, Gold, Shoebutton Eyes, Replaced Felt Pads, 23 In. 110.00
Mohair, Gold, Stick, Glass Eyes, Felt Pads, American, 18 In. 90.00
Mohair, Gold, Straight Legs, Glass Eyes, American, 20 In. 100.00
Mohair, Golden Brown, Glass Eyes, Straw Filled, Felt Pads, Bowtie, Flag, c.1935, 21 In. . .   1045.00
Mohair, Jointed, Glass Eyes, Brown Stitched Nose, 1920s, 12 In. 90.00
Mohair, Light Brown, Jointed, Glass Eyes, Felt Pads, 11 In. 55.00
Mohair, Multicolored, Glass Eyes, Felt Pads, 14 In. . . . . *Illus*   385.00
Mohair, Multicolored, Glass Eyes, Felt Pads, Pink Bow, 14 In. 385.00
Mohair, Olive Green, Swivel Head & Limbs, 21 In. 90.00
Mohair, On Wheels, Glass Eyes, Leather Collar, Iron Base, Wood Handle, c.1920, 23 In. . . .   1430.00
Mohair, Pale Blond, Swivel Head, Amber Glass Eye, Mouth & Paw Pads, 1930, 13 In. 1600.00
Mohair, Sienna, Plush, Jointed, Amber Eyes, Embroidered Mouth, Nose, c.1945, 22 In. . . .   360.00
Mohair, Tan, Glass Eyes, Mohair Pads, Rubber Nose, Red Jacket, 17 In. 360.00
Mohair, Yellow, Football Shaped, Button Eyes, Embroidered Nose, Mouth, c.1920, 25 In. . .   118.00
Mohair, Yellow, Jointed, Button Eyes, Embroidered Nose, Mouth, Claws, c.1915, 20 In. . . .   500.00
Plush, Cinnamon, Shoebutton Eyes, Felt Pads, 18 In. 145.00
Plush, Golden, Glass Eyes, Felt Pads, American, 16 In. 110.00
Plush, Panda, Black & White, Shoebutton Eyes, Fabric Pads, Red Bow, 24 In. 175.00
Plush, Panda, Shoebutton Eyes, Fabric Pads, 24 In. . . . . *Illus*   175.00
Plush, White, Glass Eyes, Felt Pads, 21 In. 30.00
Schuco, Double Face, Yes-No, 3 1/2 In. 195.00
Schuco, Janus, Mohair, Double Face, Germany, 3 1/2 In. 250.00
Schuco, Mohair, Curly, Golden, Glass Eyes, Stitched Nose, Swivel Head, 23 In. 660.00
Steiff, Alice, Tipped Mohair, Suede Pads, Red, White & Blue Bow, 15 In. 80.00
Steiff, Baby, Brown, 1984, 14 In. 120.00
Steiff, Bride, Gown, Veil, Box, 1984, 14 In. 65.00
Steiff, Chocolate Brown, Swivel Head, Amber Glass Eyes, c.1920, 17 In. 2310.00
Steiff, Dralon, White, Cozy, c.1960, 15 In. 65.00
Steiff, Groom, Tuxedo, Hat, Box, 1984, 14 In. 65.00
Steiff, Hercule, White, Medal Around Neck, 11 In. 66.00
Steiff, Minky Zotty, Draylon, Fully Jointed, Felt Pads, c.1970, 15 In. 88.00
Steiff, Minky Zotty, Draylon, Fully Jointed, Glass Eyes, c.1960, 11 In. 110.00
Steiff, Mohair, Blond, Hip Joints, Swivel Head, Shoebutton Eyes, c.1915, 16 In. 4070.00
Steiff, Mohair, Blond, Jointed, Button Eyes, Embroidered Nose, Mouth, c.1905, 9 1/2 In. . . .   440.00
Steiff, Mohair, Blond, Swivel Head, Amber Glass Eyes, Button In Ear, c.1930, 13 In. 2420.00
Steiff, Mohair, Brown, Glass Eyes, Black Embroidered Nose, Mouth, Claws, 13 1/2 In. . . .   206.00
Steiff, Mohair, Brown, Hip Joints, Swivel Head, Shoebutton Eyes, c.1915, 12 In. 2860.00
Steiff, Mohair, Cinnamon, Hip Joints, Swivel Head, Shoebutton Eyes, c.1915, 19 In. 5775.00
Steiff, Mohair, Gold, Hip Joints, Swivel Head, Amber Glass Eyes, c.1925, 13 In. 2200.00
Steiff, Mohair, Gold, Hip Joints, Swivel Head, Amber Glass Eyes, c.1930, 19 In. 3300.00
Steiff, Mohair, Gold, Hip Joints, Swivel Head, Shoebutton Eyes, c.1910, 17 In. 3575.00
Steiff, Mohair, Gold, Hump Back, Swivel Head, Shoebutton Eyes, c.1915, 20 In. 4070.00
Steiff, Mohair, Gold, Swivel Head, Amber Glass Eyes, Button In Ear, c.1920, 16 In. 2420.00

Teddy Bear, Plush, Panda,
Shoebutton Eyes, Fabric
Pads, 24 In.

Teddy Bear, Winnie-The-
Pooh, Mohair, Glass Eyes,
Mohair Pads, Rubber
Nose, 17 In.

Steiff, Mohair, Gold, Swivel Head, Amber Glass Eyes, Button In Ear, c.1920, 21 In.	2970.00
Steiff, Mohair, Honey Beige, Button Eyes, Embroidered Mouth, Nose, Claws, 14 In.	147.00
Steiff, Mohair, Honey Blond, Shaved Muzzle, Embroidered, Glass Eyes, 13 1/2 In.	150.00
Steiff, Mohair, Jointed Arms, Glass Eyes, No. 4150/93, 1960, 62 In.	1100.00
Steiff, Mohair, Jointed Limbs, Stuffed Body, Boot Button Eyes, Germany, 12 In.	1430.00
Steiff, Mohair, Reddish Gold, Swivel Head, Shoebutton Eyes, Overalls, c.1910, 21 In.	4125.00
Steiff, Mohair, Silver, Hump Back, Swivel Head, Amber Glass Eyes, c.1920, 16 In.	2860.00
Steiff, Mohair, Standing, Glass Eyes, Felt Pants, Hat, Germany, c.1947, 9 In.	448.00
Steiff, Mohair, White, Jointed Limbs, Blank Ear Button, Germany, c.1910, 12 In.	1760.00
Steiff, Mohair, Yellow, Jointed, Glass Eyes, Embroidered Nose, Mouth, 6 1/2 In.	176.00
Steiff, Wool & Cotton, Golden, Button & Tag, 1985, 20 In.	120.00
Steiff, Wool & Cotton, Golden, Button & Tag, 1985, 24 In.	175.00
Steiff, Zotty, Draylon, Fully Jointed, Felt Pads, c.1960, 12 In.	100.00
Steiff, Zotty, Mohair, Fully Jointed, Felt Pads, FAO Schwartz, c.1970, 15 In.	130.00
Steiff, Zotty, Mohair, Fully Jointed, Velveteen Pads, c.1970, 11 In.	80.00
Steiff, Zotty, Mohair, Glass Eyes, Jointed, Embroidered Nose, 1950, 11 In.	220.00
Winnie-The-Pooh, Mohair, Glass Eyes, Mohair Pads, Rubber Nose, 17 In. *Illus*	358.00

TELEPHONES are wanted by collectors if the phones are old enough
or unusual enough. The first telephone may have been made in
Havana, Cuba, in 1849, but it was not patented. The first publicly
demonstrated phone was used in Frankfurt, Germany, in 1860. The
phone made by Alexander Graham Bell was shown at the Centennial
Exhibition in Philadelphia in 1876, but it was not until 1877 that the
first private phones were installed. Collectors today want all types of
old phones, phone parts, and advertising. Even recent figural phones
are popular.

American Electric Telephone, Wall, Oak, Adjustable Mouthpiece, 2 Bells, 25 x 8 In.	230.00
Automatic Electric, Model AE40, Rotary Dial, Gold, Chrome Wheel, Art Deco, 1940	440.00
Booth, Oak, Raised Panel, Glass Doors, Double Size	8800.00
Budweiser, Beer Can, 6 1/4 In.	28.00
Candlestick, Brass, Wood Case, Dome Top, 14 1/2 x 10 1/2 In.	495.00
Chicago Telephone Supply, Wall, Crank, Oak, 2 Bells, Adjustable Mouthpiece, 25 x 9 In.	230.00
Chicago Telephone Supply, Wall, Double Box, Oak, Black Bells, 13 x 8 x 30 In.	259.00
Dean Electric Company, Oak, Wall Mounted, Long Mouthpiece, 26 x 10 In.	275.00
Ericon, Ericsson Co., Moss Green, Box, Sweden, c.1972, 8 1/4 In.	129.00
Green Giant, Little Sprout, Pushbutton, Paperwork, Pillsbury, 1984, 14 In.	85.00
Kellogg, Wall, Magneto, Bakelite Mouthpiece, Crank, 2 Bells, Oak Case, Sloped, 18 In.	100.00
Kellogg, Wall, Oak, 8 x 12 1/2 x 26 In.	200.00
Kellogg, Wall, Oak, Black Bells & Mouthpiece, c.1900, 19 In.	175.00
L.M. Ericsson, Wall, Walnut, Crest, Plated Bells, Electrical, Writing Surface, 29 x 9 3/4 In.	400.00
Sign, Bell System, Illinois Bell, Flange, 2-Sided, Porcelain, 12 x 11 In.	165.00
Sign, Bell System, Underground Cable, Do Not Disturb, Porcelain, 3 1/2 x 7 In.	54.00
Sign, Bell Telephone, Porcelain, 2 1/2 x 18 In.	110.00
Sign, Employee Parking, Bell System, White, Black Trim, Porcelainized, 12 x 18 In.	65.00
Sign, Public Telephone Booth Inside, Chicago, Flange, Porcelain, 15 x 10 1/2 In.	358.00
Sign, Public Telephone, Bell System, White Ground, Porcelain, 7 In.	110.00

Sign, Public Telephone, Illinois Bell, Porcelain, 5 1/2 x 19 In. 80.00
Sign, Telephone Office, Blue, White, 2-Sided, Porcelain, Pole Hanger, 25 x 72 In. 190.00
Sign, Telephone Pay Station, Blue, White, 2-Sided, Porcelain, Wood Frame, 11 x 21 In. . . . 90.00
Stromberg-Carlson Tel Mfg. Co., Wall, Double Box, Oak, 9 3/4 x 8 1/4 x 32 In. 288.00
Stromberg-Carlson Tel Mfg. Co., Wall, Double Box, Oak, 10 x 7 x 32 In. 200.00
Talking Machine, Victor, Model VV-IX, No. 452217, Mahogany Case, Ogee Lid, 16 In. . . . 90.00
Wall, Crank, Oak, Adjustable Mouthpiece, Foldaway Shelf, 2 Bells, 23 x 9 In. 230.00
Western Electric, No. 1317-P, Oak Case, Wall, 1895, 20 In. 380.00

TELEVISION sets are twentieth-century collectibles. Although the
first television transmission took place in England in 1925, collectors
find few sets that pre-date 1946. The first sets had only five channels,
but by 1949 the additional UHF channels were included. The first
color television set became available in 1951.

Bendix, Wood Case, Model 2025U, 1950, 19 x 18 In. 28.00
General Electric, Ivory & Terra-Cotta Plastic, Model 14T009, 12 In. 120.00
JVC, Videosphere, Spherical, Red Plastic, Model 3240, 1970s, 13 x 11 In. 160.00
Philco, Predicta, Oak Finish Pedestal, c.1956 . . . . 1668.00
RCA, Enameled Metal, Fabric, Model T-100, 1950, 10 In. 40.00

TEPLITZ refers to art pottery manufactured by a number of companies in the Teplitz-Turn area of Bohemia during the late nineteenth and
early twentieth centuries. Two of these companies were the Alexandra
Works and The Amphora Porcelain Works, run by Reissner, Stellmacher, and Kessel. Ernst Wahliss, connected with the RS & K wares,
started his own factory after 1900.

Bowl, Organically Shaped, 4 Lily Pads, Purple, Gold, Amphora, 5 x 10 3/4 In. 470.00
Bowl, Peacock, Fence, Multicolored Matte Glaze, Amphora, 5 1/2 x 12 In. 825.00
Chamberstick, Maiden & Flowers, Art Nouveau, Ernst Wahliss, 7 1/2 In. 598.00
Compote, Pierced Rim, Leaf Embossed Body, Verdigris Glaze, 6 1/2 x 8 3/4 In. 2000.00
Ewer, Art Nouveau, Applied Figural Winged Cherubs, Apple Blossoms, c.1910, 14 In. 175.00
Ewer, Flower-Like Handle, Spout, Scene, Rooster To Pounce On Spider, Amphora, 9 In. . . 405.00
Figurine, Elephant, Lioness, Amphora, 18 x 16 x 10 In. 645.00
Figurine, Nude Maiden, Standing On Shell, Art Nouveau, Ernst Wahliss, 16 In. 4480.00
Spill Vase, Futurist Cat, Ceramic, Louis Wain, 9 In. 8935.00
Umbrella Stand, Women, Gleaning Wheat, Trees, Amphora, 26 1/2 x 15 In. 2585.00
Vase, Basket Weave Body, Riessner Stellmacher & Kessel, 1890s, 15 In. 140.00
Vase, Bulbous, Organic Design, Gold, Brown, Paul Daschel, 6 1/2 In. 2530.00
Vase, Central Blossom, Purple, Magenta, Green, Gold, Ivory, Handles, Marked, 8 x 6 In. . . 80.00
Vase, Hand Painted, Reticulated Handles, Mark, 11 In. 290.00
Vase, Joan Of Arc, Eagle Helmet, Enamel, Amphora, 6 1/4 x 4 In. 3055.00
Vase, Lion's Head, Ring, Incised Flowers, 3 Handles, Marked, Amphora, 5 1/2 x 4 In. 145.00
Vase, Mermaid, Fish, Plants, Brown, Green, Art Nouveau, Schwarz, 12 In. 940.00
Vase, Organic Shape, 4 Rounded Handles, Flowers, Amphora, 7 1/2 In. 323.00
Vase, Organic Shape, Leaf Handles, Mother-Of-Pearl Ground, Amphora, 10 1/4 x 6 In. . . . 470.00
Vase, Portrait, Oval, Signed Odilox, Amphora, 10 In. 10755.00
Vase, Portrait, Twisted Waisted Shape, Amphora, 8 1/4 In. 4185.00
Vase, Spider Webs, Applied Flowers, Female Figures, Oval, Art Nouveau, c.1900, 13 In. . . 865.00
Vase, Stylized Flower, Panels, Tapered, Cylindrical, Blue, Green, Brown, Black, 16 In. 235.00

TERRA-COTTA is a special type of pottery. It ranges from pale
orange to dark reddish-brown in color. The color comes from the clay,
which is fired but not always glazed in the finished piece.

Bust, Girl, With Bunny, Artist Signed, c.1900, 15 In. 1050.00
Bust, Young Matron, Finger Waved Coiffure, Etienne Beuilly, France, 1883, 26 In. 460.00
Figurine, Aphrodite, Painted, Black Base, Late 19th Century, 22 In. 400.00
Figurine, Dog, Pug, Glass Eyes, Painted, 8 1/2 x 10 1/2 In. 725.00
Figurine, Dwarf, Drops Bowling Ball On Toe, 10 1/2 In. 175.00
Figurine, Man, Black, Sitting On Stump, Smoking, Early 1900s, 11 In. 1265.00
Figurine, Nude Female, Foot Raised On Balustrade, c.1925, 20 3/4 In. 1175.00
Figurine, Pug, Standing, Muscular Features, Curled Tail, Glass Eyes, 13 1/2 x 16 1/2 In. . . 3220.00
Figurine, Seated Male, Multicolored, Signed, John Vincent Bloom, 6 1/2 In. 185.00
Figurine, St. Ignatius Of Loyola, Hollow Back, Eugenio Pattarino, 15 In. 1090.00

Figurine, St. John The Baptist, 11 1/2 In. 60.00
Figurine, Summer, Autumn, Louis XVI Style, Marble Base, c.1885, 62 In., Pair 6610.00
Figurine, Virgin & Child, Sculpted, Belgium, c.1950, 14 In. 92.00
Foo Dog, Scribed Signatures, Fish Scale Design, Saddles, 22 x 22 In., Pair 400.00
Fountain, 2 Tiers, Bacchanalian Boy, Standing In Basin, Mexico, 1900s, 74 x 26 In. 345.00
Jar, Lid, 2 Handles, Daniel Rhodes, 7 1/2 In. 820.00
Panel, Cast Stone, Haut Relief, Putti, Bearing Vases, Napoleon III Style, 30 In., Pair 546.00
Plaque, Man, Beer Stein, JM5822, Round, 14 In. 265.00
Sculpture, Couple, Manuel Felguerez Barra, c.1952, 14 x 16 In. 1410.00
Support, Molded, Griffin, 34 In., Pair 655.00
Tile, Mother & Child, Carved, Arts & Crafts Oak Frame, 8 x 11 1/2 In. 560.00
Torso, Female, Granite Plinth, France, c.1950, 23 1/2 In. 920.00
Tub, Late Louis XVI Style, Winged, Helmeted, Female Masques, Flowers, 32 x 41 In., Pr. . 4370.00
Vase, L. Marti, Enameled, Red Figure, Handles, Ancient Greek Style, 9 3/4 In. 290.00
Vase, Nymph & Satyr, Reuben Nakian, 17 1/2 In. 805.00
Vase, P. Ipsen, Copenhagen, Patinated, Red Figure Painted, 18 In., Pair 978.00
Wine Cooler, Monk Holding Barrel On Shoulder, 20th Century, 38 1/2 In. 1645.00

TEXTILES listed here include many types of printed fabrics and table and household linens. Some other textiles will be found under Clothing, Coverlet, Quilt, Rug, etc.

Afghan, Oriental, Hand Woven, 1920s, 8 x 10 Ft. 300.00
Apotheosis Of Franklin, Tribute To Republic, Cotton, c.1785, 23 1/2 x 18 1/2 In. 675.00
Bag, Qashai, Stars, Multicolored, 1 Green Side, Southwest Persia, Late 1800s, 23 x 22 In. . 1410.00
Banner, Lady Liberty, Flag, Olive Branch, Chromolithograph, Canvas, 81 x 43 1/2 In. 3850.00
Banquet Cloth, Damask, Wedgwood Design, Leafy Border, Classical Figures, 198 In. 235.00
Bedspread, Crocheted, Pink, 1930s, 88 x 80 In. 285.00
Bedspread, Flowers, Blue Floss, White Cotton, Machine Stitch, 90 x 100 In. 295.00
Blanket, Hand Dyed, Spun Wool, Cow, Tree, Animals In Sky, 36 1/2 x 30 1/2 In. 1380.00
Blanket, Wool, Blue & White Checked, 71 x 75 In. 460.00
Blanket, Wool, Embroidered, Alternating Strips, 54 x 80 In. 46.00
Bun Holder, Scalloped Edges, White, Brown, 12 Compartments, 15 In. .... *Illus* 25.00
Bunting, Red, White, Blue, Star Pattern, Cotton, 1870-80, 214 x 23 In. 259.00
Candlewick Bedspread, Wool, Woven, Medallion, Flowers, Trees, Penn., 1800s, 80 x 67 In. 825.00
Chasuble, Silk, Gold Thread, Embroidered, Christ The Good Shepherd, 1920s 865.00
Chasuble, Velvet, Embroidered, Oak Leaves, Vines, Christ, France, 1920s 460.00
Counterpane, Linen, c.1811, 93 x 80 In. 4238.00
Cover, Dressing Table, Homespun, Linen, White, Trapunto, Flower Basket, 22 x 32 In. ... 805.00
Curtain, Flowers, Pink, Maroon, Green Floss, Wool, Satin Stitch, 25 x 56 In. 265.00
Doily, Lace, Belgian, 12 x 15 In. 250.00
Embroidery, On Silk, Peaches, Lotus, Chinese, Giltwood Frame, 40 x 41 In. 520.00
Embroidery, On Silk, Seated Men, Period Clothing, Frame, 67 1/2 x 49 In. 295.00
Embroidery, Scene, Birds, Flowers, Japan, Early 20th Century, 91 x 60 In. 590.00
Fabric, Homespun, Checked, Natural, Brown & Blue, 192 x 40 In. 4730.00
Fabric Sample, Silk, Rayon, Frank Lloyd Wright, F. Schumacher & Co., 1954, 24 x 26 In. . 230.00
Flag, American, 13 Stars, Remember The Maine, Spanish-American War Era, 27 x 42 In. ... 1495.00

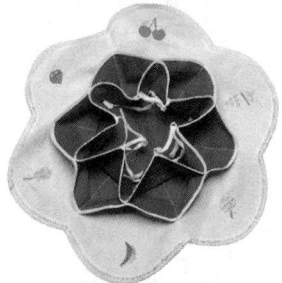

Textile, Bun Holder, Scalloped Edges, White,
Brown, 12 Compartments, 15 In.

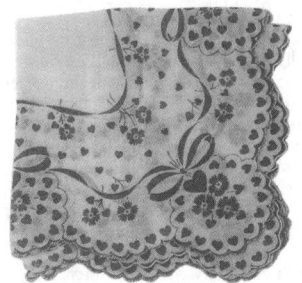

Textile, Handkerchief, Red Hearts, Flowers,
Ribbons, Wide Border, Scalloped Edge, 12 1/2 In.

Flag, American, 13 Stars, Wool Bunting, Cotton Stars, Civil War Era, 50 x 114 In. 1850.00
Flag, American, 22 Stars, 1819-20, 38 x 58 In. 14950.00
Flag, American, 24 Stars, Loop & Ties, Frame, 41 x 49 In. 1650.00
Flag, American, 34 Stars One Side, 13 Stars Other, Cotton, Hand Sewn, 1860s, 39 x 52 In. . 8050.00
Flag, American, 34 Stars, Cotton, Wool, J. Lloyd Family, Civil War, 44 x 72 In. 9500.00
Flag, American, 35 Stars, Bunting, Cotton Stars, Hand Sewn, Civil War, 59 x 92 In. 4025.00
Flag, American, 36 Stars, Wool Bunting, Cotton Stars, Hand Sewn, c.1864, 108 x 168 In. . . 2300.00
Flag, American, 37 Stars, Silk, 1867-77 . . . . 680.00
Flag, American, 38 Stars, John B. Hubbard, Post 20 G.A.R., Silk, Gold Fringe, 60 x 69 In. . 1265.00
Flag, American, 38 Stars, Wool Bunting, Inscription, J.M. Armstrong, 1876, 72 x 144 In. . . 2015.00
Flag, American, 39 Stars, Dakota Territory Into Statehood, 1889, 28 x 46 In. 415.00
Flag, American, 39 Stars, Printed Cotton, Unofficial, Dakotas, c.1876, 18 x 30 In. 2600.00
Flag, American, 40 Stars, South Dakota, 12 x 17 1/2 In. 5750.00
Flag, American, 42 Stars, Cotton, Machine Sewn, Home Made, c.1889, 37 x 62 In. 2990.00
Flag, American, 43 Stars, Wool Bunting, Appliqued Cotton Stars, c.1890, 72 x 144 In. 4600.00
Flag, American, 44 Stars, Wool Bunting, Cotton Stars, 1891-96, 102 x 174 In. 400.00
Flag, American, 48 Stars, Printed Cotton, Whipple Pattern Stars, c.1910, 14 x 23 In. 2300.00
Flag, American, Parade, 35 Stars, Arranged To Spell Free, 17 x 22 In. 11500.00
Flag, Campaign, 40 Stars, Hayes-Wheeler Jugate, Linen, 26 1/2 x 44 In. 28750.00
Flag, Campaign, Buchanan & Breckinridge N.H., Cotton, 1856, 11 x 18 In. 16100.00
Flag, Civil War, Confederate First National, 12 Stars In Circle, Silk, Frame, 18 x 32 In. . . . 3680.00
Flag, Native American Party, 26 Stars, Freedom To The American, c.1844, 18 x 27 In. 17250.00
Footrest, Round, Braided, Padded, Hanging Loop, Multicolored, Rag Stuffed, 15 In. 105.00
Fraktur, Women, Angels, Mermaids, Frederich Speyer, Pa., 1793, 13 x 15 3/4 In. 5650.00
Handkerchief, Red Hearts, Flowers, Ribbons, Wide Border, Scalloped Edge, 12 1/2 In. *Illus* 8.00
Homespun Fabric, Blue & White Plaid, Machine Stitched Ends, 100 x 105 In. 260.00
Mandarin Square, Gold Pheasant, On Blue Cloud, 1800s, 11 1/2 In. 360.00
Mandarin Square, Silver Kingfisher, Blue, Buddhistic Symbols, c.1900, 11 3/4 In. 260.00
Mattress Cover, Homespun, Blue, Red, White Plaid, Embroidered Initials, 53 x 63 In. 315.00
Mattress Cover, Homespun, Plaid, Blue & White, String Ties, 67 x 58 In. 1925.00
Needlework, Adam & Eve, Peacock, Plants, Floral Vine Border, E.B., 11 x 11 In. 165.00
Needlework, Church In Landscape, Painted Sky, On Silk, 17 x 13 3/4 In. 195.00
Needlework, Flowers, Fruit In Urn, Silk On Silk, Miss June Withrington, 1807, 9 x 8 In. . . . 765.00
Needlework, Homespun Linen, Flower Vase, E.J., 1826, Red Painted Frame, 5 x 4 In. 2090.00
Needlework, Text, Lion, Bird, Potted Flowers, Elizabeth Butler Age 11, 17 x 17 In. 275.00
Panel, 2 Immortals In Heavenly Landscape, K'ossu, 19th Century, 63 x 33 1/2 In. 1200.00
Panel, 2 Women, Child Playing With Foo Lion, K'ossu, 37 1/2 x 21 In. 330.00
Panel, Crewelwork, Branches, Multicolored, 18th Century, 51 x 44 In. 3220.00
Panel, Needlework, Gold, Flowers, Black Ground, 1800s, 38 x 18 In. 130.00
Panel, Sages In Landscape, K'ossu, 19th Century, 37 1/2 x 21 In. 300.00
Panel, Silk, Brocade, Children, Red Ground, Kyoto, Japan, 1800s, 18 x 40 In. 150.00
Panel, Silk, Brocade, Dragons, Blue Ground, Clouds, c.1800, 48 x 31 In. 575.00
Panel, Silk, Embroidered, Peacock, Pink Peony Tree, Chinese, 36 x 26 In. 115.00
Panel, Silk, Embroidered, Russet Ground, Prunus, Late 19th Century, 15 1/2 x 76 In. 135.00
Panel, Silk, Mythological Figures, Landscape, Blue Ground, K'ossu, 20 x 70 In. 690.00
Patriotic, Brown, Tan, Printed Portico, George Washington, Frame, c.1819, 27 x 21 In. . . . 2645.00
Patriotic, Printed Floral Chintz, Eagle, Shield, E. Pluribus Unum, Frame, 20 x 25 In. 259.00
Piano Shawl, Silk, Embroidered, Flowers, Multicolored, Fringe, c.1900, 50 x 50 In. 375.00
Pillow, Linen, Red, Green, Rust, Yellow Floss, Linen, Oatmeal, Satin Stitch, 20 x 15 In. . . . 205.00
Pillowcase, Linen, Oatmeal, Embroidered Pin Roses, 1923 Page From Society Embroidery 90.00
Pillowcase, Linen, Oatmeal, Embroidered Stylized Roses, Arts & Crafts, 1923, 21 x 17 In. . 90.00
Robe, Dragons, 5 Claws, Cranes, Clouds, Buddha Symbols, Gold, 20th Century 3220.00
Runner, Linen, Flower Design, Brown, Arts & Crafts, 50 In. 150.00
Runner, Linen, Oatmeal, Embroidered Red Poppies, Insects, 41 In. 265.00
Scarf, Birds, Flowers, Blue Border, Whimsical World Of Robert Sargent, 30 In. . . . . . . *Illus* 18.00
Scarf, Dresser, Trapunto, Pot Of Tulips, Catharine Lachman, Penn., Frame, 20 x 32 In. 290.00
Scarf, Mantle, Appliqued, Birds, Flowers, Calico Ruffle, Penn., c.1840, 74 1/2 x 25 3/4 In. 460.00
Scarf, Silk, Abstract Figure & Designs, Red, Purple, Gray, Peter Max, 26 In. . . . . *Illus* 50.00
Scarf, Zodiac Signs, Yellow Ground, Black Letters, Peter Max, 1970, 26 x 12 In. 75.00
Seat Mat, Woven, Flame Stitch, Sawtooth Pattern, Green, Pink, Black, 9 1/2 x 9 1/2 In. . . . 195.00
Spread, Crewelwork, George I, Flowers, Leaves, Mrs. L.V. Lockwood, 1715, 74 x 88 In. . . . 7200.00
Spread, Homespun, Blue, White, Natural, Pulled, Frayed & Bound Edges, 82 x 80 In. 3025.00
Spread, Homespun, Checked, Brown, Blue, White, Diamond Pattern, 76 x 65 In. 275.00

Textile, Scarf, Birds, Flowers, Blue Border,
Whimsical World Of Robert Sargent, 30 In.

Textile, Scarf, Silk, Abstract Figure & Designs,
Red, Purple, Gray, Peter Max, 26 In.

Stage Backdrop, Cotton, Hand Painted, c.1920, 24 x 18 Ft.	850.00
Table Cover, Woven Cotton, Multicolored Stencils, Frame, 1800s, 31 x 31 In.	1175.00
Table Mat, Embroidered Stylized Design, Lace Edge, Oval, Arts & Crafts, 33 In.	530.00
Table Mat, Linen, Black, Peacock Feathers, Flowers, Fringe, Arts & Crafts, Round, 35 In.	529.00
Table Mat, Oval, Braided, Tan, Maroon, Pink, 21 x 34 1/2 In.	275.00
Table Mat, Oval, Multicolored, Braided, 24 x 41 In.	470.00
Table Runners, Homespun, Linen, Brown, White, Blue, Checkered, 19 x 10 In., Pair	440.00
Tablecloth, Embroidered Stylized, Lace Edge, Arts & Crafts, 62 In.	175.00
Tablecloth, Flowers, Stitched, Lace Border, 46 x 52 In.	59.00
Tablecloth, Homespun, Natural Color, Pulled Fringe Edges, 72 x 55 In.	220.00
Tablecloth, Lace, Off-White, Ecru, 3 Panels, Linen, 12 Napkins, 114 x 63 In.	400.00
Tapestry, Aubusson Style, Wool, Knight, Horseback, Castle, Backing, 1800s, 78 x 101 In.	1528.00
Tapestry, Aubusson, Flowers, Salmon, Green, Ivory, 62 x 96 In.	380.00
Tapestry, Bleu Rouge, Wool, Hand Knotted, Paul Klee, 61 x 73 In.	2875.00
Tapestry, Children At Play, Arts & Crafts, 65 x 14 In.	645.00
Tapestry, Embroidered, Silk Thread, Brocade, Cranes, Among Reeds, Japan, 95 x 71 In.	3220.00
Tapestry, Flowers, Needlepoint, Beige, Pink, Green, Arts & Crafts, 46 x 68 In.	350.00
Tapestry, Hunting Landscape, With Castle, Europe, Early 1900s, 76 x 16 In.	4025.00
Tapestry, Medieval Scene, Wood Chopper, Fire, J.C. Bissery, France, 1950s, 40 x 72 In.	3825.00
Tapestry, Sisters Reclining In Victorian Parlor, Pets, Mid 20th Century, 25 x 35 In.	230.00
Tapestry, Wool, Exotic Bird, Landscape, Verdure, Flemish, 1800s, 85 x 64 In.	2700.00
Tapestry, Wool, Pavilion, Fountains, Verdant Landscape, Flemish, 1800, 95 x 99 In.	4995.00
Toile, Linen, Cotton, Goddess Of Liberty, Red Printed Designs, White Ground, 42 x 66 In.	316.00
Toile, U.S. Grant, Let Us Have Peace, Medallions, Red, Brown, Frame, 14 x 12 In.	230.00
Towel, Needlework, Mennonite, Flags, Birds, Flowers, Emma Seiningle, Ind., 49 x 34 In.	8195.00
Towel, Show, Homespun, Linen, Embroidered Peacocks, 18 3/8 x 51 In.	345.00
Towel, Show, Woven Linen, Embroidered, Fish, Alphabet, Manor Twp., 17 x 52 In.	550.00
Valance, Embroidered, Crewelwork, Vine, Flowers, Inscribed, 34 x 101 In.	3450.00
Valance, Silk Upholstery & Drapery Panels, 20 x 43 x 5 1/2 In., 7 Piece	259.00

THERMOMETER is a name that comes from the Greek word for heat. The thermometer was invented in 1731 to measure the temperature of either water or air. All kinds of thermometers are collected, but those with advertising messages are the most popular.

7Up, Co, Green, Bottle, Porcelain, 15 x 6 In.	110.00
Advertising, Winchester, Western, AA, Metal, 1960s-1970s, 26 1/2 x 7 1/4 In.	74.00
American Fence, Stands The Test Of Time, Blue, Yellow, Porcelain, 27 x 7 In.	250.00
Barq's, Drink Barq's It's Good, Bottle, 26 x 10 In.	137.00
Barq's, It's Good, Metal, 26 x 10 In.	145.00
Bayer Aspirin, New Strength & Vitality, Tonic, Blue, White, 45 In.	1650.00
Berwick Savings & Trust, Stanwood Hillson, N.Y., 11 5/8 x 3 1/8 x 1/4 In.	40.00
Bireley's Orange Drink, Not A Bubble In A Bottle, Tin, 16 x 5 In.	300.00
Bradley & Hubbard, Victorian, Desk, Meriden, Conn., c.1880, 11 In.	150.00
Calumet, Best By Test, Trade Here, Wooden, 27 In.	150.00
Camel Cigarettes, For Smoking Enjoyment, Cigarette Pack, Embossed, Tin, 13 x 6 In.	120.00
Camels, Have A Real Cigarette, Embossed Cigarette Pack, 13 1/2 x 5 3/4 In.	110.00

Carter Inx, Enamel On Metal, c.1915, 27 1/4 x 7 In. 275.00
Castrol, Green Ground, Red Letters, White Trim, Round, 12 In. 55.00
Catskill, N.Y. Dairy, Milk Bottle Shape, Wood, Cow, 10 x 3 1/2 In. 255.00
Chesterfield, Big Clean Taste, Embossed Cigarette Pack, 13 x 5 3/4 In. 110.00
Chesterfield, They Satisfy, Pack, Embossed, Tin, 13 x 6 In. 120.00
Colburn's Mustard, Wood Back, Brass Bulb Cover, 24 x 4 1/2 In. 175.00
Coulson's Cough Cure, When Others Fall, Wood, 12 In. 240.00
Cutlery By Remington, Dupont, Porcelain, 1930, 38 1/2 x 8 In. . . . . .560.00 to 695.00
Dad's Root Beer, Just Right For Dads, Bottle, Brown, Black, White, 26 1/2 x 10 In. 165.00
Doan's Kidney Pills, Is Your Back Bad Today, Graphic, Die Cut, Wood, 21 x 5 In. 247.00
Double Cola, You'll Like It Better, Blue, Red, White, Tin, 27 x 8 In. 136.00
Dr Daniels, Veterinary Medicines, Wood, 14 In. 405.00
Dr Pepper, 10-2-4, Bottle, 14 x 5 In. 330.00
Dr Pepper, 10-2-4, Bottle, 17 x 5 In. 165.00
Ex-Lax, Chocolated Laxative, Keep Regular, Porcelain, 36 1/2 x 8 In. 210.00
Ex-Lax, Chocolated Laxative, Porcelain, 39 x 8 In. 176.00
Fahrenheit & Reaumur Scales, Bronze, Oak, Horse, Shoe, England, Early 1900s 285.00
Fatima, Turkish Brand Cigarettes, Porcelain, 27 x 7 In. 205.00
Fatima Cigarettes, Pack Of Cigarettes, Yellow & Red, 7 x 27 In. 330.00
Fleet Wing Petroleum, Kennedy Bros. Oil Co., Pa., Tin Lithograph, Box, 6 1/2 x 2 In. . . . 176.00
Frostie Root Beer, Real Taste Treat, Frostie Character, Bottle, Cap, Tin, U.S.A., 36 In. . . . 138.00
Garry's Car Waxes, Red, Yellow, White, Round 1040.00
Grads Cigarettes, Image Of Graduate, Red & White, 8 x 38 In. 195.00
Hester Batteries, Start & Go, White, Black, Red, Yellow, Round 1870.00
Hick's Capudine, For Headache & Rheumatism, Blue, White, Wood, Raleigh, N.C. 330.00
Hill's Brothers, Man, Yellow Robe, Red, Enamel, Metal, c.1918, 21 x 8 3/4 In. 525.00
Hires Root Beer, Bottle, 29 x 8 In. 190.00
L&M Cigarette, Get Lots More, Tin, Embossed Pack, 1950s, 11 1/2 x 5 In. 125.00
Listerine, The Safe Antiseptic, Bottle, Wrapper, Multicolored, Porcelain, 30 In. 3100.00
Lord Sterling Cigars, Wooden, 39 x 9 In. 99.00
Mail Pouch, Chew Mail Pouch Tobacco, Sheet Steel, 39 In. 68.00
Mail Pouch, Treat Yourself To The Best, Porcelain, 39 x 8 In. 165.00
Mail Pouch Tobacco, Porcelain, Navy, Yellow & White Letters, 8 x 38 In. 248.00
Marathon Gasoline, J.B. Hollerman, Turners Station, Ky., Box, 7 In. 35.00
Marhoefer Perfect Bread, Glass, Red, White, Blue, 12 In. Diam. 110.00
Mission Of California, Bottle, Tin, 17 x 5 In. 112.00
Missouri Steel Casting Co., Joplin, Black, White, Round 715.00
Modern Appliances, Washers, Refrigerators & Stoves, Wooden, 13 In. 120.00
NuGrape Soda, 2 Bottles, Tin, 16 x 7 In. 300.00
NuGrape Soda, A Flavor You Can't Forget, 6 Bottles, Tin, 16 x 7 In. 165.00
NuGrape Soda, Bottle Shape, Die Cut, Embossed, 17 x 5 In. 165.00
NuGrape Soda, Bottle, Everybody Likes A Change, Tin, 16 x 7 In. 385.00
Orange Crush, Cap, White, Orange, Blue, 12 In. Diam. .220.00 to 300.00
Orange Crush, Naturally It Tastes Better, Bottle, Tin, 15 x 6 In. 195.00
Pennsy Supply Co., Metal, 13 x 4 In. 28.00
Phillips 66, Tires, Batteries & Accessories, White, Red, Black, Round 1320.00
Pierce College Of Business, Wooden, 24 In. 120.00
Poll Parrot, On Swing 880.00
Prestone Anti-Freeze, Red, White, Blue, Porcelain, 10 In. Diam. 2530.00
Prestone Antifreeze, You're Safe, You Know It, 36 In. 130.00
Pure One-Fill Anti-Freeze, Be Sure With Pure, Blue, White, Tin, 36 x 8 In. 358.00
Quicky, Grapefruit Kissed With Lemon, Bottle, White, Green Red, 16 x 6 In. 104.00
Ramon's Brownie Pills, The Little Doctor, Wooden, 21 In. 100.00
Ramon's Pills, Kid, Tin Lithograph, 20 7/8 x 8 7/8 In. 264.00
Rayovac, Portable Lighting Headquarters, Red, White, Black, Round 880.00
RC Cola, Go RC For Quick Fresh Energy, Bottle, Red, White, Blue, Plastic, 8 x 10 In. 35.00
Red Seal, Dry Battery, Porcelain, 27 x 7 In. 145.00
Roessner Brothers, Wood, Hagerstown, Md., 12 In. 136.00
Royal Crown Cola, Embossed Bottle, Tin, 14 x 6 In. . . . . .99.00 to 120.00
Scotch Brand Anthracite Coal, Graphics, Porcelain, 30 x 8 In. 242.00
Stelwagon Roofing Materials, Square, 3 1/2 x 3 1/2 In. 14.00
SunCrest, Bottle Shape, Tin, Die Cut, Embossed, 17 x 5 1/4 In. . . . . .90.00 to 145.00
SunCrest, More Flavor For Your Money, Bottle, Tin, 16 x 7 In. 275.00

U-Haul Rentals, Red, White, Black, Round 1210.00
Universal Batteries, Heart Of Your Car, 39 x 8 In. 130.00
Walker's DeLuxe Bourbon, Round, Glass Lens, 12 1/2 In. 77.00
Winchester Repeating Arms, New Haven, Conn., 1920s, 9 1/8 x 2 3/8 In. 1160.00
Winchester Western AA, Metal, 1960s, 27 1/2 x 7 1/2 In. 162.00
Yellow Cab & Baggage Co., Round, 6 In. 154.00

TIFFANY is a name that appears on items made by Louis Comfort Tiffany, the American glass designer who worked from about 1879 to 1933. His work included iridescent glass, Art Nouveau styles of design, and original contemporary styles. He was also noted for stained glass windows, unusual lamps, bronze work, pottery, and silver. Other types of Tiffany are listed under Tiffany Glass, Tiffany Pottery, or Tiffany Silver. The famous Tiffany lamps are listed in this section. Tiffany jewelry is listed in the jewelry and wristwatch categories. Some Tiffany Studio desk sets have matching clocks. They are listed here. Clocks made by Tiffany & Co. are listed in the Clock category. Reproductions of some types of Tiffany are being made.

Louis C. Tiffany

Ashtray, Geometric Edge, Bronze, 7 In. 206.00
Ashtray, Match Holder, Ribbed Stem & Top, Bronze, 26 In. 863.00
Ashtray, Match Holder, Venetian, Bronze, Gold Dore, 5 x 3 1/2 x 3 In. 450.00
Ashtray, Match Holder, Venetian, Sculptured Minks, Bronze, Gold Dore, 5 x 3 1/2 In. 450.00
Ashtray, Pine Needle, Green Slag Glass, Bronze 650.00
Ashtray, Removable Center, Pedestal Base, Bronze, Gold Dore, Signed, 3 1/2 x 3 1/4 In. ... 400.00
Ashtray, Ribbed, Round, Handles, Bronze, Gold Dore, 1 x 4 In. 150.00
Basket, Enameled, Bronze, Gold Dore, Red, Gold Iridescent, Pedestal, Signed, 8 x 9 In. .. 2000.00
Bill Clip, Byzantine, Stone Mounted, Bronze, Gold Dore, 7 1/2 In. 2988.00
Bill File, Graduate, Bronze, Gold Dore, Octagonal, 8 x 4 In. 650.00
Bill File, Paperweight, Pine Needle, Green Slag Glass, Signed, 7 1/2 x 3 1/2 In. 1500.00
Blotter, Abalone, Bronze, Gold Dore, Signed, 5 3/4 x 3 In. 450.00
Blotter, Graduate, Bronze, Gold Dore, Knob Handle, 2 3/4 x 5 1/2 In. 250.00
Blotter, Louis XVI, Wreath & Ribbon, Bronze, Knob Handle, 2 3/4 x 5 1/4 In. 450.00
Blotter, Ninth Century, Bronze, Blue, Green Jewels, 5 1/2 x 3 In. 650.00
Blotter, Pine Needle, Green Slag Glass, Bronze, Dark Patina, Signed, 5 1/2 In. 650.00
Blotter, Venetian, Bronze, Knob Handle, Signed, 5 1/4 x 2 3/4 In. 350.00
Blotter, Zodiac, Bronze, Gold Dore, Knob Handle, 5 1/2 x 2 3/4 x 2 In. 400.00
Blotter Ends, Abalone, Bronze, Gold Dore, Iridescent Discs, 12 x 2 1/4 In., Pair 550.00
Blotter Ends, Adam, Gold Dore, Signed, 12 x 2 In., Pair 250.00
Blotter Ends, American Indian, Bronze, Gold Dore, 12 x 2 In., Pair 300.00
Blotter Ends, Chinese Pattern, Bronze, Gold Dore, Signed, 19 x 2 1/2 In., Pair 450.00
Blotter Ends, Graduate, Bronze, Gold Dore, Signed, 19 x 2 1/4 In. 250.00
Blotter Ends, Louis XVI, Flower Wreath & Border, 1 1/4 x 12 1/4 In., Pair 350.00
Blotter Ends, Ninth Century, Bronze, Jewels, Signed, 12 x 2 In., Pair 550.00
Blotter Ends, Ninth Century, Bronze, Jewels, Signed, 19 1/4 x 2 In., Pair 650.00
Blotter Ends, Pine Needle, Bronze, Dark Patina, Signed, 12 x 2 In., Pair 450.00
Blotter Ends, Venetian, Raised Minks, Bronze, Gold Dore, 19 1/4 x 2 1/2 In., Pair 400.00
Blotter Ends, Zodiac, Bronze, Gold Dore, Signed, 19 x 2 In., Pair 250.00

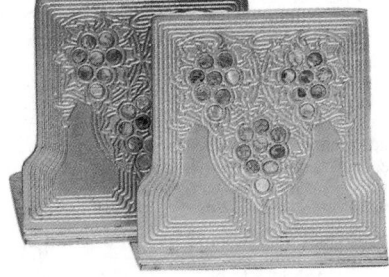

Tiffany, Bookends, Abalone, Bronze, Gold Dore, 5 1/4 In.

The old cord on a vintage phone adds value. Green cords are best. Other old forms are twisted cords, brown cords, or patterned cords called rattlesnakes.

Tiffany, Bookends, Ninth Century, Blue & Green
Glass Cabochons, Bronze, Gold Dore, 6 In.

Tiffany, Bookends, Peacock Portal, Saint Figure
In Arch, Bronze, Gold Dore, 6 In.

Bookends, Abalone, Bronze, Gold Dore, 5 1/4 In. . . . . *Illus* 3286.00
Bookends, Arch Shape, Enameled, Bronze, Gold Dore, 4 1/2 In. 777.00
Bookends, Brass, Etched Leaves, Flowers, 5 x 3 3/4 In. 1530.00
Bookends, Buddah, Curved Rim, Bronze, Gold Dore, Signed, 6 In. 750.00
Bookends, Double X, Bronze, Enameled, Signed, 6 1/4 x 4 3/4 In. 2500.00
Bookends, Figural Trees, Mountains, Shrubs, Grass, Bronze, Gold Dore, 5 x 4 1/2 In. . . 2200.00
Bookends, Medallion, Lattice, Red, Green, Enameled, Bronze, Gold Dore, 5 1/2 x 4 In. . . . 2500.00
Bookends, Ninth Century, Blue & Green Glass Cabochons, Bronze, Gold Dore, 6 In. . *Illus* 5975.00
Bookends, Peacock Portal, Saint Figure In Arch, Bronze, Gold Dore, 6 In. . . . . *Illus* 1075.00
Bookends, Persian Carpet Shape, Enameled, Bronze, Gold Dore, Stamped, 6 1/2 In. 3585.00
Bookends, Tree Of Life, Enameled, Leaves, Border, Bronze, Gold Dore, 4 3/4 x 6 1/4 In. . 3000.00
Bookends, Venetian, Multicolored, Enamel, Bronze, Gold Dore, 5 x 6 In. 2500.00
Bookrack, Grapevine, Amber Slag Glass, Bronze, Gold Dore, 14 In., Extends To 23 In. . . . 2500.00
Bookrack, Pine Needle, Green Slag Glass, Bronze, 6 x 5 3/4 In. 3000.00
Bowl, Bronze, Crackle Finish, Round Handles, Footed, Favrile, No. 407, 4 1/2 x 12 In. . . . 450.00
Bowl, Bronze, Turned Out Edge, Signed, 1 3/4 x 5 1/2 In. 350.00
Bowl, Centerpiece, Bronze, Gold Dore, Enameled, Footed, Flared Top, Signed, 4 x 8 In. . . 2500.00
Box, Card, Hinged Cover, Grapevine, Green Slag Glass, Bronze, Signed, 4 1/2 x 3 x 2 In. . 2200.00
Box, Card, Hinged Cover, Pine Needle, Green Slag Glass, Bronze, 2 Sections, 3 x 4 In. . . . 2500.00
Box, Cigarette, Hinged Cover, Medallion, Enameled, Bronze, Gold Dore, 2 x 6 In. 1135.00
Box, Enameled, Red, Black, Tamped, Bronze, 2 x 5 In. 896.00
Box, Geometric, Enameled, Bronze, Gold Dore, Signed, 6 1/4 x 3 3/4 x 1 3/4 In. 1200.00
Box, Glove & Handkerchief, Grapevine, Slag Glass, Bronze, 13 1/2 In. 4780.00
Box, Grapevine, Amber Slag Glass, Bronze, Gold Dore, Ball Feet, Signed, 3 x 4 1/4 In. . . . 550.00
Box, Grapevine, Green Slag Glass, Bronze, Signed, 4 x 3 x 1 1/2 In. 850.00
Box, Handkerchief, Pine Needle, Green Slag Glass, Bronze, Beaded, 2 1/2 x 8 In. 2500.00
Box, Heraldic, Enameled, Bronze, Stamped Cover, 4 In. 1015.00
Box, Hinged Cover, Enameled Leaves, Purple, Bronze, Gold Dore, Ball Feet, 2 x 6 In. . . . 1500.00
Box, Hinged Cover, Fleur-De-Lis, Enameled, Blue, Green, Yellow, Bronze, 6 x 5 In. 1500.00
Box, Hinged Cover, Pine Needle, Green Slag Glass, Bronze, Signed, 1 1/2 x 4 x 3 In. 850.00
Box, Hinged Cover, Zodiac, Symbols, Entwined Circle, Bronze, 6 1/2 x 3 x 1 1/2 In. 750.00
Box, Medallion, Enameled, Bronze, Gold Dore, Ball Feet, Beaded Edge, Signed, 6 x 4 In. . 1500.00
Box, Pine Needle, Amber Slag Glass, Bronze, Gold Dore, Ball Feet, Signed, 3 x 4 1/4 In. . . 550.00
Box, Stamp, Hinged Cover, Abalone, Bronze, Gold Dore, Iridescent, 2 1/4 x 4 x 1 1/2 In. . . 600.00
Box, Stamp, Hinged Cover, Pine Needle, Slag Glass, Bronze, Gold Dore, 1 5/8 x 3 In. 230.00
Box, Stamp, Hinged Cover, Venetian, Bronze, Gold Dore, Signed, 1 3/4 x 4 In. 650.00
Box, Stamp, Hinged Cover, Zodiac, Bronze, Gold Dore, 3-Section Tray, 3 3/4 x 2 1/4 In. . . 600.00
Box, Venetian, Treasure Chest, Bronze, Gold Dore, Chain, Latch, 5 1/2 x 4 x 2 1/4 In. 1500.00
Bridge Pad Holder, Symbols, Red, Black Enameled, Bronze, Gold Dore, Signed, 4 x 7 In. . 550.00
Calendar, American Indian, Raised Masks, Bronze, Gold Dore, Easel Back, 7 1/4 x 6 In. . . 1800.00
Calendar, Graduate, Bronze, Gold Dore, Easel, 6 1/4 x 5 1/2 In. 650.00
Calendar, Ninth Century, Bronze, Gold Dore, Signed, 8 1/2 x 7 In. 2500.00
Calendar, Pine Needle, Amber Slag Glass, Bronze, Gold Dore, Signed, 4 1/4 x 6 In. 650.00
Candelabrum, 3-Light, Bronze, Adjustable, 3 Favrile Glass Shades, 18 In. 10755.00
Candle Lamp, 2-Light, Gold Iridescent Glass Shades, Bronze, 17 x 12 In. 8050.00
Candle Lamp, Gold Iridescent, Ruffled Shade, Spiral Ribs, 12 1/4 In. 2000.00

Candle Lamp, Gold, Green, White Glass Shade, Pulled Feather, Favrile, Bronze, 15 In. . . . 3585.00
Candle Lamp, Gold, Pulled Leaf, Iridescent Glass Shade, Favrile, Bronze, 12 3/4 In. 7770.00
Candle Lamp, Green Glass Candle Cup, Bronze, Pulled Feathers Shade, 3-Legged, 21 In. . 8050.00
Candle Lamp, Tulip Shade, Ribbed, Green Pulled Leaves, Bronze Stand, 23 In., Pair 3450.00
Candle Lamp, Wild Carrot, Favrile Glass Shade, Bronze, c.1910, 20 5/8 In. 3585.00
Candle Lamp, Yellow & Green Pulled Feather Glass Shade, Favrile, Bronze, 18 In. 5975.00
Candlestick, 2-Light, Bronze, No. 1230, Monogram Mark, Electrified, 9 In. 1555.00
Candlestick, Bronze, Standing Beaver, Supporting Nozzle On Open Book, 8 In. 8965.00
Candlestick, Cobra, Bronze, Gold Dore, 8 In., Pair 1725.00
Candlestick, Figural, Monkey Waiter, Arms Out, Holding 2 Trays, Bronze, 5 x 8 In. 1668.00
Candlestick, Gadrooned Bobeche, Tripod Support, Slipper Feet, Bronze, 8 In. 420.00
Candlestick, Green Blown Glass Bobeches, Bronze, Signed, 17 In., Pair 1555.00
Candlestick, Green Blown Glass Insert, Root Shape Feet, Bronze, 12 3/4 In. 3290.00
Candlestick, Green Glass Insert, 3 Curved Feet, Bronze, Signed, 8 In. 2000.00
Candlestick, Pierced Bronze, Urn Shape Glass Nozzle, Tripod Base, Favrile, 10 In. 2690.00
Canister, Blue Iridescent Turtleback Cover, Bronze, Gold Dore, Cylindrical, 3 1/2 x 3 In. . 2500.00
Canister, Sailboat, Bronze, Gold Dore, Signed, 3 1/2 x 3 In. 450.00
Card Tray, Bird Of Paradise, Eating Grapes, Enameled, Bronze, Gold Dore, 8 In. 470.00
Chamberstick, Bronze, Gold Dore, Curved Arm, Raised Edge, Signed, 5 1/4 In. Diam. 550.00
Chandelier, 3-Light, Favrile Glass, Bronze, Gold Dore, Seashells, Beads, Prisms, 20 In. . . . 6575.00
Chandelier, Grape Trellis, Leaded Glass, Bronze, c.1910, 11 x 25 1/2 In. 59750.00
Charger, Abalone, Bronze, Gold Dore, Stamped, No. 3728, 14 In. 600.00
Charger, Abalone, Bronze, Signed, 12 In. 520.00
Cigar Box, Cover, Silver, Gold Decorated Copper, c.1905, 4 x 6 1/2 x 6 In. 59750.00
Cigarette Box, Heraldic, Green Leather Panels, Cedar Lined, 2 1/2 x 4 3/4 x 3 3/4 In. 645.00
Clock, Desk, Adam, Bronze, Gold Dore, 2 3/4 In. 2390.00
Clock, Desk, Venetian, Bronze, Gold Dore, Signed, 4 x 4 1/4 In. 3000.00
Clock, Desk, Zodiac, Bronze, Gold Dore, Arched Shape, Metal Dial, 5 1/4 In. 2390.00
Clock, Louis XVI, Bronze, Gold Dore, 7 x 4 1/4 In. 3000.00
Clock, Pine Needle, Bronze, Signed, 13 x 9 x 6 In. 4480.00
Compote, Bronze, Gold Dore, 3 1/2 x 6 In. 375.00
Compote, Sunburst, Bronze, Gold Dore, 3 1/2 x 6 In. 550.00
Compote, Tooled, Enameled, Bronze, Gold Dore, Signed, 10 1/4 x 3 In. 355.00
Desk Set, Geometric, 4 Piece 500.00
Desk Set, Grapevine, Bronze, 6 Piece 2760.00
Desk Set, Ninth Century, Bronze Patina, Enameled, 11 Piece 10755.00
Desk Set, Pine Needle, Bronze, Gold Dore, c.1910, 5 Piece 1910.00
Desk Set, Pine Needle, Slag Glass, Bronze, 6 Piece 7770.00
Desk Set, Zodiac, 8 Piece 1840.00
Desk Set, Zodiac, 12 Piece 2585.00
Dish, Bronze, Enameled, Multicolored, 8 x 1 In. 350.00
Dish, Lotus Shape, Bronze, Gold Dore, Stamped, 4 1/4 In. 120.00
Frame, Chinese Pattern, Bronze, Dark Patina, 7 1/4 x 8 3/4 In. 950.00
Frame, Grapevine, Amber Slag Glass, Bronze, Gold Dore, 9 1/2 x 7 3/4 In. 1763.00
Frame, Grapevine, Amber Slag Glass, Gilt Bronze, Gold Dore, 14 1/2 x 12 1/2 In. 2705.00
Frame, Grapevine, Bronze Beaded, Easel Style, 6 x 4 1/4 In. 950.00
Frame, Grapevine, Bronze, Gilt, c.1910, 14 x 12 In. 3346.00
Frame, Grapevine, Bronze, Gilt, Double, 9 3/4 x 7 5/8 In. 5975.00
Frame, Grapevine, Green Slag Glass, Easel, 7 1/4 x 6 In. . . . . 1650.00 to 2500.00
Frame, Mother Of Pearl Abalone Insets, Deco Flowers, Bronze, Gold Dore, 14 x 11 In. . . . 4255.00
Frame, Pine Needle, Bronze, Gold Dore, 6 3/4 x 6 1/4 In. 2689.00
Frame, Pine Needle, Bronze, Stamped, 10 x 8 In. 2689.00
Frame, Pine Needle, Green Slag Glass, Bronze, Brown Patina, 7 In. 1725.00
Frame, Pine Needle, Green Slag Glass, Bronze, Easel, 12 x 9 In. 3500.00
Frame, Pine Needle, Green Slag Glass, Bronze, Oval, 9 1/2 x 7 1/2 In. 2500.00
Frame, Pine Needle, Green Slag, Bronze, Patina, Easel Back, Signed, 9 1/4 x 7 3/4 In. 3200.00
Frame, Venetian, Bronze, Gold Dore, Signed, 9 x 7 In. 2500.00
Frame, Zodiac, Bronze, Dark Patina, Easel, Signed, 8 x 7 In. 1200.00
Inkstand, Abalone, Embossed Leaves, Bronze, Gold Dore, Octagonal, 3 In. 800.00
Inkwell, Adam, Bronze, Gold Dore, 2 1/2 x 4 x 3 In. 550.00
Inkwell, Art Nouveau, Curved Tray, Swirls, Bronze, Gold Dore, Glass Insert, 2 1/2 x 8 In. . 2000.00
Inkwell, Chinese Pattern, Bronze, Dark Patina, Glass Insert, Signed, 4 1/2 x 6 1/4 In. 1200.00
Inkwell, Chinese Pattern, Bronze, Gold Dore, Signed, Square 6 1/2 In. 720.00

Inkwell, Favrile Glass Insert, Reticulated Bronze, Squat, 3 1/2 x 6 3/4 In. 5676.00
Inkwell, Grape Pattern, Mother-Of-Pearl Dots, Bronze, Gold Dore, 3 x 3 3/4 In. . . .1000.00 to 1120.00
Inkwell, Grapevine, Bronze, Green Slag Glass, 3 3/4 x 6 1/2 In. 825.00
Inkwell, Grapevine, Green Slag Glass, Bronze, Beaded, 3 x 4 In. 950.00
Inkwell, Grapevine, Green Slag Glass, Bronze, Dark Patina, Signed, 2 1/2 x 3 3/4 In. 650.00
Inkwell, Hinged Cover, Abalone, Bronze, Gold Dore, Octagonal, Signed, 3 1/2 In. 750.00
Inkwell, Hinged Cover, Adam, Sunburst, Flowers, Ribs, Bronze, Glass Insert, 4 x 3 In. 550.00
Inkwell, Hinged Cover, American Indian, Bronze, Gold Dore, 5 1/2 In. 750.00
Inkwell, Hinged Cover, Graduate, Bronze, Gold Dore, Glass Insert, 4 x 2 In. 450.00
Inkwell, Hinged Cover, Louis XVI, Bronze, Gold Dore, Leaf Swag, 2 1/2 x 3 1/4 In. 1200.00
Inkwell, Hinged Cover, Modeled, Bronze, Gold Dore, Glass Insert, Signed, 2 1/2 x 3 In. .. 550.00
Inkwell, Hinged Cover, Modeled, Bronze, Gold Dore, Glass Insert, Signed, 3 1/4 x 5 In. .. 750.00
Inkwell, Hinged Cover, Ninth Century, Bronze, Gold Dore, 14K Gold Plate, 3 1/2 x 4 In. .. 2500.00
Inkwell, Hinged Cover, Venetian, Sculptured Minks, Bronze, Gold Dore, 8 Sides, 2 1/2 In. 650.00
Inkwell, Hinged Cover, Zodiac, Bronze, Gold Dore, 6 Sides, Signed, 4 x 6 In. 750.00
Inkwell, Hinged Cover, Zodiac, Bronze, Gold Dore, 8 Sides, Signed, 2 x 4 In. .....550.00 to 750.00
Inkwell, Hinged Seashell Cover, Glass Insert, Crab Shape, Bronze, c.1910, 7 1/2 In. 14340.00
Inkwell, Iridescent Blue, Silver & Blue Pulled-Feather Design, Bronze Cover, 5 In. 6025.00
Inkwell, Pine Needle, Bronze, Green, Slag Glass, Signed, 6 1/2 In. 1300.00
Inkwell, Pine Needle, Gold Matte, Carmel Slag Glass, Signed, Square 3 1/4 In. 540.00
Inkwell, Pine Needle, Green Slag Glass, Bronze, Signed, 3 1/2 x 4 In. 950.00
Inkwell, Pine Needle, Green Slag Glass, Bronze, Signed, 3 x 3 1/2 In. 550.00
Inkwell, Venetian, 2 Wells, Bronze, Gold Dore, Chain Latch, Signed, 2 x 5 x 3 In. 1500.00
Inkwell, Zodiac, Bronze, Verdigris Patina, 4 x 6 1/2 In. 500.00
Inkwell, Zodiac, Pen Trays, Green, Red, Brown, Signed, 9 3/4 x 10 1/2 In. 2070.00
Jewelry Box, Hinged Cover, Abalone, Bronze, Gold Dore, Signed, 6 1/2 x 2 1/2 In. 2000.00
Jewelry Box, Hinged Cover, Claw Feet, Bronze, Gold Dore, Dark Patina, Gold Dore, 3 x 3 In. 2200.00
Jewelry Box, Hinged Cover, Grapevine, Green Slag Glass, Bronze, 6 1/2 x 9 1/2 In. 3500.00
Jewelry Box, Hinged Cover, Pine Needle, Green Slag Glass, Bronze, 6 1/2 x 4 x 3 In. 2500.00
Lamp, 2-Light, Linenfold Shades, Frosted Panels, Molded Trim, Signed, 18 1/2 In. 3450.00
Lamp, 3-Light, Lily, Favrile Glass Shades, Bronze, c.1910, 12 7/8 In. 7170.00
Lamp, 3-Light, Lily, Iridescent Shades, Bronze, Gold Dore, Base, 16 1/2 In. 7640.00
Lamp, 6-Light, Lily, Gold Iridescent, Bronze, Ceiling, 17 In. 4025.00
Lamp, Aladdin, Green & Amber Glass, Rows Of Scallops, Cone Shaped Shade, Prunts ... 3105.00
Lamp, Bronze Base, Amber Glass Shade, Raised Leaf, Etched Border, Signed, 15 In. 6000.00
Lamp, Bronze Base, Stick, c.1910, 27 3/4 In. 3585.00
Lamp, Bronze, Favrile Glass, c.1910, 53 3/4 x 10 In. 9560.00
Lamp, Colonial Shade, Leaded Glass, Caramel, Slag, Bronze Base, 16 x 22 In. 9200.00
Lamp, Counter-Balance, Adjustable Ball-End Arm, Bronze Base, 5-Legged, 52 In. 4995.00
Lamp, Daffodil Shade, Leaded Glass, Bronze, c.1910, 27 x 20 In. 41825.00
Lamp, Damascene Shade, Iridescent Glass, Bronze Base, 12 In. 8815.00
Lamp, Damascene Shade, Iridescent Glass, Bronze Base, 55 1/2 x 10 In. 11163.00
Lamp, Desk, Grapevine, Domed Shade, Bronze, 17 1/2 x 10 1/2 In. 9560.00
Lamp, Desk, Nautilus Shade, Leaded Glass, Green, Bronze, 15 1/2 In. 11165.00
Lamp, Desk, Turtleback Tile, Bronze, Stamped, c.1910, 14 In. 11950.00
Lamp, Dragonfly Shade, Leaded Glass, Bronze, c.1910, 18 x 14 In. 47800.00
Lamp, Dragonfly Shade, Leaded Glass, Bronze, c.1910, 23 1/2 x 20 1/8 In. 41825.00
Lamp, Geometric Shade, Dichroic, Leaded Glass, Bronze, c.1910, 32 x 18 In. 45410.00
Lamp, Geometric Shade, Green, Yellow, Ribbed, 3 Sockets, Stick Base, Signed, 24 In. 34500.00
Lamp, Grapevine, Bell Shape, Slag Glass, Bronze, Harp Arm, Stick Body, 13 1/2 In. 4500.00
Lamp, Greek Key, Leaded Glass, Bronze, Gold Dore, Alligator Finish, c.1910, 22 In. 47800.00
Lamp, Green Favrile Shade, Quilted, Feathered, Bronze Base, Adjustable, 15 In. 11500.00
Lamp, Green Iridescent Shade, 50 Prisms, Bronze, c.1910, 28 x 16 In. 22705.00
Lamp, Green Pulled, Gold Iridesent Shade, Bronze, Brown Patina, Ribbed Foot, 13 In. ... 1840.00
Lamp, Hanging, 6-Light, Bronze, Viking Ball, c.1910, 39 1/2 In. 359.00
Lamp, Jeweled Feather, Leaded Glass Shade, Bronze, Gold Dore Base, 22 In. ....*Illus* 21275.00
Lamp, Kerosene, Pulled Green Feathers, Shade, Green, Purple Iridescent, 13 3/4 In. 2115.00
Lamp, Leaf, Vine Shade, Leaded Glass, Bronze Base, Gold Dore, 5-Footed, 57 1/2 In. 14100.00
Lamp, Linenfold Shade, 12 Panels, Bronze, Gold Dore, Ball Feet, Ribbed Base, 23 In. 20400.00
Lamp, Linenfold Shade, Acid Etched Bronze, Fluted Base, Gold Dore, c.1940, 13 1/2 In. ... 5875.00
Lamp, Mosque, Ivory Opalescent, Green Feather, Gold Iridescent, Wood Base, 8 1/2 In. ... 5500.00
Lamp, Mosque, Pulled Green Feather, Ivory Opalescent, Bronze, Gold Dore, 8 1/2 In. 5500.00
Lamp, Oil, Bronze, Snuffer, Stamped, 5 In. 2150.00

Lamp, Oil, Gold Iridescent Shade, Bell Shape, Bronze, Urn Base, Electrified, 15 1/2 In. . . . 5875.00
Lamp, Pine Needle, Bronze Base, Baluster, 19 1/2 In. 3450.00
Lamp, Poinsettia Shade, Geometric, Leaded Glass, Chartreuse, Bronze Urn, Base, 20 In. . . 34500.00
Lamp, Pomegranate, Mottled Green, Amber, Urn Shape, 3-Legged, Paw Feet, Signed, 24 In. 16100.00
Lamp, Spider Shade, Leaded Glass, Bronze, c.1910, 19 x 15 In. 41825.00
Lamp, Student, 2-Light, Ribbed Shades, Bronze, Applied Wire, Stepped Base, 30 In. 3740.00
Lamp, Tulip Shade, Leaded Glass, Bronze, c.1910, 25 x 18 In. 59750.00
Lamp, Turtleback Tile Shade, Platinum Chartreuse, Prisms, Bronze, Paw Feet, 28 In. 97750.00
Lamp, Vine Border Shade, Leaded Glass, Bronze, c.1910, 21 1/2 x 18 In. 19120.00
Lamp, Zodiac, 6-Sided Bronze Base, Gold Dore, Adjustable, 13 1/2 In. 5500.00
Lamp, Zodiac, Gold Iridescent, Bell Shade, Bronze Base, 2 Harp Arms, Favrile, 18 In. 4500.00
Lamp, Zodiac, Hexagonal, Bronze, Gold Dore, Adjustable, 13 1/2 In. 5500.00
Lamp, Zodiac, Iridescent Shade, Bronze, Red, Green Patina, Signed, 17 1/2 In. 3055.00
Lamp Base, Bronze, 3 Sockets, Hexagonal, 20th Century, 22 In. 3819.00
Lamp Base, Bronze, Gold Dore, Bulbous, Metal Collar, Foot Die Stamped, Favrile, 25 In. . . 5175.00
Lamp Base, Bronze, Paw Feet, Disc Base, Incised Flower, Wreath, Blue Enamel, 20 In. 2415.00
Letter Holder, Abalone, Bronze, Gold Dore, 2 Sections 1500.00
Letter Holder, Adam, Bronze, Gold Dore, 2 Sections, 6 x 9 1/4 In. 700.00
Letter Holder, Adam, Flowers, Sunburst, Ribs, Bronze, Gold Dore, 2 Sections, 9 x 2 In. . . 700.00
Letter Holder, American Indian, Bronze, Gold Dore, 2 Sections, 5 3/4 x 11 x 2 3/4 In. 950.00
Letter Holder, Chinese Pattern, Bronze, Dark Patina, 3 Sections, Signed, 8 x 12 In. 1500.00
Letter Holder, Graduate, Bronze, Gold Dore, 2 Sections, 5 1/4 x 9 1/2 x 2 3/4 In. 750.00
Letter Holder, Grapevine, Green Slag Glass, Bronze, 2 Sections, 6 1/2 x 10 In. 1500.00
Letter Holder, Grapevine, Slag Glass, Bronze, c.1910, 6 1/2 x 5 1/4 In. 1093.00
Letter Holder, Louis XVI, Gold Dore, Bronze, 2 Sections, 5 x 9 In. 1200.00
Letter Holder, Ninth Century, Bronze, Jeweled, Gold Dore, 14K Gold Plate, 10 x 2 In. . . . 2000.00
Letter Holder, Pine Cone, 3-Tiers, Bronze, Gold Dore, Amber Slag Glass, 6 x 10 In. 1165.00
Letter Holder, Pine Needle, Amber Slag Glass, Bronze, 2 Sections, 6 x 10 In. 1265.00
Letter Holder, Pine Needle, Green Slag Glass, Bronze, 2 Sections, 10 x 6 x 2 1/4 In. 1500.00
Letter Holder, Pine Needle, Green Slag Glass, Bronze, 2 Sections, Signed, 5 x 6 1/4 In. . . 1500.00
Letter Holder, Venetian, Minks, Bronze, Gold Dore, 2 Sections, 4 1/2 x 6 x 2 1/2 In. 1500.00
Letter Holder, Zodiac, Bronze, Verdigris Patina, 6 1/4 x 9 1/2 In. 560.00
Letter Opener, Abalone, Bronze, Gold Dore, Signed, 10 In. . . . . .450.00 to 550.00
Letter Opener, Chinese Pattern, Bronze, Gold Dore, Signed, 11 In. 350.00
Letter Opener, Chrysanthemum Pattern, Sterling Silver, 8 In. 75.00
Letter Opener, Grapevine, Amber Slag Glass, Bronze, Dark Patina, Signed, 9 1/4 In. 550.00
Letter Opener, Louis XVI, Bronze, Gold Dore, Signed, 10 In. 500.00
Letter Opener, Ninth Century, Bronze, Gold Dore, Signed, 10 In. 550.00
Letter Opener, Pine Needle, Bronze, Gold Dore, Signed, 7 In. 550.00
Letter Opener, Spanish, Bronze, Gold Dore, Signed, 10 1/4 In. 550.00
Letter Opener, Venetian, Bronze, Gold Dore, Signed, 10 In. 500.00
Magnifying Glass, Abalone, Bronze, Gold Dore, Signed, 4 x 9 In. 2000.00
Magnifying Glass, Adam, Bronze, Dark Patina, Beaded, 4 x 8 1/4 In. 1500.00
Magnifying Glass, Bookmark, Bronze, Gold Dore, Signed, 4 x 8 3/4 In. 1500.00
Magnifying Glass, Graduate, Bronze, Gold Dore, Bronze, 4 x 8 3/4 In. 1500.00
Magnifying Glass, Grapevine, Bronze, Gold Dore, Signed, 3 1/2 x 8 In. 2000.00
Magnifying Glass, Ninth Century, Bronze, Gold Dore, Signed, 4 x 9 In. 2000.00
Magnifying Glass, Venetian, Gold Dore, 4 x 9 In. 1500.00
Magnifying Glass, Zodiac, Bronze, Dark Patina, 4 x 8 3/4 In. 1500.00
Match Safe, Tray, Pine Needle, Amber Slag Glass, Bronze, Signed, 4 x 2 In. 650.00
Match Safe, Zodiac, Bronze, Gold Dore, Signed, 2 1/2 x 1 3/4 In. 450.00
Notepad Holder, Graduate, Bronze, Gold Dore, Signed, 7 1/2 x 4 3/4 In. 300.00
Notepad Holder, Louis XVI, Center Wreath, Bronze, 7 1/4 x 4 3/4 In. 750.00
Notepad Holder, Ninth Century, Bronze, Jewels, Signed, 7 1/2 x 4 1/2 In. 950.00
Panel, Leaded Glass, Multicolor Sections, Green Center, Square 6 1/2 In. 940.00
Paper Clip, Abalone, Iridescent Enamel, Bronze, Gold Dore, Signed, 2 x 2 1/4 In. 800.00
Paper Clip, American Indian, Raised Mask, Geometric, Bronze, Gold Dore, 4 x 2 3/4 In. . . 600.00
Paper Clip, Chinese Pattern, Bronze, Gold Dore, 2 1/4 x 3 1/4 In. 550.00
Paper Clip, Venetian, Bronze, Gold Dore, Minks, Signed, 2 1/4 x 3 1/2 In. 650.00
Paper Clip, Zodiac, Bronze, Gold Dore, Signed, 4 x 2 1/2 In. 550.00
Paperweight, Dog, Pointer, Bronze, Signed, 3 1/4 x 2 x 2 1/2 In. 850.00
Paperweight, Dog, Pug, Reclining, Bronze, Stamped, 1 3/4 In. 1016.00
Paperweight, Hound's Head, Bronze, Stamped, 2 In. 956.00

Paperweight, Owl, Bronze, Dark Patina, Signed, No. 892, 3 x 1 1/4 In. 850.00
Paperweight, Pine Needle, Green Slag Glass, Bronze, Curved Spindle, 7 1/2 x 3 1/2 In. . . . 1500.00
Paperweight, Sphinx, Bronze, Signed, 1 1/4 x 1 x 2 1/4 In. 715.00
Paperweight, Sphinx, Bronze, Singed, 1 1/4 x 1 x 2 1/4 In. 850.00
Paperweight, Turtleback, Iridescent Blue, Bronze Base, Signed, 5 3/4 In. 1955.00
Pen Brush, Abalone, Bronze, Gold Dore, Signed, 2 x 2 1/4 In. 650.00
Pen Brush, Grapevine, Green Slag Glass, Dark Patina, Signed, 1 1/2 x 2 1/4 In. 650.00
Pen Brush, Ninth Century, Bronze, Jewels, Signed, 1 1/2 x 2 1/2 In. 650.00
Pen Brush, Pine Needle, Green Slag Glass, Bronze, 1 1/2 x 2 1/4 In. 650.00
Pen Brush, Venetian, Bronze, Gold Dore, Octagonal, Signed, 2 1/4 x 3 In. 450.00
Pen Tray, Adam, Sunburst, Ribbons, 3 Sections, Curved, Bronze, Signed, 9 1/4 x 2 3/4 In. . 250.00
Pen Tray, Chinese Pattern, Bronze, Gold Dore, Handles, 12 x 3 3/4 In. 500.00
Pen Tray, Chinese Pattern, Bronze, Signed, 9 1/2 x 3 In. 350.00
Pen Tray, Graduate, Bronze, Gold Dore, 3 Sections, 8 1/2 x 2 1/2 In. 225.00
Pen Tray, Grapevine, Green Slag Glass, Bronze, Ball Feet, 2 3/4 x 9 1/2 In. 550.00
Pen Tray, Louis XVI, Ribbed Handle, Oval, Bronze, 8 1/4 x 3 1/2 In. 450.00
Pen Tray, Ninth Century, Bronze, Blue, Green Jewels, 3 1/4 x 9 3/4 In. 650.00
Pen Tray, Zodiac, Bronze, Gold Dore, Signed, 3 x 9 3/4 In. 250.00
Pendant, Iridescent Glass, Silver, 1 3/8 x 1 1/8 In. 4183.00
Penholder, Modeled, 2 Sections, Bronze, Dark Gold Dore, Signed, 4 x 8 In. 1500.00
Penholder, Ninth Century, Blue, Green Jewels, Square, Bronze, 2 1/2 In. 350.00
Penholder, Pine Needle, Green Slag Glass, Bronze, Easel Back, Hooks, 5 x 4 In. 900.00
Planter, Geometric, Bronze, Gold Dore, Signed, 8 1/2 In. Diam. 650.00
Planter, Grapevine, Slag Glass, Bronze, 4 x 8 1/2 In. 4481.00
Planter, Water Lilies, RS Monogram, Bronze, Gold Dore, 3 1/2 x 10 1/2 In. 5288.00
Platter, Bronze, Gold Dore, Upturned Edge, Signed, 8 In. 195.00
Platter, Geometric Border, Bronze, Gold Dore, Signed, 9 In. 350.00
Platter, Raised Florets, Red Enameled Center, Bronze, Gold Dore, Signed, 8 In. Diam. . . . 550.00
Postage Scale, Grapevine, Green Slag Glass, Bronze, Dark Patina, 3 x 1 1/2 x 3 In. 1500.00
Postage Scale, Pine Needle, Green Slag Glass, Bronze, Signed, 3 x 2 x 3 In. . . . .1500.00 to 1800.00
Powder Box, Curved Cover, Grapevine, Green Slag Glass, Bronze, 3 3/4 x 2 In. 2500.00
Screen, Pine Needle, Tea, Green Slag Glass, Bronze, Ball Feet, 4 x 7 In. 2000.00
Shade, Linenfold, Amber, Leaded Glass, 12 Sided, Favrile, c.1936, 5 x 9 1/4 In. 5380.00
Smoking Stand, Adam, Bronze, Signed, 24 1/2 In. 1315.00
Smoking Stand, Artichoke Molded Base, Bronze, Signed, 24 1/2 In. 1555.00
Tazza, Enameled, Bronze, Gold Dore, Heart Shape, Favrile, Signed, 7 x 6 1/2 In. 3500.00
Thermometer, Grapevine, Green Slag Glass, Bronze, 8 1/4 x 3 3/4 In. 2000.00
Thermometer, Pine Needle, Green Slag Glass, Bronze, Gold Dore, 8 1/4 x 3 3/4 In. 1800.00
Thermometer, Zodiac, Bronze, Dark Patina, Easel Back, Signed, 8 x 4 In. 2000.00
Tray, Card, Reclining Woman, Front Curved, Ribbed, Bronze, Gold Dore, 5 3/4 x 4 In. 1200.00
Tray, Enameled Grape, Bronze, Gold Dore, 7 1/2 In. 325.00
Tray, Geometric, Bronze, Gold Dore, 14 In. 400.00
Tray, Grapevine, Green Slag Glass, Bronze, Ball Feet, 4 x 2 3/4 x 3/4 In. 650.00
Tray, Iridescent Glass Mosaic, Bronze, Gold Dore, 7 3/4 In. 5380.00
Tray, Red Enameled Border, Bronze, Gold Dore, Stamped, 10 In. 295.00
Tray, Venetian, Bronze, Gold Dore, 2 Sections, Signed, 10 x 3 3/4 In. 350.00
Tray, Venetian, Sculptured Minks, Bronze, Gold Dore, 2 Sections, 3 3/4 x 10 In. 350.00
Trivet, Mosaic, Dragonfly, Signed, Tiffany Studios, 1890s, 6 x 6 1/4 In. 10000.00
Vase, Bud, Gold Iridescent Pulled Feathers, Gold Dore, Bronze Foot, 11 3/4 In. 1150.00
Vase, Bud, Gold Iridescent, Mottled Blue & Yellow, Bronze Base, Flared, 12 In. 1095.00
Vase, Curved Wreath, Raised Berries, Leaves, Fluted Rim, Bronze, Patina, Signed, 3 In. . . 1500.00
Vase, Flower Shape, Iridescent Purple, Blue Highlights, Bronze Base, 14 In. 2820.00
Vase, Flower Shape, White Opalescent, Green Pulled Feather, Bronze Holder, 17 In. 2530.00
Vase, Gold Iridescent, Baluster, Applied Lappets At Base, Favrile, 3 1/4 In. 529.00
TIFFANY GLASS, Base, Cypriote, Oval, Gold Iridescent, Favrile, 6 3/4 In. 9560.00
Bonbon, Gold Iridescent, Blue, Red, Ruffled, Stretched Edge, Favrile, 7 1/2 In. 450.00
Bottle, Green, Applied Tadpoles, Signed, c.1900, 11 1/2 In. 1035.00
Bottle, Green, Pulled Feather, Bulbous, Silver Collar, Stopper, 8 1/2 In. 1555.00
Bowl, Aqua, Diamond Quilted, Flared Rim, Pontil, 8 1/8 In. 999.00
Bowl, Blue & Purple Iridescent, Flared Rim, Favrile, 1925, 3 1/2 x 10 1/4 In. 956.00
Bowl, Centerpiece, Attached Flower Frog, Blue Iridescent, Gold Lily Pads, 13 In. . . . . *Illus* 5750.00
Bowl, Centerpiece, Blue Iridescent, Diagonal Ribs, Favrile, 10 In. 3738.00
Bowl, Centerpiece, Blue Iridescent, Swirls, Ribbed, Favrile, 10 x 3 3/4 In. 1955.00

Tiffany, Lamp, Jeweled Feather, Leaded Glass Shade, Bronze, Gold Dore Base, 22 In.

Tiffany Glass, Bowl, Centerpiece, Attached Flower Frog, Blue Iridescent, Gold Lily Pads, 13 In.

Tiffany Glass, Vase, Jack-In-The-Pulpit, Gold Iridescent, Ribbed Body, 15 In.

Bowl, Centerpiece, Gold Iridescent, Scalloped Rim, Favrile, 1800s, 4 x 13 1/2 In.	2070.00
Bowl, Flowers, Peacock Blue Iridescent, 6 Lily Pads, 2-Tier Flower Frog, 11 1/2 In.	4000.00
Bowl, Gold Iridescent, Blue, Purple, Green, Ribbed, Signed, 10 x 3 1/2 In.	510.00
Bowl, Gold Iridescent, Flared, Ribbed, Favrile, 3 1/4 x 4 1/2 In.	950.00
Bowl, Gold Iridescent, Optic Ribbed, Favrile, Signed, 8 In.	635.00
Bowl, Gold Iridescent, Protruding Ribs, Favrile, Signed, c.1900, 8 In.	865.00
Bowl, Gold Iridescent, Red, Blue, Ribbed, Ruffled Edge, Favrile, Signed, 2 1/2 x 4 In.	400.00
Bowl, Gold Iridescent, Red, Standing Ruffled Edge, Bulbous, 4-Footed, Favrile, 4 In.	450.00
Bowl, Gold Iridescent, Scalloped Rim, 8 1/4 In.	705.00
Bowl, Gold Iridescent, Scalloped Rim, Faceted, 2 1/4 x 6 1/4 In.	295.00
Bowl, Gold Iridescent, Scalloped Rim, Favrile, Signed, 4 1/2 In.	420.00
Bowl, Gold Iridescent, Scalloped Rim, Favrile, Signed, 9 1/2 In.	705.00
Bowl, Gold Iridescent, Veining To Edge, Flared Foot, Signed, 10 In.	865.00
Bowl, Gold, Purple, Applied Pedestal Foot, Favrile, Signed, 2 x 3 1/2 In.	375.00
Bowl, Gold, Red, Yellow Platinum Iridescent, Scalloped, Crimped Rim, 6 In.	230.00
Bowl, Gold, Scalloped, Favrile, Signed, 4 1/2 In.	380.00
Bowl, Green, Opalescent, Rim Veins, Footed, Favrile, 6 In.	825.00
Bowl, Laurel Leaves, Blue Opalescent, 6 1/4 In.	950.00
Bowl, Morning Glory, Butterfly, Ribbed, Laurel Leaf, Blue, 3 5/8 x 8 1/8 In.	1265.00
Bowl, Pastel Green, Favrile, Footed, Signed, 2 1/2 In.	690.00
Bowl, Pinched Rim, Gold, Platinum Iridescent, Favrile, Signed, 2 1/2 In.	200.00
Bowl, Purple Iridescent, Peacock Blue, Footed, Signed, Favrile, 11 1/2 In.	2185.00
Bowl, Underplate, Gold Iridescent, Blue, Pigtail Prunts, Favrile, Signed, 6 x 3 In.	520.00
Bowl, Underplate, Gold Iridescent, Scalloped Edge, Favrile, 6 3/4 In.	355.00
Bowl, Underplate, Purple, Blue Iridescent, Scalloped Edge, Gold Favrile, 5 & 6 In.	865.00
Bowl, White Opalescent, Emerald Green Pulled Feather, 3 3/4 x 11 In.	956.00
Bowl, Yellow Pastel, Opalescent Feathering, Flattened Flared Rim, 5 3/4 In.	290.00
Candle Lamp, Blue, Ribbed, Swirled Base, Pulled Feathers, Quilted Shade, 12 In.	2235.00
Candle Lamp, Peacock Blue, Ribbed Body, Diamond-Quilted Shade, 14 In.	6000.00
Candle Lamp, Shade, Pink & Blue Highlights, Gold Favrile, c.1910, 12 1/4 In.	1140.00
Candle Lamp, Shade, Pink & Blue Highlights, Gold Favrile, c.1910, 15 In.	1840.00
Candleholder, Blue, White Ribbing, Fluted, Signed, 4 In., Pair	2300.00
Candlestick, Gold Iridescent, Ribbed Ring, Base, Favrile, 7 In., Pair	1000.00
Candlestick, Gold Iridescent, Ribbed Stem & Base, 12 In., Pair	4995.00
Candlestick, King Tut, Blue Iridescent, Gold Interior, 10 In.	1265.00
Card Tray, Enamel, Intaglio Cut Leaves, Vines, Blue Iridescent, Violet, Gold, 6 In.	2500.00
Card Tray, Intaglio Cut Leaves, Vines, Enameled, Green Border, Favrile, 2 x 6 In.	2500.00
Chalice, Gold Iridescent, Applied Threading, Pods, Magenta, Blue, 4 1/2 In.	1035.00
Compote, Blue Iridescent, Pedestal Base, Favrile, 10 x 4 1/2 x 15 1/2 In.	3500.00
Compote, Blue, Intaglio Flowers, Pulled Feather, Clear Stem, Foot, Favrile, 4 1/2 In.	575.00
Compote, Chinese Gold Iridescent, Violet, Red, Diamond-Quilted, Favrile, 3 x 6 In.	750.00
Compote, Flower Form, Gold Iridescent, Pinched Ruffled Rim, Signed, 4 3/4 In.	1150.00
Compote, Flower Form, Opal, Green Pulled Feathers, Gold Wash, Favrile, 5 In.	1840.00
Compote, Flower Form, Pulled Green Feathers, Favrile, c.1917, 4 1/2 In.	1495.00

Compote, Gold Iridescent, Double Gourd Form, Ribbed, Scalloped Rim, 3 3/4 In. 750.00
Compote, Gold Iridescent, Leaves, Vines, Favrile, Signed, 4 In. 1175.00
Compote, Gold Iridescent, Ruffled Edge, Favrile, 6 In. 865.00
Compote, Gold Iridescent, Ruffled Onion Skin Rim, 6 1/4 In. 1725.00
Compote, Gold, Green Iridescent, Ruffled Edge, 6 In. 940.00
Compote, Gold, Purple Iridescent, Ruffled Edge, Favrile, Signed, 4 1/2 x 5 1/4 In. 1150.00
Compote, Green Opalescent, Onion Skin, Scalloped Rim, Favrile, 1954, 6 In. 805.00
Compote, Intaglio Grape Leaves, Footed, Favrile, Signed, 8 In. 2645.00
Compote, Opalescent, Turquoise Iridescent, Signed, Favrile, 7 x 5 x 3 1/2 In. 1800.00
Compote, Pink, Gold Iridescent, Opalescent Diamond Optic, Footed, 5 1/2 x 8 In. 1500.00
Compote, Stars, Opalescent, Turquoise Iridescent, Onion Skin, Signed, 3 1/2 x 7 In. 1800.00
Compote, Turquoise, Onion Skin, Clear Stem & Foot, Favrile, Signed, 7 1/2 In. 920.00
Compote, Violet Iridescent, Onion Skin, Radiating Bands, Favrile, 5 1/4 In. 850.00
Cordial, Gold Iridescent, Favrile, Signed, 3 In. 345.00
Cordial, Gold Iridescent, Wheel Carved Border, Signed, 4 5/8 In. 430.00
Cordial, Purple, Blue Iridescent, Signed, 6 In. 805.00
Creamer, Green To Blue Opalescent, Blue Iridescent Rim, Signed, 3 1/4 In. 1035.00
Cup, Gold Iridescent, Green Arrowroot, Applied Handle, Favrile, 2 1/4 In. 645.00
Cup, Green Leaf, Gold Iridescent, Favrile, Signed, 2 1/2 In. 880.00
Dish, Gold Iridescent, Footed, Ruffled Edge, Favrile, 6 1/4 x 2 1/4 In. 800.00
Dish, Ivory Iridescent, Peacock Blue Border, Favrile, Signed, 7 In. 550.00
Flower Frog, White Opalescent, Loops, 3 5/8 x 2 1/4 In. 115.00
Goblet, Amber Iridescent, Engraved Leaf, Signed, 6 In., Pair 645.00
Goblet, Blue Iridescent, Gold, Engraved, Favrile, 6 In., 6 Piece 4400.00
Goblet, Blue, Green Iridescent, Gold, Faceted Stem, Favrile, 4 In., 4 Piece 1765.00
Goblet, Clear, Blue, White Stripe, Favrile, Signed, 8 In. 645.00
Goblet, Clear, Purple, White Stripe, Flared, Favrile, 8 1/2 In. 645.00
Goblet, Gold Iridescent, Signed, 7 In. 635.00
Goblet, Gold Iridescent, Twisted Stem, No. 1237, 7 In. 865.00
Goblet, Gold, Purple, Blue, Green Iridescence, Favrile, Signed, 6 In. 520.00
Goblet, Pink, White Striped Top, Blue Foot Rim, 6 In. 315.00
Goblet, Yellow, White Stripe, Clear Twisted Stem, Flared, Favrile, Signed, 7 In. 705.00
Humidor, Bronze Cover, Gold Iridescent, Leaf, Vine, Cylindrical, 9 1/2 x 5 1/2 In. 2500.00
Jam Pot, Amber, Green Leaf, Gold Iridescent, Sterling Silver Cover, 6 1/4 In. 1135.00
Jar, Gold Iridescent, Squat, Ribs, Enameled, Favrile, 3 1/2 x 2 In. 1200.00
Liqueur Set, Gold Iridescent, Bulbous Stopper, Band Of Grapes, 11 In., 7 Piece 6325.00
Loving Cup, Gold Iridescent, Pulled Vines, 3 Applied Handles, 4 1/2 In. 2645.00
Mug, Gold Iridescent, Green Pulled, Applied Handle, Signed, 3 1/2 x 2 1/2 In. 1320.00
Nut Dish, Blue, Ruffled Edge, Favrile, 1 x 2 1/2 In. 520.00
Nut Dish, Gold Iridescent, Ruffled Rim, Favrile, Signed, 2 3/4 In. 200.00
Nut Dish, Gold Iridescent, Swirled Ribs, Polished Pontil, Favrile, 3 In. 440.00
Paperweight, Pear, Gold Iridescent, Curved Stem, Favrile, Signed, 3 x 6 In. 450.00
Plate, Amethyst Opalescent, Scalloped Rim, Favrile, 11 In., Pair 2015.00
Plate, Amethyst, Onion Skin, Scalloped Rim, Favrile, 6 1/2 In. 316.00
Punch Cup, Gold Iridescent, Intaglio Band Of Grapes, Applied Handle, 2 1/4 In. 460.00
Punch Set, Gold Amber Iridescent, Freeform Decoration, Favrile, 13 Piece 9490.00
Salt, Blue Iridescent, Ruffled Edge, Fluted, Ribbed, Signed, 2 1/2 In. . . . . .200.00 to 260.00
Salt, Blue, Gold Interior, Magenta Highlights, Scalloped Rim, Ribbed, 2 1/2 In. 290.00
Salt, Gold Iridescent, Blue, Green, Violet, Twists, Favrile, Signed, 2 In. 350.00
Salt, Gold Iridescent, Cauldron Shape, 2 Handles, Signed, 1 In. 345.00
Salt, Gold Iridescent, Flat Base, Ruffled Edge, Favrile, Signed, 1 x 2 1/2 In. 200.00
Salt, Gold Iridescent, Pinched Inverted Rim, Pontil, Favrile, Label, 2 1/2 In. 294.00
Salt, Gold Iridescent, Pink Highlights, Ruffled Edge, Signed, 2 1/2 In. 201.00
Salt, Gold Iridescent, Purple Highlights, Scalloped Rim, 2 1/2 In. 200.00
Salt, Gold Iridescent, Ruffled Rim, Pontil, Favrile, 2 1/2 In. 264.00
Salt, Gold Iridescent, Silver, Blue Interior, Round, Wide Top, Favrile, 1 x 1 3/4 In. 300.00
Salt, Gold, Blue, Pink Highlights, Ruffled Edge, 2 1/2 In. 175.00
Salt, Purple Iridescent, Footed, Ribbed, 2 1/8 x 1 1/2 In. 175.00
Saucer, Gold Iridescent, Applied Handle, Favrile, 5 In. 558.00
Saucer, Scalloped, Gold Iridescent, Scalloped, Favrile, 6 1/4 In., Pair 235.00
Seal, Scarab, Red Iridescent, Favrile, Signed, 3/4 In. 150.00
Seal, Scarabs, Gold Iridescent, 3-Sided, Beaded, Favrile, Signed, 1 3/4 In. 750.00
Shade, Candelabra, Green Pulled Feathers, Platinum On Oyster, Ribbed, 5 1/2 In. 2400.00

Shade, Gold Iridescent, Bell Shape, Diagonal Ribs, 4 1/2 In. 920.00
Shade, Gold Iridescent, Bulbous, Flared Ruffled Rim, 5 x 6 In., Pair 748.00
Shade, Gold Iridescent, Green, Blue Pulled Feathers, Scalloped Rim, Favrile, 5 In. 690.00
Shade, Green Iridescent, Platinum, Purple Raised Waves, Signed, 2 1/4 x 5 In. 2300.00
Shade, Green, Pulled Feathers, Clam Broth, Platinum Luster, Bell Shape, 5 1/2 In. 2245.00
Shade, Lily, Gold Iridescent, Pulled, Zipper, 5 7/8 x 4 1/2 In. 300.00
Shade, Lily, Green Pulled Feathers, 4 3/8 x 3 In. 1840.00
Shade, Pulled Feathers, Yellow, Clambroth Ground, Ruffled Rim, 2 1/4 x 5 In. 460.00
Shade, Tulip, Butterscotch Translucent, Crimped, Opalescent Interior, 5 1/2 In. 1440.00
Shade, Tulip, Gold Iridescent, Ribbed, Favrile, 4 1/2 x 3 3/4 In. 980.00
Shade, Tulip, Gold, Translucent, Ribbed, Crimped Edge, 4 3/4 x 3 1/4 In. 1320.00
Shade, Yellow Pastel, Opal, Pulled Green Feather, No. 841, 5 1/2 In. 1955.00
Sherbet, Gold Iridescent, Flared Rim, Spread Foot, 3 1/4 In., 4 Piece 1150.00
Tazza, Aqua, Opalescent Feathering, Translucent Stem, Border, 6 x 5 3/4 In. 748.00
Tea Screen, 3 Sections, Multicolored Swirled Glass, Bronze, Frame, 4 x 7 In. 4500.00
Trivet, Iridescent, Copper Frame, Footed, Favrile, Square 6 In. 940.00
Tumbler, Applied Threading, Pods, Peacock Eye, Purple, Blue, Platinum, 3 In. 865.00
Tumbler, Clear, Blue, White Stripe, Favrile, Signed, 5 In. 470.00
Tumbler, Whiskey, Gold Iridescent, Violet, Twist, Curved Rim, Signed, 1 3/4 In. 300.00
Vase, Aqua, Iridescent Interior, Opal Striations, Ribbed, 9 5/8 In. 1035.00
Vase, Black Iridescent, Platinum, Blue Iridescent Pulled Leaf, Vine, 5 3/4 In. 8625.00
Vase, Blue Iridescent, Purple, Gold, Pulled Feather, Signed, 10 1/4 In. 2990.00
Vase, Blue Iridescent, Swirled Shoulder, Polished Pontil, Signed, 5 In. 3170.00
Vase, Blue, Blue Stripes, Bulbous, Button Pontil, Favrile, 5 1/2 In. 1880.00
Vase, Blue, Engraved Flower Swag, Handles, Favrile, Signed, 9 In. 3055.00
Vase, Blue, Green, Green Leaf, Vine, Favrile, Signed, 4 1/4 In. 3165.00
Vase, Blue, Opal, Vertical Bands, Favrile, c.1900, 8 7/8 In. 1265.00
Vase, Blue-Green Iridescent, Pulled Heart, Vine, Signed, 21 In. 5175.00
Vase, Blue-Purple, Ribbed, Rolled In Rim, Favrile, Signed, 5 1/2 In. 1800.00
Vase, Bronze Iridescent, Amethyst, Pulled Platinum, 7 In. 345.00
Vase, Bud, Gold Iridescent, Green Pulled Feather, Footed, Favrile, Signed, 8 In. 1150.00
Vase, Bud, Gold Iridescent, Scalloped Rim, Ribbed Body, Footed, Signed, 6 In. 1116.00
Vase, Bud, Gold, Flared Rim, Pulled Blade, Cylindrical, Favrile, 20th Century, 6 In. 825.00
Vase, Egyptian Chain, Gold Iridescent, Applied Trim, 3 1/2 x 4 1/2 In. 2300.00
Vase, Egyptian Chain, Silver Gold Iridescent, Bulbous, 9 1/4 In. 5465.00
Vase, Egyptian Shape, Platinum, Purple Iridescent, Blue Ground, Signed, 3 In. 865.00
Vase, Flower Form, Amber, Pulled Feathers, White, Rum, Red, 11 1/2 In. 13225.00
Vase, Flower Shape, Brown, Gold, Mauve, Feathered, Signed, 9 In. 8625.00
Vase, Flower Shape, Gold Iridescent Veining To Edge, Ruffled Edge, 6 1/2 In. 1093.00
Vase, Flower Shape, Gold Iridescent, 5-Fold Flared Edge, Favrile, 4 x 5 1/2 In. 1800.00
Vase, Flower Shape, Gold Iridescent, 5-Fold Flared Rim, Favrile, 5 1/2 x 3 In. 1800.00
Vase, Flower Shape, Gold Iridescent, Green Striations, Dome Foot, 15 1/2 In. 3335.00
Vase, Flower Shape, Gold Iridescent, Pulled Green, Saucer Foot, 10 3/4 In. 7935.00
Vase, Flower Shape, Gold Iridescent, Ruffled Edge, Ribbed Dome Foot, 11 1/2 In. 2700.00
Vase, Flower Shape, Green Pulled Feather, Alabaster, Favrile, Signed, 4 1/2 In. 230.00
Vase, Flower Shape, Green Pulled Hearts, Vines, Signed, Favrile, 6 In. 2130.00
Vase, Flower Shape, Green Pulled Leaves, Ribbed Dome Foot, Petal Edge, 6 5/8 In. 4600.00
Vase, Flower Shape, Green, Opal, Feathered, Slender Stem, 13 In. 7130.00
Vase, Flower Shape, Opal Iridescent, Green Pulled Feather, Gold Trim, 14 In. 2015.00
Vase, Flower Shape, Opalescent, Amber Foot, Ruffled Edge, 13 1/4 In. 3450.00
Vase, Flower Shape, Pulled Feather, Green, Gold, Ivory, Folded Foot, Favrile, 13 In. 5875.00
Vase, Flower Shape, White, Gold Iridescent, Green Leaf, Footed, Signed, 5 1/2 In. 2000.00
Vase, Flowers, Heart Shape Leaves, Cobalt Blue, Gold Iridescent, 8 1/2 x 6 In. 9988.00
Vase, Gold Iridescent, Amber, Platinum, Footed, Favrile, 10 In. 1645.00
Vase, Gold Iridescent, Applied Handles, Urn Shape, Signed, 4 1/2 In. 2470.00
Vase, Gold Iridescent, Blue, Green Heart Shaped Leaves, Vines, Signed, 2 1/2 In. 2200.00
Vase, Gold Iridescent, Flared Rim, Shoulder, Ribbed, Footed, Signed, 3 5/8 In. 1175.00
Vase, Gold Iridescent, Gold Zipper & Pulled Leaves, Squat, Signed, 6 3/4 In. 7480.00
Vase, Gold Iridescent, Green Heart Shape Leaves, Vines, Favrile, 2 1/2 In. 2200.00
Vase, Gold Iridescent, Green Pulled Feathers, Flared Rim, 4 1/4 In. 1035.00
Vase, Gold Iridescent, Green Pulled Hearts, Vines, Favrile, 2 1/2 x 3 In. 2200.00
Vase, Gold Iridescent, Green Pulled Hearts, White Millefiori, Favrile, 5 In. 2415.00
Vase, Gold Iridescent, Green Vine, Cylindrical, Bulging Collar, Favrile, 12 1/2 In. 4255.00

Vase, Gold Iridescent, Intaglio Butterfly, Shouldered, Favrile, 5 In. 1150.00
Vase, Gold Iridescent, Leaves, Green, Bulbous, 8 In. 1998.00
Vase, Gold Iridescent, Molded Branch, Leaf, Oval, Tapered, Favrile, 8 3/8 In. 1725.00
Vase, Gold Iridescent, Platinum, Blue, Flared Base, Favrile, Signed, 8 In. 823.00
Vase, Gold Iridescent, Platinum, Footed, Flared, Favrile, Signed, 13 1/2 In. 3175.00
Vase, Gold Iridescent, Pulled Green Design, Slender, Favrile, 6 1/4 In. 880.00
Vase, Gold Iridescent, Raised Zipper, Blue, Pink, Collar, Bulbous, 4 In. 1800.00
Vase, Gold Iridescent, Red Highlights, Ribbed, Flared, Ruffled Edge, Favrile, 18 In. 2500.00
Vase, Gold Iridescent, Ribbed Flowers, Ruffled Edge, Footed, 12 3/4 In. 2705.00
Vase, Gold Opal Iridescent, Random Pulls, Tapered, Rolled Rim, 5 In. 1265.00
Vase, Gold, Organic Form, 2 Haphazard Ear Handles, 5 1/4 In. 1555.00
Vase, Gourd Shape, Gold, Yellow, Green, Red, Favrile, Signed, 6 In. 825.00
Vase, Gourd Shape, Pink, Blue, Yellow, Favrile, Signed, 6 1/2 In. 940.00
Vase, Green Iridescent, Gold & Blue Pulled Leaves & Vines, Favrile, 11 1/2 In. 8625.00
Vase, Green, Gold Leaf, Vines, Blue, Favrile, Signed, 2 3/4 In. 2590.00
Vase, Green, Platinum Pulled Feathers, Signed, 10 In. 1840.00
Vase, Green, Silver, Purple, Squat, Signed, 4 In. 1725.00
Vase, Jack-In-The-Pulpit, Gold Iridescent, Ribbed Body, 15 In. .... *Illus* 7480.00
Vase, Jack-In-The-Pulpit, Gold Iridescent, Veining, Favrile, Signed, 9 x 16 1/2 In. 7640.00
Vase, King Tut, Gold Iridescent, Pulled Diamond, Shouldered, Rolled In Rim, 9 In. 1955.00
Vase, Millefiori Clusters, Gold Iridescent, Brown Vines, Leaves, Favrile, 4 In. 3165.00
Vase, Millefiori, Green, Blue Iridescent Lily Pads, Vines, 6 In. 5750.00
Vase, Opal, Amber Pulled Feathers, Cylindrical Column Shape, c.1906, 5 1/8 In. 865.00
Vase, Paperweight, Agate, Brown, Green, Globe Shape, Rolled In Rim, 6 x 4 3/4 In. 8813.00
Vase, Paperweight, Orange Poppies, Green Leaves, Iridescent Amber Rim, 7 In. 17250.00
Vase, Peacock Blue, Ribbed, Dimples, Bulbous, Scalloped Edge, Favrile, 4 In. 2000.00
Vase, Peacock Blue, Round, Ribbed, Pinched Rim, Favrile, Signed, 5 In. 1800.00
Vase, Peacock Eye, Gold Pulled Feather Ground, Baluster, Favrile, 11 In. 14900.00
Vase, Pink Shaded To Cream, Pulled Gold, 12 1/2 In. 1555.00
Vase, Purple Iridescent, Corseted, Ribbed, Blue, Favrile, Signed, 5 1/4 In. 1840.00
Vase, Red, Urn Shape, Gold Interior, Green Pedestal Base, Favrile, 5 1/4 In. 7480.00
Vase, Ribbed Gourd Shape, Flared, Blue Iridescent, Green Highlights, 4 1/2 In. 1265.00
Vase, Sapphire Blue, Pulled Handles, 3 In. 865.00
Vase, Shaded Green, Grapes, Leaves, Vines, Frosted, Cameo, 10 1/2 In. 4085.00
Vase, Stick, Gold Iridescent, Bulbous Base, Favrile, 4 1/4 In. 520.00
Vase, Stick, Gold Iridescent, White Wave, Gold Zipper, Bulbous, 10 In. 2015.00
Vase, Tel El Amarna, Butterscotch, Tapered, Footed, Favrile, 11 1/2 In. 4700.00
Vase, Tel El Amarna, Egyptian Collar, Blue, Favrile, c.1910, 9 1/4 x 5 1/2 In. 10755.00
Vase, Transparent Green Ground, Blue, Platinum, Organic, Signed, 4 3/4 In. 2415.00
Vase, Trumpet, Gold Iridescent, Flared Rim, 10 In. 1495.00
Vase, Trumpet, Gold Iridescent, Ribbed Flared Base, Folded Foot, 12 1/4 In. 1880.00
Vase, Trumpet, Intaglio, Leaves, Vines, Iridescent Ribbed Foot, Signed, 13 1/4 In. 3740.00
Vase, Yellow Iridescent, Pulled, Gourd Form, Favrile, 9 1/2 In. 2875.00
Wine, Blue, Purple, Amber Stem, Favrile, 5 1/2 In., 6 Piece 1495.00
Wine, Gold Iridescent, Favrile, Signed, 6 1/2 In. 865.00
TIFFANY POTTERY, Lamp, Brown & Gunmetal Flambe Glaze, Collar Rim, 7 x 8 In. 2820.00
Vase, Blue, Green, Gray, Mottled, Textured, Matte, Tiffany Favrile, 15 x 7 1/2 In. 9400.00
Vase, Bud, Tulips, Old Ivory Glaze, 7 x 2 1/2 In. 4995.00
Vase, Embossed Leaves, Vines, Green Interior, Bisque, Signed, 10 In. 3500.00
Vase, Poppy, Bisque, Earthenware, 1910-20, 9 1/2 In. 4185.00
TIFFANY SILVER, Asparagus Dish, Underplate, Shell & Leaf Rim, Paw Feet, c.1895, 12 1/2 In. 2760.00
Bar Set, Cordis Pattern, Jigger, 3-In. Tumblers, c.1950, 3 Piece 460.00
Berry Spoon, Wave Edge Pattern, c.1884, 9 1/2 In. 290.00
Bonbon, Pierced Rose Border, 7 1/2 In. 290.00
Bowl, Molded Floral Rim, 10 1/2 In. 1016.00
Bowl, Oval, Pierced, Ribbed Border, 1 1/4 x 10 1/2 In. 145.00
Box, Figured, Cat Seated, Hinged Base, Opening At Top Of Head, 4 1/4 In. 350.00
Bread Tray, Oval, Fenestrated, Floral Borders, 11 In. 230.00
Bread Tray, Reeded Rim, Pierced Sides, 1 1/4 x 9 In. 980.00
Butter, Dome Cover, Hammered, Flared Rim, Fruit Finial, c.1868, 5 x 6 In. 430.00
Cake Basket, Round, Pierced Bands, Swing Handle, 8 3/4 In. 750.00
Cake Knife, Wave Edge Pattern, c.1884, 10 1/4 In. 260.00
Cake Plate, Molded Rim, Reeded Band, Monogram, 12 In. 460.00

Candlestick, Bamboo Shaped Stem, Rim, Base, Square, 7 In., Pair 1175.00
Candlestick, George III Style, Fluted, Bow, Swag, c.1950, 11 3/8 In., 4 Piece 6000.00
Candlestick, Oval Base, Slender Shaft, Weighted, Monogram, 9 In., Pair 460.00
Candlestick, Reeded Baluster Stem, Beaded Bobeche, Flared Base, 9 3/4 In., Pair 2300.00
Card Tray, Chased & Stippled Flowers, Raised Border, 5 x 4 In. 525.00
Carving Set, English King Pattern, c.1855, 11 & 13 1/2 In., 2 Piece 489.00
Chamberstick, Repousse, Flowers, Ferns, Monogram, 7 In., Pair 865.00
Cocktail Set, Cocktail, Sterling, Footed, 4 1/2 In., 6 Piece 1315.00
Coffee Set, After Dinner, Reeded Rim, Acanthus Leaf Handle, 9 1/2-In. Pot, 3 Piece 805.00
Coffee Set, S-Flutes, Monogram, Oval Tray, c.1890, 11 1/4-In. Pot, 3 Piece 7200.00
Coffeepot, After Dinner, Persian Style, Flowers, Leaves, Engraved, c.1891 . . . . 489.00
Coffeepot, Ribbed, Repousse Flowers, Early 1900s, 9 In. 690.00
Coffeepot, Spout, Hinged Lid, Leaf Finial, Footed Handle, Signed, 11 In. 345.00
Compote, Scalloped Flower Rim, Dipped Center, Late 1800s, 4 x 9 In. 375.00
Dessert Knife, Wave Edge Pattern, c.1884, 7 1/2 In., Pair 105.00
Dish, Floral Repousse, Stippled Ground, 7 1/4 In. 200.00
Ewer, Bacchic Infants, Grapevine, Baluster, Square Foot, c.1895, 21 1/4 In. 9000.00
Fish Knife, St. Dunstan Pattern, c.1909, 11 1/4 In. 395.00
Fish Slice, Chrysanthemum Pattern, c.1880, 11 1/2 In. 750.00
Flask, C-Scrolls, Vine, Acid Etched, Cylindrical, Oval Lids, 1902, 4 1/2 In., Pair 410.00
Golf Tee, Box, 1 3/4 In. 410.00
Gravy Ladle, Monogram, 1869 . . . . 250.00
Ladle, Florentine Pattern, Monogrammed, c.1900, 16 In. 1150.00
Ladle, St. Dunstan Pattern, Monogrammed, c.1909, 12 In. 345.00
Nut Dish, Blackberry Pattern, Engraved, c.1905, 3/4 x 4 1/4 In., 6 Piece 345.00
Pitcher, Bar, Fluid Form, Curled Strap Handle, Ice Lip, 8 In. 1300.00
Plate, Acanthus Scrolls, C-Scrolls, Shells, 1891-1902, 7 In. 235.00
Plate, Parade Of Children, Monogrammed, 1875-91, 7 7/8 In. 355.00
Platter, Oval, Impressed Mark, 1907-38, 16 In. 520.00
Punch Bowl, Wedding, Yale, Scroll & Keys Society, c.1938, 6 x 11 In. 1725.00
Salver, Man & Woman On Horse, Acid Etched, Round Corners, Square, 12 1/8 In. 1645.00
Salver, Pierced Grapevine & Leaf Border, Gilt, Paw Feet, c.1890, 10 1/2 In., Pair 6000.00
Salver, Ribbed Border, 10 In. 200.00
Serving Fork, Chrysanthemum Pattern, c.1880, 8 1/2 In. 545.00
Serving Fork, Spoon, Gramercy Pattern, Engraved, c.1922, 8 1/2 x 9 1/2 In. 175.00
Serving Fork, Vine Pattern, Sterling 400.00
Serving Spade, Grapevine Pattern, c.1872, 11 1/4 In. 200.00
Serving Spade, Wave Edge Pattern, c.1884, 12 1/2 In. 375.00
Sugar & Creamer, Martele Finish, Ear Shaped Handles, 3 1/4 In. 1016.00
Sugar & Creamer, Oval, Reeded Rims, Ear Handle, 3 1/2 & 5 1/4 In. 385.00
Sugar Spoon, Audubon Pattern, Coquille Shape Bowl, Monogram, 7 In. 405.00
Tablespoon Set, Persian Pattern, c.1872, 8 1/2 In., 3 Piece 175.00
Tea & Coffee Set, Ivy Leaves, Circular Base, Bracket Feet, Late 1800s, 7 Piece 7475.00
Tea Strainer, Marquis, Gold Wash, Monogram, 2 Handles 525.00
Tongs, Asparagus, Pierced Blade, Coin Silver, 1853, 10 1/2 In. 1425.00
Tray, Engraved Floral Wreaths, Scroll Border, Handles, Oval, c.1905, 28 In. 5060.00
Tray, Gallery, Mahogany Wreath, Line Inlaid, 1900s, 1 1/2 x 12 In. 645.00
Tray, Reticulated Border, Embossed Flowers, Shells, Oval, Signed, 11 In. 489.00
Tureen, Cover, Louis XV Style, Bombe, 4 Scroll Feet, France, 1900s, 10 1/2 In. 1920.00
Tureen, Cover, Spiraled Flutes, Leaf Scroll Border, c.1880, 13 1/2 In. 5100.00
Vase, Amphora Shape, Slender, c.1920, 18 3/4 In., Pair 7200.00
Vase, Baluster, Slender, Rippled Flutes, c.1902, 18 In., Pair 9600.00
Wine, Monogrammed L, Stamped Tiffany & Co., 4 In., 6 Piece 375.00

TIFFIN Glass Company of Tiffin, Ohio, was a subsidiary of the United
States Glass Co. of Pittsburgh, Pennsylvania, in 1892. The U.S. Glass
Co. went bankrupt in 1963, and the Tiffin plant employees purchased
the building and the inventory. They continued running it from 1963 to
1966, when it was sold to Continental Can Company. In 1969, it was
sold to Interpace, and in 1980, it was closed. The black satin glass,
made from 1923 to 1926, and the stemware of the last twenty years are
the best-known products.

    Cherokee Rose, Bell, Dinner, 5 3/4 In. 45.00

Cherokee Rose, Relish, 3 Sections, 6 1/2 In. 45.00
Cherokee Rose, Sherbet, 5 1/2 Oz., 4 1/4 In. 20.00
Cherokee Rose, Vase, Bud, Footed, 6 In. 25.00
Coralene, Vase, Black Satin, Embossed Poppies, 5 1/2 In. 100.00
Flanders, Plate, Luncheon, Pink, 8 In. 32.00
Flanders, Vase, Pink, Flared Rim, 8 In. 675.00
Fontaine, Goblet, Twilight Bowl, Clear Stem & Foot, 8 1/4 In. 150.00
Forever Yours, Goblet, Water 30.00
Franciscan Madeira, Tumbler, Footed, Dark Brown, 6 1/2 In., 6 Piece 45.00
Franciscan Madeira, Tumbler, Footed, Dark Green, 6 1/2 In. 8.00
Franciscan Madeira, Tumbler, Footed, Plum, 6 1/2 In., Pair 30.00
Fuchsia, Vase, Bud, Footed, 8 In. 43.00
June Night, Sherbet, 6 Oz., 4 3/4 In. 18.00
June Night, Tumbler, Iced Tea, Footed, 11 Oz., 5 1/2 In. 30.00
King's Crown, Candleholder, Ruby Stain 30.00
King's Crown, Compote, Ruby Stain, 5 In. 23.00
Modern, Vase, Cylindrical, Copen Blue, 12 In. 140.00
Owl, Lamp, Painted, 8 1/2 In. 495.00
Poppy, Vase, Black Amethyst, 6 1/2 In. 35.00
Twilight, Bowl, Square Foot, 10 In. 290.00
Twilight, Vase, Rounded Ribs, 7 In. 240.00

TILES have been used in most countries of the world as a sturdy building material for floors, roofs, fireplace surrounds, and surface toppings. Many of the American tiles are listed in this book under the factory name.

3 Female Figures, Green, Mottled Matte Glaze, Relief, Art Pottery, 7 1/2 x 6 3/4 In. 545.00
Bird, Leaves, Faience Painted, Multicolored, Colorado, 5 3/4 In. 235.00
Bird, Long Talons, Luster, 1900 . . . . 5779.00
Bird In Tree, Hidden In Blossoms, Tan, Green, Burgundy, Moravian, Frame, 13 x 11 In. . . 600.00
Bluebird, Grape Vines, Malibu, 8 x 16 In. 1998.00
Brown, Tan Matte Glaze, Green Crystals, Round, Marked, Flint, 6 In. 380.00
Canterbury Tales, Knight, Prioress, Doctor, Wife Of Bath, Moravian, 4 In., 5 Piece 530.00
Carved Stylized Figure, Green, Blue Metallic Ground, Square, Arts & Crafts, 8 1/2 In. . . . 590.00
Cleopatra, Green Glaze, 6 x 18 In. 700.00
Copper Enamel, Marta Lakes, 6 3/4 x 7 In. 80.00
Cottage, On Roadside, Friend To Man Motto, Waco, Frame, 10 x 13 In. 425.00
Covered Wagon, Oxen, Hillside, Multicolored, San Jose, Frame, 13 In. 750.00
Cowboy, Denim Shirt, Black Trousers, Yellow Ground, San Jose, Oak Frame, 9 3/4 In. 425.00
Daffodils, Bouquet, Potted, White, Yellow, Green, Black, Franklin, Frame, 12 1/2 In. 425.00
Fish, Bubbles, Seaweed, Turquoise, Solon & Schemmel, Frame, 17 x 17 In., 4 Piece 1400.00
Flower, Stylized, Red, Brown, Green Ground, Signed, Delahersche, 3 1/2 In. 470.00
Flowers, Blue, Purple, Green, Yellow, Flint, Marked, 4 1/4 In. 176.00
Flowers, High Glaze, Art Pottery, Art Nouveau, 6 x 6 In. 130.00
Flowers, Stylized, Green High Glaze, Alfred Meakin, 6 x 6 In. 140.00
Fruit & Leaf, Green High Glaze, Minton Hollins & Co., 6 x 6 In. 90.00
Fruit Basket, Raised Outline, Multicolored, Circular, California Faience, 5 1/4 In. 175.00
Geese, Flying, Cattails, White, Green, Brown, Blue Sky, National, Frame, 10 1/4 In. 100.00
Horse Racing, 2 Horses, Jockeys, Raised Line, Harris Strong, 12 x 24 In., 8 Piece 1200.00
Incised Trees, Riverbank, Iridescent Glaze, Signed, Gaziello, 3 1/2 x 5 In. 650.00
Kingfisher, Luster, 1895 . . . . 6225.00
Knight & Landscape, Knight & Boy On Horseback, Jose Menasque Sevilla, 5 3/4 x 11 In. . . 250.00
Landscape, House, Footbridge, Square, Claycraft, 3 3/4 In. 235.00
Landscape, Stylized, Green, Blue, Ivory, C. Pardee Works, 4 1/4 In. 2000.00
Landscape, Woman, Playing Harp, Oval, Art Nouveau, Metal Frame, 10 x 5 1/2 In. 1725.00
Madonna & Child, Blue, Gold, Black, Continental, 14 x 10 In. 115.00
Marsh, Cattails, Lavender, Cobalt, Green, Yellow Sky, Catalina, Frame, 11 1/2 In. 425.00
Men At Card Table, Outside Inn, Orange, Rust, Aqua, D & M, Frame, 13 In. 200.00
Moose, Geese, Trees, Silhouette, Yellow Ground, Franklin, Self-Framed, 13 1/2 x 8 3/4 In. . 4995.00
Ophelia, Woman's Profile, Blue Gray Glaze, United States Encaustic, 6 In. 411.00
Palm Trees, Dark Green, Lagoon Island, Blue Sky, Yellow Sun, Frame, 9 1/2 In. 225.00
Palm Trees, Small Palm Canopied By Larger Palms, Cocoa, Handcraft, Frame, 17 x 19 In. . 475.00
Peacock, Grapevine, Pastel Matte Glaze, California Art Tile, Frame, 12 x 8 In. 590.00

Persian Antelope, Red Clay, Ivory & Blue Glaze, Moravian, 6 3/4 x 5 3/4 In. 470.00
Potter At Wheel, Round, Turquoise Glaze, Sevres, 3 1/2 In. 355.00
Redwood Trees, Maroon, Blue Green Ground, California Clay Products, 8 x 12 1/4 In. 2940.00
San Jose Mission, Multicolored, Unglazed Outline, 6 x 6 In. 470.00
Ship, Rolling Waves, Multicolored, Westraven, Frame, 8 3/4 In. 200.00
Spanish Galleon, Green, Yellow, White, C. Pardee Works, Marked, 4 1/4 In. 765.00
Stoneware, Farmer, Green Glaze, Oribe, Japan, 11 x 11 In. 360.00
Summer Maiden, Enamel, Art Nouveau, Frame, Late 1800s, 19 x 16 In. 4406.00
Sunflower, Blue High Glaze, Art Tile Works, c.1881, 4 x 4 In. 70.00
Ultramarine Blue Gloss Glaze, Kensington, 6 x 6 In. 115.00
Viking Ship On Stormy Sea, Blue, Yellow, Green, Mauve, Franklin, Frame, 14 In. 550.00
Water Lily, White, Yellow, Green Leaves, Blue Water, Claycraft, Frame, 3 3/4 x 5 1/2 In. . . 175.00
Woman, Elaborate Headdress, Art Nouveau, Frame, 7 x 5 In. 470.00
Woman, Landscape, Grapevines, Art Nouveau, Frame, 6 1/2 x 11 In. 765.00
Woman, Moon, Irises, Cuenca, Johann Von Schwarz, Art Nouveau, Frame, 11 x 17 1/2 In. . 2350.00
Woman Gathering Water, Medallion Shape, Molded Design, Beaver Falls, 2 1/2 In. 45.00
Woman's Profile, Green Brown High Glaze, Medallion Shape, Beaver Falls, 3 In. 60.00
Woodpecker, Poking Holes In Tree, Blue, White, Green Ground, Mosaic, Frame, 7 1/4 In. . 70.00
Yellow & Blue Cross On Sienna, Blue, Yellow Leaf On Orange, S & S Tiles Co., 2 Piece . . 105.00
Yosemite Falls, Claycraft, 11 3/4 x 7 3/4 In. 1410.00

TINWARE containers for household use have been made in America
since the seventeenth century. The first tin utensils were brought from
Europe, but by 1798, tin plate was imported and local tinsmiths made
the wares. Painted tin is called tole and is listed separately. Some tin
kitchen items may be found listed under Kitchen. The lithographed tin
containers used to hold food and tobacco are listed in the Advertising
category under Tin.

Bed Warmer, Punched Circles, Hearts, Pine Frame, Hinged Door, Wire Handle, 6 x 9 In. . . 145.00
Biscuit, Normandie Boat, 22 In. 330.00
Cage, Squirrel, House Shape, Steeple, Flag, Side Exercise Wheel, Wood Base, 31 x 27 In. . 220.00
Candlestick, Adjustable Push-Up Rod, Scallop Grip Ring Handle, Round Base, 6 x 4 In. . . 330.00
Cheese Drainer, Plunger, Punched, Round, Feet, 19th Century, 5 1/4 x 3 In. 200.00
Cheese Press, Heart, Punched, 3-Footed, Flat, Ring Handle, 6 In. 546.00
Coffee Roaster, Fireplace, Canister, Sliding Lid, Iron Pole, Turned Handle, 51 In. 145.00
Coffeepot, 2-Piece Cone Shape Body, Hinged Lid, Brass Finial, Raised Bands, 11 1/2 In. . . 330.00
Coffeepot, Diamond Form, Curved Handle & Spout, Brass Finial, 9 3/4 In. 115.00
Coffeepot, Punched, Conical, Gooseneck Spout, Padded Handle, Lid Finial, 11 x 8 In. 715.00
Coffeepot, Punched, Flower Basket, Tulip, Intertwined Line, Brass Finial, 12 In. 1265.00
Compass Wheel, Plumed Wreath Quilt Pattern, Tin, 9 3/4 In. 990.00
Foot Warmer, Punched Eagle, Wreath, Pine Frame, New England, c.1815, 8 x 10 In. 5700.00
Foot Warmer, Punched, Walnut Frame, Wire Bail Handle, Heart In Ring, 9 x 8 x 6 In. 180.00
Ladle, Cup Shape, Hollow Handle, Loop Hanger, Embossed Bands, 3 5/8 x 13 In. 39.00
Lantern, Pyramid Shape, 4 Beveled Glass Panels, Spring Latch, Waterbury, Ct., 11 In. 546.00
Mold, Candle, 2 Tube, Taper, Strap Handle, Early 1800s, 5 1/8 x 1 5/8 In. 355.00
Mold, Candle, 3 Tube, Handle, 5 x 4 1/4 In. 715.00
Mold, Candle, 6 Tube, Loop Handle, 3 1/2 In. 690.00
Mold, Candle, 6 Tube, Oval, Loop Handle, 11 In. 120.00
Mold, Candle, 6 Tube, Penn., 19th Century, 10 & 11 1/4 In., Pair 175.00
Mold, Candle, 8 Tube, Rectangular, Strap Handle, 27 x 14 In. 900.00
Mold, Candle, 12 Tube, 2 Loop Handles, 9 1/2 In. 145.00
Mold, Candle, 12 Tube, Applied Handle, Hanger Ring, 2 Wick Holders, 10 x 6 1/4 In. 250.00
Mold, Candle, 12 Tube, Loop Handle, Hanging Ring, 6 1/2 x 8 1/2 In. . . . . .165.00 to 210.00
Mold, Candle, 12 Tube, Rectangular, Arched Footed Base, Strap Handle, 10 3/4 x 6 In. . . . 385.00
Mold, Candle, 12 Tube, Round, Crimped Top, Base, C-Shape Handle, 10 x 6 1/2 In. 990.00
Mold, Candle, 23 Tube, 15 In., Candle Box, Sliding Lid, 19th Century, 4 x 8 x 5 In. 104.00
Mold, Candle, 24 Tube, Rectangular, Arched Base, 9 1/2 x 9 1/2 In. 385.00
Mold, Candle, 36 Tube, 2 Reinforced Handles, 10 x 13 x 9 In. 300.00
Mold, Candle, 72 Tube, Tin, Square, Applied Tin Handles, 10 3/4 In. 316.00
Sconce, Candle, Arched, Crimped Cresting, Penn., 19th Century, 13 In., Pair 3825.00
Sconce, Candle, Crimped Crests, Punched Birds, 11 In., Pair 230.00
Sconce, Candle, Mirrored, 19th Century, 10 In., Pair 2350.00
Sconce, Candle, Painted, Crimped Top, Pierced Oblong Back, Early 1800s, 7 In. 355.00

Sconce, Candle, Round Reflector Plate, Impressed Spider Web, Crimped Drip Pan, 11 In. .   460.00
Teapot, Cone Shape, Raised Bands, Strap Handle, Cone Shaped Spout, 6 1/2 x 4 1/2 In. . .   35.00
Wall Plaque, Figure, Hessian Soldier, With Rifle, Punched, 8 x 5 & 10 x 6 In., 2 Piece 3235.00

TOBACCO CUTTERS may be listed in either the Advertising or Store categories.

TOBACCO JAR collectors search for those made in odd shapes and colors. Because tobacco needs special conditions of humidity and air, it has been stored in special containers since the eighteenth century.

American Eagle Tobacco Co., Amber, Label, Stork Smoking Tobacco, 6 5/8 In. 560.00
Bear, Wood, Glass Eyes, Holding Brass Ashtray, Switzerland, c.1910, 7 1/2 In. 725.00
Bison, Pottery, No. 3944, 6 In. 179.00
Bonzo, Bisque, Hand Painted, Brown, Japan, 5 1/2 In. 90.00
Bonzo, Bisque, Hand Painted, White Body, Red & Yellow Highlights, Japan, 6 In. 80.00
Figural, Black Boy Bust, Hat Is Removable Lid, 5 1/2 x 5 1/2 In.   225.00
Fraternity Student, Terra-Cotta, 6 1/2 In. 550.00
Globe Tobacco Co., Yellow Amber, Olive Tone, Barrel, Screw-On Lid, 6 7/8 In. . . . .100.00 to 560.00
Hiawatha Tobacco Works, Yellow Amber, Ground Lip, Metal Lid, Handle, 6 3/4 In. 310.00
Hunter Sleeping On Tree Stump, Terra-Cotta, 11 1/4 In. 620.00
Munich Child, Terra-Cotta, 8 1/4 In. 240.00
Pierced Rim, Applied Handles, Finial, Yellow, Black, Orange Base, Redware, 6 x 5 1/2 In. 2200.00
Pig Waiter, Terra-Cotta, 8 1/4 In. 775.00
Rectangular, Canted, Farming Scenes, Inner Lid, Delft, Dutch, c.1765, 6 1/4 In. 2040.00
Seated Figure Finial, Brass, England, c.1790 . . . .   350.00
Tree Stump, 2 Bears Wrestling On Lid, Wood, Switzerland, c.1890, 8 1/4 In. 600.00

TOBY JUG is the name of a very special form of pitcher. It is shaped like the full figure of a man or woman. A pitcher that shows just the top half of a person is not correctly called a toby. More examples of toby jugs can be found under Royal Doulton and other factory names.

Man, Seated, Green Coat, Holding Jug & Glass, Ralph Wood, 9 1/2 In. 1380.00
Man, Seated, Holding Foaming Jug Of Ale With Both Hands, Staffordshire, 9 1/2 In. 1035.00
Man, Seated, Red Coat, Yellow Buttons, Holding Jug, Staffordshire, 9 1/2 In. 980.00
Toby Philpot, Seated, Tricornered Hat, Staffordshire, 1830-40, 9 1/2 In. . . . . .395.00 to 460.00
Winston Churchill, 5 1/2 In. 140.00

TOLE is painted tin. It is sometimes called *japanned ware*, *pontypool*, or *toleware*. Most nineteenth-century tole is painted with an orange-red or black background and multicolored decorations. Many recent versions of toleware are made and sold. Related items may be listed in the Tinware category.

Beaker, Red & Yellow Swags, 4 In. 145.00
Box, Document, Black Ground, Dome Top, Brass Bail Handle, Tin Hasp, 10 x 4 x 5 In. . . .   115.00
Box, Document, Dome Lid, Stylized Roses, 19th Century, 5 1/2 x 8 3/4 In. 27025.00
Box, Document, Dome Top, Black, Red Band, Mustard Stylized Leaves, Penn., 9 In. 520.00
Box, Document, Dome Top, Black, Red Flowers, Green Leaves, Gray, Penn., 7 In. 230.00
Box, Document, Dome Top, Black, Red Swags, Yellow Drops, Tin Hasp, 6 1/2 x 3 1/2 In. .   460.00
Box, Document, Dome Top, Black, White Band, Bail Handle, Initials D/C, 9 x 5 In. 1495.00
Box, Document, Dome Top, Japanned, Flowers, White, Yellow Bands, 8 x 10 In. 220.00
Box, Document, Dome Top, Japanned, Fruit, Wire Ring Handle, Tin Hasp, 9 x 5 x 5 1/2 In.   575.00
Box, Document, Dome Top, Japanned, Ring Handle, Tin Hasp, 5 3/8 x 9 x 4 1/4 In. 290.00
Box, Document, Dome Top, Red Ground, Brass Bail Handle, Fruit, Tin Hasp, 9 x 5 x 5 In. . 1120.00
Box, Document, Dome Top, Stylized Flowers & Berries, Black, Penn., 8 In. 920.00
Box, Document, Dome Top, Swags, Leaves, Ring Handle, 19th Century, 5 3/4 x 9 x 4 In. . .   440.00
Box, Document, Dome Top, Wire Ring Handle, Japanned, 4 3/8 In. 230.00
Box, Document, Green Ground, Couch Lines, Stenciled Flowers, 6 x 9 3/4 x 6 In. 385.00
Box, Document, Japanned, Yellow Leaves, Red Bands, 4 5/8 x 8 3/4 x 4 In. 360.00
Box, Dome Lid, Flowers, Rectangular, 1800s, 6 x 9 3/8 In. 500.00
Box, Dome Top, Red & Blue Morning Glories, Green Leafy Garlands, Black, Pa., 9 In. . . .   230.00
Box, Dome Top, Red, Gold Roses, Leaves, Raised Panel, Bail Handle, 11 x 8 x 12 In. 489.00
Box, Dome Top, Urn, Morning Glories, Leaves, Stars, Black, Gold Band, Pa., 10 In. 920.00
Box, Fishing, Green, Painted Boy, Sheep, Oval, Ribs, Hinged Door, 2 Attached Straps, 14 In.   60.00
Cachepot, Copper Mounted, Parcel Gilt, Red, Flaring Square, 15 1/4 x 9 1/2 x 9 1/2 In. . . .   575.00
Cachepot, French Style, Scalloped Rim, Fruit, Swan Shape Handles, c.1900, 6 x 14 In. . . .   145.00

Tole, Coffeepot, Painted
Tulips, 11 In.

Tole, Tea Caddy, Painted
River Scene, 3 1/2 In.

Tole, Tray, Painted Flowers, Gold Vines,
Cartouche Shape, 10 In.

Cachepot, Parcel Gilt, Green, Footed, Restauration Style, Scale Pattern, 15 x 11 In., Pair ..   80.00
Candlebox, Black Paint, Cylindrical, Domed Ends, Tab Hangers, 10 1/2 x 6 7/8 In. 520.00
Canister, Slide Top, 24 x 16 x 20 In. 240.00
Coal Bin, Tapered Oval, Side Handles, Hinged Lid, Hunting Scenes, Green, c.1900, 19 In. .   2000.00
Coal Scuttle, Flowers, Black Ground, Side Handles, Figural Feet, 26 x 14 x 12 In. 170.00
Coffeepot, Painted Tulips, 11 In. . . . . *Illus*   1430.00
Coffeepot, Pomegranate, Red, Yellow, Green, Scrolled Knob On Lid Edge, 8 1/2 In. 690.00
Coffeepot, Punch Decorations, 3 Tulips, Hook Spout, Early 1800s, 11 3/4 In. 470.00
Coffeepot, Red Tulips, Yellow Leaves, Japanned, Brass Finial, 10 In. 489.00
Coffeepot, Red, Flowers, Straight Spout, Curved Handle, 8 In. 5465.00
Coffeepot, Red, Yellow Flowers, Penn., 19th Century, 10 3/4 In., Pair 3290.00
Coffeepot, Tin, Red, Pomegranate, Yellow Leaves, Japanned Ground, 10 In. 1495.00
Creamer, Red, Yellow & Green Foliage, 3 7/8 In. 230.00
Lamp, Garniture Vase, Brass Mount, Hunter Green, Louis Philippe Style, c.1900, 36 In. . . .   750.00
Lamp, Oil, Chamberstick Form, Whale Oil Burner, Red Paint, 2 In. 630.00
Match Holder, Japanned, Red & Yellow, Cutout & Crimped Crest, 7 1/2 In. 2130.00
Match Safe, Japanned, Tulip, White Band, Swags, Crimped Crest, 7 1/2 In. 575.00
Muffineer, Japanned, Tulip, Leaves, Black Graining, 4 In. 1265.00
Mug, Stenciled Gold Design, A Present, Yellow Ground, 1 3/4 In. 375.00
Mug, Yellow & Green Leaf Designs, Red Ground, 2 In. 4310.00
Needle Case, Yellow Leaf Designs, Japanned Ground With Needles, 9 1/2 In. 170.00
Pitcher, Red, Gold Leaf Designs, Green Highlights, Pa., 10 1/2 In. 1095.00
Plate Warmer, Dome Top, Flowers, Hinged Door, 3 Shelves, Black, c.1875, 30 In. 999.00
Sconce, 3-Light, Corner, Yellow, Early 1800s, 5 In. 1880.00
Sconce, Candle, Black Ground, Red Fruit, Yellow Leaves, Scrolls, Crimped Crest, 10 In. . .   2530.00
Spice Box, 6 Fitted Spice Boxes, Handle, Original Paint, 9 x 6 In. 3740.00
Spice Box, Dome Top, Berry, Leaf Ivory Band, Japanned, 2 3/4 x 4 1/4 x 2 3/4 In. 550.00
Spice Box, Dome Top, Red, Yellow Leaves, Red, Ivory Ground, Japanned, 3 x 4 x 3 In. . . .   2640.00
Sugar, Japanned, Red Cherries, Leaves, 4 x 3 In. 690.00
Tea Bin, Black, No. 11, 28 x 19 1/4 x 18 In. 180.00
Tea Bin, Marked, Number 11, 28 x 19 x 18 In. 179.00
Tea Caddy, Black Ground, Red Star Fruit, Pomegranates, Yellow & Green Foliage, 7 In. . .   200.00
Tea Caddy, Cover, Japanned, Fruit Decoration, Oval, 4 1/4 x 3 3/8 x 2 3/4 In. 195.00
Tea Caddy, Dome Lid, Flowers, Black Leaves, Yellow Bands, Red Ground, 5 x 4 In. 1035.00
Tea Caddy, Flower, Red, Green, Yellow, Dark Japanned, Cylindrical, 5 3/4 In. 230.00
Tea Caddy, Painted River Scene, 3 1/2 In. . . . . *Illus*   83.00
Tea Caddy, Red & Yellow Pomegranates, Leaves, On Dark Ground, 7 In. 115.00
Tea Caddy, Red Flowers, Yellow & Black Leaves, Red Ground, Cylindrical, 5 1/2 In. 290.00
Tea Caddy, Red Fruit, Yellow, Japanned Leaves, Black Ground, 6 3/4 In. 200.00
Tray, 3-Masted Ship, Gilt Border, Black Ground, Scalloped Edge, 24 x 29 In. 2000.00
Tray, Apple, Crystallized Interior, Berries, Red, Yellow, Blue Leaf Border, Oval, 12 x 8 In. .   4625.00
Tray, Black, Yellow, Red, Green Flowers, Raised Sides, Pierced Handles, 12 In. 500.00
Tray, Chippendale, Shaped Edge, Flower Spray, Yellow Rose, 31 x 23 In. 46.00
Tray, Fountain, Flower, Bird, Black Border, Early 1900s, 20 1/2 x 25 1/2 In. 290.00
Tray, Hoho Birds, Perched, Enamel Rocaille, Oval, c.1885, 31 1/2 In. 1763.00

Tray, Joseph, Sold Into Slavery, Curved Rim, Stenciled Flowers, Black, 22 x 30 In. 2185.00
Tray, Louis Philippe, Gallery, Allegorical Scene, Faux Bamboo Stand, 21 x 25 x 20 In. 1725.00
Tray, Louis Philippe, Saffron, Gallery, Painted Buildings, Octagonal, 21 1/2 x 18 In. 1610.00
Tray, Napoleon III, Saffron, Gallery, Military Life Scenes, Oval, 19 1/2 x 28 1/2 x 19 In. . . 1265.00
Tray, Octagonal, Canted Sides, Red, Yellow Striping, 1800s, 12 x 8 1/2 In. 10575.00
Tray, Painted Flowers, Gold Vines, Cartouche Shape, 10 In. . . . . *Illus* 165.00
Tray, Presentation, Mahogany, Dated April 26, 1824, Penn., 18 1/2 x 13 x 2 In. 1553.00
Tray, Reticulated, Apple Tray, Red Rose, Oval, 3 1/2 x 7 1/4 x 12 1/2 In. 230.00
Tray, Scenic, Painted, Oval, Late19th Century, 21 x 30 x 20 3/4 In. 1380.00
Tray, Tea, Classical Landscape, Animals & Figures At Rest, Black & Gold Border, 30 In. . . . 690.00
Tray, Tin, Apples, Leaves, Red Ground, Yellow, Black Trim, Peter Ompir, 16 1/2 In. 200.00
Tray, Wire Rim Edge, Crystallized Center, Green Flower Banding, Octagonal, 13 x 9 In. . . 9350.00
Tray, Wire Rim, Black Base, Red Ground, Flowers, Yellow Band, Octagonal, 9 x 6 In. 990.00
Tray, Yellow & Red Fruit Center, Japanned Ground, Octagonal, 8 1/2 x 12 In. 200.00
Vase, Chestnut, Rosewood, Flowering Scrollwork, Lion's-Head Mask Handles, 12 In. 300.00
Wall Sconce, French Style, Electrified, Flowers, Vines, 14 x 14 In., Pair 400.00

TOM MIX was born in 1880 and died in 1940. He was the hero of
over 100 silent movies from 1910 to 1929, and 25 sound films from
1929 to 1935. There was a Ralston Tom Mix radio show from 1933 to
1950, but the original Tom Mix was not in the show. Tom Mix comics
were published from 1942 to 1953.

Badge, Straight Shooter, Brass, Gem Luster, Red, Blue, Gold, 1937, 2 1/8 In. 175.00
Badge, Tom Mix & Tony, Crossed Guns, Pin Back, Brass, c.1930 . . . . 60.00
Belt, Buckle, Secret Compartment, Ralston, 1950 . . . . 125.00
Belt Buckle, Ralston Straight Shooter, Checkerboard Center, Brass, 2 1/4 In. 75.00
Blotter, Tom Mix Boys, Mounted Troop, Celluloid, 10 Paper Blotters, 1929, 2 x 6 In. 500.00
Button, Tom Mix & Tony, Button Gum, 1930s, 1 1/2 In. 30.00
Button, Tom Mix Circus, Celluloid, Leather Holster, Cap Gun, 1940s, 4-In. Holster 175.00
Button, Tom Mix, Miracle Rider, 1935, 1 1/4 In. 150.00
Button Set, Ralston Straight Shooters, Lithograph, 1 In., 5 Piece 50.00
Figurine, Clown, Souvenir, Tom Mix Birthplace Park, Mix Run, Pa., 1970s 11.00
Gum Wrapper, William Fox Presents Tom Mix In His Big New Hit Teeth, 1924, 3 In. 140.00
Gun, Straight Shooter, Wood, Break Open Top, Revolving Cylinder, Ralston, 1933, 9 In. . . 140.00
Outfit, Vest, Chaps, Suede, Ralston Straight Shooters, 1935, 23-In. Chaps, 16-In. Vest . . . 230.00
Photograph, Ralston Straight Shooters, Autographed, Checkerboard Frame, 5 x 3 In. 90.00
Poster, Tom Mix & Tony In King Cowboy, Cardboard, JBO, 1928, 19 1/2 x 14 In. 175.00
Poster, Tom Mix Circus, Tom Mix & Tony In Person, 1920s, 29 x 28 In. 275.00
Puzzle, Rexall Milk Of Magnesia Tooth Paste, Frame, c.1935, 20 x 13 In., 125 Piece 83.00
Ring, 14K White Gold Finish, Silver & Brass Luster, National Chicle, 1933 . . . . 5700.00
Tin, Movie Make-Up, Ralston Straight Shooters, Checkerboard Border, c.1940 . . . . 22.00
Toy, Circus Wild West Wagon, 2 Horses, Wood, Iron, Arcade, 14 In. 1870.00
Toy, Parachute Plane, Balsa Wood, Box, c.1940, 2 x 9 x 1 In. 400.00
Toy, Postal Telegraph Set, Cardboard, Metal Tapper Key, 1937, 7 1/2 x 5 In. 65.00
Toy, Telegraph Set, Electric, Ralston Straight Shooters, Box, 1940, 4 1/4 x 2 1/4 In. 100.00
Wristwatch, It's Ralston Time, Box, c.1982, 1 x 8 1/2 In. 345.00

TOOLS of all sorts are listed here, but most are related to industry.
Other tools may be found listed under Iron, Kitchen, Tinware, and
Wooden.

6 In 1, Trivet, Iron Stand, Tack Hammer, Opener, Punch, Tack Lifter, Fish Scaler 500.00
Angle Bisector, Langlais Patent, 1894 . . . . 165.00
Anvil, Peter Wright, Large Bottom Swage, 155 Lb. 250.00
Ax, Angel Wing, Iron, Hickory Handle, 21 3/4 In. 980.00
Ax, Bingham's Best Brand, Double Bitted, Embossed 45.00
Ax, Camp, Case XX, 11 In. 38.00
Ax, Camp, Keen Kutter, Hickory Handle, Lanyard Hole, 12 1/2 x 4 3/4 x 3 In. 45.00
Ax, Camp, L.L. Bean, Freeport, Maine, Child's, 10 In. 110.00
Ax, Camp, Marble's, Double Bit, Hickory Handle, 7 3/4 x 3 3/4 x 28 In. 390.00
Ax, Camp, Winchester, Leather Sheath, Shoulder Sling, 13 1/2 x 5 x 3 1/4 In. 205.00
Ax, Coachmaker's Side, Bevel Back Blade 149.00
Ax, Goosewing, 20 In. 255.00
Ax, Goosewing, Continental Decoration, Punched 6-Pointed Star, 7-In. Head, 14-In. Edge . 285.00

Ax, Goosewing, Stamped Initials, Continental	400.00
Ax, Hewing, Stubby Handle, Continental	450.00
Ax, Indian, Standing On Blade, Initials T.O.T.E., Cast Iron, 6 3/4 In.	400.00
Ax, Safety, Marble's, No. 1, Steel, Rubber, Dog, Rabbit, 1898 Patent, 2 x 4-In. Head	840.00
Ax, Safety, Marble's, No. 3, 1898 Patent, 11 1/4 x 4 x 2 3/8 In.	330.00
Ax, Safety, Marble's, No. 4, 1898 Patent, Pocket	549.00
Ax, Safety, Marble's, No. 4, Flanged Head, Wood Handle, 1898 Patent, Pocket	720.00
Ax, Safety, Marble's, No. 5, Nickel Plated Guard, Wood Handle, 10 1/2 x 4 1/2 x 2 1/4 In.	140.00
Ax, Winchester, Wood Handle, Varnished, Boy's, 28 x 6 1/4 x 3 3/4 In.	75.00
Battery, Union Battery Company, Power, Car & Plane Graphics, Dry Cell, 6 In.	209.00
Beader, Hand, Stanley, No. 66, Universal, 2 Fences, 8 Double Cutters, Box	149.00
Bellows, Blacksmith, Leather Fittings, Lancaster County, Penn.	65.00
Bevel, Stanley, No. 25, Rosewood Handle, Patent September 4, 1877, 14 In.	99.00
Bevel Square, D. Bissell Patent, Cast Iron Handle, Fold Out Wing, Adjustable Blade, 1880	1100.00
Bevel Square, Ellis & Russell Patent, Brass Flip Lever, Rosewood, 1871, 12-In. Blade	127.00
Bevel Square, H. Carter, Rosewood, Steel, 18-In. Blade	285.00
Bevel Square, L. Bailey's Patent, Cast Iron Handle, 1872, 10 In.	468.00
Boring Machine, James Swan Co., No. 2, Seymour, Conn., Shipping Crate	220.00
Boring Machine, Millers Falls	450.00
Box, Hop Roof, Stanley, No. 888, Brass Tag	95.00
Brace, Floyd & Co., Forged Iron	175.00
Brace, Henry Brown, Sheffield Plated	125.00
Brace, James Bee, Rosewood, Brass Plates, Sheffield, England, 14 In.	120.00
Brace, Joseph Goodrich, December 10, 1878	2310.00
Brace, North Bros. Mfg., No. 2100, Yankee	55.00
Brace, Pilkington Pedigor & Storrs, Wood, 13 1/2 In.	1760.00
Brace, R. Marples, Plated, Beech, Brass, Cocobolo Head, 1848 Patent	220.00
Brace & Drill Combination, Millers Falls, No. 182, Ratcheting, 1881-1935, 10 In.	190.00
Brace Bit, Winchester, No. 3543, Wood Grip & Knob, 10 In.	58.00
Branding Iron, Cattle Rustler's, Straight Line, Late 1800s, 28 x 2 3/8 In.	35.00
Branding Iron, Cooper's, Maritime Oil Co., Brass Head, Portland, Maine, 24 1/2 In.	175.00
Branding Iron, P.D.E. Koller, Wrought Iron, Signed, 1854, 13 3/4 In.	2145.00
Broadax, I. Blood, Offset Handle, Red Paint, Ballston, N.Y., 12-In. Blade, 24 In.	149.00
Broadax, J. Hicks, Eliz. Town, New Jersey	100.00
Bullet Mold, Sharps, New Model 1859, .52 Caliber, Metal, 2 Groove Cavity, 8 1/2 In.	345.00
Burglar Alarm, Conklin & Hauser, Model, Price 10 Cents, Mousetrap Type, Chicago, Box	750.00
Burglar Alarm, Reiff & McDowell, .22 Cal Blank, Nickel Plate, Phila., Pa., 1893 Patent	520.00
Caliper, Log, Gould, Grover Wheel, Scales, Brass Joints, Steel Tipped Jaws, Early 1900s	1210.00
Caliper, Log, Simon G. Noyes, Lisbon, N.H., c.1890, 36 In.	250.00
Caliper, Phoenix Saw Button, Full-Bodied, Female Profile	440.00
Caliper, Sculptor's, Curved Brass Tips, 43 In.	600.00
Caliper Rule, Sliding Barrel Measure, Belcher Brothers & Co., N.Y., Maple, Brass, 26 In.	360.00
Caliper Rule, Stephens & Co., Riverton, Conn., No. 95 1/2, Ivory, 2-Fold, 6 In.	190.00
Candlesnuffers, Brass, Signed T, England, 1700s	295.00
Carrier, Wood, Painted, Pierced Handle, New England, c.1860, 5 1/2 x 11 x 24 In.	295.00
Chest, Bench, Oak, Swing Out Panels, Drop Front, Drawers	4180.00
Chest, Bird's-Eye Maple Inlays, Mahogany Veneer	415.00
Chest, Carpenter, Trays, 20th Century, 18 x 36 x 18 In.	350.00
Chest, Cherry, Dovetailed, Bird's-Eye Maple Panels, Painted Green, 36 In.	35.00
Chest, Gentleman's, Hamacher Schlemmer & Co., Metal Vise Type, Oak, 6 Drawers	935.00
Chest, Green, Gray, Applied Moldings, Diamond On Front, Handles, 31 x 13 x 14 In.	69.00
Chest, Inlaid Star, 15 Drawers	6160.00
Chest, Joiner's, Oak, Walnut, Wainscoted, New Hampshire	495.00
Chest, M Monogram, Green Paint, Red Border, c.1875, 12 1/2 x 35 3/4 x 13 In.	235.00
Chest, Machinist, Gerstner, Oak, 26 x 16 x 9 1/2 In.	325.00
Chest, No. 2725S, Tools, Boy's Favorite	85.00
Chest, Stanley, No. 801, Sweetheart, Walnut, Pitched Roof Model, Slide Tray, 1922, 15 In.	358.00
Chest, Stanley, No. 910, Oak, 28 Tools, Packing Sheet	525.00
Chisel, Stanley, 4 Square, 1923-35, 1-In. Size, 9 3/4 In.	155.00
Chisel, Stanley, No. 25, Everlasting, Square Side, 1 1/2-In. Size, 10 In.	250.00
Chisel, Winchester, WSB 3/8, Wood Handle, 8 3/4 In.	35.00
Chisel Set, Essex Tool Co., Socket Firmer, Square Edge, Fruitwood Handle, 12 Piece	286.00
Chisel Set, Stanley, No. 60, Bevel Edge, Permaloid Handles, 1/4 To 2 In., 9 Piece	85.00

Chisel Set, Stanley, No. 110, Everlasting, No. 40 Series, Canvas Roll, 10 1/2 In., 6 Piece .. 525.00
Chisel Set, Union Hardware Co., Samson, Box, 1/4, 1/2, 1 & 1 1/4 In., 4 Piece 120.00
Chisel Set, Union Hardware Co., Samson, Wood Box, 1/4 In. To 2 In., 6 Piece 275.00
Clock Jack, Iron, England, c.1750, 14 In. 6500.00
Cobbler's Bench, Pine, Square Top, Drawer, Splayed Legs, 15 x 41 x 15 In. 95.00
Compass, Cooper's, Sandusky Tool Company, Rosewood Body, 14 In. 200.00
Compass, Marble's, No. 082, Pin-On, Brass, Box 56.00
Compass, Marble's, Pocket, Brass, 2 5/8 In. 46.00
Compass, Wrist, Marble's, Celluloid Crystal, Leather Band, Box 54.00
Cordwood Measure, T.R. Hoyt, 1887 .... 90.00
Curling Tongs, Burner, Stand, Silver Gilt, Drew & Sons, Box, 1899, 3 1/2 In. 170.00
Cutting Iron, Parallel, Norris, London, 8 1/4 In. 175.00
Dip Needle, Municipal Instrument Co., Brass Handle, Fitted Case 80.00
Dowel Machine, Stanley, No. 77, Hand Crank, Iron, 3/8-In. Cutter, 1911-69, 15 In. 550.00
Dowel Machine, Stanley, No. 77, Hand Crank, Iron, Japanned, Cutters, 1911-69, 15 In. ... 770.00
Drawknife, Watrous & Co., Elmira, N.Y., 2 Adjustable Handles, 15 In. 90.00
Drill, Bench, North Bros., No. 1005, Yankee 145.00
Drill, Hand, Stanley, No. 610, Pistol Grip, Japanned, Caddy, 1923-35, 12 In. 209.00
Entrenching, US Army, Wood Handle, Brass Throat, Leather Scabbard, 1884, 13 1/4 In. .. 350.00
Flashlight, Olin, Red Clear Cap, 6 In. 11.00
Flashlight, Ray-O-Vac, Sportsman's, Nylon Strap, Chrome Plated Finish, 19 x 4 3/4 In. ... 20.00
Flashlight, Winchester, 4 Cell, Chrome, 15 In. 40.00
Flashlight, Winchester, Copper Plated, 2 D Cell, Ribbed Barrel, 7 In. 25.00
Flashlight, Winchester, No. A-1520, Pointer, Box 260.00
Flax Comb, Iron, Forged, 1779, 14 1/2 In. 715.00
Gauge, Butt, Stanley, No. 92N, Sweetheart, Nickel Plated Beam, Rosewood, 1920-35 .... 165.00
Gauge, Cloth, Quadrant, Chrome Scale, Black Metal Arm, Brass Pillar, 22 In. 29.00
Gauge, Erlandsen, Piano Maker's, New York, 8 In. 80.00
Gauge, Marking, D.M. Lyon, Rosewood, Brass, Newark, N.J. 30.00
Gauge, Marking, Marden's Patent, J.E. Marden, Veazie, Maine, April 16, 1972, 8 In. 605.00
Gauge, Mitre, Langdon Mitre Box Co., Hand Held, Millers Falls, Mass., 8 In. 65.00
Gauge, Mortise & Marking, Winchester, No. 9778, Box 1100.00
Gauge, Mortise, E.W. Carpenter, Rosewood, Boxwood Slide 145.00
Gauge, Slitting, Round Shaft, Hand Forged Nut, Handmade 75.00
Hacksaw, Goodell Pratt Co., Framed, Rosewood Handles, 1889 Patent 100.00
Hacksaw, Henry Disston & Sons, Hand Saw Type, Fruitwood Handle, Philadelphia, 21 In. . 66.00
Hammer, Mitteldorfer Straus, Goat Head, Orange Handle, Pat. January 10, 1928, 8 1/2 In. . 110.00
Hammer, Stanley, No. 40-0, Claw, Bell Face, Atha Trademark, 15 In. 65.00
Hammer, Stanley, No. 100, Steel Head, Hickory Handle, Gold Tone, c.1940, 13 In. 110.00
Hammer, Strap, J. Houston, Bedford, N.H., c.1770, 12 In. 500.00
Hatchet, Sears, Roebuck & Co., Leather Sheath, c.1940 .... 60.00
Headlight, Winchester, Focusing, Nickel Finish, Box, 1920s 230.00
Holder, Stanley, No. 255, Cast Iron, Japanned, 1901 Patent, 1907, 16 In. 550.00
Inclinometer, Clitographe Lefebvre, Inches & Millimeter Scales, Brass, Iron, Box, c.1860 . 220.00
Inclinometer, Davis Level & Tool Co., Cast Iron, Sept. 17, 1867, 18 In. ....180.00 to 215.00
Inclinometer, Davis Level & Tool Co., September 17, 1867, 12 In. 127.00
Inclinometer, Kraengel, Cast Iron, Brass Face Plate, Eagle, Pat. August 17, 1880, 6 In. ... 550.00
Inclinometer, Kraengel, Mahogany, Buffalo, N.Y., 1880 Patent, 28 In. 2420.00
Inclinometer, L.L. Davis, Filigree, Springfield, Mass., Pat. September 17, 1867, 24 In. ... 1045.00
Inclinometer, Stanley, No. 32, Frederick Traut's Patent, Adjustable Vial 1870.00
Inclinometer, Universal Level & Tool, Frank Inclinometer, Electrified, c.1919 .... 2310.00
Jigsaw, New Rogers, Millers Falls Co., 30 In. 90.00
Jointer Gauge, Stanley, No. 386, Cast Iron, Japanned, 14 In. 120.00
Knife, Chamfer, Beer Keg, Sliding Tip 85.00
Lawn Mower, Creel, Salesman's Sample, 1876 .... 3500.00
Leather Slitter, Herrik Aiken, Franklin, N.H., Pat. March 12, 1823, 7 1/2 In. 145.00
Level, Akron Spirit Level, No. 003, Mahogany, 1887 Patent, 22 In. 20.00
Level, C.E. Jennings & Co., Cast Iron, 18 In. 255.00
Level, Corner, Davis & Cook, Cast Iron, Watertown, N.Y., Pat. December 28, 1886, 10 In. . 1485.00
Level, Engineer's, David White Co. 90.00
Level, J. & G.H. Walker, Mahogany, New York, 30 In. 80.00
Level, Machinist's, L.S. Starrett Co., No. 98, Athol, Mass., Box, 12 In. 90.00
Level, Millers Falls Co., No. 10, Rosewood, Brass Bound, 6 1/2 In. 415.00

Level, Pocket, Davis Level & Tool Co., No. 36, Japanned, 2 1/2 In. 330.00
Level, Pocket, Davis Level & Tool Co., No. 37, 3 In. 175.00
Level, Salesman's Display, Routing Around Adjustments, 15 In. 745.00
Level, Sighting, C.F. Richardson, Iron, Tripod Base, Athol, Mass., Pat. Aug. 1887, 36 In. ... 110.00
Level, Spirit, L.L. Davis, Adjustable, Gilding, Patent September 17, 1867 .... 550.00
Level, Spirit, William Johnson, Newark, 12 In. 30.00
Level, Stanley, No. 15, W.T. Nicholson's Patent, Rotating Center Vial, c.1860, 24 In. 1045.00
Level, Stanley, No. 23 S, Declivity, Adjustable, Red & Yellow Vials, Cherry, 1943, 24 In. .. 165.00
Level, Stratton Bros., No. 10, Rosewood, Brass Bound, 6 1/2 In. 330.00
Level, William Johnson, N.J., 12 In. 30.00
Level, Winchester, No. W3, Wood, Brass Hardware, 28 In. 90.00
Lock, Keen Kutter, E.C. Simmons, Logo Shape, Brass, Chain, 4 x 2 1/4 In. 50.00
Lock, Winchester, 6 Lever, Key, 3 x 2 In. 230.00
Lock, Winchester, No. W33, Brass Color, Diagonal Red Winchester, 1 5/8 In. 175.00
Measure, Hayward Bros. & Wakefield, School Desk Seat & Surface Heights, c.1900 ..... 215.00
Miner's Lamp, Winchester, 3 Cell Barrel, Wired Head Lens, Nickel Finish 65.00
Miner's Light Battery Box, Winchester, Belt Clip, 1 1/2 x 2 7/8 x 6 1/2 In. 28.00
Miter Box, Stanley, No. 360 A, Mounted On Stand 80.00
Nail Apron, Keen Kutter, White Cotton, Red Print, Val-Test Keen Kutter Logo, 17 x 7 In. . 29.00
Nail Puller, Patrick Bryant, No. 2, Chesterfield, Mass., Pat. April 10, 1849, 12 In. 145.00
Padlock, 2 Dragons, Steel, Poorman Story, 2 3/4 In. 28.00
Padlock, Acorn Shape, Steel, Poorman Story, 4 In. 140.00
Padlock, Chief, Indian, Headdress, Steel, Warded, 2 3/4 In. 55.00
Padlock, Combination, Clark, U.S. Treasury, Brass, 4 In. 700.00
Padlock, Combination, Junkunk Bros., Brass Body, Steel Shackle, 2 1/4 In. 25.00
Padlock, Corbin, 4 Secure Levers, Brass, 2 7/8 In. 15.00
Padlock, Dog Head, Steel Body, Brass Dust Cover, Smokehouse, 4 In. 95.00
Padlock, Duro, Brass Body, Steel Shackle, 1 1/4 In. 20.00
Padlock, Eagle, 6 Lever, Brass, 2 7/8 In. 55.00
Padlock, Geronimo, Round, Steel, Nickel Plated Body, Warded, 2 1/2 In. 115.00
Padlock, Kay Bee Little Rock, Steel Body, Brass Shackle, Pin Tumbler, Push Key, 2 In. 695.00
Padlock, Lock O' Fortune, Brass Body, Steel Shackle, Warded, 2 3/4 In. 20.00
Padlock, Lucky, Brass Body, Steel Shackle, Warded, 2 5/8 In. 9.00
Padlock, Reese, 6 Lever, Brass Plated Steel, Pin Tumbler, Push Key, 3 1/8 In. 11.00
Padlock, Tioga, Steel, Poorman Story, 3 In. 170.00
Padlock, Trojan, Steel Body, Brass Shackle, Pin Tumbler, Push Key, 2 5/8 In. 475.00
Padlock, W W Mfg. Co, Steel Body, Brass Keyhole, Smokehouse, 3 3/4 In. 50.00
Padlock, Winchester, 4 Pin, 3 x 2 In. 400.00
Padlock, Winchester, No. W12, Polished Brass, 2 1/8 In. ....96.00 to 270.00
Padlock, Winchester, No. W15, Cast Iron, Bronze Shackle, Key, 2-In. Shackle 180.00
Padlock, Winchester, No. W23, Cast Iron, Brass Plated, Shackle Spacing, 1 1/2 In. 115.00
Paper Cutter, Clipit, Presentation, Curved Silver Handle, Monogram RBH, c.1920, 6 In. .. 35.00
Paper Press, Little Giant Hay Press Co., Stenciled, Alma, Mich., 1900, 48 In. 300.00
Pipe Tongs, Spring Action Handle, Bowl Cleaner At Center Side, Iron, 1700s, 17 In. 588.00
Plane, Aluminum Block, Stanley, No. A18, February 18, 1913 .... 45.00
Plane, Beltmaker's, Stanley, No. 11, Rosewood Handle, 6 1/2 In. 120.00
Plane, Bench, Millers Falls, No. 7, Japanned, Number 2 Size, 1929-44, 7 In. 330.00
Plane, Bench, Stanley, No. 602, Bed Rock, Japanned, c.1930, 7 In. 690.00
Plane, Bench, Stanley, No. 608, Type 5, Bed Rock, Japanned, 1900-40, 24 In. 385.00
Plane, Bench, Winchester, No. W5, Walnut Knob, Handle, Red Logo, 14 x 2 1/2 In. 106.00
Plane, Block, Stanley, No. 9 1/2, Adjustable, 6 In. 80.00
Plane, Block, Stanley, No. 9 1/2, Type 2, Unused, Patented, 6 In. 470.00
Plane, Block, Stanley, No. 9, Rosewood Handle 1100.00
Plane, Block, Stanley, No. 110, Shoe Buckle, Type 2, 7 1/4 In. 440.00
Plane, Block, Stanley, No. 164, Adjustable, 1926-43, 9 In. 3520.00
Plane, Block, Stanley, No. S18, Knuckle Joint Block, Steel Body, 1925-42, 6 In. 60.00
Plane, Block, Tower & Lyon, Chaplin's Patent, Japanned, New York, 6 1/4 In. 265.00
Plane, Chamfer, Japanned Finish, Church Window Pattern, 1833 Patent 11660.00
Plane, Chamfer, Stanley, No. 72, Japanned, 1885-1938, 9 In. 358.00
Plane, Circular, Stanley, No. 20 1/2, Cast Iron, Japanned, 1902-17, 9 1/2 In. ....127.00 to 220.00
Plane, Coach Maker's, Curved Inlaid Brass Side Plates 1485.00
Plane, Combination, Aluminum, Box, 1915-24 .... 2970.00
Plane, Combination, Keen Kutter, No. K64, Box 990.00

Plane, Combination, P.A. Gladwin, Wood Box, Boston, Mass., Pat. April 9, 1878, 5 In. ... 4620.00
Plane, Combination, Stanley, No. 45, Walnut Case, Dovetailed, 12 In. 330.00
Plane, Combination, Union, No. 44, Adjustable, Sielgey's Patent, Green Box 495.00
Plane, Core Box, Stanley, No. 57, c.1898, 10 In. 195.00
Plane, Dado, Leonard Bailey Victor, No. 14 .... 3740.00
Plane, Dado, Stanley, No. 39 1/4, Sweetheart, Japanned, 1900-49, 8 In. 90.00
Plane, E.C. Simmons Hardware Co., No. KK 7, Rosewood Handle 66.00
Plane, Eclipse Plane Co., Adjustable Scraper, Patented Nov. 24, 1874, 9 In. .... *Illus* 1020.00
Plane, Fore, Stanley, No. A6, Aluminum, Box, 1925-38, 18 In. 3080.00
Plane, Fulton, No. 3708, No. 2 Size 145.00
Plane, Furring, Stanley, No. 340, Type 1, Pat. Apl'd For, c.1905, 10 In. 935.00
Plane, J.C. Spencer, Brass Locking Wheel, 1873 Patent, 21 In. 635.00
Plane, Jack, Sargent, No. 714, Iron, Auto Set, Box 198.00
Plane, Jack, Stanley Bailey, No. 5 1/4, Type 16, 1940 .... 70.00
Plane, Jack, Stanley, No. 605 1/2C, Bed Rock, Corrugated, Box, c.1925, 15 In. 3410.00
Plane, Jointer, Sandusky Tool Co., Imprinted, 40 In. 396.00
Plane, Jointer, Silsby Race & Holly, Seneca Falls, New York, Holly's Patent, July 6 1852 . 1100.00
Plane, Jointer, Stanley, No. 8C, Corrugated, c.1950, 24 In. 140.00
Plane, Junior Jack, Stanley, No. 5 1/4, Rosewood Handle, 1930s, 11 In. 100.00
Plane, Match, Stanley, No. 148, Tongue & Groove, Cast Iron, Nickel Plated, 9 In. 100.00
Plane, Mayo, Boss, Brass Nuts 2640.00
Plane, Miter, Julius Earlandsen, Late 19th Century 1890.00
Plane, Miter, Robert Baker, Bronze, Dovetailed, 1980 .... 759.00
Plane, Molding, A.B. Bacon, Astragal, Yellow Birch, 10 In. 1210.00
Plane, Molding, Bead, H. Chapin, Boxed, Macassar Ebony, Union Factory, Conn., 9 In. ... 1210.00
Plane, Molding, Cumings & Gale, Side Rabbet, Providence, R.I., c.1830, 9 1/2 In., Pair ... 360.00
Plane, Molding, Dog Shape, Tail As Handle, 10 1/2 In. 430.00
Plane, Molding, I. Sleeper, Double Wedges & Irons, Offset Tote, 3 1/2 In. 1650.00
Plane, Molding, Isaac Field, Yellow Birch, 18th Century 3410.00
Plane, Molding, J. Tower, Yellow Birch, Rutland, Mass., Pair 2200.00
Plane, Molding, Samuel Auxer, Handle, Ogee, Applied Fence, Lancaster, Pa., 4 1/2 In. ... 1045.00
Plane, Norris, A5, Double Screw 275.00
Plane, Norris, Gunmetal Body, Ward Blade, Rosewood, England 2310.00
Plane, Piano Maker's, Brass, Rosewood, Infilled, New York 800.00
Plane, Plow, Auburn Tool Co., Beech, Screw Lock Arms, 7 Cutting Irons 140.00
Plane, Plow, Auburn Tool Co., Boxwood, Auburn, New York 3520.00
Plane, Plow, Casey & Company, Cocobolo, Boxwood Arms, Fence 660.00
Plane, Plow, Chapin, Beech Handle, March 31, 1868 .... 600.00
Plane, Plow, Emanuel Weidler, Carpenter, Rosewood, Boxwood 17600.00
Plane, Plow, Greenfield Tool Co., No. 534, Rosewood, Boxwood Arms, Fence Boxing 240.00
Plane, Plow, H. Chapin, No. 238, 1868, 3 Arm 4180.00
Plane, Plow, H. Chapin, No. 240, Handles Screw Arm, Union Factory, 1800s 415.00
Plane, Plow, Ivory Scales, Arthington 175.00
Plane, Plow, Leonard Bailey, No. 14, Victor, Light Duty, Pat. July 6, 1875, 8 In. 4070.00
Plane, Plow, Mockridge & Francis, Brass Trunscrew, 3 Arm, Newark, N.J., 12 In. 5720.00
Plane, Plow, P.A. Gladwin & Co., Rosewood Handle, 11 In. 385.00
Plane, Plow, Solon Rust, Wooden Fence, Adjustment, Patent 1868 .... 2750.00
Plane, Plow, Stanley, No. 42 Miller's Patent, Gunmetal, 8 Cutting Irons, c.1880, 10 1/2 In. 2640.00
Plane, Plow, W. Holt, Yankee Style, Beech Body, 10 In. 220.00
Plane, Rabbet & Filletster, Union, No. 43, Box 396.00

Tool, Plane, Eclipse Plane Co., Adjustable Scraper, Patented Nov. 24, 1874, 9 In.

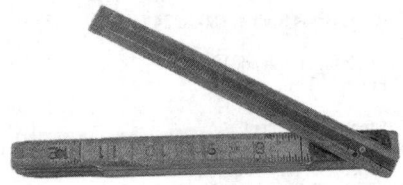

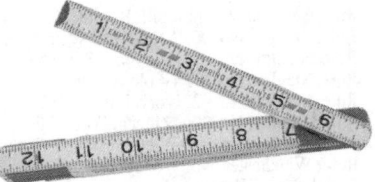

Tool, Rule, Folding,
10-Fold, 60 In.

Tool, Rule, Folding, Empire,
Spring Joints, 12-Fold, White, 72 In.

Plane, Rabbet, Record Tool Works, No. 010, Carriage Maker's, England	85.00
Plane, Rabbet, Stanley, No. 10 1/2, Carriage Maker's, Japanned Finish, c.1930, 9 In.	220.00
Plane, Rabbet, Stanley, No. 90, Steel Case, October 6, 1875, 9 In.	39.00
Plane, Rabbet, Stanley, No. 90A, Sweetheart, Box, c.1940, 4 In.	11000.00
Plane, Rabbet, Stanley, No. 93, Cabinet Maker's, 6 1/2 x 1 In.	105.00
Plane, Rabbet, Stanley, No. 196, Curved, 1912-34, 9 In.	1430.00
Plane, Sandusky Tool Co., No. 3, Smoother, Wood, Aluminum, 8 In.	550.00
Plane, Scraper, Stanley, No. 87, Cast Iron, Sweetheart, 1905-17, 8 x 2 In.	935.00
Plane, Scraper, Stanley, No. 212, Sweetheart, Box, 1911-35, 5 1/2 In.	1980.00
Plane, Scrub, Stanley, No. 40, Beech Handle, Sweetheart, 1920-35, 11 In.	90.00
Plane, Scrub, Stanley, No. 40, Rosewood Handle, 1930s, 9 1/2 In.	75.00 to 120.00
Plane, Side Bead, Mockridge & Francis, 1/8 In.	5.00
Plane, Smoothing, Millers Falls, No. 209, Chrome Plated, Tenite Handles, 1938, 9 x 2 In.	360.00
Plane, Smoothing, Munks Patent, Japanned, 1884 Patent, 6 1/2 In., 1 3/4-In. Cutter	7700.00
Plane, Smoothing, Sargent & Co., No. 407, Mahogany Handle, Conn., No. 2 Size, 7 In.	120.00
Plane, Smoothing, Stanley, No. 1, Black Japanned Finish, Patent 1892, 5 3/4 x 1 1/2 In.	1320.00
Plane, Smoothing, Stanley, No. 1, Original Box	4200.00
Plane, Smoothing, Stanley, No. 2, 7 1/4 In.	220.00
Plane, Smoothing, Stanley, No. 3, 1950s, 9 In.	55.00
Plane, Smoothing, Stanley, No. 4, Type 11, Box, 9 In.	130.00
Plane, Smoothing, Stanley, No. 604 1/2C, Bed Rock, 10 In.	360.00
Plane, Stanley, Interchangeable Sole, 3 Pairs Hollow & Round Soles, Beading Sole	4950.00
Plane, Veneer Scraper, Stanley, No. 12, Rosewood Handle, 6 1/4 x 2 7/8 In.	70.00
Plane, Winchester, No. W110, Japanned Handle, 7 1/4 In.	55.00 to 70.00
Plane, Wooden, Fruitwood, Ogee, Flat Chamfers, 1700s, 10 In.	110.00
Plane, Wooden, H.J. Harpel, Handle Tongue, Douglas, Pa.	330.00
Plane, Wooden, Israel White Panel Raiser, Skew Cutter, Adjustable Fence & Stop	90.00
Plane, Wooden, W. Martin, Flat Chamfers, S. Garrigues, Philadelphia, 1700s	270.00
Pliers, Stanley, Slip Joint, Nickel Plated, c.1920, Pair	220.00
Pliers, Winchester, No. 2489, Screw Driver End, Nickel Plated, 10 In.	40.00
Plumb & Level, Fitchburg Tool Co., Cast Iron, Filigree, Fitchburg, Mass., 8 1/2 In.	415.00
Plumb Bob, Brass, Ornately Turned, Reversible & Removable Tip, 5 1/2 In.	1870.00
Plumb Bob, Brass, Pointed Steel Tip, Wide Finial Cap, 8 In.	209.00
Plumb Bob, Clockwork Mechanism	1100.00
Plumb Bob, Engineer's, Goodell Pratt Co., Brass, Nickel Plated Cap, c.1910, 4 In.	340.00
Plumb Bob, Marples, Turnip Type, Turned Top Stem, Steel Top, 6 In.	305.00
Rake, Hay, Wooden, 19th Century, 67 x 73 In.	1195.00
Router, Carved, Walnut, 1782	935.00
Router, Mockridge & Francis, Double	375.00
Rule, Calculating, Stanley, Folding, Long's Patent, Box, c.1870, 24 In.	6820.00
Rule, Carpenter's, Stanley, No. 58, 6-Fold, Arch Joint, 24 In.	110.00
Rule, Chapin-Stephens Co., No. 036, Folding, Inclinometer, Conn., 12 In.	99.00
Rule, Drafting, Stanley, No. 96, Boxwood, Beveled, Metric, c.1890, 12 In.	2090.00
Rule, Draughtsman's, Darling Brown & Sharpe, Providence, Pat. Dec. 16, 1879, 12 1/2 In.	120.00
Rule, Dry Measure, Lufkin Rule, 3-Fold, Metric, English Scales, Mich., 1920, 24 In.	145.00
Rule, Folding, 10-Fold, 60 In. *Illus*	20.00
Rule, Folding, Empire, Spring Joints, 12-Fold, White, 72 In. *Illus*	35.00
Rule, J. Ewart, Cattle Gauge, Calculates Useful Meat, Ivory Slide, Newcastle	580.00
Rule, Keen Kutter, K690, Brass Hardware, Folding, Pocket, 12 In.	50.00
Rule, Keen Kutter, No. K690, Brass Hardware, Folding, 24 In.	20.00
Rule, Rolling, Jas. Carrington, Wallingford, Conn., Patented April 14, 1832, 14 In.	45.00

Rule, Seymour & Churchill, Bristol, Conn., 4-Fold, Ivory, Brass Bound, 1800s, 24 In. 880.00
Rule, Stanley, No. 00, 2-Fold, Ivory, Brass Fittings, 6 In. 770.00
Rule, Stanley, No. 32, Boxwood, Sweetheart, Metric, Folding, England, 12 In. 360.00
Rule, Stanley, No. 87, 4-Fold, Ivory, German Silver Fittings, 24 In. 470.00
Rule, Stanley, No. 92, Ivory, Folding, 12 In. 115.00
Rule, Stanley, No. 206, Zigzag, Wood Slide, Taut's Patent, 1902 Patent 110.00
Rule, Stanley, No. 344, Victor, Folding, Zigzag, Victor, Stanley, No. 344, 4-Fold, 48 In. . . . 99.00
Rule, Winchester, No. W84, Folding, 23 In. 145.00
Saw, Back, S. Biggin & Sons, Chamfered Back, Split Nuts, 12 In. 75.00
Saw, Barnes, No. 1, Amateur Saw, Foot Powered, c.1885 . . . . 660.00
Saw, Bead, H. Disston & Sons, Carpenter's, Philadelphia, 18 In. 66.00
Saw, Bow, Chandler & Barber, Turning Type, c.1895, 10-In. Blade 105.00
Saw, Bow, Newark, William Johnson, N.J., 12 In. 40.00
Saw, Bow, William Marples & Co., Beechwood, Lacquered 90.00
Saw, Buck, Henry Disston & Sons, Wooden Frame, Salesman's Sample, 13 1/2 x 15 1/2 In. 220.00
Saw, Cabinetmaker's Combination, January 6, 1906, 12 In. 140.00
Saw, Cabinetmaker's, Geo. H. Bishop & Co., 14 In. 50.00
Saw, Crosscut, Bluegrass Brand, No. 47, 8-Point, 26-In. Blade, 29 1/2 In. 250.00
Saw, Crosscut, Henry Disston & Sons, 9-Point, Gauge, Philadelphia, No. 12, 29 1/2 In. . . 4730.00
Saw, Crosscut, M. Barr & Co., No. IXL, 10-Point, Nashua, N.H., 16-In. Blade, 19 1/2 In. . . 310.00
Saw, Dovetail, Fenton & Barnes, Brass Back, Rosewood Handle, London, England, 13 In. . 110.00
Saw, Flooring, E.C. Atkins Co., No. 100, Curved, Applewood Handle, Etched, Ind., 22 In. . 80.00
Saw, Frame, Mortised Jointed, Rope Stretcher 60.00
Saw, Fret, Rosewood Handle, Maple Body, Brass Wing Nuts, 1870 Patent 285.00
Saw, Half Back, H. Disston & Sons, No. 8, 18 In. 605.00
Saw, Half Back, Philadelphia 1900.00
Saw, Hand, Disston & Morss, No. 43, Level, Awl, Square, Rule 935.00
Saw, Hand, Disston No. 210, Metal Cutting, Applewood Handle 28.00
Saw, Hand, London Spring Steel, No. 125, Carved Applewood Handle, 21 1/2 In. 155.00
Saw, Hand, Rip, New Haven Edge Tool Co., No. 128, 29 In. 110.00
Saw, Hand, Winchester, No. 40, Old Trusty, Walnut Handle, Carved Vine 220.00
Saw, Rip, Beech Handle, Brass Medallion 65.00
Scissors, Keen Kutter, No. 7, Straight, Trimmer, Box, 7 In. 25.00
Scissors, Wick, Barnard, Patent, 1864 . . . . .25.00 to 30.00
Screwdriver, Billings & Spencer, Billings Patent, Rosewood Handle, 1896, 5 1/2 In. 110.00
Screwdriver, H.D. Smith Co., Perfect Handle Brand, Triple Lever, Plantsville, Conn., 9 In. 35.00
Screwdriver, Jacob W. Switzer, Brass, December 7, 1852 . . . . 85.00
Screwdriver, L.S. Starrett Co., No. 557, Magazine Handle, Athol, Mass., 1907, 4 In. 65.00
Screwdriver, Winchester, Household, Lug End, Logo, 5 In. 35.00
Screwdriver, Winchester, No. 7102, Regular Pattern, Mahogany Stained Handle, 3 In. 35.00
Screwdriver, Winchester, No. 7125, Mechanics Special, Mahogany Stained Handle, 6 In. . . 35.00
Screwdriver, Winchester, No. 7160, Walnut Palm Butt Handle, Brass, 3 1/4 In. 55.00
Screwdriver Bit, Winchester, No. 2336, 4 1/2 In. 30.00
Screwdriver Set, No. 100, Wooden Case, 3 Piece 39.00
Searchlight, Winchester, No. 6920, Deluxe, Hi-Power, 3 Cell, Fixt Focus, Box 65.00
Section Liner, Drafting Tool, Both's Patent, Portland, Me., Box, 1888 . . . . 145.00
Seeder, Cast Iron, Green Paint 225.00
Set, Pedal Car, Wrenches, Pliers, Pouch, 6 Piece 90.00
Shaving Horse, Wood, Steel & Brass Wear Plates, Foot Pressure Locks, 66 In. 220.00
Shears, Tailor's, Herman Wendt, New York, 1845, 12 1/2 In. 110.00
Shears, Tailor's, R. Heinish, Newark, N.J., Pat. March 11, 1835, 13 1/2 In. 145.00
Shoehorn, Wrought Iron, Looped Handle, 9 In. 95.00
Shoemaker's Kit, Hangs On Horse's Saddle, Tools & Thread Spools, 18 1/2 x 19 x 19 In. . 475.00
Shovel, D Handle, True Temper, October 6, 1853 . . . . 30.00
Shovel, Winchester, No. 2, Plain Back, Common D Handle, Square Point, 37 1/2 In. 195.00
Skiving Machine, J.W. Chase, Leatherworker's Tool, Iron, Adjustable Head, N.H., 10 In. . . 55.00
Slick, Douglas Mfg. Co., 4 In. 130.00
Slick, H. Mellinger, 3 In. 55.00
Slick, Hand Forged, Long Handle, 6 In. 150.00
Slick, James Swan, 3 1/2 In. 120.00
Slide Rule, Quadruple, Boxwood, Imprinted Tables, Dovetailed Slides, 12 In. 429.00
Slide Rule, Stanley, No. 26, 2-Fold, 24 In. 1650.00
Slide Rule, W. Watson & Co., Boxwood, England 95.00

Tool,Wrench, Carriage, G. Flesch, Cast Patent
Date, April 18, 1876, 8 In.

Tool,Wrench, David Bradley Co., No. D89,
Bradley's Wonder, Cutout, 14 In.

Speed, Indicator, James G. Biddle, Machinist's, Timer	45.00
Spokeshave, Stanley, No. 67, Universal, Box, 9 1/4 In.	215.00
Square, Framing, Winchester, No. 9655, 12 In.	120.00
Square, Try, T.C. Crouch & Co., Rosewood, Brass, Middletown, Conn., 20 In.	130.00
Square, Try, Winchester, No. 9726, Steel	100.00
Sugar Devil, July 27, 1878 Patent	75.00
Tape Measure, Crogan Manufacturing Co., One Man, Bangor, Maine, 1915, 4 In.	130.00
Tape Measure, Iron Shape, Brass, Nickel Plate, Cat's-Eye Handle, Germany, 2 1/4 In.	180.00
Tape Measure, Lufkin Rule Co., Donut No. 986, Donut Shaped Case	198.00
Tape Measure, Stanley, No. 1266X, Direct Reading Inside, Late 1930s	495.00
Tire Inflator, Brass, Cast Iron, Wood Handle, 45 x 13 In.	330.00
Trammel, Beam, Pencil Holder, Pair	40.00
Turpentine Hacker, Cast Iron, Pear Shaped Hammer End, Hook Tool End, 21 In.	350.00
Veneer Scraper, Stanley, No. 12 1/2, Sweetheart, Japanned, Rosewood, 1905-43, 6 In.	55.00
Vise, L.S. Starrett Co., No. 86, Hand, Adjustable	80.00
Vise, Leather Worker's, Foot Lever Type, Leather, Padded Seat	95.00
Vise, P.S. Stubbs, Hand Wrought, c.1820, 1 7/8-In. Jaws	160.00
Wantage Rod, C.J. Tagiarue Mfg., U.S. Standard, Boxwood, Ivory Scale, N.Y., 36 In.	285.00
Wheelbarrow, Wooden, Iron, Red Paint, 64 In.	230.00
Wheelbarrow, Wooden, Red, Gold Trim, Iron Wheels, New England, 1900s	365.00
Wheelwright's Traveler, Cast Iron, Brass Arrow Marker	40.00
Wheelwright's Traveler, Circular, Iron, Wood Handle, Rosette, Pa., Early 1800s, 11 1/4 In.	130.00
Wire Cutters, Winchester, No. 2234	70.00
Workbench, Cabinetmaker's, 2 Vises, Maple, Oak, Ohio, c.1890, 33 x 75 x 28 In.	2485.00
Workbench, Maple, Oak, Hinged Seats, Drawers, c.1920, 64 x 28 In.	2495.00
Workbench, Stanley, Folding, Wood, Imprinted Logo, 48 In.	80.00
Wrench, Carriage, G. Flesch, Cast Patent Date, April 18, 1876, 8 In. ....*Illus*	1680.00
Wrench, Coachman's, Twist Handle Adjust, c.1830	75.00
Wrench, David Bradley Co., No. D89, Bradley's Wonder, Cutout, 14 In. ....*Illus*	1295.00
Wrench, Gem, Tower & Lyon, New York, N.Y., Nickel Plated, 4 1/2 In.	115.00
Wrench, John Deere, Open Ended, Logos On Both Sides, 11 1/2 In.	12.00
Wrench, No. 396, Hewett Patent, June 27, 1840	484.00
Wrench, Nut, D.H. Chamberlain, Boston, Mass., Pat. March 20, 1849, 14 In.	260.00
Wrench, Pipe, Keen Kutter, Steel Handle, 10 In.	35.00
Wrench, Pipe, Winchester, No. 1032, Steel Handle, 10 In.	65.00
Wrench Nut, L. Coes & Co., Dogwood Handle, 4 5/8 In.	145.00
Yardstick, Belcher Bros. & Co., Square, N.Y., 36 In.	65.00
Yardstick, W. Dickson & Son, Eagle Trademark, Brass, Feet, Wood Case, 36 In.	440.00
Yoke, Ox, Wooden, Chrome Blue Paint, Stenciled Initials S.B.F. & E.D., 38 In.	58.00
Yoke, Water Pail, Wooden, 19th Century, 36 In.	45.00

TOOTHBRUSH HOLDERS

TOOTHBRUSH HOLDERS were part of every bowl and pitcher set in the late nineteenth century. Most were oblong covered dishes. About 1920, manufacturers started to make children's toothbrush holders shaped like animals or cartoon characters. A few modern toothbrush holders are still being made.

3 Little Pigs, Marked, Goldcastle, Japan, 4 x 3 3/4 In.	110.00
Bonzo, Bisque, Green Glaze, c.1930s, 6 In.	295.00
Girl With Umbrella, Bisque, Japan, c.1930-40, 5 3/4 x 2 1/2 In.	60.00
Sailor Boy, Holds 2 Brushes, Stamped, Japan, c.1920-30, 6 x 3 x 2 In.	95.00
Wall Mount, Guy Madison, 2 Brushes, Tin Holster Holders, Die Cut, Tek	85.00

TOOTHPICK HOLDERS are sometimes called *toothpicks* by collectors. The variously shaped containers used to hold small wooden toothpicks are made of glass, china, or metal. Most of the toothpick holders are Victorian. Additional items may be found in other categories, such as Bisque, Silver Plate, etc.

Beaded Panel & Sunburst	140.00
Bedford, Fostoria	40.00
Brilliant, Fostoria	75.00
Button & Star Panel	25.00
Capitol, Silver Overlay	35.00
Carnival Glass, Marigold, Kittens	85.00
Chrysanthemum Leaf	225.00
Chrysanthemum Leaf, Gold Trim	200.00
Colonial Steps, Light Blue Opalescent	130.00
Colorado, Cobalt Blue, Gold Trim	55.00
Dalton	30.00 to 35.00
Dewdrop, Blue	45.00
Diamond Block	50.00
Diamond Lil	75.00
Diamond Spearhead, Blue	175.00
Diamond Spearhead, Vaseline Opalescent	100.00
Domino	60.00
Double Arch	40.00
Double Circle	35.00
Eagle's No. 45, Milk Glass	45.00
Empress	49.00
Empress, Green, Gold Trim	225.00
Fandango	80.00
Figural, 2 Pigs Sitting Near Red Toadstool, Germany, 2 1/2 In.	40.00
Figural, Hat, Blue & White Opalescent, Flowering Branch, Red Beetle, Hat, 2 1/2 In.	173.00
Figural, Horse With Cart	45.00
Figural, Man's Head, Beard, Brown Hat, Bisque, Painted, Germany	55.00
Figural, Pig Sitting Near Open Purse, Germany, 2 In.	50.00
Flemish	35.00
Flute, Marigold, Carnival Glass	25.00
Four Ladders	25.00
Hartford	75.00
Insulator Clay, Albany Slip, Scratch Carved Figures, 1920, 3 1/2 x 2 1/4 In.	173.00
Inverted Fan & Feather, Custard	645.00
Iris With Meander, Blue Opalescent	90.00
Ivanhoe	110.00
King's Crown, Ruby Stain	28.00
Knotty Pine Loop, Milk Glass, Footed	24.00
Ladders With Diamond	40.00
Little Lobe, Satin, Flowers	195.00
Manhattan	35.00
Manhattan, Gold Trim	50.00
Menagerie, Fish, Amber	110.00
Nestor, Apple Green	65.00
New Hampshire, Maiden's Blush	60.00
Nippon, Country Scene, 3 Handles	80.00
One-Hundred-One, Green	80.00
Orinda, Milk Glass	30.00
Palm Leaf, Milk Glass, Footed	45.00
Paneled Grape	45.00
Peach Blow, Wild Rose, Square Top	595.00
Pennsylvania	35.00
Pennsylvania, Gold Trim	45.00
Pomona, Flowers, Square Top	195.00
Pottery, Says Take Your Pick, Germany	15.00
Prince Of Wales Plumes, Ruby Stain, 2 3/8 In.	358.00
Priscilla	38.00 to 42.00
Prize, Green, Gold Trim	110.00

Punty Band, Ruby Stain, Beaded Rim	49.00
Ribbed Opal Lattice, Cranberry Opalescent	295.00
Ribbed Pillar, Pink Spatter	95.00
Rosby	35.00
Royal Bayreuth, Castle Scene, Hand Painted	135.00
Royal Ivy, Rubina	120.00
Sawtooth Honeycomb	45.00
Shell & Seaweed, White Opalescent, Enameled	100.00
Shoshone	40.00
Souvenir, Bisque, Flamingo, Myrtle Beach, Japan, 3 1/4 In.	12.00
Star In Square	80.00
Sunbeam, Cobalt Blue, Gold Trim	95.00
Sunbeam, Green	55.00
Swirl & Star Base	70.00
Thousand Eye, Blue	35.00
Vigilant	28.00
Wave Crest, Bulbous, Metal Feet	345.00
Wave Crest, White, Enameled, Petal Rim	150.00
Wedding Bells, Rose Stain	150.00
Wellsburg	45.00
Wheeling Block	65.00
Winged Scroll, Emerald, Gold Trim	395.00
Winsome	40.00
Zipper Slash	25.00

TORQUAY is the name given to ceramics by several potteries working near Torquay, England, from 1870 until 1962. Until about 1900, the potteries used local red clay to make classical-style art pottery vases and figurines. Then they turned to making souvenir wares. Items were dipped in colored slip and decorated with painted slip and sgraffito designs. They often had mottoes or proverbs, and scenes of cottages, ships, birds, or flowers. The *Scandy* design was a symmetrical arrangement of brushstrokes and spots done in colored slips. Potteries included Watcombe Pottery (1870–1962); Torquay Terra-Cotta Company (1875–1905); Aller Vale (1881–1924); Torquay Pottery (1908–1940); and Longpark (1883–1957).

TORQUAY

Cup & Saucer, Cottage, Motto, Early Sow Early Mow	80.00
Ferner, Embossed Flower Designs, Early 20th Century, 5 1/2 In.	35.00
Jug, Motto, Kind Words Are The Music Of The World, 5 3/4 In.	180.00
Spooner, Cottage, Motto, Ill Wind That Blows Nobody Any Good, 3 3/4 In.	90.00
Sugar & Creamer, Cottage, Welsh Motto, 1950s, 3 In.	110.00
Teapot, Motto, Drown Your Sorrows In A Cup Of Tea, 1867-1901, 4 1/2 In.	130.00

TORTOISESHELL is the shell of the tortoise. It has been used as inlay and to make small decorative objects since the seventeenth century. Some species of tortoise are now on the endangered species list, and old and new objects made from these shells cannot be sold legally.

Box, Dressing Table, Bone Trimmed, Padded Chamois Lining, 2 x 7 x 3 In.	690.00
Card Case, Rectangular, Checkered Design, Silver Beads, England, 4 1/4 x 5 3/4 In.	170.00
Case, Cheroot, Sliding Sleeves, Cranes, Gold, Japan, Late 19th Century, 4 1/2 In.	285.00
Cigar Case, Ivory Banded, Rectangular Shape, Silver Plate Thumb Latch, 4 3/4 In.	805.00
Cigarette Case, Silver Gilt Mounts, Asprey, London, c.1915, 3 1/2 x 5 1/2 In.	690.00
Vanity Box, Trunk Shape, Dome Lid, White Bone Edge, c.1885, 1 x 2 x 1 1/4 In.	431.00
Vase, Enameled, Flowers, Gilt Bird In Flight, Victorian, 9 1/4 In.	315.00

TOY collectors have special clubs, magazines, and shows. Toys are designed to entice children, and today they have attracted new interest among adults who are still children at heart. All types of toys are collected. Tin toys, iron toys, battery operated toys, and many others are collected by specialists. Dolls, Games, Teddy Bears, and Bicycles are listed in their own categories. Other toys may be found under company or celebrity names.

Action Figure, Captain Action, Parachute, Accessories, Ideal, Box, 1960s, 12 In.	220.00

Action Figure, Hoss Cartwright, American Character, 9 In. 55.00
Action Figure, Indiana Jones, Accessories, Kenner, Box, 1970s, 12 In. 180.00
Action Figure, Josie West, Best Of West, Accessories, Marx, Box, 1974, 9 In. 120.00
Action Figure, Mr. T, Accessories, Galoob, Box, 12 In. 35.00
Action Figure, Napoleon Solo, Man From U.N.C.L.E., Gilbert, Box, 1965, 12 In. 260.00
Action Figure, OJ Simpson, Helmet, Football, Shindana, Box, 1975, 9 1/2 In. 180.00
Adam The Porter, Pushes Cart, Windup, Germany, 1914 .... 850.00
Aero Tower, Original Box, Japan, 1930s, 9 1/2 In. 2500.00
Airplane, A.F. Airlines Air Service, Windup, American Flyer, 1920 .... 1100.00
Airplane, Air Cruiser, Pressed Steel, Buddy L, 1940s, 26-In. Wingspan 300.00
Airplane, American Airlines, AA Electra II, Tin, Plastic, Japan, 16-In. Wingspan 182.00
Airplane, Aquaplane, Tin Lithograph, Windup, Chein, Box, 8 1/2 x 4 1/2 In. 330.00
Airplane, Army Bomber, 3 Propellers, 1930-40, 24 In. 550.00
Airplane, Army Scout, Pressed Steel, Electric Lights, Steelcraft, 1930s, 22 1/2 In. 880.00
Airplane, Army Scout, Pressed Steel, Trimotor, Steelcraft, 23-In. Wingspan 1760.00
Airplane, Big Boy, Monoplane, Pressed Tin, Katz, 1920s, 24 1/2-In. Wingspan 935.00
Airplane, Boeing 747, Battery Operated, TN, Japan, Box, Late 1960s, 14 x 13 In. 135.00
Airplane, Boeing Strato Cruiser, Tin Lithograph, Marx, Japan, Box, 20-In. Wingspan 176.00
Airplane, Bomber, Jet, B-47, Electronic Control Panel, Battery, Hubco, 15 1/2 In. 88.00
Airplane, Bomber, Stuka Dive, Metal, Windup, Germany, 1937, 14 1/2 In. 1295.00
Airplane, Bomber, Tin, Propellers Spin With Wheels, Yonezawa, Japan, 14 1/2 x 19 In. ... 165.00
Airplane, Bomber, USAF Tornado, B-45, Tin, Friction, Japan, 1960s, 13 x 16 In. 165.00
Airplane, Canadian Pacific, Tin, Plastic, Battery, TN, Japan, 1960s, 14 x. 110.00
Airplane, Cessna, Plastic, Tin, Battery Operated, Bandai, Japan, Box, 1960s, 10 x 13 In. .. 90.00
Airplane, Curtiss Jenny Trainer, Tin Lithograph, Friction, Rosko, Japan, Box, 15 In. 77.00
Airplane, Dagwood, Marx, Box 1400.00
Airplane, Electra II, Tin Lithograph, Plastic, Battery Operated, Japan, 16 In. 143.00
Airplane, Fighter & Bomber Squadron, Kiddie Toy, Hubley, Box, 21 In., 5 Planes 825.00
Airplane, Fighter, Jet, F-14A Tomcat, Tin, Plastic, Nomura, Box, 13 1/2-In. Wingspan 72.00
Airplane, Fighter, Jet, F-104, Tin, Plastic, Friction, ASC, Japan, Box, 14 1/2 x 8 1/2 In. ... 145.00
Airplane, Fighter, Jet, Ride 'Em, Pressed Steel, Keystone, 1930s, 27 1/2-In. Wingspan 1100.00
Airplane, Flying Boxcar, Plastic, Marx, 12-In. Wingspan 220.00
Airplane, German Fighter, Biplane, Tippco, Germany 2195.00
Airplane, Gyroplane, Aluminum, Mecavion, France, Box, 12 In. 385.00
Airplane, Heinkel, Nazi Fighter, Lehmann, Germany, Box, 1930s 450.00
Airplane, Jet, U.S. Air Force, Tin, Friction, SG, Japan, Box, 14 1/2 In. 110.00
Airplane, Lockheed Sirius, Cast Iron, Hubley, 11-In. Wingspan 9900.00
Airplane, Lockheed Sirius, Pressed Steel, Steelcraft, 1920s, 22-In. Wingspan 1320.00
Airplane, Monoplane, Tin, Windup, George Levy, 9-In. Wingspan 248.00
Airplane, Navy Fighter, Aluminum, Folding Wings, Hubley, Box, 9 1/2 In. 264.00
Airplane, Northwest Airlines, Tin Lithograph, Friction, Alps, Japan, Box, 14 In. 358.00
Airplane, Pan American Airlines, Strato Clipper, Tin, Momoya, Box, 11-In. Wingspan 249.00
Airplane, Pan American World Airways, Pressed Steel, Marx, 1940s, 27 1/2 In. 132.00
Airplane, Paper, Tin, Kenley Co., 1919, 7-In. Wingspan 350.00
Airplane, Patrol, Tin Lithograph, Battery Operated, Cragstan, Japan, Box, 20 In. 44.00
Airplane, Patrol, Tin Lithograph, Friction, Japan, Box, 13-In. Wingspan 44.00
Airplane, Pressed Steel, Green, Orange Wings, Wyandotte, 1940s, 18-In. Wingspan .110.00 to 413.00
Airplane, Rollover Plane, Red, Tin, Windup, Marx, Box 345.00
Airplane, Seaplane, Plastic, Windup, Ideal, Box, 10 In. 77.00
Airplane, Seaplane, Tin, Windup, JEP, France, Box, 20-In. Wingspan 4400.00
Airplane, Sky Circus, Tin Lithograph, Plastic, Battery Operated, Japan, Box, 10 1/2 In. ... 33.00
Airplane, Skycruiser, Tin Lithograph, Friction, Marx, 1950s, 18 In. 132.00
Airplane, Starfire, Tin, Friction, Modern Toy, Japan, c.1950 .... 145.00
Airplane, Tin Lithograph, Battery Operated, Linemar, Japan, Box, 19 1/2 In. 330.00
Airplane, Tin, Windup, France, 14-In. Wingspan 330.00
Airplane, Tower, Tin, Windup, Celluloid Propellers, 7 In. 165.00
Airplane, U.S. Army, Tin, Windup, Marx, 18-In. Wingspan 170.00
Airplane, U.S. Mail, Tin Lithograph, Windup, Red, Yellow, Green, 18 In. 248.00
Airplane, U.S. Navy, Blue Wings, Silver Body, Wyandotte, 12-In. Wingspan 220.00
Airplane-Go-Round, Lithograph, Celluloid, Windup, U.S. Zone, Germany, 9 In. 265.00
Airport, American Airlines, Tin Lithograph, Pressed Steel Planes, Wyandotte, 12 x 16 In. .. 110.00
Airport Garage, Tin, Battery Operated, Marx, Prewar, 9 1/2 x 2 1/2 x 6 In. 215.00
Airport Terminal, Tonka, 1962 .... 525.00

Airship, Silver, Kenton, 6 In. 350.00
Airship, Tin Lithograph, Windup, Lehmann, Germany, Box, 10 In. 1650.00
Alligator, Tin Lithograph, Embossed, Swivel Action, Penny Toy, 4 3/4 In. 165.00
Ambulance, Buick, 1958 Model, Friction, Tin, Japan 195.00
Ambulance, Chevrolet, 1955 Model, Friction, Battery Light, Japan, 7 1/2 In. 120.00
Ambulance, City Hospital, Marx, 10 1/4 In. 1980.00
Ambulance, Emergency, Plastic, Pressman Toy Corp., Box, 14 x 5 x 4 1/2 In. 165.00
Ambulance, Pressed Steel, Canvas, Structo, 18 In. 1980.00
Ambulance, White, Tin, Windup, Minic, 5 In. 77.00
Ambulance, White, Wyandotte, 11 1/4 In. 150.00
Amos, Amos 'n' Andy, Taxi Hat, Walker, Tin Lithograph, Windup, Marx, 11 1/2 In. .540.00 to 875.00
Andy, Amos 'n' Andy, Tin Lithograph, Windup, Correll & Gosden, Marx, c.1930, 12 In. ... 575.00
Armchair, Doll's, Maple, Bamboo Shaping, Brass Tips On Arms, Cane Seat, 1885, 16 In. . 335.00
Artie The Clown, Driving Car, Tin Lithograph, Windup, Unique Art, 7 1/2 In. 275.00
Astro Mobile, Tin Lithograph, Plastic Fins, Friction, Marubishi, Japan, 8 1/2 In. 155.00
Atom Rocket 7, Tin, Plastic Antenna, Battery Operated, Modern Toys, Japan, 1960s, 9 In. . 160.00
B.O. Plenty, Holding Baby Sparkle, Tin Lithograph, Windup, Marx, 1930, 8 In. 150.00
B.O. Plenty, Tin Lithograph, Windup, Marx, Box, 9 In. 248.00
B.O. Plenty, Tin Lithograph, Windup, Walker, Tips Hat, Marx, 8 1/2 In. ....330.00 to 595.00
Balancing Man, Wood, Metal, 15 In. 120.00
Banjo Player, Black Man, Legs Move Up & Down, Windup, Gunthermann, 1880s 1450.00
Barbie Tea Set, Plastic, Purple, Worcester Toy Co., Box, 1961, 27 Piece 150.00
Barnacle Bill, Waddler, Tin, Windup, Chein, 6 In. ....350.00 to 425.00
Barney Google, Riding Sparkplug, Tin, Windup, Nifty, Germany, 1920s, 7 In. ....950.00 to 1320.00
Bart Maverick, Gunfighter Series, Black Gun, White Hat, Hartland, 8 In. 78.00
Bartender, Revolving Eyes, Shakes & Pours Drinks, Battery, Rosko, Box, 11 1/2 In. 152.00
Bears are also listed in the Teddy Bears category.
Bear, At Desk, VIP, Busy Boss, Battery Operated, Phone, Cragstan, Box, 8 In. 176.00
Bear, Ball Playing, Battery Operated, Japan, Box, 13 In. 523.00
Bear, Barber, Baby Bear Kicks Feet, Black Bear Barber Cuts Hair, Linemar, Box, 9 1/2 In. 465.00
Bear, Barney, Drummer Boy, Tin, Plush, Eyes Light, Walker, Battery, Alps, 11 In. 125.00
Bear, Blowing Balloon, Battery Operated, Japan, Box, 12 In. 138.00
Bear, Blows Bubbles, Tin, Plush, Plastic, Windup, Alps, Box, 8 In. 170.00
Bear, Bruin & His Ball Playing Act, Tin & Celluloid, Cragston, 10 In. 510.00
Bear, Circus, Walks With Rod, Windup, Martin Co., France 650.00
Bear, Dentist, Dentist Drills, Patients Spit, Heads Move, S & E, Box, 1950s, 10 In. .435.00 to 808.00
Bear, Golfer, Tin, Windup, Shoots A Hole In One, T.P.S., Box, 7 In. 525.00
Bear, Hungry Baby Bear, Battery Operated, Japan, Box, 9 In. 138.00
Bear, Muzzle, Clockwork, Ives, c.1880 .... 1320.00
Bear, Polar, Fishing, Laughs, 3 Fish, Alps, Japan, Box, 10 In. 254.00
Bed, Doll's, Tall Post, Stained Pine, Canopy, Mattress, Linen, 33 x 34 x 18 In. 147.00
Bed, Doll's, Walnut, Carved Headboard, Bust, Finials, 15 1/2 x 34 x 26 In. 176.00
Beetle, Tin Lithograph, Clockwork, Lehmann, Germany, 4 In. 193.00
Bell Ringer, Boy Fishing, Cast Iron, 8 In. 3300.00
Bell Ringer, Boy Teasing Alligator, Wheels, Alligator Lunges, Gong Bell Mfg. 7500.00
Bell Ringer, Ding Dong Bell, Pussy's Not In The Well, Cast Iron, 9 In. 2750.00
Bell Ringer, Dog & Cat, Cast Iron, Gong Bell Co., 1892, 9 In. 7700.00
Bell Ringer, Harold Lloyd, Tin, Germany, 6 In. 358.00
Bell Ringer, Horse Drawn Cart, Tin, Iron, c.1880, 3 1/2 In., Pair 220.00
Bell Ringer, Jonah & Whale, Cast Iron, Spoke Wheels, N.H. Hill Brass Co., 6 In. . .468.00 to 1760.00
Bell Ringer, Monkey On Tricycle, Cast Iron, 8 In. 2860.00
Bell Ringer, Monkey With Coconut, Cast Iron, 6 1/2 In. 660.00
Bell Ringer, Wild Mule Jack, Cast Iron, 8 1/2 In. 1210.00
Bicycles that are large enough to ride are listed in their own category.
Bicyclist, Perpetual Motion, Wood, Iron, Folk Art, 36 In. 1200.00
Big Parade, Plastic, Marx, Box, 12 x 16 In. 303.00
Billiard Players, Tin Lithograph, Windup, 14 In. 132.00
Bimbo, Plays Violin, Bisque, Japan, 3 1/2 In. 75.00
Black Man, Walker, Ives, c.1870s, 10 In. 2860.00
Blimp, Pony, Dirigible, Painted Green, Cast Iron, Kenton, 5 3/4 In. 303.00
Blocks, Alphabet, ELC Coffee, Box, 2 x 3 In. 198.00
Blocks, Alphabet, Hills, Union College, Village School, Wooden Box, 9 x 11 In. 1210.00
Blocks, Baby's ABC Blocks, Santa Claus, Lithograph, Box, Germany, c.1900, 11 x 12 In. . 1100.00

Blocks, Cobb House, Paper Lithograph On Wood, McLoughlin, 10 3/4 In. 1210.00
Boat, Albert Balen, Liner, Fleischman 1430.00
Boat, Battleship, Live Steam, Tin, Radiguet, 31 In. 9075.00
Boat, Battleship, Taku, Tin Lithograph, Windup, Lehmann, Germany, 9 1/2 In. 495.00
Boat, Big Bang Cannon, Cast Iron, 8 In. 275.00
Boat, Cabin Cruiser, King, Wood, Metal Trim, Ito, 30 In. 1100.00
Boat, Cabin Cruiser, Wood, Metal Trim, Brown, Stand, Japan, 30 In. 825.00
Boat, Cabin Cruiser, Wood, Metal Trim, Ito, Japan, 17 In. 660.00
Boat, Cabin Cruiser, Wood, Metal Trim, Red, White, Blue, Green, Ito, Japan, 21 In. 523.00
Boat, Ferry, Union, Bing, 16 In. 1430.00
Boat, Gun, Tin, Bing, Germany, 1909, 15 In. 1980.00
Boat, Harbour Patrol, Tin, Crank, Japan, 1950s, 10 In. 95.00
Boat, Launch, Harbor, Plastic, Ideal, Box, 14 x 5 In. 275.00
Boat, Launch, White, Carette, 10 In. 770.00
Boat, Motor, 3 Wheels, Orange Hull, Freidag, 1920s, 10 1/4 In. 5500.00
Boat, Motor, Fair Lady, Wood, Tin Trim, Battery Operated, Linemar, Box, 10 1/2 In. 121.00
Boat, Ocean Liner, Carette, 9 In. 385.00
Boat, Ocean Liner, Fleischmann, 20 In. 770.00
Boat, Ocean Liner, George Washington, Hot Air, Marklin, Box, 18 In. 10175.00
Boat, Ocean Liner, Tin, Windup, Arnold, Germany, 12 1/2 In. 385.00
Boat, Ocean Liner, Tin, Windup, Clockwork, Fleischmann Carette, Germany, 24 In. 7700.00
Boat, Paddlewheel, Adirondack, Painted Yellow, Cast Iron, 14 1/2 In. 1128.00
Boat, Paddlewheel, Priscilla, Painted Yellow, Cast Iron, 10 1/2 In. 630.00
Boat, Paddlewheel, Red Bottom, White Top, Carette, 10 In. 770.00
Boat, Patrol, Blue, Wood, Metal Trim, 33 In. 300.00
Boat, Radicon, Tin, Battery Operated, Remote Control, Modern Toys, Box, 18 In. 275.00
Boat, Red Ground, Wheels, Penny Toy, Prewar, Japan, 3 In. 138.00
Boat, Riverboat, Clockwork, Carette, 22 In. 1540.00
Boat, Riverboat, Louise, Live Steam, Bing, 19 In. 3190.00
Boat, Riverboat, Tin, Clockwork, Carette, Germany, 16 In. 2750.00
Boat, Rocket, Race, Wood, Japan, Box, 17 In. 1430.00
Boat, Scout Patrol, Tin, Painted, Clockwork, Ives, 9 1/2 In. 1870.00
Boat, Scull, 4 Oarsmen, Painted Wood, Jointed Wood Figures, 16 1/2 In. 385.00
Boat, Ski, Outboard Motor, Wood, Metal Trim, Japan, Box, 12 In. 190.00
Boat, Speedboat, Flying Fish, Tin, Crank, Lithograph, No. F-55, Asahitoy, 11 1/2 In. 248.00
Boat, Speedboat, Mercury 25, Tin, Friction, Marusan, Box, 6 In. 120.00
Boat, Speedboat, Outboard Motor, Lindstrom, 20 In. 410.00
Boat, Speedboat, Tin Lithograph, Windup, Strauss, 9 In. 468.00
Boat, Speedboat, Venture, Hornby, 18 In. 220.00
Boat, Speedboat, Wood, Brass, Mengel, Box, 12 In. 660.00
Boat, Torpedo, Pique, Live Steam, Marklin, 30 In. 23100.00
Boat, Torpedo, Taku, Lehmann, 1913 . . . . 750.00
Boat, Trailer, Motor, Tissue Paper, Insert, Tonka, Box, 1959 . . . . 1045.00
Boat, Tugboat, Neptune, Metal, Battery Operated, TN, Japan, Box, 14 In. 195.00
Boat, Tugboat, Tin, Clockwork, Ives, 11 In. 1100.00
Boat, Tugboat, Tin, TN, Japan, 15 In. 125.00
Boat, Universe Televiboat, Tin Lithograph, Plastic, Battery, Chinese, Box, 14 In. 17.00
Boat, Viking Ship, Plastic, Renwal, Box, 17 1/4 x 5 3/4 x 13 In. 330.00
Boat, Warship, Jaureguiberry, Clockwork, Bing, 1902-06, 32 In. 22000.00
Boat & Shovel, Cohn, U.S.A., Box, 10 In. 250.00
Bobo The Magician, Tin, Windup, Japan, 10 In. 300.00
Bonzo On Scooter, Tin, Windup, Gunthermann, 7 In. 1870.00
Box, Looping Plane, Marx 75.00
Boy, Playing Violin, Bisque Head, Wood Hands, Pull, Germany, 12 In. 1100.00
Boy, Playing Violin, Windup, Schuco 145.00
Boy, Riding Sled, Tin Lithograph, Painted, Clockwork, Hess, Germany, 6 1/4 In. 520.00
Bubble Blower, Boy, White Robe, Red Base, Tin, Mechanical, England, Box, 6 1/2 In. 1870.00
Bucking Bronco, Wild West, Brown Horse, Clockwork, Lehmann, Germany, 7 In. 525.00
Buffalo, Painted Eyes, Carved Ruff, Schoenhut, 7 3/4 In. 176.00
Buffalo, Wooden, Jointed, Leather Horns, Rope Tail, Brown, Schoenhut, 5 1/2 In. 248.00
Builders Supply Set, Insert, Tonka, Box, 1956 . . . . 2200.00
Bulldozer, Driver, Windup, Lithograph, Marx, 1930s, 10 In. 110.00
Bulldozer, Giant Dozer, Insert, Wishbook, Tonka, Box, 1961 . . . . 990.00

Bulldozer, Pressed Steel, Plastic, Tonka, 13 In. 6.00
Bulldozer, Robot Operater, Tin Lithograph, K.O., Japan, Box, 4 x 7 1/2 x 4 1/2 In. 770.00
Bulldozer & Trailer, Green & Maroon, Hooked Together, Structo, 14 In. 375.00
Burro, Circus, Glass Eyes, Painted Wood, 6 1/2 In. 495.00
Bus, Airport, Friction, Marx, Box, 6 3/4 In. 225.00
Bus, Army, Tin, Friction, Japan, 1950s, 11 In. 95.00
Bus, Autobus, Tin Lithograph, Windup, Lehmann, Germany, 5 1/2 In. 1540.00
Bus, Continental Trailways, Tin Lithograph, Friction, Japan, Box, 14 In. 132.00
Bus, Deluxe, Driver, Tin, Windup, Strauss, 13 In. 1100.00
Bus, Door Opens, Side-Mounted Tires, Buddy L, 29 In. 3738.00
Bus, Double-Decker, Cast Iron, Arcade, 1927, 13 1/2 In. 4125.00
Bus, Double-Decker, Cast Iron, Green, Nickel Grill, Arcade, c.1940, 7 3/4 In. .....660.00 to 800.00
Bus, Double-Decker, Cast Iron, Red, Green, Kenton, 10 In. 825.00
Bus, Double-Decker, Red, Gold Trim, Silver Radiator, 6 Rubber Tires, Arcade, 13 In. 2520.00
Bus, Double-Decker, Red, Iron Wheels, Kenton, 6 In. 650.00
Bus, Double-Decker, Tin Lithograph, Windup, Meirer, 4 In. 330.00
Bus, Double-Decker, Yellow Coach, Cast Iron, Arcade, 13 In. 1760.00
Bus, Greyhound Lines, Pressed Steel, Windup, Buddy L, Box, 16 In. 715.00
Bus, Greyhound, Cruiser Coach, Arcade, 1941, 9 1/4 In. 500.00
Bus, Greyhound, Scenicruiser, Friction, Cragstan, Box, 9 In......................... 250.00
Bus, Greyhound, Super Coach, Arcade, c.1937, 9 In. ....495.00 to 525.00
Bus, Greyhound, Tin, 1956 License Plate, Hadson, 7 In. 200.00
Bus, Greyhound, Tin, Friction, Japan, 1950s, 11 In. 65.00
Bus, Greyhound, Wood Handle, Battery Operated Lights, Ride 'Em, Keystone, 32 In. 6900.00
Bus, Interstate, Driver, Tin, Windup, Brown, Strauss, 10 In. 1320.00
Bus, Jackie Gleason, Honeymooner's Special, Tin, Push, Wolverine, 14 In. 605.00
Bus, Jitney, Driver, Tin, Windup, Strauss, 10 In. 935.00
Bus, Junior, Tin Lithograph, Chein, 1920s, 9 In. 253.00
Bus, King Leo's, Aoshin, Japan, 1960s, 14 1/2 In. 1200.00
Bus, Observatory Car, Tin Lithograph, Clockwork, Joustra, France, Box, 5 1/2 In. 550.00
Bus, Oh Boy, Tin Lithograph, 1920s, 19 In. 605.00
Bus, Pickwick, Nite Coach, Metal Wheels, Kenton, 7 1/2 In........................ 550.00
Bus, Pressed Steel, Nickel Headlights, Bumper, Buddy L 6325.00
Bus, Pullman, Royal Blue Line, Tin, Chein, Box, 18 In. 4675.00
Bus, Robot, Tin, Windup, Woodhaven, Box, 13 In. 220.00
Bus, Safety, Cast Iron, Kilgore, 8 In. 300.00
Bus, School Line, Bonnet, Tin Lithograph Skylights, Marusan, Box, 7 1/2 In. 872.00
Bus, School, Children, Tin, Friction, TN, Box, 1961, 9 1/2 In....................... 195.00
Bus, School, Painted Wheels, Dent, 8 3/8 In. 358.00
Bus, School, Tonka, Box, 1960 .... 165.00
Bus, Son Goku, Yonezawa, Japan, 1970s, 18 1/2 In. 250.00
Bus, Sound, Tin, Battery Operated, Tin Lithograph, Japan, Box, 14 1/2 In. 250.00
Bus, Tin, Driver, Window Curtains, Strauss, 1920s, 13 1/2 In. 350.00
Bus, Wolverine Express, Tin Lithograph, Driver, Passengers, Friction, 13 1/2 In. 235.00
Bus, World TV, Battery Operated, Cameraman On Roof, Alps, Japan, 1960s, 9 1/4 In. 445.00
Bus, Yellow, Rubber Tires, Cast Iron, Kenton, c.1936, 7 In. 2750.00
Busy Coolies, Start Bar, Lehmann, Box 3800.00
Busy Lizzie, Sweeps, Windup, Germany, 1920s 550.00
Butcher Shop, Wooden, Germany, 1920s, 12 x 12 In. 770.00
Buttercup & Spare Rib, Tin, Red Base, Light Blue Wheels, Pull Toy, 7 1/2 In. 550.00
Calliope, Overland Circus, 2 White Horses, Cast Iron, Kenton, 14 1/4 In. ....990.00 to 1870.00
Calliope, Royal Circus, 2 Horses, Cast Iron, Non-Mechanical, Hubley, 16 In. 3850.00
Calliope, Royal Circus, Brown Horses, Cast Iron, Mechanical, Hubley, 16 In. 2475.00
Camel, Dromedary, Felt Covered, Musical, Winding Tail, 10 In. 58.00
Camper, 5th Wheel, Inserts, Accessories, Tonka, 1970 .... 300.00
Camper, Green & Red Tin Boat, Buddy L, 12 In................................. 99.00
Cannon, Black Powder, Cast Iron, Red Wheels, c.1885, 4 1/2 x 8 In. 138.00
Cap Gun, 2 In 1, Metal, Extra Barrel, White Simulated Bone Grips, Hubley, Display Box .. 140.00
Cap Gun, 25 Jr., Cast Iron, 4 In. 6.00
Cap Gun, 101 Ranch, Cast Iron, 11 In. 94.00
Cap Gun, 6 Shot, Revolver, Embossed, 1895 Patent, 7 In. 165.00
Cap Gun, America, Shield & Stars, Cast Iron, Pat'd 1873, 8 3/4 In. 165.00
Cap Gun, Bang-O, Repeater, Chrome Plated, Tenite Embossed Grips, Stevens, Box 140.00

Cap Gun, Bronco, Metal, Plastic Grips, Kilgore, Box, 9 In. 220.00
Cap Gun, Buffalo Bill, Cast Iron, Kenton, 11 1/2 In. 94.00
Cap Gun, Buffalo Bill, Cast Iron, White Horsehead Grips, Red Jewels, Stevens, Box, 8 In. . 198.00
Cap Gun, Buffalo Bill, Cast Iron, White Jeweled Grips, Nickel Finish, Stevens, 8 In. 59.00
Cap Gun, Bulldog, Cast Iron, Kenton, 6 1/4 In. 72.00
Cap Gun, Butting Match, Cast Iron, 5 In. 523.00
Cap Gun, Cast Iron, Kilgore, 5 1/2 In. 55.00
Cap Gun, Cast Iron, Original Red Paint, Kenton, 4 In. 72.00
Cap Gun, Chief, Double Barrel, Cast Iron, 5 1/2 In. 120.00
Cap Gun, Colt.45, 6 Metal Cartridges, Hubley, Box, 13 1/2 In. 285.00
Cap Gun, Cowboy, Revolver, White, Steer Head Grips, Red Star, Hubley, 12 In. 138.00
Cap Gun, Deadshot, Cast Iron, 8 1/4 In. 165.00
Cap Gun, Dragnet, Smoking, Repeating, U.S.A., Box, 1955, 6 1/2 In. 130.00
Cap Gun, Fanner 50, Chrome Plated, White Solid Wood-Grained Grip, Mattel 135.00
Cap Gun, Fanner 50, Gold Plated, Smoking, 8 Bullets, Mattel, Box 250.00
Cap Gun, Flintlock, Hubley, Box 159.00
Cap Gun, Grizzly, Metal, Plastic Grips, Kilgore, Box, 10 In. 195.00
Cap Gun, Hero, Cast Iron, Single Shot, Checkered Grip, Stevens, U.S.A., 1937, 5 1/2 In. . . 44.00
Cap Gun, Jr. Police Chief, Cast Iron, Kenton, 4 In. 39.00
Cap Gun, Kit Carson, Repeater, Black Grips, Kilgore, Box, 9 1/2 In. 565.00
Cap Gun, Lion's Head, Cast Iron, 4 In. 165.00
Cap Gun, Lion, Cast Iron, 5 1/4 In. 110.00
Cap Gun, Long Boy, Cast Iron, Kilgore, 11 In. 120.00
Cap Gun, Monkey Cracking Coconut, Cast Iron, 4 In. 110.00
Cap Gun, Moonface, Animated, Ives 1760.00
Cap Gun, Mustang 500, Chrome, Standup Display Card, N Logo, Nichols, Texas, 12 In. . . 200.00
Cap Gun, Police Chief, Cast Iron, Kenton, 4 1/2 In. 55.00
Cap Gun, Pony, Cast Iron, 5 1/4 In. 28.00
Cap Gun, Remington Derringer, Gold Plated, Belt Buckle Flips Gun Out, Belt, Mattel 44.00
Cap Gun, Restless, Faux Stag Grips, Actoy, 9 1/2 In. . . . . .83.00 to 163.00
Cap Gun, Ric-O-Shay Jr., Steer Head Grips, Silver Star, Hubley 156.00
Cap Gun, Rodeo, Single Shot, Brown & Yellow Grips, Star, Hubley 22.00
Cap Gun, Sambo, Cast Iron, Black, Ives, c.1887, 4 3/8 In. 1020.00
Cap Gun, Scout, Cast Iron, 6 3/4 In. 39.00
Cap Gun, Sea Serpent, Cast Iron, Stevens, 1890s, 3 1/2 In. 935.00
Cap Gun, Sheriff, Cast Iron, Repeater, White Grips, Red Jewels, Stevens, Box 138.00
Cap Gun, Silver Mustang, Repeater, Chrome Plated, Nichols, Box, 8 3/4 In. 110.00
Cap Gun, Spitfire, With Clip, Nichols, Box, 1950s, 9 In. 49.00
Cap Gun, Stagecoach, Ammo, Gold & Black, Marx, Instructions, Box, 3 1/2 x 5 In. 34.00
Cap Gun, Stallion 38, 6-Shooter, 6 Bullets, Double Action, Chrome, Nichols, Box 145.00
Cap Gun, Stallion 45, 6-Shooter, Double Action, Nichols, 12 In. 230.00
Cap Gun, Stratoblaster, Space Rifle, Plastic, 3X Telescopic Sight, Renwal, Box, 26 3/4 In. . 770.00
Cap Gun, Texan Jr., White Grips, Black Steer Head, Red Star, Chrome, Hubley, Box 116.00
Cap Gun, Texan Jr., White Grips, Embossed, Cast Iron, Hubley, 1935 . . . . 110.00
Cap Gun, Western, Cast Iron, 7 1/4 In. 50.00
Cap Gun, Wild Bill Hickok, Faux Bone, Tan Horse Head Grips, Leslie Henry 90.00
Cap Hammer, Cast Iron, Patent Pending 117.00
Cap Shooter, Bear & Boy, Hammering Anvil, Pull Toy, Stevens 1430.00
Cap Shooter, Surprise Box, 2 Monkeys, Cast Iron, c.1880, 3 x 3 1/4 In. 605.00
Cape Canaveral, Atomic Missile Base, Marx, Box 77.00
Car, Airflow, Cast Iron, Hubley, 6 1/8 In. 385.00
Car, Airflow, Green, Hubley, 4 3/4 In. 450.00
Car, Andy Gump Deluxe, Cast Iron, Arcade, 7 1/2 In. 13750.00
Car, Andy Gump, Cast Iron, Disc Wheels, Red, Arcade, 7 1/8 In. . . . . .935.00 to 2300.00
Car, Aston Martin, James Bond, Battery Operated, Gilbert, Japan, Box, 11 1/2 In. 540.00
Car, Beveled Glass Windows, Rubber Tires, Driver, Carette, 12 In. 6325.00
Car, Blondie's Jalopy, Tin Lithograph, Marx, 16 In. 2420.00
Car, Blondie's Jalopy, Tin Lithograph, Marx, Box, 16 In. 2970.00
Car, Bluebird, Land Speed, Tin Lithograph, Windup, Gunthermann, Germany, 20 In. 990.00
Car, Bugotti, Tin Lithograph, Windup, Blue, Jep, France, 17 In. 1540.00
Car, Buick, Sedan, Cast Iron, Rubber Tires, Arcade, 8 In. 2090.00
Car, Cadillac Convertible, Tin, Friction, Alps, 11 In. 1570.00
Car, California 500, Diecast, Revell, Box, 11 In. 11.00

Car, Champion Racer, Drivers, On Card, Yonezawa, Japan, 7 In., 3 Piece 625.00
Car, Chevrolet, 1954 Model, Hood Ornament, Linemar, 11 In. 825.00
Car, Chevrolet, Corvette, Tin, Battery Operated, Bandai, Japan, 8 In. 55.00
Car, Chevrolet, Corvette, Tin, Friction, Bandai, Japan, 8 In. 17.00
Car, Chevrolet, Coupe, Cast Iron, Arcade, 1928 .... 1350.00
Car, Chevrolet, Sedan, Rubber Tires, Arcade, 1928, 8 1/4 In. 8250.00
Car, Chevrolet, Tin, Friction, Japan, 1955, 8 In. 145.00
Car, Chrysler, Airflow, 1936 Model, Humpback, Steel, Windup, Kingsbury, 14 In. 300.00
Car, Chrysler, Airflow, Cast Iron, Electric Headlights, Hubley, Box, 8 In. 4675.00
Car, Chrysler, Airflow, Nickel Plated Grille, Rose Color, Hubley, 4 In. 330.00
Car, Chrysler, Airflow, Nickel Plated Grille, Rose Color, Hubley, 6 In. 358.00
Car, Chrysler, Airflow, Pressed Steel, Electric Headlights, Cor-Cor, 17 In. 1430.00
Car, Chrysler, Airflow, Pressed Steel, Windup, Kingsbury, 14 In. 525.00
Car, Chrysler, New Yorker, 1958 Model, Turquoise, Tin, Chrome Trim, Alps, 14 In. 6890.00
Car, Chrysler, Town & Country, Station Wagon, Push, Tin, Wolverine, Box, 13 In. 495.00
Car, Circus, Clowns, 1964 Ford, Battery, Remote, Rico Of Spain, Box, 18 In. 650.00
Car, Coupe, 3 Doors, A.C. Williams 358.00
Car, Coupe, Cast Iron, Nickel-Plated Iron Wheels, Arcade, 6 In. 385.00
Car, Coupe, Cast Iron, Red, Nickel Spoke Wheels, Arcade, c.1933, 6 In. 550.00
Car, Coupe, Deluxe, Pressed Steel, Windup, Electric Headlights, Lavender, Girard 2310.00
Car, Coupe, Kenton, 1926, 10 In. 5225.00
Car, Coupe, Pressed Steel, Friction, Republic, 10 In. 165.00
Car, Coupe, Pressed Steel, Windup, Electric Headlights, Kingsbury, 12 In. 1650.00
Car, Coupe, Pressed Steel, Windup, Kingsbury 1980.00
Car, Coupe, Reversible, Tin, Windup, Marx, Box, 16 In. 1210.00
Car, Coupe, Soft Top, Tin, Windup, Bing, 6 1/4 In. 715.00
Car, Coupe, Tin Lithograph, Windup, Marx, 9 In. 468.00
Car, Dagwood The Driver, Tin Lithograph, Windup, Marx, Box, 8 In. ....1210.00 to 1540.00
Car, DeSoto, Airflow, Silver, Tootsietoy, 1934, 3 In. 150.00
Car, DeSoto, Sedan, Tin, Friction, Asahito, Japan, c.1950, 7 1/2 In. 110.00
Car, Dodgem, Tin, Windup, Buffalo, 11 In. 330.00
Car, Door Matic, Tin, Lithographed Chassis, Seats, Friction, HAJI, Japan, Box, 11 In. 235.00
Car, Dream, Plastic, Friction, Canary Yellow, Mattel, 1950s, 8 1/2 In. 65.00
Car, Dream, XP-1960, Plastic, Friction, Mattel, Box, c.1954, 2 1/4 x 8 1/2 x 4 In. 200.00
Car, Driver, Long Yellow Coat, Tin, France, c.1905, 8 In. 2090.00
Car, Easter, Ford, Model T, 2 Bunnies, Plastic, Pink, E. Rosen, 7 1/2 In. 110.00
Car, Easter, Hot Rod, Bunny Driver, Plastic, E. Rosen, 5 In. 72.00
Car, Edsel, 1958 Model, Sedan, Tin Lithograph, Friction, KTS, 8 In. 446.00
Car, Electro Ingenico, Remote Control, Tin, Battery, Schuco, Germany, Box, 10 In. 248.00
Car, Felix The Cat, Speedy, Wood, Tin Arms, Pull String, G. Borgfeldt, 11 3/4 In. 605.00
Car, Ferrari, Convertible, White, Lithographed Seats, Friction, Japan, Bandai, 11 1/2 In. 470.00
Car, Fire Chief, Buick, Tin, Friction, Chrome Fenders, Japan, 1959, 8 1/2 In. 120.00
Car, Fire Chief, Jeep, Pressed Steel, Tonka, 1960s, 11 In. 132.00
Car, Fire Chief, Painted, Pressed Steel, Girard, Original Box 1250.00
Car, Fire Chief, Pressed Steel, Clockwork, Electric Lights, Siren, Girard, 1930s, 15 In. 415.00
Car, Fire Chief, Pressed Steel, Lights, Siren, Hoge, 14 In. 495.00
Car, Fire Chief, Red, Cast Iron, Rubber Tires, Arcade, 5 In. 1045.00
Car, Fire Chief, Siren, Pressed Steel, Windup, Electric Headlights, Marx, 15 In. 715.00
Car, Fire Chief, Windup, Metal, Marx, 1930s, 11 In. 175.00
Car, Flivver, Model T Ford, Steerable Front, Cast Case Wheels, Buddy L, 11 In. 345.00
Car, Ford, 1955 Model, 2 Door, White, Musical, Battery, Asahi Toys, Box, 9 In. 435.00
Car, Ford, Airport, TWA, Hardtop, Tin, Japan, c.1960 .... 220.00
Car, Ford, Fairlane Victoria, 1955 Model, Black, Tin, Marusan, 13 In. 2813.00
Car, Ford, Model A, Cast Iron, A.C. Williams, 4 In. 55.00
Car, Ford, Model A, Cast Iron, A.C. Williams, 6 1/4 In. 330.00
Car, Ford, Model T, Coupe, Black, Arcade, 6 1/2 In. 650.00
Car, Ford, Model T, Coupe, Tin, Windup, Woman Driver, Bing, Germany, 6 In. 935.00
Car, Ford, Model T, Hubley, 4 In. 195.00
Car, Ford, Model T, Roadster, Hard Top, Tin, Windup, Woman Driver, Bing, 6 In. 770.00
Car, Ford, Model T, Sedan, 4 Door, Red Spoke Tires, Cast Iron, Arcade, 6 1/4 In. 196.00
Car, Ford, Model T, Sedan, Tin, Windup, Woman Driver, Bing, Germany, 6 In. .....275.00 to 495.00
Car, Ford, Model T, Touring, Red Spoke Tires, Arcade, 6 1/4 In. 259.00
Car, Ford, Mustang, Coupe, Plastic, Battery Operated, Wen'mack, Box, 16 In. 145.00

Car, Ford, Mustang, Stunt, Battery Operated, Japan, T.P.S., Box, 10 1/2 In. 245.00
Car, Ford, Sedan, Cast Iron, Driver, Arcade, 6 1/2 In. 440.00
Car, Ford, Sunliner Convertible, Tin, Friction, Reclining Seats, Bandai, Japan, 12 In. 585.00
Car, Ford, Thunderbird, 1956 Model, Red, White, Friction, TN, Box, 11 In. 435.00
Car, Ford, Venus, Tin Lithograph, Battery Operated, TN, Japan, Box, 1950s, 8 In. 225.00
Car, G-Man Pursuit, Pressed Steel, Marx, Box, 14 In. 4125.00
Car, G-Man Pursuit, Pressed Steel, Windup, Marx, 15 In. 715.00
Car, Graham Sedan, Pressed Steel, Electric Lights, Cor-Cor, c.1933, 20 In. . . . . . .1540.00 to 2750.00
Car, Hercules, Coupe, Rumble Seat, Luggage Rack, Tin, Orange, Black, Chein, 18 In. 990.00
Car, Hercules, Coupe, Rumble Seat, Luggage Rack, Tin, Red, Black, Chein, 18 In. 660.00
Car, Huckleberry Hound, Tin, Marx, 4 In. 255.00
Car, Jaguar, Tin, Battery Operated, Bandai, Japan, 10 1/2 In. 110.00
Car, Jaguar, Tin, Friction, Gray, Bandai, Japan, 1950s, 9 1/2 In. 375.00
Car, Jalopy, Tin Lithograph, Windup, Marx, Box, 7 In. 305.00
Car, Karmann Ghia, Tin, Friction, Bandai, Box, 7 1/2 In. 286.00
Car, La Salle, Tin, Windup, Wyandotte, 15 1/2 In. 415.00
Car, Leaping Lena, Tin Lithograph, Windup, Strauss, 8 In. . . . . .330.00 to 550.00
Car, Limousine, Composition Chauffeur, Bing, Original Box, 12 In. 2860.00
Car, Limousine, Driver, Tin Lithograph, Kellermann, 4 1/4 In. 300.00
Car, Limousine, Luggage Rack, Orange & Black, Chauffeur, Windup, G & K, Germany . . . 550.00
Car, Limousine, Tin Lithograph, Penny Toy, Germany, 4 In. 190.00
Car, Limousine, Tin, Carette, 16 In. 2970.00
Car, Limousine, Tin, Karl Bub, 14 In. 1760.00
Car, Limousine, Tin, Windup, Driver, 6 Discs For Curves, Bing, Box, 7 In. 1210.00
Car, Limping Lizzy, Jalopy With Driver, Windup, Marx, Original Box, 1930s 650.00
Car, Lincoln Continental, Mark II, Friction, Linemar, Japan, Box, 1956, 11 1/4 In. 5280.00
Car, Lincoln Continental, Mark II, Remote Control, Linemar, Japan, Box, 1956, 11 In. 4400.00
Car, LoLo, Tin Lithograph, Friction, Lehmann, Germany, 4 In. 385.00
Car, Lotus, Tin, Friction, Bandai, Japan, 8 1/2 In. 35.00
Car, Mercedes, Fernlenk, Tin, Accessories, Schuco, Box, 8 In. 154.00
Car, Mercedes-Benz, 230SL, 1950s Model, Remote Control, Masudaya, Box, 15 3/4 In. . . . 500.00
Car, Mercedes-Benz, Der Wagen Des Fuehrer, Hitler, Windup, Tippco, Germany, Box, 9 In. 4675.00
Car, Mercedes-Benz, Tin, Battery Operated, Remote Control, Linemar, Japan, Box, 9 In. . . 248.00
Car, MG, Wonder, Tin, Windup, Marusan, Box, 12 1/2 In. 390.00
Car, Moko, Sedan, Tin, Windup, Green, Germany, 9 1/2 In. 880.00
Car, Mr. Magoo, Battery Operated, Hubley, Box, 9 In. 275.00
Car, Mystery, Marx, 10 In. 880.00
Car, Naughty Boy, Tin, Windup, Lehmann, Germany, 5 In. 880.00
Car, Of The Future, Plastic, Friction, Marx, U.S.A., 1950s, 10 In. 145.00
Car, Oldsmobile, Rocket 88, 1960 Model, Friction, Tin Litho, Rubber Tires, 13 In. 288.00
Car, Oldsmobile, Tin, Friction, Japan, 1954, 11 1/2 In. 345.00
Car, Opel, Tin, Friction, 1950s, 11 1/2 In. 175.00
Car, Packard, Coupe, Tuner, Red, Tan Roof, Pressed Steel, 26 In. 3300.00
Car, Pierce Arrow, Interchange Body, A.C. Williams, 8 1/8 In. 660.00
Car, Police Command, 1963 Chevrolet, Siren, Tin, Battery Operated, 13 1/2 In. 120.00
Car, Police Patrol, Corvair, Tin, Friction, Ichiko, Japan, 1960, 9 In. 195.00
Car, Police Patrol, Siren, Pressed Steel, Windup, Electric Headlights, Marx, 15 In. 660.00
Car, Police, Chevrolet, Cap Fires Through Windshield, Battery, Cragstan, 12 In. 375.00
Car, Police, Dragnet, Plastic, Calling Car 99, Battery, Ideal, Box, 14 1/2 x 5 3/4 In. 275.00
Car, Police, Graham Paige, Tin Lithograph, Clockwork, Kuramochi, Japan, c.1936, 11 In. . 1045.00
Car, Pontiac, 1934 Model, Red, Arcade, 4 1/4 In. 450.00
Car, Pontiac, Woody Station Wagon, 1946 Model, Red & Blue, Box, 7 In., 2 Piece 175.00
Car, Pressed Steel, Kingsbury, 12 1/2 In. 1430.00
Car, Queen Of The Campus, Tin, Windup, Japan, 1950s 175.00
Car, Racing Set, Thimble Drome, Cast Aluminum, Roy Cox, Box, 1950s, 9 x 12 In. 495.00
Car, Racing, Astro Boy, Masudaya, Japan, 1960s, 12 In. 550.00
Car, Racing, Break-Apart, Tin Lithograph, Friction, Japan, 1950s, 6 In. 155.00
Car, Racing, Cast Iron, Black, Nickel Spoke Wheels, Arcade, c.1920s, 7 1/2 In. 415.00
Car, Racing, Cast Iron, Center Headlight, Red, Hubley, c.1932, 6 1/2 In. 1870.00
Car, Racing, Cast Iron, Silver, Fins, Rubber Tires, Arcade, c.1933, 5 1/2 In. 165.00
Car, Racing, Cast Iron, Silver, Red Trim, Rubber Tires, A.C. Williams, c.1936, 8 1/2 In. . . . 385.00
Car, Racing, Diamond, Tin, Moves, Lights Flash, Battery, Yonezawa, Box, 15 In. 1424.00
Car, Racing, Ferrari, Toschi, 21 1/4 In. 3080.00

Car, Racing, Friction, Szuki & Edward, Japan, 10 In. 125.00
Car, Racing, Golden Arrow, Tin, Windup, Kingsbury, 20 In. 1320.00
Car, Racing, Golden Jet, Driver, Friction, Bandai, Japan, 1960s, 13 In. 135.00
Car, Racing, Golden Jet, Tin Lithograph, Friction, Japan, 10 In. 55.00
Car, Racing, Jet Race, Tin Lithograph, Friction, Yonezawa, Japan, Box, 12 In. 825.00
Car, Racing, Jet Racer, Blue, King, Japan, 12 In. 275.00
Car, Racing, King, Tin, Windup, Marx, Box, 9 1/2 In. 1210.00
Car, Racing, Land Speed Record, Tin Lithograph, Friction, Japan, 1960s, 9 In. 150.00
Car, Racing, Marx 7-11, Orange & Black 575.00
Car, Racing, Mechanical Speed Racer, Tin, Marx, Box, 6 1/4 In. 605.00
Car, Racing, Oh-Boy!, Pressed Steel, Marked 110, 13 In. 530.00
Car, Racing, Packard, Pressed Steel, Friction, Turner, 26 In. 1238.00
Car, Racing, Pagco Jet, Plastic, Windup, Box, 11 In. 110.00
Car, Racing, Pressed Steel, Windup, Structo, Box, 12 In. 770.00
Car, Racing, Prop Rod, Thimble Drome, Metal, Friskies, Box, 12 In. 385.00
Car, Racing, Roy Cox Thimble Drome, Cast, Box 633.00
Car, Racing, Speed King, Sparkling, Tin, Friction, Japan, Box, 11 In. 220.00
Car, Racing, Speed King, Tin Lithograph, Friction, Japan, 5 In. 145.00
Car, Racing, Speed King, Tin, Battery Operated, Rosko, Japan, Box, 10 In. 165.00
Car, Racing, Speedway, Linemar, Japan, 1950s, 5 1/2 In. 75.00
Car, Racing, Starfire, Tin Lithograph, Friction, Marusan, Japan, 11 1/2 In. 195.00
Car, Racing, Sunbeam, Pressed Steel, Windup, Kingsbury, Box, 19 In. 2200.00
Car, Racing, Tin Lithograph, Battery Operated, Alps, Japan, 9 1/2 In. 187.00
Car, Racing, Tin Lithograph, Emmetts, 20 In. 715.00
Car, Racing, Tin Lithograph, Friction, ASC, 11 In. 145.00
Car, Racing, Tin Lithograph, Friction, Cragstan, Japan, 11 In. 120.00
Car, Racing, Tin Lithograph, Friction, TN, Japan, 11 In. 145.00
Car, Racing, Tin Lithograph, Marx, 5 In. 198.00
Car, Racing, Tin Lithograph, Windup, Lupor, 11 1/2 In. 187.00
Car, Racing, Tin Lithograph, Windup, Yellow, Red, Marx, 5 In. 132.00
Car, Radio, Tin, Windup, Music Box, Schuco, Germany, Box, 6 In. 358.00
Car, Red Devil, Driver, Passenger, Cast Iron, Blue, Jones & Bixler, Kenton, c.1910 ...... 990.00
Car, Renault, Red, Tin, Windup, Jouets De France, C.I.J., Box, 12 In. 880.00
Car, Reo Royale Coupe, Cast Iron, Nickel Driver, Yellow, Arcade, 1931, 9 In. ...2475.00 to 4400.00
Car, Roadster, Cast Aluminum, Chrome Finish, Fait Mfg. Co., 1930s, 11 In. 475.00
Car, Roadster, Driver, Pressed Steel, Windup, Kingsbury, 11 In. 1540.00
Car, Roadster, Driver, Rumble Seat, Blue, Kilgore, 6 1/4 In. 500.00
Car, Roadster, Plastic, Green, Zax, Italy, Box, c.1940, 10 1/2 In. 165.00
Car, Roadster, Pressed Steel, Clockwork, Electric Lights, Kingsbury, 1920s, 13 In. 550.00
Car, Roadster, Pressed Steel, Dayton, 18 In. 3300.00
Car, Roadster, Sheet Metal, Flywheel Drive, Steel Wheels, Schieble, 17 1/2 In. 220.00
Car, Roadster, Take-Apart, Orange & Green, A.C. Williams, 4 1/2 In. 275.00
Car, Roadster, Windup, Marx, Box, 1950s, 11 In. 275.00
Car, Rolls-Royce, Convertible, Silver, Lithographed Seats, Friction, Bandai, 11 1/2 In. 294.00
Car, Rolls-Royce, Silver Cloud, Gray, White Top, Tin, Bandai, Box, 12 In. 255.00
Car, Runabout, Pressed Steel, Wood, Red, Cast Iron Driver, Arcade, c.1908, 9 In. 880.00
Car, Runabout, Red, Cast Iron, Driver, Passenger, c.1915, 5 x 9 In. 825.00
Car, Runabout, Wood, Metal, Cast Iron Driver, Pull Toy, Mason & Parker, 9 In. 385.00
Car, Scarab, Pressed Steel, Windup, Red, Buddy L, 10 In. 715.00
Car, Sedan, Battery Operated Headlights, Tin, Windup, Marx, 8 In. 385.00
Car, Sedan, Cast Iron, Disc Wheels, Blue, Black, Kenton, c.1925, 6 1/2 In. 715.00
Car, Sedan, Driver, Windup, Cable, Plunger, Gunthermann, 9 1/2 In. 550.00
Car, Sedan, Take-Apart, Cast Iron, White Rubber Tires, Champion, 7 In. 305.00
Car, Sedan, Tin Lithograph, Clockwork, Driver, Bing, 6 1/2 In. 525.00
Car, Sedan, Windup, C. Rossignol, France, 1920s, 8 In. 485.00
Car, Space Patrol, R-10, Astronaut Driver, Lights, Tin Lithograph, Battery, Box, 13 In. 4328.00
Car, Sportsman's Convertible, Wyandotte, Box, 12 1/4 In. 825.00
Car, Steeraway, Yellow Plastic, Battery Operated, Gas Pump Bank, Irwin, 15 In. 325.00
Car, Studebaker, Sedan, Cast Iron, Green, 6 3/4 In. 660.00
Car, Stutz, 1920s Model, Sedan, Lithographed, Tin, Marx, Box, 16 In. 3575.00
Car, Stutz, Roadster, Pressed Steel, Windup, Iron Wheels, Structo, 15 In. 1045.00
Car, Tin Lithograph, Windup, Fischer, Germany, 10 In. 468.00
Car, Tin, Battery Operated, Tipp & Co., Germany, c.1925, 6 1/4 x 14 In. 880.00

Car, Tin, Windup, Remote Control, Schuco, Germany, Box, 4 In. 176.00
Car, Touring, Beveled Glass Windows, Headlamps, Green, Red Trim, Carette 6325.00
Car, Touring, Cast Iron, Blue, Removable Canopy, Red Wheels, Hubley, c.1911, 10 In. ... 2750.00
Car, Touring, Cast Iron, Kenton, 9 1/2 In. 550.00
Car, Touring, Cast Iron, Kenton, 12 In. 775.00
Car, Touring, Friction, Blue, Japan, c.1950, 8 In. 150.00
Car, Touring, Pressed Steel, Windup, Kingsbury, 12 In. 1045.00
Car, Touring, Sheet Metal, Flywheel, Stamped Steel Wheels, Schieble, 13 1/2 In. 290.00
Car, Touring, Tin, Windup, Tippco, Germany, 13 In. 880.00
Car, Triumph, Tin, Friction, Bandai, Japan, 8 In. 90.00
Car, Uncle Wiggily, Tin Lithograph, Windup, Marx, Box, 7 1/2 In. 935.00
Car, Vacationer, Station Wagon, Trailer, Boat, Motor, Tin, Plastic, Fleet Line, 5 Piece 1195.00
Car, Volkswagen, 1970s Model, Aoshin, Japan, Box, 10 1/2 In. 145.00
Car, Volkswagen, 3 Gears, Blue, JNF, Germany, Box 575.00
Car, Volkswagen, Beetle, Convertible, Pistons Light, Tin, Battery, Nomura, Box, 9 3/4 In. . 450.00
Car, Volkswagen, Tin, Battery Operated, Bandai, Japan, 10 1/2 In. 66.00
Car, Whoopee, Sheriff Sam, Tin, Plastic, Windup, Marx, Box, 6 In. 300.00
Car, Whoopee, Tin Lithograph, Windup, Marx, 8 In. 248.00
Car, Whoopee, Tin Lithograph, Windup, Marx, Box, 8 In. 880.00
Car, Wood, Tin, Cast Iron, Painted, 1897 Patent, 12 In. 975.00
Car, Woody, Station Wagon, Friction, Green, Marx 150.00
Car & Boat Trailer, Speedboat, Tootsietoy, Box, 12 In. 110.00
Car & House Trailer, Lincoln Zephyr Sedan, Hubley, 13 1/2 In. 1100.00
Car & Trailer, Mystery, Pressed Steel, Push Mechanism, Wolverine, Box, 26 In. 385.00
Car & Trailer, Pressed Steel, Clockwork Motor, Kingsbury, 1930s, 23 In. 154.00
Car Factory, Plastic, Remco, 24 In. 110.00
Carousel, Airplanes, Tin, Lever Action, Wolverine, 13 In. 550.00
Carousel, Tin Lithograph, Mechanical, Plink-Plunk Music, Gunthermann, 7 1/2 In. 540.00
Carousel, Tin Lithograph, Painted, Clockwork, Plink-Plunk Music, 13 In. 275.00
Carousel, Tin Lithograph, Spring Motor, Wolverine, 12 In. 165.00
Carriage, Doll's, Burgundy, Painted Decoration, A.C. Double Wheel, c.1866, 57 x 39 In. ... 518.00
Carriage, Doll's, Tin Lithograph, Silk Sunshade, Maerklin, Germany, c.1890, 8 In. 3190.00
Carriage, Doll's, Wicker, Bentwood, 36 In. 86.00
Carriage, Doll's, Wicker, Sleigh Ends, Rolled Top, Wood Handlebar, 32 In. 59.00
Carriage, Doll's, Wicker, Upholstered, Metal Spoke Wheels, Canopy, 38 x 25 x 11 In. 90.00
Carriage, Doll's, Wicker, Wooden Spoke Wheels, 36 x 26 x 16 In. 290.00
Carriage, Doll's, Wicker, Wooden Spoke Wheels, Handle, 29 x 27 x 14 In. 259.00
Carriage, Doll's, Wicker, Wooden Spoke Wheels, Rims, Victorian, 29 x 23 x 10 In. 58.00
Carriage, Doll's, Wooden, Painted, Leatherette Canopy, Victorian, 27 x 27 x 12 In. 258.00
Carriage, Doll's, Wooden, Painted, Upholstered, Canopy, 24 x 26 x 10 In. 890.00
Carriage, Doll's, Wooden, Painted, Wooden Wheels, Fringed Canopy, 13 In. 374.00
Carriage, Sulky, Cast Iron, Black Horse, Red Shaft, Spoke Wheels, Jockey, 8 In. 175.00
Carriage, Sulky, Nickel Plated Wheels, Kenton, Box, c.1950 .... 250.00
Carriage, Trap, Horse Drawn, Driver, Passenger, Tin, Painted, Germany 415.00
Cart, Doll's, Wooden Seat, Back, 2 Wheels, Rubber Tires, Wire Rims, 18 In. 138.00
Cart, Dray, Pressed Steel, Cast Iron Driver, Bell, Clockwork, Wilkins Kingsbury, 9 1/2 In. . 550.00
Cart, Ice Cream Vendor, On Wheels, Windup, Celluloid, Occupied Japan 250.00
Cart, News, Marklin, Box 330.00
Cart, Ox Drawn, Cast Iron, Painted 1250.00
Case, Barbie & Midge, Blue Vinyl, Plastic Handle, 1963 .... 17.00
Cash Register, Tom Thumb, Red, Decals, 1950s, 7 1/2 In. 40.00
Castor Set, Soft Metal, Pedestal, 4 Glass Bottles, Schweitzer, c.1920, 3 In. 495.00
Cat, Felix, Rocks, Chases Mice, Rolls, Wood, Platform, Nifty, Germany, 7 1/2 x 3 1/2 In. ... 675.00
Cat, Felix, Rubber Head, Wood Body, Jointed, K-E-S, 9 In. 440.00
Cat, Felix, Stuffed Mohair, Button Eyes & Nose, Back Hump, Chad Valley, 9 1/2 In. 165.00
Cat, Felix, Stuffed Mohair, Felt Ears, Button Eyes, Jointed, Chad Valley, 12 In. 90.00
Cat, Felix, Wood, Jointed, 4 In. 66.00
Cat, Felix, Wood, Jointed, 8 In. 300.00
Cat, Lapping Milk, Head, Tail Bob, String Weight, Wooden, Early 1900s, 5 1/2 In. 460.00
Cat, Squeeze Box, Papier-Mache Head, Limbs, Continental, 1800s, 6 3/8 In. 880.00
Cat, Tabby, Mohair, Fully Jointed, Steiff, c.1950, 10 In. 132.00
Chair, Doll's, Carved Wood, Curved Arms, Spindles, Oval Back Panel, c.1840, 10 In. 224.00
Chair, Doll's, Ladder Back, Maple & Ash, Rush Seat 105.00

Chair, Doll's, Maple, Cane Seat, Carved Spindles, Brass Tips, France, c.1890, 9 In. 336.00
Chair, Doll's, Oak, Ladder Back, Flared Arms, Splats, Onion Feet, 6 x 8 x 12 1/2 In. 294.00
Chair, Doll's, Walnut, Silk Upholstery, Curved Back, Splay Legs, France, c.1870, 13 In. .. 450.00
Chariot, 2 Horses, Cast Iron, Wilkins, 9 1/2 In. 330.00
Chariot, Camel, Cast Iron, Kenton, 10 In. 1210.00
Chariot, Donkey, Cast Iron, Wilkins, 9 1/2 In. 165.00
Chariot, Roman, 2 Black Horses, Silver Horse, Cast Iron, 11 1/4 In. 770.00
Chariot, Roman, 2 Black Horses, White Horse, Cast Iron, 9 3/4 In. ....385.00 to 440.00
Chariot, Uncle Sam, 2 Black Horses, Cast Iron, Hubley, 9 3/4 In. 1980.00
Charleston Trio, 3 Figures Dancing On Roof, Tin Lithograph, Windup, Marx, 9 In. 605.00
Charlie Weaver, Bartender, Shakes & Pours Drinks, Battery Operated, Box, 12 In. 170.00
Chef, Black, Key, Windup, Occupied Japan, c.1940 .... 85.00
Chicken Snatcher, Tin Lithograph, Windup, Marx, Box, 9 In. 2090.00
Chief Cherokee, Movable Indian, Accessories, Poly-Plastic, Marx, Box, 1966, 11 1/2 In. .. 125.00
Chubby Chief Elephant, Bell, Pull Toy, Fisher-Price, 1932-33, 11 In. ....*Illus* 2090.00
Circus, Humpty Dumpty, 12 Animals, 3 Clowns, 5 Performers, Schoenhut, Box, 1920 .... 2860.00
Circus, Humpty Dumpty, Tent, Schoenhut, Box, 27 x 24 In. 1760.00
Circus, Ring-A-Ling, Tin Lithograph, Ring Leader, Clown, Animals, Marx, 7 1/2 In. 880.00
Circus, Woodsy Wee, Paper On Wood, Fisher-Price, Box, Prewar, 15 In. 1320.00
Circus Set, Humpty Dumpty, 3 Clowns, Barrel, Ladder, Chair, Schoenhut, Box 220.00
Circus Set, Humpty Dumpty, Tent, Figures, Cardboard, Schoenhut, c.1920, 24 x 18 In..... 3700.00
Clarabell Clown, Mechanical, Linemar, 6 1/2 In. 375.00
Climbing Figure, Coco, Tin Lithograph, Lehmann, Germany, 13 In. 440.00
Climbing Miller, Sack, Tin, England, Box 195.00
Clock, Tin & Celluloid, Turns & Birds Move Back & Forth, Marusan, 8 In. 325.00
Clock, Wall, Tin Lithograph, Hands Move When Weights Pulled, Penny Toy, 5 1/2 In. 248.00
Clown, Dancing With Poodle, Lever, Mechanical, Embossed, Meier, 3 1/2 In. ....*Illus* 1870.00
Clown, Happy Fiddler, Sways & Turns His Head While Playing, Alps, 10 In. 325.00
Clown, High Jinks Circus, Battery Operated, Cragstan, Japan, Box, 10 In. 275.00
Clown, Hobo, Promoting Diner, Bell, Windup, Tin Lithograph, Nomura, Japan, 6 x 4 In. .. 160.00
Clown, Ko-Ko Sandwich Man, Windup, Japan, Box 175.00
Clown, Kozo, Bisque, 4 In. 125.00
Clown, O-Look, Juggler, Irwin, Box, 1930s, 13 1/2 x 4 In. 150.00
Clown, On Barrel, Parasol Spins, Windup, Tin Lithograph, Japan, 1950s, 7 3/4 x 4 In...... 202.00
Clown, On Elephant, Cast Iron, Wheels, Shimmer, 5 In. 220.00
Clown, On Motorcycle, Tin, Windup, Japan, 1950s, 6 In. 195.00
Clown, On Platform, Strums Guitar, Head Bobs, Plinkity-Plank, Distler, Windup 550.00
Clown, On Roller Skates, Tin, Windup, T.P.S., Box, 6 1/2 In. 330.00
Clown, Playing Violin, Schuco, Windup, 4 1/4 In. 125.00
Clown, Roly Poly, Blue Cone Hat, Papier-Mache, Germany, 8 In. 220.00
Clown, Roly Poly, Blue Cone Hat, Papier-Mache, Germany, 15 In. 385.00
Clown, Roly Poly, Composition, Painted, Hat, Hands On Belly, 8 1/2 In. 195.00
Clown, Roly Poly, Composition, Painted, Roly Toys, 15 3/4 In. 305.00
Clown, Roly Poly, Painted Pressed Cardboard, Germany, 11 In. 360.00
Clown, Roly Poly, Red Cone Hat, Papier-Mache, Germany, 10 In. 385.00
Clown, Rope Climbing, Composition Head, Cloth, 8 In. 187.00
Clown, Squeeze Box, Papier-Mache Head, Germany, Late 1800s, 5 In. 140.00

Toy, Chubby Chief
Elephant, Bell, Pull
Toy, Fisher-Price,
1932-33, 11 In.

Toy, Clown, Dancing With Poodle, Lever,
Mechanical, Embossed, Meier, 3 1/2 In.

Clown, Standing On Wagon, Pulled By Dog, Tin, Gama, Germany, 8 In. 495.00
Clown, The Magician, Mixed Material, Battery Operated, Alps, Box, 11 In. 165.00
Clown, Walking, Tin, Windup, Chein, Box, 6 In. 1320.00
Clown, Windup, Cragston, Box 425.00
Clown, With Suitcases, Celluloid, Windup, Occupied Japan, 1940, 5 In. 155.00
Clown & Donkey, Pull, Lithograph, 10 1/2 In. 525.00
Coach, Doll's, Painted Wood, Stencil, Leather Surrey Top, Fringe, 30 In. 440.00
Coaster Boy, Push Toy, Fisher-Price, 12 In. 385.00
Comical Clara, Mechanical, Tin, Windup, T.P.S., Box, 5 In. 220.00
Comicooky Baking Set, Box, 7 In. 85.00
Construction Set, Crane, Bulldozer, Painted, Yellow Orange, Blue, Structo 425.00
Construction Set, Hotel Statler, Lithograph, Paper, Wood, Box, Germany, 10 In. 1540.00
Construction Set, Tiny Tonka, Box, 1971 . . . . 99.00
Costume, Annie Oakley, Double Holster, Cuffs, Spurs, Leslie Henry Guns, Box 4680.00
Cow, Noisemaker, Wood Platform, Wheels, Germany, 10 1/4 x 12 In. 495.00
Cowboy, On Kneeling Horse, Arm Moves, Lasso Swirls, Windup, Tin, Marx, 1940 . . . . 120.00
Cowboy, Riding Horse, Celluloid, Tin, Windup, Occupied Japan, Box, 1940s, 5 1/2 In. 130.00
Cradle, Doll's, Mahogany, Arched Canopy, Shaped Rockers, England, 1800s, 17 1/4 In. . . . 310.00
Cradle, Doll's, Maple, Red Paint, Flowers, Arched Panels, 18 x 9 x 11 In. 690.00
Cradle, Doll's, Poplar, Hood, 12 1/2 x 25 In. 345.00
Crapshooter, Battery Operated, Cragstan, Box, 10 In. 88.00
Cream Separator, McCormick Deering, Cast Iron, Black, Arcade, 4 7/8 In. 605.00
Crocodile, Windup, Legs Move, Mouth Opens, Lehmann, Germany 550.00
Cupboard, Doll's, Cabinette, Flower Decals, Green, Cast Iron, Hubley, 13 x 8 In. 550.00
Cupboard, Doll's, Tin Lithograph, Accessories, White, Red, Wolverine, Box, 16 In. 220.00
Cyclist, Wonder, Boy Pedals Tricycle, Bell Rings, Tin, Windup, Marx, 9 In. 130.00
Dancer, Strutting My Fair Dancer, Battery Operated, Haji, Box, 9 In. 65.00
Dancing Belle, Plastic, Windup, Yellow Skirt, Tin Base, Irwin, Box, 5 In. 99.00
Dandy Jim, Clown Dancer, Windup, Unique Art, Box, 10 In. 985.00
Dapper Dan, Dancer, Tin Lithograph, Windup, Marx, 10 In. 770.00
Dennis The Menace, Plays Xylophone, Battery Operated, Japan, Box, 1960s, 9 x 9 In. 290.00
Dental Office, Tole, Cardboard, Gilt Trim, Celluloid Dolls, 1920s, 12 x 7 In. 2970.00
Desk & Chair, Doll's, Cast Iron, Green, Kenton, 5 x 2 1/2 In. 495.00
Diorama, Cat, Louis Wain, Paper, Father Tuck Series, 12 Panels 1210.00
Dirigible, Los Angeles, Cast Iron, Dent, 10 In. 440.00
Dirigible, Los Angeles, Cast Iron, Kenton, 11 In. 825.00
Dirigible, Los Angeles, Cast Iron, Silver Paint, Dent, 7 1/4 In. 90.00
Dirigible, Los Angeles, Worn Green Paint, Cast Iron, Kenton, 7 In. 358.00
Disc Harrow, Tandem, Cast Iron, Metal Discs, Arcade, Box, 6 3/4 In. 2750.00
Doctor's Cart, Patent Dates, Carpenter, 1880s, 10 1/2 In. 625.00
Dog, Afghan Hound, Tag, Steiff, 1988, 18 In. 248.00
Dog, Airedale Terrier, Cream & Amber Mohair, Floppy Ears, Steiff, 1930, 12 In. 560.00
Dog, Bulldog, Brown Wool, Button Eyes, Swivel Head, Steiff, 1910, 14 In. 840.00
Dog, Bulldog, Mohair, Excelsior Stuffing, Button Nose, Muzzle, Steiff, 10 1/2 In. 529.00
Dog, Bulldog, Mopsy, Mohair, Tag, Neck Ribbon, Steiff, c.1950, 5 In. 75.00
Dog, Bulldog, Musical, Tin, Plush, Battery Operated, Marusan, Box, 8 1/2 In. 1195.00
Dog, Bulldog, Wood, Painted, Tack Eyes, Pull Toy, Early 1900s, 10 5/8 x 13 In. 235.00
Dog, Chow-Chow, White Curly Mohair, Brown Eyes, Black Nose, Steiff, 1920, 6 In. 225.00
Dog, Cocker Spaniel, White Mohair, Black Spots, Ear Button, Steiff, 1925, 9 In. 365.00
Dog, Cockie, White Mohair, Black & Brown Spots, Swivel Head, Steiff, 1950, 13 In. 475.00
Dog, Collie, Battery Operated, Alps, Box, 8 In. 11.00
Dog, Collie, Battery Operated, Box, 7 In. 22.00
Dog, Dachshund, Black Wool, Swivel Head, Freckles, Button Eyes, Steiff, 1910, 17 In. . . . 952.00
Dog, Fox Terrier, Mohair, Glass Eyes, Embroidered Nose, Mouth, Steiff, c.1920, 10 In. . . . 88.00
Dog, Greedy Pup, Tin, Windup, Eats Candy Balls, Japan, 1950s, Box 155.00
Dog, Irish Terrier, Brown Mohair, Swivel Head, Glass Eyes, Steiff, 1915, 9 In. 1288.00
Dog, Irish Terrier, Golden Mohair, Swivel Head, Amber Eyes, Steiff, 1920, 11 In. 615.00
Dog, King Charles Spaniel, Golden Mohair, Glass Eyes, Black Nose, Steiff, 1930, 7 In. . . . 280.00
Dog, Mohair, Blond, Glass Eyes, Jointed Head, Kraemer, Germany, c.1920, 7 In. 275.00
Dog, On Wheels, Collar, Tag, Mohair, Glass Eyes, Cast Iron Wheels, Germany, 20 In. 825.00
Dog, Papier-Mache, White Fur, Glass Eyes, Wooden Feet, Pull Toy, France, c.1890, 7 In. . . 392.00
Dog, Pat The Pup, Tin Lithograph, Rubber Ears, Tail, Windup, T.P.S., 1960s, 5 x 3 1/2 In. . 50.00
Dog, Pekinese, Creamy Mohair, Black Patches On Face, Disc Eyes, Steiff, 1950, 13 In. . . . 505.00

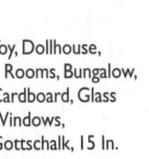

Toy, Dollhouse, Paper
Lithograph On
Cardboard, Wood,
Ta-Ka-Part, 12 In.

Toy, Dollhouse,
2 Rooms, Bungalow,
Cardboard, Glass
Windows,
Gottschalk, 15 In.

Dog, Peppy Puppy, Battery Operated, Remote Control, Rosko, Box, 9 In.	11.00 to 22.00
Dog, Poodle, Black Mohair, Steiff, c.1950s, 9 In.	55.00
Dog, Poodle, Ricki, Begging, Battery Operated, Rosko, Box, 8 In.	22.00
Dog, Poodle, Schoenhut, 5 x 7 1/2 In.	310.00
Dog, Poodle, Snobby, Mohair, Collar, Tag, Ear Button, Steiff, c.1950s, 10 In.	100.00
Dog, Poodle, Snobby, Mohair, Rhinestone Collar, Steiff, c.1950s, 16 In.	90.00
Dog, Poodle, Wooden, Jointed, Painted Eyes, Rope Tail, White, Schoenhut, 7 1/4 In.	110.00
Dog, Rin Tin Tin, Stuffed, Ideal, 22 In.	85.00
Dog, Sealyham, Creamy White Mohair, Swivel Head, Ear Button, Steiff, 1935, 9 In.	475.00
Dog, Tin, Plush Body, Battery, Eyes Light, Arks, Raises Drink, Drinks, Yonezawa, 10 In.	110.00
Dog, Tyras, Walking, Tin Lithograph, Clockwork, Lehmann, Germany, 7 In.	660.00
Dolls are listed in their own category.	
Doll Pulling Cart, Clockwork, Simon & Halbig, Box	1650.00
Dollhouse, 2 Rooms, Bungalow, Cardboard, Glass Windows, Gottschalk, 15 In. *Illus*	3300.00
Dollhouse, 2 Rooms, Bungalow, Folding, McLoughlin, c.1905, 7 x 17 In.	715.00
Dollhouse, 2 Rooms, Lithographed Red & Yellow, Accessories, Bliss, 8 1/2 In.	1760.00
Dollhouse, 6 Rooms, Gertrude Horsey Smith, Case, 1884, 16 x 12 x 9 In.	3190.00
Dollhouse, 2 Story, 2 Rooms, Porch, Balcony, Victorian, 9 x 12 1/2 x 18 In.	500.00
Dollhouse, 2 Story, 4 Rooms, Barcelona, Stable, Balcony, c.1910, 25 1/2 x 68 In.	6600.00
Dollhouse, 2 Story, Attic, White, Green Shutters, Furniture, c.1953, 48 x 58 In.	825.00
Dollhouse, 2 Story, Clapboard, Veranda, Furniture, F.A.O. Schwarz, 36 x 21 x 28 In.	705.00
Dollhouse, 3 Story, Clapboard, Balcony, Sash Windows, Spiral Stairs, 50 x 57 x 21 In.	355.00
Dollhouse, 3 Story, Clapboard, Mansard Roof, Captain's Walk, Porch, 37 x 29 x 23 In.	500.00
Dollhouse, 3 Story, Seaside Villa, Stable, Bisque Dolls, Bliss, 20 x 18 x 12 In.	4675.00
Dollhouse, Cottage, Adirondack, Log Hunting Lodge, Bliss, c.1904, 18 x 18 In.	6050.00
Dollhouse, Folding Box, Lithograph, Peter Pia Furniture, S&H Doll, 9 x 11 x 10 In.	1100.00
Dollhouse, Folk Art, Townhouse, York, Pa., Early 1800s, 22 1/2 x 19 3/4 In.	2200.00
Dollhouse, Folk Art, Wood, Lithograph, Swing-Out Front, c.1915, 13 x 8 x 7 In.	825.00
Dollhouse, Millinery Shop, Mahogany, S&H Doll, France, c.1870, 21 x 14 In.	5500.00
Dollhouse, Mother Goose, Paper Lithograph, Bliss, c.1898, 15 x 14 In.	4125.00
Dollhouse, Mount Vernon, Wallpapered Interior, Gottschalk, Germany, 19 x 21 In.	3300.00
Dollhouse, Paper Lithograph On Cardboard, Wood, Ta-Ka-Part, 12 In. *Illus*	385.00
Dollhouse, Ranch, Tin, Plastic, Furniture, Marx, Lithographed Box	110.00
Dollhouse, Red Brick Outside, Victorian Paper Inside, 21 x 18 In.	750.00
Dollhouse, Warehouse, 2 Story, Lithographed, Wood, Cart, Bliss, c.1901, 15 x 12 In.	7700.00
Dollhouse, Wood, Paper Lithograph, Bliss, c.1896, 24 x 18 x 10 In.	2035.00
Dollhouse Furniture, Bathroom Set, Plastic, Jolly Twins, Renwal, Box, 10 In.	220.00
Dollhouse Furniture, Bed, Dresser & Mirror, Commode, Chairs, c.1870	185.00
Dollhouse Furniture, Bedroom Set, Plastic, Jolly Twins, Renwal, Box, 12 In.	165.00
Dollhouse Furniture, Bedroom Suite, Fruitwood, Accessories, Schneegas, c.1900	880.00
Dollhouse Furniture, Bureau, Mahogany, Marble Top, Ormolu Finish, 10 In.	275.00
Dollhouse Furniture, Bureau, Walterhausen, Mirror, Rosewood, Kestner, c.1900, 5 In.	358.00
Dollhouse Furniture, Chandelier, 3-Light, Cherub, Gilt, Schweitzer, c.1890, 4 In.	715.00
Dollhouse Furniture, Chandelier, 6-Light, Gilt, Milk Glass, Marklin, c.1900, 6 In.	2750.00
Dollhouse Furniture, Chandelier, Hobnail Glass, Germany, Schweitzer, c.1870, 4 In.	1430.00
Dollhouse Furniture, Cupboard, Marble Top, Open Shelves, Schneegas, c.1880, 6 In.	1760.00
Dollhouse Furniture, Dining Room, Fruitwood, Accessories, Schneegas, c.1890	770.00

Dollhouse Furniture, Dresser, Pine, 5 Drawers, Porcelain Knobs, 8 3/4 x 8 x 6 In. 193.00
Dollhouse Furniture, Half-Tester Bed, Brass, Swing Arm, Marklin, c.1900, 6 1/2 In. 3300.00
Dollhouse Furniture, Iron, Curled Handle, Cathedral Trivet, 1 1/8 In. 10.00
Dollhouse Furniture, Kitchen Set, Pinewood, Nuremberg, Germany, c.1825, 36 x 17 In. .. 8250.00
Dollhouse Furniture, Kitchen Set, Plastic, Jolly Twins, Renwal, Box, 12 In. 220.00
Dollhouse Furniture, Kitchen, Dream, Deluxe Reading, N.J., Box, c.1960, 176 Piece 195.00
Dollhouse Furniture, Lamp, Hanging, Enameled Metal, Glass Globe, Marklin, 4 1/2 In. .. 935.00
Dollhouse Furniture, Living Room Set, Baby Grand Piano, Accessories 935.00
Dollhouse Furniture, Living Room, Sofa, Tables, Walnut, Strombecker, 1930s, 10 Piece .. 195.00
Dollhouse Furniture, Living Room, Tin Furniture, 3 Bisque Dolls, Victorian, 11 x 22 In. .. 450.00
Dollhouse Furniture, Mirror, Dressing, Mahogany, Victorian, 9 In. 165.00
Dollhouse Furniture, Sideboard, Mahogany, 8 In. 140.00
Dollhouse Furniture, Stove, Cook, Cast Iron, 6 Burners, Water Reservoir, 11 1/2 In. 118.00
Dollhouse Furniture, Stove, Steel, Cast Flowers, 2 Hinged Doors, Painted, 9 1/2 In. 50.00
Dollhouse Furniture, Table, Biedermeier, Accessories, Marble Top, 1850-1920, 4 In. 660.00
Dollhouse Furniture, Table, Tilt Top, Cherry, Victorian, 6 In. 66.00
Donkey, Felt, Papier-Mache, Glass Eyes, Wooden Base, Pull Toy, Germany, 5 1/2 In. 154.00
Doughboy Waddler, Tin, Windup, Chein, 6 In. 330.00
Dr. Doodle, Duck, Lithograph, Pull Toy, Fisher-Price, 8 In. 495.00
Dr. Doodle, Duck, Paper Lithograph On Wood, Pull Toy, Fisher-Price, 1931, 12 In. .... *Illus* 2200.00
Drinking Captain, Battery Operated, Japan, Box, 13 In. 165.00
Drum, Embossed, Eagle, American Flag, Red Ground, 19th Century 690.00
Drum Major, Tin Lithograph, Mechanical, Marx, 9 In. 50.00
Drum Major, Tin Lithograph, Mechanical, Wolverine, 14 In. 135.00
Drummer, Windup, Walks While Drumming, Japan 200.00
Duck, Ducky Daddles, Pull Toy, Fisher-Price, 12 In. 495.00
Duck, Nodding, Composition & Mohair, Glass Eyes, Windup, 16 x 14 x 6 1/2 In. 1155.00
Duck & Ducklings, Tin, Windup, Mouth Opens, Japan, 1950s 55.00
Duck Car, Plastic, Pull Toy, Knickerbocker Plastic Co., 10 In. 110.00
Dwarf, Walking, Tin, Windup, Chein, Box, 6 In. 1100.00
Earth Mover, Plastic, Kiddie Toy, Hubley, 14 In. 110.00
Elephant, Black In Howdah, Head Nods, Windup, Gunthermann, 1900 .... 685.00
Elephant, Cast Iron, Nodding Head, Shimmer, 4 In. 110.00
Elephant, Mohair, Fully Jointed, Shoebutton Eyes, Steiff, c.1920, 10 In. 469.00
Elephant, Ramp Walker, Cast Iron, Ives, 3 1/2 In. 110.00
Elephant, Walker, Battery Operated, Linemar, Box, 9 In. 28.00
Elephant, Walker, Battery Operated, Modern Toys, Box, 9 In. 22.00
Elephant, Windy, Juggling, Plush, Tin, Battery Operated, TN, Box, 12 In. 275.00
Elephant, Wooden, Jointed, Leather Ears, Rope Tail, Painted Eyes, Schoenhut, 8 1/2 In. .. 55.00
Elephant & Marble, Spins Umbrella With Trunk, Marble Drops, Trough, Box, 10 x 8 In. .. 278.00
Embroidery Set, Annie Oakley, Neckerchief & Hanky, Box 83.00
Erector Set, Structo, Wooden Box, 1920 .... 195.00
Farm Set, Animals, Corral, Tonka, Box, 1958 .... 770.00
Farm Set, Metal Barn, Fence, Tractor, Animals, Accessories, Marx, Box 90.00
Ferdinand The Bull, Composition, Ideal, Box, 9 In. 195.00
Ferdinand The Bull & Matador, Tin, Windup, Marx, Box, 7 In. 715.00
Ferris Wheel, 6 Seats, White, Green Base, c.1950, 23 1/2 In. 316.00
Ferris Wheel, Iron & Steel, Black, Red, Yellow, Clockwork, c.1892, 17 1/4 In. 3080.00
Ferris Wheel, Tin Lithograph, 6 Gondolas, Clown, Mechanical, Chein, Box, 16 1/2 In. ... 440.00
Ferris Wheel, Tin Lithograph, Windup, Chein, 17 In. ....275.00 to 695.00
Ferris Wheel, Tin, Windup, Chein, Box, 18 In. 715.00
Fire Engine, Hot Air, Ernest Plank, 13 In. 605.00
Fire Pumper, 2 Horses, Cast Iron, Ives, 18 In. 660.00
Fire Pumper, 2 Horses, Driver, Hubley, 1890s, 7-In. Horses, 17 1/4 In. 1095.00
Fire Pumper, 2 Horses, Hubley, 1910, 11 1/2 In. 250.00
Fire Pumper, 2 Horses, Rider, Cast Iron, Kenton, c.1900, 20 1/2 In. 865.00
Fire Pumper, 3 Horses, Cart, Cast Iron, Wilkins, c.1900, 20 In. 460.00
Fire Pumper, 3 Horses, Driver, Cast Iron, Wilkins, 12 1/2 In. 375.00
Fire Pumper, 3 Horses, Gong Bell, Dent, 1905, 19 1/4 In. 1095.00
Fire Pumper, 3 Horses, Kenton, c.1950, 10 In. 165.00
Fire Pumper, Accessories, Insert, Doepke, Box, 1952 .... 960.00
Fire Pumper, Cast Iron, Nickel Grill, Red, Kenton, 1936, 7 1/2 In. 523.00
Fire Pumper, Cast Iron, Nickel Plated Boiler, Hubley, 15 In. 3575.00

Fire Pumper, Cast Iron, Red, Gold Accents, 6 Spoke Wheels, 6 In. 345.00
Fire Pumper, Cast Iron, Red, Nickel Grill, Rubber Tires, Kilgore, 5 In. 358.00
Fire Pumper, Hercules, Tin, Chein, 18 In. 2860.00
Fire Pumper, Horse, Driver, Hose Reel, Brass Nozzle, Hubley, 1915, 12 1/2 In. 725.00
Fire Pumper, Hose Reel, 1 Horse, Hubley, 1915, 12 1/4 In. 725.00
Fire Pumper, Hydrant, Inserts, Wish Book, Tonka, Box, 1963 . . . . 715.00
Fire Pumper, Phoenix, 2 Horses, 2 Firemen, Ives, 1890s, 9-In. Horses 1995.00
Fire Pumper, Pressed Steel, Aluminum Wheels, Buddy L, 1920s, 24 In. 990.00
Fire Pumper, Pressed Steel, Pull Rod, Windup Pistons, Kingsbury 4125.00
Fire Pumper, Red, Nickel Boiler, Buddy L, 1924, 24 In. 1250.00
Fire Pumper, Structo, Box, 20 In. 660.00
Fire Pumper, Take-Apart, Cast Iron, A.C. Williams, c.1937, 6 3/4 In. 1650.00
Fire Pumper, Tin Lithograph, 3 Figures, 5 1/2 In. 300.00
Fire Pumper, Tin, Iron, Clockwork Windup, George Brown, 1870s, 7 1/2 x 10 1/2 In. 4070.00
Fire Station, Paper Lithograph On Wood, Metal Bell, Bliss, 12 1/4 In. . . . . *Illus* 1650.00
Fire Station Set, Badge, Helmets, Ladder, Ax, Ambulance, Tootsietoy, Box 475.00
Fire Station Set, Buildings, Trucks, Accessories, Wood, Keystone, Box, 16 In. 385.00
Fire Station Set, Pumper, Ladder Truck, Tin, Windup, Bing, Germany 1430.00
Fire Station Set, Pumper, Rescue Squad, Hydrant, Tonka, Box, 1960 . . . . 4510.00
Fire Truck, 2 Firemen, Cast Iron, Nickel Plated Grill, Bumper, Arcade, 9 1/2 In. 360.00
Fire Truck, 2 Firemen, Extension Ladder, Plastic, Renwal, Box, 15 In. 220.00
Fire Truck, 3 Firemen, Ladder, Rubber Tires, Cast Iron, Arcade, 16 In. 570.00
Fire Truck, 5 Firemen, Aerial Ladder, Tin Lithograph, CKO, 5 1/2 In. 330.00
Fire Truck, 5 Firemen, Aerial Ladder, Tin Lithograph, Windup, Distler, 4 1/2 In. 415.00
Fire Truck, Aerial Hook & Ladder, Structo, Box, 30 In. 550.00
Fire Truck, Aerial Ladder, Adjustable Turret, Nickel Plated, Bell, Buddy L, 40 In. 2875.00
Fire Truck, Aerial Ladder, MIC, L.A.F.D., Smith-Miller, Box 1210.00
Fire Truck, Aerial Ladder, Pressed Steel, Crank, Pull Cord, Buddy L, 40 In. 1980.00
Fire Truck, Aerial Ladder, Pressed Steel, Kingsbury, 1920s, 36 In. 1100.00
Fire Truck, Aherns Fox, Rubber Tires, Hubley, 11 In. 1870.00
Fire Truck, Big Boy, Pressed Steel, 2 17-In. Wooden Ladders, Kelmet, 26 In. 2420.00
Fire Truck, Buddy L, 1961 . . . . 395.00
Fire Truck, Cast Iron, Nickel Plated Driver, Tillerman, Ladders, Arcade, 11 1/2 In. 355.00
Fire Truck, Cast Iron, Painted, Nickel Plated, Spool, Fire Hoses, 14 1/2 In. 1020.00
Fire Truck, GMC, Buddy L, 1959 . . . . 225.00
Fire Truck, GMC, City Fire Department, Pressed Steel, Steelcraft, 1930s, 26 In. . . .2310.00 to 2420.00
Fire Truck, Hook & Ladder, Die Cast, Plastic Ladder, Hubley, Box, 7 1/4 In. 275.00
Fire Truck, Hook & Ladder, Die Cast, Red, Hubley, Box, 9 1/2 In. 415.00
Fire Truck, Hook & Ladder, Nickel Plated Wheels, Firefighters, Ladders, 7 1/2 In. 235.00
Fire Truck, Hook & Ladder, Plastic, Hubley, Box, 12 In. 80.00
Fire Truck, Ladder, Cast Iron, Nickel Grill, Red, Kenton, 1936, 7 1/2 In. 1650.00
Fire Truck, Ladder, Diamond T, Nickel Grill, Hubley, 6 1/2 In. 300.00
Fire Truck, Ladder, Die Cast, Metal Masters Co., Box, 10 In. 330.00
Fire Truck, Ladder, Driver, Cast Iron, Tin Ladders, Red, Skoglund & Olson, 16 In. 2750.00
Fire Truck, Ladder, Mack, Smith-Miller, Box 1650.00
Fire Truck, Ladder, Pressed Steel, Electric Lights, Bell, Structo, 22 In. 2530.00
Fire Truck, Ladder, Red & Silver, Hubley, 8 1/2 In. 650.00
Fire Truck, Ladders, Rope Hose, Brass Nozzle, Steelcraft, 27 In. 1800.00

Toy, Dr. Doodle, Duck,
Paper Lithograph On
Wood, Pull Toy, Fisher-
Price, 1931, 12 In.

Toy, Fire Station,
Paper Lithograph
On Wood, Metal
Bell, Bliss, 12 1/4 In.

Fire Truck, Mack, Driver, Red, Cast Iron, Arcade Mfg., 1930, 5 x 13 In. 1265.00
Fire Truck, Pontiac, Ladder, Cast Iron, Yellow Ladders, Arcade, Box, 9 1/2 In. 2090.00
Fire Truck, Pressed Steel, Buddy L, 1940s, 30 In. 175.00
Fire Truck, Pressed Steel, Electric Headlights, Kingsbury, 13 1/2 In. 1045.00
Fire Truck, Pressed Steel, Keystone Packard, 1920s, 28 In. 660.00
Fire Truck, Pressed Steel, Red, Ladders, Electric Lights, Clockwork, Marx, c.1935, 15 In. . . 770.00
Fire Truck, Pressed Steel, Structo, 1940s, 34 In. 77.00
Fire Truck, Red Steel, Gilt Transfer, Extension Ladder, Buddy L 765.00
Fire Truck, Ride On, Marx, Box, 1940 . . . . 1210.00
Fire Truck, Steam Pumper, Diamond T, Nickel Grill & Boiler, Hubley, 6 1/2 In. 450.00
Fire Truck, Tin Lithograph, Windup, Courtland, 9 In. . . . . .120.00 to 358.00
Fire Truck, Tin, Friction, Japan, 6 1/2 In. 99.00
Fire Truck, Water Tower, Cast Iron, Red, Blue Tower, Kenton, 11 1/2 In. 2200.00
Fire Truck, Water Tower, Red, Yellow Cab, Disc Wheels, International, 1930, 47 In. 2585.00
Fire Truck, Wood, Buddy L, 1940s, 15 In. 55.00
Fire Wagon, 2 Horses, Hose Reel, Cast Iron, 19th Century, 20 In. 690.00
Fire Wagon, 2 Horses, Hose Reel, Cast Iron, Dent, 21 In. 3850.00
Fire Wagon, 2 Horses, Nickel Plated Steamer, Cast Iron, Hubley, 22 In. 4025.00
Fire Wagon, 3 Horses, Driver, Firemen, Gong Bell, Dent, 1910, 19 In. 1150.00
Fire Wagon, 3 Horses, Ladder, Tin, Wood, c.1900, 48 In. 10450.00
Fire Wagon, Hook & Ladder, 2 Horses, Cast Iron, Dent, 31 In. 2860.00
Fire Wagon, Hook & Ladder, 3 Horses, 2 Firemen, Dent, 1905, 26 In. 1025.00
Fire Wagon, Hook & Ladder, 3 Horses, Cast Iron, Bell, Kenton, 1920, 31 In. 529.00
Fire Wagon, Hook & Ladder, 3 Horses, Kenton, c.1950, 11 1/2 In. 248.00
Fire Wagon, Hook & Ladder, 3 Horses, Kenton, c.1950, 16 1/4 In. 220.00
Fire Wagon, Hook & Ladder, Horses, Firemen, Gong Bell, Dent, 1915, 27 1/2 In. 95.00
Fire Wagon, Horse, Hose Reel, Cast Iron, Carpenter, 14 In. 935.00
Fire Wagon, Ladder, Painted Wood, Cast Iron, Accessories, 36 In. 605.00
Fire Wagon, Phoenix, Hook & Ladder, 2 Horses, 2 Firemen, Yellow, Ives, 1880s, 29 In. . . . 1595.00
Flintstones, Bedrock Band, Fred, Drums, Battery Operated, Alps, Japan, Box, 10 In. 500.00
Flintstones, Dino On Tricycle, Mechanical, Hanna-Barbera, Marx, Box, 4 1/4 In. 750.00
Flintstones, Dino, Hopping, Tin, Windup, Hanna-Barbera, Marx, 3 In. 145.00
Flintstones, Fred Riding Dino, Tin Lithograph, Rubber Fred Head, Marx, 8 In. . . . .250.00 to 495.00
Flintstones, Fred, Flivver, Tin, Plastic, Battery Operated, Remote, Marx, Box, 7 In. 509.00
Flintstones, Play Set, Bedrock Express, Marx, Box 220.00
Flintstones, Tank, Turnover, Tin, Windup, Linemar, 1950s, 4 In. . . . . .195.00 to 450.00
Forklift, Battery Operated, Japan, 9 x 8 In. 58.00
Fox Magician, Mixed Material, Windup, Nomura, 8 1/2 In. 195.00
Frankenstein, Lincoln International, HK, On Card, Early 1970s, 8 In. 460.00
Frog, Croaking, Tin, Windup, Japan, Box, 4 1/2 In. 110.00
Frog, Mohair, Green, Brown, Yellow, Button, Tag, Steiff, c.1960, 8 In. 45.00
Frog, Velveteen, Steiff, 4 1/2 In. 99.00
G.I. Joe, Black, Command Coat, Poncho Set, Flocked Hair, Hasbro, c.1970, 11 1/2 In. 50.00
G.I. Joe, Brown Painted Hair, Green Army Fatigues, Dog Tag, Brown Boots 70.00
G.I. Joe, Land Adventurer, Camouflage Outfit, Accessories, Hasbro, Box, 1970, 11 In. 265.00
G.I. Joe, Land Adventurer, Kung Fu Grip, Flocked Hair & Beard, Hasbro, Box, 1974 . . . . . 210.00
G.I. Joe, Man Of Action, Talking, Box, 1970 . . . . 79.00
G.I. Joe, Sea Adventurer, Flocked Hair & Beard, Hasbro, Box, 1970 . . . . 210.00
G.I. Joe, Tripwire Action Figure, 1980s 565.00
G.I. Joe, With Jouncing Jeep, Tin, Windup, Unique Art, Box, 7 In. . . . . .135.00 to 330.00
G.I. Joe, With K-9 Pups, Tin Lithograph, Windup, Walker, Unique Art, 9 In. . . . . . . .176.00 to 198.00
Gallop Cowboy, In Cart, Jumps, Pulled By Zebra, Windup, Lehmann, c.1954 . . . . 375.00
Games are listed in their own category.
Garage, 2 Cars, Tin, Windup, Lehmann, Germany 770.00
Garage, Tin Lithograph, Lehmann, Germany, 6 In. . . . . .110.00 to 176.00
Garage, Tin, Windup, Bing, Germany, 5-In. Car, 7 In. 1100.00
Gas Heater, Superior, Cast Iron, Pressed Steel, Kenton, 18 x 19 In. 468.00
Gas Pump, Cast Iron, Hose, Red, Gold Trim, A.C. Williams, 4 3/4 In. 525.00
Gas Pump, Cast Iron, Yellow, Red Trim, Arcade, 6 1/4 In. 770.00
Gas Pump, Mack, Cast Iron, Side Handle, Red, Skoglund & Olson, 6 1/4 In. 605.00
Gas Pump, Pressed Steel, Red, Glass Meter Tank, Wyandotte, 9 In. 990.00
Gas Pump, Texaco Fire Chief, Sheet Metal, Plastic, Wolverine, 30 x 14 x 12 In. 186.00
Gas Pump, Toygas, Tin, Hull Co., 10 In. 385.00

Gas Station, Bright Lite, Tin, Battery Operated, Marx, Prewar, 9 1/2 x 2 1/2 In. 385.00
Gas Station, Bright Lite, Tin, Marx, Box, 9 1/2 x 6 1/2 In. 525.00
Gas Station, Tin Lithograph, Plastic, Car, Battery Operated, Distler, Germany, Box, 6 In. . .   300.00
Gas Station, Tin, Windup, Car, Tipp Co., U.S. Zone Germany, Box, 10 In. 1320.00
George, The Drummer Boy, Tin Lithograph, Windup, Marx, Box, 9 In. . . . . .220.00 to 248.00
George Washington, Flat Figure, Hero Of 76, Paper Lithograph, Crandall, 10 In. 330.00
George Washington Bridge, Boats, Planes, Greyhound Bus, Windup, 25 In. 750.00
Giraffe, Wooden, Jointed, Leather Ears, Rope Tail, Brown Spots, Schoenhut, 11 In. 468.00
Gnome, Rubber Head, Felt Clothes, Button, Tag, Steiff, c.1950, 12 In. 300.00
Go-Cart, Lite-O-Wheel, Battery Operated, Rosko, Box, 10 In. 195.00
Goat, Hide Body, Wooden Frame, Green Glass Eyes, Cloth, Leather, Pull Toy, 14 x 15 In. . .   489.00
Goat, Mohair, Excelsior Stuffing, Glass Eyes, Felt Ears, Ribbon, Bell, Steiff, 11 In. 705.00
Goat Cart, Gray Fur, Papier-Mache Horns, Painted, Rocks, Pull Toy, 23 In. 805.00
Golden Goose, Tin, Windup, Marx, Box, 9 In. 220.00
Golf Game, Tommy Green & Cissy Lofter, Schoenhut, 1922 Patent 2820.00
Golfer, Lady, Metal, Wood, Wood Handle, Schoenhut, 26 In. 1100.00
Goofy The Gardner, Pushes Cart, Windup, Marx, 1940s 850.00
Grandpa's New Car, Tin, Windup, Japan, Box 330.00
Grasshopper, Cast Iron, Pull Toy, Hubley, 11 In. 875.00
Guitar, Wyatt Earp, Wood, Cardboard Laminate, Tricolor Stencils, 30 In. 28.00
Gun, BB, Benjamin Franklin, Wood, Metal 72.00
Gun, BB, Daisy, Buzz Barton, Model 36, 1936-41 . . . .   173.00
Gun, BB, Daisy, Cub, Model 102, Box 83.00
Gun, BB, Daisy, Gold Rush Edition, 1000 Shot Repeater, 2 Tubes Of BBs 230.00
Gun, BB, Daisy, Model 27, 1000 Shot, Lever Action, Walnut Stock, 35 1/2 In. 160.00
Gun, BB, Daisy, Model 1700, CO2, 11 1/2 In. 45.00
Gun, BB, Daisy, Targeteer, Pistol, Metal 88.00
Gun, BB, King Model E, Break Open, Repeater, Walnut Stock 190.00
Gun, Cork, Automatic, Black Enamel, Wyandotte, 9 In. 45.00
Gun, Cosmic Ray, Plastic, Blue, Ranger Steel, Box, 8 In. 275.00
Gun, G-Man Automatic, Sparking, Windup, 3 Red Jewels, Marx, 1938 . . . .   35.00
Gun, Hawkeye 50 Shot Automatic, Indian Designs, Checkered Grip, Kilgore, 4 1/8 In. 20.00
Gun, Machine, Electromatic, 50 Shot, Checkered Grips, Battery, Hubley, c.1960 . . . .   55.00
Gun, Machine, Ra-Ta-Tat, Cast Iron, Kilgore, Box 165.00
Gun, Muzzle Loader, Hand Carved, Tiger Maple Stock, Ram Rod 150.00
Gun, Pioneer Pistol, Metal Frame, Chrome Plated, Brown & Orange Grips, Box 135.00
Gun, Potato, Cast Iron, Wood Barrel, Tin Cover, 5 3/4 x 1 1/2 In. 69.00
Gun, Repeater, Horsehead Grips, Sheriff Speaking Spanish On Box 85.00
Gun, Rifle, Buffalo Bill, Clay Marble, 1885 Patent 139.00
Gun, Rocket Dart, Plastic, Red, Darts, Wyandotte, Box, 9 In. 220.00
Gun, Rocket Ship Space Pistol, Plastic, Flashing, Irwin, Box, 10 In. 600.00
Gun, Sheriff's Derringer, Die Cast, Plastic Grips, Embossed, On Card, Ohio Art 20.00
Gun, Six Shooter, Revolver, Checkered Grips, Instructions, Plastic, Ideal, N.Y., Box 11.00
Gun, Space Ray, Plastic, 3-Way Futurama, Flashes Green, White, Red, Ideal, Box, 9 In. . . .   440.00
Gun, Space, Spud, Space Scout, Instructions, Hard Plastic, 1950s 65.00
Gun, Walking Cane, Derringer Handle, Wood Shaft, Hubley, 26 1/2 In. 94.00
Gun & Holster, Cowboy, White, Bullets, Russell, Box 77.00
Gun & Holster, Double, Black, White, Red Bullets, Chrome Tacks, Buckles, Keystone, Box   145.00
Gun & Holster, Double, Colt 45, 1860 Army, 13-In. Guns 530.00
Gun & Holster, Gunsmoke, Matt Dillon, Leather, 6 Bullets, J. Halpern, Box, c.1956 . . . . . .   231.00
Gun & Holster, Mare's Laig, Dart Gun, Winchester Style, 2 Darts, 8 Bullets, 12 1/2 In. . . .   40.00
Gun & Holster, Matchless, Double, Fringe, Hubley, Box 165.00
Gun & Holster, Maverick, Single, Leslie Henry Gun, Sears, Box, 10 1/2-In. Gun 462.00
Gun & Holster, Pla-Master, Double, Herman Iskin & Co., 10 3/4-In. Texas Guns 424.00
Gun & Holster, Red Ranger, Double, Leather, Box 275.00
Gun & Holster, Ric-O-Shay, Double, Chrome Guns, Bullets, Hubley, Box 490.00
Gun & Holster, Single, Marshall, Steer Head, 3 Bullets, Hubley, Box 116.00
Gun & Holster, Smokey Joe, Hubley Texan Jr. Cap Guns, Leather, Box 170.00
Gun & Holster, Tales Of Wells Fargo, Double, Actoy, Box, 11-In. Guns . . . . .330.00 to 440.00
Gun & Holster, Texan Jr., Single, 6 Bullets, Jewels, Leather, Left Handed 110.00
Gun & Holster, Texan, Double, Leather, Jewels, Studs, 6 Bullets, Halco, Box 110.00
Gun & Holster, Texan, Hubley Cast Steel Gun, Leather, Jewel, Halco, Box, 9-In. Gun 110.00
Gun & Holster, Thundergun, Cowhide, Fur Lined, 8 Bullets, Marx 260.00

Gun & Holster, Wagon Train, Double, Diamond H Brand, 1958, 11 x 14 1/2 In. 358.00
Gun & Holster, Wells Fargo, Pony Express, Double, 6 Red Bullets, Tooled Horse Head . . . 116.00
Gun & Holster, Wild Bill Hickok, Double, Studs, Jewels, Alligator Tooled Leather 404.00
Gun & Holster, Wyatt Earp, Double, 6 Red Bullets, Leather, Actoy, 9 1/2-In. Guns 566.00
Gun & Holster, Wyatt Earp, Double, 12 Bullets, Actoy, 8 3/4-In. Guns 220.00
Gun & Holster, Wyatt Earp, Double, 12 Bullets, Leather, 11-In. Guns 329.00
Gun & Holster, Wyatt Earp, Single, 6 Bullets, Hubley Gun 230.00
Gun & Holster, Wyatt Earp, Single, 18 Bullets, Leather, Studs, Actoy, 8 1/2-In. Gun 165.00
Gun & Holster, Young Buffalo Bill, Leather, Iron Cap Gun, 1930-40, 7 1/2-In. Gun 158.00
Gun & Holster Set, Stallion 38 Guns, Leather, Gold Holster, Sheriff Stars, Nichols 330.00
Ham & Sam, Minstrel Team, Playing Piano & Banjo, Tin, Windup 978.00
Ham & Sam, Tin Lithograph, Windup, Strauss, 7 In. 605.00
Hansom Cab, Black Cab, White Horse, Cast Iron, Iron Figures, Kenton, Box, 16 In. 605.00
Hansom Cab, Cast Iron, 2 Seats, Windows, Spoke Wheels, Woman Passenger, 15 In. 175.00
Hansom Cab, Cast Iron, Kenton, 15 In. 275.00
Hansom Cab, Driver, Gray Horse, Cast Iron, Black, Arcade, 10 1/4 In. 825.00
Hansom Cab, Removable Driver, Passenger, Kenton, c.1952, 14 1/2 In. 330.00
Happy Hooligan, Cart Pulled By Donkey, Windup, Ingap Co., Italy, 1930s 1100.00
Happy Hooligan, Tin Lithograph, Windup, Walker, Chein, 6 In. 360.00
Happy The Clown, Puppet Show, Clown Sways, Changes Face, Yonezawa, 10 In. 275.00
Hayloader, John Deere, Cast Iron, Red, Green, Yellow, Vindex, 9 In. 4675.00
Hee-Haw, Balky Mule, Tin, Windup, Marx, Box, 10 In. 220.00
Helicopter, Fix-All, Plastic, Marx, Box 165.00
Helicopter, Green, Red Wheels, Windup, Japan, 5 1/2 In. 145.00
Helicopter, Red & White, Hubley, 9 3/4 In. 195.00
Helicopter, World's Fair, 1958, Brussels, Plastic, Windup, Flies Around 125.00
Helmet, Space Pilot, Plastic, Tarco, Box, 9 In. 550.00
Helmet, Tom Corbett Cosmic Vision, Practi-Cole Co., Box, 1950s 1070.00
Henry, Licking Candy Cane, Linemar, Windup, 5 3/4 In. 400.00
Henry, On Elephant, Celluloid, Windup, Borgfeldt, Box, 1930s 1295.00
Henry, On Trapeze, Celluloid, Geo. Borgfeldt Corp., Box, 6 1/2 In. 880.00
Henry & His Little Brother, On Platform, Windup, C.K. Co., Japan, Box, 1930s 1450.00
Highway Set, Hydraulic Dump, Grader, Trucks, Signs, Tonka, Box, 1959 . . . . 3025.00
Hillclimber, Speedster, Flywheel Motor, Pressed Steel, Dayton, 1920s, 12 In. 385.00
Hillclimber, Wood, Pressed Steel, Red, Green Wheels, 4 Figures, D.P. Clark, 10 1/2 In. . . . 1210.00
Hippopotamus, Wooden, Jointed, Glass Eyes, Rope Tail, Schoenhut, 8 3/4 In. 140.00
Hobo, Accordion Player, Nods Head, Monkey Plays Cymbals, Alps, Japan, Box, 10 In. . . . 394.00
Hokey Pokey, Rail Car, 2 Clowns, Windup, Wyandotte, 7 In. 120.00
Home Run King, Tin Lithograph, Clockwork, Selrite, 7 In. 660.00
Honeymoon Express, Tin Lithograph, Windup, Marx, 10 In. 90.00
Hootin' Hollow, Haunted House, Tin, Marx, Box, 11 In. 2925.00
Horse, Brown, Hide Cover, Glass Eyes, Wooden Platform, Wheels, c.1940, 32 In. 250.00
Horse, Dandy Dobbin, Pull Toy, Fisher-Price, 10 In. 385.00
Horse, Front Hoof Up, Red Saddle, Blue Blanket, Pull Toy, Germany, 14 In. 1210.00
Horse, Jumping, Clockwork, Plush, Fur Mane, Tail, Wood Hooves, Japan, 1930, 8 In. 59.00
Horse, Papier-Mache, Gray Dapple Paint, Wooden Base, Pull Toy, Germany, 7 1/4 In. 200.00
Horse, Papier-Mache, Wood, Mohair, Leather Ears, Wheels, Pull Toy, 12 In. 330.00
Horse, Platform, Gliding, Wood Carved, White, Saddle, Flax Mane, 14 x 37 x 35 In. 470.00
Horse, Prancing, Wood, Horsehair Mane & Tail, Wheeled Platform, c.1930, 35 In. 615.00
Horse, Rocking, 2 Cutouts, Seat In Middle, Painted White, 37 x 11 1/2 In. 275.00
Horse, Rocking, Appaloosa, Wood, Gray, White, High Relief, c.1950, 36 x 48 In. 575.00
Horse, Rocking, Carved, Running, Oilcloth Bridle, Saddle, 30 x 39 x 14 1/2 In. 250.00
Horse, Rocking, Cowhide Cover, 30 x 61 x 8 In. 3800.00
Horse, Rocking, Dapple Gray, Stenciled Mane, Painted Saddle, Rope Tail, 23 x 35 In. 150.00
Horse, Rocking, Horsehide Cover, Western Saddle, Glass Eyes, Springs, 36 x 50 In. 575.00
Horse, Rocking, Laminated Pine, Jeweled Eyes, Felt Saddle, 25 x 40 x 13 In. 330.00
Horse, Rocking, Painted, Horsehair Mane & Tail, Platform Base, 32 x 39 In. 770.00
Horse, Rocking, Pine, Painted, Horsehair Mane & Tail, Mid 19th Century, 24 x 46 In. 480.00
Horse, Rocking, Wood, Carved, Painted Eyes, Black Rocker, 44 In. 560.00
Horse, Rocking, Wood, Hide Cover, New England, c.1850, 43 x 15 x 70 In. 880.00
Horse, Rocking, Wood, Hide, Horsehair Mane, Tail, Platform, 1885, 54 x 46 In. 5885.00
Horse, Sparkplug, Tin, Green Base, Red Wheels, Pull Toy, 9 In. 660.00
Horse, Speckled Fabric, Leather Saddle, Wood Platform, Pull Toy, Germany 660.00

Horse, Tin, Wood Base, Wheels, 1875-80, 10 x 10 1/2 In. 575.00
Horse, White Cloth Covering, Gray Horsehair Tail, Mane, Felt, Leather, Pull Toy, 11 In. .. 290.00
Horse, Wood, Carved, Oak Platform, Cast Iron Wheels, Pull Toy, 1800s, 16 x 20 In. 750.00
Horse & Buggy, Riders, Cast Iron, Stanley, 11 In. 65.00
Horse & Rider, Celluloid, Original Tag, Japan, Prewar, 7 In. 415.00
Horse & Wagon, 2 Horses, 2 Seats, 4 Figures, Cast Iron, Hubley, 16 1/2 In. 3575.00
Horse & Wagon, 2 Horses, 3 Seats, 6 Figures, Cast Iron, Hubley, 20 In. 11000.00
Horse & Wagon, 2 Horses, Black Man On Log, Cast Iron, Kenton, 16 In. 550.00
Horse & Wagon, 2 Horses, Wooden, Metal Rimmed Wheels, 25 In. 145.00
Horse & Wagon, 4 Horses, 4 Seats, 8 Figures, Cast Iron, Hubley, 28 In. 13750.00
Horse & Wagon, Borden's Milk, Tin Lithograph, Wood, Paint, 20 In. 135.00
Horse & Wagon, Cast Iron, Wilkins, 13 In. 660.00
Horse & Wagon, Cement Mixer, Black Horse, Cast Iron, Kenton, 14 In. 1045.00
Horse & Wagon, Contractor's, Driver, 2 Horses, Cast Iron, Arcade, c.1939, 13 In. 468.00
Horse & Wagon, Covered, 2 Horses, Removable Driver, Kenton, c.1950, 15 In. 305.00
Horse & Wagon, Cowboy, Gun, Tin, Fabric, Celluloid, Windup, Occupied Japan, 3 x 9 In. . 75.00
Horse & Wagon, Dray, Driver, 2 Black Horses, Red, Arcade, 13 In. 2475.00
Horse & Wagon, Driver, Pratt & Letchworth, 1890s, 13 1/2 In. 1595.00
Horse & Wagon, Dump, Sand & Gravel, 2 Horses, Kenton, c.1950, 15 In. 305.00
Horse & Wagon, Farm, Cast Iron, Green Wagon, 2 Horses, Kenton, Box, 15 In. 303.00
Horse & Wagon, Grocery, Tin Lithograph, Chein, 11 In. 440.00
Horse & Wagon, Hay, 2 Black Horses, Cast Iron, Red Wheels, Vindex, 14 1/2 In. 2200.00
Horse & Wagon, Ice, Cast Iron, Green, Yellow Wheels 248.00
Horse & Wagon, Painted, Clockwork, Ives, 11 In. 4400.00
Horse & Wagon, Police Patrol, 2 Horses, 3 Policemen, Driver, Hubley, 1910, 19 In. 1295.00
Horse & Wagon, Sand & Gravel, 2 Horses, Cast Iron, Kenton, 10 In. 66.00
Horse & Wagon, Sand & Gravel, 2 Horses, Plated Driver, Kenton, c.1950, 16 1/4 In. 248.00
Horse & Wagon, Side Dump, 2 Black Horses, Cast Iron, Green, Red, Arcade, 14 1/2 In. 6600.00
Horse Cart, Doll's, Carriage Style, 2 Wheels, Long Shaft, Black, White, 40 x 10 In. 110.00
Hot Mammy, Windup, Fisher-Price, 7 In. 550.00
Humphrey Mobile, Joe Palooka, Comic Strip, Wyandotte Windup 475.00
Humphrey Mobile, Joe Palooka, Comic Strip, Wyandotte Windup, Original Box 750.00
Hy-Que Monkey, Battery Operated, Rosko, Box, 17 In. 248.00
Ice Box, Doll's, Alaska, Cast Iron, Food Plates, Green, Hubley, 7 1/2 In. 880.00
Ice Box, Doll's, Alaska, Cast Iron, Food Plates, Green, Hubley, 10 7/8 In. 3300.00
Ice Box, Doll's, Alaska, Cast Iron, Hubley, 5 x 3 In. 65.00
Ice Cream Freezer, Metal, Wood, White Mountain Jr., 8 In. 255.00
Ice Cream Freezer, Wood, Metal, North Bros., 8 In. 310.00
Ice Cream Scooter, 5 Cents, Tin Lithograph, Windup, Courtland, Box, 6 1/2 In. 525.00
J.F.K., In Rocking Chair, Rocks, Plays Happy Days Are Here Again, Windup, Japan, 1960s 475.00
Jack-In-The-Box, Clown, Box Decorated With Toys, Germany, 5 In. 165.00
Jack-In-The-Box, Clown, Red Box, Germany, 5 In. 305.00
Jack-In-The-Box, Happy Hooligan, Composition, Wood Box, Germany, 3 1/2 In. 1430.00
Jazzbo Jim, Dancing On Roof, Tin Lithograph, Windup, Unique Art, 10 In. 358.00
Jazzbo Jim, Dancing On Roof, Tin Lithograph, Windup, Unique Art, Box, 10 In. 440.00
Jazzbo Jim, Tin, Windup, Marx, Box, 10 In. 605.00
Jeep, Commander, Tonka, Box, 1964 .... 138.00
Jeep, Convertible, Converts To Gunship, Tin Friction, Japan, Box, 7 1/2 In. 275.00
Jeep, Jumping, Tin Lithograph, Windup, Marx, 6 In. 120.00
Jeep, Lifeguard, Red, Insert, Wishbook, Tonka, Box, 1960 .... 715.00
Jeep, Pressed Steel, Plastic Surrey Top, Tonka, 1960s, 10 In. 110.00
Jeep, Tow, Plow, Tonka, Box, 1972 .... 165.00
Jeep, Tow, Tonka, Box, 1960 .... 275.00
Jeep & Trailer, Willys, Pressed Steel, Canvas Top, Marx, Box, 21 In. 330.00
Jenny, The Balking Mule, Clown Driver, Strauss 350.00
Jewel Case, Barbie, Piano, Musical, Soft Lining, Suzy Goose, Box, 1954 .... 330.00
Joe Penner & His Ducks, Tin Lithograph, Windup, Marx, 8 1/2 In. 525.00
Joy Rider Crazy Car, Marx, 1925 .... 495.00
Jumbo, The Elephant, On Wheels, Pull Toy, Hubley, Original Box, 5 In. 175.00
Jumping Jack, 2-Sided, Plaster Face, Wooden Body, Articulated, 10 In. 230.00
Jumping Jack, 2-Sided, Plaster Face, Wooden Body, Painted, Articulated, 13 1/2 In. 430.00
Jungle Trio, Elephant Blows Whistle, Monkey Plays Cymbals, Tin, Linemar, Box, 8 In. ... 592.00
Kadi, 2 Chinese Men Carrying Tea Cart, Tin Litho, Friction, Lehmann, Germany, 7 In. 880.00

Kaleidoscope, Tubular Barrel, Walnut Stand, c.1873, 10 x 3 1/2 In. 845.00
Kaleidoscope, Wallpaper Covered, 1800s 450.00
Kestner, 264, Catterfelder Puppenfabrik, Bisque Socket Head, Wood, Composition, 28 In. . 415.00
Kid Sampson, Holding Mallet, Rings Bell At Carnival, Windup, B&R, 1921 . . . . 875.00
Kitten, Mohair, Gray, Striped, Jointed, Excelsior Stuffing, Glass Eyes, 1920, 11 In. 355.00
Knife & Badge, Deputy Sheriff, On Card, Imperial Knife Co., Box 45.00
Knitting Grandma, Cat, Battery Operated, TN, Box, 9 In. 66.00
Knock-Out Prize Fighters, Tin Lithograph, Windup, Strauss, c.1921, 5 x 4 3/4 In. 565.00
Koala, Mohair, Cream, Brown Eyes, Shaved Hands, Feet, Steiff, 14 1/2 In. 235.00
Komikal Kop, Crazy Car, Marx, 1927 . . . . 395.00
Lamb, Mohair, Green Eyes, Embroidered Nose, Mouth, Steiff, c.1950, 11 1/2 x 9 In. 150.00
Lapel Pin, Man Tipping Hat, Tin Lithograph, Pull String, Kellermann, 3 3/4 In. 77.00
Lawnmower, Cast Iron, 28 In. 200.00
Li'l Abner Canoe, Plastic, Polecat Paddles, Unique Art, 8 1/2 In. 700.00
Li'l Abner Canoe, Polecat, Paddle, Plastic, Ideal, Box, 1951, 12 In. 350.00
Li'l Abner Dogpatch Band, Tin Lithograph, Windup, Unique Art, 9 In. . . . . .350.00 to 550.00
Li'l Abner Dogpatch Band, Tin Lithograph, Windup, Unique Art, Box, 1945 . . . . 790.00
Lion, Blows Bubbles, Eyes Light, Tin, Battery Operated, MT, Box, 7 1/2 In. 125.00
Lion, Circus, Battery Operated, 10 In. 132.00
Lion, Mohair, Fully Jointed, Glass Eyes, Steiff, c.1920, 11 In. 200.00
Little Calculator, Boy In Blue Suit At Blackboard, Tin, Windup, Tip & Co. 3105.00
Llama, Cream, Black, Brown, Brown Glass Eyes, Steiff, c.1960, 16 1/2 In. 118.00
Locomotive, Ride 'Em, Pressed Steel, Keystone, 1930s, 26 In. . . . . .275.00 to 550.00
Locomotive, Ride On, 20th Century Limited, Pressed Steel, Steelcraft, 23 In. 275.00
Log Cabin, Wooden, Germany, Box 55.00
Lottery Wheel, Toys, Prizes, Cabinet Base, Wood Frame, France, c.1870, 32 In. 1680.00
Lullaby Mother, Rocking Baby, Lullaby Plays, Vinyl Hands, Alps, 10 In. 125.00
Maggie & Jiggs, Fighting, Tin, Windup, Licensed, Nifty, Germany, 8 In. 660.00
Maggie & Jiggs, Rolling, Tin, Windup, Platform, Nifty, Germany, Box, 1924, 7 In. 2250.00
Maggie & Jiggs, Wheels, Unlicensed, 8 In. 605.00
Man, On Horseback, Tin, Yellow Base, 4 Wheels, Pull Toy, Austria, 8 In. 770.00
Man, Roly Poly, Black Hat, Yellow Suit, Papier-Mache, Germany, 8 In. 195.00
Mangle, Electric, Deluxe, Buffalo Toy & Tool Works 35.00
Manure Spreader, Cast Iron, Red, Green, Yellow, Vindex, c.1928, 12 In. 3850.00
Marina Set, Trailer, Boats, Motors, Tonka, Box, 1962 . . . . 1650.00
Martin Drunkard, Tin, Windup, France, 8 In. 275.00
Merry-Go-Round, 3 Horses, Painted, Germany 303.00
Merry-Go-Round, Clockwork, Music, Painted, Gunthermann, Germany, 10 In. 1430.00
Merry-Go-Round, Playland, Tin, Windup, Chein, 10 In. 440.00
Merry-Go-Round, Sunny Andy, Spins, Tin, Spring Loaded Crank, Wolverine, 12 x 11 In. . . 340.00
Merry-Go-Round, Tin Lithograph, Windup, Chein, 10 In. 176.00
Merry-Go-Round, Wyandotte, 1952 . . . . 395.00
Merrymakers Band, Mice, Tin Lithograph, Windup, Marx, 9 In. . . . . .880.00 to 1095.00
Midget Racers, Metal, 3 Cars, Kiddie Toy, Hubley, Box, 7 In. 440.00
Mighty Kong, Kong Walks, Beats Chest, Roars, Shackles, Chains, Marx, Box, 11 In. 845.00
Mikado Family, Man Pulling Rickshaw, Tin Litho, Friction, Lehmann, Germany, 7 In. 1540.00
Milk Maid, Jointed Wood, Cloth Dress, 8 In. 715.00
Milton Berle, Crazy Car, Tin Lithograph, Windup, Marx, Box, 6 1/2 In. . . . . .350.00 to 440.00
Milton Berle, Money Car, Tin, Spinning Head, Windup, 7 x 5 In. 77.00
Mischievous Monkey, Teases Dog, Dog Barks, Tin, MT, Box, 13 x 9 In. . . . . .260.00 to 280.00
Mobile Home, Pressed Steel, Nylint, Box, 29 In. 550.00
Mobile Hospital, Air Force, Friction, Japan, c.1960, 8 In. 95.00
Mobile Power Digger, Pressed Steel, Buddy L, 1950s, 24 In. 250.00
Model Kit, Car, Alfa Romeo, Plastic, Unbuilt, MPC, 8 In. 11.00
Model Kit, Car, Austin Healey, Unbuilt, Strombecker, Box, 7 In. 65.00
Model Kit, Car, Ferrari, Plastic, Merit, Box, 7 In. 33.00
Model Kit, Car, Ford GTP, Plastic, Unbuilt, IMC, Box, 8 In. 11.00
Model Kit, Car, Formula 1 Racing, Diecast, Plastic, Unbuilt, Box, 10 In. 17.00
Model Kit, Car, Hot Rod, U-Build-It, Plastic, Nosco, Box, 10 In. 385.00
Model Kit, Car, Indianapolis 500 Racer, Diecast Metal, Hubley, Box, 10 x 12 In. 110.00
Model Kit, Car, Jaguar, Competition Racer, Plastic, Lindberg Line, Box, 9 In. 18.00
Model Kit, Car, Man From U.N.C.L.E., AMT, Box, 1967, 5 1/4 x 9 1/4 In. 150.00
Model Kit, Car, Maserati 5000 GT, Plastic, Unbuilt, Hawk, Box, 7 In. 6.00

Model Kit, Car, Mercedes-Benz, Plastic, Strombecker, Box, 12 In. 66.00
Model Kit, Car, Mercedes-Benz, Plastic, Unbuilt, Samwa, Box, 9 In. 66.00
Model Kit, Car, Miller Special, 1931 Indianapolis 500 Winner, Aurora, Box, 9 In. 45.00
Model Kit, Frankenstein, Universal Pictures, Aurora, Unopened, 1961, 13 In. 350.00
Monkey, Blows Bubbles, Tin Lithograph, Cloth, Plastic, Battery Operated, 10 1/2 In. 100.00
Monkey, Chatter, Pull Toy, Fisher-Price 50.00
Monkey, Circus, Fabric Clothes, Schoenhut, 7 1/2 In. 525.00
Monkey, Circus, Magic, Seal, Tin, Plastic, Windup, T.P.S., Box, 6 1/2 In. 72.00
Monkey, Clockwork, Ives, Box 2860.00
Monkey, Hula Hoop, Tin Lithograph, Japan, 1950s, 9 x 5 1/4 In. 75.00
Monkey, Jocko, Mohair, Brown, Steiff, c.1950, 9 In. 88.00
Monkey, Jumbo Climbing, Marx, Box, 10 In. 88.00
Monkey, Mongo, Mohair, Multicolored, Steiff, 9 In. 88.00
Monkey, On Pole, Tin, Germany, Penny Toy, 11 In. 300.00
Monkey, On Seal, Tin Lithograph, Windup, Cragstan, Japan, Box, 5 In. 75.00
Monkey, Tin, Painted, Clockwork, Red Jacket, Green Hat 495.00
Monkey, With Violin, Tin, Felt Clothes, Clockwork, Schuco, Germany, 4 1/2 In. 165.00
Monkey, Yes No, Mohair, Stuffed, Felt, Glass Eyes, Schuco, Germany, 13 1/2 In. 190.00
Monkey, Zippo, Climbing, Tin Lithograph, Marx, Box, 10 In. 55.00
Monkey & Bear Set, Monkey, 5 Bears, Ladder, Swing Set, Steiff 605.00
Monkeys, Performing, Cast Iron, Pull Toy, 12 In. 6600.00
Moon Detector, Tin, Battery Operated, Japan, 9 In. 385.00
Moon Explorer, Tin Lithograph, Windup, TT, Japan, Box, 1960s, 6 In. 145.00
Moon Mullins, Handcar, Kayo, Tin Lithograph, Windup, Marx, Box, 6 1/2 In. . . . . .550.00 to 605.00
Motor, Boat, Buccaneer 25, Battery Operated, Japan, 5 1/2 In. 248.00
Motor, Boat, Evinrude 35, Battery Operated, Japan, 5 1/2 In. 165.00
Motorcoach, Driver, Windup, Lehmann 450.00
Motorcycle, Black, Rider, Battery-Operated, Modern Toys, Box, 10 In. 635.00
Motorcycle, Harley-Davidson, Rolls, Cast Iron, White Rubber Tires, Champion, 7 In. 590.00
Motorcycle, Highway Patrol, Tin Lithograph, Friction, Japan, 1960s, 6 In. 225.00
Motorcycle, Indian Brand, Rider, Cast Iron, Yellow, Hubley, 9 1/2 In. 8250.00
Motorcycle, Motodrill, Tin, Windup, Schuco, Germany, Box, 5 In. 495.00
Motorcycle, Parcel Post, Driver, Hubley, 10 In. 2090.00
Motorcycle, Patrol, Rider, Green, Cast Iron, Rubber Tires, c.1940, 4 x 6 1/4 In. 275.00
Motorcycle, Police, Cast Iron, Rubber Tires, 6 1/2 In. 396.00
Motorcycle, Police, Sidecar, 2 Policemen, Hubley, 8 1/2 In. 875.00
Motorcycle, Police, Tin Lithograph, Friction, Haji, Japan, Box, 13 In. 35.00
Motorcycle, Policeman, Kilgore, c.1933, 4 3/4 In. 1045.00
Motorcycle, Policeman, Nickel Wheels, Blue, Champion, 5 In. 275.00
Motorcycle, Policeman, Rookie Cop, Tin Lithograph, Windup, Marx, Box, 8 1/2 In. 385.00
Motorcycle, Policeman, Rubber Tires, Blue, Champion, 7 1/4 In. 500.00
Motorcycle, Policeman, Sidecar, Blue, Hubley, 4 In. 250.00
Motorcycle, Red & Gold, Cast Iron, Rubber Tires, Hubley, 4 1/4 x 9 In. 440.00
Motorcycle, Space Patrol Super Cycle, Tin, Friction, Bandai, 12 In. 2080.00
Motorcycle, Tin Lithograph, Penny Toy, 3 1/2 In. 275.00
Motorcycle, Tin Lithograph, Windup, Technofix, Germany, 7 In. 275.00
Motorcycle, Tricky, Tin, Windup, Marx, Box, 4 In. 220.00
Motorcycle, Tricky, Tin, Windup, Technofix, Box 645.00
Motorcycle, U.S. Air Mail, Indian Decal, Driver, Cast Iron, Hubley, 10 In. 2750.00
Motorcycle, World Champion, Battery Operated, Masudaya, Japan, 1950s, 11 3/4 In. 450.00
Mouse, Cymbals, Lever, Tin, Germany, 6 In. 275.00
Mouse, Lop Ear Louie, Fisher-Price, 10 In. 165.00
Mr. Baseball Jr., Tin, Battery, Swings, Hits Ball, Original Balls, Sankei, 7 In. 575.00
Mr. Fox, Magician, Battery Operated, Cragstan, Box, 9 In. 415.00
Mr. Fox, Magician, With Rabbit, Battery, Yonezawa, Box 750.00
My Merry Jewelry Store, Merry Co., Box, 1960, 8 x 10 In. 176.00
My Merry Supermarket, Merry Co., Box, 1959, 10 x 8 In. 176.00
Mysterious Ball, Tin Lithograph, Martain, France, c.1900, 13 In. 935.00
New Century Cycle, Tin Lithograph, Windup, Lehmann, Germany, 5 In. 550.00
Noah's Ark, 40 Animals, Carved, Painted, Peaked Roof, Flower Border, 17 In. 920.00
Noah's Ark, Paper On Wood, Flat Bottom, 19 Animal Pairs, Others, People, 18 In. 770.00
Noah's Ark, Papier-Mache, Wood, Faux Thatch Roof Cabin, Steiff, 35 In. 770.00
Noah's Ark, Pine, Plaster Noah, Painted & Stamped, 28 Animals, 9 x 18 1/4 In. 890.00

Toy, Pail, Biplane Over Holland,
Dutch Girls, Windmill, Wire Bail,
T. Bros., 4 In.

Toy, Pail, Ocean Grove,
Border Of Roses, Wire Bail,
Wooden Grip, 5 1/2 In.

Toy, Pail, Sea Side, Sand,
Wire Bail, Wooden Grip,
T. Bros., 5 3/4 In.

Noah's Ark, Wooden, Flat Bottom, Painted, Animal Pairs, Bird Pairs, Dove, Germany, 24 In. 1210.00
Nutty Nibs, Native Flips Balls Into Mouth, Rolls Eyes, 3 Balls, Battery, Linemar, 12 In. .. 960.00
Odd Ogg, Play Ball, 4 Balls, Battery Operated, Ideal, Box, 1962, 13 In. 335.00
Oscar, Riding Cart, Tin Friction, France, 6 In. 550.00
Paddy & The Pig, Man In Hat On Pig, Red Blanket, Tin, Windup, Lehmann, c.1903 ...... 805.00
Pail, 3 Little Pigs, Tin Lithograph, 5 1/2 In. 250.00
Pail, Biplane Over Holland, Dutch Girls, Windmill, Wire Bail, T. Bros., 4 In. .... *Illus* 330.00
Pail, Children Playing Under Sprinkler, Tin, U.S. Metal Toy Co., 4 x 7 In. 75.00
Pail, Humpty Dumpty, Tin, Chad Valley, 3 1/2 x 5 In. 45.00
Pail, Metal, Patio Pot, Flowers, 6 In. 49.00
Pail, Ocean Grove, Border Of Roses, Wire Bail, Wooden Grip, 5 1/2 In. .... *Illus* 690.00
Pail, Remember The Maine, Tin Lithograph, Embossed Image, Candy Box, Fan 415.00
Pail, Sea Side, Sand, Wire Bail, Wooden Grip, T. Bros., 5 3/4 In. .... *Illus* 165.00
Pail, Tin, Red Ryder, Indian Chief, Hinged Handle, Ohio Art, 4 1/4 x 4 1/4 In. 40.00
Panorama, Bible, Lithograph, Wood Frame, Scroll Scenes, Milton Bradley, 11 x 6 In. 330.00
Parrot, Pretty Peggy, Battery Operated, Rosko, Box, 11 In. 130.00
Peacock, Tin Lithograph, Windup, Rubber Feet, Alps, 5 1/2 In. 110.00
Peacock, Tin, Windup, Distler, Germany, 9 In. 330.00
Pedal Car, Airplane, Airmail, Pressed Steel, Steelcraft, 1930s, 30 x 45 In. ....2200.00 to 3575.00
Pedal Car, Airplane, Navy Patrol, Pressed Steel, Steelcraft, 1940s, 36-In. Wingspan 1100.00
Pedal Car, Airplane, Rolls Racer, Airmail, Wood, Cast Hardware, 24 In. 715.00
Pedal Car, Airplane, Streak Sky, Pressed Steel, Red, White, Murray, 1950s, 46 In. 1650.00
Pedal Car, Airplane, Supersonic Jet, Pressed Steel, Murray, 1950s, 48 In. 2090.00
Pedal Car, Austin, Pressed Steel, Rubber Tires, England, 56 In. 1045.00
Pedal Car, Boat, Jolly Roger Flagship 590.00
Pedal Car, Boat, Jolly Roger, Pressed Steel, Murray, 1960s, 41 In. 770.00
Pedal Car, Boat, Jolly Roger, Pressed Steel, Windscreen, Murray, Ohio, 1967, 46 In. 1100.00
Pedal Car, Chrysler, 1941 Model, Pressed Steel, Steelcraft, 1940s, 38 In. 1870.00
Pedal Car, Chrysler, 1947 Model, Burgundy, Cream, Steelcraft, 37 In. 1540.00
Pedal Car, Chrysler, Town & Country, Wood, Pressed Steel, Steger, 1948, 42 In. 1440.00
Pedal Car, Dude Wagon, Pressed Steel, Green, Murray, 1950s, 39 In. 605.00
Pedal Car, Erskine, Toledo Metal Wheel Co., 1927-30, 37 In. 9900.00
Pedal Car, Fire Chief, Durant, Wood, Pressed Steel, Steelcraft, 1920s, 41 In. 2255.00
Pedal Car, Fire Truck, Airflow Fire Dep't., Pressed Steel, Ladders, Steelcraft, 1937, 44 In. .. 1650.00
Pedal Car, Good Humor Truck, Pressed Steel, Murray, 1955, 36 In. 1075.00
Pedal Car, Highway Patrol, Pressed Steel, Murray, 1970s, 33 In. 35.00
Pedal Car, Hot Rod, Pressed Steel, Chain Driven, Garton, 1950s, 36 In. 250.00
Pedal Car, Iron, Wood, c.1900, 48 x 20 In. 2600.00
Pedal Car, Lincoln Zephyr, Pressed Steel, Gold, Orange, Steelcraft, 1940s, 41 In. 2090.00
Pedal Car, Lincoln Zephyr, Pressed Steel, Red, Steelcraft, 1940s, 42 In. 550.00
Pedal Car, Oldsmobile, Station Wagon, Pressed Steel, Murray, 1940s, 45 In. 360.00
Pedal Car, Packard, Red, American National, 1920s, 45 In. 2200.00
Pedal Car, Pinto, Green, Murray, 33 In. 55.00
Pedal Car, Racing, Pressed Steel, Plastic Windscreen, Triang, 1950s, 47 In. 1155.00

Pedal Car, Rocket, Green, 22 x 35 x 20 In. 1095.00
Pedal Car, Skippy Line, Pressed Steel, Gendron, 1930s, 36 In. 130.00
Pedal Car, Skippy Roadster, Pressed Steel, Leather Seat, Red, Gendron, 1940, 44 In. 1705.00
Pedal Car, Skippy Series, Pressed Steel, Garton, 1940s, 36 In. 275.00
Pedal Car, Sports Car, Pressed Steel, Plastic, Music Box, AMF Radio, 1970s, 36 In. 525.00
Pedal Car, Station Wagon, Circle G Ranch, Pressed Steel, Wood, Garton, 1940s, 40 In. 525.00
Pedal Car, Station Wagon, Oldsmobile, Pressed Steel, Murray, 1940s, 46 In. ......175.00 to 300.00
Pedal Car, Thunderbird, Pressed Steel, Murray, 1960s, 32 In. ....100.00 to 140.00
Pedal Car, Tin Lizzie, Yellow, Garton, 1963 .... 1020.00
Pedal Car, Tractor, John Deere, 20 Series, With Trailer 230.00
Pedal Car, Tractor, Pressed Steel, Trailer, BMC, 1950s, 62 In. 200.00
Pedal Car, Tractor, Wooden Wagon, Pressed Steel, Chain Driven, Western Flyer, 65 In. ... 360.00
Pedal Car, Vespa, Bullet Sidecar, Pressed Steel, Blue, 41 In. 495.00
Pedal Car, Wooden Steering Wheel, Brown, Orange, Yellow, Jordan, 46 In. 375.00
Pedal Car, Zephyr, Windshield, Hood Ornament, Headlights, Steelcraft, 1940s, 48 In. 1540.00
Piano, Lithographed Angels, Bliss, 12 x 19 1/4 In. 250.00
Piano, Paper Lithograph On Wood, Paint, Schoenhut, 13 In. 70.00
Piano, Wood, Paper Lithograph, Schoenhut, 10 x 16 In. 90.00
Pianolodeon Player, Plastic, 4 Rolls, J. Chein & Co., c.1949, 20 x 20 In. 70.00
Pig, On Stick, Cast Iron, Ives 770.00
Pig, Windup, Composition, Red Bow, Descamps, Box, 12 In. 2750.00
Pillsbury Doughboy, Squeeze, 1971, 6 In. 15.00
Planetarium, Junior, Original Box, Spitz, 1950, 15 In. 45.00
Play Set, Alaska, Marx, Box 385.00
Play Set, Alaska, Marx, Box, Unopened, 26 In. 2640.00
Play Set, Bat Masterson, Indian Fighter, Unused, Box 330.00
Play Set, Captain Gallant Of Foreign Legion, Marx, Box 1760.00
Play Set, Civil War Centennial, Happi Time, Box 1650.00
Play Set, Custer's Last Stand, Sears, Allstate, Marx, Box 3025.00
Play Set, Fort Apache, Rin Tin Tin, Series 500, Marx, Box 550.00
Play Set, Gunsmoke, Dodge City, Series 2000, Marx, Box 3300.00
Play Set, Gunsmoke, Marshal Dillon's, Box 1100.00
Play Set, Johnny Ringo, Western Frontier, Marx 6210.00
Play Set, Military Academy, Marx, Box 770.00
Play Set, Rifleman Ranch, Marx, Box 3575.00
Play Set, Untouchables, Marx, Box 5225.00
Play Set, Western Ranch, Bunkhouse, Marx, Box 96.00
Play Set, Yogi Bear, Jellystone National Park, Box 880.00
Playland Whip, Bumper Cars, Windup, Tin Lithograph, Chein, 1950s, 20 x 11 In. 300.00
Playtime Set, 1935 Model Fords, 5 Cars, Trailer, Tow Truck, Tootsietoy, Box 1210.00
Police Patrol, Auto-Tricycle, Tin Lithograph, Battery, Nomura, Japan, c.1958, 9 1/2 In. ... 230.00
Political Stump Speaker, Key, Bag, Clothes, Ives, Box, c.1880s 12650.00
Pony Blimp, Green, Kenton, 5 3/4 In. 600.00
Pool Player, 3 Players, Tin, Painted, Guntherman, Germany, 9 x 8 1/4 x 7 In. 6600.00
Pool Player, Tin, Germany, Penny Toy, 4 In. 195.00
Pool Player, Tin, Painted, Guntherman 715.00
Pop Gun, Army Sparkling, Tin, Wood, Marx, Box, 24 In. 165.00
Pop Gun, King, Wood Stock, Metal Barrel, Markham Air Rifle Co. 55.00
Porky Pig, Twirling Umbrella, Holding Hat, Tin, Lithograph, Windup, Marx, 1939 .450.00 to 755.00
Potty Girl, Tin, Lever Action, Mouse Comes Out Of Pot, German, 5 In. 303.00
Power Shovel, Structo, Box, 20 In. 220.00
Powerful Katrinka, Holding Jimmy, Tin Lithograph, Windup, Fontaine Fox, 5 In. 1210.00
Powerful Katrinka, Jimmy In Wheelbarrow, Tin Lithograph, Windup, F. Fox, 5 1/2 In. 1210.00
Preacher, Black, Clockwork, Wood Podium, Ives, Box, 1880s, 10 1/2 In. 7150.00
Pushy Pat, Push Toy, Fisher-Price, 12 In. 1980.00
Puzzle Ring, Mickey Mouse & Betty Boop, 5 Different Rings, Japan 235.00
Rabbit, Blows Bubbles, Windup, Plush Over Tin, Alps, Japan, 1958, 10 1/2 In. 225.00
Rabbit, Brown Mohair, Standing, White Shirt, Gloss Eye, Steiff, 28 In. 175.00
Rabbit, Bunny Baby Carriage, Celluloid, Mechanical, Japan, Box, 6 1/2 In. 60.00
Rabbit, Bunny Magician, Battery Operated, Box, 14 In. 220.00
Rabbit, Busy Housekeeper, Vacuum, Tin, Battery, Alps, Japan, Box, 1950s, 10 1/2 In. 285.00
Rabbit, Easter, Delivery Cycle, Push Toy, Wyandotte, 1930, 5 In. 240.00
Rabbit, Happy Bunny, Yonezawa, 1950s, 14 In. 350.00

Rabbit, Nodder, Holding Saxophone, Large Horn, Celluloid, 7 1/4 In. 220.00
Rabbit, Picnic Bunny, Battery Operated, Alps, Box, 11 In. 70.00
Rabbit, Pushing Baby Carriage, Plastic, Yellow, Green Trim, E. Rosen, 9 In. 85.00
Rabbit, Roly Dolly, Composition, Painted, Schoenhut, 9 In. 340.00
Rabbit, Running, Felt, Wooden Wheels, Steiff, 15 1/4 In. 520.00
Rabbit, Smoking, Battery Operated, Cragstan, 10 In. 80.00
Rabbit, Telephone, Battery Operated, Japan, Box, 9 In. . . . . .165.00 to 395.00
Rabbit, Walker, Mohair, Mechanical, Key, 1920s, 9 In. 605.00
Radar Station, Revolving Scope, Lights, Telegraph Keys, Tin, Masudaya, Box, 10 In. 365.00
Range Rider, Tin, Windup, Marx, 1950s, 10 1/2 x 11 1/4 In. . . . . .115.00 to 250.00
Rap & Tap Boxer, Original Box, Unique Art 750.00
Rattle, Humpty Dumpty, 3 Attached Bells, White Metal, Cast Inscription, 5 3/4 In. 2.30
Rattle, Stamped Alphabet, For A Good Child, Whistle, Tin, 5 1/2 In. 66.00
Rattle Ball, Patchwork, Mennonite, Lancaster County, Pa., c.1910, 2 1/2 In. 460.00
Refrigerator, Tin Lithograph, Accessories, Pink, Marx, Box, 14 In.   110.00
Rex Mars, Rocket Fighter, Tin, Windup, Marx, 12 In. 1045.00
Rickshaw, Convertible, Passenger, Lamps, Fenders, Wire Wheels, Tin, 10 x 7 In. 1200.00
Ring, The Shadow Radio Show, Premium, Blue Coal, Glows In Dark, 1941 . . . .   650.00
Road Paver, Tonka, 1973 . . . .   99.00
Road Roller, Cast Iron, Wallworks Foundry, England, 14 1/4 In. 468.00
Road Roller, Crazy Car, Rubber Band Windup, Archer Plastic Co., 1950s, 4 1/2 In. 75.00
Road Roller, Pressed Steel, Buddy L, 20 In. 4400.00
Road Roller, Pressed Steel, Steelcraft, 1930s, 16 1/2 In. 330.00
Road Roller, Tin, Windup, Driver, Marx, Box, 8 In. 825.00
Robot, Answer Game, Does Math Problems, Tin, Battery, Ichida, Box, 14 1/2 In. 508.00
Robot, Astro Dog, Space Suit, Battery Operated, Box, 11 In. 65.00
Robot, Astroman, Walker, Tin, Rubber Hands, Windup, 10 1/2 In.   5368.00
Robot, Astronaut, Walker, Helmet Lights, Tin, Battery, Remote Control, Linemar, 7 In. . . .   1300.00
Robot, Atomic Man, Walks, Arms Swing, Tin, Windup, Japan, Box, 5 In. 930.00
Robot, Banzai, Yonezawa, Japan, 1960s, 8 In. 450.00
Robot, Col. Haphazard, NASA, Battery Operated, 12 1/2 In. 325.00
Robot, Dino, Stop, Go, Head Opens, Light-Up, Screams, Battery, 11 In. . . . . .425.00 to 480.00
Robot, Door, Tin, Lights Up, Walks, Swings Arms, Spinners Rotate, Alps, 9 1/2 In. 3800.00
Robot, Jupiter, Plastic, Tin Instrument Panels, Windup, Yoshiya, Japan, 7 In. 100.00
Robot, Lantern, Steel Gray, Shoots, Original Box, Instructions, Linemar, 1950s 5990.00
Robot, Lilliput, Walks, Claw Spring Hands, Tin, Windup, KT, Japan, Box, 6 1/4 In. 1495.00
Robot, Lost In Space, Plastic, Red & Blue, Battery Operated, Remco, Box, 13 In. 415.00
Robot, Mighty, Mechanical, Tin Lithograph, Windup, Japan, Box, 6 In. 65.00
Robot, Monster, Plastic, Taiwan, Box, 9 In. 35.00
Robot, Mr. Atom, Plastic, Battery Operated, Advance Doll & Toy Co., Box, 18 In. 335.00
Robot, Mr. Atomic, Bump & Go, Light-Up, Tin, Battery Operated, Yonezawa, 9 In. 2630.00
Robot, Mr. Mercury, Gold, Tin, Batteries, Remote Control, Marx, Box, 13 In. 675.00
Robot, Piston Action, Walks, Rubber Hand, Battery, Nomura, Japan, 9 In. 1150.00
Robot, Planet, Windup, Walks, Sparks, Japan, Box, 1960s, 9 In. 665.00
Robot, Radar, Tin Lithograph, Battery Operated, SH, Japan, Box, 1960s, 11 1/2 In. 275.00
Robot, Robotank-Z, Tin, TN, Japan, Box, 10 In. 440.00
Robot, Rocket Man, Tin, Plastic, Walks, Swings Arms, Head Light-Up, Alps, 13 In. 1540.00
Robot, Rosco Astronaut, Tin, Plastic Dome, Rubber Hands, Battery, Japan, 13 In. 770.00
Robot, Space Explorer, 11 In. 90.00
Robot, Space X70, Tulip Head, Walks, Lights Flash, Head Opens, Camera, 12 In. 1825.00
Robot, Sparky, Silver, Tin, Yoshiya, Japan, Original Box, 7 1/2 In. . . . . .675.00 to 760.00
Robot, Star, Plastic, Hong Kong, Box, 12 In. 120.00
Robot, Super Boy, Walks, Light On Helmet, Battery, Nomura, Japan, 12 In 1800.00
Robot, Super, Rotate-O-Matic, Walks, Doors Open, Gun Shoots, Tin, Plastic, 12 In. 140.00
Robot, Swinging Baby, Mechanical, Yonezawa, Box 850.00
Robot, Thunder, Japan, 11 1/2 In. 4125.00
Robot, Ultra Seven, Windup, Bullmark, Box, 1970s, 9 In. 850.00
Rocker, Doll's, Green Paint, Turned Posts, Woven Seat, 2-Slat Back, 6 1/4 x 14 1/4 In. 175.00
Rocket, Jet Mobile, Ride On, Pressed Steel, 1950s, 36 In. 250.00
Rocket Ship, Building Set, 2 Rockets, Metal, Instructions, Dan Dare, England, c.1950 . . . .   195.00
Rodeo Joe, Driving Car, Tin Lithograph, Windup, Unique Art, 7 1/2 In. 200.00
Roller Coaster, 2 Cars, Tin, Mechanical, Chein, Box, 19 In. . . . . .385.00 to 550.00
Roller Coaster, Coney Island, Original Box 2400.00

Roller Coaster, Jet, Tin, Windup, Wolverine, 22 In.	140.00
Rooster, Pulling Easter Rabbit, Cart, Flywheel, Lehmann, 7 1/2 In.	460.00
Roulette Man, Mixed Material, Lever Operated, Plaything, Box, 9 1/4 In.	165.00
Roulette Wheel, Toy Bazaar, 4 Shelves, Slanted Roof, Wood Box, France, c.1890, 24 In.	1176.00
Safari Set, Ford Bronco, Ny-Lint, Box, 1963	295.00
Sail Away, Tin, Lever Operated, Plastic Boats, Windup, Spins, Unique Art, 9 In.	165.00
Sailor, Tin Lithograph, Mechanical, Lehmann, Germany, c.1915, 7 1/2 In.	390.00
Sam, City Gardener, Pushes Cart, Tools, Windup, Marx, Box	350.00
Sandy Andy, Tin, Sand Can, Wolverine, 14 In.	1320.00
School Set, District, Painted Wood Figures, Slotted Bases, Crandall, Box	1320.00
Schoolhouse, 6 Teddy Bears At Desks, Teacher Bear, Jointed, Original Box	425.00
Schoolhouse, French Renaissance, Furnishings, 5 Bisque Dolls, c.1910, 39 x 27 In.	6600.00
Schoolroom, Cardboard, Students, Nun Teacher, 4 Desks, Lectern, France, c.1890, 17 In.	1460.00
Schoolroom, Desks, Accessories, 8 Bisque Children, France, c.1900	3850.00
Schoolroom, Wood Frame, Paper Lithograph, 7 Students, Teacher, France, c.1900, 19 In.	950.00
Schoolroom, Wood, 9 Students, Teacher, Musical, Mechanical, France, c.1890, 19 In.	2465.00
Scissors, Magician's, Tin, Lever Action, Germany	220.00
Scooter, Silver Pigeon, Tin Lithograph, Friction, Bandai, Japan, 1960s, 9 1/2 In.	265.00
Sea Lion, Performing, Tin Lithograph, Windup, Lehmann, Germany, 7 In.	140.00
Sewing Cabinet, Doll's, Wood, Flowers, Mirrored Interior, France, c.1885, 6 In.	475.00
Sewing Machine, Little Beauty, Black Finish, Red & Gilt Scrolls, Chrome Wheel, 1910	365.00
Sewing Machine, Little Comfort, Cast Metal, Wood Box, 7 In.	480.00
Sewing Machine, Singer, A Singer For The Girls, Instructions, Box	470.00
Sewing Machine, Singer, Sew Handy, Child's, 1950s	375.00
Sewing Machine, Singer, Sheet Metal, Painted, 7 In.	115.00
Sheep, Wood, Gesso, Gray Wool Coat, Wooden Base, Pull Toy, 6 1/2 x 6 In.	550.00
Sheriff Garrett, Accessories, Poly-Plastic, Marx, Box, 1973, 11 1/2 In.	125.00
Sheriff Sam, Whoopie Car, Tin, Plastic, Windup, Marx, Box, 6 In.	495.00
Shooting Gallery, Posse, Tin Lithograph, Windup, Wyandotte, 11 x 14 In.	70.00
Shooting Gallery, Tin Lithograph, Pulley, Ducks, Rotating Bull's-Eye, 14 x 11 In.	90.00
Shutterbug, Boy Takes Pictures, Walks, Turns Head, Camera Flashes, Tin, Box, 9 In.	900.00
Shutterbug, Man, Camera, Tin Lithograph, Battery, TN, Japan, Box, 1950s, 8 1/2 In.	545.00
Sign, Go, Cast Iron, Embossed, Red, Gold Trim, c.1925, 5 In.	250.00
Sign, Highway 41, Cast, White, Yellow, Red, Arcade, 5 1/4 In.	605.00
Sign, Main Street, Street Lamp, Cast Iron, Warner Bros., 5 1/2 In.	470.00
Sink, Tin Lithograph, Accessories, Marx, Box, 12 In.	99.00
Ski Ride, 2 Skiers, Tin Lithograph, Windup, Chein, 19 x 10 x 8 In.	290.00 to 695.00
Sky Rangers, Plane & Dirigible Circle Tower, Tin, Windup, Unique Art, 9 In.	300.00
Sky Rocket, Tetsujin, Bandai, 1960s, 19 In.	600.00
Slate, Lucky, Annie Oakley, Gail Davis, Self Erasing, Horseshoe, Lowe, 8 x 12 In.	55.00
Sled, Battleship, 2 Stacks, Side Wheel, Painted, Late 19th Century, 46 x 12 In.	230.00
Sled, Birds, Tree, Rose Wash, Metal Runners, 60 In.	345.00
Sled, Flexible Flyer, Racing, c.1935, 52 In.	110.00
Sled, Iron Runners, Forged Swans, Red, Blue	175.00
Sled, Lighthouse Landscape, Painted, Wood & Metal Runners, 38 1/2 x 15 In.	330.00
Sled, Old Red Paint, Yellow, Blue, White, Black, Pennsylvania, 30 In.	145.00
Sled, Pine Planks, Blue & White Flowers & Lines, Wood & Metal Runners, 39 x 15 In.	660.00
Sled, Pine Planks, Flowers, Blue Ground, Metal Runners, 14 x 4 1/2 In.	305.00
Sled, Pine Planks, Flowers, Landscape, Red Paint, Wood & Metal Runners, 31 x 10 In.	550.00
Sled, Pine Planks, Flowers, Red Paint, Metal Runners, Serpent Finials, 33 x 12 In.	605.00
Sled, Scrollwork, Roses, Painted, Late 1800s, 37 3/4 In.	295.00
Sled, Winner, Softwood, Paint, Stencil, Iron Runners, Paris Mfg. Co., Maine, 40 x 11 In.	415.00
Sled, Wood, Bird, Flowers, Blue Paint, Late 1800s, 11 x 13 1/2 x 33 1/2 In.	380.00
Sled, Wood, Horse, Red, Metal Runners, Mid-Atlantic States, c.1860, 39 x 12 In.	1920.00
Sled, Wood, Red Ground, Yellow Stencils, Iron Runners, 1920s, 24 In.	115.00
Sled, Wood, Running Horse, Red Paint, Line Detail, 27 1/2 In.	1610.00
Sled, Wood, Upholstered Seat, 48 In.	450.00
Sleigh, 2 Horses, Woman Passenger, Cast Iron, Hubley, 15 In.	1320.00
Sleigh, Doll, Wood, Iron, Flowers, Red Runners, c.1900, 15 In.	1610.00
Sleigh, Wood, Iron Skid, Turned Wood Push Handle, Winchester, 54 x 37 x 17 In.	415.00
Smiling Sam, Carnival Man, Head Shakes, Walks, Twirls Stick, Windup, Alps, Box, 9 In.	300.00
Smoky Sam, Crazy Car, Marx, 1947	395.00
Snappy, Happy Bubble Blowing Dragon, Tin, Plush, Plastic, Battery, Box, 30 In.	4465.00

Snappy Quacky, Pull Toy, Fisher-Price, 8 In. 275.00
Snick-Snack, Man Walking Dog, Tin Lithograph, Windup, Lehmann, Box, 9 1/2 In. 12100.00
Soldier, Sparkling, Crawling, Tin, Windup, Marx, Box, 7 1/2 In. 340.00
Soldier, Take-A-Part, Wood, Doepke, 1956, 9 In. 175.00
Soldier, Tin, Mechanical, Russia, 1930s 135.00
Soldier, U.S. Army Sergeant, Tin, Windup, Chein, Box, 5 In. 110.00
Soldier, Walker, Tin Lithograph, Windup, Chein, 6 In. 200.00
Soldier Set, 16th Century Knights, Lead, Britains, 9 Figures, Box 220.00
Soldier Set, Band Of The Second Dragoons, Lead, Britains, Box 250.00
Soldier Set, Coldstream Guards, Lead, Britains, New Box 99.00
Soldier Set, Drum & Bugles, Lead, Britains, Box, 6 Piece ....110.00 to 165.00
Soldier Set, Highlanders, Lead, Britains, Box, 8 Piece 660.00
Soldier Set, Infantry Marines & West Point, Lead, Britains, Box, 25 Piece 360.00
Soldier Set, Lead, Painted, Nurnberg, Germany, Box, 3 1/2 In. 99.00
Soldier Set, Mexican, Los Rurales De La Federacion, Lead, Britains, Box, 8 Piece 495.00
Soldier Set, Montenegrin Infantry, Lead, Britains, Box, 8 Piece 1100.00
Soldier Set, Navy & Army, Lead, Japan, Box, 14 Piece 165.00
Soldier Set, Reed Royal Cadets, 30 Paper Lithographed Wooden Soldiers, 5 Flags 1650.00
Soldier Set, Sovereign's Standard, Lead, Britains, Box 195.00
Soldier Set, U.S. Army Band, Lead, Britains, Box 1540.00
Soldier Set, Union Infantry, Regiments Of All Nations, Lead, Britains, Box, 7 Piece 165.00
Space Capsule, Apollo 12, Tin Lithograph, Friction, Japan, 1960s, 4 In. 75.00
Space Dog, Tin Lithograph, Silver, Red Ears, Windup, Yoshiya, Japan, 6 In. 415.00
Space Fish, Friction, Japan 270.00
Space Orbiter, Tin, Windup, Plastic Spaceships, Japan, Box, 6 In. 140.00
Space People, Plastic, Archer Plastics, Box, 8 1/2 x 5 1/2 x 1 1/2 In., 3 Piece 220.00
Space Rocket, X-40, Shooting Capsule, Siren, Plastic, Friction, HK, Box, 1960s, 9 In. 155.00
Space Scooter, Tin, Plastic, Modern Toys, Japan, Box, 1960s ....175.00 to 225.00
Space Shuttle, Columbia, Tin, Plastic, Battery Operated, Nave, Spain, 14 In. ......340.00 to 450.00
Space Tank, Spaceman, Battery Operated, Modern Toys, Japan, Box, 1950s, 8 3/4 In. 195.00
Space Trip Station, Instrument Panel, Satellites, Tin, Battery, Yonezawa, 14 In. 1500.00
Space Trooper, Tin, Windup, Haji, 7 In. 600.00
Spaceman, Fighting, Battery Operated, Box, 11 In. 175.00
Spaceship, Plastic, Red, Yellow, Irwin, 8 In. 110.00
Sparkler, Cat, Felix, Short Ears, Tin Lithograph, Pat Sullivan, Germany, 5 In. 303.00
Sparkler, Cat, Felix, The Movie Cat, Lithograph, Tin, Box 1450.00
Spreader, McCormick Deering, 2 Black Horses, Cast Iron, Arcade, 13 1/2 In. 1045.00
Spy Magic Tricks, Man From U.N.C.L.E., Gilbert, Box, 1965, 12 1/2 x 18 1/2 In. 350.00
Squirrel, Perri, Mohair, Chest Tag, Steiff, 6 In. 80.00
Squirt Gun, Automatic Water Pistol, Plastic, Kilgore, Box, 4 3/4 In. 120.00
Squirt Gun, Automatic, Black Enamel Paint, Wyandotte, U.S.A., 7 In. 30.00
Squirt Gun, Daisy, c.1933 .... 60.00
Squirt Gun, Liquid, Cast Iron, 5 In. 85.00
Squirt Gun, Repeater, Ring Trigger, Blue Finish, Daisy, c.1928 .... 90.00
Squirt Gun, Squirt-O-Matic, Water & Noise, Daisy, Plymouth, Mich. ....42.00 to 65.00
Squirt Gun, Steel Tube, Black, Wyandotte, 4 3/4 In. 28.00
Squirt Gun, Thick Ring Trigger Model, Daisy, 1915 Patent 87.00
Squirt Gun, Wire Trigger Guard, Daisy, c.1928 .... 75.00
Stable Set, Insert, Wish Book, Mini-Tonka, Box, 1967 .... 385.00
Stagecoach, Fix-It, Plastic, Ideal, Box, 15 In. 220.00
Stagecoach, Wood, Spoked Metal Wheels, 6 Windows, Domed Roof, c.1900, 15 In. 59.00
Steam Engine, Horizontal, Cast Iron, Denmark, Box, 9 In. 305.00
Steam Engine, Horizontal, Cast Iron, Hand Cranked, Red, Green, Kenton, 8 In. 3575.00
Steam Engine, Vertical, Cast Iron, Red, Green, Kenton, 8 1/2 x 6 1/2 In. 1650.00
Steam Shovel, General, Mounted On Truck, Cast Iron, Hubley, 10 In. 475.00
Steam Shovel, Hercules, Tin, Mack Cab, Chein, 27 In. 990.00
Steam Shovel, Little Jim, Marion, Pressed Steel, J.C. Penney, Steelcraft, 1930s, 20 In. 275.00
Steam Shovel, Little Jim, Pressed Steel, J.C. Penney, Steelcraft, 26 In. 8800.00
Steam Shovel, Pressed Steel, Buddy L, 1950s, 18 In. 90.00
Steam Shovel, Pressed Steel, Buddy L, 20 In. 250.00
Steam Shovel, Pressed Steel, Buddy L, 30 In. 1210.00
Steam Shovel, Pressed Steel, Electric Headlights, Structo, 32 In. 2310.00
Steam Shovel, Pressed Steel, Keystone, 1920s, 19 In. 110.00

Steam Shovel, Pressed Steel, Marx, 1950s, 12 In.	55.00
Steam Shovel, Red & Blue, Tonka, 1949	110.00
Steam Shovel, Red, Green, Nickel Shovel, Rubber Wheels, Hubley, 1934	4125.00
Steam Shovel, Yellow, Black Wooden Wheels, Wyandotte, 1940s, 18 In.	95.00
Steamroller, Cast Iron, Red, Wood Rollers, Dent, 4 3/4 In.	470.00
Steamroller, Pressed Steel, Keystone, 20 In.	1210.00
Steamroller, Pressed Steel, Steelcraft, 16 In.	195.00
Steamroller, Tin, Windup, Bing, 9 In.	385.00
Stencil Kit, Soldiers & Sailors, Baumgarten & Co., c.1915, 16 Stencils	60.00
Stove, Abendroth Bros., Cotton Plant, Cast Iron, Flowers, Accessories, 11 1/2 In.	1980.00
Stove, American ATF, Cast Iron, 4 Burners, Chimney, 11 x 13 x 6 In.	210.00
Stove, Beauty Range, Cast Iron, Steel, Cookware Set, Kenton, c.1900, 16 In.	275.00
Stove, Bluebird, Gas Range, Cast Iron, Grey Iron Casting Co., 6 3/8 In.	275.00
Stove, Buck's Stoves & Ranges, Cast Iron, Nickel, Junior, 24 In.	1100.00
Stove, Cast Iron, 4 Burner Lids, Kenton, 5 In.	55.00
Stove, Cast Iron, Nickel Plating, Majestic, Salesman's Sample, 13 3/4 In.	5000.00
Stove, Cook, Bucks Junior, Chrome Warmer, Stovepipe Frame, 22 x 12 In.	225.00
Stove, Crescent, Cast Iron, Embossed, 11 In.	115.00
Stove, Daisy, Cast Iron, Accessories, Arcade, Box, 6 In.	385.00
Stove, Eagle, Cast Iron, Embossed Eagle Head, Cookware, Hubley, 4 1/2 In.	110.00
Stove, Eagle, Cast Iron, Nickel Plated Eagle Head, Stovepipe, Cookware, Hubley, 10 In.	65.00
Stove, G.F. Filley, Charter Oak, Cast Iron, 1867 Patent, 24 1/2 In.	2090.00
Stove, Gas Range, Cast Iron, White, Arcade, 5 1/2 In.	660.00
Stove, Grey Iron Casting Co., Charm, Cast Iron, Nickel Plated, 5 In.	66.00
Stove, Grey Iron Casting Co., Choice, Cast Iron, Cookware Set, 10 1/2 In.	305.00
Stove, Hotpoint, Electric Range, Cast Iron, Copper Finish, Arcade, 5 1/2 In.	220.00
Stove, Ideal, Cast Iron, Steel, c.1894, 15 1/2 In.	140.00
Stove, Julia, Cast Iron, Flowers, Pot, Lid-Lift, Philadelphia Stove Works, 11 5/8 In.	825.00
Stove, Karr Range Co., Cast Iron, Pressed Steel, Porcelain, Blue, 12 3/4 In.	6600.00
Stove, Kent, Gas Range, Cast Iron, Blue, Kenton, c.1927, 10 In.	605.00
Stove, Little Fanny, Cast Iron, 12 In.	370.00
Stove, Little Lady, Electric, Pressed Steel, Teapot, Pot, Kokomo, Ind., 15 In.	55.00
Stove, Little Willie, Cast Iron, 14 In.	230.00
Stove, Majestic, Cast Iron, Accessories, 23 x 30 x 12 In.	6875.00
Stove, Quick Meal, Cooking, Cast Iron, 27 x 17 x 14 1/2 In.	1500.00
Stove, Radiolette, Parlor, Embossed, Silver Color, Godin, France, 5 x 3 1/4 In.	65.00
Stove, Range Eternal, Cast Iron, Steel, Engmann & Matthews, 27 1/2 In.	2420.00
Stove, Royal Esther, Cast Iron, Mt. Penn Stove Works, 14 In.	1870.00
Stove, Steel, Wood Handles, Porcelain Knobs, Electric, Beardsley & Wolcott, 15 x 7 In.	105.00
Stove, Western Electric Junior, Tin, Chrome Top, 6 Burners, 14 3/4 In.	28.00
Streamline Speedway, Bakelite Track, Tin Cars, Marx, Box, 12 x 12 In.	130.00
Streamline Speedway, Tin Lithograph Track, Tin Cars, Marx, Box, 9 x 12 In.	120.00
Street Sweeper, Driver, Cast Iron, Wire Brush, Blue, Red Wheels, Dent, 7 1/2 In.	3300.00
Street Sweeper, Tidy Tim, Tin, Windup, Marx, 9 In.	330.00 to 880.00
Streetcar, Broadway, Tin Lithograph, Folding Trolley Bar, Chein, 8 1/4 In.	80.00
Streetcar, Happy Speed, Tin Lithograph, Friction, Hadson, Box, 10 1/2 In.	590.00
Streetcar, Pressed Steel, Orange, Clockwork, Kingsbury, 9 In.	220.00
Stroller, Doll's, Bentwood, Canopy	180.00
Submarine, Tin, Painted, Clockwork, Ives, 9 In.	90.00
Sunny Andy, Kiddie Kampers, Wolverine, Box, 14 In.	770.00
Surrey, Cast Iron, 2 Horses, 2 People, Kenton, 13 In.	220.00
Surrey, Cast Iron, 2 Horses, Kenton, 15 In.	220.00
Surrey, Cast Iron, Driver, Passenger, 2 White Horses, Cloth Canopy, Kenton, 12 In.	303.00
Surrey, Fringed Top, 2 Horses, Lady Rider, Man Driver, Kenton, 1940s, 13 In.	575.00
Surrey, Fringed Top, Cloth Canopy, Wire Uprights, Kenton, c.1952, 13 In.	275.00 to 300.00
Suzy, Bouncing Ball, Mixed Material, Windup, T.P.S., Box, 5 1/2 In.	139.00
Sweeping Mammy, Tin Lithograph, Windup, Lindstrom, Box, 8 In.	470.00
Tank, Army, Windup, Painted, Structo, 11 In.	395.00
Tank, Camouflage, Painted, Clockwork, Marklin, Germany, 8 1/4 In.	415.00
Tank, Camouflage, Tin, Windup, Japan, 4 In.	140.00
Tank, Doughboy, World War I, Tin, Windup, Marx	185.00
Tank, Thunderbolt, Cap Firing, Tin, Friction, Japan, Box, 9 In.	250.00
Target Set, Fast Draw, Plastic, Mattel, Counter Display Box, 1959, 18 1/2 x 21 In.	310.00

Taxi, Aluminum, Yellow, Rubber Tires, Slik Toy Co., 7 In. 110.00
Taxi, Amos 'n' Andy, Fresh Air, Shakes, Tin, Windup, Marx, 1930, Box, 8 In. ....625.00 to 1520.00
Taxi, Brass, Dent, 5 1/2 In. 330.00
Taxi, Cast Iron, Driver, Orange, Black, License Plate No. 453, Freidag, 1920s, 5 1/4 In. ... 770.00
Taxi, Cast Iron, Freidag, 1920s, 7 1/2 In. ....3000.00 to 8250.00
Taxi, Checker Cab, Tin Lithograph, Clockwork, Chein, 6 In. 250.00
Taxi, Coin-Operated, Moves, Tin, Batteries, Ichiko, Box, 9 In. 1240.00
Taxi, Die Cast, Horizontal Grill, Rubber Tires, Orange, Black, Hubley, Box, 7 In. 220.00
Taxi, Die Cast, Vertical Grill, Rubber Tires, Orange, Black, Hubley, Box, 7 In. 140.00
Taxi, LiLa Cab, Tin Lithograph, Windup, Lehmann, Germany, 6 In. 935.00
Taxi, Lincoln Zephyr, Cast Iron, Orange, Sky Roof, Hubley, c.1939, 7 3/4 In. 605.00
Taxi, Yell-O-Taxi, Tin, Strauss, 8 In. 715.00
Taxi, Yellow Cab, Cadillac, Tin, Friction, Nickel Trim, Go-Stop Plate, Japan, c.1952, 7 In. . 55.00
Taxi, Yellow Cab, Driver, Arcade, 9 In. 750.00
Taxi, Yellow Cab, Painted Nickeled Wheels, Arcade, Box, 9 In. 4675.00
Taxi, Yellow Cab, Skyview, Folding Luggage Rack, Rubber Tires, Hubley, 8 1/2 In. 550.00
Taxi Set, Metal, Kiddie Toy, Hubley, Box, 3 Cars 935.00
Tea Set, Doll's, Cat Graphics, Tin Lithograph, 4 Cups & Saucers, Teapot, Tray, 8 x 6 In. .. 330.00
Tea Set, Doll's, China, Tray, Burgundy Embossed Box, c.1900, 9 1/4 x 6 1/4 In. 440.00
Tea Set, Flowers, China, Germany, Box, c.1900, Service For 6 .... 155.00
Tea Set, Flowers, Japan, Box, Prewar, 18 Piece 70.00
Tea Set, Flowers, Luster Ware, Japan, c.1930, Box 65.00
Tea Set, Little Hostess, China, Prewar Japan, Box 115.00
Teddy Bears are also listed in the Teddy Bear category.
Teddy Bear Parade, Paper Lithograph, Wood, Pull Toy, Fisher-Price, 1928, 14 In. .... *Illus* 2475.00
Teddy The Artist, Battery Operated, Electro Toy, Japan, Box, 9 In. 360.00
Teddy Tooter, Lithographed, Pull Toy, Fisher-Price, 14 In. 880.00
Telephone, Little Wonder, Tin Lithograph, 2 Phones, Side Crank, Box, 5 1/4 In. 275.00
Thresher, John Deere, Cast Iron, Silver Color, Green Trim, Vindex, 15 In. 3300.00
Thresher, McCormick Deering, Cast Iron, Gray, Arcade, 12 In. 605.00
Tiger, Mohair, Green Eyes, Pink Embroidered Nose, Button In Ear, Steiff, 10 In. 59.00
Tiger, Recumbent, Mohair, Steiff, c.1960, 18 In. 130.00
Tiger, Wood, Jointed, Painted Eyes, Rope Tail, Schoenhut, 7 1/4 In. 360.00
Toaster Set, Little Deb, Pressed Steel, Glass Trays, Realistic Toys, Box 65.00
Tombo, Dancing Figure, Tin Lithograph, Windup, Strauss, 10 In. 600.00
Tool Kit, Model T Ford, Good For A Breakdown, 9 Cast Tools, Oil Can, Map 440.00
Toonerville Trolley, Cast Aluminum, Nifty, Box, 4 1/2 In. 675.00
Toonerville Trolley, Cast Iron, Red, Dent, Box, 6 In. 770.00
Toonerville Trolley, Tin Lithograph, Clockwork, Germany, 5 1/4 In. 600.00
Toonerville Trolley, Tin Lithograph, Windup, Dent Hardware, Box, 6 In. 495.00
Top, Choral, Tin Lithograph, Wyandotte, 10 x 10 In. 130.00
Top, Circus, Chein, 7 x 6 In. 80.00
Top, Kaleidoscope Pattern, C.G. Wood, Box, 6 In. 165.00
Top, Sparkling, Box, 4 In. 35.00
Tractor, Allis Chalmers, Cast Iron, Rubber Tires, Red, Arcade, c.1940, 6 In. 300.00
Tractor, Caterpillar, Metal Link Track, Clockwork, Structo, 8 1/4 In. 259.00
Tractor, Die Cast, Red, Nickel Driver, Rubber Tires, Hubley, Box, 6 3/4 In. 140.00
Tractor, Farmall, Driver, Green, Red Wheels, Arcade, Box, c.1925, 6 1/4 In. 7700.00
Tractor, Ford, 9N, Cast Iron, Gray, Salesman's Sample, Arcade, c.1939, 8 3/4 In. 2200.00
Tractor, Ford, 9N, Cast Iron, Orange, Salesman's Sample, Arcade, 1939, 6 1/2 In. 2475.00
Tractor, Fordson, Cast Iron, Gray, Nickel Driver, North & Judd, 4 In. 360.00
Tractor, Fordson, Driver, Cast Iron, Blue, Red Wheels, Dent, 6 In. 3575.00
Tractor, Front-End Loader, Fordson, Green, Red Wheels, Hubley, c.1930s, 9 1/4 In. 1980.00
Tractor, Grader, Adams, Dark Orange, Doepke, 1948, 26 In. 235.00
Tractor, Huboid, Red, Pull Toy, Hubley, Box, 5 1/2 In. 195.00
Tractor, International Cultivision A, Cast Iron, Red, Arcade, c.1940, 7 In. 605.00
Tractor, International Farmall, Model M, Cast Iron, Arcade, c.1940, 7 In. 330.00
Tractor, International Harvester, Single Cylinder, Gasoline Engine, 34 x 20 x 20 In. 450.00
Tractor, McCormick Deering, 10-20, Cast Iron, Nickel Driver, Blue, Kilgore, 5 3/4 In. 1210.00
Tractor, McCormick Deering, Cast Iron, Arcade, 7 In. 165.00
Tractor, McCormick Deering, Cast Iron, Nickel Driver, Arcade, 7 In. 660.00
Tractor, Miami Scraper, Fordson, Green, Blue, Dent, Box, 10 3/4 In. 6050.00
Tractor, Oliver Orchard, Green, Red Driver, Rubber Tires, Hubley, c.1940, 5 1/4 In. 825.00

Toy, Teddy Bear Parade, Paper Lithograph,
Wood, Pull Toy, Fisher-Price, 1928, 14 In.

Toy, Trolley, Cast Iron,
Yellow Paint, 3 x 8 In.

Tractor, Steam, Heischmann, 9 In.	275.00
Tractor, Wagon, A. Chalmers, Bottom Dump, Cast Iron, Arcade, 12 In.	468.00
Tractor, Wagon, Pressed Steel, Tru-Matic, 1930s, 36 In.	550.00
Traffic Cop, Mixed Material, Battery Operated, A1, Japan, Box, 14 In.	250.00
Traffic Cop, Movable Arms, Celluloid, England, 4 1/2 In.	75.00
Train, American Flyer, Colonel, No. 4686 Locomotive, Club Car, Coach, Car, 4 Piece	4560.00
Train, American Flyer, Hamiltonian, No. 4678 Locomotive, 3 Passenger Cars	1320.00
Train, American Flyer, No. 4039 Locomotive, Baggage Car, Coach, Observation	1380.00
Train, American Flyer, No. 4684 Locomotive, 3 Eagle Passenger Cars, Standard Gauge	660.00
Train, American Flyer, No. 4687 Locomotive, Passenger Car, Baggage, Observation	2590.00
Train, American Flyer, No. 6027 Locomotive, Iron, Black, Cars, Electric, 4 x 31 In., 3 Piece	1760.00
Train, Bing, Jupiter, London North Western Railroad, 1 Gauge, 4 Piece	6600.00
Train, Bing, Live Steam, 2 Gauge, 3 Piece	4950.00
Train, Bing, No. 165 Locomotive, Great Central, Electric, 2 Gauge	2310.00
Train, Bing, No. 3238 Locomotive, Electric, N.Y. Central, 1 Gauge	2200.00
Train, Buddy L, Industrial, Locomotive, Flatcar, Tipple, Coal Car, 2 Gondolas, Milk Cans	2090.00
Train, Canadian Pacific, Cast Tin, Windup, Germany, 1920, O Gauge	395.00
Train, Carlisle & Finch, Engine, Tender, No. 131, 2 Piece	1760.00
Train, Giant, Tin Lithograph, Friction Drive, Japan, 16 In.	165.00
Train, Hornby, Tin, Clockwork, O Gauge, 20 In., 4 Piece	220.00
Train, Ives, Locomotive, Tender, Tin, Iron Wheels, Black, Red, Windup, c.1880, 6 x 13 In.	550.00
Train, Ives, Locomotive, Vulcan, Tin, Clockwork, c.1885, 7 x 9 1/2 In.	330.00
Train, Ives, No. 3243R Locomotive, Club Car, Parlor Car, Observation Car	2300.00
Train, Lionel, A.C. Gilbert Erector Hudson, Locomotive, Tender	1785.00
Train, Lionel, Erie Lackawanna, Locomotive, 6 Passenger Coaches	375.00
Train, Lionel, Freight Cars, 4 Piece	155.00
Train, Lionel, No. 8 Locomotive, 2 Passenger Cars, Box, Standard Gauge, 3 Piece	275.00
Train, Lionel, No. 224 Engine & Tender, 3 Passenger Cars, Boxes, O-27 Gauge, 5 Piece	470.00
Train, Lionel, No. 384, Passenger, Engine, Tender, Baggage Car, 2 Coaches, 58 In.	525.00
Train, Lionel, No. 2332, Pennsylvania, Locomotive, Dump Car, Tank, Refrigerator Car	775.00
Train, Lionel, No. 3330, Navy, Submarine Car	145.00
Train, Lionel, Nos. 8480 & 8482 Locomotives, Union Pacific, 7 Passenger Coaches	430.00
Train, Lucky Chug Chug, Engine, Tender, Fisher-Price, Box	275.00
Train, Marklin, No. 4021, Great Bear, London North Eastern Railway, 2 Gauge, 4 Piece	3300.00
Train, MTH, Lehigh Valley, Locomotive 4-6-4, Tender, 5 Passenger Coaches	345.00
Train, Vulkan, Engine, Plank, Live Steam, O Gauge	550.00
Train Accessory, Buddy L, Outdoor Railroad Track, 3 Piece	358.00
Train Accessory, Kibri, Freight Shed, Crane, Box	248.00
Train Accessory, Lionel, Hellgate Bridge, Standard Gauge, No. 300	550.00
Train Accessory, Lionel, Powerhouse, Standard Gauge, No. 840	1870.00
Train Accessory, Lionel, Station, Double, Standard Gauge	495.00
Train Accessory, Lionel, Station, Terrace, Standard Gauge, No. 113	550.00
Train Accessory, Lionel, Switches, O Gauge, Box	66.00
Train Accessory, Marklin, Central Station, Onion Dome, 1 Gauge	6050.00
Train Accessory, Marx, Crossing Gate, Signals, Streetlights, Control Tower	160.00
Train Car, Bing, Dining, No. 13210, London Midland Southern	195.00
Train Car, Bing, Passenger, 2 Gauge	250.00
Train Car, Bing, Passenger, Midland, 1 Gauge	220.00

Train Car, Buddy L, Outdoor Railroad Caboose, Pressed Steel, 18 In. 1100.00
Train Car, Buddy L, Outdoor Railroad Crane, Pressed Steel, 36 In. 4125.00
Train Car, Buddy L, Outdoor Railroad Locomotive & Tender, Pressed Steel, 46 In. 2420.00
Train Car, Buddy L, Outdoor Railroad Side Dump, Pressed Steel, 12 In. 1210.00
Train Car, Buddy L, Outdoor Railroad Tank Car, Yellow, 20 In. 4125.00
Train Car, Carette, Engine, Live Steam, O Gauge 525.00
Train Car, Carette, Passenger, Tin, 1 Gauge, 6 Wheels, 16 In. 195.00
Train Car, Carlisle & Finch, Boxcar, No. 1144, Paper Sides 605.00
Train Car, Carlisle & Finch, Caboose, N & M 165.00
Train Car, Carlisle & Finch, Caboose, No. 8681, Paper Sides 880.00
Train Car, Carlisle & Finch, Cattle ....65.00 to 250.00
Train Car, Carlisle & Finch, Gondola, No. 131, PRR, Blue 195.00
Train Car, Carlisle & Finch, Gondola, No. 131, PRR, Red, Paper Sides 165.00
Train Car, Engine, Clockwork, Tin, American, 5 In. 385.00
Train Car, Engine, Tinware, Painted, Stenciled, Windup, America, 1800s, 11 1/2 In. 1060.00
Train Car, Keystone, Ride On, Engine, Pressed Steel, Wood Handle, 24 In. 165.00
Train Car, Lionel, No. 25, Bumper, Illuminated, Standard Gauge, Original Box 290.00
Train Car, Lionel, No. 515, Tank, Standard Gauge 220.00
Train Car, Lionel, No. 516, Hopper, Standard Gauge 220.00
Train Car, Lionel, No. 517, Caboose, Standard Gauge 99.00
Train Car, Lionel, No. 3619, Helicopter Car 145.00
Train Car, Lionel, No. 6434, Poultry Car 45.00
Train Car, Lionel, No. 6650, Missile Launching Car 1139.00
Train Car, Lionel, No. 6801, Flat Car 45.00
Train Car, Lionel, No. 6805, Radioactive Waste Car 60.00
Train Car, Lionel, No. 8250, Locomotive, GP Diesel, Box 65.00
Train Car, Locomotive, Wood, Painted, Iron Spokes, Metal Pull Ring, 9 1/2 x 26 In. 330.00
Train Car, Marklin, Crane, 1 Gauge, Marklin 110.00
Train Car, Marklin, Tank, 1 Gauge, Tin, 8 In. 330.00
Train Car, Pullman, Pull Toy, 19 3/4 x 8 x 4 1/2 In. 275.00
Train Car, Steelcraft, Ride On, Baggage, Railway Express, Pressed Steel, 18 In. 300.00
Train Car, Voltamp Suburban, Engine, No. 2210 .... 2310.00
Train Set, American Flyer, Cast Iron, O Gauge, Box 275.00
Train Set, American Flyer, No. 9900, Burlington Zephyr, O Gauge, Box, 5 Piece 1045.00
Train Set, Buddy L, Industrial, Pressed Steel, Locomotive, 5 Cars, 2-Piece Track 2530.00
Train Set, Dorfan, Electric, O Gauge, Box 440.00
Train Set, Dorfan, No. 200, Locomotive, Tender, 2 No. 356 Pullmans, Track, Box 1155.00
Train Set, Ives, Passenger, No. 3253 Engine, O Gauge, Box 825.00
Train Set, Lionel Jr., Passenger, Orange, 3 Piece 470.00
Train Set, Lionel, Engine, No. 258, 7 Piece 525.00
Train Set, Lionel, No. 154, No. 601 Passenger Cars, Baggage, Box, O Gauge, 4 Piece 470.00
Train Set, Lionel, No. 233, Box 550.00
Train Set, Lionel, No. 629 Pullman, No. 630 Observation, 18 Track Sections, O Gauge ... 380.00
Train Set, Lionel, No. 636, Union Pacific, Electric 525.00
Train Set, Marklin, No. 1050 Locomotive, Tender, Clockwork, O Gauge, 5 Piece 605.00
Train Set, Marklin, PO-E, Electric, Locomotive, 3 Passenger Cars, 1 Gauge, 4 Piece 825.00
Train Set, Marx, Freight, No. 666 Steam Locomotive, Santa Fe, NY Central, O-27 Gauge . 150.00
Train Set, Marx, Freight, Southern Pacific, Wabash, Transformer, Track, O-27 Gauge 115.00
Train Set, Marx, Freight, Union Pacific, Erie, WECX, Transformer, Track, O-27 Gauge ... 130.00
Train Set, Marx, Honeymoon Express, Tin Lithograph, Mechanical, Box, 9 In. 90.00
Train Set, Marx, Santa Fe, Passenger, 2 Coaches, 2 Dome Cars, O-27 Gauge 115.00
Train Set, Vulkan, Plank, 1 Gauge, Box, 5 Piece 2420.00
Train Set, Weeden, Live Steam, Engine, Tender, Car, c.1890, 3 Piece 1430.00
Transformer, Star Five, Original Box, 1970s, 8 1/2 In. 235.00
Traveler, Walks, 2 Suitcases, Windup, Distler, Germany, 1920s, 7 1/2 In. 575.00
Tree, Whistling Spooky Kooky, Bump & Go, Eyes Open, Tin, Marx, Box, 14 In. 1695.00
Trinity Chimes, Cathedral Shape, Tin, Lithographed Church Interior, Chein, 1950s, 9 In. ... 55.00
Trinity Chimes, Paper Lithograph, Cardboard, Painted Wood, Schoenhut, 18 In. 220.00
Trolley, Cast Iron, Yellow Paint, 3 x 8 In. ....*Illus* 95.00
Trolley, Car, Tin Lithograph, Electric Motor, Opening Roof, Carette, Germany, 7 3/4 In. .. 360.00
Truck, A Team, Steel, Plastic, Ertl, Box, 1983, 6 1/2 x 13 In. 60.00
Truck, American Railway Express, Black, Green, Red, Decals, Keystone, 1926, 27 In. 1150.00
Truck, American Railway Express, Pressed Steel, 26 In. 880.00

Truck, Army Repair-It-Unit, Searchlight, Olive Green & Yellow, Buddy L, 1957, 15 In. 75.00
Truck, Army Searchlight, Pressed Steel, Plastic Light, Buddy L, 1950s, 15 In. 100.00
Truck, Army Transport, Pressed Steel, Canvas, Gendron Sampson, c.1940, 28 In. 2090.00
Truck, Army, Bulldog Mack, Tin Lithograph, Chein, 10 In. 248.00
Truck, Army, Pressed Steel, Turner, 20 In. 220.00
Truck, Army, Wood, Buddy L, 1940s, 13 In. 55.00
Truck, Barrel, Structo, Box, 12 In. 495.00
Truck, Bell Telephone, Accessories, Hubley, 1932, 10 In. 1980.00
Truck, Bell Telephone, Accessories, Hubley, Box, 10 In. 2200.00
Truck, Bell Telephone, Bucket, Tonka, Unopened Box, 1979 .... 248.00
Truck, Bell Telephone, Green, Hubley, 4 In. 425.00
Truck, Bell Telephone, Green, Hubley, 5 1/4 In. ....550.00 to 600.00
Truck, Camera, Pathe Camera On Roof, Pressed Steel, Marx, 10 In. 605.00
Truck, Cannon, Sonny, Pressed Steel, Dayton Toy & Specialty, 1920s, 23 In. 440.00
Truck, Car Carrier, 3 Cars, Tootsietoy, Box, 8 In. 550.00
Truck, Car Carrier, 3 Coupe Cars, Pressed Steel, Girard, Box, 22 In. 5500.00
Truck, Car Carrier, 3 Ford Model A Coupes, Green, Red & Blue, Arcade, 19 In. 1500.00
Truck, Car Carrier, Austin, Cast Iron, Arcade, c.1936, 14 In. 660.00
Truck, Car Carrier, Hertz, Pressed Steel, Tonka, 1960s, 27 In. 55.00
Truck, Car Carrier, Inserts, Wish Book, Tonka, Box, 1967 .... 440.00
Truck, Car Carrier, Race Cars, Painted, Yellow, Buddy L, 19 In. 190.00
Truck, Car Carrier, Structo, Box, 20 In. 550.00
Truck, Car Carrier, Turnpike Auto Transport, 9 Cars, Japan, Box, 1950s, 23 In. 595.00
Truck, Cattle, Structo, Box, 20 In. 495.00
Truck, Cement Mixer, Hercules, Tin, Chein, 17 In. 2970.00
Truck, Cement Mixer, Jaeger, Cast Iron, Metal Wheels, Kenton, 6 3/4 In. 690.00
Truck, Cement Mixer, Jaeger, Silver, Red & Green Frame, Rubber Tires, Kenton, 7 In. 230.00
Truck, Cement Mixer, Pressed Steel, Pull & Ride, Buddy L, Box, 36 In. 1980.00
Truck, Cement Mixer, Red & White, Tonka, 1960, 14 In. 125.00
Truck, Cement Mixer, Tonka, Box, 1965 .... 220.00
Truck, Cement, Mixer, Jaeger, Cast Iron, Nickel Plated Mixer, Arcade, 7 In. 550.00
Truck, Champion Coal, Stake, Cast Iron, Green, Rubber Tires, c.1934, 4 1/2 In. 195.00
Truck, Chemical, Mack, Bulldog, Ladders, Pressed Steel, Toledo, 27 In. 5775.00
Truck, Circus, Driver, Lion, Cast Iron, Kenton, 9 In. 1250.00
Truck, Circus, Pressed Steel, 5 Cardboard Animals, Wyandotte, Box, 18 In. 3190.00
Truck, Circus, Royal, Tiger, 2 Horses, Cast Iron, Hubley, 12 In. 1310.00
Truck, Coast To Coast, Cast Iron, A.C. Williams, 6 7/8 In. 195.00
Truck, Colonial Ham, Tin, Friction, No Ham In A Can Beats Colonial, Japan, Box, 13 In. . 250.00
Truck, Communication, Tin, Battery, Modern Toys, Japan, Box, 1950s, 12 1/2 In. 345.00
Truck, Corvair Air Express, Tin Lithograph, Friction, Japan, Box, 1961, 8 In. 280.00
Truck, Corvair Telephone Service, Tin, Friction, KTS, Box, 8 In. 305.00
Truck, Crane, Tin, Windup, VeeBee, Victor Bonnet, France, 14 In. 770.00
Truck, Dairy, Carnation Milk, Pressed Steel, Tonka, c.1955, 12 In. 138.00
Truck, Dairy, Elsie's, Beauregard Driving, Lithographed, Fisher-Price, 10 In. 440.00
Truck, Dairy, Girard, Semi-Trailer, Red, Black & Cream, 18 In. 375.00
Truck, Dairy, Marcrest, Marx, Steel, 14 In. 95.00
Truck, Dairy, Milk, Cream, Orange, Rubber Tires, Hubley, 1934, 3 3/4 In. 495.00
Truck, Dairy, Milk, Wood, Sliding Doors, 5 Milk Bottles, Buddy L, 13 In. ....90.00 to 275.00
Truck, Dairy, Pressed Steel, Rubber Tires, Sturditoy, 1920s, 27 In. 525.00
Truck, Dairy, Railway Express Agency, Drink Milk, Pressed Steel, Buddy L, 22 In. 470.00
Truck, Dairy, Semi-Trailer, Cab, 3 Trailers, Tootsietoy, Box 660.00
Truck, Dairy, Sheffield Farms, Mack, Pressed Steel, Steelcraft, 21 In. 770.00
Truck, Decker's Iowana Ham, Streamliner, Pressed Steel, Metalcraft, 13 In. 2310.00
Truck, Delivery, City, Nickel Grill, Steelcraft, 19 In. 770.00
Truck, Delivery, City, Stake, Pressed Steel, Rubber Tires, Steelcraft, 22 In. 605.00
Truck, Delivery, Curtiss Butterfinger, Buddy L, 24 In. 1650.00
Truck, Delivery, Deluxe Rider, Ride On, Steel, Pull Handle, Buddy L, 1930s, 23 In. 605.00
Truck, Delivery, Deluxe, Pressed Steel, Blue, Marx, 1950s, 14 In. 330.00
Truck, Delivery, Express Parcel, Tin Lithograph, Windup, Penny Toy, Germany, 4 In. 275.00
Truck, Delivery, Hathaway's Bread & Cake, Driver, Original Paint, 9 1/4 In. 550.00
Truck, Delivery, Land-O-Lakes, Buddy L, 26 In. 660.00
Truck, Delivery, Minute Maid, Pressed Steel, Rubber Tires, Tonka, c.1955, 24 In. 165.00
Truck, Delivery, National Stores, Pressed Steel, Marx, Unopened Box, 20 In. 715.00

Truck, Delivery, New York To Philadelphia, Cast Iron, Driver, Dent, 15 In. 4125.00
Truck, Delivery, Panel, Black Rubber Tires, Arcade, 1925, 8 1/4 In. 9625.00
Truck, Delivery, Toyland Pie Bakery, Tin Lithograph, Mohawk Toys, 6 1/4 In. 523.00
Truck, Delivery, Wyman's, Cast Iron, Nickel Plated Wheels, Arcade, 8 In. 3850.00
Truck, Delivery, Yellow Cab, Arcade, 1925 .... 9625.00
Truck, Digger, Cast Iron, Hubley, 8 In. 880.00
Truck, Ditcher, Buckeye, Cast Iron, Kenton, 12 In. 880.00
Truck, Dump, Bottom, State Hi-Way, Green, Wyandotte, 28 In. 295.00
Truck, Dump, Bronze & Yellow, Hydraulic, Structo, 1961, 18 In. 55.00
Truck, Dump, Cast Iron, Hubley, 7 In. 495.00
Truck, Dump, Coal Co., Steel, Rubber Tires, Steerable Front Wheels, Sturditoy, 26 In. 1650.00
Truck, Dump, Coal, Cast Iron, Green, Arcade, 10 In. 2860.00
Truck, Dump, Coal, Cast Iron, Red Cab, Green Body, Kenton, 1930s, 10 1/2 In. 1100.00
Truck, Dump, Coal, Mack, Tin, Windup, Marx, Box, 13 In. 1100.00
Truck, Dump, Coal, Pressed Steel, Aluminum Disc Wheels, Buddy L, 1920s, 25 In. 600.00
Truck, Dump, Coal, Pressed Steel, Marx, Box, 21 In. 385.00
Truck, Dump, Coal, Pressed Steel, Wyandotte, 11 In. 385.00
Truck, Dump, Dan-Dee, Tin, Windup, Chein, Box, 9 In. 1210.00
Truck, Dump, Diamond T, Red & Green, Buddy L, 1948, 20 1/2 In. 295.00
Truck, Dump, Die Cast, Smith-Miller, 12 In. 220.00
Truck, Dump, Gama Automatic, Metal, Friction, Germany, 1950s, 10 In. 145.00
Truck, Dump, Green, Red, Decals, Arcade, 10 3/4 In. 2500.00
Truck, Dump, Hercules, Tin, Chein, Box, 18 In. 1320.00
Truck, Dump, Hi Lift Farm Supplies, Buddy L, Inserts, Box, c.1950 .... 910.00
Truck, Dump, Hydraulic, Orange, Nylint, 1961, 23 In. 155.00
Truck, Dump, Hydraulic, Pressed Steel, Buddy L, 1950s, 21 In. 55.00
Truck, Dump, Hydraulic, Pressed Steel, Tonka, Box, 1960s, 13 In. 175.00
Truck, Dump, Hydraulic, Steel, Disc Wheels, Buddy L, 1928, 24 1/2 In. 940.00
Truck, Dump, International Hydraulic, Ride On, Pressed Steel, Buddy L, 26 In. 1210.00
Truck, Dump, International, Ride On, Pressed Steel, Pull Handle, Buddy L, 1938, 27 In. ... 1430.00
Truck, Dump, Little Jim, Red & Green, Steelcraft, 1935, 24 In. 475.00
Truck, Dump, Mack, Bulldog, Crank, 20th Century, 27 In. 2300.00
Truck, Dump, Mack, Bulldog, Pressed Steel, Boycraft Decal, Steelcraft, 1930s, 25 In. 660.00
Truck, Dump, Open Cab, Buddy L, 1926, 24 In. 265.00
Truck, Dump, Orange, Blue, Kilgore, 1930s, 8 1/2 In. 605.00
Truck, Dump, Packard, Hydraulic Lift, Pressed Steel, Keystone, 27 In. 1870.00
Truck, Dump, Packard, Pressed Steel, Steerable, Rubber Tires, Keystone, 26 In. 2420.00
Truck, Dump, Pressed Steel, Duo-Tone, Electric Headlights, Buddy L, Box, 20 In. 990.00
Truck, Dump, Pressed Steel, Headlights, Rubber Tires, Buddy L, 1930s, 24 In. 1760.00
Truck, Dump, Pressed Steel, Iron Spoke Wheels, Kelmet, 26 In. 1430.00
Truck, Dump, Pressed Steel, Rubber Tires, Green, Wyandotte 165.00
Truck, Dump, Pressed Steel, Rubber Tires, Ratchet Mechanism, Sturditoy, 1920s, 26 In. ... 1100.00
Truck, Dump, Pressed Steel, Steelcraft, 1930s, 20 In. 360.00
Truck, Dump, Red Baby, 10 5/8 In. 525.00
Truck, Dump, Red, White & Blue, Litho Grill, Art Deco, Wyandotte, 21 In. 95.00
Truck, Dump, Ride On, Steelcraft, 1930s, 22 In. 248.00
Truck, Dump, Sand Loader, Pressed Steel, Buddy L, 22 In. 385.00
Truck, Dump, Scoop, Die Cast, Smith-Miller, Catalog, Box, 12 In. 1650.00
Truck, Dump, Scoop, High Lift, Buddy L, 15 In. 140.00
Truck, Dump, Scoop, Pressed Steel, Buddy L, 1940s, 16 In. 55.00
Truck, Dump, Semi-Trailer, Red Cab, Green Dump, Wyandotte, 17 In. 355.00
Truck, Dump, Sheet Metal, Friction, Steel Wheels, Republic, 19 In. 385.00
Truck, Dump, Side Dump, Mack, Cast Iron, Red, Yellow, c.1932, 9 In. 5225.00
Truck, Dump, Side Dump, Pressed Steel, Rubber Tires, Sturditoy, 1920s, 24 In. 1320.00
Truck, Dump, Studebaker, Pressed Steel, Marx, Box, 18 In. 495.00
Truck, Dump, Tin Lithograph, Windup, Marx, 9 1/2 In. 360.00
Truck, Dump, Tip Top, Tin, Windup, Driver, Strauss, 10 In. 715.00
Truck, Easter Greetings, Tin Lithograph, Windup, Courtland, 8 1/2 In. 415.00
Truck, Easter, Pressed Steel, Wyandotte, 10 In. 1100.00
Truck, Egg, Duck Driver, Felt Arms, Pull Toy, Fisher-Price, 13 In. 660.00
Truck, Esso Motor Oil, 7 Cans, Electric Headlights, Metalcraft, 13 In. 1045.00
Truck, Express Line, Overland, 2 Trailers, Buddy L, Box, 36 In. 2310.00
Truck, Express Line, Pressed Steel, Buddy L, Box, 24 In. 3300.00

Truck, Fancy Groceries, Tin Lithograph, 1920s, 6 In. 605.00
Truck, Fast Freight, White Cab, Red Trailer, Buddy L, 1950s, 20 In. 100.00
Truck, Firestone, Structo, Red & White, Black Roof, 14 In. 75.00
Truck, Flower Shop, Friction, Japan, Box, 11 In. 550.00
Truck, Ford, Model A, Stake, Blue, A.C. Williams, 7 In. 500.00
Truck, Ford, Model A, Stake, Green, Arcade, 4 3/4 In. 200.00
Truck, Ford, Riding Academy, Horses, Buddy L, Box, 1957 .... 525.00
Truck, Gasoline, Aviation, Semi-Trailer, Nickel Wheels, Kilgore, 13 In. 4675.00
Truck, GMC, Anti-Aircraft, Buddy L, 1959 .... 250.00
Truck, Golden Apples, Tin Lithograph, Friction, Japan, 1960s, 6 1/2 In. 95.00
Truck, Gorden's Farm Delivery, Friction, Tin Lithograph, M&K, Japan, 8 1/4 In. 110.00
Truck, Grader, Adam's Motor, Metal, Doepke, 1950s, 25 In. 165.00
Truck, Gravel, Pressed Steel, Tin Lithograph, Marx, 1950s, 13 In. 110.00
Truck, Harley-Davidson, Pressed Steel, Plastic, Buddy L, 21 In. 28.00
Truck, Heinz, Pressed Steel, Electric Lights, Decals, Metalcraft, Box, 12 In. 880.00
Truck, Huber Road Roller, Cast Iron, Nickel Plated Wheels, Hubley, 8 In. 358.00
Truck, Huckster, Pressed Steel, Buddy L, 14 In. 7425.00
Truck, Ice Cream, Buddy L, 1964 .... 225.00
Truck, Ice Cream, Tin & Plastic, Friction, Japan, 1950s, 7 1/2 In. 145.00
Truck, Ice, Blue, Cast Iron, Arcade, Box, 6 In. 770.00
Truck, Ice, Hercules, Mack, Tin Lithograph, 4 Glass Ice Cubes, Chein, 20 In. 825.00
Truck, Ice, International Pure, Pressed Steel, Steering Handle, Buddy L, 28 In. 2970.00
Truck, Ice, Mack, Pressed Steel, Steelcraft, 1920s, 27 In. 605.00
Truck, Ice, Polar Ice Company, Stake, Pressed Steel, Marx, 1940s, 13 In. 275.00
Truck, Ice, Wood, Buddy L, 1940s, 16 In. 195.00
Truck, International Harvester, Red Baby, Pressed Steel, Buddy L, 1920s, 24 In. 825.00
Truck, International, Stake, Ride On, Pressed Steel, Buddy L, 25 In. 440.00
Truck, Judson Repair Co., Tin, Friction, Battery Operated, Linemar, 15 In. 468.00
Truck, Kennel, 10 Plastic Dogs, Plastic Dome, Nylint 200.00
Truck, Kennel, Ford, Ny-Lint, Box, 1961 .... 250.00
Truck, Kennel, Pressed Steel, Plastic, Dogs, Buddy L, 1960s, 13 In. 110.00
Truck, Kennel, Pressed Steel, Plastic, Dogs, Nylint, Box, 1960s, 11 In. 90.00
Truck, Kraft, Cheese, Die Cast Cab, Pressed Steel Body, Smith-Miller, 14 In. ......250.00 to 275.00
Truck, Loader, Pressed Steel, Keystone, 1920s, 17 In. 130.00
Truck, Log, Mack, Die Cast Cab, Wood Trailer, Lumber, Smith-Miller, 33 In. 415.00
Truck, Log, Orange, Hubley, Box, 7 1/2 In. 300.00
Truck, Log, Semi-Trailer, Pressed Steel, Smith-Miller, 36 In. 1045.00
Truck, Long Haulage, Tin, Windup, Strauss, Box, 10 1/2 In. 2420.00
Truck, Machine Hauler, Cast Iron, Roller, Tractor, Scraper, A.C. Williams, 28 1/2 In. 4950.00
Truck, Machinery, Pressed Steel, Buddy L, 1950s, 24 In. 130.00
Truck, Mail, Packard, Pressed Steel, Rubber Tires, Keystone, 1920s, 27 In. 550.00
Truck, Merry-Go-Around, Tin, Buddy L, Box, 13 In. 440.00
Truck, Mighty Scraper, Pressed Steel, Plastic, Tonka, 1970s, 27 In. 132.00
Truck, Military, Pulls Artillery Piece On Wheels, 2 Soldiers, Windup, 7 In. 275.00
Truck, Milk, Divco, Windup, Decals, Kingsbury, 9 In. 200.00
Truck, Motor Express, Cab Over Engine, Art Deco, Hubley, 1938 .... 3850.00
Truck, Motor Express, Structo, Box, 12 In. 330.00
Truck, Moving Van, Allied Van Lines, Pressed Steel, Cabover Cab, Tonka, 1940s, 24 In. .. 200.00
Truck, Moving Van, Allied Van Lines, Pressed Steel, Pull Rod, Buddy L, 29 In. 1045.00
Truck, Moving Van, Allied Van Lines, Pressed Steel, Tonka, 1960s, 24 In. 165.00
Truck, Moving Van, Allied Van Lines, Tin Lithograph, Friction, Japan, 6 In. 50.00
Truck, Moving Van, Allied Van Lines, Tin Lithograph, Orange, Grimland, Box, 7 1/2 In. .. 165.00
Truck, Moving Van, Allied, Kedney Moving, Private Label, Inserts, Tonka, Box, 1965 .... 880.00
Truck, Moving Van, Freight Carriers, Buddy L, 20 In. 525.00
Truck, Moving Van, Hercules, Motor Express, Mack, Tin, 19 In. 715.00
Truck, Moving Van, Long Distance, Wood, Buddy L, 1940s, 27 In. 550.00
Truck, Moving Van, Lumar Van Lines, Pressed Steel, Marx, 20 In. 550.00
Truck, Moving Van, Mack, Bulldog, Tin Lithograph, Yellow, Red Letters, Chein, 8 In. 495.00
Truck, Moving Van, Nationwide, Tonka, Box, 1950 .... 1650.00
Truck, Moving Van, Packard, Steel, Steerable Front Wheels, Keystone, 26 In. .....470.00 to 1210.00
Truck, Moving Van, Pressed Steel, Aluminum Disc Wheels, Buddy L, 1920s, 25 In. 470.00
Truck, Moving Van, Pressed Steel, Smith-Miller, Box, 20 In. 2310.00
Truck, Moving Van, Sonny, Pressed Steel, 26 In. 3850.00

Truck, Packard Circus, Sit 'n Ride, Sides Fold Down, Cages & Animals, 1920s, Keystone . 2970.00
Truck, Pickup, American Cyanamid, Fertilizer, Inserts, Box Garage, Tonka, 1964 . . . . 525.00
Truck, Pickup, Big Duke Mighty, 4x4, Tonka, Box, 1980 . . . . 65.00
Truck, Pickup, Flivver, Pressed Steel, Buddy L, 14 In.. . . . . 2090.00
Truck, Pickup, International, Cast Iron, Yellow, Arcade, 1941 . . . . 495.00
Truck, Pickup, Pressed Steel, Electric Headlights, Marx, Box, 11 In. 770.00
Truck, Pickup, Pressed Steel, Tonka, Box, 1960s, 13 In. 470.00
Truck, Police Patrol, Mack, Bulldog, Tin Lithograph, Marx, 10 In. 825.00
Truck, Police Patrol, Packard, Pressed Steel, Rubber Tires, Keystone, 1920s, 28 In. 525.00
Truck, Police Patrol, Tin Lithograph, Windup, Marx, 10 In. 1430.00
Truck, Railway Express Agency, Tin, Accessories, Stickers, Marx, Box, 20 In. 990.00
Truck, Railway Express, Pressed Steel, Electric Headlights, Buddy L, 1930s, 24 In. 600.00
Truck, Railway Express, Pressed Steel, Steerable Front Wheels, Buddy L, 25 In. 495.00
Truck, Railway Express, Pressed Steel, Tin Lithograph, Lift Gate, Marx, 1940s, 20 In. 220.00
Truck, Riding Academy, Buddy L, Box, 1961 . . . . 295.00
Truck, Road Grader, Cast Iron, 4 1/2 In. 45.00
Truck, Sand & Gravel, High Boy, Pressed Steel, Steerable Wheels, Buddy L, 26 In. 2200.00
Truck, Sand & Gravel, Pressed Steel, Opening Side Doors, Buddy L, 1920s, 26 In. 770.00
Truck, Sanitation, Pressed Steel, Buddy L, 1960s, 17 In. . . . . .185.00 to 225.00
Truck, Sanitation, Pressed Steel, Structo, 1960s, 16 In. 120.00
Truck, Sanitation, Yellow, White & Blue, Hubley, 8 1/2 In. 195.00
Truck, Sanitition, Sanitary Service, Pressed Steel, Plastic, Tonka, 1970s, 16 In. 135.00
Truck, Searchlight Trailer, Hollywood Film Ad, Die Cast, Smith-Miller, 24 In. 825.00
Truck, Semi-Trailer, Century Of Progress, Greyhound, GMC, Cast Iron, 1933 . . . . 230.00
Truck, Semi-Trailer, Die Cast Cab, Aluminum & Wood Trailer, Smith-Miller, 23 In. 330.00
Truck, Semi-Trailer, Express Line, Pressed Steel, Buddy L, 23 In. 345.00
Truck, Semi-Trailer, Express, Pressed Steel, Removable Roof, Buddy L, 1930s, 25 In. 300.00
Truck, Semi-Trailer, Fruehauf, Diecast Cab, Smith-Miller, 27 In. 275.00
Truck, Semi-Trailer, Motor Express, Deco Cab, Rubber Wheels, Hubley, 1938, 8 3/4 In. . . 3850.00
Truck, Semi-Trailer, PIE, Die Cast Cab, Aluminum Trailer, Smith-Miller, 1940s, 24 In. . . . 275.00
Truck, Semi-Trailer, PIE, Mack, Diecast Cab, Aluminum, Smith-Miller, 1940s, 28 In. 330.00
Truck, Semi-Trailer, Pine-Sol Long Haul, Private Label, Inserts, Tonka, 1970 . . . . 220.00
Truck, Semi-Trailer, Stake, Speed, Nickel Wheels, Kenton, 1930s, 10 1/4 In.. . . . . 1870.00
Truck, Semi-Trailer, Stix, Baer & Fuller, Private Label, Tonka, 1950 . . . . 2310.00
Truck, Semi-Trailer, West Coast, Fast Freight, Pressed Steel, Smith-Miller, 1940s, 21 In. . . 495.00
Truck, Semi-Trailer, Western Auto, Pressed Steel, Marx, Box, 25 In. 140.00
Truck, Service & Wrecker, Pressed Steel, Wyandotte, 23 In. 195.00
Truck, Shell Motor Oil, 8 Cans, Pressed Steel, Electric Headlights, Metalcraft, 13 In. 525.00
Truck, Shell, Pressed Steel, Buddy L, Box, 21 In. 3080.00
Truck, Sonny, Anti-Aircraft, Pressed Steel, Dayton Toy & Specialty, 1920s, 24 In. 250.00
Truck, Stake, Bronze, Tonka, 1959 . . . . 303.00
Truck, Stake, Mack, Bulldog, Cast Iron, Nickel Plated Wheels, Arcade, 5 In. 66.00
Truck, Stake, Orange, Hubley, 7 In. 1250.00
Truck, Stake, Painted, Windup, Replacement Key, Marx, 4 In. 145.00
Truck, Stake, Pressed Steel, Marx, 1950s, 14 In. 100.00
Truck, Steel Carrier, Pressed Steel, Tonka, 1950s, 24 In. 121.00
Truck, Sunshine Biscuit, Pressed Steel, Metalcraft, 12 In. . . . . .385.00 to 1400.00
Truck, Super Market, Pressed Steel, Food Cartons, Buddy L, 1940s, 13 In. 90.00
Truck, Supplee Ice Cream, Pressed Steel, Steelcraft, 21 In. 8800.00
Truck, Tanker, Benzol, Verband, Tin, Lehmann, Germany, 4 In. 50.00
Truck, Tanker, Gasoline, Green, Black Rubber Tires, Arcade, c.1930 . . . . 1320.00
Truck, Tanker, Gasoline, Mack, Hose, Driver, Cast Iron, Arcade, 1929, 12 1/2 In. 1550.00
Truck, Tanker, Gasoline, Motor Oil, Tin Lithograph, Windup, Courtland, 13 In. 130.00
Truck, Tanker, Gasoline, Rubber Tires, Blue, A.C. Williams, 6 3/4 In. 330.00
Truck, Tanker, Junior, Pressed Steel, Buddy L, 24 In. 5775.00
Truck, Tanker, Mobil Oil, Die Cast Cab, Pressed Steel Trailer, Smith-Miller, 22 In. 385.00
Truck, Tanker, Mobil Oil, Electric Headlights, Key, Citroen, France, Box, 23 In. 2310.00
Truck, Tanker, Mobil Oil, Mack, 2 Tanks, Diecast, Wood, Smith-Miller, 1940s, 34 In. 440.00
Truck, Tanker, Oil, Gas, Kenton, 10 1/4 In. 2970.00
Truck, Tanker, Pressed Steel, Buddy L, 24 In. 2200.00
Truck, Tanker, Pressed Steel, Wyandotte, 1930s, 10 1/2 In. 110.00
Truck, Tanker, Pure Oil Co., Pressed Steel, Streamlined, Metalcraft, 15 In. 525.00
Truck, Tanker, Richfield, Pressed Steel, American National, 26 In. 3850.00

Truck, Tanker, Royal Oil, Standard, Green Tank, 10 In. 1430.00
Truck, Tanker, Shell Oil, Nafta Energina Aceite, Tin, Windup, Argentina, 11 In. 385.00
Truck, Tanker, Sinclair, Pressed Steel, Green, Marx, 18 In. 440.00
Truck, Tanker, Standard Oil, Tin Windup, Driver, Strauss, 10 In. 1430.00
Truck, Tanker, Texaco, Die Cast Cab, Aluminum Tank, Smith-Miller, 15 In. 255.00
Truck, Tanker, Texaco, GMC, Buddy L, Box, 1959 .... 395.00
Truck, Tanker, Texaco, Pressed Steel, Buddy L, 1950s, 24 In. 100.00
Truck, Telephone, Structo, Unopened, Box, 12 In. 440.00
Truck, Tonka Farms, Stake, Pressed Steel, Tonka, 1960s, 14 In. 80.00
Truck, Tow, Blue, Red & Yellow, Hubley, 9 In. 195.00
Truck, Tow, Cast Iron, Nickel Plated Iron Wheels, Arcade, 12 In. 160.00
Truck, Tow, Champion, Cast Iron, Red, Blue, c.1934, 4 1/2 In. 880.00
Truck, Tow, Diecast, Pressed Steel, Smith-Miller, 1950s, 15 In. 155.00
Truck, Tow, Goodrich Silvertown Tires, Pressed Steel, Streamlined, Metalcraft, 13 In. 770.00
Truck, Tow, Hercules, Mack Cab, Tin, Chein, 20 In. 770.00
Truck, Tow, Mack, Bulldog, Tin Lithograph, Windup, Marx, 9 In. 605.00
Truck, Tow, Mack, Cast Iron, Red, Weaver Boom, Arcade, Early 1930s, 10 3/4 In. 2200.00
Truck, Tow, Mobile Repair-It, Jack, Spare Tire, Pressed Steel, Buddy L, 1940s, 28 In. 525.00
Truck, Tow, Packard, Pressed Steel, Rubber Tires, Keystone, 1920s, 24 In. 770.00
Truck, Tow, Pressed Steel, Buddy L, 1930s, 32 In. 880.00
Truck, Tow, Pressed Steel, Keystone, 26 In. 1980.00
Truck, Tow, Pressed Steel, Lincoln, 1950s, 13 1/2 In. 245.00
Truck, Tow, Pressed Steel, Red, Structo, Box, 1950s, 12 In. 155.00
Truck, Tow, Pressed Steel, Rubber Tires, Electric, Structo, 17 In. 880.00
Truck, Tow, Standard Oil, Tonka, Box, 1960 .... 2420.00
Truck, Tow, Teamsters, Pressed Steel, Decal, Original Papers, MIC, Box, 17 In. 2090.00
Truck, Tow, Weaver, Cast Iron, Arcade, 9 In. 605.00
Truck, Tow, Wyandotte, 9 In. 165.00
Truck, Trailer, Speed Stake, Cast Iron, Kenton, 6 In. 165.00
Truck, TV Service, Young Repairman, Plastic, Revell, Box, 12 In. 440.00
Truck, U.S. Army, Packard, Pressed Steel, Pull Cord, Canvas, Keystone, 26 In. 2860.00
Truck, U.S. Army, Pressed Steel, Canvas, Steelcraft, 23 In. 495.00
Truck, U.S. Mail, Pressed Steel, Sturditoy, 26 In. 1870.00
Truck, U.S. Mail, Tin, Windup, Red, White, Blue, Strauss, 8 In. 1870.00
Truck, Universal, Hayashi, Japan, 1950s, 7 3/4 In. 1200.00
Truck, Van, Box, Pressed Steel, Structo, 21 In. 660.00
Truck, Water Sprinkler, Tin, Windup, Driver, Strauss, 10 In. 990.00
Truck, Water Tower, Pressed Steel, Red, Sturditoy, 32 In. 770.00
Truck, Wooldridge, Pressed Steel, Bottom Dump Mechanism, Doepke, 1950s, 25 In. 120.00
Truck, World's Express, Diamond T, Tin Lithograph, Modern Toys, Box, 1930s, 8 1/2 In. . 2090.00
Truck, Wrigley's Spearmint Gum, Green, Buddy L, 15 In. 358.00
Truck, Wrigley's Spearmint, Railway Express Agency, Steel, Buddy L, 23 In. ....715.00 to 1540.00
Truck, Wyandotte, 1930, 15 In. 300.00
Truck, Zoo, Buddy L, Box, 1963 .... 350.00
Trumpet Player, Mixed Material, Windup, Nomura, Box, 10 1/2 In. 220.00
Turkey, Tucky, Steiff, 1961 .... 525.00
Turtle, Mohair, Steiff, c.1950s, 6 In. 45.00
Turtle, Mohair, Steiff, c.1960, 13 In. 55.00
TV Remote Control, Felix The Cat, Sony, 6 1/4 In. 75.00
Twirly Whirly, Rocket Ride, Rockets Spin & Light, Tin, Alps, Japan, Box, 13 1/2 In. 950.00
Uncle Sam, Roly Poly, Celluloid, Made In U.S.A., 3 In. 250.00
Uncle Wiggily's Bungalow, Hollow Stump, Paper, Composition, Androscoggin, 9 x 10 In. . 275.00
Velocipede Coach, Wood, Horse Head, E.W. Bushnell, Philadelphia, c.1850, 39 In. 14100.00
Ventriloquist Dummy, Black Man, Mohair Wig, Activate Through Back, 40 In. 4125.00
Victrola, Tin Lithograph, Crank Operated, Plink-Plunk Music, Penny Toy, 3 3/4 In. 275.00
Vitrine, Doll's, Burled Walnut, Glass Front, Silk Interior, c.1885, 29 In. 1065.00
Waffle Iron, Cast Iron, Wagner Sidney 110.00
Wagon, Army Service, Britains, Box 300.00
Wagon, Bakery, Black Horse, White Wagon, Cast Iron, Kenton, 14 In. 495.00
Wagon, Band, 2 Horses, Musicians, Cast Iron, Hubley, 17 In. 1980.00
Wagon, Band, 2 White Horses, Cast Iron, Kenton, 15 1/4 In. 550.00
Wagon, Circus, Band Leader's Arms Move, Pull Toy, Fisher-Price, 12 In. 880.00
Wagon, Circus, Big Six, Wild West, 2 Horses, Wood, Iron, 14 In. 550.00

Wagon, Circus, Big Six, Wood Carriage, Kenton, 15 In.	210.00
Wagon, Circus, Cage, Lion, 4 Horses, Cast Iron, Arcade, 20 1/2 In.	770.00
Wagon, Circus, Overland, 2 Horses, Cast Iron, Kenton, 14 In.	165.00
Wagon, Circus, Overland, Band, 4 White Horses, Cast Iron, 22 1/2 In.	1760.00
Wagon, Circus, Overland, Band, Cast Iron, Red, 2 White Horses, Kenton, Box, 16 In.	1045.00
Wagon, Circus, Overland, Bear, 2 Horses, Cast Iron, Kenton, Box, 14 In.	825.00
Wagon, Circus, Paper Lithograph On Tin, Spoked Metal Wheels, Gibb, 13 In.	235.00
Wagon, Circus, Royal, 2 Brown Bears, 2 Black Horses, Cast Iron, Hubley, 16 In.	3300.00
Wagon, Circus, Royal, 2 Horses, Driver, Cast Iron, Hubley, 10 x 16 In.	4255.00
Wagon, Circus, Royal, Band, 6 Horses, Cast Iron, 28 1/4 In.	6600.00
Wagon, Circus, Royal, Band, Cast Iron, Hubley, 23 1/4 In.	2200.00
Wagon, Circus, Royal, Brown Bear, 2 Black Horses, Cast Iron, Hubley, 8 1/4 In.	660.00
Wagon, Circus, Royal, Giraffe, Baby Giraffe, 4 Horses, Cast Iron, Hubley, 23 1/4 In.	7700.00
Wagon, Circus, Royal, Rhinos, Brown Horses, Cast Iron, Hubley, 16 In.	2090.00
Wagon, Farm, Large Horse, Dent, 1905, 14 1/2 In.	895.00
Wagon, Flying Eagle, Wood, Steel Undercarriage, 41 In.	110.00
Wagon, Fruit Seller, Tin, Black, Windup, Jointed, 6 1/2 In.	300.00
Wagon, Ice, Cast Iron, Kenton, 10 In.	165.00
Wagon, Log, Oxen, Black Driver, Cast Iron, Hubley, 16 In.	770.00
Wagon, Milk, Driver, Kenton, c.1950, 12 3/4 In.	468.00
Wagon, Milk, Rich's Little Milk Man, City Dairy, Tin Lithograph, Wood, c.1922, 20 In.	195.00
Wagon, Milk, White, Black Horse, Cast Iron, Kenton, 10 In.	330.00
Wagon, National, Kenton, 6 3/4 In.	440.00
Wagon, Steel, Red, Wooden Wheels, Art Deco, Wyandotte, 1930s, 8 In.	75.00
Wagon, Wood, Iron, White Star, 2 Tiers, Removable Seat, Late 1800s, 61 In.	1320.00
Walking Down Broadway, Couple Walking Dog, Tin Lithograph, Lehmann, 6 In.	250.00
Washing Machine, 3 Kittens, Crank Agitator, Tin, Ohio Art, 7 1/2 In.	190.00 to 215.00
Washing Machine, Hand Crank, Early 1900s, 8 In.	450.00
Washing Machine, Hand Crank, Early 1900s, 10 In.	400.00
Washing Machine, Tin, Kalon Radio Corp., Brooklyn, 8 x 13 In.	495.00
Water Pump, Cast Iron, Arcade, 8 3/4 In.	55.00
Western Play Time, Cowboys, Indians, Stagecoach, Plastic, Tin, Archer, N.Y., 48 Piece	85.00
Wheelbarrow, Pine, Metal Wheel Bands, Stenciled Horses, 35 x 13 1/2 In.	145.00
Wheelbarrow, Yellow, Brown, Horse, Red Wheel, 1910, 33 x 16 In.	375.00
Whirligig, Airplane, Aero Speeders, Tin Lithograph, Buffalo Toy Co., 10 In.	132.00
Whirligig, Dewey Boy, Sailor, Bearded, Blue Shirt & Pants, Holding Paddle, 15 1/2 In.	265.00
Whistle, Giraffe, In Clothes, Glasses, Monkey, Silvered Tin, Japan, 1930s, 3 1/8 In.	30.00
Whistle, Girl, Holding Clown, Golliwog, Umbrella, Silvered Tin, Japan, 1930s, 3 In.	20.00
Whistle, Girl, Holding Flowers, Hilltop, Silvered Tin, Japan, 1930s, 3 1/8 In.	20.00
Whistle, Man, Holding Rifle, Scottie Dog, Silvered Tin, Japan, 1930s, 3 1/8 In.	20.00
Wolf, Red & White Shirt, Pants, Mohair, Steiff, c.1960, 10 In.	300.00
Yeti, Abominable Snowman, Tin, Plush, Battery Operated, Remote, Marx, Box, 11 In.	845.00
Zebra, Mohair, Synthetic Fur, Glass Eyes, Ear Button, Steiff, 14 In.	95.00
Zeppelin, Graf, Worn Silver Paint, Cast Iron, 8 1/4 In.	195.00
Zeppelin, Pressed Steel, Steelcraft, 1930s, 26 In.	187.00
Zeppelin, Windup, Lehmann, Box	650.00
Zigzag, 2 Drivers, Large Wheel Apparatus, Windup, Lehmann, 1910	1350.00
Zilotone, Tin Lithograph, Mechanical, Silent Night Disc, Wolverine, 8 In.	336.00
Zoo, Britains, Box, 11 Piece	330.00

TRAMP ART is a form of folk art made since the Civil War. It is usually made from chip-carved cigar boxes. Examples range from small boxes and picture frames to full-sized pieces of furniture.

Basket On Stand, Spokes, Hanging Acorns, Geometric Chip Carved Base, 9 1/2 In.	1650.00
Box, Raised Mirror, 1880-1910, 12 x 9 x 10 1/4 In.	525.00
Box, Sewing, 2 Drawers, Velvet Pincushions, 1800s, 8 x 10 x 5 1/2 In.	325.00
Box, Stacked Chip Carved Diamonds, Pedestal, 1897, 8 1/2 x 10 In.	578.00
Box, Valuables, Maltese Crosses, Velvet Lining, Brass Side Handles, c.1910, 6 x 12 In.	115.00
Cabinet, Corner, Shelf, 2 Glass Doors, Chip Carved Top, 40 In.	485.00
Chest, Hanging, Pine, Flowers, Peaked Top, 13 Drawers, 5 Shelves, 39 x 26 x 11 In.	11800.00
Frame, Chip Carved, Multilayers, Hearts, 2 Picture Frames On Side, 20 In.	575.00
Frame, Diamond Shape, Banded Inlay, 3 Raised Areas, Worn Gold Paint, 22 In.	400.00
Frame, Wood, Chip Carved Stars, Hearts, Edges, Aged Patina, 27 1/2 x 22 1/2 In.	190.00

Mirror, Chain & Ball Whimsies, Carved Hearts & Stars, Brown Paint, 20 x 30 In.	1650.00
Mirror, Comb Holder, Raised Molding, Serrated Edges, Brown, Orange, 14 x 13 In.	275.00
Stand, Chip Carving, 31 x 12 In.	545.00
Stand, Plant, Stacked Graduated Diamonds, Serrated Edges, Pedestal, 27 x 15 In.	1320.00
Tree With 9 Birds, Chip Carved, Heart Center, Theo Demming, 1940, 31 x 25 In.	6600.00

TRAPS for animals may be handmade. One of the most unusual is the
mousetrap made so that when the mouse entered the trap, it was hit on
the head with a mallet. Other traps were commercially manufactured
and often are marked with the name of the manufacturer. Many traps
were designed to be as humane as possible, and they would trap the
live animal so it could be released in the woods.

Animal, Diamond L.S., No. 21, Double Jaws, Animal Trap Co., Lititz, Pa.	16.50
Animal, Jack Frost New-Ur-Lose, Stop Loss, Coil Spring, No. 1	35.00
Animal, Large, Iron, Newhouse, No. 14, 6-In. Jaws, 18 3/4 In.	87.00
Animal, Montgomery Double Coil Spring, No. 4, 2 x 3 1/4-In. Pan	11.00
Animal, Newhouse L.S., No. 0, Flat Link Chain, L.S. Oneida Community, 1902 Patent	122.00
Animal, North Woods Stop Loss, No. 1, Folding Guard	16.00
Animal, Pan Trap, No. 1, P.S. & W Co. L.S.	20.00
Animal, Victor Shoulder Catch, No. 91, L.S. Oneida Community, 1921 Patent	5.00
Animal, Victor, No. 3, D.L.S., Bolted Cast Jaws, Cast Pan	55.00
Coon, Metal, D.P. Trap Co., 2 x 3 x 6 In.	28.00
Eel, Basketry, Splint, 26 1/2 In.	145.00
Fly, Glass, Dome Shape, Stopper, 3 Applied Pad Feet, Cobalt Blue, 7 3/4 In.	372.00
Fly, Glass, Unique Fly Trap, Mold Blown, Pierced Top, Metal Mesh, 6 1/2 x 5 1/2 In.	116.00
Gopher, Newhouse Choker Loop, Green, Animal Trap Co., Lititz, Pa.	16.00
Minnow, Glass, Wire Frame, 12 In.	350.00
Mouse, Hell Cat, Better Mouse Trap, Eagle Lock Co.	40.00
Rabbit, A. Fenn Mark 6 Run Way, Brass Dog, England	22.00
Setting Clamp, Bear, New House, No. 5, 11 In.	424.00
Wolverine, Mountain Lion, Alaskan Jaw, No. 9, Coil Spring, 9-In. Jaw Circle	110.00

TREEN, see Wooden category.

TRIVETS are now used to hold hot dishes. Most trivets of the late
nineteenth and early twentieth centuries were made to hold hot irons.
Iron or brass reproductions are being made of many of the old styles.

Brass, Square Edge, Bail Handles, Shaped Apron, 20th Century, 12 1/2 x 21 x 14 In.	235.00
Brass, Stand, Pierced Top, Sides, Cabriole Legs, 20th Century, 12 x 17 x 11 1/4 In.	130.00
Copper, Hammered, Iridescent Mosaic Tile Inlay, Burdick, Round, 1908, 5 1/2 In.	1528.00
Iron, Heart Shaped, Leaf Engraving, 3 Footed, 10 In.	690.00
Iron, Revolving, Round, Scroll, Arrow, Tripod, Shaped Handle, 4 1/2 x 30 x 12 1/2 In.	3105.00
Wrought Iron, For Iron, Early 19th Century, 5 1/2 x 4 x 2 In.	29.00
Wrought Iron, Heart Shape, c.1800, 2 x 4 1/4 x 10 1/4 In.	264.00
Wrought Iron, Hearth, Round, Flattened Handle, Hanger Hook, 3 Leg Base, 15 x 6 In. . . .	220.00
Wrought Iron, Hearth, Round, Heart Handle, Spade & Scroll Feet, 1700s, 2 1/8 x 12 In. . .	764.00
Wrought Iron, Round, 3 Diamond Foot Legs, Scalloped Edges, 4 1/2 x 2 1/2 In.	90.00
Wrought Iron, Round, C-Shaped Center Pieces, 3-Footed, 6 1/2 x 10 1/2 In.	138.00
Wrought Iron, Spade Feet, Ring Handle, 10 In.	106.00
Wrought Iron, Triangular, Wooden Handle, c.1800, 1 1/2 x 4 5/8 x 9 3/4 In.	29.00

TRUNKS of many types were made. The nineteenth-century sea chest
was often handmade of unpainted wood. Brass-fitted camphorwood
chests were brought back from the Orient. Leather-covered trunks
were popular from the late eighteenth to mid-nineteenth centuries. By
1895, trunks were covered with canvas or decorated sheet metal.
Embossed metal coverings were used from 1870 to 1910. By 1925,
trunks were covered with vulcanized fiber or undecorated metal. Suitcases are listed here.

Bronze, Shipping Labels, Handles, Front Latch, Nude Woman, Austria, 20th Century, 5 In.	3408.00
Dome Top, Blue Paint, 1864, 30 x 42 x 24 In.	1150.00
Dome Top, Leather, Round Head Nails, 19th Century, 12 3/4 x 24 1/4 x 12 1/2 In.	80.00
Dome Top, Metal Bound, Late 19th Century, 31 x 36 1/2 x 22 1/2 In.	70.00

Dome Top, Painted, Tyrolean, Flowers, Escutcheon Front Panel, c.1900, 13 x 8 In. 470.00
Dome Top, Pine, Dovetailed Case, Iron Handles, 35 x 21 x 21 In. 259.00
Dome Top, Pine, Painted Swag, Flower, 11 x 27 x 13 In. 175.00
Flat Top, Charleston Trunk Co., Wood Slats, Metal Fittings, Early 1900s, 26 x 37 x 22 In. . 259.00
Hide Covered, Mirro, Swing Handle, Clover & Star Decoration, 2 x 4 1/4 x 2 1/2 In. 230.00
Immigrant's, Oak, 1805, 33 x 26 In. 1250.00
Leather, Brass Tacks, Tooling, Wood, Engraved Brass Plate, 24 x 14 x 12 In. 175.00
Louis Vuitton, Leather, Iron & Wood Supports, Canvas Lined, Stackable, 22 x 44 x 24 In. . 478.00
Louis Vuitton, Steamer, Leather Handles, Labels, Fabric Lined Trays, 24 x 21 x 17 In. 705.00
Louis Vuitton, Steamer, Wooden Strapping, Handles, Lined Trays, 44 x 22 1/2 x 23 In. . . . 3525.00
Louis Vuitton, Steamer, Wooden Strapping, Lined Trays, 43 1/2 x 22 3/4 x 22 In. 1295.00
Louis Vuitton, Travel Case, Fabric, Handle, Labels, Canvas Liner, 17 x 16 x 16 1/4 In. 1175.00
Pigskin, Flowers, Chinese, 12 1/2 x 28 x 17 1/2 In. 160.00
Pine, Painted, X-Form Paneling Opens To A Well, 1800s, 10 1/2 x 23 1/2 x 13 In. 705.00
Pine, Pinch Waist, Strapped, 19 x 34 In. 345.00
Softwood, Painted Flag Shield, Latch, Casters, Jas. H. Couch, Springdale, Pa., 36 In. 248.00
Stagecoach, Wood, Brass, Compartments, Coaster On Bottom, 34 x 25 x 18 In. 495.00
Wood, Dovetailed, Blue Paint, Over Red, Swing Metal Top Handle, 11 x 19 x 13 In. 405.00
Wood, Painted Fans, Rosettes, Hinged Lid, Iron Handles, Early 1800s, 13 x 30 x 15 In. . . . 2000.00

TYPEWRITER collectors divide typewriters into two main classifica-
tions: the index machine, which has a pointer and a dial for letter selection, and the keyboard machine, most commonly seen today. The first
successful typewriter was made by Sholes and Glidden in 1874.

Hammond, Model I, Curved 2-Row Keyboard, Oak Bentwood Case, 14 In. 1645.00
Hammond, Multiplex, Oak Base, 13 x 14 1/2 x 8 In. 290.00
Hammond, No. 12, Leather Case, 8 1/2 x 16 x 13 In. 248.00
L.C. Smith & Bros., No. 8, Syracuse, N.Y., 15 In. 55.00
Memo Pad, Underwood Altitude, Eagle, Typewriter, Celluloid, Cardboard, 3 x 2 In. 56.00

TYPEWRITER RIBBON TINS are now being collected. The litho-
graphed tin containers have been used since the 1870s. Most popular
with collectors are tins with pictorial graphics.

Allied Typewriter, Allied Carbon & Ribbon Mfg., Corp., New York 34.00
Carter's Ink, Carter's Dragon, Woman's Silhouette, Red, White, Black 7.00
Carter's Ink, Carter's Five O'Clock, Secretary, Powders Nose, 2 1/2 In. 28.00
Carter's Ink, Ideal Typewriter Ribbon, Orchid, 2 1/2 In. 25.00
Carter's Midnight, Boston 16.00
Flint Brand, Keelox, Rochester, N.Y., 2 1/4 x 3/4 In. 7.50
Keelox Brand 24.00
Thorobred Typewriter, Underwood Corp., Burlington, N.J. 25.00
Type Bar Brand, L.C. Smith Corona 18.00
Webster Star Brand, Hinged Lid, Boston, Mass. 18.00

UHL pottery was made in Evansville, Indiana, in 1854. The pottery
moved to Huntingburg, Indiana, in 1908. Stoneware and glazed pottery
were made until the mid-1940s.

Boot, Painted Cornucopia Of Flowers, Green, 2 1/2 In. 40.00
Bottle, Elephant, Blue, 3 1/4 In. 10.00
Bottle, Meiers Grape Juice, Maroon 10.00
Crock, Blue Lid, White Bottom, 3 In. 35.00
Figurine, Pig, Blue, 3 1/4 x 5 In. 45.00
Slipper, Black, 2 1/2 In. 15.00
Slipper, Blue, 2 1/2 In. 15.00

UMBRELLA collectors like rain or shine. The first known umbrella
was owned by King Louis XIII of France in 1637. The earliest umbrel-
las were sunshades, not designed to be used in the rain. The umbrella
was embellished and redesigned many times. In 1852, the fluted steel
rib style was developed, and it has remained the most useful style.

Advertising, Winchester Store, Arthur F. Knies, White Haven 550.00
Beach, Nylon, Steel Chair Clamp, Multicolored Stripes, 44 In. Diam. 43.00
Dusty Pink, Haas-Jordan, Black Metal Ribs, Brass Tips, Handle With Curved Plastic End . 50.00

Golf, Sailcloth, Red & White, Cloth Sheath, Polan Katz & Co., 1930s-40s, 50 In. Diam. . . .	17.00
Nylon, Dior Logo Print, Tortoiseshell Plastic Handle, Christian Dior, 31 In., 1970s	128.00
Nyltest, White Fabric, Brass Frame, Twisted Silver Metal Handle, Austria, c.1950	54.00
Orange Gold, Curved Handle, Touch 'n' Go, Protective Sleeve, PJK, 1957, 34 3/4 In.	58.00
Paper, Oiled, Block Printed Dragons & Roosters, Bamboo, 26 1/2 x 21 1/2 In.	59.00
Parasol, Embroidered Cotton, Bamboo, Wooden Handle, Bulldog's Head, c.1900, 37 In. . .	90.00
Parasol, Silk, Embroidered, Carved Wooden Handle, Folding, Japan, 1940s, 41 x 31 In. . . .	149.00
Parasol, Silk, Hand Painted Roses, Handle & Ribs Capped With Bone, 1920s, 28 1/4 In. . .	75.00

UNION PORCELAIN WORKS was established at Greenpoint, New

York, in 1848 by Charles Cartlidge. The company went through a
series of ownership changes and finally closed in the early 1900s. The
company made a fine quality white porcelain that was often decorated
in clear, bright colors.

Dish, Vegetable, Flowers, Shaker, Mt. Lebanon, N.Y., 2 1/2 x 10 1/4 x 7 In.	1150.00
Pitcher, Bill Nye, Chinese Gambler, Uncle Sam, Late 1860s, 9 3/4 In.	3968.00

UNIVERSITY OF NORTH DAKOTA, see North Dakota School of Mines category.

VAL ST. LAMBERT Cristalleries of Belgium was founded by Mes-

sieurs Kemlin and Lelievre in 1825. The company is still in operation.
All types of table glassware and decorative glassware have been made.
Pieces are often decorated with cut designs.

Val St Lambert

Candlestick, Bobeche, Hanging Prisms, 12 In., Pair	85.00
Decanter, Chamfered Square Band, Ball Stopper, 1900s, 9 3/4 In., Pair	380.00
Dresser Set, Amber Stain, 5 Piece	60.00
Epergne, 5 Cylindrical Flower Holders, Brass Frame, Cameo, 10 1/2 In.	2070.00
Figurine, Cat, Sleeping, 6 In.	235.00
Tumble-Up Set, Decanter, Tumbler Cover, Underplate, Amber Stain, 7 In.	80.00
Vase, Carnation & Leaves, Amethyst Cased, Satin Cameo, c.1900, 7 1/2 In.	520.00
Vase, Cranberry Cut To Clear, Diamond Pattern, Bulbous, Flared Rim, Signed, 9 In.	400.00
Vase, Cranberry, Gold Scroll & Flowers, Cameo, c.1915, 6 1/2 In.	260.00
Vase, Squid, Blue, Yellow Ground, Satin, Spherical, 9 In.	1175.00

VAN BRIGGLE pottery was started by Artus Van Briggle in Colorado

Springs, Colorado, after 1901. Van Briggle had been a decorator at
Rookwood Pottery of Cincinnati, Ohio. He died in 1904 and his wife
took over managing the pottery. His wares usually had modeled relief
decorations and a soft, dull glaze. The pottery is still working and still
making some of the original designs.

Bowl, Lady Of The Lake, Lady On Side, Blue, Green Matte Glaze, c.1920, 9 x 14 In.	265.00
Bowl, Mermaid, Blue, Turquoise Glaze, 8 1/4 x 14 1/2 In.	380.00
Candleholder, Green, Brown, High Gloss, Anna Van Briggle, c.1958, 3 x 5 1/2 x 4 In.	35.00
Candlestick, Brown, Incised Logo, 1914, 8 5/8 In.	545.00
Console Set, Turquoise, Mid 20th Century, 8 1/2 In., 4 Piece	160.00
Ewer, Persian Rose, Mid 20th Century, 9 In. . . . . .80.00 to 100.00
Figurine, Deer, Reclining, Maroon & Blue Matte Glaze, Marked, 4 1/2 In.	90.00
Figurine, Donkey, Maroon & Blue Matte Glaze, Marked, 3 1/2 In.	60.00
Figurine, Indian Girl Grinding Corn, Turquoise Glaze, c.1950, 6 In.	230.00
Figurine, Rabbit, Green & Blue Matte Glaze, Marked, 3 1/2 In.	60.00
Figurine, Rabbit, Maroon & Blue Matte Glaze, Marked, 3 1/2 In.	170.00
Figurine, Rebecca At The Well, Aqua, Signed, 16 1/2 In.	140.00
Figurine, Seated Woman Holding Large Shell In Lap, Green, 7 1/2 In.	259.00
Lamp, 3-Headed Indian, Sea Green To Blue, Fabric Shade, Signed, 24 In.	345.00
Lamp, Damsel Of Damascus, Mid 20th Century, 16 In.	210.00
Lamp, Panther, Maroon & Blue Matte Glaze, Butterfly Shade, Signed, Walker, 11 In.	325.00
Pitcher, Rebecca At The Well, Turquoise Glaze, Mid 20th Century, 17 In.	315.00
Pitcher, Rust High Glaze, Turquoise Rim, Incised, 9 In.	35.00
Planter, Conch Shell, Mid 20th Century, 12 In.	100.00
Plate, Grape, Blue, Green Matte Glaze, c.1907-12, 8 1/2 In.	440.00
Plate, Stylized Leaf, Multitone Blue Matte Glaze, c.1907-12, 6 In.	500.00
Snake Jug, Rose Matte Glaze, Shape 23, 1902, 6 In.	5100.00
Tile, Arts & Crafts, Trees In Landscape, Blue, Green, Brown, 6 x 6 In.	1400.00

Vase, 2 Handles, Egg Shape, Red, Lime Green Matte Glaze, 7 3/4 x 3 1/2 In. 2000.00
Vase, 3 Dragonflies, Blue, Green Matte Glaze, 4 1/2 In. 355.00
Vase, 3-Headed Indian, Green & Blue Matte Glaze, Footed, Signed, 12 1/2 In. 288.00
Vase, 3-Headed Indian, Teal Green, Red Matte Glaze, 11 x 5 In. 529.00
Vase, Arabesques, Elephant Skin Blue Gray Glaze, Squat, 1906, 5 14 x 4 1/2 In. 2000.00
Vase, Arrowhead, Leaves, Violet Blue, Rose, 17 x 12 In. 4500.00
Vase, Brown, Green Glaze, 4 1/4 In. 105.00
Vase, Cornflowers, Burgundy, Blue, Green Glaze, 2 Handles, 10 x 7 1/2 In. 4400.00
Vase, Daffodils, Green, Blue Matte Glaze, c.1916, 10 In. 560.00
Vase, Daisies, Blue, Green, Cylindrical, 1915, 7 1/2 In. 560.00
Vase, Daisies, Cylindrical, Persian Rose Glaze, 1918-19, 6 3/4 x 3 In. 265.00
Vase, Daisies, Mountain Craig Brown Glaze, 7 In. 295.00
Vase, Dogwood Blossom, Leaves, Frothy Green Glaze, 1906, 8 x 5 In. 1410.00
Vase, Dragonflies, Green Matte Glaze, 4 1/2 In. 1115.00
Vase, Egret, Dusty Rose, 16 1/2 In. 130.00
Vase, Elephant Skin Glaze, Purple, Blue, 1906, 11 1/2 x 5 In. 1880.00
Vase, Feather, Stylized, Brown Matte Glaze, Broad Shape, c.1905, 5 1/2 In. 2350.00
Vase, Figural, American Indian, Incised, 8 In. 460.00
Vase, Flowers, Carved, Waisted, Blue Matte Glaze, c.1906, 9 In. 1175.00
Vase, Flowers, Green Matte Glaze, Yellow Accent, 1906, 9 1/2 In. 1955.00
Vase, Flowers, Incised, Tapering, Blue Over Green, 1914, 10 3/4 In. 690.00
Vase, Flowers, Jet Black, Signed, 5 In. 12.00
Vase, Flowers, Leaves, Spade Shape, Squat, 1904, 4 3/4 x 5 1/4 In. 1528.00
Vase, Flowers, Stems, Maroon, Blue Matte Glaze, c.1919, 12 In. 1880.00
Vase, Flowers, Stylized, Incised, Blue, Green Matte Glaze, 8 1/2 In. 1410.00
Vase, Flowers, Stylized, Shouldered, Gray Blue Glaze, c.1914, 8 In. 690.00
Vase, Gingko Leaves, Brown Matte Glaze, 1907-12, 2 In. 529.00
Vase, Green On Green Matte Glaze, 1907-12, 5 In. 489.00
Vase, Leaf, Blue, Green Drip, Anna Van, 1950s, 5 3/4 In. 60.00
Vase, Leaf, Geometric, White Gray Glaze, Tan Ground, 6 1/4 In. 690.00
Vase, Leaf, Spade Like, Green, Marked, 2 In. 60.00
Vase, Leaves, Carved, Stylized, Maroon & Blue Matte Glaze, c.1920, 10 In. 380.00
Vase, Leaves, Flaring, Blue To Turquoise Glaze, 1920s, 8 In. 380.00
Vase, Leaves, Flaring, Mountain Craig Brown Glaze, 1930s, 8 In. 295.00
Vase, Leaves, Spade Shape, Bulbous, Frothy Glaze, 1908, 4 3/4 x 4 In. 940.00
Vase, Leaves, Stylized, Brown, Green Matte Glaze, c.1920, 5 1/2 In. 325.00
Vase, Leaves, Stylized, Incised, Maroon, Blue Matte, c.1920, 10 In. 380.00
Vase, Leaves, Yellow Matte Glaze, c.1920-30, 5 In. 645.00
Vase, Lorelei, Embossed Figure, Woman, Mid 20th Century, 10 In. 259.00
Vase, Lorelei, Glazed, Mid 20th Century, 10 1/2 In. 129.00
Vase, Mountain Craig Brown Glaze, 1922-26, 4 1/2 In. 230.00
Vase, Mulberry Glaze, 9 5/8 In. 115.00
Vase, Mulberry Glaze, Marked, 4 1/2 In. 140.00
Vase, Olive Green Matte, c.1906, 3 3/4 In. 380.00
Vase, Organic, Incised, Multitone Matte Glaze, c.1907-12, 6 In. 1645.00
Vase, Organic, Swollen Shape, Gunmetal To Green Matte, c.1910, 4 1/2 In. 1000.00
Vase, Papyrus Flowers, Bulbous, Reticulated, Frothy Glaze, 1907-11, 6 1/4 x 5 In. 3055.00
Vase, Peacock Feather, Flared, Multicolored Glaze, 1908-11, 3 1/2 In. 4700.00
Vase, Poppies, Blue, Green Matte Glaze, c.1907-12, 9 1/2 In. 940.00
Vase, Poppies, Bulbous, Blue & Green Frothy Glaze, 1908-11, 4 1/4 x 5 1/2 In. 1175.00
Vase, Poppies, Organic, Maroon, Blue Matte Glaze, 4 In. 175.00
Vase, Poppies, Shouldered, Charcoal Matte Glaze, 1902, 4 In. 2350.00
Vase, Poppies, Slender, Green Matte Glaze, c.1907, 6 1/2 In. 3055.00
Vase, Poppies, Squat, Persian Rose Glaze, 1903, 4 x 4 1/2 In. 2235.00
Vase, Poppies, Whiplash Stems, Incised, Gunmetal, Blue Matte Glaze, 10 In. 4750.00
Vase, Poppy, Maroon Matte Glaze, Shouldered, c.1915, 7 1/2 In. 980.00
Vase, Squat Shape, Carved Neck, Purple, Yellow, Brown Matte Glaze, 5 In. 865.00
Vase, Thistles, Blue Green Glaze, 1908-11, 9 3/4 In. 645.00
Vase, Tulips, Purple To Periwinkle Matte Glaze, 1903, 7 3/4 x 3 In. 2350.00
Vase, Yucca Plant, Stylized, 1930s, 4 1/2 In. 185.00
Wall Hanging, American Indian Face, Green, Blue Matte Glaze, c.1940, 4 In. 30.00
Wall Hanging, American Indian Face, Maroon & Blue Matte Glaze, Marked, c.1940, 4 In. . 90.00
Wall Pocket, Cornflower, Persian Rose Glaze, 1920, 7 3/4 x 4 1/4 In. 147.00

VASA MURRHINA is the name of a glassware made by the Vasa Murrhina Art Glass Company of Sandwich, Massachusetts, about 1884. The glassware was transparent and was embedded with small pieces of colored glass and metallic flakes. The mica flakes were coated with silver, gold, copper, or nickel. Some of the pieces were cased. The same type of glass was made in England. Collectors often confuse Vasa Murrhina glass with aventurine, spatter, or spangle glass. There is uncertainty about what actually was made by the Vasa Murrhina factory. Related pieces may be listed under Spangle Glass.

Bowl, Finger, Amber, Cranberry, Blue & Orange Spots, 6 In.	400.00
Bowl, Finger, Underplate, Orange Oil Spots, 6 In.	400.00
Finger Bowl, Underplate, Amber, Cranberry Cased, Oil Spots, Gold Aventurine, 6 In.	460.00

VASELINE GLASS is a greenish-yellow glassware resembling petroleum jelly. Some vaseline glass is still being made in old and new styles. Pressed glass of the 1870s was often made of vaseline-colored glass. Additional pieces of vaseline glass may also be listed under Pressed Glass in this book.

Basket, Daisy & Button, 7 1/2 In.	75.00
Bowl, Ruffled Edge, Internal Ribbing, 10 In.	230.00
Epergne, 1-Lily, Opalescent, Victorian, 14 1/2 In.	750.00
Jar, Cover, Greek Key, 3-Footed, 4 1/2 In.	100.00
Tumbler, Wildflower Pattern	65.00
Vase, Automobile, Conical, Embossed Stars, 6 1/2 In., Pair	200.00
Vase, Enameled Flowers, Bulbous Base, Flared Neck, 12 In.	850.00
Water Set, Heirloom, Summit Art Glass, 7 x 8-In. Pitcher, 4 1/2-In. Tumbler, 5 Piece	225.00

VENETIAN GLASS, see Glass-Venetian category.

VERLYS glass was made in Rouen, France, by the Societe Holophane Francais, a company that started in 1920. It was made in Newark, Ohio, from 1935 to 1951. The glass is either blown or molded. The American glass is signed with a diamond-point-scratched name, but the French pieces are marked with a molded signature. The designs resemble those used by Lalique.

Bonbon, Amber, Frosted, Butterflies, France, 20th Century, 1 1/2 x 6 1/2 In.	150.00
Bowl, Centerpiece, Poppies, Frosted, Round, Signed, 13 3/4 In.	60.00
Vase, Continuous Panel Of Mermaids, Clear & Frosted, Signed, 10 1/2 In.	359.00
Vase, Lobed Leaves, Flowers Heads, Raised, Engraved, 8 7/8 In.	400.00

VERNON KILNS was the name used by Vernon Potteries, Ltd. The company, which started in 1931 in Vernon, California, made dinnerware and figurines until it went out of business in 1958. The molds were bought by Metlox, which continued to make some patterns. Collectors search for the brightly colored dinnerware and the pieces designed by Rockwell Kent, Walt Disney, and Don Blanding. For more information, see *Kovels' Depression Glass & Dinnerware Price List*.

Anytime, Creamer	14.00
Anytime, Cup	12.00
Anytime, Plate, Salad, 7 1/2 In.	7.00
Arcadia, Plate, Dinner, 10 1/2 In.	24.00
Barkwood, Mug, 9 Oz.	12.00
Bits Of New England, Plate, Tapping For Sugar, 8 1/2 In.	25.00
Bits Of The Old South, Chop Plate, Down On The Levee, 14 In.	100.00
Brown Eyed Susan, Platter, Oval, 12 1/2 In.	20.00
Brown Eyed Susan, Teapot, Cover	95.00
Calico, Saucer	3.00
Commemorative, Plate, Franz Liszt, 1811-1886, Biography On Back, 8 1/2 In.	25.00
Commemorative, Plate, Peter Tschaikovsky, 1840-1893, Biography On Back, 8 1/2 In.	25.00
Coronado, Plate, Orange, 6 1/2 In.	9.00
Dolores, Plate, 7 1/2 In.	10.00
Early Days, Soup, 8 In.	10.00
Gingham, Gravy Boat	7.00

Gingham, Plate, 9 1/2 In. 7.00
Gingham, Soup, Dish, 8 1/2 In. 12.00
Hawaiian Coral, Cup & Saucer 12.00
Hawaiian Coral, Saucer 3.00
Heavenly Days, Saucer 3.00
Heavenly Days, Tidbit, 2 Tiers, 12 In. 15.00
Heydey, Cup & Saucer 10.00
Heydey, Plate, 6 In. 10.00
Homespun, Chop Plate, 12 In. 18.00
Homespun, Cup & Saucer ....8.00 to 15.00
Homespun, Plate, 9 1/2 In. 5.00
Homespun, Salt & Pepper 8.00
Linda, Bowl, Vegetable, Round, 9 In. 25.00
Linda, Chop Plate, 12 In. 31.00
Linda, Cup & Saucer 25.00
May Flower, Plate, 6 1/2 In. 15.00
May Flower, Saucer 8.00
Organdie, Bowl, 6 In. 8.00
Organdie, Bowl, Vegetable, 9 In. 28.00
Organdie, Chop Plate, 12 In. 12.00
Organdie, Creamer ....7.00 to 10.00
Organdie, Cup & Saucer 12.00
Organdie, Pitcher, 2 Qt., 11 In. 60.00
Organdie, Plate, 9 1/2 In. ....8.00 to 19.00
Organdie, Salt & Pepper 15.00
Raffia, Creamer 12.00
Raffia, Cup & Saucer 8.00
Raffia, Plate, 10 In. 9.00
Rose-A-Day, Plate, 10 In. 10.00
Salamina, Lunch Set, Rockwell Kent, 22 Piece 920.00
Sierra Madre, Chop Plate, Blue Border, 12 In. 12.00
Souvenir, Ashtray, Kentucky, Man O' War, 5 1/2 In. 28.00
Souvenir, Coaster, Texas, 4 1/2 In. 22.00
Souvenir, Plate, 48th National Convention Of Postmasters, 1952 .... 29.00
Souvenir, Plate, Carlsbad Caverns, New Mexico, Entrance, Rock Of Ages, 10 1/2 In. 19.00
Souvenir, Plate, Charleston, South Carolina, Landmarks, Red, 10 1/2 In. 25.00
Souvenir, Plate, Houston, Texas, Shamrock Hotel, Green, 10 1/2 In. 25.00
Souvenir, Plate, Kentucky, Man O' War, Churchill Downs, State Capitol, 10 1/2 In. 28.00
Souvenir, Plate, Little Rock, Arkansas, State War Memorial, Landmarks, Blue, 10 1/2 In. ... 25.00
Souvenir, Plate, Montana, Famous Scenic Views, 10 1/2 In. 12.00
Souvenir, Plate, My Maryland, Landmarks, 10 1/2 In. 24.00
Souvenir, Plate, New Mexico, Gallup, Navajo Church Rock, Landmarks, 10 1/2 In. 25.00
Souvenir, Plate, New Mexico, Land Of Enchantment, Historic Places, 10 1/2 In. 35.00
Souvenir, Plate, New Orleans, Cabildo, Landmarks, Blue, 10 1/2 In. 25.00
Souvenir, Plate, New York, Remember Manhattan, Landmarks, Maroon, 10 1/2 In. 30.00
Souvenir, Plate, Pennsylvania Turnpike, Howard Johnson's, 10 1/2 In. 20.00
Souvenir, Plate, Sacramento, Sutters Fort, Tower Bridge, State Capitol, 10 1/2 In. 9.00
Souvenir, Plate, San Francisco, Landmarks, Maroon, 10 1/2 In. 25.00
Souvenir, Plate, Santa Fe, Historical Places, Landscape, Maroon, 10 1/2 In. 20.00
Souvenir, Plate, St. Augustine, Florida, Landmarks, 1940s, 10 1/2 In. 32.00
Souvenir, Plate, St. Louis, Missouri, Map, Mary Vangelder, 1948, 10 1/2 In. 25.00
Souvenir, Plate, St. Louis, Missouri, Veiled Prophet, c.1940, 10 1/2 In. 25.00
Souvenir, Plate, University Of Notre Dame, Soren Hall, Field House, Multicolor, 10 1/2 In. ... 25.00
Souvenir, Plate, Vermont, Landmarks, Maroon, 10 1/2 In. 25.00
Souvenir, Plate, Will Rogers, Man Of Many Talents, Maroon, 10 1/2 In. 25.00
Tam O' Shanter, Cup & Saucer 12.00
Tam O' Shanter, Plate, Dinner, 10 In. 6.00
Tam O' Shanter, Saucer 7.00
Tickled Pink, Creamer 15.00
Tweed, Bowl, Cereal, 6 In. 6.00
Tweed, Cup & Saucer 13.00
Tweed, Plate, 10 In. 10.00
Tweed, Saucer 8.00

Tweed, Sugar & Creamer 15.00

VERRE DE SOIE glass was first made by Frederick Carder at the
Steuben Glass Works from about 1905 to 1930. It is an iridescent glass of soft white or very, very pale green. The name means *glass of silk*, and it does resemble silk. Other factories have made verre de soie, and some of the English examples were made of different colors. Verre de soie is an art glass and is not related to the iridescent, pressed, white carnival glass mistakenly called by its name. Related pieces may be found in the Steuben category.

Bowl, Blue Border, 3 3/4 x 9 1/2 In.	460.00
Bowl, Blue Rim, 4 1/2 x 12 In.	418.00
Compote, Signed, 2 3/4 x 6 In.	180.00
Compote, Teal Blue Border, 3 1/4 x 8 In.	240.00
Goblet Set, Opalescence, Gold Aurene Interior, 3 3/4 In., 5 Piece	645.00
Lamp, 5-Light, Lily, Bronze Base, Acanthus Leaves, Steuben, 15 In.	4025.00
Shade, Cone Shape, Steuben, 4 1/4 In.	85.00
Shade, Festoon, Ruffled Rim, Steuben, 4 1/8 In.	230.00
Shade, Flower Shape, Steuben, 4 3/4 In.	200.00
Urn, Cover, Amethyst Stemmed Plum Finial, Steuben	1150.00
Vase, 10 In.	170.00
Vase, Bulbous, Triple Stem, Rounded Base, 8 In.	575.00
Vase, Flower Etch, Flared, Shouldered, Steuben, 6 1/2 In.	575.00
Vase, Lily, Footed, Steuben, 12 In.	235.00
Vase, Opalescence, Handles, 10 1/2 In.	820.00
Vase, Quilted, Applied Blue Threading, Flared, Frosted, 6 1/2 In.	705.00
Vase, Twisted Stem, Round Foot, Ruffled Rim, 8 In.	705.00

VIENNA, see Beehive category.

VILLEROY & BOCH Pottery of Mettlach was founded in 1836. The
firm made many types of wares, including the famous Mettlach steins. Collectors can be confused because although Villeroy & Boch made most of its pieces in the city of Mettlach, Germany, they also had factories in other locations. The dating code impressed on the bottom of most pieces makes it possible to determine the age of the piece. Additional items, including steins and earthenware pieces marked with the famous castle mark or the word *Mettlach,* may be found in the Mettlach category.

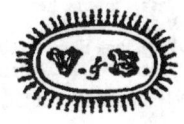

Mug, Fluted, Colorful Scene, 6 In.	55.00
Punch Bowl, Underplate, Gnomes At Wine Press, No. 2339-1028, 15 In.	193.00
Tray, Moss Green, Blue Green & White Geometric Design, 1910, 20 In.	325.00
Vase, Crystalline Green Matte Glaze, 12 5/8 In.	1093.00

VOLKMAR pottery was made by Charles Volkmar of New York from
1879 to about 1911. He was associated with several firms, including the Volkmar Ceramic Company, Volkmar and Cory, and Charles Volkmar and Son. Volkmar had been a painter, and his designs often look like oil paintings drawn on pottery.

VOLKMAR
Corona N.y

Bowl, Turquoise Blue, Open Form, Flared Sides, Footed, Marked, 5 1/2 In.	375.00
Candleholder, Crimped, Round Base, Green Matte Glaze, 3 3/4 x 5 In.	115.00
Vase, Brown Matte Glaze, Octagonal, Bottle Neck, 4 1/4 In.	264.00

WADE pottery is made by the Wade Group of Potteries started in 1810
near Burslem, England. Several potteries merged to become George Wade & Son, Ltd. early in the twentieth century, and other potteries have been added through the years. The best-known Wade pieces are the small figurines given away with Red Rose Tea and other promotional items. The Disney figures are listed in this book in the Disneyana category.

c. 1936+

Figurine, Old King Cole, 2 1/4 In.	44.00
Figurine, Rabbit, Little Laughing Bunny, Gray & White, Late 1940s, 2 3/4 In.	85.00
Figurine, Snow White & Seven Dwarfs, 8 Piece	450.00

Figurine, Squirrel, Acorn In Paws, First Whimsies, Set No. 1, 1954-58 .... 35.00
Figurine, Stoat, First Whimsies, Set No. 3, 1955-58 .... 70.00
Figurine, Watermill Factory, Whimsy-On-Why, Set No. 2, 1 3/4 x 1 1/8 x 2 5/8 In., 1980s . 25.00
Pitcher, Beefeater Gin, White Glaze, Brick Look, Decal Of Beefeater, 1980s, 5 7/8 In. 24.00
Pub Jug, Usher's Scotch Whisky, Black Letters On Cream Ground, 4 1/2 In. 45.00
Teapot, Orange, Band Of Chintz-Style Flowers Around Rim, 1920s, 6 x 7 3/4 In. 99.00
Toast Rack, Pottery, Yellow, Cow Decal On One End, Bull On Other, Marked, 3 x 6 In. ... 83.00

WALL POCKETS were popular in the 1930s. They were made by
many American and European factories. Glass, pottery, porcelain,
majolica, chalkware, and metal wall pockets can be found in many fanciful shops.

Angel, Kneeling, Blond, 1 Dressed In Red, 1 In Blue, 1950s, Pair 50.00
Applied Magnolia Twig, Pocket Form Body, Art Pottery, 1900s, 6 x 5 x 2 1/2 In. 230.00
Bean Pod Shape, Relief Leaves, Vine, Frog, Bizen, 1800s, 10 In. 230.00
Double Trumpet, Glossy White Glaze, Japan, 6 x 5 x 1 5/8 In. 45.00
Oak Leaf, Pink, 6 x 5 3/4 In. 72.00
Pink Roses, Yellow Vase, Germany, 4 x 3 In. 45.00
Red Ballet Slippers, United Ceramics, 1949, 9 x 5 In. 25.00
Red Grapes, Green Leaves, 6 In. 22.00
Upside-Down Parrot, Flowers, Red, Green, Blue, Gold Luster, 1930s 65.00

WALLACE NUTTING photographs are listed under Print, Nutting. His reproduction
furniture is listed under Furniture.

WALRATH was a potter who worked in New York City; Rochester,
New York; and at the Newcomb Pottery in New Orleans, Louisiana.
Frederick Walrath died in 1920. Pieces listed here are from his
Rochester period.

Cider Set, Pitcher, 5 Cups, Cherries, Green, Brown, Handicraft Guild, 8-In. Pitcher 4995.00
Vase, Broad Footed, Olive Green Matte Glaze, Painted Organic Design, 3 x 7 In. 1175.00
Vase, Flower, Blue, Brown Matte Ground, 4 In. 2350.00
Vase, Flowers, Leaves, Green Frothy Ground, 5 1/2 x 3 1/2 In. 5290.00
Vase, Orange Blossoms, Leaves, Tendrils, Green Matte Glaze, Bulbous, Flared, 11 x 6 In. . 16185.00
Vase, Pink Flowers, Green Leaves, Green Mottled Matte Ground, 8 3/4 x 4 1/2 In. 8225.00
Vase, Trees, Brown Trunk, Green Leaves, Green Matte Ground, 6 3/4 x 4 1/2 In. 4995.00

WALT DISNEY, see Disneyana category.

WALTER, see A. Walter category.

WARWICK china was made in Wheeling, West Virginia, in a pottery
working from 1887 to 1951. Many pieces were made with hand
painted or decal decorations. The most familiar Warwick has a shaded
brown background. The name *Warwick* is part of the mark and sometimes the mysterious word *IOGA* is also included.

Creamer, Off-White, Pink, Yellow, Green Floral Decal Border, Gold Trim 17.00
Cup & Saucer, June Bride 15.00
Mustard, Rust & Black Bands On White, c.1947, 3 x 2 3/4 In. 24.00
Plate, Bread & Butter, Pink Rose Garland, Green Leaves, 6 3/8 In. 19.00
Plate, Dinner, 22K Gold Floral Band, White Center, 10 1/2 In. 36.00
Tankard, Black Feet Chief, 1898, 13 x 6 1/2 In. 355.00
Vase, Pine Needles & Pinecones, Yellow Ground, 2 Handles, 11 1/2 In. 150.00
Vase, Pink & Red Roses, Shaded Green Ground, Twisted Twig Handles, IOGA, 10 1/2 In. . 160.00
Vase, Poinsettia, Red Overglaze, Gold Edge, Tapered, Ruffled Top, IOGA, 11 1/2 In. 135.00
Vase, Portrait, Woman, Red Shading To Black, Gold Trim, 10 1/2 In. 125.00

WATCH pockets held the pocket watch that was important in Victorian times because it was not until World War I that the wristwatch was
used. All types of watches are collected: silver, gold, or plated.
Watches are arranged by company name or by style. Wristwatches are
a separate category.

American Watch Company, 17 Jewel, c.1876, Pocket 134.00
American Watch Company, Open Face, Coin Silver Case, Spread Eagle, Pocket 201.00
Aristocrat, Hunting Case, 17 Jewel, Arabic Numerals, 14K Gold, Pocket, Size 12 .... 60.00

Bueche Girod, U.S 1904 20 Dollar Coin, Goldtone Dial, Roman, 18K Gold 825.00
Carter Howe & Co., Lotus Buds, Flowers, Trace Links, Griffin Head Seal, 14K Gold 646.00
Cartier, Open Face, 18K Gold, 19 Jewel, Blue Enamel Initials, Pocket 1880.00
Colibori, Skeletonized Movement, Gold Plated Case, Glazed Dial, 17 Jewel, c.1950 ...... 50.00
Columbus, Hunting Case, 17 Jewel, Gold Filled, Size 18, 14K Gold, Pocket 120.00
Demi-Hunting Case, White Enamel Dial, 14K Gold, Swiss, Pocket 265.00
Dent, Demi-Hunting Case, Lever Escapement, Stem Wind, London, c.1864, Pocket 470.00
Ebel, Woman's, Ring, Anti-Magnetic, 15 Jewel, 14K Gold Case & Shank, c.1953 .... 165.00
Elgin, 17 Jewel, Enamel Dial, Arabic Numerals, Second Hand, Overlaid Stars, 14K Gold .. 259.00
Elgin, Hunting Case, 15 Jewel, 14K Gold, Pocket, Size 18 .... 1100.00
Elgin, Hunting Case, Engraved, 14K Yellow Gold, c.1896, Pocket, 3 In............... 1035.00
Elgin, Hunting Case, Engraved, 15 Jewel, 14K Gold, Size 18 .... 1100.00
Elgin, Open Face, 7 Jewel, Roman Numerals, No. 2315487, Silver Case, Size 18, Pocket .. 135.00
Elgin, Open Face, 21 Jewel, Arabic Numerals, 14K Gold Filled, Pocket 239.00
Enamel, French Key Wind Movement, Portrait, Young Girl, c.1875, Pocket, 2 In. 288.00
Gruen, Pocket, 17 Jewel, 5-Sided Case, 14K Green Gold 275.00
H.N. Et Cie., Goldtone, Arabic Numerals, Jewel, Swiss, 18K Gold, Pocket 529.00
Hamilton, 16 Jewel, Nickel, No. 19183, Roman Numerals, Size 18, Pocket 485.00
Hamilton, No. 921, Dial, Size 10 Gold Filled Case, 21 Jewel, Pocket 130.00
Hampden Watch Co., Silver Case, Inscribed, To Capt. Tom, U.S. Army From C Troop 280.00
Henry Capt, White Enamel Dial, Crystal, 18K Gold, Chatelaine, France, Box 940.00
Henry Lavalette, Hunting Case, Black Enamel, Ivory Dial, Roman Numerals, 18K Gold .. 500.00
Hunting Case, Black Enamel, Roman Numerals, Swiss, 14K Gold, Pocket 530.00
Hunting Case, Feather Design, 5 Diamonds, Woman's, c.1900, Pocket 230.00
Hunting Case, Open Face, Arabic Numerals, 17 Jewel, 14K Gold, Size 16, Pocket 300.00
Hunting Case, White Enamel, 13 Jewel, Key Wind, 14K Gold, Pocket 440.00
Illinois, Bunn Special, Gold Filled, 23 Jewel, 60-Hour Mainspring 1200.00
Illinois, Hunting Case, 11 Jewel, 14K Gold, Box Hinge, Size 18 .... 1900.00
Ingraham, Dollar, Lindbergh's Flight, Statue Of Liberty, Eiffel Tower 275.00
J.E. Caldwell, Silvertone Dial, 21 Jewel, Open Face, 18K Gold, Pocket 560.00
James McCabe Of London, Key Wind, Open Face, 18K Yellow Gold, c.1828, Pocket 2519.00
Joseph Johnson, Hunting Case, 18K Gold, Key Wind, c.1875, Pocket, 1 3/4 In. 405.00
L. Gallopin, Open Face, Enamel Dial, 18K Gold, Pocket 410.00
Lancaster, Original Case, 20 Jewel, 1880s, Size 18 .... 3800.00
Lord Elgin, Open Face, 14K Gold, 21 Jewel, Manual Wind, c.1925, Pocket, 1 3/4 In. 460.00
M.I. Tobias & Co., Open Face, Gold, Pocket, 15-In. Chain 1020.00
Movado, Golf, Silvertone, Arabic Numerals, Sliding Case 235.00
Open Face, Ivorytone Dial, Roman Numerals, Nickel, Gilt Movement, 18K Gold, Pocket . 2115.00
Open Face, Judaic, Ivorytone Dial, Hebrew Indicators, 7 Jewel, 14K Gold 940.00
Open Face, Locust, Sterling Silver, Arabic, Swiss, Art Nouveau, Pocket 325.00
Patek Philippe, Silvertone, Arabic Numerals, 18 Jewel, 18K Gold, Pocket 2000.00
Pendant, White Enamel Dial, Arabic Numerals, Bow Pin, 17 Jewel, 18K Gold, Swiss 4465.00
Perret & Berthoud, 17 Jewel, Leaves & Flowers, 18K Gold, Pocket, 2 In. 529.00
Raised Gold Arabic Numerals, 14K Yellow Gold, France, c.1930, Pocket 288.00
Swiss Genova, Open Face, Silveroid Case, c.1950, Pocket 58.00
Thomas DeGaris, Open Face, Key Wind, England, c.1850, Pocket 448.00
Tiffany & Co., Longines, Open Face, 15 Jewel Escapement, Silver Case, c.1920, Pocket ... 377.00
Tiffany & Co., Open Face, 18K Gold, White Enamel Dial, Arabic, c.1925 .... 575.00
Waltham, Equestrian Design, Porcelain Dial, Roman Numerals, 17 Jewel, Size 16 ...... 2500.00
Waltham, Hunting Case, Woman's, Pendant, 14K Gold, Rope Chain, c.1888, 1 1/2 In. .. 489.00
Waltham, Model 57, Key Wind, 15 Jewel, Roman Porcelain Dial, Dennison, Size 18 ..... 1100.00
Waltham, Model 1872, 21 Jewel, American Watch Co., Size 17 .... 6400.00
Waltham, Open Face, 11 Jewel, Roman Numeral Dial, Size 18, Pocket 120.00
Waltham, Open Face, Arabic Numeral Dial, 7 Jewel, Gold Filled, Pocket 45.00
Waltham, Open Face, Railroad Grade, Riverside Movement, c.1935, Pocket 28.00
Waltham, Platinum, Diamond, Silvertone Dial, Cushion Shape Case, Art Deco, Pocket ... 823.00
Waltham, Railroad, Santa Fe Route, Double Sunk Dial, Model 1883, 17 Jewel 700.00

WATCH FOBS were worn on watch chains. They were popular during Victorian times and after. Many styles, especially advertising
designs, are still made today.

Abraham Fur Co., Fox Head, Black Enamel Bezel, St. Louis, U.S.A. 46.00
Abraham Fur Co., Fox Head, Red Enamel Bezel, St. Louis, U.S.A. 50.00

Abraham Fur Co., St. Louis, U.S.A., Fox Head, Leather Strap, G.D. Childs Co., Chicago .. 120.00
Buffalo Bill, Pawnee Bill, Nickel Silver, 1 1/2 In. 138.00
Colt Mfg. Co., Rearing Horse, Brass, Scroll & Filigree Edge, 1 5/8 x 1 3/8 In. 85.00
Dead Shot, American Powder Mills, Brass, Celluloid Insert, Leather Band, 1 1/2 In. 230.00
Dead Shot Powder, Falling Duck, Brass, Celluloid Insert, Leather Strap, 1 1/2 In. ..260.00 to 380.00
Figural, 2 Bowling Pins, Marble Ball, Silver, Engraved, 5 3/4 x 1 3/4 In. 146.00
Funsten Fur Co., Pewter, 5 Medallions, 4 Centuries Of Fur Trading, Bear, 7 x 2 In. .440.00 to 529.00
Hunter Trader Trapper, Brass, Bear In Shield, Columbus, Ohio, 2 1/4 x 1 1/2 In. 46.00
National Sportsmans Magazine, Embossed Buck, Gun, Gold Color, 1 5/8 x 1 1/2 In. 58.00
Red Man Tobacco, Indian Chief, From Good Cigar Leaf, Metal, Leather Strap, 1 x 1 1/2 In. 77.00
S. Jacobs & Co., 14K Gold, Floral Chased Case, 2 Pearls, 3 Diamonds, c.1900 .... 863.00
S. Silberman & Sons, Fur Shipper, Otter, S, Copper 70.00
Savage Arms Co., Hand Gun Shape, Nickel Plated, Indian Head, 1 1/8 x 1 1/2 In. 105.00
Shapleigh Hardware Co., DE, Diamond Edge, Diamond Shape, Copper, Silver Bezel 45.00
Smith & Wesson, Brass, S&W Logo, Revolver, Round, 1 1/8 In. 20.00

WATERFORD type glass resembles the famous glass made from
1783 to 1851 in the Waterford Glass Works in Ireland. It is a clear glass
that was often decorated by cutting. Modern glass is being made again
in Waterford, Ireland, and is marketed under the name *Waterford*.

Stemware, Sheila Pattern, Cut, 20th Century, 57 Piece 840.00
Vase, Cut Glass, Diamond Design, Stylized Leaf Border, 6 1/2 x 6 In. 316.00

WATT family members bought the Globe pottery of Crooksville,
Ohio, in 1922. They made pottery mixing bowls and tableware of the
type made by Globe. In 1935 they changed the production and made
the pieces with the freehand decorations that are popular with collectors today. Apple, Starflower, Rooster, Tulip, and Autumn Foliage are
the best-known patterns. Pansy, also called Rio Rose, was the earliest
pattern. Apple, the most popular pattern, can be dated from the leaves.
Originally, the apples had three leaves; after 1958 two leaves were
used. The plant closed in 1965. For more information, see *Kovels'*
Depression Glass & Dinnerware Price List.

Animal Dish, Kitty, Raised Letters, Turquoise, No. 5 .... 195.00
Apple, Baker, Cover, 2-Leaf, No. 67, 3 1/2 x 8 1/4 In. 65.00
Apple, Baker, Cover, 2-Leaf, No. 67, 6 1/2 x 8 1/4 In. 85.00
Apple, Baker, Cover, No. 3/19, 5 1/4 x 9 In. 105.00
Apple, Baker, Cover, No. 96, 2 3/4 x 8 1/2 In. 65.00
Apple, Baker, Cover, No. 600, 5 1/4 x 7 3/4 In. 95.00
Apple, Baker, Cover, No. 601, 6 1/4 x 8 3/4 In. 85.00
Apple, Bean Pot, 2-Leaf, No. 76, 2 1/2 Qt., 6 1/2 x 5 1/2 In. ....105.00 to 115.00
Apple, Bowl, 2-Leaf, No. 55 .... 85.00
Apple, Bowl, Kalona, Iowa, No. 6, 2 1/4 x 6 1/4 In. 40.00
Apple, Bowl, No. 4, 1 3/4 x 5 In. 75.00
Apple, Bowl, Ridgeway Cheese & Butter, No. 8, 1961, 3 1/4 x 8 3/4 In. 35.00
Apple, Bowl, Salad, 2-Leaf, No. 55, 4 x 11 3/4 In. 55.00
Apple, Bowl, Salad, Cover, No. 73, 4 x 9 1/2 In. 75.00
Apple, Bowl, Salad, Individual, 2-Leaf, No. 74, 2 x 5 1/2 In. 30.00
Apple, Bowl, Salad, No. 55, 4 x 11 3/4 In. 235.00
Apple, Bowl, Salad, No. 73, 4 x 9 1/2 In. ....50.00 to 55.00
Apple, Bowl, Salad, No. 106, 3 3/4 x 10 3/4 In. 155.00
Apple, Bowl, Soup, Dish, Inside Band, No. 44, 1 1/2 x 8 In. 135.00
Apple, Bowl, Spaghetti, 2-Leaf, No. 39, 3 1/4 x 13 In. 145.00
Apple, Bowl, Spaghetti, No. 24, 2 1/2 x 11 In. 25.00
Apple, Bowl, Spaghetti, No. 39, 3 1/4 x 13 In. ....75.00 to 95.00
Apple, Canister, 2-Leaf, No. 72, 6 3/4 x 7 1/4 In. 285.00
Apple, Canister, No. 72, 6 3/4 x 7 1/4 In. 225.00
Apple, Casserole, Cover, 2-Leaf, No. 3/19, 5 1/4 x 9 In. ....115.00 to 145.00
Apple, Casserole, Cover, 2-Leaf, Stick Handle, No. 18, 3 3/4 x 5 In. 75.00
Apple, Casserole, Cover, Square, No. 84, 6 x 8 In. 1300.00
Apple, Casserole, Cover, Tab Handles, No. 18, 3 3/4 x 5 In. ....85.00 to 155.00
Apple, Cookie Jar, No. 21, 6 x 7 In. 375.00
Apple, Cookie Jar, No. 503, 8 x 6 1/2 In. 225.00

Apple, Creamer, 2-Leaf, No. 62, 1/2 Pt., 4 1/4 In. 75.00
Apple, Creamer, No. 62, 1/2 Pt., 4 1/4 In. 65.00
Apple, Fondue, Cover, No. 506, 4 1/4 x 6 In. 800.00
Apple, Grease Jar, No. 01, 3 1/2 x 5 In. ....275.00 to 350.00
Apple, Ice Bucket, 2-Leaf, No. 59, 5 3/4 x 7 1/2 In. ....125.00 to 175.00
Apple, Mug, No. 121, 3 3/4 x 3 In. ....95.00 to 145.00
Apple, Mug, No. 501, 4 1/2 x 2 3/4 In. 400.00
Apple, Mug, No. 701, 3 3/4 x 3 1/2 In. 300.00
Apple, Nappy, No. 04, 2 x 4 1/4 In. 20.00
Apple, Pie Plate, No. 33, 9 1/4 In. 105.00
Apple, Pitcher, 2-Leaf, No. 15, 1 Pt., 5 1/4 In. ....65.00 to 75.00
Apple, Pitcher, 2-Leaf, No. 16, 2 Pt., 6 1/2 In. 65.00
Apple, Pitcher, Farmers Savings Bank, Walford, Iowa, No. 15, Pt., 5 1/4 In. 150.00
Apple, Pitcher, Ice Lip, 2-Leaf, No. 17, 5 Pt., 8 In. 215.00
Apple, Pitcher, Ice Lip, No. 17, 5 Pt., 8 In. 145.00
Apple, Pitcher, No. 15, Pt., 5 1/4 In. ....50.00 to 55.00
Apple, Pitcher, No. 16, 2 Pt., 6 1/2 In. ....55.00 to 60.00
Apple, Pitcher, No. 17, 5 Pt., 8 In. 225.00
Apple, Sandwich Plate, No. 49, 12 In. 450.00
Apple, Shaker, Pepper, Hourglass, No. 118, 4 3/4 x 2 1/4 In. 155.00
Autumn Foliage, Baker, Cover, No. 110, 6 3/4 x 8 1/2 In. 55.00
Autumn Foliage, Baker, Cover, No. 601, 6 1/4 x 8 3/4 In. 80.00
Autumn Foliage, Baker, No. 94, 1 3/4 x 6 In. 15.00
Autumn Foliage, Baker, No. 95, 2 1/4 x 7 1/4 In. 20.00
Autumn Foliage, Bean Cup, No. 75, 8 Oz., 2 1/4 x 3 1/2 In. 285.00
Autumn Foliage, Bean Pot, No. 76, 2 1/2 Qt., 6 1/2 x 5 1/2 In. 65.00
Autumn Foliage, Bowl, Salad, No. 73, 4 x 9 1/2 In. 55.00
Autumn Foliage, Bowl, Salad, No. 106, 3 3/4 x 10 3/4 In. 45.00
Autumn Foliage, Casserole, Cover, No. 18, 3 3/4 x 5 In. 125.00
Autumn Foliage, Chop Plate, No. 31, 15 In. 45.00
Autumn Foliage, Creamer, No. 62, 1/2 Pt., 4 1/4 In. ....155.00 to 165.00
Autumn Foliage, Grease Jar, No. 01, 3 1/2 x 5 In. 250.00
Autumn Foliage, Mug, No. 121, 3 3/4 x 3 In. 175.00
Autumn Foliage, Mug, No. 501, 4 1/2 x 5 3/4 In. 90.00
Autumn Foliage, Oil & Vinegar, Covers, No. 126, 7 1/2 x 2 In. 725.00
Autumn Foliage, Pie Plate, Waverly, Iowa, No. 33, 9 1/4 In. 105.00
Autumn Foliage, Pitcher, No. 15, Pt., 5 1/4 In. 125.00
Autumn Foliage, Pitcher, No. 16, 2 Pt., 6 1/2 In. 95.00
Autumn Foliage, Shaker, Salt, Hourglass, No. 117, 4 3/4 x 2 1/4 In. 95.00
Autumn Foliage, Sugar, No. 98, 4 1/4 x 3 1/2 In. 65.00
Autumn Foliage, Teapot, Cover, No. 112, 6 In. 325.00
Butterfly, Baker, Cover, No. 67, 3 1/2 x 8 1/4 In. 375.00
Butterfly, Ice Bucket, No. 59, 5 3/4 x 7 1/2 In. 500.00
Butterfly, Pitcher, No. 15, Pt., 5 1/4 In. 900.00
Butterfly, Pitcher, No. 16, 2 Pt., 6 1/2 In. 300.00
Cherry, Baker, Cover, No. 54, 6 x 8 1/2 In. 55.00
Cherry, Bowl, No. 1, 2 1/4 x 5 3/4 In. 85.00
Cherry, Bowl, No. 23, 1 1/2 x 5 5/8 In. 100.00
Cherry, Bowl, Salad, No. 23, 1 1/2 x 5 5/8 In. 60.00
Cherry, Bowl, Salad, No. 52, 2 1/4 x 6 1/4 In. 40.00
Cherry, Bowl, Spaghetti, No. 24, 2 1/2 x 11 In. 145.00
Cherry, Bowl, Spaghetti, No. 25, 3 1/2 x 15 In. 135.00
Cherry, Bowl, Spaghetti, No. 39, 3 1/4 x 13 In. ....65.00 to 105.00
Cherry, Casserole, Cover Only, No. 18, 1 3/4 x 5 In. 85.00
Cherry, Chop Plate, No. 31, 15 In. 165.00
Cherry, Cookie Jar, No. 21, 6 x 7 In. 115.00
Cherry, Pitcher, No. 15, Pt., 5 1/4 In. ....75.00 to 145.00
Cherry, Pitcher, No. 16, 2 Pt., 6 1/2 In. 190.00
Cherry, Sandwich Plate, No. 49, 12 In. 115.00
Daisy, Mixing Bowl, Wide Lip, No. 9, 9 In. 70.00
Dogwood, Bowl, Spaghetti, No. 24, 2 1/2 x 11 In. 105.00
Dogwood, Bowl, Spaghetti, No. 39, 3 1/4 x 13 In. 100.00
Double Apple, Baker, Cover Only, Small Knob, No. 96, 2 x 8 1/2 In. 25.00

Double Apple, Baker, Cover, Wire Stand, No. 96, 5 3/4 x 8 1/2 In. 105.00
Double Apple, Bean Pot, No. 76, 2 1/2 Qt., 6 1/2 x 5 1/2 In. 325.00
Double Apple, Bowl, Salad, No. 73, 4 x 9 1/2 In. ....60.00 to 85.00
Double Apple, Cookie Jar, No. 503, 8 x 6 1/2 In. 650.00
Double Apple, Creamer, No. 62, 1/2 Pt., 4 1/4 In. 250.00
Double Apple, Mixing Bowl, No. 63, 2 Pt., 4 1/4 x 6 1/2 In. 30.00
Double Apple, Nappy, Ribbed, No. 07, 3 3/4 x 7 1/4 In. 65.00
Double Apple, Pitcher, No. 15, Pt., 5 1/4 In. 275.00
Double Apple, Pitcher, No. 16, 2 Pt., 6 1/2 In. 350.00
Dutch Tulip, Baker, Cover Only, No. 67, 3 x 8 1/4 In. 35.00
Dutch Tulip, Baker, Cover, No. 66, 5 1/2 x 7 1/4 In. 55.00
Dutch Tulip, Baker, No. 68, 4 x 5 1/4 In. 80.00
Dutch Tulip, Bean Pot, No. 76, 2 1/2 Qt., 6 1/2 x 5 1/2 In. ....165.00 to 225.00
Dutch Tulip, Bowl, Fruit, No. 58, 3 3/4 x 10 1/2 In. 95.00
Dutch Tulip, Bowl, Salad, No. 73, 4 x 9 1/2 In. 155.00
Dutch Tulip, Canister, Cover, No. 72, 9 x 7 1/4 In. 185.00
Dutch Tulip, Creamer, No. 62, 1/2 Pt., 4 1/4 In. 195.00
Dutch Tulip, Ice Bucket, No. 59, 5 3/4 x 7 1/2 In. 155.00
Dutch Tulip, Mixing Bowl, No. 63, 2 Pt., 6 1/2 In. 90.00
Dutch Tulip, Nappy, Cover Only, No. 05, 5 1/4 In. 45.00
Dutch Tulip, Nappy, Cover, Burchinal, Iowa, No. 05, 2 1/2 x 5 1/4 In. 175.00
Dutch Tulip, Pitcher, No. 15, Pt., 5 1/4 In. 195.00
Dutch Tulip, Pitcher, No. 16, 2 Pt., 6 1/2 In. ....125.00 to 175.00
Dutch Tulip, Pitcher, Refrigerator, No. 69, 8 In. ....380.00 to 475.00
Eagle, Bean Pot, No. 76, 2 1/2 Qt., 6 1/2 x 5 1/2 In. 195.00
Eagle, Mixing Bowl, No. 12, 12 In. 200.00
Esmond, Bowl, Salad, Pear, Apple, No. 73, 4 x 9 1/2 In. 55.00
Esmond, Bowl, Salad, Pear, Apple, No. 74, 2 x 5 1/2 In. 40.00
Esmond, Cookie Jar, Wood Cover, Pear, Apple, No. 34, 8 x 8 1/2 In. 65.00
Fiesta, Bowl, Salad, No. 74, 2 x 5 1/2 In. 85.00
Kitch-N-Queen, Baker, Cover Only, No. 67, 3 x 8 1/4 In. 20.00
Kitch-N-Queen, Baker, Cover, Large Knob, No. 110, 6 3/4 x 8 1/2 In. 85.00
Kitch-N-Queen, Baker, Cover, Ribbed, No. 600, 5 1/4 x 7 3/4 In. 65.00
Kitch-N-Queen, Bowl, Cover, No. 131, 6 x 8 1/2 In. 105.00
Kitch-N-Queen, Bowl, Salad, No. 73, 4 x 9 1/2 In. 85.00
Kitch-N-Queen, Cookie Jar, No. 503, 8 x 6 1/2 In. 195.00
Kitch-N-Queen, Mixing Bowl, No. 64, 4 Pt., 4 3/4 x 7 1/2 In. 40.00
Kitch-N-Queen, Pie Plate, Model Market, Sam & Myrtle Inwood, No. 33, 9 1/4 In. 325.00
Kitch-N-Queen, Pitcher, Ice Lip, No. 17, 5 Pt., 8 In. 105.00
Kitch-N-Queen, Pitcher, No. 15, Pt., 5 1/4 In. 850.00
Kitch-N-Queen, Pitcher, No. 16, 2 Pt., 6 1/2 In. 200.00
Loops, Mixing Bowl, Tan, No. 5, 5 In. 5.00
Loops, Pie Plate, Blue, No. 8, 8 In. 80.00
Loops, Pie Plate, Tan, No. 8, 8 In. 25.00
Moonflower, Plate, Dinner, Black, No. 101, 10 In. 20.00
Morning Glory, Creamer, Cream, No. 97, 4 1/4 In. 600.00
Morning Glory, Mixing Bowl, Cream, No. 9, 9 In. 125.00
Morning Glory, Sugar, Cream, No. 98, 4 1/4 x 3 1/2 In. 180.00
Pansy, Bowl, Crosshatch, No. 1, 2 1/4 x 5 3/4 In. 165.00
Pansy, Bowl, Crosshatch, No. 4, 1 3/4 x 5 In. 75.00
Pansy, Bowl, Salad, Cut-Leaf, No. 23, 1 1/2 x 5 5/8 In. 20.00
Pansy, Bowl, Spaghetti, Crosshatch, No. 24, 2 1/2 x 11 In. ....115.00 to 175.00
Pansy, Bowl, Spaghetti, Cut-Leaf, No. 39, 3 1/4 x 13 In. 40.00
Pansy, Bowl, Spaghetti, No. 39, 13 In. 35.00
Pansy, Canister, Cover, No. 72, 9 x 7 1/4 In. 210.00
Pansy, Casserole, Cover, No. 3/19, 5 1/2 x 9 In. 50.00
Pansy, Casserole, Cover, Stick Handle, Raised, No. 18, 3 3/4 x 5 In. 40.00
Pansy, Chop Plate, Crosshatch, No. 31, 15 In. 135.00
Pansy, Cup & Saucer, Crosshatch, No. 40 & No. 41 .... 175.00
Pansy, Cup & Saucer, Cut-Leaf, No. 40 & No. 41 .... 45.00
Pansy, Mug, No. 61, 3 x 3 1/4 In. 185.00
Pansy, Pie Plate, Bullseye, No. 33, 9 1/4 In. 195.00
Pansy, Pie Plate, Crosshatch, No. 33, 9 1/4 In. 160.00

Pansy, Pie Plate, No. 33, 9 1/4 In. 135.00
Pansy, Pitcher, Crosshatch, No. 15, Pt., 5 1/4 In. 950.00
Pansy, Pitcher, Crosshatch, No. 16, 2 Pt., 6 1/2 In. 400.00
Pansy, Pitcher, Crosshatch, No. 17, 5 Pt., 8 In. 950.00
Pansy, Pitcher, Cut-Leaf, No. 15, Pt., 5 1/4 In. 245.00
Pansy, Pitcher, Cut-Leaf, No. 16, 2 Pt., 6 1/2 In. 55.00
Pansy, Pitcher, No. 16, 2 Pt., 6 1/2 In. 115.00
Pansy, Plate, Luncheon, Crosshatch, No. 43, 8 1/2 In. 105.00
Pansy, Plate, Salad, No. 28, 7 1/2 In. 20.00
Pansy, Sandwich Plate, No. 49, 12 In. 40.00
Pansy, Snack Plate, Bullseye, No. 30, 11 1/2 In. 20.00
Par-T-Que, Baker, Cover, Wire Warmer, No. 110, 6 3/4 x 8 1/2 In. 40.00
Par-T-Que, Cookie Jar, No. 503, 8 x 6 1/2 In. 125.00
Par-T-Que, Creamer, No. 62, 1/2 Pt., 4 1/4 In. 350.00
Par-T-Que, Grease Jar, No. 01, 3 1/2 x 5 In. 95.00
Par-T-Que, Mug, No. 121, 3 3/4 x 3 In. ....65.00 to 130.00
Par-T-Que, Plate, Dinner, No. 101, 10 In. 20.00
Par-T-Que, Plate, Luncheon, No. 102, 7 1/2 In. 13.00
Par-T-Que, Sugar, Cover, No. 98, 4 1/2 x 3 1/2 In. 75.00
Par-T-Que, Teapot, No. 112, 6 In. 325.00
Rio Rose, see Pansy
Rooster, Baker, Cover Only, No. 67, 3 x 8 1/4 In. 30.00
Rooster, Baker, Cover, Square, No. 84, 6 x 8 In. 650.00
Rooster, Baker, No. 68, 4 x 5 1/4 In. 40.00
Rooster, Bean Pot, Batman Grain, No. 76, 2 1/2 Qt., 6 1/2 x 5 1/2 In. 275.00
Rooster, Bean Pot, No. 76, 2 1/2 Qt., 6 1/2 x 5 1/2 In. 375.00
Rooster, Bowl, Fruit, No. 58, 3 3/4 x 10 1/2 In. ....85.00 to 115.00
Rooster, Bowl, Salad, Laacks Cheese, No. 73, 4 x 9 1/2 In. 95.00
Rooster, Bowl, Salad, No. 73, 4 x 9 1/2 In. 155.00
Rooster, Bowl, Spaghetti, No. 24, 2 1/2 x 11 In. 165.00
Rooster, Bowl, Spaghetti, No. 39, 3 1/4 x 13 In. 105.00
Rooster, Canister, No. 72, 6 3/4 x 7 1/4 In. 250.00
Rooster, Casserole, Cover, French Handle, No. 18, 4 x 5 In. 95.00
Rooster, Creamer, Pa. Dutch Days, Hershey, Pa., No. 62, 1956, 1/2 Pt., 4 1/4 In. 265.00
Rooster, Dutch Oven, No. 70, 4 1/2 x 9 1/2 In. ....105.00 to 275.00
Rooster, Ice Bucket, No. 59, 5 3/4 x 7 1/2 In. 165.00
Rooster, Mixing Bowl, No. 9, 9 In. ....35.00 to 85.00
Rooster, Mug, Batman Grain, No. 701, 3 3/4 x 3 1/2 In. 305.00
Rooster, Nappy, Cover, Penn. Dutch Days, Hershey, Pa., No. 05, 1957, 4 x 5 In. 220.00
Rooster, Pitcher, No. 15, Pt., 5 1/4 In. 105.00
Rooster, Pitcher, No. 16, 2 Pt., 6 1/2 In. 185.00
Rooster, Salt & Pepper, Hourglass, Sac City, Carroll, Clarinda, No. 117, No. 118, 5 In., Pair ... 525.00
Silhouette, Pitcher, No. 15, Pt., 5 1/4 In. 195.00
Silhouette, Pitcher, No. 16, 2 Pt., 6 1/2 In. 145.00
Starflower, Baker, Cover Only, No. 66, 2 1/2 x 7 1/4 In. 35.00
Starflower, Baker, Cover, 4-Petal, Large Knob, No. 96, 5 3/4 x 8 1/2 In. 65.00
Starflower, Baker, Cover, 4-Petal, No. 66, 5 1/2 x 7 1/4 In. 55.00
Starflower, Baker, Cover, 4-Petal, No. 67, 6 1/2 x 8 1/4 In. 75.00
Starflower, Baker, Cover, No. 54, 6 x 8 1/2 In. 55.00
Starflower, Baker, No. 60, 2 3/8 x 6 1/4 In. 30.00
Starflower, Baker, No. 68, 4 x 5 1/4 In. 50.00
Starflower, Baker, Open, No. 60, 2 3/8 x 6 1/4 In. 40.00
Starflower, Baker, Open, No. 68, 4 x 5 1/4 In. 20.00
Starflower, Bean Cup, 4-Petal, No. 75, 8 Oz., 2 1/4 x 3 1/2 In. 175.00
Starflower, Bean Pot, 4-Petal, No. 76, 2 1/2 Qt., 6 1/2 x 5 1/2 In. ....75.00 to 105.00
Starflower, Bean Pot, 6-Petal, Green Handles, No. 76, 2 1/2 Qt., 6 1/2 x 5 1/2 In. 195.00
Starflower, Bowl, Fruit, No. 58, 3 3/4 x 10 1/2 In. 105.00
Starflower, Bowl, No. 1, 2 1/4 x 5 3/4 In. 30.00
Starflower, Bowl, Salad, 4-Petal, No. 73, 4 x 9 1/2 In. 45.00
Starflower, Bowl, Salad, 4-Petal, No. 74, 2 x 5 1/2 In. ....35.00 to 50.00
Starflower, Bowl, Salad, No. 23, 1 1/2 x 5 5/8 In. 40.00
Starflower, Bowl, Salad, No. 55, 4 x 11 3/4 In. 45.00
Starflower, Bowl, Spaghetti, 4-Petal, No. 24, 2 1/2 x 11 In. 85.00

Starflower, Bowl, Spaghetti, No. 24, 2 1/2 x 11 In. 45.00
Starflower, Bowl, Spaghetti, No. 39, 3 1/4 x 13 In. .... 30.00 to 50.00
Starflower, Casserole, Cover, Stick Handle, No. 18, 3 3/4 x 5 In. .... 30.00 to 55.00
Starflower, Casserole, Cover, Tab Handle, No. 18, 3 3/4 x 5 In. 55.00
Starflower, Cookie Jar, 4-Petal, No. 503, 8 x 6 1/2 In. 250.00
Starflower, Ice Bucket, No. 59, 5 3/4 x 7 1/2 In. 145.00
Starflower, Mixing Bowl, 4-Petal, Deep, No. 65, 6 Pt., 5 x 9 In. 35.00
Starflower, Mixing Bowl, Value-Interstate Lumber Co., No. 5, 5 In. 25.00
Starflower, Pie Plate, No. 33, 9 1/4 In. 450.00
Starflower, Pitcher, No. 16, 2 Pt., 6 1/2 In. .... 45.00 to 85.00
Starflower, Pitcher, No. 17, 5 Pt., 8 In. .... 75.00 to 115.00
Starflower, Pitcher, Refrigerator, 4-Petal, No. 69, 8 In. 575.00
Starflower, Plate, Dinner, No. 101, 10 In. 125.00
Starflower, Plate, Luncheon, No. 102, 7 1/2 In. 115.00
Starflower, Platter, No. 31, 15 In. .... 65.00 to 105.00
Starflower, Roaster, No. 20, 4 x 10 1/2 In. 235.00
Starflower, Sandwich Plate, No. 49, 12 In. 95.00
Starflower, Tumbler, Straight Sides, No. 56, 4 1/2 x 4 In. .... 115.00 to 125.00
Tear Drop, Baker, Cover Only, No. 66, 2 1/2 x 7 1/4 In. 35.00
Tear Drop, Baker, Cover, No. 66, 3 1/2 x 7 1/4 In. 120.00
Tear Drop, Baker, Cover, Oval, No. 86, 5 x 10 In. 125.00
Tear Drop, Baker, Cover, Square, No. 84, 6 x 8 In. 95.00
Tear Drop, Baker, No. 68, 4 x 5 1/4 In. 30.00
Tear Drop, Bowl, Fruit, No. 58, 3 3/4 x 10 1/2 In. 165.00
Tear Drop, Bowl, Salad, No. 73, 4 x 9 1/2 In. .... 30.00 to 75.00
Tear Drop, Bowl, Spaghetti, No. 24, 2 1/2 x 11 In. 225.00
Tear Drop, Bowl, Spaghetti, No. 39, 3 1/4 x 13 In. 165.00
Tear Drop, Canister, Cover, No. 72, 9 x 7 1/4 In. 200.00
Tear Drop, Casserole, Cover, No. 66, 5 1/2 x 7 1/4 In. 50.00
Tear Drop, Cheese Crock, Cover, No. 80, 8 x 8 1/2 In. 425.00
Tear Drop, Ice Bucket, Cover, No. 59, 7 x 7 1/2 In. 75.00
Tear Drop, Nappy, Cover, Ribbed, No. 05, 2 1/2 x 5 1/4 In. 105.00
Tear Drop, Nappy, Ribbed, No. 07, 3 3/4 x 7 1/4 In. 20.00
Tulip, Baker, Cover, No. 600, 5 1/4 x 7 3/4 In. .... 45.00 to 80.00
Tulip, Baker, No. 96, 2 3/4 x 8 1/2 In. 115.00
Tulip, Bowl, Salad, No. 73, 4 x 9 1/2 In. 105.00
Tulip, Bowl, Salad, No. 106, 3 3/4 x 10 3/4 In. 35.00
Tulip, Bowl, Spaghetti, No. 39, 3 1/4 x 13 In. 250.00
Tulip, Casserole, Cover Only, No. 600, 2 1/4 x 7 3/4 In. 25.00
Tulip, Cookie Jar, No. 503, 8 x 6 1/2 In. 300.00
Tulip, Creamer, No. 62, 1/2 Pt., 4 1/4 In. .... 95.00 to 155.00
Tulip, Nappy, Ribbed, No. 604, 2 1/2 x 6 3/4 In. 40.00
Tulip, Pitcher, Cross Foot In Back, No. 16, 2 Pt., 6 1/2 In. 65.00
Tulip, Pitcher, Ice Lip, No. 17, 5 Pt., 8 In. 225.00
Tulip, Pitcher, No. 15, Pt., 5 1/4 In. 650.00
Tulip, Pitcher, No. 16, 2 Pt., 6 1/2 In. .... 45.00 to 95.00

WAVE CREST glass is an opaque white glassware manufactured by the Pairpoint Manufacturing Company of New Bedford, Massachusetts, and some French factories. It was decorated by the C.F. Monroe Company of Meriden, Connecticut. The glass was painted in pastel colors and decorated with flowers. The name *Wave Crest* was used after 1898.

WAVE CREST WARE

Ash Receiver, Flowers, Ormolu Feet, Handles, 3 1/4 In. 105.00
Biscuit Jar, Egg Crate Mold, Roses, 7 In. 195.00
Box, Aster, Blown Out, Embossed Floral, Metal Base, 4 1/2 In. 550.00
Box, Baroque Shell Mold, Opal, Flowers, Pink Trim, Hinged Cover, 2 3/4 x 3 1/4 In. 315.00
Box, Baroque Shell Mold, Ribbon Flowers, 7 In. 550.00
Box, Egg Crate Mold, Forget-Me-Nots, Opal Ground, Hinged Cover, 3 x 3 1/4 In. 230.00
Box, Egg Crate Mold, Opal, Forget-Me-Nots, Silk Lining, Hinged Cover, 3 x 3 In. 250.00
Box, Glove, Opal, Scrolls, Daisies, Blue Ground, 4-Footed Ormolu Base, 6 In. 1150.00
Box, Helmschmied Swirl, Flowers, 4 In. 95.00
Box, Helmschmied Swirl, Opal, Pink, Forget-Me-Nots, Hinged Cover, Round, 3 1/2 In. 230.00

Box, Helmschmied Swirl, Ribbon, Flowers, 5 In. 250.00
Box, Jewelry, Blue Daisies, Pink & White, Round, Hinged Cover, Signed, 3 x 4 In. 170.00
Box, Puffy Mold, Beaded Edges, Rectangular, 6 In. 750.00
Box, Rococo Mold, Flowers, 6 1/2 In. 400.00
Box, Rococo Mold, Flowers, Dark Green Ground, Marked, 5 In. 500.00
Box, Rococo Mold, Flowers, Ormolu Brass Mounts, Marked, c.1920, 7 x 4 In. ..... 450.00 to 520.00
Box, Swirl Mold, Enameled Flowers, Ormolu Feet, 7 1/2 In. 430.00
Card Holder, Egg Crate Mold, Enameled Flowers, 6 In. 175.00
Cigar Holder, Embossed Ribbon Border, Ormolu Feet, Handles, Marked, 3 3/4 In. 375.00
Cracker Jar, Cover, Egg Crate Mold, Pink, Brown Flowers, Bail Handle, 11 In. 460.00
Cracker Jar, Egg Crate Mold, Red & Yellow Roses, 8 In. 345.00
Cracker Jar, Floral Transfer, Silvered Mount, C.F.M. Co., 9 In. 220.00
Cracker Jar, White To Blue, Opal, Purple, Crimson Flowers, 11 In. 375.00
Dresser Box, Baroque Shell Mold, Enameled Blossoms, 8 In. 430.00
Dresser Box, Baroque Shell Mold, Pink Flowers, Green Leaves, Round, 7 In. 375.00
Dresser Box, Egg Crate Mold, Enameled Flowers, 5 3/4 In. .... 230.00 to 315.00
Dresser Box, Egg Crate Mold, Mums, Amber, Reticulated Shoulder, Ormolu, 7 x 7 In. 2415.00
Dresser Box, Embossed Scrolls, Flowers, 3 1/4 In. 210.00
Dresser Box, Embossed Scrolls, Flowers, 7 1/2 In. 260.00
Dresser Box, Enameled Violets, 4 1/4 In. 185.00
Dresser Box, Helmschmied Swirl, White Daisies, Metal Hardware, 4 1/2 In. 259.00
Dresser Box, Swirl Mold, Enameled Flowers & Fern, 7 1/4 In. 315.00
Dresser Box, Swirl Mold, Enameled Flowers, Marked, 5 3/4 In. 230.00
Fernery, Egg Crate Mold, Enameled Cherry Blossoms, 6 1/2 In. 230.00
Fernery, Embossed Leaves, Enameled Flowers, Marked, 7 1/2 In. 150.00
Humidor, Periwinkle Blue, Flowers, Script Cigarettes, Hinged Cover, Marked, 4 3/4 In. 805.00
Inkwell, Light Blue, Pink Shasta Daisies, 4 Brass Lion Feet, Hinged Cover, 4 x 8 In. 1035.00
Jardiniere, Rococo Mold, Red & Blue Mums, 4-Footed Metal Base, 8 1/2 In. 635.00
Photo Receiver, Swirl Mold, Cupid, Enameled Flowers, 4 1/4 In. 230.00
Salt & Pepper, Erie Twist Mold, Pink, Flowers 105.00
Saltshaker, Helmschmied Swirl, Flowers, Pink 35.00
Sugar & Creamer, Pink Flowers, 4 1/2 In. 405.00
Sugar Shaker, Erie Twist Mold, Opal To Pink To Yellow, Enameled Flowers, 3 1/4 In. 430.00
Tobacco Jar, Egg Crate Mold, Flowers, 5 In. 525.00
Tray, Dresser, Medallion Of Red Flowers, Cobalt Blue, Brass Rim, Marked, 7 In. 550.00
Tray, Dresser, Opal, Red Flowers, Blue Trim, Brass Rim, 4-Footed, Marked, 7 In. 635.00
Vase, Bud, Ormolu Feet, Handles, 4 3/4 In. 155.00
Vase, Enameled Flowers, Green, White, Gilt Metal Mounts, 12 1/4 In. 1060.00
Vase, Flower, Ormolu Feet, Hand Painted, 10 1/4 In. 175.00
Vase, Flowers, Ormolu Feet, Handles, 12 In. 1700.00
Vase, Iris, Blue, White, Ormolu Handles, Dolphin Feet, 12 In. 2300.00
Vase, Pink, Ormolu Feet, Handles, Marked, 8 In. 275.00
Vase, Rococo Mold, Enameled Flowers, Ormolu Base, 7 1/2 In. 260.00
Vase, Swirl Mold, Ormolu Base, Footed, 7 1/2 In. 230.00

WEATHER VANES were used in seventeenth-century Boston. The direction of the wind was an indication of coming weather, important to the seafaring and farming communities. By the mid-nineteenth century, commercial weather vanes were made of metal. Today's collectors often consider weather vanes to be examples of folk art, even though they may not have been handmade.

5 Soldiers, Silhouette, Sheet Iron, Wood Stand, 1800s, 43 1/4 x 43 1/2 In. 590.00
Arrow, Ball & Spike, Iron, United Baptist Church, Ellsworth, Maine, 41 x 49 In. 575.00
Arrow, Gilt Copper, Zinc, Turned Wood Finial, Late 1800s, 30 In. 646.00
Arrow & Ball, Iron, Copper, 36 In. 595.00
Arrow Point, Shaft, Sheet Copper, Zinc Scroll, Late 1800s, 17 1/2 x 49 In. 1116.00
Banner, Copper, Pierced Designs, Ball Finials, 4 Applied Flowers, 29 x 30 In. 1150.00
Banner, Directionals, Cut Copper, Scrolls, Piercings, Scalloping, Ohio, 51 In. 3680.00
Banner, Scrolled, Cutout Bird, Directionals, Sheet Copper, Pierced 1921, 49 x 31 In. 2350.00
Bannerette, Cutout Letter B, Copper, 4 Balls, Arrow Tipped Post, 21 1/2 x 42 In. 1380.00
Beaver, Twig, Sheet Metal, Cutout Eye, Egg Shape Stand, 1900, 23 x 31 In. 3165.00
Bull, Copper, Gilt, Flattened, Stand, 1800s, 14 x 24 In. 5875.00
Calf, Molded Copper, New England, c.1880, 19 1/4 x 21 In. 6575.00

Car, Driver, Openwork Rod & Arrow, 7 1/2 x 32 In.	176.00
Car, Roadster, Driver, 2-Sided, On Rod, Arrow, Scrolls, Stand, 1925-30, 32 In.	750.00
Colonel Sanders, Sheet Metal, Iron Stand, 1900s, 76 1/2 x 35 3/4 In.	235.00
Cow, Sheet Iron, Silhouette, Brown, c.1900, 44 3/4 x 43 3/4 In.	265.00
Dog, Hunting, Pointing, 4-Footed Iron Stand, 36 x 24 x 8 In.	550.00
Dog, Setter, Copper, Molded, Copper Rod, 1900s, 22 x 32 1/2 In.	3290.00
Dove, Zinc, Scalloped Tail, Ribbed Feathers, Stand, 14 In.	920.00
Eagle, Perched On Ball Ready To Take Flight, Copper, 1830, 18 x 23 x 55 In.	930.00
Eagle, Silhouette, Sheet Iron, Painted, c.1900, 25 x 38 In.	1880.00
Eagle, Spread Wings, Cast Metal, Openwork Rod & Arrow, 9 1/2 x 27 In.	415.00
Eagle, Spread Wings, Copper, Full-Bodied, Arrow Directionals, c.1900, 27 x 30 In.	4370.00
Eagle, Spread Wings, Copper, Gilt, 1800s, 20 1/2 x 22 1/4 In.	825.00
Eagle, Spread Wings, On Ball, Copper, Molded, 83 1/2 x 49 x 31 In.	1645.00
Fish, Pine, Sheet Iron, Tin, Late 1800s, 25 x 57 In.	1150.00
Fish, Wood, Brown, Iron Fins, Iron Rod, 1800s, 43 3/4 x 29 1/2 In.	1880.00
Fish, Wood, Original Paint, Iron Rod, Ball Finial, Patina, 1800s, 22 x 11 In.	660.00
Gabriel, Sheet Metal, Teardrop Finial, On Stand, 1800s, 48 x 49 In.	6900.00
Gamecock, On Arrow, Copper, Molded, Gilded, 1800s, 21 1/2 x 25 3/4 In.	11750.00
Gamecock, On Ball, Full-Bodied, Copper, Silhouette Tail, 1800s, 21 x 14 In.	7475.00
Horse, Electra, Trotting, Arrow, Full-Bodied, Flattened, 40 x 32 In.	1325.00
Horse, Galloping, Painted Green, Circular Stepped, Star Cut Base, 39 x 42 In.	590.00
Horse, Galloping, Zinc, 19th Century, 16 x 23 In.	400.00
Horse, Jockey, Dexter, Copper, Painted, Black, Gold, 1800s, 19 x 31 In.	5875.00
Horse, Leaping, Pine, Iron Rod, c.1900, 18 x 38 1/4 In.	9600.00
Horse, Prancing, Full-Bodied, Iron Arrow, Ball, 54 x 28 In.	230.00
Horse, Prancing, Sheet Iron, Late 19th Century, 30 1/2 x 35 1/2 In.	690.00
Horse, Rider, Copper, Zinc, Gilding, New England, c.1830, 30 x 18 In.	8915.00
Horse, Rider, Zinc, Copper, Molded, Cast, Late 1800s, 20 1/2 x 35 1/4 In.	4780.00
Horse, Running, Copper, Aged Patina, Bullet Holes, Harris & Co., 20 x 31 In.	2420.00
Horse, Running, Copper, Flat, Full-Bodied, Rod, Gilt, Verdigris, 1800s, 15 1/2 x 26 In.	2585.00
Horse, Running, Copper, Hollow Body, 16 1/2 x 41 In.	6325.00
Horse, Running, Copper, Iron, 1800s, 77 1/2 x 17 1/2 x 29 1/2 In.	2705.00
Horse, Running, Copper, Molded, Verdigris, 15 1/2 x 25 3/4 In.	2585.00
Horse, Running, Copper, Zinc, 1800s, 18 3/4 x 25 1/2 In.	470.00
Horse, Running, Ethan Allen, Zinc, Verdigris, Cushing & White, 1880-1910, 31 In. . . *Illus*	3100.00
Horse, Running, Flat, Full-Bodied, Gilt, Verdigris, Rod, Stand, c.1875, 18 1/2 x 31 In.	2115.00
Horse, Running, Lighting Rod, Copper Spiked Ball, 1900s, 73 x 23 In.	675.00
Horse, Running, Sheet Iron, Gilt, Black Paint, Stand, c.1875, 24 x 38 In.	3055.00
Horse, Running, Sheet Iron, Gold Paint, 1 Side Has Black Details, 24 x 38 In.	3055.00
Horse, Running, Sheet Metal, Serrated Tail, Mane, c.1900, 19 1/2 x 43 In.	805.00
Horse, Running, Tin, 3 Balls, Tapered Pedestal, 67 x 44 x 24 In.	690.00
Horse, Running, Wooden, Old Green Paint, Metal Base, 30 x 15 In.	3365.00
Horse, Standing, Wood, Carved, Painted, Fish Cutout Base, c.1900, 16 x 40 In.	7800.00
Horse, Sulky, Rider, Copper, Cast Brass Directionals, 63 x 36 x 19 In.	345.00
Horse, Trotting, Copper, 19th Century, A.J. Harris, & Co., 22 x 29 1/2 In.	1265.00
Horse, Trotting, Rider, Painted Green, Stepped, Star Cut Base, 51 In.	590.00
Horse, Walking, Copper, Bullet Hole, 20 1/2 x 26 1/2 In.	2310.00
Horse, Walking, Serrated Mane, Sheet Metal, Gray Paint, 21 x 28 In.	855.00
Indian, Kneeling, Arrow, Wood, Painted, c.1900, 75 3/4 x 46 5/8 In.	2938.00

Weather Vane, Horse, Running, Ethan Allen, Zinc, Verdigris, Cushing & White, 1880–1910, 31 In.

Weather Vane, Roadster, Sheet Copper, Gilt, Verdigris, 20th Century, 25 In.

Clean cast iron with coarse salt and a soft sponge. The salt absorbs oil, is abrasive enough to remove bits of food, and does not harm the pan's seasoning. Rinse; wipe dry.

Weather Vane, Rooster,
Cast Iron, Sheet Metal,
Rochester Iron Works,
N.H., 1800s, 36 In.

Indian, On Horseback, Wearing War Bonnet, Galvanized Sheet Ion, 26 x 24 In. 230.00
Mallard, Carved, Round Body, Flat Tail, Painted, Stand, 27 In. 2760.00
Odd Fellows, Zinc, 29 3/4 In. 1840.00
Oil Truck, Sheet Iron, Red, Green, Black, White, c.1950, 15 x 30 In. 690.00
Pig, Arrow, Lightning Rod, Tin, Cast Iron, Copper, Glass Ball, c.1900, 38 3/4 x 21 In. 646.00
Pig, Hollow Body, Tin, Gold Paint Trace, 21 x 5 In. 520.00
Roadster, Sheet Copper, Gilt, Verdigris, 20th Century, 25 In. .... *Illus* 2900.00
Rooster, Cast & Sheet Iron, Pierced Tail, c.1860, 32 1/2 x 37 In. 6325.00
Rooster, Cast Iron Body, Sheet Steel Tail, Red Paint, 2 Piece, 24 x 23 x 36 In. 6670.00
Rooster, Cast Iron, Painted, Swell-Bodied, Hamburg, American, 1800s, 48 x 37 In. 8400.00
Rooster, Cast Iron, Sheet Metal, Rochester Iron Works, N.H., 1800s, 36 In. .... *Illus* 9000.00
Rooster, Copper, Molded, 1800s, 23 3/4 x 22 3/4 In. 2700.00
Rooster, Copper, Red Painted Comb, Late 1800s, 14 In. 1265.00
Rooster, Crowing, Galvanized Steel, Silhouette, Wooden Base, 22 In. 575.00
Rooster, Gilt Copper, Iron Directionals, Cushing Attribution, c.1900, 77 x 24 1/2 In. 1998.00
Rooster, Iron, Glass Globe, Lightning Rod, c.1900, 25 1/2 x 20 In. ....235.00 to 380.00
Rooster, On Arrow, Brass, On Stand, 10 3/4 x 16 In. 1840.00
Rooster, Scotland Forever, Gilded Surface, Ribbed, A. Wilson, Upper Largo, 22 x 21 In. .. 1380.00
Rooster, Sheet Metal, 1800s, 18 3/4 x 17 3/4 In. 230.00
Rooster, Sheet Metal, Gilt Trace, Early 20th Century, 32 In. 4406.00
Rooster, Sheet Metal, Maine, Late 1800s, 31 1/4 In. 920.00
Rooster, Sheet Metal, Red, Yellow & Black, Wood Base, 18 x 17 In. 200.00
Rooster, Zinc, French Provincial, Hand-Wrought Iron Bracket, 1885, 26 In. 2950.00
Rooster, Zinc, Iron, Lightning Rod, James, c.1900, 34 1/4 x 32 1/8 In. 325.00
Schooner, Wooden Hull, Brass Spars, Rigging, Metal Sails, 24 1/4 x 18 1/2 In. 550.00
Sea Serpent, Sheet Copper, Yellow Paint, 1878, 10 x 19 In. 3600.00
Seal, Copper, Signed, Dated, B.A. Norling, 20th Century, 35 x 10 In. 865.00
Ship, 3-Masted, Sheet Iron, 20th Century, 26 x 19 In. 265.00
Stag, Leaping, Sheet Metal, Green Paint, Late 1800s, 37 In. 3335.00
Star & Crescent, Sheet Iron, Late 1800s, 21 1/2 x 23 1/4 In. 1116.00
Steamer, Horse Drawn, Painted, Metal, 37 In. 550.00
Sword Piercing Heart, Copper, Molded, 27 1/2 In. 1840.00
Whale, Front Fins, Wide Tail, Open Mouth, Wood, 25 x 12 In. 2590.00

WEBB glass is made by Thomas Webb & Sons of Ambelcot, England. Many types of art and cameo glass were made by them during the Victorian era. Production ceased by 1991, and the factory was demolished in 1995. Webb Burmese and Webb Peachblow are special colored glasswares of the Victorian era. They are listed at the end of this section. Glassware that is not Burmese or Peachblow is included here.

Webb

Bottle, Scent, Duck's Head Shape, White Over Cranberry, Silver Cap, Cameo, 9 In. 13225.00
Bowl, Crystal, Etched Dragons, Cameo Clouds, Bulbous, Flared Rim, 10 In. 1380.00
Bowl, Fishscale, Salmon, Creamy White, Cameo, Signed, 1 1/2 x 4 In. 460.00
Bowl, Mother-Of-Pearl, Pink, Yellow Mums, Herringbone, Ribbed, Ruffled Edge, 10 In. .. 2360.00
Bowl, Prussian Blue, Flowers, Stems, Bulbous, Cameo, 4 1/4 In. 2070.00
Bowl, Underplate, Clear, Etched, Bands Of Leafy Scrolls, Marked, 6-In. Plate 175.00
Bowl, Underplate, Cranberry, Amber Threading, Ruffled Edge, 6-In. Plate 230.00
Bride's Bowl, Cream, Opal, Hobnail, Rose Interior, Ruffled Edge, 10 In. 375.00
Cologne Bottle, Green, Water Lily, Teardrop, Lay Down, Cameo, 3 3/4 In. 2185.00

Compote, Alexandrite, Shaded To Amber, Honeycomb, Flared Wavy Rim, 4 1/2 In. 1335.00
Fork & Spoon, Ivory, Stemmed Flowers, Cameo Handles, 12 In. 805.00
Goblet, Wine, Alexandrite, Shaded To Amber, Honeycomb, Amber Stem & Foot, 4 1/2 In. . 2300.00
Jar, Cover, Prussian Blue, White Flowers, Butterfly, White Finial, Oval, Signed, 3 1/4 In. ... 2415.00
Perfume Bottle, Blue, Ferns, Butterfly, Lay Down, Silver Lid, Cameo, 10 In. 1900.00
Perfume Bottle, Cameo, Cranberry, White Flowers, Globe Shape, Silver Cap, 1 3/4 In. 1668.00
Perfume Bottle, Cameo, Prussian Blue, Ferns, Butterfly, Laydown, Screw Cap, 8 In. 1438.00
Perfume Bottle, Flowers, Butterfly, Cameo, 4 In. 1500.00
Perfume Bottle, Ivory, Flowers, Embossed Hinged Cover, Stopper, Cameo, 2 3/4 In. 1955.00
Vase, Birds Perched On Flowering Ginkgo Branches, Crimson, 7 1/2 In. 290.00
Vase, Blue, Bamboo Tree Trunks, Palms, Double Banded Rim, Squat, Cameo, 5 In. 690.00
Vase, Blue, Flowers, Tapering Oval, Butterfly, Rings, Cameo, 7 In. 1955.00
Vase, Cabinet, White Flower, Butterfly, Rose Round, Cameo, 2 In. 460.00
Vase, Cinnamon, Morning Glory Vine, Herringbone Trim, 6 7/8 In. 980.00
Vase, Coralene, Aqua Blue, Satin, Bulbous, Raised & Flared Rim, 7 1/2 In. 460.00
Vase, Coralene, Satin Shaded Blue, Gold Enameled, Tapered, Crimped Neck, 6 In. 460.00
Vase, Crimson, White Morning Glories At Neck, Bulbous Based, Waisted, 7 In. 1900.00
Vase, Flowers, Butterfly, Martele Ground, Orange To Red, Cameo, 9 1/2 In. .....3280.00 to 3525.00
Vase, Opal To Lime Green, Butterfly, Leafy Branch, Shouldered, 7 In. 400.00
Vase, Prussian Blue, White Ferns, Flowers, Butterfly, 2 Neck Rings, Shouldered, 5 In. 1955.00
Vase, Red, White Flowers, Frosted Ground, Butterfly, Cameo, Signed, 5 In. 1725.00
Vase, Reverse Trumpet, Cranberry, Tulips, Leaf Clusters, 15 In. 2875.00
Vase, Stick, Blue, Cascading Leafy Branch, Bulbous Base, 9 1/4 In. 200.00
Vase, Stick, Honeysuckle, Butterfly, Ivory, Scalloped Crimped Rim, Bulbous Base, 8 In. .. 1150.00
Vase, Stick, Opal, Enameled Flowering Vine, Frosted Overlay, Bulbous Base, 6 1/4 In. 259.00
Vase, White Flowers, Leaves, Red Ground, Cameo, 9 1/2 In. 2530.00
Vase, White, Satin, Diagonal Bands Of Ivy & Blue Flowers, Bulbous, Tapered Neck, 7 In. . 4888.00
Vase, Wild Rose, White Cased, Cranberry, Frosted, Cameo, c.1885, 5 In. 520.00

WEBB BURMESE is a colored Victorian glass made by Thomas
Webb & Sons of Stourbridge, England, from 1886.

Bowl, Silver Rim, Signed, 4 1/2 In. 130.00
Rose Bowl, Applied Leaf & Pod, Crimped Edge, Signed, 4 1/4 In. 635.00
Rose Bowl, Purple Flower, Green Hawthorne Branch, 2 1/2 In. 260.00
Vase, Branches, Lavender Blue Flowers, Leaves, 6 1/4 In. 1035.00
Vase, Bulbous Base, Ribbed, Ruffled Edge, 5 In., Pair 690.00
Vase, Hawthorne, Cylindrical, Bulbous Base, Ruffled Edge, 4 In. 145.00
Vase, Morning Glory, Cylindrical, Rolled Rim, 8 In. 805.00
Vase, Stick, Queen's Pattern, 8 In. 2185.00
Vase, Trumpet, 8 1/4 In. 405.00

WEBB PEACHBLOW is a colored Victorian glass made by Thomas
Webb & Sons of Stourbridge, England, from 1885.

Bird, Butterfly, Flowers, Bulbous, Conical Neck, 16 In. 1380.00
Bottle, Scent, Blue, White Daisies, Green Branches, 2 Butterflies, 5 In. 1095.00
Bowl, Centerpiece, Blue & Gold Branches, Ribbed, Ruffled Edge, 11 In. 1095.00
Vase, Butterfly, Branches, Blue To Cream, Pillow Shape, Crimped Edge, 6 In. 865.00
Vase, Coralene, Cranberry To Opal, Tapering, Everted Neck, 5 1/4 In. 230.00
Vase, Gold & Silver Enameled, Butterflies, Flowers, 11 In., Pair 750.00
Vase, Gold Coralene, Flared Neck, 7 1/4 In. 336.00
Vase, Stick, Applied Camphor Vines, Flowers, Bulbous Base, Ruffled Edge, 9 In. 690.00
Vase, Stick, Bulbous Base, 14 In. 520.00
Vase, Trumpet, Petaled Rim, 4 In. 345.00

WEDGWOOD, one of the world's most successful potteries, was
founded by Josiah Wedgwood, who was considered a cripple by his
brother and was forbidden to work at the family business. The pottery
was established in England in 1759. A large variety of wares has been
made, including the well-known jasperware, basalt, creamware, and
even a limited amount of porcelain. There are two kinds of jasperware.
One is made from two colors of clay, the other is made from one color
of clay with a color dip to create the contrast in design. The firm is still
in business. Other Wedgwood pieces may be listed under Flow Blue,
Majolica, Tea Leaf Ironstone or in other porcelain categories.

WEDGWOOD

Basket, Stand, Caneware, Biscuit Molded, Oval, Early 19th Century, 10 7/8 In. 940.00
Biscuit Jar, Cover, Jasper Dip, Yellow, Round, Applied Black Festoons, Handle, 5 In. 765.00
Biscuit Jar, Crow's Foot Base, Jasperware, 5 1/4 In. 60.00
Biscuit Jar, Jasper Dip, Tricolor, Classical Relief Figure, Late 1800s, 5 1/4 In. . . . .590.00 to 1000.00
Bough Pot, Cover, Moonlight Luster, Nautilus Shell, Pierced Insert, c.1815, 10 In. 2940.00
Bowl, Black Basalt, Dancing Women, Leaf Bands, 10 1/4 x 4 1/2 In. 400.00
Bowl, Black Basalt, Molded Grapevine, Impressed Mark, 11 In. 227.00
Bowl, Butterfly Luster, 6-Sided, 6 1/2 In. 480.00
Bowl, Butterfly Luster, Oriental Landscape, Mottled Orange, Octagonal, 4 x 8 In. 1725.00
Bowl, Butterfly Luster, Turquoise Exterior, Octagonal, Marked, 8 In. 1500.00
Bowl, Chalice, Fairyland Luster, Twyford Garlands, Flame Ground, c.1920, 11 In. 6465.00
Bowl, Dragon Luster, Blue Ground, Mother-Of-Pearl, Octagonal, c.1920, 7 In. 470.00
Bowl, Dragon Luster, Round & Octagonal, 8 In., Pair 540.00
Bowl, Fairyland Luster, Cobble, Dana Castle On Road, Octagonal, 1920s, 10 1/2 In. 3300.00
Bowl, Fairyland Luster, Daventry, Burnt Orange, Octagonal, 4 x 8 1/4 In. 3450.00
Bowl, Fairyland Luster, Daventry, Pinecones, Leaves, Elves, No. Z5443, 13 In. . . . . . . *Illus* 21600.00
Bowl, Fairyland Luster, Octagonal, Brown Mark, 4 In. 290.00
Bowl, Fluted Sides, Scalloped Rim, Green Matte, Keith Murray, 1937, 8 3/4 In. 650.00
Bowl, Jasperware, Lilac, White Relief, Dancing Hours, Laurel Band, 1961, 10 In. 470.00
Bust, Duke Of Edinburgh, Black Basalt, Mounted, Impressed Title, Mark, 1953, 9 In. 355.00
Bust, Shakespeare, Black Basalt, England, 1964, 10 In. 410.00
Bust, Stephenson, Carrara, Waisted Socle, E.W. Wyon, England, c.1858, 14 3/4 In. 880.00
Bust, Venus, Black Basalt, Circular Socle, Impressed Title, Marked, 1800s, 9 1/4 In. 705.00
Butter, Jasperware, Blue, Metal Base, Lid, 6 In. 70.00
Cachepot, Jasperware, Green, 8 1/4 x 7 1/4 In. 230.00
Cachepot, Undertray, Jasper Dip, Dark Blue, Classical Relief, 1800s, 5 In., Pair 1060.00
Candlestick, Black Basalt, Classical Figures, Flowers, Marked, 1900s, 9 3/4 In., Pair 235.00
Candlestick, Black Basalt, Fluted, Molded, Impressed Mark, c.1825, 12 1/2 In., Pair 650.00
Candlestick, Jasper Dip, Blue, White Classical Figures, 7 3/4 In., Pair 460.00
Cheese Dish, Cover, Jasper Dip, Black, Leaf Border, Classical Relief, c.1900, 11 In. 1115.00
Compote, Cover, Stand, Moonlight Luster, Nautilus Service, 6 3/4 x 9 1/4 In., Pair 2300.00
Crocus Pot, Majolica, Green Glazed, Hedgehog, Oval, Pierced, c.1865, 6 In. 380.00
Custard Cup, Jasperware, Blue, Applied White Latticework, Twist Handle, 2 In. 1175.00
Dish, Cover, Rabbits, Leaves, c.1872, 8 1/2 In. 200.00
Figurine, Cupid, Seated On Rock, Circular Base, Black Basalt, Marked, Late 1800s, 8 In. . 410.00
Footbath, Queen's Ware, Lop Handles, Molded Straps, Oval, c.1800, 17 In. 765.00
Hatpin, Jasper Dip, Blue, Lozenge Shaped Ball, White Border, Laurel Band, 7/8 In. 410.00
Honey Pot, Cover, Caneware, Beehive, 4-Legged Bench, Impressed Mark, 6 3/4 In. 1295.00
Ice Bucket, Jasperware, Blue, Silver Mounted, Grecian Scene, 6 In. 215.00
Incense Burner, Cover, Black Basalt, Dolphin, Festoons In Relief, Pierced Disc, 4 In. 825.00
Jar, Canopic, Cover, Black Basalt, Hieroglyphs, Symbols, c.1867, 10 In., Pair 3820.00
Jar, Cover, Fluted Body, Round, Green Matte, Keith Murray, c.1936, 5 In. 825.00
Jardiniere, Black Basalt, Classical Figures, Lion's Masks, Garlands, 6 1/4 In. 400.00
Jardiniere, Jasper Dip, Olive Green, White Classical Muses, Festoon, c.1920, 8 In. 380.00
Jardiniere, Jasperware, Figure, Sprigging, Blue, 5 In. 105.00
Jug, Flowers, Painted, Tapered Sides, Enamel, Rosso Antico, Marked, 6 7/8 In. 295.00
Jug, Jasper Dip, Crimson, Applied White Classical Relief, Garlands, c.1920, 6 1/2 In. 940.00
Jug, Jasper Dip, Crimson, Barrel Shape, White Classical Figures, c.1920, 5 1/2 In. 645.00
Jug, Jasper Dip, Crimson, Rope Twist Handle, White Classical Relief, c.1920, 6 In. 2000.00
Jug, Jasper Dip, Yellow, Applied Black Classical Relief, c.1930, 5 3/4 In. 590.00
Lamp, Sconce, 2-Light, Jasper Panel, Dancing Hours, Early 1900s, 19 1/4 In., Pair 800.00
Medallion, Jasper Dip, Blue, Frederick Augustus, White Relief, c.1775, 3 x 4 In. 1000.00
Medallion, Jasper Dip, Blue, Oval, Portrait, White Relief, 2 5/8 In., 2 Piece 353.00
Medallion, Jasper Dip, Blue, Oval, Sir Ashton Lever, c.1781, 3 1/4 x 4 In. 1175.00
Medallion, Jasper Dip, Blue, Oval, White Classical Relief, 3 x 3 3/4 In., 2 Piece 410.00
Medallion, Jasperware, Blue, Lord Hood, White Relief, Marked, c.1775, 3 x 4 In. 2350.00
Medallion, Jasperware, Blue, Marie I, Queen Of Portugal, White Relief, c.1775, 4 In. 470.00
Medallion, Jasperware, Blue, Oval, Bentley, c.1778, 3 1/8 x 3 3/4 In. 590.00
Medallion, Jasperware, Blue, Prince Ferdinand, White Relief, 2 3/4 x 3 1/2 In. 355.00
Medallion, Jasperware, White, Oval, Slave, Back Figure Relief, Late 1700s, 1 x 1 1/4 In. . . 1765.00
Medallion Set, Black Basalt, Round, Heads Of Popes, Late 1700s, 6 Piece 705.00
Mortar & Pestle, Stoneware, Vitrified, Wooden Handle, Early 1800s, 7 1/2 x 10 In. 355.00
Necklace, Jasper Dip, Blue, 19 Medallions, White Relief, Pierced Centers, 11 In. 1060.00

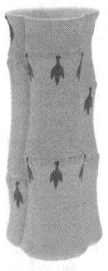

Wedgwood, Bowl, Fairyland Luster,
Daventry, Pinecones, Leaves,
Elves, No. Z5443, 13 In.

Wedgwood, Plaque, Fairyland
Luster, Imps On Bridge & Tree
House, Tortoiseshell, 12 In.

Wedgwood, Vase, Caneware,
3 Bamboo Stalks, Cream,
Brown Leaves, 7 7/8 In.

Pastille Burner, Pink Splash Luster, 3 Dolphin Feet, 5 1/2 In. 290.00
Pie Dish, Cover, Caneware, Oval, England, c.1800, 9 1/4 In. 705.00
Pie Dish, Cover, Crust Design, Grape Leaf Handle, Oval, Marked, 7 3/4 In. 590.00
Pitcher, Jasperware, White Figure, Blue Ground, 7 In. 70.00
Pitcher, Luster, Fallow Deer, 3 1/2 In. 80.00
Plaque, Black Basalt, Day & Night, Self-Framed, 19th Century, 5 x 6 1/4 In., Pair 765.00
Plaque, Black Basalt, Judgment Of Hercules, Oval, Early 1800s, 8 1/2 x 11 1/2 In. 825.00 to 1060.00
Plaque, Fairyland Luster, Imps On Bridge & Tree House, Tortoiseshell, 12 In. . . . . . . *Illus* 19200.00
Plaque, Jasper Dip, Black, White Relief, Children, Fruit, Mid 1800s, 4 x 9 In. 1295.00
Plaque, Jasper Dip, Green, Judgment Of Hercules, Early 1800s, 6 x 18 In. 2115.00
Plaque, Jasperware, Blue, Offering To Peace, Gilt Metal, Frame, Oval, 14 x 10 In. 185.00
Plaque, Jasperware, Blue, White Relief, Fall Of Phaeton, G. Stubbs, 1900s, 12 x 20 In. . . .   520.00
Plaque, Jasperware, Figural Design, Blue & White, Oval, 6 x 4 3/4 In., Pair 130.00
Plate, Argenta Ware, Chrysanthemum, Impressed, 1884, 9 In. 165.00
Plate, Bread & Butter, Majolica, Grapevine, 1874, Impressed, 5 1/2 In. 260.00
Plate, Dessert, Majolica, Green, Fruit & Leaf Border, 8 3/4 In., c.1925, 11 Piece 460.00
Plate, Fairyland Luster, Roc Centre, Twyford Border, 1920s, 10 5/8 In. 6000.00
Plate, Jasperware, Green, White Decoration, Lilac Medallion, 6 1/2 In. 1265.00
Plate, Majolica, Tulips, Ribbon Border, Impressed, 9 1/4 In. 405.00
Platter, Fish, Argenta Ware, Majolica, Oval, Scalloped Rim, England, c.1878, 25 In. 825.00
Platter, Ironstone, Peruvian Pattern, Transfer, c.1849, 15 1/2 x 12 In. 175.00
Pot, Cover, Fairyland Luster, Candlemas Pattern, c.1920, 8 1/4 In. 3820.00
Potpourri, Cover, Black Basalt, Upturned Handles, Impressed Mark, 1800s, 9 In. 940.00
Potpourri, Cover, Caneware, Smear Glazed, Loop Handles, c.1820, 8 1/4 In. 1000.00
Potpourri, Dome Cover, Jasperware, Blue & White, Dolphin Footed, 6 In., Pair 2990.00
Powder Box, Cover, Dragon Luster, Orange, Red, Purple Interior, c.1920, 5 In. 1115.00
Punch Bowl, Fairyland Luster, Poplar Trees, Mermaid & Woodland Bridge Inside, 11 In. . . .   7290.00
Punch Bowl, Poplar Trees, Interior With Mermaid Center, Woodland Bridge, 11 In. 6250.00
Ring, Jasperware, Blue & White Medallion, Black, Portrait, Bentley, c.1779, 1/2 x 5/8 In. .   825.00
Sardine Box, Jasperware, Cover, Blue & White, Silver Plated Holder, 8 1/2 In. 200.00
Sardine Box, Majolica, Asian, White, Yellow & Red Flowers, 3 1/4 x 8 1/2 x 7 In. 374.00
Tea Set, Black Basalt, Ovoid, Half Fluted, Circular Foot, 7 1/2-In. Teapot, 3 Piece 345.00
Tea Set, Covers, Black Basalt, Enameled, Painted, Flowers, Sybil Finial, 5 1/4 In., 3 Piece   355.00
Teapot, Jasper Dip, Crimson, Applied White Classical Relief, c.1920, 5 1/4 In. 940.00
Teapot, Jasperware, Blue, Grecian Scene, 4 1/2 In. 105.00
Tile, Kate Greenaway, Boy & Girl Walking In Snowy Woods, February, 1870s 85.00
Tureen, Cover, Pearlware, Impressed Mark, Early 19th Century, 17 In. 1550.00
Tureen, Soup, Cover, Pearlware, Orange Highlights, Shell Shape, 11 In. 1265.00
Urn, Black Basalt, Dome Lid, 2 Handles, Classical Shape, 1800s, 14 1/2 In., Pair 3450.00
Urn, Cover, Jasper Dip, Black, Stripes, White Dancing Hours Figures, Plinth Base, 25 In. .   1380.00
Vase, Black Basalt, Encaustic Decorated, Classical Figures, Early 1800s, 15 In. 14100.00
Vase, Black Basalt, Hercules In Garden, Lion's Head Handles, c.1868, 14 In. 1295.00
Vase, Black Basalt, Laurel & Berry Border, Swags, Wedgewood & Bentley, c.1775, 5 In. . . .   700.00
Vase, Caneware, 3 Bamboo Stalks, Cream, Brown Leaves, 7 7/8 In. . . . . *Illus*   125.00
Vase, Cover, Bronzed Black Basalt, Gilded, Playing Children, c.1885, 12 In. 4700.00

Vase, Cover, Jasper Dip, Black, Dancing Hours In Relief, Stripes, Marked, 1954, 10 In. . . .   500.00
Vase, Cover, Jasper Dip, Dark Blue, White Classical Figures, Early 1800s, 7 1/4 In. 1765.00
Vase, Cover, Jasperware, Black, Stripes, Swag, Mask Head Handles, c.1960, 8 1/2 In. 999.00
Vase, Cover, Jasperware, White, Pink & Green Decoration, 14 In. 1495.00
Vase, Dragon Luster, Mottled Blue Ground, Bulbous, Stick, 9 In. 720.00
Vase, Fairyland Luster, Baluster, Candlemas, 1920s, 10 1/2 In. 6000.00
Vase, Fairyland Luster, Baluster, Imps On Bridge, 1920s, 9 In. 7800.00
Vase, Fairyland Luster, Candlemas, Blue Interior, Trumpet Shape, Footed, 7 In. 2875.00
Vase, Fairyland Luster, Cylindrical, Torches, Flaming Wheel Border, 1920s, 11 1/4 In. 7200.00
Vase, Fairyland Luster, Daventry, 1920s, 14 In. 6600.00
Vase, Fluted Flaring, Green Matte Glaze, Keith Murray, 1930s, 7 1/4 In. 276.00
Vase, Jasper Dip, Black, Classical Muses, Festoons, Late 19th Century, 15 In. 2585.00
Vase, Jasper Dip, Light Blue, White Classical Relief, c.1867, 8 In., Pair 1000.00
Vase, Marsden Art Ware, Squat, Bulbous, Clip Decorated Flowers, c.1885, 6 In. 530.00
Vase, Moonlight Luster, Pink, Columnar Shape, 1810-15, 12 1/2 In., Pair 4945.00
Vase, Porphyry, White Terra-Cotta, Stoneware, c.1795, 7 3/8 In., Pair 1115.00
Vase, Queen's Ware, Leaf & Berry Scrolled Handles, Mid 19th Century, 10 1/4 In. 1295.00

WELLER pottery was first made in 1872 in Fultonham, Ohio. The firm moved to Zanesville, Ohio, in 1882. Artwares were introduced in 1893. Hundreds of lines of pottery were produced, including Louwelsa, Eocean, Dickens Ware, and Sicardo, before the pottery closed in 1948.

LOUWELSA
WELLER

Alvin, Vase, Bud, 8 1/2 In. 81.00
Ardsley, Bowl, Flared, 3 1/2 x 12 In. 410.00
Ardsley, Bowl, Flared, Fish Flower Frog, 12 1/2 x 6 In. 440.00
Ardsley, Flower Frog, Kingfisher, 8 1/2 In. 410.00
Ardsley, Vase, Cattails, Flared, Marked, 12 In. 150.00
Ardsley, Vase, Flared, 10 1/2 x 7 1/2 In. 355.00
Art Nouveau, Vase, Woman, Grapes, Flowers, Matte Glaze, Handle, 8 In. 235.00
Art Nouveau, Vase, Woman, Grapes, Flowers, Matte Glaze, Handle, 13 In. 440.00
Art Nouveau, Vase, Woman, Grapes, Flowers, Matte Glaze, Handle, 14 1/2 In. 410.00
Art Nouveau, Vase, Woman, Grapes, Flowers, Matte Glaze, Handle, Incised Mark, 9 In. . .   355.00
Aurelian, Clock, Jonquil, 9 7/8 In. 2070.00
Aurelian, Ewer, Yellow Pansies, Silver Overlay, 5 1/2 In. 1035.00
Aurelian, Jardiniere, Pedestal, Purple Grapes, Incised, 11 1/2 In. 690.00
Aurelian, Pitcher, Squat, Orange Blossoms, Green Leaves, 5 1/2 x 5 3/4 In. 176.00
Aurelian, Vase, Bulbous, Clover Blossoms, 5 1/2 x 3 1/2 In. 235.00
Aurelian, Vase, Tapered, Berries, Leaves, 9 1/2 x 4 In. 355.00
Baldin, Jardiniere, Brown, 9 x 13 In. 235.00
Baldin, Vase, Blue, Tapered, 13 x 7 1/2 In. 705.00
Besline, Candlestick, Berries, Leaves, Lustered Orange Ground, 11 In., Pair 235.00
Besline, Vase, Bulbous, Berries, Leaves, Lustered Orange Ground, 8 1/2 x 6 In. 470.00
Blue Drapery, Vase, 11 1/8 In. 130.00
Blue Drapery, Wall Pocket, Impressed, 7 5/8 In. 196.00
Blue Ware, Planter, Footed, Garlands, Maidens, Playing Instruments, 7 x 8 In. 205.00
Blue Ware, Vase, Embossed, Maiden, 8 1/2 x 3 1/2 In. 90.00
Bonito, Vase, Tulips, Bulbous, Marked, 7 1/2 x 4 1/2 In. 145.00
Bonito, Wall Pocket, 10 1/2 x 5 In. 120.00
Bookend, Owls, Pair 920.00
Brighton, Figurine, Blue Bird, 6 5/8 In. 863.00
Brighton, Figurine, Parrot On Perch, Impressed, 7 1/2 In. 978.00
Burnt Wood, Vase, Bulbous, Flower Band, 3 3/4 x 4 1/4 In. 82.00
Burnt Wood, Vase, Fish Design, 2 3/8 x 3 In. 69.00
Chase, Jar, Cover, White Molded Rider, Horse, Jumper, Blue Ground, 6 1/2 In. 410.00
Chase, Vase, Rider, Horse, Brown, Green, Blue High Glaze, Experimental, 7 1/2 In. 825.00
Chase, Vase, Sterling Silver Rider, Horse, Light Green Mottled Glaze, Handles, 6 In. 350.00
Chase, Vase, Sterling Silver Rider, Horse, Light Green Mottled Glaze, Tapered, 9 In. 200.00
Chase, Vase, Sterling Silver Rider, Horse, Pink Mottled Glaze, Footed, 12 In. 645.00
Chase, Vase, White Molded Rider, Horse, Blue Ground, 5 1/2 In. 175.00
Chase, Vase, White Molded Rider, Horse, Blue Ground, Bulbous, Marked, 6 1/2 In. 265.00
Chase, Vase, White Molded Rider, Horse, Blue Ground, Cylindrical, Marked, 9 In.   .235.00 to 325.00
Chase, Vase, White Molded Rider, Horse, Blue Ground, Flared, Marked, 11 1/2 In. 410.00

Chase, Vase, White Molded Rider, Horse, Blue Ground, Flattened, Marked, 8 1/2 In. 265.00 to 295.00
Chase, Vase, White Molded Rider, Horse, Blue Ground, Footed, 10 In. 410.00
Chase, Vase, White Molded Rider, Horse, Blue Ground, Paper Label, Marked, 11 In. 350.00
Chase, Vase, White Molded Rider, Horse, Blue Ground, Tapered, 7 1/2 In. 325.00
Chase, Vase, White Molded Rider, Horse, Blue Ground, Waisted, Marked, 5 1/2 In. 265.00
Chase, Vase, White Molded Rider, Horse, Blue, Pillow Form, 3 Openings, 8 1/2 In. .205.00 to 235.00
Chase, Vase, White Molded Rider, Horse, Dogs, Black Ground, 8 In. 295.00
Chase, Vase, White Molded Rider, Horse, Tan Ground, Bulbous, Marked, 5 1/2 In. 325.00
Chase, Vase, White Molded Rider, Horse, Tan Ground, Flared, Cylindrical, 11 1/2 In. 205.00
Chase, Vase, White Molded Rider, Horse, Tan Ground, Marked, 6 3/4 In. 325.00
Chase, Vase, White Molded Rider, Horse, Tan Ground, Tapered, Marked, 8 1/4 In. 350.00
Chengtu, Vase, Oval, Stamped, 6 1/4 x 3 1/2 In. 115.00
Claywood, Vase, Grapes, Faceted, Stamped, 8 x 4 In. 115.00
Claywood, Vase, Leaf & Berry Motif, 8 In. 127.00
Clinton Ivory, Jardiniere, Squirrels, Birds, Owls On Branches, Embossed, 7 x 8 In. 489.00
Cloudburst, Vase, Oval, Brown, Orange, Ivory, 10 1/2 x 4 In. 350.00
Coppertone, Bowl, Chinese Shape, 2 Squared Loop Handles, 4 3/4 In. 220.00
Coppertone, Bowl, Flower Frog, Broad Form, Incised, 11 In. 150.00
Coppertone, Bowl, Flower Frog, Lily Pad Handles, 3 1/2 x 11 In. 575.00
Coppertone, Bowl, Flower Frog, Waterlily Handles, Green, Rust, Marked, 16 In. 440.00
Coppertone, Bowl, Frog Clutching Lotus Flower, Ink Stamp, 3 3/4 x 4 In. 375.00
Coppertone, Bowl, Frog, Lotus Blossoms, Ink Stamp, 2 x 6 In. 405.00
Coppertone, Figurine, 2 Fish, Intertwined, Marked, 8 In. 3800.00
Coppertone, Figurine, Frog, 2 1/2 x 2 3/4 In. 230.00
Coppertone, Figurine, Frog, Green, Rust, 4 In. . . . . .295.00 to 315.00
Coppertone, Figurine, Turtle, 2 1/2 x 6 1/2 In. . . . . .295.00 to 530.00
Coppertone, Tile, Mottled Green, Brown 60.00
Coppertone, Tile, Stamped, 4 1/4 x 4 1/4 In. 80.00
Coppertone, Vase, Flared, Frog Perched On Each Side, 8 1/4 x 10 1/2 In. . . . . . . .1115.00 to 1410.00
Coppertone, Vase, Lily Pad, Applied Frog, Green, Rust, Marked, 7 In. 1765.00
Coppertone, Vase, Lily Pad, Carved, 2 Applied Frogs, Green, Marked, Paper Label, 8 In. . 2000.00
Coppertone, Vase, Tapered, Incised, 6 In. . . . . .160.00 to 176.00
Copra, Basket, Pink, Red Wild Roses, Impressed, 12 In. 115.00
Cornish, Vase, Blue, 2 Handles, 6 In. 115.00
Cornish, Vase, Brown, 9 In. 115.00
Dickens Ware, Jardiniere, Orange, Yellow Tulips, Impressed, 10 3/4 In. . . . . .150.00 to 230.00
Dickens Ware, Jug, 2 Fish, Bulbous, Twisted, Incised, Marked, Handle, 5 1/2 In. . . .345.00 to 355.00
Dickens Ware, Jug, Grapes On Vine, Handles, Monogram, 10 In. 220.00
Dickens Ware, Lamp Base, Iris, Impressed, 9 5/8 In. 290.00
Dickens Ware, Lamp, Dragon, Chrysanthemums, 15 1/2 In. 290.00
Dickens Ware, Mug, David Copperfield, Quotation, 5 1/2 In. 400.00
Dickens Ware, Mug, Incised, Painted, American Indian, Blue Hawk, 5 1/2 x 5 In. 175.00
Dickens Ware, Pitcher, Pears, Green, Gold Ground, Impressed Marks, 13 1/2 In. 345.00
Dickens Ware, Tankard, Deer, Tree, Impressed Marks, 11 1/4 In. 175.00
Dickens Ware, Vase, American Indian Chief, White Swan, 9 5/8 In. 865.00
Dickens Ware, Vase, Art Nouveau Flowers, Impressed Numbers, 16 1/4 In. 1955.00
Dickens Ware, Vase, Black Heart, American Indian Chief, Impressed, 10 In. 865.00
Dickens Ware, Vase, Cavalier, Monogrammed, 16 1/2 In. 405.00
Dickens Ware, Vase, Cylindrical, Etched, Painted, Golfer, Trees, 7 1/2 x 2 1/4 In. 755.00
Dickens Ware, Vase, Golfer, Lines Up Shot, Handles, Incised, 11 1/4 x 4 In. 2185.00
Dickens Ware, Vase, Kittens, Incised Monogram, 16 In. 3795.00
Dickens Ware, Vase, Lady Golfer, Shouldered, Incised, Handles, Marked, 7 In. 1295.00
Dickens Ware, Vase, Mandolin Player, 25 In. 1725.00
Dickens Ware, Vase, Monk Napping, Initialed, 10 3/8 In. 290.00
Dickens Ware, Vase, Monk Pouring Ale, Incised, 9 3/4 In. 460.00
Dickens Ware, Vase, Monk Slicing Loaf Of Bread, Impressed, 7 1/2 x 4 1/4 In. 200.00
Dickens Ware, Vase, Monk Under Brown Glaze, 3 Handles, 6 1/2 x 5 In. 375.00
Dickens Ware, Vase, Woman Golfer Swinging, Impressed, 6 3/4 In. 1725.00
Dickens Ware, Vase, Wood Duck Standing By Stream, Pillow, Impressed Marks, 5 In. 520.00
Elberta, Vase, Quatrefoil Mouth, 5 1/2 In. 138.00
Eocean, Bowl, Pink Nasturtiums, Handles, 3 1/4 In. 259.00
Eocean, Pitcher, Heron Standing In Water, Lotus Flower, 7 1/4 In. 175.00
Eocean, Pitcher, Red Cherries, Leaves, Impressed, 6 1/2 In. 140.00

Eocean, Rose, Burgundy, Signed, 13 1/2 In. 1116.00
Eocean, Rose, Pink, White, Raised, Shouldered, Marked, 11 1/2 In. 1290.00
Eocean, Vase, 6 Twisted Handles, Red Cherries, Incised, 16 In. 1150.00
Eocean, Vase, Blackberries On Vine, Monogrammed, 10 5/8 In. 315.00
Eocean, Vase, Bulbous, Painted, Cherries, 5 x 5 In. 120.00
Eocean, Vase, Bulbous, Red Berries, Leaves, 8 1/2 x 5 In. 410.00
Eocean, Vase, Daisies, Bottle Shape, Stamped, 6 3/4 In. 259.00
Eocean, Vase, Egret, Incised Mark, 8 1/2 In. 690.00
Eocean, Vase, Mushrooms, Impressed, 6 3/4 In. 460.00
Eocean, Vase, Oval, Painted, Dogwood, 9 1/2 x 4 In. 645.00
Eocean, Vase, Pink, White Berries On Vine, 6 7/8 In. 230.00
Eocean, Vase, Red, White Irises, Shaded Round, Signed, 16 3/4 In. 3105.00
Eocean, Vase, Red, Yellow Carnation, Impressed, 7 7/8 In. 345.00
Eocean, Vase, Squat Base, Long Flared Neck, Painted, Cherries, M. Timberlake, 10 x 4 In. 355.00
Eocean, Vase, Wild Roses, Marked, 8 1/2 In. 410.00
Etched Matte, Jardiniere, Grape & Leaf Branches, 6 1/2 x 8 1/2 In. 265.00
Etched Matte, Jardiniere, Grapevines, 7 x 9 In. 205.00
Etna, Bowl, Red, Twist Handles, 4 1/2 x 9 1/2 In. 115.00
Etna, Cruet, Rust Pansy, Impressed Marks, 6 In. 105.00
Etna, Jardiniere, Flowers, Impressed, 8 x 9 1/2 In. 80.00
Etna, Jardiniere, Maroon Irises, Impressed Mark, 9 1/2 x 11 In. 115.00
Etna, Mug, Carnations, Handle, Marked, 5 1/4 In. 148.00
Etna, Mug, Flowers, Embossed, Painted, 5 1/4 In. 90.00
Etna, Mug, Red Grapes, Green Leaves, Gray Background, 5 5/8 In. 58.00
Etna, Pitcher, Lavender Chrysanthemums, Impressed Marks, 10 1/4 In. 175.00
Etna, Pitcher, Red, Pink Chrysanthemums, 10 3/8 In. 115.00
Etna, Vase, Egg Shape, Pink Roses, Pink, Cream, Gray, c.1906, 14 In. 405.00
Etna, Vase, Flowers, Embossed, Painted, 6 In. 220.00
Etna, Vase, Maroon, Purple Flower, Gray To Cream Ground, 5 In. 115.00
Etna, Vase, Pink Clover, Impressed Marks, 10 1/2 In. 290.00
Etna, Vase, Pink Flowers, Beaker Shape, Marked, 6 x 4 3/4 In. 290.00
Etna, Vase, Purple Flowers, Bulbous, 7 x 3 3/4 In. 290.00
Etna, Vase, Raised Roses, Gray To Ivory To Pink Ground, Impressed Mark, 10 In. 265.00
Etna, Vase, Ruby Flowers, 5 1/4 In. 130.00
Fairfield, Wall Pocket, 9 x 5 In. 120.00
Figure, Dog, Pop-Eye, 10 1/4 x 7 1/2 In. 590.00
Figure, Frog, Seated, 5 3/8 x 6 1/2 In. 660.00
Figure, Man, Seated, Holding Hat, 4 1/4 In. 480.00
Flemish, Jardiniere, 8 In., Pair 138.00
Flemish, Jardiniere, Leaves, Impressed, 9 1/2 x 11 In. 90.00
Flemish, Jardiniere, Pedestal, Bird On Wire, 29 5/8 In. 1035.00
Flemish, Planter, Cows, Sheep, Geese, Ram's Head, 8 x 12 x 7 1/2 In. 1725.00
Flemish, Umbrella Stand, 22 x 10 1/2 In. 470.00
Flemish, Vase, Mulberry Flowering Pods, 10 1/8 In. 195.00
Flemish, Window Box, 3 Nymph's Sitting In Copse, 6 3/4 x 13 In. 2070.00

Weller, Flower Frog, Bird On Stump, 7 In.

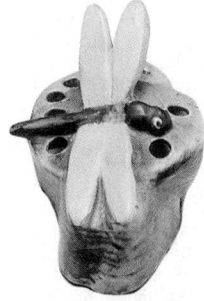

Weller, Flower Frog, Dragonfly, 4 1/2 In.

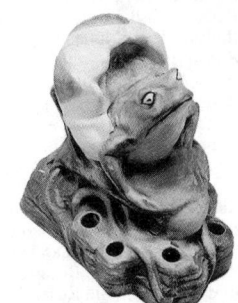

Weller, Flower Frog, Frog & Water Lily, 4 3/8 In.

Fleron, Vase, Green Matte Glaze, Ruffled Rim, 2 Twist Handles, 6 5/8 In.	185.00
Fleron, Vase, Organic Green, Rose Interior, 7 3/4 In.	60.00
Florala, Wall Pocket, Flower Panels, 9 1/2 x 5 In.	295.00
Floretta, Tankard, 2 Apples On Branch, Incised, 16 1/2 In.	520.00
Floretta, Tankard, Purple Grapes, Incised, 16 1/2 In.	430.00
Floretta, Vase, Embossed Grapes, Cylindrical, Marked, 9 x 3 1/4 In.	105.00
Flower Frog, Bird On Stump, 7 In. ....*Illus*	120.00
Flower Frog, Crab Shape, 1 1/2 x 5 In.	150.00
Flower Frog, Dragonfly, 4 1/2 In. ....*Illus*	120.00
Flower Frog, Frog & Water Lily, 4 3/8 In. ....*Illus*	120.00
Flower Frog, Frog Perched On Rock, 3 3/4 x 5 1/4 In.	560.00
Flower Frog, Girl & Watering Can, 6 1/4 In.	540.00
Flower Frog, Kingfisher On Stump, 8 3/4 In.	240.00
Flower Frog, Red Breasted Robin, 4 7/8 In.	240.00
Flower Frog, Salamander, Impressed, 1 1/8 x 4 1/2 In.	316.00
Flower Frog, Swan, 5 3/4 In.	120.00
Forest, Hanging Basket, Flared, 9 In. Diam.	325.00
Forest, Jardiniere, Footed, 7 In.	970.00
Forest, Jardiniere, Pedestal, 29 x 12 In.	1410.00
Forest, Vase, Corseted, 8 x 4 In. ....235.00 to 345.00	
Forest, Vase, Flared, Impressed Mark, 3 1/2 In.	150.00
Fruitone, Vase, Mottled Blue & Tan Matte Glazes, 9 In.	276.00
Gardenware, Frog, 8 3/4 x 9 1/2 x 12 In.	450.00
Glendale, Vase, Bird, Nest, Branches, Tapered, Stamped Mark, 10 In.	1000.00
Glendale, Vase, Birds, Nest, Impressed, 8 3/4 In.	800.00
Glendale, Vase, Bluebird On Nest, 4 In.	259.00
Glendale, Vase, Double Bud, Embossed, Bluebird, Nest, Amongst Berries, 6 1/2 In.	410.00
Glendale, Vase, Goldfinch At Nest, 7 1/4 In.	175.00
Glendale, Vase, Oval, Embossed, Yellow Birds, On Branch, 9 x 4 In.	940.00
Glendale, Wall Pocket, Goldfinches, Cherry Blossoms, Impressed, 7 1/8 In.	750.00
Greora, Vase, Divided, Fan, 7 x 7 In.	315.00
Greora, Wall Pocket, 10 1/2 In.	315.00
Group, 2 Chicks, 6 In. ....329.00 to 530.00	
Hudson, Vase, Apple Blossoms, Shaded Green To Pink, Baluster, Stamped, 13 x 4 In.	690.00
Hudson, Vase, Berries, Leaves, White, Teardrop Form, 9 x 3 3/4 In.	430.00
Hudson, Vase, Blue, Pink, Yellow Blossoms, Oval, H. Pillsbury, 7 x 3 1/4 In.	865.00
Hudson, Vase, Blue, Yellow Irises, 15 1/8 In.	3220.00
Hudson, Vase, Bulbous, 2 Large Handles, Ivory, Yellow Roses, 8 x 8 1/2 In.	1000.00
Hudson, Vase, Bulbous, Painted, Pink Tulips, 10 1/2 x 4 3/4 In.	500.00
Hudson, Vase, Chains Of Blossoms, Blue, Pink Band, Stamped, 7 1/4 x 3 1/2 In.	290.00
Hudson, Vase, Faceted, Cherry Blossoms, White & Decorated, 11 x 4 3/4 In.	206.00
Hudson, Vase, Flowers, Red, Lavender, Magenta, Incised, 6 1/2 x 5 1/2 In.	865.00
Hudson, Vase, Gourd Shape, Pink & White Dogwood, McLoughlin, 6 1/2 x 5 1/2 In.	294.00
Hudson, Vase, Iris, Cylindrical, Marked, Timberlake, 9 1/2 In.	590.00
Hudson, Vase, Iris, Purple, Red, Blue Ground, Footed, Marked, 7 In.	265.00
Hudson, Vase, Lily Of The Valley, Ink Stamp, Signed, 9 In.	748.00
Hudson, Vase, Lily Of The Valley, White, Yellow, Green, Gray To Rose Ground, 7 x 4 In.	920.00
Hudson, Vase, McLaughlin, Blue Flowers, 8 1/4 x 3 3/4 In.	176.00
Hudson, Vase, Morning Glory, Marked, Hester Pillsbury, 5 1/2 In.	825.00
Hudson, Vase, Nasturtium, Magenta, Yellow, Green, Brown, Blue, Timberlake, 9 1/2 x 6 In.	1380.00
Hudson, Vase, Oval, Painted, McLoughlin, Pink & White Dogwood, 7 x 3 In.	411.00
Hudson, Vase, Pink & White Hydrangea, Twisted Handles, McLaughlin, 15 1/4 x 7 In.	3335.00
Hudson, Vase, Pink Wild Roses, 2 Handles, Mae Timberlake, 5 1/2 x 8 In.	980.00
Hudson, Vase, Tapered, Painted, Pink & White Roses, 7 x 4 1/2 In.	235.00
Hudson, Vase, Variegated Blue & Green Matte, Yellow Iris, Cylindrical, D. England, 8 In.	560.00
Hudson, Vase, White & Yellow Roses, Bulbous, Handles, Marked, 7 3/4 In.	800.00
Hudson, Vase, White Blooming Dogwood, Impressed, 6 3/4 In.	403.00
Hudson, Vase, White Dogwood Flowers, Leaves, Branches, 2 Handles, Incised, 8 In.	748.00
Hudson, Vase, Wild Roses, Impressed Mark, 8 7/8 In.	184.00
Hudson, Vase, Wild Roses, Signed, 8 5/8 In.	575.00
Hudson, Vase, Wild Roses, Twin Handles, Signed, Ink Stamp, 6 3/8 In.	575.00
Ivoris, Umbrella Stand, Apple, 22 In.	920.00
Ivoris, Vase, Classical Style, 10 In.	80.00

Ivory, Shelf, Wall Mount, Fruit, 9 5/8 In. 175.00
Ivory, Tankard, Grapes, Leaves, Vines, Squared Handle, 10 In. 150.00
Ivory, Vase, Cupids, 4 Straight Tapered Sides, 4 Claw Feet, 13 In. 105.00
Ivory, Vase, Cylindrical, Leaf, 9 In. 58.00
Jap Birdimal, Jardiniere, Landscape, Trees, Yellow Moon, Blue Background, 10 x 8 In. 410.00
Jap Birdimal, Umbrella Stand, Landscape, Yellow Moon, 20 In. 430.00
Jap Birdimal, Vase, Oriental Person, Cobalt, Moss Green Ground, Signed, VMH, 7 x 3 In. . 115.00
Jap Birdimal, Vase, White Birds, Green Ground, Handles, Squat, Marked, 6 In. 470.00
Jardiniere, Flowers, 4 Shaped Feet, 7 1/2 x 8 1/2 In. 120.00
Jardiniere, Green Matte, Buttressed, Footed, Molded Architectural, 7 x 8 In. 489.00
Jardiniere, Lilies, Flowers, Mushroom, 5 1/4 x 8 1/2 In. 300.00
Juneau, Vase, Red Leaves, Pink Ground, Buttressed Handles, Stamped, 10 In. 230.00
Kenova, Vase, Trailing Vining Flowers, 5 7/8 In. 290.00
Kingfisher, Flower Frog, 9 x 7 In. 235.00
Kingfisher, Pitcher, Ink Stamp, 8 1/4 In. ....105.00 to 230.00
Knifewood, Bowl, Swans Under Cattails, 3 1/2 x 6 3/4 In. 290.00
Knifewood, Jardiniere, Pedestal, Daisies, Butterflies, 32 1/8 In. 2760.00
Knifewood, Planter, Birds In Fruit Trees, Stamped, 6 x 6 1/2 In. 750.00
Knifewood, Vase, Butterflies, Daisies, Teardrop Form, Stamped, 4 1/2 x 4 1/2 In. 288.00
Knifewood, Vase, Corseted Shape, Peacocks, Flowers, Trees, 9 In. 980.00
Knifewood, Vase, Daisies, Butterflies, Bulbous, Stamped, 7 1/4 x 4 1/2 In. 748.00
Knifewood, Vase, Hooded Owls Under Crescent Moon, 8 1/2 In. 1265.00
Knifewood, Vase, Squirrels, Blue Birds, Hooded Owls In Tree, 7 x 4 In. 1295.00
Knifewood, Vase, Swans & Trees, Stamped, 5 x 3 1/2 In. 1265.00
Knifewood, Vase, Swans Swimming, Forest Canopy, 4 3/4 In. 259.00
Knifewood, Vase, Tear Shape, Butterflies & Daisies, Stamped Weller, 4 1/2 In. 28.00
Lamar, Vase, Bottle Shape, Trees, Landscape, Windmills, Ships, 10 1/2 In. 525.00
Lamar, Vase, Island Palm Tree Setting, 12 3/4 In. 430.00
LaSa, Lamp Base, Pine Trees, Luster, 13 In. 489.00
LaSa, Vase, Baluster, Seascape, Trees, Water, 14 In. 1840.00
LaSa, Vase, Bulbous, Painted, Swirling Clouds, Mountainous Landscape, 6 x 4 1/2 In. 765.00
LaSa, Vase, Bulbous, Trees In Foliage, Extended Neck, 5 1/2 In. 250.00
LaSa, Vase, Landscape, 3 3/4 x 3 In. 315.00
LaSa, Vase, Landscape, Etched, Cylindrical, Signed, 9 In. 150.00
LaSa, Vase, Oval, Trees In Full Blossom, Lake, Mountain, Signed, 11 In. ....750.00 to 840.00
LaSa, Vase, Palm Trees, Oasis Mountain Scene, Silver, Gold & Red Metallic, Oval, 4 In. .. 390.00
LaSa, Vase, Seascape, Trees Reflecting In Water, Baluster, 14 x 6 3/4 In. 1840.00
LaSa, Vase, Stylized Trees, Cone Shape, Signed, 7 1/2 In. 280.00
LaSa, Vase, Stylized Trees, Leaves, Bulbous, Elongated Neck, Signed, 5 1/2 In. 280.00
LaSa, Vase, Tropical Landscape, Iridescent, 8 In. 265.00
Lavonia, Vase, Bud, Art Nouveau Woman, 10 3/4 In. 315.00
Loru, Vase, Turquoise, Brown, Flared, Notched Rim, 15 In. 290.00
Louella, Vase, Ring Handles, White Blossoms In Branches, Impressed, 7 7/8 In. 175.00
Louwelsa, Candleholder, Flowers, Brown Shaded To Tan, Double Loop Handle, 6 In. 150.00
Louwelsa, Candlestick, Nasturtium, Impressed, 10 5/8 In. 115.00
Louwelsa, Clock, Berry, 6 1/2 In. 219.00
Louwelsa, Cuspidor, Pansies, Green & Brown Ground, c.1910-15, 7 x 6 In. 270.00
Louwelsa, Ewer, Bell Flower, 11 In. 259.00
Louwelsa, Ewer, Globular, Black-Eyed Susan, 4 1/8 In. 105.00
Louwelsa, Ewer, Pansies, Brown Glaze, Bulbous, Ruffled Rim, 6 In. 69.00
Louwelsa, Ewer, Wisteria Pods Over Shoulders, 20 3/4 In. 978.00
Louwelsa, Ewer, Yellow Wild Roses, Ruffled Rim, Marked, 6 x 5 1/2 In. 115.00
Louwelsa, Humidor, Pipes, Cigars, Tobacco Leaves, Brown Glaze, Marked, Signed, 7 In. . 355.00
Louwelsa, Jardinere, Rose Blossom, 9 1/2 In. 150.00
Louwelsa, Jardiniere, Mums, 8 In. 105.00
Louwelsa, Jug, Berries, 6 In. 150.00
Louwelsa, Jug, Pansies, Squat, 3 1/4 x 5 1/2 In. 145.00
Louwelsa, Jug, Ruffled Rim, Painted, Yellow Flowers, 6 x 5 In. 176.00
Louwelsa, Jug, Whimsy, Cherries Growing From Branch, Impressed, 6 In. 220.00
Louwelsa, Jug, Whiskey, Cherries, William Hall, 7 1/2 In. 290.00
Louwelsa, Mug, Grapes & Leaves, Marked, 6 x 5 In. 105.00
Louwelsa, Pitcher, Mug, Painted, Grapes, 12 1/2 x 6 1/2 In. 235.00
Louwelsa, Tankard, Cavalier, 12 1/2 In. 259.00

Louwelsa, Tankard, Red, Orange Trumpet Flower Blossom, Vine, Cascading, 12 3/8 In. 196.00
Louwelsa, Tankard, Yellow Pears To Be Picked, 16 3/4 In. 375.00
Louwelsa, Vase, Blackberries, Impressed, Incised Marks, 16 3/4 In. 400.00
Louwelsa, Vase, Brown, White Spaniel, Impressed Mark, 12 In. 920.00
Louwelsa, Vase, Bud, Flowers, 5 1/2 In. 80.00
Louwelsa, Vase, Bulbous, Acorns, Leaves, 13 1/2 x 6 1/4 In. 175.00
Louwelsa, Vase, Chrysanthemum, Blue, Tapered, Marked, 8 1/2 In. 1000.00
Louwelsa, Vase, Clover Blossoms, 15 1/2 x 4 In. 4115.00
Louwelsa, Vase, Clover Blossoms, Squat, Stamped, 3 x 5 1/2 In. 115.00
Louwelsa, Vase, Dog, Impressed Marks, Signed, 12 1/2 In. 575.00
Louwelsa, Vase, Ewer, Wild Roses, Impressed, 9 1/4 In. 150.00
Louwelsa, Vase, Golden Peaches, Impressed, Initialed, 12 1/2 In. 345.00
Louwelsa, Vase, Grapes, Impressed, 18 5/8 In. 980.00
Louwelsa, Vase, Holly Berries, Brown Glaze, Shouldered, 7 In. 127.00
Louwelsa, Vase, Lamp, Lilies, Impressed, Signed, 26 1/2 In. 3335.00
Louwelsa, Vase, Man's Portrait, Brown Glaze, Tapered Form, Impressed, 12 1/2 In. 1410.00
Louwelsa, Vase, Nasturtium, Brown & Green Glaze, Gourd, Signed, 4 1/2 In. 120.00
Louwelsa, Vase, Old Masters, Handles, Initialed, 10 1/4 In. 690.00
Louwelsa, Vase, Orange Mushrooms, Silhouette, 10 3/4 In. 315.00
Louwelsa, Vase, Oval, Painted, Gooseberries, Leaves, 10 1/2 x 5 1/2 In. 118.00
Louwelsa, Vase, Pillow, Orange Poppies, 5 1/2 x 5 1/2 In. 175.00
Louwelsa, Vase, Pillow, Swimming Fish, 9 x 10 In. 690.00
Louwelsa, Vase, Pillow, Yellow Roses, Impressed Marks, 9 1/2 x 10 In. 185.00
Louwelsa, Vase, Poppy, Blue, Slender Form, Marked, 7 1/2 In. 765.00
Louwelsa, Vase, Red Cherries, Impressed, Incised Marks, 8 1/4 In. 127.00
Louwelsa, Vase, Red Rose, 9 In. 127.00
Louwelsa, Vase, Red, Teasel, Pink, Ivory, Purple, Red Ground, 10 1/2 x 4 In. 2235.00
Louwelsa, Vase, Red, Yellow, Carnations, 10 1/8 In. 127.00
Louwelsa, Vase, Roses, Initialed, Impressed, 8 3/4 In. 690.00
Louwelsa, Vase, Terrier, Impressed Marks, Signed, 15 In. 2185.00
Louwelsa, Vase, Wild Rose, Squat, Stamped, 3 1/4 x 6 In. 85.00
Louwelsa, Vase, Wild Roses, 15 3/8 In. 690.00
Louwelsa, Vase, Yellow Pears, Signed, 18 1/4 In. 430.00
Louwelsa, Vase, Yellow, Red Nasturtiums, Impressed, Signed, 17 In. 230.00
Louwelsa, Whiskey Jug, Red Raspberries, Monogram, Impressed, 6 5/8 In. 375.00
Louwelsea, Vase, Blue, Cherry Bough, c.1900, 8 3/4 x 3 In. 275.00
Luster, Vase, Bulbous, 3 3/4 x 4 In. 176.00
Malvern, Basket, Branch Handles, Red Flowers, Ink Stamp, 7 1/2 x 8 In. 127.00
Malvern, Umbrella Stand, Orange Glaze, 20 In. 825.00
Malvern, Wall Pocket, Tree Limb, Green, Brown, Red Flowers, 9 x 5 1/2 In. 130.00
Manhattan, Vase, Green, Signed, 6 1/2 In. 69.00
Marengo, Vase, Pink, Faceted, 9 1/2 x 3 1/2 In. 765.00
Melrose, Candlestick, 12 1/8 In., Pair 290.00
Ming Tree, Vase, Blue, White Trees, Brown Branch Handles, Marked, 8 In. 175.00
Ming Tree, Vase, Brown Matte, Green Trees, Trial Glaze, Marked, 8 In. 1880.00
Ming Tree, Vase, Green, Pink Trees, Brown Branch Handles, Marked, 8 In. 120.00
Ming Tree, Vase, White, Pink Trees, Applied Clay Bits, Brown Branch Handles, 8 In. 300.00
Muskota, Figurine, 2 Birds, Ivory, Green, 5 In. 325.00
Muskota, Flower Frog, Boy Fishing, 6 1/2 In. 150.00
Muskota, Flower Frog, Turtle, Impressed, 2 1/8 x 4 5/8 In. 375.00
Oak Leaf, Jardiniere, 8 1/2 x 10 In. 300.00
Oak Leaf, Tankard, 14 In. 115.00
Orris, Wall Pocket, Embossed, Bird, Brown & Green Mottled Glaze, 8 x 4 1/2 In. 206.00
Parian, Wall Pocket, Conical, Flowers, Geometrics, Blue, Ivory, Gray, 8 x 4 1/2 In. 205.00
Patra, Bowl, 3-Lobed, Marked, 4 1/8 In. 265.00
Patricia, Vase, Orange Swans, 3 Swan Neck Handles, 9 x 6 In. 265.00
Patricia, Vase, With Swan Handles, Cream & Light Green, 6 In. 85.00
Pearl, Candlestick, Impressed Mark, 8 1/4 In. 127.00
Pearl, Vase, Bulbous, Tapered, Marked, 5 1/2 In. 205.00
Pedestal, Umbrella Stand, 19 1/2 In. 359.00
Pumila, Vase, Brown, Flared, 10 1/4 x 6 In. 235.00
Rhead Faience, Vase, Bulbous, 3 Handles, Painted, Orange Poppies, 8 x 7 In. 1175.00
Rhead Faience, Vase, Geometric, Walking Duck Bands, Bulbous, Squeezebag, 9 x 6 In. 3220.00

Roba, Wall Pocket, Yellow, 10 1/2 In.	290.00
Rochelle, Vase, Bulbous, Painted, Blue & Yellow Flowers, Pillsbury, 6 1/2 x 3 In.	825.00
Rochelle, Vase, Stylized Flowers, Signed, 7 1/8 In.	489.00
Roma, Candlestick, Impressed Marks, 10 3/8 In., Pair	160.00
Roma, Jardiniere, Baskets Of Roses, Swags, Cylindrical Stand, 29 In.	430.00
Roma, Jardiniere, Grape & Vine Panels, Cream Ground, Marked, 9 1/2 In.	176.00
Roma, Planter, Embossed Roses, Oval, Footed, 5 1/2 x 16 In.	230.00
Roma, Vase, Paneled Grapevine, 10 In.	295.00
Roma, Vase, Paneled Stylized Dogwood, Impressed Mark, 10 In.	205.00
Roma, Wall Pocket, Printed Decoration, 8 1/2 In.	90.00
Rosemont, Planter, Bluebirds, On Branches, Pink Flowers, 7 1/2 x 9 1/2 In.	325.00
Senic, Vase, Green, Marked, 12 In.	265.00
Sicardo, Vase, 4 Lobes, Art Nouveau Flowers, Incised, 6 3/4 In.	3105.00
Sicardo, Vase, Art Nouveau, Orange Poppy, Pink, Blue Matte Ground, 5 In.	196.00
Sicardo, Vase, Berries, Impressed, 12 In.	978.00
Sicardo, Vase, Buttressed Handles, Signed, Incised, 7 5/8 In.	1265.00
Sicardo, Vase, Daisy, 3 Lobes, 4 In.	805.00
Sicardo, Vase, Flowers, 5 1/2 In.	635.00
Sicardo, Vase, Flowers, Jacques Sicard, c.1905, 4 1/4 In.	1035.00
Sicardo, Vase, Golden Flowers, Copper Color Ground, Signed, 4 3/4 In.	375.00
Sicardo, Vase, Holly Berries, Leaves, Iridescence, 6 3/8 x 8 In.	865.00
Sicardo, Vase, Iridescent Blue, Green, Purple, Gold, Squat, Twisted, 5 In.	1325.00
Sicardo, Vase, Iridescent Mottled Green, Branches & Leaves Inside, Shouldered, 4 In.	420.00
Sicardo, Vase, Iridescent Mottled Green, Tree Branches, Leaves, 4 In.	375.00
Sicardo, Vase, Moresque, Incised, 16 In.	1725.00
Sicardo, Vase, Poppy, Blown Out, Signed, 5 5/8 In.	690.00
Sicardo, Vase, Sinuous Handles, Impressed, 4 1/4 x 9 In.	1150.00
Sicardo, Vase, Squat, Gold Berries, Leaves, Purple, Green, Red, Gold, 5 x 8 In.	765.00
Sicardo, Vase, Star, 4 In.	430.00
Sicardo, Vase, Thistle, Pearlized Gold, Purple, Blue, Green, Orange Glaze, 9 x 4 In.	3335.00
Silvertone, Basket, Marked, Ink Stamp, 13 1/4 In.	460.00
Silvertone, Candlestick, 3 x 6 In., Pair	120.00
Silvertone, Console Set, Flared Bowl, Flower Frog, Candlestick, 12 In.	411.00
Silvertone, Vase, 2 Handles, Flowers, Leafy Branches, c.1925, 9 1/4 In.	259.00
Silvertone, Vase, Bulbous, 2 Handles, Yellow Daisies, 7 1/2 x 7 In.	235.00 to 265.00
Silvertone, Vase, Bulbous, Embossed, Branches, Pink, White Dogwood, 10 1/2 x 6 3/4 In.	355.00
Silvertone, Vase, Bulbous, Embossed, Lilies, 9 1/2 x 5 1/2 In.	206.00
Silvertone, Vase, Bulbous, Handles, Embossed, Yellow Daisies, 7 1/2 In., Pair	380.00
Silvertone, Vase, Bulbous, Pink Chrysanthemums, 9 x 5 1/2 In.	440.00
Silvertone, Vase, Flared, Embossed, Calla Lilies, 12 x 5 1/2 In.	410.00
Silvertone, Vase, Flared, White Calla Lilies, Pink & White Daisies, 10 3/4 x 7 In.	355.00
Silvertone, Vase, Pink & White Flowers, Handles, 10 x 5 1/2 In.	295.00
Silvertone, Vase, Purple Grapes, Ink Stamp, 6 1/2 In.	259.00
Silvertone, Vase, Squat, Flared Rim, Embossed, Pink Rose Branches, 6 1/2 x 6 1/4 In.	265.00
Souevo, Wall Pocket, Flowers, Geometric Design, Blue, Ivory, Gray, 10 1/2 x 6 In.	590.00
Souevo, Wall Pocket, Geometric Designs, Black On Brown Ground, 7 1/2 x 4 In.	118.00
Stellar, Vase, Stars, Blue, Bulbous, Marked, 4 In.	470.00
Turada, Bowl, Blue Flowers, Stylized Ivory Design, Squeezebag, Flared, 3 1/4 x 8 In.	205.00
Turada, Lamp, Oil, 7 3/4 In.	600.00
Turkis, Vase, Twisted Shape, Green, Yellow, Red High Glaze, 5 In.	50.00
Tutone, Vase, Kiln Ink Stamp, 5 1/2 In.	60.00
Umbrella Stand, Green Matte, Flowers, Raised, 21 x 11 In.	600.00
Utility Ware, Bowl, Cover, Cream, Light Blue Banded, 5 x 8 In.	12.00
Utility Ware, Casserole, Cover, Cream, Light Blue Band, 3 x 6 In.	12.00
Vase, Arts & Crafts, Green Matte, Twisted, 6 In.	460.00
Velva, Jar, Cover, 11 1/2 x 6 1/4 In.	315.00
Warwick, Bowl, Handles, Ink Stamp, 3 1/2 x 7 1/2 In.	80.00
Woodcraft, Basket, Hanging, Embossed, Owls, Apple Tree, 5 x 10 In.	120.00
Woodcraft, Basket, Hanging, Foxes, Apples, 4 3/8 x 8 3/8 In.	345.00
Woodcraft, Bowl, Oak Leaves, Squirrel Perched On Rim, 4 3/4 In.	260.00
Woodcraft, Bowl, Panels Of Squirrels In Trees, Marked, 4 x 7 1/2 In.	230.00
Woodcraft, Bowl, Squirrels Eating Acorns, Ink Stamp, 3 In.	259.00
Woodcraft, Candlestick, Owl, Double, 14 In.	645.00

Woodcraft, Flower Frog, Embossed Fly, 2 1/4 x 3 1/2 In. 315.00
Woodcraft, Lamp, Table, Tree & Vine Design, Green, Brown Ground, 18 In., Pair 400.00
Woodcraft, Mug, Foxes Peering From Tree Hole, 6 In. 400.00
Woodcraft, Planter, Foxes, Branch, 5 3/4 x 8 In. 430.00
Woodcraft, Planter, Woodpecker Perched On Side, 8 x 11 In. 750.00
Woodcraft, Vase, Apple Tree Branch, Cylindrical, Marked, 13 In. 350.00
Woodcraft, Vase, Applied Bird, Impressed Mark, 6 In. 325.00
Woodcraft, Vase, Applied Owl, Sitting On Branch, 15 1/2 x 6 1/2 In. 1410.00
Woodcraft, Vase, Blue, 6 In. 196.00
Woodcraft, Vase, Branches Of Fruit, Corseted, 12 x 6 In. 200.00
Woodcraft, Vase, Bud, Double, Entwined Branches, Stamped, 8 x 7 In. 200.00
Woodcraft, Vase, Bud, Handles, Marked, 8 1/4 x 3 In. 145.00
Woodcraft, Vase, Double, Owl Perched On Top, 14 x 7 1/2 In. 645.00
Woodcraft, Vase, Foxes In Den, 6 x 7 In. 150.00
Woodcraft, Vase, Tree Trunk, 9 5/8 In. 115.00
Woodcraft, Wall Pocket, Applied Squirrel, 9 x 4 1/2 In. 440.00
Woodcraft, Wall Pocket, Owl, 10 3/4 In. 430.00
Woodcraft, Wall Pocket, Pink Flowers, 9 x 5 1/2 In. ....118.00 to 315.00
Woodcraft, Wall Pocket, Squirrel, 9 1/4 In. 290.00
Woodcraft, Wall Pocket, Tree Limb From Tree Hole, Red Blooming Flowers, 8 7/8 In. 195.00
Zona, Pitcher, Kingfisher, Cattails, 8 1/2 x 9 In. ....235.00 to 295.00

WESTMORELAND GLASS was made by the Westmoreland Glass
Company of Grapeville, Pennsylvania, from 1890 to 1984. They made
clear and colored glass of many varieties, such as milk glass, pressed
glass, and slag glass.

Animal Dish, Eagle Cover, Lacy Base, Antique Blue, 1950s .... *Illus*   70.00
Animal Dish, Lion On Basket Cover, Milk Glass, Purple, 7 1/2 In. 94.00
Beaded Edge, Cup & Saucer, Blue Flowers, Red Center 65.00
Beaded Edge, Torte Plate, Cherries, Cherry Zodiac, 14 1/2 In. 125.00
Beaded Edge, Tumbler, Footed, Cherries, 8 Oz., 4 7/8 In. 20.00
Doric, Bowl, 4 1/4 x 12 x 10 In. 45.00
Doric, Bowl, Blue, Lace Edge, Oval, 4 x 10 x 12 1/4 In. 33.00
Doric, Candleholder, Blue, No. 23, 4 In., Pair 20.00
Doric, Candlestick, Green, 4 1/2 In. 18.00
Doric, Candlestick, Milk Glass, 4 1/2 In. 18.00
Doric, Candlestick, Milk Glass, Lace Edge, 4 1/4 x 4 1/4 In. 9.00
Doric, Compote, Sweetmeat, Green Mist, Ruffled Edge, 5 x 3 In. 25.00
Doric, Creamer, Fruit, Milk Glass, 2 3/4 x 5 In. 24.00
Doric, Rose Bowl, Cupped Lace Edge, 6 In. 45.00
Doric, Sugar, Milk Glass, 2 1/2 x 5 In. 24.00
English Hobnail, Candy Dish, Cover, Milk Glass, 7 1/2 x 5 3/8 In. 22.00
English Hobnail, Compote, 5 1/4 x 4 In. 11.00
English Hobnail, Plate, Sherbet, Milk Glass, 6 3/4 In. 15.00
English Hobnail, Vase, Ivy, Milk Glass, 7 1/2 x 5 In. 22.00
English Hobnail, Vase, Milk Glass, 4 1/2 x 6 In. 30.00

Westmoreland, Animal Dish, Eagle Cover,
Lacy Base, Antique Blue, 1950s

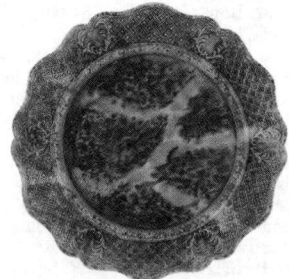

Whieldon, Plate, Embossed Lattice Rim,
Scalloped Edge, Green, Brown, 1780, 9 1/2 In.

Old Quilt, Bowl, Square, Footed, Milk Glass, 2 3/4 x 4 3/4 In.	15.00
Old Quilt, Cruet, Milk Glass, 4 1/2 x 3 1/4 In.	12.00
Old Quilt, Vase, Milk Glass, 6 5/8 x 4 1/8 In.	23.00
Paneled Grape, Planter, Milk Glass, Square, 5 1/4 In.	23.00
Princess Feather, Basket, Made From Plate, Upturned Sides, Applied Handle, 7 1/4 In.	125.00
Princess Feather, Cake Plate, Golden Sunset, 4 1/4 x 10 1/4 In.	72.00
Princess Feather, Champagne, 4 1/2 In.	10.00
Princess Feather, Cocktail, 4 1/4 In.	8.00
Princess Feather, Compote, Golden Sunset, 7 x 9 1/2 In.	85.00
Princess Feather, Plate, Golden Sunset, 12 In.	50.00
Princess Feather, Salt & Pepper, Golden Sunset	30.00
Princess Feather, Sherbet, 3 5/8 In.	8.00
Princess Feather, Sugar & Creamer	20.00
Princess Feather, Tidbit, 2 Tiers, Golden Sunset, 9 x 10 1/2 In.	65.00

WHEATLEY Pottery was established in 1880. Thomas J. Wheatley had worked in Cincinnati, Ohio, with the founders of the art pottery movement, including M. Louise McLaughlin of the Rookwood Pottery. Wheatley Pottery was purchased by the Cambridge Tile Manufacturing Company in 1927.

Vase, Baluster, Barbotine, Apple Blossom, Mottled Blue To Black, 1879, 12 3/4 In.	705.00
Vase, Green Matte, Feathered Glaze, Ridged Shoulder, 5 1/2 In.	265.00
Vase, Green Matte, Hourglass Shape Short Neck, Thick Textured Glaze, 11 In.	1380.00
Vase, Green Matte, Mottled Glaze, Elliptical Shape, Feathered Glaze, 11 1/2 In.	635.00
Vase, Green Matte, Organic Shape, 4 Handles, Charcoal Highlights, 14 1/2 In.	3290.00
Vase, Green Matte, Textured Glaze, Shouldered, 9 In.	265.00
Vase, Green Matte, Textured, Shouldered, 9 In.	295.00
Vase, Green Matte, Tooled Leaf Decoration, 3 Applied Buttressed Feet, 6 1/2 In.	1095.00
Vase, Green Matte, Tooled Leaves, 4 In.	460.00

WHEELING Pottery Company of Wheeling, West Virginia, worked from 1879 to about 1923. The firm went through a number of mergers and name changes during that time. Pottery, semiporcelain, artware, and sanitary wares were made.

Jug, Claret, Applied Reeded Amber Handle, 10 In.	.6325.00 to 7360.00
Tile, Viking Ship, Lavender Mast, Tan Ship, Blue Sky, Frame, Mark, 6 In.	90.00

WHIELDON was an English potter who worked alone and with Josiah Wedgwood in eighteenth-century England. Whieldon made many pieces in natural shapes, like cauliflowers or cabbages.

Plate, Creamware, Diaperwork & Leaf Cartouches, Tortoiseshell Glaze, c.1765, 9 In.	895.00
Plate, Creamware, Feathered Rim, Tortoiseshell Glaze, c.1780, 9 1/2 In., Pair	560.00
Plate, Creamware, Octagonal, Gadroon Rim, Brown Spatter, c.1760, 8 1/2 In., Pair	660.00
Plate, Embossed Lattice Rim, Scalloped Edge, Green, Brown, 1780, 9 1/2 In. .... *Illus*	500.00
Teapot, Tortoiseshell, Double Cone, Green, Amber, Beaded Border, Lion Finial, 6 3/4 In.	1035.00

WILLETS Manufacturing Company of Trenton, New Jersey, began work in 1879. The company made Belleek in the late 1880s and 1890s in shapes similar to those used by the Irish Belleek factory. They stopped working about 1912. A variety of marks were used, all including the name Willets.

Basket, Woven, Flared Rim, Applied Flowers, Square, Belleek, 7 1/2 In.	775.00
Chocolate Set, Pink, Gold Flowers, Ribs, Dragon Handle, Belleek, 9 1/2-In. Pot, 9 Piece	750.00
Vase, Artist Decorated, Rim Ground, 11 In.	185.00
Vase, Roses, Freeform Crimped Shape, Ruffled Rim, Belleek, 5 1/2 In.	315.00

WILLOW pattern has been made in England since 1780. The pattern has been copied by factories in many countries, including Germany, Japan, and the United States. It is still being made. Willow was named for a pattern that pictures a bridge, birds, willow trees, and a Chinese landscape. Most pieces are blue and white.

Basket, Stand, Printed, Oval, Pierced, Newcastle, 10 In.	715.00
Bowl, Vegetable, Cover, Oblong, Burleigh, 10 3/8 In.	250.00

If you wash vintage dishes in a dishwasher, use a no- or low-phosphate (under 1.7%) dishwashing product. Read the label. Also remember that lemon-oil products are not good for silverware.

Willow, Cup, 2 1/4 In.

Chamber Pot, 8 1/4 In.	450.00
Cup, 2 1/4 In. .... *Illus*	15.00
Platter, Lattice Work Edge, Oval, 20 1/4 In.	300.00
Tea Set, Child's, 18 Piece	475.00
Tureen, Cover, William Bramel, England, 9 x 13 In.	795.00
Water Set, Japan, 1940-50, 9-In. Pitcher, 7 Piece	245.00

WINDOW glass that was stained and beveled was popular for houses during the late nineteenth and early twentieth centuries. The old windows became popular with collectors in the 1970s; today, old and new examples are seen.

Leaded, Arts & Crafts, Flowers, Red, Green, Beveled, 18 x 44 In.	490.00
Leaded, Arts & Crafts, Hammered Amber, Jeweled, Frame, 32 x 14 In.	1150.00
Leaded, Arts & Crafts, Lily Pad, Cattails, Frame, 40 x 21 In.	920.00
Leaded, Arts & Crafts, Lit Candle Pattern, Original Frame, 61 x 18 In., Pair	645.00
Leaded, Glasgow Rose, Red, Green, Opalescent, Lead Frame, 28 1/4 x 24 In.	765.00
Leaded, Prairie School, 2 Chevrons, Frame, 30 x 21 In.	575.00
Leaded, Prairie School, Chevron Pattern, Iridescent Luster Top, 27 x 22 In.	590.00
Leaded, Stained Glass, Medallion & Scroll Design, Jewels, Transom, 25 x 66 1/2 In.	259.00
Leaded, Stained Glass, Woman In Headdress, Carrying Picture, 36 x 78 In.	15525.00
Prairie School, Leaded, Central Chevron, Textured Glass, 20 x 27 In., Pair	499.00
Stained Glass, Compass Design, 43 x 27 1/2 In.	1116.00
Stained Glass, Virgin & Child, Our Lady Of The Rosary, Frame, Germany, 74 x 38 In.	4600.00
Transom, Metal Rosettes, White & Red Painted, N.J., 36 x 19 3/4 In.	633.00

WOOD CARVINGS and wooden pieces are listed separately in this book. Many of the wood carvings are figurines or statues. There are also wooden pieces found in other categories, such as Kitchen.

2 Partridges, Nest Of 3 Eggs, Landscape Base, 15 In.	2185.00
Abraham Lincoln, Seated, Mahogany, Signed, Pomerville, 9 1/2 In.	2530.00
Amida, Layered Robe, Stepped Base, Clouds, Lotus, Gilt, Early 1800s, 16 In.	546.00
Angel, Kneeling In Prayer, Uplifted Wings, Painted, Gilt, 1800s, 32 In., Pair	2530.00
Ape, Articulated Arms, Painted, Rocker Base, c.1900, 31 x 34 In.	7638.00
Archangel Michael, Full-Bodied, Fiery Sword, Shield, 17 In.	690.00
Archangel Michael, Gilt, Polychrome, Spanish Colonial, 28 1/2 In.	1095.00
Archangel Michael, Polychrome, Glass Eyes, 20th Century, 21 1/4 In.	865.00
Bear, Standing, Glass Eyes, Switzerland, Post 1930, 35 In.	4025.00
Bear, Walking, Glass Eyes, Switzerland, c.1910, 6 1/2 x 12 In.	690.00
Bear, Walking, Glass Eyes, Switzerland, c.1910, 8 x 11 1/2 In.	1328.00
Bear, With Fish, Carved, Painted, 11 x 20 In.	175.00
Bird, Painted, Glass Eyes, Wire Feet, Graduated Ringed Base, 1800s, 6 1/2 x 5 In.	575.00
Bird, Red, Black Wings, Beak, Wire Legs, Round Base, Oscar Peterson, 5 x 4 In.	635.00
Black Man, Bare Foot, Short Pants, Holding Cigarette, 26 1/4 In.	2645.00
Black Man, Striding With Walking Stick, Poplar, Virginia, c.1850, 10 1/8 In.	705.00
Blackamoor, Parcel Gilt, Polychrome, Venetian, Stand, Late 1800s, 45 In.	7475.00
Bowl, Cover, Coiled Snake Biting Snake, Stylized, Yoruba, Africa, 9 x 14 In.	1175.00
Bowl, Divination, Roosters, Serpents In Beak, Painted, Yoruba, Africa, 6 x 5 3/4 In.	120.00
Bowl, Tree Trunk, Leaves, Bird, Switzerland, c.1900, 6 1/4 x 5 1/2 In.	195.00
Boy, Outstretched Arms, Animal Pelt, Basket, c.1830, 30 1/2 In.	920.00

Buddha, Seated, Brown Lacquer, Gilt, Thailand, 30 1/2 x 24 In. 460.00
Buddha, Seated, On Lotus Throne, Giltwood, 15 In. 657.00
Buddha, Seated, On Lotus Throne, Gold Lacquer, Chinese, 19th Century, 5 1/2 In. 235.00
Bust, Winston Churchill, Folk Art, F. W. Moran, Vermont, c.1965, 9 In. 1645.00
Cameroon, Standing, Long Legs, Torso, Short Arms, Africa, 59 In. 2350.00
Cat, Seated, Tabby, Raised Paw, 7 In. 3220.00
Ceres, Harvest Goddess, Oak, Full-Bodied, France, 18th Century, 55 In. 2760.00
Child, Curly Hair, Arm Raised, Polychrome Over Gesso, France, 1700s, 14 In. 1195.00
Cobra, Rearing, Hooded, Rosewood, Tiger's Eye, Opaline Glass, Anglo-Indian, 15 In. 1610.00
Cornucopia, Relief Fruit, Leaves, Pine, Red & Green Paint, Late 1800s, 20 1/2 In. 1210.00
Corpus, Loincloth, Crown Of Thorns, Halo, Polychrome, Gilt Wood, 45 In. 1610.00
Corpus, Polychrome, Painted, Spanish Colonial, 27 In. 120.00
Crucifix, Applied Metal Corpus, 19th Century, 27 In. 316.00
Crucifix, Applied Metal Corpus, Folk Art, 19th Century, 29 In. 259.00
Crucifix, Corpus, Glass Eyes, Polychrome, Spanish Colonial, 1800s, 36 In. 1495.00
Cup, Saffronwood, Salmon Ground, Flower & Strawberry Band, Joseph Lehn, 5 In. 1100.00
Doberman, Seated, Collar, Shellacked, Patina, 3 5/8 x 1 1/4 x 2 3/4 In. 495.00
Dog, Iron Bells, Dogon, Africa, 7 In. 2470.00
Dog, Seated, Alert, Painted, c.1900, 20 1/8 x 7 1/2 x 11 In. 765.00
Dove, Full-Bodied, Spread Wings, Feathers, Feet, Eyes, Painted, 9 x 1 x 2 In. 470.00
Eagle, Bald, Harvey Black, Blue Hill, Maine, 26 1/2 In. 345.00
Eagle, Gilt, Bracket Base, Pine, Lancaster, Pa., c.1820, 12 1/2 x 17 1/4 In. 8400.00
Eagle, Pine, Relief Feathers, American Shield, Arrows, Bellamy Style, 48 In. 460.00
Eagle, Red Wash Over Gilt Gesso, Pine, Late 19th Century, 16 1/4 x 32 1/2 In. 2400.00
Eagle, Scrolled Base, Beechwood, Stained, Parcel Gilt, Continental, c.1815, 9 In., Pair 865.00
Eagle, Spread Wing, Green, Black, Bellamy Style, 39 In. 460.00
Eagle, Spread Wing, Painted, Giltwood, Bellamy, c.1900, 6 x 32 In. 5020.00
Eagle, Spread Wings, Giltwood, Neoclassical Style, 8 3/4 x 18 In. 375.00
Eagle, Spread Wings, On Rocks, Brown Paint, 1800s, 11 1/2 x 30 In. 940.00
Foo Dog, Imperial Style, Garden, Flower Border, Chinese, 14 1/2 In., Pair 575.00
Foo Dog, Pups Playing With Ball, Bamboo, Chinese, c.1800, 6 1/2 In. 2760.00
Garuda, Standing On 2 Serpents With Wings, Holding Vessel, Nepal, 6 In. 140.00
Girl, Detailed Face & Hair, Simple Form Body, Pine, 14 In. 890.00
Goat Head, Black Paint, 1800s, 9 3/8 x 7 In. 150.00
God Of War, Male, Chinese, Polychrome, Gilt, 36 x 17 x 9 In. 230.00
Harlequin, Painted, 1950, Italy, 17 In. 60.00
Hen, On Nest, DeTurk, 1932, 7 x 5 In. 5175.00
Heron, White & Yellow Paint, Driftwood Stand, K.R. Coghill, Port Royal, Va., 29 In. 550.00
Horse, Eagle Saddle, Tassel Harness, 20th Century, 52 x 49 In. 635.00
Horse, Hemp Tail, Mane, Black & White Paint, 1800s, 20 1/4 x 22 1/2 In. 410.00
Horse, Leather Saddle, Harness, 19th Century, 33 x 47 In. 430.00
Humidor, Bear, Holding Hat, Glass Eyes, Hinged Lid, Switzerland, c.1890, 14 In. 3020.00
Humidor, Bear, Standing, Holding Match Basket, Ash Holder, c.1890, 14 In. 3440.00
Humidor, Owl, Black Forest, Hinged Head, Glass Eyes, Walnut, c.1900, 19 In. 8050.00
Hunter, Stag Head Cane, Powder Horn, 35 x 17 x 30 In. 175.00
Indian, Leather Fringe, Tomahawk, Painted, 10 In. 660.00
Kongo, Leaning, Hands On Hips, Painted Glass Eyes, Africa, 7 3/4 In. 1175.00
Lion, Freestanding, Painted, Signed Afrenette, 10 1/4 x 7 1/2 In. 144.00
Madonna & Child, Gilt Cloud Form Base, Painted, Ecuador, 21 1/2 In. 239.00
Man, Articulated, Hat, Suit, Striped Shirt, Painted, c.1900, 18 1/2 In. 355.00
Man, Bearded, Pinned Arms, Legs, Articulated, Painted, Stand, 14 In. 29.00
Man, Flat Brimmed Hat, Open Palm, Early 20th Century, 38 In. 748.00
Man, Holding Lantern, Ivory Head, Hands, Feet, Japan, 5 1/4 In. 518.00
Man, Standing, Hands To Abdomen, Long Head, Africa, 25 In. 206.00
Man, Wearing Shorts & Cap, Gold, Copper Paint, Oscar Peterson, c.1924, 10 In. 2015.00
Mask, Helmet Style, Pierced Eyes, Bowl Shape Hat, Yoruba, Africa, 8 x 12 1/2 In. 325.00
Mask, Helmet Style, Prominent Features, Cameroon, Africa, 16 In. 118.00
Mask, Oval Form, Protruding Eyes, Teeth, Stylized Nose, Africa, 10 1/2 In. 176.00
Mask, Square Eyes, Pointed Top, Woman, Bent Knees, Breasts, Dogon, Africa, 35 In. 880.00
Mask, Wild Boar, Red, Black, Green, White, Orange, 11 In. 470.00
Mater Dolorosa, Processional, Polychrome, 19th Century, 44 In. 2760.00
Mermaid, Polychrome, 49 1/2 In. 1525.00
Okimono, Beggar Seated, Holding Out Hand, Signed, Japan, 4 1/4 In. 546.00

Owl, Black Over Tan Paint, Relief Carved Ears & Beak, Applied Eyes, 18 In. 375.00
Owl, Black, Gold Tail, Face Detail, Blue Eyes, Metal Feet, 9 In. 60.00
Owl, On Branch, Yellow Glass Eyes, Metal Stand, Dark Patina, 13 3/4 In. 3565.00
Owl, Painted, Mustard, Black, Black Stand, Frank Finney, 26 In. 1495.00
Plaque, Eagle, Bald, On Staff, American Flag, Signed, W.A. Ramson, 1971 .... 5.00
Plaque, Eagle, Don't Give Up Ship, Gilt, Multicolor, 1900s, 10 1/4 x 28 In. 1410.00
Plaque, Eagle, Don't Give Up The Ship, 27 In. 460.00
Plaque, Eagle, Outstretched Wings, 20th Century, 24 x 43 In. 265.00
Plaque, Half Ship Hull, Pine, Varnished, Poplar Back Board, 6 x 23 In. 200.00
Plaque, Oriental Scenes, King & Court, Warriors On Horse, Back, Gilt, 26 x 16 In. 400.00
Plaque, Sperm Whale, Painted, Clark Voorhees, c.1960, 5 1/4 x 17 1/2 In. 1000.00
Quan Yin, Standing, Holding Scroll, Japan, 1700s, 15 1/2 In. 1200.00
Rattle, Bluebird & Nest, Bead Eyes, Music Box Inside, Painted, 6 In. 69.00
Reliquary, Bust, Female Saint, Gilt Wood, France, 18th Century, 14 In. 865.00
Reliquary Casket, Italy, 18th Century, 21 x 16 In. 690.00
Retablo, Holy Boy Of Atocha, Water Gourd, Seated, Oil, On Tin, 13 x 10 In. 315.00
Retablo, Southwest, La Trinidad, Jose Benito Ortega Style, 1900s, 7 x 5 In. 345.00
Robin, Painted, Walter Frederick, Prouts Neck, Maine, c.1940, 7 x 10 In. 29.00
Rooster, On Nest, Eggs In Nest, Wood Shavings, DeTurk, 6 1/2 x 6 In. 6612.00
Sage, Carrying Fish, Splint Work Basket, Rock Base, Japan, Late 1800s, 14 In. 288.00
Sage Holding Prayer Beads, Staff, 25 1/2 In. 255.00
Santo, Monk Saint, Polychrome, Spanish Colonial, 18th Century, 20 In. .... .345.00 to 575.00
Santo, Our Lady Of Sorrows, Wood Frame, Mexico, 19th Century, 10 In. 863.00
Santo, Shepherd, Carrying Lamb, Tin Flag, Painted, Gilt, Spain, 8 1/2 In. 145.00
Santos Set, Polychrome, Clothed, Man, Brown Hair, Beard, 24 In., 5 Piece 1610.00
Sculpture, Positive, Negative, James Prestini, c.1948, 8 3/4 In. 4935.00
Sign, Hand, Pointing Index Finger, Pine, Blue Paint, Gesso, 33 In. 1150.00
Soldier, Standing At Attention, Cartridge Belt Rifle, 12 1/4 In. 920.00
St. Benedict, Holding Crosier, Book Of Gospels, Chalice, 30 In. 865.00
St. Catherine Of Alexandria, Cascading Hair, Walnut, 1600s, 28 In. 9200.00
St. Francis Assisi, Multicolored, Glass Eyes, Spanish Colonial, 1800s, 14 In. 920.00
St. Francis Of Assisi, Polychrome, Giltwood, Spanish Colonial, 1900s, 14 In. 575.00
St. James, Holding Letter & Sword, Oak, Germany, 19th Century, 45 In. 1610.00
St. Jerome, Red Robe, Inset Glass Eyes, Painted, 10 1/4 In. 90.00
St. John Neopmuk, Full-Bodied, Italy, c.1950, 12 In. 260.00
St. John The Baptist, Painted, Ecuador, 12 1/2 In. 90.00
St. Joseph, Stained, South Germany, 1930s, 68 In. ....·...... 1495.00
St. Joseph, With Infant Christ, Polychrome, 20th Century, 22 1/4 In. 750.00
St. Thomas Aquinas, Multicolored, Gilt, Spanish Colonial, 1800s, 12 1/4 In. 750.00
St. Thomas Aquinas, Polychrome, Giltwood, Spanish Colonial, 1900s, 12 In. 575.00
Staff, Owl Finial, Incised Feathers, Relief Carved Wings, Tack Eyes, Poplar, 55 In. 105.00
Temple Dog, Mane, Tail, Japan, 12 1/2 In. 3738.00
Temple Lions, Seated, Japan, 5 1/2 In., Pair 288.00
Train Porter, Music Box, Head Moves, Charles Casper, Chapel Hill, c.1940, 37 In. 7500.00
Tray, Stylized, Relief Man, Animals, Yoruba, Africa, 3 1/2 x 18 In. 380.00
Turkey, Glass Eyes, Painted, Northwestern Pa., c.1907, 33 x 19 In. 2495.00
Uncle Sam, Plywood, Painted, 66 In. 58.00
Vase, Garniture, Leaf Carved, Silvered Wood, 2 Handles, 19 1/2 In. 635.00
Vase, Garniture, Pine, Ribbed, 2 Handles, Neoclassical, c.1800, 20 1/2-In. Vase 980.00
Virgin & Child, Philippino Or Spanish Colonial, 20th Century, 36 In. 489.00
Virgin Mary, Winged, Defeating Satan, Polychrome, Spanish Colonial, 25 In. 865.00
Virgin Mary Bust, Oak, Renaissance Style, German Provincial, 15 x 13 x 7 In. 1035.00
Wall Hanging, Hunting Dogs, Quail, Pine, Frame, Noah Weiss, c.1907, 19 x 20 In. 8250.00
Whale, Mounted On Conch Shell, R. Innis, South Dennis, Mass., 6 x 10 1/2 In. 460.00
Woman, Partially Clothed, Holding Basket Over Head, 50 x 24 In. 374.00
Woman, Protruding Breasts, Metal Eyes, Africa, 25 1/2 In. 295.00
Woman, Wearing Dress, Minimal Features, Red, Tan Paint, Folk Art, 9 In. 460.00

WOODEN wares were used in all parts of the home. Wood was used
for many containers and tools. Small wooden pieces are called *treen-*
ware in England, but the term woodenware is more common in the
United States. Additional pieces may be found in the Advertising,
Kitchen, and Tool categories.

Barrel, Hog's Head, Oak Staves, Iron Bands, Pine Lid, Handle, 26 x 25 1/2 In. 275.00
Barrel, Lid, Stave Constructed, Pine, Hickory, Overlapping Staves, 18 x 15 x 13 In. 375.00
Barrel, Stave Construction, Split Willow Bands, Painted Landscape, 13 3/4 x 11 In. 11.00
Bowl, 2 Horse Head Handles, Geometric Designs, Scandinavian, c.1791, 14 1/4 In. 1885.00
Bowl, Black Finish, Tapered Handle, Treen, 13 3/4 x 3 1/2 In. 430.00
Bowl, Burl Walnut, 19th Century, 18 1/2 In. 1675.00
Bowl, Burl Walnut, Tapered Sides, 6 1/2 x 14 In. 660.00
Bowl, Burl, Ash, Incised Center Ring, Raised Rim, Turned Foot, 23 x 8 In. 3450.00
Bowl, Burl, Ash, Scrubbed Surface, Flared Rim, 5 1/2 x 17 1/2 In. 1840.00
Bowl, Burl, Black Exterior, Round, Treen, 1700s, 8 3/4 x 20 In. 5580.00
Bowl, Burl, Dark Patina, Turned Rim, Foot, 9 x 2 1/2 In. 1380.00
Bowl, Burl, Molded Rim, American, 1700s, 5 x 14 In. 1100.00
Bowl, Burl, Oblong, High Curved Ends, 2 Cutout Handles, 12 x 18 x 6 1/2 In. 2530.00
Bowl, Burl, Raised Rim, Shallow Turned Foot, 14 3/4 x 5 In. 1495.00
Bowl, Burl, Scrubbed Interior, 6 1/2 x 2 1/4 In. 489.00
Bowl, Burl, Turned Rim, Foot, 3 1/2 x 1 1/8 In. 1325.00
Bowl, Chopping, Elongated, Hand Carved, Tiger Maple Handle, Label, 20 x 10 In. 90.00
Bowl, Collar, Blue Green Paint, Treen, Early 1800s, 4 1/8 x 14 5/8 In. 765.00
Bowl, Cover, Burl, Incised Lines, Inset Finial & Plugs, Footed, 4 3/4 x 4 1/2 In. 230.00
Bowl, Distressed Blue Paint, Rim, Treen, 15 x 3 1/2 In. 86.00
Bowl, Fruit, Stencil, Black & Cream Leaves, Treen, c.1825, 11 3/4 In. 59.00
Bowl, Mahogany, Branded, James Prestini, 1954, 18 1/2 x 5 3/4 In. 7050.00
Bowl, Mahogany, Stamped, James Prestini, Treen, c.1938, 10 1/2 x 3 In. 2705.00
Bowl, Old Blue Paint, Brown Interior Finish, 14 1/4 In. 288.00
Bowl, Pine, Collar, New England, Treen, Early 1800s, 9 3/8 x 27 1/2 In. 765.00
Bowl, Poplar, Painted, Red, Black Spots, Treen, 4 1/2 x 14 3/4 In. 660.00
Bowl, Treen, Bob Stocksdale, 3 7/8 & 6 1/2 In., Pair 4540.00
Brushpot, Cylindrical, Japan, 18th Century, 6 1/2 In. 605.00
Brushpot, Rosewood, Embellished, Hardstones, Tinted Ivory, Birds, Chinese, 7 In. 1035.00
Bucket, Cover, Single Piece Of Wood, Whittled Horn Peg, Treen, 7 1/2 In. 29.00
Bucket, Green Windsor Paint, Handle, c.1770 . . . . 1975.00
Bucket, Hinged Cover, 2 Iron Bands, Wire Bail Handle, 10 x 12 3/4 In. 140.00
Bucket, Peat, George III, Mahogany, Brass Bands, Liner, 12 1/2 x 13 1/2 In. 2660.00
Bucket, Red Paint, Iron Hoop, Carved Swing Handle, Early 1800s, 11 In. 765.00
Bucket, Stave Construction, 2 Brass Bands, Wire Bail Handle, Green Paint, 6 In. 635.00
Bucket, Stave Construction, Salmon & Red Paint, Willow Bands, Tapered, 10 1/4 In. 230.00
Bucket, Stave Construction, Stenciled, Tin Bands, Wire Bail Handle, 7 x 5 In. 200.00
Bucket, Stave Construction, Tapered Sides, Wooden Bands & Lid, 13 1/2 In. 230.00
Bucket, Stave Construction, Yellow Paint, Metal Bands, Wire Handle, 6 3/4 In. 170.00
Bucket, Sugar, Cover, Blue Gray Paint, Arched Bentwood Handle, 21 In. 489.00
Bucket, Sugar, Cover, Blue Paint, Tapered, Steel Tacks, Bentwood Handle, 17 3/4 In. 430.00
Bucket, Sugar, Painted Salmon, Metal Bands, Vines, Pine Lid, Porcelain Knob, 9 In. 1155.00
Bucket, Sugar, Pine, Red Paint, J.L. Lehn, Penn., 1800s, 9 x 7 3/4 In. 6325.00
Bucket, Sugar, Stave Construction, Bentwood Bands, Swing Handle, 9 5/8 x 9 In. 290.00
Butter Paddle, Burl, Ash, 8 1/2 In. 1265.00
Butter Paddle, Curly Maple, Scoop Shape, Hooked Handle, 9 1/2 In. 175.00
Canister Set, Poplar, Vinegar Graining, Stenciled, Coffee, Tea, Starch, Lids, 3 Piece 2990.00
Canteen, Old Yellow Paint, Bentwood Overlapping Staves, Brass Tacks, 10 In. 345.00
Canteen, Painted, Round, Inscription, Leather Strap, c.1800, 7 1/4 In. 1116.00
Carrier, Bentwood, Blue Paint, Overlapping Seams, Wire Bail Handle, 9 x 5 1/2 In. 460.00
Carrier, Cheese, Hardwood, Bentwood, Mortise & Tenon Construction, 14 x 17 In. 345.00
Carrier, Cheese, Windsor, Hickory Basket, Spindle, Round Top, 30 x 9 In. 460.00
Carrier, Quartersawn Oak, Tapered Sides, Cutout Handles, 20 1/4 In. 520.00
Carrier, Slide Lid, Decorated, Flowers, Oriental, Stepped Handle, 14 x 8 1/2 x 11 In. 60.00
Carrier, Walnut, Birch, Mahogany, Stars, Wheels, Diamonds, Dovetailed, 13 x 7 In. 1550.00
Cask, Oak, 3 Bands, Spigot, Tapered Sides, Bentwood Handle, 13 x 12 In. 140.00
Cheese Caddy, Mahogany, Sleigh Form, England, c.1830 . . . . 450.00
Clothespin Holder, Oak, 11 Hand Carved Clothes Pins, 1800s, 12 x 11 x 3 1/2 In. 138.00
Club, Carved, Stylized Faces, Rattan Handle Wrap, Primitive, Melanesian, 38 In. 410.00
Compote, Cover, Red & Yellow, Finger Tip Vinegar Graining, Treen, 8 In. 8340.00
Container, Lid, Fruitwood, Stamped Design, Treen, 3 3/8 x 4 In. 60.00
Container, Poplar, Red Paint Design, 3 Incised Bands, Base, Treen, 4 1/4 x 3 1/4 In. 70.00
Cup, Saffron, Blue Ground, Strawberry, Lehnware, 5 x 2 1/2 In. 2080.00

Easel, Oak, Albert Pinkham Ryder, On Wheels, Late 19th Century, 67 In. 1880.00
Figural, Autumn, Cherub, Leaf Crown, Sheaf Of Wheat, c.1800, 29 In. 9200.00
Firkin, Pine, Ocher Paint, Stave Construction, Wood Banding & Handle, 12 x 12 In. 470.00
Firkin, Pine, Yellow Paint, Lapped Finger & Stave, Wooden Bail Handle, 14 x 15 In. 495.00
Flagon, Wooden Staves, Green Paint, Iron Bands, 1700s, 2 Gal. 795.00
Foot Warmer, Dovetailed, Tin, Turned Feet, Cloth Top, Reed Handle, 5 x 8 x 7 In. 175.00
Foot Warmer, Frame, Punched Tin Firebox, Wire Bail Handle, 8 1/2 x 7 1/2 x 6 In. 90.00
Foot Warmer, Oval, Carved Rayed Circle, Cutout Hearts, Reeded Sides, 10 x 14 x 9 In. .. 290.00
Humidor, Burlwood, Mother-Of-Pearl, Brass, Pewter Inlay, Compartment, c.1915, 7 In. 259.00
Hymnal Board, Gothic Style, Oak, c.1900, 55 1/2 In. 130.00
Jar, Cover, Burl, Turned Rim & Knob, 5 5/8 x 7 3/4 In. 2530.00
Jar, Cover, Red Sponging, Dark Patina On Lid, 3 1/4 x 3 In. 115.00
Jar, Cover, Roses, Salmon Ground, Strawberries, Treen Canister, Joseph Lehn, 5 In. 690.00
Jar, Dome Lid, Poplar, Red Vinegar Design, Raised Bands, Turned Finial, 7 x 6 In. 690.00
Jar, Saffron, Cover, Red, Yellow, Green, Violas, Leaves, Treen, Joseph Lehn, 3 1/2 In. ... 750.00
Jar, Saffron, Cover, Urn Shape, Painted, Roses, Strawberries, Treen, Joseph Lehn, 5 In. ... 1150.00
Jar, Urn Shape, Lid Finial, Wire Bale Handle, Peaseware, 5 1/4 In. 175.00
Joss Stick Holder, Tree Stump Shape, Zitan Wood, 19th Century, 4 3/4 In. 196.00
Keg, Oval, Raised Concentric Rings, 5 3/4 x 4 In. 115.00
Knife Box, Edwardian, Sheraton Style, Mahogany, c.1900, 14 x 10 x 10 In., Pair 1095.00
Mirror, Hand Held, Ebony, England, c.1890, 4 1/4 In. 95.00
Mirror, Hand Held, Maple, Beveled, England, c.1890, 10 In. 65.00
Mirror, Hand Held, Maple, England, c.1890, 6 1/2 In. 95.00
Mirror, Hand Held, Maple, England, c.1890, 8 In. 125.00
Pepper Mill, Rosewood, Acorn Finial, Treen, Coil Banding, 1800s, 9 x 3 In. 35.00
Piggin, Stave Construction, 2 Bentwood Bands, Square Nails, Extended Handle, 10 x 8 In. 518.00
Piggin, Stave Construction, Red Wash, Scrubbed Finish, Medallion Handle, 8 x 11 In. 200.00
Pipe Rack, Cutout Of Flying Bird, 4 Pipe Holes, 11 1/4 x 11 In. 200.00
Platter, Turned, Stamped, James Prestini, 1948, 16 In. 2938.00
Salt, Master, Fruitwood, Footed, Base Paint, Treen, 2 3/8 x 2 7/8 In. 30.00
Scroll Weight, Prunus, Calligraphy, Zitan Wood, Jiangshang Studio, c.1752, 9 1/2 In. 605.00
Serving Tray, Walnut, Scalloped Gallery, 4 Cutout Handles, c.1750, 4 1/2 x 22 x 27 In. ... 6900.00
Shield, Hide, Oval, Painted, Red, White, Black Abstract Pattern, Africa, 43 x 22 In. 825.00
Stag, Post World War II, Germany, 12 x 12 1/2 In. 60.00
Tobacco Jar, Cover, Poplar, Carved, Incised Bands, Treen, 8 x 4 1/2 In. 495.00
Tray, George III Style, Mahogany, Oval, 20th Century, 24 In. 418.00
Tray, Inlaid, Fishing Boats, Galle, c.1900, 16 x 23 1/2 In. 1295.00
Tray, Tea, Mahogany, Inlaid, Brass Handles, Edwardian, 24 1/2 In. 370.00
Tray, Tea, Marquetry, Oval, 2 Handles, Dutch, 19th Century, 27 In. 400.00
Trencher, Birch, Hand Hewn, 42 1/4 x 13 In. 175.00
Trencher, Birch, Hand Hewn, Red Paint Exterior, Scrubbed Interior, 26 x 15 x 5 In. 520.00
Trencher, Birch, Hand Hewn, Scrubbed Interior, 12 1/4 x 19 1/2 x 5 In. 115.00
Trencher, Hardwood, Painted, Red, Rectangular, 5 3/4 x 24 x 16 In. 1610.00
Vase, Bamboo, Double Tree Stump, Prunus, Bird, Jui, Japan, 19th Century, 3 1/2 In. 805.00
Wagon Seat, Oak, Pine, Red Paint, Square Nails, Beveled Shoe Feet, 30 x 7 x 24 In. 230.00
Wagon Seat, Red Paint, Blue Medallions, Woman, Shaped Arms, 35 x 35 In. 1495.00
Wastebasket, Birch Bark, Etched Designs, Tomah Joseph, Dated 1903 .... 2090.00
Watch Safe, Hanging, Walnut, Tiger Maple, Arched Backboard, 19th Century, 7 3/4 In. .. 880.00
Watch Safe, Walnut, Scrolled Broken Pediment, Penn., 19th Century, 9 1/2 In. 999.00
Whiskey Cask, Iron Bound, Handle, Round, Bulgaria, 1800s, 12 In. 185.00
Wig Stand, Painted, England, Late 19th Century, 42 1/2 In. ....12.00 to 35.00

WORCESTER porcelains were made in Worcester, England, from
1751. The firm went through many name changes and eventually, in
1862, became The Royal Worcester Porcelain Company Ltd. Collectors often refer to *Dr. Wall*, Barr, *Flight*, and other names that indicate
time periods or artists at the factory. It became part of Royal Worcester
Spode Ltd. in 1976. Related pieces may be found in the Royal Worcester category.

Basket, Fruit, Openwork Rings, Enamel, Rosettes, Bouquet Center, c.1775, 8 In. 825.00
Bowl, Japan Fence, Flowers, Iron Red, Oval, Lobed Rim, Barr Flight & Barr, 13 3/4 In. ... 2185.00
Bowl, Painted, Gilt, Flowers, Small Sprigs, c.1770, 6 1/2 In. 270.00
Bowl, Scarlet Japan, Oval, Lobed Rim, Flight & Barr, 13 1/2 In. 1610.00

Coffee Cann, Cup & Saucer, Dragons, Rocks, Leaves, Chamberlains, c.1810, 5 1/2 In.	170.00
Cream Jug, Crackled Ice, Orange, Geometric Border, Chamberlains, c.1810, 4 1/4 In.	285.00
Creamer, Blue, White, Flowering Scrolls, Dr. Wall, c.1780	235.00
Cup & Saucer, Scarlet Japan, Prunus & Chrysanthemum Panels, Gilt Trim	575.00
Dessert Set, Pink Wild Roses, Blue Sprigs, Gilt Trim, Barr Flight & Barr, 14 Piece	1955.00
Dish, Blue Printed Carnation, Square, Shaped Rim, Insects, Blue Underglaze, 8 1/2 In.	420.00
Dish, Flowers, Shell Rim, Flared Sides, 7 1/4 In.	200.00
Inkstand, Gilt, Flowers, Serpent Handles, 2 Covered Wells, Barr Flight & Barr, 6 In.	2300.00
Inkstand, Multicolored Flower Bands, Gilt Scroll Edge, Flight & Barr, 9 1/2 In.	520.00
Jug, Sparrow Beak, Flowers, Insects, Blue Underglaze, 4 In.	415.00
Pitcher, Shaped Spout, Bulbous Body, Flowers, Reed Gilt Handle, c.1889, 6 1/2 In.	175.00
Plate, Blind Earl, Rose Branch, Flower Sprigs, Gilt Scrolls, Scalloped Rim, 7 1/2 In.	4140.00
Plate, Blue Scale Ground, Scalloped Rim, Flowers, Gilt Border, 1755-75, 7 1/2 In.	425.00
Plate, Flowers, Fluted Border, 11 1/4 In., Pair	230.00
Plate, Oriental Flowers, Fruit, Leaves, Barr Flight & Barr, 1807-13, 9 1/2 In., Pair	1320.00
Plate, Scarlet Japan, Prunus & Chrysanthemum Panels, Orange Ground, Gilt Trim, 4 In. . .	575.00
Plate, Topographical, Cathedral, Zigzag Border, Chamberlains, c.1815, 8 1/2 In.	5185.00
Sauceboat, Lettuce Leaf, Curled Stalk Handle, Flower Sprays, c.1760, 7 In.	690.00
Saucer, High Island, Blue, Island, Tree, House, Oriental Figure, Bridge, c.1753, 5 In.	5279.00
Sweetmeat, Blind Earl, Rose Branch, Butterfly, Scalloped Rim, Gilt Border, 6 1/4 In.	2760.00
Tankard, Plantation, Oriental Architectural Landscape, Blue Underglaze, 4 3/4 In.	635.00
Tea Set, Blue With Gilt Flowers, Cake Plate, 8 Cups & Saucers, Teapot, c.1780	980.00
Teapot, Cover, Globular, Painted, Flowers, Butterflies, c.1760, 4 1/2 In.	2350.00
Teapot, Stand, Flowers, Leaves, Oval, Barr Flight & Barr, c.1810, 6 1/4 In.	380.00
Teapot, Stand, Gilt Leaves, Oval, Scalloped & Fluted Rim, Flight & Barr, c.1800, 6 In. . . .	380.00
Vase, Fern, Flattened Egg Shape Body, No. 1142, 1888, 13 1/2 In.	470.00

WORLD WAR I and World War II souvenirs are collected today. Be careful not to store anything that includes live ammunition. Your local police will tell you how to dispose of the explosives. See also Sword and Trench Art.

WORLD WAR I, Banner, We've Got The Kaiser's Goat, Oh What A Headache, Stick, 9 x 12 In.	160.00
Boots, High Top, Leather, Brown, 14 1/2 In.	85.00
Doll, Doughboy, Molded Composition, Liberty Bond, Ideal, 1918, 12 In.	45.00
Helmet, Imperial German, Prussian Em Pickel Haube, Eagle Front Plate, Spike	315.00
Leggings, Canvas, Khaki, 6 Hooks, U.S. Army, Size 3, Pair	20.00
Needlework, Patriotic, Crossed Flags, Crown, Dieu Et Mon Droit, Flowers, 19 x 17 In. . . .	115.00
Poster, Buy U.S. Government Bonds, Man, Woman, Child, Flat, 1915	450.00
Poster, Fight Or Buy Bonds, Third Liberty Loan, H.C. Christie, 1917, 30 x 20 In.	190.00
Poster, Les Hymnes Allies, 2 Soldiers, Holding Hands, France, 17 3/4 x 11 1/2 In.	345.00
Poster, Over The Top For You, Buy U.S. Gov't Bonds, Riesenberg, 1917, 30 x 20 In.	69.00
Poster, U.S. Marines, 2 Marines Raising Flag, Sidney Hiesenbourg, 1913, 26 x 18 In.	330.00
Sheet Music, Give A Thought To A Buddy Of Mine, Doughboy, Bayonet, 1919	28.00
WORLD WAR II, Binocular Case, Leather, Elastic Pull Down Clasp, Strap, U.S.	30.00
Bottle, Sake, Army, Embossed Ceramic, Veteran's Prize, Japan, 1934	60.00
Bottle, Sake, Navy, Retirement, Anchor, Animals, Letters, Japan	95.00
Button, Buy War Bonds, Kilroy Was Here, 1 1/4 In.	25.00
Button, Defeat Hitler, V, Aid, Britain, USSR, China, Round, 1 In.	100.00
Button, Food For Freedom, Carrot In V, Round, Round, 1 1/4 In.	135.00
Button, Let's Go U.S.A., Keep 'Em Flying, Red, White, Blue, Celluloid, 1 1/4 In.	40.00
Button, To Hell With Hitler, Round, 1 1/4 In.	68.00
Button, Wanted For Murder, Adolf Hitler, Black, White, Celluloid, 1 1/4 In.	35.00
Button, Wanted For Murder, Adolf Hitler, Green, White, Celluloid, 7/8 In.	90.00
Button, War Bond Buyer, Rail Workers, N.J. Central, Reading Lines, Round, 7/8 In.	30.00
Button, Welcome Home Our Heroes, 3 Soldiers, 1 1/4 In.	15.00
Cap, Field, Army, Cotton Shell, Leather Sweatband, Leather Chinstrap, Japan	470.00
Cap, USAF Officers Visor, Blue Wool, Woven Band, Leather Chinstrap, Size 7 1/8	41.00
Card, Slap A Jap Club, Charter Member, 2 1/2 x 4 In.	40.00
Coat, Tropical, Wool, Khaki, U.S. Army Air Forces Sleeve Insignia, 1943, Size 34	50.00
Envelope, Hitler Mustache, Hitler Cartoon	25.00
Figure, Hitler, Hang Him In F E G, Paper, 2-Sided, 1940s, 2 1/2 x 4 3/4 In.	75.00
Figure Set, Promotional, War Bonds, 1941-45	3600.00
Flyer, Wanted For Murder, Hitler Film, 12 x 9 In.	40.00

Hat, U.S. Army Campaign, Signal Corp, Cord, Leather Sweatband, Size 7 . . . . 50.00
Hat, U.S. Army Drill Instructor, Regulation Issue, Olive Drab, Chinstrap, 1970 . . . . 40.00
Helmet, 101st ABN, Rear Seam, Swivel Bail Shell, Tactical Markings, A Straps 518.00
Helmet, Combat, M-35, Stamped Steel Shell, Spain, Size 59 . . . . 59.00
Helmet, Tropical Pith, Khaki Cloth, Woven Straw, Adjustable Straps, Japan, Size 58 . . . . . 645.00
Helmet, USMC Pith, Adjustable Chinstrap, 1944 . . . . 59.00
Japanese Hunting License, Cartoon Tojo, Snake, 1942, 7 x 10 In. 40.00
Matchbook Cover, V, Red, White, Blue 6.00
Mittens, Cotton, Olive Drab, Gray Wool Lining, U.S. Army 14.00
Now All Together, 7th War Loan, 4 Soldiers Putting Up Flag, Paper, 37 x 26 In. 28.00
Pin Dish, Milk Glass, Keep 'Em Flying, Buy Another Savings Bond Today, 3 1/2 In. 35.00
Poster, Americans All, Mexican Hat, Uncle Sam's Hat, 1943, 28 x 20 In. 345.00
Poster, Buy Victory Bonds, Hasten The Homecoming, Paper, Frame, 30 1/2 x 24 In. 75.00
Poster, Don't Talk About Troop Movements, Black, White, U.S. Government, 41 x 29 In. . 45.00
Poster, Gasoline Powers The Attack, Don't Waste A Drop, Giusti, 23 1/2 x 18 In. 220.00
Poster, Speed Up Their Finish, Eagle Attacking Hirohito, Hitler, Mussolini, F. Haase 150.00
Poster, We Have Just Begun To Fight, 1943, 22 1/2 x 16 In. 107.00
Poster, White, Black Riveters Working On Airplane, American War Effort, 28 x 40 In. 225.00
Shirt, Cotton, Khaki, Enlisted Man's, U.S. Army, Size 14 1/2 x 33 . . . . 15.00
Trousers, Field, Wool Serge, Olive Drape, U.S. Army, Size 30 x 31 . . . . 30.00

WORLD'S FAIR souvenirs from all of the fairs are collected. The first
fair was the Great Exhibition of 1851 in London. Some other important
exhibitions and fairs include Philadelphia, 1876 (Centennial); Chicago,
1893 (World's Columbian); Buffalo, 1901 (Pan-American); St. Louis,
1904 (Louisiana Purchase); San Francisco, 1915 (Panama-Pacific);
Philadelphia, 1926 (Sesquicentennial); Chicago, 1933 (Century of
Progress); Cleveland, 1936 (Great Lakes); San Francisco, 1939 (Golden
Gate International); New York, 1939 (World of Tomorrow); Seattle,
1962 (Century 21); New York, 1964; Montreal, 1967; New Orleans,
1984; Tsukuba, Japan, 1985; Vancouver, B.C., 1986; Brisbane, Australia, 1988; Seville, Spain, 1992; and Genoa, Italy, 1992; Seoul,
Korea, 1993; and Lisbon, Portugal, 1998. Memorabilia of fairs include
directories, pictures, fabrics, ceramics, etc. Memorabilia from other
similar celebrations may be listed in the Souvenir category.

Badge, 1904, St. Louis, Admissions, Copper, 1 1/2 In. 380.00
Badge, 1904, St. Louis, Juror, Gilt Nickel, Pinback, Mermod & Jaccard, 1 1/4 In. 340.00
Badge, 1904, St. Louis, Nickel Pinback, 1 5/8 In. 465.00
Basket, 1904, St. Louis, Silk Top, Palace Of Liberal Arts, 6 1/4 x 5 3/4 In. 70.00
Bread Maker, 1904, St. Louis, Universal, No. 4, Landers, Frary & Clark, 12 In. 170.00
Button, 1915, San Francisco, Celluloid, 1 1/4 In. 185.00
Button, 1939, New York, Odd Fellows Day, Celluloid, August 22, 3 1/2 In. 75.00
Button, 1962, Seattle, I Rode Alweg Monorail, Celluloid, 3 1/2 In. 25.00
Button, 1964, New York, Opening Day, Working Press, Unisphere Logo, 3 1/2 In. 159.00
Card, 1893, Chicago, Cluett, Coon & Cos., Shirts, Collars & Cuffs, Exhibit Booth 40.00
Card, 1893, Columbian, Kranich & Back Pianos, Kosmos March, Folder 44.00
Card, 1901, Pan-American, Heide's Licorice, Jujubes 40.00
Clock, 1904, St. Louis, Mantle Style, Cascades, Festival Hall, 2 Cherubs, 10 1/2 In. 2040.00
Clock, 1904, St. Louis, U.S. Government Building, Palace Of Electricity, 7 3/4 In. 4510.00
Comic Book, 1939, New York, Full Color, 96 Pages 800.00
Cuspidor, 1893, Chicago, Brass, Copper, 11 x 9 1/2 In. 360.00
Dish, 1904, St. Louis, Palace Of Electricity, Cover, 7 1/2 x 3 1/2 In. 305.00
Fan, 1904, St. Louis, Roosevelt, Jefferson, Napoleon, Francis, Wood Handle, Box, 18 In. . . 155.00
Fan, 1964, New York, Plastic, Unisphere, Fountains, Box, 7 x 12 In. 25.00
Figurine, 1900, Paris Exposition, 2 Children Playing Cards, Anchor Hallmark, 4 x 8 In. . . . 256.00
Handkerchief, 1876, Philadelphia, 13 Colonies, 37 States, White, 12 1/2 In. 60.00
Handkerchief, 1876, Philadelphia, Silk, Gold, Printed Designs, 29 1/2 x 33 In. 430.00
Handkerchief, 1933, Chicago, FDR Pictured, Red, White & Blue 155.00
Inkwell, 1904, St. Louis, Brass, Camel, 2 3/4 x 4 1/2 In. 145.00
Inkwell, 1904, St. Louis, Cascades, Festival Hall, Metal, Glass, Pen, 3 1/2 x 4 1/2 In. 455.00
Jewelry Box, 1904, St. Louis, Heart Shape, Brass, 4 1/4 x 8 x 7 In. 305.00
License Topper, 1940, New York, Heavy Metal, 5 1/4 x 10 3/4 In. 165.00
Mirror, 1904, St. Louis, Coca-Cola, Glass Of Coke, Oval, 3 In. 305.00

Needle Book, 1939, New York, 7 x 3 3/4 In.	15.00
Paperweight, 1904, St. Louis, Palace Of Liberal Arts, 4 3/8 x 2 7/8 In.	55.00
Pencil Holder, 1933, Chicago, Dog, Holds Pencil In Mouth, Cast Iron, Hubley, 2 In.	360.00
Picture, 1876, Philadelphia Exposition, Multicolored Stencil, Eagle, Spread Wings, 22 In.	2233.00
Pin Box, 1904, St. Louis, Palace Of Industries, Metal Base, Glass Top, 3 1/4 x 4 1/2 In.	175.00
Plaque, 1904, St. Louis, Imperial German, Arta Artis Vicnula, Leather Case, 4 1/2 x 3 In.	1390.00
Plate, 1904, St. Louis, Festival Hall, Cascades, Tin, Vienna Art, 10 In.	500.00
Plate, 1904, St. Louis, Jefferson & Napoleon, Eagle, Cascades, 10 In.	375.00
Playing Cards, 1893, Chicago Columbian Exposition, Columbus Landing In America	215.00
Playing Cards, 1904, St. Louis, Official Souvenir, Red Box, Samuel Cupples	195.00
Poster, 1903, St. Louis, Proclamation, President Of U.S., Frame, 32 x 45 In.	1940.00
Poster, 1934, Chicago, Century Of Progress, See, Play, Hear, 19 1/4 x 12 3/4 In.	280.00
Potlid, 1876, Philadelphia, Multicolored, Pratt, 4 1/4 In.	100.00
Program, 1939, New York, Opening Day, Trylon, Perisphere, 12 x 9 In.	75.00
Puzzle, 1904, St. Louis, Cascade, Festival Hall, Dexterity, 3 In.	159.00
Salt & Pepper, 1904, St. Louis, Palace Of Machinery, Ceramic, 2 3/4 In.	95.00
Scissors, 1904, St. Louis, Monument, Cascade, Metal, Germany, 5 3/4 In.	105.00
Sewing Box, 1904, St. Louis, Women, Tree, Celluloid, Green, Square, 6 1/2 In.	159.00
Sheet Music, 1964, New York, See The Fair, Monorail, Sphere, 1964	40.00
Spoon, 1915, San Francisco Expo Designs, Gold, Stamped	24.00
Tablecloth, 1893, Chicago, Images, Columbus, Washington, Eagle, Shield, 66 x 76 In.	90.00
Tankard, 1904, St. Louis, Grand Price Washing Machines, Goldman & Co., 10 In.	765.00
Tea Set, 1904, St. Louis, Ceylon Court, Pure Ceylon Tea, Elephant, 4 Piece	250.00
Textile, 1876, Philadelphia, Silk, Independence Anniversary, 11 x 6 In.	520.00
Tip Tray, 1915, San Francisco, Buffalo Brewing, 4 1/4 In.	230.00
Toy, 1933, Chicago, Bus, Century Of Progress, Cast Iron, Arcade, Box, 12 In.	1100.00
Toy, 1933, Chicago, Bus, Greyhound, Bench Seat, 11 1/2 In.	600.00
Toy, 1934, Chicago, Cab & Trailer, Cast Iron, 10 1/4 In.	275.00
Toy, 1934, Chicago, Cab & Trailer, Cast Iron, 11 1/2 In.	375.00
Toy, 1934, Chicago, Cab & Trailer, Cast Iron, 14 1/2 In.	475.00
Toy, 1939, New York, Bus, Cast Iron, Arcade, Box, 10 In.	935.00
Toy, 1939, Tractor Train, Greyhound, Arcade, 1939	750.00
Toy, 1964, New York, Glide-A-Ride, Tin, Friction, Japan, 9 In.	475.00
Vase, 1893, Chicago, Amberina, Trumpet, 7 In.	325.00
Vase, 1904, St. Louis, Palace Of Machinery, Blue Flowers, 10 1/4 In.	650.00
Vase, 1904, St. Louis, Women In Heat, 2 Handles, Black, 7 In.	85.00

WPA is the abbreviation for Works Progress Administration, a program created by executive order in 1935 to provide jobs for millions of unemployed Americans. Artists were hired to create murals, paintings, drawings, and sculptures for public buildings. Pieces are marked WPA and may have the artist's name on them.

Architectural Scale Model, Byzantine House, Plaster, Painted, 7 1/2 x 9 3/8 x 9 7/8 In.	200.00
Doll, All Nations, Man, Woman, Czechoslovakian Costume, 15 1/2 & 17 In., Pair .... *Illus*	378.00
Doll, All Nations, Man, Woman, France Normandy Costume, 16 In., Pair .... *Illus*	468.00
Doll, Field Worker, Modeled Head, Painted Features, Cloth, Hungarian 16 In.	140.00
Doll, Man, Modeled Head, Painted Features, Hair, Cloth Body, Slovak, 16 In.	195.00

WPA, Doll, All
Nations, Man, Woman,
Czechoslovakian
Costume,
15 1/2 & 17 In., Pair

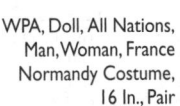

WPA, Doll, All Nations,
Man, Woman, France
Normandy Costume,
16 In., Pair

Doll, Woman, Modeled Head, Painted Features, Hair, Cloth Body, Breton Costume, 16 In. . 220.00
Mural, Oil On Canvas, Black Family, Cabin & Field, Tacked To Stretcher, 30 x 25 In. 480.00
Painting, Watercolor, Tarring Shack, Charles R. Knapp, Frame, 23 1/2 x 20 In. 1100.00
Sign, Oil On Canvas, Work Program, Recareation Project, Red, White, Blue, 46 x 39 In. .. 75.00
Tape Measure, Leather Case, Stamped F.E.R.A., Marked 60.00

WRISTWATCHES came into use during World War I. Wristwatches
are listed here by manufacturer or as advertising or character watches.
Pocket watches are listed in the Watch category.

Advertising, Colt Firearms, Water Resistant, Stainless Steel, Swiss, Box 66.00
Agassiz, Platinum, Diamond, Ivorytone Dial, Jeweled Movement, Art Deco, 5 1/2 In. 1765.00
Baume & Mercier, Woman's, 14K Gold Mesh Band, Sapphire Stem Cap 1150.00
Baume & Mercier, Woman's, 14K Gold, Oval, Ivorytone Dial, Woven Band, 6 In. 705.00
Baume & Mercier, Woman's, 17 Jewel, 18K Gold Case, Bangle, c.1965 .... 283.00
Baume & Mercier, Woman's, 17 Jewel, Gold Hands, Arabic & Baton Numerals 259.00
Birks, Ryrie, Woman's, 18K White Gold, Square Dial, Blue Hands, Diamonds, c.1930 .... 520.00
Breitling, Navitimer, Chronograph, 1960s 1007.00
Bulgari, Woman's, Stainless Steel, White Dial, Arabic Numerals 1295.00
Bulova, Accutron, 214, Electronic Movement, 18K Gold Case & Band, Box, c.1964 ...... 660.00
Cartier, Ivorytone Dial, Stick Indicators, 18K Gold, White Metal Band 765.00
Cartier, Rolex, Woman's, Oyster Perpetual, Date Aperture, Stainless Steel, Box 1530.00
Cartier, Square Goldtone Dial, Roman Numerals, 17 Jewel, Mesh, 18K Gold 1410.00
Cartier, Stainless Steel, Silvertone Dial, Arabic, Abstract, Leather 705.00
Cartier, Woman's, Diagonally Set White Matte Dial, Diamond Bezel, 18K Gold Band 6900.00
Chanel, Woman's, Black, White Dial, Roman Numerals, Onyx, Windup, 18K Gold 1295.00
Character, Big Bad Wolf, Chrome, Wolf & Pigs Bracelet, Ingersoll, 1934 .... 625.00
Character, Blondie, Dagwood, Pups, Chrome, Green Band, Danbros Watch Co., 1949 .... 1075.00
Character, Bugs Bunny, Carrot Hands, Leather Band, Warner Bros., Box, 1951 .... 1800.00
Character, Buzz Corey's Space Patrol, Chrome Case, Expansion Band, U.S. Time, 1950 .. 950.00
Character, Cinderella, Chrome, Pink Band, Ingersoll, U.S. Time, Original Box, 1950 ..... 375.00
Character, G.I. Joe Combat, Compass, Sighting Lenses, Swiss Movement, Gilbert, Box ... 330.00
Character, Garfield Cat, Cat Jumped Over Moon, Leather Band, 1978, 1-In. Dial, 8 In. ... 35.00
Character, Hoppity Hooper, Leather Straps, 17 Jewel, Jay Ward, c.1972, 1 1/4 In........ 200.00
Character, James Bond, 007, Gilbert, Box, 1965 .... 397.00
Character, Joe Palooka, Chrome, Leather Band, New Haven, Ham Fisher, 1948 .... 950.00
Character, Mary Marvel, Chrome, Red Vinyl Band, Marvel, Box, 1948 .... 989.00
Character, Mary Marvel, Chrome, Vinyl Band, Marvel Importing, Fawcett Pub., 1948 .... 875.00
Character, McDonald's, Ronald McDonald, 1984 .... 16.00
Character, Mickey Mantle, Baseball, Roger Maris, Willie Mays, All Star, 1966 .... 145.00
Character, Porky Pig, Chrome, Red Vinyl Band, Ingraham, Box, 1949 .... 994.00
Character, Texas Ranger, Animated, Leather Band, 1951, 1-In. Dial, 8-In. Strap 300.00
Character, Tom Corbett Space Cadet, Chrome, Black Band, Ingraham, 1955 ....2600.00 to 2940.00
Chase, Ivorytone Dial, Dot Indicators, 17 Jewel, 6 1/4 In. 560.00
Concord, 18K Gold, Diamond, Enamel, Alligator Band, 9 In. 705.00
Concord, Woman's, Silvertone Dial, Mesh, 14K Gold, 7 1/2 In. 355.00
Concord, Woman's, Stainless Steel, Silvertone Dial, Link Band, 14K Gold 325.00
Croton, Ivorytone Dial, Arabic Numerals, Platinum, Diamonds, 17 Jewel, Cord Band 235.00
Cyma, Woman's, 17 Jewel, 14K White Gold Case & Band, c.1970 .... 755.00
Diamond, Ruby, 14K Gold, Goldtone Dial, 17 Jewel, Swiss, 6 3/4 In. 999.00
Elgin, Woman's, Diamond Shape Dial, Blue Steel Hands, Black Numerals, Diamonds 575.00
Glycine Watch Co., Platinum, Diamonds, Arabic Numerals, 17 Jewel, Art Deco 355.00
Hamilton, 14K Gold, Silvertone Dial, Brushed Bezel, Mesh Band, 7 In. 355.00
Hamilton, Woman's, Platinum, Diamonds, 17 Jewel, 6 3/4 In. 2350.00
Hermes, Woman's, Pyramid Cover, Leather Band, Lizard Pattern, Box 1175.00
Hermes, Woman's, Stainless Steel, White Dial, Arabic Indicators 470.00
Joe Palooka, Chrome Case, Leather Band, New Haven, Box, Insert, 1948 .... 1074.00
LeCoultre, Ivorytone Dial, Diamond, Arabic, Back Wind, 18K Gold 1175.00
LeCoultre, Silvertone Dial, Numeral Indicators, 17 Jewel, 14K Gold 411.00
Longines, 25 Jewel, Automatic Wind, Date, 18K Gold Band & Case, 1970s 1225.00
Longines, Dual Time Zone, 18K Gold, Black Hands, Baton Numerals, Textured Dial 1725.00
Longines, Platinum, Diamond, Arabic Numerals, 15 Jewel 2340.00
Lucian Piccard, Woman's, Self-Winding, Diamond, 14K Gold, Swiss, c.1960, 6 1/2 In. ... 489.00
Mathey-Tissot, Woman's, 14K White Gold, Oval Dial, Disc & Dart Numerals 2530.00

Movado, Woman's, Goldtone Dial, Arabic Numerals, 15 Jewel, 14K Gold 765.00
Nivada, Woman's, Round Cut Diamonds, 18K Yellow Gold Case, Swiss . . . . .230.00 to 259.00
Normis, Woman's, Platinum, Diamond, 17 Jewel, Art Deco, c.1925, 1/2 In. 259.00
Omega, 17 Jewel, Square White Dial, Gold Baton Numerals, Crystal Dial, 14K Gold 239.00
Omega, Ivorytone Dial, Arabic, Abstract Indicators, 14K Gold 355.00
Omega, Speedmaster Professional Mark III, Date, Chronograph, c.1973 . . . . 570.00
Omega, Speedmaster, Chronograph, 17 Jewel, Stainless Steel Case, c.1965 . . . . 1040.00
Omega, Woman's, 17 Jewel, 18K Gold Case & Mesh Band, c.1975 . . . . 755.00
Omega, Woman's, 17 Jewel, 18K Gold Case, c.1970 . . . . 520.00
Omega, Woman's, 18K Gold, Silvertone Dial, 17 Jewel, Brickwork Link 500.00
Omega, Woman's, Self Winding, 17 Jewel, 18K Gold, Swiss, c.1960, 6 In. 259.00
Omega, Woman's, Square Gold Matte Dial, 40-Diamond Bezel, Mesh Band, c.1970 . . . . . . 575.00
Patek Philippe, 18 Jewel, 18K Gold Case & Mesh Band, c.1970 . . . . 3395.00
Patek Philippe, 18 Jewel, Caliber 10 Movement, 18K Rose Gold Case, c.1942 . . . . 2639.00
Patek Philippe, 37 Jewel, Automatic Wind, Date, 18K Gold Case, c.1960 . . . . 4336.00
Patek Philippe, Ivorytone Dial, Stick Indicators, 18K Gold Band, c.1960 . . . . 2705.00
Patek Philippe, Silvertone Dial, Gold Indicators Movement, Leather Band, c.1950 . . . . . . 2820.00
Patek Philippe, Silvertone, Metal Dial, Raised Indicators, Leather Band, Signed, c.1949 . . 6228.00
Patek Philippe, Tonneau Shape, 18K Yellow Gold, 18 Jewel, c.1933 . . . . 5175.00
Paul Burht, Woman's, Diamond, Sapphire, Rectangular Case, 18K White Gold, 7 In. 546.00
Pery, Woman's, Diamond, Ruby, 14K Gold, Manual Wind, c.1930, 3/4 x 7 1/4 In. 430.00
Piaget, Black Dial, Ribbed Case, Screw-On Back, 18K Gold 523.00
Piaget, Woman's, 18K White Gold, Diamond, Mesh Band, Swiss 2115.00
Piaget, Woman's, Opal Dial, Octagonal Opal Bezel, 18K Yellow Gold Mesh Band 345.00
Piaget, Woman's, Silvertone Dial, Arabic Numerals, 17 Jewel, 6 3/4 In. 500.00
Raymond Yard, Woman's, Sapphire, Diamond, Textured Band, 14K Gold 1410.00
Rolex, 18K Gold, President, Day, Date, Tree Bark, c.1970 . . . . 5175.00
Rolex, 18K White Gold, Diamond, Silvertone Dial, Chain Band, 6 1/2 In. 1295.00
Rolex, Oyster, 17 Jewel, Stainless Steel Case & Band, c.1964 . . . . 848.00
Rolex, Oyster, Perpetual, 18K Gold, 26 Jewel, Black Dial, Diamonds, c.1970 . . . . 6325.00
Rolex, Oyster, Perpetual, Air King, Stainless Steel Case & Strap, c.1962 . . . . 848.00
Rolex, Oyster, Perpetual, Bubble Back, 25 Jewel Chronometer, Gold Filled Case, c.1949 . . 660.00
Rolex, Oyster, Perpetual, Bubble Back, Auto Rotor, Stainless Steel Case, Box, c.1937 . . . . 1600.00
Rolex, Oyster, Perpetual, Bubble Back, Automatic Wind, Gold Filled Case, 1940s 1790.00
Rolex, Oyster, Perpetual, Datejust, 26 Jewel, Automatic Wind, Stainless Steel, c.1971 . . . . . 1225.00
Rolex, Oyster, Perpetual, Explorer, c.1946 . . . . 1345.00
Rolex, Oyster, Royal, 15 Jewel, Super Balance Movement, Stainless Steel Case, c.1937 . . . 425.00
Rolex, Prince, 2 Dials, Chronometer, Manual Wind, Stainless Steel, c.1949, 1 In. 4600.00
Rolex, Woman's, Cellini, Silver Matte Dial, 18K Yellow Gold Hour Lines, c.1950 . . . . 520.00
Rolex, Woman's, Oyster Perpetual, Gold Dial, 18K Gold Case & Strap, Box 8050.00
Rolex, Woman's, Princess, Platinum, 8 Diamonds, Rope Band, c.1930 . . . . 920.00
Rolex, Woman's, Textured Oval Gold Dial, Black Hands, Mesh Band, c.1975 . . . . 978.00
Silvertone Dial, Arabic Numerals, Diamonds, Emerald, Platinum, Art Deco, Box, 7 In. . . . 519.00
Tiffany, Paloma Picasso, Woman's, 18K Gold, Goldtone Dial, Box, 7 1/2 In. 2350.00
Tiffany & Co., Alarm, Silvertone Dial, Leather Band, 14K Gold, Swiss 880.00
Timex, Bing Crosby National Pro-Am, Golf, Pebble Beach, 1980, 1-In. Dial 190.00
Timex, Bob Hope Desert Classic, Golf, Hope Caricature, Case, c.1980, 1 1/8-In. Dial 200.00
Timex, Jackie Gleason Golf, Case, 1980, 1 1/4-In. Dial 200.00
Timex, Sammy Davis Jr. Greater Hartford Open, Golf, Case, 1980, 1-In. Dial 139.00
Universal Geneva, Calendar, 17 Jewel, 18K Gold, Gold Band, c.1950, 1 1/2 In. 1035.00
Vacheron & Constantin, 18K Gold, Gold Matte Dial, 17 Jewel, Florentine Band 2415.00
Vacheron & Constantin, 18K Gold, Silvertone Dial, Leather Band, Manual Wind 1410.00
Vacheron & Constantin, 18K Gold, Square Gold Matte Dial, Date Opening, 36 Jewel 1725.00
Vacheron & Constantin, 36 Jewel, 18K Gold Case & Strap, 1970s 2640.00
Van Cleef & Arpels, Woman's, Ivory One Dial, Roman Numerals, 18K Gold, Swiss 560.00

YELLOWWARE is a heavy earthenware made of a yellowish clay. It
varies in color from light yellow to orange-yellow. Many nineteenth-
and twentieth-century kitchen bowls and jugs were made of yellowware. It was made in England and in the United States. Another
form of pottery that is sometimes classed as yellowware is listed in this
book in the Mocha category.

Bank, Pig, Blue & Brown Spatter, Coin Slot, Eye Holes, 3 x 6 In. 440.00

Bank, Sheep, Molded Form, Running Brown & Green Glaze, 4 1/2 x 3 1/4 In. 862.00
Bowl, 4 x 8 1/2 In. 33.00
Candlestick, Turned Rings, Rockingham Glaze, 8 x 4 1/8 In., Pair 1320.00
Chamber Pot, Cream & Blue Spongeware Glaze, c.1900, 1 1/2 In. 90.00
Colander, Molded Relief Designs, Holes In Star Shape, White Interior, 10 In. 193.00
Creamer, Cow, Red & Black Sponged Designs, Black Tail, Head, Hooves, Ohio, 7 In. 1035.00
Dish, Rabbit, Cover, Hourglass Shape, Molded Garland, Petal Handle, 13 x 6 In. 315.00
Figurine, Dog, Spaniel, Seated, Blue Glaze, Freestanding Front Legs, 9 3/4 In. 1840.00
Figurine, Dog, Spaniel, Seated, Rockingham Glaze, 4 1/2 In. 165.00
Figurine, Dog, Spaniel, Seated, Running Blue Glaze, Crosshatched Tail, 9 3/4 In. 2415.00
Mixing Bowl, Banded Decoration, Early 20th Century, 11 1/2 x 8 1/2 In., Pair 105.00
Mold, Food, Swirl, Footed, 4 x 2 1/2 In. 145.00
Mold, Jelly, Spiral Interior, I.W. Cory, Trenton, N.J., c.1870 .... 50.00
Mug, Brown & White Banding, 4 x 4 In. 430.00
Mug, Brown Bands, Blue Seaweed, Handle, 3 3/4 In. 360.00
Mug, Relief Flowers, Ocher Accents, 3 In. 80.00
Pitcher, Hanging Game & Fowl, Hound Handle, Rockingham Glaze, c.1850, 9 1/2 In. 120.00
Potty, White Band, 2 1/2 In. 300.00
Rolling Pin 695.00
Salt, Master, White Bands, 2 3/4 In. 350.00
Teapot, Toby, Figural, Arms Are Handle & Spout, 8 1/2 In. 405.00

ZANESVILLE Art Pottery was founded in 1900 by David Schmidt in
Zanesville, Ohio. The firm made faience umbrella stands, jardinieres,
and pedestals. The company closed in 1962. Many pieces are marked
with just the words *La Moro.*

LA MORO

Bowl, Green Matte, Greek Key Design, 4 1/2 x 6 In. 150.00
Jardiniere, Brown Glaze, Scrolls, Painted Tulips, Yellow, Orange, 12 x 14 1/2 In. 206.00
Jardiniere, Green Matte, Embossed, Narcissus, 10 x 11 1/2 In. 150.00
Jardiniere, Pedestal, Brown Glaze, Painted, Tulips, Yellow, Orange, 27 In. 295.00
Vase, Neptune, Curled Handles, Mottled Blue & Brown Glaze, 18 x 13 In. 765.00
Vase, Neptune, Twisted Handles, 24 x 15 In. 645.00
Vase, Red Glaze, Black Drip, 19 In. 590.00

ZSOLNAY pottery was made in Hungary after 1862 and was characterized by Persian, Art Nouveau, or Hungarian motifs. A series of new
Zsolnay figurines with green-gold luster finish is available in many
shops today. Early Zsolnay was not marked, but by 1878 the tower
trademark was used.

Bowl, Luster Glaze, Earthenware, c.1900, 5 1/4 In. 4540.00
Figurine, Nude Woman, Luster Glaze, Earthenware, c.1900, 12 1/4 In. 2870.00
Pitcher, Handle, Tapered, Cylindrical, Oak Leaves, Acorns, Beetles, 16 In. 5290.00
Pitcher, Vase, Bulbous Shape, Painted, Applied Design, c.1890, 5 1/2 x 3 1/4 In. 90.00
Vase, Flowers, Butterflies, Gold, Pink, Blue, Green, Signed, 13 In. 590.00
Vase, Iridescent Blue, Green, Gold, 2 Mermaids, Broad Form, Marked, 10 In. 2940.00
Vase, Landscape, Luster, Egg Shape, Triangular Section Neck, c.1902, 13 5/8 In. 12000.00
Vase, Man & Woman At Shoulder, Red Glaze, 3 1/2 In. 3525.00
Vase, Metallic Glaze, Blue, Red, Purple, 7 3/4 In. 460.00
Vase, Round, Bird, Poppies, Enameled Decoration, Handles, Footed, Fischer, 14 x 11 In. .. 880.00
Vase, Silver Overlaid, Luster Glaze, Earthenware, c.1900, 8 3/4 In. 1075.00

INDEX

This index is computer-generated, making it as complete as possible. References in uppercase type are category listings. Those in lowercase letters refer to additional pages where pieces can be found. There is also an internal cross-referencing system used in the main part of the book, so if you look for a Kewpie doll in the Doll category, you will be told it is in its own category. There is additional information at the end of many paragraphs about where to find prices of pieces similar to yours.

KOVELS' LIBRARY

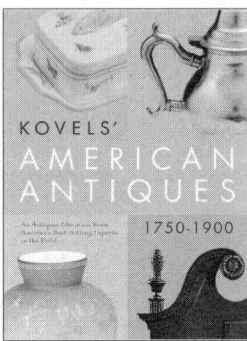